P9-CMT-367

300 YEARS OF
Kitchen
Collectibles
5th Edition

- **Every price individually brought up-to-date**

- **New mini-articles on egg scales, egg slicers, juicers, etc.**

- **New collecting online and eBay information**

- **New 16-page color section**

- **New how-to article about doing online patent research**

- **Many new sources for more information and fun related to scores of collecting specialties**

- **Many new old-time recipes**

Linda Campbell Franklin

On The Cover:

1. Tin mold, 1870s-80s, "skirt" on top protects deeply stamped design.
2. Tin cookie cutter, 1870s-80s, horse, two large finger-holes. (Chapter IV)
3. Plastic glove-stretcher/dryers, 1940s
4. Tin grater with nutmeg compartment, "Acme", 19th C. (Chapter I)
5. Cast aluminum bottle opener, hand-shaped, 20th C (Chapter VIII)
6.-a. Homespun linen blue & white table cover, c. 1860s-70s
6.-b. Homespun linen/cotton dish towel, c. 1870-80s.
7. Crocheted cotton blue & white potholder, 20th C. (Chapter VI)
8. Patented tin coffee pot, "Chesterman's", 1858-59. (Chapter XIV)
9. Tin cookie cutter, C. 1880s-90s, leaping deer (Chapter IV)
10. Tin chocolate mold with clip, chicken, 20th C. (Chapter IV)
11. White enameled cast iron pot trivet or stand (Chapter VI)
12. Pieced copper pitcher, tinned inside, braced handle, large pouring lip, 19th C. (Chapter VII)
13. Wood (probably maple) lard press, hinged, with long handles for good leverage, late 19th C. (Chapter I)
14. Forged or wrought steel implement, possibly two functions, punctured rough surface makes good grater for burned bread & slightly dished bowl, if used on other side, could be a fish "slice", the holes for draining. (Chapter X)
15. Tinned steel homemade soap-holder, homemade but fine, c. 1890s-1910s.
16. Cast aluminum cake turner, c. 1930s-40s. (Chapter XIII)
17. Copper & brass set of measures, English, mid-19th C. (Chapter V)
18. Forged iron frying pan, c. 1820s-40s. (Chapter X & XII)
19. Glazed pottery water cooler, "The Allen", late 19th C. (Chapter XV)
20. Cast iron Griswold "Krispy Korn or Wheat" pan, 20th C. (Chapter IV)
21. Cast iron ebelskiver pan, early 20th C. (Chapter IV)
22. Cast aluminum cornstick pan, 20th C. (Chapter IV)
23. Heavy tin coal scuttle, white porcelain knob, mid-19th C. (Chapter XI)

Published by

 krause publications
An F&W Publications Company

700 East State Street • Iola, WI 54990-0001
715-445-2214 • 888-457-2873
www.krause.com

Please call or write for our free catalog of publications.
Our toll-free number to place an order or obtain a free catalog is 800-258-0929
or please use our regular business telephone 715-445-2214.

Library of Congress Catalog Number: 2002107616

ISBN: 0-87349-365-6

Printed in the United States of America

Dedication

I dedicate this book to my parents, the late Robert D. Franklin and the late Mary Mac Franklin, both librarians who lighted the collecting fire within me as well as the book-writing bug, and in memory of the best flea market find I ever made – my darling Darwin the beagle, known to many by his picture on the 3rd edition. And to the firemen of New York City, with wonder and sadness, because the horrors of September 11, 2001 took place while I was working on this book. Also to my Grand Mamma, the late Willie Lee Burton; to the late Lillian Cole, pie bird pioneer; to the late Thomas Wiggins, apple parer expert; to the late Rodris Roth, curator emeritus of domestic history at the Smithsonian; to the late Pat Guthman, purveyor of the best hearth-cooking implements and hollowware; to my brother Robbie and his family; as well as to new friends made to be kept! Lighter parts are courtesy of old friends – Andrea, Terry, Frank, Brenda, Judy, Louise, Nancy, and Linda. Darker parts are courtesy of the basement. And finally to Nicky Copernicus (pictured on the back with me), Galileo Louise, Chloe Ptolemy, DuMonticello & Emitte, who share the computer room and have added paper-sorting, unfiling, nose-bounce mouse interference, and nutritious hairs to the hard drive.

Acknowledgments

Special thanks go to the publisher of the first three editions – Dan Alexander, Books Americana. Thanks also to Krause Publications for their faith in my work, and to Paul Kennedy who talked me into doing a 5th edition with generosity dosed with flattery, and Christine Townsend, who tried enthusiastically to keep me on schedule.

I am lucky to have had the assistance, encouragement, cooperation, and patience of many collectors, dealers, auctioneers, librarians, and curators. Many of them first agreed to help with the third edition. Since then I've met many more collectors, in person and on the Internet, who have undertaken to help me make many corrections, additions, rearrangements, and value assessments in areas of their particular interest, so that this fifth edition can live up to its reputation. Some of these people have written books on their own subjects, and flatter me by saying that my first books, many years ago, gave them inspiration. Several advisors have allowed me to insert notices alerting readers to their specialist subjects; this is an important source for feeding new data to me, and I look forward to serving new information to you in the next edition of this book.

My heartfelt thanks go to Joel Schiff, Georgiana Sanders, Bunny Upchurch & Kyle Goad, Pat Guthman, David G. Smith, Don & Diana Thornton, all the Holroyds of Oregon, the Moffets, Joe Young, Bill Griffiths, Wayne Smith, Teri & Joe Dziadul, Carol & Jim Bohn, Sheri & John Ficken, Donna & Bob Gaither, Leslie & Max Hand, Lois & Clark Lewis, Steve Stephens, Oveda Maurer, Ron Barlow, Clifford Boram, Meryle Evans, John & Mary Ann Lambert, Anne Serio, Ann Golovin, Joe & Jill MacMillan, Vernon Ward, the late Ray Townsend, Evelyn Welch, Peggy Wainscott, Pat Gross, Dolores Thomas, Robert Carr, Karol Atkinson, the late Marion Levy, James Trice, Bob Cahn, Georgia Levett, Litchfield Auction Gallery, James D. Julia, Jeannine Dobbs, H. H. T. Robb-Smith, Barbara Bowditch, Betty Landis, the late Phyllis Wetherall, Jens Veerbeck, John Zukatis, Carole & Larry Meeker, Greg Stahl, all the people whose names I should have included if I were more organized, and the hundreds and hundreds of readers who've written and e-mailed to share information.

Photographs include those taken by Paul Persoff of the Keillor Family Collection and other collections; those by David Arky, who did most of the photographs in the second edition; those by Jens Veerbeck of toasters; those by John Zukatis of juicers; those bought from various sources or lent for free by others; those contributed by readers; and those taken by the author.

Web site

By the summer of 2003, I hope to have a simple Web site up for this book at www.300yearsofkitchencollectibles.com

Table of Contents

(Note: NEW **COLOR PHOTO** section follows Chapter XV, on page 753)

Introduction

Who's Collecting?

Historians and scholars who study culinary history are thriving, and their number has increased greatly. "Women's work" and the psycho-sociological meaning of so-called labor-savers are popular subjects for articles and books. Academic interest means that organized collections relating to all aspects of housekeeping are increasingly interesting, respected, publicized, and valuable. There has also been a tremendous increase in the number of men collecting kitchen things. I believe that more men than women collect kitchen bygones.

A hundred, or even just 20 years ago, handmade kitchen objects were valued over machine-made things. Collectors of the old type, usually women, lived in a world ever more mechanistic, and were drawn to the opposite: Hand-carved wood, wrought iron hearth-cooking tools, and one-of-a-kind decorated crocks, because they implied a simpler way of life. In 1976 I called it nostalgic collecting of the "erstwhile quaint."

We're far from the simple, mechanical world of the 1950s; our world is now computerized and electronic. The digits operating everything are no longer the fingers of humans, but instead are the zeros and ones hidden inside computers. Most new gadgets are impossible to fix with a screwdriver or wrench, either because they are junky parts of our throwaway culture, or they're partly electronic.

Many new collectors go back just far enough to evoke their vision of a "simpler time" – but it's still a mechanical time. Nostalgia is on a much shorter time-line now. The new collector collects the "erstwhile funky" or whatever you want to call it!

The things most valued today are machine-made, mechanical or electrical, and are especially desirable if patented, and can be researched and documented.

Patent research is now a big part of the fun. (See the chapters in the back of this book on doing patent research.) The kitchen collectibles we collect, be they copper tea kettles or chrome mixers, are all tickets to the everyday life of a past – whatever past we personally prefer. With them we are able to move around in that "shadow line, that faint demarcation between a world that is vanishing and another that is inexorably taking its place," as novelist Joseph Conrad put it a century ago.

Price Guides: What Good Are They?

Think of a good price guide as an atlas of topographical field maps showing boundaries, horizons, paths, peaks, and hollows. Use it to develop unexplored areas and markets. I will never do a price guide that has "all new listings." Can you imagine a map with "all new listings?" What good would all new listings do for new kitchen collectors? They'd never know about the classic pieces, nor be able to track fundamentals over a long period, from edition to edition. A price guide at its best is a view of relative values. Going down the listings in any particular area of collecting will show you that some highly-desired pieces may be "valued" at 10 times what some other items will sell for. One thing might bring $600, while another languishes on the shelf for $6.00. It is still your job to decide for yourself how much a particular thing is worth. If you are selling it, you can look at a price guide – but be realistic, and know your market. If you are lucky, you'll get more than the estimated value. If you are buying a particular thing, you can perhaps get a ballpark idea of value from a suggested value range printed in the book, but you have to decide how much it's worth to you.

Values have been carefully reviewed by experts in the individual "fancies" of the kitchen field. They are compiled from recorded public sales, private sales, and observations, even predictions, and, yes, eBay prices are factored in, too. But remember values are different from prices. Values can't be tracked over a vast geographical expanse even though prices can be. The Internet has made the physical collecting world smaller, but there are different trends among collectors in different parts of that world at any given time. Also, as Jeff Smith of Evanston, IL, (eBayer jeffjunk) wrote me, price/value "varies drastically with where something is being sold: garage sale, estate sale, rummage sale, antique store, thrift shop, flea market, eBay, Internet online store, or collector convention." He adds that "auctions have different dynamics all their own." Editors of collector tabloids used to write about auction fever and its power to skew prices; they were talking about auctions where everyone was in the same room for a few hours. Warning: You may not be inoculated against auction fever just because you're isolated with your computer, bidding for several days in an online auction. See the Buying Online tips at the end of this Introduction.

Collectibles value/price guides aren't like those price guides car mechanics use – the ones they consult before fixing your car to see how long it'll take to whammy your ferndock, and then charge the book rate even if it takes half the time. Collectibles value guides are more like wishbooks. One of the problems of using a price guide is that it may paint a rosy picture of values to a prospective seller, but cannot provide a willing buyer. And vice versa. A willing seller ("I wish I could sell my cake pan for $$$$$") and a willing buyer ("I wish I could buy that cake pan for $$") have to get together at the same time and they have to agree on the same price for there to be a sale. Sellers can ask anything (or set any reserve price) but there has to be a sale for it to mean anything. On the other hand, it takes only one buyer who just has to have something, especially in an auction, for the price could go up way beyond reason, or (resale) value.

The natural progression of things is: First come the collectors, then collectors-turned-writers, then more collectors. People complained that my first book (and all the successive ones) made prices go up. But I counter that all sorts of new things came out of hiding, and while prices went up for the un-booked items, they leveled out for the things which time had proved were not rare, but in fact were plentiful.

Furthermore, now there are books devoted to just one subject from one chapter of my books, such as apple parers, eggbeaters, nutmeg graters, toasters, cast iron cookware, etc., etc. Those books help set new market values because they are so specific and they serve to rally specialty collectors around their subject, and along comes a club, a newsletter, a Web site and, inevitably, a new cycle of supply and demand.

"Book value" is only a record of what's already happened. You the buyer, and you the seller, can maybe get some idea of how the sale will end, but often you'll be disappointed. The best use of a good value guide is providing accurate information – and that's something the seller can use to increase the value of what is being sold. Here are some important things to keep in mind:

• Don't assume that a high price guarantees value, rarity, or resale potential.

• Don't buy something you don't know anything about hoping to make a killing.

• Don't blame the price guide if you lose money on something.

• Don't thank the price guide if you make money on something.

• Don't be annoying by saying "it's in the book with a price range of $XX to $YY" to someone who makes an offer of what they want to pay. You don't have to accept their offer.

• Don't spend more than you can afford.

Electronization Takes Command ... of Collectors

One terrific thing that's happened since the last edition is the **Internet's impact** on collecting. Anybody can host a virtual museum on a Web site, without having to have guards or a board of directors ... and often there's a "gift shop." With 24/7 access by others anywhere in the world, the Webmaster-curator can quickly build a community, and instantly add pictures of rarities, post duplicates for sale or trade, and get e-mails that offer an object, information (or even a chance to be in a book!).

Online auctions, especially eBay, have radically affected things. "The major dynamic is that collecting is now much more of a true 'market' in that for any given item there are a lot more [potential] buyers, and because kitchen items were mass-produced commodities, there are also a lot more available. So prices are truer," says Jeff Smith. "So-called 'book value' no longer has meaning. For some items (those that get notoriety) eBay's influence has been to dramatically increase prices ... for the vast majority of items on eBay, however, sellers are surprised and disappointed to find that antique store prices or book values are never reached. Many items that have too high a starting price go without even an opening bid."

"A lot of trash and reproductions are being sold online," says Greg Stahl, a collector of cast iron and aluminum toys, waffle irons, muffin pans and skillets. "I thought I could help other collectors as well as sell some of my duplicate items, so I started my site to help others identify their cast iron. Questions & answers can be posted on the site; people can buy & sell & trade." (Stahl's Web site can be found at http://griswold.auctiondesk.net/)

Everyone I talked to cautions buyers (particularly those new to the kitchen-collecting field, and those new to cyber auctions) about the large amount of misinformation lying in wait. Whether it's just ignorance on the part of the seller, or malicious intent to defraud, it's dangerous for collectors and collecting. Fortunately, eBay offers many protections for buyers and sellers. Collector Joel Schiff, who has collected cast iron cookware for decades, uses eBay and finds things. He says he always asks questions before bidding: "If there's something wrong with cast iron, it's usually discoverable through questioning, even if the seller doesn't know anything about iron. If it's cracked or warped, or missing a part you know should be there, it's fairly obvious ... or you can tell the seller how to look for it." Beginning collectors have to work harder to find out which questions should be asked.

"As far as selling on and buying from Internet auctions goes, the biggest complaint from dealers and private collectors is 'poor descriptions and inaccurate information,'" says Jack Santoro, founder of The Old Appliance Club (www.theoldapplianceclub.com). "What always happens after bad buys is we get a tremendous amount of e-mail asking for parts or help. The cold shower comes when some of those people find out they won't be able to resurrect the appliance or the cost is just too prohibitive."

Collector/dealer Carol Bohn (editor of the KOOKs newsletter, and author of a new book on nutmeg graters, both listed in the Bibliography) has always had very unusual kitchen tools for sale, especially those with moving parts, cranks, and gears. She says, "the Internet has had a big effect on my business. There used to be a big difference in prices between the West coast and the East coast, and areas in between. Now, collectors from out West don't have to take time off work or buy airline tickets, and they can check out their field daily, if they want, on eBay or other sites. For me, there's more international selling and buying." Mary Berube, Mrs. B's Antiques (www.tias.com/stores/mrsb/), says "here in New England, our rule of thumb has long been to price items at less than book so that dealers from other parts of the country can buy and make a profit. Now many dealers are selling most of their best things on eBay and only putting in the shops what is left, and the buyers stay home and buy on the computer."

Collectors/dealers Jackie and Curtis Carter, who like fruit jars, churns, and other things, comment: "The more common pieces are abundant in flea markets and antique stores, but generally overpriced. We like a bargain, and eBay is our way of getting that bargain because we determine what price we are willing to pay." Jackie adds, "We also sell on eBay because it is a way to have many people see an item at low cost to us (no rent for booth space, no maintenance, no utilities, no advertising), and the turnover rate for items is much faster than a mall booth. Some items bring more than we expect, some less, but that is the thrill of the auction!"

Asked about the availability of once common things, Carol Bohn says it may seem obvious, but we have to keep in mind that there are "no more new things from the Industrial Revolution being made! It's over!" So where we are in the collecting cycle now may mean that common things aren't selling, and people are still seeking rarities, but when the natural cycle rolls on, Bohn believes people will once again be buying – finally as rarities – things shunned now, because there just won't be many left to sell. As she said, "In about 1995 there were as many Dover or Taplin eggbeaters as you could possibly want for $20 or so. Now [2002] it's hard to find a cast iron eggbeater at all."

Cycling on for another **10 or 20 years,** we'll see eggbeaters or graters or molds made in the 1970s beginning to become more desirable and costly. So don't not buy something because it's common, cheap, or only 30 years old, if you're in it for the long run! Carol suggests meat tenderizers, vegetable peelers, jar lifters, rubber jar sealers in the original box, and any and all aluminum things (I like egg slicers, juicers, and various cast pieces) as good categories for beginners because there are still lots of them. I hope people will consider it worthwhile to collect those nice, sweet, pleasant, homey kitchen tools that aren't rare because there were so many happy users of them. These items aren't expensive because there are so many of them left, and yet are the true skeleton of the kitchen collection.

What **eBay** and other **online auctions** have done so brilliantly is to make it easy for scores of people at a time to "go" to an auction that is filled with lots which are closely tuned to their desires. Do a search for food choppers, and a typical day may turn up 15 or 20 of them in various stages of gavel-to-gavel. There may be no bids at all, ever, for a particular chopper, but the variety is about what you'd expect at a large flea or antique show, and you are still in your chair. Egg grading scales were something I wanted to check out on eBay, and within 20 minutes I saw two scales I'd never seen or heard of before, one from Australia. The 27 or so years I've spent all told just researching for my books could have been compressed into two or three years if the Internet had been available to me back in 1972. And then discoveries of hitherto unknown things would have come much sooner, and grown exponentially! Imagine: This book could have been 2000 pages long, and printed on dictionary paper, with a built-in CD-ROM and, for tired readers, there would have been an exercise video!

Web sites put up by collector organizations or by avid collectors (such as Jens Veerbeck of Germany, who has a wonderful Web site – www.toastermuseum.de or www.toastermuseum.com) actually reveal to new collectors a lot more of what's available in a field that interests them. We can now be part of a huge international community. As people learn from books, fellow collectors, and the Web, prices go way up for the really wonderful things, and way down for the common things. Some of those "common things" weren't known to be common when I did my first book in 1976, but time and attention and collector interest has opened many drawers and cupboards. While I can make no guarantee as to exactly when in 2003, I will be opening a Web site at www.300years ofkitchencollectibles.com, for updates, hopefully for message exchanges, exciting new finds, etc. Since I have never done a site, expect it to be very simple.

Just do a Web search, using a search engine like Google (my favorite by far), and type in a few words to describe what you want information on. Words like old, vintage, iron, collect, plus whatever you seek, such as coffee mills, or cooking tools, and – presto! – up come sites from all over the world, some having nothing to do with what you want, but others yielding a great deal of new information. These sites may be personal, commercial (a collector/dealer), sponsored by a club or an educational institution, or even a "history of" page put up by a company still making items in the category you

seek. Most sites have links to other sites: follow the links – it's more fun than golf! But remember that the Web is a constantly flowing, ebbing, roiling, subsiding ocean of information breaking on shores everywhere, with flotsam and jetsam as well as sunken treasures.

Rare, Not Rare, and So What?

What is "rare"? Rare is whatever the market says is rare. Until a certain number of collectors are involved, and in touch with each other, and until they "play" on the field together for a while (at least a year, but better if three or four years), nobody knows for sure what's rare. Jim Bohn, very involved in this kitchen-collecting hobby, who collects butter stamps and other things, emphasizes that rarity doesn't always translate into value. "Collectors or dealers don't know for sure what's desirable until they see that a high percentage of other collectors want a particular piece. If no one wants it, even if it's very rare, at that point there is very little value."

Rarity is proven over the long haul; so is value. That's part of the cycle, and the equation can change at any time, especially as discoveries are made, and if the right kind of persuasive hype is applied. So don't stop collecting whatever you really like – chances are it'll be rare and valuable at some point further on.

Wouldn't the early 1920s writers on bygones and old kitchen stuff, such as Mary Earle Gould, be surprised (maybe even appalled) at some of the things now avidly collected? "Golly, you mean they are collecting the toasters and graters and frying pans we used in our own kitchens?!?" one can imagine them saying; "My goodness! What's the world coming to?" But then, collectors of the 1850s would have been surprised at what antiquarians were collecting in 1920: "Oh, my, they're collecting wooden bowls and apple parers and mincing knives and things like that old corn gritter my grand-daddy made? How silly! I wonder what they think of as Art?"

Another aspect of rarity and value is directly related to the **international quality of collecting** now. Vast cargo loads of European, Middle Eastern, and Far Eastern antiques imported into the United States for the last 20 years have made it hard for similar antiques that have been in the USA for 75 or 150 years to retain their value. Nobody knows provenance anymore. Some collectors don't care, and some dealers will mislead, trying to keep the value up. Just adding the phrase "may be an early American maple sugar mold" into the description of a carved wooden mold that is actually a recently-imported, recently-carved, and pseudo-aged Chinese rice mold will cost the unwary, sometimes dearly.

If a piece of Eastern European or Scandinavian enamelware is imported by a dealer, and it looks exactly like a piece that's been handed down in a family in Ohio for 85 years, the value of both is the same on the marketplace because it is virtually impossible to tell the difference. Maybe someday provenance will be proved by an inexpensive do-it-yourself DNA test on skin secretions of accumulated fingerprints. Talk about complicated! Carol Bohn will hardly buy graniteware or enamelware now because after years of "stair-stepping value, year by year going up," suddenly the stairs are going down. If an American-made graniteware coffeepot has attained a value of $200 over the years, and a recent import that looks the same is only $50, Bohn says the "American ones will be – and have been – 'priced out of the market.'"

Buying Online – Some Tips for New Collectors

There are several online auction sites (notably eBay, which is by far the largest), involving millions of sales going on at a time. As this book goes to press, well over a thousand million auctions have taken place. Every month over seven million individuals "go" to one or more auctions on eBay—and most of them attend more than once.

Jeff Smith wrote, "I have specific strategies for **buying on eBay,** but most of those are my secrets." I agree. I may be writing this book for you, but I'm not going to give away all my hard-earned techniques for bidding. It's worth watching eBay auctions for a while and taking notes before bidding on things that usually reach high prices. Look at the bidder lists, and look up feedback for not only the seller and the buyer, but also for the under-bidders, until you have a feel for what the various players in the online auction like, end up actually buying, and the level at which they play. If you play chess, or read books on military maneuvers, utilizing such strategies probably wouldn't hurt your own auction game!

Our categories on eBay come under many headings. Go to eBay's index page (http://pages.ebay.com/buy/index.html), which lists the main categories under sections. Under the first heading, Antiques & Art, click on Ceramics, and there's stoneware, redware, yellowware, etc., with pieces including crocks, jugs, molds; click on Folk Art for a few varied items; Furniture has a section for kitchen furniture; Metalware has categories for various applicable metals; and there's just about everything in Primitives. Also under Antiques & Art's heading is Textiles, Toleware, Woodenware, and Antiques-(Post-1900). Further down are Books and Collectibles.

Just to give you an idea of how many sales are current in our categories in just those two latter areas, I'll pick out some and give the number of current auctions, as of October 2001, in parentheses. In Books, there's Cookbooks (13,599 current sales, of which many are new); in Collectibles, there's Housewares & Kitchenware (110,629). Breaking down Housewares & Kitchenware, which will inevitably include rather a lot of new items, you'll see Barware (6,249); Bottles (8,719); Flue Covers (66); Kitchenware (46,170); Metalware (12,795). Breaking it down further, in Kitchenware here are most of the categories: Bakeware (1,597); Bread Boxes (234); Canisters (1,124); Cookie Cutters (1,945); Cookie Jars (3,997); Cookware (2,388); Egg Cups (374); Graniteware (2,071); Mixing Bowls (518); Molds (1,126); Mugs (1,012); Pie Birds (235); Pepper Shakers (9,926); Small Appliances (2,340); Spice Racks, Jars (514); Spoon Rests (177); Tea Kettles (689); Trivets (590); Utensils (3,387); Other Kitchenware (7,061).

Just to give you an idea of how many seller-described "old" things are included in that count (and remember some sellers may have written "not old" which will also come up with the search) there are 16,089 "old" sales out of the 110,629 "Housewares & Kitchenware" listings; and 1,098 sales of "old" things in "Other Kitchenware."

In contrast, on eHammer, a search for "kitchen" retrieved nothing; a search for "toaster" retrieved one: a novelty salt & pepper in the shape of toaster and bread. (There were two other S&Ps.) I can't find any auction sites dealing heavily in collectible objects and antiques to report on, except eBay.

In a way, with eBay's record of listening to collectors and continually fine-tuning services and access, it just might be true that one world-wide market is the best thing for collectors. Once you are hooked, it's hard to spend less than an hour a day browsing online auctions, sometimes many more.

The best bargains and the most exciting finds are things that other buyers have **overlooked,** or that sellers have either **under-appreciated** or **wrongly-identified.** [If you read only one caption in this book, go now to IV-328.]

Mary Berube, as collector/dealer, says "When I run searches for items I try to think how someone who doesn't know what the item is would describe it." Even simple misspellings could wreck a sale! People putting a lot of items up for online auctions tend to type quickly. Most people tend to spell carelessly on the computer anyway, so you should do searches with obvious misspellings as well as correct ones. For example, yelloware (wrong) as well as yellowware (correct). And try variant spellings: for example egg beaters as well as eggbeaters. And try spelling regional pronunciations or "sounds like" variations. Also remember that English in various countries may have variant spellings; for example: mould or mold. In fact, keep a handy list of commonly misspelled words you encounter in your searches.

Search using all the tools the auction offers. And always check the box that allows a search of both titles and descriptions. On eBay you can search for the word **dog** which will pick up only the whole word dog, or you can search for dog*, and get dog, dogs, doghouse, doggy, dog-eared books, dogwood jewelry and china, and even the Doges' Palace in Venice. **To be a good seller,** you might add to your careful, honest descriptions a short list of singular and plural terms, and variant spellings to catch every buyer.

Like many collectors, Mary Berube prefers "hands-on buying" to online buying – whereas I like both kinds. Serendipitous finds are the true pleasure for me, and they occur at fleas and online auctions. I used to go to many fleas in the hot summer, but I had long conditioned myself to see things with my bare, although nearsighted, eyes. I found that having glasses on, sometimes even a hat (!) would interfere with my eyes-on searching and hands-on buying. I just couldn't see the same way.

In fact, one of the more difficult adjustments you have to make when buying online is the **loss of your sense of scale and context.** I buy mostly photographs so all are near the same size on the monitor. Photographs and other things, especially glasswares, can acquire a compelling, if misleading, inner "glow" just by being on a lit-up monitor. Color is often way off because of a low quality digital photo or scan. A very large item is shrunk to fit the monitor (and that tends to hide flaws), and small items gain impressive stature by being blown up. Keep a ruler and a yardstick near your computer for a reality check on sizes of things described in auctions.

Most of the rules here for bidders are things a good seller must keep in mind too, especially the importance of good descriptions and key words in the title to attract attention, and timing – whether it's how long your auction should be, what day it ends (Thursday nights are supposed to be good), and the ending time. You can't expect to attract lots of buyers at 3 a.m., but if you're a buyer, you might be able to take advantage of inconvenient times.

eBay is a treasure trove and a trash heap at the same time. Online auction bidders need accurate, honest descriptions and good scans because we can't use our senses of touch, smell, and hearing. The graininess of a repro cast iron piece cannot be felt with your fingertips. You can't sniff out the smell of mildew (although some sellers state, at least on eBay, "This comes from a smoke-free home"). The thudding sound given off by tapping a piece of slightly cracked ceramic cannot be heard. I'm sure that you can accommodate these shortcomings with new buying strategies, and perhaps even find some advantages. For me, the focus I gain from the isolation and intimacy of an object on the monitor at 3:00 a.m. often allows me to see details I might have missed at the flea market. But I have to admit – I still like to do it without my glasses!

Other Resources for Study

Tool Collector Groups

Organizations with very broad coverage of kitchen tools include the **EAIA Early American Industries Association** (where I got my start, and through which I found the Keillors whose collection was photographed in part for my first book), and **KOOKS Kollectors of Old Kitchen Stuff.** Both are in the United States. In the Bibliography, see the EAIA's Chronicle listing, and the KOOKS newsletter. Find **Antique & Collectible Tools Inc.'s** newsletter **Fine Tool Journal; Mid-West Tool Collectors Associations'** Gristmill; **Ohio Tool Box Newsletter**; and the **Collectors of Rare and Familiar Tools Society's Tool Shed** there, too. Many such groups exist in other countries and can be found with diligent searching on the Web.

Ephemera

A lot of what I've learned over the years came from ephemera – including trade catalogs (wholesale, manufacturer's, and store), old invoices, bills of sale, sales flyers, trade cards, labels, etc. Vital information is found in ephemera – which means here today, gone tomorrow. It was meant to be discarded after a short life of use, but lucky collectors have rescued lots of fragile paper documentation, and it can still be bought. Join and get publications from one or more of the **Ephemera Societies** listed in the Bibliography close to the back of the book. Other publications are **Paper Pile Quarterly, Paper Collectors' Marketplace (PCM),** and **Paper and Advertising Collectors (PAC).** All are in the Bibliography.

Ephemera Dealers

William Frost **Mobley,** former Ephemera Society president has a site at www.ephemeranet.com/. Another interesting site / is http://apex-ephemera.com which is sponsored by **Antique Paper & Ephemera X-change,** and PCM. It has links to merchants dealing in ephemera. Another excellent resource can be found on search engine Google's site listing 30 resources for ephemera: http://directory.google.com/Top/Shopping/Antiques_and_Collectibles/Ephemera/. An interesting online classified for all kinds of ephemera is found at www.web-pac.com/mall/default.htm.

Other sources are • **Hillcrest Books,** Miles Clark, 961 Deep Draw Rd., Crossville, TN 38555, Web site: www.oldcatalogues.com/ ; • **Harold R. Nestler,** 13 Pennington Ave., Warwick, NJ 07463; • **Kenneth E. Schneringer,** 271 Sabrina Ct., Woodstock, GA 30188, Web site: www.oldcatalogues.com/.

Cookbooks

Four centuries of cookery books reveal forgotten tools and techniques. Find middle-aged cookbooks at thrift and used book stores, library book sales, etc. Many of the online book search addresses listed in the intro to the Bibliography have cookbooks. See the Bibliography for info on **Cookbook Collector's Exchange;** and **Cook Book Collectors Club.** Three tried 'n true recipes for hard-to-find old cookbooks are: **Bonnie Slotnick Cook Books,** Box G27, 332 Bleecker St., NYC, NY 10014, located in Greenwich Village. Phone: 212-989-8962, or email: bonnieslotnickbooks@earthlink.net. The shop is open by appointment or chance, and Bonnie's phenomenal memory stores titles and want lists for years! • Dealer/scholar Jan Longone, Wine & Food Library, 1207 W. Madison St., Ann Arbor, MI 48103. Phone: 1-734-663-4894 • **Cooks Books,** 34 Marine Drive, Rottingdean, Sussex BN2 7HQ, England, is for catalogue sales of antiquarian, second-hand and some new books on food, drink, cookery, and related subjects. It is run by Tessa McKirdy. Phone: 01273 302707; fax: 01273 301651.

Food History Timeline: A marvelous online source of links to over 225 Web sites with information on food & culinary history has been assembled by Lynne Olver of the esteemed Morris County Library, Morristown, N.J. Go to www.gti.net/mocolib1/kid/food1.html. Getting to the information a different way: the sameURL address except mocolib1/kid/food2.html.

Food Trivia & Recipes. For years, the wizard of this fun site has posted answers to questions such as where to get old pans retinned and how to make seven-cheese lasagna. Uncle Phaedrus, Consulting Detective & Finder of Lost Recipes is at: www.hungrybrowser.com/phaedrus/m010302.htm.

Using This Book

The book is divided into seven broad categories, with 23 chapters having to do with food preparation processes and kitchen tasks, and patent and other research. You may be shocked to find that there are only a few pages on pots and pans, but 140+ pages on molds and food shaping. I tried to cover fields for which fewer books have been published.

Throughout the book, the common or preferred name for an item is given first. If there are alternative terms I have written either "also called a ___", or "or" followed by the term. Most of the objects were found in or used in America, but as the market grows more international, and in recognition of the fact that many hundreds of thousands of objects were imported or carried by immigrants to the United States in the last 300 years, I have continued to add "foreign" kitchen tools.

Also throughout the book are boxed paragraphs (called "sidebars") of information that can be applied to a number of objects, some in other chapters. They are in the index, so use the index at the back of the book a lot. We made it as inclusive as possible, but feel free to add index notations of your own.

Most of the value ranges have been replaced by a generalized low-ball figure and a plus (+) sign. Any value could go down, at any time, just as it may go up.

Caveats: In a book of this size, mistakes and typos are inevitable. I hope they are few and trivial, and that you won't base your buying and selling decisions solely on information and values given here. Neither I, nor the publisher, can take responsibility for either loss or fortune. Furthermore, I have listed many sources for more information, and put special notices in by collectors who have contributed a lot of time and effort to this book. These inclusions do not constitute endorsements or guarantees. Web addresses and emails change.

PREPARING

——— I. CORE, CUT, CHOP, PARE, & PIT ———

The two fundamental processes that underlie the selection of most of the implements and gadgets in this chapter are: (1) Removal of inedible or undesirable portions of the food (pits, stones, stems, rinds, and skins in the case of fruit and vegetables; bones, gristle, skin, and offal, in the case of animals, fish, or fowl); and (2) Division of the edible portions into smaller pieces for various purposes.

Some of the most popular and varied kitchen collectibles fall into this preparation category – including apple parers, cherry pitters, chopping knives, and nutmeg graters. The most ancient of cooking tools (as separate from utensils or vessels) would be put here – anything with a cutting edge or a smashing surface. In fact, you will find a surprise three quarters of the way through: A culinary collectible that is 14 million years old! Many objects in this chapter were made by hardware and manufacturing companies; see listings at the end of this chapter.

The fastest growing field of those covered in this chapter is still mechanical nutmeg graters. But while there are several hundreds of apple parers, including improved versions, there are probably under two hundred mechanical **nutmeg graters**, few of which (besides the popular "Edgar") have gone through several variations. In fact, mechanical parers are still being made, but mechanical nutmeg graters enjoyed a very short period of production, mainly in the 1860s and 1870s. Almost everyone today uses tinned ground nutmeg, or has one of the so-called "coffin" types, with the little hinged compartment for a nutmeg and a curved grating surface. While they are still being made, I know of no mechanical one being made today. At the time of this writing, there is not a book on mechanical nutmeg graters, but Carol Bohn – editor of the *KOOKS* and longtime collector/dealer – plans to publish a book (with photos and patent precis) on them in 2003 (see Bibliography). Nutmeg grater prices have risen very high, reflecting scarcity of supply and very avid demand. Since the last edition of this book, at least one grater has been discovered, and more new finds may be out there.

Implements for grinding, crushing, and mashing are among the most basic and ancient. They're a crude form of a knife, in a way; it would take a delicate, fine-edged micro-knife to cut seeds and grains for eating; a mortar and pestle are macro-mashers. Somehow "Lucy," or another very ancient ancestor, had to reduce cereals (or extremely tough roots or animal parts) into something which could be eaten. So two rocks, or a rock and a hard piece of wood, were the first mortars and pestles. Cooking wasn't even necessary – at least not at first. When it was discovered that by mashing grains, and mixing the resulting meal with liquid (water, milk and blood being the choices) before cooking, the food became something a bit more durable and also portable, a giant step forward was taken. Viewed from the start of the 21st century, surrounded as we are by toaster waffles, hotdog buns, and evocative "hunters' grain" sliced breads, it seems an amazing feat of imagination for homo sapiens [perhaps even homo erectus] to have thought up the mortar and pestle.

For many collectors, **nutcrackers** are the most appealing subgroup of kitchen collectibles in the hit or mash category. They can be viewed as refined mortars, or miniature precision clubs. Fortunately a book on nutcracker patents exists – James Rollband's *American Nutcrackers*. There is also a club, which emphasizes the old and patented nutcrackers rather than the new, made-for-collecting carved figurals. See Bibliography for info on both.

I'm putting a **Futurewatch** on two categories: Egg slicers & wedgers; and Juicers & lemon squeezers. Both are frequently listed on eBay auctions, and you may be surprised by the variety of mechanical solutions. There is a collectors club for Juicers; the club emphasizes glass & ceramic reamers, but inclues mechanicals.

Apple cider press, cast iron, red, green & black paint, "Americus," pat'd. 1872. .... **$500+**

Apple cider or wine press, cast iron heavy-legged round base, vertical screw & horizontal crank handle, staved body, embossed "M. Amendola & Co.," NYC, NY, c.1870s-80s... **$175+**

Apple corer, hand held, tin, with T handle, marked "H" on each end of handle, about 6"L, American, pat'd. by Melville Hayward Jan. 23, 1917. Don Thornton says a much earlier prototype must exist, but no patent before 1917 is known. An earlier tubular corer was pat'd. in 1884 by Brock. **$18**

Apple corer, tin tubular corer, wooden knob handle; piece inside keeps corer from going all the way through the apple – for making baked apples, "The Gem Apple Corer," pat'd. by James Fallows, Philadelphia, Jan. 2, 1877, & sold for many years.. **$18+**

Apple corer, tin, wood handle, "Boye Needle Co.," Chicago, offices in NYC & San Francisco, pat'd. Nov. 28, 1916. (Boye also made a nutmeg grater, a can opener, and still makes crochet hooks.) .... **$15+**

Apple corer, tin tube with shaped wood handle, broad at top to fit palm, spring-loaded to eject core, "Van-

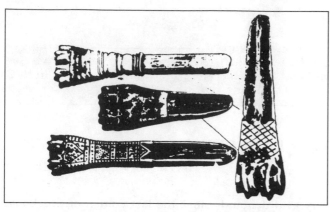

I-1. Apple "scoops" or corers. *Carved sheep metacarpal bones. Decoration style dates back at least to 1200s; these are prob. 18th-19th C. Similar ones were carved of coquilla nut.* **(B-L)** *Fancy one with hearts & "M. C." is 5"L. Courtesy Bob Cahn.* **$45+**

tage," marked "R.M.S.Co., pat. appd for." Early 20th C. .... **$45+**

Apple corer & parer combined, heavy sheet steel, nickel or tin plated. "Real-A-Peel," mfd. by Tarrson Co., Chicago, IL (another marked "Grayline Housewares, Inc." Elgin, IL), 5"L, pat'd. May 4, 1937. .... **$10+**

Apple corer & parer combined, tin & wood, hand held, non-mechanical, 2 parts – the corer fits into handle of a broad blade parer, "Dandy," American, marked "Pat'd. 1913," but doesn't match up with any known patent. .... **$12+**

Apple corer & parer/slicer combined, stamped steel, wide paring blade at one end with adjustable slice, corer has one serrated edge, marked "Jaffa's Patent No. 280,437. Price 2/8 post paid. Torquay." 9"L, English, prob. c.1930 .... **$25**

Apple corer & quarterer, best to use with already sliced apples as it is rather flimsy, very narrow outer ring of tin to hold 4 tin segmenting blades which spoke out from a circular corer, 2 vertical shanks for crosswise turned-wood handle, American, 5-3/4"H x 4-1/2" diam., last quarter 19th C. Looks very like one on right in picture below. .... **$50+**

I-2. Apple corers & dividers, *or* **quarterers.** *Pieced tin, 19th C.* **(L)** *4-3/4"H, for up to 5" apple. Collection of Meryle Evans.* **(R)** *Wood handle. 5-1/2"H x 4" diam. Ex-Keillor Collection.* **$50+**

I-3. Apple cutter or slicer. *Cast iron, steel, wood. Marked only "PATENTED" on quadrant wheel, but probably pat'd. by Daniel Davis, 2nd, March 13, 1834. 7" x 13", 19th C. The one in Thornton's book (8-2) has a fan of oblong cutting blades. Ex-Keillor Collection. That one and this are the only two known.* **$650-$750**

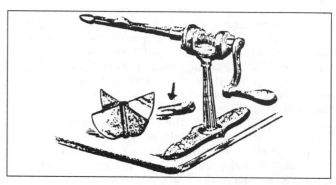

I-4. Apple corer. *"Alcott's," pat'd. by A. N. Alcott, Gowanda, NY, pat'd. Feb. 23, 1858. Converts to parer by slipping prongs (arrow) over coring shaft. Note quartering accessory. This corer was advertised, but so far none have surfaced. If found:* **$400+**

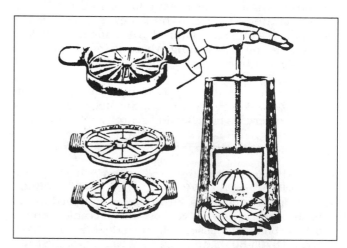

I-5. Apple corers & segmenters *or* **dividers.** **(T-L)** *Steel, 1-1/2"H x 4-1/2" diam. 14 or 18 segments. For potatoes, too; c.1905.* **(L) Rollman** *Mfg. Co., Mt. Joy, PA, for 8ths or 12ths. Tinned cast iron. c.1901.* **(R) "Westerman's,"** *with coring attachment; c.1908. Left:* **$15-$30;** **(R) $400+**

I-6. Apple corer & slicer, or **segmenter. "Climax,"** *D. H. Goodell Mfr. 10"H x 7"W. Pat'd. Feb. 16, 1869, by C. D. Read, Lowell, MA. 1870 ad.* **$400+**

Apple corer & segmenter, tin with wooden handles, hand held, quarters & cores apple with one push, American, c.1880s. **$25**

Apple corer & segmenter, cast iron frame, screw clamps, plunger presses apple down on sharp tin wheel-like plate with 8 spokes radiating from a small round hole, to make 8 segments and core in one step. The frame of this "Climax" segmenter looks almost identical to a Goodell gadget for making Saratoga potato chips, pat'd. just a few months later, but no maker's mark – probably the one pat'd. by C. D. Read, Lowell, MA, 10"H x 7"W, pat'd. Feb. 16, 1869. .... **$400+**

Apple corer & segmenter, cast iron round frame, 2 rectangular handles, "Rollman," Mt. Joy, PA, 5-1/2" diam., exclusive of frame, c.1880. .... **$20+**

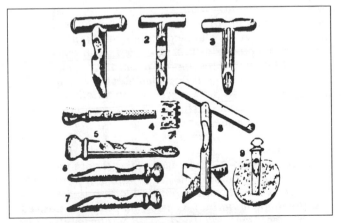

I-7. Apple corers of pieced tin. *"T" handles or wood knobs. [Note: Catalog pictures, 1-7, 9, may be much later than patents.]* **(1)** *Circa 1906.* **(2)** *7"L,* **Geuder, Paeschke & Frey,** *1925.* **(3)** *Circa 1904.* **(4) "Spengler Corer,"** *German silver or heavy tin, perforated "saw-edged" blade, 1910.* **(5)** *1905 Breck catalog.* **(6), (7)** *1920* **Central Stamping,** *6-1/2"L, one has parer.* **(8)** *Pat'd. by S. Jennie* **Renner,** *Petersburg, PA, Mar. 27, 1877. Patent drawing.* **(9) "Gem,"** *Matthai-Ingram, c.1890.* **$10-$45**

❖ NOTES ❖

German Imports – We can never estimate the vast quantities of kitchen & housewares imported from Germany at the end of the 19th C. One wholesaler in NYC, G. M. Thurnauer, made regular buying trips for about 20 years to Germany & Austria, buying wood, aluminum, tin, & china wares that were sold to retailers all over the country.

• • •

Early Mechanical Parers – The **first** widely-known apple parer, wood with a small blade and prong of iron or steel, was pat'd. by Moses Coates, Chester County, PA, Feb. 14, 1803, and presented in a drawing in Anthony Willich's *Domestic Encyclopedia,* (1803-04 Philadelphia). Willich's purpose was to present the latest knowledge about raw materials, methods, machinery, and inventions that might be applicable to "rural and domestic economy." People have reported finding obviously one-of-a-kind, handmade parers very like Coates,' so it is obvious that Willich's rural readers built their own from the drawing and specifications. Dr. Willich himself wrote about the parer that "on account of its simplicity, and the expedition with which it works, will no doubt come into general use. ... The Editor has tried the experiment with the machine, and found it to pare apples with great rapidity." The **second** parer patented was Bostonian W. Badger's "Machine for paring, quartering, and coring apples," on Feb. 10, 1809. Between 1809 and 1838 there were actually five inventors granted unnumbered patents (Badger, Cruttenden, Mosher, Pratt, & Hatcher). It is curious, therefore that the editor of *The Journal of the Franklin Institute,* for Apr. 1838, took notice of Robert W. Mitchell's "Machine for Paring, Coring, & Dividing Apples," pat'd. Apr. 13, 1838, and said it was the fourth, without ever mentioning the third. Mitchell lived in Martin's Mill (Springfield), Richland County, OH. The editor wrote "This, we believe, is the **fourth** [patent #686] obtained for the purpose; ... the apple is to be placed on a fork at the end of a shaft, or mandrel, turned by a crank, whilst the paring knife, furnished with a guard, is held in the right hand, and passed from end to end over the apple; this is then pushed towards the shaft which is furnished with knives that cut it into quarters; a centre, tubular knife removing the core." Obtained earlier, & unnumbered, but nevertheless counted by the same editor as the sixth was a "Machine for Peeling apples and Peaches" pat'd. Feb. 3, 1836, by J. W. Hatcher [Hatch in Gazette Index] of Bedford County, VA. The editor said "This ... is the **sixth** peeling machine that has been patented, and we do not think it any improvement upon the first, which was that of Moses Coates, obtained in 1803. The [Hatcher] has a spindle, with a fork to receive the apple, a second spindle with an endless screw, a cog wheel, pinion, whirl & band, & other appendages for moving the knife; the apparatus for moving the knife the only part claimed." (Ibid.). According to the late Thomas Wiggins, who was one of the pre-eminent apple parer collectors in the country, the Sargent & Foster of 1853 was the first mass-produced iron parer "readily available" to people at mid century who wanted to buy a mechanical parer, with replaceable parts.

I-8. Apple parers from Marion Levy Collection. *The late great Marion Levy let me reprint his lengthy 1979 article, "There's Fascination in Apple Parers" (The Antique Trader), in the 2nd edition. With so little room here, I can only hint at why all apple parer collectors pay him tribute. These seven pictures (and more) illustrated his historical & mechanical overview of homemade and manufactured types. "The first thing I did," he wrote, "was classify the parers into homemade or manufactured. If I had been interested in variety rather than evolution I most certainly would have concentrated on the former, as each one was distinctive, showing the ingenuity and craftsmanship of its maker. The designs were often taken from a farmer's magazine article, or copied, with embellishment, from one a neighbor had built. But for evolution one has to examine the manufactured product." Most homemade were simple lathe types with a horizontal shaft, and frequently no gear or pulley. Levy wrote that "In the 1850s, ideas of apple parers began to proliferate and they were developed along several rather definitive avenues of approach: turntable, quick return, geared segment, and lathe classes (each with many versions & subdivisions).* **Turntables:** *knife arm travels 360° per cycle.* **Quick return:** *knife pares 180°, lifts off & returns to starting point.* **Geared segment:** *Generally a stationary curved gear rack & a geared fork that is moved in semicircle by a handle (supplanting a crank).* **Lathe:** *spiral-threaded horizontal shaft with crank at one end, fork on other. In some models the apple stays stationary & parer/slicer move toward apple; vice versa for others. Levy said "Because of their simplicity & low cost, they [lathe types] ultimately outsold all" other types of parers.* **(A)** *First pat'd. parer, simple lathe with cranked axle with the fork on one end, and a paring blade attached to a "sweep."* **Moses Coates**, *Downings Field, PA, Feb. 14, 1803.* **(B)** *Homemade iron & wood parer of the* **Coates** *type. c.1810.* **(C)** *Gears or pulleys speeded up rotation. This pulley type, nearly all wood, cored & quartered. Early 1820s, type seen in Indiana & Ohio. pat'd. July 24, 1847, by Jesse* **Bullock**, *Jr., and Sewall* **Benson**, *of NYC. (This one $500+.)* **(D) Sargent & Fotser**, *pat'd. Oct. 4, 1853, by E. L. Pratt, Worcester, MA. Prob. first "practical parer with blade mechanically guided over the apple." Apple turned once per crank cycle. Notable is the spiral on the shaft, which meshes with a large gear, hence another gear, which is partially toothed.* **(E)** *Fork is geared for faster action per cycle; blade arm swivels. Pat'd. 1856 by J. D.* **Seagraves**; *mfd. Larned & Seagraves, Worcester, MA.* **(F)** *First of a* **Lockey & Howland** *turntable series, pat'd. June 17 & Dec. 16, 1856, by J. Keyes, Leominster, MA.* **(G)** *Quick return type of turntable, with the gears covered to protect from apple juice,* **Harbster Bros.** *Co. Foundry, Reading Hardware or Penn Hardware, pat'd. 1868. See Fig. I-15 for a geared segment type. All photos this page by Marion Levy.*

I-9. SOME RARE APPLE PARERS, by John Lambert. *Perhaps no other kitchen collectible has such a wide and fascinating application of mechanical principles as does the apple parer. With the advent of cast iron gears c.1850, inventors waged a furious battle to perfect the paring machine. By 1890, after well over 100 patents, home-use parers faded in popularity; most new designs were for larger commercial models. What had occupied talented inventors for over 40 years died a quiet death. The parers – arranged by age to show evolution – on these three pages are rare; most are patented.* **(A)** *Others of this gallows-like parer exist, suggesting commercial production. The 12"H post is threaded into base; crosspiece holding blade arm lifts off easily for cleaning. "**J. S.**" stamped on base front. c.1830. Pieces at left are the screw clamp.* **(B)** *A steel spiral track activates a sliding bar under a 13-1/2" wood wheel. As it turns, bar slides 2" & pulls blade across apple. At end of 1 turn, crank handle contacts lever that transfers movement through 3 different rods to push off apple. Blade snaps back as roller falls off end of track. Very early (1840s) try for full automatism.* **(C)** *Early cast iron parer-blade still hand-held, 9"H, gear teeth are round pegs. "**J. L. Havens** Cin. Oh." c.1850. This is a made-do from parts from a Havens' "Nonpareil" parer, c.1855-1870s.* **(D)** *"**E .L. Pratt Patent**" stamped in base. First mass-produced metal parer, Sargent & Foster. Commoner model has 4 round openings in gear instead of 5 spokes. 10" x 4-1/2" base. pat'd. Oct. 4, 1853.* **(E)** *"**Yankee** Apple Paring & Slicing Machine," D. F. Randall, Chicopee, MA. Pat'd. Dec. 1855. Some (without decoratively stenciled box) marked "M.S. Ault New Haven, Conn." Pared with hand-guided knife. When a latch is flipped, apple pivots 90° for slicing by whirling blades, as user turned apple with crank on small gear. Slivers drop through box into pail.* **(F)** *"**Maxam's** Patent Automatic Scroll Wheel Apple Parer. Maxam & Smith Shelburne Falls, Mass. Apr. 10, 1855." Blade is advanced across apple as follower runs on inclined spiral ridge. Blade snaps back after 3 full cranks. Intact paper label with directions. Base 4-1/2" x 9".* **(G-1 & 2)** *Pat'd. by Charles P. **Carter**, Ware, MA, Aug. 26, 1856. Some have paper labels. Circular corer/ slicer design eliminates need for threading on shaft to advance apple forward. Use of flat spring for tension & curved blade unique. Carter held other parer patents.* **(A)** *$300-$450;* **(B)** *$650-$750;* **(C)** *$100-$150;* **(D)** *$225-$245;* **(E)** *$1,000+;* **(F)** *$325-$375;* **(G-1, -2)** *$250-$285*

I-10. MORE RARE APPLE PARERS, by John Lambert. (H) *"Nonpareil Parer J. L. Havens & Co. Cin., Oh. pat'd. by J. D. Browne, May 6, 1856."* 1st all-metal clamp-on parer. Paring head on end of large coiled spring. 4 crank turns, then blade snaps back to starting position. Only 8-1/4"H, this small parer with clocklike movement pares flawlessly. Rare & choice. **(I)** *"Whittemore, Harrington & Co.'s Patent. Pat. Nov. 11, 1856 and Jan. 13, 1857."* Worcester, MA. 1st with threaded shaft to advance apple. Coring ring atop blade missing here. **(J)** Marked **"S.N. Maxam** Shelburne Falls, Mass. Pat. Apr. 1855," but really pat'd. Jan. 27, 1857, by Clarissa Hubbard for her husband, who was killed by a fall from his horse before he could submit design. 11-1/2"H parer hinged at base. Leaning right, it's cranked to right to pare. Leaning left, crank is reversed while hinged slicing knife is hand-guided toward user to slice thin rings for drying, leaving core on fork. Brittle iron, often found with broken pieces. **(K)** *"J. J. **Parker** Patent Apr. 7, 1857."* 5-1/2" gear with 4 horseshoes. Unique in that it pares apple with 1 turn of crank which hits frame & must be cranked in reverse to start over. Parker from Marietta, OH. **(L)** Pat'd. June 3, 1862, by **Jonathan White**, Antrim, NH. 9"W. Move handle across ornate crescent arc to pare apple in 1 second. Forerunner of the "Lightning," also a half-moon type but smaller. **(M)** *"Selick's Pat. Aug. 21, 1866."* Cast iron frame, poss. early commercial model. Other Selick's are wood. After paring with hand-guided blade, user shoves lever handle forward to core & segment. 8-3/4"H x 15"L. **(N)** *"D. H. Whittemore."* 8-3/4"L. Not uncommon parer with rare breaker attachment. During paring, spiral slices kept from rotating, causing them to break off in 1/4" thick semicircles. Pat'd. Aug 10. 1869; ext'd. Jan. 13, & Feb. 17. 1871. **(O)** *"Turntable,"* mfd by Lockey & How-land, Leominster, MA. pat'd. by Horatio Keyes June 17 & Dec. 16, 1856, & Nov. 22, 1870. 6-1/2"H. Unique push-off: has split frame, so after apple pared, 1/2 frame tilts back (as shown here) to bump apple against other 1/2, loosening it. Before crank reaches 12 o'clock position, small gear moves back in line to avoid crank. Rarest version, with turntable slanted 45° to keep juice & paring off gears. **(H)** $500+; **(I)** $250; **(J)** $500+; **(K)** $600+; **(L)** $350+; **(M)** $650+; **(N)** $400+; **(O)** $250+

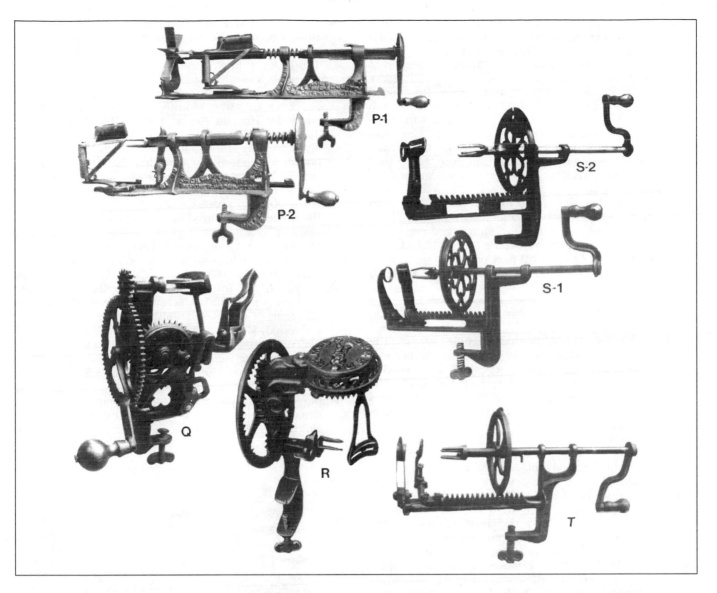

I-11. EVEN MORE RARE APPLE PARERS, by John Lambert. (P-1) *Top:* "**Missouri** *Apple Parer & Cutter. Mfd by G. Bergner. Washington, Mo. Pat. Jan. 9, 1872." 18"L in position shown. After paring, the long shaft was pushed forward with palm of user's hand to core & segment apple. George Bergner was a gunmaker & as far as we know, his parer was the only model made west of the Mississippi. Truly unusual, and prized by collectors.* **(P-2)** *Bottom: The shorter 12"L version is marked "**Missouri Peach** and Apple Parer. Mfd by G. Bergner. Wachington, Mo. Pat. Jan. 9, 1872." On most of these "Washington" is clearly misspelled with a "c." It had the added feature that pushes fruit from forks, but doesn't have a corer/segmenter.* **(Q)** *What collectors used to call "the Ultimate Union" parer, until the Ultimate Lucky Finder, Bob Grossman, found one at Brimfield in its original box (!), with label: "The **Standard**, Mfd. by Landers, Frary & Clark." Marked "Pat. Nov. 11, 1866 Pat. Apr. 6, '80," it's based on a Whittemore pat'd. Nov. 20, 1866. Highly refined device pares apple on forward movement of blade; then on reverse movement, 2nd blade (far right) slices, cores, & breaks apple into pieces for pies or drying.* **(R)** *Marked "**R. & Mc.C Speed**," & known to collectors as "Speedboy." 10-3/4"H. Poss. Canadian, it closely resembles common Reading '78 model (see I-14). Real rarity is gear lid, cast with figural resembling Gothic man with crossed arms.* **(S-1)**. *"**Oriole**," pat'd. by Robt. P. Scott, Cadiz, OH, May 16, 1871. "Scott Mfg. Co. Balt. Pat. Pnd." is mark. 12"L. Instead of rack that leans over, spiral lip has permanent gap allowing crank to be pulled back when aligned with teeth. 2-pronged fork splits old core as new apple forced on.* **(S-2)**. *Quite rare "**Oriole**" pat'd. Aug. 14, 1883. Gate has been added to open & close gap in lip. 3-prong fork.* **(T)** *Some models marked "**Jersey**," prob. because they were sold by L. A. Sayre, Newark, NJ. 12"L. pat'd. June 2, 1885. Spiral lip around main gear "worms" through teeth in rack to advance apple. Rack falls to side, so crank can be pulled back to start position. Longer-lasting than similar lathe types with threaded shafts.* **(P-1) $1,000+; (P-2) $750+; (Q) $700+; (R) $500; (S-1, S-2) $350-$400; (T) $350-$400.** *[Note: Pricing not done by collector to avoid any conflict of interest complaints. Five consultants participated in pricing these parers. All photos on these three pages are courtesy of John Lambert, who can be written (using an SASE) at 117 E. High, Mt. Vernon, OH 43050, or by email: zlambert@yahoo.com.]*

Apple corer & segmenter, tin, with 2 handles, smallest of this class of tools, used by pressing firmly down on handle, called "The Vantage," marked "S. Joseph Co." (probably the importer), & "Made in Germany," late 19th C. .... **$25+**

Apple corer & segmenter, cast aluminum, tin spoked cutters, 8 segments & small round core, big tab handles, Ludwig Mfg. Co., 5-3/4" across with handles, mid 20th C. .... **$5+**

Apple corer & segmenter, cast aluminum, tin spoked cutters, 12 segments, small round core, big cutout squarish ear handles, no marks, American or German (?), mid 20th C. .... **$8+**

Apple parer, also potato & turnip parer, cast iron mounted to wood, rather skeletal with several gears, 4 round cutouts in main gear, simple rod crank has dogleg bend, "Sargent & Foster's Patent," Shelburne Falls, MA, 10-1/2"L, metal part pat'd. Oct. 4, 1853. .... **$150-$175**

❖ NOTES ❖

Bench Parers – One of the oldest apple parers in the country is a bench type – the bench being a rather elegant plank with 3 legs, and a large 11" diam. wooden belt-drive wheel built into the bench. It belongs to The Bennington Museum, VT. Their records say it was made in West Woodstock, VT, in 1785, by Daniel Cox and his sons.

• • •

Apple Butter – "Being at the house of a good old German friend in Pennsylvania, in September last, we noticed upon the table what was called apple butter; and finding it an agreeable article, we inquired into the modus operandi in making it. To make the article according to German law, the host should in the autumn invite his neighbors, particularly the young men and maidens, to make up an apple butter party. Being assembled, let three bushels of fair sweet apples be pared, quartered, and the cores removed. Meanwhile let two barrels of new cider be boiled down to one-half. When this is done, commit the prepared apples to the cider, and henceforth let the boiling go on briskly and systematically. But to accomplish the main design, the party must take turns at stirring the contents without cessation, that they do not become attached to the side of the kettle and be burned. Let this stirring go on till the liquid becomes concrete – in other words, till the amalgamated cider and apples become as thick as hasty pudding – then throw in seasoning of pulverized allspice, when it may be considered as finished, and committed to pots for future use. This is apple butter – and it will keep sweet for very many years. And depend upon it, it is a capital article for the table – very much superior to any thing that comes under the name of apple sauce." Reprinted from "Gospel Banner," in *The Farmers' Cabinet; Devoted to Agriculture, Horticulture and Rural Economy.* Phil.: Vol. III, Aug. 1838 – July 1839.

Apple parer, bench type, wood with forged iron fork, no attached parer on this type: a sort of shaver-like parer would have been separate and held in one hand while the other hand cranked the apple round & round. American; bench is 17"H x 25"L, c.1830s-40s. .... **$300-$400**

Apple parer, cast iron, "Turntable," mfd. by Lockey & Howland, after Keyes himself mfd. it, Leominster, MA, pat'd. by Horatio Keyes, June 17 & Dec. 16, 1856. Depending on model: .... **$100-$250**

Apple parer, cast iron, 4 gear, C. E. Hudson Parer Co., Leominster, MA, Jan. 24, 1882. .... **$65-85**

Apple parer, cast iron, clamps to table, "Keyes' Patent," pat'd. by Horatio Keyes, Leominster, MA, marked June 17, 1856, & Dec. 16, 1856. An earlier version, showing only June date, was mounted to wooden board. The patent for it states that "as the prominences and cavities of the apple pass [a part that Keyes called 'the lip'], ... the cutter will be moved in a corresponding inverse manner ... and consequently the apple will be pared in a perfect manner." .... **$90-$110**

Apple parer, cast iron, commercial size, "Rival #2 96" (#2, model 96), Boutell Mfg. Co., Rochester, NY, pat'd. June 25, 1889. .... **$300-$350**

Apple parer, cast iron, cutout on gear slightly different from earlier Turntable, screw clamp nut also slightly different, "Goodell Turntable '98, No. 41," Goodell Co., pat'd. May 24, 1898. .... **$55-$75**

Apple parer, cast iron, has big ax head or keystone-like logo on gear wheel, "Keen Kutter," mfd. by E. C. Simmons Hardware Co., St. Louis, MO, pat'd. May 24, 1898. .... **$95-$130**

Apple & peach parer, cast iron, heart design gear wheel, 8 gears, Rotary Knife, "Sinclair Scott Co.," Baltimore, MD, c.1880s. .... **$100-$150**

I-12. Apple parers. (L) *Handmade, wood, iron crank, 2-prong fork. Clamps like bench-vise to table; pulley fitted with leather or cording belt. 18"H x 3-1/2" x 11", early 19th C. Ex-Keillor Collection. Top* **(R)** *Handmade, light-colored wood, perhaps maple, possibly made by experienced cabinet-maker, 2-prong forged iron fork. 6"H x 9-1/4"L. Meryle Evans Collection.* **(B)** *Straddle type, meant to be sat upon. PA German, wood painted pumpkin & dark green, cast iron gears. Needs handheld blade. 29-1/2"L x 8"W, mid 19th C.* **$250+**

I-13. Apple parer. *Seems homemade, but many examples are known, with some variations in the knife arm. Three sizes, with 6" (like this one), 7" or 8" large gear wheel, red painted wood base – some have breadboard ends. Maine, mid 19th C.* **$350-$425**

Apple parer, cast iron, heart motif wheel, very like 1858 Monroe Brothers' parer, "The Waverly," mfd. by L. A. Sayre, Newark, NJ, frame is 5-1/2"H, gear wheel is 4-3/4" diam., pat'd. Jan. 29, 1884........ **$200-$250**

Apple parer, cast iron, heavy multiple gears, screw clamps to table, "The Union," marked pat'd. Nov. 11, 1866 (date incorrect because in 1866, Nov. 11 wasn't a Tuesday. See chart of "patent Tuesdays" in Chapter XXII). Parer sold since 1864. This is the same as the "Union Apple Paring Machine" m'fd. by the Whittemore Brothers, Worcester, MA, advertised in Aug. 1865, as "patent pending." It too has several large gears, the most interesting one with cutouts in curved rays from center of gear. 1868 ad in American Agriculturist stated "The knife pares going both ways, thus saving time without increasing the speed of the apple. It throws the parings from the machine. It contains a less number of parts than any other machine in the market.".................... **$190-$250**

Apple parer, cast iron, lathe type, angled screw clamp, large gear wheel has teeth on inside which move a small gear, which turns the apple; almost round

I-14. Apple parer. *"Turntable '78," Reading Hardware Co., Reading, PA, pat'd. 1878. Marion Levy said "The gears are protected by an artistically-decorated bronzed cover. Mechanism canted at angle to improve visibility and insure that parings fall into a bucket. Besides a 'push-off' and 'blossom cutter,' it features an anti-reverse pawl to keep it from being cranked backwards."* **$60-$125**

I-15. Apple parer. *Cast iron, geared or ribbed quadrant with lever action, called a "geared segment" type. 23-3/4"L. pat'd. Nov. 2, 1880, by George R. Thompson, Quincy, IL, as improvement on his Aug. 14, 1877, patent. Pares, cores, divides & discharges core in a "single sweep of lever." Mfd. by New England Butt Co., Providence, RI, known mostly for making butt hinges. Rare & desirable.* **$1,000+**

wooden knob to crank. Very clean & modern looking. "Family Bay State," D. H. Goodell Co., based on Whittemore's patent, Antrim, NH (Whittemore's patent Aug. 10, 1869), this one late 19th & early 20th C. An Improved Bay State was made in late 1890s & early 1900s by Goodell. It has 2 of the angled screw clamps to hold the apple out over space instead of the working parts. The "Family" one was supposed to have been a "remodeled, strengthened and otherwise improved" version of the Whittemore Bay State, suitable for "hotels, restaurants, and boarding houses, or any place where any considerable quantity of apples are to be prepared." The "Improved Bay State" was "adapted for packers and evaporators of fruit or in families where an extra strong parer is needed. It is practically the same as the Family ..., except in the matter of durability. The machine is larger and stronger in every way. It has a steel screw and is fastened to the table at both ends,

I-16. Apple parer. *"Machine á peler les fruits," by French inventor Faucherre. He also invented an almond-grating machine. Screw clamps to table. Illustration from Urbain Dubois' La Patisserie d'Aujourd'hui, c.1860s. Dubois said of this picture that it was drawn too large; "in fact, it is a tiny apparatus, occupying little space."* **$125+**

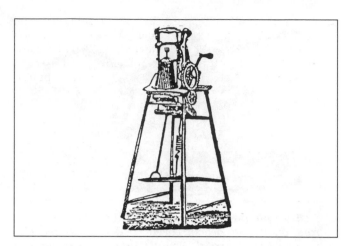

I-17. Apple parer, corer, quarterer or slicer. "Tippecanoe," mfd. by Tippecanoe Apple Paring Machine Co., NYC. Operator stood to use it; apple held upright on 3-prong fork. Looks as if it combines treadle & cranked action. Ad from Hearth & Home, 10/28/1871. We know it was advertised, but don't know if any were sold, and so far none have turned up in collections! **$1000+**

making it very firm. ... This machine has an automatic push off for removing the cores." (Joseph Breck & Sons 1902 catalog copy.) The gear wheel is also proportionally much larger to the small gear; the crank is more curved; the handle is longer. Value range for "Family": .... **$100-$150**

Apple parer, cast iron, mechanical type mounted to board, gear wheel cast with heart design used by the Monroes, in fact, almost duplicates the Monroe Brothers' apple parer, only it's slightly larger, marked "Gold Medal," American, dates on parer from 1850s, but not actually made until late 1870s. .... **$150-$200**

❖ NOTES ❖

"The pies made of the **Tomatus** are excellent. As this is a new desert [sic], those who wish to make them will slice the fruit, and pursue the same process as with a common pie made of apples." *Lancaster Journal*, PA, Sept. 6, 1822.

Apple parer, cast iron, mounted to wood, skeletal simple frame, crank mounted at right angles; one set of gears turns skinny, surgical tool-looking parer, another gear directly turns the apple stuck on the prongs, simple bent rod crank, no knob, pat'd. by J. D. Seagrave, mfd. by Larned & Seagrave, Worcester, MA (?), base is 10"L x 4"W (at its longest, parer is about 8"L), pat'd. June 17, 1856. Seagrave received another patent for a "Machine for paring apples" on Apr. 18, 1854. .... **$150-$200**

Apple parer, cast iron, openwork wheel has heart motif, apparently a real favorite of the Monroe Brothers, (James & Edwin), Fitchburg, MA. Frame is 5-3/4"H, wheel is 3-3/4" diam., frame pat'd. May 6, 1856, Sept. 9, 1858, Aug. 21, 1866; wheel: Sept. 9, 1858. .... **$190-$250**

Apple parer, cast iron, quarter circle gear rack, pares,

cores & segments, "The Thompson," mfd. by New England Butt Co., pat'd. Aug. 14, 1877, by G. Thompson. .... **$800-$1,000**

Apple parer, cast iron, red wooden plank base is original, paper label on plank, "Automatic Apple Parer," mfd. by C. A. Foster, Shelburne Falls, MA, says pat'd. 1853... **$200-$275**

Apple parer, cast iron, S curve heavy wire or thin rod crank with wooden handle, lathe type parer, screw-clamps to table, bar below threaded shaft is straight – almost resembles a plumber's wrench, "Little Star," mfd. by C. E. Hudson Co., Leominster, MA, pat'd. June 9, 1885. A slightly later model of "Little Star" – the #125 – has a completely differently-shaped bar beneath screw that curves & dips down near apple's end. About this "Little Star" was written: "The only parer in which the paring knife always faces the fruit when brought against it." (Joseph Breck & Sons catalog, 1902.) .... **$60-$75**

Apple parer, cast iron, screw clamps to table, "Reading '78," mfd. by Reading Hardware Co., PA, 11"L x 6"W, gear cover embossed with various patents: Mar. 5, 1872, Feb. 17, '74, Oct. 19, '75, Feb. 22, '76, Nov. 14, '76, May 22, 1877, and "78 USA" in center.. **$60-$100**

Apple parer, cast iron, screw clamps, spiral eccentric cam gear underneath, two cutters (this is 2nd model, according to an expert), S. N. Maxam, Shelburne Falls, MA, pat'd. April 10, 1855. Bob Cahn, The Primitive Man, showed this to me at Renninger's Extravaganza, June 1989. It was earmarked for an advanced collector. I didn't ask the price, nor would

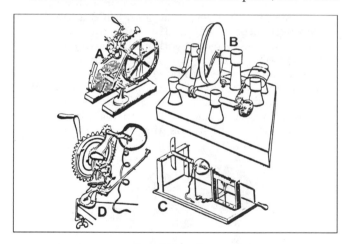

I-18. Apple parer patents. (A) pat'd. Aug. 26, 1856, by Marvin Smith, New Haven, CT. Oscillating fork. None of these has ever turned up, and although this parer was advertised in Scientific American, Jan. 10, 1857, it was probably never made, and might not have worked – although it's the same principle as the "Yankee," shown in group I-9 of rarities. **(B)** Pat'd. July 24, 1847, by Jesse Bullock, Jr., & Sewall Benson, NYC. (See I-8-C, on Marion Levy's page.) Several models of (B) exist in collections. **(C)** Parer, corer & quarterer, pat'd. June 9, 1857, by C. F. Bosworth, Petersham, MA. Probably never made. **(D)** Parer & slicer, with slicing arm for existing Maxam parer. pat'd. Jan. 27, 1857 (but says "1855" on it), by G. H. Hubbard, Shelburne Falls, MA. **(B)** **$800+; (D)** as described: **$650+**

he have told me, because it was sold. I'm guessing price range from the rarity. If I'm way off, I know I'll hear from you. If I'm low, it'll be "Where can I get one for that?" .... **$600-$700+**

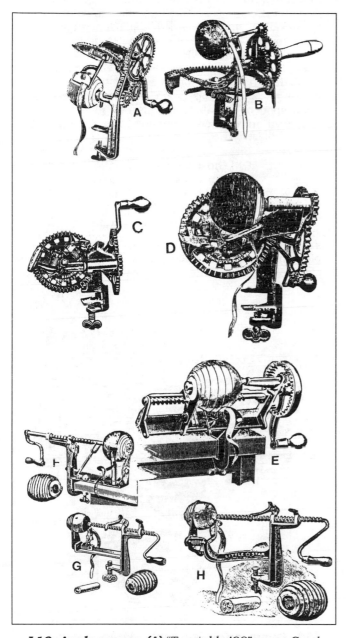

I-19. Apple parers. (A) "Turntable '98" parer, Goodell & Co., Antrim, NH. Shown with throw-off or push-off attachment. *(B)* "Lightning" apple parer, very similar to the Lightning peach parer. A Goodell parer, this one embossed "patented" on one spoke. Others have dates of Oct. 6, 1863, & Aug. 23, 1864. *(C)* C. E. Hudson, Leominster, MA. Advertised as a "throw-off" parer. *(D)* "Rocking Table" parer, C. E. Hudson, pat'd. Jan. 24, 1882, & Feb. 9, 1892. *(E)* Family size "Bay State," mfd. by Goodell Co., based on Whittemore patent of 1869. Ad from 1906. *(F)* "White Mountain," made for 90+ years by Goodell. *(G)* "Daisy," Hudson Parer Co., 1931 ad. *(H)* "Little Star" parer, slicer, corer, C. E. Hudson, redesign of June 7, 1885 patent. *(A) $55-$75; (B) $150-$200; (C) $125-$200; (D) $70-$95; (E) $100-$140; (F) $35-$65; (G) $45-$70; (H) $55-$75*

Apple parer, cast iron, screw clamps to table, unusual starfish-like spokes to gear wheel, "Hudson's Improved," mfd. by F. W. Hudson Parer Co., Leominster, MA, 7" to bottom of clamp frame, pat'd. Dec. 2, 1862. Yet another "Improved" was granted a patent on Mar. 5, 1872 to F. W. Hudson. .... **$150-$190**

Apple parer, cast iron, screw clamps to table, very large toothed gear with six 3-lobe heart cutouts, two small gears, claimed to pare the whole apple with one & a half turns of the crank, at which point you took one apple off & put another on, then turned again one & a half times, pat'd. by S. S. Hersey (his name should be cast on frame below date), Farmington, ME, pat'd. June 18, 1861. (Another patent, Aug. 30, 1864.) This was sold by Dover Stamping Co., Boston, MA, in their 1869 catalog. .... **$250-$350**

Apple parer, cast iron, turntable, screw clamps, "The Centennial," Reading Hardware Co., pat'd. by W. A. C. Oakes, Reading, PA, pat'd. Dec. 10, 1872, July 22, 1873. .... **$150-$195**

Apple parer, cast iron, turntable type, nice round knob to crank, gear wheel very open casting with four contiguous circles, screw clamps to table, "The Domestic," Landers, Frary & Clark, pat'd. by A. Turnbull & R. L. Webb, New Britain, CT, pat'd. June 10, 1873. .... **$190-$250**

Apple parer, cast iron, vertical turntable, screw clamps, round wood knob, "Transit," Hunt Mfg. Co., Antrim, NH, 19th C. .... **$250-$375**

Apple parer, cast iron, very high legs, Tippecanoe Apple Paring Machine Co., NYC, NY, c.1870s. None have turned up, but if one does, it'll be priced appropriately! .... **$1,000+**

Apple parer, cast iron, with four spoke gear wheel, one of which is elongated past rim to form handle, screw clamps to table – fancy thumbscrew, intriguing spring steel wire that curls around & has knife on end, "Non Pareil," mfd. by J. L. Haven & Co., Cincinnati, OH, pat'd. May 6, 1856. .... **$450-$550**

Apple parer, cast iron, concave gear wheel with very abstract casting pattern, screw clamps to table, activated by small gear, has push-off, "Rocking Table," C. E. Hudson Parer Co., Leominster, MA, 7-1/2"H x 8"W, pat'd. Jan. 24, 1882. .... **$50-$75**

Apple parer, cast iron with wooden handle, fixed arc, semicircular gear rack, "The New Lightning," mfd. by D. H. Goodell Co., Antrim, 7" diam. of half-circle gear, pat'd. Oct. 6, 1863, & Aug. 23, 1864, by E. L. Pratt of Boston. Great looking but not all that uncommon once you start focusing on the gear. An *American Agriculturalist* ad, Aug. 1875, states: "This machine drops parings clear of machinery, does better work than any other machine, does double the amount ... loosens the apple on the fork by the neatest arrangement ever yet invented." **$155**

❖ NOTES ❖

Whittemore's Patent – Excerpts from the "Decisions of the Commissioner of Patent" in 1871, shed some interesting light on Whittemore's application to extend his Feb. 17, 1857, apple parer patent. The examiners-in-chief reported that "No question is made of the novelty and utility of the invention." But, they add, although the application papers were incompetently and carelessly filled out, by his attorney, his application was granted. Part of his affidavit charged $1,000 as his "share of loss of Whittemore, H. & Co." The examiners say that "... all we can learn of this company is that the applicant put his patents into it as his share of the stock, and the company failed after having expended $15,000. His patents were sold with the rest of their assets, and were bought back by him, and he charges the purchase money. It does not appear that he ever disbursed a dollar of his own money on account of the company in any other way. ... The sworn statement narrates several transactions, however, from which it may be fairly and safely inferred that the invention was really worth a large sum, perhaps $50,000 or more. On one of those transactions the applicant endeavors, in fact, to form some estimate for the purpose. The right of the patent before us, and a previous patent on the same machine, were once sold for the State of New York for $1,500 per year. Both patents had then over eleven years to run, and at that rate were worth $16,500. The applicant estimates that the use of the patent for New York was worth one-tenth as much as that for all the other States, and that the whole was therefore worth at least $150,000, and this patent worth half that sum. The former patent has been already extended, and on that occasion the applicant placed the same comparative estimate on the two patents. His estimate may therefore be considered a fair one on that point." See patent research chapters at end of book.

• • •

Other parer patents granted in 1857, which may or may not represent actual production parers, are: Machine for paring apples, J. O. M. Ingersoll, Ithaca, NY, Jan. 20, 1857; Apple paring & slicing machine, G. H. Hubbard, Shelburne Falls, MA, Jan. 27, 1857; Machine for paring apples, D. H. Whittemore, Worcester, MA, Feb. 17, 1857 – this was for a board-mounted lathe type; Machine for paring apples, B. F. Joslyn, Worcester, MA, Mar. 17, 1857; Machine for paring, coring & quartering apples, C. F. Bosworth, Petersham, MA, June 9, 1857; Machine for paring apples, J. J. Parker, Marietta, OH, Apr. 7, 1857 – this was for a beautiful, rare "return" type, now worth $500+; Apple paring & slicing machine, R. W. Thickins, Brasher Iron Works, NY, July 28, 1857; it was made, in quantities unknown. Only one Thickins is known to exist as of 2002, and if you found one, it'd be worth at least $1,000+.

Apple parer, mostly wood, painted red, oblong wood base meant to be clamped (with a separate clamp) to a table edge, simple cast iron wheel, steel prong fork, steel cutting blade on parer. Looks homemade, but mass-produced in Maine, 7"H x 13"L x 6-3/4"W, mid 19th C, maybe a bit earlier. I've been told they came with 3 sizes of wheels: 6", 7", and 8" diam. This one has 6" diam. wheel. Perhaps the company who made them had a pile of assorted wheels they'd used before to make something else, so they just fit whichever one came to hand. .... **$195-$255**

Apple parer, strap-to-leg type, hand carved wood, forged iron fork, remnants of leather strap, American, 1820s to 1840s. .... **$100-$125**

Apple parer, straddle type (put it on a bench, then sit on its long board base while operating it), mostly wood, painted black, white & old orangey red in geometric design, 2 thick chunky iron gears, wood crank, Amer-

ican, prob. PA- German heritage, 29"L, early to mid 19th C. I bought this treasure at the Keillor Family Collection auction in the mid-'70s. Much, but by no means all, of that fabulous collection formed the nucleus of my first book. (See I-12). .... **$300-$375**

Apple parer & corer, cast iron, looks like an oil drilling rig, for bakeries, hotels & dried apple industry. Can be made to pare only, without coring. "Bonanza," mfd. by Goodell Co., Antrim, NH, 15"H x 16"L, pat'd. Mar. 13, 1888, but introduced June 1890. A Bonanza owned by my father, as well as one I saw in the ad, have old weld-repairs to the top "beam" of the frame – perhaps a weak spot, or metal fatigue? Is everyone finding the "Bonanza" in repaired condition?.............. **$195-$325**

Oh! those were joyous times,
The times of which we've read,
Of good old fashioned pandowdy,
Of rye-and-Indian bread.
Knickerbocker magazine June 1847

Apple parer, corer & slicer, cast iron frame, screw clamps to table, lathe action, rather like the "Little

I-20. Commercial-size apple parers for hotels, etc. All Goodell Co., Antrim, NH. (A) "Bonanza Parer & Corer." Called a "successful three-turn machine" by maker. Cast iron, mounted to board or worktable. 15"H x 17-1/2"L. Pat'd. Nov. 16, 1886 & Mar. 13, 1888 but not, I believe, introduced until 1890. A drawing used for the "Improved '98" in c.1906-1930s catalogs shows dates Nov. 24, 1886 & March 1881, but these are engraving mistakes. The '98 is described as being 21"H x 17"L. (B) "Eureka," hand or power. Pat'd. Aug. 4, 1874 & Apr. 27 & Nov. 16, 1886, sharing a patent with "Bonanza." "It has a record of 80 bushels a day by hand." Has 3 forks, so user can continuously load. (C) "Dandy," pat'd. Nov. 16, 1886 & Mar. 13 & May 8, 1888. Crank 3 times to pare, core & slice one apple. (A) $250+; (B) $550-$650; (C) $400-$500

Star," except that instead of having separate short foot above the screw clamp, this one uses cross bar of main frame, "Daisy," mfd. by Hudson Parer Co., Leominster, MA, prob. based on July 11, 1882 patent for a lathe-type parer. This was made & sold well into the 20th C. Advertisements I have for the Daisy, from various 1931 *American Cookery* magazines, state: "Cores and Slices at the same time. Three cuts and it's ready for pies, apple sauce or canning." The 3 cuts are a separate step done with a paring knife. Other ad says "... will pare, core and slice an apple in one operation – quickly.". **$50-$75**

Apple parer, corer & slicer, extremely simple cast & malleable iron lathe type, screw clamps to table, single gear without teeth that follows (?) horizontal toothed ratchet along bottom of frame, advertising probably exaggerates utility, "Oriole," Scott Mfg. Co., Baltimore, MD, c.1883. .... **$250-$395**

Apple parer, corer & slicer, skeletal cast iron, meant to be hooked up to power source, but could be cranked by hand, 3 spindles with prongs, 4 stanchions to be bolted to surface, between them & beyond is elaborate system of gears & snapping flipping levers & push offs. "Every part of the Eureka is made with an eye to simplicity, durability and strength. All its parts are adjustable, and in case of breakage can be easily and cheaply duplicated. It has a record of 80 bushels a day by hand, and 100 bushels by power. All the operator has to do is to put the apples on the fork and the machine does the rest." (Joseph Breck & Sons catalog, 1902.) You could load 3 apples at a time, but was there ever one made that would pare 3 at a time? "88 Eureka," Goodell Co., Antrim, NH, 18-1/2"H, pat'd. Aug. 4, 1874, April 27 & Nov. 6, 1886. I don't know how this differs from the "86 Eureka," touted as an improvement on the "85 Eureka." I don't know why it's the "88," if the last patent was 1886. .... **$200-$300**

Apple parer, corer, & slicer, skeletal cast iron & steel commercial model, to be bolted to tabletop, 4 high oil rig stanchions or legs at one end, large toothed gear & 5 other small gears (within the legs) turned by crank, horizontal intricate spindle works unsupported at other end, "Dandy," mfd. by Goodell Co., Antrim, NH, 18-1/4" x 19-1/2" x 9-5/8", pat'd. Nov. 16, 1886, Mar. 13 & May 8, 1888. To me it seems almost identical to the "Eureka," mfd. by Goodell Co., Antrim, NH, although that was sold prior to the Dandy patent.. **$300-$600**

Apple parer, corer & spiral slicer, cast iron, nice wooden knobby handle on crank, lathe type, originally D. H. Whittemore patent, the "White Mountain," mfd. by Goodell Co., Antrim, 6-1/2"H x 11"L, pat'd. Apr. 6, 1880, May 3, 1881. This parer, green enameled cast iron with steel shaft & wood handle, continues to be made............................... **$45-$55**

Apple scoops or corers, carved sheep bone, with knuckle as handle grip, mostly plain but for drilled dots and scored hatches, one carved with hearts & initials "M. C.," probably all are English, although poss. American examples around somewhere, about 5" to 6-1/2"L, early to mid 19th C. (Note: an "apple scoop" of coquilla nut, with puzzle ball handle, was auctioned on eBay by an English dealer.) .... **$55+**

Apple segmenter – See: Apple corer & segmenter

Apple slicer, 9 steel blades, black painted cast iron frame, apple pushed across the blades, looks like a strange xylophone & probably could be played, for those of you with a kitchenware orchestra, "Sun," C. M. Heffron, Rochester, NY, pat'd. June 10, 1890...................................... **$350-$425**

Apple slicer, wood & iron, 6 slicing blades. Apple is fitted onto prong mounted to a sliding piece of wood, & is pushed through the gauntlet of slicing blades, seemingly primitive, but mass-produced. American, 42"L, some are marked Jan. 14, 1868. .. **$300-$355**

Asparagus buncher & cutter, wood "L" shaped carrier, steel cutting blade, "Ward's Keen Edge," English, late 1800s. Some of these are showing up on eBay as "bread cutters" but the bread would have to be extremely dense. See also Asparagus bunchers in Chapter V (Measuring). **$95**

Baby food grinder, fine puréer, cast iron clamp-on frame, once painted turquoise, tin grinding drum, American or European, late 19th or early 20th C. .... **$35+**

Bean cutter, cast iron, screw clamps to table, for making French style green beans, feed one bean at a time into a sort of diagonal chute & turn crank, has 3 steel blades, removable so you can sharpen, turned wood handle, cast design of hand at bottom, "Harras No. 37," "Germany 374," 10-1/2"H, early 20th C. .... **$75+**

Bean slicer, 2 beans at a time, cast iron painted pale avocado green, "Rose," Belgian, 8-5/8"L, 20th C........ **$65**

Bean slicer, cast iron, very ornate, japanned dark brown & bronze, beans fed into hopper & pass between 2 rollers to be sliced. Screw clamps to table, American, 6-1/2"H, late 19th C (?). .... **$75+**

Bean slicer, cast iron painted blue, leaf design cast in it, screw clamp, 2 skinny bean-insertion places in back, turn crank & it turns 2 beans against cutting blade, tin cover holds beans in place & keeps them from flying out, no mark, 9"H, early 20th or late 19th C. .... **$65+**

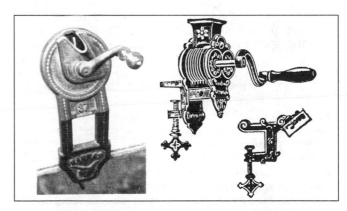

I-21. Bean slicers or stringers. Photo at **(L)** is a "Harras No. 37" bean cutter, made in Germany, cast iron, screw-clamps to table. Feed one bean at a time into chute, turn crank, and make French-style string beans. Removable steel blades. Trademark of a hand embossed on lower casting. 10-1/2"H. Courtesy Dennis Robida, Scotland, CT. **(M)** 6-1/2"H "German bean cutter," yet prob. mfd by Spong, an English firm. Exact same "slicer" in Brigitte ten Kate-von Eicken's German book on kitchenwares (see Bibliography); she writes that it's marked "gesetzltoh geschulzt" (which means patented, or registered). It has no maker's mark, but looks just like one in a Spong trade catalog. **(R)** "German Bean Stringer." Both in c.1906 NYC housewares importer's catalog. **$75+**

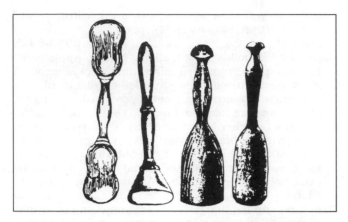

I-22. Beetles, potato pounders or mashers. *Two at right common forms, turned wood, late 19th or early 20th C. Double-headed one much less commonly found. I have found them as large as 24"L, for use in restaurants or boarding houses. Same date range. Fancy turned handle has a white ceramic "porcelain" (probably ironstone) head. It's from 1860s, and looks like a pestle for an ironstone mortar.* **$20-$75**

Bean slicer, cast iron painted blue, "The Eagle Engineering Co. Springfield, Ohio USA," pat'd. Apr. 9, 1918, 14"H. .... **$125+**

Bean slicer, oak case, iron and tin, tin slots where you feed beans in, 4 cutting blades on cutting disc, which is removable for sharpening, lid of case slides off, flywheel is perfectly balanced & it almost hums as you turn crank, no mark, 14-1/4"W, 19th C. .... **$100+**

Bean slicer & pea sheller, cast iron, screw clamps to table, green wood handle (sometimes seen in black), "Vaughn's," Chicago, IL, 12"H, early 20th C...... **$65**

Bean slicer & pea sheller combo, cast iron, interchangeable rollers of iron & rubber, screw clamp, American, 12"H, early 20th C........................... **$50**

Bean stringer & slicer, little blued steel blade, springs, "Bean-X," Orange, NJ, 6-1/2"L, "pat. pend.," c.1890s-1910s. (?). **$35**

Beetle, also called a meat fret or steak pounder, turned wood, all one piece, this one dual-purpose, having a small mushroom-shaped pestle at handle's end, American, 10"L, late 19th C. .... **$25+**

Beetle, or potato masher, handmade, one piece of maple, very dried out so it feels lighter than it should, 10-1/2"H, late 19th C........................... **$25**

Beetle, turned wood, 2 piece, with handle (sometimes painted black or dark green) that screws into large head with large age or dryness check, American or imported, 9"L, c.1900..................................... **$15+**

Beetle, turned wood, handle has nice patina, head has a few chips on business end, maybe American, unusually long: 23" and probably for a hotel, c.1890s-1910s. .... **$40+**

❖ NOTES ❖

Added value – As a rule, the beetles turned of one piece of wood bring more money than the two piece, as they are usually somewhat older. An exceptionally nice turning, nice wood or grain "figure," patina, or paint on handle of a 2 piece one, however, would add $$ too. Detracting from value would be poor surface, chipping, big dry rot, cracking.

Beetle or cracker roller, turned wood, 2 pieces (head & screw-in handle), narrow rows of ridges on face of head. Perhaps meat tenderer too? German (?), head is 8"L, handle another 5-1/2"L, c.1900............. **$50**

Beetles – See also: Potato masher; also Herb masher

Berry or fruit press, wood platform like an oil drilling rig, tinned iron saucepan-shape berry holder is perforated on bottom, short handle. Levered presser pivots in 2 places, no mark, American, 11-3/4"H x 26-1/2"L, pan about 7-1/4"diam., mid 19th C. Possibly patented rather than one-off piece........ **$100+**

Betel nut cutter, scissor action, iron blade & silver handle, in form of rooster, engraved steel around eyes & design is chiseled in, the betel nut was cut in half then the meat picked out with end of handle, made in India, 7-5/8"L, 19th C. Many of these have been imported in late 1990s. Most are not old; many sold on eBay as "rare nut crackers." Old:............... **$100**

❖ NOTES ❖

Most **betel nut cutters** are cast brass. They look Indian, most of them, but you can be thrown off guard by some simpler ones. Betel nuts are the seeds of a form of pepper plant, and the leaves, nut "and a little lime from burnt sea shells" is chewed by "East Indian natives" from India & Malay.

Boat mill – See: Herb crusher; also Spice grinder

Bread board, carved wood, motto "Speed the Plough" around border, American or English, about 9-1/2" diam., early 1900s. **$60**

Bread board, carved wood, motto "Welcome" around border, American or English, 20th C. **$50**

Bread board & matching knife, carved wood, carbon steel blade for knife, both say "Bread" – around border & on handle, English (?), early 20th C. **$60**

Bread fork, carved wood handle with wheat sheaf on one side & motto "Manners Makyth Man" on other, English (?), 12"L, late 19th C. Bread forks, if that's really what they are, are unusual. .... **$45+**

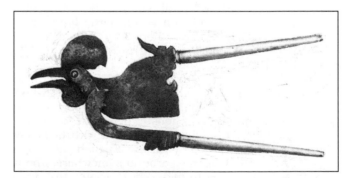

I-23. Betelnut cutter, *often mistaken for a kitchen tool. Rooster, with iron or steel blade & silver handle, 7-5/8"L, from India. Engraved steel around eyes & chiseled design. Most are brass. The nut was cut in half, then the meat picked out with end of handle. From stock of Mona Sawyer, Stamford, CT.* **$100+**

Bread fork, carved wooden handle says "Bread," 3 tine broad silver-plated fork, American?, 19th C. **$45**

❖ NOTES ❖

Bread Board Mottoes include "Give Us This Day Our Daily Bread," "Waste Not Want Not" and "Staff of Life." There are also 19th & early 20th C. bread boards from Germany, with similar mottoes in German. A few are showing up in the U.S.

• • •

Fake alert. For some years, the carved words or mottoes on knives and plates have been faked on old, uncarved knives having plain wooden handles, or on newly made but distressed wooden plates.

• • •

Blanks for Home Carvers – One dealer I talked to said that knife and board blanks were sold in the old days for people to carve themselves. This seems a reasonable assumption, when you see the variations in the carving. The carving technique for the raised block letters is basic, but results are often strikingly different, especially in spacing & size. Mottoes relating to bread abound the world over – ranging from jokes to blessings – so it is possible that this kind of carving is a tradition, at least in some countries. I have never found a document to back up this dealer's assertion, but would appreciate hearing from anyone who knows of a catalog or such, or who knows firsthand, perhaps through a family member, of this practice.

• • •

Knife Rip-offs – I thought the knives were not being reproduced, but saw a few obviously reproduced at fleas as early as 1988. (Also smaller sets for "Butter.") For example, I saw a 19th C. English bread knife, "Sheffield" steel blade, with a recently well-carved handle done in old style. The dealer's label read "Old knife, new carving." I hummed a few bars of "Your Cheatin' Heart" to calm down. You know what happened to the dealer's conscience-salving delineation of age as soon as it was sold. Although the blade was marked "Sheffield," and it was a 19th C. knife, the 1980's carving turns it into at best a new secondhand knife worth $9 to $12. This kind of irresponsible thing drives me crazy. What right do modern carvers have to take an old knife & do new old-style carving on it? The intention is only to fool everyone. "*Oh, what a tangled web we weave, When first we practise to deceive!*" – Sir Walter Scott.

• • •

Knife brand names at the turn of the century include "Comet" by Christy; "Universal" and "Aetna" made by Landers, Frary & Clark; also "Always Sharp"; the Samson "Never Crumb"; and the "Clyde." What intrigues me is that there are no bread knife (or cake knife) patents at all in the *Subject Index to Patents, 1790 to 1873*, and just 10 or 15 years after that they seemed to be a hot item.

Bread grater, heavy tinned sheet iron, slightly curved grating surface with coarse punctured holes fairly close set, wood handle, American, 12"L, early 19th C. These are still useful, and you can really work up an appetite for scraped toast. A hundred years ago, invalids were treated to toast water, made by soaking a burnt piece of toast in water, and straining off the colored water. **$75**

Reproduction Alert

Bread boards turned up in great quantities, all worn as if they'd been run over by a belt sander, bleached out too (wouldn't surprise me if a police pathologist found household bleach in the grain of the wood), I personally wouldn't advise making a big collection of these. A company called Bread Boards, in Landisville, PA, advertised "hand carved" and "beautifully crafted" 12" diam. bread boards for sale to dealers. New Sheffield boards, The Country Cottage Collection, in Elkins Park, PA, sells or sold 12" diam. "handcrafted Breadboards from Sheffield, England. These hand-carved and turned Breadboards are part of an English country tradition dating back to 1840. Carved from durable sycamore wood, known for its rich grain and hue, which mellows with age. Because each is hand-carved, no two are exactly alike." Some new Sheffield boards are carved on the outer rim, one has word "Bread," and the 5th is carved on the center of the board. (Brochure, 1987.)

Bread grater, punctured tin cylinder, fixed & braced handle, coarse grating surface, American, 10"L, late 19th C. **$100**

❖ NOTES ❖

Date Grate: Look for thickness of tin (thicker is older) & irregular, rather than absolutely regular machine punctures. By the mid 1800s punctured tin blanks were available in tinsmiths' supply catalogs, for use in making graters & probably for pie safe door panels. • Dover Stamping Co., for example, in their 1869 catalog, offered what they called "grater blanks," rather coarse, with the puncture holes exactly 1/4" apart, center to center in either direction. These could be ordered in full sheets (not given, but I believe probably 16" x 16"), half sheets and quarter sheets. A quarter sheet, presuming the above measurement, would thus be big enough to make a grater, though square, and thus unusual.

❖ RECIPE ❖

Spinach Fritters – *Boil the spinach until quite tender; drain, press and mince it fine; add half the quantity of grated stale bread, one grate of nutmeg, and a small teaspoon of sugar; add a gill of cream and as many eggs as will make a thick batter, beating the whites separately; pepper and salt to taste. Drop a little at a time in boiling lard. If it does not form fritters, add a little more bread crumbs. Drain and serve immediately or they will fall.*" Ladies' Home Journal, April 1890. A gill in the U.S. is equal to 1/4 liquid pint; in Britain it's a 1/4 Imperial pint (based on metric system), but in British dialect, a half-pint. It is possible that in early 19th century American recipes a half pint was meant. Later recipes which call for a gill require a half cup or 4 ounces.

Bread grater, punctured tin cylinder, the proportions of a large tomato juice can, with 2 appended cylindrical graters, much smaller, fixed midway up on 2 sides, bracket strap handle across top. The large grater has coarsest holes; the other 2 provide medium & fine grating surfaces. Called a "bread grater" in the 1891 *Scammell's Treasure House*, but probably useful for grating other things, too. American, 10"H, late 19th C. **$100**

Bread knife, black wooden handle, carbon steel blade, "Ontario Knife Co.," 13"L, c.1890s-1910s. **$15**

Bread knife, carbon steel, iron loop handle, "Comet," mfd. by Christy, Fremont, OH, 12"L, pat'd. Nov. 12, 1890. .... **$15**

Bread knife, carved wooden handle, says "Bread," carbon steel blade, American, 12-1/2"L, 19th C. **$15**

Bread knife, plain wooden handle, carbon steel blade with truncated tip, "Climax," American, 13-1/4"L, late 19th C. **$15**

Bread knife, steel blade, carved wood handle, blade marked "G. Gill & Sons," Sheffield, England, 11"L, 19th C. **$20**

Bread knife, steel blade, carved wood handle says "Bread," blade has trademark silhouetted twins & "J. A. Henckels Twin Works," Sölingen, German import to NYC, c.1910. .... **$15**

Bread knife, "Want Not" on wood handle, 12"L, 19th C. **$20**

Bread knife, wheat sheaf carved on handle, blade marked "Alexander E. Foulis," English, 19th C (?). **$15**

Bread knife, wheat sheaf carved on handle, carbon steel blade, all very worn, unusually short, only 8"L, 19th C. **$10**

Bread knife, wood & steel, advertises "The Pride of Brooklyn, McGarvey's Home Made Bread," no place, c.1890s-1910s. .... **$35+**

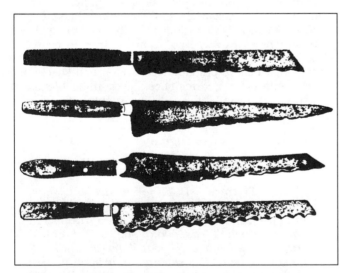

I-24. Bread & cake knives. *Scalloped & beveled cutting edges to carbon steel blades. Scallops closer-set for bread knives. Wood handles. All c.1890s to early 20th C. From top: **(1)** "Climax," 13-1/4"L. **(2)** "Tip-Top," with trademark of boy's head – the "Tip-Top Boy." 15"L. **(3)** "Victoria," American Cutlery Co., 14-3/4"L. **(4)** "Aetna" trade-name, "Universal" trademark, Landers, Frary & Clark, New Britain, CT. 14-1/4"L. Collection of Paul Persoff.* **$15-$25**

Bread knife, wooden handle, carbon steel blade, "Victor," American Cutlery Co., late 19th or early 20th C. **$15**

Bread knife, wooden handle, pointed carbon steel blade, "Tip-Top Boy," boy's head trademark, American, 15"L, late 19th C. **$15**

Bread knife, wood handle, truncated tip to carbon steel blade, "Victoria," American Cutlery Co., 14-3/4"L, late 19th C. **$15**

Bread knife & matching board, wheat carved on knife handle & around board, "Bread Knife" engraved on steel blade, English or American, 9-1/2" diam. board or plate, 19th C. .... **$85+**

Bread knives – See also Cake knife. Some can be used for both, but the basic rule is that the more widely spaced serrations or scallops are on cake knives, the more narrowly spaced ones are on bread knives.

Bread or cake knife, long scalloped carbon tool steel blade, metal handle cast with encircling bands like screw threads, marked "Lightning" & "Prussia," American, 15"L, early 20th C. **$15**

Bread rasp, heavy forged iron, rough chiseled teeth, wood handle. Shaped like mason's concrete trowel; standard bakery equipment, used like bread grater to remove burned crust, American, 9"L, late 18th or early 19th C. **$85**

Bread slicing box, heavily varnished wood, the 2 sides have 12 slots & are attached to cutting board base. Works sort of like a mitre box – the slots guide the bread knife. Simple but efficient. American or English, 5-3/4"H x 13-1/2"L, 19th C. **$125**

Butcher knife, homemade, walnut handle with brass rivets, large heavy steel blade, American, 14"L, c.1890s-1910s. .... **$15-$20**

Butcher knife, handmade brass & wood handle, brass rivets, carbon steel blade, quite heavy, American, 12"L, c.1890s-1910s. Value is in handmadeness! .... **$15+**

Butcher's steel, for sharpening knives, a long slightly tapered steel rod with faintly roughened surface, barely discernable when you run your fingernail along it, turned wooden handle, "Keen Kutter," Simmons Hardware, St. Louis, MO, 20th C. **$7**

Butter cutter, painted & nickeled cast iron, screw clamps to table edge, horizontal platform for large one lb. block of butter, which moves at preset calibrations through the levered wire cutter. It comes through 2 crossed wires which quarters it just a millisecond before it is cut into 4 pats of any thickness. Early ad shows pats falling into basin of ice water, sold by V. Clad & Sons, Phila., early 20th C. .. **$90+**

Butter slicer, cast aluminum rounded-oblong frame, with slicing wires, "Presto," 7-1/4"L. Fits a stick of butter. (Prob. Presto Mfg. Co., Ossining, NY.) **$10**

Butter slicer, cast aluminum oblong frame with tab handles & wire strung back and forth, cast aluminum base. For 1-lb. butter brick or 1/4-lb. sticks. MEDCO #44, NYC, 6-1/2"H x 9"L x 4"W, c.1930s (?). .... **$12+**

Cabbage cutter, also called a slaw board, kraut- or slaw-cutter, or cabbage plane, wood with 2 steel blades, "The Indianapolis Kraut Kutter," Tucker & Dorsey Mfg. Co., Indianapolis, IN, made in different sizes, pat'd. 1905. .... **$55**

Cabbage cutter, gray graniteware, steel blade, "Ideal," c.1900. .... **$95+**

Cabbage cutter, simple wood board with steel blade, very worn, but nice patina, American (?), 34-1/2"L x 12-1/4"W, to fit over large kraut barrel, 19th C.... **$65**

Cabbage cutter, walnut, 3 steel blades, "Disston & Morss" (Morse? Morris?), Philadelphia, PA, 24"L x 9"W, 19th C. This must have a connection with saw makers, Henry Disston & Son, but at this time I can't find info on Morss, Morse, or Morris. **$100**

Cabbage cutter, interesting swinging wood box with lid that passes over blade, describing about 15 degrees of a full circle, cast iron hinge, steel cutting blade, porcelain handle on box lid, cabbage held firmly in box, American or German, 13"H with 17" sweep to box, 19th C. **$200**

Cabbage cutter, walnut, 1 adjustable steel blade, cast iron handle, "Brady," Lancaster, PA, 25"L x 7-3/4"W, pat'd. Mar. 9, 1880, ... **$135**

❖ NOTES ❖

Added value – Homemade cabbage cutters cost more than commercial ones. Look for interesting cutouts for hanging, or interesting treatment of wood, or nice joining of sides of box, or old wrought wing nuts for adjusting blade, etc. If it has too much going for it, *caveat emptor.* Homemade, & big, it might be $225 to $575; late 19th century commercial one is worth much less.

❖ NOTES ❖

Sauerkraut – Machine for Making it. At the house of a German [in Pennsylvania] I saw a peculiar machine used for preparing sauerkraut from cabbage, and since the method of slicing the cabbage is much more efficient than with the ordinary knives used for the purpose, ... I shall here give a short description of it: a tray was made of boards ... about three feet long and seven inches wide and with two-inch sides. In the middle of the bottom of the tray was a large, square opening, extending across the tray and being about four inches wide. Across this were placed three knives parallel to one another. The width of each knife was one and a half inches. Their edges were set aslant, like the blade in a [carpenter's] plane, and in such a way that the edge of one slightly overlapped the back of the other. The cabbage was grated by these knives. On the tray was placed a moveable, bottomless box about the same width as the tray (10 in. long and 6 in. deep). ... The tray was placed over a barrel or other suitable receptacle so that the knives were over the opening of the barrel. When the cabbage was placed in the box and pushed back and forth over the knives the shredded cabbage fell into the barrel below. It is a very quick way to shred cabbage. ... This machine can be called a cabbage plane...." Peter Kalm, *Peter Kalm's Travels in North America.* English version of the 1750 book by Kalm, a botanist who worked with Linnaeus.

Cake knife, cast iron handle, carbon steel blade, "Christy," Fremont, OH, 14-1/4"L, pat'd. 1889, 1891. .... **$10**

Cake knife, corrugated cast iron handle, carbon steel blade, "Comet" mfd. by Christy, Fremont, OH, 14-1/4"L, 1890s to 1910. .... **$10**

❖ RECIPES ❖

Bubble and Squeak *– Slice of cold boiled beef; chopped potatoes; chopped up cabbage; both previously boiled; pepper, salt and a little butter; set it aside to keep hot; lightly fry some slices of cold boiled beef; put them in a hot dish with alternate layers of the vegetables, piling high in the middle."* Scammel's Treasure House, 1891.

Sour-Krout *– Take a large, strong wooden vessel, or cask resembling a salt beef cask, and capable of holding as much as is sufficient for the winter's consumption of a family; gradually break down or chop the cabbages in very small pieces; begin with one or two cabbages at the bottom of the cask; add others at intervals; press them by means of a wooden spade against the side of the cask, until it is full; then place a heavy weight upon the top of it, and allow it to stand near a warm place for from 4 to 5 days; then place the cask in a cool situation; keep it always covered up; strew anise seeds among the layers of the cabbages during its preparation."* Henry Scammel, compiler, Treasure House, 1891.

Cake knife, clear glass, in original box, "Vitex," American, c.1940s. • Glass cake & fruit knives were made in cooperation with war effort metal drives & war materials conservation. Have to be in perfect condition. Crossover interest from Depression Glass collectors. (The **Glass Knife Collector's Club** contact is Wilbur Peterson, 711 Kelly Dr., Lebanon, TN 37087.) ....,................................ **$20+**

Cake knife, clear glass, rather chunky handle, slightly serrated cutting edge, "Cryst-O-Lite," 8-1/2"L, 1930s-40s. Clear glass is not as desirable, by a long shot, as colored. And cobalt blue would be the most valuable of all. .... **$25+**

Cake knife, green glass, with flower & leaf design on handle, in its original box, "DUR-X," 9"L, 1938 (design patent #112,059). Also used for fruit, as it could not be stained by acids. **$35**

Carving fork, for meat, steel with bone handle, 2 tined, American (?), mid to late 19th C. Low value for lone pieces, without matching carving knife & steel. Well-worked handle, carved as a one of a kind piece, it has definite collector value on its own. This one does not. .... **$5+**

Carving set, carbon steel, knife, fork & sharpening steel, "Keen Kutter," by Simmons Hardware. Krossover Keen Kutterers. .... **$75+**

Cheese grater, 2 turned wood parts, with punctured tin grating surface in between. The shorter knobby part has short prongs on which to fix the piece of hard cheese (this wouldn't work for soft cheese). After putting the 2 parts together you grate by working your wrists back & forth, like wringing out clothes. Attractive pale wood. American or European, 6-1/2"L, 19th C, or early 20th. .... **$65+**

Cheese scoop, hand-machined & cut steel, ivory handle, steel shaft decorated with 4 facets surrounded by zigzags & a sort of rope or scallop design, spade-shaped concave spoon-blade has very sharp cutting edge, thumb screw holds the pusher or follower on its track inside the scoop, can be turned to lift up pusher for cleaning, English, 10-1/16"L, scoop is 1-5/8"L x 1-1/4"W, c.1840s. Not all that rare, I've seen several, but the work is individually done. Cast iron, necessarily thicker & less refined looking, obviated all the handwork needed to make such tools as this scoop. **$95**

Cheese slicer, aluminum, very musical if you pluck the wires, "Cut-Rite, No. 300" mfd. by Wagner Ware, Sidney, OH, 7"L x 3-1/8"W, "patent pending," 20th C. **$25**

Cheese slicer, plated wire bent in sort of hacksaw shape, including loop handle, thin steel wire stretched between frame is what slices the cheese, American, 6-5/8"L, c.1920 to 1949. See also: Egg slicers. **$5**

Cherry pitter or stoner, almost all wood, iron hinges. Stones 20 cherries at a time. After you load the separate hinged cherry carrier tray, you insert it into the box, fit the foller or levered press, which has 20 longish pegs, into the top so the holes line up & push out 20 pits. Pits fall out underneath, & the pitted cherries are dumped from the carrier into a bowl. Most ingenious. Pat'd. 1870, by Charles Fisher, box part is 6-1/4"H x 6-1/4"L x 5-3/4"W, 19th C. .... **$475+**

*I-25. Cherry stoner. Although this looks skillfully "homemade," it is mass-produced. It's a **Fisher's Patent Cherry Stoner,"** pat'd. by Charles A. Fisher, Philadelphia, May 24, 1870. "Five strokes stone 100 cherries" claims early catalog. Wood box with cherry-holder of wood, iron hinges, lever action. Does 20 at a time. Fit holder with cherries (like Chinese Checkers), insert into box, fit the levered follower into box, push out pits, which fall below. 6-1/4"H x 6-1/4"L x 5-3/4"W. Collection of Meryle Evans.* **$475+**

❖ NOTES ❖

The boxy **20-hole stoner** in I-25, owned by Meryle Evans, was described in my 2nd edition as "homemade." Instead, it was a handmade production piece, albeit made in small quantities. I found a picture of one in an ad in B. K. *Bliss & Son's Seed Catalog*, dated 1876. It is for "Fisher's Cherry Stoner," which will with "Five strokes stone one hundred Cherries. The rapidity and certainty with which it performs its work will make this machine a necessity in every household. Under or over ripe fruit equally well stoned, and can be done five times as rapidly as by the old way by hand, and much neater, as it leaves the fruit round and in perfect shape." The Fisher, a wooden box-like hinged device with a levered top "press" with 100 pegs, and a bottom part with 100 small holes (on which to place the cherries like Chinese Checkers), was pat'd. May 24, 1870, by Charles A. Fisher of Philadelphia, patent #103,317. The other two cherry stoners pat'd. in 1870 were by J. Marchant, Farmington, IL, April 19; and by J. N. Webster, Peoria, IL, on May 31. The clustering of dates makes you wonder if the cherry-stoner patent examiner waited until he had a stack of same-function things on his desk before examining them!

Cherry pitter, cast iron, brightly nickel plated, screw clamps to table, has interesting works: a platform with 4 little holed cups holds 4 cherries at a time; when pitter is cranked, plunger goes up & down & punches pits out, one by one, New Standard Corp., Mount Joy, PA, 10-1/4"H, "patents pending," c.1900. .... **$75-$125**

Cherry pitter, cast iron, square-cut letters & numbers, square hopper, 4 straight legs, comes apart for cleaning, mounted to board, name not marked, but pat'd. by H. Buckwalter as a "cherry-stoner," Kimberton, PA, 5"H exclusive of board, pat'd. Nov. 17, 1863. .... **$125**

Cherry pitter, skeletal cast iron frame, with 3 spraddly but insectually grasshopper graceful heavy gauge rod legs. Hopper feeds cherries against one side of the spirally-ridged or ribbed wheel turned with crank with small wooden handle, marked only with patent date, Nov. 17, 1863, pat'd. by Henry Buckwalter, Kimberton, PA,..................................... **$165**

Cherry pitter, cast iron, 3 legs, mounted to board, hopper & crank, lightweight casting, sort of cabriole legs nicely shaped with spurs like a dog's dew claws, Scott Mfg. Co., Baltimore, MD, 6-3/4"H x 12"L, 3 legs is influence of inventor Henry Buckwalter, Kimberton, PA. His patent #10,601, Nov. 17, 1863 was for a simple 3-legged tabletop stoner with a side channel (see I-27 for exact one). William Weaver's patent #54,797, May 18, 1866, claimed "certain improvements," including a "double hopper" and curved radial ribs on both sides of the pitting disk, thus being able to stone twice as many cherries as a one hopper/one-sided disk [such as Buckwalter's]. The channel exited between the two back legs. (See I-28.) .... **$125+**

Cherry pitter, cast iron, even crank knob is cast iron, 4 legs, mounted to board that has a rectangular cutout for cherries (or their stones?) to fall through, "Scott Manufacturing Co., Baltimore, MD," stem to stern 7"H x 10-7/8"L, "patent pending" (was pat'd. May 15, 1866, by William Weaver, Phoenixville, PA, based on Buckwalter's patent 3 years earlier). Four legs meant more stability. (See I-26.)............., **$75**

❖ NOTES ❖

Replaced leg – I bought a cherry pitter specifically because one leg was replaced with a wooden leg. What I didn't realize, blush, until I actually took its picture and studied *that*, was that the spout or channel was missing. It pays to look at everything and do a run-through in your mind, especially if you are highly attracted to one element to the exclusion of others. Hope this helps you someday ... remember; "Learn from other people's mistakes. You won't have time to make them all yourself."

Cherry pitter, cast iron finished in blue enamel, screw clamps to table edge, punches out 2 at a time, "Home Cherry Stoner," mfd. by Schroeter Bros. Hardware Co., St. Louis MO, 10-1/2"H x 9-1/2"L x 3"W, pat'd. Aug. 17, 1917. *House Furnishing Review* in 1918 said "It is fast and very convenient, is self-feeding, due to the rocking hopper which agitates the cherries, causing them to roll into pitting sockets. Hopper large enough to hold 12 or more cherries at a time." **$100**

Cherry pitter, cast iron painted turquoise, 2 plungers, screw clamp, Rollman Mfg. Co., Mt. Joy, PA, 14"H, c.1890s-1910s or later. **$75**

Cherry pitter, cast iron, pits 2 at a time with 2 curved rods that have ragged sharp ends. Punches pits through holes in double trough, & when pair of pitters is pulled back through a pry-off sheet of metal, the pitted cherries are knocked into a slanted wooden trough & roll into a bowl, "The Family Cherry Stoner," Goodell Co., Antrim, NH, 8"H, pat'd. 1886. According to Loris Russell, this was based on the patent of George Geer, Galesburg, IL, of Apr. 9, 1867. ..... **$65+**

Cherry pitter, cast iron, tinned finish, hopper & crank,

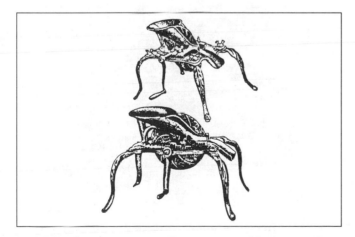

I-26. Cherry stoners. Two versions of cast iron 4-legged pitter, based on original patent (See I-30) of H. Buckwalter, Kimberton, PA, Nov. 17, 1863, as improved by William Weaver, Phoenixville, PA, May 15, 1866. Handle on crank is also cast iron. Note: one at top has wing nuts holding legs on; it's newer than other. Some marked "Scott Man'fg Co. Pat. Pending, Baltimore, MD." 7"H x 10-7/8"L. **$50-$125**

*I-27. Cherry stoner. Cast iron, 3 legs. Henry **Buckwalter's** patent, Nov. 17, 1863. Missing wooden handle to crank. Picture courtesy of The Smithsonian Institution, Museum of History and Technology. A real classic, but not rare.* **$125**

adjusted by thumb screws to adapt to different size cherries, Enterprise #2, mfd. by Enterprise Mfg. Co., Philadelphia, PA, 12"H x 9"W, pat'd. Mar. 31, 1903. The #1 was japanned, and sold for half to three quarters the price of the tinned one originally. **Lookalike alarm** – A brand new cherry pitter, styled exactly like the old Enterprise, is being manufactured (not to fool collectors). Cast into body is "CHOP-RITE Pottstown U.S.A." New price about same as for old:................................. **$30**

Cherry pitter, tinned cast iron, screw clamps, crank is not on a wheel, but at right angles & behind hopper. This one "is intended to stone cherries with the least possible cutting or disfiguring. Every good housewife will appreciate this for preserving purposes. The most satisfactory results are obtained by dropping the cherries one at a time into the Hopper immediately after Sweeper has passed the hole. With practice one can become very expert." "The New Cherry Stoner," Enterprise #12, c.1890s to c.1905+............................ **$40+**

Cherry pitter, cast iron, screw clamps to table, "Cherry Stoner No. 17," & on bottom of clamp "2884," "Enterprise" not cast on piece, 12"H exclusive of screw, Enterprise Mfg. Co., Philadelphia, PA, pat'd. Mar. 31 1903. .... **$30**

Cherry pitter, cast iron, tinned (later, c.1913, offered also in bronze japan finish), screw clamped to table, ridged wheel in center of hopper is cranked to rub stones out of the cherries, this one in its original cardboard box, "Brighton #2," mfd. by Logan & Strobridge Iron Co., sold by future mfrs., Wrightsville Hardware Co., L&S from New Brighton, PA; W.H. Co. in Wrightsville, PA, pat'd. May 15, 1866, by William Weaver, Phoenixville, PA. Made for many years after 1866, and advertised as being made by Wrightsville Hardware in 1913. In an ad from *House Furnishing Review*, March 1913, this cherry seeder is "adjustable" – like the Enterprises ones, finished in "Bronze Japan or Tinned," & "furnished either with clamp for attaching to table or with four legs." Old ones get the most money: .... **$40-$65**

Cherry pitter, cast iron, hopper has cranked rub plate, clamps on, deep spout, handle is missing turned

I-28. Cherry stoner. *Lightweight cast iron, 3 legs attached with wing nut bolts, mounted on plank through holes in feet. Marked "**Scott** Mfg. Co., Baltimore." 6-3/4"H x 12"L.* **$125**

wood knob, replacement is old wooden spool, "The New Brighton," Logan & Strobridge, c.1890s-1910s. **$35**

Cherry pitter, hand held, nickeled spring steel wire, loop-de-looped so that it fits over thumb & middle finger, fed cherries one by one with other hand, & squeezed to make sharp-ended plunger push pit out, John Houck, Chicago, IL, 7-1/4"L, pat'd. Dec. 28, 1909. .... **$25+**

Cherry pitter, hand held, small metal device with finger holes at each side, & a plunger worked with the thumb in center, has to be hand-fed, "Perfection" is name given it by a distributor, F.W. Seastrand in 1910 catalog, American, about 4"L, marked only "PAT." Earlier than 1910. .... **$35**

❖ RECIPE ❖

Cherry Bounce – Take a peck of morella cherries, and a peck of black hearts. Stone the morellas and crack the stones. Put all the cherries and the cracked stones into a demi-john, with three pounds of loaf-sugar slightly pounded or beaten. Pour in two gallons of double-rectified whisky. Cork the demi-john, and in six months the cherry-bounce will be fit to pour off and bottle for use; but the older it is, the better." Miss Leslie, of Philadelphia, Seventy-Five Receipts for Pastry, Cakes, and Sweetmeats. Appended to The Cook's Own Book and Housekeeper's Register ... by a Boston Housekeeper. Boston: Munroe & Francis, 1833.

❖ RECIPE ❖

Restarting a Mac Recipe, or, Cherries, Dried – Take large sweet cherries and stone them. The stoning can be done with a little instrument made as follows: Bend a piece of stiff wire to the shape of a rather large and long hairpin. Bind this on to a piece of wood, leaving the loop projecting about an inch. Bend the loop so that it curves over a little. The stones can be readily removed with this.

"Put the cherries into a preserving pan with well-crushed preserving sugar...in the proportion of a pound of sugar to three pounds of fruit. Boil very gently until the fruit shrinks a little, then strain them free from the syrup. Put the strained cherries on a sieve, and place them in a cool oven to dry. Do not let them cook. When they are dry enough to handle, they can be stored away. ... If preferred, the cherries can be rolled in castor or icing sugar before being stored away." Katherine Mellish's Cookery & Domestic Management, London: E. & F. N. Spon, 1901.

Cherry pitter, tinned cast iron, cranked action that pulls down vertical pit puncher, leather insert at point of impact on hopper, screw clamps to table, wooden handle (older ones natural or varnished), "New Standard #50," New Standard Works, Mt. Joy, PA, 10"H x 5-1/2"W, pat'd. in the 1870s. Also came in a 12"H size, the "New Standard #75." **$35**

❖ NOTES ❖

Lookalike alarm – A one-cherry pitter like the New Standard, also of tinned cast iron, is now being made by the White Mountain Freezer Inc., Winchendon, MA. It seems to be a variation of the John H. Webster May 31, 1870 patent for a straight-plunger style pitter. These were made over a very, very long time; I believe the ones seen with red wooden handles are as late as the 1940s. Another 1940s variation, the "50A Dandy," is made of cast iron and heavy stamped sheet metal, heavily tinned (or nickeled?), with a piston that drives pitter up and down when you turn crank. The pitter is marked New Standard Corp., Mt. Joy, but sold by White Mountain Freezer Co., Nashua, NH. (Value of 1940's one is under $25).

I-29. Cherry stoner "make-do" *or repaired piece. The* **Weaver** *patent, showing both dates, with sorrel-leaf decoration cast into hopper. Legs missing or removed purposely; body mounted to shaped wood base, 8-7/8" x 4-1/2", carved to match sinuous curves of cast iron. Iron part only 2-7/8"H; overall 6"H. [Note: Piece at one end for mounting to tabletop. Strict kitchenware dealers devalue this kind of thing; folk art and make-do collectors would snap it up.]* **$165**

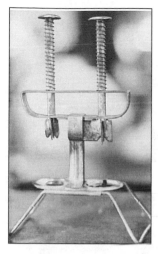
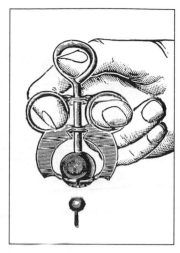

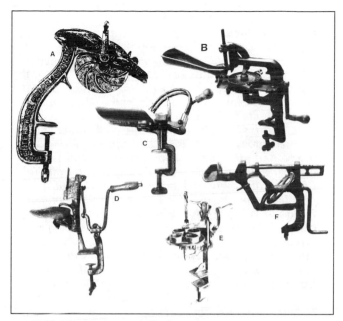

I-30. Cherry pitters or stoners. (L) *Skeletal wire & stamped sheet metal, spring-activated plungers. 8"H, no mark. Seems to pit cherry on one side, and split it on other. Courtesy Arden L. Fisher.* **(R)** *"Perfection," handheld stoner. Name given it by distributor Seastrand, c.1910 catalog.* **(L) $135; (R) $35**

Cherry stoner, red painted cast iron screw clamp frame, tall vertical shaft has large knob at top, push down spring action, one cherry at a time, oval concave white porcelainized cast iron receiver, "Excelsior 85," pat'd. 1885 (?). .... **$75+**

Cherry pitter, cast iron, long hopper, swiveling hinge above the clamp that fastens it to the table, is a sort of shock absorber while plunger-punch is in action. Hopper can be filled with about 8 cherries, which roll down one at a time for pitting, "Duke," mfd. by Reading Hardware Co., Reading, PA, 11"L, not including wooden handle on crank, "patent pending," 19th C. .... **$800-$1,200**

Cherry pitter, cast iron, screw-clamp frame, marked "Duke," this one with horizontal gear turned by crank, and notable large dished hopper with curved cutout slots, mfd. by Reading Hardware Co., Reading, PA, "patent pending," late 1800s? Exceedingly rare. .... **$1,500+**

Cherry pitter, tinned metal & wire, hand-held, "The HAND-Y," American, 3"H, c.1920s (?). **$20**

Chocolate grater, tin & cast iron, a mechanical gadget with a rectangular spring-loaded holder for a chunk or block of chocolate, has 3 rods going length of cylindrical punctured tin grating surface, 2 of which are the track for the chocolate holder, rubbed back & forth across grater in same way as this company's Edgar nutmeg grater, "The Edgar," mfd. by William J. Bride Co., Reading, MA, cylinder 7-1/4"L x 2-1/8" diam., with handle 8-1/2"L, chocolate holder is 2-7/8"H x 2" x 1-7/8", pat'd. 1891, and again Nov. 10, 1896. .... **$250**

Chopping bowl, hand carved wood, nice patina, American, 25"L x 10-1/2"W x 4"diam., early to mid 19th C. This proportion is most common – over twice as long as wide & not very deep. Old chopping bowls should show signs of vigorous cutting. The wonder is that so many look so good on the inside; maybe really badly scarred ones were burned in the fireplace generations ago. I've seen many repaired ones,

I-31-A. Cherry stoners. *All cast iron; all screw clamp to table edge.* **(A)** *"Enterprise No. 2," pat'd. 1903. No.'s 1 & 2 not adjustable for different cherry sizes, as were Enterprise 17 & 18. 12"L.* **(B)** *"Duke," Reading Hardware Co., "pat. pend." Very unusual. Swiveling hinge just above clamp functions as a shock absorber while the pitter is in operation. 11"L, exclusive of handle. Late 19th C.* **(C)** *"The Family Cherry Stoner," Goodell Co., c.1895. 8"H. Wonderful lever action plunges double pitters through cherries.* **(D)** *"New Standard No. 50," Mt. Joy, PA, 10"H, c.1900.* **(E)** *Another by New Standard Corporation, Mt. Joy. "Patents pending." Nickeled iron. All parts numbered, therefore replaceable with stock parts – the touted advantage of all uniformly cast iron appliances. Feed cherries with left hand, and as you crank, platform holding 4 cherries revolves to lie briefly under punch. 10-1/4"H.* **(F)** *Another New Standard pitter, with eccentric wheel, horizontal action. Courtesy Bob Cahn. (A), (C) & (D) Collection of Robert D. Franklin. (B) & (E) Collection of Meryle Evans.* **(A) $25-$45; (B) $1,500+; (C) $65-$85; (D) & (E) $75-$125; (F) $125-$175; (G) $1,500+**

I-31-B. Extraordinary "Duke," *Reading Hardware. Wonderful cutout cast hopper-chute at left, "pat. Pending," date not known, but prob. late 1880s. Photo & information courtesy Carol Bohn.*

Caramel Potato Cake – *1/2 cup butter, 1 cup sugar, 2 eggs, 1/2 cup milk, 1/2 cup hot riced potatoes, 1 cup flour, 2 teaspoons baking powder, 1/2 teaspoon cinnamon, 1/2 teaspoon [ground] clove, 1/2 teaspoon [grated] nutmeg, 1/2 cup grated chocolate, 1/2 cup chopped nut meats. – Cream butter and add gradually, while beating constantly, sugar; then add eggs, well beaten, milk and potatoes. Beat thoroughly and add flour, mixed and sifted with baking powder, and spices, chocolate and nut meats. Turn into a buttered and floured cake pan and bake in a moderate oven fifty-five minutes. Remove from pan and cover with Fudge Frosting.* **Fudge Frosting.** – *2 tablespoons butter, 1 cup sugar, 1/4 cup milk, 1 square unsweetened chocolate, 1/2 teaspoon vanilla. – Put butter in saucepan and when melted, add sugar and milk. Bring to the boiling point and let boil ten minutes. Add chocolate and let boil five minutes, taking care that chocolate does not adhere to bottom or sides of pan. Remove from range, add vanilla and beat until the right consistency to spread."* Fannie Merritt Farmer, A New Book of Cookery. *Boston: Little, Brown, 1915 edition of 1912 book.*

I-32-A. Chopping knives with crescent blades. *Big beauty at* **(L)** *hand-forged iron, single tang branched to 2 before inserting in wood handle. 8"H x 9-1/4"L blade, early 19th C. Top* **(R)** *Commercially made, 6-3/8"H x 7-1/2"W, prob. last third 19th C. Lower* **(R)** *Hand-forged, unusual curved wood handle fits hand comfortably. Collection of Meryle Evans.* **(L) $125; (T-R) $15 or so; (B-R) $35**

where the bottom has been chopped through, bad section cut out & hole fitted with another piece of wood, flush as possible, or a metal patch has been added. **Added value.** – Often imaginatively repaired ones bring more than those with good condition but less personality...................................... **$75**

Chopping bowl, wood with old red paint on outside, oblong, American, quite extraordinarily large at 25"L x 17"W, early or mid 19th C. Sold at a 1982 auction for $300. Now would depend on where it was sold if it would go much higher.............................. **$200+**

❖ NOTES ❖

Paint & Patina: Old paint, red, ochre, blue, green or even gray, adds to collector appeal. If not painted, a scrubbed, old patina is what you should look for. These were cut from split logs, then hollowed out with special curved cutting scraping tool called a scorp. Somewhere, twin bowls, made from the two halves of a log may exist.

Chopping knife, also called a chopper, or mincer, 2 nickeled steel half-round rocker blades set at right angles, big wooden ball knob handle painted green or red, 4-1/2"H, ball about 2-1/4", "Androck," Rockford, IL, 1930s-40s. **$7**

Chopping knife, 4 stainless steel blades set at right angles to form bell-like shape, painted wooden handle, "A & J," Binghamton, NY, 6"H x 3"W, c.1925. Knobs were painted green, yellow or red. Blue not mentioned in catalog... **$7**

Chopping knife, 3 slightly bowed, small hotdog-shaped steel blades, iron frame & wooden handle, called a tension chopper. "In this knife the blades are ... kept firm by the tension of the frame in which they are set. It does very rapid work, and is an excellent knife for fam-

ily use. Most people consider hash a very delicious breakfast dish, in spite of all the hits newspaper paragraphers have made on it, and a good implement for making it is indispensible." *Practical Housekeeper,* 1884. American, about 6"W, pat'd. 1867. .... **$45+**

❖ NOTES ❖

Stainless Steel: The Knife-Life of the Kitchen – [A] late product of steel ... is ... fast coming to the markets of the world. It is stainless steel. A steel (with an admixture of chromium) which resists rust, does not corrode or scale, and is impervious to food acids (with the exception of mustard, plus vinegar and salt which equal muriatic acid). ... The steel we now use is carbon steel. ... Think of not having to scour or polish your knives. Think of the knife having an indefinite life and always looking highly polished. Soon, too, even the handle will be made of this steel and the knife will be made of this steel and the knife will look like a highly polished silver utensil. No cleaning powders must be used to clean this steel; only warm water and soap. Its advent reminds one of the early days of aluminum utensils, doesn't it? Manufacturers are planning to make kettles, pots and pans of it, as they will wear well, and will not scale and wear as do iron ones." *House & Garden,* March 1921.

Chopping knife, fancily-shaped cast steel blade, brass inset decoration, smooth mahogany color handle, 2 tangs, English, c.1820s or 30s. **$95**

Chopping knife, brass & steel, handmade (at least it looks one of a kind & not commercial), tubular brass handle with long slit into which was slid, then soldered, the well-shaped steel blade with fancy shoulder, American (?), 4-1/2"H x 6-1/2"W, 19th C......... **$120+**

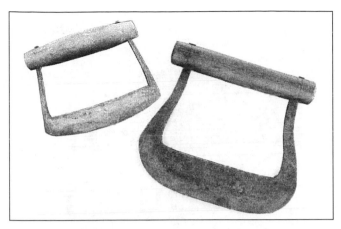

I-32-B. Chopping knives with curved blades.
Both are hand-forged steel with simple wooden grips. Visible on one at (R), you'll note score marks where maker marked where to drill for the tangs. Tangs go up through handle and are hammered flat. Usually about 5-3/4"H x 5-1/2"W, more or less. 19th C. American. **$25+**

Chopping knife, cast iron handle with cutout in top, usually painted, stainless steel rocker blade with distinct swellings at each end. This looks exactly like the "Double Action" knife, except for cutout in horizontal part of handle. I don't know if they were made by same company, 20 years apart, or if Voos got license to make them & altered handle for some purpose. Marked "Voos," American, 5"H x 6-1/8"W, c.1920s. **$10**

Chopping knife, cast iron handle with no cutout, cast steel blade shaped like baby's bottom, hence its name "Double Action." American, pat'd. Oct. 20, 1892. .... **$15+**

Chopping knife, cast steel blade, 2 tangs, forged iron handle, marked only "Cast Steel," American, 5-1/2"L blade, c.1870s. **$35**

Chopping knife, cast steel blade, cast iron shank & turned wood T-handle, blade is lightly rocked & has

very high rounded shoulders, "S. H. F.," "Bingham" (may be last name of maker or town – There were a number of Binghams in America, including three Michigan towns), prob. American, 7"H x 5-1/2"W, 19th C. **$45**

Chopping knife, cast steel blade, wooden handle, "Universal," mfd. by Landers, Frary & Clark, 19th C. **$15**

Chopping knife, cast iron stirrup-shaped handle, 2 bell-shaped carbon steel blades intersect at right angles, rocker action, "N. R. S. & Co. No. 20," (there's also a #60), (Nelson R. Streeter & Co.), Groton, NY, 5-1/2"H, pat'd. May 2, 1893. .... **$30**

Chopping knife, cast steel, quadrant handle screws to 6 "flying buttress" blades that form bell shape, taken apart for sharpening or cleaning, J. B. Foote Foundry, pat'd. 1906. .... **$25**

Chopping knife, cast steel, wood, "L. D. Wheeler," n.p. (American ? might be Wheeler Can Opener Co., St. Louis), 19th C. **$35**

Chopping knife, curved steel blade, broom-handle grip painted black, 2 tangs, "Henry Disston & Sons," the famous saw makers, Phila., 5-1/4"H x 6-1/2"L, 19th C. I've never seen one, but Henry Disston did get a potato parer patent on Nov. 29, 1859. Disston tool collectors crossover. **$25**

Chopping knife, cutlery steel blade, long tang, turned wood handle, "Mason & Parker." English, 13-1/2"L, late 19th C. **$35**

Chopping knife, deep half-ovoid blade, one tang, wood handle, marked "PERK" on blade, American, 5"W, mid to late 19th C. **$50**

Chopping knife, double blade, steel with wood handle, heart-shaped rivet head, American, 7"L, c.1870s. .... **$85+**

Chopping knife, 2 plated steel sausage-shaped blades, 2 tangs welded at one end, fit over a rod going through turned wooden handle at other end. By use of wing nut to loosen tangs, the distance between blades can be adjusted. "James F. Foster," Buffalo, NY, 6"H x 5-3/4"W, pat'd. Dec. 27, 1887. .... **$25**

Chopping knife, double bladed rocker type, black turned wood handle, loosen wing nut to take blade

I-33. Chopping knife, *with fancy cutout blade of wrought steel, and machined cast brass handle typical of English choppers of 19th C. 5"H x 7"W. I think these are usually overpriced, and should be worth half or less of great indigenous iron choppers as in I-32. Value range what's being asked:* **$150-$185**

I-34. Chopping knives, double-bladed rockers.
(L) Two heavy steel blades, ground & polished, riveted to steel shanks that encircle handle. Green enameled handle or plain wood. Kidney-bean shaped blades 6"W, pat'd. Dec. 27, 1887 by James F. Foster, Buffalo, NY, mfd. by Henry Disston & Sons, Philadelphia, late 19th C. (R) Cast steel blades, truncated ends, wishbone shank. Probably c.1870s. **$25+**

I-35. Chopping knives. (L) *Steel rocker blade, riveted cast iron handle with cutout, 5-1/2"H x 5-3/4"W, c.1890s.* **Top:** *Carved wooden handle, crescent carbon steel blade, 5-5/8"H x 8"W. Mass-produced, but probably on a small scale, and individually finished. Poss. made in St. Louis, MO.* **(R)** *A "Hachinette," from France. Carbon steel, wood, 6-3/4" x 5-1/4". Angel mark. Used by centering grip over blade's center, chopping down into smallish wooden bowl, which you continuously turned with your other hand. Think of this turning/chopping motion when you see I-58.* **(B):** *Solid steel, with all-in-one tubular steel handle, c.1890s-1920s.* **(L) $15; (T) $45+; (R) $15; (B) $25**

I-37. Chopping knife & board. *Forged iron & wood. Blade topped by cutout trotting horse, turned wood handle. 7"H x 14"L overall. Often referred to as tobacco cutters, but I believe the boards would smell if this were true of all. The fancy cut board just isn't American; perhaps French Canadian or European. Ex-Seymour Collection; sold in 1982 at Christie's. Picture courtesy of Christie, Manson & Woods International, Inc.* **$300+**

off for sharpening or cleaning, distance between 2 parallel blades is NOT adjustable – it locks in only one position. Ad from Dec. 27, 1890 *Metal Worker* has imaginary dialogue between housewife & hardware clerk: "'I do not want one of those double bladed chopping knives. You cannot wash, scour or sharpen them without cutting the fingers.' 'But,' said the clerk, 'This is one of the new Buffalo ... mincing knives which opens for cleaning and sharpening.' 'Why, that's splendid. I'll take that!' said she.'" Called a "Buffalo Adjustable," mfd. by Sidney Shepard & Co., Buffalo, NY, 6"H x 5-7/8"W blade, pat'd. Dec. 27, 1887........................ **$25**

Chopping knife, forged crescent blade, bentwood handle, American (?), 6"W, early 19th C. **$65**

Chopping knife, forged iron blade 2 long tangs, thick, slightly carved wood handle, American, 6-1/2"H x 5"W, early 19th C. **$65**

Chopping knife, forged iron, curved blade with unusually shaped shoulders leading to single shank & turned wooden T handle, American, mid 19th C. **$45**

Chopping knife, forged steel, anchor-shaped, wood handle, thin crescent moon blade, prob. American, 6"W, mid 19th C. **$50**

Chopping knife, forged steel straight-bottom blade, with turned wood handle, nicely shaped cutout for hand is almost like the top of a Valentine, American (?), 19th C. **$50**

Chopping knife, iron blade curves like sleeping dog, 3 tangs become one shank T handle, American (?), 6-1/4"H, 19th C. **$45**

Chopping knife, iron blade, very fat & curved, unusual brass tang, fat cigar-shaped T-handle grip, American, 19th C. **$50**

Chopping knife, iron with wood tiller handle off one end (just imagine the tiller of a small sailboat to get idea of shape & angle), blade's other end is fat & rounded, American, 3"H x 10"L, 19th C. **$35**

Chopping knife, ornate steel & wood, 4 brass rivets fasten handle to blade, cutout & scrolly carved wooden handle (with horn-like projections to cradle hand), almost a mirror image of fat scrolls of rocker blade, which also has a heart near the haft, birds perched on scrolled tips, European, poss. English, although some hints at German origin, 12-1/2"H, 18th or 19th C (?). I think 1830s. Somehow the handle does not look as old as I think it should for blade... **$400**

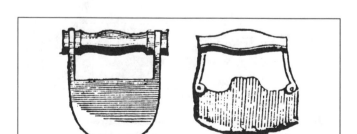

I-36. Chopping knives, *as depicted in two early cookbooks.* **(L)** *Very substantially made "meat chopper, for chopping and disjointing bones," in Warne's Model Cookery, London: 1868.* **(R)** *"Chop knife. Iron handle, steel blade." American Home Cook Book, 1854.* **$35-$65**

❖ NOTES ❖

Carpet Cutters – A type of rocking chair in the 19th C., with relatively thin wooden rocker blades rounded on the ends, were called by some wags "carpet cutters." Hence the name used for rocking chopper blades.

•   •   •

Ornately Un-American – In the late 1980s very ornate choppers began to appear regularly on the market. The blades look old; sometimes you look for more wear on the handles than is there. They are so "good" you have to wonder where did they come from. I've heard from some dealers that this ornate type is being skillfully reproduced in England for export to America. **Think English** as soon as you see fancy cutouts on the blade of a chopper, or very deep blades with profiles of roosters or animals along top non-cutting edge, or brass & iron combos; most such pieces are not American.

Chopping knife, rocker blade is thin long crescent, tang at each end of single straight wood handle, American (?), 7"W, mid 19th C. **$60**

Chopping knife, rocker blade, handles at each end, steel with turned wood knobby handles, French, 11-1/2"L, dated 1878. .... **$55**

Chopping knife, 3 stainless steel blades & wood T grip – a double set of blades, spring-loaded, brackets 3rd lower blade when wooden chopper grip is pumped down like a pogo stick, making nice springy sounds and looks very efficient. 7-1/2"H x 33-3/4"W, "Foley Chopper," Minneapolis, Pat#2,113,085, pat'd. by Melvin Higgs, Apr. 5, 1938. .... **$15**

Chopping knife, 2 steel blades, curved hotdog shape, high arching bentwood handle, not marked, but possibly a mfd. piece, American, 6"L blades, c.1880. Odd handle accounts for value. (See I-32.) **$35**

❖ NOTES ❖

Parloa's Advice – "A chopping knife with only one blade is much better than one with two blades. The blade should be almost straight across. When it is rounded a good deal, much time and strength are wasted in chopping." Maria Parloa, *Kitchen Companion*, Boston: Estes & Lauriat, 1887. It is instructive to read period literature about utensils and gadgets. While "artistically" we may admire the curved double blades, Parloa, who came with the highest credentials, founder of the original Boston Cooking School, and author of several cookbooks, obviously didn't like them.

Chopping knife, steel blade has nicely shaped shoulder & truncated ends, one tang, wood handle, American, 5-7/8"W, 19th C. **$40**

Chopping knife, steel blade with tang split at top so the Y gives extra strength to handle, like an inverted wishbone tang, prob. American, 5"W blade, mid 19th C. **$40**

Chopping knife, steel with upside down Y or wishbone tang, wooden handle, deep double rocker blades have truncated ends, American, 6"H x 5-3/4"W, early 20th C. .... **$25+**

Chopping knife, steel crescent blade, single tang with wooden handle set crooked on it, angle makes it more comfortable to use, prob. American, 5-3/4"W, mid 19th C. **$50**

Chopping knife, steel, ovoid blade pivots for dual purpose: one edge makes scalloped cuts, other minces; wood handle, filed or chiseled tooling on shaft, American, 6-1/2"H x 6-1/4"W, 19th C. **$35**

Chopping knife, steel rocker blade, 2-hander has fat wood crosswise knob at each end, marked "9," American, 9-1/2"W, 1870s. **$30**

Chopping knife, steel rocker blade in fat sausage or pickle shape, top side has small section of saw teeth, rosette rivet points on blade, basketwork-looking cast iron handle, like a heat-dissipating stove lid lifter handle, American, 6-1/2"W, 19th C. **$25**

Chopping knife, steel rocker blade with truncated ends, single tang, bullet-ended turned cylindrical handle assembled from discs of varying widths & different materials – ivory, ebony & other wood, English (?), 7"H, prob. craftsman made mid 20th C. .... **$125+**

Chopping knife, steel sausage-shape blade riveted to wooden handle 3 times the height of the blade, cutout hand hold in wood, American, 7"H x 8"W overall, early 19th C. **$60**

Chopping knife, steel & wood, 2 rocker blades with high round shoulders, ogee-shaped ends. Y-tangs at each end, turned grip, marked, "Hercules Food Ser Equip," looks 1890s, prob. mid 1920s. **$20**

Chopping knife, turned wood T-handle, single wide tang, deep nearly rectangular blade with rounded corners, marked "W. Butcher," well known iron plane maker, mid to 3rd quarter 19th C. **$50**

Chopping knife, forged blade, beautiful arrow-tipped tang, turned wooden handle, American (?), 19th C. **$50**

Chopping knife, forged iron, single tang, wide crescent blade, crude wood handle, American (?), 7-1/2"W, early 19th C. **$35**

Chopping knife, half circle forged iron blade, the top, non-cutting edge, fancifully scalloped like waves, riveted to fancy carved wooden handle rather like a saw handle, American ?, 8-1/2"H x 6-1/2"W, early to mid 19th C. **$85**

Chopping knife, nickeled steel, tubular handle, deep rocker blade with flat tangs going up to handle, very modern looking, American, 4-5/8"H x 5-1/4"W, c.1910. .... **$20**

Chopping knife, wrought iron in elongated bell shape, wood crosswise handle crammed down on short tang, American (?), 5-1/4"L, 18th C. The iron is badly pitted, the form is beautiful. I bought it at auction of Keillor Family Collection, once possibly the largest, finest household tool collection (now dispersed) ever assembled in the U.S. **$25**

Chopping knife, wrought iron, crescent blade has 2 wide tangs riveted to wooden handle, pat'd. by "B. Denton," Auburn, NY, about 6"W blade, 1850s-60s (?). **$55**

Chopping knife, wrought iron, half moon blade with longish tang, wooden T-handle, "T. Collins," about 5-1/2"W blade x 5-1/2"H, 19th C. **$55**

❖ RECIPE ❖

To Make a Cold Hash, or Salmagundi *– Take a turkey, and two chickens that have been roasted; cut the flesh from their breasts into thin slices, and mince the legs of the chickens; then wash and bone 10 large anchovies, add eight large pickled oysters, 10 or 12 fine green pickled cucumbers, and one whole lemon. Chop all these very small, and mix it with the minced-meat; lay it in the middle of a dish and the slices of the white part* *around it, with halved anchovies, whole pickled oysters, quartered cucumbers, sliced lemon, whole pickled mushrooms, capers or any pickle you like; cut also some fine lettuce, and lay round among the garnish; but put not oil and vinegar to the minced-meat till it comes to table."* Eliza F. Haywood, A New Present for a Servant-Maid; Necessary Cautions and Precepts to Servant-Maids for Gaining Good-Will and Esteem, *Dublin, Ireland: 1771.* **Pickles of nuts, fruits,** *vegetables and meats were given a lot of space in 18th C. cookbooks. The corresponding ingredients in the late 20th C. would be conveniently canned (therefore preserved) pineapple or peaches, peas or corn, ham or chicken. You would find canned nuts, in liquid, in Oriental groceries, but most Western recipes requiring nuts could be made with freshly shelled, dry roasted, or packaged nutmeats.*

Chopping knife, wrought iron, oak handle which is ovoid in section, tang inserted through simple handle then hammered over, neat little prickery shoulder point spurs just above half-moon blade, American (?), 3-3/4"W blade, late 18th C. **$135**

Chopping knife, wrought iron or tool steel half moon blade, single tang, simple turned wood cigar-shaped handle, "Isaac Greaves," Basking Ridge, NY, 6-1/8"L x 5-3/4"W, mid 19th C. **$65**

Chopping knife, wrought iron, proportionately small blade, 2 projections at top of each end of blade bent around & forged together to form handle loop, almost look as if they were originally intended to be tangs for a wooden handle before maker changed his mind, American, 5-11/16"W, early 19th C. **$45**

Chopping knife, wrought steel with wooden T-handle, half moon shaped blade, marked "Coldwell," American or English, blade is 6"W, height including blade, tang & handle is 7-3/4", 19th C. **$50**

Chopping knife & chopping board, forged iron & wood, the very thick wood cutting board cut in fancy outline, blade cut at top in shape of a trotting horse, with fat turned wooden handle "tail," prob. English, 7"H x 14-1/4"L, 19th C. .... **$300+**

❖ NOTES ❖

Figural knives, pinned into & pivoting around a chopping board, are often described as "tobacco leaf cutters," although none of the ones I've smelled have any odor of tars or nicotine. Some have been remounted to the reverse side of the board, after enough chopping has made the first surface concave. I saw a horse one at a Connecticut show in about 1984 for only $95. I don't know what kept me from buying it, but I guess the price was too low; it was appealing, but somehow it didn't grab me right. At the prices today, I guess I've lived to regret it ... a little. If it had been a serpent or a different animal, I might have leapt at the chance to buy it.

• • • •

Valuable details are anything unusual or special about hinge or pivot part; gracefulness or length or interesting angle of handle; thickness of cutting board (a full inch or inch and a quarter plank is older than the 3/4" or 7/8" thickness of today's so-called one inch

board); shape of board. Most desirable are figural knifes (often in the shape of a horse, the tail being the handle), or ones with little extra forged details or decoration. Value range: $150-$750

Chopping knife & cutting board, type that looks like food chopper but is often called a tobacco cutter, pivoting steel blade, remounted to thick chestnut block, other side of block deeply hollowed, showing where blade was mounted before, English, block 2" thick, 10-5/8"L x 6-1/8"W, 19th C. **$40**

Chopping knife – See also: Pastry knife

Citrus juicer – See: Juicers, Lemon squeezers, & Reamers

Cleaver, figural blade of carbon steel, bird head forms hook at top front of blade, flat lead handle is a replacement, probably old, of missing wooden handle. The figure probably denoted kind of meat, by kosher dietary law, to be chopped with it. Russian or Polish kosher butcher's cleaver, 4-1/8"H x 13-1/2"L, c.1890s-1910s. This one, and its mate, have a known family history, shared with me by owner Marvin Tanner. There are probably non-Jewish figural cleavers, although I've never seen any identified as such. .... **$300+**

Cleaver, magnetic tool steel, turned wood handle, "I. F. W. & S. Co.," American, 3-7/8"H x 12"L, blade 6"L, late 19th C. **$15**

Cleaver, steel blade, wood handle, marked with a steer & "Wm. Beatty & Sons," Chester, PA, only 6"L, 19th C. **$15**

Cleaver, tool steel blade with big hanging hole in top front, wooden handle, "Samuel Lee, L. F. & C." (Landers, Frary & Clark), 4"W x 13"L, pat'd. May 1886. .... **$20**

Cleaver & can opener combined, also meat tenderizer, bottle opener, bone saw, hammer. Steel cleaver blade, shaped wooden handle, other tools screwed to large front end of blade, adding desirable weight. American, 14-1/4"L, 19th C. Combo tools very collectible... **$55+**

Cleaver & tenderizer combined, steel, cast iron handle, "Tenda-Cleve," American, early 20th C. **$15**

Coconut grater, handcrafted from variety of parts made of cast iron, brass, steel, sheet metal. Upright shaft is turned iron, serrated blades act like reamer when you push half a coconut against the turning blades. Brass & wood handle. English (?), for colonial use in Jamaica or the West Indies, 7"H, mid 19th C. **$200**

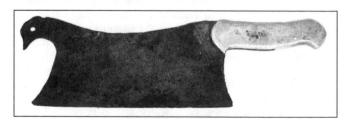

I-38. Figural cleaver. *Steel blade with zoomorphic bird head. Flat lead handle replaces original wood handle. 13-1/2" x 4-1/8", Russian or Polish, 19th C. This cleaver, one of a pair used in preparing kosher food, was brought to this country in 1903; the handle was repaired about that time. Collection of Marvin Tanner. Priceless as family heirloom; very valuable for form of blade. Figural cleavers:* **$300+**

I-39. Coconut grater. *Apparently hand-crafted from variety of parts, although manufactured ones exist. Cast iron bolt probably went through hole in table top. Brass handle with steel handle; heavy sheet metal serrated or sawtooth blades to shred an opened coconut from the inside. Quite possibly English for colonial use, perhaps in Jamaica. 7"H, mid 19th C. Located by Primitive Man, Bob Cahn, Carmel, NY.* **$200+**

❖ NOTES ❖

A Grater For Potatoes, Etc. – A reader has written in to show how a grater to prepare the potatoes for yeast may be made very easily. Place an oyster or fruit can upon the stove or near a fire, until the solder is melted; this will allow the top and bottom to be removed, and the seam to be opened. Open the large piece of tin, and with a nail punch numerous holes from the inside. A nail, which will make a ragged hole, is better than a regular punch; after punching lay the tin upon a block of rather hard wood; turn the edges, to give a place for tacks, and fasten to a board. A hole may be made in the board to hang it by. We have used such a grater for horse-radish and other purposes, and it works admirably." "Household Notes & Queries," *American Agriculturist,* NYC, April 1879.

Coffee mills – See Chapter XIV (Coffee, Tea & Chocolate)

Cook's knife, elongated carbon steel triangular blade, wooden handle, "Guelon," with trademark on blade of boy with ladder, French, 12"L, c.1920s. Worth more to a person needing a really good kitchen knife than to a collector. .... **$5+**

Cookie cutters – See: Chapter IV (Molds)

Corer, nickeled steel tube, half perforated "to reduce resistance," has effect of toothed edge around top, fitted with stop inside so core could be pushed out, turned wood knob handle, sold by Spengler Specialties, NYC, NY, early 20th C. .... **$15+**

Corer & doughnut cutter combined, tin, doughnut cutter has strap handle, corer attachment fits into hole-making inner ring, American, 3" diam. x 3-7/8"H when corer in place, c.1890s-1910s. .... **$35+**

Corer & slicer combined, metal, wood handled corer fits into handle of slicer, American, 8-3/8"L, pat'd. Oct. 12, 1915. .... **$25**

Corn cutter, a half cylinder of heavy tin about hand-sized, strap handle from top to bottom, across inside at heel end is narrow row of sharp teeth, the same distance apart as most full grown corn; above is a heavy wire which braces the cylinder & "presses out" the contents of each kernel after it is slit by cutter. As to why this would be desirable for fresh corn, the *American Agriculturist* says that the undigested whole kernel is "just as much a foreign body as a gravel-stone," therefore "careful parents and those not blessed with teeth that can crush and grind every grain, slit the kernels by drawing a sharp knife along each row, so the digestible and nutritious contents slip out." "Yankee Corn-Cutter," maker unknown, possibly patent of V. Baker for "Green corn cutter," poss., then, Otisfield, ME, maybe the one pat'd. May 31, 1870, advertised c.1872. .... **$75+**

Corn grater, a little wooden bench-like contrivance on 4 turned wood legs, iron grater teeth & blade, American, 4-1/2"H x 11-3/4"L, c.1870s-80s. .... **$100+**

Corn grater, arched steel blade with prickers, mounted over an oval hole in board, American, 12"L, late 19th C. .... **$75+**

Corn grater, crude, homemade, half cylinder of punctured tin stuck on a wooden board, dealer's tag said "Corn Gritter," which may be local usage or phonetic spelling, anyway it makes sense if you think of grits; maybe this was used for dry corn, not fresh? American, 18"L x 7"W, late 19th C. **$55**

Corn grater, wood & metal, signed "C. Frankenfield," Pennsylvania German (?), 12-7/8"L x 3-7/8"W, 19th C. **$100**

Corn husker, also called a corn shucker, corn pick, or husking pin, hand carved wood peg, leather strap, American, 4"L, 19th, early 20th C. .... **$5-$15**

Corn husker, forged steel blade, homemade leather strap to fit around hand has extra loop for forefinger, mended with WWI (?) shoelace. Pin used with the pick part to the inside of your hand, point up, so that you could guide the slightly hooked point with your forefinger & thumb, and rip down through the shucks while corn was still on stalk, to check the ripeness, or after picking before shelling. I have seen a few photos of them being held point down, as if you would stab & rip, which would be very dangerous, no mark, American, about 5"L, 19th C. Dozens of corn huskers were patented in the 1860s & '70s, most of steel & leather, and there are two books on them – see Jim Moffet and Richard Van Vleck in my

I-40. Corn graters, *or* **corn gritters** *or* **creamers,** *in the vernacular.* **(L)** *Meant to slit kernels and release innards. Pieced, soldered tin, 3"H, strap handle, marked "F. A. Walker, Boston," so either mfd or imported by them. Rare to find Walker mark on anything. Picture courtesy National Museum of American History, Smithsonian Institution.* **(T-R)** *Nicely made, wood, iron slitting teeth & scraping blade. 4-1/2"H x 11-3/4"L, 3rd to 4th quarter 19th C. Collection of Meryle Evans.* **(L) $75; (T-R) $100**

Bibliography. Thousands, maybe hundreds of thousands, were made by hand of wood or steel and leather. A few fancy ones that were patented are cornhusking gloves or mitts, to protect the hand, and quite a number of the others have some kind of protection at least for the forefinger. Some husking pins are for right or left hand, others specifically for one or the other. A pair of cornhusking gloves worth $150+; general value range: .... **$7-$15**

❖ NOTES ❖

Anyone collecting **corn-related items** would be interested in this club. In 1980, the International Corn Husking Hooks & Pegs Collectors Association formed to "collect & share information and tools that farmers used to plant, till, and harvest corn." For info: SASE to Millie Byrne, 1 Esti Court, Madison, NJ 07940. The other organization is Corn Items Collectors Association. See **Bang Board** in the Bibliography.

Corn husking hook, fixed to leather mitt, wrist strap, nickeled steel plate & hook in center of palm, pat'd. & mfd. by Clark (Edwin or Richard F.), Chicago, IL, 1910s-1920s.. **$7**

Corn sheller, cast iron arms with turned wooden T handle; tool is threaded onto the cob held in one hand, brass springs keep grooved curved-end arms around dried cob, while other hand turns sheller round & round. When half done, you switch hands, then thread another cob on. By intention, kernels go in all directions – to feed chickens. American, arms 5-1/2"L, handle 7-1/2"L, early 1900s. .... **$60+**

Corn sheller, cast iron, compact, geared mechanical with 2 large gears, hopper on top has smallish mouth but slants out to serve also as gear housing, screwed to shelf, or bench, "The Home," Livingston & Co., Pittsburgh, PA, mid 1870s..................... **$45**

Corn sheller, cast iron, cranked, adjusts for use as walnut huller, marked "Fulton," early 20th or poss. late 19th C. **$50**

Corn sheller, cast iron non-mechanical tool in shape of numeral 8; inside of each round half (one smaller than other) has 8 rather widely-spaced teeth, fits various sizes of cobs, or for both ends of large cobs, American, 4"L, pat'd. July 10, 1883. .... **$200**

Corn sheller, cast iron with lots of openwork, crank handle, screw clamps, "Black Hawk," mfd. by A. H. Patch, Clarksville, TN, c.1900. .... **$50**

Corn sheller, floor-standing model for lotsa cobs, very graceful 4 legged A frame, top chamber houses toothed disc & is shaped like point-down bellows. Large cranked wheel turns disc, cob is dropped into mouth & is forced around inside by cranking before coming out another hole, picked clean. Kernels fall out funnel bottom of body into container, pat'd. & mfd. by T. D. Burrall, Geneva, NY, pat'd. Dec. 6, 1845. He pat'd. a sheller (this one improved?) Mar. 24, 1863. A write-up in *American Agriculturist* says "We strongly recommend this machine to farmers, notwithstanding its cost, as an improvement in every respect over the common mode of shelling corn with a frying-pan or fire-shovel, by hand. Price $10 to $12." Nov. 1846................ **$225**

Corn sheller, for dry corn, cast iron frame with 5 stepped steel blades curved to fit ear, 4 wing nuts hold top half & bottom of frame together so blades can be removed & sharpened, worked by pulling ear across it; because of stepped blades you barely have to pull cob at all, longish handle could be clamped to table or work surface, supposedly Shaker, American, about 13"L, 19th C.. **$150**

Corn sheller, hand-held, scoop-like tin piece with cutter & strap handle, American, 2-1/4" x 3" x 2-1/4", late 19th C. **$75**

Corn sheller, hand-held, turned wooden handle (like small dumbbell) has 4 spring steel wires attached to center to form large coil within which is a sort of metal scraper. Corn is manually worked through center. Dollar Corn-Sheller Co., Lima, NY, adv'd. 1872. ... **$55**

Corn sheller, painted cast iron, mechanical, with 2 cranks, mounted to a straddle board, one hand to feed the corn, "Family," Harrisburg, PA, pat'd. Sept. 2, & Dec. 6, 1870. .... **$75**

❖ RECIPE ❖

Stewed Cucumber – *1 large cucumber. 3/4 pint of brown stock*; 1 oz. of butter; 1/2 oz. of flour; pepper; salt. Pare the cucumber, cut it into pieces about three inches long, then cut these in halves, lengthways, and take out the seeds. Dry the pieces well, in a cloth. Melt the butter in a stewpan, and lay the cucumber in. Fry, until it is a pale golden colour, then lift the pieces out. Stir the flour into the butter, fry together for a minute or two, then gradually stir in the stock. When boiling, put in the pieces of cucumber, and simmer until they are tender. If the stock is not flavoured enough add a little pepper and salt. When done, lift the cucumber out carefully, and lay it on a hot vegetable dish. Pour gravy over, and serve. Katharine Mellish's Cookery Book.* London: Spon; NYC: Spon & Chamberlain, 1901. * **"Brown stock,"** *the basis of many stew-like soups, etc., was made from cooked meat. Mellish's recipe included "4 lbs. of cooked meat bones or trimmings, a large carrot, 2 onions, 1 leek, 1 turnip, clarified fat, 1 stick of celery, 1/2 lb. of mushrooms, 6 cloves, 12 black peppercorns, 1 dessertspoonful of salt, 2 blades of mace, 1 bunch of savoury herbs (parsley, bay-leaf and thyme)." You made it by frying until brown the washed, dried & sliced vegetables with the clarified fat and meat trimmings. Then you add the broken up bones, mushrooms, herbs, salt & spices. Cover with cold water and boil. Skim and simmer. Strain through a hair sieve (see next chapter), and when cold "remove every particle of fat." (Something similar, or at least for a vegetarian plenty good enough, can be made with soy protein meat substitutes, lots more mushrooms & onion, and some canned pumpkin, which seems to add a versatile flavor. Or you could make a fish stock, which would be very nice with cucumber.)*

Cucumber slicer, cast iron, screw clamps to table, completely vertical round hopper or chute is cuke-sized, blades cranked, "The Patent Slicer," mfd. by Spong, London, England, 9-5/8"H, c.1920s or 1930s (?) poss. earlier. Another type is very like a cabbage plane, made of wood with a steel blade, but much smaller. .... **$95+**

Cutting board, elephant form, wood, 14-3/4"L, c.1890s-1910s. Value may depend on the party in power! **$55**

I-41. Cucumber slicer (underside shown). Ivory with silver blade. 8-1/4"L x 2-1/2"W. Beautiful tiny thumb screws adjust blade. Supposedly Asian ivory stays very white; African ivory ages to mellow golden tones. $250-$325

I-42-A. Dough scraper. Wrought iron, polished and worked by a whitesmith to take on appearance of steel. Socket handle. About 3-3/4"L overall x 3"W. Early to mid 19th C. Not an uncommon type, and very simple. Collection of Mary Mac Franklin. $55+

Cutting board, fish shape, wood with burn rings like many cutting boards have (from being used as hot pads), American, 12"L x 7-1/4"W, prob. early 20th C. $45

Cutting board, pig shape, burl figured wood with good patina, pig has rather more detail around face than usual, PA German (?), 13-1/8"L x 7-5/8"W, prob. late 19th C. Many pig-shaped boards have been made in the last 40 years or so, but all were not created equal. .... $45+

Dough scraper, forged or wrought iron, short hollow socket handle, to be fitted with jammed-on wooden longer handle, American (?), early 19th C. $70

❖ NOTES ❖

Forged or Wrought? The terms mean fundamentally the same thing; both apply to objects that are worked (or wrought) at a forge. Because the usual understanding of wrought is of something iron, black and turned in scrolls like a wrought iron fence, or wrought iron lampstand, I prefer "forged." It is not enough to describe something as "handwrought," because the metal must be specified. Copper, pewter, silver, and aluminum all can be handwrought.

•   •   •

Whitesmithed – A whitesmith worked iron past the point that most blacksmiths worked it – they beat the black out of it, so to speak, making a silvery white metal from the forged iron.

Dough scraper, brass blade, tapered tubular handle made of tin, capped with brass, copper rivets, very small, marked "J. B.," probably mid 19th C, and one of the most unusual I've ever seen. $125

Dough scraper, forged iron, like a hoe but with a hollow handle socket, for a wooden handle of any length that was useful to the cook who owned it, and easily replaced by the cook. American, 19th C. $65

Dough scraper, forged iron, skinny handle with twist at end, longish blade, American, 6-1/2"L, mid 19th C. $40

Dough scraper, machined brass, very beautiful tubular handle with bands of turned decoration, signed "P. D." by maker Peter Derr, Berks County, PA, dated 1848. Others by Derr are known. Early one dated 1832 was for sale for $375 in 1984....... $475

Dough scraper, polished forged iron, decorated with etched tulip, shaped & slightly curved iron handle,

marked with initials "C L" on blade's front, could be maker or owner, Pennsylvania (?), blade 4-1/4"W, early to mid 19th C. $375

Dough scraper, triangle of steel for the blade, a separate steel handle riveted on, American, mid 19th C. ... $45

Dough scraper, whitesmith's work, polished, planished worked iron, heart cutout, beautiful detailing on hollow tubular handle, cap knob on end, design comprised of cross-hatched lines & tiny drilled holes, American (?), 4-1/8"W, prob. 1st or 2nd quarter 19th C. $350

Dough scraper, or cake turner or short peel, forged iron, keyhole-shaped blade with punch stippled profile bust of smiling man with high arched eyebrows & standing bird, rattail handle, length of handle marked with a triple row of punched dots, Pennsylva-

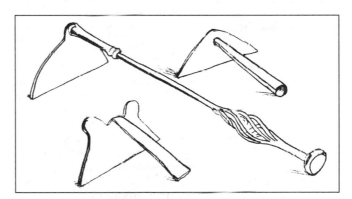

I-42-B. Dough scrapers. Long-handled one is wrought brass and iron, about 13"L, with split & twisted cage handle, with three glass marbles inside! Drawn from photo in story on a March 1990 Pook & Pook sale at Chester, PA. (T-R) This one is a simple triangle with separate tapered tubular socket handle riveted through hole in blade. About 4"W. (B-L) This one with high shoulders is drawn from one seen at a Pennsylvania show. It was made from one wrought piece, the handle being bent back between the shoulders or ears of the blade. 4-1/2"W. $900+; $125; $55+

nian in appearance, 3-1/8"L overall, blade is 5-3/4"L, appears to be mid 19th C., but I think it's a mid 20th C. fake. I suspect this only because it's too much for the money. A portrait bust? Plus a bird? Both done in unusual manner, with gorgeous keyhole shape & 1989 selling price of only $100? If real, value should be:.. **$450+**

Egg cutter & cup, stamped & enameled sheet metal, sort of a footed egg cup with egg-dome top, with thin pivoting round metal cutter with small knob. Don't know if you shell the egg first, but prob. Slices egg in half at the equator. 3-1/2"H. No marks, American (?), early 20th C. .... **$20+**

Egg cutter & cup, stamped metal, footed egg-shaped cup with hinged egg-dome top, center circular "blade" pivots to slice egg in half before opening cup. Knob on top balances top, and you eat out of both halves. Marked "C. F. Bierbach, Rochester, NY Pat'd. July 15, 1919" on underside of rim. 3-3/8"H. [Another: highly polished nickel silver finish... **$30+**

Egg opener, or egg topper, scissors style, nickeled steel (also available in silver-plated steel), 2 round loop handles for thumb & little finger, curved "blades" with a number of longish sharp teeth on inside to pierce shell of cooked egg. According to two 1890 ads, this was an "improvement" on their earlier model which had straight handles without finger loops, first made by Champion Egg Opener Co., Hartford, CT; and by 1909 made by W. R. Hartigan, Hartford, CT, then Collinsville, CT, approx. 3-1/2"L, pat'd. Jan. 4, 1887 & Dec. 22, 1903, sold at least to 1910s. (Most common egg openers are the chicken-handle little scissors, which are still being made – one by Hoffritz.).. **$6-$25**

Egg slicers

Over the years I've bought a few cast aluminum ones (along with butter and cheese slicers) because I've long had a thing for cast aluminum. Until working on the 5th edition of this book, and using eBay more than my wallet says is OK, I've discovered quite a variety in just a few weeks. As far as I know, very few people collect these now. But don't wait ... I think these will make a lot of collectors very happy! And research still needs to be done. I don't really know the full scope of the field, and so far haven't found any patents. I've put a **future-watch** on egg slicers & wedgers because I think they are handsome, varied enough for interest, small, and still quite cheap. And now you'll have an excuse for spinach with egg slices; tuna salad with egg slices; baked casseroles with egg wedges; and anything you can imagine. Hey! I just made up a recipe: make carrot pancakes (you can use the pulp from an electric juice extractor, or pulp them in a food processor) and at the last minute, add egg slices. And if those devices that allow you to make a square hard-boiled egg ever really catch on, maybe they'll start making slicers for square boiled eggs. And then ... and then...

• • •

Lookback & Brand New! – Here are the American companies that made egg slicers, as found in two sources: *Thomas' Register of American Manufacturers* of 1905-06; 1932-33; and 1946; and the 1909, 1915, and 1930 issues of the *Buyers Directory of House Furnishing Goods & Kindred Articles*, which gave model names. It was published annually by *House Furnishing Review*. (By no means should we consider the lists complete; not even all the companies we know made them bothered to list their egg slicers as a product.)

• **1905-06:** Lalance & Grosjean.

• **1909:** None listed, although it's probable that a few companies making small gadgets made them. In a 1911 article in House Furnishings Review, it was reported that George Thurnauer, the NYC importer, had "bought on a recent trip to Europe ... the aluminum egg slicer."

• **1915:** None listed, but by 1915, aluminum wares had really taken off; many companies offered aluminum things, including "novelties."

• **1930:** Allen Brothers Co., Hartford, CT; Hamilton Metal Products Co., Hamilton, OH; Thurnauer Co., NYC [imported from Germany].

• **1932-33:** Lalance & Grosjean, Woodhaven, NY; Aluminum Goods Mfg. Co., Manitowoc, WI; Standard Butter Cutter Co., NYC, NY. (Some of the following makers of vegetable & fruit slicers may also have made egg slicers, although the *Register* doesn't say so: Perfect Automatic Egg Timer & Mfg. Co., Chicago; Tucker & Dorsey Mfg. Co., Indianapolis, IN; Handy Things Mfg. Co., Ludington, MI; Acme Metal Goods Co., Newark, NJ; Bromwell Wire Goods Co., Cincinnati, OH; The Hamilton Metal Products Co., Hamilton, OH; and probably George Thurnauer Co. of NYC imported them from Germany. In addition, these makers of butter cutters, & cheese cutters, both of which used wires like egg slicers: Cherry-Burrell Corp., Chicago, IL; John B. Adt Co., Baltimore, MD; Parker Wire Goods Co., Worcester, MA.

• **1946:** William Hodges & Co., Philadelphia, PA; and Aluminum Goods Mfg. Co., Manitowoc, WI. It's still possible that the Perfect Automatic Egg Timer & Mfg. Co. was making egg slicers, as well as the other "possibles" from 1932-33. A few cheese slicer makers may also have made egg slicers: Youngberg Bros., Meriden, CT; Huot Mfg. Co., St. Paul, MN; John Clark Brown, Belleville, NJ.

• • •

Germany's Westmark – Many Westmark things are found on eBay, and their egg slicers are really handsome. The company was founded in Lüdenscheid, Germany, in 1923, and moved to Herscheid in 1932. It started as a cutlery-grinding shop run by Karl-Walther Schulte's family; but about 1932 the company decided to make mechanical kitchen gadgets of aluminum, stainless steel, plastic, etc.

Egg Slicers & Wedgers in 21st Century – A quick check of the Internet shows that several companies are making these devices, and they don't look that much different from old ones. Almost all of new egg slicers, have a round, oval, or oblong base, and a wire-strung, hinged cutter frame. Norpro, a kitchen specialty manufacturer and wholesaler in Everett, Washington, since 1973, selling all over the world, have one in cast iron (5" x 3-1/4"), and a stainless steel one (5" x 4") for eggs or mushrooms, and a stainless steel 'tong' style one which cuts wedges, and a beautifully-designed side-by-side joined unit with 2 hinged cutting frames with stainless steel wires – one side cuts slices, one wedges, and a shell-piercer (for microwave) in center; Leifheit, of Germany, makes a white plastic gadget that slices & wedges, long and narrow with hinged top that has a square and a circle cut out and strung with wires; a similar device is American, made by West Bend; a smoother, rounded-end long one is by the Italian company Pedrini, is another 2 way wedger & slicer; Amco has a stainless steel round one which cuts unusual number of slices – 16; there are a number of Westmark slicers & wedgers: an oblong white enameled steel one, a heavy formed aluminum oblong one, a combination slicer & wedger in oblong form, with two hinged slicing frames called the "Duplex," a slightly-diamond shape "Duplex Special," a 'tong' style one, hand-held, called "Columbus," a multipurpose slicer for eggs, mush-

rooms, peeled kiwi, strawberries, also tong style, called "Champion," and another oblong one called "Rundy," a tong style aluminum wedger is made by Scandicraft; there's a 3-in-1 Egg Machine, bright yellow plastic & steel, makes wedges, slices & rosettes, made in Japan for DAS; a "Two-Way" by Matfer in epoxy-coated cast aluminum, stainless steel wire; a round base aluminum slicer very like Amco's made by (?) Update International; Fox Run has one in stainless steel, oblong with wire frame; a brushed stainless steel slicer, 3-7/8" diam., no maker known; several clear & white plastic slicers with wire cutters, maker unknown. My 6-hour search of the Internet turned up these new ones. Astonishingly, there was only one each from Japan & Taiwan.

Egg slicer, nickeled metal, wires, marked in shield outline "D. R. P." (which just means a registered patent), German, 8-3/4", early 20th C. .... **$25+**

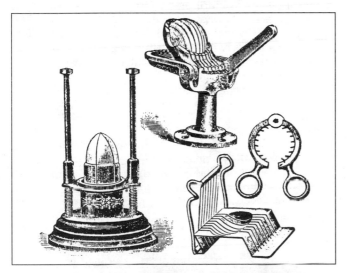

I-ES&W-A. Egg wedger, slicers & opener. (L) *Japanned & decorated cast iron, sliding cutter with 5 blades, to make 6 wedges of hardboiled egg, for use in salads; c.1870s-80s, V. Clad, Philadelphia.* **Top (R):** *Egg slicer, for sandwiches, cast iron, meant to be screwed or bolted to counter in restaurant kitchen. Lever pushes wires through egg. Also V. Clad.* **(R)** *Scissor-action device, an egg topper, "to remove a portion of the shell without crushing either the removed or remaining portion of shell. Improved version with ring handles for thumb & forefinger, instead of little short straight handles. Imported by G. M. Thurnauer, NYC, from about 1890 through 1904 at least.* **Bottom (B)** *Most common type, still made today by a variety of companies. Not very substantial, but strong enough. This one is an imported aluminum & wire slicer, of type frequently seen from 1920s on, made in metal with metal or wood slotted base. Metal more sanitary. This one from c.1927 catalog. Even in 2001, an egg slicer looks almost exactly like this one. Some more intricate, with stronger metal, and some could have their wires tightened with a little screw. The hinged wire frame is the most unchanged part.* **(L) $100+; (T-R) $55+;** *Others:* **$5-$12**

Egg slicer, plated cast iron, wire, lever action, mounted on a round pedestal base screwed to a countertop, sold by V. Clad & Sons, Philadelphia, early 20th C. **$100**

Egg slicer, sheet aluminum, hinged top with 10 wires, very cheap construction, but nifty, American, 5"L x 2-3/4"W, 1930s. Extremely similar to this, was one marked along the edge "D.R.G.M. Aust. Pat." and imported from Austria c.1910. I wouldn't be surprised if after the war an American manufacturer simply started making them. A similar one is marked "Tala," Made in England. Another "Progressus," Made in West Germany. There are many more, unmarked. **$10**

Egg slicer, well-made cast aluminum, cupped base holds egg, hinged slicer top is strung with 10 wires; by rotating sliced egg 90º you can dice it, or you can choose to make round slices or ovoid slices depending on the orientation of the egg. "Bloomfield Industries," Chicago, 4" x 4", c.1935. .... **$15+**

Egg slicer, cast aluminum, oblong base with hexagonal hinged cutter-wire frame, cupped base holds egg for round or ovoid slices, marked "Germany" near hinge, really handsome! 5-3/8"L x 3-3/8"W.... **$20+**

Egg slicer, cast aluminum (not polished) & wire, base & hinged wire-frame close to square (4" x 3-1/4"), marked "6," "Pat. Apld. For" and "Presto," a word which means "Quick" in several languages. More likely to have been made by Presto Mfg. Co., Ossin-

I-ES&W-B. Egg wedger. *Cast aluminum, round base, steel wire, and steel vertical shaft. This one has slight hitch to park the wire-frame when you pull it up to put egg in petaled cup. Marked on bottom "Regn. App. For Made in England," with "Tala" in diamond cartouche. 5"H x 2-5/8" diam. Tala dates to 1899; the company makes kitchen gadgets still – a garlic press, cake-decorating tubes; they made coffin nutmeg graters; also the simplest kind of egg slicer like one in I-ES&W-A; and garnish cutters. The wedger is prob. c.1940s.* **$15+**

I-ES&W-C. Egg wedger. *Cast aluminum, steel wire, hexagonal base, grooved vertical shaft and tip-top cutting frame. Marked "Westmark's Lukullus-6," "Germany DRP," 4-1/8"H x 3" across base, c. 1950s (?) $15+*

I-ES&W-E. Egg slicer. *Cast aluminum, octagonal cutting frame with steel wires, on oblong base, very angular Deco design. Egg can be placed sideways or lengthwise for cutting circles or ovals. Faintly embossed on frame near hinge "Germany," 1-3/8"H x 5-1/4"L x 3-7/8"W. Possibly as early as 1930s. $20+*

ing, NY than pressure-cooker maker National Presto Co., Eau Claire, WI, c.1950. Another highly polished "Presto" has an egg-shaped base, marked "4 Way Egg Slicer," and "Pat. Pend.," 3-1/2" x 5", but the egg "bed" holds an egg 3 different ways to make round, ovoid or diagonal slices, and also to dice by repositioning sliced egg; Yet another "Presto" is rectangular with truncated corners. Any of which:........ **$10+**

Egg slicer, ceramic & stainless steel (?), rather typical round hinged egg holder set into orange-glazed china dish. Handle for frame with cutting wires has small orangey plastic grip. Marked underneath on white glazed ceramic, in diamond cartouche, "Wales Slicer Belmet Products Pat Pend. Made in USA," 3"H x 8" diam., c.1930s-40s. .... **$40+**

Egg slicer, molded plastic, very finely made & substantial, oblong, hinged heavy wire frame strung with fine wires, have seen in red, and so-called "Jadite" green, Great Britain, "Hygene," c.1950s-60s.... **$15+**

Egg slicer, molded plastic & stainless steel, light pink "Melmac," round, 3-3/4" diam., American, c.1950s... **$12**

Egg slicer, wood & wire, heavy green painted frame, 10 slicing wires, no maker's name, but ink stamped on bottom gives original price, 15¢, 4-1/8"L x 2-3/4"W, 20th C. **$10**

Egg slicer, curvy wooden base, like molding, with slots for wires in heavy wire cutting frame, hinged at one end. No mark, very impractical hygienically speaking. American (?). .... **$7+**

Egg wedge cutter, cast aluminum, steel wire & spring, put boiled egg in cup, push wire blades down to cut 6 wedges, "Westmark," German, 5-3/4"L, c.1950s (?) .... **$15+**

Egg wedge cutter, cast aluminum, very simple, round footprint with vertical guide-shaft on one side, 6 petal-like forms hold egg upright, round frame with 6 crossed fine wires moved manually up and down shaft. 5"H x 2-1/2" diam, underside base marked "Regn. App. for Made in England" and in a diamond "Tala." Probably c.1950s-60s......................... **$15+**

I-ES&W-D. Egg wedger. *Cast aluminum, steel wire, tri-petal base, spring-loaded cutter frame on vertical shaft. Knurled knob on top, shapely finger/thumb plate for pushing, only mark is "Germany" under cutting frame. 4-7/8"H x 3-1/2" across, c.1950s? $20+*

I-ES&W-F. Egg slicers. *Cast aluminum, steel wires in frames, hinged at one end.* **(T)** *This one highly polished, ovoid base, egg cup part holds eggs lengthwise, crosswise, and even diagonally, marked "Presto," "11," "Pat. Pend. 4-Way Egg Slicer," 4-1/2" x 3-1/8".* **(B)** *Roughly finished, egg goes only one way – to make round slices, marked "Presto," "6," "Pat. Apld. For." Numbers don't refer to number of slices or wires. Top one may be 1950s, bottom one probably 1930s. Probably Presto Mfg. Co., Ossining, NY 9 (not the Presto company that made pressure cookers). $10+*

Egg wedge cutter, cast aluminum, steel wire & spring, tripetal footed base, from which rises a 6 petal "flower" cup to hold egg. Round cutter-wire frame held onto shaft with knurled knob. Push down spring-resisting circle strung with 6 crisscross wires, marked "Germany" underside of cutter frame, 4-7/8"H, c.1950s-60s (?).............................. **$15+**

Egg wedge cutter, cast aluminum & steel wire, largish hexagonal base with 6 flat-top petals for the egg, base has vertical guide shaft for the round wire-strung cutter frame. Unusual is fact that cutter frame pulls up on the shaft, and can be tilted back to rest in a groove. Embossed in script on underside of base: "Westmark's Lukullus" – 6", also "Germany," and "DRP." 4"H x 3-7/8"W. c.1960s (?). .... **$15+**

Egg wedge cutter, japanned & decorated cast iron, heavy stepped plinth base, cylindrical egg holder, the blades are set in a frame that slides down 2 "columns" on either side of the egg to cut it into 6 wedges. Sold to restaurateurs, but useful for families too, sold by V. Clad & Sons, Philadelphia, about 8"H, early 20th C. **$125**

Egg wedge cutter, cast aluminum & wire, spring-action 'tong'- spoon device, the top part has 6 wires and you place the boiled & shelled egg in the spoon-cup and press down the wires. "Eggwedger" by "Westmark," Germany, 20th C. Some found in the USA have been found in boxes marked "Made in Western Germany for Overseas Housewares Co., Yonkers NY USA."... **$20+**

Egg wedge cutter, cast aluminum & wire, spring 'tong' action with much smaller cup for egg than previous listing. German, 20th C. (Another has 4 plastic holder 'petals.' Another, marked "Westmark Columbus" has a 6-petaled white plastic egg cup, and spring action handle with a little lock at the hinge end.) .... **$15+**

Fish cleaner, carved wood with small steel or iron blade, handle is carved & colored portrait of woman with garters, from Belle Isle, ME, 6-5/8"L, c.1880s to 1890s. Folk art one of a kind. **$250**

Fish scaler, cast iron, "Champion," American, 20th C. **$15**

Fish scaler, cast iron, "C. D. Kenny," American, 9"L, 19th C. **$20**

Fish scaler, homemade using narrow wooden paddle carved from a piece of wood, 5 bottle caps nailed rough edge up, one cap reads "Reading Brewery Co.," others from Shenandoah Beer, Old Reading, etc., Pennsylvania, 8-3/4"L, early (?) 20th C. This is the kind of thing beginning to show up at folk art shows, with values maybe twice the kitchen-collecting market. **$20**

Fish scaler, japanned cast iron, business end is slightly curved & narrow with 34 projections, handle is long loop of cast iron, American, 9"L overall, half handle, late 19th C. **$12**

Fish scaler & knife, chromium plated steel with stainless steel blade, in shape of fish, bottom has perforated steel scaling blade, knife handle is whole back half of body & pulls out of front half sheath, "Fish-Master," "Made in U. S. A.," c.1961.................................. **$10**

Flour grinder or mill, painted heavy sheet metal, decal decoration, Arcade, Freeport, IL, c.1920. .... **$65**

Fodder & feed grinder, cast iron, several steel cutter blades, "O. V. B. Hibbard, Spencer & Bartlett," ("Our Very Best"), early 20th C. .... **$45+**

Food chopper, meat or root vegetable chopper or hasher, but called a meat cutter by the inventor, painted cast iron, tin canister hopper with wooden bottom, mounted to green painted wooden base with a cast iron ratchet gear. Crank and the hopper revolves, while the chopping blade goes up and down like a pile driver or oil rig, Athol Machine Co., Leroy Starrett, Athol Depot, MA, pat'd. May 23, 1865 by Starrett. Various sizes: No. 1, 8" cylinder; No. 2, 10" cyl.; No. 3, 12" cyl., weighs 37 lbs; No. A, 12" cyl., weighs 43 lbs; No. 4, 15" cyl., weighs 120 lbs; and two even larger commercial ones with 18" and 20" cylinders. [Note: In German Glossary Chapter XXV, you'll see translations reflecting various uses.].................................... **$125-$350**

❖ NOTES ❖

Previously invented – Mr. V. Price, of Wardour Street, Soho, London, exhibited, at the Great Exhibition, London, 1851, "A **chopping-knife** for the reduction of suet, &c., into small particles. It consists of three blades fixed side by side, to the lower surface of a flat metal frame, which is hinged at one end to a fixed metal pillar or support, and at the other is provided with a handle, whereby the blades are alternately lifted and brought down upon the suet or other substance to be chopped, which is laid upon a circular wooden dish or chopping-block. Each time that the knife-frame is raised, a hooked rod, suspended therefrom, catches into the teeth of a ratchet wheel, and turns it partly round; on the axis of this ratchet wheel is a small cog-wheel, which takes into the teeth of a circular rack or wheel, fixed to the underside of the chopping-block; and thus, at each ascent of the knife-frame, the block will be moved partly round, and made to present fresh portions of suet to the action of the descending knives." Quoted from *Newton's Journal*, XXXIX. 132. in *Andrew Ure's A Dictionary of Arts, Manufactures, and Mines*, 2nd Vol., American ed., 1854. Mr. Price also exhibited a clothes washer.

I-43. Fish scalers & combo scaler & corn grater. **(T)** *Nickeled steel, turned wood handle. A "unique culinary device ... patented 1906. ... Practically the best corn grater ever invented. For taking scales off of fish or scraping vegetables it can not be excelled. It is the first and only pineapple shredder ever."* Montgomery Ward *catalog, c.1910.* **(B)** *Japanned cast iron fish scaler. S. B. Sexton, 1930s.* **$85; $20**

Food chopper, mostly wood, probably homemade copy or repair (much less likely to be a prototype) of Starrett or Athol chopper, made up with decorative cast iron apple parer gear, also heavy simple cast 4 spoked wheel with very thick & rounded rim, that looks like a sewing machine wheel, but is the same as the Starrett wheel; the frame is cut out of quarter-inch wood, hand painted rather crudely in brown & gold (like Starrett meat & cheese press); tin tub nailed to wooden bottom, but no gear to turn the tub, you have to turn it by hand as you crank, gear reads "Reading Hardware Works," "Reading, PA," 19th C (the Athol chopper was pat'd. 1865).... **$200**

Food chopper, plated metal, screw clamps to table, works with crank, 3 discs for grating, slicing, shredding, "Kitchmaster," mfd. by Chicago Flexible Shaft Co. (which Sunbeam was part of), Chicago, IL, c.1934. Chicago Flexible Shaft started out in 1890 as a manufacturer of sheep-shearing machines! **$30**

Food chopper, tinned cast iron, screw clamps, available with 5 cutting or grinding blades & a wooden pestle, "The American," mfd. by American Cutlery Co., Chicago, IL; four sizes, viz. #10, 8-1/2"H; #20, 9-1/4"H; #30, 10"H; and #40, 12"H, c.1920.................... **$20**

I-45. Food & meat chopper, *butchers' – size No. 5, elevated on cast iron frame. 20" diam. chopping block inside the cylindrical can. From 1906 catalog.* **$225-$350+**

Food chopper or grinder, nickeled cast iron, wood handle, "Universal No. 00," mfd. by Landers, Frary & Clark, New Britain, CT, pat'd. Oct. 12, 1897, Apr. 18, 1899, & in 1900. According to a trade catalog, this came in four sizes: #00 for small families, #1 for regular family, #2 for large family which has several different blades, and #3 for hotel or market. All are about the same value, though maybe add $5 to $10 for the largest.. **$20+**

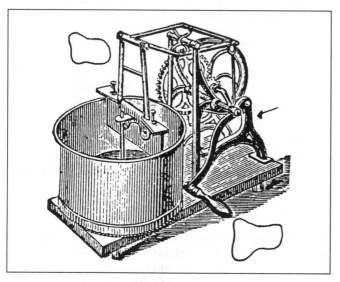

I-44. Food chopper for meat & vegetables. *Also called a "steamboat meat chopper." Also referred to as the "**American**," the "**Starrett**," or the "**Athol**" chopper. Cast iron, tin, painted wood. pat'd. May 23, 1865, by Leroy Starrett, mfd. by Athol Machine Co., Athol Depot, MA. The small arrow at right points to the place on the cast iron frame where the* **cutout** *can be checked against the two outlined shapes drawn at left and bottom right. The upper one is found on post-1877 "improved" ones. The picture here is of a pre-1877 model. There were 3 sizes – 8", 10", & 12" diameter cylinder, which rotated on ratchet underneath as chopping blade rose & fell. Makes wonderful rhythmic sound, my reason for keeping mine! Three larger ones, 15", 18", & 20" have intermittent gears instead of ratchet & pawl. This chopper was sold in Europe too, and shows up in books on English and German kitchen antiques. The smallest is the most desirable, and would bring the most.* **$125-$250+**

I-46. Cast iron working parts *of chopper in I-47. Has 3 patent dates: "June 5, 1865" (probably mistake for 1866, the date for C. A. **Foster's** patent, Winchendon, MA); "July 11, 1865," and "Jan. 31" with no year, but was 1865. Last 2 dates for A. F. **Spaulding** & S. M. **Scott's** patents, also from Winchendon, MA). 8"H x 10"L. Cast iron but for steel blade & bucket scraper. From stock of David Antinore, at Brimfield, MA. This one is missing the tin hopper with its removable wooden bottom. According to collectors Larry & Carole Meeker, www.patented-antiques.com, who have one on their Web site, the cutter blade not only moves up and down like the Starrett/Athol, but also "moves back & forth in a natural slicing motion." The parts:* **$50+;** *complete:* **$300+**

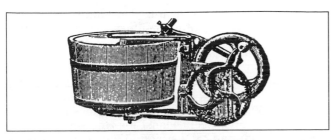

I-47. Food & meat chopper like Foster/Spaulding/Scott. *Gear wheels and top edge of chopper look identical, but there's a wooden tub instead of a tin one. This picture from* Henry Scammel's Treasure-House of Knowledge, *1890. "Indispensable where sausage & mince pies are favorites. Men who buy mowing machines and hay forks cannot afford to let their wives work away in the kitchen with old-fashioned implements when better ones are to be had for little money. If any husband refuses to buy it, let the wife cut off his supply of hash and sausages on trial, and then take severer means afterward if necessary."* **$300+**

Food chopper, grinder or mill, tinned cast iron, screw clamps, short shaft, rather large hopper, 4 "knife" discs (fine has 15 teeth, medium has 9, coarse has 3, and the nut butter cutter has close-set sharp diagonal grooves instead of teeth). "Enterprise No. 501," c.1900. .... **$20+**

Food chopper, cast iron, break away hopper, hinged in 2 halves with simple pivoting clamp, curved grinding handle embossed with words "shoulder on worm" which alone is worth collecting! Screw clamps to table, "New Standard Food Chopper," Universal Hardware Works.. **$25**

Food chopper – See also: Vegetable chopper

Food grinder, cast iron plated with brass, unusual sheet iron trough or chute, screw clamps, large hopper, side crank, retains its fine perforated metal tapered cutter insert (probably came with several, for fine, medium & coarse), "No. 1 Fruit Strainer," "Vitantonio Co.," Cleveland, OH, 9-1/4"H, pat'd. Feb. 15, 1888 (?). **$65**

Food grinder, cast iron, strong & handsome, wedges onto edge of table or shelf, no screw clamp. Top plate that rests on top of table is 2 lobed like baby's bottom or heart top, central PA, 9-1/2"H, mid 19th C. This was the only food grinder I've ever coveted. It was the late, much-missed dealer Darryl Dudash's piece. .... **$300+**

Food grinder, plated iron, hopper hinged to remove cutters for cleaning, "Russwin #2," Russell & Erwin Mfg. Co., New Britain, CT, 1902 patent............. **$30**

Food grinders, enameled cast iron, screw clamps to table, wooden crank handles, some mottled emerald green like malachite, others slightly lighter plain green enameling, one plain green one has red painted wooden handle, the other plain varnished wood, part of paper label on one reads "HARPER No. 40"; one of plain ones is still

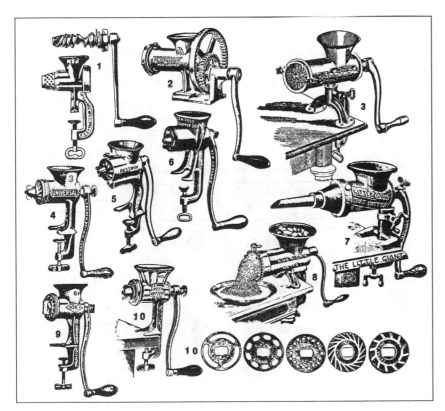

I-48. Food grinders & meat cutters. (1) "Enterprise No.2" *meat chopper for 1 lb. a minute. Not the most collectible Enterprise, but it shows the interior part, which grinds & moves meat from hopper forward. 1905 catalog shows sizes 2, 4, 6, 8, 5, 10, 12, 20, 22, 32, & 42.* **(2)** *Tinned cast iron* "Universal No. 344," *Landers, Frary & Clark. Hopper 5" x 6" diam., 9-3/4"H, "geared down to get greater ease in operation," does 4 lb. meat a minute.* **(3)** "Ellrich" *meat cutter, Ellrich Hardware Mfg. Co., Plantsville, CT, drawing marked pat'd. May 15, 1892 (has to be 1888 for "patent Tuesday"). The Metal Worker ad.* **(4)** "Universal No.3," *4" x 5" hopper, 3 lb. per minute.* **(5)** "Russwin," *originally Russell & Erwin. pat'd. Aug. 21, 1901.* **(6)** *Small* "Gem No. 20" *food chopper, Sargent & Co. 2 lb. pm. For meat, vegetables, fruit, crackers, bread, boiled eggs, cheese, nuts, raisins, figs, etc.* **(7)** "The Little Giant No. 410" *cutter. Peck, Stow & Wilcox Co., Southington, CT. Stuffer attachment. 1892 ad.* **(8)** "Great American Meat Cutter No. 112," *Hibbard, Spencer, Bartlett & Co. 1870s catalog. Case/barrel 5-1/8"L x 2-1/4" diam. plate. 2 lb. pm.* **(9)** "Diamond Edge No. 61," *with DE pierced by arrow mark. Shapleigh Hardware Co., St. Louis. 7-1/2"H, hopper is 3-3/8" x 2-5/8", 2 lb. pm. c.1914.* **(10)** "Keen Kutter No. 22 1/2," *E. C. Simmons. 10"H, hopper 3-1/2" x 4-1/2", 3 lb. pm. Four cutter plates; holed ones for chopping from coarse to fine. Reversible one does fine one side, extra fine other. c.1920 catalog. The more attachments, the more value. Form counts for something too: (2), (3), (7), and (8) have the most unusual forms. Keen Kutter items have specialist collectors whose value ranges may differ.* **(2) (3) (7) (8) $75+;** *rest:* **$20+**

in original cardboard box, "National Mincer, V. Enameled, Spong & Co., Ltd.," Harper; Spong, London, England, 9"L and 6-7/8"L mottled ones; 7-1/2"L plain green ones, c.1920s or 1930s. .... **$75+**

Food mill, and meat grinder, tabletop, zinc plated (ie. galvanized) cast iron frame, hopper & crank, a piece at bottom of shaft slides into cutout in base – a shaped & "molded" cast iron platform. Painted white, with white rubber feet, complete with various cutters & blades, in original cotton bags, "Rayflex Foodmaster," Rayflex Mfg. Co., Bridgeport, CT, about 7"H, c.1930s, but "patent pending." **$45**

❖ NOTES ❖

Galvanized Iron and Zinc Plating – Zinc-plating, also called "galvanizing," is a rust-preventing coating used for some of the same applications as tinning, but it works in a different way. When "zinc" is used in a description of a houseware, it almost invariably means galvanized iron or steel, which is iron or steel with a zinc coating. You will see the word "zinc" used sometimes in a way that makes you think an object is made of pure zinc. In the 19th century (possibly even now) sculpture was sometimes cast in pure zinc, then bronze-plated to suit the aesthetic standards of the period. I doubt if any kitchen tools are pure cast zinc. And the only zinc sheet metals are zinc alloys. Brass is an alloy of copper and zinc (sometimes tin is also added; sometimes up to 1% aluminum, which means more zinc can be added to make a pale-colored brass). Bronze is an alloy of copper and tin. "The process of galvanizing," states the unnamed author of *The First Hundred Years of The New Jersey Zinc Company* (NY: 1948), "or the coating of iron or steel with zinc to prevent it from rusting, is older than the zinc industry in the United States. As far back as 1778, in France, zinc was applied as a coating to iron utensils. In 1805, in England, a patent was taken out which recommended the use of 'nails coated with zinc' and, in 1837, also in England, the first patent on hot dip galvanizing was issued. The galvanizing industry in the United States started in 1864. ... Zinc is the most effective coating for preventing [rust] because zinc protects iron electrolytically. As a result, corroding agents in air, water and the soil attack zinc in preference to iron. ... This action is ... important when ... a small area of the base metal is exposed. ... The base [is] protected from corrosion as long as sufficient zinc remains." Zinc is sometimes called a "**sacrificial metal**" when used in this way, as it is sacrificed so that the iron is protected from oxidizing, hence rusting. • **Hot dip galvanizing and electrogalvanizing** are very different methods of applying zinc coatings, each ... suitable for certain applications." The writer adds that hot dip galvanizing is used "when the product is to be bent and formed after coating, ... wire is a familiar example of such an application." By the 1930s, at least, some zinc-plating was done by spraying on molten zinc (sometimes in conjunction with aluminum) to a thickness of at least 1/500 of an inch. • I suspect that most "zinc" or "galvanized" products known to housewares collectors – food mills, lemon squeezers, meat grinders, vegetable slicers, washboards, pails, corrugated waste cans, and so-called "linings" of dry sinks or refrigerators – are formed *before* galvanizing, and

therefore were electrogalvanized. Zinc alloy castings are found inside washing machines, refrigerators and some electrical appliances. Glass canning jars patented by metalworker John L. Mason in 1858 had the first threaded necks, and the screw-on lids for them were made of the relatively soft metal zinc, which imparted a metallic taste, but which created a good seal. In 1869, Lewis Boyd patented a glass liner (clear at first, then opalescent glass) for zinc screw-caps. • **Zincked or Tinned?** – Visual and tactile comparisons must be made with tinned, nickeled or chromed objects. Worn galvanized metal tends to look dark and somewhat mottled, and feel almost like soapstone – very smooth, yet with just a hint of drag or grab to the touch. Really corroded zinc gets a rather unpleasant white powdery film on the surface. Sort of like mealybugs on the aspidistra.

Food mill, cast iron, "Dana Mfg. Co.," (their ice cream freezers were more famous), Cincinnati, OH, c.1890s-1910s. **$20**

Food mill, cast iron, screw clamps, "Keen Kutter #11," mfd. by E. C. Simmons, 9-1/2"H, pat'd. May 29, 1906. (The #10 was pat'd. May 15, 1904.) **$20**

Food mill, cast iron, screw clamps, "Eveready #55," 8"H, 20th C. **$15**

Food mill, cast iron, screw clamps, "Rollman Food Chopper #12," Rollman Mfg. Co., c.1890s-1910s. **$15**

Food mill, cast iron, screw clamps, "Chipaway Food Grinder," 20th C. **$15**

Food mill, cast iron, screw clamps, "#7, O. V. B." Hibbard, Spencer, Bartlett & Co., (Our Very Best), 8"H, pat'd. May 17, 1904. .... **$20**

Food mill, cast & plated iron, red Bakelite™ or other molded phenolic resin handle, original box, "Acme Rotary Mincer," American, 1935. Bakelite crossover. **$35**

I-49. Food mills. *Two small cast iron screw-clamp mills. **(T-R):** "Schroeter's Improved Grater No. 100." pat'd. Nov. 1903; **Foreground:** Small painted & decorated cast iron mill, an "Improved Schroeter" almond & vegetable grater, I think a No. 10. Schroeter Bros. Hardware, St. Louis. Other types to look for are the colorfully enameled, decorative, cast iron German-made mills bearing women's names – Anna, Inge, Victoria, Carmen, Cäcilie, Amanda & Kitty, and other highly detailed design features including women's heads – make a great collection. [Note: the value depending on origin might be reversed in Europe.] German: **$50+**; American: **$85+***

Food mill, cream painted cast iron, varnished round wood pusher, marked "P. C.," 9-3/4"H, early 20th C. **$22**

Food mill, metal, saucepan-shaped, hook opposite handle, mark is old good luck symbol (backwards swastika) & "DILVER," Dilver Mfg. Co., –?– burger, PA, 8" diam., pat'd. Nov. 3, 1903 & Mar. 17, 1906. .... **$30**

Food mill, sheet iron & wood, handmade, with wrought iron handle, mounted to board, with various adjustments, no mark, American, hopper 4" diam., board 16-1/2"L, early 1800s. **$250**

Food mill, tin, 2 front teeth, green stained wooden handle, wire forms feet & handle, only 1 blade, "Moulinette," "Made in England," but a French device originally, "pat'd. in all countries," 20th C. **$30**

Food mill, cast iron, tin hopper with wood pusher, screw clamps, "Edith," German, small, early 20th C. Many German mills had rather ornate, or at least very decorative, cast frames (even though the screw clamps were very simple), and many had German women's names embossed on the frame above the crank: "Anna," "Cäcilie," "Kitty," "Lücilie," "Victoria," "Amanda," etc. **$45**

Food mill, cast iron, 2 cutters (one of which reverses coarse to fine, other is marked "Universal Bread Crumber"), "Universal," Landers, Frary & Clark, pat'd. 1897 & 1899. .... **$30**

Food or meat grinder, cast metal, steel, Winchester #W33, 20th C. Crossover interest from gun people. Winchester made several sizes, including #W11 ($40-$50), #W12 (about $60-$70), #W13, a very large one ($75-$90), #W32 ($50-$65). #W33 is valued: **$50**

Food or meat grinder, plated cast iron, screw clamps, opens to clean, Rollman Mfg Co., Mt. Joy, PA, advertised in 1902. .... **$25**

Food or meat grinder, tinned cast iron, screw clamps, in original box with different blades, "Universal #1," Landers, Frary & Clark, New Britain, CT, c.1890s 1910s. **$20**

❖ NOTES ❖

Early Hamburgers – We tend to think of hamburgers as 20th C. fast food, but as far back as 1853 the term "dodger," meaning a soft, flat, pancake sort of patty (usually made with cornmeal), was applied to a minced beef patty called a beef-dodger.

Food press, cast iron frame & sheet iron rectangular press box, decoratively painted & japanned in dark red & gold, vertical screw press action with heavy iron presser foot, perforated insert for bottom, "Starrett's Patent Food Press #1," mfd. by Athol Machine Co., Athol, MA, 9-1/2"L x 6-1/4"W, pat'd. Apr. 15, 1873. .... **$125**

Food press, potato ricer, etc., heavy tin, 4 parts, viz. straight-sided kettle with side handles, bottom & first inch up side of seeding pan is perforated; it sets down into top of kettle; another insert pan has fine wire mesh in bottom; the "plunger," as it was called by the maker, is a thick wooden disc with a sadiron type wood handle, that was "skated" around to mash food through the insert pan into the kettle. Ads state that this would "revitalize cold potatoes" as well as seed strawberries, raspberries, etc., and could be used to strain soup or gravy, etc., "Stocking's Sim-

I-50. Fruit, lard or meat presses. (L) "Enterprise," 2, 4 or 8 qts. Turn of century. **(M)** "Starrett's Domestic Press," "for corned beef, boiled mutton, tongue, boned turkey, head cheese ... and for extracting juice from fruit & berries; also for pressing lard, cottage cheese, squash, turnip, &c." Cast & sheet iron, japanned & decorated. 3 sizes: 4" deep x 6" x 9"; 5" deep x 8" x 12"; and 6" x 10" x 14". 1870s. **(R)** English-made "enameled iron fruit presser." 1895 catalog. **(L) (R)**: **$90-$150**; **(M) $125+**

plex Straining and Seeding-Press," mfd. by The 4-S-Food-Press Co., NYC, NY, pat'd. Feb. 10, 1903. **$15**

Food press, white porcelainized iron & tin, iron juice catcher, lion's paw feet, lion's head design, marked only "No. 00," French, 8-3/4"H, 19th C. "Porcelainized iron" refers to a vitreous (glass-like) enamel coating fired onto the iron. It isn't the same as "porcelain," which is a ceramic body, sometimes just called "china." **$100**

Fruit baller, 2 red wooden turned handles, nickeled steel lever handles terminate in hinged perforated cutting ring, used by pulling handles apart to cause hinged blade to scoop out ball of melon, American, 5-1/4"L, with open ring blade 1-1/2" diam., pat'd. Mar. 29, 192-? (would be 1921 or 1927). **$5**

Fruit baller, cigar-shaped red wooden handle with a stainless steel shaft out each end, one with a small bowled scoop, other with an even smaller scoop; both bowls have a small air release hole, probably Androck or A & J or the like, American, 7-3/4"L, 1940s. **$3**

Fruit & vegetable press, also called a potato ricer, japanned iron, cast iron levered handles, hopper looks like steam shovel, "Henis," mfd. by Charles F. Henis Co., Philadelphia, PA, pat'd. Nov. 1, 1881. The patent design for this, which Henis called a "Disintegrator and Strainer," had a perforated tin hopper like the steam shovel mentioned above, but the opposing presser handles were wooden paddles. Perhaps Henis manufactured them at first with wood. (I've seen many on eBay called "Juicers" or "Squeezers.") **$15**

Fruit, wine & jelly press, plated cast iron, cranked auger-like bit fits into openwork tapered part connected to large bowl-shaped hopper, 2 legged screw clamp frame. Ad copy from 1889 reads: "For seeding and extracting juice from all Fruits & Berries. Every housekeeper should have one. With this press, can be extracted the juices from Strawberries, Raspberries, Cranberries, Huckleberries, Gooseberries, Elderberries, Black-berries, Cherries, Currants, Peaches, Plums, Tomatoes, Pineapples, Pears, Quinces, Grapes, Apples, etc. The seeds and skins are discharged perfectly dry. Nothing is wasted." Enterprise Mfg. Co., Phila., 12"H x 11"L.

I-51. Fruit, wine & jelly press. *Cast iron, double screw clamp. Fruit put into hopper; when cranked through, skins & seeds came out the tip; juice poured out of the long slots whole length of horizontal nozzle-like barrel. 12"H overall x 11"L.* **Enterprise Mfg. Co., Philadelphia, pat'd. Sept. 30, 1879; sold for years. Collection of Meryle Evans. $85**

(The #46 is 19"H x 18"L and has added value.) Pat'd. Sept. 30, 1879, still for sale early 20th C. **$85**

Garlic press, cast aluminum, many 1940s-50s designs, U.S.A., Italy, Germany, Taiwan, etc. Should be collected even if value is low. New ones are made with ingenious hole-cleaners. Some of same companies who made egg-slicers in the last 40 years or so made garlic presses too. There's no mention of garlic presses either in *Thomas' Register of American Manufacturers* or the *Buyers Guide for Housewares*, up through 1946. Probably there were few garlic presses in American kitchen drawers before WWII, when returning GIs, having eaten Italian and other European cuisines that used generous amounts of garlic, wanted to find it at home too. The potential market became large enough for manufacturers to make, and importers to import, garlic presses. Garlic itself and powdered garlic was made and/or imported here by the early 1930s. .... **$1-$5+**

Grape press, tinned sheet iron reservoir in black painted cast iron frame; down-curved tapered lever; lift lever to push wood pusher or foller down; 4 wide spraddled leg rests so press fits on various sized bowls or pots; includes 3 perforated tin inserts with fine to coarse openings, "Littlefield's," (or Little Field's), English (?), 7" diam., 7-1/2"H, with 14"L lever handle, pat'd. June 16, 1868. .... **$75**

Grape scissors, forged iron, stubby blades, long handles, American (?), 5"L, 19th C. **$25**

Grape scissors, forged steel, engraved, brass spring, European?, 7"L, late 18th or early 19th C. **$25**

Grape scissors, tool steel & black painted iron, longish handles with same size loop ends, stubby blades with broad flat jaws, one edge of one has cutting blade, flat spring steel insert holds stem until it can be dropped into basket, pat'd. & mfd. by S. W. Valentine, Bristol, CT, 8"L, early 1870s. **$40**

Grapefruit corer, nickel plated steel, sharp edged cylinder with moving cutter blades inside, worked by 2 handles that stick up. Turner & Seymour Mfg. Co., Torrington, CT, 7"L, coring part 1-3/4" diam., pat'd. May 28, 1923, & Aug. 18, 1925 (?). **Overkill for grapefruit, no?** Collector Robert Rollman wrote "Have you ever heard of a grapefruit corer? What core? The size itself would preclude such activity for it would destroy half the fruit. The most common designation given in antique shops where I have seen these is a 'fruit baller.' Yet, when I tried ours on melon it did not make a very nice ball." Hear, hear. In my first book, I identified this as a baller; but I

have seen actual ads for this from the 1920s, calling it a grapefruit corer. See I-52. .... **$10**

Grater, 2 parts, cylindrical tin hopper for food, steel cutting blade is marked, turned wooden pusher, "Spong & Co.," London, 3"H cylinder, tin part 8"L, wooden pusher 9-3/4"L, 1920s-30s. **$50**

Grater, blue enamelware, demi-round with hoop handle opposite end with 2 steadying feet, 9"L, late 19th C. **$75**

Grater, blue painted cast iron & blue enameled sheet metal, clamps to table edge, Art Deco-ish geometric pattern cast into iron, wood pusher, "Helvetia," 20th C. **$65**

Grater, cast iron frame, screw clamp, cranked tin cylindrical grater for carrots, etc., pat'd. & mfd. in Montpelier, VT, by Enos Stimson, c. 10-1/2"H x 11-1/2"L, pat'd. Aug. 14, 1866. .... **$85**

Grater, enamelware, wide rectangle cut out at one end for handgrip, circular rayed pattern of punctured holes, bottom embossed "IDEAL," Czechoslovakian import to U.S.A., late 19th C. **$45**

Grater, fixed handle is not reversible for left & right handed users, wooden handle, box says "For Nuts, Cheese, Farfal & Nutmeg," Farfal is the term given to small, formed bits of pasta. "Mouli," mfd. by Moulinex, French, 8"L, "patent applied for," c.1945. .... **$15**

Grater, half cylinder of pierced copper mounted to board, unusual in copper, American (?), 22"L x 5" x 3-1/2." 19th C. **$100**

Grater, handmade, half cylinder of punctured tin tacked to long narrow wooden paddle with lollipop handle, prob. American, 15-1/2"L x 3-3/4"W, mid 19th C. **$75**

Grater, homemade mechanical grater in wooden frame, crank turns 2 flat cutout cast iron gears, which cause cone shaped punctured tin drum to revolve, sheet metal trough under grater was put on with brads, American, frame 7"H x 11" square, early 20th C. **$45**

Grater, pierced tin cylinder with wide strap handle bridging the top, this one has only 2 grating surfaces, fine & medium, but others have 3, including coarse, American (?), 7-1/2"H, pat'd. 1901. This

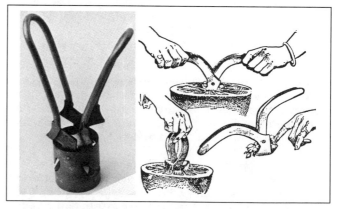

I-52. Grapefruit corer. *It is, it is. For all you doubters – see c.1927 catalog drawings at right. Turner & Seymour, Torrington, CT, pat'd. May 26, 1923, & poss. again in 1925. 7"H with 1-3/4" diam. corer. The "real" one, with wire handles, is the "hotel size." One shown in drawings is the household size, sheet metal.* **$10-$20**

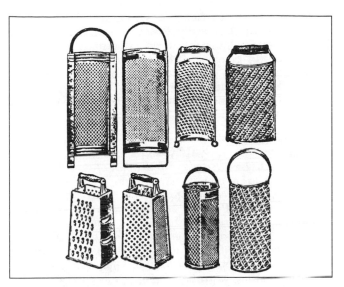

53. Tin hand graters c.1905-1920. *Most in time-honored styles dating back 200 years. (T)* **row**: *all curved, almost half-rounds, with metal or wood handles, different feet, some reinforced. (B* **row)**: *two 4-sided combination graters with strap handles, 7-1/2"H. Next a cylindrical one, the "Midget," with coarse & fine perforations. 6-1/4"H. Last a 10" x 5" (also 13" x 6") half-round.* **$10-$45**

type comes in many sizes, from just a few inches high to 16"H, maybe even bigger. Sometimes the handles are of heavy wire.................................. **$35**
Grater, pierced tin half-cylinder on wooden paddle back, American (?), 10"H x 3-1/2"W, late 19th C. Age can generally be determined by thickness of wooden back, the craft or shaping of it, patina on the tin, and hand- or machine-punctured grating teeth..................... **$50**

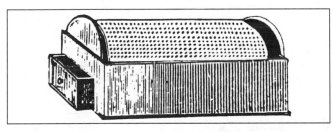

I-54. Box grater. *Line cut of one that's all tin, 13"L x 7", from c.1904-1910 Duparquet, Huot & Moneuse restauranteur catalog.*

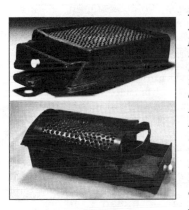

Grater, fairly thin sheet brass, punctured grating holes, plain steel handle & frame, marked "DRGM & DEP" in a diamond lozenge, German, 14-1/4"L, 19th C. .... **$85-$120**

❖ NOTES ❖

SOME EUROPEAN PATENT MARKS

Germany: **D.R.G.M** stands for *Deutsches Reichs-Gebrauchsmuster,* the pre-1918 mark meaning registered design, or "petty patent" of Germany; **DEP** or **dep** abbreviation for *deponiert* – meant a sample model had been deposited at the registry office; DEP is sometimes followed with **GES** or **Ges.** or **Gesch**, the abbreviation for *geschützt*, means protected by law or registered; **D.R.P** stands for *Deutsches Reichs-Patent*, translated "patented in the German Empire," used for mechanical (utility) patents from 1887 to 1911 (?) [I wrote in last edition that DRP came after the division of Germany after WWII, but this doesn't seem to be true.] **D.R.P.-A** means patent applied for, as does **Pat. Ang.** abbreviation for Patent *angemeldet*, which means patent pending.

France: **Bté** is an abbreviation for *Breveté*, or patentee; **DEP** is abbreviation for *Deposé*, meaning registered; *Modèle déposé* is a mark meaning that the object is protected in France for its shape; **M.M.** or **M. & M.**, means *marque et modèle*, used with Dep. – means trademark and model protected in France; **S.G.D.G.** stands for *Sans Garantie Du Gouvernement*, or, "registered" – but without guarantee or warranty by the government.

Italy: **Brevetto**, patent; *Reg.d. Modello registrato*, registered, therefore enjoying patent or trademark protection; **S.G.D.G.** stands for *senza la garanzia del governo*, with same meaning as in France.

Grater, punctured sheet brass, strap brass frame, a pronounced trapezoidal shape, reeded border (narrow ridge, size of slender reed or stalk) to grating surface done with a punch & mallet, moving it along bit by bit so rather uneven, English or German, 11"L, early 19th C to early 20th C (?)................ **$85**
Grater, punctured tin, rounded rectangle, wide tin strap, held like curry comb, American (?), 4-1/4"L, prob. early 20th C. **$15**
Grater, punctured tin with heart motif, carved wood hoop, American, 7-7/8"L x 4"W, c.1870s. **$200**
Grater, punctured tin with wide tin strap handle, oval grating surface, held like a curry comb, paper label

says "Easy to use. Grates rapidly. Safe and Sanitary for all grating purposes," "Bromwell's Greater – Grater," Saranac, MI, 20th C. Hard to find with original paper label. Such documentation is worth extra $$ to collectors. **$35**

Grater & slicer, oblong tin grating surface with alternating perforations & sharp slits, wire frame with large handle hoop at top, curled to 2 feet at bottom, stamped with mark of 2 fish, European (?), 11"H x 4-1/4"W, early 20th C. **$15**

Grater, rectangular, aluminum, large center field is fine punctured surface, top has a few rows of large pierced holes for coarse grating, bottom has pivoting potato peeler of tinned steel, going width of grater, "Triple Helper," with profile Indian head, mfd. by Chief Products, Los Angeles, CA, pat'd. but no date; c.1940s (?). **$18**

Grater, revolving, cast iron screw clamp frame, double gears, punctured tin rotating grater drum, very similar, except for shorter drum, to Enos Stimson's "Grater for carrots, etc.," American, poss. mfd. 15+ years before appearance in 1881 cookbook. .... **$60+**

Grater, revolving, rectangular wooden box with lid, tin grating drum inside, 2 drawers below, American, 9-1/2"H x 9-1/4"L, poss. late 18th C., more likely early 19th C. **$150**

Grater, revolving, tin, cast iron screw clamp frame, wood foller or pusher, "B M E No. 620," 13"H, c.1930s.. **$15**

Grater, revolving, tin & cast iron, very heavy duty large size, clamps to table, American (?), c.1880s...... **$45**

Grater, revolving, tin, wood & nickeled metal, 3 grating drums, screw clamps to table, American (?), c.1925. .... **$35**

Grater, revolving, tin & wood with very simple stamped sheet metal frame, knobless crank & 3 grating

I-56. Mechanical graters. *Wood & punctured tin.* **(L) Carrot grater:** *"For carrots, &c." Cast iron ribbed gears, counterweighted cast iron balance wheel. Revolving wooden drum has square nails driven into it. Only place to feed in food is a carrot-sized "mouse-hole" in front. No signs of use, no marks. 8"H x 7-1/2"L x 5-1/2"W. Mfd. & pat'd. by Enos Stimson, Montpelier, VT, Aug. 14, 1866. Ex-Keillor Collection. There is in the Patent Index only one carrot grater listing: Stimson's.* **(R)** *"H. P. Arthur's Vegetable Grater," pat'd. Oct. 8, 1867, Martinsburgh, NY. Stenciled on top. Wood frame, metal grater drum, wood hoop & foller & crank. 13-3/4"H to top of hopper; 19"H to fulcrum of lever. Frame 13"L x 6"W. Both Collection of Meryle Evans.* **$225-$300+**

drums, prob. American, poss. German, though not marked, 6-1/2"H, early 20th C. **$35**

Grater, semi-cylindrical brass, with iron handle, English, 14"L, early 19th C. These have become a popular "smalls" item brought in by container loads. They are usually highly polished, and quite handsome (and expensive). There is no evidence that they were ever plated. .... **$55+**

❖ RECIPE ❖

Rice with Tomatoes *– 1 teacupful of rice. 1 oz. of butter. 2 large tomatoes. A sprig of tarragon. 1 heaped tablespoonful of grated cheese. A bunch of chervil. 1 egg. Pepper. Salt. 1 large onion. Wash a teacup full of rice in cold water. Put it into two quarts of fast boiling, slightly salted water, and let it boil hard, until the grains feel tender when taken between the finger and thumb. Fifteen minutes is about the time, or rather under. Strain the rice, pour plenty of clean boiling water over it, and dry in a colander or sieve, placed in the screen or before the fire. It should be stirred now and again with a fork whilst drying, so that every grain is perfectly separate. Skin two large tomatoes, by dipping them into boiling water for a second or two, when they will peel quite easily. Mince an onion finely. Melt an ounce of butter in a pan, and slice the tomatoes into it. Put in the minced onions with the tomatoes, also the tarragon and chervil, which must be tied together, so that they may be taken out later. Add the pepper and salt, also a very large tablespoonful of grated cheese. Put in the rice, mix all well together, and break in one whole egg. Stir lightly, until it becomes quite hot. Pile it nicely on a dish, and garnish with a few nicely fried rashers of bacon and a little fresh parsley. If desired, the bacon can be omitted, and parsley only be used for garnish, but then a little chopped parsley should be sprinkled on top, as well as placing a few sprigs round the sides."* Katherine Mellish's Cookery Book. *London: Spon, NYC: Spon & Chamberlain, 1901.* [**Note:** *This is really delicious, but I put in three times as much cheese (Irish cheddar is good), and stir in chopped parsley too. Of course I don't eat bacon, but Morningstar Farm's breakfast links (veggie sausages), broiled first or microwaved, really taste good with this.*]

Grater, stamped & punctured tin, slightly curved, oval opening for hand, no mark, American(?), 9-1/2"L, c.1910... **$5**

Grater, punctured tin, "Gilmore," pat'd. 1897. .... **$5**

Grater, tin cylinder with 3 surface grades, strap handle, American, 9-1/4"H x 3-3/4" diam., early 20th C. **$10**

Grater, tin, mechanical, with 3 grating discs that insert in frame & slide back & forth to fine or coarse grate or to slice, "Safety Veg-E-Grater," Knapp-Monarch Mfg. Co., Webster City, IA or St. Louis, MO, 12-1/2"L, 20th C... **$15**

Grater, tin & wire, 2 grating surfaces, a slicer & a Saratoga (French fry) slicer, "Ekco," American, 10-1/2"L, 20th C. **$5**

Grater, tin & wire, 3 grating surfaces plus a slicer, "All-in-One," American, 10-5/8"L x 4-1/4"W, c. 1940... **$5**

Grater, tin & wire, half is a woven wire mesh, other half is machine-punched tin, "Kitchen Novelty Co." (Atlantic City, NJ), mfd. in Germany, 12-1/2"L, c.1890s to 1910. .... **$10**

Grater, tin with wire handle, "A Gadget Master Product #8," "Made in U.S.A.," 10"L x 7"W, 20th C. **$6**

Grater, stamped tin, wire handle, "Gadget Master" with three grating strips on 7" x 7" grating paddle. 20th C. **$6**

Grater, box style, wood frame fitted with drawer with porcelain knob, hand-punched tin grating surface set into frame, American, 15"L, prob. 1830s-50s. **$95**

❖ NOTES ❖

Really Dopey Inventions – I don't know where else to put this, but it's funny. From *Journal of the Franklin Institute*, Philadelphia, 1836, comes this description of Ebenezer B. Story's, Buffalo, NY, grater patent: "This grater consists of a sheet of tin perforated with holes, and placed in a box in a sloping direction, so as to make an angle of fourteen degrees with the horizon. The length of the box on the top is to be two feet one and one fourth inch. The length of the bottom is one foot eight and one fourth inch; the width ten inches, the height thereof nine inches. The size of the grater may be varied to suit the wishes of the person for whose use it is made. I claim therefore the invention of such grater, and such improvements as herein set forth and described.'" To which the editor added, "A more trifling patent than this does not often find its way to the office." Yet it did happen. Amazingly uninventive inventions were granted patents in the early days. See Patents, Chapters XXI to XXIII.

Grater, revolving, green painted cast iron, screw clamps, wooden handle, "Lorraine Metal Mfg.," 8-1/2"H, 20th C. **$35**

Grater, wood & tin, "Favorite," 12-1/2"L x 3"W, c.1910. .... **$15**

Grater-shredder, metal with green wooden handle, "Lightning 3-in-1," 8"L, c.1930s or 1940s. **$9**

Grater & slicer, double action, wood, steel, one blade makes thin julienne strips, other makes 1/4" thick slices, American, 16"L, late 1800s. **$45**

Grating machine, all wood bench-style frame & hopper, levered pusher, punctured tin drum, "H. P. Arthur's Vegetable Grater," Martinsburgh, NY, 13-3/4"H x 13"L x 6"W, pat'd. Oct. 8, 1867. .... **$85**

Grist mill, for corn, cast iron, screw clamps, Arcade, c.1900. .... **$35**

Grist mill, cast iron, clamps to work surface, big wheel with curved spokes, mill & hopper are small &

Reproduction Alert

A new tinned screw clamp cast iron mill for cereal or flour is sold by White Mountain Freezer Co. Large hopper, natural pale wood handle; it could be mistaken for an old one, although it doesn't look as old fashioned as other White Mountain mills. Price of a new one is half again as much as antique.

---

behind wheel, chute below, "Apache," mfd. by A. H. Patch, Clarksville, TN, wheel approx. 16" diam., late 19th or early 20th C. **$65**

Hasher – See: Food chopper, Athol or Starrett

Herb boats or grinders, also called herb crushers, herb mills, or spice mills. Another name for it is ship grinder. Cast iron boat, bootjack legs, interesting because wheel is wooden & its narrow edge is ribbed, & has straight wooden handles; wheel possibly replaced original iron one. Prob. Oriental, early 19th or late 18th C. • This one is shown in and credited to the kitchen of the *Whim Greathouse in Time-Life's Cooking of the Caribbean Islands*, and is probably an import from the Orient. • The value below is not just for this particular one, but for one with an iron boat & handmade wooden wheel. • Herb boat or grinder, cast iron footed boat-shaped mortar, rolling pestle wheel has 2 long wooden handles, wheel was operated by the feet in Asian countries, primarily China, where they originated (?). No marks, prob. Asian, 26"L boat, exceptionally large, 19th C. (A very small one with 10"L boat, 3" diam. wheel, was in a Nov. 1989 Garth auction. Smallest I ever heard of.) Ballast? – You rarely see herb boats; when you do they are always given an American provenance, c.1800. But clues pointing to a Chinese origin are impossible to ignore, and I find it logical to suppose them as ballast on early China Trade ships to America, beginning in 1784 with the "Empress of China" and continuing into the 1840s. Canton blue & white china was packed into the holds as ballast on tea, spices, lacquers, and silk & cotton cloth. So why not the even heavier herb mills? • Herb boat or grinder, cast iron boat on bootjack legs at each end, rolling wheel-like mill or pestle, with long wooden handles stained black, sometimes called a **go-devil**, American, European, Chinese, one is 17"L with 7" diam. wheel, early 19th C. • Philadelphia collector Ellen Blaw wrote me in 1986 saying "I have a friend who recently moved here from China ... who showed me her crusher that had been her mother's, and her mother's grandmother. It is one of the old things they brought with them from China; they use it for rice, not spices. The feet on my friends' mill are shorter, the cut out arch is not so deep. I hope this can shed some light on this somewhat mysterious item!" • The Keillor Family Collection had one about which Archibald Keillor said only that he thought it was American. He had traveled in China in the 1920s and '30s. • Carl W. Drepperd, in his *Primer of American Antiques*, wrote that these are "Chinese in origin but much used in America in the early 19th century." He goes on to say that the "operator [of the mill], barefooted, sat on a chair and rolled the wheel with [his/her] feet." Other names, according to Drepperd, are **sow & pig mill**, and **ship mill**. Another that does not have same bootjack legs, measures 18"L x 4-1/2"W with 7" diam. wheel; a third, without bootjack legs, is 13-1/4"L with 7" diam. wheel. A fourth, advertised by Stephen Douglas just as this book was going to press, has the bootjack feet or legs, the simple wooden dowel-like rod through the roller, and in their words "a most unusual embossed foliated end." This is a sort of shield-shaped tip to one end of the boat or trough, and perhaps had to do with how the grinder was operated – with the feet (?) as above? I do not believe

I-57. Herb boat, or herb crusher. Cast iron with wood handles, c.1800-1820s. *(T)* 18"L. Photo courtesy Litchfield Auction Gallery, Litchfield CT. Ex-Harold Corbin Collection, auctioned Jan. 1, 1989 for **$750.**

I-58. Herb boat, or herb crusher. Cast iron, with wood handles stained or stove-blacked. 17"L; 7" diam. wheel. Collection of Meryle Evans. Most likely Asian. See long value listings for more information. **$350-$750**

these are American-made. Herb boat or grinder, wooden brick-shape mortar has boat-shape depression cut in it, rolling hardwood crushing wheel with long side handles, like the all cast iron mill above; the Keillors believed this one was either European or Asian in origin, box 5"H x 12-1/2"L with approx. 7" diam. wheel, early 19th C. The late Archie & Myra Keillor, early stalwarts in the Early American Industries Association and discerning as well as omnivorous collectors of kitchenwares, tools, dairy implements, etc., died in the 1970s. Photographs of many pieces in their family kitchen collection appeared first in my first book, *From Hearth to Cookstove*. It was a great privilege to know them.

Most herb boats: .... **$350-$750+**

Herb boat or spice mill, cast iron, like rowboat with troughed opening at bow & wider at stern, with the effect of a seat & raised gunwhale (sides), high bootjack legs, large wheel pestle with rough wooden handles. Prob. American maybe, not Oriental, poss. PA, early 19th C. .... **$250+**

Herb mill, japanned tin, sheet iron hopper, wood drawer below, small wooden handle on crank, American (?), 7"H, 19th C. **$100**

Herb masher or beetle, turned maple with small head carved with concentric circles, American (?), 7"H, 19th C. **$35**

Horse radish grater, homemade, wooden box, punctured tin drum, sheet iron cover with simple latches (appropriated from something else), American, 14-1/8"L x 7-5/8"W, 19th C. **$65**

❖ RECIPE ❖

Melon Mangoes *– Cut a small square out of each melon; take out the seed; shred some garlic small, and mix it with mustard seed; fill the melon full; then replace the square piece; bind it up with small twine; boil a quantity of vinegar; in which, put white and long pepper, salt, ginger, and mustard seed; pour it boiling hot on the mangoes every day for four days; put a little horse radish, and flour of mustard, in the vinegar the last day; when the vinegar boils, take great care that the mangoes are well covered; you may pickle large cucumbers in the same way, they are much esteemed as a pickle."* Joseph Bell, A Treatise on Confectionary. Newcastle, England, 1817.

Horse radish grater, mechanical, screw clamp cast iron skeletal frame, cranked large tinned sheet steel disc with sharp projections, small iron shelf on left side supports radish or potato or root vegetable against vertical revolving blade. A "bike fender" shield covers half of disc nearest to user. Replaceable blade. "Distelhorst's," Chicago Nickel Works, Chicago, IL, c.1890............ **$55**

Huller or pin feather picker – See: Strawberry huller

Juicers, Citrus Juicers, Lemon Squeezers, Reamers.

Special thanks go to John Zukatis, whose personal enthusiasm and helpfulness launched my own tiny juicer collection (!) just weeks before the book was finished. John once had over 1,000 juicers, many of them cast iron or cast aluminum. Not until he was turned down on a book proposal, and started selling them, did I find him. Many of the pictures I used, and more I didn't have room for, were taken by him. Roy McDiarmid helped me with several detail & name questions, and Larry & Carole Meeker also helped. Refer to the last page of this chapter for more information.

Futurewatch: I have always ignored these. But since the advent of eBay, it is obvious that the variety and aesthetic value is very high, while for the most part prices are very low. Quantity and relatively low prices means an opportunity for collectors in search of something new! I especially like the cast aluminum pieces, mechanical and non-mechanical. Others are made of

glass, cast iron, china or porcelain, even wood, or in combination. Just the names are worth something, such as "Ex-Squeeze-It" – isn't that worth a laugh a day? Inventors generally called them "Fruit Juice Extractors," or "Squeezers," and they were for lemons, limes, oranges, or grapefruit.

• • •

Categories: Obviously all of these were meant to extract the juice in one way or another. But in order for you to be able to find what you're looking for, and to see how similar forms compare to each other, I have come up with three categories, as follows:

JUICERS: A juicer is a device with some mechanical action that squeezes juice out of a fruit, especially a citrus fruit – grapefruit, lemon, lime, orange. As expert collector John Zukatis says, "I always use the word juicer, and never call it a reamer, because a reamer is only part of the whole juicer."

JUICERS-SQUEEZERS: For the purposes of this book, a juicer-squeezer is a hand-held device that doesn't have it's own stand, and is hinged at one end, with a presser cone in one half and a convex ball or cone in the other to hold the fruit. The leverage is provided by the user's hands squeezing the handles together. Some juicer-squeezers – on the evolutionary path to the juicers – have small balance elements cast into the bottom so that they will sit flat if you put them down on a counter or tabletop.

REAMERS: Reamers in these listings refer only to the one-piece handheld devices – a reaming cone with a handle, sort of like a darning egg. A reamer requires the user to do all the work, and the reamer is basically a cup with a spout, with a reaming cone sticking up in the center, around which the user has to press & rub the halved citrus fruit. Most reamers can be used for any citrus fruit, although oranges & grapefruits are most common. See also Chapter XVIII (Electrifying work). Unfortunately, at least two premier collectors of mechanical juicers had already begun breaking up their collections (without getting a book out of them!) before I began working on the 5th edition of this book.

•   •   •

Motive forces: Squuushing by hand is the simplest way to get juice. That could be considered a motive force. Others, requiring an implement of some kind: (1) Pressure & **manual turning of fruit** against or around a ribbed cone; (2) **simple lever** which multiplies pressure on a stationary piece of fruit; (3) **Rack & pinion** vertical gear moved with a lever increases pressure in less space; (4) **Crank** with or without gears. Gears add effectiveness; and with a combination of a smaller gear to a larger gear, you "gear up" and thereby increase the movement you get with the same amount of hand motion. (5) **Hinged presses** have a hinge or pivot at one end, but they serve no motive power, just keep the halves of the juicer aligned and connected; (6) "Plier" or "scissor" action which is another form of lever, the pivot is part of the way between the ends, making plier-like jaws, and the pressure is applied by the user's strength while squeezing the handles.

•   •   •

Futurewatch on aluminum pieces, which are coming up the backstretch now. While aluminum can probably never beat cast iron, it is beautiful, and juicers are a good way to start your aluminum collection!

Squeezer Manufacturers

A lot of makers of lemon squeezers and juicers are known, but maybe some unknown pieces can eventually be found. Of course, many juicers were made in the 19th century, but the only manufacturers directory listings available start with 1905-06. What follows are lists of squeezer/juicer-makers (some glass reamers, not mechanical juicers) from two sources: *Thomas' Register of American Manufacturers of 1905-06; 1932-33; and 1946; and the 1909, 1915, and 1930* issues of the *Buyers Directory of House Furnishing Goods & Kindred Articles*, which gave model names. It was published annually by *House Furnishing Review.* In both sets of lists, given chronologically here, you will see that some known makers aren't on the lists. [Note: The *Buyers Guide* sometimes listed importers & wholesalers right along with manufacturers. Also, the model names, as given in the directories, are given in quota-

tions " " within brackets.]• **1905-06**, under "Squeezers (Lemon)": Edward S. Hotchkiss, [n.p.], Knapp & Cowles Mfg. Co. [n.p.]; Manning, Bowman & Co., and Charles Parker Co., both Meriden, CT; Landers, Frary & Clark, New Britain, CT; M. J. Bartlett & Son, and Nicol & Co., both Chicago, IL; Arcade Mfg. Co., Freeport, IL; Tucker & Dorsey Mfg. Co. (wooden ones), Indianapolis, IN; Springfield Machine Screw Co., Springfield, MA; Pleuger & Henger Mfg. Co., St. Louis, MO; John Sommer's Son, Newark, NJ; Watson Machine Co., Paterson, NJ; E. W. Bliss Co., and Union Porcelain Works, Brooklyn, NY; Sidney Shepard & Co., and West Mfg. Co., both Buffalo, NY; Max Icewenstein, and Silver & Co., both of whom made glass ones, in NYC, NY; A. C. Williams, Ravenna, OH [known to have made juicers probably as early as the 1870s]; Erie Specialty Co., and Reed Mfg. Co., both Erie, PA; Logan & Strobridge Iron Co., New Brighton, PA; Penn Hardware Co., Reading, PA.

• **1909**, under "Squeezers, Lemon": Arcade Mfg. Co., Freeport, IL ["Perfect Arcade," "Champion," "Union Drum," "X-Ray,"]; C. W. Dunlap Mfg. Co., NYC; Enamel Steel Tile Co., Bellaire, OH ["Quick & Easy," "Acme," "5th Avenue," "Samson"]; Erie Specialty Co., Erie, PA.

• **1915**, under "Squeezers, Lemon": Arcade Mfg. Co., Freeport, IL; Bogert & Hopper Co., NYC; George Borgfeldt & Co., NYC; Bridgeport Hardware Mfg. Co., Bridgeport, CT; Buffum Tool Co., Louisiana, MO ["Swastika"]; Cassady Fairbank Mfg. Co., Chicago, IL; Clipper Fountain Supply Co., Troy, NY; Erie Specialty Co, Erie, PA ["Walker's"]; E. B. Estes & Sons, NYC, NY; J. P. Fanning, Brooklyn, NY ["Fanning"]; Frank & Co., NYC; Gibbs Mfg. Co., Canton, OH; Gilchrist Co., Newark, NJ ["Yankee"]; Griswold Mfg. Co., Erie, PA ["Classic"]; C. H. & E. S. Goldberg, NYC; Wm. Goldennblum & Co., NYC; H. C. Hart Mfg. Co., Unionville, CT ["Easy"] Edwin Hills, Plainville, CT; Hotchkiss-Peck Mfg. Co., Bridgeport, CT; Indiana Glass Co, Dunkirk, IN ["Easly"]; Kingery Mfg. Co., Cincinnati, OH; Landers, Frary & Clark, New Britain, CT ["Little Giant," "Crown," "F.F.C."]; M. Loewenstein, NYC; Missouri Malleable Iron Co., East St. Louis, IL; Mosteller Mfg. Co., Chicago, IL ["Mosteller"]; Nicol & Co., Chicago, IL ["World's Fair"]; Thomas Ott & Co., Philadelphia, PA; Charles Parker Co., Meriden, CT; Peck & Mack Co., NYC; Penn Hardware Co., Reading, PA ["Penn"]; W. E. Pierce & Co., Mildford, NH; William Pratt Mfg. Co., Chicago, IL; Redlich Mfg. Co., Chicago, IL; Richardi & Bechtold, Bellaire, MI; Rocky Hill Hardware Co., Rocky Hill, CT ["Leader"]; Sargent & Co., New Haven, CT; Wm. Shimer, Son & Co., Freemansburg, PA; Silver & Co., Brooklyn, NY ["Silver's"]; Sommer Faucet Co., Newark, NJ; Stover Mfg. Co., Freeport, IL; Taplin Mfg. Co., New Britain, CT ["Victor"]; George M. Thurnauer Co., NYC [importer from Germany]; Tri-Angle Mfg. Co., Freeport, IL ["New Century," "National"]; Tucker & Dorsey Mfg. Co., Indianapolis, IN; Union Porcelain Works, Brooklyn, NY; A. C. Williams Co., Ravenna, OH; Wrightsville Hardware Co., Wrightsville, PA ["L. & S. I. Co.," "Brighton"].

• **1930**, under "Squeezers, Lemon & Orange": Basket Importing Co., NYC; California Fruit Grower's Exchange, Chicago, IL ["Sunkist Jr. Fruit Juice Extractor"]; Holmes Mfg. Co., Los Angeles, CA ["California Juice Extractor," "Holmes Juice Extractor"] Knapp-Monarch Co., St. Louis, MO; Landers, Frary & Clark, New Britain, CT; Salmanson & Baumritter, NYC; Thurnauer Co., NYC [known as importer from Germany].

- **1932-33**, under "Extractors: Lemon & Orange Juice, Etc., Glass, Metal, Etc.": Holmes Mfg. Co., Los Angeles, CA [hand power machine]; Brock Glass Co., Santa Ana, CA; Beardsley & Wolcott Mfg. Co. [metal], Waterbury, CT; Knapp-Monarch Co., Belleville, IL [manual machines]; Indiana Glass Co., Dunkirk, IN; Strite Anderson Mfg. Co., Minneapolis, MN [metal]; Central States Mfg. Co., St. Louis, MO; Tiffany Castings Co., St. Louis [squeeze type, aluminum]; E. S. Pease Factories, Buffalo, NY; Handy-Andy Specialty Co., Long Island City, NY; Richard G. Krueger, Inc., NYC, NY [reamers]; United Royalties Corp., NYC; Cambridge Glass Co., Cambridge, OH; Jiffy Specialty Co., Marietta, OH; National Capper Co., Toledo, OH [hand extractor, also combined with bottle capper]; New Standard Corp., Mt. Joy, PA; United States Glass Co., Pittsburgh, PA; Aluminum Goods Mfg. Co., Manitowoc, WI; General Grinder Corp., Milwaukee, WI; Hamilton Beach Mfg. Co., Racine, WI [who are also listed as making electric extractors.] 1932-33, under "Squeezers: Lemon & Fruit": Landers, Frary & Clark, New Britain, CT; Waterbury Button & Mfg. Co., Waterbury, CT; Nicol & Co., Chicago, IL; Arcade Mfg. Co., and Stover Mfg. & Engine Co., Freeport, IL; Tucker & Dorsey Mfg. Co., Indianapolis, IN ["wood ball"]; John Sommer Faucet Co., Newark, NJ; A. C. Williams Co., Ravenna, OH; J. E. Marsden Glass Works, Inc., Ambler, PA [glass reamers]; Wrightsville Hardware Co., Wrightsville, PA; Hamilton Beach Mfg. Co., Racine, WI [lemon & lime squeezers].
- **1946,** under "Extractors: Fruit Juice, Etc., Glass, Metal, Etc.": California Fruit Growers Exchange, L.A., CA [hand reamer, & electric]; Landers Frary & Clark, New Britain, CT [metal]; National Die Casting Co., Chicago, IL; Nu-Dell Mfg. Co., Chicago, IL [plastic]; Indiana Glass Co., Dunkirk, IN; Handy Things Mfg. Co., Ludington, MI; O. E. Thompson & Sons, Ypsilanti, MI [wooden, hand type, lime & lemon]; Strite Anderson Mfg. Co., Minneapolis, MN; Rival Mfg. Co., Kansas City, MO; Dazey Corp., St. Louis, MO; Benedict Mfg. Co., East Syracuse, NY [metal]; General Slicing Machine of N.Y., Inc., Brooklyn, NY [hand type, fruit & veg.]; Handy-Andy Specialty Co., Long Island City, NY [orange, grapefruit, lemon]; Tech-Art Plastics Co., Long Island City, NY [reamers]; Gordon Mfg. Corp., NYC, NY [hand]; R. Z. A. Mfg. Co., NYC, NY [metal heavy duty]; Renwal Mfg. Co., NYC, NY [plastic]; United Royalties Corp., NYC, NY; Kurz-Kasch, Inc., Dayton, OH [reamers]; Anchor Hocking Glass Co., Lancaster, OH [glass]; United States Glass Co., Tiffin, OH; U. S. Lock & Hardware Co., Columbia, PA [rotary]; Aluminum Goods Mfg. Co., Manitowoc, WI
- **1946**, under "Squeezers: Lemon & Fruit": Bridgeport Castings Co., Bridgeport, CT; Craft Mfg. Co., Chicago, IL [stainless steel lemon & lime]; Arcade Mfg. Co., Freeport, IL [& lime]; Tucker-Dorsey Mfg. Corp., Indianapolis, IN ["wood ball"]; C. T. Williamson Wire Novelty Co., Newark, NJ [lemon & lime]; U. S. Lock & Hardware Co., Columbia, PA; Littlestown Hardware & Foundry Co., Littlestown, PA [& lime]; Nathan Cohen, Philadelphia, PA [wooden]; Wrightsville Hardware Co., Wrightsville, PA; Hamilton Beach Co., Racine, WI [& lime].

Juicers

Juice extractor, simple "screw-in" pouring spout, works sort of like maple syrup spout. Cast aluminum, marked "Juistractor Pittsburgh PA" and patent numbers: 1,432,166; 1, 649, 755; and 1, 747, 957. These were by three different inventors, in three cities, in different years. First was Paul During's patent, Detroit, MI, Oct. 17, 1922; then Albert W. Thompson's, Miami, FL, Nov. 15, 1927; last was Charles F. Silveus, Waynesburg, PA, Feb. 18, 1930. The funny thing is, the object itself looks nothing like any of the patent drawings. There is some variety in these; in fact, the day I found this on eBay, I had found at the Salvation Army and bought it, even though I didn't know what it was! .... **$5+**

Juice extractor, yellow (or blue or green) china pitcher, modernistic sharp-edged molded diagonal swags across old-fashioned round bellied pitcher shape body; reamer sets into top & is activated to turn by pressure of your pushing half a grapefruit (orange, lemon) down on it. Ade-O-Matic Co., Los Angeles, CA, 1930. Crossover vintage design collector interest (true for many juicers)..................................... **$35+**

Juicer, bright tin, bright green painted cast iron, mixer & juicer part lift off, "Made for the Deluxe Sales Co., Inc.," NYC, 9-3/4"H, 20th C. .... **$45+**

Juicer, cast & spun aluminum, screw clamps to table edge, crank on side, several parts, including frame, very large hopper-bowl, inserted screw-grinder like a meat grinder, wooden presser. Used like a food grinder, for serious canners & jelly makers! "Victorio Deluxe Model 2," Vitantonio, Cleveland, OH, c.1920s-30s. [Two more recent versions are the

"Squeezo Strainer II," c.1950s? and "Victorio Strainer No. 200," c.1960s-70s? Wooden pusher for former has long wooden business end with knobby end; in the latter it's just a dowel rod with a short cylindrical wood end. Hopper cups much more angular and ugly in both. Finally, there's a brand

I-J&LS-1. Juicers. (L) "Streamline Juice-King," *"Rack & pinion action with lever. Red baked enamel with chrome. 9"H x 8" x 5-3/4". Chicago Die Casting Mfg. Co., Chicago. 1942 catalog.* **(R)** *"California/Florida" fruit juice extractor, for all citrus fruit. Entirely of aluminum – stamped and cast – the funnel bowl, removable strainer, reamer & frame. 13"H x 6" diam. UnID catalog page, c.1909. Possibly made by Holmes Mfg. Co., Los Angeles.* **(L) $25+; (R) $45+**

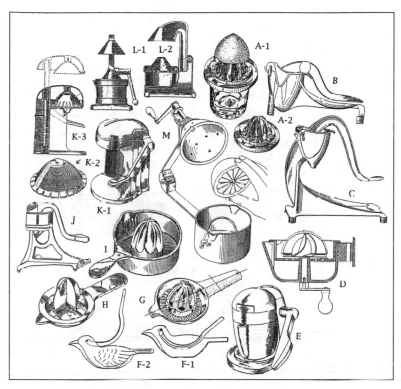

I-J&LS-2. Juice Extractor Patents & some of the inventors' pulp nonfiction. *All of these but two are known by me to have been made. The actual manufactured juicers are easy to recognize from the patent drawings. For the most part, I've cleaned up the drawings by removing all the many little arrows and numbers.* **(A-1, A-2)** *"Lemon-Juice Extractor," glass reamer, shown on tumbler, and separate. pat'd. Nov. 12, 1889, by John P.* **Manny** *of Rockford, IL, Utility Pat. #415,049. "In use I cut a lemon transverse to its lengthwise axis about the center thereof....The many projections of the extractor will necessitate but a slight oscillation of the lemon ... . The ribs ... act as wipers to free the lower edge of the half-lemon from juicy pulp. ... By experience I have demonstrated that glass is the best material ... owing to its non corroding quality and cheapness of construction."* **(B)** *"Juice Extractor," pat'd. Sept. 25, 1934, by George W.* **Bungay**, *Brooklyn, NY, Des. Pat. #93,382. No assignee. "... a new, original, and ornamental Design." (This one is the low-slung cast aluminum* **"Wear-Ever,"** *with a separate seed cup insert. (The utility patent for this one and for (C) is on the next page, in I-J&LS-3.)* **(C)** *"Juice Extractor," pat'd. Feb. 16, 1932, by George W.* **Bungay**, *Plainfield, NJ. Des. Pat. #86,217. Assignor to Household Field Corp., NYC. Cast aluminum. This is the taller* **"Wear-Ever."** *Compare to (J).* **(D)** *"Fruit Juice Extractor," pat'd. May 1, 1934, by Knut* **Larson**, *Pawtucket, RI, U. Pat. #1,957,346. "The container may be of any suitable material, as, for example, some light metal such as aluminum or enamel ware ... the reamer may be of aluminum, but it may be of some suitable non-metallic material." When this was*

finally made & became the **"Dazey Super Juicer,"** *the deep ribs of the separate reamer were straightened out (shown curved in patent drawing), and aluminum was the metal of choice.* **(E)** *"Juice Extractor," pat'd. Oct. 3, 1944, by Herbert C.* **Johnson**, *Wilmette, IL. Des. Pat. #138,983. Assignor to National Die Casting Co., Chicago, IL. This is the cast aluminum* **"Juice King."** **(F-1, F-2)** *"Portable Lemon Slice Squeezer for Table Use," pat'd. by Adolf* **Wagner**, *of Mussbach, Germany, assignor to* **Süddeutsche Metallwaren-Fabrik** *Kommandit-Gesellschaft. Pat'd .in Germany Dec. 30, 1933; pat'd. in USA Apr. 14, 1936, by Adolf Wagner, U.Pat.#2,037,553. "... a device of small dimensions which can be used on the table without a saucer. ... The lever is bent from a small strip of material ... that corresponds to the curved form of the ... container. ... the end opposite to the handle is terminated in a spout. ... The drawing shows as an embodiment of the invention a ... squeezer in the form of a bird. ... the beak forms a spout. ... The two side walls ... are cut and stamped on the outside ... so the utensil looks like a swimming sea-gull."* **(G)** *"Juicer," pat'd. Jan. 16, 1951, by Lucille M.* **Bargery**, *Minneapolis, MN, assignor to* **Foley** *Mfg Co., Minneapolis. Her patent referenced the 1889 Manny patent, and a 1949 Quam patent, as well as a seemingly unrelated 1940 Katzky patent.* **(H)** *"Combined Fruit Reamer & Strainer," pat'd. Sept. 14, 1948, by Carl G.* **Krieger**, *Mason City, IA, Des. Pat. # 150,990. This was a design patent, and referenced the Quam patent in the next image, but I don't know if it was ever made.* **(I)** *"Citrus-Fruit Juicer," pat'd. July 3, 1945, by James P.* **Quam**, *Chicago, IL, Des. Pat. #141,788. (Oddly, the utility patent for this juicer wasn't granted until Nov. 8, 1949, over 4 years later – and the filing dates were two years apart. Quam must have imagined just what his juicer would look like before he worked out the mechanics of it.) The Utility Pat. #2,487,371, has the valuable information: Quam stated "There are two general types of fruit juicers in general use. The first type includes relatively complicated machines having electrically driven reamers or having mechanically operated pressing members. The juicers of this type are relatively expensive and, being large, require a more or less permanent installation. ... The second and more common type ... includes the relatively simple glass juicers in which the orange or other fruit is turned relative to a reamer positioned thereon. Such juicers, which have long been used, are not subject to the above defects but are objectionable in that it is necessary to hold the juicer and simultaneously twist the fruit ... . This twisting movement is very tiresome and the general process is quite slow." Quam's solution was to give the juicer a "pivotal mounting" that included a "pedestal" (in other words, a lazy Susan). He goes on, in his patent claim, "The annular resilient member which is a rubber gasket-like ring on bottom ... grips the surface so that the juicer does not slip. ... The fruit ... is then cut in two and one-half thereof held firmly against the reamer. The reamer is then rotated with respect to the fruit by back and forth movement of the handle. This movement is relatively easily accomplished due to the leverage obtained from the handle and also as the back and forth pushing movement is not as tiresome as the twisting movement normally required ... . "Although the container and the reamer of the juicer are preferably constructed of aluminum it is pointed out that any other suitable material can be used." Well, Mr. Quam assigned this patent to his company, Quam-Nichols Co., Chicago, which produced the* **"Kwicky"** *juicer. Perhaps the first ergonomic juicer, but it's very hard to use, in my opinion.* **(J)** *"Design for a Fruit Juice Extractor," pat'd. May 23, 1933, by Oscar M.* **Anderson**, *New Britain, CT, assignor to Landers, Frary & Clark, New Britain. Des. Pat. # 89,942. Anderson was a Swedish subject, resident in the US. This design became the cast aluminum* **"Universal"** *juicer; I don't know the utility patent number for it.* **(K-1)** *"Fruit Press," pat'd. July 20, 1937, by Joseph M.* **Majewski**, *Jr., Kansas City, MO, assignor to Foster L. Talge doing business as the Rival Mfg. Co. This is one of 3 patents for what became the* **"Single Action Juice-O-Mat."** **(K-2)** *"Fruit Reamer," design, pat'd. Jan 23, 1940, by Joseph M.* **Majewski**, *Jr. Des. Pat. #118,640.* **(K-3)** *"Fruit Juice Extractor" utility patent, Jan. 3, 1939, by Joseph M. Majewski, Jr., U. Pat. #2,142,975. This became Rival's enameled cast aluminum* **"Juice-O-Mat."** *See how the "streamline" design differs in I-J&LS-1.* **(L-1) (L-2)** *"Juice Extracting Device," pat'd. Sept. 27, 1938, by Herbert C.* **Johnson**, *Chicago, IL; Pat. #2,131,440. This one has many similarities to the* **"Juice-King,"** *and maybe is a version of it. Johnson also held other patents that show up on the actual "Juice-King." (See I-J&LS-1.)* **(M)** *"Fruit Juice Extractor," pat'd. Jan. 14, 1930, by Clarence E.* **Elliott** *&* **Leonard O.** **Nichols**, *of Kansas City, MO. U. Pat. #1,743,661. "... a device inexpensive of manufacture in that the various parts may all be formed of die stampings and the parts readily assembled and secured together. ... The juice extractor comprises a semi-elliptic wire form ... [which] presents a blunt edge to engage the juice-containing cells of the fruit." You should read the rest of the three pages ... it's like some kind of strange science fiction about "fruit carrying members" etc. This patent became the* **"Knapps** *Orange Juicer," mfd. by the Knapp-Monarch Co., St. Louis, MO. I wonder if Leonard Nichols is the Nichols who partnered with James Quam to form the Quam-Nichols Co. of Chicago?*

If you want copies of all these patents yourself, there's a how-to on looking up patent drawings at the back of this book.

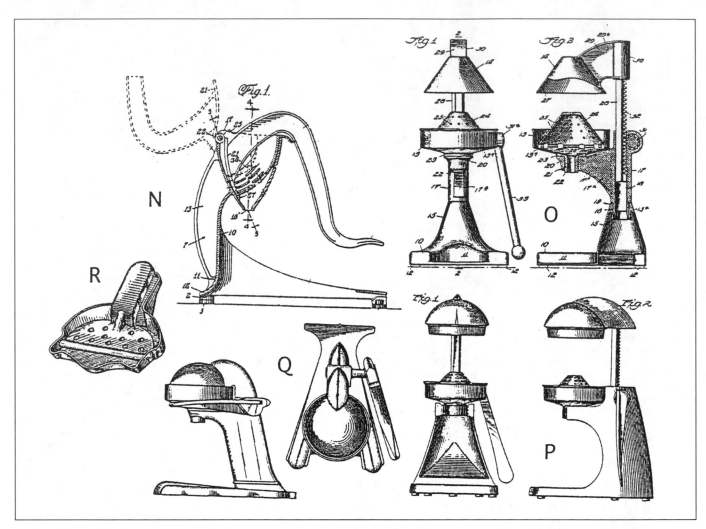

I-J&LS-3. More Juice Extractor Patents. *Continues letter-IDs from I-J&LS-2.* **(N)** *"Juice Extractor," pat'd .Nov. 1, 1932, by George W.* **Bungay**, *Plainfield, NJ, assignor to Bungay-Wolf Corp., NYC. U. Pat. #1,886,250. This is the utility patent for the* **"Wear-Ever"** *juicers in I-J&LS-2-(B) and (C). See also the Bungay-Wolf* **"Squeezeit"** *in I-J&LS-16. Bungay's intent was to "provide an operating or hand lever which will give maximum operating leverage in its various fruit pressing positions together with maximum stability ... during all such operating positions.* **(O)** *"Juice Extracting Device," pat'd. Aug. 24, 1937, by Herbert C.* **Johnson**, *Chicago. U. Pat. #2,090,913. This is a conical-top* **"Juice-King."** **(P)** *"Juice Extractor" design, pat'd. Aug. 16, 1938, by Herbert C.* **Johnson**. *Des. Pat. #110,897. This* **"Juice-King"** *much more streamlined than (L-1, -2) in I-J&LS-2, and more like the one in I-J&LS-1.* **(Q)** *"Fruit Juice Extractor," pat'd. Nov. 17, 1936, by William P.* **Koch**, *Oak Park, IL, Des. Pat. #101,957. Assigned to Chicago Die Casting Mfg. Co., Chicago. This became the* **"Orange Flow."** **(R)** *"Fruit Squeezer," pat'd. Dec. 24, 1940, by Fritz* **Katzky**, *Chicago. Des. Pat. #124,195. We've all seen this one.*

new improved model No. 200 of plastic & metal, "Victorio," by VillaWare, Cleveland, OH.] Oldest one is the main listing: .... **$25+**

Juicer, cast aluminum, screw clamps, crank turns one of 3 different-sized bladed reamers around in horizontal position over large funnel, below which is put a tumbler or bowl, "California Fruit Juice Extractor, Sr.," Strite-Anderson Mfg. Co., Minneapolis, MN, c.1929-30. (A smaller Junior model came in bright colors.).. **$40**

Juicer, wall bracket type, heavy cast aluminum with thinner spun aluminum reamer insert, crank with wooden knob, "The Speedo Super Juicer," mfd. by Central States Mfg. Co., about 5"H x 4-3/4" (5-3/4" from wall out to spout), c.1930. The wall bracket is almost always missing, alas, but sometimes you can find the whole thing at a yard sale or on eBay. **$15**

Juicer reamer, wall-mounted, cast & sheet aluminum, 4 parts: wall bracket, shallow strainer cup with holes, reamer cone with very exaggerated ribs, body or cup, with crank underneath. "Dazey Super-Juicer," Dazey Churn & Mfg. Co., St. Louis, MO, "Pat. Apl. For," application 1932; patent granted 1934........................ **$20**

Juicer-reamer, wall-mounted, cast 2-tone plastic, "Dazey Super-Juicer," so-called "streamline model," c.1941. .... **$10**

Juicer, cast metal, some alloy, wall-mounted, cup & reamer cone enameled in sunny yellow, with wall bracket. Handle knob modernized in shape, marked "Dazey Corporation," c.1950s............................ **$25**

I-J&LS-4. Juicer & reamers. *All aluminum. Big one is the funny "Handy Andy," this one with red painted base. A complete set would have a glass measuring pitcher that fits right under the reamer, and a glass, but I don't know in what color; others found with green paint, have green "Depression glass" pitcher & glass. 10-1/2"H x 6-7/8" diam. Two-part one is accessory for juicer, or could be set over a receptacle like the simple one in front.* **(L)** *As is:* **$20+; (L)** *with glass pieces:* **$70+;** *small ones* **$3+**

I-J&LS-5. Lemon squeezer. *Wood with heavily tinned male & female inserts, small 4-legged bench with hinged male lid and lever action. Closely resembles early 20th C. hotel lemon squeezer; this one probably mass-produced on small scale, mid 19th C. Picture courtesy of the National Museum of American History, Smithsonian Institution.* **$150-$225+**

Juicer, cast aluminum, wall-mounted, cup or juice container has pouring lip, deeply ribbed separate reamer cone, with a seed strainer or dam cup, crank underneath & its knob are aluminum, marked "Seald-Sweet Juicer," "L. E. Mason Co., Boston, MA," 8" x 7-1/4". Advertising claimed there were 6 different handle positions. Looks very like the Dazey, but mysterious how it connects to their patent. 1930s.. **$15**

Juicer, spun aluminum, cup sits on tiny disk feet on tabletop, has inserted seed strainer & prettily formed cone, little side crank with wooden knob, bottom marked "The Gem Squeezer" "patents pending, made by Quam-Nichols Co. Chicago." 6"H overall. Probably 1940s-50s. [Note: Here's a perfect example of something named because of popular usage, not because of its actual function or form. It just isn't a squeezer.].................................... **$10+**

Juicer, cast aluminum in "hammered" finish, simple, low-slung, long-lever type to be held over juice glass or bowl, has cup reamer insert, marked "E B A L O Y" in marked segments along top handle/lever; also "E 12-1-3." Ebaloy Inc., Rockford, IL, 14"L x 5" diam. bowl, pours from either side, c.1930s-40s. (Very similar is the Ebaloy "12-1-1" that is only 12"L, inside the top piece it says "12-2-4").............. **$15+**

Juicer, for lemons, wood, 4 legged bench, hinged top with pressing cup, long turned wooden lever, 2 inserts of heavily tinned sheet iron, possibly Shaker, mid (?) 19th C. See I-J&LS-5. .... **$150**

Juicer, cast aluminum with crude finishing, very architectural angled, openwork strut holds wide hopper cup & long lever high up, no seeding insert, just 6 holes, screwed to board, maker's name & trademark burned into wood: "Instant – Juicer, Ken Martin Co.," 8"H x 5-1/4"W hopper, 1950s.......................... **$15**

Juicer, cast aluminum, cutout frame with hopper, removable seed cup, and curved lever handle. Not as graceful as the Wear-Ever. "Universal," "Pat. Design #69942," L.F. & C. [Landers, Frary & Clark], New Britain, CT. Design by Oscar M. Anderson, assignor to L.F.& C. May 23, 1933 patent.................... **$20+**

Juicer, cast aluminum in dimpled hammered finish, angled strut screwed to green board, longish lever with wide palm-fit end, no seeder, just a toothed opening like a small shark's mouth. 7-1/2"H x 4-1/4"W hopper. No marks, c.1950s. **$15**

Juicer, cast iron, oak base painted a dark brown, lever action, definitely for oranges not lemons, no maker, 9-1/2"H, pat'd. Jan. 31, 1886. .... **$125**

Juicer, cast aluminum, four very short spraddle legs, white rubber disks on feet, long lever, separate strainer cup, "Wear-Ever Aluminum Trademark" in circle/cross on lever pivot, "T.A.C.U.CO.," The Aluminum Cooking Utensil Co., Pittsburgh, PA, Pat. #1,886,250, Design patent D-93,382, awarded to George Bungay, Nov. 1, 1932. The patent drawing is gorgeous! 4-1/2"H x 8-1/2"L. **$15**

Juicer, cast aluminum, oblong open frame with 4 little feet having black or white rubber disks, long lever, separate strainer cup, 9-1/2"H, 9"L x 5"W, "Wear-Ever Aluminum Trade Mark" in circle/cross on connecting crosspiece of frame, "T.A.C.U.CO.," The Aluminum Cooking Utensil Co., Pittsburgh, PA, Design patent D-86,217, awarded to George Bungay. Feb. 15, 1932. This "ornamental design for a juice-extractor" was assigned by Bungay to Household Field Corporation, NYC – unknown connection to T.A.C.U.Co. **$20**

Juicer, cast aluminum, simple lever action, mounted to board, cup & reamer set at angle, Rival Mfg. Co., Kansas City, MO, c.1935. .... **$25**

Juicer, cast aluminum, low-slung to be held over cup, lever pushes concave cone down over fruit, marked "Instant Juicer" "Rival Mfg. Co." Kansas City, MO, "Pat Apl'd for." c.1940s. **$15**

Juicer, cast aluminum, streamlined oblong open frame, 4 small feet, long curved lever, seed cup insert, about 9"H, "Fruit Squeezeit Juicer" embossed on front of hopper, in circle/disk on lower crosspiece of frame "Pat's Pend. Bungay-Wolf Corp. NYC".

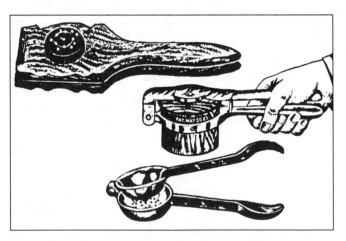

I-J&LS-6. Lemon squeezers. *Just 3 of many varieties.* **(T)** *Lignum vitae (very hard wood – in Latin the words mean* living rock*) cup & bowl in hinged paddle form, 10-1/2" x 3" (also came 13"L x 3-1/2" for lemons & 15-1/2" x 4-1/2" for oranges). Late 19th C.* **(M)** *A so-called "drum" squeezer that looks like small saucepan with lid. The "***Janes***," nickeled malleable iron frame, wooden presser, zinc-lined maple bowl. Pat'd. May 20, 1885 & sold for decades. This type looks very like a potato ricer in this line cut, but a potato ricer has a tinned cup with holes on sides and bottom. (See I-82)* **(B)** *Cast iron with porcelain-lined cup. Berger Bros., Philadelphia. 1895 ad.* **$35-$65**

Extremely similar to the Wear-Ever above, and predates it. George Bungay's patent assignment ended up with TACUC. Early 1930s. .... **$35+**

Juicer, cast & sheet aluminum, cylindrical cup-sized hopper, insert cup with holes, opening below where you place cup or glass, long curved lever like the Wear-Ever ones, two widespread tubular legs mounted to board, very robotic-zoomorphic looking! 10-1/2"H, board 13-1/8" x 5-3/8", lever handle embossed "Press-Or Midget"; embossed brass plate on end of wood base says "Lewis & Conger New York" (which was a store for kitchen supplies; See Conger article Chapt. IV.) 1930s-40s. .... **$30+**

Juicer, cast aluminum, streamlined design with stand & reamer cup and long-levered presser handle, lever marked "The Big Squeeze" "Patented." 9-1/2"H, American, 1930s-40s. .... **$25+**

Juicer, cast aluminum mounted to board, not a refined finish to either, frame straddles a receptacle of user's choice, marked on dog-leg curved lever handle "Challenge Fruit Juicer." American, 10"H, 1940s-50s. **$15**

Juicer, cast aluminum, commercial size, 3 parts: base, juice cup, stepped reamer; the 'horseshoe' base/stand's most notable feature is the row of bold embossed flowers, cup fits into ring halfway up stand, lever is gorgeous polished slim thing with small knob at top, no maker's mark, 14"H, when lever is in horizontal position, juicer is 14"L, about 25"H when lever upright, base only 5-3/4"L. Found in Quebec, could be Canadian, or American, prob. 1930s. .... **$75+**

Juicer, cast aluminum, commercial size, rack & pinion, with long lever with bullet-shaped wooden handle, black knobby grip at top to hold it steady while working it, separate cup & reamer, 21"H when lever upright. American (?), 1920s-30s. .... **$45+**

❖ NOTES ❖

New Juicers – One new juicer for restaurants, rather strikingly like the one above with the black handle, is chromed cast metal, with removable stainless steel strainer-cone & pitcher, 20-1/2"H. One very similar to the "Juice-King," with levered rack & pinion action, cast metal, in all chrome, blue/chrome, and black/chrome. 7"H. It's called the "Mighty OJ Manual Juice Squeezer." Claims 800 lbs. of pressure with the lever, but this may be an overstatement – many users have claimed it broke after a few times. Both made by Metrokane.

Juicer, cast iron screw clamp frame, cranked ball-bearing gear under reamer turns the clear glass bowl & its reamer cone. Bowl has side opening to funnel juice into waiting tumbler; bowl & reamer lift off for cleaning, American, c.1929-30. .... **$35+**

Juicer, cast aluminum, chromed & red painted cast iron (?), rack & pinion lever action type in stand, reamer cone has fine concentric ridges & small holes around base for juice, the Tilt-Top™ presser has square teeth all around edge, a cup & step-ridged reamer, "Juice-O-Mat," Rival Mfg. Co., Kansas City, MO, 7-7/8"H x 6-1/2" x 5-3/4", first pat'd. 1937. Advertised "improved models" with colored bases, etc., c.1948. .... **$25**

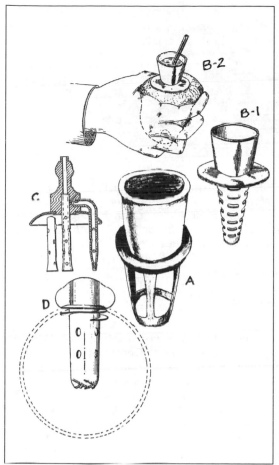

I-J&LS-7. Fruit juice extractor & patents. *All called "fruit juice extractor." In the center* **(A)** *is a cast aluminum "***Juistractor***" made to be inserted, actually forced, right through the rind or skin into a juicy fruit after it was rolled. Marked with name, and also "Pittsburgh, PA," and "US Patent Nos. 1,432,166; #1,649,755; and #1,747,957". I drew this one from one sold on eBay by* **das_kuk**, *Winona, MN. "The Cook's" transcription of the patent numbers is much appreciated. It allowed me to look up the three patents marked on the extractor itself.* **(B-1, B-2)** *Pat'd. Nov. 15, 1927, by Albert W.* **Thompson***, Miami, FL, #1,649,755. An object of the invention was to "afford facilities for holding the extracted juice so that it can be imbibed direct from the extractor without there being any necessity of transferring the juice to a cup." Also, it "can be thoroughly and effectually cleaned and sterilized when required." Thompson suggested that the tube [or straw] "may be made of any suitable material, such as porcelain, glass, or a light gauge metal." Furthermore, after insertion into the fruit, "the fruit is then grasped in the hand and is compressed toward the apertured portion of the extractor. It is obvious that the juice of the fruit will be forced through the apertures ... and thence upward into the imperforate upper portion.* **(C)** *Pat'd. Oct. 17, 1922, by Paul* **During***, Detroit, MI, Pat. #1,432,166. This drawing is harder to read, but essentially it's a device (shown here going down through the rind) with three "elbow tubes" driven into the fruit, which was palpated, then you poured (or drank?) from the "delivery tube" sticking up through the shaped handle. (I wouldn't wear a good dress with this one.)* **(D)** *Pat'd. Feb. 18, 1930, by Charles F.* **Silveus***, Waynesburg, PA, Pat. #1,747,957. This one is most easily understood because it's obvious that the cutting "blades" on the bottom would pierce the rind when pressed & twisted clockwise. It would, in an orange, "cut the entire core of the orange loose from the surrounding juice cells, the webs of the segments being also cut by this operation." Silveus also intended this to be used first as a "core remover, and thereafter to receive the juice to discharge it either into the mouth or into a receptacle." Any:* **$5+**

Juicer, cast aluminum, chrome & red-painted cast iron (?) base/stand, rack & pinion, underside of base "Single-Action™ Juice-O-Mat," cat. no. 462-C, Patent #D105,335, 2,142,975, D118,640, other patents pending. Rival Mfg. Co. **$20**

Juicer, cast & sheet aluminum, painted red enamel, similar to Rival "Juice-O-Mat," with side lever & rack & pinion to raise domed cap to place fruit inside. 3 parts: frame with gear & up & down domed presser, a juice cup with inner lip to hold the cone. Cone has raised edge and holes. Marked with *Good Housekeeping* Seal on top; marked "Streamline Super-Juicer," on bottom, pat.#2,131,440. by Herbert C. Johnson, Chicago, 1938. Design patent #195,062, "other pend." National Die Casting Co., Chicago. [Note: Was advertised as the "Streamline Juice King" by Bloomingdale's in 1938 and was available in ivory (a darkish cream, almost yellow) with red, blue, green or chrome; also red & chrome.] .... **$25+**

Juicer, cast metal frame & base, paint-enamel & chrome finish, rack & pinion lever action raises ridged conical reamer up to squush half a citrus fruit against conical upper cup-presser, should have a sheet aluminum cup to catch the juice, but rarely does, "National Juice King," National Die Casting Co., Chicago, IL, late 1930s. **$30**

Juicer, painted red cast iron stand & body, rack & pinion lever has slim, sleek black wooden handle, chrome top, separate stepped ridged aluminum reamer cone with holes & raised dished edges, perfectly fitted aluminum receptacle cup sets onto cork-lined cradle of base, 7-1/2"H, 7-3/4" x 3" at base, "The Juice-King, Model JK-35" National Die Casting Co., Inc., Chicago, 9"H, 1938 patent #2,131,440 & 1944 design patent D138,983. Cup usually not present. This squatty-but-streamlined juicer is so cute: in the closed position, with the handle forward & down, it looks like a fat lil' red-jacketed chrome dog with his face buried in the cup. Crossover retro design appeal. **$35**

Juicer, for fruit, meat & onions, a horizontal press like small bench lathe, cast aluminum frame, the retainer cup & convex plunger or press, should have shallow aluminum holder underneath to catch juice. First the retainer pivots upright to place half lemon or piece of raw meat, then put back down into horizontal position to face plunger, which is moved toward the cup by turning the wheel. "20th Century Power Juice Extractor," mfd. by the Album Mfg. Co., Freeport, IL, late 1890s, though it looks much more recent. ... **$50-$75**

Juicer, for oranges, spun aluminum with wire reamer inside, crank at top, hand held and pressure applied from handles, Knapps, 1930 patent #1,743,661, foreign patents pending, 6-1/4"H x 8"L. Inventors Clarence E. Elliott & Leonard Nichols, of Kansas City, MO. **$10**

Juicer, green painted heavy stamped iron & aluminum, 4 widely splayed legs, hopper & reamer at top, side crank turns small geared wheel, very unusual & handsome, "Universal," Landers, Frary & Clark, 10"H x 5-3/4", 1930s(?). **$35**

I-J&LS-9. Miniature reamer juicer. *Cast iron, skillet-shaped, ribbed reamer concave on underside, cast into underside is "**C. D. Kenny** Co. Teas Coffees Sugars." Mfd. by or for C. D. Kenny Co., also called Consolidated Grocers Co., Baltimore, MD (there were several foundries there.) 3" diam. pan, 1" handle, c. 1930s-'40s. Photo courtesy John Alexander, Boiling Springs, PA. Midnite Antiques; eBay user name Midnitetip.* **$125+**

I-J&LS-8. George Washington Juicer. *Cast iron with black japanning or enameling, screwed to wooden base. The unusual cast plate with George Washington's face, 13 stars, the patent date, and maker,* **G. A. Williams**, *NYC, formed part of the lever. Four legs are X-shaped cast iron, screwed to round-ended wooden base, with a smaller U cut out underneath where the juice would come out. Cup-shaped depression with one 1" diam. hole for the juice, et al. [The patent drawing for it is extremely plain, with no indication of decoration. Originally it had an insert with strainer holes for the seeds; the drawing shows a slightly rectangular piece with small holes that the inventor,* **John H. Mead**, *NYC, described as "a separate or false removable bottom, resting on the outer angle of the true bottom. This false bottom is made dishing, and is perforated by a number of comparatively small holes. A tumbler or other suitable vessel, to receive the juice of the lemon, may be set underneath the aperture." Pat. #140,785, pat'd. July 15, 1873 – unusually, it had been filed just three weeks before, and originally may have looked like the simple patent drawing. After all, it was only 3 years until the Centennial, a good opportunity to use patriotism & Washington's face to sell juicers. 7"H x 9-1/2"L x 5"W; the plate is 4-1/2" x 5". Photo courtesy Carole & Larry Meeker, who specialize in patented & mechanical antiques, as collectors & dealers. Visit www.patented-antiques.com.* **$300+**

Juicer, reamer in sort of space station stand, cranked to work, stamped aluminum & painted tin, flimsy but as cute as R2-D2, came with red or green painted base, "Handy Andy," mfd. by H. A. Specialty Co., Inc., Long Island City, NY, 10-1/2"H x 6-7/8" diam., pat'd. July 23, 1935, although on the market since about 1930. The Handy-Andy company itself wasn't in the 1932-33 directory of manufacturers, but was in the 1946 one. .... **$35+**
Juicer, reamer in top of green metal stand, crank on top, another "Handy Andy," but this is the more

valuable one. It's more substantial, and the base closely nestles a so-called "Depression glass" green measuring pitcher, and a green glass reamer cone fits into it. The crank turns the lemon or orange around on the reamer. Circa 1935................... **$95+**
Juicer, red painted cast iron horseshoe base fits around tumbler, upright part has cast aluminum cup fixed at top, rack & pinion lever raises ridged reamer, with half an orange on it, up into cup to express juice, American, 8"H, c.1940s. A company advertised the "Mighty OJ" squeezer in 1982, a new version of old one. Old:.................................... **$45**
Juicer, sheet metal with green finished wooden knob, screw clamps, a triple extractor with 3 reamers, for grapefruit, oranges, lemons, even tomatoes! American, c.1931. .... **$15**
Juicer, steel & aluminum, hand held, cup has simple wire reamer, domed lid with crank, hinged handles to be clasped firmly to increase pressure on orange inside, very small lip on side of cup for pouring juice without opening, Kwikway Products, Inc. St. Louis, MO, 6-1/2" x 4" diam. cup, 1929 patent........... **$15**

I-J&LS-10. Lemon squeezer. *Nickeled sheet iron, cast iron, and rosewood handles. Compound lever compresses a diamond-shape hinged squeeze-box on other side of the kite-shaped back.* **"The Little Giant Lemon Squeezer,"** *pat'd. May 3, 1881. 10-1/2"L; when opened fully, 16"W. See next picture also.* **$165+**

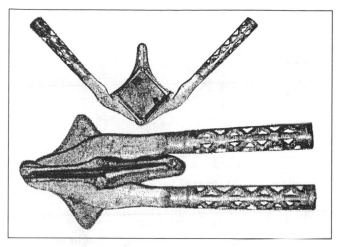

*I-J&LS-11. **Lemon squeezer.** Tinned cast iron & sheet iron, not as "bow-legged" as "The Little Giant," but possibly same maker & patentee. 9-1/2"L, reticulated hollow iron handles. Photo courtesy John Zukatis. **$65+***

Juicer, stamped aluminum, little frying pan shape with reamer cone inside, little comb-like teeth block seeds from pouring spout, sheet steel handle & pivoting base, something like a lazy Susan, rubber gasket, worked by rotating handle back & forth, "rotates on pivot base. Hold orange still ... swing handle!" Doesn't work very well, 5-1/2" diam. x 9-1/2"L overall. "Kwicky Juicer," Quam-Nichols Co., Chicago, pat'd. 1945 by James P. Quam, #141,788. .... **$15**

Juicer or reamer, aluminum, brass gears inside with stainless steel pin for reamer, wooden knob, 3 rubber feet, lift-off reamer with gear in it, "The Gem Squeezer," mfd. by Quam-Nichols Co., Chicago, IL, 6"H, 1-1/2 c. capacity, "patents pending," c.1930s............ **$20**

Juicer & reamer, mottled garnet color Catalin™ plastic (like the more familiar Bakelite™ or other molded phenolic resin), reamer part screws on & holds in place a heavy duty screen seed-catcher, marked on handle "Ex-Squeez-It" BCM, and stamped under handle "Catalan Company," Made in England, various patent numbers for different countries, c. 1930s or 1940s. Art plastic crossover collector interest here. **$55**

Juicer & reamer, green phenolic plastic, "Ex-Squeez-It," mfd. by BC M, marked "D. R. G. M.," German, 5-1/4" diam., patent #362,187 [English patent #], 1931............ **$55**

❖ NOTES ❖

Ex-Squeez-It and Ex-Plain-It! At the *U.S. Patent Full Text Database Number Search* page (see last few chapters, on patent research) I typed in the number 362187, not thinking it would do much good, since I thought it was a German patent, and I got a page with a huge machine on it. By putting the number into the "Refine Search" slot, I got a list* of 6 patents, one with the 362187 number, one with a design patent, 334,512, for a "combined storage unit and holder for a juicer and grater," patented in 1993 by a couple, Bruce & Jane Ancona, who were assignors to a hardware store I used to know in NYC, Kamensteins. I clicked on

it and got a page that showed the lipped cup & inserted reamer, but more importantly, I got a list of the "References cited" from *U.S. patents*, and *Foreign Patents*! There was 362,187, United Kingdom. It must be the juicer & squeezer in the listing above, but at this time I can't access British patents. Among the US Patents cited was an 1889 patent. Going back to the *list of 6 patents cited above, I clicked on the other patent that seemed related: #5,088,392, for a "Kitchen Unit." Open Sesame! This time, a 1992 patent by the Anconas came up, with a much longer list of *US Patent Documents* cited as references, from 1897 to 1981. So, although I haven't figured out all the intricacies of it, by entering a number in "Refine Search," I have been awarded with nine patents prior to 1960, my arbitrary cutoff date. (Although, of course, I didn't know yet if any or all of them were for juicers.) **1)** A juice extractor reamer; **2)** a reamer; **3)** a colander; **4)** another reamer; **5)** a reamer-egg separator combo set into its own lipped cup [sound familiar? and it's much neater than the Anconas' design referring to it]; **6)** an attachment for kitchen utensils "adapted to arrest the contents of the potato masher or colander which are emitted laterally ... and downwardly into a receptacle which is provided."

...continued

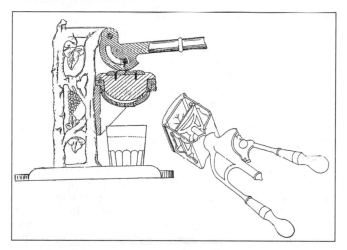

*I-J&LS-12. **Juicer patents.** I don't know if either was actually made. **(L)** A stand juicer that would be cast iron, poss. painted colorfully & realistically, the way cast iron garden fences were. Poss. mounted to wooden board, pat'd. June 18, 1867, by Oswald **Hesselbacher** & Henry **Moesta**, Detroit, MI. Pat. # 65,809. The lever is shown truncated in the drawing, but looks very powerful. **(R)** Handheld juicer, similar action to some ice cream scoops; a form of rack & pinion. Pulling handles together turns the half-round gear which moves in the teeth of the shaft which pushes the presser plate (covered in "Vulcanite," vulcanized rubber) against the end of the fruit cage, onto the plate with drip-grooves. Pat'd. Mar. 15, 1881, by Robert H. **Daley**, San Francisco, CA, Pat. #238,765. Daley wrote "My invention relates to improvements in that class of lemon-squeezers in which the follower is forced toward the bed-plate by means of a rack actuated by a segmental pinion on the end of a lever-handle." This implies that there are other squeezers similar in action to this one. If they exist: **(L) $300+; (R) 125+***

[Or...lemon juice?]; **7)** a "fruit juice extractor," mounted on a receiver; **8)** a food grater with its own receptacle, something like the nutgrinders with glass jars; **9)** a juicer/measuring cup. Because sometimes it is hard to get back to the same page, I always print out pages with promising lists of patent numbers.

Juicers-Squeezers

Juicer-squeezer, for lemons, cast iron, skinny handles with fat ends, marked "Pat. Nov. 21. 85" [1885]. 9"L x 3"W, cups 2"deep. American. .... **$18+**

Juicer-squeezer, for lemons & limes, cast metal, hand held, "Quick & Easy," Erie Specialty Co., Erie, PA, 6"L, 20th C. **$5**

Juicer-squeezer, for lemons & limes, zinc-coated cast iron, scissor action, compartment with holes to capture seeds, "Vaughn Co.," Chicago, IL, 6"L, 20th C. For an explanation of zinc and galvanizing, see a long paragraph up with the Food mill listings. **$7**

Juicer-squeezer, for lemons, tinned cast iron, hinged hand-held 2-part, with cup & rounded (not ribbed) reamer cone, and presser-cup, "Griswold No. 6," marked "367," Erie, PA, c.1910. .... **$75+**

Juicer-squeezer, for lemons & limes, heavy cast aluminum, "plier" action, marked "Acid & Rust Free," American, 7-1/4"L, early 1900s. **$7**

Juicer-squeezer, for lemons, japanned cast iron, with separate, heavily-tinned cup which can be used separately as a reamer, "American Queen," c.1906...... **$30**

Juicer-squeezer, for lemons, all maple, 2 hinged arms, with holes in the concave bowl or cup of one part, American, 10-3/4"L, late 19th C. **$45**

❖ NOTES ❖

Lemons Well-Rolled – "An old-time Philadelphia Housewife said yesterday: 'None of your new-fangled lemon squeezers for me. Anything, especially acid – squeezed through metal, such as many of the improved ones are, is very bad. The wooden ones do not have this fault; neither do those made of glass or porcelain. But they all have one fault that there is no getting rid of, and that is that the skin of the lemon is squeezed so that its flavor mixes with that of the juice. This is all wrong. There is but one way to squeeze a lemon, and that is the simple, old-fashioned way, between your fingers. Plenty of power can be brought to bear, particularly if the lemon is well-rolled first.'" *Ladies Home Journal*, Sept. 1889.

Juicer-squeezer, for lemons, wood on wooden base, hinged press, marked "The F. F. Adams Co., Erie, PA, for the Atlantic Wringer Co.," Erie, PA, 9"H x 14"L x 4"W, late 19th C. **$95**

Juicer-squeezer, for lemons, dense, well-patined hardwood, oblong board base with decorative notches at both ends, 3 fat dowel rod legs holding 2-part squeezer above base. Lower part holds perforated female cup, upper hinged part has handle at one end with same notched decoration & male presser, PA (?), mid 19th C. **$85**

Juicer-squeezer, for lemons, levered hand held type, turned wood drum set in nickel plated iron frame & handles (also came japanned for less), white glazed

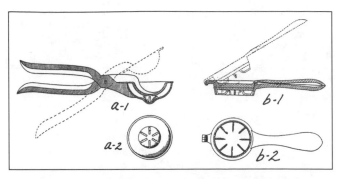

I-J&LS-13. Patents for lemon squeezer & cracker crusher. *(a-1 & a-2)* "*Lemon Squeezer,*" *pat'd. Jan. 15, 1867, by Thomas Reece & Arthur Clarke, Philadelphia, PA. Pat. #61,251. The "two cups" were meant to be "made of metal or wood or of any other suitable material. If made of metal they can be galvanized, or if made of wood they can be tinned so as to prevent corrosion." The handles are levers, pivoted close to the cups, in a manner quite familiar to squeezer collectors. (b-1 & b-2) "Cracker Crusher," pat'd. Jan. 15, 1867, by Arthur Clarke & Thomas Reece, pat. #61,163. Nice to think of the two men, possibly friends, trading lead billing with each other on alternating patents! This one, if made, could be said to make pieces of Reece's crackers. Of the two cups, one was to be "round or other suitable shape [remember, crackers came in all shapes, and there were scores of named cracker types] with "a perforated bottom to allow the cracker crumbs to pass through, or a single opening centrally located in the bottom for the same purpose." The opposing side, the crushing part, is "brought down, causing the wings to crush the crackers upon the wings in the other cup" (seen in b-2 as radiant ribs or elongated teeth). "It will be seen that this invention effectually obviates the necessity of breaking crackers with the hands or teeth, and will easily break and crush the crackers of the hardest [such as hard tack] as well as the softest kinds, and can be regulated so that they are or can be broken either fine or coarse, according to the number of teeth [wings] placed on the flanges and cup." The inventors reveal also their working out of the handles, hinged at one end: "We may hinge the sections at or near the centre of their handles ... and allow the same to be operated similar to a pair of scissors or pliers; but, on experimenting, we find that suitable purchase is had with the fulcrum at [the end]." If the cracker crusher was made, just the oddity is worth something:* **$45+**

porcelain inset, small pouring channel in wood rim, "Drum," Manning-Bowman, Meriden, CT, 10"L, late 19th C. **$55**

Juicer-squeezer, for lemons, maple, hinged male & female halves, American (?), 10-3/4"L, c.1870s to 1880s. (A similar maple one, with a porcelain insert, is 8-1/2"L.) **$40**

Juicer-squeezer, for lemons, wood (maple?), with extremely hard lignum vitae wood insert, American, 19th C. (Lignum vitae means *living rock* in Latin.) **$50**

Juicer-squeezer, for lemons, wood with white porcelain insert, mark is eagle with "S" in beak, "UPW" underneath, for Union Porcelain Works, American, 19th C. **$125**

Juicer-squeezer, for lemons, with slicer, hinged 2 part wooden squeezer, iron stand with 2 cutting blades, American, 15" x 7", c.1900. .... **$95**

Juicer-squeezer, for lemons, black painted cast iron, hinged, 2 glazed white china or ironstone reamer inserts, a loose cup with 4 holes, presser is screwed to the iron, pat'd. by T. C. Smith, NYC, NY, 8-15/16"L, marked "pat'd. Apr. 7, 1868." **$75**

Juicer-squeezer, for lemons & oranges, cast aluminum, one deep spouted cup has ribbed sides, other has ball, "Westmark LIMONA," German, 9-1/4"L, mid 20th C. Another "Westmark Limona," same size, has bright yellow plastic liner to the two cups. **$10**

Juicer-squeezer, cast aluminum, ribbed cone, ribbed spouted cup, relatively short handles, cast inside handle "Taiwan." 8-3/4"L. .... **$5+**

Juicer-squeezer, for oranges, cast aluminum, simple concave/convex cups, crude crosshatch marks on handle (to improve grip?), cast into rim "Hueva en Mexico." 10"L, last quarter (?) 20th C. **$6**

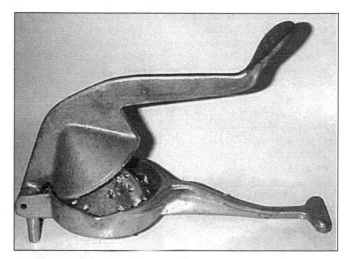

I-J&LS-15. Levered juicer, very low-slung. The "Instant Juicer" by Rival Mfg. Co., Kansas City, MO. "Pat. Apl'd for." 12"L, 1930s. Photo courtesy John Zukatis. $20

I-J&LS-14. Juicers hinged at one end. These are just six of probably hundreds made over the last 140 years. Some of these are probably 100+ years old, a few may be only 75+ years old. From the left: (1) tinned cast iron, no markings at all, 9-1/4"L; (2) tinned (?) cast iron, "Universal," mfd. by Landers, Frary & Clark, has comparatively large "cup" with spout for juicier lemons! 9-3/4"L; (3) No markings, 8"L, prob. 1920s-30s; (4) japanned (?) cast iron, totally indistinct embossed mark around rim, illegible, flattish strainer cup, 10-3/4"L; (5) brightly tinned, note ribs in both male & female parts, no marks, 9"L; (6) the "Pearl," black japanned cast iron, with wooden screwed-in half-round "reamer" – it could be replaced, presumably. Only 4 holes in the "strainer" cup. Photo courtesy John Zukatis. All c. 1880-1920. $20+

Juicer-squeezer, for lemons, black porcelainized cast iron, aluminum cup, levered hinged device, marked "LIDON," mfd. by Gilchrist Co., Newark, NJ, c.1906. .... **$15**

Juicer-squeezer, for lemons, cast iron finished in black, hinged handles, tinned cast iron reamer insert cup with spout and holed tab handle fits into bottom half, 9"L, "X-Ray 5," Arcade Mfg. Co., (perhaps they also made the "X-Ray Raisin Seeder"?). American, early 20th C. [Note: The presence of such a thing as an **X-ray** was discovered in November 1895 by physics professor Wilhelm Conrad Roentgen, at the University of Wurzburg, Germany. Within two months, people everywhere knew about them thanks to newspapers. It is probable that the use of the modern-sounding name "X-ray" was almost immediately picked up by manufacters – at least those that didn't choose "20th Century" as a trade name! .... **$50+**

Juicer-squeezer, for lemons, cast iron, 2 parts hinged, one corrugated "male," one fluted "female," not marked but from Matthai-Ingram Co., American, two sizes: 8-1/2"L & 10-1/2"L, c.1890s. **$45**

Juicer-squeezer, for lemons, cast iron frame with fancy little legs, stands on counter top, slotted concave cup, long lever handle with enameled convex presser, sold also as a nutcracker & food press, ad claimed it was useful for 12 different kitchen processes, "All – In – One," Ford Mfg. Co., Inc., Newark, NJ, about 11"L, late 19th C. **$150**

Juicer-squeezer, for lemons, cast iron, hinged, 8-1/2"L with 2-1/2" diam. bowl, late 19th C. **$45**

Juicer-squeezer, for lemons, cast iron with glass insert, "King's," English, 1882. .... **$35**

Juicer-squeezer, for lemons, cast iron with screwed-in wooden ball, & white pottery cup insert, hinged long handles, embossed "The Arcade ... Lemon-Squeezer" on top, "No.2." Freeport, IL, 8-5/8"L, late 19th C. **$45**

Juicer-squeezer, for lemons, cast iron hinged long-handled type, with unusual glass cup/reamer insert in lower half. Lower part has four little legs to hold it level, whereas most of this type were made to be held over a cup, "Williams," Ravenna, OH, late 19th to early 20th C. **$50**

Juicer-squeezer, for lemons, hinged 2 part cast iron with milk glass reamer insert, instead of more commonly found pottery or ironstone insert, American (?), late 19th C. **$75**

Juicer-squeezer, for lemons, cast iron with wooden half-ball presser inside top half, hinged long handles, "Pearl," American, late 19th C. **$25**

Juicer-squeezer, for lemons, iron, hinged 2 part, "Diamond Point," American, pat'd. July 10, 1888. .. **$55**

Juicer-squeezer, for lemons, cast iron with tinned finish, compound lever action ... when handles are pulled apart, it pulls apart a diamond- or kite-shape hinged holder for the lemon half. Perfectly straight handles all metal, reticulated with cutout triangles. 9-1/4"L. American, poss. same as next listing, pat'd. 1881. .... **$65+**

Juicer-squeezer, for lemons, cast iron with nickeled (?)finish, compound lever action ... when handles are pulled apart, it pulls apart a diamond- or kite-shape hinged holder for the lemon half. Handles much more polished than previous listing, and halfway down the ferrules hold beautiful rosewood handles. Handles slightly bow-legged; back of diamond-shaped holder for lemon marked "The LITTLE GIANT," pat'd. May 3, 1881. .... **$135+**

Juicer-squeezer, for lemons, nickeled cast iron, tin plunger & cup, horizontal reamer action activated by long lever (what maker called a "positive spiral pres-

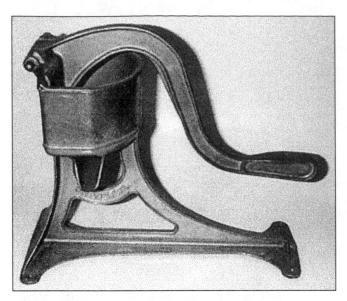

I-J&LS-17. Levered juicer. *Cast aluminum, lift-out strainer cup. Juices half of a citrus fruit up to size of a grapefruit, molded spout at bottom. 4 hard rubber feet – split as usual.* **"Universal,"** *mfd. by "Landers, Frary & Clark, New Britain, CT. "Des. Pat.#89,942," pat'd. May 23, 1933, by Oscar M. Anderson, New Britain, CT., assignor to LF&C. 9-1/4"H x 11"L at base. See also I-J&LS-2 (J). Photo courtesy John Zukatis.* **$20+**

sure"), screw clamp, small adjustable-height platform for tumbler is attached to a thin rod, "The Leader," mfd. by Rocky Hill Hardware Co., Rocky Hill, CT, about 10"L, c.1908. .... **$40**

❖ NOTES ❖

Crackers & Lemonade – At this time we don't know if either patent ever came to fruition, but two men in Philadelphia, Arthur Clarke, and Thomas Reece, were issued two patents on Jan. 15, 1867: an "Improved Cracker Crusher," and an "Improved Lemon-Squeezer." The former was a simple hinged-press device with a flat cup with big holes upon which a cracker was placed, and its opposing deeply ribbed and/or toothed crushing part, which the inventors said would "obviate the necessity of breaking crackers with the hands or teeth, and will easily break and crush the crackers of the hardest as well as the softest kinds, and can be regulated so that they can be broken either fine or coarse, according to the number of teeth placed on the flanges and cup." They added that they wanted to "construct the cup either in a round or other suitable shape." Their lemon squeezer was somewhat different from most that I have seen. Instead of being hinged at one end, theirs pivots in the middle, more like scissors, so that more pressure would be exerted on the half a lemon. They said there were to be "two cups made of metal or wood or of any other suitable material. If made of metal they can be galvanized, or if made of wood they can be tinned so as to prevent corrosion from the action of the acid." [I have never heard of **tinning wood**, but this did get a patent.] One cup is concave and has a small recess forming a bump on the outside, with slots that radiate from the center and would allow

I-J&LS-16. Levered juicer. *Cast aluminum, lift-out strainer cup. Pressure applied by the lever ... the goal of the inventor/designer of this type was to achieve the most ppsi pressure in the neatest compact space. They tried all kinds of curves, doglegs, swoops, and angles to achieve that. We know how hard some oranges can be!* **"Fruit Squeezeit Juicer,"** *"Pat's Pend. Bungay-Wolf Corp, NYC." 9"H. Note this is the same design as the Wear-Ever. And look at patent drawing in I-J&LS-3. Predates Wear-Ever. C. 1932+. Photo courtesy John Zukatis.* **$25+**

the juice but not the seeds through. The other cup is convex, and rather smaller to leave room for the lemon "without crushing the seeds." I would love to know if these were ever manufactured. **See I-J&LS-13.**

Juicer-squeezer, for lemons, sheet metal frame clamps to table, iron lever, cast aluminum perforated cup, concave glass receiver, lever rotated to press juice, arm with ring holds glass tumbler, "Walker's Quick & Easy No. 42," Erie Specialty Co., Erie, PA, c.1906. .... **$75**

Juicer-squeezer, for lemons, tinned malleable cast iron frame clamps to underside of shelf or bar, with lever in upright position so the lemon half can be put in place against reamer, which is also upright. When lever is depressed to right, both cup & lever move into horizontal position, cone & cup remove for cleaning, adjustable holder for tumbler, "Perfect," Arcade Mfg Co., Freeport, IL, c.1903. .... **$65**

Juicer-squeezer, for lemons, plated cast iron, hinged-press, long-handled: one half is cup with holes, & other half is fluted reamer, no mark, American, 7-1/4"L, 19th C. **$35**

Juicer-squeezer, for lemons, white enameled cast iron, hinged 2 part, both cups have ribbed rims. Female cup has small ring base & its handle has a projecting foot, so it can be set down on work surface & hold the juice until needed, German, about 8-1/4"L, 4th quarter 19th C. **$55**

❖ NOTES ❖

Lookalike alarm – In 1982, a kitchen supply shop in NYC advertised a hand-held cast iron lemon or lime squeezer, with lustrous black enameled finish inside & out, hinged two-part. It does not seem to have the little foot for steadying on counter. Visible in the photograph of it is a mark inside one handle, but I cannot read it. The mark almost looks like July and June patent dates, and this could be an exact cast copy of one pat'd. in 1880s.

I-J&LS-18. Levered juicer. Cast aluminum, beautiful design looks like something from Star Wars (perhaps this is Emtoo). Mounted to wooden base. Only two legs, graceful lever with pivoting presser, removable strainer cup. Handle embossed **"Press-Or Midget,"** *brass plate on board "Lewis & Conger, New York" (They were a supplier or store, not manufacturer.) 10-1/2"H on board 13-1/8" x 5-3/8"; c.1930s-40s. Photo courtesy John Zukatis.* **$30+**

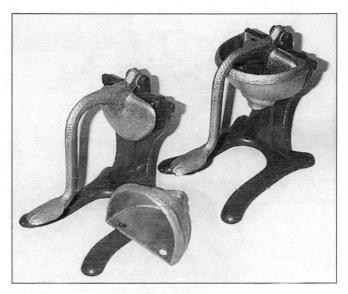

I-J&LS-19. Levered juicer, two views. Cast aluminum with red-enameled stand. Strainer cup hooks onto two projections on vertical shaft of juicer, for easy cleaning. Hammered finish to lever, presser & cup. No markings or name, alas. 8-1/4"H. American, prob. 1940s. Photo courtesy John Zukatis. **$25**

Juicer, or press, cast iron, a press with a screw to be tightened from above, juice collects in reservoir underneath, handle at side to resist torque of turning screw – for doing those really old, petrified lemons from the back of the fridge, marked "Landers, Frary & Clark, New Britain, CT," 7" x 8" x 4", late 19th - early 20th C. **$75**

Juicer, "lemon squeezer & slicer" combined, cast iron mounted to wooden board with "bite" taken out of edge at halfway point, long-legged body with high tail lever, rack & pinion mechanism, had glass or china cup insert, (this one missing) probably for restaurant or bar or soda fountain use, no marks on squeezer itself, mark is stamped into wood board: "Acme, The F. F. Adams Co.," Erie, PA, 12"H, pat'd. Dec. 20, 1887... **$95+**

Juicer, lemon wedge squeezer, silver-plated springy metal, in shape of abstract bird, lemon wedge fits between the "wings" which are then pressed together. Unmarked. 4-1/2"L, 20th C. .... **$20+**

Juicer, lemon wedge squeezer for table use, nickel-plated non-magnetic metal stamped with simple wings & feathers on side, shaped like little palm-sized songbird, although inventor, Adolf Wagner, Mussbach, Germany, wrote that it looked like "a swimming sea-gull," eyes are actually the ends of the hinge for the long curved top part of body that you open like a little box, insert lemon wedge, push down on top, juice comes out of birdbeak spout, marked "Napier," patent #2,037,553. Was awarded US patent April 14, 1936. [Note: Brand new ones are made from stainless steel, & called a "Loungin' Lime Bird" – only difference is loss of nice wing detail & vintage charm. And, just seen in stores, a stainless steel fish squeezer, same general design.] Old: **$30**

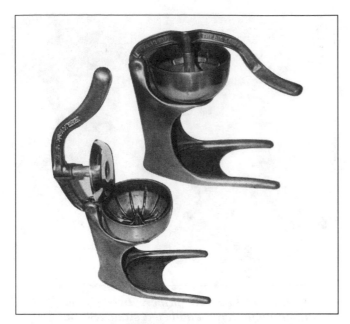

I-J&LS-20. Levered juicer, two views. *Polished cast aluminum, separate juicer bowl has a sharp narrow cone in center to spear the fruit. Pressure sort of turns the orange skin inside out. "**The Big Squeeze.**" American, ultra-streamlined, jet-age 1940s. 9-1/2"H. Photo courtesy John Zukatis. **$30+***

Reamers

Reamer (called by Wagner a "fruit juice extractor,") cast aluminum, Wagner Ware "453," like a little frying pan, with 2 pouring lips, stepped reamer has six sides, and from underneath there's a deep 6-point star concavity inside the reamer cone, 6-1/4" diam., c.1930. .... **$25+**

I-J&LS-21. Levered juicer, *about to become a hood ornament. Aluminum, mounted to varnished board. Very architectural strut support, but crudely finished – lots of machined smoothing of what must have been even cruder casting. Name on board is "**Instant Juicer**" "Ken Martin Co. Made in U.S.A." 8"H; board 10-3/4"L. American, c.1950s-60s. Author's collection. **$15***

Reamer, cast iron with chrome plating, miniature, shallow frying pan shape with 1" handle, ribbed cone, embossed on underside "C. D. Kenny Co. Teas ~ Coffees ~ Sugars," star on underside of handle. Very scarce. C. D. Kenny Co., also called Consolidated Grocers Co., Baltimore, MD, 3" diam. pan, c.1930s-40s. .... **$125+**

Reamer, cast aluminum, round dish with tab handle, seed-catcher nubs, tall ribbed reamer cone, adv. in English catalog, *George Fowler's How to Bottle,* c. 1921... **$25+**

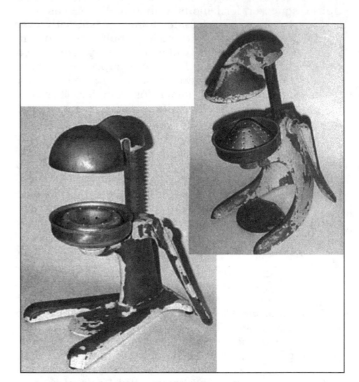

I-J&LS-22. Rack & pinion juicers. *Cast aluminum with badly flaking, peeling paint. These may actually have first been sold in the 1930s in "natural" aluminum finish; I think it was probably a marketing decision in the 1940s to paint aluminum juicers, in order to make them coordinate with kitchen decorating schemes. The all metal streamlined look was probably too "un-homey" for marketing to housewives in America. These two handsome juicers are shown in as-found condition. I plan to remove the paint and leave the beautiful aluminum finish.* **(L)** *"Orange Flow," "Chicago Die Casting Co., pat. Nov. 17, 1936, no.101,957, by William P.* **Koch,** *Oak Park, IL. John Zukatis points out that "this juicer is one of the very few that have a reversed reamer cone – the reamer is on top, and you bring it down onto the orange which is face up!" Removable fruit-holder cup. 7-1/4"H.* **(R)** *"Juice-King," pat'd. Aug. 24, 1937, by Herbert C.* **Johnson,** *Chicago. Marked with the two patents: Utility Pat. #2,090,913, Des. Pat. #110,897. "Others pending. Chicago." This has the conical top, quite a different look from the smooth round cap of later Juice-Kings. 8"H. Photo courtesy John Zukatis. Until such juicers as this and others catch the public attention, the prices are low. I paid John only $9.99 for this, but I believe they will be worth more because of design.* **(L) $20+ (R) $20+**

Reamer, clear molded glass, saucer bowl & ribbed reamer cone, "Ideal," American, pat'd. Jan. 31, 1888. .... **$20+**

Reamer, for lemons, clear molded glass, ribbed cone on base meant to set over what the inventor, John P. Manny, called "a suitable receptacle," slight dish around reamer cone, with slots to let juice through and strain out seeds, mold was embossed with "Manny's Pat. Aug. 25, 1885 Nov. 12, 1889, 2 pat.'s, Dec. 2, 90, June 29, 89." Rockford, IL. **$20**

Reamer, for oranges, lemons, limes, heavy molded glass, wide lipped saucer with flat tab handle, very pointed conical reamer in center with 3 edges or blades full length, & 3 short ones, "Easley No. 4," William F. Easley Mfg. Co., NYC, NY, 1909. ....,, **$45**

Reamer, molded glass, conical reamer has blades or sharp edges & pointed projections in waffled pattern, base has holes, edge fits over tumbler, juice goes through holes, "Easley No. 2A," Easley Mfg. Co., early 20th C., they discontinued this non-saucer style by 1910... **$45**

Reamer, molded pressed glass, transparent ultramarine, with ribbed cone, squared finger-grip, embossed "SUNKIST" on both sides, long-nosed pouring lip opposite handle, patent #68,764. Even with "multiple" chips, one sold on eBay in late 2001, for $1,059.00. .... **$900+**

Reamer, for oranges, lemons, limes, 1-piece molded glass saucer & rounded conical reamer with 4 long blades or sharp edges from top to bottom, plus 7 little pyramidal points in each of 4 sections, no handle, basket pattern & rope border, Easley Mfg. Co., c.1902................. **$45**

Reamer, & lipped pouring bowl which it fits into, clear glass, painted flowers, "Baby's Orange" on bowl, American, c.1890s-1910s. **$25**

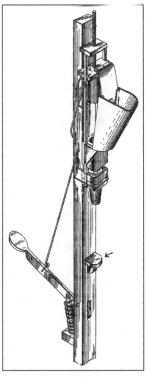

I-J&LS-23. Patent for "Lemon Presser or Squeezer" for commercial use. Pat'd. Mar. 10, 1891, by Salathiel C. Rupe, Carrollton, MO. Pat. #447,976. Mr. Rupe invented "a press adapted to be operated by foot or hand and to successively deliver, cut, and squeeze a series of lemons subjected thereto, eject the skins and pulp, strain the juice, and deliver the same into a waiting receptacle." The "standard" looks like a 2x2, which would have had to be very securely in place so as not to jiggle the receptacle on the little shelf 2/3 of the way down (see arrow). Basically, you filled the large hopper with lemons (shown whole in another of Rupe's patent drawings!), stepped on the spring-loaded pedal, which pulled on a wire secured near top to the sliding assemblage of hopper/foller-presser. It pulled the whole thing down a rod into the spout. The juice pours into the tumbler on the shelf. Who knows if it was ever made?

I-J&LS-24. Commercial levered juicer. Cast aluminum, highly finished, 14"H with lever in pictured position, and 14" across in this position. No mark; c.1930s? Photo courtesy of eBayer "eyeupsome" of Quebec City, Canada. **$75+**

Reamer & lemon slicer, die molded red plastic, figural little chef, c.1940s to 1950s. .... **$5+**

Reamer, for lemons, turned hard wood, grooved end, nice patina, American, 9"L, c.1890s-1910s. **$18**

Julien cutter, or julienne cutter, for cutting sliced vegetables into decorative little flowerettes or snowflake like patterns, to float prettily in clear soups, cast iron with 20 different cutting dies to be inserted. 4 legs (including 2 long hind legs) all with holes to screw securely to work surface, lever action with turned wooden handle on lever, imported by F. A. Walker, French (?), prob. about

I-J&LS-25. Tabletop juicer. Spun aluminum receptacle, with inserted reamer & strainer cup, crank handle with wood knob. **"The Gem Squeezer,"** mfd. by Quam-Nichols Co., Chicago, "patents pending." 6"H to top of cone. Photo courtesy John Zukatis; c.1940s (?) **$15+**

I-J&LS-26. Wall-mounted juicers. *Meant to fit into bracket permanently affixed to wall or cupboard.* **(B-L)** *Cast aluminum, including knob on crank, lift the reamer cone and the seed dam comes off for cleaning. Embossed* **"Mason Seald-Sweet Juicer,"** *L. E. Mason Co., Boston, MA, 1930s. 7"L from wall to spout.* **(T-R)** *Spun aluminum, wood knob, unscrew the reamer to take this one apart. Embossed on side of bowl* **"Speedo Super Juicer,"** *"Made in USA. Pat App. For." 5-3/4" from wall to spout. 1930s (?) Photos courtesy John Zukatis.* **$15+**

7"L x 4"H, with 1" cutting discs or dies, late 19th C. An American raisin seeder, pat'd. 1895, is very similar to this, with long stretched-out hind legs & lever action, so this cutter could have been made in the U.S.A. .... **$145+**

Reproduction Alert

A very well-carved wooden hand-held reamer, deeply grooved, with a small, delicately rounded point & well-shaped handle, 7"L, was mfd. during the 1970s, and probably still is, to sell for about $7. It was so well made and attractive that it could easily be mistaken for an earlier reamer. Advice on buying antique treen (turned wooden wares, etymologically related to the word *tree*) is very difficult, especially for simple pieces that are essentially variations on the theme of a stick! Hollowed out pieces are more likely to show signs of true age, with checks, warping, more variation in patina. Lehman's Hardware offers a similar, cheap one with a hole through the end of the handle. **Reproduction alert II.** – I've discovered on eBay that lots and lots of reproduction glass reamer juicers are in pink, clear, green. Some sellers say up front, "reproduction," but others just say "Depression Glass reamer." And we aren't in a Depression … at least not at the time this was written.

Kitchen saw, adjustable carbon steel saw blade in cast aluminum frame, very attractive modernistic form, in general outline obviously a kitchen knife; in concept like a hacksaw, "Always Sharp," mfd. by Charles Wohr, Lancaster, PA, 15-3/4"L, early 20th C. .... **$20+**

Kitchen saw, carbon steel, turned wooden handle, "Keen Kutter," Simmons Hardware, 13-1/2"L, 20th C. **$15**

Kitchen saw & cake knife combined, carbon steel with wooden handle, top edge is saw, the bottom edge is scalloped cake knife, "Victor," mfd. by American Cutlery Co., 14-3/4"L, c.1890s-1910s. **$20**

Knife, wide steel blade, rounded end, rather like a spatula but less flexible, cut out & painted wood handle is Black Americana figural black chef, American (?), 12-1/2"L, c.1930s-40s. .... **$10+**

❖ RECIPE ❖

Green Tomato Pickle – *One peck of green tomatoes sliced; one dozen onions sliced; sprinkle with salt, and let them stand until the next day; then drain them. Use the following as spices: one box of mustard [ground], half an ounce of black pepper [ground?], one ounce of whole cloves, and one ounce of white mustard seed. Alternate layers of tomatoes, onions, and spices. Cover with vinegar. Wet the mustard before putting it in. Boil the whole twenty minutes." Mrs. A. P. Hill, Mrs. Hill's New Family Receipt Book, NY: 1870.*

Knife, parer & corer combined, tinned steel, in original box, "Castello's Sixteen Tools in One," American, 8-7/8"L, 1913. .... **$10**

Kraut cutters – See: Cabbage cutters

Lard & fruit press, cast iron, Griswold #2, early 20th C. **$65**

Lard press, heavy varnished wood, nickeled iron hinge, corrugated inside 2 long paddle handles, American, 12"L, late 19th C. **$35**

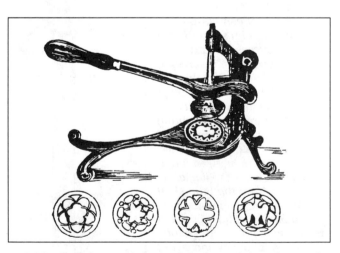

I-59. Julienne cutter *and four steel dies for it, of 16 that were offered. Note eagle pattern. To use: cut raw vegetable in thin slices; lay a slice on the disc and press handle down. Then lay a 2nd slice on disc & press, which forces 1st slice through. Meant for cutting slices of carrots & turnips, etc., in shapes for soups, garnishing, etc. Probably French. See more in Mold Chapter.* **$145+**

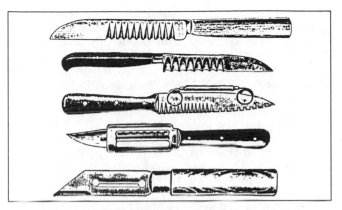

I-60. Decorating & paring knives. *A very small selection. Scalloped ones, some German, some French, for slicing Saratoga potatoes, and raw veggies & fruits into fancy garnishes or for preserving. Also for butter — even "pudding" says one ad. Middle ones have guards. Bottom one is a "razor edge paring knife." All early 1900s.* **$10+**

Lemon & lime reamers or squeezers – See: Juicers, above
Mandolines or Mandolins – See: Vegetable slicers
Marmalade cutter, cast iron, steel, wood, nice big one, probably for hotel or restaurant kitchen, "New Universal," Follows & Bates Ltd., Manchester, England, about 16"H, c.1890s-1910s **$125**
Marmalade cutter, cast iron with japanning & gold striping, raised letters picked out in gold, a sort of cone with a wood pusher to move orange peel across blade, mfd. by Follows & Bate Ltd., Manchester, England, late 19th C. **$150**
Marmalade cutter, japanned cast iron, crank handle, clamps to table, "Magic," English, about 11"H, late 19th C. **$125**
Marmalade cutter, cast iron & steel, screw clamp, cheap but serviceable, "The Rapid," Follows & Bates Ltd., Manchester, England, c.12-13"H, provisional patent #25,866/32, c.1890s-1910s. (?). **$75**

❖ **RECIPE** ❖

Orange Marmalade – *"Take twelve Oranges, two Lemons, 10-1/2 lbs. Sugar, 4-1/2 pints water. Wash the Oranges and Lemons, using a brush to remove black patches, cut into halves, and with a lemon squeezer press out all the juice into a separate basin. Strain the pips from the juice and put them into a muslin bag, and the juice into a glass bottle or jar. Finely slice the Oranges and Lemons (an excellent Machine can be seen [I-61]) and put them in a basin with the muslin bag containing the pips. Add the water to sliced fruit and let the whole stand until next day. The bag of pips should now be removed, care being taken to squeeze all the jelly from them, and then boil the Marmalade until the peel is tender. Add juice and sugar to Fruit, &c., and boil for one hour or more until it jellies on cooling. Test a small quantity in a saucer. Make the jars to contain the Marmalade hot and dry, fill them with the boiling preserve and cover at once while quite hot with Vacuum Covers, or with Parchment." Geo. Fowler, How to Bottle Fruit, Vegetables, Game, Poultry, Milk, &c. Reading, England: Fowler, n.d., revised edition c. 1922.*

Meat & cheese press, brown painted cast iron in rectangular shape, yellow stenciling, tin hopper, Starrett's, (Leroy Starrett), prob. pat'd. by J. I. Danforth, but mfd. by Starrett, Newburyport, MA (?), 7-1/2"H x 9"L, poss. another size too, pat'd. 1873, prob. Nov. 4, 1873. .... **$125**
Meat chopper, cast iron frame, turned wood crank handle, wooden tub, cranked gear wheels move blade & scraper inside tub, both up & down, and in slicing motion, pat'd. by A. F. Spaulding & S. M. Scott, of Massachusetts (2 *Patent Index* listings are: Winchester MA & Winchendon MA.) 8"H x 10"L, pat'd. June 5, 1865 (not in Index), July 11, 1865, & Jan. 31, 1865. .... **$300+**
Meat chopper, galvanized metal, screw clamp, "The Home #1," 1890s. See Zinc & Galvanizing up in Food chopper listings. **$15**
Meat chopper or grinder, tinned cast iron, height of hopper & grinder adjust with side screw & telescoping vertical frame, screw clamps to table, very similar choppers had feet for tabletop use, "The Little Giant #205," mfd. by The Peck, Stow & Wilcox Co., Southington, CT, brought out in 1890. .... **$75**

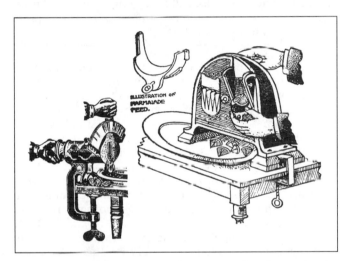

I-61. Marmalade machines, or slicers. *Both of these appeared in a c.1922 catalog/cookbook by George Fowler, London, England. **(L)** "Marmalade machine for oranges only." Double edge knife, for small families. Cast iron & steel, mounted to frame meant to screw clamp to table. **(R)** This is the "Marmalade Machine, Bean Cutter & Potato Slicer." It has adjustable blades, and two different interchangeable "feeds" or hoppers: one for marmalade, one for beans. The four blades inside could be regulated with screws inside. "To clean the machine invert it and ... immerse in a pail of water or hold it under a water tap and turn the handle of the machine. To assist in drying, pour some hot water over it, or place it near a fire. Occasionally oil knives and axle of wheel." It could be used to slice potatoes, cucumbers, carrots, French and scarlet runner beans to "any required thickness, and is just the machine to use at Christmas for slicing Almonds, Lemons, Mixed Peel, etc." Cast iron & steel, screw clamp to table. Notice the "marmalade feed" attachment-front completely open. English, probably sold for at least 30 years prior to the 1922 book.* **$125+**

Old Peck, Stow & Wilcox brochures I own show several choppers/grinders, but no 205, only a 305, as well as a 310 and a 320. An ad in a Dec. 1890 *Metal Worker* shows the No. 222. Then, a June 25, 1892, notice (op. cit) shows the **Little Giant No. 410**, tinned cast iron, with sausage stuffer attachment. We learn that: "The patterns have been changed this season so as to permit the application of a meat stuffer attachment, which can be quickly adjusted to the machine. The shape of the knife has been altered somewhat, and is referred to as stronger and less liable to break. The regular series will be known as Nos. 305, 310, 312, 320 and 322, and will be prepared for the attachments, which are not furnished with them, but which can be ordered and put on at any time. The meat cutters when furnished with attachments will be designated as Nos. 405, 410, 412, 420, and 422. Another feature of the Little Giant is that two perforated plates, with holes of different diam.s, are packed with each machine. All cutters made this season will be tinned instead of galvanized, which [adds] materially to their appearance. The company claims that the smallest cutter, No. 305, will easily cut 3 pounds of meat a minute." The notice didn't mention a 205; it was prob. introduced later in the 1890s.

Meat cutter, japanned cast iron, tabletop style with horizontal cylinder, hinged top lifts off to remove harrow blade drum & crank, bolts to table, one of O. D. Woodruff's two patents, mfd. by Peck, Stow & Wilcox, came in family or relatively small size, & medium size, Woodruff's patents date to Jan. 10, 1860 and Mar. 9, 1869. Still being sold in 1890s, possibly into 20th C. .... **$100+**

Meat cutter's glove, brass wire woven mesh glove, wrist strap, protection for left hand while cutting with right, American, early 20th C. Another crossover folk art collectible. Old ones: .... **$100+**

Meat & food chopper or grinder, galvanized cast iron, screw clamp, "Saxon," Steinfeld Brothers, NYC, NY, pat'd. 1904. .... **$35**

Meat & food grinder, tinned cast iron, little hopper, screw clamps to table, relatively long crank behind, small family size, "Enterprise #5," Enterprise Mfg. Co., c.1890s-1910s. **$20**

Meat & food slicer, cast iron, painted frame & decals, handsome & big for stores, "Enterprise," Enterprise Mfg. Co., "1881." .... **$65+**

Meat & food slicer, cast metal, cranks, "General," 20th C. .... **$15+**

Meat & food slicer, screw clamp, "Eagle," 20th C. **$15+**

Meat & food slicer, tin, wooden handle, "Dandy," 20th C. .... **$15+**

Meat & fruit juice press, plated malleable cast iron, frame has side handle for grasping with one hand, fitted into this is cup with handle, presser fits into cup & is screwed up & down with a sort of cotter pin handle above, "Walker's Quick & Easy," mfd. by Erie Specialty Co., Erie, PA, c.1905. .... **$125**

Meat & fruit press, nickeled brass with wood foller, "Wilder's," pat'd. 1906. (In 1984 I predicted some brass & flash dealer would take this piece down to the brass & buff it near to death, & price it at $100 – it happened.) Original nickeled finish: .... **$45+**

Meat grinder, cast iron, double barrel horizontal body hinged so top half lifts up, short crank, flared hopper, not marked except date, but this is an original J. G. Perry "meat-cutter," Kingston, RI, body 7"L, pat'd. March 15, 1859. .... **$150+**

Meat grinder, japanned cast iron, mounts to tabletop, long 2 part horizontal cylinder, hinged top half opens to lift out cutter drum with crank handle, "Perry's Patent No. 1," Peck, Stow & Wilcox Co., small size for families, 1890s. J. G. Perry, of Kingston, then South Kingston, RI, had 12 "meat-cutter" patents between 1859 & 1869, as well as a "meat-cutting machine" pat'd. Feb. 26, 1850. Look for ones made in the 1860s or 1870s by Perry himself, before he sold rights to P.S. & W. as well as Ames Plow Co. .... **$100+**

Meat grinder, cast iron, to be mounted to table, horizontal body, 4 feet, large mouth flared hopper, large S crank with long turned wood grip, "Perry's Patent No. 3," Ames Plow Co., 9-1/2"L, patent ext. Feb. 28, 1864, poss. made much later. .... **$135+**

Meat grinder, cast iron painted red, white enameled hopper interior, wood crank handle, only one blade (for medium – coarse), "Aalwerke #5, R AALEN," German or Dutch, 9"H, late 19th C. **$30**

Meat grinder, cast iron, screw clamps to table, "Gem Chopper," Sargent & Co., NYC, NY, large size, pat'd. March 8, 1892. .... **$50**

Meat grinder, cast metal, white porcelainized hopper, "Harras #52," German, c.1900 to early 20th C. **$35**

Meat grinder, cast & sheet iron, cranked, screw clamp, oblong hopper, short tapered perforated tubular blade, worm screw action pushes meat against & through holes, "Perfection" American Machine Co., Philadelphia, 3 sizes: #1, 2, & 3, pat'd. May 7, 1889. .... **$25+**

Meat grinder, homemade, oblong wooden box with lift-off top, forged iron cutting blades on long wooden axle inside, forged iron crank with what dealer Ron Motter, Erma's Attic, Athens, OH, said is a "bone bushing." Marked "A. F.," American (?), about 16"L, dated 1842... **$200+**

❖ RECIPE ❖

Bermuda Onions, Stuffed – Make a round hole in the upper end of each, dig out at least half of the contents; set in a dish covered with warm, slightly salted water, and bring to a simmer. Throw away the water; carefully fill the onions with minced poultry or veal, put a bit of butter in the dish to prevent burning, scatter fine crumbs thickly over the onions, and bake, covered, a half hour." Marion Harland, House & Home, a Complete Housewife's Guide, *Phila., 1889.*

Meat grinder, nickeled cast iron, screw clamps to table, thumb screw is heavy wire or small rod bent in rounded triangle – a sign of late date, different face plates for fine to coarse grinding, Chop-Rite #0, Choprite Mfg. Co., Pottstown, PA, this one late 20th C., but in production since 1870 (as "Enterprise"). The plating, the material of the knob on the crank, & the material and form of the thumb screw are all clues to age. Oldest marked "Enterprise," and would have aged dull plating, worn in many places, turned wood knob, and probably a cast iron, rather openwork fancy screw. Latest have shiny plating, plastic knob, and the above-described simple screw. Newer: $15; Early: .... **$75+**

❖ NOTES ❖

Lookalike alarm – A sausage stuffer & lard & fruit press marked "CHOPRITE" [CHOP-RITE?] is still being sold. It bolts to a tabletop or board. Lehman's Hardware, Kidron, OH, offer one in their "Non-Electric Good Neighbor Amish Country" catalog, which is now online: www.lehmans.com. They also sell parts, and say that "All Chop-Rite parts will interchange with Enterprise parts if you have the same model number."

Meat grinder, plated cast iron, very simple long barrel, widely flared hopper, spraddled 2 leg screw clamp, worm screw cutter with crank, 2 interchangeable plates with fine or medium perforations to clamp on front, barrel & hopper pull up out of clamp base when thumbscrew is loosened, "Family No. 1," Ellrich Hardware Mfg. Co., Plantsville, CT, pat'd. May 15, 1888, ... **$45+**

Meat grinder & juicer, cast iron, marked "No. 1," Canadian, 1901. .... **$20+**

Meat grinder wing nut wrench, cast iron, loop handle with elongated teardrop opening, business end almost half the length, & has a long cutout with rounded ends, & a larger round cutout midway that fits over wing nut, American, 4-1/2"L, c.1890s-1910s. **$10**

Meat grinders – See also: Food grinders; Illustration I-48; Sausage grinders

Meat juice extractor, also for fruit, tinned cast iron, large hopper, frame & hopper one piece, long tapered cylinder into which the grinding or pressing part inserts & turns; holes in bottom only to allow juice to drip into waiting bowl. Pulp or fibrin exits front into waiting receptacle, "Enterprise #21," Enterprise Mfg. Co., 12"H x 9"L, c.1880s, still selling early 20th C. Catalog of c.1905 states "The use of meat juice for medicinal purposes is a growing one, and is recommended for the aged, delicate infants and invalids, in all cases where complete nourishment is required in a concentrated form." .... **$50+**

Meat mincer, cast iron, double barrel body with large mouth, widely flared hopper at crank end, tube out other end fits onto sausage skin, or feeds ground meat to platter, latched hinged top, "Hale," pat'd. by A. W. Hale, New Britain, CT, pat'd. Mar. 15, 1859. In the early 20th C this same meat cutter was sold (and the rights probably owned) by V. Clad & Sons of Philadelphia. .... **$90+**

Meat press, cast iron, 3 parts: cup, reamer, & screw-action press, "Columbia #2," Landers, Frary & Clark, 19th C. **$85**

Meat press, cast iron frame screw clamps to table, T bar screw at top attached to press plate, removable cup is shaped like spade & set at 45º angle within frame, it has pointed front end with long slot to let out juice, "cannot clog up as in perforated pans, or soak back as is often the case. As a result more juice is obtained." "Quick & Easy," Erie Specialty Co., Erie, PA, c.1905. .... **$35+**

Meat press, enameled cast iron, cobalt outside, white inside, 2 hinged parts, corrugated inside, hollow

cast longish handles, no marks, 8"L, c.1890s-1910s............................... **$85**

Meat slicer, cast iron, painted & decorated with gilt scrolls, mounted on small piece of wood, adjustable steel blades, cast iron handle looks like turned wood – the foundry casting pattern for it undoubtedly was. American (?), 17-1/2"L, pat'd. May 15, 1894. ..... **$85+**

Meat slicer, white enameled metal, wood handle, "General #208," American, 20th C. **$35**

Meat tenderizer, also called a bovinizer, meat fret, pounder, or tenderer, hand held tool with round head fitted with 52 steel knife points; upright handle, spring-activated plate with holes through which the points pass with each downward jabbing pound, the spring pushes the plate back down, clearing the

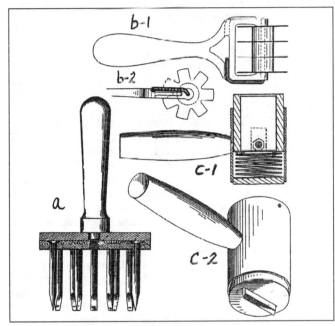

I-62. Meat tenderizer patents. *I believe all of these were manufactured. (a) "Meat Tenderer," pat'd. Aug. 14, 1894, by Daniel J. Hake, Middletown, PA, Pat. #524,436. Wooden handle, round plate fitted with 18 steel beveled or chisel-point "pins," "producing, in effect, knives." (b) "Meat Tenderer," pat'd. May 22, 1894, by Albert C. Wagner, Chicago, IL, Pat. #520,173. Rolling wheel fitted with 4 notched or toothed blades (see b-2). "In use the cutting edges are rolled over the meat with force sufficient to press them deeply below its surface and in lines crossing each other thus forming many cuts which admit a great deal of heat by greatly increasing the surfaces of the meat and thus what would under ordinary treatment be tough will when thus treated with my device become a toothsome and tender piece of meat." (c) "Meat Pounder," pat'd. Jan. 17, 1893, by John A. Carlson, Rockford, IL. Spring-loaded mallet, with a cutting blade at one end. A "plunger" inside the cylinder would push the blade out a slot; the spring would pull it back inside. "In use, when a blow is struck ... the force of the plunger upon the meat in connection with the blade, will divide the fibers of the meat." Carol Bohn believes patented meat tenderizers offer a great opportunity for collectors.* **$20+**

meat from the points, "Henis Bovinizer" mfd. by William G. Henis' Sons & Co., Philadelphia, PA, pat'd. Aug. 20, 1907. .... **$55**

❖ NOTES ❖

Henis also made a restaurant bovinizer with a long levered action, a stationary holey plate, and below it on a platform of the frame a wooden cutting board. Another device that looks something like a chopping knife with a double row of 9 very sharp steel blades, set in cast iron, with turned wood handle, was offered as a subscription premium in the May 1883 *American Agriculturist*. The maker isn't given, but it is called the "new and novel **Steakgreith**" in the ad. "Greith" is an ancient Anglo-Saxon word meaning "to make ready," a word that might have survived in some isolated American community. Perhaps the inventor used the word all his life.

Meat tenderizer, all wood with 6 sharp points carved on business end, American (?), 9"L, late 19th or early 20th C. **$15**

Meat tenderizer, Blue Onion pottery, wooden handle, European, 19th C. **$125**

Meat tenderizer, cast iron hammer with multi-toothed head, American, 7"L, 19th C. **$30**

Meat tenderizer, cast iron hammer-like instrument with grid of tiny pyramids, American, 7-1/2"L, late 19th C. **$30**

Meat tenderizer, cast iron head with 4 concentric rings of ripples, turned wood handle, hard to read name, possibly "Jachutti Co., No. 2," Philadelphia, PA, 8-1/2"L, 19th C. **$50**

Meat tenderizer, cast iron round cornered oblong frame, wooden axle rod stuck with many sharp steel blades, "Yale Meat Scorer," 8-1/4"L, patent applied for 1892. .... **$50**

Meat tenderizer, galvanized tin with wooden handle, 4 rows of deep teeth zigzags, no mark, American, 4-1/2"L, 19th C. **$25**

Meat tenderizer, iron hammer with waffled grid, wooden handle, American, pat'd. 1892. .... **$30**

Meat tenderizer, turned wooden handle, white glazed stoneware pottery with delicate blue floral decoration, round head has a waffled pattern of little pointed pyramids, European, 12"L x 3-1/3" diam., c.1890s. .... **$75+**

Meat tenderizer, rolling type, cast iron drum with sharp prickers or spikes, turned wood handles at both ends, with brass ferrules, stamped "Charles E. Miller," also some illegible numbers, probably the patent date, 12"L, c.1890s-1910s. See similar Bun divider in Molds, Chapter IV; probably made by same company. .... **$65+**

Meat tenderizer (?), rolling type, wood roller deeply carved with pyramidal points, heavy wire handle, American, roller 9-1/2"W, whole thing 12"L including handle, 19th C. [Note: Now this is thought by some collectors to be a cracker roller. But for scallopini, maybe this would do the trick.] **$35**

Meat tenderizer, rolling type, small roller has steel blades set in it, long turned wood handle, American, 9"L, 19th C. .... **$35-$50**

Meat tenderizer, head is thick cast iron 'hockey puck,' one side has wide-spaced blunt projections, other

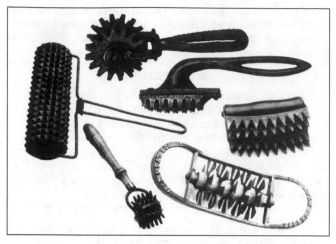

I-63. Meat tenderizers, *also called* **tenderers.** *Clockwise from top:* **(1)** *Cast iron, rolling, marked only "pat appl for."* **(2)** *"Varty Mfg. Co., Chicago, pat'd. Jan. 27, 1885. Has 2 leaf springs to push meat off prongs. From the John Lambert Collection.* **(3)** *Galvanized tin, wood handle, 4-1/2"L, 19th C. Collection of Meryle Evans.* **(4)** *"Yale Meat Scorer," patent applied for 1892. Cast iron frame, wooden rod axle, set with very sharp steel blades. 8-1/4"L. Located by the Primitive Man, Bob Cahn, Carmel, NY. Over the years, Bob Cahn has been a proven winner in recognizing & selling to collectors rarities that have greatly increased in value.* **(5)** *Small rolling one has iron blades, wood handle.* **(6)** *Recent thinking is that this is a* **cracker crumber,** *not a meat tenderizer. Lawn roller shape with toothed wood roller, wire handle, 12"L x 9-1/2"W. 19th C. Both collection of Meryle Evans. All but the "Yale":* **$35-$50+;** **(4)** *"Yale,"* **$350+**

has many sharper, closer-set ridges, wood handle, American, head 3-1/2" diam., late 19th C. **$50**

Meat tenderizer, cast iron, rocker action, has 20 pointed lethal teeth set 5 x 4, arched iron rod forms handle, American, 4" x 2-3/4", pat'd. Sept. 20, 1892. .... **$45**

Meat tenderizer, salt glazed stoneware drum head has sharp modeled points in waffled pattern, thick turned wood handle painted black, 6"L, head, 3" diam., American, pat'd. Dec. 25, 1877. .... **$125**

Meat tenderizer, stoneware head with waffled pattern, saltglazed with brown Albany slip underneath salt glaze, prob. NY state, 9"L, pat'd. Dec. 25, 1877... **$125**

Meat tenderizer, vertical turned wooden handle, head set with 14 steel chisel point blades (used in same position as hand stamp), "Pettes' Beefsteak Tenderer," pat'd. by M. M. Pettes, Worcester, MA, pat'd. March 5, 1872. .... **$75**

Meat tenderizer & ax, cast iron or cast steel(?), meant for a wooden handle, head has waffled meat pounder on one end, sharp ax on other, American, head only: 5-3/4"L, 19th C. I hate stuff like this, being a vegetarian, so may be pricing low. **$10**

Meat tenderizer & ax, nickeled steel ax or hatchet head with curved blade, opposite a tenderizing device with 3 rows of 5 thick teeth, wooden handle, comes apart for cleaning – wing nut holds head to handle, Tyler Mfg. Co., Muncie, IN, 10"L x 4-1/4", pat'd. Dec. 5, 1922. .... **$25**

Meat tenderizer, cap lifter, ice shaver & mincer combined, cast steel (?), heavy wooden handle, ice shaver part can be locked in at least 2 positions, very well-made but odd combination of functions. Bridge Cutlery Co., St. Louis, MO, 11"L, pat'd. Aug. 15, 1916. Some collectors love combo tools, perhaps because of incongruity of some, perhaps because not many are made now, so they have curiosity value. .... **$25+**

Meat tenderizer & chopper, iron, homemade from old rasp, coarse rasp teeth on one side, finer on the other, has head & handle, late 19th C. or early 20th. **$25**

Mincing knives – See: Chopping knives.

Mortar & pestle, carved gray marble, simple thick-walled bowl mortar with hexagonal sides, fat simple pestle, European (?), mortar 5"H, pestle 7-1/2"L, 19th C. (**Lookalike alarm:** A similar one made of granite sold now through the Scottish company Pots & Pans Ltd.) **$50**

Mortar & pestle, cast bell metal or bronze. There were a number of founders who cast bells & mortars. In fact, the type of flared rim this one has is called a bell mouth. English or American (?), 4-3/4"H x 3" diam., 19th C. **$100**

Mortar & pestle, cast iron, footed, 7"H x 6-3/4" diam., American, English, or German, prob. 1840s to 1860s. **$100**

Mortar & pestle, cast iron, wider than high, 8"H x 9" diam., 19th C. **$100**

Mortar & pestle, cast iron, mortar has flared sides & rim, American (?), 6-3/4"H x 6-3/4" diam., 19th C. **$100**

Mortar & pestle, cut marble, with 4 ears or nubs around flat top, for lifting, poss. English, or a French import, different sizes, 1860s-70s. Harrod's Stores, Ltd., of London, England, advertised these, in several sizes, in their 1895 retail catalog. They came in

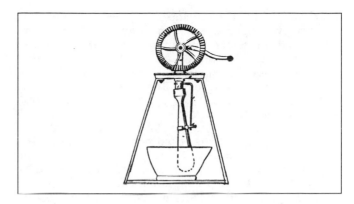

I-65. Mortar & pestle patent. *Called a "grinding & triturating apparatus" by inventor. Pat'd. Mar. 20, 1877, by Joseph J. Lancaster, London, Ontario, Canada. Pestle has rotary motion. If it exists:* **$500+**

eight diameters: 8", 9", 10", 11", 12", 13", 14", and 16". With them you could order a simple turned lignum vitae pestle with cylindrical handle part ending in larger head, which came in five sizes to suit the mortar. .... **$85-$125**

Mortar & pestle, heavy white earthenware, bowl-like with small pouring lip, glazed outside, inside unglazed, pestle with wild onion shaped earthenware head, with turned wooden handle screwed to it, sometimes marked on bottom, made by several potteries, notably Wedgwood. English, various sizes, 19th C. .... **$45-$350+**

Mortar & pestle, white stoneware mortar with slightly flared sides, rounded rim & pouring lip, wood handled stoneware pestle, Maddock's Sons, with anchor trademark, Trenton, NJ, mortar 2-3/4"H x 4-1/2" diam., pestle 6-3/4"L, late 19th C. or early 20th. **$50**

❖ NOTES ❖

Wedgwood mortar – Mortars made for druggists of marble or ironstone are expensive, but one made of Wedgwood earthenware will answer all household needs." Todd S. Goodholme, *Domestic Cyclopedia of Practical Information*, NY: Henry Holt, 1877. **Harrod's** Stores, Ltd., of London, showed a similar mortar & pestle in their 1895 retail catalog. They called its material "composition." The mortar appears to be slightly off round, but perhaps that is just the drawing, which shows a rather big pouring lip. The bowl has a very small ring foot, and the pestle is the wood and ironstone ("composition")? common to the type. This was offered in several diameters: 7", 8", 9", 10", 11", 12". The bigger they are the thicker. (I saw one about 14" diam. that was well over an inch thick. Heavy as an anvil almost.

• • •

Lookalike Alarm – Brand new white ceramic mortar & pestle sets are being made now. If you put an old & new one side by side, you'll see differences. Generally, new ones aren't quite as heavy, often they are highly glazed on the outside of the mortar, and the wooden pestle handles aren't as nicely turned, have little patina, but lots of varnish, and don't fit as neatly and snugly to the ceramic business end of the pestle.

I-64. Mortars (L). *Rev. Larry Pearson of Snellville, GA, found this marble mortar about 30 miles south of New Orleans, on the Mississippi's east bank "lying in the mud off shore near an old fort below Shell Beach. This area was settled in early days by the Spanish." In the water or mud for maybe 150 years or more, it's surprising only one oyster attached itself (atop projection on rim's far side). 4-1/2"H x 8-1/2" across at widest points. Info & photo courtesy Larry Pearson, & Cheryl & David Hitchcock. (R) Lathe-turned mortar, with interestingly-shaped carved pestle. Red buttermilk paint. 7"H x 4-1/2" diam.; pestle 9"L. Early 19th C. Collection of Meryle Evans.* **$40+; $125+**

Mortar & pestle, heavy turned tiger maple, both pieces attractively figured, small or large end of pestle can be used, American, mortar: 7"H x 6" diam.; pestle: 9"L, early to mid 19th C. **$95**

Mortar & pestle, lignum vitae, turned, with a great pedestal base, American, 7-3/4"H x 4" diam., early 19th C. **$95**

Mortar & pestle, lignum vitae, the hardest densest wood available, beautiful graining (or figure, as it's called) & patina, with slightly checked pestle, American, 7"H x 5-3/8" diam., 19th C. "A lignum-vitae mortar and pestle will last for generations, and there should be one in every kitchen." Maria Parloa, *Kitchen Companion*, Boston: Estes & Lauriat, 1887. .... **$95**

Mortar & pestle, polished cast iron, flared sides with big foot, decorative swag design around side, long handled pestle, for candy makers, mfd. by Thomas Burkhard, 1/2 pint capacity (came in 1 pt., 1, 2, 4, & 8 qt. Sizes, too), c.1870s. **$100**

Mortar & pestle, turned painted wood, with pedestal base, well worn pestle with idiosyncratic worn places on handle, American, 7"H x 4-1/2" diam., early to mid 19th C. **$95**

Mortar, ash burl, nicely shaped with small pedestal base, American, 7"H x 6" diam., early 19th or late 18th C. **$150**

Mortar, hollowed log, bottom repaired with iron bands to hold age checks together, some kind of whitish composition (probably a clay cement) in crack on inside, rather thick walls & very beat up around edges, many insect holes & some dry rot, thoroughly picturesque & "country." American, 22"H, 19th C. Many tallish slightly curved hollowed log mortars have shown up in the 1990s; I don't know where they're from. **$150**

I-66. Mortars & pestles of various classic types. *Most of upper ones are cast-bell metal, bronze, brass or iron (footed one at (R) is cast iron & called "goblet shaped" by seller). Stoneware & marble ones often have a small depression or pouring lip. Knobby projections aid steadying. Sizes from 4" to 15". 18th to late 19th C. classic forms. In some markets, cast iron would be prized much more than bell metal or bronze. Most mortars & pestles are* **$35-$65***; very large or unusual ones would bring* **$125+**

❖ **NOTES** ❖

In October 1850, the *American Agriculturist* published a letter from *M* on how "**To Make Hommony**" [sic]. The *M* stood for Maryland, where the correspondent was from. "I have so often been asked for our Maryland receipt for making hommony, that I send it to your journal, as the surest method of making it public. Some gristmills have a way of preparing it beautifully, by making a trifling addition to the machinery of the mill, which beats the hommony while the meal is being ground; but many people still prefer the old Negro way, and many mills have not the new machinery. I wish I could tell the quantity of water it takes for any given quantity ... but the negroes do everything by guess; and when I asked the man who makes it best for me, the only answer I could get was, 'jest 'xactly 'nuff ... only don't let 'em make de corn too wet, dat spiles all.'

"Take a gum-tree or oak block, and burn or dig it out to the depth of twenty inches or two feet; rub the hollow clean and smooth, and you have the mortar. A wooden pestle, equally rude, is formed, into the flat end of which drive gently (for fear of splitting it), the sharp end of a large-sized wood cutter's wedge; the broad end being thus ready for breaking and hulling the corn. The best corn must be carefully selected and shelled; moisten it well by pouring boiling water over it; when part is broken up and hulled, it should be taken out of the mortar, and fanned, again moistened with boiling water, and put in again; this fanning and moistening ... and beating to be continued until it is free from husks. Spread it out to dry, and then sift it, first through a coarse seive, which will retain only the hommony, then through a fine one, which will retain the grits. The coarse meal that remains is excellent for cakes and puddings." [Note: Now skins of the corn kernels are removed with lye.]

Mortar & pestle, turned wood, dark patina, chunky, footed mortar probably turned from a burl, worn on one edge from long rugged use, mortar is fitted with a 1/2 inch thick dowel leg, splayed downward from near the top, actually a handle to be grasped with one hand while pounding. The worn area on rim is to left of this handle, so tool was probably used by left-handed person. Pestle has thick handle with beetle-like heavy duty head & small rounded mushroom cap on other end, American, 7"H x 6" diam., pestle 7"L. Ex-Keillor Collection. **$155**

Noodle cutter – See: Chapter IV (Molds).

Nutchopper, iron & tin on wooden board base. The 8" cylinder Leroy Starrett food & meat chopper, in smallest size, was sold to confectioners and bakers as a nut chopper. **$95**

❖ NOTES ❖

Nutcrackers or Nutcracks – Although for some people, even today, a molar or a wisdom tooth is adequate for the job, probably a rock and a hard place comprised the first or earliest nutcracking contrivance. Thus we find many variations on the anvil and hammer theme. The nutcrackers we are most familiar with are mechanical – based on one of two systems: the screwed press or vise, and the levered jaw (which can work like a pliers, with the pivot somewhere between both ends, or with the pivot/hinge at one end). A levered jaw is particularly well-suited to wild and whimsical designs on the theme of animal or human mouths.

The two main types for collectors are **mechanical** and **figural**. (Actually, both types are mechanical because they have moving parts, devised to break the nut with a screwed or levered pressure.) For mechanicals, old and odd patents bring the most money, and collectors love to find variations showing development or adaptation of patents. Some patents addressed particular kinds of nuts – especially pecans and walnuts. There are many collectors of subject-driven objects (say dogs, or elephants) who seek figural and zoomorphic nutcrackers; plus there's some interest by folk art collectors – especially in subjects folk art collectors have staked out, such as alligators and the Black Americana pieces. A huge crossover interest comes from Christmas collectors, who especially like the new-but-traditional Tyrolean carved and painted figurals. If you're serious about the figurals, you must get the *Rollband* patent book to see some mid 20th C. shockers you probably thought were much older: a levered dog cracker patented in 1960; an alligator head pliers-type pat'd. 1954; a squirrel with levered tail pat'd. in 1953; a Cro-Magnon man's head, pat'd. 1950; a fabulous squirrel & log tray, pat'd. 1948; another dog with fancy cast iron base, pat'd. 1947; yet another dog with levered handle and backplate so it could also be a bookend, pat'd. 1947; a terrific alligator (a nutcrocker, heh heh), pat'd. 1934; modern alligator, pat'd. 1929; squirrel on log, pat'd. 1923; a squirrel in a bowl, pat'd. 1922; an ugly, pointy-muzzled dog head, pat'd. 1920; squirrel-head pliers, pat'd. 1920; a fat, friendly dog with levered tail, pat'd. 1912; two different squirrels from 1902 – one the wonderful folky one on a long log, and one sitting up high in tray; the best squirrel of all, levered so it cracks nuts between paws and chin, pat'd. 1902; another full-bodied dog, levered tail, pat'd. 1900; the first figural squirrel on plinth, pat'd. by F. A. Humphrey, May 28, 1878; and the first dog, with geared ratchet inside for high-lifted levered tail, pat'd. as a *"Tobacco Cutter & Nut Cracker,"* by H. Tilden, May 29, 1866. What I don't get at all (am I just too hard-headed?) is how all the similar dogs and squirrels got patents, even design patents.

•   •   •

The Nut Museum: The Web site, www.roadsideamerica.com/nut/, will give you a wonderful preview to this enchanting piece of roadside Americana. Ms. Elizabeth Tashjian loves nuts and nut history, and my sincere hope is that her unique house museum will flourish for years to come. It's at 303 Ferry Road, Old Lyme, CT, and open by appointment only. Admission is very modest and requires handing over a nut with the moolah. Ms. Tashjian has quite a collection of world nuts, art made from nuts, nutcracker sculpture in the garden, and a collection of nutcrackers. Call ahead for further information: (860) 434-7636. The **First Peanut Museum of the U.S.**, opened and operated by Shirley Yancey since 1990, is in Waverly, VA, just off Rte. 460. Mrs. Yancey displays tools of peanut farming and other goodies. And yes! I know peanuts are not nuts.

Figural & Novelty Nutcrackers

Human – Bawdy or Naughty Lady & Dancing Master Legs

Well of course these are bawdy ... may be surprising how long they've been around, and also how widely they are sold in plain view where other forms of soft porn are nowhere to be seen.

Nutcracker, bawdy legs, cast iron shapely woman's legs, large concavity in inner thighs, very unusual & more valuable because painted flesh color, original because decal was put on over paint: "Souvenir of New York City," 6"L, c.1940s-50s................... **$125**

Nutcracker, bawdy legs in frilled, knee-length pantaloons!, cast brass or bronze, no mark, 6"L, probably c.1910s. .... **$75+**

Nutcracker, bawdy legs, carved wood, 7"L, American (?), 19th C. **$55**

I-67. Zoomorphic nutcrackers. (T) Dinosaur/ dragon or griffin. Cast iron painted gold, 2-part body bolted together, saw-tooth spine ridges & tail, 13"L. Pat. #206,454 (?). Stock of Richard Ferry, Mystic Fine Arts, Mystic, CT. (B) Alligators (not crocodiles) with blunt tips. Author's (large one) silver-painted cast iron, 2 parts come apart. Scaled back, tail & lower jaw lift out revealing naked underbody & legs. 13-3/4"L. Small one cast brass in reddish hue, 2 part, riveted pivot, no marks, 7-7/8"L. Collection of Peg & Ralph Latham. All c.1920+. See text for information on 20th C. patented figurals. (T) $400+; (B) big one: $75+, small: $45+

Nutcracker, bawdy woman, carved wood, primitive-looking – sort of South Seas, Hawaiian or Filipino, sometimes described as "native woman," hands behind narrow, pointy-haired head, pointy-busty, with a hip & leg that swing out on wooden hinge w/ metal pin, not much detail except for incised lines of skirt or shorts (?) & belt, these have been sold as "folk art" for last 10 years or so, but they are fairly new, very numerous, & close to no value. 13" to 13-1/2"L......................... **$3+** (Remember that this and the next one are hand-carved, so some stylistic differences will occur within either style. Perhaps an interesting collection could be made of a lot of them, with their tiny variations.)

Nutcracker, bawdy woman, carved wood, very detailed (much better "Art" than previous listing), perhaps it's older, same general pose with skinny arms, but has a little folded short skirt very detailed, round breasts, detailed abdomen, and longish narrow face is much better carved, 13"L, Philippines, poss. around WWII as a sailor souvenir? **$30**

Nutcracker, bawdy woman's legs with high heels, cast aluminum, no mark, 6-7/8"L, c.1940s (?). ...... **$60+**

Nutcracker, bawdy legs, cast aluminum, woman's legs in long cuffed pants, on either side of hinge, where the waist is, fairly deep corrugations, no marks at all, American, 4-3/8"L, 20th C. **$30**

Nutcracker, bawdy legs, cast iron painted with gold radiator paint, rolled cuffs at ankles & similar corrugations to last listing, casting seam-gates along front & back of legs, American?, 4-1/2"L, 1930s (?) .. **$30**

Nutcracker, bawdy woman's legs, cast brass, various between 4"L and 5-1/2"L, c.1890s into early 20th C. **$90**

Nutcracker, bawdy women's legs, feet well-defined, pale-colored cast brass, two almost alike: 4-1/2"L, other 4-3/8"L, late 19th C............................... **$90**

Nutcracker, cast & turned brass, with engraved decoration, sort of whoop-tee-do dancing master's leg shaped

I-68. Figural nutcrackers. (L) *Full figure of town-crier-like figure, carved & painted wood on plinth. 8-1/2"H, collection of Priors Bank, Fulham, London, from early 19th C. book.* **(M)** *Jockey's head, in Thornhill's ad in the* Illustrated Sporting & Dramatic News, *12/1882. English.* **(R)** *Carved hardwood toothy man in moon, iron hinge in back. 5"H. Mid 19th C. Has been reproduced by Bostom Museum of Art in cast polymer resin & in brass, about 6"H with small base. This one courtesy Robert & Mary Lou Sutter, East Chatham, NY.* **(L & R)** **$225-$350+; (M) $225+**

handles, squared cracking face plate tooled with little teeth for grabbing the nut, English, range from about 3-1/2"L to 4-1/4"L, late 18th or very very early 19th C. The same people who made fire tools, andirons, bells, etc., made these heavy little crackers, which are all variations on a theme. Some have more exaggerated legs or handles than others. .... **$75-$125+**

Human – Men, Cherubs, Etc.

Nutcracker, Black Americana man in overcoat, hands in pockets over knees, painted cast iron, modeled with ring of white hair & white eyebrows like popular illustrations of "Uncle Tom," lever works lower jaw or chin, American, prob. 3rd quarter 19th C..... **$750+**

Nutcracker, Black Americana man's head, cast iron, more portrait than caricature, hair, brow, eyes, nose & upper lip have good detail, lower jaw worked by slightly curved short lever in back, head mounted to widely flared footed base, American, about 6"H, mid 19th C. .... **$950+**

Nutcracker, black man's head, caricatured Black Americana, painted cast iron in 4 parts: 2 flat halves of the head, riveted together, a lever (which comes out back of head) that works the jaw, & a diamond shape base to which all is screwed, very exaggerated eyes, lips & ears, partly painted red & white, no mark at all, American, 6-1/8"H, looks maybe c.1880s, poss. much earlier.......................... **$800+**

Nutcracker, cherub, cast brass, English (?), looks 19th C., but could be 20th C... **$75**

Nutcracker, Dickens' character, Fagin, from Oliver Twist, marked "Fagin" on one handle, "Bill Sykes" on other, also English Register #596,848. Craggy caricatured face with forefinger laid aside long nose, left hand clutches moneybag, curlicue at bottom where feet would be, English, 5"L, maybe 1930s? **$60**

Nutcracker, jester & knight, cast brass, pliers type, English or poss. American, late 19th or early 20th C. **$55**

Nutcracker, man in moon in crescent shape, mouth is pivot point, carved wood, very smooth patination, lots of expression in face, prob. Swiss or German, about 5" to 7"L, early to mid 19th C. .... **$225+**

Nutcracker, man in moon, with neat little teeth, levered mechanical, carved hardwood, crescent moon, iron hinge, English or American, moon if full would form 5" circle, mid 19th C. **$325**

Nutcracker, man who looks like Mr. Magoo, cast iron & wood, lever action, homemade wooden box painted yellow, 3-D cast iron front of man stands squint-eyed with hands in overcoat pockets, his feet inside box, mounted to a wooden back cut to fit his outline, lever works lower jaw, not marked, American, man is 7-1/2"H, 19th C. Folk art crossover interest. **$300**

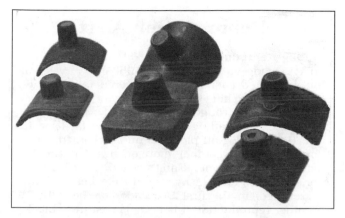

I-69. "Kneewarmer" nutcrackers – cast iron anvil part only. Note that these are "paired" only in the photo; they are all different. Made to be put over thigh near knee, while sitting, and used to break nuts with a small hammer. Size approx. 3-1/2" x 6." 2nd & 3rd quarter 19th C. Collection of Phyllis & Jim Moffet. **$75-$175+**

Nutcracker, grotesque man's head on small round collar-base, wearing liberty cap, extremely long sausage nose curves down, forked beard, carved walnut, American (?), 6-1/2"L from nose tip to back of head, 3rd quarter 19th C. .... **$200+**

Nutcracker, man's head, perhaps a comic caricature of a peasant, wearing a Phrygian liberty cap of the type worn in France before & during their revolution, large jaw with indication of teeth, forged iron, very long lever handles, French, dated 1761. This piece was for sale in early 1989 by Pat Guthman Antiques, Southport, CT. It is an example of the very best kind of iron work that you could hope to find. It is so extraordinary that it matters little if it be American, French, German or whatever, because it is art. Value range mine. .... **$600+**

Nutcracker, sailor & girlfriend, they kiss (the nut) when handle's squeezed, cast brass, 6-1/4"L, 20th C. **$60**

Nutcracker, skull & bones, nut goes between face & back of skull, bones are levered handles, cast iron has some remaining copper plating, very lean & hungry, English, 6"L, register #740410, prob. c.1920s. Crossover skull collectors vie for this. **$175**

Human – Swiss Soldiers, Tyrolean, Bavarian, Etc.

Many new, mass- & hand-produced lathe-turned, brightly painted "collectable" nutcrackers are sold today in gift shops and Christmas shops, sometimes under the misnomer "Black Forest" wood carvings. Ranging in price from about $50 to over $600, these are fun and cute but, to my mind, not of direct interest in the context of collecting kitchen tools because they are made in editions and subjects aimed at people who collect things made to be collected, not to be used. Main companies are Christian Ulbricht; Christian Steinbach; Anri; Erzebirge; Seiffener; Zims; etc. These are easily found for sale on the Internet.

Nutcracker, bearded man with skull cap, lever type, carved wood, Tyrolean, Bavarian, or Swiss(?), 19th C. .... **$275+**

Nutcracker, sailor's head with liberty cap, concave roof of mouth accommodates nut, 4 part carved base,

carved wood, European, prob. Tyrolean, 7"H, c.1860s. .... **$575+**

Animal – Zoomorphic

Nutcracker, alligator, cast iron, large detailed 'gator in 2 parts: bottom includes marshy cattails & is mounted to 3-3/4" x 10-1/2" board. Upper body has looped tail; head & jaws are angled to the left. "Blake" patent, probably later than 1853 patent. [Note: P.E.W. and J.A. Blake (Blake Brothers & Co., New Haven, CT) patented a plain, iron, levered nutcracker on Sept. 6, 1853. It was mounted on an oblong board, and had angled jaws and worked with a lever. At some point their patent was used as the mechanical basis for a zoomorphic alligator nutcracker, probably in the 1870s or '80s. This two-way type of gussied up strictly mechanical kitchen gadget is very rare, & collectors should try to find one of each of these.] .... **$250+**

Nutcracker, alligator, cast brass in 2 parts, mounted to base, American, 7-1/2"L, late 19th C to early 20th C. **$90**

Nutcracker, alligator, cast iron, detailed casting, painted dark green, with red inside mouth, looks like very old paint, 7-1/2"L, American, early 20th C. .... **$65+**

Nutcracker, alligator, cast iron with old silver radiator paint, cast in 2 parts: (1) upper jaw and naked underbody with legs & lower part of curving tail, (2) lower jaw & scaled top of body & tail, pretty good detail, no marks, 13-3/4"L, poss. early 20th C. **$75**

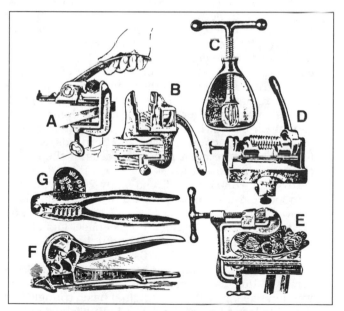

I-70-A. Mechanical nutcrackers. (A) "Enterprise," Philadelphia. c.1910. (B) "Home," Schroeter Bros. Hardware Co., St. Louis, MO. Nickeled cast malleable iron, 6"H x 4"W with 7-1/2" lever. Pat'd. c.1915. (C) Handheld "Ideal" with old-style knobbed handle. Nickeled cast iron. c.1915. (D) "Perfect" pecan cracker, Thomas Mills & Bros., Philadelphia, c.1930. (E) "Perfection," Waco, TX. Screw clamps to table. 1917 ad. (F) Levered cracker, cast iron, F. A. Walker catalog, possibly imported, c. 1870s. (G) "Harper," nickeled cast steel, c.1910. (A) (B) (D) $65+; (C) $15+; (E) $85+; (F) $45+

I-70-B. Mechanical nutcracker. Cast iron, screw clamp to table, powerful lever pushes presser against nut. Cleverly-named "Squirrel Nut Cracker," "Alex Woldert Co. Tyler, Tex and Chicago No.200F." Pat'd. May 13, 1913 & Dec. 29, 1925. 11"L with handle in upright position. Photo courtesy Tye Schwalbe, dealer in pre-prohibition breweriana, etc., online. Web site: www.cyberattic.com/ photo.cgi?schwalbe. E-mail: tyesan@webtv.net. **$45+**

Nutcracker, alligator, rather delicate & small, lever action, dark satiny cast iron, 2 parts: slender upper jaw, patterned back, slightly wavery tail, separate lower body unusual because it has shortish, pointed tail, marked "Nestor," 9"L, 20th C (?). **$125**

Nutcracker, antelope head, lever type, carved wood with set in glass eyes, long horns, very detailed carving, Tyrolean (?), 8-7/8"H x 3-1/2"W nose to ear tips, 19th C. Try to get a look at the dozens of fabulous carved wood lever crackers in Pinto's book *Treen.* (See Bibliography.) Most in his collection are human – grotesques or comic characters with gaping jaws, some dating to 16th C. Very elaborate carving of all parts. Many others are dogs, or other animals. **$750**

Nutcracker, dog, cast brass, cast (like all of them) in 2 halves, plus tail lever, rather crude & lumpy, filed roughly & bolted. Looks like St. Bernard (according to contemporaneous reports, St. Bernards & Newfoundlands were most popular breeds at the end of the 19th C.), no marks, 4-3/4"H x 11-1/2"L, looks c.1870s or 1880s, but with so many 20th C. patents that look old-fashioned going up to 1960, I just don't know. .... **$75+**

Nutcracker, dog, cast brass, on brass base, lots of hair detail, no marks, 4-3/4"H without base, 5-3/8"H with it, x 11-1/4"L, c.1870s to 1890s or is this 20th C? .... **$90+**

Nutcracker, dog, cast brass or bronze, bolted to largish wooden base, possibly not original base, triangle fold ears, big lower jaw, 6"H x 8-1/2"L, English or American. Late 19th to early 20th C. .... **$75+**

Nutcracker, dog, bronzed cast iron, on oblong stepped base, L.A. Althoff & Co., Chicago, IL, early 20th C. I

think I'd like a kennel full of the dog crackers – so many variations! **$125**

Nutcracker, dog on base, cast iron, well defined hair, advertising "L. A. Althoff," Makers of Headlights, Stoves & Ranges, Laporte, IN (or La Port?), 11"L, 20th C. This nutcracker might appeal to some stove collectors, although, for most of them, home is nowhere but on the range. It also came in nickeled finish. It is not uncommon, but prices (as with anything else), really depend on who's buying & who's selling. One with "worn nickel finish with light rust" brought only $40 at the 1989 Garth Auction, Delaware, OH. **$125**

❖ NOTES ❖

Tiny Dog Nutcracker for Dollhouses: A tiny new bronze miniature of a dog nutcracker has been recently made. An original dog on plinth was taken apart for study, the parts were carved from wood, cast, and assembled. Dollhouse size: only 3/4"H x 1-1/2"L x 1/4"W. Available from bestfriends@rockbridge.net, from the artist herself, Elizabeth Trail.

Nutcracker, dog, cast iron with copper finish, smaller than most you see, "Made in England," 8-1/4"L, marked on inside of tail "Patent No. 273,480," which was 1863 in England. .... **$100+**

Nutcracker, dog, nickel plated iron, English, 8-3/4"L, 1863 patent #273,480. (By the way, nickeled dog and squirrel nutcrackers in old designs were advertised as new products for sale in 1924 in the United States.) .... **$90+**

Nutcracker, dog with levered tail, crudely formed cast iron, English, 11-1/2"L, patent No. 273,480 marked on tail. 1863+. .... **$70+**

Nutcracker, dog, cast iron, on flat base with openwork that makes it look like sidewalk grating, marvelous jowls, "Dog Tray Nut Cracker" (for Stephen C. Foster's song, "Old Dog Tray" ?), mfd. by Harper Supply Co., North Chicago , IL, 13"L, "patent applied for," late 19th or early 20th C. A fairly simple pliers-type nutcracker was pat'd. in 1915 by J. M. Harper, so this may be his, too. [Note: Another "Tray" was enameled in rusty brown, cream, and black, with plain plinth. It's 13"L. A rather lumpy one, with plain plinth, poss. marked "Old Bobo Tray" – or "Old Dog Tray" – was for sale in 2001 and may have been one of a number of repros of rather low quality.] Openwork one:.. **$145+**

Nutcracker, dog with belled collar, cast brass, European, 5-1/2"L, looks early 19th C. .... **$125+**

Nutcracker, dog with levered tail, cast iron porcelainized in black & white, American, 5-7/8"H, on base 9-1/2"L x 3-3/8"W. Late 19th C. Dogs also exist in a cobalt blue porcelainized finish & they'd bring more. .... **$150+**

I-71-B. Dog nutcrackers. *Just 3 examples of the many versions of a St. Bernard or Mastiff type dog, most popular dog breed in 1860s-80s, although access to a new patent book makes me revise dating of many (not all) dog nutcrackers to mid-20th C.* **(T)** *Nickeled iron, 8-3/4"L, pat. # appears to be 375,460 (not same as modern-style horse #273,480; nor the dinosaur). This one English.* **(M)** *Dog on fancy base, with sheep-like fur, is nickeled iron, marked "L. A. Althoff Mfg. Co. Makers of Headlights, Stoves & Ranges, La Port, IN."* **(B)** *Cast brass, 5-3/8"H with base x 11-1/4"L. Prob. English. Biggest problem nowadays are new ones, repros made from molds of older ones. See text. Old:* **$95-$150+**

Nutcracker, dog's or wolf's head, cast iron, levered jaw, this looks very European – English or German, but it shows up in *Rollband's* patent book as a June 15, 1920 design patent, granted to A. W. & J. J. Geigand. Marked also with a pattern (?) number "1820." .... **$100+**

Nutcracker, dog – Scottie, cast iron with bright paint, skinny outline of Scottie mounted above ridged base on red wooden board, was made so that the top (mfd. in different shapes) could all use same base. New, but called a "nostalgic reproduction," although to my knowledge there is no early one it was reproduced from. 6"H x 7-1/2"L. **$9**

Nutcracker, dog with very small squirrel between front paws, cast iron on stepped plinth, triangle foldover ears, 6"H x 12-1/2"L, very unusual and desirable. .... **$85+**

Nutcracker, dragon, griffin or even possibly dinosaur, unusual, gold painted cast iron, body's 2 parts bolt together, sawtooth ridges on back & tail, English, 13"L, "#206,454" – an 1878 patent. **$400**

Nutcracker, eagle head, cast iron, on primitive 4 legged base, which is quite different from flat base of new lookalike nutcracker, American, 7"L, 19th C (?). Could this be 1920s, and made as a design variation of the point-faced dog or wolf, pat'd. 1920? **$95**

Nutcracker, eagle head, cast iron, upraised head on flat iron base, lever moves lower beak up & down, American? 6"H, 1980s. **Lookalike alarm.** – Cumberland General Store, Crossville TN, sells this one as "just like those available in the 19th century," – I've never seen an old one. New/used: $12-$15. For the old – if there truly is one:.. **$125**

Nutcracker, elephant, cast iron, painted red & black, with a little white, the red has aged to a salmon color, trunk is lever, American, 5"H x 10"L, early 20th C. **$165**

Nutcracker, elephant form, modernistic cast iron painted orange, high arched back, lever action, mid 20th C. **$150**

Nutcracker, goldfish or koi with teeth in mouth, gold painted cast iron (also found nickel plated), glued-on glass eyes (poss. not original), upper fin is spring-loaded lever, English, 8"L, Regist'd. #751,619. Prob. c.1920s. **$125**

Nutcracker, horse, modern stylized form, 2 halves screwed together, tail lever, bronzed or coppered cast iron, English, 4-1/4"H x 7-1/4"L, marked with same pat. # as dog crackers, #273,480. Crossover collectors from Art Moderne. **$300**

Nutcracker, lions' heads, a pair facing each other, cast iron, pliers type, a pronounced concavity for nut, no marks, English (?), 6-1/2"L, 19th C. [Note: Lion motif probably worth more in England than in U.S.] .... **$80+**

Nutcracker, pheasant, bronze, French, 19th C. .... **$90-$120**

Nutcracker, rabbit, cast iron, somewhat full-bodied rabbit wearing high collar & made so lever in back opens mouth to crack nut. Advertised as a "reproduction," but new design as far as I know. 9"H. **$10**

Nutcracker, rooster, cast iron, c.1890s-1910s. **$65**

Nutcracker, squirrel, carved wood, probably walnut, threaded screw action presses against nut, Tyrolean or English?, 19th C. Not as large a variety of the screw-type wooden nutcrackers as the levered ones, but others to look for include various barrels or cyl-

I-71-A. Squirrel nutcracker. Cast brass zoomorphic nutcracker; screwed press crushes nut between two slices of stump! Marked on bottom "Mod. Dep. 11AR68/88." With a large "M" & teeny "e" trademark within a circle. Very well made & beautifully finished. "11AR68/88" may be a patent date, perhaps 11 April 1968, then perhaps renewed in 1988? It's not from 1868. Photo courtesy Dieter Schulz, Germany. eBay name: fliffis; e-mail: dieter.schulz@tc-72.de. Collects old & unusual nutcrackers. **$45+**

inders with simple or fancy knobs to the screws – from a simple bird to a knob faceted like a golf ball to a standing woman. The most commonly found wood is boxwood. .... **$175+**

Nutcracker, squirrel, cast brass of very reddish hue, 2 parts with riveted pivot in jaw, no marks, lots of detail, 7-7/8"L, late 19th C or early 20th. .... **$125+**

Nutcracker, squirrel, cast iron, "Squirrel Cracker," Tyler, TX, pat'd. 1913..................................... **$125**

Nutcracker, squirrel on leaf, cast iron, American, 19th C. (Evidently this was also made in a nickeled finish at least until 1924.)............................. **$125**

❖ NOTES ❖

Some squirrel designs: A picture of five squirrel nutcrackers, from the booth of dealer Clifton Anderson, Lexington, KY, who was set up at "Atlantique City" in March 1989, makes it clear that the variations are not subtle. One squirrel, in the foreground, has the most Alert Squirrel head ... wary, tail tucked along curved back, holding a leaf on his paws, which is where the nut to crack went. Another I recognize as the reproduction I bought through the mail from someone else, smallish and very poorly cast, very furry tail, with gap between front paws. Looking at these, and at the racing, chasing busybodies in our yard, I find it impossible to call them rodents.

❖ NOTES ❖

Squirrel Lawn Sprinkler – An interesting cast metal squirrel that may or may not relate to the nutcrackers, is a lawn sprinkler from early 20th C. Other squirrel forms to look for are in chalkware.

Squirrel reproductions are being made, but I've not inspected any of them in person.

Nutcracker, squirrel on rustic branch, cast bronze or bell metal, extremely finely detailed, squirrel has funny long skinny arms & very pointed nose, lever is uplifted plumy tail widely separated from curve of back, English? or poss. American, 6"L, 19th C. This is one of the best-looking squirrels. The abstracting is very refined; the angular slender legs, the funny little ears. It sometimes seems to be a bronzed cast iron; possibly different periods? I have also seen this one with no leaf, but mounted to a turned wooden tray or plate. .... **$175-$225**

Nutcracker, squirrel on stump, cast brass, front paws holding part of the T-handle of the screw press, which crushes a nut on another stump, mark on bottom is a large "M" & tiny "e" (?) in circle, and registration marks inside oblong: "MOD. DEP. 11AR68/86". I think it must be 11 April 1968 (then renewed or whatever in 1986) because it doesn't look worn or old. But it is a great design. 4"H, possibly German. .... **$55+**

Nutcracker, squirrel sitting on hind legs on huge grape leaf, cast aluminum painted black, rather crudely cast but nice idea. The tail lifts up to lever the jaw, no mark, American?, 7-1/2"H overall, leaf 11-1/2"L, 20th C. Flat or dull black painted aluminum is almost a sure sign of rather recent origin (or recent painting). I think it's intended to fool the unknowing into thinking they've found a cast iron piece. There are c.1900 cast aluminum pieces of many kinds, however, but the novel metal, considered an attractive silvery pewter lookalike, was rarely painted, and usually in gold. **$45**

Nutcracker, squirrel, standing high, tail curled, cast iron, good detail, American, only 5"H, late 19th or early 20th C. (A newish one with not very good casting, no signs of wear, has been seen.) Old:........ **$75**

Nutcracker, squirrel, cast aluminum, called "Davy Crackit," sold by Norpro (an international wholesaler/mfr. of kitchen related gadgets), 5-1/2"H, late 20th C. **$15**

Nutcracker, squirrel with paws held palms up, on log, levered tail, silver gray painted light weight cast aluminum, brown log, green eyes, the squirrel & base case in 2 pieces down through center of squirrel & length of log, bolted together, dealer's tag says "signed H. E. Cox, Norfolk, VA," but I couldn't find any mark at all, 5-1/2"H, log 5-3/4"L, looks 1980s, and is pretty awful. **$15**

Shaped Like Things or Objects

Nutcracker, black painted cast iron, small anvil & blacksmith's hammer, probably not a reproduction of an old one, but a new idea, John Wright, Inc., Wrightsville, PA, hammer 4"L, 1960s................ **$15**

Nutcracker, blue-decorated Meissen porcelain platform frame fitted with iron screw mechanism with big porcelain knobs at each end (it looks like small decorative book press for miniature books). Meissen, German, about 6"H, 19th C. **$200**

Nutcracker, brass, "Big Ben," English, 20th C. souvenir(?). **$55**

Nutcracker, rocket-shaped, cast iron on wooden base, adjusts for different nuts, "Reed's Rocket," American, 20th C. (?). **$45**

Nutcrackers – Non-Figural - Simple kneecap & hammer/mallet ones

Nutcracker, cast iron, anvil-like contrivance, small, square, with curved undersurface to fit a seated person's knee, small short column in center has concavity for nut, used with mallet or small hammer, "Lawrence," American, about 4" square, c. 1840s. .... **$75+**

Nutcracker, cast iron, anvil like nutcracking block, fits kneecap, shield shaped with raised nut holder, fits over knee & used sitting down with small mallet or hammer, American, 3-1/2"L, 1840s-60s. .... **$75+**

Nutcracker, cast iron, 2 part, walled oblong green painted base with sort of mortar with long handled flattish plate that fits inside base, Paper label reads: "DIRECTIONS: Place cracker on a solid foundation. Place all nuts on end and hit blow with hammer or mallet. Empty the base after cracking each nut. Use 36 ounce mallet if possible until after the war." "Potter Walnut Cracker Co.," pat'd. by C. E. Potter, Sapulpa, OK, pestle about 3"L, June 5, 1945 patent #2,377,369. .... **$50**

Nutcracker bowl, turned wood, with cast iron round central "Anvil" & iron hammer, American, 7"L hammer & 10" diam. bowl, 20th C. **$25**

Nutcrackers – Mechanical
Simple pliers

Many of the nutcrackers from Europe, especially those from the 18th or 19th C., are hinged like pliers, hinged with an offset nose, or parrot-nose, jaw for the nut. These are usually carved of very heavy dense wood, perhaps boxwood or oak, with a pinned wooden hinge, and the handles are incised, cross-hatched, dotted, and chip-carved with bands of simple patterns. The handles have to be long enough to provide leverage, but because they're made of wood they can't be so long as to be cracked with the pressure of squeezing by the hand. Generally speaking, the handles will be somewhat thicker, and straighter than metal handles. Turned wood, with thick & thin places along the handle would have a tendency to break at the thinnest places. 5-1/2" to 8"L, French, English, etc. [Note: New ones are made in very similar designs ... look for ugly fakey coloring or patina, no signs of wear – from nuts or hands – generally poor quality.] Old: .... **$50+**

Crossover lever

Nutcracker, hand held crossover type, with hinge/pivot at one end, handles flip around axis to accommodate another size nut, cast iron, English, European or American, about 6"L, 19th C. There's quite a variety available. I like the cast iron ones best; others have nickeled or silverplated finishes. Range of these is between: .... **$5-$20**

Nutcracker, hand held crossover type, handmade (?) cast iron, maybe cast in multiples then finished by hand?, hinged levers, inside face of one are tiny V gouges, the other has O gouges, English (?), 6-1/2"L, c.1850s to 1900. .... **$20+**

Nutcracker, hand held crossover, pointy handles, engraved steel, English, 5-1/2"L., 19th C. **$12**

Nutcracker, hand held crossover, silver plated iron, bulbous knobs on handles, English (?), 5-1/4"L, c.1890s-1910s. **$12**

❖ NOTES ❖

It's In the Old Picture – One very similar to this, a crossover type with little rough projections on jaw parts, tapered turned handles, silverplated, appears in "Still Life with Apples, Walnuts and Holly," painted by American artist Eloise H. Stannard in 1899. You should always examine still life and genre scene pictures for objects in our collecting fields. At least you get an "as early as" date.

•   •   •

It's *In the Not So Old Catalog* – Harrod's Stores, Ltd., London, England, carried 10 different styles of this type of metal nutcrackers in the late 19th C. The turnings of the handles (or lack thereof) as well as overall decoration, and style of jaw, vary considerably. The cheapest has nicely shaped handles narrowing near the jaws, swelling out, then coming to a dull pointed end. The jaws, on both sides, have flat faces with a pattern of small nicks or gouges. The piece between the hinged jaws that determines the minimum space between the jaws while in use, is crown shaped rather than teardrop or ovoid. Slightly more expensive is one with pointed handles, two sets of turned bands, ovoid spacer, and oval grooved or fluted concavities for nuts. Another has decorated hinge pins, but wide spoon-handle levers. Another, again with oval concavity, has bamboo-like cast iron handles; another has baluster turnings with round knobs at ends; another has the crown spacer, very decorative 'rattlesnake rattle' turnings, and a zigzag line of small gouges or nicks on all faces of jaws; another is not the 2-hinge flip over type, can be used only one way, but the longish jaws are corrugated inside, with area for larger nuts near the handles. This "nut crack" came with allover fancy Renaissance chased decoration, or with chased head and plain handles. The handles of this one are the shapely ones of first type listed above. Harrod's nutcrackers came plated and plain, and were ordered through the jewelery, watch, electro plate, & cutlery department of the huge store.

Nutcracker, hand-held, crossover type, cast iron, knobbed ends to handles, corrugated parts for 2 sizes of nuts – small (like almonds) & large (like walnuts), American? 5-1/8"L., 19th C. **$12**

Other levers, handheld and mounted

Nutcracker, carved boxwood lever type, one tapered handle is L shaped, the other has pivot part fitting through bottom of L, rounded on outside with small carved double – crossed squares as decoration, ball finials, carved on one lever or handle is the name, on other is a very, very early date – surprising because the name sounds like a patent or trade name, on flat surface inside L lever is "Broughtons Cracknut," the inscribed date is "October 5, 1667," English, 5-3/8"L, 1667 (?). Dealers Michael & Jane Dunn, Claverack, NY, had this at a show in 1984. I did not get to examine it, and am taking the description from a picture appearing in *Maine Antique Digest*, April 1984. (My value range.) .... **$600-$850**

Futile Research on the "Broughton Cracknuts." – I spent several hours trying to do intuitive research on the date, the name "Broughton," and the term "Cracknut." Leads I investigated included a British regiment, originally "The Third Foot," later the "Buffs," which had the nickname the "Nutcrackers." This regiment was definitely in existence in 1667. And it fought in the Second Dutch War – one of several Restoration wars between England and Holland – which ended in 1667. With my resources, the name Broughton led nowhere, nor did I have time to really delve into the date. I did look at a very early 19th C. "every day" almanac, which details events important to England on every day of the year, but found nothing significant for October 5. One of that set of books, William Hone's *The Every-Day Book*, (the one I quote here, London: 1826), yields several squibs on nuts or nut-cracking. Sept. 14, or Holy Rood, was for nutting, signifying the "fruitfulness of autumn, and the deadly cold of the coming winter." On October 31, Hallowe'en, the Vigil night for November 1, All Saints Day, it was traditional "in many parts of England" to bob for apples and crack nuts. It is possible that the elusive "Nutcrack Night" of which I have seen only passing mention, refers to the e'en of October 31. I hate to say it, but the Web didn't provide any more information.

Nutcracker, cast aluminum, a large squarish open frame to be wall-mounted, with big lever that ratchets along outer vertical member of the frame. A totally different piece from the C. E. Potter nutcracker listed up under Simple: Knee Cap & Hammer/Mallet. But it has same patent number: June 5, 1945 patent #2,377,369........................... **$35-$50**

Nutcracker, chromed metal, hand held levered ratchet & pawl action that was advertised as working "like a car jack" but looks like a vise grip, called the "Crackerjack," mfd. by H. H. Linton, London, English, about 8"L., first made in 1948, sold for at least 15 years. **$15**

Nutcracker, cast iron, lever action, Arcade Mfg. Co., Freeport, IL, early 20th C. .... **$50+**

Nutcracker, cast iron, levered jaws stick out slightly over end, mounted to oblong wooden board, lower corrugated jaw stationary, upper one opens & depresses when curved lever is raised, pat'd. by Russel Frisbie, Middletown, CT, pat'd. May 17, 1859. Similar to the P. E. W. and J. A. Blake patents of six years earlier, which was the first pat'd. nutcracker, and extremely modern looking. [Note: Back in the 1830s, before patents were numbered in the U.S., Eli W. Blake, Johan A. Blake, and Philos Blake got a number of patents for door escutcheons, locks and mortises.]................................. **$65+**

Nutcracker, cast iron, mounted to oblong wooden board, long corrugated jaws stick out over side near one end, lever moves endmost jaw while other remains stationary. Similar to Frisbie patent; a letter by Ernest J. Rolland to *Spinning Wheel* in 1977 reported that both these nutcrackers are "often mistaken for a cork press," pat'd. by P. E. W. & J. A. Blake, New Haven, CT, base 10-1/2"L x 3"W, pat'd. Sept. 6, 1853. (See more on the Blake Brothers under a Corkscrew entry in Chapter VIII, Open & Close.) Later edition. – One of these was seen with

black painted finish, & marked "P. & S. & W. Co.," Peck, Stow & Wilcox, Southington, CT............ **$65+**

Nutcracker, cast iron with black enameled finish, mounted to oblong board, lever moves one jaw while other is stationary. Iron embossed "Sargent, & Co" and "10." American, possibly Sargent & Foster (?), 10-1/4"L, early 20th C. .... **$55+**

Nutcracker, cast iron, screw clamps to table, lever action, long slightly arched lever pulled down over small nut-holding jaw, "Enterprise," Enterprise Mfg. Co., Phila., c.1914... **$35**

Nutcracker, cast iron, screw clamps to table, long lever, "Home," American, 19th C............................... **$28**

Nutcracker, nickel plated metal rachet mechanism & lever, black enameled metal tray, in original orange & black cardboard box, "Krag's Whole Kernel Nut Cracker," American, 7"L, pat'd. Mar. 23, 1937 by G. M. Krag. **$40**

Nutcracker, nickeled malleable cast iron, screw clamps to table, pushing down lever operates worm causing longish cupped jaws to close in, jaws stepped & with opposing concavities for small, medium & large nuts, device especially meant for pecans, "Home," Schroeter Brothers Hardware Co., St. Louis, MO, 6"H x 4"W with 7-1/2"L lever, "patent pending" in 1915.... **$40+**

Nutcracker, with its own bowl, simple footed, rimmed bowl of "imitation rosewood, zebra ash or genuine mahogany," with nickeled metal high rise frame like a guillotine screwed to bottom, adjustable for 4 different size nuts, lever used to move top part down to pop nut open, "New Champion," c.1915. .... **$20+**

Screw & Vise

Nutcracker, tabletop screw type, cast brass machined to look like ship's wheel, on wooden base, American, 4-1/2"H, 20th C... **$40**

Nutcracker, carved & turned oak, doughnut shape pierced on one side by wooden screw used to press nut you've placed within hole of doughnut against opposite side, English, only 2" diam., late 19th C. I've also seen modern ones, especially in woods & finishes favored by Danish furniture makers. **$15**

Nutcracker, cast iron, nickel plated, held cupped in hand, T handle to screw, adv'g. "Cook Muffler Co.," American, approx. 4-1/2"L when screwed fully in. Frank B. Cook pat'd. this Aug. 6, 1918............. **$15**

Nutcracker, concave part of cast iron fits in palm, T handle with slightly knobby ends, screw action, this one is chrome with enameled green body, others are nickeled or even just highly polished iron, one is sort of fluted like a melon, some have narrower bodies & T bar has no knobbed ends, or have a simple looped handle, actually pat'd. Aug. 6, 1918, patentee & mfr.

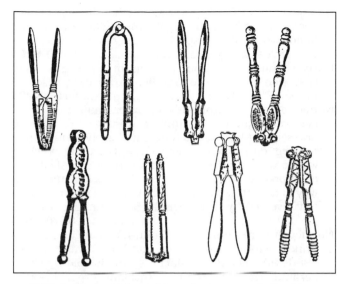

I-72-A. Nutcrackers hinged at one end; the hinge is the fulcrum, the handles are the levers. Also called nutcracks. All are nickeled or plain cast iron or steel, more or less decorative. Top row, L to R: (1) A lobster cracker; confusable, because it could be used with large nut. (2) Simple cracker with grooved area to hold nut near hinge. (3) crossover type, with reversing hinges for small or large nuts. This one accommodates several sizes. (4) Most heavy duty cracker, crossover, with grooved concavity for nut, old style of handles. Bottom row, L to R: (5) Simple non-reversing iron cracker, for smaller & larger nuts. (6) 20th C. crossover of type usually found with a set of matching nut picks. (7) Massive steel crossover, comfy handles. The little dots seen on nut face are like little prickers of steel. (8) Crossover, tooling decoration new hinge, turned handles, prob. oldest cracker in group, perhaps mid-19th C. All shown in small nut position. Many are English, c.1860-1930s. $5-$20

Frank B. Cook advertised "The Ideal"; later, without knobbed ends, "Ideal" was mfd. by Cook Electric Co., Chicago, IL, 3-1/4"W x about 5"L, sold prior to patent in 1917 ad, then 1923 ad. .... **$5-$15**

Nutcracker, cast iron, levered jaws stick out slightly over end, mounted to oblong wooden board, lower corrugated jaw stationary, upper one opens & depresses when curved lever is raised, pat'd. by Russel Frisbie, Middletown, CT, pat'd. May 17, 1859. Similar to the P. E. W. and J. A. Blake patents of six years earlier, which was the first pat'd. nutcracker, and extremely modern looking. [Note: Back in the 1830s, before patents were numbered in the U.S., Eli W. Blake, Johan A. Blake, and Philos Blake got several patents for door escutcheons, locks and mortises.] **$65**

Nutcracker, cast iron exactly like screw-clamp model, but this one screwed to a "countersunk plate" in bottom of a shallow turned wood bowl with very rounded sides & narrow foot, "All the shells & other litter fall into the bowl & are not scattered about," The Perfection Nut Cracker Co., Waco, TX, pat'd. Nov. 17, 1914, advertised in early 1917 as a "new item." This is the scarcest of the Perfection crackers. .... **$50+**

Nutcracker, cast iron, nickeled or tinned, clamps to table, looks like small bench vise, horizontal screw pushes nut against end plate, big cast T handle has swelled knobs on ends like leg bone, "Perfection," Malleable Iron Fittings Co., Branford, CT, pat'd. 1889. .... **$50+**

Nutcracker, cast iron, nickeled, screw clamps to table top & looks like small bench vise, vertical lathe type action, large T handle, slightly finer casting than earlier one, ornate letters in curve to fit frame, The Perfection Nut Cracker Co., Waco, TX, 4-1/2"H x 3-3/4"W, pat'd. Nov. 17, 1914. Another one, a little leaner, and made of nickeled cast steel, is very plain. It is marked "Perfection Nut Cracker Pat." Pecans, which are supposed to be hard to crack (perhaps to crack & get perfect nutmeats out), were Texas' biggest cash crop at the time the "Perfection" was patented................. **$40**

Combination nutcracker

Nutcracker & lemon sqeezer combination, "All-in-One," Ford Mfg. Co., Newark, NJ, 11"L, top, slotted concave cup, long lever handle with enameled convex presser, late 19th C. .... **$100-$125**

Nutcracker & picks, nickel plated (some are silver-plated), heavily knurled, 6 picks in original box, American, c.1910. .... **$6+**

Nutcracking block, kneecap – See: Nutcracker, cast iron, anvil type.

❖ NOTES ❖

Nutgrinders or choppers Look on eBay for a few weeks and you'll find quite a variety in several jar shapes & makers, paint colors, and crank knobs. As far as I can tell, all of these familiar gadgets were based on a patent by Carl A. Sundstrand, of Rockford, IL. His patent is the one found on many of the metal hopper slide sides, # 2,001,075, dated May 14, 1935. (Two years later he patented another similar gadget, a "food grater," with a cranked grating surface and a different shaped jar.) The patent drawing clearly shows a jar shaped exactly like the Hazel Atlas jar #5935 11F," so it is possible Sundstrand was already connected to the Hazel Atlas glass company.

Nutgrinder, cast iron & tin, "Climax." Glass jar, screw-on tin hopper filled with fingers that rotate when cranked, "Hazel Atlas" rounded vase-like jar, American, 1930s. .... **$18+**

Nutgrinder, tin & glass, straight-sided cylindrical jar marked "Androck 49 4" on bottom, tapered turned wood knob, 6"H, 1960s? **$5**

Nutgrinder, tin & glass, rounded jar, tin embossed "Androck Nut Meat Chopper," "pat. # 2,001,075, on bottom of jar "5935 Hazel Atlas 11F," c.1940s. ... **$7**

Nutgrinder, red tin & glass, Hazel Atlas jar somewhat pear-shaped with swaggy or drapey lines, round tops with crank. Similar ones have simple bent wire keywind crank like sardine can opener. Some marked "Federal Tool Corp." Probably 1960s+. ... **$5**

Nutgrinder, green painted metal, "Lorraine Metal Mfg. Co.," NY, c.1890s-1910s. **$10**

Nutgrinder, painted tin metal screw-on top, sliding side to hopper stamped "The Uniform Nut Meat Chopper," wooden crank knob very rounded, American, c.1940s ? .... **$6+**

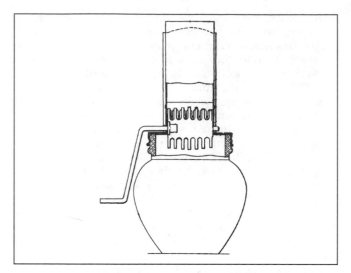

I-72-B. Nutgrinder or Nut Chopper patent. *Probably the "father" of all the nutgrinders made since the 1930s. "Nut Chopper," pat'd. May 14, 1935, by Carl A. Sundstrand, Pat. #2,001,075. The jar shown is the earliest shape of receptacle; the "fanned" teeth of steel move the nutmeats through a slotted piece between hopper & jar, and cut them into small pieces. Brings back memories of making brownies. (Sundstrand also patented a rotary grater with hopper & jar combo; the crank moved a grating drum cylinder while you pressed "cheese, crackers, chocolate, toast, cocoanut, nut meats and many other dry and semi-dry foods" against the grater. The most interesting element was the annular groove near bottom of jar, made for a wide rubber band that would encircle the jar and the edge of the bottom, and keep it from slipping.* **$10+**

Nutgrinder, orangey-red painted metal screw-on top, usually with small decal on hopper, cranked finger-like teeth, glass jar. The metal sliding side is embossed "Androck Nut Meat Chopper" on some; some have "Hazel Atlas" jars, some "Androck." 6"H, pat. # 2,001,075, made in 1940s-50s, American. .... **$4+**

Nutmeg & ginger mill, tin with little crank, looks like music box, brown asphaltum japanning, marked "Portable Ginger & Nutmeg Mill," English, 3-3/16" x 2-7/16", reg'd. Nov. 11, 1857. .... **$475-$575**

❖ NOTES ❖

Nutmeg Grater Book – See the notes for further research at the end of this chapter for information about Carol Bohn's book.

Nutmeg grater, asphaltum japanned tin, looks like miniature bug bomb gun, label reads "simple, economical, rapid and durable. Every particle of the nut used. Satisfaction Guaranteed. None wasted, easy to handle, a pleasure to use." "The Rapid Nutmeg Grater," 5-1/4"L, late 19th C. .... **$350-$400**

Nutmeg grater, big, round robust black-glazed ceramic knob (instead of the usual wood), triangular tin chute where grated 'meg comes out, storage in back, "British made," disk is 3-3/4" diam., British patent applied for, #32,492/32. .... **$160+**

Nutmeg grater, cast iron crank, wire handle, ingeniously bent so as to hold nutmeg against small grating disc, handle looks like a spark striker handle, American, 7"L, 1880s... **$150-$200**

Nutmeg grater, cast iron housing for nutmeg & other cast iron parts, wire handle, tin grating disc, no marks, 7"L, c.1870s. .... **$150-$200**

Nutmeg grater, cast iron with tin grater, shaped like small bellows, crank handle, unpin & unhinge it & it reveals brass spring-loaded catch for cartridge holder of single nutmeg, directional arrow cast in side to show which way to turn handle, 2 holes for screwing to shelf edge or cupboard side (another model marked the same way had a screw clamp frame), not marked with name, but invented by J. M. Smith, Seymour, CT, 3-7/8"L, pat'd. June 7, 1870.................................. **$475-$575**

Nutmeg grater, "coffin style," non-mechanical, brightly tinned, with lidded storage for 1 to 2 megs at top, 1980s-90s. Lookalike alarm. – This is sold by Cumberland General Store, Crossland TN, & other stores, & there's no reason to think it won't continue to be made. Old:.. **$10+**

Nutmeg grater, coffin style, tin, has lidded storage at top near hanging hole or loop, biggest variety seen in the back of these – the ingenious ways tin was poked out to create the platform inside to hold the nutmeg, mostly American, 5-1/8"L to 5-3/4"L, 19th to 20th C. Slightly fancier ones (usually with embossed designs on little lidded compartment, or with sliding lids) are English, and may bring more. .... **$10-$15**

Nutmeg grater, coffin type but very big, tin, with compartment, 2 grating surfaces on the curved front & flat back, "Acme Nut Grater," English, Register #11,467. .... **$45+**

Nutmeg grater, coffin type modified, stamped tin, has sliding lid to nutmeg compartment, back unusual in that it's stamped with an 8-rayed star, English, 6-3/8"L x 2-9/16"W, c.1900.. **$30**

Nutmeg grater, coffin type, very large, stamped & punctured tin, with storage box with sliding lid with embossed design, no marks, English, 6-1/2"L x 2-1/2"W, 19th C. .... **$45+**

Nutmeg grater, ebonized wood, or bog oak, carved to look like small champagne bottle, no marks, remnants of paper label that is illegible, European, 3-3/4"H, 19th C... **$200+**

Nutmeg grater, fancy little box grater, japanned or lacquered tin, 4"L, late 19th C. .... **$50+**

Nutmeg grater, fancy turned wood body & handle, cube of wood has working part inside, plus barrel for storing the megs, tin grater, brass side plates & cap, Champion Grater Co., invented by C. L. Gilpatric, of South Dedham, MA, but mfd. in Boston, MA, 7-1/2"L, pat'd. Oct. 9, 1866; brass cap at end of handle marked "April 2, 1867"................................,...................... **$450-$550**

Nutmeg grater, heavy cast iron with brass & wood, pinned hinges or hooks hold back on, pat'd. Jan. 30, 1877. .... **$150+**

Nutmeg grater, long tin barrel, hinged lid at end for inserting nutmeg, hinge wire is also hanging ring, grating drum made up of assembled battery of 12 toothed rings with deep & jagged teeth like harrow discs, slightly jaywhoppered, seems like overkill, stamped "The –s Davidson Automatic Nutmeg Grater," Boston, MA, 6-3/4"W, pat'd. June 2, 1908. (I've seen this given as June 9, also a Tuesday). One seen at 1994/95 show was $1,200. ...... **$750-$900+**

I-73. Nutmeg graters – some rare, some not. (A) *Simple coffin-box type, backs show 2 of many ways platform created for lidded nutmeg box atop grating surface. 5-1/4"L. Early 20th C, type still sold. 3¢ in 1905! Author's.* **(B)** *M. H. **Sexton**, Utica NY, pat'd. May 1896. Tin, nickeled spring metal holds nutmeg. 4-3/4"L x 3"W. (Larger size known).* **(C)** *Two names: "Unique" & "Monitor," pat'd. Mar. 19, 1889 by T. L. Holt. "Unique" mfd. by Steel Edge Stamping & Retinning Co., Boston; "Monitor" mfd. by New England Novelty Mfg. Co., Boston (poss. same company.) Marked "Press down lightly." 4-3/8"L x 2"W; pinkish-stained wood frame with diagonal tracks over tin grater. Photo'd as sled at the Dziaduls' at Christmastime. In England, a close-to-identical grater was patented Apr. 1, 1889 by A. J. Boult & assigned (?) to C. O. Blood. (not the same Blood who patented a flour sifter).* **(D)** *2 versions "**Edgar**." Older one at left. Edgar Mfg. Co., Reading, MA, pat'd. Aug. 18, 1891. 5-7/8"L. Green-painted wood; varnished wood. There are others, and a similar chocolate grater made much bigger.* **(E)** *Richard H. **Chinn**, Washington, DC, pat'd. July 16, 1867. No marks. All tin, sliding, spring-loaded hopper, 6-1/4"L. This is so rare, it is the only one known.* **(F)** *Nathan **Ames**, Saugus, MA, assignor 1/2 to Edmund Brown, Lynn, MA, pat'd. Oct. 13, 1857. Tin with orig. blue paint; wood spring-return pusher inside cylindrical holder. About 5-3/8"L diagonally. Patent drawing shows small loop handle; 1871 picture shows large "cup handle" of strap tin.* **(G)** *"H. **Carsley**, Lynn, Mass. Patent applied for" stamped on cylindrical holder. Pat'd. Nov. 20, 1855. 3-7/8"L. Bob Cahn.* **(H)** *Skeletal form, no mark, 7-1/2"L. Screwed pressure foot; pierced drum with holes at slight angle. Believed to be foreign, not American;* **(I) & (J)** *Two versions of same grater. Cast iron, tin, wire. 5-1/4"L (Another is 7"L). Pat'd. Mar. 9, 1886. Ex-Keillor Collection.* **(K)** *"**Gem**," rotary motion, nickeled cast iron. Caldwell Mfg. Co., Rochester, NY. 4" x 2-3/4". 1908 ad. All not attributed are courtesy Joe & Teri Dziadul, dealers in Enfield, CT.* **(A) $10-$15; (B) $850+; (C) $95-$125; (D) $65-$100; (E) $1,500+; (F) $450-$650; (G) $750-$850; (H)$300+; (I) & (J) $150-$200; (K) $75-$125**

I-74. More rare & desirable nutmeg graters. (L) *Tin & wood. Small knob in slot pulls back, spring-load pressure foot holds nutmeg against grating drum. 6-1/8"L, marked "pat'd. Dec. 25, 1877" (not a Patent Tuesday). In 1890, this design was changed – tin box part elongated to form handle & nutmeg storage, with lid on end. Spring, knob, wire crank & grating drum remained same. Mfd. under old patent by The* **Standard** *Co., Boston, called "new" by them.* **(M) "Champion** *Grater Co., Boston, Mass." Two patent dates: Oct. 9, 1866, & on end of brass cap "April 2, 1867." 7-1/2"L.* **(N)** *Tin, spring-loaded, rather crude wheel. No mark. 4-1/4"L.* **(O)** *Long tin 4-sided barrel holder with hinged lid at end. Grating drum encircled by battery of discs with deep, jagged teeth, like harrow discs. Stamped "The –S (?)* **Davidson** *Automatic Nutmeg Grater. Boston, Mass. pat'd. June 2, 1908." 6-3/4"L.* **(P)** *Two slightly different "The* **Handy**," *screw-cap ends for nutmeg storage chamber & spring-loaded hatch for 'meg being grated. Wood knobs, threads on caps, and lengths differ. 4-3/4"L and 5-3/8"L and 6-1/2"L. Late 19th C.* **(Q) "Rapid,"** *japanned tin cylinder, tapered nozzle. 5-1/4"L. Another measures 6-1/4"L. By 1906, an almost identical, much stubbier grater, called* **"Ever-Ready,"** *of nickeled brass, was only 4-1/4"L.* **(R)** *Tin, hollow tin storage handle with tiny ovoid hinged lid at end, underside, for putting 'megs in. 7-1/2"L, only mark "press lightly." Probably English, & very desirable.* **(S) Skillin & Reed** *grater, Portland, ME, pat'd. Sept. 3, 1867. Albion S. Skillin & George W. Reed; assignors of-1/2 to Henry Hanson & J. Butler. Turned wood, tin disc, springy wood pressure foot underneath to hold nutmeg in. 6-7/8"L.* **(T) "Brown & Hasler**, *Lynn, Mass. Pat. applied for." Very rare. Wood handle & presser, tin body, black paper label, gold lettering. 7"L.* **(U)** *Stamped* **"Portable Ginger & Nutmeg Mill**. *Reg. Nov. 11, 1857." English. Japanned tin, 3-3/16" x 2-7/16".* **(V)** *Wood & tin* **"Common Sense,"** *pat'd. July 23, 1867, by R. W. Whitney & Joseph P. Davis, South Berwick, ME. 5-1/8"L.* **(W)** *Pat'd. June 7, 1870, by J. M.* **Smith**, *Seymour, CT. Cast iron, hinged bellow-shaped body, spring-loaded cartridge for 1 'meg. Directional arrow cast in for crank. Could be screwed to cupboard. 3-7/8"L.* **(X)** *Tin, wood, spring "The* **Champion**" *(see (M), nicknamed "Teapot" or "Hat Box" by collectors, Hughes patent, pat'd. Feb. 27, 1877, 3-1/2" diagonal. All graters courtesy Joe & Teri Dziadul.* **(L) $200+; (M) $450-$550; (N) $750-$900+; (O) $600+; (P) $350+; (Q) $250, and with paper label might be $400; (R) $1500+; (S) $400-$500; (T) $500+; (U) $475-$575; (V) $400-$550+; (W) $275-$350; (X) $375-$475**

Nutmeg grater, long tin tube, screw caps at each end plus one 1/3 way up, like odd pocket periscope crossed with a cigar tube. Crank comes out one end, 'meg goes in hole in side, other end stores more. See also: the "Standard." American, 6-1/2"L, late 19th C. .... **$350+**

Nutmeg grater, nickel plated cast iron, hinged nutmeg holder, punctured tin disc, small crank with wood knob, black holding handle in center of disc, American, 3-3/4"L x 2-3/4"diam., c.1870s to 1880s. .... **$75-$125**

Nutmeg grater, nickel plated metal, horizontal cylinder with squared funnel below & cylindrical chimney-like hopper above, crank in end of grater barrel, marked inside a diamond "MTE & Co.," American, 3-1/2"L, 19th C, sometimes called "The Ever Ready." ... **$125+**

Nutmeg grater, non-mechanical, homemade, tin & wood, paddle shape with semi-cylindrical punctured tin arched grating surface, American, 4"L, 19th C. .... **$25+**

Nutmeg grater, oddly modern & efficiently mechanical, screwed pressure foot, pierced drum with grater punch holes at slight angle, no nonsense action, 7-1/2"L, late 19th or early 20th C. .... **$300+**

Nutmeg grater, plated metal, in cylinder shape with lift-out grater that forms top, nutmegs are stored inside cylinder, no marks, American (?), 4-1/2"L, 19th C. **$150**

Nutmeg grater, pocket, carved coquilla nut with ivory trim, shaped like a barrel. Unscrew bottom for tin grater & nutmeg storage, prob. English, though poss. American scrimshander work, only 2-1/2"L, very early 19th C. .... **$300+**

❖ NOTES ❖

Coquilla nuts, from piassaba palm of Brazil, washed up on beaches, were found by sailors, who used the richly colored, hard dense material to make intricate small carvings. These carvings and turnings, snuff boxes, patch boxes, nutmeg graters, "pretties" & tokens of love, were often trimmed with carved ivory or bone.

Nutmeg grater, pocket style, ivory with tin grater inside, caps unscrew for grater at one end, nutmeg at other, English (?), 3-1/2"L, early 19th C., or poss. late 18th. **$350**

Nutmeg grater, pocket, turned wood, bottle shape, 'meg container has screwed-on lid, rasp on end, English (?), 2-1/2"L, 19th C. **$300**

Nutmeg grater, pocket, turned wood, 3 part, little cup with knobbed lid which is fitted with punctured tin grating surface; lower part is fitted with the same (the nutmeg is rubbed between the 2 graters by twisting the top back & forth), & the grated nutmeg goes into bottom, poss. American, prob. English, 6"H, mid 19th C. .... **$175+**

Nutmeg grater, pocket type, carved wood & ivory, nutmeg-holding lid screws onto grater part, English(?), early 19th C. **$325**

Nutmeg grater, rotary action, large turned handle to hold in one hand, round tin grating surface screwed through center & screw also secures nutmeg holder. Metal crank, screwed to edge of disc, has a wooden knob & a small round presser foot to hold nutmeg while the crank is turned, "Gem," Caldwell Mfg. Co., Rochester, NY, c.1907. .... **$95-$125**

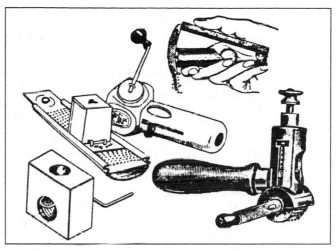

I-75. Nutmeg graters. Clockwise from one with hand: (1) The "Automatic," squeeze-action, grating on inside of curved surface. 4-1/4" x 2-1/2", nickeled steel, c.1903. "Nutmeg is placed in the hollow tube, the tube is grasped by the hand, and 'there you are.'" A bar-suppliers' catalog said "It is the only automatic nutmeg grater where you can hold the glass in one hand and manipulate the grater with the other." (2) 1924 subscription premium from American Cookery magazine. Maker not identified, but style is 19th C. (3) Patent drawing. Albert L. Platt, Oct. 3, 1893. Some have surfaced since the 4th edition of this book in 1997. (4) "Boye Sanitary" grater, Boye Needle Co., pat'd. Sept. 29, 1914. Box holding nutmegs opens when slid out of side tracking. (5) "Little Rhody," wood & tin, red & black paper label, 1880s. (1) $350+; (2) $400+; (3) $350-$450; (4) $125-$150+; (5) $200-$275

Nutmeg grater, slide & pivot action, wire frame, punctured tin, works like trombone, wooden holding handle & small wooden knob on foller that holds nutmeg against grating surface; made over a long time period with various knobs & handles, some stained green. Nutmeg could be moved "forward and back, and from side to side, preventing the grated nutmeg adhering to the surface of the Grater and bringing every part of its surface into use," said 1892 ad. "The Edgar," mfd. by Edgar Mfg. Co., Reading, MA, 5-7/8"L, pat'd. Aug. 18, 1891. These were pat'd. (as a variation of 1891 nutmeg grater of George H. Thomas, Chicopee Falls, MA by Charles F. Damon, of Edgar & Damon. One sold on eBay, with black-painted handle knobs, that reportedly was stamped "Nov. 10 1896." **Classic.** – The Edgars are a gotta-have, but as I reported last time, they've about reached their limit in this collecting cycle, & price seems to have stabilized or plateaued for the last 10 years. In the next collecting cycle, so few may be on the open market that the value may go way up. Most are at mid level of this range. .... **$65-$100**

Nutmeg grater, spring-loaded tin cylinder for nutmeg set at right angles to cranked grating disc, skinny tin tubular handle, attached with even narrower tubes, odd bridge effect of small pencil-thin tin tubes and struts (see first group picture of nutmeg graters), "The H. Carsley," pat'd. by H. Carsley,

Lynn, MA, 3-1/2"L, disk nearly 3" diam., (one without date is 4"L), pat'd. Nov. 20, 1855, but made while "patent applied for." .... **$750-$850**

❖ NOTES ❖

An anonymous tip on **grating nutmegs** appears in Aug. 1851 *American Agriculturist*, viz. "If a person begin to grate a nutmeg at the stalk end, it will prove hollow throughout; whereas the same nutmeg, grated on the other end, would have proved sound and solid to the last. This circumstance may thus be accounted for: The centre of a nutmeg consists of a number of fibres issuing from the stalk and its continuation through the centre of the fruit, the other ends of which fibres, though closely surrounded and pressed by the fruit, do not adhere to it. When the stalk is grated away, those fibres, having lost their hold, gradually drop out, and the nutmeg appears hollow; as more of the stalk is grated away, others drop out in succession, and the hollow continues through the whole nut by beginning at the contrary end, the fibres above mentioned are grated off at their core end, with the surround fruit, and do not drop out and cause a hole."

Nutmeg grater, nickeled steel, squeeze action, 2 halves consisting of tube with spring-held presser for nutmeg, & a curved backplate that has a curved rasping surface fixed at the bottom at right angles. This back plate is held against the palm, the fingers squeeze the cylinder with the 'meg – causing it to move back & forth along rasp. A spring is also in the pivot & assists "the grasping and relaxation of the fingers." German (?), called "The Automatic" in ads, 4-1/2" x 2-1/2", pat'd. c.1902.................................... **$200+**

Nutmeg grater, tall tin pocket grater, side unfolds & reveals grating surface, American (?), 2-3/4"H, 3rd quarter of the 19th C. .... **$175+**

Nutmeg grater, tin, cigar-like cylinder with a flue-like nutmeg holder, wood knob, 4-3/4"L, marked "Edw. Snyder, Massilon Ohio," late 19th or early 20th C. .... **$500+**

❖ RECIPE ❖

General Directions for Making Cake *– When cake or pastry is to be made, take care not to make trouble for others by scattering materials, and soiling the table or floor, or by needless use of many dishes. Put on a large and clean apron, roll your sleeves above the elbows, tie something over your head lest hair may fall, take care that your hands are clean, and have a basin of water and a clean towel on hand. Place everything you will need on the table, butter your pans, grate your nutmegs and squeeze your lemons. Then break your eggs, each in a cup by itself, lest adding a bad one should spoil the whole. Make your cake in wood or earthen, and not in tin." Mrs. Mary Hooker Cornelius,* The Young Housekeeper's Friend, *Boston, 1846. Twenty years after this, even longer, people were dying after being operated on by medical doctors who didn't know enough about the causes of sepsis and infection to wear clean coveralls, cover their hair, or wash their hands and instruments. It's too bad doctors didn't learn from cookbooks.*

Nutmeg grater, tin, another cigar-like cylinder with nutmeg holder rising from it, wood knob slightly fancier than other shorter one, grating surface differs too, American, 5-3/8"L, late 19th or early 20th C ... **$450+**

Nutmeg grater, stamped, pieced & punctured tin, combination grater, pie crimper & can opener, prob. "Morgan," English, late 19th C. .... **$300+**

Nutmeg grater, tin, looks like Mississippi steam boat, round tin bottom, sliding, spring-loaded hopper for nutmeg, little hanging wire loop, no mark, 6-1/4"L, pat'd. July 16, 1867 by R. H. Chinn. This is the rarest of all, only one is known as of 2001. Hard to say what the value would be if even just one more became available. Carol Bohn believes it would bring at least $1,500. However, even if a hoard of five were found, $1,500 might hold. But if 10 or more came to light, the value would probably drop back at least 25%. .... **$1,500+**

Nutmeg grater, tin, loopy wire handle, cast iron with cast iron crank, big grating disc, American, 7"L, pat'd. Mar. 9, 1886.............................. **$150-$200**

Nutmeg grater, tin, mechanical type like small Boye, but has wood knob on nutmeg housing, marked "The Del," American, 19th C......................... **$150+**

Nutmeg grater, tin & nickel plated spring metal holds nutmeg in place, swings back & forth, mark stamped on back in the tin, "M. H. Sexton," Utica, NY, 4-3/4"L x 3"W, pat'd. May 1896. This is a very desirable grater. .... **$850+**

Nutmeg grater, tin, oblong shallow piece with diagonal grating surface and with turned wooden end. Turned wooden nutmeg barrel has small wooden presser tamp that must be held against the nutmeg. The barrel slides on diagonal or transverse tracks (actually kitty-cornered) over grater, gratings fall out front. "Unique," Steel Edge Stamping & Retinning Co., Boston, MA, advertised in 1892 (maybe before); poss. rip-off of 1889 "Monitor"; or poss. is the 1889 A. J. Boult's English patent. This grater used to be (back in the 1970s & early '80s) the desirable rarity that occasionally showed up at antique shows priced above $150. It's been passed in the long stretch by all the oddities that have surfaced in last decade. See also the "Monitor" grater. .... **$165-$200**

❖ NOTES ❖

It is always possible with "**pat apple**" (Bob Cahn says that Pat Apple was the most prolific inventor in America) pieces that a patent was never granted. Examiners in the patent office were always complaining how silly some submitted ideas were, and how they exhibited no new (and therefore patentable) mechanisms or design, and in fact, how many of them didn't work. By putting "patent applied for" on your goods, however, you put a mantle of respectability on your item, and perhaps a tiny measure of protection, though the notion that someone else might copy your unpatentable invention is wishful thinking. Mystery writer Margery Allingham had her detective Albert Campion muse in *Flowers For the Judge* (a highly recommended mystery), while looking at a strange old key, that it "was squat and heavy and had that curious unsatisfactory appearance which is peculiar to old-fashioned patent devices which have never been really successful."

Nutmeg grater, interesting long, skinny tin mechanical grater, flat piece pulls down to protect grating surface, nutmeg holder is small cylinder mounted to track along folded edges, "William Bradley," Lynn, MA, 6"L in closed-up position, "patent applied for" on one; "pat'd. July 26, 1854" on another..... **$350+**

Nutmeg grater, tin, small box grater, oblong shape with flat side almost completely covered with grating surface, large hanging hole, pat'd. by W. Bradley, Lynn, MA, pat'd. Jan. 29, 1867....................... **$110-$135**

❖ NOTES ❖

1867, a Grate Year The Bradley almost starts the year off for nutmeg graters. But (1) patent was granted Jan. 8, 1867, to L. V. **Badger**, Chicago, IL.; (2) granted **Bradley**; (3) granted Mar. 5, to J. A. **Hooper**, South Berwick, ME; (4) & (5) granted July 16, to R. H. **Chinn**, Washington, DC, and to C. A. **Durgin**, NYC, NY; (6) granted July 23, to R. W. **Whitney** & J. P. **Davis**, South Berwick, ME; (7) granted Aug. 6, to L. **Von Froben**, Washington, DC; (8) granted Sept. 3, to A. S. **Skillin** and G. W. **Reed**, Portland, ME; (9) granted Sept. 24, to C. **Worden**, Binghamton, NY; and (10) Dec. 17, to W. W. **Owen** and D. **Kelly**. I have not been able to find out what was the impetus in that year. Of 27 nutmeg patents granted up through 1873, 10 were 1867 (plus the cap on another), 2 were 1866, and 4 were 1868, leaving only 11 from 1854 (the earliest specific nutmeg grater) through 1873. I tried to check tariffs, cookbooks, periodicals, but nothing popped out as significant. Any ideas? **Shoes & nutmegs.** – Several companies made nutmeg graters in Lynn, MA, but Lynn's largest industry by far were the 150 ladies' shoe factories, which in 1870 employed 20,000 people. It certainly makes me wonder if there doesn't exist a goodluck shoe-shaped nutmeg grater made in Lynn to celebrate the town's main industry!

Nutmeg grater, tin & varnished turned wood (also found with wood part stained a sort of pinky-red color), rectangular grating plate, set in braced tin frame with turned wooden end. A little straight-sided nutmeg holder with wooden screw-top, is slid back & forth over grater along diagonal edge track. Printed with direction "Press Down Lightly." Also called the "Unique" grater. Identified in old ads as "The Monitor," Boston, MA, 4-1/2"L x 1-15/16"W, "pat'd. March 18, 1889" in circle on lid of 'meg holder. The name "Monitor" may appear on paper label, if any such remains. This was distributed or possibly even mfd. by New England Novelty Manufacturing Co., which in 1890 was apparently the only manufacturer of nutmeg graters. I suppose by that time, powdered nutmeg in tins had pretty much obviated the need for the graters. [Note: This 1889 "Monitor" is very similar to the 1854 Bradley grater, listed above, and they both resemble an ironclad submarine, such as the Monitor from the Civil War. Another ingenious one, pat'd. Aug. 17, 1897, has a smokestack-like cylinder for the nutmeg, and tracks the long skinny grating surface that's like an angular tunnel. A hole in the top at one end permits insertion of nutmeg into the cylinder when it's positioned over the hole.] For the Unique/Monitor:... **$185-$225**

Nutmeg grater, tin, spring-loaded boxed housing for nutmeg tracks along edges of oblong grating surface, "The Boye," Boye Needle Co., Chicago, NYC & San Francisco, about 6"L, pat'd. Sept. 22, 1914. (Boye still makes crochet hooks.) .... **$125-$150+**

Nutmeg grater, tin & wire, strap handle, launching cylinder with spring-loaded wooden foller, wire crank with small wood knob, about 6-1/4"L diagonally, pat'd. Oct. 13, 1857 by Nathan Ames. .... **$500+**

Nutmeg grater, tin & wire, "Will grate four times faster than any other yet made," "Yankee No. 1," mfd. by Hamlin & Russell Mfg. Co., Worcester, MA, c.1884.. **$100+**

Nutmeg grater, tin, with hollow tin handle with ovoid hinged lid covering nutmeg storage & grating chamber. Only marking: "Press lightly." 7-1/2"L, probably English, late 19th C. One of the most desirable graters, and very scarce. **$1,500**

Nutmeg grater, tin & wire, "New Rapid," mfd. by Hamlin & Russell Mfg. Co., Worcester, MA, came in 2 sizes, small and large, pat'd. Dec. 25, 1877. See also the "Standard." .... **$200+**

Nutmeg grater, tin & wood, oblong wooden body with works at one end, nutmeg storage at other end has tin cap & little wooden knob on top to pull back spring-loaded pressure foot, wire crank on side turns grating cylinder against nutmeg, "Standard," Standard Co, Boston, 6-1/8"L, marked pat'd. Dec. 25, 1877; re-introduced to trade in July 1890, now with elongated box body & handle, unlike original of 1877, which had a turned wood handle. See "L" in second group photo. • Although a date is stamped on this grater, a patent search fails to turn one up – at least by me. Let's hope Carol Bohn's book will solve the mystery. The so-called patent date sometimes turns out to be the date the application was filed for consideration, but no nutmeg grater was patented in 1878 (or 1877 either). The 25th was on a Tuesday in 1877. The original "Standard" was called the "Rajah" grater in c.1880 catalog of novelties for traveling salesmen, and when advertised in Simmons Hardware Co.'s 1885 catalog.............. **$200+**

Nutmeg grater, turned wood with punctured tin disc, very nice screwed-on springy wood pressure foot, pat'd. by A. S. Skillin and G. W. Reed, Portland, ME, 6-7/8"L, pat'd. Sept. 3, 1867.................. **$400-$500**

Nutmeg grater, wood knob & tin body, black & red paper label still attached, "The Little Rhody," American, late 19th C. .... **$200-$275**

Nutmeg grater, wood, tin & wire, long wooden piece with wire & wood piece to hold nutmeg against rather big grating disc, crank comes out of center of disc, paper label on long wood piece, "Common Sense" grater, invented by R. W. Whitney & J. P. Davis, not necessarily made by the inventors, who lived in South Berwick, ME, 5-1/4"L, pat'd. July 23, 1867. .... **$400-$550+**

Nutmeg grater & cookie cutter combined – See: Chapter IV (Molds)

❖ NOTES ❖

Onion peelers are valuable but not collectable. "The earliest onion peeler I know about wore a gingham apron and sat on a chair while she peeled the onions and cried." – Henry Landis, Landis Valley (PA) Museum, in response to a query in the Early American Industries Association *Chronicle*, April 1951. The **Landis Valley Museum** is a national treasure for kitchen and tool collectors. It's on Kissel Hill Road, Lancaster, PA. Web site: www.landisvalleymuseum.org/ • Another treasure, almost beyond belief, is the ingenious cement structure built by Henry Mercer, and now the Mercer Museum, in Doylestown, PA. It, too, has wonderful collections. Web site: www.mercermuseum.org/.

Orange juicers – See: Juicers.

Orange peeler, small, curved steel blade with painted turned wooden handle. Held in the right hand, the blade is slipped under the peel & is drawn toward the thumb while the orange is turned with the other hand. (Works same way as successful 1980s orange peeler made by a man in the Midwest, featured on "*60 Minutes*" & sold through mail.) Mfd. by Robert S. West, Cleveland, OH, c.1890. .... **$5**

Oyster knife, fish shaped metal, poss. CT, 19th C. **$20**

Oyster knife, one piece of cast tool steel, square handle so it wouldn't slip easily, sword-like blade, prying edges thin but not sharp, "Stortz & Son," Philadelphia, PA, early 20th C. .... **$15+**

Paring knife, steel blade, wooden handle & brass bolster (a bolster on a knife is like a ferrule on a tool), handle marked "POTATO," American (?), 6"L, 20th C. **$15**

Pastry knife, a form of dough scraper & cutter, sometimes called a chopping knife & probably used as such, this type for dividing dough for loaves of bread, for example, or for scraping pastry board. This one is made of a single wide piece of steel, rolled top edge forms cylindrical handle, no finger cutout, American, 4-1/2"H x 5"W, c.1890s-1910s. **$15**

Pea sheller, cast iron, screw clamps, 2 sided to split the pod, goes through rollers to pop peas out, marked only with date, but pat'd. by S. Ustick, Philadelphia, PA, May 5, 1868. See a Knife sharpener entry in Chapter IX (Washing & Repair). **$85**

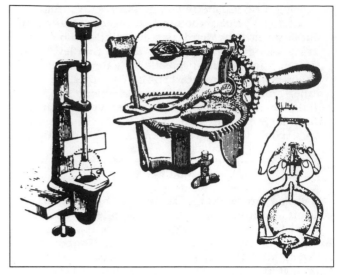

I-77. Peach stoners & parers. (L) Cast iron stoner, screw clamps, plunges and apparently cuts peach in half with blade. From F. A. Walker catalog, Boston, 1870s. *(M) "Lightning"* parer, mfd. by Goodell Co., Antrim, NH. Sargent & Co., agents (their name may appear on some gadgets like this, I don't know). Exhibited at 1869 NY, St. Louis and other agricultural fairs & won prizes. Pat'd. Aug. 17, 1869. *(R) "Rollman No.6,"* Rollman Mfg. Co., Mt. Joy, PA. "Patent applied for" in c.1901-05 catalog. **$125-$150; $50-$125; $200+**

Pea sheller, galvanized cast iron, screw clamp, downturned spout releases shelled peas, angled hopper on top, hook at bottom of frame holds small pail to catch (we wonder how well) the shells as they were expelled from rear of cranked machine, "Acme," Acme Pea Sheller Co., NYC, 7"H, patent applied for c.1880s-1890s. **$125**

❖ RECIPES ❖

Puree of Peas – Wash a pint of green peas in cold water; then put them in a saucepan with boiling water and cook 20 minutes. Have them dry when done. Press through a colander. Boil one half pint milk, add a small onion, three or four cloves and a small sprig of parsley. Rub a tablespoon each of flour and butter together. Strain the milk over the peas, put back in saucepan, stir in the flour and butter, and let boil, stirring to prevent sticking. Season with salt and pepper and serve." *Ladies Home Journal*, April 1890.

Pea Fritters – Boil a pint of green peas until tender. Mash them while hot and rub through a colander. Season with pepper, salt and a tablespoon of butter. Let cool, add the yolks of two well-beaten eggs, a cup of cream, one teacupful and a half of flour, and a half teaspoon of soda and one of cream of tartar, sifted several times with the flour. Stir and beat well. When ready to use, beat in the white of the eggs and fry, a spoonful at a time, in boiling lard." *(Ibid.)*

I-76. Pea sheller. "Acme," Acme Pea Sheller Co., NYC. Galvanized cast iron, screw clamps. Pods fell out back into pail hung on frame's hook; peas fell into dish. **$200+**

Pea sheller, sheet metal painted green, rubber feet, crank with yellow wooden knob, you roll pea pods between 2 black hard rubber rollers; presumably pods pop & peas patooie out the chute, decal label, "Holmes Pea-Sheller," Holmes Mfg. Co., Los Angeles, CA, 5-1/4"L, patent pending, c.1910s to 1930s. **$60**

Peach parer, cast iron on long wooden board base, has 2 forks, opposing each other; the large fork turns the peach, the small one turns upon the rod like a swivel when the peach is turned, and serves to hold up the outer end of the peach. The stone in each peach prevents the peach from being pushed on to one fork and held by that alone." Mfd. by David H. Whittemore, successor to Whittemore Brothers, Worcester, MA, 1860s. "The above machine," continues an 1868 ad, "is also superior for paring potatoes, and even when the potato is long and wilted, it works complete, the small or outer fork serving to hold up the outer end of the potato while it is being pared. It is also a good apple paring machine – the use of the small or sliding fork being dispensed with." Whittemore, earlier of Chicopee Falls, MA, also was issued apple parer & slicer patents. . **$150**

❖ NOTES ❖

Peter Piper Peeled a Peck of Peaches – I have at hand the Sept. 15, 1866 issue of the weekly "*Alexandria Price Current Letter-Sheet*," a flimsy-paper report on market prices of goods from *Agricultural Implements* to *Wamsutta* cotton prints, from *Ale to Shingles*, published by Knox & Wattles, Forwarding & Commission Merchants, of Alexandria, VA. A run of them for a year would be more interesting, but still, there are some tidbits. For example, "DRIED FRUIT – Demand dull. Tendency downwards. We quote: PEACHES peeled ...17@20¢ per lb. [17 lbs at 20¢ each] PEACHES not peeled ...11@12 APPLES ...10@11." It was worth peeling peaches, in other words. As a comparative, 50 lbs of new potatoes cost 60¢ whereas sweet potatoes were $8 a bushel, and New Orleans molasses was $1.30 a gallon!

Peach parer, cast iron, screw clamps, "Lightning," D. H. Goodell Co., Antrim, NH, a county fair winner in fall 1869, but pat'd. May 10, 1870. .... **$200+**

❖ NOTES ❖

Finding patent dates is sometimes hard, but it's fun. This one eluded me at first, but then I found, under **"Parer, Fork for peach,"** in the *Subject Index to Patents*, two patents with the right dates, which were for the 4 pronged fork that slips into end of peach and sort of cradles the pit or stone. They were awarded to C. D. House, Lake Village, NH, on Aug. 17, 1869, and to D. H. Goodell, Antrim, NH, May 10, 1870. Otherwise, the machine itself is like the Lightning apple parer. In the *American Agriculturist*, June 1872, there is this about a peach parer: "A continuous and urgent inquiry for a machine for Paring Peaches, has been ringing in our ears from all Peach-growing sections, for the past five years, and in response to this universal appeal, the manufacturers of the Lightning & Turn-Table Apple Parers have at last succeeded in obtaining and secur-

ing a device for Holding and Paring Peaches, which is as practical and economical as the Apple Parer, and cannot fail to come into immediate and general use." An ad in the same magazine, a year earlier, shows a detailed line cut of the Lightning Peach Parer, with the half round horizontal gear, clearly shown with patent date of Aug. 17, 1869. • I reread a letter from collector **Evelyn Welch**, from Sept. 1983, exactly six years later, and found something I must have missed before. She writes, about a non-mechanical handheld peach pitter "Sometime take a peach pitter, cut a ring around a clingstone peach with a knife, beginning at the stem hole, following the line across the peach. Take the proper sized pitter for that sized peach, slip it into the peach around the pit with the line on the peach on your left, turn pitter to side, then back around under pit, and the top will slip off. Then scoop the pit out of other half. Seems the pit has a ledge on the side and this is the professional way I was taught to cut clings at the Pacific Pea Co. Cannery (now Hunt Wesson) in Oakdale, California, when I was 16 years old (1930) and proudly earned $6 per day. We wore white cotton gloves in case the pitter slipped. We would 'ring' a lugbox of clings with the knife then pit them by the box. What I'm getting at is the story behind the need for a tool to remove pits. Pear pitting is different altogether." See Patent chapters XXI-XXIII.

Peach parer – See also: Apple parer & peach parer

Peanut shucker, wood, 2 part mill, turned on an axle by means of fancy turned handlebar-like handle. American, 19"diam. grinding surfaces, mid 19th C. **$250**

Pepper mill, or peppermill, or pepper grinder, cast iron, wall-mounted side mill like small coffee mill, c.1900.. **$35**

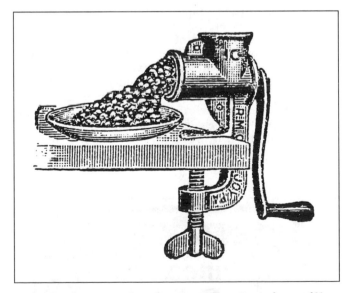

I-78-A. Peanut butter machine & spice mill. *Nickel-plated cast iron, screw clamps to table edge. "This machine is highly recommended by Mrs. S. T. Rohrer for making Peanut Butter. It will grind nuts of all kinds, spices, crackers, coffee, etc. It makes a very attractive toy for children." Rollman Mfg. Co., Mt. Joy, PA, 5-3/4"H, c.1900. In toy market, would probably be worth more.* **$20+**

Pepper mill, turned hardwood (prob. oak) base topped by complicated steel geared mechanism, including cranked bevel gears, 7-3/4"H, American or French (?), c.1944 to present (new ones offered in mail order catalogs and on eBay). Both sometimes referred to as "coffee mill" pepper grinders. Old one has large side wheel with four curved spokes, nicely turned wooden knob, brass fittings, body is deeply turned and gets slightly larger toward bottom. It's about 7-1/4"H. New one has that fakey "tarnished copper" look like those cute cheapo pencil sharpeners in the shape of various old gadgets. Light colored beechwood turned body & knob, bevel gears, globe top with sliding hatch for the peppercorns. 8"H. New: $7+; Old: .... **$45+**

Pepper mill, or possibly individual-serving coffee mill, looks like a toy coffee grinder of box type, wood, painted red & cream, made by Trösser, German maker of coffee grinders, 5-1/2"H x 3" square, c.1950s-60s. **$20**

Pepper mill, turned wood cylinder with glass liner forming effect of windows, metal crank, "Peugot" (yes, it's the bicycle manufacturer), French, 20th C. Peugot mills are still made, and still tops. **$40**

Pepper mill, dark red almost maroon dense plastic, like Bakelite, chrome top and bottom, crank knob is plastic, common barrel type used for many mills in wood, plastic, ceramic. Marked on bottom: "The George S. Thompson Corp., Los Angeles, Patent Applied For." 3-1/2"H x 2-1/8" diam. Prob. mid 20th C. Vintage design crossover...................... **$10**

Pepper mill, turned hardwood, nickeled mountings, 3-1/2" to 4"H, American, late 19th C. In the 1880s, Americans, used to using pepper shakers at table, seemed to find the French use of pepper mills a novel good idea, for flavor & to avoid adulterated packaged ground pepper. This was about 1880. Many styles of carved or turned hardwood mills were offered in the 20s.. **$15+**

Pepper mill, turned maple, novelty in shape of wine bottle, with "laser engraved" label depicting a vineyard, works in guise of corkscrew with T handle, grounds come out bottom, sold through Bloomingdales in 1983 catalog, 1980s. **$35**

Pepper mill, red plastic novelty, wonderful apple-shaped pepper grinder, crank is stem, knob is green leaf, marked "Kamenstein," a hardware & housewares company in NY. 4-1/4"H. Possibly 1960s?.................. **$20**

Pepper mill, turned wood cat figural (actually like deeply-turned chair leg, but with roundish cat head near top, painted black except for cheeks left natu-

I-78-B. Pineapple Eye Clip. "Patterson's," M. E. Mosher, Mfr., Rochester, NY. Trigger action, nickeled steel. Introduced in 1905. **$20+**

ral, white eyes, applied whiskers, 10"H, "Made in Denmark" on bottom on metal part, prob. c.1950s-60s. Crossover cat item. **$65**

Pepper mill, brass (sometimes copper & brass) cylinder with domed top, longish, slightly bent crank handle in top, very common form. Actually started out sometime in early 19th C. as a coffee mill, from Persia/Turkey. Usually has decorative bands around part of body, which is about the size of a toilet paper tube, or perhaps somewhat slimmer, and from 5-1/2"H to 10-1/2"H. Most have a knobbed catch partway down, for filling. At some point in the 20th C., people either started using them as pepper mills, or making similar ones for that use. A newish one made in Greece is marked "Atlas Pepper Mill Guarantee Made in Greece." Another new one marked "Made in Greece" is made for & sold by The Frugal Gourmet. Look for signs of wear and age if you want an oldie. New: $10+; Old: .... **$20+**

Pineapple eye snips, cast iron painted black, scissor action with attached steel blades, one a sort of scoop beak with sharp tapered end, other an open oval, with sharp top edge nearest scoop part, W. H. Collins, NYC, 5-5/8"L, 1930 ad, prob. made before that. .... **$15+**

Pineapple eye snips, looks like small pair of scissors; one hardened steel blade terminates in small spoon, other has a hollow cutter that fits into spoon bowl – as the inventor put it – "adapted to engagement with each other accurately, somewhat like the beak of parrot or an eagle," pat'd. by John F. Pack, on Aug. 27, 1901. .... **$15+**

Pineapple eye snips, or eye clips, nickeled steel curved cylinder, sort of with a pistol grip, with trigger near front that you pull to make top part of little cutter clip out the eye, "Patterson's," mfd. by M. E. Mosher, Rochester, NY, c.1905. .... **$20**

Pineapple eye snips, or pineapple eyer, simple turned wood handle, triggered snip with spring to return to starting position, one fixed piece like tiny cone, open along top side, which would be stabbed under the pineapple eye, before pulling trigger to cause cutter blade to come forward & slip into top of eye, completing the small conical excision, "Dixie," mfd. by W. H. Glenny & Co., Rochester, NY, 5-1/2"L, patent applied for c.1904. .... **$15**

Poppyseed mill, green painted iron, screw clamps, "Kosmos," 20th C. .... **$45+**

Poppyseed mill, turquoise green painted cast iron, spun brass hopper, screw clamps to table, "Standard," prob. PA, by the cherry pitter company, in Mt. Joy, 9-1/4"H, c.1890s. Thin hopper usually bent, even split. In very good condition:..................... **$50**

Potato chip machine, "machined steel with spring steel knife and lasts indefinitely" ... "unexcelled for slicing potatoes, carrots, beets, onions or any vegetable or fruit," black enameled handle, mfd. by Mebhut & Platts, Ilion, NY, 8-3/8"L, "patent pending" c. 1920s (?). $2 was original cost!... **$25+**

Potato cutter, stamped tin, counter top, for making french fries, "Maid of Honor," American, 1930s (?). See also the Whatzit cutter at end of Chapter IV (Molds).. **$15**

Potato French fry cutter or Saratoga chipper, tin cylinder with a cutting frame (like a tick-tack-toe game) to do 25 French fries or Saratogas at a time, "Silver's Sure-Cut," 4"H, c.1890s-1910s. .... **$55+**

Potato & fruit press, what other makers called a ricer, japanned malleable cast iron frame, handle & lever handle, heavily tinned plunger & perforated cup removable for cleaning, marked on top handle or lever is "Silver & Co., NY"; "Genuine Silver Press" on lower handle, Brooklyn, NY, one size only, claimed to be "the largest and most powerful," c.1880-1910. Silver & Co. claimed in early 20th C. catalog, to be "originators of the hand press and have for 30 years maintained its quality and steadily decreased its price." .... **$15+**

Potato masher, heavy twisted wire, wooden handle, American, 22-1/2"L, large hotel or restaurant size, 20th C. **$45**

Potato masher, long turned handle with little round mushroom or button end, heavy round steel head, flat disc with perforated holes in small & medium size, "Hercules," mfd. by Handy Things Co. [poss. Handy Thing Co.], Ludington, MI, c.1904. .... **$25**

Potato masher, turned upright wooden handle, flat mashing head of nickeled iron wire woven into intricate openwork "snowflake," "web," or "gear wheel" head of heavy wire. It is particularly referred to by Parloa, as follows: "Many housekeepers prefer the kind of potato masher shown below to the wooden one. In unskilled hands it gives a lighter dish of potatoes than the wooden masher, but the wooden one will be needed for other things which the wire one would not answer." *Maria Parloa, Kitchen Companion*, Boston, 1887. American, 9"L, c.1880s to 1900. .... **$25**

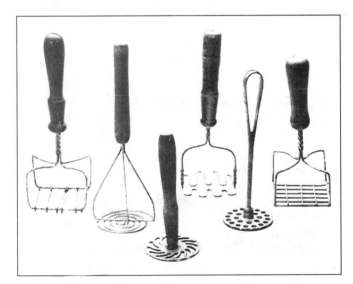

I-79-A. Metal potato mashers. *Along back row are just 4 of the scores of cleverly bent, woven, twisted, coiled & braided wire mashers, with vertical turned wood handles. Made by many makers. About 7"H to 14"H for household ones; even longer for hotel or restaurant versions. Two in front, galvanized or tinned cast iron, are called potato muddlers, and date at least to 1870.* **$10-$25**

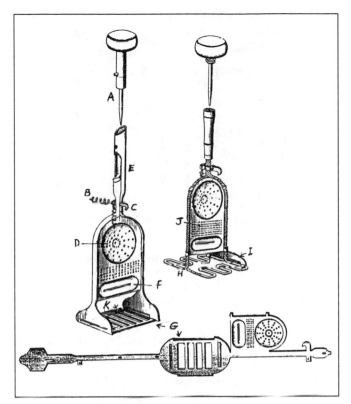

I-79-B. Combination "Kitchen Utensil" patent drawing. *If this was made, I predict it will be gobbled up by collectors at higher & higher prices; i.e.,* **Futurewatch!** *Pat'd. Aug. 14, 1917, by George Edmund Henry, Philadelphia, PA, Utility Pat. #1,237,040. A 10-in-one. "Said utensil comprises an* **(A)** *ice pick,* **(B)** *cork screw,* **(C)** *a [bottle] cap remover,* **(D)** *strainer,* **(E)** *apple corer,* **(F)** *egg separator,* **(G)** *potato slicer,* **(H)** *potato masher,* **(I)** *vegetable slicer,* **(J)** *grater,* **(K)** *pan & kettle scraper, and also dough cutter. This wouldn't be the easiest thing to use, but if Ron Popeil had existed in 1917, think of the possibilities! The lower drawing shows how most of it could be stamped from one sheet of metal, before bending & riveting. If it exists, with all parts:* **$200+**

Potato masher, turned wooden handle, heavy wire, double action: push on handle & upper set of wires goes down, A & J, Binghamton, NY, 11-1/4"H down to 9-1/2"H, pat'd. 1912. .... **$50**

❖ NOTES ❖

In 1984 there was a UPI story about an artist named Byron Randall who ran a bed & breakfast in Tomales, CA, & decorated the B & B with his collection of 389 **potato mashers**. He sold the guest house in 1989, and moved to a nearby chicken coop – presumably with his mashers, which he had started collecting because nobody else seemed to be collecting them. He told an interviewer that after that first national story, he started getting letters from people, with snapshots of their mashers which they wanted identified. Gee! I wondered why my stream of potato masher letters dried up! Maybe it was all those instant mashies I made.

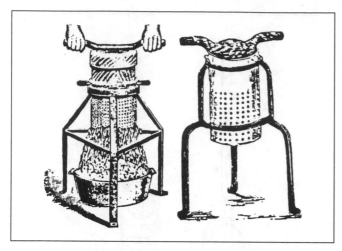

I-80. Plunger potato mashers, like big versions of potato ricers. Perforated tin cylinders, wood plungers, wrought iron stands. Sizes from 6" diam. to 9" diam. Early 20th C. **$25-$45**

Potato masher, turned wooden handle, mashing head is 2 heavy wire flat spirals, American, 10"L, c.1920s-30s. **$25**

Potato masher, turned wooden handle, twisted wire arch with 2 rows of 4 curvy zigzags, Kilbourne Mfg. Co., Troy, NY, c.1908. .... **$20**

Potato masher, turned wooden handle with round palm-fitting knob at end, with nickeled iron L shape masher blade with 2 rows of long slots cut lengthwise, bent at right angles to the handle, Androck "potato ricer," mfd. by Washburn Co., Worcester, MA, 9-1/2"L, c.1936. .... **$10+**

Potato masher, wires bent in shape of fingers, looks like glove dryer, 2 tiers of fingers set 20° or so on horizontal plane, white painted turned-wood handle, A & J, Binghamton, NY, 11"L, 20th C. **$20**

Potato masher, zigzag wire with long turned wooden handle, commercial size one, 22"L, 20th C. **$30**

Potato mashers, made of wire & wood, came in many various designs from a flat spiraled head, or a wire grid, to a slightly rocking set of 8 fingers stamped of

Reproduction Alert

This **Androck ricer** was an updated version of a somewhat older one. But the strange story concerns Virginia Nicoll of Meridith, NH, and her MMPM Company (My Mother's Potato Masher). She started in 1984 making a "reproduction" of the tool, which she says her grandmother "purchased from an itinerant peddler in rural Pennsylvania back in the 1800s." In my opinion, this masher dates back to the 1890s at the earliest, although MMPM ads say "patent circa 1882." Anyway, the Nicolls had a tool and die company make the mashing plate of carbon steel, with turned birch wood handle, and they have received a lot of publicity and enjoyed great sales. I have no idea how many of the original 10,000 ordered from the die-maker have been sold, or if they are now into the hundreds of thousands.

steel or a crisscross of loosely strung wires, most with wooden handles, some few have nickeled iron loop handles. Most are American or German, most about 8" to 10"H, late 19th through first half 20th C. .... **$10-$25+**

❖ RECIPE ❖

Imitation Spaghetti – Boil and mash potatoes, adding salt and butter, but only a tablespoonful of milk, as you want a stiff paste. Rub this through a colander into a buttered pie or pudding dish. It will fall in small, pipe-like shapes. Leave them as they lie, and, when all the potato has passed through, set the dish on the upper grating of the oven to brown delicately." Marion Harland, House & Home, a Complete Housewife's Guide, *Philadelphia, 1889.*

Potato masher – See also: Eggbeater & potato masher, Chapter II (Mix)

Potato peeler, also for sweet potatoes, parsnips, carrots, turnips or beets, large cylindrical chamber sets down into base that screw clamps to table, chamber is lined with perforated steel or carborundum to scrape off paring, reservoir of water at top of cylinder, cast iron gear in bottom, side crank, long hose-like tube that leads from base carries off ground-away peelings by the water stream coming from chamber above, American, about 16"H x 8" diam., c.1910s. **$55**

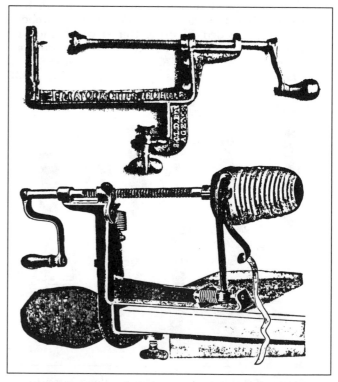

I-81. Potato parers. (T) "Saratoga Chips. 75 Cents" embossed on horizontal framework. "Sold by Agents" on screw clamp. Taylor Mfg. Co., New Britain, CT. Pat'd. June 18, 1878. Photo courtesy John Lambert. (B) "White Mountain" parer, Goodell Co. "This machine will also pare Quinces and Pears" say ads. Late 19th C. on – sold for many years. **$75+**

Potato peeler, looks like lathe-style apple parer, tiny paring blade, cast iron frame, turn the handle, stick potato on spade like prong that rotates, "Nu-Way Automatic," mfd. by Guaranty Products Co., St. Louis, MO, early 20th C. **$65**

Potato peeler, tin with gritty composition that literally sands off the peeling. Looks like a shallow oval tart pan with crimped edges, filled with the grit compo cement, with a bracket strap handle across back, "Hamlinite Peeler," maker not known, 4-1/2"L x 2-1/4"W, pat'd. July 20, 1920; prob. made for fewer than 10 years. .... **$10+**

❖ RECIPE ❖

Silver Pie – *Peel and grate one large white potato into a deep plate; add the juice and grated rind of one lemon, the beaten white of one egg, one teacup of white sugar, and one teacup of cold water. Pour this into a nice undercrust and bake. When done, have ready the whites of three eggs well beaten, half a cup of powdered sugar, a few drops of rose-water, all thoroughly beaten. Put this mixture on the top of the pie evenly and return to the oven, to stiffen a few moments. When sent to the table just cold lay a spoonful of currant jelly on the center of each piece to ornament if you wish." Mrs. M. L. Scott, Home Cook Book, 1876.*

Potato peeler, tin with wooden handle, "Morton Salt Potato Peeler," 20th C. .... **$15+**

Potato ricer, red paint enameled malleable iron lever handles, tinned perforated cup, tinned metal presser, mfd. by Handy Things Co. [poss. Handy Thing Co.], Ludington, MI, about 12"L, c.1940s.. **$10+**

Potato slicer, cast iron, tabletop, 3 knee-bent legs attached to large round slicer housing, with potato size hopper & tall vertical shaft with crank to turn blade inside, a plate could be set underneath to catch the slices of potato (or other raw root vegetables), mfd. by W. L. & T. M'Clinton (?) or W. L. & T.

I-82. Potato ricers, *or hand presses. Showing 2 basic styles: the round cylinder "drum" style, and the V-shaped one like the famous Henis press. (L) "Genuine Silver Press," Silver & Co., Brooklyn, removable cups. Strong & durable, tinned malleable cast iron. "The castings are made of a peculiar composition of iron which absolutely guarantees their unbreakability." Circa 1910. (R) 4-1/4" x 4-1/4" cup; c.1905.* **$10+**

I-83. Potato slicers. (L) *"Marguerita Macaroni" – the "only practical machine for preparing the potatoes in continuous curling strips, for boiling, stewing, or potato ribbon." Nickeled iron. Could also be used for cutting "beets, carrots, turnips, & c." for garnishing. 1914 catalog. (R) Potato slicer, pat'd. 1870, and 1871 (?) or 1877 (?). A witch in a diamond-patterned dress, stirring her brew. F. A. Walker catalog, 1870s.* **$150**

M. Clinton, (sold in early 20th C. by V. Clad & Sons), Ithaca, NY, about 15" diam., pat'd. Oct. 1-?, 187-?. (Looks like Oct. 10, 1876.)............................ **$375+**

Potato slicer, clamp on, high cast iron frame with diamond cutouts, stanchion divides into 2 arms to take shaft for crank, the other end of which is stuck into the potato, the blade is fixed at table level, supposed to slice a potato into one long continuous spiral (although it would fall apart before it could ever get as long as the old advertising picture), advertised for making Saratoga chips or cucumber garnishes, "Saratoga Potato Peeler & Slicer," Goodell Co., Antrim, NH, pat'd. 1870, 1871. .... **$150+**

Potato slicer, iron mounted on wood, potato stuck on "piston" is drawn toward revolving cranked slicing blade by long spring, sold by F. A. Walker, Boston, pat'd. by S. Walker, NYC, June 6, 1865. .... **$150+**

Querne, primitive grinding mill for seeds, grains, etc., used for the same purposes as a mortar & pestle. Small section of half a log, fitted with wooden peg feet, round hollowed out mortar portion with a millstone to fit, high bracket or goalpost frame above has rod or handle to turn the upper small millstone against the lower one, prob. Scottish, though found in 18th C. American kitchens, about 12" to 14"L x 15" to 18"H overall, 18th or very early 19th C.............. **$175-$300**

❖ NOTES ❖

Dr. Samuel Johnson defined it thus: "The **quern** consists of two stones, about a foot and a half in diam.; the lower is a little convex, to which the concavity of the upper must be fitted. In the middle of the upper stone is a round hole, and on one side is a long handle. The grinder [person operating the quern] sheds the corn gradually into the hole with one hand, and works the handle round with the other. The corn slides down the convexity of the lower stone, and, by the motion of the upper, is ground in its passage." As quoted in Webster & Parkes, *An Encyclopædia of Domestic Economy*, 1848 NY edition of English book of 1845.

Raisin seeder, 7 wires set into wood block, upright mushroom knob handle, "The Everett," Boston, 3-1/8"H x 2"W, 1880s to 1890s..................... **$50-$75**

Raisin seeder, also for grapes, tinned cast iron, screw clamps to table, giraffe neck arched frame, side crank moved a sort of saw disc inside that rubbed against the raisins, small hopper with regulating device in side, rubber rollers, "will seed a pound in 5 minutes," embossed "Wet the raisins" cast in side. "Enterprise #36" family size, Enterprise Mfg. Co., 11"H, hopper 2-1/2" x 2-1/8", pat'd. April 2 & Aug. 20, 1895; still being sold into 20th C. The No. 38, twice as expensive and somewhat larger, was for hotels, bakeries, restaurants, etc. .... **$25-$75**

Raisin seeder, black knobby turned wood handle, tinned ferrule, 7 closest tinned wire needles enclosed in a ring with wire, American, 3-1/2"L, business part is 1-1/4"L, late 19th C. Date stamped on end of handle is clearly May 2. Then a date that appears either to be 1888 or 1883 (perhaps it is 1893?) A raisin seeder was pat'd. May 2, 1871, by W.

I-85. Querne. A fairly primitive grinding mill for seeds, spices & grains. 2 round mill stones, from 6" to 10" diam. (these are 6"), the upper one turned by a handle or knob. Wood frame, 17-1/2"H x 13"L x 7"W. Swedish or Danish, 18th or early 19th C. Ex-Keillor Collection. **$200-$300**

Curtiss, Jr., of Wolcottville, CT ... this may be his. Perhaps an extension or an improvement (such as the adding of 5 more wires) of the patent was granted, and a new name "Columbian" given as a deliberate tie-in with the World's Columbian Exposition, of 1893. (May 2 came on a Tuesday in 1882 and 1893, but no raisin seeders were patented then.) Very similar is the "Columbian Raisin Seeder," with knobbed & turned wooden handle, tin ferrule & 12 wires, made in the 1890s. .... **$50-$75**

Raisin seeder, cast iron, 4 legs, levered press has 8 wires, no maker mark, known by collectors as "the headless Horseman," American, approx. 6"L, pat'd. May 7, 1895. .... **$450+**

I-84. Potato, tomato, & vegetable slicers. (1) Also called a "citron slicer" in confectioners' catalogs. "Lightning," japanned cast iron, screw clamps. 4 cutting blades to disc. 10-1/2"L, late 19th C & sold for decades. (2) "Clinton Patent," M. L. & C. M. Clinton, Ithaca NY, pat'd. Oct. 10, 1874. Japanned cast iron. For making Saratoga potato chips up to 1/4" thick, & for apples, cucumbers & cabbage. (3) "Rapid Tomato Slicer." In Valentine Clad, Philadelphia, catalog, c.1870s-1890s. (4) "Enterprise No. 49" vegetable slicer. 16"H x 11" diam. cylinder revolves. Sometimes called the "Boss." Late 19th, early 20th C. (1) $75; (2) $375+; (3) $250+; (4) $375+

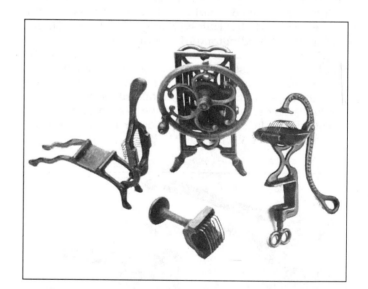

*I-86-A. Raisin seeders. Clockwise from top: (1) Nickeled cast iron, very decorative casting. (Not always plated.) 6-1/2"H x 4"W, 1870s. Appeared in F. A. Walker catalog, perhaps imported like many of their things. (2) "EZY" seeder, pat'd. May 21, 1899. "Scald the raisins" cast into other side. 5"H, clamps to table edge. (3) "Everett," from 1890s, marked "patent applied for." Wire & wood, 3-1/8"L. (4) Cast iron with 8-wire seeder attached to lever. 4 legs. Sometimes collectors call it "the **headless horseman**." Pat'd. May 7, 1895. (2) & (4) Located by the Primitive Man, Bob Cahn, Carmel, NY. (1) & (3) Collection of Meryle Evans. (1) $650+; (2) $375+; (3) $25-$45; (4) $450+*

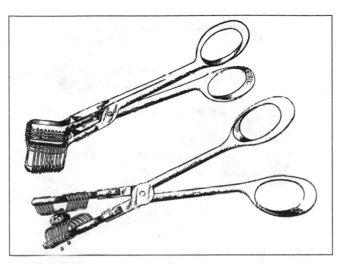

I-86-B. Raisin seeder patent drawing. *Black japanned cast iron & steel wire "Device for Seeding Raisins," pat'd. Jan. 19, 1892, by Joseph W. Calef. Pat. #467,367. Scissor action. 5-3/4"L.* **$135+**

Raisin seeder, cast iron, clamps to table, "EZY Raisin Seeder," with message to "Scald the Raisins," cast into frame, 5"H exclusive of wing nut, pat'd. May 21, 1899. All I can say is, thank heaven for seedless grapes...................................... **$375+**

Raisin seeder, cast iron, ornate, 3 legs, beautifully cast with grapes & leaves, cranked wheel, sits on table. (What is probably a later casting of this seeder was nickel plated. Price now about the same.) This was in *F. A. Walker* dealer catalog, American (?) or maybe French – see quote below. Only 6-1/2"H x 4"W, c.1870. .... **$650+**

❖ NOTES ❖

"A few days ago," wrote an editor in *American Agriculturist*, Nov. 1871, "we saw in a store a little machine which looks like a bit of European workmanship. It had a crank, and when that was turned there were all sorts of motions, evidently intended to accomplish something, but what that was we could not guess. Here was a pretty position for an editor of a household department, not to know at sight what a household implement was for. But we had our compensation. We took possession of the little machine and submitted it to one after another at the offices. At last came Mr. Judd [publisher], who has the quickest eye for 'crinkums' and the sharpest mechanical talent of any one within our knowledge. He turned the machine, looked at it in all ways, then gave up. This ingenious machine is for removing the seeds from raisins, and we have had it figured as an illustration of the wonderful mechanical ingenuity that is at work to facilitate the simple operations of the household. Every housekeeper knows that raisins are all the better for being stoned, and she also knows how tedious is the operation when performed in the ordinary manner. With this machine, the stoning is performed with comparative rapidity. It has so many parts and so many movements, that it is not easy to represent it in a drawing. The machine being fastened to the table by a clamp, the raisins are pushed one by one upon the grating. The crank being turned, the plate above comes down and holds it in place; then another plate, which contains numerous blunt needles which pass through holes as the second plate is pressed down. These needles punch out the seeds of the raisins through the grating, and to make sure that they will be removed, there works underneath this grating a blunt knife, moved by a notch on the moving wheel as it is cranked. As the driving wheel revolves, an arm comes over and pushes the seeded raisin away to make room for another. We are aware that this may seem to be complicated when shown in an engraving, but if one sees the machine in operation it appears simple enough." Thanks, I think I'll pit prunes instead.

Raisin seeder, cast iron, painted black, screw clamps to table, spring tension lever action, levered part has 5 rows of prickers, then there's a moving plate with 5 slots through which prickers fit, then a plate with oval opening with one divider across short axis, finally a fixed flat plate against which prickers hit, no mark, American, about 5"H x 6-3/4"L handle, "patent applied for" late 19th C. .... **$150+**

❖ RECIPE ❖

Indian Chutney – *For this boil 1-1/2 dozen sour apples, peeled, cored and chopped, in 3 pints of cider vinegar, adding a pound of stoned and chopped raisins, 1 pound light brown sugar, 1 tablespoon salt, 1/4 pound finely chopped ginger root, 1/4 pound chopped onions, chopped garlic clove, 1/2 pound mustard seed that has been heated in oven, and either a small fiery pepper chopped, or a shake or two of cayenne. Cook until apple is soft, stirring constantly." The Housewife, Nov. 1909.*

I-87. Raisin seeders. *Cast iron, nickeled or galvanized, screw clamps.* **(L)** *"**Enterprise No.36**," Philadelphia. Embossed "Wet the raisins" along upright frame. Rubber roller inside. Pat'd. April 2, 1895. A later patent seen on them is Aug. 20, 1895. 11"H. The No. 38 was for bakers & hotels; this for family use.* **(R)** *"**X-Ray**" seeder, composed of 38 different parts put together as true and perfect as a watch. The raison d'etre for so many parts was to make it possible to replace one part if broke, without having to buy a new one. This was the consumer ethic 100 years ago and more, before "you break it, you pitch it" wastefulness took hold. 1890s.* **(L) $25-$45; (R) $75+**

Raisin seeder, cast iron, wire & rubber, screw clamps to table, not so elegant as the Enterprise, "Lightning," American, 7-1/4"H, pat'd. 1895 & March 28, 1898. .... **$25+**

Raisin seeder, cast iron with "38 different parts," screw clamps to & arches over table, for a tray & a tumbler to fit underneath, long crank handle, X-Ray Raisin Seeder Co., American, 1880s. .... **$75+**

❖ NOTES ❖

The Seeder with X-Ray Eyes – A flyer states "The Seeder That Seeds! Finds Every Seed and Removes It! This is a model machine, composed of 38 different parts put together as true and perfect as a watch, not a single part can possibly get out of order. It will seed raisins as fast as you can drop them into the hopper and turn the crank. When we say seed, we mean it will remove every single seed! It will simply perforate the raisin and not cut it into shreds or mutilate it. Every seed will come out dry and without the slightest waste. Talk about perfection – this machine is the very acme of it. ... We will replace any defective part free of charge any time within five years!" The original price was a dollar.

Raisin seeder, iron, "The Gem," Auburn, ME, 1895 patent. (Another one, slightly lower in value, is marked "Improved Gem.") **$50**

Reamers – See: Juicers

Rutabaga slicer, or root vegetable & potato slicer, iron & brass on round wooden base, a sort of brace bit tool, blade makes "French fry" slices, or Saratoga slices, no mark, American (?), 18-1/2"H, base is 9" diam. and-5/8" thick, c.1870s (?). .... **$250+**

Sausage filler, japanned cast iron, like a curved elbow pipe with hopper & very long down-curved lever & presser at top, has long leg in back to bolt to table, short crosspiece for bolting in front, filling funnel fitted on lower end, one of three 1st pat'd. by J. G. Perry, Kingston, RI, in 1859, 1860 and 1863, mfd. by Peck, Stow & Wilcox, Southington, CT, 1890s. .... **$150+**

Sausage fillers – See also: Meat grinders

Sausage grinder, cast iron, "O. V. B." or "Our Very Best," Hibbard, Spencer, Bartlett & Co., #8, c.1890s-1910s. **$20**

Sausage grinder, cast iron, "Keen Kutter #112," Simmons Hardware, 20th C. **$35**

Sausage grinder, cast iron double cylinder type, cranked, mfd. by Russell & Erwin, New Britain, CT, mid to late 19th C. .... **$150+**

Sausage grinder, homemade & primitive, very powerful looking, wooden box with hand-forged hook latch, hinges unfortunately replaced by someone (who may have been using it right up into the 1980s) with cheapo 1950s kitchen cabinet hinges in "Colonial" hammered surface. Lift-out wooden drum inside has iron pins set in it sort of spiraling around it, on pencil marked intersections carefully drawn by maker, American, 16-1/2"L x 8" diam., early 19th C. .... **$175+**

Sausage grinder & stuffer, wood & wrought iron, tin gun, on platform meant to bridge 2 chairs, saw horses or tables; water pump-like lever works up & down to stuff casings fitted onto gun, American, 19th C. **$100**

Sausage stuffer or gun, mostly wood with tin gun & iron bolts holding gun together, wooden frame

I-88. Mechanical sausage stuffers. Top: "Stow's Patent," Russell & Erwin Mfg. Lever action in 2 sizes, for butchers or families. Pat'd. July 6, 1858 by O. W. Stow, Plantsville, CT. Lower (L) "Hale Meat Cutter" and stuffer, also R & E and in their 1865 catalog, and later in a c.1900 catalog! Grinding drums lift out. Three sizes: 5", 6", & 7-1/2" cylinders. Couldn't find Hale in Patent Index. (R) "Sausage meat cutter," from American Home Cook Book, 1854. There were several patents previous to 1854; I didn't look them up. You know how I feel about meat. Top: $200+; (L) $150+; (R) $150+

pegged, on bench frame, long lever makes it look like a sculpture of an elephant, according to dealer Lenny Kislin it was made on the Yantz Farm, Red Hook, NY, 26-1/2"H x 37-1/2"L, 19th C. With this one you pay for sculpture. **$350**

Sausage stuffer, all wood, including long box & turned screw which is cranked & slowly pushes ground sausage out end, sliding lid entire length of box for cleaning, handmade, prob. PA, 25"L x 5-3/4" square, c.1840s to 50s. **$150**

Sausage stuffer or gun, tin cylinder with strap handle & small strap loop near gun end, long snout, perforations in flat end around where snout or spout is soldered, turned wooden foller or pusher, American, about 15"L exclusive of foller, c.1850s-60s. A Jan. 1850 article in *American Agriculturist* told how to make an almost identical "sausage cutter," and said the meat "is made finer or coarser according to the rapidity with which it is fed" into the hopper... **$100**

Sausage grinder, iron, hangs on wall, 27"L, pat'd. 1885. .... **$75**

Sausage grinder, all wood, except for iron nails or spikes on revolving cranked drum inside, American, mid 19th C. **$165**

Sausage grinder & stuffer, cast iron, 2 hinged parts, catch on side holds top on, 2 cutting blades & crank handle, bolts to table surface, needs funnel or gun fitted to end, no mark except "12," American, 7-5/8"L exclusive of crank handle, c.3rd quarter 19th C. .... **$130+**

Sausage grinder & stuffer, screw clamp, tinned iron, Enterprise #38, pat'd. 1888. .... **$65**

Sausage stuffer, "Hubbard," 6 qt. capacity. **$50**

Sausage stuffer, cast iron, mounted to plank, cranked, "Wagner Stuffer No. 3," Salem Tool Co., Salem, OR, mfd. c.1900 from 1859 patent. Salem also mfd. meat presses, ham pumps & brine guns. **$75**

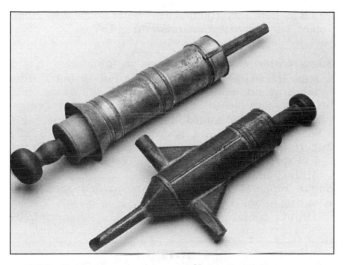

I-89. Sausage guns or stuffers. Pieced tin, wood plungers. Sausage casings (scraped intestines, yuck) fit over nozzle ends. Top (L) 29-1/2"L; takes different casing/funnel sizes. Lower (R) is 19-1/2"L. 1870s-80s. Collection of Meryle Evans. **$70-$100**

Sausage stuffer, commercial size, cast iron, hand cranked, hinged top, "Wagner Stuffer" cast in body, brass plate reads "Silver Mfg. Co.," "Salem, ORE.," 36"L, prob. the J. Wagner (Pittsburgh, PA) patent of March 29, 1859. .... **$250**

Sausage stuffer, tin & cast iron, spring loaded lever action, mounts to tabletop, shaped sort of like an urn, "Angers Perfect No. 1 Filler," Sargent & Co., late 19th C. **$75**

Sausage stuffer, tin cone with cast iron base, wooden plunger, American (?), c.1880s. .... **$70-$100**

Sausage stuffer, tin, hard maple plunger. Different size casing funnels attached by bayonet mount at end, needed 2 people or worked plunger against belly, American, each part 18"L, 19th C. **$100**

Sausage stuffer, tin & wood, hand cranked, screw clamps to table, "P. S. & W. Co., No. 112," mfd. by Peck, Stow & Wilcox Co., Southington, CT, 19th C. An 1890s brochure from P, S & W gives only one No. 112 "meat cutter and stuffer," that pat'd. by A. W. Hale, New Britain, CT, on March 15, 1859. It's japanned cast iron, works horizontally, has detachable tin stuffing tube, feeds into top & has lift-out cast iron grinding drum with swirled "Blades." Dover Stamping Co. offered Hale's machine in a 1869 catalog. Tin version a bit later. **$150**

Sausage stuffer, handmade wooden box, sliding cover, wooden works inside too, no metal, 30"L, 19th C. **$100**

Sausage stuffer, pieced tin cylinder, wood foller, casings fit over muzzle end, American, 21"L, late 19th C. **$70**

Sausage stuffer, fruit & lard press, japanned & decoratively stenciled heavy tin (one design being a basket of flowers), with lid, cast iron legs and vertical center threaded rod – with beveled gears & screw, came with removable corrugated spout or nozzle, perforated disc, interior perforated canister, # 25, Enterprise Mfg. Co., Phila., table top, canisters depicted as 4 qt. capacity, c. 16" to 18"H, pat'd. July 11, 1876, still selling early 20th C. Sizes of japanned presses – #5 = 2 qt. rack; #15 = 2 qt. screw; #25 = 4 qt. screw; #31 = 6 qt. screw; #35 - 8 qt. screw. Sizes of tinned presses – #10 = 2 qt. rack; #20 = 2 qt. screw; #30 = 4 qt. screw; #40 = 8 qt. screw. "Rack" refers to cranked rack mechanism, also on central threaded shaft... **$75+**

Shark's tooth, petrified, dark slatey brown, roughly triangular in shape, with tiny saw-tooth ridge of teeth, works perfectly to cut things up, quite easily recognizable as a naturally occurring, ad hoc saw, which works on root vegetables (and probably meat, which I don't eat, so don't know). About 3" to 5"L, 14,000,000 years old....................................... **$45**

Shredders – See: Graters

Slaw cutters – See: Cabbage cutters

Slicer for root vegetables or potatoes, japanned cast iron, horizontal action, cranked, screw clamps, choice of 4 cutting blades to fit on end, no mark, American, 10-1/2"L, c.1870s to 1890s. **$150**

Spice boat or mill – See: Herb boat or grinder

❖ RECIPE ❖

To make Tomato Ketchup – For half a gallon take a gallon of skinned tomatoes, four table spoonfuls of salt, four of black pepper, half a spoonful of alspice, eight pods of red pepper, three table spoonfuls of mustard; grind them finely, and simmer them slowly in sharp vinegar, in a pewter basin, three or four hours, strain through a wire sieve, and bottle it closely. Those who like the article may add, after the ingredients are somewhat cool, two table spoonfuls of the juice of garlic." The Farmers' Cabinet, Phila., Oct. 15, 1836.

Spice mill, japanned & stencilled cast iron, wall-mounted side mill with one flat side, cup-like hopper above, iron cup catches grounds below, crank in middle. No. 00, Enterprise Mfg. Co., c.1890s. . **$85+**

Spice mill, sheet iron, curvy hourglass shape with pronounced waist, flat top, large-knobbed crank, screw clamps to table, English (?) or American, 11"H, late 18th, early 19th C. .... **$650+**

Spice mills – See also: Pepper mills.

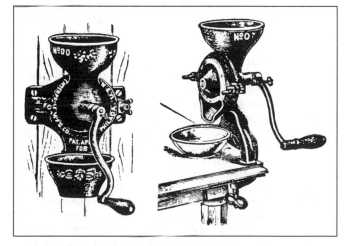

I-90. Spice mills. "Enterprise," No. OO (at left) & No. O. Decoratively painted cast iron; one is for wall, one screw clamps. c.1898. **$85+; $60+**

I-91. Strawberry huller & pinfeather picker.
"Nip-It," Windsor Stephens & Co., Waltham, MA, pat'd. Dec. 18, 1906. Nickeled spring steel. "By its use one avoids stained fingers, seeds under fingernails, crushed fruit." **$5-$8**

Spice, salt & pepper containers – See Chapter VII (Containers)

Strawberry huller, brass (maybe once nickeled), 1890s. **$10**

Strawberry huller, like tweezers, made from a fold of spring steel, narrows toward tips then opens into concave round discs with centers cut out, mfd. by A. S. Bunker, Lawrence, MA, c.1877. .... **$5-$10**

Strawberry huller, or pin feather picker, tinned spring steel pincher, "Nip-It," American, 1-1/4"L x 7/8"W, pat'd. Dec. 18, 1906. .... **$5-$8**

Strawberry huller, & pin feather puller, inch wide flat piece of nickel plated spring steel, bent to hairpin curve, uses pinching action, mounted on color printed cardboard with strawberry design, "Spee-Dee," mfd. by Kenberry, American, c.1890s-1910s. .... **$5-$8**

Strawberry huller, spring steel, stamped with strawberry design, marked "Berry Huller," American, about 2"L, c.1890s-1910s. .... **$5-$8**

❖ NOTES ❖

In the Good Old Summertime – "A housekeeper's work lies in the house. If she has a large family, the customary three meals take about all of her time, and her daily and weekly round of work takes her full time and strength, so that she has as little inclination as opportunity to go roaming abroad for exercise. Last summer, for the second time in eight years, I had my cook-stove in a shanty, or rough 'lean-to' shed, adjoining the house. How can I ever again be contented to spend a summer with the family cook-stove in a walled-up kitchen, being myself the family cook?

"No house is worth the name of home which has nowhere about it a shady porch or airy shed where a housekeeper or a hired girl can sit down in cool comfort, to shell the peas, hull the strawberries, or peel the potatoes, where she can set her ironing table, and wash her dishes without foregoing fresh breezes, and near neighborhood to grass and vines. Thoreau, who had a contempt for such treasures as most mortals love to lay up here below, observed that when a man had compassed his desire and got him a house, it seemed after all to be the house that had got him. So it is with many women – their houses keep them quite as

much as they keep the houses." *Faith Rochester, "Home Topics," American Agriculturist,* June 1876.

Sugar cutter, cast iron, clamps to table edge, has 2 legs, levered action, marked "Bartlett & Son," Bristol, England, about 9"L, late 19th C. **$65**

Sugar nippers, beautifully tooled steel, floriate design, turned knuckle guard, 9-3/4"L, early 19th or poss. late 18th C. .... **$225+**

Sugar nippers, cast steel, concentric rings around pin, leaf spring good, ball ends on handles, English, early 19th C. .... **$150+**

Sugar nippers, hand-held, lathe-turned steel, leaf spring intact, English (?), 7-1/2"L, late 18th or early 19th C. .... **$125+**

❖ NOTES ❖

"**Case-hardening of Iron**, is a superficial conversion of that metal into steel, by a cementation of it with vegetable or animal coals. This operation is usually performed on small pieces of iron, worked into tools and instruments, by putting them together with the cement, into an iron box, which is closely shut, and exposed to a red heat for several hours. Thus, the surface of the iron, to a certain depth, is converted into steel, to which a proper degree of hardness may be given, by a sudden immersion of the heated pieces into a cold liquid." Anthony Florian Madinzer Willich, *The*

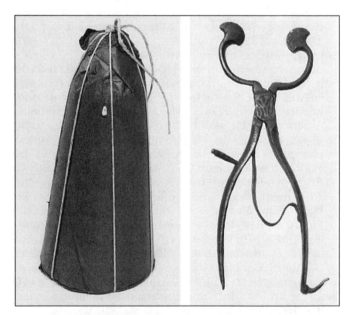

I-92. Sugar cone & sugar nippers. (L) Conical molded cake of granulated sugar, wrapped in blue paper & tied, as customary for maybe centuries in Europe, & in US in 18th & early 19th C. This one is from Belgium, but form is the same. About 10"H x 4-3/4" diam. Photo courtesy National Museum of American History, Smithsonian Institution. The blue paper wrapped around sugar loafs was re-used to dye small linens a medium indigo blue. *(R)* Prettiest nippers I ever did see. Steel, cut design at pivot, leaf spring, very stylized form. 8-13/16"L. Stock of Lauri & Bill Sweetman, Laubill Antiques, Golfstown, NH. **$65+; $175+**

Domestic Encyclopedia; or A Dictionary of Facts & Useful Knowledge, 1st American edition, Philadelphia: W. Y. Birch & A. Small, 1803-04.

•   •   •

Cutting Up Sugar – Sugar nippers were necessary because sugar came in hard molded cones, with a heavy string or cord up through the long axis like a wick, but there so that the sugar could be conveniently hung up, always wrapped in blue paper. The cones were hard and after chunks were cut or hacked off for the table, the nippers were needed to reduce the size of the pieces. I've never understood why they didn't just grate the sugar. Conical sugar molds of pottery or wood were used by pouring hot sugar syrup into them and cooling until solid. They range from about 8"H to 16"H. These molds are very rare, especially those with some intaglio decoration inside to make a pattern on the cone. The blue paper, by the way, was recycled by soaking to get the indigo color as a dye for cloth. And for laundry blueing? **"Soda for Washing.** – We have been requested by a correspondent, to publish the recipe for washing with Sub-carbonate of Soda. To five gallons of water add a pint and a half of soft soap and two ounces soda. Put the clothes (after soaking over night) into the mixture when at boiling heat, rubbing the parts most soiled with soap. Boil them one hour – drain – rub, and rinse them in warm water, after being put into indigo water, they are fit for drying. Half the soap and more than half the labor is saved by washing in this manner." *Silk Culturist*, as quoted in *The Farmers' Cabinet*, Philadelphia, Oct. 15, 1836.

•   •   •

Loaf or Broken Sugar – A bill of sale from Daniel E. Bailey, a grocer of Lynchburg, VA, dated 1839, lists two types of sugar sold to John G. Merme (?). "Loaf sugar" and "Broken sugar," the latter cost half as much. (The units of each are illegible, but probably pounds). Loaf was 20¢ a pound, and broken it was only 11¢ a pound. For cooking, the broken would have been more convenient by far; in fact, you wonder why anyone bought a whole loaf if it weren't necessary and was so much harder to use. Perhaps the fear of adulteration (intentional or insect-ional) made people want the Loaf. Other things on that interesting bill included 20 yards of "counterpane checks" for $5, 7 yards of "Blue Jeans" for $1.40, a pair of "Side Combs" for 6¢, and 6 pounds of coffee for 90¢.

Sugar nippers, or cutters, for store counter, grain painted wood box base, double arched iron frame or blade guard & wrought steel blade with decorative finial, turned knob for drawer underneath, turned handle for cutter's lever. Punctured tin plate to sift sugar before it fell into drawer, no mark, American, 4-1/2"H x 11-5/8"L x 11-1/8"W, mid 19th C. **$400**

Sugar nippers, steel, marked "P R," with tiny long-handled posnet punch mark between the initials, English or American, 8-1/4"L, 18th or early 19th C. Offered for sale by Clara Jean Davis, and as she says, "This is the first pair I've had that were signed, and I think that's rare." Very rare, and accounts for value I have put on them. .... **$175+**

Sugar nippers, steel, mounted on wooden base, American or English, 10"L, early 19th C. **$125**

Sugar nippers, steel, not finely polished, very stylized cut design at pivot, not the usual flat leaf spring but instead a pronounced S curved spring inside, American (?), 8-13/16"L, early 19th C. **$175**

❖ RECIPES ❖

Tomato Jam *– Remove all the seeds, pull off the skins, and boil the fruit with a pound of sugar for every pound. To every pound of tomato allow two lemons, rind and pulp, well boiled."*

Apple Jam *– Weigh equal quantities of brown sugar and good sour apples. Pare and core them, and chop them fine. Make a syrup of the sugar, and clarify it very thoroughly; then add the apples, the grated peel of two or three lemons, and a few pieces of white ginger. Boil it until the apple looks clear and yellow. This resembles foreign sweetmeats. The ginger is essential to its peculiar excellence."* Mrs. Cornelius, The Young Housekeepers Friend, or, A Guide to Domestic Economy & Comfort, *Boston & NY: 1846.*

Sugar nippers, steel, very nice lathe turning around pin pivot & handles, finger guard pin stuck at right angles to one handle, catch or keeper as well as leaf spring intact, English (?), 8-1/2"L, late 18th C. **Reduced value.** – The leaf spring is sometimes broken off, and often the keeper is missing. (The keeper is a catch like those found on small pruning clippers we use in the garden). .... **$125+**

Sugar nippers, tooled steel, ivory handle with brass ferrule, screwed to shaped wooden base, English (?), early 19th C. **$300**

Sugar nippers, heavy wrought iron, mounted on wood, brass ferrule and unusual wooden handle, English (?), early 19th C. **$150**

Sugar nippers, wrought iron, finely finished, steel leaf spring, finger guard peg, catch intact, nice curve to little gingko leaf-shaped blades, American (?), 8-3/4"L, late 18th or early 19th C. **$175**

Sugar nippers, wrought iron, hand held, extremely simple, leaf spring still seems fine, but I wouldn't try it out, American, 9-1/2"L, 19th C. **$100**

Sugar nippers, wrought iron, large, turned brass stanchion, base & handle of fruitwood or chestnut, English, early 19th C. **$250**

I-93. Sugar cone cutter. *For country store. Grain-painted wood box, iron arched frame or blade guard & blade. Turned wood knob & handle. Hand-punched tin plate for sifting sugar before going in drawer. Identified & located by The Primitive Man, Bob Cahn, Carmel, NY. Courtesy Mike & Sunny Kolba Collection.* **$400+**

Sugar nippers, wrought iron, not steel, very slender & sculptural, almost insect-like in appearance, American, 11"L, 18th C. **Be Careful of Old Iron.** – This has the leaf spring between the handles, but I'd never dare to try it. PLEASE PLEASE PLEASE when you examine old wrought iron pieces, don't "try them out" because all tensile strength and springiness may have been lost. And while you're at it, be very careful of cast iron, as it is easily broken under certain conditions. **$150**

Toffee ax or hatchet & hammer, cast iron, "For Toffee" cast into surface, English, 7-3/8"L, 19th C. **$50**

Tomato knife, for slicing, steel blade rather like most vegetable knives, but with tip round & wider than blade, turned wood handle, small brass bolster, marked "I*X*L Geo. Wolstenholm & Son" on blade, & chef's cap trademark containing words "Firth Stainless," "Sheffield, England," 7-1/2"L, Reg. # 747,488, July 18, 1929. .... **$15**

Tomato knife, or tomato slicer, sort of a small cleaver like tool, with turned wooden handle, stainless steel blade much shorter than other one but with even bigger round end, marked "E-B Stainless," Sheffield, England, Reg. # 809,290. .... **$15**

Tomato peeler, wood handle, scoop-like steel blade, "Ontario" stamped on handle, 20th C. **$10**

❖ RECIPE ❖

Tomato Figs – *Use thoroughly ripe tomatoes; pour boiling water over them to remove the skin; weigh them; place them in a stone jar, with an equal quantity of good sugar. Let them stand two days; then pour off the syrup; boil and skim it until no scum rises. Pour it over the tomatoes; let it stand two days; boil, and skim again. After repeating this process for the third time, they are fit to dry, if the weather suits; if not, keep them in the syrup. They will dry in a week. Pack in boxes lined with white paper, putting powdered sugar between the layers of fruit. Should any syrup remain, it may be used for making common marmalade, or for sweetening pies."* Mrs. A. P. Hill, Mrs. Hill's New Family Receipt Book, *NY: 1870.*

Tomato slicer, cast iron, round base screws to tabletop, vertical shaft with crank on top. Tomato is put into cylindrical holder with 3/8" horizontal slots, into which fit the 6 steel blades that you crank through the holder. Cuts 7 slices. "Rapid," sold by V. Clad & Sons, Philadelphia, about 9"H, early 20th C. (See picture I-84.)................................. **$350**

Tomato slicer, stainless steel rectangular frame with sharp narrow blades, with wooden 2-tone red & cream handle at one end, "Sky-line Miracle Tomato Slicer," No. 96. Also for cucumbers, eggs, carrots, cheese & butter. But oh! A tomato sandwich with mayo & fresh bread? English, mid 20th C. **$10**

Vegetable chopper, long 1/4" plywood box base, midway is bent basswood arch with slot the full length of it into which fits a carbon steel knife, looks very European, marked only "MARTA" which sounds Scandinavian, but Pinto's *Treen* claims this is English, 12-3/4"L, 20th C. **$125**

Vegetable chopper, slicer, dicer, wedger, makes 700 French fries in one minute ... you guessed it: a "Veg-

O-Matic" set, in original box with booklet, as sold on TV by Ron Popeil, beginning in Nov. 1958 (?) (Not clear if "Chop-O-Matic" was product sold that early.) A "food preparer." Plastic moderne V-8 design (V-8 in the sense of car design: a big Chevrolet-like chevron V on top) stand with room under for bowl, two upright runners or tracks for two-hand upper pusher, push food against variety of inserted cutting blades of stainless steel. Pat. #3,216,423; Chicago, IL: Ronco Teleproducts, c.1958-1963?............ **$10+**

Vegetable cutters – See also: Julienne cutter

Vegetable cutter, hammered sheet iron, fish-shaped footed base with hinged iron cutter blade in abstract form of animal's head, from India, 10-3/4"L, 19th C. type, but almost certainly mid 20th C. I bought this, hesitant a bit because of feeling it wasn't right, as a 19th C. homemade American cutting tool. Found picture of one in Pease Binder's *Magic Symbols of the World* on page 97, enabling identification. **$50**

Vegetable cutter, tin, wood paddle-shaped frame, slides back & forth, corrugated blade to cut fluted chips of root vegetables, American, 12"L, early 20th C... **$35**

Vegetable cutter, corrugated tin strip with hourglass wire handle, used to make fancy slices in root vegetables or potatoes, for soups, etc., American, small size, c.1900 to early 20th C. **$20**

Vegetable cutters, graduated set of tapered cylindrical conical cutters, in hinged tin box with conical lid, used for making decorative shapes of sliced root vegetables, there should be about 15 cutters in the box, the smallest possibly small enough to stone olives (as an early ad stated), though I'd hate to try. Seen in *F. A. Walker* catalog, Boston, also *Harrod's Stores* catalog, London – they're either American, or European, imports from 1870s. About 8"H, last quarter 19th C, poss. more recently than that. "A set of vegetable cutters will add much to the beauty of many a dish. Should be made of best tin. Boxes of graded cutters may be had. Use for stamping out vegetables, forced meat, jellies and also are valuable for coring apples and other fruit and stoning olives." Maria Parloa, *Kitchen Companion, Boston: Estes & Lauriat*, 1887. 1895 *Harrod's* catalog shows set with fancy cutters, tin crimped to form crested medallions or heraldic scrolly shapes. They could be ordered plain or fancy; the plain coming 9, 12, & 15 cutters to the case; the fancy, 4, 6, & 9 to the case................................... **$55**

Vegetable cutters, pieced tin, sort of like cookie cutters, in such designs as a shamrock, snowflake, etc., deep cutting edge, came in 20 styles, in *F. A. Walker* catalog, French (?), only about 3/4" to c. 1-1/2" across, so you are unlikely to think they're cookie cutters, c.1880s to 1890s............................... **$50**

❖ NOTES ❖

Garnishing – The art of garnishing dishes is the art of ornamenting them, and making them look elegant, and thus satisfying the eye as well as the palate. Various materials are used for this purpose. Among the most popular are cocks' combs, plovers, and hens' eggs boiled hard, prawns and small crayfish, button mushrooms glazed, stamped pieces of vegetables such as carrot, turnip, parsnip, beet root, and truffles, stoned olives, gherkins, fried croutons of bread, aspic jelly, horse radish, cut lemon and parsley. Everything depends on the artistic arrangement of the ornamentation, determined by the taste of the garnisher. Where the taste has been cultivated, or where there is a natural faculty for decoration, the task of garnishing effectively is an easy one." Henry Scammel, *Treasure House*, 1891.

Vegetable & fruit parer, smooth cast iron, horizontal lathe type, with wheel with interior gear teeth at one end, longish sharp knitting needle-like adjustable spear held & pushed fruit or veggie against revolving paring fork, (Tom Wiggins says that when doing potatoes, it's just the opposite). According to contempory ads does apples, pears, quinces, potatoes, even carrots, "The Victor," mfd. by Goodell Co., Antrim, NH, pat'd. Jan. 5, 1885. .... **$100**

Vegetable & fruit press, also colander, tinned steel "saucepan" with round bottom, perforated 3/4 of way up, to be set into heavy bent rod screw clamp frame, blade inside turned by center crank, mashing food against holes, "McCoy's Improved," mfd. by Dilver Mfg. Co., St. Paul, MN, c.1911. A very similar one made by Utility Sales Co., Davenport, IA, was advertised in 1911; it differed because only the bottom of pan is perforated, & bottom is flatter. **$25**

Vegetable garnish cutter, metal, with original instructions & envelope, "Acme," American, 20th C..... **$15**

Vegetable grater – See: Graters

Vegetable knife, almost like regular carbon steel knife with turned wooden handle, except blade not pointed, but has an attached very small concave round blade to scoop out potato eyes & "defective places from all vegetables designed for the table" (as opposed to livestock), Gilbert & Durand's Patent, F. Durand, Derby, CT, pat'd. Aug. 16, 1870 by F. Durand & W. E. Gilbert.................................... **$15**

Vegetable & nut chopper, glass jar with paneled sides, tin lid fitted with spring action plunger above, which gave the 4 blades an extra bounce, inch thick wooden disc inside jar, marked The Ernestreich Co. (possibly meant to be Ernest Reich), Chicago, IL, 10-1/2"H x 4-1/4" diam., c.1910 to 1920. See also: Nutgrinders. **$15**

I-94-A. Vegetable juicer? or Picasso sculpture! *Cast iron, embossed on the back "Minima Tutti Frutti," and "132." It is bolted to a table, and the fruit or vegetables fed into it while the screw is cranked. Body 11"L, with crank, about 19"L. Was bought by seller in Germany, but may be Italian. Information & photo courtesy Elizabeth Morrison, Houston, TX; eBay user name & email is niebo7@aol.com. Ms. Morrison travels to Germany & Poland a few times a year. Value:* **$150+**

I-94-B. Vegetable & fruit slicer, *for creating "various beautiful and attractive designs ... to make them tempting and attractive. Lattice Potatoes are exquisite garnishes; bananas sliced in these charming patterns make a most excellent dessert."* Grasgreen & Ritzinger *catalog,* c.1906-1907. **$7-$12**

❖ **RECIPE** ❖

Walnut Ketchup – *Boil or simmer a gallon of the expressed juice of walnuts when they are tender, and skim it well; add 2 pounds of anchovies, 2 pounds shalots, 1 ounce cloves, 1 ounce mace, 1 ounce pepper, 1 clove garlic. Let all simmer until the shalots sink. Put the liquor in a pan till cold, bottle and divide the spices to each."* Anthony Florian Willich, The Domestic Encyclopedia, *Philadelphia: A. Small, 1821.*

Vegetable or slaw slicer, white porcelain (china) table that slides in wooden frame, 2 steel blades, beautiful handle tips protrude from side, gorgeous elegant piece, prob. European, 14-1/2"L x 5-1/4"W, early 20th C, poss. late 19th C. See also Cabbage slicers. **$125**

Vegetable parer, aluminum frame with steel blade, "De Vault Peeler," mfd. by W. R. Feemster Co., Inc., Los Angeles - Chicago, 3"W, 1935 patent #1,990,127.. **$15**

Vegetable parer, white plastic, comes apart, one steel blade cores apples & tomatoes, other blade pares, "Item No. 990," "Made in U. S. A.," 7"L, "U.S. and World Pat's Pend." 1940s or 1950s. **$5**

Vegetable parer, corer & slicer combined, nickeled steel, wood handle set at a 45 degree angle to bullet-shaped blade, "Universal," Landers, Frary & Clark, c.1900.. **$15**

Vegetable scraper, corn grater & fish scaler combined, nickel-plated iron, turned wood handle, looks like small gardening or mason's tool, with 4 different edges: sharp beveled blade, sharp corrugated edge, comb-like edge with 6 long fork tine teeth, & curved sharp edge, sold by *Montgomery Ward,* pat'd. 1906, c.1910 catalog. Combination tools are a big collector favorite, and often bring a lot of $$$. .... **$15+**

Vegetable slicer, japanned cast iron & tin, freestanding tabletop, with encased horizontal revolving cylinder, side crank, does all kinds of vegetables, "Enterprise #49," Enterprise Mfg. Co., 16"H, cylinder is 11" diam., late 19th C. .... **$115+**

Vegetable slicer, steel, with large wood handle & press bar, American, pat'd. 1900. .... **$65**

Vegetable slicer, tin, counter top, "Morris," 1890s-1910s. **$15**

Vegetable slicer, turned wood handle, twisted wire, works like kraut slicer, "A & J Pat'd," Binghamton, NY, 16"L, c.1930s. **$15**

Vegetable slicer, deep fluted tinned blade with wire handle, hand-operated, not mechanical, American, c. 1900-1920. .... **$10**

Vegetable slicer, long wooden slide frame, steel blades, feed block of wood, hanging hole at end, "The Home Vegetable Slicer," Catawissa Specialty Mfg. Co., pat'd. 1898. Collector Dorcas Luecke copied out original paper label, reading in part: "For slicing potatoes and similar vegetables place same in front of feed block, grip handle firmly and shove through without stopping. For cabbage head pieces place the slicer over a receptacle with the end abutting against the wall or other support and [hold] cabbage in place with the hand. Avoid hot water, rinse thoroughly, and wipe knives dry. In case of accident to knives we furnish new ones at 5 cents. ... The slices being corrugated cook more evenly and in less time than if they were plain. Also slices apples for canning. Is indispensible for slicing onions, cucumbers, radishes and the toothsome raw fry and Saratoga chips. A great many dishes can be prepared with it. We claim that this is the most efficient and satisfactory vegetable slicer on the market. It is neat and convenient to handle, it is easily and quickly cleaned and ... always ready for use." **$65**

Vegetable slicer, wood frame, box for veggies slides, 6 blades with teeth, "Home Vegetable Slicer," Catawissa Specialty Mfg., Catawissa, PA, 20-1/2"L x 3-1/2"W, pat'd. Feb. 22, 1896. .... **$75+**

Vegetable slicer, zinc plated iron with wooden handle, screw clamps to table, comes apart by unscrewing halves, "Universal Vegetable Slicer," mfd. by Landers, Frary & Clark, New Britain, CT, approx. 12"H exclusive of screw, c.1890s-1910s. .... **$75+**

Vegetable slicers – See also: Julienne cutter

Watermelon plugger, iron gouging tool, 19th C (?). Used to cut out a sample plug to see if the inside was red and sweet. If not, you just stuck the plug back in. My father used one when we lived on a farm in Toledo. (Along the same line was our practice of testing corn for ripeness by pulling down a bit of husk. If it needed more time, you crumbled some pollen-bearing silk from a nearby stalk and dusted it over the silk of the husk you opened and closed it back up.) **$15**

Whatzit, tool steel blades, cast iron handle, slightly tapered blades, hinged with pin, comes apart at hinge like poultry scissors, stamped "Disston," Phila., 11"L, blades 2-7/16"W, pat'd. Oct. 16, 1877. .... **$55**

Whatzit cutting wheel, interesting handforged iron piece like a pizza cutter, which it may be; rattail handle attaches to wheel at right angle, point of axle has star shape outlined in dots punched into iron, around rim are what may be maker's name or name of place [pizza parlor?], looks like "ALBERTOS A CASIANO" or "CASIMO" or "CASA DO CASIMO," American, wheel 4-3/8" diam., dated 1975. .... **$25**

Whatzit grater, or? ... we first thought they were graters, the ones we saw at a PA & a VA flea market. Rough punctured tin. The third one solved the mystery. It too was a cylinder with torpedo-pointed ends, rectangular strap or bracket handle in middle, punched from inside before soldering to create pattern of closely-spaced bumps on outside, no holes. Dealer Ed Wilson, at Brimfield flea market, fall '87, had 3rd one plus a little wire & tin Y-shaped tool. Theirs was partly made of a Diet Pepsi can. They found out what the "grater" was at a Boston Pops concert when they saw it being played, during a reggae piece, like a washboard; It's a musical instrument! Jamaican or Bermudan or West Indian, 18-1/2"L x 2-1/2" diam., mid 20th C. **$15**

Wheat berry mill, green enameled steel box with drawer, partly nickel plated, wheat berries fed into hopper, fine to coarse settings, crank black wood knob, bracket on back, but wall half of bracket usually missing. "Wheat Krinkler," mfd. by The Wheat Krinkler Corp., Columbus, OH, 8-1/4"H x 6-1/4"W x 2-3/4" diam., c.1930s. **$50**

FOR MORE INFORMATION:

Apple Parers

You may write for more information concerning particular parers, as well as the collector club, many of whose members also collect other crank & gear kitchen gadgets and also tools. Please always enclose an SASE (self-addressed stamped envelope, preferably a #10 or business size.)

John Lambert
236 S. Main St.
Mt. Vernon, OH 43050
E-mail: zlambert@yahoo.com

James Ennenga
1621 N. 85th St.
Omaha, NE 68114
E-mail: jrennenga@ntown.net

Don Thornton
Thornton House
POB 57
Moss Beach, CA 94038
Web site: www.thorntonhouse.com/publishing.html

You can also order Don's book on *Apple Parers*, or the two on *Eggbeaters*, or other books offered by Thornton House (formerly Off-Beat Books).

Nutmeg Graters

Teri Dziadul, an antique dealer and collector since the 1960s, specializes in early kitchen accessories and hearth cooking tools. She and her husband Joe also have long had an active interest in old patented nutmeg graters, which she still offers for sale. (Joe Dziadul specializes in, and would like to hear about, unusual old tools, and golf & tennis antiques, at the same address.) To get her annual Christmas list of wonderful old kitchen & Christmas things, send a double-stamped SASE to:

Teri Dziadul
6 S. George Washington Rd.
Enfield, CT 06082

Carol Bohn, also a dealer collector, specializes in patented kitchen gadgets and tools, and also Christmas antiques. In late 2002, her long-awaited, and I'm sure definitive, book on nutmeg graters will be published by the author & her husband. It will be filled with photos, patent drawings & information. Carol drew on several fine collections as well as her own. When writing for ordering info, please enclose SASE:

Carol & Jim Bohn
501 Market St.
Mifflinburg, PA 17844

Juicers & Reamers

John Zukatis is a longtime collector and dealer of juicers & all kinds of reamers. He is selling his collection, piece by piece. He is now interested in all kinds of advertising ashtrays, and intact, old cigarette packs.

John Zukatis
John's-Jungle
Bellows Falls, VT
eBay: jnpackrats
E-mail: packrats@webryders.com

Roy McDiarmid has a very large active collection, and is seeking more. You may write or email him about unusual juicers & lemon squeezers (especially mechanicals, also old glass ones. Among other things he seeks early Griswold, Wagner, and old marked metal lemon presses on legs, such as Williams, Sammis, etc. SASE please.

Roy McDiarmid
6702 High St.
Falls Church, VA 22046
E-mail: meso@erols.com

National Reamer Collectors Association
Write: Deborah Gillham
47 Midline Ct.
Gaithersburg, MD 20878
E-mail: reamers@erols.com

Patented Antiques

My contributors Larry & Carole Meeker have a great Web site for selling "antiques of a mechanical nature." Pictures, descriptions, and lots of useful opinions about collecting abound. They also have a number of remarkable collections in a cyber museum at the same site.

E-mail: clm@patented-antiques.com
Web site: www.patented-antiques.com.

This Book

By the time this book is published I may have a modest Web site up and running. I've got the domain name, and only need to figure out how to run it. Web site: www.300yearsofkitchencollectibles.com

PREPARING

II. MIX, BEAT, STIR, CHURN, & BLEND

"Eat and run" and "grab a bite" were the only ways to eat in mankind's earliest days. The concept of fixing a meal, let alone having a meal, had to wait for tools and techniques of preparation. The most basic of those techniques involve cutting or mashing (dealt with in Chapter I).

Implements and gadgets in this chapter accomplish the next level of preparation: they change texture, taste or other attributes, mainly by creating mixtures. You might argue that eggbeaters belong in the first chapter, because the blades cut the yolks and whites. But eggbeaters are here because their purpose and their effect is to blend two parts into one.

Eggbeaters are by far the most popular mechanical device in this chapter; we are beguiled by the poetry of their motion. They look like ballet dancers, twirling and spinning. (Well, some of them are more like four year olds at a recital – not so graceful as primas, but just as spirited.) At rest, their curved blades, small waists and waiting arms promise the dance to come, and those with "aprons" are wearing big tutus! Ten years ago, when the third edition of this book came out, there was only one small book devoted to eggbeaters. Don Thornton, the author of that little beater book, has whipped up two tomes to beat all. See the Bibliography, or the information at the end of this chapter on how to order directly from the author.

Prices for eggbeaters have skyrocketed. Rarities for which only a few collectors competed a few years ago have gone from $250 to often well over $1,000. A result of high prices is that a number of previously unknown beaters have been discovered, flushed out by eager collectors, and the Internet. When a lot of collectors pursue a field, unknown examples begin to surface, even after some months or years of being hunted. This reward makes months of boring results at flea markets and online auctions seem worthwhile. (Although most collectors who 10 years ago would have concentrated almost all of their attention on one kind of object have expanded their interests in order to keep a flow of prizes coming in. That's apparently the cycle.) Thirty years ago kitchen collectors collected across the board; twenty years ago they started specializing; by the mid 1990s ultimate specialization was beginning to wane, and collectors found they really enjoyed looking for a variety of things.

Since 1998 or so there has been a further down-valuing for beaters that we thought were rarer than they really are, or that seemed more distinctive or odder than they now seem with all the many beaters known to exist. On the other hand, as time and effort have proved the rarity of others, their value has increased tremendously.

When a single-focus book is written, the role model collections on display in that book invite emulation. The demand part of the equation grows and the supply increases briefly when publicity brings the stuff out, then drops because desirable beaters are socked away in collections. Each new surge of publicity brings out a few more (for a first or serial appearance on the market). At some point, unfulfilled demand – and the high prices they bring – encourages the manufacture of fakes, forgeries and reproductions. We are not aware of any repro eggbeaters, probably because the cost of casting and/or tooling would be too expensive for the expected return possible by slowly releasing a dozen or so examples of a "newly discovered" beater. But several beaters are ripe for rip-offs; some because they would be relatively simple to manufacture (e.g., the "propeller" mixing spoon).

Patent records convince me that many eggbeaters still await discovery. Although a large percentage of patented gadgets were never manufactured, numerous patented, manufactured oddities have been found in the last fifteen years, and the possibility that they were made in commercial quantities gives hope.

If you are just beginning, don't despair. You can still collect for form, and many beaters which are classics, the basic beaters of any collection, can still be bought quite cheaply.

Unfortunately, collectors have gotten in the habit in the last decade of emphasizing rarity and awarding it top billing, all but ignoring design or form in the price structure. Maybe that's the only way the collectibles market can work, but as individuals you can collect using any criteria you want. The bottom line must be that you like something and get pleasure from having it in your collection. And you might as well, if your moolah is limited, put something other than great rarity at the top of your list.

Some collectors have enough energy and room to collect **churns**, even floor-standing models, but most people have to treat large churns more like pieces of furniture than accessories, and consider them adjuncts to other collections. It's too bad, because so much variety exists in their form, function and finish.

Mixing bowls and beater jars in this chapter are half of the whole, just as a churn body forms a whole tool only with a dasher. I find it difficult to assess clay kitchen collectibles, because ceramics have been collected for so long, and standards, rules and lingo are well-established. When I commandeer ceramics to put into a book on kitchen collectibles, to a certain extent I have to reëvaluate bowls, cookie jars, salt boxes, etc., that have already been categorized, classified, rated, and priced within another collecting context. If we are going to compete with ceramics' collectors at flea markets and antique shows, we're the newcomers who have to abide by their rules, so I suggest loading up on authoritative books on ceramic objects. You can never read too much.

Apple butter stirrer, long wood handle set at right angles to heavy oak pear-shaped blade, with curvy X cutout, good patina on handle, American, handle about 6 ft. long, blade about 6"W and 13"L, 1840s to 1860s. **$50**

❖ RECIPE ❖

***Apple butter** – Stir apples and cider all the time; you should have for the purpose a stick made of hickory wood, somewhat like a common hoe, with holes in it."* Elizabeth E. Lea, Useful Receipts and Hints to Young Housekeepers, *10th ed., Baltimore, 1859 (1st ed. 1851).*

Apple butter stirring paddle, long wood handle with paddle with largish cutout holes, used with handle horizontal & paddle in a vertical position, dragged back & forth across rim of the huge kettle, so that the paddle would stir the viscous liquid, American, 43"L, 19th or early 20th C................................ **$35**
Apple butter stirrers. – These looked the same for at least 150 years, and new ones were advertised into the 1920s, often using 1860s-1880s illustrations. Best choice are those that show use, with real good dark patina, handles polished with the wear of hands, worn paddles, repairs or interesting wooden or metal bracing, even a bit of warping gives character.... **$20-$100**
Batter bowl, yellowware, big pouring lip, acanthus leaves decoration, badly cracked, alas, mark is big deep diamond, can't read name, 13-5/8" diam.,

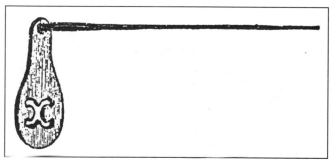

II-1. Apple butter stirrer. *This sketch appeared in the "Ladies' Department" of* American Agriculturist, *Sept. 1847. "Any handy lad of fourteen years can easily make one for his mother. The handle should be about six feet long, in order that the cook may keep from the heat and danger of fire. The other part should be of heavy oak-board, six inches broad, with two transverse slits in the lower part, and long enough to reach the bottom of the kettle, so that while it moves, the handle has need only of a steady horizontal motion." The kettle referred to, by the way, was used outdoors, and was suspended or supported above a fire; it held from a half barrel to nearly a barrel of cider. (I once made apple butter from a gallon of cider; on the electric stove, it took 15 hours!)* **$45+**

19th C. By the way, if the crack had an old repair – staples, or some kind of metal filler, for example – the value would at least quadruple................... **$10**
Batter jug, also called a batter pot or batter pitcher, brown "Albany" slip glaze, with tin lid, tin spout cover, wire bail handle with wood grip, from Havana, NY, mid 1800s. [Note that an "Albany" glaze doesn't necessarily mean Albany, let alone New York state.].. **$125-$250**
Batter jug, bulbous saltglazed gray stoneware, with funny stick-out ear handles, wire bail with wooden grip, tin cap on spout, tin lid (probably replacement, as it fits inside the opening, rather than capping the entire top opening) with strap handle, "Evan B. Jones," Pittston, PA, about 12"H, c.1870s to 1890s... **$800**

❖ NOTES ❖

Added value – For nice, but fairly common decoration, values up to $2,500 or more. For terrific human or animal subjects, with excellent drawing, good detail, verve, spontaneity, over $15,000. Repros and fakes with newly-painted decoration on old jugs abound. Many fakers are so brazen as to paint a blue design on, then coat with polyurethane! Yikes! It pays to study.

Batter jug, dark brown saltglazed stoneware, with odd clay clam shells applied on sides, as bail ears for square wire bail handle, knotty carved wood grip, tin covers on spout and top, no mark, from Bryant Pond, ME, 8-1/2"H, 19th C. **$250**
Batter jug, saltglazed stoneware, ovoid shape, rather wide applied tilting handle at base opposite the side of the pouring spout, pretty lugs on either side fitted with wire handle with wooden grip, a very desirable form. Unusual cobalt decoration of a leafy wreath encircling

II-2. Batter jugs & pail. *Three stoneware batter jugs; Notice the bails and tipping handles near bottom. Far **(L)** decorated in cobalt; **(2)** has original fitted tin spout cap and lid; **(3)** missing lid. American, mid 19th C. Generally speaking, for non-remarkable ones, the value range of plain as well as simply decorated gray stoneware is high. Brown Albany-glazed jugs probably a quarter to a half the value for gray stoneware. Far **(R)** pieced tin, came in 3 sizes: 4, 6, and 8 qts. Late 19th C. form, but in c.1904-1910 catalog.* **(L) $500+ (2) (3) $100+ (R) $150+**

a humorous big-nosed man's profile, called "Man in the Moon" by the Robackers. [Note: A similar one, with a bigger chin, also marked "Cowden & Wilcox," was owned by Donald Blake Webster, and pictured as "Punch" in his book.] Stoneware lid rather than fitted tin one, tin spout lid missing (or it's possible a cork was used), stamped with a desirable maker's mark, "Cowden & Wilcox," Harrisburg, PA, made c.1850s or early '60s. The Robacker May 1989 auction price of $10,000 for this entry was a record for batter jugs, but the price comes from the decoration not the form. Now value depends on how many similar quality decorated stoneware jugs have surfaced since 1989. Provenance, form, decoration, and the venue of the sale all affect value. Could now be: .... **$6,000 or $10,000+**

Batter jug, bulbous shape, 2 spouts, spongeware with brown, green & yellow glaze, American, 19th C. **$350+**

Batter pitcher, Rockingham flintware, yellow & brown glaze, American, 19th C. .... **$350+**

Batter pitcher, stoneware with yellow glaze, wire bail with wooden grip, American, 19th C............. **$250+**

Beaten biscuit machine, also called a biscuit brake, cast iron frame screw-clamps to table, 2 nickel-plated rollers with iron crank, cast iron base rather like a sewing machine base, with marble top. The dough is fed through the rollers, which are reset closer & closer, to really work dough until it starts to form bubbles (called "blisters") that make cracking, snapping sounds when they break. (For the sound, think of a mouthful of really old bubble gum chewed very fast.) "The DeMuth Improved Dough Kneader & Beaten Biscuit Machine," mfd. by J. A. DeMuth, St. Joseph, MO, approx. 36"H overall, table is 30-1/2"H x 36"L x 16"W; rollers are 2-1/4" diam. x 14"L, c.1890. Uncommon..................................... **$500+**

II-3. Beaten biscuit machine, or **dough kneader.** *Cast iron base, marble table top, nickeled iron rollers adjusted closer together with each successive pass-through so dough gets increasingly harder to roll through as gluten builds up & makes snap-crack sounds. 30-1/2"H x 36"L x 16"W; rollers 2-1/4" diam. x 14"L. Medallion on base reads: "The DeMuth Improved Dough Kneader & Beaten Biscuit Machine, Manf'd. by J. A. DeMuth, St. Joseph, MO." Courtesy Margaret Minich.* **$500+**

II-4. Dough brake, or beater. Wood, including corrugated ramp and roller, iron crank. Probably either homemade or limited production piece. American, mid- to late-19th C. Courtesy Mrs. A. J. Minichiello. (The name coincidence has not escaped me!) **$175+**

Beaten biscuit machine, tabletop model, mainly wood, cranked rollers, American, c.1860s. .... **$175+**

❖ NOTES ❖

Beaten biscuit machines took some of the work out of making this Southern treat – once made by beating the dough with the side of a cook's axe or hatchet, wooden mallet, or heavy rolling pin until it made cracking sounds. The biscuits keep very well, even frozen, aren't tough or crusty, but are dense & chewy. They are baked to the faintest tinge of tan.

❖ RECIPES ❖

Miss Fort's Beaten Biscuit – *1-1/2 lb. flour, 5 oz. Lard, 1-1/2 tsp. salt, 2 tsp. sugar, dissolved in 1 cup water. Blend flour, lard and salt. Mix into a stiff dough with water in which sugar has been dissolved. Work well. Beat or roll until dough blisters. Bake in moderate oven until light brown.*

Beaten Biscuit No. 2. – *1 qt. Flour, 1/2 tsp. baking powder, 1 level tsp. salt, lard size of goose egg, 2/3 cup of milk and water, half of each with 1 tsp. of sugar dissolved in milk; have dough very stiff. Beat or roll until it blisters." Mrs. W. H. Wilson,* Mrs. Wilson's Cook Book, *1914.*

Beater churn – See: Cream whip; Syllabub churn

Beater jar, green glazed crockery, "D. B. Wich Beater," American, 20th C. Blue used to be favorite color; green is gaining!... **$75+**

Beater jar, saltglazed stoneware, "Red Wing Beater Jar, Eggs, Cream Salad Dressing," 20th C............. **$85+**

Beater jar, saltglazed stoneware, blue stripe, for eggs, cream, salad dressings, made by Red Wing, advertising "You Beat Eggs, We Beat Prices, Star Grocery, Parkersburg, Iowa," 20th C. .... **$150+**

Beater jar, saltglazed stoneware, blue striped, advertising "Wesson Oil For Making Good Things to Eat," 20th C. **$75**

Beater jar, saltglazed stoneware, blue stripes, advertising motto, "Mix with Us, Save Dough, Rockwell City, IA," 20th C. .... **$150+**

Beater jar, saltglazed stoneware, marked "Holiday Greeting," Red Wing, dated 1924. .... **$150+**

Beater jar, yellowware, marked "Foremost Dairies," American, 20th C. .... **$50+**

❖ NOTES ❖

Beater jars have grown in popularity in the last 20 years or so, along with the increased interest in the beaters. The jars are mainly 20th C. saltglazed stoneware, or earthenware, usually in blue or brown, sometimes with stripes, having straight sides like crocks, approx. 6"H x 4-1/2"D. Taller than wide, they're ideal for inserting an eggbeater. Some of them even have a slightly dished interior bottom to take advantage of curved blades. The most popular ones were made by various Red Wing (MN) potteries, starting c. 1900. Red Wing jars have various finishes: "Blue Band," "Gray Line" (grayish white with blue & red bands), "Saffron," yellowware, etc. **Advertising.** – Many jars were printed with a legend, message or motto on side, advertising (or used for promotion of) a variety of retail or service businesses, mostly in the Midwest; examples include: Cairo Mercantile Co., Cairo, NE; E. C. Reed, North English, IA; Swanson's, West Union, IA; Semons, Athens, WI; Stewart Olson & Sons; Farmer's Elevator, Peterson, IA; Babers Mercantile, Hansel, IA; and Ardmore Lumber, Ardmore, SD. (See also: Rolling pins, in Chapter IV, Molds, for other advertising stoneware.) **Red Wing** is one of the most sought-after ceramic lines in this field. There are hundreds, perhaps thousands, of pieces – from flowerpots to milkjugs – that were available from this Minnesota city's potteries. See the last page of this chapter for more. • **Some other potteries** who made beater jars are A. S. Lauritson, Tyler, MN; Gross Mercantile Co., Bridgewater, SD; Frank J. Martin, Ackley, IA. Most fall within same value range, but those advertising a special crossover business may bring even more than the high end of the range: **$50-$150**

Bowls – See: Mixing bowls; see also: Bowls in Chapter VII - (Storage)

Bread machine, also called a mixing machine, a dough mixer, dough kneader, dough brake, or dough machine. Frame of cast iron, 4 arched legs, tinned horizontal body, various gears, side crank, horizontal bar to hang on to with user's non-cranking hand, top lifts off the basin; the lower part is where the kneaded dough rested or rose. Cyrus Chambers, Jr., Scientific Bread Machine Co., Phila., about 16"H, c.1890s to 1910s. .... **$125-$225+**

Bread machine, relatively shallow, broad tin bowl, with slanted sides, cast iron 3-legged frame arches up to support the handle, gear & crank, & suspend the 2 kneading blades. American, probably about 11" to 13"H, c. 1860s to 1880s. • Illustrated in 1881 cookbook, but style is at least 20 years earlier..... **$250+**

Bread maker, screw clamps to table, tin with cast iron gears, "White House Bread Maker," American, 1902. .... **$150**

II-5. Bread maker. *Heavy tin, cast iron crank & gears. "Sifts the flour and mixes 10 lbs. of best bread in 3 minutes." Scientific Bread Machine Co., Philadelphia. Pat'd. by Mrs. Lydia C. Sharpless, Phila., c.1902. Ad in* Table Talk, *April, 1903.* **$125-$225**

Bread maker, heavy charcoal tin plate, steel, cast iron. Slope-sided, shallow tin pail & lid, screw clamp iron frame, iron crank. Heavy gauge wire snaky kneader assembled as part of lid. Stamped on lid are the directions: "Put in all liquids first – then flour – turn 3 minutes – raise in pail – after raising turn until dough forms a ball – take off cross piece – lift out dough with kneader." Advertising copy of the period reads: "The process of kneading with this machine is thoroughly scientific and sanitary. It makes no difference what kind of bread flour is used. Results are always the same – better bread. Directly opposite to hand kneading is the work of the Universal. ... In hand kneading the particles of flour are necessarily pressed together, and the liquid does not thoroughly moisten each particle of the starch granules, while with the bread maker these particles are lightly held apart until thoroughly wetted ... and kneaded." "Universal No. 8," mfd. by Landers, Frary & Clark, New Britain, CT, 11-7/8"H. (Other numbers – such as No. 2, 4, No. 44 – are different heights & capacities.) Some are marked "Awarded Gold Medal St. Louis Exposition" which was in 1904. These were made for quite a long time from the 1890s on. Add $6-$10 for original paper label on pail. .... **$115+**

Bread maker, tin pail, never had a lid, screw clamp, "Universal No. 2," Landers, Frary & Clark....... **$65+**

Bread mixer, heavy tin pail, side handles, side crank turns U-shaped wire blade inside, domed crimped tin lid with wooden knob, screw clamp, labeled "Chauvauquat Bread Mixer," Polar Star, mfd. by Smith & Hemenway Co. (S. & H. Co,), NYC, NY, four sizes from two to 16 loaf capacity, c.1909. .... **$75**

Bread or dough mixer, sometimes called a dough brake, double layer of bent wood for body, nailed construction, cast iron crank, wooden knob, iron mixing blade, iron handle. Fits in crook of arm, held against body, may be American, but crank looks European, 5"H x 10" diam., 19th C. .... **$200+**

Bread rising tray, for bakers, wood, for 6 loaves, American, about 39"L x 6-5/6"W, late 19th C........ **$125+**

Bread rising trays. – Wood with trough carved out, about 3 feet long, 5" wide, these have been imported by the thousands from Europe, and sell at flea markets where other items in the booths usually include wooden high-sided wagons, bentwood boxes, and other peasantries. .... **$25+**

Butter churn – See: Churn

II-6. Batter or dough-mixing machines. *Clockwise from top right:* **(1)** *"Mixing machine" from 1881 cookbook, copied from c.1860s or even earlier cookbook.* **(2)** *Circa 1881 "****Stantan****" bread mixer, heavy tin. As liquid gets mixed into flour, cranking motion causes pan to turn by itself.* **(3)** *"****Universal No.4****," for 4 loaves. (#8 made 8.) Landers, Frary & Clark, New Britain, CT. Tinned pieced metal, with kneading rod, lid, crank, & clamp put on under the lid to provide holder for rod. Stamped on lid is: "Put in all liquids first – then flour – turn 3 minutes – raise in pail – after raising turn until dough forms a ball – take off cross-piece – lift out dough with kneader." 11-7/8"H, 1904, but sold for many years.* **(4)** *"****Universal*** *mixer for beating eggs, whipping cream or mixing soft batters ... also for cake." A curved rod kneaded heavy batter or bread dough.* **(5)** *"****Centrifugal Mixer****," The Sparrow Kneader & Mixer Co., Boston, MA. Tin & Cast iron; "stirrers" have horizontal crosspieces. Four sizes; 2 pans (5 or 10 qts.), 2 tanks (10 or 75 gallons). Flyer on flimsy paper, c.1860: "Although but a few months old, hundreds of them are in use by druggists all over, who find them invaluable for compounding emulsions and ointments heretofore made with a mortar; also, for blending powders mixed by the slow, dusty and wasteful use of the sieve. ... Each stirrer in its revolution sweeps entirely outside of its centre, and the other follows in."* **(1) $250+; (2) $125+; (3) $65+; (4) $250+; (5)$250+**

What Does He Need? A joke from the period, reported as appearing in a North Dakota newspaper: "It is reported that one of our fastidious, newly married ladies kneads bread with her gloves on. The incident may be somewhat peculiar, but there are others. For instance, the editor of this paper needs bread with his shoes on; he needs bread with his shirt on; he needs bread with his pants on, and unless some delinquent subscribers pay up, he will need bread without anything on – and North Dakota is no Garden of Eden in the winter time." *House Furnishing Review,* June 1905.

Butter fork, painted wood, 5 thick tines, looks like an Afro comb, handle is like a paintbrush's, "Mrs. Bragg's Butter Fork," not marked, American, about 6"L, late 19th C. **$12**

Butter hands – See listings in Chapter IV (Form, Mold, Shape)

Butter paddle, also called butter spade or butter ladle, carved wood with very shallow bowl & short crook-necked or hooked handle, beautiful mellow patina, 8"L, 19th C. • Added value for really good patina, signs of hand carving, exceptional figure in the grain, even knots, because they are signs of age or uniqueness. .... **$35+**

Butter paddle, carved tiger maple, all one piece of wood, standard shape, hooked handle has wonderful small man wearing top hat, seated atop handle, incised heart midway down flat shank of handle, age crack in bowl, from PA & NY border, 10-1/2"L, prob. early to mid 19th C. • More evidence of the folk art tradition in kitchenwares. This marvelous piece was discovered, & for sale by Doris Axtell, Deposit, NY, in 1985. .... **$600+**

II-7. Dough mixer. *Double bentwood, nailed construction. Cast iron crank with large wood knob, iron blade, iron side handle. This fits in crook of arm, held against body, and you apply plenty of body English to make it do its thing. 5"H x 10" diam. Mid 19th C. Collection of Meryle Evans.* **$200+**

What's a Butter Paddle For? – "For working butter, keep a wooden bowl and ladle. This last article is seldom found in New England, but always in the state of New York." Mrs. Mary Hooker Cornelius, *The Young House-keeper's Friend*, 1859. All of the familiar types (the nearly round, slightly bowled one with short crook-necked handle; the flat, straight sided, slightly rounded front edge one with angled rounded handles; and the one most resembling a spade, flat longish blade with straight edges, handle raised slightly) were shown in *Montgomery Ward's* 1895 catalog. I'm sure they were sold well into 20th C, (& perhaps today through dairy suppliers).

• • •

Bread: What Ought It to Be? "It should be light, sweet, tender. This matter of lightness is the distinctive line between civilized and savage bread. The savage mixes simple flour and water into balls of paste, which he throws into boiling water, and which come out, solid, glutinous masses, of which his common saying is, 'Man eat dis, he no die,' which a facetious traveller interpreted to mean, 'Dis no kill you, nothing will.'" Catherine Beacher & Harriet Beecher Stowe, *American Woman's Home*, 1869. Hmmm, the balls of paste sound like bagels. Speaking of beagles – some people say that stale bagels are the best teeth-cleaners for dogs!

Butter or curd paddle, carved from burl, beautiful patina, old iron repair to handle, found in NJ, 13"L, poss. 18th C. .... **$100+**

Butter paddle, carved wood, shaped like a thick, slightly scooped ping pong paddle, 9"L x 5-1/4"W, late 19th C. Really good patina might add value, but otherwise it's pretty dull .... **$25+**

Butter paddle, carved wood with shallow convex bowl, hooked handle in exaggerated angle where it joins bowl, American (?), 4-1/4"diam. with 5"L handle, 19th C. • I never even used to look at these, but have noticed lately how much variation there is in this form, particularly in handle detail & imaginative use of grain and knots. That's one of the secrets of collecting, as you know, looking for & finding variations on a theme. Bach & Bartok did it for music! .... **$50+**

Butter paddle, maple handle, wire blade, 8-3/4"L, C.1900... **$15+**

Butter paddle, maple, with hanging hole in handle, rather long at 14"L, late 19th C. .... **$20+**

11-8. Butter worker. *Tabletop model, bentwood, in simple wood frame notice the well-finished post finials, wood gears, iron handle. 13-1/2"H x 9" x 8", c.1850s-1870s. It looks much more substantial than Lilly's Patent in picture II-9, but quite possibly is that. Line cuts used in ads and furnished to editors, often idealized, simplified, or otherwise made image more "readable." Collection of Meryle Evans.* **$500+**

Butter scoop or paddle, carved lightweight pale wood, curved, slightly irregular neck, American, 8-1/2"L, late 19th C. .... **$20+**

Butter worker, for use in dairy barn or buttery, wood with remains of old blue paint on outside, a trough & 2 corrugated rollers, on skeletal frame, American, trough is 30"L, late 19th C. .... **$250+**

Butter worker, tabletop for home use, wood with corrugated swinging arm, very worn, with good patina, American, turn-of-century. The market value of all wood wares, especially dairy implements, is enhanced by a satiny patina that results from the butterfat. .... **$150+**

Butter worker, tabletop, stool-like wooden frame, bentwood holder for butter & mechanism, wooden gears, iron crank handle, American, 13-1/2"H x 9" x 8", 19th C. .... **$225+**

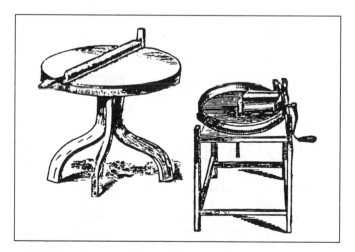

II-9. Butter workers. (L) *"California," used in a large dairy – the Point Reyes' Ranch, CA. Three-legged base screwed to floor, top revolves. Wooden knife fits into socket. Butter is put on top, cut and squeezed or squashed against table to remove all liquid, over & over then patted into molds. American Agriculturist, March 1870.* **(R)** *"Lilly's Patent," for working butter, and for adding optional salt. C. H. R. Triebels, Philadelphia, 1879, American Agriculturist ad. Probably same as sturdier looking one in photo II-8.* **$200-$500+**

Cake mixer, tin & cast iron, screw clamps to table like bread mixer, "Universal," Landers, Frary & Clark, turn-of-century.. **$125+**

Cake mixer, tin dough pail, with cast iron gears, crank & frame, screw clamps to table, "American Machine Co.," pat'd 1873.. **$125+**

Cake mixer & cream whip, tin, "Rumford," pat'd 1908.. **$15**

Cake spoon – See: Mixing spoon

Cheese curd knives were dairy tools with multiple blades to break up the curd in the process of cheese-making. American, 22"L, late 19th C. • Two types were advertised in turn-of-the-century *Montgomery Ward* catalogs: **(1)** An oblong metal frame, open at one end, with a short, turned wood handle at other, many blades set across the short axis. For cutting the curds up into fine pieces. Came in one length, 20", but five widths: 4", 6", 8", 10", and 12". **(2)** The other style is a version of a curd whip, and had 20"L blades, set 6", 8", 10", 12", 14", 15", and 20"W. These thin narrow blades, set about 3 or 4 to the inch, would swish through the curds. .... **$20-$35; $30-$45**

Cheese curd whip or whipper, 4 or 5 spring steel blades, 18"L x 1"W, set into a turned wooden handle or grip. Overall length: 24-1/2." It dates to the 1870s to 1890s.. **$20+**

Churn, barrel on A-frame stand, side crank, top loading, O. R. Flyers, Grafton, VT, about 46"H, 19th C. This type of barrel churn was called an "end over end" churn in England! • The dealer advertised this as being from 1826 (probably typo for 1876). I read listings for every Churn, every Washing Machine, & every combination patent listing in *Subject Index to Patents*, 1790-1873, also an unnumbered patents index from 1790 to 1836. No "Flyers," and no Grafton, VT. But two churns had patentees from towns called Grafton: H. D. Smith, Grafton, OH, May 5, 1868, and T. Conely, Grafton, IL, June 25, 1872. • It's possible this Flyers' churn was never actually patented. .... **$150+**

II-10. Three Dutch churn mechanisms. (1) *Large flywheel churns.* **(2)** *"At Almenaar, a churn made to go by the feet, the weight of the body being moved alternately from one side to the other, on a platform" attached by series of pivots to dasher.* **(3)** *A Gouda, Holland churn made "to work from the ceiling in a very easy way; a piece of wood, in the shape of an obtuse angle, was attached at the elbow to a pivot in one of the beams of the ceiling; the churn-stick attached to the one end" and worked by moving lever at left up & down. This article, sharing mechanical motives and marvels with Americans, adds that "in North Holland they churn using dogs in wheels, in a similar way to the turn-spits." Mechanics' Magazine, and Register of Inventions and Improvements, NYC, March 1834.*

II-11. Two-footed dasher churn. *This unusual butter churn was found in Alabama. Heavy tin container is 19-1/2"H; all wood stomping dasher is 45"L. Operates on a rope-pulley system; handles sticking out on each side are tied to a rope and pulley inside the tall housing shaft, and when handles are turned the rope operates the two feet, making them stomp the butter. Very unusual. Could be a patented piece, but could have been constructed from the kinds of how-to articles that explained the Dutch churns to readers 170+ years ago. Collection of Kyle Goad & Margaret Upchurch.* **$600+**

Churn, cast iron wheel & handle, nickeled blades, speckled blue saltglazed stoneware body, thin wooden lid with knob, no maker's name, American, 14-3/4" overall height, crock 8"H, pat'd. May 15, 1906 & Feb. 26, 1907. .... **$200+**

Churn, crank type with wooden paddles, glass jar with metal gears & screw-on lid, no mark, American, 4 qt. size, c.1900. Not a Dazey................................ **$85**

Churn, cranked, cream colored painted wood, has large crank wheel & smaller iron gear wheel above, natural finish lid, "Dazey," 18"H body, plus 12"H wheel & frame, pat'd. Dec. 18, 1917. .... **$150**

Churn, cylinder type on 4 shoe feet, wood with iron side crank, "R.W.," label shows initials over an anchor, sold through *Montgomery Ward*, American, various sizes, 1890s-1910. .... **$50+**

❖ NOTES ❖

Churn Makers – Unless incised, stenciled, or burned-in branded names remain, few ceramic or wooden churns can be identified by maker. Around 1900, many U.S. companies were making churns, including John Boyd, Chicago, IL; Creamery Package Mfg. Co., Chicago; Barber Creamery Supply Co., Chicago; D. F. Barclay, Elgin, IL; Milne Mfg. Co., Monmouth, IL; Dobson Mfg. Co., Rockford, IL; John McDermaid, Rockford; H. H. Palmer Co., Rockford; Anthony Wayne Mfg. Co., Fort Wayne, IN; I.X.L. & Goshen Pump Co., Goshen, IN; Moseley & Pritchard Mfg. in Clinton, IA; H. F. Brammer Mfg. Co., Davenport, IA; Fort Dodge Stoneware Co., Fort Dodge, IA; Ames Plow Co., Boston, MA; Bousfield & Co., Bay City, MI; Flint Cabinet Creamery Co., Flint, MI; Aspinwall Mfg. Co., in Jackson, MI; Owatonna Mfg. Co., Jackson, MI; Hilfinger Brothers (pottery), Fort Edward, NY; R. W. Fenner, South Stockton, NY; D. H. Gowing, Syracuse, NY; Wyman L. Edson, Union Center, NY; Frank L. Jones in Utica, NY; H. P. Deuscher Co., Hamilton, OH; Anderson & Carothers, Sidney, OH; Buckeye Churn Co., Sidney, OH; M. Brown & Co., Wapakonetta, OH; Standard Churn Co., Wapakonetta; A. H. Reid, Philadelphia, PA; A. B. Farquhar Co., York, PA; Prewitt, Spurr & Co.,

Nashville, TN; Vermont Farm Machine Co., Bellows Falls, VT; Stoddard Mfg. Co., Rutland, VT; St. Albans Foundry Co., St. Albans, VT; Richmond Cedar Works, Richmond, VA; Cornish, Curtis & Greene Mfg. Co., Fort Atkinson, WI; Menasha Woodenware Co., Menasha, WI; Racine Malleable & Wrought Iron Co., Racine, WI; Wisconsin Dairy Supply Co., Whitewater, WI.

Churn, cylinder type, sometimes called a bowler churn, tin in cast iron frame, square body, flywheel, mechanical movement, dated 1907. .... **$125+**

Churn, cylinder type, Tennessee "white wood" (as it was described in early catalog) box with iron hoops, iron crank, "Diamond Balance Churn Co.," named for shape of its box body, various sizes from 1 to 60 gal. (the biggest were dog-, sheep- or horse-powered), pat'd. May 28, 1889, Oct. 27, 1891 & Nov. 17, 1891. Just for a price perspective, this is for the 10 gal. size: .... **$125+**

Churn, cylinder type with side crank, ochre painted wood, rectangular hopper & wooden lid, 4 sturdy shoe feet, American (?) 21"H x 15-1/2" x 19", 1880s-1910. .... **$225+**

Churn, cylinder type, wood barrel & wood frame, crank on side, lock-on lid, "Fairy Churn," mfd. by N. H. (or H. H.) • Palmer Co., Rockford, IL, c.1880s-1900. .. **$135+**

❖ NOTES ❖

Churning – "The process of churning is necessary to force out the serous fluid from the cream in order to produce butter. This is done by agitation and in a churn. There are various kinds of churns, but the best churn is the one that will preserve the proper temperature, or the same temperature that is in the churn and cream when put into it. In warm weather, cold water for some time is to be put into the churn, and in cold weather scalding water, and also putting hot or cold water in the cream according to the season, as it is important to preserve the same temperature while churning – the best churns are those which are used in a horizontal position – such as the stationary barrel with dashers to move in the inside. A small churn is in use on this principle, and answers a good purpose, as a hole of sufficient size from one half an inch to an inch, may be made on the top, to let out the warm air produced by the agitation of the cream, and to admit the cool air. A barrel churn of this kind has been used, when 36 to 38 lb. of butter was made twice a week." *The Farmers' Cabinet*, Philadelphia, July 1, 1836, some 60 years before the Fairy Churn (listed above) was advertised, though it would answer the purpose very well.

Churn, cylinder type, wood with (original?) greenish gray paint, supposedly Shaker, 19th C. • If it were absolute that this was (1) Shaker, and (2) had the old, original paint, the churn might go for upwards of $1,000. "Paint is all" say all Shaker experts. .... **$300+**

Churn, cylinder type, wooden drum with red stenciling & cow design, American, 13"H, early 20th C. .... **$135+**

Churn, cylinder type, wooden, on frame, "White Cedar, No. 1," possibly by Richmond Cedar Works, American, 8 gal. size, c.1890s-1910s. .... **$85+**

Churn, cylinder floor model, painted cast iron frame, 4 short splayed feet support 2 wheels & crank, vertical shaft with 4 large wooden paddles, heavily tinned square-based sheet metal receptacle or body, Dazey Churn, St. Louis, MO, 2 sizes: a 2-wheel 6 gal. with 3 bars on sides of frame ; or 1-wheel 3 gal. with 1 bar on each side; on sale by 1910 – the date Dec. 18, 1917 found on it is prob. for an improvement on Dazey's April 16, 1907 tabletop tin churn..... **$150+**

Churn, cylinder floor model, rectangular wooden box, side crank at one end, fancy parlor furniture-like turned & carved legs set slightly splayed, inside is oddly shaped container with foldout lids, Julien Churn Co., Dubuque, IA (?), 1870s. **$150**

Churn, dasher type, barrel construction with tapered sides, one stave elongated to become handle, original old red paint, has lid & dasher, New England, 18-1/2"H, early to mid 19th C..................... **$350+**

Churn, dasher type, barrel with old blue buttermilk paint, wide lapped band at top, 4 iron bands, has lid & dasher. American (?), 25"H x 11"diam. at top, 1870s-80s. Many painted churns have been imported in container loads of "country" smalls from other countries... **$250+**

Churn, dasher type, bentwood, decoration in Norwegian rosemaling paint, from "Wapa Koneta," OH (town was spelled Wapakonetta, so that may have been a brand or a style name), 4 gal. size, dated 1882. It seems improbable that the decoration is contemporaneous to the churn. It was probably added in the 1950s during the rage for tôle and rosemaling paint decoration................................. **$300+**

Churn, dasher type, brown "Albany glaze" stoneware, lacks wooden lid & dasher, American, 6 gal. capacity. **$55**

Churn, dasher type, cooper's barrel-like product, wooden staves heavy tin bands, hand-forged nails, lid & dasher, American (?), 1850s. **$150**

❖ NOTES ❖

No butter, thanks – "My greatest objection, after all, to the use of butter and cheese both, grows out of the consideration that their manufacture involves a great amount of female labor, while no permanent or substantial benefit is obtained." William A. Alcott, *The Young Housekeeper, or Thoughts on Food and Cookery*, Boston, 1838, 1842.

• • •

Cream – The peculiarly rich cream of Devonshire, England, called clouted cream, is obtained by using zinc pans of a peculiar construction, consisting of an upper and lower apartment. The milk is put into the upper apartment; and after it has stood 12 hours, an equal quantity of boiling water is introduced into the lower one. At the end of another 12 hours, the cream is taken off much more easily and perfectly than in the common way, and is also more abundant and richer. ... The same principles may be applied in the use of common pans. It would be very easy, for instance, to prepare some kind of trough, of tin, perhaps, or even wood, into which the pans could be set, and hot water afterwards introduced. As a close trough would be much better than an open one, you may have a cover with holes in which to set the pans. An ingenious yankee tinman would soon make a range in this way, sufficient for a common dairy, at no very great expense. It would last indefinitely. If it is true, that you would thus get some two pounds more butter a week from each cow, the apparatus and the trouble would soon be paid for, – to say nothing of the time saved in churning. We do not see why zinc pans – which are said to be decidedly preferable to any other for the dairy – with the tin range as above, would not be quite as good as the complicated and expensive Devonshire pans. And it would be easy for a dairy woman to satisfy herself respecting the principle, without either. By using cold water instead of hot, the range would serve to keep milk sweet in warm weather." Vermont Farmer, as quoted in *The Farmers' Cabinet*, Phila., July 1, 1836.

Churn, dasher type, one elongated stave for handle, has 4 fingered wooden hoops, American (?), 12"H, early 19th C. .... **$400+**

Churn, dasher type, pieced tin, flared sides, 2 strap handles, lid with funnel, American (?), 18-1/4"H, 19th C. **$225**

Churn, dasher type, pottery, lacking lid & dasher, Catawba, NC, 19th C. **$150**

Churn, dasher type, pottery, no lid or dasher, possibly "Hewell," Gillesville, GA, 19th C. • **Added value.** – Southern origin is the big plus here. Partly this is fashion; other origins are pluses too: Texas, California, or the Southwest, for examples. .... **$250+**

Churn, dasher type, red cedar staves with white oak bands, has lid & cover, 19"H with 33"L dasher, 1980s. .... **$20-$30**

Churn, dasher type, stripped cedar with 4 brass hoops, wooden lid, dasher, sold by Montgomery Ward, American, 3, 4, 5 & 6 gal. capacity, 1890s. • Very much like new Cumberland or Lehman's

***II-12. Dasher, dash or broomstick churns.* (L)** *Gray stoneware, wooden lid & X dasher; came in 7 sizes (2-10 gals.). Old style, but in 1909 catalog. Cost from 40¢ to $1.50; lids extra!* **(R)** *Oak staved churn, with metal rim. Painted blue. Sizes holding 7, 9, 11, 13-1/2, 16, 20, 24, and 28 gallons, from $6.00 to $14.40, in catalog of D. J. Barry, 1924 – a lot later than you'd think. The blue paint must fool a lot of people. Similar churns were also made in cedar. Stoneware most valuable although a painted churn competes for high value.* **$50-$200+**

Reproduction Alert

Cedar Churns. Alert I – Old-fashioned cedar churns are being produced today and advertised "For Decorative Use Only!" and is sold through the Cumberland General Store, Crossville, TN. Their catalogue is a must for reference on variety of "country" kitchen items, still being made exactly like long ago. Dashers sold separately, and they have other churns. • Lehman's Hardware & Appliances, Kidron, OH, offer a red cedar churn also. • **Alert II.** – "An authentic reproduction from America's past. This beautiful churn is handcrafted completely of rich, fragrant cedar with brass-colored metal bands. It makes a handsome decorative item in the kitchen or by the hearth, calling to mind the simpler life of days gone by." Maybe the fragrant cedar does something to the butter, but why then were many old churns made from cedar? Maybe they aged the cedar longer? Or maybe the cedar kept the moths out of the butter? (As well as the "months" – ie. rancid age?) This 34"H churn, with slightly tapered staves, round wooden top, and "brass-colored metal bands" (probably that thin yellow-lacquered metal you find hanging treacherously off old packing crates at the dump) was advertised by Abbey Gifts of Meinrad, IN, in Oct. 1975 *Early American Life*.

churns (see below), except for the brass hoops instead of white oak bands. Dasher is virtually identical. .... **$55+**

Churn, dasher type, redware with dark olive-green glaze, turned wood dasher, simply beautiful, NC, 19th C. .... **$500+**

Churn, dasher type, saltglazed stoneware crock with ear handles, wooden lid & dasher, American, 4 gal. size, 19th C. **$100**

Churn, dasher type, saltglazed stoneware, white & blue, 2 ear handles, wood lid, American, 3 gal. size, 19th C. .... **$125+**

Churn, dasher type, saltglazed stoneware, wood lid & dasher, "Love & Fields Pottery," Dallas, TX, 20th C. .... **$175+**

Churn, dasher type, gray stoneware with blue bands, wooden lid & dasher, "Davis Brothers" stamped in clay, 14"H, 20th C. .... **$150+**

Churn, dasher type, stoneware with brown "Albany" glaze, NY state, 3 gal. size, 19th or early 20th C. .... **$125+**

Churn, dasher type, saltglazed stoneware, stoneware "2" lid, Red Wing, capacity mark #2, lofty clear red wing stencil at just the right uplifted angle, clear stenciled oval mark "Red Wing Union Stoneware Co., Red Wing, Minn" below wing. Lid: 5-3/4" diam. Churn: 12-1/2"H, 20th C. .... **$200+**

Churn, dasher type, stoneware, no lid or dasher, Red Wing, 5 gal., with typical beautiful curlicue blue "5," pair big fat leaves with curved-up ends called by collectors "Elephant Ear" leaves hanging down below straight bar, oval stencil mark below leaves [Note: "Birch Leaves" are narrower & longer, they point down, & serrated edges are more noticeable]. 20th C. .... **$300+**

❖ NOTES ❖

Churn lid value – If present, the original lid (usually wood, whether a stoneware or wooden churn) & dasher should be considered as contributing a lot to value. No lid or dasher at all subtracts value. But it is next to impossible to know beyond a shadow of a doubt if they are really original. Look for warping & patina that seem to match age. Lid should fit, after taking warpage into account. • **Red Wing** churns seem to mostly have had turned stoneware lids, although the lids would have broken more frequently than the churns themselves, and would probably have been replaced with wooden lids. The lids are marked with size number on top; some lids fit more than one size churn. Red Wing lids sell for upwards of about $75.

❖ NOTES ❖

Imperfection – Carl W. Drepperd wrote in *A Dictionary of American Antiques* that reject ceramic wares like the above churn were called **reffus wares**, and were sold cheap from what was called the "reffus box." Modern collectors, always on the outlook for personality and distinctiveness (as separate from, even sometimes opposite to, distinguished) often rummage through that box of refuse with great success. The pieces have tales to tell in their sagged lips, misshapen bellies, discolored glazes. I was at a country auction in late 1988 where a much smaller, saggy churn sold for $100; an indicator of a growing market for such things. See **Wabi-sabi** in the Index, to read more on the Japanese aesthetic of imperfection.

❖ NOTES ❖

The Milk-House of Col. M'Allister, Fort Hunter, on the Susquehanna, in 1828. "A household convenience worthy of imitation," reported visitor Judge Buel. "The Milk-house was built in the north-east side of a slope near the well, and not far from the mansion. It was composed of stout stone walls, and the roof, which rose six or eight feet above the surface of the ground, appeared to be covered with earth or tile, and was deeply shrouded with the scarlet trumpet creeper (*Bignonia radicans*), then in splendid bloom. The interior of the house, principally under ground, was fitted up with cisterns, in which water stood nearly to the tops of the pans of milk, which were arranged in them. The house was entered by a flight of steps on the south, and there was a window on the north, which could be opened or darkened at pleasure, to give ventilation. For want of a natural spring, which many Pennsylvanians consider almost indispensable in a milk-house, the water was conducted in a pipe from the well-pump, and after filling the cisterns to a certain height, passed off at the opposite side. The object was to obtain a cool temperature, in the heat of summer, which greatly facilitates the separation of the cream from the milk; this object was amply effected, with the labor of working occasionally at the well-pump." *The Farmers' Cabinet*, Vol. I, No. 1, Philadelphia, July 1, 1836.

II-13. Side crank churn. "Blanchard," mfd. by Porter Blanchard's Sons, Concord, NH. Came in 7 sizes, for from 2 to 150 gallons. With pulleys could be empowered by animals or windmills. 1875-76 flyer states that it can be operated whilst sitting down. "Women have not been as much benefited as men by the invention of labor-saving machines for the farm," said flyer, comparing sit-down Blanchard with tiresome "old upright dash churn ... which tasks the whole upper portion of the body." (Aerobically speaking, the dash provided a much superior exercise, as the Blanchard worked only "the muscles of the arms." A candidate for late-night infomercials?) **$50-$175+**

Churn, dasher type, white saltglazed stoneware with blue bands, wood lid & dasher, "No. 3" capacity mark, early 20th C. .... **$125-$170**

Churn, saltglazed stoneware, applied ear handles, overheated (or underheated?) & sagged in kiln, rugged but tired (or dashed-but-no-dasher), marked only with capacity: "No. 6," American, 18"H, approx. diam. 7-1/2", 19th C. It is very hard to price things like this. I like the crazy look of it, the personality, but the maker must have been disappointed. (You may ask, if the artist didn't like it, is it art?) .... **$200+**

Churn, dasher type, tin body, tin lid, wooden dasher. These & other dasher churns are sometimes called "broomstick churns" because of the dasher handle, which was replaceable with a screw-on type broomstick handle, American, 19th C. **$150**

Churn, dasher type, tin with flared out lip, slightly conical body, 2 handles, all with original mustard paint, American, 25"H, 3rd or 4th quarter 19th C. .... **$250-$350**

❖ NOTES ❖

Matching Toy – The tin mustard-colored churn is exactly the type of churn with flared lip, found as part of Ives' "Churning Woman" (or "Lady Churner") clockwork mechanical toy pat'd. 1874, right down to the mustard color! If you had that rare toy (which would cost you thousands to buy), you might want to pay two times as much for the real churn to use it as a pedestal base for the toy!

"Good" or "Nice." – I hope I've excised most instances of these two adjectives, because they are basically meaningless, being relative to physical & cultural contexts & viewpoint of the observer. Many ad and auction catalog writers wear out the adjectives "very fine," "important," "exceedingly good," "good" and "nice." When you are selling something, those words add nothing to the description, and are self-serving. They will not add to your eBay description line. When you're a writer, you need a new vocabulary. I have tried to use both sparingly, when I needed to imply some degree of added desirability, without being able to go into all nuances of what makes a patina good or a shape nice. Israel Sack always rated furniture he saw or sold with "good" being the lowest level acceptable to him. He used a mental checklist of attributes against which everything was measured; you have to develop your own.

Churn, dasher type, with original (or at least old) wood lid with turned knob, staved straight-sided wooden body painted light ochre, bentwood hoop at top, also iron bands, good patina & color, American (?), or poss. Canadian, 19-3/4"H x 9"diam., c.1830s-50s. **$175**

Churn, dasher type, wooden staves in old faded red paint, American (?), 18-1/2"H, 19th C. Paint adds value. .... **$225+**

Churn, dog-powered, 2 part, wood, with painted churn body, requires treadmill & big, strong dog, maybe a Newfoundland. (I'm sure the family pet, in the sense we think of it today, was much different a century ago. Sentiment was OK for lap dogs, but a bigger dog earned its keep.) American, late 19th C. .... **$250-$400**

Churns, electric – See them in Chapter XVIII (Electrifying Work).

Churn, glass tabletop, metal lid has round perforated whey screen, exposed gear to crankshaft, angled side handle with wood grip, crank handle angled to conform to lid – just misses when cranked, bulbous jar marked "Dazey Churn No. 4 Pat App For Made in St Louis MO U.S.A. Dazey Corporation," jar 9-1/4"H; lid 5-1/2"; crank & wood paddles 12"H. Somewhat older than next listing, but newer than those marked "Dazey Churn & Mfg. Co.," prob. c.1935-40. .... **$125+**

II-14. Dasher churn. Gray saltglazed stoneware with cobalt partridge decoration. Notice the beautiful spotted chest, and number "5." Impressed near one handle with mark: "T. Harrington." 18"H. Photo courtesy Litchfield Auction Gallery, Litchfield, CT. Ex-Harold Corbin Collection, auctioned Jan. 1, 1990, for $4,200.00. **$4,000+**

II-15. Dog power churns. Both are homemade versions of more expensive tread-power churns. American Agriculturist, April 1876. Compare the poor dog on the right with your hamster; or with the turnspit dog in Illustration X-93 (Chapter X).

Churn, glass tabletop, metal lid has removable perforated whey screen, with bulbous, egg-shape gear-housing paint-enameled red, wooden paddles, "Dazey Churn No. 4, Model 4," nicknamed a "Red Ball," a "football top," or a "red top" by collectors, but advertised by the company as "The New Streamlined," bulbous, bottom-heavy round jar embossed on bottom "Dazey Churn, No. 4, Pat. App For, St. Louis, MO. U.S.A. Dazey Corporation" (another has "Dazey Churn Corp."), late 1940s. (Also came in an 8-quart, #80 size, worth a bit more. So far the 2-quart #20 that was advertised hasn't showed up.)... **$115+**

Churn, glass tabletop, square jar embossed "Dazey Churn No. 40," metal screw-on lid, vertical rectangle side grip part of gear frame, red-painted turned wood crank grip. c.1950s?............................. **$75+**

Churn, glass tabletop, metal & wood, gear housing is round domed metal top painted white (came in other colors), red wood crank handle, squatter jar, much simpler than earlier Dazeys, "Dandy Deluxe Churn," designed by Jack P. Dazey, Jr., mfd. by Taylor Brothers Churn & Mfg. Co., St. Louis, MO, 1 qt. size, 1940s?... **$90+**

Churn, glass tabletop called the "fruit jar" churn by collectors because Dazey made the gear assembly & screw-on lid so that it could be used on practically any fruit jar from one quart to a half-gallon size. Very sensible, as most homes early in the 20th C would have had fruit jars, and people must have appreciated not having to order a replacement jar from Dazey. Not marked, but believed to be Dazey's. c.1930s? .... **$125+**

Churn, glass tabletop, jar with cast iron frame & gears, metal blades. "Mak-Mor Butter Machine," NYC, NY, "Makes two pounds from one pound of butter." Pat'd. May 30, 1911. • This isn't really a churn, but a way of stretching butter: you add one pint of milk to one pound of butter & end up with two pounds of butter!... **$100+**

Churn, glass tabletop type, iron gears, wood paddles, "Perfection MixMaster," American, 1 gal. size...... **$75+**

Daisy, Dazey, All For the Love of You! – These are tabletop churns for the most part, the really collectible ones usually having a glass body, [usually] iron crank & screw-on lid, & wood beater blades, sometimes with holes. Surprising numbers of these have survived, possibly because people still enjoy using them. They were manufactured in various sizes by the "Dazey Churn & Manufacturing Co.," St. Louis, MO, and were pat'd. Feb. 14, 1922. Enough variation in the glass bodies and the crank mechanism makes this a hot category for collectors! Note that sometimes people advertise these as "Daisy" or "Dazy" churns – same thing, wrong spelling. (See also the Churn, cylinder floor model by Dazey, in a listing above. Also the Churn, tabletop, tin by Dazey below.) Dazey Sizes. Various sizes found: 1, 2, 4, 6, & 8 quarts. The "gross capacity" was higher than the actual churning capacity. For 30 years or so, following a common manufacturing practice for all kinds of non-churn items, sizes were indicated by adding "0" to the quart size – the one quart is #10, the two quart is #20, etc. Often the paper label is incomplete or missing. An ad from January 1911 gives sizes as 3, 5, 7-1/2 and 9 pints, and – due out by March 1911 – 2 and 3 gallon sizes. Just to keep collectors on their toes a century later! **Dazey Prices Are a Doozie.** I have not yet been able to sort out all sizes & numbers, having not found a catalog. I hesitate printing the new prices, as everybody will think they're sitting on a gold mine, and then the bubble will burst. I believe it surely will, perhaps by the time this edition is published. The price range was pretty stable for years, inching up just a bit all the time, until recently, and although $50-$100 is still the range where some can be found, it looks like the sky is the limit for the rarest models. Value for a #10 (1-quart) depends on the shape of its glass body, and its overall condition, so it can go from $150 to $10,000+; a #20 is zooming up, now about $150. A person at a greater remove than I from the subject, should write a long, thoughtful essay on values vs. prices. I can't imagine myself ever paying that kind of money for an item produced in large or small quantities barely 75 years ago. **One Quart Rarities.** Such a little churn for so much money! The jar is only about 3-1/2" square, and the height with the mechanism is about 11-1/2"H. There are three glass jar styles for the #10 1-quart churn: (1) The oldest (c.1907) is called the "**horseshoe label**" Dazey with the name embossed in something like an arch or upside-down horseshoe shape, and has beveled rounded edges or corners, and the effect at the top is a curved arch (it's worth about $2,000+); (2) One is almost square at the top and has a bulls'-eye type circle on side of glass body (to surround a paper label – usually missing) and is called the "**bulls'-eye**" or "bullseye" (it's worth about $1,750+); some jars are marked on the bottom "Made in America," which is rarer than the "Made in U.S.A."; (3) the third is the "**slope shoulder**" or "SS" type; it has very sloping shoulders and is the rarest of the three (it can bring from $5,500 – $10,000 because so few are known). [Note that the three jar forms listed for the #10s came in other sizes too, but the #10 one-quarts are the most valuable.] "**Flowered Dazey**" or "Flower Bottom" churn is another rarity. It has an embossed, large rather simple daisy on the bottom of the jar, and

goes for upwards of $200. **Replacement whey strainer.** You can buy a replacement whey strainer (sometimes inaccurately referred to as a "fly screen") for the lid of almost any Dazey churn if yours has rusted out or is missing. Churn Castle Antiques' Wendell & Donna Stream offer them at their Web site, which also has history and values: http://showcase.netins.net/web/churns/. Their mailing address is 809 Maple Ave., Woodward, IA 50276; e-mail: xisp142@netins.net. **Dazey Company History.** There is a lot of Dazey information and many photos of churns in Thornton's Eggbeater Chronicles (see eggbeater listings). • An interest-ing Web site for Dazey company history, starting with E. B. Jones' initial small glass tabletop churn, is found at this Web site: www.geocities.com/junipercreekfarm/skills/dairy/dazey.htm.

Reproduction Alert

Cumberland General Store sells what they call "a copy of the old **Dazey**" that is "imported from Far East."

• • •

Lookalike alarm: Lehman's online catalog sells a "hand churn ... the only one made today with a glass jar ... similar to the well-known 'Dazey.'" Churns 2-1/2 quarts, has square jar with very rounded shoulders, metal gear frame, wood crank handle, and vertical metal grip at top of gear assembly to "hold the churn steady when turning." They also have a replacement one-gallon jar that's 8"H x 6-1/2" square; fits 4-3/4" lids.

Churn, glass tabletop, 4 sided jar, wooden beaters, screw-on tin lid, gear housed in red metal cone with handle grip on one side, & nice arching crank (with red wood knob) on other side. Embossed on jar is circle with smiling lion's head. "Monarch Finer Foods Churn," American (?), 9-3/4"H, c.1940s........... **$80+**

Churn, glass tabletop, with wooden paddles, "Elgin," original paper label, 2 qt. size, 20th C. .... **$80+**

Churn, glass tabletop, square jar, iron gears & lid, wood dasher-beaters, The "Premier Two Minute Butter Machine," Culinary Mfg. Co., Orange, NJ, 13"H x 4-3/4" square, c.1910. • The "Premier's" paper labels are usually intact & mostly readable. Amazing in something washed so often...................... **$125+**

Churn, "piggy" type, suspended & worked like a rocker churn, without the cradle. Pieced tin with torpedo ends, 4 little legs, rectangular built-up lid in top, with handle, American, 19th C. .... **$300-$400**

Churn, powered by washing machine, aluminum, Maytag, 15"H x 13-1/2 diam., early 20th C. Go-with for appliance collectors...................................... **$75+**

Churn, rocker style, all wood including crank & paddles, 4 legs, original blue milk paint, American, 30"H, 19th C. .... **$225+**

Churn, rocker type, in 4-legged wooden cradle, old red milk paint, supposedly Shaker, 19th C. (another color found is gray). • Shaker is always hot in the same way early American used to be, and the attribution is often given when unwarranted and unsupported by docu-

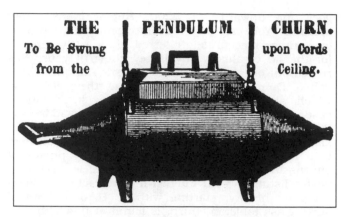

II-16. "Piggy" style swinging churn. "The Pendulum Churn," mfd. by Dairy Supply Co., NYC. Pieced tin, with "... no dasher, paddles, or inside work of any kind to injure the grain of the butter – surpasses all dash and crank churns. ... Takes up no floor room and is hung up out of the way when not in use." 1879 ad. Pushme-Pullyou action would have been fun ... for a while! **$300+**

ments or documented examples. It is hard to say if the Shakers' works will ever be sufficiently documented. Furthermore, pieces made for sale to the world at large were mass-produced, and have much less value than pieces made for community use. Study books, and visit Shaker museums. .... **$300+**
Churn, tabletop, tin body, blue painted, wooden top, iron gears & stand (or frame), 4 legs, wood dashers,

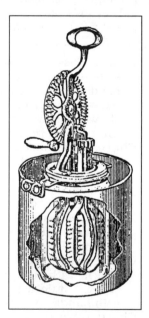

II-17. Butter merger. "Holt's Jar Cream Whip" used for adding milk to butter to extend it. "Put 1 pint unskimmed sweet milk in the 1 quart jar; add 1 lb. of butter. Pour luke warm water between jar and can. Let it stand between 5 and 7 minutes. Turn crank two minutes and you will have 2 lbs. of sweet butter." Here dasher beater is shown screwed onto inner glass jar down inside a metal can. Holt-Lyon Co., Tarrytown, NY. Pat'd. Apr. 3, 1900. House Furnishing Review ad, March 1911. A similar butter merger is the "Home Butter Merger," mfd. by the Family Butter Merger Co., in Indianapolis. It was pat'd. by Benjamin N. Hawes, Sept. 14, 1909. It also has a tin outer body, and an inner container for warm water to hasten the formation of butter. Funny enough, Family Butter Merger Co. stated in their ads a cautionary note: "Never buy a machine of any kind unless it is protected by patents. They are always frauds and may get you in trouble. Our Butter Mergers are the only ones in the world that are protected by honest patents." This, despite the fact that the Holt-Lyon was patented 9-1/2 years before! Another unsolved mystery? Either Holt or Home: **$200+**

II-18. Butter machines or Tabletop churns. (L)"The "Premier" Two Minute Butter Machine, Culinary Mfg. Co., c.1910. Square glass jar with original label, wooden paddle inside, cast iron frame & compound gears. Probably made in 1, 2, 3, and 4-qt. sizes. This one, with its shapely handgrip, was also marketed as the "Crest" churn. (R) "Dazey" churn, called the "Red Ball" or the "football" churn by collectors; marked "Dazey Churn, No. 8, 8 Qt. Model B." Bottom of glass jar notice the distinctive ridges near bottom, "Dazey Churn, Pat App For. Made in St. Louis. U.S.A. Dazey Corporation." Red paint on egg-shaped gear housing and crank handle. Jar 11-1/4"H; overall height 14-3/4". Photo courtesy Shades of the Past by Nan of Grand Terrace, CA, www.tias.com/stores/shadespast, (eBay: shadespast). (L) $125+; (R) $125+

looks like a Dazey churn, but not marked, about 18"H, early 20th C. .... **$100+**
Churn, tabletop, tin container with wooden top, 4 short legs, "Dazey Churn Co.," St. Louis, MO, 14"H x 12" square, 20th C. .... **$125+**
Churn, tabletop, japanned tin cylinder, top cranked, American, 19th C. **$125**
Churn, tabletop, turned wood, beautiful patina, American, 13-1/8"H, 19th C. .... **$300+**
Churn, tabletop tin with wood paddle, "Connfaut Can Co.," American, 21-1/2"H, 40 qt. capacity, 20th C. .... **$125+**
Churn, tabletop, tin, wood, iron, 2 handles, "Buffums Little Wonder," American, 34"H. .... **$130+**
Churn, tabletop, vivid grain painted wood, brown & ochre, American, 19th C............................. **$225+**
Churn, tabletop, wood barrel, wood blades, cranked handle, red stenciled cow decoration, "J. B. Varick Co.," 14-1/4"H x 13" diam., early 20th C...... **$175+**
Churn, yellow painted wood, floor-standing with 3 legs, lid with wooden knob, stenciled "Union Churn," mfd. by Grand Detour Wagon Co., Dixon, IL, pat'd. Dec. 20, 1864. Pat'd. by C. H. Warren & A. C. Baldwin, Tiffin, OH. **$200**
Churn & butter maker, glass tabletop, with wood paddles, has original instructions. "Home Butter Maker," American, 1 gal. size........................ **$110+**
Churn or butter maker, hexagonal glass vessel used in horizontal position, screw-on zinc caps at each end, "Churn your butter while riding across country," 7-1/2"L, "pat. appl. for," but early 20th C......... **$135+**

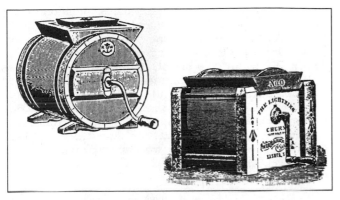

II-19. Tabletop cylinder churns. *Wood, in two popular styles.* **(L)** *Cedar, on shoe feet, marked "R.W." with an anchor; sold through* Montgomery Ward, *1890s-1910 or so.* **(R)** *"The Lightning," mfd. by Porter Blanchard's Sons, Rutland, VT, c.1890s 1910s. Both came in several sizes.* **$100+**

Churn & butter worker, wooden frame, triangular A shape supports like a swing set, and indeed, the churn can swing "when desired, but while being worked it is retained in an upright position by a board and catch," which are midway up the frame. Over the churn body, which is octagonal with slightly flared out sides, is an arched cast iron frame with a beveled gear in the center worked by a small crank. The short, slightly curved dashers are stuck at angles up and down and around the central fat wooden dasher shaft, working like a turbine. Has 2-part wooden cover. In an 1858 *Scientific American* write-up, it is claimed "This churn renders the oper-

II-21. Tabletop churn & butter worker. *"Julien – The standard churn of our country," Julien Churn Co., probably Dubuque, IA. Three sizes: holds 8 gallons (churns 5), holds 10 (churns 7), holds 13 (churns 10). Wood & metal. American Agriculturist, Jan. 1869.* **$175+**

ation of churning and preparing butter for the market very simple and easy." Pat'd. Jan. 12, 1858 by & for sale by Justin M. Smith, Lyme, CT. .... **$200+**

Churn or butter separator, cranked, wood body with iron hoops, spout on side has wood plug, wood handle, "Fayway," American, 16"H, 19th C. • How does King Kong make butter? With a Fayway. Hee hee. **$200**

Cocktail shaker, bowling pin shape, top of turned maple, unscrews from lower chromed part, American, 56 oz. capacity, same size as regulation bowling pin, late 1930s. This is the kind of thing that in the right booth at the right moderne show is just kitschy enough to get good money! .... **$150+**

Cocktail shaker, chrome coffee boiler shape with odd phallic spout, yellow Catalin™ (or other molded phenolic resin) plastic handle & knobs, black incised bands on handle, "Krome Kraft," Farber Brothers, NYC, NY, 12"H, c.1930s, after 1933 (when Prohibition ended). .... **$125+**

II-20. Tabletop churn. *All metal, painted blue, cream, or other colors. Natural wood top & turned crank handle, wood dashers, cast iron gears & crank, 18"H. "Dazey," mfd. by Dazey Churn Mfg. Co., St. Louis, MO. pat'd. Dec. 18, 1877 by Michael K. Duty (#198,363), but sold for many years, at least 20 years into 20th C. (Later ones with large flywheel at crank were pat'd. by Nathan Dazey, Dec. 18, 1917.) Came in size #s 100 to 1600, holding from 1 to 16 gallons. [Note that the "Elgin" churn, identified only with a paper label, looks exactly like this one, and has no flywheel either. Possibly Duty's patent was first made by Elgin?] Photographed stock of Country Basket, West Dennis, MA.* **$300+**

II-22. Cocktail shaker. *Realistic bell-shape. Nickeled brass, screw on cap, turned wood handle. 11"H, 20th C. Alas, although real ringing school bells would be brass (or bell metal), this one should have its nickeled finish. I wouldn't be surprised to see them showing up stripped, at higher prices. Some crossover interest from bell collectors.* **$55+**

Cocktail shaker, schoolmarm's bell shape, stainless steel, turned wooden handle screws off bell body to add ingredients; small shaker spout on side with screw cap, American, 11"H, 20th C. A full set has 4 bell-shaped glasses each with a clapper in the bottom that rings when the glass is lifted, and an 18" tray, and might bring up to $300. Just the shaker: .... **$55+**

Cocktail shaker, World's Fair souvenir, aluminum with black letters & depiction of buildings around top border. American, 1933 – same year Prohibition ended. • Crossover competition from Expo & World's Fairs collectors might add to price. .... **$200+**

Cocktail shaker set, rocket ship, chromed brass, the shaker body stores 4 cups, 1 small footed jigger cup, a lemon reamer, 4 spoons. Rocket has 4 fins at small bottom end. Top is larger diam. dome. Only mark is "Made in Germany," 12"H, prob. 1930s, after 1933 (?). • What does it really represent? Not only does it look like a space rocket, it could also be a torpedo, and given the time, who knows? However, the fact that it's marked "Made in Germany" means that at least some were intended for import to the U.S.A., which required country of origin after March 1, 1891. (**Lookalike alarm:** A new silverplate rocket shaker set, with 2 wheels under the bow, was made in the late 1990s.) .... **$950+**

II-23. Cocktail shaker set, in rocket ship shape, with parts that all fit inside! Including 4 spoons, small fitted jigger cup, 4 cups and the shaker. Notice the lemon reamer in the shallow part at left. 12"H, German, c.1930s (?). [Note: a new silverplated rocket cocktail shaker, with two wheels under the bow, was made late 1990s.] Old one: $950+

Cream separator, cast iron base, parts bolted on, heavy gauge tin top, crank, all painted in farm machinery orange, with yellow & black pinstriping, adjustable belt drive, bent wire lever regulates hole in top hopper, "Egret" in gold script, and shield shaped brass ID plate reading "Entrahmen Reinigen ZU," which is prob. Zurich, Switzerland, 15"H x 12-1/2"L, late 19th C. .... **$165+**

Cream separator, table top, "Royal Blue Jr," American, c.1900.. **$80+**

Cream separator, tin with wooden legs, uses gravity, "Marvel," 20th C............................... **$45+**

❖ NOTES ❖

Cream whip, Drink mixer, Eggbeater, Mixer or Syllabub churn? Smallish devices used for these purposes are often interchangeable, but I've tried to list them with the subject heading under which they are most noted or were most commonly advertised.

Cream whip, footed tin container, "Hodges," c.1900... **$65+**

Cream whip, squared tin blade beater-whipper, tinned cast metal gear marked "WHIPPO Super-Whip," tin lid slips over lip of glass jar marked on bottom with an "I" in an elongated diamond, 10-1/2"H, mfd. by Dover Stamping & Mfg. Co. and based on a turbine beater pat'd. Nov. 25, 1924 by Wells G. Ruggles. **$150**

❖ NOTES ❖

Hey, Archimedes! Whaddyuh call it? – I used to call this mechanism (as in next listing, and many eggbeaters) an "Archimedean screw," but this is inaccurate. The screw mechanism lifted water. The eggbeaters are a form of Archimedean drill mechanism. Here is the definition from *Hawkins' Mechanical Dictionary*, Audel's, 1909: "A hand drill for light work, whose stock is formed into a multiple spiral of quick pitch over which a nut or spool slides easily. The act of sliding the nut up and down the stock makes the latter and consequently the drill, rotate first one way and then the other, pressure being applied by a knob or ball at the opposite end of the stock." The Archimedian drill was also called a "Persian drill" in turn-of-century inventors' books on mechanical movements.

Cream whip, metal & stained wooden handle, Archimedean drill action, advertising legend on handle reads, "We have competition beaten to a froth and whipped to a cream paste. Henry Brooks, General Merchandise. James Store, Virginia," mfd. by A & J, in Binghamton, NY, 12-1/2"L, pat'd. Oct. 15, 1907. .... **$100**

Cream whip, nickeled sheet metal, long vertical shaft with wooden knob, rectangular perforated blade curves up to fit into sides of its glass mixing bowl, "New Dream Cream Whip," Kohler Die & Specialty, De Kalb, IL, about 12"L, c.1926. • Added value. – Costs the most with original shouldered glass "Utility" mixing bowl. .... **$95+**

Cream whip, tin body, 4 little strap tin legs, cast iron crank & beaters inside, "Fries," American, 8"H x 6"L x 4-1/2"W, c.1890s. .... **$100-$175**

The Census & Collecting. Don't Get Discouraged. If you think all the good stuff is probably gone, think again. Just look at the population figures for any given decade, and think how many probable owners of a corkscrew, frying pan, nutcracker, grater or cream whip those numbers imply. The rounded-off population of the U.S. in 1890 was 65,000,000 people. Even if we divide that by 6, to represent households of two adults and four children, that leaves almost 11 million homes. Of those, maybe one in 50 or 100 had a cream whip, but that's still encouraging – say 110,000 cream whips in use during the last decades of the 19th C. Even if only one in 10 survived rust, moving, war drives, and the unblushing blandishments of advertisers of "new & improved" things, there may be 11,000 of them still around. Even if there's but one in every village in the U.S., there is probably one for you. I've never bought one – one of you can have the one I didn't buy! And this hypothesis is only for something that was probably uncommonly owned to begin with. There were millions of Dover and A&J eggbeaters sold over the years; millions of frying pans; hundreds of millions of forks and spoons. • Still not convinced? **Advertising Claims & Collecting.** – In many old ads you will see manufacturers' claims about the quantity sold. For example, in a 1890 ad for the "Morgan Broiler," made by The Sun Stamping Co., it was said that "50,000 Housewives" bear out the claim that "the broiler is a demonstrated success." Even if they stopped making them that day, that still means an awful lot of those collectible broilers are possible finds!

II-24. Cream whips, egg beaters, or batter mixers. *(L) Not marked; probably same as one on (R), which is a "Fries." **(R)** 8"H x 6" x 4-1/2". Ex-Keillor Collection. Notice the differences in lids, and the wood grip on crank. One ad I have calls it the "Economy" cream and topping beater, and gives 3 sizes: 10"H x 6" x 5-1/2"; 10-1/2"H x 6-1/2" x 6-1/4"; and 12-7/8"H x 7-1/2" x 8-1/8", holding from 6 to 16 pts. Other sizes appear in other ads. An electric one, the "Dumore," looks like these, but has crankshaft hooked up to a pulley with a small electric motor. Late 19th to early 20th C, made many years.* **$100-$175**

Cream whip, turbine type, steel with nickel silver curved rectangular blade. Looks like NASA skywatch dish, with cutout gear wheel & angled wood handle. Small depression or dimple in bottom of bowl fits pivot on bottom of beater so it won't slip during use, "Dunlap's Sanitary Silver Blade Cream & Egg Whip, No Splash or Waste," J. S. Dunlap; distributed by Casey-Hudson Co, Chicago, 11"L, pat'd 1906-1916. .... **$35+**

Cream whip & eggbeater, glass & stainless steel, lid, beaters & crank all in one, "Androck," Rockford, IL, 1930s. .... **$20+**

Cream whip & eggbeater, tin cylinder with wire dasher handle, "Lightning," marked "pat'd. 1868" on the one I saw at a flea. Authority Don Thornton finds no evidence to support the name-and-date combo that I'm 999% sure I once saw. He has a white porcelain one, with metal dasher, 9"H, printed underglaze "The Lightning" "Grafton's Patent 11075 Size 1 Eggbeater," English. .... **75+**

Cream whips – See also: Drink mixers, Eggbeaters, Syllabub churns

Crock, for mixing bread, saltglazed gray stoneware, "White Hall," 18" diam., early 20th or late 19th C. .... **$100+**

Dough bowl, trough-shaped, carved wood, very smooth patina, indicating long use, American (?), 24"L x 10"W, 19th C. • In the late 1980s, at the big flea market in Hillsville, VA, I saw a large number of skillfully, but primitive-looking, carved dough troughs priced $35, which wouldn't take long to age. (I didn't see them a year or so later, and 10 years later they seem

to have been replaced with the French bread rising trays.)..................................... **$100-$200**

Dough bowl, trough-shaped, primitively-carved oak, American, 18"L x 9-1/2"W, early 19th C. • Value depends on patina, size, wood, & supposed age. "American" on a price tag often equals a lot of moolah on your bill. .... **$100+**

Dough box, also bread or dough brake, oblong pine box with slanting sides, cover has inchworm-like carved handles, American or Scandinavian, 8-1/2"H x 23"L, 19th C. .... **$300+**

Dough box, slanted sides, 4 simply turned legs, wood on outside has original dark brown paint under flaking white, American, 26-1/2"H x 41-5/8"L x 22-1/2"W, c.1870s. .... **$250+**

Drink mixer, eggbeater & cream whip, Archimedean drill action, domed snap-on metal lid with simple twisted or spiraled flat strip of metal, 4 upturned turbine blades at bottom, wooden knob at top, tall glass tumbler, "Roberts Lightning," mfd. by Dorsey Mfg. Co., Boston, MA, 12"H, c.1910s well into 1920s, perhaps later. .... **$125+**

Drink mixer or eggbeater, nickeled wire, metal, wood, Archimedean drill action, "Boun-C Beater," American, 13"L, 20th C. .... **$25+**

Drink mixer, Archimedean drill action, glass jar with tin lid, spiral tin whipper, 16"H, pat'd. Mar. 30, 1915 by Turnet H. Stough of Jeanette, PA, patent

II-25. Soda fountain drink mixers. *Cranked hand-power, not electric. (See electric ones in Chapter XVIII.) **(L)** "Quick and Easy" shaker, possibly Conant Co. Nickeled & painted cast iron, 22"H, for all beverages; c.1905 catalog. **(R)** "Coles' Shaker" or "Philadelphia" milk shake machine, 24"H, 7-1/2" x 12" base. "Each turn of the crank-wheel gives ten distinct shocks to the liquid." Coles Mfg. Co., Philadelphia, PA, in T. Mills Catalog, 1915.* **$600-$1,500+**

#1,133,413. This one is marked simply with a monogram of an "A & D" (not A & J). Maker not yet identified. Another one, same patent date, has wire finger-like beater, like a glove-drying form, worked by the Archimedean drill, and is valued approximately the same as the spiral, perhaps a bit more............ **$55+**

Drink mixer, Archimedean drill, wire with turned wooden handle, steel blades in small balloon, small pivoting "foot" on bottom seats it steady in bowl or jar, A & J, 12-1/2"L, Oct. 15, 1907. .... **$25**

Drink mixer, from a drugstore or soda fountain, nickeled cast metal, complete protective gear housing, golden oak base, "Quik Mix, A-1," base 8-1/4"H, mixing mechanism 9"H, c.1920s. .... **$150+**

Drink mixer, metal shaker & lid, "Ovaltine," early 1900s. Ovaltine, by the way, is a malt drink mix that originated in Great Britain. The American version was formulated with more and more sugar as the 20th C. progressed, but now the original version of Ovaltine, as sold nowadays in Europe, is obtainable through the Vermont Country Store, Weston, VT. They also have other old-time foods & chewing gum!.................. **$20+**

Drink mixer or shaker, for children, plastic with decals, Captain Midnight character, "Ovaltine" mixer, 20th C. .... **$45+**

Drink mixer & measure, aluminum, graduated cup shows 1/3, 2/3, and "1 cup to top"; other side marked-1/4, 1/2, and 3/4 cup, screw-on lid, marked "Smoothie Mixer & Measure" on top, 3-7/8"H x 2-3/4" diam., 1st third 20th C. **$12**

Drink or malted milk mixer, aluminum container with lid, "Thompson's Double Malted," 7"H, 20th C. **$15**

Drink or malted milk mixer, all wire frame, small sheet metal thumb piece to work Archimedean drill, for making a "Horlick's" drink. 9-1/2"L, American. Horlick's also had a malted milk plant in England, and the Horlick's "Aero Beater," similar to this one, was patented in England. .... **$20-$30**

Drink mixer or stirrer, battery-powered, chrome, in original box, 1940s.. **$10**

Drink mixer or stirrer, cast metal golf club, from a club car on the "B & O" railroad, 20th C. Two-way crossover: golf and trains! .... **$45+**

Drink mixer – jigger & swizzle sticks, chromium top hat & 4 golf clubs, very jazzee, "Chase Brass & Copper," Waterbury, CT, 1-1/2 oz. capacity jigger, mid 1930s. $1 was the original price. .... **$25+**

Drink mixer or stirrer, silver plated coil with handle, "Holmes, Edwards," dated 1889. .... **$15**

Drink mixer or stirrer, stainless steel, telescoping, "Spoonomat," 11-3/4"L, pat'd. Mar. 15, 1938. .. **$15**

Drink mixers – See also: Syllabub churn

❖ NOTES ❖

Wire Drawing – It seems impossible that something as logical as wire isn't older than it is. The useful art of wire-drawing (pulling malleable or soft metal through a small hole in a hard metal die plate to make a flexible, fine, metal thread) was known in the 1300s in Europe, and was introduced into England after 1650.

Egg whip, sheet metal, on wire frame, with large flat spoon with 4 large cutouts, also used as a pastry blender, stamped at end of handle "The Vandeusen Egg Whip, C. A. Chapman, Geneva, NY," 11"L, pat'd. Mar. 13, 1894. .... **$15-$20**

II-26. Eggbeater trade card. *"Surprise," Cragin Mfg. Co., Cragin, IL. "An Egg Beater that beats the Whites of Eggs better than any other. Cranks will not be tolerated in Egg Beaters any more. Five Dollars offered for a better Egg Beater for the Whites of Eggs. All first-class Cooks recommend them. Take one home and TRY IT, and if not convinced it is the best bring it back." Circa 1870s card; beater sold at least 30 years. In separate cut below the trade card, note the difference in braced handle from similar ones shown in next two pictures. The card:* **$7-$15**

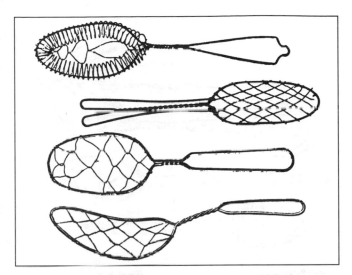

II-27. Egg whips or egg whisks. *Tinned wire, various gauges. **(T)** Spring wire coiled around rim, inner network of thin wire. **(M-1, -2)** Two variations of the "Surprise" are in what the trade called "diamond pattern" wire-weaving. **(B)** Whip in the "checker" pattern. About 8-1/2" to 10"L. Late 19th – early 20th C. See also: II-63-A & II-63-B; and Whisk pictures & listings at end of this chapter.* **$8-$20**

Egg whips or whisks, sauce whips, etc., tinned wire, usually bound-wire handles, sometimes turned wooden handles with ferrules, some have wire slip ring to adjust "ballooning" of the wire loops for beating in different size bowls, or for different needs. A sauce whip, for example, has wires bound in a longer, tighter conformation, while the egg whip has a rounder ballooning shape. American, French, etc., various lengths – about 5-1/2"L to 12"L, 1890s to the present. • Some have been made almost identically for a century or more. Unless really unusual, the price is quite low. .... **$6-$15**

❖ NOTES ❖

Eggbeater Futures: "The future for collecting eggbeaters," says Don Thornton, author of three books on eggbeaters (see end of this chapter), "is unbeatable! Internet auctions have leveled the playing field, giving all collectors a shot, at the same time, at what in the past could take two or three huge Brimfield flea markets to unearth. At the same time, however, the electronic auctions have scrambled prices, with the rarest of the rare bringing unbelievable bids in the thousands of dollars, while values of common and even scarce items have leveled off and sometimes dropped. Of course, beater treasures can still be found at flea markets and antique shows, and these traditional venues should not be ignored. The wild variety of beaters manufactured over the years," says Don, "including rotaries, ratchets, Archimedes, squeeze, rope, and water power, are out there waiting to be discovered. The dedicated collector will prevail. And just when you think you know them all, an old, unknown beater turns up, delighting the kitchen collectibles community and expanding everyone's wish list." **Great Recent Finds Spin Heads:** Don goes on, "For example, a cast-iron beauty patented by prolific beater inventor Timothy

Earle turned up in 2000. Marked 'Earle's Patent. July 7, 1863' it had been featured in a 1869 *Dover Stamping Company* catalog, but no examples had ever surfaced before. Then in 2001, the patent model for the very first rotary crank beater patented in the United States was discovered by California collector Andrew Humbert. It is Ralph Collier's patent, awarded on Dec. 23, 1856, #16,267. It launched an American beating revolution even though the beater itself was never manufactured. Fortunately, the patent model survived for a century and a half." **The World Beats Too:** "In addition," Don reassures us, "there are discoveries waiting to be made all over the world! While the rotary crank eggbeater is considered an American invention – in fact many consider it America's greatest invention – foreign-made mixers are gaining in collector popularity as more and more turn up on the Internet. These include a wild assortment from France, England, Germany, Japan, and Australia – with others sure to follow."

Eggbeater listings are divided into mechanical types, mainly Archimedean drill, and different types of rotary beaters. See also Cream whips, Drink mixers, Syllabub churns, and a fascinating Dazey Ice cream freezer in Chapter XV (Chill, Freeze).

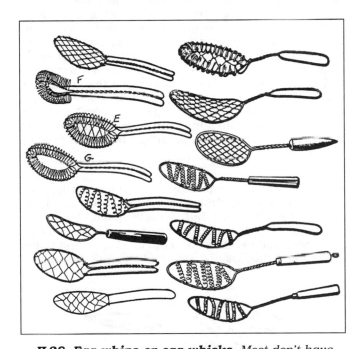

II-28. Egg whips or egg whisks. *Most don't have trade names, only the standard trade pattern names. Such standard names helped retailers order from different mfrs. The "chicken-wire" type is called "diamond" (at bottom left); closer-woven wires are "checker." Four (top right, & E, F, G) are "coiled spring" pattern, and two of those have wire lacing holding springs in place around rim. The four at bottom right, & 5th one on left, are crisscrossed smaller springs, and are called the "cross cut" pattern. Other named ones are marked with letters: "F" for "Flexible"; "E" for "Electric" (earlier known as the "Electra"); "G" for "Gem" – all from Washburn Androck catalog, 1927. Wire Goods Co., Worcester, MA, apparently had earliest patents on these; later Washburn made same or similar designs.* **$8-$20**

Eggbeaters, Archimedean

Eggbeater, all metal, a thin tin tube is the handle grip that you move up & down the twisted wire shaft to activate Archimedean drill, no maker's name, French (?), 12-3/4"L, late 19th or early 20th C. • I used to call this mechanism an Archimedean "screw," but it really is an Archimedean drill mechanism – See explanation above, preceding first "Cream whip" price entry. .... **$135-$150**

Eggbeater, nickel plated, like an Archimedean drill vegetable whip, no maker's mark, 12"L, early 20th C. .... **$45-$60**

Eggbeater, simple wire frame & blades, 2 part shaft – one adds rigidity, one is twisted for Archimedean drill action & threaded through turned wood knob, 12-7/8"L, turn-of-century........................ **$18-$25**

Eggbeater, tin, wire, & turned black wooden vertical handle, Archimedean drill, 2 wings with 4 curved ribs joined to outer circle bow of the blade. "Bryant's Patent," 13-3/4"L, 1885............................. **$175+**

❖ NOTES ❖

Counting Eggbeater Wings. Each half of a blade, as counted from top to bottom (where they are joined or are part of a continuous bent blade) counts as a wing in the old eggbeater-manufacturing lingo. A 4-wing beater means 2 blade circles – blades that come down from the top, then bell out or balloon out at the business end, then continue on back to the top. An 8-wing means 4 blade circles. Blade wings were also called members (and also dashers), so that a 2-blade, 4-wing beater could also be described as having 4 members or 4 dashers. The term "dashers" was borrowed from churn-making, and in fact a few, but not many, eggbeaters have a dashing churn-like motion, up and down.

Eggbeater, skeletal steel wire coiled in flat, vertical spiral, Archimedean drill action, 12"L. Called the "Dudley-Bryant Patent," but actually pat'd. by George Dudley, July 17, 1888, and assigned to, and mfd. by Woods, Sherwood & Co., Lowell, MA, at first. Later mfd. by Paine, Diehl & Co., Philadelphia. Bryant had

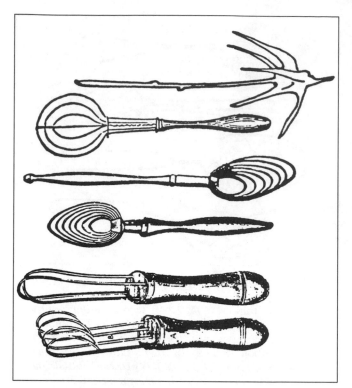

II-30. Swizzle stick & egg whips, some also called spoon egg beaters. From top: (T) is small branched twig, peeled of bark, and used by rolling shaft between hands. (2) Is a "Flat egg-whip, the best shape and easily cleaned." American Home Cook Book, 1854. (3) Next spoon one, 10-1/2"L, has long, turned wood handle with a maroon finish; Wire Goods Co., 1915. (4) Another, by Lalance & Grosjean, came with tin or wood handle, 1890. (5) & (6) Two that resemble garden tools with thick handles, are homemade ones "greatly superior to the common fork or table spoon." 10"L overall. American Agriculturist, June 1876. An American Agriculturist Nov. 1871 article on beaters said "several wire beaters are only forks in a modified form." A pear-shaped wire whisk in the article was judged "a refinement on bundles of twigs long used by confectioners and bakers." (Such twig bundles, in a very small size, have long been used in Japan in the tea ceremony.) $8-$35

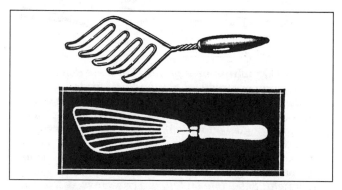

II-29. Egg whips or batter beaters. (T) Five-fingered one is tinned iron wire "Whipster," green wood handle. "Especially good for Angel Food Cakes." Washburn, 1936. (B) Other is a "batter whip," for eggs, batter or cream; choice of Blutip, green, blue or yellow wood handle. 11-1/4"L, A & J Mfg. Co., Binghamton, NY, 1930. $3+

another patent that same day, an Archimedean drill action skeletal beater with a spiral-effect stationary wire blade and a turning one within it. The Dudley-Bryant: .... **$300+**

Eggbeater, iron & steel, 4 "wing" metal blades form a pear shape around central rod shaft, turned & painted upright wooden handle, Archimedean drill mechanism, this particular one has 4 little balancing feet on circular base to settle it firmly in bottom of beater jar, "Johnson's," pat'd. Dec. 18, 1917 by Edward H. Johnson. This beater was made with several different stabilizing devices on the bottom – or none... **$55-$75**

Eggbeater, metal, turned-wood handle, side action Archimedean drill, "Batteur [de?] Bolero," French, 12-1/4"L, late 19th or early 20th C. Similar in action to the George Paine patent of June 28, 1887. .... **$170-$200**

Eggbeater or liquid mixer, tall Archimedean drill action, long shaft with only about 9 twists, wooden spool to run up and down the drill, large loop of wire for other hand, 2 small ballooned blades, with 2 little curved reinforcements that, by adding more cutting edges, make blades more effective. This "Clipper" was advertised as having a "double action" because the inner vertical blades ballooned out when the spool was at its lowest point on the drill. The round blade with curved ribs or reinforcements is the same kind of blade that's part of much older rotary "Earle's Patent." 13"H, pat'd. by Thomas Brown Aug. 30, 1887. .... **$165-$180**

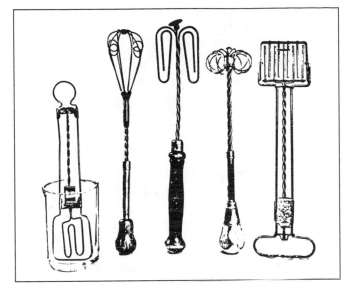

II-32. Eggbeaters & drink mixers. *All Archimedean drill. Far left* **(1)** *is* **"Horlick's"** *drink mixer in glass tumbler, 9-1/4"L, c.1910.* **(2)** *Tin, green-painted wood, wire, 12-1/4"L, German, c.1900.* **(3)** **A. & J.** *Mfg. Co., wire & wood, 12-1/2"L, pat'd. Oct. 1907. Notice the little brass swiveling cap to be centered in bottom of bowl to help keep beater in place. A smaller size (worth more) was for nursery & sick room use.* **(4)** *Tin, wood, wire, 11"L, English, no maker's mark.* **(5)** *The* **"Up To Date** *Egg & Cream Whip," 11-3/4"L, marked "April 10, 1906."* **(1) & (3)** **$30+; (2) $35+; (4)$15+; (5) $200+**

II-31. Cake whip & mixing spoons. *Also called* **vegetable servers.** **(L)** *Slotted & perforated steel spoon with shellacked wood called "antique oak-finish" handles, 11"L, Wire Goods Co., 1915.* **(M)** *Cake whip, stainless steel, handles in ivory with blue band or green with ivory band, 12-1/2"L, A & J Mfg., 1930. Many variations exist.* **(R)** *Earlier version of perforated one was called the "Perfection Cake Spoon," and sold c.1900. (See also: Mixing & cake spoons at end of this chapter; and Vegetable skimmers in Chapter III.)* **$4-$15**

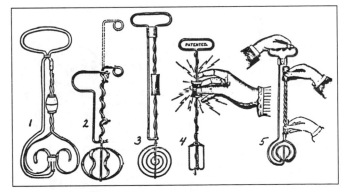

II-33. Eggbeaters & patents – Archimedean *drill.* **(1)** *Pat'd. June 2, 1885, by Charles A.* **Bryant**, *Wakefield, MA.* **(2)** *Pat'd. May 27, 1890, by Alvin Judd* **Austin**, *Shelby, NE. Entirely "wire, whereby a very cheap, simple, and durable egg-beater is produced."* **(3)** **"Dudley-Bryant"** *patent beater, pat'd. July 17, 1888 by George Dudley;* **(4)**" **Lightning Chain"** *eggbeater, mfd. by B.P. Forbes, successor to Tarbox & Bogart, Cleveland, OH. 1903 ad.* **(5)"Bryant's Patent,"** *with much tighter twisting of vertical rod that forms beater screw. They claimed 3200 revolutions a minute, by pushing 4 times up & down per second. Talk about carpal tunnel syndrome! Image from 1888 ad.* **(1) (2) (4) $250-$350+; (5)$175-$200**

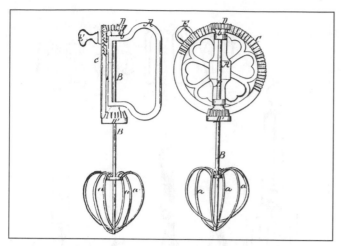

II-34. Eggbeater patent – *for a cranked rotary. Pat'd. April 24, 1866, by* **Timothy Earle.** *If this one ever turns out to have been made, the value will be sky high what with hearts and elegant compact styling, and the Earle imprimatur.*

Eggbeater & cream whip, glass jar, short wire dasher moved up & down as Archimedean drill with white china knob, "Roberts' Lightning Mixer," Dorsey Mfg. Co., Boston. 8"H, based on various 1912/1913 patents of Henry P. Roberts'. At least 3 sizes, and the 12" one worth five times as much.................... **$25+**

Eggbeater & cream whip, glass jar, metal lid, Archimedean drill, turned wooden knob on twisted wire shaft, oblong pattern of close vertical wires – described by the inventor Maurice Roberts as having

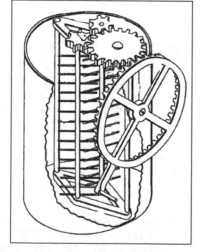

II-35. Eggbeater patent. *"A new and useful instrument or machine called the 'Egg-Cutter'" by the inventor Francis L.* **King** *of Worcester, MA. Pat'd. June 18, 1867, #65,916. King's patent drawings include this one of "the machine complete, placed in a vessel ready for use." The side gear & crank turned the smaller top gear, and the cutters "made of any thin, flat pieces of metal, so as to afford the least possible resistance when in motion, are securely soldered into slots sawed into the vertical shafts." King also claimed that if it worked as intended, "two currents" would be set in motion, and that they would be "antagonistic, and both of equal power; the egg must therefore remain almost motionless while the cutters pass through, and the egg is cut into a fluid ready for use almost instantly." King had patented a simple spoon eggbeater a year before. Compare this machine to the picture and description of the actual machine (II-36) as it was manufactured!*

II-36. Flyer for "The King Egg Beater." *This 6" x 9-1/2" c.1880's advertising flyer shows a quite different eggbeating machine from the patent of 1867. It actually is a depiction of what was marketed as the* **"Perfection Egg Beater."** *It had a tin vessel 3"H x 4" diam., and was based on Francis L. King's 1867 patent, and also Alfred C. Rex's patent of May 13, 1884 (#298,503). King's & Rex's patents both show the distinctive* "antagonistic" meshing horizontal fingers turned in different directions on two shafts connected to a gear on the top. But the finished product has a simple 9-barred gate-like structure inside that had only one shaft. Sometime after the 1884 patent was granted, in my opinion probably about 10 years later – from stylistic evidence, the tin vessel was replaced with a clear glass cup with a big glass handle. There is a wide range of value for the actual beaters: Tin vessel, c.1880s, marked "Pat Applied For": **$400+**; Glass vessel with very big handle, tin top, turned wood crank, space-saucer-like gear housing on top marked "Pat Apld For": **$1000+**; and what's probably the most recent one, with a smaller gear housing, and a glass cup with thinner bottom, but marked "Pat May 13th 1884" is, according to Don Thornton, worth by far the most: **$2,500+**. Flyer courtesy of the Arrandale Collection, Alan Arrandale, Northboro, MA. Its value: **$25+**

a "plurality of beater members." (That's what an octopus with a rug beater has.) "Simplex," mfd. by Jeannette Glass Co., Jeannette, PA, 12"H, "patent pending" – pat'd. Dec. 31, 1918............... **$85-$100**

Eggbeater, plated wire, Archimedean drill, "Skyline," English, 10-1/2"L, 20th C. .... **$12-$18**

Eggbeater & cream whip, wire with square frame at bottom filled in with rotating fork-like vertical tines, Archimedean drill, marked on thumbpiece "The Up To Date Egg & Cream Whip," 11-1/2"L, pat'd. Apr. 10, 1906 by George Flowers of Philadelphia. .... **$135-$165**

For more Archimedeans – See also: Cream whips, Drink mixers

Eggbeaters, churn cylinders – See: Cream whips; Syllabub churn

Eggbeaters, rotary (those with a drive gear rotated by hand):

Eggbeater, all metal, including heavy gauge wire handle, sheet metal gear wheel & coiled wire knob, small diam. 4-wing "balloon," "Big Bingo #70," 11"L, A & J, Binghamton, NY, pat'd. 1923, made into 1940s. .... **$15-$20**

Eggbeater, cast iron or nickel plated iron, 4 perforated tin wings (2 blades) plus heavy gauge wire with loop at bottom to capture the blades and hold in place. Name "Cyclone" is connotative of a wild "stirring" of air, pat'd. by William G. Browne, Kingston NY, 11-1/2"L or 11-3/4"L, pat'd. June 25, 1901 & July 16, 1901. • Browne's patent drawing for the *Official*

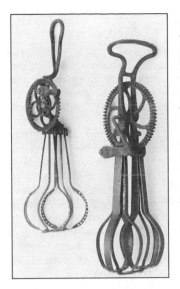

II-38. Eggbeaters – rotary. (L) *"Cyclone," Browne Mfg. Co., Kingston, NY, perforated flanges, cast iron (some are nickel-plated), 11-3/4"L (some are 11-1/2"). June 25, 1901 and July 16, 1901.* **(R)** *Taplin "Light Running" center drive, 12-1/4"L,* **Taplin** *Mfg. Co., New Britain, CT, pat'd. 1908. Notice the offset handle designed to be more ergonomically comfortable. This one came in a 10-1/2"L size also.* **(L)$50+; (R)$50-$55**

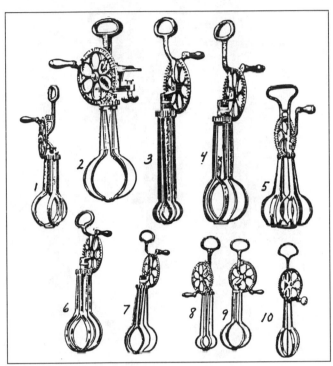

II-37. Dover – the Classic rotary! *Mostly Dover Stamping Co., Boston. "Dover" was, for a long while, a generic term for eggbeater. Patent dates are May 31, 1870; May 6, 1873; Apr. 3, 1888; and Nov. 24, 1891. Three handle styles are shown here; a fourth is rectangular. [Note that sizes in picture are not proportional.] The names are prosaic and describe size one way or the other.* **(1)** *"Extra Family Size," 9-3/4"L, Dover Cookbook, 1899.* **(2)** *"Mammoth." 1899, with screw-clamp shelf mount.* **(3)** *"Tumbler," 10-3/4"L, marked "Taplin Co., Wire Goods Co." 1915 catalog. This was to be used in a tumbler, or drinking glass. Originally, hundreds of years ago, a tumbler was just that: a round-bottomed, non-footed drinking glass that actually tumbled over because of its rounded bottom. Imbibers couldn't set it down between sips, so tumblers were very popular with pub drinkers.* **(4)** *"Hotel," 12-1/2"L, handle & wheel "chestnut bronzed" or tinned. 1915.* **(5)** *"Taplin Light Running,"* *with center drive, wide flared dashers, 10-1/2"L, bronzed finish. 1927 catalog.* **(6)** *10-3/4"L, 1927 version. Notice the handle of these later ones.* **(7)** *"Small," 8-1/2"L, described as having "chestnut bronzed" wheel & handle. 1915.* **(8)** *Another "Tumbler," 10-3/4", 1899.* **(9)** *"Family," 9"L, 1899. Blades from the 1890 model start higher & describe a bigger circle.* **(10)** *"Family," from c.1904-1910 catalog. Notice its fat wheel knob & the change in handle grip.* **(2) $350+; the rest: $45-$100**

Gazette, shows a beater very like the one manufactured, except that the handle is part of a heavy gauge metal strip forming shaft, twisted so that it was parallel, not at right angles, to gear wheel. Manufactured one has modified vertical loop handle as seen in a 1903 patent. .... **$50+**

Eggbeater, black-finished cast iron gear & crank with black wooden knob; very unusual because gear wheel doesn't stick up vertically, but is built horizontally into black screw-on lid, long, thin wire beaters that reach almost to bottom of straight-sided embossed glass jar, "Jewel 'Beater Mixer Whipper Freezer,'" mfd. by Juergens Brothers, Minneapolis, MN, about 7"H, pat'd. June 20, 1893. • Extremely rare and a very desirable addition to any collection. See II-53. .... **$500+**

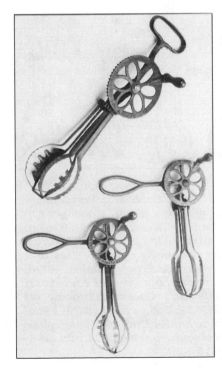

II-39. Eggbeaters – rotary. (T) *"Holt's Egg Beater," pat'd. Aug. 22, 1899, iron & tin, 12-1/2"L. Has the so-called "flare dashers."* **(B-L)** *is a side-handled "Holt's Pat'd. Flare Dasher," 8-3/4"L, iron & tin.* **(R)** *Has the same name, no fingers on the dashers, not so well made, and no flair! Collection of Meryle Evans.* **(T) $50+; (B-L) $275+; (R)$175+**

Cast Iron. It has been said that cast iron is really the art of woodcarving, because by the 1840s or so, carved wooden patterns were used by founders to create matrices or molds into which the molten metal could be poured. Gear wheel **foundry patterns** are most common, but all other cast parts had patterns too. In the mid 19th century, the economical concept of uniformly-sized parts, which could be bolted or screwed together, meant that only the broken parts need be replaced, rather than the whole tool or machine. Wooden patterns were made with lathes, drills & table saws, or were hand-carved, or both, often not from a solid piece of wood, but from laminated (glued together) layered blocks, with grain running 2 directions to make the laminate stronger and much less liable to warping. Patterns were used sometimes for many years. Small parts that stick out from the main part of the pattern were usually carved or turned separately, then glued or pegged into the main part. Patterns were varnished or painted – also to protect from warping. Painted ones are fun to collect because different parts of the pattern might be painted different colors – usually red, green, yellow & black. Each pattern was marked, usually stamped with a several digit number and one or more letters, but sometimes stenciled or painted with a number. • I have never seen a foundry pattern for a kitchen utensil or gadget, at least not to recognize it, but they probably exist (or did exist) somewhere. Occasionally a dealer at a flea market will show up with a box or pile of foundry patterns, priced from $3 up to $60 or more, having rescued discarded patterns from a foundry no longer requiring them or even defunct.

• • • •

I use the adjectives "**cutout**" or "**openwork**" throughout this book to describe castings with large "negative spaces" giving the appearance of cutouts, although the cast gear wheels are not machined and cut out after casting; only the casting model is.

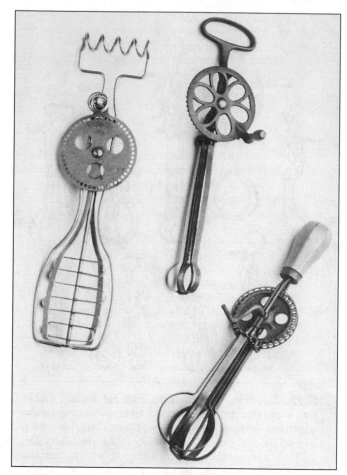

*II-41. **Eggbeaters** – rotary. **(L)** "Ram Beater"* with wiggly fingerhold grip that looks like crown. Chromed, 12"L. Sort of a combination of two of Robert A. Moore's patents (Aug. 18, 1925, which had a very tightly coiled handle grip and 2 stacked turbines, and Aug. 24, 1915, which had something rather like the wiggly cutting blades). Mfd. by Ram Metal Products Co., NYC, c. 1915-1925+. [Note that Moore's "Ram" dual-propeller turbine, not pictured in this book, would be worth $250+.] **(M)** A **Dover** "Tumbler," 11-3/8"L, iron & tin, with teensiest bow to its wings; perhaps you mixed something down inside a bottle. A bottle of cream would have had a mouth wide enough for this to fit into but there wouldn't be enough power to make whipped cream. **(R)** "Whip Well," yellow-painted wood handle, no knob on crank handle, 11"L, marked pat'd., "Mar. 23, 1920" & "May 2, 1921." Handle is different from ones marked only with 1920 patent; blade profile differs; and there's no knob on crank. The 1921 patent date was misstruck, it should have been "May 24" the same year. **(L)** $170+; **(M)** $50+; **(R)** $20+*

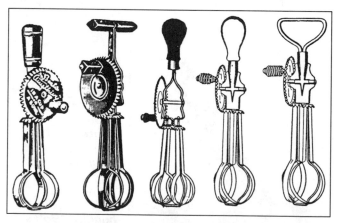

*II-40. **Eggbeaters** – rotary. Left to right: **(1)** Nickeled steel, wood, 7-1/4"L, "Beats anything in a cup or bowl." **A & J,** mfd. by Edward Katzinger Co. (which took over the original A & J). **(2)** An 8-wing, nickeled steel beater with "extra large drive wheel." Red or green angular handles. This and next 3 from Washburn **Androck** catalog, 1936. Notice the differences in handles and frames. **(3)** Also 8 wings, with green, yellow or red handle. **(4)** Four wings, nickeled steel, coiled wire knob, wooden handle in green. **(5)** One with wire spade handle, and longer shaft to wings. **(1), (2:)** $15-$35; **(3), (4), (5):** $15-$20*

II-42. Eggbeater – rotary. *The incomparable "**Aluminum Beauty**." Sometimes marked "Aluminum Beauty Beater VIKO Instant Whip." Ullman Aluminum, Division, NY. 10-3/8"L, cast & sheet aluminum. Pat'd. April 20, 1920. In reality, to a collector the value would be lower than the price you might expect to buy the best eggbeater for everyday use that there is!* **$15+**

Eggbeater, cast iron handle, wheel, gear, sheet metal four-wing (2 blades) plus central vertical rod, blades somewhat flattened at bottom to enable it to do its touted job: "Beats to the bottom of the bowl." Pat'd. by Clarence A. Taplin, Apr 14, 1903. Taplin Mfg. Co., New Britain, CT. .... **$35+**

Eggbeater, cast iron, gear wheel like Dover, grip handle, very strange beater blades – 2 heavy gauge outer wire wings (blades) with 3 fat vertical scallops, one central vertical rod with 3 horizontal wire cross-pieces that rotate within the scallops, ball bottom to fit in bowl dimple, 11"L. I'm sure this unmarked beater was another "Aerate the Egg" conceptual piece, sold through F.A. Walker (importers & wholesalers), as the "Three-Minute Egg Beater," Boston, MA, c.1880s... **$350-$450**

❖ NOTES ❖

Eggbeaters & Treasure Island – According to his classic travel book *Travels with a Donkey in the Cévannes*, Robert Louis Stevenson (of *Treasure Island* fame) in 1878, packed a little donkey named Modestine with a sleeping bag and a number of supplies for a 12-day hike in the mountains of France. He took a lamp and candles, clothing, books, a milk jug, chocolate blocks, wine, black bread, and – ta da! – an eggbeater! Probably a Dover, but I do wonder.

❖ NOTES ❖

The original Dover was patented May 31, 1870 by Turner Williams, and it was called then the "Williams Egg Beater." • An ad for The Dover Egg Beater, in *Ladies Home Journal*, March 1887, reads: "Pat. May 31, 1870; May 6, 1878. The one thing always needful in the kitchen. Always satisfactory. Popular, 4,000,000 in use. Stand first in all countries, has never had a rival. Used by all practical Housekeepers, endorsed by all teachers of cooking. Four sizes. Send for circular. Regular size sent by mail upon receipt of 50¢." • At first glance many of the Dovers look the same, but look more closely – at slight variations in the casting of gear wheel openwork petals, at blade diam., size and bowing

or ballooning of wings. Handle grips are different, too. The Dover became so popular, indeed omnipresent, that many cookbook authors made "dover" the generic term for rotary eggbeaters. One of the neatest (if not the most valuable, say $75) to find is one that has a teensy blade ballooning, about one inch across, to fit down into a tall tumbler. It has a patent date of May 6, 1873 on it. You just can't get to the bottom of the Dover story without reading Don Thornton's book.

Eggbeater, cast iron & tinned sheet metal & wire, 6-wing, clamps to shelf above bowl, "Dover Stamping Co.," Boston, MA, 17"L, the #4 hotel size called "Mammoth" (an even larger one was advertised as the "Leviathan"), c.1891. Later the "Dover Mammoth #300" was made by Taplin Mfg. Co. The "Mammoth": $350+; the "Leviathan": .... **500+**

Eggbeater, cast iron (sometimes tinned) handle, gears & frame, 6-wing – 2 tinned sheet metal blades & 1 wire blade, "Taplin's Dover Pattern Improved," Taplin Mfg. Co., New Britain, CT. There are several sizes, from 8-3/4"L to about 12"L, pat'd. Apr. 14, 1903. .... **$45+**

Eggbeater, cast iron handle & gear, 6-wing – 2 tinned blades, plus one bowed wire blade, marked "Dover Stamping Co.," Boston, MA, several sizes: 9-1/2"L, 10-1/2"L, 11-3/8"L, etc. This beater & similar ones, with improvements pat'd. July 14, 1885 by Thomas Brown, was made by Dover as well as by Standard" Mfg. Co., for probably close to 35 to 40 years, and you will find various markings, including "STANDARD EGG BEATER," and a very similar one marked "MAN-HATTAN" and "GEORGE P. BENJAMIN." This particular one, like others found not infrequently, has a mix of elements that confuse the collector. Brown's 1885 patent was supposed to refer to a steel-handled

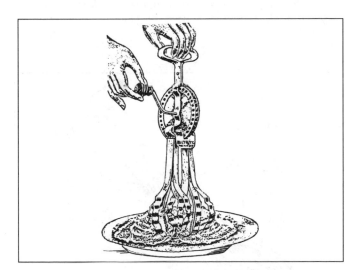

II-43. Eggbeater – rotary. *The "**Biltrite**," mfd. by Stuber & Kuck Co., Peoria, IL. Tinned steel, center drive wheel, nameplate is a "locking device holding blades permanently in place," waved beater blades "result in 50% quicker results," and the blades are "so close to plate that one egg is drawn up from a flat plate ... impossible with other makes." 1919 ad House Furnishing Review. Another "Biltrite" has a rounded upright knob handle.* **$25-$30**

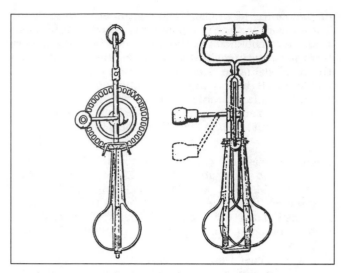

II-45. Eggbeater patent – rotary, *2 views. Pat'd. Jan. 13, 1931, by Henry J.* **Edlund**, *Burlington, VT, #1,789,224. Mfd. by Edlund Co., Inc., Burlington. 11-3/4"L and 12-1/2"L; spade or shovel grip handle that came in painted wood, also a more collectable, valuable plastic.* **$15-$20**

beater based on a Dover original, but it appears sometimes on those with cast iron handle & frame. Marked "Dover": $70+; marked "Standard": .... **$300+**

❖ RECIPE ❖

Rice Fritters – *Boil 1 teaspoonful of rice until it is tender; strain upon it 1 quart of milk; let it boil ten minutes; cool it; add flour enough to make a batter as thick as will fry easily on the griddle; 2 tablespoonfuls of yeast; let it rise 3 hours; add 2 well-beaten eggs, and cook on a heated griddle."* Henry Scammel, Treasure-House of Useful Knowledge, 1891.

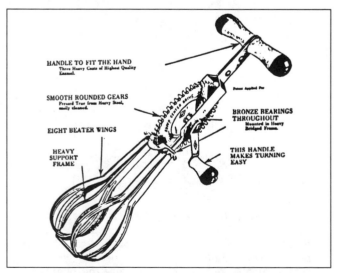

II-46. Eggbeater. *"No. 75* **Super Center Drive**" *rotary beater, nickeled steel, wood handles in Blutip, green, blue or yellow. A & J Mfg. Co./EKCO, Edward Katzinger Co., Chicago, 1930.* **$10-$15**

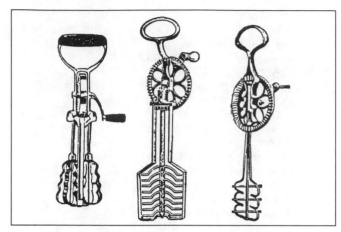

II-44. Eggbeaters – rotary. (L) *Another wavey-, scalloped- or crimped-blade type with center drive is the "Flint Mixer* **'Rhythm Beater,'**" *mfd. by Ekco Products Co., 1958. It is stainless steel, with turquoise, pink, yellow, or black handles.* **(M)** *Unnamed eggbeater mfd. by F. W.* **Loll** *Mfg. Co., Meriden, CT. Jan. 1909 House Furnishing Review. Pat'd. Oct. 9, 1906. Another has been found marked "Pat Apld For," without the protective frame around the fingered beater.* **(R)** "**Three-Minute** *Egg Beater," cast iron, Dover-like gear wheel, grip handle, 2 heavy wire blades with scallops, crosswires and vertical rod, 11"L. Sold through F. A. Walker, Boston, c.1880s, and named by them. (L)* **$6-$15**; *(M)* **$850+**; *(R) very rare:* **$850+**

Eggbeater, cast iron & tin, gear wheel with the familiar 6 petals, turned by a wooden knob, but the business end is an interesting geometric pattern of 2 curved metal wings, pat'd. by Timothy Earle, July 7, 1863, mfd. by Dover Stamping Co., as "Earl's [sic] Patent Egg Beater," "The Standard #1," or "Patent Standard Egg Beater," Earle from Smithfield, RI; Dover in Boston. Decades later Standard Mfg. Co. mfd. this "Standard." .... **$165-$200**

❖ NOTES ❖

Earle's Classic – I have no idea why the gap between 1863 patent and production, except maybe that the beater for which the patent was granted was totally different in action and appearance. It was designed with a sort of horizontal sawed ratchet for rotating the intricately ribbed blades, but was made with a rotary cranked gear and simple concentric blades. As far as I know, this first appeared in *Dover's 1869 Catalog*, which says: "This, while it is the simplest, is the most effective Egg Beater made. Held in the hand with an immovable rest, it stands firmly wherever placed and will beat eggs with greater rapidity than any other; while the price places it within reach of all. It is cleaned by a moment's rapid turning in hot water." •
Cut Me In. – In his specifications for this eggbeater, for which he was granted patent #39,134, Earle wrote: "Various devices have been employed for the purpose of beating eggs more expeditiously than by the familiar hand-process. One of these devices consists of two wire frames, one within the other, and made to revolve in opposite directions; another consists of a propeller blade which is made to rotate while a pair of beaters

have at the same time a reciprocating motion. All these machines, and all others with which I am acquainted, possess the common fault that the beaters, whether of wire or of the form of propeller-blades, do not cut the yolks and whites of the egg, but literally beat them. Now, as the albumen of an egg consists of a peculiar thick, glazy substance, it can be worked more effectually with a cutting instrument than with one which has a blunt edge. In fact, so well is this understood that housewives universally make use of the blade of a knife for the purpose."

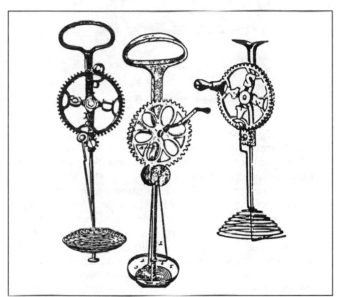

II-47. Eggbeaters & patent drawing. (L) The reality – with cast iron gear wheel spells out mfr's. initials: **"P. D. & Co."** (Paine, Diehl & Co.), Philadelphia. Notice the flying saucer-like wire dasher: "a double or compound dasher, having its two parts vibrating in opposition to each other upon the egg between them, and also reciprocating up and down against the egg in the bottom of the dish. ... It automatically fits itself to and gathers up the egg from any shaped dish whether spherical or flat bottomed inside. It whips one egg in a teacup in 15 seconds, 6 eggs in a bowl in 70 seconds." Pat'd. Dec. 1, 1885. **(M) The patent drawing.** The Dec. 1, 1885 patent, by George H. Thomas, Chicopee Falls, MA., followed by one in 1886, were the basis for the P.D. & Co. one at left, although neither of Thomas' patents show a gear wheel with the name spelled out. In fact, it looks like a Dover gear wheel. A beater that looks exactly like the patent is not known as of 2001. **(R)** The reciprocating motion, cast iron & wire **"Easy,"** was sold through Montgomery Ward, c.1895 ad. Its name is spelled out in gear wheel spokes. The "Easy" was also based on George Thomas' Sept. 28, 1886 patent. Don Thornton has seen "Easy" beaters marked with Thomas' Mar. 6, 1886 patent application date. Many "Easys" were sold: why aren't there more out there for collectors? Notice angled rods that connect dasher parts with gear wheels on all three. [Note: there were at least two other beaters with the letters or initials of the company or brand name cast decoratively to form spokes in the gear wheels: "D-O-V-E-R," and "T-H-E H-I-L-L."] **(L) $850-$1,000; (R) $1,100+**

Eggbeater, cast iron gear, two wire rabbit ear-like vertically alert handles, & tin angled blade/wings somewhat like the "Three Minute" and the "Loll" beaters, name spelled out as the spokes of cast iron gear wheel – "The Hill" in serif letters, American, pat'd. by John E. Hill Nov. 5, 1901 and Jan. 15, 1907. 11-1/2"L. Mfd. by J. E. Hill Co., Boston. Because Hill designed his beater so that the blades could be removed for washing, it's possible that this contributed, in the long run, to this beater's extreme rarity. .... **$850-$1,000**

Eggbeater, cast & stamped aluminum, solid gear wheel, 8-wing, 4 blade, plus wire, marked either "Aluminum Beauty," or "Aluminum Beauty Beater VIKO Instant Whip," Ullman Aluminum Co., Division, NY, 10-3/8"L, pat'd. Apr. 20, 1920................... **$15-$25**

❖ NOTES ❖

Rare & Precious Aluminium. Considered a precious metal on a parity with silver, an ingot of solid refined aluminium was exhibited at the Paris Exhibition in 1855, and objects as fine as a crown for the King of Sweden, and jewelry and small decorative objects were made of the metal, which could only be refined in very small quantities until almost 50 years later.

Why are there two ways to spell it? *Aluminum ... or aluminium?* For the most part American usage is the former, and European the latter. But 19th century American patents using the metal spelled it *aluminium*; as did one of the metal's earliest commercial pioneers – Charles Martin Hall – whose company was first called the Pittsburgh Aluminium Co., and by 1907 was The Aluminium Company of America (T.A.C.A.).

Early in the 19th century, The International Union of Pure & Applied Chemists used the spelling *aluminium* to conform with the historical practice of naming elements with an *-ium* suffix. So for a while scientists everywhere used that spelling.

In 1925, the American Chemical Society decided to spell the metal *aluminum*, and the American public, already familiar with that version from advertising and marks, probably didn't even notice that the word spelled their way was official! Meanwhile, most of the rest of the world continued to this day to use *aluminium*. It's one of the words useful to anyone wanting to sound European!

Eggbeater, chromed steel with wooden T handle, "Ladd Ball Bearing No. 3," Ladd Bros.; mfd. by Traut & Hine Mfg. Co. and Humphrey Mfg. Co., both of New Britain, CT, 11"L, pat'd Oct. 18, 1921 by Lavern Bordwell, marked "Other patents pending." [Note: The close vertical wings of the #5, meant for use in a tumbler, make that one worth twice the #3.] .... **$12-$15**

Eggbeater, metal with off-white egg-shaped knob handle, #72, A & J Mfg. Co., Binghamton, NY, 11"L, pat'd. Oct. 9, 1923. .... **$10-$15**

Eggbeater, heavy stamped metal, 3 narrow fold-flat upside-down heart-shaped beater blades, one fitted within the next, 11-1/2"L, "Minute Maid," mfd. by Henderson Corp., Seattle, WA, pat'd. May 13, 1930 by F. W. Henderson. .... **$115-$130**

Eggbeater, iron gear wheel, wire, tin, white porcelain crank knob, double blade fold-flat with central vertical wire shaft, "Peerless #2," 10-1/4"L, American, place & mfr. unknown. .... **$125-$150**

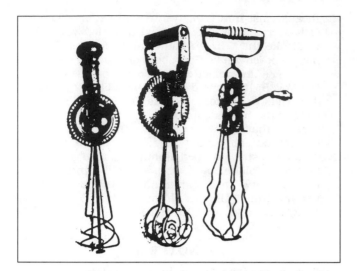

II-48. Eggbeaters – rotary wire blades. (L) *Stamped metal gear wheel with holes around perimeter, wire dashers. "Mayonnaise Toujours – Creme Chantilly – Reussis Le Roides Batteurs – CBM – Brevete SGDG." French, 12"L.* **(M)** *Spade handle, double circle "soap bubble blower" dashers. Clarence E. Elliott's "Kansas City" beater, or, as marked: "K. C. USA." In fact, it's called the "Bubble" by some collectors. Marked "Pat. 1,992,564," but actually should be 1,992,654. Pat'd. 1934.* **(R)** *Zig Zag, "Le Tourbillon," French, early 20th C. Pictures courtesy Bob Cahn.* **$65-$150**

Eggbeater, iron & tin, somewhat conical 2 bar wire frame, supporting a long central crankshaft with the handle at top, the scrolly blades horizontal at the bottom. The gear, instead of being at the top, is close to the bottom, and the curvy wings turn or revolve on the teeth of that horizontal circular gear. 11"L. "Dodge Race Course Egg Beater" is name given by collectors (only one is known to exist ... so far!), probably American, probably 1880s.................................. **$1,000 and up**

II-49. Wall-mounted eggbeater – rotary with wire whisk bows. *"Silver Wall Style No.6," mfd. by Silver & Co., Brooklyn, c.1910. Black japanned cast iron, tinned spring steel wire bows. "For hotels and restaurants. Very quick in operation, and very easily cleaned." Has a "suspended arm to which is cast a socket which fits into a corresponding pocket socket ... which may remain permanently affixed to the wall and the beater portion be removed. Large bowls or large glasses or pails or*

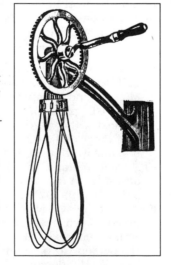

deep dishes or any other similar article may be used as a receptacle." This Silver piece has a confusing history tied in with (or rivaling) the Edwin Baltzley Dec. 15, 1885 patent assigned to North Bros. **$350-$450**

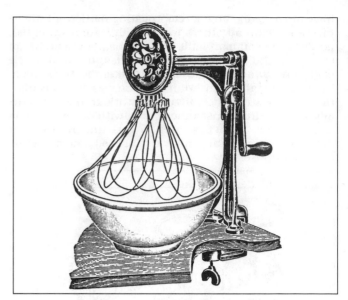

II-51. Eggbeater – rotary with container. *"Silver Hotel Egg Beater No.5," Silver & Co., c.1910. "Framework ... is heavy cast iron re-tinned with pure tin which ... makes it sanitary. The beater portion is constructed of heavy steel piano wire and will stand a great deal of hard usage. Shown ready to attach to table. Excellent for large cake mixtures, or where a large quantity of doughy mixture, eggs or mixing of any liquids or light dough is desired. It is splendid for hotels, bakers, boarding houses, and other similar places. For convenience, it disjoints at the upper portion of the arms, and is adjustable for height." Notice wheel's quatrefoil cutouts.* **$600+**

Eggbeater, iron & tin, 2 blades (4 wings) with finger-like projections – the so-called "flare dasher." "Holt's Egg Beater," Holt Lyon, Tarrytown, NY, 12-1/2"L (there is also an 11-1/2"L one, maybe others), pat'd. Aug. 22, 1899. .... **$50+**

Eggbeater, iron & tin, cast iron 6-petal gear wheel, with "fingered" blades so-called "flare dashers," but the fingers are slightly stubbier than on the bigger, vertical-handle kind. This has looped iron handle at right angles to blade shaft. "Holt's Pat'd Flare Dasher Egg Beater," Tarrytown, NY, 8-3/4"L, dated with pat'd. Aug. 22, 1899 like other one, and Apr 3, 1900, but seems to be based on Ulysses Grant Teetsell's patent of Valentine's Day, 1922. • The flare dashers seem to have grown, like mutants, out of the crimped-edge blades of "Holt's Improved Dover" beater, although they have same & later patent dates. Another with same name, same side handle, has no fingers at all, just the ripply edges, and its gear wheel has six curved spokes. .... **$250+**

❖ NOTES ❖

Eggbeater Gears – All crank & gear collectors love gears, especially eggbeater collectors. There are many kinds, some adapted by inventors from other mechanisms as various as clocks and gun turrets. Gears have to have something that will engage another gear so as to turn it, whether it be teeth that stick out and mesh with other teeth, or regularly spaced depressions into which turning gear teeth will fit. Eggbeaters have particularly interesting gears because when manufacturers kept trying to make a cheaper and cheaper product, they went to stamped, instead of cast, metal because the eggbeater didn't have to do heavy duty, precision work. Various kinds of interruptions on the smooth surface of a stamped sheet metal gear wheel were devised to perform like gear teeth. Teeth, notches, holes, grooves, bumps, beveled ridges, twisted prongs – all were made to work with a fairly generous tolerance for messy meshing. Maybe the most imaginative gear-tooth substitute is a rigid spring coil.

Eggbeater, iron & tin, with green wood T handle & knob (also came with red handles), 8 wing (4 blade circles, each half counting as a wing), A & J "High Speed Super Center Drive Beater," Binghamton, NY, 11-1/2"L, patent #2,049,727 (1936)............................. **$25-$35**

Eggbeater, nickel plated sheet metal, 4 wing, metal tubular T handle is angled 45 degrees off the gear wheel; design of everything but handle is same as Oct. 9, 1923 patent, not marked, but A & J – same gear wheel, same coiled wire knob for crank, same blades. Binghamton, NY, 10"H, 1923+....... **$15-$20**

Eggbeater, sheet metal, spade handle with wooden grip, ball-bearing gear, spectacular 3 beaters (12 wings) worked from only one geared wheel, each set of blades with vertical rod through center. Aurelius Brothers, Braham, MN, 11-1/2"L. Says only "Patent applied for," but pat'd. Aug. 28, 1923, by Paul Hazzard, #1,465,940. The patent was for a triple rotary, but with a tri-point footprint. This Aurelius has the blades in a row, for use in a wide bowl!? They must have big eggs out there! After all, the mosquito is Minnesota's state bird!............................. **$100+**

Eggbeater, stamped metal & wire, nickel plated, bottle shaped frame for the wire beater "wings" designed with back & forth hairpin curves. Extremely elegant

II-52. Eggbeater or drink mixer. *My first prize.* **"Standard** *Specialty Co., Milwaukee, WI," with "Root Mason" fruit jar. The beater is fixed to the lid, but obviously other jars could replace this one. Cast iron, tin, green glass, 12"H x 3-7/8" diam. Pat'd. June 11, 1907.* **$550+**

& modern looking, crank the simple round sheet metal wheel with 3 large holes, and its border of small holes mesh with small teeth of small gear to turn blades. Handle has coiled wire with effect of a crown. "Ram Beater," 12"H, marked "patented" but no date. Pat'd. by Robert Moore, Aug. 18, 1915; mfd. by Ram Metal Products Co., NYC. Moore also pat'd. a turbine "Ram" beater in 1925. .... **$150+**

Eggbeater, nickeled & stamped sheet metal, spade handle, gear wheel has little stamped brads as teeth – almost identical to the 1921 "Blue Whirl." "Patent ball drive," "Swift Whip," 13-1/2"L, Australian, first 3rd 20th C. .... **$45+**

Eggbeater, nickeled sheet metal, long hexagonal yellow painted wooden vertical handle, tin, wire, "Whipwell," 11"L, pat'd. Mar. 23, 1920 & May 2, 1921. Winsted Hardware Mfg. Co., Winsted, CT, 11"L,? WHIP through that egg in the 1920s & 1930s with the familiar Whipwell, Quik-Whip, & Whippit; also Whiprite Egg Beater, Champion Machinery Co., Joliet, IL (I've not found one of theirs.) .... **$30+**

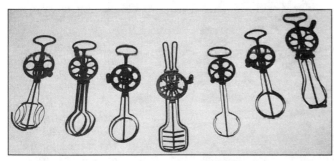

II-50. Eggbeaters – all fold-flat rotaries, *a particular love of these collectors. Left to right:* **(1)** *"Standard" egg beater, 10-1/4"L, pat'd. June 29 & Sept. 21, 1880, and March 8, 1881.* **(2)** *"Dover," pat'd. March 8, 1881, July 14, 1885, 10-1/4" L.* **(3)** *"Family," 10-1/4" L, pat'd. Sept. 26, 1876.* **(4)** *"The* **Hill,***" over 12"L. [Note that name is spelled out in the cast iron gear wheel, below the rabbit ear handle.] Pat'd. Jan. 15, 1907.* **(5)** *Marked* **"USA,"** *9-1/4" L. Some of these have slotted dashers.* **(6)** *"Manhattan," 10-1/2" L, pat'd. June 29, 1880.* **(7)** *The extremely rare "Centripetal," pat'd. June 13, 1887. Collection of Phyllis & Jim Moffet.* **$225; $75; $1,000; $850; $125; $175+; $1,000+**

II-53. Eggbeater or drink mixer. *Cast iron horizontal gear in lid, wire handle & beaters. 7-1/2"H. Glass embossed* **"JEWEL BEATER,** *MIXER, WHIPPER & FREEZER. MANF BY GRAVITY TWINE BOX CO. CLEVELAND, OHIO." Culled the* **"Household Jewel"** *in period ads, pat'd. June 20, 1893 by Henry Juergens. Some are marked "Jewel Beater Mixer Whipper & Freezer Made by Juergens Bros. Minneapolis." Photo courtesy Phyllis & Jim Moffet.* **$500+**

II-54. Eggbeaters & original vessels. (L) *Rotary "A & J" with its original clear glass beating bowl. Pat'd. Oct. 9, 1923. (R) A Liquid mixer marked with an intermingled monogram of "AD PAT. MAR. 30th 1915 2108-4," assigned to the canned milk people, Bordens Milk. Others are marked "BORDENS PAT" with the date. Wire Archimedean drill for one-hand, 3-finger mixing. $25+; $55+*

Eggbeaters, rotary, containers

Eggbeater, stamped metal, detachable skirt or apron bowl cover, green glass bowl has 4 squat, stubby feet, bowl embossed "Patent Applied for," mfd. by A & J, 12"H, pat'd. Oct. 9, 1923. Common beater, but hard to find with original bowl. Green glass is collectible in its own right. **$55**

❖ RECIPE ❖

Nondescripts – *Yolks of four eggs beaten light, one teaspoonful of salt, flour enough to form a stiff dough; beat the dough well, and roll as thin as tissue paper; cut out by a saucer, and fold twice. Cut with a knife into narrow strips, leaving them united at the extreme point. Fry in plenty of boiling lard. When taken up, sprinkle loaf sugar thickly over them. Instead of shaping as above, the dough may be cut in strips about an inch wide and four inches long, and fried as directed. The former, however, is prettier." Mrs. A. P. Hill, Mrs. Hill's New Family Receipt Book, NY: 1870.*

II-55. Eggbeater. "Silver Egg *Beater No. 4," with a "receptacle made of heavy lime glass graduated for dry or liquid measuring. The dashers or beaters are made of extra heavy Bessemer steel, re-tinned bright, the air tube is made of XXXX tin. The valve adjustment at the base of the tube is made of German silver. The tinplate cover is heavily nickelplated and polished. The handle of enameled wood." One quart capacity only. 11-1/2"H x 4-1/2" diam. Silver & Co., Brooklyn, c.1910. A few years later, the style of the wooden handle was slightly changed to be more angular, and with more turnings.* **$100-$150+**

Eggbeater, nickeled sheet metal, coil knob on gear wheel, vertical painted wood handle, panelled glass 1 pt. measuring cup with handle & generous pouring lip. • Also came with spade-handle beater. Both with aprons fitted to inside ridge slightly below lip of cup. A & J, by 1940 owned by Edward Katzinger Co. – EKCO, Chicago. .... **$35+**

Eggbeater, with all metal beater bowl, cast iron & tin beater with vertical stumpy red painted wooden handle, interesting coiled or spiraled wire around edge of gear wheel forms the teeth of the gear, openwork frame clips over edge of bowl, & supports beater. Openness provides "full vision" of name. "Ingredients can be added while beating operation is in progress," as the original ad copy reads, "Full Vision Egg Beater Set," A & J, bowl: 3-3/4"H x 4-3/4" diam.; 1-1/2 pint capacity; 9-1/2" overall height with beater, based on Oct. 9, 1923 patent; prob. made in 1930s.... **$30-$40**

Eggbeater, nickeled, with close-fitting jar lid, long 4 blades that do not balloon out at bottom, green painted wooden crank knob & T handle (this handle is cigar-shaped, not banded in the middle), Depression glass green beater jar with slightly flared sides, Ladd, New Britain, CT, 11-1/4"H, prob. late 1920s... **$55+**

Eggbeater, horizontal wire balloon blades like whisk, 2 gears, cranked on side, cast iron frame set into painted wood box or stand, with porcelain (ceramic) pan, mfd. by J. L. Newcomer, Baltimore, MD, pat'd. May 26, 1885. .... **$800+**

Eggbeater & batter mixer, white ironstone beater jar, with one side of rim raised up with a small stepped notch on either side to support cast iron beater. Gear wheel cast with 6 hearts, short handle has white porcelain knob. Extended arms off each side of shaft supports beater in its jar. Beater has wide

II-56. Eggbeaters or drink mixers. (L) *Originally mfd. as the "Silver No.3," Silver & Co., c.1910, with japanned cast iron top, nickeled gears, tinned steel piano wire bows, glass, enameled wood handle. Used also for mayonnaise or butter-merging. This one is actually "**The New Keystone Beater**," "Culinary Utilities Co." (Others may bear North Bros. name.) Scalloped iron top same as the Silver. Measures embossed on sides of glass – 1 qt. liquid (worked 3 cups); "coffee cups full" on another; Flour and sifted flour; liquids in ounces. Collection Meryle Evans. (R) "E-Z Mixer," National Mfg. & Supply Co., Pittsburg, PA. Pat'd. June 30, 1903. 32 oz., 13"H. Cast iron top with flat pad-like knob for pressing against heel of hand while mixing. No marks in metal. Lid has oil funnel hole for making mayo. This one is very rare. Courtesy Bob Cahn. (L) $225+; (R) $550+*

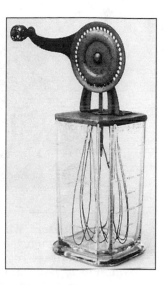

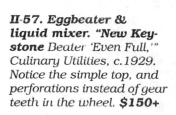

II-57. Eggbeater & liquid mixer. *"New Keystone Beater 'Even Full,'"* Culinary Utilities, c.1929. *Notice the simple top, and perforations instead of gear teeth in the wheel.* **$150+**

skirted beater blade profile, made up of interestingly twisted heavy gauge wires, & heavy central shaft that turns within a tiny cup at bottom. Beater wheel is marked, & also the ironstone jar has an underglaze design of a floral wreath & the words "Kents Improved Monroes Patent Egg Beater & Batter Mixer," (*no apostrophes*), plus a paper label (with instructions) which could be washed off, "Kents Patent" on beater, "Kents Improved Monroes [James & Edwin] Patent ...," address given as High Holborn, London, England, about 13"H, late 19th C. • The English manufacturing firm of Kent also put out a set with a beautiful footed beater jar, with same

II-58. Eggbeater with passive beater wings & pitcher. *Pat'd. glass pitcher with interior (see bird's-eye view inset) that's supposed to "do half the work" of making the liquid move around. It's "marked by a series of vertical ridges gaining in depth as they go downward and forming, on the inside bottom, a serrated cup. These vertical ridges act as passive beater wings and help to break up and beat the contents." Green or clear glass, also opaque white so-called "milk glass," and to fit the Senior or Junior beaters, which had Blutip or green wood handles. 12-1/2"H overall.* "A & J," 1930. **$40-$50**

markings. This is an extraordinary outfit – either style is highly desirable. (The "Monroe" referred to American inventor brothers – James F. Monroe, of Fitchburg, MA, and Edwin P. Monroe, of NYC – whose eggbeater got US patent in 1859. Their beater was mfd. by Dover, Boston, but looks nothing like the Kent one described in this entry.) .... **$1,000+**

Eggbeater & cream whip, tall tin cylinder with wire-rolled top and bottom, used with a heavy wire dasher that has ring loop at one end & 2 metal discs cut rather like flower petals at other, divided by washer at bottom, paper label "The Ideal Egg Beater," Ideal Coffee Pot Co., Philadelphia, PA, c.1880 .... **$100-$110**

Eggbeater/cream whips: for more that resemble this, but are activated by shaking. See: Eggbeaters, shaken.

Eggbeater or liquid mixer, green glass jar, with tin screw-on lid, to which is attached the cast iron handle, gears & the wire beater blades, "Root Mason" jar, Standard Specialty Co. works, Milwaukee, WI, 12"H x 3-7/8"diam., pat'd. June 11, 1907. • The top of the beater itself looks like a 1873 Dover. In early 1960s, I found this in a central Ohio antique shop, and felt sinful spending $16 on it ... the most I'd ever spent for anything! .... **$550+**

Eggbeater or mixer, for eggs or mayonnaise, footed glass egg-shape- bottomed vessel with flat metal lid fitted with upright iron beater frame, gear, side crank & 2 sets of wire blades inside bent to form 6 rectangular side wings that fit within slope of vessel, "E-Z Mixer," National Mfg. & Supply Co., Pittsburg, PA, pat'd June 30, 1903. [Note: This is not the same as Nathan Dazey's E-Z Butter Maker Mfg. Co. of Dallas, TX, from the same period.] .... **$550+**

Eggbeater or mixer, glass vessel with slightly flared sides, fitted tin lid with attached mixer which has tall wire handle with small wood knob at top, spiraled coil blades inside motivated by up & down action, marked "Lorraine Metal Mfg., Inc., NYC," 11-1/2"H, c. 1930s. .... **$20-$30**

II-59. Eggbeater & pitcher sets. *Also "A & J," in pint size glass pitchers. Some collectors look for the opaque green, so-called "Jadite" pressed glass pitcher with Dutch windmill design. Edward Katzinger Catalog, 1940.* **$35-$45+**

Eggbeater or mixer, "Silver's" and also "Keystone." Cast iron gear wheel with iron crank & wooden knob, set onto cast iron mansard roof-like lid with scalloped edge, over tall square-sided glass container, marked on all 4 sides with various measures, ballooning whisking wires inside flare out more in later versions. "New Keystone Beater," was made by North Brothers Mfg. of Philadelphia, who claimed they had "secured control of the machine manufactured by Keystone Beater Co., and are now [1892] the only manufacturers of it." That's from an ad in *The Metal Worker* in late 1892. Some Keystones still have the original, small chromolith paper label on cast iron top, showing a little girl looking at a mixing bowl and the beater, plus the words: "The New Keystone Beater. Reduces Work. Improves the Food. Detachable Whip. Easy to Clean. Culinary Utilities Dept., Bloomfield, NJ." Later versions of "The New Keystone Beater" had sheet metal wheel, modernized tops or lids of sheet metal, with straight edges (not scalloped). However, they kept the same glass container. Culinary Utilities was listed in directories as being in NJ and NYC. • The original cast iron "New Keystone" is very similar, and undoubtedly related, to the "Silver Egg Beater." However, the "Silver" has snake-like spokes in its cast iron gear wheel – compared to the straight ones of the "New Keystone." The cast iron "Silvers" are marked "Silver Egg Beater" by Silver & Co., Brooklyn, NY; "Silver New Egg Beater" with the image of the Brooklyn Bridge and words "Silvers Brooklyn" embossed on the jar's bottom – possibly contemporary with the beautiful, technically

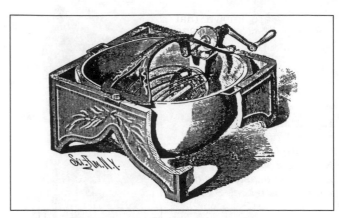

II-61. Eggbeater. *With pan and frame, this is almost a mixing machine.* **"Newcomer's** *Improved," with a chain-drive "rotary egg whip consisting of a shaft, having skeleton heads, and wires which are so curved as to make the exterior of the whip conform very nearly in shape with the hemispherical bottom of the pan. By coming very near the surface of the pan, small quantities of eggs can be whipped." Iron frame secured to wooden stand, obviously pinstriped & stencil-decorated. The small continuous chain goes from the small wheel seen fully in drawing down to a small sprocket wheel, which turns the beater. Pat'd. May 26, 1885 & mfd. by inventor, Jacob. L. Newcomer, Baltimore, MD. This picture appeared in an Aug. 1885 article in* Scientific American. *It was also pictured in an ad in the February 1885* Confectioners' Journal, *which mentioned that in the next issues there would be "flattering testimonials from leading bakers." Exceedingly rare: nobody has yet found one; but we know they are bound to be out there.* **$1,000+**

advanced bridge's 1883 opening. Both Keystone and Silver also made wall-mount mixers, some with their own jars. Silver also made plunger type beaters with round jars, but marked the same as their square ones. These had tubes through the plungers to allow finger control to introduce more air to the aerated mixture. All very scientific! A real rarity, belonging to Reid Cooper and shown in Thornton's book, is a Silver beater with scalloped edge to its cast iron top, embossed/cast on it "Horlick's." .... **$225+**

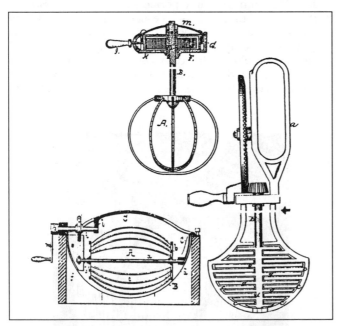

II-60. Eggbeater patents for container beaters. *All bowl-fitting.* **(T)** *Pat'd. June 19, 1877, by Eustache R.* **Dulje***, Newark, NJ. Lower* **(L)** *Pat'd. May 26, 1885, by Jacob L. Newcomer, Baltimore, MD. See next picture for finished piece.* **(R)** *Pat'd. May 8, 1877, by James H.* **Scofield***. With side handle and compact design. Small arrow points to break in drawing – original published drawing had some unspecified length cut from it at that point, common in patent drawings as they appeared in the* Gazette.

❖ **NOTES** ❖

"Silvers" Chronology – The Chronology of the Silvers/Keystone defies exactitude. The marks, names & dates in above price listing was a collaboration by Don Thornton and Linda Franklin. I'm so mixed up now I could liquify. Thornton is not convinced that the maker-name confusion relates to successive manufacturers; he thinks it is highly likely that Silver and North were contemporaneous rivals. I'll just throw in a few more notes: I found a "Keystone" in Gene Florence's book *Kitchen Glassware of the Depression Era*, 3rd ed., with what appears to be a nickel-plated lid, patent date given by Florence as Dec. 15, 1885, and the mfr. as North Brothers. The April 30, 1878 patent date found on the glass jar was actually Silver's patent for the cylindrical jar for another plunger-style beater. Some examples are known that say only "patent pending" which implies a pre-1878 beginning. • Silver & Co., etc., had at least two marks, viz: "Silver Egg Beater," "Silver New Egg Beater," with the Brooklyn Bridge and words "Silvers Brooklyn" around the bridge. • The first time I saw a Silver/Keystone depicted, it was in the of *United Profit Sharing* Co.'s 1914 premium catalog. The linecut shows the old iron gear, with "Silver & Co.'s New Beater" on lid.

Eggbeaters, rotary paddle

Eggbeater, cast iron frame & gear wheel, with odd, sweeping, back & forth motion to its oblong wire mesh paddle, "Express Egg Beater," pat'd. Oct. 25, 1887 but made into 1910s at least, because it appears in a catalog of *A. E. Rayment Supply Co.*, Rockford, IL, of that date. 11-1/2"L. Nicknamed by collectors the "fly swatter beater." • My friend, the late Ray Townsend, known to thousands of tool & kitchenware collectors, wrote about his Express beater, that "It's always reminded me of a paddle on a steamboat; and, my daughter says, when she was a kid, she used to work it so her mother would think the snow plow was going by outside and she would not have to go to school." .... **$1,000+**

Eggbeater, handmade machined brass & wire, with modestly flirtateous & charming little back & forth movement of slender gauge wire blades when crank is turned, not marked, but pat'd. by Nathaniel Miller, Stroudsburg, PA, 9-1/4"L, pat'd. April 22, 1873. • I bought this from Bob "Primitive Man" Cahn in early 1983, liking its homemade quality. Bob, who often does info follow-ups for his customers, discovered a patent awarded Nathaniel C. Miller, of Stroudsburg PA, #138,094, April 22, 1873 for this beater. (Miller's first eggbeater patent was awarded Feb.1, 1870, #99,337.) This eggbeater was too good for me, and is now owned by Mr. Eggbeater: Don Thornton. The questions remain: Was this Miller's patent model, shop model, or a copy made by a craftsman who thought it nifty, and were there ever any more?.. **$1,000+**

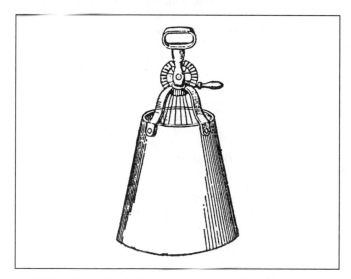

II-62. French eggbeater & container. A *"petite batteuse,"* depicted in Urbain Dubois' *La Patisserie d'Aujourd'hui,* c.1860s. **$200+**

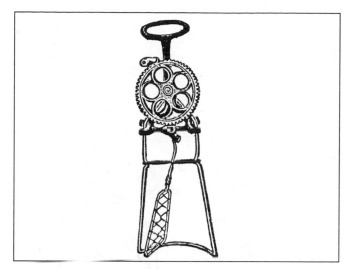

II-63-A. Eggbeater, paddle or sweep action with rotary crank. *"Express,"* also called by collectors the *"fly swatter"* beater, malleable cast iron, tinned wire, 11-1/2"L, 3" gear wheel. This picture from c. 1915 A. E. Rayment Supply Co., but beater shows up as early as a 1904 catalog of its mfr., National Mfg. Co., Worcester, MA. Actual beater is marked with patent date "Oct. 25, 1887" on the underside of the horizontal fulcrum bar, through which the shaft of the "Surprise" whip is fitted. It's not marked, but the patent number is 372,282; David T. Winter, Peabody, MA, patentee. Winter's patent states unequivocally: "I dispense with all springs, guide-rods, or adjuncts for the coiled dasher." Not only is there no "coiled" dasher, but the "Express definitely has what might be called an "adjunct" – that is, the fulcrum bar. • **Several mysteries surround the "Express." 1)** It doesn't look at all like the Winter patent. **2)** It does look like several other patents, most notably, the 1906 patent of Nicholas Stromer (see next group of patent drawings); **3)** A Canadian inventor, Dr. Edward M. Morgan, of Westmount, Quebec, patented several beaters. The first, 1904, & last, 1947, show beaters very similar to the "Express." Morgan's 1947 patent cites three other U.S. patents: his own of 1904; Winter's of 1887, and one by Stephen Coombs of Helena, MT, from 1896. **4)** The places where the various inventors lived, and where the Express was made – Worcester, MA. – are widely separated, so how did they connect? **5)** National Mfg. Co. was acquired by the Morgan Spring Co., presumably owned by Edward Morgan and located in Canada. • In 2001, at least one sold for $1,500; another for $1,026; another for $900 on eBay. **$1,000+**

Eggbeaters, scissor & squeeze, one-hand actions

Eggbeater, chromed metal, spring, & red plastic little knob or nut in top of levered grip. Name: "One Hand WIP," by Eagle Precision Mfg. Co., (also seen as Precision Tool & Die Corp.), NYC, NY, (or Long Island City, NY), 12-1/2" to 12-3/4"L, probably based on Dec. 18, 1923 patent of William Crocker, although one-hand devices had been patented since the Civil War (when many veterans lost a hand or arm). • If you didn't have to squeeze it too long, this handsome beater was very efficient: you could pour in ingredients with one hand while beating with the other. .... **$25+**

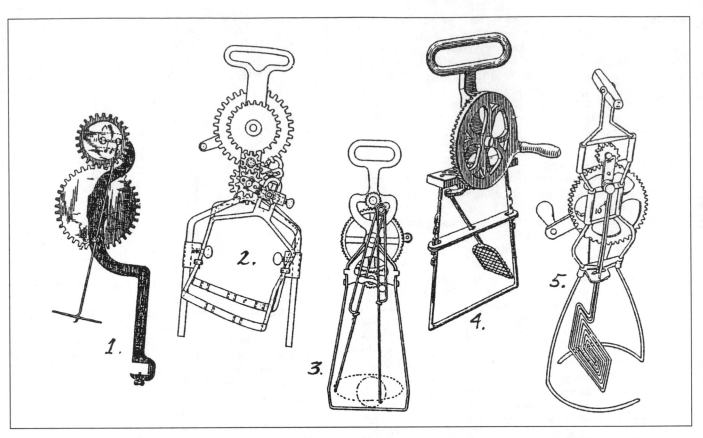

II-63-B. Eggbeaters, sweep action, with rotary cranks. *These are the eggbeaters patented from 20 years before to 60 years after the "Express." Left to right:* **(1)** *"**Egg Beater**," pat'd. Oct. 26, 1887, by David T. **Winter**, Peabody, MA, #372,282. The "vibratory dasher consists of a single stiff wire coil" and it "projects and plays up and down and swings through a regulating eye or opening in a guide-piece" halfway down the screw-clamp stand. The "laterally swinging" dasher "always remains in substantially a horizontal position, yet it describes a path nearly circular or approximately egg-shaped." He also suggests that his invention might be made with "legs instead of with a clamp."* **(2)** *"**Batter Mixer**, &c.," pat'd. Dec. 15, 1896, by Stephen H. **Coombs**, Helena, MT, #573,208. Coombs hoped that with his device, "the beaters will operate rapidly in opposite directions with both a vertical and lateral throw." The frame for the beater, with 2 side members, had adjustable guide-blocks with set screws, for guiding the side pieces of the two cranked beaters. "In operation the beaters are placed in the material to be operated upon, with the legs resting on the bottom of the vessel. ... Then by rotating the gearing the said beaters will be caused to move both vertically and in a lateral direction, one moving upward while the other is moving downward." This device "will be particularly useful in restaurants, hotels, or in bakeries, where large amounts of batter or similar material are operated upon, but of course the device is equally useful for household purposes." Imagine trying to clean that one, stuck all over with sticky pancake batter or omelette mixture!* **(3)** *"**Beater for Eggs, Cream, &c.**," pat'd. Dec. 6, 1904, by Edward Mompasson **Morgan**, Westmount, Quebec, Canada, #776,791. "My invention may be said ... to consist in providing a beater or whipper for eggs, cream, or the like having a pair of dashers revoluble in opposite directions and adapted to pass through one another during their revolution." The dashers were made of a continuous length of wire, bent into a "flattened volutoid form, the convolutions of one dasher being of different measurement to the corresponding convolutions of the other to allow the dasher ends proper to pass through one another." He said that his beater had a "carrying-frame," with "a pair of dashers having a reciprocating and oscillating movement."* **(4)** *"**Egg Beater**," pat'd. Dec. 4, 1906, by Nicholas **Stromer**, Gillett, WI, #837,432. Obviously, this is the one most like the produced "Express." The notches in the side pieces of the frame were so that the "fulcrum-bar" could be raised or lowered, in order to increase or decrease "the amplitude of the vibration of the beater, it being understood that by raising the bar the beater is made to swing through a larger arc," and vice versa.* **(5)** *"**Egg Beating Device**," pat'd. July 29, 1947, by Edward M. **Morgan**, Westmount, Canada, #2,424,703. This one looks so logical, it's too bad it wasn't made. But maybe it was! and a Canadian collector will find it. This invention called for a "fulcrum plate" with a long slot through which the shaft of the dasher could move freely. • Somewhere, in letters, or telegraphs, or perhaps even disputes settled in courts, may rest the answers to the mysteries behind the "Express" beater.*

II-64. Eggbeater – rotary paddler/sweep type.
Prototype or patent model? One-of-a-kind, hand-made, machined brass & iron wire, wooden handle, screw clamps to table or shelf edge, modest little back-and-forth or wigwag movement of the dasher to "enable a person to perfectly beat an egg in 35 seconds." 9-1/4"L. 19th C. Everyone thought this was a homemade one-of, machine shop contrivance until dealer Bob Cahn, who sold it to me, found its patent, granted May 22, 1873, to **Nathaniel C. Miller**, *Stroudsburg, PA. On Feb. 1, 1870, Miller had patented a horizontally-geared eggbeater resembling this one only in its wigwag "vibratory instead of rotary motion." Ex-Franklin Collection; now Thornton Collection.* **$1,000+**

Eggbeater, scissor action for one hand use, iron & wire, balloon wire blades like a whisk, cast around pivot is "PAT NO 1" prob. meaning pat'd, & that this one was the #1 model. 7-3/8"L. Smallest of the four Harry Jaquette (Jacquette Bros., Philadelphia), beaters, pat'd. Nov. 28, 1893. Smallest (7-3/8") and largest (20") most valuable. .... **$375-$1,000**

Eggbeater & cream whip, nickel plated sheet metal, with unusual action: fit top knob in palm, use forefinger to pull up on spring-tension hook, then release. Over & over. Good for arm-wrasslers in training, or pianists or aggie champeens. "Quik-Whip," American, 11"L, "patent pending," pat'd. by Ray Sowers, Nov. 10, 1931. (See also the one-hand Eggbeater & potato masher below.) .... **$75-$90**

Eggbeaters, rotary turbine: Turbine beaters churn liquid up from the bottom, by means of either curved, upturned blades, or slots or perforations in a single disc blade, or with a stacked series of blades.

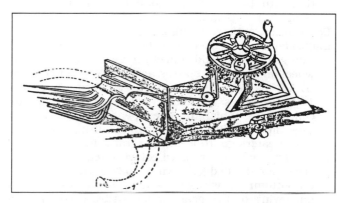

II-65. Eggbeater patent: rotary fork-beater. *Pat'd. June 16, 1891, by David A.* **Wilkinson**, *St. Louis, MO. A mechanical double fork with a horizontal gear. What a percussion instrument this would make! Probably never made, but I sure wish it had been.*

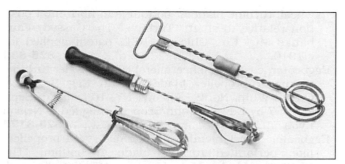

II-66. Eggbeaters for one hand use. *Left to right:* **(1)** *Squeeze action* **"One Hand 'WIP',"** *by Eagle Precision Mfg. Co., chrome & red plastic, 12-1/2"L, 20th C. Archimedean drill action;* **(2)** *beater with black wooden handle, 13-3/4"L, early 20th C. Notice the swiveling button for holding it in center of bowl. No mark, but possibly based on a Michael Rabb patent of the 1930s.* **(3)** *Fold-flat* **"Bryant's Patent,"** *from 1886, 12-7/8"L, Collection of Meryle Evans.* **(L) $50+; (M) $35-$50; (R) $200+**

Eggbeater, tin & wood, Androck's "Turbine," Washburn Co., also marked "Lutz File Company," Rockford, IL (Androck); Worcester, MA (Washburn); Cincinnati, OH (Lutz), 13-1/2"L, 1920s. .... **$18-$25**
Eggbeater, stamped metal & wire, turbine blade at bottom, "Turbine," Cassady-Fairbanks, Chicago, 12-1/4"L, c.1910-20. .... **$25-$35**
Eggbeater & cream whip, simple metal frame & handle, sort of doll-shaped, with openwork or cutout gear

II-67. Eggbeater & potato masher: one-hand, spring-powered. **"Lebanon** *Beater,"* *Seltzer Specialty Co., Lebanon, PA. Two interchangeable perforated cylinders (coarse or fine holes), with cast iron plunger that fits within the cylinder, and is attached to lower end of handle rod. Black wood handle. Looped wire adds spring action. 13"L x 2-3/4" diam. Tinned or nickel plated. Pat'd. Nov. 29, 1892 by Uriah D. Seltzer. 1892 ad. Trade cards for this tool are fairly common and sell for about $10. Value with only one cylinder:* **$450-$500**; *with both cylinders:* **$600+**

wheel, turbine blade at bottom is in horizontal position relative to shaft, "Turbine," The Cassady-Fairbanks Mfg. Co., Chicago, 10"L, patent applied for c.1910. .... **$25-$35**

Eggbeater, cast iron, sheet metal & wire, 2 tier turbine, upturned propeller blades, "Lyon Egg Beater & Cream Whip, No. 2," Albany, NY, 10"L, pat'd. Sept. 7, 1897 by Edward John Scopes, assigned to Nelson Lyon. .... **$75-$175**

Eggbeater, sheet metal, wire & wood, with propeller-like, perforated turbine blade at bottom, "The NECO," mfd. by M.A. Hougen, Minneapolis, MN, 11"L, patent pending, c.1910 to 1920................ **$35**

Eggbeater, chartreuse colored plastic handle & knob, chromed metal blades, handle set at angle to make it very easy & comfortable to grip, particularly when beating a cake for 30+ minutes. "Whirl-Whip," Los Angeles, CA, 11"L, marked "patent pending," double layer stacked blades with finger-like prongs, Maynard Mfg. Co., pre-1958, probably 1930s. The company used the phrase "whirl-whip design" in advertising. Probably meant to capitalize on earlier Whirl beaters such as the "Blue Whirl," and the "Merry Whirl," pat'd. in 1916 and 1921. The styling of all the Maynard beaters is so sleek and modern that these beaters will undoubtedly gain in popularity with crossover collectors coming in from nifty Fifties field. . **$15-$30**

❖ NOTES ❖

Visualize Whirled Peas – In the 1920s, Turner & Seymour, Torrington, CT, made Blue Whirl "Dainty Whirl" beaters, Blue Whirl "Kitchen Whirl" beaters, and "Merry Whirl" beaters – with various handle styles, pat'd. Nov. 28, 1916, and also Aug. 2, 1921 – and later the "Super Whirl." Several "Merry Whirl" beaters have been found factory-fitted with a plumber's snake instead of dashers! In the late 1920s, Androck [Washburn] made a "Whirlwind" turbine beater, nickel plated and 10-1/2"L. It was all metal except for the "ivory"-painted wooden crank knob. It was also very like their same-size regular turbine beater, except that instead of heavy nickeled iron wire it was made of flat metal. At the same time, Androck offered a set for the "Whirlwind," with a small (5" diam.) "French gray" glazed mixing bowl, with white stripes. Very moderne. These whirls are valued between $15 and $20. Other kitchen-related whirl brand names include: "Whirl-a-Whip," "Whirlbeater," "Whirlpool," "Whirlwind," "World Beater," "Super Whirl," & "Swirl Mixer," and whip brand names include: "Quik Whip," "Speed E Whipper," "Swift Whip," "Presto Whip," "Jiffy-Whip," "Whip-All," "Whip-It," "Whip-Mix," "Whip-O-Matic," "Whip-R-Well," "Whippit," "Whiprite," "Whipwell," & "Whippo." Sounds like some good vanity plates in there!

Eggbeater & cream whip, sheet metal, double slotted turbine blade, fluted disc above another that has a sort of funneling projection that would channel liquid out to edge and back over top, long central shaft, vertical wood handle is marbleized green, white & teal blue (came in red & white too), "WHIPPIT" Cream & Egg Beater, mfd. by Duro Metal Products Co., Chicago, IL, 13-1/4" or 13-1/2"L or 14"L, based on Ernest Fahlberg's Mar. 19, 1929 patent, although it was made at least four years before then. • Jane

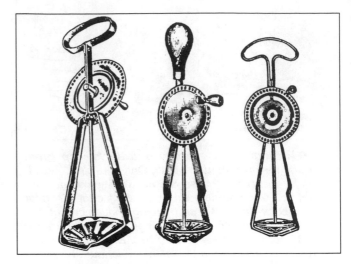

II-68. Eggbeaters & cream whips, rotary turbine. *The inventive debate over the best motion for beating an egg included strong arguments for turbine beaters. Turbines, which circulate fluids, including gas, and impart a circular motion to them (providing power in some instances), have been known at least since Hero of Alexander built a small steam-driven turbine in 120 B.C. For eggbeaters & cream whips, turbines are used to cause liquids on bottom to continually circulate upwards where they can be whipped. (L) Tinned steel, 10"L x 2-1/4" diam. of slotted turbine.* **Wire Goods Co.,** *1915.* **(M)** *Nickeled steel, wood handle is green.* **Washburn** *Co., 1936. Looks very like the Canadian "Fisher" turbine.* **(R)** *Notice the handle on this* **"Whirlwind."** *Ivory white knob. 10-1/2"L. Washburn Co., 1927.* **$35-$50**

Celehar, who did some company history research, says Duro Metal Products Co. sold Whippits in 1927 for $1, and that White & Hallock, Inc, Muskegon, MI, registered the Whippit™ trademark on Sep.18, 1928 though it was "used by their predecessor" since July 15, 1925. She explains that EKCO acquired the patent in 1945, and was selling it from then on. It's possible the patent number on my eggbeater, indicating a late-1940s patent, is a patent re-registration number. Various companies marketed the Whippit. .... **$20-$25**

Eggbeaters, rotary, whisk blades

Eggbeater, spiral coiled wire beaters, long shaft, cast iron gear wheel, odd bracebit type handle. Cast into wheel on each of 4 spokes are letters spelling name: "E A S Y," sold by Montgomery Ward, American, 1890s. • MW's ad reads "It consists of a spirally coiled wire, which in use opens and closes with exceeding rapidity, and instead of cutting the egg, as most beaters do, thoroughly aerates it." .... **$850+**

Eggbeater, cast iron, gear wheel with hearts, has screw clamp for shelf edge, & wire whisk beaters, fairly flat on bottom, the wires broadly spread at the bottom, narrowing to the gear "waist." Advertised in 1869 catalog as coming in 2 sizes: "Extra Family" & "Mammoth, for Hotels & Bakeries." Invented by James & Edwin Monroe. (Catalog misspells name with a 'u': Munroe.) Monroes Patent, mfd. by Dover Stamping Co., Boston, MA, pat'd. Apr. 19, 1859. •

II-69. Eggbeaters or cream whips – rotary turbine. (L) "*Lyon* No.2," *two-tiered turbine blades. Iron & tin, Notice the outer frame & 6-holed gear wheel. 10"L, mfd. in Albany, NY, pat'd. Sept. 7, 1897. (Very similar is the "Perfection," with double blades, a 4-holed gear wheel and no frame; it was pat'd. Feb. 22, 1898.)* **(R)** *Tin, wire,* **Cassady-Fairbank**

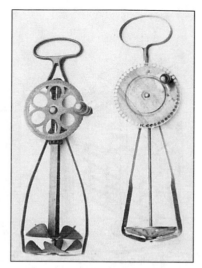

Mfg. Co., Chicago, IL, marked "patent allowed," pat'd. actually granted Nov. 13, 1917, to a Thomas Jones. Notice the simplicity of the gear wheel, with round perforated holes meshing with the teeth of the small horizontal gear not visible here. Great collecting pleasure is found in ingenious gear wheels. Collection of Meryle Evans. **(L) $125-$175; (R) $35-$50**

The patent drawing has a much simpler gear wheel, and longer frame for clamp. The beater was manufactured like patent drawing at first & "improved" with a more conventional gear and clamp by time of 1869 catalog. .... **$800+**

Eggbeater, shaken

Eggbeater, syllabub churn or cream mixer, tapered cylindrical tin body, used by shaking up & down to made the blades spin inside, sort of like a one-underpants clothes washer, only it's for one syllabub at a time. Removable turbine blades halfway down, snug-fitting lid marked "Tilden's Patent Aug. 1, 1865," 8"L x 1-3/4" diam., another is 9-1/2" x 2-1/2." Found not in *Patent Index* as syllabub churn, but as an "Egg-beater." .... **$155-$180**

II-70. Eggbeater patent – rotary turbine. *Pat'd. Nov. 14, 1882, by James T.* **Carley**, *Greenport, NY. I don't know if this eggbeater & cream whip was made, but it seems – except or short shaft & overlarge gear wheel – to be an ideal combination of turbine with revolving blades. It is so perfect, in fact, that I wager it'll be discovered in the next few years. And if it does exist, it'll bring:* **$2,000+**

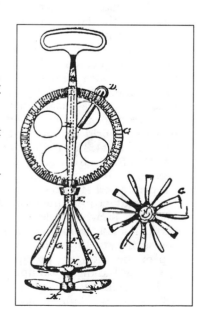

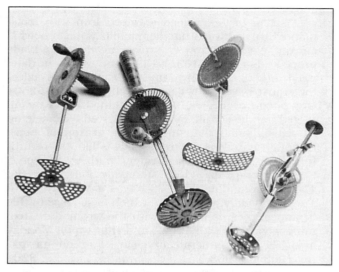

II-71. Eggbeaters & cream whips – rotary turbine. (L) "*The* **NECO**," *M. P. Hougen, Minneapolis, patent pending.* **(2)** "**WHIPPIT**" *Cream & Egg Beater, Duro Metal Products Co., Chicago. Pat. #1,705,639, white & teal blue marbled wood handle, 2 slotted dished blades & upright scraper, 13-1/2"L, 1929.* **(3)** "**Dunlap's Sanitary** *Silver Blade Cream Whip," Casey Hudson Co., Chicago, 3 patents – May 15, 1906, Feb. 26, 1907, Sept. 26, 1916. Curved perforated blade fits dimple in bottom of "Non-slip" brown-outside, white-inside glazed earthenware mixing bowl, which came with the beater.* **(R)** "**Quik-Whip**," *patent pending, nickel plated, 11"L. Unusual one-hand action: you fitted your palm to top, then used forefinger to pull up spring-tension hook, which, when released, caused perforated turbine blade to spin.* **(1) $40+; (2) $25-35; (3) $65 with bowl, $30 without bowl; (4) $95-$115**

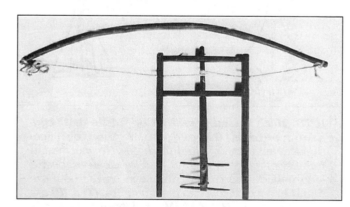

II-72. Bow drill eggbeater. *Earliest type of mechanical beater, bow drill or* **fiddle drill** *beater, works when bow is sawed back & forth. A cord passing through two small holes in support frame turns beater first one way, then the other, as it winds & unwinds on central shaft. Devices like this were used in very ancient times for starting fires, or for drilling holes. American, probably very early 19th C. Picture courtesy of the National Museum of American History, Smithsonian Institution.* **$800+**

Eggbeaters, spoon

Mixing spoon beater, tinned stamped iron with black painted turned wood handle, smallish spoon bowl is cut out leaving narrow crosspiece to which a 4 blade propeller is riveted, 10"L, to 11"L, no mark but date, pat'd. Aug. 3, 1909, by James H. Collins. See collector's must-have "propeller spoon" II-88. **$200-$250+**

Mixing spoon eggbeater, stamped tinned sheet metal, ridged handle shank, large bowl slotted like skeleton rib cage, small diamond cutout at top of bowl. Although handle is different, bowl is like the beautiful "Ideal." "The Eclipse Beater," mfd. by Stuber & Kuck, Peoria, IL, 11"L, stamped "Pat. Mar. 30, 1903." Wrong date – the 30th was a Monday, not a Tuesday. Oddly, the "Ideal," which is so close to this in appearance, is marked with the wrong date, too: mine says "Mar. 30, 1908," and that was a Monday also. The year numerals are clear – I am not mistaking 1903 for 1908. .... **$20+**

Mixing spoon eggbeater, tinned steel, deep bowl with 16 paired slots or transverse ribs, deep division down center, looks like abstract skeletal rib cage, turned wooden handle with blunt end, "Ideal," manufacturer only partly legible on mine: "Mfd. by ___ater" (or possibly ___ster"). American, 10"L x 3"W, mine says "pat'd. March 30, 1908" but really it was pat'd. Mar. 31, 1903 by Carrie Bentley. I've always thought of it as a spoon, but Bentley called it an

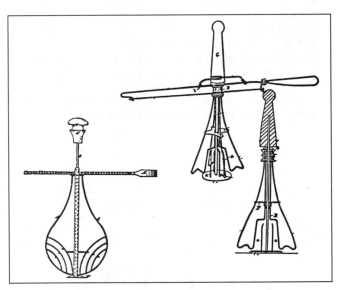

II-73. Mechanised bow drill or fiddle drill eggbeater patents. *(L) Pat'd. July 7, 1863, by Timothy **Earle**, then of Smithfield, RI. He invented a number of eggbeaters (and fruit jar closures) over a long period. The curved ribs seen on the bow are found in several collectible eggbeaters. (T) & (R) are two views of Howard M. **Brittain's** (Martin's Creek, PA) egg beater, pat'd. May 12, 1892. Action is same idea as aboriginal bow drill fire-starting tool: beater is set firmly in bowl, gripped and held in place by vertical handle, while horizontal wire bow and its spooled cord is moved back & forth to turn beaters this way then that. Brittain's was probably the patent behind a tin cylindrical bow drill beater shown in Thornton's 2nd ed., p. 264. That one has an upright turned wood handle, is 11-1/4"H, and Thornton values it at over **$400**.*

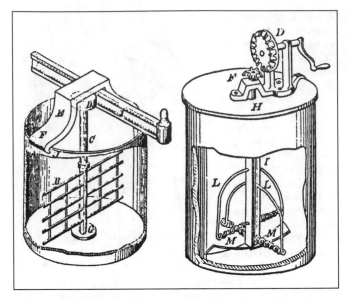

II-74. Eggbeater patents. (L) *Pat'd. Dec. 15, 1857, by John B. **Heich**, Cincinnati, OH. The "net work" beater is activated by a ratcheted bowing action. Central gear disk is described by inventor as made of India rubber, "or other elastic material, attached to the top of the rod. ... The beater is operated by the pressure produced upon the elastic disk by the motion backwards and forwards of the grooved bar" bow. From Patent Commissioner's Annual Report, 1857. Notice that the grid-like gate dasher is very like the one in the "King" beater in II-35 & 36. **(R)** Pat'd. May 21, 1867, by Marvin T. **Williams**, Milwaukee, WI. Notice the little coils on bottom horizontals of beater wings to help aerate the egg.*

"Egg Beater," so it's here. Her patent shows a continuous piece of stamped & slotted sheet metal with no wooden handle. • Classic. – I still give this pride of place in my Pantheon of kitchen collectibles, for sheer design and looks and heft. .... **$25+**

Eggbeater, waterpowered

Eggbeater, aluminum, brass, rubber, glass. Water actually circulates through the U-shaped mechanism built into the lid. Body is glass quart-size canning jar fitted with lid that's not round but sort of pear shaped (narrow extended neck in back), and inside jar are simple flared blades which revolve as the water circulates through the lid via a metal device that connects faucet & lid. The water exits out a long tube that comes out under the back neck of the lid. Round stick-on label on lid is missing, but trade name is "World Beater." Pat'd. by H. L. Thompson, Apr. 29, 1924, but mfd. prior to that by World Novelty Co., Elgin, IL...................................... **$95-$115**

Eggbeater & potato masher, 2 interchangeable cylindrical perforated steel receptacles (called a "hopper" by the manufacturer); medium & fine holes, for cooked potato or stewed apples or eggs, nickeled cast iron vertical shaft, round topped turned wood handle; the spring steel wire that connects ferrule of shaft & top of the "hopper" provides the tension & return power as handle is pumped up & down, "Lebanon Beater," mfd. by Seltzer Specialty Co., Lebanon, PA, 13"L x 2-3/4" diam. hopper, pat'd. Nov. 29, 1892 by

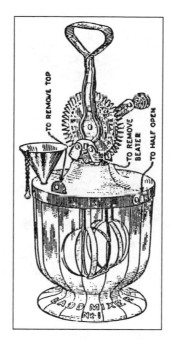

II-77. Mixing churn or *mayonnaise-maker* or *egg-beater. "Ladd #1" in quart size footed paneled bowl, showing oil funnel in 2-part, fold-back lid or apron. 12-1/2"H. The #2 is substantially larger and more impressive. This line cut is from a 1914 ad, but pat'd. 2 years later on Feb. 15, 1916, and sold for at least another 15 years. With funnel:* **$300+**

II-75. Water-power eggbeaters. *Can be attached by a hose or directly to faucet.* **(L)** *Painted metal housing on glass jar. 8-1/2"H. Turbine action of water coursing through pear-shaped lid causes beaters to turn. Discharged water apparently came out tube below the lid. Fit a quart canning jar with a screw top. Not marked, although it once had a round paper label identifying it as* **"The World Beater***, Mfd. by the World Novelty Co., Elgin, IL."* **It** *was pat'd. April 29, 1924.* **(R)** *Highly polished brass lid & metal dashers. I wonder if a company that made lawn sprinklers didn't make this beater. This one not marked except for "patent pending." It was not made to screw onto a beater jar but after attaching to faucet it could be used with any container. Pictures courtesy Glenda Clark and Phyllis & Jim Moffet.* **(L) $75+; (R) $100+**

Uriah D. Seltzer. Added value for both hoppers. .... **$450-$500; $600+**
Electric eggbeaters and electric mixers – See: Chapter XVIII (Electrifying Work)
Larding needles in case, steel in brass cylinder (or steel in japanned tin); a set of long needles in cylindrical case, used to lard in, or in effect insert or mix fat (especially strips of bacon) into lean cuts of meat before roasting, available through F.A. Walker wholesale catalog, French (?), c.1870s-80s. **$25-$45**

Malted milk mixers – See: Drink mixers; also see Chapter XVIII (Electrifying Work)
Mayonnaise mixer, blue painted cast iron, openwork heart gear wheel like so many geared objects of the late 19th C., glass jar, hole for funnel for mayonnaise oil, original blue paper label on jar, "FUPA" is the maker, (although it sounds like an acronym for 4 words beginning in F U P A, or P A F U) "Made in France," 10"H, c. 1890s-1910. .... **$500+**
Mayonnaise mixer, cast iron, clamps to table, cast iron frame supports oil drip funnel behind vertical 6-petal cast iron gear wheel; lower part is a hinged cast iron basket frame to hold a bowl (glass? ceramic? metal?), wire balloon whip blades, with two X-shaped supports to hold wires, 11"H. Only mark "PAT APLD. FOR" – 2 patents were granted Oct. 10, 1893 to Jennie De Witt Harvey, and is called by collectors "The Jennie." • This belongs to the Moffets in Illinois, and they want to know what sort of bowl it had; any information would be appreciated. . **$450+**
Mayonnaise mixer, footed glass bowl, glass lid has built-in oil "funnel" with large well & small drip hole, iron frame fastened to lid, fancy iron gear wheel & short crank knob fixed on wheel, tin blades, "S & S, Hutchinson," sometimes "J. Hutchinson," Job Hutchinson, Long Island, NY, 9-3/4"H x c.7" diam.

II-76. Mixing churn "Ladd *Beater #1," as in II-74. Pat'd. July 7, 1908, Feb. 2, 1915. Beater can be dismantled from lid. 13"H. Collection of Meryle Evans. Notice that this one doesn't have the funnel (with chain & tiny stopper) that came with it.* **$225+**

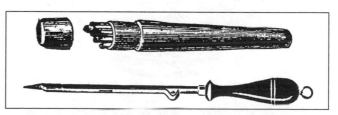

II-78. Larding needles – or "Beef à la Mode" needles. **(T)** *Brass & steel needles in tin fitted case. F.A. Walker catalog, 1870s, but sold for at least another 30 years.* **(B)** *Other is a mechanized larding needle with wooden hand, sort of like a latchhook for making rugs. c.1906-07 catalog.* **$20-$35**

II-79. Mayonnaise mixer & eggbeater. *Clamps to table, nickeled cast iron, tin, 10"H, removable beater blades – 1) thin blades, and 2) a tin paddle-scraper blade at the end of the longer shaft. It is also supposed to have a ring mount that would act sort of like a metal collar to hold the vessel. See the little light area halfway down the frame at left. That's where the vessel-support band would have been attached. This mixer also should have a funnel. No mark, no date on this one, but they are sometimes marked "**Christy Knife** Patented Fremont," Ohio. Some are found with flat rudder-like blade at bottom. Collection of Meryle Evans. See also the container-type rotary eggbeaters earlier in this chapter. As shown: $200+; with the band & the vessel: $1,200+*

II-81. Mayonnaise mixer. *Blue painted cast iron with heart cutout gear, large handle, glass jar, oil funnel hole, wire stirrer. Original blue paper label reads "VITESSE-MAYONNAISE." Trademark is a diamond with "FUPA" inside. French, c.1900. Without funnel: $250+; with funnel: $500*

footed bowl, marked "patent appl for" – patent granted later: Sept. 2, 1913, #1,071,747. ...... **$350+**
Mayonnaise mixer, called a "mixer churn" by maker, footed glass bowl, with close-fitting lid with funnel, eggbeater can be disengaged from lid, "Ladd Beater #1," "United Royalties Corp.," American, 13"H, the beater bears patent dates July 7, 1908, Feb. 2, 1915, while the glass container and fitted measuring lid or apron was patented by Lavern Bordwell, Feb. 15, 1916. .... **$300+**

II-82. Mayonnaise mixers. (L) *"Universal Mayonnaise Mixer & Cream Whipper," Landers, Frary & Clark, patent applied for. Nickeled iron top, nickeled dashers with long fingers, lid has swivel cover for oil hole. 2-1/2 to 3 c. capacity, approx. 9-3/8"H, late 19th C. This one missing 2 vertical rods that came down from the two tabs left & right on the lid & went down to a clamp-on plate under the glass vessel; also missing the funnel.* **(R)** *"S & S No. 1," or "Scientific & Sanitary." A very beautiful piece. The "S & S" forms casting design of gear wheel. Glass lid with oil funnel built in. Regular eggbeater blades. 9-3/4"H overall. This one marked "patent pending." It was patented Sept. 2, 1913, by Job Hutchinson, and mfd. by his assignee, National Indicator Co., Long Island City, NY. It was used for omelets, salad dressings, desserts, & beverages also. Collection of Meryle Evans. [Note: Another smaller "S & S" has a sheet metal gear & cup-like bowl, and is stamped "S & S Hutchinson Pat. Sept. 2, 1913" on the gear. It came with a glass funnel, and is valued at $400+.]* **(L)** *As is: $200; with rods, plate & funnel: $500+;* **(R)** *$500+*

II-80. Mayonnaise mixer & bowl. *"The **Silver** mixer came in one size only – 2 pts. Notice the oil-funnel with drop stopper for making mayonnaise. "Imported bone china" bowl, chestnut wood cover, nickel-plated brass beater. Blade is sort of half-moon shape with a few bent-up fingers. Silver & Co., Brooklyn, c.1910. $450*

Mayonnaise mixer, metal with original heavy glass quart-size jar that has 6 little feet & is embossed "The Holt-Lyon Jar Cream Whip and Mayonnaise Maker," cast iron "Dover" beater has elongated blades with slight crimping at curves, and 48 rather than 60 or 63 cogs in the large gear, long conical oil dripper funnel with little rod to regulate drip, Holt-Lyon Co., Tarrytown, NY, 15"H, 1910s to 1920. • A somewhat older one is 5/8" shorter & has 63 cogs to the gear; the conical oil dripper has a snap-strap that slips over grip of beater part. With original jar: .... **$600+**

Mayonnaise mixer, nickeled iron top, straight-sided glass handleless cup, iron gear wheel & long crank handle, wooden knob, nickeled dasher has long horizontal fingers & a set of odd vertical fingers at bottom. Lid has oil hole with its own tiny swivel cover, screw clamps to table or shelf, "Universal Mayonnaise Mixer & Cream Whip Whipper," Landers, Frary & Clark, New Britain, CT, 9-3/8"H, 2-1/2 to 3 c. capacity, pat'd. Apr. 17, 1915. About $200; but with all parts: .... **$500+**

Mayonnaise mixer, tall marked glass tumbler, metal screw-on lid has mixer blade shaft, convex perforated metal dasher is horizontal, small convexity in jar's bottom fits dimple on dasher blade bottom. "Wesson Oil Mayonnaise Maker," 11"H jar, 20th C. .... **$30+**

Mayonnaise mixer & cream whip, white porcelain footed bowl, tin lid (edge or rim only) with interior crosspiece that supports cranked beater blade of tin, tin funnel goes in hole in wide rim of lid for adding oil, imported, prob. German or English. Two sizes found: 3"H & 4"H bowl, late 19th C. .... **$150+**

Mixer, cast iron, screw clamps to shelf, green wood handle, reamer clips onto the top, "Cake Drink Mixer, Egg Cream Mixer," mfd. by New Standard Corp., Mt. Joy, PA, patent pending, c.1900. • Dealer Elissa Weitz of Lahaska, PA, said that there "supposedly is a Mount Joy bowl to use with this," and that the bowls came in a lot of sizes. However, New Standard itself advertised that practically any kitchen bowl could be used with the mixer. .... **$100+**

Mixer, nickeled metal device mounted to board, with vertical cranked wheel, metal band holds container, "Kwikmix," Schenker Mfg. Co., NYC, NY, about 10-1/2"H, pat'd. Mar. 9, 1922. .... **$300+**

Mixer, tall glass container, tin lid with snap fitting, iron shaft & 2 nickel-plated, perforated, dished, horizontal dashers, there's a spring in lid so when you pump the handle up & down it really goes to town. "Jones Wonder Mixer," Jones Tool Co., Cleveland, OH, c.1926. (See also: Syllabub churns.)... **$50-$75**

Mixer, wind-up with spring motor, clear glass container, metal top, on-off switch, American. Pat'd. July 9, 1935 by Samuel Berger. .... **$65+**

Mixer & sifter, tightly coiled springy wire, 2 handles, squeeze action makes wires go in & out, rather like a cross between a Slinky toy & an accordion. "___sse Carlson Co.," "Nifty Sifter," Rockford, IL (Andrews Wire Goods Co. was here about the same time), 8-1/2"L, pat'd. Feb. 25, 1930 by Bror N. Carlson. • Thanks, readers! Vivian Robertson sent photocopy of battered advertising card – in part reading: "A 100 uses in cooking; prevents lumping of flour, sugar and ... similar ingredients... Hotel chefs have found

II-83. Mayonnaise mixer, eggbeater, drink mixer, and cream whipper. Two slightly different examples of the **"Air-O-Mixer,"** patent pending, mfd. by Bentley-Jones Inc., Montgomery, AL. Collector Glenda Clark owns one marked with manufacturer "Bentley-Beale, Inc." Glass embossed with directions. Perforated **(L)** conical beater is of type used by makers of mixer churns & syllabub churns for at least 75 years before. Slightly domed **(R)** gridded dasher would have introduced more air into the mixture. Air-O-Mixers called "Wesson Oil Mayonnaise Maker" appeared in Wesson Oil "make your own mayonnaise" ads from late 1933 through 1934. [Note: the Air-O-Mix Corp., of NYC, was listed in a 1922 hardware trade magazine as the manufacturers of the "Whip-All" beater; perhaps that was the first trade name of the Air-O-Mix. A tin cone bottom Air-O-Mixer was also made, but the name could have been borrowed unofficially.] **$25-$55**

it indispensible in preparing gravies, sauces, cake batters ... dip into flour, sugar or other ingredients; release spring and sift into gravy skillet, stew pan, or batter bowl. ... The Nifty Sifter ... used in preparing scores of dishes where lumping will spoil the efforts of the chef." • Tiffin, OH dealer Ralph Frankart wrote me in 1984, about a woman who purchased one in 1929 in Detroit and called it a "Sprinkler." "She uses it in her baking, opens it and dips it into the sugar bowl, lets it close and by slightly opening it, sprinkles sugar on her cookies, pies, etc. Also dips it into her flour and fills it then sprinkles it on her rolling pin, rolling board, pie pans, etc. She loves it and was quite disturbed that I would not sell her mine as she wanted it as a gift for her sister." .... **$15-$20**

Mixing bowl, blue & gray saltglazed stoneware, adv'g. message for "Dentel's, Ackley Iowa," 20th C...... **$75**

Mixing bowl, blue & gray saltglazed stoneware, with cherry motif, 9-1/2" diam., 20th C. **$45**

Mixing bowl, blue & red sponged "Saffron" yellowware, wide shoulder band, narrow paneling below band, Red Wing pottery, Red Wing, MN, 7" diam. (these bowls were made in 1" increments from 5" to 10" diam., 1930s. • Value varies widely with size, presence of advertising or name, and condition, (apt to be poor for relatively porous Saffron pieces.)... **$100**

Mixing bowl, blue & red stripes, Red Wing, advertising "Rock Dell," 8-1/2" diam., 20th C..................... **$75**

Mixing bowl, blue, rust & gray spongeware, shouldered, with 6 panels, American, 8" diam., 20th C. **$70**

Mixing bowl, blue & rust sponged stoneware, for "Waddington's," Geneva, IA, by Red Wing, early 20th C. **$125**

Mixing bowl, ceramic, green with pink & blue stripes,

*II-84. **Mixing bowls.** (T-L) is wood, ranging from 12" to 37" diam. Jaburg Brothers, who sold supplies to confectioners, advertised that they would "strap Bowls and repair same." Meaning to fix cracked ones with iron bands, etc. That was in 1908, much later that we previously thought wooden bowls were being artfully repaired rather than discarded & replaced. High prices are asked for handsomely-repaired wooden bowls. (B-R) footed bowl is heavy tin, made in sizes from about 7" to 15" diam. Sold by German company, c.1904. Not shown: Jaburg also sold seamless steel mixing bowls, from 25" to 34" diam., finished black or galvanized. (T-L) $15-$200+; (B-R) $20+*

"Watt's Oven Ware," 14" diam., early 20th C..... **$65**

Mixing bowl, dark brown saltglazed stoneware, shouldered, marked "Weller," Fultonham, OH, 8" diam., late 19th C. Small dimple indent inside bottom, perfect for use with some eggbeaters. **$35**

Mixing bowl, graniteware, yellow & white marbleized, American, 9-1/2" diam., early 20th C. **$45**

Mixing bowl, green glaze, ribbed, square base goes up into round bowl, mark is shield with "9" inside circle, American, 9-1/2" diam., early 20th C. Green increasingly collectable. .... **$40+**

Mixing bowl, green glazed pottery, "Kitchen Kraft," Homer Laughlin China Co., 8" diam., c.1940s. .... **$45+**

Mixing bowl, green-glazed yellowware, square base goes up to circle, molded geometric designs, no mark, American, 10" diam., early 20th C.? If I had the '80s to do over again, I'd buy a few green-glazed yellowware bowls. What gorgeous, lively color......................... **$55**

Mixing bowl, large & relatively low, yellow glaze with green sponge decoration, gold rim, tiny crack not affecting careful use, American, 3-1/2"H x 10-3/4" diam., 19th C.. **$125**

Mixing bowl, pumpkin colored ceramic, "Watt's Oven Ware," 7" diam., 20th C.................................. **$25+**

Mixing bowl, red & cream spongeware, American, 8" diam., c.1890s-1910. .... **$50+**

❖ NOTES ❖

Lead Glazes: Caution to the Public – Mr. Editor – Sir: Will you permit me to acquaint the public ... that there is a kind of Crockery Ware, manufactured in almost every city in the Union, which is dangerous to use – and which the public will understand by the term Common Red Pottery. This ware is made of common clays from the brick

yards, and when formed, is coated with a liquid called Glaze, which is nothing less than a coat of lead. The clays being of the commonest kind, cannot be subjected to any heat in the burning that will make them safe for family use – being porous – and it is very unsafe to deposit any articles of family use in them, such as milk, butter, or in fact water, as a portion of the Lead Glazing will be extracted, and the article will, in consequence, become dangerous to use. I have noticed no fewer than ten instances within the last twelve months, of families sustaining injury by the use of such ware.

"In selecting the article of crockery that is suitable for family use, it is only necessary to ascertain that the body of the ware – the clay – has been hard burnt, which any person can understand by the sound of it – if well burnt, it will have a clear sound. The poorest kind will not ring at all, and therefore can be easily detected. An article of this kind will, in the course of a month's use, become very foul. Let any one who doubts this break the vessel, and they will ascertain the fact. There is a kind of ware, however, that is manufactured in almost every city in the Union, called stone ware, which is perfectly good for family use. This ware is formed of strong and superior clays, and undergoes a great heat in the burning, – and moreover, the glazing is not a thick coat of lead, but is accomplished by throwing salt into the kiln. All kinds of Liverpool [Ohio?] ware are adapted to all purposes of family use, being made of sound clays and well burnt. As a preventive is better than a cure, if I should be the means of preventing any person suffering from the use of the poisonous article – lead – this advertisement will answer the ends I design. [signed] C. S.," who adds "Glass may be used in all cases, and is the most beautiful and safe article extant in manufactures." *The Farmers' Cabinet* (reprinted from *The Pittsburger*), Philadelphia, Vol I, No. 7, Oct. 15, 1836.

Mixing bowl, ribbed spongeware, mottled brown & green glaze over yellow background glaze, 8-1/2" diam., 20th C... **$175+**

Mixing bowl, Saffron spatterware, with shoulder, Red Wing, with "Christmas Greetings, 1938, Protovin, Iowa," 20th C. **$75**

Mixing bowl, saltglazed stoneware, adv'g. "It pays to mix with Thoren Brothers, Rock City & Rock Grove, Illinois" on the inside, American, 6"H x 8" diam., early 20th C.? Punning advertising messages are the most fun – on mixing bowls, beater jars & rolling pins. **$85**

*II-85. **Mixing bowls.** Called schneekessel. German nickel-plated, copper (A); (B), tin (C), and glass (D) bowls. Generally between 8" to 15" diam. $10-$100*

Mixing bowl, saltglazed stoneware, Western Stoneware Co., Monmouth, IL, 10" diam., late 19th to early 20th C. **$50**

Mixing bowl, saltglazed stoneware with adv'g. message: "Farmer's Complete Department Store," late 19th or early 20th C. .... **$50+**

Mixing bowl, saltglazed stoneware, apple motif, "Watt's Oven Ware #8," "Farmer's Co-Op Elevator Co.," 8" diam., 20th C. **$65**

Mixing bowl, sponged blue & red, Red Wing, 7" diam., advertisement reads "It pays to Mix With Weisensels, Sun Prairie, Wis." 20th C. .... **$135+**

Mixing bowl, sponged, no marks, 5-1/2" diam., desirable small size, 20th C. .... **$40+**

Mixing bowl, spongeware, slight hairline crack, advertising message: "It Pays to Mix with Andrew Westin, Newberry, Michigan." 5"H x 8-1/2" diam., early 20th C. **$125**

Mixing bowl, very worn inside bottom down to the clay body, yellowware, brown mocha decoration on cream band, cream slip banded decoration, small foot, NJ, 11-3/8" diam., 19th C. Condition hurts value here. **$125**

Mixing bowl or biscuit pan, white glazed earthenware, thick sloping walls, removable & set into much deeper heavily tinned vessel with inward slanting sides, 2 strap handles with handgrip braces, little filling spout poking out on side under handle, with cap, English, 19th C. Price for 2 parts: **$175**

❖ NOTES ❖

Biscuit Pan – Hitherto consisted only of a single vessel. ... Used for beating up or whisking batters. The improved pan is formed either of metal or earthenware, inclosed within an exterior vessel, furnished with a plugged aperture, for the introduction of hot water." Thomas Masters, *A Short Treatise Concerning Some Patent Inventions...Also the Newly Improved Culinary Utensils*, London, 1850. ("Biscuit" here is in the English sense, of crackers.)

❖ RECIPE ❖

To Make Little Cracknels – *Take three pounds of flour finely dried, three ounces of lemon and orange-peel dried, and beaten to a powder, an ounce of coriander-seeds beaten and searced [sieved], and three pounds of double refined sugar beaten fine and searced; mix these together with fifteen eggs, half of the whites taken out, a quarter of a pint of rose-water, as much [quarter pint] orange-flower water; beat the eggs and water well together, then put in your orange-peel & coriander-seeds, and beat it again very well with two spoons, one in each hand; then beat your sugar in by little and little, then your flour by a little at a time, so beat with both spoons an hour longer; then strew sugar on papers, and drop then the bigness of a walnut, and set them in the oven; the oven must be hotter than when pies are drawn; do not touch them with your finger before they are bak'd; let the oven be ready for them against [before] they are done [and] be careful the oven does not colour them." Elizabeth Smith, The Compleat Housewife, 1753.*

Mixing bowl, yellow Fiesta Ware #7, mid 20th C. .. **$65**

Mixing bowl, yellow & green spongeware, gilt scalloped edge, 8-3/4" diam., American, 19th C. **$120**

Mixing bowl, yellow & green spongeware, gilt scalloped edge, 13" diam. x 5" deep, American, 19th C. **$140+**

Mixing bowls, yellow glazed earthenware with green sponge design, some have gold-glazed rim, American, range from quite small – 5-1/2" to 14" diam. & larger. The bowls tend to be relatively shallow in relation to their diam., turn-of-century.... **$45-$200**

Mixing bowl, yellowish green glaze, molded pattern of little "pillows" rather than concentric bands, mark is a shield with 8 in a circle inside it, also #4 (or possibly #14), American, 8-1/2" diam., early 20th C. .... **$40+**

Mixing bowl, yellowware, all over foliated swag design, 12" diam., late 19th C. .... **$125+**

Mixing bowl, yellowware, deep cobalt mocha decoration on band, rolled rim, very small foot, 13-1/4" diam., mid 19th C. .... **$300+**

❖ NOTES ❖

Rolled rims – A rim or edge that is described as "rolled" may actually be rolled, such as a piece of tinware, or steel – even that which has later been enameled. The term is also used to describe the look of a rounded rim, that couldn't possibly have been actually rolled – such as a turned wooden bowl or a ceramic piece.

• • •

"**Mixing bowls** come in deep yellow and light buff earthenware. Also in white stone china. Deep yellow is made of a rather soft material and breaks easily." Maria Parloa, *Kitchen Companion*, Boston: Estes & Lauriat, 1887.

II-86. Mixing bowls. (T) White semi-porcelain with wide blue band and blue pin stripes. "Heavily glazed." 4" to 13" diam., holding from 6 oz. to 7 qts., c.1895 ad. *(B-L)* is "heavy yellow stoneware, rolled edge, neat blue band decoration. Used all over the country." 4-1/2" to 15-1/2" diam., c.1895 ad. *(B-R)* "Yellow bowl," earthenware, holding from 1/4 to 12 qts. Duparquet wholesaler catalog, c.1904-1910. Age, size, condition, & glaze color determine value. Flick with your thumbnail to hear it ring (not cracked) or thud (cracked). Should be signs of wear on bottom. **$20-$200**

Mixing bowl, yellowware, deep lip, scalloped rim, ribbed melon sides, American, late 19th C. ...... **$75+**

Mixing bowl, yellowware, simple zigzag design around side, American or English, 5-3/8" diam., late 19th or early 20th C. .... **$30+**

Mixing bowl, yellowware, triple brown band, one wide, 2 narrow, marked "20" & "Made in U. S. A.," 8" diam., early 20th C. **$30**

Mixing bowl set, 3 nested bowls, yellowware, yellow with cream bands, turned setback bases, Watt's, 6 - 1/2"H x 10" diam., & 5"H x 8" diam., & 4"H x 6" diam., 20th C. Set:.......................... **$125-$150**

Mixing bowl set, Delphite glass, 3 nesting bowls in "Teardrop" pattern, Fire King, 20th C........... **$125+**

Mixing bowl nest of 3, sponged red & blue on stoneware, a Red Wing pottery, 5", 6", & 7" diam. (not complete set, as they were made on up to 10" diam.), 20th C. .... **$155+**

Mixing bowls, opaque green – "Jadite," Depression glass, nesting set of 4, actually "Skokie Green" in catalog of manufacturer, McKee Glass Co., Jeannette, PA, 6", 7", 8", & 9" diam., all relatively tall bowls, 1930s. • "**Jadite**" is the trade name for an opaque green that Jeannette Glass Co. (also Jeannette, PA) made; "**Jad-ite**" was used by Hocking, but it's such a perfect descriptive name (anyone familiar with green jade thinks translucent); collectors use it for wide range of very pale to rather richly green opaque glass. • **Looka-like alarm:** About 2001, well-made "Jadite"-looking footed cake plates, cups, bowls, etc., made in China, appeared on the market. Price for old set: .... **$75+**

Mixing machines – See: Bread machines & makers; also Mayonnaise mixers; Mixers

Mixing spoon, commercial or manufactured wooden spoon, of common type, but with head carved on end of handle, very African in style, high forehead, pronounced eyes & hair, American, 13"L, prob. 20th C. carving, but it looks awfully good, and not fakey folk. • I paid $3.50, surprise, surprise, but believe more realistic value: .... **$25+**

❖ RECIPE ❖

Another Way to Mix Cakes – Take six pieces of cane about 18 inches long; tie them fast together at one end; but, to make them open, put in the middle where you tie them one or two pieces half the length: this is called a mixing rod. Provide a tall water pot as upright as can be procured, which make hot; work your butter on a marble slab, then put it in the pan, and work it well round with the rod until it is nicely creamed; put in the sugar, and incorporate both together; add one or two eggs at a time, and go on in this progressive way until they are all used; work away with the rod with all speed; and as soon as it is properly light, (which you may know by its smoothness, and rising in the pan) take it out, and mix in the flour, spices, currants, &c. &c. with a spatter [spurtle]. This is esteemed the very best mode of mixing cakes." *Joseph Bell*, A Treatise on Confectionary. *Newcastle, England, 1817.* Spare the rod and spoil the cake, eh?

Mixing spoon, stamped & slotted metal, nickeled, green wood handle, stamped "Rumford Baking Powder," 10-3/4"L, 20th C. .... **$15+**

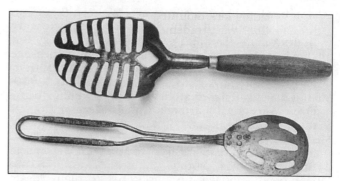

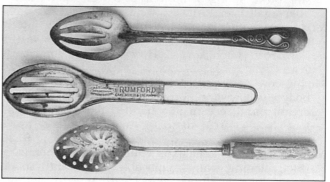

II-87. Mixing spoons or slotted cake spoons. *From the top: (1) Skeletal, rib cage-like "**Ideal**" is tinned steel, with a simple turned wood handle. 10"L. Spoon is a deep bowled shape, and is for "beating eggs, cream pan cakes, and all other kinds of cakes and batters. For mashed potatoes it can't be beat. Can also be used for lifting vegetables from the pot or eggs from the pan. Unsurpassed for mixing or stirring of fruits." Pat'd. March 31, 1903 by Carrie Bentley, marked "Mfd. by ---ster" (or ---ater). Others, 11"L, have been found with an all-in-one stamped metal handle prob. later marked "The Eclipse Beater," with the patent date, and "Mfd. by Stuber & Kuck, Peoria, IL." (Bentley's slotted spoon) was still being referenced by inventors as recently as 1997 – for a pasta-eating spoon pat'd. by Robert Pritsker. See also XIII-33, XIII-34a.) (2) Wire handle, 10-1/4"L, has "**Rumford. The Wholesome Baking Powder**" stamped into flattened part of handle. Other Rumfords are essentially the same but with bottle-opener end to handle. (3) Dark one is stamped tin, possibly German. (4) Rumford advertising one, 12"L, is worth most. It's stamped "Saltsmans Improved Royal Pat'd. Oct 6 08 RUMFORD Cake Mixer & Cream Whip." (5) Slotted & perforated one probably A & J, c.1930s-1940s. (1) $30+; (2) $15+; (3) $5+; (4) $20; (5) $3+*

Mixing spoon, stamped tin & iron, "Rumford Cake Mixer & Cream Whip," Saltsmans, 10-1/4"L, 20th C., unclear patent date on it is Oct. 6, 1908, a Tuesday. Aaron Saltsman held a patent for a slotted mixing spoon dated April 27, 1897. • Another "Rumford" mixing spoon has sheet metal bowl, with slots, and wire handle, stamped in one place to read "Rumford Baking Powder." .... **$15+**

Mixing spoon & fork combined, tinned iron with black painted turned wood handle, strange mechanical combination of fairly normal mixing spoon with small bowl & sliding fork mounted to shank, marked "L & J Novelty Co.," with trademark of "L & J" inside hexagon, Brooklyn, NY, 12-15/16"L, pat'd. 1925. ...... **$50**

Mixing spoons, slotted, tinned metal, look exactly like cat box litter scoops, in fact, such are sold for that purpose now at my local pet store, some with stamped advertising. One I have is marked "CHIEF. Lifts, whips, mixes, mashes, crushes, strains," between 10-1/4" and 11"L x 3-1/2" to 3 3/4"W, c.1890s to 1970s. Most may be 1930s or '40s. Good variety in slot patterns, just as in cake turners. **$2+**

Mixing spoons, tinned sheet iron, or nickeled iron, with various wood handles, differences in turning, finish (natural, varnished, painted, stained), & in pattern of holes & slots in the spoon bowls, various makers, including A & J, Androck, Ekco, Samson, PM, etc., American & European, all about 10"L, 1890s to 1940s. • Cast & stamped aluminum ones (mainly German) are a sub-specialty. Advertising ones with wire handles, and those with plastic handles adds even more variety to the field. .... **$5+**

Mixing spoons, called "eggbeaters" by inventors & sellers – See: Eggbeaters, spoon

Paddles – See: Butter paddle

Pastry blender, 6 springy wire half-circles, crimped into stainless steel tips mounted to wooden handle. Several styles of wooden handle – a simple rod with turned grooves, or a thicker, tapered one – the rest is

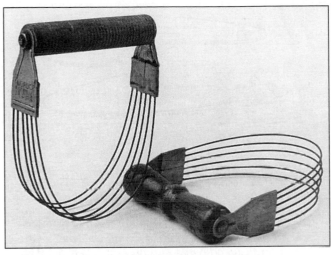

II-89. Pastry blenders. *Wire, steel & wood. 5-3/4" x 4". Both Androck, pat'd. Jan. 12, 1929. Notice the 6 wires; in catalogs & ads, there are always 7 wires. One lying flat, with shaped turned wood handle, is oldest, other with broomstick wood grip is newer. In a 1936 catalog, the handle of green or red is made of Catalin plastic rather than painted wood.* **$5-$15**

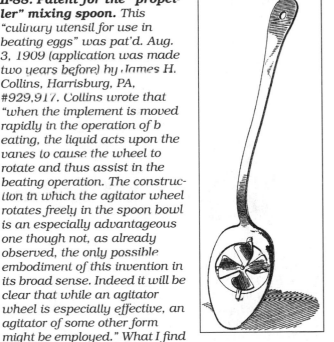

II-88. Patent for the "propeller" mixing spoon. *This "culinary utensil for use in beating eggs" was pat'd. Aug. 3, 1909 (application was made two years before) by James H. Collins, Harrisburg, PA, #929,917. Collins wrote that "when the implement is moved rapidly in the operation of b eating, the liquid acts upon the vanes to cause the wheel to rotate and thus assist in the beating operation. The construction in which the agitator wheel rotates freely in the spoon bowl is an especially advantageous one though not, as already observed, the only possible embodiment of this invention in its broad sense. Indeed it will be clear that while an agitator wheel is especially effective, an agitator of some other form might be employed." What I find particularly interesting is that this oddball patent from 1909 was being cited in patents 80 years later! It gets cited in an invention for a "High speed logic circuit and semiconductor integrated circuit device including variable impedance ... " and a "Neuro decompression device," as well as late 20th C. patents for spoons and measuring spoons. • The actual spoon, at least as it's known by collectors, has a turned wood handle, but otherwise it looks just the same. The spoon is 11"L, of tinned stamped iron, with a riveted propeller. For the spoon itself:* **$200-$250+**

basically the same. The grooved rod is probably newer one. Androck, Rockford, IL (but poss. Worcester, MA), 5-3/4"L x 4"W, pat'd. Jan. 12, 1929. • The name Androck is a combination of Andrews Wire Mfg. Co., and the location; it's unclear how and when Washburn of Worcester, MA, took on or absorbed or merged with Andrews. .... **$5-$20**

Pastry blender, also pie crust mixer & flaker, wire chopper (as described in the *Official Gazette* of the Patent Office), 6 wires in perfectly round hoop, threaded through 2 slots in the top (1 in each side) of sheet metal handle, "Lambert," pat'd. by Clara Burchard Lambert, Pasadena, CA, 4-1/4"W, #1,486,255, pat'd. Mar. 11, 1924. .... **$15-$20**

Pastry blender, like a fork, heavy nickeled iron, wooden handle, American, 9-1/4"L, patent probably either Cram's of Feb. 19, 1907 or Hayward's of Dec. 19, 1922. .... **$7**

Slotted spoon – See: Mixing spoons

Spurtle, oddly-shaped wooden stirring or scraping tool with hole in blade part, worn, some staining to end of blade, looks old but may not be, unknown origin, 13"L, looks like 19th C. • **The word spurtle** is Scottish, and refers to a cooking implement primarily used for stirring, with an edge to fit different kinds of pots, pans and kettles. They have been a longtime favorite shop project, and are so useful that one made in the 1930s of good hardwood might look about the same as one made in the 1850s. In the early 1970s, *Time-Life Books*, in their *Family Creative Workshop* series, had a chapter on making your own spurtle. • In 1973, Graham Kerr, the "Galloping Gourmet," introduced a set of five spurtles with their own hanging rack, made of hardwood. They ranged in length from about 8" to 13", and a flat spoon-shaped one had a pair of holes, and a shorter "butter knife" shaped; one had one large hole near end of the blade, and the others were without holes in the blade, but all five had hanging holes. • An

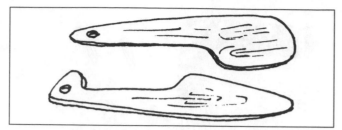

II-90. Spurtles. *Idiosyncratically-shaped carved wooden stirring paddles, adapted to various uses (like the rubber spatulas we use today) – from turning griddle cakes to stirring porridge. The verb "spurtle" means "to cover with spatterings," which is what usually happens when I make pancakes or stir oatmeal. The word is Scottish; the tool is universal. A few years ago, The Galloping Gourmet's Graham Kerr hawked carved bamboo spurtles.* **$4-$12**

1817 English confectionery cookbook, by Joseph Bell, calls frequently for a spatte, the same tool........... **$3+**

Stirrer, carved wood, turned handle with small ball knob at end, wide blade is 1/3 of full length, overall it looks like a finely-made canoe paddle, American, 13-1/2"L, poss. 2nd to 3rd quarter 19th C. .... **$40-$60**

Syllabub churns – See also: Cream whips, Eggbeaters

Syllabub churn, Tilden's – See also: Eggbeater, shaken

Syllabub churn, tin, with a tin rack (shaped like a doll stand) that adjusts in height, simple wooden knob handle, deeply conical bottom to churn, inside has a conical dasher, 9"H, marked "pat'd Sept. 14, 1875." Others found that are 12"L x 4"diam., and 11"L x 3-1/2"diam. Pat'd. by Friedrich E. Schonmeyer, Cleveland, OH. Don Thornton has one marked "Bon Ton."................. **$75+**

Toddy mixer, glass & metal, "Toddy Man," c.1930s... **$15**

Whip or whisk, for baking, wire, "Omar Wonder Flour," 20th C. Advertising adds a little value............. **$10**

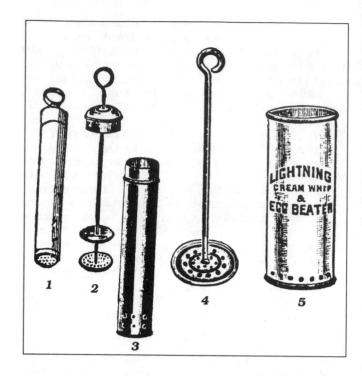

II-92. Whisk-like game of "Kan-U-Katch." *I found this picture in a c.1916 St. Nicholas children's magazine, and include it as a confusable, seen at least once marked "old whisk."* **$15+**

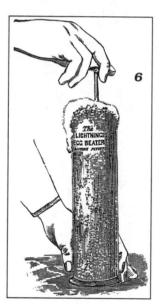

II-91. Syllabub churns & eggbeaters. *Very old type, called a **whip churn.** Above: Several patents, from at least the 1860s to about WWI. These have a perforated flat dasher. Similar-looking ones might have a conical dasher. **(1)** Was for making whipped cream or syllabub, and is from American Home Cook Book, Boston: 1854. **(2)** & **(3)** are parts of the **Matthai-Ingram** syllabub churn, 8"H x 1-3/4" diam. c.1890. **(4)** & **(5)** is the dasher & tin body of the "**Lightning** Egg Beater," also mfd. by Matthai-Ingram. Patent not known for sure, but probably Theron S. Stewart's March 27, 1888 patent. Resembles "Lightning" churns made from Saltsman's patent of July 10, 1894. It is about 5-1/2"H. "The white of an egg can be beaten in one minute to a froth stiff enough to cut with a knife."*
*Left: **(6)** "The **Lightning** Egg Beater," either "Grafton's Patent" or "Crafton's Patent." This was in an English cookbook, "Katherine Mellish's Cookery and Domestic Management," London: 1901. The tiny hole visible between two fingers at top is the air inlet in the tube that leads to the dasher; the container is "crystal glass," and Mellish says "only a little froth may rise over the top."* **$45-$70**

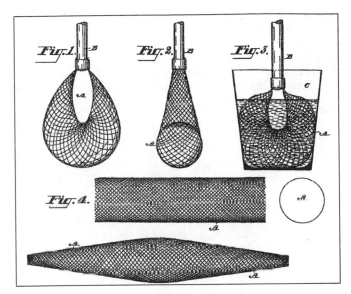

II-93. Whisk-like "culinary or egg beater." *This amazing-looking whisking beater was pat'd. by Caroline S.* **Pusey**, *Philadelphia, PA, Oct. 25, 1887, #372,043. It looks like a tiny bustle, or a hairdressing device used to plump up a chignon; in fact it was undoubtedly inspired by the material used for making such things. Pusey's specification says "…this invention is a culinary or egg beater (also a churn) constructed of elastic wires braided or interwoven to form a fabric, preferably of tubular form … having its ends turned up and secured to a suitable handle or spindle for operating." Imagine what Ms. Pusey could have done if she'd had plastic at her disposal!*

Whip or whisk, large flat metal with stenciled wooden handle, not for food, but for mixing wallpaper paste, "TIK Wheat Paste, Clark Stek-O Corp.," Rochester, NY, 14-5/8"L, 20th C. Other marked paste company whisks are known. **$10**

Whip or whisk, wire in flat snowshoe shape (Thornton calls this a "fan" shape), wire-wrapped handle, 9"L, 20th C. **$8**

Whisk, wood, tin & string, long handle you rub between palms to make it turn back & forth, small balloon blades, probably a drink mixer, American, 16"L, mid 19th C. **$15**

Whisks or egg whips, twisted wire, spoon-like in outline, with crisscross wires, springs & wires wrapped around "bowl," or a sort of chicken wire effect of wire stretched across bowl, various, some found in catalogs, like that of Androck, mostly American, about

II-94. Whisks for the baker, chef, and candy man. *Clockwise from coiled wire:* **(1)** *A roll of "Egg beater wire," for replacing whisk wires, c.1906.* **(2)** *Candy makers' "sugar spinner," 15"L, 1927.* **(3)** *Circa 1870s, with chained ring to adjust ballooning of bows to suit the job.* **(4)** *Long flat one ("snowshoe" or "fan"-shaped) with bound handle is called the "Sensible Egg Whip," and made in sizes from 9" to 15"L, over a long period. Notice the central wire, which is soldered to others and stabilizes them. (- - -) These unnumbered 3 are cream whips from Germany, c.1904.* **(5)** *"W.H.T. Patent Egg Beater," sold through candy makers' suppliers, c.1908.* **(6)** *16"L, big ballooned bows. c.1927.* **(7)** *Wood handle steel (or brass) whip, c.1908.* **(8)** *For restaurants – "Mayonnaise Whip," 5-1/2" diam. x 13-1/2"L with "four foot pole attached." Circa 1927.* **$5-$40**

12" to 13"L, mainly 20th C. Many variations are pictured. See pictures II-28 to II-30. .... **$8-$20**

Whisks, new types include: tinned steel wire with wire wrapped handles for sauces, & a more ballooning stainless steel whisk with wooden handle, adjusting ring on wires to regulate size of balloon, American or imports (mainly France & Germany), first type: 6", 8", & 10"L; second type: 12"L, new, sold in all kinds of kitchen specialty shops & departments. Approx. new value: .... **$4-$20**

FOR MORE INFORMATION

Eggbeaters

The Eggbeater Chronicles, The Stirring Story of America's Greatest Invention, (2nd edition of *Beat This*) by Don Thornton. 332 pages (enough uncovered beaters to expand the original 256 pages!), copiously illustrated with photos by Donald G. Simons & Robert S. Arnold, as well as patent drawings. One of the most remarkable parts of all Don's books is the evidence of the organized mind of a librarian or editor combined with the aesthetic appreciation of an artist. Also, Don has sought out many eggbeater patents for his all-inclusive list between 1856 and 1991, and this has sometimes meant searching indices under headings other than the old-fashioned "egg-beater." To order ($50.45 including p &h), go to Web site: www.thorntonhouse.com, or see Bibliography for address. Please, if you have eggbeater info to share, feed it to Don and he'll pass it on to me for the next edition of this book!

Ceramics & Pottery

General

A Web site with lists of many pottery/ceramic clubs and auctions if found at www.potteryauction.com/clubs-shows.html

Red Wing

Gary & Bonnie Tefft
Locust Enterprises
W174 N9422 Devonwood Rd.
Menomonee Falls, WI 53051-1302
(414) 251-1415
E-mail: LocustEnt@aol.com
Web site: http://members.aol.com/locustent/

The definitive book, *Red Wing Potters & Their Wares*, is now in its third edition. The authors have many links, and more information on their Web site.

The Red Wing Collectors Society

c/o Helen Bell
1718 W. 6th St.
Red Wing, MN 55066
E-mail: rwcs1@redwing.net
Web site: http://www.redwingcollectors.org

Churns

For information on Dazey churns and replacement parts, see long paragraph on Dazey in the churn listings.

PREPARING

III. SEPARATE, STRAIN, DRAIN, SIFT, & DREDGE

In the last chapter we mixed things; here we separate them. This preparation category includes implements that assist the cook either by allowing wanted solid foodstuff to be retained (in a sieve, colander, skimmer, etc.), or for wanted liquids or solids to be cleared of unwanted particles too large to slip through the holes, or for lumpy food to be pushed through a perforated (or screened) surface in order to render the lumps smaller, or to make them uniform in size, or to aerate them. When used with a pestle, a strainer is a form of mortar, so see Potato ricers in Chapter I (as well as the one described here).

Colanders are among the most popular utensils in this category, collected today for the material from which they are made (especially enameled iron), for their shape, and for the variety of perforated patterns. A single colander can be a thing of great and simple beauty because its form tells the whole story of its function; but a collection of different colanders, each with its particular tattoo of holes, is spectacular. The colander's lineage is ancient: bronze ones were uncovered in the archaeological digs in Pompeii buried by a volcano in A.D. 79. For collectors looking for something interesting but not expensive, colanders – partly because there are no gears and cranks – are not pricey collectibles, and the value has remained stable for years.

Most of the **cheese drainers** are in the next chapter with molds because, although they look like colanders, and the method is to strain the whey from the curds, their ultimate function is to mold a cheese once the whey has dripped out. A few did end up here. Funnels with built-in sieves (mostly vintners' or brewers' types) are here; other funnels are in Chapter V (Measuring).

Flour sifters form one of the most popular categories in this chapter. They satisfy mechanically because of cranks, squeeze handles, shakers. Many odd ones have been patented, so collectors in search of patented kitchen gadgets have created a competitive market for rare ones. Furthermore, the sifters with fun, cheerful designs enameled or color-lithographed on their sides, from the 1940s and 1950s, are a good, inexpensive collecting category because they go so well with other red, green, yellow, and blue designs and handles of the same period.

Wireware is also popular, but a confusing area for new collectors because of so many new repros and lookalikes.

Kitchen Glossary: Foot or Base? I have tried to consistently use the term "foot" (or sometimes "footed base") in the singular, when I'm writing about a sort of fixed or attached flared or convex ring or narrow band that serves as the base of a vessel, utensil or other object. The term foot has long been used in describing the bases of glass, ceramic, metal, stone, and wooden containers. A glass tumbler, for example, had to be drained in one quaff because it couldn't stand up. A drinking glass with a stem and a foot could be sipped from all evening.

Two major types of colanders are either **foot loose** or **foot fast**. (Simple colanders are foot loose and fancy free!) Foot loose means that there's a ring separate from the colander used on any surface so that a bowl-bottom colander can be set down. In China, metal rings are used with woks; in Africa, cloth rings are used for balancing baskets or clay vessels on a woman's head. Foot fast means the ring is stuck fast – soldered or riveted in place in the case of metal colanders. Some writers and antiques cataloguers call this type of fixed ring foot a "gallery foot."

More exact terms include **spreading foot** for the widely flaring incurved foot; **molded foot** for one with beading, reeding or ogee curves or other moldings familiar in wood carving and cabinetry; **round foot** for a simple convex or outcurved foot. See the illustrated glossary at the beginning of this book.

Descriptive terms haven't been codified or standardized to a high degree concerning kitchen wares, so some applicable terms must be borrowed from fields of collecting such as silver, pewter, porcelain, and furniture, as well as wood- and metal-working tools.

Metal Drives for Munitions & Material: Affect on Today's Supply of Antique Iron, Pewter, Copper & Brass Wares. – There is probably plenty of documentary evidence, so far unexplored, touching on the necessity for metal or scrap drives during (and perhaps preceding each of) the first six wars with United States' involvement, viz. the War for Independence, 1775 to 1783; the War of 1812, 1812 to 1815; the War Between the States, 1861 to 1865; The Spanish-American War, 1898; World War I, 1917 to 1918; and World War II, 1941 to 1945. Such documents presumably would be found in the National Archives, the Library of Congress, and in privately- or publicly-held collections of family papers, letters, newspapers, broadsides, perhaps even court-ordered seized records.

With the Internet, you could make some headway searching for information on, at least, the scrap-metal (and rubber) drives so well-documented for WWII. A site for citrus crate label collectors cites the loss of huge numbers of printing plates. One remembrance by Shirley Wilson, a Kansas woman, says "If you had two frying pans, you contributed one to the war effort."

The wars swallowed an incalculable number of sound household wares and tools, as well as scraps of same, pooled to recast or forge as cannon, musket balls, soldiers' canteens & eating kits, uniform buttons, army horseshoes, ironclad vessels, guns, pistols, and bullets. Basically we are talking about iron, lead, and pewter, with some brass and copper. I can't now search primary or secondary sources, but will quote from Ledlie Irwin Laughlin's *Pewter in America*, 1940, to hint at the scope of the loss. Anything said about pewter is true in spades about iron. Laughlin writes, Vol. I, p. 109, "During the [Revolutionary] war the country was combed for everything containing lead to supply munitions for the Continental troops. Little beyond the absolutely essential, and probably new, pewter would have escaped the melting-pot." In Laughlin, Vol. II, p. 69, we read that "It has been said that the dearth of Southern pewter may be chargeable to confiscation by agents of the Confederate Government of all available metal that could be used in the manufacture of munitions during the Civil War." Inexplicable to me, so far, is the vast supply of 17th, 18th, & 19th century iron, pewter, brass & copper wares found today all over Europe, which has been ravaged by war.

• • •

Meltdowns in the Pursuit of Commerce – Easily reviewed old newspapers, or "gleanings" of ads done by Dow and Gottesman, give ample proof that most, if not all, metal artisans in the U.S. solicited and bought "old iron, pewter, brass, copper, lead & tin" for melting down or reworking into new objects in more fashionable or necessary forms. These war and peace metal drives have left us with only sketchy written descriptions and incidental depictions of countless old pieces gone forever.

Meltdowns from 9/11: – The news in March 2002 is that so-called scrap iron from the destroyed World Trade Towers in NYC is being sold as salvage metal directly from the barges loaded at the site, and from the landfill where the bare ruined choirs of the WTT were being taken in late 2001. The scrap iron is being sold all over the world, and it is not impossible to imagine that in a few years we may be offered imported muffin pans and frying pans that contain cast iron or steel from the World Trade Towers.

Bean sizing sieve, also called a sorting frame, or bean sizer, square wood frame moveable at corners, crisscrossed with wood slats not tightly affixed to the frame. Adjust the sieve from coarse to finer by pulling two opposite sides out from a square shape into a parallelogram out to an elongated diamond shape – this changes the size of the interstices, or spaces, between the slats, from an inch or so down to a quarter of that. American, approx. 18" x 18", 19th C. Either handmade or limited production pieces, patina, and condition are important.............. **$100**

III-1. Ash sifter & coal sieve. (T) *"Hustler," mfd. by Hill Dryer Col, Worcester, MA. Galvanized sheet metal, horizontal cylinder with hopper at one end with crank, and perforated end that lets ashes through into bucket. 1890-1905 ad with infant imps.* **(B)** *"The Convex Coal Sieve," mfd. by Lock Haven Sifter Co., Lock Haven, PA. Heavy double-seamed sheet metal, cast iron ears riveted on for handle. The convex bottom prevents ashes accumulating in the center (most ash sifters had flat bottoms). Pat'd. Apr. 16, 1889; put on market in late fall of 1890. The Metal Worker, May, 1890.* **$10-$20**

III-2. Colanders – *foot-loose and foot-fast (soldered on). Four sizes, from 9-7/8" to 13" diam. Matthai-Ingram, c.1890.* **$15+**

Colander, also spelled in old inventory records cullender, cullinder, callender, collander, and colender. This one is pewter, wide flared sides and fairly shallow – in what would have been advertised in the 1750s as a "dish cullender" (rather than the deeper, more narrowly-rimmed "basin cullender"), foot fast, ring handles, scalloped pattern of small perforations. American (?), no discernable touchmark, 11" diam., late 18th or very early 19th C. .. **$300-$600+**

Colander, aqua enamelware, 11" diam., mid 20th C. and quite possibly European. [Note: If you want to fix an old, chipped enamelware colander, my helpful tip is to apply cosmetic repairs with nail polish –it's available in practically any color. Works great, although I don't recommend doing this to any piece you plan to sell.].. **$25+**

Colander, medium French blue enamel outside, white inside, strainer holes only in bottom in pattern of 19 little holey flowers, not evenly spaced, appearance of being very deep because of unusual proportions, 2 cup handles, rounded foot, canted sides, hanging ring midway around rim between handles, and tipping handle opposite that, 5-1/4"H x 9-5/8" diam., c.1890s-1910, Eastern European, (others seen, one red with light gray & white marbleized interior; pale yellow one, etc.). Very attractive..................... **$30+**

III-3. Colanders. *All tin, with old-fashioned styling, and possibly the cuts were already 40 years old when used in Harrod's Stores, Ltd., catalog of 1895. Clockwise from top left* **(1)***: deep bowl type, 9", 10", and 12";* **(2)** *is stamped, with riveted handles;* **(3)** *is pieced, with riveted strap handles, 8" to 10-1/4" diam., c.1895.* **$30+**

III-4. Round bottom colanders or cullenders. *All foot-fast, as most colanders are. (L) (R) (L) (R) from top.* **(1)** *"Greystone" graniteware, from 9-7/8" to 13" diam. Matthai-Ingram.* **(2)** *3-1/2" to 4-1/2" deep x 9-3/8" to 12" diam. D. J. Barry, 1924.* **(3)** *White "Sterling" enameled, 4-7/8"H x 9-1/2" to 6"H x 12" diam., Central Stamping Co., 1920.* **(4)** *Stamped tin, of large size for hotels mostly – 4-3/4"H x 13" diam. up to 7-5/8"H x 19" diam. Lalance & Grosjean, 1890, and same cut used in catalogs of 30 years later.* **(5)** *Tin version of #3.* **(6)** *Hotel colander in 3 big, sturdy sizes. "Puritan," Central Stamping, 1920.* **(7)** *Tin, in 4 sizes from 3"H x 9-1/2" to 4-1/2"H x 13-1/4". Lalance & Grosjean, 1890.* **$25+**

III-5. Slant-sided, mostly flat bottom colanders. **(1)** *"Greystone" graniteware, 9-3/4" and 10-7/8", Matthai-Ingram, c.1890.* **(2)** *Called the "Eastern Pattern" for body shape and flat bottom (?), probably not for star-point perforations. Wrought iron (though not handmade) handles, 10" to 12". Pattern offered by many companies, this one from Geuder, Paeschke & Frey, 1925.* **(3)** *Heavy pieced tin, soldered strap handles, 11-1/2" and 13-1/2", Shapleigh Hardware, 1914.* **(4)** *Flat-bottom & footless, strap handle, in 14", 16", 18", and 20", and four hole-size choices 1/8", 1/4", 3/16", and 5/16". Jaburg, 1908.* **(5)** *Tinned steel, from 5-3/4"H x 13-3/4" to 7-5/8" x 19-1/2". Pick-Barth, 1929.* **(6)** *Planished tin, 9-1/2" to 15" diam., Albert Pick, 1909.* **(7)** *9-3/4" and 11", Matthai-Ingram, c.1890.* **(8)** *Widely flared, another "Eastern" style, 12", GP & F, 1925. It's interesting to me how much variety, including hole sizes, was available to people even 80 years ago, from ordinary hardware stores. Things have certainly changed. Now it's cereals in endless variety.* **$20+**

III-6. Colander. *Perforated tin, ring foot is soldered on – foot-fast, 3-3/4" H x 9-3/4" diam. Late 19th to early 20th C. Note the seam where the collar-shaped tin pattern was soldered together before the bottom and foot were soldered on. Collection Mary Mac Franklin.* **$20+**

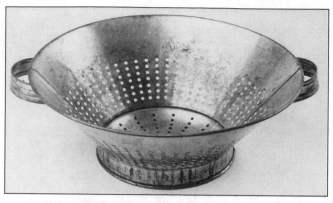

III-7. Colander. *Flared sides, brightly tinned, dished, foot fast. Note on this one that the sides have 2 seams – a pattern that saved tin. 4-1/2" H x 12" diam. Late 19th to early 20th C. Collection Mary Mac Franklin.* **$20+**

Colander, brown & white swirled enamel, prob. "Onyx," Columbian Enameling & Stamping, American, 10" diam., late 19th, early 20th C. (A sort of spotty rich brown & white enamelware line, including many flat-bottomed colanders seen in last decade, probably are European, and are valued at less than half that for American ones – at least when sold in the U.S.) .... **$85+**

Colander, dark cobalt blue enamelware, black rim & handles, elegant bowl shape, high fixed foot, prob. European, 7"H x 7-1/2" diam., late 19th C...... **$45+**

Colander, dark cobalt enamelware flecked with white, wire handles, footed, American (?), 8" diam., c.1890s-1910... **$75+**

Colander, gray graniteware, American or German, 9-1/2" diam, late 19th or early 20th C. .... **$35+**

Colander, gray graniteware, ear handles, short feet & attached drip tray, late 19th C. .... **$100+**

Colander, green speckled enamelware with cobalt blue rim & ear handles, foot fast, lovely color, 10-7/8" diam., 19th C.. **$150+**

Colander, mottled green graniteware, strap handles, foot fast, American (?), 10" diam., late 19th or early 20th C. .... **$85+**

Colander, perforated sheet iron, foot-fast, commercial but looks handmade, good condition, 10" diam., late 19th or early 20th C. .... **$15+**

III-8. Copper colanders. *Bowl-shaped colanders made of copper; (L) sold in sizes from 10" to 18", would be set down in a pot or large mixing bowl to drain, Duparquet, Huot & Moneuse, c.1902-1910. (R) One with small ball feet is tinned in and out, in 5 sizes from 10" to 14". Henry Rogers, Wolverhampton, England, 1914.* **$55+**

III-9. Colander. *Copper, with large handles making it usable with many size bowls or other vessels, on whose rim the handles would rest. 9" diam., bottom is flat and joined to sides with strong dovetail seam. Ex-Wiggins Tavern Collection of Northampton, MA. Photograph courtesy of Luella McCloud Antiques, Shelburn Falls, MA.* **Note:** *A 1986 exhibit of Shaker artifacts included a beautiful simple tin strainer, much like this, with two very large strap handles on the sides.* **$200+**

Colander, perforated tin, flat bottom has radiating holes lining up with every 3rd row of holes in sides, deeply flared, strap handles, foot fast, American, 4-1/4"H x 12" diam., late 19th or early 20th C. .... **$25+**

Colander, pierced tin, flat bottom, foot fast, tinned iron loop handles, in F. A. Walker catalog, 3-3/4"H x 9-3/4" diam., 1870s-80s.. **$20**

Colander, rounded bowl body, pierced tin, iron loop handles, nice rolled edge foot ring, separate or loose, Matthai-Ingram, 13" diam., 1890s. • **This is a hypothetical** or what-if entry. Although the catalogs offered foot loose as well as foot fast colanders, the chances of an old foot ring surviving with its separate colander bowl are slim. .... **$18-$35**

Colander, sheet iron, very large with good size holes, crudely soldered foot ring, primitive & imposing, American, 14" diam., mid to end of 19th C. This is a

III-10. Confusable – *not a colander but a* **dip basket.** *Pressed fiber dip basket for brass foundries, nickel-plating works, etc., mfd. by United Indurated Fiber Co., whose agents were Cordley & Hayes. The Metal Worker, Nov. 8, 1890. Similar things are still being sold for small-scale plating.* **$30+**

good example of the kind of object segueing out of the cheaper kitchen collectibles field into the expensive and volatile folk art market, where – presented out of context – such a piece as this qualifies as sculpture. .... **$50+**

Colander, tinned, pieced sheet-iron, large holes – indicating it's most likely a cheese drainer or "basket" as found in the next chapter with molds. This one has flat bottom, three concentric rings of holes in canted sides, stamped on both handles "R. Smith, Tunbridge, VT," 21-1/2" diam., mid-19th C........ **$350+**

Colander, tinned pieced sheet metal, hollow ear handles, small flat bottom has many holes, lower part of sides not perforated, then band of several rows of holes partway up sides, American, 14" diam., late 19th C. **$25**

Colander, white enamelware, blue rim, strap handles & foot, c.1900.. **$25**

Colander, wire mesh in tin & wire frame, wooden ear handles, also used as a purée sieve, Androck, Rockford, IL, 1936.. **$10+**

Colander, yellowware, footed, rather thick walls with pierced bottom, American, 10" diam., 19th C. .... **$150+**

Colander, yellowware, small foot, nice pattern of holes, 2 eyeholes near rim for a hanging cord, English, 10-3/4" diam., mid 19th C. • **Broken.** – Very small hairline crack may lower value by 25% or so. • **Repaired.** –

III-11. Colander-strainers of saucepan style. (T) "Mirro" aluminum, with steel hollow handle, 6-1/4" to 8-1/2" diam. Aluminum Goods Mfg. Co., Manitowoc, WI, 1927. (B) Pieced tin, large holes in slightly dished bottom only. Tubular handle, c.1870s-1900. Courtesy Lar Hothem. **$3; $15+**

III-12. Colander-strainers. (L) Tin, in 9 sizes, from 2-1/2"H x 5" diam. to 5"H x 11" diam. Saucepan style, with strap support for resting within a pan. Matthai-Ingram, c.1890. Identical pictures appeared in Lalance & Grosjean 1890 catalog, and Duparquet catalog, c.1904-1910. Lower (R) Stamped metal (quite possibly tinned copper) colander depicted in Urbain Dubois' La Patisserie D'Aujourd'hui, Paris, c.1860s-80s. The colander is being used as a support for glazed orange segments stuck on skewers to air dry. **$10+**

Conversely, if the crack had been repaired with a tin band or an intricate weaving of wire, or the use of metal staples, the value might even double! (See Chapter IX for tools for washing, sharpening & repairing housewares.)... **$150+**

Colander or strainer, dark brown glazed stoneware, smallish, roundish body with rim & base the same diam., thick arched handle like a basket, rather large holes piercing sides & bottom, PA German, 8"H including handle x 6-1/4" diam., mid 19th C (?). Probably a cheese drainer............................ **$250+**

Colander scoop, pieced & perforated tin, missing wood handle, 6"L, 19th C. **$10**

Drainer or strainer, a sort of perforated metal half-lid that fit into cooking vessel & held back the beans while pouring off liquid, "Drain-a-Way," 20th C. . **$5**

Draining pan, or sink drainer, aluminum in triangular shape, for corner of sink, "Wearever Aluminum," 1920s-30s... **$5**

Dredger, or muffineer, tin cup with pierced convex top, mug-type handle, 2 tier base, used for flour, or sugar, for dredging or coating meat with flour to make gravy, or cutlets to bake, or dusting pastry boards before rolling, for sprinkling cookies or muffins before baking (the word dredge relates to a Latin word for confection). American (?), 7"H, mid-19th C. .... **$35+**

Dredger, for flour, tin cup with handle & snug snap-on domed lid with perforations; also called a dredge, dredge box, dredging box, or drudger. American (?) – probably impossible to tell origin unless marked, c.1880s-1900. This is true because simple linecut illustrations of many kinds of kitchen tools were used for decades, sometimes by several manufacturers who would order linecuts from an engraving house, much like we can buy clip art books today.. **$15+**

III-13. Dredgers or shakers. (1) *Sugar dredger or caster, polished brass or nickel-plated brass. Jaburg Brothers, 1908.* ***(2)*** *Unidentified, probably English, mug-handled dredger, c.1870s.* ***(3)*** *Lightweight "Mirro" aluminum salt or flour shaker in paneled "Colonial" pattern (which they also offered for coffee pots and some other wares). 2-5/8"H x 2-3/8" diam. 1927.* ***(4)*** *"Dredge box," available with or without handle. Tin, or nickeled tin, or nickeled stamped brass. Jaburg, 1908.* ***(5)*** *Flat-top (others had convex top) salt or flour shaker, "Mirro," 4"H x 3", 1927.* ***(6)*** *Stamped and polished tin, high domed top, two sizes. In very old style, at least back to 1850s, this picture from 1908 Jaburg catalog of supplies for candy-makers.* ***$5-$35+***

Dredger, japanned tin cup with mug handle & slightly flared base, domed pierced lid, American or imported, in F. A. Walker catalog of 1870s or 80s. .... **$20+**

Dredger, japanned (asphaltum) tin, small handle, domed lid, American, 4"H, late 19th C. .... **$20+**

Dredger, tin, double lid – the inside one is pierced, "Steele's Dredge Box," New Haven, CT, 3-1/4"H x 2" diam., pat'd. Dec. 27, 1870. .... **$50+**

Dredger, heavy old dark tin, footed like a goblet, domed pierced lid, big strap handle on side, American, 6"H, c.1830s-60s. .... **$35+**

Dredger, grater, pastry jagger combination tool – See IV-275-A in Chapter IV, with pastry jagger listings.

Dredger, so-called milk glass, metal screw-on lid, word "Flour" painted on side, American, 4-1/2"H x 2-1/2" diam., early 20th C. **$15**

Dredger, or flour shaker, green custard glass, "McKee," Pittsburg, 1930s. .... **$30+**

Dredger, probably for cinnamon sugar, shapely pigeon breasted glass container that looks something like a fire hydrant in profile, one flat side to fit against back of stove shelf, screw-on tin lid, American, 6"H, prob. late 19th C. .... **$35+**

Egg detector, for bad eggs, heavily tinned stamped & pieced metal, very shallow but wide mouthed funnel like contrivance with a curved sharp shell-breaker ridge from the rim down to opening of the narrow neck, which forms a sort of crook-necked double elbow "S" curve, the whole raised high on 3 tall legs, sold by, possibly mfd. by V. Clad & Sons, Philadelphia, early 20th C. • The 1914 advertising in the V. Clad catalog for this says "You," meaning mostly restauranteurs, "no doubt, in breaking eggs have many times come in contact with and broken a bad or musty egg, and in most cases have spoiled quite a

number of good ones, by letting the bad one fall among them. With this Detector the chances of losing eggs by this cause will be avoided, as it contains but one egg, therefore you can only spoil one, and not from one to six or ten dozen, as the case may be, by breaking them the old way.

"By this machine you cut your shell; you do not smash it and get your batch full of small pieces. You get all out of the egg in your vessel, as there is no chance for part of each egg to run on the outside, as in the old way. You do not make a mess on your table or bench; besides, you can break eggs much faster than in the old way, thereby saving valuable time." See Egg scales in Chapter V (Measuring). .... **$50+**

Egg separator, 2 parts, enameled cast iron, cup is blue, slotted shallow yolk catcher that sets into it is enameled white, 4" diam., "T. S. Ceeton, pat'd. Oct. 8, 1891". .... **$100+**

Egg separator, cast aluminum, heavy, very astronomy- or mathematics-tool-like, small dish with outer ring, two truncated wedge handles, one small, marked "DOTTI" on top of small handle, marked "Westmark D.R.G.M. Germany" underneath, 5-1/2" diam., mid-20th C. .... **$5+**

Egg separator, stamped aluminum, lightweight, 2 large ear handles with hanging holes, 2 slots in shallow cup, 3-3/4" diam., 6-3/8"L overall, c.1915. .... **$5+**

Egg separator, stamped, slotted tin, advertising "Nathan Fletcher's Soda," American, 20th C. ..... **$5+**

Egg separator, stamped tin, thumb handle, 3-1/4" diam., advertising message "Do You Know Kemo?" on rim,

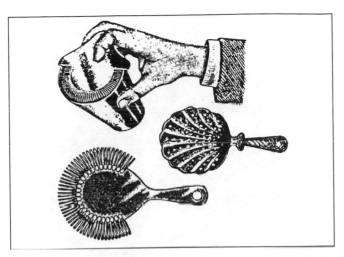

III-14. Drink strainers. (T) *Shaker strainer, nickel silver. Cherry-Bassett, 1921.* **(R)** *A Julep strainer, with shell shaped perforated bowl, with star cutout in handle. Duparquet, Huot & Moneuse, c.1904-1910. Lower* **(L)** *Coiled spring wire strainer, "fits all sizes of mixing glasses. Made of 18% nickel silver heavily silver plated." D. J. Barry, 1924.* **$5+**

early 20th or late 19th C. • Egg separators advertising dairies or egg farms, stamped of tin or aluminum, are an under-appreciated collectible........................... **$5+**

Egg separators, stamped tin, advertising "Excelsior Stove Works," another "Cinderella Stoves," early 20th C. • Added value because of stove. .... **$10+**

Egg separator, stamped tin, prettily-shaped thumb handle, "Jewel Stoves & Ranges," 3-3/8" diam., turn-of-century................................. **$10+**

Egg separator, white enamelware, single thumb grip tab handle, hanging hole, early 20th C............ **$10+**

III-15. Egg separators. (T-R) *"Degerdon's Improved Egg Separator & Saver. No loss of albumen. No waste in yolk or white." Tin, Jaburg, 1908.* **(B-R)** *"Perfect" separator. Albert Pick, 1909.* **(B-L)** *"The 1892" spun aluminum, 4-1/2" x 3-1/2", with four slots around center part. (Other companies made them with two slots ringing the center.) American Aluminum Mfg. Co., Lemont, IL, 1911.* **(T-R) $65+; (B-R) $10+ (B-L) $10+**

Fish drainer, (or some kind of combined grater-strainer?), whitesmithed (hammered, filed & highly polished) wrought iron, large slightly concave bowl in elongated trowel shape, many holes punctured rough side down, relatively short twisted iron handle, American, 15-5/8"L, late 18th C or early 19th. .... **$175+**

Fish slice, perforated tin with wooden handle, called a slice but not for slicing, it's for lifting cooked fish from a fish cooker and is perforated so juices drain out. The word "slice" relates to the elongated but broad shape (on which a typical fish would fit), American, 12-1/2"L, 19th C. .... **$65+**

❖ NOTES ❖

Flour Bolts – When searching patent indexes and records for flour sifters, don't forget that a bolt was a sifter, and some patents may be hidden to us modern folk behind old-fashioned words.

Flour sifters & bins

Flour bin & sieve, tall tin cylinder, paint enameled finish, ornamented with wheat sheaf design & name, tight fitting lid with knob on top, wire & wood crank 2/3 way down, pull out curved-front drawer near bottom, "Perfection," mfd. by Sherman, Tangenberg & Co., Chicago, IL, 25 lb capacity (also made for 50 lbs and 100 lbs), 1890s. • "Does away with barrels, sacks, pans, scoops & sieves. A few turns of the handle and you have enough for baking." Ad, March 1890. .... **$55+**

Flour bin & sifter, tall tin cylinder, painted white at some date, has tin divider halfway down, into which is set a sifter, cranked from outside front. The lower compartment has hinged door that swings out to reveal handled pan that catches sifted flour, possibly Geuder, Paeschke & Frey Co., Milwaukee, WI, 14"H x 11-1/4" diam., early 20th C. to c.1930. • **Added value.** – If this were in its original baked-on enamel finish, with stenciled decoration and word "FLOUR," it would be worth at least four times as much. It's possible that you could refinish by gently removing the mid 20th C paint, but it would be chancy... **$50**

Flour sifters, miscellaneous

Flour sifter, tin, "Hook Aston Milling Co., Flour & Feed, Mills & Elevators," Zanesville, OH, 2 cup size, early 20th C. .... **$20+**

III-16. Flour sifter. *"Tilden's Universal." Wood slant-sided box on little legs, woven iron screen sifter, leather sifter blades. 11-3/4"H x 9-1/2"L x 7-3/4"W. Pat'd. Mar. 28, 1865. Collection of Meryle Evans.* **$250-$350**

III-17. Flour or sugar sifter. *"Blood's" patent, patented as a flour sifter by A. E. and J. B. Blood, Lynn, MA. Two patents, I don't know which one this is – Sept. 17, 1861 or Jan. 9, 1866. Wood with bootjack ends, 2 wooden roller blades and wire screen bottom. Comes apart so you can clean. Body stands 8-3/4"H, with space for tray pan beneath about 9" x 10-1/2." Rocker action, pivoting at center. Collection of Meryle Evans. $250-$350*

III-20. Flour scoop & sifter. *"Earnshaw's." Tinned sheet iron, iron woven wire mesh, strap handle. 8-1/2"H. Pat'd. July 25, 1865 by J. Earnshaw, Lowell, MA. Picture courtesy of the National Museum of American History, Smithsonian Institution. $100-$150*

III-18. Flour sifter. *Tin and cast iron, woven wire mesh in bottom, 2 paddles on inside. 10"H x 7-1/2" diam. Came finished with at least two colors – green, orange. Late 19th C. Collection of Meryle Evans. $250+*

Flour sifter, tin, crank in side, "Brite Pride Visible Measure," 20th C. **$10**

Flour sifter, tin, mug style with side crank, green wooden knob on crank, "H. & Hodges," 6-1/2"H x 6" diam., with 4-1/2"L handle, late 19th or early 20th C. **$15**

Flour sifter, tin, strap handle & side crank with black wood knob, stamped into side "Special High Grade Rival Sifter, Made of Extra Heavy Grade Tin," 6"H x 5" diam., mid-20th C. **$5**

Flour sifter, tin, side crank with large green turned knob, wires form globe that turns inside concave screen, stamped on side with "Hodges" inside a large "H," 6-1/2"H x 6-1/4" diam., poss. 1940s. Very handsome, & handle special......................... **$15+**

Flour sifter, tin, wood crank knob, "Bromwell," pat. # 1,753,995; 3-cup size, 5-1/2"H, mid 20th C. **$10**

III-19. Flour scoop & sifter. *Cranked, handheld "Earnshaw's Patent." This picture from F. A. Walker catalog, 1870s. See how closely the catalog cut resembles the real thing in the next picture.*

III-21. Flour sifter bin. *Japanned and decorated tin, in assorted background colors. "Cream City" line of wares by Geuder, Paeschke & Frey, Milwaukee, 1925. $100+*

III-22. Flour sifters *of the basket type. (T) The "Handy" scoop, sifter and measure. "The Ladies are Delighted with its Convenience." Handy Mfg. Co., Chicago, 1882 ad. Lower (L) "Mystic Sifter," with crossbars and wire agitator. "Press the Sifter lightly into the flour, at the same time twist it and it will fill." 6-1/2" diam. Wire Goods Co., Worcester, MA, 1915. (R) Called the "Magic" in c.1900 catalog. Same maker. No agitator, only crossbar support.* **$30-$45+**

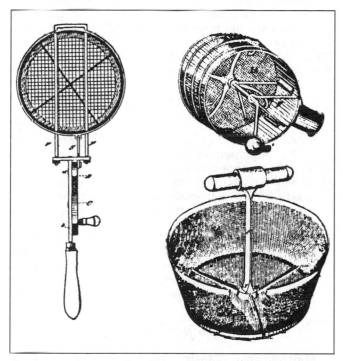

III-23. Flour sifter patents. (T-L) *Flour & meal sifter, pat'd. by C. O. Peck, Pittsfield, MA, Feb. 13, 1877. "A combined scoop and sifter, with crank, reciprocating bowl and sieve, suspended from rods" (the parallel ones going across top). Note the small crank knob partway along handle – it was turned to agitate the sieve; (T-R) Top crank with tubular side handle, pat'd. by Willoughby F. Kistler, Cleveland, OH, Dec. 9, 1884. (B-R) Basket with T-handle agitator, pat'd. by C. F. Wickwire, Cortland, NY, Jan. 30, 1877. This one was almost undoubtedly made because Wickwire was name of a wiregoods company. (T-L) & (B-R) $150-$300; (T-R) $100+*

Flour sifter, tin, green-painted wood crank knob & handle, "Bromwell," 6-1/4"H x 5-1/4" diam., c.1940s. .... **$8+**

Flour sifter, tin, braced tin strap handle, reinforced rim, side crank with wooden knob, 6"H x 6" diam., highly collectible manufacturer "Fries," c.1910. .... **$20+**

Flour sifter, tin with side crank, "New Standard," 7"H, pat'd. Oct. 15, 1918. .... **$15**

Flour sifter, tin, bracket to attach inside Hoosier style kitchen cabinet, maker not marked, American, c.1890s to early 20th C. Worth most if you have a Hoosier cabinet. .... **$40+**

Flour sifters, multiple siftings (some one-hand):

Flour sifter, double ended, 2 snug lids, funny looking sifter, white painted tin with name stenciled in blue, almost size of oatmeal carton, screen ball inside, from center of cylindrical body comes tube with wood plug through which is inserted a wire crank, "The Swan's Down Sifter" in blue on body, both lids embossed "R. E. P.," mfd. by Repath-Carver Co., Los Angeles, CA, 9-1/2"H x 4-1/2" diam., crank handle extends 4-3/4", 20th C. .... **$40+**

Flour sifter, tin, squeeze handle, scoop lip, "Triple Screen Sift-Chine" by Foley, two bands of aqua enamel around body, 5-3/4"H x 5-1/8" diam., prob. 1950s. (This is a one-hander.) **$5**

Flour sifter, tin, 3 layers of screen, "Three screens for triple sifting," squeeze action, but the best part of this sifter is the kitchen scene depicted on side: mother & daughter with doll, & son with baseball mitt. She's serving pie she's obviously just made with this squeeze sifter, utensils hang above, we see canisters, checkered floor, Venetian blinds on the window, fruit in a bowl on top of the refrigerator, all in red, yellow & white, with a little green, "Androck Handi-Sift," late 1940s patent #2,607,491. A prize '40s or '50s kitchen design. • In fact, there are many kitchy designs on Androck & other sifters of the period, which makes them great for display pieces.. **$35+**

Flour sifter, double ended tin, yellow wood handle, "KWIK," holds 5 c., 20th C............................. **$15+**

Flour sifter, tin, with green side handle, lids at each end, work it by shaking it back & forth with one hand, "Bromwell's Multiple," Saranac, MI, 7"H, 20th C. **$25**

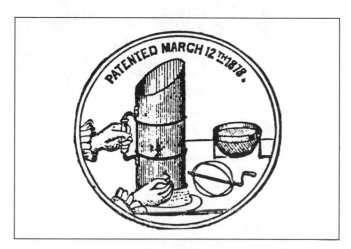

III-24. Flour sifter - fruit strainer. *"The Standard," mfd. by Washington Stamping Co., Washington, OH. Detachable bottom & agitator. Pat'd. Mar. 12, 1878. 1882 ad in The Metal Worker.* **$175+**

Flour sifter, tin, double lid (top & bottom) so you can sift twice without removing flour, simply by turning the sifter bottom side up, turned wood handle painted turquoise, "Duplex Sifter," mfd. by Uneek Utilities Co., 6-3/4"H, pat'd. 1922.................... **$15**

Flour sifters, one-hand use

Flour sifter, tin, squeeze handle type like old strength testers, "Foley," mid 20th C............................. **$10**

Flour sifter, shaker action, top rim scoop shaped, tin cylinder with flat bottom, on side is vertical turned wooden handle with wire that goes through handle & down inside to bottom of sifter to make the wire grid that rubs the flour through mesh. An 1892 ad stated, "You have heard of flour sifters that require two hands to operate! That have a round bottom which cannot be repaired! That grinds through the sieve any impurities which may be in the flour! That gives a handle which interferes with the use of the sifter as a scoop! But have you heard of the new ... sifter which is free from these objections? Shaking the sifter gently with one hand works the internal mechanism." Shaker Sifter, "Best In the World," mfd. by Sidney Shepard & Co. & C. Sidney Shepard & Co., Buffalo, NY & Chicago, IL, pat'd. July 14, 1885.............. **$35+**

Flour sifter, tin, has tubular handle enclosing a squeeze action mechanism like a strength test machine (which it may have become after a few minutes), that pulls the slotted sifter grid across the screen in bottom, 2-c. size, "The Foster," 7"H, pat'd. Dec. 1, 1914. .... **$25+**

Flour sifter, tin, lithographed advertising, wooden handle, shaking one-hand action, "Arenzville Bank ... able to do for its customers everything that a good bank ought to do." Mfd. by Erickson, Des Moines, IA, 2 c. capacity, early 20th C. **$15**

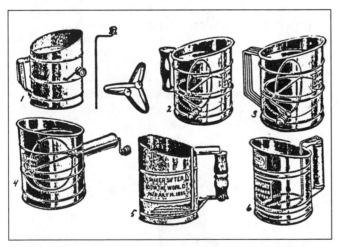

III-25. Scoop-rim flour sifters. *All showing innards. (1) "Victor," tin strap handle, shows crank and the tri-part agitator. Joseph Breck catalog, 1905. (2) and (3) are same sifters, 6-1/4"H x 5" diam., shows choice of wood and strap handle. (4) Copycat of Hunter sifter (III-27) by Savory. (5) "Shaker Sifter Best In The World," Sidney Shepard & Co., Buffalo, NY. Ripply wires on bottom move back and forth over sieve wire when you shake the sifter from side to side. 1892 ad. (6) Another shaker sifter – also called a one-hand sifter. (2), (4) and (6) all from Savory, Inc., Newark, NJ, c.1925-28 catalog.* **$10-$35**

III-26. Flour sifters with tubular handles, *and all with scoop rims. (T-L) "Reliance," with back handle, side crank. 5-1/2" x 6-1/2" x 5". Excelsior Stove & Mfg. Co., Quincy, IL, c.1916. (R) Very similar one, from Geuder, Paeschke & Frey catalog, 1925. (B) "Nesco," with crank in handle like the Hunter (see next picture). Also Excelsior Stove Co.* **$25+**

Flour sifter, tin, has shaker handle coming out of top that looks like it ought to be a crank, 2-cup style, 3"H x 3-1/2" diam., marked "Erickson Des Moines Iowa," 1920s (?)................................... **$5+**

Flour sifter, tin canister, screw clamps to shelf edge, perforated mesh bottom, spring tension dasher, 6"H, early 20th or poss. late 19th C. .... **$45+**

See also: some listings under Flour sifters, multiple siftings

Flour sifters, saucepan style

Flour sifter, tin & wire mesh in saucepan shape, tubular tin handle & wire crank, "Banner Sifter #15," Saranac, MI, early 20th C.............................. **$15+**

Flour sifter, tin saucepan style, woven mesh in bottom, rather nifty spiraling wire in bottom is cranked with knob on open top, American, 9-1/4" diam., early 20th C. A personal favorite. .... **$7+**

Flour sifters, scoop rim cylinders

Flour sifter, dark tin cylinder with scoop rim, fat tubular handle from which wooden knobbed crank sticks out, wire mesh sifting screen, "Hunter's Sifter, Standard of the World," mfd. by The Fred J. Meyers Mfg. Co., at that time in Hamilton, OH (made earlier in Covington, KY). 6-1/2"H x 4-3/4" diam. x 11-1/2"L (including handle and to tip of knobbed crank), pat'd. Aug. 5, 1879 by Jacob M. Hunter. Sold for decades. Without label: $20-$25; with paper label: .... **$55+**

❖ **NOTES** ❖

Multipurpose Classic – The Hunter is a must-have for a kitchen collection. It was advertised over 100 years ago as combining "... 12 kitchen utensils in one. It is a Mixer, Scoop, Measure, Weigher, Dredger, Rice Washer, Starch, Tomato, Wine, and Fruit Strainer. It is the most useful kitchen utensil made." A *Ladies' Home Journal* ad in Sept. 1889 reads: "Tomato-sauce, tomato soup and tomato catsup are favorite compounds. ... In no other way can they be so easily and quickly strained as with the Hunter Sifter. Owing to its construction, it can be placed in the tureen and the soup strained while boiling hot, losing little or none of its heat in the process. Bean, pea, potato, and mixed vegetable soups are strained with equal ease and rapidity." (So much for truth in advertising.) • An ad in the Jan. 1879 *American Agriculturist* said that this "Hunter's Perfection Rotary Flour & Meal Sifter" is the "only sifter in the world that can be taken in four parts to clean. 75,000 sold in 180 days. 200,000 now in use. Send 65¢ for small or $1 for large sample, or stamp for catalog." (The "small" is possibly the miniature one, though it doesn't say that.) If 1/5 of a million full-size Hunters were sold in 2 years; and they were still selling 10 years later, it's a wonder we don't all have at least 10 in our collections! After all, there are only an estimated 175,000 collectors of kitchen collectibles. • **Eggbeating too?** A Hunter belonging to Carol Bohn has the complete paper label, which reveals that the ballooned sifting blades were also intended to be removed from the sifter and used (!) as an eggbeater. Well, Carol says it works, but she is more enthusiastic than I about its efficacy! The label reads "Hunter's Rotary Flour and Meal Sifter. Hunter M'f'g Co. Always turn crank to the right. To take the sifter apart, hold agitator or wheel with left hand, turn crank to left, when unscrewed at end, pull out crank and shaft, lift agitator, take cap off end of handle and the sifter is in four parts." In my opinion, there's nothing to hold onto unless you pinch the wire shaft between forefinger and thumb and slowly turn crank while holding ballooned agitator down into bowl. You can't get up any speed at all.

• • •

Miniature Hunter Sifter – The toy/sample version came first. It is only 2-1/4"H, made exactly like the bigger one of tinned sheet iron, with a tubular handle with crank. It's stamped in relief on one side: "HUNTER'S-TOY-SIFTER (pat. May 16 71 - Apr. 7 74) BUY A BIG

ONE." It was patented eight years before the date given on the big one, and was made in Covington, KY. In the January 1889 issue of *Ladies' Home Journal* was an ad for the Hunter outlining its multiple uses. The ad went on: "...A toy sifter which shows how the large sifter works, and which will afford amusement to any little girl, will be sent free to anyone who will mention where this advertisement was seen, and enclose 2 cents for postage to the Fred J. Meyers Mfg. Co." Can you imagine that? Only 2¢! **$225+**

Flour sifter, scoop top rim, tin cylinder, wire mesh at bottom, side handle with squeeze action, "Sift-Chine" ["**Sift**-ing Ma-**chine**"], mfd. by Meets a Need Mfg. Co., Seattle, WA, c.1931. Possibly forerunner of Foley, as they also used "Sift-Chine." .... **$8-$15**

Flour sifter, scoop top rim, tin cylinder, wire mesh, wooden side handle, knobbed side crank, "Savory Sift-Chine," about 6-1/2"H x 4-3/4" diam., c.1910-20s. (See other type of scoop sifters at end of these sifter listings.) .... **$8-$12**

Flour sifter & scoop, tin, "Pillsbury's Flour," "UNIVERSAL SCOOP WITH SIFTER ATTACHMENT." 20th C. .... **$35+**

Flour sifter, grater & holder combined, metal & wood scoop shape, on remnant of paper label: "Improved Combination Sifter, F. Bucknam," Portland, ME, pat'd. May 15, 1866, #54,679. .... **$250+**

Flour sifter & scoop combined, tin, boxy shape like a square-cornered scoop, strap handle at back, with paddles inside cranked with wire crank on right side, "Earnshaw's Patent," J. Earnshaw, Lowell, MA, 8-1/2"L, pat'd. July 25, 1865. .... **$100-$150+**

Flour sifter & scoop, fine wire mesh with rim, scoop lip & strap handle all of tin. This is an oval basket elongated into pronounced scoop shape at one end,

III-27. Flour sifter classics. Scoop rims. (L) *Savory "Sift-Chine," tin body, wood handle & knob, side cranked, 1910s-20s.* **(R)** *Famous and classic "Hunter's Sifter," pat'd. by Jacob Hunter, Cincinnati, OH, Apr. 7, 1874 & Aug. 5, 1879. First mfd. by J. M. Hunter, Hunter Sifter M'f'g Co. as Cincinnati; then the No. 2 was mfd. by The Fred J. Meyers Mfg. Co. after a while. The inventor described it as a "Perfection Rotary Flour & Meal Sifter, Mixer, Measure, Scoop, Weigher, Rice Washer, Egg Beater, Tomato, Wine, Starch, and Fruit Strainer" – the "Greatest combination known," 11-in-one combination tool beloved of salesmen and manufacturers, but possibly not used as such by housewives. Inventor claimed shortly after patenting that in six months 200,000 were in use. It sold for what was at the time a high price: 75¢. Holds 3 pints, 6 cups, 1-1/2 lbs of flour. See price listings for info on the miniature. (L)* **$10-$15;** *(R) without label:* **$20-$25;** *with label:* **$55+**

III-28. Multiple sifters. *Both double-ended, for doing double sifting for lighter cakes. (Triple and even more multiple sifters were available in professional styles of sifters). (L) "Bromwell's Multiple," patent pending. Medium green wood handle. This one works by shaking back and forth in one hand. 7"H. Author's collection. (R) "Duplex," light turquoise wood handle, 5-5/8"H x 5-7/8" diam., holds 5 cups. Some marked "Duplex: Ullrich Tinware Co., Chicago," some "Uneek Utilities." Collection of Meryle Evans.* **$25-$45**

III-29. Flour sifters for extra sifting. (L) *"Triple" sifter, 4 cup capacity, 3 stacked screens, top crank.* **(R)** *"Twin-Sift," with double screen to "sift flour two times in one operation." 2 cup capacity. Both are tin, decorated with black bands & handle; ads touted "attractive yellow & black label." Trade name "Androck," mfd. by Washburn, 1936.* **$15+**

opposite which is a strap handle, "Handy," Handy Mfg. Co., Chicago, IL, about 7"L, c.1880. .... **$30+**

Flour sifter scoop shape, tin, side crank with ribbed turned wood knob, stamped "Kewpie," very small: 3-1/2"H. c.1920s? .... **$5+**

Flour sifters, tin or wood tabletop:

Flour sifter, tin body, cast iron legs, body painted green, 3 feet painted black with gold pinstriping, paper label, 3 cranked blades, screening on bottom of body, label reads "To use this sifter press down upon the crank; while putting articles in the sifter to be sifted always let the wheel rest upon the bottom." No maker's name, American, 9-3/4"H exclusive of crank, 19th C. .... **$250+**

Flour sifter, tin bucket with 3 long cast iron legs painted black, crank in open top, 3 iron paddles go around against iron screening in bottom, "The GEM Flour & Sauce Sifter," Wells' Patent, Brooklyn, NY (where J. Wells lived, not necessarily where sifter was made), bucket about 6"H x 8" diam., legs about 5"H, pat'd. Dec. 26, 1865. .... **$250+**

Flour sifter, tin pail-shaped body, brace inside & crank, 2 paddles inside, 3 cast iron legs, no mark, American, 10"H x 7-1/2" diam., 1870s or 1880s. .. **$250+**

Flour or sugar sifter, tabletop, wooden box frame with pointy bootjack legs (and sides), open top, wooden rocker crossbar handle moves the 2 connected wooden roller blades across wire screen bottom, to sift flour or sugar. 13"H x 10" square. It comes apart for cleaning, a pan to catch the sifted sugar (or flour) was slid on table underneath, paper label reads "Blood's Patent," A. E. & J. B. Blood, Lynn, MA, 8-3/4"H, with approx. 10-1/2" x 9" space underneath for a pan to catch siftings, pat'd. Sept. 17, 1861. They patented an improvement on Jan. 9, 1866. • In the 1869 catalog of the Dover Stamping Co. (which was beautifully reprinted by the Pyne Press, Princeton, NJ, 1971, in their historical catalog series), two pages are devoted to the Blood's Patent Sifter, about which it was said, "... its greatest superiority is not as a flour sifter. In preparing Squash, Apple or Pumpkin for

Pies, or other Fruits for Jams or Jellies, its value is increased a hundred fold. ... [also] stewed tomatoes, currants, grapes. ... Molasses is seldom clean enough for use, – Blood's Sifter Cleanses It Thoroughly. In the West it is used to strain Sorghum as it comes from the Mill. Those who do much with CREAM TARTAR find it invaluable. Druggists find it indispensable in sifting and straining their various Medicines. So with Glaziers, in sifting Whiting. ...." The catalog copy goes on to say that because imitators don't dare to use Blood's patent "vibrating rollers," they have "substituted various contrivances in hope to answer the purpose. Among these are Cranks, India Rubber, Bristles, Leather, Stationary Wood, &c., &c." They add that these things impart odors, wear out, get sour & filthy, and even "crumble and become incorporated with the bread or pies, constituting a violent poison."? A near perfect one was auctioned on eBay in early 2002, with the name "BLOOD'S PAT. SEPT. 17, 1861" stenciled on one side, and a complete paper label on the other side. It reads "Blood's Improved Sifter. Patented September 17, 1861. Sifts Flour, Meal, Squash, Apple, Pulverized Sugar, Whiting, Drugs, &c., with great rapidity and ease. It is the only successful sifter for general FAMILY USE ever offered to Housekeepers. It has won its way to public favor solely by its own merits. It is easily adjusted to any Pan, Box, Firkin or Barrel, or may be used upon a molding board, and is operated without putting the hands into the material. Directions.– Fit toge... central rod, and sift with a short quick stroke. Remove the central rod for cleaning. Manufactured Solely by Dover Stamping company, 88 & 90 North Street, Boston, Mass." .... **$175-$300**

Flour sifter, commercial size one for bakery or hotel, wood with brushes & screen, mfd. by J. H. Day & Co., #100, 20th C. .... **$85+**

Flour sifter, wood bin with bootjack legs at each end, screen bottom, rubber-tipped paddles, crank action, American, 10"H x 9"L, 1860s. This is very like the Tilden's. .... **$250-$350+**

III-30. Flour sifters. (L) *Cheap tin saucepan style, woven mesh, spiraled wire agitator with crank. 9-1/4"L overall, turn-of-century. Author's.* **(R)** *Tin with mesh bottom, spring tension to crank so that it presses flour through the mesh, screw clamps to shelf. 6"H, early 20th C. Collection of Meryle Evans.* **(L) $5-15; (R) $15-$35**

III-32. Gravy & soup strainers. *Enormous variety of handled strainers, some with perforated bottoms, some with wire mesh of different grades. **(1)** Gravy (L) and Soup (R) strainers, from American Home Cook Book, 1854. **(2)** Gravy, from Warne's Model Cookery & Housekeeping Book, 1868. **(3)** Copper, for gravy, high sides, flat bottom, 7 sizes from 5-1/2" to 8" diam. Henry Rogers, England, 1914. **(4)** For soup, tin, 3-1/2"H x 8", tubular handle, Geuder, Paeschke & Frey, 1925. **(5)**, **(6)** & **(7)** are "Sterling" enamelware, for gravy, "Handy," and "Soup or culinary," 4-1/4", 4" and 7-3/8" diam., Central Stamping, 1920. **(8)**, **(10)** and **(12)** are similar gravy strainers, about 4-1/2", with wood handles, from Matthai-Ingram, Central Stamping and Buhl, c.1890-1912. **(9)** "Large soup strainer," tin, perforated bottom, wire handle is 4-1/2" L. Butler Brothers, 1899. **(11)** Soup or culinary, 7-3/8", graniteware by Central Stamping. **(13)** Copper gravy strainer, conical, 5-1/2" to 8" diam. Henry-Rogers, 1914. **(14)** Deep-footed gravy, 4-1/8" or 5-1/4", looks like strainer part has own handle and lifts out. Matthai-Ingram, c.1890. **(15)** Tubular, bent handle, tinned wire, 4-3/4" to 8" diam., note hook. Sexton Stove & Mfg., c.1930s. **(16)** Soup, pieced tin, 6" and 10", Matthai-Ingram. **(17)** Gravy, tin handle, 4-1/4". Buhl. **(18)** Another deep-footed one, with perforated tin bottom – fine, medium or coarse, in 4 sizes from 4-1/4" to 7". D. J. Barry, 1924. **(19)** Soup, tin, braced tubular handle, 5" to 10", 12", & 14" diam., Duparquet, c.1904-1910. Enamelware ones in perfect condition might bring a lot more than high figure here.* **$10-$50**

III-31. Flour sifter & scoop. *"Universal" Scoop with sifter attachment, large letters say "PILLSBURY'S FLOUR," with "UNIVERSAL SCOOP WITH SIFTER ATTACHMENT" in small caps above and below. Sheet iron, wire mesh, wood, in perfect condition. Photograph courtesy of Phyllis & Jim Moffet. Was only one known at time of 4th edition, but others have been found since 1996. Still, rarity as well as the "Pillsbury" name adds value.* **$65-$100**

III-33. Soup strainer or sieve. *Note resemblance to the rocker sifter in Fig. III-17. "Kent's Patent," which "will be found most useful for procuring the transparency so much required by fashion in modern soups." Note pouring spout on corner, and the tipping handle at left. Kent manufactured many kitchen tools, including knife sharpeners, for the British market. Many were subsequently imported. This one, for example, was sold around 1905 by Duparquet, Huot & Moneuse in NYC as an "English Purée Sieve for passing soups, sauces, etc."* **$150+**

Flour sifter, wooden with metal crank, bin shape, crank in side, 11-3/4"H x 9-1/2"L x 7-3/4"W. "Tilden's Patent," pat'd. by H. Tilden, who first lived in Philadelphia, then in Boston, pat'd. Mar. 28, 1865; Tilden's 3 other patents are: May 16 & June 13, 1865 with a reissue Nov. 14; and Jan 2, 1866. Tilden – like Hunter – was another sifter inventor who also patented a toy, although his 1867 patent was a toy bow-gun. [Note: This sifter, and a few others, have a wide value range which reflects two things: location of dealer, and the relatively new interest in such things which hasn't yet found out the depth of interest, hence not its market level.]............ **$250-$350+**

Flour sifters, electric – See Chapter XVIII (Electrifying Work)

Fruit press – See Chapter I (Cut & Pare)

Funnel, copper, with filter & brass thumb piece, American, 7"L x 4" diam., late 19th C. See also: Funnels, & Pie Birds, Chapter V (Measuring). .... **$35+**

Funnel, tin, with brass screen strainer, 7"H, 19th or 20th C. .... **$10+**

Funnel, with attached strainer, which hinges & folds into bowl of funnel, the stainer being fine wire mesh in tin frame like the funnel, used with or without the strainer in place, no maker name, American, 9"L x 3-5/8" diam., pat'd. Aug. 24, 1875. .... **$25+**

Wringing Sauces through the Tammy.

Rubbing Sauces through the Tammy.

III-34. Tammy cloths. *Also called* **jelly bags** *or* **wringing cloths.** *Both pictures from* Mrs. A. B. Marshall's Cookery Book, *London, c.1900 edition. Captions are from the book – a book you should look for in antiquarian cookbook dealers for about $100. Tammy is the anglicized French word tamis, a kind of wool or wool and cotton cloth, often glazed, and used, among other things, for these strainers.*

III-35-A. Tammy cloth or jelly bag, *with turned wooden handles. Unseamed strip of heavy coarse crash cloth, probably linen or linen & cotton. Two metal rings hold it to 2 wooden "jump rope"-like handles. Put very liquid jelly, sauce or other food in cloth, hold handles and twist to squeeze out excess liquid (if making jelly), or the usable liquid (for sauces needing straining). Fully extended it's 24" L. Beautiful, warm, rusty stained color like a darling Carolina wren. 3rd quarter to late 19th C. Collection of Meryle Evans.* **$45+**

Funnel for vintner, copper, dovetail seam, brass hanging ring, fine gauze to strain out cork debris or whatever might appear in the bottle, stamped "G. E. R.," 9-3/4"L, 19th C. • The 3 initials are made with individual letter stamps, which I understand indicates it is probably an owner's initials, as a maker would have a stamp in one piece with his own 2 or 3 initials. .... **$85+**

Gravy & soup strainer, tin & wire mesh, tubular handle with ring hanger, American, 6-7/8" diam., c.1890s. These are ideal for collecting because they are found in so many variations. **$15**

Gravy & soup strainer, cobalt enamelware, elongated oval bowl, c.1900. .... **$45**

Gravy strainer or sieve, tin with brass screen, prob. American, tapers from 9-1/2" diam. down to 2-1/2", c.1900. .... **$15**

Jelly bag or wringing cloth, unseamed strip of crash (a heavy, coarse linen cloth used for towels), attached by metal rings at each end to the 2 turned wooden "jump rope" handles. Put very liquid jelly in cloth, hold handles & twist to squeeze out excess liquid. Possibly Shaker manufacture, American, 24"L fully extended, mid 19th C. • Note in the pictures the very similar one pat'd. by Frank Morton on March 12, 1867. It isn't known if he merely patented the idea of a wringer and copied a commonly-known jelly bag or not. .... **$45+**

Kettle strainer, pierced tin & wire, used to strain contents of preserve kettle when pouring from it, American, 16"L x 10"W, pat'd. 1898. .... **$15+**

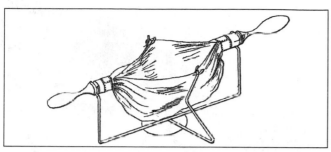

III-35-B. Strainer patent *using a* **wringing cloth** *or* **tammy cloth**. *It is actually a "sustaining frame for the purpose of conveniently pressing and straining lard, berries, cooked vegetables, &c." The inventor, Frank Morton, Kingston, MA, pat'd. this March 12, 1867. It is not known if the cloth bag and the turned handles are entirely his invention (I suspect not), but he claims them, and describes it as having "two handles made of wood or of any suitable material. To these handles is attached by means of tacks [yikes! imagine that in your jam! Like getting a staple years ago in a potato chip bag before they heat-sealed them.], or in any desirable manner, a piece of crash … to form a hammock-shaped bag." Morton described using it thusly: "The material to be pressed is placed within the bag. Now take hold of the handles, and removing the whole from the supporting frame, turn vigorously the two handles in opposite directions. This action will cause a strain to be brought upon the article under operation, and will completely dry or strain it." III-35-A is probably same.*

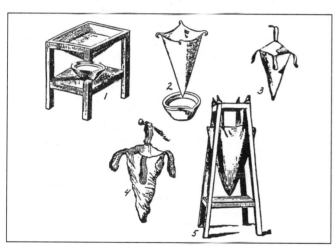

III-36. Jelly bags *plus one filtration bag. (1) and (2) are drawings from French scientist Antoine Lavoisier's book on chemistry, late 18th C. The drawings were done by his wife, Marie-Anne Paulze Lavoisier. Monsieur Lavoisier described the conical bag as made of "very close and finely woven woollen." The point of the conical bag was to concentrate the draining liquid so that it could easily be caught as it dripped. (3) A "felt" jelly bag, that's "seamless and strains jelly handsomely." Note ties to attach it to a stand like that seen bottom right. Picture of bag from* American Home Cook Book, *1854. (4) Very similar, from Warne's Model Cookery, London, 1868. (5) Jelly bag & stand, from catalog of William S. Adams & Son, London, c.1860-61. Bags are worth very little without a wooden stand with good patina. With stand:* **$45+**

Maple sugar skimmer, galvanized pierced tin cup has long wooden handle, needed because these were used to skim large pots of boiling maple sugar, American, 55"L, 19th C. Most of these were home-made and modeled after images in mid-19th C agriculture magazines; I know of only one patented one, but don't know if it went into production........ **$65+**

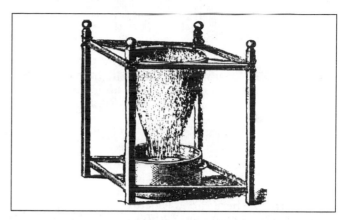

III-37. Jelly bag & stand. *More elegant, with wooden stand having turned knobs at top for easier fitting of the loops of the cloth bag. Called for to make calves foot jelly and other dishes. Urbain Dubois,* La Patisserie D'Aujourd'hui, *Paris, c.1860s-70s.* **$55**

III-38. Jelly bag strainers. *Wire with cloth. (L) Two sizes, 6" and 8" diam., with 3 or 4 legs, removable rim holds cloth. "Androck" by Washburn, 1936. (R) Two sizes – 12"H or 7"H, both 5-1/4" diam. Wire Goods Co., 1915.* **$15+**

III-39. Jelly strainer. *Pieced tin, with inner conical strainer frame for bag, and lid. Spigot at bottom. It "is made double and filled in with hot water, this heat keeps the mass limpid and a much greater amount of jelly is made from the same materials."* American Home Cook Book, *1854. The identical line cut was used in the Duparquet, Huot & Moneuse hoteliers' supply catalog, c.1904-1910.* **$50+**

III-40. Lard strainer. *Two part, tin, with cup with spout and perforated tin strainer that catches the cracklins. V. Clad & Sons, Philadelphia, c.1890-1900.* **$15+**

Meat press – See Chapter I (Cut & Pare)

Milk skimmer, stamped tin, perforations form diamond pattern, rim is crimped & turned & a sort of tab handle formed where rim is widened, American, 6-1/8"L x 5-5/8"W, 19th or early 20th C. .... **$10+**

Milk skimmer, tin, for milk or cream, stamped & pierced with perforations in a diamond pattern, hanging hole in thumb handle, Geuder, Paeschke & Frey, Milwaukee, WI, 6" x 6", 19th C. • A much older implement for the same purpose, was a **fleeting dish** or flit, a shallow dish with a ring handle.. **$10+**

Milk strainer, stamped tin, shallow perforated dish, adv'g. "Forbes Quality Coffee" in raised letters around rim, 3-1/4" diam., 4-3/8"L overall with tab, early 20th C. .... **$10+**

Milk strainer, stamped tin, small perforated shallow dish, tab handle, embossed legend "Keep Coming to Fuller's Less Expensive Store," 3-1/4" diam., 4-3/8"L overall, early 20th C. .... **$12+**

Milk strainer, tin with brass mesh, meant to fit into milk can top before pouring in contents of milking pail, American, 10-3/4" diam., late 19th or early 20th C. .... **$15+**

Molasses skimmer, homemade, aluminum sheeting formed & folded to scoop shape, then nailed to wood heel, nail puncture holes filed smooth, long wooden handle whittled to fit into hole of wooden heel of scoop-like skimmer. Dealer had 3, all from same place; one was made from an oil can, partly cut off & nailed to a wooden handle, the other was a large

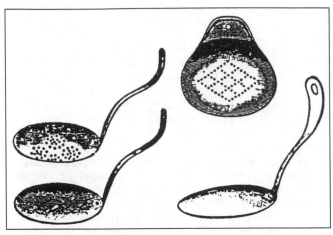

III-42. Milk skimmers. (T-R) *with extended-rim thumb handle is pierced with diapered or diamond pattern. Although surely other patterns exist, I found only this one in old catalogs of several makers. 5-3/8" x 5". Both of the other two companies here made this skimmer pattern. The two skimmers* **(L)** *with perforated and unperforated bowls, both with curvy iron handles are 4-1/2" diam. Geuder, Paeschke & Frey, 1925. Lower plain skimmer is described as having a "deep bowl," but that's relative – to other skimmers, not ladles, for instance. 4-5/8" diam. Matthai-Ingram.* **$5+**

rusted tin can. From old farm home in Campbell County, VA, near Lynchburg, 29-7/8"L, skimmer bowl 5" x 5", c.1920s or 1930s. When I bought this in about 1985, I bought it as a part of my kitchen collection, and because of Campbell connection. Now, with a houseful of folk art and found art, I'm glad I have it for those collections. It may not appeal to you, but I really appreciate having items which move along with me as I dance from collection to collection!....... **$35+**

Molasses or sorghum skimmer, perforated tin with long wooden handle, American, about 45" to 49"L, 19th or early 20th C. • These are often homemade, and those I like best. Look for interesting details or idiosyncrasies in the tin scoop part, or carving on the wood, or nifty ways of attaching skimmer to handle; also for skimmers made from old cans such as coffee cans or oil cans. .... **$35+**

III-41. Cream skimmer. *Perforated tin, turned wood handle. Nine sizes, from 6-1/2" to 10-1/2" diam., in half-inch increments. Henry Rogers, Wolverhampton, England, 1914.* **$15-$45**

III-43. Milk strainer. *Tin bowl, foot fast, with brass wirecloth bottom. 8-1/4", 9" or 10" diam., also plain one with iron wire, 10-5/8". Central Stamping Co., 1920.* **$8-$15**

"**Molasses**, or melasses, the gross fluid matter, which remains after refining sugar; and which cannot by simple boiling be reduced to a more solid consistence than that of common syrup, vulgarly called treacle." Anthony Florian Madinzer Willich, *The Domestic Encyclopedia; or A Dictionary of Facts & Useful Knowledge*. 1st American edition, Philadelphia: W. Y. Birch & A. Small, 1803-04. The sugar referred to was at the time one of several cane sugars, beet root sugar, or grape sugar. We are familiar with the term sorghum molasses, because the cereal grain *Sorghum saccharatum*, known for centuries in India, China and Africa, has been cultivated in the U.S. for about 150 years, and a sweet syrup is made from it.

Molasses faucet, tin & iron. Another molasses-related item is a suction faucet used to draw off amounts of molasses. It is geared and made of metal, and when the crank was turned it would in effect pump the gooey mess, "winter and summer, directly into a jug or bottle, without the use of a funnel. ... Free from flies and dirt." Enterprise Mfg. Co., Philadelphia, c.1885. This & next item more for grocers than housewives.................. **$35**

Molasses can, japanned tin. Half cylinder with a flat back to fit against wall, came in 10 & 20 gal. sizes. Spigot close to the bottom for measuring out smaller quantities. Matthai-Ingram made these in the late 19th C. Clean & unrusted:.............................. **$25+**

III-45. Molasses or sorghum skimmer. *Homemade, 29-7/8"L overall, with 5" x 5" aluminum bowl made from oil can. Campbell County, VA, near Lynchburg, c.1920s-30s.* **$25+**

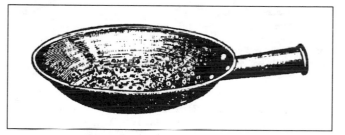

III-46. Syrup skimmer. *"For sugar planters." Perforated stamped tin, tubular socket handle meant to be fitted with long wood handle. 11-1/2" diam. Matthai-Ingram, c.1890.* **$30+**

III-44. Milk strainer buckets or pails. (L) *"The Gem Combination," mfd. by Gem Bucket Co., St. Louis, MO. Steel, with "fine brass cloth strainer which fits into a swag just below the wire in the spout, and is also held in place by the wire clasp at the back of the strainer." It has a "dairy pail bottom," which I take to mean a recessed bottom that protects the bottom from being punctured or dented or dirtied when set on barn floor. 1892 ad. Similar to many such strainer-pourer buckets.* **(R)** *"The Perfect," which "preserves milk from specks and lumps of dirt and dung, and from the atmosphere of the stable, which give the so-called animal odors. It's a seat for the milker; holds 14 quarts; cannot be stepped in nor kicked over by the cow." Dairy Supply Co., NYC. American Agriculturist, July 1879.* **$15-$40**

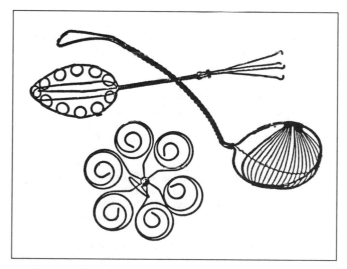

III-47. Wirewares. (T-L) *is a combination whisk or vegetable skimmer and 'grapple' for a dishcloth to clean lamp chimneys or bottles.* **(R)** *Curved across is a vegetable skimmer or server, also called a pea skimmer. Several sizes, from 4" to 5-1/2" diam. bowl.* **(B)** *is a folding 6-egg rack, for boiling & serving. All late 19th or early 20th C.* **(T-L) $45+; (R) $15-$35; (B) $65+**

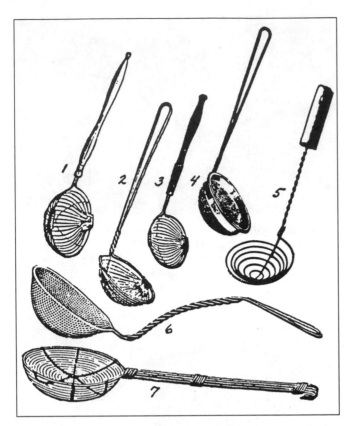

III-48. Vegetable skimmers. (1) *Wire, enameled wood handle, 4-1/2" bowl. Matthai-Ingram, c.1890.* **(2)** *This one 9-1/4"L, "Sherwood," Wire Goods Co., 1915. Other companies made nearly identical ones.* **(3)** *Red or maroon wood handle, 9-1/4"L, also Sherwood.* **(4)** *Wire handle 10" L, wire mesh bowl. Sherwood.* **(5)** *Stubby wood handle & spiraled wire, 13-3/4"L, c.1920s-30s.* **(6)** *Wire handle, two sizes – 12" or 18"L, wire mesh bowl. Sherwood.* **(7)** *With bound-wire handle. Called by some dealers a "scroll wire skimmer" for oysters, croquettes & potatoes, in five sizes, from 5" diam. x 16"L to a 14" diam. "pretzel lifter." S. Joseph, c.1927, also Sexton, c.1930s.* **$15-$35**

Muffineer – See Dredger, also Sugar shaker
Pea skimmers or vegetable lifters, fanciful wire twistings, some with wood handles, American, vary from about 13"L to 14-3/4"L, c.1870s to 1900. . **$15-$35**

I eat my peas with honey,
I have did it all my life;
Not because I like it,
But it keeps 'em on my knife!

~ A child-tickling ditty recited by my grandmother, Grace Campbell Franklin (b. c.1880), Memphis, TN, every time we had peas.

Potato ricer, or food press, zinc-coated (galvanized) cast iron frame & levered handles, heavy tin perforated cup, "Genuine Kreamer Press," 4"H x 3-3/8" diam. x 11"L including handles, c.1930s. These are often called "juicers" by sellers on eBay. See more in Chapter I (Cut & Pare). .... **$10-$15**

❖ **NOTES** ❖

Zinc coatings have a peculiar dark gray silvery look quite different from tin coating (which when new is very shiny and silvery), or from nickel plating or chroming. When corroded (by salts in a liquid or air), a powdery white deposit will occur on the surface. • See "Galvanizing" in the Index for essay in Chapter I.

Puréer, nickeled iron, no maker's name, marked "MIL. WISC." & "Pat. Appl." This could easily have gone in Chapter I.. **$20**
Salad washer, or lettuce basket, wire globe in 2 halves, hinged & with 2 twisted wire grips to hold while swinging around head (is this apocryphal?) or shaking over sink, American, 9-1/2" diam. (but they came smaller and larger), late 19th to early 20th C. .... **25+**

❖ **NOTES** ❖

Other Wire Baskets – Some wire baskets were for gathering eggs; many of those are shaped like barnyard fowl. Another type of wire basket, often mistaken for a salad washer, especially now that we have so many foreign antiques imported every year – usually poorly documented, is a snail basket for gathering snails for cooking. They are the same size or slightly larger than lettuce baskets, sometimes have a lid, a bulging body with narrowed neck. I believe that in today's antique market, a high percentage of wire wares are either contemporary reproductions from the U.S., France, Thailand, or are antique European wares.

Sieve, 2 part tin, like a ricer, perforated concave cup, the presser is convex, has tubular tin handle with a hanging loop, odd & attractive, American (?), about 7" diam., 19th C... **$45+**

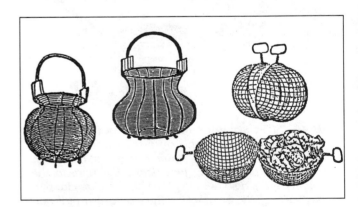

III-49. Salad washers. *Clockwise from* **(L):** *a "salad shaker" for lettuce, 8", 9", 10", 11" and 12" diam. Duparquet, Huot & Moneuse, c.1904-1910.* **(2)** *is "French Salad Washing Basket," in 7 sizes from 6" to 12". S. Joseph, c.1927.* **(3) & (4)** *Next two are a very popular long-lived ball style, in 7", 8", 9", and 10" sizes. First made by Wire Goods Co., c.1915. Advertised in a 1924 catalog, and in a 1930 magazine subscription premium ad. The ball kind is worth the least, but wire goods are very popular with collectors. See also III-61.* **$20-$100**

III-50. Sieve makers. *Unidentified early 19th C illustrations for a book of trades. Man on left is making the bentwood hoops; man at right is sewing & weaving the hair or wire. Print:* **$10.**

III-52. Sieves. *(1) Flour sieve, tinned wire mesh bottom, 11" or 12" diam. D. J. Barry, 1924. (2) Sugar sieve, brass or iron mesh, 14" diam. (3) Footed "hotel purrie sieve," brass mesh bottom, tin frame, 16" or 20" diam. D. J. Barry, 1924. (4) Stack of flour and fruit sieves, with cross wires to support the iron or brass mesh, 18" and 20" diam. (5) Stamped tin, perforated bottom, 2-3/4"H x 12-5/8" diam. Excelsior c.1916. (6) Copper sieve "for Purée" with tin frame, 12" to 16" diam. Duparquet, Huot & Moneuse, c.1904-1910, hoteliers' supply catalog. (7) Wood rim flour sieve, wire mesh, 11" or 12" diam. Butler Brothers, 1899. (8) Wood frame, iron mesh, 20", Jaburg, 1908.* **$15-$40**

III-51. Purée sieve & syrup strainer. (T) *Linecut shows how to "rub the purée through the sieve."* **To make a "Farce or Purée of Chestnuts** *– Cut off the tops of one and a half pounds of nuts and roast them for fifteen minutes, then take off the outer and inner skins and put them to cook in a pan with sufficient light stock to cover them and cook for 45 minutes with buttered paper over, when they would be quite dry. Pass them through a wire sieve, then mix with a little cream or milk, a pat of butter, a little pinch of salt and sugar, a good tablespoonful of anisette, and colour with liquid carmine to a pale salmon shade, add a dust of coralline pepper, warm and use to garnish entrées. It may also be used cold." Mrs. A. B. Marshall's Cookery Book, c.1900.* **(B)** *Sugar syrup strainer propped on wooden spoons. Urbain Dubois, La Patisserie D'Aujourd'hui, 7th ed., Paris: c.1890. (Illustration 20-30 years older.)* **$30+**

Sieve or temse, woven horsehair, all white, in 2-fingered bentwood frame, possibly Shaker, 9" diam. x 4" deep, 19th C. .... **$200+**

Sieve or temse, woven horsehair & bentwood, fastened with copper nails, pale ivory hair, probably Shaker, 6" diam., 19th C. .... **$150-$200**

Sieve or temse, woven horsehair in black & white plaid, heavily (recently?) varnished wooden frame, unfortunately the varnish even dripped on the horsehair, Shaker-style, 7" diam., 19th C, though varnish more recent. .... **$250-$350**

Sieve or temse, woven horsehair sifter, plaid black & ivory hairs, in bentwood frame with original old dark green paint, Shaker-style, 6" diam., 19th C. • Most valuable are those with the plaid effect achieved by weaving dark & light or white horse hairs. Checkered patterns valued about the same. • This one was from the collection of Greg & Linette Salisbury, sold at a James D. Julia auction, Aug. 23, 1989, for only $500. The catalog description of condition states that it "appears to be excellent throughout, even horsehair webbing is all intact and original." I have seen them with broken or missing strands (they do look as sad as old guitars or violin bows with broken sproingy strings). As has been proven over and over in 1988 and 1989, original old paint on a supposedly Shaker piece adds a so-far incalculable amount to value. Value determined by plaid and paint. A very large temse would bring high range. • One with a lapped bentwood lid for top & bottom, making a closed box, would be extremely rare, and worth probably double what a good plaid would be. One with original paint, perhaps green or the dark turkey red also called sumac (from the color of the dried seed pod in the fall) might bring half again as much......... **$800+**

III-53. Sink strainers. *Clockwise from center top (1) "Mrs. Vrooman's," blue enamel ware, wire stand, 8" x 9". It came in 2 sizes, 3 enamel colors: turquoise exterior with white inside; stone gray with mottled white inside, and plain white. It was not depicted well in catalog picture, but it has a press that pivots at bottom and pushes water out of the gooky garbage and scrapings left inside. Emeline B. Vrooman was the patentee in 1896, and she and her husband manufactured them at least through 1904, in Chicago. In 1908 it was made by Andrews Wire & Iron Works, Rockford, IL. Later by Washburn. (2-R) Next is a simple Mrs. Vrooman's with wire hangers. Best to find with the labels! Washburn Co., Worcester, MA, 1927. (3) Dark picture but really white enamel of another Washburn. Probably was also made in plain tin, because the same linecut was often used to represent various finishes. (4) White enamelware with petal-like perforations, 2-3/4"H x 9-3/4"L or 3-1/4"H x 11"L, Reed Mfg. Co., 1927. (5) Top left is a wire mesh one in style that came in various combos of galvanized wire and tin, or white or blue enameled, from 2-3/4"H x 9-1/4"L to 2-1/2"H x 10-1/2"L. Wire Goods Co., 1915.* **$10-$45**

Sieve or riddle, iron wire screening in bentwood frame, fairly crude in construction, possibly used like winnower for separating out chaff, or for mincing cooked root vegetables or potatoes, 12" diam., late 19th C. .... **$20+**

❖ RECIPE ❖

"Pureés are fashionable nowadays. A coarse and a fine sieve are needed for purée. The frame may be of wood or strong tin; the strainer of strong wires – coarse netting – being strengthened by two cross-pieces of coarse wire. Substance placed in sieve and rubbed through with wooden vegetable masher." Maria Parloa, Kitchen Companion, Boston: Estes & Lauriat, 1887. The sieve depicted in her book is quite large, perhaps 24" in diam., and is set up on wooden frame with short legs, the catching pan was slid underneath.*

Tomato Soup Patent – *"Be it known that I, James H. W. Huckins, of Boston, ... have invented a new and useful or improved composition of matters, which may be termed "**Tomato Soup**," ... to be described as follows: Take a stock-boiler that will hold about twenty gallons. Put into it fifty pounds of beef-shin to fourteen gallons of cold water. Boil it, partly uncovered, for fourteen hours. After the water has partly boiled away add a little hot water from time to time, as it may require. After it has boiled ... take it from the fire and add to it one quart of cold water. Afterward let it stand for ten minutes. Next, skim off all of the fat and strain the liquor from the meat through a fine sieve, and we shall have very nearly seven gallons of the liquor. Should there be more than seven gallons ... boil it down to the seven, but should there be a less amount, add the difference in hot water. This is called "stock." Next, take one bushel and a half of tomatoes, put them into a boiler, mash them up a little, and let them boil in their own liquor for one hour and a half. Next, strain them through a fine sieve – fine enough to stop the seeds and the skins. All the rest of the tomato must go through the sieve, after which we shall have about six gallons of the tomato liquor. If more than six gallons, boil it down ... If less than six gallons, add more tomato. Next, mix the stock and the prepared tomato together, and keep the mixture somewhat under a boiling temperature until wanted for further action. Next, prepare the following vegetables: Peel and weigh one pound and a half of onions, the same amount of turnips, one pound and three-quarters of carrots, and one pound of beets. Chop them all together quite fine. Next, take a soup-boiler that will hold sixteen gallons. Put into it three and a half pounds of butter. Next, add the chopped vegetables. Put the boiler on a hot fire, and cook the vegetables well. Next, add to them three and one-quarter pounds of flour, and thoroughly mix the whole together while hot. Next, take the boiler from the fire and let it cool a little. Next, add one ounce of black pepper, one-half a pound of fine salt, and three-quarters of a pound of brown sugar. Mix the whole well together, and add the mixture of beef-stock and tomato. The composition must now be well stirred for about ten minutes, and afterward put on the fire and stirred until it may boil. Continue to let it boil, and skim it for about five minutes, after which strain it through a fine sieve, but do not press the vegetables through the sieve. The composition will then be ready for the table, or for being hermetically sealed in cans. The amount of the preparation (which I term "tomato soup") so made will be about thirteen gallons. It is a composition containing preservative qualities, which will prevent it from decomposition for a great length of time."* Letters Patent No. 47,545, dated May 2, 1865. *That's a lot of soup!?* It touched me though, and I visualized Mr. Huckins working away with his huge boilers and his bushels of tomatoes and vegetables, and the enormous pile of bones, and the fire ... and his skeptical wife, and his daughter and son looking on, perhaps for all the 17 or 18 hours it took to make. **My** wonderful father, **Robert Dumont Franklin** (1908-2002), was, until his stroke, a wonderfully imaginative and dogged cook. He invented dried shrimp muffins; and a fried green tomato dish, and his specialty when I was growing up was succotash. I can imagine him, 150 years ago, working away to invent a new tomato soup, better than anyone had ever tasted before. And he and the family would have eaten it until it came out of their ears, all thirteen gallons of it!

III-54. Reproductions of ancient skimmers. *Bronze, in ancient designs found in Pompeian ruins in 19th C archaeological digs. These repros were made by Fonderie Artistiche Riunite, J. Chiurazzi & Fils – S. De Angelis & Fils, Naples, Italy, 1910-11. That foundry made thousands of reproductions of ancient household items, from firedogs to scales. Skimmer at (L) is about 15-3/4"L; one at (R) is about 12-1/2"L. Very easy to get fooled by such things if they're sold as genuine antiquities – or, more likely, as very "fine antiques."*

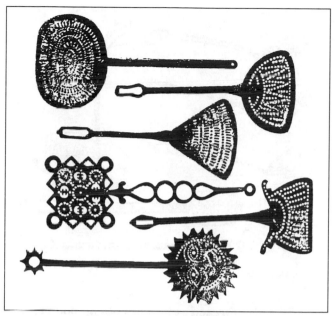

III-55. Reproduction skimmers, *in antique styles. Lengths from top: 23", 19", 19", 22", 19", and the sun face is 22"L. These were also sold as chestnut roasters. Mfd. by Pearson-Page, Birmingham, England, 1925 catalog, but possibly made for years before. This English company made reproductions of wares from the 15th, 16th, and 17th centuries. Their items are even more confusing to collectors now, especially as they are so old.*

Sieves, perforated tin, shallow with slightly sloped sides, look like gold miners' pans in movies, various perforations from coarse to fine, American, various diameters, from about 8" to 12", late 19th C. .... **$12-$20**

Sifters – See a Mixer & sifter in Chapter II; also Flour sifters this chapter. I don't just say "sifters" because a long time ago ash sifters (see picture III-1) and starch sifters were commonly known.

Sink strainer, green enamelware with attached brass plate, "Sanitary Under-the-Sink Strainer," by Kitchen Katch-All Corp., Greenwhich, OH, 1930s. .... **$45+**

Skimmer, cast aluminum, flat bowl with many small perforations in concentric rings, long tapered handle with center rib, hanging hole, marked "W3uCL," my computer can't find this in my database of metalware American companies, prob. German, 14"L x 4-3/8" diam. bowl, c.1920s. .... **$15+**

Skimmer, brass bowl, copper rivets to iron handle, American, 11"L handle, 4" diam. bowl, 19th C. .... **$50+**

Skimmer, brass bowl with iron handle, very nice looking as are most bi-metal implements, American or English, 28"L, 19th C. .... **$100+**

Skimmer, brass & forged iron, handle has heart cutout, copper rivets, American (?), 17-1/4"L, early 19th C. (?). **Watch out:** If you're paying top dollar for a bi-metal skimmer, particularly with a cutout favored by collectors and decorators, you have to be very sure you're not buying a skillful repro or a hearted-up, tarted-up, plain old piece. This goes for all bimetal implements. A well-known, reputable, knowledgeable dealer is your second best protection; your own confident knowledge is the first. .... **$300+**

Lookalike Alarm

Gold Dust Pans – Recently I saw in an 1849 business directory a sieve company advertisement for gold miner's gold dust sieving pans. I guess you might find one: look for heavy tin, and details in the edging and construction that relate to mid-19th century construction of other tinwares.

Skimmer, brass & iron with only one copper rivet holding handle on, no mark, English (?), 24-1/2"L, early 19th C. .... **$55+**

Skimmer, brass with wrought iron handle, 12-1/2"L, early or mid 19th C. Actually, brass and iron skimmers & other utensils were made well into the 1880s, probably the 1890s, so you have to judge workmanship, details, wear, style, thickness of brass, etc. .... **$125+**

Skimmer, finely worked forged iron, somewhat deep beautiful bowl with pierced pattern of holes, shaped handle with hook, signed "W. Werntz," Lancaster County, PA, bowl is 5-3/8" diam., with 13-1/2"L handle, 2nd to 3rd quarter 19th C. .... **$400+**

Skimmer, brass bowl, large, very shallow with simple large pierced design of tripartite tulip, tapered & polished forged iron handle with hook at end, the hook on same plane as handle, rather than turned under on back of handle, Pennsylvania, bowl 6-3/8" diam., with 13-7/8"L handle, early 19th C. .... **$400+**

Skimmer, pierced brass, marked on iron handle, "W. R. Boston," probably maker's initials plus place name, Boston, MA, 22"L, 19th C. .... **$150+**

Skimmer, pierced & engraved brass pan, iron handle, 22"L, 19th C. .... **$200+**

Skimmer, pierced iron with brass trim, long narrow coffin-shaped handle, spoon is quite pear shaped, handle attached to fat pear bottom end, American, 12"L, early 19th C. .... **$100+**

Skimmer, shallow brass bowl with holes pierced in concentric rings, simple forged iron handle with punched stipple decoration, Adams County, PA, 17"L, 2nd to 3rd quarter 19th C. .... **$155+**

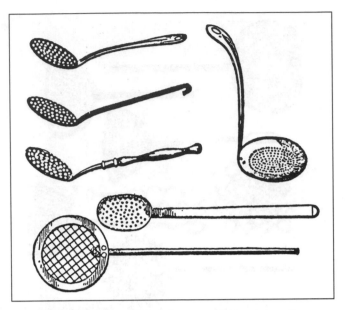

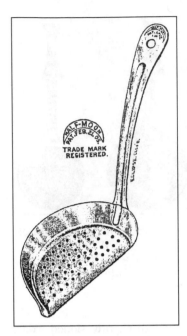

III-56-B. Skimmer.
Called the "Half-Moon Skimmer," and advertised as being for jellies, soups, milk, noodles, oysters, eggs, fish, dumplings, doughnuts, vegetables, French fried potatoes. The retail price was only 10¢, and it was mfd. by The Half-Moon Stamping Co., Cleveland, OH, and marked with a half-moon-shaped trademark. Ad from July 1905 House Furnishing Review. **$15+**

III-56-A. Perforated skimmers & egg poachers.
Three dark ones at (T-L) are all flat, with different handles. Ridged one at top is a "threaded" handle made strong with the stamped "beading"; next is a hooked "flat" handle; next is enameled wood on "long malleable shank." All in four sizes, from 4" to 5-1/8" diam. bowls. Matthai-Ingram, c.1890. (R) With curved handle is a "threaded handle egg poacher," 4-1/4" diam., Lalance & Grosjean, 1890. 2nd from bottom: One with perforated oval bowl is a "croquette spoon," and at (B), with coarsely woven wires in metal frame, is a "fried oyster skimmer." Last two from V. Clad catalog, c.1890-1900. **$10-$35**

Skimmer, shallow perforated brass bowl, riveted to forged iron handle which widens at end & finishes off with rattail hanging loop, American, 16-1/2"L with 5-1/2" diam. bowl, 19th C. .... **$155+**

Skimmer, slightly ovoid shallow brass bowl, pierced decoration of 6 point star against background of tight concentric rings of round holes, simple forged iron handle riveted to bowl, prob. PA, 23"L, 2nd to 3rd quarter 19th C. .... **$200+**

Skimmer, oak handle, imperfectly cut galvanized sheet metal disc, American, 22"L, mid to late 19th C... **$95+**

Skimmer, pieced tin, long tapered tubular tin handle, American, 15"L, 19th C. • This kind of utensil, with the well-made, tapered tubular handle, is usually advertised as "Shaker," although that may or may not turn out to be accurate. Many Shaker pieces with this kind of handle also had a fitted brace (called a boss) at the junction of handle and whatever kind of utensil it was, from dustpan to scoop. • The term pieced is not a typo for pierced. "Pieced" means composed of joined-together pieces – in this case pieces of tin. **$95**

Skimmer, tin bowl with iron handle, 18"L, late 19th C. .... **$35+**

Skimmer, tin bowl with long turned wood handle, 21"L, late 19th C. .... **$50+**

Skimmer, wrought iron, big bowl, with relatively short handle looped at end for hanging, 9-1/2"L, late 18th or early 19th C. .... **$75+**

Skimmer, yellow spatter enamelware with brown handle, American (?) or eastern European, prob. 20th C – color doesn't belong to late 19th C. **$35**

Skimmer & dipper, matched pair, brass bowls, brass shafts, delicate tapered turned wooden handles, American, 15-1/8"L, early 19th C. The pair:. **$250+**

Skimmer & dipper, matched pair, wrought iron, marked "W. Werntz," Lancaster County, PA, 19"L, 19th C. .... **$350+**

Skimmer & fork combined, metal, long handle, for stew or soup, you flipped up the skimmer to reveal the meat fork, good for poking out potatoes & meaty chunks, American, 19th C............................. **$75+**

Skimmer or butter paddle, hand-carved, figured chestnut wood, graining perfectly placed for great visual appeal, deep bowl, American, 5" across, mid 19th C. **$165**

Skimmers, blue enamelware or gray graniteware, in good condition, about 18" to 20"L, turn-of-century. .... **$30-$60+**

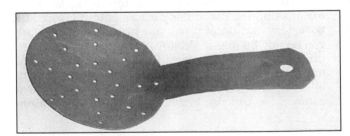

III-57. Skimmer. *Extremely simple, even crude. Sheet brass, truncated flat handle, simple 8-ray perforated pattern, marked with stamp at end of handle above hanging hole, "B. S. Porter." Although it looks like work of unskilled tinsmith, the person did have a stamp – a sign of someone in business. 13-1/2"L x 5-1/8"W. 19th C. Picture courtesy of the National Museum of American History, Smithsonian Institution. Marked name, not beauty, accounts for value.* **$100**

Skimmers & dippers, 5 pieces, all signed, brass bowls with narrow wrought iron handles tapered at hook or hanging hole ends, some pitted or split, "J. Schmidt" or "John S. Schmidt," Pennsylvania, 19" to 20"L, all are dated: 1844, 1849, 1853, 1854 & 1854. Assembled set: .... **$900-$1,200+**

❖ NOTES ❖

Skimmers for Oil Spills – What's the point of spending thousands upon thousands of hours working on a book if the author can't "file" information in it that she wants to retrieve later!?! The "Magic Mop," mfd. by Pro Diet Mop, Inc., of Belle Chasse, LA, is made of a special plastic that "attracts grease from food like a magnet." It was developed to use in ocean oil spills. Later it was made into mops used to stir hot soup and other food from which grease has to be skimmed or removed. Patent No. 3,748,682.

Soup strainer – See Gravy & soup strainers

Spout strainer, tin & wire, for teapot or coffee pot. Perfectly made deep bowl fine mesh strainer hanging from a sort of springy long hairpin that sticks into end of spout. See also Chapter XIV (Coffee & Tea). 2" diam., c.1890s. .... **$12-$15**

Strainer, also called a pea ladle, wire with crude wooden handle, bowl made up of concentric spiralling rings of wire, not criss-crossed, American, 13"L x 4-3/8"W, early 20th C? This type of strainer or skimmer with the long handle was used for serving vegetables out of pot likker. They were made from about the 1870s well into the 20th C. Some had interwoven wires done in various basketweaves, many had beautiful turned wooden handles, others had simple wire handles, which were an integral part of the strainer's outer rim. Really nice ones might bring $10 more than price of this crude one. .... **$15-$35**

Strainer, blue graniteware with white enameling inside, 2 handles, American, late 19th C. .... **$40+**

Strainer, brown marbled enamelware, 8" diam., late 19th C. **$55**

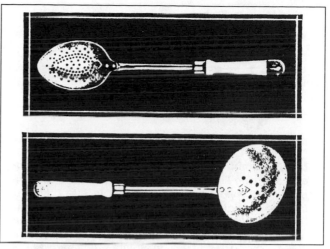

III-59. Strainer spoon & ladle. *Perforated bowls, with choice of handles. 11-1/2"L spoon has "Blutip" (cream with blue tip), green, blue or yellow handle. 11"L ladle (called that in the catalog, though we'd probably assume a ladle shouldn't have holes) in the same handle choices. Both A & J Mfg. Co., 1930.* **$5-$15**

Strainer, dark blue & white speckled graniteware, with hook on rim for hanging, American, 7-3/4" diam., late 19th C. **$65**

Strainer, extremely unusual, large perforated shallow bowl, long, "bird beak" or snipe spout off side & 40° further around circumference, turned wood handle, American (?), 13-1/4"L, 19th C. .... **$175+**

Strainer, gray graniteware, tab feet, 7 1/2" diam., 19th C. .... **$55-$65**

Strainer, pierced tin, conical bowl, tubular tin handle with ring hanging loop, could be used with pointed wooden pestle to push pulp of cooked tomatoes (for example) through, leaving seeds & skin inside strainer, American, 17"L x 8-1/2" diam., late 19th C. .... **$45+**

Strainer, pierced tin, conical bowl sets into frame that has 3 legs braced with ring near bottom, wooden pestle with long narrow conical shape, round knob

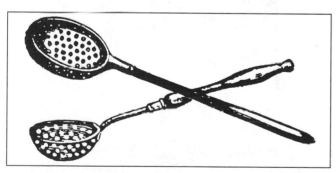

III-58. Perforated ladle & spoon. *One with apparently bigger, oval bowl is a "peculiar dipper, made of a round shallow tin pan, with a long handle, the tin being perforated to drain off the liquid." It is for putting eggs down gently into bath of pickling brine to keep for months. American Agriculturist, October 1878. Lower one is a perforated ladle with long malleable shank and delicately-turned wood handle, in 4 sizes, from 3-7/8" to 4-7/8" diam. Matthai-Ingram, c.1890.* **$15-$45**

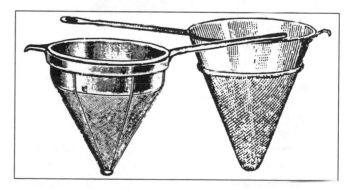

III-60. "Chinese" strainers, *in conical shape. (Another is shown in group of gravy & soup strainers.) Many companies had these, all with tin rims, iron handles, and in fine mesh. Sizes from 5" to 9" diam.* **(L)** *has wire braces, from D. J. Barry, 1924 catalog.* **(R)** *is older one from V. Clad, c.1890-1900.* **$15-$25**

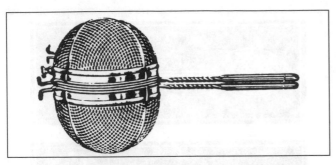

III-61. Combination salad washer & bowl strainers, *showing how two special bowl strainers with triple hooks opposite handle can be, in effect, hinged together to make a salad washer. Two sizes – 2-3/4" deep x 5-1/4" diam. or 3-1/4" deep x 6". One shown made up as washer has wire-reinforced bowl. Wire Goods Co., 1915. Most likely found singly, but a matched pair:* **$15+**

handle painted green, marked on handle "Super Sieve Pat. Febr. 14, 1928, other pat. pend. Tyler Mfg. Co. Muncie Indiana." 8-3/4" x 6" diam. at top, pestle 10"L. With pestle:.. **$45+**

Strainer, pierced tin, handmade, 11" diam., 19th or early 20th C. Country, handyman pieces such as this are extremely difficult to date. Only when something like a dateable coffee can, with the lithographed label left on, has been used for the sheet metal, can a confident dating be given. ... **$20-$40+**

Strainer, probably used in dairy, white glazed Delftware, figural bird of type seen in PA German folk decoration, Holland, 6"L, early 19th C. Figurals are extremely rare. Other forms include fish & hearts. .... **$1,200+**

Strainer, tin with wooden handle, "Wheat -?- for Breakfast," American, 13"L with handle, 20th C. .... **$20+**

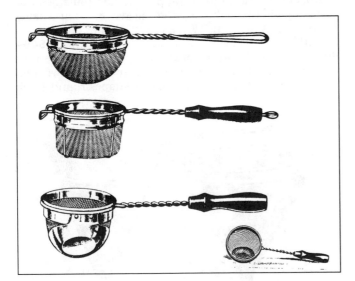

III-62. Strainers. *Three types by Wire Goods Co., Worcester, MA.* **(T)** *Round bottom, rigid rest, 1-3/4", 2-1/8", 2-1/2", 3-1/8", and 3-7/8" diam., fine mesh.* **(M)** *Flat bottom, rigid and reinforced, 2-1/2", 3-1/8" or 3-7/8" diam.* **(B)** *"Quality Dripless Strainer," Fine mesh fitted with a nickel-plated brass "drip cup," maroon wood handle. Only 1-3/4" diam., about 5" L overall.* **$5-$10; $5-$10; $15-$25**

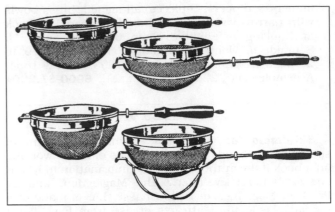

III-63. "Demountable Bowl Strainers," *with handles & wire frames, shown here with plain & reinforced bowls, maroon wood handles. 5-1/4" diam. for all bowls, which you could also buy separately. Wire Goods Co., Worcester, MA, 1915.* **$15**

Strainer, tin with wooden handle, "Ajax," made in at least two sizes, 5"L and 8"L, early 20th C. **$10**

Strainer, turquoise green & white swirl enamelware, poss. "Chrysolite," late 19th or early 20th C. .. **$75+**

Strainer or skimmer, called a pea skimmer at the time, spiralled wire with wooden handle, sold by, but not necessarily made by Dover Stamping Co., c.1870s. See also: Pea skimmer. .... **$15-$35**

Sugar shaker or caster, copper container with pierced brass screw-on lid, interesting slanted sides almost

III-64. Bowl strainers. (T) *Wire frame fits over "pan rim." In 4 sizes, from 3-7/8" to 6" diam. Wire Goods Co., 1915.* **(M)** *7" and 8", in simple 4-legged wire frame. Washburn, 1936.* **(B)** *Extension strainer with sliding wire frame, in 5", 6" or 8" diam. Also Washburn.* **$15+**

look Arts & Crafts Movement, American (?), 9"H, 19th C. See also: Dredgers. **$55**

Sugar shaker, decorated figural ceramic, "Cleminson's Girl," The California Cleminsons, CA, mid 20th C. **$40**

Sugar shaker, or muffineer, tin cup with slightly domed perforated lid, strap handle on side, marked "Fries" on bottom, 4"H x 2-1/2" diam., late 19th C or early 20th. .... **$25+**

Sugar sifter – See: Dredger, also Flour sifter

Tea strainer – See Chapter XIV (Coffee & Tea)

Vegetable strainer, called a cabbage strainer by manufacturer, a sort of combination colander & press: a handled pan with perforated bottom, and a pressure plate with lever handle which is pressed against watery vegetables to press out pot likker, then pivoted to other side whle dumping food into serving dish, heavily tinned, "New Process," Silver & Co., Brooklyn, NY, c.1890. .... **$45+**

Whatzit sifter, some sort of sifter, possibly an ash sifter, cast metal with odd finish, almost as if it were a baked-on brownish gray paint, 3 short peg feet with cork tips, looks like an old style something or other made of modern materials, like a dustpan pan with 3 walls, scoop-like handle, 15"L, 20th C. .... **$25+**

III-65. Vegetable or cabbage strainer. *"New Process," mfd. by Silver & Co., Brooklyn, NY. This is rather like a ricer for cooked potatoes, which was supposed to be in this chapter but isn't. When the press was inverted, and the press part folded back over, the food fell out onto serving dish in a sort of vegetable cake layer or huge steaming hockey puck.* **$45+**

PREPARING

IV. FORM, MOLD, SHAPE, & DECORATE

Not only am I late in coming to an appreciation of molds, so were molds late in coming to kitchens. I can't think of a single mold that is necessary, in the way a knife, pot, fireplace or stirring stick are. They are for pretty – *fer schay*: they gussy up food. This chapter is so daunting to me I've saved it for last, and don't think I haven't thought of just giving you an epic poem on fungus!

The Renaissance had decorated foods, although I don't believe the fancy copper molds typical of the late 18th and early 19th centuries were yet in existence. By 1800 or so, households of French, Italian, English, German, Russian (and undoubtably Austrio-Hungarian and Swedish) nobility could count hundreds of copper molds (or "shapes" as the English called them) in their *batteries de cuisine*. When there was a surplus of money, food and servants, and hours spent at the banquet table were considered hours well-spent, no decoration was considered excessive, no frou-frou frivolous. So what if guests only nibbled? The servants or the pigs could eat the leftovers. Confined to noble households until the early 19th century, thereafter highly decorated food became fashionable among wealthy merchant and professional classes.

By the 1870s, molds were considered necessary in every middle class kitchen. Chromolithography's advent in the early 1880s meant that cookbooks could have sumptuous, scrumptious full-page pictures, showing what food in the recipes should look like, including towering molded, decorated main courses and side dishes. While we might find it intimidating to face a foot-high molded aspic, quivering on its crystal stand, pictures would lead you to believe that the Victorians loved it. It's my feeling that labor-intensive manipulated food was inevitable ... philosophically related to a fervent Christian belief in the beauty of an ordered universe, within which humans were only doing God's leftover work by forcing everything (animals, furniture, children, clothing, buildings, landscapes ... and food) to take on shapes, appearances and functions that were unnatural, however inspired.

Well anyway, I didn't use to notice molds because at antique shows they were in with the finer things that I never looked at (furniture, crystal, porcelain), and besides, the more active mechanical things were what attracted me. It's as if molds, including copper molds, ice cream molds, chocolate molds, etc., had to wait until my attention wandered! If you are a generalist collector, like me, you will probably have experienced this kind of delayed reaction too in one area of kitchen collecting or another. (The unanswerable, but nagging question that's raised is, of course, "How many _?_ did I miss?!")

Others have been collecting all kinds of molds for 100 years. Perhaps the major appeal of molds for collectors is that **motifs and figures** are so common amongst them. There are probably hundreds of thousands of people who collect by motif – squirrels, elephants, cats, frogs, etc. I have tried throughout this book to give background information on motifs, especially information that assists further research. Many paragraphs have a bold motif heading – from stars, birds, palm trees to Kewpies.

Alternatively, the mold category may have such lasting intrigue and appeal because some of the tools used to shape food are also clever mechanical inventions that make you admire the inventors. **Ice cream dishers** are a good example. Some tools are next to useless without the inventiveness and artistry of the cook (such as jaggers for cutting out pastry shapes to decorate pies), but molds give a boost to mundane food without much effort or imagination by the cook – kind of in the way some people wear (or are worn by?) designer clothes.

It would be hard to say what is the most popular subsection in this chapter. Fancy **jelly molds of copper** have been seriously accumulated, if not "collected" as they are today, for at least 75 years, partly because of their house-decoration potential. (All that family of molds is listed under Molds.) **Cookie cutters** have been collected for at least 70 years. You could say 100 or more years, because the women who used them to make fancy holiday cookies also collected them, often on a length of twine hung up on a nail in the pantry. Cutters have recently gained widely publicized attention because of the interest folk art collectors now have in them. Of all specialties, probably only cookie cutters have more women collectors than men, but that is changing. Cookie cutters are also probably the most democratic of all kitchen fields: collectors eagerly seek old and new, and mass-produced "collectible" cutters in sets.

Butter molds and stamps got a real boost from a book a few years ago by Paul Kindig, who took the subject to a very serious level. A new book by the Van Vurens has much on manufactured butter molds. Carved wooden **cake boards** and springerle molds have gotten serious attention from high-end folk art collectors. Figural **chocolate and ice cream molds** are widely collected; here in the U.S., this is one of the few kitchen fields where a majority of pieces are European, and are known to have been imports from the start. **Ice cream dishers or scoops** have a dedicated following; astounding prices are paid for rarities, but these aren't one-of-a-kind rarities like handmade cookie cutters, because dishers or scoops have been mass-produced since the turn of the century. Their hey-day was in the 1920s and

'30s when ice cream parlors were really popular. **Waffle irons** are yet another upcoming field, mainly because of strong interest in all cast iron goods – cookwares as well as decorative pieces such as hitching posts, doorstops, garden decorations, and architectural elements.

Cast iron **muffin pans** and **cake molds** have become part of an established market with strong resale potential and probably even daily price fluctuations, as more and more collectors actively deal amongst themselves. This trend – throughout all fields of collecting – will increase as more collectors and dealers go on-line and create international Web sites. This doesn't mean that a seller can put up for sale any old cast iron piece and put a high price on it, and have any buyers. Overall, there is less and less dealing in the public marketplace; serious collectors, whether "advanced" or novice, tend to buy privately. They always hope that they will stumble over some hitherto unknown variation or rarity, online or at a country auction. As experienced iron collector Joel Schiff remarked, "Iron prices were low and slow for at least 15 years, but have never gone down. Now with the rise in value, the stock of available pieces is 'drying up,' and what might be termed the 'Griswold Feeding Frenzy' has spread to the wares of other companies (Wagner, Sidney, Filley, Wapak, etc.). Prices are rising precipitously."

How were they used? Read old patents to find out. Objects in this chapter are not always easily explicable. Even if you know their purpose, you may not know the way the riffs are played, the flourishes are performed. A great bonus to reading old patents is that there often is a paragraph about previous practices or methods. For example, to understand about holes pricked in the upper crust of a pie, we need only read a paragraph in Jay W. Butler's patent for a pie trimmer and crimper. "It has been the practice heretofore to mark the upper crust of a pie with a sharp tool cutting through the crust to permit the escape of the steam from within; while serving at the same time to initial the pie; but invariably, while baking, the crust bulged outward where cut, by the steam pressure within, resulting in total elimination of the identifying letter previously formed." Patent #907,456, Dec. 22, 1908, Jay Butler, Hermitage, NY.

Patented tools. The newest surge of interest in items in this chapter may come with the realization that so many, many of them were patented, and have mechanical parts. Several hundred biscuit and cake cutters, rolling pins and combined culinary devices, were patented between the 1850s and the 1950s, and make an exciting pursuit for collectors.

Pennsylvania German/Dutch
Background Information

References to Pennsylvania German motifs, origins, recipes, and molds are clarified in the following paragraphs; incidental information appears with the appropriate listing.

"Pennsylvania German" or **"Pennsylvania Dutch."** – Ruth Hutchison writes an interesting explanation of the "Pennsylvania Dutch" [from *Deutsch* or German] which I have not read before. "The first of the Plain Sects to sail for Philadelphia in 1683 [from the Low Countries] were the Mennonites ... followed by the Amish, Seventh-Day Baptists, Dunkards, Schwenkfelders, and Moravians. Later came the Lutherans and Reformed, so that by the time of the Revolutionary War there were so many Germanic people in Pennsylvania it was feared they outnumbered the English. Strictly speaking, there was no Germany in that day, but emigrants from the Low Countries were loosely called Germans, most of them spoke Low German, and the first of their American settlements was called Germantown." p. xi, *The New Pennsylvania Dutch Cook Book*, 1958.

Is it more accurate to use the term Pennsylvania Dutch, or to assume that that is a corruption of Pennsylvania Deutsch, therefore that it should be Pennsylvania German? Get Carl W. Drepperd's *A Dictionary of American Antiques*, and look up "Pennsylvania Dutch." In part, Drepperd says "More misinformation, erroneous claims, and wrong beliefs are current [book was published in 1952 after 10 years' compilation] in respect to the meaning of this term than any other phrase pertaining to American social history and objects that survive. What is now Pennsylvania was colonized by the Swedes and the Dutch half a century before William Penn [c.1680]. ... With Swedes, Dutch, and some Finns in residence on his arrival, Penn offered haven ... to French Huguenots, Swiss Mennonites, Amish from Flanders, Rhinish Palantinates,

Swabians, Danes, Dutch, Walloons, Swedes, and Flemings [who] arrived in the colony from 1630s to 1760s."

Drepperd says that "Pennsylvania Dutch" is more accurate and accuses numerous societies of fostering the falsehood that Pennsylvania folk arts and crafts are purely Germanic. But a *Farmers' Cabinet* of 1836 relates that 54 ships' loads of German emigrants arrived in Philadelphia in just one summer, and tells of a 1750 law prohibiting "importing too many Germans in one vessel," ostensibly to limit overall emigration. In 1677, Penn offered refuge to Quakers from the Netherlands and Germany in what was then western New Jersey, already settled by Swedes and Dutch for decades. Before he had ever seen "Pennsylvania," he invited Quakers from England and Wales to emigrate too.

The 11th edition of the *Encyclopaedia Britannica*, states that "In no other colony were so many different races and religions represented. ... Dutch, Swedes, English, Germans, Welsh, Irish and Scotch-Irish; Quakers, Presbyterians, Episcopalians, Catholics, Reformed Lutherans, Mennonites, Dunkers, Schwenkfelders, and Moravians ... most now merged in the general type." The *Encyclopaedia* says that [the language] "Pennsylvania Dutch" is a "corrupt German dialect, largely Rheno-Franconian in origin."

And More. – In *The Magazine ANTIQUES*, March 1944, a cover story explained in a note from Gregor Norman-Wilcox that in Pennsylvania of the 18th century "German" meant a "composite racial group whose homelands included Germany. ... Especially, our Pennsylvania-German colonists came from the west-German (Bavarian) Palatinate, lying along the Rhine and neighbor to the Dutch on the north." Norman-Wilcox's use in the article of the term "Pennsylvania-dutch" with a small d shows that it means just *deutsch*, not really Dutch nor yet really German.

Early Pennsylvania German Motifs. – Frances Lichten, writing in *Folk Art Motifs of Pennsylvania*, NY: Hastings House, 1954, wrote that the early motifs, not just for cookie cutters but for all the decorated arts, included: tulips or lilies, hearts, several birds (finches – the name we often see is *distelfink*, or thistle finch), song birds, doves, cocks, parrots, peacocks, and eagles, stars, geometric shapes, stags, unicorns, urns, mermaids, cherubs, and angels. She explains that the Pennsylvania Dutch only began to make decorated utilitarian wares after several generations spent establishing their farms. "A rough guess, judging by the objects which bear dates, would place this revival of the more decorative aspects of folk life somewhere around 1765." At first, traditional motifs were taken from remembered and remaining objects and furniture brought to America from Germany, Switzerland, Moravia, and other countries. Lichten explains that "In the first decades of the 19th century [the Pennsylvania German craftsman's] work began to show traces of the period decoration fashionable during the previous quarter century. Although quite out of keeping with the boldness of his traditional motifs, he adopted these ideas, [and] used them as he saw fit. ..." These adopted motifs included "certain **ornamental details** high in favor during the Empire period ... great looped draperies [used] as a frame ... rococo scrolls ..." and later "the symbols of the Romantic period – the classic column, bow-knot, rose, forget-me-not, and wreath." **Fraternal orders**, such as the Odd Fellows and Freemasons, used the column motif, so lodge decorations may have influenced, over a long period of limited exposure, non-member artisans among the Pennsylvania Germans. See a lot more on this at "Fraternal Orders: Their Symbols and Motifs" under a butter stamp listing. • **Parrots** are often depicted by the Pennsylvania Germans. The Carolina parakeet, grass green with a bright red head, was once native to Pennsylvania. Unlike some other birds, the parrot was probably not symbolic. • **Symbolic Birds.** – Cock or rooster = a Christian symbol of vigilance, and an emblem of Christ's Passion; Swan = Virgin Mary; Peacock = immortality and resurrection; Dove = innocence, conjugal affection or the Holy Ghost. The symbolisms were not necessarily known to or referred to by PA German artisans, but were copied from much older European traditional work. • **Other early motifs** include flowers, pomegranates, fish, humans, horsemen, crowns and heraldic animals. All these motifs are found in American 18th C. decorative arts, *fraktur*, *taufschien* (cut paper documents), etc., and for centuries before that in Europe and Great Britain.

❖ NOTES ❖

Buying on eBay is good for many of the items in this chapter; Cookie cutters, especially for common pieces from the 1930s to 1980s, and the occasional oddity. Cast iron and cast aluminum baking molds are another thing you can buy on eBay. As I've advised elsewhere, I suggest printing out completed auction lists from categories you are interested in. Make notes on the pages.

• • •

Mold pattern numbers were necessary when making a cast iron or aluminum mold in multiples. Patternmakers carved wooden mold patterns, complete with part numbers either carved into or incised in the wood (intaglio) or in relief on the wood's surface, so that when the mold is made of damp sand, for example, and the molten metal is poured in, the resulting food mold will have a mold pattern number and manufacturer's name, etc., either in relief, or intaglio – the opposite of what's on the carved wooden pattern. **PNs** – pattern numbers – are widely used by collectors of cast iron food molds, pans, etc.

• • •

Order of Listings. There is still some chaos in this edition. So many molds have multiple uses, or could be called a "bake pan" or a "cake mold" or something else. For a particular mold, say a *trois freres*, please consult the index at the end of the book.

Ableskiver, or Aebelskiver pan – See Ebelskiver pan
Angelfood cake pans – See Molds, in enamelware & tin sections – the spouted or tubed listings
Bake molds – also called baking molds, baking pans, bake pans, or baking tins, as well as cake molds or cake pans, muffin pans & roll pans. See Molds, Muffin pans, & Roll pans

Barley sugar mold, clipper ship design, pewter, 4-1/2" x 5", 19th or early 20th C. .... **$75+**
Bird's nest fryer, tin & wire mesh, 2 nesting bowls, with long wire handles, used by immersing in boiling fat after making a bird's nest of either cooked noodles, julienned or riced potatoes, Androck, from this maker, there was a choice of 2 diam's, 3-1/4" or 4", 1930s. • Added value. With its original cookbooklet, add about $5. .... **$20+**
Biscuit cutter, gray graniteware with strap handle, 2-1/2" diam., 19th C. .... **$65+**

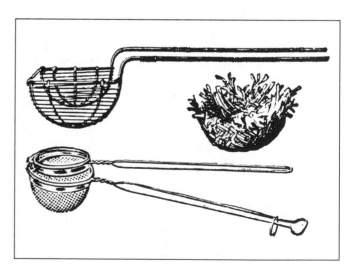

IV-1. Bird's nest fryers. For molding cooked noodles or shredded raw potatoes into shape of bird's nest, & then deep frying them. Tinned iron wire, 2 nesting baskets with long handles. **(T)** Four sizes, 3-1/2" to 6-1/2" diam. S. Joseph Co., suppliers in NY, c.1927 catalog. **(B)** Two sizes – outer bowl 3-1/4" or 4" diam. Washburn Co., Androck line, 1936 catalog. **$20+**

Biscuit cutter, tin, long fat tubular handle, closed on top & stamped: "Rumford Yeast Powder," 4"H x 2" diam., (others measure 4-1/2"H), c.1890s-1910. A very similar one was offered by Horsford's Baking Powder. It had a removable small cylinder inside for cutting "crullers" (doughnuts). .... **$40+**

Biscuit cutter, tin & wire, "Cottolene" (a cottonseed oil shortening), Chicago, IL, early 20th C. .... **$15+**

Biscuit cutter, tin with scalloped or fluted edge, strap handle. Older ones are composed of 3 separate pieces: cutter body, its soldered-on corrugated cutting edge, & a strap handle. Newer ones have stamped one piece body & soldered-on strap handle, various makers of these in 19th C, including most big tin houses, but most aren't marked, American, between 2" & 3" diam., came in various sizes, c.1870s to 1910s. .... **$15+**

Biscuit cutter, turned wood, knob handle, very thin cutting edge, traces of original white paint, American (?), 2-1/2" diam. x 5-1/2"L, could cut 3" thick dough, 4th quarter 19th C. .... **$60+**

Biscuit cutter, tin with wire finger loop, stamped with advertising message, "White Lily Flour Has No Equal," Metal Specialty Mfg. Co., (the flour from

IV-3. Biscuit cutter & roll cutter. (L) *Tin, rolls out 4 biscuits with each full revolution of wheel, wire handle, 8-3/4"L, early 20th C. Author's collection.* **(R)** *Tin roll cutter with wooden handles, to cut rolled dough into long rolls. Makes 14 rolls each revolution. Roller is 11"L overall & makes rolls 5"L. From Mennonite boarding house, Olley Valley, PA, 19th C. Collection of Meryle Evans.* **(L) $65; (R) $45**

Conrad Becker Milling Co.), Chicago, (mill in Red Bud, IL), 2-3/4" diam., early 20th C. .... **$12+**

Biscuit cutters, nested set of 3, stamped aluminum, they snap together thanks to the 2 nifty little half-round tabs punched up (the inventors called them "upstruck wings") on top of each one as handle, "Calumet Pastry Cutter," mfd. by Wearever, New OKensington, PA, 1-1/2", 2-1/4" & 3-1/4" diam., Mar. 24, 1931 patent by Leon Gage, & Joseph Weinzierl of New Kensington, PA, and Irving Wood, of Parnassus, PA, #1,797,859. Watch out for snapped-off tabs. .... **$15+**

Biscuit cutters, nested set of 9, crinkle edged cutters, in tin box stenciled in blue, "Veritas. Made in Italy for G. M. Thurnauer Co., Inc.," a big wholesale house, in NYC, that sold mostly imported European kitchenwares, from 1" to 3" diam., c.1890s-1910. These are often sold as "toy" cutters, & as such are priced high. New sets in round tin boxes are still sold in kitchen supply houses. .... **$35+**

IV-2. Biscuit cutters. *All stamped or pieced tin except 2nd row left, which is "Mirro" aluminum. All are between 1-1/2" & 3" diam. (L) to (R), row by row from top, #1 to #10.* **(1 & 2),** *1-1/2" to 2-3/4" diam., S. Joseph, c.1927.* **(3)** *Savory Tinware, Newark, NJ, c.1926-28.* **(4)** *Aluminum Goods Mfg. Co., Manitowoc, WI, 1927.* **(5)** *Geuder, Paeschke & Frey, Milwaukee, WI, 1925.* **(6)** *Sexton Stove & Mfg. Co., Baltimore, c.1930s.* **(7)** & **(9)** *Fluted edges & plain circle, Matthai-Ingram, Baltimore, c.1890 catalog, pat'd. Oct. 15, 1889.* **(8)** *Pick-Barth jobbers' catalog, 1929.* **(10)** *Deep, commercial one, 2" or 2-1/2" diam. Pick-Barth.* **$8+**

IV-4. Biscuit cutters. *From top:* **(1)** *Scalloped pieced tin, heavy duty strap handle, 2" diam., late 19th or early 20th C.* **(2)** *Rolling aluminum & wire one, advertises "Louella - the Finest Butter in America" & "Gold Seal Flour – For Best Results." Words embossed. 6-1/2"L x 2-7/8"W, c.1915.* **(3)** *Embossed stamped tin, wire handle. "White Lily Flour Has No Equal." 2-1/4" diam., mfd.. by Metal Specialty Mfg. Co., Chicago, c.1910.* **(1) $8+** **(2) $25 (3) $12+**

Biscuit or cookie cutter, round, wrought iron, simple circle with very high arched handle. American, 2-3/8"H x 2-5/8" diam., early 19th C. • This handsome wrought iron piece is in the Kyle Goad Collection, Virginia. Price range estimates probable current market value (colored by what I'd pay myself – it's that gorgeous!) .... **$100+**

Biscuit or cake [cookie] cutter, pieced tin, outer cylinder has inner cylinder with screw-on cap, spring wire coiled loosely around that, pusher plate on bottom, high arched strap handle. The pusher plate retreats up inside depending on the thickness of dough, but spring serves to push dough out. Cap screws off to fill inner cylinder with flour so that it continually dusts cutter as you sproing your way through a sheet of rolled dough. (Nice home for insects if you didn't clean it often.) Marked "D. S. Co.," Dover Stamping Co., Boston, MA, 2-7/8" diam. & almost that deep, pat'd. by George Sanderson, Boston, #78,137, May 19, 1868. The patent was originally assigned to Sanderson & to Frederick M. Baker, South Reading, MA. .... **$75+**

Biscuit or cookie cutter, stamped, pieced tin, round deep cutter with great 3-D egg-shaped knob handle as long as cutter's diam., 3 air holes, embossed "Egg Baking Powder" on the egg, Chicago, IL, 2-3/4"H overall x 1-15/16" diam., cutter itself 1-1/4" deep, (some 2"H x 2" x 1" deep), I believe c.1902-1905, but couldn't find a pertinent patent .... **$100+**

Biscuit cutters, multiple rotary type:

Biscuit or cookie cutter, rolling kind that cuts multiples, stamped aluminum with twisted wire handle, adv'g "Louella – The Finest Butter in America" as well as "Gold Seal Flour – For Best Results," American, 6-1/2"L x 2-7/8"W, c.1920s or '30s. .... **$25+**

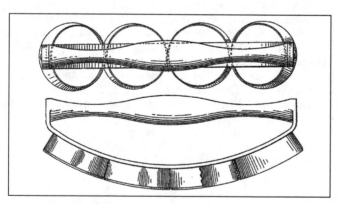

IV-5. Biscuit-cutter patent for rocker-style cutter. Held like certain food choppers, it cut 4 biscuits with one rocking movement. Pat'd. Nov. 5, 1889, by Henry T. Sidway, Chicago, IL. Actually manufactured of tin & wood, approx. 9"L, & stamped with date on curved bar to which cutters were soldered. Sidway wrote a tantalizing spec that makes you wonder if other styles were made, viz. "In the present case I have shown only a single bar with a single series of four round cutters attached; but I may employ a number of bars, each carrying a series of any number of cutters where it is desirable to cut large quantities of biscuit, and I do not confine my invention to round cutters, but include cutters of all shapes used by bakers for producing fancy cakes and biscuits." **$150**

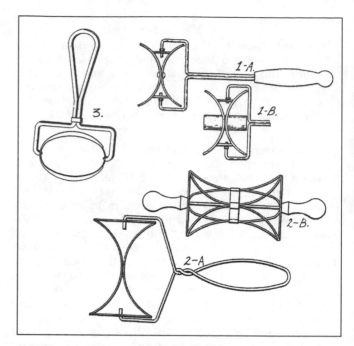

IV-6. Biscuit cutter patents for rolling multiples. **(1-A)** & **(1-B)** are 2 views of a "Cooky and Doughnut cutter" pat'd. by Theodore V. Brummett, Portland, OR, Oct. 21, 1930, #1,778,969. The first shows a cooky or biscuit cutter, with a wire shank and a turned wooden handle, typical of A & J. The 2nd image shows doughnut version with removable "cylindrical center section" in place for cutting holes. **(2-A)** & **(2-B)** are 2 styles of a "cake or biscuit cutter" pat'd. by Thomas Benton Stone, Camptown, PA, July 18, 1893, #501,903. Stone assigned 2/3 to Clarence C. Smith & Prescott A. Smith of Camptown. **(2-A)** shows a "revoluble cake cutter constructed of two rings" & a twisted wire handle. Stone's aim was to "construct a dough cutter of novel form ... which will cut the dough cleanly and clear through the sheet without ... the parts clogging up by the dough adhering thereto." **(2-B)** Stone shows a different style, a cutter formed of "three rings of wire which ... I recurve or bend ... on opposite side" which he shows with turned wood handle grips so that "cutter can rotate freely when the implement is forced by the operator over the sheet of dough in a manner similar to the well known rolling pin." The cutter part spins freely on handle shaft. **(3)** is a "cake or biscuit cutter," pat'd. by Benjamin S. Williams, Nashville, TN, July 4, 1922, #1,421,749. Cheapness & ease of use were goals, hence stamped metal (was aluminum in mfd. cutter) & wire.

Biscuit cutter, multiple rolling or rotary type, tin with wire handle, "Chicago Rotary Cutters," pat'd. May 31, 1892, by Henry T. Sidway, Chicago, #475,815. Patent drawing shows turned wood handle, and several other patentees got patents for wire-handled rolling biscuit cutters. Sidway got a patent in 1889 for a rocking biscuit cutter that did 4 at a time. Note that in British usage, "biscuit" is what we in the US call a "cookie," and what we used to call a "cake." See also the listings under Cookie cutter, multiple rolling type. .... **$65+**

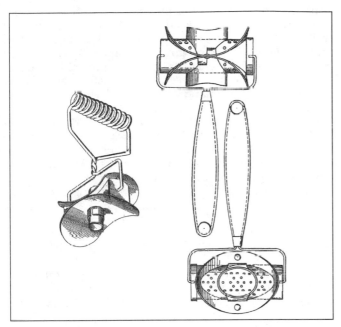

IV-7. Cutter patents for doughnuts (*as shown here*) or cookies. **(L)** Pat'd. by Charles H. Brown, Dubois, PA, Jan. 6, 1903, #717,537, one-half assigned to J. H. Smith, also Dubois. The curved blades have a fixed center cylinder, into which fits removable doughnut-hole cutter tube, which Brown says could also be used for "cakes requiring a central opening." **(T-R)** a "pastry cutter" for pastries, including doughnuts, with center hole. No, it doesn't cut ovals...it cuts circles, like all oval-looking rolling cutters shown. Pat'd. by Warner Stauffacher, Minneapolis, MN, May 26, 1942, #2,284,455. **(B-R)** more clearly shows sifting holes and filling cap (at left end of cylinder). Stauffacher's claim was to "efficiently cut dough into selected shapes...and at the same time...also applies thereto sugar, flour or other ingredients that may be desired." The cylinder is easily removed by moving spring steel wire handle apart; small cap comes off for filling.

❖ RECIPE ❖

Common Gingerbread – A pint of molasses. One pound of fresh butter. Two pounds and a half of flour, sifted. A pint of milk. A small tea-spoonful of pearl-ash, or [less] if it is strong. A tea-cup full of ginger. – Cut the butter into the flour. Add the ginger. – Having dissolved the pearl-ash [an early baking soda, with which the molasses would react] in a little vinegar, stir it with the milk and molasses alternately into the other ingredients. Stir it very hard for a long time, till it is quite light.

"Put some flour on your paste-board, take out small portions of the dough, and make it with your hand into long rolls. then curl up the rolls into round cakes, or twist two rolls together, or lay them in straight lengths or sticks side by side, and touching each other. Put them carefully in buttered pans, and bake them in a moderate oven, not hot enough to burn them. If they should get scorched, scrape off with a knife, or grater, all the burnt parts, before you put the cakes away.

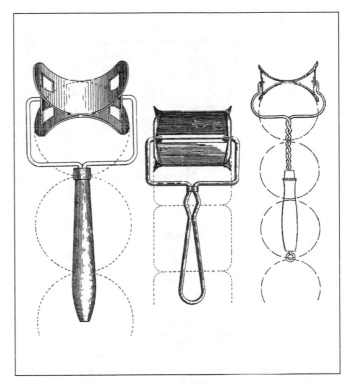

IV-8. Rolling cutter patents. (L) is another Henry Sidway biscuit cutter (See IV-5) patent, May 31, 1892, #475,815. His aim was to form two biscuits with each revolution, but he said "I do not intend to limit myself,...but contemplate changes in form and proportionn and the substitution of equivalent" parts. "For example, a separate [turned wood] handle is not necessary." He also said it wasn't necessary to make the device of stamped sheet metal, but that "it might be cast in a single piece of suitable shape." **(M)** William J. Grotenhuis, with Sidway again, Chicago, IL, Sept. 12, 1893, #504,834. This time, after two years of – I assume – successful selling of the first cutter, there's a company to which patent is assigned: Sidway Manufacturing Co., Chicago. The two end pieces of cutting drum are stamped sheet metal with 3 spoke-like deep corrugations (looking like prongs on drawing) which are cutting blades for making "rectangular round-cornered" biscuits. **(R)** a "cooky cutter" pat'd. by Gertrude H. Newman & Frederick Hills Newman, Milwaukee, WI, assignors to American Cutter Co., Milwaukee. Pat'd. Oct. 6, 1925, #1,556,019. The stamped curved blade cut cookies, but in "modified form" it had a tubular insert that was soldered in place permanently. Wire shank is twisted & inserted into turned wood handle.

"You can, if you choose, cut out the dough with tins, in the shape of hearts, circles, ovals, &c. or you may bake it all in one, and cut it in squares when cold. If the mixture appears to be too thin, add, gradually, a little more sifted flour." Miss Leslie, of Philadelphia, Seventy-Five Receipts for Pastry, Cakes, and Sweetmeats. Appended to The Cook's Own Book and Housekeeper's Register . ..., by a Boston Housekeeper. Boston: Munroe & Francis, 1833.

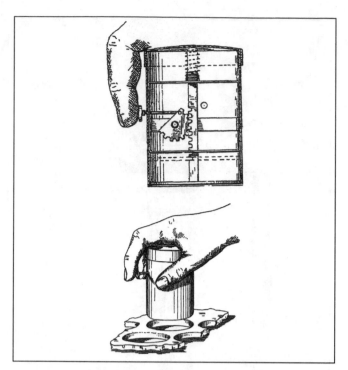

IV-9. Dough cutter patent with ejecting plunger. *The cylinder fits neatly in hand, & dough is ejected by pushing plunger with forefinger. Pat'd. by George F. Zinn, Cincinnati, OH, Sept. 16, 1902, #709,290. (This patent was cited by an inventor of the snowman cookie cutter, 1994, shown in IV-152.) As with other old patents, a clear understanding of previous practices is spelled out. Dough-cutters, wrote Zinn, "are implements used for cutting out of flat-rolled dough portions of this latter preparatory to being baked. These flat pieces may be of various shapes as to outline and more or less ornamental – as, for instance, star-shaped or simply round, as in the case of biscuits, ginger-snaps, &c. Such implements consist generally [at least by 1900] of a short tube, the shape of its side in profile being such as to produce the shape to be cut. This tube is grasped at one end and with its other open end pressed into the flat-rolled dough until the edge of the side has entirely passed through..., cutting out a piece. ... The dough-cutter is now lifted, carrying with it the piece of dough so cut out, which is presently caused to drop therefrom by shaking the implement. This method of removal is inconvenient and not always reliable or successful where the dough adheres persistently. In such cases the removal is generally accomplished by shaking the implement more forcibly until the dough becomes loose. When finally released under such circumstances, the contact succeeding its accelerated drop causes frequently the piece of dough to lose its intended shape."*

Biscuit or cracker cutter & pricker:
Look at a typical contemporary cracker – a saltine for example – and you'll see a pattern of small holes, creating the effect of quilting. The holes are created with prickers, and are to release gases while baking so they won't become pillows instead of quilts! The biscuits

with which the following implements were used were "beaten biscuits," the kind made by pounding with a rolling pin or mallet, or with a beaten biscuit machine, such as found in the pictures in Chapter II – II-3 & II-4.

Biscuit cutter & pricker, tinned iron, quite sharp edged, tall, turned wood handle painted black, 3 wires come out of ferrule on handle, American, 6-7/8"H x 2-7/8" diam., 19th C. .... **$90+**

Biscuit or cracker cutter & pricker, heavy tin with nail-like prickers inside, slightly convex cap fits comfortably in palm, mfd. by Fries & other tin mfrs. American, 1-1/2" deep x 2" diam., c.1890s-1910s..... **$55+**

Biscuit or cracker pricker, wooden knob handle with sturdy metal teeth in pattern, American, 4" x 3-1/2", late 19th C. .... **$65+**

❖ **NOTES** ❖

Biscuits – A notice in the 1837 *Journal of the American Institute* (NY: T. B. Wakeman) about Pierce's patent kitchen range, manufactured by Lockwood &

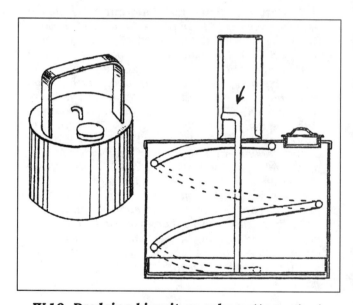

IV-10. Dredging biscuit or cake cutter patent. *This cutter was actually made, and marked "D.S. Co." – Dover Stamping Co., Boston. It has a spring-powered ejecting disk. "When the biscuit-cutter is pressed into the soft dough, the disk is pushed back toward the upper part of the cutter, where it remains until the pressure is removed from the cutter, then the action of the spring will withdraw the cutter from the dough, leaving the biscuit on the cake-board. In case it is desired to lift the biscuit from the cake-board, the disk may be held up by the crooked end of the 'stem' or 'steadying-pin' [indicated by small arrow] that sticks up out of the top surface of the cutting cylinder 'until the cutter and enclosed biscuit are in the desired place of deposit." The little snug-fit cap shown on top is used for filling open space with flour, so that "cutter may be kept constantly dusted or dredged so that it will not stick to the dough." Pat'd. by George O. Sanderson, Boston, May 19, 1868, #78,137, and assigned to himself & Frederick M. Baker of South Reading, MA.* **$75+**

Andrews, NYC, and awarded a premium at the 9th annual Fair (Oct. 1836) of the American Institute, includes a biscuit treat: "This article [the range] attracted a great attention at the Fair, and was kept in constant operation. On the sixth day of the Fair, Mr. Pierce [S. Pierce of Troy, NY] provided a dinner, and cooked in it for between fifty and a hundred gentlemen, at Niblo's. Among the articles presented at this repast, were several fine biscuits, made and stamped in twelve minutes from the sheaf! That is, the wheat in sheaf was threshed, winnowed, ground, kneaded, baked, rolled, stamped, and pricked, in the incredibly short space of twelve minutes!"

Biscuit pan, & matching cutter, rectangular brown & creamy white enamelware tray with raised edge & 12 round slight depressions, also enameled biscuit cutter with strap handle, "Onyx," Columbian Enameling & Stamping Co., Terre Haute, IN, 10"L, c.1915. .... **$100+**

Biscuit pan, stamped tin, 9 shallow oval cups, 3X3, riveted together & to a skeletal frame, thin strap handles, stamped under one cup: "8 1/2," "PAT NOV.9.69" and below it a sort of small cartouche with word MFG Co going horizontally, and some initials, poss. ending in "G" cutting vertically between the MFG and the Co. Pat'd. by John C. Milligan, Brooklyn, NY, Nov. 9, 1869, #96,605. "This inven-

*IV-12. **Biscuit or cracker stamp.** Mechanical, cast iron, spring steel with wooden block fixed with little 2-pronged prickers. Spring-load action, this knocks out pricked biscuits or crackers just short of 2" square. Stamp is 3-3/4"H. Pat'd. December 13, no year marked, but patent Tuesday the 13th came in 1870, 1881, 1887, 1892 & 1898. I think probably 1880s. Collection of Meryle Evans.* **$135+**

tion relates to an improved mode of uniting small biscuit-pans together in clusters; and consists in providing the said pans with horizontal flanges around the tops, and joining them together in rows by lapping the flanges and riveting them, joining two or more rows together, either in right lines in both directions, or in zigzag lines. ... The invention also consists in binding the whole together by wires or other bars, extending around, or along the sides of the clusters." .... **$15+**

Blancmange molds – See Molds, especially copper & tin

Border or ring molds – See Molds, especially tin

Bouche irons – See Patty iron

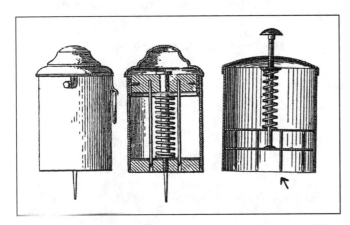

*IV-11. **Spring-action biscuit cutter patents. (L)** Pat'd. by St. George Craig, Clarksville, TN, Aug. 2, 1910, #965,991. Exterior view showing one of two bayonet catches for lid & a "perforating" pin. **(M)** another view showing interior spring. "To cut biscuits with this device the operator simply forces it down upon the layer of dough on the dough-board, and when the cutter strikes the board the operator turns or rotates the device slightly in order to cut the biscuit nicely from the sheet of dough. ... The central pin makes a central perforation in the biscuit. After the biscuit is cut and perforated... the operator relieves the pressure and then the spring forces the disk against the biscuit and thus ejects it." **(R)** "Combined Biscuit Cutter and Sticker," pat'd. by Isaac W. Lincoln, St. Joseph, MO, July 20, 1880, #230,294. This device, 30 years earlier than the one at left, actually is superior. The center plunger pin allows operator to keep it depressed until biscuit or cookie can be dropped onto a baking sheet, if desired. It makes 12 perforations [arrow points to one].*

*IV-13. **Bread dockers.** Used to mark bread before baking. **(L)** Tin & wood, in 6 sizes, from 2-1/2" to 5" diam. **(R)** "We make our bread dockers of a very heavy grade of tin, so that the letters will positively stay in place. We make these dockers in any shape & of any number of letters. They cost according to the number of letters." Both from Jaburg Brothers catalog, NYC, 1908. Words themselves would effect value because of crossover interest.* **$25-$75**

Bread baking mold, deliberately blackened tin, small isinglass window, hinged double loaf pan looks like 2 bombs or blimps lying side by side, or some kind of odd bivalve mollusk, "Ideal," mfd. by Matthai-Ingram Co., Baltimore, MD, 3-1/4"H x 12-1/2"L x 5"W (twice that for double ones), stamped with patent date near little catch: Aug. 3, 1897. • This also came in single loaf size. Original advertising claimed "Makes a crisp, moist and wholesome loaf a certainty. ... The bread is more nutritious, more tasty, and more digestible. Professor Morse, of Westfield, NJ, says bread baked in the Ideal ... is a remedy for dyspepsia and of the highest nutritive value." .... **$35+**

Bread baking mold or pan, blackened tin, 4 trough compartments for French bread loaves, early 20th C. .... **$15+**

Bread loaf pan, cast iron, double loaf, Griswold PN #960. (Note: I saw, and made a note of on-the-run at a flea market, maybe 20 years ago, a single loaf, Griswold bread loaf pan, PN 961. The collectors doubt me, but maybe out there is one. Dave Smith says, "The only PN 961 I have found is for the No. 21 Corn Bread Pan which is a later piece. They sometimes did, however, use duplicate PNs in different time periods." So keep your eyes out – if it really does exist, it's extremely rare, worth much more than even the double loaf.) Double loaf: .... **$700-$800+**

Bread pan, oblong blackened sheet iron, called Russia iron, folded corners, rolled rim, slanted sides, very substantial, ring handle at both ends, one kind was "Beaman's Patent," mfd. by Matthai-Ingram Co., 4" deep x 18"L x 12"W at top, late 19th C, into early 20th C. .... **$25+**

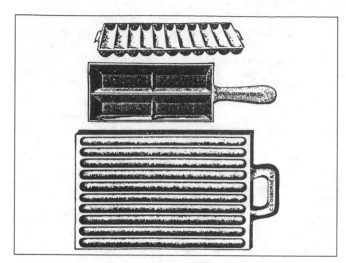

IV-15. Bread stick pan & confusable molds.
(T) *Wagner Ware Style E, cast iron, for 11 bread sticks. From 1915 Wagner catalog, Sidney, OH.* ***(M)*** *&* ***(B)*** *Both of these are solder molds for plumbers to use. Made of cast iron, & while size is not given, they are about 7" to 14"L, & were used to make sticks of lead solder. I saw one at a flea market marked "LEAD" in one of the troughs. Both apparently cast by C. S. Osborne & Co., Newark & Harrison, NJ. That foundry also made can openers, meat choppers, tools, oyster knives, kitchen furnishings, nutcrackers, nutpicks, sardine scissors, & cheese scoops, from about 1890 to c.1920. Pictures in Alfred Revill's* American Plumbing, *NY: 1894.* ***(T) $35-$55 (M) & (B) $25-$45***

IV-14. Bread pan or baking mold. *"No. 140," in corrugated spiral shape "which gives finished baked loaf a peculiar but appetizing appearance, the bread or cake may be sliced through the indentations. XX imported tin plate, 12-1/2" x 3-1/2" diam. Silver & Co., Brooklyn, c.1900. - 1910. A similar one, "The Ideal," which came in single or double loaf size, was blackened tin, without corrugations. They're almost same value. Another one, from 1927 Middleby Co. that wholesaled baker supplies, has a 4-loaf size; they say such pans are "used universally for making fig bread, also various health breads." See also IV-216, an ice cream mold.* **$25-$45**

❖ **NOTES** ❖

Russian iron – Russia iron or russian iron is a form of planished wrought iron used for roasting, baking and dripping pans. According to Elsie Hutchinson, in a book to instruct department store employees, titled *The House Furnishings Department*, 1918, it is a "special grade of sheet iron with a glossy black, slightly mottled appearance due to oxide adhering to the surface; it is produced by passing a pack of heated sheets back and forth under a steam hammer, the bit and anvil of which have indentations on their surfaces." It originated in Russia, and had an almost purple appearance, according to 19th century books.

Bread stick pan, riveted tin, 12 compartments, "Kreamer," August Kreamer & Co., Brooklyn, NY, early 20th C. .... **$45+**

Bread stick pan, cast iron, makes 22 bread sticks, 11 x 11 side by side, design based on old pan, sold through Cumberland General Store, but I may not be marked, American, 12-1/2"L x 7"W, 1980s. ..... **$10+**

Bride & groom cake dolls, bisque, painted & dressed in real cloth clothes, American (?), 4"H, 1940s. •
Futurewatch. – This is an undervalued collector field, offering a huge variety over a period of at least 100 years. A nice addition to a collection of them would include arches & altars, as well as photographs of decorated wedding cakes in bakery win-

dows. In the Jan. 25, 1989 *Antique Trader*, there was an appealing ad for 50+ sets from the 1920s on. They were from Japan, Occupied Japan & the U.S., & dealer, Shirley Rice, had them priced $15 to $35 per set, or $650 for all. • **Black Americana.** – I have not seen African-American bride & groom dolls that appear to date before the 1970s. This would be a good specialty area – especially dolls with "Afro" styled hair from the groovy '70s. I'm sure that older ones must exist, but must be rare. I'd say their value would generally be higher than "white" dolls. I assume there may be Oriental versions from after WWII – have you seen any? • **Gay couples** are a brand-new wedding cake decoration, but hard to find. • **Get 'em while they're cold.** – Many bakeries & pastry shops seem to have the same tired old brides & grooms year after year. Keep an eye on them; you might be able to buy old pieces, or trade for some brand new ones. .... **$35-$75+**

Bride & groom cake dolls, cast & painted plaster of Paris, lacy filigree base, flower arch, glass & plaster bell above heads, American, c.1910 to 1920.... **$50+**

Bride & groom cake dolls, molded plaster of Paris, painted with black, white, pink, also pearlized white paint on bride's headdress & bodice, American (?), 5"H, dated 1948.. **$25+**

Bun cutter, rolling pin cutter, tin, turned wooden handle, 18 iron blades set in large diam. cast metal roller, cuts 18 buns with each revolution of the sectioned drum, "Millers Bun Divider," (possibly mfd. by Charles E. Miller Co., See meat tenderizer in Chapter I), Milwaukee, WI, roller 7" diam., blades 6"W, pat'd.

IV-16. Bride & groom figures in automobile, cupid as chauffeur. *One of many fancy designs shown in a confectionery tools & supplies catalog. Materials not given, but probably silk flowers, gilt pressed cardboard, molded & painted plaster or bisque figures & base. This auto is so detailed it even has a crank. Dressed in cloth & paper cloth ing. 7"H x 5"W. From Joseph Middleby Jr., Inc., Boston, catalog, 1927. They also had designs with a couple in a blimp, under a lucky horseshoe, also birds, bells, bowers, & clasped hands. Detailed auto adds value & crossover interest.* **$65-$95**

IV-17. Kewpie groom & bride. *Pink celluloid doll figures, dressed in white & black crepe paper outfits glued to them, tulle veil, cloth flower bouquet, standing on flat hockey-puck cardboard disc or pillbox base. A pair I saw at a flea had a heart-shaped trellis over them made of cloth lily-of-the-valley flowers, no maker, American or German (?), dolls 3-1/2"H, overall 6"H X 3" diam., 1920s. These also came in another size, 6"H. Picture from Thomas Middleby catalog, 1927.* **The kewt Kewpies** *(take-off on "cute cupids") were created by artist Rose O'Neill about 1915, & became extremely popular. O'Neill licensed German doll mfrs. to make Kewpies; plus hundreds of thousands of hankies, jewelry, banks, post cards, etc. O'Neill did Kewpie art for Jell-O & for smaller, local dairies such as Hendler's in Baltimore), & there's lots of crossover interest today. Condition very important with easily-breakable celluloid figures.* **$30+**

Feb. 1907. Did not find patent. See also the multiple biscuit rollers & the multiple cookie rollers. **$100**

❖ NOTES ❖

Confusable: A Revolving Chip Cutter is a similar implement, on a smaller scale, with 2 turned wooden handles and a 3"W tin revolving cutter divided into eight sections, 3" x 2" – rolled back and forth and crosswise would make chocolate chips from blocks. This tool found in Dec. 1925 *Sethness Candy Maker*, Chicago. Many such cutters were patented.

Bundt cake mold or bundt pan, cast iron, cobalt blue enamel, American or German, 10" diam., early 20th C. or late 19th.. **$400+**

Bundt cake mold, cast iron, large scallops alternating with sharply-defined zigs (zags?), conical spout, American, 12" diam., 19th C. .... **$200+**

❖ NOTES ❖

Bundt: The German word *bundt* relates to the word for band or bundle, and refers to the banded effect of the flutes (such as would be found in a wheat sheaf or straw wreath, tied at intervals with twine), and probably originated as a harvest celebration cake. • **Bundt Pan Progenitor.** The well-known cast aluminum bundt pan, alternating 8 large scallops with 8 small pointed flutes, first made in 1949 as a "Nordic Ware" product by Northland Aluminum Products of Minneapolis, MN, has been reported over the years as a reproduction of a 19th C. European cast iron bundt pan, brought over – reportedly – by a European immigrant to Minnesota. Northland has now registered "Bundt" for their own use. It is not known how long ago the first bundt pan was made, probably in ceramic. Northland offers a bundt cookbook. Nordic Ware Kitchen, Highways 7 & 100, Minneapolis, MN 55416. • **Ceramic Progenitor Update.** In 1997, the June 11 issue, the *Washington Post* published an article by Marcy Goldman in the food section about bundt pans. Goldman, author of the highly-praised *A Treasury of Jewish Holiday Baking* (NYC: Doubleday, 1998), relates the history of Northland, and the account of H. David Dalquist, co-founder in 1949 of Northland, about some ladies from the Minneapolis Hadassah chapter who paid him a visit and told him about a ceramic bake mold used to make *Bundkuchens* – "party or gathering cakes." They asked if his new company could make such a thing out of aluminum, and the rest is history. Marcy Goldman's website is: www.betterbaking.com. • **Other makers**: You can get something very like Northland's bundt pan by other makers, under other names. Mirro has a "Wearever" brand "Crown Burst Mold"™; A glass version made in the Czech Republic by Kavalier Glassworks of North America, is another. Kaiser makes one of steel; Calphalon makes another of spun aluminum.

• • •

Lookalike alarm – Lehman's Hardware & Appliances, offer a spouted bundt pan, 10" diam., with 2 handles & say that all their cast iron is "produced in a family foundry – Lodge, in South Pittsburgh, TN – dating back to 1896," and that all are sand cast and "finished by hand." Like many companies now of interest to collectors, a request for information led to this reply in mid-2002: "We do not have any information about novelty muffin pans that we have made over the years." We collectors play an important role in recording the history of manufacturing – seems odd they wouldn't want to do it themselves.

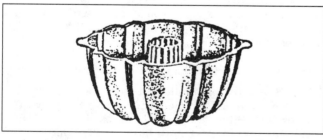

IV-18. Bundt cake mold. *Called by Wagner a "Style B" mold. Cast iron, spouted, 10" diam., Wagner Ware #310, c.1915 - 1940. All bundt pans are similar; earliest were imported from Europe in 19th C. Value depends on size & quality of casting – & sometimes on "name brand." Overall value range for such molds is $45 to over a thousand dollars for a 9-1/2" bail handle Griswold bundt pan. This one:* **$150+**

IV-19. Butter curler. *Nickel-plated, wooden handle, 8"L. From Ritzinger & Grasgreen catalog for traveling salesmen, c.1906-07.* **$5-$15**

Bundt cake mold, earthenware with brown glaze, spouted, fluted sides, crack mended with twisted wire, wire all around rim too, German or Austrian, late 19th C. • From the looks of the wire around rim, you might almost assume that these pans were sold with wire bindings, to hold them together in case of bustin' in the oven. What a mess!................. **$400+**

Bundt cake mold, finely-cast iron with wire bail, open spouted, Griswold Mfg. Co., PN 965, 4-1/2"H x 9-1/2" dia., 1st third 20th C. .... **$1,000-$1,200**

Bundt cake mold, cast iron, bail handle of type called a stop bail, a sort of ear that would allow bail to fall only on one side & on other side to be held rigid for pouring. This would make it much easier & safer to tip pan over to release cake. A stop bail of one form or another was used on many kinds of heavy cast hollowwares. Frank W. Hay & Sons, Johnstown, PA, pat'd. Mar. 10, 1891. • Except for marks, this looks just like Griswold bundt pan. Griswold made some bundts for Hay; there are various sets of markings, some with PN 965. .... **$300-$400+**

Bundt cake mold, cast iron, scalloped, solid tapered cone in center where otherwise a closed spout or open tube would be; a solid cone would have held & radiated more heat. German or other European origin, 10-1/2"D, 19th C. .... **$250+**

Bundt cake mold, cast iron, tubed, very exaggerated flutes & scallops, very deep, signs of real wear, American (?), not marked, 11" to 13" diam., 19th C............... **$300+**

Butter curler, steel & wood, curved "J" corrugated blade set in wood handle, 8"L. Used by dragging across cold butter block, to make a shallow "peel" that naturally curled. .... **$10+**

❖ **NOTES** ❖

Man & Machine Made Butter Hands – Factory-made butter hands are relatively cheap – they look machine-made too, with fairly crudely finished off beveled edges and perfectly regularly spaced corrugations. They also are flat-backed. Handmade ones are more carefully smoothed and finished, and often have somewhat convex backs. Pairs don't tend to match exactly. They bring three to four times as much money as factory made ones.

"A pair of creased wooden hands, for making butter balls, should be included in the outfit of the kitchen. With a little practice, butter may be shaped in many pretty forms, so that the dish will look very nice on the table. Be particular to select hands with fine grooves – much better results than coarse." Maria Parloa, *Kitchen Companion*, Boston: Estes & Lauriat, 1887. • "**How To Use Butter Hands.** – Let stand in boiling water for five minutes. Next put in cold water for five minutes or longer. Must be cold when used. Have large bowl half full of cold water. Cut some firm butter into pieces about the size of a hickory nut. Roll these pieces between the butter-hands into any shape you please – grooved balls, little pineapples, scrolls, etc. Dip the hands frequently in ice water." *ibid.*

Butter hands, also called Scotch hands, corrugated wood, usually maple, well-made & usually satiny from use, American, between 8" & 9"L & 2-1/2" & 3"W even 4"W, 19th C. • I used to think these were pretty much all the same. But I can report differences. Although most are within small size range, there are things a connoisseur of Scotch hands can look for. Instead of a lighter weight, dull wood, wide grooves, seek out heavier wood, pale golden satiny patina; instead of machine carved regular corrugations, look for carefully handcarved grooves; instead of pattern-cut simple paddle handles, look for more artistically formed ones, especially those that are flat on corrugated side where they must fit together, but are curved on their backs. I even like slightly mismatched pairs, perhaps perversely. Nice wooden butter hands are still being manufactured. Price for pair of hand carved ones: .... **$50-$100**
Butter hands, finely corrugated sycamore, backs of paddles convex in section, good patina, handmade, American (?), 8-9/16"L, mid 19th C. .... **$80+**
Butter hands, machine made corrugated wood paddles, for rolling butter balls, American, 9"L, 1890s-1910. .... **$20+**

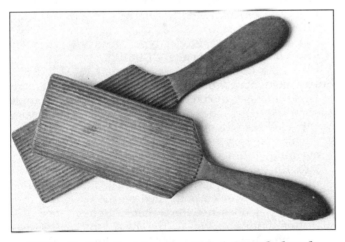

*IV-20. Butter hands, also called **Scotch hands**. Corrugated French boxwood, or rock maple, commercially made, &, though close, this is not a matched pair – note handle ends. 9-1/2"L x 2-1/2"W. Late 19th C. or early 20th C. $20-$30*

❖ NOTES ❖

Butter mold & stamp collecting tips – Do you call them "molds" or "stamps"? Technically, a butter mold is a form for butter – quarter or half pound, pound or two

pound, and may in addition decorate top surface. Box molds and plunger molds are the two basic types. Most collectors call the decorated plunger part of the mold a butter mold, but it could also be called a butter stamp. In the listing of makers, no distinction was made between molds, printers and stamps: • **Butter Mold Manufacturers.** – In the 1905-06 Buyers' Guide, of *Thomas' Register of American Manufacturers*, I found a few butter mold makers listed under molds. And though not broken down that way, there are probably others to be found in *Thomas'* section on woodenware too. • The makers are: Robert E. Turner, Lebanon, CT; Creamery Package Mfg. Co., Chicago, IL; Freeman Mfg. Co., Kalkaska, MI; Ludington Woodenware Co., Ludington, MA; A. H. Reid, Pittsburg, PA; Vermont Farm Machine Co., Bellows Falls, VT; Moseley & Stoddard Mfg. Co., Rutland, VT; & Cornish, Curtis & Green Mfg. Co., Fort Atkinson, WI.

Machine made? – You can see concentric rings, especially inside the case, that are the mark of tools used with a lathe.

Craftsmen in shops making butter molds were highly skilled, and bridged the world of one-of-a-kind completely hand carved or whittled butter stamp (much less likely to be a mold, as cases were hard to do by hand), and dime-a-dozen (though still attractive to us as collectors today) completely factory-made stamps, with templates and jigs guiding the cutting.

• • •

Subjective values Evaluating molds, especially butter molds and stamps, is very subjective. Because so much depends on appeal of particular figural motifs, a lot of the value has to be in the mind of the collector. Part of the pricing of butter molds is based on origin as well as motif. As butter mold expert Jim Bohn says, "It's like judging art – each piece is different."

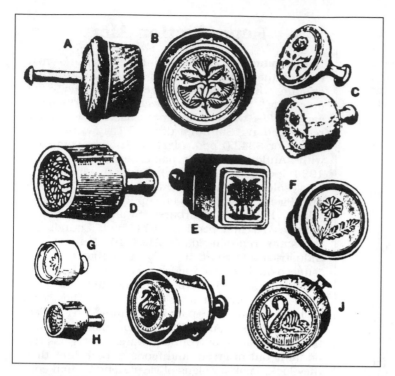

IV-22. Butter stamps, molds & cases. *All machine-carved wood.* **(A & B)** *Two views of what seller called individual "butter prints," in "Hollywood" pattern. Three sizes, for 1/2 oz., 3/4 oz. & 1 oz pats.* **(C)** *Two molds "by which butter may be put up in pound or half-pound cakes for the market. They are made of soft wood, as white-ash or soft maple, & are generally kept for sale at all country stores where willow-ware is sold.* **The manner of using them** *is as follows: When the butter is ready for making up, it is weighed out into the proper quantities, & each piece is worked in the butter-dish with the ladle into flat round cakes. These cakes are either pressed with the mold shown in the upper picture, or are made to go into the cup of the lower mold. Inside the cup is a mold with a handle which works through a hole in the upper part of the cup. The cup is inverted on to the table, & when this handle is pressed down it forces the mold on to the butter, which is squeezed into a very neat ornamental cake. By pushing down on the handle & lifting the cup, the cake is pushed out of the mold. This makes a very favorite mode of putting up fine butter for market, & is also well adapted for preparing butter for the table in houses where neatness of appearance is studied. The molds when in use should be kept wetted in cold water to prevent the butter from sticking."* American Agriculturist, *May 1872.* **(D)** *Flower pattern in four sizes: 1 oz., 3 oz., 1/2 lb. & 1 lb. From Duparquet, Huot & Moneuse catalog, c.1904-1910.* **(E)** *Wheat sheaf in square design, Valentine Clad & Sons, Philadelphia, c.1890-1900.* **(F)** *3" to 4" stamps, Joseph Breck catalog, 1905.* **(G)** *"Butter pat in Case. – This gives the butter a handsome form & print at the same time." American Home Cook Book, 1854.* **(H)** *Same as (D).* **(I)** *Swan in case, 1 oz. & 2 oz. Jaburg Brothers, 1908.* **(J)** *Swan in-1/2 oz., 3/4 oz., 1 oz., 2 oz. sizes. Ritzinger, Grasgreen, c. 1906-07.* **$40-$125+**

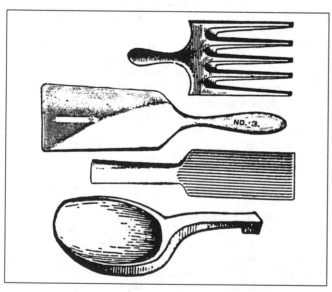

IV-21. Wooden butter tools. **(T)** *"Mrs. Bragg's" butter fork, maple, 12" x 5". Montgomery Ward catalog, 1895.* **(M)** *Butter spades, plain & grooved. The grooved one is the same as a butter hand. Joseph Breck agricultural supply catalog, 1905.* **(B)** *Butter ladle with hooked handle. Duparquet, Huot & Moneuse, c.1904-1910. Wood's patina affects value, but nothing acquires patina faster than butter or dairy tools.* **$15-$45**

Butter mold, bee, large carving on round stamp, fits into turned wood mold, plunger type, turned & carved wood, marked "Germany," 3-1/2" x 1-1/2", 20th C. .... **$45+**

Butter mold, box & plunger type, wood with nickeled brass hardware, imprints "JERSEY," early 20th C. .... **$65+**

Butter mold, cow, 2 parts: round glass (very pale greenish blue) case, molded disc or plunger prints simple standing cow, the disc is molded on top with threaded hole for screwed-in turned wooden handle, "Bomer," American, round, 4-1/2" diam., 8-1/4"L overall including handle, marked "Pat Apld for," very late 19th C. • A presumably much rarer glass cow plunger mold, depicted in Kindig's book, & belonging to him, has four cows molded on the case, as decoration. His does not have name "Bomer." See also Butter stamps – Glass & Ceramic................ **$150+**

Butter mold, cow, incised carving, cylinder with pewter bands, hexagonal shape, American, 4-1/2"H x 3" diam., 19th C. .... **$300+**

Butter mold, cow, pleasantly abstracted lathe-turned case & plunger in one pound size, a craftsman-shop production of pointy-leg cow resembling what Paul Kindig calls "Vigilant Cow," written about extensively in *Butter Prints & Molds* (See Bibliography), American, 2nd half 19th C. .... **$275+**

Butter mold, flowers, 4 with four petals each & 4 eight-pointed stars, box type, wood, marked "Porter Blanchards Son's Co.," Nashua, NH, 19th C. .... **$125+**

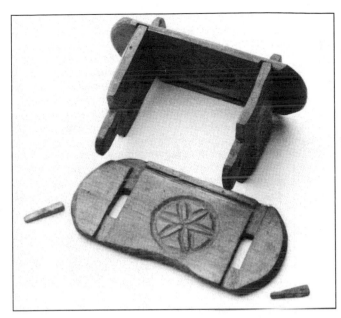

IV-23. Butter mold. *Carved wood in five parts, with holding pegs. Simple star motif. Maker's (?) mark are initials "H.Y." Block of butter would be 3-3/8" x 2" x 2-3/4". Collection of Meryle Evans.* **$125+**

IV-25. Butter molds. *Box molds of more mechanical type than one in IV-50. Note how closely carving & styles resemble springerle boards (further on in this chapter). Perhaps they were interchangeable.* **(T)** *Carved wood "Blanchard" butter mold, by maker of churns. Brass latches. Came in three sizes:-1/2 lb., marked to make two-1/4 lb. prints; 1 lb., for four prints; & 2 lb., for eight prints. This company also sold a cheaper version, which they claimed was the "same pattern as Blanchard."* **(B)** *This box did not come apart. It came in 11 sizes, making 3, 4, 6, 8, 12, 16 & 24 "cakes," from 1-1/4" x 1-1/3" (one ounce cakes) up to 3-1/2" x 3-1/3" (8 oz. cakes). From Breck catalog, 1905.* **$100-$400**

IV-24. Box mold butter stamp – How To Use. *"There is rivalry amongst fancy butter makers to excel, not only in quality, but also to offer their product in the most acceptable form, & in attractive, convenient packages. The favorite method of putting up butter for immediate sale, is that of pound cakes, ornamented with a stamp, & marked in the center, so that each can be divided into half pounds for use on the table. For this, moulds & stamps are used. This illustration shows a stamp bearing the maker's initial. Being square, the prints may be packed upon the shelves in any butter-carrier without loss of space." American Agriculturist, Sept. 1878.*

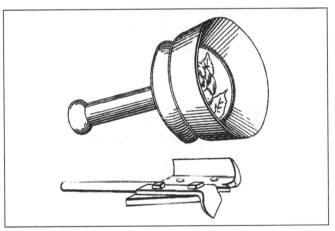

IV-26. Butter mold or stamp patent & tool to carve it *from a block attached to the lathe's chuck. John S. Bullard, Chagrin Falls, OH, pat'd. this April 17, 1866, #54,054, and assigned rights to C. Bullard & Sons, same place. It is a lathe-turned mold, & was manufactured (and mold is stamped with patent date). Bullard's specs tell about the three parts: the "shell" or casing, the handle "which is screwed or connected" to the stamp. He received a patent June 14, 1864, for the tool he used (shown at bottom). He said it made the shell smoother, and made the work much quicker. His claim for the butter stamp & shell seems mainly concerned with a legal aspect: making the mold a "uniform definite size" so that "the weight of the butter that can be put into each shell will be about the same...so as to give the exact measurement or weight which cannot be done with the old mode of constructing them."*

IV. Form, Mold, Shape, etc. 191

IV-28. Butter mold & butter stamps. (T) *Top row, 3 views: a hinged box mold, that comes apart completely. Makes a 4 or 5-lb brick, marked off by grooves made by stamps (lying in right foreground). The* **technique for use** *differs from others, & is as follows: "A pound of butter is weighed & packed into the end of the mold by means of the stamps, one of which presses the side, & the other the top, the latter having the packer's initials or trade-mark. Then another pound is weighed & packed in the same manner, & so on. In the packing, grooves are left in the butter, marking the divisions between the pounds, by which the retailer may cut it up into pieces of exact weight, each piece having been weighed previously." The finished cake with marks & divisions shown at center. American Agriculturist, May 1876.* **(M)** & **(B)** *All are of "close-grained hard wood," & all have a "hand carved sheaf of wheat" printing block. In center row left is the nickel-plated brass "Eureka," with a self-gauging attachment. Prints pounds or half-pounds, by adjusting a collar on the upright standard, which is kept in place by a clamp & screw. Center row right, with hands, is the "Philadelphia," made of cherry, screwed together with brass screws. Block has wooden stem, & mold's top is fitted with hardwood moveable cap. Pound size: 5-3/4"L x 3-5/8"W. Also came in 1/2-pound size.* **(B)** *At bottom, & disassembled just to right above it, is an "Economy" self-adjuster. Brass screws. "Cut the butter from the churn batch on the table, press the hopper full, cut surplus off smoothly with hand paddle, press block from printer by pressure on the wood stem of block, extending through the printer head block." Cherry-Bassett Co., Baltimore dairy supplier, 1921.* **$50-$65+**

Butter mold box, no pattern, wood box with iron fittings including frame & handle, 1 lb. press, American, 5-3/4"L x 3-5/8"W, 19th C. • This is a plain, functional mold, & there is one in the Smithsonian's collection. However, it is not worth $300 just because it is "in a museum."............................ **$75+**

❖ NOTES ❖

"In a museum" & "in the book" are explanatory phrases used when raising prices, but it's pretty much meaningless when the museum (Smithsonian) and book (such as mine) are known for including a wide range of things for study regardless of value.

Butter mold box, no pattern, wood, very small, marked "Munsing," American. Munsing not in Thomas' Register.. **$25+**
Butter mold, rose & other flowers in center design, hand-carved wood, square (unusual) with fluted sides, Pennsylvania (?), 5-1/4" x 5-1/2", 1850s-90s.......... **$450+**
Butter mold, carved maple round box or "shell" as the inventor called it, with butter stamp of oak leaves & 2 acorns. 6-1/2"H mold is 4-1/2" diam., stamp is 3-1/2" diam. Unusual because it was stamped with

IV-27. Butter mold for butter rolls. *After butter is worked to removed excess moisture, it is packed into a mold. The one shown here is "made of lignum vitae [an extremely hard wood], in the manner of a pair of bullet-molds. Each half being filled with the finished butter, the handles are forcibly squeezed together, & the butter is compressed firmly into a solid roll [note curved interior], which drops from the mold when it is opened. The mold is kept wetted with cold water during the operation." These rolls, which were then wrapped individually in muslin, were made to fit vertically into a large trunk-like butter box which held 30 rolls. American Agriculturist, Mar. 1876.* **$100+ (L) $325 (M) $775 (R) $750**

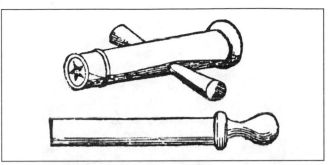

IV-29. Butter press or "French butter forcer." *Tin with insert disc with heart cutout, wooden plunger. Virtually identical to those in IV-124. "There are 12 different forms to each, that give an infinite variety to this decorative manner of serving butter." American Home Cook Book, 1854. (See also Jumble machines with cake & cookies & "Kiss Machine" with candy.)* **$100+**

a patent date across the top: "Pat. April 17, 1866." It was pat'd. by John Bullard, Chagrin Falls, OH, #54,054. Sold by a Michigan eBay seller, antiqyopo, in fall 2001 for: **$140**

Butter mold, wheat ear, 2 parts, very small rectangular box, motif carved inside, string holds halves together, paper label reads: "**Wheat-Ear Moulds.** Directions for Use. First, thoroughly soak the mould in water and then with a table knife fill in both halves of Butter Mould. Then lay a clean straw in the centre of one half, then press the two halves evenly together. Take away the top half and lift out wheat-ear on the straw." No manufacturer's name, English, overall size is 1-1/4"H x 4"L x 1-5/8"W, with 3-3/4"L wheat-ear carving, c.1900 from looks of label. .... **$75+**

Butter mold, star design, cast aluminum, R. Hall, Burlington, NC, 1/2 lb. size, 3-1/2" diam., prob. c. 1930s to 1950s. .... **$25+**

Butter press – See also Pastry tube; Cookie press

IV-30. Butter mold or stamp. *Relatively unusual paddle shape. Cow in elongated oval, rope border. Note pine tree, flower & cow's bell. 11"L x 4-1/4"W. Note dark hole which is a register hole that would match up with a short peg on [here missing] other half. Many, if not all, in paddle form are thought to be foreign. According to auction catalog, this was one of Harold Corbin's "most highly regarded" carved molds. Photo courtesy Litchfield Auction Gallery, Litchfield CT. Ex-Harold Corbin Collection, auctioned Jan. 1, 1990. Today's value probably more than price realized of $750 in 1990.*

❖ **NOTES** ❖

"Stamp" or "Print"? – Carl W. Drepperd, in *A Dictionary of American Antiques*, makes this common sense distinction between the oft-used terms stamp and print: the tool used to mark the butter is the stamp; the marked butter is the print. • In an 1890 cookbook, *On the Chafing Dish, Compliments of the Meriden Britannia Co.*, by Harriet P. Bailey (NY: G. W. Dillingham), there is a recipe for "Eggs With Macaroni: to which Mrs. Bailey adds this genteel note: "Note: – For cooking on the chafing dish, I advise always using print butter. It may seem a little extravagant. But surely when one in evening attire prepares a dish which proves to be above reproach, one may say with the March Hare, 'It is the best butter,' without losing the reputation of being an economical as well as a good housekeeper." Bailey and Drepperd didn't comment on rolling "stamps," so I have opted to call them printers.

Butter printer, rolling, flower designs, carved wood, English (?), 5-1/2"L, 19th C. • Rolling butter printers were used to make border prints at a dairy store. The large tray of butter, an inch thick or whatever, was divided off into sections, square-by-square of designs, so that so many squares could be cut off for so much poundage. This one: .... **$125+**

Butter printer, rolling, carved wood (ash?), prints a thistle & 2 star-like flowers & leaf, English, 4-1/2"L x 1-7/8" diam., 19th C. .... **$125+**

Butter slicer, nickel plated iron, 11 thin cutting wires, porcelainized cast iron base, cuts a pound block of butter into quarters, then slices them into pats, probably for hotel or restaurant use, worked by pushing wire-strung frame down using thumb tab, "Elgin #48," mfd. by Cleveland Faucet Co., 8-1/2"H x 8-1/2"L, pat'd. Dec. 31, 1901 in Canada, Sept. 1911 in U.S.A. .... **$55+**

Butter stamps – glass & ceramic:
See also glass Butter molds, listed a few pages back.

Butter stamp, wheat sheaf, rayed or piecrust border, pressed glass disc, knob handle, M'Kee & Brothers, Pittsburgh, 1868. .... **$400+**

IV-31. Butter stamps. *Both quite small. **(L)** Miniature with swan. 1-1/4" diam. **(R)** Rooster with 2 bees or stars. 2" diam. Photo courtesy Litchfield Auction Gallery. Ex-Harold Corbin Collection, auctioned Jan. 1, 1990, $275 & $250.* **(L) $150+ (R) $275+**

Butter stamp, fleur-de-lis pattern, round glass, screw-in wooden knob, French Canadian, 3-1/2" diam., 20th C. .... **$75+**

Butter stamp, geometric curved-ray design, saltglazed stoneware with large knobby handle, 23 rays around small indented circle, deeply molded, poss. OH, mid 19th C. .... **$1,250+**

Butter stamps – wood. Most butter stamps & molds are of hand- or machine-carved wood.

Butter stamp, armadillo or tortoise?, carved, crescent shape, knobby handle, looks old except for new-looking handle, subject matter makes me wary of age, 6-1/4"W, 20th C. (Note: The only other armadillo motif in this book is found on a white earthenware mold from England, c.1922.)................ **$500+**

Butter stamp, cow, detailed hand-carving of unusual rearing bovine surrounded by more typical combination of gate, overhanging branch & long grass, cable border, long handle, American, 19th C. **$400**

Butter stamp, cow with fence behind her, eager expectant horns, nice little tail, pointed udders, well-defined hooves, hair on flanks, body of mold worn, but well carved figure is perfect, American, 4-1/2" overall x 2-1/2" deep, stamp itself 3-5/8" diam., 19th C. .... **$600+**

Butter stamp, cow with pointy legs, ears & horns, in Kindig's "Vigilant Cow" style, well-cut, knob handle, American, 2nd half 19th C. .... **$500+**

Butter stamp, deer, with bent corn stalk (which he may have been eating!) overhanging him & long grass, piecrust border, American, 4" diam., 19th C. ... **$800+**

Butter stamp, donkey, with wonderfully bent front legs, slogging along on a sort of rayed ground, probably a plowed field, & with bursts of something, like leaves or flowers, filling sky, deeply carved wooden disc, chip out of one side, age cracking, very unusual motif, American, 3-3/4" diam., 19th C. ...... **$1,000+**

Butter stamp, eagle, deep carved abstract figure with corrugated border, lathe-turned one-piece blank, lathe marks evident, American, 4-1/2" diam., 19th C. .... **$400+**

Butter stamp, eagle, hand carved wood in half moon shape, very beautiful carving of benign but spread-winged eagle, wide-eyed & looking over his right wing (left wing in printed butter), details of breast &

IV-32. Butter stamps, (L) Pennsylvania style heart-shaped tulip with leaves. 2-3/4" diam. (M) Cow under tree branch, piecrust border. 3-3/4" diam. (R) Civil War soldier's bust in profile, with beard & cap. Concentric ring border: generally speaking, concentric circles as a border are lathe-turned and more recent than chip-carved. 3-1/2" diam. Photo courtesy Litchfield Auction Gallery. Ex-Harold Corbin Collection, each auctioned Jan. 1, 1990 for $355 or less. (L) $350 (M) $375 (R) $1,000

IV-33. Butter stamp. Cow with tree branch & tall grass. Piecrust border. Courtesy Joe & Teri Dziadul, Enfield, CT. $375+

wing feathers done with genius, little chips perfectly spaced for visual appeal, & long parallel curving lines to follow sweep of ruff, back of head, tail & ends of wings, two spaces filled in with rayed suns (one a moon?), initials, & a few 4 point stars between letters just inside piecrust border. • Clarence Spohn, in catalog, quotes Robacker as stating in his 1965 Touch of the Dutchland, that "The eagle pictured here has been called the most important piece of its kind in primitive woodcarving." Border has initials "S. M.," PA German, 3-3/4"H x 7-5/8"L, 19th C. • Ex-Robacker,................... **$6,000. $5,000-$7,000+**

Butter stamp, eagle with an 8 point "star," American, 2-3/4" diam., 19th C. **$450**

❖ NOTES ❖

Still a star? After eight points, I'm not sure a pointed motif is necessarily a star, but maybe it is meant to represent or allude to a star, so instead of thinking up some new word like octopunctus let's just continue calling it a star. You'll encounter this shape, sometimes reminiscent of a compass rose, on quilts too. N. B. Even with 12 points, some writers still call this a star design. Moravian stars, in 3 dimensions, have many more than 8 points.

Butter stamp, eagle with shield body, deeply carved, words "JAMES HOFMAN - SHIP BUILDER" around border, American, 19th C. • Value in relationship to ship building... **$1,000+**

Butter stamp, elliptical design with central 6-point pinwheel (or flower), flanked by a heart at each end, intricate border deeply chip-carved maple, 9-1/4"L. Several are known that are virtually identical with three small pinwheels or floriate forms between every other ray. This one may be from Nova Scotia, 2nd quarter 19th C. .... **$1,500+**

Butter stamp, fish, very fat (croppie? sunfish?) with several regularly patterned lines of waves, dentil border, 2 part, very finely carved, with separate carved & inserted knob handle (partly chewed – by piranha?),

American, found in barn in Dresden, ME, 3-3/4" diam., mid 19th C. • The detailed, well-ordered, & patterned appearance reminds you of classical Greco-Roman tiles or wall murals, especially compact puddle-sized water body hovering just behind lower fin. Perhaps the carver's inspiration was in some recently published account of an archaeological dig in the 1840s or 1850s. .... **$1,250+**

Butter stamp, fox, running, big tail brush, overhead branch, pointy enough to be a "vigilant fox" as Kindig might term it, dense, faintly yellow wood with wormholes, American, 2nd half 19th C. .... **$850+**

Butter stamp, lollipop type, double sided, unusually long handle; designs are a double heart on one side, pinwheel or fylfot design on other, PA German, 11"L overall with handle, stamp only 4-3/4" diam., mid 19th C. .... **$1,000+**

Butter stamp, lollipop type, carved from one piece of wood, double ended with 2 prints: a square print with chip-carved eagle & 4 stars separated by shank a hand's breadth long from a round print carved with 8 point snowflake-like design, American, prob. 2nd to 3rd quarter 19th C. .... **$1,000+**

Butter stamp, lollipop type, one piece carved wood, unusual because of handle angled somewhat to side instead of joining disc at right angles, simple 6 petal star flower (with small ellipses between each point) carved on both sides, simple bead border, American, 8-1/2"L, approx. 3-3/4" diam. stamp, prob. 3rd quarter 19th C. .... **$750+**

Butter stamp, lollipop type, separate turned wooden handle, nice carving of bulky cow standing on groundline that looks like cable, the words being TRADE MARK, above & below cow, maybe mid 19th C. Could be worth a lot more if the "trademark" could be traced. **$1,000**

IV-34. Butter stamps – wood & brass & redware. (L) Finely-detailed carved wood anchor with line. Long handle. 3-1/4" diam. (M) The sheep or ram here appears on a brass rather than a wooden mold. The elements of the design of this brass mold & a wooden one the same size (4-1/4" diam.), that was auctioned by Robert W. Skinner in 1880s, are virtually identical. A butter mold of brass, if kept scrupulously clean, would have the advantage of staying quite cold in hot weather. (R) Redware mold of cow under tree, facing right & with raised or repoussé [sticking up above surface] design rather than intaglio [cut down into surface] design of a carved wooden mold. 3-1/2" diam. This ceramic mold was probably made by impressing damp clay with a carved wooden mold. Butter printed with this one would have intaglio design. Photo courtesy Litchfield Auction Gallery. Ex-Harold Corbin Collection, auctioned Jan. 1, 1990. **(L) $325, (M) $775, (R) $750.**

IV-35. Butter stamp. Demilune stamp, cow & tree, cross-hatched border with wear. Collection & photograph of James E. Trice, author of Butter Molds, Collector Books, 1980. According to another expert, Jim Bohn, half-rounds have gone up in value a lot, and the cow is actually worth more than an eagle, even if this seems counterintuitive. **$1,000**
(Note: woven texture is fault of photo)

Butter stamp, Masonic building trade symbols, carved wood, carved handle, American, 4-7/8" diam., 3/4" thick, late 19th C. • Value here is tied to Masonic symbols, assuming they are *Freemason symbols.* .... **$1,500+**

❖ NOTES ❖

Fraternal Orders: Their Symbols & Motifs

The three orders expounded on here all make use of Christian symbols as well as secular symbols manipulated sometimes to hint at Christian beliefs. Because all these orders are supposedly secret and have well-guarded rites and rituals, it is not so easy to discover their symbols. Depending on the era, it has sometimes been considered a great advantage in business and politics to be a member of an order. • The ***Freemasons*** are usually dated back to the 17th C. in England, and 1733 in (Boston) North America. The 1804 *English Encyclopaedia* traces Freemasons back to the 6th C. in England, but this may be romanticizing loose guilds or fraternal orders of masons and stone- and brick-workers. Basically, Freemasons use masonry tools, viz. a trowel, crossed squares, a level, a plumb rule or bob, a mallet, a pick-axe, an iron rod. To that short list is added an All-Seeing Eye, a radiant sun, stars and comets, moon, three steps, a triangle, three triangles forming a 9-point star, three columns of various architectural orders representing Wisdom, Strength and Beauty, a checkerboard floor, a Bible as an open book, Moses' two stone tablets in round-top gravestone shape, a beehive, a balance scale, a ladder, an incense pot, an anchor and the Ark, an hourglass with wings, a scythe, crossed hammer and spade, Aaron's budding rod, a coffin, a cord, a shoe, crossed keys, crossed quill pens, crossed swords, and probably other subjects. Masonic motifs include at least one design used by non-Masons too – a square and compass arranged to make a frame – sometimes for a flexed arm and mason's hammer; these are definitely Freemason symbols when accompanied by a sun or crescent moon and letters "G" (for Geometry, or The Great Architect of the Universe, ie. God) or "A" (for Architect), but often are even when not so accompanied. • ***The Odd Fellows*** (**I.O.O.F.** – International Order of Odd Fellows) don't seem to be as old an order, so objects decorated with their symbols have values that are slightly, shall we say, younger. The Odd Fellows were around by 1745 in "isolated lodges" in England and found countrywide by 1812, according to one expert. In America, two founding dates given are 1806 and 1819, the latter – for a lodge in Baltimore – generally being the accepted date. Then in 1850-51 the Odd Fellows-related **Degree of Rebekah** was established for women. Odd Fellows seem to have the most symbols – some the same as Masonic symbols. The list includes a three-link chain that often has the initials "F," "L," "T" within the links (Friendship, Love and Truth), an All-Seeing Eye, skull and crossbones, scythe, bow, arrows and quiver, bundle of rods, a serpent, scales and a sword, crossed swords, a Bible, an hourglass (sometimes with wings), a coffin, a hatchet, fireman's pike, what looks like roman numeral III but is really a symbol for three columns or pillars representing Faith, Hope and Charity (sometimes Faith, Love and Truth – F.L.T.) as well as Wisdom, Strength and Beauty of Religion, an open tent, an altar of sacrifice, tablets of stone – Moses' 10 Commandments, a Pilgrim's sandals, staff and scrip (a satchel or bag), a shepherd's crook, a sun, an owl, a huge sheep-like lamb with a cross, half-moon, crossed gavels, baton, 5 point star, crossed quill pans, crossed wands, burning torch, and – perhaps most familiar, and most beloved by even non-Odd Fellows – a hand with heart in palm. The women's Rebekah degree of Odd Fellows uses a beehive, a dove, a moon and seven stars, a lily, and an image of Rebecca at the well. • **Knights Templar** belong to an order of knights founded during the Second Crusade about 1118, but thought by some to date back even further. In the U.S., members of some Masonic orders are called Knights Templar. The Knights use a paschal (Passover or Easter) lamb with a banner, a Maltese cross – with four equal arms that look like stylized arrowheads pointing to center, another cross with long vertical member, triangles, coffins, tents, etc. • **Other fraternal**, and "benevolent" orders include Shriners, Woodmen of America, Improved Order of Red Men, Knights of Pythias, Knights of Maccabees, Knights of the Orient, ... of Malta, ... of the Red Cross.

Butter stamp, name in very nice serif lettering around border, oval sunburst design in center, carved wood, reads "G. Haughton" & "A. Southington," New England (?), oval 5"L x 3-1/2"W, 19th C., prob. 2nd to 3rd quarter. • $325 at Garth Auction, May-5/6, 1989, Delaware, OH. Hard to explain price unless buyer had a Haughton or Southington connection.............. **$300+**

Butter stamp, name & legend around edge, geometric design in center, carved wood with knob handle, "J. CARRINGTON PAVE CASTEL," 5-1/8" diam., early 19th C. (?). • This was offered by collector & dealer Teri Dziadul of Enfield, CT, in early 1980s. Anything with a name I try to include, even if I've not seen it, because by having this all on computer I can cross reference, or at least look things up. The only other J. Carrington in my records is James Carrington, of Wallingford, CT, who patented a coffee mill in 1829. Right age, so possibly same man.................. **$350+**

Butter stamp, palm tree with stars & little amoebic odds & ends floating in sky, hand carved wood, large slightly concave (warped?) disc with short all-in-one knob on back, very unusual stylized design, dark patina, American, prob. PA, 5" diam., mid 19th C.................. **$300+**

IV-36-A. Butter stamp. *Leaping hare or rabbit, with log & grass. Very unusual and one of my personal favorites of all I've seen. Here's where subjective personal taste comes in to affect value; I might pay more for this rabbit than someone else would pay to get a prized cow – simply because I know what I like and I'll pay what I think something's worth to me. 19th C. Collection & photograph James E. Trice.* **$600**

❖ **NOTES** ❖

Palms & Xmas Trees – Christians have two sacred trees, palms and evergreens. Palms generally symbolize the birthplace of Christ; specifically His entry into Jerusalem on Palm Sunday. Criss-cross. If you always thought that "Xmas" was a slangy and improper way to write "Christmas," you'll be relieved to know that it is

IV-36-B. Butter stamp. *Very unusual big-footed baby armadillo or tortoise on demilune stamp. Notched border. A fancy carved handle seems out-of-sync with mold. 6-1/4"L, age hard to judge because style is old, but subject is perhaps unique. Courtesy Bonnie Myers, B & J's Unclaimed Treasures, Dillsburg, PA. Probably one of a kind.* **$500+**

many hundreds of years old, the X standing for "crisscross" or Christ's cross. I wonder if the common early decorative use of an X (often between straight lines above and below like a Roman numeral), wasn't used (especially by blacksmiths with their chisels and files) to signify a criss-cross, a sort of secularly-awarded religious blessing on the object. Taking this idea further, the lines may represent heaven and earth. The mark is found, sometimes in multiples, on many 17th, 18th and early 19th C. forged iron and carved wood utilitarian objects. On the other hand, because decorating hot iron with a chisel or file was not the easiest thing to do, it is possible that an X and some straight lines was just the easiest form of decoration.

Butter stamp, pineapple on a demilune stamp, turned knob handle on back, American, 7"W, mid 19th C. .... **$200+**

Butter stamp, pineapple with geometric border design, fairly crudely-carved thick pine (a nice soft wood for amateurs to attack!), with no handle, American, 19th C. (According to Mary Earle Gould's woodenware book, these handleless stamps were cookie stamps, while ones with handles were for butter. Do you think this is true?)................................. **$100+**

Butter stamp, rooster with leaves on branch, in mid crow, lathe-turned blank, screw-in handle, craftsman-shop production, nicely & competently carved wood, with simple corrugated border design, American, 3-1/2" diam., 19th C. .... **$275+**

IV-37. Butter stamp. *Elongated oval with heart & flowers, thickly carved wood. 6"L. Ephrata Cloister provenance, Pennsylvania. While appearance is somewhat crude, & design not so pleasing as certain eccentric animals, provenance & obvious PA-Dutch design add value. Photo courtesy Litchfield Auction Gallery. Ex-Harold Corbin Collection, auctioned Jan. 1, 1990, $700. Here double provenance – Ephrata Cloister & Corbin – prob. affected sale price.* **$500**

IV-38. Butter stamp. *Sitting squirrel, with nut in paw. Unusual zigzag or sawtooth border. Squirrels are a popular motif for nutcrackers, but are unusual in butter stamps. Courtesy Joe & Teri Dziadul.* **$1000**

IV-39. Butter stamp. *Demilune (literally "half moon"), carved wood with pineapple & leaves. Rope border on curve only, meaning it could be used to create a round print, without a line across center, which would mark off half-pound division. 7"W, American, 19th C.* **$550+**

Butter stamp, rose, thistle, & 3 leaf clover, single pat size, 3 finely carved designs, only 1-3/4" diam., 19th C. .... **$90+**

Butter stamp, strawberries, 2 wild ones with viney leaves, deeply carved, American, 1-1/2" diam., 19th C. .... **$85+**

Butter stamp, tulips, 3 of them with stars, hand carved wood, marked on handle "C. I.," with date, PA (?), 3-1/4" diam., dated 1827. .... **$400+**

Butter stamp & butter paddle combined, cow & 2 acorns on stamp, one piece of wood, hand carved, American, paddle is 14"L overall, stamp is 4" diam., 19th C. .... **$900+**

IV-40. Butter stamp. *Eagle stamps are among the most sought-after designs. This eagle, with odd baby-bird liplike beak, resembles Carvings by Schimmel. It is unclear if there is a clutch of arrows. And it's possible there are a couple of stars – or are those marks claws? Collection & photograph of James E. Trice.* **$600-$750+**

IV-43. Butter stamps. *Acorn motifs. Very beautiful carving & designs, but acorns are not accorded the high value placed on them by squirrels. These look like the carving stands up on the surface, but it's just a trick of light; they are carved down into the face plate. Note lathe marks on background of lower stamp. Courtesy James E. Trice.* **$125-$175**

IV-41. Butter stamps. *All eagle & shield motif, finely carved. One, 3-5/8" diam., is mounted on old paddle board – probably not a new mount; circular lines seen in photo are a clue to some extra use or technique of use. Or it might have been used as a lid for a crock of butter, making it easy to mold just before using. The one with shield body (left) is 4-3/4" diam.; other is 3-3/4". 19th C. Picture courtesy of Christie, Manson & Woods International Inc., NYC, from 1980 Brooke sale.* **Reproduction alert:** *This motif was reproduced in the 1960s; look for fine grained old wood, realistic patina, even age cracks to see if your mold is old.* **$700**

IV-44. Butter stamp. *Flower with curious curved verte-braeic stem, rope border. Courtesy James E. Trice.* **$200**

IV-42. Butter stamps. *All eagle designs, with handles.* **(L)** *Tulip-like bird is considered by many to actually be a dove. Others are known, and most have a crack in from the edge. Graceful leaf-like wings, crosshatched body, narrow piecrust border, a single star. 4-1/4" diam.* **(M)** *Eagle facing left, with shield body, long neck, flanked by laurel [?] leaves. Not an uncommon carving, but very appealing. Lathe-turned concentric 5-ring border, 5" diam.* **(R)** *Eagle & large 8-pt star, leaves. 3-3/4" diam. Photo courtesy Litchfield Auction Gallery. Ex-Harold Corbin Collection, auctioned Jan. 1, 1990.* **(L) $450-$550 (M) $200-$250 (R) $450-$550**

IV-45. Butter stamp. *Rayed flower with dandelion-like leaves. Courtesy James E. Trice.* **$75-$100**

IV-46. Butter stamps, so-called **lollipop style.** Simple geometric carvings from single pieces of wood. Probably Pennsylvania German, early 19th C. Photograph & collection of James E. Trice. **(T) $600; (B) $400**

IV-47. Butter stamp "hand stamp." "Fancy Butter" packages are, of course, of many forms, as each maker wishes his butter to be both attractive & unique. All '**print-butter**,' or butter in small packages marked with the name of the maker, is properly regarded as fancy, whether it brings a higher price than other good butter or not. Still, it ought to be good

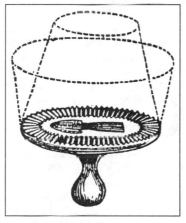

enough to sell higher than good **tub or firkin butter.** Philadelphia has long been famous for its excellent print-butter. This is generally put up upon common hand stamps in pound '**pats**,' which may have either of the two forms represented by dotted lines. Simple devices, such as a sheaf of wheat, roses, pineapples, acorns, & oak leaves & nondescript leaves are common. Monograms or single letters are not rare, with occasionally a more elaborate device.

These 'pats,' for they are patted into form upon the stamps [with a butter spade or paddle], are marketed in what are known as **Philadelphia tubs,** which are oval tubs of cedar, lined with tin, & having ice chambers in each end, having a nearly rectangular space in the center, in which the butter is packed upon shelves 2-1/4" to 3" apart. A good deal of butter is now made in rectangular, square or brick-shaped prints, & shipped in these Philadelphia tubs, or in square packages, with provision for ice in hot weather." The article goes on to extol **round butter boxes** that are made by an "ingenious application of the new kind of veneering, cut in a continuous ribbon round & round the log" & then sewing the ribbons of wood at a seam. American Agriculturist, Jan. 1880. Ultimately, price depends on appeal & quality of carving – even for these mass-produced dairy pieces. **$95+**

IV-48. Butter stamp. Hand carved from one piece, with unusual handle. Zinnia-like flower with leaves. 5-1/4"H x 4-3/8" diam. 19th C. Courtesy Joe & Teri Dziadul. **$400-$600**

Butter stamp & paddle combined, star with 6 points on stamp, carved of one piece of wood, with a small shaped shovel scoop or paddle at one end, & other end of "handle" widens out to a large disc, size of child's sand shovel, PA German(?), 9-1/2"L overall, with stamp 2-7/8" diam., 1850s-1900.......... **$600+**

Butter stamp & pastry jagger combined, cow, with wheel of jagger making leaf design, very unusual, PA German (?), 5-1/8"L overall, stamp is only 1-5/8" diam., mid to 4th quarter 19th C.................. **$700+**

❖ RECIPE ❖

Mushroom Biscuits – 8 oz. of butter, and 3 lb. 8 oz. of fine flour. Rub the butter and flour together, and mix them into a stiff paste with water; it must be made very smooth and fine; then make it into biscuits, about two ounces each; to be made round, and stamped in the middle with a butter print; prick them in the hollow with a fork to prevent blistering; bake them on iron plates in a good oven." Joseph Bell, A Treatise on Confectionary. Newcastle, England, 1817.

❖ NOTES ❖

Cake Boards & Marzipan Boards – Cake board listings and cake and marzipan board listings are together, with the somewhat similar springerle mold listings separate under the "S" listings further on in this chapter. Probably all, as well as some butter stamps, and intaglio cast iron or pewter molds, could be used for thin, fine-textured cookies using lots of super-fine sugar, such as "New Year's Cakes," speculas, gingerbread figures, as well as the fine-textured marzipan. Molds were used by applying the mold to rolled-out, slightly dried paste or dough, or by rolling dough onto a mold (if it was small) and carefully peeling it off.

Collector market for cake or marzipan boards, carved of wood in European style (even if some motifs were specifically American, such as George Washington, Columbia, and Indians) is strong – they are among the most expensive kitchen antiques – and a fairly new field of specialty. Folk art collectors have joined in since the identification of one 19th century master carver who practiced his craft in New York City – John Conger. Dealers of old American "folk art" and furniture have embraced the beautiful carved boards of Conger and others and featured them in full page ads in collector publications. According to food historian William Woys Weaver, Conger laid "out his design with a compass and trace[d] off patterns from his set repertoire," which to my mind means they are craft not art; but then, I don't call pattern quilts or pattern molded weather vanes folk art either. Be that as it may, it's in the interest of dealers and investment collectors to claim all well-carved boards as Conger's, but also to be wary of offering too many of them. Many unmarked carved boards have been attributed to Conger, especially after prices went above three or four thousand dollars! And many sellers take the imprinted housewares dealer's

IV-50. Butter stamp. *This was described by the auction house as being a "highly stylized eagle." The resemblance to an anchor is much greater. 3-1/2" diam., American, mid 19th C. Picture courtesy Robert W. Skinner Inc., Auctioneers, Bolton, MA.* **$250+**

IV-49. Butter stamp or mold-making at home! *"In reply to readers who say they can not procure the butter molds which we described in a former issue, we give directions for making them at home. The difficulty lies in getting the stamp made. Any one who can work a foot lathe, can turn the mold & the plain stamp with the handle, but the device which ornaments the stamp troubles them. To make this, take a piece of wood free from grain – a piece of soft maple or birch-root is very good – & have it turned or dressed the proper size, & a smooth face made on it. Then either draw on the face, the wrong way, or cut out letters from a printed bill or newspaper, & paste them on to the face of the mold, the wrong way, & make a border to suit the fancy, in the same manner. Then take a small, sharp gouge, like the one shown, not larger than a quarter of an inch in diameter, & smoothly cut away the wood beneath the letters, making them deep enough to show well when printed on the butter. About a quarter of an inch would be right. The depression should be neatly smoothed out, so as to make a neat, smooth print. A pretty border for the mold is a quantity of clover leaves; they may be pasted on, & the wood then cut out as before, or any other leaves would answer."* American Agriculturist, *Dec. 1872.*

name, J. Y. Watkins, as proof that Conger actually carved that mold. It is believed that Watkins not only kept on selling Conger's old stock, but that new molds were made with Conger's patterns at least until 1900. I have listed the signed and attributed and related cake boards first, then the others, no matter how old. This list is only up to 1996.

• • •

James Y. Watkins – Watkins was in business as a tinsmith in NYC, and listed in city directories beginning in 1830. His son, James Y., Jr., joined the firm in 1852 (or at least "and Son" was added to the firm's name in the *1852-53 Rode's Directory*). James Y. Watkins & Son, Inc., were listed variously as house furnishings or tinware dealers, who by 1866 were listed as dealing in "house furnishings and bakers' utensils." According to one note I've seen recently, Watkins also "made" ice cream molds; but I suspect they imported ice cream molds. The cake or marzipan boards marked with Watkins' stamp are carved with early traditional motifs and in an early style, but we don't know now how many could have been made by John Conger, or by an American or European imitator of his work.

• • •

Fakes & Frauds Bulletin – By the early 1990s the Conger touchmark, a stamped intaglio mark was "being counterfeited," according to William Woys Weaver.

• • •

New Cake Boards – With container load imports, particularly from cookie countries in Scandinavia, and with the continuing appeal of emmerlinguistication (or recountrification) in America, you will see lots of carved cake or cookie boards, many with equestrian figures, flowers in baskets, roosters, cats, pigs, etc. • Dark brown Min-Wax™ coloration, unsubtle gouges to "age" the board, and a thickness conforming to modern mill practices (often-7/8"), and the use of pine are strong clues to modern work.

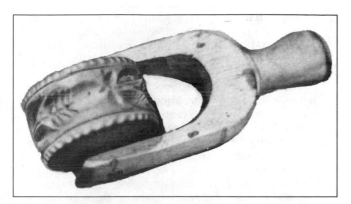

IV-51. Rolling butter printer. *Simple botanical motif & border. 5-1/2"L. Courtesy R. C. Bowen. See IV- of cookie roller which is quite similar – perhaps interchangeable functions.* **$150-$200**

• • •

Lookalike alarm & repros – The most commonly found images on carved wood cookie molds are single figures in peasant or old military costume. Many are reproductions, but in the strictest sense, most are just lookalikes "in the style of." A 1967 ad in McCall's Needlework & Crafts magazine, has photos of two long skinny boards, one carved with a man and woman, arms akimbo, both standing on little tufts of ground; the other with five images including a basket, bird and branch, windmill, and two that can't be identified. The ad reads: "Dutch Cookie Molds sent directly from Holland with foreign stamps. All the charm of old Holland is captured in these charming hand-carved cookie molds. It's a double Dutch treat for not only are they the most enchanting decorations for anywhere in the house, but they make the most delightful cookies, including farmer and wife, windmills, baskets, etc. (Recipe and history of boards included.) They will make a cherished and unique gift for every woman on your Christmas list. Antique brown elm wood, 15-1/2" x 2-1/4". $3 ea. 2 for $5.50. 4 for $10." Brochure of Cookie Mold Collection 10¢. I have no idea if they are still in business, but this company (probably but one of several that made these molds for export and for sale in Holland to tourists and housewives) was Holland Handicrafts, P.B. 74 Ridderkerk, Holland. This is a 1967 ad, so don't try to order from it!

IV-53. Twelfth-Day scene outside a Confectioner. *Probably similar to scene outside pastry shops in America for New Year's Cakes (see cake boards by Conger et al). This one in London. "From the taking down of the shutters in the morning, the pastrycook & his men, with additional assistants, male & female, are fully occupied by attending to the dressing out of the window, executing orders of the day before, receiving fresh ones, or supplying the wants of chance customers. Before dusk the important arrangement of the window is completed. Then the gas is turned on, with supernumerary argand-lamps & manifold wax-lights, to illuminate countless cakes of all prices & dimensions, that stand in rows & piles on the counters & sideboards, & in the windows. The richest in flavour & heaviest in weight & price are placed on large & massy salvers; one, enormously superior to the rest in size, is the chief object of curiosity; & all are decorated with all imaginable images of things animate & inanimate. Stars, castles, kings, cottages, dragons, trees, fish, palaces, cats, dogs, churches, lions, milkmaids, knights, serpents, & innumerable other forms in snow-white confectionary, painted with variegated colours, glitter by 'excess of light' from mirrors against the walls. This 'paradise' of dainty devices is crowded by successive desirers of the seasonable delicacies. William Hone, Every-Day Book, Vol. I. London: [1825-26]. The scene above with disconcerted customers pinned together by their fronts, illustrates the typical London boys' Twelfth-night tricks of nailing gentleman's coats to the door frame, or pinning stranger ladies & gents together. See also Yule dough in index.*

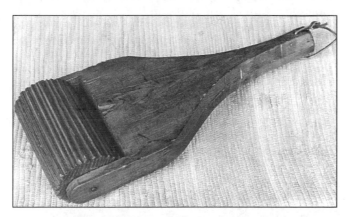

IV-52. Whatsit butter worker? cracker crumber? pastry roller? *It seems much too large for a coggling tool used by a potter to make a corrugated design onto damp clay. Hand-carved wood with roller, 17-3/4"L; roller 3-1/2" diam.; paddle-handle is 1-3/4" thick. Courtesy Alice Solomon, Schnectady, NY.* **$150-$200**

Confections Made in These Cake Boards – Marzipan, Marchpane, Massepain, or Matzabaum.

The words are, respectively, German, English, French, and Pennsylvania German. Marzipan is sort of a cross between a cookie and a candy, is always very sweet, and always has two main ingredients: confectioner's (or finely pounded) sugar and almond paste, made from ground (or pounded in a mortar) blanched almonds. A typical recipe would call for one pound of confectioner's sugar, one pound almond paste, and a little rosewater (which I assume you can buy in some specialty shop, rather than distilling it in an alembic yourself) to make the sugar and almonds into a paste, which can be molded. New recipes sometimes call for a teaspoon of almond extract. The almond paste was originally made by pounding almonds into a paste in a mortar with lots of sugar and some rosewater to sort of emulsify it to keep it from "oiling," but it's now made much more easily in a food processor – or even bought already made in specialty shops. Today, we think of marzipan as a highly colored, figural sweet in folky designs, wrapped in paper or foil. The coloring was mixed into the paste or painted on after the confection was formed. Marzipan was worked with fingers or small shaping tools like sculptors' tools, or stamped with a carved mold, or rolled with a rolling pin or pressed into intaglio carved molds such as cake boards, as well as springerle molds and butter stamps – and afterward air dried, or very lightly browned in a very slow oven. Leaving them in the oven a little bit longer results in a really wonderful toasted marchpane. • In Eliza Leslie's *Directions for Cookery*, 1848 edition, is a recipe for Almond Maccaroons, sounding very like a marzipan recipe. The recipe is reproduced in with Cake pans a little further on in this chapter.

• • •

Water marzipan – According to William Woys Weaver, marzipan molds were for New Year's Cake, a tradition borrowed from Germany, and were used to make a so-called "water marzipan" which was a less expensive non-almond version of the real thing (p.116, *America Eats*). Sugar wasn't so cheap that the mere omission of almonds could make New Year's Cake affordable for the masses.

❖ **RECIPE** ❖

New-Year's Cake – *Seven pounds of flour, sifted. Half a pound of butter. Half a pound of lard. Two pounds and a half of white Havanna sugar. – Having sifted the flour, spread the sugar on the paste-board, a little at a time, and crush it to powder by* rolling it with the rolling-pin. Then mix it with the flour. Cut up in the flour the butter and lard, and mix it well by rubbing it in with your hands. Add by degrees enough of cold water to make a stiff dough, then knead the dough very hard, till it no longer sticks to your hands. Cover it, set it away for an hour or two, and then knead it again in the same manner. You may repeat the kneading several times. Then cut it into pieces, roll out each piece into a sheet half an inch thick. Cut it into large flat cakes with a tin cutter. You may stamp each cake with a wooden print, by way of ornamenting the surface. "Sprinkle with flour some large flat tin or iron pans, lay the cakes in them, and bake them of a pale brown, in an oven of equal heat throughout. These cakes require more and harder kneading than any others, therefore it is best to have them kneaded by a man, or a very strong woman. They are greatly improved by the addition of some carraway seeds worked into the dough." Miss Leslie, of Philadelphia,* Seventy-Five Receipts for Pastry, Cakes, and Sweetmeats. Appended to The Cook's Own Book & Housekeeper's Register. By a Boston Housekeeper. *Boston: Munroe & Francis, 1833. Eliza Leslie, in the 31st edition of her* Directions for Cookery, *published 1848, gives a recipe for* "**New York Cookies**," *which she says are similar to New Year's Cakes. She describes the finishing and decorating process thusly: "...Take the lump of dough out of the pan, and knead it on the paste-board till it becomes quite light. Then roll it out rather more than half an inch thick, and cut it into square cakes with a jagging iron or with a sharp knife. Stamp the surface of each with a cake print. Lay them in buttered pans, and bake them of a light brown in a brisk oven."*

Marzipan For Christmas – Springerle For Easter – Jean Lipman, in *American Folk Art in Wood, Metal & Stone* (NY: Pantheon, 1948), wrote briefly about "carved marzipan and springerle cake molds [that] made it possible for thin Christmas and Easter cakes to be stamped in low-relief designs. The hard-wood springerle boards were carved intaglio, most often in composite groups of two to twelve patterns enclosed in separate squares, to mark the cutting lines for small individual cakes; while the marzipan boards were often designed for a single large cake. ... The finished cakes could be kept for months and, though they were so hard that it has been said it was as easy to eat the board as the cake, they were evidently a popular delicacy." (p.144)

CATCHING JOHN CONGER

Carver John Conger (probably pronounced kon'ger, with a hard "g," like the eel), was elusive for a long time, with nothing about him in standard books on folk art carvers. Most dealers advertising a signed Conger cake board, or an attributed board, said "New York State." An occasional rebel would say "Probably Pennsylvania." For all the information I was able to get, I can thank my computer (with its cross-referencing capabilities), and the wonderful microfiche collection of New York City directories at the New York Public Library, a favorite and fruitful haunt of mine while I was lucky enough to live in NYC.

When I started investigating Conger in 1990, my first lead came in an ad for a mold which was marked both "J. Conger" and "James Y. Watkins, NYC." At least this placed Conger in New York. I found my second lead in *Folk Artists Biographical Index*, edited by George H. Meyer. He cited mentions of Conger in Pauline A. Pinckney's *American Figureheads & Their Carvers* (NYC: W. W. Norton, 1940), and in Kenneth L. Ames' excellent *Beyond Necessity. Art in the Folk Tradition.* (Exhibition catalog, published by Winterthur Museum, Winterthur, DE, 1977). Pinckney's book, on a subject I had already superficially researched in hopes of finding Conger, has a lengthy list of shipcarvers and possible shipcarvers, a list on which John Conger appears with a "flourished" date of 1830. ("Flourished" is used by art historians when only one date or a very narrow range of dates is known for sure. If a piece known to be by the artist in question has a date – that becomes the "flourished" date. It implies that that single date falls somewhere within the full range of dates the artist/artisan is believed to have worked. No way of knowing if the date falls at the end, the beginning, or the middle of the supposed range.) In Conger's case, the date 1830 falls very close to the beginning of his almost 40-year NYC career. The directories I later consulted all included both "carvers" and "shipcarvers" and from that I concluded that Conger did not describe himself as a shipcarver, and was probably not one. On the other hand, *Beyond Necessity* confirmed the Watkins lead given by a 1970s ad for an attributed Conger board was marked with Watkins' name only.

Catalog item 143 in the Winterthur exhibition, was a cake board stamped "J. Conger," as well as "J. Y. Watkins, N.Y." It is in the Winterthur collection, acquisition #55.48.60. Watkins is described as a "tinsmith and owner of a kitchen furnishing warehouse," and Conger as a "carver and baker." The most recent work on Conger was done by Louise C. Belden, a research associate at the Henry Francis du Pont Winterthur Museum, Winterthur, DE. Her excellent article, "Cake Boards," in *The magazine ANTIQUES*, December 1990, depicts many Conger boards and related cake boards. Earlier, food historian William Woys Weaver wrote an article in *The Clarion*, the magazine of the Museum of American Folk Art, in New York City. It is "The New Year's Cake Print. A Distinctively American Art Form," (Fall 1989). (He later organized an exhibit for the museum.) He also researched Conger for an exhibition, and an accompanying cookbook and history, entitled *America Eats. Forms of Edible Folk Art.* (Harper & Row, 1989.) Weaver wrote that Conger used "stock motifs" (which would include cornucopias, low baskets or urns of flowers or produce, Indians, Revolutionary War soldiers, garlands of flowers or fruit, militia men on horseback, ladies and gentlemen in faux rusticant garb (à la Marie Antoinette playing dairymaid), eagles, roses, thistles, Scottish folk, and other romantic, even then old-fashioned, designs.

I received a letter from a descendant of John Conger in 1995, enclosing a photocopied page from the Conger Family geneology. From it we learn that John Conger was born October 8, 1803 in Norwich, Connecticut, where he was married in 1837 to Caroline B. Mingus. Their first child was Walter Mingus Conger, born in August 1838. From the directories I used to research the chronology that follows, it is not absolutely clear, but it seems probable that John traveled the relatively short distance to Manhattan's lower east side at about age 23 or 24 and became a carver (or perhaps an apprentice?). Then, from 1833 to 1836, it is possible that he returned to Norwich, where he met and wed Caroline Mingus, his junior by 15 years, and then the pair went back to New York City. They had four children (two survived), none named John. John Conger, master carver, died January 27, 1869, aged 65.

In constructing the following dramatization of Conger's New York City in the late 1820s and 1830s, one of the most readable, useful, and absorbing books that I consulted was Sean Wilentz's *Chants Democratic. New York City and the Rise of the American Working Class, 1788-1850.* It was published by Oxford University Press, 1984, and in paperback, with corrections, in 1986. Wilentz's book provided some of the wage figures relating to carvers, and the characterization of many Reverends of the period.

Thanksgiving week, 1989, I spent mostly in the lofty embrace of reading room 315 North in the New York Public Library, a room whose virtues I have extolled in previous books. I huddled over a microfiche machine, peering at a bright screen, to skim-read hundreds of thousands of names in NYC directories from 1815-16 through 1873-74. This collection of directories, which could be the primary source book behind a thousand books on the social history of NYC, on early trades, on the plight of widow women in the 19th century and a host of other subjects, includes the first published NYC directory, from 1799.

I not only tracked Conger through the years, but also James Y. Watkins, and a few makers of andirons, grates, stoves, and other things of interest. Time constraints forced me to stop when the object of my main search – John Conger – had been gone from the directory for three years. Watkins, and one or more of his sons, were still listed, and that is a subject which I invite anyone who wants to to pursue. William Woys Weaver, in the two publications cited above, was apparently a year ahead of me in his research into Conger & Watkins, and confectionery in America. I read in *America Eats* that Conger was not only a carver, but also a baker (making his own New Year's cakes in his own molds), and that the Watkins firm "remained in business into this century" *op* cit, p.116, and until "at least 1900" "was responsible for the continued manufacture of Conger designs." *loc* cit. Weaver also states that Conger worked in Philadelphia "for a time as a furniture carver." *op* cit, p.115, but I don't know when that was, as he was set up in NYC by the age of 24. "Why?" is a good question to ask re: whether Conger would have carved furniture in Philadelphia.

Below, with a few side trips, is my skeletal charted chronology of John Conger, based solely on the city and business directories available through a microfiche collection, and not on any census records, jury lists, or other valuable, supplementary primary sources also on microfiche and available at NYPL, nor on the research of William Woys Weaver, who came to the conclusion that Conger worked (or flourished) only between 1827 and 1835, the restrictive dates cited in an earlier reference. This tantalizingly vast microfiche collection is also at the Library of Congress, and a number of large metropolitan libraries throughout the country. If you've got about $5,000 you can buy a set of directory microfiches yourself.

The name John Conger appeared first in the 1818-19 *Longworth's Directory*, but he was an edge tool manufacturer who stayed in the directory for the next 32 years, and was then replaced by his son or son-in-law, who was called either John Conger Berry or John Congerberry. In the 1819-20 book, a John Conger, carpenter at 5 Provost Street, appeared, but he disappeared the next year. Using the directories only, it is impossible to determine if perhaps these two wood-related artisans were related – to each other, and/or to our Conger. After one appearance, the carpenter's alphabetical place was "taken" by the long-lived John S. Conger, physician, who stayed in the directory for many decades. The edge tool maker and the doctor appeared year after year as the only John Congers until suddenly, in *Longworth's* 1827-28 book, we find him, our man:

John Conger, carver, 121 Hester St., New York City. – 121 Hester Street, at the corner of Forsythe, was six long blocks below Houston Street, and only two short blocks east of the Bowery (where even today there are wholesale restaurant supply houses). It wasn't that far from some of the prettiest parts of lower Manhattan, a city then of about 175,000 people. Conger lived – probably as a boarder, or at least a space-sharer – at the corner of Forsythe and Hester, according to what was termed a "Runners' *Vade Mecum*," an address finder or guide which appeared every year in the directories. This guide was to help people locate addresses on streets which were not that infrequently renumbered, or even renamed, as the city grew and the centers of population expanded northward. According to "The Fireman's Guide" of 1834, which was a map of the city from the Battery up to 22nd Street, and from the piers and slips of the East River across to those of the North River, there was a firehouse a couple of blocks away, and plenty of hydrants within two or three. So probably Conger and his neighbors felt somewhat protected from fire. A terrible fire had raged through the area, stopping just two blocks away from 121 Hester, in 1832.

Having become somewhat obsessed with the directories, and the glimpse of life in the city where I lived for a quarter of a century myself, and knowing Hester Street just a little from the 1975 movie "Hester Street," set at the turn of the century, I made my first side trip: a short list of other occupants of the street, within a block or so of Conger. Next door at 123 Hester, for example, lived the Reverand John W. Gibbs, a man who may or may not have had a congregation in a church. His calling was not common at that time and in that area of New York, where self-styled preachers and irreligious laborers were much more easily found. Across the street at 120 Hester lived Jacob Bolmore – no occupation given in the 1827-28 directory. In the next year's directory, Benedict Bolmore, printer, was listed at 120, with Jacob as a clerk at the same address. Also the next year, although John Conger had moved on to 1 Hamersley, and carried on his business on Sullivan Street, J. D. P. Champlin & Co., business unknown, stayed on at 121 Hester, where, under some arrangement, they had shared a roof with Conger.

It is tempting to docu-dramatize Conger's place in the city-life of the time, but there is no evidence, beyond the baldest, on which to base speculations. Drama requires a protagonist (here we have Conger), and people, places, things, or social forces against which there is some kind of struggle. If a movie were made of his life, we'd have to know more about his family life, who his clients were,

his friends, exactly what characterized what we assume was his struggle to leave Hester Street. We don't know if the man ever had more than a few minutes a day to leave his work, or if he frequented one or more of the numerous porter houses or taverns, or if it took him four anxious days or a week to finish a cake board, or what else he might have spent most of his time carving. But just to indicate who his "neighbors" were, we will imagine that Conger might have stepped out the doorway of 121 to turn right, cross Forsythe, and go a few doors to see John G. Hughes, a carpenter at 113, about some mahogany or walnut wood scraps. If he went on a few more doors, maybe he encountered the whitesmith, Peter C. Cortelyou, at 110; he may have bought an apple from John Lyon, the grocer at 93; or stopped to talk to Clarissa Adams, the widow who ran a boarding house at 87, about a room; or perhaps he needed to ask David Coit, shoemaker, at 73 Hester, about fixing the only boots he had.

If he turned left when he left his abode (which was also his workplace that first year in the directory, and which may have housed several home-work artisans, or other workers), maybe he saw Thomas Gedney, the comb-maker who lived and worked at 132 Hester. Or Stephen Lockwood, whose occupation was not listed, also at 132. (Next year, the clock-manufacturer and brass founder Engell Friend also lived at 132.) Margaret Wilcox, a carpet weaver at 140, was possibly working in the cellar, trying to make the $2 or $3 a week she needed for the most frugal living, and because she was not listed as a widow, it is likely she was pretty much on her own.

Did John Conger, in fact, know any of these people the year he lived on Hester? We know he carved fancy cakeboards with formal, traditional European images of militia men and bounteous flowers; but was he doing them this early? Where would he have gotten his inspiration? Did he, in fact, come to NYC after going from his birthplace in Connecticut to live in Philadelphia? If he spent a short time in Pennsylvania, where a European folk tradition was beginning to flourish, and where many carvings and graphics comprised similar motifs, maybe his work was influenced by them. The prosaic, not to say squalid, images surrounding him in everyday life in NYC seem not to have influenced his work at all, except perhaps to make him work harder to get out. Not that there were many "good" neighborhoods at the time in NYC; only wealthy merchants and bankers lived somewhat within their own enclaves, down around Wall Street, where there were fancy retail shops as well as banking and insurance institutions.

In the area way below what is now called the "Lower East Side" – where Conger (and later with his wife Caroline) lived throughout his approximately four decades in the city – also lived most of the day laborers, jobless, and desperately poor people of New York. Pigs wandered the streets in the daytime, actually performing a sort of service by eating garbage, but creating a nuisance of more than one kind on the pavement. Hundreds of cartmen clogged the streets, pushing wooden wheelbarrows or hand barrows, or pulling hand carts, laden with whatever had to be transferred, hoping to pick up a job that would bring them from 12-1/2¢ to 25¢ a half mile (about 10 blocks). The noise must have been close to deafening – from the squealing of pigs, the crying of children, the shouts of people selling services or food, the clang and crash of hammers beating on everything from gold (to make foil), steel (to make tools), brass (to make vessels or trims or decorations), nails or pegs (to make shoes), iron nails and wooden boards (to make houses, coffins, more carts, barrels, ships), or chisels (to make carvings), the rattle of looms, and the clatter of horse-shoes and cartwheels on cobblestones.

By the next year, 1828, probably on May 1 (traditional moving day in NYC for 100 years or more, because all annual leases, as well as the quarter spring leases, were up that day), Conger had moved and was doing well enough, we suppose, to have a workplace separate from his home. It would still be nine years before he married.

There was a lot of competition in the carving trade. Although the directories do not make much differentiation between the types of carvers, a computer study of addresses of all carvers, as well as the carver-gilders, along with the addresses of cabinet makers, chair makers, and frame and furniture makers, would probably tie together some of the unknown craftsmen. Men with the dual trade of carving and gilding often worked on picture or looking-glass frames; a very few probably carved trade-signs (some of which may have been free-standing figures such as cigar store Indians). In the 1827-28 Longworth's Directory, simple carvers were apparently slightly in the majority; shipcarvers were the rarest of all the carvers.

One interesting entry I found was William Alcock, "calico-print cutter," at 8 Watts St. Later I was glad to have found him and his job description, when – after three years missing from the directory [see below] – John Conger (I believe the same one as our man) reappears as a "printcutter." Cake boards, for printing New-Year's Cakes, were widely known as cake prints. The job description "printcutter" may have referred specifically to cake prints, or it may mean than John Conger also made carved wooden printing blocks, either for a cloth-printer or a publisher – of books, broadsides, or perhaps even wallpaper.

The main publishers of the directories I used were Thomas Longworth (Longworth's Annual Almanac. New-York Register & City Directory); John Doggett, later John Doggett, Jr., later Doggett & Rode, still later Rode alone (Doggett's The New York Directory or Doggett's New York Business Directory; later Rode's Directory of New York City); and John F. Trow, compiler H. Wilson (Wilson's Business Directory of New York City, later Trow's New York City Directory).

All addresses are streets except where noted. An occasional skipped date indicates a break in the city directories not absence of listing.

DATE	NAME	OCCUPATION	WORK – ADDRESSES – HOME	
1827-28	John Conger	carver	121 Hester	121 Hester
1828-29	John Conger	carver	65 Sullivan	1 Hamersley
1829-30	John Conger	carver	15 Stanton	29 Stanton
1830-31	John Conger	carver	15 Stanton	23 Stanton
1831-32	John Conger	carver	222 Greene	222 Greene
1832-33	John Conger	carver	242 Greene	117 Fourth Av.
1833-34	not listed	not listed	not listed	not listed
1834-35	not listed	not listed	not listed	not listed

For 1834-35 only, a John Conger, baker, appears.

DATE	NAME	OCCUPATION	WORK – ADDRESSES – HOME	
1835-36	not listed	not listed	not listed	not listed
1836-37	John Conger	printcutter	211 Orange	211 Orange
1837-38	John Conger	printcutter	211 Orange	211 Orange
1838-39	John Conger	printcutter	211 Orange	211 Orange
1839-40	not listed	not listed	not listed	not listed
1840-41	John Conger	print cutter	25 Marion	25 Marion
1841-42	John Conger	printcutter	25 Marion	25 Marion
1842-43	John Conger	printcutter	25 Marion	25 Marion
1843-44	John Conger	printcutter	23 Marion	23 Marion
1844-45	John Conger	printcutter	23 Marion	23 Marion
1845-46	John Conger	printcutter	23 Marion	23 Marion
1846-47	John Conger	printcutter	23 Marion	23 Marion

DATE	NAME	OCCUPATION	WORK – ADDRESSES – HOME	
1847-48	John Conger	printcutter	23 Marion	23 Marion
1848-49	John Conger	printcutter	foot of Bank St.	foot of Bank
1850-51	John Conger	printcutter	Bank	Bank
1851-52	John Conger	printcutter	Bank	Bank
1852-53	not listed	not listed	not listed	not listed
1854-55	John Conger	printcutter	181 Bank	101 Bank
1854-55	John Conger	carver	138 Bank	101 Bank

At this point, 1854-55, the new (or renewed) listing *John Conger carver* suddenly appears as does John Conger printcutter, both listings with same home address, but different work addresses. The only problem with this is that our John Conger is not known to have had a son named John, and at the time of the directory, had been married only 17 years; so is it likely a son would be set up in his own business at the age of most apprentices? Census records or other more detailed records that are probably available in New York or Washington D.C. on microfilm or fiche might help. This is the only year when two listings with the same name and related occupations are given. It is quite possible that the names are evidence of an error in information-gathering by the compiler of the directory (*Trow's*), or that one is father, one is son, and that one or the other (probably the printcutter, whom I assume was the elder) died that year. The listing resumes in 1856-57, when John Conger was 53 years old.:

DATE	NAME	OCCUPATION	WORK – ADDRESSES – HOME	
1856-57	John Conger	cutter	138 Bank	101 Bank
1857-58	John Conger	cutter	138 Bank	101 Bank
1858-59	John Conger	cutter	138 Bank	101 Bank
1859-60	John Conger	carver	138 Bank	not listed
1860-61	John Conger	carver	138 Bank	131 Bank
1861-62	John Conger	cutter	138 Bank	131 Bank
1862-63	John Conger	carver	525 Hudson	131 Bank
1863-64	John Conger	carver	525 Hudson	131 Bank
1864-65	John Conger	carver	not listed	131 Bank
1865-66	John Conger	carver	525 Hudson	131 Bank

In 1865, for one year only, a firm appears called Conger, Smith & Heath, Tin Ware & House Furnishing Goods, at 580 Hudson as well as 400, 402, and 404 W. 15th St. The Conger in question is Walter M. Conger, of unknown relationship to John Conger. It is interesting in more than one way because John Conger's carvings have been tied, by marks, to the house furnishing establishment of James Y. Watkins. By 1865, James Y. Watkins & Son, who, after years of having at least two business establishments, including the one at 16 Catharine Street where James Y. Watkins started his NYC business life as a tinsmith in 1830, is back to only one address – the place at 16 Catharine (or Catherine) Street, three or four long blocks south of Hester, where we believe the young Conger began his career.

DATE	NAME	OCCUPATION	WORK – ADDRESSES – HOME	
1866-67	John Conger	carver	214 W. Houston	

In the 1866-67 edition, Walter Conger shows up as a maker of trays.

DATE	NAME	OCCUPATION	WORK -- ADDRESSES – HOME	
1868-69	John Conger	carver	at the rear of 94 Charlton	
1870-71	not listed (deceased)	not listed	not listed	not listed

When John Conger was not listed in the next three directories, I assumed that he was now gone for good. It was a rather strange moment when I found him missing for four years. I had so avidly followed his progress (and apparent decline), making somewhat romantic assumptions about the rise and fall in fortune as his skill – his artistry – seem to have fallen out of favor, so that his last address was in the rear of a building not far from where he began 41 years earlier. Conger's disappearance from the directories was accompanied by a sense of real personal loss for me. It wasn't until a descendent wrote me in 1995 that I learned that John Conger, master carver, died in early 1869. James Y. Watkins and his son, who had been joined, for one year only, by another son, were still working out of 16 Catharine, but the elder was living at 450 Lexington, which was up between 44th and 45th Streets, and his son was making the daily commute down to Catherine from the increasingly fashionable, if rather bucolic, West 128th Street near Fifth Avenue.

There really is nothing like these directories to give you a sort of Wellesian time trip. It is ironic, as it often is when you consider the income of the artisan, and the market value of his work 50 or 100 or 200 years later, that the current market price of one really outstanding board carved by Conger is probably more than his total life income, and probably none of it came to his descendants. It is also possible that the date chart given here will cause a re-evaluation and a certain amount of back-pedaling on prices. Note: If it is correct, as William Woys Weaver writes, that Watkins bought Conger's old stock, and continued to sell either Conger or Conger-like prints until 1900, then surely the market value will drop somewhat.

IV-54. Cake board. Elliptical lozenge shape on oblong board, side-saddle equestrienne wearing a plaid or tartan fringed skirt, fitted jacket, & small riding hat, in center floral circle, flanked by small ellipses with Colonial man at left & an American Indian at right ends of the design. Delicate cornucopias fill in the curve below. John Conger's mark. Auctioned by Litchfield Auction Gallery. -3/25-1990. American, mid (?) 19th C. (Read Conger article, this chapter, for range of dates.) **$7,000+**

Cake boards – Conger signed, attributed or related:

Cake board, basket, round carving centered on rectangular walnut board, neat saw-tooth edge frames low basket, ribbed flared sides, a lively flower arrangement of roses, tulip, leaves, composition filled in with leaves under the basket, signed "J. Conger," catalog writer speculates "possibly PA," but provenance is actually NYC, NY. 15-1/4"L x 9-1/2"W, diam. of circle is about 6-3/4", 19th C. • Sold at Richard A. Bourne Co. (Hyannis, MA) auction of Cushman Estate of Duxbury, MA, November 25-26, 1988. Price realized...................... **$1,500. $3,500+**

Cake board, boy & girl, carved walnut (?), square with round medallion depicting a boy & girl & tulips, rather Dutch in feeling – not subject treatment expected from carver John Conger to whom the unsigned board was attributed by dealer. 11-1/2"H x 11"W, medallion about 7" diam., NYC (?), probably 1st two-thirds 19th C.............................. **$4,500+**

Cake board, Columbia, carved mahogany board, elliptical overall carving barely fits within oblong bounds, no separate medallions, gracefully draped Columbia figure, surrounded by laurel (olive?) wreath, holds striped shield with legend "America" at top; spread winged eagle holds arrows in foot, & scales of justice (left pan has trade symbols & barrels, right has plow, rake, pitchfork) in beak over backs of 2 horses; other figure is American Indian in plumed headdress & cape, holding staff with Old Glory flag with 16 stars, topped by a Phrygian cap or liberty cap (originated in French Revolution), further decorated with cornucopia full of fruit, many flowers, grapes, 10 large stars, sunflower, acorns, wheel, wheat, etc. An extraordinary unsigned board as fine as "J. Conger" boards, American, 27-1/4"L x 15-1/2"W, motifs circa 1800, carving possibly mid 19th C. • **Astronomical Ellipses.** – This double-pointed shape is often called "elliptical" in ads & descriptions. Technically, only an elliptical orbit, in astronomical terms, would have the apparently pointed ends; in geometry, an ellipse is what most of us call an oval. However, in these cake board descriptions I am using the astronomy meaning. • 16 Stars. – Although there was never a flag with 16 stars, the 16th state was Tennessee from 1786 to 1803. • This extraordinary mold was sold by John Zan, Washington, NJ, in 1979, & again at auction, by Sotheby's, June 23, 1988. Catalog has a good photograph (Lot 307). American patriotic motifs add value... **$15,000+**

Cake board, cornucopia & star, carved walnut, square with chamfered & truncated corners (probably to make room for a finger to tuck under to lift the mold off the dough), round carving. Design of 5 point star in center (unusual because only 5 points), flanked by cornucopia with flowers & fruit. Above is small shield flanked by busts of 2 Revolutionary War-period military men, one has "H" next to him, other has [backwards of course] "P." This may be a centennial or 50-year commemorative for the Battle of Bunker Hill of June 5, 1775, & "P" may be Colonel William Prescott, said to have commanded "Don't shoot until you see the whites of their eyes," & "H" may be the British commander, Major General William Howe. Also in the design is a sort of barge-like ship with a flag (possibly lying off in Boston harbor). A lacy finely-scalloped border surrounds a cartouche reading "M. Hall" below the ship. This could be the name of baker Michael Hall, who appeared at least as early as 1820 & as late as 1827-28 in NY directories. Board is American, probably NY, 12" x 12", c.1820s-30s. This politico-military cake board was in the Schorsch collection sale at Sotheby's, May 1-2, 1981. .... **$6,000+**

Cake board, dog, carved wood, rectangular, with elliptical carving, nice but simple, depicting a large St. Bernard dog being ridden by small bonneted child carrying whip stick, prognathious dog panting, & with tail awkwardly curved upwards, a single tulip growing up from teardrop chip carved border, nearly to dog's belly; figures surrounded by stems with many leaves & with 15 stars, somewhat haphazardly placed, the whole resembling Conger's work only in that there is a carved ellipse. Dealer's ad states

IV-56. Cake board. *Mahogany oblong board, design within ellipse. Many symbolic & patriotic motifs, including American Indian, holding a staff with American flag, topped with a Phrygian "liberty" cap, borne in cornucopia-shaped chariot, drawn by horse toward figure of Columbia, wearing flowing dress & holding a shield & laurel wreath aloft. The shield, with stars & stripes, is inscribed "America." Above is an American eagle with an olive branch in one talon & with a pair of balance scales in its beak, left one bearing small kegs or barrels, & right one with a plow, rake & pitchfork. Large cornucopia at left, many grapes, leaves, stars fill background. 15-1/2"H x 27-1/2"L. Typical in motif, though more fussily elaborate in execution than others known of John Conger's work. There's an almost art nouveau quality in the scrolling forms – from stems, flowers, the horse's trappings to the woman's drapery, & the busy decorativeness leads me to believe this postdates the 1870s.* **Unsigned but Conger attribution.** *Photo courtesy of Sotheby's, NYC. Auctioned June 23, 1988.* **$6,000-$8,000**

IV-55. Cake board. *Mahogany, elliptical carving typical of Conger's boards. Central round medallion has footed urn or fountain with 2 doves & many flowers. The fountain/urn is obviously drawn from elaborate cast iron urns & fountains from 2nd & 3rd quarters of 19th century, such as those made by another New Yorker, Jordan L. Mott. Flanking figures are a Colonial man* **(L)** *& a milkmaid-type woman in knee-length dress & apron* **(R).** *Typical cornucopias below, roses above. 15"H x 26"L. Used for making "New Year's Cakes." Signed* **"J. Congers"** *twice. New York City, 19th C. Photo courtesy Litchfield Auction Gallery. Ex-Harold Corbin Collection, Jan. 1, 1990. Price realized then was $2950; now possibly* **$7,000-$9,000. Note:** *It's hard to guess value, partly because these don't change hands or come on the market often, & there aren't enough known, yet, to find duplicates or deduce rarity. Subject matter, size, collector provenance, & the dealer who's selling determine price. In early 1990s a Conger-attributed tiger maple board with an American eagle, Lafayette, NY state coat of arms, an American Indian, 35 stars in border & 14 stars within an ellipse, as well as an extremely rare figure of Uncle John (precursor to Sam) was for sale for $25,000.*

"attributed" to Conger; his name does help sell cake boards. NYC, NY provenance, probably, if Conger, but there's a Germanic (Pennsylvania German?) look to it. It's obvious that Conger used popular prints & graphics for design sources. 6-1/4"H x 11-3/4"L, 19th C. • Pictured in *Maine Antique Digest*, Feb. 1982, Spring Valley Antiques...................... **$4,500+**

Cake board, eagle, square board with round carving, beaded edge, features eagle standing on shield with 4 flags, grapes & leaves in woven border, decorated in background with 45 stars, signed "J. Conger," NYC, NY, 13"H x 12"W, 19th C. .... **$4,000+**

Cake board, fire truck, carved walnut or mahogany, has three Conger-like elliptical carvings lined up vertically on oblong board. Top is an elaborate eagle; middle has a fire truck similar to "The Superior" described below, but with no number & a row of XXX; bottom carving depicts a horse race, showing crowds in the stands, two horses & jockeys, & in foreground, the words "ECLIPS SUB HENBY." This extraordinary mold, probably a Conger, was advertised April 1973 in *The Magazine ANTIQUES*, by dealers John Bihler & Henry Coger, who dated it c.1825. Price then, & present location unknown. .... **$15,000+**

Fire Engine Motif Detection Story – A carved "mahogany" cake board, very like the work of "Conger," is shown in Figure 159 of Jean Lipman's American Folk Art in Wood, Metal & Stone, 1948. It's owned by the New-York Historical Society, NYC. The oblong board, 14-3/8"L x 7/8" thick, has an elliptical wheat-ear bordered cartouche with a depiction of a fire engine being pulled by three long coated firemen, with boots and hats, the first one blowing a horn. The engine has "17" on its cistern and boiler. I thought that research into early 19th C. fire companies might reveal a specific engine and engine company. I proposed to investigate three lines of enquiry: identification of (1) style of engine; (2) style of firemen's coats; and (3) style of firemen's hats, all very detailed and distinctive. • But after contacting several historical societies and fire engine museums, the only conclusive information is that it is a "goose neck" side stroke engine, with an air chamber in back, the main body being a water cistern. It is of a type dating probably to the 1820s, possibly 1830s. In addition, in a cartouche above the engine is the word "SUPERIOR." • **Charles Radzinsky**, former curator of the American Museum of Fire fighting, in Middletown, NY, wrote me that "'SUPERIOR' could be a pet or nickname given to the company and/or engine, such as 'Water Witch', 'Good Intent', 'Excelsior', etc. The rather high number, 17, would indicate that the company was in an urban rather than a rural community." I conclude from the best book on fire fighting equipment, *Enjine! Enjine! A Story of Fire Protection*, by Kenneth Holcomb Dunshee (NYC: Home Insurance Co., 1939), that the pieced hats with brim worn by the three firemen carved on the board are of the four comb type, c.1812 to 1830. Finally, the long skirted, belted coats appear to be from the 1820s. A long fire ladder is shown below the corrugated road the engine is being pulled over; in the sky surrounding the engine are six 9-point blazing stars. I conclude that the motifs of the board date between 1820 to 1830. The provenance given in Lipman (and probably the *Index of American Design*, from which the picture was taken), is "Pennsylvania"; boards marked or attributed to Conger are from New York State, but I believe this may be a Conger. There was an engine company 17 in Manhattan, that in 1832 was about 15 blocks from Conger on Hester. After 1865, Engine company 17 was close to Sullivan St. and Ludlow Place (later Houston) and a year later, Conger moved to within a few blocks of the company. Therefore, it is my conclusion that this is a Conger cake board, and that he carved it probably in 1866, making it one of his last boards. Value is difficult to assign to the fire engine board; the subject matter is highly collectible, with many thousands of dollars customarily paid for early chief's horns, ceremonial helmets, decorated fire buckets, etc. Note: In 1997, a signed J. Conger cake board, with an elliptical design on both sides: one was a very "official" looking eagle bearing a banner in its beak reading "HAPPY NEW YEAR," and the reverse was a fire truck design showing the barrel-like water tank or reservoir, the two- or four-man pumping lever (something like a see saw), laurel leaves, and a ladder lying alongside. Price unavailable.

NYC Fire Department History – An interesting historical overview can be found at this url: www.usgen-net.org/usa/ny/state/fire/31-40/ch35pt2.html. It was transcribed by Holice B. Young in March 2001.

Cake board, George Washington patriotic design, ellipse on large 14-1/2"H x 24"L mahogany board, round design within ellipse has GW in breeches & plumed tricorn hat, with his last name in banner below him, flanked by Columbia & Justice & further out by 2 cornucopias, each with one star next to it, with huge eagle & shield above GW's head (with banner reading "E. PLURIBUS UNUM," grape cluster border. In two ends of the ellipse are a sailor & an Amerindian, with boughs of corn & tulips. Outer border of 39 stars & swagged ribbon. This board, "attributed to John Conger" & dated "c.1830" by dealer David A. Schorsch, was advertised in *Maine Antique Digest*, April 1996 for an undisclosed amount. Of course, we know that Conger worked for some 35 years more, & there's no reason for assuming this is as early as 1830, although that may make it more desirable to some collectors. This is not a bargain dealer either, & because of Father of Our Country motif, it's valuable. .... **$20,000+**

Cake board, horseman, carved rectangular piece of wood, elliptical (a double-pointed shape – sometimes called a lozenge shape, an ellipse or a boat-shape) carving with round center medallion with horseman, flanked by vertical ellipses with figural carvings within, marked only "Old Rough & Ready," American, 18"H x 24"L, c.1815 motif, possibly, even probably, much later for actual carving. •The name "Old Rough & Ready" refers to Zachary Taylor, who fought in the War of 1812, & who was U.S. president in 1849-50. • **Note:** In *The Magazine ANTIQUES*, Aug. 1953, appeared a picture of a carved mahogany board, slightly rectangular, large round medallion nearly filling surface, with frontal standing figure of man with deer behind him, a memorial of Andrew Jackson, inscribed "New Orleans Jany 8," the 1815 battle, in the War of 1812, won by Jackson. This pastry mold was from the collection of Mrs. Edward R. Ferriss, St. Charles, IL, formerly a collection of George Horace Lorimer. I don't know where it is now. • "Rough & Ready" was offered for sale in 1985, by unnamed seller, who was asking $2,500 or best offer. .... **$15,000+**

Cake board, horseman, carved wood, with one side depicting large man with beard & hat riding on a

IV-57. Cake mold or cake board, Square, two-sided. One side has three men in hats, two in a sort of pugilist pose, or perhaps they're fighting to gain control of a handgun, while a third looks on. Lots of stars in a circle. Verso has a bird & a dog. *8-1/2" square. Photograph courtesy Litchfield Auction Gallery. Ex-Harold Corbin Collection, auctioned Jan. 1, 1990. Price realized, only $850. Unusual, valuable subject. $2,500 (Note: texture is fault of photo.)*

high-stepping horse, other side depicts a rooster & a soldier or militia man on horseback (a very common archetypal image, found also in American pieces), edge marked "I. W," which might be James Watkins, or possibly initials (an "I" frequently was used for "J" in America & Europe) of a European, 13-1/2"H x 10-3/4", 19th C. .... **$4,500+**

Cake board, horseman, oblong with rounded corners, horseman with lance & plumed helmet, banner behind him reads "New York Lancers," flanked by cornucopias & floral sprays, piecrust border, of the "Conger" type, American, in style early 19th C., but could be mid 19th C. or later..................... **$4,500+**

Cake board, horseman, carved mahogany (according to dealer, although some other similar boards are American black walnut), large oblong plank with elliptical carving filling most of width & length, central round medallion with horse & rider, flanked by 2 vertical ellipses with flowers, rest of space filled in with leaves & fruits of the vine, very Eastern European-looking, Slavik or Czech, but possibly carved by J. Conger or made from his pattern. Marked "J. Y. Watkins," NYC, NY, 25-1/2"L x 13-1/2"W. • Resembles J. Conger cookie or so-called marzipan boards, and all look very European. This one was advertised in the *Maine Antique Digest*, Feb. 1989, by Byron & Craig White, of Sterling, PA..... **$2,500+**

Cake board, man & woman, carved walnut, nearly square board with round carving with central figures

***IV-58. Cake boards.** (L) Carved Czech board for making decorated cake. 19th C. **(R)** "New Year Cake Board," of carved wood, with round medallion filled with horse & rider, flowers, stars & deep decorative border. The naiveté of catalog-drawing may surpass that of actual carving, at least to some extent. Mold came in two sizes, "large" for a one-pound print cake, & "small" for a half-pound print. Also offered, though not depicted, were one-pound size metal cake boards probably for springerle. Design & style is early to mid-19th C., but this picture is from Jaburg Brothers catalog of 1908 which brings probable date of many existing boards forward. Selling price of such a board might be in thousands. I can't imagine a way to know age for sure, unless owner inscribed date of purchase.* **$500**

***IV-59. Cake board.** Square with round medallion decorated with an American eagle, shield body with stripes & stars, clutching arrows, surrounded by wreaths of leaves. 10-1/4"H x 11". Photograph courtesy Litchfield Auction Gallery, Litchfield, CT. Ex-Harold Corbin Collection, auctioned Jan. 1, 1990, for $525.* **$1000+**

of man & woman in round-brimmed hats, flowers & reeded border around outside, fully carved, dealer says "attributed to John Conger," NYC, NY, size not given in ad, date estimated as "c.1810," which is probably at least 14 years too early (Conger was born in 1803) & possibly as many as 40 or 50 years too early – if, indeed, it's a Conger. .... **$2,500+**

Cake board, man & woman, rectangular walnut board with elliptical carving composed of 3 parts. In a round medallion in center is a basket of fruit, background heavily carved with flowers, flanking this are 2 vertical elliptical cartouches, within one is man with shepherd's crook & hat, other has woman with sheaf of wheat, signed "J. Conger" in two places, for John Conger, NYC, NY. 25-1/2"L x 15-1/2"W, 1820s-1860s (?). • Auctioned by Hesse Galleries, Otego, NY, Sept. 1986. Since that time, a few other similarly-carved boards have come up for sale or auction, & are usually "attributed to J. Conger." .... **$3,000+**

Cake boards, Conger – See also Springerle roller

Cake boards – probably not Conger-related:

Cake board, basket of flowers on one side is typical of late 18th or early 19th style, tulips on other side, deep carved cherry wood, thick board, beautiful patina, 7"L x 6"W, poss. early 19th C., c.1810-30, but could be later in early style – as so many Conger molds are. .... **$350+**

Cake board, cat wearing collar, tabby striped & sitting, carved board, 10"H x 6-1/2"W, poss. English, 1820s-40s. .... **$1,250+**

Cake board, corrugated very finely, with a center line so that you could break cookie in half, for sugar cookies, lightweight wood, American, 13-1/8"L, makes 3-5/8"W cookie, 1880s? .... **$75+**

Cake board, geometric, carved maple, elliptical, deeply carved geometric border in what might be called, by cut glass collectors "strawberry diamonds," center design is a 6 point star, with other tiny chip carved designs between petals or points, flanked by 2 hearts, chamfered back, Pennsylvania or Canadian, poss. Nova Scotian, 9-1/2"L x 4-1/4"W x 1" thick, early 19th C., c.1820-1840. • Occasionally these molds are labeled "butter prints." .... **$2,000+**

Pattern Glass Motifs – When trying to describe the border design, I got out my *American Glass*, by George and Helen McKearin, which depicts hundreds of pattern glass pieces. I was struck, while looking at cup plates, how similar some patterns are to butter prints; it is to be expected, as the art of woodcarving is of primary importance in making the molds for pressed glass. The period is the same too. I believe careful study would reveal many close relationships in motif and style, perhaps even traceable to a region. The McKearins say, for example, that pinwheels are typical of Midwestern (pattern-glass) designs; we think of them as Pennsylvanian when we see them on butter prints. Study! Study!

Cake board, harlequin figure or possibly Pierrot, carved wood, Dutch (?), 9"H, prob. early 19th C. ...... **$200+**

Cake board, horse & sleigh, lion, flower pot, courting couple, 3 carvings per side, European, 22-1/2"L x 4-1/2"W, early to mid 19th C. .... **$650+**

Cake board, horseman on one side, deer on other, mellow, smooth, even "greasy" feel to wood, European, 13-1/2"L, board is 1-5/8" thick, c.1800 to 1820. .... **$500+**

Cake board, horseman dandy, perhaps a Yankee Doodle, dressed up, with flowers, high boots, knee britches, roll brim hat with feather, carved wood, slightly warped plank with 2 small age or dry checks & drilled hole in each corner, dark patina, American, 1-1/8" thick x 10-5/8"H x 8-3/8"W, c.1830s-40s....... **$650+**

Cake board, man & woman, carved wood, man on one side, woman with tiered gathered skirt on other,

IV-60. Cake board. "Ancient Carving ... on an ancient oak board, two feet in diam. It represents the letters A, H, C. [backwards] in the centre, surrounded by this legend, viz. 'An harte that is wyse wyll obstine from sinnes & increas in the workes of God.' As this legend reads backward, & all the carving is incuse, it was evidently intended to give impression to something; I imagine pastry." William Hone's The Every-day Book, Vol. II, n.d. [1827 or 1828]. Hone also reproduces part of a 1778 letter from the Lord Chancellor Thurlow, from Bath, England, which says that he had received the mold from a farmer from Norfolk, England, prior to 1778.

IV-61. "Mold for ornamenting cake" patent, by Charles A. Bailey, Middletown, CT, April 5, 1887, #360,753. The "mold" is actually a wedge-shaped stamp, with a vertical turned-wood handle. Bailey claimed that although he was "well aware that it is old to provide the face of a rolling-pin with figures and designs of various characters which have a border-line formed by a flange or the like," that his invention – for ornamenting and marking the frosted surfaces of cakes – was new. It was "designed to mark the lines in the frosting along which the knife-cut is to be made in cutting the cake to serve it." First the frosting is put on, somewhat thicker than usual, Bailey explains. "It is permitted to stand a short time until it thickens a little more. After it has thickened sufficiently, I dust upon it a little fine sugar, to prevent the stamp from sticking, and I also dust the face of the stamp with starch for the same purpose." Although his drawing looks as if design is contrasting color, it is not it makes an intaglio design in the surface of frosting or icing.

European probably, hard to be certain without documentation, 17-1/4"L, board is 1-3/8" thick, looks c.1830s to 1850, but could be later. .... **$400+**

Cake board, man in kneepants & fancy hat, Dutch, 18"L, mid to 3rd quarter 20th C. • **Reproduction alert.** – Wood is stained dark brown, to resemble a harder wood, but is carved from pine. Edges of this only 1-1/4" thick board show saw marks, & back shows no evidence of hand-planing. Finally, no signs of wear. Design not as intricate as really old ones (texture of fabric, etc.) & couldn't be, because it's carved of soft pine, not hard dense walnut, bass, mahogany, or fruitwood. **$125**

Cake board, mason's tools, a square, hammer, mallet, pointing tool, compass, round shape, deeply carved, beaded border, possibly a Masonic piece, carved with initials "I. D." which are probably not the maker's initials; if they are, "I" could be old style "J," American, 7/8" thick wood, 5-1/2" diam., 19th C........ **$2,000+**

Cake board, old woman, a cat & a little dog on one side (prominent in her costumes is a big bonnet, & a pocket tied to the waist of her dress, hung from her belt, with slit opening), a plant & pot with big berries on obverse, European, 1" thick x 4" x 7", early 19th C. **$750**

IV-62. Cake board, maple sugar mold, & confection mold. *Carved wood. (L) In vertical ellipse is American Indian bearing bow in one hand & chief's feathered staff in other, 8"H x 5-1/4", American, probably prior to but near 1876 Centennial; (M) Maple sugar mold, for two cakes, each bearing banded large heart & 2 stars. 10-1/2"H x 4"W. American or Canadian, probably mid 19th C. (R) Two-sided board, with pistol on one side, tobacco pipe on other. 8-1/2" x 4". American, late 19th C. Photograph courtesy Litchfield Auction Gallery. Harold Corbin Collection, auctioned Jan. 1, 1990, $375, $350, $300. (L) $1,000+; (M) $500; (R) $600+*

> Note: Seeming woven or basketweave or finely-checked background on photos in IV-35, IV-57, IV-62, IV-63 are all the fault of multiple reproductions of the photos in three editions. The wood is smooth.

IV-63. Cake board. *Carved wood with wormholes, two-sided (see other side under springerle molds, IV-375. Large heart with flowers growing from small heart. Pennsylvania German or European. 9-1/4"H x 6-1/4"W. Signed "F. G." Ex-Keillor Collection. $1,200+*

IV-64. Cake board, *or cookie mold. Carved wood, great detail of sporty gent in plaid or checkered suit, bearing a pig on his head – cushioned by a tam o'shanter. In some ways he resembles a Scotsman. Was bought in Amsterdam. 19-1/2"H x 7-7/8"W, late 19th C. Collection of Mary Mac Franklin. $350+*

Cake board, owl & rabbit on one side, parrot & songbird on other, carved wood, signed "T. B. W. W. 20" along one side edge, prob. European, "20" may be pattern number. 11-1/2"L x 3-1/4"W, 19th C. .... **$350+**

Cake board, pickup truck from 1920s, spare tire, possibly depicts a common sight in the Great Depression, of a family moving all belongings in an old car or truck, carved wood, definitely unusual, American (?), 23-1/2"L x 9-1/2"W, 1920s or 30s. • **Unusual image.** The fact of the truck image existence, with fairly good & detailed carving, forces you to look warily at many other cookie boards with undateable images such as flowers & animals. Garth's auctioned it in 1986 for $150. Image has great crossover appeal. .... **$275+**

Cake board, woman sitting in chair spinning thread or fine yarn, carved wood, English (?), 1" thick x 2-5/8" x 3-1/8", early 19th C. (Lots of chair collectors would love this!) .... **$400+**

Cake or cookie board, animals – carved wood with figures on both sides, oblong with regal lion, head at right, tail curled up over rump, one front leg on double arch tombstone, on other side is seated cat, dark color to wood, stone marked "Koning Van Dieren." Dutch? or NY or other Dutch-settled state? 8-3/4"H x 14"L, 19th C. look; poss. 20th C. .... **$350+**

Cake or cookie board, "gingerbread mold" say ads for the reproduction. Hand carved poplar wood board, figure of periwigged Punch, in fancy striped knee britches & fitted coat, holding walking stick, exaggerated nose & chin of the famous puppet, lots of details in buttons & pattern in textile of clothing, supposed to be a replica of an "18th century original now in Van Cortlandt Manor," NY, apparently not available in cast metal as was their other replica cookie board, ad is for American Heritage Museum Collection ... from Sleepy Hollow Restorations, NY, 28"H x 10"W, advertised in July/Aug. 1978 *Americana.* • Original price was $165 plus shipping. The

IV-65. Cake ornamenting stamp & a design that could be made using it. "These little stamps **(T)** [probably nickeled brass, with wooden handles] enables any person to make the most difficult designs such as scrolls, console, valutes, etc. They are stamped direct on the cake" & were then traced over using an icing bag or ornamenting tube. Below are clasped hands, lyre, & scrolls all done with simple star or plain tubes. "A few flowers & leaves will finish the cake, however the designs will look considerably better when other tubes are used such as the star ruffler, crimper, rope, etc., especially when the shoving, swinging or pushing motion is used." Hueg's The Little Confectioner, 1921. **$35-$65**

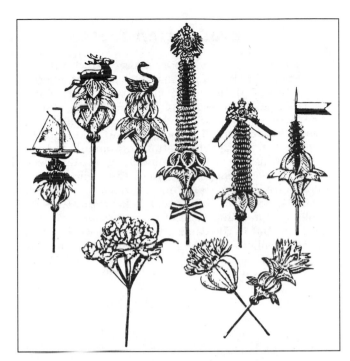

IV-67. Paper decorations, curled, twirled & colored, on sticks. For use with confections, & for roasts & joints of meat. Sailboat, buck, swan, flowers, & various towers. Bertuch, c.1904. **$5-$15+**

IV-66. Cake-decorating stencils. (T) Unidentified metal (probably brass, like most other stencils, but possibly tin), 10" diam., and others made to order. 12 designs, with which "a boy can ornament six layer cakes in one minute. **DIRECTIONS:** Place the Stencil on top of a layer cake iced with either chocolate or water icing, then sift a little xxxx sugar on top of the stencil & remove stencil carefully." Child labor! Hueg, Book of Designs for Bakers & Confectioners, 1896. **(B)** Stencils or **schablonen.** Unidentified metal. These were used very like full cake-top stencil above, but with more freedom. The paddle was held in any direction, and while or colored sugar powder was dusted on. The biggest one, at bottom, was for making palm leaves for Easter cakes; fancy big one for making grape leaves. Bertuch, Berlin, c.1904. **(T) $15-$30; (B) $10-$35+**

IV-68. Baker decorating cake. Statue of Liberty cake, on revolving stand. Note how baker supports his right hand to steady it as he makes a fancy border with icing tube. From Hueg's 1896 how-to book.

value has not gone up, but has instead gone down, even though it was nicely carved, because it is now a second-hand reproduction, and it'll be many many years before it's an antique reproduction. Very murky area of evaluation. .... **$30+**

Cake or cookie board, St. Nicholas with his miter hat decorated with a cross, long beard, bishop's crook, ecclesiastical alb or surplice, bands, & chasuble, with basket of 3 baby dolls in bunting, "hand carved" wood, reproduction or "replica of an 18th century Dutch colonial mold in Van Cortlandt Manor," American (?), 26"L x 11"W, the figure being 24"H, advertised in 1978 *Americana*. • **Reproduction alert.** – This reproduction was "also available in a polished cast metal version," which was 24"H x 8-3/4"W. The description comes from the Sept./Oct. 1978 *Americana* magazine's American Heritage catalog. The wooden one originally cost $165; the metal one (looks like cast aluminum) was under $50. The unfortunate realities are that some people will have bought these on the secondary market thinking they were getting a real antique; & that the value has gone down, not up, unlike a real antique. A copy or reproduction, at least a nameless one, can not be expected to rise in value. Reproductions by Wallace Nutting & the Stickleys excepted and that's due to the fame of Nutting & the Stickley brothers, which gives rub-off value. **$45**

Cake boards – See also Cookie mold; Gingerbread man mold; Pie top-crust mold; Springerle mold

Cake cutters – See Cookie cutters, also Biscuit cutters

Cake decorations, bride & grooms – See Bride & groom

Cake decorations, candle holders, 10 pieces (probably a full set), stamped tin, each "petaled" holder for small birthday candles has thin, long tapered point for sticking in cake, somewhat rusted overall. Very like Christmas tree candle holders, but with spikes not clips, & probably made by same people. American (?), each about 1-1/4"L overall, c.1890s-1910. .... **$45+**

Cake decorations, candle holders, painted iron flowers on spikes, American, 1890s-1910. Set of four: .... **$75+**

Cake decorations, set of four Beatles figures, plastic, in original package, 1965. Crossover collectors might pay more. .... **$55+**

Cake decorator set, or frosting tubes, plunger or syringe type, 12 different inserts or nozzle tubes to make frosting come out in stars, rosettes, pointed pixie caps, etc., with instruction book, in original box, "Ateco," mfd. by The Thomsen Co., NYC, NY, pat'd. 1925, but sold in that form for many years. • A full page 1931 ad, in *Boston Cooking School* magazine, showed an Ateco set as a premium for getting a new subscriber signed up; it included a three-tube boxed set, called "Special Set No. 700. – Aluminum syringe with three assorted Standard Brass Ornamenting Tubes ... in its attractive display box. The satin-finished barrel with its highly polished caps & brass tubes produce a fine contrast in metals which harmonize with the color combination of the box." The ad also depicted 99 other tubes you could get, "any eight as a premium" or $1 a dozen – "each [tube is] worked out to produce a certain line, scalloped border or rosette, etc., when icing is forced through them." • This is still being sold, though in a different package. I think the metal may be discernably different too. • Price for older 12 tube set: .... **$20+**

Cake decorating or frosting tubes in case, pieced tin, 6 tubes, case with conical hinged lid, French (?), case 6-1/4"L, 1870s or 80s. .... **$45+**

Cake fortune-telling charms, cast unidentified heavy metal (some kind of slush metal alloy), 15 very detailed pieces, *viz.* owl, purse, top hat, thimble, man's wedding ring, woman's ring, sadiron, heart, baby shoe, boat, button, automobile, & 3 unidentified forms, in original box that has orange, black & white label depicting a fortune teller lighting cake candles, "Made in U.S.A.," between 3/4" & 1-1/2"H, c.1930s-40s. .... **$45+**

IV-69. Decorating bulb & ornamenting tubes. *(L) Rubber bulb with threaded mouth. Various tubes & extension tubes could be used with it; it was supposed to make it easier to squeeze out icing. (R) The "Boss" ornamenting bag & tubes (bag not shown, but it was a rubber). Cloth bags also used. Before 1900, the tubes, & threaded bag screw were silverplated brass; later they were nickeled. Hueg, 1896. The book:* **$8-$20+**

These relatively late **fortune-telling charms** carry on an old tradition – for bride's parties, baby showers, birthdays, New Year's *fête*, midnight suppers, or other celebrations. Each charm was baked right in the cake, with a charm in what would become each slice. Depending on its aptness, or complete absence thereof, the chance receipt of a particular charm in a guest's slice was occasion for oohs, ahs, or guffaws. • Another set, described in Carl W. Drepperd's *A Dictionary of American Antiques* as **pudding-cake charms**, all had a tiny hanging ring. The set consisted of a pig, spoon, beaver, wishbone, nut, duck, mug, wedding band, fortune wheel, bachelor button, money bag, bell, horseshoe, donkey, seated old maid – a set less exclusively marriage-related, and suitable for general fortune telling. • A **"favor cake"** was pat'd. Nov. 16, 1943, by Mary F. Lemrow, NYC, #2,334,497, and assigned to Cushman's Sons, Inc., NYC. Her claim reads in part, "It has long been the practice, in making cakes for special occasions, to embed and conceal within the cake various articles or souvenirs, such as rings or other small metal or wooden objects. The custom has been to place such articles in the dough or batter before the cake is baked, so that when the latter is finished, the objects are entirely concealed and each remains as a surprise and favor for the person who happens to receive the slice of cake which contains it. Objection has been found in this practice, particularly in that it permits metal or other contaminating materials to come into contact with the moist dough or batter before and during the baking operation, the chief hazard being con-

IV-71. Decorated Yule Cake from Czechoslovakia (now Czech Republic). *To celebrate the birth of Baby Jesus. 19th C.*

sidered to be the possibility of poisoning or other harmful effect by reason of action between the embedded article and the moist dough. Furthermore, there is the danger that the person, such as a small child, who eats the cake, might be hurt by biting inadvertently on the embedded object, or might accidentally swallow the object. Indeed, for one or another of public health regulation, and at least in certain localities, the authorities have forbidden the sale of cakes with any hard, foreign or otherwise inedible object or material incorporated therein." Ms. Lemrow's device allowed the "desired favors or souvenirs [to be] disposed in an annular row around the outside of the upper surface of the cake." She suggests "any small objects having decorative or amusing character, such as rings, safety pins, miniature hats, shoes, ships, automobiles or the like … made of metal, wood, plastic or other appropriate material." They fit into a device that had, like numbers on a clock face, a place to put each small object, and, like a clock, a spinning dial – a "selecting device" – that pivoted in the center on a pin pressed down into the cake. Fabulous idea. Has anyone seen one?

IV-70. Decorated cakes. *Clockwise from top left the names of the cakes are:* **(1)** *basket of flowers Gâteau aux fleurs;* **(2)** *Gâteau Vénitien au sucre;* **(3)** *4-tiered Gâteau Jeanne-d'Arc;* **(4)** *cap-like Gâteau Palestine;* **(5)** *gadrooned Gâteau Moucey with plume top; &* **(6)** *Gâteau moscovite à l'ananas with pineapple top. From Urbain Dubois' La Patisserie, c.1860s-70s.*

❖ NOTES ❖

Cake Molds In general, all figural animal or Santa cake molds are here. Spouted or tubed cake molds or pans, especially those of ceramic or enamelware, are further on subsumed in the Molds listings, under their respective materials. This is because many of those molds were for a variety of purposes, not just cake.

Cake mold, 12 parts, tin, the 12 parts put together form a heart, from F.A. Walker catalog, they are mostly imported wares, in the 1870s & 1880s. • Cakes, with each part apparently equal in crumb count, could be made in other multi-part molds: floral crosses (for christenings, Easter & Christmas), a horn of plenty (for Thanksgiving), rounds & diamonds. .... **$55+**

Cake mold, heart shaped, slightly slanted sides, ring hanger, bright tin, American, 7" x 7", c.1920s. .... **$15+**

Cake mold, lamb, cast iron enameled green outside, white inside, very unusual, about 9"L, c.1890s-1910.. **$250+**

Cake mold, lamb, couchant (lying down with legs folded under body, head up), cast aluminum, along bottom of base reads "Bakers Coconut," 20th C............ **$65+**

IV-73. Cake pans. (L) *"Perfect," with removable bottom, available with or without spout. Stamped tin, two sizes, 3" deep x 9-5/8" diam., or 3-1/8" deep x 10-1/2" diam. Also made square with upside down legs called lugs. Central Stamping Co., 1920.* **(R)** *"Perfection," removable bottom, 1-5/8"H x 8-3/4" square or 2-5/8"H x 9-1/8" square. Savory, c.1925-28.* **$10-$20+**

❖ NOTES ❖

Lamb Molds: Collector Joel Schiff is one of a handful of "doctorate level" collectors of cast iron who have put in 20 plus years, maybe 50,000 hours or more, into handling, studying, comparing, researching, buying and caring for their vast collections. So I asked him about lamb cake molds, about which I know little except that I like some better than others. He pointed out to me some things maybe obvious to you but I'd never taken notice before. (1) **Legs & Feet:** Some lambs have their front legs and feet folded, or tucked under them, folded at the "knee." Some in a lying down position have the right front leg with knee up and foot forward, as if just about to stand. (2) **Handles:** Some lamb molds have big ring ear-handles on the back half, and much smaller tabs with holes on the front half; some have large ring ear-handles front and back. (3) **Holes:** Some molds have holes in the back, and some don't, and none seem to have holes in the front half.

Joel Schiff says this makes it somewhat easier to date and identify and give a value to some unmarked molds. He wrote me that "all folded feet, unmarked, non-Griswold lambs are generally $130 to $140. If it

has holes in the back it's likely this sort and this value range." I asked about the ones you see with the big ring tabs front and back, and he said, "These are almost always lambs of the 'feet forward' variety, have holes in the back, and are the earlier type of lamb molds, and almost all are from Europe. Except, of course, for the Griswold ones. In fact, says Joel, the reason Griswold couldn't get a patent on the form was because it was such an old, common – or public domain – design. These non-Griswold, old unmarked lambs are generally $225 to $300."

Cake mold, lamb, couchant with folded feet, cast iron, 2 part, Wagner but not marked, 7-3/4"H x 11-3/4"L, late 1920s on. .... **$150-$200+**

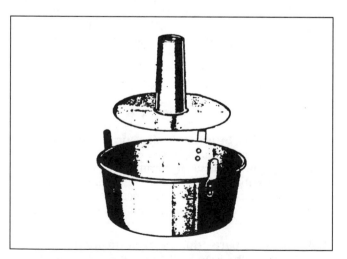

IV-72. Angel cake pan. *Loose bottom with spout that projects an inch above sides of pan, which is 4-1/8"H x 10-1/2" diam.; 3 legs assist when you turn mold upside down to get cake out. Savory Inc., Newark, NJ, c.1925-28 catalog.* **$5-$15+**

IV-74. Lamb chocolate & cake mold. *Stamped tin, legs folded underneath, slip-on clamp holds halves together, 5-1/4"H. Marked "DRGM" along plinth. German, 20th C. Photo courtesy eBayer UsedToys, Jerry Cioffi, Remember When Antiques and Collectibles, East Northport, NY.*

Cake mold, lamb, couchant feet forward, cast iron, 2 parts, American, 7"H x 13"L x 4"W, 1890s-1910s... **$130+**

Cake mold, lamb, couchant folded feet, cast iron, large ring ear handles at neck & tail, 2 part, protrusions as steadying or leveling "feet," backside flatter than front, has 3 small holes (for escaping steam or overflowing batter?), no mark, 17"L, 19th or early 20th C. .... **$275-$300+**

Cake mold, lamb, couchant folded feet, head turned to left, ears stuck straight out at sides, cast iron, looped handle at each end, Griswold PN #866 (other PN#s: #922 & #921 on insides). (These molds found as Wagner #866 also, poss. just after W bought G), Erie, PA, 8"H x 12-3/4"L, c.1940s-1950s. .... **$95-$125+**

Cake mold, lamb, couchant, heavy stamped aluminum, 2 piece, marked "Kanter," fairly good detail, about 8"H, c.1960... **$45+**

Cake mold, lamb, couchant, cast iron, 2 part, marked "Schaab Stove & Furnace Co." 2024 S. Broadway, which is not a NYC address, c.1890s-1910. It's rarity should make it more valuable than: .... **$150-$175**

Cake mold, lamb, couchant, polished cast "lustre" aluminum, 2 parts, Maid of Scandinavia Co., Minneapolis, MN, 8"H x 13"L, late 1940s on. .... **$45+**

❖ NOTES ❖

Cake molds, rabbits, etc. – The French mold and pastry-making equipment company, Letang Fils, show several rabbit molds made of *fer blanc*, which translates as "white iron" – a type of cast iron very low in carbon and high in iron. (Another series in their catalog is made of *étain* (tin). **Letang Fils** made four rabbits: • #3499, a crouching or couchant rabbit, ears tucked along the back, in three sizes: 18 cm (about 7"L); 20 cm (about 7-3/4"L); and 22 cm (about 8-1/2"L). • #3501, a trotting (!) rabbit with grass clumps, in one size only: 24 cm (about 9-1/3"L). • #3510, a sitting rabbit, ears cocked in an alert "V," in two sizes: 28 cm (almost 11"H), and 30 cm (about 11-3/4"H). • #3517, a rabbit sitting high on haunches, front feet tucked up to chest, ears straight up, in three sizes: 27 cm (about 10"H); 29 cm (about 11-1/4"H); and 31 cm (about 12"H).

Along with the rabbits, and several animals, is one lamb, couchant, #3497, in three sizes: 19 cm (7-1/2"L); 20 cm (about 7-3/4"L); and 22 cm (about 8-1/2"L). Note: A centimeter (cm) equals .39".

Reproduction Alert

According to Joel Schiff of New York, "There are reproductions of the **lamb, rabbit and Santa,** and they tend to be better castings than the usual reproductions, though not as good as the originals. The good Santa should be smooth, have a tongue in its mouth, and frequently a mold flaw 'line' down the side of his bag of goodies! The rabbit is harder to distinguish because of all his fur. The good rabbit should be smooth and have a capital "I" in the 'GRISWOLD' mark. In both, the Griswold company markings should be centered and not extend beyond the handle 'ears' inside."

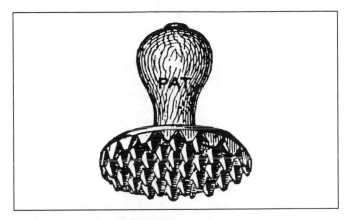

IV-75. "Rock Cake" stamp. *"The Handy,"* nickeled cast iron, wooden handle. *"This little stamp is a great time & labor saver, it makes the cakes all alike, uniform & prevents burnt edges; it does away with the fork, & is invaluable to any bake shop."* Hueg, c.1927. **$35**

Cake mold, rabbit, cast iron, 12"L, Griswold #862 & #863, 12"H, Erie, PA, c.1920s on. May be the best designed of their cake molds, fairly common still but that won't remain true. Also comes in chrome finish for slightly less. .... **$225-$275+**

Cake mold, rabbit, couchant, 2 piece redware mold, American, mid 19th C. Old redware belongs to the ceramic market; different collectors, usually, from the cast iron market............................ **$250-$350+**

Cake mold, Santa Claus, cast iron, marked "HELLO KIDDIES!!" on base at Santa's foot, tongue shows (or maybe he's eating a cookie left for him? He looks from the outside of the mold as if he's carrying a tray, but actually it's a leveling piece. PN#898, mfd. by Griswold, Erie, PA, 12"H, mid 20th C. – a late Griswold. • Best thing about this one, to my mind, is the original instruction to bake him on his face for 25 minutes, then on his back, as if he were at the beach or a tanning salon. Joel Shiff writes this was "the last of the Griswold cake molds, and I believe always has the 'overflow/steam/vent holes' in its back. So the question is, if baked on his back, is the cake sufficiently cooked as well as not generating pressure so that the batter wouldn't flow out of him? Or is it possible, though I doubt it, that there is an early form with vent holes? My feeling is that any mold without vent holes is older, and was originally intended to be cooked in separate halves, and afterward combined [with icing]."................ **$400-$600+**

Cake mold, Santa Claus from waist up, climbing out of brick chimney, heavy stamped aluminum, 2 piece, 9"H, c.1960. .... **$15**

Cake mold, Santa Claus head with floppy liberty cap on Santa, tin, slightly slanted sides, 6"H Santa head within 9" diam. pan, 20th C. • I never thought about it before, but the Santa Claus we know & feed cookies to often wears a **Phrygian cap** very like a liberty cap, & because the jolly fellow's appearance is derived from a combination of Thomas Nast's late 19th C. cartoons, & Haddon Sundblom's Coca-Cola Santa in ads, & therefore American, it is possible that his cap may have been deliberately designed by Nast as a patriotic symbol. Harrumph. Of course, it could be that the typical cap worn by skaters & skiers was the inspiration for Claus's headgear...**$55+**

Cake mold, Santa's sleigh, cast iron, 7"H x 14-3/4"L, modern fake, wholesales at about: .... **$6+**

Cake or gelatin molds – See also Molds

Cake or gelatin molds, graphic detail of body parts, stamped copper, for "adult cake," chocolate, ice cream cakes, ice sculpture, & "punch bowl frozen centerpiece" (guaranteed to thaw out party?), "Eroti™," mfd. by Delectable Fantasies, Inc., Ft. Lauderdale, FL, 12-1/2"L x 2-1/2"W; 10-1/8"L; 11"H; 10" x 7-1/2", 1983. .... **$20+**

Cake or marzipan boards – See Cake boards; Cookie boards, Springerle molds

Cake molds – See also Cake pans; & Molds, especially tubed or spouted molds that could be used for food other than; also Muffin or gem pans

Cake pan or bake mold, 2 parts, tin, a sort of pie pan, plus a very shallow "pork pie hat" inset; pan says "sponge mixture." You can put inset pan in 2 positions: "This way up for flans" with inset all the way down & the rim part placed crown up. The 2nd way, crown down, is marked "This way up for sandwiches." "Green's Two-Way Tin," English, 8-1/4" diam., registered design #77660, early 20th C. • See also Cake pan for making "Mary Ann base." .... **$30+**

Cake pan, angel food cake, with sliding door in side for loosening cake, tin, spouted, advertising "Swan's Down Cake Flour," American, small, only 6-1/2"D, c.1920s. • **Slots & Slides.** – This pan, like the Van Deusen described a few listings down, has a slide in the side. The VD has two, & the slide ends extend way up above rim, whereas the SD has but one, the slot is bigger, & it does not extend up beyond the rim. The SD slot & slide looks rather like little slot on front of file cabinet drawers where you slide in a card with name of what's in the file.................. **$20+**

*IV-77. **Lamb cake mold by Griswold,** in cast iron, seen from behind. Leveling gates on back of head & plinth. Lower photos show interior. Original box reads "One NO. 866 Griswold Early American Pre-Seasoned Quality Cast Iron Ware Lamb Cake Mold Griswold Mfg. Co., Erie, Penna, USA. Since 1865." Photo courtesy eBayer huntress-di, Diane Callahan, Elmhurst, IL. Now in Collection of Mary Copley, Gilbertsville, KY, eBaying as mulberry-mary, who collects sheep & lambs because of the nursery rhyme.*

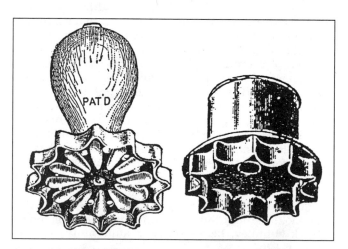

*IV-76. **Shrewsbury Cake mold & cutter. (L)** Inverted scalloped edge, with almond-shaped flower design inside. Wood knob handle. "This Patent tool will cut, crimp & finish a Shrewsbury cake at one operation, & as fast as Sugar cake can be cut out; have them all perfect & uniform far superior to hand work. For very stiff doughs this tool may be used as a mould by simply unscrewing the handle." Hueg & Jaburg both sold it, c.1908 through 1920s at least. **(R)** Tin, 3-1/2" diam. Note inverted scallops & fat handle. Jaburg, 1908. **$35; $25***

Cake pan, angel food or regular layer cake, stamped tin, 4 parts (sides, bottom ring, flat bottom, & bottom with spout) to make either spouted or plain, mfd. by Perfection, about 9" diam., late 19th C......................... **$20+**

Cake pan, gray graniteware, cast iron handles, 13" x 9", 19th C.. **$65+**

❖ RECIPE ❖

Twelfth Night Cake *– For Twelfth Night – January 6 – bake a round loaf of pound cake (put a pea and a bean in the batter) and ice with a plain icing. When firm, arrange alternately small red and white candles on the top so as to form a five-pointed star, piping a rose of icing round each candle, and garnishing with a wreath of holly." Table Talk, Philadelphia, January 1903.*

Almond Maccaroons – *Take a pound of shelled sweet almonds, and a quarter of a pound of shelled bitter almonds. Blanch them in scalding water, mix them together, and pound them, one or two at a time, in a mortar to a very smooth paste; adding frequently a little rose water to prevent them from oiling and becoming heavy. Prepare a pound of powdered loaf-sugar. Beat the whites of seven eggs to a stiff froth, and then beat into it gradually the powdered sugar, adding a tablespoonful of mixed spice, (nutmeg, mace, and cinnamon.) Then mix in the pounded almonds, (which it is best to prepare the day before,) and stir the whole very hard. Form the mixture with a spoon into little round or oval cakes, upon sheets of buttered white paper, and grate white sugar over each. Lay the paper in square shallow pans, or on iron sheets, and bake the maccaroons a few minutes in a brisk oven, till of a pale brown. When cold, take them off the papers.*

"It will be well to try two or three first, and if you find them likely to lose their shape and run into each other, you may omit the papers and make the mixture up into little balls with your hands well floured; baking them in shallow tian pans slightly buttered." Eliza Leslie, Directions for Cookery, 31st edition, Philadelphia, 1848. (See also Marzipan in Introduction to Cake Boards.)

Cake pan, round spouted mold, highish sides, 2 wide slides, like sliding doors, opposite each other in sides, which you would pull up & insert palette knife or spatula into revealed slot to loosen cake from mold, "being made solid, they will not get out of order & leak batter, as the loose bottom pans do," heavy tin, "Van Deusen Cake Molds," mfd. by C.A. Chapman, Geneva, NY, 3 sizes, up to 12" diam., 1910s. • **They stood under their pans.** – Chapman also made the "Van Deusen" molds, with slides in the sides, in oblong, square & round layer cake

IV-78. Cake mold. Cast iron rabbit, 2 halves #862, #863, 11"H (when I measured I got 12"), Griswold Mfg. Co., Erie, PA. Also came in chrome finish for slightly less. $225-$300+

---

sizes. The original ads said "The slides are made long to act as rests to turn the mould on while the cake cools, allowing the air to circulate under the cake to keep it from sweating. The cake, being stuck to the mould, will hang in it until loosened."... $10+

A **1903 ad** reads "SOME FACTS ABOUT CAKE MAKING. The old way was to grease the cake tin to keep the cake from sticking, then add flour until the cake would not settle, until it was stiff enough to stand alone, like bread. The new way is to discard the grease, and at least 1/4 of the flour, make a delicate batter and let it stick to the mold, which will support the cake while baking; and when baked invert the mold and allow the cake to hang in it to cool, which is the only way known to keep a delicate cake from settling; and when cold, loosen the cake ... with a knife."

A Clean Sweet – "The broom splint has occupied a prominent position among aids to cooking for an indefinite time, and housekeepers who are immaculate in other matters ... often take a splint from a broom with which they have, perhaps, swept the kitchen. ... A much better way is to buy a cheap little brush-broom, and keep it for this and no other purpose; one will last a lifetime." Emma Babcock, *Household Hints*, 1881.

• • •

Whose Crud Is This Anyway? • Collectors sometimes ask if it's safe to use old cake pans for baking, even if they have a bit of rust. It's safe to the user, not quite as safe for the pan, but only if you don't carefully wash and dry thoroughly after use. The solder used in such late pieced pieces is not dangerous, and rust only adds a bit of extra minerals to your cake. If you use such pieced tin pans – cake pans or muffin pans, etc. – don't scour vigorously with steel wool or a brass pot brush. Try to use a stiff dry fiber brush and then very very hot soapy water, then dry thoroughly. Hot water won't melt the solder. My rule is: If I buy an old pan with some rust and the baked-on crud that happens when fat and flour and sugar are baked, especially over a gas flame, and if I keep this pan a month before using, not only the pan but the crud too becomes mine, and harmless! It's all a matter of rationalization.

Cake pan, round, stamped tin, embossed "Free 49 cent Pan with Py-O-My Pastry Mix," 9-1/2" diam. • Another is embossed "'Py-O-My' Puddin' Cake," c.1950s. Both about: .... **$12+**

Cake pan, round, stamped tin, adv'g "Calumet Baking Powder," American, 20th C. • Others embossed "Up & Up Flour," Buffalo, NY & "George Urban Milling Co." Buffalo, NY. .... **$12+**

Cake pan, spring cake pan – called this because it springs open when the clamp is released, round, heavy tinned steel, with ring side, open in one place, with little clamp, with 3 different bottoms: (1) plain flat disc, (2) bottom with large spout, (3) what was called a "Mary Ann" base, which looks like a wide-lipped pie pan, but inserted upside down, so that when a cake was baked it would have a big depression in top for putting in fillings, like strawberries & whipped cream. "Cream City Ware," mfd. by Geuder, Paeschke & Frey Co., Milwaukee, WI, about 9" across, c.1930. • Other companies made spring cake pans. One I saw, made of heavy tin, has the same kind of wire pin going through a sort of hinge knuckle & barrel joints that some ice cream & chocolate molds have. .... **$15-$25+**

Cake pan, spring form cake pan, heart shaped, 3 part heavy tinned steel, ring opens at point, heart shaped flat bottom fits inside ring, plus clip or clamp to hold sides. "When the baking is finished & cake has cooled, all you have to do is remove the simple little clamp & the sides spring off the cake." "Cream City Ware," mfd. by Geuder, Paeschke & Frey, Milwaukee, WI, about 9" across, c.1930. .... **$15+**

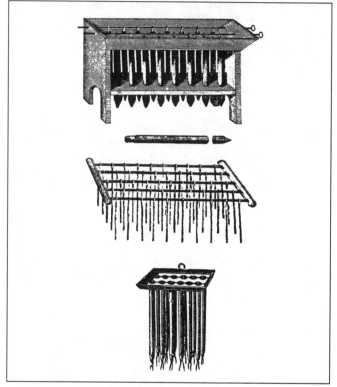

IV-79. Candle molds & candle dipping outfit.
(T) A set of tube molds, possibly pewter, set in wooden frame. Note wire rods with wicks, in place in tubes, ready for pouring in melted tallow. Note also rack strung with many wicks. Engravings from unidentified book, dated 1820, found at a print shop. (I) Candle wicks tied to sticks, the strings twisted & taken one by one & coated first with tallow to give them weight & a surface easier to coat by dipping. Next a wooden box with a sheet iron or tin bottom turned up & tacked on sides, & a lid, is put on the stove. Tallow is melted in it, deep enough for dangling wicks. Each stick with as many tallow-rubbed wicks as wanted, is dipped three or four times slowly, until no more fat hardens on them. Each stick of dipped candles (rounded ends are seen on candle) is hung on a cooling frame. When completely cool, the first stick of slim candles can be dipped again, until candles are fully built up. (Directions as well as bottom picture adapted from American Agriculturist, Nov. 1876. Interesting that pictures from 56 years before fit the instructions!) (B) A typical pieced tin mold, for a dozen candles, with hanging ring, wicks in place.

Cake pan, spring form heart, tin, spout also heart-shaped, American, 3" deep x 9" diam., mid 20th C. .... **$35+**

❖ RECIPE ❖

The London Way of mixing Cakes, used by Pastry Cooks *– Weigh down the flour and sugar on a clean smooth table; make a hole in it; and bank it well up; in this hole put your eggs; cream the butter in an earthen pan; then put to the flour and sugar, the eggs and butter; mix all together, and beat it up well with both your hands; you may work it up this way as light as a feather; then add the currants, spices, & c. Put it up in pound or two pound hoops, neatly papered at the bottom and sides; to be baked on iron sheets, in a slow oven." Joseph Bell, A Treatise on Confectionary, Newcastle, England, 1817.*

Cake pan, square, stamped tin, wire loop handle, marked "Fries," 12" x 12", 20th C. .... **$10+**

Cake pan, round, tin with spout, side handle, "Vanity Co.," 10" diam., 20th C. (Vanity only if you don't eat too much!).. **$15+**

Cake pans, a pair, tin in colorful cardboard box, with recipes too, "Kate Smith's Bake-A-Cake Kit," 9" diam., 20th C. .... **$15+**

Cake pans – See also Pie pans. Cake pans have straight sides, pie pans have flared or slanted sides

Canape or truffle cutters, at least that's the fancy name. I think I've seen the same thing in a 1950s box labeled "cookie cutters," corrugated tin circles, 9 nested cutters, in tin box, lid stamped "242" & also either "9" or "6," probably 9 for the 9 cutters inside, "Made in Germany," box 4-15/16" diam., mid 20th C. • Dealer had this for $55, priced too high because they aren't old, & are still made. The first patent I found for a canape cutter was not until 1941 (#2,271,908)... **$18-$25+**

Candle mold, redware & fruitwood, bench type with bootjack ends, 24 redware tubes (actually 1 missing), American, 14"H x 24"L, c.1830s to 1850s...... **$1,750+**

Candle mold, wooden frame with 18 pewter tubes, called by the inventor an "Improvement in Candle-Mould Apparatus," marked "Humiston," patented by Willis Humiston, West Troy, NY, patent #13,334, pat'd. July 24, 1855. .... **$1,200+**

Candle mold, tin, 4 angle feet, small handle, makes 4 candles, American, 6-1/8"H, mid 19th C. • Added value. – If it's odd, huge, small, signed, probably old, etc. – it's worth a lot. .... **$300+**

Candle mold, Pieced tin, for making 6 candles. Ribbed strap handle. Stored upside down if they didn't have a hanging ring. 10-1/4"H x 7"W, American, 1830s-1860s. .... **$125+**

Candle mold, tin, long fat single tube, top is soldered to large square flat lip that's also as stand for mold when not in use, strap handle connects tube to edge of lip, American, 21"L, mid 19th C. .... **$200+**

Candle mold, tin, round, wire handle, makes 8 candles, on plaque on front it reads "MASON'S," English (?), 6 3/8"H x 4-3/8" diam., c. mid 19th to early 20th (?) C. .... **$175+**

❖ NOTE ❖

Make Dripless Candles – *American Agriculturist reprinted this tip (from a journal called* Exchange*) on homemade candles in October 1850: "If you manufacture your own candles, immerse the wicks in lime water, in which a little nitre (saltpetre) has been dissolved, and dry them before dipping. The light from such is much clearer, and the tallow will not 'run'."*

Candy crimper, a sort of fluter or mangle for candy, cast iron & brass, an oblong iron box with hinged lid revealing horizontal brass crimper drums, & brass gears, crank in side, L.T. Yoder, Pittsburgh, PA, 9"H x 15"L x 10"W, pat'd. Dec. 3, 1883. .... **$225+**

Candy crimper, for ribbon candy, "The Champion," square-based cast iron, brass crimpers turned by a wire belt & crank, has wooden trough that folds up.

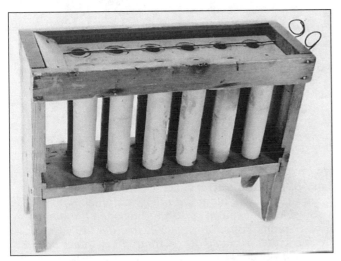

*IV-80. **Candle mold,** redware 12-tube in wooden frame. Impressed mark by maker, Alvin Wilcox, West Bloomfield, NY. 15"H x 10"L. Photo courtesy Litchfield Auction Gallery. Ex-Harold Corbin Collection, auctioned Jan. 1, 1990, for $1200.* **$1,750**

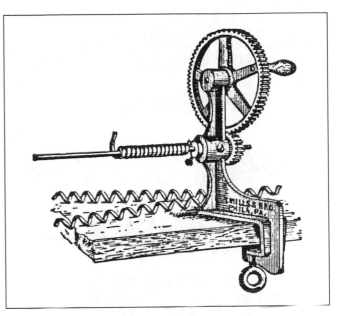

*IV-81. **Candy curling machine.** For making candies "known to the trade as 'Opera Curls.'" Thomas Mills & Bro., Philadelphia, 1930 catalog.* **$150+**

In original latched wooden box with hinged lid. Machine about 6"H, box is 7"H x 12" x 12". Pat'd. March 1886, mfd. by The Champion Candy Machine Co., Philadelphia. Still making such machines in early 20th C., so impossible to date exactly. .... **$225+**

Candy cutter, a sort of rolling pin, plated steel, barrel or drum set with 15 fixed sharp disc blades, fixed handles at both ends, used for cutting strips of candy for sticks or rolls, Sethness Co., Chicago, IL, barrel 1"L, blades set 3/4" apart, handles 2-1/2"L. (Choice of blades fixed at 7/8", 1", 1-1/4" & 1-1/2".) 1st quarter 20th C. • Sethness also made to order cutters with 24"L barrels with fixed blades set in same choice of intervals as above. They also made adjustable cutters, with "revolving brass handles," packed with 12, 15, or 20 disc blades, plus washers to separate the blades, 2 cast iron wrenches for assembling, & extra blades. The Dec. 1925 *Sethness Candy Maker,* part catalog, part recipe book (for professional confectioners). .... **$45+**

❖ NOTES ❖

Corrugated wooden rolling pin – The catalog also shows a corrugated wooden rolling pin, with turned handles, 18 sharp edged ridges set at 3/4" intervals, overall length 15", with the drum or barrel 4" in diam. It is called a wooden marker, and used to mark off rows for cutting with a knife, or for breaking apart. For more see "What're the Ridges For?" in a rolling pin entry, this chapter.

Candy cutter, for hoarhound, licorice or other hard chewy candies, looks like a miniature garden tiller or farm tool. Nickeled iron frame fitted with sharp disc blades, with a turned wooden handle. Used by rolling across spread-out pan or cooled puddle of candy to make long sticks of candy. Shorter pieces, even small lozenges, could be made by cutting across the original rows. American, last half 19th C. .... **$35+**

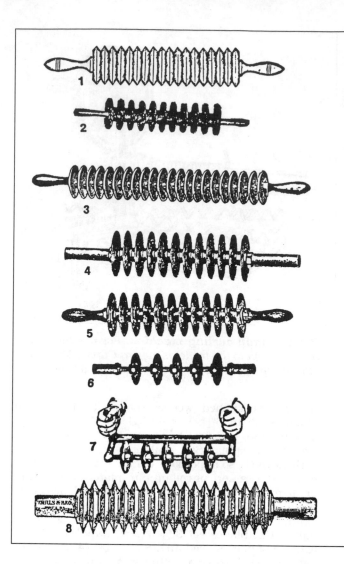

IV-83. Candy marker & candy cutters. *Most are metal, & therefore not confusable with rolling pins, although I've seen them labeled "noodle cutters." From top:* **(1)** *Turned wood corrugated pin, called a* **"marker."** *15"L x 4" diam., marking off 3/4" divisions. Sethness Candy Maker, 1925. this rolling marker is often called a cracker roller & is probably interchangeable in function with other concentrically ridged rolling pins.* **(2)** *Caramel cutter, steel blades or "knives." Could be had "adjustable," meaning you could get one with 8, 12 or 15 knives, & set them as close as desired; or "stationary," meaning with fixed blades, from 1/2" to 1" apart in 1/8" increments. Duparquet, Huot & Moneuse, c.1904-1910.* **(3)** *Bonbonschneidewalze (candy cutting roller) with tempered steel blades 3-1/4" diam. You could order with 12, 18, 26 or 35 blades (also, cheaper, one with 26 tinned iron fixed blades). Catalog of A. Bertuch, Berlin, c.1904.* **(4)** *Brass revolving handles, 12 blades with spacers, for cutting caramels & other candies. Also could be had with 6" diam. blades. Mills, 1927.* **(5)** *Adjustable steel blades, 4" diam., with spacer rings. Mills.* **(6)** & **(7)** *Movable steel cutters, for marking or cutting lengths of horehound sticks, butterscotch, peanut cakes, or bars, taffies, etc. Five 4" diam. knives (blades), with provision for adding blades.* **(7)** *Has iron frame presumably for added weight bearing.* **(8)** *Horehound stick cutter with brass revolving handles & steel blades. "Designed to meet the demand for a cutter which will cut horehound & peanut sticks & add the beveled side & rounded top to the goods. 18"L plus handles. Last three all Mills, 1927.* **$35-$100**

❖ RECIPE ❖

Hoarhound Candy. *– 7 lbs. sugar, white or brown; 1/4 oz. cream of tartar; 1 qt. water; 1/2 pint strong hoarhound tea; boil to the feather; grain against the sides of the pan with spoon, 2 or 3 minutes; then pour out onto slab; form into flat sticks, rolls or drops, with a hoarhound cutter, which are made in two styles, with movable knives or with fixed divisions." Henry Scammel, compiler, Treasure House of Universal Knowledge, 1891. "If, when the sugar is boiled, the skimmer is dipped in and shook over the pan, and then given a sudden flirt behind, the sugar will fly off like feathers; this is called the feathered stage." ibid.*

❖ NOTES ❖

Wormhole test – Back in the 1950s, "wormy chestnut" was the wood leading the pack when it came to "Colonial" old-fashioned picture frames. Lots of what was holey was actually fake. But since then, and probably for decades before, one kind of distressing done to make wood look old was the drilling of wormholes. Fake wormholes are straight; you can put a piece of

IV-82. Candy cutters. (T) *"Circular batch cutter ... especially useful in handling caramel batches." Steel knife revolves between 2 wooden handles. 6" or 9" diam. knife, "larger sizes to order."* **(B)** *"Handy chip cutter ... used for cutting chips (hard boiled candy pulled thin as paper) made in a variety of colors & highly flavored. This will cut them into uniform pieces about 1-1/2" square, while at the same time permitting them to keep flat & glossy." Two sizes: 8" block, 1-1/2"W, & a 12" block with set-in steel blades 2"W. Mills, 1927.* **$25-$75+**

paperclip wire in and it keeps going, whereas a real worm hole will wiggle around starting right under the surface, so a wire poked in will be stopped before it's gone a 16th of an inch.

Candy mold, dense, heavy yellowish wood, carvings include 2 well carved human figures, front & back views, front of figures carved at very bottom of board so the little feet could stick out in 3-D; may be **Robinson Crusoe & Man Friday** – a bearded sailor with dotted pants, & a caricatured thick-lipped "native" in short grass skirt. Dealer Teri Dziadul says these figures were used on cakes. Above are something like a corset cover or camisole, a dagger & two other small weapon-like things. On the back, the only really 3-D carvings are a pair of tiny wings! There's also a longish border design, a simple aeronautical balloon, & a sort of connect-the-dot geometric shed or hut, which probably was practice carving or a child's addition, English (?), 9-3/4"L x 3"W x 1" thick, mid 19th C. • **The book:** Daniel Defoe's *The Life & Surprizing Adventures of Robinson Crusoe* was first published in 1719, but has been a classic ever since, so it does not really assist in dating this mold...... **$400-$600+**

Candy mold, boy riding slim free range pig, an image dating back at least to early 18th C., presumably from an old nursery rhyme or song, & found in pen &

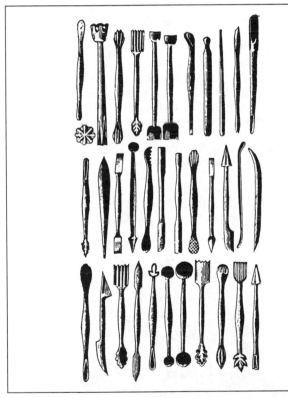

IV-84. Candy & confectionery-modeling tools. *Carved boxwood with great detail. About 4-1/2"L. Especially good for marzipan candies & modeling leaves & flowers for cake decorating. A full set included 34 tools. In top row, three round designs are meant to show what design is made by the end of the tool. Bertuch catalog, Berlin, c.1904. Value range given is for a small mixed collection of, say, 10 tools.* **$50+**

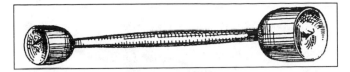

IV-85. Candy & confectionery-modeling tool. *Carved boxwood, double-ended, similar to two in top row of previous picture. 4-1/2"L. Bertuch, c. 1904.* **$20+**

ink calligraphy drawings too, one half missing, grainy wood stained dark. Looks like a modern fake – distressing on edge looks fake, too dark, it's pushing credulity to have the half that's remaining be the one with the value-adding signature initials, particularly since 2 other half-molds with the same troubling qualities have the same signature, "V. E.," on the back, supposedly PA, but looks European (motif poss. Eastern European or Dutch), 4-1/2"H x 4-5/8"W, supposed to be mid or early 19th C.; poss. 1970s or 80s. Read carefully: Probable value if old: $250-$400+ range; New: under **$25**

Candy mold, dog, carved boldly-grained wood, one half only, curly hair on body & legs, long & down-hanging curly haired ear, short bobbed tail, probably a retriever (a popular dog in the decorative arts), this one looking rather like full figure Pennsylvania chalkware, carved wood & pottery dogs of the period, but because of fortuitous "coincidence" of the remaining half having a signature, plus the fact that in same auction another mold bearing same fakey faults & signature was bought, I doubt that this is what it's maker hoped it would look like. supposed maker's initials carved on back, "V. E.," looks Pennsylvania; may be Dutch, or an American or European fake, 3-3/4"H x 5-7/8"L, supposed to look mid 19th C.; I'm afraid it's a fake from the 1970s or 80s. If it were right & old, $150+. Probable value range, because probably fake:.................................... **$25**

❖ NOTES ❖

Old dog? What do you think? – One bothersome thing about the dog mold in the listing above is the wood used, which is inconsistent with the dark color of its finish; also it is awfully distressed around edges in an unrealistic manner (and you really have to do a sort of method acting approach when examining wear and distress marks. It also just begins to approach cuteness, a deadly sin! But maybe the artisan was sentimental about the model. • Garth's Auctions, Delaware, OH, pictured all the "V. E." molds in their catalog for the April 11-12, 1986 sale, and made no representations about the molds as to age, authenticity, etc. That is an auction house to love, with apparently hundreds of neat things appearing monthly; but the buyer has to do some of the work for him-herself. Better than always having to depend on a cataloguer's opinion.

"Significant numbers of clear toy molds" began to be reproduced in 1994, according to Joel Schiff, one of my advanced collector consultants. He said that recently they've been made by the John Wright Co. and "usually marked," but that other repros are done in brass and are unmarked. The motifs most in demand are Santa, Belsnickel, eagle, Teddy Roosevelt, and Admiral Perry.

IV-86. Candy press & dropper. (T) *Mint cake press, for "pressing balls into kisses." Wood lined with tinned iron. 24"L x 12"W or 15"W. **(B)** Chocolate wafer dropper, wood, 10" x 14". Wood with hinged upper box. Both T. Mills & Bro, 1920s, but probably made much earlier.* **$75+**

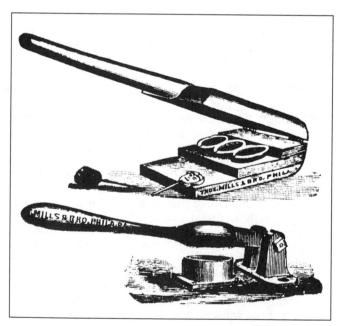

IV-87. Confectioners' presses. (T) *Sucker press, for making **lollipops**. Seven styles, including making 3 "faces on stick," a lemon slice, & oval, & a heart. Sizes of suckers varied from 1-1/2" diam. to 2-3/8". **(B) Pop Corn Ball** hand press, to make popcorn & caramel balls from 2" up to 4" diam. Also had one for making egg shaped balls. Both appear to be plated cast iron on boards. Mills, 1927.* **$75+**

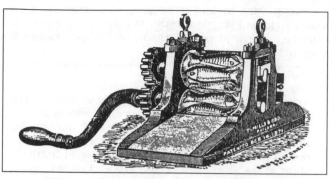

IV-88. Fruit-drop frames. *Cranked machine with patterned rollers, for imprinting boiled sugar fruit-drop candies. Fully adjustable, & with scores of patterns, all interchangeable. You had to buy a frame before you could order rollers. Rollers were from about 3-5/8"L up to 6"L, & all 2" diam. Mills, 1927 catalog, but made earlier. Good condition, with interesting rollers (note fish in lower one) would increase collectible value.* **Futurewatch Collectibles. $100-$200+**

Candy mold, man & woman, full length front views, he in long-skirted mucho-buttoned coat, with walking stick, & she in long-waisted, corseted dress, one half the mold only – back part missing, looks European – Polish or Czechoslovakian, 5"H x 5-1/4"W, 19th or 20th C.; looks older than the mold is, I'm sure. • Even when only one part is present, these candy molds can be distinguished from similarly carved wooden cookie molds by the fact that the bottom of the carving is flush with the bottom of the board. A sort of built-in funnel is formed if both halves are placed face to face & is carved so that the molten candy could be poured in. Sometimes there are small holes on background, for fitting the two halves together with small pins or pegs. When both halves are present, the value may be more than doubled. As is:... **$145+**

Candy mold, or some other kind of mold?, cast aluminum, fairly thin but nicely made, 2 rows of 4 egg

IV-89. Stick candy machine. *"Five-Cent Stick" size, adjustable for different candy thicknesses. See example of what the candy looked like. Cast iron with cast bronze rollers. This one has a hand crank, but others could be had hooked up to an electric motor. Mills, 1927.* **$150+**

IV-90. Patterns for fruit-drop rollers. *Shown is a selection from many pages of patterns in Thomas Mills' 1927 catalog. The detail is probably greater than what came out embossed on the candy itself. They were all identified by name, & by how many fruit-drops it would take to make a pound of candy. These probably weren't even big enough to be penny candies. Of particular interest to me are the heart & hand (200 to a pound), bowlegged clog dancer (there were 146 of these to a pound), face drop above fish at left, boy scout, & delightful* **Yellow Kid** *(big ears & nightgown), the first beloved comic strip character, originated by Richard Outcault about 1896. Individual rollers with multiple images range in value depending on image – of these, Yellow Kid would be most valuable by far, with crossover interest.*

IV-91. Patterns of sugar toys, *that could be made by an electric-powered "Universal" sugar toy machine, used to make transparent, brightly-colored, hard sucking candies, or decorations. "The animals turned out in this machine stand erect as if made in moulds, & run 65 to a pound. "The machine was not like the stick candy one. The candy actually passed between two revolving wheels, both of which had a pattern cut into its smooth face. The candy toys went through 'standing up,' so to speak, making their bottoms flat & smooth. Actual size of the candies ranges from 1-1/4" to 1-1/2"H. If a hoard of these candies, perfectly preserved, were to be found – in an iceberg, say – they would be collectible, & could probably be freeze-dried for permanent preservation. Mills, 1927 (but patterns found in late 19th C. Mills' catalogs also).*

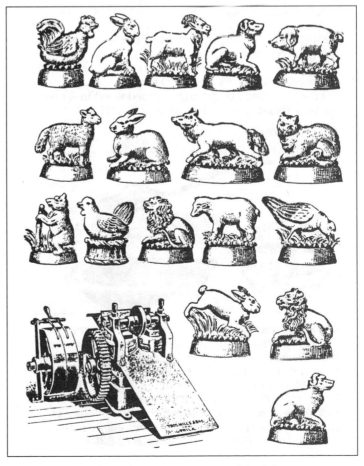

IV-93. Cream candy or possibly chocolate mold. *I still don't know what to call it, after all these years. 4-3/8"L. Looks like an egg's bathtub. Heavy cast iron with 3 legs. Something similar is shown in IV-92 for Cream eggs. Late 19th C.* **$25+**

shaped cups each, hanging hole at one end, no mark at all, American (?), 13"L x 4-1/2"W, 20th C.... **$20+**

Candy mold, sheep, couchant, 2 part, redware, with good detail, orange glaze inside, outside of mold follows form inside, with 2-1/4" peg handles sticking up from both rumps, thought by Earl Robacker to be "the only redware candy mold thus far reported" [that is, in the 1960s], PA German, 5-5/8"H x 8"L x 4-1/2"W (when both halves put together), 19th C. • Ex-Robacker, $500. .... **$700+**

Candy mold, swan in pleasingly plump shape, well-detailed uplifted perky wings, carved wood in 2 peg-fit parts, English (?), each part is 3-1/8"H x 4-5/8"W,

last quarter 19th C. • $210 at Garth's Auctions, Delaware, OH, April 11-12, 1986. .... **$200+**

Candy mold – See also Maple sugar mold

Candy molds, various designs: nickeled cast iron, shapely concoction of scrolls, curling around each other, with runnels for candy or other confection. These curled & scrolled runnels, teardrops & "S" forms are not all connected; the manufacturer's instructions say "It can be used for casting, moulding as well as baking. ... When all the pieces are casted, moulded or baked, stick them together with icing or caramel to the desired shape ... The most attractive ornament can be made out of caramel of different colors, also out of nougat, fragrant paste, gelatine paste, macaroon, sponge cake, plaster of Paris(!), etc." H. Hueg, *The Little Confectioner*, pub. c.1921. This mold was used to make showy pieces for bakery windows. H. Hueg & Co., Long Island City, NY, 14"L x 10"W x about 1" thick, pat'd. 1896, but sold for decades thereafter. .... **$75-$125+**

IV-92. Cream egg molds. *At (T-R) is "lever press for making handmade cream eggs." This came in nine sizes, making eggs that would require from 3 to 22 to make up a pound. (L) Cast brass mold, with some resemblance to chocolate "bathtub" mold in IV-128. Made eggs of 5 sizes, from 25 to a pound up to 2 to a pound. (B-R) is a cast iron mold, in 9 sizes, making eggs from 5 per pound to 1 per pound. All from Mills' catalog, 1927.* **(T-R) $65; (L)$25+; (B-R) $20+**

IV-94. Molded nougat, *meant to resemble a small footed bulge pot full of potatoes. A pretty little confection from Urbain-Dubois' La Patisserie D'Aujourd'hui, Paris, c.1860s-70s. Nougats are a sugar paste candy mixed with chopped fruits or nuts (in this case, almonds); this was made using accessory legs & bail handle.*

❖ NOTES ❖

Hueg made another **nickeled cast iron mold** that is round and has 5 concentric channels surrounding a circle in the middle. Confectioners bought these molds in various sizes, in sets of a dozen, and packed the "fragrant paste" or whatever they were molding into the circles – and then baking or whatever was needed, and assembling baskets, pyramids, cornucopias, bowls and other hollow shapes that started small and got bigger and bigger, then smaller and smaller, or vice versa. "A very slight practice will enable anyone" to make or invent similar shapes, says the 1921 booklet! I've never seen one, and from the description I think the largest of these ring molds had an outside diameter of 8 inches.

Candy pattern molds, cast plaster of Paris, various small simple shapes – buttons, lumps, elliptical discs, hearts, little bananas, lozenges, leaves, diamonds, etc., – mold patterns, used with trays of corn starch. I've never seen one that I know of, but next week? Anyway, now you'll know those cast plaster "ornaments" you occasionally see may not be architectural, but possibly are candy mold patterns, used as described below. A supplier of candy molds & ingredients, Sethness Co., Chicago, in their Dec. 1925 catalog, offered a page full of "**Plaster of Paris Starch Mould Patterns**," sold in dozen lots of one kind only – "plain, per dozen - 75¢" or "fancy, per dozen - $1." The patterns for making candy molds are interesting partly because of method of use. One maker in 1920s-30s was J. Frauenberger & Co., Philadelphia, American, European, probably 1/2" to 4" or 5"L, 19th & early 20th C. A board-full: $70+; each: .... **$3-$15+**

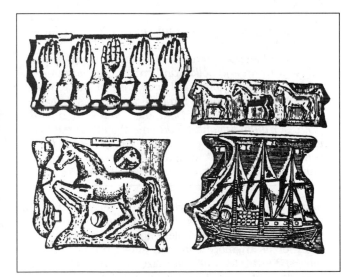

IV-95. Clear toy candy molds. *Hinged metal, making from 3 to 6 candies in small molds, & singles in larger ones. Sizes not given, but small candies come out about 1"H; larger ones up to about 3"H, or even bigger. The large ones were not made to be eaten, & were more likely to be saved (if possible) as holiday ornaments for a tree or table centerpiece (or shop window). Mills, 1927, but most of these are also found in late 19th C. Mills' catalogs.* **$75+**

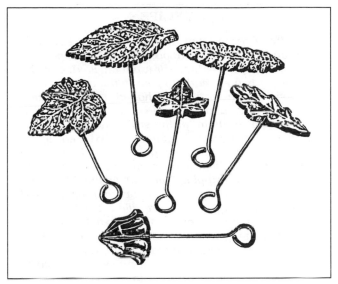

IV-96. Sugar candy stamps, *for making leaves & flowers. Embossed cast lead on wire handles, with loop for hanging. Bottom one, looking like fairy parasol, is a flower mold, the deepest one. Several companies made them, main differences are in handles. These from A. Bertuch, Berlin, Germany, c.1904.* **$10-$20+**

❖ NOTES ❖

Bon Bons – This name is given to cream goods, as described [below] in the manufacture of chocolate cream. Different varieties of shape, color and flavor are nearly all produced from the same formula. "It is necessary to have an apparatus to mould the forms of the different varieties. The impressions are made in fine pulverized starch, which is put on boards usually two feet long by sixteen inches wide, having sides one and a half inches high, which are filled with the light starch and struck off even with the edges by a straight flat stick. The **models of the bon bons** are usually made from plaster of Paris, and are glued on a flat board about one or one and a half inches apart. When starch is ready the impressions are made by gently pressing the moulds [mold patterns] that are fastened to the board their full depth in the starch until all are full. Now, having all ready, the cream must next be prepared to pour in the impressions."

❖ RECIPE ❖

Chocolate Bon Bons – *2 oz. finest assorted gum arabic, 2 lbs Icing sugar, 4 oz. Chocolate, 2 Whites of eggs. Flavor with vanilla. – Dissolve gum in a gill of hot water and strain through a piece of muslin; add the essence of vanilla; add icing sugar until the mass is quite stiff.*

"Melt chocolate with a tablespoonful of water. Work it very smooth with a spoon, stir in the 2 egg whites and icing." [Then follows a method of making bon bon drops on sugar paper sheets, squeezed from a funnel in plops.) Hueg, c.1896.

Vanilla Cream Bon Bons – *Pour a sufficient quantity [of the cream above] in a small copper pan and put it over the fire. Stir it until melted; add the vanilla. It is now ready to pour in the moulds. Confectioners use a funnel shaped vessel holding about a quart, with a handle at the upper end and a hole 1/4" in diam. at the small end, a long plug with a sharp point is fitted that can easily be moved up or down to regulate the flow of the cream. This is filled with cream, the plug prevents its escape or dripping, and by gently lifting the plug the cream is poured in each depression and shut on and off until all are filled. Let the cream remain until hard enough to handle without crushing, then empty the moulds, starch and contents in a sieve, and gently agitate until all starch is removed. Lay the bon bons in a moderately warm place for two or three days to harden, then they may be crystallized."* H. Hueg, The Little Confectioner, n.d. [c.1896].

Charlotte Russe mold – See under Molds, the Tin mold section

Cheese drainer, basket, large interstices, traces of blue paint, American, 4"H x 11" diam., mid to late 19th C. .... **$200+**

Cheese drainer, basket, tightly woven sides connecting square bottom with round top, 2 handles, Windsor style, American, 6"H x 12-1/2" diam., mid 19th C. .... **$225+**

Cheese drainer, natural wood with arrow-shaped slats leading from square base up to round hooped top rim, in so-called Windsor style, because general construction resembled that of Windsor chairs, American, fairly small example, only 5"H x 9-1/2" diam., early 19th C. .... **$300+**

Cheese drainer, skinny peeled hickory or ash spindles from square base (integral part of ladder stretchers) up to large round hoop, Windsor style, American, nice & big, 10" deep x about 22" diam., late 18th or early 19th C. .... **$300+**

Cheese drainer mold, heart shaped, punctured tin, with presser plate, & – very unusual to find – a heart shaped lid, the punctures in the bottom start as triangle in center & as each concentric row was added it got more & more swirly & rounded, American, prob. PA, approx. 6" x 6" x 2" deep, c. 3rd quarter 19th C. .... **$500+**

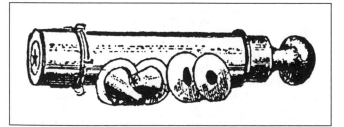

IV-97. "Kiss machine." Tin syringe with wooden pusher & various insert discs, for making candy kisses. Jaburg, 1908. See also French butter forcer (in with butter), & Jumble machine (with cookies). **$65+**

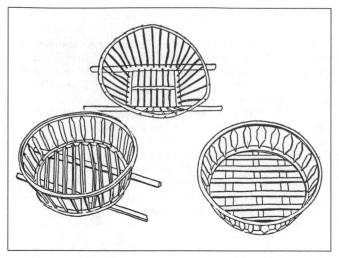

IV-98. Cheese drainer baskets & ladders, considered a type of cheese mold. These "Windsor"-style baskets were so-named because of resemblance of much of their construction to that of Windsor chairs. These baskets were lined with cheesecloth & wet cheese put in. The basket was then set over a container to catch the whey. Some had built in "ladders" *(T)*, others needed a separate ladder or pair of sticks *(L)*. When completely drained, the cheese was formed into round shapes. *(T)* Drawn from unidentified ad in Maine Antique Digest, for ash & hickory piece 10" deep x about 23" diam. *(L)* Drawn from ad of Evelyn Rue in M.A.D., 1981. *(R)* Drawn from ad of Jerard Paul Jordan in M.A.D., 1982. **$300-$1,000**

Lemon Cheese-Cake – *1 pound cottage cheese, 4 eggs (separate), 1 cup granulated sugar, 2 rounded teaspoons flour, grated rind and juice of a large lemon, 1 teaspoon cinnamon, almost 1/4 of a nutmeg, 1 tablespoon butter. – Cream the butter, add the sugar and egg yolks, and cream until light; next add the spices, flour, rind and juice of the lemon, and the cheese rubbed through a sieve or squeezed through a potato-ricer. Beat the whites to a stiff froth, stir them in lightly, and pour the mixture into a large pie-pan lined with rich pastry. Bake in a rather quick oven."* Womans Home Companion, Jan. 1901. "Quick" oven means a hot oven.

Cheese drainer mold, heart shaped, very wide at top lobes, tin, punctured & slit or slotted design of starbursts & holes, the holes nowhere near so close together as in more common slit & punctured heart molds, 3 strap feet, PA, pint-size, late 19th C. .. **$200+**

Cheese drainer mold, lobed form, rather shallow sides, 6 lobes with 3 pointed rays & three rounds, intricate concentric rings of slits, some wavery to give effect of hot sun, triangular hanging ring of wire, punctured & pieced tin, extremely unusual, PA (?), 19th C. • This one appeared in a picture in an interesting article by Mildred T. Bohne, "Tin Cheese Strainers," in *Antique Review* (formerly *Ohio Antique Review*), Feb. 1985. It is the only one I've ever seen with such an unusual shape; the most common being round, the

IV-100. Cheese mold. *Handmade tin, perforated on bottom & lower sides of cylinder. Three short conical feet. Has round tin "toller" or presser, shown at left. Both parts have loop handles. 7-1/8"H with 1-1/4"H legs; 6-3/8" diam. Pennsylvania, late 19th C. Courtesy Jean Hatt, Hatt's Hutt, Denver, PA.* **$400+**

IV-99. Cheese molds – *also called* **cheese strainers.** *(L) Fine pierced tin heart-shaped drainer-mold – like a Valkyrie's breastplate armor! With hanging ring. About 12"H. American, c.1850s-70s. For making* tsierkase, *or "pressed egg" cheese, not so-called cottage cheese (smearkase). Photograph courtesy Gail Lettick, Pantry & Hearth, NYC. (R) Pieced & punctured tin, hanging ring at top. Very unusual shape – a cloverleaf overlying a triangle. Drawn from picture in enlightening article by Mildred T. Bohne, "Tin Cheese Strainers," in [Ohio] Antique Review, 2/1985. Bohne calls these strainers a "specialized form of colander," which explains their function well.* **(L) $1,000; (R) $800+**

second most common being heart-shaped. Bohne writes that "Although they have been described as having been made for draining cottage cheese [smearkase], they were really made for ... pressed egg cheese, *tsierkase*." .... **$800+**

Cheese drainer mold, round & simple, but possibly handmade as spacing is eccentric, punctured tin hoop with flat bottom, design on bottom & sides are 5 circles of concentric rings of holes; on sides are 8 circles, marked "Weiss," American, early 20th C............. **$85+**

Cheese mold, cow, round, carved wood, American, prob. WI, 10" diam., early 20th C. .... **$125+**

❖ NOTES ❖

Cheese-Chocolate-Pudding molds – A 1927 catalog from S. Joseph, NYC, of bakers' supplies, offers several heavy stamped tin, fully 3-D animal molds in several sizes, that were described as "Imported chocolate or pudding molds, can also be used for cheese." So! The perfect definitions, distinctions & classifications which elude us as collectors, weren't even made when the molds were new!

Chocolate molds

This is a classic field of collecting and a surprising number of molds are available, dating from the first half of this century. Older ones, of course, exist also. There are a couple or more reproduced catalogs; see the name Judene Divone in the Bibliography near the end of this book. One of the appeals of closed molds is the secret treasure aspect. There is so much more detail on the inside of some chocolate molds, or ice cream molds for that matter, that I have called them the "Fabergé Eggs" of kitchendom!

Factors Affecting Prices of Chocolate Molds – Just to be old isn't enough. **Size** has a strong effect on value: large, and very large molds (over 15"H, or over 20"H) seem to get about 250% more than the 5" or 7"H molds of the same subject, condition, and approximate age. Tiny molds may also command more money than the run of the middle ones, but only if the subject is desirable. **Subject** is very important, although chocolate mold collectors seem to have a slightly different idea of what's "special" than does the outsider amateur. Some subjects are predictable, because any collectible in that shape sells well: Scotties, Teddy Bears, Kewpies, Santas (Kris Kringle, St. Nicholas, Belsnickel, Father Christmas, Sinterclaas), Poodles, Bears, Pigs, Rabbits Dressed in Clothes, and Automobiles. The mold-designers often celebrated scientific or technological objects such as dirigibles, trains and rockets, or then-current cartoon characters – much the same way that tin windup toys celebrated such things for children. It would be interesting to do a crossover comparison, form by form, with chocolate and ice cream molds and children's toys c.1900 to 1930. **Scarcity** is the other main ingredient of value. And only if you are an avid and active collector of the molds will you get a feel for what's rare. **Condition and Completeness** almost go without saying, for most chocolate molds on the market today are in fine condition. **New looking?** Dealer Don Appelquist, Suckasunny, Morris County, NJ, explains that many of "those that look new are actually old. They were never used, and never had the edges cut or trimmed, and were never mounted in the protective strapping." Rust isn't necessarily a sign of age; neither are distress marks and dings. Before you buy something, look around the dealers stock carefully. If there are a number of very similar things, especially if they are all rusted, weathered, or otherwise distressed, the stuff is probably new and reproduction. **Strap scaffolding** – Don Appelquist explained that in a candy shop, "when finished with a particular shape, having made as many as they wanted, they'd just toss the mold into a corner until needed next time." Most collectors remove the straps. **Copper and steel** – Two companies using copper and steel to make chocolate molds were Weygandt of NYC, and the American Chocolate Mould Co., in business in the 1930s and 1940s. Their molds were made of copper-plated steel that was tinned.

IV-101. Chocolate or marzipan molds. *Also meant for fondants. Stamped tin. Upper ones are "large" size, which came mounted "in plaques containing 6 moulds, all of one pattern" or with 12 the same. Size probably about 1" or 1-1/4". Lower set is "small" size, mounted same way. Probably about 3/4" to 1". From Mrs. A. B. Marshall's* Larger Cookery Book, *London, c.1902. Note flying fish – it & dolphin, lower right, would probably bring most.* **$10-$20**

❖ **MAKERS' ABBREVIATIONS** ❖

TCW = T.C. Weygandt • Ep = Eppelsheimer • AR = Anton Reiche • Som = Sommet • LtF = Letang Fils

---

Chocolate mold, Army truck with tied-on canvas covering on back, "Vormenfabriek #15371," Tilberg, Holland, 1940s (?). .... **$60-$75**

Chocolate mold, baby standing with finger in mouth, very tubby, steel alloy, AR, #17197, sold by TCW of NYC, mfd. Dresden, Germany, 6" x 3-1/8", early 20th C. .... **$95+**

Chocolate mold, baby, stark naked, one hand to mouth, one to belly, 2 part, heavy stamped tin or steel alloy, marked "Kunzig 17499, TCW," NYC, USA, Made in Germany, 12"H, early 20th C. .... **$125+**

Chocolate mold, blacksmith snippers in rectangular frame, 2 part, clamped, well stamped metal, only 5"L, 20th C. • Representations of **tools** are particularly interesting. Other tools include a hammer & a scissor-action tool that looks like pliers. Masonic emblems also include tools............................ **$35+**

Chocolate mold, Bugs Bunny, double standing figures, 2 halves hinged, within heavy frame, with old clamps, marked "Warner Bros. Productions, Inc." in molds, so name would appear on finished chocolate Bugs, each rabbit 9-1/2"H x 3-3/4"W, mid 20th C. Great crossover appeal............................... **$125+**

Chocolate mold, bulldog, sitting, tin plated nickel alloy, J.G. Laurosch, #4102, German, 5-1/4"H, 1920s-40s. • There are many **bulldog** chocolate molds – something to do with Teddy Roosevelt, who died in 1919, & was sometimes caricatured (because of his teeth & tenac-

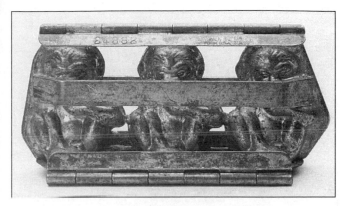

IV-102. Chocolate mold. *Heavy tin in protective frame. Hinged, marked #34882. Weygandt Co., NYC, but made in Germany. They are just 3 monkeys – not hear no evil, see no evil, speak no evil, or . . . eat no evil. Collection of Meryle Evans.* **$100-$110**

ity) as a bulldog. A popular dog of the period – maybe from a cartoon strip? Now with dogs in the ascendency as a collectible motif: .... **$55-$125+**

Chocolate mold, dromedary/camel, but no hump(s) at all, legs folded under, dimpled "hammered" (?) surface, copper. 20th C. .... **$300+**

Chocolate mold set, champagne bucket & bottle, stamped alloy, only bucket marked Ep "#4580," bucket 2-3/4"H x 2-3/4" diam.; bottle 4-3/4"H, early 20th C. Pair:.. **$100+**

IV-103-A. Chocolate molds, "or **pudding molds**. *Can also be used for* **cheese**." *Imported tin, with ribbony spring clips.* **(T-L)** *Rabbit made in 5 sizes, from-1/8 pint to 2 pts.* **(B-L)** *Lamb made in 1-1/2 pt. & 4-1/2 pt. sizes. Swan made only in 3 pint size. Worst & most unappetizing is unhappy dead pig at bottom right. How anyone could think his agonized grimace on the intelligent face of an animal more easily trained than a dog would be fun to eat beats me, but it's an ancient style and mold motif. All from S. Joseph Co. catalog, c.1927.* **$45-$150+**

Chocolate mold, Charlie Chaplin figure, well-stamped metal alloy, marked "Dépose" (deposited or registered), French, 6" x 3-1/2", c.1920s (?). • I had never seen this, nor heard of it until browsing catalogs from dealer Teri Dziadul in Enfield, CT. Her 1986 asking price: $195. Price range is mine. .... **$275+**

Chocolate mold, chicks standing on rim of nest, 2 figures, tin plated nickel & copper alloy, AR, #6543, Dresden, Germany, approx. 4-1/2" across, early 20th C. • Little "nipple" in the edge of this & many molds is called a locator, & helps to line up fronts & backs. .... **$75+**

Chocolate mold, dirigible, nickel silver, marked with name on dirigible, "Los Angeles" & "#1," German (?), 20th C. Highly collectible subject. .... **$175+**

Chocolate mold, dog – poodle or water spaniel with pom-pom poodle cut, sitting, heavy tinned nickel alloy, 2 part mold with clamps, Som #1306, Paris, 9"H, (also made 6-5/8"H), 1900 to 1950. ...... **$175+**

Chocolate mold, egg with image of Man in the Moon smoking his pipe, metal alloy, E. & Co. (Ep), NYC, 4-1/4" x 3"... **$100+**

Chocolate mold, electric iron, heavily tinned stamped metal, 2 parts with clamp, "Vormenfabriek," (reported once as Vormenfaberier – maybe a French form of name?), Tilberg, Holland (often reported as Tilbury or Tilburg), 4"L, c.1930s-40s. Unusual household image; great crossover appeal........ **$95+**

Chocolate mold, Father Christmas on donkey, early Santa character has traditional peaked cap & long robe with short jacket, 2 piece tin, German (?), 7"H, 19th or early 20th C..................................... **$195+**

Chocolate mold, fish with many fins, huge & slightly stylized, dark gray nickel alloy with partial tinning, somewhat flimsy for the length, probably for making a confectioner's showpiece, German (?), 26"L, 19th C. • **Straight Fish** – Unlike fish molds for jellies or aspics, which are curved, this mold & other fish chocolate molds are straight. I don't know the significance of the fish; obviously it's a Christian symbol, but usually

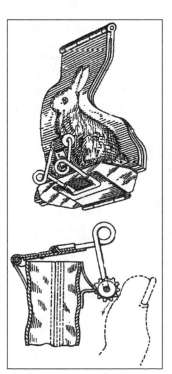

IV-103-B. Chocolate mold latch or clamp patent. *This was pat'd. as a "mold" by John D. Warren, NYC, NY, Feb. 20, 1934, #1,948,146. The top view shows a rabbit mold, as drawn by the inventor, with clamp holding base on. At bottom is a side view showing how you would roll your thumb on ribbed roller that would then go under "shoulder" & latch it closed. Warren writes in his claim, "Experience with [similar] molds ... has shown that it is very difficult to prevent the extrusion from between the closed sections of the mold of more or less of the chocolate mass in the mold cavity and the resultant formation of objectionable 'fins' upon the completed article."*

having to do with Lent, which is hardly a time to be eating a 26" long chocolate fish!...................... **$175+**

Chocolate mold, girl with watering can, 2 piece tin plated nickel alloy, Mistress Mary, English or German, 7-1/2"H, 19th C. or early 20th. • Good for a watering can collection!.............................. **$115+**

Chocolate mold, girl with watering can & large hairbow, "Little Jane," AR, #24222, Dresden, Germany, 3"H, c.1930s. • Little Jane is cute, but fortunately not so cute as the terminally-precious "Mary Jane" little-girls-with-big-bows also made by Reiche in the same period. .... **$115+**

Chocolate mold, horse, extra soldering to make a little clip with wire, horse's legs are separate, not joined or filled in, 2 part, AR #8, & #8760, 3-1/4"H, c.1890s-1910............................... **$145+**

Chocolate mold, Jack & the Beanstalk, tinned copper, good detail, no mark, 8-1/4" x 5-1/4", c.1890s-1910 (?). .... **$175+**

Chocolate mold, lamb, lying down or – in heraldic terms – couchant. Metal alloy, 2 part, Kanter Mfg. Co., Cleveland, OH, 8"H x 12"L, 20th C. .... **$100+**

Chocolate mold, lamb, standing (unusual), steel & copper alloy, TCW, #381, NY, 2-3/8"L, mid 20th C. ..... **$100+**

Chocolate mold, lion, sitting, slightly rusted metal, B.V. Vormenfabriek, #15281, Tilberg, Holland, 4-5/8"L, mid 20th C. .... **$75+**

Chocolate mold, locomotive, white metal alloy, AR, #9959, 4-3/4"H x 6-1/4"L, early 20th C. .... **$145+**

Chocolate mold, man's striped tie with looped knot, stamped heavy tin, very flat rectangular frame, marked only #12680, American, 11-1/2"L, tie itself is 9"L, 20th C.. **$40-$55+**

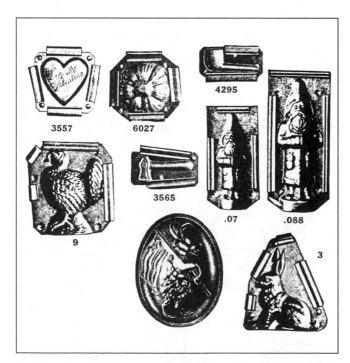

IV-104. Chocolate molds. *Variety of 2-part stamped tin molds with clips, including two standing Santas & a standing turkey. The rabbit with flag could be used to celebrate a patriotic Easter I guess. All from Mills' catalog, 1927. I left numbers on in case you find molds stamped with those numbers. Santas cost most.* **$40-$125**

IV-105. Chocolate mold. *Elephant hinged mold. Stamped "#8306" and also "20." Anton Reiche, Dresden, Germany. About 4-3/4"H. Collection of Margaret Upchurch & Kyle Goad.* **$65+**

Chocolate mold, monkey in hat, very impish, with round object (coconut?) between feet, stamped alloy, marked "H. Walter," Berlin, Germany, 5-1/4" x 3-1/4", early 20th C. (?)...................................... **$125+**

Chocolate mold, monkeys, 3 sitting in a row, but they aren't "Hear no evil, See no evil, Speak no evil," just heavy metal monkeys, a rock 'n' roll band? NYC, 3-3/4"H x 7"L in frame, c.1890s-1910........ **$125+**

Chocolate mold, mouse boldly climbing cat's leg, 2 part stamped alloy, perhaps a reference to a fairy tale, marked "G. DeHaeck Gand," Holland, 20th C. .... **$135+**

Chocolate mold, nursing bottle with baby's face on front, stamped alloy, setting or rising sun behind mountains mark, #2050, 5" x 2-3/4". 20th C.......... **$100+**

Chocolate mold, owl on branch, tin plated nickel alloy, LtF, #1599, Paris, France, 2"H, c.1890s into mid 20th C. • Made over a long period, in different alloys; hard to find........................... **$85-$135+**

Chocolate mold, rabbit, a blacksmith occupational mold, he's got one tool in his apron pocket & is standing at anvil, hammer at the ready, not marked, 1890s-1910. • From catalog of dealer Teri Dziadul in Enfield, CT, who called it a very rare subject. Extra valuable for collectors of iron, or blacksmithing tools............... **$325+**

Chocolate mold, rabbit, high sitting with basket on back, steel & copper alloy called Platina, TCW Co., #238, NYC, NY, 17-1/2"H, c.1950s............... **$350+**

Chocolate mold, rabbit, high sitting with basket on back, tinned metal, hinged at top, Ep & Co., NYC, 9"H x 4"W, Marked "Dec. 1935. U.S. Pat. No. 1,948,146," but it was actually pat'd. Feb. 20, 1934. Later date poss. a reissue date. John D. Warren got patent for the latching base.......................... **$150+**

Chocolate mold, rabbit, high sitting with one paw on basket, tinned nickel alloy, Heris, #417, Nüremberg, Germany, 12"H, pre-1950. .... **$150+**

Chocolate mold, rabbit, hiking with basket backpack, very detailed basket & features, marked "O. Darchambeau," 7-3/4"H x 4"W, c.1890s-1910................ **$150+**

Chocolate mold, rabbit in landscape, clothed & pulling wagon full of Easter eggs, "5 Miles to Go" signpost, houses, Ep & Co., NYC, entire rectangle 5"H x 7-1/2"L, early 20th C. .... **$135+**

Chocolate mold, rabbit, lady ready for church with parasol, wicker basket on back is supported by arm held behind body, beautiful curved body, apron has flipped hem, hinged on side & with 2 clips, marked "14037" & "2," AR, 7-1/4"H, late 19th C....... **$125+**

IV-106. Lamb chocolate mold. *Stamped bright tin, 5"H x 7"L x 2-1/4"W at plinth. Registration nipples & clamp-stands. Photo courtesy eBayer scollectab-at-aol.com, Fred Swan.* **$35+**

IV-107. "Froggie would a wooing-go" chocolate mold. *Front & back views. He holds a cane in one hand, and a bouquet to hand his lady love in the other. Marked "25622." Anton Reiche, Dresden. Very good tinning. 5-1/2"H overall to make a 5" frog. Photo courtesy eBayer my3sons, Lu Matis, Flemington, NJ.*

Chocolate mold, rabbit, striding on hind legs over clump of ferns, heavy stamped tin 2 parts, marked "AR #24353," Dresden, Germany, very large size: 21-1/2"H x 11-7/8"W x 5" deep, early 20th C. .... **$450+**

Chocolate mold, Santa Claus, marked "solid nickel silver," also "B-M #44," 7-1/4"H, c.1890s-1910 to c.1920s. .... **$150+**

Chocolate mold, spaceship or rocket, shiny alloy, 2 parts, relatively flat, American, 9-1/2"L x 6"W, 1960s-70s. • Don't mistake this, with 2 rocket boosters on either side, for the rocket-shaped dirigible mold, one of which is embossed "Los Angeles," & dates from late 1920s-30s. Newer one: .... **$75+**

Chocolate mold, squirrel with acorn, very bushy tail curled up over head, dark pewtery nickel silver alloy, fairly thin & light in weight, 2 parts, 15"H, c.1880s to 1920s. .... **$125+**

Chocolate mold, St. Nicholas forms in high mitred hats, multiple 3-D old-fashioned type in hinged rectangular frame, called by collectors a book mold, metal alloy, 6-1/4"W x 13"L, individual figures are about 6-1/2"H, early 20th C. .... **$125+**

Chocolate mold, St. Nicholas on horseback, with rooftop above him, 2 parts, with clamps, Dutch, 8"H x 6"W, c.1890s-1910. .... **$175+**

Chocolate mold, stag, standing with left leg poised, heavy-weight tin, marked "France 1313" with a dolphin & #48 within a diamond lozenge, Som, French, 12" x 10-1/2", 1890s-1910. Big! .... **$175+**

Chocolate mold, stars, 6 in a row, tray type, bronze-finished heavy metal, "A. F. Tool Co.," NYC, NY, 6"L x 1-1/2"W, 20th C. .... **$45+**

Chocolate mold, swan, 2 part heavy stamped tin, marked "Thos. Mills & Bro., Inc., Philadelphia," 8-1/2"H x 10-1/2"W, c.1890s-1910. .... **$145+**

Chocolate mold, swan, nickel alloy, tinned, Som, "#1756," with dolphin mark, Paris, France, 3-1/4" x 3-1/2", 20th C. .... **$75+**

Chocolate mold, swan, sitting (swimming), tin plated nickel alloy, Ep & Co., #6212, NYC, 3-1/2"L, 1919 to 1972. • According to the excellent book by Judene Divone on **Chocolate Moulds** (see Bibliography), this rather undistinguished looking mold (my judgment, not hers) was made over a very long period – 1919 to 1972. .... **$45+**

Chocolate mold, teddy bear standing (waiting to be picked up), stamped alloy, marked with new one on me, "E. I. Metro, -?- Anver," French, about 4-1/2"H, early 20th C. .... **$225+**

IV-108. Rabbit chocolate mold. *Rabbit in harness pulls wagon full of Easter eggs. Marked "VORMEN-FABRIEK" & "15243." 3"H x 5-4/5"W. Anonymous collection.*

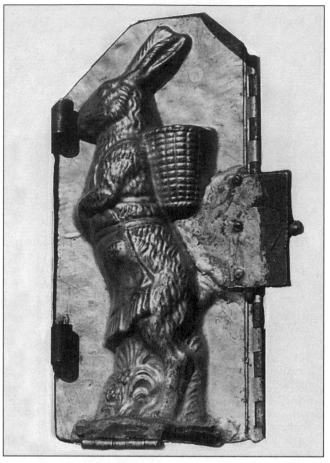

IV-111. Tiger chocolate mold. *Two views, showing either side, and also two different kinds of clips to hold halves together. Heavy, stamped tin. Marked "RIECHE & CO." & "4015," 2"H x 4-3/8"W. Anonymous collection.*

IV-109. Chocolate mold. *Standing rabbit with apron & wicker backpack. Both sides same. Hinged with one large clip. Well-detailed, 20"H. Courtesy of dealer Don Appelquist, Sussex County, NJ.* **$225+**

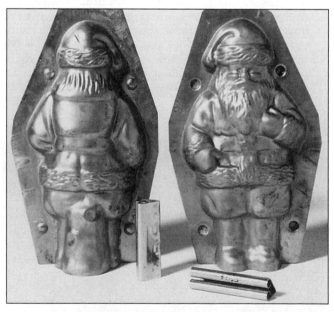

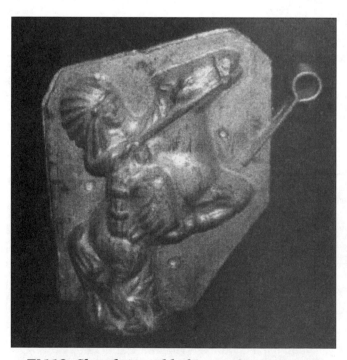

IV-110. Chocolate mold. *Santa in two parts, with registration dimples or bumps & 2 clips. Marked "76." 7"H, heavy tin, early 20th C. (Another, with 8" Santa, marked "75.") Picture courtesy of the National Museum of American History, Smithsonian Museum, Washington, DC.* **$150+**

IV-112. Chocolate mold *of Amerindian on rearing horse, not marked, but probably Anton Rieche, 6"H x 4 3/8"W. Collection of Daniel J. Beyerl, Pine River, WI.*

IV-113. Chocolate mold *of standing Amerindian in full headdress & holding well-detailed peace pipe. Two views, showing clips. Marked "H Walter Berlin Germany" with "#8621" on inside. 5-5/8"H x 2-3/4"W. Photo courtesy eBayer seller & collector robbedoes 2000, Erwin De Smet, Antwerpen, Belgium.*

Chocolate mold, television, alloy looks like stainless steel, American (?), c.1960s. • There are several really modern forms, such as radios & telephones; more & more collectors pay higher prices. .... **$65+**

Chocolate mold, toy soldier with high hat, tinned nickel alloy, Randell & Smith (?), the only English firm, or poss. American, 4"H, 20th C. .... **$55+**

Chocolate mold, turkey, tinned nickel silver, H. Walter #8635, Berlin, Germany, 4-1/2"H, c. late 1940s, early 50s. .... **$65+**

Chocolate mold, turkey, every feather shows, metal alloy, "Vormenfabriek #15292," Tilberg, Holland, 4" x 4-1/2"L. .... **$75+**

IV-114. Chocolate mold *of goggled man in Inuit (Eskimo) canoe. This is believed by some to be an Inuit Indian; by others a member of one of the expeditions (probably Perry's) to the North Pole, because features do not seem to be Indian. Marked "JKV Tilburg" and "16321." 3-3/8"H. Photo courtesy eBayer filra1, Hilde Van Heupen.*

IV-115. Chocolate mold, *two views of little boy, with oversize cap, knickers, jacket with shirt & tie. Stamped tin. Anton Reiche, Dresden, marked "17502." Overall 5"H. Photo courtesy eBayer my3sons, Lu Matis, Flemington, NJ.*

Chocolate mold, violin, stamped alloy, AR #40034, 10-1/2"L x 3-3/4"W, 20th C. .... **$125+**

Chocolate (?) molds, figurals, described by dealer in ad as "nickel plated cast iron," with "6 figures in each" of the various molds, marked "Letang Fils," Paris, 6-3/4"L x 3-3/4"W x 1/2" thick, early 20th C. • **Cast Iron?** – Although this manufacturer made chocolate molds, I don't know if these are chocolate molds, having not seen them. I'm reporting to you to add to our database. "Cast iron" seems odd to me. Subjects as described in ad: child behind hi-button shoe marked "BeBe"; small girl, fancy dress, high button shoe, "Elegante" on bottom; "Jockey" in riding clothes, crop, spurs, "Chasseur." .... **$125+**

Chocolate molds, figures of stamped metal, tray type rows of repeat images, 20th C. • Figures include sitting rabbits, turtles, ducks, roadsters, to cigars, men in the moon, kewpies, frogs & beetles. Prices vary widely according to appeal of individual subjects, as well as determined rarity. Prices range below for 5 nicely detailed frogs (modeled as if seen from above) to 4 army trucks in a row. .... **$85-$125+**

Confection mold, cast brass, round with 2 loop handles, 13 small, finely detailed cups in traditional Chinese shapes, including butterfly, chrysanthemum, koi (carp), lion head, & other flowers & forms,

IV-116. Chocolate mold, *two views of Chinese man, almost a Buddha figure, with umbrella & bare belly. Marked "SCHWARZER," and "2169." 5"H x 3-1/4"W. Anonymous collection.*

IV-117. Chocolate mold, *train engine. Marked "ANTON REICHE" & "9954" & front & back number "34." 4-3/4"H x 6"W. (See also IV-215, ice cream mold.) Anonymous collection.*

very rough casting on underside. Received with the bottom "packed very hard with sand that appeared to have grease soaked into it." This mold was reported by collector Jim Holroyd, who has shared many things with me over the years. Bought in Singapore, 9" diam. x 2" deep, looks 19th C. • Price range mine, not Holroyd's. .... **$155+**

Confectioner's mold – See Molds, tin, listing for French Pie mold

Cookie baking set, Dick Tracy comic strip motif, in original box, Pillsbury's "Comicooky," 1937............. **$125+**

Cookie boards – See Cake boards; also Springerle mold

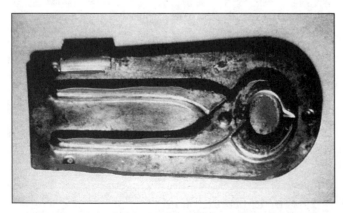

IV-118. Chocolate mold. *Stamped tin, 2 part, makes chocolate blacksmith's pincer tool. 5"H, no mark, late 19th or early 20th C.* **$35**

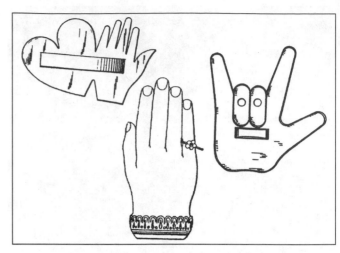

IV-119. Hand cutters *and hand-shaped confection. Left to right:* **(L)** *Heart & hand cookie cutter, flatback, strap handle, pat'd. by Marcia M. Meyers, Poplar Grove, IL, Oct. 22, 1946, design patent #145,812.* **(M)** *Design patent for a "piece of confectionery," received by Thomas Pickering Brown, Boston, MA, June 13, 1899, #31,016. Probably for marzipan, with a brass ring.* **(R)** *American Sign Language for "I Love You" indicated by this design patent received by Loraine J. DiPietro, Greenbelt, MD, April 14, 1981, design patent #258,860. Ms. DiPietro cites Brown's & Meyers' patents in her references. This one was actually manufactured by "Communicutters," in red plastic. Marked with name & patent number, also "Made in USA."*

IV-120. Old hand cookie cutters. **(L)** *Tin, strap handle, flatback with large hole. Hand motif very popular. 2-3/4"H, American, late 19th C.* **(R)** *Old dark tin, corrugated at wrist, folded-edge strap handle, small holes neatly placed in each finger & the heart. Heart-in-hand, 4-3/4"H x 3-1/2"W, mid 19th C.* **Note:** *Copies of cutter on right have been made in quantity by tinsmiths Bill & Bob Cukla, Hammer Song Country Tinware, Boonsboro, MD; each copy conscientiously & responsibly marked on back of thumb with "B. Cukla." Too bad more skilled artisans don't sign their work; when they don't, they are in partnership with any person who passes the item as antique. Size varies widely in old ones, & size, age, patina & design as well as sale venue influence price. Pictures courtesy of the National Museum of American History, Smithsonian Institution, Washington DC. Old ones:* **(L) $700+, (R) $1,000+**

Collecting Cookie Cutters

For Christmas over a hundred years ago, Pennsylvania German children in Lancaster County helped cut out and decorate foot-high cookies to stand in the front windows of their stone or brick houses. These cookie people – often gingerbread men and women iced with rows of buttons and big smiles – were a cheerful sight to snow-cold passersby. Figural cookie making was practiced in Europe at least as far back as the 16th century – most of them were made using intaglio molds rather than with cutters.

Today, the holiday tradition is carried on by a vast legion of cookie cutter collectors who make large gingerbread folk, as well as small shaped cookies, cutting the dough with old and new cutters. For most people, the joy of such cookies would be in the baking, eating, and giving of them. Collectors, however, are more interested in finding yet another whimsical lovebird or unicorn, or a different trotting horse to add to the corral-full already acquired.

Cookie cutter collectors are a democratic group who appreciate and buy cutters from all periods, from the 19th century to the present, from Europe and North America. With the phenomenally diverse forms, a huge menagerie of creatures, a galaxy of stars, a honeymoon of hearts, or a botanical garden of flowers can be assembled fairly easily.

Unlike many collectibles, the "entry level" cost of cutters is low, and because the size is small, collections of hundreds of cutters can be assembled and displayed without vast funds or space. When starting a collection, it is helpful to have a unifying theme – such as motif, material, or season.

Tin – Terne Plates & Roofs – Terne, from the French for dull, is a mixture of tin and lead, and is actually a form of pewter, according to P. W. Flower, who wrote *A History of the Trade In Tin*, 1880. Flower said that terne plates were used to line wooden packing cases of certain products that had to be kept dry or sealed from the air. • "Of the tin plates of commerce there are two general kinds: One is known as 'tin plate' or 'bright plate,' and the other as 'terne plate' or 'roofing plate.' The coating of the former is supposed to be pure tin, and the bright appearance which it presents gives it the name by which it is most commonly designated, 'bright plate.' The coating of the second kind is composed chiefly of lead, which, being dull, or dead, in appearance, gives it the name usually applied to it, 'terne,' that term being a French word signifying 'dull of appearance.' In considering tin plate for any purpose whatever, it is necessary to examine both the plate and the coating. ..." *The Metal Worker*, Sept. 23, 1882.

Tin cookie cutters of the 19th century are the most expensive type. They have many crossover devotees among folk art collectors. Old tin is relatively heavy and thick, and almost always quite darkened in color. Most old tin cutters make 3/4" to 1-1/8" deep cuts (although they can be nearly two feet in height!), and almost all have flat backs with or without strap handles attached. Backs of old ones are fairly roughly trimmed to the shape of the cutter because the tinsmith conserved every possible bit, including odd jut-outs and skinny strips, to be used for other cutters or other small projects.

Holey Tole – In old cutters there are usually several air holes or push holes cut in the flat back – which aided in getting the dough free of the cutter. Small air holes allowed air to escape that would otherwise have been trapped in the cutter above the dough. Some holes are big enough to push your finger through. **How and When Were Holes Made?** – Evidence of how things were made gives clues to their *earliest* possible date, if not the latest. So far, cookie cutter holes don't add dating data. Holes are made in sheet metal by (1) drilling, (2) drilling or punching a start hole then sawing with hack or band saw, (3) punching out or puncturing with something such as a nail, a small sharp-edged punch, or a die stamp (a form of punch). A hand-held hammer is needed to drive a nail or a small punch; and either a mechanical drop hammer is needed to provide the force required to strike a die stamp through a metal sheet, or a screwed or levered press must be used to perforate the metal. • Holes made with a punch or die can be round, heart shaped, diamond shaped, or, in fact, any shape. Most cutters have round holes, some big enough to stick a forefinger in to push out the dough, some quite small, say 1/16" across. At least one cutter from the Robacker Collection had small air holes in a heart shape, which were struck with a tiny heart shaped punch. • The holes made by any method will have a slight **burred edge**, perhaps visible only with magnification. The burr is called a "barb" or "fin," to be filed smooth. Most familiar to us kitcheneers are barbs or fins on punctured tin or brass graters, or pie safe tins. Besides a barb, there is apt to be a distortion of the metal surrounding the hole. It may be very slight, or a pronounced warp, especially with thicker metals and larger die stamps. The larger the hole the more metal resists the strike, and if that is not delivered evenly, some distortion may occur. • **Die stamps** for use by tinsmiths making cookie cutters were available at least since the early 19th C. I don't know how early a simple stamping press capable of making nickel- or quarter-sized holes in tin plate was widely available to tinsmiths. In general, assume a small town tinsmith would be restricted to small punches. A "**Machine for Punching holes in metal**" was patented by J. Sarchet in 1822. Many were patented in the 1850s to 70s. Small presses were available that screw-clamped to the workbench, using a levered ratchet. In the 1890s, and perhaps before, "The Little Giant," American Tool Co., Cleveland, was capable of making a 7/8" hole in sheet iron 3/32" thick. It was marketed to tinsmiths for "small work" – just right for cookie cutters.

Motifs – Among the most popular cookie shapes are hearts, horses, rabbits, birds, long-dressed ladies and high-hatted men, horsemen, and shapes of common household items.

Leaves and flowers are also fairly common – often these are very shallow cutters, and some have even shallower corrugated "veins" that mark but do not cut through the cookie dough. Such cutters would make cookies and also pastry plants to decorate pie tops (see also jagger-pastry stamps further on in this chapter).

Some Hints On Determining Age – In cookie cutters look for old dark tin, rather thick gauge, spotty soldering, irregularly trimmed flat backs usually without rolled edges, and other signs of hand manufacture. Spotty soldering used to be considered de facto proof of age, because it was adduced that solder in the good old days was too expensive to make a continuous solder seam. However, if a cutter was given a lot of use, and solder spots came loose, repairs at some later date would change the character of the soldering and throw off any calculations of age that were dependent on the appearance of the solder. If solder got cheaper, why couldn't a repaired old cutter have new continuous solder? • **Depth Sounding, or Dating By Shallow or Deep.** – It is possible that the old rule of thumb, that a very shallow (ie. 3/8" or less deep) always meant a 20th C. cutter, is incorrect. A large number of interesting and apparently old cutters were sold at the first and second two-day sessions of the Horst auction of the Earl F. and Ada F. Robacker Collection, May and June 1989. There were some extremely deep cutters with not any more apparent age than the larger number of cutters 1/2" or less in depth. The necessary depth would depend entirely on the kind of cookie dough being cut. To save tin, and make more economic use of scraps (which might often have been long straight strips), why make a cutter for an almost paper thin Moravian ginger cookie, for example, any deeper than it had to be to raise the flat back off the dough while cutting? One of the cutters in the sale, an almost 12"H, full length figure side profile of a woman in big shoes, small topknot, and long skirt with pinked hem (or fringe), which was very shallow, was thought by Robacker to be "probably oldest" in their collection. (That cutter brought $775.) • In the early popular collecting studies (and many of the more serious studies) of old kitchenwares, mainly in the 1920s and 1930s, many assumptions were made about many kinds of cooking utensils and tools based on hearsay, and highly colored by sloppy sentiment. Myth cannot be made Fact without direct evidence. • In the case of cookie cutters, **two avenues of research need exploring:** (1) Recipes for cookies or "cake" (50 and more years ago these cutters were called cake cutters), which would predicate the need for cutters in contrast to molds (for springerle, marzipan, etc.); and (2) Diaries, journals, receipt and account books, in which might be found reference to such popularized figures as the itinerant tinsmith who created cutters to order for a meal. • Many figural cookies dating back to the 16th century in Europe were created in carved wooden molds, not with cutters. Ad hoc cutters of some kind, such as canister lids or tumbler rims, were called for in 18th C. American cookbooks, but we don't know now at what point cutters made specifically for shaping dough, especially fancy and decorative shapes, gained widespread use.

Tin cutters are still being made by various manufacturers and by craftspeople. The manufactured ones come in a fairly small range of shapes, are able to cut 1" dough, do not have flatbacks but sometimes have handles, are very shiny and rust easily with bright orange rust.

Prices for tin cutters – For most old tin cutters from the 1890s-1910, expect to pay between about $20 to $150. I know that's a wide range, but many flower and animal cutters can be had for around $35 or less. • **The Robacker Effect** – Notable for all kinds of "Dutch country" antiques, but headlined by the unexpectedly high prices paid for cookie cutters, the first two of four Robacker Collection auctions (T. Glenn Horst, auctioneer, at Farmersville, PA, May 26-27, 1989, and then in June, 1989), had a mixed effect on the cookie cutter market. Prices achieved at these auctions are hard to translate meaningfully because of the extraordinary cutters sold, but also because of one or two extraordinary collectors who went to the heights in order to buy the cutters they wanted. It is probable that if the same cutters were re-auctioned today that prices wouldn't get so high. But this doesn't mean that they have "lost value." In a funny way, the thousands spent on the very best Robacker cutters wasn't real money! Money just had to be the medium that would draw attention to the art value of the cutters in order to elevate those cutters to their rightful place in the pantheon of kitchen collectibles. One important result of the auction and the publicity about it is that serious attention is now given to really good old tin cutters – especially attention from top folk art collectors. As to current value, more than a decade later, there are a few marketplaces where the very top dollar might be attained: the high-quality folk art show held every fall in NYC. And even then, it probably would be only some of the dealers who could ask and get prices in the thousands. Then, too, the value of a Robacker provenance is not fully calculable. A cutter known for sure to have existed at a certain time in the Robacker Collection is known for sure not to be a reproduction or fake postdating that time. With more and more fakes and forgeries and repros entering the market-stream every year, this is valuable information.

Some of the cutters sold at that auction are identified in the listings as "Ex-Robacker." Actual prices achieved may have been high because of the provenance in the famed Robacker collection. Today's estimated value range assumes that there's been some long-term bounce from the Robacker auctions. Also important to maintain the high prices is placing any cutters being sold in the highly competitive folk art market, not the "kitchen collectibles" market, although there is some crossover. Measurements given in the listings are taken from Clarence Spohn's catalog descriptions; other descriptions are entirely from my personal observation or from photographs appearing in one or the other of the Robackers' books, or articles from publications of the Pennsylvania Folklife Society. Some cookie cutters, ex-Robacker, that were small, rather insignificant in appearance or even unattractive, "late" (ie. 1920s or 30s on), or not uncommon – such as simple fish, Christmas trees, flowers, ducks, chickens, dogs, birds, bears, donkeys, lions, rabbits, stars, clubs (as in bridge), hatchets, pigs, deer, etc., – were sold in lots of 2 to 6 cutters. The lots averaged $25 or less each, just slightly over the money for similar cutters found at the average flea market or show. Another low-price factor may have been buyer burnout. A chart of highs and lows of the cookie cutter lots, mixed in with sales of other things (including hot soup and doughnuts), might show some kind of alternating cycle of alertness and eagerness to buy followed by inattention and disinclination to shell out. The figural cutters were probably PA German, but in some cases there's no known provenance, various sizes, averaging about 3" to 4"H x 2" to 3-1/2"W, most if not all are likely early 20th C. One lot of 11 cutters (only 4 had backs) went for $150, and included a hippo, Santa, angel, shooting star, etc., and obviously this lot included some unusual forms.

Stamped aluminum cutters date back as far as about 1900, but most are from 1930 on. By far the most common one seen is the little gingerbread man with a belt and buttons. These are fun to look for, because there are variations. I just found one in a cowboy outfit with holsters.

Usually the cutting edge of aluminum cutters is very shallow and not sharp, the detail is poor, and the pinch-it strap handles are punched-out slits or riveted-on strips. Some have a wooden knob riveted on. Many shapes are to be found, especially holiday shapes, and there are the so-called bridge sets with heart, diamond, spade, and club. They were also used for cutting canapes for the bridge parties, and so were deep, one-inch cutters. The price ranges from about $1 to about $8.

Plastic cutters, made in molds, date back at least 50+ years, and plastic is the most common material used today, even by companies such as Hallmark, who periodically offer "collector editions" of cutters. From the 1940s come transparent red and green cutters that make deep cuts. Opaque designer colors such as aqua or royal blue date from the 1960s on and tend to be shallow cutters. Forms are truly infinite and celebrate religious holidays, cartoon characters, and national events from the Centennial for the Statue of Liberty to the Fourth of July to presidential elections. Wilton Enterprises has sold scores of designs of metal and plastic cookie cutters and still does. Some of the fun shapes include a "Loony Tunes" set, a computer-game-inspired "Mario Brothers," and even "Teenage Mutant Ninja Turtles," and "Barbie" cutters – all created with special licenses from originators of the characters. Ekco – a long-time kitchen manufacturer – offers many cutters. Midwestern Home Products offers cutters in varied shapes. Hallmark often offers collectible plastic cutters – some of their cutters from the late 1970s and early '80s are valued between $12 and $30. This is one collecting field where things that are made "for collectors" actually have a strong secondary market. Some plastic cutters are imported from China, Japan, Taiwan, and Europe. For older plastic cutters, expect to pay 25¢ to as much as $25 or $30; new ones often come in sets, costing under $10.

Collecting Attitude, or, why collect what some people call "ugly" new cutters? First of all, I'm the first to say there are no absolutes about "beauty," and so there are many people who don't judge new cutters so harshly. And, there is more than one way to collect anything. Some of the earliest documented collectors, many hundreds of years ago, assembled oddities and curiosities of Nature and put them in curiosity cabinets. Other collectors bought (or appropriated) objects of aesthetic "merit" or intrinsic worth, including jewelry, gold decorative pieces, marble sculptures, etc. Still other collectors added only objects with religious significance (artworks and relics) to their private collections. The curiosity collectors evolved into curators of science museums; the others became connoisseurs, who based all their judgments on immutable "facts" of proportion, style, grace, finish and other establishmentarian rules (which changed somewhat with fashion, though more slowly). In the history of the United States, there have been eminent curiosity collectors like the Peale family and John James Audubon, who were scientists and artists. Also there have been many connoisseurs and pseudo-connoisseurs, of which the latter are most common and most enduring. The benefactors of many of our museums were either connoisseurs or they had lots of money and good advisors. It has not been popular outside of anthropology or sociology to collect curiosities of art until the 20th C., and even now it is often looked down upon by people who believe in a good-better-best (and not-so-good, worse, even awfuller) system of connoisseurship. (A rueful play on a dealer's appraisal of his wares as "good, better, and best" of each

form, is that it is more likely "good, better, and 'in stock.'")
• For the same reasons that a money standard is necessary, rules and calibrated values for objects need to be widely accepted, or your piece of artwork might be worthless in the very marketplace you needed it to be pricey. I mistrust any pontificant on art – fine, decorative or useful – who claims absolutes, and who says and believes "This is great; that is terrible." Absolute aesthetics are not objective, because there is no such thing as pure objectivity; this critical dilemma lies behind the ongoing argument over folk art (i.e., Yes, but is it Art?). Material culturist collectors are often as interested in the use and context of something, the reality of it, as in the aesthetics. This is not to say that material culturists don't judge objects within a group or class, but they factor in a good deal of value based on purpose or function, or even current educational potential. It is unacceptable to me that even when an old time connoisseur concedes that a thing is interesting, to her that quality is valueless.

What's in a Word? "Cookie" anyone? or "Cake"? – Once there was a clear difference, related to size, kind of dough, and effect of baking. Diminutive suffixes -ey or -y or -ie, indicate a cooky or cookie is a small cake (Dutch *koekje*). **English Usage.** – The English (but not always the Scots) call crackers *biscuits* – small, dry, flat bread or cakes; cookies are *cakes* – (according to the *Oxford English Dictionary* "a comparatively small flattened sort of bread" [no mention of sugar]; and a cookie as "a small flat sweet cake" is a term "applicable" only in the U.S. (says the *OED*). Just for fun, and not part of the discussion here, a very funny term for a tea party is quoted in the *OED*, from the 19th century English novelist Charles Reade: "cooky-shine." **American Usage.** – In *Noah Webster's American Dictionary*, 1858, a biscuit is a "kind of bread, formed into cakes, and baked hard for seamen" or "a cake, variously made, for the use of private families." According to the same American wordman, a cake is "a small mass of dough baked; or a composition of flour, butter, sugar, or other ingredients, baked in a small mass" or "something in the form of a cake, rather flat than high, but roundish." Finally, Webster says that a "Cooky" is "a small cake moderately sweet" and adds that it's a "familiar word in New England." Pennsylvania was not part of N.E. so Pennsylvanians probably called them "cakes." **Nineteenth century American cookbook authors** called cookies "cakes," and the cutters were "cake cutters." Some cakes were thick, some thin, so that is no clue. In the 1920 catalog of The Central Stamping Co., NYC, there are a number of shallow edge cutters with flat backs and handles called "Cake Cutters." These were offered in animal shapes or assorted "fancy" shapes with corrugated edges, and small inset marking designs. Marks would not stay on cookies (or cakes) that were thick or would rise and puff out in the oven. Another shown is suitable for a cookie that rises, has a deep-cutting corrugated or fluted edge round cutter and a bracket strap handle, single air hole, available in four sizes from 2-1/2" to 4" diam. It's termed a "Cookey Cutter," while the one called a "Biscuit Cutter" is slightly shallower and doesn't have the flutes. The 1914 catalog of Shapleigh Hardware Co., St. Louis, shows several very shallow flatbacks called "Cake Cutters," with small air holes, no apparent strap handles though the catalog copy says "Flat tin Handle," possibly referring to the overhanging flat backs(?). Their cake cutters have corrugated edges, with and without insets. Fancy inset ones could be ordered "extra fancy" (and weighed 25% more and cost accordingly). Shapleigh also offered animals, birds, fish, and a tantalizing unidentified "etc.," in their assorted sets of "Cake Cutters." Their cake cutters were shallow cutters with large roughly trimmed flat backs; no handles mentioned. Shapleigh showed simple round deep cutters with strap handles and termed them "Biscuit or Cake Cutters." Shapleigh's only cutter called a "Cookey Cutter" was also for biscuits; it is a simple wire and tin rotary or rolling cutter for thick dough. • **Patents for Cake & "Cooky" Cutters** – A "cake cutter," for what we now call cookies but once called cakes, and the British call biscuits, was first patented in the U.S. on Nov. 17, 1857, by George R. Peckham, (#18,647). The first patented "biscuit cutter" came along May 5, 1868, and was patented by S.E. Clapp, (#77,583). Cakes being so popular, and American moms being expected to make so many of them, certain improvements were made to enable the fast cutting out of lots of cookies in a short time. **Spring-assisted** bouncy cutters, **rolling** cutters to do multiples, and **multiple flat** cutters attached together or to a frame all made speed possible. Suddenly in 1904, the word "cooky" appears in the patent index. Alas, it's for a very boring "Cooky or doughnut cutting device" of concentric rings, patented Aug. 2, 1904, by Frank W. Gardner, (#766,178). In 1906 another "cooky mold and cutter" was patented, by Frank A. Lohmann, (#825,849), but mostly it was "cake cutters" until the 1930s. **Kinds of cookies.** – There are hundreds of kinds of cookies made with cutters and molds; some of the most important are typical Pennsylvania German cookies – especially as they relate to particular motifs, or ones with a long European tradition. Old Penn Cookies. – Ruth Hutchison, in *The New Pennsylvania Dutch Cook Book* (1958), gives 19 pages to late 19th and early 20th C. **Pennsylvania German cookies.** The selection includes raised and flat cookie recipes, from old cookbooks and Pennsylvania housewives' collections, including some that are not necessarily traditional, though widely adopted: "Moravian Brown Cookie," chilled overnight, rolled very thin and cut with "Christmas cookie cutters – men, deer, men on horseback, etc."; "*Mandelplaettchen*" or Almond Wafers, also rolled very thin and cut in shapes; "Almond Cookies" cut in "diamond shapes with jagging iron"; "*Lebkuchen*," a spice cookie of a thick dough type, chilled, rolled and cut in "hearts or diamonds"; "Spiced Ginger Cookies," stiff dough, rolled thin and cut in shapes; "Molasses Cookies," stiff dough, chilled, "rolled very thin, and cut in animal shapes"; "Butterthins," chilled, rolled thin and "cut in shapes"; and "Sand Tarts" [elsewhere called "Sand" or "Saint Hearts"] of two kinds, both rolled very thin and cut prior to baking, the second "cut in shapes – usually rounds, also hearts, stars and half moons." The rest are either drop cookies, or spooned and squashed (with tumbler bottom, wire potato masher or fork). No gingerbread boys, no zoomorphic or figural shapes. Besides what're in Hutchison: *Speculaas*, also called *Speculatius*, are very spicy, relatively low-fat stiff cookies, traditionally made in the shape of a windmill. They are also imprinted with cookie molds made up of individual images about 2" x 1-1/2" – yes, the same as Springerles. **Stiff and Spicy.** – The thinnest, stiffest, most highly spiced cookies were best suited to hang for Christmas tree decorations, especially after icing; this was traditional in Germany, Sweden and Switzerland. Such cookies were hard and tended to be preserved by the ginger in them. See also Cake boards, and Springerle molds.

Cookie cutter, angel, shown fromside, with large wing, mutton chop sleeve, long dress, tiny feet, mounted on oblong tin back, but overlaps considerably, marked only "Germany," 9-1/2"H x about 5"W, c.1891-1915. .... **$100+**

Cookie cutters, animals in set, 7 small ones in simple outline, including pig, dog, cat, deer, horse, cat-like animal with large bushy tail – another cat?, & a pointy eared, short tailed leaping animal that isn't a deer, all tin, in box, imported or American, c. 1870s or 80s. **$85**

❖ NOTES ❖

Catalog Cutters: A Lalance & Grosjean Mfg. Co., NYC, 1890 catalog has no biscuit or doughnut cutters. Under "Cake Cutters" is a 12-piece set of "retinned Animals," including a sitting cat, songbird, horse, lion, sheep (?), leaping rabbit, rooster, donkey or dog (?), eagle, pig, rocking horse, and standing man with cap and insets under arms. The set could be had in three sizes: small, medium, and large. Wholesale prices were $11.25 to $20 a gross, which might mean a gross of sets (1728 cutters), or of cutters (144 cutters). The price for the small cutters, then, were either about 8¢ a set or 8¢ a cutter. For the large about 14¢ per set, or cutter. Since this was a wholesale catalog, and it was 1890, the price was probably from 8¢ to 14¢ per set, to retail at about twice that. • A 12-piece animal set of Cake Cutters found in a 1920 Central Stamping Co.'s catalog has a rooster, mule, parrot, cat, horse, lion, sitting dog, standing dog (?), bull (or other udderless ruminant), dromedary, a song bird, and a long-necked, up-winged bird (eagle?). This set had two catalog numbers, possibly denoting size or gauge of tin. • A 1925 catalog from manufacturers Geuder, Paeschke and Frey Co., noted enamelware producers of Milwaukee, has a page of "cooky," biscuit, doughnut and cake cutters. The only cutter called a "Cooky Cutter" is tin, round with scalloped rim, "solid" back with air hole in center, and arched strap handle. It came in two sizes: 3-1/2" and 4" diam. The "Cake Cutters" came in a set of "Cream City Card Party" solid back cutters, rough cut to fit shape, hearts, diamonds, clubs, spades, air hole and no handle. These sets came in one size, respectively by shape: 2-3/4" x 3-3/4"; 2-1/2" x 2-3/4"; 2-3/4" x 3"; and 2-3/4" x 3". Also offered was a flatback star with 6 points, 3" diam.; and a heart, flatback, 3" diam. The best set? Animal Cake Cutters, 12 different designs, are a squirrel, swan, lion, eagle, duck (?), rooster, fish, cat (?), parrot, song bird, another bird, and pig. All shallow cutters, they are flatbacks mounted to flat, very rounded oval tin backs, and are approximately 3"L. Such a set, which originally came in a paper bag, would be a nice find, worth possibly $120 or so, despite a relatively recent vintage.

IV-122. Cookie cutters & mold. *Varieties of heart shapes in tin. Clockwise from top (L).* **(1)** *"Card Party" cutter, for cookies or sandwiches, in sets of four including club, spade & diamond. Ritzinger, Grasgreen catalog, c.1906-07.* **(2)** *Actually a heart mold, not a cutter, although it could be used to cut. 3"L x 2-1/2"W, fairly deep, with flat bottom, no handle of course, & no holes. D. J. Barry jobber catalog of housefurnishings, NYC, 1924. The following three are commercial bakery types, with thick palm-fitting handles:* **(3)** *is 3" across, with interior trefoil design. Central Stamping Co., 1920.* **(4)** *Three sizes, 2-1/2", 3-1/2" & 5-1/2" across. Jaburg, 1908.* **(5)** *Another scalloped one, 2-3/4" x 3" or 3" x 3-1/2", Jaburg.* **(6)** *Nested set of 7 cutters. Bertuch, Berlin, Germany, c.1904.* **$10-$40**

IV-123. Tin heart baker's cutter. *Commercial bakery cutter with scalloped edge. One advantage of big handle is extra air intake to drop those cookies out faster, plus it fit in palm of hand for more ergonomic comfort. Stamped 3-1/2 in two places on handle. Measures 7/8" deep x 3" x 3-1/2", & heart is 3-1/4" x 3-1/4". Late 19th or early 20th C.* **$15-$25**

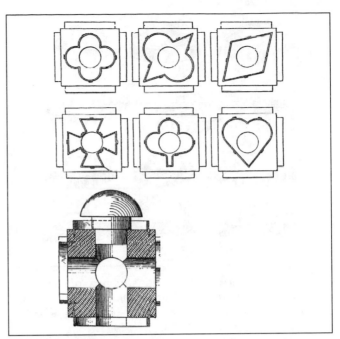

IV-121. Multiple cutters-in-one patent, *by Humbert D. Valle, Philadelphia, PA, May 31, 1938, #2,119,260. Called by Valle a "dough cutting device," the claim was for a cube shaped body with a different cutting die or blade on 5 of 6 faces, and a handle on the 6th. Not shown (because patent drawing was harder to understand) was a totally cubular "pastry cutter" with a different cutting die on all 6 faces, a design patent granted Roland J. Hartenberger, Sheboygan, WI, Sept. 25, 1934, #93,396. (See also IV-152.)*

Cookie cutters, animal set of 12: bird, cat, chicken, dog, duck, goat, goose, horse, pig, pigeon, sheep, & swan, simple tin outlines, original printed cardboard box, "Barnyard Cooky Cutters," American, 1930s. ...... **$40+**

Cookie cutters, animals from farm set, tin, 12 in original box with color picture of farm scene, American, 20th C. • Added value for M.I.B. (mint in box) – sets in original boxes are desired by many collectors, although, of course, boxed sets are not comparable in value to older, handmade, non-commercial cutters. Graphic box really adds value.................. **$65+**

Cookie cutter, automobile of 1930s type, tin, flatback, strap handle, American, 4"L, 20th C. • Automobiles were a fairly popular motif for early 20th C. cookie cutters & ice cream molds. I have also seen carved wooden cookie boards with the open top roadster type of car & a spiffy driver.......................... **$50+**

Cookie cutter, bird, a small distelfink (gold finch or "thistle" finch – favorite food for all types of finches is thistle seeds), tin, flatback, prob. PA German, 3"L, late 19th C. .... **$25+**

Cookie cutter, bird, backward-looking, of type found in Pennsylvania German fraktur & other decorated paper documents as well on decorated stoneware, dark tin, flatback, PA (?), 4-1/2"L x 5/8" deep, 19th C. .... **$85+**

Cookie cutter, bootjack, tin, flatback, American, 3-1/4"L, c.1890s-1910...................................... **$45+**

Cookie cutters, bridge cutters or what traditionally were called hearts, rounds & diamonds, i.e., heart,

IV-124. *Cookie cutters.* All stamped aluminum, with riveted handles. "Mirro," mfd. by Aluminum Goods Mfg. Co., Manitowoc, WI, 1927 catalog. **$3-$8**

diamond, spade, & the trifoil club, tin, set of 4 in original box, rather deep cutters, with strap handles, these were also sold as sandwich cutters, for those little crustless dainties served at bridge parties, American, approx. 3" diam., 1920s-1930s. .... **$35+**

❖ NOTES ❖

German playing cards – Suits on German cards are an acorn, a tulip-shaped leaf, a heart, and a decorated ball. The card suits of the U.S. and Germany correspond thusly: acorn = club; leaf = spade; ball = diamond. I don't know if bridge party cookie cutters pertained in Germany.

Cookie cutter, bugler on horseback, in military charge position, tin, flatback, one of a very popular subject group, the genesis of which probably goes back to 17th C. carved cookie boards found in several European countries, PA German, 7"H x 6-1/4"L, prob. 4th quarter 19th C. .... **$650+**

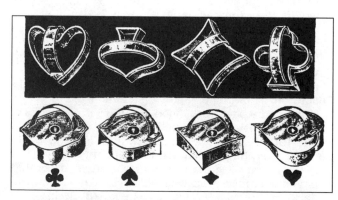

IV-125. *Sandwich cutters,* or large cookie cutters. Pieced tin. **(T)** Simple strap-handled backless set of card suits, from S. Joseph catalog, c.1927. **(B)** Flatbacks with air holes. Ritzinger, Grasgreen catalog, c.1906-07. For singles: **$10+**

IV-126. *"Bridge set" or "card party" cookie cutters,* all pieced tin. **(L)** All approximately 2-3/4" x 3", but heart is biggest at 2-3/4" x 3-3/4". Flatbacks, trimmed roughly to follow outline. **(R)** Card party set plus a star & a crescent moon. About 2-1/2" x 2". Savory, c.1927-28. Singles: **$5-$15**; Sets: **$25-$65**

Cookie cutters, buildings – a set of 4 deep, tin, backless & strapless "cookie cutters" called "Cookie Village," consisting of 4 building-shaped cutters, including a hip roof & a salt box house, a church, & a meeting house (the latter 2 with steeples). Directions tell how to make 24 different buildings, by combining shapes (which you would fasten together with icing). You could make a 3-D building because you were using "firm plain cake, baked in one inch layers." Trees & bushes could be made for your cake village by using only the steeples. It was suggested that you could freeze the village, by wrapping each building in plastic, for future use. No mark on cutters, box with directions is clearly marked: "Fox Run Craftsmen," Lambertville, NJ, cutters 2-3/4" to 4"H, c.1960s. .... **$30+**

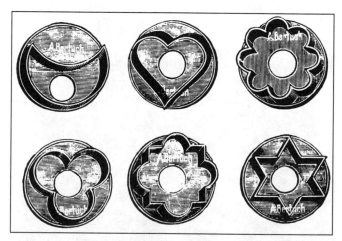

IV-127. *Cookie cutters.* Flat round backs give uniformity, rolled edges. For making tea cookies. The scalloped one top right is a *"Bolivar"* cutter. I have not been able to track down just what a Bolivar cookie/cake is – Simon Bolivar, the South American leader who died in 1830, seems an unlikely eponym. Although linecuts from their catalog shows "A. Bertuch" on cutters themselves, this was probably to restrict use of the linecuts by others, not proof that cutters were so-marked. Catalog of A. Bertuch, Berlin, c.1908. Singles: **$10-$20+**

Cookie cutters, cartoon characters Dagwood, Blondie, the children, dog Daisy & her puppies, yellow plastic, Educational Products Co., Hope, NJ, c.1948. In original box. Singles: $5+. Set: .... **$100+**

Cookie cutter, cat, sitting, tin, no handle, stamped "Davis Baking Powder," 7/8" deep cut x 4"L, early 20th C. .... **$25+**

Cookie cutter, cat, slightly pregnant, suspicious but eminently feline, short legs, shortish tail, head turned to gaze from almond eyes. The detail inset in the face created with small curls or loops of tin soldered inside outline of head, 2 very large finger push-out holes in flat back, PA German, 3-3/4"H x 7-3/4"L, 1870s-1900. .... **$550+**

❖ **NOTES** ❖

New Meows – An amusing pieced tin, flatback cookie cutter, which should be called "The Owl and the Pussycat Combined," a sort of 2-legged cat with large head and round inset eyes, inset beaky nose, and a bird-like tail, appears in *The International Cook's Catalogue*, (Random House, 1977). The cutter, which is 4-1/2"L x 3-1/4"H x 1/2" deep, is (at least in 1970s) imported from South America, where it was used to the make a *galletita* honey and cornmeal cookie, in the form of a *gatito*, or little cat.

Cookie cutter, Christmas tree, tin, no back, strap handle, with tiny narrow brace across cutter where trunk branches out, has a handmade look, but I've seen 2 exactly alike, German(?). Phyllis Wetherill writes that the brace is typically German, 1-1/8" deep x 5"L, 1890s-1910. .... **$25+**

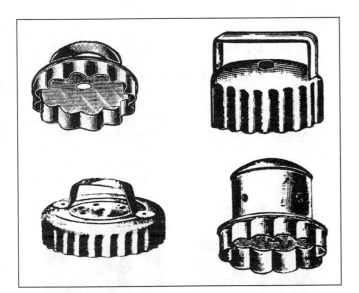

IV-128. Cookie cutters. All with scalloped edges, & one – bottom right – called a "Bolivar" cutter by distributer. Clockwise from top left. (1) Pieced tin, flatback with strap, 3-1/2" or 4" diam. Buhl Sons hardware, c.1919. (2) Seamless stamped tin, bracket handle, 2-1/2", 3", 3-1/2" or 4" diam. Central Stamping Co., 1920. (3) Baker's style of "Bolivar" cutter, Jaburg catalog, 1908. (4) Stamped aluminum with riveted handle, 3-1/4" diam., Aluminum Goods "Mirro." $5-$15

❖ **NOTES** ❖

The **Christmas tree**, because it is an evergreen, has been a Christian symbol, a sacred tree, at least as far back as the early 17th C. Many people believe its pagan origins go much further back, and that the evergreen was adopted, for obvious reasons, by Christians. The other sacred tree to Christians is the palm.

❖ **NOTES** ❖

Traditional New Years motifs – During at least the last half of the 19th C., from various items I've seen, German decorators or artisans consistently used 4 motifs: a gold horseshoe, a pig, a 4-leaf clover, a money bag, and a lady bird or lady bug. In addition, bells are frequently seen, but this is almost universally a symbol of change, including the coming of the New Year. I think we might find that cookie cutters in these shapes, perhaps even a lady bug.

Cookie cutter, corncob, tin, flatback, 6"L, 19th C. .... **$55+**

Cookie cutter, crescent moon & heart, tin, fat cylindrical handle with palm-fitting convex cap, for bakery use, 5" diam., c.1920s to 1930s. .... **$50+**

❖ **NOTES** ❖

Woodstove Christmas Cookies In the 19th Century – "At least a week before Christmas all the tin cooky cutters were brought from the cellar and scoured with wood ash until they shone. There were forms of every shape and description – birds, stars, hearts, horses, and other animals. No one wanted to miss a chance at cutting out these lovely cookies. Usually mother would permit the children to use her thimble to cut a hole in the center of the cookies. The dough remaining in the thimble was baked into 'thimble' cookies, as the children called them. Often a dozen or more kinds of cookies were baked. The recipe book was in constant use. There were biscuits, sand tarts, ginger, and spice cookies. ... Store baskets, wash baskets, and lard cans were brought out and filled with newly-baked goodies. Many were needed, depending on how large one's family was or where he lived. If you lived in the city there was much company and many visitors to be treated. The poor had to be remembered and some cookies must be given to the friend who had lent mother a special cooky cutter." Katharine D. Christ, "Christmas in Pennsylvania," *Historical Review of Berks County*, Winter 1960-61.

Cookie cutter, deer, leaping, tail up, tin, flatback with 3 air release holes, PA German, 9-1/8"H x 12-1/2"L, c.1870s-90s. "Leaping deer" often translated as *springerle*. .... **$600+**

Cookie cutter, dog, standing large breed – Newfoundland? St. Bernard? heavy gauge tin, with folded top edge, strap handle, deep cutter, American, 6"L, mid 19th C. .... **$95+**

Cookie cutter, dog – Scottie, shallow stamped aluminum with green wooden knob handle, American, 1930s-40s. **$10**

IV-129. Cake cutters. Pieced tin with strap handles. Pretzel cutter, 3-7/16", & almond-cookie cutter, 3-1/4" diam. Bertuch, c.1904. **$40+**

Cookie cutter, dog very like a Scottie, running pose, tin, flatback with strap handle, some age, probably machine made, American, 3"H x 4-1/2"L, c.1930s-40s. .... **$20+**

❖ NOTES ❖

Dog Dates – The dog cutter above is the kind of cutter you could probably research to narrow down the date, if it is indeed a Scottie. Unfortunately, there are fashions in dogs. To all dogs who ever were and ever will be, I apologize for not listing you! Mixed breeds are my favorites (I have three now), and they may make up the majority of the decorative canine collectibles we see – they are just dog, all dog. If you love dogs, you'll enjoy *The Bark Magazine*, which celebrates all dogs..2810 Eighth Street, Berkeley, CA 94710; (877) 227-5639; e-mail: bark@thebark.com. Web site: www.thebark.com.

1880s-90s: Surprisingly, the most admired dogs in America in the 1880s and 1890s were the huge St. Bernards and Newfoundlands, because of Victorian sentimental feelings about dogs which heroically saved lives, at least in legend. This accounts for how many of them you see on old trade card illustrations and dramatic lithographs of a huge dog saving a drowning child. A fair number of them were treasured pets, going by old cabinet cards and other photos. At the same time, one of the most commonly found dogs in photographs with family members was the pug, which saved lives by making their owners laugh. **1900:** Beginning in 1900, "Nipper," the quizzical white dog – part bull terrier, part fox terrier – with a well-placed masking spot, was featured by the Gramophone Co. in ads listening to a record player, or, as the ads had it, "His Master's Voice." (The touching story of this dog is very interesting, and is found at many sites, notably www.ais.org/~lsa/nipper.html). At around **1900-1915**, if you go by old photographs, an extremely popular dog was the American Staffordshire bull – usually white with a prominent black mark, often over the eye; this dog breed is often nowadays confused with the pit bull. Hollywood had a great effect on dog popularity. **1920s - 1940s:** When were Scotties really popular? In the 1920s and increasingly so in the 1930s, and they were used as a motif in everything from weathervanes to boot scrapers to pocketbooks and slippers. The most famous Scottie was Fala, President Franklin D. Roosevelt's favorite pet, who often traveled with the President and was in a comic strip. Fala was given to Roosevelt Christmas 1940, lived with Eleanor after the President's death in 1945, and died in 1952. 1920s on: Shepherds (led by Rin Tin Tin in a 1923 movie) began to move up the charts. **1930s:**

Scotties were overtaken by Fox Terriers, probably due to Skippy, the winsome, fearsome, lively barker featured as "Asta" in the 1930s' 14 Thin Man movies with Myrna Loy and William Powell. 1950s: Cockers and Poodles were popular in the 1950s. 1960s on: Advertising, TV shows, TV commercials, cartoons, and movies have much effect on dog fads. Collies, Beagles, Chihuahuas, Bull Terriers, and mixed terriers.

• • •

18th & 19th Century – Very popular dogs featured in decorative arts (particularly ceramic figurines), in the 18th and 19th C. were (1) the little "Comforter" or lap Spaniel, with big eyes, floppy big ears, and silky hair; (2) the Pug, another small, baby-faced dog meant for lap or silk cushion; (3) an intelligent working dog, the standard Poodle, whose poodle cut was known by the 19th C. at least (from France), and whose tight curls, long ears, and cocky tail made great models for works of art or craft; (4) the watersport Retriever, a large dog also depicted with ringlets or curls; and (5) the Water Spaniel, another similar-looking breed.

• • •

Dog Days in Early Pennsylvania? Although some advanced collectors of cookie cutters believe strongly that dog motif cutters didn't naturally fit into the early PA German repertoire of motifs, I believe that if they used dogs in watercolors, on quilts, in wood carvings (think of Mountz) and chalkware figures, why not cookie cutters? Cats may be another story; they are much less common in all decorative art until this century, though sometimes featured in portraits of people, or paintings of kitchen or barn interiors.

Cookie cutter, dromedary (one hump, not two like a camel), used for Christmas cookies, tin, flatback, fairly thin sheet tin, shallow cut, 3-1/2"L, American, prob. early 20th C. .... **$30+**

Cookie cutter, dromedary, tin, no backing, just arched strap handle from hump to belly, 2 legs show, offered as mail order premium by "Dromedary Cocoanut" which was mfd. by The Hills Brothers Co., NYC. Sold for 10¢, or 5¢ through 1915 ad. .... **$25+**

Cookie cutter, Dutch boy, odd small circles (that made holes) under his arms, tin, strap handle, turned edge, American (?), 5-1/8"L, late 19th C. or early 20th. .... **$45+**

Cookie cutter, eagle with spread wings, tin, flatback, 6-1/4"W x 1/2" deep, late 19th C. .... **$65+**

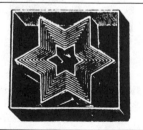

IV-130. Nested cookie or cake cutters. Hearts, 6-point stars, 6-petaled flower, squared 'flower.' Ten cutters per box, sizes range from 1-1/4" to 4". S. Joseph, c.1927. Nested plain rounds & scalloped rounds, called "paste cutters" were sold at least as early as 1860. Set: **$65-$85+**

IV-131. Cake cutters. Assorted fancy shapes, crimped or corrugated edges, flatbacks. Some with interior flower shapes. Central Stamping Co., 1920 catalog, but using much older linecut that may date to 1860s. Set: $65-$85

Cookie cutter, elephant, possibly related to P. T. Barnum's "Jumbo," tin, flatback with strap handle, PA German, desirable size – 6-3/8"H x 9-7/8"L, prob. 4th quarter 19th C. .... **$500+**

Cookie cutter, elephant, tin, strap handle, American, 9-1/8"W, 19th C,, prob. 1880s. Jumbo the Elephant may have been the inspiration for this large cutter, which sold in NYC at a Pier Show for $250 or so in the mid 1980s. .... **$650+**

❖ NOTES ❖

Elephantine Chronology – Most famous American elephant was **Jumbo**: In 1883, circus entrepreneur Phineas T. Barnum bought a large African elephant from the London Zoological Gardens for exhibition in the United States. People were wild for Jumbo, and he not only came to be used as a wonderful advertising image (you'll see many 1880s chromolith trade cards with large elephants, some named Jumbo), but his very name became synonymous with very big. The next time you buy a jumbo-sized box of detergent, you've got P.T. Barnum to thank! The word "jumbo" itself is of uncertain origin although it sounds vaguely Indic, but has been used to mean something very big since at least the 1880s; it's possible that Barnum simply chose a word that already implied large size in colloquial usage. • Barnum's wasn't the first elephant in the United States (even though wooly mammoths roamed the continent thousands of years ago). Probably the **first** was a three year old female, who arrived in 1796, and was exhibited along the Eastern seaboard for an unknown length of time. • Probably the **second** was a four year old male, exhibited in the same area, including Philadelphia and Newburyport, from 1797 for an unknown period. This elephant, whose name was not given in the early newspaper report I read of him, was advertised as eating 130 pounds of food a day, and drinking "all kinds of spirituous liquors; some days ... 30 bottles of porter, drawing the cork with his trunk." Where were the teetotalers when we needed them? • The **third** elephant was "Old Bet," who was brought to America in 1815 by a sea captain and sold to early circus-man Hachaliah Bailey who exhibited her around Putnam County, NY. • **Political elephants.** Later elephant cookie cutters may be related to the symbol of the Republican party, an interesting political comment.

Cookie cutters, fairy tale set of five plastic cutters & embossers (pressed designs), in original box, Hansel, Gretel, witch, pine tree, gingerbread house, American, 1947. .... **$85+**

Cookie cutter, Father Christmas (one precursor of what we call Santa Claus) with toy bag on back, beard & cap, long skirted robe, small feet, mounted to but overlaps the oblong flatback, tin, marked only "Germany," 9-1/2"H x about 5"W, c.1891-1915. .... **$350+**

❖ NOTES ❖

The **Belsnickel** is another Christmas character depicted in cookie cutters. By custom, the costumed Belsnickel came on Christmas Eve to decide which children had been good or bad (shades of Santa). "If one lived in the country, he expected to see ... a weird-looking hobgoblin with a long beard and a blackened or false face, dressed in old clothing ... often ... torn and ragged. In one hand the Belsnickel carried a whip or a bundle of switches, and in the other a bag of nuts, snitz [dried apples], and occasionally candy.

"The Belsnickel always asked whether there were any children living there who had been naughty. Those who had recently raided the cooky basket or forgotten some chore had real cause to be frightened. ... Before he left, he would open his bag and strew his nuts, snitz, and candy all over the floor. ... Invariably, as a boy tried to get the candy, the whip would come down on his shoulders. ... Sometimes ... he left a switch for the parents to use." The origin of the Belsnickel comes from *Pelz*, meaning fur, because **St. Nicholas** was always represented as a person dressed in a huge fur cap and a fur-trimmed suit. He, too, carried, thrown over his shoulders, a bag in which he had presents for good children. His servant, **Knecht Rupert**, had a blackened face and always carried a bundle of switches which he left for naughty children. "The city Belsnickel was a somewhat different character. Often more than one Belsnickel visited a home. Sometimes there were as many as five or six in a group, led by a leader. Their visit was much the same as to their country cousins, except that these visitors, instead, looked for cookies as a treat. The city Belsnickels were dressed in all sorts of costumes and disguises. Among the group one was likely to find clowns, Indians, harlequins and anything imaginable. Often they carried a musical instrument such as a hand organ, accordian, guitar, trombone, banjo or musical bones." Katharine D. Christ, "Christmas in Pennsylvania," *Historical Review of Berks County*, Winter 1960-61. The English counterpart of these musical characters were **Christmas Mummers**, who still parade in Philadelphia. Many cookie cutters are found in the shape of Indians, humorous characters, and musical instruments; probably these cutters refer directly to the Belsnickel tradition. See also Cookie cutter, Santa.

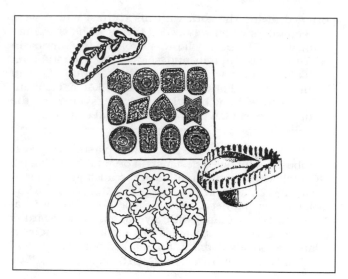

IV-132. Cake cutters. *From top:* **(1)** *Fancy leaf with tulip inside, from Henry Scammell's Treasure-House of Knowledge, 1891.* **(2)** *"An assortment that shows a few of the many designs in cake cutters made of tin, to give fancy forms to cakes. They may be had of all house furnishings stores, & are among the luxuries of the kitchen – very nice where they can be afforded, & they are not very costly. The effect is pretty when different or even a single fancy form is used." Scammell's.* **(3)** *Bakery version of a veined leaf cutter with a fat handle. Came in two sizes: 1-3/4" x 3-3/4" or 2-1/4" x 4-5/8". Joseph Middleby, Boston, 1927.* **(4)** *Round tin box of assorted flower shapes. Sometimes these sets are mistaken for toy cookie cutters. F.A. Walker catalog, c.1870s. Singles & sets:* **$15-$75+**

Cookie cutters, figural set, airplane, star, heart, chicken & clover leaf, 5 miniature cutters in original cardboard & tin box, Dixon Specialities, Inc. (or Specialties?), NYC, NY, box only 1-3/8" deep x 2-1/2" diam., c.1940s. Set: .... **$40+**

Cookie cutters, figurals – tin, old. Animal, human & object forms, tin flatback that fits the simple outline perfectly, shallow cutting edge, a few have strap handles, factory-made, little detail. This kind of cutter is just primitive enough to look homemade, but it isn't. (Though probably they were handmade to some degree.) American, two general groups of sizes, about 3" to 4"L & about 4" to 7"L, c.1890s-1910s. Each: .... **$10-$50**

❖ NOTES ❖

When **Form Adds Value** to factory-made cutters. Variables include collector interest in and charm or appeal of individual forms, detail (though for most cutters there isn't much), size, condition. Large, well-detailed popular forms always win, and bring prices 3 to 4 times as much, within this rather narrow field of factory-made cutters. For some examples, a boring eagle might be $20, while one of the same size with a little more zest might be as much as $55; an armless long-skirted woman might be $20, while one with arms and a hat might be $65; a fat simple chicken with no cluck might be $10, while a rooster with a big tail or

cocky head tilt could be $45. Think Quirk, Personality, Attitude! You get the idea.

Cookie cutter, fireman, poised while working, simple but effective profile, flatback, tin trimmed only approximately to fit outline. As with many cookie cutters it is hard to recognize the subject until you study it (& others), PA German (?), 7-1/4"H x 3-3/4"W, 1870s-1900. .... **$350+**

Cookie cutter, fish, fairly ornate, tin, square or bracket strap handle, rectangular flatback with turned edges, American, fish is 5-1/2"L, makes only 1/2" deep cut, back is 6-1/2"L, late 19th C. .... **$30+**

Cookie cutter, fish, simple & stylized, with crimping top & bottom to represent fins, punched up half-moons as tab handle on back, tin, flatback size of playing card, American, cuts 1/2" deep, 4"L, late 19th C. **$35**

❖ NOTES ❖

Few Fish Flaunt Flair – I've never seen a really really nice fish cutter; most are very shallow cutters, and have open mouths, top and bottom fin and tail, but nothing particularly well-shaped. Also, I don't know why, most of the ones I've seen have very poor soldering, and are coming apart. I can imagine a more intricate one, perhaps with nifty crimped edges to fins and tail. • Fish cookies are almost certainly Christian religious symbols, Christ having been a "fisher of men" and also because "He divided the loaves and the fishes to feed the multitude. "

Cookie cutter, flame, very stylized, of the advertised stove, back stamped with ornate scrolled border & name, strap handle embossed with legend, stamped tin, shallow cutter in shape that looks like ruffle top tulip, "Garland Stoves & Ranges," & "The World's Best," 3-5/8"W, late 19th C. .... **$30+**

Cookie cutter, gingerbread boy, a classic form, though this one is a more than insipid cutter, tin, strap handle attached to flatback, American, 5"H, late 19th C. .... **$10+**

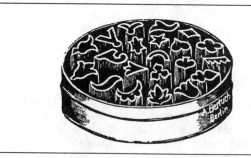

IV-133. Nested cookie or cake cutters. *Leaves, flowers, & a few useful abstracts. Tin, in tin box. Sold in sets of 1, 2 or 3 dozen cutters. A. Bertuch, Berlin, 1908. These were very small, & same or similar ones were sold as canape cutters & vegetable cutters (for decorating broth soups). Many of these round tin boxes of small cutters are still being sold, & were made at least since the 1940s, & probably continuously since 1900 or before. See Vegetable cutter pictures near end of chapter.* **$30-$50+**

GeeBees – English and European gingerbread bakers from the early Middle Ages (13th C.) into the first third of the 19th C. often made gingerbread men as well as other gingerbread forms. In fact, according to Max von Boehn in *Dolls & Puppets*, a revised edition of which was published in Boston in 1956, "The gingerbread doll had a tenacious life ... [and] the shapes which it assumed remained the same for centuries." According to Dan Foley, in *Toys Through the Ages* (Philadelphia & NY: Chilton Books, 1962), "So popular was gingerbread in England that there were fairs where only gingerbread and toys were sold. Each year in Birmingham, two gingerbread fairs were held until well into the nineteenth century. ... Long lines of market stalls, filled with gingerbread in every imaginable shape and form, were interspersed with booths filled with toys." He goes on, "Gingerbread men were called 'husbands' at the English fairs, and were often referred to as 'Jim Crows' in nineteenth century America" where they had become popular since the 18th C. Foley cites Nathaniel Hawthorne's *House of Seven Gables* as a literary source for the mention of gingerbread elephants! Another popular and historical form for gingerbread was the edible horn book, modeled like the wooden or ivory ones, a sort of abecedarian paddle, sometimes with numbers, formed in ceramic or carved wooden molds before baking. Such gingerbread horn books were all said to be decorated with gold leaf, and were given children as rewards, or inducements for learning.

Andrew W. Tuer, in *History of the Horn Book* (©1897, reprinted 1968 by Benjamin Blom, Inc.; & 1979, Arno Press) devotes a chapter to **gingerbread horn books**. He writes "Halfpenny gingerbread was made of flour, sugar, and treacle. In a white variety of cake stamped from the same moulds there was more sugar and the treacle was omitted. Pieces of gold foil were dabbed on both sorts. ... The white cakes being sweeter and dearer – they sold for a penny – were considered better and were ... given as ... rewards. It may be noted here that confectioners sold a white gingerbread of a better class of flour, butter, ground ginger, lemon rind, nutmeg, and loaf-sugar." Tuer believed the molds for gingerbread horn books dated to the mid 18th century.

Cookie cutter, gingerbread boy, shallow stamped copper anodized aluminum, on original printed card, Color Craft Co. #89, Indianapolis, IN, 5-7/8"H x 3-1/2"W, prob. 1960s-70s. .... **$3+**

Cookie cutter, gingerbread boy with barely discernible features (meant for the purchaser because the impression made on cookie dough would be fleeting to say the least), very shallow stamped aluminum, green painted strap handle riveted on, no marks, American, 5-7/8"H x 3-1/2"W, originated c.1930s, but made for a long time. .... **$3+**

Cookie cutters, gingerbread or "spice bread" (pain d'épices) – made by Letang Fils, Paris, & shown in their catalog from 1912. They show outlines, plus interior lines delineating clothing, buttons, accessories, ribs, hair, scales. Wonderful forms: bishop, gentleman, countryman, rabbit, dog, soldier, Arab, lady with buttoned 3/4 coat & flower, lady with ornate clothing, lion, donkey, fish, gingham dog (!),

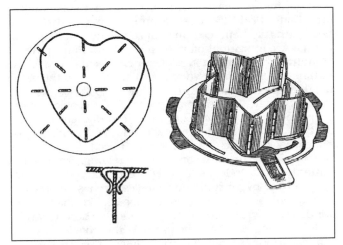

IV-134. Adjustable-design cookie cutter patents. *Not necessarily practical, but a cool cutter concept.* **(L)** *"A device for cutting out biscuits, cakes and other similar articles made from sheets of dough," pat'd. by Charles H. Hawbolt, Portland, ME, July 27, 1909, #929,215. The cutting strip was to have ends soldered together, and be flexible enough to be bent into different shapes – here as a heart. Little clamps (one is shown from side, below cutter) would hold strip's edge while cutting. One clamp stuck out from bottom of disk at each point where you see a slot in drawing. The inventor wrote, optimistically, "The strip is so placed on the disk that one or more of the spring clamps will catch it and the other clamps will be avoided. By a little manipulating this can generally be done. ... One clamp is sufficient to hold the cutting strip in some cases but two clamps will often be used." **(R)** This one, pat'd. by Axel Herbert Carlson, May 1, 1934, #1,957,319, looks more likely. It was to be formed of parts stamped or pressed out in multiple & "easily and quickly assembled" by an economical manufacturer. It required no soldering & little riveting. Of main interest is that sections could be arranged into a shape by a rivet in the pivot slot, and held in place by "frictional engagement." I hope this was actually manufactured & you find one!*

pirate, Chinese man, four little men in hats, & four little grinning pigs. Each: .... **$50-$80+**

Cookie cutters, hands, old dark tin, flatbacks with strap handle, American, from 2-1/2"H to about 7"H, strips forming cutting edge about 3/4"W, at least, 19th C. Hand-shape cutters are extremely desirable, as are full figure & well-detailed human forms (particularly men, because of their legs & thus more detail).. **$350-$1,000**

❖ **NOTES** ❖

Value-adding details Simple outlines of inanimate objects, geometric forms, and some animate forms like some leaves, flowers and fish, are worth the least. Start adding details and the value goes up, sometimes disproportionately. This more complicated detail can be in the outline itself or within the outline or both. **The Outline Itself.** – Detail is added with a closer following of the natural outline, *viz.* sawtooth or serrated leaf edge, fingers on a hand, heels on shoes, a bun, crimps or curls on a head, a zigzag hem, coattails, apron strings, a tongue in the mouth, individual hairs on a tail, a nut in the paws of a squirrel, etc. **Within the Outline.** – Details inside the outline are sometimes added with strips of tin the same depth as the outline, the ends of the strip joined, used to cut out small details or portions of the cookie. Sometimes the strips are not as deep as the outer cutting edge so that linear marks are made on the surface of the baked cookie which would, whether iced or not, make the form more readable or more interesting. Same depth cutter types include small curls of tin to cut out holes for eyes or buttons, or rounded triangles, arches and rectangles to cut out under arms akimbo, basket handles or windows. A variation of this includes short meander strips cutting all the way through the cookie, used to make a strong but small mark, going all the way through the cookie, but short so as not to jeopardize the integrity of the cookie. A little "E" of tin, for example, was used to make a human ear. **Shallower marking types** include simple strips bent in a curve to indicate the line of an animal's back leg, or the veining of a leaf, or to give dimension to the points of a star, or define petals on a flower, or make a heart shape within a geometric or figural outline. Sometimes crimped tin strips are used • **Final note:** Many stark and simple cutters, with little detail, are worthy of study and collection, and can be more dramatic artistic statements than those with more detail. Beware of the cute detail. • If you want to collect cutters, study general books on folk art long and hard, and keep referring back to them after you've been out and have seen some cutters. If you aren't born with a sense of what folk art is, you can acquire it. You can also apply aesthetic knowledge and intuition achieved by studying all other kinds of art and design – from Japanese netsuke to African masks to the paintings of Miro to the wire art of Alexander Calder. A successful collector has gut feelings, backed up with exercised brains!

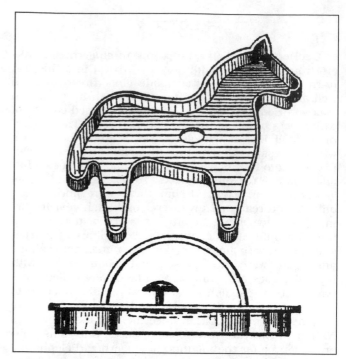

IV-135. Horse cake-cutter patent & tool. *Pat'd. by Henry Erzinger, Amana, IA, April 24, 1877, #190,018. Erzinger's horse cutter patent claimed to "furnish means whereby the process of shaping by hand each individual form of cutter is changed, so that any number of duplicates can be formed from a single pattern." He called for a supporting block with a central bolt to which a "blank piece of tin" is punctured and placed over a central bolt and "be seated directly upon the block." The pattern is then laid upon the blank and secured by the bolt. A narrow strip of tin, which becomes the dough-cutting edge, is soldered on at right angles, following the outline of "forming pattern." Erzinger said that any design could be used for forming pattern – "any animal, bird, game, fish, miniature men and women, and even any article, such as a boot, a pipe, &c. Representations of leaves, plants, and, in brief, any design, may be used." He shows his combined tool which he himself used when making cutters: a handle, provided with a soldering-edge for soldering a cutting strip to main [back] plate, and a hook, to be stuck into "the slot of the pattern after the cutter is taken from the supporting block" to remove it from the design pattern. It is more than highly likely that many old cookie cutters found now by collectors were made by Henry Erzinger! It also helps explain the air-release hole and its placement. Take out some of your cookie cutters & examine them closely for **signs of a bolt** having held a back plate in place through a central hole.*

Cookie cutter, hatchet, with inscribed notation "George Washington's hatchet he used to cut down his Dad's favorite cherry tree," tin, signed "Robt. P. Frey," Cleona, Lebanon County, PA, 6-3/4"L, dated 1973. .... **$25+**

Cookie cutter, hatchets, a pair in one cutter, tin, fat cylindrical palm-fitting handle with convex cap, for commercial bakery use, 5-5/8" diam., c.1920s to 1930s. .... **$55+**

Cookie cutter, hatchet, stamped aluminum, green wood knob handle, one air hole in blade, 3-3/4"L x 2"W, cheap & not rare, but very appealing because it depicts a tool. c.1940s. .... **$3+**

Cookie cutter, heart design, corrugated tin, commercial bakery type, with large fat cylindrical handle that fits in the palm of the hand, convex cap on handle, stamped "3-1/2" in 2 places on handle, no maker's mark, (Jaburg Brothers was one company making them, NYC), measures 3"H x 3-1/2"W, heart itself measures 3-1/4" x 3-1/4" x 7/8" deep, early 20th C. .... **$20-$45+**

Cookie cutter, heart, interesting spring-action push-off rod that goes through the strap handle & is attached to the pusher plate inside, tin, American, heart 3" from point up to crack between lobes, late 19th C. to 1915s. .... **$115-$145+**

Cookie cutter, heart, corrugated around outside, with inset in center to mark design of 3 petals, tin, flat-back, strap handle, lots of little holes in back, American, 3-1/8"W at largest part, late 19th C. .... **$45+**

Cookie cutter, heart, deep cutter, no back or handle, homemade from old turquoise, printed tin "Maxwell House" coffee can, American, 1-3/4" deep x 3-1/2"L, c.1940s. Folk art crossover appeal. .... **$35+**

Jingling Itinerant Tin Peddler Theory – In older popular books on folk art, especially Pennsylvania Dutch, you often find the jingling itinerant tin peddler theory of cookie cutter origins, or **JITPTOCCO**. So far I haven't traced it to its first appearance; but somewhere someone first wrote, in effect, as Jean Lipman did in the following: "It must have been a red-letter day for the *hausfrau* when the itinerant tinsmith came by with his jingling cart and made her some newly designed cooky cutter, while the whole family watched his nimble fingers at work with shears and solder." (*American Folk Art in Wood, Metal & Stone*, 1948). • In Earl F. Robacker's booklet about cookie cutters, he says, "The tinsmith, traveling from place to place, soon exhausted his ready-made stock, and profitably extended his trip by manufacturing a variety of buckets and pots and pans at farmsteads where they were needed. ... The smaller bits which fell from the shears were used up ... in such items as children's toys ... and cooky cutters." Robacker goes on at some length describing motifs, and then: "In later years, with the passing of the tinsmith's jingling cart, a specimen set of cutters would often be put on display at a general store, and orders received there." (*Home Craft Course, Pennsylvania German Cooky Cutters & Cookies*, Plymouth Meeting, PA: 1946). • Margaret Coffin wrote: "In the country the tinker was apt to travel on horseback, saddlebags filled with solder, old lead, and a soldering iron, a spoon mold, a clock dial mold, and bits of tinplate ... [to repair] a teakettle, mend a hole in a pan, or cast a spoon. He made cookie cutters to order to fit the [housewife's] fancy." (*History & Folklore of American Country Tinware, 1700-1900*, NYC: Galahad Books, 1968. • Jeannette Lasansky's *To Cut, Piece & Solder, The Work of the Rural Pennsylvania Tinsmith*, (1982) includes so much in-depth information, interpretive of 10 tinsmiths' account books and cutters, that it could be called a book on cookie cutters, even though it covers all kinds of tinwares. According to her, even in the 1750s many Pennsylvania smiths had a shop. A 1793 ad for "gingerbread cutters," cited by Lasansky, gives a shop address. Lasansky does not, as far as I know, mention itinerant cookie cutter makers.

The 1832 Tinker – "Here comes the Tinker, – surgeon-general of pans and kettles in all the alleys and courts about town, as well as in all the villages in the neighbourhood. Yet, till the establishment of large manufactories, and the making of articles by wholesale, and the keeping of them in warehouses and shops, the tinker was a man of no small importance: and the people had to wait his pleasure before they could cook their dinner. At that time, if any one wanted a pan or a kettle, the plan was to send for the tinker, who travelled with all the materials and tools necessary for his purpose; and, erecting his apparatus by the hedgeside in the summer, or in any shed or outhouse in the winter, the tinker worked away as blithe as a lark, well knowing that he should not be grudged his price, and a mug of ale to lighten his labour. ...

"The tinker, and the other men of the travelling workshop, learned to make the people themselves much more handy than they are now; and that was of far more advantage to them than would at first be believed. A labourer now, whether boy or man, has lit-tle opportunity of seeing the whole of any thing made; and workmen in the great manufactories are not much better; very much of the work [which used to be made by a tinker] is done by machines. ...

"When the tinker went about in full employment, all the boys came to assist with his little furnace and forge; and there they learned to do many useful things...

"But can't the boys go and learn of the tinker still? [Now the tinker] has very little to teach them. ... He used to be an iron-founder and a brass-founder; had ... crucibles for melting his metals, bellows for blowing his fire, and hammers and pincers. He also knew how to mix his metals – could have made a fine-toned bell out of an old tin pot and copper kettle; and work up all the old tin, copper, and brass, for use again. He [made] solder and could give the seam of the kettle the degree of firmness that you wanted; if you wanted a kettle to stand a strong heat, the brass, zinc and copper filings were mixed in a moment, and iron was so firmly joined as to bear a red heat. ... Now the tinker has only a pot of coke, blown by means of holes in the bottom, a soldering iron, some soft solder and a pinch of rosin; and therefore his employment is as inferior as himself" (*Pinnock's Guide to Knowledge*, London, Sept. 8, 1832.)

Cookie cutter, heart with corrugated edge for a Valentine, bracket or strap handle on flatback, not real deep, or uncommon, poss. PA, 3" x 3", late 19th C.......... **$35+**

❖ NOTES ❖

Age Wrinkles – The earliest method for corrugating sheet metal was with the use of a corrugating or crimping swedge – a sort of little molding anvil to fit onto an anvil; an iron piece, cast with the requisite pattern of hills and valleys against which the metal could be hammered, thereby taking on the corrugations. • As far as I can determine, **corrugating or crimping machines** for tinsmiths were not patented until 1854. Therefore, cookie cutters (or other tinwares) that have extremely regular corrugations are almost undoubtedly from the 2nd half of the 19th C. or later. These hand-operated machines (one of which a friend and I found on the

IV-136. Cookie cutter. *Farm draught horse, old tin, flatback, very large pushout holes, 5-1/2"H x 6-1/8"L, 1870s-80s.* **$75+**

streets of NYC in the 1970s) look rather like large fluting machines, or some kind of interesting laundry mangle. The two rollers have corrugated surfaces, and the distance between the rollers is adjustable. The sheet of tin (or brass or other sheet metal) is fed through while the machine is cranked. • A very simple tool, actually a pair of **long-handled tongs** with special jaws with diagonal grooves on the inside, was available and advertised for "tinners, stove dealers, galvanized iron and cornice makers, and all workers in sheet metal." Tedious to crimp 200 feet of cornice for a house, maybe, but just the ticket for a cookie cutter. – **"Packham's Pipe and Sheet Metal Crimping Tongs,"** advertised in *The Metal Worker*, Aug. 12, 1882. • Packham Crimper Co., Mechanicsburgh, OH, also had a cranked crimper which did the same jobs, only faster – a machine screw-clamped to the work table, had 2 narrow rollers and so could only crimp a narrow band of metal or the edge of something – perhaps 3" or 4"W. It was also advertised in 1882. • A tinsmith from Ohio wrote *The Metal Worker*, Sept. 9, 1882: "to suggest that all **my brother chips** [the nickname amongst themselves for tinners and tinsmiths] buy a machine specially devised for **crimping stove pipes**. It costs so little money that it is within the reach of every one, and a tool of this character is far preferable to a combination tool. A machine especially designed for the purpose is expensive only in the first cost. Experience demonstrates their great utility in the tin shop. Devices of this kind are very generally sold in the trade, and may be ordered from any tinners' suppliers. It also promotes morality, for it saves a lot of swearing over ill-fitting stove pipes."

• • • •

Corrugations Not So Old – I had once thought that these were at least 100 years old; they all look so old-fashioned, folky Victorian, dark and beat up. A very nice 3" shallow-cutting heart "Cake Cutter," flatback, strap handle, corrugated edge, and even shallower, 3 petal inset marking design, appears in the 1920 manufacturers' catalog of The Central Stamping Co., NYC, NY. Central Stamping also had an assorted set of 12 fancy cutters, the simplest of which were a corrugated oval and a corrugated hexagon. There were also a diamond, 2 rounds, a square, an oblong, a 6 point star, an egg shape, and an oval with corrugated edges, all with insets, and finally an 8 point star with plain cutting edge. It's reasonable to assume that other companies made this type of cutter, possibly only hearts, diamonds and other geometrics, but possibly leaves and other designs too. They are probably dark because they were either scrubbed too hard, or the tin plating was very thin; the rust and the dings came from neglect or hard usage. • "The less expensive tin cake cutters in their multitudinous designs are very inexpensive and good tools. they are keen cutting and light and durable." Ethel R. Peyser, *House & Garden*, June 1922.

Cookie cutters, heart in hand motif, a Shaker as well as a PA German motif, signifying "hearts to God, hands to work." Old dark tin, flatbacks with or without strap handles, air holes for releasing dough, relatively deep cutting edges, American, range from about 2-1/2"H to 6"H, mid 19th C. to 1890s or so. ..... **$700-$1,500+**

IV-138. Cookie cutters. *Three tin flatbacks with small air holes offered by Joseph Middleby, in jobber's catalog, 1927. A "large man" cutter was 10-1/4"H; a "small" man was 5-1/2", whereas a large animal was only 5"H.* **$25-$45+**

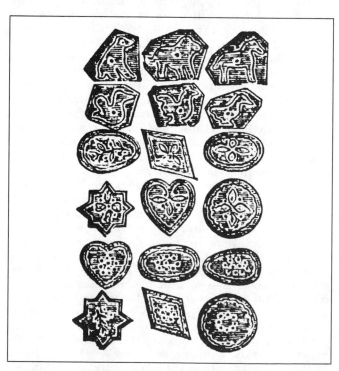

IV-139. Cookie cutters. *Assorted fancy animals & geometrics, flatback tin. They could be had plain, or with "fancy centers" (that made indentations but did not cut through), as most are here. Animals (like lion & horse at top) came in 3 approximate sizes: 2-3/4"H, 3-1/2"H & 4"H. Matthai-Ingram, c.1890.* **$20-$55+**

IV-137. Cookie cutter. *Tin horse on rough-trimmed conforming flatback. One of animal, bird & fish forms in Montgomery Ward catalog, c.1895. 4¢ original cost!* **$25-$45+**

Hearts in Hands are the second most avidly sought type of cookie cutter, after the full human form (mainly men) or vice versa, depending on the collector. Look for old tin of relatively thick gauge, signs of hand manufacture such as the edges of the strap handle meticulously but not machine turned. **Reproductions** of the example in the Smithsonian, made by tinsmiths Bill and Bob Cukla, of Hammer Song, Boonsboro, MD, are marked on the back of the thumb "B. Cukla." • James Barnett, the master tinsmith of the Old Dominion Tin Shop, makes a heart-in-hand cutter. Contact him at P.O. Box 203, Wytheville, VA 24382, (540) 223-0540. E-mail: tinner@hotmail.com. Web site: www.olddominiontin-shop.com. • Other makers' reproductions should be marked, but may not be. You can do a Web search for cookie cutters and find a lot of sites.

Cookie cutter, horse facing right, rectangular flatback, no handle, 2 air holes, American, 8" x 6", c.1870s to 1880s. .... **$150+**

Cookie cutter, horse, long skinny & very short, facing left, very shallow cutting edge, tin, long bracket strap handle, American, horse is 3"H x 6"L, late 19th C. .... **$100+**

Cookie cutter, horse with high rump, high head & 4 little legs like the drawings in that charming 1963 book *A Leg At Each Corner; ... Guide to Equitation*, by Norman Thelwell, tin, small thumb size strap handle, one tiny nail hole to string on cord probably, as it's not big enough to function as an air release hole, American, 5-1/2"L, late 19th C. .... **$100+**

Cookie cutter, horse with very short, slightly bent legs, tin, homemade, primitive, rather deep 3/4" cutting edge, American, 7"L, late (?) 19th C. • Full figure horses are really popular forms; less desirable are horse heads. .... **$150+**

❖ RECIPE ❖

Ginger Horse-Cakes – One quart of flour, one pint of best Orleans molasses, one cupful of sugar, tablespoonful and a half of ginger, two small teaspoons of soda, half a cupful of sour cream, and a heaping tablespoonful of lard. Sift the flour first, and then sprinkle the ginger well through it, add the sugar and molasses, putting in lastly the soda dissolved in the cream. Obtain from a tinner a cutter shaped like a horse, for cutting out the cakes." Gertrude Strohm, *"Pies and Small Cakes,"* The Universal Cookery Book, *NYC: 1888.*

❖ NOTES ❖

Old Cookie Cutter Shapes – Ann Hark and Preston A. Barba, in *Pennsylvania German Cookery*, Allentown, PA: Schlechter's, 1950, give a recipe borrowed from Mrs. Robert A. Wertman Sr. for **"Bellylaps** – An old-time Christmas cooky."** Made of flour with lots of dark molasses, a small amount of butter, two eggs and some baking soda, they are rolled out to "about 1/4 inch thick on a lightly floured board. In the olden days it was customary to make large cookies of this particular dough and they were cut into the shapes of hearts, stars, eagles, horses and their riders." Bellylaps were also called belly-guts.

•   •   •

Batallion Day – Like the Civil War reenacts popular with some people today, there was an annual Battalion Day held in many Pennsylvania communities between 1783 and 1862. This day of parading, training and militia exercises, included cavalry troops outfitted in uniforms at least similar to those of the Revolutionary War. So cookie cutters (and carved cake or marzipan boards), or any other decorative use of the horse-riding soldier, could as easily be inspired by latter day Battalion exercises as by the War of Independence. For more, see J. Ritchie Garrison's "Battalion Day: Militia Exercise and Frolic in Pennsylvania Before the Civil War," *Pennsylvania Folklife*, Winter 1976-77, Vol. XXVI, No. 2.

Cookie cutter, round band of tin, 12" diam., enclosing 16 different outline cookie cutters – duck, dog, bird on a branch, tulip & daffodil. All the cutters are soldered to one another so that all the various cookies (& the oddly shaped scraps left over) could be cut in one step. A number of them were seen in the late 1970s & early 1980s, mid to late 20th C. .... **$5+**

Cookie cutter, leaf, corrugated outer edge, inset marking veins, with big cylindrical palm-fitting handle with convex cap, for commercial bakery use, tin, unusual because marked: "Wood & Selig" (or Selic?) – could be maker, dealer or bakery, NYC, 4"L x 2-1/4"W, cutter 5/8" deep, handle 2-3/8"H & cap dome, x 2-1/8" diam., c.1890s-1910 to early 20th. .... **$25+**

Cookie cutter, leaf, corrugated outside & 4 inset vein markers, tin, strap handle, Pennsylvania European-heritage style, 4-3/4"L x 2-1/2"W, shallow cut, late 19th C. .... **$15+**

Cookie cutters, leaves & flowers, tin, flatbacks, shallow cut, with corrugated outside edges as well as even narrower corrugated interior inset strips for marking leaf veins or little pedula designs, once thought to be indubitably Pennsylvania German, & perhaps the first ones were. But they are found in later general manufacturers' catalogs, sometimes described as "Cake cutters," American, about 2" to 4"L x 3/8" to 1/2" deep, 1870s to 1920s. .... **$15+**

Cookie cutter, lion, very simple flatback, tin, 3-1/2"L, 20th C. **$15**

❖ NOTES ❖

Lions may originally have been borrowed from heraldry by cookie cutter makers; or they may be a religious symbol (the lion and the lamb shall lie down together; or a symbolic representation of Christ by a lion); or they may reflect an interest in the lion seen in early menageries or circuses. Probably the first African lion brought to America was the "Lyon of Barbary," which arrived in 1716 for exhibition in New England.

Cookie cutter, male figure, standing strong man, arms down, feet out, heavy sheet iron or terne plate (a heavier tinplate with higher percentage of lead), flatback with air holes of 3 sizes at head, shoulders, chest, belly, thighs & ankles, unusual in that they are symmetrical, which adds to visual appeal, or rather doesn't distract, as the holes in a cutter this big are very obvious, two strap handles behind knees & behind heart, American, unusually tall at 18-1/4"H, mid to late 19th C. A spectacular sculptural piece with great appeal to folk art collectors, & sold as such over a decade ago by dealers Roger Ricco & Frank Maresca. The piece was shown a few times, & the price kept going up................ **$5,000+**

Cookie cutter, man, hunched & elderly, skinny walking stick, imagine making a cookie & not breaking off that walking stick, tin, flatback, PA German (?), 7"H x 4-1/4"W, late 19th C. Great folk art piece.. **$450+**

Cookie cutter, man in derby or bowler hat, full standing, soldered tin strips that form the cutting edge in 2 parts – top half of his body overlaps bottom half & solder joints are just below waist level on both sides, no strap handle, no back, "Nutbrown Product," a mark found on a number of housewares from manufacturer Thomas M. Nutbrown, Blackpool, England. About 5"H, mid 20th C. Fairly common............ **$20+**

Cookie cutter, man on horseback like a Revolutionary War Hessian soldier, tin, flatback, marked "GHESCINERE MENIN"(?), Belgian (or French, German, or Alsatian?), 11"H x 9"W (tail to nose), 19th C. • Ex-Dziadul. One of several marked this way...... **$300+**

Cookie cutter, man, standing, tin, fat cylindrical handle with convex cap on end, for commercial bakery use, marked "Germany," 5-1/4" diam., c.1920s to 1930s. .... **$80+**

Cookie cutter, man, tin, flatback closely trimmed except between thighs & between back arm & back, an example of Black Americana called the "Runaway Slave" by Robackers & in auction catalog, obviously intended to be a running black man, with crimped hair on top of head, full lips. Small curl of tin for eye, another for ear, but not much detail in extremities. The figure, with its curved torso, appears naked, or at least there are no ridges or other indications of hems or cuffs. PA German (?). Pennsylvania was destination for many runaway slaves. 12-1/8"H x 7-1/2"W, prob. 3rd or 4th quarter 19th C. • Ex-Robacker, $7,400, paid by a very discriminating collector of cookie cutters who planned

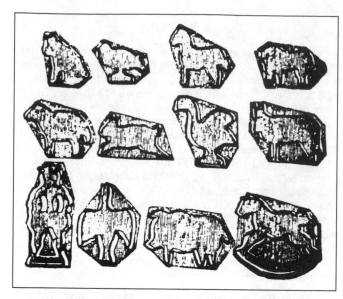

IV-141. Cookie cutters. *Tin, flatback with backs cut roughly to conform to contour. Sold in 3 sizes, small, medium & large. These, like other mass-produced but early cutters, are easily mistaken for handmade one-of-a-kind cutters. Lalance & Grosjean, 1890.* **$20-$55**

to write a book celebrating the folk art forms. The almost unimaginably high price reached in 1989 cannot be used to make judgments about any other cutters. The high price achieved for a very fine cutter cannot be very useful in determining the probable market value of any but the most closely comparable cutters. .... **$7,000-$8,000+**

Cookie cutter, man, tin, rather primitive, standing but no hat or cane, this not my idea of a gingerbread man, American, 7"H, 19th C. • Some of these almost look like political figures. Humorous caricatures of

IV-140. Cookie cutters. *Four of 12 assorted "fancy animals" that were offered in a box for 80¢. Strap handles. All animals have a folky rather than a mass-produced look. Ritzinger & Grasgreen, c.1906-07.* **$25-$35**

Reproduction Alert

"Runaway Slave" Reproduction alert – Within a couple of months of the sale in 1989, an enterprising person in Spencer, NC, created a lookalike cutter (that doesn't really look like the original), without consulting the owner of the superb original, quickly turned out an awkwardly-drawn (but perhaps well-executed) rip-off, in the same size, in "a rich, aged patina," and supposedly in a "marked and numbered limited edition" for $24.95 ppd. Thank heaven it's marked and numbered (I don't know how many are in the edition), and let's hope the marks are permanent and deep. In the original, the lines flow as if Picasso or Matisse had drawn them; in the copy, the back leg is bulging and muscular, the front one skinny, the fingers look like hooves, and the head is tiny and with a hatchet-like projection off the back, whereas the original has gorgeously simple crimped hair, and a robust face. The inset ear on the new is oversized and poorly positioned; that on the original is a sort of squiggled "C" and in good proportion.

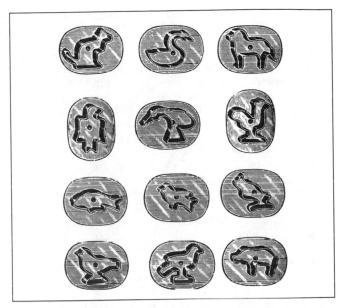

IV-142. Cookie cutters. *Tin, solid oval backs of uniform shape give a more mass-produced look. About 3-1/2", small air holes. Packed 12 in a paper bag. Geuder, Paeschke & Frey, 1925.* **$15-$30+**

people as well as animals were popular with PA German cookie makers. **$175**

Cookie cutter, man with hand raised to reach for something, small curl of tin for inset eye, tin, flatback, PA German, 9-7/8"H x 5-5/8"W, 3rd or 4th quarter 19th C. Great! • Ex-Robacker, $425. .... **$500+**

Cookie cutter, man with hat, interior inset strips or curls of tin making line of his arm, also eye & ear, tin, flatback, together with a simple cutter of man in hat, PA German, 7-1/4"H x 3-5/8"W, & 7-5/8"H x 3-1/2"W, 3rd or 4th quarter 19th C. Hatted men cutters are extremely desirable, particularly in anything over 6"H. • Ex-Robacker, for both cutters, $425. For both now:...................................... **$700+**

Cookie cutter, mermaid with up-curled tail, nice & robust, tin, flatback, PA German, 5-3/8"H x 5-5/8"L, prob. 1870s-1900.• Ex-Robacker, $450. .... **$500-$600**

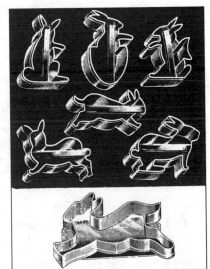

IV-143. Rabbit cookie cutters. *All tin. Strap handle, backless ones at top are about 3-1/2"L. Bottom one, with flat tin back, was about 6"L. It was offered in sitting, running & standing positions also, & was called a "gingerbread rabbit cutter." S. Joseph, c.1927.* **$15-$35+**

Old Catalogs for Research – Nothing is so helpful to the collector as old, illustrated manufacturers', wholesalers', and retailers' mail order catalogs. Especially nice is a small importer's catalog, c.1906, of the firm of Ritzinger & Grasgreen, NYC. Depicted in it are two of an "assortment of 12 Human Figures In Box," which sold (retail or wholesale not specified) for 80¢. They are tin outline cutters, top edge rolled, no flatback or strap handle. Two figures are depicted: The woman's ankles and heeled boots show under her hem, she wears a wide brimmed hat; the man's suit coat is just a bit longer than nowadays, with a more pronounced waist, and he wears a flat-crowned had. They were probably imported from Germany. The company also sold a 4 piece set of Sandwich Cutters, tin, flatback, strap handles, with air release holes in the center, in bridge sets, club, spade, diamond and heart. The set sold for $1.20 – a high price then. The look of the cutters, with flat backs only roughly trimmed to shape, makes it easy to assume that many of the cutters sold as cookie cutters today may have originally been intended for cutting crustless luncheon sandwiches. There is also a deep cutter set of Card Party Cutters, "Hearts, Clubs, Spades, Diamonds," tin with rolled top edge, heavy duty strap arched handle. Another set offered by Ritzinger & Grasgreen is an "Assortment of 12 Animals in Box" for 80¢. Depicted in the catalog are 4 cutters, tin outlines, no backs, 3 with narrow strap handles (much narrower than the strap handles for the Humans. They are: an eagle, cat, dog and fish (no handle).

Cookie cutter, rolling – See Biscuit cutter, multiple rolling type; Cookie cutter, multiple rolling type (at the end of the cookie cutter listings); and amongst Rolling pin combinations

Cookie cutter, rooster, carved wood, cutting edge also wood. It wouldn't really cut, per se, but would smuush the form out from the rolled dough, PA German (?), 4-1/2" x 4-3/8", 19th C. • Ex-Robacker, $250. .... **$250+**

Cookie cutter, rooster, of type sometimes called a "maple sugar mold" – tin with wooden back, PA German, 5-1/2" x 6-5/8", 1870s-1900. • Ex-Robacker, $750. .... **$500+**

Cookie cutter, rooster with high perky tail with 4 squared off feathers, long open beak, 2 oblong legs with no feet, round bumptious rear end, iridescence to tin (possibly coated with something?), 4 small air holes & several small holes up in tail feathers, beak & legs, old type tin flatback, marked "A. J. B.," poss. PA, 5"H x 4"W x 5/8" deep, dealer tag said "not old." Prob. late 1970s or even 1980s. .... **$12+**

Cookie cutters, round, 4 graduated cutters with corrugated edges, in box with lid, all made of tin. "Merridale Works," English (?), box 4" diam., 20th C. .... **$20+**

Cookie cutter, round with scalloped edge, tin, fat cylindrical handle has convex cap on end, for commercial bakery use. This one was called a Bolivar cutter by at least one company. (They also made a Shrewsbury cutter with inverted scallops.) Maker's name not marked, but Jaburg Brothers was one maker/importer, NYC, NY, 4-1/2" diam., early 20th C. A number of cookie cutters that would make Bolivars were patented, although not using that name.

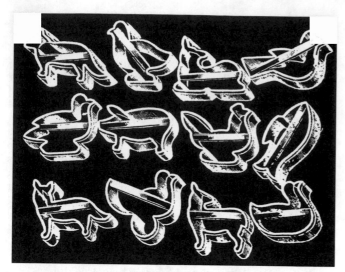

IV-144. Animal cake cutters. *Leaping rabbit was only one of many backless cutters offered by Jaburg, which included in "small" a horse, basket, scissors, pitcher, trumpet, bear, parrot, star, camel, & cat. A "small rat" & a "large man" were offered side by side. Other designs were "Jumbo" (elephant), horse & rider, Liberty Statue, Men & Women, watch, padlock, & eight sizes of hearts. The boxed set of 12 shown under the rabbit was also sold, & possibly made, by Central Stamping Co. The same linecuts were used over & over, & by several manufacturers at the same time. It is hard to say how much more (or less) primitive catalog pictures are than cutters themselves. These pictures, Jaburg Brothers, 1908.* **$8-$35**

For another scalloped-edge cutter, see Cookie cutter & doughnut cutter combo. .... **$20+**

Cookie cutter, sand tart round, tin with corrugated outside cutting edge, inner ring plain, for ring "sand tart" cookies of type traditionally hung on indoor Christmas trees, strap handle, American, 3" diam., late 19th C.. **$10+**

Cookie cutter, Santa Claus, tin, flat oblong back is not cutaway to follow outline, which is more usual. The figure's detailed outline includes hem of greatcoat; he carries small Christmas tree on his right shoulder, stands on block assumed to be the top of chimney, all in all the form & stance is very like Christmas post cards & other holiday images of Santa, this cookie would require much decorating in different colors to make form interesting. PA German, good size: 11"H x 5-1/2"W, late 19th C. See also Cookie cutter, Father Christmas. • Ex-Robacker, $850. .... **$900+**

Cookie cutter, Santa Claus with toy pack on his back & what cataloguer Clarence Spohn (& the Robackers) call a tsipfel cap, a liberty cap (though that's not the translation), tin, flatback, "handle missing, solder loose," PA German, 9-1/2"H x 6"W, prob. 4th quarter 19th C. • Ex-Robacker, $375. .... **$500+**

Cookie cutters, Santa Claus & detailed Christmas tree, tin, strap handles, a pair, detailed, American, 9"H, 1890s-1910.. **$150+**

Cookie cutter, Santa related motif of St. Nicholas with mitred hat & long staff, tin, flatback, no handle, stamped with illegible name – MENIN is most likely, French, Belgian, German, or Alsatian (?), 11"H, 19th C. • Dealer Teri Dziadul. Teri & I think possible variations of the visible letters are: "GHESCINERE MENIN" (or MERIN or MEKIN), or GHESCUIERE MENIN (or MERIN or MEKIN – note how all have same diagonals). (See a horseman cutter, & a woman cutter.) **$800**

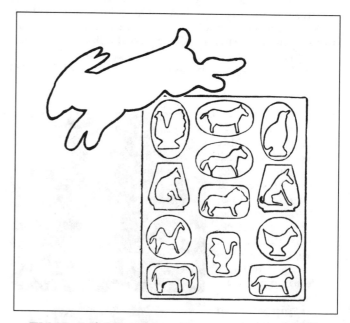

IV-145. Animal cake cutters. *Assorted set in two approximate sizes – 1" & 2-1/4". Tin, strap brace handles, boxed. S. Joseph, c.1927. Singles:* **$15-$35.** *Set:* **$80-$100**

Cookie cutters, shoes, a highbutton pair, tin, flatback with trimmed edges, strap handles, prob. PA, 4-1/2"H, c.1880s to 1900. • **Shoes** have been a symbolic love token for a long time (witness the old shoes tied on the back of the going away car). These cutters maybe were a token of love or, even more likely, a 10th wedding anniversary gift.. **$125+**

Cookie cutter, song bird, a small unidentifiable species, early heavy dark tin (probably terne – see cookie cutter introductory essays) with the satiny feel described by some writers as "greasy," flatback, no handle, prob. PA, 4-3/4"L x 2-1/2"W x 3/4" deep, 19th C. .... **$60+**

Cookie cutter, squirrel with small loop that cuts out eyehole, plus inset strips for detail in tail-brush, tin, flatback, solder very bright (repair? late cutter of old tin? Probably the former), PA German, 7"H x 5-3/8"W, 1870s-1900. • Ex-Robacker, $350. .... **$450+**

Cookie cutter, star, 5-pointed, unusually deep, flatback tin, strap handle, American, 2-1/2" deep x 4" diam., 19th C. • The tin is so sharp & the sides so deep that it's possible these were used for something other than cookie cutting. Can't think what, though............. **$40+**

Cookie cutter, star, Moravian 10 point, tin, American, 2" diam., late 19th C. • For delicate Moravian ginger cookies, thin as cardboard & crisp as chips (great with coffee ice cream)....................................... **$25+**

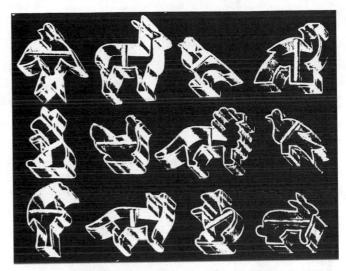

IV-147. Cake cutter set. "Noah's Ark" assortment, 3-1/2"L. Could be had with or without handles. Shown here with what appear to be braces across body for strength. (They also made rabbit set in an earlier picture, which shows handles clearly.) S. Joseph, c.1927. Singles: **$15-$35**

Cookie cutter, tobacco pipe, modern briar type, tin, flatback, for Father's Day? American, 5-1/2"L, this one prob. 20th C., though pipes with a long stem much earlier.. **$35+**

Cookie cutter, tulip, tin. Imagine an oval doughnut cutter, which would make a tulip motif center hole instead of a round or oval one. The outer cutting edge is a ribbon of tin forming an oval, with a small central tulip with curved stem, 3 petals in design we think of as Pennsylvania German. This little tulip cutter is mounted to a capped cylinder which forms the handle, & this cylinder is held in place in the oval's center by 2 strap braces on the long axis, prob. American & commercially made, not PA German, 5-1/2"L oval, early 20th C. .... **$95+**

IV-146. Cake cutter sets. (T-L) is a **"Noah's Ark Set"** of 1" deep x 3"H cutters, that came in an "attractive cellophane wrapped box." In at least the first half of the 19th century, and earlier, children in Christian homes were not allowed to play with toys on Sunday, ecept for carved wooden Noah's Ark sets, after the Old Testament story. Perhaps these cookies are somehow an offshoot of that. **(R)** Standing tall is Savory's "Ginger Bread Man," who was 9-1/2"H x 5-3/4"W x 2" deep. I believe he must have had a flatback to which the features were soldered (or possibly that's the artist's improvisation to help sell cutters. Savory, c.1925-28. **(B-L)** Small set, with 12 designs about 3"H or long, from Buhl Brothers Hardware Co., Detroit, c.1919. Singles: **$15-$65+**

✥ RECIPE ✥

Kindergarten Sandwiches – *Remove crusts from a white and graham loaf and cut each in thin slices, lengthwise. Shape with round, round-fluted, elliptical [oval], cutlet-shaped, square or oblong cutters. Spread one-half the pieces generously with butter, which has been worked until creamy. From remaining pieces cut out shapes, using small flower, animal or fancy cutters, and refill cuts thus made with similar [matching] cuts of bread of contrasting color. Put together and wrap in cheesecloth wrung out of hot water to keep moist until serving time." Fanny Merritt Farmer, A New Book of Cookery. Boston: Little, Brown, & Co., 1915 edition of 1912 book. • I found the "Kindergarten Sandwiches" instructions confusing, even when looking at the picture in the book, so will describe in other words. The "graham" bread is a dark whole-grain bread, and the other bread is white. A tulip "insert" cut out of dark bread is inserted into the identical cutout space in the white bread – like assembling a jigsaw puzzle from two identical sets, one light, one dark. Other sandwiches were* *done as mosaics, held together with butter. Peering closely at the picture of the various cutters in Farmer's book, you see they're are all tin, but different ages and origins. Some are deep-cutting, some shallow cutting, some flatback, some backless, some with a bracket strap handle, some with no handle. The most complicated one is the tulip and oval, which does two cuts at once.*

Cookie cutter, tulip with curved stem with 2 small non-tulip leaves, very graceful form, strong & simple, 3 point large petals, tin, flatback, PA German (?), approx. 6-3/4"L x 4-1/8"W, 1870s-1900. ..... **$110+**
Cookie cutter, twins, females, tin, outline with no detail, no back, no handle, American, 3-5/8" x 3-3/8", 1890s-1910. This cutter may have extra value because there may be a story behind the twins. See below......... **$55+**

❖ NOTES ❖

Twins – Here's something to look for, a Biddendens "bun" mold, as described by Carl W. Drepperd in *A Dictionary of American Antiques*. He says that from the 16th to 18th C., carved molds depicting the charitable **Chulkhurst twins**, Elisa and Mary, of Biddenden, England, who were joined at hip and shoulder, were used to mark the buns (probably some form of cookie) that were distributed to the poor, under the terms of the twins' will. The legend, if it is that, dates back to the 12th C.

Cookie cutter, Uncle Sam. Marvelous tall proud figure, with 5 little curls of tin for buttons down his coat front, one curl for the eye, a sort of E scroll of tin for the little ear, each finger delineated, unusual flatback, in that – according to cataloguer Clarence Spohn – it is the back of a tin wall sconce that was used. The edges of the backing are turned, & there is a little impressed bead molding around part of perimeter. PA German, 12-1/4"H x 4-1/4"W, 1870s-1900. • Ex-Robacker, $3000. .... **$1,500+**
Cookie cutter, Uncle Sam, walking tall, in swallow tail coat that projects slightly over edge of flatback, high crowned hat, beard, skinny legs with heeled boots, oblong flatback, very shallow cutter, one large push-out hole in hat, 2 small air release holes in body, PA German, 12-5/8"H x 3-1/8"W, 1870s-1900. • Ex-Robacker, $725......................... **$1,500+**
Cookie cutter, Uncle Sam, with flying coat tails & high hat, wonderful profile full figure, apparently old dark tin, flatback, American, 12-1/2"H, 19th C. A real one, & you'd have to be sure of yourself, would probably bring: .... **$1,500+**

Reproduction Alert

Uncle Sams are widely reproduced, that is to say faked, now, to capitalize on the rage for folk art. You have to develop a feel. If they look too good, they are. If the drawing or outline seems just too hokey pokey folky, it is. If it's real cute, give it the boot. If it looks too distressed, it is. If the crudeness is overwhelming, it probably overwhelmed its 1970's or 80's maker too. The rotter.

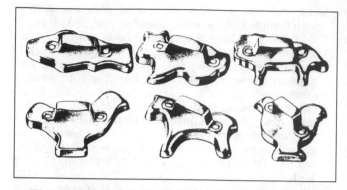

IV-148. Cookie cutters. *Stamped aluminum with riveted bracket handles, about 4". "Mirro," Aluminum Goods Mfg. Co., 1927.* **$3-$10**

Cookie cutter, woman in a long dress, copper, flatback, 2 large push-out holes (bigger than air holes & useful for thin dough cookies that might not drop out of their own weight), very plain geometric female form, with a small circle for head, larger circle for upper body, large triangle for skirt, no arms. Sounds boring, it is, sort of, but still it has more zip than can be described, if you think A R T. American, 8"H, late 19th C. • **Copper** is popular with modern crafts people, but was also used by cookie cutter makers in the 19th C., much less often than tin. .... **$125+**
Cookie cutter, woman, small, tin, flatback, "GHESCINERE MENIN" (? See St. Nicholas cookie cutter above), Belgian, French, German, or Alsatian (?), 6"H, 19th C. • Cutter was Teri Dziadul's; value mine: .... **$400+**

❖ RECIPE ❖

Making Moravian Christmas Cakes *– With your sleeves rolled up and your aprons on, you and Mother begin to roll and cut out. Mother seems to get along well from the first, but at your end of the table there is more or less trouble. ... Your first tinful looks pale and ragged beside Mother's perfect, crinkly ovals ... later you get the knack. All the extra boards are needed to hold the cakes. ... While Mother tests the oven, to see if the heat is low and steady, you survey with pride the hearts, stars, crescents, diamonds, squares, circles and different geometrical shapes, but you think more fondly still of the animals and the men and women that will be made after dinner. ... The afternoon baking is somewhat different from the morning session. You have packed the cakes away in the deep can, and have run over to borrow Mrs. Reed's animal cutters. It takes all Mother's skill to move a long-eared rabbit from board to tin, and the elephant with a curled trunk is troublesome too. There are horses, dogs, cats, roosters, ducks and many others. You are quite occupied holding your breath and making Ahs! and Ohs! as each cake is successfully or unsuccessfully placed. Mother does not make as many of these delightful creatures as you could wish, and when it comes to the men and women cakes there is just one apiece for each of you children. Baking this last batch is more work for both Mother and you, but neither of you minds the extra trouble. You remove them from the tins with* care bordering on reverence, and place them on top of the 'common' ones: not a few lose their limbs and have to be put in the boys' pile of 'brokens.' When the last fragile cookie is stored away and the lid closed over it you and Mother feel that the busiest, happiest and most profitable day of the year is past." Annie M. Stein, Ladies' Home Journal, Dec. 1909. • *This informative little fiction whimsy had a* **Moravian molasses cookies recipe**, *calling for 1 qt. of molasses, 12 oz. of butter and lard, 12 oz. of brown sugar, 1 oz each of soda, ginger and cinnamon, 1/2 oz. each of cloves and orange peel, and 4 lbs. of flour. The soda was mixed with a TBS of milk, and when all the other ingredients (except flour) were stirred into a sticky mass, the soda was added: "How the mass puffed up!" The flour was added last, mixed in, and the mixture covered and set to get cold, before rolling and cutting.*

Cookie cutter combination tools:

The simpler combos were for making cookies & biscuits, two kinds of cookies, or cookies, biscuits and doughnuts. The more complex involve grating or other processes that would end up as cookies (or other pastries). See also Rolling pin combinations.

Cookie cutter & doughnut cutter, strainer & apple corer combined, ingeniously pieced tin & mesh, being essentially a cylinder of tin, one edge of which is corrugated or fluted, the other straight, in between a piece of mesh, & sticking out of the side at right angles is a 3"L corer tube. Further on around the edge sticks out a short tube used to cut the holes out of doughnuts. American, 6"L (including corer), 3" diam. main cutter, late 19th C. • Nothing like these interesting combination tools to get a walkin' hawker's, traveling salesman's or agent's attention. They may have cost the salesman 2¢ wholesale, & he could sell them for 15¢. What a sales pitch too!... **$300+**

Cookie cutter & doughnut cutter combined, tin & wire, round cutter with wire handle sticking out side &

IV-150. Gingerbread boys. (L) *Shiny thin tin, fairly recent manufacture, 8"H.* **(R)** *Stamped aluminum, with details that probably wouldn't show on finished cookie. Has strap handle created by slitting back. 5-3/4"H, 1940s.* **$3-$8**

going through from one side to the other so that the wire supports a small doughnut hole cutter to be used with the plain cutting edge. Flip it over & it makes scalloped edge cookies, which some writers say is the traditional style of cutter for a Pennsylvania German cookie called an "Apee." American, 6-1/2"L x 3" diam. Probably one of Simon J. Harding's patents. One, #848,823, was from April 2, 1907 & had a wooden handle; a wire & tin one, #1,598,717, was issued Sept. 7, 1926, but looks older. The earlier one, when Harding lived in Pennsylvania, was assigned to Fred. D. Harding, of West Baldwin, Maine. The later one shows Simon Harding living in West Baldwin himself. .... **$85+**

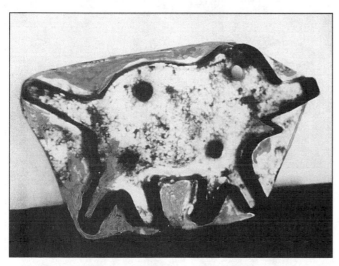

IV-149. Cookie cutter. *A large flatback tin elephant, probably "Jumbo." Strap handle. Shallow cutter, exuberant trumpeting position. 9-1/8"W, 19th C. Collection of Charismatic Studio.* **$200-$400+**

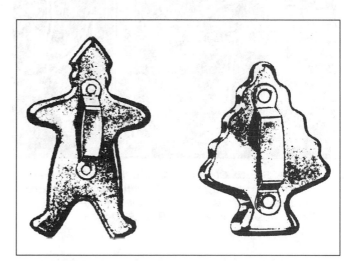

IV-151. Gingerbread boy & tree. (L) *Here bracket handle is riveted on, & there are no features. 6" x 3-3/4".* **(R)** *The tree is about 3-1/4", & catalog pictures were not to scale. "Mirro" Aluminum Goods Mfg. Co., 1927.* **$3-$8**

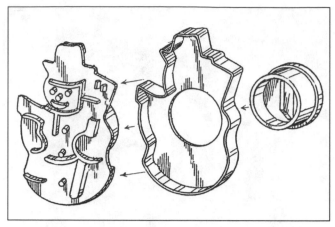

IV-152. Snowman cutter patent. *A modern patent, which cited a number of old patents from 1902 to 1989, including one each by George Zinn (see IV-9); and Humbert Valle (see IV-121). Pat'd. by Robert F. Sadler, Rochester Hills, MI, Apr. 19, 1994, #5,303,473, assigned to Superior Piston Ring Corp., Detroit, MI. The inventor claimed, in the wonderful language inventors have used from the beginning, "A device for cutting and engaging a doughy material having a deformable consistency, ... transferring the shape from a first location to a second ... and disengaging the shape." The drawings show three parts in an exploded view.*

IV-154. Men & women cutters. (T) *Part of what Ritzinger & Grasgreen refers to as an "assortment of 12 human figures." 3"H, without handles. About 1908.* **(B)** *Tin man & woman with brace handle, 3"H, S. Joseph Co., c. 1927. Slight variations from top one, but essentially the same. I wonder what they were holding? Songbooks? Bibles? Cookies? Pairs:* **$50+**

IV-153. Santa Claus & Angel. *Tin profile cutters with rolled top edge (for stability) & strap brace handles. Santa is 4-1/2"H; not-to-scale angel is 5"H. S. Joseph catalog, c.1927.* **$10-$25**

IV-155. Cookie cutters. *Molded light blue plastic with fine interior details. Santa is 5"H; Christmas tree, 4-1/2"H. (These came in other colors.) Stanley Rome Products, 1950s-60s.* **$1-$3**

Apees – *A pound of flour, sifted. Half a pound of butter. Half a glass of wine, and a table-spoonful of rose-water, mixed. Half a pound of powdered white sugar. A nutmeg, grated. A tea-spoonful of beaten cinnamon and mace. Three table-spoonfuls of carr-away seeds. – Sift the flour into a broad pan, and cut up the butter in it. Add the carraways, sugar, and spice, and pour in the liquor by degrees, mixing it well with a knife; and add enough of cold water to make it a stiff dough. Spread some flour on your pasteboard, take out the dough, and knead it very well with your hands. Cut it into small pieces, and knead each separately, then put them all together, and knead the whole in one lump. Roll it out in a sheet about a quarter of an inch thick. Cut it out in round cakes, with the edge of a tumbler, or a tin of that size. Butter an iron pan, and lay the cakes in it, not too close together. Bake them a few minutes in a moderate oven, till they are very slightly colored, but not brown. If too much baked, they will entirely lose their flavor. Do not roll them out too thin. The top of the oven should be hotter than the bottom, or the cakes will lose their shape." Miss Leslie, of Philadelphia,* Seventy-Five Recipes for Pastry, Cakes, and Sweetmeats, Appended to The Cook's Own Book and Housekeeper's Register ...., *by a Boston Housekeeper. Boston: Munroe & Francis, 1833.*

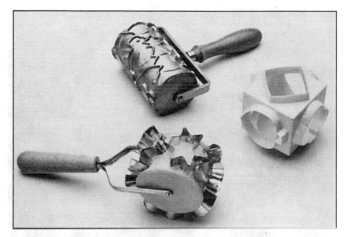

IV-156. Multiple cake cutters. (T) *Rolling cutter, heavy cast metal drum, many contiguous designs, bird on branch, elf, bear, bell, rabbit, chicken, chick, Christmas tree, etc. Natural finish wood handle, 7-3/4"L, no marks, c.1960s-80.* **(R)** *Plastic cube is by EKCO, with 4 bridge club motifs (heart, spade, diamond, club), plus half moon & star. 3-1/2" square, 1980.* **(B-L)** *Roller has yellow plastic drum on which are a cross, 6-pointed star, shamrock, circle, heart & a whatsit. 9-3/4"L, yellow wood handle. Marked "Made in Hong Kong." Early 1980s.* **(T) & (B-L) $45; (R) $15+**

❖ NOTES ❖

Apees Anyone? Ann Hark and Preston A. Barba, in *Pennsylvania German Cookery*, Allentown, PA: Schlechter's, 1950, write that A.P.'s are spelled "apees, apeas, apise and apiece." Marcus B. Lambert in his *Pennsylvania German Dictionary* enters it as "Eepies," and relates it to the French *épice* (*pain d'épice*, spice bread or gingerbread)." Ruth Hutchison's *The New Pennsylvania Dutch Cook Book* (1958), repeats a story from John F. Watson's *Annals of Philadelphia*, that in early Philadelphia, a "young woman named Ann Page had made the first of these cookies, scratching her initial on each one, hence AP's." The apee story may be yet another apocryphal pastry origin story, the most famous being about Sally Lunns. Stories: (1) They were first made by a young English woman named Sally Lunn; or, (2) They are of French origin, and because of their golden top crust and white underneath they were first called "Soleil et Lune" (sun and moon). • **Patented sun & moon cookiers:** Although not named "Sun & Moon" or "Apee" as such, an ejecting "pastry cutter" that made "circular and crescent-shaped biscuit or pastries" was patented by Jennie Boiarsky, Charleston, WVa, Nov. 22, 1927 (#1,649,803).

Cookie cutters, multiple cutouts:
There are various types of cutters making multiple cutouts. Stationary, rolling, rocking. Many are patented (see illustrations).
Cookie cutters, multiple cutters that make several different cookies at once, an auction lot of 3 made of tin. Most, if not all, are probably patented. (1) The

most unusual is the combined flour container (according to Earl Robacker), nutmeg grater and 4 cutters. Body of grater is cylindrical, with oblong raised grating surface along one side. With the lid on, on both ends is a fancy cutter, inside lid is a 3" heart cutter, and finally, with the lid off, a round cookie could be cut with the cylinder's rim. (2) Another unusual one was a cube with different cutters on each of the 6 sides; (3) was a large oval cutter for making 13 different cookies at a time, American, poss. PA German, 1st is 4-1/2"H x 3-1/8" diam.; 2nd is 4-1/2" square; 3rd is 11-1/4"L x 7-1/2"W, the combination piece poss. 1870s to 1900; others 20th C. • Robacker May 1989 price for the lot of three cutters was $800. • A similar, but more **complex combination cutter** than (1), is depicted in Brigitte ten Kate-von Eicken's *Küchengeräte um 1900*. It consists of a japanned tin cylinder, with a perforated domed lid on one end, a fine grater and a medium grater soldered lengthwise on opposite sides of the can, with a finely crimped round fluted cookie cutter on the end, a bracket strap handle going from close to the bottom to near the top, and opposite the vertical handle is a tin bracket with a fluted pastry jagger wheel. A stamped brass (?) medallion attached to the can above the jagger is not completely legible in the photo, but it appears to read "–RGAN COMP/ MANDAL6 (or MANDAL'S)/LONDON," with a lot more that is completely illegible. Clearly it is English. It looks 1870s to 1890s, and is probably same age as the one in Robacker sale. An American collector says it's called a "**Kitchen Magician**," which may be a later appellation. Value range for complex tin combination baking tool cutters: .... **$175-$250+**
Cookie cutter, multiple rolling type, rolling, sheet metal, white wooden handle, "Rollemout" by Ameri-

IV-157. Rolling multiples cookie cutter, *in stamped tin with aluminum handles. Marked "DRGM" & "Made in Western Germany." 4-1/2" handle-to-handle with approx. 3-1/2" wheel with five riveted cutters. Photo courtesy eBayer Nybadhabit @aol.com, Lisa Beh.*

can Cutter Co., Milwaukee, WI, 20th C., "Patent Applied For." • The late Phyllis Wetherill, cookie cutter queen, showed a Rollemout with twisted wire handle in her profusely-illustrated book on 20th C.. cookie cutters (see Bibliography). I don't know which handle is earliest. .... **$20+**

IV-158. Cake cutters. *Top* **(L)** *combination tool: apple corer, biscuit cutter, doughnut maker, fluted cookie cutter, strainer or sifter. You made doughnuts by first cutting with plain round, then cutting center with small tube seen at top. 6"L x 3" diam., late 19th C.* **(R)** *deep star-shaped tin cutter, 4" diam., 3-1/2" deep overall, cutter itself an unusual 2-1/2" deep.* **(B-L)** *lathe-turned pat'd. wooden* **doughnut cutter,** *4-1/2"L x 2-3/8" diam. Late 19th or early 20th C. All Collection of Meryle Evans.* **(L) $125+; (R) $35+; (B-L) $65+**

IV-159. Cookie cutter rolling pin, *with three shapes: heart, star & oval (which made a round cookie). Soldered & pieced tin, nifty knob handles, 7"L. No marks, c.1870s-80s. Collection & photo of Carol Bohn, Mifflinburg, PA.* **$225+**

Cookie cutter, multiple rolling type, tin, wire handle, 3 interchangeable barrels for making diamonds, waffling, or swirls, in original box, mfd. by Guirier, c.1930s. .... **$35+**

Cookie cutter, multiple rolling type, makes a diamond, heart, club & spade, green wood handle, body of roller & cutters are crimped & riveted tin, no maker name, makes 1-1/4" cookies, overall length 6-1/8", marked with patent #1,855,663. Pat'd. as a "Rotary cutting device," by George J. Bregman, Cleveland, OH, Apr. 26, 1932. .... **$40+**

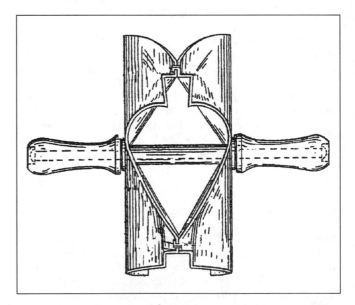

IV-160. Rotary cookie cutter, *pat'd. by George J. Bregman, Cleveland, OH, Apr. 26, 1932, #1,855,663. Different because axis of turning goes through cutting blade cylinder. It's easy to imagine a sort of galumphing gait as a "rotary cutting device" rises up over long cutters, and descends quickly, even if inventor claimed that "the device can be rolled smoothly and rapidly over a mixing board ... having a sheet or strip of dough spread thereon." However, against all odds, it was actually made, in aluminum, with black wooden handles, & is supposedly stamped "FOLER" – which I think could be a misreading of "FOLEY."*

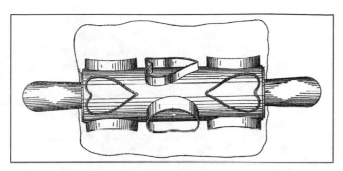

IV-161. Cookie cutter rolling pin patent. *Pat'd. Oct. 31, 1865, by Isaac N. Pyle, Decatur, IN, #50,732. "I have invented a new & improved combined cake-cutter & rolling-pin." The pin was an ordinary rolling pin of "any desired size or length. It may be of the ordinary kind, having its handles formed out of the same piece of wood or made separately, and rigidly secured to it; but I prefer to make the rolling pin without handles, and insert a rod in each end, and place the handles upon the rod, a hole ... having previously been made through them, and securing them with a nut on the end of the rods." The cake cutters are made on a cylinder that will "envelop or partially envelop" the rolling pin, which you provide. "It will be understood that the roller is to be used as an ordinary roller for rolling out dough into sheets; that it can then be rubbed off & enveloped in the case. This can then be rolled over the sheet of dough, & the cakes will be cut out quickly & accurately. The cakes so soon as cut drop out of the cutters more readily than when ordinary flat-surfaced cake cutters are used." Official Gazette of the U.S. Patent Office. In picture, odd oblong shape represents rolled out dough. Pyle said that of course it was understood that "several different cases, bearing different designs" could be used in succession, providing many varied cookies. If this was ever made, which is not known, it would have a high value:* **$300+**

❖ NOTES ❖

Periodical research – I have not been able to track down a copy of the periodical, but in the September 1925 issue of *Industrial Education Magazine*, there is a how-to article by an H.W. Paine entitled "Rotary Cookie Cutter." (At that time, rotary cookie and biscuit and doughnut cutters were well-known.) I know there is an article, although I've not found it or read it, because of the *Readers' Guide to Periodical Literature* subject and author index, which is in most if not all public libraries, and lists articles that appeared in magazines from last part of 19th C. to date. – The problem is that the library probably does not have a full set of the particular magazine you want to see. So make a list and contact used magazine dealers and look at flea markets and house sales.)

Cookie molds, cast iron:
There are many reproductions of these on the market; most are a gritty silvery or gray iron, and they date from the mid to late 20th century. Old ones are very dark gleaming black, with very fine and well-defined casting, with a very satiny smooth finish to the finger. • Iron collector Joel Schiff terms these **press & roll-over molds**, "to distinguish them from cookie/biscuit/muffin pan molds. Old ones (often from England) were frequently large, very smooth & with classical motifs such as the pineapple, the Odd-Fellows chain links, Greek urns & lyres, basket of flowers, & bird-on-a-branch."

Cookie mold, basket of berries, cast iron, oval, gritty silvery look to iron which indicates it is a modern cheap reproduction, American (?), 5-3/4"L. If this were really an old mold, it would be from the mid 19th C. This dates to the mid to late 20th C. At most: .. **$10+**

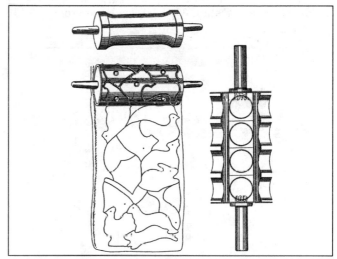

IV-162. Two rotary cake cutter patents. (L) *is a waste not, want not cutter pat'd. by Edward Stumpf, Jersey City, NJ, July 10, 1906, #825,775. At top is "body or core" of cutter, awaiting cutting "sleeve" to be slipped onto it. Below is thing in operation, with cutting sleeve which has flanges or "cutting ribs" "arranged in form of an endless or annular irregularly-filamented web (simulating a spider's web) extending continuously around the surface. ... The filaments form a series of figures which vary in shape as desired. [Here] I have shown the filaments, ribs, or flanges properly shaped ... to form ... the shapes of the heads or bodies of various birds and animals." Stumpf claimed that there would be no waste dough, and hence no need to remove "small intervening portions of dough." **(R)** Pat'd. by Edward A.C. Petersen, Chicago, IL, Jan. 26, 1892, #467,828. Again, cutters could be in "any desired shape, with any fanciful kind of a cutting-edge, and they can, if desired, have a central cutter ... for making doughnuts." Petersen wrote that "I prefer to removably secure the cutters to the cylinder, so that they can be removed and replaced by others of another design, and as a convenient way of attaching them to the cylinder I have ... adapted [the cylinder] to receive lips or flanges on the cutters." You had to remove one handle & end disk to remove cutters.*

Cookie mold, basket of holly, cast iron oval, casting gate in back, not in middle, mostly ground down flat, Christmas holly in theorum-like low, flared sides basket, no mark, prob. American, 5-7/8"L x 4"W x 1/4" deep, c.1840s to 1860s. .... **$150+**

Cookie mold, bee skip or skep, flat cast iron oval, prob. NY state, 19th C. A bee skip is a coiled & bound rush, straw or reed hive, placed on a wooden stand – a bench or table. They look like upside-down rush baskets with a hole in the side. .... **$150+**

Cookie mold, bird on branch, carved granite, two-sided, with flowers & monogram on other side, very rare, 4" x 6-1/2" early 19th C. Folk art collectors find stone carvings very desirable. .... **$250+**

Cookie mold, bird on branch with 5 stars, oval, cast iron, no handles, possibly a wafer mold – at least it could make thin wafer like "cookies." 5" x 3-1/2" oval, mid 19th C. Molds meant for cookies, without the reins or long handles of wafer molds, & resembling secular wafer molds in their designs, were made by foundries in NY state & probably elsewhere. **$250**

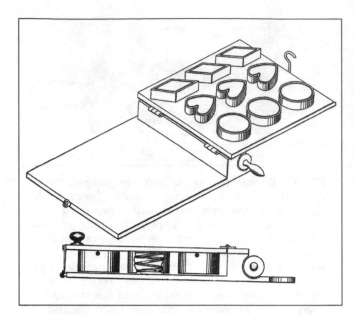

*IV-164. **Cake or biscuit cutter & "molding board" patent,** another version, another inventor. Pat'd. by Alexander P. Ashbourne, Oakland, CA, Nov. 30, 1875, #170,460. The hinged board has a hinged cover to which cutters are affixed. The dough is rolled out or laid on part at left, then cover is shut down upon it & "instantaneously" will cut cakes or biscuits. The lower image is a section drawing showing spring inside each cutter. A presser plate or ejection plate cut exactly to fit inside each cutter ejects the cut dough, leaving it on board. A cleaning nightmare, but definitely easier to use than Shrote's. After latching cutting lid to board, it could be hung on wall from that backboard; rolling pin fits into cutout endpieces, as seen.*

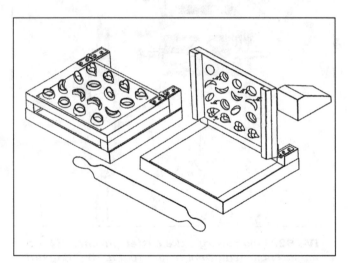

*IV-163. **Cake cutter & cutting board patent,** two views & rolling pin. Pat'd. under title "Cutting and panning cakes" by John H. Shrote, Baltimore, MD, Oct. 11, 1859, #25,767. **(L)** Perspective "view of the invention ready to cut the dough into cakes and to deliver the cakes on the pan for baking." **(R)** Another perspective view with the cutter board elevated [in upright position] in the act of discharging the scraps left on it after cutting out the cakes and depositing them on the pan." The wooden rolling pin is ordinary. Shrote explained the construction as having tin cutters in any desired shape soldered to a sheet of tin, and then a board "with corresponding holes cut through it, onto which the cutters are firmly attached." It seems to work by rolling out dough to desired thickness, then laying dough on the sheet of cutters & rolling the pin over it "sufficiently hard to cut the cakes." Shrote claims that then they fall at once down on the pan which is placed inside the bottom frame. Then you raise the frame, knock it against the block (seen behind) to dislodge scrap dough & start over. Frankly, I'd have to see it to believe it! The inventor reserved the right to make the complicated cutting plate of pieced & soldered tin & wood out of a single cast iron piece.*

❖ NOTES ❖

Date By State, or Star-gazing – The look of the bird mold is c.1840s to 1860s. But if you use a star chart as it relates to each state entering the Republic, it could mean this dated to 1788, when the 5th state (Connecticut) through the 11th state joined the union.

Cookie mold, butterfly, flat cast iron oval, Albany, NY, 5-1/2"L, early 19th C. Extremely unusual motif. .... **$225+**

Cookie mold, cornucopia, cast iron, rounded oval, central cornucopia holding melon, pineapple, grapes, fat leaves spilling out, 2 star-like X marks, border entirely made up of small dots, rather close together, perhaps done by a stove foundry, looks like casting from Troy or Albany, NY, 4"L, c.1840s. .... **$150+**

Cookie mold, lyre, cast iron, oval, gritty silvery look to iron which indicates it is probably a modern cheap reproduction, American (?), 5-1/4"L. If old, mid 19th C.; if new, prob. mid 20th C., worth under $10. .... **$30+**

Cookie mold, Odd Fellows, cast iron, oval with hanging hole, Odd Fellows symbols: 3 chain links (Friendship, Love and Truth), hatchet, fireman's pike, 3 columns or pillars, hand with heart in palm, crossed swords, bow and arrow, American, 6-13/16"L x 5"W, 19th C. • This thing looks like a firemark, but if it

IV-165. Cookie mold. Cast iron, oval, intaglio fruit & berries in a basket. Casting gate on back is mostly ground down. 5-7/8"L x 4"W x 1/4" deep. Possibly Albany or Troy, NY, 19th C. $150+

Reproduction Alert

A very rounded **oval pineapple mold**, cast iron with enough matt black paint finish to hide any gritty surface (if it exists) front and back, is marked on the back with a permanent molded identification. In a small oval are initials "OSV" surrounded by words "Old Sturbridge Village," plus another mark with illegible numbers or letters, plus numbers "5-50." This mold has a fairly large hole all the way through near the top for hanging. It is probably cast from a mold made from an original in their collection. If you've never been to Old Sturbridge in Massachusetts, do go; it's a wonderful place. And you could always "do Brimfield" before or after, as it's just a few miles away. **$30+**

were it would have more than one hole, as it would have to be screwed or bolted to a building wall. For more information on Odd Fellows, see a listing regarding Fraternal Order motifs in with the butter stamp listings. .... **$175+**

Cookie mold, Odd Fellows, cast iron, rounded oval, I.O.O.F. symbols almost the same as the other one, 3 linked chain, bow & 2 arrows, crossed swords, heart in palm of hand, & 3 pillars, no hanging hole. American, 6"L x 4-1/2"W, 19th C. .... **$175+**

Cookie mold, pineapple, cast iron, oval, Albany Foundry Co. (?), Albany, NY, 6"L x 4 1/2", looks much earlier in 19th C. than this company, which was est. in 1897. .... **$150+**

Cookie mold, pineapple, cast iron, oval, gritty silvery look to iron which indicates it's probably a modern cheap reproduction, American (?), 6"L, if old, mid 19th C.; if new, prob. mid 20th C.

Cookie mold, urn, cast iron, rectangular, intaglio design of neo-classical Greek urn with flowers; assumed to be NY state, but not marked. 4" x 2-3/4" mid 19th C. (?)... **$150+**

Cookie mold, or marchpane mold, or even springerle mold. Good old cast iron, elliptical shape with a narrow channel around outside, plus 20 round concave dimples framing unusual subject – child on footed chamberpot or thundermug with handle, child has small pointy feet, almost look like boots with little heels, finely modeled, iron is right: very smooth &

silky to feel, finely grained, no marks, prob. American, prob. NY state, maybe Troy or Albany – stove foundry towns. 5-3/4"L x 3-3/8"W x 1/2" deep, from look of child & chamberpot, I believe c.1840s-1850s.
• Most of these molds which are right, & not grainy gray repros, may have come, as popular supposition has it, from New York State, possibly an Albany foundry, or even The Albany Foundry Co., in existance only from 1897-1932, though late 19th C. or early 20th seems very late. Mold found by dealer Ed Boeyink, of Hilton, N.Y., between Albany & Syracuse, in a long-held private collection. .... **$300+**

IV-166-A. Cookie or marchpane molds. "Marchpane" is the English equivalent of marzipan. Cast iron, elliptical or oval intaglio designs. Upper (L) Unusual design of boy with pipe in his mouth, sitting on chamber pot. 3-1/2" x 6". Border design of dots. The author's version is quite similar, though 1/4" smaller, & child has no pipe. Mary Mac Franklin mused whether or not these molds might have been used for making sweet rewards for successful toilet training – pipe version for a boy. This is probably oldest of the three, &. appears to be c.1840. (T-R) Songbird on branch, dotted elliptical border. 3-1/4" x 5-1/4". (B) Cornucopia, grapes, dot border, 5-3/4" x 4-1/4". Photo courtesy Litchfield Auction Gallery. Ex-Harold Corbin Collection. Auctioned Jan. 1, 1990, $275; $170; $185. Now: (L) $350; (T-R) $150; (B) $150

Reproduction Alert

Odd Fellows reproduction alert – Odd Fellows molds are being reproduced. Get to know what old cast iron and new cast iron look like. Remember, most new cast iron is not made with virgin ore, but from all kinds of scrap iron, including whole engine blocks with other metals involved. Graininess, relatively light weight, slightly blurred details, somewhat lighter metal color & no patina are alarm signals that scream newness.

IV-166-B. Cookie or marchpane molds. *Swan in a circle, surrounded by dots, on oval mold, 4-3/4" x 5-3/4"; pineapple in Pennsylvania German style, though probably New York State. 6" x 4-1/2"; & oval with acorn & leaves, 4" x 5-3/4", the last being thickest of all six molds auctioned. mid 19th C. Photo courtesy Litchfield Auction Gallery. Ex-Harold Corbin Collection. Auctioned Jan. 1, 1990, for $180; $85; $160. Now: $150-$250*

❖ NOTES ❖

Cookie molds of cast iron. N.Y.C importer/dealer George Thurnauer, 1890s-1910s, advertised 7 square or rectangular molds, 5 oval ones & 3 rounds. I wonder if the oval ones are the cast iron ovals with single designs seen in such quantity at antique shows in the late 1980s.

Cookie mold, bear, glazed redware, large bear with fur, claws & teeth all delineated, American, 3" x 5", early 19th C. .... **$300+**

Cookie mold, oblong tin mold, with 3 clamps along top, in section it is the shape of a spade (as in cards), & is for making icebox cookies, the dough of which was chilled then sliced. Heart-, club- & diamond-shaped molds were made too. This kind of metal mold was usually lined with paper (antique cookbooks say letter paper or parchment), to make removal easier. American, about 12"L x 2" across, prob. "Ateco Ice Box Cookie Mould" – "Mix 'em! Freeze 'em! Slice 'em! Bake 'em! – no fuss no bother no rolling pin." August Thomsen & Co., 1920s-1930s........................... **$15+**

IV-167. Cookie mold. *Round, wood, deeply-carved mason's tools, including a hammer, mallet, chisel, & square. Also initials "I. D." (or J.D.") 5-1/2" diam. x 7/8" thick. Dealer thought it might be a butter mold instead. I disagree.* **$300+**

❖ NOTES ❖

Sliced or Icebox Cookies – These cookies cannot be mixed and baked immediately because they require thorough chilling in the refrigerator. Their great advantage for the small family, which likes its cookies fresh, is that the dough can be kept on hand and the cookies sliced and baked as needed. It is because the dough can be used over a period of a week or more that we suggest a fairly large recipe even for the small family. Icebox cookies are always of the crisp, buttery type.

❖ RECIPE ❖

Butterscotch Cookies – *(45 to 60 Cookies) 3-1/2 cups flour. 3 teaspoons baking powder. 1 cup butter or other fat. 2 cups brown sugar. 2 eggs. 2 teaspoons vanilla. 1 to 1-1/2 cups chopped nuts. – Sift the flour and baking powder together. Cream the fat; stir in the sugar gradually; add the unbeaten eggs one at a time; add the vanilla; mix well; stir in the dry ingredients. The mixture will be a stiff dough.*

"The cookies may be shaped in several ways as follows: (a) In butter cartons. Stand 1 pound butter cartons on end and pack the mixture firmly into the corners. (b) In a cracker box. Waxed fiber boxes need no lining; tin boxes should be lined with heavy waxed paper with the ends extending beyond the edge of the box. Pack the dough firmly into the box. (c) With floured hands shape the dough into rolls about 2 inches in diam., wrap the rolls in heavy waxed paper, twisting the ends. The roll will settle to an elliptical shape on standing.

"Place the molded dough in an efficient refrigerator for several hours or until it is very hard. Remove the chilled dough from its wrappings; place on a molding board covered with heavy waxed paper; cut into slices about 1/8 inch thick. Place on a baking sheet (greasing is not necessary because of the large quantity of fat in the dough); bake on the top shelf in a moderate oven (375° F.) for 10 to 15 minutes." Marjorie Heseltine and Ula M. Dow, Good Cooking Made Easy & Economical. *Boston: Houghton Mifflin, 1933.*

Cookie molds – See also Springerle mold

Cookie mold pan, cast aluminum, very light color & bright, 18 cups with 9 tulips & 9 scalloped rounds, Wilton Enterprises, Woodridge, IL, 1980s. • The Wilton Cookie Maker Fancy Cookies booklet, 1984, Wilton Enterprises, Inc., includes several catalog pages of aluminum baking pans, plastic cookie cutters, tartlet molds, cookie racks & sheets, icing & pastry bags & tips, mini muffin pans, & at least 6 cookie mold pans, 5 have 18 cups, one has 16, for Viennese, Bavarian, Marseilles (16 cups), Barcelona, Venetian & Parisian cookies. The catalog is worth as much as the pan; Wilton is a whole collecting category......... **$15+**

Cookie or jumble press, or butter press, or pastry tube, pieced tin, wing like side handles, nicely buttressed, turned wooden plunger with nicely flared out top, 5 plates to insert in business end, to create cookies in different shapes, from a half moon to a 10 point star, European (?), c.1870s. **$65**

Jumballs – 8 oz. of Jordan almonds, 2 lb. 8 oz. of searched [sierced, sieved] sugar, about two whites of eggs. – Blanch and beat the almonds until there is not any particle of the almond to be seen; then rub in with the pestle two pounds of the sugar with whites of eggs; beat them well until smooth; that done, divide the paste into three parts, one for white, one pink, and the other yellow. The pink must be coloured with the best lake finely ground; and the yellow with strong prepared saffron; stiffen each with part of the sugar left; then put them through a jumball mould; and make them into rings about the size of a dollar. Lay them on dry paper, and bake them in a very slow oven. N.B. A **jumball mould** should be made of brass, in the shape of a butter squirt, with a star at the end, half an inch in diam.." Joseph Bell, A Treatise on Confectionary, New-castle, England, 1817. [Lake is lac, the same red resinous secretion of the tiny scale insects lacs that's used to make lacquer.]

Cookie press, fat metal cylinder with plunger, & set of 6 cutout metal inserts to form everything from stars & flowers to corrugated rounds, made by icing decorator people, Ateco, The Thompsen Co., N.Y.C, N.Y., c.1940. Lots of these around, from 1940s to at least 1960s. .... **$15+**

Cookie press, tin cylinder with wood plunger with 2 little side handles, also called a pastry tube or syringe, late 19th C. **$65**

Cookie press, tin tube, wood plunger but no handles, American, 12"L, early 20th C. .... **$25+**

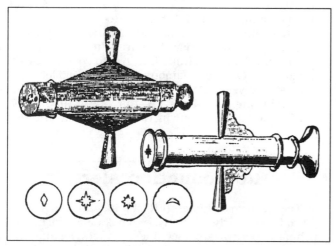

IV-168. Jumble machines, or **jumble syringes** for making cookies known as jumbles, which William Woys Weaver describes as "any kind of cookie twisted into rings, knots, or even bows." **(L)** Syringe in four sizes, came with 2, 3 or 4 insert discs (all seen below). Jaburg, 1908. **(R)** Pieced tin, wood plunger, various fancy-holed inserts. F. A. Walker import catalog, c.1870s. This style of jumble press required both hands (to hold side handles) & a belly to push it against (which was achieved by eating jumbles). See listings for Pastry tube. **$85+**

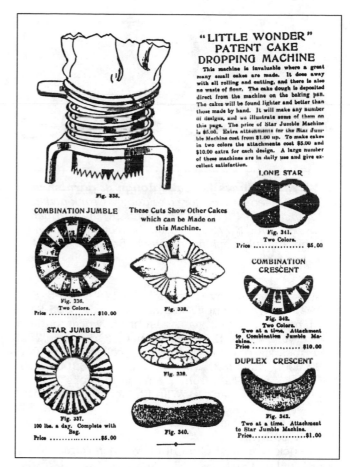

"LITTLE WONDER" PATENT CAKE DROPPING MACHINE

This machine is invaluable where a great many small cakes are made. It does away with all rolling and cutting, and there is also no waste of flour. The cake dough is deposited direct from the machine on the baking pan. The cakes will be found lighter and better than those made by hand. It will make any number of designs, and we illustrate some of them on this page. The price of Star Jumble Machine is $5.00. Extra attachments for the Star Jumble Machine cost from $1.00 up. To make cakes in two colors the attachments cost $5.00 and $10.00 extra for each design. A large number of these machines are in daily use and give excellent satisfaction.

COMBINATION JUMBLE
Fig. 336.
Two Colors.
Price $10.00

These Cuts Show Other Cakes which can be Made on this Machine.

Fig. 335.

Fig. 338.

LONE STAR
Fig. 341.
Two Colors.
Price $5.00

COMBINATION CRESCENT
Fig. 342.
Two Colors.
Two at a time. Attachment to Combination Jumble Machine.
Price $10.00

STAR JUMBLE
Fig. 337.
100 lbs. a day. Complete with Bag.
Price $5.00

Fig. 339.

Fig. 340.

DUPLEX CRESCENT
Fig. 343.
Two at a time. Attachment to Star Jumble Machine.
Price $1.00

IV-169. Cookie press or "Cake dropping machine." A little metal stand with bag. Spring action. Came with various inserts to make all different jumbles & cookies shown. Jaburg, 1908. **$35+**

Corny Advice – The American Agriculturist, Sept. 1846, published a tip on "How to Boil Green Corn," with advice on eating it too. "The proper state in which to eat green corn, is, at the time that the milk flows upon pressing the kernels with the thumb nail. It is best when boiled in the ear with the husks on, the latter of which should be stripped off when brought to the table. The ears should then be covered with butter, with a little salt added, and the grains eaten off the cob. Over-refined people think this vulgar, and shave them off, but in so doing they lose much of their sweetness."

Corn bread skillet, cast iron, frying pan shape with short handle & teardrop hanging hole, 8 dividing ridges to create 8 wedges, hole in center, mfd. by Lodge, South Pittsburgh, TN., 1" deep x 9" diam., late 20th C. New versions have a hole in the center of the pan. .... **$25-$35**

Corn bread skillet, cast iron, sectioned in wedges, marked "Corn Bread Skillet" on back, American, 9-1/8" diam., 20th C. .... **$20+**

Corn or wheat stick pan, cast iron, 7 sticks with well-formed kernels, "Best Made Wheat & Corn Stick Pan, No. 1270," marked "S. R. & Co." (Sears, Roe-

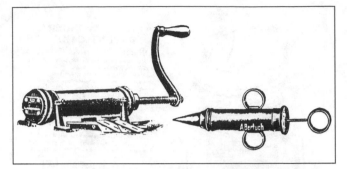

IV-170. Syringes for cake dough & garnishes. **(L)** *A "Queenspritze," for cake dough. Crank action, 12 inserts. 14"L x 3-1/2" diam.* **(R)** *A "Garnier-spritze," only 3-7/8"L, & could be worked with one hand (thumb pushing plunger). Bertuch, c.1904.* **$55+; $35**

buck, but mfd. by Griswold). 13-1/8"L x 5-5/8"W, 1927 design patent #73326...................... **$95-$135**

Corn or wheat stick pan, cast iron, wheat pattern, Griswold #282, Erie, PA, 20th C. (Griswold #2800 corn stick pan is valued by collectors $1,000-$2,000!) The #282:............................... **$200-$250+**

Corn stick pan, cast iron, 7 alternating cobs, marked on one cob on back "BoWlin Ft. Worth" [Texas], 12"L x 5-1/2"W... **$7+**

Corn stick mold, gray graniteware, 5 cobs, American, early 20th C................................. **$125+**

Corn stick pan, cast aluminum, Wagner Ware, Sidney, OH, pat'd. 1920. .... **$25-$45**

Corn stick pan, cast aluminum, "Krusty Korn Kobs," Wagner Ware, tea size, 7-1/8"L x 4-1/8"W, mid 20th C. Not common but still cheap. .... **$35-$45**

Corn stick pan, cast aluminum, 7 ears alternating direction. The slight irregularities of each cob make me sure original casting patterns were real ears, probably of hard seed corn, Mullins Non-Ferrous Castings Corp., St. Louis, MO, 20th C....... **$20-$30**

Corn stick pan, cast aluminum, odd cob-shaped cups but no kernels, just 3 long ridges in each cup, makes 7 sticks, medallion on back: "Wearever, No. 22–," "Made in U.S.A.," 13"L x 5-1/2"W, 20th C... **$15-$20**

Corn stick pan, cast iron, "Krispy Korn Mold," Wagner, Sidney, OH, 3 sizes: (1) Tea size, 7-1/8"L x 4-1/8"W; (2) Senior size, 13-3/4"L x 6-7/8"W; & (3) Junior size, 11-5/8"L x 5-7/8"W.
1920s. .... **(1) $50-$65; (2) $50-$60; (3) $20-$35**

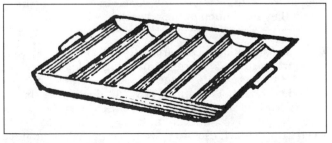

IV-171. Corn cake or roll pan. Called a "**Russia Iron Roll,** *or corn cake pan. – Gives a handsome brown soft under-crust." Russia iron is heavy sheet iron, not cast iron. This appeared as a kitchen necessity in* American Home Cook Book, *1854.* **$65+**

Corn stick pan, cast iron, 5 ornate cobs with curly silk tassels at ends & scrolly husks, in wide bordered rectangular frame with fancy scroll handle at each end, stamped "John Wright" on back, with button affixed to one handle reading "Classic Gourmet," Wrightsville, PA, ©1984.

Corn stick pan, cast iron, 7 alternating well-modeled corn cobs, in original lithographed box (sometimes found with wraparound cardboard label instead), "Junior Krusty Korn Kobs, #1319," (I've seen this reported as #1319D), "patent pending," Wagner Ware, Sidney, OH, Junior size is 11-5/8"L x 5-7/8"W, pat'd. July 6, 1920, but made for many years. In the box: .... **$100+**

Corn stick pan, cast iron, 7 cobs facing same way, Griswold "Krispy CORNORWHEAT Stick Pan #262," also marked "825" & "13," Erie, PA, 8-1/2"L x 4-1/8"W, 1927 design patent #73,326, made for many years.. **$75-$95**

Corn stick pan, cast iron, 7 well-defined head-to-toe ears, Griswold "Krispy CornorWheat Stick Pan, No. 270," also marked "#636," Erie, PA, 13-1/8"L x 5-5/8"W, 1927 design patent #73,326. .... **$200-$250**

Corn stick pan, cast iron, 7 well-defined head-to-toe ears, Griswold "Krispy CORNORWHEAT Stick Pan, No. 280," with same patent as #270. 14"L x 7-5/8"W, c. 1927+.. **$800-$1,000**

Corn stick pan, cast iron, 7 head-to-toe cobs, in original printed cardboard sleeve, advertising blurb reads: "Corn Cake Pan, Griswold Early American Quality Cast Iron. There's nothing like iron to cook in. By the makers of Griswold famous cast iron skillets. For almost 100 years, Americans have known Griswold." Griswold Mfg. Co., Erie, PA, this one c.1953. (Only $3.50 bought a new one in 1973.) .... **$55-$65**

Corn stick pan, heavy molded glass, 7 cobs alternate directions, Wagner Ware, 13"L x 6"W, according to collector Jim Holroyd, between 1942 & 1947. Use of glass due to WWII metal drives. (It's probably safe to assume most of the glass ones date to the same period.) .... **$35-$65+**

Corn stick pan, molded glass, "Beauty Bake," 20th C. .... **$35+**

Corn stick pan, molded glass, 6 ears, half of each ear made up of gracefully pulled back husk, "Miracle Maize," American, 12"L x 6-1/4"W, "Pat. Pend.," 20th C. See also Wheat bread mold. **$55**

Corn stick pan, chrome-plated cast iron, 7 cobs all same direction, Griswold "Crispy Corn Stick Pan," "No. 283," & at bottom, "931," 1930s. Although less common, chrome not as desired by collectors. .... **$120-$140**

Corn stick pan, poor reproduction, cheap cast iron, 7 cobs all pointing same way, each letter of misspelled words on back impressed separately in the casting mold, marked "No. 252 CRISWOLD CRISPY COR-NORWHEAT SNICK PAN" also "625," & address "ERIE PA USA," but made in Taiwan, 8"L x 4"W, 1980s (?). • When imported, they have a tiny gummy gold & black sticker on the front, reading "W. E. RHYNE CO., Made in TAIWAN." Stickers fall off in heat. You would buy one of these "CRISWOLD" pans only for your study collection. .... **$2-$4**

Corn stick pan – See also Wheat bread mold pan

Cracker crusher or roller, wood, handles, corrugated drum or barrel, with corrugations going around the circumference of the drum, used to crumb crackers. 11"L, 1890s-1910. Also used to crumb dry bread. See also Rolling pins "What are the ridges for?"....... **$35+**

Cracker pricker, fat wooden knob with 12 iron pins or "nails," American (?), 4-1/4"H x 2" diam. 19th C. .... **$65+**

Cracker pricker, or biscuit prick, carved wood, one piece palm fitting knob & rather elongated body, 7 thick pins or nails, American (?), 5"H, 19th C. • Necessary for soda crackers or biscuits & for beaten biscuits to prevent huge blisters or air pockets forming during baking. .... **$65+**

Cracker pricker, or biscuit prick, double-ended, fairly intricately carved body, with simple geometric designs; the two heads have pricks carved from the wood in two different designs & lengths, 7-1/2"L, c. 1870s.. **$75-$100+**

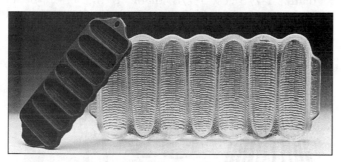

IV-172. Corn stick pans. (L) Cast iron, "Griswold Krispy cornwheat Stick Pan #262," Erie, PA. 8-1/2"L x 4-1/8"W. Makes 7 one-way sticks. (R) Molded heavy glass, Wagner Ware. 13"L x 6"W. Makes 7 which-a-way sticks. Which makes me wonder out loud, why did muffin & roll pans always make odd numbers? For luck? Collection of Meryle Evans. $65-$95; $45+

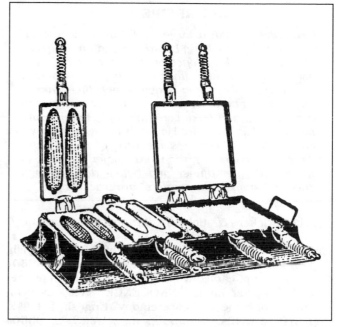

IV-173. Corn dog baker. "Krusty Korn Dog" baker, also sandwich toaster (grill) or steak fryer. *"A big money maker! For use on gas, gasoline, oil or coal stoves. 'Krusty Korn Dogs' are novel & delicious. The hot dog is baked inside corn batter, which as it bakes, moulds itself to resemble an ear of corn 6-3/8"L & 1-1/2" diam. Easy to make: Red hots are first fried in butter, then placed in korn dog' sections together with required amount of batter, they are then quickly & thoroughly baked together. Baker is made of cast iron, smooth japanned finish, with heavy, sturdy wire coil pan handles. Heavy lifting handles at each end."* Frame is 2-1/2"H x 10-1/4" x 21-1/4"; fryer pan (R) is 3/4" deep x 8-1/2" x 8-3/8". You bought frame, & a fry pan (griddle), & a pair of "Krusty Korn Sausage Dog Pans," each of which made two, separately to suit your business. In Pick-Barth wholesale catalog of many makers' hotel & restaurant supplies, 1929. See also weiner dog baker IV-417. For whole set-up: **$550-$800+**

Cracker pricker & cutter, cast iron, spring steel with wooden block that has little 2 pronged prickers stuck in it. Spring-loaded action, fat palm-fitting handle, it not only cuts out square crackers but makes the pricked marks in them essential to their success. American, made crackers just shy of 2" square, marked "Pat'd. Dec. 13." Tuesday, patent-granting day, fell on Dec. 13 only 3 times in the possible time frame – 1864, 1870, 1881, 1887, 1892, 1898, 1904, and 1910, etc. My patent subject index goes only to 1873, & it is not in that under any kind of biscuit, cake, dough or pastry cutter, so – although the appearance is 1870s, I go with 1880s or 1890s. Now somebody else can do the rest of the legwork. (See IV-12)...................................... **$135+**

Cracker pricker & stamp, carved wood, 3 nails to punch holes through cracker, depicts marvelous burning house with raging flames, house has big gothic window with tiny leaded panes, English, 1 9/1" x 1-1/4", c.1820-30s. .... **$450+**

Crackers – *Take a large cupful of bread dough; roll out on the molding-board; spread on it a piece of butter and lard together, as large as a goose-egg; sprinkle a little flour over it; fold it up, and pound with something heavy a long time; take a small piece at a time; roll out very thin; stamp with a clock key, and bake very quickly."* Henry Scammel, compiler, Treasure House of Universal Knowledge, 1891. (Note: In some turn of the century American cookbooks, the word "wafer" is used, to be served after dinner and before dessert, with cheese. I suspect the "wafers" are crackers.)

Cracker prickers & stickers – See also Biscuit cutter & sticker; also Pie markers

Cracker stamp, carved wood basket of flowers, English, 1-3/4" x 1-1/4", c.1840s.............................. **$250+**

Cracker stamp, carved wood depicting sheep, 6 pricker nails, cracker name "INNOCENCE," religious symbolism for some kind of ceremony? English, 1-3/4" x 1-3/8", c.1840s. .... **$350+**

Cracker stamp, carved wood, double arched top like 2 tombstones, name of cracker "VICTORIA," English, 2" across. Looks like it could date from Queen Victoria's 1837 ascendency as late as the 1860s or so. ...... **$300+**

Cracker stamp, carved wood, looks like a dumbbell, or a doggie bone, English (?), 1-7/8" across, mid 19th C. .... **$175+**

Cracker stamp, carved wood, makes 6-point star plus many pricker holes, American or English (?), 2-3/4" diam., 19th C. .... **$150+**

Cracker stamp, wood carved with rose & thistle, name of cracker carved too: "UNION," from Great Britain – the rose signifying England, the thistle Scotland, 1-7/8" x 1-3/16", early 19th C..................................... **$200+**

Crimpers – See Jaggers & Crimpers & Trimmers. Some are combined jaggers (which cut) & crimpers (which squushed & sealed edges); see also Sandwich sealer; and Tart sealer

Croquette mold, tin, conical shape, 2 halves pinned lengthwise to release molded ground meat (ham, chicken, veal, fish) form to roll in crumbs before cooking, possibly made by Silver, marked Brooklyn, NY, 4-3/4"L x 3" diam. at open end, c.1880s. According to Richard Hooker, who wrote the amusing, informative *History of Food & Drink in America*, meat choppers in the 1860s & '70s "opened to the housewife & entire school of dishes based on chopped foods: croquettes, timbales, patties, loafs, ..." etc.. **$15+**

Croquette mold for drumsticks, hinged plier-type cast aluminum, long handles, pivot near the drumstick shaped "spoon-scoop" ends, incised "Chicken Sans Volaille," also "BK1" on one handle, "AMPCO" on other. 8"L x 4-1/2"W. 1950s? .... **$15+**

Cutlet molds, pieced tin, shaped like cutlets or big fat commas, deep straight sides, used to shape a mixture of minced meat, spices, onion & egg into shape of lambchop or drumstick, etc., before cooking, but not used to bake the cutlet in, American or European, about 5"L x 1" deep, from c.1870s to 1900. • I've never seen the leg of mutton mold, made of pieced tin in the appropriate shape but with slanted rather than straight sides, but one was advertised in

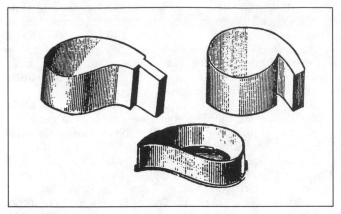

IV-174. Cutlet cutters & mold. *Two punctuation mark-like cutters, pieced tin, from F. A. Walker catalog, 1870s. I don't know if they had a flatback. Two sizes, probably about 4" & 6"L. Bottom one is a mold, in same catalog as heart mold in with heart cookie cutters. Tin, 4" x 2-1/4". The top ones might be used to cut shapes from whole, as opposed to ground, meat.* **$12-$20**

the F. A. Walker catalog of 1886. I suppose it is much larger, meant for forming a meatloaf for a family rather than an individual serving............... **$10+**

Croquette mold – See Drumstick croquette mold

Dariel mold, often spelled dariole in old catalogs, a little tin cup – slightly flared cylinder, flat bottom, rolled edge, side seam, for a particular kind of small cake or custard, very like a small tartlet cup found today in the frozen food section of grocery stores. F. A. Walker's 1870s catalog also called them "individual jelly cups" ("jelly" meant a gelatinized sweet or savoury, not a big blob of grape jelly). The same Walker's catalog also had a cut of what looks exactly like a bouche iron, but called a dariole mold – a turned wooden handle set at right angle to corrugated, flared, solid cast iron mold to be dipped in batter before quickly deep frying. That type of mold molds on the outside rather than the inside. American or European, 2"H x 2-1/4" diam., last half 19th C. • F. A. Walker, in an 1886 sales brochure, advertised three sizes of dariel molds, viz. 1-3/4"H x 1-3/4" diam.; 1-7/8"H x 1-7/8" diam.; & this one. Not all had equal height & diam. • Added value. – Tinned copper would bring a bit more.................. **$7-$15+**

IV-175. Small molds, *for dariols & one bouche cup (bottom center). Stamped & pieced tin. Center of one at left is oval.* Mrs. A. B. Marshall's Larger Cookery Book, *1902.* **$15-$25**

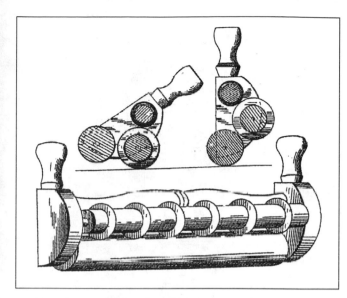

IV-176. "Combined rolling pin and dough cutter" patent, by Charles S. Goodnough, Nough, TN, July 3, 1894, #522,465. Above are two views of cutter from side, in use, with cutter blades rolling on surface, and with rolling pin or roller on surface. Big drawing shows "improved household implement by means of which dough can be rolled into sheets and then cut into strips for making cake, biscuit, &c., in a rapid manner." Another combination was pat'd. two years later by William M. Pugh, Indianapolis, IN, assignor of half to Edward Pfeiffer. August 11, 1896, #565,635. In Pugh's case, the cutter was an attachment slipped onto a common rolling pin. The slipped-on cutters he showed made square biscuits or cakes.

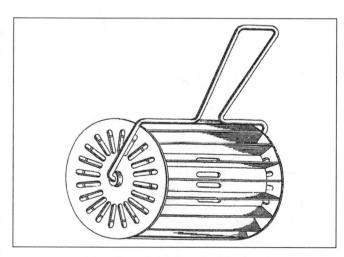

IV-177. Rotating cake cutter patent, to make many long thin strips for making ladyfingers, etc. Pat'd by Bryce B. Smith & George L. Gay Jr., Kansas City, MO, assigned to Smith. Jan. 7, 1908, #875,960. Inventors claimed it was "especially adapted to the cutting of doughnuts, ladyfingers, etc." Obviously a different kind of doughnut! Of interest are long slot-like air-holes. Air-holes were a big concern ... because getting cut dough to drop off a cutter on its own accord was important.

IV-178. Doughnut or cruller cutter, top & underneath view. Fluted or crimped & pieced tin, strap handle, actually pat'd. Oct. 1, 1889, by George W. Knapp, Baltimore, MD, #412,100. The "Oct. 15" date shown in catalog linecut was undoubtedly a mistake by linecut engraver. Matches a similar biscuit cutter. Knapp's actual patent emphasized that it had no soldered parts, & there was no handle. From F. A. Walker catalog, c.1890. **$15-$25+**

Dough board – See Pastry board
Doughnut cutter, 2 part, with insert for cutting doughnuts, tin, "E-A Company Flour Always All Right," Waseca, Minnesota. 2-3/4" diam., 20th C. ..... **$20+**

❖ NOTES ❖

Dunkin Oly Koeks – As long ago as 1809, in *History of New York*, Washington Irving described some tasty treats in "An enormous dish of balls of sweetened dough, fried in hog's fat, and called dough nuts, or *oly koeks*." [The latter is the Dutch term.] See also Ebelskiver pans.

Doughnut, cake, biscuit & "cookie" cutter, appears to be piece of lathe-turned wood, from side it's like a short ninepin or beetle, hollowed inside to make a thin cutting edge plus hole cutter, American, 4-1/2"L x 2-3/8" diam. Marked "Pat. Mar. 26, 1907." Pat'd. by Vernon T. Littlefield, Bangor, ME, assignor of 1/6 to Harry A. M. Rush, 1/6 to James A. Rush, and 1/6 to Eugene Rush, all of Millinocket, ME, (#848,561). Littlefield's specs are of great interest because while it has always been assumed by me that this was a dedicated doughnut cutter, apparently the center hole cutter was a separate piece which was fit or "seated frictionally" into a socket inside. "For cutting biscuits and the like the auxiliary cutter is detached from the body of the main cutter." I wouldn't advise trying to pry off the "auxiliary cutter" if it is there; it might be warped firmly in place. And who knows, it's possible later versions may have been made with and without the socket to avoid any problems with fitting the center cutter into the socket. Added value: patina & smoothness, ... **$85+**
Doughnut cutter, multiple rolling or "rotating" type, with aluminum cutting blades with small tubes, for cutting 2 doughnuts in one revolution, twisted wire & turned wooden handle available in different colors. This was one of a set of 4 for making "cookies, doughnuts, rolls, scones & tarts." From editorial copy in *House Furnishing Review*, Jan. 1930, we learn about "rotating cutters having detachable

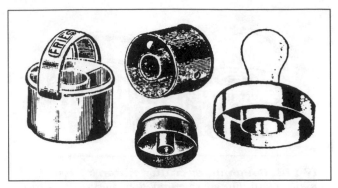

IV-179. Doughnut cutters. *Clockwise, from top.* **(T-L)** *Tin, strap handle, deep cutting, no top, one size only, 3" diam. Marked "Fries." From Sexton Stove & Mfg. catalog, c.1930.* **(T-C)** *Next is heavy tin one with rounded palm-fitting top, deep cutter, for bakeries. 3". Pick-Barth catalog, 1929.* **(R)** *Combination cookie & doughnut cutter, with detachable center cutter. Aluminum, white painted wooden handle, 3"H overall x 2-3/4" diam. "Mirro," Aluminum Goods Mfg., 1927.* **(B)** *Solid back tin one, either 3" or 3-1/2" diam. Geuder, Paeschke & Frey, 1925.* **$10-$25;** *with name stamp:* **$15-$20**

blade for cleaning & edges flanged at a varying pitch so that the cutting edge cuts vertically, straight through the dough, leaving no dough sticking to the blades." And also the advice that the doughnut "Item [is] somewhat seasonal. Best buying months are February, March, April, September, October & November." ... "Six foot counter space is sufficient for demonstration." "Rollemout," by The American Cutter Co., Milwaukee, WI, being made at least by 1928. Price for one from set only: .... **$25+**

Doughnut cutter, stainless steel with wood T-handle, "The Saturn," 1930s. .... **$15+**

Doughnut cutter, tin, fluted sides with strap handle, center hole cutter soldered on, handle soldered on, but main body is stamped, American, 3-1/2" diam., marked "Pat'd. Oct. 1, 1889." (Note: The linecut of this cutter which appeared in several catalogs shows the date "Oct. 15, '89" stamped into the cutter. It was probably a mistake by the linecut engraver.) The patent, by George W. Knapp, Baltimore, MD, #412,100, was for a "cake-cutter" of stamped tin or sheet metal and no handle. Knapp's major claim was to avoid soldering, because that "way of constructing them, besides being expensive, is objectionable, in that after a little use the top plate often becomes detached from the rim, and ... the crevices on the inner side, where the said parts are united ... form a lodgment for the dough, and is ... difficult to keep clean." So whether or not it was with Knapp's approval or knowledge, this doughnut cutter, with a soldered handle & hole cutter, was made by adding something to the simple cake cutter. .... **$65+**

Doughnut cutter, tin, long cylindrical handle, end closed, marked "Rumford," 3-7/8"H x 2-1/2" diam., c.1890s-1910. .... **$25+**

Doughnut cutter, tin, strap handle, doughnut holer cylinder has 3 struts holding it to outside cylinder, mfd. by Fries, 3"H overall, cutting part 1-1/2"H x 3" diam., early 20th C. .... **$25+**

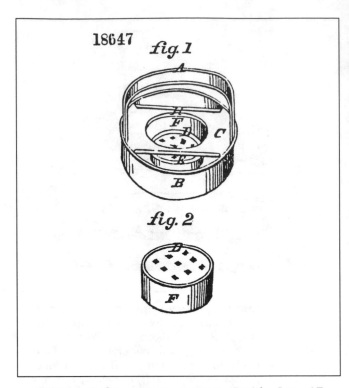

IV-180. Cake cutter patent. *Pat'd. Jan. 17, 1857, by George R. Peckham, Worcester, MA, #18,647. Has a separate insert in center so that doughnuts, or kind of jumble cookie that was ring-shaped, could be made. Note air holes & neat, safe rolled edges. Official Gazette.*

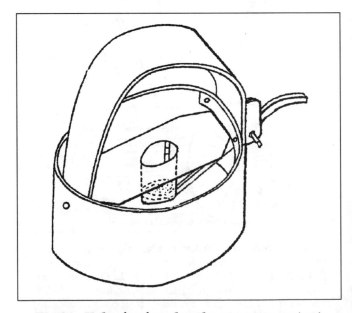

IV-181. Hole-ejecting doughnut cutter patent, *showing ejecting trigger, which was fitted through slots in central cutter, & was used to eject center dough. Pat'd. by Alfred E. Johnson, Racine, WI, June 7, 1921, #1,380,560.*

IV-182. Doughnut & cake cutter patent. Pat'd. by Uriah D. Seltzer, Lebanon, PA, June 6, 1893, #499,149. Above shows tool, which I believe I've seen, with double cutters, in 2 sizes. Below is with doughnut cutter insert. The handle at an upward oblique angle made it comfortable to hold in that position; slightly flipped over, handle would angle down. **$65+**

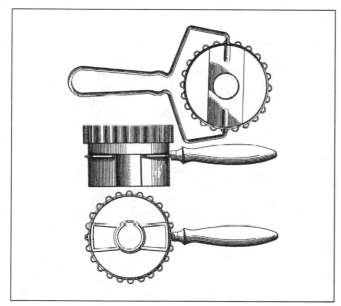

IV-183. Cake & doughnut cutter patent, awarded Simon J. Harding, Harrisburg, PA, Apr. 2, 1907, #848,823, assigned to Fred D. Harding, West Baldwin, ME. All 3 views are from one patent; Harding wanted to provide a "reversible cake-cutter adapted to cut the cake-dough either round or scalloped and either with or without a central hole or opening." Something "simple, inexpensive, and efficient." **(T)** Least expensive – bent "stout wire" handle, with sheet metal transverse bar that carries central cutter. **(M)** A side view showing "crimped or corrugated" cutting edge & center cutter flush with plain cutting edge & turned wooden handle. **(B)** Top view of (M) showing a rigid transverse piece, rather like a skeletal bow-tie, "preferably made of a casting of brass or other suitable material."

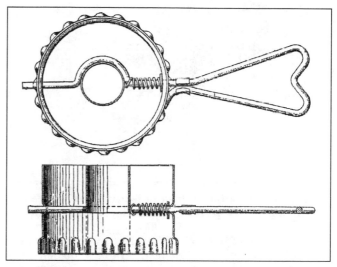

IV-184. Cake cutter with plain & fluted cutting edges, pat'd. by Simon Joseph Harding, West Baldwin, ME, Sept. 7, 1926, #1,598,717. Harding is still at it, 20 years later! The upper view shows a top view with doughnut-cutter; lower shows a side view – with fluted edge & plain edge. The inner cutter was soldered in place to the rod, and by twisting handle & inner rod, center cutter could be flush with plain or fluted edge; a spring & washer holds in place the bent rod to which inner cutter is fixed.

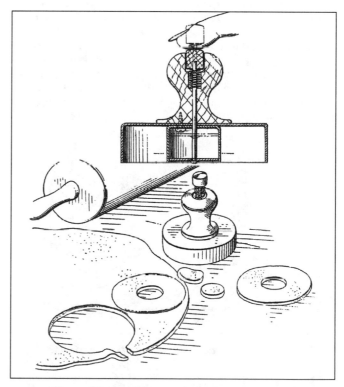

IV-185. Doughnut hole dough remover patent, awarded George W. Frazier, Warren, OH, Jan. 29, 1957, #2,779,097. (Frazier applied for the patent April 1954.) The familiar ejecting "plunger plate" seen in much earlier patents (see IV-9, IV-10, IV-11, IV-164, IV-235) is also spring-activated. The plunger plate is removable for cleaning.

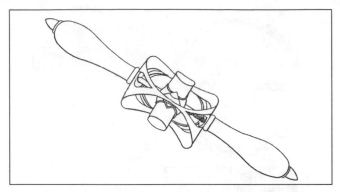

IV-186. "Revolving hand-biscuit and confec-tionery-cutter patent," *pat'd. by Seth E. Clapp, Cambridge, MA, May 5, 1868, #77,588. Assigned to patentee & John J. Ridgway. Cut 3 with each revolution. "In the drawings, I have represented my invention as it appears when used for cutting jumbles, that is, round cakes having the centre cut out; but for many purposes I remove the centre-piece, and use the other part for cutting biscuits, crackers, &c." Removal of center cutter piece meant user had to unscrew a long bolt which went through from tip of right handle.*

Doughnut cutter, tin, strap handle with center ridge for strength, edges folded over, a straight-across strap is strut for cylindrical hole cutter, American, 1-1/8" diam., 1890s-1910.. **$15+**

Doughnut cutter & apple corer combined, tin, strap han-dle, the separate corer is removed from cutter's "hole" for use in making doughnuts, American, 3-7/8"L x 3" diam., c.1890s-1910.. **$20+**

Doughnut mold, hinged cast iron, long handles with wooden grips, looks like 3 leaf clover, makes 3 dough-nuts, filled then held in boiling fat, "Ace Cloverleaf Donut," Ace Co., St. Louis, MO, 20th C...... **$55-$100**

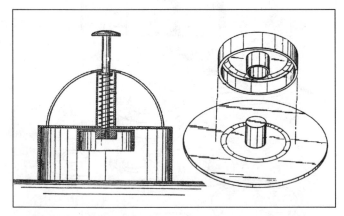

IV-187. Spring-activated cutter patent, *by James Collins, Central City, Gilpin County, Colo-rado Territory, Apr. 18, 1876, #176,217. Could be used two ways: make a simple round cut by not depressing central cutter, or depress it to make a cake with a hole in it. This patent was cited 102 years (!) later by Herve L. Fournier, South Attleboro, MA, in his springless patent for a "mold for forming a hamburger patty" (Aug. 15, 1978, #4,106,162) along with patents from 1919, 1940, 1953, etc.*

Doughnut press, aluminum, spring-loaded plunger releases dough into boiling fat, 8-1/2"L, "D. R. M., Manitowoc, WI," with recipe booklet. c.1930s. **$15**

Drumstick mold – See Croquette mold for drumsticks

❖ NOTES ❖

Ebelskiver or aebelskiver pans are of Scandinavian origin, at least in name. They are cast iron, round with a relatively short frying pan type handle, and have seven ball-like cups (I've never seen one with more or fewer cups). • They are also called "muffin molds," "egg poachers," "apple pancake pans," "Danish cake pans," and "olie-koeck pans" – for "fat cakes" or fritters. For the latter, I'm indebted to William Woys Weaver, and his highly-readable cookbooks that are full of social his-tory. On page 69 of *The Christmas Cook* (Harper Peren-nial, 1990) he writes "Several nineteenth-century foundries in this country sold an implement they called an *olie-koeck* **pan**. Many signed examples bear the names of J. M. B. Davidson & Shear, Packard & Com-pany of albany, New York, or Griswold of Erie, Pennsyl-vania. This pan is the same as the egg and *Krapfen* pans made in Germany." Ebelskivers are apple pan-cake balls made with apple slivers and batter.

❖ RECIPE ❖

Ebelskiver Recipe *– According to Rebecca Wood, who wrote the wonderful cookbook* Quinoa the Supergrain, Ancient Food for Today, *here is the way to make these "apple sliver pancakes." You make a smooth batter like pancake batter (she adds cardomom), then heat the ebelskiver pan (she spells it ableskiver) over medium heat. "Thoroughly oil wells. Fill each well 5/8 full of batter and allow to cook for several minutes or just until the surface contacting the pan has browned. With a bamboo skewer (or knitting needle or nut pick), pierce and lift the cooked side up to a right angle. The batter pours out to form a second surface. When the new surface browns, turn again. A total of four turns* *produces a round and hollow ball." She adds a small slice of apple (or other fruit) before making the first turn.*

Ebelskiver pan, also referred to as a "muffin mold" or an "egg poacher," with 7 round-bottomed cups set in frying pan-like straight sided frame with short handle, marked both "Griswold No. 32," & "962," Erie, PA, cups 1-1/4" deep, pan is 1-3/4"H x 9-1/4" diam. with 4-3/4"L handle, as early as c.1918 or as late as the 1960s. .... **$35-$65**

Ebelskiver pan, cast iron, 3 peg feet, 7 cups, eye ring in handle, prob. Scandinavian, 7-3/8" diam., 11"L, c.1850s-70s. .... **$100+**

Ebelskiver pan, heavy cast aluminum, plastic handle, 7 cups, marked on back "Ebelskiver Pan" also "Apple Pancake Balls," Northland Aluminum Products, Inc., Minneapolis, MN, 9" diam., 20th C. This is the one sold under the "Nordic Ware" trade name. .... **$25+**

Ebelskiver pan, cast iron, round with short frying pan handle, 7 cups, no feet, only mark is "8," 1-1/2" deep x 9" diam. x 5-3/4"L handle, 19th C. .... **$35-$55**

Ebelskiver pan or muffin pan, cast iron, 7 shallow flat bottom cups, more like muffin pan, short frying pan handle has teardrop hanging hole, the bottom is really great – instead of being perfectly flat, it reveals the shape & position of each cup, & has interesting hollows & negative spaces. Two molds were required to cast this – one for top & one for underneath. That's not so unusual, but shapes of cups underneath are. American, 9-1/4" diam., 6-1/2"L handle, c.1890s-1910. .... **$75+**

Ebelskiver pan – See also Plett kaker

Egg pan, with 12 round cups, often called a muffin or gem pan but patented as an egg pan, cast iron, marked "N. Waterman," patented by Nathaniel Waterman, Boston, MA, pat'd. April 5, 1859, patent #23,517. Waterman was a fairly prolific inventor, beloved of collectors. Others of his patents include a coffee maker, a foot warmer, a match-stand, a sad iron & a waffle iron. • This egg pan patent ended up covering baking pans of different shapes & sizes,

IV-189-A. Ebelskiver pan or egg poacher. *Cast iron, 7 cups, no feet. Only mark is "8." 1-1/2"H x 9" diam. with 5-3/4"L handle. I like this one much better than Griswold, especially its bottom. Courtesy Jean Hatt, Hatt's Hutt, Denver, PA.* **$45-$65**

IV-189-B. *Detail of Ebelskiver in IV-189-A.*

despite the drawing of the 4-3-4 cup pan in the *Annual Report of the Commissioner of Patents* for 1859, the design for which the patent was granted. • See David Smith's article on cast iron pans for more on Waterman. .... **$75+**

Food mold – See Mold listings. This huge field includes molds suitable for cake, pudding, jelled sweet or savory dishes, aspics, & more.

Fortune cookie press & baker, cast iron, bright finish, works like wafer or pizzelle maker, hinged square with double wood handles. Metal part 7-1/2" x 6-1/4" inside divided into 3" diam. depressions for dough; exterior highly decorated with Chinese temple & cook. In original box with paper fortune strips. 1960s-70s...... **$45+**

❖ NOTES ❖

Fortune-telling & Divination – It's not uncommon to have food imprinted with a symbolic message, a proverb, perhaps a blessing, so fortune cookies aren't such a wild idea. And getting something on a paper slip is at least as old as raffle tickets. A random draw of a slip would tell you if you won the toaster, the car wash, the dinner for two. • Although no one believes that **fortune cookies** originated in China, there is a story that 700 or 800 years ago Chinese warriors fighting the Mongol invaders,

IV-188. Ebelskiver or aebelskiver pan. *Also called a* **muffin pan**, *or an* **egg cooker**, *but really for ebelskivers, which are apple-chip pancakes. Cast iron, Griswold No. 32, #962, Erie, PA. Seven cups, 1-3/4"H x 9-1/4" diam., with 4-3/4"L handle. Cups are 1-1/4" deep.* **$35-$65+**

in disguise as monks, put secret messages about military maneuvers inside rice cakes to hide them. Then, supposedly, 800 years later, the idea occurred again to a restauranteur in San Francisco to bake wontons with messages inside. Not very likely that the idea waited so long. • But the *I Ching*, or *Book of Changes*, which is a 1200-year old system for telling truths about life, by throwing sticks or coins and looking up the pattern in one of the five books, constitutes an early counterpart to fortune-telling, and the *I Ching* has been known for centuries. • To read about **moon cakes**, filled pastries made in the shape of various things and animals, and filled with sweet or savory fillings, and to read about a Chinese use of Moon Cakes with a message inside, to overthrow the Mongols, go to this Web site: www.cnyantai.com:88/english/ytfq_en/festivals_1.htm. • An article about the **Mee Mee Bakery** in San Francisco, relates the story that a restauranteur, Makota Hagiwara, manager of Golden Gate Park's Japanese Tea Garden, invented fortune cookies in 1909, but didn't patent them. Shortly thereafter, they began to be manufactured and marketed as Chinese fortune cookies. • Another theory is that Chinese moon cakes were the forerunners. • At least 350 years ago, inventors were making clockwork, wind-up mechanical **automata**, in the form of people or animals. The most well-known in this country would be the gypsy fortune teller figures in carnival arcades, such as seen in Tom Hanks' movie, "Big." You would put a coin in and get a fortune back on a slip of paper. These were first made in the late 19th century. Go to this Web site if you are interested in automata; it tells the story behind that 16th C. figure: www.blackbird.vcu.edu/v1n1/nonfiction/king_e/ prayer_1.htm.

Fortune-telling cake charms – See Cake fortune-telling charms
French pie mold – See Molds, tin

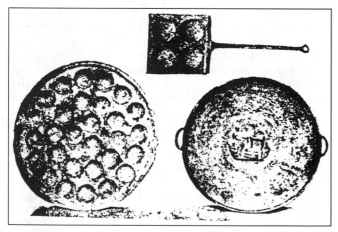

IV-190. Ancient egg poachers & basin. *Cast bronze reproductions of cookwares found at Pompeii, during excavations at different times in the 19th C. (The basin at right, with bas-relief decoration of swimmers, was excavated June 5, 1880.) Large pan at left is 29 cavities for eggs & measures 19-1/8" in diam. The long-handled square pan for four eggs measures 17-1/4"L. They were offered in "Pompeii or Herculanum" finishes. J. Chiurazzi & Fils & S. De Angelis & Fils, Fonderie Artistiche Riunite, Naples, Italy. Catalog from 1910-11.*

IV-191. Stovetop fortune cookie maker, *like a pizzelle iron. Complete with original colorful box, recipe booklet & paper fortune strips. Bright finish cast iron or steel plates with wooden handles, four 3" diam. baking wells inside. Metal plates about 7-1/2" x 6-1/4", and have fancy raised design of Chinese building, "Fortune Factory," & Chinese calligraphy. 1960s-70s. Fortune cookies have never been part of traditional Chinese cuisine, & were probably developed by some very clever restauranteur who baked or fried some sweet-dough wonton wrappers after folding them, and thought of putting something fun inside, like any other kind of fortune-telling device, to encourage customers to come back. It's not uncommon to have food imprinted with a symbolic message, perhaps even a blessing, so fortune cookies aren't such a wild idea. Photo courtesy ebayer son-yatats, Sonja Sherrill, Canada; Collection of Jenni Undis.* **$45+**

Fritter baker – See Ebelskiver pan
Frosting tubes – See Cake decorator set
Fruit or melon ballers – See entries in Chapter I (Cut)
Gem pan – See Muffin or gem pan
Gingerbread man mold, heavy cast aluminum, 2 part, very 3-D, on his base it says "Gingerbread Man," very exaggerated features of man – possibly meant to be an African-American chef, hence might be appropriate for a "Black Americana" collection. 8"H, maker unknown, ad found in *American Home*, Feb. 1949. .... **$75+**
Gingerbread molds – See Cake boards; also Cookie boards
Goffering or gauffre iron – See Wafer iron
Gugelhupf mold – See Molds, ceramic, spouted or tubed, pudding or Kugelhopf; see also Molds, copper
Hoarhound cutter – See Candy cutter
Ice cream cones & wafer molds:
Ice cream cone baker's mold, 6 cast iron heavy conical forms, hinged "cover," handle, 1880s? Rare. .... **$350-$450**

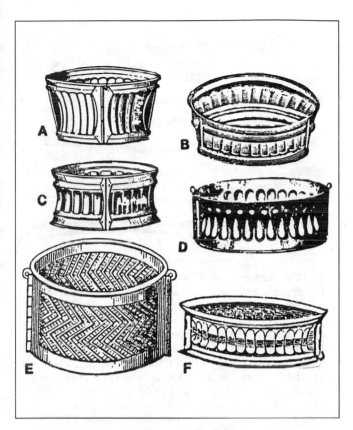

IV-192. French pie or pâte molds. *All hinged, most relatively shallow compared to diam.* **(A)** *German hinged mold, simple flutes, in 5 sizes, from 5-1/2" to 8" diam.* **(B)** *Similar, with ring border, ranges from 5-1/2" to 8-3/4" diam.* **(C)** *Another German one in 8 sizes, from 4-3/8" to 9-3/4" diam. All Bertuch, Berlin, c.1904.* **(D)** *Oval "pie mold," planished tin. 11-1/2", 12" & 13-1/2" diam. John Van Range Co., Cincinnati, 1914.* **(E)** *Round, herringbone design, two sizes. English, from Mrs. A. B. Marshall's Cookery Book, c.1887-1900.* **(F)** *"French Oval Meat Pie Mould. – Opens at one end." American Home Cook Book, 1854.*

Ice cream wafer mold, cast iron, 3 piece, patterned to make a waffled design, with "ICYPI MADE IN USA" in pattern, ICYPI, mfd. by Automatic Cone Co., Cambridge, MA, 1920s. • These molds were not necessarily used by each soda fountain owner, because already prepared & baked wafer sandwich "holders" could be bought in large quantities already made. They are open on one end only to receive a slab of ice cream made using the ICYPI mechanical ice cream dipper. (ICYPI is pronounced I-Cee-Pie & usually spelled IcyPi by the company.) • See also the ICYPI ice cream disher under ice cream disher listed with other sandwich or slab dishers. See also Wafer irons............. **$350-$400**

ICE CREAM DISHERS & SCOOPS
Listed by type, starting with simple non-mechanical scoops.

Non-mechanical variety:
Ice cream disher, bowl of cast aluminum with colored anodized aluminum cap at end of tubular handle, non-mechanical. The "Roll Dipper" disher is filled with liquid that is supposed to chemically keep it warm enough to help scoop out very cold ice cream.

IV-193. Ice cream cone fryer. *Cast & plated iron, wooden knob handle. Batter: 1 lb. soft flour, 4 oz. confectioner's sugar, 3/4 pt. beaten eggs, 3/4 pt. milk. Mix flour, sugar & eggs with an egg beater very good, then add milk gradually. In meantime have your oil heated to 370° to 375°. Put your spring iron in the oil, allow to get hot; then dip the iron into the mixture, but don't let the mixture run over the iron. Then take the iron out & put in the heated oil; in a few seconds the cake [cone] is baked. Take out & give it a knock on a piece of wood to remove the cakes from the iron. Put the iron in the oil again for a few seconds. Knock the adhering oil off, & continue the same way as before. If mixture gets thick, add a little more milk & eggs. A nice showy cake which has a fine taste if eaten fresh, but it will be dry the next day." Pat'd. 1903 or before. H. Hueg catalog, 1910.* **$125-$175**

7"L, designed by Sherman Kelly, mfd. by Zeroll Co., Toledo, OH, 7"L, 1934 to present day. Called by the Museum the "Roll Dipper," this was chosen by the design curator to be in the Museum of Modern Art's Design Collection, NYC. Zeroll changed its name in 1953 to Roll Dippers, Inc. Other disher-dippers made by them in the 1940s & '50s are the "Nuroll" & "Roldip.".. **$10+**
Ice cream disher, bowl of cast aluminum, non-mechanical, has smaller bowl & longer handle than the later award-winning "Roll Dipper," cap on end has blue finish, probably too early to be anodized, "Zeroll #30," Toledo, OH, 1934 patent #1974051....... **$15+**
Ice cream disher, bowl of cast aluminum, non-mechanical, no special fluid in handle, "Nuroll," Toledo, OH, made by Zeroll Co., 1950s............................. **15+**

IV-194. Ice cream cone baker. *Called a "Standard Cone Oven," used on any style stove. Came with wooden conical roller for rolling into cone as soon as taken off the baker. T. Mills, 1915. Value depends on category of collector. Ice cream collector:* **$75-$125+;** *waffle iron collectors:* **$150+;** *cast iron pan collector's evaluation:* **$75-$120**

Ice cream disher, bowl & handle cast aluminum, hollow & filled with "non-toxic anti-freeze." 7"L x 2" diam. scoop, "The Anti-Freeze Scoop," "Made in Japan," c.1950s.. **$10**

Ice cream disher, bowl of cast aluminum with ridged cigar-shaped handle & a bowl clunkier than similar "Roll Dipper," non-mechanical, marked "PROGRES-SUS" (Note: Some letters may be indistinct – mine reads only "...ESSUS"), made in Italy, 7-1/2"L, c.1960s.. **$5+**

Ice cream disher, bowl of unidentified metal with wood handle, non-mechanical, "Arnold," pat'd. 1928. **$20**

Ice cream disher, nickeled brass, wooden handle, New Gem Mfg. Co., Newark, NJ, (affiliated with C. T. Williamson Wire Novelty Co. – the corkscrewers), c.1932-1940. .... **$35+**

Banana split elongated bowl, mechanical:

Ice cream disher, banana split type, elongated oval bowl of nickeled nickel silver, thumb piece, black painted wooden handle, "Hamilton Beach #34," actually the Gilchrist #34 after HBCo. bought Gilchrist (1931), 30 scoops to a quart, bowl approx. 3-3/4"L x 1-3/8"W x 7/8" deep, c.1931-1934. .... **$550-$650**

Ice cream disher, banana split type, long oval, nickeled brass, wooden handle, long thumb lever, "United Products Co., Inc.," Chelsea, MA, 11-1/2"L, bowl 3-1/4"+L, 1930s. .... **$500-$650**

Ice cream disher, banana split type, nickeled brass, wood handle, elongated oval disher, earlier version marked "Gilchrist #31" – just like round-bowl one. 11-1/2"L, pat'd. 1915. .... **$550-$650**

Bowl-shaped round cup, mechanical:

Ice cream disher, bowl cup, nickeled brass, wood handle, "Philcone Disher," 10"L, 1930s. (For eating ice

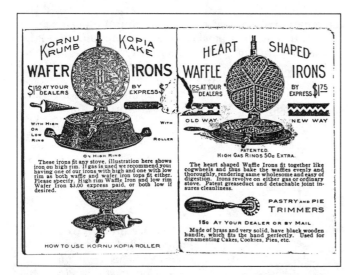

IV-195. Wafer & waffle irons. *For stove top.* **(L)** *Kornu Kopia Krumb Kake wafer iron set in choice of high or low frame, with a fancy quasi-religious old-fashioned design. Note conical & cylindrical wooden rollers that came with the wafer iron, to roll hot & still-soft wafers into cones or cylinders, for filling with ice cream.* **(R)** *5 waffles are heart-shaped. Also advertised was a brass pie trimmer with turned wood handle. Booklet from Alfred Andresen & Co., Minneapolis, c.1905. Booklet worth about $30 in ephemera market. Wafer iron (L):* **$75-$125***; Waffle iron (R):* **$45-$65**

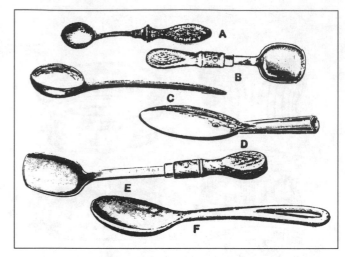

IV-196. Ice cream dishing spoons. *Also called* **ice cream spades.** *(A) nickeled metal, wood handle, round bowl, handle marked "Crandall & Cudahy," in Duparquet, Huot & Moneuse catalog, c.1904-10. (B) Tinned steel, shank riveted to wood handle. 2 sizes: 10"L & 12"L. From Pick-Barth, 1929. (C) All metal, round bowl. D, H & M, c.1904-10. (D) Oval paddle, tin, D, H & M. (E) Long-handled, "spade bowl," 10", 12" or 14"L, D. J. Barry catalog, 1924. (F) Spade bowl, all metal, nickel-plated cast metal (brass?). 11-1/2"L. Pick-Barth, 1929.* **$5-$20**

cream whilst listening to Fibber McGee & Molly on your Philco radio.) .... **$40-$65**

Ice cream disher, bowl cup, nickeled brass, wooden handle, 30 dips to a quart size, "Indestructo #31," mfd. by Benedict Mfg Co., East Syracuse, NY, 10-1/2"L, 1920s... **$60-$80**

Ice cream disher, bowl cup, cast aluminum bowl, cast metal quadrant gear & thumb lever, steel scraper inside bowl, clumsily shaped turned wood handle, no marks, prob. American, 8-1/2"L, bowl 2-1/2" diam., c.1950s-60s... **$10+**

Ice cream disher, bowl cup, cast aluminum, thumb press lever to release ice cream by making the little 'golf tee' prod in bottom of bowl knock it out, squared handle, made in Japan, 7-1/2"L, 1950s........................... **$3+**

❖ **NOTES** ❖

Futurewatch – While cheaply made, these odd mid 20th century **mechanical dishers** are some of the collectibles in this field to be looking for, even though they are nowhere near as exciting & well-engineered as the older ones. A lot of them have a handle like a screwdriver. I must have a dozen different ones, picked up at yard sales & thrift shops, all under $3. Names include Scoop Master, Maid of Honor, Peerless, Croford, Progressus, Nevco, Baskin Robbins, Tranco, Lightning, Action Scoop by Kamkap, Bonny Pro. Co., Arnold C. Eichin (anodized aluminum), Shore Craft, Alpine Brand (Italian), Androck, and a really neat red & yellow all-plastic (with metal thumb-piece spring for release) by Lloyd Disher Co. They won't ever gain great value, but as interesting adjuncts to your valuable dishers they offer a lot.

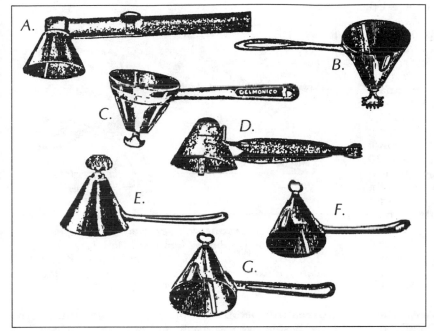

IV-197. Ice cream conical or cornet dishers. *A cornet is sort of a small cornucopia – both come from a root word meaning horn. Paper cornets (like those pointed-bottom disposable paper cups) were used in 18th & 19th C. for nuts or sweetmeats. All dishers shown here have a blade that scrapes out inside. Most are simplest mechanical type – the* **"key scraper,"** *with a blade (sometimes called a knife) inside that is scraped around the inside of the cone by twisting the "key." All conical types seem odd now because the resultant conical scoop of ice cream faces the wrong way to fit into a wafer-like cone, but this style predates the baked cone, & was used to serve a conical serving of ice cream in a dish. All are about 7" to 8-1/2"L. From top:* **(A)** *"Chicago" disher, nickel plated, one size only, 16 to a quart. It has a spring-loaded scraper activated by thumb piece on long tubular handle.* **(B)** *"Clad's Improved," of seamless drawn steel, German silver knife, 4, 5, 8, 10, 12 & 16 to a quart.* **(C)** *"Delmonico Improved," cast iron handle, heavy spun brass bowl, all nickeled, interior cup removable. 6, 10 & 12 to a quart.* **(D)** *Kingery's "Rapid," one-hand squeeze type – blade moves when you squeeze double handle. One squeeze makes the 2 crossed scraper blades (in effect 4 blades) turn & release ice cream. One-handed kitchen utensils, which probably started after the Civil War, when amputees needed such utensils, are an interesting broad-spectrum collectible. The "Rapid" has a nickel-plated spun brass bowl & blade, "Bessemer steel spring," in 4, 5, 6, 8, 10, 12, 16 & 20 to a quart. (A, B, C, D) from Albert Pick catalog, 1909, mfd. by Kingery Mfg. Co., Cincinnati, OH, pat'd. Sept. 4, 1894.* **(E)** *"K-W-Cone" disher, mfd. by Keiner-Williams Stamping Co. Tinned bowl, malleable cast iron handle, with long slot. Several sizes. Cherry-Bassett catalog, 1921, pat'd. Nov. 7, 1905.* **(F)** *&* **(G)** *are two versions of "Clewell" disher & measure:* **(F)** *Tin bowl, cast iron handle with small hanging hole, German silver knives, made in "standard sizes." Mfd. by V. Clad, Philadelphia. This one from an 1892 ad.* **(G)** *Bowl is seamless drawn steel. Note handle with long slot opening. 4, 5, 6, 8, 10, 12, 16 & 20 to a quart. In 1915 & 1924 catalogs. (Note: Around 1909, Erie Specialty Co. (later C. L. Walker Co.) made two key-scrapers. Their #184 had a wooden handle; 184A had simpler bent wire handle. The key looks like top of old skate key or clock key with two holes. Blades were removable.) (D) Kingery "Rapid"* **$150-$175***; the rest:* **$15-$75**

Ice cream disher, bowl cup, cast aluminum with golf-ball dimples cast in grip handle, "Scoop-Rite," patent pending, c.1940s. .... **$15-$20**

Ice cream disher, bowl of chrome plated brass, black Bakelite™ handle, Model #66, by Hamilton Beach Mfg. Co., Racine, WI, pat'd. 1920, with these handles prob. 1930s. • **Black Bakelite**™ looks like hard rubber & is one trade name for the generic molded phenolic resin plastic. Catalin™ is another. .... **$22+**

Ice cream disher, bowl of chromed brass, wood handle, Hamilton Beach "No-Pak" #31, 103"L, pat'd. 1932. (Please don't encourage strippers by buying "deplated" ones.) .... **$60-$75**

Ice cream disher, bowl cup, nickel-plated brass, 2-way finger action, springless model referred to as "Dover Springless," or "Double Flip," Dover Mfg. Co., c.1928. .... **$75-$95**

Ice cream disher, bowl cup, nickel plated brass, has unique slicing mechanism – when finger lever is operated a blade slices off excess ice cream, giving a perfect half-round mound of ice cream, called "The Perfection" & the "New Method" disher in trade advertising although a much older "New Method" disher that measured portions was being sold in 1915. Thumb lever marked "Dover Mfg. Co."

with patent & place, Dover, NH, 10-15/16"L. Two models: 1) with a single finger lever, 2) a double with a lever for thumb & one for fore- or middle finger. Pat'd. 1924 & 1928. • Some sold through Perfection Disher Co. of Boston, hence trade name. Single: $600-$700; double lever: .... **$650-$750**

Ice cream disher, bowl cup, nickeled brass, fat wood knob on top, round cylindrical disher part has central vertical shaft, worked by pushing down on knob with palm, Fro-Zon Mfg. Co., Schenectady, NY, pat'd. Feb. 24, 1925. .... **$500+**

Ice cream disher, bowl with point, probably nickeled brass, with plain-shaped wood handle, thumb lever with spring return. The bowl has a small pointed protrusion on outside – advertising copy from a June 1919 "Soda Fountain," reads "Our Service Disher has every good point any other disher ever had & a few points no other disher has. Once you see this disher with the point, the point will get you & you will 'get the point.'" Further: "Make a hollow in the top of the ice cream with the point on the back of the disher. Serve the syrup on the top of the cream where it will do the most good. Make every drop count. A little less fruit & syrup served this way looks like more & gives better satisfaction. All the syrup served this way is eaten with the cream & none is left in the bottom of the dish." Service Commodities Mfg. Co., Chicago, IL, c.1919+. .... **$500-$750+**

Ice cream disher, bowl cup, nickeled brass, round bowl with scraper, spring & small thumb lever, flat, knurled metal handle (called by collectors "beavertail handle") embossed with patent date, manufacturer & trade name, "Clipper Disher," mfd. by Geer Mfg. Co., Troy, NY, 9-1/4"L, pat'd. Feb. 7, 1905 by Rasmus Nielsen. Nielsen pat'd. at least 10 dishers, some conical, some round, before 1921. Round: $200-$300; conical: .... **$300-$400**

Ice cream disher, bowl cup, nickeled brass, marked "Dairy Fresh," 20th C. • According to Wayne Smith, this is a **fool-the-collector item** made in Taiwan (origin noted on removeable paper label), that can be detected by shoddy workmanship. .... **$7+**

Ice cream disher, bowl cup, nickeled brass, knurled metal handle that looks borrowed from a screwdriver, spring-operated with thumb lever, marked: "Myers Deluxe Disher," Chicago, IL, pat'd. May 19, 1936 by Louis Myers. .... **$30+**

Ice cream disher, bowl cup, nickeled brass, shaft screwed into end of red painted wooden handle, not well made but interesting for the extreme simplicity of the gearing. A tight spring inside handle, thumb piece has 5 holes & a little gear has 5 teeth; as you push thumb lever against teeth they move the scraper, Japan, 8"L, 20th C. .... **$7+**

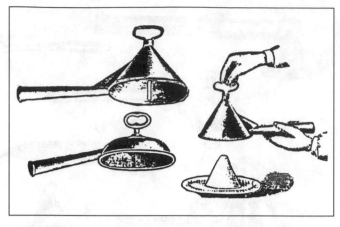

IV-199. Ice cream key scrapers. *Two types, tin with capped tubular handles. One has conical bowl, braced to handle (shown in use at right). Other makes rounded serving. The latter is much rarer. Bertuch, Berlin, c.1904.* **$25-$45+**

Ice cream disher, bowl cup, nickeled aluminum bronze, with small gear, rack & spring halfway up shaft to bowl, rosewood handle, quite simple, even modern in look, hard to find, mfd. by Gem Spoon Co., Troy, NY, 10-1/2"L, sizes in 6, 8, 10, 12, 16, & 20 dips to the quart, pat'd. by Bernice J. Noyes, May 7, 1895. The **Noyes' Gem** was possibly the first round bowl.

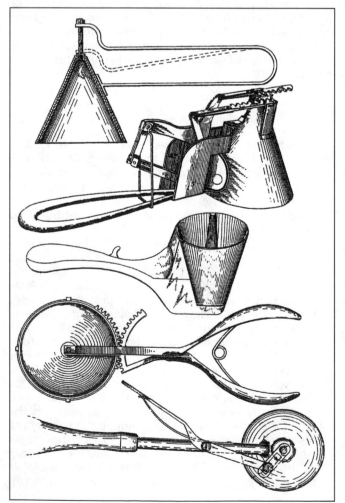

IV-198. Patents for cornet dishers. *All Pennsylvania, all 1896 or 1897. Top to bottom:* **(1)** *Pat'd. as a "mold" by Alfred L. Riggs, Knoxville, PA, June 9, 1896, #561,727. "The operator grasps the handle and uses the mold as an ordinary dipper. When the same is filled with the cream, it is held on the plate or saucer ... and the upper half of the handle is forced downward ... causing the rod carrying the cutters to revolve by reason of the lug engaging in the spiral groove. This loosens the cream and allows it to fall out into the plate."* **(2)** *Pat'd. by Arthur W. Lockwood, Everett, PA, Dec. 21, 1897, #595,954. The odd mechanism at left is a "bell-crank lever," used by depressing with the thumb, which produces a "semirotation of the shaft."* **(3)** *Pat'd. by James E. Crea & William H. Crea, Allegheny, PA, July 20, 1897, #586,807. Small trigger pulled back with thumb (spring inside handle) when you wish cutters to release ice cream inside bowl. "The entire mechanism controlling and actuating the cutters is concealed so as to prevent the substance upon which the disher is being employed from coming in contact therewith."* **(4)** *Upper view of "Mold and disher" pat'd. by Alfred L. Cralle, Pittsburgh, PA, Feb. 2, 1897, #576,395. Segmental rack gear operates cutter when handles are squeezed. Note spring between handles, which returns them to open position.* **(5)** *"Mold and disher" pat'd. by Thomas F. Rankin, Allegheny, PA, assignor of a half right to Joseph A. Buttress, same place, Oct. 12, 1897, #591,635. This one has a turned wooden handle, meant to be made "preferably" from aluminum. Simple thumb lever mechanism moves pivoting link on top of the cone, thereby turning the scraper blades to release the dip.*

disher, & predates the similar Gilchrist #31, which was a decided improvement since the mechanical part was moved farther away from the ice cream itself. .... **$50-$60+**

Ice cream disher, bowl, thumb lever with quadrant gear activated roll-over, cast aluminum with German silver plated bowl, "Unique," bowl size "8," Mosteller Mfg. Co., Chicago, IL, pat'd. July 3, 1906. • Buyer had choice of "best white metal," or cast aluminum; both had German silver/nickel-plated bowls. Thumb lever with quadrant gear, 6, 8, 10, 12, 16, & 20 scoops to a quart – ie. the #6 would make the largest scoops. #8 value: .... **$1,000-$1,400**

Ice cream disher, bowl cup, nickeled brass, wood handle, lever action, "Trojan No. 16," by Gem Spoon Co., Troy, NY (later Newark, NJ, after the '20s), c.1911. .... **$60-$70**

Ice cream disher, bowl cup, nickeled brass & copper, squeeze action moves scraper inside bowl, Gilchrist #30, 10-1/2"L, c.1915-1930. .... **$30-$40**

Ice cream disher, bowl cup, nickeled brass, wooden handle, thumb lever with tiny gear, rack & concealed spring, #31, mfd. by Gilchrist Co., 11"L, pat'd. March 23, 1915. • This is the most common make & common size (#31) or model of all dippers – reflective of its great popularity when made. It was not patented until 7 years after Raymond Gilchrist filed for a patent, but was sold for many years beginning in 1908. The bowl in this model came in nine sizes: 6, 8, 10, 12, 16, 20, 24, 30, & 40 scoops to the quart. This Gilchrist remains a classic. .... **$30-$45**

IV-200. Ice cream measure. "Perfection" was one name used; "Philadelphia" was a later name. Actually a Clewell patent of May 3, 1876, mfd. by Valentine Clad, Philadelphia, PA, in two sizes: 1 pint & 1 quart. This footed goblet shape with handle is from a 1915 catalog. Spun brass, nickel plated outside, silver plated inside (probably meaning German silver), with nickel-silver blade that scrapes out the portion. In cutaway linecut you can see the key in the base. An 1892 V. Clad ad mentions only German silver. The Cherry-Bassett Co., calling it a "Philadelphia" measure, has two versions – one "heavily tinned," & one silvered inside, nickeled out. $25-$75

❖ NOTES ❖

Still a Classic – For a long time the price range of $65 to $85 held at fancy antique shows, but these Gilchrist #31s had become a sort of token kitchen tool that was displayed with the pressed glass & Staffordshire. Real ice cream disher collectors know how common they are, & more exciting novelty dishers, manufactured originally in much, much smaller quantities, have grabbed the bucks.

Stripped to Death – The Gilchrist ice cream servers have been the victims of nickel strippers for almost 20 years. It's a real bugabear of mine, the stripping of the original nickel plating from cast brass dippers. It's like taking the old finish off furniture. The price of these dippers was going up & UP, & not only in the '70s & '80s but still some dealer ads reflect the trend towards stripping, & unabashedly say "brass ice cream scoop." Such is the power of the golden-glow metal; brass glisters like gold, whereas nickel has no glamour unless it's on an old stove. I've often seen a Gilchrist #31 with its original plating, if somewhat worn, for $25 to $30. In the next booth, a highly polished, buffed, stripped one may be as high as $85 – Hey! It's real brass! It is NOT a good investment to buy one like that.

The **gear & rack** provided "alternate rectilinear motion ... to the rack-rod, by the continuous revolution of the ... spur-gear, the spiral spring forcing the rod back to its original position on the teeth of the gear, quitting the rack," in terms taken from *Mechanical Movements*, first published in 1868, renewed in 1896, reprinted in 1933 in a "Century of Progress" special edition.

Related collectible – Look for the *Saturday Evening Post*, June 27, 1953, with a colorful cover by American artist Amos Sewell. The genre depiction of an outdoor children's birthday party shows a harrassed mother holding what appears to be a Gilchrist #31.

Ice cream disher, bowl cup, cast aluminum, one piece scoop, with spring action thumb button in bowl's center, Decatur Lloyd Disher Co., Decatur, IL, 1940. .... **$10-$20**

Ice cream disher, bowl cup, original nickel plating, thumb lever has only mark: "16-to-a-Quart," 20th C. .... **$12+**

Ice cream disher, bowl cup, pewter-like cast aluminum & nickel-plated steel, #16, Bohlig Mfg. Co., St. Paul, MN, pat'd. Oct. 6, 1908. Martin Bohlig's patent uncannily resembles an 1884 patent. Extremely unusual disher used for filling ice cream cones; when handle is squeezed the bowl divides in half, opens like a steam shovel bucket & drops the ice cream through bottom into cone. Very rare. .... **$900-$1,100**

Ice cream measure/packer-type disher, meant to fill cardboard cans of hand-packed ice cream that used to be commonly available at ice cream parlors. Looks like a mechanical bulb-planter. 9-1/2"L overall with 3-1/4" diam. x 3-3/4"H cylinder. Marked "The Excelsior," Stamford, CT. Also "Pat Ap For" & "Keep in Water when not in use." 20th C. .... **$100-$150**

Conical or cornet, mechanical:

Ice cream disher, conical, what was called a cornet disher in the old parlance, key wind, heavy tin & galvanized metal, key at top turns the cornet itself rather than the scraper inside (reverse is true on most if not all other conical dishers), #10, American, about 8"L, Naylor's Patent of June 19, 1888. .... **$45-$55**

Ice cream disher, conical disher with vaguely heart- or valentine-shaped key, tin with tubular steel handle with brass cap on end bearing name & date, "Clewell's V. Clad Maker," mfd. by Valentine Clad Co., Philadelphia, 8-1/2"L, pat'd. May 3, 1876... **$35-$50**

Ice cream disher, cone or cornet disher, heavily nickel plated, one handed kind with fancy looking embossed squeeze handles (like tongs) with a spring at the end. Handles look like those grip strengtheners you get at sports stores, "Kingery's Rapid," Kingery Mfg. Co., Cincinnati, OH, 8-1/2"L, pat'd. Sept. 4, 1894. One expert collector says this can go to $250-$350 if undamaged & in fine condition. .... **$150-$175**

Ice cream disher, cone disher, loop handle, ornate key release, tin & iron, "K W" in oval of key, Keiner-Williams Stamping Co., Richmond Hill, NY, 7-1/2"L, pat'd. Nov. 7, 1905.................................. **$20-$25**

Ice cream disher, cone type, with key mechanism, key is letter "G," tinned steel, loop handle, Gilchrist Co., Newark, NJ, 7-1/2"L, c.1915-1931............ **$20-$25**

❖ NOTES ❖

Cornet Key Names – The four initials or monograms found on the keys of this type of disher – known to me or Wayne Smith in his excellent first book on dippers are: KW, BK, W, and G. Keys are plain open ovals, slightly fancier geometric open forms, or very fancy casting – like Delmonico's scroll. We would love to know of any other initial keys. I'd like to say also that although I read books, and talk to collectors, and try to learn, any mistakes I make here are due to too little knowledge on my part, and in no way can they be dished up to my advisor Wayne Smith.

IV-201. Three types of mechanical ice cream dishers. (T) *Cast aluminum, thumb-lever spring action prod knocks ice cream out of bowl, 7-1/2"L, made in Japan, 1950s.* **(M)** *Longest one is a* **Dover Mfg. Co. #20** *slicing dipper, wooden handle, nickeled bowl. This has a leveling cutter that flattens scoop before it comes out. 10-1/2"L.* **(B)** *Cornet disher with key-wind, heavy tin, marked "#10." In this case, key at top turns cornet-shaped bowl, not the scraper inside, although the reverse is true of most (or all?) others. Pat'd. 1883 (?). Last two collection of Meryle Evans.* **(T)** *$10+;* **(M)** *$600-$700;* **(B)** *$40-$50*

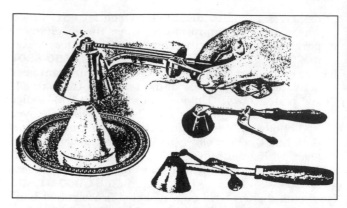

IV-202. Mechanical cornet dishers. *All with thumb levers that move blade within.* **(L)** *Large one is* **"Gilchrist's No. 33 Pyramid"** *disher. "Bowl & scraper all made of German silver (nickel). Phosphor bronze spring fully concealed. Press button (arrow points to it) to take entire thing apart for cleaning or repairing. Six sizes: 6, 8, 10, 12, 16 or 20 to a quart.* **(R)** *Disher under the hand is* **C. L. Walker Co.'s "Quick & Easy"** *disher, formerly made by Erie Specialty Co., then by C. L. Walker Co., the president of which was Edwin Walker. Pat'd. about 1904 (?). As made by Erie: nickel-plated copper bowl; German silver knives; some seem to have had cast bronze, other malleable iron, handles. In the beginning, c.1904 when made by Erie, it came in only 6 sizes: 5, 6, 8, 10, 12, & 16 to a quart; later in 9 sizes: 6, 8, 10, 12, 14, 16, 20, 24 & 30 to a quart. Walker's was written up glowingly in trade press, although some copy came directly from the company. The "Quick & Easy" tradename was used for Walker's key-scrapers & thumb-lever dishers.* **(B-R)** *Bottom disher is the* **"Dandy."** *Two qualities – silver plated or tinned, with wood handle. 8, 10, 12, & 16 to a quart. First two illus. from 1919 ads in The Soda Fountain trade magazine; "Dandy" from Albert Pick catalog, 1909.* **$100-$150**

Ice cream disher, cone disher, metal, "Safe-T-Cone," American, early 20th C.............................. **$10-$15**

Ice cream disher, cone or pyramid-shaped disher, nickeled brass, wood handle, Gilchrist #33, with thumb lever like the #31, & concealed reciprocating gear & notched rod atop the pyramid, Newark, NJ, 10-1/2"L, pat'd. Sept. 1, 1914. • This one came in 6 sizes: 6, 8, 10, 12, 16 & 20 scoops per quart. .... **$75-$100**

Ice cream disher, cone shape, nickeled brass, spring on top of cone, pulled by pressure on long wide thumb lever, turned wood handle, "Quick & Easy #486," Edwin Walker's patent, mfd. by his company – Erie Specialty Co., Erie, PA, 10-1/2"L, pat'd. May 11, 1915, but inventor filed application 5 years earlier, so it's possible at least some were made before the patent was granted. • In 1909, this Quick & Easy was advertised as being made of cast aluminum (called by Erie "our cast aluminum near-silver metal" that "remains white like silver, insuring clean, attractive service"), & it came with a tiny little one-cone tray – #487 – used while filling cones, that looks like a miniature griddle with frying pan handle. Apparently you released the cone of ice

IV-203. Ice cream disher. *"Gilchrist #30," with squeeze action. Nickeled brass & copper – sometimes called "bronze metal," 10-1/2"L, c.1915-1930.* **$35-$50**

cream, big end down on the little tray, then maneuvered the ice cream into the baked cone. The sales copy reads amusingly: "The distinctive feature of this cone disher is that the bottom of the cone is so shaped that the ice cream sets down solidly in the cone when released from the disher ... This gives the appearance of having served the customer with an unusually liberal amount of ice cream." Unlike other "Quick & Easy" models, this one was solely for filling cones. .... **$275-$325**

Ice cream disher, cone-shaped nickeled "seamless pressed copper cup," German silver (scraper blades) "knives," nickeled malleable iron handle (three years later, in 1907, the handles were described as being cast bronze – the whole disher being heavily nickel-plated), thumb lever operates a rod atop cone which pulls knife or scraper around inside cone, ad states "This Disher is used at the St. Louis Exposition," "Walker's No. 186," pat'd. by Edwin Walker, mfd. by Erie Specialty Co., Erie, PA, six sizes of scoops-to-the-quart: 5, 6, 8, 10, 12, 16. By 1907 it was made up to size 20, advertised 1904. See listing above for Walker's patented 1915 brass disher. • Walker's dishers also included a shallow round cup one, #386, with levered thumb piece, almost like this one, & a simple key top conical one of tin (#184), & cast aluminum models........................... **$350-$550**

Ice cream disher, conical bowl, plated brass, "N. & Co., Delmonico," 8"L, c.1890s-1910. .... **$75-$100**

Ice cream disher, conical metal dish, squeeze action handle, wire spring plier type, 10"L, "Squeeze Action," Pat'd. April 9, 1901, American. Rare......... **$350-$450**

IV-204. Ice cream disher. *Classic Gilchrist's #31, thumb lever. Made in nine sizes: 6, 8, 10, 12, 16, 20, 24, 30, & 40 to a quart. Also sold for dishing out mashed potatoes! Nickel-plated "bronze metal." From 1930s catalog. CAUTION: This & one above are the ones dealers like to engolden, by removing necessary nickel plating.* **$35-$55**

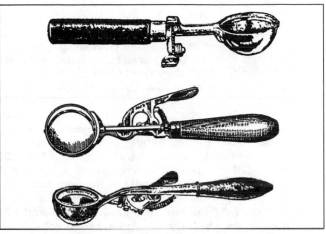

IV-205. Ice cream dishers. (T) *"Arnold," with nickel plating. End of handles marked with code colors for size. (So you could see them when they sat immersed in that bucket of disgusting bath-water scummy mess.)* **(M)** *The "Philcone," identified as a "patent chromium plated disher," in Jaburg catalog, 1915. Small-scoop sizes only, 12, 16, 20, 24 & 30 to a quart.* **(B)** *"Gem" disher, with bowl made of "aluminum bronze, heavily nickel plated." Rosewood handle; 6 to 20-to-the-quart sizes.* **$45-$65**

IV-206. Ice cream disher. *"Service" disher. The distinguishing feature is the pointed piece on top, & their ads are filled with word play on "the point." But it's a great idea: "Make a hollow in the top of the cream with the point on the back of the disher. Serve the syrup on the top of the cream where it will do the most good. Make every drop count. A little less fruit & syrup served this way looks like more & gives better satisfaction." Heh heh. (Even today, food service trade magazines are full of ideas to convert "less" into "more" visually, adding perceived value & making it possible for menu prices to be jacked up. Canners & bottlers are doing it now – take a look at apple sauce jars.) Service Commodities Mfg. Co., Chicago. Ad in The Soda Fountain, 1919.* **$500-$750**

Ice cream disher, cast metal, pointed conical bowl, spring-loaded catch in handle, handle & bowl split apart when catch is released. 7"L. Only mark "Pat. Pend." Larry Meeker says this is "a sleeper because they aren't marked & aren't in Smith's book." Before the Internet they used to bring $1,000; now considered a bit more available & currently bring: .... **$600-$800**

Ice cream disher, conical disher, tin with heavy wire handle, key-scraper, no mark, American, 7-5/8"L, c.1890s-1910. • Wire handle is unusual, as most have a sheet metal or cast handle. .... **$20-$25**

Ice cream disher, conical, heavy tinned sheet metal, stamped sheet metal handle with long hole, key release/scraper is relatively big oval, no mark, American, 7-3/8"L, late 19th C. .... **$20-$25**

Novelty shapes – heart, cube, tube, etc. mechanical:

Ice cream disher, heart-shaped bowl, nickeled metal, shaft, & thumb lever, simple turned wood handgrip is stained red, makes heart-shaped servings, mfd. by the inventor, **John Manos**, Toronto, OH, 11"L, pat'd. Nov. 17, 1925. Marked "Patented Nov. 1925" on back of heart-shaped pusher plate. Mr. Manos had molded glass heart-shaped dishes made in New Moundsville, WVa (a big glass center) to go with the ice cream; & because they would have suffered much higher casualties from use, the dishes are valued at about $100 each. • Price has skyrocketed for these dishers, & Wayne Smith, who actually had the great honor & pleasure to talk with Mr. Manos himself, reports directly from the inventor's mouth that there were only 1,000 made. • One of my concerns is that as the price goes up, it'll be profitable for a very skilled person to make fakes. After all, it's not platinum, so the material cost would be small, & it's not even really all that odd, except for that beautiful heart-shaped dipper bowl. One man in 1987 advertised his standing offer for $2,500 for one. One sold at a Gaithersburg, MD auction in February 1988 for $3,000. At a Noel Barrett auction in New Hope, PA, in April 1988, someone paid (including 10% premium) an astounding $4,620. At an auction in St. Louis, MO, in 1989, one brought $5,500. For a while, Wayne Smith was carefully tracking the selling prices of the heart dishers; 15 sold between 1988 & 1989, & 10 more were sold by 1991, with an average selling price of $3,450. Since then, prices have leveled off, with an occasional "bargain" in the $2,000 range. These high prices are, obviously, for dishers in Good+ condition, with no damage. It's impossible to say now whether this is a temporary stall in a price rise, or a signal of a downturn. At a Colorado auction in about 2000, one in the original box brought an unheard-of $12,000. Auction fever? If Manos' recollection is accurate, that only 1000 were made, this situation offers an almost unparalleled opportunity in any field of collecting to track the market for an appealing, attractive, strongly-designed durable item over a period of years! We know that 1000 could not have survived. To be neither optimistic nor conservative, say that between 1925 & 1940 half, or 500, were lost, melted for scrap, destroyed, or thrown out by accident. Then there would have been, in 1940, 500 awaiting disposition. Maybe 50 of those are accounted for. If you collect ice cream implements, specializing in dishers, you would see that old pool of possibles drying up in the sun, like a rain puddle in August. So my feeling is, the price hasn't really started to go down yet. Wayne tells me that there are over 1000 known collectors now in this field, which is rapidly expanding. A small percentage of those people would be able to afford to pay so much money for something. So who knows what the price range might become? In 1996 I wrote "who knows how long it will take an entrepreneur with criminal intent to make, say, 10 copies?" and lo and behold: Larry Meeker writes that "I cannot confirm this, but I've heard that my own worst case scenario has happened and that there has been a made-up heart disher offered for sale on the Internet." Wayne Smith writes that "About 1997, a few (I believe fewer than five) copies of the heart dipper were made by a skilled craftsman & actually were sold as reproductions for $2,000+." I was told that they were marked in an inconspicuous place with the letters "ST." The wood handle is also slightly different from the original. Good advice would be to know where your dipper came from. The price is really crazy, but it's hard to know what to say or if there's an absolute rule to apply to what you will be asked to pay, or what you "should" pay................................... **$5,000-$7,500**

Ice cream disher, cube, stainless steel, makes small 1-1/2" cube of ice cream, "P C Server," mfd. by Prince Castle Co., c.1950s. .... **$150-$250**

Ice cream disher, tubular novelty, nickeled metal, wood handle, 9-1/2"L lever, long cylinder makes a tube of ice cream that is inserted in chocolate covered "bun" – the dessert is called a "cold dog." Canadian, pat'd. 1926. .... **$600-$750**

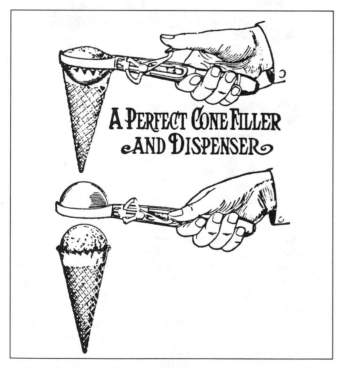

IV-207. Ice cream disher. "*Unique,*" *mfd. by Mosteller Mfg. Co., Chicago.* "*A perfect cone filler & dispenser, made in sizes 6, 8, 10, 12, 16 & 20 to Quart.*" *Two styles, one of white metal, one of aluminum, both with German silver bowls. Ad in Iron Age, 1909.* **$1,000-$1,400**

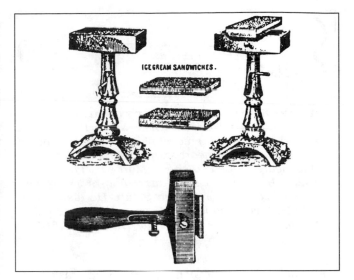

IV-208. Ice cream sandwich molds. *"Pan-American," for "the very latest form in which Ice Cream is sold at Soda Fountains, Cafes, etc., is the Ice Cream Sandwich, composed to two oblong Biscuits with a thin cut of Ice Cream between them." (T) Style One is shown in 2 views with fancy cast iron base, 9"-10"H; (B) style two was handheld, 5"L. Apparently "mold" holds wafer or biscuit in place while ice cream slab is put on & topped. Thomas Mills, 1915 catalog. (T) $400-$500; (B) $100-$200*

Sandwich, slab, or pie a la mode, mechanical:

Ice cream disher, pie a la mode novelty, triangular wedge-shaped aluminum disher with angled wooden handle, "Pi-Alamoder," mfd. in St. Louis, MO, pat'd. by Harlan Gardner & Alvin Olafson, Aug. 10, 1926. .... **$1,250-$1,500**

Ice cream disher, sandwich scoop, cast aluminum handle, stainless steel body, "Rainbow Ice Cream Dispenser Cake Cone Co., Inc.," St. Louis, MO, 10"L, sandwich part 2-7/8" x 3-3/8", 1920s. . **$300-$400**

Ice cream disher, sandwich type square disher, nickeled brass, nice big cog gear wheel, small thumb lever, wooden handle, "The 'Polar-Pak' Disher," mfd. by Philadelphia Ice Cream Cone Machinery Co., Phila. 10-1/2"L, pat'd. July 26, 1932. • Production started upon or before patent application was filed in 1928; disher is marked "Pat. Apl'd For.".............. **$350-$400**

Ice cream disher, sandwich disher, rectangular with spring inside handle. "Ergos," nickel-plated brass, 3-3/4" x 2" x 5-1/2", English, 1920s..... **$150-$200**

Ice cream disher, sandwich disher, adjustable to make three slab sizes, nickel silver (alloy), long shaft, wide-set thumb/forefinger lever, wooden handle, ads called it "Mayer's Handy Ice Cream Disher," marked on front "Mayer Mfg. Corp.," Chicago, IL, 12"L, "Patent pending" appears in a 1915 ad. • "Mayer's Handy" is very like the Jiffy Dispenser dipper, but doesn't have slightly curved disher, the wooden handle is slightly different proportion, & the thumb lever is not just slightly bent, it is cast & machined. The "Jiffy" (see below), which was sold by a Chicago company, & pat'd. in 1925, is undoubtedly closely related. .... **$125-$175**

Ice cream disher, sandwich style, "German silver" (old name for nickel silver, which was an alloy of copper, zinc & nickel, used for flatware & some hospital equipment), nearly square, slightly bowed disher, wood handle, thumb lever, "Jiffy Dispenser Co.," distributed or possibly mfd. by Jiffy Sales Co., Aurora, IL (Jiffy Sales in Chicago), 12-1/2"L, pat'd. Feb. 17, 1925. .... **$125-$175**

❖ NOTES ❖

Ice cream sandwiches were very popular in the 1920s, especially as a soda fountain novelty. However, people could make their own at home with waffles and by slicing a brick of ice cream, which was slightly larger than an unquartered pound "brick" of butter or lard. Until bulk ice cream was available, these sandwich dippers were not especially useful in a home kitchen; sales pitches were directed to soda fountains and ice cream parlors. More than two dozen styles of sandwich dippers were made during the 1920s! All are highly collectible. If price for more common mechanical dippers has remained on a plateau or even gone down, the novelty shape dishers have often gone way up.

Ice cream disher, sandwich style, square disher of nickel silver alloy, with levered push-out, wooden handle, "ICYPI" (the trademark, pronounced "Icy-Pie," was patented in 1926), Automatic Cone Co., Cambridge, MA, 10"L, 2-1/2" x 2-1/2" slab, c.1926. This disher was used to fill "ICYPI" wafers – a special sandwich wafer with three sides enclosed to prevent dripping. It was, in effect, a flattened, square cup. This popular ice cream treat was eaten by millions from about 1924 to 1930. • Note: ICYPI is pronounced I-Cee-Pie & was usually spelled IcyPi by the company. • An early ad for the Automatic Cone Co.'s "ICYPI" named the Pioneer Ice Cream Cone Mfg. Co. as the manufacturer; perhaps they meant of the wafer itself, not the dipper. (See Ice cream wafer mold above, with Ice cream cone baker's mold.)....................... **$125-$175**

Ice cream disher, sandwich style, square disher of nickel silver, levered push-out, wooden handle, "McLaren's ICYPI," McLaren Consolidated Cone Corp, Dayton, OH, 10"L, 2-1/2" x 2-1/2" slab. In 1929, McLaren Co. & also United Products Co. (Chelsea, MA) were licensed by Automatic Cone Co.,

IV-209. Slab disher, marked "ICE CREAM PIE" and "United Products Corp. Chelsea MASS." Nickel-plated brass, 7-3/4"L x 2-3/4"W, making slices or slabs about 2-1/2" x 2-1/2" x 5/8" thick. Photo courtesy eBayer dace925, Donna Buys, Dace Avenue Antiques, Sioux City, IA, & Ruben Johnson, South Sioux City, NE. Collection of Steve Brown, Fremont, NH. **$250+**

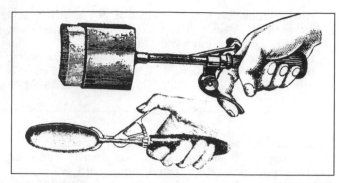

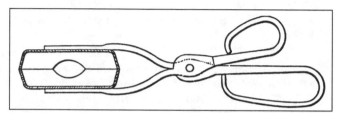

IV-210. Novelty ice cream dishers. (T) *Slice molder,* **"Handy,"** *mfd.. by Mayer Mfg. Corp., Chicago, c.1910s. Not a thumb lever, but a forefinger lever, as shown.* **(B)** *Banana split disher* **Gilchrist #34,** *long oval, 3-3/4"L x 1-3/8"W, 20 per quart. Both in Mills catalog, 1915.* **$500-$600; $550-$650**

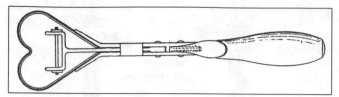

IV-212. Heart-shaped disher patent. *Pat'd. by John Manos, Toronto, OH, Nov. 17, 1925, #1,561,558. Brightly nickel-plated cast brass novelty disher, 11"L; heart-shaped servings for special heart-shaped dishes. Marked "Pat. Nov. 1925," but only on some according to ice cream disher book author Wayne Smith. He also says only 500 were made, based on an interview with Manos. Turned wooden handle.* **$5,000-$7,500**

IV-211. "Mold for Ice-Cream, Jellies, &c." *patent. Pat'd. Aug. 19, 1873, by Edgar Mason May, Fond Du Lac, WI, #141,882. Looks very modern. A sectional view of scissor-action mold – a round "pan or cup" with open ends facing each other. "Each cup has a curved piece cut from one side, so that when they are closed together they resemble a round box with an opening in the periphery." It was to be used by holding open & dipping in [ice] cream, "or other substance to be molded, taking up as much as can be held. They are then forced together, pressing the cream into a compact mass, the surplus passing out through" that hole in the periphery! Cast or sheet metal, inner surfaces "corrugated, carved, or ornamented in any manner." Official Gazette of the U.S. Patent Office.*

Cambridge, MA, to manufacture the highly successful ICYPI. .... **$150-$175**

Ice cream disher, sandwich/slab type, German silver, heavy wooden handle, makes a rectangular slab, "Sanitary Mould Co.," pat'd. 3/17/1925. .... **$400-$500**

Ice cream disher, sandwich type, nickeled brass scoop, rectangular, broad & slightly curved or bowed, turned wood handle, thumb lever action, no marks, American, 12-1/2"L, c.1930s. • This is like a cross between a Jiffy & un-curved Mayer sandwich dishers. Wooden handle is shaped differently, as is the position & shape of the thumb lever. ..... **$125-$150**

Ice cream disher, sandwich type, nickeled brass, spring inside handle, used to hold while being made, & then to serve ice cream sandwiches, "Reliance," 4-1/2"L, 2" x 3-1/2" slab. American, c.1920s. .... **$100-$150**

Ice cream measure, pieced tinned heavy sheet iron, footed goblet shape with generous strap handle on one side, key (which is hidden in concave base or ring foot) turns 2 scrapers that go all way up inside of cup. Opposite the handle is an attached medallion, unfortunately rather smashed & illegible, "Clewell," mfd. by Valentine Clad, Philadelphia, pint-size: 5-1/2"H x 3-1/2" diam., May 3, 1876 is the date on the medallion. (The same patent date, May 3, 1876, as their disher). Used to measure ice cream for take-home consumption. Made in one quart & one pint sizes. • Several companies made this type of measure, unfortunately few were marked. The "Perfection Ice Cream Measure," which was essentially the same as the Clewell except it was "made of hard spun metal, silver plated inside & nickel plated outside" with a "tempered nickel-silver" blade inside, was advertised by Thomas Mills & Brother, Inc., of Philadelphia, along with "Clewell" cornet ice cream disher, in their Catalog #31, late 1920s. Unmarked: $25-$75; marked: .... **$50-$125**

Ice Cream Molds

Most are a somewhat soft, gray, heavy metal called **"pewter,"** although it's not the same proportionate mix of metals used in the 18th century for plates and hollowware. They are not made of lead. Many **"white" metal alloys** that could be formed with great detail were made in the 19th century as substitutes for pewter. The molds are mostly two-part, hinged, and heavy, or relatively thick – so that they would hold the cold temperature longer while unmolding the ice cream. Many molds – perhaps most – are not as antique as we think they must be in this age of prepared foods and frozen novelty desserts. Prices have risen dramatically in the last decade or so, as have prices for all kinds of molds. • **Figural, Animalistic, Zoomorphic, Novelty** – In art-talk, something made in the shape of a human figure is called figural; if it's an animal or bird form it's animalistic or zoomorphic. In collector talk, "figural" usually broadly means something that has the shape of a human, animal, inanimate object or natural object. An ice cream mold, either for making a flag or a flamingo, might be termed "figural" or, sometimes, "figurative." The word "novelty" is also often used instead of figural. I use the term figural throughout because it is the more widely (mis)used term; it is easier than zoomorphic; and animalistic is sometimes used to describe something sensual or even bestial, as opposed to what is "spiritualistic" in humans. Read the daily news for your dose of human spiritualism and its opposite.

Some molds achieved their full effect only when accompanied by "decorations" of composition or printed paper or wire – such as leaves, stems, hats, golf clubs, flags, sails, and tablewares. Krauss and also Jo-Lo offer these in their 1930's catalogs. There were also paper favor companies, like Dennison's, and novelty companies who offered extremely inexpensive little decorations.

Holidays. With the 20th century came the commercialized commemoration of more and more holidays. Special cards, decorations, objects, and also ice cream molds were made to help people celebrate (and to help companies sell more merchandise in seasons besides Christmas). This is especially true beginning in the 1920s.

Confusables. Models or "Chalkware"? It is interesting when looking at ice cream mold catalogs from the early 20th century how many of the big molds (often represented by colored plaster or "composition" models made in the various molds – used for display by the ice cream shoppe taking party orders) remind you of ceramic "cottage" figurines, or of chalkware. Most would not fool a chalkware collector, but people just getting started with carnival chalks, which are cruder and have more popular-culture subjects, might find these models (if they indeed have survived and surface in the market) very confusing. Especially the traditional animals – squirrels, rabbits, cats, pigs – and the holiday figures like Santa or George Washington. At this point, I have no idea of the probable collector market for these models, and am not aware of a collector group for them, but I believe they should be collected, and may command prices, if colored especially, higher than the molds themselves! My Krauss and my Jo-Lo catalogs show some really fabulous pieces. Jo-Lo's 1930's catalog even gives the price for each mold and also each model. (See also Candy pattern molds.)

Evaluating Molds. When looking at ice cream molds, remember that any damages in soft pewter (holes, small cracks, hinge damage) reduce value dramatically. Look for good condition and fine interior detail. Interesting shapes or "collector cult" subjects add value too – subjects such as Christmas, teddy bears, Amerindians, character figures.

Old Style or Reproduction? – Tantalizing evidence exists in the 1932-33 *Thomas' Register of American Manufacturers*, that old-style ice cream molds were being made in the early '30s by a company called Reproductions Co., Boston, MA. Alas, when you turn to the manufacturers' alphabetical listing, this company is not given. I tried "Ice Cream Mold Reproductions Co." and "Boston Reproductions," to no avail.

E – K – S. There are the big three – a handful of early 20th century American companies whose marks are almost always abbreviated to initials on the molds themselves, plus the style or design number, usually three or four digits, and abbreviated to single initials by collectors (for ads and collection lists). These are Eppelsheimer & Co., NYC & Brooklyn, a.k.a. "E & Co. N. Y.," or E; Krauss Co., Milford, PA, a.k.a. "K" or "Krauss," or K, established in 1860; and Schall & Co., NYC, a.k.a. "S & Co.," or S., the oldest company. (Note: Eppelsheimer &

Co., in 1945 *Thomas' Register*, was listed as belonging to Warren Bros. Corp, Cranford, NJ.)

Krauss's catalog states that any molds made of "pure tin" would cost 20% more than the pewter. An article in *The Spinning Wheel*, Sept. 1965, by Duncan B. Wolcott, says that in 1965, moldmaker Walter Perry, who worked at Fr. Krauss in Milford, PA, uses **"61% tin and 39% lead"** for his molds. This is cause for great concern, if true. Mr. Wolcott also writes "If the [owner] plans it as an ash tray, will it lie flat? If he wants it for decoration or as a conversation piece, it should to a certain extent tell its own story. Many of today's collectors of pewter ice cream molds are actually using them to make up their own fancy individual ice cream desserts." Krauss also claimed that their moulded hinge construction was "exclusive" to them. "Unlike the common practice of soldering the hinge to the metal mould, we have perfected a manufacturing method of actually moulding the hinge as part of the mould itself ... which makes for a much stronger and truer hinge construction."

Other American Mold Makers: There are many unmarked molds, whose makers we cannot at this time identify. There are other molds which may or may not be marked by the following makers. In the **1905-06** *Thomas' Register of American Manufacturers*, I found: W. H. Sweeney Mfg. Co., Brooklyn (who made cake, ice cream, jelly, pudding molds); • Crandall & Godley, NYC; • Eppelsheimer & Co., NYC; • William Hart, NYC (who also manufactured carved cake boards with engine turnings, springerle molds, jelly molds, and copper pans as early as 1876); • Lalance & Grosjean Mfg. Co., NYC; • Valentine Clad & Sons, Philadelphia; • Thomas Mills & Bros., Pittsburgh. • **1932-33** *Thomas' Register*: • Cherry-Burrell Corp., Chicago (later Cherry-Bassett); • Reproductions Co., Boston; • Fr. Krauss & Son, NYC (I don't know the relationship to Krauss Co., Milford, PA); • James Y. Watkins & Son, NYC (known to us from the John Conger cake boards); • August Kreamer, Brooklyn, who made many kinds of kitchenwares – although I had not been aware of their ice cream molds. • Eppelsheimer & Co., Brooklyn; • Victor V. Clad, Philadelphia; • Thomas Mills & Brother, Inc., Philadelphia. • In the **1945** *Thomas' Register of American Manufacturers* are the following listings, some of which carry over from earlier directories: • Cherry-Burrell; • Ueding Ice Cream Mold Mfg. Co., Vincennes, IN; • Warren Bros. Corp., Cranford, NJ; • August Kreamer, Brooklyn; • Grimm Mfg. Co., Cleveland, OH; • Victor V. Clad; and • Thomas Mills & Bro., Inc., Philadelphia. • **Others:** One name known from a mold & a search of city directories is Jacob Ernst ("J. Ernst, N. York") a mold-maker in New York from 1858 through 1872. • Not found in the *Thomas'* directories, but known: • Jo-Lo (Joe Lowe Corp., Brooklyn), c.1930s catalog; • T.TCW Co., NYC, 1930s and 1940s, imported molds from Europe, and made their own – for ice cream & chocolate; • "D. & Co." – not known, prob. 20th C.

European mold makers. Some of these are taken from catalogs in my collection, others from molds themselves. French: • M. Cadot et Cie, Paris (founded 1826; catalog c.1900), marked "C C" on each mold. The double "C" appears within the trademark image of an old cranked ice cream freezer that looks exactly like a wishing well. Well ... I wish for some ice cream too, *n'est-ce pas?* • E. Compiègne, successor to Cadot, c.1904, also marked "C C" on each mold, tin and pewter molds. • A. Anthoine, Paris, late 19th C. catalog, probably in business from 1860s on, pewter and tin molds. • H. Trottier, Paris, (large geometric or vase-shaped tin molds, late 19th C. • Maison Letang Pére & Fils, Paris, using the mark "L.G.," early 20th C. catalog, but in business since 1832. German: "Joh: Reinöhl" for Johannes Reinöhl, Ulm • A. Bertuch, Berlin, (tin and pewter molds). • Herrn Gustav Krieg, Hanburg, late 19th C. to –?– (I have c.1914 catalog). Austrian: "GE, Austria" is mark on one mold I've seen; I don't know the company; English. Harton & Son, London, known to be working in 1878 - c.1890. Successors to Harton & Watts, pewterers, London, prior to 1878. • Biertumpfel & Hepting, London, fl. 1860s (Maltese cross and orb mark). • A. B. Marshall, London, c.1860s -?. Mrs. Marshall ran a cooking school, wrote many cookbooks, and had a huge culinary supply store in London, which may have also handled imported wares. Note: It's a good idea to remember, if you are researching European molds, that sizes in French and German catalogs are given in centimeters and litres. A centimeter (cm.) is .39 of an inch; a litre (lit.) is approximately 1.06 the size of a quart and therefore approximately equal to 2.12 pints.

•　　　•　　　•

French patent marks. Objects with the mark "*Breveté S.G.D.G.*" indicates patent protection for technical aspects. Marked "*Déposé,*" the object has a patent for its design – its shape or trademark name.

German patent marks. The mark "*Gesetzlich Geschütz*" or "*GG*" means "protected by law." The "*DRP*" mark is the equivalent of our utility patent; "*DRGM,*" registered design, is the equivalent of our design patent.

•　　　•　　　•

1838 Ice Cream – To the editor of the British *The Magazine of Domestic Economy*, July 1838: "Mr. Editor, – Can you give me any practical directions for making Ice creams? I have this year an opportunity of procuring ice in a rough state, but being unacquainted with the management of it for cream, &c., I shall be obliged by your giving the necessary directions through your valuable Magazine; also as to what vessels are necessary for the general use of ice in a small family." The editor replied: "Sorbetieres or moulds for cream or fruit-ices, are made of two sorts of materials, block-tin and pewter; of these, the latter is the best, the substance to be iced congealing more gradually in it than in the former; an object much to

be desired, as when the ice is formed too quickly, it is very apt to be rough, and full of lumps like hail, especially if it be not well worked with the spatula; the other utensils necessary for this operation are, a deep pail, with a cork at the bottom, and a wooden spatula about nine inches long; being so far provided, fill the pail with pounded ice, over which spread four handfuls of salt; then having filled the sorbetiere, or mould, with cream, &c. put on the cover, and immerse it in the centre of the ice-pail, taking care the ice touches the mould in all parts; throw in two more handfuls of salt, and leave it a quarter of an hour; then take the cover from the mould, and with the spatula stir the contents up together, so that those parts which touch the sides of the mould, and consequently congeal first, may be mixed with the liquid in the middle; work this about for seven or eight minutes; cover the mould, take the pail by the ears, and shake it round and round for a quarter of an hour; open the mould a second time, and stir as before; continue these operations alternately, until the cream, or whatever it may be, is entirely congealed, perfectly smooth, and free from lumps. Take care to let out the water, which will collect at the bottom of the pail, by means of the cork, and press the ice close to the sorbetiere with the spatula. When the cream is iced, take it from the pail, dip the mould in warm water, but not to let it remain an instant; dry it quickly, turn it out, and serve it as soon as possible."

•　　　•　　　•

Ice Cream Molds – Note on How To Read the Listings: For brevity, I've used the standard number notation style of mold collectors – the initial of three big makers: **E (Eppelsheimer), K (Krauss), S (Schall & Co.)**, hyphen, style number. • Some listings have no maker, no number – for them, what information I have is included. • Unless otherwise noted, molds are "pewter" – or whatever pewter-like alloy passes for pewter. • Unless otherwise noted, molds are the individual serving size – which varies, but is relatively small (usually 7-10 per quart) compared to a table service mold (holding 1 or 2 pints) or a banquet or centerpiece mold (which held 3 or 4 pints or more). • I have chosen to list only the figural or zoomorphic molds rather than the geometric, architectectonic ice cream molds, which look more or less like other food molds. Most of them were made in heavily double-tinned sheet iron, partly stamped perhaps, but using the technique of piecing. That type of mold is mainly from the 19th C.

Ice cream mold, airplane, 8 to the quart, E-1132, (larger one, 5 to a quart, is E-1131, c.1930s. Jo-Lo had same one, same numbers, & offered a "gum paste aviator" at $12 per 100.) **$75**

Ice cream mold, apricot, hinged 2 part, only mark is a gouged "X" in hinge, late 19th C...................... **$35+**

❖ NOTES ❖

How to put Ice Cream into Moulds – "Rub your moulds very bright; then fix on the top and bottom with writing paper; take off the top, and fill the mould with the frozen ice cream already prepared; it must be forced

in very tight that no holes may appear when turned out; then lay on the writing paper, fix on the top, and immediately cover it well over with salted ice, go on in the same way until the whole is put into moulds; then lay them on one side, upon ice, in a tub with two bottoms; cover them well over with salted ice, which must be pressed tightly down; and in one hour it will be hard enough to turn out; but should it be wanted in a shorter time, a little salt petre beat small, and mixed with the salt, will be of great advantage to it. **To put Ice Cream into Shapes, to represent ripe Fruits.** – Your apricot moulds being ready for use, open them, and colour the inside a pale yellow, with a small brush; then take another brush, and dip it in lake finely ground, colour the sides of the mould, in part, with it; then take a small bit of whisk, dip it in the **lake**, and spot the mould a little with it; after which, fill both sides very full, and put them together; wrap the shape in strong brown paper, to keep the salt from penetrating the opening of the mould; then immerse it well in salted ice. N. B. Peach, pear, or pine apple, must all be coloured in the same manner, well bedded with ice, beat small, and salted properly, as before." Joseph Bell, *A Treatise on Confectionary*, Newcastle, England, 1817. (**Note:** "Lake" was a red colorant.)

• • • • •

To Turn Ice out of Shapes – "When you wish to turn out your shapes, have every thing in readiness to receive them, and never turn it out before the moment it is wanted; take each mould and wash it well in plenty

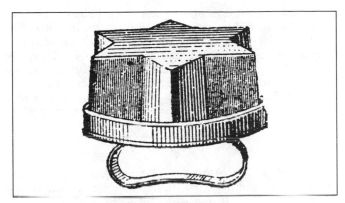

IV-214. "Bombé Sarah Bernhardt" mold. *Not all bombé molds are shaped like bombs. Some are conical; this one is a 6-point star, made of tin, with a close-fitting lid. It appears in Urbain Dubois' La Patisserie d'Aujourd'hui, published over long period, with illustrations from early editions, c.1860s-80s. A Sarah Bernhardt bombé, named after the French actress of the last half of the 19th C., had peaches, maraschino cherries, & vanilla mousse. (It is not in Hering's.)* **$40-$70**

of cold water; then rub it dry with your towel; take a strong knife, and force off the top; rub the top very clean; then take away the paper, and place the top on; do the same with the other end; after which, take the mould between both your hands, (having previously taken off both top and bottom) and let the shape of ice drop on to the dish you serve it up to the table upon; repeat this with every mould, do it in as short a time as possible, and serve it to the table immediately. N. B. The ices in natural shapes must be turned out in the same way, and laid upon the dish, when you may put a natural stalk into each, and garnish them with their own leaves." *Ibid.*

IV-213. Bomb or bombé molds. *All for iced dessert dishes – ice cream, iced pudding. biscuit glacé, etc. I don't know what made this style so popular, maybe it was some exciting anarchist movement; it goes back at least two centuries. Clockwise from upper left:* **(1)** *"Bomb," tinned copper, two sizes – 1 pint & 1 quart. Note fuse opening. Pick-Barth, 1929.* **(2)** *Tinned copper, from William S. Adams, London, c.1860-61.* **(3)** *"Bombé Enflammée" mold, A. Anthoine, Paris, c.1900.* **(4)** *"Boulet," in four sizes, holding 1/2 litre, 1, 1-1/2 & 2 litres. Anthoine, c.1900.* **Note:** *An invaluable book for research into dishes is* Hering's Dictionary of Classical & Modern Cookery, *trans. by Walter Bickel, published in Germany. I have a 1974 edition. There are almost seven pages of recipes for Bombe, "a special ice concoction moulded ... & deep frozen. The mould is lined first with plain ice cream & the center filled with a bombe mixture of different flavor, to which may be added diced fruit & other ingredients. [Just like iced biscuit.] Fruit should be macerated in liqueur & sugar before being added to prevent it freezing too hard. Bombé mixture is made by whisking egg yolks with a syrup of 28 deg. first hot & then cold, blended with whipped cream & the desired flavor." Just for one example: "Zamora: lined with coffee ice: filled with Curacao-flavored bombé mixture."* **$55-$200+**

Ice cream mold, baseball player, K-555, 8 to a qt. (They also sold little baseball bats to go with the players, for $3 a gross!). **$150**

Ice cream mold, basketball, showing segmented construction & lacing, Jo-Lo-1150, 8 to a quart, 1930s.. **$45**

Ice cream mold, battleship *Monitor* with turret top, for those Civil War Veterans or Widows luncheons, could get cannons & flags, Jo-Lo-1068. .... **$125**

Ice cream mold, bicyclist in knee britches & billed cap on bike, oval plinth, white iron, #3506, about 8-1/2"H, Letang Fils, Paris. **$225**

Ice cream mold, bicyclists – lady riding is K-431; man riding is K-551. She is 7 to the quart; he is 8 to the quart! Each:.. **$225**

Ice cream mold, boar or wild pig, E-647. May somehow relate to Teddy Roosevelt's hunting prowess. **$65**

Ice cream mold, little boy climbing fat tree stump taller than he, round base, white iron, #3493, about 9"H, Letang Fils, Paris. **$200**

Ice cream mold, bridge sets – the lady having a bridge party could serve various playing-card related ice creams with her bridge cookies! Krauss made rectangular "cards" on which were molded a Queen, a King, a Jack, or an Ace in any suit – ranged K-432 to K-447 or, for smaller ones, ranged K-526 to K-541. Then you could apply little "spots" or suit emblems, including hearts (K-355), spades (K-353), clubs (K-356), diamonds (K-354); or you could serve a bowl with one each of the largish 11-to-a-quart heart (K-213), spade (K-211), club (K-214), & diamond (K-212). For someone with the time or the maid, these could be gaily colored just like a playing card. Value range given for one card mold, with suit figure in relief:.... **$30-$35+**

❖ NOTES ❖

Freezing • Coloring • Decorating – "The best results are obtained by using soft ice cream which works well into all parts of the mold and produces a finished model, perfect and distinct in every detail. FREEZING is done in a hardening room or with brine which is a mixture of three parts ice to one part salt by weight. If used in brine, it is advisable to seal the seams of the mold with butter or wrap the mold in wax paper to prevent the salt penetrating to the cream. In ten to twenty minutes the Ice Cream Form should be hard enough to remove from the mold by immersing in cold water and carefully lifting the form out of the mold. Hot water will destroy fine detail. COLOR EFFECTS are obtained by using different flavored ice cream, such as Vanilla for white, Pistachio for green, Strawberry for pink, Chocolate for brown, and so forth. These flavors are pressed into the various parts of the molds with a small knife or spatula. COLORING is also done by Painting, Spraying or Dipping the hardened Ice Cream Form into a certified food color. Color designs of rare beauty and attractiveness may be obtained by using one of the methods mentioned or a combination of them. The appearance of Ice Cream Forms may be further improved by the addition of "**fixtures**," such as artificial leaves, flags, ribbon, and so forth, some of which are suggested throughout this catalog. FANCY DECORATING with a tube, using ice cream or whipped cream is always attractive. It is advisable to do this work in a hardening room. Every tray, container or wax paper should be thoroughly chilled before placing an Ice Cream Form thereon so as to avoid the possibility of melting the resting side of the form." Joe Lowe Corp., Brooklyn, NY, 1930s catalog.

Ice cream mold, Brownie character with acorn lid cap, fat tummy, hands at side, K-389, 8 to a qt. **$135**
Ice cream mold, Buddha, #476, maker unknown. Ewwwwh, who would want to eat Buddha? **$55**
Ice cream mold, buffalo on round (nickel-like) disc, S-586 .... **$115**
Ice cream mold, bust of Admiral Byrd in his parka, 2 part tin, E-1165, 8 per quart, 1930. .... **$175**

❖ NOTES ❖

South Pole Crossover – A sales letter from Eppelsheimer, dated June 1930, reads: "THE BYRD ANTARCTIC EXPEDITION RETURNS TO THE UNITED STATES DURING JUNE. It is expected that Admiral Byrd will tour the entire Country, giving lectures about his Expedition to the South Pole. There will doubtless be Banquets in his honor in every City he visits. Be prepared to supply Fancy Forms of Ice Cream of the BUST OF BYRD in his 'Parka' (fur-coat), mold No. 1165

and BYRD'S SHIP 'THE CITY OF NEW YORK', mold No. 1164. Molds for making the Fancy Ice Cream Forms, capacity 8 per quart, price $3 each, Display Models 60¢ each, less your usual discount. ORDER YOUR SUPPLY NOW." The **display models** mentioned were molded composition figures that showed how the ice cream in a particular mold would look; they'd be extremely collectible; I don't think I've ever seen one for sale, but Eppelsheimer offered them as a sort of advertising premium to confectioners or ice cream parlors who ordered a quantity – usually a dozen – of a particular mold.

Ice cream mold, cat, large sitting realistic cat with head turned & front paw on ball, Jo-Lo-10, table service or centerpiece size holds 3 pints. The mold model for this, once painted, would fool many people into thinking it was a carnival chalkware piece...... **$350**
Ice cream mold, cat sitting on the lower curve of the Man in the Moon, on his beard, looking into his quizzical face, Jo-Lo-1180, 8 per quart. Wonderful image... **$150**
Ice cream mold, cat – called "Puss in Boot" but not the fairytale character; instead, a cat in a big boot, head showing only, K-178. (Note: This design was also made in a large centerpiece size, numbered K-2, that held two quarts of ice cream & would bring four times that of individual mold, even more.) **$120**
Ice cream mold, cat quartet on oval "stage" with 4 animated, well-modeled cat figures playing guitar, cello, flute & one holding music book & singing, Bertuch-593, holds nearly 2-3/4 pints, c.1904. .... **$425**
Ice cream mold, cherries, 4 to a mold, K-108. As accessories, they sold a gross of leaf-&-stem pieces for $1.50. .... **$35**

IV-215. Melon molds. *Used for iced desserts & puddings.* **(T)** *The warty "Musk Melon" mould is tin, hinged, & came in 4-1/2", 5-1/2" & 6" diam. S. Joseph, c.1927.* **(M)** *Plain melon, holding 1-1/2 pints. Mrs. A. B. Marshall's The Book of Ices, c.1900-02.* **(B)** *Two views of hinged pewter ice cream melon mold, for "fruits glacés." Urbain Dubois, c.1860s-80s. More familiar to us are melon molds in a half-melon shape, pictured in IV-325 & IV-326.* **$60-$100+**

Ice cream mold, clown figure, hands in pockets, K-624. For $2.25, they sold 100 clown hats to set on the unmolded ice cream serving. **$75**

Ice cream mold, cow, head turned, low haunches, hinged 2 part centerpiece mold, "L. G." in oval, mfd. by Maison Letang Pére & Fils, Paris, France, late 19th C. **$200**

Ice cream mold, cradle – woven wicker basket on rockers, with babe & blanket inside, 3 piece, K-344. A hundred "baby faces" (printed paper) could be bought for $4.50. .... **$125**

Ice cream molds, cup & scalloped saucer, 2 different molds. Cup is K-205, with capacity of 6 to a quart; Saucer is K-198; capacity 10 to a quart. (Note: The saucer could be used to hold other "spot" or small molded bite-size ice creams – flowers, fruits, hearts, eggs, etc. For the pair: **$125**

Ice cream mold, "Darkey," (I apologize for using the term that Jo-Lo used), a Black Americana image of man sitting on sack or carpet bag, Jo-Lo-1053, 9 to the quart, 1930s. Very collectible for the reasons that make it such a painful image of some awful history in this country. It sure makes you wonder who sat down & enjoyed ice cream made in these molds – some good ol' boys & segregationists? **$150**

Ice cream mold, "Darkey stealing turkey," Jo-Lo-1089, 8 to a quart. This one is an even worse example of Black Americana from the 1930s – not that long ago, really. The further into the 21st C. we go, the more horrible, sickening & unfathomable the dark American past seems. Maybe the field should be termed "UnAmericana Noir" collectibles. **$150**

Ice cream mold, dog (retriever? poodle?), large & seated on oval plinth, with very deep tightly curled mane, long ears, body shaved close except for muffs on front feet, mane & tail, huge head, ponderous (or patient?) visage, pewter, small stamped maker's mark of old cranked freezer (resembles a well), "C C"

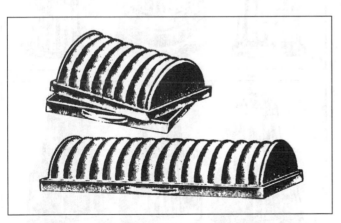

IV-216. Ice cream mold. Looks like a tin quonset hut. Shown in 1 pt. & 2 pt. sizes. "An entirely new idea is worked out in the Silver Ice Cream mold. The housewife may send the receptacle to the **cream saloon**, *& have the ice cream packed in ready to use, or it may be packed in at home. In each instance it assumes the shape of the pan & makes a splendid appearance. The cream can be sliced at the sections. The results are very dainty & appetizing. ... It can be used also for gelatine, custards, etc." Compare with fig bread mold (IV-14) at beginning of chapter, which was also Silver & Co., Brooklyn, c.1910.* **$45-$65**

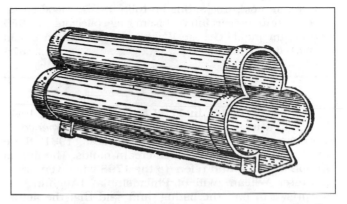

IV-217. Ice cream mold. Tin, long "bridge party" club motif, for slicing. Cherry-Bassett, 1921. **$35+**

& "Marque Fabrique," according to catalog #13 it was in the #969 series, mfd. by M. Cadot et Cie, Paris, France, 3 pt. capacity, pre-1900. .... **$350**

❖ NOTES ❖

Curly dogs – I have a c.1900 catalog of ice cream molds made by E. Compiègne, successor to Cadot. It says that "*tous les moules portent ma marque C. C.*" – all molds marked C. C. • They had a poodle couchant, with curly ears – much more obviously a poodle, which was originally bred as a retriever. Also a very short-haired hound dog, lying down with head pointed up. Letang Fils of Paris had nearly identical molds, which they advertised in their 1912 catalog as for "cake or ices."

Ice cream mold, dog – a sort of poodle with curly mane, sitting on hexagonal plinth, Bertuch-607, holds 3/4 pint, c. 1904. .... **$100**

Ice cream mold, eagle on a disc-like medallion approximating USA national seal, American, late 19th C. **$85**

Ice cream mold, eagle, standing & looking over his left shoulder, lead, 2 part with 5 pinned clamps, linecut in F. A. Walker catalog shows mark of a tiny castle stamp, imported, c.1870s or 1880s. **$130**

Ice cream mold, electric light bulb, pointed tip in Mazda style, Jo-Lo-990, 8 to a quart, 1930s. Some crossover interest. (Another bulb with standard shape, #1112, was also offered.) **$50**

Ice cream mold, elephant on grassy oval plinth, trunk curled under, Bertuch-559, large capacity of almost 4 quarts, banquet size, c.1890s-1910. Really awe-inspiring. **$750**

Ice cream mold, Eskimo figure (probably from same period as the Admiral Byrd bust, K-510. (This has also been listed as "Arctic explorer" S-510.). ... **$125**

Ice cream mold, female near-nude figure, K-401. (Note: This was not included in their "occasion index" – no, not under Maritime, nor Valentines – not even with the mold they called "Foxy Grandpa" K 594!) 7 to a quart. **$150**

Ice cream mold, fireman, K-340. You could order little firemen's hats as decorations, for $4.50 per 100. (That's about the price we pay for 16 party napkins. Too bad we can't get these cute little decorations now!) **$150**

Ice cream mold, frog sitting on tulip, K-578. Good cross-over (or hop-over) interest from frog collectors. **$65**
Ice cream mold, George Washington's bust on shield with flag, K-456. .... **$75**

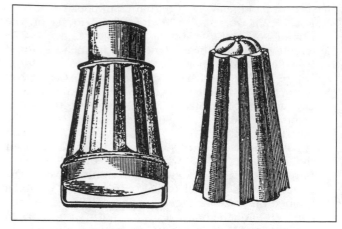

IV-219. Ice cream or ice pudding mold. **(L)** *is tin mold, balanced on its bracket strap handle. The cylinder seen at top serves to hold mold upside down while filling, & helps protect stamped copper ornamental turk's-head top if mold is handled carelessly during use.* **(R)** *is "shape produced" by mold. This one was made in 1, 1-1/2, 2, 3 & 4-pint sizes. Mrs. Marshall's Book of Ices, c.1902.* **$40-$60**

❖ NOTES ❖

Ice Cream Molds in 1798 & 1803 – In Ledlie Irwin Laughlin's massive, instructive *Pewter In America*, 3 volumes in one, American Legacy Press, 1981, there are but two references to ice cream molds. The first is in Vol. II, p. 54, and refers to the 1798 will inventory of pewterer William Will of Philadelphia. Laughlin was surprised to find the listing, and said that the actual form itself, with a Will touch [mark], had not been found as of then (1940). In Vol. III, p. 111, Laughlin also transcribes a July 25, 1803 newspaper advertisement placed by NYC pewterer, George Coldwell. It reads: "Ice Cream Moulds, a few pair of pewter Ice-Cream Moulds are now finished and now offered for sale at the subscriber's work-shop No 7 Beekman-street. They contain one gallon, are well made of the best materials, very strong and infinitely more durable than those made of Tinned Iron. ...." Coldwell then enumerated his other products. Laughlin again states that as of the time of publication (1970) of Vol. III, he had yet to read of any other pewter ice cream molds, nor had he seen any [to recognize, we must add]. Such molds may so differ from what we might assume such a mold would look like (for example, it may look like a pudding mold, or a pail with a lid) that we may never know if we've seen one or not.

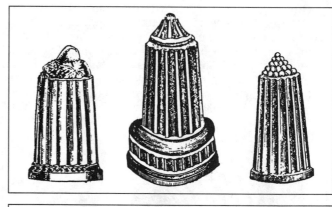

IV-218. Pyramid ice cream molds. None look like Egyptian pyramids, but influence is there from the exciting archaeological digs in Egypt at various times in 19th C. **(L)** *Fancy patterned mold, 1 litre or 2 litre sizes, Anthoine, Paris, c.1900.* **(R)** *Looking like a stack of witch's hats, this style was made round (as here), square & octagon, with 1, 2 & 3 rings. Jaburg, 1908.* **(C)** *Stamped & pieced tin swirled like soft ice cream, with lid. Imported, possibly from England. 1-1/2 quart size: 6"H x 6-1/2" diam.; & 2-1/2 qts.: 8-1/2"H x 8" diam. Joseph, c.1927.* **$40-$75+**

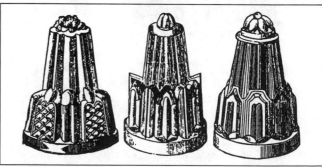

IV-220. Ice cream or ice pudding molds. Top row, all "pillar molds," of tin, possibly with stamped copper tops. **(T-L)** *"Fruit Top," in 1, 1-1/2, 2 & 3-pt. sizes;* **(T-M)** *"With plinth" is sole description. 2 & 3 pts.* **(T-R)** *"Cherry top" in 1, 1-1/2 & 2 pts. Made to put maraschino cherries in. All from Mrs. Marshall's Book of Ices, c.1902. Bottom row: ornate stamped tin molds, 1 quart sizes, with nooks for fruit, lady fingers, etc. Probably all imported from England, c.1870s-90s. See also IV-330.* **$60-$110+**

Fruit Ice Cream Recipe – "Ice-cream is prepared by mixing three parts of cream with one part of the juice or jam of raspberries, currants, etc. The mixture is then well beaten; and after being strained through a cloth, is poured into a pewter mould or vessel, adding a small quantity of lemon-juice. The mould is now covered, and plunged into a pail about two-thirds full of ice, into which two handfuls of salt should be previously scattered. The vessel containing the cream is then briskly agitated for eight or ten minutes, after which it is suffered to stand for a similar space of time; the agitation is then repeated, and the cream allowed to subside for a half hour, when it is taken out of the mould and sent to table." Anthony Florian Madinzer Willich, The Domestic Encyclopedia; or A Dictionary of Facts & Useful Knowledge...., *1st American edition, Philadelphia: W. Y. Birch & A. Small, 1803-04.*

Ice cream mold, George Washington's hatchet, marked "G. W." in case you thought it might be Carrie Nation's, #243. .... **$35**

Ice cream mold, George Washington's profile bust on hatchet head (or, as Krauss put it in a sort of guillotinish way, "George Washington's head on an ax"), K-336. .... **$75**

Ice cream mold, hand with fancy cuff, S-289. A favorite sentimental decorative motif from the 1840s on, especially in the 1880s-1910s. **$65**

Ice cream mold, Kewpie on little mound w/ word "Kewpie," E-1115, early 20th C. (Jo-Lo has this with same number). For more on Kewpies, see the first entry under "Bride & groom figures," this chapter. • Kewpie Krossover interest is strong. **$135**

Ice cream mold, lettuce head – "Romaine," K-549. ..... **$35**

*IV-221. Jelly & Cream molds. Copper, with lining inserts, so that a different color or flavor could be put into center of mold, & would show in horizontal slices when served. **(T)** "Alexandra," came in 2 sizes. That's Imperial Russia's Empress Alexandra, beautiful wife of Czar Nicholas. **(R)** "Brunswick Star," also came in 2 sizes. Mrs. Marshall's Book of Ices, c.1902. Design registered in England in the 1890s. For mold & insert: **$175-$300***

*IV-222. Ice cream molds – Transportation. By theme is just one way to collect molds. The detailed drawings from catalogs are idealized versions of what ice cream would look like when molded. Lots of exaggeration was allowed artists: Although many molds have great detail, not all of it shows on ice cream. Accessories like wheels, flags, canes, etc., had to be added, & were made of paper, wood or metal. **Top** two pewter molds, for 1-1/2 & 1-1/3 litres, from Bertuch, Berlin, c.1904. See also IV-117, a chocolate mold. **Bottom** two, in individual sizes of 7 to a quart are also pewter, pictures from Duparquet, Huot & Moneuse catalog, c.1904-1910. Bicycle also made in large 4-pint capacity. All train, & bike motifs have good crossover interest. (See also IV-16, a cake decoration.) Molds: **$95-$150***

Ice cream mold, lion couchant on lid of rectangular box mold, double-tinned pieced & stamped sheet metal, Bertuch-525, Berlin, capacity of 1-1/2 litres, or 1-2/3 pints. c.1904. .... **$90**

Ice cream mold, lion, standing, 2 part lead mold with 6 pinned clamps, F. A. Walker catalog linecut shows mark of a tiny castle & some illegible initials on this mold, European (?), c.1870s, 1880s. ..... **$100-$135**

Ice cream mold, locomotive – old steam type with barrel-like boiler body, whistle, cab, K-477. (Note: A generalist price guide lists a set that includes a locomotive, tender, & two passenger sleeping cars, no number given, valued at over $500. The only trace I can find of anything but locomotives is a passenger car & locomotive from Bertuch, Berlin.) **$120**

Ice cream mold, locomotive – old steam type, centerpiece size, Jo-Lo-155, holds 4 pints. **$300**

Ice cream mold, mandolin, K-547, an instrument very popular among the college crowd in the 1920s (not to mention, Tiny Tim!). **$95**

Ice cream mold, Max & Moritz, a pair from German cartoon & book fame. Mold has a sort of "soap bar" plinth, with the 2 caricatured boys from the waist up, Bertuch-573, holds about 1-1/2 pints. Crossover interest. **$175**

Ice cream mold, Mikado – Japanesey full length figure in flowingly draped kimono. This celebrated either the very popular comic opera by W.S. Gilbert & A.S. Sullivan from the late 19th C., or generally the craze for Japonism – a style movement in the late 19th C. **$155**

Ice cream mold, Miss Liberty (sometimes called Miss

FANCY ICE MOULDS IN PEWTER.

No. 42.—DUCK. No. 43.—SWAN.

1 quart, £1. 2s. 0d. 2 pints, £1. 0s. 0d.

No 44. No. 45. No. 46.
DOVE. BUNCH OF GRAPES. CAULIFLOWER

1¼ pints, 15s. 0d. 1 quart, £1. 4s. 0d. 1 quart, £1. 4s. 0d.
No. 47.—HEN. No. 48.—FISH.

1 quart, £1. 0s. 0d. 1 quart, £1. 0s. 0d.
No. 49. No. 50. No. 51.
PINEAPPLE. BASKET OF BUNCH OF
 FLOWERS. ASPARAGUS.

1 quart, 19s. 0d. 1 quart, £1. 4s. 0d. 1 quart & ½ pint, £1. 4s. 0d.
SPECIMEN PAGE FROM 'BOOK OF MOULDS.'

IV-223. Ice cream molds. Pewter, various designs from a sample or "specimen" page of Mrs. Marshall's touted Book of Moulds. *Late 19th C. The hen on nest, swan, & fish probably would be worth most, and you have to figure in size also.* **$75-$175+**

Columbia), be-draped & standing on globe & wearing crown, hinged 2 part centerpiece mold, marked "Joh: Reinöhl" for Johannes Reinöhl, Ulm, Germany, c.1860s-70s. (This is not Statue of Liberty.) .... **$200-$250**

Ice cream mold, pedestal, square column with base & top, suitable for placing a small molded ice cream (of course, molds made by different companies were mixed & matched to create still-lifes & vignettes) or a composition "party favor" piece such as a composition bust of Lincoln or a cupid. K-571. .... **$30**

Ice cream mold, pie slice in wedge shape, 8 to a quart, Jo-Lo-1097, 1930s. Wouldn't this be fun to make in layered fruit ice creams, & then put a pie a la mode wedge of ice cream on top using a novelty disher? **$40**

❖ **RECIPE** ❖

Ice Pudding – 1 pint of milk. 1/2 pint of whipped cream. 8 eggs. 4 oz. of castor sugar [granular like what we now buy in bags as opposed to fine confectioner's sugar]. 1/2 lb. of crystallised fruit. Lemon peel. A wineglass of kirsch [cherry brandy] or noyeau syrup [unidentified, but I suspect it is unfermented juice from fresh fruit]. Put one pint of new milk into a stewpan, with four ounces of castor sugar and the thinkly peeled rind of half a lemon. Bring to a boil, and simmer for five minutes. Strain it on to the beaten yolks of eight raw eggs.

Return the mixture to the stove, and stir until it thickens; but on no account let it boil. Rub it through a fine hair sieve or tammy, and put aside until quite cold. Freeze, as directed, but when of the consistency of batter, add half-a-pint of whipped cream, also half-a-pound of any nice crystallised fruits cut up small, and a wineglass of kirsch or noyeau syrup. Mix well, and continue freezing. Fill a fancy mould with the frozen mixture, and put it in an ice cave*, or pile round with ice until wanted. This pudding is a pale yellow, from the yolks of the eggs, and there are coloured specks on the surface where the pieces of crystallised fruits show." Katharine Mellish's Cookery Book, *London & NY: Spon, 1901.*

* *An **ice cave** is a small ice box with insulated walls.*

Ice cream mold, Radio Corporation of America "His Master's Voice" double joined medallions, with Nipper & phonograph & motto on right disc, & RCA with lightening bolt on left. Jo-Lo-1168. It's shown in their 1930s catalog, with the caption "Specially designed for the Radio Corporation of America through one of the large Ice Cream Manufacturers." There is no indication that this mold (probably an individual mold about 7 to 9 to the quart) was not available to the general public. I believe this would be a very valuable mold, with great crossover interest. .... **$400+**

Ice cream mold, shoe, 3 part, late 19th C. The form of a shoe has long been a love token. .... **$60-$65**

Ice cream mold, lady's slipper with back & heel (another was a backless slip-on mule with heel), 3 piece, "899A," 20th C. **$35**

Ice cream mold, snowman – much more a human figure than the rotund pile of balls we're used to, arms folded across chest to hold an accessory broom, a hat could be bought too, Bertuch-578, holds nearly 1-1/4 pints, c.1904. .... **$115+**

IV-224. Ice cream molds – Pigs. Two tin styles on bases. **(T)** 1 litre $22, & 3/4 litre #1149. From Fabrique Spéciale de Moules en Etain ... Marque c.c., *Paris France catalog, 1900. The "C.C." mark had a well with bucket & initials "C.C." I will refer to molds from that catalog as "Marque C.C." from here on out.* **(B)** *This tin mold is from the same catalog, but you can see the design is different. It is advertised as the #832 "1/2 Glace" style; which I assume may mean there's dimensional modeling on only one side?* **$100-$150+**

IV-225. Ice cream molds – Horses. Top **(L)** appears to be the sea god Neptune, borne on waves in a chariot. It & large horse at **(R)** are 1-3/4 & 1-1/4 quart sizes. The jockey on left is 7 to a quart. First three tin molds all sold through Duparquet, Huot & Moneuse, early 20th C. Jockey lower right is pewter, 1-1/8 litres (A dry litre is about 9/10 of a quart; a liquid litre is just over 1 quart. Ice cream must be halfway between.) Bertuch, Berlin, c.1904. **$150-$225+**

Ice cream mold, squirrel sitting, large 2 pint table service mold, K-27.. **$135**

❖ NOTES ❖

Chalkware Confusable – When I saw the plaster model made in the above large squirrel mold, I realized that it is quite possible that many of the so-called "carnival chalkwares," perhaps even the "19th century chalkwares" so hotly collected now may actually be ice cream mold models. Especially reminiscent are this squirrel, a cat, a lamb, a Santa, & a rabbit standing with paw on stump.

Ice cream mold, Struwelpeter, stamped tin, marvelously detailed figure of 19th C. German folktale bad boy "Struwelpeter" – literally shock-headed Peter, with a shock of long straw like hair sticking out all over in a bush. Everything Struwelpeter was told not to do he did; he was used in morals & manners tales as an example of what happened if you didn't behave. Bertuch-564, little over a pint capacity, c.1890s-1910. See IV-240. .... **$125**

Ice cream mold, Statue of Liberty, centerpiece size, metal, 2 part, Jo-Lo-150, 10 pt. capacity, c.1930s-40s. • In their catalog, they also offered this design on a pedestal, for sale or rental, with a 26 pint capacity for large parties or banquets. It was 37"H. The mold was $30; for $10 you could get a display model made in it. .... **$350+**

Ice cream mold, wheat sheaf, stalks forming pedestal base, with the top very rounded, 2 part, Biertumpfel & Hepting, with Maltese cross & orb mark, London, design registered July 22, 1868. .... **$100**

Ice cream mold, Whistler's Mother – oval framed medallion showing woman in chair, drapery, picture on wall, & word "Mother," Jo-Lo-1187, 8 per quart. Really unusual. **$130**

Ice cream mold, "Yellow Kid," the raggedy little street waif created by cartoonist Richard Outcault, whose strip ran in Hearst newspapers beginning in 1896 & was probably first popular American cartoon character. K-476, c.1890s-1910. .... **$175**

Ice cream mold or freezer, pressed glass cylinder, domed glass lid, perhaps has inner cylinder (?) of glass, wire clamp frame, exactly like the Fox mold, but advertised as is the Dazey as a "freezer," & not described well enough to know if there is an inner chamber. Ad reads "No cranking, no gear, no dasher, no rust, no crank, no metal, no wood, no labor, just VELVET ICE CREAM." Reassuringly, it "Makes Ptomaine Poisoning impossible." "The Sanitary," mfd. by Consolidated Mfg. Co., Hartford, CT, about 9"H, advertised Jan. 1909, still in business 1915. .... **$150+**

Ice cream mold or freezer, pressed glass cylinder with slightly domed lid, footed base, tin inner chamber open at both ends, false bottom has small hole fitted with white glazed stoneware stopper & rubber washer, which is where you would use wooden dowel pusher to push ice cream out the open top. Wire

IV-226. Ice cream molds – Lobsters, dolphins & a shrimp. The dolphin, or dauphin, molds, a symbol of French royalty, were probably used for "Crownprince" bombés, with a hazelnut & kirsch mixture. Big lobster was described in catalog as a "Glace entière" as opposed to a "Demi-glace" (or half mold). Anthoine, Paris, c.1900. Small lobster found in Duparquet, Huot & Moneuse c.1904-10 catalog, in very small sizes, from 9 to 20 to a quart, & in a 5 pint size. Shrimp is #1090 in Marque C.C. catalog, 1900. Upper dauphin, #1180, is 2, 1-1/2 & 1-1/4 litres. Marque C.C. Large dauphin, #101, in 1 litre size. Anthoine, c.1900. Small lobster & shrimp: **$75-$125**; Large molds: **$125-$275**

IV-227. Ice cream molds – Dogs. *Mainly poodles or retrievers. Top* **(T-L)** *#13, glace entière, tin. Marque C.C., 1900.* **(T-M)** *#3 in Series No. 969, tin, glace entière for 9 centilitres. Marque C.C.* **(T-R)** *#83, Anthoine, c.1900. Bottom* **(B-L)** *#8, Series No. 969, tin, glace entière, Marque C.C.* **(B-M)** *"Chien loup," No. 82, Anthoine.* **(B-R)** *Poodle with ball, #52, demi-glace, Anthoine.* **$135-$300+**

clamp, which is also handle, holds lid & stopper on, marked "G. H. Fox" & patent dates, invented by George H. Fox, Bangor, ME, 8-1/2"H x 3-1/2" diam., pat'd. Feb. 14, 1899, & July 15, 1902. .... **$150+**

Ice cream mold or freezer, pressed glass cylindrical vessel, inner vessel (possibly tin, less probably glass, unclear from old ad picture), wire clamp to hold lid on & wire pusher to push round ball of molded ice cream out of inner cylinder for slicing, called a "freezer" in ad, "The Dazey Glass Freezer – The Freezer that Freezes Without Motion," probably mfd. by the churn people, probably about 9"H, depicted in *House Furnishing Review* as a "latest model" in 1911. ...... **$150**

Ice "freezing tray," for making decorative ice cubes, rubber. An interesting one with 24 cups in hearts, spades, diamonds & clubs, was patented by Leo James Gold, Los Angeles, CA, Nov. 8, 1932 (Design #88,226). I don't know if it was ever made, but it's something to keep your eye out for.

IV-234. Ice cream molds – Eagles. **(L)** *Small, 7 to a quart. Duparquet, Huot & Moneuse.* **(R)** *#0256, lead or pewter, with clamps, size not given. F. A. Walker, 1880s.* **$70-$150+**

IV-233. Ice cream molds – Lions. *Top* **(T-L)** *Lion couchant, with paw on ball (globe). #10, 9 centilitres. Marque C.C.* **(T-R)** *Another regal lion, #103, holding 1-1/2 or 3 litres, Anthoine. Middle* **(M-L)** *#84, Anthoine.* **(M-R)** *More realistic cut of a mold, showing two hinged parts & clamps. Lead or pewter mold, from F. A. Walker import flyer, c.1880s. Bottom* **(B-L)** *Box mold, tinned sheet iron, holding 1-1/2 liter. Bertuch.* **(R)** *Two sizes, 9 to quart, & 3-1/2 quarts, Duparquet, Huot & Moneuse.* **$100-$350+**

IV-228. Ice cream molds – Cats. *Top* **(T-L)** *Pewter Cats' Quartet, cats & podium, holding 2-1/2 litres. Complete with music stand. Apparently instruments were extra. Bertuch, c.1904.* **(T-R)** *#14 in Series No. 969, glace entière. Marque C.C., 1900. Bottom* **(B-L)** *&* **(B-M)** *, #74 & #75. One on left is a wild or jungle cat. Both Anthoine c.1900.* **(B-R)** *Cat with ball, small size – 11 to a quart. Duparquet, Huot & Moneuse, c.1904-10. The quartet:* **$250+**; *others:* **$135-$300+**

IV 229. Ice cream molds – Squirrels. (L) #18, *Series No. 969, glace entière, Marque C.C., 1900.* **(M)** #84, *Anthoine, Paris, 1900.* **(R)** *Small one in several sizes, from 7-10 to a quart, 20 to quart, & 2 pints. Duparquet, Huot & Moneuse, c.1904-10. See also squirrel nutcrackers in Chapter I.* **$85-$225**

IV-231. Ice cream molds – Rabbits. *Top* **(T-L)** *12 & 20 to quart; also 3 pint size. Duparquet, Huot & Moneuse.* **(T-R)** *Pewter, 2 pint size, Mrs. Marshall's Book of Ices. Middle* **(M-L)** #16 *in Series No. 969, glace entière, Marque C.C. Bottom* **(B-L)** #78, *Anthoine.* **(B-R)** *Standing in cabbage patch, pewter, 1-1/4 litre size. Bertuch.* **$90-$150**; *big one:* **$175-$250+**

IV-230. Ice cream molds – Chickens. *Top* **(T-L)** *Hen on high basket,* #818, *Marque C.C.* **(T-R)** *Hen on basket nest* #55, *demi-glace, Anthoine.* **(B-R)** *Rooster,* #49, *sold glace entière & demi-glace. Anthoine. I left out one that shows rooster mounting hen – hey! what occasion was that one for?* **$90-$175+**

IV-232. Ice cream molds – Elephants, *perhaps based on Jumbo.* **(L)** #559, *pewter, 2-3/4 litre (almost 4 quarts) although looks teensy here. Bertuch. You could also order a canopy accessory.* **(R)** #73, *Anthoine, not sure of size.* **(L)** **$300-$450;** **(R)** *If large, same as other. If 2 to 4 to a quart:* **$70-$90**

Jaggers & Crimpers & Trimmers – A jagger is a pastry cutter, generally one that makes a jagged (actually zig zag) edge. They are also called pie wheels, pie rimmers, pie jiggers, pie cutters, trimmers, jagging irons, gigling irons (very archaic term), jiggers, and probably other names. Often jaggers are combined with tools that crimp or corrugate edges of dough in order to seal it – for example, the upper and lower crusts of a pie, or the edges of a tart. Those tools are called pie or pastry crimpers, or sealers.

Jaggers could be used to cut or trim off the pie crust dough that hung over the edge of the pie pan, or to cut shapes out to lay on top in lieu of a top crust, or to cut strips for a lattice top. Of course jaggers could be used to cut other dough, such as for making free-form cookies. Some jaggers are made with separate crimpers (which squush and corrugate and seal the top and bottom crust edges together, for pies or tarts; sometimes the jagging wheel and the crimper are all in one wheel. Some jaggers – usually scrimshaw ones – have two fork-prong prickers for making steam release in the top crust. Some jaggers are made with a pastry stamp at the other end, a sort of small curvy cookie cutter used to cut out leaf shapes, used especially for the tops of savoury pies.

Generally there are two kinds of collectors for pie jaggers and pastry crimpers – the patent collectors who seek patented late 19th C. pieces, and the folk art collectors who favor scrimshaw if they're rich, and old, interesting design, especially with old paint on handles, if they aren't so rich. Prices haven't really moved a lot – jaggers are a neglected corner (or outer edge) of both folk art and kitchen collectibles.

• • •

Crimped pie crusts – The ridged or corrugated edge of the pie, after being crimped, is what gives the name piecrust edge to quite a large number of butter stamps. On the other hand, a piecrust table, in furniture talk, is one with the kind of riffled edge given to a pie edge by pinching with the fingers & thumb. A modern "piecrust trimming and scalloping device" was patented by Mary Di Domenico, Chicago, IL, on Dec. 25, 1951, (#2,580,081). What a Christmas present! It was designed to create a sealed edge that somewhat resembled the hand-pinched riffling. I don't know if Domenico's trimmer was ever made. (See IV-263.)

JAGGERS & CRIMPERS
ALUMINUM

Crimper & trimmer, & marker, nickel plated shank, red wood handle, ingeniously stamped aluminum wheel – little prongs pushed out from disc (inventor called them "a plurality of lateral projections") to give a crimping effect when rolled; used in horizontal position, the same circle of prongs could be used to make steam holes in upper crust. "Vaughn's Pie Trimmer & Sealer," Chicago, IL, 5-1/2"L, pat'd. May 10, 1921 by Evelyn L. Simpson, of Waterville, ME, #1,377,974. The original patent had simple all metal handle & was pat'd. as a "pie marker and trimmer"; this one prob. c.1940s. .... **$15+**

IV-235. Ice cream mold – 3-Leaf Clover – or Card Suit Club. One of a number of similar molds, all marked "Pat. Pend. John W. Ladd Co. Distr." on arched handle. Has a plunger plate operated by spring rod under handle. Three others are a heart, a spade & a diamond; another is a Masonic symbolic tools – crossed divider & square. All are about 5-1/2"H, and the shapes measure about 3" x 2-3/4". Photo & information courtesy Larry & Carole Meeker, dealers & collectors of patented antiques. www.patented-antiques.com

Jagging wheel & dough scraper combined, wheel-to-point is 4-1/8"L, pat'd. May 10, 1921 – but is a variation on Evelyn Simpson's patent #1,377,974. .... **$55+**

Jagger or crimper, cast aluminum, wooden handle, "Dandy," American, 6"L, pat'd. April 22, 1925. ... **$15+**

Jagger or crimper & trimmer, cast aluminum, relatively large wheel with corrugations & cutting edge, short pointed handle with large hanging loop, "Ateco," mfd. by August Thompsen & Co., NYC, NY, c.1920s. .... **$15+**

Crimper, aluminum, "Juice Tite Pie Sealer," 5-1/2"L, 20th C. .... **$15+**

Crimper, pie sealer, aluminum, "Just-Rite," Minneapolis, MN, 20th C. **$10**

IV-236. Ice cream molds – Baskets. Top (T-L) Basket of Fruits, with split pomegranate on top. 3 pint capacity. (T-R) Wheatsheaf, 8"H, 1 quart. (B-L) Basket of flowers, 1-1/2 pints. (B-R) Smaller fruit basket, only 1-1/2 pints. All from Mrs. Marshall's Book of Ices. English, late 19th C. $65-$125+

IV-237-A. Ice cream molds – Flowers, *Hinged pewter. Beautiful detailing in 3-part lily mold, 5-1/4"L closed. No marks. Author's collection. Two-part carnation & tulip molds, collection of Meryle Evans. Late 19th into early 20th C. Made for long time.* **$50-$65+**

IV-239. Statue of Liberty ice cream mold. *Huge mold, 37"H in two sections, statue & base. The company rented this mold to be used for banquets. What we're actually seeing here is a photograph of "composition* **display model**" *– a plaster casting that showed what mold would do. Joe Lowe Corp., "Jo-Lo" line. Brooklyn, c.1930s.*

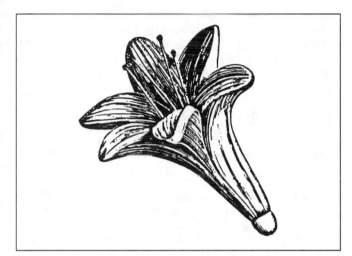

IV-237-B. Catalog shot showing lily mold *in IV-237 closed up. Two sizes: 7 to a quart, or 3-pint capacity. Duparquet, Huot & Moneuse catalog, c.1904-10.*

Crimper & trimmer, aluminum sealer, plastic cutting wheel, wood handle, "Dual Purpose," American, 20th C. .... **$15+**

Crimper & trimmer, cast aluminum, would trim as it corrugated the pie's edges to seal the top crust to the bottom one, no mark, American (?), 4-3/4"L, 1920s or 30s. .... **$15+**

BONE: (See also Ivory; Scrimshaw)
Jagger, bone wheel with turned maple handle, 4-1/2"L, 19th C. **$55**

IV-238. Ice cream molds – pewter gnomes. *#633, two of them at tavern table, holds 1 litre in all. #632, gnome pushing large nut . . . uphill?, holds 1-1/8 litres. Bertuch, Berlin, c.1904.* **$135-$200**

IV-240. Ice cream molds. *More fantasy figures in hinged pewter molds.* **(T-L)** *#578 Snowman, in 1-1/4 litre size. Broom & hat extra.* **(T-R)** *#564* **Struwelpeter,** *or Shock-headed Peter, antihero of cautionary morality stories used to teach children manners & behavior in Germany. 1 litre.* **(B-M)** *#591 Bacchus, holding 1-1/2 litres. All Bertuch, c.1904.* **$125-$200**

IV-241. Jagging iron. *Probably all metal, maybe cast & sheet iron, or brass. Drawn from tiny sketchy engraving in original kitchen interior print in Bartolomeo Scappi's* Opera di M. Bartolomeo Scappi, *a 1570 Italian cookbook. There's a trestle table holding a mound of dough or flour, rolled-out paste with a long slim rolling pin resting upon it, a craved wooden tool like a big molar tooth, used as a dough marker, & a clumsy, large jagging iron with serrated wheel & relatively short shaft, with knops at center & end.*

Jagger, bone, simple carving, American, 4"L, mid
  19th C. **$60**
Jagger, turned wood with bone wheel, steel pin, American,
  5"L, 19th C. **$35**
BRASS:
Jagger, brass shaft, small brass cutting wheel, big
  crimping wheel is cast iron, American, 6-1/2"L, late
  19th C. .... **$75+**
Jagger, brass shaft & small brass wheel, cast iron seal-
  ing & trimming wheel, no marks, 6"L, late
  19th C. .... **$40+**
Jagger, brass shank & fancily fashioned wheel, turned
  wood handle has original hang-up ring, American or
  English, 7-1/2"L, 19th C. .... **$125+**

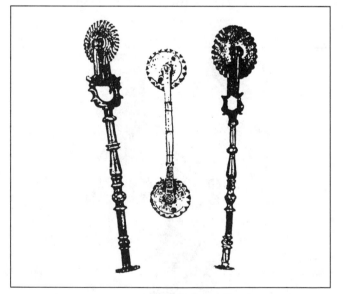

IV-242. Jaggers. (L) & **(R)** *Cast iron long ones from Italy, 17th C., many tiers of turned knops & rings. Pieces on end are semi-circular cutters (see next picture.) 8-1/4"L.* **(M)** *is smaller, two-wheeled brass one, 18th or early 19th C., 5-1/2"L. Note drilled holes in brass one; these are often found, & I can only assume it had something to do with cost-per-ounce, either making or shipping costs. Courtesy Hillman Books.* **(L)** & **(R)** *$165+,* **(M)** *$50+*

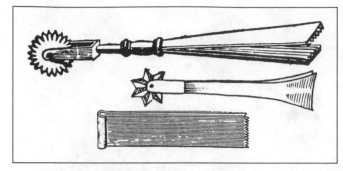

IV-243. Jaggers & pastry pinchers. (T) *a "paste jigger," with smallish wheel & long pincers, corrugated lengthwise on inside. Hard to say what material, either brass or iron are springy. Linecut from* Warne's Model Cookery, *London & NY: 1868.* **(M)** *Drawing adapted from paste-pincher depicted in Mrs. Beeton's Everyday Cooking, 1872 edition.* **(B)** *A spring steel pincher, from Duparquet, Huot & Moneuse catalog, c.1904-10. Pincher:* **$85+; (M)** **$35+; (B) $10+**

Jagger, brass, lightweight brass wire shaft or frame, split
  to take a light sheet brass wheel at each end, American, 4"L, late 19th C. Possibly patented. See illustrations of patented jaggers & pie rimmers. .... **$35+**
Jagger, brass shank, steel wheel, large but delicate,
  turned wooden handle, American or English, 9"L,
  2nd quarter 19th C. .... **$75+**
Jagger, brass wheel, forged iron shank, wooden handle,
  American, 8"L, early to mid 19th C. .... **$45+**
Jagger, cast brass, wheel at one end, curved semi-circle
  cutter at other, turned brass shank, English or
  French, & imported in the late 19th C., between
  about 4 -1/2"L & 7"L, 19th C. • An all brass jagger, 4-
  3/4"L, with a slightly knopped shank, curved stamp
  at one end & small jagging wheel with 4 drilled holes,
  was auctioned by Garth's in Sept. 1989. It was
  marked "Germany" – first I've heard of. .... **$20-$45**

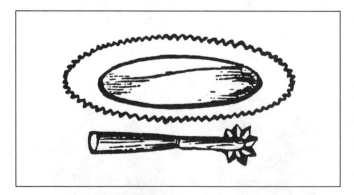

IV-244. Jagger & pie. *Simplified jagging iron with a pie crust showing serrated edge, taken from Henry Scammell's* Treasure House of Useful Knowledge, *1891, a book compiled, often without credit, from all existing books available to the editor. The style of this engraving seems very old, even 18th C., & it is possible that jagger was meant to have a pincing end, rather than what appears to be a horn or wood handle.*

Brass Jaggers from India (?) – There are, upon examination, a great variety in these, even though most have the knop or thickening in the center of the shaft, & the smallish corrugated or jagged wheel, & the cutter or stamp at the other end. I have seen some rather crudely cast & finished ones, with extremely flimsy pins holding the wheels in place, that appear to be of recent manufacture. With all the brass coming in from India, that's my suspicion, though I've not seen "Made in India" marked on any of them. The best ones, most to be desired, have leaf stamps instead of simple corrugated curves. These stamps were used to cut out pastry leaves to be applied to the top crusts of tarts or pies. The curved pieces could be used to cut out circles or ovoid shapes, as well as sawtooth-edged elliptical leaves. • There are several patents which look very like some of these brass jaggers.

Jagger, cast brass, nickel plated & very heavy, piece probably one-off machinists' work, American, 6-1/4"L, c.1890s-1910 .... **$95**

Jagger, brass wheel & shank, black painted wood handle, Alfred Andreson & Co., Minneapolis, MN, 20th C. **$25**

Jagger, cast & machined brass, unusual long straight shank with slight knob at end, American or European, 6"L, 19th C. **$45**

Jagger & crimper, brass, American, pat'd. 1871. I haven't been able to locate the patent by searching subject indices; a page-by-page search of actual *Offi-*

IV-245. Jaggers & pincer. (T-R) *is a wood-handled jagger, from Lalance & Grosjean, 1890, as well as Duparquet, Huot & Moneuse, c.1904-10, catalogs. Other three pictures – pinchers, jagger with turned wood handle, & latticed pastry of some kind – from chapter on little cakes & petits fours, in Urbain Dubois's* La Patisserie, *pictures c.1860s-80s.*

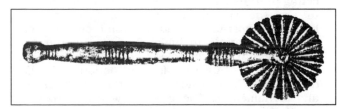

IV-246. Jagger. *Carved whalebone, 6"L, early 19th C.* **$150+**

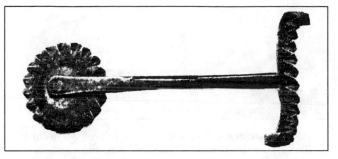

IV-247. Jagger. *Brass, with unusually curved cutter at one end. 6-1/4"L. Early to mid-19th C.* **$50+**

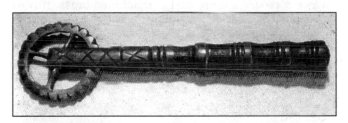

IV-248. Jagger. *Cut pewter wheel, 4 spokes, set in turned & carved wood handle in old red paint, possibly overpainted on old green. 6-3/4"L, probably American, 1720s-1750s.* **$300+**

cial Gazette pages may be necessary; I suggest 1871, 1872 & 1873. There's always a possibility it was never patented. **$65**

Jagger & crimper, heavy brass handle or shaft, 2 brass wheels at one end plus steel edge sealing stamp or edger at other end, patented as an "improved pie rimmer" by Jonathan Stephen & William Zeller, Womelsdorf, PA, 5-1/2"L, pat. # 57,990, pat'd. Sept. 11, 1866. .... **$125+**

Jagger & pastry stamp, brass wheels & stamp with turned wooden handle, American, or English (?), 6"L, 19th C. .... **$45+**

IV-249. Jaggers. *A pair of double-wheeled brass jaggers. (T) cast one with substantial knopped shaft, wheels not drilled out; (B) sheet brass wheels, 4 holes each (which may have had something to do with diecutting technique of making the wheels), & having a much thinner shaft – actually brass rod split at each end to accommodate wheels. 4"L each. 19th C. Courtesy Barbara Canter, Livingstone, NJ.* **$45+; $35+**

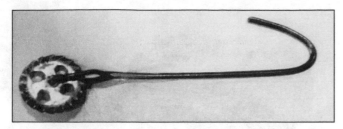

IV-250. *Jagger. Stamped brass wheel, something like those in previous picture, set into split iron square rod (nail stock?), that's hooked at end for easy hanging up. 5-7/8"L, 19th C.* **$25-$35**

Jagger & pastry stamp, cast & machined brass, turned beechwood handle, cruciform with 2 stamps & wheel, English, 11"L, 1830s-50s. **$150**

Jagger & pastry stamp, cruciform baker's tool, cast brass, includes jagging wheel, diamond shape stamp with 16 points laid out in rows of 4 x 4, round stamp also has 16 points, English, 7-5/8"L x 3-7/8"W, c.1810s... **$300+**

COPPER:

Jagger, wheel is a copper coin, Quebec, Can., 1852, wooden handle............................... **$150+**

Jagger, copper, heavy copper or bell metal wheel & shaft, turned wooden handle, very pretty, wheel drilled out with 4 holes, English (?), 6"L, 2nd quarter 19th C. (?)................................... **$135+**

IRON:

Jagger, iron shank, brass wheel, wooden handle, American, 7-1/2"L, mid 19th C. **$55**

Jagger, cast iron shank with knops & the effect of turning, forged iron wheel, turned wooden handle, probably a one-off blacksmith's piece, American, 5"L, 19th C. • A knop is like a knob only it's not on the end or top of something, but somewhere in the middle. **$120**

Jagger, cast iron, wooden handle, quite simple, American, 9"L (which is exceptionally long, & indicates this may have been used in a bakery), late 19th C............ **$100**

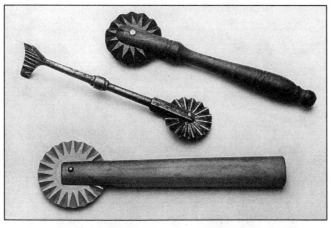

IV-251. *Jaggers. (L) "Ivory" colored plastic wheel, asparagus green shaped plastic handle, beautifully simple, c.1915-20s. (M) Machined brass, commercially made, possibly Russell & Erwin one mentioned in IV-254. 3rd quarter 19th C. (R) Turned wood with ebony-like wheel, 19th C. All between 4-1/2" & 5-1/4"L. The most valuable is the plastic one.* **(L) $100+; (M) $45+; (R) $35+**

IV-252. *Jaggers & pie sealer. Left to right: (1) Fat wood handle, thick, machined steel wheel, 6-1/4"L; (2) Nickeled steel shaft & wheel, black, turned wood handle; (3) Blue & white Meissen or Blue Onion porcelain wheel, light-colored handle, possibly boxwood, Dutch (?) (4) Steel handle, brass shaft, nickel-plated brass wheel; (5) turned wood handle, steel shaft, architecturally cut, steel wheel with very small serrations – possibly not a jagger but bookbinder's tool. (6) Next, very heavy cast brass, nickel-plated. Dealer thought a machinist might have made it for his wife; (7) last, pie sealer, turned wood handle, brass ferrule, wire axle, corrugated wood crimper roller. This might be potter's coggler. Courtesy dealer Lenny Kislin, Bearsville, NY. Most valuable are (2), (3) & (6).* **$65-$200**

Jagger, forged iron with file-decorated shaft & faceted ball knob end, one wheel, sometimes called a gigling iron in very old cookery books, American, 8-1/8"L, late 18th C. .... **$200+**

Jagger, forged iron, simple, forged or possibly drawn wire rod in square shape (nail stock?), which has been split at one end to admit a brass jagging wheel with 4 drilled out holes, & pinned through, handle end bent into sharp hook for quick hanging, very utilitarian, American, 5-7/8"L, poss. early 19th C. • **Holey Wheelies** – I cannot figure out why the holes are cut in the wheels, surely not for decorative purposes. The only thing I can think of is that even that little bit drilled out would mean saved brass (the filings or dust could be melted) or saved weight for shipping... **$75**

Jagger & crimper, also called in ads a pie crimper & ornamenter, cast iron, with longish flat handle with 2 heart cutouts (top to top), corrugated wheel, 5 fork-like prongs to pierce upper crust to let steam out while baking, "Cinderella," mfd. by Mr. G. J. Capewell, Cheshire, CT, 1870s, but can't find patent. • **Handy to Have in the House.** – "A well stocked house-furnishing store is to us a most interesting and instructive place to visit. It is wonderful to see the various contrivances for performing household operations, and the numerous little conveniences that go to make domestic matters run smoothly, but are classified under the general head of 'Notions.' ... [A rather] fanciful notion is the 'Cinderella,' which is a trade name for a new Pie crimper and Ornamenter. The grooved wheel is used for printing rosettes, and also to run along the edge of the pie to crimp it; on the other side, opposite the wheel [not at the other end of handle, but on the flip side], is a set of blades which cut ventilating holes in the crust in the form of a star. Manufacturer also makes tack hammers and various other articles handy to have in the house." *American Agriculturist*, Dec. 1876. .... **$25+**

Jagger, wrought iron wheel, turned wood shank, American, 6"L with 2" wheel diam., early 19th C. **$75**

Jaggers, forged iron, 8 different ones, wheels of different "gauges" of teeth, very simple rod handles, a few with half circle cutters on one end, two with faceted knobs at end, American or European (maybe Italian), 6" to 8"L, with wheels 1" to 1-1/4" diam., 1820s-1870s. For collection of 8: about $500. Singles:............ **$80+**

IVORY: (See also Bone; Scrimshaw)

Jagger, ivory – elephant not whale or walrus ivory, inset with ebony pins, metal hook on end, nothing special to look at, but the material counts, 7"L, mid 19th C. .... **$95+**

PEWTER:

Jagger, pewter wheel, heavily carved wooden handle with old old red paint, possibly old green paint underneath, American (?), 6-3/4"L, early to mid 18th C., or even older.................................. **$300+**

PLASTIC:

Crimper & trimmer, big brass wheel, black molded phenolic resin handle, steel shaft, American, 20th C. .... **$55+**

Jagger, plastic – marbleized asparagus green Catalin plastic handle, with carved "ivory" plastic jagging wheel, steel pin, American, 5-1/4"L, 1930s. • The rage for interesting, well-designed plastic, partly fueled by *Art Plastic*, by Andrea DiNoto (see Bibliography), has caused prices for especially nice, or particularly interesting plastic kitchen wares to go up. **$100**

Jagger, plastic & aluminum, butterscotch yellow molded Catalin plastic handle, cast aluminum shank, bronze or copper well-defined corrugated wheel, American, 7-1/2"L, 20th C. **$80**

❖ **NOTES** ❖

Marketing information from *House Furnishing Review*, Jan. 1930 says that the "Relative popularity of colors is as follows: Green, 60%; red, 25%; yellow, 15%." Apparently blue was not a choice in 1930 (or any other time?).

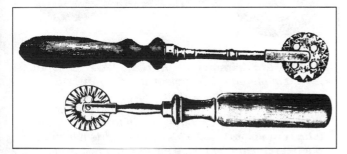

IV-253. Commercial jaggers. *For bakeries.* **(T)** *Brass wheel, drilled holes, long shaft, turned wooden handle. 7-1/2"L with 1-1/8" wheel.* **(B)** *Shorter, stubbier, 6-3/4"L, 1-1/8" wheel with finer serrations. Both S. Joseph catalog for bakers, c.1927.* **$65; $45**

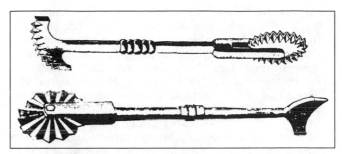

IV-254. Jaggers. (T) *cast brass, with long curved paste cutter for making circles, ovals, ellipses, leaves, etc. Five knops in center of shaft. This picture is from 1908 Jaburg Brothers catalog for confectionery supplies. The style is very old. Similar ones, differing in workmanship, number of knops, length of cutter, style of serrated blades, & style of straddling shaft for wheel.* **(B)** *picture is from John Van Range, Cincinnati, catalog of 1914. Similar one-knoppers appear in 1865 catalog of Russell & Erwin Mfg. Co., New Britain, CT, & Lalance & Grosjean, 1890, as well as a 2-knopper made by Ekco, with 1" wheel, about 1925, & many modern cheap imports, prinicipally from India. Caution: The lightweight, fairly crude ones are often way overpriced, & should be under $25. Pictured ones:* **$35-$55**

PORCELAIN:

Jagger, turned rosewood handle, with all-white porcelain wheel, English (?), 19th C. .... **$75+**

Jagger or crimper, turned wood handle in unvarnished pale wood, blue & white Meissen wheel, Dutch or German, late 19th C.................................. **$125+**

SCRIMSHAW:

Figural whale & walrus ivory & bone. Especially prized are pieces with double wheels & a pricker – sometimes in the form of a unicorn horn. (See also Bone; Ivory)

Jagger, scrimshaw piecrust edger in form of horse with an elongated, curved fish or whale's tail, the head is fairly small and as abstract as Cycladic art from over 3000 years ago, the front legs arch downwards and grasp a jagging wheel, the 6 spokes of which are cut in such a way to create 6 hearts, American, 5-3/4"L, early 19th C. • At early 1980s auction of Barbara Johnson's scrimshaw collection, the jaggers, many architectural or geometric in style, went for high prices, from $750 to $1,700. Others, highly ornamen-

IV-255. Jagger with ornamenter. *A very old style, back to the 1600s, wheel with a cutter that worked like a cookie cutter to make pastry leaves. Such leaves ornamented the top crust, or were baked, then laid upon the filling. Probably brass, English or French. Note knop (a mid-shaft knob) in center. F. A. Walker, Boston, import catalog, c.1870s.*

tal but not figural or zoomorphic, ranged from only $275 for one with a broken prong on the pricker part, to $1,550. • At another auction about the same time, some whale ivory and walrus ivory jagging wheels, none of them figural, realized only $225 and $650. Geometric was in, figural wasn't. Depending on the subject of the scrimshaw pieces, values have risen 100% to 1000%. • At Richard A. Bourne Co.'s auction in July 1989, of the Jeffrey Cohen Collection of maritime antiques, two scrimshaw unicorn jaggers, each with a long bifurcated horn pricker, & front legs that straddle wheel, sold for $8,000 & $10,000, plus 10% premium for buyer. .... **$2,000+**

Jagger, scrimshaw: carved whale bone with whale tooth wheel, mermaid with long wavy hair, smiling, slightly Negroid features so she almost resembles African carving, 3 brass nails hold on arms, American (?), 9-5/8"L with 2-1/16" diam. wheel, early 19th C. .... **$2,000+**

Jagger, scrimshaw, with detailed horse's head with bridle, leg-like extensions grasping wheel, the spokes of which are the 5 points of a star, American, 6"L, early 19th C. • This one sold for $500 at auction a few years ago. .... **$2,500+**

Jagger, whale bone scrimshander work, sailor with hands on his midriff against his double-breasted buttoned jacket, straddling large fluted wheel (looks like

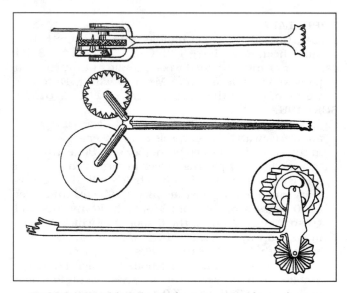

IV-256. Double-wheel jagger & pie crimper patents. (T) & **(M)** *Top two show two views of a "pie crimper" as it was titled or "improved pie-rimmer" as called within the claim; pat'd. by Jonathan Stephen & William Zeller, Womelsdorf, PA, Sept. 11, 1866, #57,990. The rimmer consists "of a handle provided at one end with a rotary cutter secured to an irregular or ornamental roller & corrugated wheel, & at other end with a* **butter cutter or print.**" *That's the first time I've seen that little curved thing called a butter cutter!* **(B)** *A "pie rimmer" pat'd. by Neal N. Brown, Reading, PA, Nov. 26, 1867, #71,274. Brown describes his as having a "curved marker" for "marking the pastry" at one end. A "crimped roller" and a cutting roller are at other end, tool to be used "in the usual manner." Method of affixing wheels constitutes the newness claimed. See also IV-274.*

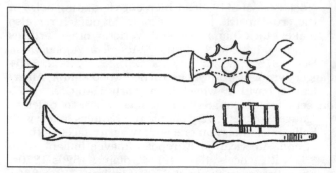

IV-257. Pastry crimper patent, *two views. Pat'd. by Jerome Redding, Charlestown, MA, & John B. Coe, Boston, MA, April 14, 1868, #76,813. They also call it an "improved pastry-jigger." It looks different from other jaggers/jiggers. The notched shank is to be used as a "gauge" & also a marker. "The wheel is mounted loosely on a pin projecting from an extension from the shank, and this continues beyond the wheel making a guide for running against the edge of the [pie] plate, and for thereby keeping the wheel at a uniform distance from such edge, as its teeth roll around the piece of pastry. This guide may be made plain, or it may branch laterally, and be furnished with teeth to indent the paste." (See also IV-263.)*

he's riding a unicycle), wears little black cap, a skimmer, eyes appear set in of ebony, but are possibly carved & painted, American, 6-1/2"L with 1-3/4" diam. wheel, c.1850s.................................... **$4,000**

Jagger, whale bone scrimshander's work, determined-looking mermaid, arms nailed on with tiny nails, long hair down back, American, 6"L, early 19th C. **$2,000**

STEEL:

Jagger, steel shank & wheel with bone handle, American, mid 1800s. **$55**

Jagger, turned steel handle shaped like turned wood handle, brass shaft, nickeled brass wheel, American, 7-3/8"L, late 19th C. **$125**

IV-258. Pie trimmer & marker. *Wood & metal. "This simple little instrument trims off the surplus pie-crust that projects over the plate, and at the same time neatly ornaments the border. It is one of the indispensable conveniences of the kitchen after it has once been used. Pies can be made without it, but if ornamentation does not add to the nutriment, it pleases the eye and aids digestion, and* **pies are not famous for being the most digestible articles in the world,** *no matter how carefully made." [Bold-face emphasis mine.] Scammell's Treasure-House of Knowledge, 1891.* **$15+**

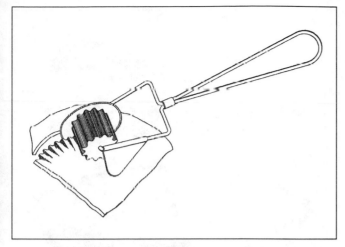

IV-259. Pie cutter & crimper patent. *Pat'd. by Alexander H. Stillwagen, Pittsburgh, PA, March 10, 1908, #881,738. Simple tin plate & wire tool that was manufactured. Tool turned sideways to use fin-like triangular cutter blade to make slots in top crust, or for trimming. (See IV-267.)* **$15**

Jagger, steel, machined shaft & handle, brass wheel, very finely made, American (?), 7"L, early 19th C. **$150**
Jagger, steel wheel, hand carved & turned wooden shank, with original dark worn red paint, American, 8"L, late 18th or early 19th C. • To identify these really old ones, study books on furniture styles, candlesticks & andirons, as they will give you a feel for the look of late 1700s turnings. Here, it's partly old red paint, partly magisterial (as in sceptre) look that increases value. .... **$500+**
Jagger, steel, replica of early 19th C. figural jagging wheel in the collection of Metropolitan Museum of Art, NYC, & created by them in their workshops. Roughly "S" shaped shank, with a simple bird at one end, a fishtail at the other, 10-1/2"L, 1980s. This is a reproduction sold through the beautiful Metropolitan Museum (NYC) catalog in the early 1980s for $170. Very hard to figure a resale value for this, because it's a reproduction, not an original. The price had to be high for the reproduction because of

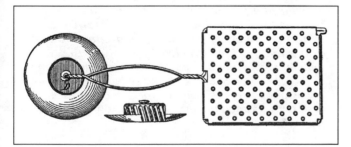

IV-260. Combination pastry knife & rasp *"for rasping the dried and burned edges from cakes and otherwise plumbing them up preparatory to glazing or frosting, which may also be utilized as a common grater." Spoken like a bricklayer! Small linecut shows angled corrugations on crimping wheel. Pat'd. by Frederick A. Tobler, Los Angeles, CA, Aug. 15, 1905, #797,088.*

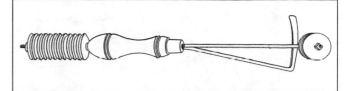

IV-261. Pastry cutter & crimper, *pat'd. by Wallace R. Marie, Boston, MA, April 13, 1869, #88,883. Patent assigned to Thomas A. Mitchell, Washington, DC. Marie wrote that he had "invented a new and useful Machine for Cutting and Crimping Pastry and Cake, called 'The Combination Pastry and Cake-Cutter and Crimper.'" Rod & handle & crimping element at far left held together with a threaded screw & nut. I hope this was made, I love the look of it.*

the work involved in making it, but my feeling is that it is like new furniture in an old style, after you've had it a day it's simply second-hand furniture & it'll take a generation (more like 50 years) to become valuable again. I'd be very wary of such pieces, as the price for an original of this type might be in the high hundreds. I believe the Museum marked theirs. Anything offered you should be carefully examined with a magnifying glass – standard collector equipment. Get as powerful a one as you can find. Repro resale value: .... **$65+**
Jagger, wrought steel, lathe turned, American or English, 7-3/16"L, mid 19th C. • Sometimes you will see the term **engine turning**, but strictly speaking that is lathe turning done on an eccentric lathe, one

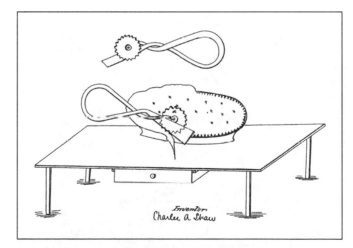

IV-262. Pie crimper in use on table, a patent *by Charles A. Shaw, Biddeford, ME, Nov. 6, 1860, #30,592. My favorite patent drawing in this book. Don't you love the scale of it? This is why I love patent research. The crimper is a simple bent wire & crimped sheet metal device. The wire at one end is attached to a small cog wheel; at other end it's "flattened, forming the blade or trimmer." Shaw writes, "I am aware that a wheel with cogs is an old device; and that a crimper with a guide or tailpiece has been used ..., but what I claim as new ... is the knife and wheel when combined to crimp and trim a pie at one operation, constructed as specified."*

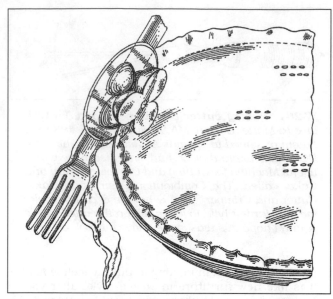

IV-263. "Piecrust trimming and scalloping device" patent, *given Mary Di Domenico, Chicago, IL, Dec. 25, 1951, #2,580,081. One way to crimp a pie crust is by pinching it with fingers & thumb, giving dough a little twist. This 1951 invention (applied for in 1949) could be "mounted upon the handle of a fork, the tines of the fork may be used for piercing the pie crust for the holes to permit escape of the vapor generated in baking the pie." The device trimmed & scalloped the edge. Di Domenico's patent cites 5 much older patents: Stephen's #67,601 (1867); Brown's #71,274 (1867); Redding et al. #76,813 (1868); Clem's #820,553 (1906); and O'Brien's #868,359 (1907).*

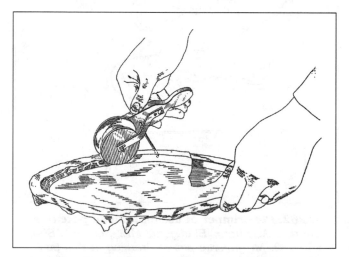

IV-264. Pie trimmer patent, *awarded John S. Croxford, Newport, ME, July 23, 1907, #327,151. One claim is that this cutter can "conform to the shape of the pan ... and permit cutting disks to adapt themselves to pie-crusts of different thicknesses." Looks to me like a waste of time – you first cut lower crust, then place upper crust on, trim it & press the two together. Note that dirty right thumbnail! Yikes!*

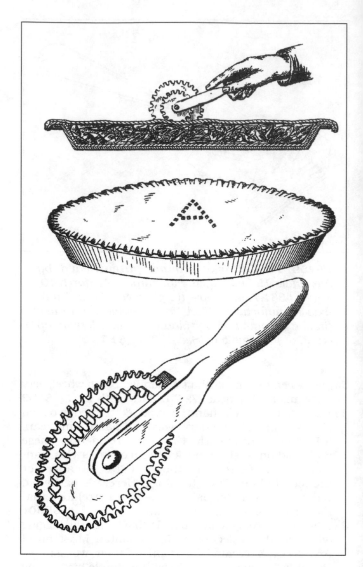

IV-265. "A pie may be trimmed, crimped, marked, and punctured," *with this device pat'd. by Jay W. Butler, Hermitage, NY, Dec. 22, 1908, #907,456, assigned one-half to Henry J. Walz, Buffalo, NY. "It has been the practice heretofore to mark the upper crust of a pie with a sharp tool cutting through the crust to permit the escape of the steam from within; while serving at the same time to initial the pie; but invariably while baking, the crust bulged outward where cut ... resulting in total elimination of the identifying letter." Butler claims that his invention would puncture "the crust with small openings ... [and] in this manner cutting of the crust is avoided and consequently it cannot bulge outward." Of course, there's also a rotary disk with "crimping-teeth and a narrow peripheral flange" for cutting.*

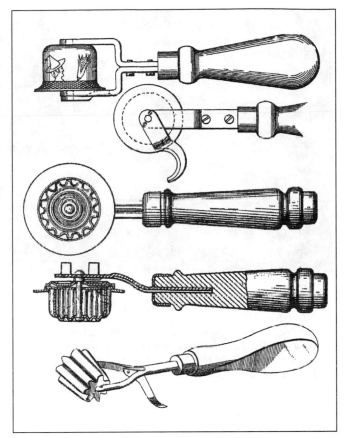

IV-266. **Pie crimpers & trimmers**, *three patents. From top:* **(1)** & **(2)** *Maybe the most interesting is this Hallowe'en motif device, pat'd. by Marius H. Heighton, Ravenna, OH, Sept. 7, 1926, #1,599,129. It was to have interchangeable rollers with ornamentation, or "occasional illustrations suitable to the occasion or period in which the pie ... will be employed." Second image shows it from the side, with a slightly-offset, hooked trimming blade.* **(3)** & **(4)** *This crimper, "conveniently made entirely of sheet metal" [except for the $$ turned wooden handle] – "simple and cheap" to make was pat'd. by John C. Forster, Pittsburgh, PA, Apr. 28, 1925, #1,535,300.* **(5)** *Pat'd. by Robert H. Berkstresser, York, PA, May 5, 1903, #727,269. "The revolvable crimping-roll is ... loosely journaled ... and may be of solid or hollow formation ... of a frusto-conical form" with deep corrugations. The "trimming-knife" acts as a trailer, set at an inclination, which guides the device as it's moved around the pie crust.*

that could turn designs not concentric to the center axis. Spiral turned borders, fancy rosette-like turnings, etc., are engine turned......................... **$250+**

❖ RECIPES ❖

Almond Filberts – *1 lb. of Valentia almonds, 1 lb. searched [sierced or sieved] sugar, about 2 yolks of eggs. – Blanch and beat the almonds very fine with yolk of egg; mix in the sugar and yolks, and beat them into a smooth paste with the pestle; roll the paste out thin, and cut it up with a proper cutter in lengths; then cut it so as to leave three points on each side; place a small almond on the middle*

point, and one opposite (being previously made wet with yolk of egg and water); roll them up, and put two across each other, and one on the top, which will form a filbert. Work up all your paste in this way; place them on a clean iron plate dusted with flour: bake them in a slow oven. NB. A proper cutter for filberts must be made of tin, in a zig-zag shape, with nine points on each side; when the paste is cut by it, it will make three nuts." *Joseph Bell, A Treatise on Confectionary, Newcastle, England, 1817. Imagine an oblong of pastry with 9 points of a zigzag on each side; cut this in thirds. And that's as far as I can get with this. If rolled up, with crosswise almonds sticking out, I imagine it looking rather formidable. Bell was Confectioner to the Prince of Wales and the Duke of York, before writing the book.*

•   •   •

Dough-Nuts – *Three pounds of sifted flour. A pound of powdered sugar. Three quarters of a pound of butter. Four eggs. Half a large tea-cup full of best brewer's yeast. A pint and a half of milk. A tea-spoonful of powdered cinnamon. A grated nutmeg. A table-spoon ful of rose-water. – Cut up the butter in the flour. Add the sugar, spice, and rose-water. Beat the eggs very light, and pour them into the mixture. Add the yeast, (half a tea-cup or two wine-glasses full,) and then stir in the milk by degrees, so as to make it a soft dough. Cover it, and set it to rise. When quite light, cut it in diamonds with a jagging-iron or a sharp knife, and fry them in lard. Grate loaf-sugar over them when done." Miss Leslie, of Philadelphia, Seventy-Five Receipts for Pastry, Cakes, & Sweet-meats.* Appended to The Cook's Own Book & Housekeeper's Register ..., by a Boston House-keeper. *Boston: Munroe & Francis, 1833.*

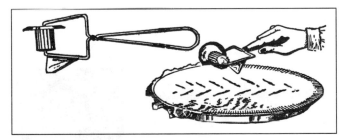

IV-267. **Crimper & pie cutter.** *"Ideal," from Seastrand salesmen's catalog, c.1929. This is the crimper in IV-259, pat'd. by Stillwagen, March 1908, #881,738. "Why not save time by using the Ideal? The only perfect pie cutter & crimper; it not only makes a cleaner cut & a neater crimp, but it presses both crusts firmly together, thus preventing the rich juices from boiling over." Wood & wire & tin, with edging trimmer.* • *About a similar cutter, was written "This simple little instrument trims off the surplus pie-crust that projects over the plate, & at the same time neatly ornaments the border. It is one of the indispensable conveniences of the kitchen after it has once been used. Pies can be made without it, but if ornamentation does not add to the nutriment, it pleases the eye & aids digestion, & pies are not famous for being the most digestible articles in the world, no matter how carefully made." Scammell's Treasure-House of Knowledge, 1891.* **$25+**

Jagger, machined steel wheel, fat wood handle, American, 6"L, late 19th C. .... **$60+**

Jagger, steel shank with very architectural turnings & planes, small-toothed wheel, turned wooden handle is possibly 19th C. replacement, American, 7-1/2"L, 1st to 2nd quarter 19th C. **$150**

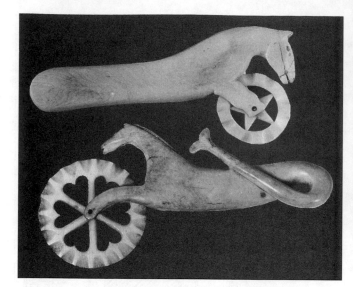

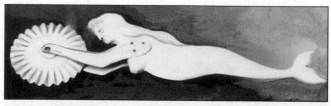

IV-269. Scrimshaw mermaid jaggers. (T) *Mermaid holding large wheel. Carved whalebone. Arms nailed on with tiny nails. Courtesy Sidney Getler, American Folk Art, NYC.* **(B)** *Carved whalebone mermaid holding large, beautifully-carved wheel. Flowing hair, lots of face detail. Slightly Negroid features on smiling face. Three brass nails holding on arms. 9-5/8"L, wheel 2-1/16" diam. Courtesy Neil Blodgett, Higganum House, Higganum, CT.* **(T) $2,000+; (B) $2,500+**

IV-270. Scrimshaw jaggers. *Sea horses.* **(T)** *Carved whalebone, star-shaped spokes to wheel. 6"L, early 19th C. Picture courtesy of Robert W. Skinner Inc., Auctioneers, Bolton, MA.* **(B)** *Carved whalebone, fishy tail, heart cutouts on wheel, 5-3/4"L. Picture courtesy of the National Museum of American History, Smithsonian Institution.* **$2,000-$2,500+**

TIN:

Crimper & trimmer, tin, wire, corrugated wide wheel, "The Ideal," maker unknown – possibly the inventor. Marked "Pat'd March 10, 1908." Pat'd. by Alexander H. Stillwagen, Pittsburgh, PA, #881,738. .... **$20+**

Crimper & grater & cutter combined, tin, tinned steel, wooden crust crimper wheel at one end, middle part punctured for grating nutmegs, probably, fatly-pointed tip used to trim off excess dough around edge & to slash steam slits in top crust, American, 6-7/8"L, late 19th C. .... **$75+**

IV-268. Scrimshaw jagger. *Upstanding sailor of carved whalebone, with ebony hat, high button shoes, pupils & buttons. He straddles the jagging wheel like a unicycle. 5-3/4"H. Courtesy Neil Blodgett, Higganum House, Higganum, CT.* **$4,000+**

IV-271. Jagger. *Cast pewter rabbit or leaping hare, resembling cast pewter chocolate molds made by 19th C. makers such as Anton Reiche, Dresden, Germany. Charming, almost feminine look, 6-1/4"L, looked old – although nowadays there are so many "collectibles" made by so-called limited edition companies, something similar could be made recently. That said, I wouldn't be surprised if this was made as a sideline by a chocolate mold manufacturer in Europe in 2nd half of 19th C.* **$500**

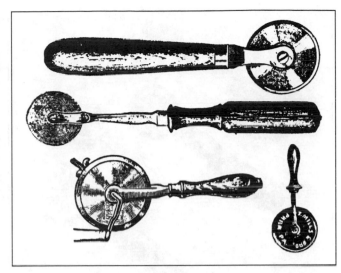

IV-272. Pastry & pizza cutters. *Sharp steel blades, in a variety of wooden handles. From top:* **(1)** *From Jaburg, 1908.* **(2)** *Long shafted one, in 3 sizes: 7-1/2"L with 1-1/2" wheel; 8"L with 2-1/4" wheel; 8-3/4"L with 3-1/4" wheel. S. Joseph, c.1927.* **(3)** *Lower left, a large-wheeled cutter, 6" diam., with gauge; &* **(4)** *right, a 4" or 6" diam. cutter, larger sizes to order. T. Mills, 1930. For candy, pizza, bread dough, etc.* **$5-$35**

IV-273. Pie crimper & ornamenter, *cast iron. "Cinderella," invented & mfd.. by Mr. G.J. Capewell, Cheshire, CT. Cast aluminum. Face of wheel used for printing rosettes; & also crimp; on the other side, opposite the wheel ... is a set of blades which cut ventilating holes in the crust in star shape. American Agriculturist ad, Dec. 12, 1876. The broadside valued at about $10. The tool:* **$25+**

WOOD:

Jagger, turned fruitwood with ebony wheel, French (?), 4-3/4"L, c.1880s. Added value. – One with really nice turning might bring a few dollars more, but this is a commonly found variety, & may even be made today. .... **$35+**

Jagger, carved bird's eye maple, handle & wheel, American, 4-1/2"L, late 19th C. .... **$45+**

Jagger, grain painted wood handle, metal, "Ridgely," American, late 19th C. .... **$35+**

Jagger, hand carved wood, big wooden wheel, American, 8"L, 1860s or 70s... **$50**

Jagger, lathe turned wood, 2 wheels of different size corrugations, one at each end, American, 8"L, mid 19th C. .... **$75+**

Jagger & pastry stamp, carved wood, very smooth, satiny patina, abstract flower incised on shank, stamp at one end is serrated, possibly American, more probably English, 6-3/8"L, mid to late 19th C........ **$165+**

IV-274. Pie rimmer, crimper & pastry cutter. *Pat'd. Sept. 11, 1866, 5-1/2"L, brass. Mfd.. by Jonathan Stephen & W. Zeller, Womelsdorf, PA. Illustration is from flimsy printed broadside that advertised the rimmers. Note little footstool on which the infant stands. Such little painted stools are found in many "country" collections. It would be fun to collect all the items seen in a period picture like this. (See IV-256.)* **$125**

❖ **NOTES** ❖

Cornerfolds – "The handsomest way of ornamenting the edge of a pie or pudding is to cut the rim in large square notches, and then fold over triangularly one corner of every notch." Miss Leslie, of Philadelphia, *Seventy-Five Receipts for Pastry, Cakes, and Sweetmeats.* Appended to *The Cook's Own Book & Housekeeper's Register ...,* by a Boston Housekeeper. Boston: Munroe & Francis, 1833.

❖ **RECIPE** ❖

Rhubarb Pies – *Gather a bundle of the leaf-stocks, sufficient quantity – cut off the leaf and peal [sic] the stock of the thin epidermis – cut in quarter inch pieces, and lay them into the crust – cover well with sugar, and add nutmeg, orange peal and spice to taste. The flavor is equal, and many deem it preferable to gooseberries. The pie-plant is perennial, herbaceous and very hardy. A dozen plants will afford a family a constant supply."* The Farmers' Cabinet, *Philadelphia, Aug. 1, 1836.*

Jaggers & crimpers – See also Crimpers

Jelly molds – See Molds. Especially the tin & copper ones

Jumble press – See Cookie press, also Pastry tube

Krum Kake – See Wafer irons

Kugelhopf mold – See Molds, kugelhopf, tubed or spouted, in ceramic & copper sections

Lady finger cutter, stamped tin, strap handle, 2 air holes, American (?), 2-7/8"L x 1"W, 19th C..................... **$35**

IV-275-A. Combination tools: dredgers, graters & dough cutters. (L) *Pieced tin, japanned finish, brass medallion appears to say "-organ – Comp. Mandal 6 LONDON." (Probably "Morgan.")* Sugar shaker or dredger, shape cutter (corrugated bottom), nutmeg grater, lemon grater or zester, & pastry jagger. Late 19th C. **(R)** *A nearly identical piece pat'd. as an "Improved Dredge-Box, Cake-Cutter & Grater," by Sydney Cooke, Bayonne City, NJ, April 26, 1870, #102,225. Cooke describes his invention thus: "The lid of the box is a doughnut-cutter; the bottom of the box is a corrugated cake-cutter; the raised graters are attached to the sides of the box, one for nutmegs, & the other for lemons, &c. The grates being raised from the surface of the box prevent the holes in them from getting clogged. The jagger iron or knife is attached to the front of the box." Official Gazette of the U.S. Patent Office. I do not know the story of how the Morgan one came to be licensed (or not).*

IV-275-B. Spice box & cake cutter patent. *Another, even simpler "spice box and cake cutter" (as patent was titled – either by Patent Office or Inventor) was pat'd. by George D. Bayley, Lebanon, NH, Feb. 17, 1863,*

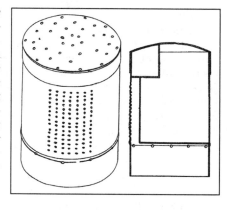

*#37,716. Bayley's claim, headed "Improved dredging-box, with grater and cake-cutter attached," said "My present invention consists of a **new** article for kitchen use, in which are combined a grater, a dredge-box, and a cake-cutter. These three articles, which are in frequent requisition by cooks and particularly by cake-bakers, are now usually made separate, the three articles occupying much more room on the table where the cook works, and being more liable, one or other of them, to be out of reach than they will be when combined in one article." He goes on to say that the cylindrical dredge-box has a perforated lid to be filled with flour. A grating surface is on the side – for nutmegs, and* **(R)** *under the lid you can see a small interior compartment for a nutmeg, & a larger compartment for the flour. Note bottom of flour compartment about 1/4 way up from bottom, which serves as cake or biscuit cutter.* **$300+**

IV-276. Crimpers & jagger. *Top left to bottom right:* **(1)** *Large all wood wheel, set in wooden handle, 7"L, homemade? Collection of Meryle Evans.* **(2)** *galvanized tin edge-sealer with plain wood handle, 6-1/2"L, possibly homemade with kitchen tool handle, or could be a pat'd. tool, although I didn't find a matching patent drawing. Late 19th, early 20th C.* **(3)** *cast aluminum, very cheapo, something like "Cinderella," 4-3/4"L;* **(4)** *Cheapest of all is "Vaughn's Pie Trimmer & Sealer," pat'd. May 10, 1921. Aluminum wheel with crimping prongs bent up out of stamped wheel, green painted wood handle. 6-1/2"L. c.1940s-50s.* **$10-$35+**

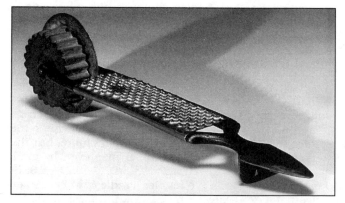

IV-277. Crimper & grater combined. *Tin, wood & cast metal. The grater was probably used for nutmeg. The pointed end may be a can opener, or for making slashes in top crust before baking, or a jar opener for cutting seal of a fruit jar full of preserved fruit. 6-7/8"L, American, late 19th C. Picture courtesy of the National Museum of American History, Smithsonian Institution.* **$55+**

IV-278. Spouted mold. *Redware, glazed inside & out. Handle on one side. 3-1/8" deep x 9-1/2" diam. American, mid 19th C. Ex-Keillor Collection.* **$200-$300+**

Lady finger sponge cake baking tray, stamped tin, oblong tray with 6 elongated peanut shaped, or as the catalog says, "finger shape" cups, in Harrod's Stores catalog, London, England, 11"L, late 19th C. .... **$45+**

Lady finger or madeline mold (both are a sort of small sponge cake), sheet tin, rather crudely made, 6 small elongated ovals, corrugated at each end, riv-

IV-280. Nineteenth Century Pastry Kitchen with Molds. *Unidentified highly-detailed print, showing kitchen layout similar to those found 300 years before the mid-19th C., as well as today. From (L), traveling around wall: cupboard with rolling pin, dredger, can with scoop; L-shaped range with 3 grated openings, above which is a metal drip hanger rack with 7 stirring spoons, and above them are bracket shelves loaded with molds & sieves. In middle of back is some kind of oven. Then more molds, with a balance scale on table at right rear, & a large dresser with molds, a glass dome protected, molded confection, & a churn in near right corner. Probably English or French, probably about 1870-80.*

eted to flat sheet, handle on one end, American or German, 9"L, each cup 4-1/4"L, 19th C. **$50**

Lady finger pan, tin, stamped with elongated peanut shape cups, "Kreamer," Brooklyn, NY, early 20th C. **$30**

Lady finger pan – See also Sponge cake tin

IV-279. Cake mold showroom from 1890s-1900, as depicted in back advertising section of most of Mrs. A. B. Marshall's cookery books. Eat your heart out, mold collectors! Swans, fish, fancy molds are the stock in the cases. The women in foreground appear to be writing letters, but perhaps they are copying out recipes, or writing orders. One ad in her cookbooks was for Marshall's "BOOK OF MOULDS, which may be had gratis on application, or is sent post free to any address. It contains 68 pages and over 400 engravings. Illustrating, in different sizes and designs, about one thousand kinds of moulds." Following this image were sample pages from the book, some of which are reproduced in this chapter. Alas, Book of Moulds has not been found, yet, as described.

IV-281. A Yule Dolly or Baby Cake or Dow [dough] Dolly, *from 19th C. Czechoslovakian journal. The leaves represent a sprig of rosemary, which might have been gilded, held by image of Christ child in swaddling – all made of dough. The Yule Dolly was made all over Europe & the United Kingdom in 18th & 19th centuries, and undoubtedly long before.*

❖ RECIPE ❖

Apple Bread – *Boil a dozen good-sized apples that have been peeled and cored, until they are perfectly tender. While still warm, mash them in double the amount of flour, and add the proper proportion of yeast. The mass should then be thoroughly kneaded without water, as the apple juice will make it sufficiently soft. It should be left to rise 12 hours, then formed into loaves, and baked when quite light. Apple Bread was the invention of a scientific Frenchman, and it has always been highly commended for its healthfulness."* Ladies' Home Journal, Sept. 1896.

Loaf pan, white enamelware with cobalt trim, 8"L, 20th C. • Sometimes these look suspiciously like some kind of sterilizing container from a medical supplier. **$20**

IV-282. Baking mold, or backform. *Leering man's head – mythological. Copper, 10-5/8" diam., German, mid to late 19th C. Picture courtesy Waltraud Boltz Auctionhouse, Bayreuth, Germany.* **$500**

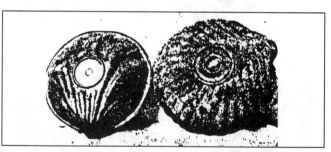

IV-283. Ancient molds reproductions. *Cast bronze cake molds, originals of which were found buried under volcanic debris at Herculaneum* **(L)**, *& at Pompeii* **(R)**, *almost 1800 years after the eruption of Vesuvius destroyed the towns in minutes.* **(L)** *Scallop shell-shape. Original 2" deep x 8-1/4" diam.* **(R)** *Scalloped with more detail. 2-7/8" deep x 8-3/4" diam. They both have simple round bottoms, & the reproductions were only made with a polished finish. From catalog of Fonderie Artistiche Riunite, of J. Chiurazzi & Fils & S. De Angelis & Fils, Naples, Italy, c.1910-11.*

IV-284. Dessert made in "biscuit mold," *which you might think could mean an unglazed ceramic mold, or one in which biscuits or cookies (or cake) were made. But, many copper molds are called "biscuit molds." In French catalogs, similar-looking molds were described as being "pour biscuit ou pour glaces." A particular type of frozen dessert was called an "iced biscuit," made of different colors & flavors of a frozen meringue, puréed fruit & whipped cream, put into various nooks or compartments of biscuit molds. I also believe from my reading of some old catalogs that indeed some biscuit molds were meant for a cake-like dessert. This picture from Urbain Dubois' La Patisserie, c.1870s.*

Lollipop mold, cast iron, makes 5 octagonal lollies, with room for stick, American, 5-5/8" x 10-1/2" x 3/8" deep, late 19th C. (?). **$200**
Lollipop mold, makes 24, heavy stamped metal, American, 20th C. **$55**
Lollipop or sucker mold, 2 part stamped metal, rough square with image of hen on basket, place for round stick in bottom, American (?), 3" x 3" square, c.1930s (?). .... **$5+**

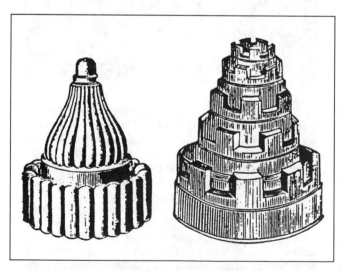

IV-285. Macedoine molds. *Imported copper, 6-1/4" & 6-3/4" diam. at bottom. A* **macedoine** *is chopped fresh fruit, soaked in kirsch & maraschino cherry juice, mixed with cream & chilled. Duparquet catalog, c.1904-10.* **$100-$175+**

IV-286. Kugelhopf or gugelhupf cake mold.
*Stamped copper, tinned inside, 4" deep x 10" diam.
Very small 6-point star opening in spout. Probably
German, 1890s-1910. A* **gugelhupf** *cake has a
yeast dough mixed with seedless raisins, grated
lemon peel, chopped almonds. The mold is first
greased with butter, coated with chopped almonds
& bread crumbs, filled about half full, put in a
warm spot to raise the dough, then baked. Served
sprinkled with powdered sugar. Collection of Mary
Mac Franklin.* **$100+**

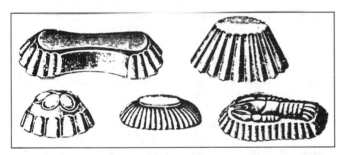

IV-287. Madeline molds. *Small molds of stamped
tin. S. Joseph, c.1927.* **$8-$12**

**IV-288. Madeline
molds.** *Stamped tin,
from F. A. Walker
catalog, c.1890.
Probably imported.*
$7-$30

Madeline molds, stamped in tin in geometric, natural &
figural shapes, individual serving sizes, used for
baking the rich small sponge cakes – recalled so well
by Marcel Proust in his 7-volume novel *Remembrance of Things Past*, 1913-1927. They are rather
like poundcake, served plain or ornamented with
frosting, nuts or fruit. Also called a dariole mold. No
mark, French (?), a few inches wide, 1870s to 1880s,
poss. earlier, but known from F. A. Walker catalogs.
• A horse's head, a rose, shells, a bunch of grapes, &
a fluted flaring cup are among the forms known.
Note: The traditional shape for madelines was a
scallop shell, or a shallow fluted cup, but importers
& dealers seem often to have felt free calling various
things by the same name (not just madelines). See
also a Muffin pan further on.......................... **$18+**
Maple sugar mold, all tin, with corrugated cups riveted
to rectangular tin pan, American, 9"L x 6-1/4"W,
small cups. 19th C...................................... **$45+**
Maple sugar mold, carved block of wood set into tin
stand or frame that holds it up as if on an easel, mold
is heart-shaped, American or Canadian, 6-1/4"H
with frame, mold itself is 4-1/4"W, 19th C. .... **$175+**
Maple sugar mold, carved wood, 2 hearts & a crescent
moon, American? 15"L x 3-1/2"W, 19th C. ... **$125+**
Maple sugar mold, carved wood, a blue jay or cardinal
with crest, American or Canadian, 5-1/2" x 6-3/4",
20th C. .... **$55+**
Maple sugar mold, carved wood, beaver design, Cana-
dian (?), 8-1/2" x 3-1/4" early 20th C............. **$125**

Maple sugar mold, carved wood, squirrel with thick curled tail, 6-1/2" x 5-1/4" 20th C............... **$125+**

Maple sugar mold, carved wood with 3 designs – sunburst, heart, tulip, American or Canadian, 17"L x 5"W, 19th C................................. **$125**

Maple sugar mold, chip carved thick wood, one end cut away except for wedge shaped handle (large part out), 3 cakes made in shallow fluted cups, Canadian or American, 11"L x 2"W, mid 19th C.............. **$55+**

Maple sugar mold, deeply carved wood, oblong plank, 3 hearts, with sides & bottom of cups further decorated with carving, Canadian (?), somehow doesn't look American, 22"L x 7"W, early 19th C....... **$175**

Maple sugar mold, for making sugar pyramids, very tall & narrow, all wood, 4 side pieces are acute triangles held together with simple wooden clamp: a square cut out of oblong piece of wood, meant to fit down over assembled sides & be wedged in place, so mold could be filled at big open base end. The wedge also served as a sort of flange so the mold could be put in a rack or frame to harden, Canadian, about 10"H x 4-1/2" square at base, 19th C.......................... **$85**

Maple sugar mold, hand carved, long & skinny, makes 14 hearts, 42"L, makes 2"H hearts, 19th C. .... **$135+**

Maple sugar mold, heavy terne plate tin, prints 12 figures, *viz.* cornucopia, fleur-de-lis, pear, heart, daisy, oak leaf, shell, bell, fish, moon, flag, automobile & strawberry, "Jaburg Bros.," NYC, NY, 6" x 6-1/2", c.1930s (?). .... **$125+**

Maple sugar mold, oblong of wood, 14 carved figures, including horse, diamond, 6 pointed star, hearts, houses, anvil, etc., very precisely & carefully cut, in contrast to many observed maple sugar molds with rather crude carvings, American, 32"L x 7"W x 2"

IV-290. "Fancy Patty Pans *for baking ornamental tea cakes."* *These were probably indistinguishable from madeline molds.* American Home Cook Book, 1854. **$8-$15+**

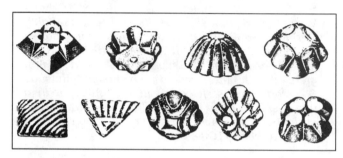

IV-291. Petits fours molds. *Small, & pretty much similar designs as madeline molds, only somewhat deeper.* S. Joseph, c.1927. **$8-$15+**

thick, 19th C. The houses add particular interest. (Even more valuable are the rare house-shaped molds in 3 dimensions. These are in 2 or 4 parts; inside carving includes doors, windows, chimneys, etc. They're probably earlier than flat ones, & may be Canadian.) This one offered by the Jorgensens of Hallowell in 1983. Value range mine............. **$550+**

IV-289. Madeline molds. (T) *set, stamped tin, from Pick-Barth catalog, 1929. A few sample sizes: top left one is 4" x 2-1/8"; star one at right is 2-7/8" diam.* **(B)** *set, imported tin molds, from G. M. Thurnauer & Bro., NYC dealers & importers.* House Furnishing Review *ad, Jan. 1903. Singles:* **$5-$10**; *Sets of 10-12:* **$50-$100**

IV-292. Maple sugar mold – both halves. *Carved wood, horse, beaver, fish, square with plus & minus signs(?). Note pegs & holes, for holding halves together. Each half is 18"L x 4-1/2"W x 1-3/4" thick, Canadian or American, late 19th C. Photo from Jeannine Dobb's Country Folk Antiques, Merrimack, NH.* **$750+**

Maple sugar mold, sheet tin, 7 individual shallow cups with hexagonal exteriors, round interiors, riveted together (this is the reason for the hexagonal edges) & giving the appearance of a piece of honeycomb, thin strap handle (I identified this as a muffin pan in last edition), American, 9-1/8" diam., 19th C. • Maine collector Joanne Wilson wrote to tell me that hers was "given to me by a lady who said it was used as a maple sugar mold on the farm where she grew up." I accept this new attribution, as it does seem too shallow for muffins, though not for some kind of small cake or cookie. .... **$45+**

Maple sugar mold, strawberry, carved wood, American, 9-1/4"L x 5-1/2"W x 1-3/4" thick, 19th C. .... **$135+**

Marzipan mold, also called a marchpane or massepain mold, heavy tin plated, 2 hinged sections, 3" x 3", German, 19th or 20th C. **$50**

Marzipan mold – See also the many Cake boards, & Springerle boards & molds

---

Molds for Aspics, Blancmange, Food, Jelly, Pudding, etc.

I have grouped almost all the molds here which tend to have more depth than cake molds, or are useable for a variety of foods and might sometimes be termed "food molds," or are known as jelly molds or pudding molds. Not included, generally speaking, are cake, candy, chocolate, cookie, ice cream molds. There are also a few molds under "Bake molds" which might also fit here. The greatest concentration in this long listing is for either Jelly molds or Pudding (sweet or savoury) molds.

FANCY MOLDED FOOD

Each of the finely detailed nooks and crannies in food molds (stamped, or hand-beaten repoussé, or formed by piecing small shapes of copper or tin, or molded in ceramic) could be filled with a piece of food or a spoonful of differently-colored gelatin so that when turned out the surface of the fancy dish would be beautifully patterned. Little slices of carrots or lady fingers or olive slices or biscuits all had their places – usually after the entire mold was coated on the inside with clear jelly. Very contrived artifice, but in its way attractive – at least in chromolithographs of 19th century cookbooks. Molded puddings and blancmanges might be decorated with bits of fruit, and with a sauce or icing dribbled decoratively over the peaks like snow.

A Modern View of Artifice – Famous ex-patriot American cookbook author, French food expert, and artist Richard Olney (*Simple French Food*, 1974; *The French Menu Cookbook*, 1970) told his interviewer, William Rice, for an article in *The Washington Post*, Dec. 12, 1974, that "... to be appetizing as well as attractive, food should always look like food, and we may be grateful that the chilly bits of baroque architecture with sumptuously inlaid facades of jewel-cut truffle, egg-white, and pimiento mosaic belong largely to the past."

TYPICAL MOLDED FOODS & Why They Set Up in Shapes

Molds are not a necessary part of cooking. They are used to form food which will set up in one way or another, and hold its fancy shape when you turn it out (unmold it) and serve it. Molded foods are, literally, set pieces – that is, "an often brilliantly executed artistic work characterized by a formal pattern," as the *American Heritage Dictionary* defines the term.

Aspic is the word usually used for a meat or fish flavored jelled dish. It is made with something called "aspic jelly" which is gelatin, like any other, but savory, and cooked with onion and spices of choice and strained. It sets because of the gelatin. Sometimes aspic jelly was poured in a thin layer over some meat dishes, or was chilled and cut into fancy shapes to garnish a galantine dish.

Blancmange or Blanc Mange is a sort of pudding dessert – in some old books it may be classified as a pudding or a custard or an iced dessert. In a way it's all three. It sets up because of cooking milk and starch together with other ingredients. Starches included corn, rice, or arrowroot starch, or wheat flour. Some old recipes call for Irish Moss, which is Carrageen moss, a seaweed, from which a mucilaginous gummy substance can be extracted when it's cooked in water or milk. Carrageen is harvested today, and used widely in commercial foods. After being cooked in a saucepan or double boiler, a blancmange is poured into molds, chilled then turned out for saucing and serving.

Breads, cakes & muffins take shape because their ingredients include some form of starch, sometimes gluten, and liquid, and sometimes egg, and because they tend to expand during cooking. They will take the form of whatever they're baked in.

Custard sets up because of cooking egg and milk together, but it is usually eaten right out of custard cups or glasses, and is not turned out. Or it is cooked, then poured into puff paste, and baked. An exception would be custards such as flan which are turned out of the cup in order to pour on the caramelized sauce. • Mrs. A. P. Hill, in her *Receipt Book* of 1870 wrote about the difference between **puddings and custards**, "Puddings are baked without crusts and usually in deeper vessels; are generally served hot and eaten with sauces. Custards ... as a general thing, are baked in rich paste, and usually served cold."

Ice cream, Ices and other **frozen desserts** set up because they are frozen – more or less assisted by the particular combination of ingredients. A century ago ice cream was either made with a custard base or with a gelatin base – both of which aided the binding. Today we get ice cream with lots of "fillers" including natural and artificial gums.

Jellies – that is, jelled or gelatinized dishes, set up by the use of gelatin or isinglass (a gelatin made from the air bladders of certain fish). Jellies are either sweet and based on fruits, or a savoury aspic of fish, meat, or vegetables. "Jelly" is a basic, presumed to be neutral in flavor, so aspic jelly defines what has been done to the basic jelly. Fruit jellies used today for toast, set up mainly because of fruit pectin, found in apples, crabapples, and other fruits; some writers define this kind of jelly as strained jam.

Mousses set up because of the gelatin into which whipped cream and other puréed ingredients are whipped, and may be sweet dishes or savory. They are served chilled, and have a lot of air in them so they seem very light and fluffy. Soufflés are also whipped, but using a lot of egg whites.

Puddings set up because of the combination of ingredients cooked together, always some kind of starch (even as crumbled bread or crackers), and usually milk and egg. Rice flour, or pounded rice, is particularly sticky, as is oat flour. Puddings may be hot or cold, sweet or savory. See also Custards.

TURNING OUT A MOLD

In an 1838 copy of *The Magazine of Domestic Economy*, published in London, is this query and answer: "Sir, – Every housekeeper, however practical, must, if candid, admit many failures in practice; one of my greatest is, that my jelly, of which I have to make much, never turns well or tolerably from the mould; though it is filled from cold water, of white stone ware, of each figure, &c., yet it never takes any form. The jelly is as invariably stiff, clear, and good, but some witchery always spoils its appearance. Can you help? – We do not quite understand what our correspondent means; but we believe the sum of her complaint to be that her jelly does not turn out well from the mould.

"A jelly-mould may be made either of common tin, block tin, or of white earthen or stone ware. [Note no mention of copper!] If of one or other of the two first-mentioned materials, before the jelly is turned out, the outer surface of the mould should be rapidly wiped with a napkin dipped in hot water; if the mould is of earthenware, it should itself be dipped for an instant up to the edges in hot water. The jelly will then turn out well, provided it be well set, cold, and stiff."

Turn-out Two – "Take a pan or basin of hot water, of a temperature that you can only just bear your hand in. Dip the mould in, lift it out very quickly, and turn the shape out – this is with a tin or copper mould. An earthenware mould takes a little longer for the heat to get through." Katharine Mellish, *Cookery Book*, London & NY, 1901.

FOOD MOLD PARTS

The naming of parts of many collectible kitchen things is difficult, because sometimes manufacturers' terms are too technical or can't be understood intuitively, or because collectors and writers have used terms (which may or may not be accurate) for so long that they are understood widely.

The **parts of a food mold** (which itself is called a shape in England), in order of importance to the value, are the **top**, the part with the stamped design, which will be on top of the finished molded food; the **sides** or **base**, which is the deep part forming the walls of the mold, and which may or may not be stamped or hammered with its own designs or shapes; the **skirt**, which is a sort of shallow mirror image of the base, and which rims the top so that the mold may be set upside down while the food congeals or becomes firm; and, in some molds, a ring hanger; **feet** or similar levelling projections that perform the same function as the skirt, to make the mold stable while the food is setting (these are found almost always on fish molds); and lid. In the middle of some molds you may find a tube or a spout. The **tube** is capped, sealed or closed so that steam or spurts of liquid can't come out in the middle of the mold; a **spout** is open so that it can spout. Both kinds would allow heat or cold up into the center of the mold to more evenly gel, freeze, or bake the contents. Note that some redware spouted molds have evidence of being used with a cork to suit a particular use. As a mnemonic, visualize a closed mailing tube and an open coffee pot spout.

KINDS OF MOLDS

Blancmange molds. Usually, blancmange molds are geometric tin or copper molds, possibly indistinguishable from other food and jelly molds in these listings. Basically, these intricate, relatively thin-gauge metal molds were used in forming dishes which were not baked or cooked in them. The only time I've really labeled them "blancmange" molds is if the mold could be matched up to an old catalog or cookbook picture so labeled. Sometimes, not only can I not tell the fine differences between similar molds, I wouldn't try, because so many 19th C. molds were used for all kinds of food. They were also used for flummery, and the tall tiered architectural types were also called ice-cream pagodas or ice cream towers. Most are so tall that I can't imagine how they were served. Would you like to divide a tapering tower of frozen flummery into 12 precise portions before it all precipitously toppled? (Alliteration T. Agnew might have liked to try.)

Border or ring molds. These were oval or round, in various serving platter/plate sizes. Some were used to form a ring of cooked rice (which is sticky enough to take a molding) or mashed potatoes, or even some kinds of mashed or puréed vegetables like green peas. They were set around meat, or another kind and color of vegetable. Other ring molds were used for jellies or mousses or fancy ices.

Cake & bake molds. The main kind treated in this section are the fluted or turban head spouted or tubed ceramic molds, with a few tubed or spouted molds in other materials. For shapes such as lambs or rabbits see at the beginning of this chapter under Cake molds or cake pans. It's hard at this time to differentiate between pudding and cake molds of the same type. In Germany, many ornate stamped copper or tin molds that we are accustomed to think of as jelly molds are called bake molds. For Sponge Cake molds – see ceramic, tubed or spouted molds.

Individual molds. Most are for single servings of jellies, or little cakes of various kinds. Deeper ones are for either; the very shallow ones are meant to be used in quantities for making little shaped cakes or dessert elements like lady fingers, madelines, sponge cake – and often these little cakes were used to line the inside of much larger molds to create extravaganzas of dessert. You will note how each decorative element around the border of a pieced or stamped tin or copper geometric molds are exactly the size, say, of a lady finger.

Jelly molds. The most prized of these are 18th or early 19th century, elaborate pieced copper molds, well-tinned on the interior. Later ones are pieced or stamped tin, or stamped copper, or a combination of both metals in order to take advantage of copper's ability to take a finer-detailed design. Copper must be properly and completely tinned on the inside before use. Most of the metal molds have a simple rolled-edge 'skirt' or raised edge ringing the design in the top, so that the mold would stand steady (upside down) while the gelatine set. These skirts serve the double purpose of protecting the fancy designs in the tops. Architectural and geometric designs could be rested on their peaks or hills or other "high" spots, without needing a skirt. See also Cake and bake molds above.

There are also lovely ceramic jelly molds, which also have a skirt. They have several advantages for molded food – they take and hold a hot or a cold temperature, and their glaze helps in the unmolding process.

To ornament Jelly – "Jelly put into moulds should be particularly strong; a little stock from isinglass, mixed with the calf feet stock, will be of great use, when you intend to introduce fruit; fix your moulds in salt; then fill them half full of jelly; let it stand until set; place on it a large strawberry, just plucked, with the leaf and stalk on; fill up the mould with the jelly; you may also introduce in another mould cherries, and in another peaches, and so on; this, however, can only be done when fruit is in season; when it is not, wafer paper painted as such, or in landscapes, and laid upon the dish, and your shape of jelly turned upon it, have a very good effect." Joseph Bell, *A Treatise on Confectionary*, Newcastle, England, 1817. (Translation: Use extra strong gelatin when using fresh fruit (like now, the cautions against using fresh pineapple, as opposed to canned). Set the moulds down in a bed of salt – to stabilize, and to chill (think ice cream makers). When the first layer is set, put in the fruit – if nothing's in season, then fill the whole mould with the flavored gelatin, and paint fruit or a landscape (!) on a thin piece of paper, put it on the serving dish, and unmold the gelatin. If it's as clear as it's supposed to be, the painted fruit or landscape will show through the mound. Gadzooks!

Pudding molds. Most pudding molds were used either to bake a pudding, or to steam a pudding. This meant it had to take oven heat, or would have to be set down in a larger container with water, which would steam when hot. However, a good number of pudding molds were used the same way gelatin molds were used – the ingredients were mixed and cooked in a saucepan, then transferred to the pudding mold to be chilled and set. Tin and ceramic molds are most common. There are sweet dessert puddings (some served cold, some hot) as well as savoury puddings meant to be eaten with main courses, something like our "stove top stuffing." Many pudding molds have a spout (open) or tube (closed) in the center so that they could be cooked through and through at a more even rate. That kind of

IV-294. Dessert jelly ad. "Bro-Man-Gel-On," mfd. by Stern & Saalberg, NYC. Ladies' Home Journal, 11/1902.

open-center mold also works best for some cakes (think of angelfood cake or sponge cake). Some of the most desirable of all molds, and particularly of pudding molds, are late 18th, early to mid-19th century Pennsylvania German redware molds. One of the most spectacular ones I've ever seen was a huge (16" or 17" diam.) fluted mold that had been broken and repaired with metal staples and wire.

Vegetable or rice molds. Sometimes elaborate molds were used to mold cooked rice or puréed vegetables, not necessarily with anything added to make it take the molding. Presumably the dish was served hot. These were advertised in the 1870s, and were very architectural tin molds indistinguishable from blancmange or ice cream or jelly molds.

American Made Copper Molds. Practically at the last minute, after reading 60 years' worth of NYC directories on microfiche, I found an extremely important listing in *Trow's Directory* for 1866-67, which is confirmation of what seems logical – that some copper molds were made in America. The expanded listing in question is for Louis Ottenheimer, at 404 E. Houston, and 295 Second Street "near Union Market," NYC. It reads: "Ottenheimer Louis, tin, brass and copper works. Copper tea kettles, stew pans, sauce pans, confectioners' pans, the only manufacturer in this country of Copper Sponge Cake and Jelly Moulds; copper and brass urns for porterhouses, various styles; brass and copper drainers, copper funnels; tin, brass and copper measures."

Arrangement of listings. I have first divided the molds into the material they are made from – aluminum, cast iron, ceramic, copper, copper and tin, enamelware, glass, and tin. • Then I have tried to indicate what kind of mold each one is. I've listed the sort of generic "unknowns" or undifferentiated simply as molds, and they come first in each section. Motifs are often highlighted for your shopping convenience!

IV-293. Molded gelatin (jellied) dessert, made with Rich's "Tryphosa" brand jelly mix. They had great flavors, including mint & coffee & wine (like Madeira). Turn of the century booklet.

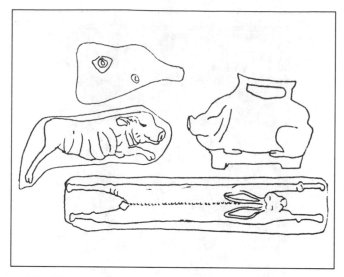

IV-295-B. *Outline drawings of animal molds in 295-A.*

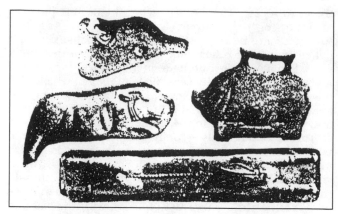

IV-295-A. Ancient animal-shaped molds. *Pictures not to scale vis a vis each other. These are old cast bronze reproductions of pastry & other molds found in excavations at Pompeii during 19th C. Two at (L) are a leg of ham, 13-1/2"L, & a whole dead pig, 20-1/2"L. At right is a pig with handle, only 7-7/8"L. At bottom is a horrible flayed hare, each detail of its poor backbone dotting the length of the mold. 26-1/2"L. All were made at Fonderie Artistiche Riunite, by J. Chiurazzi & Fils & s. De Angelis & Fils, Naples, Italy. From their catalog, 1910-11.*

ALUMINUM MOLDS:

Jelly mold, aluminum, stamped heart shape individual size, marked "Jell-O," American, 20th C. Stacked sets are more valuable than singles. Set:......... **$10+**

Jelly mold, stamped aluminum individual size cup with rolled rim, slightly flared sides, & large embossed block capital letter in bottom, mfd. by The Barnard Co., Boston, MA, 1/4-pint size (also came 12 to a quart), c.1910. Added value – A single one wouldn't be worth much, but a set of six or 12 or especially 26 would be nice. Value would be affected also by the particular initial, whether or not it suited you. Originally you could order whatever initial you wanted... **$7+**

Jelly molds, copper-toned stamped aluminum, set of 5, most with fluted or pleated or scalloped sides, all with wire ring hanger, in various shapes with rather mushy-formed "soft" stamped design, *viz.* pentagram with bunch of grapes, heart with 3 cherries & twig, square with pear [hey! a pome, if not a pomme], diamond with seahorse [huh? an inedible motif], & a triangle with a crab. "Add a unique touch of beauty to your kitchen with these smart, new ... molds ... & the charm of decorating with copper color will be only part of the fun. You'll love them just as much for those distinctive gelatin salads & desserts they mold so beautifully. They're specially formed to hold more of that fancy topping, too," reads the ad. West Bend Aluminum Co., West Bend, WI, c.1958. • These have a certain value for a study or nostalgia collection, & they add interesting sidelight to the decayed art of making fine food molds. But they won't ever really be the "antiques of the future" as they look so ... well, awful................ **$5+**

Jelly molds, set of 4 individual stamped aluminum, anodized copper on outside, patterns stamped on tops are acorn & oak leaves, daisy or sunburst, 4 leaf clover, thistle & leaves, maker not known, offered as premium by Knox Gelatine, 5 oz. size, 1972. These are rather like the ones in preceding listing, but maker is unknown. A set is also known that says "Jell-O." Value for either set: **$7**

Jelly molds, a set of 8 individual, stamped aluminum, fluted sides, for congealed salads or iced desserts or even Jell-O, American, 3-1/2" deep x 4" diam., 1930s or 40s. Came with two tall wire racks each holding four filled molds for the refrigerator. Two racks & 8 molds:... **$10**

BRASS MOLDS:

Jelly mold, frame with 10 wonderful stamped fat well-detailed fish in 2 rows, all facing same direction, brass & tin, probably for individual fish mousses, English or American, each fish 5"L x 2"W, overall dimension is 10-1/2" x 10", late 19th C........ **$125+**

CAST IRON MOLDS:

Generally, cast iron is for baking, but iron holds cold temperatures as well as hot, so it is also useful in making some candies & even jelled dishes, which must be "set." The downside is that cast iron molds would be much more difficult to heat just enough to unmold, unless it is quite thin.

Mold, cast iron, oval, "M. & H. Schrenkeisan," NYC, NY, about 2-1/2" deep x 7-1/2"L, late 19th C. ...... **$50+**

Mold, heavy thick cast iron, in bath tub shape without legs, probably candy – dealer thought it was a chocolate mold for cream eggs, cast on bottom is only "1 lb," American, late 19th C. .... **$25+**

Mold, heavy cast iron, amazing finny detail on curved fish, American, 2-3/8" deep x 12-13/16"L at widest, mid 19th C... **$175+**

CERAMIC MOLDS:

Mold, bake or pudding?, yellowware ceramic, oval with flat inside bottom, fluted sides, recessed inside foot, drippy brown Rockingham glaze outside, stamped clearly on bottom, advertising "L. B. Patterson Fire-Clay Ware Manufactory, Pottsville, PA," almost 4" deep x 9"L x 7"W, 19th C. .... **$165+**

Mold for blancmange, gray glazed pottery, very decorative molding with recipe for a blancmange pudding printed on side, advertising "Brown & Polsons Corn Flour," English, 7" x 5-1/2" x 5", c.1890s-1910. .... **$85+**

Mold, red stoneware not glazed on outside, pale yellow glaze inside, green around chipcarved edge, figural of baby (Baby Jesus) in swaddling clothes, face rather well detailed, bundling has pattern of flowers. Although this is a newborn baby (which seems like Christmas), the bread baked in it is for Easter, or perhaps Lent, at least in Germany. Several versions of the ceramic *Wickelkinder* (swaddled babies) are depicted in German books on old kitchenwares. One has curly hair, a fluted ruff, & the swaddling is criss-crossed with a ribbon tied with a bow. A stamped tin one shown in one book, which looks like a chocolate mold, & dates to the end of the 19th C. Southern Germany, 12"L x 5-1/2"W, c.1830s-40s. .... **$200+**

❖ NOTES ❖

"1825-26 Yule-Dough, or dow [sic], a kind of baby, or little image of paste, was formerly baked [in England] at Christmas, and presented by bakers to their customers, 'in the same manner as the chandlers gave Christmas candles.' They are called yule cakes in the county of Durham. Anciently, 'at Rome, on the vigil of the nativity, sweetmeats were presented to the fathers in the Vatican, and all kinds of little images (no doubt of paste) were to be found at the confectioners' shops.' My correspondent, Mr. Brand, who mentions these usages, thinks, 'there is the greatest probability that we have had from hence both our yule-doughs, plum-porridge, and mince-pies, the latter of which are still in common use at this season. The yule-dough has perhaps been intended for an image of the child Jesus, with the Virgin Mary,' he adds, 'it is now, if I mistake not, pretty generally laid aside, or at most retained only by children.'" William Hone, *The Every-Day Book*, Vol. I, n.d. [1825 or 1826]. Yorkshire bread doll. Lesley Gordon, *A Pageant of Dolls* (NYC: Wynn, 1949), says that in the Yorkshire district of England, a "bread doll" was made "as nearly as possible to look like a real baby, with fingers and toes marked on it and a small dab of dough for a nose; this doughy infant was lightly baked and dressed in real white babyclothes."

Mold, cauliflower design, cream colored earthenware, "Alcock," English, 8"L, last quarter 19th C...... **$75+**

Mold, pudding or bake?, brown glazed ceramic, celebrating the American Centennial, molded mark "1776-1876" inside, American, 1876. .... **$125+**

Mold, pudding or bake?, yellowware, ear of corn, American, 4-3/4"H x 8"L x 6"W, 19th C. .... **$75+**

IV-296. Ceramic molds. A page from S. Joseph catalog, c.1927. These are fairly heavy creamware or stoneware, well-glazed; star, turtle, lobster, corn, fish & melon all came in more than one size. The turtle mold would be most valuable: **$100-$125**; the rest: **$75-$100**

IV-297. Cornucopia or Horn of Plenty molds. For various foods. All are hinged. *(T-L)* shows a dessert, decorated with a molded cornucopia, from Urbain Dubois' La Patisserie. *(T-R)* Simple mold at top, made in 4 sizes, from 5-1/2" to 10-1/4"L, Duparquet, Huot & Moneuse, c.1904-10. *(B-L)* Decorated one at bottom is copper, 6-3/4"L, & imported (from Germany?), also D, H & M. *(B-R)* With gadrooning & braced curly tail is "French Horn of Plenty," 10-1/2"L with 7" opening, for ice cream. S. Joseph. **$65-$125**

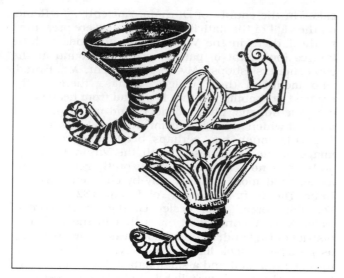

IV-298. More cornucopias, *a popular form because it symbolizes bounteous harvests, plenty, prosperity. Ribbed one upper* **(T-L)**, *6-3/4"L.* **(B-R)** *with flower horn is much larger, about 10-3/4"L.* **(T-R)** *Small one was made in 4 sizes, from 4-3/4" to 11"L. All Bertuch, c.1904.* **$65-$125**

❖ RECIPE ❖

Corn Meal Pudding, No. 1 *– One pint of sifted meal, one tumbler [6-8 oz.] of good molasses, one pint of sweet milk [ie. not buttermilk], a quarter of a pound of butter, grated lemon peel or powdered mace to flavor it. Boil the milk; while hot, pour it upon the meal, and mix well. Warm the butter. Stir to the molasses half a teaspoonful of [baking] soda. Beat the eggs separately; add the eggs when the mush is cold. Mix all well. Bake in a buttered dish. Eat with a rich liquid sauce."* Mrs. A. P. Hill, *Receipt Book, NYC, 1870.*

Mold, corn design, ironstone, American or English, 10"L, 19th C. **$75**

Mold, corn design, cream earthenware, English, 6"L, late 19th C. .... **$60+**

Mold, custard or pudding using milk?, ironstone, large size oval, fluted base, rare image: cow with man milking her, English, 19th C. **$300**

Mold, so-called crown mold because of very deep molding (just as deep, wide molding along the ceiling is called crown molding), cream glazed ceramic, English, 3-3/4"H x 5-3/4"L x 4-1/4"W, mid 19th C. .... **$70+**

Mold, fish for a Lenten dish?, brown glazed redware, an unidentifiable, slightly curved, scaly fish with pleasant smile & pronounced double caudal or tail fin, no other fins, very primitive, somewhat lumpy ungraceful form, PA German, 11-5/8"L x 4-1/2"W, 19th C. .... **$300+**

Mold, redware fish, slightly curved with bifurcated short tail, no fins, large exaggerated scales & smiling expression, Pennsylvania, 19th C. .... **$300+**

❖ NOTES ❖

No More Breaks – "To prevent Glass, Earthen, Potter's and Iron[stone] Ware from being easily broken ... put dishes, tumblers, and other glass articles into a kettle; cover them entirely with cold water, and put the kettle where it will soon boil. When it has boiled for a few minutes, set it aside, covered close. When the water is cold, take out the glass. Treat new earthen ware the same way. When potter's ware is boiled, a handful or two of bran should be thrown into the water, and the glazing will never be injured by acids or salts." Mrs. Cornelius, *The Young Housekeepers Friend or, A Guide to Domestic Economy & Comfort,* NY or Boston, 1846.

Mold, rabbit design, earthenware, "Meakin," English, mid 19th C. .... **$85+**

Mold, redware glazed inside with dark brown, lots of detail, rooster with squirrel-scroll tail, small feet underneath hold it steady, American, rooster is 11-1/2"H x 11"W, mid 19th C. • Ex-Jacqueline Hodgson Collection. .... **$800+**

Mold, glazed pottery, oval with flutes inside & scalloped rim, design is a tall footed urn, 4 feet on mold formed as flower petals, English, only 2"H x 6-1/4"W x 5-1/4"W, early 19th C. **$75**

Mold, brown glazed pottery, slightly oval, fluted sides, very detailed swan, high tipped up tail, with reeds, English (?), about 7"L x 6"W x 3" deep, late 19th C. .... **$125+**

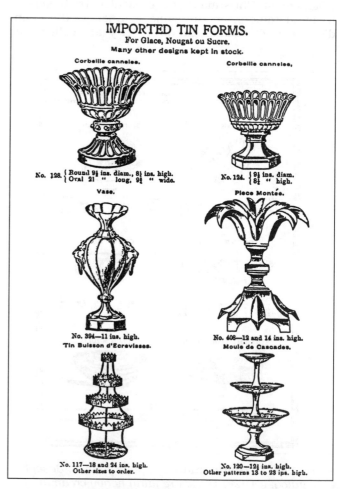

IV-299. Molds for glacé, nougat, etc. *Tall urn & fountain "forms" for a variety of fancy desserts. Page from Duparquet, Huot & Moneuse, c.1904-10.* **$200-$350**

Mold, jelly or aspic, armadillo design, white vitreous earthenware, "Shelley," Longton, England, c.1922. ... **$200+**
Mold, jelly or aspic, white ceramic, asparagus bunch, Minton #41/6, English, mid 19th C. .... **$125+**
Mold, jelly or aspic, saltglazed stoneware, basket of flowers, German, 20th C. .... **$45+**
Mold, jelly or aspic, white glazed ceramic elephant, white body clay, English, 2" deep x 6-1/2" x 4-3/4", mid 19th C. .... **$225+**
Mold, jelly or aspic, buff glazed heavy ceramic, deep molded bunch of grapes in top, American, 3 3/4"H x 8"L x 7"W, mid 19th C. .... **$75+**
Mold, jelly or aspic, ceramic, grape cluster, brown ringed earthenware, English, 7"L, 19th C. .... **$75+**
Mold, jelly or aspic, lobster, oval, earthenware, German, 19th C. .... **$95+**
Mold, jelly or aspic, ceramic, glazed stoneware, rectangular, fun design made up of concentric borders of round tennis balls with crossed tennis rackets on top, "Copeland," English, c.1890s-1910. ...... **$250+**

❖ NOTES ❖

CERAMIC MOLDS – SPOUTED or TUBED – user's choice. I use the term "tubed" to mean a closed or capped tube, because I have several times seen such redware molds with an old cork stuck in the end of the tube. It was deemed useful to use one mold for different baking jobs – one requiring a closed tube, the other a spout. A mold set down in water for steaming might be corked or have a closed tube, so that water wouldn't percolate up and splish-splash on the food. A mold used in the oven to bake a cake allows the heat to rise up in spout and cook from the center out as well as the outside in. Tube is closed; spout is open.

Cake mold, also called a sponge cake mold, brown glazed earthenware, fluted, spouted, with side handle, American, prob. PA or Shenandoah Valley of VA or WV, 3-1/8"H x 9-1/2" diam., 19th C. Any piece with clear provenance from a known potter would be worth much more than an anonymous piece like this. .... **$125+**

IV-300. Biscuit, creme or jelly mold. *Stamped copper lion, tinned inside, oval, 7-1/4"L. Bertuch, Berlin, c.1904.* **$300+**

❖ NOTES ❖

Sponge Cake – A. H. Rice and John Baer Stoudt, in *The Shenandoah Pottery*, first published in Strasburg, VA, by The Shenandoah Publishing Co. in 1929, and reprinted in Berryville, VA in 1974, call this kind of glazed earthenware spiral fluted spouted mold a "Spiral sponge cake mould," in their catalog of Alvin Rice's huge personal collection.

• •

The meaning of sponge cake may differ from region to region, and from period to period, because while I can find Pennsylvania German (closely related to Shenandoah Virginian) recipes for sponge cake, they are all to be baked in square or oblong loaf pans. It is angel food cake which calls for the spout. And in one book, something called "Glory Cake," which is like angel food cake except that the yolks are used also, separated from the stiffly beaten whites. This cookbook is Ruth Hutchison's *The New Pennsylvania Dutch Cook Book*, NY: Harper & Bros., 1958. It was originally published in 1948.

Pudding or kugelhopf mold, pottery with medium brown glaze, wheel thrown, fluted & spouted afterward, spout is corked with obviously contemporaneous cork, American, 3-3/4"H x 7-1/2" diam., 19th C. .... **$125+**
Pudding mold, ceramic, glazed & handpainted, apple design in relief, fluted sides, spouted, American (?), only 3-3/4" x 4-3/4", 20th C. .... **$35+**
Pudding mold, redware with unusual black glaze, Turk's head design, spouted, widely-canted sides, American, 11" diam., 19th C. .... **$150+**
Pudding mold, earthenware, spouted, has handle which made it easy to handle when very hot, American, 9-1/2" diam., mid 19th C. .... **$125+**

❖ RECIPE ❖

Brown Betty Pudding – *Take a cup of grated bread crumbs, 2 cups fine-chopped tart apples, 1/2 cup brown sugar, teaspoon cinnamon, one tablespoon butter, cut into bits. Butter a deep pudding dish, and put a layer of apples on bottom; then sprinkle with sugar, cinnamon, and butter and cover with bread crumbs. Put in another layer of apples, and proceed as before until ingredients have been used, having a crumb layer last. Cover the dish and bake for 3/4 hour in moderate oven, then remove the cover and brown the top. Serve with sugar and cream."* Maria Parloa, Kitchen Companion, *Boston: Estes & Lauriat, 1887.*

Pudding or cake mold, glazed earthenware, a mottled brown finish, conical spout, large swirled flutes, stamped "John Bell," Waynesboro, PA, 4"H x 10" diam., c.1860s-70s. The earthenware & stoneware made by John Bell & his brother Samuel Bell is possibly, taken as a whole, the most desirable pottery in the history of America. John Bell's figural pieces, dogs, & especially lions, bring many many thousands of dollars the rare occasions they come to auction. Most Bell pieces are safely (alack alas but also fortunately) in museums or private collections. ...... **$500+**

Pudding or cake mold, Turk's head with spout, cream-ware, American, 9" diam., 19th C. .... **$90+**

COPPER MOLDS:

Mold, copper, round with 2 handles, 9 shaped cups, very Oriental in feel, a fish, shell, leaf, melon, etc., sold as "French" but a new one bought in China was shown me recently, 12-1/4" diam., dealer said c.1760; I think prob. late 19th C. to recent times. • The dealer's price of $1,400 was based on belief it was "18th C. European." Value range is based on my belief it is much newer than dealer said. .... **$85+**

Mold, confection or candy?, heavy copper, tinned inside, well-defined thistle design, only mark is "194," 1" deep x 2-1/8" diam., late 19th C. .... **$10+**

Mold, blancmange, relatively thin pieced copper with tinned interior, 8 sided, very architectural, English (?), only 6"H, late 19th C. .... **$200+**

Mold, jelly or blancmange, 3 tiers, very architectural, copper, tinned inside, stamped "N & G 529," 4"H x 4" diam., late 19th C. • Dealer William Davis said that manufacturers used some very fine contemporary designers to design the molds, & that they also used architects. He said he had one mold that looks like the top of the Chrysler Building in NYC! .... **$165+**

Border or ring mold, copper, stamped, tinned inside, rustic & exaggerated twiggy bird's nest design, English, 6-1/2" diam., late 19th C. .... **$300+**

Border mold, copper, heavily tinned inside, geometric oval, makes an oval food "frame" for other food – say rice around peas on a platter. 7"L, late 19th C. Note that not all border molds were oval, although plat-ters are oval. Many were round & were used on a big plate. **$110**

Jelly mold, pieced & stamped copper, tinned inside, architectural, each tier soldered together, tall "chef's hat" effect, 6-lobed top with swagged sides or base, marked only with stamped number 38, probably an inventory number, English, 8-1/2"H, c.1860. Inven-tory numbers were either scratched on the mold, or were stamped using different combinations of single digit stamps, made of iron & looking like a nailset or punch except that a small backwards number is on the tip. .... **$700+**

Jelly mold, stamped or beaten into form, architectural, each of 4 tiers pieced & soldered together, copper, tinned inside, tall & with a sort of scalloped Jell-O mold look on top, marked "206 C," English, 8"H x 6-1/2" diam., c.1860. .... **$375+**

Mold, blancmange mold, heavy pieced copper with tin lining, 6 columnar pieces form structure, 15"H, 1850s to 1870s. .... **$300+**

Jelly or blancmange mold, copper, 3 tiered, the 2nd tier is fat columns into which lady fingers would fit nicely, top tier of fat turban twists, stamped with numeral "1," also initials of owner, "J. A. C.," English, 9"H x 8" diam., c.1860s. .... **$500+**

Jelly mold, pieced copper, heavily tinned, hanging ring, corn design stamped in bottom (what becomes top of food), English, 8"L oval, late 19th C. .... **$85+**

Jelly mold, copper with heavily tinned inside, fluted sides, cornucopia in top, oval, 1-1/2" deep x 4-1/2"L x 3-1/2"W, late 19th C. .... **$65+**

Jelly mold, copper, tinned inside, crown-like with chain link effect on top, 5 lobes to sides, stamped "M 443," no other mark, English, 5-1/2"H x 5" diam., c.1860. .... **$300+**

Jelly mold, copper, tinned inside, shallow oval mold in 3 tiers, diamonds on top, marked "Moulton Paddocks" & with initials "E. C.," possibly the owner's initials, English, 2"H x 6-1/2"L, mid 19th C. .... **$115+**

Jelly mold, fish, copper, tinned inside, 3-1/2"L, late 19th C. .... **$55+**

Jelly mold, fish, stamped copper, tinned inside, "Kreamer," Brooklyn, NY, early 20th C. .... **$50+**

Jelly mold, copper with dovetail seams, scroll-petaled flower on top, round edges, slightly dented, stamped in mold, at least the top, marked only with #15, English, 6-1/2"H, mid 19th C. .... **$165+**

Jelly mold, pieced & seamed copper, tinned inside, braided border & 8 tall fluted risers, unpolished old patina, only mark is "435," stamped in so it's either maker's mark or inventory mark from large kitchen, English, 6"H x 5-1/2" diam., c.1840s to 1860s. .... **$250+**

Jelly mold, copper, tinned inside, oval ring, gothic arches, stamped with the #198 & a maltese cross & orb, sign of a Birmingham works, English, 2-3/4"H x 6"W oval, c.1870s to 1890s. Birmingham, England was a great copper mold manufacturing center from about 1840 to about 1910, according to mold dealer William Davis, of Wilmington, DE. Traditionally, Bir-mingham has been known for several centuries for brass working. .... **$250+**

Jelly mold, copper, tinned inside, oval, makes hearts at the top of columns, pieced, with dovetailed seam, no mark, English, 6"W oval, c.1870s to 1880s. ..... **$250+**

Jelly mold, copper, pieced & stamped, dovetail seam, tinned inside, high base or sides shaped like a fez, couchant lion on top, looking up, simple skirt, no discernible mark, English (?), 4-3/4"H exclusive of low lion, 7"L, c.1850s. .... **$600+**

Jelly mold, copper, tinned inside, rose design stamped in top, 7"L x 5"W, late 19th C. .... **$65+**

Jelly mold, seashell design, copper, tinned inside, 3-1/2"L, late 19th C. Could also be for a madeline. .... **$35+**

Jelly mold, starflowers, copper, tinned inside, individ-ual size, 3-3/4" diam., late 19th C. .... **$45+**

Jelly mold, copper, simple design, besides the makers' mark, another mark is an 8-point star. The numbers "11/11" are also scratched in, probably a personal inventory number, perhaps meaning this mold was number eleven out of a set of eleven, other marks are a stamped Maltese cross & orb, & "#458," Bir-mingham, England, 4"H, mid 19th C. .... **$165+**

❖ NOTES ❖

Marks on Molds – Quoting dealer William Davis, of Wilmington, DE, the molds were marked because "they were very expensive when they were new. I have one with the coat of arms of the Duke of Bedford, one with those of the Earl of Selburne; these molds were marked and had inventory numbers too. Very frequently on the Birmingham ones, you'll find a star stamped in the side. This was a craftsman's signature, but I've not been able to identify the maker." He showed me another signature comprised of a cluster of 4 periods, a half moon, and a tiny 8-pointed star.

Aspic Jelly – *Aspic jelly is largely used in cold entrées such as boned chicken or turkey, game, vegetables or fish, the material being molded in the jelly. This means that the aspic must be brilliantly clear and of firm consistence. It also presupposes a foundation of strong stock made of veal or lean beef according as the finished jelly is to be of a light or dark color. For one quart of good strong stock allow one box of granulated gelatine, two tablespoonsful of strained lemon juice, the whites of three eggs, one scant cupful of white wine, a bay leaf, two cloves, one dozen peppercorns, two sprigs of parsley, a sprig of thyme and one-quarter of a cupful each of chopped onion, celery and carrot. "Put three-quarters of the cupful of wine, the seasonings and chopped vegetables into a saucepan, cover and simmer for ten minutes, then strain. Soak the gelatine in one cupful of the stock; when soft and swollen put into an agate [graniteware] saucepan with the lemon juice and the remainder of the stock, heat slowly; when warm season to taste with salt and cayenne. Whip the whites of the eggs to a soft froth, dilute with the liquid strained from the vegetables, add to the soup and bring rapidly to the boiling point, stirring constantly. Now put aside the spoon, let boil very gently for three minutes, draw to the side of the fire and let stand untouched for twenty minutes. Strain through doubled cheesecloth wrung out in cold water, being careful not to squeeze or the jelly will be clouded. Add the reserved wine and it is ready to use." – That is, to gently stir in the bits of meat or vegetables, to put into a mold, and chill until gelatinized firmly. Cornelia C. Bedford, "Housekeepers Inquiries," Table Talk, Philadelphia, January 1903.*

Pudding mold, so-called beehive type, copper, with brass screw-on base, ring handle on snug lid, concentric lines inside are tinning lines, according to dealer William Davis, no mark, 5-1/4"H x 4-1/2" diam., 1840s to 1860s (?). • I asked Delaware dealer William Davis about the tinning, and he said that in some instances the makers "began with tinned sheet copper; in others they were dipped. Frequently you'll find them tinned both inside & out. I had an eagle mold, the exterior was originally tinned but in the cleaning I had it removed – much more attractive." If all jelly or pudding molds had been tinned outside, I'd take the same purist stance on removing tinning that I do on "brassifying" ice cream dishers, which were tinned for health reasons. The molds did not have to be tinned on the outside, & if the housekeeper was willing to devote the time to polish them, because of their beauty, fine. .... **$225+**

Pudding mold, beehive mold, large rounded copper bowl on disproportionately tiny pedestal foot of tooled brass that screws on so it can stand upright, snug-fitting lid with ring handle, marked only #6, English, 6-1/2"H, mid 19th C. • One similar to this had a bayonet fastening for the lid. .... **$165+**

Pudding mold, beehive type, copper, with small cast brass pedestal screw-on base, brass ring handle on snug-fitting copper lid, tinned inside, looks like a lifesize upside down artichoke, marked "F. W. & Co. #1100," English, about 7"H overall, late 19th C............. **$165+**

Pudding mold, copper, cylinder with slightly slanted shape, bayonet mounted lid with bracket strap handle, tinned inside, marked only with the Birmingham orb & Maltese cross, & "#195," English, 5-3/8"H exclusive of strap handle x 5-1/2" diam., 1840s to 1860s (?). **$225**

Pudding mold, copper, tinned inside, hanging ring, marked "Christian Wagner," German, 11" diam., c.1890s-1910. .... **$125+**

COPPER MOLDS – TUBED or SPOUTED:

Kugelhopf or gugelhupf mold, spouted (with a little cruciform opening in the spout, instead of being fully open with rolled rim), stamped copper with tinned interior, German, 4" deep x 10" diam., late 19th C. • Kugel or gugel is the German word for ball (the same word is used for glass Christmas balls); the hopf or hupf is harder to figure out – it means to hop. A funny story mold collectors tell is that kugel is actually kugl, the hood of a Capuchin monk, who made a cake shaped like his hood and it was sooooo gloriously good that he danced with joy! This kind of mold is surmounted by a ring of balls or round shapes, with successive layers less round. This one is a traditional kugelhopf mold, the word is used also for many different spouted or tubed stamped copper molds, even ones with grapes or flutes or swirls. One distinction might be made – the center may be tubed or spouted, but the diam. of the center part is relatively wide compared to angelfood cake pans. • **Older kugelhopfen.** Older molds from the late 18th or early 19th C. are simpler, smaller (about 7" or 8" diam.), the ball or flute or other motif is partly hammered, partly pieced, & the molds have brazed seams. .... **$150+**

Mold, copper, tinned inside, flared sides, tubed turk's head, poss. American, prob. European, 11" diam., mid to late 19th C. .... **$135+**

❖ NOTES ❖

To ornament a Spunge Cake, as a Turban. Provide a copper mould in this shape, and bake a spunge [sic] cake neatly in it; when cold, ornament it with some handsome borders on the foldings, cutting off the bottom part of the border to make them represent rich lace; then fix one or two feathers on the side, which will give it a neat effect." Joseph Bell, *A Treatise on Confectionary*, Newcastle, England, 1817.

Mold, spouted, copper, tinned inside, stamped turban-like pattern makes it look like a Bundt pan, small metal ring for hanging, no mark, German, English or American, 5"H x 10-1/2" diam., late 19th C. • Aspics, & what were called "jellies" & other congealed or jellied foods were made in such molds. .... **$175+**

Mold, spouted, copper, very simple fluted design, no marks at all, 10-1/2" diam., mid 19th C......... **$145**

Mold, spouted, with 6 fluted cap-topped towers, heavy pieced copper, tinned inside, English, 5"H, c.1830s to 1850s (?). • For collectors, the apparent aristocrats of copper molds are the architectural ones, the more sky-reaching & cloud-breaking the more fun, but actually these are later than the highly prized molds from early Victorian times. Extreme gothic aspirations, & thin gauge copper, date English molds to the 1880s or 1890s. .... **$225+**

Mold, heavy copper, pieced & hammered, spouted, Masonic (?) hammer mark & a "5S" over a "C," American (?), 19th C. .... **$250+**

Mold, heavy gauge copper, tinned inside, tubed oval, fluted sides, top has turk's head effect, looks as if it has been wire brushed which lowers its value, marked "LAGRE 448 M. TEBE. DE," Belgian or French?, 11" **$300**

COPPER & TIN MOLDS:

Jelly mold, copper & tin, ear of corn deeply embossed on copper top, tin sides & skirt, American (?), 5-1/4"L, 19th C. **$110**

Jelly mold, copper, tin skirt, corn design, oval 4" deep x 4"W x 6-1/2"L, 19th C. **$125**

Jelly mold, tin sides & skirt, deeply repoussé copper top, grape bunch, 5-1/2"L, late 19th C. **$85**

Jelly mold, pieced & stamped tin, copper top, oval, "picket" flutes around sides, seamed at each end, top is very high profile stamped copper lion couchant but looking over left shoulder (couchant sinistral? as opposed to couchant dextral) with distinctly bewildered expression, this lion polychromed in old paint, metallic gold, shades of deep yellow, black, with red inside mouth & red border, very unusual & attractive, English, 5"H x 7-1/4"L, mid (?) 19th C. • The paint, which I believe is period & original, accounts for about half the probable market value. .... **$600+**

Jelly mold, copper & tin, lion design, deep tin sides, shallow tin skirt, English, 7"L, 19th C. .... **$225+**

Jelly mold, tin skirt to support mold upside down while gelatin setting, tinned copper oval mold with slightly slanted sides, fairly common pineapple design, English or poss. American, 6-1/2"L x 5"W x 5" diam., late 19th C. or early 20th. .... **$75+**

Jelly mold, copper with tin sides & tin skirt, rose design, 4" deep x 4"W x 6-1/2"L, 19th C. ..... **$125+**

Jelly mold, shallow tin skirt with tin plated copper mold, thistle pattern, almost as common as the pineapple, 8-1/2"L, English, 19th C. **$110**

Jelly mold, tin with tinned copper mold part, wheat sheaf & sickle, prob. American, 19th C. • Motif adds value. .... **$125+**

ENAMELWARE MOLDS:

Mold, enamelware, fluted gray graniteware, American (?), 2-1/2" deep x 7" diam., late 19th C. **$65**

Pudding mold, dark brown & white mottled enamelware, European, 2"H x 12-1/2" diam., c.1890s-1910. .... **$50+**

Pudding or cake mold, gray & cobalt blue agate enamelware, slope sided, possibly Columbian Enameling & Stamping Co.'s "Dresden," Terre Haute, IN (?), 11" diam., late 19th C. or very early 20th. .... **$125+**

Pudding mold, gray graniteware, a melon mold with plain tin close-fitting flat lid, 7"L, 19th C. Very attractive, & much less common than the all tin melon mold. **$155**

Pudding mold, melon type, gray graniteware, flat tin lid, "L & G Mfg. Co. No. 60, Extra Agate," mfd. by Lalance & Grosjean, Woodhaven, NY, late 19th C. • An 1898 ad reads: "Cooking Utensils are Safe is stamped with trademark ["AGATE" nickel steel ware]. Because to each article is attached chemist's certificates [a blue label], guaranteeing that it is free from arsenic, antimony, lead or any other poisonous ingredient." .... **$165+**

Pudding mold, cobalt enamelware, melon type with flat tin lid, last quarter (?) 19th C. .... **$175+**

ENAMELWARE MOLDS – SPOUTED OR TUBED:

Cake mold, angel food cake, octagonal blue & white swirled enamelware, with spout, no mark, American or European, c.1890s-1910. .... **$150+**

Cake mold, angel food cake, pale aqua & white enamelware, spouted, American (?), 9" diam., early 20th C. .... **$125+**

Cake mold, octagonal, cobalt enamelware, spouted, American (?), c.1890s-1910. .... **$150+**

Pudding mold, gray graniteware, spouted Turk's head, American (?), 19th C. .... **$90+**

Mold, gray graniteware, spouted Turk's head, only 6-1/2" diam., late 19th C. .... **$45+**

GLASS MOLD:

Jelly mold, pressed glass, for gelatin dish, oval, clear glass, paneled sides, English, 3-1/2"H x 7"L x 4"W, late 19th C. (See also Butter molds; and an Ice cream mold.) **$100**

TIN MOLDS:

Tin jelly molds are most common. Mass-produced of stamped & pieced tin, usually oval, with a fluted base or side wall, most have a simple rolled-edge raised edge ringing the top design. There are a variety of well-defined, deeply-stamped designs that include flowers, fruits, vegetables & animals, as well as geometrics. They were imported in great numbers in the 1870s, '80s, and '90s from France, Germany or other countries, in various sizes holding 1/2, 1, and 1-1/2 pints, 2 pints, and 2 quarts. These are usually found rather darkened, & with very little bright tinning showing. Similar, but more expensive (originally and now) molds are made all of tin except for the top where the decorative motif is stamped; some of these are made of copper, which took a deeper & more detailed stamp, & would avoid any tendency to rust in the creases or soldered joints. They were also more decorative, although more work for the housewife. See also Copper & tin molds.

Bake mold, for little gems or cookies, 12 heart-shaped cups made of rolled-edged strips of tin, each cup separate and riveted to blued steel flat sheet iron, no handle, prob. American, 13-1/2"L x 6-1/4"W, each heart 2-1/2"L, late 19th C.............................. **$45+**

✤ RECIPE ✤

Royal Hearts – *1 lb. Valentia almonds, 1 lb. 8 oz. beat sugar, 8 oz. flour, 10 eggs and 6 yolks. Beat the almonds fine with yolk of egg; then add the sugar; mix it well with a spatter; keep adding one egg at a time; when beat well up, mix in your flour gently; set tin rims in the shape of hearts, neatly buttered, on paper placed on an iron sheet; fill the rims three parts full, and bake them in a slow oven." Joseph Bell, A Treatise on Confectionary, Newcastle, England, 1817. • A* **spatter** *is a stirring implement described by Bell as "made of ash or elm, resembling a large wood spoon, only flat on each side." Ibid. Undoubtedly the same wooden tool is the Scottish spurtle – See the Mixing chapter.*

✤ RECIPE ✤

Queen or Heart Cakes – *One pound of sifted Sugar, one pound of Butter, eight Eggs, one pound and a quarter of Flour, two ounces of Currants, and half a Nutmeg grated. Cream the butter as in 'Twelfth Cake' [Put the Butter into a stewpan, in a warm place, and work it into a smooth cream with the hand"], and mix it well with the sugar and spice, then put in half the eggs, and beat it ten minutes – add the remainder of the eggs, and work it ten minutes longer, – stir in the flour lightly, and the currants afterwards, – then take small tin pans of any shape (hearts the most usual,) rub the inside of each with butter, fill and bake them a few minutes in a hot oven, on a sheet of matted wire, or on a baking plate, – when done, remove them as early as possible from the pans." William Kitchiner, The Cook's Oracle, London, 1827. By the way, "Queen or Heart Cakes" is correct, although a card-player might suspect the "or" should be "of."*

Bake mold, looks like some kind of muffin mold, heavy tin, oblong shape, 6 "V" troughs side by side, triangular in section, for making "Waldorf Triangles," or "Golden Rod Cake," or "Orange Slice Cake" and many other fancy cakes, not marked (one company making them was Jaburg Brothers, NYC), about 13-1/2"L x 3-1/2"W, late 1890s to c.1920s. This size baked six one-penny sticks; another with only three "V" troughs make 10¢ size "Golden Rods.".......................... **$35+**

Blancmange molds, a pair, tin, deep scalloped base with octagonal "lighthouse" structure atop, tightly fitted lids on bottom, poss. English or French import, poss. American, 11-1/2"H x 5" diam. at base, c.1870s. Pair:.................................... **$175+**

Blancmange mold, high tin structure consisting of very pointed central pinnacle surrounded by 2 tiers of lower pointed peaks, European or American, 11"H, c.1870s.. **$140+**

Blancmange or ice cream mold, pieced tin, straight sides with rolled edge, clumsy but charming corrugated cup in center with 6 small very pointed cones, one in each of the 6 large scalloped compartments around the center, American, 19th C........... **$125+**

✤ RECIPE ✤

Ground Rice Flummery – *boil 1 quart milk, except that portion which you have reserved to wet a heaping teacup of rice. Stir this in when the milk boils up; put in 1 teaspoon of salt. When it has thickened, stir in a table spoonful or two of dry ground rice, let it boil up again all around, and take it off the fire as soon as you think the dry rice has become scalded. Have ready a bowl or blancmange mould, wet with a spoonful of milk or cold water, into which pour it. If it is of the right consistency, it will turn out after 15 or 20 minutes in good shape. Eat with sugar and milk or cream. For this and all similar milk preparations, peach leaves are better than any spice [to add an almondy flavor]. Boil in the milk 1/2 dozen fresh leaves from the tree. Remember to take them out before you stir in the rice." Mary Hooker Cornelius,* The Young Housekeepers Friend, *Boston, 1846. • Note: Some flummery recipes use gelatin, but their distinguishing ingredient is almost always rice meal or flour. Katharine Mellish's cookbook (Cookery and Domestic Management. Including Economic and Middle Class Practical Cookery.* London & NY, *1901) contains a recipe for "Corn Blancmange."*

✤ RECIPE ✤

Almond Charlotte – *Blanch and chop fine one large cupful of almonds. Melt three tablespoonsfuls of sugar in a frying pan – do not add any water – throw in the almonds and stir until browned, then turn out to cool and pound them quite fine. Put them in a double boiler with one cupful and a half of milk and heat slowly to the scalding point. Beat together three egg yolks and two-thirds of a cupful of sugar, add some of the hot milk, mix and turn into the [double] boiler, stirring until the mixture begins to thicken. Add one-half of a box of gelatine which has been soaked in one-half of a cupful of cold water and stir until it is dissolved; take from the fire, strain and set aside until beginning to cool and thicken. Add one pint of thick cream whipped to a solid froth, stir lightly until mixed, then turn into a fancy serving dish or into individual molds." Cornelia C. Bedford, "Housekeepers Inquiries,"* Table Talk, *Philadelphia, January 1903.*

✤ RECIPE ✤

Charlotte Russe – *Whip one quart rich cream to a stiff froth, and drain well on a nice sieve. To one scant pint of milk add six eggs beaten very lightly; make very sweet; flavor high with vanilla. Cook over hot water [ie. in a double boiler or bain marie] till it is a thick custard. Soak one full ounce Cox's* *gelatine in a very little water. When the custard is very cold, beat in lightly the gelatine in a very little water. When the custard is very cold, beat in lightly the gelatine and the whipped cream. Line the bottom of your mold with buttered paper, the sides with sponge-cake or lady-fingers fastened together with the white of an egg. Fill with the cream; put in a cold place, or in summer on ice. To turn out, dip the mould for a moment in hot water. In draining the whipped cream, all that drips through can be re-whipped." Miss Neill, in Gertrude Strohm's The Every-day Cook-Book, 1888.*

Cake mold, hearts, 3 on long oblong tray, tin, Ekco #52, American, 29"L overall, each pan 9"H x 8"W, 20th C. .... **$35+**

Charlotte Russe mold, small, stamped & pieced polished tin, bottom has small disc-like flat foot, rest of bottom is fluted, not actually distinguishable from jelly molds or blancmange molds, & often in old catalogs you will see the same linecut used on different pages, to depict different items! These came in small individual sizes & in larger sizes more suitable to the recipe given above. French, English or American, 3-1/2" deep x 3" diam., late 19th C. .... **$5-$15+**

French pie mold, or pâte mold, also called a confectioner's mold, round, stamped tin, hinged opposite the clamp, French, came in several sizes through the F. A. Walker catalog: 7", 9", 10", & 12" diam., 1870s. • Some of these had fluted sides, some were stamped with fruit & vine designs or other designs. The ring was in 2 parts so the sometimes concave designs on the sides could be released; rings were either hinged & pinned, or pinned in 2 places. .... **$40+**

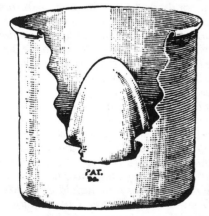

PATENT CHARLOTTE-RUSSE PANS.

Advantage over old style.

No paper cups are needed, no sponge cake sheets to be baked, no cutting nor trimming, no leakage, no waste, no lining of paper cups. No laying out with lady fingers. Simply fill the pans with sponge cake mixture, when baked remove them from the pans, and fill them with whipped cream. The cake itself forms a regular cup with large hole in centre to receive the cream, these pans will pay for themselves in a very short time, 15 cents each, $1.50 per dozen.

IV-301. Charlotte Russe pan, or mold. Stamped metal, probably heavily-tinned. Pat'd. 1896. From H. Hueg's The Little Confectioner, c.1900, but made for several decades after. $15+

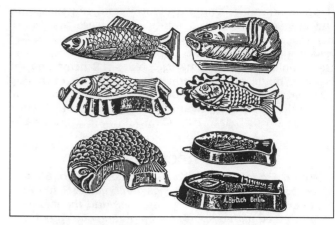

IV-302. Fish molds for various foods, including iced, jellied & biscuit. Most of these probably for fish-flavored aspics or mousses. All about 7-1/2" to 13"L. (T) Top two are from Mrs. Marshall's Cookery Book, c.1902; (M) second row right is from S. Joseph, NYC, c.1927 & eye is same scalloped-edge design as Czechoslovakian fish mold in photo IV-305. Rest from Bertuch, Berlin, c.1904. $35-$75

Jelly or blancmange mold, stamped & pieced heavy tin, 3 tiers, architectural in appearance, hanging ring at rim, poss. American, 9"H, 19th C. .... **$75+**

Jelly mold, stamped tin, shape of stack of corn cobs, American, 1870s. An unusual version of the corn mold. .... **$85+**

Jelly mold, pieced tin, round, sides or base made in 3 parts, soldered to top, interlinked crabapple design on top, scored lozenges on sides, marked near ring hanger, initials that look like a capital "N" superimposed on a "C," also numbers 32 & 6, no country of origin, 3-1/2" deep x 8-1/8" diam., late 19th C. .... **$30+**

Jelly mold, fish, stamped tin, for congealed (jellied, or gelatinized) dishes, although at least one dealer said it was for baking Lenten bread. American or German, 19th C. .... **$30+**

❖ NOTES ❖

Decorating with figural molds: "The Accolade of the Pudding Mold. – Every year the harassed interior decorator is driven well nigh distracted in a vain endeavor to find some new idea in decoration. What shall it be? Eagerly he searches London, Paris, Berlin and Vienna in the chance hope of discovering some novelty that will fit in with the general furnishing scheme and make one room look different from a hundred others. ... Now an enterprising few, instead of scouring the foreign marts and exhibitions have stayed at home and looked around their own homes for inspiration. And at last they have found it. ... Strangely enough, the kitchen has been the chief source of inspiration; so the following suggestions for decoration are well within the reach of the slenderest purse.

"One of the most amusing of these ideas is the way in which the ordinary tin pudding molds can be used for decorative purposes. ... [Especially] interesting is the use of large jelly or pudding molds as mural decorations. For this purpose the molds selected should be rather important in design. Fortunately many enchanting patterns are obtainable. Some show fruit nestling in beds of vine leaves, while others reveal fantastic looking fish, such as one sees in old Japanese prints. Then there are animals – rabbits, chickens, and even squirrels – charming accessories for a child's room. More novel are the molds patterned in geometrical designs – a type particularly well suited to rooms furnished in the modernist taste. Hung upon the wall or above the mantlepiece, gleaming like dull silver and covered with unusual designs, they look like native masks or ... modern sculpture." Derek Patmore, *House & Garden*, Aug. 1928.

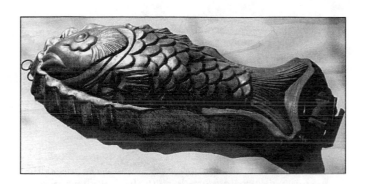

Jelly mold, stamped tin fish, simple head, wide flat edges, wire leveling leg, stamped "CF," also numbers "499" over "3," "AUSTRIA," 2-1/4" deep x 9-1/8"L x 4-1/4"W, c.1900 to 1920................................. **$45+**

Jelly mold, stamped tin, fish-shaped, fancy head, "G. M. T. Co., Czecho-Slovak," 1-5/8" deep x 9-1/4"L x 3-3/4"W, c.1900 to 1920. .... **$65+**

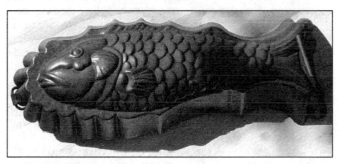

IV-303. Fish molds, *in animated curves.* **(T)** *called a "Dresden carp mold," stamped tin, with hanging ring at center, 8" or 11" diam. size, from S. Joseph, NYC, c.1927.* **(B)** *Stamped tin, 11" & 12" diam., from Bertuch, Derlin, c.1904.* **$45+**

IV-305. Fish molds, *for aspics, etc.* **(T)** *Stamped tin, leveling "leg" at tail end, marked "Germany," c.1900-1920. Probably a Bertuch mold from Berlin. 2-3/4" deep x 13-1/2"L x 5-1/2"W.* **(M)** *Stamped tin, simple head, wide flat edges. Wire leg at tail end. Stamped "Austria," &. "CF" (?), also #499 over a #3. I cannot identify maker. 2-1/4" deep x 9-1/8"L x 3-3/4"W. Early 20th C.* **(B)** *Stamped tin, somewhat more detail, unusual eye. Stamped on side "G.M.T.Co. CZECHO-SLOVAK," 9-1/4"L x 3-3/4"W x 1-5/8" deep. Early 20th C. All three Ex-Collection of late NYC food stylist Grace Manney.* **$45+**

Jelly mold, stamped tin, fish-shaped, stamped on leveling "leg" at tail end is "Germany," 2-3/4" deep x 13-1/2"L x 5-1/2"W, c.1900 to 1920s................................. **$45+**

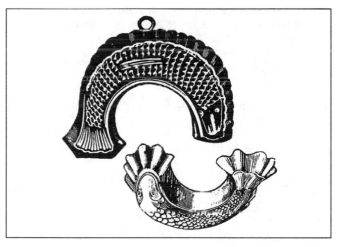

IV-304. Molds for biscuits, cremes, etc. *Copper. Many of these made in several sizes. All sizes range from 4" to 8" diam. Bertuch, c.1904.* **$45-$200**

❖ NOTES ❖

Schooling Adds Value – I have to say, the more fish molds I see and the more I think about hanging them together in all their variety on the wall, the more I like them. Each one may be not be worth that much, or even be all that exciting a form, but imagine a school of 20 or 30 of them, swimming across the wall! Gee! I can hardly wait.

❖ RECIPE ❖

Fish Jelly – *"Take a two-pound haddock, one onion, and half rind lemon; just cover with water, and boil; remove all the bones and skin; flake the fish, or pound it in a mortar, with a tablespoonful of butter, pepper and salt to taste. Put back the bones, reduce the liquor to one pint, add a quarter of a packet of gelatine (previously dissolved in a quarter of a tumbler of cold water). Make some veal forcemeat, without suet, roll in small balls, and drop into boiling water; they will cook in seven minutes. Decorate a mould with the balls and rings of lemon, mix the strained liquid with the pounded fish, and, when nearly cold, pour into the mould. Hard-boiled eggs may be made over in this way."* Gertrude Strohm, The Universal Cookery Book, 1888. *If you do not like the idea of veal, for humanitarian or any other reasons, you can use ground turkey, or decorate the mould with mushroom caps and forget the meat except for the fish. I'm sure if you are really inventive, you could make tofu fish – otherwise known as tofunna fish or tofinny fish.*

Jelly mold, stamped & pieced tin, grape bunch design, 3-1/4"L x 2-3/4"W, 1890s-1910. .... **$15**

Jelly mold, tin, 2 part, with strap handle on lower section, strawberry, cherry, apple, pear, grapes & plum design, obviously for a conjealed fruit salad! "Kreamer," early 20th C. .... **$35+**

Jelly mold, stamped & pieced tin, round geometric, with castle turrets around sides & a pattern of blocks in the top, also called a town mold, because of its resemblance to an abstract medieval walled town, in an F. A. Walker catalog, most of whose things were French or English imports, 1870s to 1890s. ..... **$70+**

Jelly mold, tin, sharp edges almost as if it were to be a cutter, shape is outline of pineapple, bottom is separate & pushes through the shape, no mark, 2-13/16" deep x 7-1/4"L, c.1890s-1910. .... **$45**

Jelly mold, stamped & pieced tin, pineapple top, drape or "peacock eye" sides or base, simple skirt, American or English, mold depth 4-7/8", skirt is 6" x 7", c.1890s-1910... **$40**

IV-306. Jelly molds. *Ovals with various embossed designs. 6-1/2" to 7-1/2"L. Material not mentioned, possibly stamped steel as some others on same page of catalog, or possibly copper with tin lining, or maybe just tin. S. Joseph, c.1927. Part of value relates to subject; part to material. Stamped steel would be unusual, but probably not as valuable to collectors as copper.* **$35-$85**

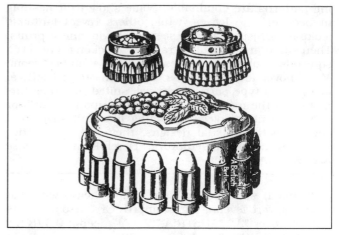

IV-307. Jelly molds. *Two at top have protective rims, to keep designs from being banged, & also to enable mold to stand firmly, upside down, for filling & while setting. Tin with fluted skirts. Sizes from 1/2 to 2 pints, & 2 quarts. F. A. Walker catalog, 1880s. Bottom mold, with grape bunch on top, is also oval, in 2 sizes – 8" & 8-5/8"L. Would be fun to do a 21st century dessert with simulated lipsticks in various shades! Bertuch, c.1904.* **$125**

Jelly mold, stamped tin, scroll shape, marked "SCT Co.," German, about 5-1/2"L, 20th C. .... **$15+**

Jelly mold, stamped & pieced tin, round, 4 pieces soldered – the skirt & the simple fluted side or base made of 2 pieces, & the top, which is an embossed shell design, bordered by rope, marked "France 296," 4" deep x 6-1/4" diam., c.1890s-1910.............. **$25+**

Jelly mold, tin, oval with short skirt, 6 point star design, an individual mold size, for a fancy jellied dish, English or American, 2-1/2"H x 3-7/8"L x 2-1/4"W, 19th C.. **$45+**

Jelly mold, tin, thistle design on top, fairly well-defined stamping, sides stamped in unnamed pattern, could be called "peacock eye" or "drape," made of 3 parts soldered together – the sides or base, the skirt or protective raised edge around fancy stamped top, & the top, American or English, mold depth 3-3/8", skirt 5-1/4"L x 3-3/4"H, c.1880s. .... **$35+**

Pudding molds, heavily tinned, so-called melon style (imagine half an elongated acorn squash) with close-fitting flat lid that has an oval wire ring handle that folds flat, some of these are found marked "Kreamer," (made in Brooklyn, NY), others unmarked, American (poss. also English), various sizes, typical one is 6-1/2"L x 5"W x 3-3/4" deep (stamped 3 on lid), another is 7"L x 5-1/2"W x 4" deep, another 10"L x 5-5/8"W, late 19th C. to early 20th. • The **handles** are sometimes missing, & the molds are sometimes found still brightly tinned outside, but rusted inside, where dampness was trapped by the tight-fitting lid. Most have an oval wire loop soldered to the body of the mold so that you could grasp lid & body with your left & right hand & pull apart. If the ring was once there & is now missing (you can see the evidence by bits of solder in a roughly rectangular shape), subtract about $5 to $7. Extra large sizes cost the most. .... **$50-$85+**

Pudding mold, melon shape, tin, 3 clips, marked only with 14 in a diamond & 127 on other half, 5-1/2" deep x 6" diam., 19th C. • I got the sparse description from an ad, so this is a hypothetical entry. I imagined a flat-top mold until reading that Henry Eppelsheimer, of the famous ice cream mold company, had patented a full-round "pudding and ice-cream mold" on Nov. 10, 1885. His patent drawing looks like tops of 2 flat-lid melon molds fitted together, both with elongated oval wire handle. • I think this one isn't Eppelsheimers (theirs have no need of clips), although it is possibly a full round... **$55+**

Pudding mold, stamped tin, flat close-fitting lid with round turban or turban squash mold, American or imported, about 6" or 7" diam. x 4" deep, c.1870s or 1880s. .... **$45+**

Trois freres bake tin, round with low sides, top stamped with very swirly design, sometimes called a "trois freres" mold after 3 French pastry chefs, French, 2" deep x 7-1/2" diam., late 19th C........................ **$45+**

Vegetable or rice mold, pieced tin, an assemblage of pointed spires, almost spikes, the overall outline fitting into a cone shape, meant for molding cooked mashed root veggies or cooked rice, from F. A. Walker catalog, European (?), probably about 6" to 8"H, probably came in 2 or 3 sizes, late 19th C................ **$75+**

TIN MOLDS – RING OR BORDER:

These molds, like tubed or spouted molds, are also open in the center.

Border mold, tin, extraordinary form composed of 7 swirled (like soft ice cream) & pointed cones, wire hanging ring, German, 9" diam. (came in various sizes with different numbers of cones), c.1890s-1910.. **$125+**

Border or ring mold, stamped tin, marked "KREAMER 2," 9-1/2"L x 6-1/4"W oval, mfd. by A[ugust] Kreamer, Brooklyn, NY, early 20th C. Kreamer's oval rice mold came in three sizes, & you could get them with snug lids. .... **$55+**

Border or ring mold, tin, with ring handle, "15" is only mark, 2-1/4" deep x 6" diam., 1890s-1910. .... **$25+**

Border mold, stamped & pieced tin, fruit design on top, plain sides, American, 10" diam., early 20th C. .... **$35+**

IV-308. Jelly mold. Stamped & pieced tin, pineapple design, rim. Mold depth 4-7/8"; overall 6"H x 7"L. Ex-Collection of Grace Manney, NYC food stylist. **$45+**

IV-309. Jelly molds. Sampling from ad of stamped tin molds sold by J. & C. Berrian, NYC. Ad in History of Prominent Mercantile & Manufacturing Firms in the U.S., *Boston: 1857. The molds:* **$20-$65+**

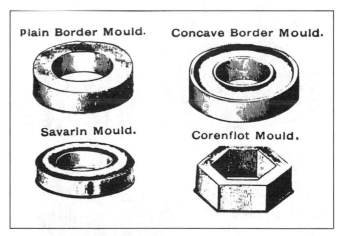

Plain Border Mould.   Concave Border Mould.

Savarin Mould.   Corenflot Mould.

*IV-310. Border molds, also called **ring molds**. For forming rings of one kind of food (such as rice or a salmon mousse) around another kind or color. These are all pieced tin. "Plain" came in rounds from 5-1/2" to 9-3/4" diam., & in ovals from 6-1/4" to 10-1/4"L. "Concave" in similar but slightly smaller dimensions. "Savarin" came in rounds, from 1-1/2" to 11-3/4" diam., & in ovals, 6-1/4" to 11-3/4"L. It was used for making a Savarin cake, soaked in spirits while still warm, but served cold with a cold sauce. Hexagonal "Corenflot" came 3-1/2" to 10" diam. Duparquet, Huot & Moneuse jobbers' catalog, c.1904-1910.* **$15-$35**

IV-311. "Breton" border mold. *Six lobes, offered in two sizes (not given, but probably about 7" & 10" diam.). One page of "moulds for entrées, sweets, savouries, &c." Mrs. A. B. Marshall's Larger Cookery Book of Extra Recipes, London, c.1902. (Mrs. Marshall, in addition to writing cookbooks, had a cooking school, & a large shop for culinary tools. Her books all have advertising pages in the back, all identified as coming from her Book of Moulds, a catalog of 68 pages. One mold dealer in NYC has seen a large book of moulds; cookbook dealers here & in England have turned up only one much smaller one. The search continues in 2002.) The mold:* **$35+**

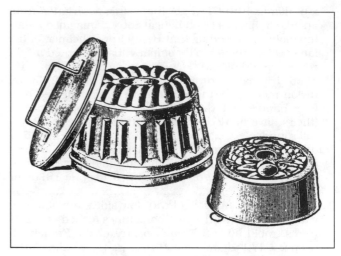

IV-313. Covered border molds. *Metal not mentioned – could be stamped tin or stamped copper that's tinned inside; probably tin.* **(L)** *2-quart.* **(R)** *3-1/2 quarts, fruit wreath design, lid not shown. S. Joseph Co., c.1927. The copper mold value might be two or three times as much as tin:* **$25-$45+**

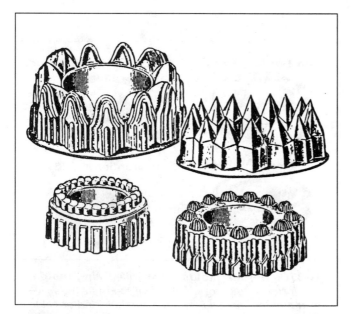

IV-312. Border molds. *All "imported tin." Clockwise from top (L):* **(1)** *Came in rounds, 8" or 8-3/4" diam., or ovals, 10-1/4 or 11"L.* **(2)** *Rounds in 7", 8" or 8-3/4" diam., or ovals, 7", 8" or 22"L.* **(3)** *Oval only, 5-1/2", 6-1/4" or 7"L.* **(4)** *Round only, 7", 8" or 8-3/4" diam. Note in last two, especially, how one color of food could be pressed into knobs on top. All from Duparquet, Huot & Moneuse catalog, c.1904-1910. Size & condition greatly affect value.* **$25-$75+**

IV-314. Jelly molds. *Stamped & pieced tin.* **(L)** *Round, interlinked crabapple (?) design bordering top, scored lozenges on skirt. Skirt in 3 parts, soldered to top. Marked near hanging ring, looks like capital "N" superimposed on a C or H, with "32" & "6." No country of origin, could be pre-1892 if imported, or turn-of-the-century if American. 3-1/2" deep x 8-1/8" diam.* **(R)** *Round, tin, shell design bordered by rope. Simple fluted skirt of 2 pieces soldered. Marked "France 296," 4" deep x 6-1/4" diam. Ex-Collection of NYC food stylist Grace Manney.* **$45+**

Border mold, tin, deep design of 13 connected hearts, American (?), 8-1/2" diam., prob. early 20th C. .... **$135+**

Border mold, tin, scalloped perimeter with plain inside ring, 9" Cake pan, round, stamped tin, Turk's head, 9" diam., 20th C. **$25**

TIN MOLDS – other TUBED or SPOUTED:

Price is determined by shape (an octagonal or hexagonal mold usually costs more than a simple round one), apparent age, condition, general look, & workmanship if handmade.

Cake mold, tin, fluted, tubed with closed end, American, 7" diam., early 20th, late 19th C. Lots of cake & pudding molds turn out cakes or puddings with open centers. The tube or spout in the center of the mold allowed the heat (dry, steam or hot water) to cook contents more evenly. .... **$25+**

Mold, tin, spouted with 9 sections shaped like Mr. Softee™ ice cream cones, the flat-bottomed kind, hanging ring, American or imported, 9" diam., 19th C. .... **$150+**

Mold or cake pan, round, 3-part, 2-way, deep tin cylinder, fitted either a bottom with built-in tapered spout, or a plain bottom, "Gem," mfd. by American Machine Co., Philadelphia, PA, pat'd. July 29, 1890. ...... **$35+**

Mold, heavy pieced tin, very carefully made, tubed, 8 pronounced scallops, large diam. tube, ring hanger, American (?), 2" deep x 6-1/2" diam., 1890s............... **$20+**

Mold or cake pan, octagonal with tube, factory blackened tin, American, 13" diam., 19th C. or early 20th. .... **$25+**

Mold or cake pan, pieced & hammered tin, side wall has very graceful flare with 10 generous scallops & folded rim, slightly conical seamed spout soldered to bottom. This is unusual because it was made in only 2 pieces instead of 3. Starting with a large round tin "doughnut" with a hole only 1-7/8" diam. in center, it was hammered or beaten up into pan with flat bottom & scalloped sides. Usually there is a seam or two on the side, as well as a seam around the bottom where the sides were joined, then a separate spout soldered on too. American, poss. VA, 3-1/2" deep x 10-1/4" diam. at top, 7-3/4" at bottom, 1870s, poss. earlier.......................... **$55+**

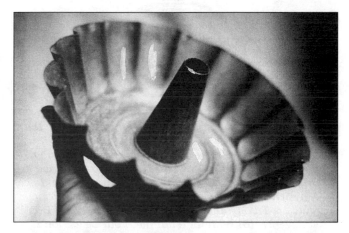

IV-315. Fluted mold, with spout. Stamped tin, with spout soldered on separately. 7-1/2" diam. 1890s-1910s. Not valuable but oh it's made so well! **$15-$25+**

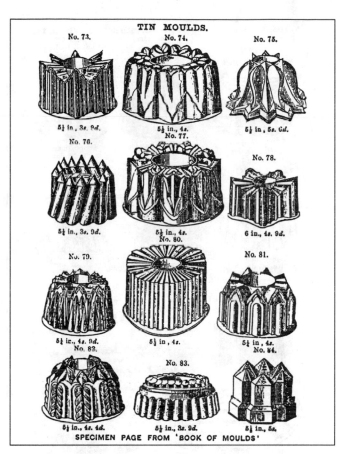

IV-321. Specimen page from Marshall's Book of Moulds. *Tin molds in fancy shapes, mostly for jellies, from Mrs. A. B. Marshall's Cookery Book, London, c.1900 edition.*

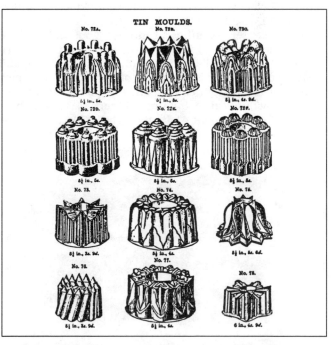

IV-322. Specimen page from Marshall's Book of Moulds. *From Mrs. A. B. Marshall's Larger Cookery Book of Extra Recipes, London, c.1902 edition.*

IV. Form, Mold, Shape, etc.   329

IV-323. Specimen page from Marshall's Book of Moulds. *Molds for hot & cold entrées & savories, as well as a copper bombe mold. From Mrs. A. B. Marshall's Cookery Book, London, c.1900 edition.*

Mold, "Savarin" cake mold, after famed chef Brillat-Savarin, used for other dishes too, ring-shaped, tin, large center opening, rounded "bottom" (which becomes cake's top), no mark, European or American, 9" diam., 1890s-1910. .... **$25**

Mold or cake pan, pieced tin, 6 point star, spouted, hexagonal flat bottom & very angular points, rolled rim, for individual cakes, Jaburg Brothers, NYC, NY, about 1-5/8" deep x about 4" diam., early 1900s, ... **$20+**

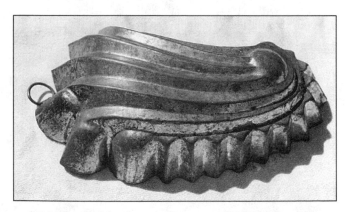

IV-324. Mold. *Stamped tin scroll, hanging ring, marked "SCT Co., Germany." 7"L, 20th C. Ex-Collection of NYC food stylist Grace Manney.* **$25-$35**

IV-325. Melon mold. *Very unusual mold with ribbed copper body, wrought iron handle. Note leveling foot where handle joins body. 18"L overall. European probably, early 19th C. Ex-Wiggins Tavern Collection, Northampton, MA. Photograph courtesy Luella McCloud Antiques, Shelburn Falls, MA.* **$400+**

IV-326. Melon molds – for Pudding & Ice Cream. *Tin, oval. Three versions (you'll note that some never did have handles on body).* **(T)** *"Pudding Mould. – Who likes boiled pudding can have it dry & light if cooked in one of these moulds."* American Home Cook Book, *1854.* **(M)** *"Fancy Quart & Two-Quart Ice Cream Mould." Cherry-Bassett, 1921.* **(B)** *With wire handle. Four sizes: for 2, 3, 2-1/2 & 4 pints. From 6-1/2" x 4-3/4" x 3-1/2" up to 8" x 6-1/8" x 4-1/8". Central Stamping Co., 1920. An even larger range of sizes, from 2 to 8 pints, was offered by Duparquet about 1904.* **$45+**

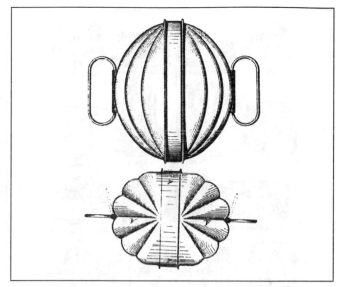

IV-327. Melon "Ice cream & pudding mold" patent. Pat'd. Nov. 10, 1885, by Henry Eppelsheimer, NYC. Eppelsheimer, of course, was connected to the well-known American ice cream mold firm. This melon has two convex halves, with one serving as a snug-fitting "lid" to the other. Official Gazette of the U.S. Patent Office. **$65+**

IV-328. Melon pans for baking. Size not given, but a commercial bakery pan, stamped tin. The melons are probably about 5"L each. Jaburg, 1908. **$45**

IV-329. Pudding mold. Round tin **"Turk's Head"** or turban mold. (Could also be a turban squash – related to a melon!) I call this one the laughing jockey. F. A. Walker catalog, c.1890. **$35+**

IV-330. "Hall of the Mountain King" molds & others. Stamped, pieced tin. Actually **(T-L)** is a "Jelly or Blanc Mange Mould," also for ice cream. American Home Cook Book, 1854. **(T-R)** is a "Vegetable & Rice Mould," #229, for making decorative spires of cooked, mashed root veggies or rice. F. A. Walker catalog, c.1890. Nearly identical molds are still made, & sold in such all-inclusive kitchenware stores as Bridge's in NYC. (See also IV-220.) **(B)** Bottom row are tall tin molds resembling skyscrapers, columns, towers. **(B-L)** an imported mold, probably from England, c.1910s. It came in 3- & 4-pint sizes. **(B-M)** Stamped & pieced tin, came in 5 sizes, from 2 to 6 pints. **(B-R)** Advertised as a "patent design" that came in 3 sizes – 2, 3 & 4 quarts. Last two designs from Lalance & Grosjean catalog, 1890. **$75-$100**

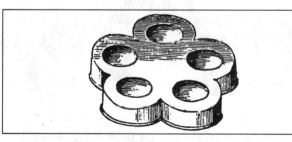

IV-331. Piccolo mold, "... for making a fancy jellied dish called Little Piccolos. Line molds with 1/8" thick lemon jelly, & after lining, fill up top parts with 2-colored creams, using forcing bags and plain pipes for purpose, & partly fill up the bottom part of the moulds with finely-shredded blanched sweet almonds & pistachio nuts; in the centre of each put a little liquid jelly, then close up the moulds, place them on ice till set, & turn out on wet foolscap paper. Serve on a little plate, with chopped jelly around edges, & pour over a pale green cream made of whipped cream mixed with lemon jelly, rum, 'Noyeau' syrup, & coloring." From Mrs. A. B. Marshall's Larger Cookery Book, c.1902. Picture from her 1900 book. **$65**

IV-332. Pudding molds. (L) *Stamped & pieced tin, imported by Duparquet, NYC. 4-3/4" diam. Big flat bracket handle on lid. Hearts add value. C.1904-10.* **(R)** *Heavy tin, spouted, clearly showing bayonet mount for lid. Four sizes, from 1-1/8 to 2-3/4 litres. Bertuch, c.1904.* **$40-$75**

IV-333. Steamer molds, *for pudding & bread. All three, with spouts or plain, are for steaming pudding or brown bread. Bottom two have* **bayonet mount** *(put on & twist to secure) lids. Tin, in many sizes.* **(B-L)** *Spouted ones, mainly for pudding, are for 1 to 4 quarts.* **(B-R)** *Plain one, from 1-1/2 pints to 4 quarts, from 4" x 4" to 8" x 6-1/2".* **(T)** *Made by Dover Stamping Co., c.1899 (& before & after); others from D. J. Barry 1924, Kreamer, etc.* **$35+**

IV-334. Jelly molds, *& others, from William S. Adams & Son, London, ad in Francatelli's Cook's Guide Advertiser, c.1860-61.*

MUFFIN PANS – CAST IRON:
Muffin baker, cast iron, 7 very shallow straight-sided indentations rather than cups, as this was for making muffins of the English muffin type, not the delicatessen bran muffin you may have visualized. Iron is heavily encrusted from use (a good sign when dating pieces), "JOHNSON" cast on handle, American, 10-1/2" diam. with 6-1/4"L handle, 19th C. These are often called "pancake pans" because small flapjacks can be made in the cups, and the design is quite similar to the Scandinavian plettkakers. I am calling it a muffin baker after seeing a nearly identical one pictured in the 1872 *New Cyclopedia of Domestic Economy*. Such a pan took the place of separate muffin rings (tin hoops sort of like tuna fish cans with both ends open), which were laid upon a hot griddle, and the batter poured in. The all-in-one version was both more and less convenient. .... **$50-$65+**

IV-335. Rice boiler, *or* **pudding mold.** *Fluted, tubed, close-fit lid with strap handle. Tin. F. A. Walker, c.1890. Condition very important – most old ones severely rusted.* **$45+**

Gems – "These are the simplest form of bread, and if properly made are certain to be light and sweet. A hot oven and hot pans are prime essentials, and there must be no delay between making and baking. The coldest water, ice-water preferred, should be used. Use either whole-wheat or Graham flour, three parts of flour to one of water. ... For a dozen gems allow one large cup – a half pint – of ice water, one even teaspoon of salt, and three cups of flour. Stir in the flour slowly, beating hard and steadily, not less than ten minutes. The pans should have been set on top of the stove, and oiled or buttered. Fill them two thirds full, and bake about a half hour." Mrs. Helen Campbell's recipe, in Good Housekeeping Discovery Book, No. 1, 1905.

Muffin mold or gem pan, cast iron, shapely oblong with 13 variously shaped shallow cups, including 2 hearts, one at both ends, 2 6-point stars, one next to both hearts on the long axis, 4 rounds in corners plus one in the center, & 2 scalloped cups on each side, cut-out tab handles at both ends, looks right, nice satiny smooth dark iron, no marks, American, 16-1/2"L x 8-1/2"W x 3/4" deep, late 1800s. .... **$95-$130+**

Cleaning New Iron-Ware – I do not remember to have seen directions anywhere for preparing new cast-iron utensils for service in cooking. I know I had a deal of trouble with my first stove furniture, and whenever I have anything of the kind to deal with now I wonder if there is not some better way than I have learned. I have just been tackling a new set of iron gem-pans. I filled them with ashes and water and left them standing during the forenoon. I heated them on the stove before emptying them, and then gave them a good washing and rinsing. I think they will do for use to-morrow morning. I usually scour new kettles with ashes, then rub them over with a little grease, and wash them well with suds. To-day a lady told me that it was a good way to wash new irons with sour milk. I had no sour milk to use, but I do not see the philosophy of it. It is not rust with which we have to deal in cleaning new iron, but a fine sand, used in the casting." Correspondent to Editor, *American Agriculturist*, June 1874. Note: Wood ashes and water form a somewhat mild lye.

Muffin or cookie pans, cast iron, fancy cups, in wide-bordered rectangular frame with fancy scroll handles, (a) 5 toy soldiers in same frame, (b) a number of small figural cups, "Classic Gourmet Series," mfd. by John Wright, Wrightsville, PA, © 1984.................. **$15-$25+**

Muffin pan for gems (a small, shaped muffin), cast iron, 8 shallow cups: leaf, house, rooster, spade, 6 point star, petaled flower, crescent moon & club, plus 3 small diamonds between the rows, newly made but not a reproduction of an old design, sold through Cumberland General Store, possibly marked, 14"L x 6"W, shipping weight with package is 6 lbs., 1980s................................. **$10**

IV-316. Spouted cake molds, *all called* **turban molds,** *or* **Turk's head** *molds, despite differences in fluting.* **(T-L)** *Stamped tin, made in six sizes, from 3-3/4"H x 7-1/4" diam. to 4-1/4"H x 11" diam. Matthai-Ingram, c.1890. (R)* **(T-R)** *Similar one with less-angled flutes, to be had with or without spout. Stamped tin, 4 sizes, all somewhat smaller than previous one. Savory, Inc., c.1925-28.* **(B)** *Unusual ovoid flutes, stamped & pieced tin, made in 3 sizes, from 7-7/8" to 10" diam., holding 2, 4, 5 & 6 quarts. Lalance & Grosjean, 1890.* **$30-$45+**

IV-317. Cake pan, *for small cakes. Six-point star, pieced tin, spouted. Three sizes, plus smallest one, probably about 5" across, came 12 fixed on a frame. Jaburg, 1908. The sizes of many of these cake & candy molds were described in early catalogs by retail price of cake or candy baked within. For example, this one came in penny, 5¢ & 10¢ sizes, referring to the little cake's price. Crossover interest from folk art collectors, who might pay more.* **$20-$35**

IV-318. Baba cake, *shown in* Ryzon Baking Book, *1916. Advertising cookbooklet for baking powder maker.*

IV-319. Baba cake mold. *Stamped & pieced copper, heavily tinned. Another name for this, from German, is "Old German pound cake mold." Came in 8 sizes, in 3/4" increments, from 6-1/4" to 11-3/4" diam. Bertuch, c.1904. A similar one of heavy copper, 11" diam., marked with patent date of 1870, has been reported.* **$100+**

IV-320. Sandtorten molds. *These have similar tops (or bottoms) for almonds, but one has high plain sides, one has low fancy sawtooth or gear-like sides. Both from 8" to 13" diam., pieced tin. S. Joseph Co., c.1927.* **$45-$85+**

❖ NOTES ❖

Similar Bake Molds & Repros – There's an 8-cup cast iron ornamental mold for gems or muffins with a pear, beet, two leafs, an apricot (?), cherries, pomegranate, and a Turk's head (whorled, and resembling a Turkish turban). Originally made by Schofield Mfg. Co., NYC, c.1890-1900, the mold cost 75¢. The mold was also made in a 6-cup size, and the flat top frame into which the cups were cast has a scalloped edge that conforms to the cups' outlines. • A repro, with oblong body with a ridge on the edge and fancy handles was offered by *McCall's* magazine in about 1984, for $16.95. It is 15"L x 7-1/2"W x 1-3/4" deep. • In the 1990s, other fancy molds in cast iron were offered mail order from catalogs, and include an oblong saguaro cactus pan (15-1/2" x 5-3/4" x 1"); a 6-cup "Tex-Mex" motif pan with star, wolf, cactus, armadillo, pea-pod-like crescent moon, and sun (11" x 7-1/4"); a 7-cup Christmas pan with Santa, bell, tree, star, bow, cherub, and holly sprig (12" x 7-1/2"); and another Christmas one with four reindeer, snowman, tree and sleigh (12-1/2" x 8"). New fancy and figural molds may become collectors items, so you may want to sock them away where they won't rust.

IV-336. Reid's cake pan design patent, *pat'd. July 18, 1871, by Adam Reid, Buffalo, NY, #D5,132. Reid wrote "The nature of my design for cake-pan consists in combining a variety of patterns and shapes ... There can be no doubt but that the combining of a variety of patterns into one baking-pan makes it more convenient and much more desirable." It ended up just as in the picture he submitted: hearts, stars, plain & scalloped cups. He specified that "in the ends of pan are openings, into which the ordinary stove-cover handle fits, so that it can be moved the same as a spider on the top of the stove." This is the "Reid's Patent" that is sometimes referred to in molded marks in handles of certain cast iron pans we usually call* **muffin or gem pans**. **$125-$175**;

Muffin or other bake pan, cast iron, skillet shape with 6 heart-shaped cups, one center cup in shape of 6 point star, raised rim, side handle with pointed end & elongated hang up hole, Emig Products, Inc., but I don't know if marked, Reading, PA, 8-1/2" diam. with 6-1/2"L handle, weighs 4-3/4 lbs., from 1966 catalog. .... **$40+**

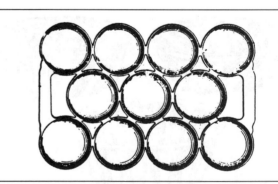

IV-337. Egg pan & cake baker patent, *by collector-revered Nathaniel Waterman, Boston, MA, April 5, 1859, #23,517. His objective was to invent "a new or Improved Egg-Pan or Article for Cooking or Baking Eggs." Eleven cups, with flat bottoms, to be cast of iron. Waterman believed that the design of cups was necessary in order to allow for a strengthening (& convenient) handle at each end. "Open spaces are left between the cups to allow the currents of heat to pass upward between them so as to equalize the heat against their surfaces. The metallic connections of the cups serve as conveyors of heat from cup to cup." Official Gazette of the U.S. Patent Office.* **$40-$60**

Egg 'O My Heart – F. A. Walker, the NYC supplier and importer of housewares, showed a cast iron "egg fryer" in an 1870s catalog. From the linecut picture it appears to be exactly the same as the Emig pan above. Walker's catalog also had a stamped tin "egg fryer," with no handle, very shallow rolled rim, cups for 18 eggs. $8 to $12 for recent ones.

Muffin or gem pan, actually patented as an egg pan, cast iron with gray graniteware on inside of 8 oval cups, N. Waterman, (Very unusual to find enameling inside a marked Waterman piece.) Boston, MA, pat'd. Apr. 5, 1859. (When ill-cast or worn, date looks like 1853 or 1858.) The problem here is that there isn't much of a following for enameled cast iron ware among collectors. In fact, some collectors have been known to remove enameling. Yikes! sez the purist. The value to enamelware collectors would probably be quite a bit higher................. **$85-$125+**

Muffin or gem pan, cast iron, 11 shallow cups in 3 rows, curved handles at ends, "R. & E. Mfg. Co.," Russell & Erwin Mfg. Co., Nathaniel Waterman patent, 13"L x 8-3/4"W, each cup is 3-1/4" diam. x 1" deep, pat'd. April 5, 1859, but made by R & E some years after that. • This was actually patented as an "Improved Egg Pan" and described as a "new or improved manufacture of baking pan, or arrangement of cups, and a handle at each end of the series, all connected together and cast or founded in one solid piece of metal and with heat passages between the cups." This pan was not only made by Russell & Erwin, but also Hibbard, Spencer, Bartlett & Co., who made two sizes: (1) 11 cups 2-3/4" diam., & (2) 11 at 3-1/4" diam. See article on Cast Iron Muffin pans by David Smith following this chapter...................... **$45-$60+**

Muffin or gem pan, patented as an "egg pan," sold as gem pan by Russell & Erwin, cast iron, 12 round cups, interesting to examine handle ends, as slight roughness at 2 "bulge" points, both ends, make you

IV-338. Cake or egg baker. *This one follows almost exactly Waterman's design. Cast iron, marked "W & L Mfg. Co.," pat'd. 1867. So far I've been unable to ID "W & L," but I believe it must have been a short-lived (?) company owned by Nathaniel Waterman & someone unidentified. (See also CIBP-1 in David Smith's article following this chapter.) Picture courtesy of the Smithsonian Institution, Museum of History & Technology.*

IV-339-A. Baking molds or gem pans. (T) *Darkened tin made up of shallow, flat-bottomed round cups stamped into hexagon modules – here 7 have been riveted together, but modular format meant that any number of them could have been assembled in a honeycomb fashion. A bent tin strap handle attached. 9-1/8" diam., pat'd. Nov. 9, 1869, by John Milligan. (This mold design has sometimes been called a maple sugar mold.) See IV-339-B. Another design has been found, with shallow oval cups, 3 x 3 in a roughly rectangular shape, riveted in a frame & stamped under one cup "8 1/2 PAT NOV. 9.69" & a logo of some kind reading "Mfg Co" with 2 or 3 other letters going vertically through. **(B)** Tin, seven scallop shells stamped in circular modules, riveted together, & further strengthened by a circumferential band of tin, 9" diam. Late 19th C. Collection of Meryle Evans.* **$35+**

think these could have been cast in long rows & snapped apart at the handles, then ground smooth. Nathaniel Waterman patent, mfd. by R & E Manfg Co., #6, 10-3/4"L x 7-1/8"W, pat'd. April 5, 1859 – often looks like "1858" or "1853." Joel Schiff says that "sometime between the 1880s and 1900, the overflow gate – and hence the mark – was moved from the bottom of the pan to the side rim; the side rims were also being used as access gates or conduits for the molten metal to flow into greater numbers of mold forms during a single pour. These could, then, indeed be 'snapped off' and ground down when preparing the final product." .... **$35-$45+**

❖ NOTES ❖

Soap molds? Collector Beth Kidder, of Normal, IL, wrote me in 1988 to report that she had three similar cast iron molds, one each with round, oval, & oblong wells, all shallow, & all bought at local antique stores. The one with oblong wells "appeared not to have been used for baking, but it did have a light allover coating of a whitish substance which behaved like soap. The insides are pretty rough. ... I first heard these pans [all three styles] called soap molds in spring 1987," writes Beth, "at a privately operated museum called Little Norway, Rte 1, Blue Mounds, WI, 53517. The museum is a preserved pioneer homestead, built by the Norwegian immigrant Austin Haugen. I questioned the guide about the pan, and she was quite definite in her identification of it as a soap mold." Beth's husband suggests that people may have used baking molds, or gem pans, as soap molds because they worked so well for that purpose. • You are in luck: In the cyber age, Little Norway, in the Valley of the Elves, has a Web site: www.littlenorway.com/

Muffin or gem pan, cast iron, 12 round bottom cups, what Griswold called a "golf-ball pan," tab handles, cutouts between each cup, Griswold No. 9, 10-1/8"L x 7"W, c.1920s-30s. Griswold also made a 6-cup golf-ball pan, the No. 19, which brings $100 to $200 more than the 12-cup. .... **$75-$100+**

Muffin or gem pan, cast iron, 12 very shallow fluted turk's head cups, cutout tab handles, Griswold #14, 13-1/8"L x 8-1/2"W, c.1920s on. .... **$600-$700**

Muffin or gem pan, cast iron, 5 hearts surrounding single star, has one short, holed, handle with opening for a pot-lifting tool. Griswold's "Heart-Star #100," 7-3/4" diam., c.1926 or later. • The game of bridge became extremely popular in the 1920s, & all sorts of kitchen- or cooking- or serving-related things used bridge motifs. Yes, I know; stars aren't taken from playing cards. (A smaller version of this pan was also made, #50, only 6-1/2" diam. & only 1/2" deep cups, which is valued by avid collectors $1,200-$1,500.) The small-

est, & the largest, are often worth the most. For the #100: .... **$600-$700+**

Muffin or gem pan, cast iron, 8 cups arranged 3, 2, 3, with 2 clubs, 2 diamonds, 2 spades & 2 hearts, called a "No Trump" mold (I have also seen it referred to as a "Grand Slam" mold). Shallow flat-bottom cups, almost square pan has cutout handles inside outer rim, rather than projecting out. About 9-1/2"L x 7-1/2"W. Not marked, but made by Lodge. American, 1930s-40s. Collector Jim Holroyd says some variation of these card suit pans were made by several foundries, although they don't look the same. Joel Schiff says newer ones by Lodge are up to a half-inch smaller than old ones. **$100**

Muffin or gem pan, cast iron, 8 figural fruit & vegetable cups, *viz.* pear, squash, apple, beet, turnip, cherries, & unidentifiable ones, & scrolled handles, 13"L x 8"W, Wright, 20th C. Possibly one of Wright's oldest molds, in continuous production up to about 1999, and called the "harvest pan." Newer ones have smaller and less detailed cups. Oldest have a casting gate mark. Collector Jim Holroyd sent me a picture of his, which has 3 very small holes which appear to be drilled down the center of the long axis. Newer: $45+; oldest ones with casting gate mark: .... **$165+**

Muffin or gem pan, cast iron, oblong with flat top, 8 cups (they also made a 6 gem pan) with deeply & neatly molded fruits all in a general round configuration: quince or pear, peach, cherries, leaves, rosette, & something like a pomegranate (?). Outside on the two long sides of the pan the edges scallop around the cups. Triangular cutouts, one at each end, between the end cups, no handles. The Schofield Mfg. Co., c.1900 brochure depicts this & calls it "Our Ornamental Gem Pan ... made of finest gray iron." About 13"L x 8"W, c.1900..... **$250-$400**

❖ NOTES ❖

Schofield's brochure states "They need no recommendation, as all housekeepers know that **thin cast-iron** bakes more evenly than tin or sheet iron, and the beauty of the design sells the 'gem.' The poor man's table, neatly arranged, is more appetizing than the richest luxuries improperly placed." c.1900

• • •

New cast iron looks entirely different from old wares, even after use, or even if old piece with which you make comparisons was never used. New: grayish, and grainy, poor casting edges, etc. And it doesn't cook well either. Often deliberately rusted, the rust is bright orange and powdery – you could use it for blusher.

• • •

Old Gray Iron Ain't What She Used to Be. I don't know how literally we can take it, but there were companies casting at the end of the 19th C. who advertised "cast gray iron." But the older gray iron wasn't so terribly grainy or gritty. I don't know all (any?) of the secrets of making gray iron, but here's something on the subject from the Mar. 22, 1890 *Metal Worker*: "Aluminum in Cast Iron turns the combined carbon to graphite – that is, [it] makes the white iron gray and also [closes] the texture of the metal. [Aluminum] makes the metal more fluid and susceptible of taking a better polish and retaining it. Aluminum will also increase the tensile strength of many grades of cast iron and aids in obtain-

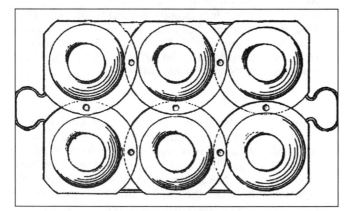

IV-339-B. Milligan's riveted pan patent. Pat'd. by John C. Milligan, Brooklyn, NY, Nov. 9, 1869, #96,605. "The pans made of sheet-metal in dies by striking up, generally of round form, and according to my improvement with wide flanges, which I make use of for connecting pans together in clusters by lapping said flanges, and riveting them together, as many as may be required, in any preferred order of arrangement, either in right lines in both directions, or in any other lines." This patent is somewhat unusual because he had applied for it only about 45 days before.

ing sound castings free from blow-holes. It has been used in preparations from 1/10 of 1% to 2%, with good results, with various grades of cast iron." 1990s+. Note that recyclers of metal, notably in Japan, melt down entire car engines creating an "alloy" that would contain iron, aluminum, brass, chrome, copper, steel, and possibly more.

• • •

Batter Pans in 1824. From a Charlotte, NC newspaper, as gleaned by James H. Craig (*The Arts & Crafts in North Carolina, 1699-1840*), an advertisement placed by Edward M. Bronson, who had a sheet iron & tin plate factory in Charlotte, reads "... Batter pans, of every description, Hearts, Diamonds, Scollops, &c. &c. ..." I suspect these were individual muffin molds, and as such would be the earliest I've found evidence of. Gosh! Get me a time machine! So many places to go; so little time. Muffins, of course, were known much much earlier, but were rather like what we know as English muffins, and were cooked in muffin rings on a griddle. Similar, or perhaps even identical, were flan rings, tin hoops set flat on a cookie sheet or flat pan and used for baking flan (custard). • See "Royal Hearts" recipe at beginning of this chapter, in with Bake mold entries.

Muffin or popover pan, cast iron, 11 cups, Griswold spelled it "Pop-Over," Griswold #10, Pattern #949 (sometimes reported as 949-B), Erie, PA, 11-1/8"L x 7-5/8"W (given in company catalog as 11-1/4" x 7-1/2"), 20th C., ads for the pan in 1973 look just the same as earlier ones. • In 1919, Griswold's full page ad in *House Furnishing Review* depicted one 11-cup pan with two large holes in both handle ends, and stated "Griswold cast iron gem and muffin pans are made in 17 different shapes. Being heavier and thicker they retain the heat more evenly and longer than ordinary pans." In 1973, the price was only five dollars! .... **$45-$60**
Muffin pan, or corn bread pan, cast iron in shape of frying pan with handle & 3 short triangular legs, 7 shallow ebelskiver-type cups, one in center, casting gate in center on bottom, no marks, prob. American, 7" diam. with 4-1/4"L handle, c. mid 19th C. .... **$100-$150**
Muffin pan, cast iron, 12 flat bottom cups, many smoothed-off casting marks on back, marked with either a "9" or a "6" on back, also patent date, 12"L x 7-3/16"W, pat'd. April 8 (1913 or 1919?)......... **$30+**
Muffin pan, cast iron, 12 flat bottom cups, nicely formed interstices between cups, rather than the rough & sloppy ones found on repros, only mark: "F" on back of handles. 11"L x 6-3/4"W, late 19th C. .... **$30+**

Muffin pan, cast iron, 13 cups include 2 hearts, 2 six point stars, 5 rounds & 4 fluted rounds, "Reids Patent," 16-1/2"L x 8-5/8", sometimes reported to have been pat'd. Dec. 1870. But the design patent #5132 that I have a copy of says "pat'd. Jul. 18, 1871" by Adam Reid. Collector Jim Holroyd's pan is marked with the July 18 date on one handle, & "Reids Patent" on the other. Collector LuAnn Funk writes that she has this pan, & on one handle it says "Reids Pan" (rather than Pat.), & on the other it says "Dec. 1870." It's the little variations that make a lot of collectors bigly happy! .... **$160-$185+**
Muffin pan, cast iron, 8 cups – leaf, clover, crescent moon, chicken, spade, 6-point star, house, scallop, & 3 smaller diamonds down center, heart shaped handles at each end, 14"L x 6"W, mid 20th C. to 1980s.. **$25+**
Muffin pan, cast iron, 8 shell-shaped muffins or gems, rather shallow, 19th C. (?). The shell-shape was originally for making the little Madeline cakes – this might be for that too, although I think mostly of tin pans not cast iron. See also Madeline mold earlier in this chapter.. **$65+**
Muffin pan, cast iron, bar handles, "G. F. Filley #10," mfd. by Excelsior Stove Works, St. Louis, MO, late 19th C. This was Filley's most common non-standard form.. **$100-$150+**

❖ NOTES ❖

Giles F. Filley, Pioneer In Stove Trade – Mr. Filley was born in 1815, and went to St. Louis from Connecticut, in 1836. "Upon his arrival he sought employment with his brother, O. D. Filley, who was then conducting a tinsmith's shop. ... Later Giles F. Filley was taken into partnership with his brother, assuming a third interest in the business. In this connection he remained until 1841, at which time he [decided] that there was not enough in the business for two, and so he retired. In that same year he came to NY with the intention of buying trinkets to take to Oregon for the purpose of trading with the Indians. It was his original intention to take one of Astor's boats from NY to Astoria, OR, but changing his mind he purchased a stock of crockery, which was shipped to St. Louis, where he opened a crockery store in 1842, remaining in that business until 1849.

"In 1848 he concluded to engage in the business of manufacturing stoves, and in December of that year ground was broken for a stove foundry, the molding floor of which was 80 x 100 feet, and the warehouse 30 x 100 feet. The first casting was made in the foundry on Sept. 1, 1849. ...

"The first stove made by Mr. Filley was what is known as a step stove, called the Prize Premium, and was sold to Stark Mauzy of Brunswick, MO. The first Charter Oak stove was turned out on March 18, 1852, and was purchased by a man who, coming along the street and seeing the stove standing on the sidewalk, asked Mr. Filley if it was for sale. Informed that such was the case, he purchased the stove and took it home to his farm, some miles back of Clarksville, MO. The first bill of Charter Oak stoves was afterward sold to C. G. Jones of St. Louis, MO, who was then conducting a stove store. ... At the time Mr. Filley took up his resi-

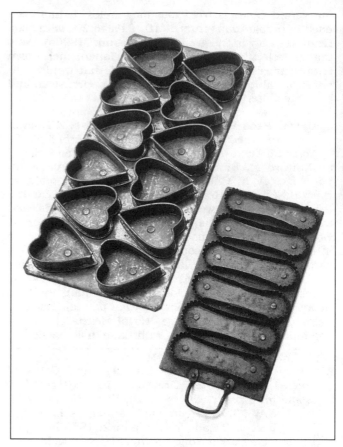

IV-341. Baking pans. *Pieced & sheet tin.* **(L)** *12 hearts riveted to oblong blued steel sheet. 13-1/2"L x 6-1/4"W, each heart is 2-1/2"L. Maker unknown.* **(R)** *Other one makes 6 ladyfingers, with fluted ends. Mold 9"L exclusive of handle; cups 4-1/4"L. Both late 19th or early 20th C. Collection of Meryle Evans.* **(L) $75-$150; (R) $40+**

dence in St. Louis that city had a population of about 7300. The first theatrical performance was given in the upper part of an old salt warehouse, the entrance being by an outside stairway. The chandelier for this theater was made in Mr. Filley's shop and Mr. Filley personally superintended the work of putting it in place. It was a tin chandelier with petticoat lamps." *The Metal Worker*, Feb. 27, 1892.

Muffin pan, cast iron, 6 cat/kitten cups, sitting, standing & playing, 11-1/2"L x 7"W, with scrolled handles. Offered in 1997 catalog of catscats, Web site: www.catscats.com. Foundry unnamed. Future collectible. .... **$30+**

Muffin pan, cast iron, makes 12 cakes or muffins in troughs, mold almost identical to 19th C. Nathaniel Waterman patent "French Roll" pan, made for many years by Hibbard, Spencer, Bartlett & Co., This one "Griswold #11," Erie, PA, 12-1/8" x 6-1/8", 20th C. .... **$35-$55+**

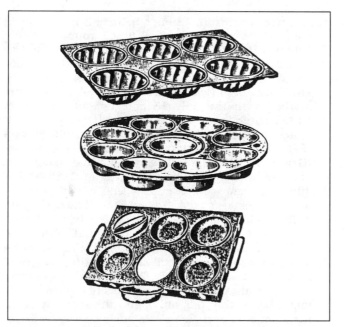

IV-340. Baking pans, *of stamped tin.* **(T)** *"Turk head pan," in 3 sizes: 11" x 7-1/4" with 6 cups; 14-1/2" x 7-1/4" with 8; & 14-1/4" x 11" with 12. Cups all same size. Geuder, Paeschke & Frey, 1925.* **(M)** *Unusual round "biscuit pan," on frame. Plain cups, 2-1/4" x 1-1/8" deep. Only one size, with 9 cups, 9-1/2" diam. Central Stamping Co., 1920.* **(B)** *Oblong pan with detachable shallow flat bottom cups. Stamped tin. Delphos Can Co., Delphos, OH, a company that made oil cans & dustpans. Ad in* House Furnishing Review, *Jan. 1906.* **$35+**

❖ **NOTES** ❖

Griswold Collectors Caveat. In a way, compared to all collecting fields except stamps and coins, and maybe dolls, new heights have been attained in knowledge of details and minute differences by collectors of Griswold (and to a lesser extent, Wagner). It is way way beyond me, partly because my cataloging instincts are more than satisfied by working on my books. So you won't find details like "slant TM" (meaning slanted trademark), or very much detailed notation of pattern numbers, especially what they signify (like "the 400 series indicates this was a ___," or "the 866 didn't appear on earlier ___," etc.).

Lookalike alarms – muffin pans. All of these are probably good bets for futurewatches. A 1980s muffin pan, cast iron, round with 7 mixed motif cups: 2 plain, 2 fluted, 2 hearts, one star cup in center, maker not stated in catalog, 9" measured across handles, 8" measured diagonally without handles, that was sold through (among other places I'm sure) Cumberland General Store, Crossville, TN. In 1983 they were selling it for $7. It seems to be going in the secondary market now for much more. Hearts: Another, actually more attractive, with 9 heart-shaped cups (outside rows both go one way, inside row goes opposite direction, so all 9 fit neatly together, shaped sides, handles at both ends. It is 9-1/8"L x 7-1/2"W, was in Lehman's Hardware 1989 catalog. Probably the Lodge foundry made them – that family-owned foundry, founded in the late 1800s, has been making interesting bakeware and specialty items for decades. Another possibility is John Wright Co. foundry. Lehman also offered a 13"L x 7-3/8"W muffin pan with ribbed handles at each end, design of what looks like 11 interlocking exotic animals. Other muffin pans in the 1989 catalog: 8 teddy bears, & is 15-1/4"L x 7-1/2"W; 8 fruits & vegetables, 15-1/8" x 7-1/2"; 26 letters, highly decorative for making alphabet cookies, 14 5/8"L x 7-5/8"W. Finally, one more, with ribbed handles, but double-sided, is 13-3/4" x 6-7/8", & allows you to make a gingerbread house & a gingerbread man & woman. One side makes a "Victorian home" & the spicy couple; the other side makes a log cabin, & 2 more folks.

Oldest Continuous Foundries in the USA. Which is it? Both Lodge and Wrightsville Hardware claim to be America's oldest continuously-operated maker of cast iron products. Lodge Mfg. Co., Box 380, South Pittsburgh, TN 37380, (423) 837-7181, can also be visited online at www.lodgemfg.com, and from there you can request a catalog, or go to their online shop to see various things. Their 2002 Web site shows gem-like bake molds with cactuses, stars, and perch. John Wright Co., Wrightsville Hardware, PO Box 269, Wrightsville, PA 17368. Figural bakeware – in 2002 this included the gingerbread house, the intricate flower muffin pan, the harvest pan, toy soldier pan, and a 9-heart muffin pan – can be seen online at www.jwright.com/index.cfm? CategoryID=27 & do=list.

Muffin pan, rusted cast iron, overall shape is a sleigh, interior cups are in Christmas motifs: gift stocking, Santa's head, star, tree, snowman, toy soldier, no marks, possibly John M. Wright, Wrightsville, PA, 7"H at highest point x 15-3/4"L, c.1970s or 1980s. • It looks neat, but it sure isn't worth the $350 a dealer at Brimfield had on it...................... **$25-$40**

MUFFIN PANS – ENAMELWARE

Muffin pan, cobalt & white swirl enamelware, 8 shallowish cups stamped (before enameling) in rectangular sheet metal, rolled rim, small hanging hole at one end, 1880s or so. **$100**

Muffin pan, gray graniteware, 12 cups, joined by metal strips, marked "Agate Nickel Steel Ware," Lalance & Grosjean, c.1890s-1910. .... **$55+**

Muffin pan, gray graniteware, Turk's head, 8 cups, late 19th C. .... **$65+**

Muffin pan, blue & white mottled enamelware, 8 cups, "Iris," Hibbard, Spencer & Bartlett, Chicago, IL, early 20th C. .... **$100+**

MUFFIN PANS – SOAPSTONE

Muffin pan, soapstone block with 9 cups, from a Vermont dealer, prob. VT, 1-3/4"H x 11-3/4"L x 7-1/2"W, late 19th C. .... **$100-$125+**

MUFFIN PANS – TIN or SHEET METAL

Muffin pan, or muffin tin, interesting raised rectangular tin tray has wire end handles, sides ventilated with penny-size holes, 6 shallow round cups set into holes in tray, Delphos Can Co., Delphos, OH, c.1905.. **$15+**

Muffin or madeline pan, stamped heavy tin, 7 scalloped cups riveted together, crude strap frame, American, 9" diam., c.1890s-1910. .... **$40+**

Muffin pan, or madeline pan, stamped tin, 7 scallop shell cups riveted together within circular frame, still rather brightly tinned, American, 9" diam., 19th C. ...... **$35+**

Muffin or gem pan, stamped tin, 12 cups soldered into frame, ring in one corner to hang up, no discernable mark, late 19th C. .... **$25+**

Muffin pan, pieced tin, 8 cups held together in thin flat tin frame, mfd. by Geuder, Paeschke & Frey, 1" deep x 14-1/4"L x 7-1/4"W, c.1890s-1910. .... **$35+**

Muffin pan, sheet iron, 12 cups, "Lockwood," Cincinnati, OH, 1900-10. .... **$25+**

IV-342. Noodle cutter. Hand-cranked, table top. "Vitantonio Mfg. Co., Cleveland, OH." Pat'd. Feb. 13, 1906 & March 2, 1920. Cast iron, tin & wood, roller attachment shown here, the "Zigzag #6," is iron, tin & has white rubber around axle. Pasta maker is screwed to piece of wood which would be clamped to table top. 7"H x 7"W. Company still making similar machines. Most for those with extra attachments. **$85+**

Muffin pan, tin, 12 cups, "Minute Maid," American. .... **$15+**

Muffin pan, tin, "Pillsbury Health Bran," 20th C..... **$15+**

Muffin pans – See also Bake molds; Corn stick pans; Tart pans

Noodle cutter, called a "Pot Pie Noodle Cutter & Lifter" by dealer, corrugated tin wheels with wire handle, rolls along & cuts ruffled-edge lasagna-like noodles, pat'd. by FELDT, Jamestown, NY, 8"L, no date, but looks c.1880s or 1890s. .... **$75+**

Noodle cutter, iron, wood & brass, mechanical, "Teek 1," German, c.1890s-1910. .... **$65+**

Noodle cutter, metal, turned wooden handles, dated 1932. .... **$10+**

Noodle cutter, metal, wood, crank action, "A A L Werke," & "Mark AAL," German, 20th C. ...... **$100+**

Noodle cutter, or noodle pin, a noodle cutting turned wooden rolling pin with sharp edged corrugations. German (?), 14"L, late 19th C. (?) or early 20th? .... **$25+**

Noodle cutter, 7 rolling straight blades opposite 7 rolling zig zag blades, adjustable because the blades are mounted on a sort of lazy tong, accordian action frame. Fully extended it is 25"W, meaning it could cut wide lasagna noodles from a large piece of rolled dough; folded tight it's 11"W, for narrower noodles. You could use the blades on either side. German, late 19th C... **$22+**

Noodle cutter, rolling type, wire handle & frame, 14 sharp blades with plate to push cut noodles off blades as it is turned, "The Ideal," Toledo Cooker Co., Toledo, OH, c.1910. .... **$25+**

Noodle cutter & pasta maker, cast iron frame with 4 long legs, mounted to wooden base, iron crank, kneading rollers like a mangle or wringer action, white rubber on axle of cutter attachment, set with blades, "Vitantonio Mfg. Co.," Cleveland, OH, 7"H x 7"W, pat'd. Feb. 13, 1906, March 2, 1920. • I saw great ad in 1983 *Gourmet Retailer*, for Vitantonio, depicting Angelo Vitantonio & his "first American pasta machine." The company is in Eastlake, OH, now, still importing & manufacturing Italian cookery

IV-343. Pancake griddle iron. *"U Like 'Em" multiple griddle. Polished cast iron that "will not absorb fat." Reversible so "no turning of cakes required." Each 6" diam. pan works independently. Made in 3 sizes, for 4 cakes (originally 49¢), for 6 cakes (71¢) & 8 cakes (97¢). Mfd. by Griswold; in Albert Pick catalog for hoteliers, 1909.* **$250-$375**

IV-344. Pastry "board" made of slate. *Also called a* **dough board.** *This beautiful thing with arrow tab handle is made of slate not wood. Hole for hanging cord. 17-1/2" diam., American, probably Pennsylvania, possibly early 19th C. Bigger than most I've seen. Picture courtesy of Robert W. Skinner Inc., Auctioneers, Bolton, MA. Slate pastry boards are still being made, but quality and finish look different.* **$300+**

items – pizzelle irons, ravioli makers, cavatelli & gnocchi makers, tomato strainers, etc. .... **$85+**

Noodle making machine, cast iron with wood, screw clamps, cranks, no mark except "patent pending," 6-3/4"L, late 19th C. (?). .... **$30+**

Noodle pin, for ravioli, carved wood, long body has 10 spool-like sections with corrugations around circumference & 4 long ridges end to end, 2 short turned handles. Two flat pieces of dough with the filling in blobs inside were rolled with this to seal the filling in the little squares of pastry. After drying a little they were broken apart & cooked in rolling boiling water, Italian, 24"L, 20th C. .... **$18-$25**

Pancake pan – See the first Muffin pan listing; also Plett kaker

Pastry boards with matching rolling pins – See Rolling Pins

Pastry board, oak covered with tin, T. Mills & Brother, Philadelphia, PA, 23" x 14", 1890s-1910. • Mills made confectioners' & candy makers' tools..... **$100**

Pastry board, thick plank cut slightly oval, very slightly warped, but beautiful dark patina from all the butter rolled on it, small hanging handle with hole, American (?), 19" diam., 19th C.............................. **$165**

Pastry or dough board, slate, very short arrow-shaped handle, with hanging hole, Pennsylvania, 17-1/2" diam., 2nd half 19th C. Geologist Noel Moebs informs us that the slate dough or pastry board is "made from a very fine & unique type of slate that is still being quarried in Pennsylvania's Pen Argyl by Anthony Dally & Sons, Inc., & others." • I saw several in 1983 & 1984, and only one since; it was stuck in the window of a photocopying place on lower Broadway in NYC. I wondered at the time if they were being made now? They all have a lovely mellow slate patina, thin (about 1/2"), and were pretty much all the same diam., but varied widely in price, from $80 on up. • I suspect that these pastry boards doubled as hot plates (see the historic paragraph next). And, hey! Why not chalkboards for messages? ...... **$300+**

❖ NOTES ❖

Black boards. "A Black Board should be in every kitchen, not to mark with chalk, but to place pots &

kettles on when removing them from the fire. Make it about a foot square, & one inch thick. It need not be washed often merely for looks, as the corners will be unsoiled. Its use will save the tables, floor, sink, etc., from many unsightly marks." *American Agriculturist*, March 1865. **Slate shingles** – I have several old slate shingles on countertops in my kitchen. Beautiful color, and they protect wooden and other surfaces.

Pastry board – See also Dough board. And, if you're using the term to mean a mold, look also under Cake board

Pastry stamp, cast & lathe-turned brass, like a small meat tenderizer with 6 small pyramidal points on head, turned wood handle with original hanging ring, very heavy, English, 7-7/8"L x 4-1/4"W, c.1820s to 1830s. .... **$275+**

Pastry tube, also called a pastry syringe, or cookie press. White metal cylinder & funnel nose, wood plunger, German (?), late 19th C. .... **$45+**

Pastry tube, or cookie press, tin cylinder with wooden plunger, star-shaped opening, American, 10-1/2"L, late 19th C.......................... **$45+**

Pastry tube, or cookie press, tin, small cylinder, with side wings used to hold it while pressing the plunger. Could be filled with several different flat tin discs that have cutouts in various shapes – stars, rosettes, etc., through which the dough was expressed in fancy shapes for making drop cookies in something besides blobs. Also used as a butter press for fancy pats, American, c.1870s. .... **$45+**

Pastry tube – See also Cookie press

Pâte mold – See Molds, tin section, French pie mold listing

PATTY IRONS, BOUCHE IRONS, ROSETTE MOLDS & TIMBALE MOLDS

All the molds here are used by dipping into a bowl of batter, which adheres to the mold, then dipped into boiling fat or oil for a few seconds. Some make little cups to be filled with sweets or savories, some make lacy little cakes that could be sprinkled with confectioners' sugar.

Patty iron set, cast iron, with long handle, 4 molds: 2 deep cups, 2 lacy open ones, in original box, Griswold Mfg. Co., Erie, PA, about 9"L with handle, early 20th C. .... **$55-$75**

Patty irons, cast iron, in original box, "Mrs. Wheelock's," American, 1920s. .... **$35+**

Patty irons, cast iron, set of 2 deep cupped ones in original box, with one screw-in heavy wire handle. One cup heart-shaped, one fluted round. Patties were cooked in deep fat, then filled with cold or hot, savory or sweet fillings – very nice for luncheons! Mmmm, wish I had me one right now. Griswold, Erie, PA, round cup: 2-1/4" diam.; heart about 2-7/8" across, c.1926 on................... **$35-$45+**

❖ NOTES ❖

Brown, Then Serve – Even a scrap of newspaper found in a box can provide tidbits to spice up your general knowledge. A very yellowed piece torn out of a January (!) issue of an unidentifiable Richmond, VA paper, dated probably c.1900-1905, has this delightfully odd tip: "**A Brown Luncheon.** – Just to vary the monotony of life there is the 'brown' luncheon. The creamed lobster is served in cups covered with brown tissue paper, the browned chops, browned fried pota-

toes, and browned rice croquettes on plates decorated with a design of brown oak leaves and acorns. The ice cream is chocolate frozen in shape of large English walnuts and the little squares of white cake bear the design of a leaf in tiny chocolate candies. The courses are served from large wooden trays ornamented in pyrographic work decorated in brown leaves and the water is poured from a little brown jug. All the decorations are brown, shading from seal to orange. The candles are yellow with autumn leaf shades. The name cards are placed inside little boxes decorated with pyrographic work and suitable for jewel boxes. The hostess wears a gown of panne velvet in the shade of brown known as 'burnt onion' and the maid's apron and headdress are decorated with brown bows."

Patty iron or patty mold, cast iron, heart, individual, Griswold #2. According to collector Joel Schiff, the patty & rosette irons (which are probably all 20th C.) were commonly sold in sets, unlike bouche & timbale case irons which were sold individually........ **$20-$25**

Patty iron or mold set, cast iron, in original box, cast iron, little kettle with thin wire bail handle for boiling oil, right size for dipping in the batter-coated lacy rosettes & patty irons, also a cast iron rosette, a mold with concentric rings with 4 spokes, a heart, & a patty shell or case mold, 2 screw-in threaded wire rod handles about 7"L. Chromolithograph inside box lid shows kettle on little electric hot plate. Griswold Mfg., Erie, PA. Oil kettle is 2-1/2" deep x 5-1/8" diam., c. 1940s-50s from box image. .... **$85-$135**

Patty or bouche iron, also what was later called a timbale iron, cast iron with iron shaft ending with wood handle, at right angles to shaft is screw-on bouche iron, shaped like a small cupcake (fluted, corrugated or plain). The iron was used by dipping it in bouche batter to coat the bottom & sides of the iron, then quickly dipping it in deep hot fat to make a little fluted shell or case for stuffing with crab meat salad or other ladies' delicacies. Skilled users could dip the forms of an entire mold to just the right depth in the batter, & so make 4 cups at a time. American, or French import, about 8" to 10"L, c.1870s-1890s. Much more recent ones were made at least into 1950s. New ones: $8-$20; Old:................. **$35-$50+**

❖ NOTES ❖

Old & New – The older bouche irons have nicely-turned wooden handles and decorative ferrules, everything seems carefully machined and decoratively designed. Newer ones, including some from the 1920s and later, have the simplest forms: most conspicuous is the iron rod shaft with a right angle bend and machine screw threading on the end. Often seen at fleas, but old ones are the real prizes.

•   •   •

Bouche or Dariole Batter – "Take two tablespoons of flour, drop two eggs into it, and mix with enough milk to make a batter, similar to fritter batter. Heat iron in boiling lard; then dip iron into batter, take out and leave on iron till batter drops off." Recipe accompanying the linecut of a tool that appears twice in an 1886 F. A. Walker catalog, under the names Bouche Iron as well as Dariole Iron.

From **Thailand** comes a similar device, with longish wood handle and 2 brass heads (one a small fluted cup, one a corrugated cup) which are dipped in hot oil, then in batter, then back in boiling oil. The 2 little pastry cups "float away" from the mold, according to *The International Cooks' Catalog*, NY: Random House, 1977.

Rosette iron set, cast iron in original box, the star & wheel molds were dipped into thinnish batter, then plunged quickly into a deep pot of very hot cooking fat, cooked for a minute, dropped off the molds & drained on paper, making light crispy confections in the same shape as the molds, & served after dusting with powdered sugar, "Manufactured for Alfred Andresen & Co.," Minneapolis, MN, this one, from the box's design, is mid 20th C. They are a much older form. .... **$45+**

❖ NOTES ❖

An Alfred Andresen ad in *Ladies' Home Journal*, Dec. 1906, shows **Rosette Wafers** being cooked in a steaming stovetop sauce pan. They are described as the "daintiest, crispest little morsels that ever tempted an epicure, or delighted the fastidious. Light as a summer zephyr, and delicious as ambrosia. You can make

IV-345. "Timbale sheet." Twelve relatively deep cups riveted on sheet tin, made in four sizes. Sheet 8" x 6" with cups 1-3/4" x 1-1/2" up to 10" x 7-1/2" with cups 2-1/4" x 2". Sold through D. J. Barry catalog, 1924. Used in U.S. for making little pastry cups to be filled with sweet or savoury fillings. (In England, timbales were almost always little layered aspics, which could also be made in dariole cups or "little bombé" moulds. Mrs. A. B. Marshall's Cookery Book, c.1900-1902, gives several aspic Timbale recipes.) In Fannie Farmer's Boston Cooking-School Cook Book of 1896, none of the timbales are aspic – & range from mounds of rice to creamed seafood in little baked pastry cases. For example: "Rice Timbales. Pack hot boiled rice in slightly buttered small tin moulds. Let stand in hot water ten minutes. Use as a garnish for curried meat, fricassee, or boiled fowl." Another Fannie oddity: "Macaroni Timbales. Line slightly buttered Dario moulds with boiled macaroni. Cut strips the length of height of mould, & place closely together around inside of mould. Fill with chicken, or Salmon Force-meat. Put in a pan, half surround with hot water, cover with buttered paper, & bake thirty minutes in a moderate oven. Serve with Lobster, Béchamel, or Hollandaise Sauce." **$45+**

forty of them in 20 minutes at a cost of ten cents with this simple little iron and the thinnest batter. A distinct novel delicacy for breakfast, luncheon and afternoon tea sold by leading dealers at 50 cents per set." They offered to send a free recipe booklet, "illustrated in eight colors," plus an "interesting catalog of culinary novelties," and all you had to do was send your dealer's name. I wish it would work now; I'd love to have an early Andresen catalog (which itself, incidentally, would be worth about $35 to $50).

Rosette irons, cast iron, set of 2 in original cardboard box, the "shallow pattern" openwork rosette irons, heavy gauge wire screw-in handle with wooden grip, Griswold, (there were several makers of these), Erie, PA, round rosette is 2-5/16" diam.; scalloped one (which looks like 4 hearts, arranged points in) is 3" diam., c. 1926-1960s (?)........................... **$35-$55**

Rosette & timbale mold combined, cast aluminum molds in set, screwed onto Y-shaped handle that looks like slingshot or wishbone, simple hotdog-shaped turned wood handle, meant that 2 could be dipped at once. One fluted round & one fluted

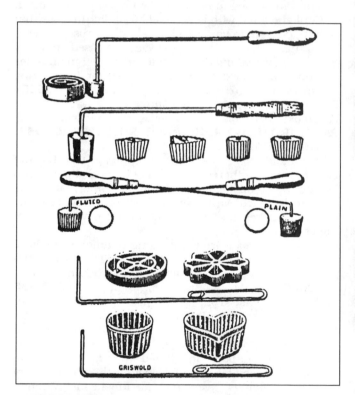

IV-346. Patty, rosette, timbale, or bouche irons. For making little pastry cups, about 2"H, that could be filled with cremes, mousses, & savouries. From top (1) one with spiraled iron is a "Coiled Spring Cake" or sprungfedern iron. Turn-of-century catalog. (2) A plain & 4 fluted cups or "case fryers," is nickel-plated, from S. Joseph, c.1927. (3) Crossed timbale irons, nickel-plated, could be had as plain or fluted rounds, ovals, hearts, diamonds, spades or clubs. From Sexton Stove & Range Mfg., c.1930s. Both 2 & 3 would be used by Fannie Farmer to make pastry cases for Cream Oysters or the like. (4) & (5) Last two sets from Griswold. These you often find in original boxes. **$20-$60**

IV-347. Patty, Rosette, Timbale set. "Enjoy 'Old World' pastry treats!" Cast aluminum, about 3" diam. Double stemmed handle meant you could make 2 at a time. By this time "timbale" had stretched to include case molds much wider than deep. Probably A. Andresen. Gift shop ad in House Beautiful, April 1964. **$12+**

square timbale or patty shell mold, plus one star & one wheel-like rosette mold. Patty shells could be filled with anything from fruit or custard to creamed chicken, very popular for luncheons, American, molds each about 3" diam., 1960s. .... **$15-$20+**

❖ NOTES ❖

Modern rosette maker – Shown in an early 1980s kitchenware catalog is a cast aluminum dessert rosette set, for making "waffle cookies and fruit filled patty shells," shrink-wrapped on printed card, mfd. or imported by Fairgrove, place illegible. It consists of slightly bent rod with handle, a patty iron with heart, spade, diamond and club, a butterfly and an 8 petal flower, the three things to be screwed to the handle.

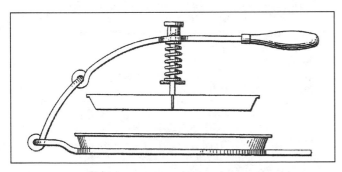

IV-348. Pie cutter patent. Pat'd. by Clarence B. Lewis, Los Angeles, CA, Apr. 9, 1907, #850,022. A hinged & levered device, with a spring return action, having "any number of radially-arranged [spoked] cutter blades. Any number of blades may be employed, and they may be of any size and shape, but I preferably employ six when the device is to be used for cutting pies, and shape them ... [to cut wedges] ... so that they will fit the pie pan which rests upon the base-plate."

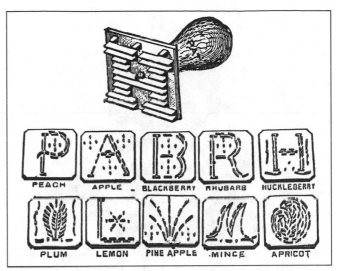

IV-349. Pie markers, for bakeries to mark flavors on two crust pies. **(T)** Pie stamp, for putting initials on upper crust & puncturing it to let steam escape. Full set of 7 letters: A, C, H, L, M, P, R. in H. Hueg catalog, c.1900-1921. Let's see: Apple, Cherry, Huckleberry, Lemon, Mince, Peach, Rhubarb? **(B)** This set from same period, not only has letters (P, A, B, R, H, L, & M), also has picture designs to mark other pies with same initial letters as basic ones. Jaburg, 1908. Singles: **$5+;** Sets: **$20+**

Rosette wafflet molds – according to manufacturer the pieces in this cast aluminum set are "combination rosette and patty shell" molds, includes rod handle that screws into the 8 different heads – club, heart, diamond or spade rosette or patty – also available in a scalloped edge cup or flower, "Century," mfd. by U. S. Utilities, Chicago, IL, c.1933................. **$15-$30**

Pie birds or vents – See Chapter V (Measure & weigh)

Pie crimper or pie jagger – See Jaggers, Crimpers & Trimmers

Pie divider, tin, rim turned up, big strap handle, looks like a huge cookie cutter that cuts wedges, cuts only 5 pieces in an 8" pie, no maker's mark, American, about 4-1/4"L, 20th C...................................... **$30**

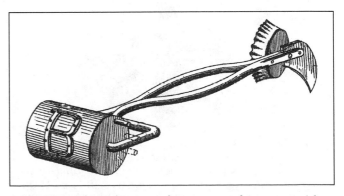

IV-350. Pie printer, crimper & trimmer, pat'd. by Frederick K. Booth, Reynoldsville, PA, Dec. 31, 1901, #689,848. The printer roll has "the design or figure in relief thereupon, and points projecting above said figure or design at intervals." The thing that looks like a bottle cap is a crimper.

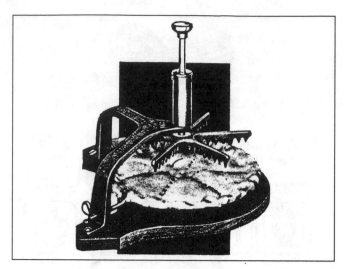

IV-351. Pie & Cake marker. *For professional bakers to mark portions. Screwed to wooden base, spring-loaded punch. Nickel-plated, or polished cast aluminum. It marked a dotted line where to cut pieces, & could be fitted with markers for from 4 to 12 slices for different sizes of pie or cake tins. D. J. Barry, 1924.* **$20+**

Pie pans:

Pie pans have slightly flared or canted sides; cake pans are sized the same but have straight vertical sides.

Pie or cake pan, tin, round, slightly flared sides & wide rim, embossed "PY-O-MY Dutch Apple Cake Mix Baking Pan," 1-1/2" deep x 9" diam., early 20th C. .... **$10+**

Pie pan, tin, rectangular, stamped "Free 49 cent pan with your initial purchase of new Py-O-My Pastry Mix," 20th C. .... **$10+**

Pie pan, blue & white swirl enamelware, 9" diam., c.1890s-1910. .... **$15+**

Pie pan, cobalt blue & white agate enamelware, 10" diam., early 20th C. Another, only 8-1/2" diam., all white interior, slightly less. .... **$15+**

IV-352. "Cottage stamp." *"In place of moulding the Cottage in six pieces, mould them in one piece, place same in pans, when half raised dust them lightly with Rye flour & stamp with this tool." In Hueg & Jaburg catalogs, early 20th C. "Cottage" is hard to track down. It's probably the same as "Cottage Pudding," a cake-like confection, which Marjorie Heseltine, in Good Cooking, from early 20th C., says to bake in a pan & cut into squares. The stamp is for bakeries.* **$25+**

IV-353. Pie pans or plates. *Shallow (with exception of (4), with slanted sides (layer cake pans have straight sides). From top: (1) Scalloped, stamped tin, in one size, 8-9/16" diam. x 1-1/8" deep. Savory, c.1925-28. (2) Perforated tin, 9-3/4" x 1-1/16", also Savory. (3) "Greystone" gray graniteware plate in 5 sizes, from 7" to 11" diam. Also came in slightly deeper versions, 9" to 11" diam. Matthai-Ingram, c.1890. (4) A "Greystone Lebanon" pie plate, for deep dish pies. 7-3/4", 8-1/2" & 9-1/2" diam. The "Lebanon" referring to an area of Pennsylvania. Also Matthai-Ingram.* **$5-$30+**

Pie pan, green & white swirl enamelware, 9" diam., 20th C. A cobalt & white swirl, 8", is same price range. .... **$15+**

Pie pan, pale blue & white swirl enamelware, 12" diam., early 20th or late 19th C. In turquoise, a bit more desirable. **$15**

Pie pan, stamped tin, "Goldblatt Brothers," 20th C. ... **$7+**

Pie pan, stamped tin, shallow very slightly slanted sides, attached metal cutter pivots from center, to cut pie out of pan, "Clipper Pie Plate," L. E. Brown & Co., Cincinnati, OH, 8" diam., c.1880s. .... **$7+**

Pie pan, tin, flared sides, embossed "Manning" in script, 7-3/4" diam., early 20th C. .... **$6+**

Pie pan, tin, slanted sides, embossed "New England Table Talk Flaky Crust – Mother's Only Rival," 1-1/4" deep x 9-5/8" diam., early 20th C. **$10**

Pie pan, tin, slanted sides, advertising would make you think it a cake pan, "Presto Self-Rising Cake Flour," pat'd. 1924. .... **$10**

Pie pan or pie plate, stoneware with brown glaze, corrugated edge, American, 9" diam., 19th C. .... **$85+**

❖ **RECIPE** ❖

Shrimp Pie – *"Take a quart of shrimp, clean picked from the shells; if they are very salt in the boiling, season them only with a little cloves and mace; but if they want salt, shred two or three anchovies very fine, mix them with the spice, and season the shrimps. You may make a good crust, because they do not want much baking; put a pretty deal of butter over and under them, one glass of white wine, and sent it to the oven." Eliza F. Haywood, A New Present for a Servant-Maid; Necessary Cautions & Precepts to Servant-Maids for Gaining Good-Will & Esteem, Dublin, Ireland: 1771.*

Pie pan or pie plate, (usually the ceramic ones are called plates), PA German redware, with message in yellow slip, "A Good Apple Pie is the Best of All," PA, 9" diam., late 19th C. .... **$650+**

Pie plate, spongeware pottery, "The Pure Food Sanitary Cooking Ware," American, early 20th C. .... **$135+**

Pie plate, stoneware, bright blue glaze inside only, maple leaves molded along sides, outside not glazed, "Cookin Ware," Neu-Deel Economy Health Cookin Ware, Canadian (?), 9" diam., "Patent Office R & G," prob. 2nd quarter 20th C. .... **$25+**

Pie top-crust mold, redware pottery, nearly square with hanging hold in top left corner, Detailed round design in relief of eagle standing on a shield, arrow underneath, rope border, the outer wide border being 8 demilune swags. It was in the famed titus Geesey Collection in Wilmington, DE, & was depicted on the cover of September 1953 *Spinning Wheel Collectors'* magazine, & described within as being "possibly" made from an intaglio carved wooden cake board. The article also states that this mold was used to imprint the top pie crust. I never

IV-354. Plett kaker, or Pancake pan. Also referred to as a "muffin baker" in the 1872 New Cyclopedia of Domestic Economy. "Muffin" as in the flat "English" muffin; some collectors call these "biscuit skillets" – perhaps in European sense of sweet biscuits, called cookies in U.S. Cast iron, 7 very shallow cups, with "JOHNSON" cast on handle. 10-1/2" diam. with 6-1/4"L handle. Lower picture shows interesting appearance of bottom. Note heavy incrustation. Ex-Collection of NYC food stylist, Grace Manney. $50-$65

IV-355. Plett kaker, or Pancake pan. Cast iron, 7 very shallow flat-bottom cups, 3 legs. From ad of NYC dealer, J. & C. Berrian, in a book on prominent manufacturers of U.S., 1857. $125+

heard of such a thing before, but maybe! Probably Pennsylvania German, probably early 19th C. Probable value: .... **$1,200+**

Pizzelle iron – See Wafer or pizzelle iron

Plett kaker or pancake pan, sometimes called in the U.S. a biscuit skillet, cast iron, 7 shallow flat-bottom cups & skillet handle with teardrop hanging hole, marked "Western Importing Co." (successor to Alfred Andresen), on bottom near handle. Andresen used the name along with his own to mark company products. Because this piece has only the Western Importing Co. mark, it's likely that this dates after Andresen's departure from the company in 1906. Cups 2-1/4" diam., overall 8-3/4" diam., prob. 1906+. • A "*plett*" is a Scandinavian word for "spot" – hence, small pancakes, maybe what we'd call silver dollar cakes. These pancake molds are rather plentiful, & only recently are collected – primarily, according to Joel Schiff, "as a result of Andresen's involvement with Griswold, who actually manufactured their forms from about 1904 on. Andresen originally imported & used other companies to make their wares. .... **$35-$40+**

Plett kaker or pancake pan, cast iron, like griddle with 7 extremely shallow flat-bottom cups bigger than the ebelskiver cups, slightly raised edge, short upcurved handle with teardrop hanging hole, Griswold Mfg. Co., PN 34, after a Swedish type of pan, 9-1/2" diam., with cups only 1/4" deep, each cake 3" diam., made c.1918 on, for many years................ **$40-$55**

Popover pan, cast iron, 11 deep, slightly slant-sided flat-bottomed cups, Wagner Ware #01 B, Sidney, OH, cups are 1-7/8" deep, 11"L x 7-1/2"W, 1890s-1910. .... **$30-$40+**

Popover pan, cast iron, marked "Griswold" & "Wagner Ware." It has been said that because Wagner bought Griswold in 1957, for a while both names appeared on some pans. But a Wagner Ware supervisor told

Dave Smith that the double marked pieces were done in 1972 to phase out the Griswold trademark. Two years later, in 1974, General Housewares bought out the merged company. This pan, prob. 1972+. .... **$25-$40**

Popover pan, cast iron, tab handles, 2 casting gates on bottom, no mark, 8" x 12"L, c.1890s-1910. ..... **$40+**

Popover pan, or gem pan, cast iron, tab handles solid not cutout, 11 cups, Wagner Ware, marked "B" on center cup on back, Sidney, OH, 11-1/4"L x 7-5/8"W x 1-7/8" deep, late 19th C. (?). .... **$35-$45**

❖ RECIPE ❖

Graham Gems – *"To one quart of Graham flour add one half pint fine white flour; enough milk or water, a little warm, to make a thick batter; no salt or baking powder; have the oven hotter than for biscuits; let gem-pans stand in the oven till you get ready; beat batter thoroughly; grease your pans; drop in while the irons are smoking hot; bake quickly a nice brown." Henry Scammel, compiler, Treasure House of Useful Knowledge, 1891.*

*• **Graham flour** was named after the Reverend Sylvester Graham (1794-1851), an American who was the first to recognize the value of eating whole-wheat flour, bran and all. He spent a lot of his life trying to encourage housewives and cooks to use his flour, which we now welcome as high fiber. He was ridiculed as a mad faddist by some, but did attract a large, enthusiastic following. Many 19th C. recipes called for graham or "entire wheat" flour.*

Pretzel cutter, also called a bretzel cutter, tin like a cookie cutter, flatback, strap handle, 5" across x 4", cuts out the dough in the crossed-arms-within-heart shape that is basically the pretzel shape, for

*IV-356. **Popover pans.** These are referred to as **"corn bread"** pans in Hibbard, Spencer, Bartlett's catalog showing "Waterman's Cast Bake Pans." They're called a "Gem Pan" in Griswold's catalogs.* **(T)** *#10, 11 pans, 2-3/4" diam. each. 1880s.* **(B)** *#10, cakes 2-1/2" x 1-3/4". Griswold, early 20th C.* **$35-$50**

*IV-357. **Rice ball boilers.*** **(T-L)** *Perforated tin, for balls of "fried" farina, from Urbain Dubois, c.1860s-80s.* **(T-R)** *"Wire pea or vegetable boiler, for beas, beans, rice, boils dry & when taken out no grains are left in the pot." Small one at far right is a "tea boiler." American Home Cook Book, 1854.* **(B)** *Tinned screen or wire gauze, in one size, 5-1/2" diam. Washborn "Androck" line, 1936.* **$10-$25**

deep fried dough. Not technically a pretzel, which is made by hand, by rolling out a long "snake" of dough, & bending it around into the heart & crossing the ends & laying them on the edge of the heart (a pretzel is supposed to represent praying arms). Late 19th C. or early 20th. .... **$35+**

Pretzel cutter, cast aluminum, very grainy & poorly made, late 20th C. .... **$5+**

Pudding molds – See Molds, in various materials

Pudding pan, blue & white swirl enamelware, rectangular, 12"L, late 19th C. **$30**

❖ RECIPE ❖

Indian-Meal Pudding – *One cup of yellow Indian meal, one quart and a cupful of molasses, one generous tablespoonful of butter, one teaspoonful of salt, one pint of boiling water, half teasponful each of cinnamon and mace. Scald the salted meal with the water. Heat the milk in a farina-kettle [a double boiler]; stir in the scalded meal, and boil, stirring often, for half an hour. Beat the eggs light; put in the butter and molasses, stirred together until they are several shades lighter than at first; add the spice; lastly, the batter from the farina-kettle, beaten in a little at a time, until all the ingredients are thoroughly incorporated. Grease a pudding-dish; pour in the mixture, and bake, covered, in a steady oven, three-quarters of an hour. Remove the lid, and brown. This is the genuine, old-fashioned New-England 'Indian' pudding. Eat with sauce, or with cream and sugar. It is very nice." Marion Harland, Universal Cookery Book, 1887.*

Pudding pan, gray graniteware, shallow, slightly flared sides, "Chef-ette Enameled Ware" on red paper label, American. .... **$55+**

Rice ball, large perforated 2-part spun aluminum ball, clip fastening, chain to hang off pot's side, American, 7" diam., 20th C. .... **$10+**

Rice ball, tin & wire screening ball, 2 parts unscrew, wire handle locks over edges to hold halves together, chain & hook for edge of pot, American, 5-1/4" diam., marked with date, pat'd. June 17, 1930. .... **$10+**

Rice boiler mold, stamped & pieced tin, flat-bottomed, tubed with slanted out fluted sides, close fitting slightly convex lid with big strap handle, small wire ring catches to attach lid, American or European import, about 5" to 7"H x about 3" to 4" diam. at top, c.1870s to 1880s. • These look like pudding molds, & may have been used as such, but advertised by F. A. Walker in their catalog as rice boilers........... **$55+**

Rice cake mold, carved wood paddle, good luck symbol & calligraphy, Chinese, 7"L, poss. 19th C., more likely a 20th C. sort of export souvenir. • These started showing up, in vast quantitites, about 1982 or 1983. Many of them do not have Chinese characters carved in them, but typically Chinese motifs such as koi (goldfish/carp), butterflies, chrysanthemums & fruit. They come in a sort of butter paddle shape, or in truncated & elongated ovals, often with hanging hole with leather thong tie. The first wholesaler ads for them listed them in six styles: (1) a long narrow one, 12"L x 1-3/4"W with 10 small images; (2) 8-1/2"L x 3-1/2"W paddle, with sort of flower clam design; (3) 8"L x 3"W, paddle, irregular head, with curvy fish design; (4) 12"L x 2-1/2"W board with four fruity designs; (5) (6) 12"L x 3-1/2"W boards with either 2 strange flower-fruit butterfly carvings, or 2 fish. Nothing in ad identified them as being Chinese, but they were called "Molds, 75-100 years old," & were priced $23 to $32 each, with 50% discount if you bought 10 or more, which meant that a dealer could then resell them for about the wholesale for one. It didn't take many months before they began appearing. The resale price is often very high, if there is but one on display, as much as $85 or $95. Asking price usually at high end of range............... **$15-$45**

Rice cake mold, large oblong paddle with smallish handle, probably used for some kind of rice confection, 6 carved out cups including 3 different fish, a bird, also 2 plant-like flowers, Chinese, 13"L x 6"W, late 19th C. (?). • **Caution:** This is the largest of the Chinese rice cake molds, which have been sold all over the United States since about 1983 as, variously,

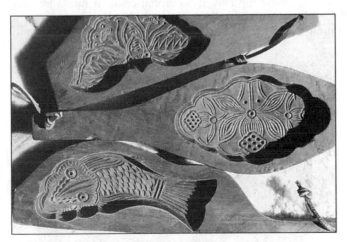

IV-358. Rice molds from China. Carved wood paddles, with typical Chinese motifs of fish, butterfly & lotus flower. Usually called "sugar molds" by dealers who don't know or aren't telling. These are actually imported from China, & may be old in some instances. Photograph from stock of Mary Colborn, Murrysville, PA. $15-$45

maple sugar molds, cookie molds, or candy molds. This is not to say they are not nice molds, but you could be paying a premium for "early American" when it's probably "late Chinese.".............. **$30-$40**

❖ COLLECTOR HINT❖

Stop, Look, Listen ... and Read – Some antiques people think that out of a given number of collectors, a very few are graced with "the eye," an ability to see and know what is good, to pick the treasure from the dross. Furthermore, some of the antiques experts firmly believe that you're either born with it or you'll never have it. I don't entirely believe that, although there is an element of natural talent involved. Lots and lots of studying, of subjects as diverse as Japanese woodblock prints, African masks, Fauvist paintings, Egyptian jewelry, Shenandoah pottery, Victorian valentines, Thonet chairs, and Christmas glass ornaments, will never be wasted. But you must absorb yourself in each subject, sit on the sofa with a pile of library books from call number 700's shelves, and look at all of them, back and forth. Don't say "I don't like African masks." Look at pictures of them, or best, real ones in museums, until you do like them. Don't say "Fiesta Ware is cheap and ugly." Look at it until you appreciate what there is about it that's perfectly done. This is not to say you have to like everything, or that everything is worthy of praise. But everything you study, go in with a Zen "don't know" mind. The open mind, the clean slate *tabula rasa* mind, will allow you to learn something you can apply to your butter molds, churns, tin trays, copper tea kettles, cast iron griddles. You will find yourself choosing, and knowing why. • I used to think that to study a piece (or to analyze your motive for wanting it) took the fun out, spoiled it, maybe even prevented its purchase (to question is to doubt). Now, because I know there are many ways to study a piece or a field aesthetically, socially, historically, functionally – I know that study can only add to the pleasure. Harry Rinker wrote in a column on "Collectibles" in early 1989 that the "fun" of collecting is in the chase, not in the piece itself. If he really means that, I am diametrically in opposition. In collecting, a little (or no) knowledge is not only the dangerous thing, the foolhardy way, it's self-defeating in the long run, because the fun of the chase is diminished by a lack of awareness – of the other hunters, as well as the hunted. Then, after your treasure is up on the wall, mounted with the other trophies, there would be nothing to reflect on, no new way to re-appreciate, or re-evaluate. • So keep on reading and looking, and exercise your own "eye."

Ring mold – See above in Molds, tin border molds

Roll cutter, brass & iron, it rolls with 2 handles, like a rolling pin, cuts dough into oblongs, English, 4-3/4" diam. rolls or biscuits, English patent #16798 (19th C., prob. c.1880s).. **$85+**

Roll pan or bread stick pan, cast iron, 11 long troughs, 2 lengthwise casting marks, filed down, catty-corner on back, no maker mark, 13-1/4"L x 9-1/4"W, 19th C. .... **$45+**

Roll pan, cast iron, makes 12 French rolls in trough-like cups rounded on bottom & oblong in outline, in 2 rows 6 x 6, very similar to what Griswold called a

IV-359. *"Elementary method of rolling layered pastry."* From Urbain Dubois La Patisserie, late 19th C. Note completely straight, slim, "French" rolling pin. This pin created perfectly-even thin pastry.

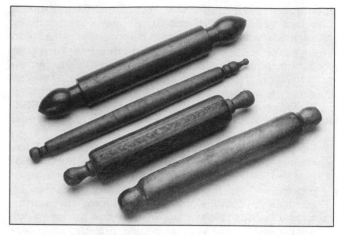

IV-360. **Rolling pins.** *Fancy carved wooden pins, well-turned from one piece of wood. One with variegated wood, third from top, with bulbous handles & thick barrel, is possibly a Shaker piece. Note 2 different ends on long French pin – undoubtedly made to order for a cook with special needs. From about 15-1/4"L to 18-1/2"L. 19th C. Collection of Meryle Evans.* **$60-$125+**

muffin pan. American, dated 1850. No U.S. patent that year for bake pan, roll pan, muffin pan, gem pan or bread pan. This is very handsome, but according to Joel Schiff is the "most common pan in the United States"! .... **$25-$40**

❖ NOTES ❖

American Agriculturist, Jan. 1868, had one of these illustrated, with a short article called **"Gems or Aerated Rolls.** – The only convenient article for cooking Gems is a French roll pan for baking, and we cannot warrant success in anything else. The pans are made of cast iron, and can be had at the large hardware and furnishing stores in the cities at about $4.50 per dozen, and 75¢ single. Put the pan upon the stove, heated nearly to redness. Take one cup of water, one cup of milk, and three cups of flour, of the best quality. Stir in the flour gradually, and with a spoon beat the mixture five minutes briskly. The object of the beating is to get as much air as possible into the batter. Put a piece of butter of the size of a pea into each of the moulds, and fill about two-thirds full with the batter. Put immediately into a very hot oven, and bake for 20 minutes, or until nicely browned.

"This form of unleavened bread is the best article for breakfast or tea we have ever found in that land of good housekeepers, Eastern Connecticut. It is exceedingly light, palatable, and nutritious, excellent for invalids and dyspeptics, and quite as good for people in sound health. They are so nice that we hope our readers will try the article for themselves. We bear no ill-will to hop growers, or venders of soda, saleratus, and other salts, but we have no doubt that the Gems once introduced into a family would greatly diminish the use of these unwholesome articles in cookery, and help to promote health and good digestion." (What I don't understand, is how you take this 2/3 full red hot pan weighing 4 pounds or so and get it quick into the hot oven.)

Gems – Occasionally the word gem is associated with "aerated roll" – meaning a non-yeast roll whose dough is raised with saleratus or baking powder, or by being "air whipped."

Roll pan, cast iron, very shallow, makes 8 oval rolls, only mark is "No. 5" on back, 7-3/8"W, c.1890s-1910. .... **$25**

❖ NOTES ❖

Confusable – What looks in pictures like a roll pan for making 4 oblong rolls, & may look like one in real life (or it may be much smaller), is a solder mold. It is oblong with flat long handle coming from one end, the pan divided into 4 shallow oblongs. It is marked "C. S. Osborne" on the handle. I found it in *Alfred Revill's American Plumbing,* NY: Excelsior, 1984. The resemblance in picture is striking enough to add. See IV-15. (Also very similar to baking pans, and approx. the same size, are cast iron molds with conical cups; these are assayers' slag molds, and have various numbers of cups (often 6) in an oblong frame. One has frying pan handle off one end, and 2 rows of 3 cups. Another has a long single-file row of 6 conical cups; it has a wooden handle at one end. These crucible molds were used to melt finely-ground ores to determine the percentage of

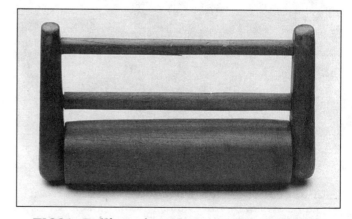

IV-361. **Rolling pin.** *Of type called a* **draalhus** *by Pennsylvania Germans. Heavy wood with double-barred handle for extra strength & good grip. 11"L x 6-3/4"H as shown. 19th C. Collection Meryle Evans.* **$175-$250**

gold or silver in a particular prospector's sample. Collector Jim Holroyd told me about them, sharing information he'd got from Jack Ward.)

Roll pan, flat tin sheet with 6 curvy roll cups riveted to sheet, Silver & Co., Brooklyn, c.1916. .... **$15+**

Roll pan or Vienna baker, for what are called "Vienna Rolls," cast iron, 6 cigar-shaped cups set rather farther apart than usual, Griswold #26, about 12-1/2"L, c.1890s-1910 or early 20th C. • Wagner's was almost the same, 12"L x 6-1/2"W. Value range related to whether it is marked #6 or #26, & the company marking. Griswold higher than Wagner. .... **$50-$100**

Roll pan or Vienna baker, heavy tin, 9 oval shallow cups set in frame, with end handles, mfd. by Lalance & Grosjean Mfg. Co., late 19th C. .... **$20+**

Roll pan, cast iron, 11 shallow cups set 4 x 3 x 4, handle brace at each end, W & L Mfg. Co. (Warnick & Leibrandt), 19th C. .... **$25+**

ROLLING PINS

Rolling pin manufacturers. From several directories, with whatever information is in the directories. *Thomas' Register of American Manufacturers, Buyers' Guide* **1905-06.** • Wm. R. Hartigan, Collinsville, CT; Williams & Marvin Mfg. Co., Deep River, CT; • John Sommer's Son, Newark, NJ; • Ohio Tool Co., Columbus, OH; • *1909 House Furnishing Review Buyers' Directory.* • Escanaba Woodenware, Escanaba, MI • Wm. R. Hartigan, Collinsville, CT • Imperial Mfg. Co., Cambridge, OH "White Opalite" trade name; • Richard & Bethold, Bellaire, MI • plus an unspecified number of "woodenware" manufacturers. • *1930 House Furnishing Review Buyers' Directory.* • Brush Pottery Co., Zanesville, OH; • Hinkle Leadstone Co., Chicago, IL; • J. Shepherd Parrish Co., Chicago; • Stoware, Inc., Stowe, VT; • G. M. Thurnauer Co., NYC (prob. imports from Germany); • *1932 Thomas' Register of American Manufacturers.* • J. Shepherd Parrish, Chicago (wooden); • Stephenson Mfg. Co., South Bend, IN (wood); • H. A. Stiles & Co., Boston; • Munising Woodenware Co., Munising, MI; • Sandvik Saw & Tool Corp., Minneapolis, MN (creased, rolling); • Koons Bros., Grooville, NY; • Bogert & Hopper, Inc., NYC (wooden); • E. B. Estes & Sons, NYC (wood); • G. M. Thurnauer, NYC; • Carolina Wood Turning Co., Bryson City, NC; • Imperial Mfg. Co., Cambridge, OH (glass & wood); • Brush Pottery Co., Zanesville, OH; • C. Prouty & Co., Eldred, PA; • H. Sheldon Mfg. Co., Elkland, PA; • N. Cohen, Philadelphia; • Wm. Hodges & Co., Philadelphia (springerle); • Royal Mfg. Co., Philadelphia (wooden); • United States Glass Co., Pittsburgh, PA (glass); • Roy Bros., East Barnet, VT (wood); • Artwood Products Co., Inc., Morrisville, VT (enameled handles); • Stoware, Inc., Stowe, VT; • *1945-46 Thomas' Register of American Manufacturers.* • J. Shepherd Parrish Co., Chicago (wooden); • H. A. Stiles & Co., Boston, MA; • Munising Wood Products Co., Marquette, MI; • Norman Products Co., Newark, NJ; • Anchor Equipment Co., NYC (wood); • JB. F. D. Co., NYC; • Bogert & Hopper, NYC (wooden); • P. M. C. Mfg. Corp., Phoenicia, NY; • Carolina Wood turning Co., Bryson City, NC; • Imperial Mfg. Co., Cambridge, OH (glass & wood); • Owens-Illinois Glass Co., Toledo, OH (glass); • Nathan Cohen, Philadelphia (wooden); • William Hodges & Co., Philadelphia (springerle); • George Marnhout Co., Philadelphia (wooden); • Royal Mfg. Co., Philadelphia (wood); • Red Jacket Pencil Co., Nashville, TN; • Sanders Mfg. Co., Nashville; • National Clothes Pin Co., Montpelier, VT; • Verdwood Products Co., Morrisville, VT (enameled handles); • Stoware, Inc., Stowe, VT.

Rolling pins come in a wide range of styles and sizes. Some are truly just "pins" (like a sailor's belaying pin), slightly tapered at each end, used by rolling with the palms of both hands at each end. Some of these are quite long and thin, others fatter and short. Then there are the revolving barrel pins that have handles, which are gripped in one position and pushed away or pulled toward the cook, across the dough. The barrels are made of various materials. I've divided the listings into sections according the material. See also some information in the Cake board listings; also in the Pastry board listings. See also Noodle cutters, also Cracker rollers.

ROLLING PINS – advertising:

Rolling pin, blue & white pottery, advertising "W. E. Neyland," Goliad, TX, late 19th C. .... **$150+**

Rolling pin, brown pottery, adv'g. "Thompson's General Store," Grand Junction, IA, 19th C. .... **$160+**

Rolling pins, pottery, printed with advertising. Most are 1890s-1910. •"Robert F. McAfee, Dealer in Groceries, Augusta, IL"; • "John M. Merriot" (possibly John H.), Mt. Vernon, Iowa; • "J. F. Reily Groceries, Hardware, Implements, Buggies & Wagons," Seaton, IL; • "Dawson Furniture," Ziegler, IL (that one with blue stripe); • "Thompson's General Store," Grand Junction, IA, (brown stripe); • "Killian's," Wahoo, NE (brown stripe); • "Peterson & Anderson," Pomeroy, IA; "Joseph Reuter, General Merchandise," Gilbertville, IA; • bank or flour mill advertising maxim, "Save Your Dough"; • brown bands & letters, "O. O. Hartley, Home of Quality Groceries, Phone 53, Roseville, IL," c.1890s-1910; • with brown stripe, "Perry & Buchanan General Merchandise, Quasqueton, IA; • with brown stripe, "White Swan Flour," Garrison, IA; • white & blue pottery, "Ernest Nelson Sells the Flour that Makes the Dough Hump Great." Value range mostly based on desirability & subject of advertising, meaningfulness of place, & condition & decoration, is range for others noted.. **$110-$185+**

Rolling pin, salt-glazed stoneware with blue border with flowers, wooden handles, advertising message "Compliments of Berks County Democrat, a Newspaper," Boyertown, PA, 8-1/2"L excluding handles, late 19th C. • This one has extra appeal to crossover collectors because it advertises a newspaper. .... **$275-$350**

Rolling pin, white pottery, "Kelvinator" – yes! the fridge people, the pin to be chilled before using, American, 20th C. .... **$75+**

Rolling pin, milk glass, wooden handles, advertising "Pekin Coal Fuel Co.," Pekin, NE, 19th C. Very unusual because most advertising pins are ceramic. ...... **$100+**

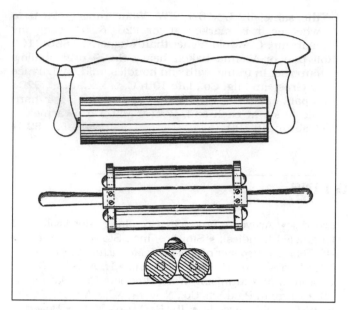

IV-362. Draalhus single roller & double roller patents. (T) *A patented version of rolling pin in IV-361. This one pat'd. by George A. Twele, NYC, NY, May 10, 1881, #241,253, assigned one-half to Henry C. Twele, NYC. His claim was for the way the "peculiar form of a handle" was connected to the rolling-pin, which* **can be operated by one or both hands.** *[Bold face emphasis mine.]* **(B)** *Top view & end-on view of a double roller pat'd. by Albert L. Taylor, Springfield, VT, July 16, 1867, #66,909. Taylor wrote in his claim: "The ordinary single roller does not spread the paste or dough evenly if passed over the later in one direction only. It is necessary to roll the paste or dough first in one direction and then in the other, in order to get it of uniform thickness throughout, and this is attended with a considerable expenditure of time and labor. My improved device can be manufactured at a trifling advance over the ordinary single roller ... [as] they do not require to be as large in diameter. I would remark that more than two rollers may be employed, but two will answer equally as good a purpose as three or more." See a photo of real thing in IV-364.*

Rolling pin, wood, with pyrographic, or hot poker work, adv'g. "Custers Mills, Milton, PA," late 19th C. ... **$75+**

ROLLING PINS – aluminum, cast iron – See Rolling pins, misc. metals

ROLLING PINS – ceramic, non-advertising:

Rolling pin, blue & white china, with blue painted wooden handles, "T. G. Green & Co., Ltd.," English, 18"L, late 19th C., early 20th. .... **$85+**

❖ RECIPE ❖

Shrewsberry Cakes – *"1 lb. butter, 1 lb. sugar, 2 lb. flour, and a few caraway seeds. – Rub the butter in with the flour; then put in the sugar and seeds, and mix them up into a paste, with a little milk; roll them out thin, cut them with a small round cutter, and bake them on iron plates in a good oven." Joseph Bell, A Treatise on Confectionary. Newcastle, England, 1817.*

Rolling pin, blue & white Delft faïence barrel with windmill scene, very heavy, has turned wooden handles & rod, English, German or Dutch, 9-3/16"L (overall 17-5/8"L), c.1870s. • This is quite possibly a noodle roller, a *Nüdelrolle*, because of ratio of the barrel length to overall length. .... **$350+**

Rolling pin, blue & white sponge decorated salt-glazed stoneware, wooden hadles, American (?), 15"L x 5-1/4" diam. (a very fat or thick roller drum, possibly for noodle dough), 19th C. ... **$165+**

Rolling pin, blue-decorated white pottery, with Dutch windmill scene, turned wooden handles, English or Dutch, 15"L, 19th C. • **Caution:** Sometimes the handles have been replaced. If the pottery shows wear, even small chips or hairline cracks, but the handles look unused, you shouldn't have to pay as much. .... **$250+**

Rolling pin, ceramic, to be filled with cold water, "Petit Point Rose" design, has original stopper, Harker China, American, 20th C. .... **$60+**

Rolling pin, crockery decorated with wildflowers, type found from Rodman, IA, also Milwaukee, WI, late 19th, early 20th C. .... **$145+**

Rolling pin, ironstone, long turned wooden handles, American (?), 9-1/2"L x 3-3/4" diam. pin, 4"L handles, 19th C. .... **$150+**

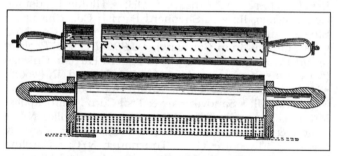

IV-363. Flour-sprinkling rolling pin patents. (T) *Pat'd. by Anson B. Fowler, Shelton, Washington, Feb. 15, 1896, #599,171. "It is understood that it is very desirable to automatically sprinkle flour upon the dough, especially when the latter is freshly mixed." The perforated pin is made of sheet metal, with an inner & outer shell, one within the other "and one turntable on the other, for bringing their perforations in or out of register." He also said there was to be an "agitator within the inner shell, for agitating the flour contained therein." The thing came apart for filling & cleaning – a pin mount held one of the handles & its attached cap in place, and when removed, the cap could be used as a biscuit cutter. (B) Pat'd. by Morton Harloe, Hawley, PA, Dec. 12, 1905, #807,075. His name is definitely Harloe not Harlowe. This patent has a trough and dredger "for flour or sugar by which the dough may be more or less covered while it is under manipulation on the molding-board." It works because as the roller revolves it causes the dredger to also revolve "so that the contents of the dredger are tumbled, as in a tumbling-box." Harloe encourages, "A little experience gives great facility in the use of the rolling-pin, so that the dredger may be made to drop just as much flour (or fine sugar, as in rolling out cookies) as is needed." See IV-364 for the real thing.*

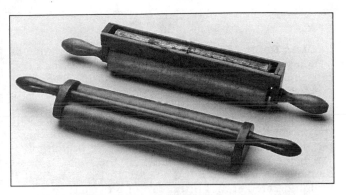

IV-364. Patented rolling pins. (T) *Has its own compartment of dusting flour above in mesh cylinder. 20-1/4"L. This is Harlowe's [sic] "Do No Stick" pin, pat'd. Dec. 12, 1903, seen in lower IV-363 patent drawing.* **(B)** *Double barrels or rollers, & beautifully formed handles, is 20"L, with rollers 11-3/4"L x 1-3/4" diam. It is "Taylor's Patent Combination Rolling Pin" pat'd. July 16, 1867. June Sprigg says it is a Shaker pin. The instruction sheet reads "The advantage of this Roller is, it will do the work in half the time it can be done with the single roller. It is worked with the greatest ease." See also IV-362 for Taylor's patent & IV-363 for Harloe's [sic].* **$200-$300; $175-$250**

Rolling pin, white porcelain, with painted ship, *The Harkaway* & painted motto reading "A present for my cousin Rose Godsmark, 1861" ... also "When this you see, remember me, & bear me in your mind. Let the world say what it will, speak of me as you find." (NO, it did not say "... as your friend.") Open at one end, English, 1861. • Retyping this into the computer, something about the ship's name makes me wonder if this was sort of a generic seaman's gift, that he could get painted with his lady's name. "Harkaway" sounds more like a romantic story than a ship ("Hark! I'm away.") Can anyone out there report another pin like this one? Or news of a real ship by that name? .... **$225+**

Rolling pin, salt-glazed stoneware, wooden handles, motto "May peace and plenty/ Dwell on England and shore/ And there remain/ Till time shall be no more." English, late 19th C. .... **$200+**

Rolling pin, white salt-glazed stoneware with blue floral & scroll bands near ends, T. G. Green & Co., Ltd., English, 18"L, 19th C. .... **$200+**

Rolling pin, yellowware, wood handles, 11"L barrel, plus handles, American, 19th C. Rolling pins are unusual in yellowware. .... **$250+**

ROLLING PINS – enamelware:
Pastry board & rolling pin, white enamelware, mounted to wall with iron brackets, board hinges down out of way & brackets fold inward, pin has turned wooden handles, Barnes Mfg. Co., Mansfield, OH, 27" x 28" with 6"H backplate, c.1914. .... **$350-$450+**

❖ NOTES ❖

Enamelware pastry boards are uncommon. The only patent I could find was granted Isabella Youart, Troy, OH, July 13, 1886, #345,470. She wrote about her "pastry-board having an iron base and porcelain facing

... applied to the iron in like manner as it is now applied to iron kettles and other cooking utensils. ... Such pastry-board will be ... found both sweeter and cleaner, for the reason that all dough of which pastry is made contains lard or butter and greases whatever it comes in contact with. ... My pastry-board can be as readily cleaned as the marble 'board' used for a like purpose, but it can be made much cheaper than a board made wholly of marble." She adds a good idea, that "If desired, the board may be constructed with a clamp or groove, to catch on the table, for the purpose of preventing the board from slipping about when in use."

ROLLING PINS – glass:
Rolling pin, amber glass, freeblown, knob ends – one with pontil, prob. American, 16"L, 19th C..... **$125+**

Rolling pin, amethyst glass, freeblown with 2 knob handles, American, 15-1/2"L, 19th C. .... **$130+**

Rolling pin, clear glass, metal axle, turned wood handles, "Gem," 19-1/2"L, 20th C. .... **$90+**

Rolling pin, cobalt blue glass, enameled ship design, English, 13-3/4"L, dated 1854. • You see so many with ships & flowers, you have to wonder how the decorative painting survived on so many. These pins, reported to be sailors' love tokens, were probably never actually used in the kitchen, but were decorative parlor pieces. I actually believe they were 19th C. seaside souvenirs from the coast of England................. **$235+**

Rolling pin, marbleized or swirled cobalt blue & white glass, knob handles, American, 17-1/2"L, mid 19th C. .... **$145+**

Rolling pin, marbleized or swirled pink & white blown glass, knob handles, American, 16"L, mid 19th C. .... **$200+**

Rolling pin, milky, almost opalescent white Bristol glass, English (?), 13"L, 2nd or 3rd quarter 19th C. • Nineteenth C. opaque white glass (often called "milk glass," a term a lot of glass collectors don't like), is sometimes called Bristol glass, although it was made, wrote Hampden Gordon (*The Lure of Antiques*), "... in London & Stourbridge, Sunderland and on the Tyneside as well as at Bristol."............................... **$135+**

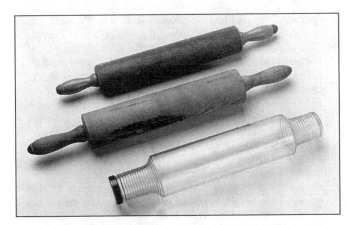

IV-365. Rolling pins. *Two wooden ones, with separate turned handles & an axle rod. 16-1/4"L & 18-1/2"L. Glass bottle pin has screw-on metal cap, & was meant to be filled with cold water or shaved ice. Many old old pins were glass – they could be chilled & this makes rolling fine pastry easier; c.1900 for wood; 1930s for glass.* **$15-$35**

Rolling pin, milky pastel green "Jadeite" glass, American, 1930s... **$250+**

Rolling pin, "Bristol" type opalescent white glass, turned wooden handles, Imperial Glass Mfg. Co., Cambridge, OH, 19"L, pat'd. July 26, 1921. (Still being made & sold in the 1940s.) • Rollers in opaque white glass (that people inaccurately call "milk glass") that is found with enameled & gilded decorations are also called by what is almost a generic term – Bristol glass, but was made probably at even more places than the decorated blue glass. .... **$135+**

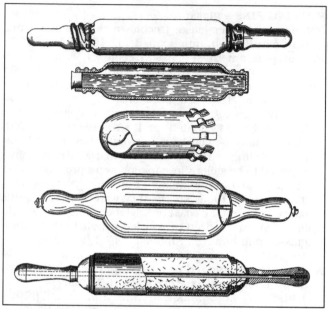

IV-366. Three patented glass rolling pins. *From top:* **(1)** *top three are all drawings from patent by Charles L. Sanford, Washington, PA, June 18, 1907, #857,308, one-half assigned to Okey J. Morrison, Ripley, WVa. Sanford's claim stated that his idea was "to provide a rolling pin having a compartment or chamber for the reception of a cooling medium" that would keep the dough from being tough. The cylindrical body (2nd down from top) is "preferably formed of glass" and would hold ice water. The stopper is clearly seen at the left end. The cylinder has threaded ends, & handles of metal with notches were Sanford's preference. These either looked like the handles on the top drawing & would slip over ends and be crimped into place, or they would look like the handle with a big hole (3rd down).* **(2)** *(seen 4th down from top) is a much simpler glass pin, pat'd. by Joseph Nath, Lancaster, NY, May 22, 1883, #278,258. A central rod or shaft goes through the pin & extends out into turned wooden handles. The inside of the handles was carefully hollowed out to exactly fit the knobby ends of the glass pin. The handle could be unscrewed & the glass body slid off for cleaning. The problem, it seems to me, would be warping of wood due to water, & then it wouldn't fit & would leak.* **(3)** *At bottom is a patent of Rollo M. Vick, Alliance, OH, Mar. 1, 1910, #950,775. At least he provided for gaskets inside the handles, but the rod still has to go through holes at each end of the glass pin.*

❖ NOTES ❖

Glass Rolling Pins are Cool. One inventor, Rollo M. Vick (see IV-366) explained very well the need for a cold pin, and why inventors used glass, marble, even concrete (!) as materials. Vick wrote in the claim to his patent of March 1, 1910: "In rolling dough it is of importance that the rolling-pin coming in contact with the dough be cool and more especially in the working of pie dough, owing to the fact that if the rolling-pin is warm the heat or more specifically the warmth has a tendence to injure the ingredients in the dough. It is well understood that butter, lard or other like materials are used for the purpose of shortening the dough. If a warm rolling-pin is applied the heat or warmth has a tendency to cause the particles of butter or lard to move toward the surface of the dough upon which the rolling-pin is applied, leaving the center or inner portion of the sheet of dough without the necessary amount of shortening material and when the dough is baked the center portion has a tendency to become hardened and tough." A number of inventors came up with ways to make a glass pin that could be filled with ice water – most of them just seemed to be trying to fix handles to the things, because all-glass pins with glass knob handles and a cork had been used for many years, possibly a century or more.

Rolling pin, white "milk" glass, well-turned wooden handles have plain wood knob close to pin with gripping part stained green, National Mfg. Co., Cambridge, OH, patented but I can't read the date. Presumably 1890s-1910.............................. **$85+**

Rolling pin, clear glass with screw-on black-painted metal lid, step-down ribbed glass handles, meant to be filled with ice water, American, 14-1/4"L x 2-3/4" diam., c.1920s-30s.. **$15+**

Rolling pin, clear glass bottle type, with white painted screw-on metal cap, "Roll-Rite," with the Good Housekeeping Institute Seal of Approval printed on cap, American, 14"L x 2-1/2" diam., 20th C. .... **$22+**

Rolling pin, clear glass with wooden axle rod & turned wooden handles, this one not a bottle, American, says pat'd. July 28, 1921, but the 26th was Patent Tuesday that year.. **$25+**

Rolling pin, custard glass, aluminum screw-on cap, American, 1930s. **$85**

Rolling pin, green glass, fat & short, with small knob ends, European or American, 5-1/2"L, 19th C. .... **$80+**

Rolling pin, green glass, freeblown, lots of bubbles, American, 15"L, 19th C. .... **$65+**

Rolling pin, purple blown glass, heavy, knob handles, English or American, 15-1/2"L, 19th C. .... **$200+**

❖ RECIPE ❖

*"**Best Scotch Bread** – 1 lb. butter, 1 lb. sugar, 1 lb. 8 oz. flour, 4 oz. cut almonds, 4 oz. lemon. – Cream the butter; then mix the other ingredients with it into stiff paste; you may cut it in different shapes; put caraway comfits and citron on the top; and bake it in a slow oven. *** **Scotch Bread, another Way.** – 1 lb. 8 oz. butter, 1 lb. sugar, 2 lb. flour, a little mace. – The butter to be rubbed very fine with the flour;*

then add the sugar and spices; make it into stiff paste, with a little cream; roll half of it out, and lay upon it cut almonds, citron, and caraway comfits; then roll out the other half, and lay it upon the top; press it down; mark it in diamonds; cut it any shape you please; and bake it in a slow oven. It is most commonly cut in small diamonds, and mixed with rout biscuits." Joseph Bell, A Treatise on Confectionary. Newcastle, England, 1817.

Rolling pin, blue & red spattered opaque white glass, white glass inside so possibly of a type called Nailsea, freeblown, double ball-knobbed, English, 14"L, 19th C. .... **$250+**

Rolling pin, blue & white loopy Nailsea glass, English, 20"L, 2nd or 3rd quarter 19th C. .... **$250+**

Rolling pin, clear glass with blobs of cobalt with blood red & brown glass blobs too, big knob ends, salt still inside, cork intact, prob. Nailsea, England, 14"L, prob. 2nd or 3rd quarter 19th C. • A story started up in the late 1980s that these glass salt pins were used by sailors to "smuggle" salt. .... **$250+**

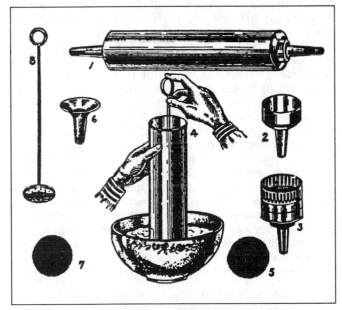

IV-367. Rolling pin combination tool.** Pieced tin, with everything needed to cut cookies (2) & (3), make doughnuts (using both ends of funnel 2), churn syllabubs (4), funnel (2), strain (5) & (7) [different meshes that don't show here], & roll dough (1). From Seastrand catalog, c.1912. **Matchsafe & bait box collector Max Hand** was trolling on eBay for "early bait tins" one evening. One listing that came up was "Early Tin Bait/Cricket Box" and Max thought it sounded interesting. The item was described as an early tin bait holder for crickets. The seller, reports Max, described how it worked by saying that you kept the crickets in the round cylinder, and when you needed one, you simply pushed down on the plunger and that forced the cricket out the funnel opening in the other end." You guessed it: It's this rare rolling pin combo, and Max ended up winning the auction, pretty sure it was an antique kitchen tool and interested in it as that. **$300+

Rolling pin, green & white Nailsea glass, big thick white swirls, freeblown, knob ends, prob. really from Nailsea, England, 14"L, 2nd or 3rd quarter 19th C. .... **$275+**

Rolling pin, Nailsea glass, red with white loops, knob at each end, unusual & very desirable in red or cranberry, English, 14-1/2"L, prob. mid to late 19th C. ...... **$175+**

Rolling pin, Nailsea-type glass, aquamarine with white loopy swirls, a handle at each end, remnant of ribbon hanger, prob. English, but poss. American, 9-1/2"L, prob. mid 19th C. .... **$200+**

❖ NOTES ❖

Nailsea & Bristol Glass – British antiques author, Hampden Gordon, wrote a no-nonsense, easy to follow, small book, *The Lure of Antiques. Looking & Learning Today,* published first in 1961 by John Murray, London. The chapter "Variety in Old Glass" gave tips on Nailsea and Bristol glass, invaluable to those who fancy glass rolling pins. Nailsea glass is "... but a species of bottle glass, which was taxed at a lower rate ...," writes Gordon. Then, with but one passing reference to rolling pins, he explains that the glass-house at Nailsea was founded in 1788 by J. R. Lucas (a bottle maker from Bristol), and that typical "early work" was dark green with "splashes and loops of white." He goes on, "The style was changed in 1810 ... [with a new owner], and "clear glass took the place of green with loops and stripes in white and pink and blue and other popular colours. ... About 1830, came the style in which the coloured loops are massed closely together, concealing the clear glass. Dating is very difficult; for the later Nailsea patterns, and particularly the quaint conceits such as walking-sticks and pipes and rolling-pins with inscriptions – great favourites on the fairgound – were still immensely popular in late Victorian days." He goes on to say that the term "Nailsea" is almost a generic term for the white-swirled novelty glass that was made not only at Nailsea, but at Warrington, Stourbridge, and other glass-making towns.

Rolling pin, Bristol glass, translucent rich blue with ship & other decorations in gilt, poss. Bristol, England, or other English glass center, 14"L, prob. early to mid 19th C. • Practically all these rich cobalt blue rolling pins with traces of enameled decoration, are called Bristol glass. According to Hampden Gordon (*The Lure of Antiques*), painted blue, emerald green & purple glass were all done at Bristol, Sunderland & "a number of other places." It's a field in which too little knowledge can do you in. Over a period of more than 100 years, the blue color was achieved several different ways, according to the supply of varying qualities of the cobalt mineral (or substitutes) with which a blue color could be created in glass. .... **$235+**

Rolling pin, opaque "black" or extremely dark green "Nailsea" glass with what appears as light blue & white splashes throughout, knob ends, prob. English, 12"L, 2nd to 3rd quarter 19th C. .... **$150+**

Rolling pin, turquoise green Bristol glass with gold & red painted floral decoration, cork missing, English or French Bristol, 15"L, c.1870s to 1880s. .... **$185+**

Rolling pin, very heavy glass, old style fat drum with fat knobby short handles, filled with bath salt crystals,

"Clean Bath Salts," mfd. by the Clean Perfume Co., Chicago, 13"L, c.1890s-1910 to c.1915 (?)....... **$35+**

ROLLING PINS – marble or stone:
Many repro, or rather new, marble pins are available today, often with turned wood handles and highly polished finish.

Rolling pin, marble, all one piece including handles, very heavy, thick & cold, 16"L, 19th C............. **$35+**

Rolling pin, marble with no handles, very smooth (but not finished like a statue would be), American (?), 17"L x 3" diam., prob. 19th C.......................... **$35+**

ROLLING PINS – misc. metals:
Rolling pin, aluminum, "Mil-Bar Co.," Canton, OH, 20th C. .... **$25+**

Rolling pin cast iron, for candy makers because the iron can be so well chilled, wood handles, American, 24"L, early 20th C., or poss. late 19th. .... **$45+**

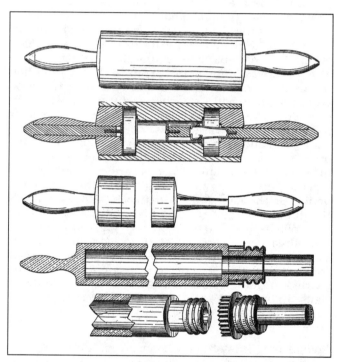

IV-368. Patented combination rolling pins. (T)
1st three drawings are patent granted Albert J. Roof, Peoria, IL, May 19, 1868, #78,135. It was to be made hollow at the center, with the hollow enlarged at each end & "fitted to receive and hold the cake-cutter and vegetable-masher, the handles of which become the handles of the rolling-pin. The vegetable-masher was spring-action. Apparently Roof made these because he wrote "I sometimes form the handle of the vegetable-masher in the same manner" as I form the handle of the cake cutter, ie. in two parts, the outer one of which is a hollow cylinder, that revolves around the inner part. (B) 4th & 5th drawings are the patent of Jane L. Landrith, Marshfield, OR, July 14, 1891, #456,042, for a "rolling-pin combined with other implements," for the use of bakers. It combined "separably a cake-cutter, pie-crimper, and edge-dresser, and a dredge-box for flour" – all in compact form. The pin itself had a "hollow vitreous [glass-like] cylindrical body" with a "handle made of sheet metal having a foraminated cap on one end" with an internal thread.

Rolling pin, nickeled metal pin, turned wooden handles, plus something inside that makes it rattle, perhaps lead shot to make it weigh more?, American, 15-1/2"L, c.1920. • Another similar one, same value, has green stained wooden handles & is 15-3/4"L. .... **$15+**

ROLLING PINS – plastic:
Rolling pin, molded plastic, fixed handle arched across from one side to other, round red frame set with 8 white rolling cylinders, like cigar tubes of different lengths, side by side at right angles to the handle, which was held to push multiple rollers to & fro', "Magnus New Style Rolling Pin," mfd. by the Magnus Harmonica Corp., Newark, NJ, about 10" diam., c.1940s (?). • Yep, the harmonica-makers made this. The copy on the colorful box states "Like Magic. Rolls the Dough with one Hand. Fluffier, Tastier Pies & Pastries." It doesn't have a lot of heft, but all those rollers, & the pressure of the hand directly above the center, does work. .... **$45+**

❖ NOTES ❖

ROLLING PINS – tin or tin & wood: Tin pastry boards & rolling pins sets were made by several companies. However I didn't find any patents for the sets, and only one patent for a tin pastry board with the curved bottom to hold a roller. That was granted Forrest Victor Braymer, Blooming Valley, PA, Sept. 11, 1906, #830,764. Braymer wrote about that edge: it "is ... of substantially U shape ... to describe a substantial semi-circle, and this tends to stiffen the board and serves at the same time as a receptacle for particles of flour or dough and also for a rolling pin." It had a hanging ring loop at the top. There was also an 1893 patent, but I missed it this time around! • The sets either have all-tin "boards" & rolling pins of wood with tin covering on the drum, or they have wood-baked tin boards & pins similar to the others. Prices have reached at least $875 on occasion, but then more came out of the woodwork so the price may not hold. They are highly desirable, and unused, with paper label, add another $100 or $150 on top of the value range given for the next four.

Rolling pin & pastry board, set that could be hung on the wall. The board is wood, with a working surface of tin. According to 2 partial paper labels on the back, "The metal plate ___ ___ the manufacture of th___ is a special composition ___ finished in pure palm of ___ therefore necessary before using the first time to wash it with soap and warm water to remove any oil that may have been left on the surface. The ___ of the board is made of ___lv ___ veneer, with the grain ___ crossed, and then ___ saturating entirely [with] pure boiled oil, this ___ it from spliting [sic] or ___." At the bottom is a wooden ledge, sort of like found on a blackboard, with 2 metal spring clips to hold the wooden rolling pin. The pin has 2 spool-turned handles. The American Bread & Pastry Board Co., Cambridge, OH, about 25" square, c.1890s-1910. .... **$550+**

Rolling pin & pastry board, all sheet tin, ring loop at center top for hanging on wall, bottom edge turned up to hold tinned pin (wooden handles), paper label reads "Union Manufacturing Co.," Cambridge, OH, 19th C. **$750**

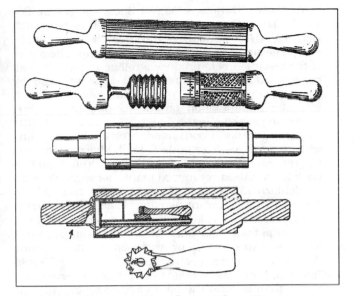

IV-369. More combination rolling pin patents. *Top **(T)** 2 pictures are patent of Frank Prentis, Grand Rapids, MI, Nov. 17, 1885, #330,421, assignor of two-thirds to James Tallman & Herman Prentis, same place. This block-tin or wood veneer cylindrical pin contained "a beefsteak-pounder, a potato-masher, a nut-meg grater, horse-radish grater, and biscuit-cutter." The thin-stemmed, weak-looking corrugated thing was the meat pounder when used on its side, and a potato masher when used vertically. **(B)** Bottom 3 pictures are patent of Charles E. Phillips, Abington, MA, May 30, 1865, #47,979. The rolling-pin contained "various utensils used in the preparing of pastry, cake, &c., thus economizing space and saving of the time usually spent in collecting the separate articles when scattered about in different directions, as they are often apt to be for want of a proper receptacle to contain them." Enclosed within, seen in the section drawing (2nd from bottom) is a tantalizingly familiar-looking **nutmeg grater**. Below it is the "toothed roller or **pastry-cutter**" which would slip inside the pin. "One end of the roller is made of tin or other metal, and so formed as to fit over the roller and to serve, when detached from it, as a ring to cut out biscuits, &c." Its other end (where small arrow points) is a smaller diameter, and has a detachable wooden handle stuck into it. When that handle is removed, the smaller diameter is used to cut holes out of doughnuts, etc.*

Rolling pin & pastry board, tin with tin rolling pin, partial label on back: "The Metallic Board – Only All Metal Bread & Pastry Board," American, 21-1/2"L x 8-1/2"W, pat'd. 1893. .... **$650+**

Pastry board or sheet, tin, wooden back, trough of wood at bottom to hold rolling pin, which is missing, paper label on back "The Non-Absorbent Bread & Pastry Board," American, 21"L x 21-1/2"W, c. 3rd quarter 19th C. If this had the tin & wooden rolling pan with it it would be a lot more expensive. **$375**

Pastry board or sheet, tinned sheet iron, holds rolling pin in curved bottom edge, hangs on wall from little wire ring, American, 23" x 16", late 19th C. or early 20th. May be the Brayer patent. .... **$300+**

ROLLING PINS – wood:

Rolling pin, carved tiger maple all one piece, with 2 long handles, American, 21"L including both 4"L handles, 19th C. • I've seen several, & of course maple was the best wood after lignum vitae for rolling pins, because of weight & dense grain, which meant protection from moisture & cracks, & both resisted absorption of ingredients that might make the pin smelly or unsanitary.......................... **$80+**

Rolling pin, double rollers with oval-ended frame & simple turned handles, maple, beautiful patina, paper label "Taylor's Patent Combination Rolling Pin." pat'd. by Albert L. Taylor, Springfield, VT, rollers 11-3/4"L x 1-3/4" diam., overall length 20-1/2", pat'd. July 16, 1867 (#66,909). • This pin, because of the simplicity of form & shape of turned handles at each end has been incorrectly attributed by other writers to the Shakers. It is also not the only double roller. • As the original spiel had it, "The Advantage of this Roller is, it will do the work in half the time it can be done with the single roller. It is worked with the greatest ease, as the Combination Rollers give double the surface bearing, & one roll following the other – making the Pastry of uniform thickness, & perfectly smooth & even finish." Original price was (you'll have to dust yourself off now!) only 50¢. .... **$200-$300+**

Rolling pin, hardwood with turned bone handles, prob. American, 15"L, 19th C. .... **$175+**

Rolling pin, heavy, thick lignum vitae which is the hardest of all woods & nearly as dense as iron, meant to last forever. Probably a commercial baker's pin, American (?), 16"L, 4-1/2" diam., 19th C. **$85+**

Rolling pin, heavy wood with heavy frame & 2 vertically-held handles at ends, the type called by the PA Germans draalhus, American, 11"L x 6-3/4"H including upright handle frame, prob. late 19th C., & prob. patented. .... **$150+**

Rolling pin, maple with handles on axle rod, probably bakery or hotel kitchen ware, American, 27-1/2"L, early 20th C. .... **$50+**

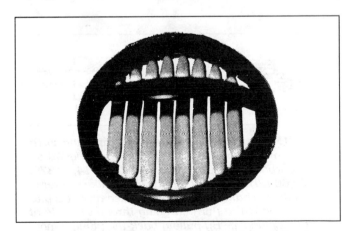

IV-370. Rolling pin. *Really odd red & white plastic one. The "Magnus," mfd. by Magnus Harmonica Corp, Newark, NJ. Arching handle across 8 rollers makes it a one hander. Great conversation piece, or use for duet performances with a harmonica player. Photograph & information courtesy of great cookie cutter collector, Evelyn King.* **$45-$65**

Rolling pin, tapered wood, name marked in pyrography or hot poker burned letters, "Pie Maker," Harrisville, NH, 1890s-1910. .... **$50+**

Rolling pin, turned & carved wood, barrel connected by a sort of stand-up frame with vertical ends as gripping handles. These uprights carved rather like simplified human forms. They're connected lengthwise not only by the pin's axle, but by a plain wooden dowel & a carved dowel, PA, 14"L x 5"H including pin & handle, 19th C. .... **$175-$250+**

Rolling pin, turned from one piece of maple, including handles, American, 14"L x 3-1/2" diam., 19th C. .... **$25+**

Rolling pin, turned maple, button or mushroom knob at one end, American, 12-1/2"L, 19th C. • I believe these dense wooden pins, with one knob only, could also be used as pestles of a sort for such things as cooked apples or potatoes, although this is just a hunch. I suppose if the patina at the rounded no-knob end is different from the rest of pin, that might be considered evidence of such use. A string could be tied around the knob for hanging. .... **$35+**

Rolling pin, turned maple, nylon ball bearings, length marked off in centimeters & inches, Rowoco Inc., Elmsford, NY, 18"L x 3-1/2" diam., early 1980s. .. **$5+**

Rolling pin, wood with iron rod, turned handles painted green, set at right angles to pin itself, marked only "D. R. G. M.," German, 10-1/8"L with 5-1/2"L handles, pre-1918, prob. early 20th C............................. **$65+**

❖ NOTES ❖

The initials **D. R. G. M.** are found on some German collectibles – prior to 1918 – and stand for *Deutsches Reichs-Gebrauchsmuster*, which meant that any trademark shown was a registered trademark of Germany. After 1918, and until the division of Germany after WWII, I believe at least one official mark used was *D. R. P.: Deutsches Reichspatent*.

Rolling pin, wooden pin with wooden rod & handles, also wood & perforated sheet metal self-dusting compart-

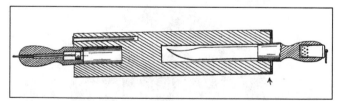

IV-371. Patented rolling pin combination with knife, and "soda dispenser"! Pat'd. by Jonathan L. Scarborough, Oliver's, TN, Oct. 14, 1879, #220,669. The thing at left that looks like a corer is actually a "chamber intended for use as a receptacle for soda. The thin rod going through handle at left is a plunger. "By pulling back the plunger more or less any desired quantity of soda can be measure out." Soda (baking soda) was used in making biscuits & crackers. The thin rod going into the body of the pin at left top is a knife-sharpener. The little arrow at right points to the metal "band" which fits over the right end of the pin & makes a biscuit or cake cutter when pulled off.

ment above, "Harlowe's Do Not Stick," American, 20-1/4"L, "pat'd. Dec. 1903" (or "1905"?). This was pat'd. Dec. 12, 1905 by Morton Harloe (note name difference), Hawley, PA, #807,075. Harloe wrote "The object of the invention is to produce a rolling-pin which shall carry a trough and a dredger for flour or sugar by which the dough may be more or less covered while it is under manipulation on the molding-board, thus preventing sticking to the dough." .... **$200+**

Rolling pins, turned wood, handles or knobs all in one with pin, interesting woods & knob shapes, unusual lengths, American, from about 14"L to 20"L, 19th C. • Look for variations of turned maple, for example, with particularly nice knobs. These may have mostly been one-off turnings meant as gifts. Some were commercially produced. • Added value. – Add another $20 or so if some feature is extra ultra – for example, extra long, or extra thick, or with extra nifty turning details, or great deep patina. .... **$50-$85**

Rolling pin, hard wood, ridged or corrugated lengthwise rather than around the pin's circumference, this one carved of one piece of wood including handles at each end, nice patina, American, 14"L, this one poss. as early as mid 19th C. • See also Noodle cutter; also one Candy cutter entry & picture this chapter. ... **$45-$85**

❖ NOTES ❖

What're the Ridges For? In *Tri-State Trader* of Aug. 5 and Sept. 3, 1985, collector William Baader and Ralph and Terry Kovel had a rolling pin fight about what ridged pins were for. • Is one with ridges around the circumference for crushing crackers or stale bread to make crumbs? • The Kovels, using Doreen Yarwood's *The British Kitchen* as their source, say it is for rolling out oat cakes (and allows "a current of air to pass beneath the oatcakes" Yarwood). • Baader claims it is for crushing oats to make oatmeal, using Edward Pinto's *Treen and Other Wooden Bygones* as his expert source. • I say it is what it's used for. Many of us (at least in the 1950s) rolled graham crackers for pie crusts, or wheat cereal flakes for fried chicken or even Saltines for topping tuna casseroles. I've seen these ridged pins – whether corrugated lengthwise or around the circumference, used to pound meat (and therefore it could be called a tenderizer). Pins with the lengthwise ridges are also used for making croissants or other pastry with lots of butter that has to be layered into the dough. • Pierre Franey's column on Kitchen Equipment in *The New York Times*, 2/21/79, describes one thus: "The French-made Tutové pin, which has [longitudinal ridges the length of] its barrel and is excellent for distributing butter in puff paste, costs four or five times as much as...[another pin selling for $10 in 1979]."

Ridges around the circumference. – An ad in the July 1897 *Woman's Home Companion*, depicts a rolling pin with a barrel about the same length as either of the two handles, ridged circumferentially. The ad copy reads "Noodles now made easily by the Lightning Noodle cutter. 'Cuts 'em quick and fine.' The cooks delight. Sent to any address for 35¢. Household Supply Co., Toledo, O."

Patented annular corrugations. – William L. Stanley, Cambridge, OH, received a patent Dec. 1, 1903, (#745,923) for a "rolling-pin." It is interesting on many fronts. First, he was from Cambridge, and didn't patent a glass pin. Second, the pin has knurled corrugations.

Third, his invention "relates to a metallic rolling-pin, and in its general form it comprises a cylindrical body formed of sheet metal, with annular corrugations to strengthen the same." A "tubular shaft" went through the length of the pin, and a "spiral bracing rod" was pushed through and "bears against the inner walls." Handles are at each end. Unfortunately, Stanley doesn't mention French pastry, or crackers, only that the corrugations added strength.

Rolling pin, wood with decorative carvings – See Springerle rolling pin

Rolling pin confusables, 2 types: (1) Wooden pin, with 6 corrugations & tapered ends, an axle & 2 handles, about 24"L. It is a very old leather tanner's tool for working the "bloom" off hides. (2) All-wood or wood & hard rubber pins with a waffled pattern, about 16"L; which are antique spot reducers or massagers. American, (1) late 1700s to early 1800s; (2) late 1800s. .... **$200-$300 & $45-$100**

Rolling pin footstools seem to have been made in three periods: (1) early 19th century with "Windsor" style turned legs. These are probably all English, & are painted like Windsor chairs – green or black, with ochre or gold pin striping on legs; (2) late 19th century with carpet piece tacked onto barrel of the large pin; (3) from the 1950s or so, in fake "olde fashioned" maple varnish & tacked-on carpet on the pin. The oldest pin stools are very rare, & generally speaking are probably the largest (up to 22"L, & about 9"-10"H). The 1870s-1890s ones are somewhat smaller & "fancier," but still seem to have been made with a real rolling pin with turned legs set in at a slightly less exaggerated splay. The 20th century ones are comparatively puny, & are obviously made to be footstools, rather than adapted from real pins. Newest (3). $35-$55; (2): $100-$125; (1) oldest: .... **$300-$400**

Rosette molds – See Patty Irons & Rosette Molds

Sandwich sealer, turned varnished wooden handle, chrome plated or stainless steel metal bracket & wheel, which has double tread design, for making fancy "tea & open sandwiches, delicious canapes for

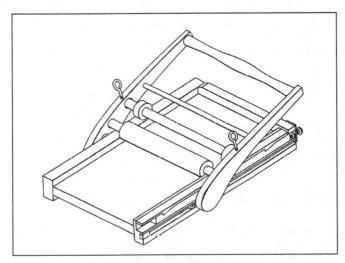

IV-372. "Bread machine" roller patent. Pat'd. by Nelson Long, Watertown, NY, May 26, 1868, #78,800. The roller's height was adjustable so that different thicknesses of dough could be rolled.

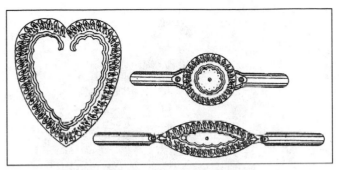

IV-373. Short bread mold patent, pat'd. by Simon Scott, Wellington, New Zealand, June 26, 1906, US Patent #824,445. Unusually, an actual street address – 127 Cuba Street, Wellington – was given in patent! It's for molds used in "manufacture of short-bread and similar cakes." The mold was to be made of gun-metal & mounted on a wooden back with two handles. "Cells forming part of the pattern of the mold are shaped to imitate the crimping accomplished by the thumb and finger of an operator making cakes by hand."

your luncheons, teas, & meetings ... helps make turnovers, ravioli, pierogi, kreplach, strudel, dumplings. Free recipes furnished." "Krimpkut Sealer," mfr. unknown, adv'd. by Gemini House, Buffalo, NY, 1968 ad. • Originally this tool, guaranteed to make you a "Sandwich Queen," cost only $2.15 ppd. .... **$5+**

Sealer or crimper – See Jaggers & Crimpers & Trimmers; also Tart sealer

Snow cone set, molded plastic & metal, snowman figure of white on white snowbank base, red plastic roller goes in hopper in top of head, eyes, nose & teeth of plastic "coal," red plastic shovel & funnel, red crank in back turns perforated metal cylinder against ice cube, shaved ice supposed to come out front & cascade picturesquely down front into snowbank so it could be shoveled into cups; set includes red & yellow squeeze bottles with flavoring syrup, small Dixie conical cups, in original box, with illustrated instruction folder, "Frosty Sno-Man Sno-Cone Machine," marked Hasbro, mfd. by Hassenfeld Bros., Inc., Central Falls, RI, 9-1/4"H, c.1952.................................. **$10-$15+**

Soap molds – See a listing under Muffin or gem pans for speculation on this extra use for such molds

Souse mold, for pork head-cheese (which dates back in America to at least 1801, from cookbook evidence). Cast iron, round with 2 handles, scalloped border design with sow's head including ears, in good

IV-374. Souse mold, *for a kind of spiced, pickled pork-head dish, yuck. Cast iron, 8-1/2" diam. x 2-3/4" deep. Photo & collection of David G. Smith.* **$150-$175**

detail, American, prob. PA (?) 11" diam., late 19th C. to early 20th. Joel Schiff says he has never seen either a sprue or a gatemark on some 50 or more souse mold heads he's seen. He believes they originated in the south, & were probably introduced closer to 1920 than 1900. He asks if I have any documents to help date the earlier-looking souse molds, but I don't, except a pig head mold (side view rather than head on) of bronze found at Pompeii, & dating to the first century C.E. .... **$150-$175**

IV-376. All cast metal springerle mold. Heavy metal like pewter. Makes 15 individual designs, measures 5-3/4" x 3-1/2". House with well, dog, church, another church, bird, grapes, raspberries, 2 beeskips on bench, elk (?), duck in pond, heron, berries, hunter with gun & rabbit, man cooking over gypsy kettle, woman holding a boot (?) in one hand. Courtesy Lenny Kislin, Bearsville, NY. $250+

Souse mold, painted cast iron, pig's sad face, ears down, natural pink tones in what looks like old paint (see also a painted lion mold in copper & tin molds, above), scalloped frame, loop handles cast in top & bottom, American, 8-1/2" diam. plus 1-1/4" handles, late 19th C. .... **$150-$175**

❖ NOTES ❖

"Where a pig can be a pig." The worst thing I've seen in a grocery store ever is an arrangement of styrofoam trays with pigs' heads under the shrink wrap. It almost made me sick. I wouldn't eat pork, or beef, or lamb, or veal, or mutton (and haven't for 19 years) if you paid me a million dollars. Think about it: A pig is more intelligent than a dog, by far, and can be trained and housebroken (even to use a litter box), is affectionate and naturally clean. Why not try soy protein "bacon" and "sausages" … it's very good. And, if you know of any pigs needing sanctuary, contact this wonderful non-profit **sanctuary called PIGS, Inc.,** POB 629, Charles Town, WV, 25414. E-mail: pigsanct@aol.com. Web site: www.pigs.org/

Sponge cake tin – See Molds, tin, ladyfinger pans, etc.

Springerle Boards & Rollers

Springerle boards are intaglio carved (that is, carved into rather than carved relievo – raised relief, where the background is carved away, leaving the design raised like a cameo). They are generally smaller than cake boards, although large ones were made, with border lines carved into the mold that would indicate where the individual springers were to be cut after molding and before baking. Some springerle boards are of cast iron or pewter.

Springerles – also spelled Sprengerlies – According to William Woys Weaver springerles are a so-called "water marzipan" a cheaper non-almond version of marzipan (p.116, *America Eats*). • "The beauty of [these baked springerle] cookies, with their detailed designs in high relief, veritable cameos in dough, charms young and old," wrote Ann Hark and Preston A. Barba, in *Pennsylvania German Cookery*, Allentown, PA: Schlechter's ("Publishers for the Pennsylvania Germans since 1810"), 1950. They went on to say that the word *springerle* means "charger or horse" in "South German"; other sources say it means "small jumping horse" in German. Yet other sources say it means "leaping deer" – and perhaps as many deer as horses are depicted on the molds we know. *Sprengen*, related to the *sprengerlie* spelling found in an American cooking magazine of 1903, means both to blow up and to gallop! Hark and Barba note that "the man on horseback is a familiar figure among our old Christmas cooky cutters" and the image is common on cake boards and springerle molds too. They write that the "beautiful designs [are] delicately engraved into pearwood or some other hard or close-grained wood. Most of them are imported from Germany and are occasionally for sale in our large department stores."

Springerles: Wood to Iron and Pewter – I have read in various sources that these were sometimes cast from patterns made from original carved wooden springerle molds. Would be especially good for bakery which could soon wear out a wooden mold. These metal springerle molds are also found in a heavy cast metal something like lead that is probably zinc. A book by Katherine Morrison McClinton states that marzipan molds were first made in carved wood, then of tin and cast iron. William Woys Weaver says that in the last half of the 19th century, bakery supply companies had made cast iron, and, later, pewter copies of the old carved molds.

What do you make of this? The Smithsonian was offered a puzzling mold with these same images. It is cast iron but with a strange variegated iridescent color appearing on underside that makes you suspect impurities or unorthodox casting methods. On the mold's topside are 12 intaglio images laid out 3 across by 4 down: an apple basket, pear, turkey or peacock, cornucopia, bird in branch, oak leaves with acorn, fruit tree branch, horseshoe with blacksmith's hammer, large bird on branch, bushel basket with apples, grape leaves, tall cross – identical to the images described on a cast iron mold listed toward end of these listings. On

IV-377. All cast iron springerle mold. 12 squares, slightly irregular, each cookie would be about 1-1/8" x 1-3/4". Basket with 3 apples, pear with 2 leaves, turkey or peacock, cornucopia, bird in branch, oak leaves with acorn, fruited branch, horseshoe with blacksmith's hammer, large bird on branch, tall basket with apples or peaches, grape leaves, a cross. *Courtesy Lenny Kislin, Bearsville, NY. Now in Joel Schiff Collection.* **$400+**

the underside of this relatively thin metal slab, in relief, are the same images, backwards so to speak. Furthermore, four short peg feet, almost like casting sprues, extrude from the four corners. There is considerable appearance of damage to the underside image of the tall basket where the peg leg is joined, and also to the cross cookie, but it occurred before the casting was made, so may have been on original metal casting from which this apparent copy was made. Overall dimensions are slightly larger than the main one priced in the preceding entry, viz. 8-3/16"H x 4-13/16"W; each cookie about 1-15/16"H x 1-7/16"W. The collection from which the mold came was rather old and select, so if this is a reproduction, it has some age. My suspicion is that the upper and underside images are somehow indicative of the exact method of production, a method that remains unknown.

Sources for Springerle Designs – It is hard to find identification of, or exact sources for, the designs, but if you keep your eyes open all the time, serendipity and diligence will sometimes give you clues. **Catchpenny prints**. I picked up a Dover Publications book, 1970, called *Catchpenny Prints. 163 Popular Engravings from the Eighteenth Century*, from the cheap wood engravings originally published in London by Bowles and Carver, in the late 1780s and early 1790s. A man with a whip, seen on one mold, is identified as a waggoner [sic] in a very similar picture in the catchpenny book. A man with a tall ladder is usually identified as a "Lamplighter," but sometimes I believe they may be chimney sweeps, at least if there is any hint of a long brush. **Trades people**, including butchers, shoe-makers, hat-makers, coopers, carpenters, etc., are somewhat common designs on springerle boards. **Costume fashions.** A good reference book on costume, including hair styles, shoes and hats, would be very valuable for collectors who specialize in decorated pieces or figural items. **Bird Watching.** Catchpenny prints and chapbooks for children are full of birds. The Dover reproduction of 1780s-90s catchpenny prints, in one book, must have 100 bird pictures, tail up, tail down, straight beak, finch or parrot-like beak, open beak, closed beak. Each bird is labeled, but it is very difficult

IV-375. Springerle board. Carved fine-grained wood, 9-1/4" x 6-3/4"W, signed "F. G." American, Pennsylvania German, 1860s-70s. Carved on both sides – other side is a much plainer heart, seen in IV-63. Note great variety of motifs, including man playing pipe while sitting on bench under a tree with curving branch (think of those butter molds), & St. Nicholas & his reindeer. Ex-Keillor Collection. **$500-$1,000**

to decide which bird was used by the springerle mold carver. Some birds are more likely to have been used than others because of fable and song, *viz.* swan, peacock, turkey, sparrow, magpie, robin, wren, nightingale, duck, and goose. More unusual waterbirds such as cranes (herons?) and sandpipers are found on some items, like decorated stoneware.

• • •

"**Sprengerlie** – Each nation has its own way of celebrating the advent of the New Year, some custom in private or public life. In this initial number for 1903 we illustrate a cake familiar to all Dutch and German housewives – sprengerlie. A very rich, sweet dough is rolled out and stamped with molds of quaint or familiar objects. Not long ago we were privileged to see two such molds at least a hundred years old; one was of iron, a four by six-inch oblong, with a dog on one side and a basket of roses on the other; the second was of some hard wood – a six-inch ellipse – and showed a reindeer with branching horns. The aged housewife who owned them also gave a practical exposition of the manner in which the dough was rolled on the molds, carefully detached then baked. Some modern molds are similarly made, but it is better when purchasing to buy a regular sprengerlie pin. This rolling pin is of hard wood and has the figures carved in it. In all cases the figures are sunken so that the patterns stand in relief on the dough. These cakes are very popular in various sections of the country, and molds or pins can be obtained from or through any first-class house furnisher. For the dough cream together one-half of a pound each of butter and sugar. Sift in one-half of a teaspoonful of salt and three-quarters of a pound of fine pastry flour, then add gradually two well-beaten eggs and one scant teaspoonful of vanilla. This will make a stiff dough (if the eggs are small a few drops of cold water may be added), which is turned out on a board and thoroughly kneaded. If flat molds are used the dough is rolled down to half an inch, laid on the mold and rolled until the even surface is but half as thick, carefully peeled from the mold and laid on a slightly-buttered flat pan. With a sprengerlie pin on hand, the ordinary pin is preferred until it is rolled almost thin enough, then the special pin is applied and the cakes cut apart with a jagging iron. When on the pan they are brushed with unbeaten white of egg and are often sprinkled with 'hundreds and thousands,' sugared caraways or carda-

moms or similar tiny confections. The oven should be very moderate so that the cakes when done will not be much deeper in tint than a straw color. If placed in a tightly-covered tin box or pail they will keep crisp for a long time." *Table Talk*, Philadelphia, January 1903.

✧ RECIPE ✧

Springerle Cookie Recipe – *A basic recipe for these cookies, requires 2 eggs, a cup of sugar, grated lemon rind, 2 cups of sifted flour with about a half teaspoon of baking powder, and 2 teaspoons of aniseed (it is this and the lemon that give the distinctive taste and fragrance). All the recipes suggest beating the eggs first, then slowly beating in the sugar and adding the lemon rind. Then you start adding the flour and baking powder. Finally, add the aniseed. The dough shouldn't be too soft; if it seems soft, stiffen by kneading in a little more sifted flour, and roll out thin (a quarter inch thick) and lightly flour the surface. The mould has to be pressed onto the dough carefully to leave its impression. You can cut the cookies apart before baking, especially if you use a mold that doesn't have the dividing lines. Some molds are so made that the whole set can be baked whole and broken after being baked and cooled. The ones with a groove between each design probably should be cut before drying; the ones with a ridge, sometimes relatively wide, between each design can be left until after baking. Carefully lift the printed dough with a couple of spatulas or cake turners, and shift to greased then floured tin baking sheets. Cover with a dry towel overnight, so that they have a chance to set and dry out. They will bake in about 15 minutes at 325°, and should not be allowed to get brown.*

Using a Springerle Board or Mold – A springerle board is usually used lying flat on a work surface, with the rolled dough pressed or rolled into it. It is sometimes used the other way, with the dough rolled out and the mold pressed down on the dough, and lifted off. Either way, the individual designs were cut apart with a jagger or knife, or baked whole to be broken apart, depending on the kind and depth of dividing line between each design.

Springerle board, carved hard wood, vertical rectangle with 12 designs, including woman in gathered skirt, holding 3 part burden on head; rooster; woman sowing seeds from apron; an arch of some kind with tree; cherry or current branch; bird on fruit tree branch; 2 handled posset cup or tyg with odd plant (?); alert deer; sprightly flower; man with whip, probably a wagoner; hunting horn with 2 tassels; & woman in native costume with brimmed hat, & multi tiered gathered skirt, next to tree. The individual cookies have very narrow frames, separated by a narrow channel or runnel – the type to be cut apart before drying & baking. European, about 6-1/2" x 4", prob. 3rd quarter 19th C. ...... **$150+**

Springerle board, carved maple wood, 8 patterns laid out in 2 x 4 formation, including animals, fruit, flowers, German or poss. German American, 8-1/2"L x 3-1/2"W, 19th C. .... **$145+**

Springerle board, carved walnut, large ornate wreath design of flowers & birds, "Harman's Bakery," Brunswick, ME, 9" square, early 20th C. • If you're reading this & wonder why this isn't called a cake board or marzipan board, I can't answer you. I'm confident it's interchangeable. See also an entry under Pie top mold..................................... **$175+**

Springerle board, carved wood, 6 designs: rooster, house, fruit compote, dog, shore bird, grape bunch, European (?), 7"H x 3-1/4"W, 1890s-1910........................ **$100+**

Springerle board, carved wood with 5 geometric designs on one side only, handle with hanging hole, European (?), late 19th C. .... **$75+**

Springerle board, carved wood with a cherry, grapes, sailboat, poss. American, 5-3/4" x 3", 1890s-1910. .... **$100+**

IV-378. All cast metal springerle. *Probably cast pewter. 7-1/2"H, with musical, fruit, & household scenes. Note woman arranging flowers, 3rd down on far right. Late 19th C.* **$150+**

IV-380. Another commercial springerle mold, *carved wood. With from 1 to 12 pictures, costing wholesale, from $2.50 to $8.64 a dozen!!! S. Joseph, c.1927.* **$55+**

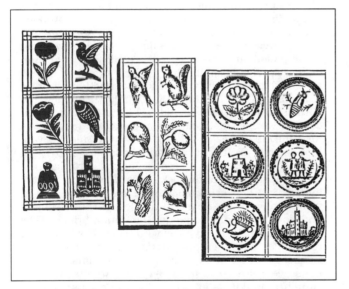

IV-379. Commercial quality carved wood springerle boards. (L) *"Wooden cake prints or Springerle Moulds," 6 prints to block, available "plain" or "fancy" (I don't know which this is), Ritzinger, Grasgreen c.1906-07.* **(M)** *One of several designs, which could be had on boards with from 2 to 12 designs, for 15¢ to 80¢ each.* **(R)** *More fully detailed round designs on bigger board, but price was still under 80¢. Both from Jaburg catalog, 1908. Collector value now is higher than it should be for something mass-produced & machine carved.* **$55+**

IV-381. Springerle rolling pin patent. *Pat'd. by Louis Blaul, Lancaster, PA, May 16, 1876, #177,319. "A highly-spiced delicious small cake, having the upper side ornamented by raised figures of various objects, is known by the name of springerly.' The tedious process for giving the embossed figures, by pressing the prepared dough into intaglio molds, neatly and deeply carved into wood for the purpose, is greatly simplified by the use of my newly-invented embossing rolling pin ... The blocks heretofore used, engraven at a considerable cost, might be stereotyped, which, in itself, would be an improvement for multiplying the intaglio molds, but the tediousness in their use would still remain; but by means of dies or other modes in use,* **to have them formed in pure tin or other metal, backed up on the inside and formed into a cylinder,** *provided with a central shaft and handles...could be produced at a trifling cost to supply the trade, embracing every variety of design and ornamentation." [Bold type emphasis mine.]*

IV-382. "Rolling pin for marking gingerbread *and other pastry." Design patent granted John Holt, Gardner, ME, Dec. 10, 1861, design #9,532. "The configuration of the two outer spaces consists of six V-shaped grooves around the pin." In the center, at left, are "two shields" with stars & scrolls; center right is "a representation of foliage." All cut into surface.*

Springerle board, hand carved wood, images on both sides (as they usually were), designs include angel, pecking chicken, steamboat, castle, tricorn hat, unusual & small, 19th C. .... **$165+**

Springerle board, machine carved wood, 4 squares on pale maple wood, American or European import, early 20th C. .... **$35+**

Springerle board, or confectionary mold? Carved wood, long & skinny, on one side is a woman carrying water, a ship, a mermaid, & a lion, on other side are 37 small carvings, mainly fish, some people, a dog, birds, griffin, European, 18"L, board is 1-5/8" thick, looks c.1800 to 1820 .... **$200+**

Springerle board, worm eaten fruitwood, carved on both sides, rooster, boar, squirrel & heart on one side, a cat, dog, horse & lion on the other, European, 5" x 9" prob. early 1800s, poss. even late 18th C. .... **$550+**

Springerle board, carved boxwood (?), 6 images laid out 2 x 3: foamy beer mug (?), long-skirted bustled lady with fan, a cupboard, a pig, a boy bowling or playing bocci, with 3 balls in pile behind him, & finally a stepped thing like a plant stand with tiny unreadable objects on the 3 shelves, European, 5-7/8"H x 4 -1/8"W x 1" thick, 1870s when bustles were "in" or skip to mid or late 1880s. .... **$185+**

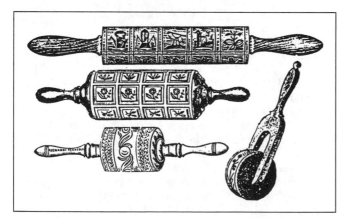

IV-383. Springerle rolling pins & cake *marker. Some called **"New Year's or Springerle Rolling Pins."** (1) Top one has 12 designs, from Middleby, 1927. (2) Has many designs, this one has 24; picture cheats a bit on perspective. Jaburg Bro., 1908. (3-L) & (4-R) from Germany. All late 19th C. to early 20th. No way to know how long a pattern could have been made in same way.* **$125-$200+**

Reproduction Alert

I had quite a start when I found an ad in Dec. 1973 *Early American Life* for a "Beautiful **springerle cookie mold** ... an exact reproduction of 18th century Pennsylvania German original. Makes 12 cookies picturing 12 different craftsmen. Mold is of heavy metal mounted on hand-finished cherry-wood. Also serves as a handsome and indestructible kitchen wall plaque. History and our own springerle recipe included. $15 ppd. The House-On-The-Hill, South Strafford, Vermont 05070." Now. Do I have a repro? Probably. The small, dark and rather sharp ad photo shows the same 12 images, but there appear to be slight differences in the shapes of things, esp. the Fisherman's net. And mine is not mounted on cherry, and there are no signs of a once-attached hook for hanging on the kitchen wall. It's scary and very maddening; you buy something because it looks so right, then a bully kicks sand in your face with a 1973 ad.

Where to Get Springerle Reproductions Now, for use. In danger of being closed forever, The-House-On-The-Hill was bought and moved by collector-enthusiast Caroline K. Kallas years ago to Villa Park, IL, POB 7003, 60181. Phone: (630) 969-2624. There's a good Web site too: www.houseonthehill.net/. Kallas offers all kinds of cookie-related things, including cutters, rolling pins, and all kinds of supplies on the Web site. There are also many links, and she keeps the site really up to date. You can order her catalog ($3 ppd) as a reference and as a positive impetus to make your own springerle! The most helpful thing Ms. Kallas told me, in a letter, is if you find screw heads in the back of the wooden plaque, this indicates the metal face is screwed on and old – newer ones are glued onto the wood. Newer, pot metal molds, are first copper- then nickel-plated. Kallas's very fine, good-looking replica springerle molds are glued to a cherry wood back plate and have a brass hanging ring in the top edge. Subjects include the "Guildsman" (or Trades) mold (7-1/2" x 4-1/2"); "Musical and Variety" mold, flowers and trades and musical instruments (7-1/2" x 4-1/2"); the "Swan" mold, swan, bird, boater, fruit, churner and house (6" x 3-1/2"); "Petite," house, dog, church, church, bird, grapes, fruit, bee skeps, goat on rocks, swan, peacock, flowers (5-3/4" x 4"); "Cornucopia," with cornucopia, flower, game beater, goat; "Heart," heart design with lovebirds and flowers (3-1/2" square); "Der Kinderbringer (The Child-bringer)," winged angel with baby (4" x 2-5/8"); 6 round designs – grapes, birds, flowers, birdhouse, female gardener (6" x 4"); 6 ovals designs, anchor, house, lovebirds, etc. (6" x 3-1/2"); "Architectural," 9 churches, buildings (6" x 6-1/4"); 15 designs, animals and people (8-3/4" x 4-3/4"); and others (mostly religious) imported from Switzerland. • For wax reproductions: Historic Waxcraft, 176 Elmerston Rd, Rochester, NY 14620.

Where else to get Springerle & other cookie molds for use. Wooden molds that each are individual freehand-and-router carvings by Gene Wilson are offered by Gene and his wife June at HOBI Handcrafts, POB 25, Belleville, IL 62222-0025, Web site: www.cookiemold.com. They also offer beautiful shortbread and gingerbread molds, butter molds, and cookie stamps. • Don D. Dillon Carvings, 850 Meadow Lane, Camp Hill, PA 17011, (717) 761-6895; no Web site that I can find. Catalog: $1.00, but please send SASE.

IV-384. Whatsit press mold – for tortillas? *All wood, bent & carved. 16"L x 6-7/8" diam. Practically without mark or stain, none inside, so probably not used. No drainage holes for cheese. No bloodstains, so not for meat patties. Collection of Meryle Evans.* **$65+**

Springerle mold, ceramic block, flat with 35 separate small impressed images, German, mid (?) 20th C. reproduction. .... **$25+**

Springerle mold, cast metal plate, probably zinc, attached to oak board. This one has 12 designs laid out 3 across by 4 down. The designs show tradesmen or craftsmen and their tools & products. Amazingly detailed images of Butcher (sausages, cleaver & chopping block); Cooper (barrel); Tailor (sitting cross-legged, 'tailor' fashion, on his table, scissors); Wheelwright (wheel & plane); Blacksmith (horseshoe & anvil); Stone Carver (blocks, pick & square); Druggist (scales & apothecary chest); Fisherman (net); Lamp-lighter (ladder); Carpenter (adze & sawbucks); Shoemaker (boots & shoes); Clockmaker (carrying case clock reading 10 to 2). All with dividing ridge, & herringbone chip-carved edges, American (?) or European – nothing here to rule out either. Measures 7-5/8"L x 4-3/8"W. Cookies are 1-15/16" x 1-3/5". Metal is 1/8"+ thick, mounted to board (no screws visible) almost ,5/8" thick, prob. repro from 1970s-80s, although it looks c.1840s-50s.
• There is some crossover interest from tool collectors.
• Price range is for an authentic old one; divide by 5 or 10 for value of repro. .... **$350+**

Springerle mold, cast metal, probably zinc, with 12 designs, L to R: crossed guitar and cornet; 3 berried plant; squirrel on stump eating nuts; lyre and laurel wreath; clump with 3 flowers; bird (magpie, mockingbird or nightingale?) on branch; dairymaid in long gathered skirt with ruffled bottom, carrying 2 pails; wild flower with 6 leaves and single stalk with tiny flowers; woman in long 2 tiered gathered skirt, possibly arranging flowers in pot on 3 legged stool; man (lamp lighter?) with tall ladder, hand in belt; lily of the valley type plant; and man in skirted hunting coat with gun under arm walking toward tree. Each design has chip carved herringbone frame, & was meant to be cut apart before baking. European, 6-1/8" x 3-3/4", mid 19th C. (?). .... **$175+**

Springerle mold, cast metal sheet with 12 rectangular designs, 3 across by 4 down with dividing ridges & chip carved edges, mounted to oak board. The very heavy dark gray metal is not lead or iron, but probably cast zinc, as the detail is very good, & zinc was similarly used for electrotyping & printing plates. Designs, L to R: log church & pine tree; peacock (?) on shed roof (?); 2 grape bunches; strawberry plant; table with 2 bee skeps & 6 bees; downhill mountain goat; swan on pond; wild turkey (?); branch with 5 five-petal flowers (jasmine?); man in hat, gun under arm & dead rabbit; butcher with sausages & butcher's block; short-skirted woman (man in skirted coat?) in kitchen with posnet, dead fowl & a fish in each hand & utensil rack (?), American (?) or European for American market, 3-5/8"L x 4-7/8"W. 1-5/16" x 1-1/4" cookies. Metal is 1/8"+ thick, mounted to board almost 5/8" thick, prob. 1840 to 1860. • The originals of these molds were probably carved wood, used to make casting models for metal molds. The cast metal ones, whether zinc or iron, reveal their carved wood origins. Price range for old ones: .... **$175+**

Springerle mold, cast pewter mold mounted to wooden back for stability, 12 rectangular designs include people, plants & animals, European, 7-1/2" x 4-1/2", 19th C. (?). .... **$165+**

Springerle mold, heavy cast metal, probably zinc, makes 15 individual cookies to be cut or broken apart, designs are laid out 3 across x 5 down, & include house with well; dog; church; another church; bird; grapes; raspberries; 2 bee skeps on outdoor table; elk (?); duck in pond; heron; berries; hunter with gun & rabbit; man cooking over gypsy kettle with hanging implements; woman holding something in one hand (broom?) & something unidentifiable in other hand, motifs could be English, American or German, 5-3/4"H x 3-1/2", mid 19th C. (?). This old one is not cast aluminum. .... **$175+**

Springerle mold, unidentified heavy cast metal, rectangle divided into 6 pieces including 2 birds on branches; perky flower; odd domed building; building with thing on top like TV aerial but possibly a lighthouse; & something like a mug on top of a drum; all these descriptions are based on a picture in a 1917 ad of imported metal molds brought into NYC by Otto Thurnauer, German, c.1917. • Turn-of-century dealer Thurnauer lists seven rectangular or square molds, five oval ones & three rounds. Are the old oval ones the cast iron ovals with single designs seen in such quantity at antique shows in the late 1980s? • See also Cookie mold. (Note: The Thurnauer firm still imports kitchen things – I bought a tin mold recently with their stamp.). .... **$150+**

Springerle mold, cast iron, 12 squares laid out 3 across by 4 down, each square slightly irregular in outline, depicts basket with 3 apples; pear with 2 leaves; turkey or peacock; cornucopia; bird in branch; oak leaves with acorn; fruit tree branch; horseshoe with blacksmith's hammer; large bird (parrot?) standing on branch; tall bushel basket with apples; grape leaves, a high cross; a stunning collection of images, European or American, each cookie would be about 1-1/8" x 1-3/4", mid (?) 19th C. .... **$150+**

Springerle molds – See also Cake boards; Cookie molds; Pretzel mold

Springerle roller or rolling pin, carved drum (or barrel) about 3"L, with two turned handles about 3-3/4"L. Design of roses & leaves. Marked "J. Conger," one of only two Conger examples of this form that I have record of. The other appears on p.110 of *America Eats* by William Woys Weaver and belongs to the Henry Francis du Pont Winterthur Museum. Its design is also of roses & leaves, with a decorative edging motif on both ends of the barrel comprised of

IV-386. Baking molds, of small size, 3" to 4" – for patties or tart cases. Stamped tin. See others farther on in chapter. From A. Bertuch catalog, Berlin, Germany, c.1904. **$25+**

a sort of lacy border on either side of a narrow band of dots. That one is 12-3/8"L overall, 3" diam. (Note: See the cake board listings for a lot more on Conger. Note: For using a springerle roller, see the recipe above for "Sprengerlie.") .... **$1,000+**

Springerle rolling pin, carved wood, relatively fat short barrel divided into 16 segments with flowers, animals, butterfly, fruit, other designs, yellow painted wood handles, American or European import?, c.1930s. (With original cookbooklet, maybe a bit more.) .... **$65+**

Springerle rolling pin, carved wooden wheel in slingshot-like handle, pineapples & leaves, with metal pin axle, German (?), 5-1/2"L, 19th C. Look for well-carved designs, in unusual subjects, just as you would for butter molds. Rarest are those with 4 or 5 different designs, not a band of repeats. Look also for well-formed handles, old patina (butter & age contribute), condition, & size. .... **$75+**

Sugar cubes, gift box with white sugar cubes decorated in colorful sugar frosting, include candlestick, angel, snowman head, white wreath, green wreath, Christmas star, Star of Bethlehem, bells, Christmas tree, candy cane, poinsettia, praying angel & full-figure snowman, 1940s-50s. .... **$5+**

Tart pan, fluted sides with ring holder, gray graniteware, only 3-3/4" diam. x 1-1/4" deep, 19th C. .... **$45+**

Tart pan, sheet metal, "Parkersburg Iron & Steel Co.," WV, 1890s-1910. .... **$15+**

Tart pan, cast aluminum, 12 tart cups with fluted flared sides, unusual looking because the edges of the cups actually raised above the flat tray, almost like a sculpture of tarts. "Nordic Ware No. 206," Minneapolis, MN. 15-1/2" x 10-1/4". .... **$12+**

Tart sealer, cast aluminum with wooden knob, spring-loaded action works scalloped inner ring to seal the tart while outer ring cuts round outline. Could be used for ravioli or tortellini too. Marked "Tart Master," approx. 4" diam., pat'd. 1938. • A new "Tartmaster" [one word] was being made in the 1970s (still may be); looks the same except that knob is now a metal cap. Directions read "Roll out a sheet of dough, place small mounds of filling at regular intervals, cover with a second layer & then, with a quick push of plunger, punch out tarts or ravioli." ..... **$8+**

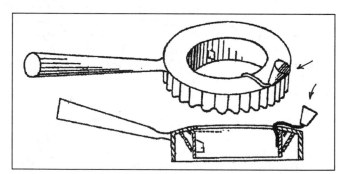

IV-385. Tart or cake cutter patent, awarded James H. Winslow, Lynn, MA, April 14, 1875, #164,667, assignor of two-thirds of his right to May & Withey of the same place. "It is well known that in the manufacture of tarts the dough or pastry forming the crusts is usally made separately, the upper crust or rim of the tart being cut in the form of a ring and afterward placed upon the lower crust or bottom of the tart preparatory to baking and filling with the jelly." His invention made it quick & easy to place upper rim or crust upon lower one. There's actually an inner cutter which is rotated by a little handle sticking up that looks like a funnel (see arrow).

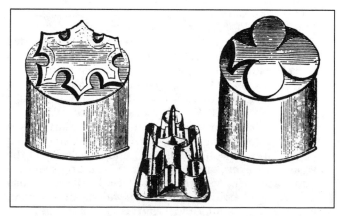

IV-387. Vegetable cutters. In this chapter, because while they are cutters, they are meant to create special shapes. Pieced tin. The pictures are primitive, as are many old catalog linecuts, but they show that you can cut a shamrock or 6-point star from a slice of root vegetable. Came in 20 styles, used for decorative veggies for inside molds, or for soup. F. A. Walker catalog, c.1890. Other vegetable cutters & julienne cutters are in Chapter I. **$15-$25**

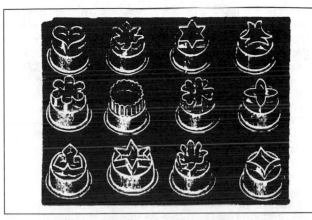

IV-388. Vegetable cutters. *Set of tin cutters, showing available designs (note shamrock, etc.). Came in three sizes: 7/8", 1" & 1-1/4" diam. Ordered as "macaroon cutters," the same set was made in 2" & 2-1/4" diameters. S. Joseph, c.1927. For a set:* **$55+**

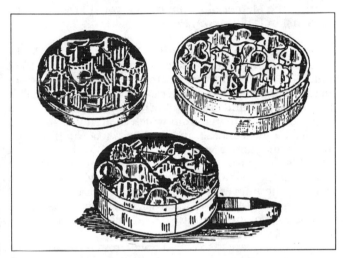

IV-389. Vegetable cutters. *Three more sets, in round tin boxes. Top 2 sets are from S. Joseph. 1-1/2" cutters & 2" cutters. Bottom set of 12 cutters, very like others, is in a tin box only 3-1/2" across. "Can use either end of cutters." This was given as a subscription premium for 1930 American Cookery magazine.* **$45+**

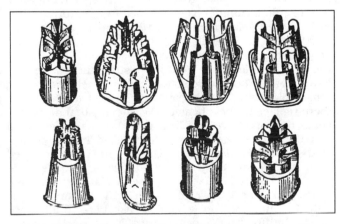

IV-390. Vegetable or "garnishing" cutters. *Also for pastry. Came in 50 patterns, in sizes 1", 1-3/16", 1-5/8", 1-3/4" & 2-1/8". Duparquet catalog. Per cutter:* **$15-$20+**

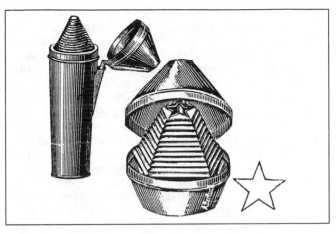

IV-391. Nested garnish cutters. (L) *"Column cutters" or corers. Nested, tin, made in various shapes. Only about 7"H overall. F. A. Walker, c.1890s, but made before. Probably imported from France.* **(R)** *Many shapes, all geometrics. This shows a star set. For vegetables or pastries. Bertuch, c.1904.* **$50**

IV-392. Vienna roll stamp, *for making vienna rolls the right way, marked in 5 sections. "May also be used for hot cross buns." Used when yeast dough is "half proved." You mark them, turn them over, wash with water, & bake. Hueg, c.1905.* **$15+**

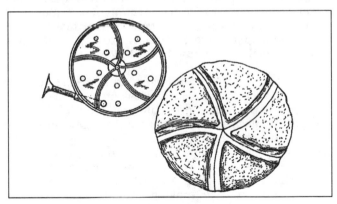

IV-393. Vienna roll-shaping implement. *Pat'd. by Eugene Mitschler, NYC, NY, Oct. 21, 1913, Pat. #1,076,509, as a "dough-shpaing implement ... a device adapted to be used for the production of breakfast rolls which are known in the trade as 'Vienna rolls, [which] are provided in their tops with a plurality of radially extending grooves or indentations." (Drawing at right.) To use this strange device: "A lump or ball of dough is placed upon a support, the implement with its open end put on top of it and forced [downward]. The air displaced by the dough escapes through the perforations in the disk and cover. The [spring-return] push rod is forced inward, thereby ... forming radially extending grooves in the top of said lump or ball." Yummy!*

Tortilla iron, looks like a cast iron stovetop waffle iron, low frame with very flared base, cutout short side handle like a skillet's, hinged press with long iron rod handle, used like a waffle iron only it bakes a thin cornmeal batter to make one tortilla at a time, not marked, American, or poss. Mexican?, 1870s to 1900. • These were probably made in cast iron up to the 1960s or '70s, then in cast aluminum, worth considerably less to collectors. .... **$45-$65+**

Truffle cutter – See Canape or truffle cutters this chapter; also Julienne cutter and Vegetable cutters in Chapter I (Cut) with 10 tiny, very fancy tin cutters with reinforced edges, designs inclosettes, scrolls, & forms that look heraldic, "J. Y. Watkins," a house-furnishing shop in NYC that began in the 1830s when Watkins set up as a tinsmith. By the late 19th C., the firm was a wholesale supplier, & most likely an importer of European k" diam., c.1870s-90s. • Importer F. A. Walker advertised a single deep-cutting vegetable cutter, tin, flatback, in one of the almost figural "heraldic" designs found in the Watkins box. No size is given, but Walker was in business from the 1870s probably to c.1900. These could also be used for cutting out shapes in very firm jellies that would be used to decorate galantines or to insert in jelly molds before pouring another color of jelly. .... **$45-$65+**

Vegetable cutters – The majority are still, in this edition, in Chapter I (Cut); there's always the 6th edition! See Julienne cutters, also Vegetable cutters, also a couple of illustrations

Vegetable or rice mold – See Molds, tin, ring or border

Vienna baker – See Roll pan or Vienna baker

Wafer Irons and Waffle Irons

These are easy to tell apart. Wafers are "wafer thin," more or less crisp; waffles are thicker and "waffled" with a grid of little "niches" – square or other shape, such as hearts or diamonds – in an all-over pattern. Early wafer irons and early waffle irons both may have long handles, called reins. In fact, some 20th century wafer and pizzelle irons also have long reins. Wafer irons make one round wafer at a time, whereas waffle irons may make just one, or make several break-apart waffles that are divided into wedges or squares or hearts, etc. In addition, there are "Hotel Waffle Irons," for hotels, restaurants or even large boarding houses, that were large two-burner cast iron rectangular frames, in which three or more 2-plate hinged "pans" making 3 small waffles each were arranged so they could be flipped individually to match orders. Other hotel irons were large oval or rectangular frames to fit over two burners or range eyes, which made six or more breakapart cakes. Pizzelles are a type of wafer, and their molds are found below in Wafers.

•   •   •

Wafer types. We are accustomed to seeing pictures of round wafer irons with ecclesiastical or eagle and star motifs; the former probably used for religious ceremonies or occasions. Political or patriotic ones are harder to relegate, and yet there are proportionately many of them. (Perhaps some are skilled 1876 reproductions?) • Albert H. Sonn, in his three-volume *Early American Wrought Iron*, NY: 1928, wrote that wafer irons were "used in making of holiday or wedding wafers"; those with heart and flower motifs were probably for weddings. (Early heart-shaped waffle irons with reins probably were too.) • Dr. Henry Mercer's "Wafer Irons," an article in Vol. V, *Bucks County Historical Society* publications, 1920, outlines six types of wafers: (1) ecclesiastical, (2) domestic, (3) documentary, (4) medicinal, (5) fish, and (6) confectioner wafers. This was related by Richard H. Shaner in his fact-filled article "Waffles and Wafers," *Pennsylvania Folklife*, Summer 1962, Vol. XII, No. 4, pp.20-23. Shaner adds that the ecclesiastical ones were probably most common, because they were still being used in the 20th C. He wrote that in 1920, "there were still Catholic churches in the area [Pennsylvania Dutch country] which were still making wafers from 18th century styled wafer irons." An extensive collection of wafer irons can be seen at the Mercer Museum (which you'll love for many reasons) in Doylestown, PA.

•   •   •

Volcanic lava wafers – An letter from John W. Wells to the *New York Pennsylvania Collector* in June 1984 relates a fascinating fact. In the early 19th C., and for many years thereafter, American and English families made the "Grand Tour" of Europe, and included a climb of Mt. Vesuvius, from which molten volcanic lava would be descending in rivulets. According to Mr. Wells, some guides would "lift up a gob of molten lava with his 'wafer iron' ... squeeze it for a moment, and out would drop a small slab of congealed, glistening lava bearing the impression of the iron." He has one about 3" x 4", a quarter of an inch thick, that reads "Salvatore Madonna" on one side and "1832" on the other.

•   •   •

Wafer irons are also called **oble irons** (probably from the German *oblaten*, or else an example of a phenomenon in the English language, of a dropped "n" word, in this case noble iron. Another example is the word apple, which was originally napple).

•   •   •

Goffering or gauffre irons or goofer irons – This use of the word goffer was a big surprise to me, because I never heard the term goffering iron used for anything but a ruffle-ironing implement used in the laundry. But in Silas Bent's *Machine Made Man*, (Farrar & Rinehart, 1930), p.26, is the following: "there were toasters, and boat-shaped troughs wherein coffee could be ground with two handled discs. And for pastries there were 'goffering irons.' These were stands bearing metal pods with removable discs, which could be heated in the coals; then replaced, they heated the metal so that pastry could be ironed over it." In a way this makes sense, if you think how wafers were first rolled into a conical shape to receive ice cream. Other words, in corrupted French or -?- are *gaufriers*, or *gaufrettes*, or goffer, and the word *oublie* for the wafer itself (related to German *Oble*). • **Or Vice Versa?** To further confuse things, some 19th C. catalogs, from which storekeepers could order, used "Gauffre Irons" to mean waffle irons, along with "Wafer Irons" for those. See also the lengthy section on ice cream in this chapter.

WAFER IRONS:

Wafer iron, for hearth, cast & forged iron, intaglio design of heart within rectangular frame of criss-crossed lines, long handles called reins, marked "S. M. /ID ED," American, 5" x 8" head, 31-1/2"L overall, dated 1787. Originally in the Keillor Collection. ...... **$1,000+**

❖ NOTES ❖

Wafer iron, for hearth, with 13 stars – I reported this in the last edition, fully believing that I had seen one & carefully counted the stars. I checked all my files & was unable to come up with original source documentation. Advanced collector Joel Schiff wrote me regarding this: "I have seen seven or eight of these, in three different styles. All had 16 stars. If this is a legitimate wafer iron, it would be very very rare, & probably worth significantly more than the 16 star variety." Would probably be worth upwards of $3,000. Let us know if you have evidence of a wafer iron with 13 stars.

• • •

Dating by the Stars – Antiquastrology. There was never, officially, a flag with 16 stars, but at one time there were only 16 states. The state was Tennessee, and it was the 16th state from 1796 to 1803, when Ohio became the 17th state. There were 13 stars to the first American flag, under the First Flag Act of 1777 and back to 13 stars on coins from the 1820s, 1830s, 1850s, 1860s and 1890s; there were 12 stars in the Bon Homme Richard flag of 1779; there were 15 stars in the flag under the Second Flag Act in 1795 and 15 stars on 1794 and 1797 Liberty coins; and 20 stars in the design under the Act of 1818. This is useful information so far as it goes. Check a world almanac or encyclopedia if you are trying to determine origins or dates from the number of stars on a piece. Even then it could be a commemorative or patriotic piece that refers back to a date or period, rather than contemporaneous to it.

Wafer iron, for hearth, cast iron, Great Seal of the U.S. design with eagle & shield with 16 stars, "lips" or head 5-1/4" diam., overall length 27-1/2", long rein handles, American (?). (Tennessee was admitted in

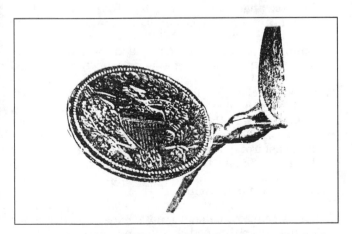

IV-394. Wafer iron detail. Wafer irons were used to make thin, crisp cookies called wafers. Cast iron, wrought handles. Eagle with shield body & 13 stars, possibly as early as 1800. 27-1/2"L x 5-1/4" diam., American. Ex-Keillor Collection. **$1,200+**

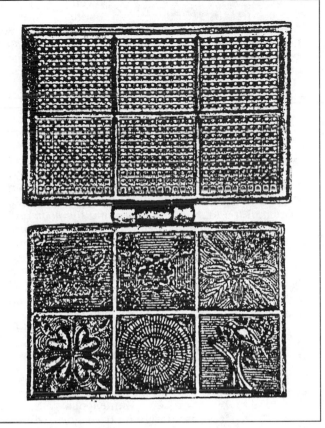

IV-395. Waffle-wafer iron detail. Showing mold head only. Cast iron, forged iron handles. Commonly found, but quite appealing, an iron with rectangular heads for making a sort of waffled wafer combo. Thicker than wafers. 6 designs. Note bird in tree & various flowers. This one marked "H. & M." Others have been brought back from German trips, & found with no marks. Iron expert Joel Schiff says this is "generally thought of as Swiss." **$150+**

1796, & the 17th state, Ohio, in 1803.) However, as Joel Schiff wrote me, "While clearly not made before 1796, the 16 star types may have been made primarily in England, up to & even after the war of 1812, as an export item." One such iron was advertised in 1984 bearing the makers' mark "POPE & JONES" in a small oval, near where the each rein handle is joined to its disc. .... **$1,000+**

Wafer iron, for hearth, cast iron plates (sometimes called lips), long forged iron reins or handles, with figure 8 loop attached to one, a knob on other, the plates with finely detailed eagle & striped shield with 16 stars, "E Pluribus Unum" in ribbon banner in eagle's mouth, one foot holding 8 arrows, one holding olive branch, American, 6-1/2" diam., 31-7/8"L, c.1796 to 1803 – or later. .... **$1,500+**

Wafer iron, for hearth, cast iron with forged reins, flower surrounded by concentric rings, American, 28"L, c.1800 .... **$350+**

Wafer iron, for hearth, forged iron with brass stamps inside the "lips" to ensure very fine detailing in finished wafers, & fast even heating, American or English, 2-1/2" x 4-1/2" wafer disks, & 14-1/2"L handles, 18th C. or very early 19th C. .... **$350+**

Sweet Wafers – *Two ounces of butter, half a pound of sugar, half a pound of flour, five eggs, beaten separately. Bake in wafer-irons well greased, and roll over a knife."* Mrs. A. P. Hill, Mrs. Hill's New Family Receipt Book, *NY: 1870.*

Almond Wafers – *Ingredients, 1/2 lb. of sweet almonds, 1/4 lb. of sifted sugar, 1 oz. of flour, and 2 eggs. Blanch and cut the almonds small, moisten them with the yolks and whites of eggs previously beaten. Sift into them the sugar and the flour, and mix the whole together with two drops of essence of lemon peel. Lightly butter a clean tin [apparently a square or rectangular baking pan], and spread the mixture over it as thin as possible. Bake it a light brown, and cut it with a knife, before it is cold, into long squares; roll them immediately on pieces of wood, to make them round and hollow. They are usually served to garnish creams."* Webster & Parkes, An Encyclopædia of Domestic Economy. *1848 NY edition of 1845 English book.*

Wafer iron, cast iron, "Kornu Kopia Krum Kake" (or Krumkake) by Andresen, Minneapolis, MN, early 20th C. Ornate cross design on both sides, with center cartouche containing name. Meant to set down in low or high cast iron, 2-handled frame to set over heat source (high frame if gas, low if wood). These were meant to be removed from the iron when baked (a couple of minutes) & quickly rolled into a cone –

IV-396. Wafer iron detail. Cast & wrought iron. Note design with wreath of leaves around border, & a sort of urn or vase design with stylized flowers. This one is usually known by collectors as the "Easter Lily" pattern, and is found on 20th C. wafer irons & Krumkake irons. Compare with next picture. This photograph courtesy of the National Museum of American History, Smithsonian Institution. Probably not as old as assumed from style of reins, & may even be early 20th C. – as in catalog shot from Duparquet in next picture. **$150+**

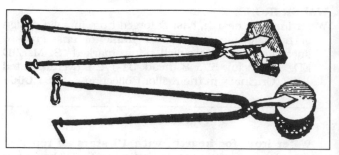

IV-397. Gauffre & wafer irons. Probably similar combination as previous picture, rectangular one making a waffle, or "gauffre" in France. William Adams & Son, London, c.1860-61 ad. **$100-$200**

or a "cornucopia" using a separate tool that's an iron cone with a handle, that looks like a gardener's dibble or planting stick. .... **$95+**

Wafer iron for "Krumkake" wafers, cast aluminum, low frame with wooden-handled 2-headed mold. Same pattern as Griswold and Wagner wafer irons of wreath around an odd clump of flowers like bleeding hearts which is sometimes called the "Easter Lily" pattern. "Nordic Ware" mf'd. by Made By Plastics for Industry, Minneapolis, MN, c.1960s(?). Wafer Krumkake area is 5-1/4" diam., frame fits 8" burner. .... **$15+**

Wafer iron, nickeled cast iron, floral wreath surrounding odd flower design that looks like bleeding hearts inside plates, long rod-like reins, in a frame that itself has a sort of "frying pan" handle, just like a waffle iron of the period. PN# 895, 995, and base #894, "The Griswold Mfg. Co., Erie, PA, Patented JUNE 29, 1880" but made for at least 30 years. .... **$450+**

Wafer iron, cast iron with long reins, hinged, on base, plates decorated with flowers & wreath like the Griswold, "WAGNER MFG. CO. SIDNEY O. PAT'D FEB 22, 1910," made for another 30 years or so. .... **$175+**

Wafer irons called Pizzelle irons:

The word pizzelle is from the Italian word *pizze*, meaning round and flat. It is found with many spellings: *piazelle, pazella, pizzele,* and *pizelle.*

Wafer iron, of type called a pizzelle iron, for use on the hearth although modern, cast iron, with long handles, rectangle with diamond pattern waffling, Baccellieri Brothers Mfg. Co., Philadelphia, 20th C. These were made in iron up to 1950 or so, thereafter in aluminum. A pizzelle is a crisp Italian hazlenut or anisette wafer that looks like a lacy doily when sprinkled with confectioner's sugar after baking. .... **$45+**

Wafer or pizzelle iron, for hearth though modern, cast steel, rectangular, long handles, Ciunta Brothers, Philadelphia, 20th C. .... **$35+**

Wafer or pizzelle iron, for hearth, forged iron long handles, cast iron plates with simple waffling criss-cross design, 23"L, late 19th C. or maybe early 20th C. .... **$55+**

Waffle irons, for hearth:

Waffle iron, for hearth, cast iron heart shaped head, forged reins & catch to hold ends together while baking, heart shaped waffles, no mark, American, 21-1/2"L x 5-1/4"W, early 19th C. .... **$350+**

Waffle iron, for hearth, cast iron, hinged 2 part with long handle, one part has small 1/8" lip that holds other half more securely in place, head is lovely 12 scallop edged circle, which when waffles are broken apart reveal that they form 6 hearts, simple waffling pattern, prob. American, 10-5/8" diam. head, 20-1/2"L overall, 19th C. .... **$250+**

Waffle iron, for hearth, cast iron with forged iron handle, the iron is star shaped, with small stars within the waffling grids. These small stars look punched; ironware collector Joel Schiff believes they were swaged, that is, while the cast iron was hot (or after reheating), the waffling grid was hammered on a sort of miniature anvil-like swage block with a small star design. I'm not sure the apparent accurately placed stars could have been achieved that way. American, prob. PA German, 6-1/2" diam. waffle, 34-1/4"L overall, late 18th C. • Ex-Robacker, $1,550. .... **$1,250+**

Waffle iron, for hearth, long forged iron reins & rectangular plates with diamond waffle grid, "scissor" or pivot point levered handles rather than type with hinged head. Marked "Chatham," (probably B & W Co., or B. W. Co.), Chatham, -?- (Chathams in GA, CT, IL, IA, KY, MA, PA, NY, NC, VA), 24-1/2"L, early 19th C. .... **$175+**

Waffle iron, for hearth, forged iron handles, cast iron mold, beautiful decoration along top edge of one half of the mold's back depicts 2 Hessian soldiers on horses, & a pine tree, inside is simple waffling grid, no maker's mark, American. Head 6"W x 4-1/4"H, overall 26"L. Looks 18th C., but may be 19th C. or even later revivalist, though fine.................... **$250+**

❖ RECIPE ❖

Rice Waffles – *Boil half a pint of rice and let it get cold, mix with it one-fourth pound butter and a little salt. Sift in it one and a half pints flour, beat five eggs separately, stir the yolks together with one quart milk, add whites beaten to a stiff froth, beat hard, and bake at once in waffle-irons."* Mrs. S. C. Lee of Baltimore, in Practical Housekeeping, 1884.

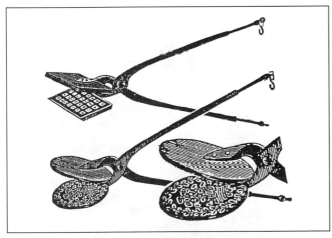

*IV-398. **Waffle iron & wafer iron & detail.** Cast heads, long wrought handles called reins – note clips at end that hold the handles together.* **(T)** *Simple waffle iron at top, 6" x 3-1/2" head.* **(B-L)** & **(B-R)** *this one particularly interesting because by blowing up the small, small picture in Duparquet catalog, c.1904-10, you see that wreath & urn design is same as Smithsonian one, which may help bracket date from 1840s to c.1910.* **$100-$200**

*IV-399. **Wafer-cum-waffle iron,** cast with wrought-iron reins, or handles. 27"L x 5-1/2" diam., simple concentric rings, a ring of waffling projections, a central rosette. Photo courtesy of the National Museum of American History, Smithsonian Institution.*

❖ NOTES ❖

Nathaniel Waterman's "New Ornamental configuration or design for the half plate of a Waffle baker." Prolific and kitchen-friendly inventor Waterman got Design patent #578, July 5, 1853, for a "waffle-plate or mould" that combined elements from waffle iron and wafer irons (*viz.* the semi-pious words). His design, divided into quadrants by crossed bars, had a rim around the outside in which are "raised letters in reverse, they being those of the words, Faith, Mercy, Truth, and Grace, one of the said words, being represented in each quadrant, within which latter are also numerous frustro [??] pyramidal projections that are elevated on the plate. The other half, presumably to be hinged to the ornamental plate, is not shown, probably meant to be made the same, with the same design, as the plate shown.

Waffle iron, for hearth, rectangular cast iron head has rows of small dimpled squares for grid (looks like aerial view of city streets, from 10 miles up), set at right angles to long wrought reins, one ending with knob, other with free-moving loop to work as catch, marked "B. W. Co." also "Chatham" (see another above), approx. 15"L overall, head 6" x 4", early 19th C. • "At auctions kitchen furniture is popularly supposed to go for a song ... these things are usually sold in lots and a person needing a waffle iron and muffin rings may find himself in possession of coal scuttles and dish-pans." *Appleton's Home Books*, 3 volumes, NY, 1881, 1884............................. **$175+**

Waffle irons, range or stove top:
High frames were for gas or coal or vapor stoves; low frames for wood.

Waffle iron, cast aluminum, handle replaced with piece of heavy black insulated cable, lid has smiling sun face, waffling pattern comprised of 6 stars & a crescent moon in each waffle, slightly corroded, "Mazie Lee," 8-1/8" diam., 20th C. A "techtique" make-do!...................................... **$30+**

Waffle iron, cast aluminum high frame, multi-purpose outfit that makes waffles & if you use the frame with

IV-400. "Waffle furnace." *Of range-top type. Cast iron, with removable iron & handled low frame. This one is "A very ingenious article, making four good-sized waffles with less labor than is required in making one with the ordinary iron" [ie. at the time, the long-handled, or reined, kind]. From* American Home Cook Book, *1854. The artist drew quadrant grid sketchily.* **$65-$100+**

omelette pans, it cooks eggs too. Wagner Ware #8, 20th C. I love aluminum, but it isn't anywhere near as valuable to most collectors. .... **$140-$165+**

Waffle iron, cast aluminum, oblong, makes 2 rectangular waffles, very simple grid with squares with a dimple in each, short stubby black painted wood handles, "Waffle Iron For Armstrong Table Stove," S. S. Co., Huntington, WVa, 6-1/4" x 5-1/4" exclusive of handles, which are 3"L, early 20th C. .... **$30+**

Waffle iron, cast iron, hearts, diamonds, flowers, low frame, 2 part mold, long forged iron handles, Warnick & Leibrandt 8, 9", Philadelphia, PA, 3rd quarter 19th C. This probably is a long-handled conversion from their more commonly-made stove top waffle irons. Joel Schiff says you can still get these in PA for about $55; elsewhere:...................... **$75-$100+**

Waffle iron, hinged waffle part only, frame missing, cast iron, turned black painted short wood handles, grid of 4 simple parts, "Crescent Waffle #8," Fanner & Co., Cleveland, OH, late 19th C. .... **$35-$65+**

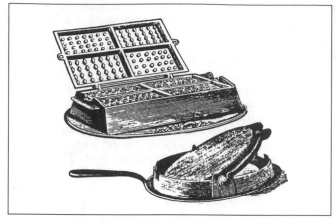

IV-402. Waffle irons. (T) *This is, as catalog states, a "square" iron, for stove tops. For 1, 2 or 4 cakes. Similar to IV-352, but not as nice because it only has diamonds & rounds.* **(B)** *Pennsylvania "card pattern" [known, but not shown in linecut], round, low frame, flipped with lid lifter tool. Four sizes (6" x 7", 7" x 8", 8" x 9" & 9" x 10" – sizes which I think refer to diam. of the iron & then frame) were offered by Stuart Peterson, 1875 & Leibrandt & McDowell Stove, 1861.* **(T) $100-$200; (B) $45-$55**

Waffle iron, rectangular 2 part hinged mold that sets into 4 legged frame with side handle, makes 3 waffles with patterns of little squares, little diamonds & little hearts, maker not marked, American, 5"H x 8"L x 5"W, c.1870s. .... **$125+**

Waffle iron, sits over range eye, 2 big looped bail handles, 4 waffling patterns, hearts, stars, diamonds & rounds, hinge is gorgeous cast leaf, New England Butt Co., Providence, RI, 9-3/4" diam., makes 7" diam. waffles, mid 19th C. New England Butt Co., who were named for the butt hinges they made for doors, also made the various iron wares of Nathaniel Waterman. .... **$175-$225+**

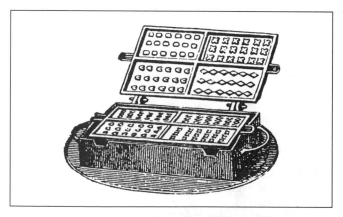

IV-401. Slightly later stove top waffle iron. *Cast iron 4 designs – hearts, diamonds, squares, X'es. Maker unknown, but Dave Smith thinks could be Savery. The linecut shows that each rectangular waffle has a different pattern on front & back. Ad of J. & C. Berrian, wholesalers & retailers of house furnishings, NYC. 1857 ad.* **$150-$250**

IV-403. Waffle irons, *All could be flipped in their frames to evenly heat top & bottom.* **(L)** *This one in "new style," with fleur-de-lis designs, low frame for range or stove top,* **(T-R) (B-R)** *others with frames elevated on 3 or 4 legs, & with what were called "patent revolving" designs. All probably by Nathaniel Waterman.* Russell & Erwin *catalog, 1865.* **(L) $45-$60; (T-R) $130-$160; (B-R) $130-$160**

Waffle iron, square, cast iron, on low stand or frame (worth more than the high frame #11), 4 square waffling grids, Griswold #11 – "The American Waffle Iron," early 20th C. (High frame worth a lot more.) ..... **$150+**

Waffle iron, stove top, cast iron, hearts with center star motif grid, bail handle on frame, coiled heat dissipating handle on hinged mold, Griswold #18, pat'd. May 18, 1920 & July 11, 1922. .... **$150-$175+**

Waffle iron, cast iron, "X" geometric pattern with name inside, "Giles F. Filley," St. Louis, MO, prob. 3rd quarter 19th C. .... **$95-$125+**

❖ NOTES ❖

1884 Waffling. Here's what Mrs. S. C. Lee of Baltimore, wrote in her 1884 *Practical Housekeeping* about waffle irons: "The waffle iron is a very peculiar machine. The waffle is put in, locked up, baked on one side to a lovely brown, turned over, prison and all, until the other side is a still lovelier brown, and then released steaming hot ready for the table."

Waffle iron, cast iron, mfd. by Bridge & Beach Stove Co., dated 1865, but poss. made over long period. .... **$85-$150+**

Waffle iron, cast iron, 2 piece with bail handle, Wagner Ware, 1920. • An ad in the Dec. 10, 1892 *The Metal Worker*, claims that Wagner had just brought out the "only bailed and detachable hinge waffle iron in the market." Depicted in the ad is a low frame mold, the socket joint hinge opposite the 2 turned wood handles, arched bail crosswise. Patent for such a bailed waffle iron was given to Wagner July 26, 1892. ..... **$45-$65+**

Waffle iron, cast iron, 3 pieces, low frame with extra decorative frying pan handle, the 2 part waffle iron has openwork casting to dissipate heat, Majestic Mfg. Co., No. 885M, St. Louis, MO, 16"L with handle, pat'd. 1908. (Much later, Majestic made electric waffle irons.) .... **$150-$200+**

IV-404. Waffle irons. *Stove top styles, cast iron.* **(T-L)** *Small one from Matthai-Ingram, c.1890, in sizes 6" x 7" to 9" x 10".* **(T-R)** *Big one from M. L. Filley, Troy, NY, c.1880.* **(B)** *Bottom one, with apparently fancy face that is probably just a bad drawing of diamonds, from unidentified 1880s cookbook.* **(T-L)** *$45-$65;* **(T-R)** *$200-$300+;* **(B)** *$45-$100*

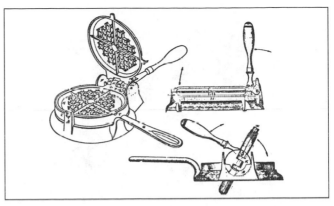

IV-405. Waffle iron patent. *Pat'd. by Alexander S. Patton, Columbus, OH, Aug. 23, 1881. Shows in several pictures the particular type of "hinge journal" used for turning mold in frame, & the upright handle that made opening the lid easy. Official Gazette of the U.S. Patent Office.*

Waffle iron, cast iron, design of little girl & garden (Mistress Mary? not contrary enough to not get her waffles?), 2 hinged round plates, quite possibly this was made by Stover, the windmill company, 20th C. • Friend & collector Linda Fishbeck of Texas found this, the dealer said it was a waffle iron, & she didn't buy it, feeling there was something wrong about it. Sounds to me, some years later now, that it was probably just missing its frame, & that it possibly could even be late 19th C. In the future, one sure thing to look for would be the two side "pegs" that would fit into slots in the frame. .... **$60+**

Waffle iron, cast iron, flower, heart & diamond design waffling plate, 2 part with stand, Francis Buckwalter & Co., Boyer's Ford, PA, pat'd. Aug. 9, 1910. Also known as the "Pennsylvania card motif." .... **$45-$65+**

Waffle iron, cast iron, frame has 2 high arched handles, hinged 2 part mold fits down in, has marvelous recipe for potato waffles in pretty hand printed-looking letters cast intaglio on flat lid: "**Kartoffel Waffeln.**" A translation of the recipe: 1/2 lb. cooked grated potatoes, 1/4 lb. meal, 1/2 litre warm milk, 3 eggs, 50 grams butter, 20 grams yeast. Recipe is only marking, prob. German not PA German, 11" diam., late 19th C. I think this is fabulous, though not very valuable, except to recipe collectors, cookbook collectors, Mr. Potato-head, and writers? ... **$90-$130+**

IV-406. Waffle iron patent. *Pat'd. by J. T. Lambert, Detroit, MI, April 17, 1877, assignor to Detroit Iron & Brass Mfg. Co. "Handle may be used to lift lid or reverse position of the iron." Official Gazette of the U.S. Patent Office.*

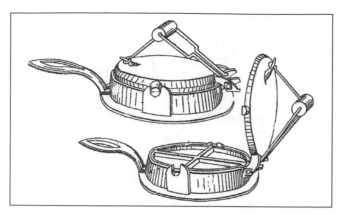

IV-407. Waffle iron patent. *Pat'd. by Cornelius Swartwout, Troy, NY, Aug. 24, 1869, #94,043, assigned to himself, Joseph Foxell, Thomas Jones, & Edward W. Millard, all Troy, NY. Mainly patent is for this "handle, connected with and forming part of a waffle-iron, by means of which the same may be readily turned over without danger of slipping, and without the possibility of burning the hand."*

Waffle iron, cast iron, high frame, Wapak #8, mfd. by William H. Howell Co., Geneva, IL, 20th C., marked with the Wapak Indian. High frame were for gas or coal or vapor stoves; low for wood. .... **$175-$250**

Waffle iron, cast iron, high frame, Harwi #8, American, early 20th C. .... **$30+**

Waffle iron, cast iron, low frame, Favorite Piqua #8, Favorite Stove & Range Co., Piqua, OH, 1890s-1910. "Favorite" line introduced 1892. For crossover handle type: .... **$75+**

Waffle iron, cast iron, low frame, 2-part hinged round mold fits into it, simple square grid, Dover Stamping Co., about 8" diam., c.1870s. .... **$75+**

Waffle iron, cast iron, low frame, 2 parts, hinged, 2 side handles on frame, mold divided into 4 wedges, design is fleur-de-lis & crosses, Norths, Harrison & Chase, #7, 8, Phila., late 19th C. Common. .... **$45-$80+**

❖ NOTES ❖

WWI Waffles. It was your patriotic duty during WWI to eat waffles. Early ads in 1918 & 1919 really pushed them as food, so that they could sell more waffle irons. What I don't understand is how they managed to get the iron to cast the waffle irons with; what about metal drives? In Sept. 1918 trade publication, *House Furnishing Review*, a Griswold ad stated "With housewives all over the country absorbed in menu problems, this is the time to feature your kitchen-ware!" Since this was aimed at retailers, they added "Our advertising, appealing to 550,000 readers, stimulates waffle-hunger." Stover, meanwhile, claimed that people were "Living on waffles."

Waffle iron, cast iron, low frame with flat top, convex underside side handle, 2 part hinged waffle mold fits into this, extremely plain, not marked, American, makes 8" diam. waffle, overall length including handle 18-1/2", c.1860s or 1870s................. **$65-$85+**

Waffle iron, cast iron, low frame with slightly up-angled frying pan handle, hinged round waffle mold set down inside with lifting ring upright on lid; you would need an extra tool, perhaps some kinds of stove lid lifters would work, to open it up, oh bother it all, must we have waffles again? Lid of waffle mold has beautifully crisp design of small daisy-like flower or stylized sun in center & a half inch band of radiating lines around rim, not marked, American, frame is 9-1/2" diam. with 5-1/2"L handle, makes 6-1/2" diam. waffles, c.1870s or even 1860s. • From the look of the casting, my hunch is this was cast by a stove maker, probably in Troy or Albany, NY, & possibly as early as the 1850s. There was a waffle iron patented by C. Swartwout of Troy, NY, Aug. 24, 1869. A really early waffle iron patent was a design patent granted Nathaniel Waterman of Boston, on July 5, 1853, but this isn't his. • There were, I believe, no more than 5 waffle iron patents, including a design patent, granted before 1873. But I'm sure that many waffle irons were made, especially simple ones to go with specific ranges or stoves, without a pat'd. design. .... **$65-$100+**

Waffle iron, cast iron, low frame with very wide flange to accommodate a variety of range eyes, frying pan handle, 2 part, hinged mold has no handles but for a little tab with hole for lifting tool, hearts, diamonds, rosettes, circles & Xs – what the dealer called "Deck of Cards" pattern, more commonly known among collectors as the "Pennsylvania card pattern," Orr, Painter & Co., No. 6-7, Reading, PA, mold is 5-15/16" diam., c.1890s-1910. • Another, slightly larger, marked No. 7-8, with broken hinge, was priced $25. What use is a broken one? .... **$45-$65+**

Waffle iron, cast iron, low frame with wide flange, longish "frying pan" handle, mold is hinged, 2 part with no handle, 4 designs: heart with 3 small diamonds inside; simple scrolls with 3 small diamonds between; 5 radiating broken lines; & a pattern of rather widely spaced small diamonds. Top mold has same 4 designs, only they're rotated 90° on the axis so that each waffle would have different patterns front & back. Lid has small iron ring near edge for

IV-408. Waffle iron. *Griswold #9 "French Waffle Iron," for doing four pairs at a time. Hotel or restaurant (or large family) model. Note stubby wooden handles – short but sufficient. 22-1/2"L x 11-1/2"W, pat'd. June 29, 1880. Ad in* The Metal Worker, *June 20, 1890. Lower end for regular square waffling design; higher for this "stylized spiderweb" waffling design. Full range of value given by cast iron consultants:* **$1,000-$2,000**

lifting with small pot hook, unfortunately this has no mark at all but is the same waffle iron as the marked "Augur & Lord" in next listing, American, 8" diam., 9-1/2"L handle on frame, mid to 3rd quarter 19th C. .... **$50-$75**

Waffle iron, cast iron, round, 3 parts: flanged frame, hinged mold making 4 wedge waffles decorated with small hearts, diamonds, scrolls, ridged rayed lines. Augur & Lord, Chester, CT, 8" diam. mold, mid to 3rd quarter 19th C. .... **$50-$75**

Waffle iron, cast iron, medium high frame with 2 part waffler, makes 4 small waffle wedges with pattern of fleur-de-lis & crosses, North, Chase & North, #6, 7, Philadelphia, 5-3/4" diam., 11-3/4"L with handle, late 19th C. Common pattern. .... **$55-$80**

Waffle iron, cast iron, range top, very low frame with flat rim, frying pan side handle, 2 part hinged mold fits into it, nice casting of scrolly wreath around center design of concentric rings on lid, American, 8" diam., 14"L overall, marked "8/9/1910." Common pattern. .... **$40-$55**

Waffle iron, cast iron, range top, very low frame with frying pan handle, 2 part hinged mold, Orr Painter & Co. 7 & 8, Reading, PA, makes 6-3/4" diam. waffle, 13"L overall with handle, 19th C. Common pattern. .... **$45-$65**

Waffle iron, cast iron, round, 3 parts, wide flanged low frame with "frying pan" handle, hinged mold making 4 waffles in different patterns: small outlined hearts, small diamonds, small squares with pattern that could be interpreted as "SS" on surface, & small circles with pebbled surface, 8" diam. x 15"L with handle, John Savery's Son & Co., NYC, NY, c.1880s. (See also the waffle iron above for Armstrong Table Stove.) .... **$65-$85**

IV-410. Heart & star waffle irons. *Everybody wanted in on the sweetheart act. These are Griswold's "Heart & Star Waffle Irons," low & high frame, with 5 hearts surrounding a star, & a tiny star within a bigger one. The lid looks like a five-leaf clover! (Note: Griswold also made a 5-heart design, the lid of which looked like a 10-scallop-petaled flower, for Western Importing Co. after 1904. It had a wooden side handle, & a nifty cut-out cast iron handle on frame. It's worth under a hundred.) Cast iron, from c.1925 flyer with recipes. The handle design helped dissipate heat. The heart-star design was patented May 18, 1920 & July 11, 1922. (The later heart-star is worth more than the earlier all heart, at least in cast iron.)* **$150-$250**

Waffle iron, cast iron, round (despite rectangular measurements given in their catalog, as transcribed below), 3 part with low frame with side frying pan handle, 2 part hinged mold fits into it, Matthai-Ingram Co., came in 4 sizes: 6" x 7", 7" x 8", 8" x 9", & 9" x 10". c.1890s. .... **$45-$55+**

Waffle iron, cast iron, round head, 6-point PA-German flowers on one side, waffled grid on other, no mark, PA or German, 20th C. .... **$25-$45**

❖ NOTES ❖

"Among iron goods used in the kitchen are frying pans, waffle-irons, roll-pans, griddles for batter cakes, large iron pots, etc. Sometimes some of these things are so highly polished that they only require to be washed in soap and water and rubbed dry. ... **Griswold's American Waffle-irons** are most satisfactory. They are comparatively new." Maria Parloa, *Kitchen Companion*, Boston: Estes & Lauriat, 1887. The text illustration is of a cast iron waffle iron, low frame, short "frying pan" handle with hanging hole, hinged mold has very short handles, the baking surfaces divided into 4 parts with simple waffling pattern of small raised square blocks with dimples.

Waffle iron, cast iron, round or square high frame, Wagner Ware #8, c.1890s-1910. Round: $50-$75; Square: .... **$95-$125**

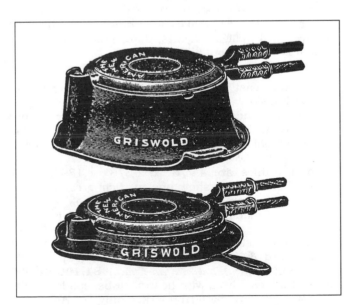

IV-409. Waffle irons. *Griswold's "The New American Waffle Iron," probably both based on June 25, 1893 patent, as described in wholesaler's catalog.* **(T)** *High or "deep" frame, "specially adapted for vapor stoves," came in one size, "8D," with round "pan" 7-3/4" diam., according to Buhl catalog.* **(B)** *Low frame style for wood stoves came in "8" & "9," with "pan" diam. slightly less – 7-3/4" & 8-5/8", Buhl catalog, c.1912.* **(T)** **$75-$100;** **(B)** *higher end for those with skillet handle (not shown)* **$55-$85**

Waffle iron, cast iron, short handled, makes 5 heart-shaped waffles, riveted-on leather handles probably replacements, marked "MUSTAD #4," European, inside diam. 6-1/4", handle 7"L. Prob. mid to late 20th C. Joel Schiff believes this is still in production. .... **$35-$55**

Waffle iron, cast iron, small, flared, wide-flanged frame, hinged 2 part mold, wood handles, "Buster Waffle No. 8" cast in script on lid, depicts Buster Brown facing his dog Tige, who sits up to get a treat. Mfd. by Andrew M. Anderson & Co., Chicago, pat'd. 11/13/1906. • One is depicted in Steve Stephens' "*Cast Iron Cookware News*," Nov. 1990 issue; it has coiled-wire, heat-dissipating handles. Crossover cartoon collector might pay the most. ..... **$450-$1,000**

Waffle iron, cast iron, frame that sets over range is rounded corner square, but the waffling plate is rectangular & divided into three break-apart "gridded fields" per plate with 3 different waffle designs – hearts, squares, diamonds, Griswold #1, c.1890s-1930s. When you see such a wide value range, it's partly due to a constantly self-correcting Griswold market. .... **$450-$700**

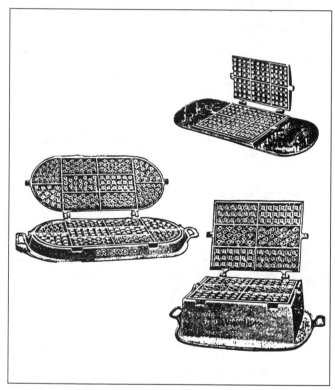

IV-411. Waffle irons. All multiple range eye frames. (T-R) By John Van Range Co., Cincinnati, 8" & 9" made "to fit on all our Pacific, Maggie, Chimney Corner, & No. 130 Single Oven Ranges, but no other range." Of course they thought this meant people would want their waffle iron so much that they'd buy the range too – but that's a poor marketing strategy! (L) Griswold #7, 17-3/4"L x 7-1/2". Came in three sizes, this one smallest. #9 was 21"L. The littlest kids in the family probably begged for the "ends." 1909 catalog. (B-R) Griswold #00, 10-1/4" x 7-3/4", makes 6 waffles with waffling patterns in hearts, squares, diamonds & rounds. (T-R) $75-$200; (L) in 3 sizes: $800-$1,200, $1,000-$1,500, $1,000-$2,000; (B-R) $525-$650

IV-412. Waffle iron. "Yum Yum" waffle iron, a Griswold hotel iron, the nickname was the cataloguers' (Albert Pick, 1909). While "French" one sat over a stove, this one has its own stove. Other irons, say those from the "French," would fit this frame also. Three sizes: 2 pans, 4" diam., frame 14-1/2" x 11-1/2"; or 3 pans, 4" pans, 20"L x 11-1/2" frame; or 4 pans in 22-1/2" x 11-1/2" frames. Pat'd. 1901, 190-? Values without gas stove: (2 pans) $500; (3 pans) $700; (4 pans) $1,200

❖ NOTES ❖

Griswold #02 & #0: The Griswold #2 is similar, only slightly smaller, and also makes 3 break-apart waffles with three patterns (front and backs different) and it's worth about $600-$800. The Griswold #0, slightly larger than the #1, makes four different break-apart waffles, in 4 designs: hearts, diamonds, squares, circles. It is worth about $500-$700.

Waffle iron, cast iron, elongated oval frame with long oval hinged waffle pan, divided into 10 break-apart waffles – the curved ends were divided into two wedges with rounded edges, & the central section made 6 oblong waffles. Hearts, squares, diamonds & circles. Griswold #7, pan is 17-3/4"L x 7-1/2"W, & most waffles are 4-7/8" x 2-3/8", c.1890s-1910. Smith & Wafford show one in their great book on Griswold, complete with simple wire hook to lift lid. Griswold made this in 3 sizes, the largest is 21"L x 9-1/2". The #7 originally cost $1.35; the #8 cost $1.60; the #9 cost $1.95. Now? Eat your heart out, Standard & Poor! (#7) $800-$1,200; (#8) $1,100-$1,500; (#9) .... **$1,100-$2,000**

Waffle iron, cast iron, with hearts, clubs, spades & diamonds waffling pattern, marked only "7," American, 20th C. .... **$35-$45**

Waffle iron, cast iron with stand, hearts & diamonds waffling pattern, Abbott & Lawrence, 8-1/2"L, late 19th C. .... **$45-$65**

Waffle iron, cast iron, with wonderful logos forming waffling pattern for 4 pie-wedge waffles, "Keen Kutter No. 8," E. C. Simmons Hardware, St. Louis, MO, 20th C. Reproduction alert. – There are repros of this. Look closely, because it's a pretty good copy. .... **$120-$150**

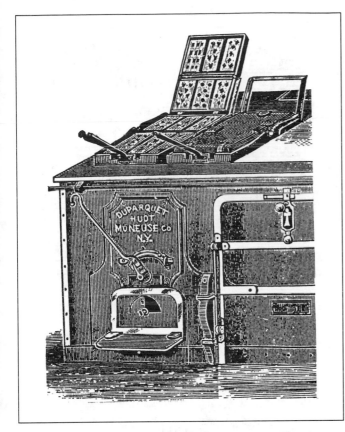

IV-413. Waffle irons built into range. This is a "griddle & waffle range combined," all sheet iron & cast iron. Range itself 4 feet long, with 2 waffle irons (one shown here closed, one open) & a griddle 21" square (you see corner at right). Duparquet, Huot & Moneuse, NYC, c.1904-10. Waffling patterns are hearts, diamonds, rounds & squares. The 6 waffle irons themselves would be valued at least $450+. The whole set-up with range might be valued at more than $3,000.

Waffle iron, commercial use, cast iron, makes 12 waffles, I have no idea what this looks like, having only read about it in a trade journal of 1892. Called "The Hotel Mammoth," mfd. by Stuart & Peterson Co., Philadelphia, adv'd. Sept. 24, 1892, *The Metal Worker.* This is something of a hypothetical entry, because I've never seen one. Collector Joel Schiff has one which he believes is twice as large!! & he's never seen or heard of another. (I bet many of them went into war materiel.) As a rule, large commercial wares didn't get the same attention from collectors as regular family sized, or toy sized, until fairly recently. They do give you a lot of bang for your buck. .... **$300+**

❖ NOTES ❖

Waffles and Catfish. "Any one familiar with the suburbs of Philadelphia, may have seen at various small hotels near the Wissahickon, the notice posted in a conspicuous place, 'Catfish and Waffles.' Why such a forlorn little fish with such a repulsive name, except to Philadelphians, is associated with waffles, we are unable to discover. With flap-jack it would do very well,

for what visions do flap-jacks suggest of elegant supper tables and shining silver. But the delicious waffles which are so seldom seen on private tables nowadays, bring to mind our childhood and grandmother, with her solid, old-fashioned silver, and well do we remember the little silver basket, with its equal parts of powdered sugar and cinnamon, the proper thing to spread is here offered for the benefit of those who do not know **how to make these** just right: 2 cups of milk; 2 eggs; 3 cups of flour; one teaspoonful of cream-tartar; one-half teaspoonful of soda; one saltspoonful of salt; one tablespoonful of melted butter." *American Agriculturist,* October 1883.

Waffle irons, electric:

Waffle iron, electric, aluminum base, chromed lid, shaped wood handles painted black, 3 Bakelite™ (or hard rubber?) feet, temperature dial in lid has mica covering, "Bersted Model 242," Bersted Mfg. Co., Chicago, IL, 12" overall diam., 8-1/4" diam. grid, 1930s.. **$30-$40+**

Waffle iron, electric, chrome all over except plastic side handles on octagonal base & hinged lid, various controls on base, "Wafflemaster," Waters-Genter Co., Minneapolis, MN, 1931. .... **$25-$35+**

Waffle iron, electric, nickeled cast metal, hinged mold raised off simple flat base, turned wooden spade handle on side, huge outlets in top & bottom plates for electric cord, General Electric Co., about 9" diam., maybe a bit more, 1922-1923. .... **$25-$35+**

Waffle iron, electric, nickeled metal, fancy cutout pedestal base, side lifting handles, another handle for domed top plate of mold, "Universal," Landers, Frary & Clark, c.1920s. .... **$35-$45+**

IV-414. Electric waffle iron. One of earliest – very early 20th C. General Electric #293079. Cast iron frame & waffler. Note spiral "cool" handles, & two sets of screw-in power plugs that went into lightbulb sockets. Photo courtesy General Electric Corp. This is a good example of what's now being called a "tech-tique." $600+

Gingerbread Waffles – *2 cups flour, 1 tsp ginger, 1-1/2 tsps cinnamon, 1/2 tsp salt, 1 tsp baking powder, 3/4 tsp soda, 1 cup molasses, 1/3 cup butter, 1/2 cup sour milk or buttermilk, 1 egg, well beaten. – Mix the dry ingredients. Put molasses and butter in a saucepan, let come to boil and remove from heat at once. Cool, then add milk and egg. Add mixture to dry ingredients and beat until light and smooth. Bake immediately on an Electric Waffle Iron which is not quite so hot as for ordinary waffles, for molasses burns easily. Serve with honey or sweetened whipped cream." Recipe from Waffles, Brooklyn Edison Co., Inc. Bureau of Home Economics, n.d. [c.1935 to 1940]. Included in this little booklet was information on: Saturday morning junior misses' cooking classes; how to arrange a waffle party for your club; and even Lamp Shade Making Classes. In those days, they had to urge the surge.*

❖ NOTES ❖

A New Piece of China – "The waffle plate is a great addition to the table ware. It may be had in plain china or handsomely decorated; the former costs one dollar, the latter from two to three dollars. The perforations in the top admit the escape of the steam so that the cakes may be kept warm yet free from moisture. The deep bowl gives ample space for the half-dozen circles of delicious brownness." *The Housewife*, NY, July 1891. This is a deep, widely flared bowl or dish, with perforated flat china top with knob handle.

IV-415. Electric waffle irons. *Two more "techtiques."* **(T)** *"Westchester Automatic, Catalog #149Y183," by General Electric. Chromed finish, black enamel stripes, "old ivory marblette" handles & pendent drop handle. Fibre feet. Detachable cord. 11-3/4" diam. base. The rim you see is to catch batter overflow – great idea! From 1935-36 catalog.* **(B)** *The "Handy-hot" iron, No. 4704-H, by Chicago Electric Mfg. Co. Square overflow tray. 7-1/4" cast aluminum grids, chromium finish on outside, "rich looking walnut finished" handles. Chicago Electric catalog, 1938. Really cool Deco look.* **$80-$135**

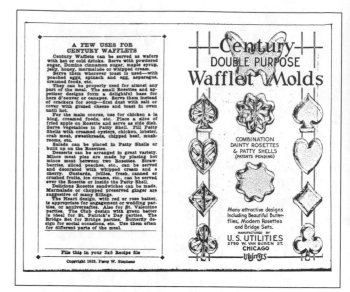

IV-416. Wafflet mold recipe booklet, *published for U.S. Utilities, Chicago, 1933.*

IV-417. "Weiner Dog" baker patent. *This picture is from the June 1930 issue of Science & Invention, in their "Yankee Brains at Work" column about new inventions. This is Patent #1,742,945, issued to Peter S. Banff. "Relates to an electrical cooking device designed primarily for that type of sandwich termed 'hot dog.' However, it may be adapted for producing any article of food to which it is applicable." The "hot dogs" or weiners on plate look like big animal crackers, but child appears to be eating a hot dog. "The invention consists of an electrical cooking device with an open bottom upper casing & an open top lower casing, each adapted to contain a heating unit," & 2 facing molding plates detachably connected to lid & lower part of mold. See also IV-173. Wow! Bow Wow! Wonder if it was ever made? If so, probable value:* **$1,000+**

Waffle iron, electric, nickelplate, porcelain-top insert in top lid, Deco ridged fan-shaped handles on tray base, and pendent handle on upper lid, thermometer set into center, 3 hearts & pink flowers design on top, 13" diam, marked "SuperElectric, Superior Electric Products, St. Louis Missouri," c.1930. .... **$35+**

Waffle iron, electric toy, nickel-plated, wreath & bows "engraving" around lid, black wooden knob to pedestal base, simple waffling grid, only 3"H x 4-1/2" diam, at base, to make 3 3/4" waffles! Plenty big enough for a stack. No marks. .... **$45+**

Whatzit cutter or mold, stamped & pieced tin, partly corrugated deep sides, shaped like horseshoe & looks like a mold or some kind of cutter, "Acme Potato Implement Co.," Traverse City, MI, 1-7/8" deep of which 3/4" is corrugated, 5"L, c.1890s-1910. .... **$25+**

Whatzit mold, or possibly something else, heavy cast iron, 3 legged, looks like a bath tub for an egg, & in fact has been advertised by at least one dealer as a toy bath tub, American, 4-3/8"L, c.1880s. • **What Kind of Mold?** If this is a mold for chocolate, you would end up with only a half egg that might have to be joined to another half egg. Its weight & thickness argue against its being a chocolate mold, but stranger things have been true. I thought it was possibly something like a spoon rest when I first bought it, but that seems doubtful. See IX-93. .... **$25+**

Wheat stick pan, cast iron, 7 ears of wheat all same direction, two little knob feet on bottom at each end, "Puritan No. 1270," also marked #1513 on bottom, 13-1/8"L x 5-1/2"W, 20th C. .... **$95+**

Wheat stick pan, also called a wheat bread pan, cast iron, makes 6 same-direction wheat sticks showing beautifully-delineated grainy head of wheat stalk. The oblong frame is cutaway around both ends of each cigar-shaped wheat stick, making a sort of thin, lengthwise "rail." Marked on non-hole handle "GRISWOLD," & underneath: "No. 27, Whole Wheat Stick Pan Griswold Erie, PA., U.S.A. 638," 10-7/8"L x 5-7/8"W, 1926 on.

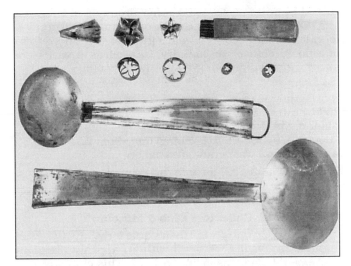

*IV-418. **Wax-flower modeling tools.** Pieced tin. This is an example of the kind of **confusable** item often mistaken for a cooking tool. Shown are dippers for molten wax, plus forms for cutting out petals. 19th C. Picture courtesy of the National Museum of American History, Smithsonian Institution. See also Vegetable cutters & nested cookie or cake cutters. A set approximately this size: $75-$125+*

(Another one, the same size, same No. 27, has on back "Wheat & Corn Stick Pan" & the well-used design patent #73,326. • Griswold also made a solid-frame 7-wheat stick pan as No. 2700; & to further confuse things, there's a "Merit" 7-stick wheat pan with "No. 1270" on its back. This is a very, very exacting, precise field of collecting, & you absolutely must have *The Book of Griswold & Wagner*, by David G. Smith & Chuck Wafford. See Bibliography.).......... **$200-$275+**
Wheat stick pan – See also Corn stick pan

FOR MORE INFORMATION

This is such an enormous chapter, with so many avid collectors, that there is new collector info all the time. I advise subscribing to newsletters, and doing regular Google searches online for clubs, dealers, newsletters and books in your specialty.

CAST IRON COLLECTORS

Joel Schiff

This collector wants to buy unusual pieces of cast iron cookware to add to his collection, especially iron molds. Joel has helped me with identifying & researching ironwares for 20+ years. Transcribe e-mail address with care!

321 E. 12th St.
NYC, NY 10003
Phone: (212) 353-1805
E-mail: cstirnckwr@aol.com

David Smith

This collector, who wrote the cast iron baking pan article in this chapter is very interested in cast iron broiler pans. Dave also has a newsletter.
"Kettles 'n Cookware" full of information & bonhomie.
Drawer B

Perrysburg, NY 14129
E-mail: panman@panman.com
Web site: www.panman.com

The Meekers, Patented Antiques

A Web site for selling "antiques of a mechanical nature." Also a number of remarkable collections in a cyber museum at the same site.

Larry & Carole Meeker
E-mail: clm@patented-antiques.com
Web site: www.patented-antiques.com.

Joanie Baldini
654 W. 26th St.
Erie, PA 16508
E-mail: thespider1@aol.com

Wagner and Griswold Society

WAGS – for collectors of cast iron kitchenware – was formed after consulting with many collectors, by collector-dealer-enthusiast Greg Stahl, who himself seeks cast iron toy kitchen items & cast iron & aluminum gem & muffin pans. The WAGS mission is to share information & the enjoyment of collecting cast iron &

cast aluminum cookware & other products of Griswold Mfg. Co. & Wagner Mfg. Co., & other manufacturers & foundries. Many collectors are interested in more than one manufacturer or foundry, as well as a variety of forms, not all of which are strictly for cooking.

Greg Stahl
R & G Antiques
290 Chestnut St.
Clinton, MA 01510
Phone: (978) 368-6646 (evening: 6pm–9pm EST only)
Web site: www.wagnerandgriswold.org

See also Chapter XII for info. on enamelware collectors.

COOKIE CUTTERS CLUBS & NEWSLETTERS

Cookie Cutter Collectors Club & Museum

"Cookie Crumbs" is their quarterly. CCCC was founded by Phyllis Wetherill with an appeal to readers in *Women's Circle* magazine in 1972. This club has several regional organizations.

Contact for club: Darlene Farrell
504 Louann St.
Pittsburgh, PA 15223
E-mail: blocmagu@bellatlantic.net
Contact for newsletter: Joyce Moorhouse
E-mail: asmjem@connect.com

"Cookies"

"A Bi-Monthly Newsletter Devoted to Cookies & Cookie Shaping," has been going strong since 1972. Founding editor, the late Phyllis Wetherill, did it through 1994. As of late 2002, the Web site was under construction.

Contact/editor: Rosemary Henry
9610 Greenview Lane
Manassas, VA 20109
E-mail: editor@cookiesnewsletter.com
Web site: http://members.tripod.com/Cookies Newsletter/

CAKE & BUNDT SPECIALISTS

Bundt Pans

Lots of recipes & information, on Web site of food writer & baker Marcy Goldman, author of *A Treasury of Jewish Holiday Baking* (Doubleday, 1997), and *The Best of Betterbaking*.com (Ten Speed Press & Random House, 2002).

Contact: Marcy Goldman
Web site: www.betterbaking.com

Casanova

Cake & Sugar Artists of Northern Virginia is a group of professionals and other enthusiasts, with a great Web site full of cake ideas, information, news, and best for all of us: links.

E-mail: casanova@wizard.net
Web site: www.cakeclub.com/

SPRINGERLE MOLDS

See within listings in chapter.

ICE CREAM CLUB & BOOKS

Club for you who scream for ice scream!

Join the club & get the high calorie newsletter *The Ice Screamer.*

Contact: Don Snyder
Box 465
Warrington, PA 18976

Wayne Smith's Ice Cream Dippers

Separate Price Guide. An indispensible book. Please use an SASE.

Contact/author: Wayne Smith
Box 418
Walkersville, MD 21793

Ice Cream & Chocolate Molds Catalog Reprints
Dad's Follies

This couple have collected & sold ice cream molds and chocolate molds for three decades. Along the way, they got a number of catalogs, which they have had reprinted because they "felt this information would be invaluable for other collectors." They have many offerings.

Contact: Lorry & Bruce Hanes
40 Kingston Court
Gibsonville, NC 27249
E-mail: DADSFOLLIE@aol.com
Web site: www.dadsfollies.com

PIZZELLE WAFERS

This is a great site with all kinds of historical pictures, folklore, and current information on where to find new irons for use and tips on using them. There's even info and pictures of a very collectible electric pizzelle iron patented in 1956 by the DeMarcos.

The Perfect Pizzelle
Contact: Hilary Versagli
E-mail: info@pizzelle.com
Web site: www.pizzelle.com

MUSEUMS
Johnson & Wales University Culinary Archives & Museum

This museum, an adjunct to the University for culinary & hospitality industry professionals, was started in 1979 with over 7500 antique cookbooks, and culinary memorabilia from famed Chicago chef & author Louis Szathmary. It has grown to a banquet of cookbooks, art work, menus, food ads, etc. Revolving exhibits until larger quarters are finished. The University has campuses in several states.

Contact/curator: Barbara Kuck
315 Harborside Blvd.
Providence, RI 02903
Phone: (401) 598-2805
E-mail: museum@jwu.edu
Web site: www.culinary.org/

Jell-O Museum

History of Jell-O, complete with trivia that will amuse you.

23 E Main St.
LeRoy, NY 14482
Phone: LeRoy Historical Society, (585) 768-7433
Web sites: www.jellomuseum.com/ or www.iinc.com/ jellomuseum

Kraft Foods Jell-O Web page

Invented in 1897, now owned by Kraft, Jell-O gets a colorfully-illustrated company history online.

Web site: www.kraftfoods.com/jell-o/history/

DAVID G. SMITH
11918 Second Street
P.O. Box B
Perrysburg, NY 14129

Advanced collector David G. Smith – The Pan Man – has a spectacular collection of old cast iron cookware. He also publishes the newsletter "Kettles 'n Cookware," and is co-author with Chuck Wafford of two books on Griswold & Wagner wares (see Bibliography). Mr. Smith carefully cleans, weighs, measures, catalogs and photographs each piece as it is acquired. All the photographs in this special article commissioned for this book were taken by Dave. Anyone wishing to correspond directly with him may use the address in the pan! Or see the FOR MORE INFORMATION section just preceding this article. Dave is also interested in cast iron broiler pans. Perhaps we'll get an article for the 6th or 7th edition of this book! Website: www.panman.com

Cast Iron Baking Pans

by David G. Smith

Muffin pans, gem pans, popover pans, breadstick pans, cornstick pans, and French roll pans – baking pans with numerous compartments are called by many names. The names of the pans were influenced by era, culture and cookbook recipes, and then designated by the manufacturer. A muffin pan by one maker might be called a gem pan by another.

Cast iron baking pans were made in many hundreds, perhaps thousands, of foundries in the world. Some of the largest and most notable foundries that manufactured baking pans in the United States are Wagner, Sidney, OH; Griswold, Erie, PA; Favorite Stove & Range Co. (Favorite Piqua), Piqua, OH; Wapak, Wapakoneta, OH; R & E (Russell & Erwin) Mfg. Co., New Britain, CT; G. F. Filley (Excelsior Stove Works), St. Louis, MO; and Lodge Mfg. Co., South Pittsburg, TN (which is still making cast iron wares). The identity of the makers of the baking pans illustrated in this article

has been determined by markings on pans, reference to old trade catalogs, and/or design characteristics.

Standardization of Pattern Numbers & Letters: The five pattern numbers – usually referred to by collectors as PN or p/n – which were standard with many manufacturers are PN 3 (See CIBP-3, -63 and -82); PN 5 (CIBP-5, 71, -80); PN 9 (CIBP-9, -52); PN 10 (CIBP-10, -42 through -44, -73); and PN 11 (CIBP-11, -48, -49, -74). For the purposes of this book, PN will be spelled out as pattern #, to avoid any misadvertent confusion with the size number, identified with No. – abbreviation for "number."

For the most part, foundries participated in this standardization of style numbers. Two major exceptions were Wagner, which preferred a letter designation; and G.F. Filley, which, except for one pattern, was very creative with their designs and did not follow the industry norm. Filley's two pans that did conform were their No. 5 and No. 3, which were like the Waterman No. 7 (See CIBP-71.)

❖ Nathaniel Waterman and R & E Mfg. Co. ❖

If any one person influenced the design and manufacture of baking pans, it was Nathaniel Waterman of Boston, MA. Waterman established in September 1825 a large kitchen furnishings jobbing house that sold many kitchen and housekeeping items. "Waterman Furnishing Store" at 5 & 7 Essex Street, is listed as a house-furnishing store in the 1869 Boston Business Directory, along with F. A. Walker & Co., at 83 & 85 Cornhill, and Edward W. Noyes & Co. at 1827 Washington, whose names are familiar to readers of this book. Waterman's goods included French-style coffee biggins, waffle irons, water filters, tea kettles, "ventilated refrigerators," and gridirons – under the name "Waterman's Patent." In 1858, Waterman designed and patented a series of roll pans to be used "for baking bread in small rolls." That patent was followed by his April 5, 1859 patent for an "Improved Egg Pan" which had openings between the cups "in order to allow currents of heat to pass upward between them, so as to equalize the heat against their surfaces."

Subsequent Waterman Roll Pans had this "egg pan" modification, and bear the April 5, 1859 date. Waterman designs set a standard, which was followed by many foundries. The most common series found today are numbered from #1 to #11, and are marked either "Waterman - Boston," or "R & E Mfg. Co." The R & E Mfg. Co. was the Russell & Erwin Mfg. Co. (later Russwin) of New Britain,

CIBP-1. Roll pan. *" R & E Mfg. Co. No. 1." Also marked " Patent April 5, 1859." Eleven round very shallow cups. 12-1/2" x 8-5/8"; cups, 3-1/8" x 5/8" deep.* **$25-$40**

[Edit. note: *This pan is very close to the Smithsonian-owned one that appears to be marked "W & L Mfg. Co." After looking at a number of the "R & E" pans under a loupe, I finally found one with wear marks that distorted the "R & E" just enough that it might somehow have been read as "W & L." This is only a clue – not a final judgment. LCF. See IV-338.]*

CT, which specialized in building hardware. As was common in the 19th C, indeed in the 20th, inventors either sold sole rights or licensed other companies to manufacture their inventions. Designs were (and still are) pirated too. Notable foundries besides R & E apparently produced the Waterman patented designs but they were not marked as such. Some of these are included in the illustrations of the Waterman Series in CIBP-1 through CIBP-11. Marked "Waterman" pans are not as plentiful as those marked "R & E Mfg.," and are therefore more desirable.

CIBP-5. Roll pan. "N. Waterman Boston" No. 5. Also marked with April 5, 1859 patent date. Eight rounded oval cups. 12-1/4" x 7-3/8"; cups 4-1/8" x 2-3/4" x-3/4" deep. **$30-$40**

CIBP-2. Roll pans. (T) Underside of an otherwise unmarked "No. 2." Eleven round cups. 12-1/2" x 8-5/8"; cups, 3-1/8" x-5/8" deep. **(B)** "Detroit No. 6," with same handle as other. Eleven shallow cups in openwork frame. 12-5/8" x 8-1/2"; cups, 3" x-5/8" deep. Other makers call this a "No. 2". **$25-$40**

CIBP-3. Roll pan. Underside of a "No. 3," showing small round "foot" to each cup. Eleven round cups. 12 -3/15" x 8-11/16"; cups, 3-1/8" x-3/4" deep. **$35-$45**

CIBP-6. Roll pan. "N. Waterman Boston" No. 6. Also has April 5, 1859 patent date. Twelve rectangular cups with rounded corners. 12-3/4" x 7-7/16"; cups, 3-1/4" x 2-1/8" x 9/16" deep. **$35-$45**

CIBP-4. Roll pan. "R & E Mfg. Co. No. 4." Other handle marked with April 5, 1859 patent date. Eight elliptical cups. 13-7/8" x 7"; cups, 4-1/8" L x 2-3/4" W x-3/4" deep. **$30-$40**

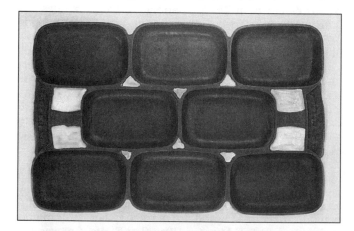

CIBP-7. Roll pan. "R & E Mfg. Co. No. 7." Russel & Erwin Mfg. Co. Patent date April 5, 1859. Eight rounded rectangular cups. 11-3/4" x 7-11/16"; cups, 3-1/2" x 2-1/2" x 11/16" deep. **$35-$45**

CIBP-8. Roll pan. *"N. Waterman Boston" No. 8. With April 5, 1859 patent date. Eleven oval cups. 13-9/16" x 6-11/16"; cups, 3-3/8" x 2-5/8" x-5/8" deep.* **$30-$40**

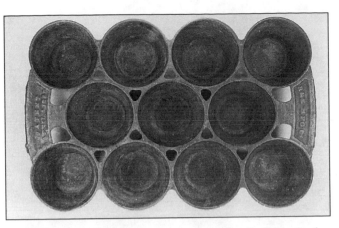

CIBP-10. Popover pan. *"R & E Mfg. Co." Marked with patent date, that appears to say 1858, not 1859. Eleven cups with flat bottoms & flared sides. 12-3/8" x 8-1/8"; cups, 2-3/4" diam. x 1-3/4" deep.* **$35-$45**

CIBP-9. Roll or muffin pan. *"R & E Mnfg. Co." No. 9 "golf ball" pan. Also marked with April 5, 1859 patent date. Twelve round cups. 10-1/2" x 6-5/16"; cups, 2-5/16" diam. x 1-3/4" deep.* **$30-$40**

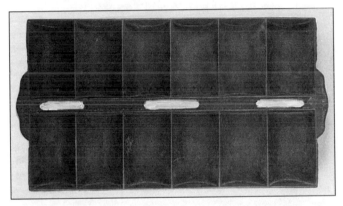

CIBP-11. French roll pan. *"No. 11." Marked on handles with "Patent Apr 5, 1859." (This is Nathaniel Waterman's patent #23,517.) Twelve trough-shaped cups. 13-1/4" x 7-1/4"; cups, 3-3/8" x 2" x 1" deep.* **$20-$30**

⁕ Wagner ⁕

Wagner Mfg. Co. of Sidney, OH, used a lettering system to identify their styles. In addition, they used a four-digit catalog number. Though the pan may not be marked with "Wagner" or "Wagner Ware," the letter or a combination of letters and numbers identify the piece as Wagner. The illustrations from CIBP-12 through CIBP-24 were all listed in Wagner's 1913 and/or 1924 catalogs.

The 1924 Wagner catalog had this to say about the "Krusty Korn Kob" mold (**CIBP-23**): "One of the most delicious and popular hot breads today is the 'Krusty Korn Kob' made in the Wagner mold. This mold produces delicate, crisp, golden brown cornbread, shaped just like an ear of corn, but infinitely more delicate and appetizing than old fashioned cornbread."

There were three sizes of the Krusty Korn Kob mold (**CIBP-24**). They are the "Krusty Korn Kob, Senior," which is 13 1/4" x 6 7/8"; the "Krusty Korn Kob, Junior," which is 11 5/8" x 5 7/8"; and the "Tea Size," which is 8 1/2" x 4 1/4".

CIBP-12. Gem pans. (T) *"Wagner Ware" – "Little Slam Bridge Pan." Twelve figural shallow cups with three in each card suit. Widely spaced in solid rectangular pan with no handle, but with small hanging hole. 10-3/4" x 7-5/8"; cups, 2" x 2" x 1-1/4" deep.*

CIBP-15. Gem or popover pan. "Wagner Ware," style "Q." Five flat-bottom cups. Recess for stove lid lifter. 7-1/2" x 5-5/8"; cups, 2-1/2" x 1-1/2" deep. Cups are easy-cleaning: where sides join bottoms is rounded. **$45-$50**

CIBP-12. Gem pans. (B) *Another very shallow cup pan. Wagner, style " A," c.1900-1920. Eleven flat-bottom shallow cups. 11-3/16" x 7-5/8"; cups, 2-3/4" x-5/8" deep. Value range for (T) is for nickeled finish & plain iron.* **(T) $100-$125 ; (B) $35-$45**

CIBP-13. Gem pan, *commonly called a* **popover pan**. *"Wagner Ware," style " B." Note small hanging hole at both ends. 11-5/16" x 7-11/16"; cups, 2-3/4" x 1-3/4" deep.* **$30-$35**

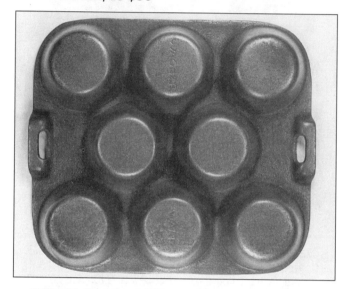

CIBP-16. Gem pan. "Wagner Ware," style "R." Eight flat-bottom round cups. 8-1/2" x 7-3/8"; cups, 2-1/2" x 1-1/2" deep. **$45-$50**

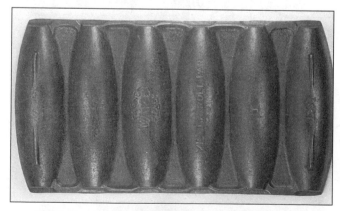

CIBP-14. Vienna roll pan. *"Wagner Ware Sidney," style "I," also marked "Vienna Roll Pan" and with a 4-digit catalog number. Six fat cigar-shaped cups in solid frame. There is also one with an open frame. 11-1/2" x 6-1/2".* **$65-$80**

CIBP-17. Gem pans. (L) *"Wagner Ware," style "S," pattern #1428. Eleven flat-bottom round cups in solid frame with stove lid lifter recesses. 10-3/4" x 7-1/4"; cups, 2-1/2" x 1-1/2" deep.* **(R)** *Wagner Ware" – "Little Gem," style "C." Marked "pat. pending" on underside. Twelve round flat-bottom cups in openwork frame. 9-5/8" x 7-1/8"; cups, 1-3/4" x 1-1/4" deep.* **$30-$40; $125-$150**

CIBP-18. Gem pan. *"Wagner Ware," style "T," commonly known as a* **"turk's head"** *or "turk head" pan, for the supposed resemblance to an ancient Turkish-style turban. Twelve cups in openwork frame, with handles. 14-7/8" x 10"; cups, 2-3/4" x 1" deep.* **$55-$75**

CIBP-19. Gem pan. *"Wagner Ware," style "K" (which may or may not appear on the mold), with five swirl-fluted cups, also sometimes called a "Turk's head" pan (more accurately, costume-wise, than the pan in CIBP-18, because the swirls more closely resemble the turban referred to). Unusual because of almost nonexistent frame. 7" x 5"; cups, 2-1/2" x-9/16" deep.* **$350-$500**

CIBP-20. Gem pan. *"Wagner Ware," style "L." This style is usually* <u>not</u> *marked. Six bowl-like round cups. 6-3/4" x 4-1/2"; cups, 2-1/4" x 1" deep. Unmarked:* **$75;** *marked:* **$150**

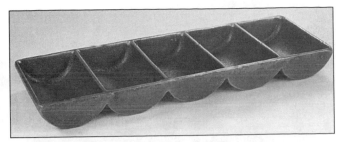

CIBP-21. Gem pan or French roll pan. *"Wagner Ware," style "O." This style may or may not be marked – marked are rarer. Five trough-shaped cups. 9-3/8" x 3-1/8"; cups, 3-1/2" x 1-3/4" x-7/8" deep.* **$100-$150**

CIBP-22. Gem pan, *with a short handle. "Wagner Ware No. 2." Three flat-bottomed cups like the popover pan cups. Including handle: 6-5/8" x 5 3/8"; cups, 2-1/2" x 1-1/2" deep. [Ed. NOTE. This looks to me like a cloverleaf, and is the most charming pan that I've ever seen. LCF.]* **$250-$350**

CIBP-23. Cornstick mold, *also called a* **cornbread mold.** *"Wagner Ware Sidney" – "Krusty Korn Kob" – "Reg. in U.S. Pat. Off." – "Pat'd July 6, 1920" and with the catalog number "1318," plus the little outline cross. Seven well-delineated cobs, alternate directions. Tab handles with hanging holes. The "Senior" size: 13 1/4" x 6 7/8". (Note: There's another "Krusty Korn Kob" senior-size pan (catalog number 1319), marked "Pat. Pending," "Wagner Sydney." Has narrow oblong handles without holes & is worth about twice the "1318."* **$50-$60**

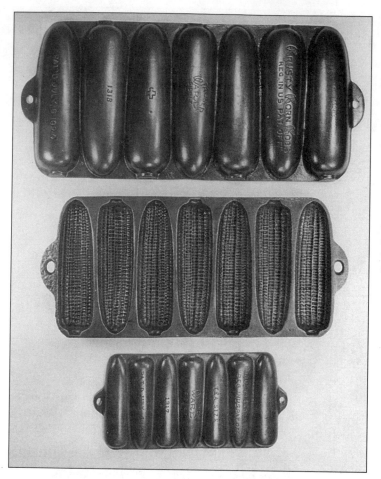

CIBP-24. Cornstick molds, *showing the three sizes of "Krusty Korn Kob" pans. From top: "Senior" depicted in CIBP-23; "Junior," 11-5/8" x 5-7/8"; and "Tea Size," 8-1/2" x 4-1/4". All have 7 alternating cobs.* **$60; $20-$35; $50-$65**

✛ Lodge ✛

The Lodge Mfg. Co. has been located in South Pittsburg, TN, since 1896. [**Ed. note:** At least one source gives an 1872 date, and the sign at the entrance to the town says "1873". LCF] Lodge is still producing cast iron cookware, and other items. While Lodge did use a catalog numbering system, not all their baking pans are numbered. Some are marked with a letter.

There are two significant differences between the letters used by Wagner and those used by Lodge. The letters used by Wagner are usually located in the middle of the pan and are intaglio – they give the effect of being incised or indented into the surface because the original casting mold from which the pans were made had raised letters. Letters on a Lodge pan are usually raised, usually on the end or in a corner, and they also appear to have been placed at random. These letters were molders' marks, and used for quality control purposes. CIBP-25 through CIBP-33 are all of Lodge pans.

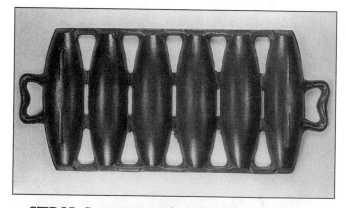

CIBP-25. Gem pan, or Vienna roll pan. *Lodge Mfg. Co. No. 18. Six fat cigar-shaped cups or sections in open frame. Handles almost like truncated hearts. 13-3/4" x 6-1/4". (See also CIBP-14.)* **$75-$100**

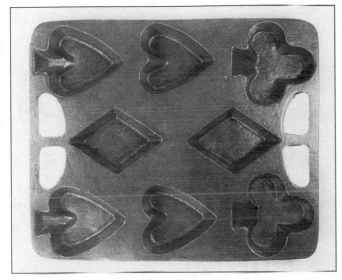

CIBP-29. Muffin or gem pan. *Lodge's largest turk's head pan, No. 20. Twelve fluted cups in open-work recessed frame. 16-1/8" x 11"; cups, 3-9/16" x 1-1/16."* **$45-$60**

CIBP-30. Muffin or gem pan. *Lodge turk's head pan, marked "R" on raised circle on back. Six fluted cups in solid, recessed frame, with bifurcated T-handles. 12" x 7"* **$35-$45**

CIBP-26. "Bridge" pan, *for making gems or little cakes in shape of card suits. Lodge No. 26, style "D." Eight flat-bottom shallow cups, hearts, diamonds, spades & clubs, in rectangular solid frame with generous cutouts for fingerholds at both ends. 9-7/8" x 8-3/8."* (**Note:** *a later version, slightly smaller & unpolished, was still in production at least until 1997: [***Edit. note:*** *But latest 2002 catalog doesn't show it. They do have 2 novelty bake pans: the "Perch Pan" with 5 alternating fat perch muffins, and the "Saguaro Cactus Pan" with 5 2-armed cacti. LCF]* **$75-$100**

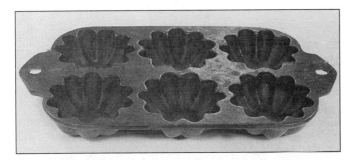

CIBP-27. Muffin or gem pan. *Lodge, style "R" turk's head pan. Six deeply fluted cups in solid, flat-top frame, with tab handles with hanging holes. 9-3/4" x 5-3/8"; cups, 2-1/2" x-3/4" deep. This one's still being made. Old ones:* **$35-$40**

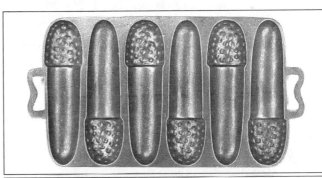

CIBP-31. Stick molds. (T) *The Acorn pan. Six cups in the form of the typically elongated acorns of the magnificent southern Live Oak tree. (This pattern has been vulgarly known as the "penis pan" among some collectors, and supposedly was withdrawn from manufacture for that reason.) This example is a particularly fine casting.* **Caution: reproductions** *are being made of this pan. 11-3/4" x 6-3/8"; cups, 6-1/8" x 1-5/8" x-5/8" deep.* **(B)** *Cornstick mold. Lodge, "V." Five cobs facing same direction in solid rectangular frame with arched handles the full width of the frame. 9" x 5-3/8."* **$200-$350+; $20-$30**

CIBP-28. Muffin or gem pan. *Another Lodge turk's head molds, the No. 19. Six fluted cups in openwork recessed frame with the "truncated heart" handles. 13-3/4" x 8"; cups, 3" x 1" deep.* **$45-$60**

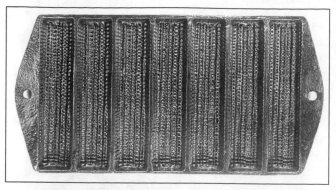

CIBP-32. Cornstick molds. *Both Lodge, but not marked. Identified by the typical full-width triangular Lodge handles. Both have cobs all facing same direction.* **(T)** *Seven stick pan: 12-1/2" x 5-1/2".* **(B)** *Unusual nine stick pan: 15-5/8" x 5-1/2" may be only 25 or 30 years old. [Edit. note: Lodge's 2002 catalog shows 2 styles of cornstick pans. A "mini" with 7 cobs alternating directions, holed tab handles more like Wagner's, 1/2" H x 8" L x 4" W; and 3 sizes similar to (B) in this illustration, although the cobs are shown in the catalog sketch as looking more like pickles or cucumbers. There's a 5-cobber, 1" H x 8-1/2" L x 5-1/2" W; a 7-cobber, 1" H x 12" L x 5-1/2" W; and a 9-cobber 1" H x 15-1/2" L x 5-3/4" W. You can order a catalog online at* **www.lodgemfg.com.** *LCF]* **(T) $15-$25; (B) $45-$55**

CIBP-33. Cornstick mold. *No marks, but because of the shape of the handles, the texture of the casting, and the general shape of the pan, it is believed to have possibly been cast by Lodge. Seven square-ended cobs ... but not cast in the same direction. From L-R: Cobs 1, 2, 3, 6, and 7 are facing same direction; Cobs 4 and 5 are turned the other way. 11-3/4" L x 6-1/8" W; cobs, 5-7/8" x 1-1/4" x-5/8" deep. Note: Since this picture was taken, the collector has found another one, almost identical, marked "CAHIL" in a diamond cartouche, and "1507." It is slightly smaller: 11-1/2" x 6"; cobs, 5-5/8" x 1-1/4" x-5/8" deep. [Edit. note: There was a Cahill Co., a foundry specializing in fireplace furnishings, in Chattanooga, TN, at least in the 1930s. See CIBP-78, -79, and -80 for information on pieces supposedly made by "Chattanooga Iron." LCF]* **$50-$80**

✣ Griswold ✣

"The line that's fine at cooking time" – Griswold slogan in a 1935 catalog.

In 1884, the Griswold Mfg. Co., Erie, PA, began manufacturing hollowware (the trade's name for cooking utensils, and found spelled as either one or two words). Early Griswold baking pans, when marked, were marked "Erie," but many were not marked either "Erie" or "Griswold." They are identifiable as Griswold, however, by a three-digit pattern number. Many of these pattern numbers appear to have been inscribed by hand in the mold (see further on **CIBP-53, -54, -57**). Griswold identified their baking pans by two methods: a style or catalog number, and a pattern number. For example, a #22 Breadstick pan is also identified by pattern #954.

Of all the manufacturers, Griswold produced the greatest number of patterns, including variations. It is the variety that make their molds so interesting and challenging to collectors. My books on Griswold and other founders' iron wares have a great deal of information on marks, and show several hundred Griswold pieces.

Variations of the cornstick pan took several paths. (1) a difference in the designs of the kernels and cobs (**CIBP-34 through CIBP-38**). (2) Notice that all the cobs face in the same direction, with the exception of pattern #270 and pattern #280. (3) Size is also a variable. Most of Griswold's cornstick patterns came in two sizes: pattern

#272: 13-3/4" x 5-3/4", and pattern #282: 14" x 7-5/8", but the one in **CIBP-34** came in three sizes.

There was also a 8-1/2" x 4-1/8" "Tea Size," pattern #262, of the "Crispy Corn or Wheat" pan, shown at the bottom of **CIBP-39**.

Griswold also made "Puritan" wares. The kernel design of the Puritan (**CIBP-40**) is almost identical to the "Griswold" shown above in **CIBP-37**, but the angular-edged shape of the Puritan pan's handle is different from other cornstick pans, and the pan is also slightly smaller.

The Griswold No. 27 and No. 28 "Wheat Stick Pan" vary in size, and in marking. Both sizes may be marked either "Wheat & Corn," or "Whole Wheat." Judging from the quality of lettering, I believe the "Whole Wheat" marking is earlier. **CIBP-41** illustrates both the size and lettering variations.

Without a doubt, the most common style muffin pan, whether Griswold or any other company made it, is the No. 10 eleven-cup popover pan. Griswold made several variations, of which **CIBP-42, -43**, and **-44** illustrate but three. There were also variations in Griswold's No. 18, six-cup popover pan (**CIBP-45, -46, -47**).

Many foundries produced a No. 11 muffin or roll pan. Griswold – being true to form – had its own variations (**CIBP-48, -49**). Another variation was a so-called half-sized version (**CIBP-50**). A larger version of their No. 11 was the No. 15 (**CIBP-51**). They also made a No. 16 – a "half-size" of the No. 15, but not illustrated here.

Often referred to as the "golf-ball pan" is Griswold's No. 9, pattern #947, pan. In this instance, Griswold made design variations with the same pattern number. **CIBP-52**, **-53**, and **-54** are all marked pattern #947. CIBP-53 is one of Griswold's early pans. **CIBP-54** was probably made for a chain store's distribution.

Even the plain No. 22 Breadstick pan is interesting because of variations (**CIBP-55**).

A fancier Griswold pan is the "Heart-Star." See Griswold's and another company's versions in **CIBP-56**.

Another Griswold variation to look for are two pans with the same pattern number but different style numbers. The No. 6 Vienna Bread pan, pattern #958 was later designated style No. 26, with the same pattern #958 (**CIBP-57**). To add to the confusion, there's a No. 26 Bread Pan (**CIBP-58**), but it is pattern #960.

Griswold made several other baking pans. Not all had variations. See CIBP-59 through -66.

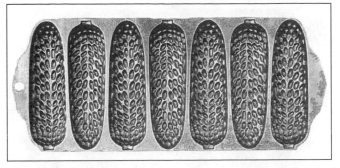

CIBP-36. Stick mold, called the "Crispy Corn or Wheat Stick Pan." Griswold pan with seven all-purpose corn or wheat ears, alternating directions, and hanging hole in only one handle. This type came in two sizes. No. 270: 13-1/4" x 5-3/4"; and No. 280: 14" x 7-5/8". No. 270: **$200-$250**; No. 280: **$800-$1,000**

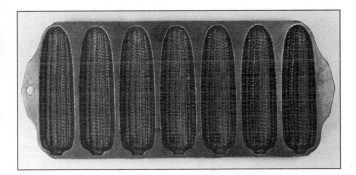

CIBP-34. Cornstick mold, called the "Crispy Corn Stick Pan." Griswold pan with seven cobs all facing same direction, and hanging hole in only one handle. This type came in three sizes. No. **273**: 13-1/4" x 5-3/4"; No. **283**: 14" x 7-5/8"; and No. **262**: 8-1/2" x 4-1/8." No. 273: **$30-$45**; No. 283: **$150-$200**; No. 262: **$75-$95**

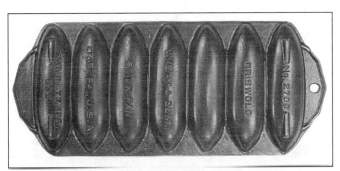

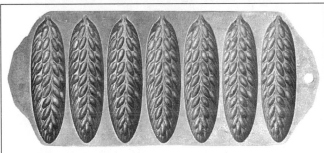

CIBP-37. Stick mold, called the "Wheat and Corn Stick Pan," cups & bottom. Seven elliptical ears facing same direction. 13-1/4" x 5-3/4". Two pattern numbers, #2700 and #1270, the latter of which is not marked "Griswold," but rather "S.R. and Company Best Made"— made for Sears, Roebuck & Co. #2700: **$250-$350**; #1270: **$100-$120** (Note: The similar #2800 would be the real find! Seven elliptical ears, pan measures 13-1/2" x 7-1/4" W (1-1/2" wider than the 2700), with same patent number but different pattern number: "633." It would be valued $2,000-$2,500.)

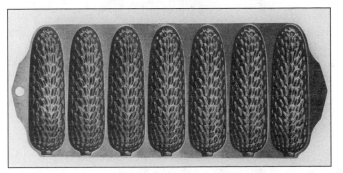

CIBP-35. Stick mold, called the "Crispy Corn or Wheat Stick Pan." Griswold pan with seven sort of all-purpose cups (neither much like ears of corn or wheat) all facing same direction, and hanging hole in only one handle. This type came in two sizes. No. 272: 13-1/4" x 5-3/4"; and No. 282: 14" x 7-5/8". No. 272: **$150-$200**; No. 282: **$200-$250**

CIBP-38. "Wheat Stick Pan," *marked "Griswold" on one handle. Six ears of wheat, all facing same direction in open frame. Note the hair-like silk in the design of the kernels. One handle has hanging hole. Pan came in two sizes: No. 27 is 10-3/8" x 5-7/8"; and No. 28 is 12-5/8" x 7". Either size:* **$200-$250**

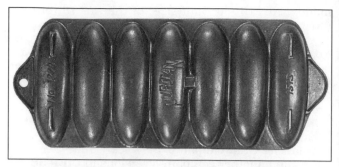

CIBP-40. Stick pan, *in "Wheat and Corn Stick" pattern #1270. This one made by Griswold, but marked with a name they used, "Puritan" and "1533." Rounded tab handles, one with hanging hole. Note: although the pattern number is the same as the one Griswold used in making the pan for Sears, the handles are quite different.* **$95-$115**

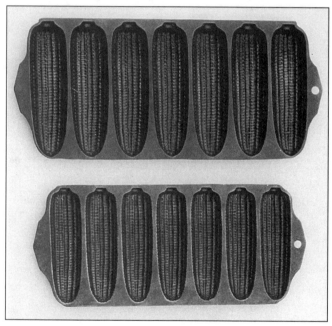

CIBP-39. Cornstick molds. *Griswold's "Crispy Corn or Wheat" stick pans, showing comparison of the three sizes. All have seven cobs facing same direction.* **(T)** *14" x 7-5/8";* **(M)** *13-1/4" x 5-3/4"; and* **(B)** *the "tea size" (pattern #262), 8-1/2" x 4-1/8," which is 1/4" narrower than Wagner's "tea size."* **(T) $150-$200; (M) $35-$45; (B) $75-$95**

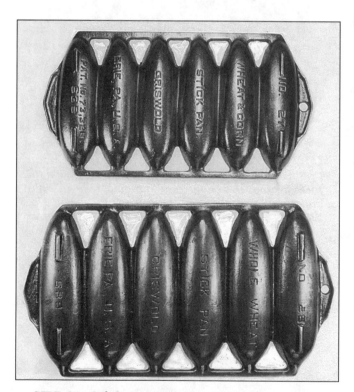

CIBP-41. Stick pans, *by Griswold, with size and marking variations. Both have six sticks in open frames.* **(T)** *pattern #638, is No. 27, "Wheat & Corn Stick Pan" – "Griswold" – "Erie, PA, U.S.A." – Pat. No. 73, 326. It measures 11" x 6"; cobs, 5-3/8" x 1-1/2" x-1/2" deep;* **(B)** *pattern #639, is No. 28, marked "Whole Wheat." 12-5/8" x 7"; cobs, 6-3/8" x 1-3/4" x-5/8" deep.* **$200-$250**

CIBP-42. Popover pan. *"Griswold's Erie" No. 10, pattern #948A. Eleven flat-bottom cups in openwork frame. 11-1/4" x 7-3/4"; cups, 2-1/2" x 1-5/8" deep.* **$35-$40**

CIBP-43. Popover pans. (T) *"Griswold" – "Erie, PA U.S.A.," No. 10, pattern #948. Eleven flat-bottom cups in mostly solid frame with large fingerholds at both ends. 11-1/4" x 7-3/4"; cups, 2-1/2" x 1-5/8" deep.* **(B)** *"Best Made No.10" – "S. R. and Co." Pattern #1253. Eleven flat-bottom cups in openwork frame with large fingerholds. This was made by Griswold for Sears, Roebuck & Co. 11-3/16" x 7-1/8"; cups 2-9/16" diam. x 1-1/2" deep.* **(T) $35; (B) $45-$50**

CIBP-44. Popover pan. *"Griswold" – "Erie, PA U.S.A.," No. 10, pattern #949B. Eleven flat-bottom cups in mostly solid frame with large fingerholds at both ends – note difference in their shape and those of CIBP-43, top. 11-1/8" x 7-5/8"; cups, 2-1/2" x 1-3/8" deep.* **$20-$30**

CIBP-45. Popover pan. *"Griswold's Erie No.18" marked on handles. Six flat-bottom cups in openwork frame. 8-1/2" x 5-1/2"; cups, 2-1/2" x 1-5/8" deep.* **$95-$125**

CIBP-46. Popover pan. *"Griswold's Erie No.18." Six flat-bottom cups in openwork frame that differs substantially at handle ends from CIBP-45, therefore in length. 9-1/8" x 5-1/2"; cups, 2-1/2" x 1-5/8" deep.* **$75-$100**

IV. Form, Mold, Shapes, etc.   389

CIBP-47. Popover pan. *"Griswold," No. 18. Pattern #5141. Six flat-bottom cups in openwork frame with yet another handle style. 9-1/8" x 5-1/2"; cups, 2-1/2" x 1-5/8" deep.* **$65-$85**

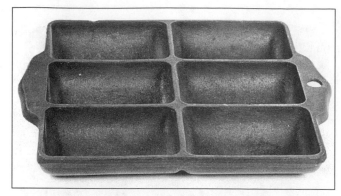

CIBP-50. French roll pan. *Griswold No. 17. So-called "half-size" version. Six troughs. 7-1/2" x 6"; cups, 2-7/8" x 1-3/4" x-7/8" deep.* **$85-$95**

CIBP-48. French roll pan. *Griswold, No. 11. Twelve closely-regimented trough-shaped cups. 12-7/8" x 6-1/8"; cups, 2-7/8" x 1-3/4" x-7/8" deep. Frame is closed rather than partially cutout as in CIBP-11 (the early one from 1859, which overall seems more delicate and graceful).* **$35**

CIBP-51. French roll pan. *"Griswold" No. 15, pattern #6138. Twelve rather deep troughs, narrowly separated. 14-3/8" x 7-1/2"; cups, 3-1/2" x 2" x 1-1/4" deep.* **$150-$195**

CIBP-49. French roll pan. *"Griswold" No. 11. This version has a dividing "aisle" of a half inch between the two rows of six trough-shaped cups. 12-7/8" x 6-5/8"; cups, 2-7/8" x 1-3/4" x-7/8" deep.* **$45**

CIBP-52. "Brownie Cake Pan," *also familiarly called "golf ball muffin pan." Griswold No. 9. Twelve bowl-like cups in skeletal frame. No hanging hole in handle, but none needed with those cut-outs. 10-3/8" x 7"; cups, 2" diam. x 1" deep. Underside of each ball has a word or part of a word. 1925-1930s.* **$125-$150**

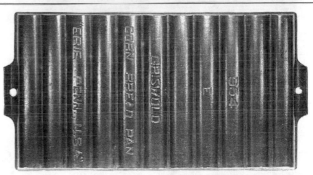

CIBP-53. Muffin pan. Griswold pattern #947, marked at both ends on crosspieces in what appears to be hand-drawn numerals. Ten bowl-like cups in open frame. 9-1/2" x 7-1/8"; cups, 2" x 1" deep. c. 1890. [**Ed. note**: It's unusual to find a muffin pan of any kind with 10 cups. The more usual was 9 or 11 or 12 cups. There was certainly room for one more cup in the center row. But then, why did they make 11-cup molds, divisible only by one or eleven? Could this be some numerological tidbit that we don't know about? LCF.] **$150-$200**

CIBP-55. Breadstick pans. (T) Griswold No. 22, pattern #954. Eleven long troughs. 14-1/2" x 7-3/8"; cups, 7-1/8" x 1-1/8" wide. **(B)** Marked "Corn Bread Pan" on bottom. Griswold, pattern #954-E. Eleven long troughs. 14-1/2" x 7-1/2"; cups, 7-1/8" x 1-1/8" wide. [**Ed. note**: This is the type of baking mold that bears close resemblance to cast iron molds with series of thin (or fat) troughs used by plumbers to cast lead sticks. I saw one just before this book went to press, and it was marked "LEAD" on one of the troughs, which may or may not have been customary. See IV-15. LCF.] Note: The No. 23-pattern #955, same size as the pattern #954-E, is worth two and a half times as much as the No. 22s. **$35-$50**

CIBP-54. Muffin pan, another in the **"golf ball"** pattern #947. Griswold, 12 cups, 10-3/8" x 7-1/8"; cups, 2" x 1" deep, c.1890-1920. **$75-$100**

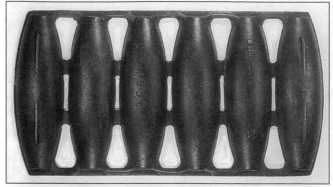

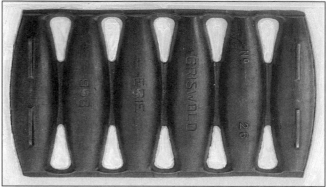

CIBP-56. Baking or Gem pans, in two versions of a "Heart-Star" design. **(T)** Griswold No. 100, pattern #960. Five fat hearts with star in center. Short tab handle. 7-3/4" across including handle. Cups, about 2" x 1" deep. A 1925 Griswold flyer said "Use ... to bake gingerbread and simple cakes for the children's lunches. Also nice for jello and fudge molds. Just as easy to make as in any shape pan!" **(B)** This one is not Griswold, and is an unmarked pan with skillet handle with teardrop hanging hole. Six hearts surrounding 6-point star, recessed in round frame. 9" diam. plus 6" L handle; cups, approx. 2-1/2" x 2-1/2" x 1" deep; star is 3-1/2" W. **(T)** Size No. 100:**$600-$700; (T)** Size No. 50: **$1,200-$1,500;** **(B) $85-$125** [**Ed. note:** Re: **(B)** This unmarked heart-star pan is almost surely an Alfred Andresen Co. pan, in almost continuous production since it was first featured in ads around the turn of the century. Another similar one was made by Emig Products as early as the 1960s. Old ones have a casting "gate" mark on bottom, and are worth the most. LCF].

CIBP-57. Roll pans, in the Vienna roll pan style, both are pattern #958, with six fat elliptical stogie-shaped cups. 12-1/2" x 6-7/8"; cups, 6-1/4" x 1-5/8." Note differences in lettering, and in the pairs of casting gates at each end. **(T)** Griswold No. 6, c. 1880s. Not always marked "Griswold," and worth more if it is. **(B)** Griswold No. 26, c. 1915-1930s. [Edit. note: When you look at the two Vienna Roll markers, IV-392 & IV-393, it is hard to understand why two such different rolls are both called "Vienna Rolls." LCF] **$75-$150**

[Edit. note: There is one, rare, really fabulous Vienna Roll Pan, the No. 1, It has raised lettering inside "VIENNA ROLL PAN No. 1." It's 11-1/2" L x 3-3/4" W, and with the little gatelegs on the bottom, it looks exactly like one of those herb crushers or "herb boats" used for grinding herbs and spices, and pictured in Chapter I. To see the Griswold one, see p. 120 in Smith & Wafford's The Book of Griswold & Wagner, 1995. LCF]

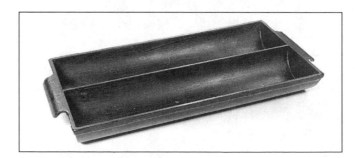

CIBP-58. Bread pan. "Griswold Erie" No. 26, pattern #960. This bread pan is listed in a 1905 Griswold catalog. Two long trough-like sections for two loaves. 13-7/8" x 6-1/2"; loaves, 12-1/8" x 3" W x 1-3/8" deep. Note undercurve of the handles at both ends. With the pattern number only it's worth less than with "Erie No. 26." **$800-$1,000**

CIBP-59. Muffin or gem pan. *Griswold No. 8, pattern #946. Eight flat-bottom shallow cups in openwork frame. 12-3/4" x 6-3/8"; cups: 3" x 7/8" deep. Note the slanted Griswold logo or trademark in the large outline cross within circles.* **$175-200**

CIBP-60-A. Muffin or gem pan. *Griswold No. 6, pattern #944. Twelve rectangular cups with rounded corners. 13" x 7-3/4"; cups, 2-7/8" x 1-7/8" x-1/2" deep. Marked "GRISWOLD ERIE PA U.S.A. 944" on the underside of the 4 center cups. & "No. 6" (with "o" underlined under one handle). The "R" and the "W" in GRISWOLD are slightly tilted in a modern-looking lettering. Not shown is the earlier one, c.1890-1910, unmarked except for pattern number "944" under one handle & "NO. 6" under other. The quality of casting of examples of this later one varies widely, affecting value. c.1910-1930.* **$195-$250**

CIBP-60-B. Muffin or gem pan, *two views, top & underside of Griswold No. 7, pattern #945. Eight flat-bottom rectangular cups with rounded corners, openwork frame. 11-3/4" x 7-7/8"; cups, 3-9/16" x 2-3/8" x-5/8" deep. [Edit. note: I've seen tiny differences in cup measurements – have seen reported as 3-1/2" x 2-1/4" – which may just be misreading of ruler, or rounding off. LCF]* Added value: *worth more with pattern number than without.*

CIBP-60B Underside *marked "No. 7" under one handle, "945" under other. Not all are marked with pattern number. With pattern #:* **$150-$200;** *without pattern #:* **$85-$100**

CIBP-61-A. Muffin pan. *"Erie No. 8," mfd. by Griswold. Pattern #946. Eight flat-bottom cups in skeletal frame. Marked "ERIE" under one handle, "946" under other & "No.8 MUFFIN PAN No.8" along center strip. 12-3/4" x 6-3/8"; cups: 3" x-7/8" deep, c.1890-1920.* **$195-$250**

CIBP-61-B. Gem or muffin pans. *Similar Griswolds.* **(T)** *Griswold No. 2, pattern #941. Eleven flat-bottom shallow cups in openwork frame. Note the curve or convexity on underside of end handles. 12-1/2" x 8-1/2"; cups, 3" x-5/8" deep. The No. 2 is not known to be ever marked "ERIE" or "GRISWOLD." c.1880-1900.*

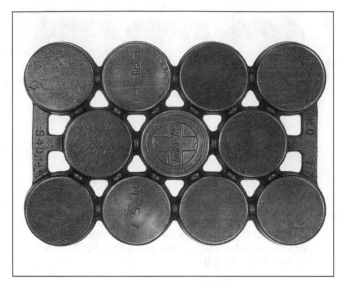

(B) *Griswold No. 1, pattern #940. Eleven round flat-bottom cups in openwork frame. Note flatness on underside of end handles. 11-1/2" x 8-1/2"; cups, 2-9/16" x-3/4" deep, c.1890-1910.* **(T) $175-$200; (B) $175-$200**

CIBP-64. Gem pans, *in different turk's head designs with radial fluted cups.* **(T)** *Griswold No. 130, pattern #634. Six cups in solid frame. Marked on underside of one large tab handle; hanging hole in other. 10" x 5-1/2"; cups, 2-5/8" x-7/8" deep.* **(B)** *Griswold No. 14, pattern #641. Twelve cups in openwork frame. Note handles tabbed onto two end cups. 13-1/2" x 8-5/8"; cups, 2-1/4" x-7/8" deep.* **$500-$700; $600-$700**

CIBP-62. Gem pan. *Griswold No. 12, pattern #951. A very delicate, beautiful pan. Eleven flat-bottom, straight sided cups in interesting rectangular frame that conforms to 4-3-4 arrangement of cups. 11" x 7-1/4"; cups, 2-1/4" x-3/4".* **$175-$200**

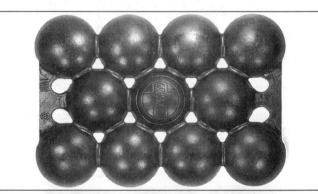

CIBP-63. Gem pans – sometimes called "golf ball" pans. **(T)** *Griswold No. 3, pattern #942. Eleven bowl-like cups in openwork frame. 12-1/2" x 8-1/2"; cups, 2-3/4" x-3/4" deep. Note trademark.* **(B)** *Griswold No. 19, pattern #966. Six cup* **"golf ball"** *pan in very openwork frame. 7-3/4" x 4-5/8"; cups, 2" x 1" deep.* **(T) $185-$400; (B) $450-$500**

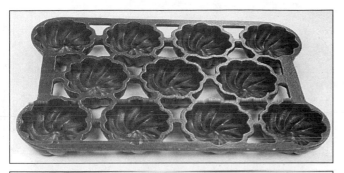

CIBP-66. Muffin pan. *Griswold No. 140 "Turk Head" or "Queen Cake" pan, pattern #835. Twelve fluted flat-bottom cups (they look like stamped aluminum Jell-O molds). 12-5/8" x 8-1/4"; cups, 2 5/8" x-7/8" deep. (This pattern also came in the No. 240 size, which is 14-5/8" x 10"; cups, 2-3/4" x-7/8" deep, and has a raised rim, worth about $200-$250.)This one:* **$150-$200**

CIBP-65. Muffin pans. (T) *"Griswold" No. 20, Pattern #953. "Turk Head" pan, with swirled radial flutes. Eleven cups in openwork frame, the outer corners round to encompass the corner cups. 10-3/8" x 7-1/8"; cups, 2" x-3/4" deep, c.1900-1930.* **(B)** *"Detroit No. 33." Eleven turk's head cups in openwork frame. 10-3/8" x 7-1/8"; cups, 2-1/4" x-3/4" deep. [Edit. note: Did Griswold copy "Detroit," or vice versa? Or did Griswold produce this pan for "Detroit," which was maybe the stove company? LCF.]* **$250-$600; $85-$125**

⁙ G. F. Filley ~ Excelsior ~ W. C. Davis ⁙

Baking pans marked "G. F. Filley" were manufactured by the Excelsior Mfg. Co., St. Louis, MO. The Excelsior Stove Works, incorporated in 1865 as the Excelsior Mfg. Co., was founded by Giles F. Filley. This explains the pans being marked with his name. Excelsior also made "Charter Oak" stoves and ranges.

Excelsior's 1884 catalog illustrates a line of "Excelsior Bakers' or Gem Pans," in No. 1 through No. 8, and No. 10, No. 11, and No. 12. It lists no No. 9; does one exist? The catalog also lists a No. 15, but with no illustration.

For the most part, Filley designs (CIBP-67 through -74) were very creative and did not follow the trade's standardization. The exception is their No. 5 (CIBP-71). Filley pans are greatly desired by collectors.

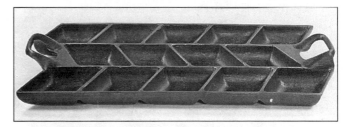

CIBP-67. Muffin or gem pans. (L) *G. F. Filley No. 2, mfd. by Excelsior Mfg. Co. Hexagonal honeycomb design, quite possibly used for some kind of honey cake. Fourteen cups in oblong shape with zigzag sides. Two upraised handles with large openings. 12-3/8" x 7"; cups, 2-1/4" x-1/2" deep.* **(B)** *G. F. Filley No. 1. Fourteen diamond-shaped cups set in sort of herringbone pattern. 13" x 6-5/8"; cups, 2-1/4" x 2-1/8" x-3/4" deep.* **(T)** **$300-$350;** *(B)* **$325-$375**

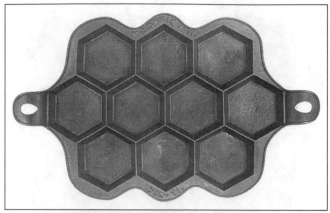

CIBP-70. Baking pans. (T) *G. F. Filley No. 12. Fourteen bowl-shaped cups in solid frame. 12-1/4" x 6-5/8"; cups, 2-1/4" diam. x-7/8" deep.* **(B)** *G. F. Filley No. 10. Eleven round cups with raised bottoms, in solid frame with cup-conforming outer edge. 12-1/2" x 8-1/2"; cups, 3" x-3/4" deep. [Edit. note: Possibly used for making a small sponge-cake that would be served upside down, the shallow depression caused by the raised bottom in the mold filled with berries. In today's grocery store, you'll see packaged sponge-cakes of this type sold with strawberries. LCF.]* **(T) $200-$225; (B) $100-$150**

CIBP-68. Gem or muffin pans. *More in honeycomb hexagonal patterns. These by W. C. Davis, Cincinnati, OH.* **(T)** *Ten cups in roughly rectangular frame. Elongated tongue-like tab handles. 14-1/2" x 9-1/8"; cups, 3-1/8" x 1" deep. This pan was also made with thirteen cups ($275-$300).* **(B)** *Seven cups in roughly round pan, with elongated skillet handle with teardrop hanging hole. 9-5/8" diam., plus 5" L handle; cups, 3-1/8" x 1" deep. Higher value is for marked pans.* **(T) $200-$225; (B) $150-$175**

CIBP-71. Muffin or gem pan. *G. F. Filley No. 5. Eight flat-bottom oval cups, with Filley's typical upraised handles, and cup-conforming pan sides. 11-5/8" x 7-1/8"; cups, 3-5/8" x 2-3/8" x-3/4" deep.* **$100-$125**

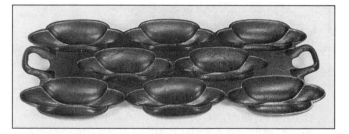

CIBP-69. Muffin or gem pan. *G. F. Filley No. 4. Eight 4-petaled oblong cups – a unique shape amongst gem pans – with edge of frame conforming to edge of side cups. 14-3/8" x 6-5/8"; cups, 4-5/8" x 2-3/8" x-5/8" deep.* **$250-$300**

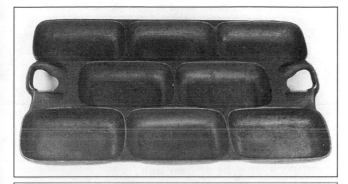

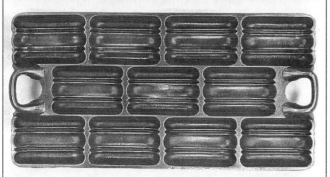

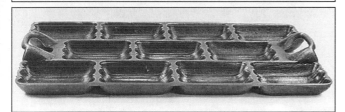

CIBP-72. Muffin or gem pans. (T) G. F. Filley No. 3. Eight simple rectangular flat-bottom cups with rounded sides & corners. Same angled upwards openwork handle grips. 11-3/4" x 7-5/8"; cups, 2-1/4" x-1/2" deep. **(M)** & **(B)** Two views of G. F. Filley No. 7. Eleven ribbed rectangular cups. 12-1/2" x 6-3/8"; cups, 3" x 2" x-9/16" deep. **(T) $100-$150; (M) & (B)$350-$450**

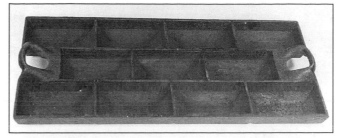

CIBP-73. Muffin or gem pan. G. F. Filley No. 8. Eleven rectangular flat-bottom cups with canted sides. 13-1/8" x 6-1/8"; cups, 3-1/8" x 1-7/8" x 1" deep. **$225-$275**

CIBP-74. Baking pan. G. F. Filley No. 11. Eleven round cups [with bowl-like bottoms and a rounded molding ring around top half of cup that will result in a sort of 'foot' or ring around the cake, that would be served upside down. 12-1/4" x 8-1/2"; cups, 3" x-3/4" deep. **Note:** There's also a G. F. Filley No. 6, with eleven oval cups & the same molding ring. It's 12-1/2" x 6-1/2"; cups, 3" x 2-1/4" x-9/16" deep (The No. 6 would be worth $185-$215.) For the No. 11: **$150-$200**

✤ Barstow ~ Favorite ~ Other Foundries ✤

The following baking pans (CIBP-75 through -92) are from various other foundries. Some have marks identifying the company, some do not. Some companies were prominent, some obscure. Encouraging to collectors is the fact that the variety goes on and on.

CIBP-75. French roll pan. Unmarked. Unusually large, with twelve trough-like cups with interesting cutouts in the "aisle" between the rows. Shapely handles look like the ends of draughtsman's T-squares. 16-1/4" x 8-1/4"; cups, 3-3/4" x 2-1/4" x 1" deep. **$45-$75**

CIBP-76. Muffin pan. *This example unmarked, but other known examples have been marked "Barstow Stove Co.," which was a 19th and early 20th C stove foundry in Providence, RI. Twelve parallelogram cups set in an interesting pattern, with sides raised almost-1/4" above top surface of solid frame. No real handles, but because of angling of the cups, two cattycorner handles are effected. 11-1/2" x 7-1/2"; cups 2-1/2" x 2-1/2" x 1" deep.* **$100-$150**

CIBP-77. Popover pan. *"Favorite pop-over pan," mfd. in Piqua, OH. This is the largest of the popover pans. Nine cups in openwork frame with side handles. 10-1/2" x 10-1/2" plus handles that extend from edge of frame about 1-1/2". Cups: 3-1/8" diam. at top x 2-1/2" deep. Weight, 8 lbs, 12 oz.* **$350-$400**

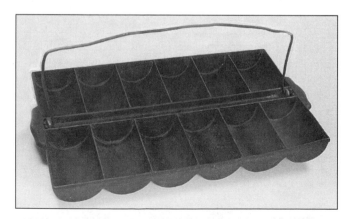

CIBP-78. French roll pan. *Barstow Stove Co., Providence, RI. Twelve trough-like cups with bracket-shaped wire bail handle, hooked into holes in the "aisle" between the rows. Note angular shape of end handles. 14-1/8" x 8-1/4"; cups, 3-3/4" x 2-1/8" x 1-1/4" deep.* **$45-$65**

CIBP-79. Muffin or gem pan. *A No. 2, identified by fellow collector Chuck Wafford as made by "Chattanooga Iron." Eleven flat-bottom cups with rounded sides and cup-conforming frame edge. 12-5/8" x 8-5/8"; cups, 3" x-5/8" deep. [Edit. note: There was a Chattanooga Iron & Coal Co., in Chattanooga, TN, that made cast iron radiators; there was also a Chattanooga Stove & Foundry Co. In addition, see CIBP-33 for some information on Cahil Co. LCF.]* **$45-$70**

CIBP-80. Muffin or gem pan. *A No. 5, identified by fellow collector Chuck Wafford as made by Chattanooga Iron. Eight oval flat-bottom cups with rounded sides; solid frame whose outside shape conforms to the layout of the cups. 12-1/4" x 7-1/4"; cups, 3-3/4" x 2-1/2" x-3/4" deep. [Edit. note: Talk about restrained design and pure elegance. If the Japanese can be attracted to antique American kitchen utensils as a hot new collectible for the 21st century, this pan and the next, also by Chattanooga (?), may do the trick. LCF.]* **$50-$80**

CIBP-81. Muffin or gem pan. *A No. 8, identified by fellow collector Chuck Wafford as made by "Chattanooga Iron." Eleven oval flat-bottom cups in simple frame. 13-1/8" x 6-5/8"; cups, 3-1/8" x 2-1/4" x-3/4" deep. [Edit. note: There was a Chattanooga Iron & Coal Co., in Chattanooga, TN, that made cast iron radiators; there was also a Chattanooga Stove & Foundry Co. LCF.]* **$50-$75**

CIBP-82. Muffin or gem pan. *Unmarked No. 3, but from its appearance, probably from a southern foundry in the US. Eleven round flat-bottom cups in solid rectangular frame with oval handle openings (note raised edges). 13-1/8" x 9"; cups, 3" x-3/4" deep. (This design is found also in a smaller size, the No. 6, also with eleven cups. 12" x 8-3/8"; cups, 2-5/8" x-1/2" deep.)* **$50-$70**

CIBP-84. Gem pan. *Unmarked and maker unknown. Crudely molded (or perhaps only crudely cast) oblong pan with eight oval cups with the stepback ring that will form a rim to hold a few berries or syrup or whatever. Simple tab handles. Cloverleaf cutouts are interesting. 14-7/8" x 8-1/8"; cups, 4" x 2-1/2" x-3/4" deep.* **$65-$75**

CIBP-83. Ebelskiver or applecake pans. (T) *Hollow iron socket handle to accommodate a long wooden handle. Marked "NAC & Co." Seven bowl-shaped cups set in round recessed pan frame. 9-3/4" diam. with additional 7-3/4" L handle. Cups, 2-1/2" diam. x 1-1/4" deep.* **(B)** *This example is exactly the same size, and is also marked "NAC & Co." It has a rigid bracket handle of heavy steel wire, and was cast with reinforcements, specifically for taking this handle. Otherwise it is the same as the one above. [Edit. note: " NAC & Co." has not been identified. It is probably some precursor or variant of Northland Aluminum Co., Minneapolis, MN, even though this pan is made of cast iron and Northland is known for their cast aluminum ebelskivers. LCF.]* **(T) $60-$85; (B) $60-$70**

CIBP-85. Vienna roll pan, *of type called a* **corn pone pan** *by some manufacturers. Completely unmarked. Four very fat cigar-shaped cups in openwork frame. No handles. 12-1/2" x 6-1/2"; cups, 5-7/8" x 2-5/8" x 1-1/8" deep. [Edit. note: This looks like a Griswold No. 4 "ERIE bread pan to me & maybe other iron beginners. That may explain why you see them priced with a wide range of values up to $400+. This piece, however, is in David Smith's collection, and he does not identify it as Griswold. The experience of handling and owning hundreds, even thousands, of cast iron pieces gives advanced collectors almost subliminal clues to identification that a casual collector or a writer like me cannot have. LCF]* **$100-$125**

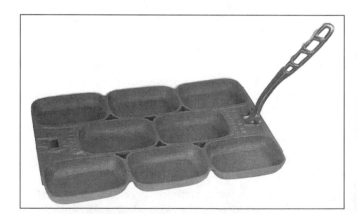

CIBP-86. Roll or muffin pans, "French Roll" type. **(T)** Marked only "No. 14" under handle, but this is a Griswold pan, c.1890. Twelve rectangular flat-bottom cups in very modern-looking frame with slotted openings between the cups. 12-1/2" x 6-5/8"; cups, 2-1/2" x 1-7/8" x-3/4" deep. **(M)** Roll pan. "Shepard" – "Buffalo," No. 12. Twelve rectangular flat-bottom cups in frame with vent slots. Note cutout in left handle that accommodates stove lid lifter. 15-3/4" x 6-3/4"; cups, 2-3/8" x 1-3/4" x-3/4" deep. **(B)** Marked "French Roll Pan No 11." Twelve trough-shaped cups in ventilated frame. 12-3/4" x 7-1/2"; cups, 2-3/4" x 1-7/8" x-7/8" deep. When found marked "Erie" it's worth much more. **(T) $500-$600; (M) $125-$175; (B) $45-$65+**

CIBP-87. Roll pan. Unmarked. Six oblong flat-bottom cups with canted sides, tab handles. 10-7/8" x 9-1/4"; cups 4-1/2" x 3" x 1" deep. [Edit. note: As a folk art collector, and a generalist collector, I am often attracted to handsome pieces that may or may not be valuable to a specialist collector. This pan is so perfect in form that I would rank its design with the best minimalist art of the 1980s or with nearly any Shaker cupboard. Therefore, I agree with the few who value this pan from $150-$200+ – it is art. **An important point to make to new collectors: Ultimately, the best rule of thumb vis a vis prices is pay what feels right for you.** A dealer, of course, must pay less than what his customer will pay. LCF.] **$50-$75**

CIBP-88. Muffin or roll pan. Shepard Hardware, Buffalo, NY, No. 7. Mf'd. c.1880. Eight oblong cups with rounded corners, in openwork frame with square recesses at ends to accommodate a stove lid lifter, not supplied with the pan. 11-1/2" x 7-1/2"; cups, 3-5/8" x 2-3/8" x-5/8" deep. **$60-$85**

CIBP-89. Roll pan. *Unmarked. Unusually large pan, with ten oblong cups with canted sides. Note fancy raised handles. 15-1/2" x 9-1/4"; cups, 4" x 1-1/4" x 1-1/4" deep.* **$65-$85**

CIBP-90. Muffin pan. *Schofield Mfg. Co., NYC, c.1890.* **Rare** *fruit and vegetable pattern, figural cups in openwork frame. 9-1/8" x 6-5/8."* **$250-$400**

CIBP-91. Gem or cake pan, *or* **shortbread** *mold? Unmarked. Nine cups with crosshatched or lightly "waffled" bottoms; fancy, sort of pleated sides, joined to form the largest possible open spaces between cups [which is probably a clue to use, as this would allow more hot air to circulate]. Cups, 2-1/2" x 2-1/4" x-1/2" deep; handle, 2-1/2" L. [Edit. note: I don't think it's a candy mold, having seen nothing like it in any of the numerous trade catalogs I've searched. The cups are too big anyway. LCF. Since the last edition, collector collector Joel Schiff has come to believe this is a shortbread mold, which makes sense to me because of waffled grill in bottom. Schiff values it at around $200. Me too. LCF]* **$75-$95**

CIBP-92. Gem or muffin pan. *Unmarked. Rounded oblong frame with handles; twelve cups, with 9 flutes instead of the more usual 10 flutes. 15-3/4" x 10-1/2"; cups, 2-3/4" x 1" deep.* **$45-$65**

✦ Reproductions of Baking Pans ✦

by David G. Smith

Reproductions and copies are increasingly a problem in today's antique and collectibles market, as originals become more difficult to find, and rareties become more and more valuable.

Unfortunately, reproductions are sometimes sold as originals. For the novice, and sometimes even the experienced collector, it is difficult to recognize the difference. There are some indicators which can help you determine an original from a reproduction.

(1) Rust, & **(2) Baked-on Food.** Many originals, even if rusted, will have an accumulation of years of burned-on food and grease. Also, rust on an old piece will probably be uneven. This is caused by the protection the encrusted food has given parts of the metal. Rust on a new reproduction will usually be even, and often is bright orange.

(3) Casting Quality. Craftsmen who carved the molds and cast the originals were proud of their work. Their products were precise. Today's mass-produced reproductions, for the most part, do not get the attention of human hands. The illustration, CIBP-93, below, shows a forgery of the Griswold pattern #262 Tea Size Corn Stick Pan. Note how grainy the iron of the reproduction is (lower right) compared to the old original (upper left).

(4) Patina. Older iron has a patina, a satiny smoothness, which new castings don't have. Look at CIBP-94 and note the difference in the detail of the kernels between the authentic original (top) and the reproduction (bottom).

(5) Modern casting technique. Note the excess left by the breathing hole pin CIBP-94, bottom. In one modern method of casting, breathing holes are punched into the cast to allow air to escape when the molten iron is poured into the mold. When the air escapes, the molten iron rises in these holes. These projecting "pins" are then broken off or ground down.

(6) Inaccurate copying. CIBP-95 illustrates an attempted copy (possibly of Far Eastern manufacture), not a reproduction. This pan is marked "CRISWOLD" (with a "C" not a "G") and says "SNICK" (with an "N" not a "T"). It also has the pattern #252 (with a "5") instead of #262 of the Griswold original. This pan is commonly seen; there may be others. Buyer beware!

(7) Grinding and finishing. Older, original castings were, for the most part, precise, therefore required very little "cleaning" – filing or grinding. Shoddy molding of repros is compensated for by grinding off excess

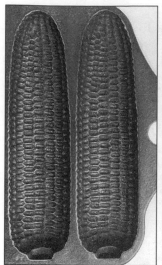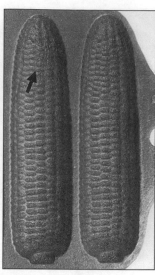

CIBP-94. Details of Interiors of stick pans in CIBP-92. (L) *Detail of two cobs from authentic Griswold No. 262 from previous illustration. Note relatively smooth surface of frame and handle, sharp detail of kernels, clean hanging hole.* **(R)** *Detail from repro Griswold. Note fuzzy kernels, ground-off breathing hole pin (arrow), evidence of other grinding on the handle, and the partly filled-in sloppy hanging hole.*

metal, but sometimes the reproduction-maker doesn't even bother with that. CIBP-96 shows the edge of an original casting at top, compared to the reproduction edge, bottom.

(8) Weight or Heft. Another sign of a reproduction relates to weight. Repros tend to be much heavier than old originals. The original in CIBP-96, top, for example, weighs 3 lbs, 6 oz. The reproduction, bottom, weighs 4 lbs, 14 oz – over a pound & a half more! If a pan feels too heavy for its size, it may very well be a reproduction. Below (CIBP-97 through CIBP-100) are some other old pans commonly reproduced, along with their weights and sizes.

(9) Signs of wear. Wear is a good indicator of an original. Being pushed in and out of an oven over a period of years polishes high points on the bottom of a

CIBP-93. Stick pans – Authentic vs Reproduction. (L) Authentic *Griswold No. 262 "Crispy Corn or Wheat" pan.* **(R)** *Reproduction of same. This would be easier to see if you could lay the pieces down side by side. Get out your magnifying glass (What! You don't have one?) and notice that even with the "graininess" due to the printing process in this book, you can still see that the one on the left has a smoother finish.*

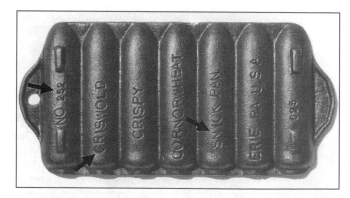

CIBP-95. Stick pan – Reproduction, *laughably inaccurate, not uncommon, reproduction. Note misspellings in "Criswold" and "Snick" as well as incorrect pattern number.*

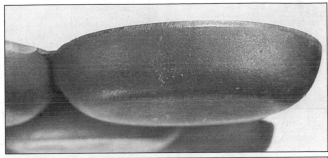

CIBP-96. Details of cup edges, *comparing the grinding-off of an* **authentic** *pan* **(T)** *and a* **reproduction (B).**

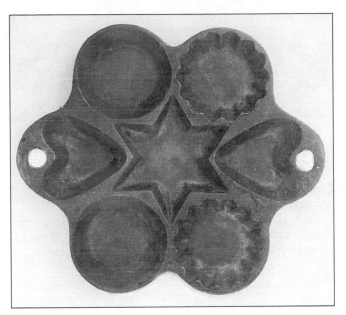

CIBP-98. Muffin pan – Authentic Half-size. *An authentic, half-size version of Reid's Pat. However, it is not marked or dated, and it's not been learned when these were first made. They have been in production for quite a while. The casting quality is the same as the large original pan. Seven cups: 2 fluted, 2 hearts, 2 plain rounds, surrounding a single 6-point star. 9-1/4" x 8-1/8"; weighs 2 lbs, 4 oz.* **$60-$80+**

muffin pan. CIBP-101 illustrates these wear points on the bottom of the eight-cup fruit and vegetable pan.

Final judgment. Just one of the nine indicators of an original (encrusted food, uneven rusting, high quality casting, patina, weight, signs of wear) is probably not sufficient to positively determine what is an old original from what is a reproduction. The newer the repro, the easier the task becomes. One complication are old and heavily-used reproductions from 60, 70 or 80 years ago. A combination of several indicators is a pretty good indication you've got a repro.

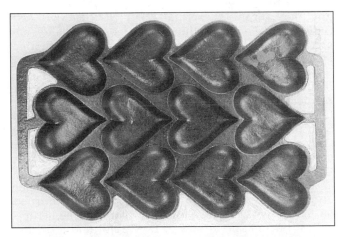

CIBP-99. Muffin pan – Authentic. *This is an authentic original in the twelve-cup heart pattern pan. 13-1/4" x 8-3/8"; weighs 4 lbs, 12 oz.* **$95-$125**

CIBP-97. Muffin pan – the Real "Reid's Pat." *One of the most famous. An authentic, original "Reid's Pat.," dated "July 18, 1871." It is 16-1/4" x 8-3/4", & weighs 4 lbs., 11 oz. The reproduction of this pan is not marked & dated.* **$125-$165**

CIBP-100. Muffin pan – Authentic. *This is an authentic original of the often-seen eight-cup fruit and vegetable pan. 16-5/8" x 8-1/4"; weighs 4 lbs, 9 oz. This has been reproduced for a long time – at least 40 years. One of the reproductions is found with a tiny white enameled button identifying it; that was the early John Wright repro. Later Wright repros don't have the button.* **$145-$185**

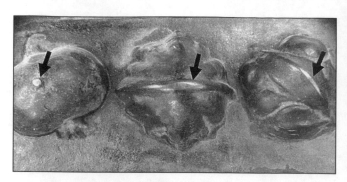

CIBP-101. Detail of CIBP-100, *showing bottom of the fruit & vegetable pan cups. Notice how wear polishes the high points.*

Cleaning and Preserving Iron
✛ Preserve the Patina Above All Else ✛
by David G. Smith

It is no easy task to clean a muffin pan, or any other iron cooking utensil, which has an accumulation of many years of burned-on grease, or rust from years of neglect. The result is worth the effort. If you have optimism and perseverance, the rest is elementary!

The first consideration is to preserve the patina. In cast iron, the patina is the natural smoothness of the surface, smoothness that has developed through years of use, especially by the slow absorption of oil or fat, and the high heat. To preserve the patina, do not use anything abrasive; especially DO NOT SANDBLAST. Sandblasting destroys the old finish and the value, and often gives a pitted, grainy look that is no better than that of reproductions.

Soften & remove burned-on food. – The first step of the cleaning process is to soften and remove the burned-on grease. This can be accomplished by applying an oven cleaner. Apply it as directed on the can, with plenty of fresh air, and let it set for several hours. Oven cleaner can burn your skin, so wear rubber gloves, best are the heavy-duty ones widely available at home improvement centers.

After a few hours, wipe the deposit off and apply another coat. Repeat the process until all the burned-on grease is removed. Stubborn spots can be scraped with a putty knife or spoon. Be careful not to dig into the iron. [**Edit. notes:** Some collectors are very happy with sand-blasting, although it requires great caution and skill and is irreversible. Some collectors will not use anything chemical on their old iron, and advise using wood or glass (like a heavy shard from a bottle) to scrape the metal. Proceed very slowly and cautiously when scraping and protect your hands and eyes. LCF]

After removing burned-on grease, you may discover rust underneath.

Remove rust. – The most difficult task is removing rust. The best way to remove it is with a wire brush. If you have an electric drill, many shapes and sizes of wire brushes are available – some are quite fine. Power brushing is much easier than hand brushing, but it is hard for some people to gain fine control over the brush, which may skip and bounce if it gets caught in a corner or cut-out. Do not use a coarse brush on a smooth surface. A coarse brush will scratch the surface, and destroy the patina. Use a fine brush first. If this is not adequate, cautiously try a coarser brush. [Edit. note: Again, many collectors hate wire brushes in all forms and descriptions, but particularly the big unwieldy coarse ones often used to refinish (ie. ruin) old furniture. I've seen experienced people use a fine wire brush mounted on an electric motor, with beautiful results. I would advise practicing – maybe on a few of those repros you wish you hadn't bought. I tried using a fine brass-wire brush that was a suede brush for shoes on heavily rusted old andirons, and ended up with a sort of golden sheen that now won't come off. LCF].

Severe, crusty rust may not come off with brushing. Crusted rust pods resemble barnacles. They can be broken by scraping them with a spoon or putty knife; then use the brush to remove them.

I do not like to use a rust-removing chemical (such as naval jelly) because it leaves the iron a dull gray and destroys patina. I have used it in severe cases – it does work. After removing the rust, I scrub the pan in a detergent with a brass brush to remove iron dust and the rest of the grease. After thoroughly drying the iron, you are ready to cure and preserve it.

Cure the iron. – There are several methods you may use to cure and preserve an iron piece. Some use vegetable salad oil, some peanut oil, and some mineral oil. All will protect against rust, and none are poisonous.

I prefer to cure a pan with solid Crisco, which works better than the oil. Apply it to the pan and put the pan in the oven at about 225°, and leave in for about 30 minutes. Remove the pan and wipe off the excess grease. Replace in the oven and leave for another 30 minutes, then shut off the heat and let it cool down. I think you will be pleased by the results. Vegetable oil –

such as corn or peanut oil – tends to leave a sticky film on the pan, making it unsuitable for curing pieces meant for display only.

Considered only from the viewpoint of rust prevention, I have found that mineral oil works best. Wipe it on liberally and let it soak in for a few days, then wipe off. The mineral oil accents the patina and also tends to darken the color of the iron. It is also consumable, so you can cook with the pan later if you choose.

Care after use. – After you have baked with a cured pan, don't scour it. Merely rinse it in clear hot water and wipe it out with a paper towel. [**Edit. note:** Don't think you can get rid of burned food by letting the hot pan sit in water or by boiling water in the pan on the stove. This will result in lost patination and food in that pan will tend to burn more easily the next time. LCF] Stubborn deposits may be dislodged by scraping with a spoon (start with a plastic or wooden spoon before resorting to metal). After the pan is clean and dry, apply a protective film of Crisco – it doesn't take much. [**Edit. note:** I bought a smallish, beautiful, smooth, perfectly-patinated griddle to make pancakes on. One day I put it on the front, smallish burner on the electric stove to heat and turned away to finish prepping my breakfast. I heard a loud CRUNNNKKK sound and found that the pan, which had seemed to neatly fit the burner was, in fact, so close in size that as it expanded in the heat, so had the coils of the burner until the pan slipped down around the coils. Finally, the pressure on the ridge underneath the pan caused it to crack in half. This took only a couple of minutes. Be careful! LCF]

"CARE OF CAST IRON"

by E. Lillian Hutchinson

From her book *Department Store Merchandise Manual*, New York University Housefurnishings Department, NYC: 1918

"... New cast iron ware, which is to be used for cooking, should be coated on the inside with tallow and allowed to stand for a few days, then heated until the fat melts, and washed in hot water and washing soda. Rinse in hot water and wipe dry, rubbing very hard." p. 11

More Views on Care & Cure

Greg Stahl's excellent Web site, www.wagnerandgriswold.org , offers other collectors' views of how to take care of all the problems found on old cast iron pieces.

MEASURING

V. WEIGHT, AMOUNT, SIZE, QUALITY, TIME, & TEMPERATURE

Clocks and scales are the best-established categories in this chapter, but not necessarily from a kitchen collector's viewpoint. In fact, kitchen clocks of old or new vintage are hardly collected at all. I think a **future-watch on kitschy figural kitchen clocks** might be in order for the new century.

Scales relating to food handling have a well-established market. Those with polished brass faces or interesting cast iron bases lead the category. Scales are, however, for most advanced scale collectors, the only dip in the ocean of kitchen collectibles that they've ever taken. Strictly speaking, many scales aren't kitchen collectibles at all, but are considered an attractive go-with and therefore belong in this book. Scales are primarily an important specialty in the scientific instrument collecting field, and have been featured as men's antiques for decades. It may seem amazing to us in the United States, but many European people collect only the weights used for scales.

Egg scales are virtually ignored by most scale collectors, but with kitchen collectors they are very popular, and getting more and more expensive. Just one evening's search on eBay brought up 50-some egg scales, with about 12 different makes.

Many cupboards and pantries have been raided by collectors who have preferred (at least until very recently) not to acknowledge kitchen antiques as a serious and worthy field. The contents that have been kidnapped this way include most decorated tinwares (sometimes appropriately called tôle), most polishable brass and copper wares, and all woodenwares that could be attributed to the Shakers, or that could be given the name **treen** (also trein), which is a Scottish word for something made of wood. Although there is much disagreement about what treen includes, it usually applies to objects of turned wood, sometimes called turnery. Another theory of the word's origin is that it means something made from trees. At any rate, the way you will find turned and carved cider funnels or fine, old scoops (or butter paddles, from Chapter II), will be to conduct your own raid into the treen market, which is altogether more posh than ours.

Another category in this chapter that has enjoyed a good deal of cachet is **measures** – most particularly liquid measures of copper (remember the unfortunate Law of Polishing: shine = decorative value) or pewter. Copper is considered here but not pewter, because that field of collecting is long established and requires years of specialized study. Green Depression glass measuring cups are also borrowed from glass – a specialist collecting field about which I know little. I don't (or I should say that I can't) do glass.

TABLE OF EQUIVALENT MEASURES

Not only do you need equivalent measures when working with very old or foreign recipes, but some of the kitchen antiques you collect were catalogued using metric measures or unfamiliar units. Sometimes you're at a flea market with no way to measure something: use a dollar bill, your own first thumb joint, lipstick tube, or Altoid™ box, and translate when you get home.

WEIGHTS:

1 dram	1/16 ounce
1 ounce	16 drams
1 pound	16 ounces
1 pint	1 pound

(*"A pint's a pound, the world around."*)

LENGTH OR SIZE MEASURES:

1 inch	25.4 millimeters, or 2.54 centimeters
1 foot	30.48 centimeters
1 yard	3 feet, or 36 inches, or 0.91 meter
1 meter	39.24 inches, or 1.09 feet
1 centimeter	0.39 inches
1 USA dollar bill	2-9/16" x 6-1/16"
First joint of thumb	1-1/4" to about 1-3/4"
#10 business envelope	4-1/8" x 9-1/2"

COOKING MEASURES:

1 drop	1/60 to 1/76 teaspoon
15 drops	1/4 teaspoon
1 pinch	1/8 to 1/4 teaspoon
1 teaspoon	76 drops, or 1/3 tablespoon
1 tablespoon	3 teaspoons
1 dessert spoonful	2 teaspoons
1 cup	16 tablespoons, or 8 ounces, or 1/2 pint
1 tumbler	6 to 8 ounces
1 wineglass	4 to 6 ounces
2-2/3 cups	1 pound (brown sugar, oatmeal, corn meal)
1 pint	2 cups (a pound of butter, flour, granulated sugar)
1 quart	4 cups, or 2 pints
1 goose egg butter	2 heaping tablespoons
9 large eggs	1 pound

DRY MEASURE VOLUME, U.S.:

(British Imperial is about 1/5 more)

"A dry measure" may be marked with some of the same quantities – pint, quart, gallon, barrel – as are wet or liquid measures when filled, but the weight and cubic inches differ. For example, one dry pint has 33.6 cubic inches; whereas one wet pint has 28.875 cubic inches.

1 pint	1/2 quart
1 quart	2 pints
1 peck	8 quarts, or 1/4 bushel (Peter Piper picked a lot!)
1 bucket	2 pecks, or 1/2 bushel
1 bushel	2 buckets, or 4 pecks or 64 pints
1 quarter	8 bushels
1 chaldron	36 bushels
1 barrel	2 kilders (or kilderkins), or 4 firkins
1 puncheon	2 barrels, or 4 kilderkins, or 8 firkins

LIQUID OR FLUID MEASURE, U.S.:

(British Imperial is about 1/5th more)

1 ounce	1/16 pint	29.574 milliliters
1 gill	4 ounces	0.1183 liter
1 pint	16 ounces, or 4 gills	0.04732 liter
1 quart	2 pints	
1 pottle	4 pints	
1 gallon	8 pints, or 4 quarts	3.7853 liters

1 bucket	2 gallons, or, informally, 5 quarts or more
1 firkin	72 pints, or 9 gallons (See page ___)
1 bushel	74 pints
1 kilderkin	2 firkins, or 144 pints
1 runlet	1 kilderkin, or 2 firkins, or 144 pints
1 wine barrel	31-1/2 gallons, 119.24 liters or 252 pints
1 beer barrel 136.27 liters	36 gallons
1 oil barrel 158.98 liters	42 gallons
1 hogshead	63 gallons, or 7.2 firkins, or 9/10 puncheon
1 butt or pipe	126 gallons
1 tun of wine	252 gallons
1 tun of beer	259 gallons, or 28.8 firkins

CONVERSION EXAMPLES:

You know:	Multiply by:	To find:
Inches	2.54	centimeters
Feet	30.48	centimeters
Fluid ounces	29.57	milliliters
Cups	0.24	liters
Gallons	3.79	liters
Centimeters	0.39	inches
Liters	1.06	quarts
Liters	0.26	gallons
Liters	4.23	cups

Asparagus buncher, cast iron, painted dark red, mounted to oak board, has end board or plate, a U-shaped cradle for stalks, and spring-loaded hinged piece to form bunch, "The Philadelphia Buncher," 5-1/2"H x 8-1/2"L exclusive of board, looks late 19th or early 20th C. .... **$95+**

Asparagus buncher, cast iron top of frame, slightly scrolled cutout wood adjustable for bunching the asparagus, brass spring clips and ratchet thumb catch (probably "The Philadelphia" model), manufacturer unknown to me, "PHILA." is the only mark, buncher hoop is 4-3/4" diam., base is 11-5/8" x 10", 3rd quarter to late 19th C. .... **$100+**

V-2. Asparagus bunchers. (L) Oldest style of French bunchers, a type probably dating back at least four centuries, consisting of "two pairs of wooden scissors with curved blades, to each short arm of one of these is fixed a wooden rod, which passes through a hole in the corresponding arm of the other, allowing the two to be placed at the desired distance apart." A string is used to hold the rods in place after the 'scissors' are opened to the right size. (R) Conover's buncher, wood, hinged with lever (partially visible in vertical position), with brass strips inside. The fattest butt end of the stalks are pushed against the endboard at right. Both pictures from American Agriculturist, May 1876; and Feb. 1876. $55+; $100+

V-1. Asparagus buncher. Cast iron hoops, hinged, mounted to oak (?) base. Joseph Breck & Sons catalog, 1903-05. $95+

The **hinged buncher**, mostly of wood, with springy brass partial hoops in a wooden cradle, flat wood end piece against which to thump the bottom of the stalks, is depicted in the February 1876 *American Agriculturist* as "Conover's Asparagus Buncher." The article gave advice on sorting by size and washing before bunching, and advised standing the finished bunches (held in the buncher until they could be tied in 2 places with string) on wet hay if they had to be "kept for some hours before packing" for market. This magazine was full of advice on marketing, such as it is easy to grow the food but hard to market it. For example: a delicious, juicy watermelon couldn't be sold in New York City markets because it was too hard to carry under your arm, too big for a market basket, and New Yorkers refused to hoist them on their shoulders to carry home! After several years of disappointing sales, someone finally came up with a sort of book-strap device with a wooden handle (shades of those nifty things we used to get attached to suit boxes), to provide what nature had neglected to provide: a way to carry a watermelon. • In another article from 1873, the editor noted that if one wanted to sell produce, one had to "conform to the customs of that market ... If a lot of loose asparagus, or strawberries in the large trays used in Cincinnati, were sent to the New York market, they would probably find their way into the garbage-cart." This is probably still true. I am dismayed by huge trays of strawberries (such as are found 125+ years later in Charlottesville, VA) and wish for the small box style of New York City.

Bean sizer or bean sorting frame – See Chapter III (Separate, Strain, Drain, Sift and Dredge).

Beer measure, copper slant-sided pitcher-like container with long V neck lip or spout originating at bottom, flared foot, strap handle, inset panel with 4 small arched glass windows down one side, hinged lid with small perforated hatch in middle, manufactured by E. Ketcham & Co., NYC, NY, 2 qt. capacity, c.1877. .... **$130+**

V-3. Beer measures. *Copper, with glass viewing or indicator window, hinged flat lid with vent holes, strap handles.* ***(L)*** *A 2-quart size from Duparquet, Huot & Moneuse hotel & restaurant supply catalog, c.1904-1910.* ***(R)*** *One with a braced handle from the Manning & Bowman catalog, 1892. It came in 2, 3 & 4 quart sizes, either planished (hammered & polished for fine finish) copper or nickel-plated copper. The catalog says it has a "strainer for pouring from bottom." These are found in other c.1900 catalogs.* **$150+**

Bucket, for dry measure, tin, with handles, "Franklin," 1/2 bushel capacity, late 19th C. .... **$20+**

Bucket, dry measure, wood with old green paint, American, 2 gal. capacity, 19th C. • "**Bucket**. The term is applied, in the South and West, to all kinds of pails and cans holding over one gallon." John Russell Bartlett, *Dictionary of Americanisms. A Glossary of Words and Phrases* usually regarded as peculiar to the United States, Boston: 2nd ed. 1859 (1st ed. 1848). .... **$80+**

Candy scoops & thermometers – See: Scoop, candy; Thermometer, candy

Clock, battery, decorated china plate, 6 herbal bouquets, Arabic numerals, General Electric, 9-1/2" diam., c.1960. .... **$10+**

Clock, ceramic, Black Americana, Aunt Jemima, works' mfr. not known to me, pottery by Red Wing, MN, 20th C. .... **$175+**

Clock, electric, blue & white Delft china plate, Dutch scene, English, German or Dutch, 20th C. ..... **$45+**

Clock, electric, colorful yellow china octagonal plate with blue & green flowers in border, center is clock face, Arabic numerals, insignia of windmill, "Cretonne," by Irving Miller & Co., NYC, NY, 9" diam., 1930. ..... **$15+**

Time Isn't Ageless – "To the casual observer, today's smart kitchens seem perfect in their charm. Gay, sparkling, they are a whirl of matching color ... harmonious in every detail ... except the offending clock! Sometimes a crude, ungainly alarm; often a makeshift relic of other days. ... Miller has created an enchanting array. Clocks, bright as butterflies ... perky-fresh and in perfect tune with the kitchen scene. Designed in a cheerful 'cottage-y' mood, these delightful timepieces are of gleaming porcelain ... so charmingly right for the kitchen, so easy to keep twinkling and clean. ... Either with the 8-day lever movement (which does away with the pendulum nuisance) or the new electric movement (which need never be wound or regulated)." Sept. 1930 ad, *House & Garden*.

Clock, electric, molded avocado green "antiqued"-looking plastic, in shape of hutch cupboard, with 3 little metallic plastic copperoid plates on top shelf, a pot & 2 candlesticks on 2nd shelf, clock face on front of lower doors, Arabic numerals, mfd. by Spartus, 12"H, 1960s? • More charm than you'd think. Another version was made in wood tones, with blue & white plastic Delft-looking wares, plates, etc., on the shelves & wonderful blue & white coffee pot. I wonder how many versions Spartus did. .... **$7+**

Clock, frying pan, keywound with regulator, a real stamped sheet steel frying pan, decal image of North & South America as voluptuous women's figures, mfd. for Expo in Buffalo, NY, a "Cold Handle Acme" pan, mfd. for the Pan-American Exposition Co. by the New York Stamping Co., NYC, 26"L including handle, 13" diam., clock itself ©1899 for 1901 fair; but pan pat'd. Nov. 14, 1876. There was at least one more Pan-Am pan clock, but this is the most valuable... **$1,000+**

Clock, frying pan, black painted cast iron, sides have hammered look with bronzed finish, outside bottom of pan cast with raised numbers, painted white,

*V-4. **Teapot electric clock.** Stamped steel, finished in choice of colors: ivory, white, green, red or blue. 7"H x 8-1/2"W with 4" dial. Mfd. by Sessions. Advertised in various ladies magazines in 1941. See also V-101.* **$35+**

electric or battery (?), unclear from catalog, Emig Products, Reading, PA, 8" diam., 21 x 12"H overall, c.1966.? • Wholesale price then was $13. Asking price now isn't much higher. .... **$20+**

Clock, frying pan, cast iron, quartz battery motor, loop hanging hole, 2 pouring lips, 4 Arabic numerals & 8 dots as well as the hands are finished brass, has second hand, sold (& mfd.?) by Clock Wise, Inc., Andrews, NC, 6" diam. frying pan bottom/clock face, advertised in 1983. .... **$20+**

Clock, frying pan, electric, enameled iron & tin, white pan, red screwed-on handle, red knife & fork (minute) hands, modern-looking sans serif Arabic numerals in white on white, "Made in Great Britain," c.1950s. In just a few years this has doubled in value because of great crossover interest in designy stuff from the 1940s and 1950s. .... **$125+**

Clock, frying pan, sheet metal, with knife & fork hands, this one German, early 20th C. .... **$125+**

Clock, frying pan, electric, molded plastic with copperoid finish, "Model 504," Herold Products Co., Chicago, IL, c.1950s. .... **$30+**

Clock, frying pan, electric, stamped tin, Sessions, Forrestville, CT, c.1920s. .... **$35-$55**

Clock, frying pan with inset clock. A nickel-plated, cast iron promotional piece for dealers. Hung by hole in short handle, with the bottom of the skillet facing out. 8-1/2" diam. Cast with large-letter legend around clock, "ERIE UP TO TIME" and "We Sell Hollow Ware," Griswold Mfg. Co., Erie, PA, 1900 to early 20th C. High value because it's made by Griswold. Crossover advertising collectible................ **$3,500+**

Clock, milk can figural, battery-operated, molded plastic, finished in a sort of brushed pewter or old tin look. Great thing about the casting is it successfully imitates a banged-up old milk can, with dents. Face with large Arabic numerals is on a flattened front, has sweep second hand. Called the "Milkmaid" clock in ads, "Seth Thomas" on face; inside, cast into plastic, it says "Ronthor R 60 3464," & "Seth Thomas 2436," NYC, NY, 11"H x 7-3/4"W, 1973 ad. ...... **$10+**

Clock, pumpkin, 3-D stamped tin, round face has some 3-D modeling, painted in shaded orange, with black Arabic numerals, 2 hands. I saw this in an ad only, which doesn't mention works – probably some form of 7-day windup. Advertises in bold lettering on face: "None Such Mince Meat [&] Pumpkin-Squash Like

Mother Used To Make," American, 10" diam., early 20th C. .... **$1,000+**

Clock, refrigerator in shape of Monitor Top, electric works, heavy cast metal, painted white, black, fake hinges on 2 doors, clock face on doors. Warren Telechron Co. mfd. this Electron clock for The General Electric Co., Ashland, MA, 8-3/4"H x 5"W x 3 1/8" deep, advertising piece made from 1928 to early 1931. • Refrigerator collector Russell Wilson adds that these clocks were "an exclusive premium item given to managers (dealers) of G.E. appliance stores selling the Monitor Top." There were, according to G.E., only 21,460 clocks made altogether during the years 1928 to 1931. .... **$525+**

❖ NOTES ❖

According to Russell Wilson, there were four types of these **GE Monitor Top clocks** made in 1928, 1929, 1930 and part of 1931, alike at a cursory glance, but differing in case, movement and numerals. For example, he said that the nameplate above the clock shrank on later models from 3-3/8"L to only 1-9/16"L; the coils of the condenser "monitor top" went from 16 down to 14 and vertical fins were added; numerals changed size too; and later movements were marked "Model No. M-1," with a serial number prefix "A." Wilson also said that a cast iron penny bank, 4-3/4"H, also exists. • Edwin P. Mampe, writing in the National Association of Watch & Clock Collectors Museum's *The Bulletin*, knew of two versions of the clock: an earlier one with longer nameplate, larger Arabic numerals, legs indented at the joint with a box so they appear separate, and the 16 condenser coils on top permanently affixed to the case. A later type has no indentation where the legs join and has a 14-coil condenser bolted to case and thus replaceable.

Clock, shelf, gingerbread oak case, brass works, key wound, William L. Gilbert Clock Co., original paper label "Tiger," Winsted, CT, late 19th C. .... **$175+**

Clock, teapot, chubby figural, stamped metal, electric movement, Arabic numerals, came in white, green, red or blue finish, Sessions, 7"H x 8-1/2"W, c.1940.. **$35+**

Clock & inkwell combined, cast brass with cast round face, decorated with flour sacks, brooms, barrels or kegs & groceries, advertising 50th anniversary (1863 to 1913) of Joseph Spidel Grocery Co., mfd. by Mercedes, American, 1913. .... **$450+**

Coffee measure, metal, with sliding back wall to adjust capacity for 2, 4, or 6 cups, "Dix Coffee Meter," pat'd. 1908. See also p. 686 .... **$30+**

Coffee measure, tin, Bokar, 20th C. [Note: Some people may be collecting the plastic coffee measures from coffee cans, which go back at least 60 years.] ... **$5+**

Dinner chimes, mahogany rectangular base with molded edges, 4 bell metal oblong keys mounted to base, raised above it a little, to be hit with little wooden ball on a stick. My grandmother, Grace Campbell Franklin, had one of these on her sideboard, and when we visited it was the greatest honor to be asked to ring the dinner chime. I usually played a version of "My dog has fleas." Originally such chimes came with a tune booklet – even "bugle calls" could be played on the chimes. Who knows –

one tune might mean "Liver Tonight, Stay Upstairs," another "Buttered Biscuits Going Fast," another "Soup's On, Come Immediately." One company, Kohler-Liebich, made "Liberty" chimes, Chicago, IL, 1910s & 1920s. Others probably much earlier. .... **$25-$75+**

Dry measure, bentwood, hand-forged lap nails, painted old gray, American, 9-3/4" diam., 19th C. .... **$75+**

Dry measure, bentwood, turned wood side handle, copper rivets & nails, American, 3-1/2"H x 5-1/2" diam., 19th C. .... **$85+**

Dry measure, bentwood with copper rivets, for measuring dry weights as opposed to liquid amounts, "C.A. Wilkens," Henniker, NH, 8-3/4" diam., 20th C. .... **$75+**

Dry measure, bentwood, with cover, supposedly Shaker, Maine, 8" diam., 19th C. Covers rarely found. .. **$175+**

Dry measure, bentwood with tin binding, American, 5-1/4" diam., 1 qt. size, mid 19th C. .... **$65+**

Dry measure, dark green painted bentwood, 9" diam., late 19th C. Blue paint seems to be most popular; then green, red, mustard, and lastly, white calcimine. .... **$135+**

Dry measure, bentwood with old mustard paint, 7-1/8" American, 19th C. .... **$135+**

Dry measure, oak bentwood, "Daniel Cragin," Wilton, NH, 11-1/2" diam., 19th C. • Another by same maker, only 5-3/4" diam.: add 10% to 20% to value, because of rarer size. .... **$175+**

Dry measure, bentwood, copper nails, looks like saucepan with exaggeratedly uptilted handle, American, 6-1/2" diam., 19th C. .... **$150+**

Dry measures, for grain, nested set of 4, old blue painted bentwood, American, 6" diam. to 12" diam., late 19th C. .... **$500+**

Dry measures, set of 4 round graduated measures, bentwood, American, 6", 7", 9", and 11" diam., late 19th C. .... **$175+**

Egg alarm timer, aluminum insert rack to put in the pan with eggs, in original box with instructions; very soft, soft, and medium; whistles when egg is done, 20th C. .... **$22+**

Egg scales – See: Scale, egg grading

Egg tester or candler, pierced tin cylinder with strap handle, resembles a drinking cup, has hole in top for holding eggs to be candled using candle inside, "The Family Egg-Tester," American, 3"H, pat'd. March 13, 1876. .... **$65+**

V-5. Egg timers. *At first glance, these appear identical. Both are obviously plaid, undoubtably Mauchlin ware. (L) Called an "egg glass," in "Scotch Wood," glass bulb. From 1870s-80s F. A. Walker kitchenware catalog. (R) 3"H, in c.1909. A. Pick catalog.* **$65-$125**

V-6. Egg timers. (L) *Japanned cast iron pedestal-based frame with swiveling glass bulb, imported or American. Could be anywhere from about 4"H to 7"H. From F. A. Walker catalog, 1870s-80s. (R) Also called a "time-glass for boiling eggs." Three turned wooden posts, wood disks for top and bottom, glass bulb. Virtually identical linecuts found in c.1870s-80s F. A. Walker and c.1909 Duparquet, Huot & Moneuse catalogs. (L) $125+; (R) $65+*

Egg tester & scale, green-painted oblong metal box with porthole on top at one end for candling with an electric light; mounted on it is a simple egg-grading scale very like the Brower upright (the one with the flower-petal-like egg cup for all sizes of eggs), American, c. 1940s. .... **$85+**

Egg timer, Black Americana, tin, color lithographed, so-called "Mammy," 3 hooks for potholders, 3 minute timer, American, early 20th C. **$155**

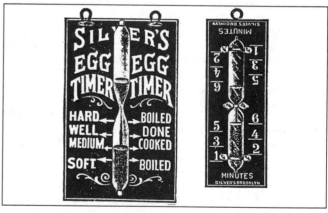

V-7. Egg timers. *Also called in latter years "telephone timers." (L) "Silver's Revolving Egg Timer," to hang on kitchen wall. Heavy printed fibre board with glass bulb containing fine white sand. Printed marks. (R) Brooklyn Egg Timer "is made of Bohemian glass with a sifted clear yellow imported time glass sand, that is absolutely reliable, never clogging, never stopping, and always indicating the correct time at the graduated points on the enameled board." 8-1/2"H x 1-1/2"W. These two are from the c.1910 catalog of Silver & Co., Brooklyn. (A similar one, valued at perhaps a third the value of the Silver's, is a 1920s German import, enameled metal frame (red, white or blue) which could be hooked at either end on wall.) A good go-with for Silver's eggbeaters.* **$85+**

V-8. Egg timers. *Though similar in form, (L) is of turned wood, with portholes for viewing the sand bulbs, From S. Joseph catalog, c.1927; (R) is of pieced tin, japanned with background color and a few sprigs. Ritzinger & Grasgreen import catalog, c.1906-07. They look somewhat older than they are, but catalog linecuts were used for decades sometimes, and these could have been made for 50 years prior, at least.* **$65+; $85+**

Egg timer, cast iron frame with pedestal base, shaped like a cheval mirror, with small glass bulbs pivoting inside, from F. A. Walker catalog, American (?), or European import, about 4"H, c.1870s-80s. .. **$125+**

Egg timer, Mauchlin ware (wood with red plaid finish), simple square top & bottom with 4 corner columns, glass hourglass bulb inside this cage. Scottish or German imitation, early 20th C. Early pieces of Mauchlin are highly collectible now................ **$65+**

Egg timer, turned wood frame with old red paint, small glass bulbs inside, American, 4"H, 2nd to 3rd quarter 19th C. .... **$95+**

Egg timer, cast white metal, painted figural Amish woman with churn, glass bulbs off to side on pivot, John Wright, Inc., Wrightsville, PA, 2"H x 3"W, c.1963. (Other vintage figurals and novelty timers are a 4-1/4"H yellow-glazed windmill, c.1950s; a wonderful German porcelain maid in black short dress, white apron & cap, holding the old, double-bulb glass timer with orangey sand, marked "11341"; and a German-made porcelain Scotsman in kilt & red jacket, with white crossbands – the base marked "foreign" and "260.") .... **$35+**

V-9. Egg timer – "The Signal." *This was found in the Feb. 1882 American Agriculturist. "A short while ago we [the editor] visited Messrs. Baldwin & Co., Murray Street [NYC], for novelties. Among other things ... is the Signal Egg-timer. In this the sand-glass is suspended in a frame; ... and when sufficient sand has run into the lower part of the glass, its weight turns the glass and the hammer, shown at the top, falls down and strikes the bell below, informing the cook that the time is up. Below is a wedge-shaped counterpoise; by moving this, the alarm will be given at the end of two, three, or four minutes."* **$275+**

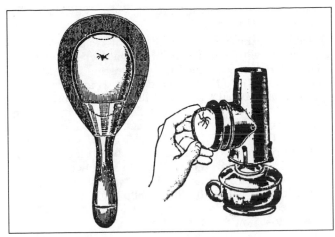

V-10. Egg tester. (L) *Turned wood with cup for egg, encircled by a sheet tin or cardboard "frame" with a hole in the center about the size of the eggs tested. Black cloth or ribbon fills in space around edge of egg. The idea is to completely block light from escaping around edges of egg, in order to intensify the effect of the light shining through it. "A fresh or infertile one [is] perfectly clear, while a fertile one that has been incubated two days will show the embryo, as in the engraving. Infertile eggs may then be taken from the nest." American Agriculturist, early 1870s. I always had thought egg candling was done prior to selling the eggs. This implies that it's done when gathering, to leave fertile, viable eggs with the hen. (R) "Prairie State," pieced tin with small spirit lamp, a mirror inside reflects light through the egg. Joseph Breck catalog, 1905. The "spider" you see on the eggs is the embryonic chick.* **$40+; $100+**

Egg timer, wall mounted, figural milk bottle back plate of enameled tin, attached flip timer with small glass bulbs, American, 6"H, c.1890s-1910. .... **$100+**

Egg timers, or egg glasses, figure-8 hourglasses but measuring a few minutes not an hour (or more), within frames of cast iron or turned wood, sold through F. A. Walker catalog, poss. European import, probably about 3" to 5"H, c.1880s................... **$65+**

V-11. Egg detector. *Pieced tin, wire. Note arched piece in left of "dish" – this is the cutting edge. "By this machine you cut your shell; you do not smash it and get your batch full of small pieces. You do not make a mess on your table or bench; besides, you can break eggs much faster than in the old way, thereby saving valuable time." V. Clad & Sons pamphlet, c.1890-1900.* **$100+**

❖ NOTES ❖

Futurewatch: Novelty and figural clockwork timers are good go-withs for novelty salt & pepper sets. There is a large variety; to me the most interesting for a kitchen-collector are those that give a double whammy: such as the salmon plastic Fiestaware pitcher timer, and the various Revere™ ware plastic tea kettles, stockpots, etc., finished to look like stainless steel. There are also animals, and foodstuffs like a hamburger, an ear of corn, and a hard-boiled egg with the top sliced off to show the yolk. These would be a good thing to start accumulating, preferably left in packaging (I can't resist putting mine on a 130-year old shelf, like a Lilliputian kitchen). Definitely keep them from being used, and from airborne grease. Cost now $1.99 and up.

Folk art sculpture, saxophone, made up of soldered-together tin kitchen utensils: funnel, flour sifter, grater, and lots of tin ice cream spoons as the buttons & plates, almost full size, probably for hardware store display, American, very early 20th C. (Lavines say 1910). • Dealers Jim & LuAnn Lavine in Geneseo, IL, advertised this in early 1989. Value range mine................. **$800+**

❖ NOTES ❖

Funnels – So far these aren't avidly collected, but as we know, a collection of types, rich with variation, can be very attractive. A century ago, the word "tunnel" was sometimes used instead of funnel. In fact, the word "tunnel" is related to "tun", a large cask for wine, and one meaning of a tunnel was a pipe to draw off fluid from a tun! "Three tunnels are needed – a grocers tunnel for filling preserving jars, and one large and one small for filling bottles, jugs and cruets." Maria Parloa, *Kitchen Companion*, Boston: Estes & Lauriat, 1887.

Funnels, ceramic:
Fruit jar funnel, green sponged yellowware (unusual form in ceramic), small handle, American, 3"L x 5" diam. at top, wide neck, 19th C. **$110**
Funnels, enamelware:
Fruit jar filler or funnel, mottled gray graniteware, turn-of-century. • See: Fruit jars & related items in Chapter XVI (Can, Dry and Preserve).............. **$15+**

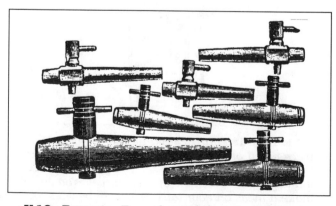

V-12. Faucets. *Turned wood faucets, leather- or cork-lined. For use with coopered vessels. J. Breck catalog, 1905.* **$3+**

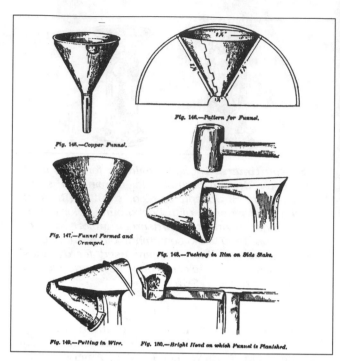

V-13. Steps in making a funnel. *From a series on the "Art of Coppersmithing" by long-time coppersmith John Fuller, Sr., in trade paper The Metal Worker, June 14, 1890. (Fuller's articles were from his book published c.1889.) "Copper funnels were generally made brown, in size from pint to gallon. Let us make one to hold a half gallon; that is, one into which a half gallon of liquor may be dumped without running over. It will be found that an 8-inch cone whose slant height is equal to its diameter will hold approx. a half gallon, Imperial measure. Funnels have always been of one style, and formed of one-half a disk whose radius is equal to the diameter of the mouth of the funnel." After assembling, it was scoured, tinned inside, and the outside rubbed with "Spanish brown." Note dovetailed seam; also crimped or furrowed neck providing air-escape route. Approximate value for late 19th C, pieced copper, 8" to 10"L funnel:* **$35+**

Fruit jar funnel, for canning jars, white enamelware, wide untapered neck, no mark, American (?), 5"L, late 19th or early 20th C. .... **$110+**
Fruit jar funnel, large-throat size for canning jars or bulk meals & grains, also called a grocer's funnel, wide neck & mouth, cobalt & white swirled enamelware, 6" diam., late 19th C........................... **$75+**
Funnel, blue & white mottled enamelware, white interior, small strap handle, 5"L x 4" diam., turn-of-century. Same approximate value for one in blue & white swirl enamelware. .... **$55+**
Funnel, gray graniteware, crimped bottom, small side handle, 6"H, early 20th C. Another with elliptical mouth, same size. .... **$25+**
Funnel, white enamelware, small with relatively long neck, 4"H, early 20th C............................... **$5+**
Funnels, glass:
Funnel, amethyst glass, flared sides, rolled lip, American (?), 5"L x 10" diam., early 19th C... **$150+**
Funnel, glass, bottom of neck is quite sharp, somehow looks like laboratory equipment, and it's not marked

"Pyrex," which you would expect if it were a kitchen piece, 20th C (?). .... **$5+**

Funnels, metal – aluminum, copper, tin:

Fruit jar funnel, for canning jars, spun aluminum, coffee-cup like handle, wide cylindrical neck to fit into top of canning jar, 4-1/2"H x 5" diam., late 19th C. .... **$3+**

Funnel, spun aluminum, fat bowl, ring handle, shapely neck, about 4-1/2"H, late 19th C. The fat bowl is the charm & value. .... **$3+**

Funnel, wide-mouthed, unusual brass in oval shape, American, mouth is 5" x 6-1/8", neck is 2" x 3", funnel is 7"H, 1860s. .... **$35+**

Funnel, for brewers, copper with wire hanging loop, Eastern Bottlers Supply Co., 11"L x 9-1/4" diam. at top, c.1880s to 1900. .... **$35+**

Funnel, copper for bartenders, advertising "Lash's Bitters," late 19th, early 20th C. .... **$65+**

Funnel, copper & tin, large tumbler-shaped cup with rolled rim, abruptly narrowing neck, "Schuyler's Improved Safety – Static Proof Filtering Funnel No. 1," Schuyler Mfg. Co., Springfield, OH, 8-1/2"H x 5-1/2" diam., cup is 5"H, early 20th C. "pat. pending." I'm not convinced this is a kitchen piece – why the "static proof"? Maybe it's some kind of commercial piece that facilitated free-flowing contents. Or, it may be related to the late 19th, early 20th C. fascination with the powers of electricity – and was made by a company trying to cash in on that. .... **$30+**

Funnel, copper, tinned inside, American (?), cone-shape tapers from 6-1/2" diam. at mouth down to 2" at neck, late 19th C. • This is lovely, but it's the kind of puff 'n buff piece which is as much Brasso™ as anything else! I know I sound crazed on the subject of stripping and over-polishing brass and copper, but it drives me crazy. On the other hand, if a dealer has just re-tinned an old copper piece, I will pay extra, because it now costs over $1 a square inch to have it done. .... **$30+**

❖ NOTES ❖

Scour with Sour – By the way, an old-fashioned way to polish copper was to keep a little saucer of sour milk (or buttermilk) near the stove, for wiping the copper pots every day. It tends to make a pinkish finish, at least at first. Try it; it almost always works, especially after a vigorous first-time cleaning.

Funnel, copper, with brass spout & stopper, "Straiter," Boston, MA, pat'd. Dec. 5, 1893. .... **$45-$55**

Funnel, copper with brass thumb piece that closes funnel, bulbous shape, "Straiter," Boston, MA, holds almost a quart, pat'd. 1890. • See also Strainer funnels in Chapter III (Separate, Strain, Drain, Sift and Dredge). .... **$65+**

Funnel, handwrought copper, dovetail seam construction, American, 10-1/2"L, early 19th C. .... **$95+**

Funnel, for lamps, copper, embossed with name, a store premium or giveaway, for filling lamps with kerosene. (Coleman lamp funnels known in tin too; worth something less.) "Coleman Lamp & Stove Co." with paper label for "Steve's Furniture," turn-of-century. ... **$30+**

Funnel, pieced tin, interesting "around the corner" shape, 2 elbow joints that allow funnel to fit into hole otherwise inaccessible, looks like a Dogpatch hearing aid for Mammy Yokum, no mark, 14-1/2"L measured

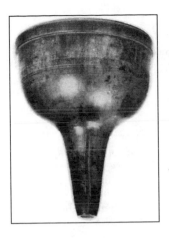

*V-14. Cider funnel. Turned wood, with 5-1/4"L neck. From 1983 Linden sale at Christie, Manson & Woods International Inc. Rather than round, oblong is the more usual shape for cider funnel bowls. Probably early 19th C. **$135+***

sort of diagonally, 5-1/2" diam., late 19th C. Folk art crossover interest; why, oh why, didn't I buy it when I saw it!?! .... **$75+**

Fruit jar funnel, pieced tin, ring handle, early 20th C. .... **$6+**

Funnel, tin, with long cylindrical handle, capped & hooked, possibly for filling candle molds, American, 6" deep x 4-3/4" diam., overall length 13-1/4", early 19th C. .... **$45+**

Funnels, wood:

Funnel, cider, carved from one piece of wood, American, 18" x 8-1/2" oblong x 3-1/2" deep, with 1" diam. hole in center of the oblong bowl, early to mid 19th C. • These large, oblong (rather than round) cider funnels are very unusual looking, often primitive in style. They were meant to fit across the top of a cider keg. Prices range considerably, not so much because one is that much nicer than another, but because of dealer knowledge, demand of collector, and general market conditions. A few cider funnels

*V-15. Fruit jar funnels. Obvious distinctive feature is large diameter neck. (Bag-filler funnels are really big and have very large neck openings too.) Top **(L)** is plain, pieced tin, strap handle, shortish neck, 4-3/8" diameter cup with 2" diameter neck. Top **(R)** "Greystone" graniteware, same dimensions. Both Matthai-Ingram catalog, c.1890. **(B)** is spun & polished aluminum, riveted handle, with 1 pint capacity. 5-3/8" diameter cup; 2-1/8" diameter neck. "Mirro" Aluminum Goods Mfg., 1927. (If you thought aluminum was a post-20s thing, you'll be surprised to know there were many spun aluminum wares from about 1890 on. The older ones are noticeably more attractive than later ones, but value might be only a dollar or two more.) **$10-$60+***

V-16. Measuring funnel. *"Improved candy funnel," heavy tin, spiral spring ("no stick needed"), originally for confectioners. "Lately it found its way into restaurants and hotels for laying out griddle, wheat and buckwheat cakes." Henry Hueg, The Little Confectioner, c.1900-1921.* **$25+**

have dates or initials carved on them, which adds to the value, as do any finishing touches. Folk art crossover interest... **$95+**

Funnel, cider, carved from two pieces of wood, oblong with rounded corners, has separate wooden spout fitted into center of bottom, American, 18-1/2" x 9" oblong x 4-1/2" deep, early 19th C............... **$125+**

Funnel, cider, carved from one piece of wood, oblong wooden trencher (a sort of side-walled plate) with hole in bottom center, American, 21" x 8" oblong x 3" deep, early to mid 19th C............................ **$135+**

Funnel, for maple sap, barrel construction with iron band, American, 12"H x 11-1/2" diam. with 6"L cylindrical neck, 19th C. .... **$90+**

Funnel, turned wood, with nice lip, rather deep, nicely rounded bowl, tapered neck, American, 5-1/4"L, early 19th C.. **$135+**

Funnels, combination tools:

Funnel, corer, cookie cutter & grater combined, pieced tin, funnel has scalloped mouth for cutting cookies, the small end has sharp points for coring, the strap handle is partly punctured for grater & has one edge with saw-teeth (I don't know what for). American, 5-3/4"L x 3-1/2" diam., "pat. appl. for," c.1890s to 1915 (?). Collection of Carol Bohn. .... **$145+**

Funnel & dipper combined, tin, with 6 parts that fit together in various ways to create a funnel, sifter, dredger, measure, tea or coffee strainer, colander, ladle, clothes sprinkler, egg poacher, or funnel cake

V-17. Measuring funnel patent. *"Combined graduated measure and funnel," pat'd. Oct. 2, 1877 by Simon Schippert, Burlington, IA. Has a stop valve to plug the mouth of the neck (seen within cutaway), activated by the thumb lever. Pieced tin. Official Gazette.*

V-18. Measuring funnel combination tool, *called a "Combination Funnel Jigger," quadruple silverplated Britannia. Graduated inside to show 1/2, 1, 1-1/2 and 2 ounces. "Produced by one who has many years of experience in dispensing drinks, and he found a constant need for an article that would combine both all the uses of a graduated jigger and Pousse Cafe and Float making contrivance. ... It will make one dozen Pousse Cafes as easily as one. It is almost instantaneous in making a brandy, or other float ... and dispenses with the old-time method of using a spoon in order to float a liquid." A. Pick, 1909. See also the "funnel droppers" a few in V-32 and V-33.* **$40+**

maker – considerably more than its name implies. The 6 parts are (1) main body or bowl, with handle, and bottom with screw threads; (2) funnel neck soldered to flat plate that fits hole in bottom of bowl; (3) screw threaded ring, like a canning jar ring; (4), (5), & (6) discs of perforated tin or wire mesh to provide various porosities. "Five-in-One," American, 5-1/4"H x 4-3/8" diam. x 8-1/2"L including long handle, c.1890s into 1910s...................................... **$130+**

Funnel & measure combined – See: Measure & funnel combined

Hourglass, glass funnel-like bulbs in wood frame, gilt & blue paint. (See also: Egg timers.) American (?), 7"H, early 19th C. .... **$150+**

Hourglass, simple 6-corner wooden cage-like frame, turned wooden columns at each corner, 2 glass flask-shaped bulbs fastened at waist with chamois leather, sometimes called a **bottle glass**, American (?), 8-5/8"H, early 19th C or late 18th. .... **$150+**

V-19. Measuring funnel. *"Burke's Patent," copper that's tinned inside, strainer piece inside pouring nozzle. Two sizes: to measure from 1/2 pint to 1 quart; and 1/2 pint to 1/2 gallon. 1920s.* **$25+**

Hourglass, wood frame in old blue paint, glass with sand, American, mid 19th C. • Added value: Old blue color more $$ than red; this one has nice detailing besides and a certain lopsided charm. [Note: New wooden-frame primitive hourglasses are being made; I saw one painted mustard, with reddish sienna polka dots on eBay.].....................$95+

Hourglass, wooden frame with rounded glass bulbous funnels joined at the small ends, 7-1/2"H, late 18th, early 19th C...$125+

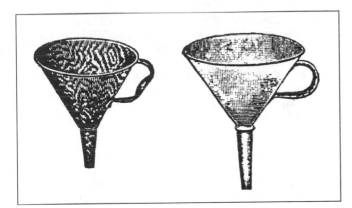

V-20. Funnels. (L) *Graniteware with large riveted side handle with grip, in 1 quart and 1/2 gallon sizes. Available through the Sethness Co. candymaker's catalog, maker unknown. 1925.* **(R)** *White enameled steel without a seam, imported from Czechoslovakia. Five sizes: 3", 4", 4-3/4", 5-1/2" and 7-1/8", with capacities from 3 to 32 ounces. Pick-Barth catalog, 1929.* **$10+**

V-21 Funnels. *Clockwise from deep conical one at* **(L)**: *Copper or brass, with strainer, in two weights – "light" and "strong" and six sizes from 1/2 to 2 pints.* **(T)** *– a large brewers' funnel, "brown" copper, with shapely bowl, in five sizes from 1/2 to 4 gallons.* **(R)** *Copper or brass, with strainer, in six sizes from 1/4 to 2 pints.* **(B-R)** *– a pewter strainer funnel, in two qualities: "best" and "common," five sizes from 1/4 to 2 pints. All four from catalog of Henry Rogers, Wolverhampton, England, 1914.* **$15-$100**

V-22. Combination funnel, measuring cup/dipper, strainer, jar filler. *Spun aluminum. Has long "saucepan" handle, and the neck is a curved conical shape. Maker unknown, but from the Ritzinger & Grasgreen import catalog, c.1906-07.* **$15+**

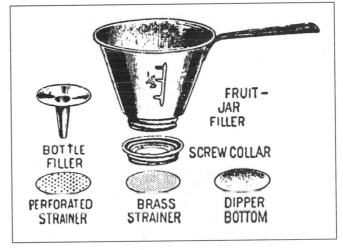

V-23. Combination funnel. *Another, this one in pieced tin, with one brass strainer. Also from Ritzinger & Grasgreen catalog.* **$15+**

V-24. Percolator funnel, *to put in top of coffee pot so that the flange held it in place. Cloth filter inside. 4-1/2" diam. Graniteware mfd. by Matthai-Ingram, c.1890.* **$45+**

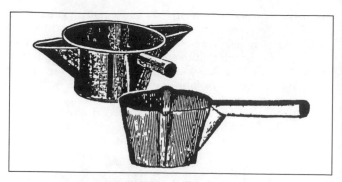

V-25. Funnel with stove polish. *You bought it with a quarter pound of C. W. Hart & Co., Troy, NY, paste stove polish inside. "All will readily perceive the convenience of the tube of the funnel, which serves as a handle, thereby making it possible to polish a stove without soiling the hands." You certainly didn't rub the funnel on the stove, and would need a brush too. "After the Polish is out of the Funnel, it can be used as a household article, always ready and convenient; therefore we utilize all, both the box and the blacking." Ad in The Metal Worker, Oct. 7, 1882. Collector value now is related to finding one with the marked tin cap or lid. Otherwise it's just a tin funnel with fluted neck.* **$25+**

Lamp funnel – See: Funnels, copper
Liquid measures are sometimes called **measuring pitchers** because they look and function like a pitcher, usually with a tapered body, wraparound lip & strap handle.

V-26. Droppers for candy-making. *Sort of a cross between a measuring funnel and a ladle, but put in this chapter because of relationship to droppers and fillers seen in other pictures. **(T-L)** is a "copper sugar dropper," in sizes from 5" to 10" diam., tapered tubular handle without capped end. Bottom **(L)** is a "copper mint dropper, with one or two lips," 4" to 10" diam., also tubular handle. They are in the Duparquet, Huot & Moneuse c.1904-1910 catalog. **(T-R)** is one of early chemist Lavoisier's laboratory instruments – made of copper or silver, for making a solution of salts in water. It dates to the 18th C. **(B-R)** is from a German confectioners' supply catalog of c.1904, a "Giesspfannen" [pouring pan] with two lips. A. Bertuch, Berlin. It is probably the same as B-L. Biggest have more decorative value, and valued as such.* **$50-$125**

V-27. Custard dippers or pie fillers. *Heavy pieced tin. **(T-L)** is from Duparquet, Huot & Moneuse, NYC, catalog c.1904-1910, and has extremely pronounced spouts. It came in 1, 2, and 3 quart sizes. **(B-R)** has braced tubular handle, and was available in 1 and 1-1/2 quart sizes. It's from the Jaburg Bros. candy-making supply catalog, 1908.* **$50-$125**

Liquid measure, brass can, strap handle, American (?), 1 pint capacity, mid 19th C. .... **$45-$60**
Liquid measure, copper, flared complete wraparound lip, strap handle with semi-cylindrical inset for better grip, dinged, "Fleming Apple Distillery," Fairmount, NJ, 7-1/2"H, late 19th C. .... **$45-$65**
Liquid measure, copper, wraparound pouring lip, strap handle, American or English, 1 qt. capacity, 19th C. Sets of these were sold by candy makers' suppliers, at least as late as 1925. Copper ones were offered in six sizes, from 1 pt. to 1 gal., by the Sethness Co., Chicago. Theirs had a completely wraparound lip that was wider at the pouring front than over the handle. The largest one, which sold for only $2.50 in 1925, also had a strap handle with part of the loop filled in to make a handgrip........................... **$65+**
Liquid measure, copper, simple cylinder with strap handle, close-fitting lid with strap handle, "Stevens & Duncklee," Concord, NH, 5-1/2"H x 5" diam., holds 52 oz. – an odd amount, neither here nor there, being 6-1/2 pts. or 3-1/4 qts. Possibly relates to a standard measure used for some now-unidentified liquid. Probably 4th quarter 19th C. .... **$50+**

V-28. Pumpkin pie filler. *Pieced tin, with braced handle, two spouts, and a flared funnel-like hopper at top; 2, 3 & 4 quart capacity. The catalog had absolutely no explanation of how it's used, but at least you'll recognize one if you see it! Jaburg Bros., 1908. Has "folk art" appeal.* **$75+**

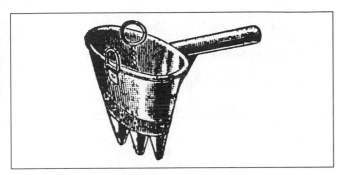

V-29. Three-nose funnel, *for making butterscotch wafers. Pieced copper, with valve control ring visible coming up out of mouth. Braced tubular handle. Thomas Mills confectioners' catalog, 1930.* **$115+**

V-31. Multi-nose or spouted funnel, *or "dropper for cream work," to be used in filling cream-filled pastries. Pieced tin, bail handle, seen curving around just above the 10 spouts. Turned wood handle above operates the bank of rubber stoppers. This could be had in "any size to order." Thomas Mills, 1930.* **$85+**

Liquid measure, copper, tinned inside, wraparound lip, reinforced strap handle, big dent in one side, no marks, American or English, 7-1/2"H, 1 qt. capacity, 19th C. .... **$25+**

Liquid measures, copper & brass, elongated necks & widely-flared bodies (like skirts), English (?), 1 qt. & 1 gal. capacity, 19th C. Value for pair:......... **$200+**

Liquid measures, set of 3, tin-lined copper with small attached brass labels & brass strap handles in rounded rectangular shape, English (?), 1/2 pt. size is 3-3/8"H x 3-1/8" diam.; 1 pt. – 3-7/8"H x 3-5/8" diam.; 2 pts. – 4-3/4"H x 4-1/2" diam., mid (?) 19th C. Value range is for each, the way measures are usually found. .... **$35+**

Liquid measures, copper, tapering body & wraparound lip, strap handles, set of 6, M. Smith," English or American, early 19th C. .... **$200+**

Liquid measure, gray graniteware, "NESCO," St. Louis, MO, 1 gal. capacity, 1st quarter 20th C. .... **$40+**

Liquid measure, gray graniteware, graduated stepped thirds, wire handle, American, 1 c. capacity, c.1890-1910. .... **$20+**

Liquid measure, gray graniteware, pouring lip, slanted sides, 2 qt. capacity, late 19th C. .... **$25+**

Liquid measure, gray graniteware, riveted handle & lip, American, 1/2 pt. capacity, c.1890s-1910. ...... **$25+**

Liquid measure, gray graniteware, straight sides, applied flaring wraparound pouring lip, strap handle, American, 2 qt. capacity, turn-of-century. (Pint size about 1/3 value, quart about 1/2.) .... **$35+**

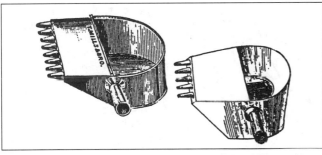

V-30. Multi-nose or spouted funnels, *also known as "A. B. Runners" [no, I don't know why], "Candy Droppers," or in German, Giesspfannen, or pouring pans. Five- to 8-spouters were depicted in several confectioners' supply catalogs. A c.1904 Bertuch catalog from Berlin offered them with 4, 6, 8 and 10 feststehenden Röhren, but depicted only a 5-spouter. Duparquet, Huot & Moneuse (c.1904-1910) also had a 5-spouter (with a beveled front edge like Bertuch's (R) and 4, 6 or 8-spouters. The 1925 Sethness candymaking catalog picture (L) actually shows a Thomas Mills' runner with 8 spouts; Sethness offered only 5-spouters, but a 1930 Mills' catalog says they could be had with 4, 5, 6 or 8 spouts ... or "any size to order." Sometimes described as a "rare candle mould filler," which it isn't, although it is rare.* **$125+**

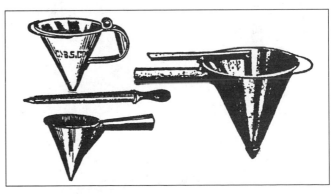

V-32. Funnel droppers. *All pieced tin. (T-L) from Sethness 1925 catalog, apparently mfd. by C. & B. S[ethness]. Co., with braced handle. 6" diam. at top, 3/8" opening. (B-L) Another that also came with a funnel stick , Thomas Mills' c.1915. The cone of this one came in four diameters and heights: 6-1/4" x 7"; 7-1/2" x 8-1/2"; 7" x 10"; and 10-1/2" x 12". (R) The biggest one in the picture is also Mills' – from 1930. It has a spring-lever built-in funnel stick, and was advertised as useful also "for cordial work." (A cordial was a filled candy, like chocolate cherries.) The funnel stick is used to push the creme material through the hole. See also the measuring funnels V-16 -19.* **$30+**

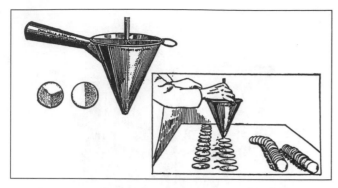

V-33. Funnel dropper. *For making cream wafers in 2, 3 or 4 colors (note dividing partitions within body of funnel). Pieced tin, capped tubular handle. Mills, 1930.* **$30+**

Liquid measure, pieced tin, stepped sides, upside-down truncated cone, strap handle, marked "Kellerman's" (the mfr.?), & "U. S. Standard," & "J. Coover," "Harrisburg, PA," 6-1/2"H, embossed 1 qt., 1 pt., 1/2 pt., & 1 gill, pat'd. Oct. 22, 1872. Coover, of Chambersburgh, PA, invented method for forming sheet-metal measures... **$45+**

Liquid measure, tin, bail handle, shaped like a small coal scuttle, marked "Pour Chaque Litre" & "Can-

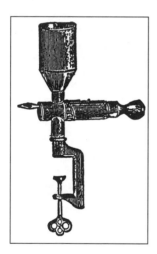

V-34. Cake filler, *or* **cream puff filler.** *Screw clamped to work table, mostly pieced tin. For a small set-up – in a shop with limited demand. Jaburg Bros., 1908.* **$85+**

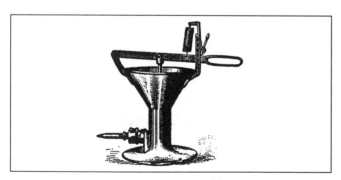

V-35. Cake filler. *The great headline in the catalog is "THE ANGER FILLER," which sounds like a short story by Ray Bradbury! A cream puff filler which would "deliver large portions" or could be "regulated down to the smallest, which is 60 parts to a pound." about 16"H? Jaburg Bros., 1908.* **$65+**

neleure Correspondante," French, 1 decilitre capacity, mid to late 19th C. .... **$35+**

Liquid measure, tin, flared wraparound lip, strap handle with brace, American, 8"H, 8 c. capacity, 19th C... **$15+**

Liquid measure, tin, high pouring rim, blobs of spelter or solder on it with marks stamped in the blobs, its size on a brass plate, and word "JOB" under plate. Square or bracket strap handle, strangest marks are letters stamped near handles, front & back: "Y Q A R C D F G H K M N P Q" (it's possible that "R" was a poorly punched "B"). Only 2"H x 2" diam., marked "1 deciliter," 19th C. • As to the meaning of the string of 14 letters, I wonder if it indicates that the measure had been inspected 14 times, and each time the inspector used a different letter punch to indicate it had passed inspection? .... **$60+**

Liquid measure, tin, wraparound lip, generous strap handle, can part is perfectly cylindrical, marked with 3 ridges to divide it into fourths, looks like a coffee can, Matthai-Ingram was one mfr.; I'm sure many others made similar wares, American, 4 sizes: 1 pt., 1 qt., 2 qts., & 4 qts. The 1-qt. size is 5"H x 3" diam., c.1890 to 1910. .... **$15+**

Liquid measures, set of 6, pieced tin, slightly conical, wraparound lips, large strap handles, only one of which (the 2 gallon size) is reinforced, F. A. Walker catalog, American or imported, 1/4 pt. to 2 gal. capacity; that is, approx. 3"H to 15"H, c.1870s-90s. .... **$25-$55**

Liquid or dry measure, stamped tin, "Kreamer," 4 c. capacity, c.1900. Kreamer stuff is widely collected.. **$25+**

Liquid or dry measures, set of 4 graduated cups with thumb tab handles, stamped tin, "Maryann's Accurate Measure," Chicago, IL, 1/4 c. to 1 c., 20th C. For the set: .... **$15+**

V-36. Measuring device patent. *Pat'd. Aug. 2, 1887 by Elijah Truman, Parkersburg, WV. "The measure provided with a chamber closed on all exterior sides and partially covering the top of the measure, and having a discharge-nozzle, and a [spring-controlled] hinged cover to that portion of the top of the measure not covered by said chamber." Truman claimed as worthy of a patent "the combination of a measure having pins or axles below its center of gravity, and a support having standards provided with notches at different heights to receive the axles of the measure." The drawing alone makes this worth putting here. It's as surreal as a Man Ray or other Dada drawing. Patents were granted for many useless things; sometimes it seems as if patent examiners were charmed by the drawings as much as anything! If this were ever made, or if a patent model exists, I believe the collector value would be* **$400** *or more. Official Gazette of the U.S. Patent Office.*

V-37. Measures. (L) *"Straight ale measure" in choice of "best pewter" or "common pewter," and in 1/2 pint, 1 pint or 2 pints.* **(R)** *Wine measure, in "best" or "common" pewter, and in "gun-metal." Many more sizes here: 1/16, 1/12, 1/8, 1/4 and 1/2 pint, 1 pint and 2 pints. Henry Rogers, Sons & Co., Wolverhampton, England, 1914. A full set of seven would be a good find, and would be over $200.00, despite lack of age.* **$60+**

Liquid measure, tin, with scrolly cast iron side handle, upside down conical shape with stepped divisions marking off 1 gill, 1/2 pt., 1 pt., 1 qt. Big flared fixed foot, I say prob. English, because on one 2-day trip to PA I saw at least a dozen of them, 6-3/4"H x 5-1/2" diam. at top, late 19th C. .... **$35+**

❖ NOTES ❖

Collector hint: Keep track of how many examples of a form you see in one group shop, one market, one show, one antiquing trip, especially if it's something you don't think you've seen before. You can often tell when a container-load has just arrived and, from other things in the booth or show, maybe even where it originated.

Measure, varnished, dark reddish brown wood-fiber & glue composition, rather thick-walled, cylindrical with raised edge for pouring lip opposite tin strap handle, bound with thin wire in 3 places, Indurated Fibre Ware, Cordley & Hayes, NYC, 9"H, late 19th or early 20th C. .... **$45+**

Measure & funnel combined, called in catalogs a **utility measure**, a slightly tapered vessel, with strap handle hand grip, fitted with most of a funnel instead of pouring lip, copper, tinned on inside, American, 1 gal. capacity, late 19th into 2nd quarter 20th C. • A similar one was sold, in pieced tin in 5 sizes from 1/2 pt. to 1 gal., by the Matthai-Ingram Co. The funnel attachment, as they called it, made it easy to fill small-mouthed vessels or to direct the stream in a particular place in a larger-mouthed vessel. The tin ones would bring only about half what the more "decorative" copper one would bring. .... **$25-$45+**

Measuring cup, spun aluminum, "Swans Down Cake Flour Makes Better Cakes" embossed on side, American, 1 c. capacity, 20th C. Something with a name is always worth a little bit more. .... **$10+**

Measuring cup, cobalt blue & white mottled enamelware, "McClary," Ontario, Canada, 1 pt. capacity, early 20th C. .... **$75+**

V-38. Measures. *Copper, tinned inside, with brass handles. From 3-3/8"H to 4-3/4"H – 1/2 pint to 2 pints, marked on small brass plates. Collection of Mary Mac Franklin. Set:* **$125+**

Measuring cup, gray graniteware, heavy, applied pouring lip, strap handle, "Granite Iron Ware," mfd. by St. Louis Stamping Co., St. Louis, MO, 1 c. capacity, pat'd. May 30, 1876, May 8, 1877. .... **$30+**

Measuring cup, embossed green Depression glass, Kellogg's, American, 1 c. capacity, 1930s. .... **$20+**

Measuring cup, embossed green Depression glass, 3-way pouring lips, straight sides, Hazel Atlas, 1 c. capacity, c.1930s. .... **$20+**

Measuring cup, embossed green Depression glass, one pouring lip, sides flare up slightly, Hazel Atlas, 1 c. capacity, c.1930s. A lot of notice is given to the wares of Hazel Atlas on eBay sales. I believe it must be a full collecting category. .... **$20+**

Measuring cup, embossed green Depression glass, sides flare, modernistic or Art Deco stepped angular handle, rather tall, 3 pouring lips, c.1930s. ..... **$45+**

Measuring cup, glass, "Faultless Diamond Starch," American, 1 c. capacity, 20th C. .... **$5+**

V-39. Spirit measures. *Sometimes called "haystack measures." Both in the brown-finished copper described in Figure V-14. They could be had in many sizes: 1/8, 1/4, 1/2 and 1 pint, 2 or 4 pints, 1, 2, 3, 4 or 5 gallons. The* **(L)** *one is termed a "bottle necked" measure. H. Rogers, 1914. The value here is not in real age, but in the ancient form.* **$45+**

Measuring cup, heavy colorless glass, no pouring lip, marked on one side 1/4, 1/2, 3/4, & 1 c.; on other side 1/3, 2/3, & 1 c., "Sellers," to go with their cabinets, pat'd. Dec. 8, 1925. .... **$30+**

Measuring cup, stamped tin, "Rumford Baking Powder," 20th C. .... **$15+**

Measuring cup, stamped tin, "Cottolene" (shortening made from cottonseed oil), American, 1 c., early 20th C. .... **$15+**

Measuring cup, stamped tin, embossed advertising message "Drink Barrington Hall Coffee," 1 c., 20th C. **$10+**

Measuring cup, tin, deep wraparound lip, strap handle, American, 5"H, 2 c. size, late 19th C. .... **$10+**

Measuring cups, small tin flared side cups with tab handles, set of 4, "Mary Ann's Accurate Measure," mfd. by Katzinger Co., Chicago, measures 1/4, 1/2, 1/3, and 1 c. 1930s-40s (?). .... **$12+**

Measuring cup, turned maple, double ended with cups at each end, American, only 3-5/8"H, late 19th C. .... **$65+**

❖ NOTES ❖

Measuring lines in pans – I have seen cooking pans of bell metal and possibly also sheet iron (I can't recall now) with concentric rings on the inside bottom, as well as the sides. I thought it was some accident or evidence of the manufacturing process. But when I read in one of Soyer's 19th century cookbooks about frying, and read to "place into the pan any oleaginous substance [viz. butter, lard], so that, when melted, it shall cover the bottom of the pan by about two lines. ..." I realized that the lines, even on the bottom, might be used for measuring. (It is also possible that a "line" is a unit of measurement, somehow related to line as a measure of length equaling 1/12 of an inch. In that case, Soyer would mean covering the bottom of the pan with lard enough to be 1/6 of an inch deep when melted.)

Measuring spoon, 4-way flip-over tool, stamped metal, 2 spoon bowls measure 1 tbs. and 1 tsp., flip over & small concavities on back of bowls measure 1/2 tsp. and 1/4 tsp., advertising "Dr. Price's Baking Powder," 4-3/8"L, "patent pending," 20th C. .... **$12+**

V-40. Measures. *Pieced tin, partially wraparound lips, braced or reinforced handle for largest, 2-gallon, size. Smallest is 1/4 pint. F. A. Walker catalog, c.1890; same cut used to depict "Old Time" measures of heavy tin plate in the Matthai-Ingram catalog also c.1890. Each:* **$25-$55**

V-41. Measures. *Quite similar to those in V-40, except that they are made of heavy tin with copper lips, and all, including the smallest, have reinforced strap handles. Sizes 1 gill, 1/2 and 1 pint, 1 quart, 2 quarts and 1 gallon. Duparquet, Huot & Moneuse, c.1904-1910. Extra value is for the "decorating" value of the copper. Each:* **$30-$90**

Measuring spoon, aluminum, peculiar instrument with flat center handle strip, with propeller-like swiveling spoons at each end, measures 1/4 and 1/2 tsp., 1 tsp., and dessert spoon, "Level Measuring Spoon," mfd. by Barnard Co., Boston, MA, "patent applied for" c.1920s. .... **$35+**

Measuring spoon, for coffee, molded yellow or red plastic, with Mr. Peanut™ handle. He stands on tablespoon coffee measure, and has smaller cup atop his head, Planters Peanuts, 20th C. .... **$65+**

Measuring spoon, silver-plated metal, beading around handle, with hanging hole, bowl of tablespoon-like spoon engraved with concentric oval rings for different measurements, with "Armour's Extract of Beef" engraved on bowl, picture of can of beef extract on handle, with label engraved "Armour & Co.," Chicago, U.S.A., c.1905. .... **$15+**

Measuring spoon, tin, "A & P," 20th C. .... **$5+**

V-42. Measures. *Heavy tin, shown in 3 sizes:* **(L)** *2 quarts, which has a beautiful curved and reinforced handle to allow for pouring approximately four pounds of fluid,* **(R)** *1 pint,* **(M)** *1 quart, all with flared wraparound high lips. (A gallon size, with similar handle to 2-quart, was also available.) Notice the ribs or ridges denoting divisions within. Lisk Mfg. Co., 1896.* **$15+**

Measuring spoons, stamped "malacca" tin of extremely simple construction, the handles of the three sort of riveted together with an open brass ring – like a grommet, "Original," Landers, Frary & Clark, New Britain, CT, measured in teaspoons and drops: 1/4 tsp. or 15 drops; 1/2 tsp. or 30 drops; and 1 tsp. or 60 drops, pat'd. July 10, 1900. LFC showed the spoons at the Mechanic's Fair in Boston, fall of 1898, and said the three measurements "form the complete spoon measurements for any recipes." Also that the set "will hang by the eyelet on any convenient nail in your pantry when not in use." Ah, the simple claims of old-fashioned ads! I believe this may be the "original," of what we now take for granted. .... **$20+**

V-45. "Utility" measures, or **combination measures,** *described in various catalogs as being a measure with an attached funnel. These appeared in several catalogs from about 1890 well into the 1920s (and probably later). Top one, shown being used to fill a bottle, is of pieced tin, in 5 sizes: 1/2 and 1 pint, 1 quart, 2 and 4 quarts. Matthai-Ingram, c.1890. Lower one is of polished tinned steel, with "tinned steel rests" on the bottom, reinforced handle. It came in 3 sizes: 1, 2 and 4 quarts. "Puritan" line, Central Stamping Co., 1920. Another one, almost identical but made of copper and available only in the 1-gallon size, is found in the Sethness publication of 1925. Value range for tin only; add from 50 to 100% for a copper one.* **$25-$45+**

V-43. Measure. *Graniteware, gray & white. Completely wraparound lip, reinforced strap handle. Maker unknown, but was available in 4 sizes from Sethness: 1 pint, 1 quart, 1/2 gallon and 1 gallon. 1925 catalog, but probably virtually unchanged for 30 years before that. The graniteware enamelware market has dropped somewhat because there are so many recent imports of old enamelware from Europe. The assurance of American provenance has become problematic.* **$60+**

V-46. Measure. *Stamped & pieced tin, wraparound lip, strap handle, embossed graduations of 1-quart size. 5"H x 3" diam. Maker unknown, c.1900.* **$15**

V-44. Vinegar measures & funnel. *Each piece scarped, hollowed, and finished from one piece of wood, (not identified, but possibly maple or ash) in catalog of Joseph Breck, 1905. Style of all pieces is like much older examples. A set consisted of a pint, quart, 1/2 gallon measure and the funnel. Approx. value range for measures might tend to be higher than that for a funnel, which was probably about 7"H. Much of asking price would be based on patina and condition, and the presumption of great age that could be based on style and patina. Each:* **$35-$75+**

V-47. Measure. *Copper, 5-gallon size only, with two tipping strap handles near the bottom, flared wraparound lip-rim or flange, swinging strap handle with reinforcement at center. Graduated with ribs. Sethness, 1925. Original price was $9.75 – talk about inflation!* **$45+**

V-48. Measuring cup. *Molded lime glass, "annealed to prevent breaking from extremes of heat or cold. Graduated in thirds and fourths. Style called the "Brooklyn." "One may hold it up to the light and see just the exact measurement." Silver & Co., c.1910.* **$25+**

Oven thermometer, 2-part, heavy stamped brass-finished (or brass?) sheet metal with asbestos on bottom, & tilted upright frame with mercury thermometer, in original box, chromolithograph picture on front shows turn-of-century, aproned woman putting food in oven with her thermometer, & legend "Always Use a Taylor Thermometer for Uniformity in Cooking & Baking." Also is an illustrated cookbooklet, *Taylor Homeset Cookbook. Bake & Cook the Thermometer Way,* with recipes. Woman on cookbook cover is of later date, but same box was probably used over a long period. "Taylor," model #5928, Rochester, NY, c.1920s. • Added value: If the

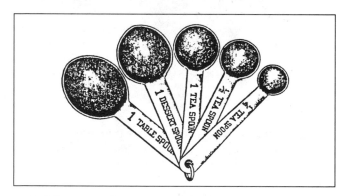

V-49. Measuring spoons. *Aluminum, on a ring, a set of five including the midway measurement* **"dessert spoon,"** *widely known in England, but not here anymore, although 19th C American cookbooks use that measurement. Mfd. by the E. A. Fargo Co., Taunton, MA. An ad in* House Furnishing Review, *May 1915.* **$7+**

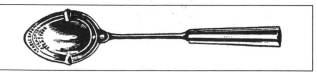

V-50. Measuring spoon. *A nickel-plated stamped steel mixing spoon with measuring graduations marked on bowl. Green plastic handle. Two sizes: 8-1/2"L & 10-3/4"L. "Androck" line, Washburn Co., 1936.* **$5+**

box were in good condition with a vibrantly colored (instead of faded & scuffed) picture, the set would sell for two or three times as much................. **$10+**

❖ NOTES ❖

Pie Birds, Vents & Chimneys – The earliest picture I've seen of a pie vent was in a very early (probably pre-1710) chapbook/cookbook. (See Illustration X-1 in Chapter X.) But I suspect that if I read Italian, I'd discover some kind of pie vent in use at least as early as the sixteenth century. In the 1890s there were a number of "pie funnels," "crust supports and ventilators for pies and pastry," "pie chimneys," "pie tubes," and "pie vents" patented in Great Britain and here. They may have been invented to cash in on a serious pie fad. Or to replace earlier specific pie vents, or modified ceramic or glass funnels used for the purpose of venting steam from a two-crust sweet or savory pie as it baked. **The two requisites** that help you recognize a pie vent, or even a figural pie bird, are an **arched opening in the base**, and a **vent-hole above the crust level** – mouth, eyes, trunks, hats, chimneys, etc. There are many 3-1/2" to 6"H ceramic figural pieces, which could be confused – until you note that they have no arched base and no definite vent-hole. Expert Lillian Cole dated the beginning of zoomorphic or human figurals (mainly in ceramic, a few in glass) to the 1930s, beginning with a blackbird. There are now many different blackbirds, almost the fabled "four & twenty blackbirds" baked in a nursery rhyme pie. Most of them look fairly similar and few are marked, although they come from potteries in several countries. There are dozens of other designs – most are the same motifs for which there are thousands of collectors, including: hens & roosters, clowns, chefs, ladybugs, elves, pigs, dragons, snowmen, dogs, penguins, fish, owls, elephants, Santa's, opera singers, bluebirds, cats, Wise Men, Mexican women, mushrooms, frogs, English "Bobbies," "Mammies," Dutch girls, angels, waiters, zebras, pelicans, ducklings, goslings, whales, bears, turtles and more. Some advertising pieces or licensed characters – like Donald Duck – may cost a lot, partly because of crossover interest. Most pie birds are collectible for under $50.

My friend, the late Lillian Cole, started a newsletter for pie bird collectors about the time the third edition of this book came out. Lillian's collection numbered over 400 different birds (or other animals or people), most of which she believed were American-made. She probably knew more about them than anyone – partly because she had a detective's instinct, and had incredible luck in tracking down the potteries & people, in the U.S. and abroad, who made pie birds. See club information at the end of this chapter.

Pie bird, Black Americana figural so-called "Mammy" with exuberant bandana turban, ceramic, American, about 4-1/2"H, c.1920s-30s............................ **$50+**
Pie bird, ceramic, figural blackbird, in original box. The bird was positioned in the pie, a slit was cut in the top crust & it was put, serape-fashion, over the bird. Steam was supposed to be vented from within the pie, although it is possible that they didn't work as well as they were supposed to. This bird is marked "Royal Worcester." English, 4-1/2"H, 20th C.... **$30+**

❖ NOTES ❖

Humongous Pie on Wheels – The following appeared in the *Newcastle Chronicle*, 6th January 1770, in England: "Monday last was brought from Howick to Berwick, to be shipp'd for London, for Sir. Hen. Grey, bart., a pie, the contents whereof are as follows: viz. 2 bushels of flour, 20 lbs. of butter, 4 geese, 2 turkies, 2 rabbits, 4 wild ducks, 2 woodcocks, 6 snipes, and 4 partridges; 2 neats' tongues, 2 curlews, 7 blackbirds, and 6 pigeons: it is supposed a very great curiosity, was made by Mrs. Dorothy Patterson, housekeeper at Howick. It was near nine feet in circumference at bottom, weighs about twelve stones [168 pounds], will take two men to present it to table; it is neatly fitted with a case, and four small wheels to facilitate its use to every guest that inclines to partake of its contents at table."

Pie bird, figural goose, pink ceramic, English,
  20th C. .... **$40+**
Pie bird, pink ceramic figural of the "Pillsbury Twin,"
  Pillsbury, 20th C............................. **$30+**
Pie bird, chef on a sort of pedestal, all white glaze,
  England... **$35+**
Pie bird, black chef, in green clothes, c.1940s. (Other
  color clothes worth a third or half.) .... **$150+**
Pie bird, crested head, blue glazed, eyes are the vents,
  20th C. .... **$35+**
Pie bird, Donald Duck, cream color with pale blue
  sailor hat, bright yellow base & beak, marked "Walt
  Disney" and "Donald Duck," 1940s. .... **$150+**
Pie funnel, white china with wide brim, mfd. by Nut
  Brown, England, c.1920s. .... **$35+**
Pie vent or funnel, also called a pie chimney, white china,
  marked "Gourmet Pie Cup" with a crown, English,
  1880s-90s. • There are several stoneware or white pottery pie vents, from England, Germany & the U.S.
  Names to look for are "Roe's Rosebud Patent"; "Cascade"; "The Improved Pie Funnel"; "Whitaker's";

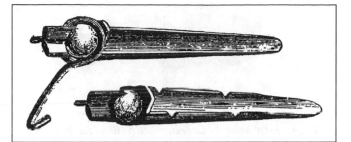

V-52. Sap spouts. (T) *galvanized cast iron Eureka sap spout of 1869;* **(B)** *"improved" Eureka from 1870, mfd. by inventor, C. C. Post, Burlington, VT. "In the improved one, the bucket hangs by two points, so that it cannot swing like a pendulum, and in two narrow notches, so that it cannot twist nor wabble [sic]."* W. J. Chamberlain, Hudson, OH, wrote in "Maple Sugar Making," American Agriculturist, *Feb. 1871: "Last year I recommended a wooden sap spout ... because it was, on the whole, better than any metallic one I had then seen. I find four or five different kinds are used in Vermont, but only one appears to me preferable to the turned, bored, and notched- in- three- places one in general use [in Ohio]. That is Post's Eureka."* The marble-like *"hemisphere'hugs' against the outer edge of the hole" in the tree.* **$4+**

"Wilkinson's"; and "Foulds' & Smiths.'" There are also glass & aluminum funnel vents. .... **$30+**
Room thermometer, stamped & painted tin, shaped like
  an urn, American, 1st quarter 20th C. .... **$15+**
Room thermometer, wall-mounted, stamped sheet metal
  painted red, shaped like round teapot, has 2 simple
  hooks at bottom for hanging potholders, "Tel-Tru,"
  Tel-Tru Thermometer Co., Rochester, NY, 5"H x 7"W,
  c.1930s to 1940s... **$20+**

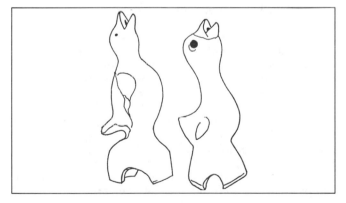

V-51. Pie birds. *Pastel-colored glazed china,* **(L)** *a blackbird or songbird, 5-1/8"H; the* **(R)** *one in the form of a baby bird asking for food is much heavier than the other, 5-3/8"H. 20th C. For those of you who wondered if you would recognize a pie bird vs. a bird figurine, note the cutouts in the base. Ex-collection the late Lillian Cole. The value range for these is very wide, depending on where you find them. (See the book in my Bibliography by Ellen Bercovici, Bobbie Zucker Bryson & Deborah Gillham for good views of many pie birds.)* **$35+**

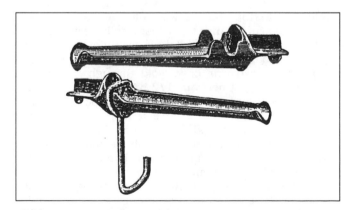

V-53. Sap spouts. *Here are C. C. Post's Eureka spouts after another 13 years! "The Sugar Maker's Friend. Over 6,000,000 sold, to replace various kinds." About 3-1/2"L. Note that he went back to the wire hanger for one style. The price in 1871 was described by Mr. Chamberlain as "high" at $4.00 for a hundred spouts. By the time of this ad, in American Agriculturist, March 1883, the price was $4.25 and $4.50 per hundred. You could order a sample for three 3¢ U.S. stamps. Sounds like a postage cut would spur business growth a lot better than a tax cut!* **$5+**

V-54. Sap spout. *Galvanized malleable iron, the "Breck" spout – "the invention of a practical sugar maker." Guaranteed not to break from being driven into the bored sap hole in the tree, and the cast-in hooks were made to "withstand the strain of high winds" which often caused buckets to twist off the hooks. They also sold the "Concord," "the common spout used largely in New Hampshire and Vermont, made of wood and steel." Joseph Breck, 1905.* **$4+**

Scale, balance, equal arm balance type, tin & iron, center post like a dinner horn, closed end possibly weighted with plaster or sand, beam is cast & looks European, 2 tin pans hung with string, probably homemade of assorted parts, American, 21"H, mid 19th C. Crossover folk art collectible. .... **$650+**

Scale, beam or balance, iron, chain hangers, tin pan, American?, 14" x 24", 19th C. .... **$25+**

Scale, candy, spring balance for countertop, cast iron, brass pan, counter top, "Brandon," American, about 14"L, pat'd. 1867. .... **$100+**

Scale, candy of the spring balance type, tin base, brass pan, white enameled dial, Hanson Brothers, Chicago, IL, 12"H, late 19th C. .... **$85+**

Scale, candy or confectioners', unequal arm balance type, black painted cast iron, abstract fishtail or bird foot base, with 3 toes, brass pan, Fairbanks & Co., Philadelphia, PA, 1870s-80s. Fairbanks also used a lot of red paint on cast iron bases. .... **$160+**

Scale, countertop, sometimes called a platform scale, unequal arm balance type, cast iron base with fishtail that keeps base stable, flat platform (for putting basket, box, bag or pieced brass pan of goods), oval brass pan with fixed ring base, sold through *Montgomery Ward* catalog, American, 1/2 oz. to 25 lbs. capacity, dated 1892. • Platform scales of this type are unequal arm balance scales & have a long, calibrated bar sticking out to the side, with a hook at the end from which a weight can be hung, plus a movable sliding weight that slides along the bar (like the scale at the doctor's office). The most commonly seen base design has an exaggerated fishtail (a sort of 2-toe chicken foot) sticking out at the bottom in the same direction as the bar; it helps keep base stable. .... **$125+**

V-55. Spice scale. *Of the hanging equal arm balance type. Japanned & pinstriped cast iron arm,* **(L)** *tin weight pan and scoop* **(R)** *for the loose spice being weighed. These cost only 75¢ for small size, or $1.25 for large, in Jaburg catalog, 1908.* **$45+**

❖ NOTES ❖

Egg Grading Scales. Of all the regrets I have about collecting, I feel now that maybe the biggest mistake I made was not going after a wide variety of egg grading scales, usually called egg scales. Made to weigh eggs one at a time, from the smallest pullet's eggs to a large turkey's, these scales probably reflect a design aesthetic closer to various modern art movements of the 20th century than any other single category of kitchen collecting. Think Alexander Calder and his mobiles and stabiles! Think Jean Tinguely and his "junk" sculpture! Think Marcel Duchamp and his kinetic sculpture! Think David Smith and his gigantic welded steel sculptures! If you like egg grading scales, you must look at books of these artists' work; you'll be amazed.

• • •

When I was a child ... in Toledo, Ohio, we had chickens and nice eggs from them (although the rooster always attacked my mother), but we still went to a woman who sold eggs near my grade school, Glann School. I recall going around back to the cellar entrance, where she sat in a very dark little room (where I can now figure she was candling eggs as well as weighing them), and I recall shelves, and paper egg boxes. We never kept our eggs in the refrigerator; it wasn't necessary because they were so fresh and the happy chickens were bug-eating free-range.

10 Favorite Egg Grading Scales

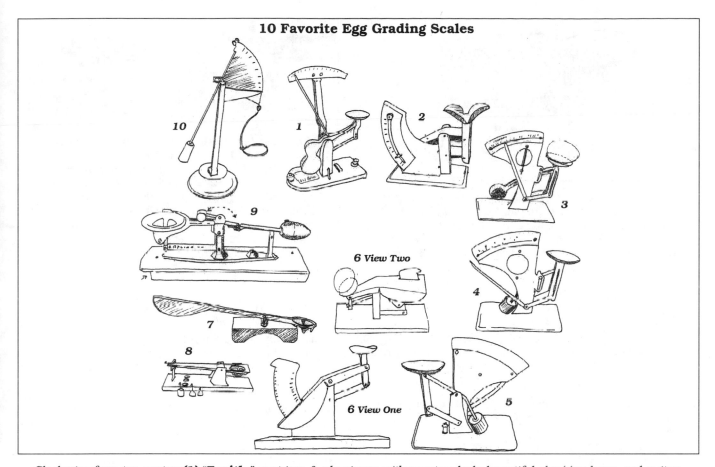

Clockwise from top center: **(1) "Zenith,"** *cast iron & aluminum with spectacularly beautiful sky blue base, red guitar-shaped weight, and silvery aluminum dial and egg pan. 8"H. The knobby things at both ends are rubber bumper stops.* **$65+**; **(2) Brower,** *which could be called the "Brower Flower" for the petal-like egg cup which could hold eggs from the smallest chicken to large turkey eggs. Pale green stamped sheet metal. (See also V 78).* **$65+** *depending on condition.* **(3)** *The* **"Mascot"** *with the "yo-yo" weight. Note the cut porthole & its cotterpin balance – just what the Jiffy-Way has. Black-painted stamped sheet metal base & frame, aluminum pan, 6-1/2"H x 6"L x 2-3/4"W.* **$20+**; **(4) "Mascot"** *with the cylindrical weight like the Oakes, possibly a bit older than the yo-yo.* **$25+**. *(Note: Others have been seen, virtually identical, called the "Oakes 'Premiere.").* And wait 'til you find a "Mascot" with the skeletal sheet metal frame [not shown], marked on the dial "Prospectus Mfg., Co., Minneapolis, Minn." Whoo-wheee. It would be $100+;* **(5)** *the* **"Oakes** *Sanitized Equipment for every poultry need," Oakes Mfg., Co., Tipton, IN, seen from the back so you can see how the weight works. Note that it does not have the cotter pin balance & porthole. Same balance weight as (4), black-painted sheet metal, aluminum egg pan, 5-1/2"H x 6-1/4"L x 3-1/2"W,* **$30+**, *one painted red, with four bright colors demarking the weight zones, just under the dial band, is newer, but still probably pre-1950s.* **$25+** *(I've seen another with just red paint, no multi-color – very attractive);* **(6)** *View I: This is a peculiar scale, called the* **"Unique,"** *probably because of the fact the dial is what moves up and down through a slot in the frame. View II: Specialty Mfg., Co., St. Paul, MN [Note: Another seems to have been made by the Steel Edge Stamping & Retinning Co., Boston, MA, probably as a result of a licensing deal or company takeover? And a red-painted one is marked the "National Egg Grading Scale.] 6"H x 7-1/2"L x 2-3/4"W, prob. 1940s+,* **$18+**; **(7)** *The* **"Oakes No. 555,"** *which is completely different. Doesn't look like it would work, but if you set it up on a shelf so the half-oval balance can work freely, it does. Red-painted galvanized cast metal base, galvanized steel arm, only 1-3/4"H x 11-1/2"L – just right for a narrow shelf at eye level. 20th C.* **$15+**, *with original box,* **$30**; **(8)** *The* **"White Line Grader,"** *green-painted stamped sheet metal & wood, White Mfg. Co., Gardena, CA, pat'd. July 25, 1922. It has three lead weights of varying sizes, which came in cutout depressions in the wooden base, and also supposed to have three copper discs like washers which could be added to a weight before hooking onto the end of the balance beam-arm.* **$75+**; *slightly older ones, red-painted sheet metal, never had the X-cutout basket suspended in the wide end of the balance arm, but had a wire basket instead. It was called the "Gilt Edge." Pat'd. in 1918, #125181, by O.C. White. Very desirable, particularly with original box and paper label on bottom, and all parts & weights.* **$85+**; **(9)** *The* **"Magic Egg Scale,"** *Reliable Mfg. Co., Los Angeles, CA, cast metal, aluminum, and lead-like heavy weight, metal base, very, very Art Deco, and wow! – that ovoid weight with its own adjustment. The weight at the fulcrum, where I've drawn the arrow arc, can be moved to either side of the fulcrum. 3-1/2"H x 8-1/2"L, 1930s. [Note: A less complicated one is simply called "The Reliable," and "Poltriquip Ltd., Los Angeles," and some have an ID plate reading "Reliable Egg Scale – See Weight Chart – Reliable Mfg. Division of James Mfg. Co., Log Angeles, Calif., USA."]* **$50+**. **(10)** *Unbelievably beautiful upright pendulum scale, which I drew from a photo on the scales-and-weights Web site. It is marked only "egg grader," and the cast metal and the wonderful flag-like pendulum are painted dark blue. I love it! About 9"H, English, probably late 19th or early 20th C.* **$250+**

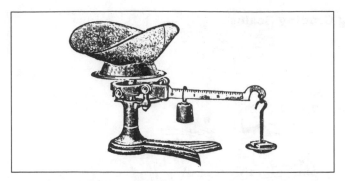

V-56. Spice scale, *or candy, grocers' or counter scale. At any rate, an unequal arm balance-scale with a single beam. Black enameled cast iron with gold pin-striping, brass beam, cast iron weights and poise (the movable weight along the beam), and choice of brass or tin scoop (pan). Note the scoop pan in the picture has a high flared foot; the thing looks almost like a fancy hat. Round plate upon which the scoop sits is 8" diam.; scoop is 18"L x 8-1/4"W. Mfd. by Fairbanks – a high quality scale, & the price in the 1910 Norvell-Shapleigh catalog reflects that: $15.50 with the brass pan; a buck & a half less for tin.* **$150+**

Scale, egg grading, cast iron weight & balance painted red, cast iron base painted sky blue, aluminum egg pan & scale, brass pointer, very sculptural & aerospacey, "Zenith Egg Grader, #1002," also marked "1-F," Earlyville, NY, 8"H, early 20th C. .... **$65+**

Scale, egg grading, brass with lead weights movable along the balance arm, mounted to oblong wooden base, "P.D.S. Pool Grader, Australia" on a rectangular celluloid ID plate. 3-1/4"H x 11-1/2"L, early 20th C. .... **$300+**

Scale, egg grading, black painted sheet metal, "Mascot," American, one with yo-yo weight, 6-1/2"H, c. 1930s-40s. .... **$20+**

Scale, egg grading, metal, "Val-A," American, 20th C. .... **$20+**

Scale, egg grading, metal, "Montgomery Ward," American, c.1900. .... **$18+**

Scale, egg grading, metal, made in Toledo, OH, 20th C, could this be Toledo Scale Co.? **$15**

Scale, egg grading, painted sheet metal, red, green & white, "Jiffy-Way," "World's Largest Manufacturers

V-57. Counter scale. *Japanned cast iron, bronze pinstriping, one type of so-called **"fishtail" base**, tin scoop pan, single beam, 25-pound capacity. Possibly a "Howe" scale; offered in A. Pick catalog, 1909. The price then was only $3.60.* **$125+**

V-58 Counter scales, *arm balance scales with single beam.* **(L)** *"Little Detective Pattern," probably Fairbanks, black japanned cast iron with brass beam. Tin scoop 12" x 6-3/4". Capacity 25 pounds. Norvell-Shapleigh 1910 catalog.* **(R)** *Painted and striped cast iron columnar base, capacity to 36 pounds, available with tin or brass scoop for the round plate. Available through, and possibly manufactured by, the John Van Range Co., Cincinnati, 1914.* **$175+**

of Egg Scales," Owatonna, MN, 5-3/4"H x 7-1/8"L, pat'd. 1940 & still being made. • This is by far the most commonly found egg grading scale. It is a spring balance scale like many postal scales. Indeed, many egg grading scales are like postal scales, and at least one, in England, was made two ways, with a dial for weighing letters, and one for eggs. In the Jiffy-Way, the weight of the egg depresses a spring, which makes a pointer move to the calibration mark. New they cost about $18.00; hard to tell if red is more popular or valuable than green. Old Jiffys, if you can recognize them, don't bring much more than new. .... **$15+**

Scale, egg grading, polished metal, mounted on wooden board, has clip to hold egg, no mark, 20th C. . **$65+**

Scale, egg grading, sheet metal base with spun brass egg cup, very simple modern frame, thumb screw adjustment, beautiful engraving of numbers on the scale, no marks, 9-7/8"H, 20th C. This is art, not just an egg scale. .... **$100+**

Scale, egg grading, stamped aluminum, the fulcrum emits a wonderfully soft, slithery sound as the egg is weighed, "Acme Egg Grading Scale," Specialty Mfg.

V-59. "Union scales," *platform countertop, with single beam and slotted cast iron weights that slip over hanging weight rod. Painted and decorated cast iron, with pieced scoop (tin? brass?). Capacity from 1/2 ounce to 240 pounds. Jaburg catalog, 1908. The original cost was only $4.00, which seems absolutely impossible now.* **$100+**

V-60. John Wanamaker's Candy Department, *"from a photograph – showing four National Cash Registers in use,"* but also a unequal arm candy scale in foreground. From ad in Century, c.1880.

Co., St. Paul, MN, 4 1/2"H x 10-1/2"L x 3-1/2"W, pat'd. June 24, 1924. • Some egg grading scales, like this one, are very like some postal scales, and are classed as pendulum balances. This one is fairly common, but it's a real classic. .... **$15+**
Scale, egg grading, tin box mounted to wooden base that's painted green, cup for egg, directions printed on it: "It is necessary that this scale is set level to

V-61. Cake scale, or platform scale with dial. Decorated cast iron, with oblong marble platform. Wonderful fluted columns. It came in three sizes: capacity 5 pounds, measured in 1/2 ounce increments; capacity 10 pounds, measured by 1 ounce; and capacity 20 pounds, by 2 ounces. Mfd. by John Chatillon & Sons, NYC; sold through Jaburg, 1908 catalog. **$175+**

V-62 Cake scale, of equal balance "trip" type. Japanned and decorated cast iron with 8" x 10" cool marble plate for the cake (or fudge?) being weighed. Jaburg, 1908. **$135+**

V-63. Scale, called a *"ball scale"* by Thomas Mills & Bro., in 1930 catalog. It is impossible to read the name plate because it wasn't engraved as real words, but it may have been made by Mills – and from the looks of it, long before 1930. Ornate cast iron with ball-shaped poises. Nickel-plated brass scoop. It could also be had with a plate (or platform) instead of a scoop. Capacity five pounds by quarter ounces. 1930 price with scoop was relatively high: $22.00. **$175+**

weigh correctly. Clamp furnished is used when definite grade is desired. Place clamp on dial at grade wanted, and it will act as a stop to indicate for any ... [weight]. This speeds up grading." "Reliable, Automatic Dial Egg Scale," Reliable Incubator & Brooder Co., Quincy, IL, 13"L, early 20th C. .... **$50+**
Scale, egg grading & tester – See: Egg tester & scale
Scales, equal arm balance type sometimes referred to as a "balance scale," for countertop, cast iron base with hexagonal pyramid flanked by lyre shapes, pieced tin pan with fixed ring base, full set of 7 cast iron weights, in *F. A. Walker catalog,* American or import (?), about 6"H excluding pan, c.1880s. • A countertop equal arm balance scale has a base that supports a sort of seesaw beam, each end of which has a platform. On one platform (or four-"fingered" support) goes the pan with the goods; on the other goes a weight or selection of

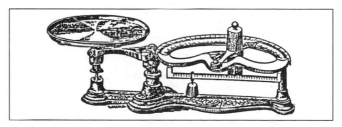

V-64. Counter scale, a *"double graduated"* 'arc scale' that combines with Utility, both Beauty, and Convenience. Its primary object is to save the annoyance and expense [of] the loss of weights. It works [like] ordinary counter Scales, but in lieu of the plate for the ... weights, has a Graduated Arc, with a **Permanently Attached Weight,** through which an Index is passed, which [moves] over the Arc and denotes with great accuracy the weight of the commodity in the opposite dish. The scale is peculiarly adapted to Druggists, by having upon the Arc, a scale of Apothecaries' weights along with the ordinary Avoirdupois scale ... with an outer and inner index. ... The scale is also manufactured for Grocers, Tea Dealers & Confectioners." Buckelew & Waterman, Philadelphia, c.1840s-60s. **$350+**

weights in pounds & ounces, until the two platforms balance. This type is also sometimes called a **platform scale**, a **country store scale**, a **countertop scale**, or (if it's small enough) a **candy scale**. It should not be called simply a "balance scale" because all scales are balances – they are equal arm balances; unequal arm balances; spring balances (either platform or hanging); and pendulum balances. See the technical leaflet *"Scales and Weighing Devices"* that Albert R. Eaches wrote for the American Association for State and Local History... **$150+**

Scale, equal arm balance, countertop for candy, cast iron with brass pan, set of cast iron weights, "Dayton Style No. 166," (probably Dayton Standard Scale Co., Dayton, OH), late 19th C. • Most candy scales are of the class called equal arm balances. They have a calibrated beam with arms of equal length, one end supporting a pan or scoop or platform for the thing being weighed, and a platform on which to pile weights that will counterbalance exactly that which is being weighed. Instead of being suspended from a hook, the calibrated beam is, in effect, suspended on its fulcrum, like a teeter-totter. When you are trying to remember just what kind of scale is a candy scale, visualize eating candy while playing on a seesaw. .... **$75+**

Scale, equal arm balance for candy, cast iron, painted black, with gold pinstriping, with brass pan, weights missing, no mark but date, 1915. • So-called candy scales, or countertop equal arm balances, are the most collectible scales at this time, because of the decoration & form of the cast iron part, and the presence of a polished brass or interesting pieced tin pan or scoops. .... **$125+**

Scale, equal balance arm scale of unusual type, for candy or confectioners, cast iron stepped base, flat pan at one end, interesting half-circle horizontal graduated arc with a sliding weight on bar below arc, Buckelew & Waterman, Philadelphia, prior to 1867, but I can't find patent. • This one is an equal balance arm scale, but the platform or pan for what is being weighed is balanced by a permanent weight, which causes a pointer to show weight on a calibrated arc. In addition, below this arc is a small, calibrated beam with a small sliding poise, which is used to weigh the bottle or jar or small container that is to be filled. This prior weighing automatically adjusts the pointer on the arc. It really is quite ingenious, but I'm glad we don't have to use them at salad bars! $275+ • The 1867 advertisement for this scale states that, "this novel invention combines

V-66. Counter scale, *equal arm balance with plate, weights and scoop. Black japanned cast iron with fancy lyre-like Federal-inspired design. Weights 1/2 ounce to 4 pounds. This illustration from the F. A. Walker catalog, c.1890s. An identical linecut appeared in the 1875 Stuart, Peterson & Co.'s manufacturer's catalog, so they may have made them. Either this was the most popular style of scale at the turn of the century and several firms made them, or the artists doing the linecuts for catalogs all drew the same one just a bit different.* **$150+**

with Utility, both Beauty, and Convenience. Its primary object is to save the annoyance and expense attendant upon the loss of weights. It works upon knife heads, as in ordinary Counter Scales, but in lieu of the plate for the reception of weights, has a graduated Arc, with a Permanently Attached Weight, through which an Index [pointer] is passed, which latter, moving over the Graduated Arc, denotes with great accuracy the commodity in the opposite dish [on the opposite platform]."

Scale, equal arm balance, countertop or "grocery" scales, green painted cast iron, brass scoop pan, Fairbanks, 11"L x 6-1/2"H, dated 1877.......... **$75+**

Scale, equal arm balance scale, countertop – sometimes called a country store scale, black finished cast iron with red & gold trim, tin pan, brass beam, American, late 19th C. .... **$175+**

Scale, equal arm balance type, countertop, red painted cast iron base, tin pan, with 1 lb. & 2 lb. weights, very handsome, Southwark Hardware Co., Philadelphia, PA, late 19th C. .... **$175+**

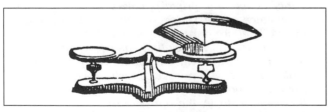

V-65. Counter scale, *equal arm balance type. Cast iron, meant to be used with weights piled on plate at left. The picture, of an "improved weighing balance," comes from the 1854 The American Home Cook Book, which had many illustrations of recommended kitchen equipment.* **$135+**

V-67. "French scales," *equal arm balance, with brass plate and index pointer. Capacity 4 and 5 kilograms. Imported from France, and sold by Duparquet, Huot & Moneuse, NYC, through their 1904-1910 catalog.* **$150+**

❖ NOTES ❖

Scales of the **hanging spring balance** or **hook balance type** are probably the most commonly found scales at flea markets and antique malls. This is because so many of them, in a range of sizes, were used in Europe, Great Britain and North America – by grocers, butchers, farmers, feed stores, seed stores and housewives, and because they are so well made that a century or a century and a half later, they just keep on going! Those weighing up to 12 pounds are the commonest household size; up to 24 pounds worked for families and small tradesmen. Those with 50-pound capacities are commercial or at least for business use. "Landers, Frary & Clark" is the most common brand name scale found today in the U.S. "Salter's" is the commonest in England; "Chatillon" is a French name, but it's an American scale. Other makers include "Royal"; "Eagle Warranted"; and "Excelsior," mfd. by Sargent & Co. All those in a certain weight capacity group are pretty much worth the same thing, unless there is something unusual about the brass face – fancy design or collectible advertising.

• • •

Hanging spring balance scales use a spring, but the weight hangs off the spring (with a hook) rather than being placed on top of it to depress it, as in a dial scale. The face or dial of the scale, on which the pointer registers the weight, is usually long and rectangular and often brass, but it can be round, like a dial scale's face. There has to be a hanging ring at top, so the scale can be hung near where it's to be used. From the bottom comes a ring & hook, from which is hung the food to be weighed. A complete set might also have a round platform with a fixed bail handle to hang off the hook (some of these have porcelainized platforms and nickeled brass frames & bails), or a pieced tin pan with chains to hang off the hook.

In Albert R. Eaches' Technical Leaflet #59, "Scales and Weighing Devices," he writes: "A spring balance is a weighing device which utilizes the physical distortion of a piece of metal." In this case it's a steel spring, inside the cylindrical scale body, that is "distorted" or pulled to a looser spiral by what is hung from it, causing a little pointer to move on the calibrated face.

Asher & Adams' *Pictorial Album of American Industry*, published in 1876 as a gala advertisement and history for the U. S. Centennial, has a piece on the New York scale manufacturer Thomas Morton, in which they surveyed the "origin" of [hanging] spring balances, also called hook balance scales. "Since the invention, nearly half a century ago, of the spring balance by one George Salters, of West Bromwich, England, we suppose no article of a mechanical nature in itself has obtained so universal a practical character as this. Scarcely a butcher or grocer in any country ... but finds its utility second only to his knife and hatchet. ... When spring balances were first introduced in America our people had but little confidence in them. The principle of springs was deemed unreliable, but they soon began to work their way forward. As soon as their real value was known, competitors in the field ... sprang up with great rapidity, and the market was flooded with unreliable scales and balances. ... In 1842, in conjunction with Mr. A. A. Bremner, Mr. Thomas Morton introduced to the American public the first domestic made spring balance, the construction of which was based upon Salter's method. This was a hook balance scale to weigh up to 24 lbs. From that day to this the principle [of these scales] has remained intact, though the number of varieties of spring scales now made by Mr. Morton amounts to more than 150, rising from balances that will weigh a ten cent stamp – which, by the way, weighs only a quarter of a dram – up to heavy instruments capable of weighing accurately 2,000 lbs. at a time. ... Mr. Morton's goods rank with the best. None but the very best iron, steel and brass that can be bought are used in his manufacturers. ... As a striking evidence of their excellence it might be remarked that one of the Morton & Bremner spring scales has been in use in the Boston market for the last twenty years, and has never faltered or required any repairs whatever." One of the scales pictured with the above is a jockey chair, a very elegant armchair without legs, hanging from a large round dial decorated with an eagle and the date 1866 – what a great, big bathroom accessory!

Scale, hanging spring balance, oblong brass face, 12 pound, "Landers, Frary & Clark," New Britain, CT, mid to late 19th C. .... **$40+**

Scale, hanging spring balance, for ice, iron with brass face, (Landers, Frary & Clark, as well as Wilson Mfg. Co., made ice scales of this type), American, c.1900.. **$40+**

Scale, hanging spring balance, brass face, iron, "Frary's Improved Balance #2," mfd. by L, F & C, 50 lb. capacity, late 19th C. .... **$45+**

V-68. Counter scales, *equal arm balance scales with the lyre base, almost identical to the Stuart, Peterson/Walker scale. (T-L) "Hatch Pattern Even Balance" from the 1910 Norvell-Shapleigh Hardware Co. catalog. "a low priced scale for family use. 8-pound capacity, japanned cast iron frame 12-1/2"L, tin scoop is 16-3/4"L x 9-1/4"W. Original price $4.20. (B-R) "Iron Bearing Bakehouse Scales," cast iron. With the weights, in the 1908 Jaburg catalog, this was only $2.75. Hard to believe. – H. G. Wells, where are you when we need you!* **$150-$250+**

V-69. Counter scales. *Japanned and decorated cast iron frame, seamless stamped brass scoop 13"L x 6"W, rubber tips on the "fork" that holds the scoop.* Thomas Mills *catalog, 1930.* **$155+**

Scale, hanging spring balance, brass & iron, "Chatillon," NYC, NY, 8"L x 1-3/8"W, 25 lb. capacity, pat'd. Dec. 10, 1867, Jan. 6, 1891, Jan. 26, 1892. ... **$45+**

Scale, hanging spring balance, cast steel, brass base & iron pan, "Class Two, Salters Improved Family Scale, No. 50," Silvers Patent, English, 14"H, late 19th C. .... **$125+**

Scale, hanging spring balance, iron ring, iron hook, brass face engraved with measurements, "Salter's Improved Spring Balance," mfd. by Salter & Co., West Midlands, England, 50 lb. capacity, 2nd to 3rd quarter 19th C (?). • "Salter's improved Spring Balance. – A very neat form of the instrument [known as the spring steelyard] has been recently brought before the public by Mr. Salter, under the name of the Improved Spring Balance. The spring is contained in the upper half of a cylinder behind the brass plate forming the face of the instrument; and the rod is fixed to the lower extremity of the spring, which is consequently extended, instead of being compressed,

V-70. Counter scales, *also called* **even balance trip** *scales. Cast iron are enameled or japanned, and decorated, seamless brass scoops.* **(T-L)** *described as being "without tare beam," which means that you could not adjust it to take the weight of the commodity's container into account when weighing for contents. It came in four sizes.* **(B-R)** *is a tare beam, and came in three sizes. Both from the 1908 Jaburg catalog for professional confectioners and bakers.* **$135+**

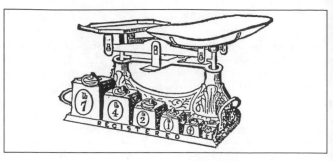

V-71. Scale, or "weighing machine." *The "Registered" style, in three sizes, 1/4 ounce to 14 pound capacity; 1/4 ounce to 7 pound capacity; and 1 ounce to 4 pound. Cast iron, ornate, japanned base, octagonal scale plate, slightly dished pan.* Harrod's Stores *catalog, London, 1895.* **$250+**

by the application of the weight. The divisions, each indicating half a pound, are engraved upon the face of the brass plate, and are pointed out by an index attached to the rod." Captain Henry Kater, *The Cabinet Cyclopaedia.* Conducted by the Rev. Dionysius Lardner. Volume on Natural Philosophy. Mechanics. London: Longman, Rees, Orme, Brown, & Green, 1830. The engraving in the book looks exactly like the Salter's scales so often seen. It should be noted that the hook is forged iron; on later examples, the hook would be a heavy drawn wire, cut into a point and bent. (By the way, Salters made an egg scale unlike almost any other; it looks sort of like the family scale in V-84, but with an eggcup on top! It would be worth several hundred dollars, I believe.) .... **$70+**

Scale, hanging spring balance, iron with brass face, "Peck's," (Peck, Stow & Wilcox, CT), c.1890-1910... **$45+**

Scale, hanging spring balance, iron with large crested brass face, decorated with checkerboard design top and bottom, legend reads "COW CHOW MAKES MORE MILK AT LESS COST, Don't guess – Use this Purina Milk Scale," Ralston Purina, (coincidentally there was a Ralston Scale Co.), American, face is 10-1/2"L by an unusually wide 4-1/2", weighs to 30 lbs, 20th C. Who wouldn't want one of these?... **$450+**

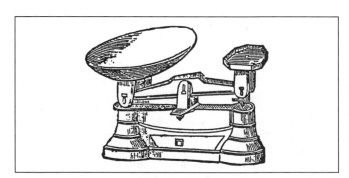

V-72. Scale, *or "weighing machine." Called "Family" style in England, although an American "Family" style scale was probably always a dial scale like those in V-84, -85, -86. Very simple cast iron frame, octagonal weight plate. Same three capacities as the "Registered" in V-71. Also from Harrod's, 1895 catalog.* **$135+**

V-73. Scale, *with weights arrayed along front of cast iron frame. "As one of the great elements of success in cooking is preciseness in the proportions of ingredients, the cook should never be without a good pair of scales, and she should keep them in thorough order. In delicate dishes an unequal proportion of an article inserted only to impart a certain flavour, will ruin the dish. The necessity as well as use of scales is therefore obvious." Picture and quote from* Warne's Model Cookery and Housekeeping Book, *compiled by Mary Jewry. London: 1868. (***Lookalike alarm** – *an "antique style" scale with brass scoop, finished in black, with imperial brass weight, is being sold for use and decoration today as the "Staffordshire scale" in Great Britain.)* **$125+**

Scale, hanging spring balance, green painted steel case, "Viking #8910," Hanson Scale Co., 13"L, 100 lb. capacity, 20th C. .... **$60+**

Scale, hanging spring balance, red, black & green finished iron, with white enamel face, 2 pointers, marked "Hanson Dairy" (not the name of a particular dairy, but a "dairy scale" by Hanson Scale Co.), American, 6-3/4" diam. face. .... **$150+**

Scale, hanging spring balance, brass plate, steel & iron, "Excelsior Improved Spring Balance," mfd. by Sargent & Co., American, about 6"L, 25 lb. capacity, late 19th or early 20th C. .... **$65+**

Scale, spring, also called a dial scale, a kitchen scale, or a family scale, this one the boxy kind with pan or platform on top, meant for kitchen or household use, green painted iron, red & white enameled face, red pointer, tin pan, "American Family Scales," turn-of-century to 1920s.. **$45+**

Scale, spring, for kitchen or household use, cast iron & stamped sheet iron, "Simmons Hardware Co.," 20th C. Crossover Simmons collectors. .... **$75+**

V-74. Scale scoop, *for bakehouse scales. Heavy tin, pieced construction, footed. Came in three sizes: medium, large and extra large. 1908 Jaburg supply catalog.* **$15+**

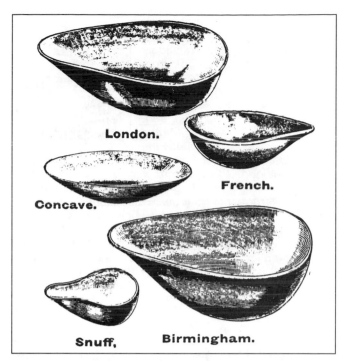

V-75. Scale pans or scoops. *All obviously unseamed (which means stamped) and probably brass. The five styles – London, Birmingham, French, Concave, and Snuff – were all offered in the 1914 Henry Rogers, Wolverhampton, England, catalog. Collectors will pay extra for brass pans, even if originally the scale had a tin pan, or if the brass pan was nickeled.* **$15+**

Scale, spring, kitchen balance with large brass dial face, "Arlosa Coffee," 20 lb. capacity, early 20th C. Advertising piece. .... **$100+**

Scale, spring, kitchen or family scale, the boxy base with a large dial face on front, with the weight pan or forked support (almost like an upraised hand with fingers outspread) that holds a scoop or pan on top, sheet iron, partly painted, "Winchester," turn-of-century. You've got competition from Winchester collectors. ...... **$275+**

Scale, spring, kitchen or household type, iron base, "Cat Tail," sold through *Sears & Roebuck,* American, c.1890-1910.. **$35**

V-76. Trade card, *for Fairbanks scales, NYC. Chromolithograph card from 1880s, depicting the showroom, with several gents looking over various sizes and types. For the card:* **$15+**

V-77. Weights, *of several types.* **(L)** *Weights, for bakehouse scales. Five materials, available singly or in sets of 8 or 9, from 1/2 ounce to 4 pounds or 1/4 ounce to 4 pounds. The five were nickel-plated brass, solid brass, cased brass, zinc, or cast iron. 1908 Jaburg catalog. Value mostly for sets of matching*

weights, even if the sets are incomplete. Per weight, with maybe a bit added for solid brass weights: **$2-$10;** **(L-M)** *"Nest of Brass French Weights" in wooden box, in kilograms.* **(R-M)** *"Nest of Iron American Weights," stacked, 1 ounce to 8 pounds. Duparquet, Huot & Moneuse, c.1904-1910. A full set of 10 French ones would be worth between* **$40-$100.** *For an iron set:* **$40-$100+.** *Far* **(R)** *Bell weight, in 10 sizes, from 1/4 ounce to 7 pounds (skips 5, 6 pounds). All in Henry Rogers, Wolverhampton, England, 1914 catalog. Individual bell weights:* **$35-$100+**

Scale, spring, metal with white face, red pointer, "Pelouze," 12"H x 6-1/2" diam. dial, 20th C. ... **$35+**

Scale, spring balance, cast iron 3-legged frame, round cast iron faceplate, very finely cast with calibrations, weighing platform on top, "Novelty Scale," "Turnbull's Patent," American, 7-3/4"H, 12 lb. capacity, pat'd. July 24, 1877. Just fabulous; this is the kind of neat cast iron piece that appeals to "iron" collectors, who dip in and out of many specialty fields of collecting – from garden to stable, hardware to kitchen, still banks to doorstops. .... **$250+**

Scale, spring balance, family type, very graceful minimalist cast iron base, round deeply engraved brass face, beautifully formed shallow bowl is the attached weighing pan, "Salters Family Scale, No. 50, Class II Improved," about 13"H, weighs to 15 lbs., late 19th or very early 20th C. Pure sculpture............... **$135**

V-78. Egg grading scale. *Brower Mfg. Co., Quincy, IL, light green-painted sheet metal, flower-like egg pan would hold small chicken eggs up to large turkey eggs. 6-1/2"H, American, 20th C. Photo courtesy Ebay seller oldseahag4911; collection now of Kathy L. Smith.* **$50-$100+**

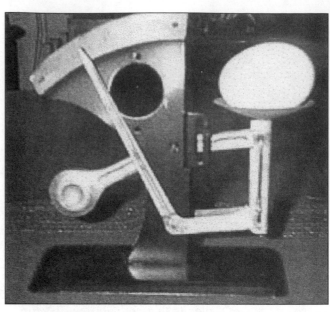

V-79. Egg grading scale. *"Mascot" with yo-yo weight. Black painted sheet metal, aluminum egg pan. Photo courtesy Marge & Bud Streed, Moose Lake, MN.* **$20+**

Scale, spring balance, family type, fancy cast iron, "Sutler #49," 12-1/2"H, c.1890s.................... **$130+**

Scale, spring balance, countertop (despite brand name this is not the standard old fashioned "family" style scale), heavy sheet iron, finished black, very fancy dial plate, legs, flat platform, "Novelty Family Scale," sold by Montgomery Ward, Chicago, IL, late 19th C. .... **$65+**

Scale, spring balance, family or dial type, painted sheet metal, square base, round dial, square flat platform, American Family Scales, 9-3/4"H x 6" square, pat'd. 1898, mfd. for years. Condition of paint is important here; these rusted easily, so inspect for repainting over rough, bumpy rust areas. .... **$35+**

Scale, spring balance, family scale type, sheet metal painted black with fancy trim, brass dial, tin pan, "Columbia," Landers, Frary & Clark, 24 lb. capacity, c.1890s-1910. .... **$45+**

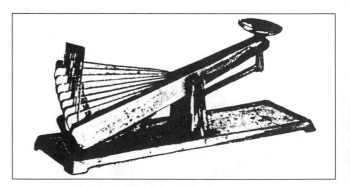

V-80. Egg grading scale. *"Acme Egg Grading Scale," mfd. by Specialty Mfg. Co., St. Paul, MN, aluminum. 4-1/2"H x 10-1/2"L x 3-1/2"W, pat'd. June 24, 1924. This one, to me, is very desirable aesthetically and aurally. The sound of those weight blades clicking into place until balance is reached! Oh me!* **$18+**

V-81. Egg grading scale. *The most commonly found kind – mainly because it's been made continuously since being patented in 1940. "Jiffy-Way," green or red painted heavy sheet metal, 5-3/4"H x 7-1/8"L. Patent #2205917. Jiffy-Way Inc., Owatonna, MN – "World's largest manufacturers of egg scales." 1-1/2 ounces to 2-1/2 ounces.* **$15+**

Scale, spring balance, family type, slanted dial, stamped steel body enameled blue with pin striping, tin scoop fits on claw, "Triner Perfection," mfd. by Allsteel Scale Co., Inc., NYC, 24 lb. capacity, 10"H x 6"W, pat'd. May 1, 1906. Interesting looking. .. **$35+**

Scales, spring balance, or dial scale, red painted cast iron base, brass pan & glass dial face, "Eureka," style C, 18"H x 15", pat'd. Oct. 5, 1869. • These spring balance scales have a base below the weighing platform or pan, and a large clock-like dial on the side of the base with an index pointer that indicates the weight. These usually have a little fine tuning wheel for resetting zero.......................... **$225+**

Scale pan, pieced tin, oval with its own foot ring attached to the flat platform of balance scale, American (?), 4" deep x 14-1/8"L x 8"W, late 19th or early 20th C. • Hard to evaluate because it is part of something else & might be worth a lot to someone trying to set up a spring balance scale. .... **$15+**

Scale, spring with beam, countertop, cast iron, brass scoop, 2 iron weights, includes scoop, 20th C. **$75+**

❖ NOTES ❖

Steelyard scales, from the class of scales known as **unequal arm balances**, are the oldest type of scale, and examples from many parts of the world are known. It consists of a long flattened beam suspended from a hanger hook attached close to the thicker, shorter arm of the beam. There is a hanger hook underneath the short arm, from which the thing to be weighed is hung. The long arm of the beam is calibrated, in pounds or ounces, or metric units, and has on it a weight called a poise, which can be slid along the long arm to balance whatever is hung from the hook at the other end. The poise may be cast iron and somewhat decorative, and a steelyard scale might have several different poises. According to Albert R. Eaches, who wrote the invaluable Technical Leaflet #59, *"Scales and Weighing*

Devices," for the Association of State and Local History, these unequal arm balance scales got the name steelyards "when steel was first imported into England." He also explains that another type of unequal arm balance scale very like a steelyard, and sometimes even called a steelyard, should actually be called a weighmasters beam scale. These can be identified by the rather large swooping hooked end (looks almost like an antique ice-skating blade) of the short arm of the beam, and by two sets of calibration and two "separate poises to correspond" to these calibrations.

Scale, steelyard, or stillyard type, wrought iron, long rod with weight, hook at other end for the goods, nice detailing. When not in use, steelyard scales tend to look like a pile of iron bars & hooks. They only really come to life when they are hanging up & have the movable poise placed so it can balance the weight of the end with the hook or hooks, or when actually weighing something. For display, some scale collectors hang a heavy weight from the hook meant for the goods. According to Carl W. Drepperd, a small steelyard scale is called a **steel foot**. American, 25"L, 18th C. .... **$75+**

Scale, steelyard, iron & brass, "Detector," American, 23"L, late 19th or early 20th C. .... **$35+**

Scale, steelyard, iron, with an iron weight that has a raised star design cast on it, American, 25 lb. capacity, late 19th C. .... **$25+**

❖ NOTES ❖

Steelyard caveat emptor – Being imported now from Turkey are a steelyard scale with single hanging dished pan, and an equal balance scale with two pans hanging

V-82. Egg grading scale. *Another Brower, painted sheet metal, leveling device is a small steel ball that rolls freely within a riveted area visible through plastic window, works something like a carpenter's level. 5-5/8"H x 8-1/4"L x 3-3/8"W, Quincy, IL, 20th C. Photo & descriptive details courtesy of Jennifer Hamilton (Ebayer: jenabee).* **$22+**

from the beam, which is suspended by a chain and hook. All the pans are hung with three chains and are made of copper and iron. Three sizes of each are being imported: of the first type, a 21"H with 8" pan; a 24"H with 10" pan; and a 27"H with 12" pan, ranging from $60 to $125.50 in price. Of the second type, a 17"H with two 5" pans; a 20"H with 8" pans, and a 27"H with 10" pans, ranging from $67.50 to $142.50 each. The ads of one of the two import companies never mention country of origin and explain, "Some items have minor dents and old repairs that do not reduce their value." This company also sells various straight-sided pots, round-bottom pots, waisted pots with bails, flared-side shallow pans with covers (all preceding have 2 handles); also 3 sizes of copper "egg pans" with round cups, also plates, bowls, frying pans and long-handled pans with braces. In many sizes. One company sells by the piece; the one that mentions "Turkey" sells by weight.

Scoop, adjustable, tin, has lever you push to shove back plate out, smooth-working, American (?), 10"L x 4"W, 19th C. .... **$35+**

Scoop, adjustable, tin, inventor must have been still working on this one when he quit. You have to sort of wriggle the back plate out with your fingers, like a back plate in a really old style filing cabinet drawer. No marks, American (?), 13-1/2"L x 4-7/8"W, 19th C. .... **$125+**

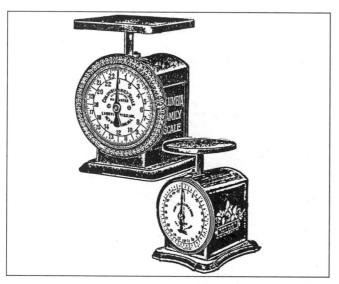

V-83. Family scales, also called **dial scales.** Both enameled and decorated sheet iron with flat platforms and round dials on front, all weigh to 24 pounds. **(T-L)** "Columbia", mfd. by Landers, Frary & Clark, New Britain, CT. In six models: black enamel; white enameled dial, square steel top; white enameled dial, steel top, tin scoop; brass plated scale; brass plated with white enameled dial and steel top; and the most desirable one – brass plated body, brass dial, brass scoop, steel top. Joseph Breck catalog, 1905. **(M)** "Favorite," mfd. by John Chatillon & Sons, pat'd. July 16 [?], 18--, "silver-plated" brass dial, "handsomely ornamented." 24-pound capacity. In 1924 D. J. Barry catalog. **(R)** Stamped sheet iron, white painted dial, 11"H with 8" diam., pan or tray attached on top, "The Daisy," maker unknown from the ad. **$35; $35+; $135+**

V-84. Family scale. Cast steel or iron with brass base and iron pan. "Class Two, Salters Improved Family Scale, No. 50," 14-pound capacity, about 14"H. English, late 19th C. Salters is one of three big names in scales, the others being Chatillon and Fairbanks. **$135+**

Scoop, apple butter, carved wood, all one piece, open D-handle, American, 4-1/2" x 11-1/2", late 19th C. .... **$125+**

Scoop, candy, a crude measure, pieced sheet brass, attached handle, small size, late 19th C. • Some of these were made by candy scale makers, & match the pieced sheet brass scale pans. .... **$25+**

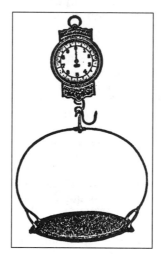

V-85. Hanging spring balance scale. Fancy japanned cast iron case with large white enameled dial, 7" diam., with graduations enameled in black. 13" diam. pan suspended from tinned bow & swivel. Overall 31"H. 10-pound capacity. Norvell-Shapleigh, 1910 catalog. **$100+**

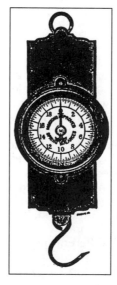

V-86. Hanging spring balance scale. This is the most commonly found type of old scale; at least one appears at every show and flea market. This one is iron with brass face to the spring-housing, steel spring, white-enameled dial in front. Mfd. by Morton & Bremner (formerly Thomas Morton), NYC. In Asher & Adams Pictorial Album of American Industry, 1876. **$50+**

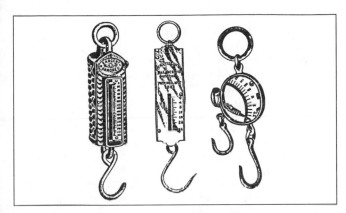

V-87. Hanging spring balance scales. (L) *"Sargent Armored," black japanned steel case for spring, nickeled brass dial on both sides, steel spring, tinned steel hook & ring, 9-1/2"H x 2-1/2"W, overall length 14", 200-pound capacity in 5-pound graduations. Norvell-Shapleigh Hardware Co., 1910 catalog.* **(M)** *"Chatillon's Balance No. 2", iron case with curved back and nickel-plated brass front; also available with flat back, and a much broader index pointer. 25-pound capacity by 8-ounce increments. D. J. Barry catalog, 1925.* **(R)** *Called a "German Crab" scale in the Norvell-Shapleigh catalog, which refers to the side hooks, because its capacity is 300 pounds, in 5-pound graduations – not the thing for weighing crabs. Spring steel frame 3-3/4" x 3-1/2", overall 10-1/2"L, polished brass demilune face with stamped lines & numbers, polished wrought steel hooks and ring.* **$45+**

Candy scoop, japanned tin, tapered sides, small with braced tubular handle, late 19th or early 20th C. .... **$12+**

Scoop, carved & stained wood, probably walnut, folk art piece with largish oblong bowl, the handle is a gorilla with a snake twisted around it, supposedly made by an elderly black sailor, coastal New Jersey, 9-1/8"L, mid 20th C. • I also bought a box with a sliding lid by the same man, a master carver with a sense of humor. Both pieces show a remarkable resemblance to some East African carvings. .... **$350+**

Scoop, carved wood, long bowl & longish handle, huge dry-wood or age check in wood is mended with tacked-on strap iron, bowl mended with waxed string – actually the two halves sewn together, American, 12"L, 19th C. This is a very collectible repaired piece. .... **$100+**

V-88. Spring balance scale, *and standard. Nickel-plated brass. Maker not shown, in catalog shot but probably Chatillon. Could be had with a double-faced dial, and the arched standard could be bought separately. Jaburg 1908 catalog.* **$200+**

Fig. 1.
—The Folding Family Scale.
Folded Flat Against the Wall.

Fig. 2.
—Scale Unfolded and Ready for Use.

V-89. Fold-away scale. *Called in the Metal Worker article about it a "folding family scale," but the term "family" is most usually associated with spring scales with platforms or pans above the dial. Ornamental cast iron bracket, brass pan, unequal arm balance type with poise and loose weights, 50-pound capacity by 1/2-ounce graduations. Mfd. by Folding Scale Co., Beloit, WI. "Heretofore persons having a family scale have been troubled by having no regular place for it that would not at times make it an inconvenience. This new device overcomes that difficulty, as the scale can be folded up against the wall or door to which it is attached. The Metal Worker, May 31, 1890.* **$250+**

V-90. Ancient steelyard scales. *Excuse the poor quality of the picture: it is adapted from a 1910 catalog with shadowy photographs, of a foundry in Naples, Italy, that specialized in reproductions of ancient bronzes found at Pompeii and Herculaneum. Cast bronze. Two have hanging pans, one has a hook. This type of scale has changed little in 2000 years; the weights have changed (see Figure V-91). In this lengthy catalog, the date the archaeological find was made, and measurements of the originals are given. These steelyards were found the 31st of July, 1888, at Pompeii.* **(L)** *45 cm. or about 17-3/4"L;* **(M)** *40 cm. or about 15-3/4"L;* **(R)** *50 cm. or about 19-3/4"L. They were available in 2 finishes: blackened cast bronze (Herculaneum) or verdigris or green (Pompei). Center figural* **weight** *for steelyard of ancient Pompeian type. Cast bronze, woman's bust, with waved hairstyle and draped bodice. It appears that a hook was cast on top of the heads – this one represents the weight of the scale at right – and hooked through a ring that hung from a chain fixed to the steelyard beam. The size is probably about 5-1/2" to 6"H. My drawing adapted from J. Chiurazzi & Fils-S. De Angelis & Fils catalog, 1910-11.*

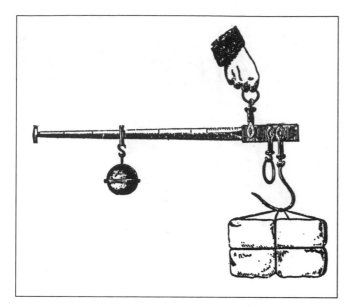

V-91. Steelyard scale. *The round moveable weight is at* **(L)**, *the package being weighed is at* **(R)**. *Illustration (taken from a schoolbook of 1905, entitled* Natural Philosophy), *explains that the steelyard scale, also known as the* **Roman balance**, *"has no great sensitiveness" and is based on the principle of a lever. The fulcrum is the pivot point on the beam below where the hand is holding the hanging ring. The arm or beam to the left of the fulcrum is "graduated into equal parts," and the weight is moved along the sharp edge of the arm until a position is found in which it just counterbalances the load. The weight of the lever itself is allowed for in the graduations. For this type of manufactured scale the value is much less than that for a comparably-sized hand-forged one.* **$45+**

Lookalike Alarm

Somebody is making cast aluminum streamlined scoops today. Lehman's Hardware & Appliances, Kidron, OH, offers 5 sizes in their *"Non-Electric Good Neighbor Amish Country" catalog.* • Old ones (of any type of scoop) will show damage to the lip of the scoop, the front edge that pushes against whatever is being measured out may be nicked, especially smoothed, even thinned out somewhat. I saw a picture of one in a circa 1900 magazine that was said to have measured "over two and a half tons" of coffee beans during the preceding year, and the long "lower lip" of the scoop had been worn down and shortened so much that essentially the scoop was a can with a handle at one end. **Alarm II:** There were nicely made & good-looking pieced brass scoops, very old-fashioned in design, being made in the 1980s by Brasscrafters, Syosset, NY, about 16-3/4"L. They are so well made that they could easily be mistaken as antiques. I don't know about any permanent marks. It is always a good idea to get on the mailing list of such catalog houses as Yield House (which specializes in the country look), and keep a clip file of info on new pieces. That's why I never turn down even a 1950s or 1960s magazine such as *Good Housekeeping* or *House Beautiful*; I search the back pages for small display ads showing items which are likely, just 20 or 30 years later, to be taken as antique. **Alarm III:** Furthermore, in the 1990s and into the 21st C., with the proliferation of dollar stores and cheap goods coming in from China by the ton, it will inevitably happen that you'll end up with a piece or two in your collection. Hey! What's the remedy? You gotta shop, shop, shop all the time; and shop doesn't mean buy ... just look.

V-92. Candy scoop. *Molded glass. From D. J. Barry 1924 catalog, but probably had been made for at least 30 years at that time.* **$45+**

Scoop, cast aluminum, fairly smooth, rounded handle, marked "Wagner Ware" on handle, 11-1/4"L x about 4-1/2" deep, c.1930s (?). ...... **$8+**

Scoop, cast iron, sharply truncated cylinder with longish handle, meant for washing or cleaning compound, marked "4 ounce OAKITE," mfd. by Oakite Products Inc., NYC, NY, 6"L, late 19th C. ...... **$30+**

Scoop, coffee beans, cast aluminum, "Barrington Hall Coffee," 20th C. ...... **$5+**

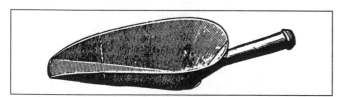

V-93. Scoop. *Flat-bottomed, self-balancing, pieced brass, which could be had nickeled for a quarter extra. Tubular capped handle. Sizes 00, 0, 1, 2 & 3 (measurements not given, but probably ranging from about 5"L to 10"L). Jaburg 1908 catalog.* **$10+**

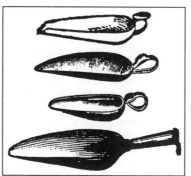

V-94. Scoops. *From the top:* **(1)** *"French sugar scoop," from* American Home Cook Book, 1854. **(2)** *Thumb scoop, tin with ring handle, in 2 sizes: 5"L x 3"W and 6"L x 3-1/4"W. Buhl Sons c.1919 catalog.* **(3)** *Spice scoop with ring handle, tin, in 3 unstated sizes, and* **(4)** *Tea or candy scoop with tubular handle, tin, in 2 sizes. Both from 1924 D. J. Barry catalog.* **$10+**

V-97. Tea scoop. Seamed brass with big rounded bowl, turned ebony handle. Four sizes that measured from 2 ounces to 1 pound of loose tea leaves. Henry Rogers, Wolverhampton, England, 1914. **$65+**

V-98. Flour scoop. Pieced tin, braced tubular capped handle, reinforced upper rim. Came in 2 sizes – small and large. Jaburg, 1908 catalog. **$15+**

V-95. Scoops in advertising. *The struggle to find a catchy advertising phrase has long been with us. (Now we would probably say "scoop this up." Brass scoops in set of four, tubular capped handles, crimped back plate, apparently flat-bottomed self-balancing. These were manufactured by William Wrigley, Jr., & Co., Chicago & Philadelphia, the chewing-gum makers! They were offered as a "necessity in every retail store," and available as a free premium when the dealer sent in order for 120 five-cent packages of gum. Advertising card, printed in blue, c.1900. The scoops, singly:* **$10+**

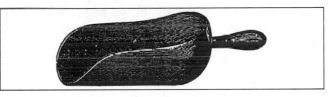

V-99. Sugar scoop. *Cast solid aluminum, 3 sizes: 11"L x 4"W; 12"L x 5"W; and 14"L x 5-1/2"W. Thomas Mills 1930 catalog.* **$8+**

Scoop, coffee beans, tin, "Martinique Coffee Scoops Them All," Oct. 19, 1897 .... **$15+**

Scoop, coffee beans, probably for grocers, cast aluminum, "Blue Diamond – Sunbeam Best Coffees," 12"L x 4-1/2"W, 20th C. .... **$20+**

Scoop, flour, carved from one piece of wood, rounded short handle. American (?), 6-1/2"L, late 19th C. • Small hole at end of handle, as well as handle's rounded shape, are evidence that this was at least partly lathe-turned, so probably from a manufactory. .... **$25+**

Scoop, flour, carved maple, nice long oval bowl with curved handle, American (?), 12-1/2"L, early 19th C. .... **$85+**

Scoop, flour, carved wood with fingerhold grip, primitive, very smooth finish, American (?), 7"L, 19th C. .... **$40+**

Scoop, flour, metal bowl with thick wire handles, handles stamped "Airy Fairy Kwik Bis-kit Flour," also "Airy Fairy Cake Flour," American, 7-1/2"L, early 20th C. A campy gotta-have. .... **$22+**

Scoop, flour, stamped metal, "Trisco Flour," 5-3/8"L, early 20th C. .... **$10+**

Scoop, flour, tin with turned wooden handle, American, 7"L, late 19th C. .... **$10+**

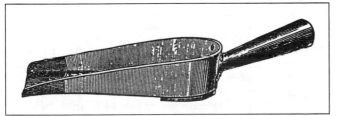

V-96. Looks like a scoop – *but it's a* **bankers' money shovel.** *Copper, flat bottom, steel lip like certain dustpans, tubular handle is copper (available also in turned ebony), protective heel like a shoe! The size is not given, but presumably about 10"L or longer. English. Henry Rogers, Wolverhampton, England, 1914 catalog. This is sure to show up in the containerloads from England. Now you will know what it is!* **$40+**

V-100. Scoop or dry measure. *Carved from one piece of wood. Marked "TOLLARD" – which could as easily have been the store in which it was used as the maker. Short hooked handle. 15-1/4"L. c.1860s-80s. Picture courtesy of Christie, Manson & Woods International Inc.* **$135+**

Scoop, heavy, galvanized crimped sheet iron, brass rivets, cast iron heel, wooden handle, 8"L, early 20th C. .... **$15+**

Scoop, tin with tubular handle, braced underneath at attachment. (This brace was called by tinsmiths the "boss.") American, 9"L x 4-1/2"W, 19th C. .... **$15+**

Scoop, turned wooden handle, bentwood cup is elongated half-round, brass nails like those used for pantry boxes, Shaker manufacture, 14"L x 6-3/4"W, 19th C. .... **$160+**

Sorghum meter or faucet, metal and wood, to be fitted into a keg, metal, pat'd. 1878. .... **$20+**

Spigot for cider barrel, wood with pewter key, marked "John Sommer's Best Block Tin Key," English (?), 19th C. .... **$8+**

❖ NOTES ❖

Futurewatch: Thermometers are certainly an unexplored collecting area, as far as I know. There is a great variety available, including candy, meat, deep fat, and oven types, as well as those with a kitcheny motif, and wall-hung room temperature thermometers. Some companies besides those in listings include: "The Acme" oven thermometer, mfd. by Evans Stamping & Plating Co., Taunton, MA, early 20th C; oven thermometers by Ingram-Richardson Mfg. Co., Beaver Falls, PA, and Rochester Mfg. Co., Rochester, NY, both from the 1920s-1930s.

Thermometer, cast iron corncob, cast in 2- or possibly 4-part mold (possibly made from real cob), painted black, hand-engraved brass face along length is flat, rest of cob is fully dimensional, American, 10-1/2"L, c.1870s. Wonderful for folk art, corn, cast iron collectors. .... **$250+**

Thermometer, candy, tin with brass face, marked "Spirit, Boil, Simmer, Heat, Temple, Freezing" (stages for sugar cooking), mfd. by J. Kendall & Co., 6-1/2"L, 19th C (?). .... **$30+**

Thermometer, for candy, copper, "Moeller Instrument Co.," Brooklyn, NY, c.1900. .... **$55+**

V-101. Room thermometer. Red-painted, stamped heavy tin in teapot shape. "Tel-Tru" Thermometer Co., Rochester, NY. 7"W, c.1930s-40s. (For you who are looking for backgrounds for photos – this is water-spritzed chipboard, an excellent mottled background for dark objects.) See electric kitchen clock V-4. **$20+**

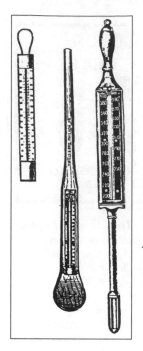

V-102. Candy-makers' thermometers. (L) for hard candy, with 5"L stem, 14-1/2"L overall. (M) "Wood stirring paddle with thermometer," this one at least we know was mfd. by Thomas Mills. 36"L. (R) Copper-cased with glass, 12"L, 14"L or 18"L. (M) "Improved boiling thermometer," turned wooden handle, in 2 sizes. First, for caramels, hard candy, etc., has a 14"L stem and is 32"L overall. All from 1930 Mills catalog. **$12+**

Thermometer, for candy & jelly, long palette-knife-shaped calibrated metal plate with glass tube, and with marks giving stages in candy-making, tapered turned wooden handle, large hanging loop at end, Taylor Instrument Co., Rochester, NY, Toronto, CAN, mid 1930s. .... **$12+**

Thermometer, for candy & jelly, metal with light green wooden handle, "Taylor," c.1940s. .... **$12+**

❖ NOTES ❖

Handy Oven Thermometer – "Many test their ovens in this way: if the hand can be held in from 20 to 35 seconds, it is a quick oven, from 35 to 45 seconds is moderate, and from 45 to 60 seconds is slow. 60 seconds is a good oven to begin with for large fruit cakes. All systematic housekeepers will hail the day when some enterprising, practical 'Dixie' girl shall invent a stove or range with a thermometer attached to the oven so that the heat may be regulated accurately and intelligently." *Practical Housekeeping*, 1884. • Thomas Masters of London invented what was probably the first oven thermometer about 1850. It was a glass ring with mercury and an indicator guide telling what to put in the oven when the mercury reached a particular point on the guide.

Thermometer, for oven, porcelainized iron in white, light blue, light green or orange, tall vertical tombstone shape set on flat round base, glass tube with degrees from 100° to 600° marked off, "Bake-Rite Portable Oven Thermometer No. 115," mfd. by American Thermometer Co., St. Louis, MO, 5-1/2"H, late 1920s, early 1930s. .... **$12+**

Thermometer, for oven, modeled almost exactly like the "Bake-Rite" but available only in white porcelainized metal, tombstone-shaped vertical face with glass tube, set on stamped round base marked with maker's name, registers from 200° to 800°, & is also marked from "slow" (at 300°) to "hot" (at 500°): is the extra 300 degrees for people who fire pottery in their ovens? Taylor Instrument Companies, mid 1930s. .... **$5+**

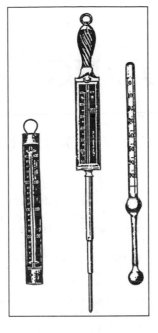

V-103. Thermometers. All have mercury stems. (L) Confectioners' thermometer, copper case. 12"L. Stamped maker's name looks like W. L. Imhagen & M. Espe, NYC. 1925 Sethness catalog. (M) Dough-mixing thermometer, turned wooden handle. 7"L case, approx. 21"L overall. Pat'd. April 24, 1894. Made by Homann & Maurer (sp?), Rochester, NY. In 1908 Jaburg catalog. (R) Syrup hydrometer, also known as a saccharometer. Glass. Also Homann & Maurer. Sethness 1925 catalog. $12+

Thermometer, printed metal, "Ward's Vitovim Bread," Ward Baking Co., NYC, etc., early 20th C. • A store thermometer, although no doubt some would have been found just outside the kitchen door, maybe on the icebox porch...................................... **$100+**

Timer for toaster, green marbleized plastic, chrome, green cord, to be hooked up to a Hotpoint toaster, "Hotpoint," Edison General Electric Appliance Co., Chicago, IL, 1930s. • An interesting explanation for the name The General Electric Co., is found in Orra L. Stone's History of Massachusetts Industries, 1930. He says THE is a formal part of the name and is an acronym for Dr. Elihu Thompson and Dr. Edwin J. Houston, who were co-founders of the American Electric Co., est. 1879 in Philadelphia, and a predecessor to GE, plus Thomas Alva Edison, whose Edison General Electric Co., est. 1881, merged with American Electric to become The G. E. Co. (This may be an apocryphal tale.) [Note: See about novelty timers in the egg timer section a few pages back.]......... **$125+**

Utility measure – See: Measure & funnel combined

COOPERED WARES – HOW BIG?
Or, Twenty-Nine Firkins of Beer on the Wall

In everyday eighteenth-century life, a knowledge of such exact measures as barrel, hogshead, tub or firkin was vital to any citizen who bought, sold or bartered grain, butter, ale, soap, tallow, cider or any other dry or liquid stuff that was measured out in supposedly uniformly sized coopered (staved & bound wood) containers. Many of these containers (at least the smaller ones) are found in kitchen and country store collections today.

In America's earliest days we used British standards of measure. Later the legal capacity of coopered vessels differed (and still do) in England and America. To take just one early eighteenth-century liquid product – ale or beer – and give its rounded off, old time British measures: one tun of ale equaled about four hogsheads or almost seven and a quarter barrels, or fourteen and a half kilderkins, or close to 29 firkins. A tun of ale held

about 259 gallons, a firkin held only a little over nine gallons. A keg was a small ale or beer cask that held 10 gallons or less, so it was an inexact measure that might easily coincide with a firkin. (A cask usually referred to a generic coopered container, just as today we often use "barrel" to generally mean a big coopered container, or "keg" to mean a small one.) A kilderkin and a runlet had the same measurements – almost exactly 16"H x 20" diam.; a firkin was half that in both dimensions; a butt was twice as big.

FOR MORE INFORMATION

Piebirds

Piebirds Unlimited
POB 192
Acworth, CA 30101-0192
Web site: www.hometown.aol.com/asworthd/Piebirds Unlimited.html

Scales

The International Society of Antique Scale Collectors
Bob Stein
800 W. Adams St., Ste. 821
Chicago, IL 60606
Web site: www.isasc.org

Thermometers

Thermometer Collectors of America
Warren D. Harris
6130 Rampart Dr.
Carmichael, CA 95608

HOLDING & HANDLING

VI. TRIVETS, STANDS, & RACKS; ALSO POTHOLDERS

Is it a **trivet** or is it a **stand**? Trivet is the choice in common English usage – even for something with four legs. Trivets are three-legged, vaguely triangular stands meant for sadirons, and the word itself means three legs, but people are used to calling any sort of cooling stand a trivet. Most of the trivets and stands here are for hot pots or hot dishes. Most are technically stands, not trivets because they have four or more legs. Over the objections of some, I'm going to use the familiar word "trivet" for most of the pieces in this chapter. **New trivets:** Mostly I don't get into these, but I've had an art project idea in mind for about 7 years (to make a gate out of welded-together aluminum kitchen things & gadgets & spoons). Well! Imagine my surprise upon going into Bed, Bath & Beyond in November 2001, and finding two cast aluminum trivets: One in high silvery finish, made as if a whisk, a cake turner, & a slotted spoon were welded together. This one made in Thailand for Copco has a hanging ring and 4 little peg feet with rubber covers. 9"L x 6-1/2"W. The other one has a sort of wavery picture frame around a fork, knife, & spoon, welded together with lots of open space. Meant for a hot dish. This one isn't marked, but the tag says "Via"/"Design Ancona"/ "Made in China." 9"L x 7-3/4"W. Future collectibles.

Wire pieces are increasingly popular and have finally earned their own book (see Bibliography). Many round, flat wire stands are actually countertop cooling racks for baked goods – either taken out of the pan, or left in. The wire itself drew heat off the bottom of the pie pan, but it also allowed cooling air to circulate; others are stands for teapots to be used at table, and they protect the finish. Wire can be twisted and bent into the desired scribbly design. It can be easily soldered (so many wire stands are a combination of soldered and twisted wires). It could even be twisted in spirals around lengths of wire, making the heat conduction potential even greater. The most wide-open and unexplored stands and trivets are homemade – of scrap copper, steel, tin, even wood.

This isn't a big area of collecting, and people are most familiar with the trivets or stands meant for sadirons. Hand-forged trivets are often very valuable. And some of the trivets for cast iron roasters or other pots and pans are important to collectors of Griswold, Wagner, etc. Oddly, many of those trivets are used inside the utensil to hold up tired roasts. Some are made of cast aluminum, to match the hollowware they were meant to be used in. Griswold, like many 20th C foundries, also made old style sadiron trivets in lacy cast iron – those are worth under $40. If Griswold had been thinking of collectors, surely they would have made a limited edition trivet or stand of their wonderful Griswold spider in a web. If that had ever been made, it might be worth more than $500. But they never did, so if you see one, you know it isn't a Griswold. (There is a very interesting 8-spoke spider-web-with-spider, cast iron trivet, with webbed handle, 6" diam., marked "Rd. No. 96845," which I believe is English. It's worth upwards of $125.) A fun go-with to look for is a 1954 catalog from Lily Mills Co., Shelby, NC: "*Wrought Iron Crochet*, Book #74" which has 23 patterns for objects to be crocheted in black yarn, including several trivets!

Hot mat, variegated woods in pinwheel design, some think it to be Shaker because of the variegated woods (used for rolling pins & table mats), 8" diam., came in other sizes, 1920s. New ones are made with strong fishline.. **$20-$25**

Jelly maker's stand, cast iron, sort of like a trivet bench, 4 legs, top has 2 large holes – for 2 kettles, American, about 26"L, 19th C. .... **$150+**

POTHOLDERS
Or, Another Way to Handle a Hot Pot

A long time ago I discovered that the cheapest, most colorful, easily-found kitchen collectible is the potholder (sometimes spelled pot holder). The commonest is the woven rag strip kind made on a little square loom that is at least 60 years old. Most of them have no distinctive feature at all, but occasionally one with interesting color is seen.

The three most collectible types are (1) unique (not pattern) 19th century quilted and/or appliquéd cotton or wool ones, or needlepointed wool ones, often in the shape of a butterfly or bird (so that wings can be folded around the handle). The old printed calicoes and chintzes make this type a good go-with for a quilt collection. Some of these old potholders are actually meant to be used in the parlor, when pouring tea from a hot teapot. (2) 20th century (c.1900-1950s) figural appliqué, done in ginghams and calicoes, and usually made from a pattern, or at least a how-to article in a ladies magazine. (3) 20th century crocheted potholders: geometrics (c.1900-1950s), and figurals (c.1900-1950s, but mainly the '40s and '50s). Some crocheted pieces have very intricate, virtuoso stitches that make the flat potholder into a 3-D work of textile art.

The colors most commonly found in the last two types are red and white; then green and white; then red, green, and white; and finally colors like blue, yellow, and pink. The first three combinations reflect the color schemes most favored in kitchens in the 1930s and '40s, schemes which also inspired the implement handles in red, green, white and, much more rarely, yellow and blue. Hanging loops were part of the holder in the late 19th century on, and rings seem to be a 20th century feature. Small circles of celluloid, called a "bone ring," were stitched to an edge through the 20th century; brass rings were also used. These rings are barely an inch across – they were used to make cafe curtains. Crocheted holders often have a ring crocheted only from the yarn, or crocheted over a "bone" or brass ring.

Every motif fad – from palm trees to seafood, from barbecue to tropical fruits – that was used for dishes, lamps, aprons, wallpaper, shelf paper, cabinet decals, juice glasses, bridge tallies, etc., also found expression in potholders. Crochet pattern books, with cheerily attractive finished potholders shown in color photography or duotone on the covers, were put out by such yarn and thread makers as Coats & Clark's, American Thread Co., and The Spool Cotton Co., in the '40s and '50s. A needlework magazine with patterns for everything from tablecloths to bedroom booties was *"The Work Basket,"* published about 40 years, until 1971. These magazines and pattern books are great research sources, and fun go-withs.

The introduction to a 1947 American Thread Co. potholder pattern book says "More Pot Luck – So many handicrafters loved our *Star Pot Holder Book No. 32*, with recipes, that we decided to design another book with the same idea, but with oh-so-different patterns.

We hope you'll like them – they look so bright and sparkling when made with Star Brand Cottons." So a recipe for "Crab meat au gratin" is accompanied by a fish-shaped potholder, and another with a crab double-crocheted on a plain square. Accompanying a "Cheese cake" recipe are – you guessed it – "Panties Potholder #5512" and a "Slip Pot holder." "Indian Pudding" gets three designs, a "Navajo" geometric, a "Log Cabin" design something like the pieced-quilt pattern of that name, and "Indian Circle", like a pinwheel.

The 20th century holders are usually a lot dirtier and stained than the older ones, which weren't really meant for day-to-day kitchen use. Fortunately, the crochet yarns tend to be 100% cotton, and color fast to a high degree. They can be washed very successfully. An elderly needlewoman of my acquaintance is known to all her friends as a person who can always get an old textile clean. The "magic" potion she usually uses is "Biz™" or "Super Biz™" powdered detergent. A few tips: don't soak overnight (even strongly set dyes can begin to run); do it in stages – be somewhat timid at first. Soak a little, scrub with your fingers a little, rinse a lot, squeeze in a towel, and dry quickly. And do it again if the stain hasn't come out. Sometimes a paste of detergent and water can be applied to a stubborn stain, left to do its work for a short few minutes, then rinsed out. As for scorch? Nothing gets it out completely.

At least three articles have been published on this unheralded, but increasingly popular, field of collecting. The first was "Handle with Care," by Cathy Cook, former editor of *"Country Accents® Collectibles. Flea Market Finds,"* in the Summer 1996 issue. Another article cited by Cook is by social historian Rachel Maines: "The Evolution of the Pot Holder from Technology to Popular Art," *Journal of Popular Culture*, July 1985. An online article, "A Passion for Potholders," is found at www.countrycollector.com/ccsummer98 /potholders.html. Another appeared in *Martha Stewart LIVING* sometime in 2000 or 2001.

Potholder, appliquéd cotton, Black Americana cook or chef, American, 1940s or so. Probably not a pattern piece. **$20**

Potholder, appliquéd cotton, pig motif, 20th C. **$10**
Potholder, appliquéd cotton, hearts and diamonds, red & green on white, brass hanging ring at corner, c.1930s. **$5**

VI-1. Potholder. *Appliquéd cotton cat, handsewn, with simple embroidery. Thin and barely stuffed at all – obviously for decoration.* **$10+**

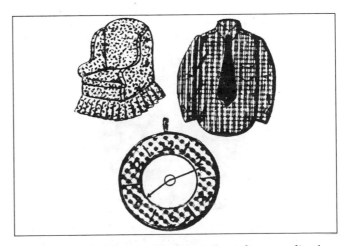

VI-2. Potholders. *Gingham & calico appliqué, handsewn, with simple embroidery. Picture from McCall's Needlework magazine, Summer 1941.* **$7+**

Potholder, appliquéd cat's head, very fanciful, c.1930s... **$10**

Potholder, appliquéd & embroidered cat's head, c.1950s... **$8+**

Potholder, crocheted thick cotton yarn, deep red & green, with interesting wiggly woven look to top side, brass hanging ring sewed on corner, 4" x 4", c.1920s... **$10+**

Potholder, for teapot in parlor, needlepoint in dark green & red, brown polished cotton backing, design is a rebus poem, pictures given here in parentheses: "Except the (Tea Kettle) Boiling (B), Filling the (Tea Pot) Spoils the (T)," prob. American, close to 6" square, c.1830s to 1850s. .... **$125+**

Potholder, embroidered cotton cutout, depicts a house, c.1920s to 1930s. **$15**

Potholder, crazy quilt silk & satin, embroidered, probably for parlor use while pouring tea or coffee, c.1870s to late 1800s....................................... **$25**

Potholder, bargello needlepoint, backed with printed cotton, geometric pattern, c.1880s. **$15**

Potholder, appliquéd & cutout felt, odd, typically Amish, color combinations modern-art in appearance, cotton flannel baking, all bound in red cotton tape, c.1880s to 1890s. The Amish are making potholders now, in the old way, and probably with old material or artificially-aged material. Hard to tell from the old ones but not worth as much. .... **$20+**

Potholder, tan wool flannel, red cotton tape binding, tiny red braid machine stitched in floral pattern on front, back plain (another example done on gray wool flannel), supposed to be Amish, c.1880s to 1890s.. **$15+**

Potholder, chicken with stuffed upstanding neck & head, body folds around handle of teapot, mustard & ochre cotton sateen, green floss knots around neck, blue eyes, Mennonite, 5-3/8" diam., c.1900-1920s...... **$60**

Potholder, needlepoint, pink, red, & blue, tree of life, printed brown calico backing, Mennonite, 5-3/8" x 5-5/8", c.1870s... **$55+**

Potholder, printed cotton & muslin butterfly, the wings to be folded around the handle, 6"W wingspread, c.1920s. .... **$7+**

Potholder, crocheted cotton, caricature face of an Oriental, yellow with red lips & black hair, yarn pigtail braided & attached, 6" diam., c.1940s-1950s. .. **$20**

Potholder, fine needlepoint on canvas, one side is a rebus with ombré shaded lettering in red on green background, with black kettle picture, reads "Genie put the [kettle] on & we will all take tea," obverse has flowers, vases, dog, cat, pair of scissors & a wreath on black background, English (?), 5" x 4-3/16", c.1860s to 1880s. • Being a rebus collector, this attracted my attention immediately. It is a fine piece of needlework, as well as being a puzzle, and has crossover appeal to various kinds of collectors. .... **$125+**

Potholder, appliquéd in layers & embroidered, Black man's face, with frayed fringe hair, red wood jersey lips, white jersey eyes, flappy ears, not a nice caricature, but interesting handicraft in Black Americana mode, 8" diam., c.1890s to 1910s.................. **$70+**

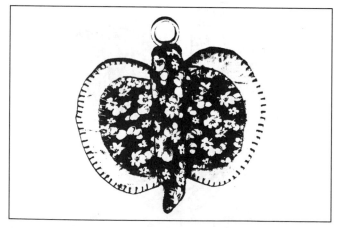

VI-3. Potholder. *Colorful appliquéd cotton, hand-sewn, butterfly's body has extra stuffing. What's called a "bone" ring of celluloid. 1930s or '40s.* **$5+**

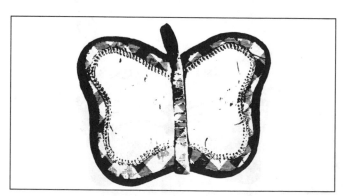

VI-4. Potholder. *A simple gingham butterfly with corded edge. Handsewn. Same idea, different species of butterfly! 1930s or '40s.* **$5+**

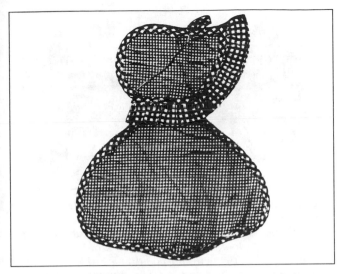

VI-5. Potholder. *Cotton gingham checks in two sizes, both red & white. Machine sewn. Probably 1950s.* **$5**

VI-6. Potholders. *Really well-done crocheted holders with crocheted flowers done right on the background pieces. Red, green, yellow & white – very 1940s.* **$20+**

Potholder, for handle of parlor teapots, velvet parrot without wings, only body, tail & simple head with beak, body folds over the handle, green velvet with pale tan silk lining, embroidered with mother-of-pearl button eyes, poss. English, certainly High Victorian, 7"L, c.1880s to 1890s.? Another one, an inch longer, was teal blue velvet with beige silk lining. .... **$35+**

Potholder, Black Americana needlepoint with simple depiction of a dancing black man & woman who nearly fill the space, also "Any holder but a Slave holder," reputedly made for Frederick Douglass by Lena Irish, 5-1/2"H x 6-1/2"W, c.1860s-70s. • Dealer Bernie McManus, Woodbury House, Woodbury, CT, offered this punning piece in 1985, along with a letter by Douglass. In Feb. 1989, Windham Antiques in Shepherdstown, WV, advertised a "potholder by freed slave (NC, circa 1865), red, black, white cross-stitch on gray wool (Confederate uniform)," red binding and hanging loop. It has a dancing Black man and woman very small in center, and the same motto, but with all 6 words with initial capital letters, and measures 5-1/2" x 6". .... **$250+**

Potholder, crocheted bear-head, black, crocheted contrasting trim that looks like rick-rack, appliquéd felt eyes, 1950s. **$10**

Potholder, crocheted cotton bunch of bananas, yellow & brown, brass ring, 1950s. **$5**

Potholder, crocheted cotton, white with red outlines, little house shape with colored windows & door, crocheted hanging ring as chimney, about 5"H, patterns for these advertised 1940-1941 .... **$7+**

Potholder, appliquéd cloth, blue & white gingham around edge, white cotton center, red stitching, a clock face with every other numeral, tab hanger at top, 5" diam., pattern appeared for this in Summer 1941 *McCall's Needlework* magazine. • In the same how-to article appeared a wonderful cozy little armchair-shaped potholder of calico. Also a great man's shirt with red tie, the sleeves and shirt tails forming irregular outline on basic round shape. I've never seen either one, but would like to! **$10**

Potholder, crocheted cotton, round, with appliquéd flowers & leaves crocheted separately from red, green, & yellow cotton. Hanging ring of metal. American, 6" diam., c.1930s 40s. .... **$8+**

Potholder, printed cloth, adv'g. "Reddi Kilowatt," c.1920s-30s. • See Chapter XVIII (Electrifying Work), for more on Reddy. .... **$15+**

Potholder rack, plywood cutout, Black Americana theme, a painted "Mammy" with blue & white gingham checked apron & kerchief of cloth, white thumbtack eyes, paper glued-on lips, thumbtacks in legs to hold 2 potholders, American, 7"H-1/4" thick ply, c.1940s. .... **$25+**

Stand, cast iron, sand casting of a real hand, hanging (?) hole in wrist, American, 18th or early 19th C.? This was seen in a dealer's (Rose W. Olstead, Madison, NJ) ad in *The Magazine ANTIQUES*, July 1962. I suspect the price then was under $50. If you found such a piece now, if it was determined to be old, the price would be much higher, and it would be for sale by a folk art dealer. .... **$700+**

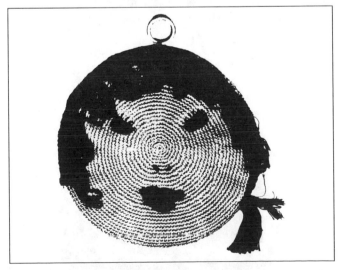

VI-7. Potholder. *Crocheted caricature of Oriental woman's face. Yellow with red lips & black eyes & hair. Braided pigtail. C.1940s-'50s.* **$20+**

Stand, for pots, and combination tool including meat tenderizer, tack hammer, stove lid lifter, pot lifter (hook fits around bail handle), pie crimper, candleholder (the last 2 dubiously efficacious), found in cast iron and cast bronze-like metal. Basically round, with 4 deep ridges (the tenderizer) shooting off at an angle, 2 round candle- or finger-sized holes, one longish curved piece (lid lifter), 3 short hooked pieces off bottom, viewed from right angle, it's an [unintentional] caricature of Groucho Marx. This is almost always found at fleas and shows on the tables of people dealing in knives, guns, Nazi memorabilia, camo-junk, etc., and is usually labeled "brass knuckles," which it most assuredly isn't. "6-Way Trivet" is one; another American one is the "Seven Way Kitchen Aid," pat'd. by W. H. Thayer, May 24, 1881.. **$60-$85+**

Trivet, also called a dish rest, cast iron, round with side handle, 3 legs, heart motif with radiating spokes, heart end to handle, American, 11-3/8"L x 6-1/2" diam., marked "1829" on handle. This has been reproduced by Virginia Metalcrafters in brass and iron. Old iron one:........................... **$150-$175**

VI-10. Potholders. *More red & white crochet from the 1940s. The one on the left actually somewhat resembles the wirework teapot trivet stands. The dress, which looks like a doll dress (Yo! Barbie, eat your heart out!), actually couldn't be a doll dress because the stitches connect back to front. Both with crocheted-over "bone" (or celluloid) rings.* **$2-$5+**

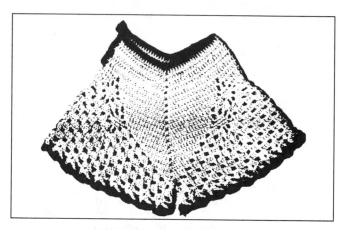

VI-8. Potholder. *There are those "Cheese cake" panties! This red & white pair is actually nicer & fancier than the Star pattern book version. This is probably the most commonly found crochet motif. c.1940s-'50s.* **$4+**

VI-11. Potholders. *These are partly handmade – the fruit appliqués are sewn to squares of a manufactured dishcloth. Lined with layers of cotton, bound with cotton tape, and machine stitched around edges, with a loop made from the extra 2" of tape. c.1950s.* **$3-$5**

VI-9. Potholder. *Crocheted red & white cottage, c.1940.* **$7**

VI-12. Potholder. *Cotton terrycloth souvenir of the 1939 World's Fair in Flushing, NY, showing the Trylon and Perisphere that towered over the exhibition buildings. 1938/39.* **$20+**

VI-13. Trivet. Called a *"farrier's whimsy"* in the auction catalog. Steel and brass; a horse (or pony) shoe, fitted with three high-laced boots as feet and decorated with miniature farrier's tools – anvil, tongs, hammer, etc. Approx. 5-3/4"W x about 1-1/2"H. Photo courtesy Litchfield Auction Gallery, Litchfield CT. Ex-Harold Corbin Collection. **$700+**

Trivet, brass, fire bar type that hooked onto the fire bar that went between 2 andirons, stylized thistle design, English (?), 19th C. .... **$150+**

Trivet, cast brass woman's head, Bradley & Hubbard, Meriden, CT, 3rd to 4th quarter 19th C. **$75**

Trivet, cast iron, round with heart & rays design, 8" diam., late 19th C. This is the kind of design reproduced widely. Use every bit of your iron-age-detecting knowledge before buying. .... **$45+**

Trivet, for Dutch oven #6, round, cast iron, pattern of round holes, "Griswold #204," Erie, PA, 12" diam., turn-of-century. [Note: #205 through #211 are all Griswold Dutch oven trivets in different sizes.] .... **$20-$35+**

Trivet, expanding, for hot dishes, copper & brass, prob. originally nickeled, "Manning-Bowman," American, 1st half 20th C. .... **$20+**

Trivet, for kettle or pot, cast iron square, 4 legs riveted on, at the knee of each leg is a flattened oval medallion

VI-14. Trivet or stand for pot. Intricate cast iron, japanned finish (similar iron doilies often seen in enameled finish, white, blue or black). Russell & Erwin, mid 1860s. **$45+**

with a relief profile of a Roman warrier in helmet, all 4 the same, openwork top plate spells out name, "Houchin's Patent," NYC, NY, but T. W. Houchin lived in Morrisania, NY, 2-1/4"H x 5-3/8" square, prob. 1870s to 1890s.? (Another Houchin trivet, probably for a portable kettle or other little vessel, has very delicate cast iron top, probably brass plated or bronzed, is only 3-3/4" square with 3 shaped 1-1/4"H brass legs, round cutout design in top spells out H O U C H I N. (It is worth only $7 to $15.) .... **$75-$100**

Trivet, probably for pot, cast iron with bronzed finish, skeletal triangle with 3 longish feet, marked on underside "Thos. W. Houchin Co. 1898," NYC, 1-1/2"H x 4-1/4" sides, TOC. .... **$20+**

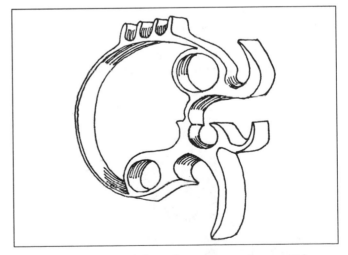

VI-15. Stand or trivet for pots, and a **combination tool.** This was patented May 24, 1881 by W. H. Thayer as a *"seven-way"* tool. It is often called a brass knuckle by those who don't know. Its seven functions are **(1)** trivet, **(2)** stove lid lifter, **(3)** pot bail hook, **(4)** meat tenderizer, **(5)** pie crimper, **(6)** bottle opener, and **(7)** candleholder. It is found most commonly in cast brass, and is worth a bit more in cast iron. **$60-$85+**

Trivet, for pot, beautiful cast iron in interesting flat-top piece with large hole cut in center, outside edge basically round with projections where 3 legs attached, largish tab handle (shaped like a porringer handle) has a hanging hole, English (?), only 2-5/8"H x 4-1/2"W at widest part, mid 19th C. (?). .... **$35+**

Trivet, for pot, cast iron, advertises "Cinderella Stoves," early 20th C. **$45**

Trivet, for pot, cast iron, letters form openwork design, "J. R. Clark Co.," Minneapolis, MN, late 19th C. or early 20th. **$35**

Trivet, for pot, cheap metal cast to resemble bamboo, back bears motto "East or West – Campbell's Soups Are Best," Campbell Soup, c.1970s (?)............... **$5+**

Trivet, for pot, white enameled cast iron – a permanent doily, very ornate openwork, the center a sort of flowerette composed of 6 hearts joined at the points, the outside frame composed of 12 looped and rococo scrolls arranged so that 2 form a unit, all surrounded in delicately scalloped edge, peg feet, American, 18" diam., prob. 1860s to 1880s.............. **$45**

Trivet, for pots, cast iron, this one also called a simmering cover, to use on cook stove, Walker & Pratt Mfg. Co., "W & P," 7-3/4" diam., 19th C. **$15**

Trivet, for roaster, oval with 6 little tab feet, cast iron, with pattern of three sizes of round holes, Griswold #7 (it came in 4 sizes: 3, 5, 7, & 9), "Oval Roaster Trivet" #276. .... **$90+**

Trivet, orange painted cast iron, advertising "Grain Belt" beer, early 20th C. .... **$35+**

Trivet, wire in a spiral, cross pieces form legs with a rivet, American, 6" diam., c.1890s to 1910s. **$15**

Stand, wire, for hot dishes, round, tight spiral of thin wire, reinforced and soldered by eight spokes radiating from center, with 8 little loops underneath as feet, several makers among the wire novelty companies, American, about 6-1/4" diam., late 19th or early 20th C. Variations. – This type has many variations, sometimes unsoldered and held together only by little twists of wire at each intersection of spiral and spoke. I have seen them as large as 8" diam.; others may be larger. Other variations of thin twisted wire stands include some that look like daisies, with each petal having its own little bent loop foot, and some with many spokes or rays without

the spirals but using heavier wire, twisted sometimes from two strands. See also the wire baskets in the next chapter. Usually these bring: .... **$15-$25**

Trivet, a real forged iron horseshoe, backed with disc of sheet metal from which a large V has been cut, with 3 forged short peg legs, American, 4-1/2"L, late 19th or early 20th C.? I bought this for $2 from a dealer who said it was an "ashtray," but that is way under the money. And, no, I didn't argue................. **$75+**

Trivet, for pot or kettle, a real wrought iron horseshoe welded to sheet iron, 3 feet, American, 19th C.? There are enough of these, all one of a kind, to make a very handsome collection...................................... **$100+**

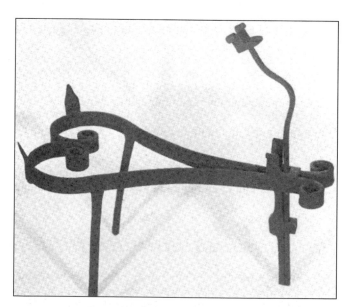

*VI-17. **Trivet for frying pan**, or other long-handled pan. Forged iron, heart shape, long legs. Upright piece supports handle of pan – if it tilts up (which handles of most hearth utensils did to make them easier to hold and move for a person standing at the hearth). Continental European, possibly French or Portuguese. Late 18th or early 19th C. Photograph courtesy of Pat Guthman Antiques, Southport, CT.* **$650+**

*VI-16. **Trivet**. Cast iron, spoked heart design. Dated "1829," which makes it very desirable, as well as the hearts on its face & handle. 11-3/8"L x 6-1/2" diam. Picture courtesy of the National Museum of American History, Smithsonian Institution. [Note: Virginia Metalcrafters made a repro of this in brass in the mid-20th C.* **$150+**

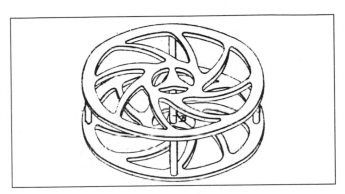

VI-18. Stand patent. *Pat'd. Dec. 8, 1885 by Joseph P. Hurley, Philadelphia, PA, #332,201. Called a "Kitchen utensil" by Hurley, and claimed to be "a new article, ... a metallic stand for kitchen utensils, consisting of two plates with connecting legs, all cast in one piece." I have a cast brass drain cover that looks almost exactly like this, although the center hole is much smaller and was meant for a screw. It has three stubby feet, and except for the fact I actually removed it from a drain in a building being razed, who would know? This from the* Official Gazette *of the U.S. Patent Office. If it were made:* **$25-$45+**

Trivet, wrought iron in a tight coil, with handle, quite heavy, 10"L including handle, early 19th C. ..... **$65+**

Trivet, for pot, wrought iron pony shoe mounted to black painted copper plate cut to fit shape, 3 wrought booted feet with rounded toes & heels, boots resemble riding boots, American (?), 1-1/4"H x 4-7/8" x 4-7/8", early 19th C........................ **$200+**

Trivet, for pot, wrought iron, heart-shaped, with a scroll & heart inner design, 3 boot shaped feet, like riding boots, stamped with a small eagle punch mark & a flower on the handle, maker's name marked too, "J. English," PA (?), 10-3/4"L x 4-1/4"W, early 19th C.? Ex-Robacker Collection. Sold at Horst Auction, June 1989 for $1,600. It is very hard to predict what pieces originally from famous collections will sell for the next time around, especially if the new collector is not famous. See the essay on Composition of Price. Because of the marks, the hearts, & the boots:.................................... **$700-$1,500+**

❖ NOTES ❖

The Composition of Price – Why did the Robacker heart & boot trivet sell for so much? Surely a record for a trivet or stand. There are many elements that went into the price, which may or may not be the secondary market value for this trivet; I believe that factors (1) & (2) probably contributed to the price realized.

(1) It came from a **famous, published collection**, the Robacker Estate, and gains value from association, and from the fact that it had presumably been bought by a knowledgeable couple who wouldn't have bought a reproduction or fake. (2) It was **sold at auction**, where the pace and fever of selling are conducive of high realized prices. (3) **It is marked.** It not only had a maker's name, "J. English," but also a stamped American eagle with a shield & banner and a clutch of arrows. So far, nothing is known about the maker. (4) There was a

valuable **multiplier motif** in the design, in this case cutout hearts – usually good for multiplying the price by 5 or 10 times or more, meaning that without it, the price might be 1/10th to 1/20th. (5) There was at least one **figural element** in the design. For me, personally (thanks to my 12AAAA understanding), the most enchanting factor is the boot feet. I already own one nice trivet with cast boot feet. I saw another trivet or stand, probably Pennsylvanian, in the Keillor Collection, when I was doing my first book; the Keillors' was 13"L, with a cutout cock or rooster, a very graceful & shaped handle and is truly the most wonderful of the three, and I wish I owned it. I also wish that I could see all three next to each other; it'd be useful to compare the shape and exact size of all the boots. (6) **Size** is the most easily overlooked factor in the composition of price; whether a piece is unusually large or small – especially if you are looking at pieces in a catalog or book. In this instance, it is large. The one we are discussing is nearly a foot long – a good-sized trivet, quite impressive.

Trivet, wrought iron, round long triangle outline, with pointed piece almost like steeple from point of trivet up into open space, topped by cutout bird form (like a weathervane), 3 feet in shape of boots, all pointing away from slightly curved skinny handle. This was in the Keillor Collection, auctioned in 1976, and may be one of the finest trivets ever seen on the market, American or poss. French, 2"H x 13"L overall, early 19th C. .... **$700-$1,600**

Trivet, for pots or kettles, forged iron, with hearts in center, plus a 2-hearted handle, American, 12"L, date difficult to call? Old Hearts. With the heart motif's popularity, and proliferation of fake forged iron pieces of all kinds, this could be as recent as 1988. This one has convincing signs of wear, cleaning, polishing, & use, both on bottoms of feet, and on surface, and may be early 19th C. .... **$100+**

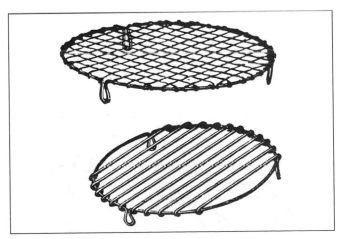

VI-19. Kettle bottoms & meat rests. *A form of trivet, and often identified as such. They were meant to be used inside a pot or kettle. Both are tinned iron wire. The upper mesh one, with wires welded to the round frame, came in 6", 7", 8", 9", and 10" diam. The bottom one was only made in 7" and 8-1/2" diameters. The Washburn Co., Worcester, MA. "Sno-Cap catalog, 1927.* **$6-$10**

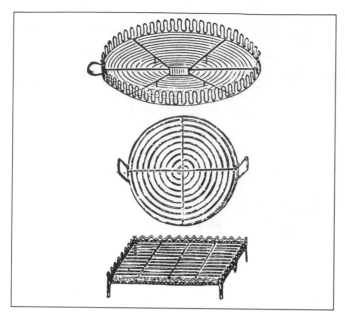

VI-20. "Grates." *Much older than the ones in VI-19 are these three pastry or confectioner's grates, meant for cooling baked goods.* **(T)** *This came in sizes from 6" to 16" diameter;* **(M)** *Simpler center one was made in 5-1/2" to 15-3/4" diameters (or any size "to order".* **(B)** *This came 9" x 13", 10-1/2" x 15", and 12" x 16", or any size to order. From professional suppliers Duparquet, Huet & Moneuse, NYC, c.1904-1910. The form, and probably the linecuts used to illustrate the catalog, are from the 1860s or 1870s.* **$20-$45**

Trivet, cast & wrought iron, 3-legged hearth style for pots, also called a brandelette, brandiron or brandise. American (?), 10"H, 18th C. .... **$150+**

Trivet, for hearth, revolving, forged iron, American, 11" diam., high legs, very early 1700s. The trivet, without a handle, is much rarer than the similar form, the revolving broiler (See Chapter X [Hearths] for those.) .... **$200-$300+**

Trivet, for hearth, with adjustable fork or handle support that works on the pawl & ratchet idea, forged & twisted iron "running man" piece with adjustable height to support fork or stirring spoon. Two long legs on either side of circle of trivet, one leg near end

VI-21. Pot stand. *Twisted iron wire, originally tinned, 6-1/2" diam. Probably French, but could also have been made by Sherwood of Worcester, MA. Called also a "teapot stand." American Agriculturist, November, 1872.* **$20-$30**

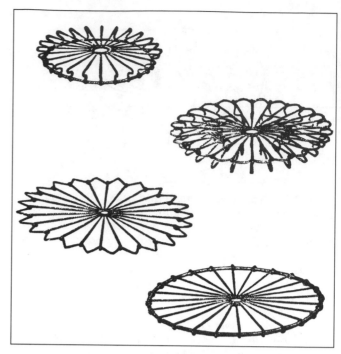

VI-22. Tea or coffee pot stands. *Twisted wire in various shapes, available in different sizes. Mfd. by Sherwood, Worcester, MA, mid 19th C. & made for a long period.* **$20-$45**

of handle, very handsome form that looks like what sculptor Alberto Giacometti would have done, if he'd made 18th century cooking utensils. 7-5/8" diam. x 24-5/16"L. Found in house on the Connecticut-Massachusetts border, 18th C. .... **$575+**

Trivet, for hearth, wrought iron with sliding support for saucepan handle, 3 penny feet, 22-1/2"L, 18th C. .... **$350+**

Trivet, wrought iron, round with 3 legs & a long handle, for hearth use. American (?), 6"H x 8" diam., with 11"L handle, late 1700s or early 1800s.................... **$300+**

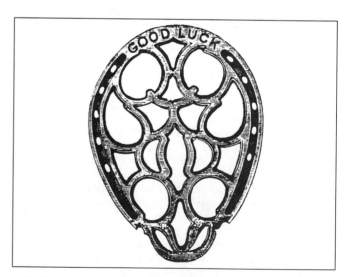

VI-23. "Tea or coffee pot stand." *Called that in the catalog, but looks more like a sadiron stand. Nickeled cast brass horseshoe design, with expected "Good Luck." Heinz & Munschauer, Buffalo, NY, 1882 catalog.* **$70+**

HOLDING & HANDLING

This is literally a catch-all chapter – maybe because almost everyone has some kind of container collection. It's been said that women are great collectors of containers – boxes, jars, trunks; maybe there's a physiological basis for what is often an obsession! This chapter also has more kinds of things valued by "crossover collectors" (folk art, ceramics, baskets, glass, wooden wares) than probably any other.

To figure out which aspect to pursue yourself is "like trying to use a straw to drink from a fire hydrant," as some wag said about Congress and its legislative agenda. Probably half the stuff at any flea market or antique show might be classified as a container of some kind. Open or closed.

There are several subjects here that I've decided not to include to any extent: **Cookie jars** are very specialized, prices are difficult for an outsider (i.e., non-collector) to track meaningfully, and there are several books and collector clubs. You can do a search online. I am also excluding licensed-**character lunchboxes** for similar reasons, and in fact include very few – but all true antique ones. **Novelty salt & pepper shakers** have several colorful books, and a club, as do **candy containers**. See the end of this chapter for more information on clubs and contacts.

Two areas where there's elbow room for collectors, and on which a **Futurewatch** has been placed, are **berry baskets** and **candy boxes**. Low to mid-range prices are still the rule, but by the time this 5th edition is published, I may have to eat my berries. A broad, and deep, collecting base is essential to the long life and success of any collecting field, and is rather like a mountain lake fed by springs from the bottom and rain from the top.

Some areas are ripe for attention, but may be too limited in scope for a broad following. If there isn't enough variety (in price as well as appearance or material), there's no fun. **Collapsible cups**, and **string holders** are of interest, but I think probably only the latter might have enough variety to sustain a collector market.

Finally, I've included a sampling from two long-established collecting fields – **birdcages**, and **candlesticks** – because of their obvious connection to the kitchen and the running of a household. In college, where I lived in a boarding house, our wonderful cook Melba Hamlet kept her parrot in a corner of the kitchen. Many birdcages are showing up at antique shows; a good many, I believe, originating in England and Europe as part of the trend toward commissioned container picking done by dealers who don't actually go overseas to shop themselves. There are also many, many Far Eastern reproductions of the big "condo" birdcages – probably 99% of the big green and big purplish-brown ones are modern fakes. Candlesticks are merely glanced at in this chapter – just a hint of what might be added to a collection of useful household objects.

Finally, for me the most exciting and fully satisfying area of collecting in this chapter are **repaired pieces**, sometimes called "**make-dos**" – as in "Use it up, Wear it out, Make it do, Or do without!" It is a vast field waiting to be plowed and discovered. Gently, now ... gently. Tools as well as pitchers or bowls were repaired to extend their lives, and a lot of rather fancy glass that got broken was made into something else. I suspect that housewives themselves did a lot of it – they were accustomed to using a soldering iron during canning, and there was always a kitchen drawer with twine, tack hammer, awl, baling wire, soldering iron (see the canning chapter), nails, heavy staples, and other odds and ends that could be ingeniously used to repair something. This chapter contains short catch-all essays on **Japonisme**, **matches**, **fibreware**, **tin**, and **tinplate sizes**.

ABC plate, ironstone, transfer printed in black underglaze, depicts 2 small boys playing with small whips & a spinning top, decorated with red, green, yellow, & blue, "Mekins," English, 5-1/4" diam., mid 19th C. .... **$150+**

ABC plate, ceramic, decorated with Palmer Cox's Brownies, American, pat'd. Feb. 11, 1896. • Palmer Cox wasn't the only Brownie artist. He was the originator, but Brownie illustrations for ads were drawn by a team signing off as "Marr & Richards, Eng [graving]. Co., Milwaukee." So look for that name as well as Cox's. .... **$150+**

ABC plate, stamped tin, alphabet border, nifty train design with cloud of smoke from smokestack, American, perhaps mid 19th C. • Lots of potential crossover interest here................................. **$135+**

ABC plate, stamped tin, low relief, embossed sans serif alphabet letters, depicts girl & boy (both skirted) running with hoops, lots of landscape, American or English, toy – only 3" diam., prob. 1840s-60s. Wide value range due especially to kind of show at which it is sold. .... **$75+**

ABC plate, stamped tin, depicts General Tom Thumb in primitive depiction, tight military clothing with sword at side, arms crossed across chest, big shoulder epaulettes – like Napoleon Bonaparte without the tricorn; in fact, Charles Sherwood Stratton, the midget whom P.T. Barnum showed beginning in 1842 when he was only four, wore Napoleonic outfits on occasion. Napoleon died in 1821, but the memory of the "little general's" victories & final defeat was good for Barnum's advertising. Stratton died in 1883. Plate only 3" diam., American, prob. c.1850s............. **$75+**

ABC plate, stamped tin, rolled rim with upper case letters, lower case letters surround profile portraits identified as "Oscar" & "Josephine," the man in military uniform with epaulette & Napoleonic curly short hair, the woman with a bead choker, & neo-classical hairdo with trailing tendrils on shoulders. This was a puzzle until I turned to the 11th ed. Encyclopædia Britannica, which revealed Swedish King Oscar I & his wife Josephine; he reigned from 1844 to 1859. Swedish, 6-1/2" diam., prob. 1844 to 1859, or later to commemorate something. ..... **$75+**

❖ NOTES ❖

Rolled rims – A rim or edge that is described as "rolled" may actually be rolled, such as this piece of tinware. The term is also used to describe the look of a rounded rim, that couldn't possibly have been actually rolled – such as a turned wooden bowl or a ceramic piece.

ABC plate, stamped tin, serif alphabet letters around wide rim, depicts small dead Cock Robin lying at feet of large sparrow with bow; legend "Who killed Cock Robin. I said the sparrow with my bow and arrow, I killed Cock Robin" appears around picture. Could be American or English, no words that prove British spelling, 8-3/4" diam., mid 19th C up into early 20th C. (This plate was offered in an 8" size by L. H. Mace Co. of NYC, for 36¢ a dozen.).................. **$85+**

ABC plate, stamped tin, serif letters, delightful depiction of elephant & his name, "JUMBO," prob. American because the famed elephant Jumbo, exhibited by P. T. Barnum beginning in 1883, was most famous there, but could be pre-1883 English because Barnum bought Jumbo from the London Zoo, 6-1/4" diam. A 6" diam. stamped tin "JUMBO" plate was offered by Central Stamping Co., NYC, in their 1920 catalog. See Elephant chronology in Chapter IV (Molds). .... **$75+**

ABC plate, stamped tin, somewhat runover looking, serif letters around rim, bust of George Washington, with name "Washington" underneath & 13 stars arched overhead, American, 6-1/8" diam., 19th C. The condition depresses value here.............................. **$55+**

VII-1. ABC plate. *Stamped tin, round (though depiction is oval), Jumbo, an elephant famed in the 1880s. 6" diameter. Central Stamping Co., 1920 catalog.* **$75+**

VII-2. ABC plate. *Stamped tin, 6" diameter, Cock Robin depiction. This one probably late 19th C. This was offered in mail order catalog of Butler Brothers, 1899. It was offered in other catalogs through the 1920s, along with "Hi-Diddle-Diddle" nursery rhyme. Butler offered an undescribed one called "Harvard."* **$65+**

ABC plate, stamped tin with rather ugly alphabet letters around rim, depicts cat playing fiddle, dog dancing, cow jumping over moon, dish & spoon hand in hand, legend reads "Hey Diddle Diddle," American or English, no words to check British spelling, 7-3/4" diam., mid 19th C. • Obviously this type of plate was made over a long period. Only by collecting a few and comparing them can one discover the differences. Even if somewhat flattened, dinged & bent, and with plating loss, the value is still about $50. A perfect specimen would be somewhat suspect because these were plates used by very small children, and no doubt banged on highchairs. Simple repro ABC plates with just letters around rim are commonly found. **$85**

VII-3. Shipping basket. *I need to set the record straight: this is not for fruit, as was thought until recently! Wood splints woven in flared shape almost like a standing cornucopia. What it really kept safe was not fruit (and why I thought that fruit wouldn't topple it over I don't know) but the cornucopia-like giant "morning glory" horn of an early Victor gramaphone. About 25"H. Photo of piece sold years ago by Arne Anton, American Primitive, NYC. Value as rare early recording go-with:* **$450**

VII-4. Peach basket & bushel basket, (L) "standard Jersey & Delaware" type (there was also a "Michigan" type made without the hoops, holding 1 peck). Wood veneer with 3 hoops, came in 2, 4, 6, & 8 quart sizes. • "The fruit-dealers in Chicago have a little 'dodge,' which we never saw elsewhere. Each basket of peaches is covered with a piece of tarletan or millinet, of a bright rose or scarlet color, which gives to the fruit a most attractive appearance, and at the same time prevents handling; this is put [also] over pears and other fruit." American Agriculturist, Nov. 1875. *(R)* Elm staves, oak bottom & handles, galvanized iron hoops. Originally cost $4 per dozen! Both pictures are of old type baskets, From D. J. Barry & Co. catalog, 1924. **$25+; $45+**

Apple basket, oak staves painted yellow, wood bands, round double bottoms, wire bail handle with turned wood "spool" handle, poss. Edgerton Mfg. Co., Plymouth, IN or Paoli, IN, half-bushel size, prob. early 20th C. Two 1920's catalogs show nearly identical baskets, natural finish oak. Established in 1849, Edgerton possibly made same baskets over a long period. They'd be surprised at today's prices. .... **$150+**

Apple box or basket, for market, nailed wood with slanted sides, painted green, 10" x 13", late 19th or early 20th C. **$135**

Apple butter jar, stoneware, dark brown Albany slip glaze inside, mug shape with round lip & slightly limp, applied "mug" handle, impressed mark, "F. H. Cowden" with place, "Harrisburg, PA," 7"H, c. 3rd quarter 19th C. **$135**

❖ NOTES ❖

Confusable – The apple butter jar above looks very much like a stoneware **chamberpot**, except that the mouth is slightly smaller than the largest circumference of the vessel's body, whereas in a chamberpot, the mouth widens out slightly. I would rather collect apple butter jars than chamberpots. In "The Shape of Stoneware," an article by James Mitchell, of the William Penn Memorial Museum (Harrisburg, PA) in *Early American Life*, Oct. 1978, we are told that "Sanitaryware is generally not found made from stoneware, but chamberpots are sometimes encountered. There are at least three marked examples. ... One dated "1776" was excavated from the site of the James Morgan Pottery in Cheesequake, Middlesex County, NJ. ... Another marked "Charlestown" belongs to the Smithsonian. ... The third is marked "Hawthorne Pottery Co [Hawthorne, PA]" and is in the ... William Penn Memorial Museum."

Apple tray, tôle – painted tin, square bottom, widely-slanted arch-topped sides, intact original paint in red, green, and yellow, on dark asphaltum background, prob. CT, 13" x 8", mid 19th C. .... **$950+**

Apple tray, tôle, oval, amber crystalized inner bottom, large hand hold cutouts at both ends, simple flowers & leaves in red, salmon, pink, yellow, green, black, & white, American, 2-3/4" deep x 12-5/8"L x 7-3/4"W, early to mid 19th C. .... **$1,500+**

Apple tray, tôle, rectangular bottom with high arched & slanted ends & slanted sides, crystalized & colored gold inside on bottom, sides japanned dark brown with flowers & leaves in yellow, white, blue, red, & black, in extremely good condition, American, 2-3/4" deep x 12-5/8"L x 8"W, mid 19th C. (See more on trays at end of chapter.) .... **$1,500+**

❖ NOTES ❖

Market Forces Change Evaluations. In the 1970s, these rare tôle pieces would probably have brought a lot more. There are still very exclusive, fancy antique shows selling very high-ticket items. But it is my feeling that the old-style knowledgeable (and rich) collector willing to pay for such a relatively unshowy piece is just about non-existent today. Now people with tons of money want pieces that declare their value more spectacularly. Even a small, modest 19th C folk art painting would have more show-off value; as would a small Oriental rug. In addition, as many of the old collectors died, their collections were bequeathed and absorbed into museum or historical society collections. Who knows if the value will ever come back up to 20th century levels?

Barrel, made from hollowed tree trunk, American, 30"H x 19" diam., early 19th C. Folk art crossover interest. ,,,,,,,,,,,,,,,,,,,,,,,,,,,,,,,,,, ... **$150+**

❖ NOTES ❖

American? It was probably safe until the 1980s to say that certain types of **rustic wooden pieces** were American. But every year since then, at every flea market, there is more and more evidence of rustic wood such as barrels, tall narrow churn-like receptacles, and baskets that originated in the Far East or Europe. Without microscopic examination of cellular structure, or unless I dug it out of the ground myself, I wouldn't be too confident about provenance for many wooden things. If you see them at their first dispersal point – say a big country flea market where dealers from all over the country shop – with a lot of similar items all with the same-colored dust, you can probably count on their being imports. And P.S. How many **borer beetles** have you seen recently? Injected boric acid products help.

Basket, for berries, round, vertical strips of prettily cut-out wood veneer bound with wire, wood bottom with hole, crimped tin edge (some found with wooden hoop at top), often called a "Shaker" basket but many examples have a non-Shaker manufacturer's name stamped on the bottom – "D. Cook's," with patent date, or "L. Cook & Co.," with place name. Others stamped "Union Manufacturing" & place, New Haven, CT, at least two sizes, pint (4-3/4"H) &

quart (taller & much bigger in diam.), pat'd. July 12, 1859, but prob. made over a long period. ..... **$125+**

Basket, for berries, wood splits, galvanized tin rim, American, one half pint size, 3-1/8"H, late 19th C. • Dealer Mickie Carpenter of Lousiville, KY told an amusing story about the "spice balls" she often fills such baskets with in booth displays. Her friend Kathie Hill makes the balls of ground spices mixed with a cementing-paste of some kind, and stuck with cloves. Once she had a small bowl full at a show and a man wandered into the booth, picked a spice ball up and bit into it, and made a very sour face. "Do you have anything I can spit this into?" he asked. She told him there was a waste can down the aisle, but allowed the taste alone to chastise him. The basket: .... **$145+**

Basket, for berries, flared sides, very small but not delicate. Bottom is round wood disc with hole, strips of split wood almost as thin as veneer tacked to disc and to strip that forms rim with small-head brass tacks, American, only 2-1/2"H x 4" diam., c.1860s-80s. .... **$75+**

Baskets, for berries, 2 very unusual, charming round, smoothly turned, bark baskets. Sides gently flared, with very skinny high arched cutouts, little finger size, from base up. Most appealingly, both baskets have been repaired. One with a small tin patch bent over the round rim, and tacked; the other with cord actually sewn back & forth across a long crack. Impressed in a 3/4" band close to the top is the name. "Mellish Patent," mfd. by Baird & Roper, Norfolk, VA, 4"H x 5-1/2" diam., pat'd. Feb. 23, 1869. .... **$150+**

Baskets, for fruit, various brands & very utilitarian, (1) thin split wood, constructed with 3 crisscross strips joined at base and bent up to form sides, purple stained band of wood at top, (2) essentially the same as 1st but slightly different look, name stamped in purple, (3) wooden bottom, crisscrossed narrow strips of wood, bound with wire, one marked "Webster," Webster Basket Co., Webster, NY, one half peck, turn of century to c.1930s or 1940s. .... **$10+**

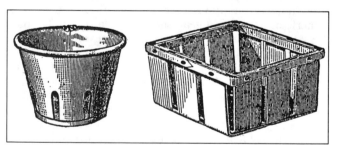

VII-5. Fruit baskets. (L) "Mellish" *patent, for berries, peaches, etc., in various sizes. Wood bark with unusual appearance. Illustration from David Lyman ad in* American Agriculturist, *July 1868 and later. Mellish baskets also manufactured by Baird, Roper & Co., Norfolk, VA, and advertised in same magazine after May 1870. Very hard to find – I've only seen two in 10 years. (R) Square, veneer with nailed rim, meant for strawberries. "Thoroughly ventilated, remarkably attractive when filled with fruit – and can box." Capacity one quart; they also made crates to hold from 12 to 96 quart baskets! American Basket Co., New Haven, CT.* American Agriculturist, *June 1865. (L) $150+; (R) $10*

The Rochester Berry Basket.

[Patented 1870.]

1 quart.   1 pint.   ⅓ quart.

The best ventilated and neatest Basket made.

Fits in Beecher Crates.

VII-6. Berry baskets. Interesting wood veneer construction, nailed rims, Pat'd. 1870. Collins, Geddes & Co., Moorestown, NJ. Ad in American Agriculturist, *May 1872.* **$65-$125+**

Basket, for fruit, decorative, not utilitarian, twisted wire, 4 very unusual cabriole legs, bowl with 8 fancy petals with scrolls inside, American or French, about 9-3/4" diam., 1870s to 1890s. .... **$250+**

Basket, for fruit display on sideboard or dining table, delicate, lacy twisted wire, sometimes painted dark green, very dark red, or white, 3 ply wire pedestal base, handles, French or American, 14"H, 1870s-80s. Like wirework egg stands meant for table use, these could be imports from France, not American, even though the USA had several thriving wiregoods firms. .... **$165+**

Basket, for fruit, woven, looped, soldered wire, a footed compote with swags around top, for all the world like a line drawing of a cut glass compote, showing where the fancy wedge cuts would be made by the cutter, American, about 8"H (these are hard to measure sometimes because wire squushes), 1870s to 1890s. .... **$155+**

Basket, for gathering fruit or vegetables, round wooden bottom, with a sort of picket fence of tongue depressors, wire-bound, forming flared sides, folding wire & wood handles, Shaker, made in KY, 14-1/2" diam., 19th C. Two others seen are one with rectangular bottom (with slightly rounded long sides) & handle at each end, 20" x 12-3/4", and elongated oval-bottomed one with very flared sides, 32"L x 20"W. Ovals up to twice the price for rounds. .... **$250+**

Lookalike Alarm

A good design can't be improved, and **wire things** have eye appeal matched only by pen & ink drawings. Giulio Cappellini, a designer in Milan, Italy, has a line of accessories called "Filo di Ferro" [wire of iron]. He makes "reinterpretations" of French wire fruit dishes, high footed compotes, low baskets, stemmed candleholders (for votive candles in glass jars), and various plate & platter trays – all of exquisitely twisted iron wire. To my eye, especially in photographs, they look just like the pieces from 100+ years ago; soon, differences will be impossible to detect.

VII-7. Berry & fruit baskets. *The baskets in the last picture were advertised as fitting "in Beecher crates." Here are some real Beecher Basket Co. baskets. Various shapes and sizes, pat'd. May 31, 1864; Dec. 17, 1872; and Feb. 26, 1878. Westville, CT. American Agriculturist ad, May 1878. Thirteen years before, C. Beecher & Sons, advertised their widely-acclaimed "Veneer Fruit Basket," being "neat, stylish, durable and cheap." As well as close-nesting when empty. It was similar to the 1864 patent basket shown at bottom, only sides didn't curve at all.* **$20-$100**

VII-8. Useful gourds. *Ad placed by Waldo F. Brown, Oxford, OH, to sell his gourd seeds and a booklet. Note two baskets made from the gourd, which he said could be grown to hold 2 gallons! American Agriculturist, Feb. 1892. Old containers made from gourds are often found varnished, but you should see the beautiful painted ones and I'm not talking about the Mexican tourist pieces, but 19th C. utilitarian pieces! Basket made from gourd:* **$30+**

VII-9. Berry basket. *Wood veneer, wood bottom, sheet metal rim. Type often called a "Shaker" basket, but it probably isn't. Many are marked "D. Cook's," or "L. Cook & Co." or "Union Manufacturing, New Haven, CT." Pat'd. July 12, 1859, but made over long period. 4-3/4"H.* **50+**

Basket, half-bushel size, oak splint, a zinc hoop plus wooden hoops & bottom, bentwood oak handle grips with both ends cut to pointed wedges & driven into woven bands near top, extremely handsome, perfectly made, American, late 19th C. .... **$150+**

Basket, hickory splint with wooden handles, bushel size, American, late 19th or early 20th C. Patina costs! .... **$95+**

Basket, homemade from green-painted motor oil can, cut from rim down close to bottom so sides could be made to flare out, edges bent around copper wire rim, high arched copper wire handle, basket 6"H, can from c.1920s-30s. Folk art crossover. **$65**

Basket, miniature splint, 2 handles, very finely made & detailed, American, only 3-1/2" x 3", mid 19th C. .... **$175+**

Basket, tin, footed, with twisted, corrugated rim, base & handle, American, 11-1/2"H, c.1870s. • Tin household objects or items of apparel from shoes to baskets to hats to chairs were commissioned from tinsmiths as 10th Anniversary gifts. Surprisingly few have surfaced, although many are hidden away or on display at museums. The more detail the better. The value remains surprisingly low ... at least to me. I think they are splendid pieces. .... **$450+**

VII-10. Berry basket. *Very similar to VII-9. Wood veneer splits, galvanized metal rim & hoop at bottom. Only 3-1/8"H. Courtesy Mickie Carpenter.* **$50+**

Perhaps a Futurewatch? – On Jan. 1, 1988, the Litchfield Auction Galleries, CT, sold the James & Nancy Clokey collection of folk art, including **10th Anniversary tin pieces**. I wish I'd been there. The *Maine Antique Digest* reporter summed up the disappointing take by saying that the Clokey's "enthusiasm never rubbed off on others." I, and everyone else who might have smidges of the Clokey's *joi*, so overestimated what the pieces would bring that I (we?) didn't bid. A square basket of woven strips of tin, with a fancy wrapped hoop handle and edges, and four sproingy loops at each corner, filled with polychromed stone fruit (which alone should have brought the price) sold for only $425, plus 10% premium. A punch decorated pudding mold sold for $900 (plus 10%); the decoration probably accounted for most of the money. A life-size Windsor chair, all tin, went for a shockingly low $525 (plus 10%). A cake box, round with slanted sides, domed lid with nifty funnel finial and applied 3-D tin flowers, which MAD reported the Clokeys paid over $4,000 for when they bought it, went for a paltry $1,200 (plus 10%). I don't know what this bodes for the future of Anniversary Tin, but surely it isn't true market value. See also the sidebar entitled "1875 Tin Anniversary" in Chapter XIII (Turn, Spoon, Flip & Dip).

Basket, wire in form of chicken, very intricate weaving, wires are close together, painted tin trim: red comb, yellow eyes, with wooden beak, carrying handle of heavier wire, prob. American, 8-1/2"H x 12"L, 19th C.

VII-11. Wire baskets: *fruit compotes, cake stand, flower-holder centerpiece. The linecuts are all "Sherwood's Standard White Lustral Wire Ware" from the catalog of Woods, Sherwood & Co., Lowell, MA, as it appeared in a book from 1876. In 1872, the same linecuts were used in an article on "tinned twisted wire" household goods, based on French originals, in Nov. 1872* American Agriculturist. *So many wire baskets are being made today, for decorative purposes, that it takes some doing to find an old one … and recognize it. Be careful.* **$95-$200**

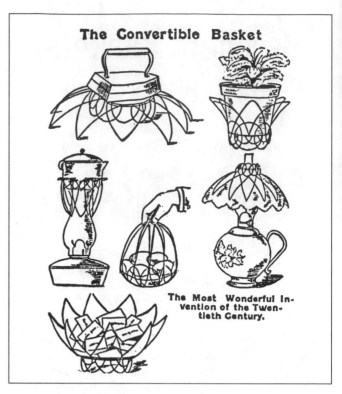

VII-12. Convertible basket, *made of nickeled iron wire, and used as a lamp shade, flower stand, egg boiler, hanging lamp, ladies' work basket, [sad] iron stand, card holder, cake stand, fruit basket, etc. Novelty catalog of A. E. Rayment Supply Co., Rockford, IL, c.1910-20s. (One of these, looking confusingly but appropriately old, was for sale for $265 in 1997!)* **$35+**

Cheep chicken. – This isn't the common 1950s chicken basket, perfectly rounded & made from somewhat heavy wire not too close together, soldered joints. That kind shouldn't be more than $15. This one:................ **$275+**

VII-13. Market basket. *Dyed straw, 14"H x 14-1/2"L, Tennessee, 1930s-40s. Collection of Mary Mac & Robert Franklin.* **$25+**

VII-14. Beer pot or pitcher. Graniteware, reinforced strap handle, wire bail handle with turned wood. Lalance & Grosjean Mfg. Co., NYC, 1890. $65+

Basket, woven splint, miniature melon, very finely made, Tennessee, only 5-3/4" across, c.1850s. .... **$325+**

Basket, woven splint (& reed?), large, straight-sided, colored green, blue, orange, & yellow with potato stamp designs, American – possibly Native American, 20"H x 24" diam., 19th C...................... **$600+**

Batter jugs – See Chapter II (Mix, Beat, Stir)

Beater jars – See Chapter II (Mix, Beat, Stir)

Berry box tray, green painted wood, very flat with low sides, high arched bentwood handle, meant for holding 12 berry boxes, American, 1-1/4"H sides x 17" x 12", 19th C. • These came in various sizes & proportions, but most seem to have been meant for 8 or 12 small square berry boxes. Some had four little block feet, one at each corner. Many were left unpainted, but old green, gray, blue, and red are found. .... **$125+**

Berry container, also for dried fruit, made of wood fiber, dipped in paraffin, used with a special sealing tool, square or oblong, round air holes in top & lids, "Seal-Tite Weis Fibre Containers," mfd. by American Container Co., NYC, NY, five sizes, from half-pint to quart, 1918.................................... **$20+**

❖ NOTES ❖

Early Paper Containers appeared in the Jan. 7, 1888 *Chamber's Journal*: "An attempt now being made on an extended scale to introduce **bottles** made of paper into this country [England] merits some passing notice. The paper-bottle industry, which has achieved considerable success in Chicago, and is gradually extending throughout the United States, has not yet obtained any development on this side of the Atlantic. Foremost amongst the advantages accruing from this new adaptation of paper is the fact that the bottles are unbreakable;

Lookalike Alarm

To cash in on country-look lust, some entrepreneurs have recently made up crude berry box trays from old crates or other weathered old wood. You get a feeling for them after a while, but many have tell-tale, freshly- sawn edges, easily visible.

whilst the cost at which they can be placed on the market is considerably lower than that of articles of the same size in glass, stoneware, or tin. A great saving in weight is moreover effected, a desideratum of no small moment where cost of carriage of large numbers has to be taken into consideration; whilst the cost of packing is reduced to a minimum, for breakage in transit, which is a constant source of loss with glass bottles, is obviously impossible. Special machinery is employed in the manufacture of paper bottles. A long strip of paper of requisite thickness having been formed into a tube by bending around a circular 'mandrel,' is covered externally with an outer glazed sheet, bearing any printed labels to be employed; the tube is then cut into short lengths, to the ends of which are added tops, bottoms, and necks of paper – or of wood, if special strength is desired – nothing further being necessary beyond pouring in and lining the insides with a composition, which on setting will effectively resist the action of acids, spirits, inks, dyes, &c." Milk cartons are taken for granted now; only in last few years are milk bottles making their reappearance – even in chain grocery stores. They keep milk colder so it lasts better.

Berry pail, blue & white swirl enamelware, with lid, straight sides, 7"H, turn-of-century................ **$95+**

Birdcage, brass cage, molded opaque white "milk" glass cups, cast iron stand with small bird design on base, American or German, mid 19th C. Required equipment for many late 19th C. or early 20th C. kitchens was a bird, plus cage. Housewares stores & departments stocked birds & cages; unfortunately, the practice continues in some stores today......... **$175+**

Birdcage, brass wires & sheet brass, arched top, simple bottom with 4 squatty feet, scrolly hanger on top "Colonial," mfd. by American Cage Co., Racine, WI, 1920s.. **$50+**

VII-15. Birdcage & ground squirrel (chipmunk) cage. (L) Wheel cage with painted iron wire and stamped tin front & trim. 19"H x 13-1/4" x 6-1/2" body (tray base is 16-1/4" x 12"). (R) Enameled iron wire & stamped & perforated sheet metal, 18"H x 11" x 7-3/4". Both in catalog of Norvell-Shapleigh Hardware Co., St. Louis, 1910. $90-$175+

VII-16. Pen & ink original drawing. *"The Warm Weather – Terrific explosion of a Ginger Beer Truck." Signed "K. Gregory", c.1880. A somewhat more refined & finished version appeared in a Harper's of the period – this may have been a first sketch, or a loose copy. 11-1/8"H x 8-1/4"W. A primitive, spirited drawing. Note corkscrew in vendor's hand, and the exploding thick stoneware ginger pop bottles, which are about 7" to 9"H. The simple, mass-produced tan & ochre bottles are worth about $30-$45. The drawing:* **$150+**

VII-17. Stoneware bottles. (L) *A Gin bottle, with handle, made by Wingender, in NJ, cobalt blue flower & bands, 10"H.* **(M)** *a root or ginger beer bottle, big lip, initials in cobalt blue "D B", 10"H.* **(R)** *Another Wingender gin. Photo courtesy Litchfield Auction Gallery, Litchfield CT. Ex-Corbin Collection, 1990 sale.* **$125-$225**

VII-18. Pickled food bottle. *Green glass in "**Cathedral**" pattern, with gothic arched hexagonal sides. 13"H, American 19th C, mold-blown. Photo courtesy of Robert W. Skinner Inc., Auctioneers, Bolton, MA.* **$300-$600+**

Birdcage, globular pumpkin form, tin top, bottom & center band, bars of tin going from "North Pole" to "South Pole," conical finial on top with wire hanging ring, top, band & bottom painted blue, bands/bars painted white, a lovely form but awful to think of a bird living out its life inside this. Birds should live outside, in their natural habitat. No mark, prob. New England, 14"H, early 19th C. .... **$200+**

Birdcage, heavy green, ochre & red painted tin, tin roof in peaked form, decoratively pierced with tiny quatrefoils, wire sides, no marks, American, 18"H x 15"L x 9"W, 19th C. .... **$125-$150**

Birdcage, high beehive or haystack shape, iron wire, longitudinal wires bound by latitudinal wires twisted at each intersection, very deep straight sided pan, almost like a cake pan, bottom, hanging ring of wire at top, not painted, American (?), about 13"H x 10" diam., prob. mid 19th C. .... **$150+**

Birdcage, japanned & decorated perforated & plain tin, brass wire, in shape of large mansion with mansard "French" roof with widow's walk on top, large arched "entry," with 2 interior staircases, solid back, on scalloped base with 4 conical feet, Heinz & Munschauer, Buffalo, NY, about 16"H x 12-3/4"W x 8-1/2" deep, c.1880. .... **$225+**

Birdcage, on pedestal stand, round with double dome top, brass wires finished in colored enamel, large brass finial, stand looks like bottom four-fifths of a floor lamp from same period, it is marbleized with paint, Crucet Mfg. Co., NYC, NY, early 1920s. • They offered in their ads a booklet I'd love to see: "Lovely Cages." The ads' claims pack a lot of decorating value into a birdcage: "Introducing a harmonious assortment of exquisitely decorated cages with pedestals to match decorative surroundings of home. There is a wide variety of finishes to suit exacting, individual tastes or requirements, among which are: New dandelion and black ivory and colors. Roman gold and marble effect. Antique walnut and gold. Black and gold. These alluringly new and charming cages are a decided relief from ordinary, unsightly bird cage in general use. You will have a pride in the lasting beauty of the distinctive Crucet." .... **$75+**

Birdcage, pierced & pieced sheet metal, art deco, large canister cylinder, snap-on bottom, witch's cap conical

VII-19-A. Novelty bar bottles. *All are molded figurals with etched details. From left to right:* **(1)** *Mermaid;* **(2)** *Portrait bottle of champion heavyweight pugilist* **Jim Jeffries**, *who boxed from 1896 to 1904, and 1910 to 1921. This design shows "champion ready for an engagement," probably was done after his first retirement. Bottle has etched tights, body is painted flesh color. Catalog states "best and only representation of a pugilist made in the form of a bottle." Crossover appeal for boxing collectors.* **(3)** *"Never Rip" decanter ... "They like to pour from it." A touch of soft porn, as in many late Victorian things.* **(4)** *Elephant's head & trunk, "cleverly gotten up for back bar display." All from the hotel & bar supply catalog of Albert Pick & Co., Chicago, 1909 (with some items going back to 1905).* **(1) $75+; (2) $500+; (3) $85; (4) $75+**

top, sides and top all cutout so as to form a pattern of oblongs divided into 3 triangles, each triangle with diagonal lines going different direction from its neighbors, very effective & looks somewhat like abstractions of spider webs – a motif popular in the 1920s & '30s. Little sliding door for bird egress & entrance, & for filling water & feed dishes. This one almost well-

VII-19-B. Bottle stoppers. *Figural heads, all mounted to corks.* **(L)** *Dour Uncle Sam, of "elegant china bisque ... finely colored."* **(M)** *Carved wooden bulldog, decorated with pyrography.* **(R)** *Best: comical colored rubber clown, whose tongue protrudes when squeezed. This might be a* **Futurewatch!** *I've never seen any of these. All of these were commercial, and meant mostly for bars or restaurants. Albert Pick, 1909. Lots of crossover potential in this type.* **$10-$35+**

VII-19-C. Bottle stoppers. *Molded colored celluloid. Modernized versions, with more detail, of familiar carved & painted wooden stoppers – many of them also from Germany. Albert Pick, 1909. Most valuable in pairs. Each:* **$30+**

enough made to look like a professional commercial craftsman made multiples of the design, but not quite. I think it's a one-off piece made skillfully in a home workshop. Prob. American, 18"H x 12" diam., prob. late 1920s or early '30s. Folk art. .... **$250+**

Birdcage, slightly peaked roof, wire sides, unusual feature being a sort of canopy of tied-back curtains actually made of polka-dot painted cutout tin, zigzag bottom, meant to hang from a holder, French, mid 1930s. Kitsch appeal, plus! **$150**

Birdcage, stamped, japanned & decorated tin, wire, reticulated footed pedestal base also stamped with human figures, hexagonal dome-topped cage with reticulated gallery 2/3 way up, "cornice" decorations at corners made of stamped metal, Heinz & Munschauer, Buffalo, NY, 18"H x 9" diam., c.1880. • Many cages from this period are **painted in vivid color** combinations of cobalt blue, a bright medium green, an almost fire engine red (or a maroony red), and a sort of acid yellow. The blue is sometimes chalky in appearance; exactly like bright blue paints used by kindergartners. Some cages are decorated with small floral decals on the peaks; they resemble lithographed paper-covered dollhouses of same period................................. **$250+**

Fake Alert

The most commonly-found repro (or, rather, outright fake) **birdcage** is the big (36"H x 28"L x 9" deep), dark green or brown, three-domed, wood & wire bird condo, with a fake clock above the arched front door. Asian-made, deliberately aged and distressed to make it look antique; it's been imported by the thousands, along with fake carousel horses, wicker baby buggies, hobby horses, ad nauseum. Gift catalogs offer them retail for $300; antique dealers have them for up to $500. The intent is to bilk the gullible, not house the homeless, my opinion of the "value" of this cage is a big ZERO. Don't encourage them & don't buy 'em, please.

Bottles – There are thousands of types of bottles that would be found in kitchens from the 17th C on. I can't possibly cover the subject here. Best to join a club (see last page of this chapter), and buy books on the types of bottles that appeal to you.

Bottles, for pickles, mold blown green or aquamarine glass, all with collared mouths, molded in the Gothic arch sided style called "cathedral" jars, ranging from pale green to rather dark green, collection of 5, as follows: (1) short squat one with 3 arches, extra decoration on front, plain arch in back has columns on either side, 8-1/4"H; (2) 4 sides, 3 arches with extra designs, 8-1/2"H; (3) 8 sided jar with arches, 11"H; (4) dark green, 4 sides with upside down crown around neck of jar, very simplified designs on body, 11-3/8"H; (5) large version of first one, crude mold, lots of bubbles, 4 sides, 3 arches filled with designs, 14-1/4"H. Quite extraordinary range of sizes. American, mid 19th C. • According to Steven Van Rensselaer, who wrote *Check List of Early American Bottles* and *Flasks* (Southampton, NY: *Cracker Barrel Press*, 1921), "It is probable that most of the glass works made them, but it is known that they were made at the Willington Glass Works [in] East Willington, CT." • Individual prices might range from $250 to $800. This set: .... **$2,200+**

Bottle carrier, green painted sheet iron, holds 6 bottles around outside, one in center, cap end of bottles fit into "dimples" in lid, kept cool with packed ice, for Nehi bottles, mfd. by Universal Container Co., Toledo, OH, about 8-1/2"H x 7-1/4" diam., 20th C. Crossover appeal for soda collectors................ **$75+**

Bottle carrier, soldered wire, 6 bottle "silos" 2 x 3 formation, high arched twisted wire carrying handle, from an F. A. Walker catalog, (also came in 2 & 4 bottle sizes), French?, c.1870s. .... **$150+**

Bowl, burl, deep, waxy-feeling wood, 2 small checks [dryness or age cracks, naturally occurring as wood dries out], one check filled with an old repair composition material, bowl slightly warped, American, 4-1/4"H x 11" diam. at widest part, late 18th or early 19th C. Another hard-to-provenance type of wooden antique. .... **$750+**

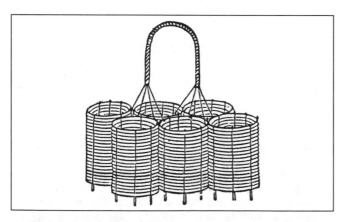

VII-20. Bottle carrier. *Tinned iron wire, twisted & soldered, made for 2, 4 or 6 bottles. From F. A. Walker catalog, 1870s-80s. SEE also VII-146.* **$95+**

VII-21. Burl bowl. *Old, original red paint on exterior, about 16-1/2" diameter but slightly warped as usual. First half 19th C. Photo & information courtesy Jeannine Dobbs'* Country/Folk/Antiques, *Merrimack, NH. A sublime form, good-sized.* **$2,000+**

Burls are abnormal, though not harmful, protuberant wart-like growths occurring on the trunks & large limbs of trees and are usually found on hard- or semi-hardwood trees, though they can occur on any tree. The cause is "imperfectly understood," to use woodmensch Albert Constantine Jr.'s phrase. Speculations as to cause include injury (fire, frost, nail holes or other violent physical contact), and irritation from bacteria, fungi or viruses, says Constantine. I have heard people explain them as the effect of wasp stings; Constantine relates the belief that woodpeckers may cause burls to form. • Different writers list **different trees** as most probable to have burls, especially those burls valuable to wood turners or cabinetmakers. Most lists include walnut, oak, cherry, sugar maple, mahogany, myrtle (ie. acacia), thuja (ie. thuya), various ash, yellow poplar, olive, mountain laurel, arbutus (ie. madrone burl), birch, Norway burl birch, English elm, redwood, and box. Early settlers and 19th C artisans in Europe and the United States prized highly figured burls, especially for making bowls. American Indians used burls to make bowls, some with handles carved in figural or animalistic forms. • According to Constantine, some species of burls **check and warp** easily, maybe even requiring repair before using. This may explain why some burl bowls are so decidedly warped & cracked. Most burl wood can be very highly polished, sometimes without the addition of any wax or oil. • To read more about wood, and to better understand color and figure (pattern of eyes, swirls & loops) of all woods, I recommend *Know Your Woods*, by Albert Constantine, Jr., (NY: Charles Scribner's Sons, 1959; revised by Harry J. Hobbs, 1975). Constantine is a name well known to 20th C wood artisans, because the firm has supplied craftspeople with woods, veneers, & other materials for many years.

Bowl, burl, large, well-figured oval, 2 small handles are part of rim, very good patina, small crack with old repair done with metal staples ("staple" in this context doesn't mean Swingline™), not signed, but known to be from Bergen County, northeastern NJ,

6-1/2"H x 19"L x 15"W, early 19th C......... **$2,000+**

Bowl, burl, lathe-turned bands on outside, cracks fill-fixed with solder, American, 15" diam., early 19th C. .... **$1,500+**

Bowl, burl, birds'-eye maple (?), 2 bands turned around top, American, 5-1/4"H x 13-3/8" diam., early 19th C. .... **$750+**

Bowl, burl, oval shape, finely figured, old iron staple repair holds short age check, American, 19"L x 15"W x 6-1/2"H, late 18th or early 19th C. See picture VII-110 for several prized mended pieces. .... **$2,300+**

Bowl, burl, small age check or crack in rim, very good patina, American, 5" deep x 10" diam., 19th C. • Many burl bowls with a rounded lip or rim are described as having a "rolled" rim, a term only for metalwares where the metal has actually been rolled, usually around a wire core, to give stability.................................. **$750+**

Bowl, burl with old tin patch repair, American, 9" diam., 19th C. .... **$500+**

❖ NOTES ❖

Wood knots – "In the back country ... cups, bowls, and trenchers were cut out of wood and served every-day table purposes. White ash knots were used for ... bowls and constantly the woodworkers were grubbing around the forests for knots in old sugar maples, soft maples, ash, beech, and birch trees. A single large knot would make a whole nest of bowls. Such wood was referred to as 'dish timber.'" Richardson Wright, *Hawkers & Walkers in Early-America*, 1927.

Bowl, cast iron, American, unusually deep, 7" deep x 9" diam., 2nd to 3rd quarter 19th C. .... **$175+**

Bowl, cast iron, deep, with rounded rim and ring base, American, 3-1/2" deep x 9" diam., 18th C. • You see very few of these advertised for sale. The only dealer I ever knew of who consistently came up with them

VII-22. Burls still growing on tree. *This particular tree is near Mt. Crawford, VA, in the Blue Ridge area. In many places in Virginia and New Jersey (two states I personally know of) there are huge trees growing with a full supply of burls.*

is Clara Jean Davis of Concord, NH. She is a direct descendent of Joseph Jenks (Jencks), first iron founder in America...................................... **$300+**

❖ NOTES ❖

Iron bowls are fabulous. One dealer described one of hers as having "a ring like bell metal." Clara Jean Davis of Hopkinton, NH, has said about her offerings that they were nicknamed "poor man's pewter." Another dealer called hers a "slave bowl." In my *300 Years of Housekeeping Collectibles*, page 205, you'll see two cast iron bowls that were called "wash hand basins" in the 1861 trade catalog I found the pictures in. One is bell-shaped with flared rim and with a small foot, and came in three sizes: 3-1/4"H x 8-1/2"; 3-1/2"H x 9-1/2"; and 3-3/4"H x 10" diam. They could be had in plain cast iron, tinned, or porcelainized. The other one is proportioned more like a mixing bowl, with small foot, and came in five sizes, plain or tinned: 3-3/4"H x 9-1/2"; 4-1/4"H x 10-3/4"; 4-5/8"H x 11-3/4"; and 5-3/8"H x 13-1/2" Both styles were from Leibrandt & Mcdowell Stove Works and Hollow-Ware Foundries, Baltimore & Philadelphia. • Most cast iron bowls were made without a foot, some did have a narrow ring base. Most have slanted straight sides or slightly rounded sides; the earliest have round sprue marks on bottom, later ones (late 18th, early 19th C) have straight sprue gate mark. No recorded marks are known on American ones (English ones are usually marked). They come in varying heights from about 3" to 4-3/4"H, and varying diameters from about 7" to 12", 18th or 19th C. Generally valued upwards of $100.

Bowl, called a Scotch bowl or Scotch kettle, cast iron with forged falling bail handle, long casting gate on bottom, irregular reinforcing band around outside, just under slightly flared lip. The Scotch bowl did not necessarily have a lid that came with it, although if you've cooked oatmeal, grits or Cream of Wheat™ you'll recall how the bubbling surface sends up small volcanic eruptions of scalding hot meal bubbles to burn your stirring hand. Not marked, American, 2-7/8"H x 10-3/4" diam., c.1830s to 1850s. • According to Carl W. Drepperd's *A Dictionary of American Antiques*, a cast iron, cup-shaped cooking pot about the size of a Scotch bowl but without the flared sides, is called a Yankee bowl. .... **$100+**

Bowl, for eating, turned wood, slightly warped, with faded old blue paint on outside, it has acquired a lovely patina inside from "wet" food, oils & greases, American, 7" diam., early 1800s. .... **$175+**

Bowl, probably for fruit, painted turned wood, tulip on grayish old rose background, probably Lehnware, named for Joseph Lehn (also found spelled Lehne), Lititz, Manheim Township, Lancaster County, PA, 5"H, mid 19th C (Joseph Lehn lived 1798-1892, & worked c.1856-1892). • For comparison, see entry for Sugar bowl, turned wood, made by Pease. .... **$950+**

Bowl, turned wood, rather thick, old gray paint on outside, American, 17-1/2" diam., mid 19th C. • My theory about all **old gray paint** seen on 19th C pieces is that when you mix lots of leftover colors together and add white, it is always a shade of gray, and therefore old batches of mixed paints were used up in painting utilitarian pieces (including a surprising number of kitchen chairs). Otherwise it seems odd to pick gray, unless it was because it didn't show dirt. For modern collectors, it's a boon – grays seem very contemporary & cool & allow the form to lead. **$325**

Bowl covers, for storage in refrigerator, made of "washable, airtight oil silk, with Lastex bands," looks like rubberized parachute silk. A complete set would include a zippered pouch for bread & small covers for bottles and jellies, Blossom Mfg. Co., NYC, NY, late 1930s.. **$2+**

Bowl or trencher, hand-hewn thick wood in oblong shape, with old red paint on outside, American, 29"L x 13" x 6" diam., early 19th C. • Size, age, patina and paint = added value............................... **$275+**

Bowls for mixing – See Chapter II (Mix, Beat, Stir).

Box, bentwood, straight lap with copper tacks, constructed with wooden pegs, wire bail handle with wooden grip, original varnish in golden color, stamped "Weston Sherwin & Co.," Winchendon, MA, 2-3/4"H x 4-3/4" diam., 19th C. See also Pantry boxes... **$550+**

Bread box, a sort of quonset hut, with roll-up lid, painted tin with little design of long-skirted woman with parasol, painted ivory with green trim, ivory with red, or white with red, "Betsy Ross Roll-A-Way," mfd. by E. M. Meder Co., c.1935. These jumped in price about the 1990s, when retro-styled kitchens became popular & people started buying fresh-baked bread or making their own in bread-makers. .... **$35+**

Bread box, for diner or big household, holds 4 loaves stacked on end, tin, & with baked-on white enamel, lid has knob and hole, word "BREAD" stenciled on, motto reads "The All Welded, Rigid, for strength and durability. Built like a bridge," English, provisional patent #29069/24. Others are white or green; a white one with no stenciling:............................ **$60+**

Bread box, japanned tin, imitation oak graining design in ochre and brown, wire handles, stenciled "BREAD," flat top, side wire handles, hasp closing, Matthai-Ingram Co., American, came in nests of three: 10", 11" and 12" deep x 13-1/4", 15-1/4" and 16-1/2"L x 9-1/2", 10-1/2" and 11-1/2"W, late 19th C. • Separately, maybe $25-$40 each. For original nest of three:.. **$100+**

VII-24. Bread raiser. "With ventilated cover." Heavy tin, riveted strap handle, four sizes in same odd-seeming choice of quart capacities – 10, 14, 17, and 21. Small ones suited for families, the largest for hotel kitchens or bakeries. Approx. sizes: from 6-5/8"H x 14-5/8" diameter to hold 10 quarts, to 8-1/4"H x 19-1/4" diameter (21 quarts). Central Stamping Co., 1920. Very similar bread raisers were made by Sexton Stove in Baltimore, Savory of Newark, NJ, and Geuder, Paeschke & Frey Co., Milwaukee, WI, in the 1920s-30s. Graniteware ones may bring a lot more. **$75-$125**

Bread box, square tin box, punctured with holes & slits, roof-like lid with cast iron handle at top, design on front of box rather like pie safe tins, stars in each corner as spandrels, band across center has initials, probably of owner, "K. M. B.," prob. PA, 15"H x 14" square, mid 19th C. A "folk art" piece........... **$500+**

Bread & cake box, painted tin, two white porcelain knobs, roll-top with cake drawer below, 2 wire side handles, stenciled "BREAD" and "CAKE." (This came in ivory, white, blue, green, gray, red or yellow painted tin.) C. B. Porter Co., American, 14-1/2"H x 16"L x 11-1/2"W, turn-of-century, early 20th C. **$50**

Bread & cake box, tin japanned in brown, words "Bread & Cake" in yellow stencil, has roll-top front lid, fold-down wire handles at side, "Kreamer," 13-1/2"H x 12"L x 11"W, 20th C. **$90**

Bread raiser, gray graniteware, with tin lid, small base, 16" diam., c.1890s-1910. (This form more often found in all of tin.) .... **$125+**

VII-23. Bread box. "Roll-A-Way" style with choice of decorations. This one is "Early American Girl Moderne," in ivory with green trim, or ivory with red trim, or white with red. "Betsy Ross Moderne" was not shown in ad. Mfd. by E. M. Meder Co. 1935 ad. Bread boxes, especially from the '30s and '40s, are increasingly in demand because of the millions of people using their own bread machines. **$35+**

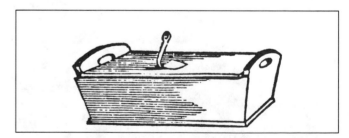

VII-25. Bread trough & dough scraper. Oblong wooden box with slanted sides. This was used the way the raisers were later used. I just love these old pictures from American Home Cook Book, written "by an American lady." NY, 1854. The crooked-handle scraper is not described, but it appears to be one of the wrought iron ones – a sort of dough hoe. I've never seen a carved wooden dough scraper, but it could also be that. **$125+**

Buckets & Pails. Both buckets and pails are for carrying, as well as measuring, dry or wet materials, even though we've gotten used to thinking that both are meant only for holding water (especially for mopping). Informally, a bucket of liquid would hold at least 5 quarts; more formally two gallons. A dry bucket measure held about the same. A pail is understood to more likely contain liquid, but it's about the same size and capacity. Interestingly, the word "pail" is thought to come originally from the Latin word *pagina* meaning "page." See also Milk pail, Slop Jar, Firkin, Piggin, here and in Chapter V (Measuring).

Bucket, cobalt & white enamelware, wire bail, wood-grip, late 19th C. Condition important – most are found rusted out. **$95**
Bucket, composition wood fiber & glue, wire & wood, bail handle, "Indurated Fibre Ware," agented by Cordley & Hayes, later called "Fibrotta," NYC, NY, 9-1/4"H, 1883, 1884, 1885 and 1886 patents, company still in business in 1915. .... **$55**

Fibre Ware History – After years of thinking Cordley & Hayes were manufacturers, I read in *The Metal Worker* that they were agents for The United Indurated Fibre Co., Lockport, NY. • "A good substitute for wooden pails is what is called wood-pulp ware. Pails, dishpans, wash-bowls, etc., are made of this. [It is] light; no hoops to rust or loosen, and can be kept dry and clean easily." Maria Parloa, *Kitchen Companion*,

VII-26-A. Pails & a "Dutch bucket." *Left to right:* **(1)** *Staved wooden pail of cedar (10, 12 or 14 qts. or pine (12 qts only). Iron bound, wire bail, wood grip. Duparquet, Huot & Moneuse 1904-1910 catalog.* **(2)** *Pieced tin, flared sides, wood grip, in 6 qt. (6-1/4"H), 8 qts. (6-3/4"H) and 10 qt. (7-7/8"H) sizes. Savory, Inc., c.1925-28. Tin one least valuable, although even rusted ones sometimes priced high.* **(3)** *Graniteware water pail in 12 qt. size only. From Sethness Co. catalog, 1925.* **(4)** *This is the "Dutch bucket," and the name is possibly because it is not really a bucket (see Index for other examples of using the word "Dutch"), or because it actually is in the shape of a style of bucket or pail from Holland. Pieced tin, footed, japanned on outside, 4 sizes from 8 to 14 quart capacity. Matthai-Ingram Co., Baltimore, c.1890.* **$25-$50**

VII-26-B. "Milk-Jug and Water-Pail." *An 1858 cautionary morality fable in the form of a conversation:*
MILK-JUG:
Water-pail, how can we two agree?
What are you, pray, sir, compared to me?
You'd better be gone, to drudge about,
For, if you stay, I shall turn you out.
WATER-PAIL:
My dear little Jug, mind what you do;
Fine things are brittle, and so are you.

The milk-jug thought always of his worth,
He look'd so handsome upon the hearth;
But the cook she crack'd him,
which made him leak,
And he lay on the dust-bin that very week;
But the plain old water-pail held his own
Full three years after the jug fell down.

Picture Fables, *drawn by Otto Speckter, translated from German rhymes of F. Hey. NY: Appleton, 1858.*

Boston: Estes & Lauriat, 1887. Other products were fruit bowls, keelers, slop jars, commode pails, spittoons, cuspidores, mats and trays. • **Other fibreware companies** were The Standard Fiber-Ware Co., Mankato, MN, who made a line of pails and basins, etc., of flax fiber c.1891; and Delaware Hard Fibre Co., Wilmington, DE, c.1905. The wares varied considerably, and included things to be left outside, filled with water! Anything in this somewhat vulnerable pressed wood-pulp composition is rare, because it first lost its protective varnish after long exposure to water and hot sun, and then would crack. • An **especially odd item** is a deep, straight-sided **basket with high hoop handle**, the entire body being perforated. This was made in the 1890s for industrial use. They were called "dip baskets" and meant for dipping into molten plating metal (tin, nickel, copper, etc.) by brass foundries, nickel-plating works, etc. They replaced stoneware baskets because they were thought to be more durable.

Bucket, emerald green & white swirled enamelware, bail handle with wooden grip, turn-of-century. Desirable color. .... **$100+**
Bucket, extraordinarily bold, handsome small wooden bucket, painted dark green, with three wide lapped fingers in rather high relief, two large arched lugs for pegged bentwood bail, said to be Shaker, about 7"H x about 7" diam., 19th C. • The 1988 price ($3,050) is

what George Morrill paid at a Mike True auction. Collector & auctioneer Morrill, said "When you find impeccable color, you just have to go for it." .... **$3,000+**

❖ NOTES ❖

"A Rightness in Green." – Cornelius Weygandt wrote in *The Heart of New Hampshire; Things Held Dear by Folks of the Old Stocks* (NY: Putnam's, 1944), a delightful chapter entitled "Why Woodenware is Painted Green: for Leslie Joy." He searches, wonders, and asks all around; he notes that "Most cooperage is left unpainted, fully three-quarters of it. If twenty-five percent is painted, fifteen of that ... is green, five madder red, and five a blue so light it is almost gray, a blue even lighter than the Amish blue of barns and houses in Pennsylvania Dutchland." He describes many pieces of painted "cooperage" in his collection, some "painted the characteristic dark green." One is a "spice box seven inches long, five inches broad, and three inches high. It is oval in shape and redolent of ... spices. ... Its top and bottom are pumpkin pine and the sides of both base and cap look and feel like brown ash. The sides are pegged to top and bottom. Each is one piece of thin brown ash bent around on itself and sewed together with linen thread. ... Some folks would write it down as Shaker made, but there were good artisans aplenty in the long ago outside the Shaker communities as well as within them. Its sides, rubbed in places, reveal a green much lighter in color than the characteristic dull dark green traditional for such pieces. This lighter green is, perhaps, a priming coat." Finally, Weygandt talks to a "lady of Newbury across the Connecticut in Vermont" who says "There has never been any question in the matter. Since Vermont has been Vermont it has been proper to keep white sugar in green buckets, brown sugar in red buckets and soft maple sugar in unpainted buckets." Weygandt concludes by suggesting "... there seems, somehow, a rightness in green for cooperage."

Bucket, coopered wood painted with diagonal smoke graining, iron bound at bottom, middle and near top, bands daubed with paint, falling wire bail with simple wood grip with beading at each end – a subtle detail that probably translated into a few hundred $$$ of total, it's perhaps the punctum, or telling point. Joseph Lehn, 9-1/2"H, 19th C. Lehnware is highly prized. .... **$4,500+**

Bucket, for sugar storage, not to hang on a maple tree, slanted sides with fitted & turned staves, 3 decoratively painted bands, lid has rounded edge, turned bands on flat top, possibly original white porcelain mushroom knob with screw, painted with orangey salmon background, white, red, yellow, green, & black leaf & vine decoration, what's now called "Lehnware," made by Joseph Lehn, Lititz, PA, 8-1/2"H x 7-1/2" diam. at top, mid 19th C. .... **$1,000+**

❖ NOTES ❖

Joseph Lehn's Turned Wooden Wares & Where Lehn Came From – Lita Solis-Cohen, in her *Maine Antique Digest* report on the Musselman auction of 1985, wrote that Lehn was a "farmer-woodworker from Hammer Creek Valley, Elizabethtown Township, Lan-

caster County, ... active from 1850 to 1890." I can't find any Gazetteer that locates an Elizabethtown Township in Pennsylvania. **Carl W. Drepperd**, in an article in May 1954 *Spinning Wheel* speaks of Lititz (or Litiz, Manheim Township, Lancaster County), as an "old Moravian Community," and, furthermore, places Joseph Lehn at a hamlet called Clay, "some four miles north of Litiz," where he made a "fairly scrumptious living as a wood turner, selling plain turned things. Then he had the idea of painting the woodenware somewhat after the manner of tinware painters of an earlier day." He also used Staffordshire wares and "Gaudy" wares for motifs. Drepperd tells us that Lehn's special favorite was his own design of pussy willows. **Mildred T. Bohne**, in *Ohio Antique Review* (now *Antique Review*), June 1984, wrote that Lehn settled in Clay, "close to Ephrata," and that he started making barrels about 1856 to supplement his farm income, and also small turned woodenwares. She goes on to say that "his small shop was at the back of the house he built at Hammer Creek, a little south of Clay." [Notice how we keep inching south?] Bohne describes many of the forms, from buckets to small covered spice & saffron containers and trinket containers in the shape of footed goblets, and also explains that Lehn "had trouble keeping up with his decorating" and resorted to a combination of paint and decalcomania, and that he also "contracted out some decorating to William Helich, an Ephrata chairmaker, and to John Sechrist."

Bucket, for sugar, wood staves with bentwood hoops & pegged handle, double band at bottom, close-fitted bentwood frame lid, marked on lid "Our Centennial Best, 1776-1886," 12"H x 12-3/8" diam. at base, 1876. Added value for mark & commemorative origin. .... **$150+**

VII-27. Butter boxes. *"Bradley's" patented boxes, made of spruce or oak veneer "sewed together," tin bands at top and bottom. Used after scalding, by packing tightly with butter, overlaid with a disc of wax paper. American Agriculturist, Jan. 1880. A matched set, even an assembled one, is worth more than the sum of single prices because of decorative & completist appeal. Each:* **$45-$125**

VII-28. Butter jar or crock. *Stoneware, with applied ear handles, slightly domed lid with self knob. Made in 11 sizes: 1/4, 1/2, 1, 2, 3, 4, 5, 6, 8, 10, and 12 gallons. The ones made in bigger sizes, from 15 to 50 gallons, were for meat, and did not have lids. Duparquet, Huot & Moneuse, hotel supplier, c.1904-1910 catalog.* **$40-$150+**

Bucket, or sugar firkin, original bluish green paint, staved, bail handle of split ash, bent to hoop, wooden cover, branded on bottom "D. C. & G. Bissell," American, 11-3/8" diam., 19th C......... **$150+**

Butter box, pine bentwood, bentwood strap handle, iron hardware locks when box is lifted! American, 12" diam., 19th C. .... **$125+**

Butter carrier, round bentwood with original blue paint, wire bail handle, wooden grip, American, 9-3/4" diam., c.1890s-1910. When it comes to value, blue's the hue that is true!.. **$150**

Butter carrier, with cover, red painted wood, with wire bail handle, 12" diam., 19th C. .... **$125+**

Butter crock, also called a butter pot, saltglazed stoneware with indigo blue on bluish gray, depicts Utica's characteristic bird on branch, marked "White's Utica," Utica, NY, 3 lb. size, 3rd quarter 19th C. .... **$300+**

❖ NOTES ❖

Stoneware Investment – The most valuable American or Canadian saltglaze stoneware dates to late 18th or early 19th C, and has **incised** decorations filled in with cobalt blue or brushed with blue before stage in firing when salt is thrown into top of the kiln. These pieces are very rare. Not so rare are stoneware forms with elaborate "**quill traced**" cobalt decoration (liquid slip applied through the narrow opening of a quill fitted as a sort of funnel into the mouth of a "slip cup," a small, squushed-sided bottle filled with liquid slip, powdered cobalt mixed with a flux and a binder and some water, and used sort of like modern day tubes of fabric decorating fluids, by drawing with tip of quill, leaving a trail of blue slip. The commonest cobalt decorated wares have **brushed** decorations, distinguishable because the lines tend to be broader, softer and reveal strokes of the stiff brushes used. Birds, animals, flowers, anthropomorphized suns, moons & stars, and often humorous portraits of people are all found in all three types of decoration, though mainly the 2nd & 3rd types. While collectors like crocks and jugs that have maker's stamp impressed in clay before firing, or marked in blue under the glaze, wonderful stoneware forms can be found that are unmarked. It is advisable to study books that offer advice, and to pick up and look at and think about stoneware that is available for sale at antique shows, auctions and flea markets, and always to ask questions. • The best book to my mind is Donald Blake Webster's *Decorated Stoneware Pottery of North America*, Rutland, VT: Charles E. Tuttle, 1971. It will be hard to find, and worth whatever you have to pay if you intend to seriously collect stoneware.

Butter crock, apricot saltglazed stoneware, with original lid & wire bail handle, 9" diam., late 19th C. .... **$175+**

Butter crock, blue & cream saltglazed stoneware, original lid, wire bail handle, 10-1/2" diam., late 19th C. .... **$150+**

Butter crock, brown "Rockingham" glazed pottery, with original lid, 8-1/2" diam. x 6-1/2"H, 3rd to 4th quarter 19th C. The shiny medium-brown glaze may have originated in England, but the term is often used regardless of provenance...................... **$100+**

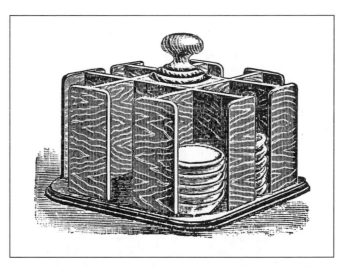

VII-29. Butter chip holder. *You're right, it looks just like a poker chip holder. We don't know which came first. Wood (looks to be some kind of plywood), holding 6 stacks of butter chips or patties on what appear to be little pans or saucers. From V. Clad & Sons, Inc., c.1890-1900 pamphlet. For a restaurant, but I couldn't resist!* **$45+**

VII-30. Butter dishes. *Both in "Perfection" granite ironware with choice of white metal or nickel plated mountings & protection bands. Both have two small hooks on lip to hold butter knife. Manning, Bowman & Co., c.1892 catalog.* **$125+**

VII-31. Cake box. "The japanned tin boxes keep cake, bread, &c., perfectly fresh without the undesirable moisture of the stone jar." American Home Cook Book, 1854. Thirty years later, similar ones were being offered by the kitchen supplier F. A. Walker, Boston. **$50+**

Cake box, also called a cake tin, chromolithographed tin, round with close-fitting lid, three extremely collectible images for added value: Santa Claus holding a bird toy, with a teddy bear & a Golliwog in his toy pack, border of holly leaves, one of the best ever, "Rich Iced Christmas Cake," Debus Bakeries, 3-3/4" diam., c.1910s to 1920s. The Golliwog is most of the value here.................................... **$225+**

Cake box, for Christmas fruitcake, lithographed tin, depicts an Art Deco Santa Claus, American, 1930s. **Added value.** – Generally, the most collectible boxes have Santa images, especially if the art is in a very pronounced style, such as art deco, where image of Santa has been manipulated to fit art style............................... **$40+**

Cake box, round with hinged, slightly domed lid with hasp closing, very deep & looks like a hat box, japanned & stenciled with scrolls & word "CAKE," from F. A. Walker catalog, American or imported, deep relative to diam., c.1870s......................... **$50**

Cake box, stenciled tin, red background, black & gold design, slant-front drop lid with porcelain knob,

VII-32. "Pastry closet" or cake safe. Sometimes called an "upright cake box." Round corner, black or white japanned stamped tin, 6 compartments. 15-1/2"H x 11-1/4" x 10-1/8". Central Stamping Co., 1920 catalog. **$45+**

VII-33. Cake & pie box. "A new idea in making a receptacle for pie and cake. In this box may be placed pie and cake in separate compartments perfectly safe from insects of all kinds, and yet thoroughly ventilated and aerated by its patented construction." One size only: 8"H x 12-1/2" square. Three finishes: brown japanning with gold stenciling; oak grained with gold; white enamel with gold. Silver & Co., Brooklyn, NY, c.1910 catalog. In perfect condition: **$85+**

marked "CAKE BOX," with Schepp's Cocoanut advertising inside lid: "The object of this can is to serve as a Cake Box – the convenience of which will be readily seen at a glance. The cover opening in front and letting down, does not necessitate the trouble of pulling the box out from under the shelf and almost any Lady would cheerfully pay twice the price of one in preference to the unhandy old style box. "PRICE 60 CENTS." Early 20th C. • A two-shelf Schepp's box, with blue finish, was also made, worth just about the same. Price depends heavily on condition, as it does for all chromolithographed tin containers. .... **$75+**

Cake box or safe, japanned & stenciled tin with cast iron carrying handle on top, 2 shelves, swing-out door that could be ordered with a lock, from F. A. Walker catalog, poss. imported from Europe, or American, about 24"H (?), c.1870s. .... **$95+**

Candle box, brown japanned tin, cylindrical shape with shield-shaped back with hanging holes, not uncommon, prob. American, 19th C. These were still being made & sold or used at least as late as 1910, in North America, the U.K., & Europe, as well as countries such as Australia. .... **$150+**

Reproduction Alert

A "handcrafted reproduction of [**candle**] **box** used in 1800's," made in copper (natural or burnished), plain tin, "pewter finished tin," or "raw tin for toleware painting" were all available from Craft House in Tiverton, RI. This candle box was a long cylinder with hinged, pierced lid with single hasp, 2 tabs with holes for hanging on wall, and was 13-1/2"L x 4-1/2" diam. They were offered for $16 and $9.25 in Dec. 1973, and $20.75 and $12 in Oct. 1975 editions of *Early American Life*.

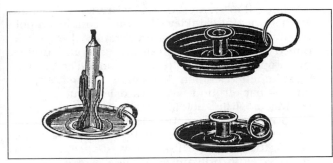

VII-34. Candlesticks. *Japanned stamped tin, all with black finish. At* **(L)** *is a "save-all" with the bottom of the candle accessible to the saver of scrap candles.* **(T-R)** *is 6-1/2" diameter with deep saucer base for runny candles.* **(B-R)** *came in two sizes: 4-7/8" and 5-1/2" diameter. Central Stamping Co., 1920 catalog.* • *In an English cookbook from about 1904, I found a shopping list in the hand of the mistress of the house. It said "servants' clock, milk?, and candle sticks." I pictured simple tin candlesticks like these.* **$25+**

Candle box, heavy tinned sheet iron, in cylindrical shape with hinged lid, not of common store-bought style (such as one with shield-shaped back), American, 18"L, early to mid 19th C......................... **$300**

Candle box, wood in old red paint, base molding, open with no lid, skinny high backplate with large round top and hanging hole, looks like a doughnut on a stick or a lollipop, American, 11"H x 12"L x 7"W, early 19th C. Caution: easily faked............... **$250+**

Candle box, wood with grain painting, slanted sides, old cut nail, cutout half moon in arched (sometimes called a 'tombstone') back board, American (?), 6"H x 11"L, 19th C. .... **$250+**

Candlestick, cast iron, 2 parts: square base about 1"H, fluted column for candle, no mark, American, 5-3/4"H, c.1840-60s. **$175**

Candlestick, hogscraper type, tinned sheet iron, hanging hook, marked "Merriam, Harris, Wheeler, and Merriam," American, 5-3/15"H, marked "Patented 1853" on thumbpiece, pat'd. April 2, 1853.................. **$125+**

Candlestick, sheet iron with touch of brass, a push-up type referred to as a hogscraper stick as well as a wedding band stick (now being widely reproduced); the former for resemblance to a butchering tool, the latter for narrow brass band about 5/8 the way up from bottom. (Much rarer are hogscrapers with double bands.) This stick has most commonly found marked, "SHAW," on push-up thumbpiece. Birmingham, England, 6-1/2"H, mid 19th C. • A rarer version has an iron ring instead of the brass. ...... **$125+**

Candlesticks, pair of hogscraper type, tinned sheet iron, broad inverted saucer-like base, push-up in shaft, marked "S. T. Barnes," Columbus, OH, only 5-1/2"H, pat'd. July 19, 1853... **$175**

Candlestick of type called "chamberstick," white enameled stamped steel, blue edge, small ring handle on saucer base, short candleholder with wide flared flat rim, marked underneath with a medallion with balance scales, "KJAB," the "Scale Brand" mfd. by the Kockum Enamel Works, imported by Markt & Co. of NYC, made in Sweden, 6-1/4" diam., turn-of-century.. **$55+**

❖ **NOTES** ❖

Enameling Process – "When the vessels in the stamping works are of the right shape they are sent to the magnificent enameling department. It is here that the ware receives its ornamental, porcelainous [sic] appearance. The various utensils are first placed on large carriages and run into the enormous ovens, in which process a quantity of oil and other matter is thrown off. They emerge from this heat black and ugly, and are then dipped into tubs of stain and are afterward boiled and washed quite clean. "They are now ready to receive their first coating of enamel, and afterward to be enameled white or blue. In order to receive the first coating the vessels are dipped in a thick, creamy enamel paste, but this first coating, however, must be burned in, and for this purpose, after being thoroughly dried, they are placed on iron cars and run into red-hot ovens, in which they remain from eight to ten minutes.

"The wares are once more placed in the enamel to obtain the outer coating; the edges of white wares are coated blue, the handles of water cans, etc., are coated and all the other articles are given their proper appearance. By a most ingenious method the so-called granite effect is obtained in the coating. This is brought about by the vessel being dipped in enamel, the specific gravity of which is different, so that when the vessel is lifted out the enamel runs off, gets hard and certain attractive markings appear. Once the vessels have been fully enameled they are once more burned, this time becoming quite hard and glossy. They are then assorted and sent to the warehouse. The daily output from the Kockum factory [established in 1859, and also maker of "Flag Brand" wares] is as high as 20,000 vessels." *House Furnishing Review*, Feb. 1907.

Candy box, heart-shaped cardboard, lid covered with padded red satin, die-cut white paper cupid glued on top, red satin ribbon edges, no name, 5" across, 1910s or '20s (?), maybe later. Condition is all, unless the candy is still good, heh heh. .... **$15+**

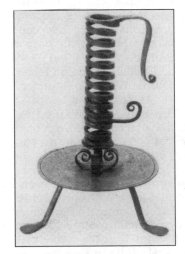

VII-35. Candle holder. *Forged iron "pigtail" holder, on tripod base. 10"H. Maker's mark on rim of underside of base, "Samuel Yellin." Philadelphia, early 20th C. [Yes, the 1900s, not a misprint. Yellin was considered one of the finest artisan blacksmiths ever, and created many works for architects to install in homes they built. For a book on Yellin, see author Jack Andrews in the Bibliography. And do a Web search for more info on his prized work. Photo courtesy Litchfield Auction Gallery, Litchfield CT. Ex-Harold Corbin Collection, auctioned Jan. 1, 1990. Price realized: $2,100.* **$5,000+**

VII-36. Candlesticks. *I found a 1925 Pearson-Page Co., Ltd., catalog of "cast and sheet brass reproductions," art and novelty items. Pearson-Page was in Birmingham, England; the catalog bore the NYC importer's name. Many of the pieces are now labeled "antiques," but I know different. Clockwise from top* **(L):** *(1) Pan type of sheet brass, riveted handle, 5-5/8" diameter. (2) 7-1/2" diameter pan. Note thumb rest on curled handle. (3) 7" diameter pan decorated with chased designs around floor of pan and on handle. Shallow sides have perforated design.* **(B-R)** *(4) 8-1/2" diameter pan with square strap handle, probably a new art style, not a reproduction.* **(B-L)** *(5) Version of chamberstick, 6-1/2"H x 7" diameter pan. Could be had plain or with chased decoration.* **$40+**

Candy box, heart-shaped cardboard, top is chromolith of exuberant roses in turquoise vase, gilt paper on edges, box maker unknown, held Schrafft's candy, 2 lb. box, 13" across x 1" deep, 1940s. .... **$10+**

Candy boxes, cardboard. Some covered in printed or colored paper (desirable motifs include "pretty ladies" & certain animals like cats, pigs, bunnies), some have satin or other cloth or paper ribbons, some are shaped (hearts probably best), some with paper-hinged lids, some retaining paper lace flaps inside, various candy makers, but not all have a name & were possibly identified with paste-on paper label, American, German, English, French, Swiss. Sizes from miniatures (like little Whitman Sampler™ boxes) to large 10 lb. chocolate boxes, late 19th C to 1950s. **Futurewatch.** – This may become an attractive collecting field. Old candy boxes have been used as perfect containers for trinkets, buttons, pencils, greeting cards, etc., and have often been just too good to throw away. Candy box manufacturers' catalogs and old candy advertisements would round out a collection. Price range for boxes only. **Schleicher Paper Box Co.** – A selection of rectangular ones from just this one manufacturer's catalog: 1 lb., 2 lb., 3 lb., & 5 lb. decorated boxes, some with overhung lid & bottom. (1) Allover spider web stained-glass look & trompe l'oeil (fool the eye) ribbon; (2) moiré sunray stripes behind buxom lass; (3) 2 tone background with chromolith woman in pic-

ture hat; (4) art nouveau scrolly "frame" with snowy sleigh scene; (5) twinkley Christmas candles in holly wreath; (6) art deco teal & orange design with framed pretty lady portrait; (7) overall subdued "raindrops in pond" pattern & trompe l'oeil ribbon; (8) silhouetted Indian horseman against sky; (9) bubbles background with Beardsleyesque girl; (10) be-fringed "girlie" holding breast (gadz, who would you give this to?); & more. "Masterbuilt," F. J. Schleicher Paper Box Co., St. Louis, MO, company est. c.1900, these boxes c.1930s. • Most spectacular are square ones in brilliant colors like Lautrec posters, mostly of women. • Original prices for all types, wholesale, ranged from about 4¢ each for simplest litho ones, through 18¢ each for pretty ones, to 90¢ each for a 2-layer Christmas candle rect. one 5 lbs. Most expensive were red satin-covered heart-shaped boxes, some of which, the 2-layer 5 lb. kind, with hand painting or embossing, cost as much as $2 each wholesale. Prices applied on lots of 100 boxes. The candy probably cost less than the boxes. Condition is of major importance in pricing old candy boxes. .... **$5-$50+**

Candy bucket, miniature turned wooden bucket with flat lid, bound with wire, with wire bail handle, originally filled with maple sugar hearts, "Sap Bucket," Maple Grove Candies, Inc., St. Johnsbury, VT, 21 oz. capacity, c.1930. .... **$10+**

Candy container, cobalt blue glass, form of a dog, poss. 1940s-50s, as most early ones were clear colorless glass. .... **$50+**

Candy container, molded clear glass Scottie dog, tin cap, J. C. Crosetti Co., Jeannette, PA, 2-1/2"H, 1962. .... **$50+**

Candy container, glass kettle with 3 little feet, paper cover, "Boston Beans Candy," mfd. by T. H. Stough Co., Jeannette, PA, 1st quarter 20th C. .... **$150+**

Candy container, molded clear glass rabbit, marked "J. H. Millstein Co.," Jeannette, PA, 6-1/2"H, "pat. appl. for" (prob. 1st quarter 20th C.). .... **$200+**

❖ **NOTES** ❖

Embossed marks – According to William C. Ketcham, in "The Collectible Glass Candy Container," *Americana*, July 1976, "... since 1912 the manufacturers of the containers have been required by law to emboss their names – Victory Glass, Eagle Glass, & J. B. Higbee Glass are a few of most common ones – on their bottles." I suppose this had to do with some Food & Drug law.

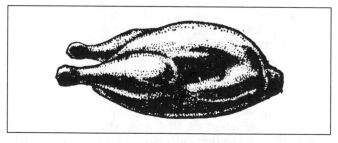

VII-37. Candy box. *Papier-mâché turkey, "colored to represent a roasted turkey." Bottom opening. 4"L. From Slack Mfg. Co. novelty catalog, c.1925. Originally cost $9.50 for a gross.* **$65+**

VII-38. Candy boxes, *for Christmas. Lithographed cardboard, frosted with mica sprinkles for snow. Candy fits into opening in bottom of each. Originally cost $5 a gross. From Slack Mfg. Co. novelty catalog, c.1925. Each:* **$50-$100**

Candy container, molded glass rolling pin, metal cap, turned wood handles, "V G Co." (Victory Glass Co.), Jeannette, PA, 7"L, holds 3 oz., early 20th C. .... **$125+**

Candy container, molded glass vacuum cleaner, wire handle & tin wheels, "Dolly Sweeper No. 2862," West Brothers, Grapeville, PA, 3"H x 2-1/4"W, early 20th C. .... **$300+**

Candy container, papier-mâché in shape of roast turkey, opening is in bottom with cloth tape hinged cover, 4-3/8"L, late 19th or early 20th C. .... **$90+**

Candy container, papier-mâché turkey, molded & painted, Pulp Reproduction Co., Milwaukee, WI, 5-1/4"H, 1st third 20th C. Sometimes found in folk art dealer booths............................. **$90+**

Candy container, extremely realistic miniature smoked ham, polychromed papier-mâché, smoothed out with plaster, with hanging hole in "bone" & a twist of cord knotted through it, German (?), 4"L x 2"W, late 19th C. .... **$95+**

VII-40-A. Candy boxes & cool slang. *For fancy chocolates or candy assortments. All were oversized for actual contents held – meant to fool recipient. Chromolith paper covers in "beautiful assortment of art pictures," with real ribbon. One at left, 15-1/2" x 9", has classy deep flange. Catalog says "This is positively the* **biggest flash** *on the market." Two at right came in 3 sizes: 1/2 lb. box, 10-1/2" x 4-1/2"; 1 lb. box, 10" x 6"; and 18 oz. box, 12-1/2" x 5-1/4" which "looks like a 2 lb. box." From Slack Mfg. Co. novelty catalog, c.1925.* **$5-$20**

VII-39. Candy boxes, *for Hallowe'en. All in orange & black, cardboard & tissue. The ones in the top row are small size; the lower row has big ones. From Slack Mfg. Co. novelty catalog, c.1925. The big cat & pumpkin, and cat, pumpkin & owl in front are worth the most.* **$40-$150**

VII-40-B. Paper candy cases, *or cups for candy or other small confections. Fluted or pleated colored paper in a variety of forms – mostly kitcheny things. Note the heart; the "staved" keeler at right of 2nd row; the coffee cup; the low pail, bucket or firkin; the washtub; the basket! All from Duparquet, Huot & Moneuse catalog, c.1904-1910, from which hoteliers and confectioners bought supplies.* **$3+**

VII-41. Canister set. *Yellowware, "Dandy-Line," mfd. by Brush-McCoy Pottery Co., Zanesville, OH. Included spice containers (on top row), those for sugar, salt, butter & flour, tea & coffee, and also bread & cereal & cake jars, rolling pin, mixing bowls, milk pitchers, and nappies (the smallest bowl on table). Various kinds of knobs and handles, not really matching. Ad in* House Furnishing Review, *Aug. 1915. Full set of 15 pieces probably at least:* **$700+**

Candy container, full-size hen, tail up & head down in pecking position, head comes off at neck, painted paper and glue composition, extremely well-detailed, German (?), 12-1/2"L, c.1890s-1910............ **$300+**

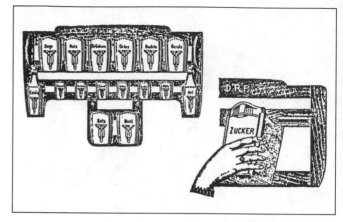

VII-42. Canister set. *Decorated china with patented rack with built-in metal lids. Made in Germany and imported by housewares wholesaler G. M. Thurnauer, NYC.* House Furnishing Review, *Aug. 1910.* **$125+**

Candy container, red, white & blue paper, in shape of George Washington's hatchet, marked "I Cannot Tell a Lie," poss. imported, prob. American, early 20th C. .... **$25+**

Canister, embossed stamped tin with stylized overall chrysanthemums in *Japonisme* style, truncated conical top with close-fitting lid, japanned in bronze color, American, 6-1/4"H, 19th C. .... **$15+**

Japonisme

This French word describes a style of decorative arts (or decoration on useful objects) that show direct influence of various arts of Japan, as well as China and the rest of the exotic Orient. "Japanese" motifs such as chrysanthemums, butterflies, fans, parasols, & bamboo, are found on Japanese screens, kimono cloth, inlaid metalwork, and other domestic goods; the same motifs can be found in westernized versions that Japanese artisans devised for export to Europe and U.S. since mid 19th Century. These imports were further westernized & interpreted (diluted or exaggerated) by Western artisans who used them as models for making goods for their consumers. *Japonisme* as a movement is usually dated from the 1870s to 1890s, although some people push up the tail end of it as far as WWI; a design movement with some similarities is "The Eastlake Style," named for aesthetician Charles Eastlake, whose influential theories about good design and applied decoration were widely subscribed to. Both correspond somewhat in period & inspiration to the flowering of art nouveau.

Activating The "Japanese Movement" – Nineteenth century American interest in Japanese-like decorative motifs actually began with Commodore Perry's 1850's voyages to Japan, which were meant to open trade with Japan. This interest became a very popular fashion in the 1870s, long before Gilbert & Sullivan wrote *The Mikado* (which was first seen, in London, in 1885); the musical only fanned the flames. The Centennial Exhibition in 1876 also added to interest in Japanese style.

Enamelware Decoration – By 1890, such a huge manufacturer as Manning-Bowman satisfied popular demand for the look with a large selection of enamelware designs influenced by Japanese motifs; at about the same time, David Block, a New York manufacturer of stamped tin housewares, sold "Chinese Pattern Embossed Goods," which were Western forms the surfaces of which were covered with a dense Westernized hodgepodge of Oriental motifs. Many late Victorian artisans in all fields adopted the coloration of *Japonisme*, especially vivid colors against dark backgrounds. Examples are seen in black velvet crazy quilts & chromolithographic commercial arts such as trade cards or greeting cards. By WWI, the "Movement" was over, having been supplanted by the Arts & Crafts Movement, and early stirrings of art deco.

Japanning is Something Different – Japanning is much older than *Japonisme*, and it is another thing entirely, though much of it is characterized by vivid coloring against a dark background, adapted from Oriental lacquerware color schemes. By the early 1600s, imported Chinese Coromandel screens & lacquered furniture were known in the West, including Britain, where some of the finest early japanning was done. Many of these Oriental wares had dark (black or brown) or "Chinese" red backgrounds, with decorative motifs in color & gold or bronze, plus inlays of colored stone or mother of pearl. Imitation "Japan" finishes were applied to papier-mâché & wooden furniture & trays, as well as sheet metal coal vases, trays, coffee urns, etc. In the 18th century, fashionable ladies in

England and America (and probably in Europe) took up japanning – that is, "the Art of covering bodies by grounds of opake colours in varnish, which may be either afterwards decorated by painting or gilding, or left plain. ... ," according to Robert Dossie, in Handmaid to the Arts, published in 1758. Ground [background] colors were browns, reds, maroons & blues.

"Japanning" is defined in the 1854 *Dictionary of Arts, Sciences and Manufacturers*, by James Smith, as "the art of varnishing in colours, and is frequently combined with painting ... [on] wood, metal, paper, and leather." But in practice, by mid-19th C, "japanning" mostly meant semi-translucent, heat-resistant lacquers on tin, like most pieces in this book. Oxidized tinted linseed oil or baked-on asphaltum (a sort of petroleum) were used. Dark maroon-y brown is commonest color. Other colors included red, crimson, pink, yellow, green, blue, white, black, and a browny-black "tortoise shell." See Chapter XIV.

Chinoiserie or de Chine – These are French terms used in the decorative arts to describe Western decorative motifs considered or supposed to be typical of, or related to, Chinese arts. Western artisans got inspiration from Chinese porcelains (some of which were made by Chinese potters in designs and with decorations, ordered by Western importers (especially those in Holland), and even based on European designs: a real cultural exchange twice over. • For the most part, Chinoiserie motifs are only "supposéd" – that is, they are often not authentic, but are based on exotic decorations taken more from European engravings in travel books about China than from real Chinese arts. The term is related to *Japonisme*. • In applied decorations, there are many Chinese and Japanese motifs common in name, if not in appearance, including depictions of Nature (flowers, bamboo, birds, water) and of manmade objects (fans, kimonos, stools, vases). • One marked difference is that Chinese arts have more motifs which appear geometric or abstract, and Japanese arts may have more even, allover patterns. • Cross pollination, ie. the influence upon Oriental art by Western arts, and vice versa, back and forth, as well as the cross cultural influences between China and Japan and the rest of the "Orient" (including India) is common to both decorative movements – Japonisme and Chinoiserie.

❖ NOTES ❖

Bug Out – "Tin cans of meal and sugar, stone jars of salt ... Tin boxes are best receptacles for food that would attract mice and weevils. They are, to be sure, more expensive than wooden buckets, but they are lasting and perfectly secure. Should have labels, and if they are made to order, have labels painted on them at the same time. Such boxes as cracker manufacturers use will answer this purpose and may be obtained through the grocer." Maria Parloa, *Kitchen Companion*, 1887.

Canister, japanned tin, hinged dome top, stenciled "TEA" or "COFFEE," 6"H, American 19th C. .... **$30+**

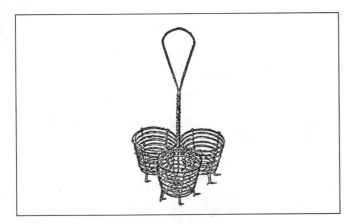

VII-43. Table caster patent, *for small bottles – oil, vinegar, perhaps a bottled catsup or sauce too. Pat'd. Nov. 10, 1874, by Daniel Sherwood, Lowell, MA, assignor to Woods, Sherwood & Co., who were huge manufacturers of wire goods. This was the patent drawing, but it looks like the catalog line-cuts too. It also closely resembles a wire egg-boiler rack. The real thing:* **$65-$100**

Canister or pantry set, 10 emerald green glass jars, slanted ribs, rectangular, metal screw-on lids, name labels for Cereal, Flour, Sugar, etc., mfd. by Owens Illinois Glass Co., Toledo, OH, c.1920s or very early 1930s. A Greenie's Dream Set! **$250**

Canister for cookies, looks like small corrugated garbage can but was described as an "artistic shape," it's impressed "COOKIES" on side, came in 4 colored glazes, green, canary, ivory or blue, "Kolorkraft No. 344," mfd. by Brush Pottery Co., Zanesville, OH, about 8"H, introduced Dec. 1928. **Color Fashions.** – The jar was an editorial feature in *House Furnishing Review* in February 1930. At the time it was said that "Colors harmonize with kitchen and pantry. Colors available and their relative popularity is as follows: Green, 65%; canary, 20%; ivory, 10%; blue, 5%." (This was to guide the retailer in his ordering). Furthermore, "Best quantity buying months are those preceding the spring, Thanksgiving and Christmas seasons."... **$55**

Canister set, also called a cereal set, decorated earthenware, sort of ovoid rectangles, domed lids with huge hand grips, glazed with light cream background with a sort of happy-go-lucky plaid effect in blue and black in horizontal band near tops, entire set has 15 pieces, often you find just the big 6, marked on the fronts: "Tea, Coffee, Sugar, Rice, Barley, Farina," or maybe 7, with the "Salt" box with hinged wooden lid. Jug-like cruets are marked "Vinegar" and "Oil." Six half-size smalls are for spices: "Ginger, Cloves, Nutmeg, Cinnamon, Allspice, Pepper." imported from Czechoslovakia, early 1920s. .... **$150+**

Canister set, glazed china, red & white checkerboard design below, with much smaller diagonal checkerboard border, oblong, with china lids, marked on front in French for contents, the largest canister being for SUCRE (sugar). Very attractive, even when worn. French, the smallest about 4-1/2"H, the largest about 8"H, c.1920s (?). Each about: **$50**

Canning jars – See Chapter XVI (Canning)

Carrier boxes for cutlery – See Cutlery tray

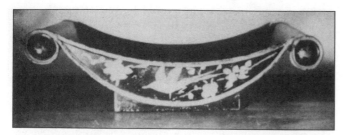

VII-44. Cheese cradle. *Tôle – or japanned tin, with birds & flowers in ochre, white and gray on dark ground. A lovely form that almost looks like a doll-size Roman lounging chaise. 14" x 6". The form looks Welsh (Pontypool or Usk); the decoration too. Courtesy The Abrahams, Langhorne, PA.* **$500+**

Cheese baskets – See Cheese drainer baskets in Chapter IV (Molds).

Cheese box, bent basswood, painted in shades of yellow, for storage, American, 9"H x 15-3/4" diam., 19th C., perhaps early 20th. .... **$150+**

Coffee can, tin pail with fitted lid, lithographed elephant, wire bail handle, "Elephant Coffee," Jewitt & Sherman Co., 4 lb. can, c.1890s (?). Example of using familiar & famous Jumbo the elephant, to imply large quantity & perhaps exotic quality.. **$95+**

Coffee can, wonderful barrel-shaped lithographed tin can, fitted lid, "Cafe Gruzerio Extra," Rio De Janeiro, Brazil, 5 lb. can, late 19th or early 20th C....... **$60+**

Collapsible cup, also called a collapsion cup, divided into telescoping sections of nickel plated brass, engraved with scrolls, 5 telescoping bands, marked on top in fancy script "Vest Pocket Cup," Scovill Mfg. Co., Waterbury, CT, pat'd. Feb. 23, 1897........ **$15+**

Collapsible cup, metal, Rumpp & Son, (a leather goods firm; this probably had a leather case), Philadelphia, PA, late 19th C.. **$15+**

Collapsible cup, metal with depiction of couple on tandem bike, these are also called cyclist cups, American, late 19th or early 20th C. Crossover interest. ..... **$35+**

❖ NOTES ❖

"Why Go Thirsty? – Michigan laws forbid the use of public drinking cups. Probably you have noticed that when traveling, and made pointed remarks about the lawmakers, which didn't relieve your thirst in the least.

VII-46. Creamery vessels. (L) *Milk jug or ewer for 3 quarts of milk, earthenware, unglazed outside. German type; made also in 19th C., U.S.A. Lid fit into top like butter crock top.* ***(M)*** *Large milk vessel. "Filled with milk and set into water in pans or tubs – or other crocks. ... Water is renewed as often as ... convenient. The outside is so porous that the water, if it once wets the surface, is continually drawn up by capillary attraction. It evaporates all the time, thus notably cooling the milk."* ***(R)*** *Process called "Slipping the cream," whereby "after the milk is two days old, in ordinary weather, the cream may be loosened from the sides of the pan," and slips from the pans into a cooler that has a spigot at the bottom. American Agriculturist, May 1880.*

No one need go dry. An aluminum collapsible drinking cup that will slip into a handbag, a traveling bag, or a coat pocket, solves the thirst problem, and enables the possessor to laugh at the laws. We can furnish these cups in any desired quantity at figures that will net you a comfortable profit." *Hardware News,* published monthly by Buhl Sons Co., Detroit, MI, April 1912. Probably other states had similar laws.

Collapsible cup, nickel plated Britannia, 3 narrow & one wide telescoping band, footed base like a wine goblet, engraved, Meriden Britannia Co., Meriden, CT, 1886-87. .... **$20+**

VII-45. Cracker or pretzel jar. *Sponged decoration in blue on white ironstone. Nickeled copper bottom & top rims, and nickeled brass hinged lids. 7-1/2"H x 12-1/4" diameter. Late 19th C. Courtesy The Abrahams, Langhorne, PA.* **$225+**

VII-47. Stoneware crock. *Gray glazed stoneware, 10"H , wire bail handle with turned wood grip, 10"H, c.1900. This is plain, well designed, & serviceable, but there's no oomph and no decoration to add value.* **$20+**

VII-48. Public drinking cup, as depicted for c.1908-1910 campaign to improve sanitation in public places. The cups this caricatured were simple enamelware or tin cups, or dippers such as we've seen being used in movies. Frightening health campaigns helped companies like Dixie Cup, who made one-use throwaway cups, as well as the collapsion cup companies, who made cups for each person to carry around with them. This from an "Educational Sheet" distributed by the Minnesota State Board of Health, published by Pioneer Press, St. Paul, MN.

VII-49. Collapsing or portable drinking cups. From left to right: **(1)** & **(2)** "Vest pocket drinking cup, shown closed with embossed lid, and fully extended. Stamped metal, nickel-plated. "Indispensable for fishing and picnic parties, tourists, etc." Rayment catalog, c.1910-20s. **(3)** "**Collapsion cup**," "pure white metal, finished in the finest style; warranted non-corrosive; holds half-pint; incased in screw top nickel case." Robert H. Ingersoll & Bro., NYC. c.1900 ad. **(4)** Embossed aluminum, polished finish, 2-1/2" diameter at top. "Mirro" made by Aluminum Goods Mfg. Co., c.1910s. **$6-$15**

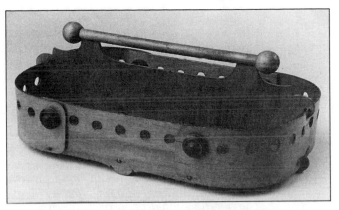

VII-50. Cutlery tray. Cutout bent veneer finished in silky honey-color, turned wood grip and bull's-eye knobby decorations, green baize bottom lining, 2-1/2"H exclusive of handle & centerboard x 11-1/4"L x 7-1/2"W, c.1890. Since the publication of the 3rd edition, the Smithsonian has acquired a wonderful sewing stand made like this. If any of you have seen other pieces that seem to be of the same type, please let us know! **$225+**

Collapsible cup, nickeled brass, pat'd. by John Lines, mfd. by Scovill Mfg. Co., Waterbury, CT, pat'd. Feb. 23, 1897. .... **$15+**

Collapsible cup, nickeled brass, very small – good for one shot, embossed flowers & scrolls on cover, American, only 1"H, perhaps a traveling medicine cup? Pat'd. Dec. 23, 1896............................ **$20+**

Collapsible cup, tin, 3 telescoping bands, engraved lid, name "Clement" engraved on lid, which could be owner, late 19th C. There was a Clement Mfg. Co. that made cutlery, etc., in Northampton, MA.............. **$15+**

Comb pocket or rack, also called a tidy rack or simply a tidy, wall hung, heavy embossed brass, with flowers, scrolls & sentiment "Remember Me," arched top with 2 holes for hanging, American, 13"L, 19th C. • Nice to think of this as a love gift, given by a person courting a cook or a maid!... **$125+**

Comb rack, tin with embossed design of mermaid, 10"W, 19th C. See also Tidy racks. .... **$35+**

Comb rack, embossed tin, design of Japanese fans & ribbons, 3 pockets & a mirror set on angle in center, hung on wall, American, 6-3/4" x 7", turn-of-century.. **$30+**

Comb rack, for comb or oddments, carved & painted wood, with relief motif of horse in pasture, and young girl, on other side of fence, some painting, American, 16"W, c.1910s. .... **$150+**

Crock, saltglazed stoneware, 2 applied ear handles, flat rim with slight lip, pale ochre or tan glaze with black and cobalt blue decoration, of bosomy bustle-y young woman, from knees up, walking small black dog, who has just made his contribution to the footpath, with large very pretty script remark, "Oh my?" [question mark rather than exclamation mark], a wonderful example of humor, though, of course, a strange subject for a food crock, although possibly this was for vegetable scraps bound for the compost heap, also stamped "J. B. Pfaltzgraff & Co.," York, PA. 7-1/4"H x 8" diam., last quarter 19th C., prob. late 1880s. Pfaltzgraff began business c.1840 and is

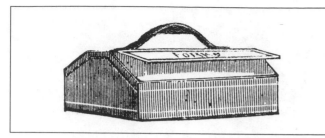

VII-51. Cutlery tray or knife box. *Japanned tin, hinged lids on either side, handle with reinforced grip. "A knife box should be large enough to hold the knives and forks in every day use, and nothing more. ... The handle should be large and sensible, and the partition through the middle of the box always separates the knives from the forks; there should be a lid to each side, to keep out the dust." American Agriculturist, Aug. 1879.* **$55+**

still in business. • Robacker, May 1989, auction price. It's the humorous figures that brought most of the money – an absolute folk art prize....... **$19,000**
Crock, saltglazed stoneware, blue quill-traced, very calligraphic decoration of bird, Millers, Boston, MA, 3 gal. capacity, mid to 3rd quarter 19th C. (?)........... **$600+**

❖ **NOTES** ❖

"Apples, in small quantities, may be preserved by the following. First, completely dry a glazed jar, then put a few pebbles at the bottom, fill it with Apples, and cover it with a piece of wood exactly fitted, and fill up the interstices with a little fresh mortar. The pebbles attract the moisture of the apples, while the mortar excludes the air from the jar and secures the fruit from pressure." Anthony Florian Madinzer Willich, *The Domestic Encyclopedia; or A Dictionary of Facts & Useful Knowledge,* 1st American edition, Philadelphia: W. Y. Birch & A. Small, 1803-04.

VII-52. Cutlery tray. *Wood, slanted sides, well-shaped centerboard handgrip, painted in bright colors like a game board. 14-3/4" x 7-3/4". In booth of Stephen Score, Essex, MA – a high-end dealer who's recognized this as folk art. Wide value range reflects the importance of where a piece is for sale. A very high price could be expected at one of the big Americana antique shows. The lower price might be expected at a small regional show – and believe me, stuff is still coming out.* **$700+**

Crock, saltglazed stoneware with 2 flowers in blue, marked "J. Fisher & Co." (Jacob Fisher), Lyons, NY, 3 gal. capacity, late 19th C........................... **$175+**
Crock, stoneware, gray with blue band 5/8 of way down side, with legend, "WESSON OIL – For making good things to eat." 5-1/2"H x 4-1/4" diam., 20th C. .... **$95+**

❖ **NOTES** ❖

Cutlery trays – also called knife boxes, knife carriers, knife & fork trays, cutlery trays, cutlery boxes, carrier trays, flatware trays, silverware trays or spoon boxes – from the 19th & early 20th C. mostly seem to be divided into only two compartments. Rarely can an old one be found with three sections, though the 20th C. plastic or wooden cutlery trays we keep in our kitchen drawers always have 4, and sometimes 5 or 6 sections. Certainly knives, forks, and spoons were all in wide use during the 18th and 19th centuries, and people were accustomed to use different tableware for salads, meats, fish, desserts, bread, etc. The fact that the commonest name seems to be a cutlery tray does not mean they were only for knives.

Cutlery tray, bentwood oval with copper nails, straight lapped, original (?) light green paint, bent nail or wire hinges for the 2 center-hinged lids, 3-arch centerboard has handhold cutout, possibly Shaker, 2-7/8"H handle, body is 3"H x 12-3/4"L, c.1870s (?)........... **$250+**
Cutlery box, bentwood, unusual, round-sided box, with thickish wood bottom and 4 sections formed by 2 cross-piece dividers, one of which serves as centerboard with handhold cutout, held together with small nails or brads, prob. European, poss. English, almost certainly not American, about 4" deep x 11" diam., prob. mid 19th C. **$135**
Cutlery tray, bentwood with border decoration of cut-out holes, bottom edge cut so as to form 4 feet in middle of sides, turned wood "curtain rod" grip handle, lapped ends fastened with nails and turned balls of wood, green baize lining of both compartments, highly decorative, American, 4-1/4"H at center x 11"L x 7-1/4"W, 19th C. The Smithsonian, Museum of American History, Domestic Division, has a sewing stand made the same way, with near-

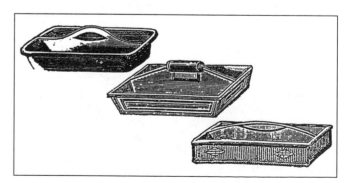

VII-53. Cutlery trays. (T-L) *stamped sheet metal;* **(M)** *pieced sheet metal japanned & pinstriped, with tubular grip;* **(R)** *wicker work, lined with tin. All from 1895 catalog of Harrod's Stores, Ltd., Brompton, England.* **$45+**

matching features, probably made by the same, unknown, company. .... **$250+**

Cutlery tray, cutout wood, carved twisted rope or cable edging, handle carved to look like a twisted 3 strand rope, simple cutouts resemble hearts & acorns, canted sides, American (?), 11"L, 19th C. ..... **$150+**

Cutlery tray, dovetailed pine, faint traces of red paint, high double arch centerboard with heart cutout, American, 11"L, 19th C. **$200**

Cutlery tray, flat base which forms low foot, deeply canted sides set back from edge of base, cutout centerboard, painted blue inside, American, 11"L, late 19th C. .... **$150+**

Cutlery carrier (?), indurated fiber ware, divided pan, perhaps a utensil or cutlery carrier for clearing the table, cutout centerboard for hand grip, marbleized green-blue and cream paint on outside, cream inside, American (?), 4"H x 8-13/16" diam., c.1870s.. **$85+**

Cutlery tray, inlaid, stamped & stained design in top ridge of handle, high centerboard carved with 2 stars, circles & heart, 2 scrolls, dart designs with shields, nice molded foot, American, 10-1/2"L x 8-1/2"W, mid 19th C. .... **$350+**

Cutlery tray, made of woven wire & a sheet metal frame, 2 sections, American, 10-1/4"L x 6-3/4"W x 2" deep, c.1900. (This is the type that was made in a miniature size [about 3"L] for use with doll cutlery. Nice to have both)! **$50**

Cutlery tray, painted pine with imitation graining in shades of ochre & brown, very fanciful with knots & extreme grain pattern, American, 13"L x 6-1/4"W, mid 19th C. The graining qualifies it for some folk art collectors.................................. **$250+**

❖ NOTES ❖

"Folk Art" Caveat: "Folk art" is a catch-all term meant to describe a certain naïveté in vision or execution, and it's sometimes used to lend distinction (and extra $$) to things better or more accurately described as "handmade" or "crude" or "old magazine craft project style." Folk art is the exceptional, not the ordinary, artwork of "folk"; the emphasis is on art. A wonderful African American folk artist named Abraham Lincoln Criss, originally of Virginia, had a big sign in his yard that said "Folk's Art," which I thought was a pretty darn good way to put it. It is practically impossible to come up with an all-purpose definition. You must develop your own taste and eye for it; conjure up a vision of all the handmade objects you have (or have seen) which were made by people who considered themselves craftsmen or artists, but whose work doesn't fall into the mainstream of academic art of the period in which they worked. Then sift out what you believe to be the very best examples – the pieces that are definably art, which have something about them you may not be able to describe in words. You probably have a few pieces that qualify as folk art. The secret is to refine your own taste even if you can't define it out loud. When someone else, like me, tells you it's folk art, never take our word for granted. Start at the beginning & figure out why.

Cutlery tray, pieced tin, horizontal tubular handle soldered to centerboard, American, 11-3/4"L, c.1850s to '70s(?). Fairly common. .... **$125+**

VII-54. Dish cover or fly screen. *Woven wire, with thin band of tin around base, and tin disk and knob on top. The advertisements claimed the tinned sheet metal had a "blue steel coloring." It is blue, but is not blued steel, which means something else and was known at the time to protect steel from rusting. You do see blued steel gun barrels, and blued steel clock & watch hands, among other things. 11" diam., American, c.1900.* **$30+**

Cutlery tray, pine, old red paint, molding nailed to top edge, high arched centerboard, handle cutout, American, 12"L, 19th C. .... **$125+**

Cutlery tray, pine with geometric pattern pressed into sides & ends (looks like pyrography, but probably done like the steamed & pressed wooden kitchen chairs), cutout handle, American, 2 1/2"H at sides x 11-3/4"L x 7-1/4"W, early 20th C. .... **$20+**

Cutlery tray, red stained pine, straight sides, centerboard carved with simple alligator as grip, with head & tail curved slightly up, prob. American, 19th C. .... **$400+**

Dinner pail, stacking sections, pieced tin, lower straight sided pail with short oil can like spout holds a deep pan with slightly flared sides, then a pie pan like piece, then domed lid. Wire bail with wood grip to lower pail, metal clip strap holds parts together & can be locked with small padlock or kept closed with a peg, W. F. Janeway, Columbus, OH, 1890s. • The editor of *The Metal Worker*, May 28, 1892, described the pail thus: "The pail is used for tea or coffee, the lower pan for the main dinner and the shallow pan for pie or cake. It is made of heavy stock, nicely finished. The pail is also furnished without the strap or shallow pan. ... The pail is designed for miners, railroad men and others who carry a large quantity of tea or coffee. Instead of being obliged to remove the dinner in the mine, and getting dirt into it, the miner can drink his fill by drawing it through the spout, as the spout terminates in a hole at the bottom of the pail. The lock strap prevents the cover being knocked off when hitting the pail in getting off and on cars, and prevents the dinner being stolen, by locking the pail. The large space for carrying the coffee is referred to as a desirable feature, and a great improvement over a flask, or a shallow receptacle attached to the lid of the pail. The point is emphasized that drawing the coffee through the spout is much pleasanter and more desirable than drinking from a pail or cup also that with this spout there is no danger of any of the coffee being wasted. The lock strap and spout add but 15¢ at retail to the price of a pail. These pails are sold so they may be retailed at 45¢ to 75¢, according to the size of pail and number of pans." .... **$30-$55+**

Dinner pail, tin, 4 stacking compartments that set down into each other, high wire rack handle, from F. A. Walker catalog, c.1890s. • "The tin pail is a badge of work, generally honest work, always productive work, and work is the root of all that we have. We, the people, the rich, the society people, the literary people, the talkers and writers who make so much fuss in type and pretend to rule – or ruin – the world, all depend on the workers who are represented in force in 'the tin pail brigade.'" *The Metal Worker*, Sept. 2, 1882. .... **$55+**

Dish covers or fly screens; called fly walks by the Shakers. Wire screening, stamped into dome shape, with narrow japanned tin frame & disc for black-painted turned wood knob, made in rounds or ovals, to fit plates, dishes, pans, etc., Japanning was red, green, blue or asphaltum brown, perhaps other colors I've not seen, Matthai-Ingram was one manufacturer, American, Matthai-Ingram's nested sets all about 5" to 7"H; ovals 8" to 18"L; 6" to 14" diam. rounds, c.1870s to 1910s. • Other manufacturers of the period were: Bromwell; Gibbert & Bennett; Frederick J. Myers; Joseph Scheider; W. H. Sweeney; Wickwire Brothers. All the products probably were very similar. These have gone up incredibly. Range covers most asking prices: .... **$40-$95**

Dish covers, heavy pieced planished tin, high-domed, oblong or oval in shape to fit over serving dishes or platters, with cast iron handles that are sometimes heavily tinned, American, 19th C. .... **$40+**

Dog biscuit canister, round cylinder, snug lid, enameled in bright red, black silhouette of Scotty in beg-

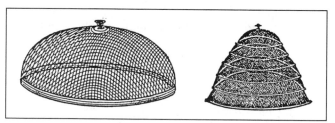

VII-55. Dish covers. *Also called* **fly screens** *or* **fly covers.** *People who have these always price them very highly, but the price is unwarranted. They were made over a very long period.* **(L)** *A cover in oval shape, is made of "closely knitted wire, blue steel coloring." It was "especially adapted to Free Lunch Counters," and came in 10", 12", 14", 16", and 18" lengths. Round ones came in a series from 8" to 14" diameter. From Albert Pick catalog, 1909. At* **(R)** *is a stack of "wire dish covers. – To cover meats, pastry, milk, butter, &c., from dust, flies, &c., in the pantry or on the table." The picture is from the* American Home Cook Book, *1854. Prices sometimes crazily high – I've seen them marked over $100.* **$30+**

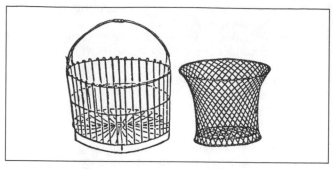

VII-56. Egg baskets, *for gathering.* **(L)** *Iron wire, in 5 sizes (6", 7", 8", 9", and 10" diameter), is from Duparquet, Huot & Moneuse catalog, c.1904-1910.* **(R)** *Retinned wire, looks like wastebasket, even in dimensions – 15"H x 12" diameter at top. "Keeping eggs in our wire basket has the advantage of locating broken ones instantly." From Albert Pick catalog, 1909.* **$40+; $65+**

ging position, labeled "Biscuits," American, 7-1/4"H x 7" diam., c.1930. • Scotty crossover collectors will bark your shins for this one. .... **$40+**

Dog feeding dish, crockery glazed in green, with depiction of dogs, 20th C. .... **$25+**

Dog feeding dish, heavy glass, with glass lid for putting in fridge, if you know a dog that wouldn't gobble it all up at once! Red logo & adv'g, "Ideal Dog Food," 20th C. .... **$35+**

❖ NOTES ❖

Ever wonder about **dog food**, when it started? Here's an historical tidbit or kibble: "One of the oldest industries in Chelsea [MA] is the Austin Dog Bread & Animal Food Company ... a subsidiary of the Loose-Wiles Biscuit Company, 2nd largest in the U.S. ... In 1864, following a serious fire in Lynn, C. F. Austin & Co. moved to Chelsea, manufacturing ship and pilot bread. In 1885, regular biscuits were manufactured with dog bread as a sideline, but in 1908, when part of the plant was removed to Boston, the Chelsea division became principally noted for its dog bread and animal food. ... It is said that the first dog bread ever manufactured in the United States was made by this concern, the process of manufacture being similar to that used in the general baking industry. Three large ovens consume approximately 100 barrels of flour a day and more than 500 pounds of cereal. Fresh meat is an important part of the ingredients. The modern equipment, consisting of flour mixers, ovens, meat boilers, conveyors, cylinder, kibbling and automatic weighing machines, etc., produce the bulk and package commodities, which are distributed throughout the U. S. One-third of the product of dog bread flakes, dog bread, puppy bread and cat food is shipped in packages." Orra L. Stone, *History of Massachusetts Industries*, Boston: S. J. Clarke, 1930, Volume II (of II).

Dog feeding dish, yellowware, with nipple-shaped protrusions up from the bottom, made especially for weaning puppies, who would learn to suck 'n' eat at the same time, American, 9" diam., 19th C. • Only one I ever saw. .... **$150+**

VII-57. Flour bins. *Japanned tin, with more or less decoration, in gold.* **(L)** *Black background with gold Japanese influenced motifs, c.1880s.* **(M)** *Japanned brown, 50 lb. capacity. Buhl Brothers, c.1919.* **(R)** *Black with simple border design, in three sizes: 15"H x 10-1/2" diameter; 21-5/8"H x 12-1/2" diameter; 27-1/8"H x 15". Central Stamping Co., 1920.* **$50-$150+**

Dog feeding trough, cast iron, rather thin walls, very smooth dark finish, really looks like a miniature hog trough, with 2 divisions – for water & kibbles, no marks, American or English, 15"L, late 19th C. • This looks very old and finely made. I thought it was much older, until I found reprint of the Harrod's Stores, Ltd., 1895 catalog, which shows a very similar one. Harrod's offered 4 sizes: 12"L without the division, 15"L, 18"L and 24"L, all with the division. I did see a tag saying "Cat trough" on a small one at a PA group shop. .... **$55+**

Dog & cat feeding dish holders, cast iron finished black, figural dachshund with short tail; cat with curled tail; both bodies are horizontal and flat with 2 holes for stainless steel bowls; 5"H x 18"L x 6-1/2"W. Mfr. is unknown, they were offered in the mail order catalog of the *2001 Humane Society of the U.S.* (www.hsus.org). I believe these are guaranteed to go up in value because they are dear to our hearts & well made. .... **$40+**

Feed pan, heavy galvanized sheet metal, round, fluted flared sides, looks like large fluted cake mold, mfd. by Milcor Steel Co., Canton, OH, 3-1/2" deep x 17" top diam., c.1930. .... **$10+**

Firkin, wood, painted mocha, finger-lapped, American, 9-1/2"H, 19th C. .... **$75+**

VII-58. Flour canister, *3-part, with sifting tray inside. Tin-lined copper, 7"H x 6-3/4" diameter, wooden knob. 19th C. Collection of the late Mary Mac Franklin.* **$75+**

❖ **NOTES** ❖

History in Small Things – "I embrace the common, I explore and sit at the feet of the familiar, the low. Give me insight into today, and you may have the antique and future worlds. What would we really know the meaning of? The meal in the firkin; the milk in the pan; the ballad in the street; the news of the boat; the glance of the eye; the form and the gait of the body." Ralph Waldo Emerson, "*American Scholar*," 1837.

Firkin, wood with dark green paint, finger-lapped construction, probably for liquids, American, 12"H, 19th C. .... **$125+**

Firkin, wooden staves, painted putty color, 4 wood bands with copper fasteners, wooden bail handle, made by cooper, probably Shaker manufacture, American, 9-1/2"H x 9-1/2" diam., 19th C. ... **$200+**

Firkins – See also Buckets & Pails; also Chapter V (Measuring)

Fly screens – See Dish covers

Fruit jars – See Chapter XVI (Canning)

Ginger beer bottles, tan saltglazed stoneware, banded in ochre (usually top half is ochre), thick flat mouth, rather roughly finished. Used for holding explosive homemade drinks that built up pressure and needed to have the corks tied down. The overhanging lip serves to anchor the string or twine. These bottles are a common type often seen at flea markets. American, English, about 7" to 9"H, 19th C. .... **$15+**

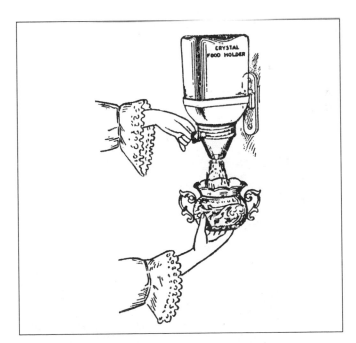

VII-59. Food holder. *"Crystal," mfd. by Ware-Standard Mfg. Co., NYC. For sugar, coffee, rice, salt, Indian meal, hominy, etc. Clear glass in metal bracket. This one shown with wall bracket; also was made to slide into brackets mounted to underside of shelf, so that they would hang down from the shelf. Made in 3 sizes, for 3-1/2, 7 and 14 lbs. of dry food. "Turn the knob and the food runs out." Ad in* House Furnishing Review, *May 1905.* **$50+**

❖ RECIPES ❖

Ginger Beer (superior) – *To six quarts of water add one ounce of cream of tartar, and two ounces of white Jamaica ginger; boil it ten minutes. Strain it; add to the liquor a pound of loaf sugar. Put it on the fire; let it simmer until the sugar is dissolved. Pour into an earthen vessel, into which has been put two ounces of tartaric acid and the rind of one lemon. When lukewarm, add half a tumbler of strong hop yeast. Stir all well together, and bottle; tie down the corks tightly. Use in a few days."* Mrs. A. P. Hill, Mrs. Hill's New Family Receipt Book, NY: 1870.

• • •

Imperial Pop - *Three ounces of cream of tartar, an ounce of bruised ginger, a pound and a half of loaf sugar, half a tumbler of lemon juice, a gallon and a half of water, a wineglass of yeast. Shake well together; bottle, and cork well."* ibid.

• • •

Ginger Beer – *Boil together four gallons of water, one pint of hops, twenty races of ginger, beaten. Boil briskly half an hour; keep the vessel covered; strain; sweeten with good molasses. When tepid, add a pint of brisk yeast. Cover it closely with a thick cloth until morning; then bottle, and cork tight. Scald the corks, and drive them in, and tie down with twine. Keep in a cool place. It will be ready for use the third day. Less yeast may be used if the taste is not liked."* Ibid.

Implement rack, also called a utensil plaque, blue & white enamelware, trough along bottom edge, late 19th C. .... **$130+**

VII-60. Lehnware goblets. *Carved & painted wood.* **(L)** *Red & green paint, with snake wrapped around it, 3"H.* **(R)** *Flowers & vines, typical of Joseph Lehn, Lancaster County, PA. 2-1/2"H. Photo courtesy Litchfield Auction Gallery, Litchfield CT. Ex-Harold Corbin Collection, auctioned Jan. 1, 1990 for $550 & $400.* **$1,000+; $900+**

VII-61. Herb tray. *Japanned tin, iron central handle, compartments. Picture from ad of William S. Adams & Son, London, in Francatelli's Cook's Guide Advertiser, c.1860-61.* **$85+**

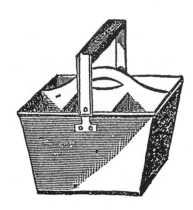

VII-62. Housemaids' box, *for carrying little cleaning tools, polishes & rags, pieced tin, high handle in addition to the centerboard with the handgrip cutout. Japanned to resemble oak. From Harrod's Stores, Ltd. 1895 catalog.* **$75+**

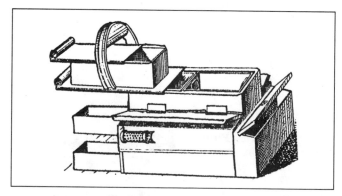

VII-63. Housekeeper's safe patent. *Pat'd. Feb. 10, 1880, by Ebnezar H. Sturges, Wing's Station, NY. It has many compartments, not only for cleaning tools but for cooking tools too. The top box is for knives. Spices were apparently meant for the hinged compartment in the front, where the nutmeg grater is mounted. Official Gazette of the U.S. Patent Office. If ever made:* **$200+**

Implement rack, fancy scribed & carved wood, European, 28"L, late 19th C. • These are often termed "utensil racks," but actually a utensil is a hollow-ware cooking pot or such, and these are really implement racks. .... **$125+**

Implement rack, gray graniteware, somewhat shield-shaped, with spoon, dipper & skimmer, 19"H, turn-of-century. .... **$125+**

Implement rack, tall with drip catcher at bottom, utensils: ladle, tasting ladle, small ladle or gravy spoon and skimmer, teal blue enamelware, all have a gold pin stripe on handle, inside of bowls are white, European, late 19th or early 20th C. .... **$225+**

Implement rack, turquoise enamelware, no mark, prob. European import, early 20th C (?). .... **$95+**

Implement rack, wall hung, with high, stepped backplate and shallow oval drip catcher, strap bar near top with skimmer, tasting spoon, ladle and dipper hanging from it, all matching teal blue & white enamelware with fancy gold pinstriping, skimmer holes are concentric & close-set, prob. European import, late 19th C. • **Gold trim** was used in Europe, but as far as I know, not on American enamelwares. .... **$200+**

Implement rack, white enamelware, wall mounted, with matching small & large ladles & 2 skimmers, 21-1/4"H, c.1900. .... **$95+**

Implement rack, with implements, japanned tin, black-finished wood-handled meat fork, cake turner, can opener, carving knife, cake knife, strainer-spoon, sharpening "steel," paring knife, mixing spoon, cleaver. "Perfect Kitchen Set," American, 23"L, 20th C. .... **$150+**

VII-65. Implement racks, *also called* **utensil plaques** *in Europe. All imported from Germany, c. 1904. "German manufacturers of house furnishings have devised a great variety of racks or sets for holding articles of kitchen utility. They are decorative and practical, some bearing appropriate designs in the panels, while others are plain, the panels finished in Delft tile. The woodwork is of grained oak or of a softer wood heavily enameled in white. ... The vogue for these sets has gained great headway abroad, and the demand is also extending in this country. The sets pictured retail for from $4.50 to $6.50, with all the accessories." The only metal one is at lower right, with the curved dripping trough at bottom. Though the article, in House Furnishings Review, doesn't mention Thurnauer, it was probably that NYC firm that imported these. The printed-on German words for spices & staples didn't seem to deter sales in the U.S. Without implements:* **$50+**; *with:* **$150+**

Implement rack, wood, scrolled crested top, forged iron hooks, prob. not American, a bit too ornate along top, 24-1/2"W, early 19th C, perhaps late 18th C. These have been faked and imported from Indonesia (where lots of wood & iron Colonial-looking stuff is made for stylish gift shops) & elsewhere. ...... **$150+**

Implement rack, wooden framed round plate-like wall hung piece with round Delft tile in center, wooden piece at bottom has 6 holes for handles of tools, including skimmer, ladle, spoons, etc., German, c.1904. .... **$125+**

Jar, earthenware, glazed with a reddish brown, cream body clay, charmingly marked in nice big letters on side "PLUMBS" [sic], English, 5-1/4"H, mid 19th C. .... **$150+**

Jug, gray saltglazed stoneware with cobalt scrolling & leaves, "New York Stoneware Co.," Ft. Edward, NY, 2 gal. capacity, c. 3rd quarter 19th C. **$165**

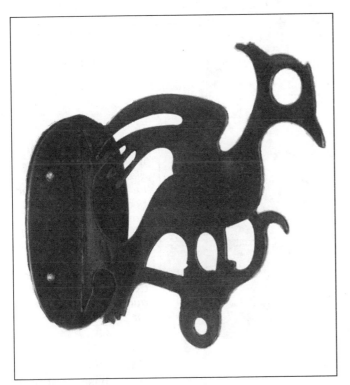

VII-64. Implement hook, *bought with ladle probably not original to it. Heavy brass, cutout in large-eyed bird form. Oval plate to be mounted to wall or woodwork of fireplace surround. 7-1/4"H x 8"W. Early 19th C. English. Collection of the late Mary Mac Franklin.* **$325+**

❖ NOTES ❖

Jug Stoppers Add Value – A hand-carved wood jug stopper can be worth more than the jug itself, if it's good folk art and figural. Some to hope for are a Black man's head, a dog's, cat's or mule's head, or a coiled snake (perhaps made from a root). Doris Axtell, dealer in Deposit, NY, advertised an exceptionally large one in May 1989 that sounded great: "carved wooden hand & wrist jug stopper, old natural patina, well-defined sculpture, 7-1/4"L overall." She had it at $750, and if you had the right jug (as sculpture base), you'd really have something. See color photo section.

Jug, hammered copper, pewter lined (looks like tin), shaped somewhat like water pitcher, but with back & front pouring lips, with crosswise falling bail high arched handle, based on Russian design, B. Paleschuck, NYC, NY, 7"H, 2 qt. capacity, early 1930s, poss. based on 19th C. form. .... **$50+**

Jug or pitcher, hammered heavy gauge brass with 3 copper bands, tall, with very slanted sides, flat bottom, high arching lip is balanced by nicely arched handle, foreign looking & "reminiscent of old world ties is this Russian pitcher jug," also made in copper with brass bands, Adolph Silverstone, Inc., another Allen Street brass company like Palechuck, NYC, NY, 9"H, one qt. capacity (also 12"H, 2 qt. capacity), early 1930s, prob. based on 19th C. form. ...... **$40+**

Jug, pieced copper, tin lined, unusual shape with the body having slightly slanted sides for most of its height, narrowing in dramatically, then rising straight up again for high neck, tiny lip, forged iron handle riveted at rim & curves down to narrowing part of body. Jug actually "looks" foreign, and it is a

VII-69. Jug. *Definitely a plumber's whimsy, as it's made of lead. Softened lead worked like clay to make decoration around neck and handle. I forgot to measure it, but seem to recall about 7" or 8"H. Courtesy Lenny Kislin, Bearsville, NY.* **$300+**

VII-67. Jug with frame. *"Brackett's Revolving Jug," stoneware jug in cast iron frame making it easy to pour from. A beautiful, elegant form. Probably 1870s-80s. This was sold way under the money to my mind in 1985, for only $150. Photo courtesy Penny Sanders, Sanders Auctioneers, Wilton, NH.* **$650+**

VII-66. Make-do "Bail for a Water Jug." *Drawing in* American Agriculturist, *April 1881, showing how "a jug, having lost its handle, was provided with a substitute in the form of a bail, as follows: Two wire 'rings' were made, one to go below the largest part of the jug, and the other and smaller one near the neck. These were held together by four wires passing between them. 'Ears' were put on opposite sides of the upper ring, and a stout wire bail attached; this bail was provided with a wooden handle through which the wire passed. From experience we can say it is more convenient to carry than a jug with the ordinary, one-sided handle." A repaired piece like this would probably sell for upwards of* **$225+**

VII-68. Jug. *Redware with brown crackle glaze, provocative lady's leg in high laced boot forms the angled handle. 8-1/2"H. 19th C., New England. Photo courtesy Litchfield Auction Galleries, Litchfield CT. Ex-Harold Corbin Collection, auctioned Jan. 1, 1990, for $450.* **$750**

Syrian form, 11-1/2"H, 7" diam. at base, 3" at neck, made c. 1930 from much older form.............. **$25+**

Jug, saltglazed stoneware, applied handle at neck, 2 peg-like projections on either side, halfway down body, that fit into cast iron swing frame, so that the jug can be tipped to pour without picking it up, rather like modern whisky-pouring bottles in

VII-70. Jugs. (L) Shoulder jug, for liquor. Four sizes, from 1 qt. to 2 gal. capacity. Sure seems amazing that there was an actual type of jug to go with those "hill-billy" cartoons from 50+ years ago. **(M) "Common shape"** jug, "the kind that has been in use for many years. The demand for this old-style jug is ever increasing." In 7 sizes, from 1 qt. to 5 gal. **(R) Bailed jug**, "a new style." 2-1/4" diameter opening, 3 sizes – 1/4, 1/2 and 1 gal. (SEE VII-47.) From Albert Pick catalog, 1909. Makers unknown. **$40-$100+**

frames, "Brackett's Revolving Jug," American, c.1880s (?). • Sold at auction by Sanders Auctioneers & Appraisers, Wilton, NH. .... **$650+**
Juice dispenser, octagonal painted tin base, decals of lemons & grape clusters, brass fittings, 2 glass containers, ice goes inside to chill drinks, American, 30"H, late 19th, early 20th C. .... **$500+**

✤ **RECIPE** ✤

Miss Matilda's Ginger Cakes – Three quarts of flour, one teacup of lard, one quart of molasses, one tablespoonful of soda beat into the molasses, half a teacup of sour milk, the same of water, and three tablespoonfuls of ginger. Roll half an inch thick; cut in any shape, and brush over with the white of an egg." Mrs. A. P. Hill, Mrs. Hill's New Family Receipt Book, NY: 1870.

VII-71. Keeler. Staved shallow tub, made in pie or cedar. Came in 4 sizes: 9-3/4", 12", 15", and 16-1/2" diam. Duparquet, Huot & Moneuse, c.1904-1910 catalog. • At first, this kind of coopered staved shallow tub (such as seen here) was a "keeler" – a cooler – used in a brewery, or probably also in a dairy. By the 1850s, the keeler or "keeler tub" was a tub in which dishes are washed. **$65+**

Keeler, staved wood, with 2 handles, low sided tub for cooling liquids, American, 5-1/2"H x 12-1/2" diam., very early 19th C. .... **$165+**
Lard jar, gray saltglazed stoneware with funnel top, American, one-half-gal. capacity, 19th C. .... **$55+**
Lunch box, a sort of suitcase that looks like an old camera box of the period, imitation pebbled leather-ette with strap handle, side folds down to reveal 3 heavy tin square trays, an oblong flask, & spirit lamp, "Bon-Vee-Von Lunch Box", mfd. by Union Luncheon Box Co., NYC, 7"H x 8"W x 5" deep, c.1903. • Boy! Those bon vivants really used to do lunch! .... **$50+**
Lunch box, bentwood, oval, well-fitted lid, swing handles, American, 8"L x 5"W, 19th C. .... **$50+**
Lunch box, brown pasteboard with leather strap handle, a tobacco box, "Sensation," late 19th C (?). Crossover interest. .... **$50+**
Lunch box, called a tine, bentwood oval, lid swivels on peg at one end and then snaps when you push down on the little knob-like projection with your thumb and pull up on lid with your fingers to make lid come up, painted black then carved through to wood, Norwegian, 10"H, 19th C. • Norwegian tines

---

Reproduction Alert

Not only are collectors being confused by recent imports of elderly **Turkish copper and iron** cook-wares, we now have a further Middle East Muddle. I have seen a few jugs (which I thought of as pitchers) generally answering the description of the pieced copper jug above. I could tell they came from a slightly Eastern-influenced country – they actually look Moorish, and could date to the 15th or 16th centuries. Not long ago, I found a 60-year old editorial note about one in the Sept. 1930 *House Beautiful*, as follows: "One day when poking around among some odds and ends of old Syrian copper [seen in profusion in the late 19th and early 20th C. on Allen Street, NYC] I came upon the original of a jug [as described above]. I said I thought that copies of it would be both good-looking and extremely useful. I hoped it would be ready to show you early in the summer, when you might have used it as a water pitcher or as a vase for field flowers, but the business of copying takes time, and fall is now on the way. Perhaps, after all, it is just as good now to hold sprays of bittersweet, or honesty, or even to have fitted up for a lamp base. ... The proportions are excellent. It is of lustrous copper lined with pewter [?] (in case you want to use it as a water pitcher) and it is fitted with a handle of half-polished iron. With very little work, and the right shade, this could be converted into a stunning and important-looking lamp. The price is $7.75 ... at B. Paleschuck, 22 Allen St., NYC." Paleschuck was established in 1897, and sold real antiques and also made reproductions of antiques, mostly from Russia and the Middle East, made of brass, copper, pewter and iron. Paleschuck was but one of many similar companies.

VII-72. Tine. *A Norwegian lunch box, bentwood oval with vertical wooden supports at each end, lapped, 10"L, painted black then carved through to make design. Lid swivels on a sort of wooden button at left end. Others are very colorful, and may have a swinging strap handle. 19th C., but a form that goes back much further. Courtesy R. C. Bowen.* **$250+**

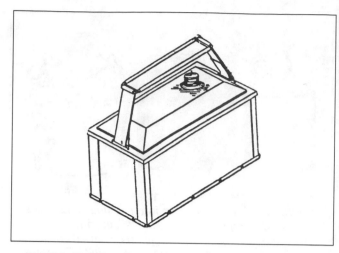

VII-74. Folding lunch box patent. *Pat'd. Nov. 4, 1884, by Alfred Brown & Alvin Lightner, Kansas City, MO. Sides and end are hinged, and the cover has slots for the straps of the handle. Official Gazette of the U.S. Patent Office.*

VII-73. Lunch carriers in disguise: (L) Lunch satchel *for seamstresses & excursionists, etc. "In outward appearance it is not to be distinguished from any other Leather Satchel for the use of working men and women, bookkeepers, clerks, engineers, conductors, drivers, school-teachers, dressmakers, seamstresses, excursionists, and all persons whose business requires their absence from home during the dinner-hour. It will hold a sufficient quantity of meat, vegetable, bread, and pie, coffee, tea or milk for one person's dinner, properly secured in their places, without napkin or paper, perfectly ventilated, and with an independent arrangement for heating them. They are made in different colors and in two sizes." Disguised brought-from-home lunches seemed to be important at the time. Peck & Snyder ad in Century Monthly, March 1883.* **(R) Best seller!** *This is a tin box made to look like a book, and is japanned in assorted colors, in "imitation of Morocco Leather." The spine reads "MID DAY EXERCISES." This has some extra appeal because there are collectors of book-shaped objects. 2-1/4" x 7-3/8" x 4-7/8". Lalance & Grosjean catalog, 1890. Before reading this, if you'd seen one, would it truly have had as much appeal as it does now? This is why I have so much background info – it adds to the long run appeal of any antique.* **$25+; $45+**

VII-75. Dinner carriers. (L) *carrier in style called "decked." That is, the compartments – 2, 3 or 4, depending on how many courses – stack. Tin. From F. A. Walker catalog, 1890s.* **(R)** *Dinner pail, "New England" style. "Sterling" gray enamelware, by Central Stamping Co. Wire bail with wooden grip, and lid, which "shuts over outside" has wooden knob. Three sizes, holding 1-3/4 qts, 2-1/2 qts or 3-1/4 qts, and that's a lotta lunch. 1920.* **$35+; $65+**

VII-76. Sandwich box. *Tin with hinged lid. I'd like to find a source for these, newly made. They would be very useful. From Harrod's Stores 1895 catalog.* **$20+**

came in various shapes, from slightly oval to very oval, to round and rectangular. Most were decorated with a hot poker in stylized designs. Some were colored. Some were painted, then carved through to the light wood underneath. .... **$275+**

Lunch box, embossed in small diamonds & japanned tin, book-shaped box, with name on spine, hinged lid (front cover), "Larrabee's Lunch Box," 8-1/2"H x 5-1/2"W x 3" deep, late 19th C. (?). .... **$50+**

Lunch box, litho'd tin, "Sensible Tobacco," turn-of-century? It may seem strange now, in the increasingly smoke-free atmosphere of the 2000s, but some tobacco tins 100 years ago were especially designed to have a second life as lunch boxes. Some names to look for include "Winner Cut Plug," "Just Suits," "Pedro," "Redicut, "Dixie Queen," Patterson's," "U.S. Marine Cut Plug," and "Union Blend." Crossover interest of course. .... **$45-$100+**

Lunch bucket, brown & white mottled enamelware, wire bail handle, prob. "Onyx," Columbian Enameling & Stamping Co., c.1890s-1910. .... **$120+**

Lunch bucket, gray graniteware, 3 parts, with bail handle, American, c.1890s-1910. .... **$135+**

Lunch bucket, tin with 2 inner trays, cup fits onto oval domed lid, wire bail handle with wood grip, "Lisk," Canandaigua, NY, 9-1/2" x 6-3/8" oval, late 19th C. .... **$60+**

Lunch or dinner pail, tin, wire bail handle, 2 compartments, plus lid is a flask for hot coffee (or tea), the opening is capped with a tin mug, giving the whole thing the name "cup-top kettle," American, late 19th C. .... **$55+**

Lunch pail, better called a dinner pail, gray graniteware, miner's type with tray & cup inside, wire bail handle, late 19th C. .... **$75+**

❖ NOTES ❖

Dinner Pails – In the 1850s & '60s, "the dinner pail was a simple two-quart tin pail, with a cover. The food was packed in it as well as the space would permit and the skill of the housewife would allow. And sometimes it was a queer mess when lunch time came around. The bread-and-butter slices at the bottom of the pail, and the corned-beef sandwich that made the next layer, were saturated with the juices of the apple pie and mince pie on the top, which had gradually settled

and become compressed by the joltings of carrying, and the entire dinner tasted of a conglomeration of flavors that only exactive hunger could render palatable. No provision was made in this miscalled dinner pail for the reception of drink or the carrying of a knife and fork and spoon. If these were carried, they were bestowed in pockets in the clothes, as was also fruit, or else were made up into a separate parcel.

"The first true dinner pail came years after this makeshift had proved inadequate. It was a pail with removable compartments – or at least one removable receptacle. About half way from top to bottom was a projection to receive a cup fitting the interior of the pail, the cup to hold coffee or tea, while the lower space received the solid food. On top of the cover was a cylindrical ring that was a receptacle for salt, or salt and pepper in desirable proportions, and this ring was covered with a half-gill cup, with handle, into which the coffee or the tea might be poured. Subsequently were added a plain disk or diaphragm of sheet tin to separate the bread from the pie, or the dry from the moist, and on the outside of the pail were fixed tin straps that served as sheaths to a fork, spoon and knife.

"But a still more important advance has been made. If one will take a run west of New York to Paterson, NJ, and beyond, and can spend time at prominent railroad centers, or the mining regions of Pennsylvania, he will observe workmen departing in the morning carrying a tin trunk of considerable size. With some curiosity he will inquire what these peddlers are vending, and will be told that these tin trunks contain rations for one and sometimes two days. These trunks are arranged for hungry men. They are divided into partitions, each with its cover, and each cover nearly air-tight. At one end is the removable receptacle for drink." *The Metal Worker,* Sept. 2, 1882.

Match dispenser, cast iron alligator with lots of detail, "Monon Route," late 19th C. .... **$325+**

VII-77. Lunch kit. *Black finished steel box with sliding compartment, steel & aluminum bottle, tinned steel drinking cup, with extra nested aluminum food trays to fit inside. 7-1/2"H x 10"L x 5"W. D. J. Barry catalog, 1924. In the 1970s and '90s there was crossover appeal to faddish teens, to use as pocketbooks, and it'll probably happen again.* **$25-$40+**

VII-78. Dinner pail, with trays & pie plate. "Saulson," in 2 sizes, 6-1/2" x 6", and 6-3/4" x 7-1/8". Central Stamping Co., 1920. **$25-$40+**

VII-80. Lunch box. Mickey Mouse, color lithographed tin, with "Bull Dog" wire handles, mfd. by Geuder, Paeschke & Frey, Milwaukee, in 1935. 4-3/4"H x 8-1/4"L x 5"W. This is the earliest known comic character lunch box, and while it has an interior tray, it never had a thermos bottle. It was made by a firm that had specialized in tin- and enamel- wares of many kinds for at least 55 years. Photo and collection of Robert Carr. Value range mine, not Carr's. **$1,200+**

VII-79. Lunch box. Chromolithographed tin, oval, close-fitting lid, swing strap handle. This small box pictures characters from Peter Rabbit, as illustrated by Harrison Cady. Mfd. by Tindeco in the 1920s. A similar, more commonly found box has square corners. This one is 2-1/4"H x 4-1/2" x 3-1/2". Photo and collection of Robert Carr. Value range mine, not Carr's. **$175+**

VII-81. Make-do "catch-all." A hanging repository for "burnt matches, bits of thread, paper, etc., made from the broken top part of a footed goblet. All the rage in 1874-1875, so much so that "crockery stores were beseiged for broken goblets, and when none were left, it is hinted that some storekeepers broke them on purpose." American Agriculturist, March 1875. The article told how to make a pincushion of the bottom half, then how you could use the top part too, with bits of cardboard, silver paper, crocheted bag & tassels. **$35+**

VII-82. Spill cups, *an early version of match hold-ers for long matches called spills. These particular 1920's repros don't predate striking matches, but were meant for "Colonial" decoration, all the rage at the time. Embossed, pieced sheet brass, with fleur-de-lys, Adams' wreath, heraldic device. All 10-1/2"H x 5"W. From Pearson-Page 1925 catalog. My mother had one with a tall skinny bottle in it, with water, for flowers.* **$25+**

Match holder, 2 fluted urns, mostly black painted cast iron, 3 parts, crested fancy openwork backplate, urn fronts riveted on, striking panel with light colored gritty substance between feet of urns, white inside flutes, wall hung, American, 7-1/2"H x 5-1/2"W, (another is 6"H), pat'd. Jan. 16, 1867, but not in *Subject Index to Patents.....................................* **$85+**

Match holder, 2 pockets with openwork shield back-plate, flowers & scrolls, wall-hung, cast iron, 5-1/2" x 6 -1/2", late 19th C (?). .... **$95+**

Match holder, for the mantle as an ornament, a minia-ture hearth with crane & swinging kettle, sheet brass, double pockets – for used & unused matches, English, about 6"H x 3-1/8"W, late 19th C... **$155+**

Match holder, frying pan, handle up, half an egg shell sticks out from middle of pan, oxidized silvery fin-ish, wall hung, black enameled cast brass, 7-1/2"H x 4-1/2"W, c.1890s..................................... **$125+**

Match holder, wall hung, crimped tin resembling pair of scallop shells under cylindrical pockets for matches, striking surface below, originally japanned or painted, often found in sort of salmon color; one sold by big catalog house, Butler Brothers, at the turn-of-the-century, had a crested stamped back-

---

Reproduction Alert

Urn holders have been reproduced in cast brass, and is in a 1989 catalog of a reproduction wholesale company in Massachusetts. The striking panel does not have any grit. One clue not always applicable, is that antiques that are made of cast iron are often reproduced in cast brass (partly because work can be cheaply done in India, and other countries), but mostly because brass is con-sidered decorative by a broader market whose pri-mary interest is in decoration, not collecting. Remember: "All that glisters is not" old!

VII-83. Match holder patent. *Pat'd. Mar. 13, 1877, by J. A. Kratt, Buffalo, NY. Wall-hung, carved wood, fancy backplate, 2 turned half-cups. The feature claimed by the patentee is the fact that the "box plate" is hinged to a back-plate, and is "provided on the rear side with a friction-surface." I can see the spilled matches now.* Official Gazette.

plate with striking panel between 2 pockets with a scalloped top, and scallop shells underneath. It was called the "Twin," and came in assorted colors of "enameled" tin. Another type had the 2 shell deco-rated open pockets, mounted to a back plate of brass-finished tin, which I think was probably a transparent yellow japan or varnish. This one, pat'd. in 1859, is the most valuable of this style. American, 4-1/2"H x 7"W, another is 4"H x 8"W, c.1860s-1910. The fairly common scallop shell match pockets are a de rigeur classic for kitchenarians. .... **$30-$85+**

❖ NOTES ❖

The History of Lucifers & Matches up to 1882 – "The 50th anniversary of the invention of matches by three Austrians was recently celebrated in Vienna. The inventor of the lucifer match lives in every country under the sun, so Austria will do as well as another. Fifty years ago [1832], in England, matches had only reached the stage known as 'lucifers,' and were clumsy and inconvenient. Fox, Burke & Dr. Johnson used to light their candles with flint & steel, though practice probably made them more skillful than we would be at such an operation. About the beginning of the century long brimstone matches took the place of tinder. About 6 inches long, tipped with sulphur, they caught fire easily from the spark of a flint.

"In 1825 an apparatus called the 'eupyrion' was used in most cities. This was a large-mouthed bottle contain-ing sulphuric acid, soaked in fibrous asbestos, and the matches, about 2 inches long, were tipped with a chem-ical combination, of which chlorate of potash was the principle ingredient. When the match's end was dipped in the acid & rapidly withdrawn, fire was produced, but the acid was inconvenient, the matches easily spoiled by damp. Next came the 'pyrophoros,' the pneumatic tinder-box, and Doberlenier's hydrogen lamp.

"In 1832 the first friction match was made. It was jokingly called a lucifer. Lucifers were substantially the same as present matches, pulled through a piece of sandpaper. Since then, it has been altered from a silent to a noisy match ... the safety fusée, which ignites only when rubbed upon chemically-treated paper. This safety match was patented in England in 1856." *The Metal Worker*, Nov. 4, 1882.

The first American friction matches, or lucifers, were made by Daniel Chapin & Alonzo Dwight Phillips of Massachusetts. Phillips received a patent on phosphorous friction matches on Oct. 24, 1836. The nickname "lucifer" was apt: the head was coated with a composition of powdered chalk, phosphorous, brimstone & glue. **Boon or bonfire?** The friction match saved trouble except when two of them accidentally rubbed together and caught on fire. Safety matches required a special striking surface, so open-top match holders (as differentiated from match safes – match holders with a lid, especially if self-closing) could be safely used? In 1858, a short cautionary tale in *Scientific Artisan* went like this: "Were I an insurance agent, remarks a writer in an exchange, I would make it an imperative rule, that every house insured by me should be provided by metal or earthen boxes, in which matches should be kept. They are often seen lying loosely upon the shelf or in the closet, where a careless servant, or an unthinking child or even a mischievous mouse, may produce disastrous results with them. A little incident has made me very careful in this matter. One day, when about closing my room, I hastily threw a key into a drawer where were several loose papers and miscellaneous articles, and closed it; but just as it was closed, there was a glimmer of light within the drawer, which attracted my attention from its novelty. Opening it, I found that the key had struck the end of a friction match and fired it." • The 1881 edition of *Practical Housekeeping*, advised that "The only proper place to put matches is in a metal box with a self-closing lid." Then the 1884 *Practical Housekeeping* advised that "**Friction Matches** – should never be left where the mice will get them, as they carry them to their nests, and sometimes ignite them. They are poison to children, and are dangerous to women, who

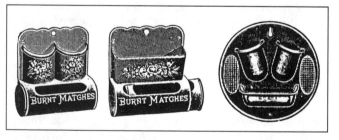

VII-84. Match holders. *(L)* & *(M)* *These were advertised as "safety match safes" because of the cylindrical "receptacle at the bottom to hold" burnt matches, and which was effectively closed by turning the inner cylinder. The term* **match safe** *usually refers to a fireproof receptacle in which the unburnt matches are kept, with a lid that would contain fire if by rubbing together they ignited. These japanned and decorated tin ones were pat'd. Aug. 6, 1895, and sold by Dover Stamping Co., Boston. (R) Stamped sheet steel enameled in "dull gunmetal finish." 5-3/4" diameter. The Washburn Co., Worcester, MA, 1927. Some of collector appeal comes from colorful decoration.* **$45+**

VII-85. Match holders. *All wall-hung, and all stamped tin, japanned in variety of colors, (L) type called a "twin," with scalloped bottom & "assorted colored enameled pockets." Linecut differs only slightly from a 1899 Butler Brothers catalog that sold theirs for 17¢ a dozen, wholesale! (R) Two with lids, properly called* **match safes**. *(B-R) is "self-closing." Three sizes: 5" x 4-1/2" x 1"; 3-3/4" x 2-1/2" x 1-5/8"; and 4-1/4" x 2-3/8" x 3". Central Stamping Co., 1920.* **$25-$50+**

ignite them by stepping on them, and endangering their clothing from fire." Of course, a match safe wouldn't take care of all the dangers.

Match safe, blue japanned tin with golden pinstriping, American (?), 3" x 4", 19th C. .... **$65+**
Match safe, cast iron, "Self Closing," mfd. by D. M. & Co., New Haven, CT, 19th C. .... **$75+**

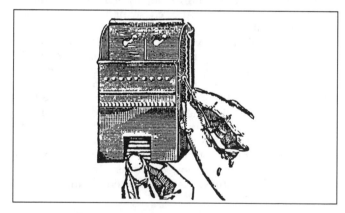

VII-86. Match safe. *"Lusk," with choice of oxidized copper, nickel plated, or brushed brass finish. Two advertised features were a "spark guard" along side that protected against flying sparks, and also that a "Lusk will save its cost many times over in keeping the wall paper and polished woodwork from being marred by matches, as the scratcher is always handy." In traveling salesman's supplier catalog put out by F. W. Seastrand, c.1910s. Great thing about reading original catalog copy is the glimpse into everyday life long ago. Here you can imagine the loutish, ne'er-do-well striking his matches on mama's pretty flowered wallpaper until she was ready to scream. Then here comes a knock at the door, and it's the traveling salesman!* **$50+**

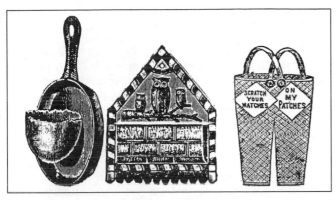

VII-87. Match holders. *(L) Fry pan wall-hung holder, black-enameled cast brass, with egg shell given an oxidized "silver" finish. (M) Owls on stone wall were a popular Victorian motif. Both from Montgomery Ward catalog, c.1895. (R) "Just out and the funniest novelty of the season. A perfect pair of miniature pantaloons, but five inches in length, made from the finest Cassimere.* A pair of silk suspenders attached to the buttons on pants can be used to hang it on the wall. It will hold a full box." Sandpaper patches 1-3/4" across. A. E. Rayment Supply Co., c.1910-1920s. * Cassimere is, and was, a wool twill used for men's suits. (L) $125+; (M) $75+; (R) $125+*

Match safe, cast iron, bin with lid, embossed flowers on sides, spring dispenses matches, "IDEAL," 5" x 3", 19th C. .... **$75+**

Match safe, cast iron, with lid, in shape of fireplace, American, 1871. Being dated adds value for many collectors. .... **$150+**

Matchbox holder, boxy cat, painted wood, with metal buttons for eyes, painted nose & whiskers, and the upward curving tail serves to hang it to wall, American, 20th C. • I have seen enough of these, all slightly different, to be sure it was one of those home workbench projects described in a magazine, around the 1920s or '30s. Anyone know exactly? **$25-$65+**

Milk bottle, molded glass with large round cream top embossed as baby face. Those without the baby face, but with large round cream top and sloping shoulders are also called bubble tops, or Mae Wests. "Brookfield Dairy," small half-pint size, early 20th C. .... **$75+**

❖ NOTES ❖

Glass cleaning collector hint – At a flea I overheard a dealer telling a customer to try Efferdent™ or other cleanser for false teeth inside a bottle with discoloration or fogging. I wouldn't try it on a great rarity, not until you try it on something else. Some people use bits of copper shaken inside; I've used bee-bees. • A set of old ice cream dishes I have are discolored and opalescent from being washed in a dishwasher by the previous owner (a no-no for old glass). But they look great, almost frosted, with ice cream in them!

Milk bottle cover, stamped metal, convex ring that fits down inside mouth of milk bottle to increase the tightness of seal, marked "Frigidaire" with their crest 3" diam., early 20th C. .... **$15+**

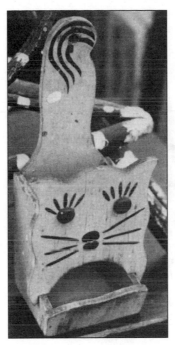

VII-88. Matchbox holder. *Cutout plywood, green with black trim, furniture leg skids for eyes. Typical of home craft project holders, usually animals or people. 1920s-40s. Cats probably valued highest, if folky. $25-$45+*

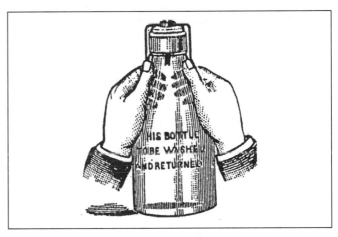

VII-89. Milk bottle. *"Warren," Pat'd. Mar. 23, 1880, mfd. by Warren Glass Works Co., NYC. Advertised American Agriculturist, 1882. $25+*

VII-90. Milk can server. *Provided an "attractive pitcher that harmonizes with the most richly appointed table service." Probably stainless steel. Pat'd. 1915 & 1916. Liquid Container and Server Corp., Los Angeles, CA. $30+*

VII-91. Milk pail & teapot. (L) *Teapot cobalt blue enamelware with gold trim & white flowers, hinged lid. Probably European, late 19th C.* **(R)** *Pail in plain gray enamel, turned wooden knob, bail handle, about 10"H. Courtesy Mainland Antiques, Mainland, PA.* **$75+; $60+**

Milk holder, for condensed milk – meant to turn a can into a table cream pitcher, silverplate, figural fox on lid, inside lid is adv'g. for "Wisconsin's Fox Brand Condensed Milk," late 19th C. .... **$75+**

Milk pail, blue ombré (shaded light to dark) enamelware, wire bail, probably Shapleigh Hardware Co., late 19th or early 20th C. **Added value.** – Green "Shamrock" ombré finish worth a bit more, & purple "Thistle" ombré worth half again as much. .... **$125+**

Milk pan, pieced tin, handmade, slanted sides, 3-1/2" deep x 15" diam. at top, late 19th C. .... **$12+**

Milk pan, redware with brown glaze, relatively shallow compared to diam., slanted sides, American, 16-1/2" diam., 19th C. .... **$175+**

❖ NOTES ❖

Earthenware vs. Stoneware, or Lead vs. Salt. – "Before the glorious Revolution ... here and there were scattered Potteries of Earthen-ware, infamously bad and unwholesome, from their being partially glazed with a thin, cheap washing of Lead. The best of Lead-glazing is esteemed unwholesome, by observing people. The Mischievous effects of it, fall chiefly on the country people and the poor everywhere. Even when it is firm enough so as not to scale off, it is yet imperceptably eaten away by every acid matter: and mixing with the drinks and meats of the people becomes a slow but sure poison.

"It is wished the Legislature would consider of means for discountenancing the use of Lead in glazing Earthenware, and encourage the application of the most perfect and wholesome glazing, produced only from Sand and Salts ... A small bounty, or exemption, on this might be sufficient to the end. But, what if public encouragement was to be given on homemade Stone-ware, rather than on Earthen-ware? In Stoneware, Lead is never used; no other glazing need be used for stone than what is produced by a little common salt strewed over the ware, which operates as a flux to the particles of sand that stick on the sides of the Ware, whilst it is in the furnace.

"Stoneware is now scarce and dear amongst us, as the housewife knows. This is owing to its great bulk and low value, that scarcely affords to pay the freight." *Pennsylvania Mercury*, Feb. 4, 1785.

Mustard pot, brown & tan earthenware in jug shape, "As You Like It" lettered underglaze on side, after Shakespeare. 5"H, English, c.1900. .... **$25+**

Napkin rings. – Made of many materials, viz. carved wood, molded plastic, woven straw, but most spectacularly, Victorian silverplate, especially figural ones, little sculpturinos with animals and/or people cleverly disporting themselves on a platform (sometimes wheeled), including a cylindrical holder for the cloth napkin. This is a highly specialized field, especially the silverplated figurals, which I will not attempt to include in this book. Look for Dorothy Rainwater's books on silver & silverplate, some published by Schiffer, and Victor Schnadig's *American Victorian Figural Napkin Rings*, Wallace-Homestead, 1971, out of print. American, European, Oriental, c.1850s (?) through present time. "**Napkins** are never supposed to appear a second time before washing, hence napkin rings are domestic secrets and not for company." Todd S. Goodholme, *Domestic Cyclopedia of Practical Information*, NY: Henry Holt, 1877. .... **.25¢-$500+**

VII-92. Milk pail holder. *(Not for use with milk pail of type in VII-91.) Hoop iron with riveted knee pieces, homemade, not commercially sold. American Agriculturist, July 1873, had directions for making it. Workmanship of individual piece would determine value.* **$25**

VII-93. Molasses pitcher. *Japanned pieced tin, strap handle, flip lid. Two sizes: holding 1 or 2 pints. Central Stamping Co.;1920 catalog, but easily thought to be much older.* **$35+**

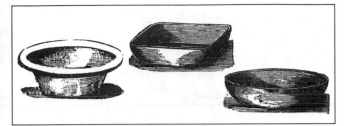

VII-94. Two nappies & a pudding dish. *Lipped, square and round, all earthenware. "Very neat milk pans, made of yellow or whiteware, are sometimes used and are by far the best round shallow pans. They are called by the trade 'nappies,' and are round or oval. The convenient sizes hold 4 to 6 quarts; the 8-quart ones are heavy to handle. The round ones with a lip were formerly made extensively for the southern trade, but less so now. Square dishes of the same ware are called 'puddings;' they are rectangular with somewhat rounded corners, and in common use as pudding dishes, but are admirable milk-pans when small quantities of milk only are kept." American Agriculturist, May, 1880.* **$40-$100**

Newspaper rack, not for newstand use like I always thought, but for a "hubby" who buries his face in the paper at table. "Keeps the daily news out of the breakfast butter. So good-looking that even wives like it. In English bronze, or brass and copper" reads the ad. A tabletop easel of wire, with a cutout silhouette of a cock, & word "NEWS," Chase Brass & Copper Co., Waterbury, CT, mid 1930s. .... **$125+**

Pail, blue & white agate enamelware, with tin lid, wire bail handle, late 19th C................................... **$55+**

Pail, deep blue & gray enamelware, cover, wire bail handle, probably Columbian's "Dresden," 19th C. .... **$125+**

Pail, marbleized midnight blue & white enamelware, 19th C. .... **$75+**

Pail, straight sided, with pouring lip, copper, with thick copper bail handle, American, 4 gal. capacity, mid 19th C. .... **$150+**

VII-95. Nappy or nappie. *Yellowware, in 10 sizes, from only 3" to 12" diameter. Note slanted sides. In modern dictionaries, the general definition of a nappie, or nappy, is a small, shallow, slant-sided bowl used for cooking, said to derive from a Middle English word, nap, meaning bowl. (It's also a nickname for napkins, hence for diapers.) Some sources say they are for cooking, and some nappies have fluted bottoms or sides. Obviously, from the quote in the previous caption, to some people nappies were milk pans of a fairly large size. Although 20th C. ads show glass nappies, most are ceramic. This linecut from Duparquet, Huot & Moneuse hotelier supplies catalog, c.1904-1910.* **$40-$150+**

VII-96. Nursing bottle. *Burr patent "medallion feeder," glass flattish bottle, glass 'straw,' rubber tube & nipple. Embossed eagle in medallion, M. S. Burr Co. From Butler Brothers 1899 catalog. This type of flask-like nurser, though not this brand, dates to at least the 1830s. The tubes may have been made of bone or pewter or porcelain. Nipples were bone, wood, ivory, pewter (hopefully without lead) and finally rubber in the last half of the 19th C.* **$125+**

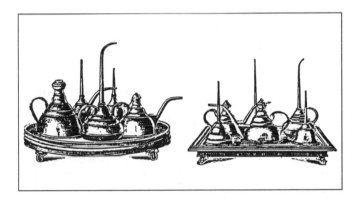

VII-97. Oiler sets – confusables. *Here because they're as elegant as cruet sets for the dining room, and possibly confusable. (L) Engineers' oiler set with oval tray and set of 4 oiler cans. Two sizes: trays 14" x 8-1/2" and 16" x 11-1/2", the larger having 5 cans. They could be had in brass or nickeled brass finishes. Note little wheeled casters on the trays. (R) Set on either 14" x 9" tray with four cans or 17-1/4" x 11" with five. Both are McNab & Harlin Mfg. Co., NYC, 1898 catalog. (Note: There are rather elegant pieced tin cans with small spouts seen at antique shows & fleas that turn out to be 1990's olive oil cans from kitchenware catalogs. These non-kitchen oilers are valuable – there are many collectors. Values for singles:* **$10-$40**; *for sets:* **$55-$125+**

Pail – See also Bucket; Slop jar

Pantry box, bentwood painted robin's egg blue, 2 finger laps, 5-1/2"L oval, 19th C. Storage for bulk or loose food such as meal or flour or crackers.......... **$200+**

Pantry box, bentwood, deep green paint, 3 finger laps, 1 finger lap lid, 7" diam., 19th C. Value is in color & finger laps. .... **$500+**

Pepper pot, turned wood, pedestal base, English, 6-1/4"H, early 19th C, poss. late 18th. (Pepper pots were also made of tin, and looked like flour dredgers.)...... **$225+**

VII-100. Pantry boxes. *These are all simple painted bentwood boxes, rather like hatboxes in design. None have the fancy and valuable finger-lapped construction. They range in size from 8" diam. to 14" diam., and are colored in soft, almost chalky, old paints: dark red, mustard yellow, ochre yellow, and a sort of medium blue. Staining from contents can be seen at the bottom of the one on the far left. American, c. 1850s-70s. An assembled set sampling all the possible colors (including other reds, blues, and greens, as well as gray & off-white) and sizes, from the smallest (perhaps 3" or 4" diam. up to 20" diam. or more, might comprise 20 or more boxes, and be worth upwards of $4,000. Singly:* **$125-$600**

❖ **NOTES** ❖

Changes in Climate – One thing I worry about, when there's nothing else, is all the old, old treen that's recently been imported into the USA from abroad, where climatic conditions are quite different and have been for centuries. Suddenly a nice old turned wood pepper pot finds itself sitting in a hot Arizona or Baltimore collection, unprepared for the considerable change in humidity and temperature. What happens to it? Does anyone have personal experiences to share with recent imported wooden smalls?

Pepper Box.

VII-101. Pepper boxes & a salt "box" *These were also called* **casters** *– a container to be shaken, hence to cast out from, a condiment.* **(L)** *Made in pieced & stamped tin, or better, in Britannia metal. From Harrod's Stores, Brompton, England, 1895 catalog.* **(T-R)** *is a relatively flat-top salt "box," 3"H;* **(B-R)** *is dome-topped pepper box, 3-3/4"H. Both in Duparquet, Huot & Moneuse catalog, c.1904-1910.* **$10-$50**

VII-102. Pepper bottle –" *... a charming, life-like representation of a funny, knowing little pug dog. It is entirely of frosted silver, and will never fail to receive admiring attention. The pepper is shaken out through the tiny holes in the top of the dog's head."* *Original cost only $2, in novelty silverplate catalog, c.1883-84. Value range assuming bottle really made of silverplate. Huge crossover interest from pug collectors.* **$125+**

Pickle bottles – See Bottles, for pickles
Pickle jar, stoneware glazed inside and out, levered bail clamp-on lid, Weir Pottery Co., Monmouth, IL, 14"H x 8" diam., 19th C. into early 20th C. In a 1902 ad in *Ladies Home Journal*, a note was added at bottom of ad that **"Heinz, the pickle man**, has just ordered

VII-103. Picnic or market baskets. (L) *Called a "chip-basket," which is "made of neatly interwoven wooden splits, with strongly-framed flat covers, which shut down closely, and are fastened by catches." Rounded corners. American Agriculturist, May 1871.* **(M)** *Refrigerator basket, made of rattan, with layer of asbestos (!) and layer of felt between rattan body and inside metal lining. Ice compartment shown at near end, which is removable for cleaning. Called the "Everybody," and came in 2 sizes: 12"H x 21" x 10", or 14-1/2"H x 22" x 10".* **(R)** *is woven of ash, plywood top, lined of material, and "made for the sole purpose of keeping out sand and dirt." 11"H x 19-1/2"L x 11"W. Both in 1930s Abercrombie & Fitch catalog of outdoors goods.* **$30-$60+**

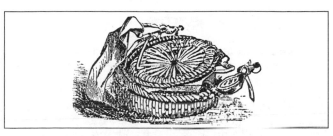

VII-104. Hanaper. *I found this word by accident, along with the hard-to decipher picture of a round canteen-shaped basket with wide cloth shoulder strap. It was in the 1903 Century Dictionary Encyclopedia. A Middle English word, hanypere, or Old French word hanapier, hannepier, etc. meaning "a case for a* **hanap** *or drinking-cup, or for other vessels. ... It was often made of wickerwork, and sometimes covered with leather." It is obviously where the word hamper, used for a picnic basket, came from.*

500,000 Weir Jars." The H. J. Heinz Co., by the way, founded in 1867, has a museum of artifacts and memorabilia numbering in the thousands. It is at company headquarters in Pittsburgh, but is so far not open to the public, alas. .... **$40+**

Picnic or automobile lunch kit, blackened tin, in wood case, "Model 4 Auto-Cook-Kit," by Prentiss-Wabers Products Co., Wisconsin Rapids, WI, 5"H x 16-1/2"L x 9"W, early 20th C. • Automobilia collectors are probably well aware of such things, but it's a new branch of kitchen collecting. .... **$50+**

Pie carrier, plywood, homemade, 7 tiers of cutout "C" pieces of plywood, plus full circle top & bottom pieces, American, 20"H x 10" diam., c.1950s. .... **$15+**

Pie rack, 4 tiers, twisted wire, not painted black (as some repros are), no mark, problematic to date.

VII-105. Picnic basket patents. (L) *"Lunch-box," pat'd. July 26, 1881, by Sarah A. Hoskins, Bangor, ME. With a "hinged & folded table, each leaf of which has a pair of hinged legs crossing one another." Fitted compartments.* **(R)** *"Refrigerator-basket," pat'd. Oct. 28, 1884, by John R. Hare, Baltimore, MD. "a waterproof bag [is] placed between the felt filling and the wicker-work casing" to act as an insulator. Official Gazette of U.S. Patent Office. (NOTE: Well-fitted-out picnic baskets, many from England, go for upwards of $65.)*

VII-106. Picnic basket. *Handsome form, said to be Shaker. Tightly woven ash splint over reed. 10"H x 16"L, 2 lids, woven handle slightly unraveled. Late 19th. C. probably.* **$120+**

Could be late 19th, could be 1980s. • Reproduction alert. – I see them advertised all the time, but haven't examined any. Common sense would tell you to look for signs (using a magnifier) of wear – pie pans scraping in and out for years, scuff marks on bottom from being moved, polishing marks. From other repro wire pieces, I know they use wire of the same gauge for uprights and rests. Don't pay for a descriptive tag that tries to assure you "early" or "old," unless you are sure. If old: .... **$45+**

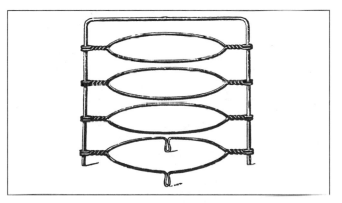

VII-107. Pie holder & cooler. *Tinned wire, made in 5 styles. The 4-plate style was made with light gauge and heavy gauge wire. This one, from a 1915 catalog, is exactly like one that has been in our possession for over 30 years, maybe even 35, and is probably old because it predates the repros seen everywhere now. Ours measures 10-3/4"H x 12-1/4"W at bottom. Pie plate rings are 7-11/16" outside diameter. The wire is 3/16" diameter. Line-cut is of a style dating to the late 19th or early 20th C. Other styles in catalog are made entirely of heavy gauge wire, for 6, 12 and even 24 pie plates for a bakery. From catalog of Wire Goods Co., 1915.* **Caution:** *Some reproductions of these are sometimes hard to tell, being of heavy wire. Most are painted dull black, but then so are some of the old ones. Ones with bright orange rust are undoubtedly repros, as are any with some kind of heart twist. I can't guarantee a description of an old one, but I'd say if you have one you've had for at least 30-35 years, or if you find any now for more than 4 pies, they're probably old.* **$20-$100**

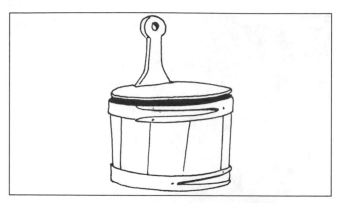

*VII-108. **Piggin**, with lid, which is unusual. 9-1/2"H overall. Early 19th C, either North American or European. Patina and original exterior paint add value.* **$150-$400**

Pie rack, iron, mounts to wall, dated 1874. (Sorry I have no more information on this, but material and presence of patent year adds value to what's already collectible.)... **$100+**

Piggin, for liquids, staved pine, ash "buttonhole" hoops top and bottom, overlapped & fastened with wooden button-like peg, the distinguishing feature making this a piggin is the one elongated stave handle, this one beautifully shaped like long-stemmed mushroom, to give the hand a good purchase, has unusual flat cover with flange inside, finished outside & in with dark brown stain, possibly walnut stain (?), New England (?), or poss. Canadian, 6"H x 9"diam. plus 4"L handle stave, early 19th C. **Piggins** are described sometimes as small wooden buckets. The elongated stave for the handle, for most of them, is quite simple & it may have a hanging hole in it. They are not often found with their lids. See salt box picture VII-115. .... **$200+**

Pitcher, repaired Bennington-type brown glazed stoneware, originally one of the pitchers with molded old man's face under lip. Handle broken off, repaired neatly with wide tinsmithed bands (with turned edges) forming a sort of harness around the body of the vessel, with a wide braced tin strap handle. Prob. VT pitcher, with New England (?) repair, 12"H, pitcher maybe 1840s to 1860s, repair poss. 1860s to 1880s. .... **$500+**

*VII-109. **Pitcher**, missing its original handle, economically repaired with soldered tin. Drawing was sent to American Agriculturist, July 1885, by C. F. Alkire, Madison County, OH. Value depends on artfulness of repair, as well as original interest & value of the pitcher.* **$125-$500+**

❖ NOTES ❖

Handles for Pitchers – A jug or pitcher without a handle is often considered past its usefulness. An economical person, believing a few pennies saved are equal to so many earned, may re-handle a jug or a pitcher with great ease, in the manner shown in the engraving. ..." (a thin tin harness around neck & under belly, vertical strap in front, strap handle connects top & bottom band.) *American Agriculturist*, July 1885.

• • •

Repaired pieces are now in great demand. A book, *Waste Not, Want Not: The Art of the Make-Do* was published in 1986 about the broken goblets, lamps, pitchers, etc., repaired or fitted out with new parts of different materials; such pieces are called fractures or make-dos. In the book there is heavy emphasis on pincushions made from broken goblets or hurricane lamp bases, and not a lot of other types of things. The book was available from the author, Don Naetzker, 205 S. Main St., Fairport, NY 14450. If you write, use an SASE.

• • •

The name "make-do" comes from the thrifty ditty: "Use it up, Wear it out, Make it do, Or do without." I think the repaired piece, or the one made into something else (maybe, "make it do a new service"), has an ancient lineage. The mid-to-late Victorian urge to make a kickshaw or gimcrack out of every possible material object, from acorn to felt scraps, from ribbon to paper lace doiley, fed into this lineage & added things like the pincushions mentioned above. (I bought one recently with a goblet foot & stem, ground off at top of stem, & fitted with a human hair-filled pillow in old patterned silk.)

• • •

1875 Pretties: The *American Agriculturist*, a journal for farm families published in NYC, had an article in March 1875 on **"How to Make a Catch-all.** - Some clever person has contrived a use for broken goblets. They were so popular near last Christmas, that crockery stores were beseiged for broken goblets, and when none were left, it is hinted that some store-keepers were so obliging as to break them on purpose. Here [a picture of the goblet top and its broken off stem & foot, and a picture of a sort of crocheted hanging basket on a wall hook] you have a picture of the fractured article – the bowl and the foot. Of course, you all know how to make a pincushion of the base of the glass; and now I am going to tell you how to utilize the upper part. Take a strip of silver perforated cardboard, 9 holes deep (cutting it through the 1st and 11th row of holes). Measure the top of the goblet, and allow the strip to lap over 1 or 2 holes. Fit it snugly, now [needle] work upon the cardboard in any colored worsted you like, the 'Roman Key,' or any other pattern ... through the holes." Then you crochet the bag and make a tassel, and you can "hang it up by your bureau or other convenient place for burnt matches, bits of thread, paper, etc." Sort of like a small wall wastebasket. Hmmm. See VII-81, also picture XVI-20, "Uses for Old Tin Cans" in Chapter XVI.

• • •

Damages & Sitters: I love the terms used by sellers & collectors to describe damage to ceramic, glass, metal. Besides hairline cracks and dings, nicks and chips, are two probably solely for glass: flea bites and chiggers – both of which mean tiny nicks. Often it doesn't seem to dampen value very much. And if it's a lot of damage, but on one side only, the item can become a shelf piece, also called a sitter.

Plate, deep dish, almost a bowl, cast iron, marvelous patina, American, 4" deep x 7-3/4" diam., late 1700s, early 1800s. .... **$130+**

Porringer, cast iron, fanned or ribbed openwork short handle, shallow recess underneath bottom edge, long casting gate on bottom, "Kenrick #0" marked on bottom, along with size, West Bromwich, England, 4-1/8" diam., 1/2 pint, the smallest size, early 19th, late 18th C. Many porringers marked "Kenrick" are found in this country, as well as coffee mills & a few other ironmonger wares. Alex Ames, in his book on old iron, identifies the first "Kenrick" maker as Archibald Kenrick, of West Bromwich, who established his foundry in 1791, and is still in business as A. Kenrick & Sons. Distinctive openwork fan-ribbed handle was probably copied by American founders. .... **$125+**

Porringer, cast iron, openwork ribbed fan handle, "Kenrick," English, 6-3/4" diam., early 19th C. .... **$135+**

❖ NOTES ❖

Portable pantries were an intermediate product with self-contained storage units, usually with an inte-

VII-110. Repaired pieces. *This is one of my favorite pictures in the whole book. These were from an exhibition of repaired pieces, "On the Mend," held by Bonnie Grossman, The Ames Gallery of American Folk Art, in 1988. As she wrote, "examples are leather-patched, tin-patched, gut-sewn, stapled, and glued with sawdust paste." Also as Bonnie wrote, these are very "endearing" pieces, comfortable to live with. Photograph by Ben Blackwell. All objects courtesy Ames Gallery of American Folk Art, 2661 Cedar St., Berkeley, CA, (510-845-4949; e-mail:_ amesgal@home.com) and are valued upwards of $250 each.* • *Of related interest is the Japanese Zen Buddhist aesthetic concept known as* **wabi-sabi.** *It celebrates the beauty of objects that are imperfect, incomplete, and impermanent. A book explaining this design tenet is Leonard Koren's* Wabi-Sabi for Artists, Designers, Poets & Philosophers, *Stone Bridge Press, 1993.*

VII-111. Porringer – two views. *Cast iron, half-pint size and so marked on underside. Mfd. by the ubiquitous West Bromwich, England, founder, A. Kenrick, with distinctive fan-like tab handle. 4-1/8" diameter, long casting gate. Some in this size are marked "No. 0" but this one appears to be marked "No. 3." Photo courtesy of Oveda Maurer Antiques, San Anselmo, CA.* **$125+**

gral flour sifter, and some with a windup clock. *Before the advent of portable pantries, housewives and cooks stored staples and spices in assorted canisters, tins, bins, bags, boxes, drawers, and various racks and shelves – on the wall, floor, table and pantry. After these useful store-alls came the "Hoosier"-type, moveable work station – a sort of media center for cooking, where everything was stored within in various drawers and canisters, and where the housewife had built-in work surfaces – even pastry boards. The "portable" pantry was so-called not because it was put on a buggy and taken somewhere, but because it was moveable, and could be placed on any table or cupboard shelf that suited the individual. Of course, preparations for a big church social would have been made easier if the lucky church lady in charge could commandeer somebody's portable pantry for temporary use in the church kitchen! And who knows which came first: the housewife's portable pantry or the cowboy's chuck wagon?*

Portable pantry, also called a security safe, black japanned pieced tin, countertop, with almost turret-like bins on either side of large central rounded "silo" part which contains 5 stacked spice containers, lids out, coffee mill on right side, compartments in bottom with white porcelain knobs, center bottom door labeled "The Kitchen Secretary," American, about 40"H, 19th C. .... **$800+**

Portable pantry, black japanned tin, wheat design stamped in the tin, big bins on top for coffee, flour & corn meal, coffee grinder on right side, flour sifter in center works by moving lever left & right back & forth, 6 spice canisters with double lids, including inner shaker lid, in "stacked" position, lids out, down center, 2 heavily-encrusted compartments at bottom, almost as if used as an oven, but that couldn't be, mark so worn & rubbed it can't be read (except by infrared maybe?), probably a "Queen Safe," 50"H x 36"W, late 19th C. .... **$800+**

Portable pantry, tin, black with gold & silver decorations, bins in top, central vertical row of 6 spice cans, coffee mill on right side with crank, shelves for pies (?) below, waist high, marked "Queen Safe" in large serif letters, mfd. by Cincinnati Stamping Co., Cincinnati, OH, 42"H x 29"W, late 19th C. ... **$800+**

Portable pantry, dark asphaltum japanned tin with ochre stenciling in Japanese-derived (Japonisme) bamboo and birds and butterflies motif, basically straight sides with front slanted out at bottom, usual bins for flour & coffee beans, with built-in flour sifter & coffee mill (crank on side), 5 vertically stacked spice canisters in center, compartments below for flour, sugar & meal, marked "Manufactured for the Standard Cabinet Co. by B. Hunt Stamping Works," Kansas City, MO, 34"H x 26"W, pat'd. 1893. Collector Mike Murrish of California sent me the information on this one............. **$800+**

Portable pantry, japanned black tin, with stenciled letters & bouquets of roses, also containers or canisters stenciled GINGER, CLOVES, CINNAMON, SPICE, MUSTARD, TAPIOCA, RICE, HOMINY, BARLEY, and one that's unreadable, crank on side for coffee mill, lower bins labeled CAKE & BREAD, the 2 above those for SUGAR and MEAL, with flour sifter in center, "Security Safe," 38"H x 31"W, pat'd. 1900 and 1901. .... **$900+**

Portable pantry, japanned & stenciled tin, sort of Chinoiserie designs, top has 2 half-round bins with hinged lids on top that reveal compartments for flour sifting & coffee grinding with pans to catch the

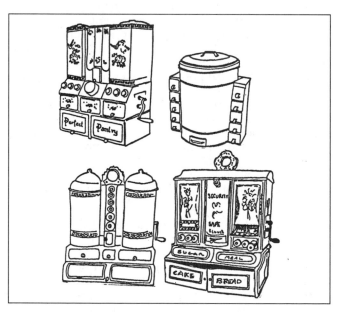

VII-112. Portable pantries. *Clockwise from upper (L). (1) "The Perfect Pantry," pat'd. 1904. Some have a clock frame on top, although I believe the user supplied the clock. (2) Maker unknown, flour compartment in center, with sifter built in, spice containers along sides. (3) "Security Safe," pat'd. in 1900 and 1901, 38"H x 31"W. Japanned dark brown with flowers and gilt stenciling. (4) Possibly a "Globe Cabinet," though similar in some respects to the "Queen Safe." 42"H x 31"W x 21" deep. Note opening for a clock, and also curved fronts of lower compartment. What's different from named examples I've seen are the two different-sized round spice compartments down center. Value goes down, and identification is hard, when pantries have been re- or over-painted.* **$500-$1,200+**

grounds, doors in bottom section reveal 2 sifters (flour & sugar[?]), center section has vertical row of spice canisters with screw-on tops, divided compartment below has 2 small pans like miniature loaf pans, originally there was a mirrored door covering the spice containers, there seems to be storage for baking pans or implements too, stenciled in script on lower doors is "Globe Cabinet," 41"H x 27"W, on a wooden base possibly added later, with 8"H legs, 1880s-1890s. Collector Geraldine Hoven is to be thanked for description & pictures of this heretofore unknown portable pantry, which was her grandparents' in Iowa.. **$900+**

Portable pantry, japanned tin, painted with flowers, butterflies, etc., compartments for all staples – flour (with sifter), sugar, etc. – spices, coffee (with grinder), unusual swing-out scale on side, missing the clock. Scale marked "F & C" on face; cabinet marked "The Standard Cabinet Co., B. Hunt Stamping Co., Kansas City" [MO], early 20th C. ..... **$800+**

Portable pantry, set on table, or well-braced shelf, not hung on wall, japanned & flower stenciled tin with name on 2 lower doors covering shelves, bins or containers for flour, corn meal, sugar, built-in coffee grinder on right side with crank sticking out side, white porcelain knobs on doors & spice canisters, clock in center top, "Perfect Pantry Co.," St. Louis, MO, about 50"H, pat'd. 1904....................... **$800+**

Portable pantry, simple black finished tin with stenciled labels for various compartments, 2 tall side "silos" flank center section with 6 stacked spice containers with double lids (one for shaking), topped with opening for clock (I've never actually seen one with the clock intact; maybe you had to furnish your own? or maybe you put a portrait of the cook in it!), 2 match safes, lower compartments for flour, meal & sugar, coffee grinder on right, bottom compartment like most of the portable pantries has hinged lids with curved fronts that make base larger & steadier, stenciled "Portable Pantry" on front, 42"H x 31"W x 21" deep, 19th C. .... **$900+**

Portable pantry, simplest most economical kind, white painted metal chest with hinged cover, compartments inside hold 5 lbs sugar, 5 lbs. flour, 3 lbs coffee, on front are 3 pull-out small catch drawers, with crank for flour sifter, & lever for releasing sugar & coffee, "Service Master," 10"H x 15"W x 8" deep, 20th C. .... **$125+**

❖ NOTES ❖

***Salt: A World History** – The Magnificent Story of How a Common Rock Has Shaped Civilization,* by Mark Kurlansky, may leave you thirsty, but not for more information, as he has brilliantly told the 10,000-year old history of salt and humans in over 475 pages. See Bibliography.

Salt box, blue enamelware with wooden hinged lid, prob. imported in 1880s-1900 from Germany, late 19th C. .... **$125+**

Salt box, gray & cobalt saltglazed stoneware, wall hung, round with flattened back, the German "SALTZ" written on front, German, late 19th C. .... **$100+**

Salt box, green-glazed ceramic, box with chamfered corners & scalloped backplate with hanging hole, varnished, stained wooden lid, marked only "SALT," Bavaria, c.1900-1930................................ **$115+**

VII-113. A "Salt" – a container called by what it contains. *Turned, then chip-carved wood in abstract form of pineapple or osage orange, perhaps even a sort of inside on outside pomegranate. Green paint on outside, red inside, 5"H. Photo courtesy Litchfield Auction Gallery, Litchfield CT. Ex-Harold Corbin Collection, auctioned Jan. 1, 1990, for $750.* **$900-$1,250+**

Salt box, wall hung, copper with glass insert, hinged cover, "Kreamer," Brooklyn, NY, 9"H, early 20th C. .... **$125+**

Salt & pepper dispenser, glass silo-like containers on green plastic base, has center plastic control panel with a black & a white push button to open plugs in bottom of respective containers, Imperial Metal Mfg. Corp., Long Island City, NY, 2"H x 2 3/8"W, pat'd. Aug. 5, 1939. .... **$15+**

Salt & pepper shakers, Catalan™ colored plastic, pepper is yellow with black top, salt is red with green top – each is half a cylinder & fit together into a little round tray that holds them together, American, in all 2"H x 1-1/2" diam., c.1930s. .... **$20+**

Salt & pepper shakers, paneled glass, slightly tapered sides, screw-on chrome cap has built in shaker device to keep holes clear, "Never-Klogg" mfd. by Reiner Products, Inc., NYC, NY, c.1929-30. ..... **$15+**

Salt shaker, shapely molded clear glass jar with screw-on white metal lid with knob in top. Twist knob back & forth & it moves spiraled wire auger inside jar, "Kant-Klog," Humboldt Mfg. Co., Brooklyn, NY, c.1915. .... **$25+**

Salt shaker, known by collectors as a Christmas Salt because of patent date, a bright blue clear blown molded glass honey pot or barrel shaped jar, screw-on pewter or Britannia lid with high acorn knob that

VII-114. Salt box. *Two colors of turned wood, with bull's-eye backplate hanger, hinged lid. Word "Salt" in little ribbon design on front. Imported from Germany by G. M. Thurnauer, NYC. Ad in* House Furnishings Review, *Jan. 1911.* **$90+**

VII-115. Salt boxes. (L) *Turned wood, no lid, painted to simulate ceramic mocha ware (which may have been what some graniteware designs were meant to resemble), with gilt rim. Only 3-1/2"H. Photo courtesy Litchfield Auction Gallery. Ex-Harold Corbin Collection, auctioned Jan. 1, 1990 for only $175.* **(R)** *A wall-hung salt in the form of a piggin, with one long stave forming the hanger handle. Wood, iron hoops. Norwegian, 12"H overall & 4-3/4" diameter, mid (?) 19th C. Picture courtesy of the National Museum of American History, Smithsonian Institution. This one would have more value in the U.S. if it were made here.* **(L) $450+; (R) $150+**

you twist to turn the inside agitator device, like little metal fingers, some pointing down, some up, to break up damp salt, marked on lid, "Dana K. Alden. Boston." Glass by Boston & Sandwich Glass Co.; agitator by Alden Salt Caster Co., Sandwich, MA, and Boston, MA, respectively, 2-1/2"H, pat'd. by Hiram J. White, Dec. 25, 1877. • These came in different colors, and in a taller paneled shape. There were sets with a pepper shaker too, sometimes found in a caster with ring handle. There are other old versions, patented by other inventors. Value is partly determined by color. Range for the type: .... **$275-$600+**

❖ NOTES ❖

Salt & pepper shakers – figurals or novelties. There are as many figural S & Ps as grains of salt in one of them. Most are molded plastic or ceramic, some are cast slush or pot metal. These novelties seem to have started in the 1930s when kitchens began to get fun, with bright colors, lots of motifs used in decals, curtains, potholders. Before then, clever push-button mechanical devices were in demand. Many figurals are under $20 a pair; exceptions would be for certain name brand or character advertising pieces, but they'd be worth a lot more only if rare. A hint at what's available follows: 2 little Schlitz beer cans in cardboard 2 pack, lithographed tin, 1957; China boy chef, adv'g. Tappan Ranges. Stainless steel hotplate, plastic knobs & 2 burners, 2 very realistic glass drip coffee makers, 1950s; • Die molded colored plastic, Aunt Jemima & Uncle Mose F & F Mold & Die Works, Dayton, 5-1/2"H (also 3-1/2"H size); • Pair of opera glasses, knurled focus knob which actually controls whether the salt or the pepper side is open, c.1903; • "Milk glass" Monitor top refrigerators, cork plugs, tiny GE stickers, made for, if not by, General Electric, c.1930s; • Black & white plastic washer marked "laundramat" (for salt) & front load dryer (pepper), red plastic non-fuctional indicator lights, clear plastic windows in doors, rubber plug in bottom, "Ideal Models," Detroit, MI, 4"H, 1950s-60s. (This set worth up to $30+); • Copper & chrome finish molded plastic frying pans, 1960s; Molded plastic nude female forms, a lá Venus de Milo, one black & one white, marked "H. F. & Co." in diamond, 4"H, 1940s (worth up to $25+); • Plastic washing machine with wringers, machine body is a sugar bowl, wringers are salt & pepper, "Made in U. S. A.," "patent pending," c.1950s; • red & white plastic power mower with black rubber wheels, when you pull it the eccentric bends in the wire axle under the shakers alternately pushes up the pepper shaker then the salt; in original box, "Tiny Power Mower" but no maker's name, c.1950s; • Cast white metal, 2-wheel countertop coffee mills crudely formed, black & white, colored tulip & heart decorations, John Wright Inc., Wrightsville, PA, c.1963. • Other 1963 Wright castings are sadirons, a woman & cow, woman or man in rocking chair, a horse & buggy, and boy & wheelbarrow;? Cast white metal (also called pot or slush metal) coffee pots, white with red & green decoration, mid 20th C; • Cast white metal dog/salt, cat/pepper, adv'g. "Friskies," Dayton, OH, 20th C., worth $30-$40; Yellow dog & black cat, colored features, supposed to be Fido &

VII-117. Salt shaker. *The "Crown," with device that could be lifted to pull rods up through holes to break up clogged salt. (By the way, you can put a few big grains of rice in a saltshaker, and that prevents most clogging.) Heavy glass, with silver-plated brass embossed top. H. & H. Mfg. Co., NYC. House Furnishings Review ad, May 1907.* **$25+**

Fifi, for Ken-L Ration, F & F Mold & Die Works, Dayton, OH, 20th C, common, but real works of plastic art; etc. Most of these are: **$10-$30+**

Slop jar pail, white enamelware, wire bail, white pail cover, 20th C. • Pails with lids were often used as

VII-116. Salt box & match safe. *Red & white checkered enamelware, probably German, possibly French, late 19th C. Photographed in booth of Steve Smith, Country Bumpkin Antiques. You will often find these staples canisters from Europe with the German or French words for the contents on the front – such as "Salz" or "Sel." Fairly common to find these or similar attractive checkered pieces because of increasing numbers of imported antiques. The more that are imported, the less "rarity" eye appeal they have, hence the lower the collector value. For the pair:* **$150-$250**

VII-118. Saltshaker. *Another anti-clogging one called the "Kant-Klog." "Crystal" and "non-corrosive white metal." Humboldt Mfg. Co., Brooklyn, NY. House Furnishings Review ad, Oct. 1915.* **$25+**

slop jars, kept on kitchen counter near sink for scraping dishes into. Some food was put in as slops for pigs, although some pig farmers decried this practice. Some liquids used to make vinegar, including cider, hard cider & leftover wine, were put in separate jar or pail, left to turn to vinegar via the action of that gooey blob called "mother." .... **$25+**

Slop jar, gray graniteware, slightly rounded body, with wire bail & wooden grip, lid. Kept in the kitchen next to the sink, these held dish scrapings & veggie juice & parings used to "slop" the pigs, although there was disagreement about how much "garbage" was really good for a pig. 12"H, turn-of-century. .... **$75+**

Soda glass or hot toddy glass holder, also called a zarf, a sort of open rack with handle, nickeled brass, cup handle, used in soda fountains & bars, American, about 3-1/2"H, late 19th C. through mid 20th C. .... **$8-$15**

Soup tureen, stamped & pieced tin with ornate cast iron finial & handles, lid has a "bite" opening in edge for ladle, from F. A. Walker catalog, American, or English (?), came in several sizes: 3, 4, 6, 8, and 10 quarts. One example seen is 10"H x 15-1/2"L x 9-1/2"W oval, c.1870s. .... **$125+**

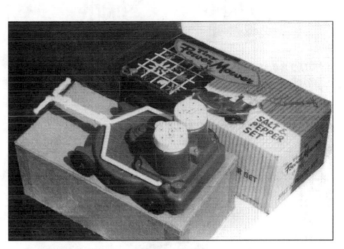

VII-122. Salt- & pepper shakers. *Novelty plastic power lawnmower in original box. Red & white plastic, black rubber-like wheels. Says "Tiny Power Mower," but no maker's mark or origin. When you push mower, the eccentric axle underneath alternately pushes up the pepper then the salt. 1950s.* **$20+**

VII-119. Salt & pepper dispenser. *Glass containers screwed into green plastic stand. Two buttons: push white one to release salt; black one for pepper. 2"H x 2-3/8"W. Imperial Metal Mfg. Co., pat'd. Aug. 5, 1939, #1,772,041. There are several varieties of this type.* **$15+**

VII-120. Salt- & pepper shakers, *originally meant for lunch kit or picnics. Spun aluminum. 2"H x 1-5/8" diameter, "Mirro." Mfd. by Aluminum Goods Mfg. Co., 1925 catalog.* **$4-$8**

VII-123. Slop jars. *All "Greystone" enameled ware by Matthai-Ingram, c.1890.* **(L)** *Has tin lid, wire & wood bail, tipping handle near bottom.* **(M)** *Two handles, footed;* **(R)** *bailed & footed. "Slop" was not contents of chamberpot. It was, in the toilette set, for the used wash water from the basin; and in the kitchen, it could either be the soggy remains on a plate – to be "slopped" to the pigs, or more discretely, it could be only leftover vinegar, wine, apple or grape juices, which with what's called "mother," turn into vinegar.* **$55+**

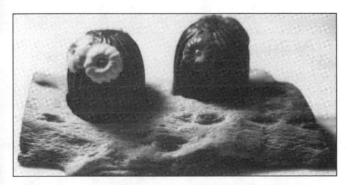

VII-121. Salt- & pepper shakers. *Cactuses of molded plaster, painted green, with red and yellow flowers. 2"H, they sit in base made of real cactus wood. Souvenir of Benson, AZ, c.1940s. Value may increase slightly with renewed interest in Western motifs.* **$10+**

VII-124. Soda glass holders, or zarfs, *two views each. Both are adjustable, and made of nickel plated spring brass. Bottom one has a base or foot. From Cherry-Bassett Co., Baltimore & Philadelphia, 1921 supply catalog.* **$5-$10**

VII-126. Soup tureen. *Tin, with cast iron handles and lid finial. "Bite" out of lid for ladle. 10"H x 15-1/2"L x 9-1/2"W oval. Ex-Keillor Family Collection. The exact same tureen, even with the vertical lines on the body (which I thought were shading), appeared in the F. A. Walker catalog from the 1870s. It was available in five sizes – for 3, 4, 6, 8, and 10 quarts. (Another very similar tin vessel, with rim foot, in 4, 6, 8, 10, 13, and 18 quart capacities, was in a catalog meant for hoteliers, c.1904-1910.)* **$200+**

VII-125. Soup tureen. *"Patent Perfection Granite Iron," round tureen with nickel-plated or silver-plated mountings. 6-pint or 8-pint capacity. Manning, Bowman & Co., c.1892. See also VII-146.* **$250+**

❖ NOTES ❖

Soup Tureens in Museum – The Campbell Museum collection of soup tureens, in Camden, NJ for 20 years, was donated in 2000 to the Winterthur Museum. About 125 of the most significant pieces – out of hundreds of American & European tureens, ladles, spoons, trays, etc., made of ceramics, pewter, silver, etc. – are on display in Winterthur's new Dorrance Gallery, Route 52, six miles north of Wilmington, DE. Call 302-448-3883 for visiting information. The collection toured the country for two decades, and the Dorrance family, which has been connected with Campbell Soups since 1876, funded the new gallery at Winterthur – considered by many to be the U.S.'s premier museum of antique home furnishings.

TIN AND TIN-PLATING

"Tin-plate, or tinned plate, or, as the French people call it, fer blanc or white iron, is a material which, in a converted shape, is familiar to everyone under the name of tin; but outside of those unfortunate enough to be engaged in the manufacture, or are fortunate enough to deal in or convert this useful metal, few, indeed, of the world are aware that their so-called block-tin tea pot, kettle or dish-cover, is made of nine parts iron, and one part tin.

"Tin plates vary in size, in substance, in toughness, and in the nature of their coatings: in sizes they vary from a sheet of 10" x 14", suitable for a one-pound tin of provisions, to a sheet of 40" x 28", adapted for roofing purposes in the western states of America; in substance they differ from a sheet of taggers, as thin as paper itself, to a plate of ten times that thickness, adopted for the dish covers of ordinary use. ... Coating varies with the purposes for which the tinplates are required, the lightest covering is sufficient for mustard & biscuit purposes; the heaviest possible coating is [best] for dish-covers, which have to stand planishing in conversion, and will be subsequently subject to the inevitable ceaseless "rubbing" of every careful household." P. W. Flower, *History of the Trade In Tin,* London: G. Bell & Sons, 1880.

Tinware Origins & Tin Tariffs – It's hard to tell the origin of some tin items because until the early 1900s there were almost no tinned iron or steel plates (or sheets of what we call tin) manufactured in the U.S. We didn't have the rolling mills for it, and probably 99% was imported as raw material for hundreds of stamping and/or piecing tinware factories in the U.S. Virtually everything from pie pans to cans for peaches to pails and pudding pans were made of imported plates or sheets of tinned iron (or steel). Many tin housewares were imported from Europe or England ready to sell.

William McKinley, a Republican Congressman (elected president in 1897), introduced a protectionist tariff bill, which passed in the fall of 1890 and went into effect March 1, 1891. It had at least three provisions of interest to collectors:

(1) country of origin must be marked on all import items.

(2) imposition of a higher tariff on import tin plate, and

(3) a huge tariff on import enamelwares.

Collectors have been thankful for the country of origin provision, although it is of limited value to us when glued paper labels are allowed to satisfy the law.

The imposition of the tin plate tax occasioned long editorials and heated fights in the House because it would raise prices of American-made finished goods made by an estimated 5% to 25%. Republicans hoped to use the tariff to encourage the infant industry of rolling tin plate in this country (sort of an early "trickle down" theory). Democrats argued that the increase of prices on canned goods & housewares would be an "unfortunate burden for the working man." One of many long *The New York Times* articles in 1890 laid out a chart of examples of how prices would rise. A four-quart coffee pot now costing 20¢ would cost 18¢ with no tariff at all, but 23¢ with the new tariff. An 11-1/4" colander costing 15¢ would be 14¢ or rise to 17¢. A 4" pie plate now 5¢ could cost 4¢ or rise to 7¢. An **1890 ad for Wanamaker's**, Philadelphia, said "Tinware is advancing in cost, and very soon the manufacturers [!] will have their way and you and we will have to pay very much more. In view of this ... we made some time since a large purchase of kitchen tinware at what was a low price then and would be far lower now. Bread Raisers, 10 qt., with cover & ventilator in lid 58¢; tin-frame Flour sieves 9¢; tubed Cake molds 10¢; small Tea Kettles 20¢; Japanned Nutmeg Graters 1¢; Japanned Nests of Spice Boxes 30¢...."

Shortly after the McKinley Tariff went into effect in 1891, a budding industry of rolling and plating iron & steel plates needed to grow quickly to satisfy enormous demands of tinsmiths & factory makers of pots, pans & cans.

A year after the Tariff, the following article appeared in Jan. 1892, *The Metal Worker*: "**Tin Plate Sizes.** – Tin-plate manufacturers are still feeling their way with reference to sizes and gauges and nomenclature in general. A few concerns are turning out 14 x 20 and 20 x 28 plates of IC and IX gauge [a common grade and a better but not best grade], but greater thought is being given to the wants of the consumers in this matter than any one outside of a very small circle would suppose.

"No one seems inclined to erect tin plate works which shall be restricted to the sizes of plates heretofore current, which would make it impossible to produce larger sizes on occasion. All want to turn out whatever a consumer may desire. 1892 will, no doubt, decide many of the questions, which are still open. Gauge designations have already been partially established upon a basis differing from that of British manu-

facturers." Next the journal listed all the "tin-plate works in operation and projected" – a scant 32 of them, mostly in Ohio & Pennsylvania.

To give the other side, the journal quoted from a circular sent out by a group of tinsmiths and factory owners: "If the tin-plate industry can be transferred to this country within a reasonable time and without damage to our business and the hundreds of thousands of workmen employed at our factories, and if we can get raw material as cheap as that obtained before the increased tax was levied on it, we will be the greatest beneficiaries. ... Since the bill passed, we have had to pay over ten million dollars more for the tin plates we use in our factories and workshops, and every year the tariff will add over 15 million to the cost of our material.

"At the present moment [Dec. 10, 1892], ... the present output of American rolling mills and platers ... is less than 1% of the entire [requisite] of tin plate in America.

Tin Plate or Sheet Tin Sizes May Be Clues to Age – All the major writers on tin agree that imported sheets of tin plate were small from the 1700s to about 1890. They disagree, however, on exact sizes of imported sheet tin during that period, although it's hard to compare exactly because of different reference dates. Most if not all tinwares used in America prior to the 1720s, at least, were finished wares imported from England (sometimes made with German or Bohemian tinplate). A knowledge of maximum sizes would possibly help in judging age of large pieces. You can make your own rough paper patterns of pieced wares, or measure with a cloth tape measure. The six sources quoted below are listed chronologically by their period of research. W. D. John & Anne **Simcox**, 20th century historians of tinplate industries; Jeannette **Lasansky**, a 20th C. historian of craft processes; Shirley **Spaulding DeVoe**, a 20th C. domestic historian; Andrew **Ure**, an early 19th C. encyclopedist; Philip William **Flower**, a late 19th century historian of industry; and *The* **Metal Worker**, a late 19th C. trade newspaper. (See Bibliography for works.)

Lasansky:
c.1720s-1840s tin plates: 16" x 16"
1915 Standard: 14" x 20"

"Terneplate [roofing tin plated with a lead & tin alloy, not for cookware] came ... as large as 28" x 40". These larger sizes meant that some shapes could be cut out in one piece, but generally the tinsmith was always restricted in this regard, having to make many of his forms out of seamed pieces" (p.76, Lasansky's *To Cut, Piece, & Solder*).

John & Simcox: Their studies included tinplating in early Bohemia, France, and Wales, leading to Pontypool.
c.1697-c.1760s (?) single size: 12" x 9"
c.1697-c.1760s (?) doubles: 18" x 12"

DeVoe: She relied on a size chart from c.1817, of imports from Wales & Germany.
c.1817 Common size: 10" x 13-3/4"
c. 1817 Heavier plate: 15" x 11"

"When or if the early tinsmith ever used a tin sheet larger than 15 x 11," DeVoe writes, "cannot be determined, but it was probably first imported when tin was admitted duty-free by the Tariff Act of 1833" (p. 126, DeVoe's *The Art of the Tinsmith, English and American*).

Ure: Writing about English tin plate sizes, which at that time were imported to the United States.
1838 Standard, "Common No. 1":   10" x 13-3/4"

1838 Other sizes:
    9-1/4" x 10-1/4"
    9-1/2" x 12-3/4"
    12-1/2" x 16-3/4"
    5" x 11"
    3-3/4" x 10"

The standard was marked on crates "C1" & called "Common No. 1." A box of 225 Common No.1 plates weighed exactly 100 lbs.; it thus was the standard for measuring other plates. C1 comprised the thinnest iron plate, coated with thickest layer of tin – best to resist rust. The only other box of tin plate that weighed exactly 100 lbs. was a box of "Waster's Common No. 1" – small "seconds." All other grades and sizes were measured in qrs. (quarters of 100 lbs.), and lbs. (pounds). The biggest plates ("Common Doubles") came 100 to a box weighing 3 qrs. 21 lbs. (96 lbs).

Flower:
1870 plates for cans: 10" x 14"
1870 plates for roofing: 40" x 28"
(p. 156, *Flower's History of the Trade In Tin*, 1880).

The Metal Worker: This was an American trade paper, and they described English tin plates of the time. They used the terminology "Common No. 1" in "XXX" (best grade) sizes, but instead of just one size there are nine!

Surprising to find so many small increments – not much would have been left over for cookie cutters or children's toys if the figuring was so close.

1892 Standard, or Common #1:

10" x 14"	14" x 14"
10" x 10"	15" x 15"
11" x 11"	16" x 16"
12" x 12"	20" x 20"
13" x 13"	

1880 Tin Containers – "We have not referred to the large uses for tea and coffee, matches, tobacco, jams, and bonbons, soup, fish, arrowroot, revalenta, baking powder, blacking, and the many other articles in daily use, which handsomely covered with paper labels, or still more handsomely finished by the new decorating process [direct lithography on tin], are to be seen in shop windows wherever you pass, for it would be useless, and wearisome to follow in detail the almost endless purposes [for tin plate]." Philip William Flower, *A History of the Trade In Tin*, London: G. Bell & Sons, 1880.

Spice box, 6 containers inside, all tin, "Kreamer," Brooklyn, NY, turn of century. • Very interesting, rare Kreamer piece...................................... **$100+**
Spice box, 6 round cans, oblong japanned heavy stamped tin box, cast iron handle on hinged lid, hasp closing, American (?), 9"L x 6-1/8"W, c.1890s.. **$100+**

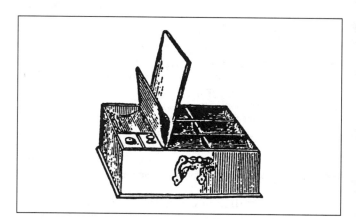

VII-128. Seasoning box. Japanned tin, hinged lid, cast iron handles. William S. Adams & Son, London, ad in Francatelli's Cook's Guide Advertiser, c.1860-61. **$150+**

Spice box, japanned & pinstriped tin, 2 hinged lids on either side of center handle, each open to reveal 3 compartments, Dover Stamping Co., 19th C. **$150+**
Spice box, japanned & pinstriped tin, oblong two-tier chest, with small collapsing cast iron handle on top, 10 almost square drawers – 5 on each side (3 above, 2 slightly larger below), all stenciled with name, the bigger drawers for commonly used spices like salt, pepper, sugar, etc., Dover Stamping Co., 6-1/2"H x 9-1/2"L x 6-1/2"W, 1860s to 1880s. .... **$200+**
Spice box, japanned & pinstriped tin, oblong, hinged hasp-closing lid, cast iron handle, round, 7 round stenciled containers: Ginger, Cloves, Pepper, Allspice, Mace, Nutmeg & Cinnamon, American, mid 19th C.... **$165+**

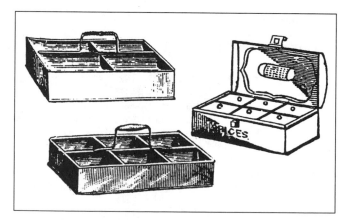

VII-127. Spice boxes. (T-L) is a "Cooks' tin spice box" that came with 4 or 6 compartments. Duparquet, Huot & Moneuse, c.1904-1910. (R) "The Spice Box. – Has six separate boxes that take out, so that whole or ground spices may be kept nice and separate." Note the nutmeg grater in the lid. American Home Cook Book, 1854. (B-L) "Extra heavy XXXX tin, highly polished, heavy wired edges top and bottom." 3"H x 9-1/2" x 12-1/2" with 4 compartments, or 15"L with 6. Pick-Barth catalog, 1929. **$50-$150**

Spice box, japanned & pinstriped tin box, stamped lid imitates wood molding, with hasp lid that has nutmeg grater clipped inside, containing 6 square tin containers with stenciled names "Mace, Allspice, Cloves, Cinnamon, Ginger, Nutmeg." American, box: 10"L x 7", individual tins: 2-3/4"H x 3-1/4" x 3-1/4", late 19th C. **Hasp closings** are a remnant of earlier days when spices & tea were actually locked up, albeit in portable (therefore easily stealable) small containers.. **$150**

Spice box, japanned tin, rectangular stamped tin, inside hinged lid is a little scoop, 6 containers for Allspice, Cinnamon, Ginger, Mace, Nutmeg, Cloves, 8-1/2" x 6-1/2", American (?), 19th C. First I've seen with a scoop. **$150**

❖ NOTES ❖

"**Nutmeg & Mace**, as we know them, are the dried seed or stone of the Nutmeg fruit, which is one of the most beautiful fruits that nature produces. It is about as large as a peach, and of a pale orange color. While ripening, it splits open lengthwise into halves, showing within the fleshy, bright, orange-crimson network of the Mace. Although a part of the Nutmeg fruit, it is considered and handled as an individual spice. Next, inside, is a brown shell of no market value. Within this shell is the center or seed of the whole fruit – the Nutmeg itself. Both the Mace and the Nutmeg are dried in the sun, and then graded for quality and size. As there is comparatively a small amount of Mace in each Nutmeg fruit, Mace is much higher in price than Nutmegs. The flavor is also much more delicate." Jos. Middleby, Jr., Inc., *Bakers' Supplies* catalog, 1927.

• • •

Nutmeg's History – A book tracing the history of nutmeg from about 1000 C.E. on, was written by Giles Milton, and published in 1999. It's entitled *Nathaniel's Nutmeg: Or, the True and Incredible Adventures of the Spice Trader Who Changed the Course of History*. See Bibliography.

Spice box, japanned tin with gold pinstriping, side handles, hinged lid with knob on edge, 16 spice canisters, for all the usuals, plus Saffron, Laurel Leaves, Mustard Seed, Kimmel, & Sundries, mfd. by Silver & Co., Brooklyn, NY, 3"H x 8-1/2"L, c.1909..... **$150+**

Spice box, japanned tin with gold & red pinstripes on asphaltum background, 6 square cans for Nutmeg, Cloves, Mace, Ginger, Allspice, Cinnamon, plus nutmeg grater inside lid, American (?), 9"L x 6-1/8"W, 19th C. .... **$135+**

Spice box, lithographed tin, red, white, & yellow with gold pinstriping, "Nutmeg, Ginger, Cloves" marked on outside, hinged cover holds clip-in nutmeg grater, box has 4 spice containers, American or European, 5-1/2" diam., 19th C. .... **$125+**

Spice box, tin with asphaltum japanning, domed lid with brass knob, inside partitioned into wedges for 6 loose spices, nutmeg & grater fit in hole in center of wedges, American, 6-1/2" diam., third quarter 19th C. .... **$135+**

Spice box, tin, round, domed hinged lid, cast iron fancy knob, hasp closing, japanned with gold pinstripes, divided into 6 wedge compartments, with central tube for nutmeg & grater, about 9" diam., English

(?), probably made for 30 or more years, it appears in Harrod's 1895 catalog. .... **$135+**

❖ NOTES ❖

1840: "For **spice boxes**, it is best to keep different sorts in small, separate painted tin boxes, each with tight lid and handle to hang it by, to nails driven along the edge of dresser shelf. Each box to have name painted on side. These are better than large boxes, in which, not withstanding the division, the spices are very apt to get mixed." Miss Eliza. Leslie, *Housebook*, 1840.

1887: "**Spice boxes** come in many forms. Little boxes labelled with various kinds of spice are fitted into one large box. If they were well made they would be very desirable, but they are so poorly made it is difficult to take covers off or put them on. The illustration [of an oblong tin box with two "roof top" lids, hinged at center or "peak," inside divided into 3 compartments per side, hasp closing] shows good one with three compartments on each side; the only objection being that the spices are not so well protected as in the case of little boxes within one large box. However, one does not keep much spice at a time in these pantry boxes, and the saving of time and patience is a consideration." Maria Parloa, *Kitchen Companion*, Boston: Estes & Lauriat, 1887.

1918+ Spice Boxes: Lots of spice boxes, cabinets & containers of all sorts were imported in the 1870s through the teens, especially from Germany, so that trade stopped with the WWI. After that, probably the wide availability of packaged spices in small shaker tins obviated the need for the old fashioned spice containers, although you could still get sets in glass and tin.

Spice box, round tin box with 7 small containers, "Chautauqua," American, late 19th C. Chautauqua was an interesting adult educational social movement that began in 1874 and went into the 20th C. People went to Chautauqua, in upstate SW New

VII-129. Spice caddy patent. *Pat'd. Oct. 14, 1879, by William B. Hartley, Washington, D.C. "The invention consists in a caddy consisting of a main or stock receptacle or vessel constructed of suitable material, and of any desired capacity, to hold the articles [tea, coffee, spices] in bulk, [and] being provided at the bottom with a series of hoppers, each with a sliding partition or cut-off, beneath which are arranged a series of removable drawers of varying sizes." Official Gazette, U.S. Patent Office.*

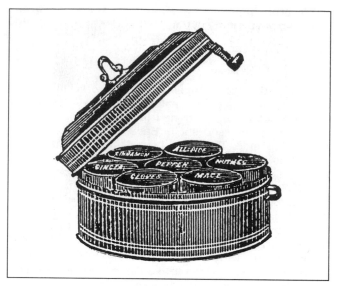

VII-130. Spice box. *Dark japanned tin, hinged hasp-closing lid, iron finial. Round box with 7 containers, all stenciled: "Ginger, Cloves, Pepper, Allspice, Mace, Nutmeg, Cinnamon." F. A. Walker catalog, c.1880s.* **$165+**

York, for tent lectures and thousands of people attended over the years. A sort of Woodstock combined with summer school. The name would have been familiar to most Americans. .... **$90+**

Spice box, round, with gold decorations & japanning, 4 cans inside for Ginger, Allspice, Cloves & Nutmeg, "The Model Spice Box" on center of lid, framed by flowers & leaves, very small, only 4-3/8" diam., 19th C. .... **$125+**

Spice box, tin, punched (but not punctured) tin design on hinged lid, inside are 4 compartments with largish round open center for nutmeg & grater, tin ring legs, very delicate & pretty, American, 3-1/4"H x 6-3/16"L x 3-11/16"W, mid 19th C. .... **$225+**

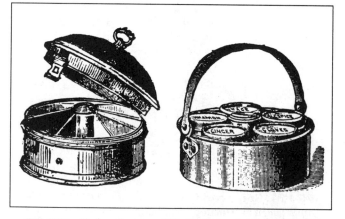

VII-131. Spice boxes. (L) *Japanned tin with gold border, radiating compartments, hinged close-fit lid with cast iron finial, hasp. Center hole, where axle would be in a wheel, is where nutmeg grater fit. (R) Open spice basket-type carrier for canisters. Decorated in "art colours with gold border." Both from Harrod's Stores, Brompton, England, catalog of 1895, but much older style.* **$125-$175**

VII-132. Spice boxes. *Both from Silver & Co., Brooklyn, catalog of c.1910. (L) Spice & condiment box, with hinged lid and drawer has 12 spice boxes and a compartment for 6 bottles of extracts for flavoring. Tin, finished brown & gold, oak-grained & gold, or white and gold, with white porcelain knobs and 2 handles. 8"H x 10-1/2" x 11-1/4". (R) Round spice box is "neat, roomy" and has 8 small canisters. 3"H x 10" diameter in brown japanning with gold, oak grained with gold, or white with gold. An 8" diameter one was offered in brown only. There are specialized Silver & Co. collectors.* **$125-$175+**

VII-133. Spice cabinets. (L) *Ash with oil finish, 8 small marked drawers, shaped backplate for wall-hanging. 18"H x 12"W. Sold originally through Montgomery Ward, c.1895, for only 90¢. (R) Wooden with carved fancy arched pediment top. Eight marked drawers. Imported from Germany, and with English spice names, by G. M. Thurnauer, NYC, 1903. These aren't rare, were mass-produced, but they have the look that appeals to collectors & decorators.* **$125+**

VII-134. **Spice cabinet.** *Simplest wooden type, 6 marked drawers, varnished finish. 13"H x 9"W x 5" deep. D. J. Barry catalog, 1924, maker unknown.* **$75+**

Spice box, tin, with stamped design of morning glories, 4 spice compartments & 2 graters for bread & nutmegs. American (?), c.1890s-1906 (?). The decoration of this may have been influenced by the great popularity of the so called morning glory external Gramophone™ horn by Victor, which had a short life between about 1903 and 1906 (pre-Victrola™ with internal horn). Some came in metallic finish, but somewhere gloriously painted to look just like a giant 24" diam. morning glory! (See also picture VII-3.) .... **$115+**

Spice boxes – See also Spice tray

Spice cabinet, 8 drawers, stenciled tin on gray background, arched top, American (?), 19th C. ..... **$150+**

Spice cabinet, red painted tin, 8 drawers, scalloped top edge, wall hung, late 19th C. .... **$150+**

VII-135. **Spice cabinets.** **(L)** *Another imported carved wooden one, this with 4 small feet, to set on top of table or counter. It had tinned, embossed name plates – here, the catalog linecut was fudged so that the words (which I believe are in German) can't be read. G. M. Thurnauer & Bro., NYC, House Furnishings Review, Jan. 1911.* **(R)** *Japanned tin, bronzed or "fancy decorations." Made in 2 sizes, with 6 or 8 drawers. Jobber's ad in House Furnishings Review, Aug. 1913, maker unknown. This is the tin cabinet you'll sometimes see described, inaccurately, as "Pennsylvania German" or "early tin." Still, the look is great.* **$150-$200+**

VII-136. **Spice & pasta cabinet,** *advertised as a* **"pasta 'n pizza rack."** *Philippine mahogany, earthenware drawers are hand-painted. 13"H x 11"W. This is hard to value. On the one hand you can say "it's only about 45 years old" (advertised in House Beautiful, Sept. 1960), and think of it as rummage sale material worth under $25. Or you could say, "it's already only about 45 years old, but awfully cool."* **$75**

Spice cabinet, tin, wall hung, 8 drawers, nicely-shaped pediment top, American, 13-1/2"H, 19th C. . **$200+**

Spice cabinet, for wall, bronze japanned tin, sort of art nouveau arched top, 6 drawers labeled Vanilla, Ginger, Cloves, Cinnamon, Pepper, Nutmeg; American or European, c.1890s-1915. .... **$150+**

Spice box, tin-banded varnished round bentwood box with 8 individual bentwood boxes inside. Stenciled "SPICE" on lid of outer box & names of spices on containers, American, 3-1/2" deep x 9" diam., 3rd quarter 19th C. **$200**

VII-137. **Spice tower or turret.** *Stacked spice boxes, turned wood, pale honey-color hardwood. Decalcomania labels in light yellow with black engraved letters for Cinnamon, Ginger, Cloves, Nutmeg. 7 1/8"H. English, 19th C. Courtesy R. C. Bowen. (Another one has 5 boxes: Cloves, Nutmegs, Cinnamon, Allspice, and an unlabeled one. 9-1/2"H overall; each box is 1-1/2" deep x 2-1/2" diameter on inside. English, 19th C.)* **$175+**

Spice box, thin quarter sawn maple bent into round, tin rim to lid and bottom, 7 round canisters with spices marked on lids, largest, for Cloves, in center, bottoms of canisters marked Patent Packing Co., Newark, NJ, pat'd. Aug. 31, 1858. This is one of at least 3 versions of bentwood boxes with seven canisters. **$200**

Spice box, varnished thin wood with metal bands, black stenciling on lid of outer box, lids & sides of all 8 inner boxes, American, 9" to 9-1/2" diam., pat'd. 1858. You often see **orphaned** spice containers from expensive sets, which would have 8 containers in the big box. (The singles are relatively cheap – $15 to $20.) .... **$175+**

Spice box, hickory split round box, varnished, 7 round spice containers inside, all stenciled, 8" diam. box, 19th C. .... **$145+**

Spice box, mechanical, figural, painted & brass-mounted wooden box shaped like book lying on table, side handle on "spine," dial selection on top, little carved & painted man on one end raises lid of little keg to reveal your choice, English, 18th C. **Crossover collecting** competition with automaton & folk art collectors. Offered for sale in early 1986 by Pat Guthman Antiques & Accessories for the Kitchen & Keeping Room, of Southport, CT. Value range mine. .... **$1,200+**

Spice cabinet, 7 drawers, wood, with scroll-shaped pewter or white metal drawer labels which meant they could be written on with a graphite pencil. Bottom drawer marked "Nutmeg Grater," small, mid to late 19th C. .... **$250+**

Spice cabinet, hanging, 6 drawers, pine with white porcelain knobs, stamped tin labels, American, 12"H x 8"W, late 19th C. .... **$125+**

Spice cabinet, maple, 6 drawers with white porcelain knobs & whitish pewter-like or Babbitt labels which allowed penciled IDs to be wiped off, American (?), mid 19th C. .... **$275+**

Spice cabinet, oak, 16 drawers, wall hung, late 19th or early 20th C. These are way over-priced, but the market seems to bear it. They were sold in *Sears & Montgomery Ward* catalogs at the turn of the century for a couple of dollars! .... **$150+**

Spice cabinet or chest, dark green painted wood, dovetail construction, 8 drawers, countertop not wall hung, American, 19"H x 27-1/2"L, 2nd quarter 19th C. .... **$550+**

Spice cabinet, pine, early green & red paint, 8 butt-joint drawers in simple frame, American, 11"H x 9"W, mid 19th C. .... **$350+**

Spice cabinet, various woods with original yellow paint, 6 labeled drawers for "Bay Leaf, Allspice, Cinnamon, Ginger, Cel. Seed, Mus. Seed" (Celery and Mustard), shaped backboard, American, early 19th C. . **$650+**

❖ NOTES ❖

What Was In Old Spice Boxes? – The term "Spice box" seems to limit the contents, but these cased sets of small drawers were useful for saving many kinds of treasures. In the early 1980s, I bought a small beat-up leather-bound book published in 1807 that was an account of the shipping trades of Russia, Prussia, Sweden, Denmark, and Germany, with a bit on the United Kingdom and even the United States. Particularly interesting is a list of merchandise imported in 1802 into Hamburg, Germany – at that time the busiest port in Europe. The list goes on for pages, always edifying and intriguing for its glimpses and whiffs of trade and the social scene almost 200 years ago. A selection from that list gives some idea of what might have been in the drawers of an 18th century spice box:

Amber	Medicines
Beads	Natural curiosities**
Buckles	Perfumery
Buttons	Pepper
Cassia*	Quills
Cinnamon	Saffron
Cloves	Sealing-wax
Incense	Snuff & snuff boxes
Lemon peel	Tinsel
Mace-bloom	Watches
Mace-nuts (Nutmegs)	

*Cassia is a tropical plant bearing pods that were used as a cinnamon substitute.

**Natural curiosities consisted of fossils, shells, stuffed birds, petrified wood, bones, skulls, mounted insects, geodes, meteorites, attractive mineral specimens, etc.

Spice cabinet, dovetailed wood, old dark wood finish, 12 drawers with nice turned knobs, counter top or wall hung, American, 17"H x 19"W x 6-1/2" deep, early 19th C. **Fake colors.** – Unfortunately, the rise of craft stores has encouraged people to put fake old paint finishes on newer wooden pieces. Rubbed, scrubbed, nicked, and marred they are hard to detect. And there are even paints put on in two layers that fight each other to make crackles or alligatored finishes. You have to get a feel for the true old colors; the modern "olde" colors tend to be "antiqued" (dulled, grayed) versions of colors. .... **$500+**

Spice cabinet, walnut with brass knobs, hanging, 6 drawers, American (?), 11-1/2"H x 8"W x 8" deep, 1870s. .... **$175+**

Spice cabinet, wood, 6 small drawers, one wide drawer at bottom, celluloid drawer labels (could be written on with pencil & washed off for changes) in imitation or as a modern adaptation of older ivory or pewter labels, American (?) or German, late 19th C. **$250+**

Spice cabinet, wood, arched backplate, white porcelain knobs, 9 small named spice drawers, a shelf above & 2 long drawers at bottom for tea & coffee, wall hung, Pure Food Co., Cincinnati, OH, 24"H x 10"W, turn-of-century. .... **$275+**

Spice cabinet, yellow varnished natural wood, marvelously shaped & engineered, wall hung, with 6 tin & wooden drawers, paired 2 x 2 with centerboard between for a double bow front, shaped backplate, pin goes through from top to bottom on both sides & round compartments pivot out on it, pat'd. by J. T. Carter and J. Park, Lowell, MA, 9" to 10"H, pat'd. Dec. 10, 1867. .... **$500+**

Spice cabinet or chest, wood, outside grain painted dull brown, with gold pinstripes, inside (surprise!) red & green with yellow varnished drawer fronts, 2 doors with one remaining knob of turned ivory, lock missing, 12 drawers inside, 10 with paper labels with ink handwritten names "Cinnamon, Pudding Spice, Nutmegs, Carraway Seeds, Black Peppers, Mace, Cloves, Cayenne Pepper, White Pepper, Long Pepper," English, 10-1/2"H x 12-5/8"W, c.1840s to 1860s. .... **$500+**

❖ RECIPE ❖

Currie – Imitation of the India Currie – 3 ounces coriander seed, 3 ounces turmeric, 1 ounce black pepper, 1 ounce ginger, 1 ounce mustard, 1/2 ounce lesser cardamoms, 1/4 ounce each of cayenne pepper, cinnamon and cummin. Pound fine and mix well." Mrs. Cornelius, The Young Housekeepers Friend, or, A Guide to Domestic Economy & Comfort, *Boston & NY: 1846.*

Spice chest, and Pasta 'n Pizza Rack. Wall hung, Philippine mahogany chest with crested backplate, 2 long earthenware-fronted labeled drawers full width at bottom, for linguine & some other spaghetti, above that 2 half-width drawers for macaroni & noodles, 4 small spice drawers at top for oregano, bay leaf, rosemary & basil. All "hand-painted under glaze with Venetian gondolier designs," European for American market, 13"H x 11"W, c.1960. Tacky then, fab now! **$75**

Spice & condiment containers, glass with PA German designs, possibly an incomplete set with only 5

pieces: marked "Cocoa, Salt, Spice, Sugar, Nutmeats," American, 4-3/4"H, 20th C. .... **$35+**

Spice container, green ribbed glass, screwtop aluminum lid, Hazel Atlas, who also made canning jars, 20th C. • A set of six would cost more than six times the single price: .... **$10+**

Spice containers, glass with metal shaker tops, set of 6, McCormick & Co., Baltimore, 2nd quarter 20th C. When they tore down the old McCormick building in Baltimore folks said you could smell the cloves for miles! .... **$35+**

Spice containers, tin, lithographed in blue & white with Dutch scenes, 5 square cans, 3"H x 2-1/2" square, 20th C. Set: .... **$30+**

Spice & cookie set, Black Americana Aunt Jemima, colored plastic, American, 20th C. **Aunt Jemima** is a created human food character (like Betty Crocker or Ann Page); she was advertising every time she was seen. She is probably the oldest of the females – 100 years old in 1989. Set includes cookie jar, cream & sugar, 6 spice containers, a large & a small set of salt & pepper shakers. Usually seen as individual pieces. .... **$300+**

Spice containers in rack, 9 containers, wood rack, "Black Cat" ceramic, American, mid 20th C. The cat does it. .... **$50+**

Spice rack, black painted cast iron one shelf with flying eagle above, 8 labeled glass jars with stoppers, "Ironmaster," possibly made by H. E. Hitt, Roslyn, PA, 15"L, c.1968. .... **$30+**

Spice rack, turned & varnished wood wall rack, with fancy cut pediment and 2 small drawers at bottom, made with small feet so it could be kept on counter, fitted with 6 blue & white porcelain spice jars with little knobbed lids, German, c.1904. .... **$125**

Spice rack, wire in shape of crossed spoon & fork, with 4 hooks for hanging 4 china chefs with painted faces, paper labels & hanging loops on top of chef caps, "Made In Japan," 3-1/2"H x 9"L, chefs are 3-1/2"H, c.1950s. .... **$45+**

Spice rack, with 12 milk glass square shaker jars with black metal lids, Griffith Laboratories, Chicago, IL, each jar 4-3/8"H, patent #2,107,697 (1938), being advertised in early 1940s. This also came with green lids & lettering; Griffith made a set with little honey-pot-shaped jars with lift-out shaker piece under lid. **$115**

Spice rack, with 8 jars, painted red wire rack for wall or countertop, square white glass jars with blue Dutch figures & scenes plus the spice names fused into the glass, Frank Tea & Spice Co., Cincinnati, OH, c.1941. The one I seem to find by itself is "Pepper" with the windmill. Singly they go for about $3. The original price was $1.25 for all, but now for a racked set: .... **$30+**

Spice shaker, bulbous big-breasted blown-mold glass, metal shaker lid, flat backside to sit on stove shelf, c.1870s-80s. .... **$30+**

Spice tower, 3 sectioned varnished turned wood, decal labels are light yellow with black engraving, this one for "Mace, Cloves, Nutmeg," English, about 6"H, last quarter 19th C. **$175**

Spice tower, turned wood, lovely light yellow color, 5 stacked powderbox-size containers, all screw together, one on top of the other. This particular tower has Cloves, Nutmegs, Cinnamon, Allspice & an undesignated box, English, different sizes & number of boxes, this one 9-1/2"H, with each con-

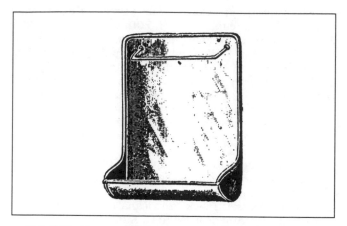

VII-138. Spoon dripper or **utensil- or implement rack.** *A wall rack for hanging ladles, tasting spoons & basters. Copper, 28"H x 21"W. Mfd. by Henry Rogers, Sons & Co., Wolverhampton, England, 1914 catalog. Likely to be sold as older than it is – the form may be 40 or 50 years earlier.* **$90+**

tainer 1-1/2" deep x 2-1/2" diam., 19th C. .. **$175+**

Spice tower, varnished wood, lid & base painted or stained red, green paper labels engraved with black, stripes on lid & base, 3 tiers: Nutmegs, Mace, Cloves. Very unusual coloring. English, 19th C. .... **$175+**

Spice tray, japanned tin, 6 canisters with slightly convex shaker lids in carrying tray with low sides & strap handle, English (the flat-topped set, very similar, was American), c.1860s-70s..................... **$50+**

Spice tray, japanned tin, strap handle, 6 small round cans with snug lids, American (?), tray is 5-1/2" x 4-3/4", cans are 2-7/8"H x 1-3/4" diam., late 19th C........ **$50**

Spice tray, japanned tin tray has crimped railing, high crimped & scrolled strap handle, holds 6 japanned canisters, lots of soul, American, 8"H x 7-1/2"L, 1850s-70s. .... **$100+**

Spoon rack, tulip poplar, painted red, carved pinwheels & geometrics, wall-hung, holds 5 spoons, New England, 18th C. .... **$1,200+**

Spoon rack, wood, with drawer below, late 19th C. Only the really remarkable 18th C. ones, with interesting chip carving, and excellent patina, bring a lot. Some of the ones seen now are not very old, certainly not very well (or attractively) made. Look at construction methods in drawers, and especially look at back, for signs of machine sanding/planing, or for much older and perhaps slightly uneven hand planing or shaving. .... **$35-$45**

Storage containers, mostly for the refrigerator, molded polyethylene plastic the inventor first called "Poly-T," with snap-on lids, also other forms, "Tupperware™," originally called "Wonder Bowl," named after inventor Earl Silas Tupper, Orlando, FL, 1931 to present. Price range for resale "collectible market" – not new. .... **.50¢-$4**

❖ NOTES ❖

Tupperware: An entertaining *Washington Post Magazine* article, Jan. 22, 1989, written by Vic Sussman ("I was a Middle-Aged Tupper Virgin"), tells about Tup-

perware International's Museum of Historic Food Containers, where, he says, "you can inspect everything from prehistoric vessels to the latest in Tupperware." The museum was founded by Brownie Wise, the woman who invented the party system for selling Tupperware, and she called it the "Museum of Dishes." It's at Tupperware World Headquarters, Box 2353, Orlando, FL 32802. Call ahead for further information: (800) 366-3800.

String holder, black painted cast iron, oval wall plaque with arched bracket with hook, holding round 2 part ball with oval holes, "old-fashioned" but probably not strictly a reproduction, but an adaptation. Tolerton & Warfiled Co., Sioux City, IA, advertised c. 1900 a cast iron ball, hinged 2-part twine holder, suspended from hook or bracket (?) by hoop of wire. Mfd. by Emig Products, Reading, PA, 4" diam. x 8"L, weighs 1-3/4 pounds, c.1966. Price in the 1960s was $3 for a pair, wholesale. The secondary market asking price now, which may not really be "value," is much higher... **$25+**

String holder, cast iron, beehive shape, one of more commonly found forms, but quite desirable, American, mid to late 19th C. **Reproduction alert.** – Detail in repros is not good, usually has flat black paint, is slightly lighter in weight than it looks like it ought to be... **$150+**

String holder, cast iron, black finish, in shape of gypsy kettle with 3 little legs & wire bail handle, advertising motto embossed on both sides, "Use Jaxon's Soap," American, 4-1/2"H x 4-1/2" diam., late 19th C. or early 20th.................................. **$175+**

String holder, cast iron, gypsy kettle shape, 3 peg feet, openwork cast iron lid that fits down just inside rim, the openwork design actually comprises 3 "S's," adv'g. "S. S. S. for the Blood," American, about 4-1/2"H, late 19th C. or early 20th. .... **$165+**

VII-139. String holders, or **twine boxes.** *(L) Brass ball, nickeled, on stepped base. (M) Nickeled brass with embossed design. (R) Cast iron, on stand. Finished with copper or with japanning. All from Jaburg Brothers catalog, maker unknown, 1908. In a store or bakery, there would be spools of regular twine, as well as colored, gold and silver tinsel twine, were available.* **$125-$200+**

VII-140. String holders. *Two hanging types, two counter tops types. All are cast iron, either japanned or finished in black paint. Most are about 3-3/8" diameter.* **(T-L)** *and* **(T-R)** *from Albert Pick catalog, 1909; others from D. J. Barry catalog, 1924. Considering lack of age on these, I think they are usually overpriced.* **(B-L)** *and* **(B-R)** *The only one with a name is the "beehive," 4"H x 4-1/2". Thomas Mills & Bro., c.1930.* **$95-$150+**

VII-141. Sugar bucket. *Staved wood, bentwood hoops and handle. Fitted lid. 9-3/4"H x 10-1/2" diameter at base. From Massachusetts, 19th C. Photo courtesy of the National Museum of American History, Smithsonian Institution.*

String holder, cast iron, nickel plated, round with heavy wire frame with counterweight, so after string is pulled & cut, it rights itself to pull back extra twine, marked only: "Pat. Sept. 9, 1890." .... **$100+**

String holder, cast iron, unusual fish shape, American (?), prob. 3rd or 4th quarter 19th C. .... **$150+**

String holder, cast iron with old red paint, sphere or globe on high foot, surmounted by comic open mouthed woman's face with hole for string. American, 8-1/4"H, 19th C. .... **$350+**

String holder, hand holding twine ball, cast iron, American, late 19th C. .... **$200+**

Sugar bowl, gray graniteware, with Britannia mountings, nice round body, high domed lid with finial, 19th C. .... **$175+**

❖ NOTES ❖

White metals – What is often called "pewter" in modern dealers' ads is either an unnamed white metal (as described in the mfrs' own catalogs) or Britannia (sometimes seen spelled Brittania), which was a British, and later American, white metal substitute for pewter (and very close to it in composition & appearance), that contained no lead, but rather tin, antimony & copper. An American white metal compounded of the same 3 metals, invented about 1825 by Isaac Babbitt, of Taunton, MA, was known as "Babbitt Metal."

Sugar bowl, milk glass in shape of Monitor Top refrigerator, adv'g. General Electric, c.1930s. .... **$90+**

Sugar bowl, nickeled stamped metal base with 3 stamped cabriole legs, side ear handles, bowl is molded glass, rather like a melon with scalloped flutes, flat top, sliding lever in base releases sugar, "Sanitary," mfd. by Ideal Sanitary Sugar Bowl Co., NYC, NY, 2 lb. capacity, c.1915. .... **$50+**

Sugar bowl, painted tin, double stepped foot ring, slightly domed lid has 3 tiny joined tin cylinders for a knob, black ground with red, yellow & green flowers, super looking, American, 3-3/4"H x 4" diam., early 19th C. .... **$500+**

Sugar bowl, robin's-egg blue enamelware & black trim, including knob, rim & handles, probably Lisk Mfg. Co., Canandaigua, NY, 4-1/2"H x 4" diam., 20th C. .... **$125+**

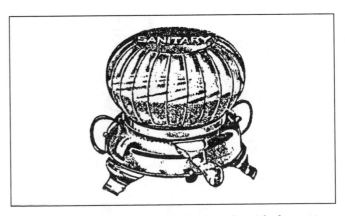

VII-142. Sugar bowl. *"Sanitary," with lever to release measure of sugar. Holds 2 lbs. Clear glass with nickel-plated base. Ideal Sanitary Sugar Bowl Co., NYC. 1915 ad.* **$100+**

Sugar bowl, with fitted lid, beautifully patinaed turned wood in bulbous shape, nice finial, called Peaseware, made by Hiram Pease, (& other Peases?), Painesville, Lake County, OH, 4-1/2" x 5", worked c.1850-1890. .... **$350+**

❖ NOTES ❖

Peaseware – The turned wood containers made by Pease(s) closely resemble woodenware covered bowls by other makers such as Paine. Some are footed goblet shapes, like the Lehnware trinket & saffron containers, and open eggcups. Some, with small flared footed base, have thin wire falling bail handles with simple wooden grips, with slightly convex lids with (mostly) acorn finials of wood. At some point, the company was Pease & Brown. Products of this partnership are rising in value, especially large lidded pieces, which may bring up to $1,500. (At this time, collectors value more the distinctive, colorfully painted turned & footed woodenwares of Joseph Lehn of Lancaster County, PA, which can bring more than $3,000 for certain covered forms.)

Sugar dispenser, green Depression glass jar, cylindrical shape, conical metal lid, mechanical measuring unit inside, "One Spoon At a Time," c.1930s. Also came with clear glass, called "crystal" by Depression glass people. .... **$150+**

Sugar jar, yellowware with turned bands, lid with set-in knob, Brush-McCoy Pottery Co., Zanesville, OH, 10 lb. size, c.1915. .... **$50+**

VII-143. Syrup pitchers. *Also called simply **syrups**. All but first have "patented central spout and cut-off," from Manning, Bowman c.1892 catalog. Clockwise from **(T-L): (1)** Decorated enamelware one, with separate drip plate, with nickeled or silvered mountings. **(2)** "Pearl Agate" in assorted soft tints in mauve, brown, green, etc. **(3)** "Decorated Opal," with Grecian finial. **(4)** Chased quadruple silver plate. **(5)** Another chased design, nickel or silverplate.* **$150-$250+**

VII-144. Tin containers. (L) *A mini top hat, painted tin, and not a container except when upside down. 3-1/4"H.* **(R)** *Pieced tin in form of farrier's anvil, the lid having a horseshoe-shaped handle. Decalcomania transfer shows horseshoeing scene. English tea container, 6-1/2"H. Photo courtesy Litchfield Auction Gallery. Ex-Harold Corbin Collection, auctioned Jan. 1, 1990, for $425 & $450.* **$450+**

Sugar server, clear glass, "Tilt-A-Spoon," early 20th, late 19th C. .... **$30+**

Sugar server, old-fashioned looking heavy glass bottle with nickel trim, fat bottom, narrow neck, cast-in narrowing part in neck to measure out one teaspoon of sugar each time you turn it over, "Sanitary," c.1915. .... **$25+**

Tidy rack – See Comb rack

Tray, elongated oval, reticulated sides pieced from 2 sheets of tin, large half-moon cutouts for handles at both ends, black japanned ground & painted with flowers in red, yellow & green, of a type of decoration & workmanship known to come from workshops in Stevens Plains, ME, 13-1/2"L x almost 4" deep, c.1820s-30s. You'd have to really know your stuff to buy these decorated tin American pieces. Starting before 1900 and going into the 1950s, classes were held in decorating tin trays and boxes, and similar commercial products have been sold for 100 years. Best to leave to museums, unless you are sure! .... **$650+**

❖ NOTES ❖

Tôle peinte collector hint – If you are going to buy painted or decorated objects of household decoration, especially things made of tin, elegant enough to be termed tôle in this country, you must carefully read a how-to & history book long out of print. It is Esther Stevens *Brazer's Early American Decoration*, Springfield, MA: Pond-Ekburg Co., 1940, 1947. It is an extraordinarily fine and useful book on painted decoration on tin, papier-mâché, wood, etc., used to make trays, chairs, floors, apple trays, bellows, candle sconces, coffee pots, dower chests, etc. Brazer covers subjects such as gold leaf and "floating" color, various kinds of graining -- smoked, feathered, sponged, feathered or brushed, and has especially valuable information on "How to collect designs" [in order to reproduce them yourself], "searching for an old design beneath outer prints," "faint traces," etc.

This book was intended to assist the skilled home-crafts person to successfully decorate the surface of many kinds of decorative accessories as well as furniture, and has detailed drawings and patterns, which might help identify a piece you aren't sure of. Pieces done then are now 50+ years old, and with ordinary wear & cleaning could fool just about anybody.

Tray, japanned and flower-painted tin, raised slanted gallery around edge, called octagonal because it's a rectangle with 8 corners), also called a coffin tray, pieced from 2 sheets of tin (vertical seam on minor axis), near perfect unrestored condition, possibly Zachariah Stevens, Stevens Plains, ME, 23"L, c.1830s...... **$750+**

Tray, japanned, stenciled & painted tin, with fruit compote still-life in theorum style, rectangular with rounded corners, broad convex rim with handle cut outs in elongated ovals with small heart-points toward center, very good condition with some alligatoring to varnish, attributed to Emma J. Cady, East Chatham, NY, early 19th C. .... **$850+**

Tray, tôle, with flowers, Pennsylvania-European heritage motifs, not strictly PA Dutch, 18"L, late 19th C. .... **$100+**

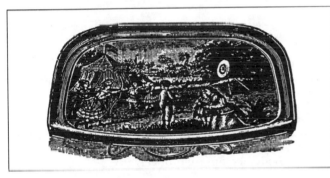

VII-145. Child's tray, *for clipping to table edge. Assorted colors and fancy designs on chromolithographed stamped tin, spring steel clip. This one shows children playing outside on lawn, somewhat dangerously with bows and arrows. 15-3/8" x 10-1/2". Central Stamping Co., 1920, in design from 19th C.* **$35+**

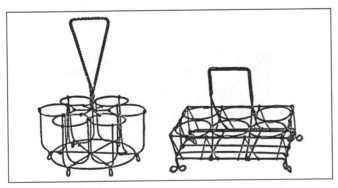

VII-146. Tumbler and bottle carriers. *Made of tinned wire, plain with twisted handle at* **(L),** *for 4, 6 or 9 bottles, or all twisted construction* **(R)** *for 2, 3, 4, 6, 8 or 12 tumblers and ranging in size from 6-1/2" x 3-1/2" up to 12-3/4" x 9-1/2", Wire Goods Co., "Sherwood" products. 1915. SEE also VII-20.* **$50+**

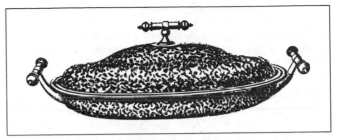

VII-147. Vegetable dish. *"Patent Perfection Granite Ironware," with white metal mountings. Came in 3 sizes, 11"L, 13"L and 15"L. Manning, Bowman & Co., c.1892. SEE also VII-125.* **$155+**

Tray, or waiter, tin, with crystalized center and japanned, stenciled and painted border design of large grape leaves, spiral tendrils, outer border is a chain of comma or teardrop shapes, elongated octagon (rectangle with truncated ends to make 8 corners or sides) or coffin tray, no handle cutouts, could be NY, CT or PA, 32"L x 17"W, 2nd quarter 19th C...................... **$850+**

❖ NOTES ❖

Crystal Gazing – Provenance of this waiter, or serving tray, is hard to know because crystalization was used by tin decorators in 3 states. Grape leaves (vineyards?) may be clues. Earl Robacker, who thinks Pennsylvania, wrote that "the effect of crystals [is] obtained by washes such as aqua fortis and sal ammoniac before the varnish was applied in japanning." **"Moirée Metallique,** called in this country [U.S.A.] crystallized tin-plate, is a variegated primrose appearance, produced upon the surface of tin-plate, by applying to it in a heated state some dilute nitro-muriatic acid for a few seconds, then washing it with water, drying, and coating it with lacker. The figures are more or less beautiful and diversified, according to the degree of heat, and relative dilution of the acid. This mode of ornamenting tin-plate is much less in vogue now than it was a few years ago." Andre Ure, M.D., *A Dictionary of Arts, Manufactures, and Mines; Containing a Clear Exposition of Their Principles and Practice.* NY: Appleton & Co., 1854, in 2 volumes reprinted from the "last" corrected English edition. "Less in vogue now" may be 1830s or '40s. Ure explains **chemical aspects** of this decorative technique in his "Tin-Plate" entry: "It seems that the acid merely lays bare the crystalline structure really present on every sheet [of tin plate], but masked by a film of redundant tin. Though this showy article has become of late years vulgarized by its cheapness, it is still interesting...to practical chemists. The English tin-plates marked F answer well for producing the Moirée, by the following process. Place the tin-plate, slightly heated, over a tub of water, and rub its surface with a sponge holding one part of common salt or sal ammoniac in solution. Whenever the crystalline spangles seem to be thoroughly brought out, the plate must be immersed in water, washed either with a feather or a little cotton (taking care not to rub off the film of tin that forms the feathering), forthwith dried with a low heat, and coated with a lacker varnish, otherwise it loses its lustre in the air. If the whole surface is not plunged at once in cold water, but...is partically cooled by sprinkling water on it, the crystallization will be finely variegated with large and small figures. ... A variety of delineations may be traced, by playing over the surface of the plate with the pointed flame of a blowpipe." *Ibid.*

Tumbler, blue & white swirl enamelware, 20th C. A **tumbler** in fairly modern usage means a drinking glass without a stem, or a footed base. But a few hundred years ago, a tumbler was a drinking glass made with a rounded bottom that would actually tumble over if you tried to set it down. Whether it was to make you drink less or more, I don't know.................................. **$10+**

Utensil racks – See Implement racks

Utility rack, red enamelware with gold trim & with white lettering on each of 3 separate cups for dishwashing chores: "Zeep, Zand, Soda," meaning Soap, Sand & Soda, Dutch, 20th C........................ **$150+**

VII-150. Wine coolers. *Bottom (L) is oldest. It's japanned tin, with cast iron handle. From American Home Cook Book, 1854. Other two are from Duparquet, Huot & Moneuse, 1904-1910 catalog. (T) is japanned tin; (R) is galvanized sheet metal for one bottle.* **$65+**

Utility rack, wall hung, white enamelware with blue lettering marking contents of each of 3 separate cups, "Zand, Soda, Zeep," materials used in washing dishes, pots & pans. Dutch, turn-of-century. • Mine's in the bathroom, with combs in one cup, toothbrushes in another, and I have temporarily shelved the 3rd cup, as the hole provides a "holster" for a hair-drier. .... **$100+**

Water pitcher, blue & white mottled enamelware, bulbous body, ice lip, turn-of-century. .... **$75+**

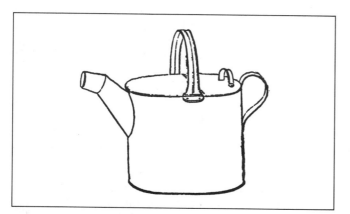

VII-148. Water can. *Not a watering can for gardens, but a hot water can for adding hot water to wash basin, or for other uses. Enameled sheet iron, white inside & out. Harrod's Stores, Brompton, England, 1895 catalog.* **$100+**

VII-149. Water pitchers, *for hot and cold water. Wild designs, "painted in bright and subdued colors; superb adjuncts to summer or city houses." F. A. Walker, 1886 catalog supplement.* **$50-$200+**

VII-151. Oooops! *Center picture is from a humorous story in Century magazine, June 1878. The officer from the War of 1812 has fallen backwards "plump into the sour-tub." The term **sour-tub** does not appear in any dictionary of Americanisms I have. I suspect it may be the same as (R) yeast tub, from the Duparquet, Huot & Moneuse catalog, c.1904-1910. It was made to hold 12, 16, 24, 30, 35, and 40 gallons. (T-L) A **yeast pail**, holding 10, 12, 14 or 16 quarts. Both of oak staves.*

❖ NOTES ❖

Date Enamelware By Weight – One clue in dating enamelware is the weight of the underlying steel or iron. Reproductions or lookalikes, as well as most regular wares made since the end of WWI, are rather considerably lighter in weight than older pieces. If you recall, in the 1970s a lot of bright new wares, in very colorful blue, turquoise, green, red, orange or yellow, were imported and sold in warehouse stores specializing in fun, inexpensive, household wares. If you have such a piece, compare its heft with that of a piece you are trying to date. New pieces also seem to make a sort of tinny scratchy sound when pulled across a stainless steel sink or other resonating surface. **Using the Five Senses + One:** You can develop a list of sensory tests for many categories of collectibles: sound (when struck with wooden spoon, tapped with fingernail, dragged on a metal surface); feel or touch (the surface, especially when you can run your thumb opposing your middle finger on the inside and outside of something); appearance of shape, color, signs of wear, damage, decoration, or surface – a magnified surface examined with high power loupe or magnifier will reveal many secrets; weight or heft; and even taste and smell sometimes. And always use your common sense.

FOR MORE INFORMATION:

ABC PLATES & MUGS

ABC Collectors' Circle
E-mail: drjgeorge@nac.net

ABC Plate & Mug Collectors
67 Stevens Ave.
Old Bridge, NJ 08857

BASKETS

Note: A search on Google for basket collector clubs yields over 17,000 listings. Be forewarned, however: most of these are manufacturer-related, or are for collectors of baskets made for collectors – not the same thing as baskets made over centuries for use. Adding the word "antique" doesn't help much. I'm afraid you'll have to sort through listings to see what you want.

CANDY CONTAINERS

Candy Container Collectors of America
Contact: Betty MacDuff
2711 De La Rosa St.
The Villages, FL 32162
E-mail: epmac27@aol.com
Web site: www.candycontainer.org

BOTTLES & JARS

Old Bottle Club of Great Britain
(Umbrella organization for regional clubs)
Elsecar Heritage Centre
Nr Barnsley
S Yorks S74 8HJ
England
Federation Of Historical Bottle Collectors
Web site: www.fohbc.com/

Federa Of Historical Bottle Collectors

This non-profit organization helps collectors find bottle sites, shows, and clubs in Canada, the U.S., and some other countries.

Web site: www.fohbc.com/

Canadian Bottle Collector

This site, run by Rob Sturrock, is a good way to find out about bottle collecting in Canada.

E-mail: primex@portal.ca
Web site: www.geocities.com/Eureka/Promenade/4600/

Antique Bottles Collectors Haven

This site has links to all kinds of information, from bottle classification to newsletters to clubs. Highly recommended.

E-mail contact: Reggie Lynch: rlynch@antiquebottles.com
Web site: www.antiquebottles.com/

Collector's Clubs In New Zealand, Australia

This site has all kinds of collectibles represented, with a few bottle and glass clubs.

Web site: www.thecollector.com.au/collecto1.htm

National Assoc. Of Milk Bottle Collectors
Box 105
Blooming Grove, NY 10914

Folk Art In Bottles

Extraordinary site with scores of whimsy bottles with carved objects or scenes inside. Ultimate recycling of whiskey jugs & bottles, medicine flasks, you name it. Collector Susan D. Jones created the Web site, and is interested in hearing from anyone with direct knowledge of carvers.

E-mail: sdjones@sdjones.net
Web site: http://sdjones.net/FolkArt/bottlestory.html

YAHOO CLUBS

As you probably know, Yahoo has thousands of sites for collectors of just about anything under the sun. They are online "talk" sites, with hosts, and e-mailed messages back and forth between members. Go to the following "hobby" site to find your way to your favorite subjects. Sometimes membership is limited in number because of volume, so don't give up.

Web site: http://ca.dir.clubs.yahoo.com/Hobbies

COOKIE JARS

One fun thing on their site is a contest for the ugliest cookie jar; until you've seen them, you can't imagine!

American Cookie Jar Association
Contact: Sandi Philips
E-mail: books@hibek.net
Web site: http://cookiejarclub.com

Cookie Jar Collectors Club
595 Cross River Rd.
Katonah, NY 10536

Cookie Jar Newsletter
Contact: Joyce
RR-1 Box 504
Walterboro, SC 19488

GLASS

A generalized Web site with live links (remember, though, that Web site addresses change) is found at:

http://members.tripod.com/Elizabeth_Swift/links. html

This site includes clubs for Anchor Hocking, Fry, and Pyrex as well as specific forms such as bottles and reamers. Also information on museums, and on repros and counterfeits.

INFANT FEEDERS & NURSING BOTTLES

American Collectors Of Infant Feeders

Contact: JoAnnn Gifford
1849 Ebony Dr.
York, PA 17402-4706
Web site: www.acif.org/home.htm

MATCH SAFES & HOLDERS

This does not include matchbooks. There is cross-over interest from tobacciano collectors.

Max Hand

Collector of early (1850-1920) cast iron & metal match holders.
406 Jefferson Dr.
Charlotte, NC 28270-3653
1-800-849-0343
E-mail: maxrhand@aol.com

International Match Safe Association

Note: There is an excellent, extensive bibliography on the Web site for this collectors' club.

Contact: George Sparacio
POB 791
Malaga, NJ 08328-0791
Association e-mail: imsa@matchsafe.org
Personal e-mail: mrvesta1@aol.com
Personal Web site: http://members.aol.com/mrvesta2
Assoc. Web site: www.matchsafe.org/

METAL WARES

There are various pewter collectors' societies; for the most part I've steered clear of pewter because it is a very select, old field of collecting as precise and unknowable to an outsider as is silver. Look for The Pewter Society or Pewter Collectors Club of America online.

Antique Metalware Society

Objects made of non-precious metals & their alloys, with emphasis on the study of domestic artifacts. A Journal and two newsletters are published every year.

POB 63
Honiton. Devonshire
EX14 1HP England

SALT & PEPPER SHAKERS

Novelty Salt & Pepper Shakers Club

Contact: Lula Fuller
POB 677388
Orlando, FL 32687-7388
E-mail: ilfuller@aol.com

The British Novelty Salt & Pepper Collectors Club

Coleshill Clayton Rd.
Mold Flintshire
CH7 ISX England
Quarterly newsletter.
Web site: www.ezeeweb.co.uk/shakers

SALTS & SHAKERS (NON-NOVELTY PIECES)

There are many regional collector societies for open salts; listed here is only one, a national society that's been around for years.

Antique & Art Glass Salt Shaker Collectors Society

A group who collect all sorts of antique salt shakers, including the patented Christmas salts, the Mt. Washington salts, etc.

Membership Chairman AAGSSCS
1775 Lakeview Dr.
Zeeland, MI 49464-2108
E-mail: ccglass@cbantiques.com
Web site: www.cbantiques.com/ssc/

MUSEUMS

The Museum of Beverage Containers & Advertising

1055 Ridgecrest Drive
Millersville, Tennessee 37072
Phone: (800) 826-4929
E-mail: mbca@gono.com
Web site: www.gonocom/vir-mus/museum.htm

The Salt Museum

Cheshire has been a major center of salt processing for two millennia.

162 London Rd.
Northwich, Cheshire
CW9 8AB
Phone: +44 (0)1606 413 31
E-mail: cheshiremuseums@cheshire.gov.uk
Web site: www.saltmuseum.org.uk

HOLDING & HANDLING

——— VIII. TOOLS THAT OPEN & CLOSE ———

In this chapter are the ingenious devices used to open – and close – cans, bottles and jars. As Christine Frederick wrote in 1929, in *Selling Mrs. Consumer,* "The modern housewife is no longer a cook – she is a can-opener." But Mrs. Consumer's problem, undoubtedly from the beginning, was finding a can opener that actually worked well and kept on working. Elsie Hutchinson, who wrote a guide for salespeople (*Department Store Merchandise Manual*) in 1918, had this to say: "Can openers are of many styles and there are few satisfactory ones."

Can openers – rigid and mechanical – are probably more widely popular with American collectors than are corkscrews. There is great variety in mechanical types – from one moving part to a series of gears. A new/old concept of can opener was recently advertised on TV: the "Safety Can Opener," which easily shears off the lid with the rim intact! According to the ad, you can re-use the lid to close up "pet food cans." There are many simple rigid openers with no-nonsense utilitarian handles that are actually levers – the inventors described using these like a "brake," pushing it forward and back down, forward and back. The minority of can openers have figural handles.

As more and more collectors specialize in can openers, prices continue to rise, albeit very slowly, and not for all, or even most, openers. When unknown types are discovered, and other collectors find out, this will set off a search for multiple examples. The numbers so far are encouraging. When collectors Joe and Jackie Young started back in the 1970s, they thought "How many more could there be?" after their first 25 or so. Now, 5,000+ can openers later, they still don't know, and the world's their oyster ... can! A much newer collector, Bill Griffiths, has well over 1,000 openers, most of them from the United States.

Can openers make a good field for a beginning collector because of variety, quality, quantity, and price. For some reason, prices are still very reasonable. The Youngs have copies of over 1,600 U.S. patents, and 500+ English patents, and haven't started to get copies of European patents. All of this sets the ideal collecting scene because there is also an opportunity to trade up and to specialize. I keep expecting a club, and, please, at least one book on them, because it's such a richly rewarding subject, but as of 2002 there's nothing. Get crankin', you guys!

Arguably, the most elegant collectibles in this chapter are **corkscrews** (long ago called wormes, scrues, or bottlescrews), which have been collected for many years. A newly-coined word for lovers of these clever metal pigtails is "Helixophile." Whether or not it is true today, I believe that corkscrews first gained their cachet because of the wine found within most bottles with corks. Anybody who would pay $4,000 or $20,000 or even more for an historic, aged bottle of wine (whether or not it would be potable), would want the very finest antique corkscrews. Today's collectors look for interesting patented screws. W. C. Fields said "We lost our corkscrew and were compelled to live on food and water for several days." Such a thing would never happen if you had a large corkscrew collection!

Collectors of **bottle openers** generally fall into two groups, those seeking patented, simple or combination-tool openers, especially those bearing advertising (and which may be shaped like something); or those looking for more decorative figural openers. Nowadays, "bottle opener" refers almost exclusively to a prying tool for opening crown caps, which began to be used in 1894. According to many corkscrew collectors, what they are most into is quality and rarities. Most of them aren't what we'd call "kitchen collectors."

Jar openers. The only ones here are a few meant for pickle jars or peanut butter jars, etc., with tightly screwed-on lids. Jar wrenches, on the other hand, are usually considered a "go-with" for collectors of canning or fruit jars, and other related canning equipment, and are to be found in Chapter XVI.

Rubber grippers. Nowadays, "jar opener" often refers to those CD-sized discs of flexible textured rubber or vinyl which help you open a jar with – almost – your bare hands. They are printed with advertising messages as promotional giveaways. But some are almost 100 years old, and care must be taken not to rip or crumble the rubber. Probably someone, somewhere, is collecting them.

Crossover collecting really hits its stride here because of all the figural and zoomorphic designs. eBay has opened up a lot of crossover collecting because of the ease of searching among the 500,000+ items being newly listed every day. Just by typing in the word "dog" or "alligator" or "baseball," one can find several pages, sometimes over a thousand auctions, which may relate to their theme.

Combination tools. Can opener, bottle opener, corkscrew, and glass cutter combos are all listed together following can opener listings.

Bar set, molded white plastic & metal, skeleton & bone figurals, bottle opener, corkscrew, 6 drink stirrers – all skull atop femur bone, "Name Your Poison," 1950s (?). Motif has crossover appeal for Halloween & skull collectors. .... **$45+**

Bottle cap, steel, rubber seal, knurled knob, "Sta-a-liv," for use with fizzy soda bottles. American, 1947-48. ...... **$1**

❖ NOTES ❖

Go, Gyro! I just had to include this because of the ephemera that came with it. My friend Brenda "keep-it-for-at-least-20-years-then-consider-getting-rid-of-it" Woodward sent me an old flyer from the **Gadget-of-the-Month Club,** Hollywood, CA, whose motto was "easier living for everyone ... thru new products." On one side we see "the best gadget of 1948" – the 1948 "gadget of the year" – "Sta-a-liv" bottle cap for a dollar each. On the reverse is a set of four plastic "Levelors" – self-leveling skids for chair legs, etc. – "adjustable to meet almost any kind of 'unbalanced situation' in your home."

• • •

Figural fizz-savers I like are little vacuum pumps that suck the air out of half-full bottles of soda pop. They really do work. Disney and other licensed cartoon characters form the figural heads.

• • •

Bottle cappers are divided into two types: (1) foil crimpers were used to crimp a tin foil cap over a cork already in a bottle, and (2) cap crimpers were used to put on crown caps – the metal caps with crimped edges so widely used today in all parts of the world that it seems incredible that they weren't patented until 1894! **Cap crimpers** are common, and simple versions are still being made and sold to home brewers. Mostly, their value is connected to their present-day usefulness. Most bottle cappers found were for semi-commercial use, not for home use. For the home bottler of anything fizzy, from hops beer to ginger beer, a simple levered bottle capper made easy work of bottling a couple dozen bottles of home brew. I recall in the 1960s sitting on the floor with a friend in Memphis, surrounded by the strong odor of new brew, passing bottles to him to be capped with the small device on the floor between his knees. Cheers! Gimmer.

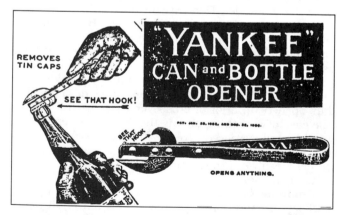

VIII-1-A. Bottle & can opener. *Nickel plated "Yankee." Pat'd. Jan. 28, 1902 & Dec. 26, 1906, and mfd. by Taylor Mfg. Co., Hartford, CT. (See also the Combination tools further on.)* **$5-$10**

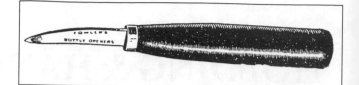

VIII-1-B. Bottle opener. *Steel blade in black-painted wooden handle, with ferrule. Very much like patented oyster openers. This is an English one, "Fowler's Bottle Opener," pictured & described in a c.1922 catalog/cookbook by George Fowler, London, England, in which Fowler wrote "Lacquered metal covers may be removed by forcing a skewer, the point of a pair of scissors, or Fowler's Bottle Opener between the covers and the bottles, or by cutting the rubber with a sharp pen knife; this will allow air to enter the bottles and the covers are then easily removed without being damaged." There were a number of oyster openers patented in the 19th C., and this relatively short, pointed blade is rather like several of them.* **$15+**

Bottle capper, cast iron, lever action, countertop, "Big Ben," English, c.1880-1910. For use with a tin foil cap which was placed over the cork. .... **$35+**

Bottle capper, rather decorative cast iron, mounted to oak oblong, simple knurled lever is pulled to crimp tin foil caps on corked bottles, embossed "CAPPEE," Manning & Bowman Co., c.1901. .... **$50+**

Bottle capper & cork press combined, cast iron mounted to wood, lever used to press three sizes of corks and/or to crimp a foil cap within a rubber-lined cylindrical opening. "Gem Capper," American, "pat. appl. for," early 20th C. .... **$65+**

Bottle corkers – See Cork or corking press, cork drivers

Bottle, jar & screw cap opener combined, rubber gripper to protect & assist hand, "EZY-GRIP," Sieberling Latex Products Co., Akron, OH, early 20th C.... **$1+**

❖ NOTES ❖

Bottle openers: The English call these openers **crown cork openers,** after the shape of a bottle cap, which within living memory was lined with cork for a tight seal. (Remember making badges or pins of Coca-Cola caps by prying out the cork, and pressing the two halves back together with a thin layer of clothing in between?). The crown cap (crown cork) was invented by William Painter of Baltimore, in 1894. For some reason, Americans call the double-ended can & bottle opener a church key, but I don't know of anyone who calls other can and/or bottle openers that. Do you?

BOTTLE OPENERS, advertising or utilitarian

Bottle opener, also called a cap lifter, adv'g. "Rumford," early 20th C. .... **$10+**

Bottle opener, "Baltimore Cork & Screw," MD, 1908. .... **$20+**

Bottle opener, wall-mounted with 2 screws, cast and tin plated iron with red lettering: "Coca-Cola," "The Starr X," pat'd. 1925. .... **$10+**

Bottle opener, cast steel, "Anchor Opener," 4"L, c.1910... **$7+**

Bottle opener, double-ended, flat steel, adv'g. "Stone Malt Co.," 7-1/2"L, 20th C. .... $7+

Bottle opener, flat plated steel, key-like double-ended with open mouth cap lifter, and peanut-shape cutout that's marked "Pat. Feb. 19, 1901. A.W. Stephens Mfg. Co., Waltham, Mass." on one side, "Trade > Picnic < Mark Reg. U.S. Pat. Off." on the other. Pat'd by F. W. Lyons, Louisville, KY, 3-1/8"L. Many are known, most adv'g. beer. These could be ordered by a brewery stamped with any name or slogan, so the collector fun is finding new names. Research into the pre-Prohibition brews helps date. Marked examples include "Duquesne Silver Top Beer," "East Tennessee Brewing Co.," "Grand Rapids Brewing Co." ...... $20+

Bottle opener, flat steel, adv'g. Coca-Cola's "Sprite Boy," late 20th C. .... $5+

Bottle opener, steel business end, nicely tooled, with turned wood handle, "Havell," Irvington, NJ, 5"L, c.1900. .... $10+

Bottle opener, steel, green painted wood handle, dated 1933. .... $5+

Bottle opener, plated steel flat cutout of baseball player, the toe of one lifted foot creates the "hook" for opening, pat'd. 1914. Clever figural advertising piece with crossover appeal. .... $75+

Bottle opener, pointing hand, flat plated steel, "Effinger Beer," Baraboo, WI, 20th C. .... $45+

BOTTLE OPENERS, figural, souvenir, or decorative

(See boxed Reproduction sidebar near end of this classification.)

Bottle opener, alligator, polychromed cast iron, 20th C. These are widely reproduced – especially the awful racist ones. Old: .... $25+

Bottle opener, alligator & black man, cast iron, obnoxious racist Black Americana, undoubtedly American, alas, and even worse, it's 20th C. Widely reproduced. Old: .... $35+

Reproduction Alert

At one time the **Coca-Cola openers** were hot; then someone claimed to have found a huge warehouse supply, and then (or simultaneously because the story of finding them was a scamming ruse) someone started reproducing them, so the value hasn't risen. In early 1989 I noticed an ad for a repro, which may have first been offered long ago. A company in Clarksville, AR, adv'd. "Coca-Cola cast iron wall type bottle openers $21 doz.," but we don't know if this is a new repro, or by now a "Warehouse find" of an old cache of old repros. Arggh. Collectors were not in a position to watch one particular item over the long crucial period between, say, 1960 and 1990, because it wasn't their specialty, or they weren't old enough! I've never wanted one of these openers, but used to see at least 10, in original boxes, every Saturday during the 1960s that I went to Englishtown Flea Market in south central New Jersey. To see them still for sale, for the same price or a little more, is proof that when something is available in large quantities, and has nothing going for it beyond the name, it just won't increase in value.

❖ **NOTES** ❖

Collectibles That Offend – There's no right way to deal with these things. For a collector, many things do not come with intrinsic moralities or value judgments. I know what I wouldn't want around the house, and that includes offensive racist things, Nazi collectibles, animal traps of all kinds (you'll note I have never put a mousetrap into any of my books – I hate them), and meat-tools of the kitchen. *De gustibus non est disputandum*; it's your choice, of course.

Bottle opener, automobile jack, iron, American, c.1915-25. .... $35+

Bottle opener, baseball cap, cast metal, painted black & orange, souvenir of "Mets," NYC, late 20th C. .... $10+

Bottle opener, billy goat with great horns sits atop opener, polychromed cast iron, 20th C. .... $30+

Bottle opener, bottle-shaped, flat nickeled-steel with small hanging hole at bottom for key chain (?), "Deppen Brewing Company Reading PA, Queen Quality" incised above depiction of a glass with foamy head, Oddly, there's the design of a corkscrew also incised on it which creates a little added value, "Pat'd March 12, 1912," American, 3-1/4"L. .... $25+

Bottle opener, brass with antler handle, mid 20th C. Most of this type I think of as "icky chic." .... $15+

Bottle opener, steel with horn handle, sterling silver applied decoration, American, 7-1/4"L, pat'd. 1864. .... $65+

❖ **NOTES** ❖

Antlers or Tusks – An antler is a renewable resource; people walking through the woods in early spring can find deer antlers wherever deer live. A tusk – whether it's an elephant, walrus, rhinoceros, or boar tusk – as well as a buffalo or cattle horn, is not renewable, and requires the savage mutilation, and painful death, of the animal from which it is taken. For me, it is bad karma to have anything obtained in the brutal way all tusks are obtained. Doing research in 19th century business directories for NYC, and other cities, I found horrifying and truly sickening illustrated ads for ivory, showing "natives" fighting with elephants, blood and gore pouring from wounds in the elephant, the native triumphant in his fight to obtain the ivory tusk for the decorative trades in the Western and Eastern Worlds. Old directories list many men whose occupation is described as "turner, in ivory and wood." It's imperative that the vast numbers of people who make up the collecting world become responsible and respectful "harvesters."

❖ **NOTES** ❖

Plastic – Although 40 or so years ago I absolutely hated plastic, thinking it beneath consideration because it was a fake something else, I believe that the reason I have come to appreciate plastic objects so much in the last decade is because they may represent a saved elephant, a spared tree, a cow that wasn't turned into a pocketbook. Think about it. And to be honest, some plastic is beautiful in itself, especially when it's not imitative.

Bottle openers, chromium, very stylized art deco/modernist, the figures of each style are mounted to a large C-jaw which is the business end of the opener. A rearing horse, a Scottie, an elephant, etc. American, c.1931. .... **$45+**

Bottle opener, clown's head with open mouth as opener, cast iron, painted colorfully with polka-dotted tie, wall mounted, poss. made by John Wright Inc., or maybe earlier by another company, 4-1/2"L x 4"W, weighs 14 oz., when finish is worn it looks like a 1930s piece. This design is in Wright's 1963 catalog. **Old ones** from 1920s or '30s get up to $75 or more, but there are so many now 30- and 40-year-old repros that it's hard to advise how to buy. 1963 wholesale price was 60¢. See the lobster bottle opener for hints on evaluating new things. .... **$15+**

Bottle opener, dachshund, cast brass, no mark, c.1950s. .... **$45+**

Bottle opener, dachshund, nickeled-iron, adv'g. "Medford Lager Beer," German (?) made for American brewery?, 20th C. .... **$55+**

Bottle opener, dog with open mouth, cast brass, probably Riverside Brass, Canadian, mid 20th C. .... **$25+**

Bottle opener, drunk or lovelorn cowboy embracing a cactus, cast iron, painted, souvenir type, 20th C..... **$20+**

Bottle opener, drunk & palm tree, cast iron, painted, 20th C. **Drunks aren't funny,** but they are collectible. The palm tree drunkard is rarer than the lamppost ones. While the original price might have been a dollar, now the asking price is much higher. Widely reproduced. **$25**

Bottle opener, drunkard leaning on signpost, colorfully painted cast iron, poss. made by John Wright Inc., Wrightsville, PA, 4"H x 2-1/2"W, weighs 7 oz., in 1963 Wright catalog, but possibly theirs is repro of earlier one. **Souvenir type:** Sign was painted with different place names, such as St. Petersburg, FL, or Hershey, PA. More common is the drunk on lamppost, which usually did not have a place name. That one weighs only 6-1/2 oz. The 1963 wholesale price of either was 40¢. Asking prices now are partly dependent on place name. .... **$20+**

Bottle opener, fireman's helmet, painted cast metal, red with white shield area that has detailed decal, to use you set the hat, with its oval white metal ring opener (marked "bottle opener") over the crown cap and pry up. Ring also marked "Scott Prod Inc Newark NJ," 1-7/8"H x 3-1/8"L x 2-5/8"W, c.1930s-40s. .... **$75+**

Bottle opener, fish, painted cast iron, 5-1/2"L, 20th C. .... **$30+**

Bottle opener, guitar, heavy metal, with opening in body of guitar, Japan, c.1960s. Groovy pop culture crossover. .... **$10+**

Bottle opener, lizard (or baby alligator?), realistic small figural of cast bell metal or bronze painted in shades of brown; curled tail with a loop near end works as the cap lever, looks European from fineness of detail, poss. Austrian? (Vienna?), 4-3/4"L, early 20th C. If this were a **Vienna Bronze,** and the dealer knew it, the price would be four times the asking price of $50. Wide value range relates to venue of sale: .... **$55-$175**

Bottle opener, lobster, red painted cast iron, possibly a reproduction of an early 20th C. opener, poss. made by John Wright Inc., Wrightsville, PA, 3-1/2"L x 2-1/4"W, Wright's weighs 7 oz., shown in 1963 Wright catalog. The **difference in real value and asking price** for

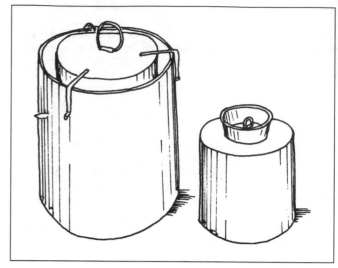

VIII-2. Early cans. *Both of pieced tin plate.* **(L)** *"Cotton's Preserve Can," pat'd. Dec. 21, 1859 by P. H. Cotton, Demopolis, AL, patent #22,351. Lid slightly concave to form recess for melted wax or sealing cement poured in to make airtight. Bent wires hold lid on while cement hardens.* **(R)** *"Manley's Preserve Can," pat'd. Aug. 3, 1858 by E. Manley, Marion, NY, patent #21,078. According to* Scientific American, *no can "surpasses this one for cheapness ... simplicity and perfection." Slightly concave top is removed to put food in; can then placed in hot water to expel air from inside; cover replaced & center cup fitted into top to hold the cement. "To open the can ... pour hot water into the cup, which melts the cement."* Scientific American, *Feb. 26, 1859 and Sept. 25, 1858.* **$30+**

reproductions is very difficult to determine. By now, those Wright pieces which are assumed to not be reproductions, that were designed new for 1963, are 40 years old, easily qualifying under any criteria as collectibles. The difficulty comes when a piece is a reproduction, for it would take much, much longer than 40 years to become valuable in its own right. 1963 wholesale price was 30¢. .... **$20+**

Bottle opener, nude with arms stretched above head, cast brass & steel, 4"L, mid 20th C. This motif fits in with lots of 1950s collectibles, many of which are tacky, which is a big collector field. **$75**

Bottle opener, nude with upstretched arms, white metal, brass (?) plated, marked "Herbert," prob. mfd. by Herbert Specialty Mfg. Co., makers of toys & novelties, Chicago, IL, 4-1/2"L, 1st third 20th C. **$75**

Bottle opener, pelican, painted cast iron, souvenir type, mid 20th C. **$15**

Bottle opener, shark, cast aluminum, American, 1930s. .... **$25+**

Bottle opener, steer head, handsome very Cubist sculptural form – somehow goes with Picasso's *Guernica* painting, cast iron with bronzed finish, no mark, 7"L, 1920s-30s. .... **$75+**

Bottle opener, parrot or macaw on perch, cast iron, painted in bright colors, may or may not be reproduction, poss. made by John Wright Inc., 5"H x 2-1/2"W, weighs 7-1/2 oz., 20th C. • **Reproduction alert?** – If there was an "original" it may date to 1920s or 30s, but there definitely is one in Wright's 1963 catalog for 40¢. .... **$18+**

Bottle opener combination tools – See Combination tools following the can opener listings.

Bottle opener for milk bottles – See Milk bottle opener.

Bottle stoppers – See Chapter VII

Bottle opener combination tools – See Combination tools following the can opener listings.

Bottle opener for milk bottles – See Milk bottle opener.

Bottle stoppers – See Chapter VII

❖ NOTES ❖

Reproduction Figural Bottle Openers. Many openers in this figural class are being widely reproduced, some are even reproductions of reproductions done in the 1960s of openers from about 40 years before that. That includes the wall-mounted ones and the hand-held ones. The castings are horrible, but don't show up well in scanned images on eBay, for example. I don't believe that any but the most non-observant sellers really think they are selling antiques. The metal is very grainy – undoubtedly mixed scrap metals were melted down for these and other cast iron collectibles. Remember that nowadays, cast iron may have many other metals in it because car engines and other mixed metal scrap is melted together, meaning there is some percentage of aluminum, brass, copper, zinc, and steel mixed in. The edges are rough, or are crudely filed down; openings are filled in with sloppy overruns of molten metal; painting is sloppy, crude and often "antiqued" in that telltale way with a faint orangey glaze over everything, meant to look as if the iron has rusted through the paint. **Aluminum paint-em-yourself repros:** A long-time collector of figural openers, Dale Deckert of Orlando, FL, announced in 1996 that he was going to try to reproduce over 40 figurals originally made by Riverside Brass of Canada, from their "plates." Instead of cast iron or brass, they will be cast aluminum, ready to paint or plate by the purchaser. These include an alligator, various birds including parrots, cats, dogs, donkey, elephants, fisherman, fish, goat, lamb, liquor bottles, raccoon, squirrels, etc. Deckert made the *2002 Guinness Book of Records* for having amassed 20,884 bottle openers. Hmmm.

A Brief History of Canning
– or, Bully Beef For You, Too!

You can't find two histories of canning that give all the same names, dates, and information. I am footnoting this article (a version of which appeared in my newsletter, *Kitchen Collectibles News*, Jan/Feb 1985), to facilitate retracing the various authors' research. See footnotes following article and table of patents.

It is agreed, however, by all sources, that in 1809 – in response to General Napoleon's challenge to find a way to keep food fresh, or safe to eat, for his fighting troops – the concept of the supposedly long term, airless preservation of food became practical. The French confectioner, chef, pickler and bottler Nicholas Appert won a 12,000-franc award by devising a way to put food up in glass containers. In 1810, he published the results of his studies, to fulfill the stipulations of the awarders. At the same time, the Englishman Peter Durand was awarded a patent for his technique of putting food up in glass containers, but he included tin cannisters in his patent.[1]

Those early glass, wide-necked canning jars or bottles were filled with food, immersed up to the neck in a bath of boiling water until the contents were also boiling, then corked with waxed corks. The corks were then secured with wire. But the bottles cracked easily during the boiling process, or were broken later, and they were not perfectly sanitary because of the porous corks, which would admit bacteria (a danger unknown to Appert or Durand). Certainly not a handy way to preserve food for soldiers in the field or sailors on the high seas.

In 1811, Englishmen Bryan Donkin and his partner John Hall – mentioned in a few sources – patented a similar technique, and then in 1813 or so[2], they changed to handformed tin canisters. Through a smallish hole in the top, minced or diced food was put into the cans, the cans were set in boiling water baths (like a French *bain marie*) until the food boiled. A little cap-like disc was set on the hole and soldered in place. Though Donkin and Hall worked about the same time as Appert and Durand, it was this unheralded pair who actually set up the first factory for canning meat; in 1818, the products were being sold – including to career officers who could afford this luxurious new convenience food.[3]

Meanwhile, in America, tin-canning of fish was begun in New York City about 1819[4], and glass jar "canning" was patented in 1825[5] by Ezra Daggett and Thomas Kensett. The reported dates are fuzzy, but the two men's names are certain, as is that of William Underwood, who about the same time began putting up vegetables in glass jars. One source[6] says that all three changed from glass to tin in 1839.

Can-makers, who frequently were also the food processors who filled the cans, went from small enterprises that could turn out a few score cans a day, by hand, to factories that could produce hundreds of cans. The Winslow Brothers of Portland, ME, had a can factory in the 1840s[7] that made cans with a filling-hole only 1-1/2" across. Each worker could make about 60 cans a day. By the end of the 1850s, there were machines involving stamping of one-piece blanks that boosted production to 1,000 cans a man (though not necessarily in the Winslows' operation). A man named Colonel Silas Ilsley made cans in Brooklyn[8] in the 1860s, as did Joseph Campbell (Soup's on!), and Abram A. Anderson in Camden, NJ.[9] Two Libby brothers and their partner Archibald McNeill moved from Portland, ME to Chicago – where the stockyards were – and began canning corned beef and other meats in 1872. Business was booming in canned goods, and the early pioneers of canning often became big

1. Bragdon, Charles R. *Metal Decorating from Start to Finishes*, Freeport, ME: Bond Wheelwright Co., 1961. Page 81.

2. Clark, Hyla. *The Tin Can Book*, NYC: New American Library, 1977. Page 13.

3. Ritchie, Carson I. A. *Food in Civilization. How History Has Been Affected by Human Tastes*, NYC/Toronto: Beaufort Books, 1981. Page 144.

4. Clark. Page 11.

5. Bragdon. Page 81.

6. Bragdon. Page 82.

7. Bragdon. Page 82.

8. Clark. Page 11.

9. Bragdon. Page 83.

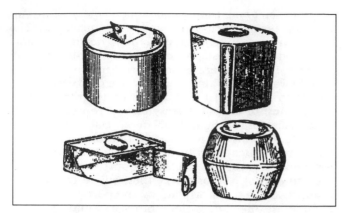

VIII-3. Early cans. *Pieced tin; various kinds of air-tight openings.* **(T-L)** *a "rip patch can" from 1875, which required a hole to be opened, and a hook to pull off squarish patch.* **(T-R)** *A squarish can with canted sides, called a "pyramidal can," 1879.* **(B-L)** *a "rip side can," 1879, and* **(B-R)** *a fruit can with bulge-pot sides and large opening for lid, 1879. Drawings adapted from* Wonders of Modern Industry, *1938.* **$30+**

names in canned goods later – names still known today from the grocery store shelves!

But there's more to the story between the 1830s and the 1860s. One reason for the popularity of canned foods before the Civil War was the large number of people traveling westward, including Gold Rush miners. About 30 years after the gold-panning Forty-Niners rushed across the American continent, Philip William Flower wrote his *History of the Trade in Tin*[10], and described huge rusting dumps of empty tin cans left by the miners and other westward-ho'ers. He also told of the astounding number of tinned goods leaving the major canning city of Baltimore in just one year: 45-million one-pound cans, primarily of oysters and peaches!

Early hole-and-cap cans sometimes had rings soldered on with the cap, and when yanked with a hook they pulled through the relatively soft solder and reopened the hole. The problem was how to get the food out of the small hole. (To digress – once on an ill-planned trip from New Orleans to Memphis, in my adventurous twenties, all we had in the car were a couple of cans of baked beans, a

heavy jackknife, and no money even for 15¢ McDonald's. But we had a nice roadside picnic by punching a hole in the cans and drawing out the beans, one at a time, with September-stiff weed stalks. Very ad hoc, very subsistence, very memorable.)

Because there were many different ways to close up cans, in factories or home kitchens, there were many different ways of opening cans too – using simple tools meant for other uses, like chisels, hammers, and punches – but no specific can-opening tools at first. By 1854, it is known that C. S. Osborn had marketed his can opener, without a patent as far as we know in 2002. By 1858 there was undoubtedly a usable can opener. A patent model exists, although production has not been proved, of Ezra J. Warner's can opener of January 5, 1858.[11] Warner's patent was entitled "Instrument for Opening Cans," but in his specifications, Warner wrote that "The advantages of my improvement over all other instruments for this purpose consist in the smoothness and rapidity of the cut." Although some other collectors think this may mean only an improvement over chisel-and-hammer, I believe it goes further and implies that there were previously-patented "instruments for opening cans." Warner emphasized the money-saving advantage of having his cutter piece of the tool be replaceable if it got damaged. He also claimed that "...the piercer will perforate the tin without causing the liquid to fly out, as it does in all those which make the perforation by percussion of any kind." His invention had a steel "piercer bar," and a "curved cutter of cast steel" with a looped bar of steel that could "swing or rock" into position, and would be "held against the surface of the tin, while the curved cutter will be forced between its parts and cut the tin smoothly through" when "worked in the manner of a brake."[12] The hair-pin like "loop" could be adjusted so that the blade would fit on either side of the loop or inside it; was an improvement over something else specifically meant to open cans. By the 1870s, some newer styles of cans could be opened by cutting the thin tops off with a knife, or by pulling off a tin strip – a lá Quaker Oats boxes – to loosen a cap.[13]

---

10. Flower, Philip William. *History of the Trade in Tin.* London: G. Bell & Sons, 1880.

11. Young, Joe. "Some Notes on Early Can Openers," *Kitchen Collectibles News*, March/April 1985. Page 23.
12. United States Patent Office, *Specifications of Letters Patent No. 19,063*, Jan. 5, 1858.
13. Clark. Page 19.

First Ten Years of U.S. Patented Can Openers
1858-1868

The function of invented can openers – when they worked – was to open up a hole in the lid and enlarge it enough to get the contents out. Because the early cans usually had a patented closing, and came in a wide variety of shapes and sizes, there may have been need only for simple hooks, punches, or even just "hot water" to open cans such as the Manley in VIII-2-(R). Ezra Warner, and a number of other early patentees, specifically mention the disadvantage of hitting something hard enough to make it punch a hole in the lid because the contents would then splash out of the hole.

Collector Joe Young wrote up a list of the first 10 years of can opener patents granted in the United

States for an article in my newsletter in the 1980s. I combined his list with one that I had assembled in an earlier issue of the newsletter. Since the mid-1990s when the 4th edition of this book was published, the list has increased, with examples found during searches of the *Official Gazette of the Patent Office*. Jim and Phyllis Moffet, who are probably the most successful finders of unknown kitchen tools of all kinds, live very near a patent depository library and use it frequently. They uncovered several can opener patents for Joe Young.

I used to live in Toledo, OH, and NYC – both depository libraries. Now I only have a subject index of patents from 1790-1873 published many years ago. Searching this index is tedious. I looked under "can opener," "combination tool," "kitchen tool," "wrench," and others that looked possible; then I ran them through the patent number search online [see how-to near end of this book], but none of them "canned" out.

INVENTOR'S NAME	RESIDENCE	DATE	NUMBER
1. Ezra J. Warner	Waterbury, CT	1/05/1858	19,063 **
2. William C. Dick	New York, NY	11/01/1864	44,856
3. Charles A. Ruff	Providence, RI	3/07/1865	46,709
4. Samuel D. Lecompte	Leavenworth, KS	9/19/1865 Reissue 2/4/1868	50,011 *** RE2,851
5. Eben T. Orne	Chicago, IL	3/13/1866	53,173 ***
6. W. K. Baldwin	Chicago, IL	5/15/1866	54,668
7. O. J. Livermore	Worcester, MA	6/26/1866	55,878
8. Seth P. Chapin	Atlantic, NJ	7/17/1866	56,368
9. John Willard	Norwich, CT	8/21/1866	57,422 ***
10. J. Osterhoudt	New York, NY	10/02/1866	58,554 **
11. William McGill	Cincinnati, OH	1/08/1867	61,080 ***
12. S. O. Church[a]	West Meriden, CT	1/15/1867	61,161
13. Sineus E. Totten	Brooklyn, NY	1/22/1867	61,484
14. Thos. A. McFarland	Meadville, PA	5/21/1867	64,891
15. Frederick Seymour	Nashville, TN	6/18/1867	65,957 ***
16. W. L. Hubbell	Brooklyn, NY	10/22/1867	69,996
17. William H. Forker	Meadville, PA	10/29/1867	70,188
18. George A. Dickson	Woodcock Twnsp, PA	12/24/1867	72,464
19. Mark T. McCormick	Meadville, PA	4/07/1868	76,490 ***
20. Nathaniel F. Stone	Chicago, IL	4/14/1868	76,669
21. Charles F. Ritchel	Chicago, IL	5/12/1868	77,916 ***
22. F. S. Wyman	Chicago, IL	7/28/1868	80,326
23. Guy C. Humphrey[s]	Washington, DC	11/17/1868	84,122

a. Is it possible that the expression Church Key came from this?
** Patent models for these are known to exist.
*** Examples of these can openers are known to exist.

NOTE: The listings, which cover the first 10 years, were patented under various names, most commonly "Can opener" or "Tin can opener," although the patent subject index, and the patents themselves may have different headings. See list of headings below. • C. S. Osborn's can opener dates to 1854, and was made in Newark, NJ, but so far a patent for it has not been found. This may be the case for others.

Patent titles: (1) "Instrument for Opening Cans"; (2) "Improved Tool for Opening Tin Cans"; (3) "Improved Knife for Opening Tin Cans"; (4) "Instrument for Opening Fruit Cans"; (5) "Improved Tin-Can Opener"; (6) "Improved Machine for Opening Tin Cans"; (7) "Improved Can-Opener"; (8) "Improved Implement for Opening Sheet-Metal Cans and Boxes"; (9) "Improved Instrument for Opening Tin Cans"; (10) "Improved Method of Opening Tin Cans"; (11) "Improvement in Cork-Screws"; (12) "Improved Can-Opener" and within the text he calls it a "New Device for Opening Fruit Cans, &c."; (13) "Improvement in Can Opener" [sic]; (14) "Improvement in Can-Opener"; (15) "Improved instrument for opening sheet-metal cans"; (16) "Improvement in Can-Opener"; (17 "Improvement in Machine for Opening Cans"; (19) "Improved Tool for Opening Cans"; (20) "Improvement in Can-Opener" [sic], and Stone refers to Lecompte's patent; (21) "Improvement in Can Opener" [sic]; (22) "Improvement in Can-Opener," and Wyman refers to Lecompte's and also Chapin's patents; (23) "Improvement in Sheet-Metal Can and Box-openers."

❖ NOTES ❖

Can Opener Manufacturers in *Thomas' Register of American Manufacturers* and *House Furnishing Review Buyers Directories*. Note that it is very likely that companies other than those listed in *Thomas'* or *House Furnishing Review* made can openers. Small companies with very limited local distribution were perhaps left out. I always suspect that a commercial publications might have not listed some companies if they didn't advertise. Note that *Thomas'* list is alphabetical by state; *HFR* by company; also *HFR* gives some brand names – in parentheses here. A number of the listings in *HFR* are probably importers, not manufacturers, but I have no way of knowing; also it's likely that some of the listings from NYC and Chicago are showroom addresses, not where the actual factories are. Note also that I own all the *Thomas'* cited (the first was reprinted and is in the Bibliography), and that I just bought what was available to me. It is a yearly directory, still publishing, and unimaginably fascinating. The *HFR* listings were the ones I was able to see (and photocopy) at the New York Public Library, when the volumes were still intact, before being put on microfiche and making them extremely hard to use. Note the tiny number of listings in the 1930 *HFR* – especially compared to the one in 1915!

Thomas' **– 1905-06.** This list is from the *1905-06 Thomas' Register of American Manufacturers, Buying Guide.* • Bridgeport Hardware Mfg. Co.; and • Knapp & Cowles Mfg. Co., Bridgeport, CT • W. L. Barrett, Bristol, CT • L. D. Parkhurst, Danielson, CT • Brown & Dowd Mfg. Co., Meriden, CT • Landers, Frary & Clark, New Britain, CT • A. S. Henn & Co., New Haven, CT • American Cutlery Co.; and • Radecke Mfg. Co., Chicago, IL • Illinois Cutlery Co., Decatur, IL • Paxton Hardware Co., Paxton, IL • Sinclair Scott Co., Baltimore, MD • New England Specialty Co., North Easton, MA • Springfield Machine Screw Co., Springfield, MA • J. F. Bigelow Mfg. Co., Worcester, MA • Goodell Co., Antrim, NH • Kraeuter & Co.; C. S. Osborn & Co. [printed E. S. Osborn in directory]; and Frederick Sharp, all of Newark, NJ • Union Mfg. & Specialty Co., Buffalo, NY • Peck, Stow & Wilcox Co.; and Sargent & Co.; and Smith & Hemenway, all NYC • P. Kron; and N. R. Streeter & Co., Rochester, NY • Gibbs Mfg. Co., Canton, OH • Fred J. Meyers Mfg. Co., Hamilton, OH. Philadelphia Novelty Mfg. Co., Philadelphia, PA • Wrightsville Hardware Co., Wrightsville, PA • Stowell Mfg. & Foundry Co., South Milwaukee, WI. **HFR – 1909.** F. M. Bower Co., NYC • Bridgeport Hardware Mfg. Co. ("Matchless"), Bridgeport, CT • Brown & Doud Mfg. Co., Meriden, CT • The W. G. Browne Mfg. Co. ("I X L," "None Such," "Clipper," "Best"), Kingston, NY • Chick & Braconier, ("Chick") Rockford, IL • The Ellis Mfg. Co. "Dandy," "Ever Ready," "Little Giant"), Milldale, CT • Fletcher, Terry & Co. ("Sprague"), Forestville, CT • Fremont Crescent Metal & Mfg. Co., Fremont, OH • Graef & Schmidt, NYC • Handy Things Co. ("Handy"), Ludington, MI • Imperial Mfg. Co., Greendale, MA • F. W. Loll Mfg. Co., Meriden, CT • A. F. Meisselbach & Bro. ("Columbia"), Newark, NJ • Ontario Knife Co., Franklinville, NY • Phoenix Hardware Mfg. Co. ("Phoenix"), Homer, NY • Wm. Shimer

Sons & Co., Freemansburg, PA • Sitterly Novelty Works, Auburn, NY • Smith & Hemenway Co., NYC • Superior Mfg. Co., Detroit, MI •The Taylor Mfg. Co. ("Yankee," "Little Gem," "Nifty"), Hartford, CT • Ira F. White & Son ("Woods," "Sure Cut"), Newark, NJ **HFR – 1915.** American Cutlery Co. ("The Only"), Chicago, IL • Andrews Wire & Iron Works ("Chick," "North Pole," "Androck"), Rockford, IL • Arcade Mfg. Co., Freeport, IL • Arnold Woodenware Co., Cleveland, OH • Ault Wooden Ware Co., Cincinnati, OH • Bell Mfg. Co., Amsterdam, NY • The Beveridge Mfg. Co. ("Joy"), Baltimore, MD • John Bing, NYC • Bradley & Farnham ("Dandy," "Ever Ready," "Excelsior," "Hercules," "Little Giant," "Peerless"), Middlefield, CT • Bridgeport Hardware Co. ("Imperial," "Up-to-Date," "No. 5"), Bridgeport, CT • W. G. Brown Mfg. Co. ("The Best," "None Such," "I. X. L.," "Shear Cut Clipper," etc. [what *HFR* said]), Kingston, NY • Browne & Dowd Mfg. Co. ("Never–Slip," "XXX," "Diamond," "Crescent," "Sprague," "King," "Star"), Meriden, CT • Buffum Tool Co. ("Swastika"), Louisiana, MO • Cassady-Fairfank Mfg. Co., Chicago, IL • Cronk & Carrier Mfg. Co. ("Perfect"), Elmira, NY • George L. Curtiss Co., Southington, CT • Dean Wire Goods Co., Worcester, MA • Dover Stamping & Mfg. Co. ("Never Slip Monarch"), Cambridge, MA • Elles Mfg. Co., Milldale, CT • Fischer Bros. & Corwin, Newark, NJ • Fletcher Terry Co. ("Sprague"), Forestville, CT • Frank & Co., NYC • Fremont Crescent Metal & Mfg. Co., Fremont, OH • C. H. & E. S. Goldberg, NYC • Wm. Goldenblum & Co., NYC • Goodell Co., Antrim, NH • Graef & Schmidt ("Twin Brand"), NYC • L. F. Grammes & Sons, Allentown, PA • Grey Iron Casting Co., Mt. Joy, PA • Hamblin & Russell Mfg. Co. ("Ideal"), Worcester, MA • Handy Things Co. ("Handy"), Ludington, MI • Hardware Specialty Co. ("So Easy," "Ever Ready," "Clean Cut," "Picknick"), Chicago, IL • The Irwin Mfg. Co. ("Slick-Ope"), NYC • Knickerbocker Mfg. Co., Belleville, NJ • Kraeuter & Co., Newark, NJ • Landers, Frary & Clark, New Britain, CT • Lawrence Hardware Co. ("Hercules"), NYC • P. Lowentraut Mfg. Co., Newark, NJ • Mackie-Lovejoy Mfg. Co., Chicago IL • A. F. Meisselbach & Bro. ("Columbia"), Newark, NJ • G. E. Meissner & Bro., NYC • Nicol & Co. ("I. X. L."), Chicago • Norlund Novelty Co., Williamsport, PA • Ontario Knife Co., Franklinville, NY • C. S. Osborne & Co., Harrison, NJ • Parker Wire Goods Co. ("Ideal"), Worcester, MA • Peck & Mack Co., NYC • Perfect Specialty Co. ("Perfect, Jr."), Detroit, MI • Phoenix Hardware Mfg. Co. ("Phoenix"), Homer, NY • Plainfield Hardware & Mfg. Co. ("Easy"), Plainfield, NJ • A. P. Read Co. ("Read's"), Chicago, IL • Reading Saddle & Mfg. Co. ("Reading"), Reading, PA • Richard Stephen Co. ("S.R."), Southbridge, MA • Rockford Metal Specialty Co., Rockford, IL • Rocky Hill Hardware Co., Rocky Hill, CT • S. & I. Co., Springfield, MA • Schatz Mfg. Co. ("Acme," "Kan Kut"), North Poughkeepsie, NY • Shapleigh Hardware Co. ("Diamond Edge"), St. Louis, MO • J. M. Sherwood Co., NYC • Wm. Shimer, Sons & Co., Freemansburg, PA • Smith & Hemenway Co., NYC • I. S. Spencer's Sons, Newark, NJ • Sperry & Alexander Co. ("Centaur"), NYC • Sterling Hardware Co. ("Sterling"), NYC • N. R. Streeter & Co. ("Tip-Top,"

"Streeter's," "New Sprague," "American," "Suprise" [*sic.* May or may not have meant Surprise]), Rochester, NY • Superior Hardware Mfg. Co. ("Perfect"), Detroit, MI • Taplin Mfg. Co., New Britain, CT • Taylor Mfg. Co. ("Yankee," "Nifty," "Little Gem"), Hartford, CT • G. M. Thurnauer Co. ("Columbia," "Delmonica"), NYC • United Royalties Corp., NYC • Ira F. White & Son ("Sure Cut," "Bull Dog," "Woods"), Bloomfield, NJ • Wrightsville Hardware Co. ("Hopper"), Wrightsville, PA. *HFR 1930.* American Cutter Co., Milwaukee, WI • Edlund Co., Burlington, VT • Everts & Zuver, NYC • Samson-United Corp., Rochester, NY • G. M. Thurnauer Co., NYC • Utility Mfg. Co., Baltimore, MD • Vaughan Novelty Mfg. Co., Chicago. *Thomas' – 1932-33.* From *Thomas' Register of American Manufacturers.* Paschall Tool Co., Los Angeles, CA • Apex Mfg. Co., Oakland, CA • Star Can Opener Co., San Francisco, CA • Pugsley & Morrison, Yuba City, CA • H. C. Cook, Co., Ansonia, CT • Ellis Mfg. Co., Milldale, CT • Humphrey Mfg. Co.; North & Judd Mfg. Co.; Taplin Mfg. Co.; Sargent & Co.; and Voos Co., New Haven, CT • Turner & Seymour Mfg. Coop., Torrington, CT • Waterbury Button & Mfg. Co., Waterbury, CT • A & J Kitchen Tool Co.; Alto Mfg. Co.; Boye Needle Co.; Frederic Greer Co.; Indestro Mfg. Co.; Mackie-Lovejoy Mfg. Co.; Reliable Mfg. Co.; Vaughan Novelty Mfg. Co.; and P. C. West Mfg. Co., all Chicago • Arcade Mfg. Co., Freeport, IL • Moline Iron Works, Moline, IL • Gellman Mfg. Co., Rock Island, IL • Halsey Mfg. Co., Evansville, IN • Sinclair-Scott Co.; and Utility Mfg. Co., Inc., both Baltimore, MD • The Everredy Co., Frederick, MD • Hamblin & Russell Mfg. Co.; and Washburn Co. Wire Goods, both Worcester, MA • Enderes, Inc., Albert Lea, MN • R. Brownson & Co., Hastings, MN • Bouquet-Brownson Co., St. Paul, MN • Bunker-Clancey Mfg. Co., Kansas City, MO • Central States Mfg. Co.; Dazey Churn & Mfg. Co.; and Surety Mfg. Co., all St. Louis, MO • Goodell Co., Antrim, NH • White-Stumpfl Cutlery & Hardware Mfg. Co., Bloomfield, NJ • C. S. Osborne & Co., Harrison, NJ • Havell Mfg. Co., Irvington, NJ • Acme Metal Goods Mfg. Co.; William Johnson Inc.; and Newark Hardware Mfg. Co., all Newark, NJ • Ontario Knife Co., Franklinville, NY •

P. M. C. Mfg. Co., Kingston, NY • Louis A. Boettiger Co.; Consolidated Tool Works, Inc.; Gordon Mfg. Co.; J. A. Henckels; United Royalties Corp,; and Edward Weck & Co., all NYC, NY • Samson-United Corp., Rochester, NY • Morse Mfg. Co., Syracuse, NY • Braunschweiger Bros., Toledo, OH • United Sales Corp., Portland, OR • Grey Iron Casting Co., Mt. Joy, PA • Gem Stopper Co.; and Wm. Hodges & Co., both Philadelphia, PA • Forster Mfg. Corp., Pittsburgh, PA • Ennis Mfg. Co.; and Reading Saddle & Mfg. Co., both Reading, PA • Wrightsville Hardware Co., Wrightsville, PA • Edlund Co., Burlington, VT. *Thomas' – 1945.* From *Thomas' Register of American Manufacturers.* National Machine Products, Los Angeles, CA • Humphrey Mfg. Co.; North & Judd Mfg. Co.; and Taplin Mfg. Co., all of New Britain, CT • Voos Co., New Haven, CT • Turner & Seymour Mfg. Co., Torrington, CT • A & J Kitchen Tool Co.; Ace Mfg. Co.; EKCO Products Co.; Edward Katzinger Co.; Mackie-Lovejoy Mfg. Co.; Reliable Mfg. Co.; Swing-A-Way Steel Products; Vaughan Novelty Mfg. Co. (Vaughan advertised in *Thomas'* that they were the "world's largest manufacturer of openers for cans & bottles, with 50 different kinds & 14 types" that would "open any shape of can having standard rims"); and Zim Mfg. Co., all from Chicago • Moline Iron Works, Moline, IL • Sinclair-Scott Co., Baltimore; The Everredy Co., Frederick, MD • Hamblin & Russel Mfg. Co.; and Washburn Co., both Worcester, MA • Foley Mfg. Co., Minneapolis, MN • Rival Mfg. Co., Kansas City, MO • Dazey Corp.; and Steel Products Mfg. Co., both St. Louis, MO • Goodell Co., Antrim, NH • Acme Metal Goods Mfg. Co.; Newark Hardware Mfg. Co.; and C. T. Williamson Wire Novelty Co., all Newark, NJ • Regina Corp., Rahway, NJ • Uneeda Notions Mfrs., Long Island City, NY • Louis A. Boettiger Co.; Cahil Mfg. Co.; Graef & Schmidt, Inc.; and United Royalties Corp., all NYC • Allen Metal Products, Yonkers, NY • L. F. Grammes & Sons, Allentown, PA • Thompson Mfg. Co., Erie, PA • Wrightsville Hardware Co., Wrightsville, PA • Grey Iron Casting Co., Mt. Joy, PA • Reading Saddle & Mfg. Co., Reading, PA • G. G. Greene Mfg. Co., Warren, PA • Edlund Co., Burlington, VT • J. W. Speaker Corp., Milwaukee, WI.

Can opener, black painted cast iron, thick ring at business end, longish handle with large hang-up hole, circular blade, marked only "MARVEL," 7-1/4"L, blade is 2-5/8" diam., early 20th C. .... **$45+**

Can opener, black painted cast malleable iron, all vertical, loop handle, double blades in shape of arrowheads, "Heysinger's," 5-1/4"L, pat'd. Oct. 24, 1876. .... **$55+**

❖ NOTES ❖

Bull openers – One early major canned food was tinned beef, also called "bully beef" (at least by the British Army), but surprisingly, the first known patented can opener shaped like a bull, was pat'd. in 1875 by J. A. Wilson, of Chicago, IL. His and others of these openers – strong as a bull themselves – utilize a play on words. There are many variations, and they make a fun collection. Look for variations in expression, eyes, horns, hair detail, collar (not often present), tail, body shape, as well as variation in finish (plain iron, gilded,

bronzed, black). Because they are included in present-day container-loads of "smalls" from England, I assume that many of them are English. Perhaps they were exported from the U.S. to England? An example depicted in Evan Perry's *Collecting Antique Metalware* (London: Hamlyn, 1974) has a spike cast with the head, and the steel blade is marked with an undecipherable ironworks' name, plus "Sheffield," a famed center of cutlery manufacturing, and silver-plating, in England. One avenue of exploration would be for evidence that American manufacturers pirated the word "Sheffield" to imply fine-quality cutlery steel.

•   •   •

Two different sides. In the next listing, where the two screwed-together halves exhibit different carving details, one explanation is that the mold maker didn't use the same carving technique for both halves. It's more likely that a large manufacturing set-up would require many more than one carved mold casting model. Therefore, more than one carver would have made the models, and halves could have gotten separated, or one might be damaged, or the halves might be carelessly kept, and so castings from two disparate halves might end up together.

Can opener, bull's head with looped tail handle, cast iron (sometimes nickel plated, sometimes bronzed), English. Usually about 6" to 6-1/2"L, c.1870s through WWII at least. .... **$65+**

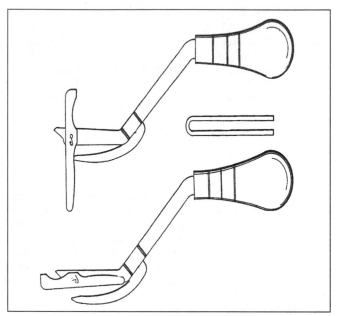

VIII-4. First known can opener patent, *called by the inventor "Instrument for Opening Cans," two views. Pat'd. Jan. 5, 1858 by Ezra J.* **Warner***, Waterbury, CT, #19,063. The tiller-like handle held the hand comfortably above but behind the working parts. The cutter blade is the curved piece at bottom; the piercing bar is the wide piece with truncated end from which is pivoted the swiveling piece Warner calls the "looped or swinging bar," shown vertical in* **(T)** *and horizontal in* **(B)***. Warner writes in his specs, "To use this instrument, I swing the loop bar substantially to the [vertical] position ... take hold of the handle, and press the point of the piercer-bar through the tin in the desired place, turn the instrument and insert the point of the curved cutter through the perforation already made, [at which time the looped, shaped bar goes to a horizontal position on top of the can, and the blade works up and down between its two sides], and work the handle in the manner of a brake. When the handle is moved up, the loop bar will be held against the surface of the tin, while the curved cutter will be forced between its parts and cut the tin smoothly through, and when the handle is moved down, the instrument may be pushed forward for another cut, and so on, thus allowing the operator to cut as fast as he can move his hand." He claimed also that "the piercer will perforate the tin without causing the liquid to fly out, as it does in all those which make the perforation by percussion of any kind." Warner also said that "a child may use it without difficulty, or risk." The cutter was removable so it could be replaced, or, presumably, sharpened. The patent model is known of this cutter, but so far no one has found a production piece.*

Can opener, bull's head & partial body, cast iron in 2 halves, very pronounced horns, particularly when seen from front, upper jaw's crosswise ridges look like teeth from side; blade & spike are one piece & screw in; interestingly, while the horns & ears are the same, the hair on the 2 halves is different – little details like this make this small area of collecting very interesting, spike is marked "H L 43," English, 6"L, late 19th to early 20th C. .... **$65+**
Can opener, bull's head with very curly hair, cast iron, 6"L, 19th C. .... **$60+**
Can opener, bull's head & partial body, cast iron in 2 halves, spike & blade one piece screwed in to head, not much detailing in casting, English, 6"L, late 19th C. or early 20th C. .... **$50+**
Can opener, bull's head & partial body, cast iron in 2 halves, spike cast in top of head, pleasant round eyes & ears, long hairs go straight back in line with body, English, 6"L, late 19th C. to 1930s? ...... **$65+**

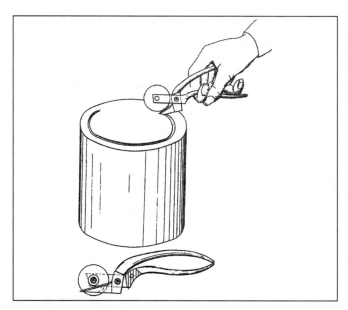

VIII-5. Second known can opener patent. *William C.* **Dick***, New York City, pat'd. this Nov. 1, 1864, as "Improved Tool for Opening Tin Cans," patent #44,856. It was comprised of a "pointed cutting-blade" attached to one shank or jaw, and "a grooved jaw attached to its other shank, in such a manner that the pointed cutting blade can be easily run through the top or any other part of a tin can, and by the action of its cutting-edge against the groove of the other jaw the sheet metal is readily and easily broken, and a hole can thus be cut in the pan large enough to give access to its contents." Dick claimed that "very little power is required to operate" it, and "a child is enabled to cut an opening in an ordinary tin box or can." Note: it seems hard to believe that once someone (Warner) had patented an "improved can opener" that there wasn't another one patented between 1858 and 1864 when this one was patented. Somewhere in there is a find waiting to be made – perhaps an early version of the simple opener issued by the U.S. Army (see VIII-38) – because the Civil War was underway during this period. Neither a patent model or production model is known.*

Can opener, cast iron, "Indestructo," early
20th C. (?).. **$10+**
Can opener, cast iron, "King," pat'd. 1895. .... **$15+**
Can opener, cast iron, "A. S. & Co., Columbia," – NY? or
PA? or CT?, pat'd. July 25, 1899. • There were many
towns & villages named Columbia all over the U.S.
by this time, the most likely manufacturing centers
for can openers being in NY, PA or CT. (Collector Bill
Griffiths has one marked "Columbia," like a Keen
Kutter handle & blade, with design patent by Meisselbach, Sept. 26, 1893. See the manufacturers' list-
ings above.).. **$70+**
Can opener, cast iron, cigar-shaped wood handle
stamped with name "Keen Kutter," Simmons Hardware Co., c. World War I. Griffiths has two with similar blades, different handles. Also another that has
a bottle opener. Crossover Keen Kutter collector
interest. .... **$45+**
Can opener, cast iron, counter top, possibly for a restaurant, maybe a big family's kitchen, with an eagle
on the top, mounted to heavy block of wood. This is
a double opener that will open short cans on the
side, taller cans in the back. Long curved lever
works a small blade in the front to open a tuna fish
size can, while the back blade is large & sort of heart
shaped. I thought this was Enterprise, because of
the eagle, but it doesn't appear in any known Enterprise catalog. 7-1/2"H; lever is 12"L. Bill Griffiths
believes this is probably the Williams' patents of
Jan. 8, 1878, and Oct. 29, 1878. .... **$600+**

VIII-6-B. Can opener patent. *Pat'd. May 21, 1867
by Thomas A.* **McFarland,** *Meadville, PA, patent
#64,891. For opening oyster, fruit and other tin cans
– "a cheap, simple, and effective implement for cutting an opening in a can by a single blow" by its
"curved pointed teeth" which enter the lid easily,
and as it is forced downward "the cutting continues, the cutting edges expand until they meet ...
and thus punch out a ... disk or plug" of lid. McFarland wrote "I am aware that it has been proposed
to open cans by the use of a single cutter operating
like the single blade of a shear; ... also that cutters
have been used in combination with separate
spring handles sliding through a ring, and thus
compressing the cutters to cut a plug out of a cork."
Official Gazette. This and most other patent drawings that follow represent pieces that might or might
not have been manufactured. Values for these
patent "ghosts" are speculative. If it exists:* **$45+**

❖ NOTES ❖

Heavyweight Champion Can Opener – Bill Griffiths wrote me about a really rare model of the Enterprise: instead of an eagle, it has a figure of the famous
heavyweight champion boxer John L. Sullivan on top.
Champion for an entire decade, 1882 to 1892, Sullivan
fought the last bare knuckle title bout in 1888. This is
probably a commemorative piece, either from 1888 or
1892. Crossover knockout appeal. It's worth at least:
$1,000+

Can opener, cast iron, handle has cross-hatch knurling
pattern like Disston tools, adjustable blade, no
mark, maybe Disston, 5-1/2"L including blade,
poss. #2080, pat'd. April 19, 1887................. **$20+**
Can opener, cast iron, adjustable blued steel blade,
round ridged wheel with crosspieces (looks just like
miniature steering wheel), center pin was punched
into can's center, then cutting blade moved to position
at edge of can – whatever the can's diameter (within
reason). Name & date cast into crosspieces: "Hopper's
Can Opener," about 4-3/8" diam., marked "Pat. Dec.
22, 1896." This was Charles S. Hopper's first can
opener patent.. **$95+**
Can opener, cast iron, longer steel blade with greater
adjustability, looks pretty much same as earlier version, slightly finer-looking casting of outer wheel-
like ring with 4 spokes and sort of scalloped edges as
if they were very worn gear teeth, marked on cross-
pieces "Hopper's Can Opener," with date, pat'd. Oct.
3, 1899. This was Hopper's second patent. 4-1/2"
diam. [Note: Another, probably later, version is identical but for the marked snappy new name, "Safety
First." Mfd. by Cuspidore Mfg. Co., Newark, NJ, and
possibly others.].. **$75+**

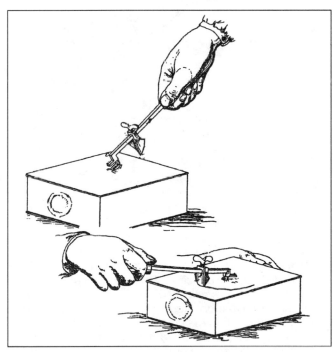

VIII-6-A. Can opener patent. *Frederick* **Seymour,**
*Nashville, TN, pat'd. this June 18, 1867, as "Improved
Instrument for Opening Sheet-Metal Cans." Patent
#65,957. This one is very like some later can openers
with its adjustable cutter. Seymour writes in his specs
that the disk cut from the tin was "preserved from
dropping into or escaping out of the can." This and the
VIII-7 show what we would call a box, but which was
used for preserving some kinds of food. A production
model of this opener is known.*

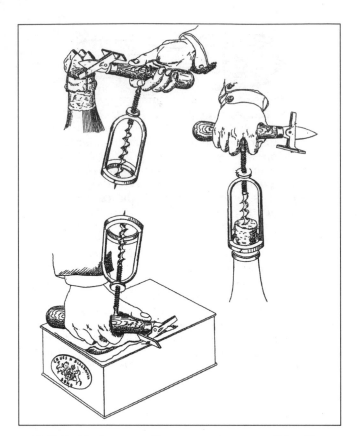

VIII-7. Corkscrew & can opener combination patent, *Jan. 8, 1867, #61,080. William C.* **McGill** *patented this device as an "Improvement in Cork-Screws" used "for Cutting Wires, Drawing Corks, &c.," with an adaptive use for opening cans. The sketched embossed label or cartouche seen on the end of the box says "Cross & Blackwell Bros.," a famous company from the U.K., but McGill was from Cincinnati, OH. A production model is known.*

Can opener, cast iron loopy handle with tool steel blade, "Peerless," 6-1/2"L, Schofield patent, Feb. 11, 1890 (same patent date as "Delmonico"). [Note: The "Peerless" combo bottle & can openers/knife sharpeners below in "Combination tools" are a different patent. Another interesting note: Collector Alan Wilder has a can opener like this that definitely is marked "Fearless" and "Made in U.S.A." A mystery to investigate.] .... **$15+**

Can opener, cast iron, skinny short snake of curved metal with blade, with screwed on simple cutting blade, "The Delmonico," 7"L, pat'd. Feb. 11, 1890, by Schofield (same date as one of "Peerless"). Collector Joe Young says the manufacturer probably tried to capitalize on the name of the popular NYC restaurant. He and his wife also have a champagne tap marked "The Delmonico." .... **$15+**

Can opener, cast iron, mechanical, "Bunker Clancy," late 19th or early 20th C. Please ID this for me if you can. .... **$25+**

Can opener, cast iron, mounted on its original card, "Vaughn's Safety Roll Junior," Chicago, IL, 20th C. .... **$12+**

Can opener, iron, with corkscrew, "Opens All," mfd. by Vaughan, 1930s. Just one of many Vaughn openers .... **$10+**

VIII-8. Can opener. *Called a* **sardine opener,** *"to open tin boxes of sardines, preserved meats, preserves, &c." Wood & steel, and surprisingly modern in design. American Home Cook Book, 1854; this opener may actually be an English import, as its appearance in that book predates the first patented American can opener by four years. See the English can openers in VIII-36; their handles are turned in much more modern style, but the works appear very similar.* **$10+**

Can opener, cast iron, openwork handle has sliding blade to adjust to different can sizes, "World's Best," Pittsburgh, PA, 6-3/4"L, pat'd. June 6, 1899 by Frederick C. Smalstig, Allegheny, PA. Collector Bill Griffiths has this with 4 different logos. • Very similar to the "U.S. Can Opener," and because both were made in Pittsburgh, probably one is an improvement or later edition of the other. .... **$40+**

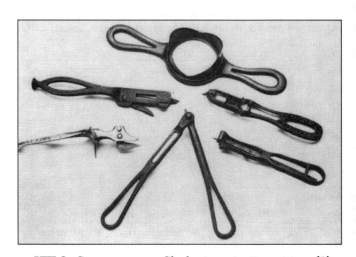

VIII-9. Can openers. *Clockwise, starting at top:* **(1)** *Cast iron & steel, 2 handles, pushed into lid then rotated to cut off whole top. 10"L.* **(2)** *Cast iron & steel, sliding adjustment for blade, embossed* **"World's Best,** *Pittsburgh, PA," 6-3/4"L, pat'd. 6/6/1899 by Frederick C. Smalstig, Allegheny, PA.* **(3)** *Cast iron & steel, (very like #2) marked on it:* **"U.S. Can Opener,** *Made in Pittsburgh PA, Pat'd. May 7, 1895." 6"L. Collector Joe Young says this is a Smalstig & Mayer patent of 8/4/1896.* **(4)** *Cast iron, 2 pivoting handles. Poke tip in, swivel it around. Marked only "patent applied for." 7-3/4"L.* **(5)** *Nickel plated cast iron, steel, 6-1/2"L, "The* **Safety,"** *Coles' patent, May 12, 1914.* **(6)** *Cast iron, pointed tip at right was punched into can's top by tapping on little knob at other end with small hammer. 7-5/8"L. Unmarked, but identified as the* **"Elgin Wood"** *(Toronto, Canada), Wood (or Woodward?) patent, Aug. 19, 1890. All six located by the Primitive Man, Bob Cahn, Carmel, NY.* **(1) $200; (2) $40+; (3) $40; (4) $45+; (5) $30+; (6) $40+**

Can opener, cast iron, sliding blade adjusts to fit different size cans, not very spectacular to look at, but still a nice one, "U.S. Can Opener," Pittsburgh, PA, 6"L, Smalstig patent, May 7, 1895................... **$40+**

Can opener, cast iron ring, with ratchet clamp to hold can, separate cutter on another pivoting ring, long loopy handles, "Champion," maybe a Peterson patent (?), pat'd. 1873..................................... **$85+**

Can opener, cast iron; the knob at end opposite sharp pointed blade serves as place for tapping with hammer to drive point in before starting to cut, very graceful & interesting, unmarked, American, 7-5/8"L, late 19th C. .... **$35+**

Can opener, cast iron & tool steel, vertical mechanical type, 2 blades – one rounded, one straight for sardine cans, lever attaches to either of 2 pivot points, seems to be marked either "Bleakley" (?) or "Blakesley" (?), American, about 16" to 18"H, pat'd. May 1888 (?). Collector Bill Griffiths says it doesn't fit either Blakesley patent he knows – April 28, 1891, nor June 25, 1869. I don't have a picture, just notes from an antique show. I don't think this is a "phantom" can opener, and am listing it in hopes of clearing up mystery... **$125+**

Can opener, cast iron, has adjustable blade in sliding frame, big "nail head" or spike on end to pound hole into can top, and a great screw-action works, with rat-sized "Mickey Mouse" ears on a disc, "Baumgarten," American, 9-3/4"L, 1896. This description is

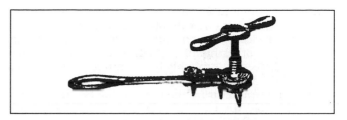

VIII-11. Can openers. (T) Cast iron mechanical type, with large turning screw something like Baumgartner opener. Spikes & blade underneath. Marked only "Pat. Appl. For" on handle. 7-1/2"L. This is either the patent of Oscar E. **Braconier** (Rockford, IL), Dec. 8, 1908, or the **Lyons** patent of Dec. 4, 1888, depending on who you ask! Collection of Peggy Wainscott. *(B)* The **Baumgartner** side cutter, pat'd. in Canada, 1896. As shown 9-3/4"L. Ex-Keillor Family Collection. A similar opener with 3 "ears" is marked "ABC PAT NOV 27, '94" – fits a Bien patent, but looks different. **$150+**

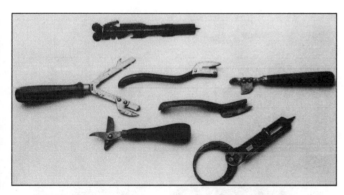

VIII-10. Can openers. From left (1) Most unusual is the Y-shaped slingshot-like one. Steel, turquoise wood handle. 7-1/2"L. This had 2 different handle styles. Both marked "Pat. Pend." *(2)* To me, neatest is top combo: knife sharpener between eye-like wheels, glasscutter, can & jar or crown cap bottle opener. *(3)* Center, serpentine handle, painted cast iron, steel blade. "The **Improved Peerless**, Austria, U.S. Patent Pending"; *(4)* Just below it, also with curved handle, is cast iron "**Delmonico**," with crosshatched handle, pat'd. Feb. 11, 1890 by Schofield; *(5)* at right: simple, fat wood handle, large blade, mfd. by **Cassady-Fairbanks**, Chicago; *(6)* Combo tool with circular jar wrench, mfd. by "J. C. **Forster** & Son, Pittsburgh." Pat'd. Sept. 13, 1910. 6-3/4"L. *(7)* Big blade & pivoting guide, shaped wood handle. Meant primarily for opening square or oblong cans, as of sardines. c.1880s. Probably a **Sprague** variant, pat'd. Jul. 21, 1874. Collector Bill Griffiths has one with a cast iron loop handle. All Collection of Meryle Evans. *(1) $10; (2) $15+; (3) $15+; (4) $15; (5) $20; (6) $15+; (7) $30+*

from the only one I've handled – from the Keillor Family Collection – back in 1973, so I can't check. Collector Bill Griffiths writes: "A similar opener, with 3 ears on top is marked 'ABC Pat Nov 27 '94.'" He says that a "Baumgartner" opener in his collection has part of a patent date near the center hub "Nov 2....," and wonders if the ABC and this "Baumgartner/Baumgarten" patent are the same. .... **$150+**

Can opener, mechanical, cast iron, with handle something like a skillet handle, fitted onto end with a vertical screw, & several sharp points underneath, similar to the Baumgarten patent opener, only mark is "Pat Appl For," American, 7-1/2"L, c.1900. Lyons' patent, Dec. 4, 1888.................................... **$100+**

Can opener, cast iron with gritty cast no-slip surface on handle, simple pointed blade, curved handle, no marks, 6-3/4"L, c.1900. .... **$12+**

Can opener, malleable cast iron with 2 long, openwork, two loopy pivoting handles, one has adjustable blade in it to fit the size of the can; poke tip in center, adjust blade to match the lid's radius, and while holding one handle stationary as a sort of lever against which you can push, you swivel the other handle with the cutting blade around, American, 7-3/4"L, marked "patent applied for," late 1880s. • See next two entries... **$35+**

Can opener, malleable cast & sheet iron, with 2 openwork "loop" handles, opposite each other on the outside of the cutting blade, a full circle of sharpened iron, push down circular blade on can lid & rotate entire opener, while pushing downward, no mark, but surely the one mfd. by Lehman, Bowman [seen as Bolen in at least one record] & Co., of Decatur, IL, 10"L, advertised c.1890 as their "No. 3," so fits with the John Kaylor patent date of May 7, 1889. .. **$80+**

Can opener, malleable cast iron, with 2 pivoting loopy handles – upper one with steel cutting blade that you push in circle around can top, with lower ring as guide, the other handle, which is attached to a ring-shaped piece that roughly fits within top of can, has a point at end opposite handle. That pointed piece is a punch for puncturing the can top to start the cutting and to hold the can. Ad copy says this is a "double lever patent can **opener & holder, combined.** You hold the can firm with one handle, while you cut the top out with one stroke with the other." A little rickety – from age or imperfect manufacture, but terrific looking. Ads identify this as "Lehman #9," mfd. by G. W. Lehman & Co. (later? Lehman, Bolen & Co.), Decatur, IL, 8-1/2"L with ring 3-1/4" diam., no mark except John Kaylor patent date, May 7, 1889. .. **$85+**

❖ NOTES ❖

Malleable cast iron – I feel uncomfortable using this term without a clear understanding of how to look at something and know if it's plain cast pig iron or malleable cast iron. The latter has less carbon in it than pig iron but more than wrought iron, and is extremely "malleable" or workable by hammering or rolling. When I have found documentation for an object, such as an ad, booklet or flyer, and the metal is described as "malleable cast iron," I have added it to the description (of what I count as only 25 pieces in this whole book). One source describes it as an "alloy of steel." Another has a simple definition that states "Malleable iron is able to be shaped or formed by hammering or pressure." An editorial answer to query in the May 31, 1890 *Metal Worker*, says that "The work of making malleable iron castings necessarily involves considerable time, and they cannot be turned out with the rapidity of gray castings." This was to explain the higher cost. The most important aspect when using malleable cast iron for a can opener which had to be tapped into the can lid, is that it can keep its strength and integrity when subjected to "hammering or pressure." Therefore, an object with a lever action, for example, could hold up well without fracturing like ordinary cast iron might, and without tending to bend, as some wrought iron might if the pressure were great enough. An economic advantage is that casting is cheaper than forging, and scrap is an integral part of the alloy. • Many, probably most, modern objects made of cast iron, unless otherwise noted, are made with re-founded scrap cast iron. This scrap, which is composed in great part of old cracked car engine blocks, will not be "picked over" before founding, and so will also contain small quantities of aluminum and brass.

Can opener, countertop for restaurant, cast iron with deep-blue painted spool-like wooden handle, "Heavy Duty Can Opener, No. A-123," also No. 134, mfd. by Dazey Churn Co., St. Louis, MO, 12-1/2"H x 11-1/2"W, 20th C. .... **$50+**

Can opener, crowing rooster, cast iron, American, 20th C. .... **$15+**

Can opener, fish, cast iron, blade set in with screw to remove for sharpening, English, 5"L, late 19th C. .... **$80+**

Can opener, fish, like a sardine, with slender slightly curved body, dark-green-painted cast iron, very

VIII-12. Can opener. *Cast iron mechanical type. Looks like a Nardi steering wheel! Marked* "**Safety First**." *Mfd. by the Cuspidore Mfg. Co., Newark, NJ; there may have been other manufacturers too. This is Charles S.* **Hopper** *(Philadelphia, PA) second patent, of Oct. 31, 1899. (Hopper's first patent was Dec. 12, 1896.) 4-1/4" diam. Collection of Peggy Wainscott.* **$75+**

exaggerated and beautiful scales & front fins, gills bold too, large ring around eyes (where blade can be unscrewed for cleaning or sharpening), rather small tail ending in large ball, no mark, English, 4"L, c.1870s. .... **$90+**

VIII-13. Can opener. *Cast iron, V-blade, cast eagle on top. (Mounted to wood for stability here.) This is a double opener – small short cans cut on side seen here; taller cans in the back. Snaky lever works small blade in front to open a tuna fish-size can. Large, heart-shaped blade in back. Only 7-1/2"H with 12"L lever. (Eagle once made me wonder if this were an Enterprise Mfg. Co. product, but the U.S. Centennial spawned many patriotic motifs.) Pat'd. by Chas. M.* **Williams**, *Bethel, KY, Jan. 8, 1878. Collection of Meryle Evans. (Note: A less elegant, somewhat newer V-opener exists, with open diamond shape on top, that may be the H. J. Schmidt patent, Aug. 12, 1913, where eagle is here. $300+. See text for amazing John L. Sullivan version!)* **$600+**

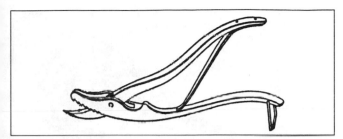

VIII-14. Can opener patent. *Pat'd. May 29, 1877 by David F. Fetter, NYC. A "pair of spring-pliers, with a slotted convex jaw, notched or serrated on either side of the slot, and pivoted therein; a curved blade having concave cutting-edge, terminating in an upwardly-turned point; the handles authoritatively thrown open by a spring, and held together, when not in use, by a wire loop at their extremities." Official Gazette. Compare this with the Wheeler Patent Co. opener in the next picture.*

Can opener, flat wood handle, brass ferrule, marked "T N & S," English, 6-1/2"L, c.1890s-1910. .... **$20+**

Can opener, flat wood handle, bulbous head, brass ferrule, cutting blade marked "Wynn & Timmins," English, 6"L, c.1900 .... **$20+**

Can opener, flat sided shaped wood handle that's flat sided – probably flattened after turning on lathe, steel blade, "Midget," American, 6-1/8"L, (another reported was only 5-3/4"L), White & Winkler patent, July 19, 1904. .... **$20+**

Can opener – called a sardine opener, for sardine cans, tempered tool steel blade in turned wooden handle, with distinctive & typical sardine-opener's long evil-looking blade, prob. American, about 8"L, 1870s. (Some sardine openers have a scissor action, and have a leaf spring between the two handles to facilitate cutting.) .... **$20+**

Can opener, sort of like sardine [can] shears, a levered, 2 handle iron & steel cutter which gnawed its way through the tin after a starter hole was made, tension of handles achieved with a leaf spring. They claimed it could be used for cutting stovepipe also.

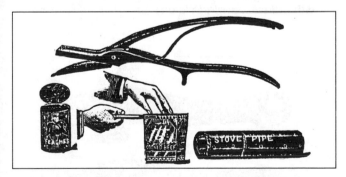

VIII-15. Can opener. *Cutlery steel blade, malleable iron handles, steel spring. Mfd. by **Wheeler Patent Can Opener Co.**, St. Louis, MO, and introduced in mid 1890. Looks very like the Fetter patent. Makers claimed the Wheeler "is the only can opener that will cut off the top of paint pails. ... It cuts stove pipe, tin pipe, &c." Also cut square cans (center corned beef can below). The Metal Worker, 1890. $30+*

VIII-16. Can opener. *One of three malleable cast iron openers pat'd. May 7, 1889 by John Kaylor, assigned to G. W. Lehman, Decatur, IL. This is the **Lehman No. 3**. After point at bottom left side of ring is stuck into top of can near the edge, the opener is "pressed down upon the top of the can until the spur [blade] penetrates the top. Then the moving handle is rotated and the top is cut off." Mfd. by G. W. Lehman & Co., later Lehman, Bowman & Co. Their No. 1 and No. 2, with wingnuts on top, are seen in VIII-17. $85+*

Wheeler Patent Can Opener Co., St. Louis, MO, introduced 1890.. **$30+**

Can opener, green enameled wood handles, one to hold, one to turn, steel mechanism & blade, "Edlund Junior," mfd. by Edlund Co., Burlington, VT, 6-1/4"L, pat'd. April 21, 1925, May 12, 1925, June 18, 1929. .... **$12+**

Can opener, hardened steel hooked blade, simple turned wood handle, ferrule, "Handy," mfd. by Handy Things Mfg. Co., Ludington, MI, Franken patent, June 11, 1895..................................... **$15+**

Can opener, iron, "The Jewel." Found with several different logos. Pat'd. July 10, 1923. .... **$15+**

Can opener, iron, "Lowe," early 20th C.(?). .... **$10+**

Can opener, iron, loop-handled, with corkscrew folded inside handle, "Dixie," 1930s............................. **$5**

Can opener, iron, with gears, "Enbay," early 20th C.(?). .... **$20+**

Can opener, iron with wood handle, "Clean Cut," early 20th C.(?). .... **$10+**

VIII-17. Can openers. *Two **Lehman** top openers, with wingnuts, based on Kaylor patent of May 7, 1889. No. 1 **(L)** is at top of piece of stationery dated July 8, 1890, No. 2 **(R)** appears on a business card. From photocopies of ephemera in the Phyllis & Jim Moffet Collection. The ephemera almost as valuable as the real things. $85+*

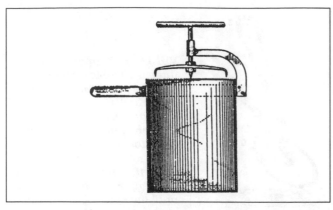

VIII-18. Can opener patent. *Pat'd. Aug. 30, 1887 by William J.* **Hammer***, Boston, MA. A "spring clasping-holder" with handle, and a "standard extending over the top with a pointed turning rod sliding through" it, and a "knife," with a blade at each end, moved by the turning handle above. Looks extremely efficient. Official Gazette.*

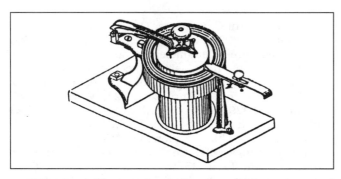

VIII-19. Can opener patent. *Pat'd. Dec. 29, 1885 by Charles W.* **Acker***, Watertown, NY. Patent application was accompanied by a patent model. This one includes a frame into which the can sits, while the blade is carried by a rotary ring above. Official Gazette.*

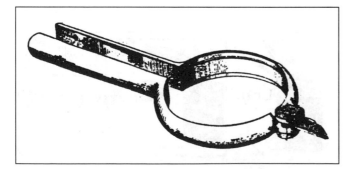

VIII-20. Can opener patent. *Combined jar-wrench & can-opener, pat'd. June 9, 1885 by Alexander* **Van Slyke***, Fort Plain, NY. The wrench part is easy to see, but heaven knows how it cuts a can's top unless the handles are used like levers to advance the blade seen at the fulcrum. (More jar wrenches in Canning chapter.) Official Gazette.*

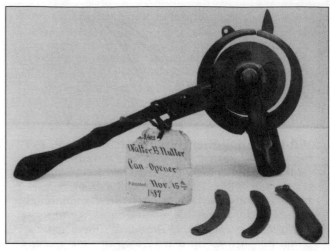

VIII-21. Can opener patent model. *Cast iron, adjustable. According to tag, the patent was applied for on Nov. 15, 1887 by Walter B.* **Nutter***. Appears to fit over top of can, and worked with rotary motion. Pieces in foreground look like size adaptors – one on right may be a blade. Picture courtesy of the National Museum of American History, Smithsonian Institution. Possible value if opener was ever made: $300+. Value of patent model:* **$1,000+**

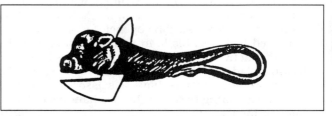

VIII-22. Can opener *or* **tin opener***, as it would be called in its native England. Cast iron bull's head, with looped tail. Spike & blade one piece of steel, adjustable or removable for cleaning. 6"L. 19th C. There are many variations on this – enough for a herd. Many have spikes cast as part of iron body, with adjustable blade (lower "jaw") of steel.* **$65+**

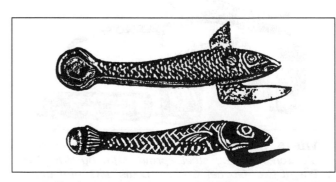

VIII-23. Can openers. *Cast iron fish.* **(T)** *Adjustable blade & spike-in-one. Probably English. 5"L. Late 1800s.* **(B)** *Well-defined scales and eye, original dark green paint. Only 4"L. Meant for opening sardine or herring tins. English. 3rd or 4th quarter 19th C.* **$75+**; **$90+**

VIII-24. Advertisement. *Franco-American can shows one version of a can ready-made for easier opening. One tactic used to complement the search for better can openers was to make cans themselves easier to open. Century, May 1893.*

VIII-25. Can opener. *The "Best Yet," mfd. by Hasbrouck Alliger, NYC, pat'd. Jul. 29, 1890. Malleable iron, steel blade. Point is driven into the top near center, then it's levered down to almost horizontal position to force chisel-like blade into rim. Then, holding the*

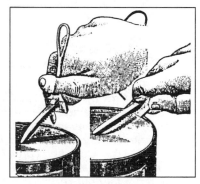

two parts firmly in the right hand, while holding the can in the left, one "carries the two handles around in a circle" as one either cuts off one's left thumb or the can's lid. Alliger claimed "It is so shaped that the blade will not work up, and [it] has no thumbscrew ... but fastens in the desired place by an automatic lock." The Metal Worker, Aug. 30, 1890. **$30+**

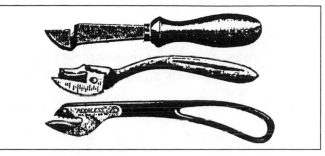

VIII-26. Can opener. (T) *"The **Acme**," mfd. by the Goodell Co., Antrim, NH. "The blade is alluded to as being made of extra quality steel, and not to be confounded with the Cheap John affairs, of which there are many. ... It is designed to open any shaped can; to cut close to the edge, allowing the contents to be removed without breaking. The bend in the blade allows the handle to come down on the outside of the can, to secure a long leverage and a long cut." Wooden handle. Made by one of the best companies, so it probably was good. The Metal Worker, Jul. 5, 1890.* **(M)** *"The "**Stand-by**," steel blade riveted on, not adjustable. c.1899.* **(B)** *"**Peerless**," pat'd. Feb. 11, 1890, by Scofield. An editorial note in House Furnishing Review, Jan. 1903, stated "This is truly an age of little conveniences and ... here is one of those little devices that save the housewife time and trouble, and probably her husband much profanity." Nickel plated, cutlery steel blade riveted to loop handle, toothed gripper "to prevent slipping."* **(T) $10+; (M) $5+; (B) $15+**

Can opener, iron & wood, "A & J Miracle," Binghamton, NY, 6-1/4"L, 1930s. The all-metal one is slightly less. .... **$10+**

Can opener, nickeled steel shaft, tempered steel blade, turned wood handle, "A & J," Edward Katzinger Co., Chicago, IL, 8-1/2"L, 1940. .... **$10+**

Can opener, syrup cans, metal, with little lifting spout slightly inset to catch drips, "For Karo Cans Only," very small, pat'd. 1935. .... **$15+**

Can opener, nickel plated iron, very modern-looking, with graceful curve, & relatively big head, "The Safety" marked on end of handle, American, 6-1/2"L, Cole's patent, May 12, 1914. .... **$30+**

Can opener, pistol-shaped, loop handle, cast iron, adjustable steel blade, American, 8-1/4"L diagonally, Way & Clarke patent, Mar. 9, 1886. ...... **$85+**

Can opener, plated & black painted cast iron, adjustable, long shaft with round head with 3 big ribs, "ABC," 7"L in closed up position, 9-1/2"L fully extended, Blen patent, Nov. 27, 1894. .... **$125+**

Can opener, rearing horse, cast iron, American, 20th C. .... **$55+**

Can opener, screw clamps on shelf or table edge, nickeled iron works with horizontal gears, blue wood knob, "Blue Streak," Turner & Seymour Mfg. Co., Torrington, CT, 4"H x 7"L, pat'd. Oct. 1, 1921, Aug. 8, 1922, & Apr. 10, 1923. Sold into 1930s. • Patented 7 years before 1st wall-mount opener. .... **$20+**

Can opener, several small triangular steel blades to puncture can, turned wood handle with mushroom-like knob, J. Kaufman, NYC, NY, 6"L x 3-1/4" diam., Kaufman patent, Sept. 6, 1870....................... **$95+**

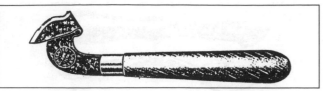

VIII-27. Can opener. *"Handy," made of hardened steel, for round or square cans. An "improved" version of original pat'd. June 11, 1895, by Robert Franken, Pico Heights, CA. Mfd. by Handy Things Mfg. Co., Ludington, MI, and sold originally for only a nickel! House Furnishing Review, Jan. 1903. It's sometimes marked, sad to say, "KKK" – for Kalifornia Kan Kutter.* **$15+**

Can opener, skeletal steel frame, point at smaller end for sticking in center of can, then the cutting blade can be moved along slide of shaft to fit can's radius, then whole thing is rotated to cut off most of lid, marked on sliding blade part "Hercules" with Hawks' patent date, Aug. 12, 1902. (See the "Peerless" openers too.) • I wonder what the tetanus or botulism death rates were when such openers were in wide use? At least nobody trade-named an opener "The Lockjaw." .... **$15+**

Can opener, steel blade & malleable cast iron, 2 parts, with long handle & toothed piece, plus a shorter handle with chisel-like blade. The tip of long piece is stuck into middle of can, then the chisel blade is moved along the teeth until the blade lines up with edge of can. It is then stuck into can top at edge, and pushed down to lock into position. Then it is pulled around the can top, presumably while turning the can counterclockwise with left hand. Could be used only with right hand, and does not live up to name at all. "Best Yet," Hasbrouck Alliger, NYC, NY, pat'd. Jul. 29, 1890. .... **$30+**

Can opener, steel, long black painted wooden handle, "Sterling," 7-1/2"L, Duncan patent Aug. 26, 1902. .... **$20+**

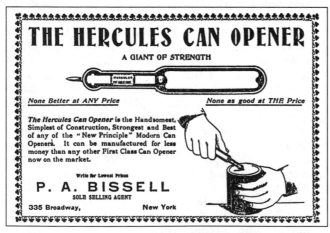

VIII-28. Can opener. *"Hercules" – "A Giant of Strength." Pat'd. Aug. 12, by M. L. Hawks. Skeletal steel with adjustable blade position. Manufacturer unknown, although a company named Bradley & Farnham was making a "Hercules" can opener at about that time. House Furnishing Review, Feb. 1904.* **$15+**

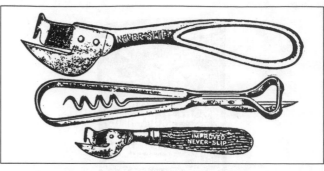

VIII-29. Can openers. *(T) All-metal loop handle version of the "Never Slip" – one of many similar openers meant to give a good grip and a leveraged cutting angle. Browne & Benton patent, May 17, 1892, mfd. by Dover Co.; (M) simple all steel "King" combo corkscrew & can opener. A cheaper version of it (not shown) is the "Dean." (B) Wooden handled "Improved Never-Slip" version, pat'd. 1895. All in April 1905 catalog of Joseph Breck & Sons, Boston.* **$10+; $5+; $5+**

Can opener, steel, of type sold at the grocery now, a real cheapo type that actually works well, "Tilt-Top O-Matic," American, 3"L, c.1920....................... **$5+**

Can opener, steel with turned wood handle, brass ferrule, riveted 2-part blade with snub "nose" marked "ERIE, 227,761." Mfd. by Griswold Mfg. Co., Erie, PA, c.1930s according to David Smith. The number, which looks like a patent number, is for a pump in 1880 .... **$150+**

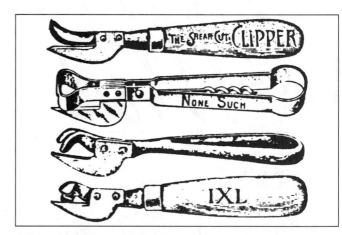

VIII-30. Can openers. *Variety, two all metal, two with wooden handles – all made by same company, W. G. Browne Mfg. Co., Kingston, NY, who also made ice picks, potato mashers, tack hammers & "The Cyclone" eggbeater. (T) "The Shear Cut Clipper;" (M-1) "None Such" with crown cap opener & fold-out corkscrew. (Browne's best seller – "The Best" – opened crown caps & corks too, and it looks like the "None Such" except there's a bottle cap hook on top.) (M-2) All metal one with a tack puller; (B) "IXL." House Furnishing Review, Oct. 1902. (Note: There's a "Clipper" patent from 1926, but this one was pictured & named 24 years earlier.)* **$10+**

VIII-31. Can opener. *"Sure Cut," long shank with sliding blade, wooden handle, for round & square cans. Pat'd. Jul. 19, 1904. by White & Winkler. Mfd. by Ira F. White & Son, Newark, NJ. Came in several different sizes. House Furnishing Review, May 1906.* **$15+**

Can opener, steel with turned wood handle, and sliding piece on shaft, "Vulcan Cut Can & Bottle Opener," American, 8-7/8"L, 1910. .... **$15+**

Can opener, steel, wood handle, "Sure Cut," came in several sizes, White & Winkler patent, July 19, 1904. .... **$15+**

Can opener, steel & wood, mark on blade is a small diamond with "SR" inside, also a shield that says "Our Label" above it, and "M. P. B. D. BM. & S. W. U. of N. A." which John Lambert, a few years ago, guessed might stand for "Massachusetts Professional Bottlers and Professional Bottle-Makers Brotherhood & Skilled Workers Union of North America." Inside is motto "Unity, Mutual Assistance and Education." Marked by manufacturer's (?) name: "S. Richard, Southbridge, MA," 5-7/8"L, late 19th C. Collector Bill Griffiths has two, only one with the shield & initials. Did Richard make them for different groups?........................ **$25+**

Can opener, tinned or nickel plated steel with turned wooden handle, painted turquoise (some found with

VIII-32. Can opener. *"Joy" – "One Shove Does the Act" (sounds like a "Lieutenant Columbo" episode!). Metal with wooden grip. If kept sharp, it probably worked very well. Mfd. by Beveridge Mfg. Co., Baltimore, where tin-canning got started 150 years ago. House Furnishing Review, Feb. 1915.* **$50**

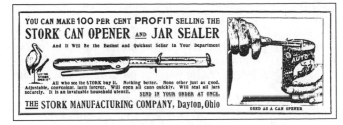

VIII-33. Can opener. *"Stork" combo can opener & jar sealer. All metal. Consists of a movable slide inserted in a handle. One side has flanges to grip the jar top when lever in handle is pressed. Mfd. by The Stork Mfg. Co., Dayton, OH. House Furnishing Review, May 1905.* **$10+**

clear lacquered finish), shaped like a slingshot "Y," 7-1/2"L, marked "Pat. Pend." – prob. 1930s. **$20**

Can opener, unusual 2 steel blades, deep V-shape, fitted to horizontal suitcase grip turned wood handle, the whole thing pushed into top of can, "One shove does the act," as the ad said. "This is not the usual or average cheap 'cut around the edges' can opener or one that 'pulls around in a circle.' The Joy Can Opener cuts out a complete circle with one shove or one downward pressure and leaves a tiny part of the opening uncut, which acts as a hinge, so that the cutout part can be pressed back again, for a covering." "Joy Can Opener," mfd. by W. E. Beveridge Mfg. Co., Baltimore, MD, not adjustable for different size cans, would make cut about 4" diam., c.1915. **$50+**

Can opener, wall mounted, "Dazey," by Churn company, St. Louis, 20th C. .... **$15+**

Can opener punch, red & yellow painted wood bottle-shaped tool with little metal punch to open can, "Pet Milk Irradiated Can Opener," 4"L, early 20th C. • See? People could have had to worry about "irradiated" food 70 or so years ago, but then it seemed healing, magic. I wouldn't eat it if you paid me............................ **$15+**

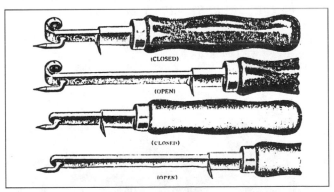

VIII-34. Can openers shown closed & open. *(T-1, T-2) Combined with a bottle opener, "Peerless," nickeled carbon steel, turned wood handle enameled black. (B-1, B-2) The "So-Easy." Houck patent. Mfd. by Hardware Specialty Mfg. Co., Chicago, IL. House Furnishing Review, Jan. 1914. The LeCompte patent of 1865 is very similar to the "So-Easy," except that the adjustment for diameter is made by sliding two parts of the shaft closer or further apart and setting with a thumbscrew, whereas here the shaft evidently retracts into the wooden handle.* **$15+**

Combination tools – mainly bottle & can openers & corkscrews, with a variety of extras: knives, spoons, glasscutters, jiggers, etc. It was a popular concept by inventor, manufacturer, and marketer to combine as many things as possible in order to increase opportunities for sales. Some of the wildest patents in the history of the U.S. Patent Office are combinations (many include beds!): Combined bedstead, chair, secretary & wardrobe; combined call bell & slop jar; combined birdhouse & clothesline support; churn & washing machine; headrest & umbrella; etc.

Bottle opener & cake server combined, possibly for weddings? Wire and sheet metal, the most peculiar combination ever, 11-5/8"L, pat'd. Nov. 24, 1914. .... **$35+**

Bottle opener & can opener combo, fish, cast metal, adv'g. "C. G. Richardson Oils, Gas & Machinery," Patten, ME, late 19th C. .... **$35+**

Bottle opener & can opener combo, cast aluminum bird head long curved upper beak, unlike a pelican, with curved tapered handle, marked "PELI-CAN-OPENER Mfd. B. Harrah, Cannondale, Conn.," 6-1/2"L, pat'd. 1936. .... **$20+**

Bottle opener & corkscrew combo, adv'g "Green River Whiskey," 20th C. .... **$15+**

Bottle opener, crown cap opener, corkscrew & hammer combo in shape of small hammer, black finish on steel, 4"L x 2-1/2"W at head. The hammerhead itself is fairly thick and weighty. American, c.1920s? Some crossover hammer appeal. .... **$15+**

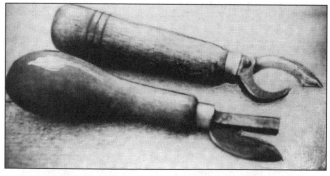

VIII-35. Can opener. "Slick-Ope," *very similar to* "Sure Cut" *in VIII-31. Adjustable, sliding blade on shank has locking device. Pat'd. Nov. 1, 1910, by Hall. Mfd. by Irwin Mfg. Co., NYC. House Furnishing Review, 1915.* **$15+**

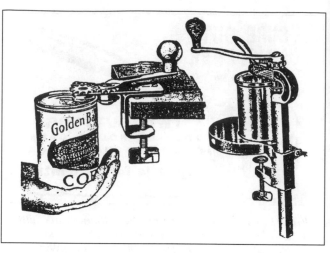

VIII-37. Can openers. (L) "Blue Streak" *shelf-clamp opener. Nickeled steel, blue wood knob, household size: about 4"H. Pat'd. early 1920s. (R)* "Hotel Blue Streak," *with metal stake & adjustable platform to support large heavy cans, about 7"L (plus crank). Mfd. by Turner & Seymour Mfg. Co., Torrington, CT, 1920s. Illustrations from c.1927 S. Joseph catalog of kitchen & bar wares.* **$20+**

Bottle opener, knife sharpener, & glasscutter combo, cast iron, "Apex," c.1900. .... **$15+**

Bottle opener & mechanical adv'g. pencil combo, blonde wood pencil body printed "Hausman Mfg. & Sales Co." with address & 1950s phone number, "Chicago 51, ILL," metal tip for pencil lead, metal end with hooked opener & eraser, early 1950s.. **$5+**

Bottle opener & slotted spoon combo, wire & sheet metal, 10-1/2"L, pat'd. Feb. 23, 1915. .... **$15+**

Bottle opener & stirring spoon, nickeled finish, wide slightly dished spoon. Long handle with notched opener marked "Compliments of SEVEN-UP BOTTLING COMPANY Springfield, Illinois," 7"L. The name "7-Up" was adopted in 1936 by the Bib-Label Lithiated Lemon-Lime Sodas mfd. by the Howdy Co., founded in 1929. This probably dates to late 1930s or early 1940s. A fascinating Web site on **"The History of Pop"** is found at: www.usfirehouse.com/Soda History.htm .... **$25+**

Bottle opener & stirring spoon, exactly like the one above, wide ovoid slightly-dished spoon marked "LIQUID 'CREMO' MALT," tubular handle stamped with address "Two doors north of Ogden Ave. Phone-Crawford 3232," 7"L, American, c.1930s (?), Cremo was also an ale and beer, but was also a "health drink" c.1905. .... **$15+**

Bottle opener & spoon-stirrer combo, iron, "Firestone." .... **$10+**

Bottle opener, wrench & meat cleaver combo, iron, "Kitchen Klever Kleever," American, I'm sure. Late 19th early 20th C. As in Leave it to Klever Kleever – a sort of homey horror show. .... **$25+**

Bottle & can opener, steel with black painted wooden handle, "Peerless," 8-3/4"L, Houck patent, Oct. 29, 1912. .... **$15+**

Bottle & can opener & knife sharpener combo, cast iron, exaggerated fish-bird fantasy shape (as if drawn by abstract artist), "Peerless," 6-1/2"L, pat'd. Aug. 12, 1902, Mar. 31, 1903. .... **$20+**

VIII-38. Can opener. The "P-38," U.S. Army issue. Steel, hinged triangular blade. Stamped "USA **Shelby Corp.**" 1-1/2"L. According to Joe Young, this was first pat'd. in 1886. During WWII they were sold to the Government by the barrel. (In the 1935 Thomas' Register of American Manufacturers, a hinge company, Shelby Metal Products Co., Shelby, OH, was listed – probably it's the one that by WWII became Shelby Corp.) Collection of Jim Holroyd, Oregon. **$3+**

Bottle & can opener, knife sharpener, glass cutter combined, cast & sheet iron, long & very neat with 2 knife-sharpening emory wheels at one tip, the eyes of an insect, less like a fish than the other combo openers, this is like a 6-1/2" length of backbone, "The Improved Peerless," Austria, "patent pending" in U.S., probably after 1903. .... **$15+**

❖ NOTES ❖

Glaziers' combo tools – with a can opener or not? The next two listings are here because of an ongoing disagreement. The only arguments are about whether these combination devices with putty-can-opening in their repertory should be listed as can openers in a book on kitchen tools. I maintain they do, because a housewife's daily encounter with cans weren't all with cans containing food. They had to open cans of wax, and paraffin, and paint, and putty to fix glazing, which might be in window or in kitchen cupboards. Interestingly, Sineus E. Totten's 1867 "improvement in can opener [sic]" looks like a putty knife with a small hook at one end of the squared-off blade, and quite possibly he meant it at least in part for glaziers to use. By the way, Totten assigned the rights to his invention to himself and a partner – the aptly named C. L. Topliff. Housewives were also advised to have tack hammers in a kitchen drawer, which may explain why so many combo tools have small hammers. With them they could fix upholstery, close wooden boxes, and hammer fitted lids back onto cans.

Bottle & can opener, knife sharpener & glazier's tool combined, mostly cast iron, American, 5-1/2"L, pat'd. June 8, 1869 by S. G. Monce, Bristol, CT as a "Glass-cutting tool." Monce later patented another "glazier's tool" July 1, 1973. The late Marion Levy led me to this idea. He identified the parts, left to right: tiny roundel glass cutter at tip, tapper, 2 nippers (top edge), knife sharpener, putty knife with spacer pins, and corkscrew to pull cork on linseed oil bottle to be mixed with whiting to make the putty. But then the putty may also by then have come in a can, so ...? • Combo can opener/ knife sharpeners were also patented by F. W. Echternach & M. J. Welch of

VIII-39. Can opener. "Edlund Jr.," steel, painted wood handle. Made over many years, and 1930 version almost exactly same as this 1944 version. Substantial, works great, not too sanitary. Lots of handle variants. **$5+**

Philadelphia, Feb. 6, 1872 with the added feature of a "fork cleaner"; and S. C. Stokes, Manchester, NH, Feb. 15, 1872. .... **$15+**

Bottle opener, can opener & corkscrew combined, also knife sharpener & glasscutter, cast iron, American, pat'd. Aug. 17, 1875 by Woodward, as marked on frame. This is especially interesting because of the tiny peggy "feet" underneath the neck of the "arrowhead" blade and at the other end too. This combo tool is a mirror image, almost, of one in previous entry, and is owned by collector John Lambert. .... **$35+**

Bottle & can opener, corkscrew, glasscutter, knife sharpener combination, cast iron, with wire screw, no marks, English. 5-1/2"L, late 19th C. Evan Perry, author of a Shire Album book, Corkscrews & Bottle

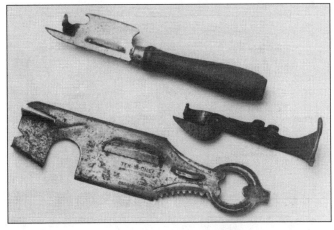

VIII-40. Combination can openers. From top: **(T)** Can opener, crown cap opener & -?-, wood handle, c.1930. **(M)** Small c. 1915 **"Norlunds 3-in-1"** with knife sharpener wheels center shaft, broad head to tap other end into can. **(B)** Wide nickeled **"Ten-in-One,"** mfd. by New Jersey Patent Novelty Co., c.1910. It scales fish, opens bottles, slices carrots, severs twine, chops veggies, does screwdriver duty, and more. **$15+**

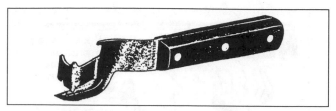

VIII-41. Combined can & crown cap opener.
"Nuform," carbon steel & cocobolo wood handle,
modern beveled design. Its makers, *The Lo-Vis Co.,
Kalamazoo, MI,* were given the Good Housekeeping
Seal of Approval. *House Furnishing Review, Jan.
1917.* Probably went out of business during war, or
turned to making other things. **$5+**

Openers (see Bibliography), said about a similar
multi-purpose tool that it was "the nastiest corkscrew ever issued." (His example was very like this,
except that it also had a screw gauge and a 3" ruler,
was 6-1/2"L, and had a British patent.) .... **$20+**
Bottle & can opener, knife sharpener combined,
hooked iron blade with knife sharpener sticking up
sort of like wings above, wood handle, Boye Needle
Co., Chicago, about 7-1/2"L, pat'd. Sept. 10, 1912 &
Dec. 18, 1917 (?). Bill Griffiths has one with the
Sept. 1912 date, also "Aug. 12, 1913." He also has a
different-looking Boye, with dates Aug. 19, 1913
(Morrell patent), Apr. 6, 1920, & June 15, 1920.
Boye made nutmeg graters, apple corers, screwdriv-
ers & various needles, and still makes crochet
hooks, etc. .... **$25+**
Bottle, can opener, knife sharpener combo, steel, "Nor-
lunds 3-in-l," O. A. Norlund, Williamsport, PA, 4-1/2"L,
c.1915. .... **$15+**
Bottle & can opener, knife sharpener combo, wood
handle, iron top, "Sharp Easy," Premier Mfg. Co.,
Detroit, MI, pat'd. 1922. .... **$25+**

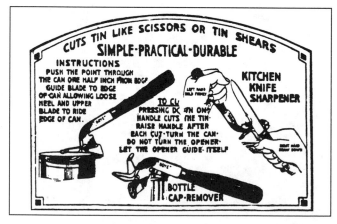

VIII-42. Combination can opener. *A bottle opener
& knife sharpener combo tool made by The* **Boye**
*Needle Co. (whose nutmeg grater is more notable).
Pat'd. Sept. 10, 1912 and Aug. 12, 1913. (Although
an ad shows a different date: Dec. 16, 1917.) This
is a little double-sided printed flyer that was sent
out with the products. • A non-scissors model from
Boye bears patent dates Aug. 19, 1913 and May 6,
1920.* **$15+**

VIII-43. Combined can & bottle openers. (T)
*8"L, a 2-way type with sliding knife on long
shank. (B) 6-1/2"L. Nickeled metal & painted handles in choice of green, yellow, red, green with
ivory band, and yellow with blue band. Both
Washburn Co., "Androck" line catalog, 1936.* **$5+**

Bottle & can opener combined tool, with fish scaler,
screwdriver, chopper, carrot slicer, etc., steel, "Ten-
In-One," New Jersey Patent Novelty Co., Passaic, NJ,
7-1/2"L, c.1900. Extremely clumsy & weird; if Evan
Perry ever saw this one, I'm sure he'd say that it was
the "nastiest" combo tool he'd ever seen. And it
doesn't do windows, because there's no glasscutter
on it! .... **$15+**

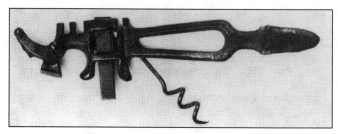

VIII-44. Combination novelty glazier's tool. *This
one happens to be the* **Monce** *patent of June 7,
1869. It's 5-1/2"L and is complete as shown.
According to the late Marion Levy, whose apple parers appear elsewhere in this book, from L to R are
glass cutter roundel, tapper, 2 nippers (for edge of
glass), knife sharpening stone, corkscrew for pulling
linseed oil bottle cork, and at end, the arrowhead
shape, putty knife with "two spacer bars." • Almost
identical are the* **"Excelsior** *Glazing Tool," on which
the arrowhead-shaped end was termed a "putty
knife"; the* **"Centennial** *Combination Tool," with
glass cutter, knife sharpener, can opener, wrench,
tack hammer, tack puller, screw driver and needle
straightener." Both made by the New England Novelty Works, F. R. Woodward, proprietor, Hill, NH.
These, and two other products (viz.* **"Our Household Tool"** *had the "arrowhead" as an ice pick and
a can opener), had glass cutting element patented
by Woodward on Aug. 24, 1875. • Another variant
was a cast iron can opener, knife sharpener & polisher, called a* **"Centennial Novelty,"** *but pat'd. four
years before (Feb. 6, 1872) by F. W. Echternach & M.
J. Welch, Philadelphia. • Yet another is depicted in a
novelty catalog aimed at traveling salesmen,
c.1880. It is a more streamlined version based on
Clark's glasscutter patent, called a "Combination
Novelty Tool," "consisting of glass cutter (which
could be used as a paper pattern cutter too), scissors & knife sharpener, glass nippers, can opener
(the "arrowhead"), and graduated wrench (the long
slot in the center).* **$20-$40**

Bottle & can opener combination, nickeled steel parts riveted together, corkscrew secured in looped handle, hook to remove crown caps, "Yankee," pat'd. Jan. 28, 1902 and Dec. 26, 1906, Taylor Mfg. Co., Hartford, CT. Looks very like the "Best" by W. G. Browne. .... **$12+**

Bottle & jar opener wrench, sheet steel, "4-in-1," J. C. Forster & Son, Pittsburgh, PA, about 6-3/4" or 7"L, pat'd. Sept. 13, 1910... **$15+**

Bottle opener & corkscrew combined, nickeled steel, looks sort of like can opener except the cap-lifter part isn't at all sharp, screw folds within open loop handle, pat'd. by H. A. Chippendale, American, c.1890s-1910... **$125+**

Bottle opener & corkscrew combined, the so-called "Volstead" figural, shape of stern top-hatted man (**Andrew Volstead**, who authored the Prohibition Act) with beaky nose, black hat, huge shoes, clasped hands, corkscrew pivots up out of tail coat in back when head is twisted, now and piece on chest are bottle opener, hat comes off and reveals small space – for a jigger of liquor (?), base marked "Old Snifter" and mfr.'s name "Demley," American, c.1919 to 1933 (period of Prohibition). Many corkscrews incorporated a similar caricatured image of what some people say is Senator Volstead, and others, notably Don Bull, say the skinny, dour, beaky-nosed caricature was based on the political cartoons of Rollin Kirby, for the *New York Morning World*. It's possible that Kirby had Volstead in the back of his mind. .... **$175+**

Corkscrew & jigger combined, so-called Senator Volstead figural, "Old Snifter" with beaky nose, corkscrew pivots up in front when head is turned, hat comes off as jigger, "Old Snifter," mfd. by Neghaur, NYC, NY, c.1919 to 1933 (era of Prohibition), ... **$175+**

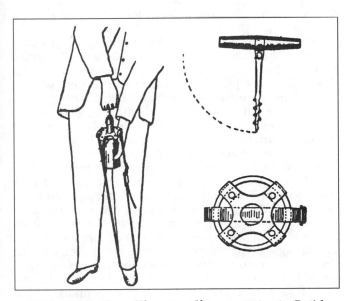

VIII-45. Cork-pulling appliance patent. *Pat'd. Dec. 2, 1890 by Alfred J. Parker, NYC. Composed of a flexible strap (to put foot through) passed through a "flexible yoke" (spoked piece lower right) with a hole in center for the bottle's neck. The appliance was to be used to aid the person pulling the cork by holding the bottle secure. I doubt if it was ever produced.* Official Gazette.

Corkscrew in a coffin-shaped, silky-cloth-lined black cardboard box, the "Old Snifter" corkscrew, a shot glass & bottle opener. Paper label on front of coffin says "Born 1919 Died _____" left blank because the end of Prohibition wasn't known when this was patented. Marked on coffin "Patent applied for, Copyright 1932." 1-5/8" diam. x 6-1/2"L x 2"W at widest point. Sold in Feb. 2002 on eBay auction by eBayer cybid for:... **$331**

Corkscrew, bottle opener, spoon & jigger (hat), silver-plated figural combo, very detailed casting – two sides with Old Snifter/Volstead's body on one side clasping his jacket together & holding drink glass & on other side he grasps lapel with one hand, other hand stuck under lapel. Marked inside mouth from one side "W. B. MFG. CO." in a shield-shaped cartouche, and other mouth marked "Pat. 8 – 16 – 32 USA." 9-3/4"L. Sold on eBay in March 2002 by eBayer jonnnboy for: **$196**

Corkscrew, cap lifter, cigar cutter combo, folds up along figural handle, greenish mottled celluloid alligator, marked "D Peres, Germany," 4-1/4"L, prob. c. 1890s-1910.. **$800+**

Bottle opener, corkscrew & jigger combined, chromed brass, handle unscrews to reveal screw & bottle opener, Chase Brass & Copper, with centaur logo, Waterbury, CT, 1930s. **Chase's flashy deco home bar** products (ice buckets, shakers, trays, etc.) and other kitchen-related things, are a popular separate field for collectors. Not all bright chromed cocktail accessories are Chase. West Bend, Farberware, Manning-Bowman, and a Canadian company, possibly Riverside Brass (?), made similar wares. **$20**

Can opener & corkscrew combined, nickeled steel, screw folds up into space between handle loop, a style commonly seen today, & prob. being made from original design, "Browne Line None Such," mfd. by The Browne & Dowd Mfg. Co., Meriden, CT, Fenn patent, Nov. 3, 1908. The trade name situation a century ago was quite different from today's, and several companies might use the same or similar names, for all kinds of products. "None Such" was a popular name – like "Uneek," "Non Pareil," "Ne Plus Ultra," "Best Yet," "None Better," etc. – and was used by at least five companies for such widely different products as blankets, mince meat, canned corn (see the Lehman Can Opener picture), can openers, and chain pumps, to name a few!......................... **$15+**

Can opener & jar wrench combined, sheet steel, "4-in-1," mfd. by J. C. Forster & Son, Pittsburgh, PA, about 6-3/4" or 7"L, Forster patent, Sept. 13, 1910. .... **$20+**

Corkscrew, bottle & can opener, fork combination, iron, marked "B.M. Shipman Importer New York," and "Bon Accord Mackerel" "Bon Accord Herring," 6-1/4"L, American, c.1900.................................... **$35+**

Corkscrew, fork, & 2 narrow blades, both very slim, one nearly 3-1/2"L with tapered point like nail file; other only about 1-3/4"L with truncated end, when folded up the whole tool is very skinny, only 4"L. Fork has 3 long prongs or tines in late 18th, early 19th C. style. Steel blades & worm, brass handle that tools fold into. Mark illegible, but looks perhaps Arabic according to eBay seller. .... **$200+**

Corkscrew, hammer, hatchet, jar wrench, ruler, etc. – "15 Tools in One," Jenkins' 1930 patent. .... **$100+**

VIII-46. Cork-extractor patent. Pat'd. Aug. 9, 1881 by Frederick Mann, Milwaukee, WI. A tubular sheet metal handle with long slot. Cap at left is removed & the vertical slender arm or rod on left is taken out from inside tube, passed through the slot, and cap is somehow used to fix it to tubular handle. The right arm "pivots and swings" or can be made to be detachable and kept inside also. If this looks feasible to you, you must be knocking the tops off bottles to open them now. Official Gazette. If it exists, the value should be quite high because of construction and material. **$45**

Corkscrew, can opener, bottle opener, jar opener, tack lifter, hammer, scissor sharpener, knife sharpener, nippers, pipe wrench, wire stripper, tongs, nut cracker, file, & several hexagonal wrench cutouts, multi-tool combo, prob. cast malleable steel, pat'd. by Erik Nylin, 1909, American. .... **$250+**
Corkscrew combos – See also Corkscrew, Folding Combinations – Bows or Harps.
Corkscrew & cork combined, cork with wire passed through the cork from top to bottom, bent at ends, probably not as airtight as needed for wine, invented by William H. Towers, poss. mfd. by The Union Pin Mfg. Co., Boston, MA, 1862. • Towers also invented a machine for opening oysters, a new kind of broom, and a straight pin that wouldn't fall out. .... **$25+**
Corkscrews are continued following Cork drivers, Cork presses, Cork pullers.

❖ NOTES ❖

Cork, which grows principally in Spain, Portugal, Algeria, and other Mediterranean countries, is not wood per se, but the bark of an evergreen oak, *Quercus suber*. A cork tree reaches sufficient maturity after 15 years that two or three inches of its thick bark can be stripped off without killing the tree! After eight more years, another crop is ready, and this harvesting can go on for 80 or more years. Cork has been used since ancient times – but not always for stopping up bottles and jars. All the writers on corkscrews speculate on just how long "corks" have been used – thus necessitating all sorts of cork cutters, compressors, drivers, and extractors, including corkscrews or bottlescrews. Tools are only needed for really tight-fitting corks, and it is hard to know how early cork's great compressibility was taken advantage of. A fascinating article appeared in the January 21, 1854 issue of Great Britain's *Chamber's Journal*, in it, the author relates a story told by the ancient Roman natural historian, Pliny the elder, about a Roman courier who escaped the Gauls by putting pieces of cork under his arms and swimming the Tiber River. He further writes, "The ancients kept their wine in casks and jars which were stopped with pitch, clay, gypsum, potter's earth, and other substances; and the wine was drawn from these vessels into open cups or pitchers, which were brought to table; but when, in the fourteenth century, it became customary to keep wine in small bottles, then did also become prevalent the method of securing these bottles with small bits of cork-bark, which bits very soon acquired the name of corks. ... it is very compressible and elastic; and is easily cut – hence cork possesses remarkable qualities for bottle-stoppers." [Vol. I, No. 3.] Another writer, Henning Webb Prentis Jr., in his 1939 Newcomen address on Armstrong cork, contradicts the *Chamber's* article. "The poet, Horace, is quoted as having told a friend, about 25 B.C., that on the occasion of a coming anniversary banquet he expects to 'remove the cork sealed with pitch' from a jar of a rare vintage of forty-six years earlier."

•   •   •

Old Corks Recycled – A long article in *The Metal Worker*, Aug. 5, 1882, on the secondhand bottle market in America, includes some new (to me) information on corkselling. "That bottles should be used again is not so much of a wonder when considered, but that old corks should be is something to marvel at. In a low, wooden building in Mulberry Street old corks are made 'as good as new.' This is the only place in New York where they are dealt. The dealer buys the corks by the barrel, and pays from $1 to $3. His trade is mostly in champagne corks. The best and cleanest of these he sorts out and sells to American champagne makers [who, the article explains, also bought used foreign champagne bottles, being unable at that time to make them strong enough in America]. The bottom of the cork where the first bottler's brand appears is shaved off and the name of the second stamped on them. These corks were cut expressly for champagne bottles, and as they can be bought much more cheaply than new ones, the bottlers purchase them. The old cork dealers obtain 25 cents a dozen for them, and make a handsome profit.

"The broken and dirty corks go through a peculiar process. They are first subjected to a sort of Turkish bath to clean them, and after they are dried are cut down. They are put in a machine and turned, while a sharp knife runs across them and takes off a portion. They can be cut to any size, and with the solid surface removed look as bright as when new. The corks cut down are purchased by root beer and soda water makers, who use smaller bottles. They can save a considerable amount by purchasing old corks, which, as it is easy to see, will do as well as new ones. The 'old cork man' is rushed with business. The champagne and root beer and soda water bottles take all the corks that he can furnish. He gets his supply at the hotels and elsewhere ... No demand has yet developed for small corks. The druggists are compelled to use new corks, but the dealer talking on the subject thought that manufacturers of ink, mucilage and the like, might use old corks as well as not." I wish the article had mentioned what they did about corkscrew holes.

•   •   •

Corking apparatus – "We have recently seen in the [NYC] House-furnishing establishment of J. H. Baldwin, a German contrivance for compressing the corks in bottling. It is essentially a conical tube with a plunger. The apparatus is set upon the neck of a bottle, the plunger lifted, and a cork introduced at the opening [partway down the tube]. The cork drops into the cavity which tapers downwards; it is lined with metal. By striking upon the top of the plunger with a mallet, the cork is driven downwards, and so much compressed in its passage, that it enters the neck of the bottle with ease. Good corks should be procured and soaked in warm water, to render them pliant, and then be pressed and driven in with a wooden driver; a flat piece of heavy wood or a mallet will answer. In filling the bottle it should not be so full that the cork will touch the liquid, as the bottle will be broken in driving the cork. There should be a space of an inch or more between the surface of the liquid and the bottom of the cork; this will prevent breaking." Editor, "The Household," *American Agriculturist*, August 1870. Refer to these instructions for the next 10 listings.

Cork drawer – See Cork puller or drawer

Cork driver or corking press, turned wood (looks sort of like a nautical belaying pin), 2 part, with copper insert in bottom tapered part, opening is fitted over bottle with a soaked cork put in the side opening, not marked, 10-1/4"L when completely closed, German (?) late (?)19th C. Similar drivers still being made in Germany. .... **$150+**

Cork driver, turned wood with rich patina, metal lined, has four sections, including a plunger rod with its fat wood knob – confusable because it looks like a whimsy, a toy, or a musical percussion instrument. About 9"L, late 19th C. **$250**

Cork driver or corking press, turned walnut with simple shape, arched opening in side, tapered "chute" partially copper lined, marked "F. Amos," 10-1/4"L, English (?), mid 19th C. .... **$275+**

Cork driver, turned wood with great patina, overall bottle shape, wide cavity opening, stamped on side "The Star" "John Summer's Patent," late 19th C. **$225+**

Cork driver, turned wood, highly polished finish, "Best Star of Bottling," John Sommers, Newark, NJ, 11-3/4"L unextended, pat'd. Aug. 25, 1885. .... **$175+**

VIII-47. Cork puller or drawer. "Yankee-6," cast iron in choice of finish: bronze or nickel plate. Fancy casting of mechanism housing. Bottle is clamped into position underneath, and handle is worked up & then down. There was also a "Yankee-7," also to be clamped either to counter, shelf or work board. Its handle started in vertical down position, and was moved up only, but traveled the same overall distance as the #6. The bottle clamp was optional. Mfd. by the Gilchrist Co., Newark, NJ, early 1900s. **$125+**

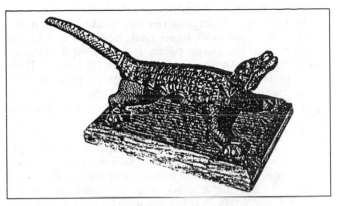

VIII-48. Rotary cork press. Cast iron, wooden base, rotary motion compresses cork to reduce its diam. long enough to stick it in bottle neck. A. Pick & Co. hotel & bar supplies catalog, c.1905-09, but press design may be much older. **$125**

Cork driver or bottle corker, turned wood, non-bulbous plunger top – actually it's shaped like a tapered cork, very graceful reeding. Bottom of plunger has screw-on pewter cap, tapered interior is brass lined. 12"L extends to 17", German, c.1870s. .... **$175+**

Cork driver, turned maple, "Redlich Mfg. Co.," Chicago, IL, early 20th C. into 1930s. .... **$75+**

Cork driver or corking machine, cast iron with some fancy embossing, painted & pinstriped, screw clamps, lever with big wood knob, "Yankee." Works by holding the bottle by its neck in exact position to receive the cork, which is put in a sort of "hopper," and plunged downward by force of the lever. About 13"L, late 19th C. .... **$125+**

Cork driver or corking machine, malleable cast iron, unattractive industrial design, but very efficient for setting corks at any depth. Screw clamps to shelf or counter, one lever sets cork, one lever holds bottle, "Corkee," pat'd. Feb. 19, 1901. .... **$75+**

Cork driver or corking machine, cast iron, screw clamps to shelf, horizontal dog-leg lever to built-in cork compressor connected to bottle clamp underneath, another cranked lever drives cork. "Invincible," c.1910. .... **$75+**

Cork press, alligator with head looking up and tail lever up, regular pattern of warty stripes to represent the hide extends in diminishing size from neck to end of tail, red-painted cast iron, hinged at chest, holes drilled in feet so that it could be screwed to countertop or a plank, would press four sizes of corks. By

VIII-49. Cork press. Figural alligator, well-detailed cast iron. Mounted to shaped oak board, screwed through feet. Does four sizes of corks. Picture courtesy James & Phyllis Moffet. **$900+**

"press" is meant compression. A water-soaked cork slightly larger than was needed would be put in the press to compress it so that it could quickly be inserted in the bottle before it expanded to its original cut size. American, 3rd quarter (?) 19th C. There are **at least three different alligator presses.** This one has a variation where the "warts" end partway up the tail, to be taken over by a sort of crosshatch knurling (VIII-48). Another is perfectly charming, truly a cute little 'gator modeled much less realistically, with the three "sections" all the same length: head & jaws, body, and tail. Also does four corks – probably for pharmaceuticals, not liquor. These are all essential for a good alligator collection, which would also include a lawn sprinkler and a couple of nutcrackers. .... **$900+**

Cork press, cast iron in shape of playful setter dog, undoubtedly made by same company that made the head- and tail-up alligator presses. Does four sizes of corks. American, c.1970s-1900. I've never seen one of these, but it was pictured in the September 1971 issue of *Spinning Wheel*, p. 44. .... **$350+**

Cork press, cast iron, mounted to wooden base, half-circle cradle with levered 6-spoked 4-1/2" diam. ridged wheel. Called a "rotary" cork press, marked "Enterprise Mfg Co Phila" on one side, and "Pat Aug 7 1868 No. 2" on other side. Overall 6"H x 12"L including lever arm. It originally sold for 50¢. The most commonly found type but very handsome design. .... **$125+**

Cork press, cast iron finished with japanning or bronze, leaf-like design to lever, 3 legs with mounting holes, 3 corks. Russell & Erwin, c.1875.. **$125+**

Cork press, cast iron, japanned or bronzed, 3 scrolly legs, leafy top with shapely lever, does 4 corks, including very small one for pharmacies. Originally cost only $2.25 per dozen, wholesale! Probably Russell & Erwin, c.1875.................................... **$150+**

Cork press, cast iron, "Whitall-Tatum," Philadelphia, 19th C. into early 20th. Probably for pharmeceutical bottle corks.. **$65+**

Cork press – See also Bottle capper & cork press

Corking machines – See Cork driver or corking machine

Corking presses – See Cork driver or corking machine

VIII-51. Corkscrew. *Figural "Old Snifter" caricature of Senator "Prohibition" Volstead. Corkscrew tail, bottle opener hook under chin. Hat removes – not big enough to hold much but a sniff! Painted cast metal (brass?). Many versions of this, some without cap opener or removable hat, c.1920s-30s. Read extended price entry under the Figural Corkscrew entries.* **$85-$150+**

Cork pullers don't just grab the cork and pull it out, as the name may seem to apply. They incorporate a corkscrew, but use a (usually) levered action to facilitate pulling out the cork after the screw has engaged it.

Cork puller or extractor, iron & wood, looks much like a button hook with a T-handle, a groove along the stem allows air back inside so that a vacuum isn't set up that spews out contents when opened. 3-1/2"L, marked "B.J. Greely," Benjamin J. Greely, and patent # "379,010 PAT MAR 6 88" marked on stem. American. .... **$115+**

Cork puller, nickeled steel (advertised also as coming "silver plated," but was it really silver?), extremely simple small device that mounts vertically to wall, cupboard or door jamb. You hold the bottle in place, then raise the lever so the centercut screw enters the cork, then lower the lever to withdraw cork, "Yankee #1," Gilchrist Co., c.1890s-1915. (The Yankee #2 of steel mounted to a shelf edge with a screw clamp.).. **$35+**

Cork puller, nickeled cast iron (also found bronze-plated), with fancy scrolled design on sides. Mounted to shelf, counter or other horizontal sur-

VIII-50. Corkscrews. *The cheapest kind, but perfectly efficient for many kinds of corked bottles. These came with single ring of wire for the fingerhole, or double ring for strength. Simple one at top could also be had with two kinds of tubes. Center one has wooden tube with no printed advertising. The wholesale price was $3.75 for 250 of them. At bottom is one showing printed wooden tube, meant as giveaway. They were only 25¢ more! Made at Albert Pick & Co.'s Pennsylvania factory. A. Pick, 1905-09.* **$1-$10**

VIII-52. Bawdy folding corkscrews, *more politely called "lady legs." (L) "Leg puller," enameled striped stockings in red & white, blue & white, etc. Crucible steel worm. 2-1/2"L folded; 5"L open. One example of popular type. Original wholesale price was $7.25 a dozen! (R) Folding lady. "An imported novelty, beautifully enameled in colors." Tempered crucible steel worm. The real one has almost as much of a dour expression. The legs look just like the catalog cut. Both from catalog of A. Pick, 1905-09. (L) $110+; (R) $300+*

face, has bottle holder clamp, upward lever action, "Yankee #7," The Gilchrist Co., Newark, NJ, c.1892. (There's also a Yankee #6 that's pretty much the same but it operates with an upward then downward motion of the knobbed lever. Originally they cost about $1.95 – this is another one of those time-machine shopping list items.) .... **$95+**

Cork puller or cork drawer, cast iron, fancy embossed design, bronzed or nickel-plated, screw clamps to shelf or counter edge, has device to hold bottle (like one in picture of the "Yankee 6"), lever is pulled up to draw cork out. "PULLMEE," probably Manning Bowman/ Freeport Novelty Co., c. 1913. ...... **$115+**

Cork puller, or cork extractor, mechanical, for bars or restaurants, cast metal, screw clamps to bar edge, "Edie Patent," Smith & Egge Mfg. Co., Bridgeport, CT, pat'd. Feb. 4, 1890 by Alexander Edie. ... **$125+**

Cork puller, cast iron, overall fancy embossing, nickeled finish only. Attachment so that cork can be half or fully pulled. "SHOMEE," marked "Freeport Novelty Co.," as well as "Manning Bowman," "Meriden, CT." early 20th C. .... **$100+**

Cork puller, cast iron, screw clamps to shelf or bar, angled lever with long turned black wood handle, embossed brass facing plate with vines & flowers, "Champion Bar Screw," mfd. by Chas. Brown & Sons, San Francisco, pat'd. 1896. .... **$200+**

Cork puller, screw clamps to table edge, for bar or buttery, nickeled cast iron, steel, wooden knob on crank, nicely eared wingnut on clamp, helical worm, "Infanta No. 8," pat'd. 1895. .... **$175+**

Cork puller reproduction alert, screw clamps to bar edge, cast brass with lots of cupids, replica of 1890s cork puller, one lever clamps to bottle neck, larger one, with turned wooden handle like the "Champion," used to draw out cork, recorks by reversing motion, says "VINTNER" in vertical letters on main body, c.1985. **Alert #2.–** A simpler version, of cast aluminum & called the "Estate" has knurled bottle clamp that looks like the old "Yankees" but lever like the "Champion," mounted to vertical iron rod and board, instead of screw clamp, is less than half the price. Well-made enough to probably pass for much

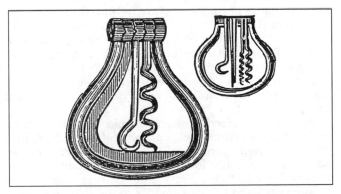

VIII-53. Corkscrews. *Combination folding harp or bow pocket types. Large one (L) is a "Champagne Opener," and has button hook (nothing to do with bottle-opening) and a curved wire-cutting blade in addition to worm; (R) smaller one has extra worm, and a pick. F. A. Walker catalog, 1870s. Value related to how many tools, from one to at least 10. These: $35+*

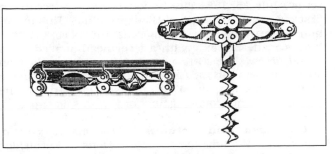

VIII-54. Corkscrew. *Another folding type, the "Handy Pocket Cork Screw," mfd. by the Little Giant Letterpress Co., NYC. Nickel-plated. You worked it by holding the tip of the screw worm to the cork with one hand, then pulling up on upper half of handle, which "forces the screw down." It would, of course, if it worked at all, force it straight into the cork without screwing. The Metal Worker, Jul. 28, 1892. $20+*

VIII-55. Corkscrews. *(L) A so-called **self-puller** with cap to fit over mouth of bottle. (R) A flat twist helical worm, and slender wooden handle reinforced with a metal ring at each end. About 6-1/2"L. D, Huot & Moneuse catalog, c.1904-10. $4+*

older, if the wood and metal is distressed. New price from *Wine Enthusiast* mail order catalog in 1985: **$159.90**

Cork puller, screw clamps to edge, mostly for bar or restaurant use, fancy openwork cast iron, nickel plated usually, lever, "Phoenix," 1887. .... **$175+**

Corkscrew, "bar screw" – See Cork puller.

Corkscrew combination tools – See Combination tools following the Can opener listings; also Corkscrew Folding Combinations – Bow & Harp, in with the Corkscrews.

❖ NOTES ❖

First American Corkscrew Patent – The late Raymond Townsend wrote an article in *Fine Tool Journal*, Sep/Oct 1989, saying that it has been incorrectly thought that the earliest American corkscrew patent is that of Philos Blake (a nephew of Eli Whitney from New Haven, CT), granted March 27, 1860. [Note: Actually, Joe Kane, *Famous First Facts*, wrote that the first was rec'd by M. L. Byrn, #27,615, on March 27, 1860. Same date. Hmmm.] According to Ray, the first was George Blanchard's combined nutmeg grater & corkscrew, July 15, 1856 (see under Nutmeg graters in the first chapter). The claim of Blake was that "This invention is a new and improved manufacture of cork extractor, as made not only with a lever head applied to its lifting screw, but with a lever screw nut applied on such screw and to the cap of the heck stand, in such a manner that it may rotate and screw on the lifting screw and either rotate against or within said cap."

• • •

Corkscrew Manufacturers in *Thomas' Register of American Manufacturers* and *House Furnishing Review's Buyers Guides*. Listings were mostly under Corkscrews, a few from Cork Pullers in both. [Note that *Thomas'* is alphabetical by state; *HFR* is alphabetical by company, and also includes some brand names – here in parentheses.] *HFR* has perhaps a disproportionate number of companies from NYC but that usually proves to be the showroom address not the address of the factory. *HFR* also lists importers, not always differentiated in their directories, nor here. For more notes on these directories, see the Can Opener Manufacturers listing at beginning of Can openers.

Thomas' – 1905-06. This list is from the 1905-06 *Thomas' Register of American Manufacturers, Buying Guide.* • Meriden Britannia Co.; and Meriden Cutlery Co., Meriden, CT • Humason & Beckley Mfg. Co., New Britain, CT • Hills Edison, Plainville, CT • R. Wallace Sons Mfg. Co., Wallingford, CT • Empire Knife Co., Winsted, CT • R. Blackinton & Co., N. Attleboro, MA • National Mfg. Co., Worcester, MA • Rockwell-Clough Co., Alton, NH • Wm. Crabb & Co.; and C. T. Williamson Wire Novelty Co., both of Newark, NJ • Gorham Mfg. Co.; and Parks & Parks; and Smith & Hemenway Co.; and J. H. Walbridge & Co., all of Troy, NY; Erie Specialty Co.; and Reed Mfg. Co., both Erie, PA. **HFR – 1909. Corkscrews:** Dame-Stoddard & Co., Boston, MA • Erie Specialty Co. ("Quick & Easy"), Erie, PA • Graef & Schmidt, NYC • Robert Murphy & Sons, Ayer, MA • Rich Radigan & Co., NYC • Smith & Hemenway ("Peerless," "Reliable"), NYC • Arthur W. Ware & Co., NYC • C. T. Williamson Wire Novelty Co., Newark, NJ. Cork Pullers: Arcade Mfg. Co. ("Champion," "Daisy," "Triumph," "Favorite," "Clipper," "Handy," "Standard," "Phoenix," "Arcade"), Freeport, IL • Erie Specialty Co. ("Samson") • The Gilchrist Co., Newark, NJ • Hugo Reisinger, NYC. **HFR – 1915.** Arcade Mfg. Co., Freeport, IL Basket Importing Co., NYC • John Bing, NYC • R. Blackington & Co., North Attleboro, MA • Louis A. Boettiger Co., NYC • George Borgfeldt & Co., NYC • Briscoe Mfg. Co., Detroit, MI • W. C. Browne Mfg. Co., Kingston, NY • Browne & Dowd Mfg. Co., Meriden, CT • Cassady-Fairbank Mfg. Co. ("Trinity"), Chicago, IL • Clough Corkscrew Co., Alton, NH • George L. Curtis Co., Southington, CT • Dame, Stoddard & Co., Boston, MA • J. R. Dawson Mfg. Co., Philadelphia, PA • Erie Specialty Co. ("Quick & Easy," "Walkers"), Erie, PA • Frank & Co., NYC • C. H. & E. S. Goldberg, NYC • Graef & Schmidt, NYC • Edwin Hills, Plainville, CT • Humason & Beckley Co., New Britain, CT • Irvington Mfg. Co., Irvington, NJ • J. E. Kennedy ("Universal"), NYC • M. Loewenstein, NYC • G. E. Meissner & Bro., NYC • Meriden Cutlery Co., Meriden, CT • R. Murphy & Sons ("R. Murphy's"), Ayer, MA • New Era Cork Extractor Co. ("New Era"), Jacksonville, FL • Charles Parker Co., Meriden, CT • Peck & Mack Co., NYC • G. M. Thurnauer Co. [they were importers mainly from Germany],

NYC • Universal Metal Specialty Co., ("Universal"), NYC • R. Wallace & Sons Mfg. Co., Wallingford, CT • Ira F. White & Son Co., Bloomfield, NJ • Wiebusch & Hilger, NYC • Windsor, Stephens & Co. ("Always Handy"), Waltham, MA • C. T. Williamson Wire Novelty Co., Newark, NJ. **HFR – 1930.** The only listing is G. M. Thurnauer Co., NYC. **Thomas' – 1932-33.** Voos Co., New Haven, CT • Autoyre Mfg. Co., Oakville, CT • Waterbury Button & Mfg. Co., Waterbury, CT • Vaughan Novelty Mfg. Co., Chicago • Rockwell Clough Co. (they made adv'g., pocket, miniature, medicine bottle, etc., corkscrews), Alton, NH • Hoegger Inc. (also bottle openers), Weehawken, NJ • C. T. Williamson Wire Novelty Mfg. Co., Newark, NJ • P. M. C. Mfg. Co., Kingston, NY • Louis A. Boettiger Co.; and J. A. Henckels, Inc., both NYC. **Thomas' – 1945.** From *Thomas' Register of American Manufacturers.* • Voos Co., New Haven • Vaughan Novelty Mfg. Co., Chicago • C. T. Williamson Wire Novelty Co., Newark • Louis A. Boettiger Co.; and Graef & Schmidt, Inc.; and Hill Adv'g. Specialties Co., all NYC. Cork Pullers were made by Arcade Mfg. Co. of Freeport, IL, and C. T. Williamson Wire Novelty Co., Newark, NJ.

• • •

Corkscrews – When was the first? – The 1854 *Chamber's Journal* writer who wrote on cork didn't speculate on the age of corkscrews. Recent writers date the first corkscrew to the late 17th century, when it was called a "bottle scrue" or "steel worme." I like to speculate that it was around much, much earlier. Several factors assist me in my theory: the ancient knowledge of cork's properties; the ancient manufacture of relatively small bottles; the ancient consumption of wine and beer; and – essential to my premise – Archimedes' invention of a giant screw to draw up liquids from wells, or flooded areas. I believe that all this practical knowledge would naturally have led to the idea of a small-scale tapping screw that could be used, like a champagne tap is used now, to draw out fermenting or sparkling wine, and on from that to a screw to draw out a tight cork. Failing proof of that, I bet that older examples of the wrought iron L-shaped corkscrews (see VIII-57) used by cellar masters, may date at least to the 1500s, possibly even earlier.

Corkscrew-collecting hints – For most collectors, the aristocrats of corkscrews are **patented mechanical** ones from the 19th century; next in desirability would be rigid wrought iron or other metal ones dating back to the 17th or 18th centuries – pure functional form that you could imagine Leonardo da Vinci using. Least costly, though widely and popularly collected, are late 19th century and all 20th century corkscrews, figural and mechanical.

In any mechanical corkscrew collection, the patient and patented search for improvement is evident, and while handmade and one-of-a-kind screws are valuable additions to a collection, the patented examples excite the most collector interest. All sorts of mechanical movements used in huge engines of the Industrial Revolution are found on a small scale in corkscrews: rack-and-pinion gears, wheels, levers, cams and clutches.

The screws themselves vary, although most people call all of them "worms" or "screws." These are the **types of worms:** (1) single wire helix (spiral), and the rarer (2) double or duplex helix (one is much shorter than the other), (1) and (2) are found in relatively lighter or heavier gauge wire; (3) augured worm screw (looking like a cross between a wire helix and a wood screw); (4) fluted wire helix (which is made of relatively heavy gauge wire and has a channel or "flute" scoring the outer side of the entire worm's length); (5) bladed worm (on this, the outer side of the wire helix or spiral has a sort of sharp edge or blade to it); (6) center- or solid-cut worm – sometimes called an Archimedean screw – (which has, in effect, a straight center shaft with a spiraling blade the entire length, at first easily confused with the bladed worm until you get the hang of it); (7) steep-pitched center worm – called a "speed worm" – (which is like 6 but with fewer spirals per inch [s.p.i.] so the "pitch" or angle of the blade edge is greater); (8) cyphered wire helix (which I can't find a definition of, but in pictures it is a peg-and-worm two-part tool, the "peg" has a straight center shaft, around which fits a tightly-fit spiral wire worm. (9) flat twist worm is a term appearing in a c.1904 Duparquet, Moneuse & Huot catalog to describe a corkscrew that looks like it could be a center-cut worm or a bladed worm. •

Other variations have to do with size and finish: (a) taper: un-tapered worm, or (b) tapered worm (much less common, and refers either to the tapering of the wire itself, or tapering of the radius of the spirals); (c) point: pointed (terminated by drawing the tip into a point that lines up vertically with the shaft), or (d) tip: not pointed (but simply terminated in the spiral so the point – yes, there is a pointed end – is of the same curve and pitch as the helix/spiral); (e) radius: screws with different turning radiuses; and (f) pitch: different pitches – what I call s.p.i. or spirals per inch. (The fewer s.p.i., the faster the worm could be screwed through the cork); and finally, (g) length: the length of the screw or worm varies, depending on the intended use (*viz.* wine corks or medicine bottle corks, pocket, pantry, picnic, or wine cellar, etc. "A turn short" is a phrase used sometimes by collectors and dealers, when a screw appears to be shorter than it ought (as if broken off, then re-sharpened, for example).

Finally, there are many other terms to describe the **forms or types:** barreled, open cage, spring barrel, bell-cap, moving bell, spiked flange, swivel-over collar, duck bill cap, flared moving bell, Columbus type expanding frame, sprung frame, split-ring frame, folding, folding fulcrum, bow or harp, picnic; handles: eyebrows, twisted wire, T-handle [which can be wood, metal, bone, ivory, horn, plastic], 2-finger pull, 3-finger pull, 4-finger pull, ring, figural; mechanical principles: double-levered, rack and pinion, spring action, concertina, screw and lever; and additional features: cap lifter, pick, brush, wire cutter or breaker, wax cutter.

Note that all these different mechanisms and forms were organized by me for this book back in the mid-1990s. You may find it a useful beginning, or you may prefer the more recent, and ongoing, classification system developed by advanced collectors, and listed with the "For More Information" listings at the end of this chapter.

Inventors – Three English corkscrew inventors, whose corkscrews are avidly collected are: Sir Edward Thomason, who patented what he called the "King's Screw" in 1802; William Lund was probably the most prolific inventor of corkscrews, his designs vary considerably in mechanical principle; and James Heeley. The four most famous American names are C[ornelius] T[itus] Williamson – inventor and founder of a long-lasting company, and his son and successor, William A.

Williamson. The third is William R. Clough, whose simple ring-handled, one-finger, wire and wood corkscrews, each with its own cylindrical wooden "sheath" meant to be stamped with an advertising message, are ubiquitous. The fourth is Edwin Walker, who patented many types of corkscrews, including an 1894 extractor or cork puller which incorporated a corkscrew. The entire field, American and European, is vast, and only a hint of the range is given in this chapter.

Corkscrews – Advertising & Souvenir

Some are folding or figural. Most of these are considered common by longtime corkscrew collectors, but oftentimes the advertising collectors will pay two to three times the values listed here just to get one they don't have. In my experience, which over 30 years has been to look at all kinds of things even if I wasn't searching for a particular item to buy, I have seen only two or three "Listerine" corkscrews, for example, therefore from my point of view as a generalist they are rare.

Corkscrew, cheap metal, very small folding type, worm folds into handle loop, red-painted sheet metal loop handle printed "Carter's Ink," pat'd. 1894. Crossover writing materials collectors............................ **$30+**

Corkscrew, sheet metal painted yellow, "Panopepton," almost identical to Carter's one, may be same age & patent. .... **$15+**

Corkscrew, adv'g. folding type, flimsy yellow & black printed tin, "Listerine," mfd. for them by unidentified novelty company, about 1-1/2"L folded, c.1900 to 1920s.. **$10+**

Corkscrew, adv'g. type in printed wooden tube sheath, "Kellerstrass Distilling Co., Kansas City," 1900. .... **$15+**

Corkscrew, steel, painted wood handle adv'g. "Welch Grape Juice," bell-cap, c.1887 Williamson patent, prob. early 20th C. .... **$25+**

Corkscrew, disguised within World's Fair key that opens, "Century of Progress," 1939. Crossover from Fair collectors. .... **$65+**

VIII-56. Corkscrew. *A simple one with turned, stained wood handle, hardened steel wire, attached to handle by winding. More expensive versions upgraded step by step: nickeled wire, varnished wood; then tempered steel, brace, and imitation rosewood handle; then "best tempered steel," wire cutter and polished hardwood. They were mounted to a card, 12 at a time, and originally wholesaled for from 30¢ per doz. to $1.75 per doz. Butler Brothers catalog, 1899.* **$5+**

Corkscrew, steel in wooden tube, small, meant for the corks in flavoring extract bottles, advertising printed on tube: "Chamberlain's Pure Extracts," c.1900....... **$10+**

Corkscrews – Figural & decorative

Note that all the Senator Volstead or Old Snifter corkscrew combinations are up in the listings of Combination Tools, right after the can opener listings. Note that some Folding, Advertising, and Lever corkscrews are also figural.

Corkscrew, alligator of carved staghorn, steel worm, prob. American because of motif, early (?) 20th C. .... **$150+**

Corkscrew, antler tip handle with sterling silver fittings, very small and may have had a sheath for pocket, 3"L, 19th C. .... **$65+**

Corkscrew, baby's upper torso, cast brass, French, c.1900. • Why a baby? It's the infant wine-lovin' Bacchus. .... **$85+**

Corkscrew, boot, sterling silver pocket screw in shape of high boot complete with pull-up straps, and wear wrinkles at ankle, corkscrew with bottle-opener looped bow at top pulls out of boot, marked "R. Blackington, Attleboro, Mass," and on bottom of heel is "Sterling," the hallmark, "738 Pat. Apl. For," boot 2-1/2"H; overall height 3-3/4", early 20th C. These sometimes sell for three times as much as the lowball value....................... **$50+**

Corkscrew, bottle shape, nickeled, brass plate label with engraved logo, date & "Anheuser Busch" beer, mfd. by C. T. Williamson Wire Novelty Co., Newark, NJ, dated 1897. Unscrew top half of bottle to reveal worm with tiny button release that folds out to right angles with bottle. 2-3/4"L. Early beer collectible. Brings less than I'd think it should, but it's fairly common....................... **$30+**

Corkscrew, bullet shape, very similar to the Busch bottle. Bottom half unscrews so worm can be pulled out & flipped into position, marked on bottom "Williamson Co Newark NJ Pat Sep. 4, 1900." Seems possible that the patent was for the mechanism only; the bullet may have related to the Spanish American War or much later, during WWI. .... **$40+**

Corkscrew, cat with screw as the tail, brass & steel, 3-3/4"L, c.1910. To a cat collector this might be a real prize. .... **$45+**

Corkscrew, Cheshire cat, cast brass & steel, English (?), late 19th C. For a cat collector, great; for a Lewis Carroll collector, super!.................... **$100+**

Corkscrew, clown head, molded plastic – very moderne, 4-1/2"L, 20th C. .... **$45+**

VIII-57. Corkscrews. *Called* **cellar corkscrews.** *Forged iron, twists at top provided leverage for turning. Italian, late 18th C. 6-3/4"L and 8-3/8"L. Collection Hillman Books.* **$100+**

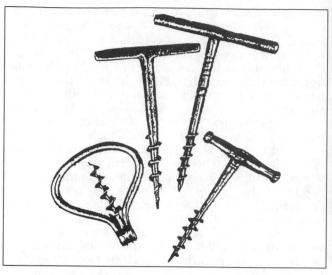

VIII-58. Corkscrews. *All forged iron, all helical worms. European, probably Italian.* **(L)** *Folding harp with a center cut worm, 2-7/8"L folded. The "T"-handle ones are 4-3/8"L, 4-5/8"L and 3-1/2"L. Mid to late 18th C. Collection Hillman Books.* **$95+**

Corkscrew, donkey, nickeled-cast steel, very Deco design of animal with all legs folded beneath, and looking back over shoulder at the screw, which forms long upright tail, 2-3/8"L, English, Reg. #180446, 1933............................... **$45+**

Corkscrew, elephant head, ivory handle, glass eyes, sterling silver ferrule, English, 8-1/8"L, c.1900........................... **$85+**

Corkscrew, grotesque head of cast brass, steel helical worm, head is mythological hairy beast adapted from Durham Cathedral door-knocker, poss. a souvenir, marked only "DURHAM," English, 7-1/4"L including hanging ring on head's top, c.1930s................. **$70+**

Corkscrew, key of heavy cast brass, shaped like a very old-fashioned, ornate door key, probably a sommelier's corkscrew – the key signifying his control of the locked door to the wine cellar. (The key may just stand for hospitality, say some.) There are many varieties of these, from many countries: Italy, Germany, Bulgaria, France, and the form is still used, so most you find are probably not old. This one marked "G E A Bochum," European, late 19th C (?). (See also the key under advertising corkscrews.) .... **$75+**

Corkscrew, pixie figure carrying lantern, cast copper, simple helical worm screw, English, 6"L, late 19th C. .... **$60+**

Corkscrew, sailing ship, cast brass, 20th C., prob. 1950s............................. **$25+**

Corkscrew, Shriner's cap, cast aluminum, 6"L, 20th C. .... **$65+**

Corkscrew, sommelier, man dressed as aproned waiter or sommelier holding green bottle, looks like carved and painted wood, but is pour-molded powdered wood & resin composition, head and shoulders pull out to reveal corkscrew and bell cap, "SyrocoWood," mfd. by Syracuse Ornamental Co., Syracuse, NY, 8"H, c.1940-50s. I really think Syroco is yucky, especially the pieces stained to look like wood instead of being painted, but who cares! A lot of collectors love it for the variety of forms............. **$85+**

❖ NOTES ❖

Syroco. Collector Larry Meeker wrote me that the Syroco™ figural corkscrews, produced in Syracuse, NY, during the 1940s and 1950s, are currently "very collectible and the prices have steadily climbed. The more common ones," he writes, "such as the waiter and old codger bring up to $150 while rarer variations such as the clown and Indian bring $300 to $800." Meeker cautions strongly that you have to watch for condition problems, and especially what are called **"marriages"** – the putting together of whole parts of broken pieces in order to create a piece that looks perfect and whole. • Another collector says that the "Golden Knight" and the Indian Chief Syroco™ corkscrews are extremely valuable, by which I imagine he may mean over $800. • You can go to **Don Bull's virtual museum,** right to this URL, and see Syroco™ corkscrews: www.bull-works.net/virtual/syroco/syroco.htm .

Corkscrew, sommelier, carved & painted wood, a formally-dressed wine-serving man, with steel, European (?), 20th C. (?). .... **$80+**

Corkscrew, squirrel, steel helical worm, cast brass acorn with huge-tailed squirrel perched on nut, hanging ring at top, English (?), 6-1/2"L, late 19th C. .... **$125+**

Corkscrew, steel with boar's tusk handle, silver & ivory trim, European, late 19th C. .... **$95+**

Corkscrew, tomahawk or hatchet, wood handle, iron works, American (?), c.1900. .... **$45+**

Corkscrew, tree stump figural handle made of iron, 6"L. .... **$35+**

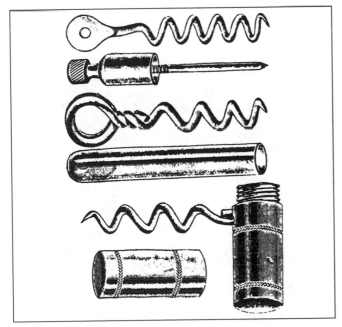

VIII-59. Corkscrews. For "vest pocket." All nickeled steel. Top (1) & (2) two are the screw and the cap for it, to be assembled by putting the rod through hole and using as handle to twist. Nickeled steel, 3"L. (3) Is simple heavy twisted wire & metal tube, 3-1/4"L. At bottom is (4) a neat one with screw kept inside, then fitted into position for use. 24"L in tube. A. Pick, 1905-09. $15-$25+

Corkscrew, Viking ship with mythological Griffin heads, remove single sail to reveal screw, nickel- or chrome-plated cast iron, 3-1/2"H x 4-1/4"L, 20th C. .... **$35+**

Corkscrews – Folding

For other folding examples, see also Advertising corkscrews, and also all the Combination tools listed right after the can opener listings, and the Corkscrews in the listing section after this one.

Corkscrew, folding, nickel-plated, when folded the worm retreats into the folding T-handle, "The Handy, Patented Feb. 24 1891," Mfd. by Little Giant Letterpress Co., NYC. (See VIII-54.) .... **$20+**

Corkscrew, folding, "The Davis," pat'd. 1891....... **$15+**

Corkscrew, folding bawdy lady's legs, plated metal with enameled red & black stockings, 5-1/2"L when folded, German, c.1900. .... **$110+**

Corkscrew, Gay 90s' lady's legs, slightly bent at knees, wearing red & white striped stockings of celluloid (they also came in charcoal-gray stripes and green stripes), partly nickel-plated, with high top laced boots, very elegantly risqué, mfd. by Severin R. Droecher, German patent #21718 Jan. 1, 1894, patentees Steinfeld & Reimer, 3"L. Many had striped or colored celluloid riveted to metal legs. The more flesh showing, the higher the value. The smallest lady legs are under 2"L and bring up to $800 or so. (See similar idea in the naughty lady nutcrackers in Chapter I.).................................... **$200+**

Corkscrew, Gay 90s' lady's legs, slightly bent at knees, folded, has striped stockings from boot-top to just above knee, thigh enameled "flesh" color, 2-1/2"L, Graef & Schmidt, German, c.1910. (Also came in red/white, blue/white, green/white stripes, and wholesaled for 59¢ each!) .... **$140+**

Corkscrews, Folding Combinations – Bows or Harps

The most common folding corkscrew is the "bow" or "harp" style, which is more or less like a horseshoe-shaped hoop or bow of steel, the two ends joined on either side of one or more tools, in a tight fit so the tool swivels out to be used. They're usually about 2-3/4" to 3" folded. See the picture VIII-58, the one on the far left. • These can be **found with from 1 to 10 different tools,** a sort of man's chateleine, and early ones may go anywhere from $20 to $50 per tool. One recently on eBay is German, and came in a small leather snapped pouch, which looked like the 1940s-50s. It had 9 tools: corkscrew, can opener, drill, screwdriver, cap lifter, hammer, knife, awl, saw, and sold for under $60 – about $10.50 per tool.)

Corkscrew, buttonhook & pick combined, steel frame, folding tool in harp or bow, French or English, 3-1/2"L, 19th C. .... **$50+**

Corkscrews – "Functional"

Not figural, decorative, levered, mechanical, and of course we hope all corkscrews function.

Corkscrew, brass barrel with turned ivory handle with black bristles, 6-1/4", "Thomason," English, mid (?) 19th C.. .... **$500+**

Corkscrew, brass & bone or ivory, with dust & cobweb brush in one end of handle, Thomason type, English, 7-3/8", mid 19th C. Estimated at a 1983 Christie's sale to get $80 to $120, because such corkscrews had brought that before, this one got $440. Often auction prices are reported in trade papers with "Caution: Auction Price," but auctions can go anywhere – up or down – depending on the people bidding. .... **$500+**

Corkscrew, brass shank with large ring below turned wood T-handle, helical worm, marked "The Twin" on ring, Wolverson patent, reg. #310265, English, 1877. Very elegant. .... **$125+**

Corkscrew, cast iron, wood handle, Archimedean screw in cage, cast iron, wood handle, 1883. .... **$65+**

Corkscrew, forged iron, very elegant L-shape for cellar use, long worm, Italian, 9-1/4"L, 18th C. ...... **$100+**

Corkscrew, Archimedean screw, steel, "Diamant J P Paris" [J. H. Perille], c.1900.......................... **$120+**

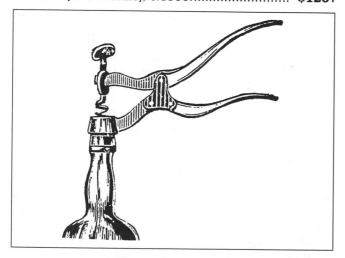

VIII-60. Corkscrew. *Mechanical "Lund's Lever" 2-part, 2-step opener. The 2 parts are plier-like lever and the screw, the shaft of which has a hole that fits over hook at top of plier/lever. The 2 steps are: screw the 3-1/2"L worm into cork, then fit bell cap over mouth of bottle and hook lever through hole in worm. The screw part is commonly orphaned, and mistaken for small pocket corkscrew. English. In importer F. A. Walker's catalog, 1870s, but pat'd. 1855.* **$125-$175**

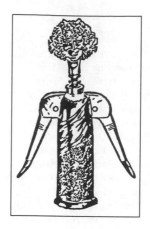

VIII-61. Corkscrew. *A modern figural: Bacchus, mfd. by Godinger, cast brass. Circa 1983-84.* **$25+**

Corkscrew, for beer bottle, wooden cigar-shaped T-handle, nickeled shaft, short bell-shaped cap lifter of iron, design pat'd. by William A. Williamson, for Anheuser-Busch, pat'd. Dec. 13, 1898. Very common form, made over long period. .... **$15+**

Corkscrew, steel & wood, with cap that fits over bottle mouth, "W. Williamson" patent, American, 5-3/4"L, pat'd. 1887... **$15+**

Corkscrew, "peg & worm" pocket or traveling type, polished cut steel with some lathe turning, and faceted peg, English, 4"L, 19th C. • **Peg and Worm.** – The "peg" is the handle, a cross piece with a knob or handle (in this case) either plain or decorated; the peg fits into the twist at the end of the screw. These came in little tubular sheaths, making them safe to carry about in trouser pockets. $65-$95 for really simple peg & worms. This turned steel one:.. **$125+**

Corkscrew, coil spring on shaft, Sommer's patent. .... **$300-$500**

Corkscrew, sliding cone, Curley's patent....... **$300-$500**

Corkscrew, "The Magic," 1883 patent. .... **$200-$300**

Corkscrew, Edwin Walker's 1891 patent. .... **$100+**

Corkscrews – Levered: Single, Double, Compound

Corkscrew, lever action, cast iron with brass maker's plate, "The Royal Club," pat'd. by Charles Hull, English, 1864... **$300+**

Corkscrew, lever – Bacchus' head with wild curly hair, double lever type, levers are arms, the "body" that fits over bottle neck is cast brass to look like Greek tunic, with grapes, mfd. by Godinger, c.1983............... **$30+**

Corkscrew, iron, 2 parts, a plier-like single lever, with a bell cap to fit over cork, and with a worm or screw that fits on the end. The worm was twisted into the cork, and then the plier-lever was hooked on. The screw is commonly found by itself, having lost the plier part that it fits into, "Lund Patentee London" on one side along with a crown & shield, other side marked "The Patentee 24 Fleet St & 57 Cornhill London," English, patent #736, pat'd. 1855. • Classic. – Watney & Babbidge's Corkscrews for Collectors says variations of Lund's Lever were made by "a number of firms over the years," & sold through the "Army and Navy Catalogue" as late as 1925-26....... **$150+**

Corkscrew, single lever, steel with turned wood handle painted black, pat'd. by Alfred Sperry, Wallingford, CT, 8-1/2"L, marked "Patd May 22, 1878." One sold by eBayer past-possessions in March 2002 for:... **$1,610**

VIII-62. Corkscrew.
Turned bone handle (possibly ivory), dark bristle dust & cobweb brush intact, cast & turned brass cylindrical sheath covering mechanism. Thomason type. Patented, 19th C. English. 7-3/8"L as shown. Picture courtesy of Christie, Manson & Woods International, Inc. **$400+**

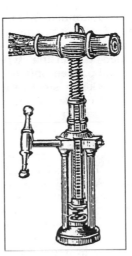

VIII-64. Corkscrew. *Double lever corkscrew with ratchet wheel, and side turning handle, in the style of the King screw. Probably steel with bone or wood handle, fitted with dust brush. From F. A. Walker import catalog, 1870s.* **$150+**

Corkscrew, lever, single – steel, single arm pump lever type works like handle of water pump, marked "W.W. Tucker," Hartford, CT, pat'd. Sept. 3, 1878. .... **$800+**

Corkscrew, lever, tangent lever mechanism, iron, originally enameled black, brass, separate worm is iron with metallic copper finish, "Spong & Co.," London, England, 7-3/8"L, registered Nov. 4, 1873........ **$125+**

Corkscrew, compound lever type – multiplied leverage achieved by two- or three-jointed criss-crossed arms, called **"concertina"** or **"lazy tongs,"** named the "American Reliable Concertina," c.1890s-1910. (Lazy tong corkscrews come in many incarnations – most are common and sell for under $50.) .... **$165+**

Corkscrew, compound lever type with crisscrossed arms with 4 lever points, also called "lazy tongs" or concertina type corkscrew, big oval ring grip at top, forged steel with bronze finish, marked "Patent Wier's Patent 12804, 25th September 1884," mfd. by James Heeley & Sons, English, 14"L fully extended. "Weir" or "Wier"? This is widely described as being spelled WEIR, but I've seen it on actual corkscrews as WIER. Maybe there are both? A classic. This corkscrew, bronzed or nickel-plated, was sold as late as 1939-40 in Army & Navy Stores Limited catalog, London, England. We suppose it was offered for a

long time after, too. (A 5-3/4"L repro one, with same bronzed finish, marked "Guild of Sommeliers – in vino felicitas" is fairly recent, but still brings a decent price of over $35.) .... **$100+**

Corkscrew, nickel plated metal, cap fits over bottle's mouth & cork, action consists of a compound lever – a "jointed extension" like a lazy tongs, with 3 crossed or zig zag arms, used by screwing in worm, then pulling on handle, which pulls cork as it extends, "Zig-Zag Corkscrew," American, late 1920s. • Probably related to the French one in more than name & works.. **$75+**

Corkscrew, compound lever (lazy tong or concertina) style, steel, marked "Zig Zag, No. 38," on handle, also marked "Bte S.G.D.G. Fr & Et. M & M. DER," French, 10-1/4"L fully extended, 1870s. These are still being made exactly the same. Old:........... **$75+**

❖ NOTES ❖

Marks on French Items – *Bte* is an abbreviation for *Breveté*, or patentee. S. G. D. G. stands for *Sans Garantie Du Gouvernement*, or, registered, but without warranty by the government. In this case, it seems to say registered without warranty by the government of France. *Et* is probably *Etranger*, meaning foreign. M & M stands for *Marque et Modele* meaning trademark and model were deposited.

VIII-63. Corkscrew. *Another of Lund's patents from 1855. Bone crossbar handle, steel cage, helical worm, hanging ring at top, missing the dust brush. About 7-1/4"H as shown. English.* **$125**

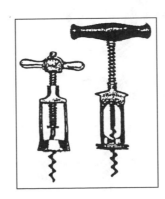

VIII-65. Corkscrews. (L) *"The Challenge," French-style, locking "fly nut" at top, cast steel open cage, helical worm. 6-1/2"L fully extended. (R) Steel & wood "Columbus," with spring around shank between cage & turned wood handle – referred to as a "sprung shank" type. 6-1/2"L. The "Challenge" worth $20 to $40 more than other. Full range of value:* **$85+**

Corkscrew, compound lever concertina, miniature just shy of 2"L, marked "VINS FAMY," (Famy is a winery), French, perhaps 1920s-30s?......................... **$50+**

Corkscrew, compound lever modified "concertina" type like two very long arms held akimbo, then only one more pair of shorter "elbows," nickeled steel, oval ring handle, steep pitched center cut screw, "The Irresistible," pat'd. by Armstrong, English, late 19th C. .... **$135+**

Corkscrew, mechanical double lever type, bronzed steel, broad-shouldered levers (in down position), wing-nut-like top, steel helical worm, marked "Heeley's Patent A-1 Double Lever 1888," and "James Heeley & Sons, 5006 Patent Double Lever," English, 6-1/2"L, 1888. Marvelous & graceful looking........................... **$150+**

Corkscrew, lever, cast & machined brass, with cog & rachet mechanism, and wingy top that looks almost like a maple tree seed, has a collar to grasp top of cork, Rosati's patent, Italy, 6-1/2"L, 20th C. ... **$45+**

Corkscrew, lever, shiny tinned iron, "Magic Lever Cork Drawer," English, 5-3/4"L in closed position (levers down), c.1890s-1910, marked "pat. appd for."... **$125+**

Corkscrew, lever – nude "bionic" man, brass with red faceted glass eyes, looks more like a hood ornament than a corkscrew. Mid- late 20th C. Yuck (I say that now, but from experience I can say, yesterday's "yuck" is often tomorrow's "yummy")............... **$35+**

Corkscrew, lever – sommelier, double lever type, silver plated metal, little man's body fits over neck of bottle, modeled with wescot & sommelier's medallion on chain, shoulders are where the levers pivot, the levers are his 2 arms, round bald head with big ears, called "Pierre le Sommelier," French import, 8"H, c.1980. .... **$25+**

Corkscrew, lever – owl's head, with large eyes, plated metal, lever type, the 2 lever arms rather like wings, the words "HOOTCH-OWL" cast into body, pat'd. by R. G. Smythe, American, pat'd. 1935. Crossover owl interest. .... **$225+**

Corkscrews – Mechanical other than Lever

Corkscrew, clutch mechanism, steel with open barrel cage, turned wooden (or fancier bone) handle, Coney & Co.'s "THE KING" (not Thomason's King's Screw), Birmingham, England, pat'd. 1904. Handle affects price. .... **$150-$250+**

Corkscrew, double-action mechanical type with so-called "hermaphrodite raising screw" that goes one

VIII-67. Jar opener. *Malleable iron, thumb-screw adjusts tension. Paper label "Best," Portland, ME. 3"L. "Pat. Appl.," early 20th C., maybe 1920s.* **$15+**

way then another, steel screw, brass barrel ornately decorated with the fruits & plants of wine & beer making, turned bone handle. Also has intact brush at one end of T-handle, Thomason patent, English, 1802. .... **$450-$650+**

Corkscrew, so-called "Italian Grinder" type with bladed worm, open barrel, really neat crank at right angles, with nearly 4"L shaft and upright rounded wood knob, used by placing over bottle mouth, holding to angular wing grip at top with one hand while cranking like a coffee mill with the other. A very handsome reproduction, marked "David Maniago," 6-1/2"L, late 20th C. .... **$75+**

Corkscrew, rack & pinion mechanism, blued steel (some have brass barrels or cages) with lathe-turned bone-ivory handle at top, plain steel smaller side handle, "King's Screw," or with only "King's" capitalized. Patented in 1802 by Sir Edward Thomason. Two English makers of are Mapplebeck & Lowe, and Dowler, English, about 7"L (hard to measure mechanical in a uniform way – open, half open or closed). 19th C. Those with double bone or ivory handles cost more. Messrs. Watney & Babbidge, in *Corkscrews for Collectors* (see Bibliography), say at least 24 manufacturers have been identified as making Thomason's "King's Screw," which is highly regarded as one of the handsomest and finest of the rack & pinion types. (Those with double bone or ivory handles cost more.).................... **$450-$650+**

Corkscrew, rack & pinion type, long steel frame with turned wooden handle, brush intact, "London Rack, Lund Maker, Cornhill & Fleet Street, London," mid 1800s... **$200+**

Glass cutter combination tool – See Bottle & can opener, knife sharpener & glazier's tool combined.

Jar opener, cast iron, "H. L. Jenney," Greenfield, MA, undated late 19th C., "Pat. Appl'd For." .... **$35+**

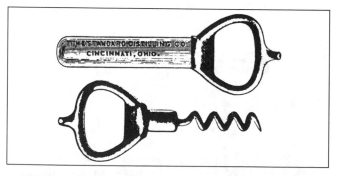

VIII-66. Corkscrews, *and crown cap opener combined. Protrusion is a wire breaker. Pocket advertising type, shown with & without printed wooden tube. (Also came with metal tube.) A. Pick, 1905-09.* **$10**

❖ NOTES ❖

"Pat. Appl'd For," which dealer Bob Cahn, Primitive Man, always refers to as "that famous inventor – Pat Apple," was marked on gadgets, or used in advertising, in an attempt to protect them at least long enough for the inventor to make some money. Sometimes it wasn't even true; but usually it seems to have meant production could go on for a few months or even one or two years, before a patent was granted (or possibly rejected, something the inventor would hardly emboss on the side of his invention). Similarly, "Pat. Pending" was supposed to mean that the patent had been applied for, and the inventor was optimistic of its chances. But it isn't a guarantee that the patent was applied for, nor an indication that it was granted. Patent dates found embossed or stamped on a device may or may not be the actual date the patent was granted. • The date may also be the date the patent was applied for, usually many months prior to the granting. • There's also the chance that the date is accidentally wrong, perhaps an error during marking. • A real United States patent date is always a Tuesday. See the chapters on Patents at the end of the book.

Jar opener, iron with screw-action adjustable hook, "Best," mfd. by H. & E. Sanborn, Portland, ME, 3"L, "patent applied for," c.1920s (?).......................... **$7+**

Jar opener, mechanical, tinned cast iron, meant to be wall mounted with (missing) bracket, vertical frame with "faucet" knob to screw one of 2 corrugated jaws to fit lid, "#A100" on moving jaw, "Speedo," Central States Mfg. Co., St. Louis, MO, 6"L, c.1900 to 1912 "patents pending." Worth a lot more with wall bracket. .... **$20+**

Jar opener, or jar wrench, nickeled iron oblong frame for geared jaws, which are set by turning the cigar-shaped wood handle clockwise until the jaws fit the jar lid, then turning the other way to twist the lid off, handle painted red or green, or varnished, "Top Off Jar & Bottle Screw Top Opener," Edlund Co., Burlington, VT, gear moves jaws from 1-1/8" to 4-3/8"; width of metal part of tool is 1-5/8". 1933, but made

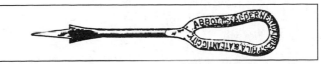

VIII-68. Milk bottle cap lift. *Steel, handle stamped with name of dairy. Cherry-Bassett Co. catalog of supplies for dairies, 1921.* **$3+**

for some years, with various handles, at first wood, later plastic. .... **$5+**

Knife sharpener & glass cutter – See Combination tools..

Milk bottle cap opener, iron, "Jack Spratt," c.1890s-1910. .... **$4+**

Milk bottle opener, metal with wood handle, adv'g. "White Lily Milk," 5"L. .... **$5+**

Milk bottle opener, to open paper cap wires, looks like a cross between a buttonhook and a pick, embossed with the dairy's name, 1920s?-30s? • As a child in the '40s, how I loved to open (with my bare fingers) the wires on those pleated paper caps. The wires went in a kitchen drawer, like the twisties do now, for future repair jobs. My parents still use an aluminum pan lid that lost its ring, that Daddy fixed with two of those milk bottle wire twists.................. **$5+**

FOR MORE INFORMATION

BOTTLE CAPPERS

Robert Rauhauser
POB 324
Thomasville, PA 17364-0324

BOTTLE OPENERS

Just For Openers

Emphasis on beer & soda advertising openers & corkscrews

Contact: John Stanley, editor of newsletter
POB 64
Chapel Hill, NC 27514
Organization e-mail: jfo@mindspring.com
Web site: www.just-for-openers.org/

Figural Bottle Opener Collector's Club
Contact: Mary Link
1774 N. 675 E.
Kewanna, IN 46939
E-mail: marylink@pwrtc.com
Web site: www.fbocclub.com

CAN OPENERS, BEER CAN OPENERS & CORKSCREWS

Joe Young

Can openers & corkscrews wanted from around the world. Correspondence invited and all inquiries answered.

POB 587
Elgin, IL 60121-0587
Phone: (947) 695-0108
E-mail: jandjyoung@mindspring.com

Bill Griffiths

Old & unusual can openers wanted, also related materials.
E-mail: griffithsbc@worldnet.att.net

Jim & Phyllis Moffet

The Moffets huge collections of mechanical kitchen antiques inspire many. They would be interested in unusual can openers.

POB 200
Modesto, IL 62667-0200
Phone: 217-439-7358

Patented Antiques
Carol & Larry Meeker

The Meekers specialize in patented antiques & seek to buy corkscrews & can openers.

E-mail: clm@patented-antiques.com, or
clm@antiqbuyer.com
Web site: www.patented-antiques.com

CORKSCREWS

International Correspondence of Corkscrew Addicts

Their president is called the "Right" – as in, "I'd rather be right than president." Their international membership is limited to 50, with a long waiting list – an organization that's obviously very exclusive. The first Right was Brother Timothy of the Christian Brothers. If you seriously collect corkscrews, you may want to get on the list by writing the Right (as of 2002).

Helgir Solheim
Nedre Prinsdalsvei 48, 1263
Oslo 12, Norway
Phone: 47-2-261-2854
E-mail: solhelix@online.no
More ICCA info @ Don Bull's
www.corkscrewmuseum.com

Canadian Corkscrew Collectors Club

Open membership.
Contact: Milt Becker
One Madison St.
East Rutherford, NJ 07073
Phone: (973) 773-9224
E-mail: clarethous@aol.com [note no "e"]
E-mail: CCCCdues@aol.com

Golden Gate Corkscrew Collectors

A San Francisco area club; also have information on a software program developed especially for corkscrew collectors – but not for Macs, alas.

Contact: Dean Walters & Vintage Antiques
Phone: (415) 459-6393
E-mail: dean_w@pacbell.net
Web site: http://home.pacbell.net/dean_w/ggcc.html

or

Fred O-Leary

Phone: (408) 996-3101
E-mail: fsoleary@aol.com

Don Bull

See also Bull's books in the Bibliography, and the extensive list of related books on his Web site of his Virtual Corkscrew Museum. Also seeks beer can openers.

POB 596
Wirtz, VA 24184
E-mail: corkscrew@bullworks.net
Web site: www.corkscrewmuseum.com

Corkscrew Glossary

A multi-lingual glossary of corkscrews, good if you are buying from Europe, is found at this very long URL.

http://www.google.com/search?q=cache:78al-jnR-bxs:www.tuerler.net/corkscrew/documents/dict_de.pdf+brevetto+19th+century&hl=en

Corkscrew Classification

Four long-time collectors have compiled a "universal system to classify corkscrews." These self-termed "helixophiles" are Fred Kincaid, Frank Ellis, Fred O'Leary, and Joseph C. Paradi. They divided all the corkscrews into 12 classes, subdivided by types; then by styles.

Web site: www.corkscrewnet.com/WorkingWithCS/Classification/SCReWSystem.htm

Short Corkscrew Patent History

This is one of many interesting related sites with the short history of everyday objects. Includes European patents.

Web site: http://inventors.about.com/library/weekly/aa122000a.htm

CORKSCREW MUSEUMS OR COLLECTIONS ON VIEW

Brother Timothy's Collection

Part of it is on display at this West Coast Napa Valley facility, a cooking school of great renown, where you can eat and drink wine.

Culinary Institute of America's Greystone
2555 Main Street
St. Helena, California, 94574
Tour reservation: (707) 967-2328

Korkenzieher Museum Der Welt

Small private German museum.
83708 Kreuth-Enterbach
Tegenseer Strasse 32
Germany

Musée Du Tire-Bouchon

Domaine de la Citadel Winery
84560 Mènerbes
France
Contact: Yves Rousset-Rouard, Proprietor,
Phone from North America: 011-33-04-90-72-41-58

Musée Le Secq Des Tournelles

Part of the Museum of Fine Arts of France, this enormous collection of iron and steel objects, including some corkscrews, was begun by Henri Le Secq des Tournelles. The huge book showing his collection was reproduced in paperback several decades ago.

Housed in St. Laurent Church
Rouen, France
Web site: www.discoverfrance.net/France/Museums/Secq-Tournelles.shtml

HOLDING & HANDLING

IX. WASH, REPAIR, & SHARPEN

This short chapter has tools and racks used for washing dishes and draining them dry; others for sharpening knives (although a few combination can openers and knife sharpeners are found in the previous chapter).

Knife sharpeners, which have the most variety, are probably the most popular tools here. If you include the contrivances used for cleaning or polishing knives, there's something for everyone – from an 18th century knife-cleaning or scouring box, to a strange revolving wooden drum, like some magician's trick machine, with slots for the knives.

My personal favorites are the **soap savers**, but I'm afraid the field is quite small. I prefer the homemade ones, but they're hard to find.

A surprise field, closely related to advertising collectibles, and just a tiny bit out of my purview, is comprised by the small flat chromolithographed sheet metal **pot scrapers**. Some astoundingly high prices, over $400, were achieved at an auction where a number of them were sold about 1985. Few of them show up on eBay, and most of those are the Penn Stove advertising ones.

A good book on **brushes** has yet to appear. I have about 200 brushes, and maybe 30 broom & brush catalogs. The variety is awesome, so it is a great futurewatch.

See the repaired pieces in Chapter VII, Containers.

Cutlery trays – See Chapter VII, Storage & Containers

Dish drainer, 2 piece, wire with sheet metal soap tray, c.1900. .... **$25+**

Dish drainer, all wire, for 12 plates, resembles today's dish drainers except for wire trough at end for cutlery, "Loop Weld Model No. A-4," by Marlboro Wire Goods Co., 3-7/8"H x 18-3/4"L x 12"W, c.1910. Note that Marlboro also made one for 15 plates that's 19" x 12-1/2". • A child's toy version was made exactly the same way and just as well, differing in the number of loops & plate arches. It's only 6-1/8"L x 3-5/8"W. It's valued at about $100. The bigger ones:............. **$30+**

Dish drainer, blackened tin & wire, with fold-down cutlery draining trough with 8 drain holes along gutter of it, wire rack lengthwise down center for plates & saucers, Androck No. 199, 3-7/8"H x 19-1/2"L x 12"W, early 20th C. • Rusts like crazy, but if lightly rusted, you can fix it up. • There was, in the 1870s or so, a wire rack that looks like a dish drainer, but was advertised as a dish warmer, pictured sitting over 2 range eyes, lids on. This sheet metal one would have served well to warm plates, but then it wouldn't have had the cutlery compartment.... **$50+**

Dish drainer, round dish drainer, very substantial heavy plated wire, wide metal rim to help hold shape, round cutlery basket in center, Utility Mfg. Co., Baltimore, MD, about 15" diam., c.1920s. Probably it was round so that it could be used by setting down in a deep dishpan to rinse, then the whole shebang could be lifted out and set on stove or sink to drain... **$35**

IX-1. Kitchen interior with sink & stove. *Charmingly exaggerated spaciousness. Note slanted sink drain. Hot & cold running water. Mosely Folding Bathtub Co., Chicago, IL, 1896 catalog.* "We have heard of a dish-washing machine, and seen an engraving. After it was invented, and pictured in one of the papers devoted to inventions, that was probably the last of it, for we never heard of one in use, and never expect to. The great trouble about a machine is that it can not think, and will give the same treatment to a delicate China saucer that it would to a large heavy platter. Dish-washing does not demand a high order of intellect, but it requires some thought." *American Agriculturist, July 1875.*

Dish drainer, round, open woven wire, detachable cutlery holder suspended in center has much finer wire mesh bottom. When I first saw one of these I mistakenly thought it was just a discard from an old dishwashing machine, and by "old" I thought maybe the 1950s. Androck, Washburn Co., 5-1/4"H x 15" diam., c.1930s. .... **$35+**

Dish drainer, soldered wire, T-shape with cross bar for flatware, or tumblers if tall narrow loops used,

longer piece has loops for plates, American, 16"L, c.1890s to 1910s.. **$45+**

Dish drainer, pine with woven wire screen & wooden dividers, American, 1880s. .... **$55+**

Dish drainer, water- & soap-bleached pine, 2 rows of nearly vertical dowel pegs to hold plates, a third of the drainer has cross pieces of dowels for flatware, small white rubber knobs on 4 feet, American, 2-3/4"H x 17-3/4"L x 11-1/2"W, 1890s to 1920s (?)......... **$55+**

Philosophy of Dishwashing

by Christopher Morley

"But I am forgetting my duties as host," said Mifflin. "Our dessert consists of apple sauce, gingerbread, and coffee." He rapidly cleared the empty dishes from the table and brought on the second course.

"I have been noticing the warning over the sideboard," said Gilbert. "I hope you will let me help you this evening." He pointed to a card hanging near the kitchen door. It read:

> ALWAYS WASH DISHES
> IMMEDIATELY AFTER MEALS
> IT SAVES TROUBLE

"I'm afraid I don't always obey that precept," said the bookseller as he poured the coffee. "Mrs. Mifflin hangs it there whenever she goes away, to remind me. But, as our friend Samuel Butler says, he that is stupid in little will also be stupid in much. I have a different theory about dish-washing, and I please myself by indulging it.

"I used to regard dish-washing merely as an ignoble chore, a kind of hateful discipline which had to be undergone with knitted brow and brazen fortitude. When my wife went away the first time, I erected a reading stand and an electric light over the sink, and used to read while my hands went automatically through base gestures of purification. I made the great spirits of literature partners of my sorrow, and learned by heart a good deal of *Paradise Lost* and of *Walt Mason*, while I soused and wallowed among pots and pans. I used to comfort myself with two lines of Keats:

> *'The moving waters at their priest-like task*
> *Of pure ablution round earth's human shores—'*

"Then a new conception of the matter struck me. It is intolerable for a human being to go on doing any task as a penance, under duress. No matter what the

work is, one must spiritualize it in some way, shatter the old idea of it into bits and rebuild it nearer to the heart's desire. How was I to do this with dish-washing?

"I broke a good many plates while I was pondering over the matter. Then it occurred to me that here was just the relaxation I needed. I had been worrying over the mental strain of being surrounded all day long by vociferous books, crying out at me their conflicting views as to the glories and agonies of life. Why not make dish-washing my balm and poultice?

"When one views a stubborn fact from a new angle, it is amazing how all its contours and edges change shape! Immediately my dishpan began to glow with a kind of philosophic halo! The warm soapy water became a sovereign medicine to retract hot blood from the head; the homely act of washing and drying cups and saucers became a symbol of the order and cleanliness that man imposes on the unruly world about him. I tore down my book rack and reading lamp from over the sink.

"Mr. Gilbert," he went on, "do not laugh at me when I tell you that I have evolved a whole kitchen philosophy of my own. I find the kitchen the shrine of our civilization, the focus of all that is comely in life. The ruddy shine of the stove is as beautiful as any sunset. A well-polished jug or spoon is as fair, as complete and beautiful, as any sonnet. The dish mop, properly rinsed and wrung and hung outside the back door to dry, is a whole sermon in itself. The stars never look so bright as they do from the kitchen door after the ice-box pan is emptied and the whole place is 'redd up,' as the Scotch say."

Christopher Morley, The Haunted Bookshop, *1923.*

Dish mop, cotton thrum with slender broomstick handle, Shaker construction, 9"L, mid- to late 19th C. • Thrum is the word for loose ends of warp threads, left when the finished weaving is cut off the loom – hence for short pieces of scrap thread or yarn. .... **$40+**

Dish mop, turned wooden handle, cotton mop head tied on. In 1904, *House Furnishing Review* commented "Not one housewife in 25 knows how useful a ... dish mop is in the kitchen. ... Women who as girls were taught to immerse their hands in hot, greasy dish water are not prone to leave the beaten path of drudgery. They say the old way is good enough. As most of us have graduated from the tallow candle and the stage coach to the electric light and trolley car, why not improve in the same ratio in

minor things?" In the same article, the largest American manufacturer was identified as J. H. Estes & Sons, Fall River, MA, with 4 styles, 5 sizes each. This company began making them c.1900. • We often see dish mops at antique shows labeled "Shaker." Indeed, the Shakers made dish mops, using cotton **thrum** or the warp weaving threads cut off the looms. The simple turned wood handles and the bound cotton threads used in all the early ones would make it hard to know which were Shaker, which were J. H. Estes or other company. **$10**

Dish scraper – See Plate or dish scraper.

Dishpans were often made in enamelware in the late 1800s to early 1900s, although the finish chipped and cracked easily. Dish pans almost always have two handles (heavy wire, strap, ear), have a relatively broad flat bottom, deep slanted sides, and are at least 12" diameter, smaller ones without handles were some other kind of basin – a child's wash basin, or a pan for making a pudding. Very similar are washbasins, used with a pitcher, in rooms without running water. In imitation of fancier ceramic pieces, some wash basins were footed, or had a small flared base, and had sort of rounded or "bowled" sides. The flat part is smaller in diameter than that of a dishpan. Collectors of enamelware are well-organized, and buy and sell frequently, making the market hard to track for an outsider. In determining value, condition is very important, color is next, unless the pan has a very unusual rare color, but is not in near perfect condition. Manufacturer marks are also important to collectors. Value by

IX-3. Dish drainer. *Water & soap-bleached wood with dowel pegs, 2-3/4"H x 17-3/4"L x 11-1/2"W. White rubber feet. American, 1890s.* **$55+**

color, listing (A) body colors & (B) rim/handle color:
Blue & white mottled; dark blue: .... **$100+**
So-called "end of day" swirls of white, pale green, light blue, brown; black: .... **$175+**
Cobalt blue spots & blobs on white; black: .... **$125+**
Dark green & white in short jabby swirls; black: **$125+**
Brown & white speckly, white inside (attractive, but relatively new & lightweight); white: .... **$30+**
Red & white speckles & lines; red & white: .... **$65+**
Gray graniteware (looks like stone); gray: .... **$30+**

Dishpans or washbasins – See paragraph on iron bowls in Chapter VII

Dish warmer, usable also as a drainer, all wire oblong trough-shaped rack, made so it's flat on top, with vertical slots for a dozen or so plates or shallow dishes, to be set over 2 lidded range eyes for warm air to rise & dry or warm plates, American, 15"L, mid to late 19th C. .... **$200+**

Dishcloth holder, wire, 4 hooked fingers, the handle end is a coil and twist of the wires, a slip ring makes the fingers hold cloth in a tight grasp, American, 10-3/4"L, c.1890s. .... **$15+**

Dishcloth holder & cork puller combined, wire & wood, slip ring & 4 wire prongs which grasp cloth, American, 12"L, c.1880s to 1910. .... **$15+**

Dishcloth holder & vegetable skimmer combined, wire, with 4 hooked prongs at one end, an openwork twisted wire spoon at other end, slip ring to tighten prongs, American, 12"L, c. 1890s-1910. .... **$15+**

Dishwasher, tinned sheet iron, wooden lever handle, basket inside, "Whirlpool Sanitary Dishwasher," mfd. by Hershey-Sexton Mfg. Co., pat'd. July 28, 1914. • A "Whirlpool" washer was being made by the Nineteen Hundred Corp., of Binghampton, NY, in early 1930s. I can't find any better clues to maker. .... **$65+**

❖ NOTES ❖

To Wash Dishes – Dishes should be rinsed in clear, hot water after having been washed in soap suds. It is necessary from a sanitary point of view [because] the caustic alkali is corrosive and unwholesome, and the grease often impure. A rack made of narrow strips of half-inch board is a device frequently used for draining dishes, thus saving the trouble of wiping them. This rack placed on a shelf inclining towards and adjoining the sink holds the dishes securely while they are dry-

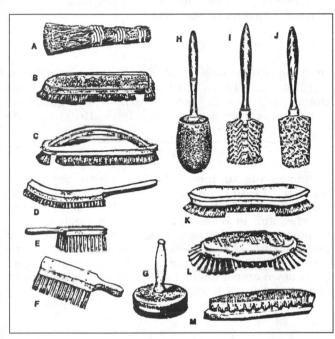

IX-2. Brushes, mostly for cleaning. *(A)* Sink *brush, bound natural fibers.* **(B)** *Scrub brush, wooden back. Note gap between bristles & different angle & set of bristles.* **(C)** *Stove brush, arched wood handle. Note gap.* **(D)** *Curved plate brush, made with 2, 3, 4, or 5 rows.* **(E)** *Baker's wash brush.* **(F)** *Steel wire brush for kitchen tables & butcher blocks. (A) - (F) all from Duparquet wholesale supply catalog, c.1904-1910.* **(G)** *Puree sieve brush. Looks like sign-painter's stencil brush. Jaburg Bros., NY, 1908.* **(H)** *Glass-washing brush, of "best Russia boar's bristles, drawn with copper wire."* **(I)** *Another, of horsehair, for tumblers. "Each little bunch ... bound with copper wire."* **(J)** *Another for tumblers, also Russia bristles. These 3 styles came in 3 sizes: "pony," "medium," and "large." Albert Pick & Co. wholesale catalog, 1909.* **(K)** *Yeast tub brush, of tampico (a plant) fiber. 11"L x 2-3/4"W. Jaburg & D. J. Barry catalogs, 1908, 1924.* **(L)** *"Imperial" ox fiber scrub brush, 11"L x 6"W. Barry, 1924.* **(M)** *"Boxwood scrub-brush. – To clean beautifully unpainted wood, table tops, meat and pastry boards." American Home Cook Book, 1854. Prob. most valuable would be H, I, & J.* **$6-$30**

ing. Milk is a substitute for soap in the kitchen. A little put into hot water will soften it, give the dishes a fine gloss, and will not injure the hands. China and glass (when very dirty) are best cleaned with finely powdered fuller's-earth and warm water, afterwards rinsing it well in clean water. All china that has any gilding upon it may on no account be rubbed with a cloth of any kind, but merely rinsed, first in hot and afterwards in cold water, and then left to drain till dry. Cups and saucers which have become stained with coffee or tea can be easily cleaned by scouring them with baking soda." Henry Scammell, *Treasure-House of Knowledge*, 1891.

Dishwashing brush, glass cylindrical bottle to be filled with soapy water, one threaded end has a turned wood handle that is hollow but has remnants of red rubber – probably a squeeze bulb; the other threaded end has screw-on zinc cap with small perforations on top, & a wood doughnut-shaped brush set with tampico fiber bristles, embossed on glass "CLIMAX Dish Dash Washer," American, 10"L, "pat. pending," c.1920s. • Collection of Carol Bohn. Price range mine. .... **$75+**

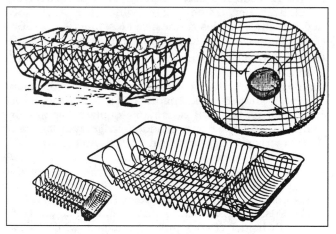

IX-4. Dish drainers & dish warmer. (T-L) Dish warmer or dryer. Galvanized iron wire rack, to hold plates, and "set upon stove or in front of a fire, or over a hot-air register." American Agriculturist, *March 1872.* **(T-R)** Dish drainer, round, wire, with mesh cutlery drainer in center. 5-1/4"H x 15" diam. Pat'd. in 1901 by Marie L. Price, Chicago, who assigned one third rights to Bertha A. Price. Pat. #646,128. Similar one with detachable silverware basket, was sold through Washburn-Androck in 1936, as something "good for country trade as drainer will fit inside round dish pan for draining dishes." (Note that this would require a dishpan at least 16" diam.) **(B-L)** & **(B-R)** Toy & full size of same drainer. "Loop Weld" iron wire, Marlboro Wire Goods Co. 3-7/8"H x 18-3/4"L x 12"W. Child's sample version, on original cardboard mount, is only 6-1/8"L x 3-5/8"W. Usually for two or three pennies, postage included!, readers of ladies' magazines such as the Ladies' Home Journal, could order miniatures for their little girls. Such miniatures, made carefully and with all the parts miniaturized, were used in a way as a mail order sales force – the intent was to sell the housewife a full-sized version. Both c.1910-15. **(T-L) $35+; (T-R) $35+; (B-L) $100+; (B-R) $30+**

IX-5. Dish Dryer. "*Androck #199.*" *3-7/8"H x 19-1/2"L x 12"W, with fold-down perforated cutlery drainer tray. From Washburn Co., Andrews Division, catalog, 1936. A similar blackened "charcoal" tin one had an attached wire cutlery basket instead of tray.* **$45+**

Draining pan for sink, royal blue & white enamelware, 12" diam., c.1890s-1910. .... **$55+**
Draining pan for sink, white enamelware, triangular to fit into sink corner, 3 short legs, c.1890s-1910. .... **$45+**

❖ **NOTES** ❖

Homemade drainer – An idea which has proved "most reliable in my own home, I send along. A round piece of tin which one can easily procure, when punched full of holes (which you can easily do with hammer and nails) makes a capital arrangement to put in the opening of the pipe which leads from the butler's pantry sink. This of course prevents many things from going down and stopping up the drain." *The Housewife Magazine*, Feb. 1910, NYC: A. D. Porter.

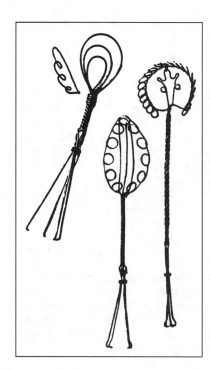

IX-6. Dishcloth holders & vegetable servers. *Twisted wire, slip-ringed prongs. Longest one is 13-1/2"L. No perfect chapter for these combination tools – see others in Chapter III. One at* **(R)** *Collection of Meryle Evans.* **$15+**

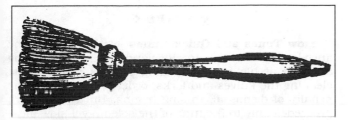

IX-7. Dish swab. *Type often described as "Shaker," because of short cotton pieces called* **thrum.** *Turned wood handle, cotton strings. The one shown was store-bought at a "house-furnishing store," but the circa 1870s description that follows is for a home-made one. "The swab may be made on any smooth round stick, about a foot long, and an inch in diameter. About two inches from one end cut a groove; take candle-wicking, white carpet-chain, or even strips of strong cotton cloth, and cut or fold about eight inches in length; tie this material firmly into the groove at the middle, and turn down and tie firmly at the end of the stick, and you will have a 'machine,' which will last many weeks, and go into boiling soap-suds, or even lye, without cringing." $5-$30*

Gloves, "India rubber," gauntlet style, apparently stitched together, Goodycar's India Rubber Glove Mfg Co., NYC, NY, advertised 1870. (I don't know if any of these could have survived, but if you thought gardening or dishwashing rubber gloves were fairly new, look at the date on these! • By at least 1901, Faultless Rubber Co. of Akron was making molded rubber gloves, which you could order by glove size, and finger length – long or short. • "Rubber gloves for kitchenette and kitchen use save the hands and are worth their weight in radium. If more women used them the housework problem would be less like martyrdom. They preserve the hands' health and beauty." Ethel R. Peyser, "Tinware, Rubber and Paper for the Kitchen," *House & Garden*, June 1922. People do collect rubber stuff: bathing caps, bathtub toys, dog toys, galoshes, and fill them with soft poly-fiber to keep them from collapsing in on themselves!... **$7-$15**

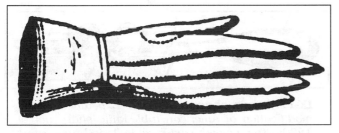

IX-8. Rubber glove. *From 1870* American Agricul-turist *ad of Goodyear's I[ndia] R[ubber] Glove Mfg. Co., NYC, in business at least since 1866. I don't know if you'd ever find a pair not dried out or shrunk in on themselves and sticky, but a collector of rubber bathtub toys & hot water bottles suggests treating them with Neat's Foot Oil and carefully stuffing with polyester fiber fill from a craft store's pillow-making supplies. A pair would be worth probably more than twice as much.* **$7+**

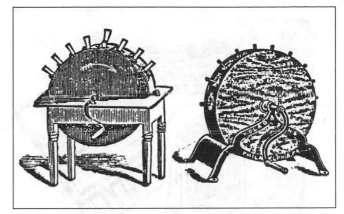

IX-9. Rotary knife cleaners. (L) *Cranked machine (the interior moved, not the outer part with the knives stuck out of holes), on table-like frame. "Knife-clean-ing machine. – By the use of which knives need never be put in water, and are kept bright with less time or trouble than in the old fashioned way." American Home Cook Book, 1854.* **(R)** *"Kent's" patented rotary cleaner, originally pat'd. in England. Made to hold 3, 4, 5, 6, 7, 8, 9 or 10 knives, including a carving knife. This one is tabletop style with cast iron frame and wooden drum. Very similar one mfd. in England by Spong & Co. Sold well into 20th C. for hotels and res-taurants. This picture is from V. Clad catalog, c.1890.* **$150-$350**

Knife cleaner, cast iron square frame screw clamps to table. A crank at side turns 2 geared & cranked felt covered rollers, making them rub together; they adjust for even snugger contiguity with 2 set screws. The device is used by inserting tip of knife blade between rollers, then turning crank, probably while pushing blade all the way through. I imagine the felt rollers were possibly dressed with some kind of scouring material too, pumice or brickstone. This scouring powder probably fell off the rollers into the bottom of the device, which has sides that form an inch deep well. The felt was in round discs, like washers, put on (like beads on a string) the rollers' axles. I guess so that individual ones could be replaced if badly cut or worn. Pat'd. as a "Machine for Scouring Knives, Etc." by G. M. Morris and J. Newton, Watertown, CT, base 4-3/8" square, rollers approx 2" diam. and 2-1/2"L, overall height 7-1/2", including screw clamp, only mark is the patent date, Dec. 4, 1855. • **Detective Serendipity Identifies Whatzit.** – I got this at auction, and thought it was a pea sheller – that pea pods were cranked through the presumably once-soft felt rollers, popping them open so the peas would fall in the well. Oh dear, such fantasizing. The 1855 patent date was too early for the *Official Gazette* which didn't start until 1873. The thing wasn't listed under Pea Shellers in my subject index to patents up to 1873. By chance, browsing in a Patent Office book, picturing agricul-tural and mechanical patents of 1855, I found a rec-ognizable drawing of a knife scourer, and it immediately made perfect sense! Nice to identify a Whatsit. **$50**

Knife cleaner, polishing-stone blade, green wooden han-dle, probably A & J, 7"L, c.1930s to 1940s. .... **$5+**

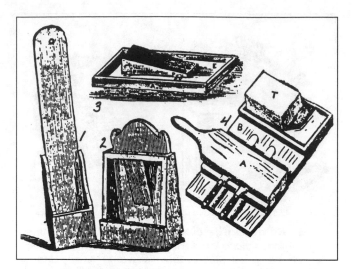

IX-10. Knife scouring or cleaning boxes. *Also called* **knife boards.** *A bath brick or other suitably fine grit was kept in the box-like part; knives were laid on the long part of* **(1)**, *or slanted part of* **(2)** *and* **(3)**, *and rubbed with rag, brush or large cork. Knives polished by moving back & forth between leather-covered hinged parts of* **(4)**, *while pressing down to make tight fit. All between about 16" to 26"L.* **(1)** *and* **(2)** *F. A. Walker catalog, c.1870s.* **(3)** *and* **(4)** *both from American Agriculturist, June 1876 and Aug. 1875. It was advised to "wipe knives with woolen cloth after rinsing." This was to impart a bit of anti-rust lanolin to the metal. Old paint, attractive patina and decorative cutouts, etc., would add value.* **$40-$150**

Knife cleaner, tabletop style, cast iron frame with wooden drum slotted for inserting knives so several can be done at once. Inside, a rubber roller (like wringer) polishes blades, with aid of a polishing powder, "Kents," London, England, various sizes for different numbers of knives, pat'd. 1882; Kents' common "Improved Patent" was pat'd. 1890. • In *Knights' Cyclopaedia of the Industry of All Nations* (London, 1851), appears this: "... a machine has been invented to perform the operation of cleaning table-knives; in which the cleaner has simply to turn a handle, instead of bestowing arm-movement in a somewhat laborious way. There are two rival patented machines for this purpose, Kents' and Masters'; both relate to a machine which was invented by an American, and was introduced into this country [England] ... by the parties above-named. The machine consists of a flat cylinder, or drum, in the inside of which are brushes placed in contact; holes are made around the drum, in which are placed from four to twelve knives, according to the size of the machine. The blades of the knives pass between the brushes; and when the brushes are made to rotate by a handle worked from without, the blades of the knives are exposed to an amount of friction sufficient to clean their surfaces." .... **$150-$350**

Knife cleaner & polisher, cast iron frame, screw clamps to table edge, other screws adjust distance between white rubber fat rollers, works like a mangle, "Spong's UneeK," English, about 9"L, 19th C. .... **$125+**

Slow Tunes and Quick Tunes – "I have heard the anecdote attributed to Rowland Hill; who, being annoyed at his footboy singing profane songs whilst cleaning the knives and forks, ordered him, under the penalty of dismissal, to sing hymns. But as the work proceeded only to the tune of the solemn yet slow measure, Mr. Hill was compelled to tell the boy to return to his old style of profane music, otherwise his knives and forks would not have been ready for dinner." Alfred John Dunkin, to British periodical *Notes and Queries, 3rd Series, Volume VII*, April 8, 1865.

Knife & scissor grinder, japanned cast iron, screw clamps to table edge, "sapphire" carborundum wheel is turned by crank, & with each turn passes through cooling water compartment below. Both of the 2 wire clips, one on each side, are put in position for one side of knife blade (but are raised out of way when doing scissors). 3 toothed gears "gear up" action so that one turn of crank turns wheel 6 times. "Clipper," mfd. by Montgomery & Co., NYC, wheel 4" diameter x 1" thick, entire grinder about 7"H, 1890. .... **$35+**

Knife scouring board or box, also called simply a knife board, used for cleaning blades, painted wood with bath brick in compartment, heart cutout at top end, prob. PA, 38"L x 5-1/2"W, mid 19th C. .... **$150+**

Knife scouring box, pine with original green paint on outside, simple box attached to footed scouring platform, American, mid 19th C. .... **$150+**

Knife scouring box, wood, long board with compartment at one end for bath brick powder or other abrasive that was spread on board so that when the flats of the knife blades were rubbed up & down, sort of á la razor stropping, they would be polished. American, 34"L x 5-1/2"W (they vary in length from about 30" to 40", and in width from about 4-1/2" to 6"), 19th C.

• **Added value.** – Those with old painted surfaces outside, fancy cutting to sides of compartment, or hang-up hole in fancy cutout (especially a heart), could bring up to five times as much as this: . **$100+**

Knife sharpener, bentwood drum, vertically mounted (like a one man band's drum beat with the foot

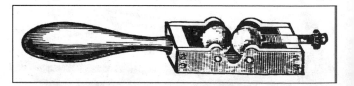

IX-11 Razor sharpener. *The "Expeditious" is a modification of American table-knife sharpener of 1830s. Two smooth cast steel balls in brass frame with ivory handle; blade was drawn between the balls, which were 3/4" to 1" diam. and had a hole drilled through the center. Screw at right "added for the purpose of keeping the balls in contact, and if the pivots are ... a little loose in frame, the balls may be turned and again fixed. The balls are made as hard as possible, and polished in a direction opposite to that of their axes." Journal of the Franklin Institute, 1837. Crossover interest from razor collectors.* **$50+**

IX-12. Knife sharpeners. (T-L) *Has three cast iron legs, and spring steel in bottom allows adjustment of two crisscross sharpening bars. 6"H. Pat'd. Oct. 1891.* **(T-R)** *Is small & homemade, wood handle with 2 squares of steel screwed to wood, the wood almost cut through by many sharpenings. 5-1/2"L. Late 19th C.* **(B)** *One in foreground is turned wood with 2 crisscrossed, adjustable steel sticks. 7-1/4"L.* **(T-L) $65; (T-R) $35; (B) $20+**

pedal) on iron frame, iron crank, with leather polishing leaves inside on a wheel. Used with polishing powder, mildly abrasive, "Self-adjusting Stag," mfd. by Spong & Co. Ltd., English, tabletop model, (others floor standing and more expensive), late 19th C. • Spong also made the earlier "The Servant's Friend Patent Knife Cleaner," circa 1880. .... **$165+**

Knife sharpener, cast iron with 3 legs, spring steel in bottom allows adjustment of the 2 bars that sharpen, American, 6"L, pat'd. Oct. 1891. .... **$65**

Knife sharpener, for scissors too, cast iron fishtail-like piece at one end with sharpening stone, attached to a longish pointed "steel" [a rod with very fine cross-hatched surface texture] for sharpening large chef's or butcher's knives, mfd. by Goodell Co., about 13"L, c. 1890s-1910... **$35+**

Knife sharpener, homemade tools with 2 squares of steel screwed to wooden handle, resembles a patented sharpener of same type, American, 5-1/2"L, late 19th C.. **$20+**

IX-13. Knife sharpeners. (L) *"Silver Duplex," silver & Co., Brooklyn, c.1910. Small screw-clamped cast iron frame, 2 steel sharpening sticks.* **(R)** *Nickeled steel with knobby wood handle. J. B. Foote Foundry Co., 1906.* **$25+**

IX-14. Knife sharpeners & scissor sharpener. *Clockwise from top:* **(1)** *"Clipper," for knives & scissors. Shown with wire clip for doing knives. Cranked, screw clamped to table, pat'd. May 18, 1886. Widely advertised 1880s to 1910s.* **(2)** *"Handy" sharpener for scissors. Eastman & Co., NYC. 1895 ad.* **(3)** *"American," mfd. by Mossberg Wrench Co., Mfrs of Novelties, Attleboro, MA. Pat'd. Feb. 23, 1892. Two discs between which blade was pulled.* **(4)** *"Peerless" combo sharpener & can opener. Early 20th C.* **(1) $35; (2) $10+; (3) $15+; (4) $10+**

Knife sharpener, iron & carborundum, "Winchester," New Haven, CT, early 20th C.......................... **$65+**

Knife sharpener, iron with wood handle, "Eversharp," Tungsten Tool Co., NYC, NY, early 20th C. ..... **$20+**

Knife sharpener, large bench style, has 6 carborundum sticks in a wheel at top, adjustable, red painted cast iron with black & yellow pinstriping, oil can attached, "Blankner's Knife Sharpener," mfd. by Blankner Knife Sharpener Co., Cleveland, OH, 9-1/2"H x 11"L, "patent pending" (c.1880s), and marked on wheel 0-5-4-3-2-1. • I don't know why, but these numbers may work like the number used to designate printings in books, and which are removed one by one each time book goes back to press. .... **$175+**

Knife sharpener, simple turned wood handle with screwed-on adjustable steel pieces, brass tip, American, 7-1/4"L, late 19th C. .... **$25+**

Knife sharpener, looks homemade, brass with some iron, stamped with individual letter stamps to read "M A R Y E Z I L," only 3-5/8"L, late 19th C. (?)................. **$25+**

Knife sharpener, metal, adv'g. "Crescent Hill Milk," 1920s.. **$10+**

Knife sharpener, metal, "Sharpeit," mfd. by Dazey Churn Co., St. Louis, pat'd. 1925. .... **$25+**

Knife sharpener, metal, "Lil Sharpy," mfd. by Milwaukee File Co., WI, late 19th or early 20th C. ..... **$10+**

Knife sharpener, nickeled cast metal, 2 sharpening stones, screw clamps to table, lever works the 2 upright "Y" sharpening stones mounted to metal, H. L. Johnson, 6-7/8"H, pat'd. July 24, 1888 & Sept. 2, 1890. .... **$65**

Knife sharpener, nickeled steel with wooden knob handle, J. B. Foote Foundry Co., Frederickstown, OH, about 5"H, 1906... **$25+**

Knife sharpener, steel frame & "roof"-like housing, "corundum" wheel, wall mounted, access through 2 guide slots on top, crank turns wheel, "Wulff Knife Sharpener," Hone-Rite, 1941 patent #2,257,407........... **$10+**

Knife sharpener, tabletop, iron frame with iron water trough to catch the water used to cool as it worked, cranked grindstone, mounted on wooden plank base, American, 8" diam. grindstone, (other sizes from 6" to 12" diam.), c.1890s-1910................ **$35+**

Knife sharpener, turned wood handle & frame, partly cut through from use, 2 small square iron plates bolted in position to create a V-opening for sharpening knife, loosen them & rotate edges of plates, American, 5-3/8"L, mid 19th C. to 1870s........ **$20+**

❖ NOTES ❖

Stove & Knife Sharpener Combined – A candidate for most unusual, although very logical, combination tool is F. & L. Kahn's c.1890 range or stove top of cast iron, with a special beveled edge in the front to be used like a knife sharpening steel to clean up burry edges of a knife. Sturdy – that's for sure. The ads claimed "Always ready. Always Sharp! Always useful." Kahn, I believe, sold rights to stove companies to manufacture their own stoves or ranges with the Kahn's patented edge.

Plate or dish scraper, hard white rubber, green rubber handle, "Daisy," mfd. by Schact Rubber Mfg. Co., Huntington, IN, 5-3/4"L, 1933 patent #1898690. .... **$5+**

Plate or dish scraper, rubber with wood handle, "A & J," but mfd. by company that took over A & J, Edward Katzinger Co., Chicago, IL, c.1940........ **$5+**

Plate or dish scraper, white rubber blade in stamped metal holder, turned wooden painted handle, marked "WB/W," I think it's probably Waterbury Button & Mfg. Co., (thought by Don Thornton to be Washburn Bros.), Waterbury, CT, 5-3/4"L, c.1925. • A number

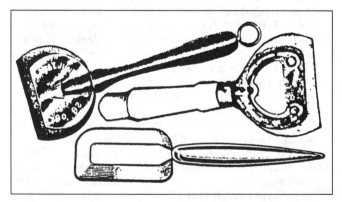

IX-15. Plate or dish scrapers. (L) *"Foskett's," wood, tin, rubber, 5-3/4"L, pat'd. June 26, 1906. Sold through Wire Goods Co., Worcester, MA, 1915 catalog.* ***(M)*** *Wood handle, tin riveted clamp for rubber blade. Marked "WB/W." (Perhaps Waterbury Button & Mfg. Co., because hard rubber buttons were common at the time; or, Washburn Brothers.) 5-3/4"L, c.1925. I buy these scrapers all the time because they look so much like small African sculptures when held blade side up.* ***(B)*** *Rubber with green wood handle, 9-1/2"L. Androck, 1927.* **$3+**

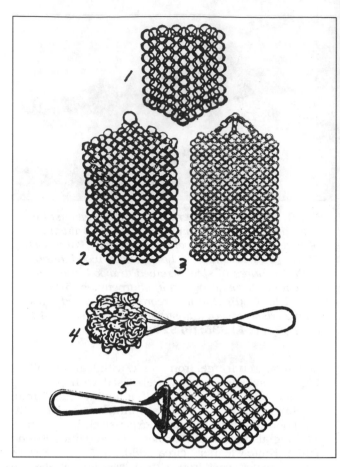

IX-16. Pot chains or pot scrubbers. *Not shown to scale; assembled from various catalogues. All chain mail – iron rings linked into flexible pads (or a ball with a handle).* ***(1)*** *Double rings, 4 sizes, from 3-1/2" x 5-1/2" to 8-1/2" x 11", with 1/2" or 3/4" rings. Washburn Co., 1936.* ***(2)*** *13" x 7", double mesh, hanging ring. Matthai-Ingram, c.1890.* ***(3)*** *"In some parts of the country, a pot-scrubber made of iron rings, as shown, is used, but it is by no means so well known as it ought to be. We do not know who the manufacturer is, but it is for sale at some of the hardware stores in New York City." American Agriculturist, July 1877. Over a century later, in the 1980s, some were being made in midwest by an elderly man who had made them in a factory ages ago.* ***(4)*** *Also Matthai-Ingram.* ***(5)*** *"Sensible," all nickel plated, iron handle is also a scraper. 5/8" double rings, 5-1/2" x 3-1/4". Excel c.1916 catalog, and Washburn, 1936. Caution: Various styles are being reproduced.* **$30+**

of hard rubber & metal plate scrapers were made by different companies. Lasher Mfg. of Davenport, IA, made one around 1909-1910 with turned wooden handle, half moon metal plate with rubber scraper part, called the "Kitchen Kumfort." Around 1915 Cassady-Fairbank Mfg. of Chicago made the "Foskett" scraper, almost identical in form. .... **$5+**

Polish, for aluminum, paper canister with silvery printed label, "Silver-Seal Polish, esp. prepared for Silver-Seal Kitchen Equipment," mfd. by Century Metalcraft Corp., Detroit, MI, (Chicago office named on label), early 20th C. **$10**

Metal Polishing Recipes – *"Common irons may be brightened by rubbing them first with a rag dipped in vinegar and the ashes, then with an oily rag, and after that with scouring paper, rotten stone, or white brick; but, if possible, red brick should not be used, for it makes sad work. This method of cleaning serves for all sorts of common irons or brasses, tho' some prefer goose-grease to oil, or any other sort of grease, and do not use scouring-paper to brasses. If these should be very fine steel stoves and fenders, they should be first rubbed with oil, then with emery, till clear and bright, and next with scouring paper, which is an excellent thing to rub irons with that are not in constant use, every two or three days." Eliza F. Haywood, A New Present for a Servant-Maid; Necessary Cautions and Precepts to Servant-Maids for Gaining Good-Will and Esteem, Dublin, Ireland: 1771. Whew! and for a wage of a few pounds a year!*

Pot cleaner, stamped sheet steel, parallelogram almost square, with short handle from one corner, 2 corrugated edges, one edge with bristles set along it, "The Korker Sink & Pot Cleaner," about 4" square, c.1890s-1910. .... **$15+**

Pot cleaner, wire rings like chain mail, wire loop handle, some have iron loop handle, made first in the late 19th C., but now widely reproduced. • "The 'chain-cloth' a net work of steel rings resembling an old fashioned reticule is of great service in cleaning burned kettles." Todd S. Goodholme, *Domestic Cyclopedia of Practical Information*, NY: Henry Holt, 1877. Chain mail fabric is now being sold for interior decoration for about $100 a square foot! These chain mail scrubbers are widely reproduced. .... **$30+**

Pot mender, tube holding a small sharp metal reamer and white metal (relatively soft) rivets. Only a hammer was needed. Paper label on tube reads: "For tin, enamelled & Aluminum ware. Saves money – double life of ware. Directions. Rivets in the handle. Ream hole to fit rivet. Hammer in place...." Arco Sanitary Mender, 7"L, 1910. .... **$9+**

Pot menders, soft metal patches with tiny rivet or bolt, small triangular wrench, mounted on chromolithographed card, "Mendets," Collette Mfg. Co., Amsterdam, NY, different sizes & different number of patches, pat'd. 1922, several different cards through the years, and still being made. .... **$5+**

Pot menders, wooden box with little metal discs and special "wrench," "Mendets," pat'd. 1922. .... **$5+**

*IX-17. **Pot menders.*** "Mendets," Collette Mfg. Co., Amsterdam, NY. A metal patch, a tiny "bolt," and a small triangular wrench, mounted on chromolithographed card. This one c.1940. Fun to collect a variety from different periods; in 1908 they called them "Collette's Patent Patches." By 1910 they had name "Mendets." They're still sold, but card graphics are ugly. **$5+**

❖ NOTES ❖

Pot scrapers are idiosyncratically-shaped metal pieces, with or without handles, used to scrape cooked-on crud and crust off the inside contours of various shapes of pots and kettles. The most collectible are small flat pieces of metal, approximately 2-7/8" x 3-3/8", plain, or lithographed with advertising (sometimes on both sides) for stoves, flour companies, various foods, etc. They usually are found in one of three shapes (see IX-21) that have curves and corners meant to fit any shaped pan. Collector Karol Atkinson, who wrote an article on pot scrapers for my second and third editions, has only found two different manufacturers' marks on the advertising type: W. D. Beach Co., Coshocton, OH; and Passaic Metal Ware Co., Passaic, NJ. Crossover collector interest has raised the asking price of two sought by graniteware collectors – the NESCO, and the "Royal Granite Ware" – to over $350 sometimes! The one with a fabulous color depiction of a sack of Red Wing Milling flour, with the wonderful red wing, has also greatly increased in value because it's desired by Red Wing ceramics collectors. One that has eluded Atkinson is a lithographed tin one depicting Buster Brown, and advertising "Buster Brown Bread," made by Schmidt's Bakeries, Harrisburg, PA.

Pot scraper, green, cream & black lithographed sheet tin, advertising type. "Mount Penn Stove Works, Penn Pots & Pan Scraper, Fits any corner of pot or pan," printer/mfr. W. D. Beach Co., Coshocton, OH. This and one for Henkel's Flour are two most common scrapers. • Of all the pot scrapers, this is the only one I run into fairly often. Still – this, like anything else – won't get less rare with time. .... **$75+**

Pot scraper, lithographed tin, "Royal Granite Ware," late 19th C. This qualifies as an advertising piece, and is highly desirable to enamelware collectors. .... **$250+**

Pot scraper, nickel plated steel, shaped to fit crevices & corners of pots and pans, marked "Jack the Scraper," mfd. by Bauer Utensil Mfg. Co., Cleveland, OH, c.1914. That name alone is collectible! .... **$15+**

IX-18. Scrapers of various kinds. (1) and **(2)** are **dough scrapers. (1)** *Wood handle, 5", 6", 7", or 8"W;* **(2)** *Tubular handle, all iron, 4", 5", or 6"W. Duparquet, Huot & Moneuse, c.1904-1910.* **(3) Candy-makers' crystallizing pan scraper.** *Sethness, 1925.* **(4)** *often sold as chopper, but is kettle or* **pan scraper***, all steel, tubular handle. T. Mills, 1930 catalog of candy-makers' supplies.* **(5)** *Bench or* **butcher block scraper***, all steel.* **(6) Broiler scraper***, triangular blade, wood handle.* **(5)** & **(6)** *look quite old, and the forms may be, but they both are in a c.1904-1910 catalog. Most valuable is probably* **(6). $15-$45**

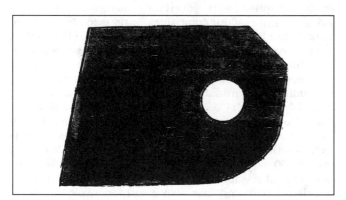

IX-19. Pot, pan and kettle scraper. *Note that this is almost exactly the same as the potscraper shape most commonly found with lithographed advertising. The early date of the following story by a magazine editor predates the chromolithed scrapers it so resembles by 25 to 35 years. "A curious thing came by mail. It was a piece of galvanized iron, of about 2 inches length, and had attached to it a label which read: 'Pot, Pan, and Kettle Scraper. Please accept, with the compliments of the season, from John Furbish, dealer in kitchen furnishing goods, stoves, etc., Main street, Brunswick, ME. December 25, 1871.' It seems that Furbish did not, as many stupid people do, go and patent a simple thing. He had tried it, found it good, had a lot made, and gave one to every holiday customer. The piece of sheet-iron is so shaped that it will meet all possible angles, and save no end of knives and spoons. ... First rate, and I wish I had had one before." American Agriculturist editor, May 1872.*

Pot scraper, tin, triangular with hang up hole, no advertising – possibly scoured off long ago, late 19th C. .... **$15+**

❖ **NOTES** ❖

"A clam shell is more convenient for scraping kettles and frying pans than a knife. It does the work in less time." Emma Babcock, *Household Hints*, 1881.

Pot & kettle scraper, heavily-tinned stamped sheet metal with Y-shaped handle, pivoting oblong scraping blade fastened to the Y, stamped "F. E. KOHLER & CO. PAT June 6, 93 Canton O USA." American, 1893. .... **$10+**

Scissors sharpener, adv'g. "Monarch Malleable Ranges," c.1890s-1910 to 1920s. .... **$35+**

Sink brush, tin, steel wire bristles, simple wood handle, fan-shaped, also cleans crevices in pots & pans, marked "Y-R," mfd. by Rice Mfg. Co., New Durham, NH, 9-1/4"L x 4"W, pat'd. Feb. 27, 1900......... **$10+**

Soap cleanser canister, green paint enameled metal canister with shaker holes in top, side embossed

IX-20. Pot & pan scraper. *"Instantly cleans pots, pans, pails, cake tins, cake griddles, dough boards, etc." Picture copyrighted 1909 by "Peale Hdw. Co." or possibly "Pease Hdw. Co." From door-to-door salesman's catalog, F. W. Seastrand, c.1910s.* **$6+**

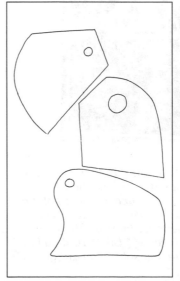

IX-21. Pot scraper shapes. *Actual reduced tracings of three types in the Karol Atkinson Collection.* **(T)** *Small hanging hole, approx. 3-1/2" across.* **(M)** *Larger hanging hole, commonest shape ("Admiral Coffee," "Ward's Remedies, Extracts, ...," "Mt. Penn Stove Works," "Red Wing Milling Co.," "Sharples," and "Dove Brand" ham & bacon.) Approx. 3-7/8" across;* **(B)** *Small hanging hole, most curvaceous shape, "Junket" dessert powders is in this shape. Approx. 2-9/16" x 3".*

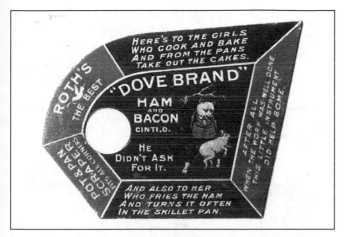

IX-22. "Pot & Pan Scraper Fits All Corners."
Chromolithographed sheet metal (tinned steel), flat,
approx. 3-1/2" across. "Dove Brand" ham & bacon,
Cincinnati, OH. Picture courtesy Karol Atkinson
Collection. Rhymes in segments along edges tell
how it's used: "Here's to the girls/ who cook and
bake/ and from the pans/ take out the cakes./
And also to her/ who fries the ham/ and turns it
often/ in the skillet pan./ After all/ when the work
was well done/ this little instrument/ did help
some." c.1910s. **$175+**

with image of Dutch Girl, screw-on bottom is black,
"Old Dutch Cleanser," c.1930s-50s. .... **$20+**
Soap cleanser canister, tin, color lithographed, "Bon
Ami" 12 oz. capacity, 1940s. • When I was about two
and a half, I started a combined scrapbook and
sketchbook. The color ads for the Bon Ami chick –
"Hasn't scratched yet" – were my favorite, and the
scrapbook is full of Bon Ami ads. .... **$35+**

IX-23. Pot scraper. "Sharples Tubular Cream Separator." Beautifully color lithographed scene.
Reverse is in cobalt blue and depicts the separator.
Approximately 3-1/2" across. Picture courtesy
Karol Atkinson Collection. 1909. • These are essentially advertising collectibles, which is why the values are so high for examples in extremely good
condition. **$200+**

IX-24 Pot scraper. Color lithographed sheet metal.
"Red Wing Milling Co.," Red Wing, MN. A name
known to many collectors of decorated stoneware
crocks, jugs, and beater jars from all the consor-
tium of Red Wing potteries. These are another
crossover collectible, sought by three schools of collectors – kitchen, advertising, Red Wing. Picture
courtesy Karol Atkinson Collection. **$325+**

Soap saver, homemade sheet steel, nice perforated box
with long handle, fill with soap scraps to swish in
dishpan, American, 13-3/4"L, c.1890s-1910. Some
folk art crossover interest. .... **$45+**

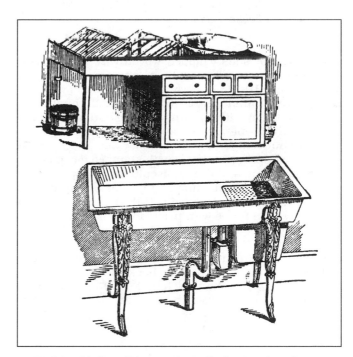

IX-25. Sinks. (T) "Wash Sink for Kitchen," suggested to improve the "unpleasant features" of dish
washing. Sink is "lined with sheet-iron instead of
zinc, and is made with two divisions." Removable
wooden racks. American Agriculturist, April 1883.
(B) "Sanitas" kitchen sink, fancy cast iron legs
(which are now very valuable to restorers). From
Alfred Revill's American Plumbing, NYC, 1894.

IX-26. Sink brush. *Wire with wood handle. Marked "Y-R," pat'd. Feb. 27, 1900, mfd. by Rice Mfg. Co., New Durham, NH. 9-1/4"L.* **$10+**

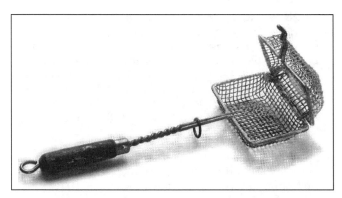

IX-27. Soap saver. *Wire mesh box, twisted wire handle with slip ring, wood grip. 10"L, c.1920-40s. Disshul Collection.* **$7+**

Soap saver, or suds whipper, woven wire like a bustle making 2 fat pillows with a long wooden handle, American, 10-5/8"L, early 20th C. .... **$10+**

Soap saver, round perforated tin box, 2 equal parts held together with slip ring on long spring wire handle, Matthai-Ingram Co., about 11"L, pat'd. Sept. 14, 1875, but sold for decades. .... **$15+**

Soap saver, spring steel wire with stamped mesh holder for soap scraps, 2 round biscuit-shape halves of the soap compartment clamped together by slip ring on long wire handle, American, 19th C. .... **$8+**

Soap saver, tin frame with twisted wire handle & hanging loop, wire mesh container for the soap, 3-1/2" x 2-1/2" with 7"L handle, c.1890s-1910. .... **$15+**

Soap saver, wire mesh box, wooden handle, box is hinged 2 parts, with little hook closing that slips under ring on shaft of handle, 10"L, c.1920s to 1940s. .... **$10+**

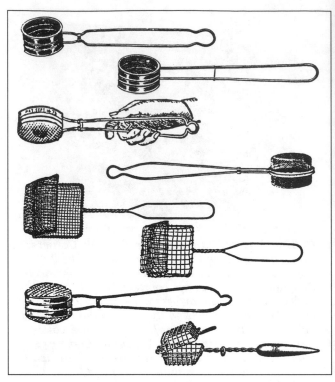

IX-28. Soap savers. *Soap scraps are put into the boxes or cages, and tool is swished through dishwater to make suds. Work great. Left to right from top:* **(1)** & **(2)** *Tin with fine wire mesh, 2 different handles. Both are 1-1/2" deep x 2-3/8" diam. x 12"L. Wire Goods Co., 1915.* **(3)** *Matthai-Ingram, pat'd. Sept. 14, 1875, c.1890 catalog.* **(4)** *"New Standard," from unidentified c.1900 flyer.* **(5)** & **(6)** *Tinned wire, different meshes offered.* **(5)** *Came in 4 box sizes, 11"L or 16"L.* **(6)** *Only in wide mesh, 8-1/2"L overall.* **(7)** *With "cups of wire gauze," was described in* American Agriculturist, *1881.* **(8)** *Welded wire, tinned, green handle, 10-1/2"L. Washburn, 1936.* **$10-$30**

Soap shaver, tin with wire arch handle, looks like a vegetable grater but the openings are like little crescent moons or smiles, embossed "Sunny Monday – Saves Soap & Labor," 10-3/4"L x 4"W, c.1900 to 1920. .... **$15+**

Stove blacking brush, iron handle, black bristles, "People's," c.1890s-1910. .... **$18+**

Stove polish can, colorful lithographed tin, depicts devils cavorting on black iron cookstove, "X-Ray Stove Polish," c.1890s-1910 to 1910s. .... **$35+**

Stove polish can holder, or Blacking tin holder – See IX-39, XI40a.

COOKING

X. HEARTH & FIREPLACES

The increasing interest in practical hearth-cooking and the revival of walk-in fireplaces built to order by specialists, make it necessary to have some coverage of the subject in this book. In addition, to understand the goals of the late 19th century and 20th century cook (and collector), you do have to have some background in hearth-cooking.

Most pieces – hollowware utensils and implements here are from the 18th and 19th centuries. Some that are very old and were meant to be used in hearth-cooking were carried over to cast iron cooking ranges, so if you don't see something here, you might find it in the next chapter. Ranges were coming into use by the first quarter of the 19th century in some urban houses, even though the old-fashioned hearth-cooking techniques were still being practiced late in the 19th century in many rural homes. I've put the **hollowwares** and the **"sad" (or flat) wares** like griddles in this chapter, while many **implements**, such as flesh forks, toasting forks, or tasting spoons (although they started life as hearth-cooking implements) are in Chapter XIII. Old tea kettles used in the hearth are in Chapter XIV, Coffee & Tea.

The major caution about collecting hearth-cooking tools – from whirling broilers to spiders to trammels-relates to **provenance** – where the thing originated. The overall effect of the flooding of the American antique market with dealer-imported "containerloads" of old hearth metalwares is that prices of all unmarked, unattributable pieces are more or less depressed. Overseas, I don't know what the effect is – especially now with the attempted homogenization of the European Union.

A good percentage (not calculable at this point, but probably as much as 75 to 85 percent) of old forged iron, cast bronze, or cast iron pieces for sale in the United States today were brought over in the last 30 years from Europe and the Middle East.

The first wave of modern immigrant hearthiana came, as did the Mayflower, 380+ years ago, from the British Isles; then wares from Germany, Holland, Italy, France, Scandinavia, the British Isles, Poland, Russia, Czechoslovakia, and even China, began to come in with waves of immigrants. Around 1900, vast quantities of wares were imported from Germany, especially, to satisfy consumers in the U.S. Brass Russian wares were imported and sold on Allen Street in New York City (where they still can be found in small shops).

In about the 1980s-90s, the great bone-yards of old iron that must lie in every cellar and outbuilding in Portugal was discovered, resulting in a good deal of Portuguese iron coming to the U.S. to be sold as decorative items, and to a lesser extent, to collectors. Much of it is quite attractive and well-made. In fact, "decorative" is the quality of much of the container-loaded old iron that enables American collectors to recognize it as European. Where a simple curve might have been used on an American pot rack, for example, a splendiferous (splendi-ferrous?) scrolly crest would more likely have been the choice of a European artisan.

And finally, in the 1990s and early 21st century, imported containerloads of Middle-Eastern wares (mainly from Turkey), and Chinese metal antiques further confuse the new collector. Since about 1990, an alarming number of outright fakes have been imported from Indonesia. They're pretty good craftspeople, too.

The application of **decorative motifs** to everyday household items, such as those made by the Pennsylvania Germans, came relatively late; the delay is attributed to the lengthy struggle just to meet purely utilitarian needs. So, too, did decoration for art's sake come late to other immigrant communities throughout this country.

When one blacksmith might have to do for an entire village, pounding out necessaries like horseshoes, trammels, and cranes, does it stand to reason that he would have labored an extra amount of time to add curliques and furbelows, while six horses that had thrown their shoes waited out front?

Regardless of provenance and age problems, the future for this field looks bright. Many collectors actively use their collections, and it's an interior decoration idea still in the ascendancy. The field still needs sorting out. We are faced, somewhat more directly than is often the case, with the questions of how much value do we place on provenance – how much are origins worth; how much extra value do we chauvinistically place on American origins; how much information will we demand from dealers who sell us old iron trammels and three-legged kettles? From a somewhat academic point of view, I think origins mean a lot, for two reasons. Not only are we usually asked to pay a premium for things "made in the U.S.A." (or the American Colonies, if they predate the Revolution), but our clear view of the background of a thing is obscured when either we aren't told where it is from, or when its origins are deliberately misrepresented. I feel it is necessary to continually stress the substance of things because I value meaning as much as – perhaps more than – appearance.

Collector/dealer Erik Gronning says "American cast and wrought pieces bring much higher prices than European items – at least in the U.S." He notes that in the last few years "there has been a new interest in early 18th century American wrought iron – especially things from the Hudson River Valley and Connecticut." In a way, though, I suspect that collectors all over are especially interested in identifiable pieces made near their particular home base – Georgia iron in Georgia, Quebec iron in Quebec, Virginia iron in Virginia, Irish iron in Ireland, etc.

It's Later Than You Think – I have acquired an 1895 Harrod's catalog from Great Britain, which offers many hearth-cooking pieces virtually identical in appearance to old ones – tin kitchens, cranes, bird roasters, etc. These weren't reproductions; they were meant to be ordered by a country crofter living in a home that was already 200 or 300 years old, or by a colonial living in more "primitive" conditions halfway around the world.

Olde Wordes – This chapter has more unfamiliar words, probably, than any other. Just as this book was being finished in early 2002, I found a wonderful **online glossary** at thousandeggs.com. See the end of this chapter for more.

Adapter ring, looks like legless pot stand or trivet. Forged iron ring with a long, angled-up handle with hanging loop, meant to fit over hole or eye of an early range to support handleless utensils of different circumferences. A versatile handle, useful in late 18th or early 19th C on the brick ranges of the time, which had iron tops pierced with rows of holes (or eyes) for the utensils. These tops were set into the top of a brick structure, which was the firebox. The fire was fed through doors set in the brick; ovens, drafts, and dampers were also brick-set. This kind of cooking range was something midway between a fireplace or hearth and a cast iron cooking stove, where the firebox too was made of iron. American or European, about 19"L overall, 8"diam. ring, late 18th or early 19th C. .... **$35+**

Ale boot, shoe-shaped, pointed toe, pieced copper, strap handle, pushed into hot ashes to warm ale, American, late 18th C. .... **$275+**

Ale boot or shoe, pieced copper, hinged fitted lid, strap handle, tinned inside, English, 7-1/2"L, late 18th or early 19th C. .... **$350+**

Ale shoe, pieced tin with cast white metal knob on hinged cover, English or American, 9"L, early 19th C... **$235+**

Ale warmer, conical, copper with wrought iron handle, tinned inside, English or American, 11"L, early 1800s or even late 1700s. .... **$250+**

❖ NOTES ❖

Copper caveat – "When taken into the human body, copper acts as a violent emetic, and is generally considered as poisonous; though it has occasionally been prescribed by physicians, it is always an unsafe and hazardous remedy. Hence, the greatest precaution is necessary in using this metal, of which so many kitchen utensils are manufactured. Besides the most scrupulous attention to cleanliness, it is extremely improper to leave any liquid to cool in a copper vessel; for this metal is more easily decomposed by liquids, when cold, than in a heated state.

"In order to prevent the deleterious effects of copper, the vessels made of it are usually covered with tin, on the inside. Nevertheless it is justly complained, that the tinning of copper vessels is not sufficient to defend them from the action of the air, moisture and saline substances; because, even when strongly coated, they are liable to rust [sic]. This may be remedied by a thicker coating of tin; and a manufacturer of this kind was established a few years hence in Edinburgh; in which ... the surface of the copper is made very rough ...; then a thick coat of tin is laid in, and the copper hammered smooth as before." Anthony Florian Madinzer Willich, *The Domestic Encyclopedia*; or *A Dictionary of Facts & Useful Knowledge*. 1st American edition, Philadelphia: W. Y. Birch & A. Small, 1803-04.

New Iron Falsely Aged & Its Telltale Rust. – Lester Beitz wrote in an August 1975 article in *Early American Life*: "[Recently] I came upon sets of the renowned Hessian Soldier & General Washington cast iron andirons in the same shop – which made me mighty suspicious. ... Close examination revealed ... top quality recasts, complete with that peculiar rust effect, circa 1974, caused by immersion in a solution of vinegar & nitric acid, caustic soda, sal ammoniac, or car battery acid – any number of concoctions which produce the desired effects. ... the overly large, thin flakes of rust resulting from such treatment are ... a dead giveaway." This is true of lots of iron, not just andirons; odd how new

X-1. Kitchen scenes, c.1690-1700. Both English, from an early chapbook [cheap book]. Two spits & a legless bulge pot are seen in the first picture. Note plate rack & small-paned windows, which would not have appeared at the time in America. Note the apparent pie funnel in the bottom picture (above cook's right hand.) Undated chapbook entitled A Choice Collection of Cookery Receipts, printed c.1700 at Newcastle, England.

iron's rust seems to always come out orange, and much of it very fine powder. Hey! Use it for a blusher!

Andirons & Firedogs – According to Alice Morse Earle, *Customs & Fashions in Old New England* (Scribner's, 1893): "The andirons added to the fireplace their homely charm. **Fire-dogs** appear in the earliest inventories under many names of various spelling, and were of many metals – copper, steel, iron, and brass. Sometimes a fireplace had three sets of andirons of different sizes, to hold logs at different heights. **Cob irons** had hooks to hold a spit and dripping-pan. Sometimes the 'Hand-irons' also had brackets. **Creepers** were low irons placed between the great fire-dogs. They are mentioned in many early wills and lists of possessions among items of fireplace furnishings, as, for instance, the list of Captain Tyng's furniture, made in Boston in 1653." Creepers apparently once had at least four meanings in early America that are all related to our subject here: (1) A Dutch oven; (2) "An iron used to slide along the grate in kitchens." Noah Webster, *An American Dictionary*, 1858; (3) "An instrument of iron with hooks or claws, for drawing up things from the bottom of a well, river, or harbor." ibid.; and (4) "A small, low iron, or dog, between the andirons" – given as an obsolete meaning in *Webster's New International Dictionary*, 1931.

Andirons, for baking potatoes in hearth, also called oven andirons, cast iron, no upright post, mainly comprised of horizontal log supports – hollow slant-sided "tunnels" with slide-out drawers or ovens for 4 to 6 potatoes. Both bars have a high-toothed ridge cast the length of the top – like a stegosaur's spine plates – to hold logs. See X-5. No marks mentioned, American, about 5" or 6"H x about 5" or 6"W, about 14" or 15"L, poss. as early as the 1st quarter 19th C, but could be 2nd, even 3rd quarter. These unusual andirons were pictured in an article on "Pre-Stove Cooking," by Edwin C. Whittemore, in *The Spinning Wheel*, March 1965, and have never appeared in any other publication, nor has been seen by anyone I've ever talked to. I am guessing at dimensions from the photograph. They are a wonderful idea, and somebody ought to make them now for use in living room fireplaces........ **$450+**

✧ RECIPE ✧

Apple Butter Making – *In the Sept. 1847 American Agriculturalist, writer E. S. notes "The large copper kettle (my kettle holds half a barrel of cider) three-quarters full of new sweet cider, made from sound apples, is set over the fire before five o'clock in the morning. I let it boil two hours, and then put in as many apples, which were peeled, cored, and cut up the night before, as will fill the kettle, and at the same time, I throw in about two quarts of nicely cleaned peach-stones, which by sinking to the bottom, and being moved about incessantly by the stirrer, prevent the fruit from settling and burning, which would spoil the whole. I take care in selecting the apples to secure a large proportion of sour ones; for, as the cider is sweet, unless this precaution be taken, the sauce will have a vapid taste that nothing can remove. ... On the hearth, around the fire, I place numerous pans and pots of apples and cider, simmering and stewing, which I empty into the kettle as fast in succession as the contents boil away enough to make room for them; but after twelve o'clock I never allow any more to be added to the mass. The boiling must be continued steadily until the whole is reduced to a smooth, thick marmalade, of a dark, rich brown color, and no cider separates when a small portion is cooled for trial.*

"From the moment the first apples are put into the boiling cider, the whole must be stirred without a moment's intermission, otherwise it will settle and burn; but the handle of the stirrer must be passed from hand to hand as often as fatigue or inclination makes a change desirable.

"My kettle holds half a barrel of cider, which, with the first apples in it, begins to boil about nine o'clock in the morning, and the whole is done enough by eight o'clock in the evening, when a sufficient quantity of powdered all-spice, cloves and cinnamon may be added to season it to your taste. The apple-butter must be dipped out as soon as possible when it stops boiling; for, if it cools in the copper or brass, it is in danger of becoming poisonous, as may be detected even by the unpleasant taste imparted by the action of the acid upon the copper. I prefer sweet stone, or earthen-ware pots to keep it in, but where the quantity made is very large, a barrel may be employed."

Apple butter kettles, hammered copper, flat bottom, side ear handles of iron, American, range from 15 or so gallons up to 40 gallons or more. Imagine lifting this, full or empty. You couldn't! 2nd quarter 19th C. See also stirrers in Chapter II, Mix, Beat. ...... **$400-$800**

X-2. Art as "Kitchen Maid" and "Cook Maid," made up irresistibly of kitchen tools. The real master of this style was a 16th C. Italian artist, Archimboldo. See chapter on implements for his version. Kitchen Maid has teakettle head, tong upper body, coal "skuttle" skirt, ash shovel and poker arms. Note brush tucked into band on the scuttle. The Cook Maid has lid head, and colander face, bellows upper body, frying pan and gridiron arms, soup kettle or cauldron lower body, peel and flesh fork legs, but I don't know what her shoulders are. From William Hone's The Every-Day Book, Vol. II, London, 1827.

X-3. Adapter ring. *A ring of flat iron with a long handle used to adapt the opening in an early brick raised-hearth range to a vessel somewhat smaller than the opening. Something similar, a stand with legs (bottom left) was used to hold a legless cooking vessel over coals in the hearth.* **$35+**

X-4. Ale or beer warmers. (T) *two conical ones are of copper, with bow handle or turned wood handle. Sometimes called **ale spikes**. Came in 1, 2, 3, and 4 pt. sizes; Henry Rogers Sons & Co., Wolverhampton, England, 1914. **(B-L)** & **(B-R)** Other two, with and without lids, are called **ale boots**, ale shoes or ale slippers, also made of copper, although some sheet iron ones are known. The shoes were easier to use than the conical ones, which had to be held, or stuck into some kind of trivet or stand. **(B-L)** about 9" to 11"L exclusive of handle; **(B-R)** is 6"H x 18"L overall. It is from the reproduction catalog of Pearson-Page Co., Birmingham & London, England, 1925. Only old ones worth much.* **$150+**

❖ **NOTES** ❖

Black Teeth & Apple Butter. A. M. Thomas, of Flemington, NJ, wrote a query to *Americana* magazine in July/Aug. 1989, about the effects of making apple butter in cast iron. She wrote "of the experience of a woman in this area who made apple butter in a large ironware pot, only to find that her teeth turned black after she ate the apple butter. A food scientist at Rutgers University explained that tartaric acid from the apples combined with iron from the pot to produce iron tartrate salts." Maybe all those witches depicted cooking over a pot, grinning through their black teeth, were fond of butter of apple, not eye of newt.

Apple roaster, dark heavy gauge old-looking tin reflecting oven, 3 shelves, shaped feet, 2 little strap handles on side, about the size for pippins, American, only 7-3/8"H x 6"W, mid- to late 19th C (?). Made in 1700s & throughout entire 19th C. .... **$300+**

Apple roaster, tin hearth reflector, on top is a bracket strap handle, 2 shelves, upper shelf is perforated with long eye- or almond-shaped slots, the only such roaster that dealer Joe Dziadul has ever seen. American, 9-1/8"H x 9-5/8"W, early 19th C. .... **$500+**

Apple roaster, tin & iron, wooden handle, looks sort of like a silent butler or a fat-hooded dustpan, American, c.1870s. .... **$135+**

Apple roaster, tin, open front reflecting oven with adjustable tray, American, early to mid-19th C (?). .... **$300+**

Ash shovel, wrought iron, curved bifurcated ram's horn handle, 18"L, early 19th C............................. **$75+**

Bannock board, thick plank of unidentified wood with smooth face, set with stubby wooden handle in back that props it at about a 40-degree angle, used for making corn meal cakes called bannocks. American (?), 12"L x 8"W, handle 6"L, early to mid-19th C. It's gotta have some oomph to sell at all. .... **$40+**

❖ **NOTES** ❖

BANNOCK (Gaelic: bonnach. Irish: boinneag.)
In Scotland, a cake of oatmeal, baked on an iron plate.
Behind the door a bag of meal;
And in the kist was plenty
Of good hard cakes his mither bakes;
And bannocks were nae scanty.
Scotch Songs, II. 71.

•   •   •

Bannocks defined: "In New England, cakes of Indian meal [cornmeal], fried in lard, are called bannocks." John Russell Bartlett, *Dictionary of Americanisms. A Glossary of Words and Phrases usually regarded as peculiar to the United States.* Boston: 2nd ed.1859 (1st ed. 1848).

❖ **RECIPE** ❖

Recipes for Bannocks – (1) *"Into one pint of Indian meal stir a pint of buttermilk; 1/2 teaspoon of salt; one teaspoon of molasses; one of butter; and add two well-beaten eggs; one pint of wheat flour; thin with milk to a thin batter; last, stir in two* large teaspoons of soda dissolved in hot water; pour into buttered shallow pans; bake one hour in quick oven which bakes top and bottom brown." This recipe, which sounds like corn muffins, appeared in *Treasure-House of Useful Knowledge*, compiled by Henry B. Scammel, who pirated recipes from many earlier cookbooks.

(2) *"To one quart sour milk, put a teaspoon of salaeratus, dissolved in water; warm the milk slightly, beat up an egg, and put in corn meal enough to make it thick as pudding batter, and some salt; grease a pan and bake it, or you may put it in six or eight saucers."* Elizabeth Lea, Domestic Cookery, Baltimore, 1851, 1859.

❖ NOTES ❖

Author's Bannocks: When I made bannocks (on a plank in front of a huge fire), I used the "Irish Bread" recipe below, substituting cornmeal for half the flour. They were rolled to about half an inch thickness, and slapped on the board rather smartly. They cooked through, "to the heart," before they lost their precarious hold on the plank. If I tried them again, I'd experiment with using a little brown rice flour or oat flour (from health food stores), which are quite sticky.

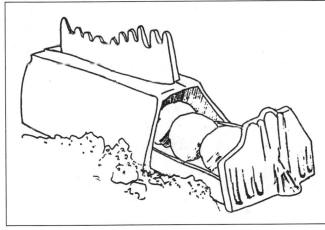

X-5. Andiron bake oven. *Cast iron, with sliding oven "drawer" for baking potatoes or other food. It is relatively low and rather short, appearing to be about a foot to 15"L in the photograph. This drawing is taken from the only picture I've ever seen of this type of andiron – it appeared in "Pre-Stove Cooking," by Edwin C. Whittemore, Spinning Wheel, March 1965. The brontosaurus ridge holds the logs above and also conducts heat from every point touching the burning log. Hot ashes are pushed up against the tunnel. Possibly as late as mid 19th C, but probably much earlier. Collector Joel Schiff saw a recently-made adaptation of this made of gritty cast iron, and with a cast woman's head bolted on to the front of the drawer. It was not a good casting at all, sharp edges and no finish, and yet the dealer asked $600.* **$450+**

❖ RECIPE ❖

Irish Bread – *4 cupfuls flour, 1/2 cupful butter, 1-1/2 cupfuls milk, 1/2 teaspoonful salt, 3 teaspoonfuls Calumet baking powder. Mix the ingredients to a soft dough; roll an inch thick, shape into cakes, six inches across, with a large cooky cutter, and bake on a hot griddle. Before taking from the fire, be sure they are baked to the heart. Split in two, butter and serve hot."* Sidney Morse, Household Discoveries, c.1909.

❖ NOTES ❖

Fire-Cakes – "There never was anything that tasted better than my mother's 'fire-cake,' – a short-cake spread on a smooth piece of board, and set up with a flat-iron before the blaze, browned on one side, and then turned over to be browned on the other. (It required some sleight of hand to do that.) If I could only be allowed to blow the bellows – the very old people called them 'belluses' – when the fire began to get low, I was a happy girl." Lucy Larcom, in *A New England Girlhood*, Boston: 1890.

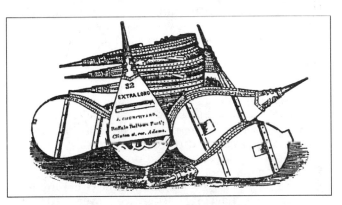

X-6. Bellows. *"Buffalo" bellows, mfd. by Joseph Churchyard, Buffalo Bellows Factory, Buffalo, NY. Under his direction, "skilled work men" made "warranted bellows of the Eastern, Southern and Pittsburgh Patterns ... of the best materials." He also repaired them. Ad in Thomas' Buffalo City Directory, 1866.*

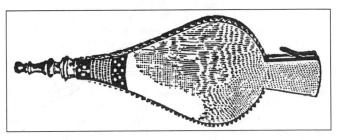

X-7. Bellows. *"Antique oak" in six sizes, and "complete assortment of other styles." German import advertised by George M. Thurnauer & Brother, NYC, Nov. 1909. Many companies, even in the early 1900s, made bellows in a deliberately old-fashioned style, some complete with painted boards & fancy trims.*

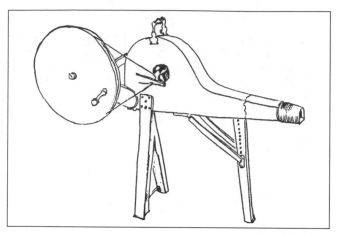

*X-8. **Standing bellows.** Mechanical type with adjustable front leg to deliver the blast where it was needed. 27"H x 38"L, probably English, early 19th C. From ad of James II, in James Robinson's gallery, NYC.* **$3,000+**

Bellows, new leather, wooden body painted yellow with stenciled & painted flower decorations, new leather, brass nozzle, prob. American, 18-1/2"L, early 19th C. This pair was $275 at Garth Auction, May 5-6, 1989, Delaware, OH. (At the same sale, another decorated bellows, with fruit & leaves, and the old leather, in very worn condition, reached $175.) ..... **$300-$700+**

❖ NOTES ❖

Buying Bellows. Leather condition isn't as important as the painted decoration – original early-1800s brilliant red, yellow, black and green paint decoration, simple geometrics, or theorum-like still-lifes, or town scenes such as might be found on an old Baltimore or Hitchcock chair, add hundreds to value, and fine examples may bring over $1,000. Erik Gronning adds "Some bellows have reached prices over $20,000 – especially ones made at the end of the 18th century by Samuel McIntire. One bellows sold recently for $25,000. Paint decorated ones that are American are very valuable," at least to American buyers.

• • • •

The Dealer Factor. Selling price starts with the object itself, but its level depends on the dealer who ends up advertising or showing the piece. Nationally-known dealers can get three, four, even ten times what a hinterlands dealer could get. This is true of all colonial or early American antiques. To some extent, selling on the Internet (for example, on eBay) levels the playing field.

Bellows, various types: (1) small, hand-held decorative leather & painted wood, turned handles, brass trim, for parlor use; (2) larger, simpler wood & leather, for kitchen hearth or small blacksmith's hearth; and (3) mechanical bellows, key-wound or cranked, wood & metal without accordion action, more like a fan. All 3 types are collected; at present, mechanicals are very desirable. For example: iron fitted, wood-cased belt-drive type in 2 parts: a sort of bellows-shape body, awkwardly held in left hand by short turned wood handle or set on hearth pointing brass "hose" nozzle at

embers, upper wheel cranked to motivate fan blades in lower part, drawing air in side vents & exhaling it from nozzle, French, 21"H, early 19th. .... **400-$2,000+**

Bird roaster, heavy gauge tin reflecting oven with triangular sides with strap handles, looks like a pup tent, the back pivots at the crest of the "tent" and flips to cover open side, so you don't have to take the birds off the 2 hooks to turn them, you simply flip the reflecting back & turn the roaster, American, 7"H x 8"L, 19th C. .... **$200+**

Bird roaster, tin, very simple arched top with 4 hooks, no legs or feet, American, 10"H x 10"W x 8" deep, 19th C. .... **$200+**

Bird roaster, tin, with hooks inside, short strap legs & strap handles, American, 7"H x 11"L, 19th C. By birds they didn't mean chickens or Butterball™ turkeys, but very small field birds like quail or partridge, or songbirds. Yikes. .... **$250+**

Bird roaster, tinned sheet iron, seen from side looks like bent over "L," generously looped strap handle, 6 hooks in pairs of 2, one pair top center, 2 pairs on lower row on either side of top pair, hooks reinforced on backside of this small reflecting oven, rimmed drip pan below, American, 11-1/2"H x 9"W x 4-1/4" deep, early to mid (?)19th C. .... **$300+**

❖ NOTES ❖

Age Will Out? – Just when you feel a little secure about the probable age of these old **reflecting ovens**, you find, as I did, a copy of the wonderful 1895 Harrod's Stores, Ltd. (London) catalog, reprinted by St. Martin's Press in 1972. (The actual title of the reprint, which is probably how you'd find it at the library, is *Victorian Shopping.*) Over a thousand pages with terrific linecuts of everything anyone would want for house, home, body, yard, barn or buggy. • There are several tin reflecting ovens, called generically "Broilers," in the Ironmongery & Turnery department pages. (For their "Cheese Toaster" see another entry in this chapter.) A pup tent-like "Game Oven," with hinged front lid, three wire hooks, and a strap handle on the two triangular ends, could be ordered 9"W, 11"W, 12"W or 14"W. Another, not pictured, but described as "strong," came in three sizes: 11"W; 13"W and 15"W. Presumably "strong" means thicker gauge tin as well as more substantial structure. Also available was an "Improved Broiler" oven with rather tall squared body, hinged domed hood with strap handle, four wire hooks, and a heavy wire hook support to hang on fender bar. It came measuring 9"W and 12"W. Another was a "Cheese Oven," with hood and strap handle fixed to a large rectangular double pan. Another, the "American Oven," was made of tin, a large rectangular box, with a lift-out tray with wire handles, set onto a shelf, about 2/3 way up from bottom, hinged lift-off hood or lid, and the most distinguishing feature, a sheet of tin set at 15° from front to back, which reflected the heat to the underside of the shelf and tray. Behind this reflector, rather like underneath a flight of stairs, is an open space supported by side pieces of tin. Another was Harrod's "Dutch Oven," with open straight front, round back and domed lid, strap handle on top, three hooks over a reticulated removable shelf midway from top to bottom. Long pins at both ends allowed you to take this partly apart for cleaning. It came 9"W, 10"W, 12"W and 13"W. • Harrod's shipped all over the world – from Smyrna to Switzerland, from Tahiti to Tripoli. In 1895 they did not ship to the United States, as "Parcel Post [is] not in operation." Hmmm.

Bird roaster, wrought iron, dangle type which was hung on crane by its own hook, with sliding hoop with 2 hooks, poss. NY state?, 16"L, 18th or very early 19th C. • I'm glad we don't eat little birds that fly by nowadays. Imagine hooking a robin, a lark or

X-9. Bird roaster, reflecting oven. *Pieced tin, 4 hooks under hood, strap handle. Drip pan has two birdbeak pouring spouts at corners. 10"H. Photo courtesy Litchfield Auction Gallery, CT. Ex-Harold Corbin Collection, auctioned Jan. 1, 1990, for $375.* **$450+**

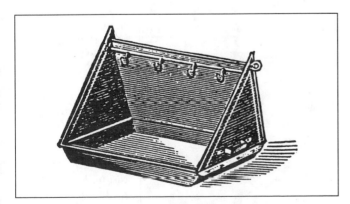

X-10. Bird roaster, *of reversible type. Sheet tin. Hooks for 4 birds; small bracket handles on sides. Nowhere near as desirable as one in X-9. From F. A. Walker import catalog, 1870s-80s.* **$150+**

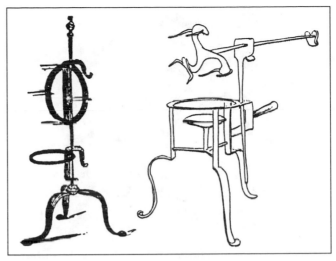

X-11. Bird roasters. (L) "Toaster and Trivet." *Picture from* Warne's Model Cookery and Housekeeping Book, *London: 1868. Wrought iron, and it looks as if it may even have a brass finial.* **(R) Bird roaster or bird spit.** *Wrought iron, with small drip or grease cup. Note Isle-of-Man type motif of the whirling spit, and the heart at the other end. Drawn from ad of* Milk Street Antiques, *Portland, ME. Value range mine not Milk Street's.* **$600-$1,500+**

a nice fat chickadee to such a thing. Yuck. I don't eat chickens anymore. (In my books, you never know where you'll read a plea for vegetarianism, do you?) .... **$450-$650**

Bird roaster trammel, wrought iron and brass, marked with stars & other punched designs, stamped all over it is "PATENTEE PATENTEE PATENTEE," French, 18-1/4"L at its least extension, adjusts in half-inch increments, mid 19th C. .... **$400-$600+**

Bird trammel, 2 hooks, for hanging a large trussed bird from for roasting, American or English, adjustable from 16" to 23" fully extended, 18th C. .... **$300+**

X-12. Bird spit. *Tripod base with pronounced snake feet. Wrought iron, interesting 'easel' hanger with six double spits. 30"H, 18th C. Photo courtesy Litchfield Auction Gallery, Litchfield CT. Ex-Harold Corbin Collection, auctioned Jan. 1, 1989, for $1,600.* **$1,500-$2,000+**

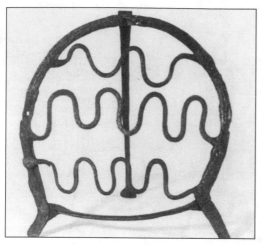

X-13. Scotch broiler, also called a **brander.** Easel-back upright broiler, forged iron, serpentine grids. Probably Scottish, 18th C. Photograph courtesy of Pat Guthman Antiques, Southport, CT. The late Pat Guthman had a large and very fine selection of kitchen-related antiques, almost exclusively related to hearth or early brickset range cookery, and wrote a food column in the Newtown Bee's "Antiques & Arts Weekly," Newtown, CT. The shop is still open – see last page of this chapter. **$900+**

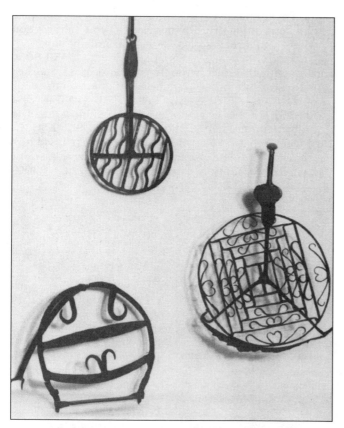

X-14. Various hearth broilers. All forged iron. Top two are meant to sit flat. One at right has very decorative, probably European, hearts and scrolls, and 3 legs. Bottom left is another brander or Scotch broiler, startlingly anthropomorphic. All late 18th C. Photograph courtesy of Pat Guthman Antiques, Southport, CT. **$350-$1,000**

X-15. Whirling broiler or rotary grill. Forged iron. Note serpentine grid and rattail hanging loop. 18"L x 9" diam., American, 18th C. Ex-Keillor Family Collection. See also the revolving gridirons. Many pieces in the Keillor Family Collection were bought by Archie Keillor in the U.K. when he was on buying trips for the antiques department of the great NYC store, B. Altman's. **$600+**

Brander or Scotch broiler, also called a brandiron, a grill or gridiron held nearly vertical to the fire on a sort of easel. Wrought iron, 15"H, six serpentine & flat bars, probably Scottish, late 18th C. .... **$450-$600+**

Brander, or Scotch broiler, wrought iron, horseshoe-shaped standing tripod type, American, 15-3/4"H x 12"W, late 18th, early 19th C. The design of the near-vertical broiler face & tripod, and condition of the iron contributes to value. Added value given by penny feet & extra iron scroll. .... **$250+**

Broilers, stationary

Broiler, wrought iron, front legs with penny feet, back legs are double-toed, beautiful long handle with rattail loop, American, 18th C. .... **$400-$600**

Broiler, wrought iron, 4 serpentine bars, very simple feet, handle ends in "doughnut" hole, American (?), 17"L, early 19th C. .... **$275-$375**

Broiler, wrought iron, 4 short feet, ram's horn handle, American (?), 30"L x 17"W, 18th or 19th C. **$300-$400**

Broilers, whirling or revolving

Called rotary or rotating broilers or whirling broilers, also rotary grills, rotary gridirons – ingenious pieces with a frame, legs and handle that remain stationary when placed on the hearth, while the round grid of the broiler

X-16. Whirling broiler. Forged iron, with upright handle in center, and hooks for hanging small birds (?) around rim of wheel. French fleur-de-lys design, probably French, or possibly French Canadian. 16" diam., late 18th C, probably prior to the Revolution. Courtesy Sestienne Collection. **$900+**

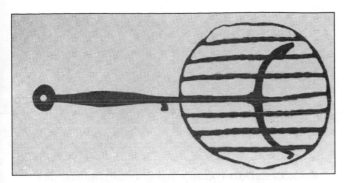

X-17. Whirling broiler or grill. *Forged iron with unusual twisted-for-strength grids. Very nice penny diamond handle. Photograph courtesy of Pat Guthman Antiques, Southport, CT.* **$450+**

can be rotated to evenly expose all parts of the steak or other cut of meat to the hot coals over which the broiler may be placed, as well as to the flames within the fireplace. (See also Toasters, pivoting; Toasters, revolving.)

Broiler, rotary, cast iron wheel with 19 spokes, each fluted or runneled with a concavity – a sort of grease arroyo – directing hot drippings to reservoir in handle, next to broiler, 3 legs, hanging hole in handle, handle marked only "PATENT," American, 12" diam., 25-1/4"L overall, c.1830s. Cast iron is unusual for a revolving broiler, but not for a patented broiler. Casting made it a production piece. .... **$250-$450**

Broiler, rotary, wrought iron, round, wavy grid, American (?), quite small, 7" diam., 19th C. .... **$300+**

Broiler, rotary, alternating scalloped & straight bars, 3 legs, American or English, 3"H x 11" diam., 11-3/4"L handle, early 19th C. .... **$550+**

Broiler, rotary and upright – a sort of merry-go-round grill, wrought iron with fleur-de-lys pattern formed by flat bars of iron making the grill's surface with unusual scalloped "fence" or edge around circumference, short penny feet, European, prob. French, 10" diam., 18-1/2"L overall, 18th C. .... **$650+**

Broiler, rotary, wheel-like grill with radiating spokes fairly close together, lubricating grease cup below center pivot pin, "Y" handle – the 2 arms of the Y support the grill, plus nice long handle with grease catching cup, forged iron, 3 feet, American, 13-1/2" diam., 25"L overall, prob. 18th C. **Lookalike alarm.** – This has been reproduced with a brass center nut & bolt. .... **$450+**

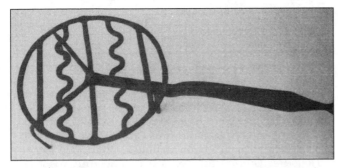

X-18. Whirling broiler or grill. *Forged iron piece, with alternating straight and serpentine bars. Late 18th or early 19th C, probably American. Photo courtesy of Oveda Maurer Antiques, San Anselmo, CA.* **$450+**

X-19. Cauldron or caldron. *Riveted bronze, from ancient Ireland, 8th C. The illustration is from an article "The Old Poetic Guild in Ireland," by Charles de Kay, Century, April 1890. The story told in the article is about a "band of poets" who traveled all around and carried with them a "Large pot, or caldron, called* **'The Pot of Avarice.'** *This was the sign of their intention to claim food from the chief they visited, although in legend it was meant for the gold and silver they expected as prequisites. ... From a caldron like this one, king, poet, and hero obtained their porridge, their boiled beef and mutton, and their venison, which they ate without forks, using" short knives and their fingers. This one is one of several in the Dublin Museum.*

X-20. Hearth scene, *with large cast iron cauldron in background on 3 long legs, cast iron tea kettle* **S-hook** *hanging from chain probably hanging from* **lug pole** *rather than crane, ash shovel and tongs in foreground. The little story told in this 1858 children's book is remarkably humane. The little mouse explains she has stolen sugar to feed her babies, and the lady smiles and says "Well, Mouse, you may keep your prize;/ For I am going, just like you,/ To feed my child, who is hungry too." Picture Fables, drawn by Otto Speckter, from German Rhymes by F. Hey. NY: Appleton, 1858.*

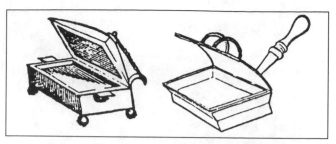

X-21. Cheese toasters. (L) *"Cheese toaster to make Welsh Rarebits, with double bottom for hot water."* American Home Cook Book, 1854. *(R) Cheese toaster, with wooden handle, from F. A. Walker catalog, 1870s-80s. Both of pieced tin.* **$125-$250**

Broiler, rotary, forged iron, very plain with neat perky upraised handle, long legs, American or English, 3-3/4"H x 12-3/8" diam. with 14-3/8"L handle, early 19th C... **$475+**

Broiler, rotary, grids made from square bars turned at angle so a sharp edge is along the top, English (?), 24-1/2"L x 12-1/4" diam., early 19th C. ...... **$250+**

Broiler, rotary, wrought iron, round broiler or grill has alternating straight & undulating flat bars, 3 feet, longish handle, American, Canadian or English, 13" diam., 18th or early 19th C. • This type, with the wavy & straight line design, is most common, and apparently added just a touch of decorative quality to satisfy the original customer. There are many variations on the wavy straight theme. French whirling broilers or French Canadian ones tend to be fancier, and incorporate variations of fleur-de-lys for the broiling surface..................................... **$450+**

Camp stoves – See Chapter XI (Stoves).

Chestnut roaster, cast iron, iron legs, European or poss. American, 4" deep x 12-1/2" diam., mid 19th C. .... **$175-$225**

Chestnut roaster, copper pan with pierced design in cover, twisted wrought iron shaft and wooden handle, American (?), 13-1/2" diam., 18th C. • Collector Erik Gronning says the best way to tell the difference between a chestnut roaster pan and a bedwarmer is the size of the holes: larger holes, usually, for the roaster, small, usually, and sometimes shaped like commas, for the latter......... **$500-$750**

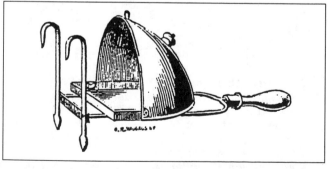

X-22. Cheese roaster or toaster – reflecting oven. *Hangs on fender of fireplace, for roasting birds, chops, apples, or for melting cheese – perhaps on a porringer of soup. From F. A. Walker catalog, 1870s-80s.* **$300**

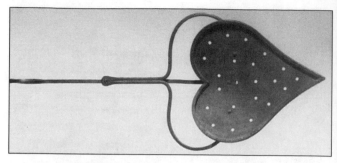

X-23. Chestnut roaster. *In extremely unusual heart shape. Long thin handle, twisted for strength. 28-1/2"L. Pennsylvania, 18th C. Photo courtesy Litchfield Auction Gallery, Litchfield, CT. Ex-Harold Corbin Collection, auctioned Jan. 1989 for $900.* **$1,000+**

Chestnut roaster, like a bed warmer, sort of, hexagonal pieced brass pan with a pierced lid, long flat handle, very shapely and with cutouts, English or poss. American, early 19th C................................. **$300+**

Chestnut roaster, pierced brass, long wooden handle, prob. English but could be American, 17"L, early 19th C. .... **$275+**

Chestnut roaster, steel with decorative engraving, wooden handle, English, or poss. American, 12" diam., c.1810-1830. Not the usual metal, which helps separate it out from all the brass ones. **$300+**

Clock or clockwork jack – See Bottle jack, X-72; also: Jack, clock; and picture of Smoke jack, X-52

Cook pot, also called a flesh pot, cast iron, very globular body, high straight-sided neck with triangular ears, forged and twisted iron falling bail, very long splayed legs, very handsome, American, 14-1/4"H, late 18th or early 19th C. .... **$200-$275**

❖ NOTES ❖

A cooking pot is one form of **cast iron hollowware**, or hollow ware. Kettles, tea kettles, skillets, posnets, saucepans, porringers, spiders, Dutch ovens, the bowls of large ladles, and other wares with "hollow" insides are called hollowware. Some had to be cast in two, three, even four parts because the mouth or rim was smaller in diameter than the belly or middle. The term is also used for pewter, silver, brass, bell metal, copper and bronze wares. **Sadware** is applied to cast objects that are flat and cast in a one-part mold (or a relatively flat mold), as opposed to hollowware. Griddles, sadirons (or flat irons) are sadware.

Reproduction Alert

Chestnut roaster reproduction alert – Arthur Todhunter, NYC, NY, made "quaint & useful gifts," mainly for use around the fireplace, that were "reproductions of Old England and Colonial wrought iron work and fire place furnishings." In a Dec. 1921 *House & Garden* ad, we see a "chestnut roaster," which is a round brass pan, pierced lid with slight convexity to center of it, with what appears to be a simple turned wooden handle. The size is not given, but is probably about 20" to 30"L.

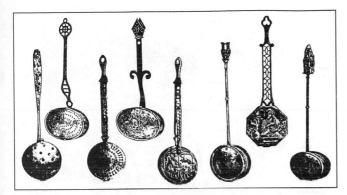

X-24. Box style chestnut roasters. *"For fireside decoration." All are reproduction, revivalist, or meant-to-look-old decorative brass items made by Pearson-Page, Birmingham, England, 1925 catalog. You could choose a brightly polished or an "old colour" finish. Upper row, left to right: (1) "The Battersea," 20-1/2"L; (2) "The Bishop," 20-1/2"L; (3) "The Musician," made round, square or octagon, 22"L. Bottom row, left to right: (4) "The Christy," 17"L, the oldest-looking one; (5) "The Graham," 16"L; (6) "The Wells," 16"L; (7) "The Colchester," 18"L; (8) and the oval "The Stratford," 19"L. Value range is for exactly what they were made to be – decorative items, with no claim to authenticity. They are, of course, almost old enough to be considered "antiques," if you call a repro "antique." These are quite beautifully made.* **$75-$225**

Crane, cast iron, simple and small, American, late 19th or early 20th C. This is not strictly a fake or reproduction, but is a revivalist piece that was made to satisfy decorators' demands during a renaissance of Colonial accessories that got underway in the 1880s-90s (again in the 1920s; and again in the 1950s). The iron is usually flat and smaller gauge than old ones, and very uniform the whole length, showing little if no hammering. Contemporary blacksmith artisans make cranes too, slightly more irregular and ruggedly forged than the outright decorator crane, but still not like the old ones. Also you'll not see any signs of wear. (A **"blanket crane"** was always wood (iron would have rusted and stained the blanket) and swung out from fireplace and was used for drying blankets, or heating them to wrap up a person with the ague.) Newish crane: .... **$125-$150+**
Crane, forged bar iron, curved bracket, very, very simple, American (?), only 19"L, 19th C. .... **$200-$350+**
Crane, forged iron, curved brace, very simple, American or European, brace is 34"H, crane is 26"L, prob. 18th C. .... **$300-$400+**
Crane, forged iron, simple design with ram's horn tip to tapered bar, American (?), 21"L, 19th C. **$300-$450**

❖ NOTES ❖

Cranes start at under $75 for simple small ones of late manufacture. **Added value.** – The bigger, more interestingly forged cranes bring more, up to $2,000+ if anything zoomorphic or figural has been done with the iron. • The will inventory of Jacob Alleweins, Berks County, PA, who died in 1781, listed a brass crane – very unusual.

Reproduction Alert

Yes, that **little crane** that doesn't look old is wrought iron, but it is easily perceived as new. The iron is merely a scrolled piece of perfectly uniform 3/4"W, 1/8" or 3/16" thick flat wrought iron bar.
• A **1970s fireplace crane & barbecue grill set**, comprised of a vertical tension bar, a fixed fire bowl of sheet iron (like a big 24" diam., shallow, slightly round-bottomed pan), above which is a grill (round with 10 cross bars of plated iron wire), above the grill is the scrolled bracket crane with hook, from which to suspend a cooking pot. Sold as part of this 5-piece set was a small gypsy kettle with 2 quart capacity – a cast iron 3-legged, round-bottomed pot with the old type casting band around the widest part, wire bail handle. The whole set was made by Malone's Creative Products (formerly Malone's Metalcraft) of McMinnville, TN, prior to 1973, and sold for $49.50. The little pot or kettle could be bought separately for $8.50. The June 1973 ad states that they made "hundreds of other items," so I wish I had a catalog.

❖ NOTES ❖

Lug-poles, a sort of stationary crane: "The lug-pole, though made of green wood, sometimes became brittle or charred by too long use over the fire and careless neglect of replacement, and broke under its weighty burden of food and metal; hence accidents

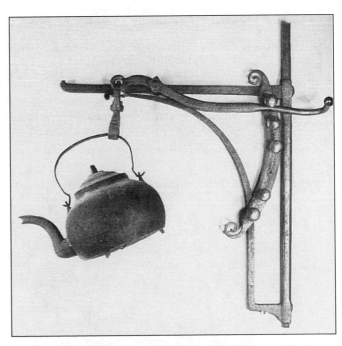

X-25. Quadrant crane & kettle tilter, *with tea kettle. Forged iron, beautifully detailed and well-finished. Lever caught under one of six pegs (one missing). 18th or very early 19th C. Photograph courtesy of Pat Guthman Antiques, Southport, CT. Value range is solely mine.* **$2,000-$3,000+**

became so frequent, to the detriment of precious cooking utensils, and even to the destruction of human safety and life, that a Yankee invention of an iron crane brought convenience and simplicty, and added a new grace to the kitchen hearth." Alice Morse Earle, *Customs & Fashions in Old New England*, Scribner's, 1893.

Cranes, forged iron, a pair of floor-standing cranes with penny feet, T-bar, American or English, 35"H, 18th C. Very rare. Erik Gronning reports that these were "also used as coffin supports." .... **$2,500-$3,000+**

Creeper – See a Spider entry, p.596

Curfew, from the French *couvre-feu*, or fire-cover. Also called a sleeper. A sort of half-dome, or quarter sphere – think of a baby buggy hood. They are usually at least 10" across, sometimes larger, made of sheet brass, copper or iron. This one is forged sheet iron, somewhat pitted, with a vertical twisted forged iron handle from the top down to the bottom, with a curl at the bottom tail. This hearth essential was pushed against the back or side of the fireplace, with the glowing embers of a wood fire within, to shut off the air. In the morning, the curfew was removed and the fire could be quickly restarted with a few puffs of the bellows. American (?), 10"H x 13"W, late 18th or early 19th C. .... **$175-$300**

❖ NOTES ❖

Curfews with added value – Although I prefer iron, there will probably be more brass ones shown (mostly European imports), and as their decorative value is considered greater, their price would be higher by at least 10% to 100% over that for the iron. Early *repoussé* ones, from the 17th or 18th C, are very desirable and rare, and may bring up to $2,000, according to Erik Gronning.

Curfew, wrought iron, 2 penny feet, gooseneck curved handle in back, American, 9-1/2"H x 10-1/2"L, 18th C. .... **$165-$225**

Dangle spit, steel, horizontal serpentine wing-like governor at the top of a steel vertical rod with 6 holes at 1" intervals, with a much thinner rod with a small hook at its top and 3 very sharp bigger hooks at the

X-27. Curfew, or coeuvre-feu. Used to cover hot coals in fireplace. This one illustrated an article in William Hone's The Every-Day Book, *1825-26. About it was written: "It is of copper, rivetted together, as solder would have been liable to melt with the heat. It is 10" high, 16" wide, and 9" deep. The Rev. Mr. Gostling, to whom it belongs, says it has been in his family for time immemorial." Appears to have a repoussé design.*

bottom to hold the meat or game bird to be roasted. The small hook at the top could be set into one of the holes to adjust the height off the fire. The whole thing was suspended by a stout twine or cord from the edge of the mantle, and it was set in rotary motion by twisting, so that when released, it would twirl as it unwound, thereby winding itself up again. English or American, 16"L fully extended, early 19th C. • **Added value** from any file or engraved decoration, or a date or initials............ **$375-$575+**

Dippers – See Chapter XIII (Implements)

Double boiler, inner copper kettle with bail handle suspended on an "S" pothook from high double-arched fixed bail handle of outer iron kettle. Possibly for hearth use as well as range-top. American, 16-1/2"H overall x 13-1/2" diam., c.1830s to 1850s. .... **$350+**

Dutch oven, cast iron, 3 footed, ear handles to use with pot lifter hooks, lid with raised edge to contain coals, lid has a few triangular "chips" along edge, marked only "Baltimore," 8-1/2"H x 12" diam., early 19th C. • Dutch ovens **marked "Baltimore"** show up fairly

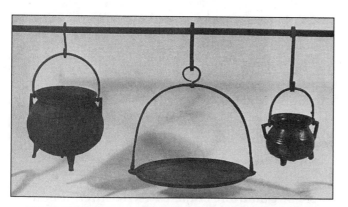

X-26. Standing crane with utensils. Cast iron pot at left, cast and wrought girdle plate, and wonderful 18th C English cast bronze pot. Photograph courtesy of Pat Guthman Antiques, Southport, CT. Unusual crane is the type used in pairs to hold coffins.

X-28. Double boiler. Copper kettle inside, with forged iron bail handle, hung from "S" pothook in double arch of fixed handle of outer iron kettle. Could be used with a crane in the fireplace, and later on a range. 16-1/2"H overall x 13-1/2" diam. 1830s-50s. Ex-Keillor Family Collection. $800+

often. It is not known who made them, but there are three good possibilities: William Baer & Co., established prior to 1817, or the Cast-Iron Manufactory (which might have also been called Baltimore Cast-Iron Manufactory), established by 1803, and Hayward, Bartlett & Co., established 1844. The look of these is definitely early 19th C, so the latter is perhaps the least probable choice. .... **$200-$250**

❖ NOTES ❖

Perhaps or Maybe: Why Ifs, Ands & Buts Are Necessary – Throughout this book I have tried to be as accurate as possible, about provenance or dates. You will notice lots of question marks in parentheses after dates and places. You will also find a good number of "looks like" or "possibly" [poss.], or "probably" [prob.], and a few "perhaps." The appeal of objects with marks and patent dates obviously lies in the surety, which such identification gives the collector. In fact, I believe that's why the two most popular fields of collecting worldwide, all totaled, are stamps and coins, because they have dates, provenance, and well-established historics. Our field has its marked pieces too, but probably more pieces are mysterious and require research and study.

Dutch oven, cast iron, 3 peg feet, deep raised edge on lid, small interior flange to make a good fit in kettle, very handsome, particularly in this big size, American, 11"H, early 19th C. For some comments on a utensil called a creeper, see some notes under Spider. With the lid (original or at least dating from same period and perfectly fitting), the value increases another 20%-25% .... **$200-$250**

Dutch oven, cast iron, forged falling bail handle, 3 stubby legs, nice deep flange or raised edge on lid, American, 6-3/4"H x 9-1/4" diam., early 19th C....... **$250-$350**

Dutch oven, cast iron, forged bail handle, 3 legs, high lipped lid, American, 14" diam., early to mid 19th C. .... **$200-$250**

X-29. Dripping pan and ladle. *Sheet iron, placed under spitted meat to catch the drippings, which were used for making sauces, gravies, soups, or for rendering for a purer fat. Warne's Model Cookery, London, 1868.* **$85+**

Dutch oven, & lid, sometimes called a braising pot, bake kettle, camp oven, or bake oven, cast iron, with 3 short legs, raised edge on lid, small interior flange to keep lid in place. "Kentucky Stove Co.," KY, 10" diam., early 19th C. .... **$350+**

❖ NOTES ❖

Dutch ovens. These were called *four de campagnes* in French, literally country oven. Many recipes in Alexandre Dumas' classic *Le Grand Dictionnaire de Cuisine* call for such a utensil, and called for the "braising pot" to be set in hot coals with the special lid with raised edge to be piled with coals. Close reading of some recipes seem to indicate that the *four de campagne* sometimes referred to what was called a tin kitchen in America. So perhaps the confused American usage of the term "dutch oven" dates to a similar French ambiv

X-30. Dutch oven in use. *Somewhat romanticized illustration from the 1880s of a somewhat earlier housewife piling hot coals on the dished lid of her long-legged dutch oven, to bake something within. Note stationary crane in fireplace, with chain trammel – the most primitive kind. Also the ring atop the andiron. Its mate also had a ring, and a spit could be suspended thus between the andirons.*

X-31. Dutch oven. *Cast iron, bail handle, 3 shortish legs, very well-fitted and undoubtedly original lid with deep flange. 8-3/4"H x 9-1/4" diam. American, probably early 19th C. Picture courtesy of Robert W. Skinner Inc., Auctioneers, Bolton, MA. • It has been claimed by at least one writer that the Pilgrims, who spent some years in Holland before departing for the new land, brought "Dutch ovens" with them and used them on shipboard. An old oval Dutch oven would bring twice this or more.* **$200-$400+**

X-32. Cooking pot, *something like a Dutch oven, which may or may not have the distinctive high flange on lid. This charming illustration, is but one of at least 32, in a French book about a Monsieur Vieux Bois (Old Man Wood), who has many household adventures. Apparently the food cooking in this pot caught on fire, and was ruined, so Monsieur Bois carried it up on the roof so the dog could eat it. We all have known such dogs, n'c'est pas? Odd as it seems, there were dogs that either lived, or stayed, on the roof of their family's dwelling. Occasionally on eBay a photograph from the late 1800s showing such a dog is sold. Unfortunately, the bookshop where I found this in NYC tears many non-valuable books apart and sells the pictures as decorations. But those of us who use the pictures as part of our research, as well as those who just love an intact book, squirm at such practices.*

X-33. Dutch oven. *Cast iron, very unusual with the raised handles for the bail. Late 18th or early 19th C. Photograph courtesy of Pat Guthman Antiques, Southport, CT. • Advanced iron collector Joel Schiff believes the odd bail handle had an added loop on either side, to slip over the ear handles, and then be secured with a pin or wedge, sort of like a cotter pin.* **$600+**

X-34. Dutch ovens or French bake pans. *Clockwise from* **(T-L)** *"French Bake Pan of wrought iron, to put fire or embers on the cover if needful." American Home Cook Book, 1854.* **(T-R)** *"A Bake-kettle, or Skillet." "When cooking stoves came in, the bake-kettle, or covered skillet, went out, and with it went a large part of what was good in our American cookery. How many of your readers [American Agriculturist, Sept. 1870] ever saw a bake-kettle? Probably only those who enjoy the blessing of a wood fire to cook by. Just send an artist down to the backwoods of Maine or away "out west," and have a drawing made of this most capital kitchen utensil. "Pioneers" will know what I mean; it is a shallow kettle with a lid, which has a turned-up edge, and upon which coals are placed; and the thing to be cooked is "between two fires."* **(B-R)** *Cast iron, unground, shallow or deep pattern, in sizes from 8" to 14" diam., from 2-1/2"-3-1/2" diam. for shallow and 3-1/2"-5-1/4" diam. for deep. National Stoves & Ranges, c. 1916. Note triangular ears, generally thought to be a sign of great age.* **(B-L)** *"French bake kettle," cast iron, note there is no flange at all on the lid. Henry N. Clark, Boston, MA, 1884 catalog.* **$125+**

X-35. Dutch oven/skillet. Called simply "skillet" in the catalog. Cast iron, "plain finish, unground." "Furnished in deep or shallow patterns." Seven sizes, from 8" to 14" diam., from 2-1/2" to 3" deep for the shallow ones, and 3" to 3-1/4" diam. for the deep ones. National Stoves & Ranges. c.1916. **$150+**

alence. **Why "Dutch"?** – One reasonable explanation for the name is given by Louise Peet and Lenore Sater in *Household Equipment*, NY: John Wiley, 1934, 1940. They wrote: "Dutch ovens were brought to America by the Pilgrims. As is well known, the Pilgrims spent some years in Holland before coming to America. The Mayflower was a tiny vessel and baggage limited. The dutch oven could be used for such a variety of cookery that it took the place of several other pots and pans and was, therefore, a favorite utensil of the early settlers."

The word "Dutch" is sometimes used to indicate that something is a substitute for something else. A *Dutch wife* (or husband) is the long torso size or bolster pillow that you use to drape your arm and knee over when sleeping on your side. *Dutch gold* is golden in color, but is actually a cheap alloy, tombac, made of copper and zinc, which is beaten to a foil and used to gild certain toys or knicknacks. A *Dutch treat* is not really a treat, because you are paying for yourself. A *Dutch uncle* is a person who isn't your uncle, but takes it upon himself to reprehend you. And a *Dutch oven* is a substitute for a built-in bake oven. The chief characteristic is the raised edge around the lid – meant to hold hot coals so that while the oven sat on the hearth, or in the embers, getting heat from below, it was also getting heat from above.

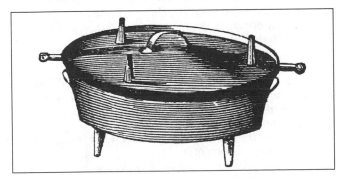

X-36. Biscuit baker. Cast iron, very like the Dutch oven. 12" and 14" diam., from Stuart, Peterson & Co. catalog of cast iron hollowware, 1866. No explanation is given; time travelers are supposed to know these things. See three legs on lid, and the two little stubby knobs obviously used to flip it over. This could be used with both parts upside down, or the way shown here. **$500+**

• • •

Yankee bread is very good or very bad, according to the manner in which it is made. We commend it to dyspeptics. The Indian meal should be either bottled or sifted." *The Farmers' Cabinet,* Philadelphia, Aug 1, 1836. ***What's Meant by "Iron Pan"?** –I can't guarantee what is meant by "iron pans." Although from the context it sounds as if an iron pan might be a cast iron gem or muffin pan, the recipe is way too early for that. So I believe them to be sheet iron, flat-bottomed pans, rather deeper than pie pans but with slightly flared sides, which are rarely found today. It is possible that they are cast iron Scotch or Maslin kettles of some kind, especially as the other utensil of choice is a kettle. ****"Iron kettles"** I'm presuming to be a Dutch oven. Another possibility is that iron pans and iron kettles are the same thing, and both refer to Dutch ovens, because Beecher & Stowe in their 1869 *The American Woman's Home,* list among requisite iron wares, "a Dutch Oven, called also a bake-pan." As for "bottled cornmeal," I'm confident that this was a dialectical version of "beetled," or pounded. A beetle is a pestle-like wooden implement with a big head and a handle. And a very old low German word for maul is *bötel*.

Firebacks – Out of the scope of this book, firebacks are important in restoring old fireplaces or building new ones to 18th century appearance. Cast iron firebacks with various figural and decorative designs, some with dates, were set up in the back of the fireplace to reflect heat back toward the fire (making it hotter) and the room. Reproduction firebacks are available from Country Iron Foundry in Naples, FL. (941) 434-2181; www.firebacks.com.

Fish broiler, flips like swiveling hearth toasters, wrought iron footed frame with spikes to hold fish, even a small arch under handle to hold it up off hearth, American (?), 18th C. .... **$450+**
Fish grill, forged iron, elongated grid, long handle, prob. American, 30-1/2"L x 3-1/2"W, early 19th C. .. **$200+**
Flesh forks: See Flesh fork in Chapter XIII (Implements)
Frying pan, forged iron, long handle, American (?), 10" diam. with 11"L handle, early 19th C. .... **$100+**

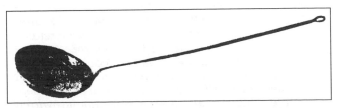

X-37. Frying pan. Wrought iron, 50"L x 14-1/2" diam., American, 18th or early 19th C. Ex-Keillor Family Collection. **$200+**

"Frying pan" or "Skillet"? Terminology varies – What started out as a clearer-cut difference between a frying pan and a skillet in the 18th C, based on the form, became at some time a regional difference in language usage not catalogued anywhere. In my experience Ohio and New York people say *frying pan*, Tennessee folks say *skillet*. Then there's a chronological difference; a skillet in the 18th C and early 19th C is more like what we might think of as a saucepan with legs. And a frying pan was also called a *spider*. Besides place and age, there's **trade terminology**: the names used by the manufacturers. Griswold, from Pennsylvania, used "skillet" as did Ohio's Wagner. Your choice. See the paragraph "Skillet or Posnet?" further on.

Frying pan, cast iron, three 2"H legs, American, 10-1/2" diam., early to mid 19th C. These 3-legged ones could have been used on an early brickset range, too. Added value: all hearth-cooking frying pans with feet are worth more than flat ones. Fireplace frying pans have long handles. The value difference doesn't apply to 20th C frying pans like certain rarities of Griswold or Wapak, which are worth more to their collectors than any hearth cooking pan. .... **$100-$200+**

Frying pan, cast iron, three 2-1/2"H legs, forged iron replaced handle that was riveted on to chipped edge of pan, long casting gate, this isn't a new pan but there is an odd gray glittery look to the iron on the bottom, possibly because of heat generated by weld-

X-39. Girdle plate or griddle, hanging type with swiveling trammel ring. Deep rim, with chip (not a pouring lip), crudely cast iron. 16"H x 13" diam., American, late 18th C. Photo courtesy of Robert W. Skinner Inc., Auctioneers, Bolton, MA. **$300+**

ing to replace handle, after pan cracked and original cast handle broke off, marked only "No. 8, 12 in." on bottom, American, actually 11-1/2" diam., overall length with new handle is 21-5/8"L, early to mid 19th C (?). .... **$90-$150+**

Frying pan, & lid, cast iron, pan has three 2-1/4"H legs, lid has raised edge like for Dutch oven, marked "1 N," G. T. Glascook & Son, Greensboro, NC, 12" diam., mid (?)19th C. .... **$65-$90**

Frying pan, repaired sheet iron, hand wrought handle is extremely long, the 2 repairs to pan – one a rectangle of brass, one of copper – are riveted on, American, pan 14" diam., handle about 38"L, late 18th or early 19th C. By virtue of its repair, this has become a folk art piece, and its value no longer relates solely to it as a utensil. .... **$400+**

Frying pan, wrought iron, rattail handle, American, 12" diam., 14"L handle, early 19th C. .... **$95-$150**

Girdle or griddle plate, cast iron, no legs or feet, rigid bail handle by which it was hung on a pothook from a crane, American (?), 14-3/16" diam., c.1830s. .... **$150-$250+**

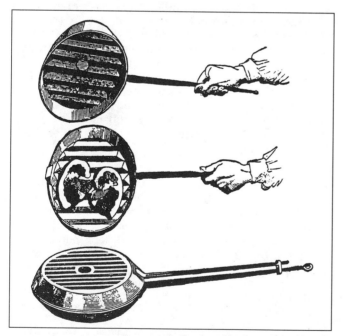

X-38. "Captain Warren's Bachelor's Frying Pan." *"Invented by Captain Warren" and it retains heat because of the heavy flutes inside. "It shuts and can be turned over from one side to the other, as the cook pleases." Note how long wrought iron handles have a slip right – exactly like that on long-handled waffle irons, from which Captain Warren may have received his inspiration. From* Warne's Model Cookery, *London, 1868. See also XII-25 for more Captain Warren!* **$300+**

Flannel Cakes or Crumpets *– Two pounds of flour, sifted. Four eggs. Three tables-spoonfuls of the best brewer's yeast, or four and a half of home-made yeast. A pint of milk. – Mix a tea-spoonful of salt with the flour, and set the pan before the fire. Then warm the milk, and stir into it the flour, so as to make a stiff batter. Beat the eggs very light, and stir them into the yeast. Add the eggs and yeast to the batter, and beat all well together. If it is too stiff, add a little more warm milk.*

"Cover the pan closely and set it to rise near the fire. Bake it, when quite light.

"Have your baking-iron hot. Grease it, and pour on a ladle-full of batter. Let it bake slowly, ... when done on one side, turn it on the other.

"Butter the cakes, cut them across, and send them to table hot." Miss Leslie, of Philadelphia, Seventy-Five Receipts for Pastry, Cakes, and Sweetmeats. *Appended to* The Cook's Own Book and Housekeeper's Register ...., *by a Boston Housekeeper. Boston: Munroe & Francis, 1833.*

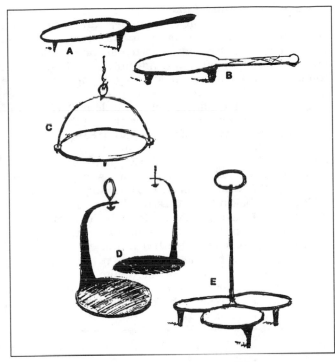

X-40. Girdle plates or griddles. (A) (B) *Cast iron, Pennsylvania. 11" diam., early 19th C. Three legs, with leg under handle nearly twice height of other two, intentional, I'm sure to get more reflected heat when placed on hearth. Simple crisscross on handle of **(B)** is cast in; it has no rim. **(C)** Full-bailed plate, with short feet. Cast and wrought, with side ears for the bail. 15-1/2" diam. Early 19th C. **(D)** Both are quarter-hoop hanging girdles, probably English or Scottish. Forged iron, with plates almost 17" diam. One on right, missing part of the ring bolt, sold at 1986 auction for $700. **(E)** Cast &forged iron, hearth-standing or hanging, central handle, late 18th, early 19th C. (E) Was drawn from ad of Pat Guthman Antiques, Southport, CT.* **$125-$700**

Girdle plate, cast iron, half-hoop fixed handle with large ring on top end, to be hung from crane. English or Scottish, small size, only 9" diam., early 19th C. .... **$250-$400**

Griddle or girdle plate, also called a backstone [bakestone] in old inventories, forged iron, fixed bail handle with swivel ring, American, 10" diam., mid to late 18th C. .... **$20-$300+**

X-41. Gridiron or grill. *Forged iron, with grease trough. Late 18th, early 19th C. Probably American. Photograph courtesy of Pat Guthman Antiques, Southport, CT.* **$350+**

X-42. Hearth utensils. (T-L) *Skimmer of brass with iron and wood handle, c.1800-1820; **(T-R)** grill or gridiron hanging at top right, c.1790-1810. Bottom row: left to right: **(L-1)** Small cast iron bowl; **(L-2)** large cast iron bowl; **(L-3)** small posnet or skillet, cast iron, c.1820s-30. **(L-4)** Long-legged cast iron frying pan, c.1830. Picture courtesy of Georgia G. Levett, Levett's Antiques, Camden, ME. Probably the bowls are worth the most.* **$125-$450+**

Griddle, cast iron, long handle, 3 longish legs – 3-1/4"H, American, 12" diam., 2nd quarter 19th C. .... **$150-$200+**

Griddle, cast iron, round with short "keyhole" shaped handle with hanging hole, no legs, cool, smooth, seductive, slate-like finish, American (?), 11-3/4" diam. with 2-1/2"L handle, very early 19th C. .... **$90-$120+**

✧ RECIPE ✧

Best Batter Cakes, or Mush Cakes *– Beat the yolks of eggs very light, add one pint milk, two pints mush almost cold, 1-1/2 pints flour, one tea-spoonful salt, three table-spoonsful melted butter. To be well beaten together. Just before frying them, whip the whites to a strong froth, and stir it lightly into the batter. For frying all kinds of batter cakes, use no more lard than is necessary to make them turn well.... But the usual mode is to boil homminy twice a week, and put it into a wooden or stone vessel, and set it in a cool place to prevent its becoming musty. When wanted for use, take the quantity necessary for breakfast or dinner, and having put a small quantity of lard into an oven, let it become hot; put in the homminy and mash it well, adding some salt; when well heated it is ready for the table. Some persons allow it to bake at the bot-*

tom, and turn the crust over the hominy when put on the dish. Be careful to have no smoke under the pot while boiling, or when frying for the table. Few things require more care or nicety in their preparation than hominy. (These pints were all measured with the common tin cup.)" The Farmers' Cabinet, Devoted to Agriculture, Horticulture and Rural Economy. *Philadelphia: Vol. II, No. 1, Aug. 1, 1837.*

❖ NOTES ❖

Bucket Double Boiler – "Let me suggest for the comfort of those who stir [mush] an hour or two, and then labor a great while to wash out the pot in which they boil it, that all this trouble may be saved by cooking it in a tin pail, set in a pot of boiling water, and after it has cooked, letting it cool in the same, after which it will slip out in a mass, leaving all clean behind it. Whosoever tries this plan will never try the old one again, for it prevents the possibility of burning the mush, and dispenses with all care and trouble except occasionally to replenish the water in which the pail is set to boil." *Farmer and Mechanic, April 1853.*

Griddle, forged iron, 3 longish legs, long handle with hanging hole, found in Virginia, 11-11/16" diam., overall length 23-1/4", late 18th or early 19th C. .... **$300-$350**

❖ NOTES ❖

1865 – "I looked over a whole **batch of recipes** sent in by readers, and though I don't doubt they are good of their kind, it is the kind that don't suit me. The only thing the title of which tempts me at all is **Johnny cake**. I open the recipe, and find that though the mixture may be good, it is baked in an oven! Shade of my grandmother! a Johnny cake in an oven! Don't you see that when it is baked in an oven, though it may be something good, it isn't Johnny cake? That must be baked on the middle piece of the head of a flour barrel (Beach's brand preferred), with a hole in the northeast corner. The cake is placed on this, and set up against a flat iron in front of a bed of hickory coals, to bake, and nothing short of this can be Johnny cake – but as I sometime intend to make a cook-book, I won't say anything more about it. – If I do make a cook book, I won't have any mince pies, any sausages, nor cakes, nor puddings, nor anything sweet, nor any saleratus; but just you wait and see what I do put in." A Bachelor, "Household Department," *American Agriculturist, Feb. 1865.*

•   •   •

Jonakin, **Jonikin** or "**Jonny Cake** derives its name from *Jaunny*, the name of Pequots and Narragansets for Maise or Indian Corn. As this was a new grain to the Pilgrims, they very naturally adopted the Indian name, and called the bread made of it Jaunny Cake. After these once powerful Indian tribes were destroyed and forgotten, the origin of this name was forgotten also, and from similarity of sound, became corrupted into Jonny Cake." *Journal of the American Institute, NYC, March 1839, p.336.*

Superior Johnny Cake – The following receipt will make a Johnny cake fit for an alderman, a mayor, an editor or any other dignitary in the land: Take one quart of milk, three eggs, one tea-spoonful saleratus, one tea cup of wheat flour and Indian meal, sufficient to make a batter to the consistency of pancakes. Bake quick in **pans*** previously buttered, and eat warm with butter or milk. The addition of wheat flour will be found a great improvement in the art of making these cakes." *The Farmers' Cabinet, Aug. 1, 1836.* (***Pans** aren't further identified. *Subject-Matter Index of Patents for Inventions,* has an intriguing early patent for a "baking-iron," records of which burned in fires at patent office 1836 or 1877, which was granted E. Skinner on Oct. 1, 1830. Was a baking-iron a Dutch oven with lid? a dripping pan? "**Journey Cake.** – Pour boiling water on a quart of meal, put in a little lard and salt, and mix it well; have an oak board with a rim of iron at the bottom, and an iron handle fastened to it that will prop it up to the fire; put some of the dough on it, dip your hand in cold water and smooth it over; score it with a knife, and set it before the coals to bake." Elizabeth Ellicott Lea, *Domestic Cookery, 1859.*

❖ RECIPE ❖

Johnny-Cake – Sift one quart of Indian meal into a pan; make a hole in the middle, and pour in a pint of warm water, adding one teaspoon of salt; with a spoon mix the meal and water gradually into a soft dough; stir it very briskly for a quarter of an hour or more, till it becomes light and spongy; then spread the dough smooth and evenly on a straight, flat board (a piece of the head of a flour-barrel will serve for this purpose); place the board nearly upright before an open fire, and put an iron against the back to support it; bake it well; when done, cut it in squares; send it hot to table, split and buttered." Mary Stuart Smith, Virginia Cookery-Book (as reprinted in G. Strohm's 1888 Universal Cookery Book).

Griddle, forged iron, to hang from crane, with bail handle and swivel ring at apex of arch of handle, American (?), 14-1/2" diam., 19th C. .... **$175-$250**
Griddle, rotating, wrought iron, long handle has heart shaped loop, 3 peg feet, American, 25"L, 19th C. .... **$175-$250**
Griddle or girdle plate, forged iron, fixed forged iron handle forms quarter circle hoop, swivel ring to hang from trammel or pot hook, 3 peg feet, American, 13" diam., 18th C. • If Jonathan Winters were writing the copy for this, he'd make a crack about needing a girdle after you'd eaten a few of the flapjacks made on this, but actually **girdle**, meaning encircle, is the word origin. **Metathesis** – transposition of letters, such as "r" and "i" to make girdle into griddle – was typical for the English language for centuries, and is seen in the way words from some other languages, French, Italian, German, are changed when they join the English language. .... **$175-$300**
Gridiron, cast iron, 3 legs, long handle, drip cup midway along handle, cast along back of handle is the name, each word looks as if it were carved on sepa-

X-43. Hearth utensils. *"The sow came in with the saddle, The little pig rock'd the cradle/ The dish jump'd up on the table/ To see the pot swallow the ladle./ The spit that stood behind the door/ Threw the pudding stick on the floor./ Odsplut! said the gridiron, Can't you agree?/ I'm the head constable, Bring them to me."* [*"Odsplut" is a very old way to swear "God's blood" without actually saying it.*] Mother Goose's Melodies, 1833.

rate narrow plaques that could be used in the casting mold arranged in a horizontal line or stacked, depending on requirements of various castings, "Campbell Foundry Co.," Harrison, NJ, 28-3/8"L x 16-5/8"W, c.1850s...................................... **$150+**

❖ RECIPE ❖

1884 Steak *"Place the steak on a hot, well-greased gridiron, turn often so that the outside may be seared at once; when done, which will require from five to ten minutes, dish on a hot platter, season with salt and pepper and bits of butter ... A small pair of tongs are best to turn steaks, as piercing with a fork frees the juices. If fat drips on the coals below, the blaze may be extinguished by sprinkling with salt, always withdrawing the gridiron to prevent the steak from acquiring a smoky flavor. Always have a brisk fire, whether you cook in a patent broiler directly over the fire, or on a gridiron over a bed of live coals. ... A steel gridiron with slender bars is best, as the common broad, flat iron bars fry and scorch the meat, imparting a disagreeable flavor."* Practical Housekeeping, Minneapolis, 1884.

❖ NOTES ❖

Some **English foundry names** which may appear on hollowwares or other cast iron wares, from the 18th & 19th Cs are: Baldwin, Son & Co., Stowport; "Beatrice" – John Harper; Carron Co.; Coalbrookdale, Abraham Darby, Shropshire; Cockrane & Co.; A. Kenrick; Walter Macfarlane & Co., Saracen Foundry, Glasgow; Richard Rowbotham, Providence Foundry; and J. & J. Siddons, West Bromwich.

Gridiron, cast iron, enameled white inside, 3 legs, grease cup, "A. Kenrick & Sons," also either numeral 9 or 6, West Bromwich, England, 1-1/2"H legs, 21-3/4"L including handle, mid to 3rd quarter 19th C. .... **$95-$150**

Gridiron, cast iron, grease drip basin in back, 2 short front feet, short handle, American, 13" x 16", 19th C. .... **$80+**

Gridiron, cast iron, grease trap and spouted to pour, grid is 10 runneled strips, two legs in front, one in back, shortish handle, American (?), handle about 6"L, mid 19th C. .... **$55+**

Gridiron, forged iron, almost square top with 12 very slightly concave bars, long front legs, back legs curved and much shorter, detachable grease catcher hooked along back edge, longish, upcurved handle with large ring at end, American (?), grid is 11-1/4" x 12-1/2", overall length 23", late 18th or early 19th C. .... **$350+**

Gridiron, forged iron, simple rectangular grid of flat bars, short leg in each corner, the hind legs are a bit shorter than the front, medium-length fishtail handle with grab bar along top, detachable grease catcher like hook-on trough along back edge, American, 17"W x 23"L overall, 18th C. .... **$400+**

❖ NOTES ❖

Short Legs – I have three theories of why one of three legs, or two of four, would be considerably shorter than the others: (1) they were worn, broken off, or burned off by accident; (2) they were intentionally ground down so as to tilt the utensil and collect, pool, or puddle juices or

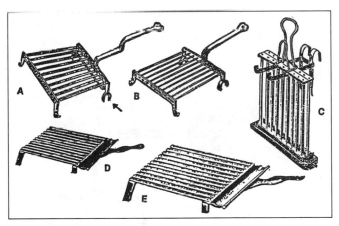

X-44. Gridirons or grills. *None all that old.* **(A)** *"Fluted gridiron," fluted steel bars, "fat pan" or grease trough along back edge, under bars. Notched back feet to hook onto fender; 7, 8, 9, 10, 11, & 12 bars.* **(B)** *"London gridiron," a more economical model in same range of sizes.* **(C)** *"Double-hanging gridiron," with tinned iron wire (or with wrought iron, tinned all over "after made.") 8", 9", 10", 11" & 12" (or for wrought one, 10, 11, 12, 13, & 14 bars).* **(A-C)** *from Harrod's Stores, Ltd., Brompton, England, 1895 catalog.* **(D)** *"Heavy gridiron" in iron, 6 sizes, from 8-1/2" x 12" to 13" x 16 3/4", the smaller three for families, others for hotels. Duparquet, Huot & Moneuse, c.1904-1910.* **(E)** *Tinned sheet iron, 15-1/2" x 9-1/8" to 16-3/4" x 13". Lalance & Grosjean, 1890.* **$75-$200+**

fats to assist in basting or making gravy or sauce; or, (3) they were shortened intentionally so that face of utensil (and food on it) addresses the heat (coals or flames) more directly. These shorter legs are found on griddles, grilles, spiders, and various saucepans and skillets. (By the way, one old meaning of **pot-leg** is of a short piece of iron, such as a broken-off or ground-off pot leg, used as shrapnel-like shot in a shotgun.)

Gridiron, or "cooking furnace gridiron," as the inventor called it. Round, has runneled (fluted or concave) bars or ribs, gravy trough "all around, on the outer edge, having a spout on one side for discharging the gravy," handle on one side. "It may be made of cast-iron, or wrought, or sheet-iron, or any other material, and may be varied in form, size, or shape, as convenience may require, with, or without legs, for so I make them," wrote the inventor, Jonathan Powers, Lansingburgh, Rensselaer County, NY, who pat'd. it Aug. 10, 1829. • The Editor of the *Journal of the Franklin Institute* commented about this **gridiron**: "We are again at a loss to know what is intended to be patented. It certainly cannot be a round gridiron, as these have been made by the thousand. The fluted, or concave bars, and gravy trough, we have known for upwards of forty years [ie. c.1780s]: these, therefore, are not new. But, as the patentee has not chosen to tell his claim, it is not our business to do so; we therefore leave the discovery to others." It would obviously be hard to know if you'd found a Powers' gridiron, but I include all this as instructive of workings of the patent office, and of the infinite potential for finding interesting pieces, perhaps signed somewhere..... **$200+**

Gridiron, wrought iron, 2 penny feet plus foot at base of long handle, fixed grid, New England, 2-1/4"H x 19 18/"L, late 18th or early 19th C. .... **$250+**

Gridiron, wrought iron, 4 small peg feet, long handle, American, 10-1/2" x 11" rectangle, with 11"L handle, early 19th C. .... **$250+**

X-45. Revolving & stationary gridirons. (T-L) Cast iron, 12" diam., catches grease underneath. **(M-R)** Rectangular slightly convex, cast iron. Both Russell & Erwin, 1865. **(B-L)** "Revolving enamelled gridiron with fluted bars to convey the gravy to the cup" [which is seen mid-handle]. American Home Cook Book, 1854. **$150-$225+**

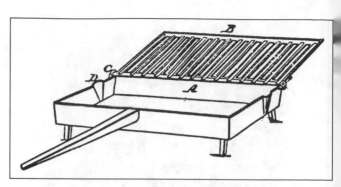

X-46. Gridiron patent. *Pat'd. Nov. 14, 1836, by Amasa Sizer and George Sizer, Meriden, CT.* **"Combined gridiron and spider."** *"The nature of our invention consists in uniting a gridiron and spider in one instrument in such manner that both may be used together or each separately at the same time, the juices of the broiling meat being conducted into the spider or when the spider is separately used, into a receiver placed within it. To enable others skilled in the art to make, and use our invention we describe its construction as follows: The form may be square, circular, or oval when open for use, or a half square, or parallelogram, or a semicircle when folded. The model deposited in the Patent Office is semicircular when folded. The spider **(A)** and gridiron **(B)** are each cast whole in separate castings, and united in the following manner. The spider is formed with legs and a handle, and on each end of the spider around the corners of the side approaching the fire is a projecting ear **(C)**, having a staple of wire set in the casting to receive the pintle or gudgeon of the gridiron, and on which it turns. Near each of these ears is a spout **(D)** on each end. The gridiron is cast with fluted bars, and rim, on the end of the bar, which joins the spider, gudgeons or pintles are extended, which when connected" form a hinge. When the two parts are used separately, and at the same time, a narrow tin pan is placed under the edge of the gridiron and within the basin of the spider, to receive the drip. When folded, the tin pan may be used as a chafing dish."* Official Gazette, *patent #78!*

Grill, or broiler, forged iron, large square with shaped flat forged iron handle with rattail, the grill bars alternating plain with little loops & hearts, the whole giving an effect of iron ribbon cleverly tied, French or Belgian, or poss. French Canadian, about 12" square, handle 10"L, late 18th C (?).... **$800-$1,000**

Grill, revolving or rotary – See Broiler, rotary

Grisette, wrought iron, long canoe-shaped rather shallow bowl, with long forged iron handle set at right angles from middle of long axis, the handle terminating in a right angle bend forming a supporting leg, this was used in the 18th C for dipping lengths of rush into melted fat, to coat the stalks as crude "candles," American, 'boat' bowl is 7"L x 3"W x 1" deep, handle 21"L, 18th C. **Confusable.** – This is here because it could be mistaken for some kind of fish cooker or cooking ladle; or for a herb crusher (see Chapter I). .... **$550-$700**

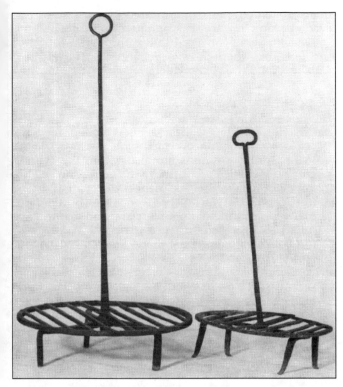

X-47. Standing gridirons. *Wrought iron. 18th C, prob. American. Photograph courtesy of Pat Guthman Antiques, Southport, CT. Each:* **$650+**

Gypsy pot or kettle, cast iron, with 3 casting ribs around circumference, cast in 3-part mold, American, 11-3/4"H x 12-7/8" diam., early 19th or late 18th C. .... **$275-$375**

❖ **NOTES** ❖

Preparing Hominy for the Table – It must be thoroughly washed in cold water, rubbing it well with the hands; then washed in the same way in warm water, changing the water several times. Put it into a large pot of cold water, and boil steadily eight or ten

X-48. Grill. *Wrought iron, well-finished. Heart decorations add much to value. 26"L overall x 13"W. Probably English, late 18th C.* **$450+**

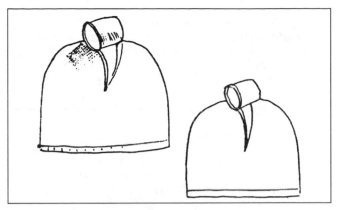

X-49. Hoe blades. *Forged iron, potentially used for baking hoe cakes in front of coals or fire. When laid down, the shank socket would serve as a little foot that would raise one end toward the fire. Blades about 6" to 8"W.* **(L)** *is a* <u>Virginia</u> *style weeding hoe;* **(R)** *is a* <u>Carolina</u> *style hoe. Both made as "plantation" hoes in Sheffield, England, c.1816.*

hours, keeping it closely covered. Add hot water frequently while boiling, otherwise the hominy will burn and be dark colored. When hominy beans are used, one pint to a gallon of hominy, to be put in when the hominy is put on. If it is put on the first thing in the morning, and kept briskly boiling, it will be ready for dinner at two o'clock. Season with butter and send it to the table hot. (These pints were all measured with the common tin cup.)" *The Farmers' Cabinet, Devoted to Agriculture, Horticulture and Rural Economy.* Philadelphia: Vol. II, No. 1, Aug. 1, 1837.

Hake, forged iron, an "S" hook for hanging pots or kettles from crane, American (?), 6"L, 18th or early 19th C – but hard to date now because so many are being made by artisan blacksmiths. With these, the best you could hope for would be something zoomorphic, for example, the hook ending in a snake's head or dog's head. Multiply price below by 30X to 100X if you should find such a thing. .... **$20+**
Ham hook – See Hook, ham or meat
Hearth warming shelf, wrought iron bracket, hung on nails in side of fireplace, American, 9"H x 13"W, 18th C. These are extremely rare, and might be mistaken for regular wall bracket shelves. .... **$275+**
Hoes, forged iron or steel, broad-bladed, tilted sockets without their long wooden handles, sometimes struck with maker's mark, American, early to mid 19th C. .... **$15-$45+**

❖ **NOTES** ❖

Hoe downs & ups – Looking at a modern hoe, it is not easy to imagine propping one up at such a slant in front of the fire that a corn cake could actually be slapped upon it and baked. But the 19th century had a variety of hoes, for purposes such as weeding or grubbing, with shank sockets set at different angles, and blades of different dimensions. Hoes varied from region to region too. I have not yet seen a perfect description of a hoe suitable for hoe cakes.

Virginia Hoe Cake – *Pour warm water on a quart of Indian meal; stir in a spoonful of lard or butter, some salt, make it stiff, and work it for 10 minutes; have a board about the size of a barrel head, (or the middle piece of the head will answer,) wet the board with water, and spread on the dough with your hand; place it before the fire; prop it aslant with a flat-iron, bake it slowly; when one side is nicely brown, take it up and turn it, by running a thread between the cake and the board, then put it back, and let the other side brown. These cakes used to be baked in Virginia on a large iron hoe, from whence they derive their name."* Elizabeth E. Lea, *Useful Receipts and Hints to Young House-keepers, 10th ed., Baltimore, 1859 (1st ed. 1851).*

❖ NOTES ❖

Hoe Pones – E. Scott Boyce, in *Economic and Social History of Chowan County*, North Carolina, 1880-1915, published by Columbia University, 1917, wrote about this odd cooking utensil of the 1880s: "The 'hoe-cake' – a pone of corn-bread baked on a hoe that had already lived out is usefulness as a farm utensil – in Chowan had not yet passed into the realms of fiction." [p.223 of this really neat book.]

Hook, forged iron, 4 points, flattened, dealer Dorothy Lyon said she was told it was used for roasting small game birds and the flattened ends were supposed to keep the juices from dripping, American, prob. Richmond, VA, 9"L, late 18th or early 19th C. **$90-$110**

Hook, ham or meat, braided wrought iron, with eye at top and but one hook. Sides or large cuts of meat (such as hams) were hung in smokehouse from these. Sometimes the meat was rubbed in ashes, or wrapped in cloth before hanging. 9"L, American, late 18th, early 19th C. .... **$75-$100**

Hook, ham or meat, braided wrought iron, 4 hooks, - 1/2"L, the hooks reach out 10"W. Impeccable provenance: it was formerly in the Keillor Family Collection, found installed in the chimney of a house built in Plymouth, MA, in 1711. .... **$400+**

Hook, ham or meat, forged iron with 4 graceful hooks, ring for hanging at top. Made from 2 twisted lengths of bar iron, heated & pounded together. Could be from anywhere; no stylistic details to tie to a country, 24"H; each hook 7-1/4"H, prob. late 1700s, early 1800s. Hard to date. So many turn up, you wonder if somebody has a blacksmith in the backyard. ... **$75+**

❖ NOTES ❖

The Smoke-house of Col. M'Allister in 1828, Fort Turner, on the Susquehanna, above Harrisburg. "A convenience worthy of imitation," reported visitor Judge Buel. "The Smoke-house was a wooden octagon building, perhaps 16 feet in diameter, perfectly tight, except the door-way. The peculiarities of this building were, it was set a foot or more above the ground, and was perfectly dry, and bacon, hams, &c., were kept hanging around its walls all summer without becoming damp or mouldy, or being injured by flies; and in the second place, no fire was admitted into the building, the smoke being conveyed into it through a tube from the outside, where it was generated." *The Farmers' Cabinet*, Vol. I, No. 1, Philadelphia, July 1, 1836.

Hook, pot – See Pot hook

Hot water kettle – See Tea kitchens

Jack, type called bottle jack, brass with forged iron hook, rotary action provided by a clockwork movement, spring wound, concealed within the cylindrical bottle shaped drum above the hook. The key hole for winding is in the side, near the bottom of the cylinder. "Salter's Warranted Economical Bottle Jack," mark is a mariner's knot pierced by an arrow, & the initial "S," English, 12"H, c.1820s (?). A Mr. Salter (probably the same one) made brass-faced hanging spring balance scales. .... **$375+**

Jack clamp for bottle jack – or mantle clamp, also jack rack, cast & worked brass, a simple screw clamp, sliding jack hook, acorn finial to screw, English or poss. American, late 18th or early 19th C. (Those in elegant whitesmithed steel about same value.)...... **$250-$375**

X-50. Bottle jack.
Japanned sheet iron, or brass (which were much more expensive). Clockwork inside, but named for its overall shape. From Harrod's Stores Ltd., Brompton, England, 1895 catalog. They also cleaned and repaired bottle jacks, as probably many clock repairers did too. See also the reflecting oven Meat screens, which were made for use with bottle jacks, X-69-71. **$225+**

X-51. Clock jack.
Skeletal iron frame, brass front. 8-11/16"H excluding governor wheel at top. Cast iron weight. Photographed from stock of Mark & Margery Allen, Putnam Valley, NY. **$1,500+**

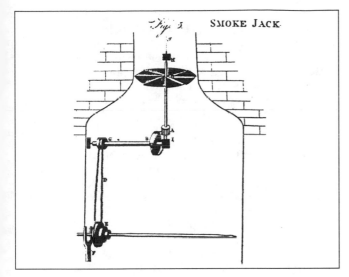

X-52. Smoke jack. *18th C drawing cut (by dealer, not me) from unID book of plates. "A. Bell" was the engraver, and this is the "Smoke" plate, No. CCCCLXXI, so it was a big book. Note gears. This interesting invention worked by using the heated air (smoke) updraft which turned the vane, which turned the shaft which turned the spit – all in the house that Jack built! Archie Keillor told me, when I worked on my first book, that you could only collect these in your mind – by catching a sight of one when peering up an old chimney in an English manor home.*

Jack, clock or clockwork, brass & iron, iron weight, English, 8-11/16"H exclusive of wheel at top, early 19th C. The value of some of these relates to venue of sale; also crossover interest from collectors of clocks and scientific tools. .... **$675+**

Jack, clock, forged iron, spoked wheel, scrolled front plate, arched wall bracket, 3 gears and spool, American or English, 14"H, late 18th or early 19th C. At auction, this and similar clock jacks might bring upwards of $5,500, according to Erik Gronning, who avidly follows such sales. .... **$3,000+**

❖ NOTES ❖

Planetarium stove – In the *Journal of the Franklin Institute ... and Mechanics' Register* [Philadelphia], of 1839, appeared a report of a patent obtained July 12, 1838 by Samuel Pierce of NYC for an "Apparatus for Roasting Meat and other Articles." The *Journal* editor writes as follows: "This apparatus is denominated the 'manifold roaster, or planetarium stove,' and the patentee says, 'the main object of my improvement is to combine together a number of spits, or jacks, each of which is to sustain a joint of meat, a fowl, or other article to be roasted; and each of which spits is to be suspended by a hook over its appropriate dripping pan, the whole of which spits may be made to revolve simultaneously by wheel work, properly geared, either before an ordinary fire, or more perfectly by being placed around a stove constructed for that purpose; in which latter case the spits not only revolve on their own axes, but have an orbicular revolution round the stove. The effect of the heat is, in either case, to be promoted by means of reflectors. When the planetarium stove is complete, and in

operation, its external appearance is that of an ordinary cylindrical stove of large diameter, the external cylinder being a case (usually made double) which surrounds the stove, and which also surrounds the system of spits which revolve round said stove." Pierce went on to claim that the originality of this invention was in the multiple vertical spits revolving simultaneously. I'm not convinced this was anywhere near the first of this type, although the older English ones seen in pictures were horizontal spits.

Jack, clock, steel, cast, wrought & machined brass beautifully scrolled front plate, clean clockwork, the word "jack" in the name, standing for the assistant or spit turner who is no longer necessary, English, 18th C. .... **$1,200-$1,500+**

Jack or spit engine, clockwork mechanism for driving spit, brass face, wrought iron frame, English (?), 18th C. • Appearance, workability (or at least repairable condition), completeness add value.............. **$1,500-$2,500**

Jack & crown spit, also called a spit engine, cast & machined brass, forged iron, marked "John Linwood," English (?), 18th C. .... **$1,200-$1,500**

❖ NOTES ❖

A **spectacular mechanical spit** was reported in William Hone's *The Every-Day Book*, 1827: "The most singular spit in the world is that of the Count de Castel Maria, one of the most opulent lords of Treviso. This spit turns one hundred and thirty different roasts at once, and plays twenty-four tunes, and whatever it plays, corresponds to a certain degree of cooking, which is perfectly understood by the cook. Thus, a leg of mutton à lá anglaise, will be excellent at the 12th air; a fowl à la Flamande, will be juicy at the 18th, and so on. It would be difficult, perhaps, to carry farther the love of music and gormandizing."

Jack & spit, standing floor model clockwork jack, timer bell, vertical oblong housing for works, lion's paw feet to 4 short legs, carrying handle on top, cast iron & steel, cranked to wind, can motivate 3 long spits, one end hooked to jack, other supported on wrought iron stand, French, 48"H, early 19th C. • I don't know maker of this, it's not marked, but another French one, with clockworks inside a small 4 legged pedestal base, that drives a spit in a tin reflector oven with rounded back, and tapered tubular tin legs, was made in the mid 19th C by Viville of Paris. Not only did the spit turn, but some system of "rotating spoons" kept basting the meat as it turned. The clockwork has bells that ring when it's winding down. It was exhibited at an antique show in 1988 by Larry Melvin, Springfield, OH................ **$2,200+**

Kettle, also spelled cettell, or kittel in old records, this one of cast iron, 3 short feet, slightly flared out sides, reinforced with one inch wide wrought iron band near top, American (?), 7-1/2"H, 18th C. Every once in a while you see such pieces with the wrought band, which may be as narrow as 3/8"................................ **$150+**

Kettle, cast iron with 3 legs, heavy twisted forged iron bail handle, domed lid, 3 longish feet, circumferential ribs or ridges, bulge-pot type that looks like a "gypsy kettle," American, 6-1/4"H x 4-1/4" diam., late 18th C. .... **$275-$350**

Department of Transportation & Sanitation Department find new uses for landfill! I read of a 17th & 18th C practice called "**kettlin' the roads**," which involved dragging old, cracked, and probably holey, iron kettles and pots behind a sleigh in order to break up the coating of slick ice on the tracks of sleigh runners on snowy roads.

Kettle, with lid, heavy copper with wrought iron swing handle, slightly convex bottom, meant to hang on a fireplace crane, American (?), 15" diam., early 19th C. .... **$200-$375**

Kettle, cast iron, with 3 legs, rare in this small size – only 4"H, American, early 19th C. .... **$250+**

Kettle, cast iron, round bottom, ribbed, 3 feet, American, 10" deep x 17" diam., 19th C. .... **$95+**

Kettle, cast iron, "gypsy" type with bulging body, 3 very short legs, rounded bottom, slightly flared lip, falling wire bail handle, 2 ribs around circumference, "J. A. Goewey," Albany, NY, 12-1/4"H x 11" diam., mid 19th C. .... **$100+**

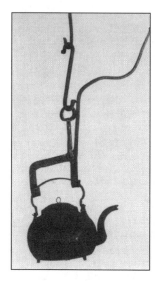

X-53. Kettle tilter with kettle. *Forged iron with cast kettle. Photograph courtesy of Pat Guthman Antiques, Southport, CT. (See also a quadrant crane with kettle & kettle tilter X-25.)* **$600+**

X-54. "A simple feed cooker." *A large cast iron kettle, "large enough to admit the chine [rim] of a meat barrel or tierce, and arranged with a fire-place beneath it. A number of holes are bored in the bottom of the barrel, and two strong rings are affixed to the sides. The barrel is placed upon the kettle, fitting closely inside the rim, and is filled with roots and meal. A close cover is fitted to the top, and the contents of the barrel are cooked by the steam from the kettle. The barrel may be lifted off when the feed is cooked, by means of a small crane and windlass, and placed upon a wheelbarrow to be carried where it is to be used." Imagine doing that every day! American Agriculturist, June 1878.*

Reproduction Alert

A small, rather clumsily **cast iron "gypsy" kettle**, with 3 fat peg legs widely splayed, wire bail, and (if all parts are accounted for), a brass lid and brass firestarter rod, was advertised as the "always useful Cape Cod lighter," for $4.95, by H. Wiener, NYC, NY. The ad date is Nov. 1937, *House Beautiful*. • **Alert II.** – In 1930, one of the more lame Colonial rip-offs was an ashtray & cigarette holder combo of wrought iron. It consisted of an awkward little 3 legged tray with 2 resting places for cigarettes, above which, by means of a thick ungainly bent iron rod with hook, hangs a "Gypsy's Pot" of cast iron. Overall the piece is only 8-1/2"H; the pot is about 3-1/2"H, and has a wire bail handle, 3 splayed peg legs, a pronounced ridge around widest part of belly, some roughness in the casting (covered with black paint), and a lid which hangs from a little dogleg jag on the main hook. As is often true, the *House Beautiful* ad copy says a lot: "An Ash Tray of Distinction combining unique charm with usefulness, the 'Gypsy's Pot' is an ash tray sure to please any smoker. The cast iron pot for cigarets is a miniature replica of America's first cast iron pot [Saugus?!?]. Forged-iron stand holds a removable tray. Finishes: Chinese Red, Black, Jade green, Rusty Iron or Copper .... $3.50." This piece has some collateral value in a collection; it is intriguing, after all, to see how far Colonial Revivalists would go!

Lookalike Alarm

The Spring-Summer 1970 *McCall's Needlework Magazine* has an ad showing a **tiny-looking bulge pot and a little hot water kettle**, both cast iron. The pot has tiny peg feet, and both have fitted lids and wire bail handles. They held "delicious preserves – wild huckleberry in pot, seedless blackberry in kettle." They were "about 4" high," and originally cost $7.95 each, postpaid. Available from House of Webster in Rogers, Arkansas. I'm sure many of these have come on the market as antique toys or the ubiquitous "salesman's samples." (See X-67.) **Lookalike alarm 2.** –Lehman's Hardware & Appliances, Kidron, OH, offer a full range of hammered copper kettles with extra bottoms brazed in, cast iron or cast brass lug ears, and steel bail handles, in their "*Non-Electric Good Neighbor Amish Country*" catalog. These are apple butter kettles and flat bottom kettles; the former come in 8, 10, 12, 15, 20, 25, 30, 40 and 50 gallon capacities, from about $175 to $450+. I believe the stamped trademark is "MAKERS" on the side. The flat bottom kettles come in 1, 2, 4, 6, 8, 10 quart sizes, and 3, 5 and 8 gallon. They have a "tough, tarnish & weather-resistent polyurethane coating" which must be removed with paint remover for cooking. • Price range is for fairly small antiques; $$$ goes up in quantum leaps for large ones.

❖ NOTES ❖

Spun brass & copper kettles – Until about 1852, copper and brass kettles were made by hammering sheet metal over a form, or by a combination of hammering and piecing (usually with a dovetailed joint). But in 1852, an inventor named J. F. Flanders was granted patent #8627 for a new method, a patent he granted to Roys & Wilcox, whose names appear on the bottom of many kettles made by this wonderful new way. It was described in the report of the *Commissioner of Patents* for the year 1852: "An automatic machine for performing, on a large scale, the well known metallurgic operation of spinning up cups, platters, and such like articles, from a flat disk in a lathe, is worthy of notice. In this machine, large copper kettles, known in the shops as brass batteries, and usually shaped by repeated blows of a small hand hammer, are formed with great rapidity, and with a beauty and finish never attained by the handmade article. A species of burnisher, sometimes provided with a friction roller, is forced, by means of curved slots acting in connexion with screws and guides, to travel in tolerably close contact with the exterior of a revolving conical mandril formed of cast-iron. The flat sheet of metal is clamped upon the apex of this conical-former, revolves with it, and is gradually, by the action of the burnisher, forced to conform exactly to its shape. Several formers, each deviating more from a disk, and approaching more nearly to the form of the finished kettle, are used before the operation is completed, in order to bring the metal gradually, and by successive stages, into its new shape, and avoid all straining that might be injurious to the finished article.

"This contrivance is now in use. Its productions will speak for themselves, and will, on account of their superior beauty, have the preference over the old article, even if the inventor should not reduce the price to that extent which the labor-saving qualities of his machine would fully warrant." p. 385, *Ex. Doc. 65, 32d Congress.* Washington: Robert Armstrong, Printer, 1853.

• • •

"Kettle-pots." This term was used in the mid-18th century by at least two American metal-workers to describe their wares in advertisements. Mary Jackson of Cornhill, Boston, MA, and Thomas Russel of Boston, both used the term. Both were founders of hollowware in brass.

Kettle tilter, also called a tipper or a lazy elbow, idle back, used to assist the cook in pouring from a heavy kettle (especially a tea kettle or hot water kettle) suspended over a fire in the hearth, wrought iron, no marks, English or American, late 18th C. They are a very desirable collecting category and go for:............ **$500+**

Kettle tilter, forged iron, monkey-tail handle, American or English, 19-1/2"L, 18th C......................... **$500+**

Kettle tilter, forged iron, swivel loop to hang from hook, pleasantly curved handle, American or English, hard to measure exactly, but about 8-1/2"H x 14"L, 18th or early 19th C... **$500+**

Kettle tilter, forged iron, swivel ring and brass knob on end of curved handle, poss. American, more prob. English, 21"L, 18th or early 19th C. .... **$500+**

Kettle tilter, forged iron, swivel ring, shapely brass knob on handle and swivel ring, English (?), 23"L, c.1800. .... **$500+**

X-55. Plate warmer or dish warmer. *Sheet iron with japanned finish, & with cast iron cabriole legs with lion's paws. Cast handles at sides. This kind was slightly more versatile than the closed top kind, although heat escaped out of the top. American (?), mid 19th C. Courtesy William Hodges.* **$450+**

Kettle tilter, forged iron, swivel ring top with acorn finial, nice swoopy thin handle, American (?), about 13" across, late 18th or early 19th C. .... **$500+**

Ladles – See Chapter XIII (Implements).

Meat hooks – See Hook, ham

Meat screens – See Reflecting oven – meat screen

Mulling iron, forged iron, wooden handle, paddle-like end, American (?), 16"L, 18th or early 19th C. .... **$125-$175**

Mulling iron, wrought iron, a hook at one end, a sort of curved blade, almost a paddle, at the other end, English or American, 18"L, 18th or 19th C. .... **$125-$175**

Peels – See Chapter XIII (Implements)

Plate warmer, also called a hot closet, sheet iron cabinet, plain decoration, tall and cylindrical with door, small chamber at bottom with air vents, not for putting in charcoal – the air vents just drew rising hot air from hearth up into cylinder, American (?), 3 feet H x 13" diam., early 19th C. .... **$375-$550**

Plate warmer, sheet iron cabinet with original red paint with flowers in ochre, cast brass side handles, elegant slim cast iron cabriole legs with penny feet, arched top, door, prob. English, 32"H, c.1800 to 1830. .... **$650+**

X-56. Plate warmer. *Japanned & decorated tin, most of decoration and finish burned off. With sheet iron legs bolted on. Brass decorative side handles. 28-1/2"H x 13-1/4"W, 2 inserted shelves. Other side open to the fire. Probably English, late 19th C. Photographed at booth of Jill Oltz, Mountainville, NJ, at a Pier show in NYC.* ***$300-$450+***

X-57. Plate warmers. *Both japanned tin with decorative cast iron legs & handles. Both with open backs to fire; probably imports from England at the time of their use.* **(L)** *From ad of J. & C. Berrian, NYC dealer, in* History of Prominent Mercantile & Mfg. Firms in the U.S., *1857.* **(R)** *From F. A. Walker catalog, 18701-80s.* **$450-$600+**

Plate warmer, japanned sheet metal cabinet with domed top, shaped like a firescreen, 2 wire shelves inside, in F. A. Walker catalog, American (?), c.1870s. **$350**

Plate warmer, sheet iron cabinet with cast iron legs bolted on, brass side handles, most of japanned and painted decoration burned off long ago, 3 shelves, nice front door (facing out to room) & open of course in front though braced with bars of metal, prob. made at the Usk, Monmouthshire works in Wales, 28-1/2"H x 13-1/4"W, c.1800- to 1815. .... **$675+**

Plate warmer, tin & cast iron cabinet, 3 well shaped cabriole legs with lion's paw feet, mostly open at top with wide inner lip, one shelf, side handles, no door, American (?), about 28"H, early 19th C. .... **$475+**

Plate warmer, japanned tin cabinet with bronzed cast iron decorative trim, high cast iron cabriole legs, lion's paw feet, English (?), 30"H x 15"W, 19th C. **$475**

Plate warmer rack, wire & forged iron, concentric wire rings form platform, meant to hang in fireplace, American (?), 15" diam., early to mid 19th C. **$200+**

❖ NOTES ❖

American Makers of Posnets, Skillets, Sauce-pans, etc. I've been working for years on a database of workers and manufacturers of metal kitchen utensils and other wares, including bells, from the early 17th C to about the 1940s. It is a work in progress, so this can't be considered definitive. The following are names either known from 18th & early 19th C newspaper advertisements, or that were found on one or more objects known to museums or collectors/dealers, and are the makers of posnets [p], skillets [sk], frying-pans [fp], sauce-pans [sp], kettles [k], and some other things which might be unfamiliar and which I'll spell out. I've listed them **in roughly chronological order**; a date such as "fl. 1740" means "flourished 1740," which means that only one working date is known – perhaps from a dated piece or an early newspaper advertisement. • Mary Jackson, later Mary & William Jackson, Cornhill, Boston, MA, fl. 1730-1760, pots, pans, "kettle pots," [k], [s], cast brass. • Lawrence [or Laurence] Langworthy, Newport, RI, fl. 1731, "footed skillet," worked in brass, cast iron, sheet iron. • Massaponex Furnace, Colonel Alexander Spottswood, prop., near Fredericksburg, VA, fl. 1732, pots, [s], "country castings," cast iron. • Jonathan Jackson, Boston, fl. 1736, [s], [fp], [sp], brass, copper, iron. • Samuel Powell, came from England to the Brethren's Shop in Bethlehem, PA, c.1740s, a possible because he cast "various wares" in bell metal. • Thomas Russel, Boston, fl. 1740, [k], [s], [fp], [sp], "kettle-pots," brass, copper. • Richard Clarke, Boston, fl. 1741, pots, [k], [s], cast iron. • Benjamin Harbeson, Sr., Philadelphia & Lancaster, PA, fl. 1760-1795, copper sheet metal wares. • Nathaniel Austin, Charlestown (Boston), MA, fl. 1763, [k], [fp], [k], cast brass, cast iron. • Richard Collier ("R.C."), Boston, then Providence, RI, fl. 1763, [sp], [fp], metal. • Isaac Zane, Jr., Marlboro Furnace, Frederick County, VA, c. 1767-1795, [s] & "pott ware" [ie. hollowware]. • Peter Curtenius, NYC & "West of NYC," fl. 1763-1787, [s], [k], "pye pans," cast iron. • Mount Hope Furnace, Morris County, NJ, c.1772-1825, [k], [s], "griddles with and without legs," etc. • "O. I." ["I" poss. for "J"], Pennsylvania (?), fl. 1780-1800, deep skillet with 3 legs, cast iron. • Joseph Webb, Boston, fl. 1781, [s], "fry-kettles," cast iron. • William Whall, Boston, fl. 1789-1796, a possible because he cast unidentified forms in cast iron & brass. • Lafayette Furnace, Stafford, CT, fl. 1790-1837, [s], other hollowware, cast iron. • Bourbon Furnace, John C. Owings & Co., Prop., Bourbon County, KY, fl. 1791-1797, pots, [s], cast iron. • John Taylor (mark is "J" with backwards "N" "Taylor", or "In. Taylor," [note that when type was sorted by a printer, if they ran out of "J"s, they substituted "I"s], Richmond, VA, fl. 1793, [p], cast bell metal or bronze. • Richard (?) Austin (or Auston) & Robert Crocker, Boston, MA, fl. 1795-1800, [p], cast bell metal, bronze • Dewsbury Crawley, NYC, fl. 1797-1804, [sp], stew pans, wrought iron. • I. Wingrees, 18th C, a wrought sheet iron skillet or fry pan was found on a sunken ship, the "Philadelphia." • Crabb & Minshall, Baltimore, MD, late 18th C, [sp], copper. • Robert Streeter & Co., (American?), late 18th C, 3-legged skillet, cast bell metal. • Caleb Allen, Boston, then Providence, RI, fl. late 18th - early 19th Cs, made & mended [k], [fp], [s], [sp], various metals. • David Lamborn, London Grove Township, Chester County, PA, fl. late 18th - early 19th Cs, porringers, [s], iron. • Warner, Philadelphia, fl. late 18th to early 19th Cs, [p], bell metal. • "W. C.", "Newport C." [prob. Connecticut], fl. late 18th to early 19th Cs, [p], cast bronze. • "W.H.", no place known, fl. late 18th to early 19th Cs, [p], cast bronze. • Henry Reigart, Philadelphia, fl. 1803, [sp], [k], copper. • James Davis, Boston, MA, worked 1803-1828, then merged with Joseph W. Revere to form Revere Copper Co., 1828-1900, [p], bell metal or bronze. • Baste & Youce, Danville & Shelbyville, KY, fl. 1806-1817, [sp], coppersmiths, then commenced brass founding as "Alte & Co." • Caleb Allen, Boston, then

Providence, RI, fl. late 18th to early 19th Cs, [fp], [k], [sp], brass & copper. • "N. S.", possibly Nathaniel Starbuck, fl. late 18th to early 19th Cs, [p], cast iron. • "Wasbrough," (American?), fl. late 18th to early 19th Cs, [p], cast bell metal. • John Savery [or I. Savery], Carver, MA, fl. 1812-1826, then Albany, NY, 1826-1834, hollowware, 3-legged, long-handled pot, cast iron. • Joseph Bruin, Lexington, KY, fl. 1816-1820, a possible because he cast bells & other unidentified things in bell metal & brass. • Daniel Curtiss, Albany, NY, fl. 1822-1850, a possible because he cast "various wares" in bell metal & brass. • Edwin Porter, Newbern, NC, fl. 1829-1839, [sp], iron. • Pickens & Littlehole, Boston, fl. 1830, hollowware, [k], [s], spiders, cast iron (?). • Savery & Co. [sometimes Savory], Philadelphia, fl. 1838-1867, 3-legged pots, [sp], etc., cast iron.

Posnet, cast iron, rather shallow, with 3 short legs and long handle, American, 3"H including legs, 7" diam. bowl plus 6" handle, 18th C. .... **$150+**

Posnet or skillet, bell metal, long handle, 3 peg feet, "Austin & Crocker," Boston, MA, 18th C. Sold at the 1980 Garbisch collection auction for $3,100. Price related to the metal, the mark, the great rarity, and a prestigious and renowned collector (of folk arts). • American bell metal posnets with the names cast into the handles, now bring over $2500 ... at least to American collectors. .... **$3,100+**

Posnet or skillet, cast bell metal or bronze, 3-legged with long handle, used like a saucepan, marked "Wasbrough No. 6," 7"H x 7-1/2" diam. with 11-1/2"L handle, 5-1/4"H legs, 18th or very early 19th C. . **$1,500+**

Posnet, cast iron, 3 feet, slightly upslanted side handle, no mark, American (?), 5"H x 5" diam., early early 19th C. One way to collect these is to look for variations in handles and feet, or to get a range of sizes (maybe starting with the darling miniature ones about 2-1/2"H), or – this appeals most to me – to get only repaired ones. **$150**

Posnet or skillet, cast iron, 3 legs, long handle, **repaired** in very entertaining way: one leg seems to have dropped out leaving hole, or else broke off, and hole was ground out, then a bolt was stuck through the hole with a washer, and it was all hammered up

X-59. Posnet & Closeup of handle. (T) *Cast bell metal, 3 long legs, long flat handle slightly tapered at end, flat on top, round in section. Made by Robert Crocker & Richard (?) Austin, Boston, late 18th or very early 19th C. 8-1/2"H x 8-3/4" diam. x 19-5/8" L including handle. Picture courtesy of the National Museum of American History, Smithsonian Institution, John Paul Remensnyder estate. (B) "Austin & Crocker, Boston" in very unusual floriate scroll border. Picture courtesy National Museum of American History, Smithsonian Institution, John Paul Remensnyder estate.* **$3,000+**

around to fit the curve of the pot, then a pin, sort of like the cotter pin idea, was driven through a hole in the bolt to hold it tightly in place, American, 5-1/4" diam., with handle 11-1/16"L, legs are 1-1/4"H, early 19th C. • I love things like this, but paid only $19 for it. I honestly don't know if I would have bought it if it had been much more; I have very deep pockets but very short arms when it comes to collecting. My advice is go for the old, old repairs, as they are truly unique and add worlds of romance to a piece. .... **$175+**

X-58. Posnet. *Cast bronze, 3 legs, one under handle longest by far so tilts forward. Long horizontal handle flat on top, half-round in section. Cast along top of handle: "W. C : NEWPORT. C [?]." 9-1/16"H x 8-1/16" diam. x 17-5/16"L with handle. Picture courtesy of the National Museum of American History, Smithsonian Institution, John Paul Remensnyder estate.* **$2,500+**

X-60. Posnet. *Cast bell metal. Maker, known more for andirons, is James Davis, who was working c.1803-1828. Marked "J. Davis Boston." Photographed from stock of Jay Kohler & Louise Rozene, Sunset Mountain Farm, Amherst, VA.* **$2,500+**

X-61. Posnets. *A delightful family of unmarked cast bell metal posnets in five sizes. Note brace, which may be an old repair, to handle at far right. Posnets are relatively deep and have flat bottoms (skillets have rounded bottoms). Photograph courtesy of Pat Guthman Antiques, Southport, CT. Assembled set:* **$5,000+**

❖ NOTES ❖

"Skillet" or "Posnet"? Both the posnet and skillet were used rather like saucepans. A posnet is probably the smaller of the two. You do not find clear distinctions in old inventories or even cookery books, and certainly no exact sizes given anywhere. • Alice Morse Earle, writing in a chapter called "Table Plenishings," in *Customs & Fashions in Old New England* (NY: Scribner's, 1893) has rather a lot to say about posnets, although a lot of it is now discounted because of her tying posnets and porringers together. It's possible that 300 years ago they weren't so careful. Generally we think of porringers as something to eat out of, and a posnet as a small cooking utensil. The etymology Earle relates is interesting: A **posnet** "was spelt, in various colonial documents, posned, possnet, posnett, porsnet, pocneit, posnert, possenette, postnett, and parsnett. It is derived from the Welsh *posned*, a porringer or little dish. In 1641 Edward Skinner left a 'Postnett' by will; this was apparently of pewter. In 1653 Governor Haynes, of Hartford, left an 'Iron Posnet' by will. In the inventory of the estate of Robert Daniel, of Cambridge, in 1655, we learn that 'a Little Porsenett' of his was worth five shillings. In 1693 Governor Caleb Carr, of Providence, bequeathed to his wife a 'silver possnet & the cover belonging to it.' By these records we see that posnets were of various metals, and sometimes had covers. I have found no advertisements of them in early American newspapers, even with all their varied array of utensils and vessels. Fancy the name fell quickly into disuse in this country." p. 141 of Earle's book. See also the paragraph "Frying Pan" or "Skillet"? with listings for frying pans, above. • A very interesting site, run by the Lord Stefan li Rous (aka Mark Harris) (http://www.florilegium.org/) relates old and new food tidbits from cookbooks, etc., includes this perfect description of a classic posnet, termed a "skillet" in the recipe. From *Le Menagier de Paris* (Janet Hinson, translator, is a recipe for "Crepes in Tournay Style." "First, you must have the use of a brass skillet holding a quart, of which the top is no wider than the bottom, even by a very little, and the edges should be 3 or 4 fingers tall and half a finger thick." To measure in fingers means the width, not the length, of fingers. Another citation on the same site is from the late 14th century cookbook *The Forme of Cury. A Rollle of Ancient English Cookery*, by Samuel Pegge, which calls for a posnet when making "cryspes," ie. crisps – a crispy sweet cookie-like crepe dessert. • **What is a posnet now?** A dot com company providing point-of-sale payment options has the name, so if you do a Google search without adding the words cookery or kitchen, chances are you'll get POSnet.com.

Posnet or skillet, cast iron, 3 tall tapered legs, long handle, marked "N. S." (possibly Nathaniel Starbuck), American, 12"L including handle, 18th or very early 19th C. .... **$1,500+**

X-62. Bulge pot, *of type colloquially called a* ***"gypsy kettle."*** *Cast iron, squat bulging body, 2 vertical seams, long casting gate on bottom, 3 longish legs, 3 vertical bands in relief around circumference. Marked on side "No. 1. 2 QTS. SAVERY & Co. Philadelphia." 6"H x 9-5/16" diam. Photo by Jennifer Oka. Picture courtesy of the National Museum of American History, Smithsonian Institution, John Paul Remensnyder estate.* **$375+**

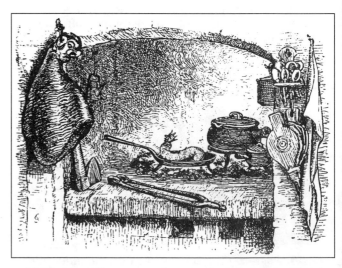

X-63. Hearth scene, *showing anthropomorphized food and utensils. Sausage is cooking in a frying pan over the coals. The covered vessels in rear are not identified. One on stand is probably made of heavy earthenware; smaller one with lid looks like a small skillet with lid, of cast iron. From Picture Fables, drawn by Otto Speckter, 1858.*

X-64-A. Pot, or "gypsy kettle." *Cast iron, 3 legs, twisted forged iron bail, domed lid with loop handle. 6-1/2"H x 4-1/4" diam. beautiful small size. American, late 18th C. Picture courtesy of Robert W. Skinner Inc., Auctioneers, Bolton, MA.* **$450+**

X-64-B. Gypsy kettle or pot, *cast iron, 2 vertical seams, bail handle. A little beauty. Early 19th C. Photo courtesy of Oveda Maurer Antiques, San Anselmo, CA.* **$350+**

Posnet or skillet, cast iron, nice deep bowl with 3 legs, flat top handle, American, 5-1/2"H x 6-5/8" diam. plus 6-1/2" handle, 18th C. .... **$175+**

Pot, also found spelled pott in old records, this one cast iron, bulbous body, 3 legs, with cast iron cover with generous curved loop handle, wrought bail handle, straight sprue gate mark on bottom, American (?), unusual height-to-width ratio: 10"H x 8" diam., 18th C. This is a wonderful piece offered for sale several years ago by Clara Jean Davis of Concord, NH. She loves old iron and it shows in the pieces she finds. .... **$175-$225**

Pot, cast iron, with lid, oval shape with plump rounded sides, forged bail handle, English (?), or poss. American, about 11"L the major axis, late 18th or early 19th C. .... **$155+**

❖ NOTES ❖

Iron imports in 1775 – A NYC importer named George Ball advertised in the newspaper in 1775 that he had just received some "useful and wholesome iron utensils, so much recommended by physicians for their safety, and so generally and justly preferred to copper, by all the best housekeepers in England, for two of the best reasons in the world, viz. that they are entirely free from that dangerous, poisonous property [verdigris], from which so many fatal accidents have been known to arise amongst those who use copper vessels, and because they never want tinning." He goes on to enumerate the imports, including "Tea kettles from three quarts to six, four-gallon pots with covers, to five quarts, pie pans, two gallon oval pots, stew pans and covers, of several different sizes, fish kettles of six different sizes, with strainers, saucepans, from six quarts to one pint. For cabin use on board of shipping, they are far preferable to copper, as no danger (however careless the cook, or long the voyage) can possibly happen from using them, as too often has through these causes, from the use of copper. They are all wrought according to the most approved pattern now used in London." Ball had no doubt of a warm, anglophilic reception to his ad: the British used New York City as its base of operations during the Revolutionary War from 1776 to 1783. New York had been a British stronghold since the 1660s, after taking over from the Dutch; about two thirds of the population was either British or Loyalist. The New York area did become the site for many battles between Americans fighting for independence and British forces.

X-65. Bulge pot, two views. *with pieced tin slightly domed lid. Cast iron, wire bail handle, 3 short feet. 9-1/2"H x 10-3/4" diam. Note that wonderful pieced edge at bottom of lid photo. From stock of Jean Hatt, Hatt's Hutt, Denver, PA.* **$375+**

Pot, "gypsy kettle" type with globular body, sometimes called a bulge pot in some founders' price lists, flared rim, pitted cast iron, 2 lug handles of triangular shape with "elbows" that are almost straight out from side and partly curved inside, 3 circumferential or horizontal mold rings on belly and one around flared neck, as well as a "latitudinal" or vertical casting line from the "equatorial line" to the rim on both sides between the handles, long casting gate on bottom, 3 tapered legs that are flat on side facing in and deeply rounded on outside, this example with beautiful especially high, full half-circle wrought bail, which – when up – exactly copies the curve of the unusually large and high arched handle riveted to the flat, hammered sheet iron lid, which is probably original. No mark, American, 7-1/8"H x 7-3/4" diam. at top, legs are 1-5/8"H, late 18th or early 19th C. • For me, a good deal of the charm (and value) of this particular pot lies in the lid, and the matched arches of lid and bail...................... **$175+**

The most authoritative writing – all new articles and books included – I've found on dating really old iron pots and kettles was done by John D. Tyler, Curator of Science, Industry, and Technology at the Pennsylvania Historical and Museum Commission. He wrote two similar articles, one in *The Magazine ANTIQUES*, Aug. 1971, and another in the April 1978 *Early American Life*. The latter is somewhat more helpful, because it has a chart of the lug or ear handles. Both have a lot of information tying English and American technology to evidence found on the pots themselves – casting mold & seam lines, and sprues & casting gates (the former round and older, the latter a narrow oblong) through which the molten iron was poured into the molds. Tyler says that the rounded legs are typically American; the "triangular" ones English. We can all wish there were a Tyler book to read and reread.

Pot chain, or trammel chain, forged iron, to hang pot over fire, hook at each end, 25 nice big round links, by using the hooks in different ways the effectual length of the chain is changed, could be American or European, 41"L, 18th C. See also Trammels. .... **$100-$300+**

A superstition reported in William Hone's *The Year Book* (London, 1845 edition), reports: "Professor Playfair, in a letter to Mr. Brand, dated St. Andrew's, January 26, 1801, mentioning the superstitions of his neighborhood, says: '... mischievous elves cannot enter into a house at night, if, before bed-time, the lower end of the crook, or iron chain, by which a vessel is suspended over the fire, be raised up a few links.'"

X-66. Bulge pot in use. *"To bed, to bed, says Sleepy-Head; Let's stay awhile, says Slow; Put on the pot, says Greedy-Gut, We'll sup before we go."* Mother Goose's Melodies, 1833. *Many of these moralistic fable books for children have delightfully detailed engravings or woodcuts, which show such things as dress and household accoutrements. Note here what appears to be either a frying pan or a bed warmer leaning against the surround. Note the figural andiron of man in tricorn hat.*

X-67. Miniature 20th century pot & kettle. *These minis of cast iron may look like 19th or early 20th C miniatures or toys, but were mass-produced and filled with preserves: wild huckleberry in the bulge pot, seedless blackberry in the kettle. Both about 4"H with wire bail. From House of Webster, Rogers, AR, advertised in* McCall's Needlework, *Spring-Summer 1970.*

Pot hooks, also called racking crooks, forged iron "S," hooked over pot chain, trammel, crane, or another pot hook, with a bail-handle or hoop-handle kettle, pot or griddle hung from the lower crook. Alice Morse Earle, in *Customs & Fashions in Old New England* (1893), writes "In earlier days the great lugpole [made of green wood, to withstand the heat & flames], or, as it was called in England, the backbar, stretched from ledge to ledge, or lug to lug, high up the yawning chimney, and held a motley collection of pot-hooks and trammels, of gib-crokes (or jibcrokes), twicrokes, and hakes, which in turn suspended at various heights over the fire, pots, and kettles and other cooking utensils" (p.130). Cotrall is another term. American or European, from about 6"L to 9"L, any age up to end of 19th C. • **Reproduction alert.** – I suspect many of the ones found laid out on hopsacking for the unwary are newly-forged. Look at the "grain" of the beaten iron, the texture, and particularly the two tips, which should not look as if they'd been snipped off with very powerful cutters. The blacksmith of the past might have used pincers, but would have cut, then hammered again to finish the tips. • If you ever see an old pot hook with a snake's head, buy it. • Some of Earle's terms are not to be found in 19th century dictionaries and glossaries of Americanisms, of which I have not a few. I believe croke is a corruption of crook, and a gib-croke would be a side hook. I think twicroke could be either a 2 hooked crook, or possibly a twisted hook. Hake is a kind of fish, but probably here it's a corruption of hook. .... **$20+**

Pot lid, copper with relatively short forged iron handle with hanging hole chiseled out, leather, wood or horn gasket to insulate iron handle where it is riveted to the lid, copper rivets, tinned inside, raised edge to fit saucepan rim, marked "M. W.;" inventory numbers "226, 7225, 2573;" plus initial "E" scratched lightly on surface near handle, English, 6-

3/4" diam., 3-5/8"L handle, early 19th C. • Another one marked "M. W.," bought at same time, is much smaller (4-1/2" diam. with 2-1/2"L handle), and has one number the same, "7225," with some scratchmarks under the first two making it look like a "5," and a small "6" under the long number, probably left over from some other time, plus the "E." • It was only when closely examining these lids, which my mother had owned for years, preparatory to photographing them and writing these descriptions, that I noticed the faint scratched inventory numbers, and the heat-insulating gasket on the larger one. Close examination when you clean or draw something seems to work better to uncover unnoticed details than just looking at it. That is, until you learn how to look. .... $25-$40

❖ NOTES ❖

Collector Tip – You know those little black plastic hooks that some socks come attached to at the store? Well, don't let the cashier throw them away. They are perfect for hooking over wrought iron dutch crown pot racks to hold extra pieces that aren't too heavy.

Pot lifter or pot bail, wrought iron, 2 "hinging" or swiveling curved arms with hooked ends, forming a sort of wishbone shape, used to hook under ears of kettle or pot, for lifting. 14"L, late 18th or early 19th C. • With a huge iron pot full of boiling food, I'd hate to have to depend on a pot bail. Besides childbirth, accidents at the hearth – especially catching on fire, or other burns – were a leading cause of women's deaths in the 18th C. .... $65-$150

X-68. Pot hook. *Best one ever. Finely whitesmithed steel hook with beautifully shaped long slender forearm and hand grasping where loop comes around. 5-15/16" x 4-1/4", American (?), early 19th C. Photo by Jennifer Oka. Picture courtesy of the National Museum of American History, Smithsonian Institution, John Paul Remensnyder estate. There would be much excited crossover interest from folk art collectors if this were actually for sale!* **$1,000+**

To extinguish Ladies' Clothes, catching Fire – We often hear, and read in newspapers, when one of those deplorable accidents has happened, which generally deprive us of the youthful and most lovely of our kind, dry recommendations, that ladies, whose dresses may catch fire, should lie down. This, though undoubtedly the right method of extinguishing a flame, is better illustrated, and imprinted more deeply on our recollection, by the following experiment. Take two pieces of muslin, (the article which usually catches fire), or paper, or any other light ignitable substance, and having set on fire the lower part of both, hold one piece upright , as female dresses are worn; it will burn out in about one minute, blazing up to a great height, where the neck and face may be supposed to be burnt. Meantime, fling the other piece of burning muslin on the ground; it will burn slowly, the flame at no time ascending more than an inch or two, and although the burning article might not be moved -- as must happen when a living person is enveloped in it – nearly ten minutes would elapse before it would be consumed. In short, it is evident that a perpendicular female dress, though fifty feet high, would burn out with a destructive flame in less than a single yard of the same material laid in a horizontal position. It results, therefore, from the foregoing experiment, that as soon as a lady's dress is discovered to be on fire, she should instantly lie down; and she may then call for assistance, or confidently set about extinguishing the flame herself. N.B. A current of air always prevails near the floor, particularly between the door and fire-place, and therefore it must be kept in mind, not to run out of the room, nor to open a window, in such cases, as that would be fatal." *The Young Man's Book of Amusement, Containing the Most Interesting and Instructive Experiments In Various Branches of Science.* London: 1850.

Pot lifter, wrought iron, 2 hinged arms ending in inward bent flat & wide hooks that could fit under outside lip of pot or kettle, or under some types of ear handles, American, prob. PA, 15"L each arm, 18th C. .... **$95+**

Pot lifter, wrought iron, 2 hinged & slightly curved arms with hooks at ends, meant to fit any size pot or vessel with ear handles, American (?), each arm 13"L, 18th or very early 19th C........................ **$75+**

Pot or kettle lifter, forged iron, 2 long arms twisted partway for tensile strength, hung on ring, arms end in curved pieces that act as your curved fingers would to fit under rim of pot, Pennsylvania, 17-1/8"L, mid to late 18th C. .... **$165-$200**

Pot pusher, forged iron, 3 legs and curled handle, semicircle cradles pot and makes it easy to push pot steadily and farther into the hot coals on floor of fireplace, rather ornate, American (?), 5"H x 6"W, 18th C. Very simple ones, go for between $60 and $90. Fancier ones, perhaps with long handles or bold penny feet are: .... **$165+**

Pot pusher, wrought iron, chiseled zigzag decoration on handle, English or poss. American, 6-1/8"W at farthest reach of 2 arms, which means it wouldn't push a very big pot, early 19th C or late 18th C. .... **$125-$175**

Pot pusher, wrought iron, pot-fitting wide open "horseshoe" of iron, with the ends bent into legs, short twisted handle supported by another leg, used to push posnets or bulge pots or other cooking vessels deeper into the coals or hot ashes. The height, of course, couldn't be so great as to push against the pot above about the lower third of its height. American (?), 3-1/2"H x 7-1/4"W x 9"L including handle, 18th C or very early 19th C. .... **$165+**

Potato rake, for pulling potatoes from ashes in fireplacc, (or some kind of scraping tool, like for scraping out pumpkins), forged iron, straight toothed blade curved around so it would fit inside something like a pumpkin, longish handle with rattail end, American (?), 13"L, early 19th C. .... **$145+**

❖ NOTES ❖

At Walden Pond – In Henry David Thoreau's 1854 *Walden, or Life in the Woods*, in the "House-Warming" chapter, we read "The next winter [1846] I used a small cooking-stove for economy, since I did not own the forest; but it did not keep fire so well as the open fireplace. Cooking was then, for the most part, no longer a poetic, but merely a chemic process. It will soon be forgotten, in these days of stoves, that we used to roast potatoes in the ashes, after the Indian fashion. The stove not only took up room and scented the house, but it concealed the fire, and I felt as if I had lost a companion. You can always see a face in the fire."

Reflector or reflecting oven, also called a Yankee baker (by Henry Thoreau), or a tin kitchen, small, tin, horizontal blimp shape, 4 V-strap legs, crank for spit at one end, 2 strap carrying handles on top, oval hinged lift-down door in back to check progress of food, English or German, 12-1/2"H x 14"L exclusive of crank, late 19th C. .... **$450+**

Reflector oven, heavy tin plates soldered together, with spit, strap handle and strap legs at each corner, basting door in back, American, 16"H x 20"L, late 18th or early 19th C. .... **$550+**

*X-69. Meat screen – reflecting oven, sometimes called a **tin kitchen**. Of type specifically for a hanging jack of some kind, especially a bottle jack. This one has a dangle spit with 6 weighted rods – a flywheel – spoked out to assist the backward and forward spinning. Sheet iron with crown-like or harped superstructure. We see it as we would from the fire, the door in back is for the cook to view the proceedings and to baste. Vertical forged iron spit with hooks. Front left leg propped up on wood support indicating piece was either customized to fit a particular hearth, or that one leg has broken, or possibly that the other three legs were lengthened. c.1790 to 1840. Picture courtesy of the National Museum of American History, Smithsonian Institution. **$700+***

X-70. Meat screen – just 100 years old. Note striking resemblance to one from Smithsonian Collection in X-69. They may have to revise estimated age. This one came in three widths, 19", 21", and 24". Note lid on grease trap. Harrod's Stores, Ltd., Brompton, England, 1895. **$700+**

X-71. Meat screen. Tin, with bottle jack in place. William S. Adams & Son, London, c.1860-61 ad in Francatelli's Cook's Guide Advertiser. Note that all of these have a basin-like depression in the bottom for drippings. **$500+**

Reflector oven, heavy tin, with spit, American, 17"H x 25"L, 19th C. If you want to read a very old-fashioned, but sweet, storybook, featuring as the protagonist one of these neat old reflecting ovens, look for *The Tin Kitchen*, by J. Hatton Weeks, published in New York and Boston by Thomas Y. Crowell & Co., in 1896. The protagonist – a tin kitchen – relates the job of cooking an old gander as brown and juicy as possible for the parson's visit. .... **$475+**

Reflector oven, tin, meant for biscuits with 2 shallow shelves, American, 14"W, c.1840 to 1850. .... **$150+**

Reflector oven, tin, with strap handles on top, 4 strap legs, spit & crank handle, "back door" for basting, American, 10"H x 12"L, 1830s-40s. In many old cookbooks, these are confusingly also called "Dutch ovens." .... **$450+**

Reflector oven or tin kitchen, heavy sheet tin, cranked spit, door in back, 4 short strap legs, pour-off grease spout at side bottom, American, 17"H x 19"W, 19th C. .... **$450+**

❖ NOTES ❖

In **1797, a Tin Plate worker** by the name of Dewsbury Crawley, of New York City, advertised in the paper

*X-72. Meat screens & bottle jacks. You may
think I've got too many of these, but I found it fascinating that something so ancient-looking could be
relatively new. Both are tin, with clock-wound bottle
jacks in place. (L) "Roasting screen and jack. The
screen is adapted to the ranges and cooking stoves
in general use. The jack is wound up and runs so as
to keep the meat constantly turning til cooked."
American Home Cook Book, 1854. (R) "Roasting
oven with jack." Two sizes – 18"W and 24"W ovens,
jacks able to turn 25 lbs and 40 lbs. Note key for
bottle jack on floor. Duparquet, Huot & Moneuse,
hoteliers' supply catalog, c.1904-1910. $650+*

that "a very capital improvement [has been made] on
the tin roasting ovens so universally in use, by making
easy what was thought the most difficult task in using
them, [the former mode of basting] which by the
improvement is done on the top by means of a hopper
and strainer, which causes the fat to drip gradually on
the victuals roasting." I've never seen one; I'm sure we
could recognize it by the built-in hopper and strainer in
the top. • At the time Crawley was working, **tin was
imported** in small plates, measuring about 8" x 14",
from Wales for the most part. This is why really early tin
kitchens are made of pieced-together plates if they are
over 14"L. For more [conflicting] information on sizes of
tin plate, see pp. 497-98. • Tin plate [and copper]
worker Dewsbury Crawley advertised in the *New York
Daily Advertiser*, that he had for sale some "**Curious
wrought Iron Kitchen Furniture**. ... stew pans, sause
pans, fish kettles, steam kettles, large pots &c. These
articles are tinned on the inside in a peculiar manner,
have bright iron covers, and [are] otherwise constructed
for use and ornament in the kitchen and are not to be
equalled in this city, and are preferable as to whole-
someness, which no one will dispute who knows the
distinct properties of copper and iron." October 6, 1797.

Reflector oven or tin kitchen, heavy sheet tin large cylinder, on 4 high iron legs, spit crank in side, hinged
door in back for basting, etc., not marked, 38"H,
c.1820s to 1840s. .... **$475-$650**

❖ NOTES ❖

Reflecting Ovens & Dutch Ovens – You will find in
some early cookbooks & other writings, as well as ads
by some 20th century dealers, that a tin kitchen
reflecting oven is sometimes called a "Dutch oven." The
underlying meaning of "substitute for oven" makes
both uses appropriate. I use "Dutch oven" only for a
cast iron kettle with a lid with raised edges. Recently I
found that John Russell Bartlett (famous for *Bartlett's
Familiar Quotations*) defined "Dutch oven" in the 1889
(4th) edition of his *Dictionary of Americanisms*, whereas
he did not in the 1859 (2nd) edition. Bartlett wrote in
1889: "**Dutch Oven.** A tin screen placed before a
kitchen range, or open wood fire, within which is the
meat to be roasted." He doesn't define tin kitchen in
either edition. • An English book from the **1860s**, in its
American edition of 1870, has three line engravings of
types of **reflecting ovens**. **(1)** "The well-known **Dutch
oven**" is a reflecting oven with a rounded back and
back sides, therefore having a half-circle 'footprint'. "It
is usually made with a little dripping-pan in the bottom, and it has a [slotted] shelf in the middle to place
anything upon that requires to be warmed or browned;
a small meat cut, or a bird, may be roasted by removing this shelf, and suspending the article by one of the
hooks, which are made to turn to expose the different
sides of the meat." **(2)** Next "The **Yorkshire oven**.".. differing from the Dutch in "being higher in proportion to
its width, giving more room for anything suspended to
be roasted; and by a slit in the handle, the meat may
be moved farther from the fire, or nearer to it. There is
likewise a door in the back for access to the meat. The
shelf is only placed occasionally. ..." The back side of
this one is flat, and it is the top that is a rounded arch
from side to side. **(3)** Last is "**The American oven** ... an
improvement on the Dutch. By means of a bottom
slanting upward, and the top slanting downward, the
reflection of heat is still stronger. In this case, the meat,
or other article, is laid in an iron tray, which is movable, and may be lifted out by two handles, the top [of
the oven] moving back on hinges; beneath the false
bottom is a place for warming plates. This apparatus is
coming much into use, being found extremely convenient for roasting & baking bread, cakes, &c." (Note
that Carl W. Drepperd, in *A Dictionary of American*

*X-73. Reflecting
oven. Called in
English catalogs a
"Dutch oven," which
was another common
name for a tin kitchen
reflecting oven. Came
in four sizes, from 9"
to 13" W. Harrod's
Stores, 1895. SEE
also the Bird roasters.
Because we know
these were made very
late in the 19th C,
and probably into the
20th, the valuing of any piece depends on appearance,
patina, source, and practical need – maybe the buyer is
cooking on the hearth at home. $150+*

Antiques, (Doubleday, 1952), used the term "American oven," saying that it was invented in America c.1790.) American collectors usually see types (1) and (3), especially the slanted one. It may not always have a slanted bottom, with a hidey-hole or sort of plate shed behind.

Reflector oven or tin kitchen, tin, angled "reflective" back, strap handle and 2 strap back legs, front legs twisted wire, extentions of the wire that went around edge of whole body, over which tin was folded at the edge, pouring spout at bottom right, forged iron spit, American, 14"W, mid 19th C. .... **$275-$350+**

❖ NOTES ❖

A utensil suitable for summer, or shipboard or camp cooking, was the **Salisbury portable kitchen**, an enclosed brazier invented in 1780 by an Englishman, William Redman. He described it thus: "For roasting, boiling, or baking of any kind of provision. The body or furnace is made oval or round, of wrought or cast iron, tin or copper. Within it is placed a grate for the fire, and in the upper part a pot for boiling with water or steam, or a plate for baking. Underneath the fire is a vacuity open in the front, serving as a receptacle for the ashes and admitting a current of air to pass through the fire, thereby carrying off any smoke or dust through a tube or funnell affixed. A front is fixed to the furnace before the fire, which joins close to a reflector, purposely to confine the heat so as to roast and boil, or do either separately with a very small quantity of fire. The reflector is made of tin, brass, or copper. A spit goes through it, and at the bottom a dripping pan is so fixed as to draw off the gravy, that the meat may be easily basted at a door which is made on the top or any convenient part. A gridiron may be fixed occasionally in the place of the spit for broiling, with an additional reflector placed obliquely underneath it, or occasionally an iron plate may be placed in the reflector for the purpose of baking. They may also be made with two reflectors, to fix to the same body, for roasting two or more joints at once." Abridgments of *Specifications Relating to Cooking, Bread-Making*, and *The Preparation of Confectionery A.D. 1634-1866*. London: Office of the Commissioner of Patents, abridged edition, 1873.

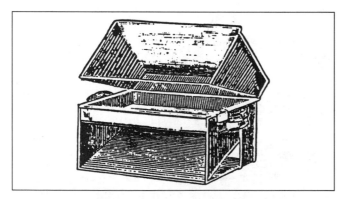

X-74. Reflecting oven, *also called here a "**Dutch oven for baking before the fire.**" Tin, boxy, not very attractive. F. A. Walker catalog, 1870s-80s.* **$125-$175**

Lookalike Alarm

Just when you thought you were safe with a sure oldie. Harrod's Stores, Ltd., the great London department store, depicted one of these "**Meat Screens, for Bottle Jack**" that looks like it ought to be a couple hundred years old, not a hundred! But there it is, in their 1895 retail catalog. It has a sort of lyre-shaped tin rack above the round dome top that was for suspending the windup jack. It also has a lidded grease or fat well in the bottom, the tubular tin legs are braced, and it was offered in three sizes: 19"H, 21"H and 24"H. They also made one they described as "Extra strong, with enclosed Bottom for Hot Closet, to order, 21 in. 24 in." These were almost twice as expensive. I guess a "hot closet" is a sort of warming oven compartment under there, probably with access from the back, just like the hinged door in the back of the meat screen.

X-75. New England kitchen interior, *as depicted on frontispiece of Esther Allen Howland's The New England Economical Housekeeper, and Family Receipt Book. Worcester, MA: S. A. Howland, 2nd edition, 1845. Note light walls and well-lit room. This is obviously not a very old house; neither is it new or it would have a brick- set range if not a cooking stove. Note dead animals hanging on walls – yikes. At **(A)** is a spit leaning against work counter. She is probably going to spit the goose, and fix it with a skewer, lying on counter. At **(B)** far back is black cast iron kettle hanging on crane. **(B)** At hearth, placed out a short distance, is a tin kitchen, a reflecting oven of good size, while foreground shows requisite bountiful-harvest basket with spilled veggies. At **(C)** are more iron 3-legged pots under the work table.*

X-76. Reflecting oven – "Tin kitchen." *Sheet iron, made from rectangles of tin soldered together, indicating an early date – late 18th or early 19th C. They were known and documented by the late 18th, and were considered novel and very useful. Wrought iron spit could be used at three different levels. There are tiny slots in the spit and they took the ends of skewers which secured meat to the spit. 13-1/4"H x 18-5/8"L. Picture courtesy of the National Museum of American History, Smithsonian Institution.* **$750+**

Reflecting oven – tin kitchen, with bottle jack, pieced sheet iron, tall domed oven on 4 cylindrical tin legs, balloon shaped tin structure above, of strap tin, supports windup jack inside, flywheel inside has 6 counterweights, door in back for basting or checking doneness, sometimes this type of vertical tin kitchen was called a niche screen roaster, and the English called it a meat screen for bottle jack. This one American, about 30"H, c.1790 to 1840. ..... **$1,000-$1,500+**

Revolving toasters – See Toaster, revolving

Roaster, steel, iron & brass, square shaft, fully adjustable for distance to fire, hung over grate, handle unscrews, 6 hooks, English (?), approx. 18-1/4"L, early 19th C. .... **$250-$350**

Roaster, wrought iron vertical frame with penny feet, adjustable hooked rack, brass finials, "Bainbridge," English or American, 31"H, dated June 22, 1833 – not a patent date, because that year, June 22 was

X-77. Tin kitchen. *Pieced tin, four iron hooks, spit and crank. Back door opens to allow basting. Came in three sizes, 20", 24", and 26"W. F. A. Walker catalog, 1870s-80s.* **$400+**

X-78. Salamanders. *Wrought or cast iron. They were heated to red hot in the fire, then set over a dish to radiate the heat and brown a meringue, pudding, or whatever else needed it. Even in 1891, they were still being called for in recipes, although you could use a "hot stove lid" instead.* **(T)** *Wrought iron, 34"L, 6-1/2" diam., English, 18th C. Ex-Keillor Collection.* **(M)** *Drawing to show how used.* **(B)** *Newfangled style, adjustable in height – it probably turned on a threaded post. Warne's Model Cookery, London, 1868.* **$125-$300+**

Sunday, and patents aren't issued on Sunday no matter what country. The name sort of "sounds English," but lots of 18th & 19th C American names did, too! A cursory search of the index to the *Official Patent Gazette*, for numbered & unnumbered patents, fails to turn up a Bainbridge. .... **$600-$700**

Roasters – See also Broilers, Gridirons, Grills, this chapter

Roasting fork – See Chapter XIII (Implements)

Rotating broiler – See Broiler, revolving

Salamander, wrought iron, file decorated, short knee-out legs at joint of disc & handle, American, 16"L, 18th or very early 19th C. .... **$350+**

Salamander, forged iron, beautiful trifed feet, English (?), 6-1/2" diam. disk, 34"L, 18th C................ **$250-$350**

❖ NOTES ❖

A **"wrought iron" salamander** was offered in five (unstated) sizes in the Harrod's Stores, Ltd, of London, 1895 retail catalog. It is a bit thicker looking than the old ones, with a nearly round head & neck, with a thinner long handle with knob at the end. Apparently some could be ordered with a stand, and these salamanders have a different neck, with a hole through it that slips over the top of the stand. The stand has a heavy stepped base that suports a shortish vertical rod about the same thickness as the salamander's handle. You could thereby heat the salamander, slip it on the stand on your work table, and pivot it over your meringue or whatever it was you were lightly browning, and leave it there while you tended something else. • When you read catalogs, particularly those from the very late 19th C or early 20th, you cannot believe how many things you supposed long gone by then were still offered for sale and actual use. This is not the same as reproductions or fakes meant for decoration.

Chocolate Custard *– Scald a quart of milk; stir in 4 heaping tablespoonsful of grated chocolate and simmer two minutes to dissolve it; beat up the yolks of 6 eggs with 1 cup of sugar; add to the milk and chocolate; stir for one minute; then add vanilla flavoring and pour into your custard cups, which should be waiting in pan half full of boiling water in the oven; cook until you see that the custards are done; let them cool and then grate sweet almonds over the top; make a meringue of the whites of the 6 eggs and a little sugar; pile it on the top of each custard; grate more sweet almonds over that; set them in the oven to brown a little, or brown by holding a salamander or hot stove lid over them." Henry Scammel, compiler, Treasure-House, 1891 (filled with recipes from unidentified older sources).*

Saucepans – See Skillet
Scotch broiler – See Brander
Skewer holder & skewers, forged iron, ring top to boldly-shaped rack, American, 8"H, 18th C. .... **$700-$1,000**

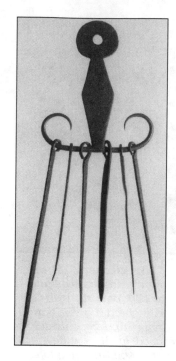

X-79. Skewer rack & skewers. *Wrought iron, early 18th C. Picture courtesy of the Smithsonian Institution, Museum of History & Technology.* **$600+**

❖ **NOTES** ❖

Skewer value – Provenance and attractiveness are important to skewer rack values. A plain unexceptional example, relatively late, would bring $75-$100 at best. An early Pennsylvania German rack, with skewers, in some unusual or desirable design like a heart would bring lots more – perhaps more than $1,000. One or two cautionary notes: you can't know if skewers are original to a particular rack, so you should neither pay for "matching," nor should you expect it. Blacksmith's marks may identify maker or owner. • **Reproduction alert.** – Also, there's a high probability of finding recently-made holders and skewers, made not with the intent to deceive, necessarily, but as part of Colonial Revivalism. 20th C blacksmithing craftsmen's books usually include a skewer design or two. There's no way to tell the difference if someone clever means to trick you. Some collectors feel that there's a general falling off in the buying of the simple forged iron early pieces because of this fact that they can be easily reproduced. Then aged with only a little more care and skill. Such collectors go on to say that perhaps this explains the fast-track approach of later 19th C patented gadgets, etc., which cost a lot to reproduce and are therefore not. (So far.) The cost of molds and the whole casting process probably means that until antique cast iron things start selling for $1,000 or more, we won't have many reproductions of things with moving parts, although cast iron toys have been profitably reproduced for years.

Skewer rack & skewers, holder is tulip pattern with wide arms, all 4 skewers have end bent for hooking to holder's arms, 2 are twisted for strength, one has very very sharpened point, American (?), holder 4"H x 4"W, early 19th C. .... **$400-$600+**
Skewer rack & skewers, the rack also called a skewer fraime, wrought iron, familiar elongated diamond with bull's eye above, upcurving horns or arms, 5 assorted skewers, no mark, American or European, holder or rack is 6"H, skewers range from about 5-3/4" to 11"L, late 18thC for rack, skewers may be 18th & 19th C. • Look for special forms & beautiful detailing in rack. Be healthily suspicious of figural or zoomorphic or animalistic rack forms, such as open-beaked birds or eagles. Probably too good to be true........ **$350-$500+**
Skillet, cast iron, with 3 legs, American, only 6" diam., 18th C or early 19th. These skillets look like what we would think of as a saucepan with legs. A hearth skillet has been described as a utensil shaped like a shallow kettle, that is, pretty much cylindrical with the mouth being about as large in diameter as the bottom. (A silver skillet, on the other hand, used for warming liqueurs in the 18th C, has a mouth slightly smaller than the largest diameter of the body.) .... **$125+**

X-80. Skewer rack & skewers. *Forged iron with very fine cutting & filing. Thought to be possibly from East Windsor, CT, c.1760. Drawn from photograph of piece exhibited at Wadsworth Atheneum. From unidentified private collection.* **$600+**

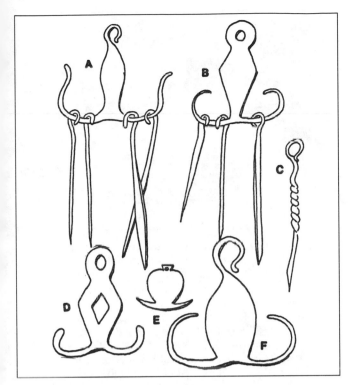

X-81. Skewer racks & skewers. *Wrought iron, 18th & 19th C forms. Almost all skewer holders or racks are variations on two themes: (B) and (D) a diamond shaft, or (A) and (F) somewhat bulbous shaft and with upraised arms. (E) The tulip-like form of is very unusual, but probably wouldn't have the presence to command a top price. Value depends on age, size, and design. Don't worry about a "matched" or "original" set of skewers, because even in the 18th and 19th C a set would be built up of various skewers made for specific purposes. Special forms & beautiful detailing, such as extra fine rattail loops or twisted (C) iron add value. For racks:* **$175+**

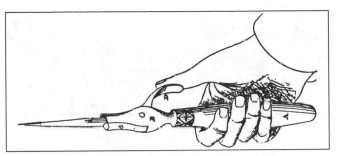

X-83. Skewer pullers patent. *Pat'd Oct. 30, 1877, by F. A. Will and Julius Finck, San Francisco, CA. Consists of a handle, a permanent jaw, a movable jaw operated by the thumb-lever. Shown with skewer stuck in it.* Official Gazette.

Skillet, cast iron, 3 peg feet, cast into handle is "13 IN," also "Cleveland TN," 13" diam., 2nd quarter 19th C. .... **$175+**
Skillet, cast iron, 3 stubby feet, long handle, shallow rounded bowl, American (?), 19th C............. **$125+**
Skillet, forged iron, 3 legs, American (?), 6"H x 6-1/2" diam. x 5"L handle, late 18th, early 19th C. From the small size of so many of the very early skillets, the following reference is puzzling: • "Some three families cook and bake in one skillet, called the **cook-all**." W. Faux, *Memorial Days*, London: 1823. .... **$125+**
Skillet, forged iron, perfectly round-bottomed, 3"L legs, long handle, American (?), 5-1/2"H x 7-1/2" diam., with 3"L legs, 11"L handle, mid to late 18th C. A skillet for hearth cooking very rarely had a flat bottom, unlike a spider. .... **$275+**
Skillet, forged iron with long handle, dished bowl, 3 stubby feet, American (?), 4" diam., 18th C. • In a fascinating book entitled *History Cast in Metal. The Founders of North America*, by Clyde A. Sanders & Dudley C. Gould (n.p.: Cast Metals Institute, American Foundrymen's Society, 1976), the authors show a cast

X-82. Skewer racks & skewers. *Even commercial sets might have well-shaped racks. (L) Iron, from Henry Adams & Son, London, c.1860-61 ad. (R) "Steel skewers. Round, 3" to 9". Oval, 3" to 11", and 4" to 12"." Look at that rack. Would you guess Duparquet, Huot & Moneuse, c.1904-1910? Although they could just have picked up an earlier linecut to use in their catalog. Still, the style looks early 19th or late 18th C.* **$125-$200**

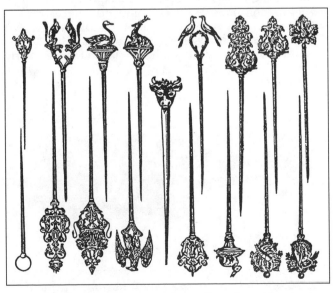

X-84. Fancy skewers. *All are French, with possible exception of center one, the bull's-head, which came from Mrs. A. B. Marshall's Cookery Book, London, c.1900. The others from Duparquet, Huot & Moneuse, c.1904-1910.* **$22+**

X-85. Skillets. *Cast iron, rounded bottoms, 3 legs, long handles flat on top, half round in section. Used sitting over raked coals in fireplace. 18th or early 19th C. Picture courtesy of the National Museum of American History, Smithsonian Institution.* **$150+**

iron pot, bellied body, triangular lug handles, three longish feet, which they describe as an English-made posnet. They go on to say that a four-legged pot was a skillet, or, in Northern England, a **stufnet**. I have yet to see the absolutely dependable definitive explanation of a skillet or posnet... **$250+**

Skillet, wrought iron, long handle, 3 long legs, "G. W. Ibach," PA. 17-1/2"L including handle, 5"H, 18th or very early 19th C. .... **$300+**

Skillet, ring handle, iron, "W. Foster, #8," early 19th C. **$200**

Skillet, forged iron with pouring spout and fixed arched handle with trammel ring, American, 12-1/2"H including handle x 12" diam., 19th C. ... **$200-$275**

Skillets, cast iron, set of 6 in different sizes, long handles and 3 legged, to use on hearth. American, late 18th C. This rare & wonderful set was sold by Lillian Blankley Cogan, one of the earliest dealers in kitchen "primitives," in 1988 for only: **$1,800**

Sleeper – See Curfew

Spider, also called a speeder colloquially, cast bell metal, long handle angled up at 40 degrees off the horizon, 3 long splayed peg legs, handle marked "20 Warner," American or English, about 7"H x 7-1/4" diam. with 9-1/2"L handle, late 18th or early 19th C. .... **$350+**

X-86. Skillet – note the round bottom. *Cast iron, long, more angular legs & handle. Longish casting gate on bottom. 4"H x 13-3/4"L overall. Picture courtesy of the National Museum of American History, Smithsonian Institution, John Paul Remensnyder estate.* **$300+**

X-87. Skillets & spiders – all with legs. *All cast iron.* **(A)** *"Lipped frying spider," in light or medium weight, both in 4 sizes, 8", 9-1/2", 11", and 12-1/2" diam.* **(B)** *"Biscuit spider with lid." Also in light or medium weight, and 11", 12" or 13" diameters.* **(C)** *"Plain cake spider." Light or medium, four sizes from 8" to 12-1/2" diam. All from Russell & Erwin Mfg. Co., New Britain, CT, 1865.* **(D)** *"Shallow spider" [flanged lid make it also a Dutch oven) in six sizes from 8" to 13" diam.* **(E)** *"Skillet," which came nested in 3 sizes (not given); and* **(F)** *"Deep spider," in six sizes from 8" to 13". Note flat-top handles and half-round undersides of handles. Also note the flanged lid – making this also a Dutch oven. Stuart, Peterson & Co., 1866 catalog. See Chapter XII also.* **$155+**

Spider, probably so named for the typically long legs, wrought iron, 3 legs, flat bottom, repaired, American, prob. PA, 6"H x 6-1/2" diam. with 10-1/2"L handle, 18th or early 19th C. .... **$120-$145**

Spider, cast iron, 3 short peg legs, flat bottom, American, 9" diam. with 5-1/2"L handle, mid 19th C........ **$125+**

Spider, cast iron, 3 legs, long handle, straight sides, flat bottom, American, 5"H x 10-3/4" diam. pan, 9"L handle, 18th C. .... **$125+**

❖ NOTES ❖

Creepy spider – A "creeper" is described in W. Scott *Boyce's Economic and Social History of Chowan County:* "The principal cooking utensils, even of most of the best families, were a pot, a creeper (a spider) or two, a long-handle frying pan, a tea-kettle, a griddle, and two or three wornout hoes" [p.222]. It sounds the same as a Dutch oven, but is a spider according to Boyce. He writes that "most baking ... was done in the creeper. ... To bake in the creeper, it was set on the fire and coals heaped on the lid. It was in this receptacle that was cooked that famous dyspepsia-producing Southern dish known as 'hot biscuit.' The much-prized apple and peach 'jacks' (kinds of pies – the New England 'turnovers') were cooked either in this or in the frying-pan" [p.223]. while "some few had big ovens for baking sweet potatoes, and some were baked in creepers, but probably the bigger half was roasted on the hearth before the fire ... or in the hot ashes." loc sit. He further describes "The creeper at this time [1880s] as a heavy cast-iron pan some 3" or 4" deep, covered with a lid, [that] stood on three legs about three inches high. The handle was from 12" to 15" long." W. Scott Boyce, *Economic and Social History of Chowan County*, North Carolina, 1880-1915, submitted as a doctoral thesis at Columbia University, and published in NYC in 1917. It is a marvelous book, with many valuable nuggets of information.

Spider, wrought iron, flat bottom, long handle, "Whitfield" marked on handle, American (?) or English (?), 8"H x 14" diam. with 17"L handle, early 19th or late 18th C. .... **$100-$200**

✣ RECIPE ✣

Spider Food !

Poached eggs – *Have ready a kettle of boiling water, pour it in a pan or speeder, which is set on coals; have the eggs at hand; put a little salt in water, and break them in, one at a time. Let remain till white is set and take them out with an egg spoon."* Elizabeth E. Lea, Useful Receipts and Hints to Young Housekeepers, 10th ed., Baltimore, 1859 (1st ed. 1851).

X-88. Spit set-up in hearth. Basket spit, spit-dogs & clock jack. *A clockwork jack, with heavy weight to drive it, (like a tall-cased clock.) It moved the chain, which moved the pulley wheel, which turned the spit – on which was the roast that Jack turned. Spit height adjustable by hooking it on at different levels of the andirons. Cup-like tops were for caudle cups, to heat milk & mead or other hot drink. From ad of now defunct B. Altman & Co., June 1957. Longtime buyer for Altman's antiques was a wonderful Scotsman, Archie Keillor, who traveled all over the world looking for things. It was his family collection that was featured in my first book on old kitchen things, now out of print. I'm sure he found these items.* **$4,500+**

✣ RECIPE ✣

New England Fire Cakes – *Make a pie crust not quite so rich as for puff paste. Cut off small pieces and roll out thin about the size of a breakfast plate, as nearly round as possible. Have a griddle over the fire, and bake a nice brown, turning it when done on one side and browning nicely on the other. When done, put on a plate and butter it well. Have ready another cake, and bake, piling one upon the other, and buttering each piece, until all you have made are cooked. Serve them quite hot, cutting down through all the layers. This is very nice if, as you butter each piece, preserved strawberries or raspberries are spread upon each layer. It is an old-fashioned New England cake, and in olden times was cooked in iron spiders, propped up before the kitchen fire; hence its name. It is a very nice short cake, to be eaten hot, for supper or breakfast."* Mrs. F. D. J., in Home Cook Book, 1876.

Spider, wrought iron with 3 legs, flat bottom, American, 7-3/4" diam., late 18th or early 19th C. **$125-$150**

Spit rack, wrought iron with penny feet (round & flat, usually somewhat bigger than a modern American penny – more like an English penny in size. They were formed by hammering flat the terminals of the legs.) Adjustable vertical spit with hooks, American or English, 28"H, 18th C. .... **$750-$1,000**

Spit, basket, also called a cradle spit, forged iron, a cage-like "basket" of iron centered on long spit rod, for holding any roast meat which might come apart if just skewered to a plain spit. This one complete with hinges & pulley, English (?), late 18th C. (Note: Another kind of spit with provision for holding the roast was called a spit with **holdfast**, a fixed two-pronged fork onto which the spitted meat was rammed.) .... **$700-$1,000**

Striker, for striking against a flintstone to make a spark to start a fire, would be kept in an early home in a tinder box (probably tin or wood), with a stone, a piece of charred linen. This striker is slightly different from most I've seen – flat narrow bar of forged iron, bent in a very tight hairpin curve with both tips curled in at the open end, American

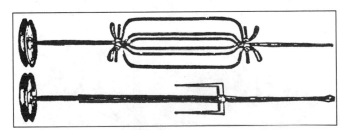

X-89. Spits. *Wrought iron.* **Basket or cradle spit & "spit with Holdfast."** *The basket or cradle type was used to hold small game birds or animals or joints of other meat, which it was better to keep unskewered so that it would remain moist inside instead of dripping out all its juice. The one with the holdfast was supplemented with skewers, which went through the meat and through holes (which you can't see here) in the thicker part of the shaft. From William S. Adams & Son catalog, London, c.1860-61.* **$150+**

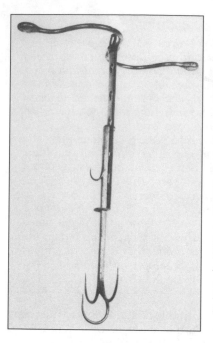

X-90. Dangle spit. *Probably for birds. It was hung from a cord (which had to be replaced every so often from charring), and then twisted. The longish curved wings or governors helped to keep it twisting and turning, first one way then the other. Steel, 16"L fully extended (shown here about half extended), American, early 19th C. Ex-Keillor Family Collection.* **$700+**

X-92. Turnspit dog in his cage. *Depicted in* The Comic Offering; or Ladies' Melange of Literary Mirth for 1835. *London: 1835. Oh, yeah – Hah hah*

or European, 3-3/4"L, 18th or very early 19th C.
• **Other strikers** I've seen include something almost as wide open as a small horseshoe with no attempt to finish off the tips at the open end; rather loosely curved striker with one "arm" decidedly shorter than other, both tips curled; and various strikers with file and chisel decoration. The value range below would not include the decorated ones, which would add another $25-$100 to the high value. .... **$40-$95**

Striker, forged iron, flat, form appears to be a "rocking fox," the rocker blade with both ends curled rather tightly, like old ice skate blades, incised lines to indicate the separation of 2 front legs and 2 back legs, also the eyes and mouth, brush tail out straight behind, prob. European, but if American (?), poss. Connecticut or Virginia?, not Pennsylvania, 2-3/4"H x 4-7/8"L, early 19th C (?). • This is the first figural striker I've ever seen, so don't know how to judge it. The dealer is from CT, at a VA show; a lot of interesting iron in his booth, but people say most of his wares are Portuguese; iron is getting all mixed up nowadays. .... **$275-$400+**

Tea kitchen, a sort of kettle, also called a covered cauldron, copper, tinned inside, slightly round-breasted body, sturdy bail handle with pivot ring, small central opening with lid, copper and brass spigot sticks out straight from side, right at bottom, spigot as long as kettle is in diameter, to be hung on trammel or pot hook in fireplace for ready supply of hot water, English, 10"H x 10-1/2" diam., late 18th C.
• A slightly later variation of this was adapted, or

X-93. "The Turnspit." *Illustration from the magazine* Frank Leslie's Boy's & Girl's Weekly, *Aug. 7, 1869. "Not long since, a wheel in a circular box was brought from an old house to a railroad station in England, with a lot of old trumpery. The other articles attracted little attention, but this puzzled the group. There were old men and women, too, but none remembered seeing such a thing in use. At last, a blacksmith of a neighboring village said it was a turnspit's wheel, such as he remembered to have seen in use. It seems a hard lot for the dog to be kept at his work for, perhaps, three hours, till the joint was done, and we do not wonder the custom at last fell into disuse." Special short-legged, barrel-chested dogs were bred for this. The illustration here is a somewhat simplified engraving of a Thomas Rowlandson print, which shows more details.*

X-91. Spit driven by dog power. *"Dog-Wheel. – Both the turnspit-dog and apparatus for cooking are now nearly out of use. The example here was sketched in Glouscestershire about five years since."* Hone's Every-Day Book, *1850. What a horrible thing to do to a dog. And probably breathing smoke the whole time.*

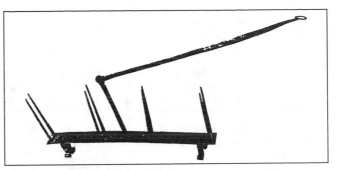

X-95. Pivoting toaster. *Wrought iron, 30"L x 13"W, possibly English, early 19th C. Ex-Keillor Family Collection. All you had to do was pick it up by the long handle, do a neat sort of flip with the handle, and set it down again.* **$500+**

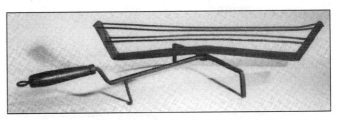

X-96. Revolving toaster, *also called a* **toe toaster,** *because instead of leaning over to turn it, you could turn it with your foot. Wrought iron, wooden grip on handle, possibly mid 19th C. Wooden handle grip is the puzzler – it just doesn't look old. Picture courtesy of the National Museum of American History, Smithsonian Institution.* **$400+**

frame 13"L with 13"L handle, early 19th C. So many of these flip over types are appearing at fleas and shows that I believe most are probably coming in from Europe in container loads. .... **$350+**

Toaster, pivoting or swiveling, the kind you have to pick up the handle & move it to swivel the toast frame, very decorative wrought iron arches and handle, American (?), more likely French Canadian or European, late 18th C. .... **$400+**

Toaster, pivoting or swiveling, wrought iron, 4 rectangular arches, American (?), late 18th C or early 19th . A really fine American toaster of the pivoting or revolving type could bring up to $2,000.... **$350+**

❖ RECIPE ❖

*A recipe for a "**Method of Making Toast Water**" appeared in the Aug. 1851 issue of American Agriculturist. "Take a slice of fine and stale loaf bread, cut thin, (thin as toast is ever cut,) and let it be carefully toasted on both sides, until it be completely browned all over, but nowise blackened nor burned in any way. Put this into a common, deep stone or China pitcher, and pour over it, from the teakettle, as much clean boiling water as you wish to make into drink. Much depends on the water being actually in a boiling state. Cover the pitcher with a saucer or plate, and let the drink cool until it is quite cold; it is then fit to be used. The fresher it is made, the better, and of course, the more agreeable. The above will be found a pleasant, light and*

X-94. "Kitchen Fire-Place at Windsor Castle." *"The open fire-place measures 6 x 8 feet in size, the products of combustion passing up the chimney in such a way as to operate a kind of fan wheel [smoke jack], which is connected by means of belting and gears and revolve with the long spits placed before the fire. On these spits are various kinds of joints and poultry, while beneath is a large pan for the purpose of collecting the drippings from the various kinds of food in process of cooking."* The drawing is an engraving, made from a pencil sketch that a "gentleman connected with the [stove-making] firm" of Rathbone, Sard & Co., Albany, NY, made on a trip to England in 1889. The Metal Worker, *April 5, 1890.*

created, for use on top of a range, with the spigot sticking out off to side of range, as supply of hot water. This type is generally somewhat larger, and because it stood on its own, was made to balance more safely by being taller and having shorter spigot relative to diameter. • The 1895 Harrod's Stores catalog depicts two of these, cylindrical bodies, slightly domed top, with fitted lid with strap bracket handle, long spigot spout, falling wire bail handle. Made of cast iron or "London Wrought Iron," they were called Tea Kitchens or Boiler for Fire in the Harrod's catalog. In cast iron, there were three sizes: 2, 3 & 4 gallons; in wrought iron: 2 & 3 gallons. ... **$350-$500+**

Tin kitchen – See Reflecting oven, Tin kitchen

Toasters, fixed

Toaster, fancy brass single slice toaster for hearth use, probably for tea time in the parlor, with pivoting lazy elbow handle, scalloped-edge heavy gauge brass plate with 2 curved arches of brass rod to hold bread, English almost undoubtedly, c.1830s....... **$175-$225**

Toaster, forged iron, long slightly arched handle fixed to pair of footed arches with hook support underneath for one thick slab of bread, English, 12-1/2"L x 5"W, 18th C. .... **$375-$425**

Toasters, pivoting or swiveling

Toaster, pivoting, also called a flip toaster, forged iron, 2 sets of 3 twisted arches, European (?), toaster *highly diuretic drink. It is peculiarly grateful to the stomach, and excellent for carrying off the effects of excessive bile."*

Toaster, pivoting, wrought iron & wire, 4 pairs of arches, arched penny feet on toast frame, American or European, 40"L overall, early 19th C........ **$400+**

Toaster, swiveling type with long handle, forged iron, heart design supports, from Maine coast, frame is 12-5/8"W x 5-1/4" deep, with 18-5/8"L handle, late 18th C. .... **$550+**

Toaster, pivoting, wrought iron with 4 twisted arches on footed frame, can be flipped at swivel-hinged junction of long handle and toaster, American (?), late 18th , early 19th C. • The fancier the iron work on these, the more likely they are to be English or European. Most have iron handles; occasionally you find one with a wooden handle.................... **$700+**

Toaster, revolving

Toaster, revolving, or toe toaster, so-called because instead of having to lean over to turn the toast, you could just give it a tap with your foot and the rack would turn to face the other way. Forged iron, with unusual sprouted corn stalk-shaped supports for

*X-99. **Revolving toaster.** Wrought iron, with unusual "corn sprout" supports for bread, in addition to double arches. Late 18th or early 19th C. Picture courtesy of the National Museum of American History, Smithsonian Institution.* **$750+**

the bread, within the double arches more commonly found, American, late 18th or early 19th C. • You're never too old to learn: I learned the toe toaster term by accident, watching an episode of "Reading Rainbow" in August 1987, which featured a visit to Sturbridge Village in Massachusetts............. **$250-$350**

Toaster, revolving, wrought iron with 2 sets of double arches, nice handle with hanging eye, American, 19"L, early 19th C. .... **$550+**

Toaster, forged iron, revolving, double arch holder on frame with long handle, 2 sets of double tree-like sprays of iron within arches that hold bread into holes, one on each side adjusts for various size of slices, American, c.1770s. .... **$950+**

Toaster, rotating type, frame has 4 sets of double rams' horns to hold 2 slices of bread, 4 little deep knee-bend legs, and very unusual tiller handle rising up for convenient handling, wooden grip, signed "N. B." New England (?), 8-1/2" x 12", late 18th C. .. **$950+**

Toasting forks – See Chapter XIII (Implements)

Tongs, forged iron, one arm is twisted, small head, American, prob. PA, 17-5/8"L, mid to late 18th C. .... **$150+**

Trammel, chain, forged iron, 50"L, early 19th C. .... **$120-$180**

Trammel, chain, strong twisted wrought iron hook, 70"L, early 19th C. .... **$150-$225**

Trammel, for fireplace, wrought & polished steel, nice filework decoration, swiveling hook, English (?), 13" to 21" closed & open lengths, late 18th, early 19th C. .... **$350+**

*X-97. **Revolving toaster.** Wrought iron, strong spirals, extremely well-made. 3-3/4"H x 11"L overall x 7"W. American, early 19th C. Ex-Keillor Collection.* **$650+**

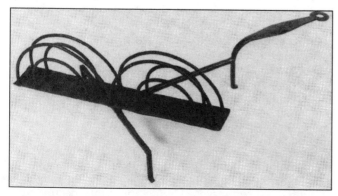

*X-98. **Revolving toaster.** Wrought iron, with two sets of four arches, big and small. 19"L, early 19th C. Ex-Keillor Collection.* **$575+**

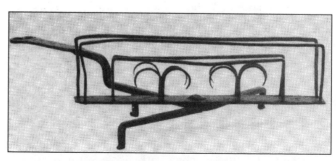

*X-100. **Revolving toaster.** Wrought iron, another one with the "corn sprouts." Ram's horn handle. 17-1/2"L x 13-1/2"W, American, late 18th C. Picture courtesy of Robert W. Skinner Inc., Auctioneers, Bolton, MA.* **$650+**

❖ NOTES ❖

Polishing Metals – "The polishing of metals differs according to the kind of metal and the kind of manufacture; [but] there are some general principles to be attended to as being common to all, of which it [is] useful to have a clear idea. All polishing is begun, in the first instance, by rubbing down the surface by some hard substance that will produce a number of scratches in all directions, the level of which is nearly the same, and which will obliterate the marks of the file, scraper, or turning tool … first employed. For this purpose **coarse emery** is used, or **pumice and water**, or sand and water, applied upon a piece of soft wood, or of felt, skin, or some similar material. When these first coarse marks have been thus removed, they next proceed to remove the marks left by the pumice-stone of finely powdered pumice-stone ground up with olive oil, or by finer emery and oil. In some cases, certain polishing stones are employed, as a kind of hard slate, used with water. To proceed with the polishing, still finer powders are used, as **Tripoli** & **rotten-stone**, which is still finer, and is found only in Derbyshire. **Putty of tin** & **crocus martis** are also used for high degrees of polish. But the fact is, in respect to polishing, that the whole process consists … in removing coarse scratches by substituting those which are finer & finer, until they are no longer visible to the naked eye; and … if the surface be examined by a microscope, it will be seen that what appeared without any scratches is covered … with an infinity of them, but so minute that they require a high magnifier to be discovered. The operator … who understands this principle, will … vary his polishing substances according to the nature of the article he wishes to polish. … His polishing material must be able to scratch, in a coarser or finer manner, the substance he is desirous of polishing, for wearing down is only effected by producing minute cuttings or scratches. It is evident … that great care must be taken to have the last polishing material uniformly fine, for a single grain … of any coarse substance mixed with it will produce some visible scratches instead of a perfectly polished surface. … Polishing materials: coarsest are emery, sand, glass-paper, whiting, or chalk, putty of tin, & black-lead" usually mixed with oil. Webster & Parkes, *An Encyclopedia of Domestic Economy*, 1848 NY edition of English book of 1845.

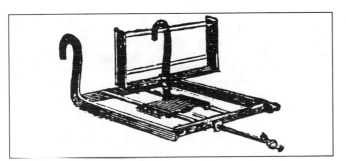

X-101. Fender toaster or trivet. *Described in Warne's Model Cookery, London, 1868, as an "improved revolving toaster, also available as a hanging Trivet, for Kettle, Saucepan, or Plate." Hmmm.* **$150+**

X-102. Trammel. *Wrought iron, finely done. Saw-tooth style with crane ring, extension 45" to 61"L. Probably American, early 19th C. Ex-Keillor Family Collection. The faint numbers you may see at top of "blade" are Keillor's acquisition numbers, not a mark.* **$450+**

Trammel, forged iron, 2 piece flat bar iron, one with holes, one with rod to fit into any hole of other part, with hook at bottom, American, adjusts from 35"L to 60"L, so for very large fireplace, late 18th C. Unless these have some kind of spiffy form or decoration or hook or look, they are really rather dull. I like the saw-tooth trammels much better, or the hand wrought chain ones. .... **$300+**

Trammel, forged iron, chain with long hook, knobbed lugpole hook, American or English, early 19th C. See also Pot chain. .... **$350+**

Trammel, forged iron, saw-tooth style, for big fireplace, American (?), 32"L to 41"L extended, late 18th or early 19th C. .... **$325-$450**

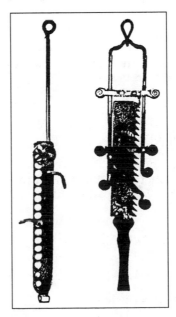

X-103. Trammels. *Both wrought iron, 18th C, probably not American. (L) Pawl & ratchet type, with crank action. 36"L as shown. (R) Elaborate saw-tooth style, probably earlier than other one. 56"L as shown. Ex-Keillor Collection.* **$250+; $900+**

X. Hearths & Fireplaces 601

Trammel, forged iron, saw-tooth type, simple keeper attached to hook through rattail loop, 11 usual-sized teeth, somewhat (and appealingly) different in angle and size, American, 21-1/4"L extends to approximately 32"L, early 19th or late 18th C. Auctioned at Garth Auction, May 5-6, 1989, Delaware, OH. . **$350+**

Trammel, possibly for a lamp, steel, English, 20-7/8"L sans hook, dated with individual punches or stamps, "ANNO 1774." .... **$325+**

Trammel, saw-tooth ratchet, cut out of heavy sheet brass, with a cutout flat finial decoration of a cock, English (?), extends 20" to 35"L, looks 2nd to 3rd quarter 19th C. • It's possibly a containerload import piece, or maybe it was a decorative piece made in the 20th C because there's something about it that just looks wrong & fakey. .... **$200-$300**

Trammel, very large wrought iron saw-tooth type, large hanging ring at top, 24 relatively small saw-teeth (the 12th down broken off), decorative keeper and hook, heart cutout in crested top of the wide 'blade', very unusual low relief decoration top to bottom of vines & tulips, poss. PA German, 47"L unextended, early 19thC (?). .... **$1,200+**

Trammel, wrought iron, hook & eye type, adjustable from 31" to 47"L, early 19th or late 18th C. ... **$350-$450.?**

❖ NOTES ❖

Valuing Trammels. Many trammels go for under $100 because they don't excite much visual interest unless they are very fine examples. But look again: workmanship, when you lean over and study them or clean them, begins to add up to higher value. Of course, you have to love iron. Several trammels would have been found hanging from the lug pole or crane in early kitchens, some are surprisingly long. Added value. – Some are very decorative, with scrolling curves and fanciful sawteeth or hook-and-eye elements; chains can be gussied up too. The finest go for upwards of $2000.

Trammels' Provenance Trampled in Container Loads. – Many, maybe most, antique trammels for sale in the U.S. today probably just arrived on these shores from England or Europe. Is there a difference if a French trammel got here in 1780 or 1980? You have to decide.

Trammel – See also Bird trammel

Trivet, for hearth, with adjustable fork or handle support that works on the pawl & ratchet idea, forged & twisted iron "running man" piece with adjustable height to hold fork or spoon, 2 long legs on either side of circle of trivet, one leg near end of handle, very handsome form that looks like what sculptor Alberto Giacometti would have done, if he'd made 18th century cooking utensils. Found in house on the Connecticut-Massachusetts line, 24-5/16"L, trivet is 7-5/8" diam., maybe mid 18th C. .... **$700+**

Trivet, for hearth, wrought iron with sliding support for saucepan handle, 3 penny feet, 22-1/2"L, 18th C. .... **$400+**

Trivet, wrought iron, round with 3 legs & a long handle, for use on the hearth, American (?), 6"H x 8" diam. with 11"L handle, 18th or early 19th C............ **$275+**

Trivets not for hearth use – See Chapter VI (Trivets, Stands, Etc.).

Wafer & waffle irons for hearth use – See Chapter IV (Molds).

FOR MORE INFORMATION

IMPLEMENTS & HOLLOWWARE TO BUY

Dealers advertise in collector newspapers such as *Maine Antique Digest*, Waldeboro, ME, with photographs of interesting pieces. You might want to keep a scrapbook of such ads.

Erik K. Gronning

Advanced collector & dealer interested in buying unusual hearth-cooking utensils and tools. He will also try to answer questions about objects in your collections.

6645VT Route 7A
Shaftsbury, Vermont 05262
Phone: (802) 375-6376
E-mail: erikgronning@earthlink.com

Oveda Maurer Antiques

I got several really good photos of things from this dealer several years ago. She deals in early lighting and hearthware, ceramics, etc.

Contact: Oveda Maurer
34 Greenfield Ave.
San Anselmo, CA 94960
Phone: (415) 454-6439
E-mail: omaurer@earthlink.net
Web site: www.ovedamaurerantiques.com

HEARTH-COOKING CLASSES

There are hearth-cooking teachers around the country. For hearth-cooking classes in your community, contact your historical society, or any restoration village nearby. I only have classes for North America, but if there are classes in Europe, Australia, New Zealand, or elsewhere, let us know for future editions.

Alice Ross Hearth Studios

Old-style traditional techniques learned at a hot hearth, hot stove, hot smokehouse, or hot brick oven. Make it the centerpiece of an American/ NYC vacation! Ms. Ross is a pioneer of teaching hearth-cooking, and now offers woodstove cooking, etc. – all with lively measures of social history. There are some 32 different, mostly 6-hour, classes. My faves are "Baking Day 1 & 2," "The English Pie" (sweet & savory), and "Pastas, Noodles & Dumplings," with early German & Italian recipes and lots of my favorite gadgets. If you want to learn a cuisine, Alice probably teaches it.

Contact: Alice Ross
15 Prospect St.
Smithtown, NY 11787
Phone: (631) 265-9335
E-mail: aross@binome.com

Susan Lucas
Heritage Workshops
Newlin's Mills
219 S. Cheney Rd.
Glen Mills, PA 19342

Historic Deerfield
Contact: Grace Friary
Box 321
Deerfield, MA 01342-0321
Phone: (413) 775-7127
E-mail: grace@historic-deerfield.org

Old Sturbridge Village
Early 1800s cooking.

1 OSV Rd.
Sturbridge, MA 01566
Phone: (800) SEE-1830
Web site: www.osv.org

Plimoth Plantation
17th century cooking.

POB 1620
Plymouth, MA 02362
Phone: (508) 746-1622
Web site: www.plimoth.org

Heritage Toronto
Spadina House
285 Spadina Rd.
Toronto, Ontario
M5R 2V5 Canada

BLACKSMITHING, ETC.

There are probably many places to learn blacksmithing around the world, in many communities. Here is only one.

Conner Prairie
Blacksmithing & occasional hearth-cooking classes.

13400 Allisonville Road (at 131st St.)
(Off Exit 5 from Interstate 69, near Indianapolis)
Fishers, IN 46038-4499

Phone: (800) 966-1836
Web site: www.connerprairie.org/inside/contact.html

MEDIEVAL WORDS

Thousand Eggs

Other glossaries are listed in this book, but this one pertains especially to the hearth-cooking tools and methods. An extensive "glossary of medieval & Renaissance Culinary Terms" will help you track down meanings in old cookbooks. Ms. Renfrow has written two books at this time: *Take a Thousand Eggs or More* (400 adapted 15th century recipes); and *A Sip Through Time* (400 ancient & 17th –19th century recipes for all kinds of drinks.)

Contact: Cindy Renfrow
7 El's Way
Sussex, NJ 07461
Web site: www.thousandeggs.com/glossary.html
URL for the books: www.thousandeggs.com

MEDIEVAL COOKBOOKS, BIBLIOGRAPHIES, ETC.

Poison Pen Press

A site for books by various publishers, especially on medieval cookery and other domestic aspects of the Middle Ages & Renaissance.

951 Coney Island Ave. Ste. 111
Brooklyn, NY 11230
Phone: (800) 838-5257
E-mail: devra@poisonpenpress.com
Web site: www.poisonpenpress.com/

BIBLIOGRAPHY

A bibliography compiled by librarian Kirsti S. Thomas with books in several languages, mostly published in last four decades and many are likely to be found in libraries. Most have adapted recipes for modern use.

Web site: www.drizzle.com/~celyn/mrwp/feast.txt

COOKING

XI. STOVES & RANGES

Stoves are not really collected the way other kitchen things are. Most people who are fervently interested are what are known as **collector-users**. Occasionally you see a news story about this or that celebrity who has paid a fortune to have a restored antique stove installed in a magazine-ready glam kitchen. Whether it's a "Garland" in bright "Freedom Red," from 1953, or a 1930s British "Aga," it has great practical value as well as collector value.

They aren't really collectors, but there are many hundreds of people in the U.S. seriously into old stoves – especially those for cooking. Thank heaven the collectors and collector-users came along at the right time; and fortunately an adequate supply of stoves survived wartime metal drives, and modernizations of dwellings to keep us supplied.

Antique cook stoves and **ranges** probably have a slight edge on popularity, but there are some fantastically beautiful parlor heating stoves that deserve more attention, especially ones that look like large sculptures of urban Victorian buildings. Imagine how beautiful they looked with the mica windows glowing from the fire within, looking as if a party were going on in every floor of the house.

Futurewatch: A related category is hot water radiators with built-in warming ovens, from the late 19th to early 20th centuries, meant for cold, high-ceilinged dining rooms where eating dinner took an hour or more. These are going to be the hardest things to find; they haven't been given the sort of safety net that a lot of other old things have (either because they weren't important enough to notice and throw away, or they were too useful or too noticeable to discard). Probably several million radiators, many of them attractive works of cast iron art, have been junked or melted down in the last 80 or 90 years, gone forever.

Some people collect **stove parts**. I knew somebody in NYC who used to climb into dumpsters (where they throw all kinds of eminently-collectible stuff when renovating old buildings) to dig out cast iron gas-stove jet rings, which come in cast forms as varied as flowers in a garden, or coronets at an 1890s gathering of the crowned heads of Europe. When I lived in NYC, I often rescued porcelainized cast iron knobs, drop pulls, and handles, even decorated oven fronts, while walking my dog.

Some people collect **stove tools and accessories** – from ash shovels and lid lifters to scuttles and stovepipe "flue stops" or flue covers. I've seen enough **flue stops** (those things that look like brass luncheon plates) to know that there is a satisfactory diversity and range to give a collector a run for the money. A lot of **stove lid lifters** are competently-designed, even handsome, and some are figural. I've only got one – a cast iron female figural one described in this chapter (see XXXX XI-41), which I was fortunate enough to see listed in an *Antique Trader Weekly* classified. Another desirable one is a bent Victorian lady's leg with booted foot.

An adjunctive category is **camp stoves**, appealing, perhaps, because of the ever-increasing interest in hearth cooking and in and portable "stoves" from braziers to chafing dishes. You might find a wrought iron one at a militaria show, from a dealer in Revolutionary War or Civil War equipment, but you may be competing with reenactment afficianados.

Smart collectors, no matter what their specialties are, will not depend solely on specialist dealers within their fields, but will imaginatively try to find connections to other specialties where treasures may lie hidden. For you, it might be a dumpster, a gun show, or a scrap yard, that will yield up something grand – maybe even a splendid "**kitchen piano**," a period nickname for magnificent ornate cooking ranges – their ebony gleam coming from locomotive black finish, the twinkle coming from the nickeled trim.

Clifford Boram's article "What's My Stove Worth?" follows the listings in this chapter. That's the last word; and truly, you must read the last words in that article! For me, evaluating old stoves is almost like the antique car market. There isn't any Blue Book. The variables due to location alone are enough to make every deal dependent on its own particular terms. Any errors in the values of the ranges and stoves in this chapter of the book are solely my own; Boram's article are solely his own, based on long experience.

There is a lot of material to help you with further information at the end of this chapter.

Ash sifter shovel, wood & wire, instead of steel blade with the typical shovel rounded shoulder, it's made of welded heavy wires, going lengthwise and joined at shoveling edge, and at top, steel "ferrule" fasted to long wooden handle, for shoveling through ashes to clear out clinkers or unburned debris from furnaces, or perhaps even large stoves. Androck, 50"L overall, "blade" is 14"L x 8-1/2"W, 1930s. • These were made by different wire goods companies, some with patterns of braced crisscrosses – very graphic, but all for same purpose. The handles are often missing or broken. (Note: A shorter wire shovel, used to sift dug-up potatoes from their surrounding dirt, but almost identical in looks, is a potato scoop. Its handle is 30"L and the shoulder of the blade is solid steel, so the wires were shorter.) Ash sifter shovel: .... **$15+**

Blacking box holders – See Stove blacking holders, and XI-39 & XI-40.

Camp stove, very small portable type called Revolutionary War soldier's stove, penny feet, sheet iron & forged iron, wood handle, a sort of modern day Sterno™, American, 6-1/2"H x 5" diam., 18th C to early 19th C. .... **$650+**

Camp stove, wrought iron with turned wooden horizontal side handle and hanging ring, 4 small penny feet, rectangular body or firebox, with rack or grid above, plus 4 corner supports for pot, works like a brazier – as a portable fire. American, 5-1/4"H x 6"W x 12"L, late 18th or early 19th C. .... **$650+**

XI-1. Camp stove, to be used like a brazier. These could be used by anyone needing a small portable stove. Wrought iron with turned wooden handle. For use with charcoal. Four resting pads on the corners of the top accommodated whatever needed heating, and raised it slightly above level of detachable grill. 5-1/4"H x 12"L overall x 6"W. This type is late 18th or early 19th C.; later ones were cast iron. Picture courtesy of Robert W. Skinner Auctioneers, Bolton, MA. $650+

XI-2. Brazier or camp stove. Cast iron footed body with wire bail. Lift-out grid has heart with radiating lines (symbolizing warmth of heart). 7-1/2"H x 10-5/8" diam. Sold at Ada F. & Earl F. Robacker auction, Horst Auctions, July 21-22, 1989, for only $275. See also the spoked heart trivet in Chapter VI. **$450+**

Camp or folding "pocket" stove, black painted hinged and folding sheet metal 3 sided base, with stamped brass & tin fuel cup, in original box, with directions: "Use only Alcohol, pour in slowly through the wire gauze, one or two table-spoons full and light it. The Best Folding Pocket Cook Stove in the World." "Climax Patent Folding Pocket Cook Stove No. 888," Houchin Mfg. Co., NYC, NY, 4-1/2"H x cup 3-1/2" diam., trademark reg. May 18, 1875, with patents earlier & later. • Pat'd. Sept. 17, 1872, May 4, 1875, July 27, 1875, Jan. 29, 1878, Mar. 20, 1883.... **$35**

Carbonite camp stove, boxy iron body, supposed to burn a special fuel, 4 squatty, fat-knee cabriole legs, adjustable air vent on side, single hole on top fitted with lid notched for lid lifter, wire bail handle, turned wooden grip, "Carbonite," The American Safety Fuel Co., NYC, 10"H x 10-1/2" square, with 6" hole & lid (also came in 7" or 8" sizes), early 1890s. .... **$150+**

Charcoal stove, a more modern camp stove, one burner, cast iron fire/coal vessel with flared sides and wide flared lip with 6-point star-like openwork grill that sits just inside the flared lip; vessel sets on wonderful little cast iron 4-legged hearth, wire bail handle, Griswold's "Eldorado No. 2," c.1895-1910s. .... **$600+**

❖ NOTES ❖

Requisites for Efficiency – Mrs. Cornelius, in the *Young Housekeeper's Friend*, Boston & NYC: 1846, listed among the requisites (mainly iron) for an efficient kitchen, a "Portable charcoal furnace, of iron or clay, useful in summer for washing, stewing, etc." These portable stoves, or braziers, could be used outdoors, or in a breezeway, in order to not heat the house more than was necessary. • **Traveling tinsmiths** used similar, maybe identical, portable charcoal furnaces for melting solder, and most farmers had one to perform certain mending chores.

Charcoal or other portable stoves – See Portable stoves.

Coal carrier, also called a stoker, brass with wood & wire carrying handle on side, like little suitcase, sheet iron bottom, small knob slides in slot to regulate vent opening in top, several marks stamped on lid, "Girodon & Cie. Fabnts. Déposé a Villeurbanne

XI-3. "Improved coal-scuttle." For a base-burner stove or top-fed stove. Amount of effort required to raise to a pouring level (note tilting handle on right side near bottom) was much less than a conventional scuttle because it did not need to be "lifted through a large part of a circle." American Agriculturist, Feb. 1881. **$40+**

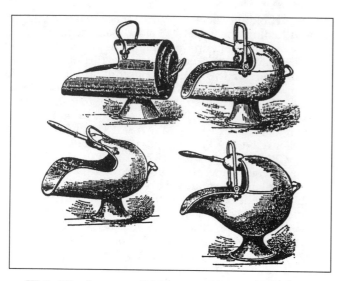

XI-4. "Coal scoops." I have no idea why these are scoops and similar ones are hods. The primary difference seems to be the rounded, hooded tops. These illustrations accompanied a series of practical articles, "Art of Coppersmithing," serialized in The Metal Worker, from John Fuller's 1889 book on the same subject. These copper coal containers, "considered an adornment for the parlor," were made in these traditional shapes some 40 years before Fuller related his long experience in crafting all manner of copper household articles. The names, clockwise from top left are "The Florence," "The Nautilus," "The Boat," and "The Royal." The Metal Worker, *Nov. 15, 1890. Value would depend on condition and material (copper would be highly prized.)* **$35-$125+**

Lyon; Breveté en France" & "A l'Etranger Stoker S.G.D.B.," Lyon, France, 1-7/8" deep x 7-1/4"L x 5-1/2"W, c.1870s (?). • *Breveté en France* means Patented in France; **S. G. D. B.** stands for *Sans Garantie Du Gouvernement*, or, registered with, but not warranted by, the government. This is more likely to be collected for its decorative value & very small size. My mother, Mary Mac Franklin, kept a sort of potpourri in hers. .... **$115+**

Coal hod, wood with tin interior, cast brass handles, English, mid to late 19th C............................ **$65+**
Coal hod or scuttle, japanned & tôle-decorated heavy sheet tin with original tin liner, for the parlor, flowers & scrolls on black background, cast brass handles on side, nice feet, slanted hinged lid, this was the type of coal vase called a purdonium, back stenciled "Mfd. by Sidney Shepards Co.," Buffalo, NY, 23"H, 3rd quarter 19th C. Decorators' crossover interest. Imported European coal hods are sold as decorative items. .... **$200+**

❖ NOTES ❖

1890s Coppersmith Explains: John Fuller Sr., author of occasional articles in a series called "Art of Coppersmithing," in *The Metal Worker*, wrote about "coal scoops and coal hods" as well as "coal scoopettes" (yuckette word!), in Article XVIII, Nov. 15, 1890. • See XXXX XI-5. • Some interesting terminology is used, which may either explain or confuse our notions of what's what. A number of horizontal coal containers with long "lower lips," like pelicans or pouters, all have flared feet and Fuller calls them all "coal scoops." Only two designs are called "coal hods" – one is a vertical cylinder with tipping handle, arched falling handle and a roller coaster top edge to form a scoop mouth when held horizontally; the other looks almost identical to another that is called a scoop. Finally, the little scoop shovel used to remove coal from a receptacle is called a "scoopette." All the designs, which Fuller encourages metal workers to make, have names. As usual in his articles, Fuller mixed past & present tenses: "Coal scoops were made in a number of fashions, among which, besides the common hod, were the round mouthed scoop; the square mouthed or flat bottom; the Tudor; the Florence; the Nautilus; the Royal; the Boat; and the Helmet. Some of these names are variable, according to the factories in which they are made, while others have had the same name from the time they were first designed. The hod has always been a hod, and the common round mouth shape [he calls it a hod] has never received any other cognomen."

Fuller goes on to say, in the only clue I've found to dates, that "We will now endeavor to describe the manufacture of several scoops in which we participated some forty years since [*ie.* c.1850], and while there have been deviations made during this long time ... it would seem that nothing of any marked importance has been introduced to inconvenience one from resuming work as of yore." Most of the designs he describes measure 12" diameter at front, 13-1/2" at back, and are 18" long. He writes that "the ears may be cast or wrought" and the tubular handles are bent of 3/4" pipe, "filled and bent, then filed and burnished." (pp. 28-29.)

Coal scuttle, not antique, hammered & pieced rounded copper body with brass base, large gravy-boat-type pouring lip, lion's head fittings for swinging handle, blue and white Delft porcelain hand grips on back handle & large swinging handle, supposed to be a "traditional Dutch Coal Scuttle," made in Holland, three sizes: 9-1/2"H, 12-1/4"H, 15-3/4"H, all measured to lip, sold through the mail in 1973 ads in *House Beautiful*, etc. The value now is for the look, not as antique.. **$65-$125**

Coal scuttle or vase, japanned & stenciled tin, highly decorative, cast iron feet & handle on pull-down bin front, counterweighted so as to be self-closing, holds small supply of coal for parlor heating stove, from F. A. Walker catalog, English (?), c.1870s. • Chance of finding one with japanning & stenciling intact, and without major dings & dents, equals that of finding a Model-T in factory condition.................. **$115-$150+**

Coal scuttle or vase, pieced sheet metal in lighthouse shape, painted black, flower-like pressed white glass knob on tight fitting lid, bail handle with wooden grip, little decorative cast iron feet, American, 13-3/4"H, c.1870s to 1880s. .... **$55-$70**

Coal scuttle or vase, tôle (decorated tin), footed helmet-shaped basket with high arched handle, domed lid

XI-6. "Patent Hand Revolving Pan," *or confectioner's nut roaster. "It will pay the Retailer to manufacture Cream, Jordon and Burnt Almonds, which can be made fresh everyday. The goods made in this pan are more like the Hand-made goods. The sugar coating does not become so hard and brittle. This pan will also do three times the work of the old-fashioned swinging pan. ... Put one in your store window and set a boy to work making goods." Broadside signed by Thomas Burkhard, date unknown, but looks to be 1860s-80s. I looked under everything I could think of in the Patent Index to find exact date, but couldn't find anything.* **$300+**

with cast iron finial, cast brass lion's head side handles, could possibly be a **chestnut urn**, used to carry hot chestnuts to the table, but none depicted in book on Pontypool & Usk japanned wares shows a handle like this one, from Pontypool or Usk, or Wolverhampton, 25"H, c.1800 to 1810....................... **$500-$750+**

XI-5. Coal vases. *Japanned and "handsomely ornamented." (L) Three cast iron fancy feet, fire iron attachment in back, and a half-cylindrical "vase" decorated in Japanese motifs, after the high (and low) fashion of the day. The "japanned" finish, by the way, does refer to the country Japan, but only because of its attempted resemblance to the fine lacquer finish used by generations of Japanese artisans. Japoniste motifs, also imitative, decorated all kinds of minor and major decorative arts in America, beginning with the 1850s opening of Japan to U.S. trade, and then in full bloom after the 1876 world fair. Mfd. by Heinz & Munschauer, noted for their birdcages, depicted in 1882 catalog. (R) Patented self-closing vase, cast feet, from F. A. Walker import catalog, 1870s. Valuable only if finish is in very good condition.* **$115-$150+**

❖ NOTES ❖

1838 American Coal Scuttles – "Thomas Darby & Son, 160 Bowery [NYC], exhibited specimens of brass and copper coal scuttles, at the late fair, and obtained a premium. Mr. Darby claims to have first carried this manufacture into successful operation in this country, and offers them of as good quality and as cheap as the imported. They are articles required in almost every family. We hail the successful commencement of the manufacture of every new article of general use and necessity, as the commencement of a new era in the history of our productive industry, and the name of the pioneer should be enrolled on the catalogue of benefactors. Let any one just ask the question – what will be the difference to the country, whether a coal scuttle is made and sold here, or imported from England and sold. It is, simply, that in the one case the money is in the country, and in the other, it is out of the country. We hope every American will purchase Mr. Darby's coal scuttles, as long as he sells as good and as cheap scuttles as the imported." From a report, in the Dec. 1838 *Journal of the American Institute* on the 11th annual Fair, Oct. 1838, sponsored by the American Institute, NYC, which fostered knowledge of invention and the improvement of manufactures.

Coal shovel, cast iron, for stoves, "Boss," Indiana Stove Co., c.1890s-1910s. .... **$25+**

Coal shovel, heavy cast iron, "DMI Co.," American, late 19th C (?). The only companies I could find fitting this at all were "Detroit - Michigan Stove Co.," from the 1930s, and Matthai-Ingram, much earlier. .... **$10+**

Coal tongs, cast iron, small & decorative, c.1890s-1910s. .... **$15+**

Coal tongs, cast iron with spring in hinge, possibly mfd. by Matthai-Ingram, American, 12"L, late 19th C. .... **$20+**

Conjurer, also spelled conjuror, a magical portable cooking stove & vessel in one, of heavy tin plate, shaped like a cake carrier or bandbox Round, sheet iron bottom part or stand is ventilated with holes & has a small "hearth" or fire place let into one side. Above is a close-fitting container for food, with slightly-domed close-fitting lid with strap handle. American, prob. early 19th C. .... **$200+**

Conjurer kettle, or camp kettle, heavy tin tea kettle in odd shape – a very very short cylinder with flat bottom, flat top with small biscuit cutter lid, curved spout comes out of top, with normally sized & placed forged iron handle. This was supposed to set down into a tall cylindrical portable sheet iron stove, with very short strap iron feet, in the base of which was built a small fire over a draft hole. Conjurers, or conjurors, were meant for cooking in non-kitchen settings, and were said to require but 3 sheets of paper to cook a steak. English (?), 8" diam., mid 19th C. Price range for kettle, which in a pure sense, is incomplete – not being with its conjurer. .... **$50+**

❖ NOTES ❖

Conjurers, Necromancers, & Chafing Dishes. I am indebted to A. H. T. Robb-Smith, Woodstock, England, who wrote me years ago about these devices to see if I had anything to add to research he had done, a skimming of which I have used here. It seems clear that a conjurer is related to a brazier or chafing dish (see Chapter XII). Behind them all was the idea to cook with a small, economical amount of fuel. The conjurer was very like the necromancer that probably preceded it, and was an ad hoc quick cooker fueled by strips of burning paper. Also related are portable cast iron ship-board stoves, called a caboose, cabouse, or camboose, for which a Dutch oven, in turn, was sometimes substituted. Etymologically this is intriguing because it is believed that the word "caboose" is of Dutch origin. Robb-Smith found a description of a necromancer in the first edition, **1747, of Hannah Glasse's** *The Art of Cookery*: "Take a large pewter or silver dish, made like a deep soop dish, with an edge about an inch deep on the inside, on which the lid fixes (with an handle at top) so fast [snugly] that you may lift it up full, by that handle without falling." She says layer it with 6 lbs. of mutton, onion, turnips, etc., cut into thin strips, cover with boiling water, close it up, and "hang the dish on the back of two chairs by the rim, have ready three sheets of brown paper, tare each sheet into five pieces, and draw them through your hand, light one piece and hold it under the bottom of the dish, moving the paper about; as fast as the paper burns light another, till all is burnt, and your meat will be enough; 15 minutes just does it." (p.51.) In **1797, Patent conjurers** were adv'd. by NY tinplate

worker Dewsbury Crawley, exactly like the English Conjurers or "little cooking vehicles" made by the "real and first inventor [viz. Lloyd, London]." He added that it would be convenient for ships' masters "as it will enable them to cook in the cabbin. Also on fishing parties as the fish may be cooked immediately without a fireplace or cabouse." Also in **1797, Thomas Passmore**, Philadelphia Quaker, advertised his "exclusive right of making ... the Conjurer," adding "... it is perfectly innocent and harmless." None of his were "More than 12 inches in diameter." **Eliza Acton's** *Modern Cookery*, **1845**, describes a block tin apparatus with a sheet iron base, into the "aperture" of which you put "a sheet or two of paper" for fuel; steaks or chops within cooked in 8 to 10 minutes. Chafing dishes, fueled by alcohol lamps, are related to ancient braziers – footed, handled firepans for cooking & heating rooms, & to conjurers, etc.

•   •   •

The Conjuror, or Camp Kettle – "Some years ago, an apparatus of this name was very generally sold in London, where some may yet be found at the ironmongers, and is remarkable for the expedition with which a small piece of meat may be dressed in it; sufficient for one person may be done in less than five minutes; and a pint of water can be boiled in the same time, the only fuel being half a sheet of thick brown paper. In the interior of a cylinder of sheet iron, an iron cone ... perforated, is placed over a hole in the bottom. A shallow dish of tin, with its [flat] cover, holds the meat, suppose a beefsteak, and fits exactly into the top of the cylinder. There is a little door on the side, through which the paper wrapped round the cone is set fire to; the door is then shut. The heat of the flame being confined altogether within the cylinder, very soon cooks the meat, an effect which is assisted by the steam being confined by the cover of the dish. The smoke passes off by a pipe. ... This little machine has been found extremely useful, not only in fishing or shooting parties, and other occasions where a dinner might be required at a distance from home, but likewise in numberless instances in the house where cooked meat or hot water may be wanted quickly, and when it is inconvenient to light a fire, particularly in summer. It is, perhaps, impossible to carry economy, convenience, and expedition farther than by this apparatus; but it must be admitted that by this process the meat is neither roasted, fried, baked, nor stewed; but it is completely done, and, with proper management, very palatable for those who have a good appetite." Webster & Parkes, *An Encyclopædia of Domestic Economy.* 1848 NY edition of English book of 1845. Sounds for all the world like a microwave oven!

Cook stoves – See section: Ranges & Stoves, this chapter

Drying oven, tall oblong box with small smokestack on top, galvanized iron, 2 sets of double doors, stacked one over other, reveal drying or baking shelves, used on top of range or stove, "Zimmerman Fruit & Vegetable Dryer & Bake Oven," mfd. by Zimmerman Fruit Dryer Co., Cincinnati, OH. In May 1880 there were "over 11,000 in use." .... **$45-$75**

Fireless cooker, metal box with 2 wells containing original soapstone heater discs (the most common material because it holds heat so well), 2 lids, with clip fasteners, stones were heated on range then put in the cooker, then the special deep pan was set over

XI-7. Fireless cooker. *"Caloric – the Auto Cook,"* Caloric Fireless Cookstove Co., Grand Rapids, MI. 17"H x 36"L x 15"W, "solid quartered oak, furnished complete with German-made enamel ware, patent revolving bar-lock covers." On casters. Ladies' Home Journal ad, April 1906. The collector value here is quite a bit due to the oak, which is a nice go-with for quarter-sawn oak tables and chairs in today's family room kitchens. **$75+**

the disc, "Thermatic," American, c.1890s-1910s. • Because some of these were insulated with straw, at least the homemade ones, they were also known as haybox cookers. .... **$50-$100**

Fireless cooker, oak chest with 2 lids, each covering a metal lined well with a soapstone disc at the bottom, which were heated in or on the stove, plopped in, the food in cylindrical vessels put in on top, for slow cooking without fire! This one with its original vessels & their lids, "Caloric" – "Hygienic, Scientific, Economical," Caloric Fireless Cook Stove Co., Janesville, WI, 14"H x 29"L x 15" deep, the vessels shy of

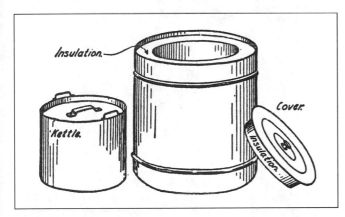

XI-8. Fireless cooker. *"Two vessels, one inside the other, separated by sawdust, asbestos, or other poor conducting material. Foods are heated in the usual way to the boiling point or to a high temperature, and are then placed in the inner vessel. The heat of the food cannot escape through the non-conducting material which surrounds it, and hence remains in the food and slowly cooks it." Bertha M. Clark, General Science, NY: American Book Co., 1912.* **$20-$30**

12" diam., early 20th C. .... **$75+**

Fireless cooker, wooden box with all aluminum inside, including pots, pans, racks & lids, 2 holes with soapstone heater discs, "The Ideal," Toledo Cooker Co., Toledo, OH, early 20th C. • They also made cookers with wooden boxes, & steam cookers. .... **$35+**

Fireless cooker, oak box like blanket chest, 3 wells, enamelware kettles with lids that lock on when twisted like a bayonet mount, "The Auto Cook," mfd. by Caloric Fireless Cook Stove Co., Grand Rapids, MI, 17"H x 36"L x 15"W, c.1905. .... **$50+**

Fireless cooker, metal box printed to look like wood, 3 holes with aluminum lining, single chest lid, "Rapid," mfd. by William Campbell Co., Detroit, MI, c.1919. .... **$25-$45**

Fireless cooker range, looks like small apartment stove, electric powered rather than the heated stone type, pull-out drawer or bin below with insulated box that looks like old-fashioned fireless cooker, oven above that with Pyrex™ window, hotplate-grill style top. The usual concept behind a "fireless cooker" is that the food is partly cooked on some other stove, prior to being put for finishing in the cooker. This "Campbell's Rapid", invented by William Campbell, is combo range & cooker, with a thermostat that turns electricity on and off as needed to maintain the temperature. The fireless cooker part is in the lower pull-out bin. There's an oven above that, and a stove top grill on top. William Campbell Co., Alliance, OH, & Georgetown, Ontario, Canada, c.1925. .... **$75+**

❖ NOTES ❖

Flue stops – An ad in *The Metal Worker*, April 12, 1890, shows a flue stop trade-named the "Crystal," made by Haslet, Flanagen & Co. of Philadelphia, and patented July 19, 1887, Sept. 4, 1888; and April 9, 1889. They were packed for wholesale trade 12 to a box, half "gold," half "silver," and were 8-3/8" diameter. The one in the ad has a gadrooned border surrounding a picture of an old mill, bridge and trees. • A supplier's catalog put out by Buhl Sons Co., Detroit, c. 1919, shows several "Flue Stops." Two have stamped brass frames, with a sort of egg and dart design to the brass part, the centers, as shown in the catalog, both have a snowy scene of a tall steepled church. Another, "The Royal," which has a double figure-8 spring wire fastener on the back which popped into the stove pipe hole, was available either in a brass finish or "fancy assorted [lacquered] colors." The 2nd flue cover, "The Perfect," came in a brass finish, with "fancy assorted centers." This cover had two spring wire ears, sticking out both sides, which were bent into the stove pipe opening. A third type, "The Gem is a Flat Stop which can be papered over if desired. It has a Patent Fastener at the center" (the double figure-8 wire one). It came painted gray with "fancy assorted centers" – presumably the same cheap chromolith landscapes, etc., that the other(s) came with. • Any of you who have been in a store offering supplies for wood-burning stoves have seen modern flue covers. They are stamped metal, very yellow; they are brass-plated rather than brass, or may have an off-white or beige baked-on paint finish, with exceedingly ugly, poorly-printed color pictures glued on the centers. You could do better with a picture cut from any magazine – which is what I think the advertiser meant by "can be papered over." • **Hand-painted covers.** Most desirable are those with oil-painted scenes or images painted on the centers, amateur but charming, and some qualify as folk art.

Flue cover, also called a chimney hole cover or flue stop, very decorative cast iron, probably made by a stove foundry to match a particular line of stoves, late 19th C. These have gotten very collectible, as more people collect "architectural elements." The cast iron ones are highly desirable. .... **$65+**

Flue cover, japanned tin, brown color, put in place when cook or heating stove was dismantled for summer leaving hole where stovepipe would ordinarily go. Although it has nothing to do with flues, the trade name reflects the marketing magic of an exciting new source of power: "Electric," American, 14-1/2" diam., pat'd. Jan. 7, 1890. .... **$5+**

Flue cover, brass colored metal frame, hanging brass-color chain, 2 girls in bonnets under glass, 19th C or early 20th C. .... **$15+**

Flue cover, brass frame, chromolith depiction of lovely girl in garden, German, late 19th or early 20th C. .... **$15+**

Flue cover, brass frame, chromolithograph of dancing Victorian children, music by a bug orchestra, American, litho prob. German, 9-1/2" diam., c.1880s. • This cute conceit, of the cheerful bugs playing music, is found on all kinds of color lithographed commercial art of the period. It always amazes how peculiar some Victorian art is. Dancing bug pictures nowadays would be featured in the before panel on a Raid™ ad, I'm afraid, or a movie by Disney. .... **$25+**

Flue cover, brass frame, color depiction of English countryside with lots of teensy flowers, only 5" diam., c.1900. .... **$7+**

Flue cover, brass frame, decoratively stamped border, chromolith picture of Little Boy Blue, American, 9" diam., c.1890s-1910s. .... **$15+**

Flue cover, brass frame, litho of 2 curly-headed little girls, clip back, American (?), 7-1/2" diam., late 19th or early 20th C. .... **$15+**

Flue cover, brass frame, litho of 2 girls on a lake, swans around the boat, clip back, German (?), c.1890s-

XI-9. Flue covers, for covering hole in wall where stovepipe (usually parlor or heating stove) goes through, when the stove is taken down for the summer. (T-L) Stamped tin, with brass-like finish, cheap chromolith picture. From Lalance & Grosjean, 1890. (R) A similar one, called a "crystal flue stop ... the handsomest now on the market. Gold and silver finish." Pat'd. July 19, 1887, Sept. 4, 1888, and April 9, 1889. Haslet, Flanagen & Co., Philadelphia. The Metal Worker, April 12, 1890. (B-L) "Gold lacquered, wide flange" flue stopper, with "fancy picture." 8-1/4", steel spring to snap into hole. Wheeling Corrugating Co., 1921. $10-$15+

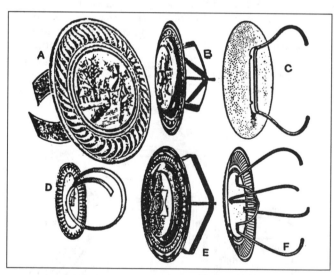

XI-10. Flue covers, showing different types of hoops. (A) Spring steel. Sears & Roebuck, c.1900. (B) "Higgins Perfect" flue stops, with 5/8" double hoops, brass-lacquered embossed cover, 6" diam. (C) Androck Folding, with flat cover for papering over. Green enamel finish. (D) "Gold lacquered" disc with no picture, single coiled flat spring. Central Stamping Co., 1920. (E) A "Higgins Single Hoop Star Cover," embossed and "brass lacquered," no picture. (F) "Edward's Tip-Top" flue stop, with double folding spring steel hoop, colored pictures, embossed metal disc, lacquered. brass 9-3/4" diam. B, C, E, and F all from The Washburn Co., Rockford, IL, catalog from 1927. $7-$15+

1910s. • These fancified brass frame flue covers were available with stove pipe collars that has matching stamped flanges. .... **$10+**

Flue cover, brass frame, lithograph of wintry church scene glued in center, American, 8-1/2" diam., c.1890s to 1920s. .... **$7+**

Flue cover, brass frame, lithographed picture of horses & stable, American (?), c.1900. .... **$7+**

Flue cover, brass frame, reverse painting of sylvan scene on glass, prob. late 19th C. .... **$65+**

Flue cover, brass frame, stamped & beaded border, chain hanger, well-done, "naive" hand-painted snow scene in oils, depicts shed, bar, trees, lots of snow, & large black dog walking across center of scene, American, large – 12" diam., late 19th C. ..... **$125+**

Flue cover, brass frame, with beading around outside, oil painting of pug dog inside, no mark, 12" diam., c.1890s-1910s. • You compete here with crossover dog & folk art collectors, so if you find something like this that's cheap, it's probably because those collectors haven't yet harvested the flue cover field. .... **$125+**

Flue cover, tin frame, stamped with design, center picture painted in oils of child feeding cat, 19th C. .... **$12+**

Flue cover, glass & color-tinfoil, brass chain hanger, depiction of kitchen with little girls paring apples by hand, prob. European, big 12-1/2" diam., late 19th or early 20th C. • Not very many flue covers have kitchen depictions, as the fancier ones were meant to cover the hole when the parlor stove was knocked down for the summer. .... **$45+**

Flue cover, glass & colored tinfoil, brass hanging chain, religious depiction of 2 children watched over by an angel, European, 12" diam., late 19th or early 20th C. .... **$15+**

Flue cover, tin, chromolithograph picture of garden girl with red roses, spring clips to hold in hole, 8" diam., c.1890s-1910s. .... **$10+**

Flue cover, tin, stamped & painted, with chromolith farm scene on paper center, 19th C or early 20th C. .... **$10+**

Flue cover, tinsel frame in dark blue, brass chain, center depicts young woman with water jug, Belgian, late 19th or early 20th C. • I believe that the flue covers with chains are as a rule older than the spring clip ones. They fit in better with the Victorian conceit of hanging as many decorative things on the wall as possible. .... **$20+**

Flue cover, tinsel frame, rich red color, brass chain hanger, chromolith family scene in center, European, early 20th C. .... **$15+**

Flue cover, brass frame, small blond boy's portrait bust wearing red winter cap, American or European, 8"

diam., c.1890s-1910s. .... **$10+**

Flue cover, brass with glass cover, depicts bust of young girl surrounded by flowers, 19th C. ...... **$30+**

Grate shaker, ornate cast iron tool, used to move the grate & shake out the ashes & small clinkers to the floor of the stove's firebox for cleaning. Bements Stove Co., late 19th or early 20th C. .... **$7+**

Oven door, for bake oven, cast iron with hinged plump heart with sliding vent & motto "Heart of the Home" cast on it, dealer Emanon Corner Antiques says it was made in Ringoes, NJ, first half 19th C. • It has high collecting value for several reasons. First, the heart and the motto. Second, because it is not just decoration, as more and more colonial revivalists have bake ovens and walk-in hearths built in their 21st C homes, to use for cooking the old way. Price range mine, not Emanon Corner's. .... **$700+**

Oven door, cast iron, fancy casting, "F. Earl Landis, Brunerville Foundry," Brunerville, Land County, PA, late 19th C. .... **$75-$125+**

Oven door, for built-in hearth oven, cast iron, strap latch, pintail hinges, draft plate, design of 5 fluted fans, "Lincoln Foundry," Bath, ME, 11-1/2" x 15", early 19th C. These so rarely come on the market it's hard to tell what might happen to the prices. Some doors have cast designs that appeal to folk art collectors. .. **$475+**

Portable oven, sheet steel & cast iron, nickeled hinges & fittings, see-through glass window in drop-down door shows 2 shelves in one oven, came in two sizes – 13-1/4"W (#125), and 21"W (#140), "Bolo," mfd. by Griswold Mfg Co., Erie, PA, c.1920. Another Bolo I've read about but not seen is about 22"H x 13-1/4"W, two ovens connected by a flue. • In the 1930s, Griswold made a "pie oven," with a black finish, slightly smaller than the #125 Bolo, worth about the same. .... **$115+**

Portable canal boat stove, cast iron, 2 burners, 3 legged, small hearth, American or English (?), 18"H, late 19th C. .... **$400+**

Portable stove, for fishing vessels or whaling ships, small cast iron wide-lipped fire pot with inset rack for putting cooking vessel on, forged iron bail handle, fits on base that has 3 legs and a little hearth, American, 9-1/2"H x 13" diam., 19th C. See also the Camp stoves, esp. the Griswold one. .... **$300+**

Radiator, ornate cast iron, meant for dining room with 2 compartments called hot closets built right into it for keeping food warm, spectacular item – and think how many are rusted out in dumps or melted down during two World Wars. American, late 1880s to 90s. **Futurewatch.** I predict that even as this book is being printed there will be a number of people discovering & collecting ornate old steam & hot water radiators, and the salesmen's samples of them. ..... **$450+**

"Range" or "Cook Stove"?

Like many people, I tend to use the word "stove" somewhat indiscriminately, even when I might actually mean "range." It's easy to learn the difference between a mid-19th century range and stove, but not so easy in the 20th century, when the two terms often seem to be a regional choice meaning the same thing.

For centuries, and into the 19th century (and much later in many parts of the world) cooking was done in fireplaces or on hearths. In the 18th century came what are called **brick-set ranges** – actually an "arrangement" such as a row, or, say, a set of three holes by two holes in the brick top of a brick cabinet or box, with air intake at floor level, and cast iron doors for the oven(s), for feeding the fire, and for taking out ashes and coals. Pots and griddles could be set over, or down into, the holes (called range eyes, or boiling holes), or raised above them. (See the adapter ring picture X-3 in Chapter X.) Many, perhaps most, brick-set ranges were built into the old brick fireplaces where cooking was done at an earlier time; others might be built along a wall.

After brick-set ranges, the next new idea developed in the second quarter of the 18th century, with cast iron **five-plate stoves** or **jamb stoves** that were European in design. The plate stoves were a sort of cooking box assembled and bolted together from "plates" of cast iron, and set on a hearth. The plates are more or less decorative, and some resemble cast iron firebacks. These plate stoves could be broken down and moved, unlike brick-set ranges, and were a step toward mass-production. The carved wood casting models could be plunked into damp casting sand over and over and cast again and again, and presumably a person with one broken stove plate could order another. (Cast iron can't be mended by welding.) In some sect communities (see XI-14 and -15, XI-8 and -9) brick-set and plate stoves remained in use close to the 20th century. By the 1740s or so, six-plate stoves, or close stoves, with legs came in, and also Benjamin Franklin's small free-standing stove which had a much larger hearth area – about as much as a fourth of the total length of the stove. Twenty years later came ten-plate stoves, which had an oven and hinged doors on either side.

Cast iron ranges and step-top cook stoves came next, around 1815; they could be set all the way or partly into the old fireplace to make use of flues and chimneys. This is when I think the nomenclature problem began. A wide fireplace could take a free-standing "leg base range," or a "cabinet base range," and a really wide fireplace could accommodate a cook stove.

To help visualize these: a range is an oblong with one of the long sides against a wall or existing fireplace back; and a cook stove is an oblong with a short side against wall or fireplace. The three interrelated, telling differences between a range and an older cook stove are (1) positioning and layout of oven(s); (2) placement of oven door(s); and (3) placement of flue.

According to stove/range expert Cliff Boram and the stove industry (never called the "range industry"), what defines a **range is** its smoke collar for the flue(s), which is on the back long side of the top, and a front-opening oven door on the side where the cook would stand. A range may have four, six, or eight holes, or "range eyes." (Or even more for hotels.) The stove industry actually used both "stove" and "range" in advertising copy for ranges, but not vice versa.

A **cook stove** – according to Boram and the 19th century stove industry – has its smoke collar (hence, its flue) on the back short side of the top, with the oven running through the short axis, with a door on either end of the oven, so that if the cook stood in front of the stove, she would go around to either side to open the oven. And it appears that a cook stove usually has only four holes. (A box stove has one, or maybe two.) By the late 1880s, cook stoves with eye-level, raised ovens were available.

Nowadays, depending on what part of the country you live in, you call your gas or electric cooking-station either a stove or a range. And if you cook on a wood-burner, you probably call it a "wood stove," even if technically it's a range. Just to complicate things, in England the word **"cooker"** was widely used for what appear to be both ranges and stoves. Also, some dealers, who primarily are in business to help people who want one old stove to use in their kitchens, aren't as fussy about terminology as collectors.

• • •

Gobbledecook in 1829 – To share with you the charm of technical journalism from 175 years ago, I will transcribe a few paragraphs on an invention granted John J. Hess from an 1829 issue of the *Journal of the Franklin Institute* [Philadelphia]. "For an Economical Cooking Stove; John J. Hess, Philadelphia, March 19 [1829]." The inventor claims "This stove consists of seventeen pieces, or plates, independent of eight doors, and three grates, all resting upon four feet, which, when properly applied, and put together, form a perfect, whole, and entire construction, capable of performing, with rare economy, a great variety of cooking operations, together with numberless other services in housewifery, being heated by a very small portion of wood, or anthracite coal." The *JFI* editor advises that "The foregoing is the exordium of the specification, and the following is its peroration." Then back to Hess: "With this apparatus, and attentive care in its operations, great economy must be preserved in the consuming material used for fuel. Steam is generated from the boilers, and when received into proper vessels, can be applied to all the delicate cookery of luxurious dishes, without the aid of assistants; and important advantage to families. Boiling water is always in readiness; and with the same fire, baking of meats, and bread, or fruit, roasting, broiling, stewing, frying, boiling, and fricaseeing, are expeditiously going on, at one and the same time!"

The editor adds "There is a something so stimulating in the foregoing enumeration of properties and results, as to make us wish to anticipate the usual 'hour of prime'; and had we one of Mr. Hess's stoves, we certainly should hurry the cook. As it is impossible to describe this stove without engravings, and as most of our readers, like ourselves, are more inclined to partake of a good dinner than to study the means of preparing it, we will merely give them the address of the patentee, who resides at No. 237 North Second Street, Philadelphia, who is prepared to gratify the taste of those who will apply to him."

• • •

An article in *The Metal Worker*, June 4, 1892: **"What is the cost of a stove?** Perhaps there is no question put to stove manufacturers that admits of so many and so widely differing answers as this. Some stove makers stoutly maintained that their stoves cost 4¢ per pound and upward; other concerns ... sell their stoves at 3¢ per pound, and figures even lower than 3¢ are talked about." (Cook stoves weighed from about 300 pounds up to 475 pounds or more.) The largest cost by far was for the actual iron castings of the stove parts – about 20% of the total cost. Mountings & trim accounted for about 9% of the total, with plating & buffing an additional 3-1/4%. Copper or enameled iron hot water reservoirs & their fittings were a little more than 1% of the total. Remember that at this time, a big cast iron stove with nickel trimming could be bought retail for under $20; less fancy ones, with fewer niceties, sold for under $15. Would they laugh to know that a cook stove originally costing 4¢ per pound, or $14 for a 350-pound stove might cost $4 or $8 per pound now?

• • •

Range, range in the home – A complaint aired March 1839, in the *Journal of the Franklin Institute of Philadelphia*, goes "The greatest objection to the kitchen ranges devised by various ingenious projectors, is the want of simplicity. Cooks will not take the trouble of learning to use them, or, which is necessary, to keep in order the various novel articles by which they are accompanied." By the 1870s, probably most cooks were either supplied with simpler ranges, or experience as their teacher.

. . .

Taking Down Stoves – "Some people do not know when to take down a heating stove. The good wife may be one such, for a day that is warm enough to thaw out the flies is a suggestion to her that the heating stove should go. She tells her husband that the time has come to call the tinner to come at once. The husband is so full of fear that she will mention the subject of garden and ask him to bring home infantile cabbage plants, that he is only too glad to have stoves the only 'spring' subject. Unfortunately, he neglects to tell the tinner. The fire has died out in the stove and the evening is cool, so he sits by the kitchen stove.

"The next morning is rather cool, so the wife allows a fire to be made. For a few days all goes well, but then the sun comes out like a Fourth of July parade, and then there is no use of talking, the stove must go. As usual, he forgets to inform the tinner, and when he comes home he is told that no further foolishness will be allowed.

"The husband hunts up an old coat and a hat that the tramps would not take as a gift. The kitchen table is used for a pedestal, and on this he stands. The wire that holds the pipe to the ceiling is removed with care, and then as the wife and hired girl stand with outstretched arms, the stove pipe is detached from its surroundings. Two joints of the upright pipe slip out, and as they fall our man tries to catch them, and in so doing tips the pipe in his hands and gives wife and hired girl a deluge of ashes. The room resembles the crater of a volcano retired from active business.

"After much tugging and lifting the stove is got as far as the back kitchen by placing a pair of roller skates under it. The carpet is swept and the table is returned to the kitchen. It is then discovered there is no stopper in the chimney; when found, it must be put in, so the kitchen table has another journey. All goes well for a few days, until a cold wave. At last the tinner is sent for, and soon the stove is again in position, where it remains until all doubts about the weather are set to rest. After ice cream has been in vogue for some time, the tinner and his men come and in a few moments take down and away the stove and its pipes. There is no dirt on the carpet, and the hired girl's hair is free from ashes. This family has concluded that the proper person to transport stoves is the stove man." Signed "Tin Chips," as quoted in *The Metal Worker*, April 23, 1892. The subject of taking down or putting up the stove with the seasons had high humor value for Victorians and early 20th century folk. Many post cards, and lots of stereoviews treated the subject.

Pricing Old Stoves & Ranges

Prices for most of the stoves shown here reflect value for stoves that have been restored and are in good working order. Added value for stoves completely re-nickeled; even more for those first copper-plated, then nickeled, which adds a certain soft warmth to the silvery metal. Generally speaking, if you want to buy a nice-looking, somewhat ornate, nickeled-and-shined cast iron range or stove of the late 19th century, rebuilt so that it all works, you can expect to pay at least $3,500. The fanciest of these kitchen pianos may have colored enameling (blue is especially desirable), fancy re-nickeled trimmings, overhead ovens, ornate hob shelves – the works, and if they have been rebuilt or refurbished, expect to pay between at least $5,000 and $12,000 or more. These prices are mainly for coal or wood stoves. For most early 20th century gas ranges, expect to pay up to $4,000, depending on the features, the color, the size; some may be a lot less, some a lot more. Wood & coal stoves can also be converted to work with gas or electricity, while retaining the outward appearance of its original state. Add about $1,000 to $2,000 for conversions. The days of finding a fabulous-looking 100 year old relic from a bygone kitchen for under $100 (and it wasn't all that long ago) are past. • Heating stoves such as parlor stoves and base burners, from the mid- to late-19th century, with some of the same trim and pizzazz of the cook stoves, generally cost less than cooking stoves – partly because hardly anyone would be able to use them. I bought one, an intricately-cast cylinder about 32"H, enameled cast iron with lion's heads, in order to make a sort of Japanese garden light with a big candle inside. Now for the lifestyle to go with it!

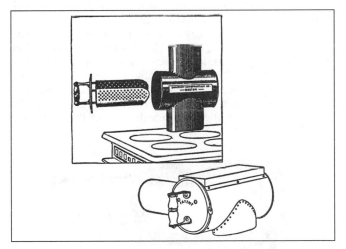

XI-11. Garbage carbonizer, to fit in stovepipe "between the stove and the flue of the chimney, and becomes a permanent fixture. It is a horizontal cylinder about 1/3 larger in diam. than the stovepipe. One end is removable, and attached thereto, on the inside, is a semi-circular pan or scoop, perforated along both sides and having solid ends and a tight bottom." The scoop is filled with the garbage and slid into place, where the heat eventually carbonizes it. "The carbon which remains is utilized as fuel," wrote Fannie Merritt Farmer from her Boston Cooking School, in praise of the gadget. Mfd. by New England Sanitary Co., Boston. American Kitchen Magazine, *April 1896.* **$5-$15**

So many Trojans – According to the 1860 U.S. census, Troy, NY, had three brass and bell founders, three iron works, eight stove manufacturers and 20 tinware manufacturers. That year, in the entire United States there were some 290 cast iron stove and hollowware foundries, at least among those counted in the Census. Think how many hundreds of thousands of collectible objects were made that year alone!

Cook stoves in 1847, In the *American Agriculturist* of Nov. 1847, comes the following lamentation, along with kudos for a new cooking-stove. "Stoves are now so generally used all over the Middle and Northern portions of the United States for cooking, that one is to be found in almost every dwelling. Common as they are, the mass of them are defective, and in many cases very poor. We feel that we are doing a great service to our readers by recommending them to the use of proper stoves for cooking, particularly the planters of the South whose system of economy in cooking is very bad at present, incurring a vast deal of labor and expense for fuel, to say nothing of the imperfect manner in which it is often done. In fulfillment of our promise in the October [1847] number, we would now call attention to Granger's iron-witch airtight cooking-stove ... the main object of which has been to get as perfect and convenient an implement as possible, and at the same time to have it simple and without complication of flues, dampers, &c. The front of the stove is lined with brick, which keeps up that steady even heat, which is so desirable in baking, and in which particular cast-iron ovens are found so defective. By means of the brick in this stove, the baking is more like the old fashioned brick-oven, which it is universally acknowledged bakes in the best manner. A summer-furnace on the hearth is also attached to the stove with two boiler holes on which any and all the boilers fit. The furnace will be found very desirable for summer use, when but little fire is wanted; as a few chips or charcoal will do the cooking. The furnace can also be used at the same time with the stove, giving six boiler holes. A gridiron is also well fitted to the hearth for broiling, by raking the coals directly from the fire-chamber on to the grate. The

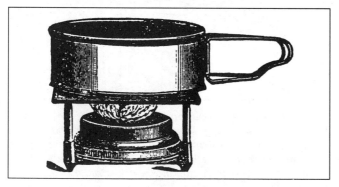

XI-12. **Portable**, or **pocket stove.** *"Houchin's Improved Patent," with gridiron and boiler (with folding handles) holding nearly one quart, which can be used as a drinking cup. Will "boil water in five minutes to make 2 or 3 cups of Tea, Coffee, or Chocolate, Boil Eggs, Stew Oysters, etc." Fueled with two tablespoonsful of alcohol; "the Lamp being filled with indestructible packing will not spill or explode." Houchin Mfg. Co., NYC. 1877 ad.* **$35**

XI-13. **Dining room radiator – two views.** *"Perfection," mfd. by Michigan Radiator & Iron Mfg. Co., Detroit. Shown open, it reveals the oven or "hot closet" above with a slotted shelf, and the smaller one below. Top "oven" is about 18"H x 21"W. Radiator came in seven sizes, from 35" to 65"L. The Metal Worker, Aug. 23, 1890. Since 1991 I have seen three of these installed in old houses.* **$450+**

grate in the fire-chamber is omitted, and the wood is burned directly on the bed of ashes, by which means the fire can be covered up and kept over night, which cannot be done on a grate; the expense of purchasing new grates is thus avoided." • The conservation of fuel that so occupied the minds of some 19th century editors & inventors was not based on any ecological or environmental beliefs or ideals. It was purely a matter of economics, of supply & transport. Heavily-populated areas, especially, needed to use as little fuel, wood or coal, as possible. How I wish, as I write this in 2002, that the U.S. had a president dedicated to preserving the natural resources of this beautiful country, instead of giving them all away to big industry.

North Carolinian Cook Stoves. E. Scott Boyce wrote, in *Economic & Social History of Chowan County, North Carolina*, 1888-1915 (NY: 1917) that in the studied area, by 1915, "probably 90% of home owners and 50% of all other families now have sewing machines; for cook-stoves, the percentage is about 98 and 75, respectively." So some people were still cooking over fires, probably still using the "creepers" Boyce wrote about [see Chapter X].

Designing Stoves: "How Solids Suggest Modern Products. – The cube and its elastic variations, called in geometry by the incredibly awkward name of 'rectangular parallelepipeds,' will probably be the most useful [in designing]. Stoves, refrigerators, kitchen cabinets, even the kitchen sink, are generally variations of these forms." Harold Van Doren, *Industrial Design, A Practical Guide* (NYC: McGraw-Hill, 1940).

Right and Left-Hand Ranges – It is somewhat difficult to tell just what the custom may be in different parts of the country or among different manufacturers or dealers. Ranges are made of several kinds. Some are double ranges with a fire-pot in the center and an oven on each side. Others are single ranges with a fire-pot on the left side and oven on the right. Other single ranges are made with fire-pot on right and oven on left. ... The one in ordinary use has the fire-pot on the left, oven on the right. The question arises, is this a right- or a left-hand range? As the vast majority of people are right-handed, it seems ... natural to suppose that the range most widely used would be constructed so as to be most convenient for them and would therefore be a right hand range. Yet this view is not taken by many manufacturers, who curiously enough regard the range in common use as a left-hand range, insisting that the location of the fire-pot fixes the name. Fuller & Warren's catalogue, for instance, says about their Diamond B range: 'This range has the fire-box constructed at the right side of the oven, hence it is termed a right-hand range, and for that reason it can often be used to advantage when a left-hand range or cook stove could not be used conveniently.'

"This peculiarity in naming ranges gives rise to a great deal of uncertainty in filling orders. One stove manufacturer, whose ranges are all made with fire-pots at the left, says that when he is asked by a customer for a left-hand range he invariably replies that he does not make them. While all his ranges are really left-hand, according to [Fuller & Warren's usage], he knows that his customer is seeking a range of a different type from those in common use, even if he does not use the term 'left-hand.' Other manufacturers, however, do not reason in the same way, but fill the order according to their own acceptation of the term. ... Among dealers it is very probable that the custom exists of calling a range right or left hand according to the oven.

"It would be most interesting to have the opinions of the trade on this question in nomenclature and their reasons for adopting the name ... they regard as correct. ... What say you? Is a right-hand range one with the oven on the right or the fire-pot on the right, and why?" Editor, *The Metal Worker*, March 15, 1890.

Cook stove, cast iron, oblong box, rather fancy 'bath tub' legs, 4 holes on top, oven & firebox doors on side, no maker's or founder's name, American, c.1840s-50s. .... **$1,000+**

XI-14. "Mennonite Woman cooking at a Hearth." *A raised hearth, almost a range. Note hams and sausages hanging high up to be smoked; also the trivet or stand on which the center utensil rests, with the fire underneath. The flat-bottomed frying pan at right has three rather tall legs and a long handle. The tall, round-bottomed pot at left also has legs. "The most primitive cooking arrangement was seen in Harvey County [Kansas]. This is merely a block of adobe or masonry, 2 feet high, built in the base of an ordinary chimney. Cooking is done by building straw and corncob fires under each vessel, like persons camping out."* Article on Mennonites, based on observances of Mr. H. Worrall, Shawnee County, KS, in American Agriculturist, *Dec. 1878.*

Cook stove, of type called a covered wagon stove, though not old enough to be for a covered wagon, cast iron, oval with slanted sides, flat top with 2 eyes, looks sort of like bath tub with little grate in side, 4 short legs, mfd. by Fischer Leaf Co., Louisville, KY, 12"H x 18"W x 12" deep, pat'd. 1879. .... **$350+**

Cook stove, cast iron, small oven, 4 burners, large flat hearth, 4 legs, design of front is like 6 fluted columns close together, "Summer and Winter Cooking

XI-15. "Interior of Mennonite Kitchen." *Also in Kansas. Note adobe or brick cooking range at right, and wash or laundry range at left, and the ubiquitous huge basket of corncob fuel. What look like ovens in the ranges are "fire doors" through which fuel was added. Baking ovens are seen as dark rectangles in the back wall, which is actually part of the main chimney. According to the* American Agriculturist, *Dec. 1878, one Mennonite settler asserted: "Americans burn money; we burn straw." Still true, alas.*

XI-16. Brickset range. *"Union Range," which won many medals and awards at the world's fair in London, and at others in U.S. and Canada. Moses Pond & Co., Boston, MA. Ad in* American Portrait Gallery, *1856. Note ovens, large oval boiler at left on range, and huge hot water kettle. Standing at right is a hot water heater, with pipes leading to upstairs!*

Stove No. 4," invented by famed stove designer Philo Penfield Stewart, Troy, NY, 41"H x 36"W, pat'd. Sept. 1838 (he was still patenting stoves 20 years later).. **$3,500+**

Cook & parlor stove, cast iron, actually a parlor stove but known as a dining room helper because the top is a small oven, "Oven Parlor No. 7," mfd. by Newberry, Filley & Co., Troy, NY, c.1854 to 1858............... **$2,000+**

Cook stove, electric, cast iron boxy body, flexible tubes coming up from back to attach to wall mounted box with switches & dials, ancient styling for hinges on oven door, 4 eyes, the lids of which make an even or flush working surface stove when not in use, oven has inner glass windowed door, "Carron," English, c.1912. Other electric items are in Chapter XVIII. For its design curiosity value: .... **$700+**

Range, cast iron, completely refurbished, re-nickeled, & painted with black high temperature paint (what used to be called "locomotive paint"), marked "Glenwood F" and "Glenwood Range #108," Perry & Co., Albany, NY, c.1906. .... **$2,500+**

❖ **NOTES** ❖

Nickel-plating – At Brimfield, MA, flea market, regular dealer Dave Erickson, of Erickson's Antique Stoves, explained nickel plating this way: the plater grinds & polishes the surface to be plated, then puts a heavy copperplate layer on & buffs that. The copper gives a warm glow to the nickel tone, & also is a "primer" to fill in minor imperfections. A good nickel-plater always puts the copper on first, then nickels the surface. Poor nickel-plating is obvious when you sight down the nickeled part from an extreme oblique angle and you see ridges, ripples, sanding & filing marks. Erickson sells completely restored, antique gas, woodburning and electric stoves and ranges.

Range, cast iron, "Imperial Clarion 8-20," mfd. by Wood & Bishop, Bangor, ME, late 19th C. .... **$2,500+**

Range, cast iron, nickeled copper, 6 burners, oven, warming oven, hot water reservoir, and all original accessory tools, "Copper Clad," 5 feet high, 19th C. .... **$4,500+**

Range, cast iron, nickeled iron decorative pieces with

XI-17. Range & stove. *Cast iron.* **(L)** *a brickset range, probably set into old high walk-in fireplace recess. Two flues – one at each back corner. Note decorative castings on doors. Cast by Sanders & Wolfe, successors to A. T. Dunham & Co., Troy, NY. Range pat'd. 1853.* **(R)** *a cook stove. Note hearth and decorative casting. Also Sanders & Wolfe, 1855 or 1856 ad.*

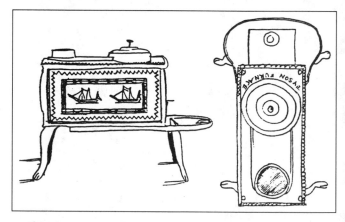

XI-18. Box or close stove, *with six plates, and four legs, but otherwise identical to a three-legged one that once belonged to trade-catalog-cataloguer Lawrence B. Romaine. Cast iron, 16"H x 23"L x 13"W, cast by Tyson Furnace, Plymouth, VT, dated 1839. This one was drawn from an Old Brookfield Tavern, Danbury, CT, ad in* The Magazine ANTIQUES, *from Nov. 1929.* **(L)** *The side view shows the ships that gave it its name "Mayflower" stove.* **(R)** */Bird's-eye view. The 3-legged version is depicted in Josephine Peirce's* Fire On the Hearth, *published in 1951. "Very rare" in 1929 ad, and "very popular design, possibly made other places [besides at Tyson], according to Peirce.*

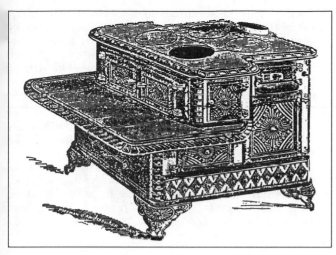

XI-19. Cook stove. *Cast iron, ornate all over in designs not dissimilar to pressed glass designs from the same period, which came from molds also. Mold-makers and other kinds of carvers all drew on patterns common to furniture, architectural ornament, woven Jacquard textiles, etc. See more on space-filling patterns in the mini-chapter on pie safes. Maker of this cook stove not mentioned, but I believe this is the "New World Air-Tight" cooking stove, mfd. by Vose & Co., Albany, NY. From a dealer's ad in Johnston's Detroit City Directory, 1857-58.*

acorn motif, very substantial base with cabriole legs, oven above, fold-down nickeled shelves on either side of flue, refurbished, "Crown Acorn," mfd. by Rathbone, Sard & Co., Albany, NY, 61"H x 64"W, pat'd. April 18, 1907 & Sept. 17, 1907. ..... **$5,000+**

Range, white gas/gasoline, beautiful blue porcelainized iron, nickel trim, "Quick Meal," Ringen Stove Co., early 20th C (in the late 19th & early 20th C, the maker's name was "Quick Meal Stove Co." .... **$3,800+**

Range, white gas/gasoline, cast iron, sheet iron, 3 side-by-side large burners & oven, burns white gas. Has white porcelainized panels on doors, ornate nickel trim & on the fancy versions there are small grill work doors that flip down to reveal niches for warming a bun or two or for keeping salt & pepper shakers, or perhaps a flour dredger, or some crackers to keep them crisp. Towel rack on side. A smaller one has one oven, no storage cupboard, no salt & pepper niche. All have a japanned tin & cast iron fuel tank & filter, with 4 cocks with air intake valves, connect with rubber tubes to the burners & oven, "Quick Meal," Ringen Stove Co., pat'd. Sept. 15, 1903, Mar. 31, 1908, Dec. 21, 1909. Collector Dewayne Ziegler has explained to me that "the long tubes on the end fill up with gas. Pull them out, light them, and shove them in a hole in your burner." Sounds like no easy feat to me!... **$3,000+**

Range, cast iron, very square & geometric "Eastlake" designs typical of designs on paper goods from the same period, no really rounded forms, exhibits the mold-makers' jigsaw gingerbread rather than more voluptuous hand-carving, oven, large water reservoir at side, nice hob shelf with cutout brackets, "Happy Thought," mfd. by Pittston Stove Co., Pittston, PA, dated 1884. Call it good karma or conversation piece, this stove has got a great collectible name. (There was also a "Grand Happy Thought," for the power of positive cooking.)......................... **$4,000+**

Range, ornate cast iron, warming ovens above, urn pedestals on either side of flue, 6 holes, water reservoir on side, "Grand Windsor," Windsor Stoves and Ranges, in Montgomery Ward catalog, and made at one of their foundries, late 19th C. .... **$3,500+**

XI-21. "Anti-clinker" stove, *the "Fearless No. 8" made by Rathbone, Sard & Co., Albany, NY, 1873. Called a "plain top" cook stove, it is shown here without the reservoir for hot water and the warming closet which would be attached at the right side. Clinkers are rock-hard pieces of coal which will not ignite, and had to be removed.*

XI-20. Air-tight stove, *toted by Uncle Sam-like figure, on top of advertising flyer dated 1872. C. H. Tyler, a dealer, referred to himself as "U. R. Uncle," and was located on Davis St., in Greenfield, MA.*

What's In a Name? – I suspect that there are other collectors, like me, who would pay extra, a sort of premium, because something had a really great name right on the front. A personal short list of favorite names for cooking stoves or ranges include: "Legal Tender," "Busy Bee," "Early Breakfast," "Merry Christmas," "Reindeer," "Shoo-Fly," "Alligator Range," and your choice of "Woman's Rights" or the "New Cinderella."

Range, gas, cast iron, 6-burner, two ovens, vertical broiler, warming closet above side oven, fully restored "Magic Chef," c.1937. • A few years ago, this would have been valued about the same as a comparable range by another maker. According to Clifford Boram, "there have been a number of magazine articles about antique gas ranges in the last few of years. They all illustrate the big Magic Chefs, so all the free-spenders have been paying through the nose for them." Demand has driven the price. Boram reports the following prices for fully-restored ranges (remember not all will get this much): 8-burner: $12,000+; 6-burner: .... **$6,000+**

Range, gas, wood or coal. Finished in light gray blue (almost like so-called Wedgwood blue) enamel over the cast iron, re-nickeled, fitted with safety pilot for gas, given fiberglass insulation. Gas oven & broiler on right above door with built-in temperature gauge, a wood-stove oven below with temperature gauge in door, range eyes fueled by gas, United Premier Boston Stove Foundry, Reading, MA, c.1926. .... **$3,500+**

XI-22. Kitchens of "Notable People," *abbreviated from article in* The Metal Worker, *Feb. 8, 1890, detailing importance of the "French range" instead of a stove, for the wealthy.* **(T-L) "Fred Vanderbilt's Kitchen,** *showing end of servants' dining table." Frederick Vanderbilt, 459 Fifth Avenue, NYC. "This kitchen is an old-fashioned one, is below the street and is dark and damp. Gas is burning all day long. The servants when at dinner sit at two long tables in the kitchen. There is no chef here. His place is occupied by a French woman, who has the girth of a typical cook." I bet the servants of "Fred Vanderbilt" were a diseased, unhappy lot.* **(T-R)** *"Kitchen of* **W. W. Astor.** *"William Waldorf Astor, 8 E. 33rd Street, NYC. The kitchen "is comparatively small, but there is a separate dining-room for the servants, so the chef has it all to himself. Here the cooking dishes are of porcelain, the French cook considering porcelain more wholesome for use than copper. Hardwood floor, polished to the smoothness of glass."* **(B-L) A. M. Palmer's** *kitchen, 25 E. 65th St., NYC. "The most beautiful, light and clean kitchen imaginable, and in it is a cook who makes one think of the old days when in mother's kitchen at home he reveled in doughnut horses and gingerbread men. It is typical of those of New England, with its oaken floor and shining tins, and one looks instinctively for the cat that should be purring before the fire."* **(B-R)** *"Kitchen of* **Cornelius Vanderbilt.** *" 1 W. 57th St., NYC. It was the largest private kitchen in New York, and considered very fine. Floor of brown & white marble; pressed brick walls, one side and end with glass-doored cupboards. "This kitchen is beautifully lighted, as it is in the front part of the basement, on a level with the street, and has two very large stained glass windows." German chef used copper because "copper is cleaner than anything else."*

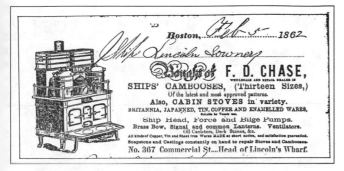

XI-23. "Ship's camboose," or *caboose,* or **cabin stove**. This is the remaining top third of sales receipt of F. D. Chase, Boston, MA, dated Feb. 5, 1862. Note the fairly high brass rail or gallery which kept the utensils from falling off.

Range, gas, colorful enameled cast iron, main body in white with a Chinese red trim (manufacturer called it "Mandarin Red"), long red legs, ovens to side with heat control on inner side wall over range top, Estate Stove Co., Hamilton, OH, c.1928. • Estate also made electric ranges, and color combinations were a rich "King's Blue" and white, and "Jade Green" and white. You could get the oven and broiler on left or right side of range surface......................... **$2,000+**

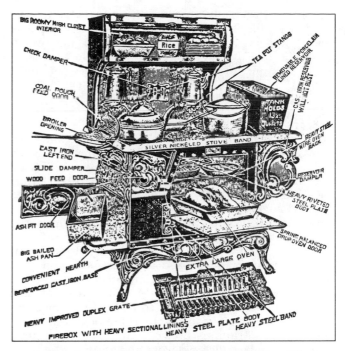

XI-25. Leg base range, with parts identified, *from a c.1895 Sears' catalog page. Was accompanied by lots of text extolling virtues.*

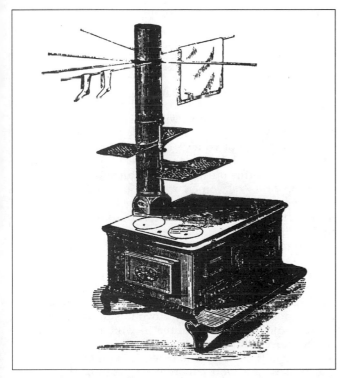

XI-24. Range with attachments. *Drying & towel rack, of walnut or maple rods, fits on stovepipe. The shelves, also were fitted to the pipe, and available in sets of 2 or 4, were meant for "dishes while taking up dinner," for keeping plates warm, or for raising bread. "Always Handy" accessories mfd. by American Manufacturing Co., New Haven, CT. American Agriculturist, Dec. 1874. Possibly a Vose "wide oven" stove.*

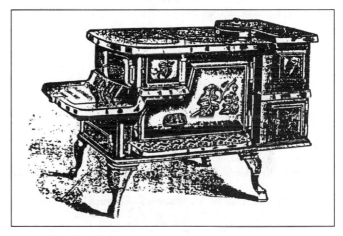

XI-26. Cook stove. *"Original Troy Charter Oak." M. L. Filley, Troy, NY. 1882 ad in The Metal Worker, reading "We offer our celebrated Charter Oak, manufactured by us since 1854. Entirely remodeled and with the improvements usually found in first-class wood stoves. In altering it we have retained all the good features that have made this stove so famous, and added those that experience has shown the trade demanded."*

❖ NOTES ❖

Stove Coloring – "Retail store equipment used to be painted red in most instances and for a time there was a fad in scales and meat grinders for gold lacquer. Machine tools were painted at the whim of the manufacturer until the conglomeration of hues in factories became absurd. ... When the cast-iron stove was replaced by the more modern sheet-metal variety, the industry went chiefly to white. For a period of four or five years white in turn gave way to a variety of pastel colors, applied with fancy crystal, cloud, and woodgrain effects. This fad finally ran its course, and white again became the overwhelming choice of most women." Harold Van Doren, *Industrial Design, A Practical Guide*. NYC: McGraw-Hill, 1940.

•   •   •

More color in Kitchens – About a year ago colored kitchen utensils burst upon the horizon, pots and pans as well as the handles of flat ware assuming such gay tints as vermilion, sea green, ultramarine and daffodil yellow. As a result, kitchens bloomed, decoratively speaking. Housewives, proud of their softly tinted walls, hangings and pots and pans, brought their guests into the kitchen to demonstrate the superiority of this colorful room over the all-white interiors of yore. The cook, stimulated by all this novelty, looked contentedly around and cooked a better meal, and even the family cat blinked more contentedly on a hearth made of brightly-hued tiles. Now a manufacturer has gone a step further and created colored plumbing fixtures. Enameled sinks for kitchens are now available in such engaging tints as horizon blue, West Point gray, spring green, lavender, old ivory and autumn, the latter being a deep, pinkish beige tone." Editorial, *House & Garden*, Aug. 1928. Just two years later, someone of the same ilk was saying that "severity should, perhaps," be the rule for the kitchen. That engaging whimsy drained out very quickly.

•   •   •

Color & Current Value – People who buy an old stove are attracted to great color, especially since most of today's stoves are clinically sterile and white. Red, rich blues, and ultramarines will cost more – but what a cheerful centerpiece for the heart of your home!

Range, gas, looks almost like a fancy sideboard or buffet for dining room, oblong box on slightly cabriole legs, enameled in tan, with fronts of ovens & control panels in black & white marbleized enameled iron, green Bakelite™ pendant pulls on all doors & utensil drawer, extremely handsome, "Magic Chef Patrician

XI-27. Humorous post card. That stove is giving all it's got! But what I love are the sleeping chickens, which "Paw" has to turn to face the wall before retiring. Published by Asheville Post Card Co., Asheville, NC, in the 1950s, and an example of stove-related non-advertising paper available to collectors. **$2-$5**

OH! WHAT A DIFFERENCE!

THIS IS THE WAY OUR FATHERS USED TO COOK.   THIS IS THE WAY WE COOK.

XI-28. Modern cooking, as depicted in The Metal Worker, *June 18, 1892. At left is a hot old smoky wood stove, with what appear to be corncobs [now coming back as a clean fuel] all over floor, a squalling baby fallen into the coal hod, and the chauvinist husband stalking out instead of helping. A "Fire King" gas stove, mfd. by A. Weiskittel & Son, Baltimore, with tin plate from the factory of Coates & Co., Baltimore, has made everyone happy.*

Model," mfd. by American Stove Co., St. Louis, MO, late 1920s. $200 was the original price!..... **$3,000+**
Range, gas, streamlined clean design, 4-burner, white enameled steel, pendant or drop pulls, broiler drawer under 6 control dials, "Magic Chef," American Stove Co., St. Louis, MO, c.1934......... **$1,000+**

❖ NOTES ❖

An old ad for the above "**Magic Chef**" range started off with words sure to shrivel the heart of a collector of today: "The Modern Housewife discarded the old Coffee Mill Years Ago ... Isn't it about time to discard that old-fashioned range of yours? The sound of the old coffee mill is no longer heard in the modern kitchen. Progress has relegated this outmoded appliance to the junk pile. Yet thousands of women who wouldn't keep a coffee grinder in the house, except as a relic, continue to use a gas range that is just as out of date. Don't cheat the junk pile and yourself any longer. ... Replace the antiquated range with a modern automatic Magic Chef."

•   •   •

"Smoothtop" ranges – These are a 1930s transitional form made to assist cooks who were used to 19th and early 20th century wood/coal stoves that had a flat smooth top, closed by stove lids and the "cut long center" and the "short center" – which fit around the round stove lids, like a jigsaw puzzle, to make a perfectly smooth surface. The new "Smoothtop" ranges are gas ranges, and you can remove parts of the smooth top to reveal the gas ring below, or even – for slow-cooking – set the pan down on the cover, with the gas fire going below it.

Range, peach enameled cast iron, nickel trim, 2 warming ovens above, oven & broiler below, 6 eyes with one having smaller eye in middle of lid, 2 lids in center lift out along with the fat "I" shaped piece between them, to open up a long, round-end oblong suitable for a 2 hole gridiron or boiler, etc.. "Copper Clad," early 20th C. Unrestored. .... **$1,500+**

Range, gas, cast & sheet iron, box with fancy side valves, "The Sun Dial," mfd. by Goodwin Meter Co., South Carolina Power Co., SC, c.1946. .... **$250+**

Simmering cover, cast iron round "trivet" to set into range eye to reduce heat, openwork 6 wedge design, with slots for lid lifter, marked "Simmering Cover, W & P Mfg. Co.," Walker & Pratt Mfg. Co., 7 1/2" diam., c.1890s-1910s. .... **$30+**

Stove-ware adjuster, cast iron, looks like miniature stadium, with step down sloping levels inside, open at bottom, 3 square feet so it sits stead on flat surfaces, adapter used to make various "round bottomed" utensils fit gasoline and oil stoves, small tab on side with notch for lid lifter. Ads say "Specially adapted to fit all size round bottom ware and round Waffle Irons. ... Also equalizes and retains the heat under all cooking utensils." Griswold Mfg. Co., about 10" diam., advertised 1892. .... **$30+**

Stove blacking, in tin container, red, white, & blue label with flag design, "The Union Blacking," c.1890s-1910s. .... **$15+**

Stove blacking holder, also called a blacking box holder, cast iron, 3 peg feet, open handle, scrolly biparte end, dog's head on spring-tensioned slider, 9"L x 2-3/4"W, marked "J. & W. Cairns," and "1857," pat'd. Jan. 13, 1857, by J. &W. Cairns, Jersey City, N.J, pat. #16,374. An almost identical one, minus the dog, was patented by G. W. Taylor, Springfield, VT, June 1, 1867. • This has been advertised by a dealer in "country items," as a "rare mechanical four-way trivet," which it isn't. .... **$125+**

Stove-blacking holder that looks like a trivet, adjustable, cast iron, 3 feet, figural head like a bulldog or even odd human, adjustable with thumb screw, and has lip to fit over edge of pan (?) or something to hold it securely, J & W. Cairns, 10"L x 2-3/4"W at widest point, pat'd. Jan. 13, 1857. .... **$125+**

Stove door, cast iron, depicts man clearing wood, "Leibrandt & McDowell Stove Co.," Philadelphia & Baltimore, mid 19th C. .... **$200+**

❖ NOTES ❖

Stove knobs – Most knobs, pendant drop handles, and bracket handles are either nickeled cast iron, or nickeled iron wire coils (such as made by the Troy Nickel Works), or are cast iron enameled in white. I still think that if you can't save the stove, save the knobs. In NYC it is not so common as it once was to find a stove thrown out on the street for pickup that day by the Sanitation Department, and most stoves are vintage 1920s, but there are still goodies to pick up.

Stove knobs, nickeled cast iron, one an elongated blimp shape with the pointed tips of metal, the middle half transparent blue glass; the round one having an orb of blue glass fitted into a metal base with 2 arms for holding bolt through glass, "Jewel," Greene & Mallett, manufacturers of stove trimmings, Troy, NY, came in 10 sizes and styles, and also in amber glass, Jan. 1892 ad in *Metal Worker*. It's likely these would be sold not as stove knobs but as bureau knobs. The blue color especially desirable to collectors. Each: .... **$5-$15+**

XI-29. Gas range. *"Caloric," in pale green porcelainized finish with ivory trim, in kitchen with marbled dark forest green & white floor. Note stacked ovens, warming closet above them, and overall streamlining of design. House & Garden, 1930 ad. An article in* House Beautiful *of the time said "The kitchen range may be said now to have reached the robot stage, since it works with the minimum of human control or manual guidance! The mere pressing of a button or manipulation of cock or switch, and the 'die is cast' for an economically cooked meal. The first thing that strikes the beholder is their modern air! The new ranges have taken unto themselves a new beauty! In some cases, we admit there is an effort at ornament which defeats itself in over elaboration and bewildering design and mottlings, but on the whole, every manufacturer has models beautiful enough to capture the eye of the most fastidious. Whereas we used to have woeful black, squatty, graceless ranges, to-day we have console models, with legs slender but firm, and with cabinets as attractive as are many chests of drawers. We have them enduringly enameled in white with gray, blue, green, and other colored trim, and finished in chromium rather than nickel." "The Robot of the Kitchen,"* House Beautiful, *May 1931.*

Stove lid lifter – also called a democrat, or a stove dexter, cast iron, design of heat-dissipating handle formed of handsome cutout letters, "ESTATE #33," American, 10"L, c.1890s-1910s. .... **$12+**

Stove lid lifter, cast iron, nickel plated, coil handle and head of Jack Frost at the business end, "Alaska" brand, mfd. by Troy Nickel Works, Troy, NY, about 10"L, late 19th to early 20thC. .... **$35+**

Stove lid lifter, cast iron in form of slender, attenuated but voluptuous long-haired and long-gowned woman wearing a crown, which, with her upraised arms, forms part of the pot lid lifter at her head end, the stove lid lifter being at her foot, odd monobut-

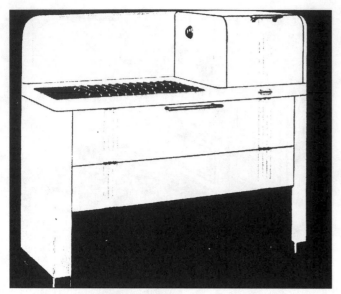

XI-30. Oil-burning range. *"Perfection #R-869,"* by Perfection Stove Co., Cleveland, OH. The ad doesn't mention oil, but touts kerosene. Ultimate simplicity – probably would be collectible by moderne collectors seeking a look. Farm Journal & Farmer's Wife, *May. 1939.*

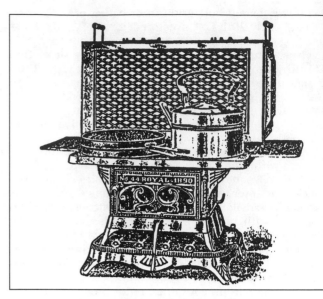

XI-32. Oil stove. *"Royal #44,"* mfd. by The Perry Stove Co.'s Argan Stoves & Ranges, Albany, NY. Nickel-plated cast iron. Pat'd. 1890. This was a small stove, but size isn't given in ad. The Metal Worker, *June 28, 1890.*

tock rear, unmarked, American, 8-5/16"L, c.1850s or 1860s. .... **$250+**

Stove lid lifter, cast iron in form of Victorian booted lady's leg, unmarked, 9"L, American, c.1850s or 1860s. Not for your home range. It'd be interesting to know what market these were aimed at.... **$250+**

Stove lid lifter, nickeled cast iron, working hook end is a bull's head, handle is tight coil to dissipate heat and stay cool, hence name, "Alaska" brand, sold through Montgomery Ward as well as other stores, mfd. by Troy Nickel Works, Troy, NY, about 10"L, late 19th C. .... **$25+**

Stove lid lifter, openwork cast iron, the central motif being a heart outline, with a sort of fish outline coming from between the lobes, & a sort of banner from the point, there being useful tips at both ends, the banner or streamer contains the initials "J P A" & date, mfd. by J. P. Abbott, Cleveland, OH, 1882 .... **$45+**

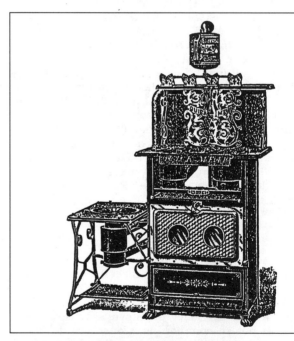

XI-33. Gasoline stove. *"Quick Meal Cabinet Range, #924,"* mfd. by the Quick Meal Stove Co., St. Louis, MO. Among the features may be mentioned glass tubes which show the dripping of gasoline when the stove is in use, German silver needle points and a rim on the gasoline burner top extending over the burner drums and tubes, thus protecting them against the dripping from cooking vessels. All the pipes are anti-rusting material. [This model] is a new pattern, nicely japanned and ornamented." The Metal Worker, *Feb. 6, 1892.* This kind of stove may be in "low demand" among stove collectors, but I imagine there are collectors of japanned wares who would love to have it – functioning or not – in their kitchens.

XI-31. Tabletop gas stove. *"No. 2 Junior,"* mfd. by Cleveland Foundry – who also made the oil range in XI-30. Ad in The Metal Worker, *Feb. 6, 1892.* (Note: This is one, commonly understood meaning of "tabletop." Stove makers in the early part of the 20th C sometimes used "tabletop" range to mean a flat-top range with nothing, such as an oven, raised above the cooking surface.) **$40-$50**

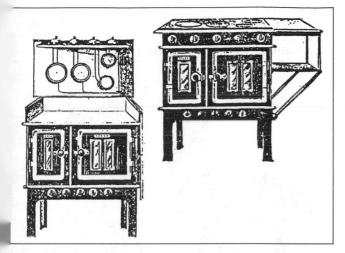

XI-34 Electric cooker [stove], two views. "Gilbert," mfd. in England. *(L)* View with hinged shelf down at side, and top raised for work surface, showing underside of the four round "boiling discs." Note controls for each of discs. Two ovens – one with two heating elements, one with three – explain the row of five control dials. *(R)* In position for cooking. Picture from Maud Lancaster's *Electric Cooking*, 1914.

XI-35. Electric cooker [stove]. "Electroyl," mfd. by Purcell & Nobbs, London, England. Picture shows how it is set up in front of a fireplace, with some kind of crinkled stuffing filling the hearth opening. Cast iron frame, steel oven, with oven 23" x 16" x 16". Two 8" boiling discs flush on top, also one 6", and a griller/toaster. The area between the top and the oven is a "hot closet" or warming oven, for keeping plates and food warm. The control panel is mounted to the wall. Maud Lancaster's *Electric Cooking*, 1914.

XI-36. Two photographic stereoptican card panels, making entertainment out of what was a no-joking-matter affecting many husbands and wives in the 19th and early 20th centuries. *(T)* Busy one shows wife admonishing husband, who's ready to throw soot-caked elbow pipe on floor. Note: flue cover is already in place (above wife's head); also ladder, mad wallpaper, coal hod. "Have patience, dear, don't swear" caption is repeated on back in several foreign languages. ©1897 by Strohmeyer & Wyman, pub'd by Underwood & Underwood. *(B)* Simpler one is posed so the man has stovepipe legs. "Oh, Dear! Don't Swear" is the caption. ©1892 by B. L. Singley, pub'd by Keystone View Co. How-to columns advised an aid to a "felicitous putting up" by numbering both ends of each section of pipe. Several more versions – mainly photographic – of the cards exist. For photographic ones: **$6-$15+**

Stove lid lifter, cast iron with coiled wire loop handle, "Stover," late 19th C. .... **$7+**

Stove lid lifter, crudely finished cast iron, marked on one "Horn" with initials M A, American, 9-3/8"L, c.1890s-1910s. .... **$7+**

Stove lid lifter, cast iron, in combination with a pot lid lifter at other end, quite simple form, made by an unknown stove company, American, 9"L, 19th C. There were a number of combination stove tools patented, some with various curved projections for lifting pot lids, carrying bail handled pots, pulling tacks. .... **$10+**

Stove lid lifter, coppered cast iron, handle is thick tube with a number of holes cast in it to help disperse heat by helping air circulate around it, fairly straight long shank, "The Zero," sold through Montgomery Ward, late 19th C. .... **$7+**

Stove lid lifter, wrought iron bar, handle split into 6 narrow strips then loosely woven together to form heat dissipating handle, really beautiful, American, 14"L, early 19th C. .... **$125+**

Stove lid & trivet, cast iron in slightly raised design of sort of ruffley-edged nautilus shell, on the underside are 2 short peg feet plus the slot where you stick in the lid lifter which forms the third foot, extremely handsome piece of cast iron, marked on back "K O

XI-37. Parlor stoves, *with fancy cast iron finials. From the "Madison Square Series," mfd. by Southard, Robertson & Co., NYC. Madison Square lies just north of 23rd Street, east of 5th Avenue, and it was a fashionable area. These stoves were "very moderate in price" in 1890 when advertised, but would cost a small fortune today, especially the building-shaped one with the horse. spectacular & highly desirable, especially now that there's been an upsurge of interest in collecting building-shaped banks, souvenirs, lamps, etc. A dancing gypsy with tambourine tops the other stove. Note low-set foot rails which look like carrying handles. In fact, at least one turn of the century parlor stove maker, Moore, advertised "Easy to carry; invert the foot rails and use them as carriers." Collectors for these would probably come from the folk art sector as much as the true stove collecting population.* **$3,000-$10,000+**

118," might be Kiechle & Oberdorfer stove company or even the O. K. Stove Works, 9-1/16" diam. 19th C. .... **$30+**

Stove name plate or plaque, from oven door, multicolor enameled metal rectangle, "Glenwood," 8" x 10", c.1890s-1910s. .... **$12+**

XI-38. "Heating Stoves of 1990." *In the trade magazine* The Metal Worker, *Aug. 16 1890, was printed a teasing piece on parlor or heating stoves of the future, based on the un-stovelike appearance being exaggerated beyond reason by contemporary stove designers. An abridged version of a spoof newspaper account, supposedly from 1990, of the purchase of this stove in the shape of a Newfoundland dog (cast iron with glass eyes on a nickel-plated base) follows: "I, being in need of a new base burner, called on Jones & Johnson for the purpose of purchasing a stove. Upon entering, I was bewildered at the glittering array of samples of artistic stoves spread before me. The place would hardly be taken for a stove store on account of the peculiarity of the designs. One would sooner imagine he was in a zoo or taxidermist's place of business, or possibly Barnum's winter quarters. There were cook stoves in the form of turtles, alligators, camels; heating stoves representing Bismarck, General Washington, Uncle Sam, dogs, cats, bears, tigers, elephants, lions, and, in fact, almost every conceivable object. The huge elephant stove is for school houses and public institutions. ... One beautiful pattern was George Washington. Standing as he did, he looked as if he might indeed be the father of the world. He was mounted on a platform or box with the word 'Liberty' in large raised letters across the front of the ash-pit section. His right hand rested on the Western hemisphere of a bronze atlas which was placed at his side. His left hand held a statuette of the Goddess of Liberty Enlightening the World. The look upon his face was that of success achieved. A gentle pressure upon his right shoulder would cause his head to fall back, exposing the top into which the fuel was put to replenish the fire." The George Washington heating stove was actually made – and sold as a "dumb radiating stove" (meaning that it didn't "speak" for itself, and furnished heat created elsewhere. A garden statue in the same design was also made. Made by their inventor, Alonzo Blanchard, from the 1840s, and later by J. L. Mott Foundry, they have sold to collectors for upwards of $1250. Any other fanciful form described above, if it had ever been made, would be worth many thousands to collectors of cast iron, folk art and dog art – perhaps* **$15,000 or more!**

XI-39. Stove blacking box-holder patents. (1) indicating the round can with dotted line, pat'd. Jan. 13, 1857, and mfd. by J. & W. Cairns, of Jersey City, NJ. It was made, and is cast iron, with three peg feet and a figural dog head on the slider (not shown on the patent drawing). 9-3/4"L. Pat'd. Jan. 13, 1857, by J. & W. Cairns, Jersey City, NJ, pat. #16,374. **(B)** showing spring tension slider, is G. W. Taylor's patent #60962, of Jan. 1, 1867. Springfield, VT. Official Gazette. The dog holder: **$125+**

Stove name plaques, cast iron oval or oblong cartouches, with the name of the stove model, and/or the stove founder, and/or the place where made, mostly about 3" x 8". Not commonly found, not usually collected, but some are very appealing, like "Oriole" "Balto. MD." .... **$5+**

Stove ornament or "urn," brass plated cast pot or slush metal, marvelous standing Indian with feather headdress, framing him is sort of wreath of elongated pin oak leaves, stands up on round base, doesn't need to be on a stove for great effect, "Round Oak" stoves, Doe-Wah-Jack, 11"H, very early 20thC. • There are several versions of this, some with the Indian figure, some with urns or other shapes surrounded by stylized oak leaf wreath. .... **$160+**

Stove urns, cast iron, footed open top compote-like vessel that fit on hob shelves of some stoves, and were filled with water, which evaporated, humidifying the dry kitchen. Some were enameled inside; some were nickel plated or "bronzed." No foundry mark on many of these, although sometimes there's a part number cast in, American, about 5-1/2 to 6-1/2"H, about 6" diameter, mid to late 19th C............. **$65+**

XI-41. Stove polish ad. "X-Ray," mfd. by Lamont, Corliss & Co. Ladies' Home Journal, Oct. 1904. (Wilhelm Konrad Roentgen discovered X-rays in 1895, and it was so revolutionary an idea that companies grabbed the name even though it had nothing to do with their product, just as slightly earlier companies had used the word "electric" to attract attention. A raisin seeder in the first chapter is called the "X-ray" seeder.) Blacking wasn't just a cosmetic, or a way to hold heat; it protected against rust.

Stove pipe oven, or drum oven, blued sheet iron, fits into stovepipe and hot air passing by bakes biscuits or cookies, there's a crank in the back to clear the pipe of soot, "Sootless Sue," mfd. by Stratton & Terstegge, Louisville, KY, 1890s-1910s. .... **$45+**

Stove pipe plate, cast iron, "Adams," American, pat'd. 1897, 15-3/4" diam., rim 6-1/4"W. .... **$45+**

Stove pipe trivet, airy fine cast iron, very openwork design within round frame, of 6 stars, touching at points to each other and frame, one projection, just like a lid lifter, fits into ring that goes around pipe. Ring could hold several. no mark, American, 6-5/8" diam., late 19th C. **$100**

XI-40 Stove blacking box. A homemade wooden box, 4"H x 7"L, with a screw-on cover with handle, and a place for a cake of polish, the brush, and the "mixing plate or dish" marked "E" for mixing in the naptha or gasoline. "The cover has an opening (C), which comes directly over the mixing dish. Across this opening is placed an old knife blade, or a bit of iron filed sharp. The cake of polish is pushed across this blade until a sufficient quantity for use is scraped off, and falls directly into the dish, where it is to be mixed."

XI-42. Stove polishes in cans. "Black Silk" paste "to be mixed with naptha, benzine or gasoline." "Vulcanol," was a cream ready for instant use. These were applied with special blacking brushes, sometimes called daubers, which look rather like the shoe blacking brushes you can still buy. Offered by Excelsior Stove & Mfg. Co., c.1916.

XI-43. Stove door. *Oval, cast iron, "Liberty & Union," with 26 stars, which would date it to between 1837 (when Michigan became the 26th state) and 1845. 11"H x 13"L. Photo courtesy Litchfield Auction Gallery, Litchfield CT. Ex-Harold Corbin Collection, auctioned Jan. 1, 1989 for $450.* **$550+**

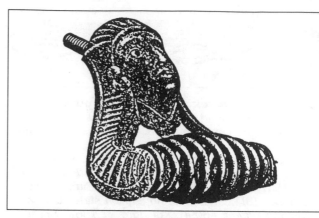

XI-44. Stove handle. *"Alaska. Always Cold," mfd. by Troy Nickel Works, Troy, NY. All their coiled handles were called "Alaska," as a trade name, and they had at least three choices of figurals at the end of their heat-dissipating handles: a bull's head symbolizing strength (?), a Jack Frost (?) head, symbolizing cold, and this Egyptian's head, symbolizing desert heat. Note echo of the coils in the stylized hairdo. Ad in The Metal Worker, Aug. 6, 1890.* **$30**

Stove plate, from early cook stove made up of plates, like a prefab house. Depicts 2 tall men with guns, wearing Liberty caps, and 2 bearded men in frock coats shaking hands, from the Hudson River Valley, NY, 24"H x 25-1/2"L, late 18th or early 19th C. .... **$1,500+**

Stovetop oven – actually a sort of cooking utensil, shaped like a cake carrier, aluminum with iron bottom & wire rack, with thermometer in lid, "West Bend Ovenette," by West Bend Aluminum Co., West Bend, WI, 10-1/2" diam., c. 1940s. • In NYC, I could bake a pair of sweet potatoes in this much faster than I could clear out the cast iron wares I keep in my oven. A mouse lived in the oven too, sometimes, and I hated to disturb him. .... **$5+**

Stovetop oven, heavy tin, has heat indicator in lid, "Bake Queen," early 20th C. .... **$5+**

Stovetop oven, tin, rack inside, one half of the oven, sides and top, is on a pivot and swings around inside other half, no mark, American, 6-1/2"H x 10-3/4" diam., 19th C or very early 20th. .... **$35+**

Stovetop oven, tin with copper bottom, 2 door, "Conservo," Schwarzbaugh Co., Toledo, OH, 20th C. • Some people call stovetop ovens "Dutch ovens;" other people call reflector ovens "Dutch ovens." I've reserved the name for the cast iron kettle with a lid with high flanged sides (see the Hearth chapter.).................. **$15**

Toasters – See illustrations XI-50, XI-51 and XI-52

Trivet, attaches to back of stove for a place to put a teapot, cast iron, deer design, American, early 20th C. .... **$75+**

Trivet or hot plate, folding, nickel plated cast iron, to be wall mounted near stove, marked "A. Cast 14," 8" diam., 19th C. **$65**

"What Is My Antique Stove Worth?"

by Clifford Boram

(A version of article was appeared in "*The Antique Trader Weekly*," Feb. 8, 1984. It's been revised by its author. Read it to understand the difficulties of stating "market value" for stoves, and all kinds of kitchen antiques. See how to reach Mr. Boram at the end of these combined stove chapters.)

"What is my antique stove worth?" If people answered your question with, "It's worth whatever you can get for it," you'd think they were being evasive or flippant. But let's take a closer look at your question, to see if it's asking too much.

The question seems to say, "I'm not familiar with the market for antique stoves, but I take it for granted there's a going price for stoves like mine, regardless of circumstances, if only I can find out what it is." The market for antique stoves is too thin for a consensus on a going price to emerge. In a market this thin, even the

experts are at sea. The difference between a greenhorn and an expert is the greenhorn feels flustered by being at sea in an unfamiliar market, and the expert is accustomed to being at sea. In the course of long experience, the expert has become resigned to the very unhelpful truth that an antique stove isn't "worth" something; it's only worth something to somebody.

Eight factors (all with sub-factors) to consider when trying to place a value on a stove are: Time, Place, Artistry, Age, Rarity, Material, Type, & Condition

TIME is one of the circumstances that influences a stove's price. In 1972, before the energy shortage and the suddenly renewed popularity of old stoves, they were being sold for scrap at one cent a pound. Later, their increasing popularity happened to coincide with a period of high inflation when the price of all collectibles was being driven skyward. In 1982, when inflation

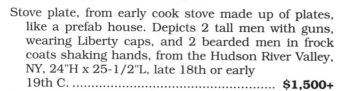

WIMSW-1. Wood- or coal-burning cook stove.
*Example:"Valley Queen." Such a stove can retail for about **$800** when fully restored. At a country auction, the rusty, neglected veteran, complete but with some warped and cracked parts, would bring about **$50**. (Ed. note: Prices here are subject to all factors mentioned in text of Clifford Boram's article. Any discrepencies between his and my valuations in Chapter XI should be decided in favor of Boram, with reference to actual market conditions in your community.)*

WIMSW-2. Range. *An attractive all-cast-iron range from the 1890s will often be priced at over $2000 in a restorer-dealer's shop. Baut this 1891 "New Adonis" range, Buckwalter Stove Co., is so spectacular that it deserves a price of **$3,000+**.*

appeared to be under control and a recession had made many buyers tight-fisted, the price of antique stoves edged back down. Whoever wants the best price must time his sale to the economic cycle.

Time of year also influences prices. Spring is the worst season to sell your stove; demand is slight. Late August through December are the months of heavy demand. Antique stove restorer-dealers are often overstocked and short of money in July, so they're only buying at bargain prices, if at all.

Time is also a factor in another way: are you in a hurry to sell your stove, or can you afford to wait for the right buyer to come along? If you have to sell the stove by tomorrow, you'll pretty well have to take whatever an antique dealer will give you for it, which is often surprisingly little. A dealer who specializes in dolls and glassware won't offer as much for your stove as one who trades in hard goods. And no dealer's offer will be even close to the price he expects to get by waiting – a year or more, if necessary – for the right buyer.

PLACE also impacts price. There's a thin but continuous stream of desirable stoves being shipped to the lucrative Pacific Coast market. Prices in the Midwest are comparatively very affordable. New England is a hotbed of interest in antique stoves. Interest is near zero in the deep South, and Southerners are taken aback when they hear New England prices. Although New York City is notorious for its high prices on antiques, the demand for antique wood/coal stoves is small, because New Yorkers can't store fuel, firewood is prohibitively expensive, and few people have chimneys or flues. In New York City, antique wood/coal stoves usually are only used as decorative pieces, and their bulk and weight keep them from being popular even for that purpose. However, antique gas ranges are used and appreciated there.

Place also matters where restorer-dealers aren't evenly spaced in a region. A restorer-dealer in Rhode Island tells us he never has to pay more that a few hundred dollars for even the most desirable unrestored stove in perfectly good condition. With no other

restorer-dealers competing for stoves in his area, he has the market to himself. Farther north in New England, where there's more competition, restorer-dealers have to pay more.

Place also makes a difference when an antique stove is being sold in its own hometown. A stove made by Madison Stove Works in Indiana, is just another out-of-state stove to a buyer in Iowa. But take it back to Madison, and the demand will be greater for an object of local interest. The same holds true in much lesser degree for stoves sold in their home state.

ARTISTRY is an important influence on an antique stove's price. There are plenty of people, especially older and less educated ones, who fail to realize the beauty (if any) in their old stove. Either they sell the stove at a scandalously low price to the first bargain-hunter who happens to come along, or they're flabbergasted to see the high price it brings at auction. By contrast, there are other people, not educated about old stoves, who have heard of an antique stove that brought a premium price and who are quite incensed when someone offers them a realistic price for their very plain and uninteresting one. In general, a stove that's generously ornamented with raised designs on the castings and has some nickel-plated parts is worth more than a plain one. The more translucent mica windows it has, the better. One or more ceramic tile cameos attached to the castings are another desirable feature. And the less sheet metal, the better. Desirable options like a high warming-closet, water reservoir, and gas side attachment on a wood/coal range also add to the value.

If the stove was originally cast from fresh patterns, the designs will have a crispness that may add a little to the price. Many stoves were cast from old, cracked, and carelessly-repaired patterns. The traces of these defects often show on the castings, and may lead a choosy buyer to pass the stove by.

AGE influences the price of a stove, but it's not completely true that the older a stove is, the greater its value. There was a golden age of stove-making, say

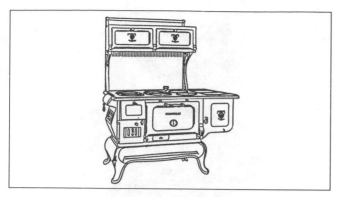

WIMSW-3 Range. *This porcelainized cast iron range, a 1922 "Peninsular," is typical of the plain style that became the predominant favorite in the early decades of this century. Restorer-dealers often price these very common ranges well* **below $1,000** *in Midwest markets;* **below $1,300** *in New England.*

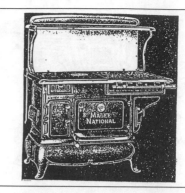

WIMSW-5 Range. Wood-, coal-and-gas combination range. *New England restorer-dealers have lately been getting* **$2,000+** *for fine combination ranges like this 1927 "Magee National." In 1984, at the wrong auction in Indiana, an unrestored one in average condition sold for $15 because no-one in the crowd was interested in cooking. The buyer was an elderly woman who needed something to heat her garage.*

from 1870 to 1910, during which art and technology both reached a peak. An 1820 stove is interesting, but not as efficient or useful as the improved 1890 models. A 1930 stove is just as useful as an 1890, but not so pretty. Most people who admire old stoves want to use them too. If a stove isn't very useful, the people who would want to buy it are fewer, and the price suffers. Hardly anyone is a really serious stove collector, the great bulk of demand comes from admirers who have only a few stoves at most.

The golden age of stoves ended as stoves became smoother, plainer, and easier to wipe clean. In general, stoves with a porcelain finish are more modern, and hence less desirable, than the bare-iron "black" stoves, but some of the earliest porcelainized ranges, still shaped in the old style, are raving beauties that will make your eyes pop. White is the least desirable color for porcelain. Chrome trim, rather than nickel, is the sure mark of a stove too modern to qualify as an antique.

RARITY of a particular stove may have a modest influence on its price, but perhaps not in the way you'd expect. Rarity may be undesirable to a buyer con-

cerned about the parts situation. A kitchen range by the Majestic Mfg. Co., of St. Louis, MO, may command a premium over an equivalent model by the Cedar Grove Stove Co., of Cedar Grove, WI, (a small and obscure manufacturer). Majestic parts are available; Cedar Grove parts would have to be fabricated. Certain common makes, such as Glenwood and Monarch, have a reputation for quality that gives them preference over an unknown make.

The only time rarity helps the price of a stove is when the buyer is looking for a particular type or model. For years, a serious collector has been searching for a hay-burning stove, and has been willing to pay a premium price for it, because it's the only type he doesn't have. The Nott's Patent stove would be another such example. Its historic significance as the first base-burner combines with its rarity to make it prized by collectors.

Some types of antique stoves are more in demand than others. Base burners are the most admired type, because of their beauty. The 1900 to 1915 base burners are most often seen for sale, but once you've met an 1890 square base-burner, you'll know why it commands a higher premium. Cottage parlor stoves, cooking stoves, and the upright, steel-jacketed "oak" stoves rank third. Laundry stoves and sheet-steel air-tight heaters go begging, and are so common that there's some agreement on a correct price. One restorer-dealer offered to bury another's house in oval air-tights for $25.00 to $30.00 apiece!

MATERIAL counts too: restorers prefer cast iron stoves, which are bolted together and hence easy to take apart for repair. Steel ranges, on the other hand, are riveted together. If their sheet steel panels are rusted through or otherwise damaged, most buyers just aren't interested.

FUEL type effects value. Wood-burning and coal-burning stoves are usually most in demand, but a wood and gas combination range often receives a modest premium over a comparable wood-only range because of its greater utility: a wood-burning range makes the kitchen uncomfortably hot in summertime. (ED. note: Older houses, c.1870s-1930s, in warmer parts of the country often had a "summer kitchen" out-

WIMSW-4 Range. *Numerous rivet heads identify steel ranges like this 1899 "Majestic #251." They're exceptionally difficult to restore, but in top condition they can bring over* **$1,200** *at the right auction.*

WIMSW-6 Base-burner. *Dealers have been known to ask* **over $5000** *for a fully-restored square base-burner, such as the classic* **1904** *"Art Andes." The "piggyback" oven, seen at center back, is a desirable option.*

WIMSW-7 Base-burner. *The 1886 Argand round temple-like base burner with the Roman warrior finial is awesome, though many round base-burners are plainer and too small to be really spectacular. Note the piggyback oven here, too. Value probably* **$5,000+.**

WIMSW-8 Base-burner. *The 1931 "Columbian Art" reflector base-burner typifies the twilight of the base-burner era; the desirable Victorian fancywork has been smoothed away, leaving only a handsome structure that priced even* **below $2,000** *would have trouble finding a buyer in some markets.*

WIMSW-9 Heating stoves. *Two extremes of the oak stove desirability spectrum are shown by* **(L)** *E. Bement & Sons' 1892 "Capital Oak" and* **(R)** *Auto Stove Works' 1937 "Sun." The "Capital Oak" is blessed with mica windows, fancy ornamentation and even a cast iron jacket — a deluxe option preferable to the "Sun's" sheet steel jacket. Larger skirt rails and a pair of nickel-plated wings beside the feed door would also be desirable in Bement's stove, but those features belong to the 1900 to 1930 era. Even though the "Sun" is now over 60 years old, its Art Deco styling denies it any claim to an antique premium above its utility value; it's a modern stove. (Ed. note: Always the optimist, I keep thinking that perhaps there exists a stove of that period which inadvertently rather than deliberately was artfully designed. And I have to say I like those stepped legs.)*

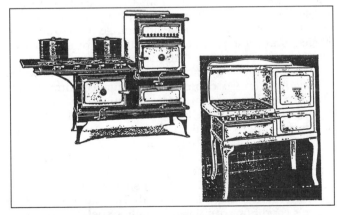

WIMSW-10 Gas ranges. *The recent surge of interest in gas ranges has driven some prices over $3000+ for fully-restored, top-of-the-line models. It should be obvious that the 1921 double-oven Chambers* **(L)** *is infinitely more desirable of the two shown here. The 1928 Tappan* **(R)** *shows the routine antique gas range configuration. A price of $150 for a good unrestored one would be a realistic minimum price paid by a dealer. Even later gas ranges, from the 1930s, with no high structure, are so close in form to modern ones that they have trouble commanding a significant antique premium. See the note in Chapter XI on the "Magic Chef" phenomenon.* **(L) $3,000; (R) $150+.**

WIMSW-11 Various low-demand stoves. (B-L) *Large black one is a kerosene range. Top row (T-L) to (T-R) are a sheet iron oval "Air-Tight," a kitchen heater, and a cast iron circulator. (B-M) cast iron laundry stove and (B-R) gasoline range with its small fuel tank raised above. (Ed. note: Perhaps it's the influence of collectors who want, in effect, whatnot shelves for their collectible utensils, but the kerosene and gasoline stoves sometimes find appreciative buyers — in some regions, by non-stove collectors. Collectors as a rule, don't want them. Many laundry stoves are very handsomely designed, and are considered natural adjuncts to sadiron collections. Wherever in this book that you see "Ed. note" that means written by and expressing the opinions solely of the author of this book — Linda C. Franklin.)*

side the main house. It might have been as simple as a banged-together sort of shed. Anything to get the main kitchen stove's heat away from the house.) There has lately been increasing interest in antique gas ranges, which are at a considerable advantage in metropolitan areas, and which some cooks find more satisfactory than the modern type. Antique gas heater stoves have lately become popular because of environmental restrictions on woodsmoke emissions. The first, tentative demand for antique electric ranges has begun to appear in a few areas. Significant demand for antique kerosene ranges is limited to Amish country. Gasoline or white gas ranges go begging.

In evaluating a stove's condition, first see if its defects impair its beauty. Some buyers, who only want a stove for show, will disregard the most shocking internal damage, if only the stove looks good. To take account of a stove's condition, run down this **checklist:**

1) Is there **rust?** Are the rust pits so deep they'll be a problem to fill? Any parts rusted through? (Remove ashes and soot to be sure.)

2) Are there any **cracks** in the cast iron?

3) Have any hooks, tips, etc., been **cracked off?**

4) Are any parts **warped** or **burnt out?**

5) Is the **firebrick** (if any) intact and sound?

6) If there's a porcelain finish, has it been badly **chipped?**

7) Are there any bolt holes or mounting tabs that suggest **missing accessories** or controls?

8) Do all parts fit together nicely? Is anything **loose?** Do moving parts **work smoothly?**

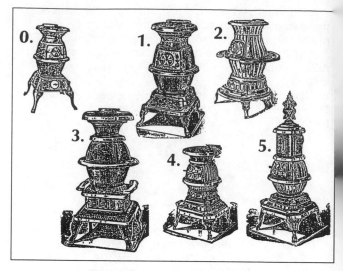

WIMSW-12 Cannon or "pot-belly" stoves. *These too are considered of low value to most antique stove collectors. Popularly called "pot-belly" stoves, but termed* **cannon, globe,** *or* **egg stoves** *by the industry, most of these were among a manufacturer's cheaper goods comparatively plain and simple stoves with no pretensions to the fancy, nickel-plated, mica-windowed parlor stove category that antique enthusiasts admire and pay high prices for today. Plenty of first quality, heavy, and substantial cannons were made too, but they were for depots, schoolds, offices, and other commercial situations, rather than for homes. Only a few achieved parlor stove features. Within the cannon category, it's possible to distinquish differences in desirability, and hence value. Lowest in interest and value is the utterly utilitarian and totally uninteresting little cannon, picture* **#0** *above. Such a stove's value depends entirely on its usefulness, not on the fact that it may be 70 years old. It would generally bring less than* **$40** *at auction, although you might see it priced at more than* **$100** *in a shop.* **#1,** *still low scale of desirability, is the sort of cannon most often seen. It has a bit of ornamentation, and isn't unattractive, but it lacks any features that would make it stand out from the crowd.* **#2,** *with its ribbed design and fender ring, begins to be more desirable.* **#3,** *with both foot rails and a fender ring, is a fine, handsome cannon, as connons go, but would beneft still more from cheery mica windows in its feed door, through which to view the fire.* **#4,** *an artistic jewel among cannons, has mica windows in its feed door and three mica doors just above grate level. Its foot rail, deep ribs, and rich, angular design also contribute to its great desirability. It would be a bargain at* **$300+,** *especially in its larger sizes. Occasionally a sheet metal* extension drum *or even a cast iron extension containing a self-feeding magazine for coal would be added to the top of a cannon stove,* **#5** *has one [not the ornamental "urn" on top, but the cylindrical part below that], and is thus a* base-burning cannon. *The ornate extension must be considered desirable, although it makes this stove more spectacular and odd than beautifully proportioned.* **$150+**

9) If **repairs** have been made, are they **neatly** and **professionally done,** or are they crudely finagled with putty and incorrect substitution of materials or parts?

10) Are the **correct stove tools** (ash shovel, soot rake, poker, lid lifter, and grate-shaker handle) included, and are they marked with the stove's name? Is there a teakettle or other hollowware marked with the stove-maker's name? Is there an original manufacturer's catalog or official cookbook showing the stove?

11) Is the **stove's history known?**

Still Want To Know What Your Stove Is "Worth?"

• What about asking an antique stove restorer-dealer for an appraisal? Many will appraise a stove by mail, from a photo, if you tell them about its condition in detail. There may be a charge of $10 or more for this service. But appraisals are only appropriate and useful for estate tax calculation, insurance inventory valuations, or divorce settlements, where you must have a figure, regardless of market reality. This real-life anecdote that shows why appraisals aren't appropriate for practical situations like deciding the price for an actual transaction: Recently, an insurance firm retained a professional antiques appraiser from Oregon to appraise the value of a household lost in a fire. Photos from some years before were all she had to work with. A 1926 gas range with a wood-burning side had been in the kitchen. After showing the photo to several professional antique stove restorer-dealers on the West Coast, she got appraisals ranging from $300 to $5,000.

• What about auction price comparison? Normally, auction prices are lower than retail prices. Dealers get a lot of their wares at auction, and mark-up may be nearly 200%. If collectors attend the same auction, they may bid some prices up to the retail level, or even higher. The auction price for a certain stove isn't necessarily the price you should charge for yours.

• What about price guides? There are too many variables relating to your stove for an antiques price guide to help.

• What about prices on stoves at an antique stove restorer-dealer's shop? He's based the prices on a number of factors, including cost of restoration supplies, overhead, hours of labor; utility value of a new stove of equivalent size and type; and the decorative/artistic desirability of the antique. Most of these factors have a going price, but the art value doesn't. And it's the one that matters most to a buyer. That's why some types of stoves aren't worth restoring. When a dealer is also a collector, he may like some of his stoves so much that he really isn't interested in selling them, and may put an unreasonably high price on them. It's his way of saying, "If you're crazy enough to pay me that kind of money for my stove, I'd be crazy not to accept; otherwise it's a keeper."

So What Do You Do To Arrive at a Price to Sell?

The foregoing observations aren't meant to keep you from examining the market, just to keep you from being intimidated by it, and to help you understand that in a market this thin, you are the market, to a surprisingly large degree.

• Figure out what the stove is worth to you; how much worse-off would you be without it? That's your minimum price. Be sure to take into account the stove's desirability.

• Find the right high-incentive buyer with enough income to let her pay generously for what she wants. The time and effort you put into finding her has a lot to do with the final price.

• Help this buyer decide her maximum price for the stove by asking how much better-off she'd be with it, or the price above which she'd be disappointed and want to decline the deal.

• Have her write her maximum price on a slip of paper while you write your minimum on another, and exchange papers. The correct price is half-way between your minimum and her maximum, and you'll both be equally pleased.

This is negotiation, the most satisfactory pricing technique in a thin market – one lacking high volume and demand. There's no reason why the burden of setting the price should be borne entirely by the seller! But a warning about this strategy: First, make the buyer understand that once the papers have been exchanged, no further negotiation is going to take place. Don't let an unscrupulous person get away with stating a false low maximum that will inevitably be less than your minimum so that he or she can then raise it to your minimum level. A maximum less than your minimum means that person is not the right buyer.

For More Information

STOVE INFORMATION

Antique Stove Information Clearinghouse

This is a service (basically archivist Clifford Boram's one-man show), that offers made-to-order catalog photocopies and other historical information. Boram is Historian for the ASA (Antique Stove Association). His advice and help has been invaluable to me for almost 20 years. Many ironware collectors have bought photocopies of the hollowware sections of old stove catalogs in the enormous collection available through ASIC. (Note: the street address has changed slightly from the last edition.) Please, always use a self-addressed stamped envelope!

Contact: Clifford Boram
421 N. Main St.
Monticello, IN 47960-1932
Phone: (574) 583-6465 (Let it ring!!)

ORGANIZATIONS

Antique Stove Association

This organization for serious stove people as well as those approaching the subject obliquely by collecting cast iron cooking utensils, etc., was hosted by the late Macy Stern, of Houston, Texas, for years. Lest you think there are hundreds of stove collectors in the USA, Cliff Boram cautions, "Please keep in mind that there are only about two dozen serious antique stove collectors in the whole country. Stoves are so heavy and bulky that they don't collect well. The great majority of serious antique stove people are either restorer-dealers or owner-users." Boram is an owner-user with nine stoves, including a "parts stove" backing up one in use, four which are apart and being worked on, one "serving as a filing cabinet, one for sale cheap, and one pile of junk." Macy Stern's categories of members included "Collector, Restorer-Dealer, Library, Owner-User, Pattern-maker, Re-porcelainizing Shop, and Toy Stove collector." A number of collectors of kitchen wares, stove accessories, lid lifters, and advertising items also belong. • A commercial quarterly newsletter with classified ads, historic and practical articles, and guides to museums, etc., serves stove buyers and sellers, and is now also the association's newsletter, and can be subscribed to without joining ASA.

Contact: Caroline & Craig Royske
Newsletter: "Antique Stove Exchange"
POB 2101
Waukesha, WI 53187
Phone: (262) 542-9190
E-mail: ase@ticon.net
Web site for ASE: www.theantiquestovexchng.com/

The Old Appliance Club

Not just stoves, but all kinds of appliances. See more following Chapter XVIII, "Electrifying Work." TOAC is affiliated with Antique Stoves, listed under Dealers. Newsletter: The Old Road Home. Mr. Santoro has a manual called "How To Purchase the Right Vintage Stove," and offers a full year of free consultation with the purchase of it.

Contact: Jack Santoro
P.O. Box 65
Ventura, CA 93002
Phone: (805) 643-3532
E-mail: toac@sbcglobal.net
Web site: www.theoldapplianceclub.com

DEALERS IN OLD STOVES

Just a few dealers in old stoves, known to me, are listed here. One way to locate an old stove near you is to join the Association, or subscribe to "ASE" where you will surely locate a dealer. Or try your local appliance dealers, metal scrap yards, even classified ads in your newspaper. Or do a search online to find a stove you really want.

Erickson's Antique Stoves

Fully restored, functional gas, wood, and electric stoves.

Contact: Dave Erickson
2 Taylor St., Box 2275
Littleton, MA, 01460
Phone: (979) 486-3589

Macy's Texas Stove Works

Once a woman named Macy Stern was asked to buy used appliances for about 500 apartments. Her client took the newer pieces, leaving Ms. Stern with heavy older stoves and ranges, etc., which led to Macy's Texas Stove Works. She defined "classic" or "vintage" ranges as those made since the 1930s, while "antique" ranges were made earlier. The late Ms. Stern admired them all, but you probably won't find a wider array of interesting 60 and 70 year olds at an A.A.R.P. meeting! A full range of gas and electric ranges – Chambers, Anderson, Magic Chef, Tappan, Roper, Royal Chef, Glenwood, etc. – old enough to have belonged to the grandmothers of those of us who are

"vintage" ourselves! MTSW restores, rebuilds, and fabricates parts for old ranges, and also parlor stoves, including re-porcelainizing. The man who did Ms. Stern's restoring, repairing and fabricating is Kenny Johnson, who now is the enthusiastic owner of MTSW. One service he offers is porcelainizing old stoves in the color a customer wants – even if it's just changing white to off-white!

Contact: Kenny Johnson
5515 Almeda Rd.
Houston, TX 77004
Phone: (713) 521-0934
Web site: www.macysclassicstoveworks.com

Good Time Stove Co.

An antique stove dealer's interesting website with lots of valuable information on cooking and heating stoves.

Contact: Mr. Richard "Stoveblack" Richardson
Box 306 Route 112
Goshen, MA 01032-0306
Phone: (888) 282-7506
Web site: www.goodtimestove.com/htm/
stovehistory.html

Antique Stove Heaven

Amazingly, while typing this chapter, I had the TV on and saw Mr. Williams talking about several old stoves. He stressed the importance of checking the lining of ovens, etc., the sound condition of the pipes feeding gas to the burners, and explained that various missing or damaged parts can be fabricated. He said that if you see a stove for sale, how much you pay should include everything including cosmetics – check how much new porcelain and/or re-chroming needs to be done.

Contact: Winsor Williams
5414 Western Ave.
Los Angeles, CA 90062
Phone: (323) 298-5581
E-mail: winsorstove@aol.com
Web site: www.antiquestoveheaven.com

Antique Stoves

Allied with Jack Santoro of The Old Appliance Club, this is a good mid-continent source to buy old stoves dating from 1750 to 1950s, and stove information.

Contact: Edward Semmelroth
410 Fleming Rd.
Tekonsha, MI 49092
Phone: (517) 278-2214 (M-F)
E-mail: sales@antiquestoves.com
Web site: www.antiquestoves.com

The Stoveworks

Antique & new stoves and restorations, serving western Canada, near Calgary, Alberta.

Box 3368
114-1 Street Ave. N.
Airdrie AB T4B-2B6
Canada
Phone, in Canada: (403) 948-2238
Fax: (323) 298-0029

Or visit our South Bay location at:

1428 Pacific Coast Highway
Harbor City, CA 90710
(310) 326-0030

XI-45. Stove lid lifter. *Spectacular voluptuous female form, cast iron. Surely not for a housewife's cook stove; probably for the stove on a railroad caboose or the like. 8-5/16"L, c.1850s-80s.* **$250+**

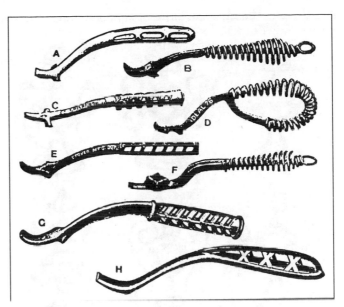

XI-47. Stove lid lifters. *(A) - (F) are from Excelsior Stove & Mfg. Co., c.1916. (A) and (C) are cast iron with a "coppered" finish. (B), (D), (E) and (F) are nickeled cast iron. (F) is a combination lifter and grate shaker. (G) and (H) are openwork castings of cast iron, offered in "coppered" finish. Heinz & Munschauer, Buffalo, NY, 1882.* **$5-$15+**

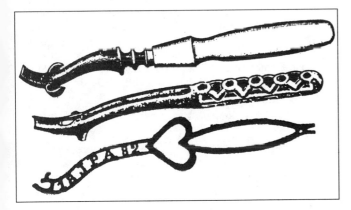

XI-46. Stove lid lifters. *(T) japanned cast iron shank, brass ferrule, and red-stained turned wood handle, 11"L. The two little curved side arms are for lifting pails. From unidentified catalog page, c.1870s-90s. (M) a "cool handle" one, nickeled cast iron, mfd. by Cleveland Foundry, OH. 1892 ad. (B) a heart-and-ellipse one, openwork handle, cast iron. Letters in cutout form are "J.P.A." flanked by "18" and "82." Mfd. by J. P. Abbott, Cleveland, OH, in 1882 ad, claiming this is "the best, the handsomest and easiest selling stove lid lifter is the Abbott Cold Handle." Although it doesn't mention it, the bifurcated end (B) was probably meant as a tack claw. Crossover folk art interest in hearts. (T) & (M) $5-$15+; (B) $65-$100*

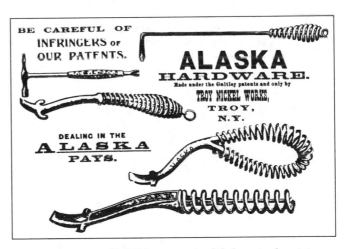

XI-48. Stove lid lifters, etc. *(T) four tools at top comprise the entire ad of Troy Nickel Works, Troy, NY, who made the cool coil "Alaska" line. The bent tool at top is a poker. The small hammer is for tacks – note tack-pulling tip to handle. Hardware News, Feb. 25, 1895, but made much earlier. (B) a coiled-wire lifter – perhaps one of those "infringers" of patents warned against by Troy. It was mfd. by L. M. Devore, Freeport, IL. He calls it a "non-heating wire handle." The Metal Worker, 1892.* **$5-$15**

XI-49. Stove urns, *of stamped metal trimmed with delicate cast handles & finials.* **(T-L)** *available from 5-1/2" to 8-1/2"H; next one* **(T-M)** *7"H;* **(T-R)** *8-5/8"H and 9-1/4"H;* **(B-L)** *10-5/8"H and 11-3/4"H;* **(T-M) 11-1/4"H and 12"H; (B-R)** *12" and 13" H. They made more – up to 14-3/4"H. National Stoves, Ranges & Furnaces, of Excelsior Stove & Mfg. Co., Quincy, IL, c.1916. Another crossover – some people buy these as objet d'art, even if they aren't interested in stoves. Most desirable are figural finials, that may bring five times as much as the above. Some stove urns actually held water, to help humidify the room.* **$20+**

XI-50. Whatzit that's not a cook stove accessory. *This is here because of slight resemblance to the similarly well-cast, beautifully patinated cast iron accessories that went around a stovepipe. Collector Joel Schiff and I believe that this is probably Korean or Vietnamese (something similar though a single "dish" is called le hap in Vietnam). Cast iron, 2 parts: what you see is all one part – the central "bowl" (not a brazier because there's no vent holes in bottom) has five dogwood-like "petals" that tilt slight down toward the cups cast at each tip. The little points have a tiny groove that has to be just decorative because you couldn't pour out of one without spilling the other four. Marks on back of bowl look like numbers in reverse, and read from right to left 073342 or 073345, with a definite Oriental character at each end. Center bowl: 6-5/8" diam.; overall diam. is 19", hole in underneath part is 5-5/8" diam., and has 5 slots to keep bowl from rotating, when you set this iron "flower" down into it. Dealer Lenny Kislin, Bear, NY, had this at a Pier show in NYC. It's probably 20th C.* **$350+**

COOKING

XII. POTS, PANS & HOLLOWWARE

This chapter is fairly short, but space is so restricted, and good books exist for two major fields: cast iron cookware; and vitreous enameled iron or steel – usually called "graniteware," after a popular stone-like mottled gray finish. Graniteware ("agateware," or, most accurately, "enamelware") has been collected for decades. While most collectors of cast iron seem to be men, most enamelware collectors are women. Enamelware is not really durable, because the glassy fired-on surface will shatter or chip easily, but there is an amazing variety of forms and colors. Floods of imported enamelwares over the last decade have frosted the prices for all enamelware, especially unmarked wares.

Cast iron cookware is a well-established, active, competitive market. It's cool, calm, and collected. It's durable, solid and smooth. Above all, it's heavy – so heavy that if you were hanging on to a few pieces of it you couldn't be blown away. Iron is literally in the blood. A sufficiency of it makes you healthy; a deficiency makes you anemic. In 1989, about the time the cast iron market took off and gathered hundreds of strong collectors, there was even a men's cologne called "IRON."

There's more variation, and a wider spread in value of cast iron pots and pans than in any other field of kitchen collecting. This is because its collectors track rarity and prices all the time, closely. The comparative rarity and desirability of different sizes, and variations in marks by the same foundry, add complicated levels to this field. Some nine inch (#9) skillets (frying pans) might be worth a tenth of a particular #13, or the right combination of large block lettering, logo, and smoke ring (the raised ring on bottom) might make a #2 worth $3,000 or more. A pot with a certain style of logo on its bottom may be worth four times what the same pot with a different style logo is. If you expect to collect and pay fair, going prices for things you want, buy all the books (look in the Bibliography for roman numeral XII in the left column), join organizations, go to conventions, read the message boards on Web sites. Always ask questions and make notes.

Other metal cooking wares shouldn't be neglected. Copper is the most generally-admired metal, mainly for its decorative appeal to non-collectors. There's some info on tin here, and in Chapter VII (Containers). Aluminum has many fans (I love cast aluminum), as does brass. There are lots of books in the Bibliography, some related to other chapters, on various metal wares.

Aetna – See a Chafing dish entry

Bain marie pans, copper, set of 6 deep cylindrical pans, forged iron handles, sizes 8-24 oz., c.1830-1880s.. **$650+**

Bain marie with pans, literally a water bath, called a bambury in England, heavy tin, 6 high-sided saucepans, all with lids, 2-eye size for cook stove burners, American, mid 19th C................................. **$250+**

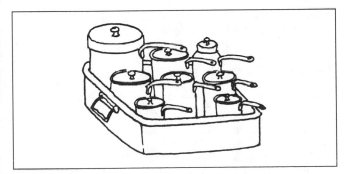

XII-1. Bain marie set. *Tall, straight-sided pans, long handles, for setting in large pan called a "box" of water. Bain marie means "bath pool." This set, copper with iron handles, from* Mrs. A. B. Marshall's Cookbook, *London, c.1900.* **$450+**

Bake pan, hammered sheet iron, no seams, oval with slightly flared sides, no handles, very stark design, American (?), 2-3/4" deep x 13"L x 11-3/4"W, late 19th C. .... **$35+**

Bean pot, with lid, cast iron commemorative piece, lid has cast iron knob & baked bean recipe is cast inside the lid, simply: "1 tablespoon mustard, 2 teaspoons salt, 1/2 cup syrup, 1/2 cup sugar, 2 lbs beans, 1 lb pork, 4 onions." On top of lid is cast name, place & date, "Alabama Pipe Co., Anniston, AL," 5-1/2"H x 8-1/2" diam., marked also "Christmas 1954." .... **$65+**

Berlin kettle, style sometimes called a bean pot because of ear handles on a bulbous body. Cobalt blue & white swirl enameled iron, black rim & trim, wire falling bail, slightly domed lid with large round cobalt-enameled knob, American or European, 5-1/4"H x 6-3/4" diam., late 1800s-1910s. .... **$175+**

❖ NOTES ❖

Berlin kettles, or **Berlin saucepans.** A type of tightly-lidded kettle, very globose with round bulging sides, ear lugs & a wire bail handle, was widely known in the 19th & early 20th centuries as a Berlin kettle. (It's possible the term is even older, & that it was once applied to certain thin-walled bulbous cast iron cookwares, perhaps made of Berlin iron from the Royal Foundry at Berlin, Germany. Berlin iron was described as "very fusible" & used for fine castings, including jewelry.

Berlin kettles were imported by the hundreds of thousands, in sheet iron, tin, aluminum, & enamelware. When WWI broke out in July 1914, nothing much was done in the USA about the name "Berlin." I don't know how many German-made housewares continued to be available for import here. Britain & Canada entered the war in August 1914; they had stopped importing German goods. The U.S. entered the war in April 1917, but not until 13 months later was a general appeal made to housewares dealers to stop using the word "Berlin" or any other word associated with Germany. • June 1918 saw the beginning of a series of *House Furnishing Review* articles entitled "Over the Top" about "Made in Germany" style or brand names. Monarch Aluminum Ware Co. of Cleveland instigated a campaign that exhorted American manufacturers & retailers to rid the housewares trade of all German-made goods, & of names such as "Berlin," and – within a few months – to remove the word "Delicatessen" from stores, & "Wiener schnitzel" from menus. Most successful was the first campaign.

Excerpts from six letters written by officers of various companies who made "Berlin-type" kettles follow: (1) "It's the 'Paris' Kettle now – 'Berlin' ousted! Aladdin Aluminum cooking Utensils will have no more 'Berlin' Kettles or Saucepans." 2) "Having entirely discarded the trade name 'Berlin' we will designate them as 'Washington Kettles,'" declared Monarch. (3) "We call the Berlin Kettle the 'Victory Kettle,'" wrote a retailer. (4) "We changed the name of our Berlin goods to 'Convex' Kettles, Saucepans, etc. ... While we have no objection to 'Washington' Kettles, there is no significance in this, whereas 'Convex' describes just what the kettles are," said the Republic Stamping & Enameling Co. (5) "We have changed the name of our Berlin Kettles to 'Liberty Kettles,'" said Enterprise Aluminum Co. (6) "I would

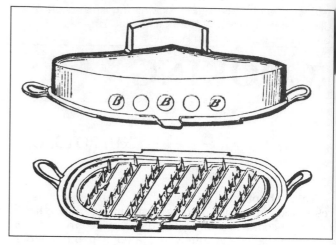

XII-3. Broiler or ***Gridiron*** patent. *Pat'd. Sept. 30, 1856 (#15,799) by William Bennett, NYC. His claim was for the "pins or elevators attached to the bars of the gridiron, used in connexion with the ventilating cover."*

suggest they call them 'U.S. Saucepans,' Pots, etc., or 'Yankee Saucepans,' Pots, etc." signed, A retailer.

Something which sent chills up my spine were the many signed letters reprinted, in part, in *The Metal Worker*, signed by men with markedly German-heritage names: Hippenstiel, Wilhelm, Wesselmann, Danziger, Fleischman, Arnstein, Kauders, Eisenberg, Lobsitz – on and on they went, with suggestions for "driving out the Hunns," for naming chamberpots "Friederich," for "eliminating everything of a German nature," etc.

The Armistice was signed not long after, but by October 1918, the editor of the trade journal *House Furnishing Review* was reported "The 'Berlin' saucepan was the first to go, and the 'made in Germany' slogan will not again adorn the shelves of our American house-furnishing and hardware stores." He then went on to warn retailers against stocking their shelves with "unbranded goods of unknown quality of the peddler type" because they might have German origins. • Not too long after at least some manufacturers were back to using "Berlin Kettle," undoubtedly because it had been used for so many years. Collectors use the term today.

Broiler, heavy stamped sheet iron, round, for stovetop use, 4 parts: bottom plate or lid, corrugated top plate or lid, & 2 important middle parts with crosswise & concave or grooved bars or ribs; all parts hinge together, longish handles on top & bottom, tab handle on top plate, "The Morgan," Sun Stamping Co., Kalamazoo, MI, late 1880s-c.1900............ **$35+**

❖ NOTES ❖

Learning From Old Ads. A printed broadside, penciled "Rec'd May 8th, 1889, Wed' Morn'g" by a long ago owner, is all about the "Morgans Odorless Frying-Pan & Broiler combined Styled A," patented July 19, 1887. The flyer was sent out by "Sole Manufacturers & Patentees," Morgan Mfg. Co., Kalamazoo, & is just two years earlier than the ad placed by Sun, who may have bought the manufacturing rights. It is clearly pictured & has but three parts: a very shallow "extra fine grey" cast iron frying pan bottom

XII-2. Broiler & fry-pan combined. *"Tracy's The Triumph," Maltby, Henley & Co., Rocky Hill, CT. Stamped steel frying pan-lid detaches. Broiler is cast iron with grooved ribs. One of many such openwork stovetop broilers. 1890 ad.* **$150+**

with two hook-like hinges sticking out opposite the handle, a central broiling plate, also cast iron, with grooved bars set crosswise to the handle, & with two tabs with holes that fit over the hooks on the lower pan, plus a stamped tin lid, slightly domed. The text claims that this is "A Blessing to Every Housekeeper! As 57,000 Now Using Them Gladly Attest!" It goes on to say that this Morgan (I'm sure Style A is different from the one made by Sun a little later) is "adapted to cooking steak, meats, oysters, eggs, onions, and vegetables of all kinds, toasting bread, &c., over gas, oil, wood, coal or gasoline fire. Prevents the grease from spattering the stove, retains the juices and substance of food, making it more palatable, and does its work in less time than any Frying Pan or Broiler made." The name "is on bottom of every Pan." An acrostic poem further touts their "contrivance rare."

Much of comfort, strong and real,
Or of good we all may feel,
Rises from some handy spring
Governed by some Patent Thing.
And, of these, we give to man,
Now an improved Frying-Pan.
    Oh! So?
    Yes. Guess
    What may its advantage be.
    There! Look!
    Do you cook?
    Read within and you shall see.
Much of odor comes to man
From the common frying pan.
    'most all this, as we connspire,
Goes right down into the fire. ...
    Oh! So!
    Don't it go,
    Speeding on through room and stair?
    You bet!
    It can't get
    Out of our contrivance rare.
Come, save all this nasty scent.
Order one and be content.

XII-5. Broilers. *Cast iron. Note handle differences.* **(1)** *Patent for meat-broiler having "concave-convex central portion with closed corrugations from the crown" down to circular channel around edge. Pat'd. July 5, 1881, by Hosma W. Libbey, Cleveland, OH.* **(2)** *Two-part, marked only with patent date "AUG 77." Not visible are the small holes in perimeter, between grids & grease "moat." It's probably the "Favorite" from Piqua, OH.* **(3)** *10" diam. "Favorite" – a "gasoline broiler also useful for a camp fire." 1910s. Info courtesy Robert Knutson of MN.* **(4)** *Three-part Griswold "Erie Double Broiler," with "solid cast iron body, base-ring & tin cover." Convex closed grid sets into channeled base ring that collects drips & grease. From Albert Pick catalog, 1909.* **(5)** *Griswold one-part open-grid boiler for gasoline stoves. Picture from The Metal Worker, 1890.* **$05+**

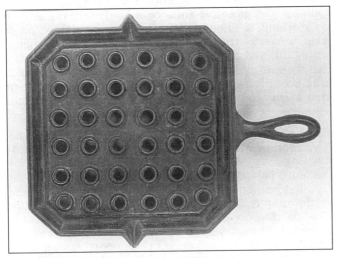

XII-4. Broiler. *Cast iron, 10" square, truncated corners, 4"L. handle & 2 pointed pouring lips. Collector believes the company also made a round one because it looks so similar. Dated Feb. 26, 1876. Photo courtesy David G. Smith.* **$150+**

Broiler, stovetop, cast iron, 2 parts hinged, both with handles & grooved parallel bars, but viewed from above, the bars cross diagonally to form diamonds not squares, "Russells Patent," 10-3/4" diam., marked "April 9, 1887." .... **$65+**

Broiler, stovetop, cast iron, one piece, convex with handle & pouring lips, underneath is concave & stepped like a stadium, each stage has perforations & 4 depressions that line up with ever larger depressions at each stage & then with the pouring lips; marked underneath & on top "Brooklyn Broiler," Silver & Co., Brooklyn, NY, 10-1/2" diam., pat'd. April 7, 1894. .... **$85+**

Broiler, stovetop, cast iron, round, slightly convex with little oblong tabs sticking up in concentric rings, small hole in center is the vent, with riveted-on short shaft & small cast iron disc, grease trough around edge, small pointed pouring lip, frying-pan-like handle, missing its original domed sheet iron cover with handle, cover would be marked with name & mfr. "North," Cleveland Foundry Co., Cleveland, OH, 10-1/2" diam., marked on disc & handle "Pat'd. July 19, 1887." As is: .... **$45+**

Broiler, tin, wire mesh & turned wood, "authorized" brass ID plate on side reads "American Broiler," mfd. by S. Bower's American Broiler Co., 11" diam. plus

7"L handle, pat'd. July 21, 1868 (#80,125) & Oct. 19, 1869 (reissue #3,684) by S. Bowers, of Penn Yan, NY, & then Elmira, NY. It was sold by, & even possibly made under license by, Lalance & Grosjean; E. Ketcham; Russell & Erwin; & N. E. James. ..... **$35+**

❖ NOTES ❖

Patented Broilers. Many of the stove- or range-top broilers, patented in the 1850s into the early 20th century, were claimed to solve the problem of smoke from burning splattered grease, by use of specially designed covers & patterns of grooved grill bars. Some of the ribbed or barred broiling surfaces were slightly convex, with runnels in the bars draining into a sort of grease moat encircling the pan's edge. Some broiling surfaces were an openwork grill, allowing flames to go up between the bars to the meat, bread, etc. Some versions were more like frying pans, but with ridges cast into the bottom to hold the meat up out of the grease. All had at least two detachable parts; often one part would serve as a frying pan by itself. These American broilers were mostly patented between 1862 & the 1910s.

XII-6. Broiler, 2 versions. *Hinged, 2-part cast iron with broiling bumps. "Henis Patent Self-Basting," first pat'd. Aug. 12, 1879.* **(T)** *Originally came in 4 sizes: #8 round, for #8 stove [that means the eye hole was 8"]; #9 round for #9 stove; #11 oblong, 9" x 11" to fit on two eye holes; and #15 oblong, 15" x 9" for "large family." Picture from ad of Paine, Diehl & Co., 1888.* **(B)** *This was the improved version, somewhat more substantial, mfd. by Royal Mfg. Co., Ltd., Philadelphia – "sole manufacturers of improved 'Henis.'" 1903 ad.* **$45+**

Broiler, stovetop, "Triumph," Tracy's Broiler & Fry-Pan Combined – "Complete Breakfast Outfit." Cast & sheet iron, It was made by Haltby, Henley & Co., Rocky Hill, CT. 2 hinged parts – a tinned sheet iron frying pan separable from cast iron broiler with "arched, grooved ribs, through which the juices of the meat flow into the outer channel." After removing from stove, you'd pour off grease from the channel, then reverse pan so contents remained in pan, which could be used as a regular frying pan too. Probably late 1880s. .... **$65+**

Broiler, stovetop, cast iron, pattern of "self-basting" bumps & ridges inside, "Royal Improved Henis," mfd. by Royal Mfg. Co., Philadelphia, c.1903. .... **$45+**

Broiler, cast iron, arched grooved ribs in big herringbone or chevron pattern feed into outer grease channel, 2 pouring lips, slightly raised frying pan handle with hanging hole, no lid. "Dundee," mfd. by Dundee Mfg. Co., Boston, advertised as early as 1923 & as late as 1930. .... **$35+**

Candy kettle, copper, dovetailed seam, convex bottom, heavy iron handles, no mark. American (?), 19" diam., mid 19th C. Candy kettles & a few other professional cook's wares were made throughout the 19th C. & early 20th C. almost the same, & if unmarked are hard to date... **$135+**

Chafing dish, or hash dish, chaffern, or chaffing dish (in some 18th & early 19th C. records), stamped & pieced tin, oval pan with cabriole legs, 3-tube camphene burner, American, 10"H x 12"L, mid 1800s......... **$75+**

❖ NOTES ❖

Tin Down South – C. F. McCoy, in *Eighty Years Progress of the U.S., 1781-1861*, published in NY in 1864, gave an account of traveling in the South, & finding out that most things – from buggies to furniture – were made in the North. McCoy writes, "I asked at a tin shop, and they said their stoves, and gas fixtures, and lamps, and japanned work, and block tin were from the north, but that their tin ware was made in their own shop, though out of English plate and with northern solder." • In fact, throughout the 19th C., at least foundries, & possibly tinware manufacturers, as well as clothing & shoe-makers listed among their products, wares for the "Southern Trade." How those metalwares differed from Northern wares, it's never stated, but we know about clothing & shoes that much of it was shoddy goods, so it is not impossible to imagine that lower quality iron & tinwares were sent south too.

Chafing dish, copper, 3 parts: stand, pan & lid, "Empress Ware," pat'd. 1907. .... **$65+**

Chafing dish, nickeled brass, simple chased round-bottomed pan with turned wood side handle, domed lid, 3-legged high frame over alcohol burner, Manning, Bowman & Co., Meriden, CT, c.1902. .... **$35+**

Chafing dish, or alcohol gas stove, as maker called it, nickeled brass, very Arts & Crafts look, platform base with 4 stately, columns, denatured alcohol stove within, pan above looks like domed temple roof, mfd. by Buffalo Mfg. Co., Buffalo, NY, c.1908. .... **$55+**

Chafing dish, tin, oval, alcohol pan below, a type also called an allblaze dish or allblaze-pan, American or import (?) by company such as F. A. Walker, 6-3/4"H x 16"L oval, c.1870s. .... **$225+**

Aetnas. Closely related to allblaze chafing dishes are aetnas or etnas – tall vessels meant for heating small amounts of liquids or mulling them, which sat above (or somewhat within) a saucer or container filled with flammable spirits. Aetnas are shaped like coffee pots; or are cylindrical with domed lids; or are heavy tin inverted cones, pouring lip & hinged lid, & a small strap handle soldered at one end only. All three types are shown in F. A. Walker catalog of the 1870s.

•   •   •

The Chafing Dish. "Its Vogue Signalizes a Nation's Progress, and is Indicative of Good Cheer and Success," was published in *House Furnishing Review*, Sept. 1904. Lots of tantalizing references to ancient civilizations and chafing dishes appear in the article, with quotes attributed to famous long-dead writers. From ancient classical Roman writer Seneca (c.4 BC-65 AD): "Daintiness gave birth to this useful invention in order that no viand should be chilled and that everything should be hot enough to please the most pampered palate. The kitchen follows the supper." From the 15th century, a quote from Sir Francis Bacon's treatise on "Physiological Remains," in which Bacon compared metal alloys. "Make proof," he wrote, "of the incorporation of silver and tin in equal quantity, or with two parts silver and one part tin, and ... observe whether it will endure the ordinary fire which belongeth to chafing dishes, posnets and such other silver vessels." Skipping 300 years, the article goes on, "It appeared in America in 1720. The colonists having overcome the difficulties incidental upon the making of a new country, began to appreciate and to desire the luxuries and adornments of refined living. The father of a rich bride of the day, who desired to give his daughter 'a truly elegant outfit,' in the list of household furnishings he ordered from England, included '6 small brass chafing dishes, 4 shillings apiece.' From which fact may be inferred that the hospitable hostesses of that time were wont to give chafing dish parties, as do the entertainers of this enlightened century." The writer goes along in this rather smarmy vein, and finally writes that the chafing dish "... is a boon to the journalist who, after his nightly toil, enjoys a repast in his own home." This echoes what Eliza Acton wrote in 1845, in *Modern Cookery*, that the conjurer "... is an especially convenient mode of cooking for persons whose hour of dining are [*sic*] rendered uncertain by their avocations."

•   •   •

1929. "When Maidens Were Wooed Over the **Spirit Lamp.** – The turn of the century gave us a new leaf; we manifested domestication: America entered into the Chafing Dish Era. ... One wonders what has become of all the chafing dishes. In some old-fashioned parlors they are still displayed. They are gathering dust in many an attic. Give them another ten years of neglect, and antique dealers will be selling them as Early American. Yet there is many a woman in America today who, on sight of a chafing dish, finds her eyes clouded with tender remembrance, for in her time the chafing dish was the first step that led to the altar. Women were known by their skill in casually cooking up tasty bits. These romps of twenty years ago knew full well they were being judged once they lit the spirit lamp, and young men, after the dumb fashion of callow youth,

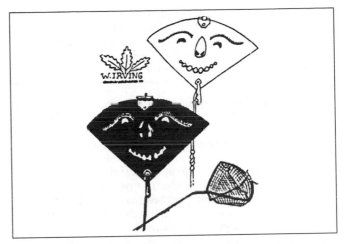

XII-7. Corn popper folk art. *Sheet steel, forged iron handles with strengthening twist, heavy wire baskets. Marked with a tree-oak-leaf stamp & name "W. Irving." Other Irving pieces known include a "Saratoga Jabber," & "Saratoga Frizzler" – for French fries. These two, slightly different corn poppers are for hearth use, or backyard cookouts. Courtesy Aarne Anton, American Primitive Gallery, NYC.* **$1,200+**

found themselves more and more enmeshed as savory odors arose. ..." Richardson Wright, "The Chafing dish Era," *House & Garden*, Oct. 1929.

Conjurer – See Conjurer in Chapter XI (Stoves)
Cooker, a conjurer-like contrivance, & a puzzler until I found a documentary reference to it (see below). My notes are sketchy, having been taken on the run at a flea market some years ago: "sheet iron pan or fire vessel, slightly bulging sides, grate inside, vent on one side & chimney-like pipe on round opening in top is missing a lid or some kind of vessel." It was invented by someone named Spiller, English, prob. late 1840s. .... **$100+**

Batching It – In *Knights' Cyclopaedia of the Industry of All Nations*, published in London in 1851, is this note on page 657: "In the so-called '**bachelor's kettles**,' of which Spiller's is a recent specimen, the problem seems to be to determine in how short a space of time, and with how little trouble, can a frugal meal for a person be prepared. Spiller's apparatus consists of a kind of saucepan, with a small opening on one side to admit air, and a flue fixed in the opposite side to let off smoke. A very shallow tea kettle forms the cover to this saucepan. In the middle of the saucepan is a small iron grating, and on this grating is placed one of those small net-work arrangements of sticks which constitute 'patent firewood' and which are now sold so cheaply at one farthing each. This wood being kindled, and the kettle placed over it, the heat is so confined as to make the water in the kettle boil by the time the wood is consumed. With some of these contrivances a kind of small frying-pan is sold; and by using a larger piece of patent firewood, time is allowed for a small dish of savory cookery after the water has boiled: the kettle being quickly replaced by the pan. There is a certain amount of usefulness in the contrivance, which makes it available for others besides the 'bachelors' whom the patentee seems to have had in his thoughts."

Cooker, heavy cast aluminum, domed aluminum lid, bottom edge "flares" out, distinctive flat "broccoli-flowerette" side handles, knight's head in plumed helmet mark, sometimes has sword across head, "Guardian Service," mfd. by Century Metalcraft Corp., 1930s. • Mrs. Edith Spangler, of Pennsylvania, wrote me, "I am one of the people who helped to put on those **dinner parties for Guardian** Services from 1936 into the forties, 'til they started the glass lids. But at first they made it and called it 'Silver Seal.' My husband ... put on chart talks after the meal. We had a good sale [of the pieces]. We usually had between 15 and 20 for a meal. Ingredients were a big roast, potatoes, carrots, rice and pancakes and graham cracker pudding, everything prepared on top of the stove." • Some collector interest now that may grow. .... **$20+**

Corn popper, aluminum pan with crank in lid, Kwikway Products, Inc., St. Louis, MO, pat'd. 1927. .... **$15**

Corn popper, long handle, hinged box – half of wire mesh "like the ordinary popper, to be used when the corn is preferred popped dry," the other half of sheet steel, for popping with seasoning, "More's Reversible," mfd. by C. A. Chapman, Geneva, NY, c.1908. .... **$15**

Corn popper, metal, enameled orangey red lid with 2 wooden knobs, crank is heavy rod, bent so as to stir the popcorn around inside, wood handle is painted orange; it snaps off its bracket on the side to go inside for storage, 7" diam., 20th C. .... **$8+**

Corn popper, shallow round tin pan, with screen dome "lid," long handle with litho cutout of Mickey Mouse halfway down handle, eagerly holding the release catch that opens the popper, rim & handle painted red, pan is 8" diam., overall length is 19-1/4". 1930s. • Rarely found in good condition, & those are fought over by crossover Disney collectors.................. **$765+**

❖ NOTES ❖

Where Was Orville? – An interesting early newspaper story about corn poppers goes as follows: "**The First Cornpopper Laughed At.** – In the winter of 1837, Mr. Francis P. Knowlton of Hopkinton, New Hampshire, purchased of Mr. Amos Kelley a sheet of wire netting from his manufactory on the main road, and constructed the first cornpopper ever made. The various parts were cut the required shape and sewed together with wire. Mr. Knowlton then made some for Judge Harvey and Judge Chase, which they sent to various parts of the United States as curiosities. Thinking he could see a field of usefulness for the newly-conceived article, Mr. Knowlton made several and took them to Concord to a hardware store, hoping to introduce before the public a useful utensil and to receive a reasonable remuneration. His production was scorned and ridiculed by the proprietors and they refused to have anything to do with it.

"He gave up and Mr. Amos Kelley began pressing them into shape out of wire and they slowly grew in favor." *New York Times*, Aug. 3, 1890, from a story in the *Concord People and Patriot*.

• • • •

In Orra Stone's *History of the Manufacturers of Massachusetts*, 1930, he wrote that a Samuel Ayers of Worcester, MA, "was of an ingenious turn of mind and invented and fashioned most of the tools and devices he used in wire working. He is said to have been the first man to press a corn-popper into shape from wire mesh cloth." [p.1769. Stone doesn't tell where he got this information, nor when Ayers made his poppers.]

Corn popper, tin with crank handle, shaped like a saucepan, raised bottom, "E-Z Corn Popper," 9" diam., early 20th C. **$15**

Corn popper, tin, wooden handle, "Lightning," 20th C. **$25**

❖ RECIPE ❖

Pop Corn Pudding – *Pop some corn nicely, then roll it as fine as you can. One pint of corn to one quart of sweet milk; add a small piece of butter, one teaspoon salt, beat two eggs with enough sugar to sweeten the milk; mix all together. Bake 30 minutes." From a periodical,* The Housewife, *NY: A. D. Porter Co., Aug. 1904.*

Custard kettle, cast iron outer kettle with bulging sides, block tin inner kettle sets down inside a hole in the top of the outer one, turned wooden handle, lid with little bracket strap handle, tapered tubular iron handles on outer vessel, angled slightly up, American or English, 7-1/2"H, c.1850s-1900...................................... **$125**

XII-8. Cruller or potato fryers for deep frying. *Also called **frying baskets** or **double fry pans**. Heavy wire or perforated metal baskets suspended in various sizes of pans. **(L)** Pat'd. July 8, 1879 and mfd. by Matthai-Ingram, Lalance & Grosjean, etc. **(R)** Up to 20" diam. wrought steel, Duparquet, Huot, Moneuse, c.1900-1910.* **$75-$150**

Hasty Pudding – "*Boil in a pot or kettle about six quarts water, leaving room for the addition of the meal; mix in a pint bowl full of Indian meal [corn meal] and cold water with a large spoonful of salt. When the water boils, stir this into it. After 30 or 40 minutes, stir in four or five handfuls of dry meal, and let it boil as much longer; then add a little more dry meal and boil 20 minutes longer. Taste it to see if it is salt enough. Stir it very often to prevent its burning. Most people make it too thick and do not cook it half long enough. Boil it, altogether at least two hours. When taken out, it should be so soft that it will in a few minutes settle down smooth in the dish. If you wish to fry it when cold, put a spoonful of water into each cup, pan or dish into which it is to be put, to keep it from sticking.*" Mrs. Cornelius, The Young Housekeeper's Friend, or, A Guide to Domestic Economy & Comfort, Boston & NY: 1846.

Hasty – Pudding Sauce – "*1 cup hot milk, 1 cup sugar, 2 eggs, 1 tablespoon butter. Stir the butter into the boiling milk, add the sugar, and pour this on the beaten eggs. Return to the custard kettle and stir until it begins to thicken. Flavor with vanilla, adding, if you like, nutmeg, and set in hot, not boiling, water till needed.*" Marion Harland, House & Home, a Complete Housewife's Guide, Philadelphia, 1889.

XII-9. Double or farina boilers & valved saucepan. *Clockwise from top center:* **(A)** *"French Milk Sauce Pan," with valves in lid.* **(B)** *Milk saucepan, tin with thick, white earthenware inner pan. Still being sold today, in nearly same form, also imported from France. This picture from an 1870's-80s Walker import catalog.* **(C)** *"Sauce Pan & Potato Steamer," from American Home Cook Book, 1854.* **(D)** *Farina boiler for custard, corn starch, milk. Note spouting for water in lower part.* **$55-$125+**

Block tin – As the term is used in old kitchen furnishing lists, block tin refers to thin sheets of tin-coated iron, not the actual "block" or ingot of partially refined, nearly pure tin. (Stream or Grain tin was finer still.) Often the authors of 19th C. cookery books specified block tin utensils as the best for the money. What they meant is revealed in a later book by Elsie Hutchinson: "The best tin plate is dipped twice; this is called 'block tin,' or 'retinned ware.'" The House Furnishings Department, NY: Ronald Press, 1918, 1922.

Double boiler, gray graniteware, with lid, American, late 19th or early 20th C. If a color, add as much as $200 .... **$55**

Double boiler, shaded dark-to-light blue ombré enamelware, may be Shapleigh Hardware's "Bluebelle Ware," early 20th C. **$65**

Double boiler, tin, copper bottom, bracket strap handle lid, 8-3/16"H, c.1850s .... **$75+**

Double boiler, tin outer mug-like water container with cast pewter (or Britannia) trim & handle, inner pewter pot with spout has brass bottom, bail handle, finial on cover, "Manning Patent," Meriden, CT, design elements late 18th C.; but this prob. dates from 19th C. .... **$150+**

Double boiler egg cooker, heavy copper, tinned inside, brass handles, nifty yellow molded plastic chick on top peeps when eggs are done, only words stamped on metal are "Fill to this line with cold water." Fill upper compartment with water to one of the three depths marked for soft, medium or hard boiled, then put eggs in the lower part & cover with cold water, then put top on for cooking. The chick is supposed to peep; mine is silent. Not marked, was sold through Lewis & Conger retailers, prob. through other firms too, American (?), 5-1/2"H parts together, c. late 1920s to early 1930s. Originally $1.50 .... **$30**

Dutch oven, cast iron, "Barstow Stove Co., No. 2," 7-3/4"H, 19th C. .... **$45+**

Stove Makers' Hollowware – Generally speaking, stove collectors are not interested in hollowware, and so not much cross-referenced information is available to collectors. (See information resources at end of Chapter XI.) You'll often find tea or water kettles with a stove maker's name; other hollowware, such as griddles, frying pans, Dutch ovens, etc., are less commonly found with a stove maker's name. An article in The Metal Worker, June 4, 1892, says that the contribution of hollowware to the total cost of manufacturing stoves was very small, but even so it represented an area where penny saving was possible. In the 1890s, a big cast iron stove with nickel trimming could be bought retail for under $20; less fancy ones, with fewer niceties, sold for under $15. Pretty astounding. • The article elaborated on hollowware: "There are numerous establishments that do not make hollow ware, but prefer to buy. The cost of hollow ware which this concern makes and sells with its stoves will, therefore, appear strange to some of our foundry readers. Nevertheless, we present the figures [for making & finishing hollowware in the stove foundry] in this case just as we find them. [Labor involved in] grinding hollowware ... costs 26/100th of 1% of the total stove cost, while the supplies used amount to 29/100th of 1%, making a total of 65/100th of 1% of the total cost of stoves [sold with hollowware]." In other words, for a stove costing $20, the hollowware was estimated to cost only 13¢.

• • •

Hollowwares meant for use on the stove were also called **stove wares**. The terms are used to describe all cooking utensils with "hollow" insides, as opposed to flat pieces like griddles. Everything from skillets and frying pans to tea kettles and roasting pans, made of cast iron, brass, copper, tin, aluminum, enameled iron, etc., could be called hollowware. The term was commonly used by iron founders (spelled as one or two words) to describe their cast iron wares, which they may have cast in different parts of the same foundry as they cast stoves, stove lids, sadirons, etc. The prevailing theory about the word sad iron, by the way, is that its name means heavy or solid iron. Another is that it was the same as the term used by pewterers, who used sadware to refer to flat wares, like plates. According to Ledlie Irwin Laughlin, in *Pewter In America*, the "hammerman," whose job was to take a plate after it was turned on a lathe, and hammered it out, was also called the "sadware man." The word flat iron is supposed to refer to the fact that the iron was cast in one piece, not as hollowware, although some sadirons are hollow. Read more in the hearth cooking section, under Cook pot.

Dutch oven, cast iron, large deep kettle with 3 very short legs, snug lid with flared raised edge, arched iron handle, falling wire bail, well-finished & smooth, "Griswold" #13, 9-qt. capacity, as late as 1973. • It was selected for an editorial feature on old-fashioned kitchen wares in *House Beautiful*, in 1973; the editor wrote "Early American deep kettle can hang over a campfire and hold enough food for the whole Scout troop." The price for it then was only twenty dollars!...................................... **$450**

Dutch oven, cast iron, slightly slanted sides, large cast ear handles, heavy wire falling bail, completely flat lid with high arched handle. Original brochure reads "It is adapted for many purposes, and will be found a very useful utensil in the kitchen. It is superior to any other roaster for roasting meats, etc., and can be used very conveniently on gasoline stoves." The kettle looks at least 20 years older than indicated by the brochure & the reference to gasoline stoves. On lid: "Wagner, Sidney, O, 9," c.1893 brochure. See also Dutch Ovens in Chapter X. **$55**

❖ NOTES ❖

Precious Iron – "Every person knows the manifold uses of this truly precious metal; it is capable of being cast in moulds of any form; of being drawn out into wires of any desired strength or fineness; of being extended into plates or sheets; of being bent in every direction; of being sharpened, hardened, and softened at pleasure. Iron accommodates itself to all our wants, our desires, and even our caprices; it is equally serviceable to the arts, the sciences, to agriculture, and war; the same ore furnishes the sword, the ploughshare, the scythe, the pruning hook, the needle, the graver, the spring of a watch or of a carriage, the chisel, the chain, the anchor, the compass, the cannon, and the bomb. It is a medicine of much virtue, and the only metal friendly to the human frame." Andrew Ure, *A Dictionary of Arts, Manufacturers, and Mines*. Volume I. NYC: D. Appleton & Co., 1854 (First published in London in 1839; this edition "reprinted ... from the last corrected & greatly enlarged English Edition" of 1853.)

❖ RECIPES ❖

Corn Bread – "The south has long been celebrated for its grateful corn bread, cakes, muffins and hominy. In consequence of an invitation in the Cultivator, a young lady in Tennessee has kindly sent us the following directions for making these domestic delicacies of the table, for which we respectfully tender her our acknowledgments. – Plain Corn Bread. – Six pints [corn] meal, one tablespoonful salt, four pints water; thoroughly mixed with the hand, and baked in oblong rolls about two inches thick. Use as much dough for each roll as can be conveniently shaped in the hand. Many persons use hot water; in winter it is certainly best. The bread is better to be made half an hour or more before it is baked. The oven must be tolerably hot when the dough is put in. All kinds of corn bread require a hotter oven and to be baked quicker than flour." [Possibly to be baked on baking sheet of iron, or large sheet iron drip pan.]*

Light Corn Bread – Stir four pints meal into three pints tepid water; add one large tea-spoonful salt; let it rise five or six hours; then stir up with the hand and bake in a brisk oven. Another method is to make mush, and before it grows cold, stir in half a pint of meal. Let it rise and bake as the first.*

Corn Cakes – Six eggs well beaten, one pint milk, one tea-spoonful salt, two pints mush almost cold, two pints meal, and three table-spoonsful melted lard. Grease the [Dutch?] oven and put one large spoonful of batter in each cake. Do not let them touch in baking.*

Corn Muffins – Made in the same way as corn cakes; grease the muffin hoops and heat the oven slightly, before putting in either corn cakes or muffins. A better muffin is made by substituting two pints flour instead of meal. (These pints were all measured with the common tin cup.)" The Farmers' Cabinet, Devoted to Agriculture, Horticulture and Rural Economy. *Philadelphia: Vol. II, No. 1, Aug. 1, 1837.*

Ebelskiver pan or egg poacher, gray & brown enameled cast iron, 7 cups, "frying pan" handle, "Crown F.," prob. European, c.1890s-1910. See also Chapter IV (Molds) .... **$40+**

Egg boiler, wire basket with slanted sides, all wires spoked out from center of flat bottom, high central handle of 4 twisted wires with loop handle, The Wire Goods Co., Worchester, MA, basket 2-1/2" deep x 6" diam., overall height 6", 1910s. **$20**

Egg boiler & holder, folding wire for 6 eggs, has springy stand of same wire, American, 7-1/2"H x 6" diam. when completely open, late 1800s-1930s........ **$45+**

XII-10. Egg poachers & boilers. (1) *Tin, 3-cup stack, loose cups in arched iron frame. "Egg poacher. – Break an egg in each cup and submerse the whole in hot water," American Home Cook Book, 1854.* **(2)** *"Upright egg poacher or dropper with sauce pans to fit." ("Sauce pans" are the little perforated cups.) Tin, in sizes to hold 3, 4 or 6 cups. F. A. Walker, 1870s-80s.* **(3)** *Poacher, thin stamped aluminum, "Quality," mfd. by E. A. Fargo Co., Taunton, MA, 1915 ad.* **(4)** *"Maryland" poacher, tin, with automatic "catch" at top of handle. Used in a stew pan or skillet, c.1890. See also #15.* **(5)** *Stamped tin, with 5, 10, or 20 cups. Central Stamping Co., 1920.* **(6)** *Spring-lift cups, tin, for 3 or 6 eggs. Very similar to Silver & Co. one pat'd. Nov. 3, 1885. This from 1909 supplier catalog.* **(7)** *Cast iron rings with detachable handle, to be used in "frying pan, basin or on a griddle." Paine, Diehl & Co., 1888.* **(8)** *"Egg poacher, with a loose inside frame, and ladles to hold eggs." Warne's Model Cookery, London, 1868.* **(9)** *"Plymouth Rock" boiler, nickeled copper stand, tinned egg stand for 6 eggs. Alcohol lamp underneath for table cooking. Albert Pick catalog, 1909.* **(10)** *Tin with iron handle, from F. A. Walker 1870s-80s import catalog.* **(11)** *"Ideal" boiler, Specialty Co., Warehouse Point, CT. 1893 ad. "You've wanted it for years – perhaps unconsciously," says ad, predating Freud's "id" by a decade at least!* **(12)** *Coddler, 2-tier frame holds 12 eggs. Wings are halves of hinged lid. Manning, Bowman, 1892.* **(13)** *Coddler from American Home Cook Book, 1854.* **(14)** *2-tiered wire boiling stand, for cooking & then serving at table. "Sherwood's Patent" – "useful & ornamental in a high degree," tinned iron wire, c.1870. Sizes made for from 4 to 12 eggs. Was pat'd. as an "Egg stand & boiler" by Edward P. Woods & Daniel Sherwood, Lowell, MA, Nov. 12, 1867, #70,769. Assigned to their wire-goods manufactory, Woods & Sherwood.* **(15)** *Spring in upright tube holds rings onto perforated base. Manning, Bowman, 1892.* **(16) & (17)** *1868 ad for the Sherwood one-level 6-egg stand.* **(18)** *Folding wire boiler stand easily kept in drawer, c.1910s.* **(19)** *Egg poacher patent by E. C. Townsend & A. Washburne, NYC, Jan. 30, 1877. "A series of perforated receptacles with movable [clip-on] bottoms" (see arrow pointing to hatch bottom!), which "permits the removal of their contents through the lower ends." (1), (2), (3), (5) $15+; (4), (6), (7), (10), (15), (18) $10+; (8), (9), (11), (12), (13) $25+; (14) $75+; (16), (17) $45+; (19) if made, $35+*

Egg coddler, heavy tin square box on 4 cast iron fancy feet, vertical center handle & side handles are cast iron, hinged 2-part lid folds out from center, from F. A. Walker catalog, imported or American (?), made in various sizes for 8, 10, 12 or 16 eggs, c.1870s......... **$60+**

Egg coddler, tin, oval lidded vessel & lift-out rack that suspended up to 16 eggs over boiling hot water, American(?) or French or English import, 7"H x 9"L x 7"W, 19th C. .... **$145+**

Egg fryer – See Muffin or other bake pan in Chapter IV (Molds).

Egg poacher, 8 stamped aluminum parts, including straight-sided pan with handle, like frying pan, set-in disc with 5 large cutout holes for egg cups & one small hole (for finger?), 5 stamped round-bottomed cups with hook handles, lid with wooden knob, "Quality," mfd. by E. A. Fargo Co., Taunton, MA, c.1915. .... **$20+**

Egg poacher, brightly tinned cups inside for 5 eggs, tight fitting lid with balloon-shaped wire knob made of 2 cross-arched pieces, paper label on lid reads "The Savoy Steam Egg Poacher," mfd. by Republic Metalware Co., late 19th C............................. **$45+**

Egg poacher, heavy tin, steam vent handle upright in center between 3 perforated poaching cups, "... can be used in an ordinary stew pan as well as a skillet. A little automatic catch at the top of the standard holds the rings while the cooked eggs are removed with a knife." "Maryland," mfd. by Matthai-Ingram, various sizes, this one the 3-egg size, late 19th C. .... **$20+**

Egg poacher, heavy tin, upright dog-tail-like handle stamped "S & Co." (Silver & Co.), Brooklyn, NY, 3 eggs, 6-3/4"H, pat'd. Nov. 3, 1885. • "Silver & Co.'s (41 B'way, NY) new egg poacher will be found of great value. Place it in a pan of boiling water, with a teaspoon of salt to pint of water. Let water boil two minutes, draw back pan where water will hardly bubble, and break an egg into each ring. Let the eggs stand for about three minutes and they will be done. Always be sure to have the poacher hot before eggs are put in, and it must be in the water when the eggs are broken into it. One can use muffin rings, and keep the shape of the egg round; but this new poacher is so convenient one can hardly do without it." [Picture caption:] "The rings are joined. By compressing A [short upright lever] against handle – rings lift up and pan can be scraped of egg."

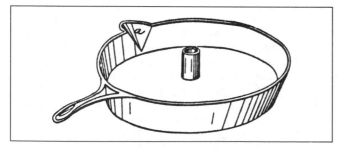

XII-11. Frying pan patent. *Pat'd. Sept. 20, 1864, (#44,346) by S. B. Sexton, Baltimore. Cast iron with integral venting tube or flue. Use with a domed lid. Sexton manufactured stoves & hollowwares into the 1930s. This was definitely made: Joel Schiff found one at the Brimfield flea market, and although it was cracked, he bought it.* **$75+**

Maria Parloa, *Kitchen Companion*, Boston: Estes & Lauriat, 1887. .... **$35+**

Egg poacher, nickeled metal (probably brass, as this company made lots of bathroom accessories), with vertical shaft with knob on end set into low round frame that holds 3 egg cups with handles & perforated bottoms, mfd. by H. & H. Mfg. Co., NYC, NY, c.1904. .... **$30+**

Egg poacher, stamped tin & iron, frame has central upright handle and 3 little feet, 3 separate perforated cups with little tab handles to lift them out of the frame, from F. A. Walker catalog, imported or American, c.1870s. .... **$20+**

Egg poacher, tin, 8 parts: an insert frame holds 5 egg cups with handles, pan, lid has centripetal cluster of loops of tin for a knob (I've also seen wire loops), "Buffalo Steam Egg Poacher," (paper label: "Savoy Steam Egg Poacher"), mfd. by Republic Metalware Co., Buffalo, NY, 3"H x 10-3/8" diam. plus 6"L handle, late 19th C. • Back in a Dec. 1897 *Ladies' Home Journal*, this poacher was advertised by the Sidney Novelty Works of Chicago, seeking agents, and combining with it a **cooker for cereal** that would fit, within a ring, into the same pan. Also available were extra deep custard cups to use instead of the egg cups. The cost was 50¢ for the poacher, 50¢ for the cereal cooker and 25¢ for the custard cup set. These were described in the ad as aluminum, and it is possible that Sidney Novelty was using "Buffalo Steam Egg Poacher" as a generic description of a type of egg poacher. .... **$45+**

Egg poacher, tin, tubular handle in center with thumb lever to press which drops platform down away from the rings to let the finished eggs slide off, 2 egg size, American, late 19th C. .... **$20+**

Egg poacher, triangular with long handle, cobalt enamelware with white inside, 3 egg size, European (?), c.1890s-1910... **$50+**

❖ NOTES ❖

Breakfast c.1890. Eggs weren't all they ate for breakfast in late Victorian times. A summer breakfast (for the middle or upper class) might consist of pieces of melon, shredded wheat with sugar & cream, salted cod "a la Francaise," broiled lamb chops, sautéed new potatoes, crumpets [like English muffins], and coffee. Or you might have peaches instead of melon, eggs not lamb chops, and fried eggplant instead of potatoes. Plus cereal and rolls. It's interesting to me that even in the 1890s, menus for breakfast didn't call for orange juice.

Etna – See aetna

Farina boiler, like a double boiler with pouring spout in lower vessel, lid has strap handle, inner & outer vessels have a long side handle, F. A. Walker catalog, American (?), c.1870s...................................... **$18+**

Fish kettle, also called a fish boiler, oval, copper with iron handle, NYC, 13-1/2"L x 8"W, late 19th C. .... **$125+**

Fish kettle, pieced, planished tin, large oval kettle has high wire bail handle the long axis, insert of perforated tin with 2 wire handles on the long sides, domed lid has strap handle, Matthai-Ingram Co., 6-3/4"H x 17"L x 9-1/2"W, late 19th C...................................... **$30+**

Fish skillet, oval, with lid, cast iron, rare to find with lid, Griswold #15 (the #13 didn't ever have a lid). Erie, PA, 2-1/2" deep x 15"L x 9-3/4"W. 1940s-50s. With lid: .... **$450+**

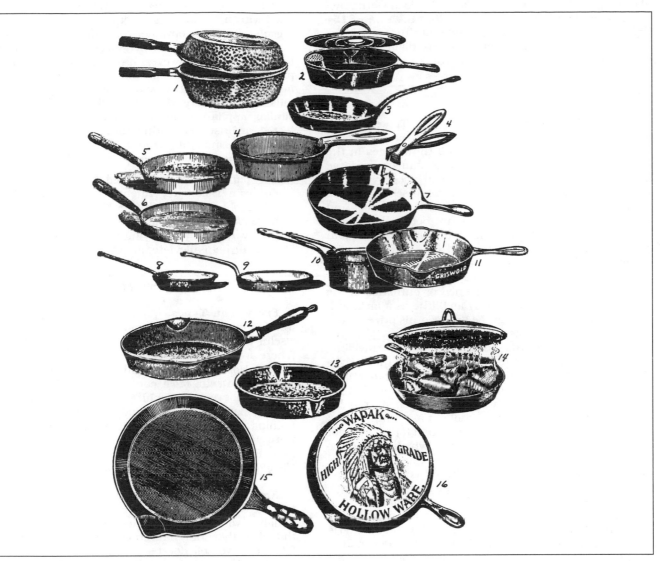

XII-12. Frying pans, fry pans, or **skillets.** *Cast iron except where noted. By the time of stovetop cooking, the distinctions once made between frying pans, skillets & spiders were practically non-existent, although the term "spider" began to lose ground by the 1890s.* **(1)** *Chicken fryer, hammered cast aluminum. 1939 ad.* **(2)** *"Improved frying skillet," with perforated flue built into side. Mfd. by Brewington, Bainbridge & Co., Baltimore, 1890 ad.* **(3)** *Copper frying pan, made 5"-12" diam. Duparquet, Huot, c.1904-1910.* **(4)** *"Excelsior" detachable handle, 2-part, pivoting, depicted converting a cake pan into a fryer. Would make a cake, pie, pudding, dairy, or any other handle-less sheet metal pan into a frying pan, or could be used to facilitate removal of any such pan from the oven. Excelsior Handle Co., Augusta, KY, 1882 ad. Rare to find Kentucky-made pieces.* **(5)** *Omelet pan with sloping sides, and* **(6)** *sauté pan with straight sides. Both from Warne's Model Cookery, London, 1868.* **(7)** *Has heat-equalizing ring on bottom. Sizes 5-10, ie. 7-5/8"-11-1/4" diam. Sexton, Baltimore, Md., c.1930s.* **(8)** *Omelette pan, and* **(9)** *sauté pan, and* **(10)** *"Fricandeau" pan, for a French style of cooking potatoes – with interior draining basket. All William Adams, London, c.1860-61.* **(11)** *Griswold fry pan made from 7-1/2" to 11-3/4" diam., c.1909 ad.* **(12)** *"Spider or skillet," wood handle, 2 lips, 5 sizes from 8" to 11-1/2" diam. Shapleigh catalog, 1914.* **(13)** *"Stove spider," ground cast iron, 5 sizes from #6-#10. Matthai-Ingram, c.1890.* **(14)** *Self-basting "Chicken, steak & chop braiser" skillet. Griswold, 1929 catalog.* **(15)** *"Common spider, ventilated handle," made in 6" to 10" diam. Henry N. Clark, Boston, 1864.* • *Note that while manufacturers measured the diameter on the bottom, because their pots, pans & frying pans had to sit over, but not drop into, stove eyes, collectors measure across the top, not counting the lip(s). This leads to a great deal of confusion to "outsiders" or newcomers to the cast iron field, and shows up in eBay auctions.* **(16)** *Idealized drawing of Wapak Ware Indian on skillet bottom from a 1915 ad supposedly showing a #13, but Joel Schiff believes that Wapak never made a #13 Indian frying pan. What's actually in the center bottom of the skillet, is a smallish round medallion with the Indian head. This Wapak Indian skillet in #4 size is being reproduced, poorly, today. Wapak Ware, Wapokoneta, OH.* • *Value of most frying pans depends on the maker, the size, & the marking, and most frying pans you see are usually from $10- $30, and are sold for their utility, not as collectibles. Rarities can bring in the thousands – buy the books and join the clubs if you intend to spend the bank on old cast iron frying pans!* **(2) $70+; (3) $40+; (4) $15; (5), (6) $30+; (8-10) $35+; (11) (14))** *wide range for Griswold, must read Griswold books.* **(15) $50-$75;** *(16 size #13, if it does exist):* **$850+;** *(16 #4 size)* **$400-$600+;** *(16 #11 size)* **$200+**

Flan pan, fluted metal, "Dr. Oetker," "Made in Germany,"
11-3/4" diam., late 19th or early 20th C. .... **$15+**
Fry kettle, tin, long wooden handle fits through 2 ear
handles on each side, American, 16" diam.,
19th C. .... **$20+**

❖ NOTES ❖

The 1832 Tinker – "Here comes the Tinker, – surgeon-general of pans and kettles in all the alleys and
courts about town, as well as in all the villages in the
neighbourhood. Yet, till the establishment of large
manufactories, and the making of articles by wholesale, and the keeping of them in warehouses and shops
... the tinker was a man of no small importance: and
the people had to wait his pleasure before they could
cook their dinner. At that time, if any one wanted a pan
or a kettle, the plan was to send for the tinker, who
travelled with all the materials and tools necessary for
his purpose; and, erecting his apparatus by the hedgeside in the summer, or in any shed or outhouse in the
winter, the tinker worked away as blithe as a lark, well
knowing that he should not be grudged his price, and a
mug of ale to lighten his labour. ...

"The tinker, and the other men of the travelling
workshop, learned [*sic*] to make the people themselves
much more handy than they are now; and that was of
far more advantage to them than would at first be
believed. A labourer now, whether boy or man, has little opportunity of seeing the whole of any thing made;
and ... workmen in the great manufactories are not
much better; very much of the work [which used to be
made by a tinker] is done by machines. ...

"When the tinker went about in full employment, all
the boys came to assist with his little furnace and forge;
and there they learned to do many useful things ...

"But can't the boys go and learn of the tinker still?
[Now the tinker] has very little to teach them. ... He
used to be an iron-founder and a brass-founder; had ...
crucibles for melting his metals, bellows for blowing his
fire, and hammers and pincers. He also knew how to
mix his metals – could have made a fine-toned bell out
of an old tin pot and copper kettle; and work up all the
old tin, copper, and brass, for use again. He [made] solder and could give the seam of the kettle the degree of
firmness that you wanted; if you wanted a kettle to
stand a strong heat, the brass, zinc and copper filings
were mixed in a moment, and iron was so firmly joined
as to bear a red heat. ... Now the tinker has only a pot
of coke, blown by means of holes in the bottom, a soldering iron, some soft solder and a pinch of rosin; and
therefore his employment is as inferior as himself" Pinnock's *Guide to Knowledge*, London, Sept. 8, 1832.

❖ NOTES ❖

• Is Zinc Safe? – In the *Washington Post Magazine*,
April 30, 1989, Robert Brunier of Silver Spring, MD,
wrote a letter to the editor questioning an earlier article
on a chef, who talked about making risotto in "pots
where outside it is copper and inside is zinc." Brunier
says "I would hate to learn that one of your readers
tried to prepare risotto ... [in such a pot]. I doubt that
the metallic taste would be so exciting. ..."

"Chef Ricchi may have been referring to copper pots
lined with tin, a much gentler and kinder kind of cooking utensil. Zinc containers ... can cause food poisoning" by interacting with acidic foods (such as
tomatoes). Zinc, however, has long been the preferred
plating for dairy utensils. W. T. Flanders, in *Galvanizing and Tinning*, 1916, wrote that "Laundry machinery,
milking machinery, dairy utensils, water heaters, and
similar appliances subject to corrosion can be protected against decay due to electrolysis by sprayed
deposits of zinc suitably located." (p.104.)

Frying pan, cast iron, marked "Stuart, Ferancee-HP
For Iron Deficiency Anemia," American, 4" diam.,
late 19th or early 20th C. • This pan's makers must
have claimed that the minute iron particles making
their way from your frying pan to your fritters would
cure, or help alleviate, anemia...................... **$15+**

❖ NOTES ❖

Frying Pan Types – "A common short-handled cast-
iron frying pan that can be put in the oven is a necessity.
Useful for hash, spider corn-cake, baked omelets, etc.
[There are] three other varieties of fry pans – which come
in sets. Housekeepers should have some of the pans in
at least two sets. Most common is the French polished
fry-pan, (not really French). Smooth, light, well made and
cheap. Many sizes; 20¢ and up. For an omelet-pan,
nothing compares with the pans of English hammered
ware. Heavier than, but similar in shape to the French
pan. [But] the handles are longer." Maria Parloa, *Kitchen
Companion*, Boston: Estes & Lauriat, 1887.

•   •   •

Broken Skillets – "About four weeks [ago] we sold
two No. 8 skillets to a person who about two weeks ago
bought two more and yesterday another one, stating
that the other four had cracked without having had a
fall. Now, we sell dozens of skillets every year, yet we
never had any such complaint before. They could not
have been of a bad lot for we have some of the same
which are all right. If you know of any reason by this
should happen, would you oblige us by a reply in *The
Metal Worker*? NOTE. – We fancy the trouble may have
been from the way in which the skillet was used rather
than in the quality of the skillet itself. If inquiry is made,
it may be found that the skillet was put suddenly on to a
hot fire in such a way as to heat the bottom very rapidly,
while the sides and all the metal exposed except the center remained cold. It is also possible that the skillet was
heated very hot and cold water poured into it. In fact
there is a variety of ways in which unequal expansion
might break the skillet, without the person who was
using it realizing that the treatment was doing the damage." *The Metal Worker*, Dec. 16, 1882.

•   •   •

Soyer on the Frying-Pan – "Introduction. – This useful utensil, which is so much in vogue in all parts of the
world, and even for other purposes besides cookery – for
I have before me now a letter, written on the back of a
frying-pan, for want of a table; but in your letter you
suggest the necessity of paying particular attention to it,
as it is the utensil most in vogue in a bachelor's residence. I cannot but admire your constant devotion to
the bachelors: you are always in fear that this unsocia-
ble class of individuals should be uncomfortable. For my

part, I do not pity them, and would not give myself the slightest trouble to comfort them, especially after they have passed the first thirty springs of their life.

"You will ... find, in these receipts, that the usual complaint of food being greasy by frying, is totally remedied, by sautéing the meat in a small quantity of fat, butter, or oil, which has attained a proper degree of heat, instead of placing it in cold fat and letting it soak while melting.

"I will ... having my frying-pan in one hand and a rough cloth in the other, with which to wipe it (considering that cleanliness is the first lesson in cookery), initiate you in the art of producing an innumerable number of dishes, which can be made with it, quickly, economically, relishing, and wholesome. But I must first tell you, that the word fry, in the English language, is a mistake; according to the mode in which all objects are cooked which are called fried, it would answer to the French word *sauté*, or the old English term *frizzle*; but to fry an object, it should be immersed in very hot fat, oil, or butter, as I have carefully detailed to you in our '*Modern Housewife*.' To *frizzle, sauté*, or, as I will now designate it, semi-fry, is to place into the pan any oleaginous substance, so that, when melted, it shall cover the bottom of the pan by about two lines; and, when hot, the article to be cooked shall be placed therein. ...

"I prefer the pan, for many objects, over the gridiron; that is, if the pan is properly used. As regards economy, it is preferable, securing all the fat and gravy, which is often lost when the gridiron is used.

"All the following receipts can be done with this simple batterie de cuisine, equally as well in the cottage as in the palace, or in the bachelor's chamber as in the rooms of the poor." Alexis Soyer, *A Shilling Cookery for the People*, London, 1854.

Frying pan, cast iron, "Fat Free Fryer #1102" or "Wagner Greaseless #1102" mfd. by Wagner Mfg. Co., Sidney, OH, 12" diam., "Pat Appl For," late 20th C.......... **$45+**

Frying pan, cast iron, deep sides, with original Black Americana printed paper label showing "Mammy" cooking chicken, "Old Virginia Chicken Fryer," 12" diam., 20th C.. **$25+**

Frying pan, sheet iron, original colored label with Black Americana picture of "Mammy" & black man cooking, "Pullman," c.1890s-1910. .... **$25+**

Frying pan, cast iron, fancy cast handle probably matched stove, pouring lip, nice rounded rim, unmarked American, 2-1/4" deep, just shy of 12" diam., 1880s to 1890s................................... **$45+**

Vagaries of the Kitchen

"'Twenty-seven religions have I found in this country!' writes a French tourist, 'and but one gravy!'

"Had the satirist been familiar with the machinery of the average American kitchen, he might have added – 'and that is made in the frying-pan.'

"Our housewife may be unversed in the matter of steamers, braising and fish-kettles. The chances are as ten to one that she never owned a gridiron, and would laugh a patent 'poacher' to shrillest scorn. Were any, or all of these given to her, and their uses enlarged upon intelligently and enthusiastically, she would shake an unconvinced head and brandish her frying-pan in the face of anxious innovators and disgusted reformers. A convenient implement? Hear her testimony and behold her practice.

"For breakfast, her family is nourished, be it winter or summer, upon fried bacon, or salt pork, fried mush and fried potatoes. The bacon is cooked first; done to a slow crisp, and set aside to 'sizzle' out any remaining flavor of individuality, while she gets the mush ready. The meat comes out, and the slices of stiffened dough go in, first to absorb, then to be ... (still slowly) cooked by the hot fat. All the fat is soaked up before the cold, boiled potatoes, cut into clammy 'chunks' are put in. In fact, the last relay of mush is scorched to the bottom of the pan, and the bits of pork, clinging to the sides, are unsavory cinders. A great spoonful of lard sets all that to rights, and is just melted when the potatoes are immersed in it. Browning, under this process, is an impossibility, but a few outside pieces burn satisfactorily, and the rest smoke as the contents of the invaluable utensil are dished. Breakfast is ready...

"The colander – the most efficient check upon that Lord of Misrule, the frying-pan – inasmuch, as by its use, some of the reek and drip may be got rid of before the food is served – is seldom in our housewife's hands, except when squash or pumpkin-pies are to be made. Least of all does she think of employing it in serving vegetables. ...

"I was more hopeful, ten years ago, than I am now, of possible reformation among the reigning autocrats of the culinary department. 'Mother' is joined to her sooty idol, the FRYING-PAN; to her family pie crust, to boiled tea, to undrained beets, and drained (instead of wiped) china.

"The one ray of light comes from the fact that some of our young girls are beginning to look upon cookery as a practical science." Marion Harland, *House & Home, a Complete Housewife's Guide*, Philadelphia, 1889.

❖ NOTE ❖

Recipe for Gumbo – "There are tricks in the art of molding as well as in all other trades, says a correspondent, writing from a city in the northern part of the Empire State [probably Troy or Albany, NY]. A prominent stove man was recently discussing the subject of molder's tricks, one of which is the manner in which he does away with imperfect castings, for it is well known that the molder has to pay for careless handiwork, and this he does not relish. In order to get over this a molder invented a paste or composition, but just what it is the stove man did not know. It is called 'What is it,' or some designate it by the euphonious, although perhaps not classic, term of 'gumbo'. When a large flaw is found by the tricky molder in his casting, he applies a dose of 'gumbo', which is supposed to be a composition of iron filings and a sort of paste." "Odd Plates," in The Metal Worker, Feb. 27, 1892.

Frying pan, sheet metal, "Pan American 1901" for expo in St. Louis, 1901. • See Clocks in Chapter V (Measure & Weigh). .... **$15+**

Frying pan, stamped iron, "cleaned and finished," cold handle, 1 pouring lip, "Acme," New York Stamping Co., NYC, pat'd. Nov. 14, 1876, Feb. 5, 1878. ..... **$7+**

Frying pan, stamped sheet metal, small pouring lip at side, nicely shaped hollow stamped & embossed handle with name and dates, "The Central," 7" diam. with 8"L handle, pat'd Jan. 5, 1875, Nov. 27, 1877. ... **$7+**

Frying pan, very shiny white or silvery metal, nickel & chrome alloy called "Nirosta," handle rather longer than usual for frying pans, tip of handle is sort of pointed, teardrop shape hanging hole, 2 pouring lips, Industrial Alloy Products Corp., prob. WI, 1-1/2" deep x 8-1/2" diam., with 7"L handle, c.1930. ..... **$7+**

❖ NOTES ❖

"Kitchen **utensils in solid nickel** come from France. They are beautiful, smooth and almost indestructible. They are cast without the slightest groove or seam, and are made very solid. They come without covers; I suppose, because of the expense. The articles are costly at first ... but with proper care will last a lifetime. There is nothing to break or peel off and mingle with the food." Maria Parloa, "Household Helps & New Ideas," *Ladies' Home Journal*, May 1900.

Frying pans – See also Skillet; also Frying pans in Chapter X (Hearth Cooking)

Griddle, cast iron, oblong for use over 2 range eyes, Griswold #746-A9, 10" x 22"L, c.1890s-1910. .... **$85+**

Griddle, cast iron, hinged, makes 3 griddle cakes, fits over 2 range eyes, c.1870s. **$50**

Griddle, cast iron, hinged oblong 2 part griddle, one side plain, other segmented in 3 parts, "The Canton Cake Griddle," Cornman Cake Griddle Co., Mechanicsburg, PA, 13-1/2"L x 5-1/4"W, pat'd. Apr. 28,

XII-13. Griswold's "Erie" spider logo. Spider is another word for frying pan. From an 1890s ad in trade magazine for the founders, Erie Hollow-Ware Works, Griswold Mfg. Co., Erie, PA. The actual "spider" spider has two pouring lips in rim, and a frying-pan shaped spider & web in a round center medallion, with "Erie" and "8" marks. Spider-marked pans: **$1,000+**

XII-14. Soapstone griddles. Iron rims, bail & ear handles. Used for grease-free, even cooking, especially good for pancakes. (L) "Hodges' Superior," William Hodges & Co., Philadelphia, c.1880s-1920. (R) From 12" to 16" diam. Buhl Sons, c.1919 hardware catalog. **$30+**

1898. .... **$65+**

Griddle, cast iron, hinged top lid divided into 4 sections, rectangular & fits over 2 eyes, handles at each end, "Jeffery Patent," pat'd. by E. A. Jeffery of Trappe, MD, mfd. by Tuthill & Avery, Easton, MD, about 20"L including handles, pat'd. Aug. 27, 1867. .... **$150+**

Griddle, cast steel, side handle, marked "Solid Steel, 10" on handle, also maker, Wrought Iron Range Co., 12-1/8" diam., 19th C. **$35**

Griddle, rectangular with angled up "frying pan" handle, green agate enameling over iron, American or European, c.1890s-1910. .... **$100+**

Griddle, soapstone in heavy metal band, VT or VA, c.1890s-1910 or more recent .... **$25+**

❖ NOTES ❖

Lookalike or Real Thing? – If something is made for 100 years, the same way, you can't say that the latest ones are reproductions or fakes. When the material has been changed, you can date the object. In a 1942 *House & Garden* ad, an "Old Fashioned Vermont **Soapstone Griddle**" is featured: "Modern Gadgets Have Not Improved ... Grandmother's Griddle." "Never in all these long years has anything been devised to better it. Remember how it hung in the woodshed ready for those special feasts of golden brown pancakes dripping with butter and maple syrup? Here is an old fashioned Vermont soapstone griddle, and it doesn't smoke because no grease is used on it." 12" diam., only $2.95 ppd. The metal frame and two oval wire handles aren't described, but look like tinned iron. • A late 19th C catalog of Hibbard, Spencer, Bartlett & Co. depicts an oval, iron-rimmed soapstone griddle, with oval wire handles, in two sizes: 9" x 18" and 10" x 20". Both are very thin. (They also show a soapstone foot warmer, a thick block with a wire carrying handle inserted in holes in the side, which came in five sizes: 6" x 8", 7" x 9", 8" x 10", 8" x 12", and 10" x 12".) I don't know when the griddles stopped being made, but they are frequently found at flea markets and "country" shows. • By the way, a small long-closed quarry in Schuyler, VA, 30 miles from Charlottesville, with notably hard and good quality soapstone especially suitable for making stoves began to be quarried again in 1989. The company which reopened the quarry is a Finnish firm,

TuliKivi, which makes soapstone wood-burning stoves and cooking utensils.

•   •   •

Greaseless Griddles. "To do away with the grease on the griddle for baking cakes, have the ordinary iron griddle ground smooth on a grindstone and rubbed off with a piece of fine sandpaper wrapped around a block of wood. If the griddle be rubbed with a turnip, the desired smoothness will be obtained and the unpleasant smoke done away with." Henry Scammel, compiler, *Treasure House of Useful Knowledge*, 1891.

Griddle greaser, fork-like device of steel wire, black painted wooden handle, slip ring to hold 2 parts together after grease-laden cloth (?) inserted, marked on ferrule "Oblosser Sanitary Greaser Holder," Oblosser Mfg. Co., Bloomsburg, PA, pat'd. Feb. 5, 1910. .... **$10+**

Griddle greaser & cake turner combined, plated steel 2 part implement with turned black-painted wooden handle. An unperforated turner blade, with thumb piece on top of shank to fold the small griddle greaser jaws out of the way, or to put them down in working position, wire slip ring holds jaws closed to hold greased cloth, marked "Specialty Works" (ie. Catawissa Specialty Works), Catawissa, PA, prob. 1880s. .... **$25+**

Griddle greaser & scraper, cast iron, tin with cloth lard pad, long looped handle, cup for lard with push-on

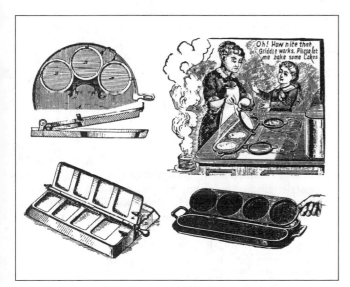

XII-15. Griddles for multiples. *The two at left are patent drawings:* **(T-L)** *was pat'd. March 16, 1880, by Ira W. Snyder, Varna, NY. The round underplate has 3 separate openings on one side of its diameter, plus a hinged "auxiliary plate" covering the 3 circles.* **(B-L)** *This one was pat'd April 28, 1885, by Francis L. Carpenter, Hartland, VT. Considering the origin of the inventor, it's quite possibly soapstone.* **(T-R)** *"Schofield's Patent" in plain or porcelainized cast iron. Sized to make 3 or 4 at a time; separately hinged pans. Pat'd. Jan. 25, 1881 & improved April 20, 1886.* **(B-R)** *"Reversible griddle," cast iron, straddles 2 stove eyes or holes. Flip 4 at once, which may have created problems because center of griddle not quite as hot. Maker unidentified. American Agriculturist, Oct. 21, 1871.* **$65+**

tin cap with cloth head, on other side of cup is small scraper for cleaning griddle before using, "W. H. Bixler," Easton, PA, 7-1/4"L, pat'd. July 22, 1873. • How To Use a Bixler Griddle Greaser. – "To prepare the greaser for use – Fill the bowl of No. 2 [the cast in cup], then place upon it the perforated cap No. 4, over this cap lay the circular piece of cloth, and then put on and press up tightly the spring ring No. 3, which holds both cloth and cap in place. Be sure and press up the rang far enough to prevent its scraping the griddle. After the cloth is first put on, rub a little lard on the outside before using." .... **$25+**

Gridiron, cast iron, side handles, grease drip catchers all 4 sides, American, 19-1/2"L x 9-1/2"W, 1860s. .... **$65+**

Gridiron, cast iron, grilling bars have runnels (concave ruts) for grease run-off, oblong, fits 2 range eyes, pouring lip at side of one end, decorative outside shape, no mark but date, 24-1/2"L, "Pat'd. July 24, 1860" by J. S. Brooks & L. B. Grover of Rochester, NY. .... **$150+**

❖ **NOTES** ❖

"Gridiron – With this primitive utensil a great deal may be done in the way of cooking, but it requires care, or otherwise great loss of food and money will be sustained; a few minutes' constant attention, when the article is on the gridiron, will save at least twenty per cent, and the palate will feel more gratified. I use two kinds of gridirons, each costing very little; one is of cast iron, to go on the fire, and the other is of iron wire, made double, to hang from the bar of the grate before the fire, made so as not to too much press the object cooked within it. The principal care in this, as in all kitchen utensils, is never to put them away dirty; always wiping the gridiron clean after it has been used, and again before you use it, and a place kept where it should hang." Alexis Soyer, *A Shilling Cookery for the People*, London: George Routledge & Sons, 1854.

Gridiron or grill, portable, in metal suitcase, heavy sheet metal oblong bench-like thing on folding legs, ventilating slots along 4 sides, one piece grill top fits down over bed of coals, Androck, 1930s. **$25**

Gypsy kettle – See Bulge pot, Chapter X (Hearth)

Ham boiler, tin lined copper with cast iron handles, close-fitting lid, oblong & deep, rounded corners, American, 7"H x 12-1/2"L x 7-5/8"W, c.1860s to 1880s. • Ham boilers were also used for cooking turkeys and fish. • For Hams or Turkeys – "An ordinary wash-boiler, thoroughly cleaned, may be used, with care in cleansing both before and after using." *Practical Housekeeping*, 1884. .... **$125+**

Hot water kettle – See Chapter XIV (Coffee & Tea)

Jelly pails – See Preserve kettle

Kettles – See Preserve kettle

Lid, for large oval platter, copper, tinned on inside, with brass ring handle, very Victorian. Possibly hotel ware, and turn-of-century, not marked, American or European import, 10-1/2"L x 7-1/2"W, 19th C. See also Pot lids, this chapter. .... **$45+**

Necromancer – See Conjurer

Omelette pan, cast aluminum, 2 parallel turned wooden handles both with hanging rings, hinged in middle to make it easy to quickly cook one side of the omelette, then the other. "Griswold," "Erie PA," 11" diameter open, c. 1920s-30s. .... **$100+**

Oyster broiler, wire, double frame of twisted wire, looks like those toasters we used at camp for roasting hot dogs or hot dog buns, American, late 19th or early 20th C. (See also a Gridiron entry in the Chapter X.) .... **$20+**

Pancake machine, Black Americana, cast & sheet metal, with color litho'd image of Aunt Jemima at top, mint, unused condition, adv'g. "Aunt Jemima Pancakes," Quaker Oats, small stove size, 1940s. • Flat-jacks, flap-jacks and slap-jacks are other late 19th C names for pancakes. .... **$350+**

Patty bowl, cast iron, looks like small kettle, with wire bail handle, for heating oil for quick cooking, "Gris-

XII-16. Ham boilers. *Tin-lined heavy-weight copper, cast iron handles.* **(L)** *7"H x 10-1/2"L x 6-1/2"W.* **(R)** *7"H x 12-1/2"L x 7-5/8"W. Both American, probably 1870s-90s. Courtesy Collection of Mary Mac Franklin.* **$90-$125+**

wold #871," Erie, PA, 3-1/8" deep x 7-1/2" diam. across top, 20th C. .... **$100+**

Peanut & almond roaster, looks like horizontal cylindrical coffee roaster, & would probably work for coffee too, sheet iron oblong box with hinged rounded top, inner cylinder of heavy wire cloth screening, cranked at one end, the whole on an oval base which would fit on 2 range eyes, mfd. by Thomas Burkhard, approx. 22"L, c.1870s. .... **$125+**

Pie pans – See Chapter IV (Molds).

Poaching pan – See Egg poacher.

❖ NOTES ❖

Date By Lids – To an extent, dating can be approximated by the type of lid. Often the older covered pieces have enameled bodies, but the lids are of stamped tin, sometimes with wooden knob or even cast iron knob. Finials of cast iron or wood, on an enameled lid, are generally older than all-in-one enameled lids & knobs. • Handles can help date a lid too – scrolly cast iron handles are oldest, dating as far back as the early 1870s, turned and painted wooden handles second oldest (or the same age as other cast handles such as used by Manning-Bowman), and enamelware handles probably only since end of 19th C.

• • •

Futurewatch – This kind of pot lid (not the transfer printed ceramic kind from England, which have been collected for decades) would make a fabulous collection, & they are much undervalued & perhaps even unnoticed. You could start with an early one like this, include a nice copper one with iron handle, go on up through the interesting 1930s tin or aluminum ones. See also a couple of pot lids in Chapter IV.

Pot lid, dark tin, slightly concave with wide edge to fit lips of several small pots, cast iron acorn finial knob, American (?), 4-1/2" diam. with 1/2"W lip or edge, early 19th C. **$10**

Pot lid, heavy cast aluminum, has lip & 2 "scallops" to cover a skillet's or kettle's pouring lips, 3 zigzag concentric rings inside dome, with small, medium & large zags, "Wagner Drip Drop No. 9 Skillet Cover," Wagner Mfg. Co., pat'd. Dec. 4, 1917, Feb. 10, 1920, Mar. 8, 1921 & Mar. 4, 1922. .... **$5+**

Pot lid, heavy, cobalt blue blob agateware, lip to fit inside pan or pot, enameled inside & out, 7-3/8" diam., late 19th C. .... **$5+**

Pot lid, stamped galvanized tin, rigidity given by big-petaled daisy pattern stamped on surface, with instructions, "To keep foods warm stand pots on this utility cover." "No. 10," but no other mark, 10" diam., 1936 design patent #11078. .... **$3+**

Pot lid, stamped tin, concentric ribs or rings that give it strength & rigidity when standing the second pot on it, "Stand another pot on this cover. Keeps foods warm – saves burner space." "Safety Ring Pot Cover, #9," mfd. by Ekco, 9" diam., 20th C................. **$3+**

Potato baker, cast aluminum in zeppelin or egg shape in 2 parts (around middle, not lengthwise), wire clamp, spike inside one half to hold potato, for stovetop cooking, marked with a "TMW Co." monogram, with large "W," which I believe is a 1920s mark for The Wisconsin Mfg. Co. A 1948 ad found by my friend collector Georgiana Sanders describes it as the "Top-O-Stove" baker of heavy cast aluminum, mfd. by Na-Mac Products Corp., a subsidiary of William B. Warner & Co., Inc.; TMW Co., (later mfd. by Na-Mac), Manitowoc, WI; Na-Mac in Los Angeles, CA, large potato size, c.1920s-1950(?). **$25**

Potato baker, cast iron, pale green enameled iron cover, "The Master Bake Pot," American, pat'd. 1918....... **$35**

Potato baking rack, tinned wire, like a wire toboggan with spikes at ends of cross pieces to hold 12 potatoes, "Jaxon," mfd. by J. B. Timberlake & Sons, Inc., Jackson, MI, about 14"L, patent applied for in 1911..... **$5+**

Potato baking rack, heavy sheet tin in long strip to slide into oven, set up on down-turned edges, large holes for balancing potatoes on end, no spike or hook to hold them, wire handle, Gier & Dail Mfg. Co., Lansing, MI, pat'd. Aug. 1, 1909. .... **$5+**

Potato baking rack, tin strip with down turned edge to form sturdier base, wire loop handle at one end for pulling out of oven, the 6 thumbprint size projections of tin are punched up vertically to form "prickers" for baking potatoes to be stuck on, the whole thing then slid into oven, "No Burn" or "Handi Kuick" & made by at least 2 manufacturers, Dier & Dail Mfg. Co., & Springfield Specialty Co., respectively Lansing, MI and Springfield MA, 15-1/4"L x 2-1/8"W, both pat'd. Aug. 1, 1909, & made for at least 10 more years. • Springfield Specialty advertised in 1911 that they had a huge sign painted on the side of a brick building (not clear if in Brooklyn or Manhattan), that they suggested you should look for "the next time you cross the Brooklyn Bridge." It was a strange painting with potatoes lined up to be baked, mountains in the background, with the legend "The New Sensation ... Bowery, Coney Island" plus a depiction of the "Handi-Kuick." Makes you wonder if traces of it might not still be there. .... **$10+**

Potato boiling pot, or spaghetti kettle, a cross between a coffee boiler & a large preserve kettle, gray & white mottling, very round body, large lidded deep V-neck spout (presumably for pouring off starchy water) opposite a good-sized vertical tipping handle, lid with strap handle, falling wire bail handle has wood grip, American, 7-1/2"H, c.1890s-1910.......... **$125**

Potato or cruller fryer, heavy tin, lower vessel like a long-handled frying pan that has an arched support with a hook from which to suspend perforated inner vessel in boiling fat, in the Montgomery Ward catalog, about 12" diam., 2"deep, pat'd. July 8, 1879. .... **$10**

Preserve kettle, also called a jelly pail, spun brass, marked only "#13, Connecticut," c.1860s or 1870s. .... **$90+**

❖ NOTES ❖

A blacksmith's daybook of 1835, offered for sale by bookseller Jim Presgraves of Bookworm & Silverfish, Wytheville, VA, contained one especially provocative entry for "hooping brass cittle," which could mean forging an iron hoop-like bail handle, or perhaps forging an iron hoop or band to go around the body of a kettle to reinforce it. Most receipts or journals filled out by blacksmiths are more mundane, with shoeing horses being the most common job mentioned.

Preserve kettle, spun brass (that's what Hayden invented a technique to do), heavy falling bail of forged iron, brass ears and copper rivets, lip is rolled, sides slanted

out a bit more than usual, marked "H. W. Hayden's Patent," this one made by Hussey & Co., Pittsburgh, PA, 7-1/8"H x 10-1/4" diam., pat'd. Dec. 16, 1851, extended May 24, 1870. • Carl W. Drepperd, in *A Dictionary of American Antiques*, wrote that Hayden's 1851 spinning patent wasn't an abrupt change from hammering the metal (or battery work) to shape it and make it thin. He briefly describes a lathe process called skimming or skum work, done in the early 19th C. It is easy to imagine how layers of metal were removed, probably from a relatively thick & heavy cast piece, with a cutting tool. .... **$95+**

Preserve kettle, spun brass, forged iron bail handle, "H. W. Hayden's Patent" but no manufacturer's name, prob. Waterbury, CT, 15" diam., pat'd. Dec. 16, 1851, reissued May 24, 1870, Feb. 13, 1886.............. **$125+**

Preserve kettle, sometimes called a fruit stewer, described in dealer's ad as "brass plated copper," which doesn't sound right to me, although sometimes a new bottom was put on old kettles, and perhaps the marked bottom was put on another copper kettle, with iron bail handle, stamped "E. W." or "H.W. Hayden's Patent" with date, & "Mfd. by the Ansonia Brass Co.," 9"H x 12-1/2" diam., pat'd. Dec. 16, 1851 by Hayden, but probably made somewhat later..... **$95+**

❖ NOTES ❖

General Directions for Preserving Fruit and Making Jellies – A kettle should be kept on purpose. Brass, if very bright, will do. If acid fruit is preserved in a brass kettle which is not bright, it becomes poisonous. Bell-metal is better than brass, and the iron ware lined with porcelain, best of all." Mrs. Cornelius, *The Young Housekeepers Friend, or, A Guide to Domestic*

Preserve kettle, spun brass, riveted ear handles, copper rivets, much lighter than cast brass kettles or buckets, "American Brass Kettle Manufacturers," "No. 10" on ear handles, "No. 5" on kettle bottom, 12" diam., second half 19th C. .... **$95+**

❖ NOTE ❖

To Clean Brass Work – *Take 1 ounce of oxalic acid, 3/4 pint of New England rum, and 3/4 pint of oil. Put mixture in bottle, cork it close, and let it stand two or three days before using it. It should be shaken occasionally. Rub the brass with a clean woolen cloth, dipped into a small quantity of the liquid, then rub it with dry rottenstone with another cloth. The bottle should be labelled as poison." Mrs. Cornelius,* The Young Housekeepers Friend, or, A Guide to Domestic Economy & Comfort, *Boston & NY: 1846.* • *Rottenstone is a decomposed siliceous or flinty limestone. I believe that modern brass polishers could use the finest grade of powdered pumice, which is used by cabinetmakers for the French polishing method of finishing wood, or perhaps even common lime used for gardening.*

Preserve kettle, brass, forged iron bail handle, marked on bottom "The American Brass Kettle Manufacturers," 6-3/4"H x 10-1/2" diam., c. 3rd quarter 19th C. .... **$70-$90**

Preserve kettle, cast brass, cast ears & iron bail handle with loop in mid-arch to hang on pot hook from crane, not marked, American, 10" diam. and heavy, second half 19th C. .... **$85+**

Preserve kettle, brass with fixed flat iron handle, no mark, American (?), 6"H x 12" diam., early 19th C. .... **$125+**

Preserve kettle, cast brass, wrought iron bail handle, American, 8" diam., 19th C. .... **$125+**

Preserve kettle, hammered brass, forged iron falling bail handle riveted on, American (?), 2-3/4"H x 5" diam., almost small enough to be a toy, but I don't know, mid 19th C. Crossover miniature. .... **$130+**

❖ NOTES ❖

The Journal of the American Institute published a report on their Ninth Annual Fair NYC of October 1836, including something on brass kettles that were awarded as a premium. "**Brass kettles**, manufactured by Israel Coe & Co., Wolcottville, Litchfield Co., Conn. A letter to the managers [of the Fair], says: – They are particularly worthy the notice of the managers and patronage of the public, the factory being the first and only establishment of the kind in America, erected at a vast expense and risk. The enterprising mechanic, Israel Holmes [sic], who conducts the concern, has made two or three voyages to England; and, at the risk of his life, obtained workmen to carry on the manufacture from England, where there are but one or two establishments, which are carried on with the utmost secrecy. It has been in operation about one year, and turns out of the solid metal about one ton per day, superior to those imported from England, and selling in market readily at a higher price, on account of their superiority. They are hammered entirely from the solid metal, without rolling. Since their commencement, the Yankees have taken hold of the work, and now do the labour equal to the imported workmen, and finish much better kettles; and a part is now done by machinery, of our own invention, which is there done by hand."

Preserve kettle, copper, with lid, riveted, no handle on kettle but lid has small brass handle, American (?), 13-1/2"H x 13" diam., 19th C. .... **$125+**

XII-17. Preserve kettles & pots. (1) *Cast iron with porcelainized exterior & inside – necessary to use with fruit & tomatoes. Ring below rim is tipping handle.* **(2)** *Brass kettle with iron bail, made from 8"-13" diam. (1-4 gallons). In candy-supplier Jaburg catalog, 1908, maker unidentified. Can't know if it was spun brass, though by that time it could have been.* **(3)** *Spun brass preserve kettle, made in sizes 2-14 gallons, iron bail, c.1900. The form, and the method of manufacturing dates to H. W. Hayden's Dec. 16, 1851 brass-spinning patent. And even the linecut for the catalog has emphasized the concentric rings inside.* **(4)** *"Sterling" gray enamelware, 10 sizes up to 15" diam. Pouring lip, tipping handle, falling bail with wood grip. Central Stamping, 1920.* **(5)** *Cast iron sugar kettle, much larger than appears here. Sizes to hold 8-80 gallons. Hibbard, Spencer, Bartlett, c.1870s-90s.* **(6)** *"Triumph" cast iron, Patton Mfg. Co., Columbus, OH & Jeffersonville, IN, 1890 ad. Note use of tipping handle.* **(7)** *Large cast iron bulge-pot-shaped cauldron or farmers' boiler kettle, John Savery's Son, NYC, 1882 ad.* **$30-$200+**

Preserve kettle, sky blue & white swirled enamelware, "Solid Steel," Cleveland Stamping & Tool, OH, 9" diam., early 20th C. **$65**

Preserve kettle, cobalt blue & white enamelware, bail handle with wooden grip, drain spout, clamp for holding lid on, American, 10-1/2"H, 19th C. .... **$75+**

Preserve kettle, blue & white swirl enamelware, wire bail handle with wooden grip, one ear handle, enamelware lid, 10" diam., c.1890s-1910................ **$25+**

Preserve kettle, dark turquoise & white swirl enamelware, white inside, bail handle, about 5 gal. capacity. .... **$50+**

Preserve kettle, heavy ceramic crock in kettle shape with slightly rounded bottom, set down within and suspended on the edge of a bottomless sheet iron outer cylindrical straight sided kettle with falling bail, sheet iron lid with wire handle, meant for slow cooking of cereals or vegetables, Universal Cooking Crock Co., NYC, NY, pat'd. Oct. 25, 1881. .... **$45+**

Preserve kettle, or baking kettle, cast aluminum, rounded bottom, domed lid & wooden knob, wire bail handle, ear handles that "form a perfect check for the bail, so that when emptying the contents of the vessel burning of the fingers is prevented" (says a 1911 ad), Wagner Ware, Sidney, OH, six qt. capacity, c.1925. .... **$45+**

Preserve kettle, cast iron, bail handle, "Holland's Mfg. Co.," small 5" diam., 19th C. .... **$55+**

Pressure cooker, black cast iron, enameled white inside body & lid, straight sided low kettle with 2 loop ear handles, lid sets on, and is fitted with an interior flange, but does not fit with bayonet mount or screw clamps or anything else, on top of lid is a nice handle knob cast with lid, and 2 release valves (?), one like a little spigot, the other with a hinged cap that reveals a hole through the lid, marked "*C. H. Umbach Blettgheim 11 Garantie,*" German, 5"H x 11" diam., late (?) 19th C. • This one is pictured in Brigitte ten Kate-von Eicken's *Küchengeräte um 1900,* a wonderfully illustrated book on (mostly) German kitchen wares. The German term *Papinscher Topf* refers to the Frenchman Denis Papin, who invented the digester, the earliest pressure cooker........ **$125**

XII-18. Various kettles. All "Favorite Piqua" hollow-ware, mfd. by Favorite Stove & Range, Piqua, OH, 1890 ad. The regular & low kettles are virtually identical to those made by Wagner Mfg. Co., Sidney, OH. Scotch bowls are for cooking porridge. All have tipping handle-rings. These all from an ad in The Metal Worker, Sept. 27, 1890. **$40-$150+**

RIMMED KETTLE. — FLAT BOTTOM KETTLE. — RIMMED POT. — REGULAR KETTLE. — LOW KETTLE. — REGULAR BULGED POT. — SCOTCH BOWL.

Lookalike Alarm

At least one heavy cast aluminum pressure cooker resembling the old style with the wonderful wingnuts, is made today in four sizes: 10-1/2 quarts, 15-1/2 quarts, 21-1/2 quarts and 41 1/2 quarts. There are 6 screw clamps. Petcock and gauge are on the lid. The new one sells for between $50 and $100.

Pressure cooker, cast aluminum, "American Steam Pressure Cooker," 20th C. **$25**

Pressure cooker, cast aluminum, black plastic handle fixed to pan part, with a small tilting grab handle opposite, black plastic handle for the lid is detachable, red plastic valve on top of lid, "Wear-Ever," Aluminum Cooking Utensil Co., New Kensington, PA, 4 qt. capacity (they did a 7 qt. one too), late 1940s. .... **$25+**

Pressure cooker, cast aluminum, black plastic handles to lid and pan, lid slightly raised from rim, with pressure valve sticking up on top, with rack and recipe booklet, "Mirro-Matic," Aluminum Goods Mfg. Co., 4 qt. capacity, late 1940s. .... **$15+**

Pressure cooker, cast aluminum, wooden handles, the lower one with finger grip corrugations, lift-off steam release valve with small black rubber bulb in top, "Presto Cook-Master," National Pressure Cooker Co., Eau Claire, WI, 4 qt. capacity, late 1940s. • Presto cookers came in other sizes too, including 3 and 6 quart, plus a shallower one called a "Fry-Master" & a large canner. Values all about the same.......... **$15+**

Pressure cooker or soup digester, heavy planished tin, clamp-on lid, bail handle, American, 1870s.... **$25+**

Pressure cooker, copper bottom, "Conservo Cooker," American, pat'd. Feb. 5, 1907........................ **$45+**

Pressure cooker, tall straight-sided vessel of cast aluminum, slightly domed lid with large thumb-screwed clamps, large pressure dial upright in center of lid, wire basket inside, came with shallow vessels which could be stacked within, Economy Pressure Cooker Co., Lincoln, NE, 10 qt. capacity (other sizes included 14, 18 and 30 qts.), 1920s. .... **$15+**

Pressure cooker, which they called a saucepan, cast aluminum, red plastic gauge on top, centered on sliding clamp piece, 2 black plastic handles, black rubber gasket, "PressureQuick No. GM 3B," General Mills, Minneapolis, MN, 4 qt. size, patents pending, 1940s.. **$15+**

Pressure cooker or digester, heavy cast iron, lid screws down with 5 swivel clamps that drop out of way to open lid, gaskets on each steam cock, heavy wire bail handle with turned wood grip, "Windsor 'A' No. 10," Montgomery Ward Co., 10"H, c.1890s-1910. See also XVI-3 .... **$15+**

Roaster, kettle with lid & rack with holes to lay food on in kettle bottom, cast iron, inside lid are 2 concentric zig-zag circles to cause condensation to drip back into food while cooking, "Drip Drop Roaster Wagner Ware #8," has pattern number 1268B cast on bottom, mfd. by Wagner Mfg. Co., pat'd. Dec. 4, 1917, Feb. 10, 1920, Mar. 8, 1921 and Mar. 14, 1922. .... **$45+**

Roasting pan, 2 part oblong, sheet iron, shallow lower pan with slightly slanted sides, top is hinged to it & is a dome like a Quonset hut, cast iron sliding vent on one end, "Crown," S. & Co. (Silver & Co.?), NY, 8-3/4"H x 16-1/4"L, pat'd. Dec. 6, 1892. Silver pieces highly collectible. .... **$35+**

Roasting pan, blackened tin, upper & lower halves same size & sides flare, wire handles, folded corners, little bumps for feet stamped on bottom half, "Black Beauty Sanitary," EKCO, 6-1/4"H x 12"L x 8"W, 20th C. .... **$15+**

Roasting pan, cast aluminum straight-sided oval vessel with tab handles at each end shaped like flat broccoli flowerettes, high domed glass lid with longish flat "knob" on top, for stovetop roasting, "Guardian Service," mfd. by Century Metalcraft Corp., 1940s. ... **$15**

Roasting pan, cobalt enamelware with large gray spatters, fixed in one place with a Mendit, "Savory," mfd. by Republic Metalware Co., (not Republic Stamping & Enameling Co., Canton, OH.) Buffalo, NY, 20th C. • Fun to find Mendet-mended wares!................ **$15**

Roasting pan, dark blue & white speckled agateware, repaired with a "Mendet," pan has no maker's mark, 13-1/2"L, early 20th C. • This is the most commonly found color. For collectors of enameled iron, the Mendit detracts from value. For collectors of social history, it adds to charm.................................. **$15**

Roasting pan, light blue enamelware, "Savory," Republic Metalware, 17"L, c.1890s-1910. Great color. .... **$115+**

XII-20. Lids. *Various metals – stamped aluminum, dimpled charcoal tin, stamped tin, cast aluminum, cobalt & white enameled sheet metal. Upper* **(L)** *is a "Safety Ring Pot Cover," by EKCO. "Stand another pot on this cover, keeps foods warm – saves burner space." Dimpled one under it with big-petaled daisy ribbing is another utility warming lid, design patent #11,078 (?). Cast aluminum one with zigzags inside is a "Wagner Drip Drop No. 9 Skillet Cover C-509." Pat'd. Dec. 4, 1917, Feb. 10, 1920, Mar. 8, 1921, & Mar. 4, 1922.* **$1-$8**

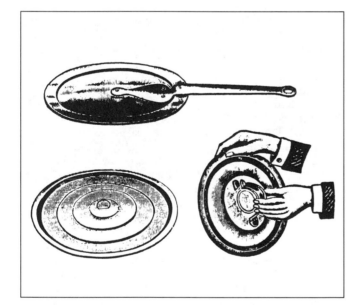

XII-19. Lids. *Top lid is very old style, often mistaken for early 19th C.; tinned copper "hotel sauce pan cover" with iron handle, made from 5-3/4" to 9-1/4" diam. Central Stamping Co., 1920; similar ones sold well into 20th C. by hotel & restaurant suppliers.* **Lower (L)** *Stamped tin, stepped for rigidity & for some adaptability to pan sizes, ring handle, came in 19 sizes in 1/2" increments from 6-1/2"-15-1/2" diam. Savory, c.1925-28.* **Lower (R)** *"Original Lasher Spring-in-handle" pot cover. You got a rack of many sizes of stamped tin covers & used a single spring steel handle to fit any of them. Lasher Mfg. Co., Davenport, IA, 1909. Complete set in rack would be worth more.* **$1-$15+**

XII-21. Pottery cookwares. *Top* **(L)** *Stoneware stew pan, glazed white or black inside. F. H. Weeks, Akron, OH, 1895 ad.* **(T-R)** *A* **petite marmite** *or small pot, to hold 1, 2, or 3 portions for cooking. In 3 sizes: 3-1/2", 4-1/2", & 5-1/2". Duparquet, Huot, Moneuse, c.1904-1910.* **(B-L)** *&* **(B-R)** *Both are "Boston Bean Pots," holding from 1 qt. to 2 gallons. Glazed inside & out. c.1910.* **$20-$50**

Roasting pan, sky blue & white enamelware, big oval, top & bottom same height, 2 metal vents, one at each end, turned to let out varying amounts of steam, Reed Mfg. Co., Newark, NY, 8-1/4"H x 17-1/4"L, pat'd. May 2, 1911. .... **$115**

Roasting pan, mottled green agateware, rectangular rather than oval, flat lid, American (?), 20th C.. **$55**

Rum warmer or ætna, also spelled etna, also called a toddy warmer (see which), planished tin, inverted cone with pierced lid, set into a sort of saucer for burning spirits & used for heating or mulling small amounts of liquids quickly, English or American, mid to 3rd quarter 19th C. **$75**

Saucepan, cast iron in sort of truncated inverted cone shape, the casting seam around the "equator" of the body, riveted on is partially cylindrical bent sheet iron long handle at about 5 degrees up from horizontal, marked only with "2 QTS" and place, Marietta, PA, mid to 3rd quarter 19th C. **$65**

Saucepan, copper, cast iron handle with copper rivets, restaurant size, with matching lid with long handle, "D. H. M. Co.," Duparquet, Huot, Moneuse, NYC, NY, 11-3/4" diam., c.1890s-1910. .... **$165**

Saucepan, copper, tinned inside, deep, with flat lid also made of copper, long iron handles on both pan & lid, New York, late 19th C. • These look quite old because the classic form couldn't be much improved! **$135**

XII-22. Roasters & bakers. Also called **roasting pans.** (T-L) "Crown," sheet iron, tinned cast iron handles, 4 sizes, 14"-19"L, for 7 to 16 lb. turkeys. Mfd. by Silver & Co., Brooklyn, c. 1910. They made 2 other styles: a "Brooklyn," and a "Royal." (T-R) "Model" roaster, oval, seamless, self-basting, gray mottled enamel with black handles. Two sizes: 15-3/4"L & 17-3/4"L. Available with fish racks. Central Stamping Co., 1920. (B-L) "Excelsior," blackened sheet iron, 10" to 19"L, mfd. by M. F. Koenig & Co., Hazleton, PA, 1890 ad. (B-R) The "Brownie" self-basting roaster, heavy sheet iron, 4 sizes: 14"L to 17-1/8"L, originally cost from 23¢ to 33¢ each. Albert Pick catalog, 1909. **$10-$40**

Saucepan, copper with iron handle, probably for restaurant or hotel use, as most of this company's wares were. Marked on both pan & lid "D. H. & M. Co." (Duparquet, Huot & Moneuse), 9-1/2" diam., late 19th C. **$75**

Saucepan, dovetailed copper with forged iron handle, copper lid with brass finial, originally tinned inside, American, 7"H x 6" diam., 19th C. **$95**

Saucepan, for use in a bain marie, copper, high sides & cylindrical, slightly up angled cast iron handle, dove tail seaming, tinned inside, American (?), 5-1/2"H, c.1840s to 1850s. **$75**

❖ NOTES ❖

Dovetail seam construction offered a much stronger braze or solder, as there were that many more edges to be joined together. Next time you're straddling a fine racing bike, look down and see where the upright "head tube" that holds the handlebar's stem joins the horizontal or angled cross bar of the frame under you. The cross bar or "top tube" under you fits into a very fancily scrolled pipe called a "head lug" (there's also one under the seat called a "seat lug." The opening socket in the lug where the cross bar is inserted is often made with a decoratively jagged edge that affords an extra soldering or brazing point to make the joint much stronger. In cabinetry, the dovetail affords more gluing surface.

Saucepan, enameled steel, with slightly slanted sides, handle with hanging hole, white enamel bottom & inside, the sides have colorful ombré vertical bands with white between, French, 7" diam. plus 6"L handle, early 20th C. .... **$15+**

Saucepan, stamped & polished aluminum, handle with hanging hole, "Mirro Aluminum," various sizes, c.1918. • A colorful cookbooklet put out by Mirro in 1918 suggests **Date Your Aluminum.** To prove the economy of any utensil is very easy, if the date be scratched upon it. Just buy any Mirro Utensil & date it with the month & year of purchase. Long before it has begun to wear out you will know that Mirro is amazingly economical." I've never seen a piece scratch-dated this way, but would all of you look & see? The picture in the booklet shows a woman scratching the date with a nail, up near where the handle is joined at the rim. .... **$2+**

❖ NOTES ❖

Futurewatch – For the be all & end all in saucepa-nache, look for a **"New! Self Stirring Saucepan,"** advertised in ladies' magazines in early 1973. Enameled in "flame" or "yellow," and lined with Teflon™, this 3-quart saucepan has a "battery-operated rotary [stirrer] concealed in the cover, to keep sauces, soups, custards, puddings, cereals cooking evenly and [to] prevent burning." The pan, which could be used with a gas or electric stove, had a straight black plastic side handle, a bottom with rounded sides, a slightly domed lid with the battery pack & little motor that would cause the stirrer sticking down from the center to turn. Originally it was $28.95, maker not given, unless it was Riverdale Industries, NYC. 1990s' price would be very low, although if as new, M.I.B., & if it does work, it may gain on its 1973 price.

XII-23. Saucepans, etc. – most are age-deceptive old forms. *Note how the handles are either nearly horizontal or angled up. This affected how they were set up on the range … those used on back burners would most likely have up-angled handles to reach easily. The same forms lasted many decades.* **(1)** *Copper or wrought iron, pouring lip. Tapered tubular handle that may be a socket handle, Harrod's Stores, London catalog, 1895.* **(2)** *"London" shape, iron or copper, no lip. Also Harrod's.* **(3)** *"Sugar boiler," prob. tinned copper, straight sides, William Adams, London, c.1860-61.* **(4)** *Planished block tin, lipped, and* **(5)** *block tin with straight sides, both Harrod's.* **(6)** *Top copper saucepan with matching lid, horizontal handles, 5"-20" diam.* **(6)** *Bottom copper saucepan is a "half saucepan." If it were cut down even lower it'd be a plat à sauté. Both Duparquet, 1904-10.* **(7)** *"Puritan" hotel seamless pan, from 2-1/4 to 33 quarts. Central Stamping, 1920.* **(9)** *Cast iron, tinned or enameled inside. From 1 to 20 quarts, tubular handle; and* **(10)** *Casserolet, looks huge here but really is only 1-1/2"H x 3-1/4" diam. Both Duparquet, Huot & Moneuse, NYC, early 1900s.* **(11)** *Cheap stamped tin, iron handle, 4-quart size; and* **(12)** *tin stew pan, 3-quart. Both offered through Butler Brothers wholesale catalog, 1899.* **(13)** *Copper boiler; and* **(14)** *set of copper saucepans & lids. All Duparquet, meant for restaurant or hotel use.* **$3-$125+**

Saucepan, with lid, turned wooden knob, enamelware, white inside, black rim. The outside & lid spectacularly enameled in irregular quarter-sized blobs of sky blue, interspersed like a conglomerate rock with brown & white mottled agate. The manufacturer called this finish "Duchess"; collectors call it "Turtle," "Chickenwire" or "Tortoise," mfd. by Vollrath Co., Sheboygan, WI, 4-7/8"H including lid, c.1900 to 1910s.. **$135+**

Saucepans, set of 4, copper, tinned inside, with forged iron handles, all with dovetailed seams, slightly slanted sides, largest marked with dealer's name: "Temple & Crook Ironmongers Matcome St. S.W.," London, England, smallest is 3-3/8" diam. with 3-1/4"L handle; the largest is 5-3/4" diam. with 6"L handle, late 19th C. • If you figure about $55 to $70 each, the price for the set would fall between about $250 & $275, with another $25-$50 added because it is a set, although only one is marked. .... **$275+**

Saucepans, "triplicate" set of 3, very heavy cast aluminum, a large round divided into thirds, for wedge-shaped pans, with projection on outside curve for the single slip-in handle used for any of them. Domed lids with wooden knobs. Wagner Ware, c.1925........ **$75+**

❖ NOTES ❖

Aluminum healthy? Wagner claimed about these & others in their line that they "are especially designed for waterless healthful cooking. They are of thick aluminum – process hardened – made to stand the steady heat in waterless cooking, which would destroy an ordinary utensil or burn the food. They are thick enough for the purpose intended – and no thicker." The advertising in the flyer I refer to also mentions "the new health cooking." • From the beginning of its use for kitchen wares, c.1888, aluminum has been given bad health reports, possibly coming from makers of tin, iron or enameled steel wares. (Enamelware was attacked in the late 19th C. for causing appendicitis. Flaked enamel supposedly lodged in that vestigal organ.) In the 1960s, reports in alternate health magazines, like *Prevention*, warned of effects of aluminum in foods, particularly acidic foods. Many people scoffed. In the 1980s, some reports linked Alzheimer's & aluminum. I'd just as soon never use it again.

Scotch bowl or kettle, sometimes called a Yankee bowl, cast iron with forged falling bail handle, long casting gate on bottom, irregular reinforcing band around outside, just under slightly flared lip. Scotch bowls did not necessarily have a lid, although if you've cooked oatmeal or grits you know how the bubbling surface sends up small volcanic eruptions of scalding hot meal to burn your stirring hand. Unmarked, American, 2-7/8"H x 10-3/4" diam., c.1830s to 1850s.. **$45**

❖ RECIPE ❖

Cracked Wheat – One pint of the cracked grain; 2 quarts of water; boil in a smooth iron pot over a quick fire; stir in the wheat slowly; boil fast; stir constantly for the first half hour of cooking, or until it begins to thicken; lift from the quick fire, and place the pot where the wheat will cook slowly for an hour longer; keep it covered closely; stir now and then, and be careful not to let it burn at the bottom. When ready to dish out, it is a neat way to have molds moistened with cold water; cover lightly and set in a cool place; eat warm or cold with milk and sugar." Henry Scammel, compiler, Treasure House, *1891 – a collection of uncredited earlier recipes from many cookbooks.*

Skillet, cast aluminum, interesting chain link design handle which is decorative & also dissipates heat very effectively, too many links to be Odd Fellows piece, many marks include maker's name, "Wilton," monogram "RWP" or "RPW," Roman numeral III, Indian head profile facing left, also "1892," marked "Columbia, PA," but Wilton is supposed to be in Mt. Joy, PA. Small, 7" diam., relatively long handle, 1892 could be a date for start of company. Otherwise, mid 20th C. (?). • Possibly 1940s or later souvenir? I'm sorry for not buying this one, as it certainly seems unusual & cheap ... the dealer marked it only $15... **$30**

Skillets, cast iron or aluminum, Griswold, Erie, PA. Please refer to Smith & Wafford's book, & reported sales on eBay, etc. It is too exact a science for me to evaluate Griswold skillets or frying pans. Most range from $40 to $60; however, rarities of size & marking may bring over $1,000. All I can say is that while there are many beautiful cast iron skillets made by companies besides Griswold, the attention to detail & the finishing is extremely beautiful on Griswold.

❖ NOTES ❖

Fine Finishing. I was reading a little catalog pamphlet, called *The Griswold Erie Cook Book,* that's mostly about a food cutter, & featuring some recipes. It's not dated but was published in the 1910s (?), though parts were probably previously published pre-1900. In it I came across a statement that brought out all my protective instincts – toward all founders of cast iron cookware. Under a linecut of an "Erie" frying pan, Griswold makes this claim: "Griswold Cast Cooking Utensils Is In a Class by Itself. Until we conceived the idea of an extra finished ware, all ironware was known as common (Statesprison) ware. Griswold 'Erie' Ware is made from a special mixture of iron, after models skilfully designed, distributing the proper thickness of metal where it is necessary to insure the best possible results in cooking dainty dishes, & prevents burning of food. We make a complete line. Send for Bulletin No. 40." I have never heard cast iron wares generally (& disparagingly) referred to as a class of prison-made ware, even if a few state penal institutions did have stove & hollowware foundries.

•   •   •

Texas Prison Ware. T. Lindsay Baker, Texas historian & windmill collector, wrote about one such prison-related furnace & foundry in his *Building the Lone Star. An Illustrated Guide to Historic Sites,* published by Texas A & M University Press. 1986. The first furnace was called "Old Alcalde Iron Furnace," at Rusk Penitentiary, est.1886 & running until 1894, when it was replaced by one operating until 1909. It was outside the prison walls & produced pig iron for the foundry within "to manufacture a wide range of iron goods.

Some of these were made solely for penitentiary use, & others were sold commercially. Among these products were heating stoves, ranges, sadirons, ... grates, ... and a wide variety of hollowware."

Skillet, cast iron, very rare because of mark which features a skillet-bodied spider, big on its web, the only word is on bottom of depicted pan-spider: "Erie" & "8." Griswold #8, Erie, PA, c.1890s. Punning logos were very popular in advertising in the 1880s & 90s, & not so much again until the 1950s. This logo is very rare, according to David "Pan Man" Smith, whom I thank for bringing it to my attention. The spider has also been seen on a teakettle....................... **$1,250+**

Skillet, cast iron, square for frying eggs, handle comes out of one corner, Griswold, 4-3/4" square, mid-20th C. (Added value. – Rarer, & larger, Griswold square frying pans have the handle coming out of the middle of one side, not the corner, but they are 9" square. They're worth $250+.) Small one:... **$35+**

Skillet, copper, tinned inside, iron handle fastened with copper rivets, marked "D. H. & M. Co." (Duparquet, Huot & Moneuse), NYC, NY, 2-1/2" deep x 13" diam., handle 14"L, c.1890s-1910. .... **$65+**

Skillet, old deep "saucepan" style, copper, dovetail seam, wrought iron long handle, stamped "Smith & Anthony Co." on body, & "S & A Co." on handle, also "Boston, MA," 11-1/2" diam. with 13-3/4"L handle, mid 19th C.. **$125**

Skillet, old deep "saucepan" type, copper with wrought steel long handle, stamped "Colony R. I.," prob. American, 10-1/2" diam. with 11-1/2"L handle, mid 19th C. .... **$75+**

Skillet, purple & white swirl enameled stamped iron, white inside, very heavy, all-in-one handle stamped & folded, large hanging hole, 20th C **$150**

Skillet, red porcelainized cast iron, Griswold #709, c1930s.. **$45**

❖ NOTES ❖

Chip Off the Old Skillet – Some advanced collectors of iron consider it okay to chip off damaged porcelainized finishes to reveal the pan underneath. (I don't know what enamelware collectors feel about it.) While it is true that the pan intended for enameling starts off the same as the pan for normal finishing, it rubs me wrong to alter a finish at all. It's a mystic iconic sort of notion, but I say that this chipped red pan came out of the factory with its enamel intact, was bought & used that way, & therefore might be said to have at least a teensy bit of red enamel soul that doesn't deserve shattering. Hah.

Skillet, & self-basting lid, yellow enameled cast iron (harder to find than red), Griswold #8, 1930s. .. **$50**

Skillet, or frying pan, cast iron, with smoke ring cast in bottom that lifts the pan 1/8" or so above stove plate, so there won't be a hot spot. According to collector Joel Schiff, the better term is heat ring because its main purpose is to trap the heat, not prevent the smoke from coming out into the room. Griswold #1 "411," (very close in size to the #0, found in this book under toys), Erie, PA, about 4-3/8" diam., c.1890s to 1900. • A wanted ad in *Antique Trader Weekly* offered $500 for this particular size with "smoke ring." There have reportedly, by the end of 1989, been only three of this size found, so your guess is as good as mine as to how much the really avid collector might pay – as well as how many more there may be out there. • Steve Stephens, editor of *Cast Iron Cookware News*, says that the pattern number, 411, indicates this is a toy. .... **$500-$600+**

Skillets – See also Frying pan; Omelette pan

Soup pot & cover, copper with dovetail construction, forged iron handles to both, "L.F.D & H." NYC, NY, 12"H, 19th C. .... **$125+**

Spider – See in Chapter X (Hearth Cooking)

Stand, stovetop, or slow cooking trivet, meant to be placed between pot & burner's flame, cast iron with radiant "spokes," the 2 half-round parts are notched to fit together at rim & form a round, embossed "Woman's Friend," New London, CT, pat'd. 1870. .... **$15**

Steam cooker, heavy metal, with 2 stacked doors, removable metal shelves inside, to hold various size pans or roasters, or even corn or potatoes with no pan at all, copper pan-like bottom for water, upright wooden carrying handles on sides at top, steam vent in top, set on stove top to steam cook, Toledo Cooker Co., who also made fireless cookers, 21-1/2"H x 12" square, pat'd. Feb. 5, 1907. .... **$25**

Steam cooker, tin with copper base, tin domed lid with strap handle, nickeled brass whistle, "The Ideal Steam Cooker," Toledo Cooker Co., Toledo, OH, 16"H, pat'd. 1900. .... **$45+**

Steam cooker, pieced tin with heavy copper plate on bottom of lower reservoir pan, above which is fixed a cylinder into which fits a tin cup for the food to be heated or cooked, "The Arnold Automatic Steam Cooker," mfd. by Wilmot Castle & Co., Rochester, NY, 8-3/4"H, pat'd. July 8, 1879, May 9, 1882 & Sept. 2, 1882. .... **$100**

❖ NOTES ❖

Cook Me Tender. In the March 1839 *Journal of the Franklin Institute* came this news of a "Novel Mode of Cooking Tough Meat, so as to render it Tender." – It was stated to Dr. Hare, by Mr. Jacob Perkins, now of London, that an old fowl, or a tough piece of meat, might be made tender by exposing it to the temperature

XII-24. Steamer insert *for pot or kettle. Adjustable aluminum, shown in open position. Imported from Germany, by George Thurnauer & Brother, NYC, 1912 ad.*

XII-25. Steam slow cookers called "Warreners." (L) *"Captain Warren's Everybody's Cooking Pot." Outer bulge shape belies inner vessel which has slanting sides. Vent tube in lid shown below (see arrow) connects with metal tube that passes diagonally through inner vessel from outer water-holding vessel, sort of like the one at right. This one from* American Agriculturist, *Jan. 1871.* ***(T-R)*** *Oval, bulgey "Warren's Patent," from Harrod's, 1895. Made for 3, 4, 5, 6, & 8 gallons, from 14" to 18". Also made with straight sides and round, not oval.* ***(B-R)*** *Another type, with separate compartments for meat & 2 vegetables.* American Agriculturist, *June 1871. See also X-38 in the Hearth Cooking chapter for more Captain Warren.* ***$20-$50+***

of boiling water for a considerable length of time, the meat being placed in a vessel into which the water did not enter. The experiment was tried by Dr. Hare on a tough piece of beef; the apparatus used by him consisted of two vessels, one placed within the other, the space between them being filled with water, & the beef being closely covered in the inner one. The water was kept boiling for nearly twelve hours, & the results verified the statement of Mr. Perkins; the meat was rendered tender & with the aid of proper condiments, an excellent bouillie was obtained. Steam, of course, might be substituted for the boiling water, as the requisite degree of heat would be obtained by causing it to pass round the vessel containing the meat." • "Bouillie" became in England, "bully" beef – a tenderized, cooked beef put up in cans. Which were then opened using cast iron can openers in zoomorphic form of steer's head & shoulders. See also Chapter VIII (Can openers & Corkscrews).

•　　　•　　　•

Tin caveat – "Before the advent of the Kingly Aluminum and the Queenly enamels, agates, granites, etc., tin was used extensively in the kitchen, but now the cooking utensil is very rarely tin and rightly so. Tin melts at a comparatively low temperature [450˚ F] and is besides affected by acids. That is why baking, stewing, etc., are not to be done with tin utensils plus acid food. The dark rings on baked apples cooked in a tin dish show very plainly what acid and tin do in combination. ... There are some householders who have tin ware left over from the past. To those we say, don't let it worry you; as they die out replace them with better, if you care to, but be loyal to what you have used if they have served." Ethel R. Peyser, *Cheating the Junk-Pile*, NYC, Dutton, 1922.

Stewing pot, cast iron, round bottom with 3 stubby peg feet, squat keg shape with flared rim, stop bail handle (ie. an ear cast so as to prevent bail from falling both directions), tipping handle, "Triumph," Patton Mfg. Co., Columbus, OH, 1890s. .... **$45+**

❖ NOTES ❖

Chinese Ironware – The pot above is marked, but it will probably come as a surprise to you, as it did to me, that cast iron cooking wares (shapes unknown) were exported from China. A short news item in *The Metal Worker*, Oct. 7, 1882, explains: "The manufacture of iron pans at Amoy, China, a large industry, is in the hands of two houses – a monopoly. The sale of iron pans in China is said to be enormous, and the export of the same from Amoy, principally to the Straits Settlements [British protectorate settlements on or near Malay, including, most notably, Singapore and Malacca. They were inhabited by mixed populations of Europeans, English, Eurasians, Chinese, & various natives], increased from 1,242,639 pounds in 1880 to 1,420,864 pounds in 1881. It was ascertained that the pans could be manufactured at Amoy, shipped abroad, and sold for one-half the price charged by the monopolists, and two men, an Englishman and a German, started foundries at Amoy with that fact as their goal. The local authorities, however, took a 'furious stand' against the invasion of the foreigners, and Peking officials have under consideration a request from Amoy to

XII-27. Pots & pans of blue enameled ware. *"Complete outfit ... true blue." Sets sized for the range-eye sizes of 7", 8" and 9". Teakettle, coffee pot, Berlin kettle (bottom right), saucepan, pudding pan (top left), double boiler (bottom left), dish pan (center), soap dish (top right), basting spoon & soup ladle (crossed in front of dish pan), Windsor dipper (in dish pan), two pie plates (for baking pies in). $4.58 for all, Sears Roebuck, 1908. In perfect condition, probably 200 times as much or more.*

prevent the prosecution of the enterprise by foreigners, so surely calculated to reduce the Chinese monopolists to the necessity of paying their laborers European starvation day wages."

Toaster, stovetop, blackened sheet iron, square flat tray with partly perforated tin pyramid inside wire frame with stamped metal platform on top for coffee pot or pan, a 1906 *Ladies' Home Journal* ad stated that "the slices are soft and palatable and possess that rich, nut-like flavor not obtainable by any other toaster," "Vulcan," mfd. by William M. Crane Co., NYC, NY, c.1906. .... **$7+**

Toaster, stovetop, blackened sheet iron square tray, slightly raised sides "catch the grease for basting if the user desires to heat meat of any kind." Attached to tray's center is large perforated tin cone within the 4-legged frame that holds a coffee pot; bent wire holds bread on 4 sides, mfd. by Wilson Toaster & Specialty Co., Minneapolis, MN, about 7" square, c.1903. .... **$7+**

Toaster, stovetop, pyramid style, tin, "Silver's Brooklyn Toaster," Brooklyn, NY, 7-7/8"H x 5" square, pat'd. Oct. 28, 1902. .... **$10+**

Toaster, stovetop, round perforated sheet steel plate, with pattern of radiating dots, with simple wire pyramid above that could be folded flat, "Wolff Visible Toaster," pat'd. 1920. .... **$10**

XII-26. Stock pots with brass spigots near bottom. (L) *"Gotham," seamless agateware (enamelware), stamped tin cover, two lug handles, brass strainer inside, 10-1/4" to 15-1/2" diam. Central Stamping, 1920. **(R)** Choice of copper, brazed iron, or seamless steel, snug lid with its own set of lug handles. English, c.1900, but in style going back at least to 1840s. $60-$150+*

XII-28. Potato baking rack. *Stamped tin with cutout & bent-up tabs to stab into potatoes, wire handle, 15-1/4"L, c.1900. $35-$60*

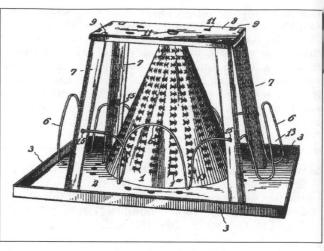

XII-29. Soup digesters, *an early form of* **pressure cooker. (L)** *Papin's Digester – "La Marmite" – a cylindrical vessel ["M"] with a firmly screw-clamped lid. "To close the vessel hermetically, sheet lead is placed between the edges of the cover and the vessel. In the cover there is a hole which is closed by a rod kept in place by a cylindrical guide ["u"] which presses against a lever. Pressure may be regulated by means of a weight ["p"], movable on the lever [between "d" and "b"]. The lever is so weighted that when the pressure in the interior is equal to six atmospheres, for example, the valve rises and the vapour escapes. The destruction of the apparatus is thus avoided, and the mechanism has hence received the name of safety valve. The digester is filled about two-thirds with water, and is heated by a large Bunsen burner." Denis Papin, French scientist, invented this digester in 1679 – over three hundred years ago! Picture from D. Atkinson's* Natural Philosophy, *1905. That lead seal! And we worry about cooking in aluminum?* **(T-R)** *This Digester produces "a larger quantity of wholesome and nourishing food" than any other. This was claimed because in it bones and gristle could be softened completely, for eating in a soup. Argghh! Two size ranges given as from 1 to 8 quarts, and from 4 quarts to 8 gallons.* American Home Cook Book, *1854.* **(B-R)** *Cast iron, 2 to 6 gallons, Duparquet, Huot catalog for hoteliers, 1909.* **$30-$400+**

XII-31. Stovetop toaster patent. *Pat'd. by George R. Wilson, Austin, MN, Sept. 13, 1898, #610,668. Wilson's specs read in part, "The object of the present invention is to ... provide a simple, strong, and durable one designed to be used in connection with an oil, gas, or similar heater, and adapted to conduct all smoke, gases, and odor from such a heater to the top of it and prevent them from coming in contact with the bread. A further object is to provide a device capable of uniformly toasting bread and adapted to prevent crumbs from falling into a burner and enable them to be readily removed ... to clean the toaster. ... Another object ... is to provide a toaster which will be adapted to form a support for a pot or analogous receptacle, so that it may be readily employed for making tea and coffee and for cooking." The "conical radiator" was made of sheet metal; the detachable brackets of wire. See also XVIII-32-B.*

XII-32 Stovetop toasters. (T-L) *"Worcester," tin & wire, folds flat, 8-7/8" diam., Washburn Co., 1936;* **(T-R)** *"Jim's Toaster," convex tin bottom with wire, heat-throwing cone. Does 5 slices. Excelsior Stove & Mfg. Co., c.1916;* **(B-L)** *"Kitchen Kumfort," 2-sided, steel, with perforated radiator base, 5"H x 8-1/2" diam. Washburn Co., 1927;* **(B-R)** *"Brooklyn Bread Toaster," heavy sheet steel, wire supports on 4 sides, 6"H x 8" square, Silver Co., Brooklyn, NY, c.1910.* **$3+; $7+; $5+; $10+**

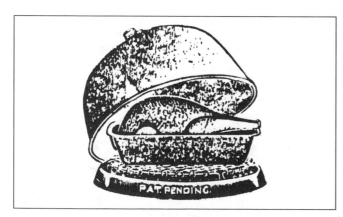

XII-30. Stovetop oven. *"Kantburn Kooker," or ovenless baker. Sheet metal. Also mfd. by Stanley Savage Mfg. Co. 1913.* **$15+**

Toaster, stovetop, round sheet steel base with 4 wide bracket risers (leaving flat space on top for plate or coffee pot or another slice of bread), with wire display-rack-type supports for 4 slices, most different is a tightly woven wire cone, point up, caged inside, "Radiant Incandescent Wire Cone," Washburn Co., about 5-1/2"H, late 1920s. .... **$10+**

Toaster, stovetop, sheet steel & wire, 2 slices only – bread forms sides of pup tent that's attached to round perforated base, supposed to be used on gas or gasoline stoves, "Kitchen Kumfort," Washburn Co., Andrews Division [Androck], 5"H x 8-1/2" diam., late 1920s. **$7**

Toaster, stovetop, slightly rectangular straight-sided pan with many perforations, frying pan-like handle at one end, 2 heavy wire rods above, on which to rest the bread, "Nichthauser & Levy," NYC, NY, about 10"L & 9"L handle, c.1904. .... **$7**

Trivet, for inside pots to support a roast or fish, green enameled cast iron, in snowflake-like lacy pattern, 3 short legs. These are also found in white, black, gray or blue in many designs. 8" diam., 19th C. **$25**

Water reservoir, stovetop, thinnish cast iron with perfectly smooth finish, oblong with square corners, fits 2 range eyes, hinged 2-part lid, picnic basket style, that not only lifts off completely, but unhinges with simple movement, lid is perfectly smooth & flat on top, inside with other identification of model numbers, etc., it says "KEEP TANK FILLED WITH WATER." No maker's name, only "MOD 65 66 33 NO 20 MOD 40 NO 22 RES. COVER. TRI-REG-REN MOD 85-87...," etc., American, 10"H x 17"L x 10"W, c.1890s-1910. .... **$45+**

Waterless cooker, aluminum, straight-sided vessel with side handles, 3-legged rack inside holds 2 semi-circular pans with round, highish-sided pan on top, close-fitting lid with 4 clamps, made in 4 models: "American," "Favorite," "Kitchen Craft," & "West Bend"; cover marked "The Waterless Cooker," mfd. by West Bend Aluminum Co., West Bend, WI, sizes for large or small families, late 1920s. **$10**

FOR MORE INFORMATION

With a computer you can do amazing searches for information & sites. I use the search engine www.google.com & find almost too much! Asking for sites related to cast iron & Griswold, for example, brought up many sites. I have only put the ones I'm familiar with here.

ORGANIZATIONS

National Graniteware Society
Contact: James Cox or Cindy Cox
POD 9248
Cedar Rapids, IA 52409-9248
Phone: (319) 390-7867
E-mail: info@graniteware.org
Web site: www.graniteware.org
Quarterly newsletter & convention, etc.

Griswold & Cast Iron Cookware Association
Emphasis is on Griswold, which is the focus of many collectors of cast iron. At the time this book goes to press, the newest contact information was not known, but you can get info from any of the three cast iron collectors – Stahl, Schiff, or Smith – listed below.

Web site: www.gcica.org
(At time of this writing, it loaded very slowly & then froze my computer, but could just be me.)

Wagner and Griswold Society
WAGS – for collectors of cast iron and cast aluminum kitchenware – was founded, with help from other collectors, by collector enthusiast Greg Stahl, who seeks cast iron toy kitchen items & cast iron & aluminum gem & muffin pans. One bonus will be an active message board where you are encouraged to share information.

COLLECTORS OF CAST IRON

This collector wants to buy unusual pieces of cast iron cookware to add to his collection, especially iron molds like in Chapter IV. Joel has helped me with identifying & researching ironwares for 20+ years.

Joel Schiff
321 E. 12th St.
NYC, NY 10003

Phone: (212) 353-1805
E-mail: cstirnckwr@aol.com

David Smith
This collector, who wrote the cast iron baking pan article in Chapter IV is very interested in cast iron broiler pans. He also has a newsletter "*Kettles 'n Cookware.*"

Drawer B
Perrysburg, NY 14129
E-mail: panman@panman.com
Web site: www.panman.com

Greg Stahl
Web site for Cast Iron Collectors

R & G Antiques
290 Chestnut St.
Clinton, MA 01510
Phone: (978) 368-6646
(evening: 6pm - 9pm EST only)
Web site: www.wagnerandgriswold.org

Greg Stahl
R & G Antiques
This site has cast iron for sale, but more to the point it has an active message board where you are encouraged to ask for information & a Sell/Trade/Want Board. It's run by collector enthusiast Greg Stahl, who seeks cast iron toy kitchen items & cast iron & aluminum gem & muffin pans.

290 Chestnut St.
Clinton, MA 01510
Phone: (978) 368-6646 (evening: 6pm – 9pm EST only)
Web site: http://griswold.auctiondesk.net

See also sources listed at end of Chapter XI (Stoves).

MUSEUMS

Wyandot Popcorn Museum
History of popcorn & poppers & commercial popcorn & peanut machines. Marion has yearly popcorn festival.

Contact: George K. Brown
169 E. Church St. – Heritage Hall
Marion, OH 43302-3819

Phone: (614) 389-2948
Web site: www.wyandotpopcornmus.com/

RETINNING COPPER

Atlantic Retinning & Copper Repair, Inc.

Copper pots & pans should never be used when the tin wears off, even in places. Here is a very useful source; you can calculate your cost, and you can print out mail order forms. The charge is by the inch, and Mr. Gibbons suggests measuring a saucepan, for example, with a tape measure from the rim, down the side, across the bottom, and up to the opposite rim.

Contact: Jamie Gibbons
560 Irvine Turner Blvd.
Newark, NJ 07108
Phone: (973) 848-0700
Web site: www.retinning.com/index.html

Fante's

Retinning service & all kinds of kitchen pots & pans.

1006 S. Ninth St.
Philadelphia, PA 19147
Web site: www.fantes.com/copper_cookware.htm

Guardian Service

Replacement lids, pressure cooker parts, cookbooks individual pieces, old & new wares, even Guardian Service aprons.

Contact: Ivin Bernstein
2110 Harmony Woods Rd.
Owings Mills, MD 21117
Phone: (410) 560-0777
E-mail: Vettelvr93@aol.com
Web site: http://members.aol.com/vettelvr93

Guardian Service Cookware Discussion Group
E-mail: guardian-service-cookware-subscribe@ egroups.com

COOKING

XIII. IMPLEMENTS THAT TURN, SPOON, & FLIP

The title of this chapter says it all. These are hand-held, minimally-mechanical cooking tools (correctly called implements, not utensils) of the most basic type. These tools are extensions of the cook's hands, that help the cook move food or food particles from one utensil or container to another. Many are variations on a spoon theme (spoon, ladle, dipper); others are forks of various types and sizes; most of the others have blades – narrow or wide, metal or wood – that will slide under cooked food so that it can be turned over or retrieved from kettle, griddle or oven. There is a lot of enamelware in this chapter; read cautions in Chapter XII.

There are some things that might have appeared in this chapter but were moved to a chapter more related to function. Some butter paddles are in the Form, Mold & Decorate chapter; skimmers, as well as wire vegetable skimmers or "pea ladles," are all in the Separate & Strain chapter; scoops are in the Measuring & Weighing chapter.

The **most avidly-sought item** in this chapter is the **doughnut lifter** seen in XIII-16. In fact, anything with the littlest bit of mechanical element, even a simple hinge, adds value for alot of collectors, so some flesh forks, pie lifters, egg lifters, etc. are popular. **Cake turners** are still the most generally popular category within this chapter for collectors of 20th century kitchenwares. The enormous increase in collectors of metal and wooden Colonial and hearth-cooking implements has meant more interest in ladles and cooking spoons, although I know of no one who collects them as a category. Collectors of enameled implements are legion; primarily they are material collectors, not form collectors.

Barbecue spatula, looks like a long-handled cake turner. Brand new but seems collectible: rectangular stainless steel blade is cut out with abstract chef's head & toque, red plastic handle has a push button that makes the tool say "clever comments." Mfd. by Wee Talk! Inc., adv'd. 1996. Sold new for $14.99. .... **$15+**

Basting spoon, or baster, heavily tinned iron, deep bowl, possibly mfd. by Lalance & Grosjean, Woodhaven, LI, NY, 19"L, c.1890s-1910. .... **$6**

Basting spoon, speckled black & white agateware, deep bowl, pointed end, American or European, 13"L, c.1890s-1910. .... **$20+**

Basting spoon, though rather shallow bowl, cast aluminum, marked "Mueller & Co.," Hagen, Germany, 14"L, c.1890s-1910. .... **$5+**

Beefsteak tongs – See Tongs

Butter hands – See Chapter IV (Mold & Shape)

Cake server, wide trowel-like tin blade but otherwise with same stamped embossed wire handle as cake turner or spatula of same make, both adv'g. "Rumford, the Wholesome Baking Powder," possibly mfd. by Pilgrim Novelty Co., American, early 20th C. Value varies because it gets priced as a "Rumford" collectible, or just as a simple cake server. .... **$10+**

XIII-1. Asparagus holder. *"Champion" wire tongs, 3-1/2", 4-1/2", 5-1/2" diameter. Asparagus actually cooked in holder. Mfd. by A. H. Brinkmann & Co., Baltimore, MD. House Furnishing Review, 1903. See Chapter V for Asparagus bunchers.* **$15+**

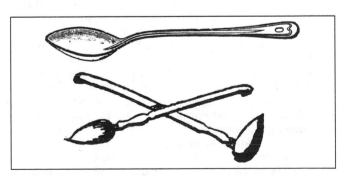

XIII-2. Basting spoons. *Distinguishing feature of most is a rather shallow bowl with horizontal long handle. (T) Stamped steel with "threaded" handle – a ridge stamped in lengthwise for strength. 10", 12", 14" or 16"L, Central Stamping Co., 1920. (B) Crossed "French Basting spoons are deep and with side handles," American Home Cook Book, 1854. Probably iron. Note shaped handles & hooked ends.* **$5-$20+**

XIII-3. Cake turners or short peels. *All are forged iron. (**L**) Heart-shaped shoulders, turned wood handle, possibly newer than others. 16"L. Mid 19th C. Collection of Meryle Evans. (**M**) & (**R**) have hooked handles. (**M**) Has spatulate blade, 17-1/2" L, (R) has cut & filed decorated handle with abstract heart or arrow point near middle. Oblong blade unusual. 22"L. Both late 18th, early 19th C. Photo courtesy Litchfield Auction Gallery, Litchfield, CT. Ex-Harold Corbin Collection, auctioned Jan. 1, 1989, for $425.* **$135+; $175+; $350+**

❖ NOTES ❖

Cake Turners – All the cake turners on the next few pages are meant for flipping pancakes, hence their name. Pancakes are also called "griddle cakes." The turners are also used for turning anything cooked on a griddle or even in a frying pan – from English muffins to fried eggs.

• • •

"Cake turners" or "Spatulas." Cake turners are often called spatulas, although this is technically incorrect, or at least debatable. On the one hand, when you talk about the shape of some fingertips, or certain petals or leaves, they are spatulate if they broaden at the tip in a spade-like way. That is the classic cake turner blade shape. A [pan] **cake turner** has a blade which is almost always longer than it is wide, about 5"L x 4" or 4-1/2"W, and the blade is also almost always slotted or perforated with a number of holes. A cake turner is used to flip food like flapjacks (flatjacks, pancakes, hotcakes), fried eggs, grilled cheese sandwiches, crab cakes or banana fritters. Many people specialize in the numerous cake turners of the A & J Co., later Edward Katzinger Co. (now EKCO), or of Androck. • For the most part, a **spatula** is like a wide, flexible or limber dinner knife blade, only bigger – about 1-1/4"W. The long, slender blade is rounded on the end, and the most common kitchen uses are icing cakes, or scraping work surfaces or grills, or cleaning the curved insides of bowls. Some spatulas are also perforated, but longness and flexibility are the basic attributes. • What we might take as our final arbiters, the manufacturers catalogs of the 19th & 20th centuries, are divided on terminology. • Finally, what does it matter? Lots of people think I nitpick about words, not just kitchen words,

but I believe that if you want people to be able to understand exactly what you mean, you have to use exactly the correct word.

• • • •

Shrove Tuesday Flapjacks & Pancake Bells – William Hones 1845 edition of *The Year Book*, for Feb. 3, Shrovetide, relays a quote from "Taylor, the water-poet, in his works, 1630" – "Shrove Tuesday, at whose entrance in the morning all the whole kingdom is inquiet; but by that time the clocke strikes eleven, which ... is commonly before nine, then there is a bell rung, cal'd the pancake bell, the sound whereof makes thousands of people distracted, and forgetful either of manners or humanitie; then there is a thing called wheaten floure, which the cookes do mingle with water, egges, spice, and other tragical, magicall inchantments; and then they put it, by little and little, into a frying-pan of boiling suet, where it makes a confused dismall hissing, untill at last, by the skill of the cooke, it is transformed into the forme of a flip-jack call'd a pancake, which ominous incantation the ignorant people doe devoure very greedily."

Cake turner, (or small peel, perhaps even a dough scraper, though without the latter's customary angled handle). Whitesmithed iron, nifty large hanging ring, American, prob. PA, 12-1/4"L, late 18th C..... **$135+**

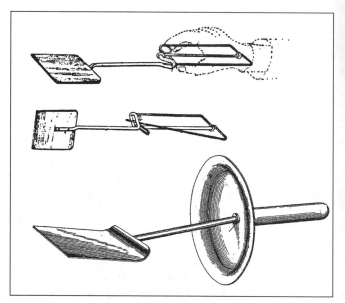

XIII-4. Cake turner patents. *(**T**) Two views of a cake turner with a mechanical flipping action. Pat'd. April 14, 1891 by Randall W. Stephens, Honesdale, PA, assignor to William D. Muir. Stephens claimed "The edge of the cake-lifting plate is inserted under the cake in the usual manner and the latter lifted above the bottom of the skillet. The thumb is now employed to press upon the spring-terminal ... [which] oscillates the handle, giving the plate a partial turn. This turn serves to invert the lifter and throw the cake face down upon the skillet." A new wrestling move! (**B**) En guarde! "Cake turner or similar article," pat'd. July 10, 1900, by Amanda C. Ericson, Victoria, IL, #32,918. "At the juncture of the shank and handle is a relatively-large bell-shaped or dished guard or shield." For those ferocious flapjacks!*

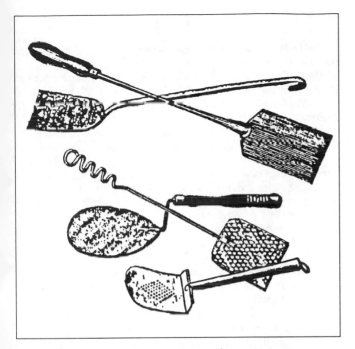

XIII-5. Cake turners & egg slices. *Cake turners also often called* **spatulas.** *Crossed implements at top:* **(T-L)** *All metal egg slice with hooked handle. 17"L, c.1904-1910;* **(T-R)** *Wood handled one is 21"L – a "hotel" cake turner. c.1901-10;* **(M-L)** *pear-shaped nickel-plated blade is the "Kitchen Kumfort Trowel," with rubberoid tiller handle. "The old fashioned turner was originally invented to lift and turn cakes on an old fashioned flat griddle. Now as the number of articles which are either fried or cooked in hot fat, such as croquettes, meat balls, omelets, etc., have increased, the cake turner has been used to handle such articles simply because there was no other utensil at hand. Experiments with a turner having the handle elevated about two inches from the blade resulted in [this] lifter." Lasher Mfg. Co., Davenport, IA, 1911 ad.* **(M-R)** *Is the "Jewel," with "flat serpentine handle that gives a good grip" (and, not incidentally, acted as a heat sink because heat had to travel further on curves). Steel, Arcade Mfg. Co., 1905.* **(B)** *Egg slice, blade 4-3/4" x 4-1/8" with perforated blade, c.1904-10.* **$15+**

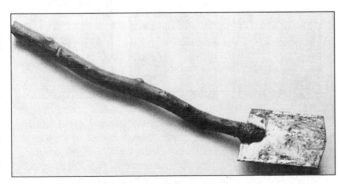

XIII-6. Homemade cake turner. *My personal favorite. Made from flattened & trimmed tin can, whittled stick, wire & a nail, 16"L. Found by Oregon collector Jim Holroyd, at "a camp on the Skyline Trail in the Oregon Cascades, c.1965."* **$20+**

Cake turner, polished, filed, shaped & decorated forged iron, handle has round hanging loop, copper inlaid along handle, small blade with very rounded shoulders & tips, no cutouts, marked "B. H" with date, PA. Blade is 4" x 3-7/8", with 12"L handle, dated "1821." (Ex-Robacker Collection.) .... **$800+**

Cake turner, or keyhole spatula, blade of whitesmithed iron is shaped like a fat, large keyhole, there's a cutout cross in the "ball" of blade, American (?), 8-3/4"L, very early 19th C. .... **$85+**

Cake turner, keyhole spatula, twisted forged iron handle, all filed & polished whitesmith's work, pretty silvery appearance, American, 11"L, very early 19th C. • This keyhole shape, sometimes called a thistle shape (with bulbous part down), was used in much later cake turners too – especially in enamelware. .... **$125+**

Cake turner, forged iron, smallish flat blade with marvelous wing-like shoulders, long shaft that is straight for first few inches, then twisted with big-fat & little-tight twists, rattail loop at end, American, 17"L, 18th C. .... **$275+**

❖ NOTES ❖

Whitesmith or Brightsmith Work – The silvery surface comes from being worked, filed, polished, planished and hammered. The hammering & polishing, which gave the surface a very fine texture, is called planishing. Sometimes the smith who did this work was known as a whitesmith or brightsmith. • According to Carl W. Drepperd, in *Primer of American Antiques*, originally a whitesmith was the same as a whitster, who was a "Planisher – one who hammered iron white," and only later did a "whitesmith" come to mean a worker in tin, tin plate, or any other white metal.

• • •

White Sediment on Iron – Every once in a while I come upon an old iron piece with this white substance, which really isn't powdery. I wondered if it's a sort of flux used when working the iron, and if its presence indicates a piece was never finished, and therefore never used. Anyone know? Here's another possibility, just found in a Southern recipe book: **"To Prevent Rust** in Iron Utensils." – "To prevent their rusting when not in use: Mix half a pound of lime with a quart of warm water; add sweet oil until it looks like cream. Rub the article with this; when dry, wrap in paper, or put over another coat." Mrs. A. P. Hill, *Mrs. Hill's New Family Receipt Book*, NY: 1870.

• • •

"Forged" or "wrought"? These terms mean the same thing, although "wrought" is the more common. A blacksmith or whitesmith uses a forge to heat the metal he's going to hammer (or sometimes chisel) into shape. That blacksmith is a "wright" who wrought. I believe that because "wrought iron" has been so common, and used by all and sundry to describe all sorts of neo-Colonial hammered iron pieces, that today's dealers are more inclined to use the word "forged," just to set their wares apart. Furthermore, "hand-forged" and "hand-wrought" are used to distinguish generally older pieces from those made with mechanical hammers.

Cake turner, forged iron, whitesmithed, polished & filed yet dark in color, shapely strong handle, end has teardrop hanging hole, shovel-shaped rectangu-

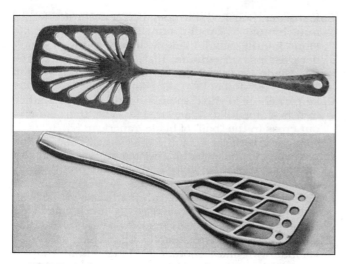

XIII-7. Cake turners. Both cast aluminum.
(T) Marked "Royal Brand" & "Made in Germany."
12-1/2"L, c.1910. **(B)** Angled straight-front blade.
Word "Aluminum" appears in hammer-shaped
mark on back, also "D.R.G.M. Germany."
10-1/4"L, c.1910s. **$10-$15+**

lar blade with rounded shoulders, slightly flared
sides, bold cutouts of rather large diamond near
center with four round holes near each corner,
signed "E. P. Sebastian" on handle. Edward Sebastian was noted for openwork "spatulas." Host, Berks
County, PA, blade 6-1/4" x 5-1/2" with 14-1/2"L
handle, c.1850s-80s. • Ex-Robacker Collection, auctioned by Horst May 1989, for $1,400 – in good part
because of the Robacker provenance......... **$1,000+**
Cake turner, forged iron with wide flat blade, relatively
short handle, American (?), 13-1/2"L, mid
19th C. .... **$95+**
Cake turner, forged & polished iron, long handle with
small heart cutout in end near rattail loop, American;
PA (?), 18-1/2"L, early 19th C............................ **150+**
Cake turner or peel (for removing bread from oven),
nicely shaped wrought iron blade with heart-top (or
shoulder-padded) shoulders, turned wood handle,
shortish shaft, American, 12"L, 19th C. .... **$125+**
Cake turner or peel, very small round disc blade, interesting long handle with short chevron & bulls eye
hole, marked "Levi Lewis," prob. PA, 14-3/4"L,
19th C. .... **$175+**
Cake turner or peel, whitesmithed forged iron, well-
formed shoulder, initials "A. W." inlaid in brass on
handle. From near Stroudsburgh, PA, 13-13/16"L,
early 1800s. Marked pieces very desirable.... **$300+**
Cake turner, or perhaps peel, forged iron, whitesmithed
& polished, long handle with broad end & rattail
loop, decorated with cut lines & bull's eyes. Round
blade has cutout 6 point star or petaled flower, 3/4"-
wide border decorated with 6 bull's eyes, American,
20-1/2"L overall, blade is 4" diam., 18th C. Good
size & decoration. .... **$300+**
Cake turner, forged & polished iron, unusual sideways
rectangular blade almost size of playing card, with
rounded corners, thin graceful forged iron handle,
with small hanging loop, fine inlaid brass floral
designs. PA. Blade 4" x 5-1/4"W, with 16"L handle,
dated "1854." • Price achieved at May 1989 Horst
auction of Robacker collection: $325........... **$500+**

❖ NOTES ❖

Fake Brass Inlays – Jeannette Lasansky, (Oral Traditions Project, Court House, Lewisburg, PA 17837) is
author of several meticulously researched books on old
Pennsylvania crafts. In "Collectors notes," Nov. 1980
The Magazine ANTIQUES, she shared her discovery of a
number of fake brass inlays found in a disparate group
of 18th or early 19th C. forged iron implements from
different collections. The faking was done at some point
after 1860 (determined from fluorescence analysis of
the brass involved), and probably in the 20th C. Pieces
included cake turners, flesh forks, tasters, ladles and a
skimmer, all common forms, with stylistic differences
in the design of the forged iron. The significant thing,
what brought Lasansky's attention to the fraud, is that
"On all the pieces the brass-inlay technique is identical
and the motifs, repetitive."

The **three types of decoration done by the faker**
are (1) narrow bands with minimal engraved design; (2)
wide bands with engraved initials and/or dates (Lasansky says they are all from 1823 through 1829); and (3)
wide bands or inset "lozenges" with images (hearts,
eagles or tulips) engraved on them. From the pictures
shown in that article, of pieces in the Titus Geesey Collection at the Philadelphia Museum, and the Abby Ald-
rich Rockefeller Folk Art Center, Williamsburg, VA, it
seems that without Lasansky's eagle eye, and the sharing of artifacts made possible by exhibits, photographs
and books, we would never have known. The engraving
is of the bright cut variety from the early 19th century,
and the style of letters, numbers and pictures mimics
the eagerness and slight primitiveness of examples of
authentic period engraving. It's scary. Ive not seen an
update, though Lasansky asked collectors and curators to closely examine their collections. One thing

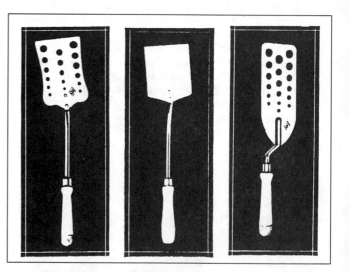

XIII-8. Cake turners. All nickel-plated steel, with
turned wood handles with "three coats of highest
grade enamel" in 2-tone Blutip colors. All made
with choice of holes or no holes. **(L)** Perforated
blade with "shoulders," 13"L. **(M)** Plain small one is
11-1/4"L. **(R)** Long perforated "kitchen tool" with
tiller handle, 11"L overall. All "EKCO," Edward
Katzinger Co., Chicago, in "A & J Blutip Kitchen
Tools" catalog, 1930. A & J was division of EKCO.
$5-$15

apparent from the pictures is that the pitting, scarring and surface distressing of the polished iron of the handles of the various implements is in sharp contrast to the virtually untouched surfaces of the brass inlays. • I must stress that no item from the Earl F. & Ada F. Robacker Collection was said to have a fake 20th C. inlay, and the sharing of Lasansky's observations is not meant to impinge on the value or authenticity of any inlaid piece auctioned by T. Glenn Horst.

Cake turner, handsomely formed tin, tiny pie-wedge cutouts, stylized heart & bird decorations, ribbed cylindrical handle with little strap hanger, possibly a 10th Wedding Anniversary gift, found in Bradford or Sullivan County, NY, 13-3/8"L x 2-1/2"W at widest point, c.1860s to 1880s. .... **$200+**

❖ NOTES ❖

1875 "Tin Weddings – Passing an extensive house furnishing store twice daily, we most always give a glance at the show-window. Some months ago we saw a most beautifully fashioned shoe on exhibition, which appeared to be made of the finest planished tin. We wondered what it could be for; it was too large for a smokers ash-receiver, and could hardly be an article for kitchen or table use; several days after, and before we had time to step in and solve the matter, there appeared by the side of the shoe an elegant fan of the same material, at least so far as fine workmanship could make a tin fan elegant; this added to the mystery, but in a day or two all was made plain by the displaying of a card reading 'Articles for Tin Weddings.' All that we know of 'tin weddings' is that the tenth anniversary of marriage is by some people celebrated, as a sort of burlesque upon silver weddings, by a party, at which the guests made presents of tinware. The presents were formerly of useful articles, but now it seems that the burlesque itself is travestied, and much ingenuity is expended in making articles for tin weddings which can be of no possible use to those who receive them. Quite a large number of these articles are now imported from France; two of these have already been named above; besides these we found on inquiry there were ridiculous bouquets of tin flowers; preposterous necklaces, and other jewelry of skillful workmanship, but all of the same cheap material; a tin saw and other tools for a mechanic; instruments supposed to be emblematic of the medical profession, and other curious, expensive, and equally useless articles are offered. Now we believe in innocent amusement, and if any fun can be had out of a tin wedding – if the parties most concerned are so disposed – so be it, but there should be some sense even to our nonsense, and we must say that we regard this matter of tin shoes, tin bouquets, and the like, as carrying the matter just a little too far." – Anonymous editor, *American Agriculturist*, July 1875, NYC, where the espied tinwares store was. The editor would be astounded at the high regard some collectors today hold these "nonsensical" tin objects. See Chapter VII.

Cake turner, probably a 10th Anniversary piece, not for use. Described by the Robackers as a "Pie peel," but the blade isn't large enough. The blade is bent to create angled-up shoulder, & is crudely soldered to long dented cylindrical handle, the only redeeming feature being the punctured tin decoration (& that done with no finesse) comprised of a squat, typically Pennsylvania German heart, with the initials "L" and "S" inside, the heart surmounted by a wavy line indicating a leaf scroll with a small flower in the center, PA, 21-5/8"L, with blade about 6-1/4"L x 4 1/2"W, late 19th C. (Ex-Robacker Collection.) .... **$500+**

Cake turner, homemade, a flattened tin can side, carefully cutout in a truncated wedge shape, front edge bent, nailed to a peeled & partly whittled stick, extremely well-worn, great patina on handle, wire wrapped around handle as a sort of ferrule, Oregon, 16"L, found around 1965, dates poss. to c.1940s. • Found by collector James R. Holroyd of Oregon, discarded at a camp on the Skyline Trail in the Oregon Cascades. .... **$20+**

Cake turner, also called a kitchen trowel by manufacturer, ovoid unperforated blade, nickel plated steel, tiller handle "Elevated about two inches from the blade," in trowel fashion, rubberoid handle grip, "Kitchen Kumfort Trowel," mfd. by Lasher Mfg. Co., Davenport, IA, about 10"L, patent applied for by 1911. .... **$15+**

Cake turner, wrought iron handle with brass blade, perforations in blade form the initials "L. H.," which were probably those of the owner (or recipient of this handmade gift). American, 9-7/8"L, 1850s to 1870s. .... **$225+**

Cake turner, brass with forged iron handle, "F. B. S.," Canton, OH, 14-1/2"L, pat'd. 1886. • The style of these looks much older, and there are lots of them around, accounting for wide value range, because they look much older, & some people may not be aware of supply. .... **$45+**

Cake turner, tinned sheet metal, wire handle stamped flat with embossed design and "Rumford," blade simple with small heart-shaped hole near the riveted joint of handle & blade, "Rumford Baking Powder" adv'g. piece, possibly mfd. by Pilgrim Novelty Co., American, 10-3/4"L x 2-3/4"W, c.1914 (?). • This same turner without an adv'g. message is worth less. .... **$18+**

Cake turner, enameled sheet iron, white with pale blue pattern of "Chicken wire," tubular handle, hanging ring, blade spatulate in shape with rounded "shoulder," pattern of perforations is two double rows of stylized wheat berries along outside blade edges, American (?) or European, 13"L, c.1890s-1910. • This came in various color combinations. The "Chicken wire" effect adds a lot to value here; one with black or dark red handle & plain white blade would be a fourth or third as much. .... **$95+**

Cake turner, nickel-plated steel with wire shank, blue & ivory painted wood handle, Perforation pattern is center straight line of holes flanked by an outward curving line of holes on each side, "Blutip," A & J, Binghamton, NY, 14-1/4"L, c.1940s. • Price reflects poor condition of paint. The two-tone ones, especially with ivory, seemed to flake off in big chips more readily than the red or green finishes. Even in good condition these don't bring much. .... **$5+**

Cake turner, oblong tin blade, sharp front corners, rounded corners at heel of blade, 2 elongated corrugations lengthwise on blade – according to the ads, "So the cake cannot slide sidewise." Paint-enameled turned wood handle, mfd. by Handy Things Co., Ludington, MI, blade is 3-1/2"L x 2-7/8"W, overall length 11-1/4", c.1904. • Remember, "cake" refers to pancake, not layer cake. .... **$7+**

Cake turner, perforated tinned steel & wire, the heavy wire handle wiggles & snakes off at the tip, an elegant solution to heat dispersal problem. "A good cook will quickly see the merits of this cake turner. The grease passes through it instantly and leaves the food light and tempting. The handle gives a firm, cool grip and is easily cleaned," say the ads of the time. mfd. by Arcade Mfg. Co. (famed toy makers), Freeport, IL, 14-3/4"L, c.1905. .... **$20+**

Cake turner, stamped sheet metal, handle riveted to simple blade, round shoulder, no finesse to design, but it wouldn't look bad in that bouquet-of-turner-tulips stuck handle down in a crock, no mark, American, 13"L, c.1890 to 1900. .... **$5+**

Cake turner, tin, adv'g. "Quick Meal Ranges," for Ringen Stove Co., but prob. not made by them, early 20th C. .... **$15+**

Cake turner, tin & green finished wood, blade is stamped with ridges to add rigidity and is perforated with highly decorative pattern of holes that form a heart reminiscent of Pennsylvania German designs, American, 11-3/4"L, 20th C. .... **$5+**

Cake turner, tin with knobby turned wooden handle, baked on white enamel finish with 1/6th of handle at end dipped in rich medium blue, wire shank, shapely shouldered blade with 3 graduated rows of perforations, "Blutip," A & J Mfg. Co. (Div. of Edward Katzinger), Binghamton, NY, 13-1/4"L, c.1930. .... **$5+**

Cake turner, tin with wire, has 3 long oblong blades with large holes, they are stacked 1 2 3, but when fanned out when you pull the thumb release they almost triple the width of the useable blade. This way you can adjust the width to suit the griddle or frying pan you are using as well as the pancake or omelet, marked "Coradon," (the one in Jane Celehar's book was made by Gadget Mfg. Co.), NYC, 12-1/2"L, blade: 6-1/2"L x 2-5/8"W, spreads to 8-1/2"W, pat'd. Dec. 8, 1936, by Minnie Greene & Lois Udey. .... **$12+**

Cake turner, tinned blade, embossed handle, "Aurora Ice Cream," early 20th C. .... **$12+**

Cake turner, tinned iron, adv'g. "Ira Egger General Merchandise," American, early 20th C. .... **$7+**

Cake turner, tinned iron with bottle opener handle, adv'g. "Clyde Milling Co.," Clyde, KS, early 20th C.......... **$7+**

Cake turner, tinned iron with bottle opener handle, adv'g. "Farmers Mercantile Co.," pat'd. Nov. 24, 1914. ... **$7+**

Cake turner, tinned metal, heart-shaped blade with very small heart cutout, bottle opener at other end of handle, looks rather like a Rumford turner, adv'g. "Metropolitan Furniture Co. – A Good Place to Trade," American, pat'd. Nov. 24, 1914. .... **$20+**

Lookalike Alert

Flap the Jack, Mac, Lookalike alarm – Lehman's Hardware & Appliances, Kidron, OH, offers a very similar one with stainless steel blades in their *Non-Electric Good Neighbor Amish Country* catalog. • Another mechanical type has a trigger that you pull which flips the blade; talk about a "lazy elbow" (as the nickname goes for kettle tilters from hearth cooking days)!

Cake turner, tinned steel blade in pear shape with straight front edge, slightly elevated tiller handle with turned wood grip, Cronk & Carrier Mfg. Co., Geneva, OH, 12-1/2"L x 4"W, c.1920s. .... **$7+**

Cake turner, tinned steel blade, wire shank, turned wooden handle. The blade is unperforated & if the turner is held upright, blade up, it looks like an abstract tulip. In fact, if someone could come up with an unobtrusive base, which would hold unaltered cake turners much as a flower frog holds roses and carnations; you could have a very wonderful bouquet of cake turners. I'm afraid the base would either obscure the handles, however, or the handles would have to be drilled. How about drilling a block of clear acrylic? Hmmm ... Aarne Anton, wanna try? ... marked "WB/W," I believe this is probably Waterbury Button & Mfg. Co., Waterbury, CT, 14-1/4"L, c.1910-30. .... **$10**

Cake turner, tinned steel blade with as many perforations as a sieve, nicely turned wooden handle left natural, American, 15"L, c.1910. .... **10+**

Cake turner, tinned steel blade with rounded "Fins" at the back end, 3 rows of perforated holes, center one straight, side ones curved out, stamped "Stainless" (which it wasn't), so they crossed that out & stamped it "Rustless" (which it wasn't either), A & J Mfg. Co., Binghamton, NY, 13-1/4"L x 3-1/2"W, c.1935. • Some of value is in social history aspect of the stamped marks. .... **$7+**

Cake turner, tinned steel long oblong blade with 2 sizes of perforations forming diamond pattern, pronounced shoulder to blade, turned wooden handle, American, 12"L x 3"W, c.1920s........................ **$7+**

❖ NOTES ❖

Brand names – The reality of collecting is that people still pay more for "Brand names" than unmarked pieces, but I firmly believe that in the long run this is a less successful way to collect. Remember that unknown art always has to be discovered.

Cake turner, tinned steel with wood handle, odd extremely rigid near-round blade with truncated end & no perforations, American, 14-1/4"L x 4"W, c.1910s. .... **$7+**

Cake turner, cast aluminum, angled slots in blade, 4 holes at front edge, marked "Aluminum" inside a hammer's outline, also "D. R. G. M." (for Deutsches Reichs-Gebrauchsmuster), German, 10-1/4"L, early 20th C., prior to 1918, when the mark "D. R. G. M." was superceded... **$10+**

Cake turner, cast aluminum with sort of rayed design or perforations, hanging hole in handle, "Royal Brand," German, 12-1/2"L x 3-3/4"W, I used to think these were c.1930s; now I think c.1910s. .... **$15+**

❖ NOTES ❖

Country of Origin Marks – Part of the widely-debated McKinley Tariff Act, passed by the 51st Congress on October 1, 1890, is of interest to all collectors. From Chapter 1244, Section 6: "That on and after the first day of March, 1891, all articles of foreign manufacture, such as are usually or ordinarily marked, stamped, branded, or labeled, and all packages containing such or other imported articles, shall, respectively, be plainly marked, stamped, branded, or labeled in legible English words, so as to indicate the country of their origin; and unless so marked, stamped, branded, or labeled they shall not be admitted to entry." The name "England" often appeared stamped on export china after 1875, and many English potteries marked "England" after 1880, but all did after 1891.

Cake turner, shapely tinned steel blade with 3 parallel rows of large to small graduated perforations, wooden handle, A & J, Binghamton, NY, 13-1/4"L, 1930s. • These A & J cake turners came in a variety of sizes and patterns of perforations. Size & paint condition on wooden handle determine value. ... **$5+**

Cake turner, tinned steel, wire, wood, blade has pretty design of radiating petal-like lines and small holes, shapely shoulder to blade, marked "WB/W," probably Waterbury Button & Mfg. Co., 12-1/2"L x 3-1/8"W, c.1915-20. .... **$10**

Cake turners – See also Barbecue spatula

Cooking implements, set of 4 in original box, sheet metal with green wooden handles, "Samson Cutlery," Rochester, NY, 20th C. See also Implement racks in Chapter VII.............................. **$20+**

Cooking set, handcrafted, cleaver, large spoon, carving knife & sharpening steel, flesh fork, handles are assembled bands of ivory, pipestone [catlinite] & onyx. American, c.1960s............................. **$100+**

Cooking spoon, metal, adv'g. "Monarch Stoves," c.1890s... **$20+**

Cream dipper or ladle – See Dipper or ladle for cream

❖ NOTES ❖

Dippers are often found made of "ready-made" raw materials like burls, coconuts, gourds, or coquilla nuts. A very nice collection could be made of these. Dried gourd dippers were made by many so-called "Native" cultures as

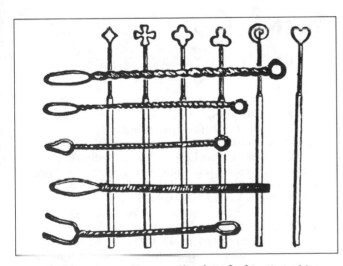

XIII-9. Bon Bon dips or dipping forks, tinned iron or brass wire, to lift candies out of coating. Plain ones from candymakers' supplier S. Joseph Co. catalog, c.1927. Fancy ones from T. Mills, Philadelphia, 1930. Almost identical ones date well back into 19th C. $4-$20

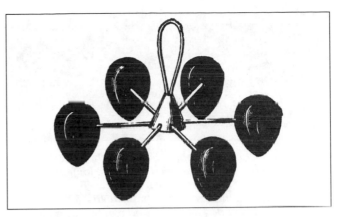

XIII-10. Candy egg dipper, or egg hook, for coating cream eggs with chocolate. Heavy tinned wire, with hanging loop (to hang on rack). "Small" to accommodate 6 eggs, for 1¢, 2¢, 3¢ or 5¢ eggs; and "large" for 4 eggs of 10¢ size. Mills, 1930. $8+

well as by country North Americans. An old gourd dipper from Mexico or Central America might be expected to have some decoration carved into its surface, or a more colorful dyed wool cord, or perhaps the gourd itself might be painted on the outside. If you're interested in growing gourds to make dippers, birdhouses, bowls, rattles, rainsticks, etc., the organization for you is the **American Gourd Society**, 317 Maple Ct., Kokomo, IN 46902-3633. Web site: www.americangourdsociety.org/.

• • •

Out Of Your Gourd – W. Scott Boyce's *Economic and Social History of Chowan County, North Carolina, 1880-1915*, published in NYC by Columbia University, 1917, says about 1880s country people: "They improvised by far the greater number of their own dippers, occasionally from conch shells, more frequently from cocoanut hulls, but largely from the common gourd, which was cut, scraped, boiled, scrubbed, and sunned to remove the 'gourdy' taste and smell – said taste and smell, however, in spite of all these efforts, remaining to a more or less degree just as long as there was a piece of the gourd" [p.109].

Dipper, carved ash burl, beautiful patina, turned handle, American, bowl is 3" deep x 6" x 5-1/2", slightly warped oval, unusual 13"L handle, early 19th or late 18th C. .... **$175+**

Dipper, coconut, small, highly polished after stripped of husk, turned wood long handle set at about 30° angle, pointed tip, pewter ferrule, marked "Cleveland Brothers, Providence, RI," mid 19th C. .... **$250+**

Dipper, dried gourd of ornamental variety, long skinny neck, large hole cut out of main body, scraped clean & then dried, old cord through hole at tip of natural handle, gorgeous patina, American, 10"L, 19th C. .... **$85+**

Dipper, dried gourd, polished, ornamental variety, big bowl, curved neck with enough hook to end to hang over edge of bucket, American, 8"L x 3" deep, 19th C. .... **$65+**

Dipper, brass bowl, forged iron handle hooked on end, American (?), 15-1/4"L, late 18th or early 19th C. Brass is soft & dings easily, so a certain amount of wear is okay.. **$200+**

XIII-11. Cheese scoop. *Steel mechanical scoop, bone or ivory handle (shaped like table knife handle). Tiny rivet has cut decorations & facets. Thumbscrew (small piece where arrow points) holds follower on track inside spade-like scoop and can be turned to lift follower for thorough cleaning. 10-1/16"L overall; scoop 1-5/8"L x 1-1/4"W. English, 19th C. Courtesy Louise Bibb of Virginia.* **$55**

Dipper, often called a cocoa dipper, characterized by round cup/bowl, small bowl relative to overall size, & rim that's very slightly smaller than widest part of bowl. Enameled gray & black mottled outside of round-bottom bowl, black rim, black inside bowl, turned wood handle painted black, set into socket fixed at about 40° to bowl, prob. American, cup 3-5/8" diameter, 11"L overall, late 19th C .... **$75+**

Dipper, gray graniteware, "Windsor" style, rolled rim, long tubular handle riveted on at almost 45° angle. A "Windsor" has a flat bottom, and somewhat slanted sides, so that the dipper almost looks like a very small if long-handled saucepan. American (?), 13"L overall, c.1890s-1910.................................... **$35+**

Dipper, agateware, mottled gray, "Windsor" type, large straight-sided & flat-bottomed bowl with slightly angled, turned wood handle painted black, four sizes, from 4-1/4" diam. x 3" deep, to 6-3/4" diameter x 3-3/4" deep, handles 5"L, American, 1880s-90s. .... **$45+**

Dipper, tin, of flat-bottomed type called a cup dipper, smaller than a "Windsor," stamped tin, slightly bulging sides, rolled rim, long forged iron handle with hanging hole, set about 45° angle to edge of cup. This kind of dipper could be filled, then set down without spilling, with the handle propped against something. Matthai-Ingram Co., 5-1/8" diam. cup, 14"L handle, late 19th C. .... **$15+**

XIII-13. Dippers. (L) *Pieced tin, both with flat bottoms and braced tubular handles. Top has long handle with shovel-like half-loop handle. 1-3/8-quart capacity; bowl 3-5/8"H x 6-1/2" diam. Central Stamping Co., 1920.* **(R)** *Bent maple with turned maple handle & pine bottom. Copper tacks hold lap joint together. Shaker, mid to 3rd quarter 19th C.* **$15-$30; $250+**

Dipper, gray graniteware, bent-tip flat handle, deep but small bowl, a few dings & chips, 12"L overall, c.1890s-1910. .... **$5+**
Dipper, robin's-egg blue enamelware with black trim, black enameled tubular handle, probably Lisk Mfg. Co., Canandaigua, NY, 14"L, 20th C. .... **$25+**
Dipper, mottled brown & white enamelware, a few slight dings, possibly "Onyx," Columbian Enameling & Stamping Co., or European, 5-1/4" diam. bowl, handle 14-1/2"L, late 19th C. In last decade thou-

XIII-14. Dippers, *most with round-bottomed bowls. From* **(T-L): (1)** *Tin, tubular handle, 2 qt. size. From Butler Brothers catalog, 1899.* **(2)** *Large water dipper in "Pearl Agate," which came in different pale colors, all with black-enameled wood handle, nickel or silver plated fittings. Manning, Bowman & Co., c.1892.* **(3)** *Smaller gray enamelware handle, very like the previous one, but not so well made – at least, original wholesale price was 5¢ each, as opposed to $1.10 each. Butler, 1899.* **(4)** *"Copper dipper," with tubular socket handle. Sizes from 4" to 10" diam. Duparquet, Huot & Moneuse, c.1904-1910.* **(R)** *Flat-bottomed one is "Windsor" type, agateware, turned wood handle; 4 sizes from 3"H x 4-1/4" diameter to 3-3/4"H x 6-3/4". Lalance & Grosjean, c.1890. Copper & agateware worth most; tin least.* **$15-$125**

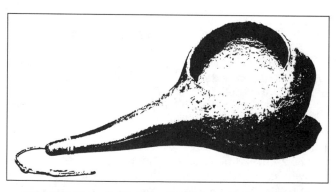

XIII-12. Gourd dipper. *Dried gourd. Late 19th C. Picture courtesy of the National Museum of American History, Smithsonian Institution. Value for similar pieces:* **$50-$120+**

XIII-15. Suds dipper confusable. *Pieced tin, for laundry work. Tin, two sizes, 3-5/8" x 6-1/2" and 4"H x 6-7/8". Savory, Inc., Newark, c.1925-28.*
$15-$30

sands of mottled brown & white enamelwares have been imported from Europe. They look great, but the collector price support just isn't there. .... **$15+**

Dipper, forged iron, stamped on handle is maker's name, "H. W. Weaver," 23-1/2"L, early 19th C. **$75+**

Dipper, forged iron, huge round-bottom bowl with 2 qt. capacity, long handle with hooked end, American, 24"L handle, early to mid 19th C. .... **$75+**

Dipper, forged iron, rattail handle, American, 15"L, early 1800s. .... **$60+**

Dipper, pieced tin with tubular handle set at angle, American, 9-1/2"L, 2-cup capacity, 19th C. .... **$30-$38**

Dipper, tin, unusual for the stamped message: "Stolen from State Bank," Springfield, MN, looks c.1890s-1910. .... **$18+**

Dipper, tin, flat tinned iron handle with hook at end, American, 14"L with 5" diam. bowl, 19th C. .... **$15+**

Dipper, tin, long handled, tubular handle, with half-moon mount, blue paper label with black printing states "Made of Best Quality Charcoal-Plate, Warranted not to rust," "Reed One-Pint," mfd. solely by the Reed Mfg. Co., Newark, New York (not NJ), 14"L, dipper is 5-1/8"W x 3-1/4"H, pat'd. Nov. 17, 1896. .... **$15+**

Dipper or ladle for cream, for using with milk bottles, tin, small conical bowl, vertical wire handle with slight curved hook on end, looks rather like a candle snuffer in form and size, mfd. by C. A. Chapman, Geneva, NY, c.1908. .... **$7+**

Dipper/ladle for cream, stamped tin, American, dated 1924. .... **$7+**

Dipper/ladle for cream, stamped tin, "Sweet Clover Condensed Milk," 20th C. .... **$7+**

Dipper/ladle for cream, stamped tin, for milk bottles to dip off cream that rose to top before homogenization, small like a gravy ladle for table use as it had to fit down in mouth of milk bottle, "Cream Top," pat'd. Sept. 2, 1924, Mar. 3, 1925. .... **$7+**

Dipper & skimmer, a pair, forged iron, polished, filed and decorated, stamped on both handles is maker's name, "W. Werntz," 19"L, early 19th C. .... **$150+**

Dippers – See also Ladle.

Dipper & skimmer, a pair, wrought iron, narrow handle with hooked end, large shallow bowls, the skimmer pierced with concentric rings of small holes, the handles inlaid with brass bands, engraved with initials "T. L." and "1823" (see note below), American,

19-1/4"L. • This pair sold at Garth's Auctions, Delaware, OH, April 11-12, 1986, for $1,200. Probable value range now is extremely difficult to assess. If they are a recently-decorated iron pair, they're good only for a study collection, and valued under $30. If they are legitimate (and I'm not doing anything here but speculating that they might not be) the range for a pair with brass inlay would be:... **$1,000-$1,500+**

❖ NOTES ❖

Uh-oh, the Dreaded "1823." – While the two implements may be genuinely old (and they do have authentic-looking distressing, pitting, tiny scratches, etc.), the inlaid brass date & maker bands are possibly modern en-forgings, to coin a phrase. Jeannette Lasansky did some work on the modern addition of faked brass inlays to old implements. She found that the faked dates all fall within the limited range of 1823 through 1827.

For other skimmers – See Chapter III (Strain & Sift).

Doughnut lifter, bowed or curved slender wand of wood, with turned handle, for poking into kettles of boiling fat to remove doughnuts when they are just so, Mennonite, 30"L, 19th C. **$100**

Doughnut lifter, scissor action multi-lever type with 4 long hooked prongs, cast iron & wire. Used to "Turn, lift & remove doughnuts & such from the hot cooking oil." American, about 10"L, pat'd. April 14, 1908. (The "Mazola" oil version made of stamped tin & wire valued about $175+.) .... **$300+**

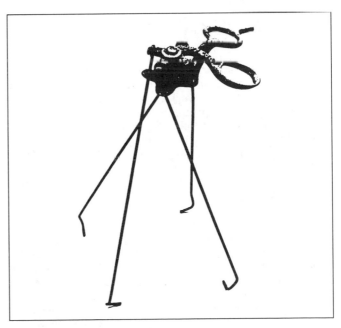

XIII-16. Doughnut lifter, *scissor action with cast iron body & iron wire grippers used to "turn, lift and remove doughnuts and such from the hot cooking oil." 8"H, pat'd. April 14, 1908. Should have been in the Disney movie* Dark Crystal *– as a moon-water-strider. Collection of Meryle Evans. This is a wide value spread, but they are uncommon, and most kitchen collectors want this **classic** for their collections! A stamped tin version, marked "Mazola" is valued about $175.* **$300-$350+**

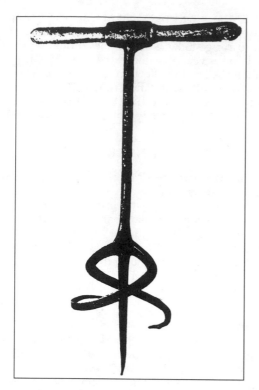

XIII-17. Dried fruit lifter or sugar auger. *Looks like a whirling dervish. Malleable cast iron, wood handles, 16-3/4"L. Pat'd. July 27, 1875. Used to extricate stuck-together dried apricots or apples from a keg or barrel, or similarly, for damp-stuck sugar. Stab it in & twist. Collection of Meryle Evans.* **$125-$175**

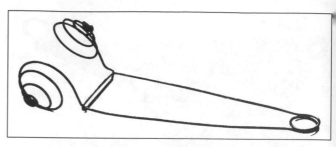

XIII-18. Egg lifter. *Or* **egg tongs.** *Spring wire, for retrieving hard-boiled eggs – or dumplings! 12-1/2"L, c.1890-1920. Collection of Meryle Evans.* **$25+**

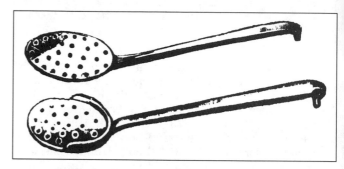

XIII-19. Egg slices, *or slicers. Completely tinned perforated copper blades & iron handles.* **(T)** *Nine sizes, from 3" to 7" diam.* **(B)** *Only two sizes: 4" and 4-1/2" diam. Henry Rogers, Sons & Co., Wolverhampton, England, 1914 catalog.* **$25**

Dried fruit or sugar auger, or dried fruit loosener, forged iron, with wooden crossbar handle (like on an old push lawnmower), two twirly prongs with straight pointed prong extension of handle, looks like a dancing post hole auger, pat'd. by H. J. White, sometimes called the "Hiddleson's Dried Fruit Auger," agented by S. W. Sheldon, NYC (but we don't know where made), 16-1/4" to 17"L (measured examples), pat'd. July 27, 1875. (In the last edition, I said 1873 or 1875, because the mark wasn't clear. Now I've seen 2 more that also appear to say 1873, so it is possible that a fault in the casting was made. July 27 was on Tuesday in 1875, and Tuesday is patent-awarding day in America.) • Also called a **sugar devil,** obviously because of its whirling dervish appearance. (Or ballet dancer, for the gentler soul.) Also called & used as a "Fruit lifter," to tear into a keg of hard sugar, or stuck-together dried fruit, to break it up. .... **$125-$175+**

Dried fruit or sugar auger, wrought iron, 2 curved out-and-in prongs, wooden T-handle like old lawnmower handle, pat'd. by William McCormick, Blair, NE, about 16"L, pat'd. May 23, 1876. • Another type was made by Enterprise, Mfg. Co. in Philadelphia, PA. It has a "T" handle, long shaft with crosspiece at bottom with short prong in center, and 4 curved short wider blades along the bar. Enterprise prob. 1890s. .... **$125+**

Egg lifter, spring steel wire, squeeze action, the 2 clasping ends are concave coils of wire, like an insect of some extreme ectoskeletal kind, American, 12-1/2"L, c.1890s to 1920s. .... **$25+**

Fish slice, enameled steel, cobalt blue tubular handle which is relatively short compared to white blade, diamond pattern of 9 perforations in center, blade and handle stamped out of one piece, some dimension given to blade, handle curled to make tube, American or European, 11-1/2"L, c.1890s-1910. .... **$65+**

Fish slice, perforated tin with wooden handle, wire hanging ring, design is a fabulous outline of fish with 2 fins, gill, eye in the small holes on blade, American, 12-1/2"L, late 19th C. .... **$125+**

Flesh fork, for hearth, forged iron, twisted handle with elongated chevron, rattail loop, 3 tines – 2 outer straight & simple, center one partly split or reticulated – finished by whitesmith, American, 18-1/2"L, late 18th or early 19th C. The word "flesh" means meat. .... **$150+**

XIII-20. Fish slice, *also called a* **fish carver.** *Shape of blade fairly typical of fish slices. Tin with turned wood handle, perforated design of fish, 12-1/2"L, late 19th C. Very unusual. Collection of Meryle Evans.* **$125+**

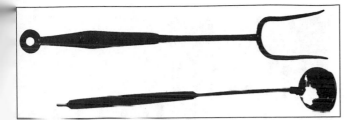

XIII-21. Flesh fork & tasting spoon. *Forged iron fork, late 18th C. Brass bowl & iron handle spoon, c.1800. Picture courtesy of Georgia G. Levett, Levett's Antiques, Camden, ME. Each:* **$100+**

Flesh fork, forged iron, 2 prongs, long handle is arrow shaped – from arrowhead point (where it joins tines) to fletch. At end of handle is heart with small hanging hole; smaller heart punched into flat surface near end of handle, American, 16-1/4"L, early 19th C. .... **$450+**

Flesh fork, forged iron, 2 tines, shaped handle, end shaped like fletching on an arrow (the trimmed feather part), prob. PA, 16-3/4"L, early 19th C. .... **$450+**

Flesh fork, forged iron, 2 tines, elongated chevron & bull's eye handle, American (?), late 18th or early 19th C. .... **$150+**

Flesh fork, forged iron, 2 tines, elongated diamond & bull's eye end to handle, plus heart, very decorative, signed "Nathan Putnam," prob. PA, dated 1749. .... **$550+**

Flesh fork, forged iron, very long handle with figural finial of man's head with pop eyes & pork pie hat, large hanging ring cutout a few inches below head, 2 tines, not signed, prob. PA, 29-1/8"L, prob. 1840s-1870s. • Offered for sale in 1981 by David A. Schorsch, Greenwich, CT. Upscale folk art piece. .... **$3,500+**

Flesh fork, wrought iron, 2 prong, with arrow shape handle or shaft, terminating in marvelous generous heart with a small hanging hole. Almost too good to be true. American (?), PA (?), 16-1/2"L, 19th or poss. late 18th C. .... **$350+**

Flesh fork, forged iron, ring handle, 2 long tines, American (?), 21"L, early 19th C. • Impossible, I believe, to determine origin of these pieces. There have now been so many brought in by dealers from other countries in the last few years. .... **$65+**

Flesh fork, planished forged iron, light-color, whitesmith work, 2 tines, ring handle, American (?), 15"L, early 19th C. .... **$65+**

Flesh fork, wrought iron, unusual with four tines of type found on much later dinner forks, rattail hanging loop, decoratively marked handle, 21"L, 18th C. or early 19th C. .... **$275+**

Flesh or meat fork, tinned sheet metal, "Rumford," American, 20th C. .... **$15+**

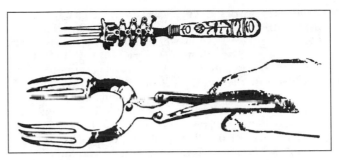

XIII-22. Forks *with mechanical actions.* **(T)** *Sandwich fork, with lazy-elbow push-off. Blue & white Meissen handle, came in small and large size. Ritzinger & Grasgreen, importers, c.1906-07.* **(B)** *"Duplex Serving Fork," wire spring, steel tines, nickeled handle. "For lifting vegetables from boiling water; for lifting fruit jars in canning; for serving." 10-1/2"L. Washburn Co., 1927.* **(T) $20+; (B) $10+**

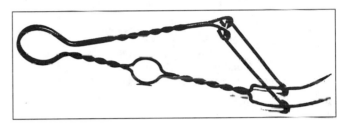

XIII-23. Fork *with push-off, for serving hot potatoes, or meat slices. All wire, 9-1/4"L, pat'd. June 6, 1895. Collection of Meryle Evans.* **$20+**

XIII-24. Flesh fork. *Forged iron, 3-tined, twisted & stepped handle with chevron echoes space in reticulated center tine. Perfect rat-tail loop. 18-1/2"L. Late 18th C. Picture courtesy of Robert W. Skinner Inc., Auctioneers, Bolton, MA.* **$150+**

Flesh fork – See also Roasting fork

Fork, cast iron handle with simple scroll design, meant for table, American, 7-1/2"L, mid 19th C. Love that cast iron. .... **$15+**

Fork, twisted wire, ingenious push-off action when handles are squeezed, 2 tines, American, 9-1/4"L, pat'd. June 11, 1895. .... **$20+**

❖ NOTES ❖

Fork Feeding – *The Young Lady's Friend* (Boston, 1836) advised: "If you wish to imitate the French or English, you will put every mouthful into your mouth with your fork; but if you think as I do that Americans have as good a right to their fashions as the inhabitants of any other country, you may choose the convenience of feeding yourself with your right hand armed with a steel blade; and providing you do it neatly and do not put in large mouthfuls, or close your lips tight over the blade, you ought not to be considered as eating ungenteely."

• • • •

Naughty Forks – "Forks were not generally used at table until the reign of James I, in England [r.1567-1625]. They were, however, known in Europe long before this. The first fork mentioned in history belonged to a Byzantine lady, who, on coming to Venice as a bride in the middle of the 11th century, brought with her a golden 'prong' as it is called in the pamphlet describing it. This fork, which probably had only two prongs, evidently caused a great sensation, for St. Peter Damian, afterwards Bishop of Ostia, mentioned it in a sermon, wherein he severely rebuked the lady for her luxury and extravagance in actually taking up her food with a golden prong, when God had given her fingers for that very purpose.

"The preponderance of patties in these [Medieval] menus is probably due to the fact that fingers then supplied, to a great extent, the place of knives and forks. Spoons were used, but knives were not general till about 1563, and forks were not commonly used in England until 1611." Excerpt of "Medieval Cookery," reprinted from *Gentlemans Magazine*, in *House & Garden*, Oct. 1906.

Implements – See Implement racks in Chapter VII (Storage & Container).
Ladle, brass bowl, iron shaft with turned wood handle, American, 16"L, 19th C. .... **$75+**

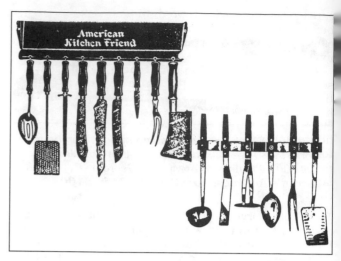

XIII-26. Implement sets. (T) *"American Kitchen Friend," "our new flat handled kitchen outfit," with japanned tin rack, tinned steel blades, wood handles, brass rivets. Imported, probably German. Thurnauer wholesaler ad from* House Furnishing Review, *Dec. 1909.* **(B)** *Almost 50 years later: "Flint Stainless Steel Kitchen Tools – tall, tapered, and terrific. So good they're guaranteed for fifteen years." From "Flint" line of EKCO, mfd. by EKCO Products Co. 1958. Racked sets:* **$60+; $15+**

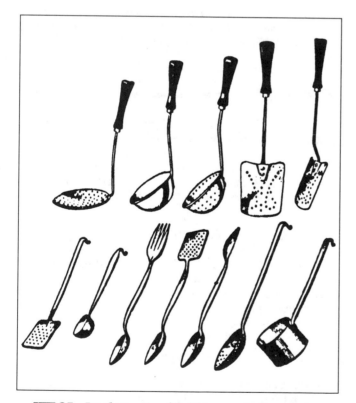

XIII-25. Implements. (T) *Skimmer, ladle, strainer ladle & cake turner (view show crooked handle) are stamped aluminum. "Mirro," Aluminum Goods Mfg. Co., 1927.* **B)** *Catalog describes from left to right:* **1.** *"Slice" or cake turner with tinned-copper blade.* **2.** *Sauce Ladle.* **3.** *Spoon with Fork.* **4.** *Spoon with Slice.* **5.** *Double Spoon.* **6.** *Pierced Spoon.* **7.** *Stock Ladle. "All tinned iron, William S. Adams & Son, London, England. c.1860-61. Sets:* **$20-$40; $50-$70**

❖ **NOTES** ❖

"Ladle" or "Dipper"? – Euphony? Capacity? First of all, 20th century dictionaries don't seem to make much of a thing about defining the differences. In fact, the terrific *Webster's Second* even gives as one of the definitions of dipper – "A ladle," and for ladle, they say it is used to ladle out or dip out liquids – from soup to molten iron! In fact, popular usage over a long period seem to decide the question of whether it's a ladle or a dipper. "Soup" and "Punch," for example, seems to be coupled with "ladle"; while "Chocolate" and "water" go with "dipper." Did someone long ago decide that "Soup dipper" sounded strange? And how'd you like to gaze up into the night sky at the "Big Ladle" There is, to some extent, a hint of quantification about the two words, so that "dipper" implies a smaller amount (dip, sip, nip, pip), while "ladle" implies a greater amount. • Richard H. Thornton, in *An American Glossary, Being An Attempt to Illustrate Certain Americanisms Upon Historical Principles*, London: Francis & Co., 1912, lists "Dipper" with the meaning "A ladle," first citation of usage 1801. He doesn't give "Ladle" its own listing. • John Bartlett's *Dictionary of Americanisms. A Glossary of Words and Phrases Usually Regarded As Peculiar to the United States*, Boston: Little Brown, 1887, defines a dipper as "A vessel, generally with a handle, used to dip water or other liquor." "Ladle" is not accorded a definition. In the 1859 edition of Bartlett's book, "dipper" is not listed. • Checking out the *Oxford English Dictionary*, I found (as also cited in Bartlett), that the first printed reference to "dipper" belongs to George Mason's *A Supplement to Samuel Johnson's Dictionary*. In 1801, Mason said a dipper was "A spoon made in a certain form. Being a modern invention, it is not often mentioned in books." So he gave no printed earlier source, but by inference we can assume it to be earlier. It's not that a word "dipper" hadn't existed before, it's just that the meaning was different. The *OED* cites a 1611 use – for a person who dips, or moistens (as in Dippin' Donuts).

Get a handle on the differences. – Nowadays, it seems that the primary difference lies in the angle of the handle. Both dippers and ladles have handles long in relation to bowl size, but the ladle's handle is set either at right angles (90°) to the bowl, or on the same horizontal plane as the rim of the bowl. A dipper seems to be set at between 15° and about 40°. Size of bowl probably has something to do with the definition, ladles being generally larger than dippers. • See also the "Windsor" style dippers and the "cup" style in the listings above.

Ladle, brass bowl, rattail iron handle, marked "J. Whitman," Reading, PA, 20"L, c.1800 to 1830. .... **$250+**

Ladle, brass bowl with flat steel handle with hanging hole at end, unmarked, American (?), 13"L, 19th C. .... **$125+**

Ladle, brass bowl, wrought iron handle has ring loop at end, American (?), dated "1835." .... **$250+**

Ladle, cast aluminum, marked "G. M. T. & Bro." (G. M. Thurnauer, listed in *Thomas' Register* as a "Manufacturer," this was probably made in Germany for Thurnauer? & imported, as most GMT wares were, c.1900-1910. .... **$10+**

XIII-27. "Instruments of Human Sustenance: Cooking." *Etching done in 1569 by an artist in "circle of" Guiseppe Archimboldo – the Italian artist who specialized in surreal assemblages of objects or fruits to resemble human figures. Painting which inspired etching was done by Giovanni da Monte Cramasco. Part of the verse translates "This is not an image, this is not a figure. It is the noble makings in the art of cooking." Photo courtesy of The Metropolitan Museum of Art, Elisha Whittelsey Collection, The Elisha Whittelsey Fund, and Harris Brisbane Dick Fund, by exchange, 1977.*

XIII-29. *Ladles & packers for dairies.* *Wood, in familiar forms we see today often described as mid or early 19th C. All from **1921** Cherry Bassett Co. catalog of dairy supplies except top right, a hooked-handle butter ladle "in the New York Style." 1905 catalog. (T-L) Is "transfer ladle" for ice cream or butter. • Other pieces include butter hands, dairy & factory size ladles, from 12" to 16"L, butter fork 11-1/4"L. • A striker for tubs or printer looks like a rolling pin in picture; 27-1/2"L. • Also assorted square & round dairy packers, etc. Value range shown is what it should be for such recent items, but wear & patina may make age impossible to determine, and even with such mass-produced items, there's always the chance that some inadvertently handsome piece of wood was used and now looks older. See also Chapter IV (Molds).* **$10-$50**

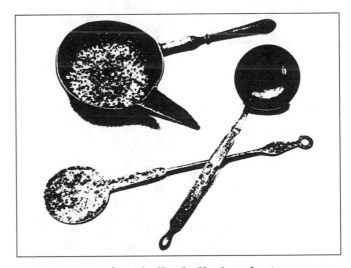

XIII-28. *Strainer ladle, ladle & cake turner or peel.* *(T) Wonderful long-beaked tin strainer has wood handle set into tubular socket. 13-1/4"L overall. (R) Brass ladle has steel or whitesmithed iron handle, marked "8" only. 13"L. (L) Cake turner or short peel is steel, marked "Levi Lewis," 14-3/4"L. Early 1800s. Strainer ladle is best piece. Collection of Meryle Evans. (T) $225+; (R) & (L) $100-$150*

XIII-30. Ladles. (L) *From "Androck Balanced" line. Oval with pouring lip at each end, nickel plated, upright handle with tapered enameled wood grip. 10-1/2"L, with handle in choice of green, yellow, red, green with ivory band, or yellow with blue band. Washburn Co., 1936.* **(T-R)** *Tinned iron "French Gravy Ladle," 3 sizes with bowls 1-3/8" deep, from 2-3/8" to 3-1/8" diam. Sexton Stove & Mfg. Co., Baltimore, c.1930s, but this is much older cut.* **(R-M)** *Tin soup ladle, threaded handle, bowl 3-3/4" diam. Central Stamping Co., 1920.* **(R-B)** *Welded iron handle with hook, tinned all over, 4 sizes from 3-1/4" to 4-1/16" diam. Savory, c.1925-28.* **$5-$20**

XIII-31. Syrup ladles. *Above are two pan-like ladles, tinned, with riveted iron socket handles to take long wooden handles.* **(T-L)** *Advertised for "sugar planters." Matthai-Ingram, c.1890.* **(T-R)** *More common spouted form for syrup ladles. From* Urbain Debois' La Patisserie D'Aujourd'hui, *Paris, c.1860s-90.* **(B)** *Copper with socket handle for any useful length of wooden handle & 2 spouts. Iron bail. 7"H x 9" diam. Ex-Wiggins Tavern Collection, Northampton, MA. Courtesy Glenna Fitzgerald. Photograph Luella McCloud Antiques, Shelburne Falls, MA.* **(T-L & T-R) $40-$60+; (B) $125+**

XIII-32. Leg of mutton holder. *Nickeled steel or iron, wood handle. Fitted over end of bone and tightened, this allowed you to hold it securely for carving. Ritzinger Grasgreen importers' catalog, c.1906-07.* **$8-$15**

Ladle, cast aluminum, ovoid bowl, long upright handle with short prong off side about 4 inches from end, to hook on side of kettle, German, 10-3/4"L, c.1910-1915. .... **$10+**

Ladle, cast aluminum, ovoid bowl, with one side distinctly more rounded than other side, long handle has cast-in ridge in center, set upright at almost right angles to bowl. Type sometimes only marked with country of origin, "Made in Germany," 10-3/4"L, c.1910-1915. .... **$10+**

Ladle, dark blue spattered enamelware, 13"L, late 19th C. .... **$25+**

Ladle, enamelware, long black hooked handle, bowl is white inside, outside with blue blobs with brown & white veining called "Turtle," "Tortoise" or "Chickenwire" by collectors, but "Duchess" by manufacturer, Vollrath Co., Sheboygan, WI, c.1900. • "Now architects and decorators decree that beauty belongs in the kitchen too! ... even pots and pans can be interesting and attractive." Vollrath ad, 1928. .... **$50+**

Ladle, pewter bowl with socket-fitted turned wood handle, American (?), 15"L, mid 19th C. .... **$125+**

Ladle, possibly a tallow spoon, wrought iron, wonderful upcurving long handle with arched foot toward end, rather deep bowl with pouring spout that rests perfectly horizontally on hearth or table, American, 4-1/2"D bowl, 19-1/2"L overall, 18th or very early 19th C. • This is another rarity found by Clara Jean Davis. My description is adapted from her sale list, in which she also said "Rather crudely made, doubtless a country blacksmith, however, interesting work... Done all in one piece of iron pounded out to make the bowl... Most likely used as tallow spoon. Very early iron, impure, likely 18th C." .... **$200+**

Ladle, tan enamelware with green trim, 1930s.... **$10+**

Love spoon, carved wood, painted & decorated, 5 glass windows set into wood over 4 printed blue & brown calico scraps plus a damask pink & white scrap;

XIII-33. Lifter. *Twisted wire. 15-1/4"L, c.1900. Courtesy Carol Bohn, Mifflinburg, PA.* **$25-$35**

carved hex signs, little XXX borders & a tree of life, plus the initials, are picked out in red paint or lacquer (possibly mixed with sweetgum or wax), Welsh, 11"L, 18th or very early 19th C. • I think this is the most extraordinary Welsh love spoon I've ever seen, I guess it's the charm of the little pieces of material set under glass that does it for me **$1,500+**

Marrow spoon, carved & decorated wood (possibly cherry), American (?), 10"L, late 18th C. .... **$85+**

Marrow spoon, very fine grained wood with good patina, lathe turning on end of handle, American or English, 11-1/4"L, late 18th or early 19th C. .. **$85+**

Meat fork – See Flesh fork.

Olive fork, for pickles, cherries, olives. Nickeled iron, long rod looped at one end to make a grip, end split to make 2 short sharp tines, mounted on original card, "No. 185-M," "Just the Tool for Small Mouth Bottles," American, 8"L, c.1915. .... **$2-$5**

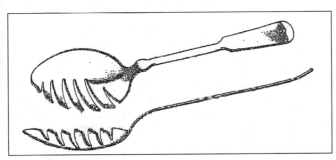

XIII-34. Spoon patent, *2 views. This was pat'd. Apr. 21, 1908 (#885,444) by Alonzo W. Cram, Haverhill, MA, as a "Mixing-spoon." "At one side the bowl is provided with a series of curved blades, the said curve being the same as the rest of the bowl. The said blades are gradually twisted longitudinally thereof and start at the inner end where the blades connect to the bowl of the spoon." He claimed that the during mixing "the material being beaten or mixed is caused to travel upward over the inclined blades, and thus is more thoroughly beaten." Cram had two entirely different slotted mixing spoon designs in the same patent application, and all three designs were granted the same patent! I don't believe I've ever come across that before. (The 2nd spoon has the same handle, but a full spoon "bowl" with 5 crosswise slots; the 3rd has 3 longitudinal slots – Cram's patent predates the Oct. 1908 patent for the Rumford slotted spoon seen in II-87.) I put this patent here, instead of in Chapter II, because of its relationship to two other patents, one shown in the next picture. A design patent, #1906, was granted March 1, 1864, to Webb Harding, Cambridge, MA. It was for a* **Macaroni Spoon.** *The Patent Office has lost the picture, but here is part of Harding's description: the bowl's "proportion and contour is similar to the common spoon, has deep serrations or spaces cut or formed in its edges along the sides and point or forward end thereof, such spaces leaving pointed and curved teeth ... The serrations do not extend to the whole depth of the bowl." Harding's design, according to his specs, had finger-like tines around all edges of the bowl. (See also the Mixing spoon eggbeaters listed in Chapter II; and the slotted Mixing spoons, especially the "Ideal").*

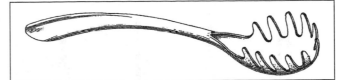

XIII-35. Pasta spoon patent. *This was pat'd. Oct. 29, 1957, by Robert O. Nelson, Chicago, IL, assignor to Cameron Inc., Chicago. Patent #2,810,957. We have all seen this mid-20th C. spoon, called a "Food Serving Utensil" by Nelson, but its design goes way back to the 19th C. Nelson specifications contain cited references to other patents, including one to Cram's patent 50 years earlier! Nelson wrote that his device performed the "various functions of a spoon, a ladle and a fork." "There are many designs for ladles which are used to serve particular types of liquid foods. There ... are many designs for forks for serving such foods as spaghetti, tossed salads and the like. There are also many designs for spoons having particular functions. ... If a housewife is to prepare and serve a wide variety of foods, it becomes necessary for her to have her utensil drawer cluttered with a great many serving utensils. The present invention will effectively handle spaghetti, macaroni, tossed salads, sauerkraut (with or without the juice), cooked vegetables such as beans, corn, peas and the like."*

Olive or pickle fork, twisted wire, American, 10"L, prob. late 19th C. .... **$3+**

Peel, carved pine, somewhat charred on blade end, nice used patina on handle, for removing bread from oven, American, 51"L, 19th C. .... **$135+**

Peel, carved wood, probably pine, European (?), blade only 13"L, with 5"L handle, late 19th C. .... **$65+**

Peel, for bread or pies, wrought iron, long handle with a fat ball end, American (?), 48"L, late 1700s... **$150+**

Peel, made in one piece instead of joined handle, wooden, with very long bakery handle, front edge of blade straight & thinned, 54"L, c.1800. .... **$175+**

Peel, wrought iron, fat knob on end of long handle, American (?), 51"L, late 18th or early 19th C. • This peel, being 51"L, is obviously not going to be confused with a cake turner, but that is a possibility for short-handled & small-bladed peels. In fact, I don't know how to tell you it couldn't be a cake turner. And who knows? Maybe those skilled cooks back in the 1780s or the 1810s used small peels for all kinds of purposes. .... **$150+**

Peel, forged iron, long handled with ram's horn finial. This is most unusual, with a church & cemetery actually painted on the peel's blade, in what appears to be about 50 to 70 years after the peel itself was made, American (?), about 50"L overall, with 10" x 8" blade, c.1740-90. Ex-Violette de Mazia Collection. .... **$2,000+**

Peel, wrought iron, ram's horn handle, wide blade, "Londonderry" (NH?), 35"L, late 18th C. .... **$200+**

Peels, wrought iron, long ram's horn handle, the commonest type found, ranging in size widely. American (?), 22"L; 25"L; 29-1/2"L; 35"L, early 19th C. • 1st price range for about 2 feet long & under; 2nd range for 2 feet & over, esp. over 4 feet long. .... **$40-$85; $95-$250+**

XIII-36. Short peels or cake turners, and one baker's shovel 2nd from right. Forged iron, late 18th or early 19th C. From 10-1/2" to 14-1/2"L. Ex-Linden Collection. Photo courtesy Christie, Manson & Woods, International Inc. Each: **60-$150+**

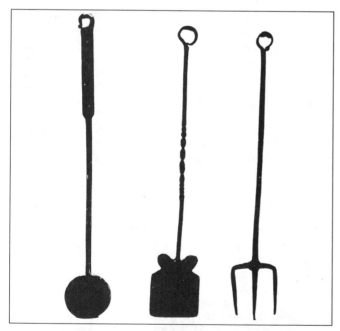

XIII-37. Tasting spoon, cake turner or peel, flesh fork. Forged iron. **(L)** Tasting spoon with incised zigzags, whitesmith finished handle, 18"L. **(M)** Cake turner with wonderful winged shoulders to the blade, 17"L. **(R)** Fork with 3 tongs, 16-3/4"L. Sold at auction in early 1980s for **$125; $600;** and **$75.** American, late 18th or early 19th C. The most remarkable piece, the cake turner, would probably be valued above **$350,** but we don't know the reason behind its high price a decade ago. Photo courtesy Robert W. Skinner, Inc., Auctioneers, Bolton, MA.

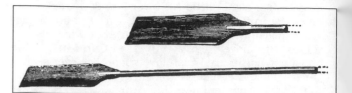

XIII-38. Peel blade & peel for bakers. Replaceable tapered blades, which wore down & chipped along front edge, came in five sizes: 6", 8", 10", 12" and 14" wide. Replacement handles were – get this! – 12 feet long, and slipped into blade socket. c.1904-1910. Very similar wooden pieces, albeit narrower in blade, were candy stirring paddles & scrapers. Many were from 36" to 46"L. **$20-$40**

Peels – See also Cake turner or peel

Picnic fork, shaped thin wood with 3 stubby tines, pencil writing on back from souvenir-saving child reads, charmingly, "September, 8, 1942, Sun Set Large" [sic], mark burned into handle "Bentwood Forks," with a daisy, American, 4-7/8"L, c.1941. • **Futurewatch:** Believe it or not, this is a nice little sub-field for collectors – wooden picnic spoons and forks. I have quite a number of them, but this is the first marked one.. **$1-$3**

Pie lifter, forged iron, 2 widely-spaced tines to support the pie (I'd not want to depend on it when taking a hot one from the oven), twisted handle, broken-ring loop at end, American, 14"L, c.1840s. .... **$150+**

Pie lifter, blackened sheet steel, like a big oblong pan or cookie sheet, & possibly used as such, rounded front end like some oven peels have, very low raised sides, the end, or handle, raised at about 45° angle with end curled under, embossed on handle "I. W. MCNESS," American, 15"L x 10"W, looks early 20th C., but may be later. .... **$45+**

Pie lifter, heavy spring steel wire with cast iron fingers, & sliding hook that slides along handle & grips pie pan, American, 16"L, pat'd. 1883. .... **$85+**

Pie lifter, tinned metal combination tool, with long handle with crown cap opener at one end, & narrow rounded cake-serving knife flat blade, with small heart cutout, at other end. Stamped into the two narrow parts of handle's shank is "Use Omar Wonder Flour. Puts Magic In Your Baking," early 20th C. .... **$35+**

Pie lifter, hexagonal tin platform to support pie, green wooden handle, adjustable side grips, "Sure-Grip," American, 20"L, c.1910-20s. .... **$45+**

Pie lifter, wire with wooden handle, a sort of fork, with 2 long prongs that fit under the pie plate, American, 17-1/2"L, 19th C... **$45+**

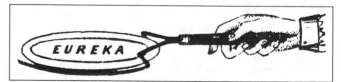

XIII-39. Pie plate lifter. "Eureka." Wooden handle with 2 wire prongs with stamped tin support for pie plate. Heinz & Munschauer's, Buffalo, 1882, who were famous for their birdcages. **$45+**

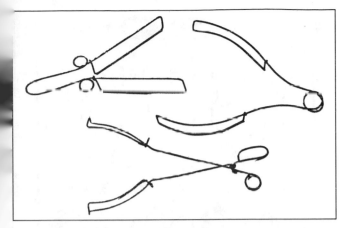

XIII-40. Wire pie plate lifters. All wire & spring action. (T-L) Has finger & thumbholes, and works okay as long as pie isn't heavy. (And what pie, sigh, isn't?) 14-3/4"L. (T-R) Slightly springier; no stronger. 14-3/4"L. (B) Is least trustworthy. I wouldn't carry a mud pie with it. 16-1/2"L. Collection of Meryle Evans. **$45+**

Pie lifter, wooden handle, heavy gauge wire, c.1890s-1910. .... **$45+**

Pie lifter & lid lifter combined, hinged cast iron, with hook ends, openwork casting in handles, 8"L, c.1880s.. **$95+**

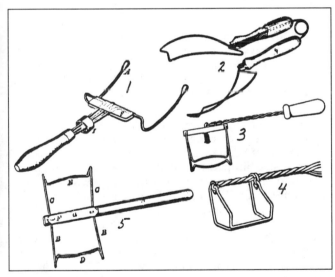

XIII-41. Plate lifter patents. (1) "Improvement in Forks for Handling Heated Plates." Pat'd. Nov. 11, 1856. G. W. Hyatt. (2) A "plate or dish lifter" pat'd. Nov. 6, 1877, William Beattie, Portage, WI. Looks like a grip strengthener. (3) "Pie turner," pat'd. Sept. 27, 1887, George H. Thomas, Chicopee Falls, MA. Has "spirally-grooved rod" (dark part between the "plate engaging arms"). (4) "Pie plate holder," pat'd. Sept. 22, 1874, Joseph L. Daugherty, Newry, PA. To fit in narrow column of Official Gazette, his handles were cut off in drawing. Even so, it still looks unworkable. (5) Plate Lifter, pat'd. March 5, 1867, Daniel Welch, Lowell, MA, assignor to H. A. Hildreth, Lowell, & W. J. Johnson, Newton, MA. One jaw fixed, other adjustable "to accommodate itself to varying plates."

Pie lifter or hot pan lifter, heavy wire flapping wings or arms, black-painted turned wood handle, spring action thumb piece to work the arms, which we hope won't flap while you carry your blue ribbon pie from oven to table, American, 12-1/2"L x 6"W (each wing), late 19th or early 20th C. .... **$75+**

Pie or hot plate lifter, heavy spring steel wire arms & long double-shaft wood handle, looks like it ought to have something to do with clothes hangers. But it grips around opposite sides of pie plate (or other hot plate), "Triumph," sold through Montgomery Ward, or imprinted with adv'g. for a store, American, 13-1/2"L, c.1890s. .... **$45+**

Pie or cake slice segmenter guide, wire, sets down over a pie or single layer of cake to create a guide for a separate (not included) knife to cut 8 equal wedges, c.1890s-1910. .... **$35+**

Pie server, metal, left in pan under the pie during baking, wedge-shaped & bent to conform to sides of pie pan, Shera Corp., Hohokus, NJ, for a 9" pie pan, but the peculiar thing is that it is so wide it only allows for 5 wedges, "Patent applied for," c.1940s (?). .... **$5-$10**

---

*"An apple-pie without some cheese
Is like a kiss without a squeeze."
Old English rhyme*

Pie server, tinned metal, green wood tiller handle, cutouts in blade, adv'g. "Rumford," manufacturer not known, early 1900s. .... **$10+**

Punch bowl hook, twisted steel wire with large curve at one end to fit over edge of punch bowl, smaller end is hooked for punch cup, plated in nickel, made by mfr., C. T. Williamson Wire Novelty Co., Newark, NJ, early 20th C. .... **$2-$3**

Roasting fork or roaster, forged iron, looks like a sort of lizard skeleton, with 2 straight prongs flanking a central wiggly one, 2 penny feet not far from forked end, a beautiful if damaged ram's horn loop at end, American, 26"L, late 18th or early 19th C. ..... **$350+**

Roasting fork, for hearth, brass & steel, 3 tines, telescoping handle with some turning & detail, hanging ring, English (?), 12" extends to 20"L, 19th C. • For a while in the late 1970s you saw a good number of

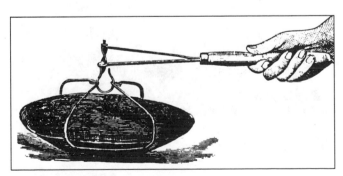

XIII-42. Pie turner & lifter. "Locke's Automatic," W. E. Thomas & Co., Boston, MA. "The wire jaws are put around the pie plate, and the weight of the pie when lifted causes it to turn, on account of the ingenious spiral attached to the handle. I'd call this "Tenterhooks Hopeful Pie Lifter." The Metal Worker, Nov. 15, 1890. **$75+**

these at antique shows; they don't appear much anymore, maybe the sources have dried up. See also Flesh fork. .... **$95-$150+**

Sauerkraut auger, very like a sugar auger, probably interchangeable, iron & wood, with twirled tongs that were stuck into kraut barrel, twisted, & used to bring up big batch of dripping sauerkraut to transfer to pot or serving dish, American, 3rd quarter 19th C. .... **$150-$225+**

Serving fork, aluminum, graceful bold handle of twisted aluminum rod, with tendril & bud terminal, "Buenilum – Made in U. S. A.," 8"L, c.1940s. There are several pieces in this neat pattern. .... **$10+**

Skewers & skewer frames – See Chapter X (Hearths)

Skimmers – See Chapter III (Strain & Sift)

Spatula, embossed metal, message is "Merry Christmas, Happy New Year," 10"L, 20th C. **$25**

Spatula, embossed metal, (name has been seen spelled two ways) "Swans Down Makes Better Cakes," also "Swansdown," Igleheart Brothers, Evansville, IN, 12"L x 1-1/4"W, 20th C. .... **$15+**

Spoon, carved from horn, very old repair with riveted iron bands, American, 7"L, late 18th or early 19th C. .... **$75+**

Spoon, for stirring powdered seltzer into water, long handle, marked "Bromo Seltzer Cures Headache!" c.1920s. **$25**

Spoon, pressed wood fiber, end of handle has 4 crosses marked on it, shaft stamped "Sanispoon," mfd. by American Container Co., NYC, NY, 5"L (they also made a 3-1/2"L one), 1918. .... **$3-$5**

Spoon, wrought iron, round bowl, rattail back attachment where handle is forged to bowl, American (?), 7"L, late 18th C. .... **$55+**

Spoons – See also Taster; also Chapter II (Mix)

Spoon & fork combined, scissor action, carved of whale baleen with ivory pin, English or American whaling vessel product, 8-1/4"L, second half 19th C. .... **$125-$150+**

Spoon & ladle set, blue & white speckled enamelware, hanging holes in both handles, 20th C. For the pair: .... **$55-$90+**

XIII-43. Woodenware street seller print. *The man holds a grass rake. Note woman's woodenwares, from (**L**) to (**R**): Mixing spoons; knobbed chocolate mullers; –?–, perforated spoons; rolling pins. Unidentified engraving, "Publish'd as the Act directs June 1773. Published by John Heywood & Son. Excelsior Works, Manchester. [England]."*

XIII-44. Spoons, ladles, tableware. *All cast aluminum, "Clover Brand." Mfd. by W. Seibel, Metmann, Germany, who also made Britannia wares. House Furnishing Review, March 1914. Small tableware:* **$3+;** *implements:* **$10+**

Spoon rest, stamped aluminum, instructions: "Place on kitchen table or range. Easy to clean. Unbreakable. Burn proof." American, 20th C. .... **$2-$3**

Spoon rest, stamped tin, with loop hook for side of pot or pan, egg shaped bowl with 7 drain holes, adv'g. "Rumford the Wholesome Baking Powder," 3"L, early 20th C. .... **$30+**

Suckit spoon, a spoon & fork combination – one at each end, light-colored whitesmithed iron, shallow bowl, Pennsylvania version of an English form, 16-3/8"L with 2-5/8" diam. spoon, early 19th C. .... **$500+**

Taster, also called a tasting spoon, for hearth use originally, but a type of spoon still in use, forged iron, smallish bowl, long straight shank widening at end, rattail hook, incised with zigzags & highly polished or planished by whitesmith, also called a brightsmith, American, 18"L, late 18th C. .... **$125+**

Taster, forged iron, long straight handle ends in rattail loop, shallow turnip-shaped bowl, American, 21"L, early 19th C. .... **$75+**

Taster, ovoid bowl, very long handle with ridge up center, set in almost horizontal position to bowl, for right-handed cooks to pour from small end of bowl into mouth, "Made in Germany," 13-1/2"L, c.1910-1915. .... **$15+**

Taster, small brass bowl, riveted to forged iron long handle, American (?), about 18"L, early 19th C. .... **$100+**

Taster, tinned brass (called latten) bowl, forged iron handle riveted to bowl in 3 places, very attractive shape to tapered flat handle with hooked end, crudely engraved, and dated, American, 7-3/4"L, "1862." .... **$375+**

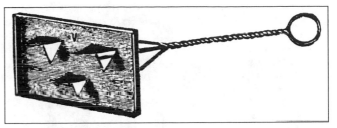

❖ NOTES ❖

Pennsylvania? – Everyone likes to know where a piece comes from, and some places are "sexier," hypewise, than others. Pennsylvania as provenance has been very popular for a long time; Ohio, South Carolina, Alabama, Georgia, Texas, West Virginia and Tennessee are upcomers. And there are probably many more out West, though we in the East are last to hear about it. But you have to think: People everywhere used utensils and implements, and there was a constant emigration, generally westward, all through the 19th century – when most of our antiques were made. The combination of brass and iron often proves to be Pennsylvanian; but the tasting spoon above could be a "country" piece from practically anywhere.

Taster, tinned brass (latten) spoon bowl, wrought iron handle, American, 7-3/4"L, dated "1862." • **Added value.** Pricier with tinning & date. Other tasters, with brass or copper bowls, might bring slightly less. A taster has a somewhat shallow & perfectly round spoon bowl, riveted to the perfectly straight handle that lies along same horizontal plane as the bowl. A shallow bowl means the food to be tasted didn't have to be cooled a long time (& the cook didn't have to eat a lot). .... **$185+**

Taster & scraper (?), forged iron, with spoon at one end, a sort of cake turner, scraper at other end, marked "C. Monk," American (?), 7"L, 19th C. .... **$50+**

Toasting fork, 3 ply heavy twisted wire, decorative handle, of a sort of toasting fork made in England in the 1800s; but dealer found it in Ohio & said that 3 strands & the heaviness of the wire were "typical of Ohio work," so prob. Ohio, 17-3/8"L, c.1860s to 1880s. • I happen to have bought this one, & like it a lot better than the ones I've seen that were admittedly English imports. The wire is more substantial. .... **$150+**

Toasting fork, 3 tines, decorative long handle, forged iron, 23-3/8"L, c.1820s to 1830s. .... **$175+**

Toasting fork, for hearth cooking, wrought iron, wooden handle, 3 tines, American (?), 55"L, early 19th C. or late 18th C. .... **$100+**

XIII-45. Roaster & toaster. Forged iron. **(T)** Serpentine tine makes it useful as roaster. Damaged ram's-horn handle. 26"L, late 18th C. Ex-Keillor Collection. **(B)** Toasting fork, 3 prongs, 22"L. Early 19th C. See Hearth chapter. **$250-$350+**

XIII-46. "Home-made Toasting Fork." "A fork that will hold bread, cakes, muffins, or even chops, steaks and slices of bacon, that are to be toasted, before a fire, may be made of any refuse piece of tin, as the bottom of a sardine box, or the side of a fruit can. A piece of tin of convenient size, 6 to 8 inches long, and 3 to 4 inches wide, for instance, is flattened out; the corners are cut off, and the edges are turned up as shown in the engraving. This is done to make it stiffer, so that it will hold its shape. Three angular [triangular] pieces are then cut and bent up, and three wires are fastened into the holes, and then twisted to form a handle. This is a little useful thing for the boys to exercise their ingenuity on." American Agriculturist, July 1877. See also the Potato baking rack in the Stove chapter. **$10-$20**

Toasting fork, forged iron, long handle with ball finial, 3 crooked tines separated from handle by flat cutout heart which looks as if it would be a heat deflector, but is probably just a decorative way to join tines to handle, prob. English 22"L, 18th C. • This piece was imported by B. Altman & Co., NYC, probably found by Archie Keillor, who traveled & bought for the store's antiques department. Advertised for $29.95 in a 1957 ad. Oh for a time machine! .... **$250+**

Toasting fork, forged iron, simple form with 2 tines, supporting arch forms 2 short legs, loop at end of handle acts as leg, American (?), 15-1/4"L, 18th or early 19th C. .... **$200+**

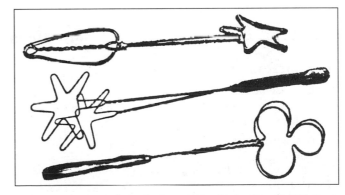

XIII-47. Toasting fork patent & toasters. All for holding a slice of bread (or piece of meat) over a heat source – stove or campfire. **(T)** Patent drawing of 5-point star "Toaster & broiler," all wire, with squeeze handles, pat'd. Sept. 18, 1877, by Samuel Poole, Brooklyn, NY; **(M)** Star toaster, wire wood, 19"L x 5-1/8", c.1910. Courtesy Carmille S. Zaino. **(B)** Wire, wood, cloverleaf, 16-1/2"L x 4-3/4"W, late 19th C. Ex-Keillor Collection. When used, these left a lighter pattern on the bread slice, so a decorative design was a selling plus. **$35-$75**

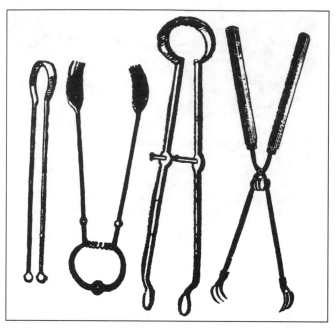

XIII-48. Beefsteak tongs & multi-purpose tongs.
(L) Simplest pair from American Home Cook Book, 1854. "To turn a steak, to avoid puncturing holes with a fork, which lets the juice escape." (M-1) are "spring tongs," 18"L, from Duparquet, Huot & Moneuse, c.1904-1910. (M-2) Next to last are from Warne's Model Cookery, ed. by Mary Jewry, London: 1868. (R) For "taking various articles out of boiling water, roasting oysters, taking fish out of brine, ... as a dish-washer, and particularly to wash out the inside of fruit jars, pitchers." Spring activated, long wooden handles. "Ladies' Favorite," mfd. and invented by Mr. G. J. Capewell, Cheshire, CT. American Agriculturist, Dec. 1876. $40-$70

Toasting fork, forged iron, turned wooden handle, brass hanging hook, 4 prongs describe a cubic space, American or English, 26"L, 19th C..... **$175-**

Toasting fork, twisted 2-ply wire handle forms hanging ring at end, little metal sleeve or collar pulls down to release or open its prongs, English, 20-1/8"L, c.1880s (?). **$45-**

Toasting forks, set of 4, all forged iron with 2 tines (1) The tines on the "Marshmallow fork" are long very slender, slightly curved, with suggestion of hooks at ends, the rod of the shaft is twisted 1/3 of way up from tines, and looped handle is twisted around shaft. (2) The "Little Colonial Fork" is very lightweight, has short tines, loop ring with tip twisted around shaft, which has another twist above tines. (3) The "Twist rod fork" is made of a length of iron rod, the ends forming the tines, a loop for hanging, the shafts 2 wires twisted in 2 places to hold together. (4) The "Twist handle fork" has beaten tines to flatten and broaden them somewhat, loop handle, 2 twists to shaft. A "Colonial" set for "Bungalow & camping parties." The Arden Forge, Arden, DE, respectively: 30"L, 15"L, 24"L and 30"L, adv'd. in Sept. 1923 *House Beautiful.* • **Lookalike alarm.** – You'd not know which were made by Arden Forge (I'm sure other Colonial Revival forges made similar forks for fireplace or campfire), unless you found in original packaging with name. But this listing will alert you to the fact that even the least of old kitchen implements were replicated or approximated by 20th century commercial companies. Similar forks were still being made in 1990s. • Resale price range for 20th C. set. .... **$20+**

Tongs, for cooking, metal, adv'g. "Ney's Restaurant," Bad Axe, MI, early 20th C............................. **$10+**

Tongs, iron, adv'g. "Only Gas Costs Less," early 20th C. .... **$7+**

Whatzit spoon & fork, wooden spoon at one end, 3-tined fork at other. Spoon is like a scoop & when dealer accidentally set implement in sunny place, tallow came out. The chip carving forms zigzags, hole in broad part of fork for hanging up, English (?), 20-7/8"L, with 6"L tines, mid 1800s (?). .... **$75+**

For More Information

AUCTION HOUSES

Garth's Auctions

You really won't believe the things they come up with! It's just astounding.

2690 Stratford Rd.
POB 369
Delaware, OH 43015
Phone: (740) 362-4771
E-mail: info@garthsauction.com
Web site: www.garthsauction.com

Horst Auction Center

This auction house is mentioned frequently in this book, especially in this chapter and the Hearth chapter. They specialize in primitives & household tools. Even household goods sales turn up great things because of the auctioneer's location. Clarence Spohn, who's also mentioned frequently in this book, has been their cataloguer & historical consultant for many years.

Contact: T. Glenn, Tim, or Tom Horst
50 Durlach Rd.
Corner of Rte. 322 & Durlach Rd.
Ephrata, PA 17501
Phone: (717) 738-3080
E-mail: sale@horstauction.com
Web site: www.horstauction.com

Litchfield County Auctions

This house is also cited a lot in this book; they have fine art & antiques auctions, which can be previewed online.

POB 76
940 Route 202
Bantam, CT 06750
Phone: (860) 567-4661
E-mail: lca@litchfield-auctions.com
Web site: www.litchfield-auctions.com

DEALER/COLLECTOR

Carol Bohn

This collector/dealer specializes in patented kitchen gadgets, particularly nutmeg graters, about which she is writing a book. If you are looking for an odd and rare gadget, ask her if she's got one for sale!

501 Market St.
Mifflinburg, PA 17844
E-mail: cjbohn@sunlink.net

Patented Antiques

Contact: Larry or Carol Meeker
Phone: (530) 620-7019
E-mail: clm@patented-antiques.com
Web site: www.patented-antiques.com

MUSEUMS & COLLECTIONS

The Anthropology Department at the California Academy of Sciences houses the **Rietz Food Technology** Collection. Containing approximately 1,700 items, this collection was assembled by Carl Austin Rietz, an inventor and executive in the food industry. His interest in the industry led him on travels around the world to collect objects used in the production, processing, storage, presentation, preparation, and serving of food.

Web sites:
www.calacademy.org/research/anthropology/utensil/index.html

http://www.calacademy.org/research/anthropology/tools/ (This site has Victorian kitchen & table tools... English...my book not cited.)

COOKING

XIV. COFFEE, TEA & CHOCOLATE
with a lot about enameled wares

Well, it's about time to take a break and have a cuppa. This chapter has two of the most popular collecting fields in it: **coffee mills** (or grinders), and **enamelware** teakettles and coffee pots. Many people who collect food-related items are attracted to coffee, tea, and chocolate. They use books on coffee-growing, or the tea ceremony or the history of the chocolate trade, to broaden the historical and social interest of their collections. Trade cards and candy wrappers are an important part of chocolate-collecting.

The ever-growing market in exotic blends of imported coffees, and the proliferation of specialized coffee bean shops is accompanied by increased interest in coffee utensils and gadgets. Apparently there are many new theme collectors of coffee-related stuff ... including caterers, and owners of the bean shops. They like to assemble old roasters and mills, sometimes for window-decorating potential, which is not to say they aren't truly interested in the objects themselves. There has been a shift in collecting from primarily late 19th or early 20th century mills to much earlier pieces. Consequently, prices have gone up across the board. There are a lot of collectors of vintage coffee cans, and coffee scoops or measures advertising a coffee brand – some for grounds, some for instant – are good go-withs. By 1900, there were over 200 companies that imported and sold coffee. By 1932, there were about 350. I don't know how many had their own brands, and how many of those would have had coffee measures, but the outlook is promising for a lot of collectibles!

Enamelware (more popularly, if less accurately – "graniteware") prices rose quickly in the 1980s and early '90s, but as explained in the Introduction to this book, floods of foreign enamelware imports have dampened prices except for marked rarities. Still, among the most desirable and expensive enamelware pieces are coffee pots, teapots or kettles. Chocolate pots are high on collectors' lists. I won't try to get into the intricate whys & howmuchfors, but suggest you join the club and buy the books. See the end of Chapter XIII for more information.

There's still room for entry level collectors of things in this chapter, such as smaller pieces like coffee measures, chocolate muddlers, tea balls, tea steepers, and tea strainers. And look for orphaned teakettle whistles, especially figural ones.

❖ NOTES ❖

Chocolate muddlers or mullers of the Spanish type called a *molinillo* (meaning mill), are a sort of combined stirrer & small pestle, carved of wood with loose concentric rings. See drawing in XIV-1. (Note that long-handled narrow spoons of silver or silverplate, used by inserting into the spout of a chocolate spout, are also called muddlers.) For centuries these wooden ringed stirrers, have looked just about the same, probably since the Spanish explorer Cortez had chocolate with Montezuma. They are a form of puzzle-carving because the rings are carved loose – freed, so to speak – from the stick that forms the body, and the rings cannot be removed unless broken! Many found now in the U.S. were made in Mexico within the last century. A molinillo is used by rotating between the palms, which creates a froth. Anyone who's tried to stir melting chocolate, or dry cocoa into milk knows how hard it is to avoid clumping; a molinillo or muddler fixes that. Wooden ones are about $5-$35+.

Chocolate grater – See Chapter I (Cut & pare)
Chocolate molds – See Chapter IV (Molds)

Chocolate pot, copper with steel handle, with possibly original wood muller (or muddler), English, 7"H, mid 18th C. .... **$500+**
Chocolate pot, in its own nickel plated castor, brown & white agateware with nickeled collar, lid & spout, "Manning Patent," Manning & Bowman, American, 11"H, c.1890s-1910. .... **$600+**
Chocolate pot, pear-shaped body, cast & machined brass, 3 brazed-on short legs with fat ball feet, side handle of heavy ebonized turned wood, hinged spout lid, lid with finial & thumb hinge, French or Swiss, 8-7/8"H, c.1730s. .... **$350+**

❖ NOTES ❖

Finials or knobs for tea or coffee pots, were shown in 1869 Dover Stamping Co. catalog, which also showed many tinsmiths' supplies, as well as housewares. Dover offered a "bright bird," a simple dovelike bird on grass; a "bright acorn," a pair of acorns sticking up from leaf; several round and rosette models were offered in a choice of finishes: "black" (sheet iron without tinning) or "bright" tinned.

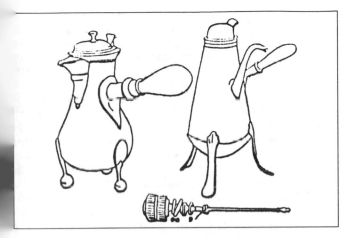

XIV-1. Chocolate pots & a molinillo. Both have typical rounded bottom, which accommodated the muddler (stirrer). **(L)** Cast & turned brass, pyriform body (sometimes called "pear-shaped") with 3 ball feet, side spout, hinged lid with thumb-piece, ebonized wooden handle, 8-7/8"H. Probably French or Swiss, c.1730. Drawn from ad of reknowned brass antique dealer, Rupert Gentle, Wiltshire, England. **(R)** Pieced tin with hinged lid, slender gooseneck side spout, wooden handle. Probably American, early 19th C. Drawn from ad of Pat Guthman Antiques, Southport, CT. **(B)** Mexican all-in-one piece carved wood **molinillo**, **muller** or **muddler**, about 8-1/2"L. The three rings marked with "•" dots are loose, and twirl when the stick, held vertically, is rubbed between the palms. The rings do not slip off end. Note corrugated wide bands at bottom. Chocolate, of course, originated in South America. Pots: **$500+**; **$300+**; muddlers: **$5-$35+**

XIV-3. Box mills. (L) "No. 1050 Improved." mfd. by John M. Waddel Mfg. Co., Greenfield, OH. "This is designed for a good, low priced mill, with burr and shell so constructed as to grind coffee very fine. The point is made of a new feature in this mill, consisting of a device for firmly locking the grinding shell and large retinned hopper to the box, holding the shell firmly to its place and making a bearing for the burr shaft." Open the door and a round tin receiver cup automatically slides out – this feature was typical of Waddel mills. From writeup in The Metal Worker, Aug. 16, 1890. **(R)** An English box mill, with raised hopper, wooden box with ornate cast iron top & slanted sides, shallow drawer. Marked on medallion above door, but I can't read. Both Kenrick (West Bromwich, England) and T. & C. Clark (later named Wolverhampton & Clark, Wolverhampton, England) made similar box mills. This one is probably a T. & C. Clark. From Harrod's Stores 1895 catalog. **(L) $140-$180; (R) $125-$150+**

XIV-2. Box type coffee mill also called **lap mill** or **French mill.** Cast iron with closed-top hopper, tin drawer slides underneath. Key at side for taking apart for cleaning. Screwed to oblong board with shaped ends and 3 holes at each end, perhaps for fingerholds for carrying? Mill 6-3/4"H exclusive of crank; base 5-1/2" x 5-7/8", Pennsylvania, mid 19th C. Courtesy of the late Darryl G. Dudash, Alaquippa, PA, who had a great eye & is sorely missed. He specialized in Pennsylvania cast iron. **$350-$450**

XIV-4. Box mills. Clockwise from top: **(1)** "Favorite No. 700." raised hopper with cover, and with handle for firm grip, wood box-jointed body with drawer, box 4-1/4"H x 6-1/4" square. Pat'd. 1880 & 1888. **(2)** "Imperial No. 147." sunken hopper with hinged cover, white walnut box, cast iron top finished with "French gold bronze." 4-3/4"H x 7" square, pat'd. 1888. **(3)** Simplest type of raised hopper box mill, "No. 257," japanned iron open hopper, hardwood box, 3-1/4"H x 6" square. 1-3 are Manning, Bowman & Co., Meriden, CT, from the 1892 catalog. **(4)** "Universal No. 110," mfd. by Landers, Frary & Clark, New Britain, CT. Black enameled sheet steel with iron handle & crank. 8-1/2"H. Both in ads from 1905. The colorful one is more attractive than the plain one, but has a narrower value range. **(5)** "None-Such," mfd. by Bronson-Walton Co., Cleveland, OH. Chromolithograph-ed decorative box with scene of coffee-drinkers. Domed hopper & top crank. **(1-3) $95-$150; (4) $75-$150; (5) $200-$400**

Coffee biggins – See section Coffee Biggins, Boilers & Pots after Coffee Mills

Coffee boilers – See section Coffee Biggins, Boilers & Pots after Coffee Mills

Coffee cup, china, large size, with caricature of NYC's Boss Tweed and a spoofing quote, on other side, from the time of the Tammany Hall political boss's downfall. In tradition of 200 years of politically-related engravings & plates & cups: "I am not greedy, but I like a lot." American, early 1870s. Crossover political, also NYC collectors. Price probably less in areas of the country with no interest in Boss Tweed, although his name became nationally synonymous with political graft................... **$325+**

Coffee cup or mug, graniteware, white background with dark green (or black?) transfer picture of pine tree, etc., adv'g. "Dickenson's Ace Clover, Extra-Recleaned, A Trade Winner" & "Dickenson's 'Pine Tree' Timothy Seed, Average Purity Test, 99-1/2%, It Stands Alone" (the lone pine tree symbolizes this). Dickenson's, American, 19th C. They must have made a lot of these, because you see them fairly regularly. .... **$45+**

Coffee drip maker – See section Coffee Biggins, Boilers & Pots after Coffee Mills

Coffee & hot beverage urns – See Urns

Coffee makers – See section Coffee Biggins, Boilers & Pots after Coffee Mills

Coffee measure scoop, stamped & pieced tin, rolled edge, shaped like a trowel but with flat triangular bottom, short tubular handle opposite pointed end. Embossed on the 2 sides: "McLAUGHLIN & CO. THE LARGEST ROASTERS OF" and "FINE COFFEES IN THE WORLD," "PATENTED OCTOBER 19, 1897." 14"L x 6-1/2"W at widest point. W. F. McLaughlin & Co., Atlanta, GA. See also Chapter V. .... **$100+**

Coffee measure or scoop, stamped aluminum, adv'g. "Schillings Best," for A. & C. Schilling, coffee wholesalers, San Francisco, CA, c. 1910s-30s.......... **$10+**

Coffee measure, tinned stamped sheet metal & long wire handle, flat-bottom bowl stamped "COFFEE MEASURE CASWELL," & shaft of handle flattened & stamped on back "Above all others National Crest Coffee." End of handle forms a sort of pear-shape hanging hole, which was probably also a tool to help open a coffee tin. A variation has the motto stamped on the flattened pear-shape end; & some have been reported with no stamping on the handle. 9"L – 10"L, Geo. W. Caswell Co., San Francisco, c.1920s-30s. **$10**

Coffee measure, tinned stamped metal, flat-bottom 2" diam. scoop bowl stamped "Coffee Measure," handle stamped "For MFA Coffee," 5-1/2"L overall, American, c. 1920s-30s.............................. **$5+**

Coffee measure, stamped aluminum, flat-bottom & long handle, like toy frying pan, stamped "Coffee satisfaction is assured by A&P COFFEE SERVICE," & a long handle: "one level measure to each cup." 5-1/2"L, c.1940s (?). .... **$5+**

Coffee measure, cup of dark brown Bakelite™ (or other molded phenolic resin plastic), very Deco stepped design with zigged-edge tab handle, marked inside "Cory Reg U.S. Pat. Off. 1/2 Ounce," and on the bottom "Glass Coffee Brew Corp. Chicago." Only 1-3/4"H. As one eBay seller ("tutibud") remarked, design is like that for little Akro Agate cups. 1930s-40s (?) .... **$10+**

Coffee measure, small square red plastic scoop, bottom embossed with the trademark logo of man in nightshirt, coffee cup raised to lips, "HILLS BROS COFFEE GUIDE," 2" square, tiny tab handle, Hills Brothers, NYC, c.1950s. (?) .... **$15+**

Coffee measure, tin cup, 2 stamped fill lines, stamped on front opposite strap handle: "For One Quart" & "Barrington Hall The Baker-ized Coffee" & "For One Pint" & "Economy Without Sacrifice," 3-1/2"H, early 1900s.. **$6+**

Coffee measure, tin cup with rolled rim, variable measures – a swiveling flat plate could be stuck into one of 3 narrow slots to measure 2, 4 or 6 cups, stamped "DIX COFFEE METER," and "PAT SEPT.1 '08." American, 3-1/4"H x 2-1/8" diam. Some are stamped on side with name of a firm, such as a newspaper or grocery, that gave them out as premiums. .... **$22+**

Coffee measure scoop, (or spice scoop?), robin's-egg blue enamelware on outside, white inside, strap handle, no marks, only 3-1/2"L, c.1920s........ **$30+**

Coffee Mills Or Grinders

1905-06 Coffee Mill Makers. The following are from *Thomas' Register of American Manufacturers, Buyers' Guide*, 1905-06. Something I found interesting was that although some made both, a number of spice mill makers did not make coffee mills. On the other hand, a number of food companies imported tea, coffee and spices. • Charles Parker Co., Meriden, CT Landers, Frary & Clark, New Britain, CT • Peck, Stow & Wilcox co., Southington, CT • Woodruff & Edwards Co., Elgin, IL., Arcade Mfg. Co., Freeport, IL • Ames Plow Co., Boston, MA • Jonathan T. Nove Mfg. Co.; and • George L. Squier Mfg. Co., both Buffalo, NY • Jabez Burns & Sons, NYC • Jonathan Chatillon & Sons, NYC • Fairbanks Co., NYC • Lane Bros. Co., Poughkeepsie, NY • S. Howes Co., Silver Creek, NY • L. J. Miller, Cincinnati, OH • Bronson-Walton Co.; and • Fanner Mfg. Co. both Cleveland, OH • Sun Mfg. Co., Columbus, OH • Waddel Wooden Ware Works, Greenfield, OH • Coles Mfg. Co.; and • J. C. Dell & Son (electric); and • Thomas Devlin & Co.; and • Enterprise Mfg. Co. of PA; and • Henry Troemner, all of Philadelphia, PA • Reading Hardware Co., Reading, PA • Howe Scale Co., Rutland, VT. **1909** *House Furnishing Review Buyers' Directory*, with trade-names. • Arcade Mfg. Co., Freeport, IL, "Bell," "Crystal," "Telephone," "Jewel," "Monarch," "Home," "Imperial," "Favorite," "King," "Arcade" • Bronson-Walton Co., Cleveland, OH, "B-W Steel" • Coles Mfg. Co., Philadelphia, PA • Enterprise Mfg. Co., Philadelphia • Landers, Frary & Clark, New Britain, CT, "Universal," "Crown" • National Specialty Co., Philadelphia • Charles Parker Co., Meriden, CT • Peck, Stow & Wilcox, NYC • Southern Foundry & Machine Works, Fredericksburg, VA • Sun Mfg. Co., Columbus, OH, "Sun" • Waupaca Novelty Works, Waupaca, WI • Woodruff & Edwards Co., Elgin, IL, "Elgin," "National" • Wrightsville Hardware Co., Wrightsville, PA. **1915**

House Furnishing Review Buyers' Directory, with trade-names. These are from a combined listing for coffee and spice mills. I've tried to differentiate. • Abbe Engineering Co., NYC • Arcade Mfg. Co., Freeport, with "71 varieties of Family Coffee Mills" • Arnold Wooden Ware Co., Cleveland, OH • John Bing, NYC • George Borgfeldt & Co., NYC • A. & F. Brown Co., NYC • Buckeye Steropticon Co., Cleveland, OH, "Oplex" wall-mounted mill • C. C. Clawson, Flagtown, NJ • Coles Mfg. Co. & Pennsylvania Lawn Mower Works, Philadelphia • A. J. Deer Co., Hornell, NY (electric) • Thomas Devlin Mfg. Co., Philadelphia • Engle Coffee Mill Co., Newton, IA • Enterprise Mfg. Co., Philadelphia, "Enterprise" • Fanner Mfg. Co., Cleveland, "Star," "Ever Ready" • Frank & Co., NYC • C. H. & E. S. Goldberg, NYC • Hobart Electric Mfg. Co., Troy, OH, "Hobart Electric" • Howe Scale Co., Rutland, VT (electric) • Lalance & Grosjean Mfg. Co., NYC • Lane Bros. Co., Poughkeepsie, NY, "Swift" • Landers, Frary & Clark, New Britain, CT, "Crown," "Universal" • G. E. Meissner & Bro., NYC • National Specialty Mfg. co., Philadelphia • Nordyke 7 Marmonn co., Indianapolis, IN • Chas. Parker Co., Meriden, CT • Peck, Stow & Wilcox, Southington, CT • Rice & Danziger Inc., NYC • Silver & Co., Brooklyn, NY, "Silver" • Steiner Mfg. Co., St. Louis, MO, "Steiner" electric • Steinfeld Bros., NYC, "Model," "Steinfeld," "Eclipse" • Sun Mfg. Co., Columbus, OH, "Sun" • G. M. Thurauer Co., NYC, imports • Waddel Woodenware Works Co., Greenfield, OH • R. W. Whitehurst Co., Norfolk, VA • Wilmot Castle Co., Rochester, NY • Woodruff & Edwards Co., "Elgin National" • Wrightsville Hardware Co., Wrightsville, PA. **1930** *House Furnishing Review Buyers' Directory*, with trade-names. Huge drop-off in numbers, and not known if all four were coffee mills or spice mills only. • Basket Importing Co., NYC • Landers, Frary & Clark, New Britain, CT • Ben S. Loeb Inc., NYC • George M. Thurnauer Co., NYC, importer. **1932** *Thomas' Register of American Manufacturers, Buyers' Guide.* This listing is for household mills only. • Parker Bros., Meriden, CT • Charles Parker Co., Meriden, CT • Arcade Mfg. Co., Freeport, IL • Freidag Mfg. Co., Freeport, IL • Hussmann-Ligonier Mill Co., St. Louis, MO (electric) • Enterprise Mfg. Co., Philadelphia (hand & electric) • Wrightsville Hardware, Wrightsville, PA • York Electric & Machine Co., York, PA.

❖ NOTES ❖

"**A French coffee-mill**, which is simple and durable, is a necessity where filtered coffee is made. This will grind coarse or exceedingly fine. Easily adjusted and so simple that a child can use it." Maria Parloa, *Kitchen Companion*, Boston: Estes & Lauriat, 1887. • Note: A "French" mill was another way of saying a box or lap mill with a hopper above the box, not within it.

Coffee mills, box type

Also called table mills, lap mills or French mills, but many early catalogs called them "box mills" to differentiate them from wall-mounted side mills, or those which clamped to a table top.

Coffee mill, box type, mahogany (or cherry?), pewter hopper, cast iron crank handle, "Selsor, Cook & Co.," Philadelphia, 3rd quarter 19th C. .... **$125+**

❖ NOTES ❖

Friction & Anti-Friction Box Mills. I turned to MacMillan's wonderful tome on mills and got date info & place from it. Furthermore, apparently I've seen a marked mill (probably at a Pennsylvania flea market which I used to attend many times a year – before PA's pigeon shoots) but Joe found his references in a catalog; I wish he'd seen it rather than me! Listed, but not described in the 1870 catalog, are two basic types of Selsor, Cook mills: "Friction" and "Anti-Friction." Turning to one of my books on **mechanical movements** (used by inventors), I learned that friction was one way of driving one wheel with another. The surface is sometimes gritty, or faced with rubber or leather, to give it some grab. Another way to get grab, and increase the amount of touching surfaces, was to V-groove the wheels around their circumference, so that instead of-1/2 inch-wide area of each wheel touching, the surface would be doubled, by having V-grooves with two 1/2- inch sides. This "frictional grooved gearing" was said to be "comparatively recent" in the 1868 book.

As to "anti-friction," the only thing I could find in this book is an "anti-friction bearing" – the drawing clearly shows ball bearings. • See also a listing for a Carrington's wall-mounted side mill in that category, below.

Coffee mill, box type, cast iron, pat'd. by J. R. Adams, (#75,259), NYC, NY, Dec. 1, 1867. .... **$135+**

❖ NOTES ❖

Barbed Wire Connection – Joseph F. Glidden, who invented barbed wire, may have had an Adams' mill. Stephen L. Goodale, *Chronology of Iron and Steel*, (Pittsburgh: Pittsburgh Iron & Steel Foundries, 1920), wrote about Glidden's two 1874 patents for barbed wire: "The first barbs were made on an old coffee mill, and the wire was twisted with the crank of an old grindstone. The barbs were put on one at a time, and set in place with a hammer. It was first manufactured under the name Barb Fence Co., at De Kalb, Illinois." (p. 185).

Reproduction Alert

The extremely simple box style with bowl-like hopper & box joints, is being made today, & one that's being sold by Cumberland General Store of Crossville, TN has "satin black finish" cast iron, is 6"H x 4" square, & sells for about $35. • **Alert II.** – Lehman's Hardware, Kidron, OH, offer a 7"H x 4-3/4" square box mill with "dovetailed corners" (which are actually box jointed). • **Alert III.** – A 1968 ad in *McCall's Needlework & Crafts*, shows a box-joint wooden coffee mill, drawer with wood knob, ornate cast iron top, top crank with white porcelain knob, handle grip, hopper inside box, described by "The Country Cousin" dealer as "Decorative coffee mill really works, has a hand-rubbed antique walnut finish. 7" high. $9.95. ppd."

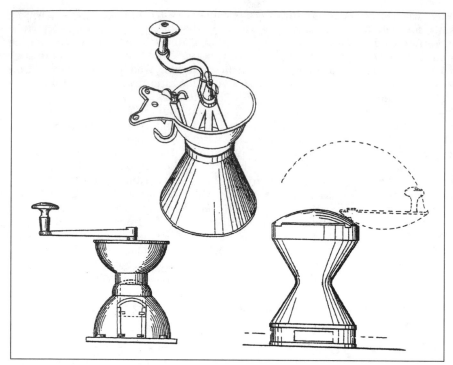

XIV-5. Coffee mill patents. (T) *Patent granted L. R. Livingston & Calvin Adams, Pittsburgh, PA, on Sept. 25, 1840 (#1,795) for "Manner of Constructing Mills for Grinding Coffee, &c." The inventors claimed to have improved the construction of "metallic mills" by forming the hopper, the shell within which the nut operated, and the "arch pieces and collar" that supported the spindle in a one-piece casting. They also claimed as new the manner of constructing the "part by which the mill is fastened to a table, or shelf," and also the part, which regulated the feed, by elevating or lowering the nut. As you can see, a thumbscrew secured the mill by tightening the plate that slipped over table or shelf and the hook that was underneath. Although the patent drawing looks similar to the other two patents in this group, actually the lower part is "a tin receiver which may slip on to the outside of what they called the shell." At right,* **(R)** *is John R. Adams' (NYC, NY) patent of "Improvement in Coffee-Mills," granted Dec. 17, 1867 (#72,259), though applied for in July 1865. The Civil War undoubtedly affected its design, as it would have been – as Adams said – compact and easily packed away. It was very ingenious – the lid "is hinged to an arm extending from the top of the shaft, to which the grinder is secured, said lid being provided with a handle secured to its inner surface in such a manner that, when the lid is opened, it takes the place of the crank, by which the grinder is set in motion, and when the lid is closed, the whole mill is brought in a compact form, which can easily be packed or stored away in a small space." The body "is made in the form of a double cone ... the upper cone forms the hopper, and the inner surface of the lower cone forms the concave grinding-surface, which corresponds to the grinding-cone." "The lower ... body is cylindrical, and [has] an aperture through which the ground coffee can be discharged. This aperture is opened or closed by a ring, which swivels." At lower left* **(L)** *is Thomas W. Brown's "Improvement in Coffee-Mills," dated July 19, 1870 (#105,545) and reissued Sept. 27, 1870 (#RE4,130). Brown, of Boston, assigned the patent to Charles Parker, Meriden, CT. He wrote that the object of his invention was "to produce a cheap and durable mill; and the invention consists in forming the base or receptacle of the mill and the runner-chamber in one and the same piece, whether the hopper be also cast thereon or formed in an independent piece." The adjusting screw is on the under side of the mill. Brown claimed that the manufacturing cost would be simplified and greatly reduced by casting the base and runner-chamber in one piece, and even more reduced by casting the hopper and "central support in the same piece" with the others. But he added, "In some cases a brass or copper hopper is preferred to iron, and in such cases the hopper may be formed separately and secured to the runner-chamber."*

Coffee mill, box type, cast iron & wood with box joints, hopper & crank on top, very plain, may be a cheap proprietary model made for a mail order house, American, c.1890s to 1910s. .... **$25+**

Coffee mill, box type, cast iron & wood, side crank out of side of wooden box instead of more usually seen out of top of hopper, side handle, "Parkers Columbia Rapid Grinder, No. 260," sold through Montgomery Ward catalog, Meriden, CT, 1 lb. size, c.1890s. A very desirable mill. .... **$175+**

Coffee mill, box type, dovetailed wood, japanned cast iron, "Parker's Union Coffee Mill No. 25," 6-1/4"H, c.1908. .... **$50**

❖ NOTES ❖

Parkers & Coffee Mills. Edmund Parker and Herman White of Meriden, CT, got three patents on June 22, 1832 for a Coffee Mill & Spice Mill. This was before patents were numbered. On Feb. 7, 1860, John Parker and Edmund Parker, got patent #27,065, for a "Coffee Mill," which was a side mill. On October 29, 1861, Edmund Parker, Meriden, CT, got patent #33,599 for "Improvement in Coffee-Mills." On May 5, 1868, Charles Parker and Edmund Parker, Meriden, CT, got patent #77,649, for "Improvement in Coffee-Mills," a box mill, and assigned it to Charles Parker Co., a company that stayed in business making coffee mills at least until 1932, (and bathroom fixtures by then); and appears in the 1945-46 *Thomas' Register of American Manufacturers* as makers of machinists' vises and bathroom accessories. Parker Brothers was another company in Meriden making coffee mills (and firearms) in 1932; but no longer at all in 1945-46. So sometime between 1932 and 1945, both Parker companies stopped making coffee mills. • **Social history**, economic history, and coffee mill history can be deduced from these excerpts from their specifications: 1860: "As is well known, these implements are almost always to be used by persons of but little discretion, as servants, and

continued p. 690

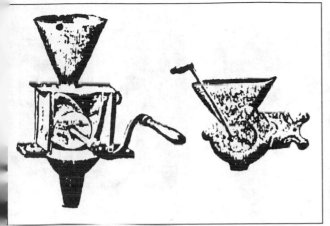

XIV-6. "Mr. Garnet Terry's Mill" & another old one. (L) *A hand mill, for coffee beans, spices, etc., of wood and sheet iron. Invented by Londoner Garnet Terry, c.1800-01. Illustration published in Anthony Willich's The Domestic Encyclopedia, 1803-04, which was a practical work meant for men who were used to making most of their own tools and household items. **(R)** Coffee or spice mill, "but will grind grain of any kind. It is sold without a frame, and is so constructed as to be fastened to a post or board in any part of the house, or it can be attached to a simple frame." Sheet iron with revolving cast iron corrugated "plates" which could be ordered separately. From article in* Journal of the American Institute, *Sept. 1841. Its most recognizable features for a search are the apparently straight crank handle, and the 2-fingered back-plate for screwing to wall. It predates 1841, so it could be Ammi Clark's mill, Berlin CT, pat'd. Aug. 4, 1833. But it looks like the #2 side mill of the Lane Bros.-Swift Co., based on a patent by Beriah Swift, Washington, NY, Aug. 16, 1845 (#4,149). The patent drawing for Swift's mill doesn't look like this, so the interior milling surface – with concentric rows of teeth alternating with furrows – was possibly the part used in the #2. It may have been manufactured and in circulation before a patent was applied for or granted.* **$200+**

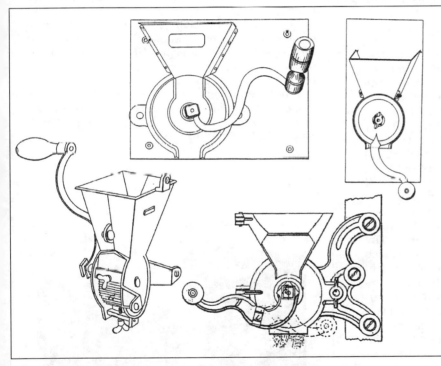

XIV-7. Side mill patents. (T) *John Luther, Warren, RI, pat'd. this "Coffee-mill" Aug. 11, 1843 (#3,215). This mill is constructed of a "circular flat plate or shell of cast iron with a rim around its edge, grooved on its inner surface." This is screwed to a back plate after placing the cast iron grinding wheel inside. Then the "narrow extremity" of the sheet iron hopper is stuck down into the top of the grinding shell, and it is screwed to the back board. An adjusting screw in the back adjusts a "gate" inside the hopper, "so as to fill up more or less space." Another screw passes through the back board and "presses against the wheel which by being turned one way or the other increases or diminishes the space between the wheel and the shell." A lot to go wrong with this one! And forget about cleaning it.* **(T-R)** *Charles R. Edwards, Suspension Bridge, NY, pat'd. this "Improvement in Spice and Coffee Mills," March 1, 1859 (#23,082). It's cast all of iron, or of iron with a tin hopper, and has no back except the board ("or whatever the mill shall be fastened to"). Bottom* **(B-R)** *Andrew J. & George W. M. Vandegrift (Cincinnati, OH) patent for "Improvement in Grinding-Mills," May 17, 1870 (#103,106). "Mills of this class have been imperfect in not ... being conveniently opened and closed, and not having ... a jointed crank, capable of being folded up." The Vandegrifts claimed a regulating "temper-screw" that wouldn't work loose because of a "friction-washer." Also "we are aware that folding cranks have been used in tape-line reels, and, perhaps, in some other small instruments, but in such instances the handle of the crank has folded to the center, and fitted in a chamber or cavity formed for the purpose in the end of the shaft." The hopper's top is closed with a plate of sheet-brass or other metal. Left* **(B-L)** *Hiram Twiss (Meriden, CT), got this patent for a "Mill for grinding coffee and other substances" June 19, 1837, (#243). It's the oldest in this group, and like all mills its grinding surfaces are slightly different, the way, and form of, the parts are cast are claimed as improvements, and the inventor tries to solve problems such as grounds coming out the sides, and regulating the grind coarser or finer. Twiss had a new twist, however ... a thing he calls the "clearer" that "may be formed in various ways and of different materials. I have sometimes used a piece of tin, a piece of leather, and a brush and found either would effect the object. I have also used a piece of leather made fast between two pieces of tin 2-1/2" long and 1/4" wide secured by solder at each end and placed 1/8" apart to receive the piece of leather." This is fastened to the mill to press with its "curved end moderately upon the cylinder ... where the ground substance is discharged." It was supposed to discharge the ground substance as soon as it's ground!*

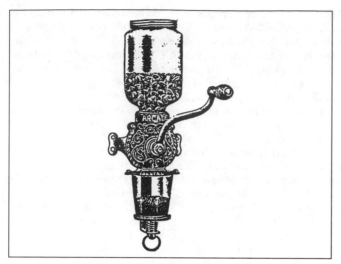

XIV-8. Wall-mounted coffee mill. *"The Crystal." so-named because of glass hopper/canister and receiving cup. Ornate cast iron mill. Arcade Mfg. Co., Freeport, IL. Ad in* Thomas' Register of American Manufacturers ... Buyers' Guide, *1905-06. (When complete with the Arcade glass cup receiver this value is highest.)* **$125-$150+**

continued from page 688

therefore should be so constructed as to avoid the possibility of being injured by careless handling or adjusting." 1861: "In the old mills it is well-known that as the hoppers become partially emptied the coffee is constantly thrown out in this way, and it is almost impossible to get the last grains through at all, as they roll over and over until by chance falling into a favorable position to get the first nip and thereby become cracked, all which defects my improved guide-brace overcomes, as a single grain is as readily ground as when the hopper if full." 1868: "The bottom board of these box-mills has been heretofore necessarily put on with screws, inasmuch as from time to time it is desirable that the grinding parts should be taken apart to be cleaned. The bottom had then to be unscrewed, (four screws,) as also the bed (two screws) and the hopper, (two screws,) to separate the parts. By our improvement the hopper is taken off by turning it partially around. Then, by introducing the hand through the opening for the drawer, and turning the bed a little, it is readily taken out. As thus the bottom may be put on with nails, it will be seen that at least eight screws are saved in the construction, thereby reducing the first cost, as well as greatly facilitating the cleaning, inasmuch as no tools are required for taking the mill apart."

Coffee mill, box type, chromolithographed tin depicts coffee plant on front & convivial scene of man & woman drinking the brew on the sides, sunken hopper with crank, small drawer, "None-Such mfd. by Bronson-Walton Co.," Cleveland, OH, c.1904. Larry Meeker emphasizes that "condition of the color printing is crucial to the value" of this type. .... **$200-$400**

Coffee mill, box type, dovetailed hardwood, entire top is cast iron finished in bronze lacquer, sunken hopper has pivoting cover, handle on top, "Imperial Mill No. 705," mfd. by Arcade Mfg. Co., Freeport, IL, box 5"H x 6" square, c.1903-04. .... **$95+**

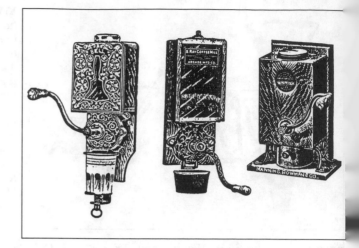

XIV-9. Novelty & canister-top coffee mills. (L) *"Bell," ornate cast iron front to oak box. Glass receptacle inside.* **(M)** *"X-Ray." with glass box above ornate cast iron mill. Ads in* House Furnishing Review, *1908.* **(R)** *"The Telephone Mill." for coffee or spices. "Made of hard wood, highly finished and nickel trimmed, and is the only boxed mill which can be fastened equally well on Table, Shelf or Wall. ... It is easily regulated to pulverize if desired." Name plate says "The Telephone Mill. Ring Up For Coffee. Freeport, Ill." Arcade Mfg. Co., appeared in* Manning-Bowman 1892 catalog. *Original price in 1890 was only $2.50. More desirable one has fancy cast iron front. Arcade Mfg. Co. made 70 "different varieties of coffee mills and 400 house furnishing specialties."* **(L) $400-$500; (M) $125-$180; (R) $450-$600**

XIV-10. Coffee mill. *"Lone Star Side Mill" which "may readily be attached to the face of a door, window casing, or the wall" and may be "folded up when not in use." Projects 4" from wall when folded. John M. Waddel Mfg. Co., Greenfield, OH, article in* The Metal Worker, *June 14, 1890.* **$250+**

XIV-11. *Coffee mill.* Shelf or table-mounted. Cast iron with bell-shaped hopper. Maker not known; picture from Harrod's Stores 1895 catalog, London. **$100+**

XIV-12. *Coffee mills.* Various grinding & pulverizing styles of cast iron mills mfd. by Enterprise Mfg. Co., Philadelphia. Early 20th C. catalog. Note that top one is "adapted for Steamboats, Butchers, Lumber Camps" and will "granulate 3/4 pound of coffee per minute." (And, presumably, make hamburger & sawdust too!)

XIV-13. *Coffee mill.* **(L)** "Double Grinding" mill for tabletop use. Decorated cast iron. Silver & Co., Brooklyn, c.1910. It came in two sizes, which affect price. It gets its name by being "a new departure in 'Grinding Mills.' Has two inlets for the Coffee Bean and two outlets for the Ground Coffee." Adjustable for coarse to powdered grinds. **(R)** "Crown No. 11." mfd. by Landers, Frary & Clark, New Britain, CT. Painted & decorated cast iron, 12-1/2"H, drawer in base. From Pick catalog, 1909. (L) #1: **$250-$350**; (L) #2: **$350-$400+**; (R) good condition: **$250+**; (R) poor paint: **$90-$125**

Coffee mill, box type, forged iron box on base plate supporting 4 corner columns with brass fleur-de-lis finials, large capacity high mortar-shaped hopper also houses mill, with serpentine scroll supports & side handle of flat iron also shaped like fleur-de-lis, central crank has turned wooden knob, French, 16"H. If for home use, certainly not for small family (although Emile Zola drank 40+ cups a day), late 1600s or early 1700s............................. **$650-$900**

Coffee mill, box type, "French style" with raised hopper, wood with ornate cast iron top, bad condition, with warped wood, poor finish, drawer knob missing, American, 19th C. • Even with everything wrong, still can bring some money as a decorative shelf piece or "sitter." .... **$25-$40**

Coffee mill, box type, grain painted tin in bold red & black, hopper filled at top, but bottom has a snap-on hinged lid which you open to release the ground coffee from the box, sort of like how you empty crumbs from a toaster, marked only "P B" on front, in block letters, "P.B. Machina Accaiai [or Acciaia]," Italian, 4-1/2" square, late 19th C or early 20th C. • The dealer had another like it, somewhat smaller, rather dully finished in brown paint, for much less... **$90+**

Coffee mill, box type, heavy cast iron, square with slightly slanted sides, 2 cast-in flanges for bolting to board or table, cast iron drawer, brass hopper, brass oval medallion with regal looking rampant lion, "A Kenrick & Sons Patented Coffee Mill," England, 6-1/2"H, prob. c.1860s to 1880s. .... **$125-$150+**

Coffee mill, box type, cast iron, wood, side handle on side & crank on other side, drawer, "Arcade IXL," proportion somewhat different from most box mills, being 11"H on a 7-1/2" square base, Arcade Mfg. Co., Freeport, IL, late 19th C. .... **$150+**

Coffee mill, box type, low wooden box with box joints, cast iron mill, hopper inside, cranked on top with "self adjusting spiral spring drawer for grounds," "Chicago Double Grinder, No. 60," Chicago Coffee Mill Co., IL, pat'd. Oct. 19, 1886, but began making in 1890. .... **$90+**

Coffee mill, box type modern style, dark maroon Bakelite™ (or other molded phenolic resin plastic), nickel plated handle, metal works inside, wooden knob, "The PE-DE Coffee Grinder," *"Dienes-Reform D. R. G. M. R. P."* German, 8"H, 1930s. • The last two letters, R. P., stand for *Reichspatent.* The D. R. G. M. stands for *Deutsches Reichs-Gebrauchsmuster* (or Registered Trademark of Germany). Dienes-Reform means Reformed Office. The whole mark (Reformed Office of German Registered Trademarks and Patents) might have been used between WWI, when D. R. G. M. was used by itself, and WWII, after which Germany was divided. .... **$85+**

Coffee mill, box, modern style, marbled dark brown Bakelite™, upright somewhat chunky cylindrical hopper/grinder rising up from oblong receptacle bow-fronted base, marked in circle on top "DMR" and "Ver Diesel Motoren Rostock." 9"H overall; base about 5-1/2" x 3-1/8". Reportedly mfd. by a company (DMR) who built diesel engines, in Rostock, Germany, early 1930s. .... **$60+**

Coffee mill, box type, ornate cast iron top & dovetailed wood, tin drawer with wooden front & knob, top handle, "Challenge Fast Grinder," Sun Mfg. Co., Greenfield, OH, 1 pound size, late 19th C. • In 1891 Jno. M. Waddel Mfg. Co., also of Greenfield, OH, sent out letters informing dealers that the Sun Nov-

XIV-14. Coffee mills. (L) *Enterprise Mfg. Co. No. 8, with double cast-iron flywheels, brass canister/hopper (sometimes nickel-plated), eagle finial, bulbous cast iron mill housing hinged in center. Three sizes in this style: 8, 10, & 210, which would grind 1 lb., 1-1/2 lbs., & 1-3/4 lbs. per minute. Offered in Duparquet, Huot & Moneuse catalog, c.1904-1910. (Note: from the same period, an almost identical red & gold one [except for decorations on the cast iron mill-housing] is Landers, Frary & Clark's "Crown No. 80." which has a nickeled hopper/canister.)* ***(R)*** *"Swift Mill," Lane Brothers. Large, double-wheeled mill, painted cast iron with drawer in box base. About 22"H. Early 20th C. ad, but mill dates to 1870s.* ***(L) $400-$1,000; (R) $350-$600***

XIV-15. Coffee mill, *on high stand. Ornate, painted & decorated cast iron. Enterprise Mfg. Co., Philadelphia, late 19th C. This is so coveted by collectors that even one in poor condition (mainly paint, but may include dents & dings to hopper) brings serious money. Poor:* **$600-$900;** *good :* **$1,500+;** *excellent:* **$3,000+**

elty Works of Greenfield was infringing Waddel's patents on their "Greenfield" mill. .... **$70-$100**

Coffee mill, box type, with wide shelf base & lid, cast iron sunken hopper, lid, crank & top grip, door below swings out to reveal tin pan on little shelf that pivots out when you open the door, "Greenfield Coffee Mill, No. 91," mfd. by Jno. M. Waddel Mfg. Co., Greenfield, OH, 9-1/2"H, prior to 1890. See the similar mill by Sun Mfg. Co. .... **$120+**

Coffee mill, box type, plain, pale beech wood, drawer below, chrome-plated stamped sheet metal top, chromed top crank, German, c.1961. This box mill was offered new in *House Beautiful* ad; also cherry or walnut. The 3 woods cost $4.95, $7.95 and $8.95 originally. .... **$15+**

Coffee mill, box type, stamped steel with black enamel finish, sunken hopper, crank on top, wood knob, "Universal #109," Landers, Frary & Clark, New Britain, CT, 5-1/4"H x 5-1/4" square box, pat'd. Feb. 15, 1905. .... **$75+**

Coffee mill, box type, very ornate beautifully carved wood, probably mahogany, decorated with angel's heads at each corner of the lower box part, then carved into tower part housing mill works, with acanthus leaves coming down from top, 4 tiny feet, iron screw-on top with graceful iron crank with turned wood knob, ring handle on little drawer. This mill – with the almost furniture-like look, and the tall tower broadening out with undulations into the little box – is what is called a "Louis XIV" type mill because that is when this style appeared, marked "Tivelier Jeune" [Tivelier Jr.], St. Etienne, France, 10-3/8"H, c.1830s-1850s. .... **$400-$600+**

Coffee mill, box type, wood & cast iron, original red paint, pin-striping & other decoration on iron, "Landers, Frary & Clark," New Britain, CT, 12"H, late 19th C.............................. **$200-$250**

Coffee mill, all cast iron tabletop or lap type, 2-piece, twist-apart (top half twists off lower part – a sort of bayonet mount), very decorative with careful, clear casting. Landers, Frary & Clark. Fragile, so condition is all. .... **$300+**

Coffee mill, box type, wood & iron, original paper label on box, "Home Coffee Mill #767," mfd. by Arcade Mfg. Co., pat'd. June 5, 1884. .... **$90+**

Coffee mill, box type, wood with chamfered top, turned cast brass tower, called a "collar," forged iron crank with turned wood knob, iron decoration on 4 sides of box, & brass ring handle on little drawer, Austrian or Hungarian, about 8"H, early 18th C......... **$350+**

Coffee mill, box type, wooden, cast iron finished with thin copper plating, sunken hopper, crank in top, "Parker's National Coffee Mill No. 430," only 4 1/2"H, c.1900s 1910.............................. **$75-$100**

Coffee mills, electric

Coffee mill, electric, cast iron painted white, with glass jar, looks almost like some modern flashlight & bird-feeder combined, "KitchenAid," division of Hobart Mfg. Co., Troy, Ohio, 1938. (Note: Oddly to me, because it isn't the original finish, Larry Meeker explained to me that one of these that's been restored & repainted in "slick automotive enamel with pinstriping" brings between $100 and $150!) .... **$60-$80**

Coffee mill, electric, enameled cast iron base, screw-on clear glass bean holder above, a glass tumbler marked off in measures sits under chute in left side, "KitchenAid," early 1940s......................... **$40-$50**

❖ NOTES ❖

Wartime dates – It is problematic to date any American, Canadian, English, French or Italian product to the years of the World Wars. • WWI had been going on for three long years before the U.S. declared war against Germany. I suspect that all metals, as well as glass & cloth, were in short supply for making housewares in any involved country between 1914 & 1918. Ads in trade magazines such as *House Furnishing Review* reflect the trade restrictions imposed on products of the Central Powers. • WWII really started long before Germany invaded Poland in 1939. I'd like to read a study of trade practices between what became the Allied Nations and the main Axis powers, Germany & Italy, starting, say, in 1935. At any rate, the war was almost two years old when the U.S. landed troops in Iceland, and over two years old when we declared war in December 1941. Probably a great percentage of manufacturers of household appliances and wares suspended domestic production to turn to suitable war materiel manufacturing. Strategic raw materials were severely restricted. Many ads of the early 1940s talk about what goodies would come after the war was over. Any products made of vital materials (iron, steel, copper, rubber, etc.) that were sold in the U.S. between c.1940 and 1946 may have been made before that period. I don't know what the government did during the **metal & rubber drives** when objects made of metal or rubber were solicited from the general populace ... whether or not they asked the same thing of manufacturers & their warehoused finished products. In a September 1944 ad in *Better Homes & Gardens*, the headline is "War or no war – Mrs. Jones keeps 'selling' KitchenAids! KitchenAid has gone to war – but enthusiastic KitchenAid users haven't stopped 'selling' their friends. What do they say? They say that a KitchenAid is more than a kitchen 'gadget.' It's a kitchen machine, strong enough and powerful enough to take the elbow-grease out of the really hard ... jobs – mixing, mashing, juicing, whipping, and such. ... They say – but why go on? The fact remains there still isn't a single KitchenAid to sell. But someday there will be – and then remember to talk to a KitchenAid user before you buy any mixer."

Coffee mill, electric, enameled cast iron, with glass top, "KitchenAid No. A-9," Hobart Mfg. Co., Troy, OH, 1938. .... **$55+**

Coffee mill, electric, for supermarket (and U.S. Navy!) use – known to mill collectors as the "Big Pot," in shape of big fancy coffee pot with high domed lid &

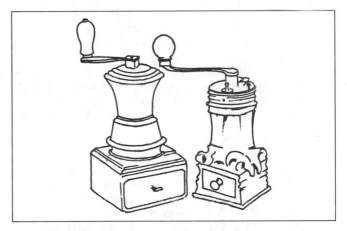

XIV-16. Coffee mills. *Small cylindrical mills of wood, about 7" to 9"H.* **(L)** *A simple turned wood mill made in the Provence district of France, in very early 18th C. It was supposedly based on earlier Italian models.* **(R)** *Carved wood mill from the 18th C. It looks as if it could have been made by a furniture or frame-carver. Both are drawn from a wonderful article, "Les moulins à café," by Edith Mannoni, that appeared in the French magazine* Art & Décoration, *Aug./Sept. 1982. It is filled with unusual mills, mostly unfamiliar to American collectors.* **$125-$200+**

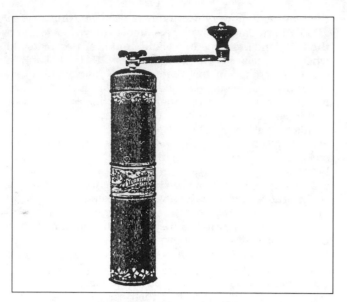

XIV-17-A. "Turkish" style coffee mill. Actually marked *"The Turkish Coffee Mill"* on decorative center band. *"Patterned after Oriental models, heavily japanned, has black enamel finish, and is handsomely decorated. The grinders are of highest grade & grind the coffee to a fine powder, which is especially suited for making 'after dinner' coffee."* 13"H, mfd. by Landers, Frary & Clark, picture from Albert Pick catalog, 1909. Look also at the listings for Pepper mills in Chapter I (Cut, Grind). According to Joe MacMillan, there's a great variety of old & new ones, & wide value range. **$45-$150**

curved short "duckneck" spout, has 4 grinds – coarse, boil, perk & drip. Panel lights up in back to tell what grind to use: "Extra fine (maybe put through twice?) for glass maker, fine for drip, medium for perk, coarse for pot." "American Duplex Electric Coffee Cutter," mfd. by American Duplex Co., Louisville, KY, 30"H, c.1936-1940. • It is one of 350 reportedly made. I've actually seen several for sale; maybe a store chain (or a fleet) suddenly closed up a few years ago, releasing these into the atmosphere? • **Duckneck spout.** – What better name for a short, almost vestigial gooseneck spout than duckneck?.. **$500-$1,500+**

Coffee mills, globe

Coffee mill, tabletop, dark burnt orange-painted cast iron globe mill with curved top crank with fat wood knob; top-hinged lid to drawer compartment, in slant-side base, is embossed: "Grand Union Tea Company." GUTCo was in Brooklyn, NY; mill mfd. by Griswold Mfg. Co., Erie, PA, for Grand Union, 10-3/4"H, c.1920. Much of the value is due to Griswold collectors, not mill collectors. (Note: In the 1920s Griswold also made a virtually identical mill, bearing "The Griswold Mfg. Co. Erie PA." embossed on the drawer front, with black wood knob. This style eliminated the need for a hinged lid. It's worth $1,000+ to Griswold collectors.) GUTCo mill: .... **$500+**

Coffee mill, cast iron globe on iron strut-like frame, half-lid hinged in flat top, large ungainly crank comes out of side. Globe is embossed with concentric rings around the longitude lines from North Pole to South Pole, and its two halves are bolted together. Marked

on the globe, above the crank shaft "ADAMS" and on the opposite side "CENTENNIAL." A very petite mill only 6-1/2"H to lid; "belly" of globe only 3-3/4" across, crank handle about 5-1/4"L. This was located by the archaeologist of iron, Bob Cahn, and is in the collection of Neuman & Bogdonoff, NYC. Another was advertised by Golden Lane Antiques, New Oxford, PA, in 1994. The "Centennial" is most surely the U.S.A.'s in 1876. The mill itself looks rather English, but the "Centennial" refers to America's. I think this mill was a design patent of 1874 or '75. .... **$500+**

❖ NOTES ❖

Mill Inventors Named Adams: According to a compiled Index and Guide to the *Early Unnumbered Patents from 1790-1836*, an inventor named R. W. Adams of Marlborough, VT, patented a "grist-mill" on Dec. 8, 1808; and an inventor named W. Adams, of Guilford, NC, patented a "grist-mill" on July 18, 1827. I wouldn't have considered grist-mills, except that there was an 1833 patent for a

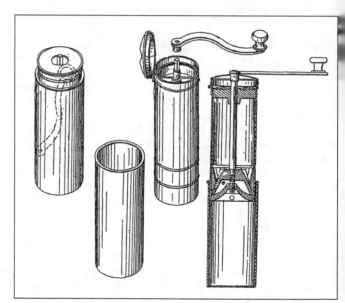

XIV-17-B. Portable coffee mill patent. Samuel H. Witmer, Cincinnati, OH, pat'd. this June 28, 1864 (#43,374), & assigned it to Mahlon M. Wombaugh, also Cincinnati. His *"Improved Portable Coffee-Mill"* is *"adapted for camp and mining uses"* because of compactness and light weight. A cylindrical box held the "telescopic" mill, which Witmer said was 2"diam. x 6"L, and would hold two ounces of coffee, sufficient *"when properly ground, for a mess of four or five men."* Perhaps a military background led him to say that after removing the winch, the mill *"may receive its charge of berries, and will be ready for immediate service the moment the men rest for a meal or bivouac."* To use, it could be *"held between the knees, or in the left hand merely"*; when stowed in the cylindrical box, it could be kept in a pocket. Left to right: **(1)** cylindrical box with handle inside & lid; **(2)** receptacle for grounds part of mill; **(3)** the lid off, crank out ready to be put on shaft, and hopper upper half, that holds the beans to be ground; **(4)** Fully assembled, showing mill parts inside center.

"grist and coffee mill." An inventor named Isaac Adams got 3 patents for a hulling machine – "machine for breaking the husks of coffee berries"on Jan. 13, 1835, and 2 patents for the same on Jan. 13, 1836. To me this doesn't sound like a coffee mill, which grinds the berries after they've been freed from the hulls. Patent office typos may account for the dates. (Isaac Adams also got several patents for power printing presses in 1830 and 1836.) By the way, another Bostonian, T. Ditson, also got a patent for "breaking outer husks of coffee-berries" on the same day, same year. • A "coffee-grinding mill" was patented by L. R. Livingston & Calvin Adams, Pittsburgh, PA, Sept. 25, 1840 (#1,795). • Another mill was patented by John R. Adams (#72,259) on Dec. 17, 1867. • Then there was a mill patented by Calvin Adams, July 18, 1876.

Coffee mills, screw clamps to table:
Coffee mill, clamps to table, wood & iron, "S. H. Co." (Simmons Hardware), St. Louis, MO, c.1890s-1910... **$145+**

XIV-18. Biggin coffee makers. *When the factories of Manning-Bowman & Co., at Meriden, CT., were remodeled in the early 20th C., a "vault was discovered that had become bricked up at some time in the past and forgotten. In this vault were found a large number of coffee percolators and other household apparatus, which was made by Manning-Bowman & Co. as far back as the Civil War." (The company was started back in 1849.) Shown here, and in the cited article in* House Furnishing Review, *Aug. 1911, are* **(L)** *a* **combined French biggin & drip percolator***, pat'd. in 1873. The coffee was "extracted by pressure of a wooden block forced down by wet coffee grounds."* **(R)** *"A nearer approach to the modern coffee* **percolator***, made by Manning-Bowman in 1875 and patented in 1876. It proves quite conclusively that contrary to general belief [in 1911], the percolator is not a recent contraption. This model has a center tube with spray top, and a water spreader on the cover to distribute the water that is forced up through the tube. It differs radically from the present day percolators in the fact that the water, after it is poured in the funnel shaped aperture on the side" is percolated only once through the grounds, instead of "making a continuous percolation as the modern ones do."* **$150+**

XIV-19. Biggin "French coffee pot." *Graniteware with planished tin. White metal or nickel-plated mountings. Made in 5 sizes – from 2 to 6 pints. Manning, Bowman & Co., 1892.* **$150+**

Coffee mill, screw clamps to table, cast iron, decorative decal, "Universal #30," Landers, Frary & Clark, c.1890s-1910. .... **$45+**
Coffee mill, japanned & stenciled cast iron, like the #00 but with screw clamp, hopper built in, but a bowl must be put below chute during use, "Enterprise #0," Enterprise Mfg. Co., 11-1/2"H, c.1898. .... **$45+**

Coffee mills, "telephone" novelty

Coffee mill, telephone novelty type that looks like an old oak wall crank telephone dating only a few years before the mill itself, wall or shelf mounted, ornate cast iron front to wooden box, "Telephone Mill," mfd. by Arcade Mfg. Co., Freeport, IL, 13"H, pat'd. Sept. 25, 1888, April 15, 1890, & April 11, 1898. .... **$450-$600+**

XIV-20. Biggin coffee pot patent. *Pat'd. Dec. 29, 1885, by Philip A. Covington, Fort Worth, TX, assignor of one-half to Albert H. Iverson. "A coffee-pot having a cone-shaped chamber perforated and provided with an upright tube, a perforated cup surrounding the same, a flaring cap connected to the tube and bottom of cup, a perforated retaining-plate, and a condensing-vessel formed with a convex bottom." For making a type of percolated coffee.* Official Gazette.

Coffee mill, telephone novelty type, wall-mounted, all wood with side crank, Brass plate gives name & dates, "The Telephone Coffee Mill," pat'd. (2 years after Arcade's desirable telephone mill) by F. J. Hollis, Kansas City, MO, 16"H x 6-1/4"W, April 18," 1892. .... **$600-$800+**

Coffee mills, wall or side mount

These have the hopper and mill found mounted to a board, or not, and are usually called "side mills." They have an iron frame with 2- or 3-arm projections through which the mill could, if desired, be first mounted to a board and then to any upright surface: a wall, the side of a cupboard, or even a door frame.

❖ NOTES ❖

An 1841 article (*Journal of the American Institute*) on **side mills** – the design of which hardly changed for 60 or 70 years – says "It is sold without a frame, and is so constructed as to be fastened to a post or board in any part of the house, or it can be attached to a simple frame."

❖ NOTES ❖

"Wood back" mills – Lots of side mills are found mounted to a board, sometimes with three holes in a staggered pattern on one side. This way, the mill could easily be put up on the side of a cupboard, or the wall of a pantry or kitchen, and moved more readily. Joe MacMillan terms these "wood back" mills.

Coffee mill, cabinet side mount, cast iron, folding handle, marked "Geo. W. M. Vandegrift." Andrew J. & George W. M. Vandegrift, of Cincinnati, OH, received patent #103,106 on March 20, 1866, for a "grinding-mill for Coffee, Spices, &c." Among their claims was that this one was conveniently opened for cleaning, and had a jointed crank that could fold up. They also suggested that the opening in the front of the hopper be closed with "the insertion of a plate of

XIV-21-A. Biggin coffee pot. *"Chesterman's," stamped & pieced tin, with fabulous air vent in crosspiece, with original cork stuck in it. Cast iron handle. Embossed stamped brass oval is the label – such stamped brass plates are found on many things, including many coffee mills of the period. Pat'd. 1859 & 1860. 9-3/8"H. See next picture.* **$175+**

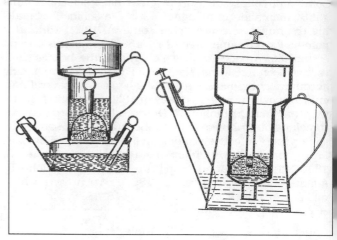

XIV-21-B. Two Chesterman patents. *Both of these patents were given William Chesterman, Centralia, IA. (L) This one was pat'd. July 19, 1859 (#24,795); on top is a "vessel" on a perforated bottom, "which serves to expose eggs or other similar substances to the heat of the vapor and steam...so that [they] are ready cooked" with the coffee itself. The patent also had provision in the central portion for a tied-on flannel strainer, which is also used as a "piston," & an "air tube" on the right, which builds up pressure so that "not a particle of the flavor or aroma...can possibly escape." (R) This one was pat'd. Jan. 24, 1860 (#26,889), and unusually, the inventor states exactly what patent this one is an improvement on: his own, of exactly 6 months before. He writes "In order to be able to take out the grindings from my pot without danger of mixing some of it with the liquid coffee I have now arranged the piston packed strainer in a separate movable cylinder which fits into the new or stationary cylinder of the pot so that the strainer forms an adjustable bottom ... and in removing this cylinder the strainer together with the grindings is taken out at the same time." Whew! Obviously, after it went into production a few more changes were made in the design. • See also the infuser pots in XIV-34.*

sheet-brass or other suitable metal." Collectors consider this very desirable. .... **$350-$550+**

Coffee mill, japanned & stenciled cast iron, wall mount side mill with hopper above balanced by receiving cup below, crank in middle, one of their many "rapid grinding and pulverizing mills possibly usable as spice mill, "Enterprise Mfg. Co. #00," 9"H, hopper holds 4 oz., "pat. applied for," shown in their 1898 catalog-cookbook. .... **$30+**

Coffee mill, wall-mounted side mill (hereafter "wall/side"), sheet & cast iron, painted black & mounted to natural-finish wood block that's partly carved & painted so that it "mirrors" shape of the sheet iron hopper front, brass ID plate reads: "Wilson's Improved Patent Coffee-Mill," mfd. by Increase Wilson, or Wilson's Foundry, New London, CT, mill and hopper are 6"H, hopper is 4"W, crank is 4-1/2"L, 1840s to 1860s (?). • The only dated Increase Wilson coffee mill patent I found was March 6, 1818, and this mill is based on the old patent, though the mill itself isn't anywhere near that old. .... **$95-$200+**

Coffee mill, wall/side, looks rather like the Wilson mill but backplate is cast iron as is the hopper, & there is a thumb-screwed "friction piece" called a "collet," a sort of washer to regulate coarseness of grind, marked "James Carrington, Wallingford, CT," pat'd. April 9, 1829 (pre numbering). • From a record of Carrington's patent claims in the *Journal of the Franklin Institute*, April 1829, comes this, which might help explain our question (see above) over "friction and anti-friction." "I claim as my invention,

XIV-22-B. Breakfast with Nathaniel Waterman: his "Cafetière, or Apparatus for Making Coffee." Mr. Waterman, of Suffolk County, MA & later Boston, is well-known to collectors of kitchen things. He held the famous patent for the "egg-pan" muffin pan (#23,517). Also a match-stand, a sad iron, a foot warmer, a gridion, a portable cooking stove (#5,675), & possibly many more. This Cafetière was pat'd. Feb. 26, 1850 & combines a coffee holder placed within the interior of the "decoction pot," a "spring expander to preserve the coffee when wet, in a close body, and at the same time, to afford to it room to expand without the production of such a condensation of it as would tend to injuriously prevent the flowage, or percolation of the water through." **(M)** Shows the hot water reservoir [above] and the coffee holder "as they appear when removed from the lower pot which holds the decoction." **(R)** On Sept. 8, 1863, Waterman got a patent for a coffee-boiler which resembles the much earlier one, having also a spring & an upper hot water reservoir. Most interesting to me is the change of the spout & handle, undoubtedly in response to changing fashion.

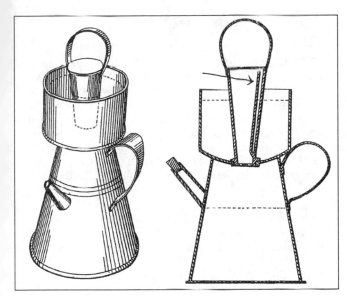

XIV-22-A. "Apparatus for Making Coffee and Tea." Pat'd by Antoni Bencini, Milton, NC, Sept. 27, 1838 (#952). I love the look of this – good, clean, modern Italian design! Only over 160 years ago. Bencini had invented a new way of making coffee or tea, and used a "common coffee pot of any given size with a receptacle or condenser affixed on the top of the said coffee pot holding about one third of the quantity of the main pot." The condenser/receptacle has a screw-threaded hole at the bottom and a stopper (the narrow tapered inset) which screws into it "so as to prevent the cold water from passing into the body of the pot until necessary." That stopper is "hollow with a division [the thing that looks like a rod near the side], ... and a small hole near the bottom of the stopper for the steam to pass through into the cold water in the [upper] receptacle." A "cork or wooden stopper" was put in the pouring spout while boiling. Here's Bencini's description of how the pot is used (and you probably couldn't describe the use of a Mr. Coffee™ any better!) "Any given quantity of ground coffee or tea is put into the pot which shall then be filled with boiling water to the strainer of the spout [that dotted horizontal line, otherwise unexplained] which should be so fixed as to make it two thirds full. Then screw in the stopper and fill the receptacle with cold water and set it on live coals for boiling. Let it boil until you discover steam artistry from the top of the receptacle/condenser…in fifteen or twenty minutes. Take it from the fire, unscrew the stopper so as for the water which has received the evaporation and flavor of the coffee or tea to pass into the body of the pot, then unstop the spout and it is ready."

and as very important improvements, the cast iron plate and hopper, and the collet in the plate in aid of the thumb-screw, to regulate the machine. By means of the friction piece, or collet, that screw will hold its place, and not yield to the motion of the crank, or be subject to wear by friction; and the runner, having a more extensive bearing, will run more true, perform its work more perfectly, be less liable to get out of order, and the whole machine being thus made of iron, not only assumes a more elegant form, but is free from shrinking, warping, and other effect of weather".................................. **$165-$200**

Coffee mill, wall/side, cast iron works in heavy stamped tin housing or body, triangular tin hopper, mounted on wooden board with three holes. Marked "S.J." looks c.1890s-1910. • I saw this a long time ago, and my flea-market notes weren't any more detailed. A search in Joe MacMillan's rewarding opus on mills led, finally, to an "S. J." The description fits with a "pressed sheet metal" side mill on p. 632 of MacMillan, mfd. by Theodore Frank Parker, who was in business, c.1891, with a man named "S. J. Goff." There's more to the story I'm sure, and we hope you will come up with more info! .... **$85+**

Coffee mill, wall/side, cast iron bean box above iron mill housing, spring & screw clamp holder below for cut crystal container for the grounds. Ornate casting

XIV-23-A. Biggin "French coffee pot." *Nickel-plated copper, "extra well made and the up-to-date thing." Hinged cover, ebony [perhaps ebonized] handle. 1 pt. or 2 pts. From Albert Pick catalog, 1909. You know if you see one in an antique shop now, the nickel [oooh, icky proletarian] plating will have been surgically removed to reveal the copper & improve price.* **$65+**

depicts a hand bell surrounded with Art Nouveau scrolls, etc., & the word "BELL," one of 70 styles mfd. by Arcade Mfg. Co., in their "Crystal" line, Freeport, IL, c.1908. .... **$400-$500**
Coffee mill, wall/side, on board, sheet iron hopper, cast iron mill & "S" crank, no lid on hopper, but doesn't appear there ever was one, embossed "L. Holts Improved Coffee Mill," eagle & banner saying "Patent." Looks 1850s; no patent record for a Holt between 1790 and 1873 – under "Coffee-berries, Machine for breaking," "Coffee mill," "Mill," "Grinding machine," "Grinding-mill," or "Grist-mill." • According to MacMillan, this should be "E. Holt" ("E" for Elias, although my notes say "L"). Elias Holt worked with Charles Parker: In 1829, Charles Parker "went into business for himself. He contracted with [Patrick] Lewis & [Elias] Holt [Meriden, CT] to deliver a certain number of coffee mills every month." Unfortunately for this mystery, those

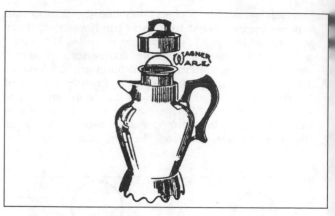

XIV-24. Drip coffee pot. *"French style," cast aluminum, 3 parts with inner basket, 3-pt. capacity. Mfd. by Wagner, Sidney, OH. "It makes coffee without boiling by the French [drip] method. It keeps coffee hot for a long time. The pot also is a beautiful pitcher. It will keep lemonade, etc., cold for a long period. It may be used for ice water by putting the cracked ice in the basket." 1930 ad. Similar pots with the scalloped bottom edge were made by other companies.* **$75+**

mills were box or lap mills, not side mills for mounting to the wall. Help!................................. **$85+**
Coffee mill, wall/side, screwed to board, sheet & cast iron, cast iron crank, marked "P. S. & W. Co. No. 6," Peck, Stow & Wilcox, CT, 5-1/2"H, 3rd to 4th quarter 19th C. .... **$75+**

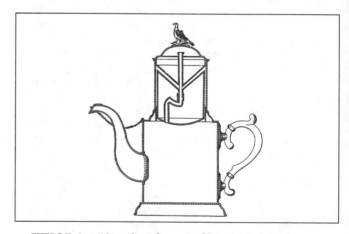

XIV-25-A. "Condensing Coffee-Pot" patent. *E. Hall Covel, NYC, NY, got this patent Feb. 8, 1859 (#22,856); it is for a class of pots "in which the vapor from the water in which the coffee is boiled is condensed in a separated chamber, and returned to the body of the pot to retain the aroma of the coffee, and consists in providing a largely increased amount of surface, against, or in which, the vapor of the boiling coffee is condensed, to be returned to the body of the pot to mingle with its contents, and in placing a water valve in the steam pipe of the pot to act as a safety valve, which ... allows the steam to escape ... if the boiling should be so intense as to create steam more rapidly than could be condensed." This explanation is very clear & may explain other condensing coffee makers in this chapter. Note the bird finial – it appears to be a hawk or eagle.*

XIV-23-B. Biggin coffee maker, *and possibly a lamp filler, both in pieced tin. Note the delightful* **zigzag brace** *to the long spout at right. 19th C. Photograph courtesy Oveda Maurer Antiques, San Anselmo, CA.* **$125+; $100+**

Coffee mill, wall/side, screwed to piece of wood, which is then screwed to the wall, japanned cast iron, "Sun No. 94," Sun Mfg. Co., Greenfield, OH, c.1900. .... **$100**

Coffee mill, wall/side, tin & iron, "Parker #60," Meriden, CT, c.1860s to 1900 • This looks like the "Eagle" side mill pat'd. by J. & E. Parker, Meriden, on Feb. 7, 1860 (#27,065), and so marked on round stamped brass ID disc on hopper. The "Eagle" came in four sizes: #50, #60, #70 & #80, and sold in the Dover Stamping Co. catalog of 1869. .... **$65**

Coffee mill, wall/side, wood, drawer & crank have white china knobs, signed "I. D. Post, Lahaska, PA," last quarter 19th C. **$225**

Coffee mill, wall/side, unusual fold down type, adjustable mill parts, deep hopper & crank of cast iron, these 3 basic elements fitted to a wooden platform which is hinged to fold up against the wall. It would have to be mounted somewhere where a receptacle could be placed, & may have seemed more ingenious that it was in practice, "Lone Star," J. M. Waddel Mfg. Co., c.1890. Very desirable. .... **$250+**

Coffee mill, wall/side, wooden box with iron lid & with one glass side for viewing the beans above the cast iron mill housing and crank, simple iron receptacle for grounds below. Advertised as "A reliable grinder at a very low price ... for customers of limited means." "X-Ray Mill," mfd. by Arcade Mfg. Co., Freeport, IL, c.1908. .... **$125-$180+**

Coffee mills, wall-mount canister top

Coffee mill, cast iron, decorated tin cylindrical hopper (like upside down bottle screwed into top of iron body), "Regal #44," Landers, Frary & Clark, early 20th C. .... **$60+**

Coffee mill, mounted on board, iron, large glass canister with red lettering "Koffie," Dutch (?), c.1890s-1910. .... **$90+**

XIV-25-B. Coffee boiler & teapot & biggin. (L) & (M) Enameled graniteware, with paint-enameled turned wooden handles, gadrooned domed hinged lids. St. Louis Stamping Co., St. Louis, MO. Ad in The Metal Worker, Aug. 20, 1892; (R) Biggin, for drip-style coffee making, which was also known as "French style." Graniteware and tin, from Matthai-Ingram catalog, c.1890. **$125-$150**

XIV-26. Souvenirs of huge coffee pot in Winston-Salem, NC. Black-painted cast pot (spelter or zinc) metal, and cast brass version, both 5-1/4"H. I suspect brass one is older, maybe from the 1930s. **$5-$15**

Coffee mill, cast iron with glass canister, marked "Crystal No. 3" on glass, mfd. by Arcade Mfg. Co., Freeport, IL, c.1890s-1910. • **Arcades** are the most commonly found coffee mills, in various models & sizes. Having "Crystal" on the glass canister adds value, as they are easily broken, and could be replaced with other glass jars. .... **$125-$150+**

Coffee mill, cast iron mill housing & crank & bracket, finished in black, white or blue enamel, clear glass upper bean container has screw-on lid on top & its bottom screws into iron center part, with clear glass grounds holder below, "Enterprise Mfg. Co. #100," 14-1/2"H, early 20th C. With bracket: ... **$200-$300**

Coffee mill, Delft blue & white pottery, iron works & crank, Dutch, English or German – prob. the latter, 1930s. .... **$75-$100**

Coffee mill, painted or bronzed japanned cast iron, oblong upper box holds beans above grinder, cast iron front has shield cutout with glass window to show beans, below mill is spring-tension screw with plate that holds cup or can tightly against bottom of mill to catch grounds, "Golden Rule Blend Coffee. The Finest Blend in the World," Citizen's Wholesale Supply Co., Columbus, OH, 17-1/2"H, early 20th C. .... **$225+**

Coffee mill, red & black sheet tin canister & cup, cast iron mill housing, "Aroma #9," Bronson & Walton Co., Cleveland, OH, early 1900s. .... **$85+**

Coffee mill, mounted to board, blue, red, green & white lithographed tin oblong canister above, depicts fat Dutch girl & sea scenery, cast iron mill & catch-can below in bracket, marked "Holland Beauty" under woman's image, mfd. by Bronson-Walton Co., Cleveland, OH, pat'd. July 9, 1901. Value is mostly in fine condition lithographed tin canister. .... **$95-$125+**

Coffee mill, screwed to board, oblong lithographed sheet metal canister top, in exaggerated grainy wood design, oval glass viewing window, below is plain cast iron mill housing & crank, with grounds cup that matches top, "Oplex #10," mfd. by Bronson Walton Co., Cleveland, OH, pat'd. July 9, 1901, other patents pending. • Fancier version has little cast iron support for the catcher cup, which received the grounds. ...... **$70-$80**

XIV-27. Post card of "The Big Coffee Pot" in Winston-Salem, NC. Color lithograph, reprinted over fairly long period. This one was mailed in 1940. The conical coffee pot itself, with the braced crooked neck spout and handle with reinforced grip, is made of painted tin and was erected in 1858 near where it still stands today, the junction of South Main St., Old Salem Rd., and Brookstown Ave. in Old Salem. Tinsmith-merchants Julius & Samuel Mickey, who wanted to attract customers to their roofing, tin and stove business, had it built (or perhaps built it themselves). Fortunately, it lasted through two metal drives and various vicissitudes. The pot, probably based on a Moravian style, is 7'3"H x 27" diam. at top & 64" diam. at bottom. It is calculated that it would hold 740-1/2 gallons of coffee. • If you want other big signs & wayside attractions, there is the giant sheet metal coffee pot (24 feet high) & cup, in Davidson, Saskatchewan (see photo at Craig Thom's site: ***www.thom. org/gallery/statues/SKDVcoffeepot/);***) a giant waitress to serve you, at Martha's Café (see Thom's photo at ***www.thom.org/gallery/statues/ IDBFmartha/***). Too late to see it now, but there was a 25 foot high steaming A & P coffee cup on Broadway in NYC many years ago; it was the work of Douglas Leigh, who created many huge electric signs at Times Square.

Coffee mill, screwed to board, oblong lithographed tin canister above, cast iron mill housing, canister marked "Silver Lake" with four-leaf clover, mfd. by Bronson Walton Co., c.1901-1905. • The works & the shape were, I think, patented July 9, 1901. I'm sure that different styles or decorations for the lithographed canister were introduced at least yearly. (Note: an embossed glass canister version of the "Silver Lake" sold on eBay in 2001 for over $500.) .... **$75+**

Coffee mill, green lithographed tin canister, "Lightning No. 2 Belmont Hardware Co.," green catch-cup... **$300-$500**

Coffee mill, mounted on oak board, tin rectangular canister above black-painted mill, red, red & white, lithographed with coffee cup, "Bouquet Roasted Coffee O. V. Tracy & Co., Syracuse, NY," red receiver can or catch-cup. .... **$400-$600**

Coffee mill, sheet metal & cast iron, screwed to board, oblong box with a small drawer below the mill to catch the grounds, & a larger storage drawer for the coffee beans on the side, cast iron S-crank handle, brass plate on mill's hopper embossed "John Luther's Coffee Mill, Warren, RI," 12"H x 16"L overall, "Pat'd Aug. 11, 1843" (#3,215). .... **$200+**

Coffee mill, sheet steel canister painted black, cast iron crank & grinder, wood knob, green & white label on can, "Universal, #0012," Landers, Frary & Clark, 13-1/4"H, pat'd. Feb. 14, 1905. .... **$75-$90**

Coffee Mills, Urns, with Single or Double Wheels, Countertop

Some for home use, but mostly for stores: These are sometimes called "uprights," but I prefer "wheelers." According to Larry Meeker, these have been "avidly collected for years. Lately one of the notable trends is to pay a premium for models in 'super condition.' Mills with fantastic original paint, and pristine, vivid decals can command previously-unheard of prices today. The same holds true for unusual colors and rare models. Condition can be very subjective. We've all heard 'it's in great condition for its age,' but for collectors paying top dollar, good condition isn't enough; they demand something close to 'near mint' before they get their wallets out. Watch this happen time after time in auction results: a typical fair condition #2 mill will bring $200 or so; a really nice one will bring $500-$600+; and one of those minty nice ones can go to $2,000 or more."

Coffee mill, for home use – upright like the "wheelers" but no wheels on this smallest model, cast iron, painted black with some fancy gold striping trim & stencils, open top urn body-hopper breaks [comes apart] at fattest part, where crank is, for cleaning, etc. Drawer in base has white porcelain knob. Capacity of hopper is only 4 oz. of coffee, "Enterprise #1," American, 12-1/2"H, crank 6"L, c.1890s-1910. • $2.25 was the original cost. Good condition: .... **$275+**

Coffee mill, cast iron with original paint & stenciled designs, double wheel, drawer below, body "breaks" in center, hopper lid surmounted by eagle, "Enterprise #7," 21-1/2"H, 17" diam. wheel, dated 1873, still selling, with replacement parts, at least as late as c.1905. .... **$600-$800**

❖ NOTES ❖

Replacement parts for coffee mills – Every part was replaceable. Perhaps of most interest to the general collector is the fact that 20 eagles were offered, from 25¢ each for the small mills up to 60¢ for larger ones. Looking closely at catalog pages, you can see differences in eagles: (1) Flying with wings spread wide & up-curved; (2) flying, wings out in downstroke position; (3) standing with wings way out; or (4) tucked in partway, heads left, heads right. What a warehouse-find these spare part eagles would be!

Coffee mill, cast iron & wood, double wheel, painted blue, "S. H. Co." (Simmons Hardware Co.), St. Louis, MO, 13"H, late 19th C. • Larry Meeker reports on a "Keen Kutter" crossover phenomenum: "One of these Simmons Hardware 'Koffee Krusher' Keen Kutter #2 size mills brought the incredible sum of $4,500 at the annual Keen Kutter collectors' auction in Missouri in 2001. Others have not done quite as well on the internet auctions." .... **$300-$450**

Coffee mill, countertop type with double flywheels, painted & decorated cast iron mounted on wooden base, hinged lid for hopper, drawer below, "Coles No. 2," 9-3/4" diam. wheels, mfd. by Coles Mfg. Co., Philadelphia, PA, c.1906. • Coles made smaller & larger mills, for coffee & spices. .... **$500-$800**

Coffee mill, countertop, cast iron, double wheel with openwork 5 petal flower gear design, shapely body painted red and black, with gold pinstripes, wheels, with name cast around outside rim, rich dark blue with letters picked out in gold, the vase-shaped hopper above is painted light & dark blue with design of sun's rays in red on top, instead of being polished brass. Eagle & flag decals on body. "Elgin National Coffee Mill," 26"H, 1880s to c.1890s-1910. .... **$600-$900**

Coffee mill, countertop double wheel type, openwork wheels with 6 petal flower, red painted cast iron, brass knobs on pull out drawer, & hopper lid, wood crank handle, marked on wheel "John Wright, Wrightsville, PA," 11"H x 7"W, advertised in 1973. .... **$200-$300**

Coffee mill, countertop for commercial use, red painted cast iron, spectacular double wheels, stately plinth base, cylindrical bean hopper with domed lid, with blue & yellow paint trim, & applied landscape & portrait bust decals on hopper & grounds box, "Lane Brothers & Co. #15," Poughkeepsie, NY, 29-1/2"H, wheels 16-1/2", pat'd. Feb. 9, 1875. ... **$900-$1,300**

Coffee mill, counter or tabletop, small 2 wheeler, painted cast iron, mfd. by "Swift," Poughkeepsie, NY, c.1890s-1910. .... **$350-$450**

Coffee mill, countertop for home, painted & decorated cast iron, double wheel, drawer in base, breaks apart in middle, no eagle on hopper top, "Family Mill No. 2," Enterprise Mfg. Co., 4 oz. hopper, 12-1/2"H, 8-3/4" wheels, late 19th C. Condition very important. .... **$400-$1,100**

Coffee mill, countertop store model, 2 wheels, cast iron, original red & black paint, "Landers, Frary & Clark," New Britain, CT, 10-1/2" diam. wheels, c.1890s-1910. .... **$400-$600**

❖ NOTES ❖

L, F & C in Colors. Landers, Frary & Clark produced one of the most varied lines of color combinations: two-tones – red & black, black & white; and all green, all black, and all blue models. Larry Meeker writes that the original condition, not retouched, or repainted, plays a huge role in determining value.

Coffee mills, countertop, painted & decorated cast iron, nickeled brass hopper, "Enterprise Mfg. Co." Mills with these hoppers are denoted by model numbers with fractions. The "2-1/2," for example, had a large hopper, while the "2-1/4" had a smaller hopper. Meeker reports these can go for: ..... **$1,200-$2,000**

XIV-28. Coffee pot. *Pieced tin, squared short curved spout, unusual fanciful curve to handle. Brass mushroom finial to convex lid, 10"H. Pennsylvania, mid 19th C. Courtesy Carol Bohn, Mifflinburg, PA. While this one is not decorated on the surface, the extra* **wiggle** *in the handle adds great sculptural charm, which many people pay extra for. (See XIV-23-B, -31, -33 for more odd spout braces. What a wonderful collection theme that would be!* **$350+**

Coffee mill, double wheel store model, countertop but with funnel opening to lower compartment instead of drawer, painted & stenciled cast iron, eagle on top same as others, "Enterprise No. 12," Enterprise Mfg. Co., 32"H with 25" diam. wheel, late 19th C., but sold into 20th C. .... **$600-$1,000**

Coffee mill, store model for countertop, cast iron painted red & stenciled, with 2 large daisy petal-spoked wheels, convex round hopper has domed top, with cast eagle on top, white porcelain knob on drawer below, regulated to grind coarse or fine, "seventy-five turns by hand will granulate a pound of Coffee as fine as required" ... "and by power (larger Grinders being supplied) fifty turns." "Enterprise Mfg. Co., #9," wheels are 19-1/2" diam., overall 24"H, c.1890s-1910. This is the 4th from biggest overall size of this type with lower drawer. • The larger are the #10, 28"H, 19-1/2" wheel, concave flared urn hopper; #209 & #210, which both have 25" diam. wheels. #209, 33"H, has an iron wheel, a fat urn-shaped hopper surmounted with an eagle with wings spread. #210, 37"H, is even more spectacular, as it has a nickel-plated hopper, in a concave-sided urn-shape, surmounted by eagle with wings partly folded down. •

There are also smaller ones. The full range of capacity is 1-3/4 lbs. to 7-1/2 lbs. coffee. • Then there are floor-standing models with their own fancy cast iron bases. For those, the added value is considerable, probably triple, the countertop styles............. **$500+**

Coffee mill, cast iron, 2-wheel countertop, #200 Chas. Parker, Meriden, CT, 8-1/2" diam. wheels. • Larry Meeker reports that "Charles Parker mills have eclipsed 'Enterprise' mills in collectability." .... **$750-$1,200**

Coffee mill, cast iron, 2-wheel countertop, #3000 Chas. Parker, 10-3/4" diam. wheels..................... **$1,000+**

Coffee mill, cast iron, styled in a way that makes it look like a large floor mounted mill (at least in a photo), but is a countertop that's only 16"H, wheels are 10-1/2" diam., unusual hopper with a sliding door. Chas. Parker #202. Ultra rare................................. **$1,500+**

Coffee Mills, Floor-Standing Double Wheelers

Coffee mill, floor model on 4 legs, ornate cast iron base in original paint, huge double flywheels, flared vase-shaped hopper is right, I believe, but looks rather small for the wheels, stepped dome lid with wings-up eagle, "Enterprise #18," 5 feet 8"H, 31" wheels, c.1890s-1910. • I've seen one advertised as size "18-1/2"; I think this must be a model with a nickel-plated brass hopper, as described above by Larry Meeker. • If you think you'll buy one through the mail, it weighs 233 pounds, and was originally "packed in two crates and one box.".................................... **$1,500-$2,000**

XIV-29. Coffee pots – wriggled & punched. *Both Pennsylvanian pieced tin with inverted cone bodies and crooked-neck spouts.* **(L)** *Pot with flared footed base. Its funnel-like conical hinged lid, which gives it a slightly comical appearance, is very uncommon. Note extra brace to handle. The style of decoration is called* **"wriggled."** *Signed with serpentine maker's mark, early to mid 19th C. 10-3/4"H.* **(R)** *A jauntier pot, 11-3/4"H, has maker's smoothly domed lid. Its decoration called* **"punchwork."** *Signed in beautiful capital serif letters by* "W[illoughy] Shade for Mary Shade," *and dated March 18, 1848. We do not know who Mary was, but such coffee pots were usually, if not always, presentation pieces given to brides.* • *In* **wriggleswork,** *the graving tool was skidded across surface, making a jiggedy mark to outline & fill shapes of flowers, leaves, etc.* • **Punchwork** *is done with a punch, but although it is hit hard enough to make a dimple on the tin's surface, it is not allowed to puncture or pierce it. Photograph courtesy Sotheby Parke-Bernet, NYC.* **$2,700+**

XIV-30. Pieced tinwares, *including coffee pots, & unusual conical vessel. Compare the dark pot in very back with pot in XIV-28. Note the two-handled cup or sugar bowl, & the punctured tin cheese mold in foreground. Photograph courtesy Oveda Maurer Antiques, San Anselmo, CA. Sugar bowl, oil can, maybe:* **$125+** *; coffee pots:* **$250+**

Coffee mill, floor-standing model on intricate cast iron base, 2 wheels. Cast iron with brass hopper & tall finial, "John C. Dell & Son," American, 33" diam. wheels, pat'd. 1884. Dell mills very rare. .... **$1,500-$2,000**

Coffee mill, floor-standing store model, 2 wheels, cast iron with all original black & red paint, "Elgin National," mfd. by Woodruff & Edwards Co., Elgin, IL, 65"H x 27-1/2"W, c.1890s-1910......... **$1,300-$1,600**

Coffee mill, floor-standing store model, ornate lyre base, double flywheels (the petal spokes of which are much fatter than on the Enterprise), large brass hopper with eagle finial, all original red paint, "Elgin National Coffee Mills," 60"H, c.1890s-1910. .... **$1,000-$1,300+**

Coffee mills, miscellaneous

Coffee mill, cast iron, 4 legged, frame screwed to long board with 3 fingerholes at each end, huge crank, tin drawer slides underneath between the legs, key at side to take works apart for cleaning, cup-shaped hopper, an extraordinarily handsome mill, not marked, Pennsylvania (?) or maybe Austrian (?), mill is only 6-3/4"H (exclusive of crank) x 5-1/2" x 5-7/8", mid 19th C.................................... **$250+**

Coffee mill, cast iron, brass, looks something like a cannon with an "S" crank where the cannon ball would come out, drawer below, "Persepolis Coffee Grinder," Metropolitan Brass Foundry, NYC, according to Joe MacMillan, prob. made only between 1902-1910. .... **$800-$1,000**

Coffee mill, cast iron cup or hopper & bracket to screw to board, this example mounted to thick wooden paddle, porcelain knob on crank, saw-toothed opening in bottom of hopper, marked "ADAMS" on handle, opposite the word "PATENT," 12-1/2"L with 4-1/2" diam. hopper, date "1840" on underside. • Dealer Bob "Primitive Man" Cahn found it. He discovered that ADAMS also made paint mills of a portable kind (perhaps also larger sizes). • Again, Joe MacMillan to the rescue: This was patented by Calvin Adams, Pittsburgh, PA, on Sept. 25, 1840, #1,795. .... **$400+**

Coffee mill, very primitive wooden body with punched iron decorative sides, wide flaring hopper with top crank, the whole thing mounted to seat-sized paddle. It is, in fact, a seat, to be straddled while working. Turkish, 18th C. .... **$350-$550**

the #750, as above, & the #550 with a crank, instead of a flywheel, which was also 17-1/4"H. The ID number is on the hopper................... **$200-$400**

❖ NOTES ❖

Turkish Imports – I include a Turkish mill because in the last three or four years of the 1980s, lots of kitchen antiques began showing up in flea markets, imported from Turkey. At the time of this writing, most of these antique imports are copper frying pans with interestingly braced iron handles, or similar saucepans, or the more familiar exotic coffee pots. Some wholesalers are pricing these by the pound. In addition, around the turn of the century, many wares, mostly copper and brass, were imported to the U.S., and sold chiefly by dealers in NYC's brass district, down on Allen Street. This was true well into the 1960s, and people shopped there for samovars for 60 years or more. Turkey shared a border with Russia, so it is likely that some Turkish wares showed up in the emigré shops. Other Turkish coffee mills are much fancier, reflecting ancient Byzantine and Persian crafts of inlay and mosaic; some are made of several kinds of wood, even with bone decoration and brass fittings. A star and crescent moon decoration easily identify a piece as Turkish, but this symbol was not adopted for their flag until 1936. I don't know how long ago the symbols were popularly used. • To confuse things, a popular American fraternal order, the Shriners, use as their emblem a Turkish scimitar (curve upwards) with a downpointing crescent moon with a 5-point star pendent from the scimitar's blade. The Shriners wear a fez, which is also Turkish. Some decorative arts of American origin have the scimitar insignia or emblem.

Turkomania – In 1743, a young (and presumably attractive) Turkish ambassador arrived in France. This excited the French to an even higher excitement about all things Turkish – a fad that had been around for two or three decades. Everything Turkish was desirable: rugs, book designs, music, theater, coffee – and, presumably, coffee mills. Ersatz potentates and sultanas had their portraits painted in turbans and Turkish costumes. The end of the fad coincided with the Revolution, at the end of the 19th century. • **Pepper mills.** See also the listings for Pepper mills in Chapter I (Cut, Grind).

Coffee mill, wood base, vertical post that supports sheet iron 5-1/2" diam. hopper with snap-on hinged lid. Sometimes called a "post mill." Below the hopper are the horizontal works in a cylinder, with side crank; very delicate looking. George Washington had one almost the same which is now in the Smithsonian, possibly made by an artisan from the illustration & description in the famed 1750s *Diderot's Encyclopedia*. French or even poss. American, about 23"H, late 18th C. .... **$600-$800**

"Coffee" mill, stump- or box-top, cast iron, with one wheel, simple angular open cast body, shallow wide hopper, for cracking bones, shells, corn, etc., for poultry feed, "Enterprise #750," 17-1/4"H, with 19" diam. wheel, c.1890s-1910. • **Confusable.** – "Coffee" is in quotes, because this Bone, Shell, Root, Bark, Salt & Corn Grinder is sometimes confused with a coffee grinder. Enterprise made 3 of these grinders – one wall-mounted, the #650, which was 11"H; and

❖ NOTES ❖

1846. "If you use a coffee-biggin, let the coffee be ground very fine and packed tight in the strainer; pour on boiling water, stop the spout of the pot, shut the lid close, and place it upon a heater kept for the purpose. This is made at table." Mrs. Cornelius, *The Young Housekeepers Friend*, or, *A Guide to Domestic Economy & Comfort*, Boston & NY: 1846.

1884. "Two cylindrical tin vessels, one fitting into the other; the bottom of the upper one is a fine strainer, another coarser strainer is placed on this with a rod running upwards from its center; the finely ground coffee is put in, and then another strainer is slipped on the rod, over the coffee, the boiling water is poured on the upper sieve and falls in a shower upon the coffee, filtering through it to the coarse strainer at the bottom, which prevents the coffee from filling up the holes of the finer strainer below it." *Practical Housekeeping*, Minneapolis: 1884.

Coffee Biggins, Boilers, Percolators & Pots

The original drip coffee maker, was invented by a Mr. Biggin c.1800.

Coffee biggin, French style, tall cylindrical body, enameled a soft sage green with black chicken wire design overlaid, with rows of white dogwood blossoms, partially fluted nickeled white metal mountings – spout & handle, tall white metal insert & domed lid, enameled white inside, Manning, Bowman & Co., Meri-

XIV-31. Tinwares. *Note low-originating straight spout on coffee pot at right. But for me, of special interest is the funny spout and its* **serpentine brace** *on the vessel at left. It appears to be an oiler or lamp filler of some kind. (Cup or sugar bowl is same as one in previous picture.) This dealer always has unusual metalwares. Photograph courtesy Oveda Maurer Antiques, San Anselmo, CA.* **$125+**

den, CT, capacity 2 pints, c. 1880s. • Price on highly decorative pieces is hard to determine. Partly this is because many advanced collectors prefer the subtleties of plainer wares, while the "outsider" assumes the fancy ones ought to bring the most. .... **$375+**

Coffee biggin, gray graniteware pot with gooseneck spout, tin cylindrical vessel (the biggin part) with domed top, this one from Matthai-Ingram catalog and American, others imported, came in different sizes for capacities from 1/2 to 5 qts., this one about 8"H plus another 5" for tin part, c.1870s or 1880s. .... **$175+**

Coffee biggin, tin, cast white metal handle originally painted black. A cork stopper is kept in a little dead end funnel on straight spout's bridge or brace strut, except when it's transferred to spout when coffee has to be kept hot inside, "Chesterman's Coffee Pot," William Chesterman, Centralia, IA, 9-3/8"H, pat'd. July 19, 1859, & Jan. 24, 1860. .... **$175+**

Coffee biggin, silvery plated (tin? Britannia? not nickel) copper, straight-sided cylindrical lower body, slightly smaller diam. drip top, curved handle, straight spout, large round knob on lid, American, prob. CT, 11"H, mid to 3rd quarter 19th C. .... **$200+**

Coffee pot, a sort of combined French biggin & drip percolator, conical metal body with long straight spout originating near bottom of pot, fancy open-work scrolled cast iron handle, long "stove pipe" drip cylinder, with wooden rod or pressure block used to force hot water through the grounds placed in the perforated interior strainer, Manning-Bowman & Co., Meriden, CT, pat'd. 1873. .... **$135+**

Coffee Boilers

These have tapered sides and big bodies, with smallish V-neck spouts. Typically seen in cowboy movie campfire scenes.

XIV-32. Coffee pot. *Paint-decorated tin, (I don't know the color, which would be important in determining value – see text for relative color values). Short straight spout, hinged lid with curled-tin knob. Note diagonal piecing seam under handle, indicative of small sheets of tin. Note also the faint light circle behind the flowers: this is thought by some to be near-proof of Pennsylvania origins, and yet coffee pots having this circle and with exactly this kind of border near the top, are said by others to be typical of Connecticut provenance. Generally speaking, it seems that the straight spout tends to be Connecticut, while the crooked spout is Pennsylvanian. Remember: wares were made in CT for "Western" trades, & peddled in NY & PA. 8-7/8"H, 19th C. Picture courtesy of the National Museum of American History, Smithsonian Institution.*

XIV-33. Coffee pot? *At least so identified by the Smithsonian. I believe it may be a large lamp filler or even an olive-oil can. At any rate, a tinsmith's work of art. Funnel top (for making drip coffee? for safer filling with the lamp oil?). Hinged lid, strap handle,* **swag-braced spout.** *I think it's a lamp filler because of the smallness of the spout's tip, and the angle of the spout. 11"H, 19th C. Picture courtesy of the National Museum of American History, Smithsonian Institution.* **$275+**

Coffee boiler, blue agateware, wire bail handle, fixed side handle, tapered body, American, 10"H x 8-3/4" diam. base, late 19th C. .... **$135+**

Coffee boiler, blue & white swirl enamelware, with small V-neck lip or spout, American or European, late 19th C. .... **$75+**

Coffee boiler, gray graniteware, with typical V-neck lip or spout, "Granite Iron Ware," mfd. by St. Louis Stamping Co., St. Louis, MO, 8-1/2"H, pat'd. May 30, 1876, May 8, 1877. .... **$125+**

Coffee boiler, mottled blue enamelware, enamelware lid with wooden finial, enameled handle, American or European, late 19th or early 20th C. .... **$75+**

Coffee boiler, tin with wide strap handle, plus small strap "tipper" opposite lip to ease pouring, from F. A. Walker catalog, imported or American, different sizes, including 6, 8, 10 & 12 qt. capacity, c.1870s................ **$65+**

❖ NOTES ❖

1878, 1978, 2078? The Tin Pan Nuisance – 'If I were Duke of this country,' began a friend, as we rode through an elegant section of the country, 'I would punish with banishment every man or woman who threw tin trumpery into the street.' – 'Amen,' said I, 'and send them out of the country with a string of oyster cans for a necklace.' This was no new spectacle – we had seen the like a hundred times before – but in this instance it was especially aggravating. There was a large country-house, with a beautiful lawn extending to the fashionable avenue, and at one side to a public road, not fashionable, but greatly traveled, and in a small ravine that made a gap under the fence and opened into the roadside gutter, was tumbled a mélange of old tin-ware – coffee and tea-pots, pans, cups, watering pots, innumerable fruit and vegetable cans, and broken crockery. It was an ugly blotch on the otherwise fair beauty of the place. ... What to do with such old trumpery, that cannot be burnt, seems to be an unsolved riddle with the majority of country people. In cities, the housemaid stuffs it in a barrel, which the ash and garbage-men carry away. In the country, it is commonly pitched into some out of the way place, under porch floors, into vacant cellars, under currant bushes, etc., but always where in some moment it will be discovered. ... "So far as I know, there is no better way to dispose of broken and worn out wares, than to put them into a well dug for the purpose – one which has a cover, and which, when full, can be earthed and grassed over. Such a receptacle has its advantages – one always knows where to look for old basins and pans, if they are needed, for broken pottery when pieces are required for drainage, while bits of glass are thus put forever out of the way of children's feet.

"The sight of old tin 'lying around loose' [must] have a charm for some people, judging from the way they distribute it in their backyards and front ditches. A man's back-yard is his private property; if he chooses to make it a hideous looking place, it is his own affair; but the man who makes a public highway the receptacle of his trumpery, should be prosecuted by the Commissioner of Roads, and punished as a polluter of public morals. It is as manifest [an] indelicacy to allow such broken & worn out domestic utensils to public view, as to throw old shoes in the street." – MWF, *American Agriculturist*, April 1878.

Coffee boiler, white & brown speckled enamelware, nickeled base & lid, wood finial & fancy handle, Manning, Bowman & Co., 9"H, pat'd. 1889. ... **$225**

Coffee boiler, white & sky blue marbleized enamelware, bail handle & turned wooden grip, American, 13"H, c.1890s-1910... **$225+**

Coffee boiler, thresher's boiler type – that is, a very big one for the harvest crew, green & white swirl enamelware, American (?), c.1890s-1910.............. **$200+**

Coffee drip maker

Coffee drip maker, individual size, aluminum, little non-folding legs, one of which serves as handle,

XIV-34. "Infuser for tea or coffee," two views. *"By the insertion of the stopper into the spout of the pot, the water poured into the [upper chamber] infuser is retained there until it has dissolved all the desirable properties of the tea or coffee. By withdrawing the stopper the prepared beverage is allowed to run into the pot, from which it may be served in the usual way. This infuser is made in three styles – tin, enameled ware and stoneware, and it comes in various sizes." Imported from Europe by G. M. Thurnauer & Bro., NYC wholesalers of housewares. Article in* House Furnishing Review, *July 1905. • See also Chesterman's pot in XIV-21-B.*

snug-fitting lid, put coffee grounds in cup, which is marked with measuring line on side, pour water in, put lid on, no maker name, 3"H x 3-7/16" diam., 1940s. • My mother's note inside reads "In the early days of WWII, a teacher at Hutchinson School (Memphis, TN) gave me this to send to my mother to make her one-cuppa." .... **$10+**

Coffee makers

Coffee maker, electric drip style, chrome 4 legged urn, the sides flaring up & out, drop ring handles on each side, 2 side-by-side spigots – one for coffee, one for hot water to "dilute to taste" or for making tea, "Edicraft Menlo Siphonator," mfd. in the Laboratories of Thomas A. Edison, Inc., Orange, NJ, 9 cup capacity, c.1930. • The original cost was $45 – a very high price in Depression years. For $42.50 more, you could also get a sugar holder, creamer & a sort of truncated oval tray to match. • For other electric wares not related to coffee, see Chapter XVIII (Electrical Gadgets & Appliances)...................... **$45-$65**

Coffee maker, electric, chrome globe, Pyrex lid. 15"H overall x 10" diam. "Labelle Silver Co., Brooklyn, NY, Cat No 1955A, Automatic," c1955. .... **$25+**

Coffee maker, for dining room, on stand with 4 cabriole legs, over alcohol lamp, all copper except for "fishbowl" glass globe top through which passes the vertical tube which circulated the boiling water through the grounds, "Empress Ware, No. 2," New York Stamping Co., Brooklyn, NY, pat'd. March 2, 1893 and Sept. 17, 1895. • Very similar pieces with alcohol lamps were made by other companies. Manning-Bowman made the "Meteor Circulating Coffee Percolator," with a sort of sugar bowl-shaped glass top; another was the "American Coffee & Tea Extractor," by Buffalo Mfg. Co., Buffalo, NY, advertised in January 1903; a third was the "Auto Vac Glass Coffee Filter," maker unknown, advertised in 1917; then the "Paramount Percolator," NYC, with a glass top and bottom, advertised in 1915; a fifth was advertised by F. A. Walker, "housefurnishers" in Boston who imported many of their goods. This was the "French Steam Coffee Pot," of copper or silver-plated copper, with a glass sugar-bowl like top part. It came in sizes from 2 cups to 20. Sternau, a NYC company known to us for "Sterno," made a handsome coffee maker outfit on a stand with columns at each corner of the stand & a sugar bowl-shaped top part. Sterno got a Feb. 17, 1865 patent for the fuel part, and a Nov. 10, 1908 patent for the rest. • All such decorative wares were aimed at the new market that liked to cook at the table – newly servant-less hostesses, who could also set up chafing dishes, waffle makers, and other pieces, heated by alcohol lamps or electricity.. **$45-$65**

Coffee maker, tin with turned wood handle, strainer inside, American, c.1910 to 1915. .... **$15-$20**

Coffee maker, vacuum type, 2 globular glass sections, glass rod filter, black phenolic plastic handle & lid, small black measuring scoop, Cory Glass Coffee Brewer Co., Chicago, IL, early 1940s. In a way, the most collectible part is the measure. .... **$15+**

Coffee maker, 2 fishbowl-shaped glass globes, one above the other, scalloped red plastic "skirt" for the lower globe, part of the handle assembly, cover of top globe is also red, has odd little tabletop "gas" stove, with 2 handles, called the "Bride's Special," with "Pyrex" glass, "Moldex" plastic, mfd. by The Silex Co., Hartford, CT, about 18"H, late 1930s. • Silex made several models – gas & electric – at the time. A fancy "De Luxe Lido" model had chrome instead of the "Moldex" & a sort of saucered chrome base. Another model, the "Buffet Service," for parties, had 2 bottom pouring pots, with one top globe. This model came on a 2 burner electric stove with black plastic base & small black handles at each end. .... **$15+**

Coffee maker, "Pyrex Vaculator," 2 glass globes one on top, plastic handle, 10"H. Sits on top of the 3-3/4" diam. "Silex Candlelight Coffee Warmer," of glass with chrome top. .... **$15+**

Coffee percolators

Coffee percolator, aluminum, green Depression glass percolator lid, turned wood handle, 4 little feet, no mark, 14"H, 1930s. .... **$18+**

Coffee percolator, stamped aluminum, paneled sides, domed percolator lid set with green glass, turned wood handle, V-neck spout, "A. A. W. Peerless Co., The Better Ware," American Aluminum Ware Co., Newark, NJ, 9"H x 4-7/8" diam., c.1915-1930. .... **$15+**

Coffee percolator, stamped aluminum, slanting sides rounded at bottom, percolator lid, clear glass, somewhat straightened out gooseneck spout, C-shaped black-finished wood handle, No. 69, Landers, Frary & Clark, 7-1/2"H x 5-3/4" diam., c.1915-1930. .... **$15**

Coffee percolator, aluminum with faint gadrooning in "Colonial" pattern, footed base, gooseneck spout, glass percolator top, black-painted shaped wooden handle, looks top-heavy, "Wagner Ware," Sidney, OH, c.1915 (?). Very similar to the Griswold one next, but slightly looser, sloppier design. **$70**

Coffee percolator, aluminum, footed base, gooseneck spout & fancy black wood handle, "Pyrex" percolator top, Griswold Mfg. Co., Erie, PA, c.1920. Based on Valentine D. Pfirman's patent #1,257,110, Feb. 19, 1918, assigned to Griswold. This was at the height of the first American "colonial style revival" of the 2oth C.; at least two more were to come – the 1950s & the 1970s. .... **$135+**

Coffee percolator, cast aluminum chunky gadrooned style called "Colonial," short V-neck pouring lip, "The Griswold Mfg. Co. Erie PA, USA," c.1934. .... **$70**

Coffee percolator, copper & brass, urn shaped with wooden handles, finial & spigot handle, nice footed base, on stand, Manning & Bowman, 13"H, pat'd. 1906. .... **$85-$110**

Coffee percolating drip type, nickeled copper, straight sided cylinder with beading around top edge, straight tapered spout set midway up, vertical bracket handle of ebonized turned wood, ball valve in spout is a real marble, very fine wire mesh (called wire gauze) filter compartment gets filled with grounds & put down in pot, then strainer with vertical pipe – the "air tube" – put in on top of filter. Domed cover with knob. Medallion on side: "Marion Harland Tea & Coffee Pot," mfd. by Silver & Co., Brooklyn, NY, 4 cup capacity, c.1890, but made over a 30 year period or more. • This also came in polished copper (tinned inside), or in what they called "Old English" finish, which was not defined in catalogs or ads. Possibly a sort of dull pewtery finish? This pot was also advertised with curved "question mark" handle. .... **$35+**

Coffee percolator, dark blue spattered enamelware, early 1900s. .... **$75+**

Coffee percolator, light blue speckled enamelware, "Universal," L. F. & C., Landers, Frary & Clark, pat'd. first in 1894. .... **$165+**

Coffee percolator, red & white swirled enamelware, glass insert in lid, 20th C. Red & white enamelware is high among the most sought-after colors. . **$150+**

Coffee percolator, pale green enameled iron, nickeled copper lid & trim, paneled body, tubular handle painted black, aluminum basket, glass top, called in catalog the "High Pattern-Cold Water Type," glass insert in lid is "Fire King," function of the odd little tippy pedestal base was to draw heat up, separating the pedestal from the top is some kind of insulating material, Reed Mfg. Co., Newark, New York (not NJ), 9-7/8"H, 6 cup capacity, c. 1927. (It also came in white.) This particular color, sometimes called **"closet green"** by stove manufacturers, was called "blue" in the Reed catalog. A little Fire King crossover interest. .... **$45+**

Coffee percolator, straight sides, green & tan enamelware, green glass in lid, all interior parts present, American, 1930s. **$35**

Coffee percolator, with rather fat slant-sided metal body, long tapered straight spout originating near bottom, simple strap handle above which is an attached tin funnel – the aperture through which water is poured into a sort of pocket inside pot. Above is a short cylinder, with hinged lid, where the grounds are & where the tube with perforated top terminates. Pour water in, it's forced up tube & percolates out strainer through coffee grounds. A 1911 article (below) told the difference between this early percolator & later ones: in the 1875 one, the water only dripped through one time, instead of over & over. Manning-Bowman & Co., Meriden, CT, for sale in 1875, but pat'd. in 1876. .... **$100+**

❖ NOTES ❖

Archaeological Find – In a large ad featuring a brand new percolator for 1911, come three tantalizing paragraphs in small print, entitled "A Chance Discovery and Its Meaning. (1) While making changes in our factory at Meriden a short time ago, workmen opened up a long forgotten vault in the wall. (2) In the vault were a number of Manning- Bowman Coffee Percolators made from 1865 to 1876. Weird productions compared with modern designs, they show the wonderful progress we have made in Coffee Percolator building since 40 years ago. (3) The next time you are in Meriden, or New York, do not fail to drop in and inspect them." Oh boy, wouldn't you love to have that time machine now?

Coffee percolator, yellow enamelware with green trim, glass top, 20th C. .... **$30+**

Coffee percolator, plated metal tripod base, double-globe glass coffee maker in 2 parts -- the filter part & the serving part, both decorated with leaves, scrolls & chrysanthemums in "silver deposit" on clear glass. The glass parts sit over alcohol heater in base, or can be used on a gas, coal or electric stove, "Auto Vac Glass Coffee Filter," mfd. by Auto Vacuum Freezer Co., NYC, NY, c.1917. .... **$35+**

Coffee percolator, tin, perfectly cylindrical shape, with a perforated grounds cup insert, percolating funnel tube, slightly tapered straight spout originating near

XIV-35. *"Student's coffee pot."* Brass and tin, with wood side handle. 2, 4, 6 and 8 cups. From F. A. Walker catalog, c.1870s. **$45-$60+**

bottom, slightly domed lid with pretty little cast metal finial, graceful question-mark shaped handle. Manufacturer's brochure states that "In using a new pot a slight taste of tin impairs the flavor of the coffee. After a few times using, (or after boiling coffee in the pot a few hours) this entirely disappears." Also stated is that the 2 extra pieces, filtering cup & tubed funnel, "are of a form easily kept clean, durable, and, if necessary, easily repaired or renewed by an ordinary tinsmith." "The Windsor," mfd. by Hubbard & McClary, Windsor, CT, 9 sizes -- from one to 16 qts., c.1870s. .... **$30-$45+**

Coffee percolators, electric

Coffee percolator, electric, 2 glass globes with red phenolic plastic handles & swingaway or swivel lid for lower globe, black plastic base, percolating tube goes up through center, very handsome, "Silex" glass, "Automatic Coffee Percolator" mfd. by General Electric, c.1940s (?). Crossover interest from modernist collectors. .... **$85-$100+**

Coffee percolator, electric, chrome plated brass & copper ball on high flared foot, with funny tapered perky spout, balanced on opposite side by arched white plastic handle, knurled knob on lid, "Table Electric" by Chase Brass & Copper Co., Inc., division of Kennecott Copper Corp., 7 cup capacity, c.1937. • A non-electric companion was a teakettle, a large chromium ball, same kind of tapered spout, much smaller ring foot, white plastic handle forms arches a few inches from spout to backside, describing an arch approx. 1/5 of kettle's diam. .... **$65+**

Coffee percolator, electric, chromium-plated copper vase-shaped footed body & creamer & sugar, all have pendant red-maroon Bakelite™ drop handles. "Keystoneware" set with tray. Marked "Hatfield," "125V," "BAKELITE-MADE IN USA – 250 V." 13-1/4"H x 9-1/4"W including handles. Early 1940s. .... **$40+**

Coffee percolator, electric, round, Labelle Silver Co., Brooklyn, NY, 1950s. .... **$20+**

Coffee percolators – See also Percolator urn

❖ NOTES ❖

Burnett's Coffee Clearer A Woman's Invention. A patented combination of Cod Fish Skins and White of Eggs. The Best article for Settling Coffee. Eggs saved and no patent coffee pots needed. At a daily expense of less than-1/2¢ per family." Feb. 1889 ad of Joseph Burnett & Co., Boston.

•   •   •

"Extracts from unsolicited letters" used in manufacturers' brochures make informative reading. Some **Hubbard & McClary** extracts are transcribed here: "I have never seen, before, a coffee-pot which suspended the coffee midway between the top and the bottom, and then sent a continuous circulating current of water down through the ground powder, ascending by a separate channel to be again sent down through the grounds, and so on, over and over, until the nutritive matter of the ground coffee was so thoroughly leached and extracted as to leave the grounds about as tasteless as sawdust. This is just what your coffee-pot does." * * * "I weighed out one ounce of ground coffee, and placing it in the pot I added six cups of boiling water and boiled it five minutes; the result was six cups of coffee, which was consumed without any settling material, and which was so strong as to excite comment from the family, which was kept in ignorance of the way it had been prepared. The grounds, when collected and dried, changed from the original dark, to a light brown color. These exhausted grounds I placed in a paper marked 'A'. I next secured a quantity of grounds from the common coffee-pot, after breakfast, and dried them to a deep brown color. I then weighed out one ounce of these, which I placed in a paper 'B'. I next placed 'A' in your pot, and adding six cups of boiling water, I boiled it five minutes; the result barely colored the water, and no recognized taste of coffee was perceptible in the liquid. Cleaning out the pot, I put in 'B', – added six cups of boiling water, and boiled for five minutes; the result was a TOLERABLE cup of coffee – wanting in richness, but quite as good as one gets on steamboats or at R.R. stations, and fully confirming your declaration, that at least one-third saving in the coffee required may be effected."

•   •   •

Tinkering Made Easy – "Holes in sauce pans or other tinwares, is a small thing. Those who will take the trouble to learn, can easily do small jobs at soldering, but many have not the needed gumption, and spoil the job. These will find the 'Magical Patching Plate' a great convenience. It is a thin sheet of solder prepared for the purpose, from which a bit is to be cut out large enough to well cover the hole; the surface of the ware is scraped bright, the patch put on, a poker or other hot iron held upon it, and when the solder melts, the job is done." *American Agriculturist*, 1877.

Coffee pots -- Aluminum

Coffee pot, aluminum with Bakelite™ or other molded phenolic resin handle, 2 part, top is "biggin" drip container, lower has V-neck pouring spout. (Another version, reportedly only 11"H, has green wooden finial and handle.) "Drip-O-Lator, The Better Coffee Maker," Enterprise Aluminum Co., Massillon, OH, 12"H, pat'd. by R. F. Krause, Jan. 14, 1930.... **$20+**

Coffee pot, polished cast aluminum, sort of egg shaped body, flat on bottom, in what manufacturer called a "graceful Dutch shape," hinged stepped lid made with perforated strainer appendage that fits exactly over small lip or spout, turned wooden handle, "which can readily be replaced if accidentally charred" (and I've seen quite a few with the handles charred on the lower end). "Monarcast," mfd. by Monarch Aluminum Ware Co., Cleveland, OH, c.1915. .... **$20+**

Coffee pot, so-called French style (Biggin dripper), cast aluminum in 4 parts, viz. lid (which looks like a fat biscuit cutter), perforated drip insert, urn shaped pot with black handle & funny fat little spout or lip up at top rim, separate sort of flared ruffled base, "makes coffee without boiling" by putting ground coffee in the cylindrical insert and pouring in water. Wagner Ware, 3 pt. capacity, 1930. • A nearly identical pot, except for a more traditional gooseneck spout & rounder handle, was reported by collector Mozelle Bamber, of MA. Hers, which is marked on the bottom "Super Maid Cook-Ware," is 10-1/2"H or 11-1/4"H on base, which is about 4" diam. Another collector from New Hampshire wrote to report one that is unmarked except for "Made in Canada." .... **$30+**

Coffee pots -- copper & nickeled copper

Coffee pot, copper, hinged lid, green Depression glass insert in lid, mark is indistinct, looks like "MERID–," could be name Meriden or possibly the place, Meriden, Ct., 1925. .... **$15+**

Coffee pot, copper, roundish body, wood finial & handle, Manning & Bowman, makes only one cup, late 19th C. .... **$30+**

Coffee pot, copper with brass hinge, wood finial on lid & wood handle, brass ferrule on handle, crooked neck spout, "James S. Shaw Co.," 5-1/2"H, 19th C. .... **$70+**

Coffee pot, slant-sided, copper, tin lid with unusual copper ring finial, wire bail with wood grip, American, mid 1800s. .... **$75+**

Coffee pot, copper, with brass trim, & nifty turned wood handles painted black, American, 11-1/2"H, c.1890s-1910. .... **$45+**

Coffee pot, copper, with Britannia (pewter-like) lid, gooseneck spout & handle, very fancy, American, late 19th or early 20th C. .... **$75+**

Coffee pot, hammered copper, pewter lined (looks like tin), foreign-looking pot with round globular lower body, small ring foot, topped by slightly flared high neck with big beak spout, domed lid, thin handle curves out from near rim and 'falls' inward to middle of globe, a reproduction based on a Russian pot from sometime in 19th C, which in turn reflects Middle Eastern & Turkish influence, B. Paleschuck, NYC, NY, 10"H, one qt. capacity, early 1930s, based on 19th C form. .... **$25+**

Coffee pot, nickel plated copper, covered spout, turned wood handle & knob on lid, "Rome 4" on bottom, Rome, NY, early 20th C. .... **$20+**

Coffee pots – electric

Coffee pot, electric, chrome, with sugar & creamer to match, "Edison General Electric Hotpoint," 20th C. .... **$25+**

Coffee pot, electric, chrome with tan handles & spigot, shaped like a football, "Forman Brothers Inc.," Brooklyn, NY, 2nd quarter, 20th C. .... **20+**

Coffee pot, electric, copper, makes 4 cups, 20th C. **$35**

Coffee pot, electric, floral patterned china, chrome base & spigot, matching creamer and covered sugar bowl, (china by Fraunfelter) "Royal Rochester," mfd. by Robeson Rochester Corp., (Zanesville, OH), Rochester, NY, pat'd. Aug. 12, 1924. .... **$135+**

Coffee pots -- enamelware

Coffee pot, black & white enamelware, American, large size, c.1910 to 1930s. .... **$4?**

Coffee pot, blue & white enamelware in slant-sided shape, with moss roses on both sides, doesn't look like Manning-Bowman wares, prob. European, late 19th C. .... **$145+**

Coffee pot, blue & white enamelware with flower design, tin lid, gooseneck spout, European or American, late 1800s. .... **$155+**

Coffee pot, bluish-gray graniteware, tin top with wooden finial, unusual one-cup size, late 19th C. .... **$85+**

Coffee pot, robin's egg blue & white agateware, gooseneck spout, American, 19th C. .... **$125+**

Coffee pot, sky blue & white speckled enamelware, gooseneck spout, bail handle with wood grip, late 19th C, early 20th. .... **$150+**

Coffee pot, teal & white swirled agateware, 11-1/2"H, c.1890s-1910. .... **$200+**

Coffee pot, turquoise & white spattered enamel with deep blue trim, American, late 19th or early 20th C. .... **$250+**

Coffee pot, dark turquoise enamelware, with gooseneck spout, European or American, c.1890s-1910. .. **$150+**

Coffee pot, peacock blue & white enamelware, gooseneck spout, American, early 20th C. .... **$150+**

Coffee pot, brown graniteware with a few chips. 12"H, 19th C. Nice color, but a shelf piece or sitter, as they say, although that refers more accurately to something with a rusted out bottom, or a hopelessly calcium-clogged inside. .... **$25+**

Coffee pot, brown speckled enamelware, with Britannia mountings, including lid, handle & spout. Protective band around base is brass – undoubtedly once nickel-plated, probably Manning, Bowman & Co., c.1890-1900. .... **$155+**

Coffee pot, brown & white agateware, white metal lid, copper base, shell & column motif on throat of spout & handle, probably Manning & Bowman, 10"H, late 19th C. .... **$275+**

Coffee pot, brown & white spattered agateware, domed "golden" pewter lid, spout & handle, golden-colored tin "skirt," possibly colored by japanning. American, 11-3/8"H, late 19th C. .... **$300+**

Coffee pot, brown & white speckled enamelware, gooseneck spout, nickeled white metal mountings, probably Manning, Bowman, late 19th C. .... **$150+**

Coffee pot, brown & white swirled enamelware, gooseneck spout, probably "Onyx," Columbian Enameling & Stamping Co., c.1890s-1910. .... **$150+**

Coffee pot, dark brown enamelware flecked with white, hinged lid, possibly "Onyx" by Columbian Stamping, or possibly Manning, Bowman & Co., or even none of above, and, instead, European, early 20th C. ...... **$95+**

Coffee pot, cobalt enamelware, with gold trim, gooseneck spout, prob. European, late 19th C. ..... **$135+**

Coffee pot, gray spotted graniteware – two-tone, pewter spout, base, trim, handle, crown collar & lid, American (?), 8-3/4"H, 19th C. .... **$135+**

Coffee pot, gray graniteware, tin lid with white porcelain knob, hollow cast iron handle was originally painted black, American (?), 8-1/2"H, late 19th or early 20th C. .... **$95+**

Coffee pot, green & white striped enamelware, small size, European, prob. Czechoslovakian, early 20th C. to 1930s. .... **$135+**

XIV-36. Coffee pot – Turkish style, easily confused with a butter melter or some other saucepan. Copper, in the "Turkish pattern," made in six sizes, holding from 1 to 6 cups. Henry Rogers Sons & Co., Wolverhampton, England, 1914 catalog. **$20-$30**

Coffee pot, lavender or mauve (hey! what would you call **mauve**? Oscar Wilde said it was pink trying to be lavender; and Thomas Beer, who in 1926 wrote *The Mauve Decade*, about the 1890s in America, said it was "pink turning to purple." Some dictionaries say mauve is lilac). Anyway, pale browny lavender speckled enamelware, tin spout & tin lid with turned wood finial, wood handle, probably Manning & Bowman, American, 9"H, late 19th C........ **$250+**

Coffee pot, mulberry enamelware, lighthouse shape, black-painted turned wood handle & wood finial, 9"H, c.1890-1900.......................... **$250+**

Coffee pot, pink agateware with hand-painted petunias, nickeled brass & copper trim including breast-band, spout, lid & base, probably Manning & Bowman, late 19th C. .... **$225+**

Coffee pot, purplish brown enamelware, domed enameled top, turned wooden handle, possibly Manning, Bowman & Co., 9"H, late 19th C. .... **$185+**

Coffee pot, enamelware with colorful depiction of Statue of Liberty, ornate pewter spout, domed lid & handle, American, Statue of Liberty Commemorative, 1886. • Would Have Been Great Investment – Offered in 1982 for sale by Al & Nancy Schlegel, Willow Hollow, Penacook, NH. The price then was only $225. It would most likely have jumped to double in 1986, for the centennial of the statue. Probable value now: .... **$1,000+**

Coffee pot, enamelware with white background & floral design, white metal mountings at collar, gooseneck spout, base, handle, (these were also offered with nickel plated mountings at a slight extra cost), Manning-Bowman, pat'd. June 5, 1883, registered Jan. 13, 1885. .... **$225+**

❖ NOTES ❖

1906 "New Art Enameled Ware. Beautiful Creations That Prophesy Great Developments in Ornamental Novelties of Steel. – It is refreshing to turn away for a brief while from ... ordinary enameled ware ... & contemplate the possibilities that lie in enameled ware as an article for decorating & beautifying homes. Not much of the latter is yet shown in this country, & probably none of it will ever be made by the American manufacturer whose mind runs more toward the question of profit than the production of truly artistic wares.[!] But the Austrians have devoted considerable time of late to the making of beautifully decorated vases, pitchers, urns, mugs, etc., that at first glance can scarcely be distinguished from pottery or fine china, although made of drawn steel.

"It is decorative in every sense of the word and possesses all the charm of ... ceramic ... [plus] indestructability, for this new art enameled ware can be dropped to the floor or knocked about with impunity. ... [On display at a NY firm, Stransky & Co., is a collection of] various kinds of enameled ware that are sold in foreign countries. In America, the housewife is satisfied with her white and white, blue and white, gray mottled, etc., but abroad ... tastes are more exacting, and each country demands its own particular designs.

"In Japan, for example, the vogue is for flowery patterns in all the pleasing colors of the Sunrise Kingdom, and the Stransky collection contains a series of basins bearing characteristic pictures. Some are purely floral, but others portray boating scenes and sketches of Japanese life, every detail being worked out even more minutely than is possible on pottery.

"If the limits of this article permitted, it would be highly interesting to describe separately the enameled ware fashions of each country: China, Little Asia, Turkey, Singapore, Siam, the Balkan States, Hungary, etc., all have their individuality, running the gamut from the fantastic dragon patterns of China to the thick, heavy designs of Russia. It is amazing how well the colors are produced, and the effect of real china is so cleverly simulated that even a trained eye could be readily deceived. The Stransky collection will be appreciated by those of the trade who are interested in something more than enameled ware which sells at nineteen cents, marked down from a quarter." *House Furnishing Review*, Feb. 1906.

❖ NOTES ❖

Coffee pots, tin – painted, punched & plain: Color & Added Value. – Generally speaking, blue background is $$$$$, red is $$$$, yellow $$$, black $$, & brown $.

Crooked-spout Coffee Pots – A pattern for fraud. In the mid-1980s, an expert in early painted tin (sometimes called tôle) noticed something chilling. Libby Spencer, writing in *New York-Pennsylvania Collector*, December 1985, recounted the sighting, within a four week period, almost a dozen painted tin, crooked-spout coffee pots – which are considered rare. Further, all were black, with flowers & scrolls in red, yellow and green. All had the cutback spout tip that looks like an open bird beak. All had hinged domed lids with small mushroom finial. All had a braced strap handle. All had orangey rust. All had "signs" of wear – not too little to look new, not too much to turn off a sucker who'd want to pay $800 to $1,000 to add one to a collection. The value of a real, 150-year old pot of this type, could be well over $1,000 – definitely a critical-mass to trigger fakers, especially if there's only one fabricator to make them, and one "fence" to pass them off to dealers. Using a common market equation, the cost of something is multiplied by about two to arrive at wholesale, and multiplied by either four or five to arrive at retail. In this case, it would imply a cost of between $200 and $250, and a wholesale price to an unsuspecting (we hope) dealer that would include another $200 to $250 –

or $400 to $500. Not only is the collector, and the hobby, a loser, but so is the poor schlub talented enough to make such a thing, and desperate or crooked enough to be willing to. I'm sorry, but my advice is don't buy this form unless the provenance is absolutely fool-proof. The value ranges are as they were reported or seen in the last few years. The plain colored ones are probably OK, and possibly the brown asphaltum ones are OK, unless the faker thought he better sprinkle in a few more common examples. Probably the descriptive phrases printed above in bold type ought now to raise hackles.

Coffee pot, lighthouse shape, decorated tin, or tôle. Dark brown japanned background (least desirable color) with polychromatic flowers, & swagged border, strap handle with grip, crooked spout, stepped low dome lid with brass knob finial, amazingly unworn finish, American, 10-5/8"H, 19th C. pot with period decoration, though faked finishes are known. • Brought $3,700 at Garth's Auctions, Delaware, OH, April 11–12, 1986. .... **$3,000-$4,000**
Coffee pot, lighthouse shape with crooked neck spout, domed lid with brass knob, braced strap handle with grip, painted tin with flowers, fruits, leaves in color on black asphaltum background, American, 11-1/2"H, mid 19th C. .... **$900+**

❖ NOTES ❖

Black grounds – "Black grounds may be formed on metal, by drying linseed oil only, when mixed with a little lamp-black. The work is then exposed in a stove to a heat which will render the oil black. The heat should be low at first, and increased very gradually, or it will blister. This kind of japan requires no polishing. It is extensively used for defending articles of ironmongery from rust." James Smith, *The Dictionary of Arts, Sciences and Manufacturers.* Vol. II, p. 795. Boston: Phillips, Sampson & Co., 1854.

The Kin-Hee Coffee Pot

is a triumph of genius. It is unlike other Coffee Pots. If you can boil water you can in one minute make Coffee in it fit for a king. By actual test it costs only seven-tenths of a cent per cup. It is, therefore, the best to drink and the least expensive.

Demonstrated at Pan-American Exposition

This shows the coffee pot upside down, the top filled with boiling water and coffee submerged. It stands for one minute, straining cloth is put on, then the bottom. Then the entire pot is turned right side up and the coffee is ready to serve. A child can do it. *Patented May 22, 1900.*

XIV-37. Coffee pot. *"Kin-Hee" pot, mfd. by James Heekin & Co, Cincinnati, OH, and in Canada, The Eby, Blain Co., Ltd., Toronto. They also sold a mocha-java coffee blend in 1 lb. cans.* **$20+**

Coffee pot, lighthouse (tapering toward top with straight sides) style, tin with black japanning, crooked neck spout, slightly domed hinged lid with brass knob, American, poss. CT, 10"H, 19th C. Not as desirable to collectors as would be one with either a red background, or painted decorations over the japanned background. .... **$325+**
Coffee pot, lighthouse style with perky – even impertinent – pieced, crooked neck spout & extra large curved handle, dark brown japanning & polychrome flowers, brass mushroom finial to lid, American, 10-5/8"H, 19th C. Not as desirable as one with red or blue japanned background color. But surface is very good, & looks original. .... **$2,500+**

❖ NOTES ❖

Spouts – I use the term crooked neck or crook-neck, or crooked spout only with an angled spout having a seam at the elbow (to mix similes), occasionally at "wrist" also. Sometimes these are called cock's head spouts. Many crooked spouts on copper teakettles look just as angular, but do not have a circumferential elbow seam. These are called gooseneck spouts, and there is a wide latitude in the use of the term. Some goosenecks are more stuck-out, curious, and aggressive than others, more ganderish; some are more graceful and plump at the bend; others are small and timid, perhaps goslings? The crooked neck spout is, I'm sure, tinsmiths' version of coppersmiths' gooseneck spout, which could not be copied exactly, because it was impossible to hammer out the extreme angle in tin plate, and keep the plating's integrity.

Coffee pot, lighthouse type with tapered sides, painted tin with scrolls & flowers on dark green ground, somewhat worn, nice scrolled strap handle, deep conical lid, very handsome, American, 11"H, mid 19th C. .... **$1,200+**
Coffee pot, painted tin or tôle, decorations in perfect condition, red, yellow & green on black asphaltum ground, braced strap handle, attractive finial, American, looks mid 19th C. .... **$1,500+**
Coffee pot, engraved tin, with designs including tulips, eagle, flag, peacock, vines & leaves, PA German, prob. mid 19th C. .... **$3,000+**

❖ NOTES ❖

Punched tin is not punctured tin. It refers to a very rare form of decoration, done by tapping a small punch along the outlines of flowers, urns, birds, eagles, on what will be the inside of the vessel, in order to make a raised beaded line.

Coffee pot, punched tin, slightly battered but still graceful crooked neck spout, design of small pot with large tulip & leaves punched on one side (perhaps on both?), braced strap handle, traces of "old black paint & light rust." Pennsylvania, 11"H, mid 19th C. • Sold at Garth's, July 28, 1989 for: **$2,600**
Coffee pot, punched tin, simply decorated with strong tulip and leaves on upper part of body, flowers with

6 petals below, spiraled ring border around flared foot, crooked spout, braced strap handle, nearly flat lid with button finial, out & in body pieced from 2 truncated cones (also called an inverted cone body by some cataloguers), the shorter below, joined at the "waist," 1/3 way from bottom, marked with two initials "A" and "R," probably those of owners, Pennsylvania, about 10"H, dated 1867. • This piece from the Lamb collection was sold at Pennypacker's in 1976. Price then was $2,300. A similar pot, 11"H, with punched design of flower pots with tulips, very attractive curve to spout, was in the Richard Withington March 4, 1989 auction at Andover, MA, and sold for a low $1,100. .... **$3,000+**

Coffee pot, for students, tin with brass trim, wooden handle sticks straight out halfway down cylindrical body, straight side spout attached at bottom of pot, looks sort of like an espresso coffee pot, from F. A. Walker catalog, four sizes: 2, 4, 6 and 8 cup capacity, c.1870s or 1880s. .... **$45+**

❖ NOTES ❖

F. A. Walker – Importers & Manufacturers. I have always thought that F. A. Walker was only an importer & wholesaler. But here's an enlightening news item from *The Metal Worker*, Oct. 21, 1882. "Messrs. F. A. Walker & Co., 83 Cornhill, Boston, manufacturers and refinishers of brass goods, have a very fine display of brass fenders, fire screens, fire sets, coal vases, tea urns, placques, brass-trimmed bellows, &c. Several specimens of Benerez brasswork shown by this firm are very fine indeed, and attract marked attention."

Coffee pot, large tin one with unusual copper bottom that comes 2 inches up sides. The copper protected the tin solder & conducted heat better besides, American, 19th C. .... **$45+**

XIV-38. Tea & coffee pot. "Marion Harland" pot, mfd. by Silver & Co., Brooklyn, NC. In their c.1910 catalog. Made of copper with ebonized wood handles. Could be had in plain, nickel-plated or "Old English" finish. Tinned inside. It was sort of a percolating infuser. Marion Harland ran a cooking school in the late 19th C., and wrote cookbooks too. *Historically important.* **$35+**

XIV-39. "Self-pouring" tea or coffee pot. "Royle's Patent," this "Boston No. 1" model was sold by Paine, Diehl & Co., Philadelphia, out of their 1888 catalog. It was probably made for them by William Vogel & Brothers, Brooklyn. The patent was granted April 3, 1888 in America, but two years earlier in England. There, the self-pourers were made by James Dixon & Sons, Sheffield, for the patentee, J. J. Royle, Manchester. Wherever made, most seem to be made of Britannia metal, which could be left plain, or plated with nickel or silver. Meriden Britannia Co. and The Boston Co. were other makers in the US. It was sometimes called a "**mother's helper**" because "mother" (the person designated to pour tea at tea time) needed only pull up the pump in the top of the finial, place the cup under the spout, and push the piston down. I imagine it took a bit of practice. **$100+**

XIV-40. Canal or barge coffee pot, "gaudy" decorated, with glazed applied posies. Rockingham ceramic called "barge" or "canal craft," used on British canal barges. Besides the flowers and the mini-pot finial is the legend "A Present from a Friend" on the side. 10-1/2"H x 6-1/2"W, English, 19th C. Ex-Keillor Collection.

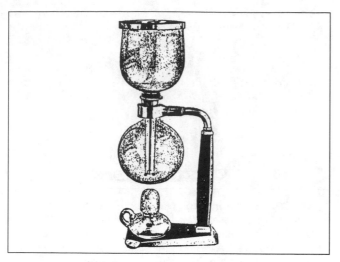

XIV-41. Coffee & tea filtering system. *"Boston,"* all glass, mfd. by The Silex Co., Boston, MA. Came in 4 and 6 cup sizes. House Furnishing Review, May 1917. **$95+**

XIV-42. "Tricolator" coffee maker. *Filtering percolation pot, the "Norfolk" 9-cup electric. Mfd. by Tricolator Co., Inc., NYC, who had at least two dozen styles, with glazed & decorated china pots, Pyrex™ pots, & metal upper parts. 1933 brochure.* **$40-$100+**

Coffee pot, pieced tin, tall & thin, extreme conical body with funnel top, strap handle, hinged lid with strap handle, curved spout support from neck where cone meets funnel, for drip coffee, extraordinary piece. American, 12"H, early 19th C. .... **$500+**

Coffee pot, pieced tin with diagonal seams, straight spout with thin brace at top, slanted sides, braced handle. If this is not early 19th C., at least it was made from small pieces of tin. (Tin was only available in small sheets during 18th & early 19th C., imported, mostly from England. But nothing would stop a frugal tinsmith from using pieced scrap tin from larger, later sheets.) Style sometimes called "Shaker," American, 9-1/2"H, early 19th C. • See also Reflector oven in Chapter X (Hearths); and information on tin plate in Chapter VII, (Storage). .... **$250+**

Coffee pot, straight-sided, tin, with copper bottom, turned wooden handle painted black, American, late 19th C. .... **$45+**

Coffee pot, tin, 3 loop tin finial on the lid, prob. CT, 6"H, c.1830s to 1850. .... **$125+**

Coffee pot, tin, conical shape with straight side spout, strap handle, simple but very unusual, the design as

XIV-43. Coffee percolator-urn, *and server. Chrome, electric, mfd. by Labelle Silver Co., Brooklyn, NY, c.1950s. It's possible that this company is related to Silver & Co. And it's possible you can see me taking the photo at a NYC street fair.* **$95**

spare & elegant as the sleek Italian designs of 100 years later, American, 8-3/4"H, prob. 2nd quarter 19th C. .... **$95+**

The Thirteenth Annual Report of the Commissioner of Labor. *1898. Hand and Machine Labor,* Volume 1 (Washington: GPO, 1899) compares **two methods of making a 2-quart coffee pot** from tin. The conical pot above is about the same age as the "primitive" one described below. "Under the modern method the bodies of the pots were cut with a steam cutting machine in 15 minutes. Under the primitive method the tin was cut with stock shears by hand and required 4 hours, but before the tin could be cut ... it was necessary to mark it out, and this required an additional ... 2 hours and 40 minutes, so that ... the hand work required nearly 27 times as long as the machine work." The "primitive" method dates to 1840; the machine method to 1895. *The Report* lists one tinsmith's 30 production steps – using tools from an awl & hatchet stake to swage & peening hammer – in order on the left below. The 22 steps for machine-making, taken by 27 different workers (with 18 job descriptions), are in the right-hand column.

1840 PRODUCTION STEPS "Primitive Method"	1895 PRODUCTION STEPS "Factory Method"
marking out bodies of pots	cutting out bodies
cutting out bodies	perforating for spouts
turning top edges for wire	edging bodies for wire
putting in wire	forming bodies
peening down top edges	grooving bodies together
swaging bead around tops	wiring top
forming bodies	notching bodies for hinge
cutting out handles, spouts, rims	boring bodies for bottom
forming spouts	cutting out bottoms
turning edges of handles for wire	double-seaming bodies
putting in wire and forming hinges	cutting out spouts
peening down edges of handles	forming spouts
cutting out hinges; forming tin lips on hinges;	cutting out handles
forming handles	beading handles
marking out covers	forming handles
cutting out covers	cutting out covers
raising covers	drawing covers
turning edges of covers	crimping covers
peening down edges of covers	notching covers
putting knobs on covers	punching covers & putting in knobs
soldering spouts and seams in bodies	soldering all seams*
turning edges for bottoms	testing pots
marking out bottoms	plus overseeing establishment;
cutting out bottoms	furnishing power; and
edging bottoms	firing boiler [for steam power].
snapping on bottoms	
peening down edges of bottoms	
double-seaming bottoms	
soldering all seams.	
*Note that soldering was also done by hand in the factory setting of 1895.	

Coffee pot, tin, finial is a grape cluster, brass ID plate with an eagle reads "The National Tea and Coffee Pot Company," "J. B. Smith's 1859 Patent," "Milwaukee, WI," with a patent number, either 22,737 or 22,787 – a patent I cannot find by name or number. The 22,000 number range is okay for January 1859, but the patent index shows no 1859 patent issued to a J. B. Smith. Pot also marked with other patents: Nov. 19, 1867's #71,236 & #71,237. • J. B. Smith patented this & at least two more coffee pots – in 1868 & 1872. • A clue is found in the index of re-issued patents. George R. Chittenden, Chicago, and Charles A. Smith, Milwaukee, assignees of James MacGregor, Jr. (of Troy, NY), got a re-issued patent for McGregor's "improvement in coffee-pots," RE3,176, Oct. 27, 1868, following a 7-year extension of the original patent issued McGregor on April 11, 1854 (#10,752)............................... **$85-$100+**

Coffee pot, tin, brass ID plate reads "The Young America," American, dated 1859. • There's a town in Minnesota, known to devotees of sweepstakes, called "Norwood Young America," and it dates back at least to 1861, but I couldn't find, among the several coffee pots patented in 1859, any from that state. Probably related to the Smith pot............................... **$100+**

Coffee pot, tin, lighthouse (or slanted sides) shape, with domed lid & ring finial, wire bail handle, great braced handle, 3 qt. capacity, American, early to mid 19th C. • Even plain, this is quite a looker, especially the braced handle. A lot of modern designers – even (or especially?) architects – could learn something by studying such a coffee pot as this.................... **$75+**

Coffee pot, tin, "out-and-in" hourglass body of 2 different height truncated cones, the bottom one upside down, joined at the large ends around the "waist" in a sort of collet, with crooked spout originating in lower part, braced strap handle with grip, hinged high conical lid with scrolled double ring finial, rather high foot. Elaborately decorated with an eagle (?) & foliage in wrigglework or wriggle work, accomplished by tapping a small chisel-like tool with a mallet or hammer so that it makes tiny bounces or skips & cuts a sort of chased zig-zaggy line in the metal somewhat similar to brightwork engraving on silver. This is probably the most highly desired type of tinware, more than painted tin, and is sometimes called wrigglesware. Unmarked, but if Lasansky is correct, "M.B." is the maker, therefore prob. PA, 10-3/4"H, 19th C. • According to Jeannette Lasansky, in her *To Cut, Piece, and Solder*, "Only one maker of tinware used this [wriggle work] technique ... unfortunately ... [his] identity ... remains a mystery – only two of his pieces have initials (M.B.), and none are dated." (p.72) Her book shows four pieces. .... **$5,000-$7,000**

Coffee pot, tin with fluted spout, delicate mushroom finial on lid, cast iron handle with spur lid rest, beautifully made, elegant detail, American, late 19th C...... **$125+**

Coffee or teapot, pieced tin lighthouse shape body, made of 8 soldered vertical strips, thin strap handle, straight spout originates almost halfway up body, American, mid 19th C. .... **$125+**

Coffee or teapot, straight sides, Britannia trim and curved fluted spout, fancy handle, celadon green enamelware body with blue & pink morning glories with green leaves, Manning-Bowman, Meriden, CT, 9"H, 1890s... **$250+**

❖ NOTES ❖

"Where the ebullition is most violent." – "Among the new inventions that may prove of advantage to housekeepers is a contrivance known as a 'percolator,' though the term does not accurately describe its operation. It consists of a small cage or basket of perforated tin or of fine wire-gauze attached to an air-tight tin float. The float forms a sort of cover for the cage and is easily detachable. A bent wire at the top of the float serves as a handle. The finely-ground coffee, as much as required, is placed in the cage, and the whole is then lowered into the water. The float keeps the coffee near the surface of the water where the ebullition is most violent, and the strength is very quickly extracted." Appleton's *Annual Cyclopaedia & Registry of Important Events of the Year* 1887. The writer goes on the say that the "cage" of coffee grounds in effect "floats" so that water can keep being passed through it, instead of the grounds sinking to the bottom, waterlogged, if in a "cambric bag" as of old.

Coffee roaster, cast iron, 3 part, pot with 3 legs, wire bail handle, pivoting agitator with tall vertical handle, slotted lid, pat'd. by F. Humphrey of Philadelphia, mfd. by I. A. Sheppard & Co., marked Philadelphia, PA (Baltimore was another Sheppard location). Size #1: 5-1/4"H x 8-1/2" diam., pat'd. Mar. 13, 1866 (#53,148)............................... **$275+**

Coffee roaster, cast iron frame with 3 legs & thin wire bail, side handles that are held clamped together by the slip-on long dogleg crank, cast iron 2 piece globe shaped container rests in frame, looks like something from a planetarium, "Woods Patent," mfd. by Roys & Wilcox & Co., Berlin, CT, ball: 6-1/2" diam. with 5-1/4"L handles; frame: 2-3/4"H x 9" diam., pat'd. by Thomas R. Wood (Cincinnati, OH), April 17, 1849 (#6,345). This is one of the most desirable coffee roasters of all. • Another very similar one seen is

XIV-44-A. Coffee roaster. Cast embossed marks: "Woods Patent, Roys & Wilcox Co., Harrington's Import, Berlin Ct. Pat'd. May 17, 1859." Oddly, the T. R. Wood's Patent was granted April 17, 1849, so actually this is dated as J. D. Harrington's patent, not Woods.' Wood lived in Cincinnati, OH; Harrington in Rochester, NY. The word "Import" is another mystery. The unknown missing "chapter" might be found by searching the Official Gazette for the not-infrequent reports on infringement suits, etc., between 1849 and 1859. Cast iron, hinged 'cannon ball' in frame, with bail handle & 3 legs. Ball has long handles, which clamp together by the crank. Frame 2-3/4"H x 9" diam.; ball 6-1/2" diam. with 5-1/4"L handles. Courtesy the late Darryl G. Dudash, Alaquippa, PA. Prices vary widely; range given here is general average. **$800+**

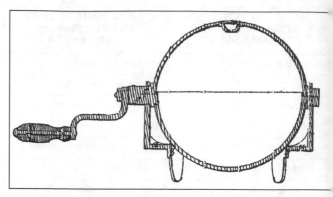

XIV-44-B. Wood's coffee roaster patent. Thomas R. Wood, Cincinnati, OH, pat'd. this roaster April 17, 1849. Wood desired to "adapt the apparatus to the boiler holes of cooking stoves, ranges, and furnaces, instead of requiring a separate furnace as heretofore." He also wrote "instead of making the vessel which holds the coffee of a cylindrical form," I make it "of a spherical form" so that it could be adapted to the boiler holes. One half of the sphere "fits onto a rim on the other" half, and the halves were made so as not to come apart except when the movable half is above the other. Wood's rim also had a flange that was to project down into the cook stove hole, and the flange had legs long enough "for the apparatus to rest on when placed on the floor." Wood's roaster had wire bails attached to each side of the rim plate to carry the roaster. It had a little cast-in thumb & finger piece "in a recess" in the upper sphere to lift the top half off. Note the two ways the handle crooks or curves.

marked "Roys & Wilcox," plus a patent date of May 17, 1859, pat'd. by Josiah D. Harrington, Rochester, NY, #24,024; it was featured in the 1869 Dover Stamping Co. catalog. A handsome example was for sale by a dealer with a very discerning eye and fabulous iron stock. His price was $900 in late 1988. For the Woods: .... **$800+**

Coffee roaster, for hearth, sheet iron cylinder with sliding "trap" door, long crooked crank handle out of one end, short iron rod out of other, fit into spit holder or other iron frame, Canadian or American, 20"L tip to tip, cylinder itself is 8-3/4"L x 6-1/4" diam., sliding hatch opens to 2-1/2", c.1840 to 1860. (Note that Griswold did similar pieces, much later.) ...... **$275+**

Coffee roaster, for hearth, sheet iron, cylindrical, long shaft & wooden handle knob, American (?), 50"L, early 19th C. .... **$250+**

Coffee roaster, heavy cast iron, straight sides, top crank that moves the 4 stirring "fingers" inside, 2 large upright fixed ring handles, looks like a cross between an ironclad Civil War submarine & a pirate's chest, not marked, American, 11"H x 8-3/4" diam., mid-19th C... **$450**

❖ RECIPE ❖

Dandelion Coffee – sent in by a reader of an British periodical, *Cottage Gardening*. "Dr. Harrison, of Edinburgh, prefers dandelion coffee to that of Mecca; and many persons all over the Continent prefer a mixture of succory* and coffee to coffee alone. Dig up the roots of dandelion, wash them well, but do not scrape them, dry them, cut them into the size of peas, and then roast them in an earthen pot, or coffee roaster of any kind. The great secret of good coffee, is, to have it fresh burnt and fresh ground." (*I don't know if **"succory"** is the same as "chicory" in this instance. Food writer Waverley Root says that "succory" sounds as if it ought to be a stand-in word for "chicory" but that it actually means suet. Oh, gag me with a spoon ... in my coffee? I think it's a word for dandelion root, probably unknown to Waverley Root.) *American Agriculturist*, Sept. 1846.

Coffee roaster, heavy sheet iron, saucepan or frying pan style with long handle, fitted lid with small oval trap door, crank in top, American, 8" diam., (another of these is 7-1/2" diam. x 2-1/2" deep, overall length 16" including handle), c.1850s or 1860s. Looks very like the one depicted in *The American Home Cook Book of 1854*. **Reproduction alert.** – This saucepan roaster has been reproduced in heavy steel, with same long handle.. **$150+**

Coffee roaster, key wound clockwork mechanism, sets over 2 range eyes, cast iron frame, tall housing of works at one end, long horizontal wire mesh cylinder holds beans, hemi-cylindrical pieced tin cover with strap handle fits down over the wire canister, diagonal revolving plates inside move the beans around, "American Coffee Roaster," pat'd. by C. A. Mills, Hazel Green, WI, 9"H x 18-1/2"L, pat'd. April 28, 1863

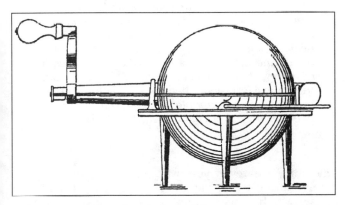

XIV-44-C. Harrington's coffee roaster patent. *Josiah D. Harrington, Rochester, NY, pat'd. this "machine" May 17, 1859 (#24,024). He claimed that the "nature of this invention" consisted in "constructing the machine as to make it more convenient and efficient in practice, and to allow of the parts of which it is composed being made available for other purposes," although he didn't mention what other purposes. The divided handle is hollow, to "reduce weight" (and probably heat) and also the crank (which appears to go through the hollow of the handles) "not only serves to hold the two halves of the ball together while rotating, but also to lift up one half of the ball when moved." The roaster rests in "vertical bearings" on the plate which rests over a cook stove hole when in use, and placed on the long-legged "trivet" when not in use. The trivet makes it appear useful in a hearth too. Handle & knob look more like the finished product in XIV-44-A.*

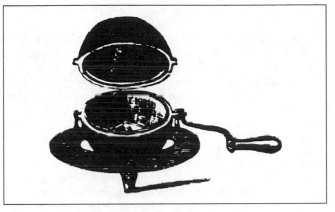

XIV-44-D. Coffee roaster. *Similar to the Wood's & Harrington Patents in previous 3 pictures. The legs are short & the crank has a curve like Wood's original 1849 patent, although the plate that rests over the stove hole is apparently wider than any of the others. This one was depicted in F. A. Walker & Co.'s catalog, 1880s. Another one, with a straight handle more like Harrington's, was depicted in the 1866 Dover Stamping Co. catalog.* **$700+**

(#38,320) & Nov. 7, 1863 (#50,878). In the original specifications, the "totally sheet-metal" coffee mill was operated with a clockwork mechanism. Mr. Mills wrote "The frame and upright plates may be cast iron, the vessel of sheet metal, and the wheels of the clock mechanism may be of cast or wrought metal, the teeth being cut. I do not, however, confine myself to any particular material or mode of manufacture." The improvement two years later had a "wire-cloth" receptacle, a "detachable lid or cover," and two "driving springs" for the clockwork mechanism so that it could be wound while operating. .... **$950+**

Coffee roaster, sheet iron & brass, aluminum, alcohol heating lamp in base, clockwork action, corrugated drum inside bounces beans around, snap lid, looks like a percolator inside, detachable crank looks like a Victrola handle. has 2 speeds, "Rapide" & "Lente" plus "Arrette" (stop), French, c.1890s-1910. . **$200+**

Coffee roaster, sheet iron can with sliding lid & round, flat cast iron frame with oblong, walled box-frame for the cylinder to sit in, & a tapered channel on one side for inserting an iron lid-lifter-like handle, fits over range eye, sliding door in top of canister body, bent-rod side crank, Griswold Mfg. Co., Erie, PA, cylinder is 8"L x 5-1/2" diam., plate is 9" diam. Looks c.1880s, but Dave Smith, a Griswold expert & author, dates it to c.1910. Having the inserted lifting handle is the clincher for the highest value. .... **$1,000-$1,500**

Coffee roaster, sheet iron, lid with hinged trapdoor for beans, brass gear in center operates iron stirrers inside, American, about 2" deep x 10" diam., mid 19th C. .... **$350+**

Coffee roaster, sheet iron, pan shape, fitted lid, lower handle is a pointed shaft, as if it once had wooden handle. no mark, American(?), pan is 7-1/4" diam., 20-1/4"L overall. mid 19th C. .... **$125+**

Coffee roaster, sheet iron pan style, hinged trapdoor opening in fixed lid through which blades inside are visible, cast iron crank has old repair, marked "#22," American, 19th C. .... **$125+**

Old Repair – When it doesn't qualify as a make-do, or a repaired piece with some quirkiness or idiosyncracy or charm in the repair (which may add value), an "old" repair still takes away less value than a recent repair. As to whether or not it is an old or new repair, you must examine all the elements – method, metal, condition – to decide. Because cast iron is so friable, and pieces tend to crack or break off, legs, stanchions, rods, wingnuts, finials & handles all tend to "go missing," as they say in British mysteries. Old repairs are likely to be frankly repairs; modern repairs, by collectors or dealers, are likely to be much less obvious, and may be cast in iron from a matching part, or from another piece, or even from a carved pattern mold. It is not bad form to ask if anything is a replaced part, or at least to examine things for which you are paying a lot with a magnifying glass, and to request a full description on your receipt, noting replacements or repairs or refinishing.

•   •   •

"LUTE – A Matter to Mend Broken Vessel. – Take any quantity of white of eggs, and beat them well to a froth. Add to this soft curd cheese, and quicklime, and begin beating a-new all together. This may be used in

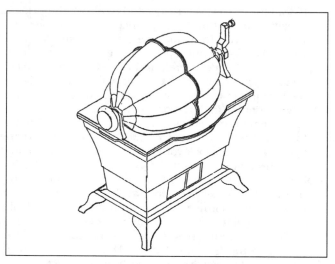

XIV-45. Coffee roaster patent. *Samuel Pierce, Troy, NY, pat'd. this wonderful pumpkin-like roaster Aug. 14, 1855 (#13,447). Troy was the center of stove-making at the time, and Samuel Pierce, first of Peekskill, then Troy, patented several stoves. I don't know if this was ever made; I hope so. He wrote "The distinguishing characteristic of my improvement consists in making the interior surface of a spheroidal roasting vessel of a series of longitudinal angular parts projecting inward, and alternating with coextensive, concave, hollow parts, swelling outward; to completely stir and mix the coffee as the vessel is revolved during the operation of browning or roasting the coffee ... the external form of the* **vessel to resemble that of a muskmelon.*** *The casting was in two halves, then "permanently fastened to each other" with rivets. Finally, Pierce's patent said he wasn't claiming "a cylindrical or a spherical roasting vessel with a portable furnace or other heater" only the shape of the vessel. Wow Wheee!!! If it exists:* **$1,500+**

XIV-46. Coffee roaster which avoids inequal torrefaction. *"The gratefulness of the beverage afforded by the coffee bean depends upon many circumstances, which are seldom all combined. The nature of the soil, the climate, seed, mode of culture and cure, influence greatly the quality of the fruit. But when all these particulars concur, and the berry is of the finest sort, it may be ruined in the roasting." So wrote Andrew Ure, in A* Dictionary of Arts, Manufactures & Mines, *1854. The illustrated commercial roaster was developed by William Law of London, who "conquered the difficulties" of roasting evenly in a sheet metal cylinder by inventing "the globular roaster, actuated by a compound motion like that of our earth. This roaster, with its double, rotary motion, is heated not over an open fire but in an atmosphere of hot air, through a cast metal casting. The globe is so mounted as to revolve horizontally, and also from time to time vertically, whereby the included beans are tossed about and intermingled in all directions. Inequality of torrefaction becomes impossible." Afterwards, the coffee is ground between two flat millstones, and is "thereby capable of giving out all its virtues to either boiling or cold water."* **$1,000+**

mending whatever you will, even glasses, and will stand both fire and water ... Another, for the same purpose, which resists water. – Take quicklime, turpentine, and soft curd cheese. Mix these well together; and, with the point of a knife, put of this on the edges of the broken pieces of your ware, then join them together." James Cutbush, *The American Artists Manual,* or *Dictionary of Practical Knowledge.* (Philadelphia, 1814). • **Mending With Brads.** – The most common (or at least visible) repair found on any ceramic wares utilizes the brad, a metal staple-like object made of a fairly soft metal. At a recent auction I saw a lovely Willow Ware soup tureen on a stand, with a high domed lid which had a very old brad repair that held the two halves together. The brads, about 10 of them, were set fairly close together, just under an inch apart, and were about 5/8" wide straddling the break line. The technique is probably very ancient, and probably found in every country where ceramics exist. In the Oct. 1946 *National Geographic Magazine,* on p. 540, there's an interesting picture of an Afghanistan workman sitting on a pad on the floor, holding a broken cup with the toes of one foot while he uses a beautiful bow drill to

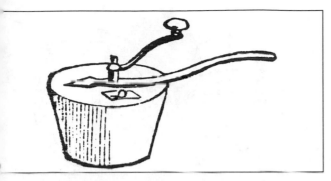

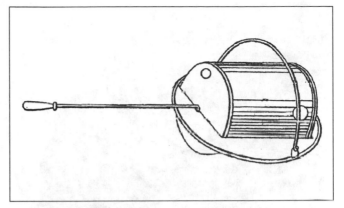

XIV-47-A. Coffee roaster, *saucepan type. Sheet iron with cast iron crank and probably wrought iron long handle. Depicted in* American Home Cook Book, *By an "American lady," 1854. Directions said to add "to each pound of coffee one table-spoonful of water. The coffee will thoroughly roast without being burned." In early 1997, a tinned sheet iron roaster with "illegible names on cover & base," 9-1/8" diam. x 3-1/4" deep, that looks simi-lar to this one except for the hole in the lid, was advertised by a group shop in New Hampshire. Either may have been the Trissler & Brecht.* **$150+**

XIV-48-A. Abel Stillman's cylinder roaster. *Still-man, Poland, NY, got patent #1,919, Dec. 28, 1840, for this very typical cylindrical coffee roaster made to fit over a stove hole like "the common griddle." He said the cylinder was of sheet iron, from five to ten inches in length "and about the same in diameter." The shaft extends out one end just far enough to rest on the bearing in the plate; it extends out the other end 18" or more, and a "handle or crank" is fitted to it "for the convenience of the operator." In the end of the cylinder toward the handle "is a small hole in which is a plate of mica or other transparent sub-stance" so that the operator can view the coffee while it's roasting.*

"bore small cavities into either side of the crack. Brads of soft copper are hammered in, binding the pieces. From Iran to Tientsin [85 miles S.E. of Beijing, China], this is a common repair." The article, *Back to Afghani-stan,* is by Maynard Owen Williams.

Coffee roaster, stove top, sheet iron oblong box, shal-low, with longish handle with ring at end. Hinged lid has pierced holes in it, American, about 20"L includ-ing handle, 19th C. • The pierced lid gave Mary Earle Gould pause, in *Antique Tin and Tole Ware,* and she thought this might have been a "fire carrier" or "coal carrier" but certain stains inside led her to

believe it might have served a double duty. She also had heard it might be a corn popper. Although she didn't mention any names, she wrote that some of these had been found with manufacturers' names stamped in the metal. .... **$135+**

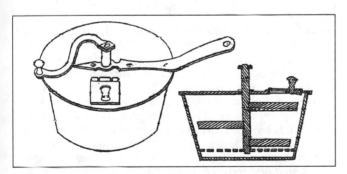

XIV-47-B. Coffee roaster patent. *This saucepan type roaster was pat'd. April 30, 1850, by W. H. Trissler & Elias Brecht, Fairview, PA, (#7,329). They claimed that the top of the vessel extended just enough to "form a flanch [sic]" or flange that would rest on the edge of the hole of the cook stove. The roaster "is composed of a water tight vessel, having a perforated false bottom located" just above the true bottom. The crank rotates the* **(R)** *"stirring wings" inside. A little water was placed in the bottom, and as it evaporated the "vapor will penetrate and expand the coffee grains."*

XIV-48-B. Coffee roaster – cylinder in frame. *"Patent Flue" roaster to use on cookstoves or ranges. Cast & sheet iron, high carrying handle on top, crank at one end. Mfd.. by Stuart, Peterson & Co., of Philadelphia, PA, and Burlington, NJ, who made stoves and stove hollowware. They made this roaster in 4 sizes: one is round to fit a 8" or 9" hole; others ovals to fit two 6" holes, two 7" holes, and two 9" holes. 1875 catalog picture. There is a great similarity in this style of roaster to confection-ers' roasters used for "burnt" almonds, and other nuts.* **$275+**

XIV-49. Coffee roaster – cylinder in frame,
*"American Coffee Roaster," pat'd. April 28, 1863
(#38,329) and Nov. 7, 1865 (#50,878), by C. A.
Mills, of Hazel Green, WI and then Bristol, CT.*
Clockwork *mechanism wound by key seen at
right. Sets over 2 eyes of range. You load the heavy
wire canister with coffee beans, set it into the cast
iron frame, slip tin cylindrical cover over it, wind it,
and let 'er roll. 9"H x 18-1/2"L. Collection of Meryle
Evans. Mills claimed in his 1863 patent that what
he mainly claimed was the clock-mechanism and
the fan enclosed within the cylinder, used as a
blower to keep the key-wound spring cool.* **$950+**

XIV-50-A. Coffee roaster missing its lid. *Cast
iron, 3 short peg legs. 5-1/4"H x 8-1/2" diam. Pat'd.
March 13, 1866 (#53,148) by Fenton Humphrey,
and mfd. by I. A. Sheppard & Co., Philadelphia. See
the next illustration for a description of the lid. A
very similar roaster, based on the N. Linden (Chicago) patent, Nov. 15, 1870 (#109,228), was made
with a heavy sort of "doughnut" cast iron lid with
the center opening covered with a tin lid with strap
handle. The Linden dasher had a pair of blades
reticulated like a backbone. Picture courtesy of the
Museum of History and Technology, The Smithsonian Institution. Add another $100 for lid.* **$475+**

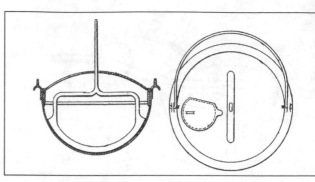

XIV-50-B. Coffee roaster patent, *which could be
used as a kettle for cooking other things. Fenton
Humphrey, Philadelphia, PA, pat'd. this roaster
March 13, 1866 (#53,148).* **(L)** *A side view showing
the stirring piece which Humphrey called a "pedal" in
that it could be attached by a wire one end of which
was held in the operator's hand to give an oscillating
motion to it. The kettle part, made of cast iron, with a
wire bail handle, was placed "over a slow fire." The
lid* **(R)** *was domed, probably made of heavy sheet
iron or tin, it set down into the rim of the vessel, and it
had a longitudinal opening in the center for that
"pedal" shaft; and an irregular-shaped, covered
opening (left of the slot) whereby a "common tablespoon" could be used to "bring some of the grains to
the light, where its complexion can be seen."*

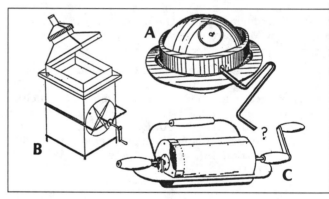

XIV-51. Coffee roaster patents. (A) *Pat'd. Nov. 8,
1881, by George A. Bridler, Middletown, PA. This
patent application had a model – perhaps you'll be
lucky enough to find it. Note the resemblance to the
Woods/Harrington patents. This is a "two-part roasting-vessel provided with a [round] door and a cranked
stirring rod with double circular flanged base support,
which is reversible. I put a question mark at the end of
the crank, not knowing how it was supposed to end,
and assuming it was longer in the straight shaft
where it first comes out of the frame.* **(B)** *Pat'd. Aug. 2,
1881, by Henry A. Leher, Cape Girardeau, MO. The
claim, for which Leher got his patent, seems very silly
– he showed the wooden handle separate from the
crank, and said that it had a socket. The sheet metal
oblong box has a revolving cylinder within.* **(C)** *Cylinder in frame. Pat'd. Dec. 1, 1885, by Matthew J.
Clark, Clermontville, OH. A metallic cylinder in 2 separate longitudinal sections, riveted together, each section "provided with an inwardly-projecting flange
formed integral with the section." In addition, one end
of the cylinder has a "detachable head" or cover. All
pictures from Official Gazette.*

XIV-52. Coffee roasters – cylinders in frames. *Somewhat similar types made of sheet iron with round cast iron frames to fit over range eye, and cranked cylinders.* **(L)** *"Imperial Family" roaster, by T. B. C. Burpee, Philadelphia. Ad in Century, Oct. 1892.* **(R)** *I've been assured that this is the "Griswold Coffee Roaster," although not identified as such in Albert Pick catalog, 1909. Catalog lists 3 sizes, with cylinders: (No. 1) 6"L x 5-1/2" diam.; (No. 2) 8" x 5-1/2"; and (No. 3) 9-1/2" x 7". These correspond with Griswold. Note that the long handle at left is a sort of lid lifter that fits into slots on the round plate of the frame: that's a Griswold feature. But there are two discernable differences: (1) that right-hand short crank. The Griswold has a bent rod crank. But this may be a commercial adaptation; and (2) the opening in the cylinder under the sliding lid is on the wrong end and is the wrong shape for a Griswold. 85 years ago these cost under $2!* (L) **$250+;** (R) *if not Griswold:* **$250+;** *if Griswold:* **$1,000-$1,500**

XIV-54. Coffee roaster. *Pit bottom style, meant to sit down into eye of range. Heavy cast iron, with crank in lid that stirred beans with four "fingers." Hinged lid, upright lifting rings. 11"H x 8-3/4" diam., looks English, but may be American, mid 19th C. Collection of Meryle Evans.* **$275**

XIV-53. Portable coffee roaster, *all-in-one stove with revolving cylinder* **(L)** *"suspended on a crane over fire, and can be swung outward for filling or discharging," as shown here. Made for hand-cranking or power-hookup. "Hyde's Patent" – July 1, 1862, and Feb. 2, 1864. Came in four sizes, for roasting No. 1: 20-30 lbs.; No. 2: 30-60 lbs.; No. 3: 75-135 lbs.; and No. 4: 150-270 lbs. Wow! This picture from Duparquet, Huot & Moneuse hotel supply wholesale catalog, c.1904-1910.* **(R)** *Edward J. Hyde, Philadelphia, PA, pat'd. this combined roaster &. stove July 1, 1862 (#35,758). The stove has an "ash drawer" at bottom, a grate, a draft-flue (the hole opening in back), & an adjustable lid-like piece "which serves as a fuel-door, and may be thrown up so as to convert the stove into an open 'Franklin,' or thrown down so as to make it a 'close' stove."* **$450+**

XIV-55. Coffee roaster. *Sheet iron with holding handle and crank handle. The crank turned the bevel gears in the center of the top, turning the stirrer "fingers" inside. Note trapdoor. 9" diam., 20"L overall. Picture contributed by The Primitive Man, Bob Cahn. I believe this may incorporate the Rufus J. Morton (Big Lick, NC) patent of March 23, 1880 for a "stirrer for coffee-roaster."* **$275+**

Coffee scoops – See Coffee measure

Coffee urns – See Urns

Conjurer kettle – See Conjurer kettle in Chapter XI (Stoves)

Funnel for percolators, enamelware, looks like long cone divided so the top half is like a coffee cup with handle, then a wide flange or lip almost like a saucer, then long conical neck with very small opening at bottom. The flange allowed the percolator funnel to rest on rim of various size coffee pots, to turn them into percolators. Unmarked Matthai-Ingram, about 6-1/2" or 7"L x 4-1/2" diam., c.1890s................................. **$35-$50+**

Hot water kettle – See Tea or hot water kettle. Technically speaking, all teakettles are actually hot water kettles because you heat water in them, then pour the hot water over the tea into a teapot to steep.

Molinillo or muddler – See Chocolate molinillo

Percolator urns – See Urns

Percolators – See also Coffee percolators

Tea ball, perforated spun aluminum acorn with chain, 1920s or 1930s.. **$5-$7**

Tea ball, sterling silver, in shape of tiny fancy teapot, hexagonal body with canted sides, classical handle, high domed lid lifts off for tea leaves, the whole body perforated with fine holes, The Watson Co., Attleboro, MA, about 1-1/2"H, c.1930. .... **$35+**

Teakettles – aluminum

Teakettle, cast aluminum, high bail handle with wooden grip, Colonial style, "Wagner Sidney, O," 5 qts., c.1902 to 1920. .... **$60+**

Teakettle, cast aluminum, lid swivels sideways, neat little filling hole & lid at top of spout, falling wire bail handle with turned wooden grip, flat bottom, "Colonial Design, Safety Fill #8," Griswold Mfg. Co., Erie, PA, 9-3/4" diam., 6 qt. capacity, pat'd. Sept. 9, 1913............ **$65+**

Teakettle, cast aluminum, side-swiveling lid, wire bail handle with wood grip, "Colonial Teakettle," Wagner Ware, 6 qts., pat'd. 1902. .... **$65+**

XIV-56. Tea or hot water boiler, of early type that was originally made to hang inside fireplace, although it would work on a range top too. The bail with eye on this 20th C. one meant it could be hung on a hook somewhere convenient. Copper, with tinned iron heavyweight bail, long spigot. Henry Rogers Sons & Co., Wolverhampton, England, 1914 catalog. **$175+**

XIV-57. Tea or hot water boiler, also sometimes called a **hot water urn**. Copper, slightly tapered body, long tapered spigot. Flat lid with bracket handle, forged iron bail handle with swivel ring in center. Smithsonian dates between 1854 and 1894, but we see from XIV-56 that it could be much later. 11-1/8"H exclusive of bail x 21-1/4"L overall with faucet. Picture courtesy of the National Museum of American History, John Paul Remensnyder estate. **$250+**

Teakettle, cast aluminum, sliding lid, turned wood handle with wooden knob, oblong shaped kettle, very dramatic, "Wagner Ware Grand Prize Teakettle," 12-5/8"L x 8-7/8"W, pat'd. Sept. 28, 1916. .... **$70+**

Teakettle, cast aluminum, smooth sides, slightly domed swivel or swingaway lid, flat bottom, wire bail with turned wood grip, "Griswold #6, 8-7/8" diam. at bottom, c.1920.. **$100+**

Teakettle, cast aluminum, rounded body with small flat part under spout, hinged lid, short fat gooseneck spout, coiled wire bail, "No. 330," Wear-Ever, T. A. C. U. Co. (Aluminum Cooking Utensil Co., sales division of Pittsburgh Reduction Co.), 8-1/4" diam., 1903-1915. .... **$30+**

Teakettle, cast aluminum with highly polished finish on rounded body, lovely iron wire falling bail handle in "chef's hat" profile characteristic of kettles from the early 19th C., coiled grip, long inquisitive gooseneck spout, "Wear-Ever," T. A. C. U. Co. (The Aluminum Cooking Utensil Co.), 9" diam., c.1920. .. **$30+**

❖ NOTES ❖

Contenders for First Aluminum Casting – A 1917 article on Griswold in *House Furnishing Review* states "During the period 1890 to 1894, the Griswold Manufacturing Company in conjunction with the original Pittsburgh Aluminum Company – now the Aluminum Company of America – first made, in an experimental way, aluminum ware. This aluminum ware was cast in sand molds, and was the first cast aluminum ware known to have been made in the world. A few of these first pieces of cast aluminum ware were offered to the trade during those years, and after long years of service, they have still been found to be in perfect condition.

"A process of hardening the surface of aluminum ware was later discovered. After casting, by a secret electrical treatment, the surface is tempered, hardening and closing all the pores of the metal. This 'tempered surface,' as it is called, is positive proof against discoloration or absorption, and the ware remains for all time a silvery gray." The article adds "the first big trade on Griswold cast aluminum tempered ware came through their London office" and only later became known all through the world! • Auburn Hollow Ware Co., of Auburn, NY, made at least one exhibition piece of cast aluminum – a teakettle, and it may have actually been the first cast aluminum kitchen piece made. This was reported in *The Metal Worker*, April 30, 1892 (with "Wax" instead of "Ware").

Teakettle, cast aluminum, very modern style, low arched handle, large hole in molded spout, for filling & pouring, "Magnalite #4135," mfd. by Wagner Ware, 10" diam., c.1930s. .... **$55+**

Teakettle, or hot water kettle, cast aluminum, side-swiveling lid, short coffee-boiler style V-neck lip or spout, wire handle with wooden grip, very simple slanted straight sides, looks thick & it is, Wagner Mfg. Co., 10" diam. at base, c.1910. .... **$50+**

Teakettles, cast aluminum, various styles, mfd. by Griswold, Wagner or Wear-Ever T.A.C.U. Co. (The Aluminum Cooking Utensil Co.), about 8-1/4" to 10" diam., 1903 to about 1915. • When I wrote my first book in the early 1970s, I only knew one person who collected them, Paul Persoff, my photographer. He used to buy them at the Englishtown (NJ) flea market for under $5. General ball-park range for this type of kettle: .... **$35-$75**

Teakettle, cheap, thin aluminum with nifty molded black plastic chef's head whistle-stopper, copper bottom, cane-wrapped handle, "Raineland" with 3 stars, 7-3/4"H, 20th C. .... **$15-$18**

Teakettles – Chromium

Teakettle, chrome body, copper bottom, strap handle painted red, plastic bird's head whistle, "Revere," 20th C. .... **$25+**

XIV-58. Tea kettle. Cast aluminum, wood, bail handle. 10" diam., c.1910. Wagner Mfg. Co., Sidney, OH. Collection of Paul Persoff, who photographed my first book so long ago. **$45+**

XIV-59. Tea kettle. Cast aluminum, wood. Note small filling hole with its own lid, and larger swiveling lid, good for cleaning lime deposits out of interior. 8-1/2" diam., 4 quart size. "Colonial Design, Safety Fill," mfd. by Griswold, Erie, PA. Pat'd. Sept. 9, 1913. Collection of Paul Persoff.

Teakettle, chromium plated solid copper, red strap handle, copper bottom, very Art Deco design, cast white metal bird whistle, "Made in U. S. A.," 20th C – similar to the Revere one. .... **$25+**

Teakettles – Copper

Teakettle, brass & copper, possibly stripped of original nickel plating, forged iron bail with turned wood grip, white porcelain knob on lid, 5-1/2"H including knob, late 19th C. .... **$40-$55**

❖ NOTES ❖

Cleaning Copper With Love Apples – While waiting for dishes to be served in a restaurant in NYC's Chinatown, we used to amuse ourselves cleaning pennies with the Louisiana Hot Sauce™ that was a standard condiment on the table. The darkest penny will turn bright and pink (and unshiny) in seconds. Earl Proulx, in his *Yankee* column, "Plain Talk," Dec. 1987, gives a tip on cleaning a very darkened copper bath tub: "For the inside of the tub, scour it with ketchup."

•   •   •

Arsenic & old copper – "As arsenic frequently enters metallic compositions, especially those of copper and tin, it were much to be wished, that such compound metals could for ever be banished, at least from our Kitchens." Anthony Florian Madinzer Willich, *The Domestic Encyclopedia; or A Dictionary of Facts & Useful Knowledge...*, 1st American edition, Philadelphia: W. Y. Birch & A. Small, 1803-04.

Teakettle, copper, beautiful slender gooseneck spout, fixed handle, domed & ridged lid with high acorn finial, mid 19th C. .... **$150+**

Teakettle, copper, dovetail seam, gooseneck spout, signed "J M W E," English (?), 19th C. • A **dovetail seam** is just what it sounds like – small "fingers" of the copper alternating from either side of the seam. The reason for it is that it increases the total area of brazing, thus strengthening the seam. See also the Mold chapter.. **$175+**

Teakettle, copper, dovetail seam, high dome lid, pit bottom, little hinged cover for spout, no marks, but hinged lid on spout prob. means English, 8-1/4"H, 2nd quarter 19th C..................................... **$165+**

Teakettle, copper, dovetail seams, forward thrust gooseneck spout, extremely well-formed falling strap handle of copper, more in profile of a bowler hat than a chef's hat, a few dings, marked "G. Ebert," PA, 6-1/2"H exclusive of handle, 19th C............................. **$400+**

Teakettle, copper, gooseneck spout, "Finnemore, Granbrook" (might be Cranbrook), 5 qt. capacity, early 19th C. .... **$225+**

Teakettle, copper, gooseneck, with brass finial, unsigned (look on flat of handle usually for stamped

XIV-61. Teakettles. *Both copper with barrel handles.* ***(L)*** *"New Shape Round" kettle, made in capacities from 2 to 10 pints.* ***(R)*** *"Range" kettle "with well,"* *(ie. a pit bottom kettle). Made to hold from 6 to 12 pints (skipping 11). Henry Rogers Sons, Wolverhampton, England, 1914 catalog.* **$85-$150+**

maker's name), prob. PA, marked "5," 1830s-40s. • Marked wares bring highest prices............. **$275+**

Teakettle, copper, highly polished, turned wooden grip on wire bail handle, porcelain knob on lid, "Majestic," c.1890s-1910. .... **$65+**

Teakettle, copper, on stand, with alcohol burner, meant for sideboard or tea table, Swedish, c.1890s-1910. .... **$95+**

Teakettle, copper, pieced, with horizontal seam at "equator" or widest part, cast brass handle frame & handle, no marks, 2 qt. size, 9" diam., mid 19th C. or earlier. .... **$75+**

Teakettle, copper, ringed around & shaped like a woven straw-grass bee skep, bird's head whistle in spout, early 20th C. .... **$35+**

Teakettle, copper, tin inside, shaped like a squatty bell, with a very wide (impossible to tip over) base & a narrow opening, strap handle with grip, very large coffee boiler V-neck type spout, close fitting flat lid. I've never seen a real one or even seen a picture of an old one of which this is supposed to be a replica. An ad featuring this **reproduction** has explanatory notes. "A replica of those [the copper captain's kettles] used aboard Nantucket Whalers during the 1800's. Used in the Captain's private pantry for warming his tea or grog." Landfall Collection, S. Norwalk, CT, Feb. 1975, *Early American Life* magazine. American-made (?), 10"H including handle, 10" diam. at base, c.1975. • A ship's decanter has a squatty, wide-bottomed body so that the center of gravity is as low as possible. I believe this ad is legitimate & that old kettles like this, dating to the early to mid 19th C., probably exist. Price range is for repro, which sold for $47.75 ppd. in 1975. .... **$30-$55**

Teakettle, copper with brass trim, bail handle with black finished turned wood grip, wooden knob on lid, marked "Rome" where handle is attached, Rome, NY, 1898. • Possibly originally nickeled, as many are found that way, or maybe they were offered both ways. .... **$55+**

Teakettle, copper with gooseneck spout, falling handle, "J. Gable, Lancaster, PA," 14-3/8"H with handle upright, "1843." Marked, dated & good form = high price. .... **$450-$600**

XIV-60. Tea kettle. *Copper, tinned inside, brass mushroom finial on domed lid, falling handle of flat copper forming chef's hat shape. This one rakish by being bent – whether that was the intention of the maker or early user or an accident we don't know, but it did make it easier to pour from; I know, I went through the motions of pouring from it. Marked in relief on top of handle "John W. Schlosser." This exact type of small brass finial is also found on early- to mid-19th C. cabinet-work, such as spice chests, and were used as pulls for the small drawers. They were probably bought by the gross from a brass foundry in Connecticut. When handle is up – 11-3/4"H, early 19th C. Photograph by Jennifer Oka. Picture courtesy of the National Museum of American History, Smithsonian Institution, John Paul Remensnyder estate. Value guide is very general – marked copperwares highly collectible, but to a small select market. This "value" is not meant to set a price on a John Schlosser tea kettle, nor on a piece in the Smithsonian's collection, nor on any other particular marked American kettle.*

XIV-62. Teakettles. *Square ones, seamless copper with gooseneck spouts, meant for gas stoves. (L) To be had with barrel or ebonized wood handle. (R) To be had with amber or "opal" (opalescent glass) handle. Made in several sizes, from 4 to 12 pints. Also Henry Rogers, 1914.* **$95-$150+**

Teakettle, copper, with hollow copper handle, acorn finial on lid, gooseneck spout, English, late 19th C. .... **$95-$125**

Teakettle, copper with iron bail handle, wood grip, lid with strap handle, short duckneck spout, marked "Old Colony," sounds like a Colonial Revival reproduction, (possibly Old Colony Foundry, in which case it'd be Bridgewater, MA), 7-1/2"H x 9-1/4" diam., c.1920s. .... **$35-$50**

Teakettle, copper with iron whistling bird in spout, late 19th C. For me, 90% of the value is in that bird! .... **$65-$80**

XIV-63. Teakettle. *Copper, tinned inside, tapered body, crooked neck spout, falling strap handle in good chef's toque profile, domed lid, brass mushroom finial. Marked on handle "C. Kiefer, Lancaster, PA, 1848." 12-11/16"H with handle up x 13-3/8" overall length. Photograph by Jennifer Oka. Picture courtesy of the National Museum of American History, Smithsonian Institution, John Paul Remensnyder estate.*

XIV-64. Teakettle. *Copper, oval cylinder with flat bottom & top, gooseneck spout, fixed handle with barrel grip flanked by small spurs. Small lid with turned wooden knob plus an opening on opposite side, which is the top of an inverted funnel. It's a sort of double-boiler vessel within the outer pot. 10-1/4"H overall x 10"L. Embossed medallion fixed on top says "The Cyprus No. 341. 1879. Patented Jan. 28." Probably English. Photograph by Jennifer Oka. Picture courtesy of the National Museum of American History, Smithsonian Institution, John Paul Remensnyder estate.*

Teakettle, copper with simple scrolly handle, gooseneck spout, acorn finial, PA, prob. Philadelphia, 2 cup size, late 18th or early 19th C....................... **$125+**

❖ NOTES ❖

Finial Shapes – The "Silver" chapter of *The Complete Encyclopedia of Antiques*, compiled by *The Connoisseur*, edited by L. G. G. Ramsey, Hawthorn Books, 1962, has a short entry on finials, applicable to silver wares, but – after factoring in a time lag for decorative elements being adopted for other metals, and an even longer lag to reach America – we can use the facts when we study other metals. The **timetable for silver finial shapes,** according to Ramsey: Early 18th C. = acorn; Rococo Period, Mid to Late 18th C. = flame and pineapple; Classic Period, Late 18th to Early 19th C. = urn, pine cone. For application to American copper teakettles, you would probably be safe adding 50 to 100 or so years to the widespread use of acorns; then a much shorter time, say 30 to 50 years for the flame and pineapple; by the time you get to urns and pine cones, the period is only about 15 to 25 years behind in America compared to Great Britain or the Continent. As with all such "rules" of thumb, it's not true in every case.

Teakettle, copper, with unusual (probably replacement) green & white enameled lid, gooseneck spout, "Majestic," American, 5 qt. capacity, c.1890s-1910....... **$55+**

Tea or water kettle, copper, tinned inside, dovetail seams, lid with brass acorn finial, gooseneck spout, marked "J. C. & W. Lord," Birmingham, England, 7"H x 5-3/4" diam., late 19th C. **$145**

Tea or water kettle, nickeled brass & copper, gooseneck style, "Gilchrist," large size, 1903................... **$35+**

Tea or water kettle, nickel-plated copper, crescent shaped so that it can be placed on top of stove, against the stovepipe. 7"H x 14" diam. Maker unknown; seen in Albert Pick wholesale catalog, 1909.................... **$75+**

Teakettles – electric

Teakettle, electric, chrome-plated metal, very modern in appearance. Electrical element is in back end of handle, & the kettle could also be used stovetop like any other teakettle. "Speedmaster," (Waters-Genter?, hence Minneapolis?), 1930s. .... **$35+**

Teakettle, electric, silver plated copper in hammered finish, 8 sided & footed, with plain fat gooseneck spout, high rattan-wrapped handle, acorn finial made of oak, designed by Peter Behrens, Germany, 1909.................................... **$450-$600**

Teakettles – enamelware

Teakettle, blue & white swirl agateware, white lining, swivel lid, "Wrought Iron Range Co.," St. Louis, MO, 4 qt. capacity, late 19th C. .... **$175+**

Teakettle, cobalt blue enamelware, marked only "Iron Range Company," probably same as "Wrought Iron Range Co.," (St. Louis, MO), late 19th C....... **$135+**

Teakettle, cobalt enamelware, in small size sometimes called a Five-O'clock, American, late 19th, early 20th C. .... **$50+**

Teakettle, cobalt & white swirl agateware, 19th C. **$130+**

Teakettle, deep green agateware, white enameled interior, gooseneck spout, high domed hinged lid, "Made in Yugoslavia," early 20th C. .... **$50+**

Teakettle, gray granite, bell-bottomed, gooseneck, bai̇ handle, 19th C. This particular one is a "shelf," o̤ should I say "hob" piece, as the bottom has holes al̤ over it. .... **$1?**

Teakettle, whistling type, steel body decoratively enam̤eled as worried setting hen, handle arches over lid̤ spout has cast phenolic resin chicken head, the comb̤ attached with a rachet device thumb-activated to pul̤ back for pouring, wings delineated in black lines or̤ white body, "TeaBird™," M. Kamenstein (NYC), bṳ made in Taiwan, 2-1/2 qts. capacity, 1986. • **Futurewatch.** – Anything with figural detail, whethe̤ it's useful or useless, will probably have collector value sometime in the future. Original price of this is $30̤ Discounted to $23 in 1989. By the mid 1990s there̤ were many figurals – various cats, birds, fruits, etc.̤ for new retail under $50. Secondhand market in perfect condition, possibly close to that. But wait 50̤ years, and never use it, and it may gain 200% on your̤ investment. Or it may not. .... **$20+**

Teakettle, mottled green agateware, tiny flakes chipped off, early 20th C. Condition lowers value. **$35**

Teakettle, tan with green trim enamelware, probably Vollrath, 1930s... **$30**

Teakettle, very architectural looking, beige enamelware with black trim & black interior, chrome handle with Art Deco Bakelite™ (or other molded phenolic resin) knob, canted back handle with plastic grip, strainer holes in spout, no mark, 8-1/2"H exclusive of handle, c.1930s. .... **$45-$60**

Teakettle & teapot, matched pair, shaded blue ombré enamelware, American, 6"H & 6-1/2"H, early 20th - late 19th C.. **$175-$265**

Teakettle, teapot & coffee pot set, sky blue enamelware, cobalt knobs, coffee pot's glass lid made by H. C. Fry Co., Rochester, PA, 20th C. .... **$165-$250**

Teakettles – iron: cast, enameled, sheet, stainless steel

Teakettle, white enameled iron, cobalt handle & knob, on bottom in black is a transfer print of a dreaming woman in a corset, with title "Dream of Comfort,"

XIV-65. Teapot. *Gray graniteware with white metal (probably Britannia) spout, handle, lid, breast-band and base rim. Late 19th C. From the collection of Susan Kistler, Lenhartsville, PA.* **$125+**

XIV-66. Teapot. *"Patent decorated pearl agateware,"* mfd. by Manning, Bowman & Co., in their 1892 catalog. Pat'd. in 1883. This style was one of several occasion-related pieces. People could pay extra and really personalize them – this one says *"Grandma's Birthday."* Value is partly in the sentiments. **$200+**

adv'g. "The Specialité Corset," and on bottom in cobalt is mark "20 C III," 7-5/8" diam., early 20th C. • For a similar motif, see the "Mademoiselle Worth" pitcher in the Container chapter. I think that if corset collectors (they do exist!) discovered these pieces the prices would go up. **$150**

Teakettle, blue & white enameled heavy cast iron, late 19th C.• A lot of these big kettles are actually water kettles, meant to heat water for tea (or anything else). .... **$75+**

Teakettle, deep blue & white enamelware over cast iron, low & squat, "Wrought Iron Range Co.," St. Louis, MO, 7" diam., 4th quarter 19th C. ..... **$85+**

Teakettle, brown & white enameled cast iron, European or American, 2 qt. size, c.1890s-1910.. **$125+**

Teakettle, deep midnight blue enameled cast iron, low & squat of the type sometimes called a bachelor kettle, fixed handle with wooden grip, very short pouring lip or spout, American, 8" diam. base, late 19th C. .... **$50-$75**

XIV-67. Teakettle. *Cast iron, globular body with wonderful spout. Fitted tin lid, wire bail, 3 short legs. Photograph courtesy Pat Guthman Antiques, Southport, CT. Maybe not "classic," but even better because it's so exuberant and idiosyncratic.* **$265+**

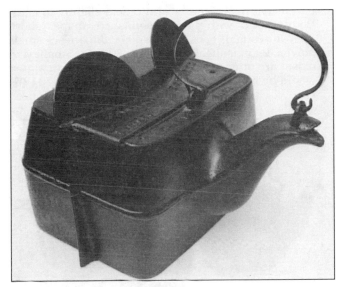

XIV-68. Teakettle. *Cast iron, oblong, with Mickey Mouse ears. These fins actually form, along with the rib down the sides, a partial heat seal. The kettle was made for a specific type of stove, and was stuck partway into its heat box. The collector was told, when he bought it, that it "came off a barge on the Erie Canal." Such stoves may have been used on canal boats.I was told this was patented as a **boiling kettle**, Feb. 23, 1869, (#87,306), by Stephen Spoor, Phelps, NY, and mfd. by him. The 1869 boiling kettle looks totally unlike this kettle; it's just a plain pot. Oddly, the marking seen on the lid "Spoor's Patent #5114," is untraceable so far. I've searched the patent index for every permutation of kettle, and tried searches of 5,115, 5,411, 5,144, and many others! There is no such patent, or reissue, or design. Photograph courtesy of David Smith. (See his article following Chapter IV, on cast iron muffin pans, etc.)* **$225+**

Teakettle, red enameled thin metal, little aluminum snap-on whistle with turned wood knob, you have to take whistle off to pour, no mark, 6-7/8" diam. across bottom, c.1930s or 1940s................... **$10+**

Teakettle, cast iron, odd square shape with 1"W flange angled from back to front down sides and top, meant to fit into a specific base burner, forged iron bail handle hooks to end of spout and to hinge of lid, "Spoor's Patent #5114," mfd. by Stephen Spoor, and by license by A. Ingraham & Co., Troy, NY, 7"H x 6"W x 10"L including spout, c.1850. See the picture, XIV-68 for the puzzle of the patent number. Makes me wonder if it isn't a patent by A. D. Spoor of Coxsackie, NY; several of his stove patents date before numbering, to the 1830s. • **Classic.** – This is a spectacular must-have for teakettle collectors. Spoor also designed & patented a sort of flanged inserted niche that went into the stove, & could then be used as a shelf with a tea steeper or a flat iron or a square frying pan. .... **$225+**

Teakettle, of a size and shape that make it look like a teapot, cast iron, black, very pebbly surface like a warty toad, fine polished surface, small round lift-off lid with cast knob, the round smooth forged bail handle is somewhat bigger around than might be expected (at least from a Western point of view) and is thickest in the center and tapers slightly to ends. Body round with faintly squashed shape, short, almost vestigal, gooseneck spout. Japanese, small, maybe 2 pt. capacity, 19th or 20th C. Smallest & oldest are priced in the upper range; brand new ones would be much less: .... **$125+**

XIV-69. Teakettles. *"Ripley's New" kettles, from 1860 announcement that patent was being extended to March 14, 1867. "The objection for many years existing to the use of the old fashion Cast Iron Tea Kettle, owing to the difficulty in moulding the spout, its liability to clog or fill, especially when use of lime water is made, were fully removed by the production of the Kettle in the above, which was the invention of Mr. Ezra Ripley, to whom letters patent were granted on the 14th of March, 1846 (#4,417). The breast of the Kettle may be so shaped as to prevent any possibility of filling with sediment, and ensuring the greatest rapidity of pouring. The cost of moulding is reduced at least six cents per Kettle, a very material difference from former prices. The pattern may be made in any shape desired, but will be composed of two parts, the spout being connected with the body of the Kettle. Each part of the pattern can be removed from the green sand core separately, leaving the cores of the spout and body of the Kettle together in one entire core, which prevents the old necessity of setting a dry sand core for the spout. The pattern may be made to part vertically or longitudinally at the option of the manufacturer. The spouts being spacious admit of being enameled with the inner surface of the body if desired. ... We are prepared to dispose of foundry rights; patterns and Flasks can be furnished on reasonable terms." Signed Ezra Ripley, Fuller, Warren & Co., Troy, NY, March 15, 1860; a circular sent to "stove and hollow ware manufacturers." Ripley got two more teakettle patents: July 9, 1867 (#66,521) & July 14, 1868 (#79,860).* **$150+**

❖ **NOTES** ❖

Japanese Nambu Ironware – Such iron wares a[s] the kettle above are considered among the finest [of] Japanese crafts, and are the so-called Nambu iron ware, made from a peculiarly ferrous sand (probabl[y] part volcanic material) in the northernmost part of th[e] main island. Nambu iron is also used for cooking ware including hollowware & griddles. The kettles, at leas[t] are beginning to show up regularly at antique shows[.] The iron sometimes has a very dark brown color. Th[e] teakettles are finely made, and there is little that woul[d] alert the first time viewer of some examples that the[y] are Japanese. There is an almost bell-like ringin[g] sound when you put the lid back on that differs fro[m] the clunk or dull ring of most Western cast iron. I don'[t] know if the Japanese iron workers add(ed) somethin[g] to the metal. Sometimes the lids are made of brass[,] bronze, or (rarely) copper, in addition to iron. I hav[e] never seen one without a pebbly or hobnailed surface (known as "hailstone" finish, according to Joel Schiff)[.] The craft continues, and newly-made "hailstone" Japa-nese teakettles are sold in import food and housewares shops. For export to the U.S., they should have country of origin marked somewhere. In addition, modern ones may have an enameled color finish on outside, or a white-enameled, or tinned interior, sometimes an aluminum strainer insert, and the casting gate has been ground off, as opposed to snapped off. • A very charming **miniature** of this already small teakettle is actually a water vessel, perhaps an inch or so in height, used by Sumi painters and calligraphers to moisten the ink blocks. They have a tiny regulating hole, which the user covers with forefinger, while holding lid on too. By removing the finger briefly, the pressure inside is relieved and the water comes out the tiny spout. These antique miniatures (a teapot is only one form the little water vessel may take, some are figural animals or birds or mythological beings) are sold for upwards of $400. I saw one for $800. In Japanese metal work, as in so much else of their artisanry, the master whose name is signed in a teensy mark, makes up much of the value. This is a very sophisticated market.

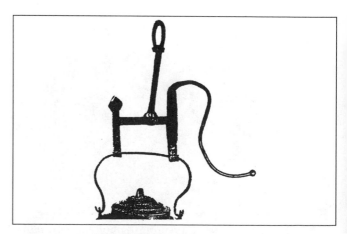

XIV-70. Kettle tilter. *Wrought iron, swivel ring at top, "S" curved handle with ball tip, approx. 14"L. Late 18th or early 19th C. Ex-Keillor Collection.* **$375-$450**

XIV-71. Tea- or water kettle. *Cast iron, pit bottom, hinged lid, coiled heat-dissipating bail handle. Nice squat, bulbous body. Squared gooseneck ("swan" as in England) spout. Marked "M'Dowell, Phila. PA." 8"H overall to slightly domed lid x 12" diam. Part that fits down into range eye is 9" diam. x 1-1/2"H. Courtesy of dealer Jean Hatt, Hatt's Hutt, Denver, PA.* **$125+**

Tea or hot water kettle, cast iron, pit bottom, magnificent & beautiful round body, short gooseneck spout, falling forged iron bail, hinged lid lifts up, hinge opposite spout, the flattish lid has name, plus a beaded design in a circle, "Abbott & Noble," Philadelphia, 10-3/4"H x 9-1/2" diam., late 19th C. .... **$325+**

Teakettle, bulbous cast iron body, 3 short feet, gooseneck, forged iron handle, no maker's mark, American, late 18th or early 19th C. .... **$150+**

Teakettle, cast iron, swiveled or pivoted copper cover, gooseneck spout, American, 9"H, 19th C. .... **$80+**

XIV-72. Closeup of spout of XIV-71. *Note marks of filing to smooth out casting lines; also the small knurled knob to lid.*

XIV-73. Teakettle. *Enameled cast iron, deep midnight blue, barrel handle. American, late 19th C. Courtesy Darwin Urffer.* **$55+**

Teakettle, cast iron with tin cover, heavy bail handle, long gooseneck spout, American, 5-1/2"H, late 19th C. .... **$55+**

Teakettle & kettle tilter combined, called a tipping kettle, cast iron, nearly straight sides, simple slightly domed lid with ring finial; the curved lever on top, right above spout, is the attached kettle tilter. Forged iron bail handle with ring top, at right angles to the spout, allows it to be hung from trammel or pot hook. Prob. New England, about 15"H x 12" diam., late 1700s to early 1800s. Signed ones bring even more. .... **$600+**

Tea or water kettle, cast iron, bail handle marked with place and date, Vermont, 3 qt. size, "1875.".... **$90+**

Teakettle, cast iron, "Rhine Mfg. Co.," 19th C. .... **$45+**

Teakettle, cast iron, 3 very short peg feet, long casting gate on bottom, very pronounced angular gooseneck, forged bail, vertical casting seams on both sides, circumferential casting seam around middle, and including lower part of spout, domed lid with riveted cast brass knob (not necessarily original), no mark, American, 7"H, 2nd quarter 19th C. The value here is in the age, the nice form, & especially the spout. .... **$200-$250+**

Teakettle, cast iron, "Foxell, Jones & Millard, Troy, NY," 1870s. .... **$75+**

Teakettle, cast iron, "bowler hat" profile wire bail handle, domed lid with spoked ridges out from squared finial, pit bottom, "Higgins, Foxell & Martin," Troy, NY, c.1860. .... **$95+**

Teakettle, cast iron, brass cover, fixed handle, poss. English because of the brass lid, 19th C. .... **$95+**

Teakettle, cast iron, bulbous with gooseneck spout, small feet, iron handle, prob. American, mid-19th C. .... **$175+**

Teakettle, cast iron, enameled, swirled cobalt blue & white, bail handle, short "duckneck" spout, marked "St. Louis Stove Works," MO, early 20th C., poss. late 19th C. .... **$75+**

Teakettle, cast iron, flat bottom, duckneck (short fat gooseneck) spout, casting line curves down &

around close to bottom at back, falling bail of nickeled wire with heat-dissipating coil for hand grip, swivel lid covers entire top, and pivots at back where handle is attached, with knob at opposite edge. The center part of the lid, like a mesa, rises up & has sizeable flat top – touted as being a place where you could set something else to keep it hot, "Favorite," Favorite Stove & Range Co., Piqua, OH, advertised July 1890. • This line was available in pit bottom style, & in various finishes: plain cast iron, "milled" iron, galvanized, nickel plated, & nickel plated with white porcelain enamel inside. .... **$65-$95**

❖ NOTES ❖

Wagner Too? – In Jan. 1892, an editorial notice in *The Metal Worker* told about a new company's new line of "high grade hollow ware, high polish or nickeled finish, including a teakettle available flat bottom or pit bottom, in seven sizes from 8 to 30 gallons. The linecut used to illustrate the kettle is as close to identical as possible to the linecut showing the Favorite Piqua kettle 18 months before, considering that two different firms of cut engravers made the pictures. In addition, a low kettle with bail, round tipping handle and 3 peg feet is shown; it is also the same as an earlier Favorite, though engraved by a different firm. The use of the same linecuts was widespread in retail catalogs, but one wonders what's the case here? Did Wagner copy Favorite's kettles themselves, detail for detail? Did they only make a similar one and require of their engraver to furnish them with "an engraving like this one here" ... tossing the Favorite one on the artist's desk? No mention is made in *Metal Worker* about the similarity; but this is no surprise as many trade magazines then, as now, were a mix of advertising, editorial puffery, editorial posturing, and serious facts.

Teakettle, cast iron, flat bottom, hexagonal dome on flat flanged lid, forged bail, marked "B" on bottom & a large "4" on side, American, 5-1/2"H exclusive of lid, mid 19th C.. **$75+**

Teakettle, cast iron, forged bail with turned wood grip, swiveling or pivoting hinged lid, pit bottom, heavily incrusted on outside, marked on lid "John A. Goewey, #8," Albany, NY, 19th C...................... **$75+**

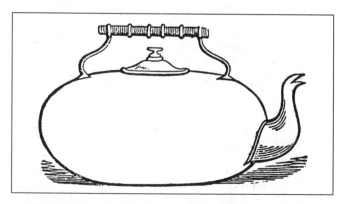

XIV-74. Tea kettle. *Depicted without a caption in American Home Cook Book, 1854. Probably brass. A charming plump shape, and interesting handle grip.*

Teakettle, cast iron, forged iron handle, swiveling li[d] with no knob, 3 short peg legs, long straight castin[g] gate on bottom is filed down, on side is a sort o[f] palm leaf decoration cast in, marked only "S. C." which may be Spencer Cole, poss. CT, poss. late 18th C. or early 19th C. .... **$300-$40[0]**

Teakettle, cast iron, gooseneck spout, marked only "Bro[m]wich," Bromwich (or West Bromwich), England where at least 2 iron foundries were: Siddons and Kenrick. This one has 2 qt. capacity, mid 19th C...... **$80+**

❖ NOTES ❖

Using a Gazetteer – Because from the form there was some question in my mind when I first saw this many years ago if it was American or English, I checked a very useful reference book I bought called *The Centennial Gazetteer of the United States*, by A. von Steinwehr, published by J. C. McCurdy & Co. in 1875. It contains "a geographical and statistical encyclopædia of the states, territories, counties, townships, villages, post-offices, mountains, rivers, lakes, etc., in the American Union," and can be checked for place names from the 18th Century through 1875. Bromwich seems such a John Updike/Connecticut-type name, but as of 1875 there was no Bromwich or West Bromwich anywhere in the "Union."

Teakettle, cast iron, gooseneck spout, forged bail, "J. J. Siddons West Bromwich," England, 2 qt. capacity, 19th C. .... **$75-$100**

Teakettle, cast iron, gooseneck spout, forged iron bail handle unusual in that it's fixed in place – that is, it's not a "falling bail." American, 7-1/2"H overall, very small 1-1/2 pt. capacity, early 19th C... **$175+**

❖ NOTES ❖

Pit bottoms & flat bottoms – The "pit" referred to is a hole in the top of a range or cook stove, which is covered with a lid that can be lifted out to gain direct access to the fire's heat. A piece of "pit bottom" hollowware has, in effect, two bottoms: the lower bottom, which has a smaller circumference, to fit down into the hole, fire hole, or range eye; and the flanged part that rests on the flat area around the hole or range eye. Another way of making the hole smaller so that flat bottom hollowware won't fall through is to use an adapter ring (See adapter ring picture, X-3 in Hearths). • A flat bottom pot or kettle is flat all the way across the bottom, and is generally a little newer than a pit bottom pot or kettle.

Teakettle, cast iron, pit bottom, chubby body with short duckneck spout, flat falling bail handle connected to the levered lid with small thumb piece, "S. W. Ransom & Co. # 8," pat'd. by A. Ransom & R. D. Granger, Albany, NY, Mar. 19, 1861. .... **$75+**

Teakettle, cast iron, pit bottom, swivel lid with finely embossed scrolls on it, "A. Bradley & Co., Pittsburgh, PA," 1866... **$75+**

Teakettle, cast iron, pit bottom, hinged lid, flat forged bail, "I. A. Sheppard & Co., Baltimore, MD" (another Sheppard foundry was in Philadelphia), mid 19th C. • According to Leander Bishop's book on early manufacturing, Baltimore had, in 1860, ten iron foundries (including stove makers), five brass founders, and 37 tin, copper, and sheet iron wares manufacturers. • This is an interesting piece because of the combination of attractive elements: it's cast iron, with a pit bottom, and instead of a heavy iron wire bail handle, it's got a wrought or forged iron handle. .... **$100+**

Teakettle, cast iron, pit bottom, ornate scrolled casting on top of sides, 3 tiny peg feet, forged bail, slightly domed lid with tab handle, no mark, American, 7"H exclusive of lid, 2nd to 3rd quarter 19th C. ..... **$75+**

Teakettle, cast iron, pit bottom, swingaway lid, flat bail handle, neat shape with a sort of decoy-like swooping line, no number or mfr.'s mark, American, 11" diam. including spout, late 19th C. .... **$85+**

Teakettle, cast iron, straight sides, high gooseneck spout, almost serpentine in its curves, with fabulous very wide flat "tu-tu" flange partway down sides - making the kettle a variety of pit bottom for range top, falling bail forged strap handle, American, early 19th C., transition from hearth to range .... **$225+**

Teakettle, cast iron, pit bottom, swingaway pivoting lid, short stubby spout, small separate washer-like disc fits in depression at back end of lid where forged bail hooks on to lug, "Joseph Bell & Co. #9, Wheeling, WV," pat'd. (prob. by B. H. Menke, Cincinnati), June 23, 1863. .... **$125+**

Teakettle, cast iron, shallow pit bottom, swivel lid, fat spout, falling forged iron bail, "Bussey & McLeod," stove makers, Troy, NY, 8"H, pat'd. Jan. 1, 1861. .... **$85+**

XIV-75. Teakettle. *Cast iron with forged iron handle, bronze lid. 5-1/4"H x 6" diam. Early 19th C.* **Japanese.** *"The Accomplished & Lucky Tea-Kettle," a Japanese folk tale about an old teakettle living at the Morinji temple in Jōshin Province. "One day, when the priest was about to hang it over the hearth to boil the water for his tea, to his amazement, the kettle all of a sudden put forth the head and tail of a badger. What a wonderful kettle, to come out all over fur!" The priest called in the novices to see it, and whilst they were staring, the kettle jumped up into the air and began flying about the room. The priest and his pupils chased it, and finally knocked it down and forced it into a box, "intending to carry it off and throw it away in some distant place, so that they might be no more plagued by the goblin." Unfortunately, a tinker who did work at the temple came by, and the priest thought he might as well make a little money for the kettle by selling it to the tinker. When he took it out of the box, it looked like an ordinary kettle; the tinker paid 20 copper coins for it and left for home. During the night, the tinker was disturbed many times by noises, and was frightened by the sight of the kettle covered with fur, but it always resumed its kettle shape. The tinker decided to set up an exhibition at a traveling show, along with musicians and other performers, and he became rich when all the great nobles of the court came to see the dancing kettle. "At last the tinker grew so rich that he took the kettle back to the temple, where it was laid up as a precious treasure, and worshiped as a saint." Published in* Scribner's Monthly, *Oct. 1873, and taken by them from Mitford's Tales of Old Japan.*

XIV-76. Teakettle. *Cast iron, small globular body with 3 short feet. Cast in 3 sections, see vertical & horizontal seams. Crook-neck spout, flat forged falling bail, stepped dome lid – intriguingly chained to handle. "A. T." cast on side. 6-1/8"H x 12-1/4"L. Prob. 1830s. Photograph by Jennifer Oka. Picture courtesy of the National Museum of American History, Smithsonian Institution, John Paul Remensnyder estate.*

new iron pot before cooking in it; scour well with soap and sand, then fill with clean water, and boil one or two hours." Practical Housekeeping, 1884.

Another recipe for seasoning: *"The best way to prepare a new iron kettle for use is to fill it with clean potato-peelings, boil them an hour or more, then wash the kettle with hot water, wipe it dry and rub it with a little lard; repeat the rubbing for six times after using. In this way you will prevent rust, and all the little annoyances liable to occur in the use of a new kettle." Emma Whitcomb Babcock, Household Hints, NY: Appleton, 1881. See more on this subject in Chapter IV, Molds, and the Cast iron muffin pan sub-chapter.*

Teakettle, cast iron, swivel lid, forged handle, casting gate on bottom, "Wisher & Co.," Philadelphia, PA, 1 gal. size, 6-5/8"H, number "50" on bottom, pat'd. 1861..... **$75+**

❖ NOTES ❖

"Among the ... **colonists** of New England many domestic **utensils of Iron,** with which the humblest dwellings are now [1868] supplied, were quite unknown. Others were comparatively rare, and were prized accordingly. The inventories of property, and the wills of many persons of good estate, particularly enumerate such articles as Iron pots, of which one or two appear frequently to have comprised the whole stock. These were often bequeathed to some member of the household as a mark of esteem. The exclusive use of wrought-iron tea-kettles, and the extreme rarity of iron vessels a century ago [1768], are evidences of the limited product of cast-iron

XIV-78. "Toddy kettle" & gas lamp heater. The "Union Attachment" bracket fits to the gas fixture and provides a place for a smallish (and definitely light weight) teakettle. Mfd. by Standard Co., NYC. The Metal Worker, July 8, 1882.

ware, even in the parent country, whence the colonists were supplied with such things as were then in common use. The profusion of such wares in every department of culinary service at this time is the result of comparatively recent improvements in this branch of metallurgy, and is due to the substitution of coke, and still more of anthracite, for charcoal in the reduction of ores." pp 488-89, Vol. I, Leander J. Bishop, *A History of American Manufactures from 1608-1860.* (Philadelphia, 1868).

Teakettle, cast iron, pit bottom, swivel lid, short spout, wire falling bail handle, "Hardwick Stove Co.," Cleveland, TN, late 1800s. .... **$65+**

Teakettle, cast iron, pit bottom, swivel top, forged falling bail handle, long casting gate on bottom, "Ohio Stove Co.," Portsmouth, OH, 19th C. .... **$65+**

Teakettle, cast iron, tapered sides, half circle hinged lid on top, forged bail, short duckneck spout with flat beveled underside, 4 qt. capacity, "Leibrandt-M'Dowell" (stove company) on lid, Philadelphia, PA, late 19th C.... **$75+**

Tea or hot water kettle, cast iron, hinged top, coiled wire heat-dissipating handle, squared gooseneck spout, pit bottom, "M'Dowell," Philadelphia, 8"H to slightly domed lid x 12" diam., pit bottom is 1-1/2"H x 9" diam., 19th C. .... **$125+**

Tea or hot water kettle, cast iron with brass handle & lid, marked "Cannon Deepfields," English, "No. 2, 5 pints" on bottom, mid 19th C. .... **$100+**

Teakettle, galvanized cast iron, pit bottom, swoopy curved pouring spout with out-thrust lower lip, falling bail handle with heat-dissipating "Alaska" coil grip, Matthai-Ingram, came in No's. 6, 7, 8 and 9, c.1890s. .... **$35-$50**

❖ NOTES ❖

Seeger & Guernsey's Cyclopaedia of the Manufactures and Products of the United States, published in 1890, gives a very long list of **stove & range founders;** then a long list of makers of cast iron **hollowware,**

XIV-77. Tipping kettle. Cast iron, bail is flat forged iron. American, early 19th C. Photograph courtesy Pat Guthman Antiques, Southport, CT. **$400+**

some of whom also made stoves. It is probably by no means complete, but might be interesting to see here, and to check against your own collections. • Abendroth Brothers; Albany Stove; Belleville Stove; Samuel Booth; Bouton Foundry; Bramhall Deane; Broadway Machine Co.; Budke Mfg. Co.; Chamberlain Stove Co.; Cleveland Co op Stove Co.; Clipper Mfg. Co.; Columbus Iron Works; Cribben, Sexton; Culter & Proctor Stove Co.; Defiance Machine Works; Great Western Stove Co.; Griswold Mfg. Co.; Highland Foundry; Hill, Whitney & Co.; Hoy & Co.; F. & L. Kahn & Bros.; Keokuk Stove Works; Lithgow Mfg. Co.; Magee Furnace; Manning, Bowman & Co.; Marietta Casting Co.; Marietta Hollow Ware & Enamelling Co.; Mount Penn Stove Works; Ohio Stove Co.; Patton Mfg. Co.; J. S. & M. Peckham; Rathbone, Sard & Co.; John Savery's Son; I. A. Sheppard & Co.; Standard Mfg. Co. (Add Sidney Hollowware Co., Sidney, OH, which sold to Wagner in 1898.) • A few years later, in *The Buyers' Guide [of] Thomas' Register of American Manufacturers*, NYC: **1905**, the only listings are Atlanta Stove Works, Georgia; Blacklock Foundry Co., South Pittsburg, TN; Marietta Casting Co., and Marietta Holloware & Enamelling Co., both of Marietta, PA; Mobile Stove & Pulley Mfg. Co., Alabama; Phillips & Buttorff Mfg. Co., Nashville; and Wagner Mfg. Co., Sidney, OH. (To which we must add the most obvious omissions: Griswold Mfg. Co., Erie, PA; Wapak, Wapakoneta, OH, which had begun just two years before; The W. C. Davisa Favorite Stove & Range Co., Piqua, OH.)

Teakettle, sheet iron, unusual inner & outer bodies, pipe vent connects hole in bottom center of outer body & passes through inner body at angle, with exit & entry holes brazed to seal; pipe vent ends up at one of holes around the rim near the lid. It draws heat up through the water in the inner kettle, working something like a percolator. Kettle has straight spout in 2 sections, with holes around lower section (part of outer pot) evidently to increase air draft & efficiency in heating the water. Nicely-shaped fixed bail handle, like handles from American 1820's kettles, turned wooden grip & hanging ring of wire, lift out lid in center of top of pot, like an ironclad battleship with its air holes & heavy sheet iron. "R. Wall, #568," Grove City, PA, about 6-1/2"H including lid x 10" diam., c.1880s or poss. a little earlier? .... **$150-$175**

XIV-79. Electric teakettle, *on Art Nouveau-styled stand, mfd. by "Simplex." From* Maud Lancaster's Electric Cooking, *1914.* **$45+**

XIV-80. Electric teakettle. *"Speedmaster," with "independent electric heating element, but is so constructed that it may also be used on any stove the same as the ordinary type of kettle." From* The Electric Home, *E. S. Lincoln, 1936. The styling is so "thirties," & hence collectible.* **$35+**

❖ NOTES ❖

The Journal of the Franklin Institute of Philadelphia, Aug. 1828, reported on an "**Improvement in the Tea Kettle,** and other vessels for culinary purposes" as follows: "A Mr. Gordon, of London [England], is manufacturing tea kettles, and other culinary vessels, which are said to be very economical; the improvement consists simply in enclosing vessels of the ordinary kind, such as tea-kettles, stew-pans, &c., with an outer casing surrounding their sides, but open at the bottom, for the flame of a lamp [alcohol or spirit] to act upon it. When heat is applied to vessels so constructed, the plate of air between the cases becomes highly rarified, and the heat, having no tendency to descend, accumulates in the upper part to such an intense degree, as to be capable of melting a rod of glass if passed up the cavity. In vessels of the usual construction, the greater part of the heated air escapes without producing any useful effect; in these, however, it is detained, and the water may in consequence be boiled in a very short space of time. The chief advantages of the new construction are, therefore, economy of heat, or of the inflammable matter employed in producing it, economy of time, and convenience; the value of these may be variously estimated by different individuals, but all will acknowledge that they are important."

Teakettle, stainless steel body & spout in round-topped wide-bottomed cone shape, with ring of embossed dots just up from bottom, high straight spout terminated by red plastic bird whistle, high 3/4 round handle, part of which has Wedgwood-blue plastic handgrip with finger holds on underside, & red balls at each end, designed by American architect Michael Graves for Alessi, 2 qt. capacity, ©1985. • An editorial note in 1986 said that 25,000+ of these $100 to $125 kettles had been sold in the first three or so months since its introduction late August 1985. .... **$100-$150**

Teakettles – tin

Teakettle, heavy pieced tin, gooseneck, has "chef's hat" or popover-shaped outline to the fixed upright handle, typically American. 5-1/2" diam. at bottom, sides cant slightly outward as they go upward. 9-3/8"H including handle, prob. 1st quarter of 19th C. .... **$135+**

Teakettle, pieced tin, long straight high angle spout, hinged lid, strapwork falling bail handle, strapwork ring finial on lid, American, 6-1/4"H x 3-3/4" diam., mid 19th C. .... **$65+**

❖ NOTES ❖

Early Tin – "The Dutch or Irish emigrant far away in his tent on the boundless prairies of the West, the boatman barging down his cotton over the bosom of the Mississippi, the Father of Waters, the rough miners of Nevada fighting with nature to extract the virgin silver from the heart of the Rocky Mountains, all require tinware in its rudest form, a tea-pot, a kettle, a pannikin, a wash-bowl, and requiring them are well aware that they will find them ready when desired at the nearest country store. ... There is no doubt that the immense modern increase in the manufacturing and consumption of tin plates has resulted from the rapid increase of population in the U.S.A." P. W. Flower, *A History of the Trade in Tin*, 1880. [The "plates" are flat sheets of tin plated iron, not dinner plates.]

Teakettle, tin, with range eye pit bottom made of copper, strap handle, domed lid, American, late 19th C. .... **$65+**

Teakettle, very low & broad, gooseneck spout, wide falling strap handle, stamped & pieced tin, "for oil stoves," Matthai-Ingram, 8-1/2" diam., 3 qt. capacity, c.1890s.. **$35+**

XIV-81. "The Clock That Makes Tea." *"Most people seem to think that America has cornered the world market on Yankee inventive genius, but it remains for our British cousins to cap the climax of inventions intended to permit the weary sojourner on this terrestial ball to roll over and take another nap again" by means of the clock teapot. "Johnny Bull likes his cup of tea upon rising, [and with this] the clock wakes him up, lights a lamp, boils a pint of water, pours the water into handy teapot, puts out the lamp, and rings a gong announcing that tea is ready." This was in* House Furnishing Review, *Feb. 1908, and whether it's true or a ruse, I don't know. But they've got 'em now!*

Teakettle bracket, backplate is cutout heavy gauge copper in form of simple 2 handled ewer, 4 holes to screw to wall. Coming from center is a swinging bracket that pivots full 180°, sliding hook for teakettle or teapot handle, English (?), 6-3/16"H x 6-1/8"W, with 7-7/8"L swinging bracket, c.1850-1870s. **$250**

Tea & coffee pot, shiny tin plate, black wooden handle and knob, marked only "Extra Tin Plate," American, 2 qt. capacity, c.1890s-1910. .... **$25-$35**

Teapot, advertising, miniature size, saltglazed stoneware, 2 color decoration, "Van Dyke Coffee & Tea Co.," early 1900s...................................... **$145+**

Teapot, 3 metals – tin, brass and copper. Brass finial on lid, footed & very graceful, 19th C....... **$85-$100**

Teapot, black & white speckly enamelware, with Britannia collar & lid, strainer inside gooseneck spout, 8-1/2"H, 19th C... **$150+**

Teapot, blue glazed earthenware, lid chipped & repaired, double wire bail handle with black painted turned wood grip, no marks, 5-1/2"H to finial top, 19th C. .... **$350+**

Teapot, blue & white swirl agateware, hinged lid, 7"H, late 19th or early 20th C. .... **$165+**

Teapot, Britannia metal, wonderful melon-ribbed shape, small curved feet, marked "James Dixon," early to mid 19th C. .... **$85+**

❖ NOTES ❖

In 1836, the *Journal of the Franklin Institute* published a short report of interest to people trying to date Britannia (and other metal) teapots. "Tea-pots made by steam. **Britannia metal tea-pots** are now made by steam; the round bodies are spun, and the wooden handles and knobs are cut up by powerful steam engines. A good workman can spin twenty dozen of potbodies in a day." A complex melon shape like this might possibly have been made using a spun blank.

Teapot, canal boat or barge china, with dark brown glaze and thickly decorated blue flowers and birds, and pink & white flowers, very small teapot finial on lid, medallion or scroll on front reads "A Present From A Friend 1790," English, 12-3/8"H, 1790. This colorful pot is an example of many decorative, exuberant "folk" pottery wares used by the thousands of people who lived on the barges & flat-bottomed boats that plied up & down the vast inner canal system in England. The pieces date well into the 19th C. .... **$575+**

Teapot, cinnamon colored enamelware, white inside, turned wood handle with black finish, nickeled brass lid & base with wood knob, Manning-Bowman, 6-1/2"H to top of finial, pat'd. May 21, 1889. .... **$250+**

Teapot, cobalt enamelware, white flower decorations, gold trim, hinged lid, European, 7"H, c.1890s-1910. .... **$175+**

❖ NOTES ❖

Czechoslovakian Enamelware – It took a while, but American collectors of enamelware seem to finally have wholeheartedly welcomed European wares made from the mid 19th century up through the early 1930s to their collections. These are wares imported in the waning years of the 19th century and up to WWI, wares imported during a short resumption of trade, and finally wares only recently imported by containerload, specifically for the collector market. This latest wave of importing will probably include old marked pieces once made for possible export (viz., after 1891, bearing name of country of origin), as well as more truly antique pieces dating back as far as the mid 19th C. While there were probably hundreds of European enamelware manufacturers in the late 19th C., there were only a handful in all of the United States, and none that I know of in Canada. • For today's collectors (perhaps enamored of other "gaudy" wares), **Czechoslovakian** pieces are especially interesting, having been made in really spectacular patterns & bold colors, with skilled, confident painting, peasant or "country look" designs. Sometimes sets are found, recently imported to the U.S. Plaids in cobalt blue & white, or red & white, colorful polkadots, flowers, leaves, stripes, geometric border patterns, often with contrasting colors for spout, handle and finial, are very desirable. Trade journal ads, c.1900, showed imported German, Austrian & Swedish imported wares. • A provision of the 1890 **McKinley Tariff Act** raised an already stiff tariff on imported enamelware. Although American enamelware brought in $4 million yearly, *The New York Times* commented: "It is not very durable, the base being of iron, and the profit is very heavy." Of "Bohemian" enamelware they wrote, "nearly all ... foreign ware is ... blue & white ... more attractive than the mottled [American] graniteware." Steel-based imports were considered three times as durable. McKinley's tariff raised the 45% rate already in effect. In 1890, stores stockpiled foreign enamelware to sell at prices lower than would be seen again for a long time. • In 1890, St. Louis Stamping Co.'s Imperial Decorated Iron Ware was touted as "closely approximating French china in weight and grace of form ... The ... original color decorations in flowers, &c., are in pleasing contrast with the pure white enamel surface." • Chapter VII (Containers & Storage) has more on the Tariff Act.

Teapot, decorated china, hinged metal lid with large finial knob with hole in it, odd spout turns down like a faucet, "Royle's Patent Self Pouring Teapot," mfd. by Doulton Potteries, Manchester, England, 7-1/2"H, pat'd. 1886 in England by A. J. Royle. • **Classic.** This fabulous piece was advertised as "a boon for mothers of large families" (as most families of the time were). You didn't have to pick up the teapot to pour the tea; instead, you merely lifted the lid, put your finger over the hole in the finial knob, then closed the lid and the tea came out the downturned spout. Woe to the M.O.L.F. if she'd forgotten the cup. An article in *Spinning Wheel* in Oct. 1969, showed examples made of Britannia, by Meriden Britannia Co., and told about one marked "Asbury-Paine Mfg Co., Phila. PA" with a patent date of April 3, 1888. This patent date is the American one, and was used on self-pouring teapots made of various materials. (See XIV-39) .... **$100+**

Teapot, enamelware, white background with gorgeous raspberries, blackberries & leaves in brilliant colors, pewter lid, copper bottom rim to protect from chipping, Manning-Bowman, 9-1/4"H to finial top, pat'd. May 21, 1889, in late 1890s catalog as are others. .... **$325+**

XIV-82. "Bird teakettle." *An old idea in a new design – the whistling plastic (or metal in older ones) bird in the spout that whistles when the water is boiling. This stainless steel one with colored plastic handle & bird designed by architect Michael Graves, copyrighted 1985. In mint condition:* **$200**

Teapot, "end of day" enamelware with swirls of several bright colors, predominately cobalt & red, with orange & yellow, American (?), small, 19th C. **$250+**

❖ NOTES ❖

"End of Day." – The popular, but not necessarily accurate, term for swirled multicolored enamelwares (as well as blown glass wares) is "End of Day" pieces. I have not seen documentary contemporary evidence that would back up a somewhat romantic notion that the dog-tired artisan, at the end of a 10- or 12 hour workday, would be lively enough, and adequately enough supplied with "leftovers," or even allowed, to work past quitting time to make a whimsical end of day piece for a loved one. I am speculating here, just as everyone else does, but it is possible that the first few of this type of thing became so much the rage that artisans everywhere wanted to make or were asked to make such things during regular working hours. Diaries, documents, worksheets, inventories – all would help answer our questions. Do you keep a diary? • More subtle color mixtures don't bring the high prices that brighter ones do.

Teapot, globe-shaped, blown-molded glass, with engraved floral spray on sides, press-molded lid with knob, "Pyrex," English, 5-1/2" diam.; 1-1/2 pt. capacity, c. 1930. • This earliest Pyrex teapot is the only one with engraved flowers. .... **$125+**

Teapot, gray graniteware with pewter cover, spout, breast band & handle, copper bottom, footed, handle is scrolled, domed lid with nice finial, body is a beautiful, nearly round form, American, late 19th C. **$200**

Teapot, gray graniteware with tin spout, handle, lid, breast-band & base rim, American, 19th C. **$225**

Teapot, japanned tin, big foot, stamped inside lid with mark – probably maker's not owner's – carpenter's dividers straddling a rising sun, also initials "W & S," American (?), 14"H, c.1840s. .... **$400-$500**

Teapot, nickeled copper, double walled, wood handle, decorative nickeled cast pot-metal finial on lid, "Sweeney Mfg. Co.," Brooklyn, NY, 3 pt. size, early 20th or late 19th C. .... **$35+**

Teapot, olive drab green enamelware, white inside, pewter handle, nickled brass base, wooden "heat sink" where handle joins lid, "Quality # 5," mfd. by Manning-Bowman, Meriden, CT, 8-3/4"H, late 19th C........... **$200+**

Teapot, pale green & white marbleized enamelware, gooseneck spout, "Elite," marked Austria, c.1890s-1910. .... **$175+**

Teapot, spun aluminum with wooden handle, chain that feeds through finial of lid is attached to small domed tea ball perforated with circles of holes, looks like "The Little King" of comic strip fame, "Merit," American, 7-1/4"H x 8-1/2"W including spout and handle, c.1920s. **$20**

Teapot, very bulbous shape, bright blue agateware, with Britannia trim – lid, spout, part of handle, Manning-Bowman, 1889.................................... **$125+**

Teapot, white & blue speckled enamelware, also called speckleware, possibly United States Stamping Co., Moundsville, WV, 1st quarter 20th C............ **$175+**

Teapot, yellow enamelware with red poppies & green trim, gooseneck spout, prob. European, 20th C. .... **$50-$70**

Tea set, with teapot with brave straight spout & long gently-arched ribbed plastic handle, sugar bowl with round lid, creamer, designed by Russell Wright for Chase Copper & Brass, Waterbury, CT, c.1930s. Designer's name is the $$-maker here; there are many collectors of his table settings. ...... **$225-$300**

Tea steeper, cobalt blue enamelware, early 20th C. (?).. **$35+**

Tea steeper, dark green enamelware with white loopy streaks or swirls, white inside, "Chrysolite," American, c.1890s-1910. .... **$85+**

XIV-83. "Tea & Coffee Urns in Batteries," *meaning in a connected group. Copper & brass with nickel plating overall. Made in 4 set sizes: 3-gallon urns, 5, 8 and 10 gallons. S. B. Sexton Stove & Mfg. Co., Baltimore, c.1930s. It's not much of a leap of imagination to think of them as The Ladies Come To Tea (and eat a lot of cookies). Value hard to give; they would probably be worth most as second-hand restaurant supplies, bought to put into use. Required house-room (the "real-estate-factor") has to be calculated when pricing large items of no particular use.* **$100-$400**

XIV-84. "Canteen" urn. *Nickeled copper, shaped like barrel on stand. Two-gallon capacity, so just the right size for a big house-party. From Albert Pick 1909 catalog.* **$150-$350**

Tea steeper, white enamelware with blue trim, c.1890s. .... **$15+**

Tea strainer, gray graniteware, c.1890s-1910. ...... **$20**

Tea strainer, tin with red wooden handle, depicts teapot & cups on the strainer cup, 1930s-40s....... **$15**

Tea strainer spoon, silverplate, adv'g. "Tetley Tea," 20th C. **$25**

Tea strainer & stand, nickeled metal, Main Tool & Mfg. Co., (Brooklyn, NY?), 20th C........................... **$10**

Tea urns – See Urns

Trivet, for teapot at table, ornate cast iron, with name around edge, "Midget," American, 3-3/4" diam., c.1890s-1910.. **$35+**

Trivet for coffee or teapot, cast iron, lacy doily design, 5 little feet, "Griswold Trivet," mid 20th C........ **$100+**

Urns – Coffee, Hot Beverage, Tea

Coffee urns

Coffee urn, chrome plated, orange Bakelite™ (or other molded phenolic resin) handles & spigot handle, "Champion," looks c.1930s & is probably English or European. .... **$40+**

❖ **NOTES** ❖

Coffee urn – called an **argyle** in England, copper body, tinned inside, with slender vertical open top cylinder into which fits a heated cast iron slug (looks like a sash weight) that would keep the coffee hot. Cast brass handles & spigot, side handles have opalescent knobby white glass grips, spigot has more opaque white knob, square base, 4 small feet, high decorative rather churchy dome lid with high copper finial, King Manufactory, Hull, England, 16"H, c. mid 19th C. **$275+**

Coffee urn, copper, brass spigot, wooden handles, on stand with solid fuel burner underneath, mfd. by Sternau, NYC, c.1890s-1910. .... **$255+**

Coffee urn, electric, chrome plated brass & copper ball, on fluted base, white plastic handles, knob on top, spigot handle, and ring base with 4 small ball feet, looks like a little robot baby, but would "put poise in your parties." "Table Electric" by Chase Brass & Copper Co., Inc., division of Kennecott Copper Corp., 25 cup capacity, c.1937. • Crossover interest from Art Deco, Art Moderne, & Chase name brand collectors................. **$65+**

Coffee urn, electric, nickel plated, very ornate, with matching creamer & sugar, "Universal," mfd. by

Landers, Frary & Clark, only 11"H, patents from 1910 to 1920s................. **$35+**

Coffee urn, for restaurant or hotel use, copper with brass trim & handles & spout, very lovely graceful form, American, 21"H, c.1890s-1910. ...... **$200-$225**

Coffee urn, heavy polished aluminum, electric heating unit concealed in slightly flared perforated base, tall with 2 body sections, each with black plastic side handles, domed lid with black plastic knob, glass viewing tube above spigot, West Bend Aluminum Co., West Bend, WI, made 48 cups, late 1940s. **$15**

Hot beverage urns

Hot beverage urn, for restaurants & hotels, copper & brass, "Mason's," American, 18"H, including little

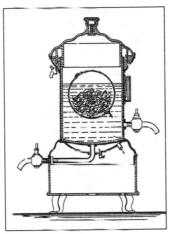

XIV-85. Coffee urn patent. *The Duparquet & Moneuse hotel supply company, whose early 20th C. catalogs I've plundered for this book, had two individuals who got at least one patent. Elie Moneuse & Louis Duparquet, NYC, NY, got patent #92,987 for this urn on July 27, 1869. "In the coffee-pots or urns heretofore made, a difficulty is experienced in coating the inside of the copper vessel with suffi-cient thickness of melted tin to prevent the same being rapidly worn off in using or cleaning said vessel.... We make use of a ... lining made of block-tin rolled out into sheets, fitted accurately into the inside of the copper vessel, and the two united at the joints with solder. This lining is much more perfect and durable." In other urns, they say, the cover is set down inside with the rim in a water-vessel, and the condensa-tion of vapors and aroma is lost by running into this water-vessel and being thrown out with the dirty water. Moneuse & Duparquet "place an annular water-vessel around outside the upper end of the urn, with a cock to allow the water to be drawn off, for replenishing, or other-wise. This water ring receives the flange of the cover" while a second flange from the cover "sits within the urn so that all the aroma and vapors from the coffee are retained, and condense on the inside of the cover and inner flange and run back into the coffee." The cover has a valve to allow air to pass in when the coffee is drawn from the cock [on the right] and a pipe and cock "coming in at the lowest part of the urn" [lower left] is where "the thicker coffee or sediment" is drawn off. A steam pipe (which they say could be replaced with a lamp or a gas pipe) provides the heat underneath. Finally, "It has been usual to place the ground coffee in a bag, or stationary strainer. This is frequently left above the coffee in the urn, and ceases to be useful. The strainer is difficult to clean out, and pouring boiling water through the coffee in the strainer involves considerable loss of the aroma while the cover is off. ... We employ a perforated metallic globular coffee-holder formed of two half-shells, hinged or clasped together, so that the coffee is first placed in this holder and the shells shut together, the boiling water is supplied into the urn, and then the coffee and holder are dropped into the hot water and the cover put on. Thereby the aroma is retained, and the coffee always remains in the liquid."*

feet, c.1890s-1910. These were used for hot water, coffee, even clam broth. Some of these were nickel plated. .... **$150-$250**

Hot beverage urn, for restaurant or hotel, copper with brass fittings, brass spigots, domed covers with knobs, American, 20"H x 18"W, c.1890s-1910. .... **$400+**

Hot drink urn, for restaurant. Nickeled copper & brass, ornamented with "jewels, surmounted with ruby glass 'Hot Drinks' sign with jeweled metal mounted frame." "The Princeton." (They also had "The Harvard," and "The Cornell," but no "The Yale.") Seen in Albert Pick catalog, 1909. Very flashy and neat. .... **$400+**

Percolator urns

Percolator urn, alcohol burner below, plated metal, antique style body with rounded belly, cabriole legs, side handles, glass percolator top, "Universal Perco-lator Co.," Landers, Frary & Clark, 12"H, pat'd. 1907-1910. .... **$135+**

Percolator urn, electric, chromium plated paneled Georgian style urn, ebonized wood handles & spigot handle, on 3 legged base, Royal Rochester Co., No. E639, mfd. by Robeson Rochester Corp., Rochester, NY, 15"H, c.1930s. .... **$30-$45**

Percolator urn, electric, copper, tinned inside, with straight-sided "milk can" style urn, glass dome, black Bakelite™ (or other phenolic resin plastic) side handles & spigot handle, on rather heavy brass tri-pod stand, "Universal," mfd. by Landers, Frary & Clark, New Britain, CT, pat'd. May 22, 1899. This almost looks Arts & Crafts, and the period is right, so possibly it has some extra value now to the avid A & C collector. .... **$75-$110**

Percolator urn, electric, nickel plated, on 3 long cabri-ole (so-called "Queen Anne") legs, glass percolating top with high domed metal lid & finial, plug screws into bulb socket, Simplex Electric Heating Co., Cam-bridge, MA, 01906.......................... **$45+**

Percolator urn, electric, silver plated, octagonal base, octagonal paneled urn, Georgian style (of late 18th or early 19th C.), "Automatic Percolator," Hotpoint, Edison Electric Appliance Co., 12"H, c.1930s. **$50+**

Percolator urn, electric, nickeled brass & iron, glass, turned wood, handsome metal urn with spigot, sur-mounted by sugar-bowl shaped glass percolating bowl, lion's paw feet, side handles, "Type ECP," mfd. by General Electric, c.1918-1919. .... **$60+**

Tea Urns

Tea urn, a sort of English samovar, brass urn is round, tinned inside, set up on 4 pillars, square base, alcohol burner below bolted to base, English, 14"H x 7-1/2" diam., c.1840s. In silver this form might be as much as 40 years older............................. **$175+**

Tea urn, brass plated globe on straight legs, sort of Art Deco or Arts & Crafts space station, strips of bam-boo wrapped around spigot, heating alcohol lamp below, Austrian, early 20th C. .... **$175-$200**

Tea urn, copper with brass handles, spigot & trim, on 4 legs, English, 21"H, late 19th C. .... **$165+**

Tea urn, tin, grape cluster molding, cast iron handles, brass spigot, American (?), 15"H, c.1870s (?). .... **$100-$125+**

Water kettles – See Teakettles

Whistle for teakettle, stamped & pieced brass, bird has a "stem" to fit into spout, American, 3-1/2"H, pat'd. 1923. .... **$25**

GENERAL CATALOGS

Cumberland General Store

This catalog company, which also sells online, specializes in "old time general merchandise," which includes a lot of kitchen things. In 2002, their 250-page catalog is only $4 – a worthy investment. They carry everything from cook stoves to coffee mills.

1 Highway 68
Crossville, TN 38555
Phone: (800) 334-4640
E-mail: info@cumberlandgeneral.com
Web site: www.cumberlandgeneral.com

Lehman Hardware & Appliances

This is a company I mention throughout this book because they sell so many things close to or the same as they were 100 years ago. Lehman's specializes in non-electric, simple-tech tools, and their main market is the Amish, and are "located in the middle of the largest Amish settlement in the world." People all over the world can order online, or get the print catalog.
P.O. Box 41
Kidron, OH 44636
Phone: (888) 438-5346
E-mail: info@lehmans.com
Web site: www.lehmans.com

ANTIQUE DEALERS

Oveda Maurer Antiques

I got several really good photos from this dealer several years ago. She deals in early lighting and hearthware, ceramics, etc., and is now on the Internet!

Contact: Oveda Maurer
34 Greenfield Ave.
San Anselmo, CA 94960
Phone: (415) 454-6439
E-mail: omaurer@earthlink.net
Web site: www.ovedamaurerantiques.com

COFFEE COLLECTOR CLUBS

Association of Coffee Mill Enthusiasts

A quarterly newsletter, *Grinder Finden*, conventions, etc. Special thanks to Joe MacMillan for the impetus he gave with his great book to this growing field. The A.C.M.E. organization will be reprinting MacMillan's book.

Contact: Lucy Fullinwider
POB 5761
Midland, TX 79704
E-mail: aeL4@surfnetusa.com or acmeman@erols.com

Online Club

Serves as a forum for Q&A, photos, links, etc. There's some rigamarole signing up with yahoo groups; I can't hack it.

Web site: http://clubs.yahoo.com/clubs/coffee millenthusiasts

COFFEE COLLECTORS WEB SITES

These sites can sometimes help you identify something and get an up-to-date value from items shown for sale on the site.

Michael L. White

POB 483
Fraser, CO 80442
Phone: (970) 726-0448
E-mail: mwhite483@rkymtnhi.com
Web site: www.rkymtnhi.com/grinder
Web site: www.rkymtnhi.com/grinder/classif.html

Extremely useful to the collector is his explanation of the classifications of mills (found at the second Web site cited here). This collector/dealer also has several good links to Web sites of help to beginning collectors. White's books are in the Bibliography, and highly recommended.

Millmania

Contact Judith A. Sivonda
375 Congdon St.
Middletown, CT 06457
E-mail: millmania@att.net
Web site: www.millmania.com

This is the personal site of the secretary of the A.C.M.E. She co-authored a book with Mike White, and it can be ordered from his site or hers!

PATENTED ANTIQUES

These collectors'/dealers' coffee mill information, and want list, are on the first of their two Web sites (the one for their own collecting wants, the other for patented antiques for sale, sometimes including coffee mills). Coffee mills are just one of many passions – plan to spend an hour or more on their sites!

Contact: **Carole & Larry Meeker**
Phone: (530) 620-7019
E-mail: clm@antiqbuyer.com
Web site: www.antiqbuyer.com/coffee.html
Web site: www.patented-antiques.com

COFFEE & TEA MUSEUMS

Bramah's Museum of Tea And Coffee

40 Southwark Street
London SE1 1UN
Tel. 020 7403 5650
E-mail: e.bramah@virgin.net
Web site: www.bramahmuseum.co.uk

Kaffee Museum

Verein für Kaffeekultur
Contact: Kurt Falkner
PastorstraBe 14/5/13
A-1210 Vienna, Austria
E-mail: info@kaffeemuseum.at
Web site: http://kaffeemuseum.at

UCC Coffee Museum

Ueshima Coffee Company
6-6-2, Minatojimanakamachi
Chuo-ku, Kobe-shi, Hyogo-ken
Japan
Phone: 078-302-8880
Web site: www.iko-yokobe.com/k-sisetu/ucc.htm

Twining Teapot Gallery
Norwich Castle Museum
Castle Meadow
Norwich NR1 3JU
England
Phone: 01603 493625
E-Mail: museums@norfolk.gov.uk
Web site: www.norfolk.gov.uk/tourism/museums/castle.htm

CHOCOLATE COLLECTOR WEB SITES

Martin Mihal

This collector in the Czech Republic collects chocolate wrappers, and he has links to English, European, Mexican, and other collectors.

E-mail: choco.mamih@post.cz
Web site: http://mujweb.atlas.cz/www/chocolate/enmain.htm

CHOCOLATE HISTORY

Web site: www.chocolate-artistry.com/recipes.php

CHOCOLATE MUSEUMS

The following are only a few of the many sites that turn up during a Google search.

Wilbur Chocolate's Candy Americana Museum

48 N. Broad St.
Lititz, PA 17543-1026
Web site: www.wilburbuds.com

Chocolate Factory And Museum

Érico Choco-Musée
634, Rue Saint Jean
Faubourg Saint-Jean Baptiste
Quebec, QC Canada G1R 1P8
Phone: (418) 524-2122
E-mail: info@chocomusee.com
Web site: www.chocomusee.com

Gremi Chocolate Museum

According to this museum, the first European chocolate factory was founded in Barcelona in 1780.

Gremi Provincial de Pastisseria de Barcelona
E-mail: gremi@patisseria.com
Web site: www.pastisseria.com/htm-a/museu.htm

Cologne Chocolate Museum

Offering guided tours in several languages & some special events. (doing a Google search allows you to request an instant translation to English)

Imhoff Stollwerck Museum
Rheinauhafen 1a
50678 Cologne
Germany

Phone: +49(0)221/93 18 88-0
E-mail: bankett@schokoladenmuseum.de
Web site: www.schokoladenmuseum.de

Museum of Cocoa and Chocolate

Contact & founder: Mrs. Jo Draps
House of the Dukes of Brabant
13 Grand-Place
1000 Brussels, Belgium
Phone: 0032 (0) 514 20 48
E-mail: info@mucc.be
Web site: www.mucc.be

PRESERVING

XV. CHILL & FREEZE

A very early way to preserve food was by lowering its temperature (in ice or cold water) to stop decomposition; some anthropologists even believe that the early humans who followed the Ice Age "harvested" mastodons and other animals that had been preserved (perhaps even for thousands of years) in glacial ice.

Prior to about a 150 years ago, people built springhouses and/or ice houses. Springhouses utilize a natural year-round spring – lively rather than sluggish – which either courses underground or above ground. A springhouse might be a small 6 x 8 foot outbuilding made of stone, brick, logs, and built into a hillside; or it might be a much larger space, with room for benches, even a work table, built sometimes in a cellar under the house. For the convenience of the housewife, springhouses best had raised troughs through which the water flowed, but sometimes a channel was cut at floor level. Stoneware crocks, jugs and stoneware pans were set into the troughs so that the water would flow past and keep the contents cold.

Ice houses are below ground ice "wells" lined in brick or stone, with a drain at the bottom running downgrade for some distance, or percolating down into a sort of tank. They usually had a built-up thatched wooden roof, and, if well-made, a vestibule with a northern-facing door to the outside, and a door into the well, to act as an air lock. Inside, huge chunks of sawn or chopped lake or pond ice, or even "dry" snow, were rammed compactly into place on a bed of clean, dry straw. Then the top of the ice was insulated with straw or marsh grasses or whatever relatively clean vegetable matter could be used to protect the ice from the air, overlaid with boards. Ice stored in the winter could be expected to last well into the summer. Some of these wells or pits had thick stone or brick dome roofs, insulated on top with thick layers of earth and sod. A ladder was kept inside. Stored ice was used to cool drinks and make desserts, as well as to preserve food, especially meat. Somewhat more common methods of preserving food for long spells were smoking, salting, sugaring, and drying. (See next chapter.)

The most popular collectibles within this chapter are small **ice chippers**, **shredders**, **shavers**, and **ice tongs**. Prices haven't moved very much in these categories since the mid 1980s, except for 18th or early 19th century forged-iron ice tools, which have become much more expensive (as have their cousins, the hearth tools). I have placed a **Futurewatch** on **ice cube trays** – aluminum, rubber, and any other material I'm not aware of.

The least popular category is still iceboxes and refrigerators – which implies nothing about their artistic or historic merit, merely (and it ain't so mere) their size. For most people, one or two iceboxes is the limit; many people seek decorative oak ones that go with Arts & Crafts or Mission furniture or Art Moderne decor. They use them as bars or storage cabinets in their living or dining rooms.

You may have expected to find ice cream molds, and dishers or scoops here, but they're in Chapter IV with other molds and shapers. Ice cream freezers are here.

Freezer, fabulous streamlined design with 2 round deep cylinders flanking a finned motor, all in white enameled steel, colored top lids on both compartments, "no food more than 9 inches away from all-surrounding source of cold," 1945 ad states. "You store two units with food. You use the food out of one unit. When this is consumed, you turn it off and start using the food in the second unit." "Deepfreeze," mfd. by Deepfreeze Division of Motor Products Corp., North Chicago, IL, interior of compartments 30"H x 18" diam., overall 41-1/4"H x 65-5/8"L x 26-11/16" diam., began making c.1938.......................... **$125+**

Ice ball "cubes," large aggie-marble-sized stainless steel balls, filled with a liquid that holds cold. Marked "Pat. No. 1,641,139 Fifth Ave. B. Altman & Co. New York." Alas, this appears not to be a utility or design patent number, so I can't dig out more info. 1-1/2" diam. Prob. late 1950s. Set of 6: .... **$5+**

Icebox – See Refrigerator (icebox), and Refrigerator (electric).

❖ NOTES ❖

"Iceboxes" is what I always assumed iceboxes were called until gas or electric **"refrigerators"** came in. But many advertisements for, and catalogs of, "iceboxes" used the word "refrigerator" way back in the 19th century. In fact, I wouldn't be surprised to learn that the term "icebox" didn't come in until we needed something to differentiate a refrigerator that was loaded with ice to make it cool, and a refrigerator with coolants. • As for the patent record (from the beginning up to 1873), there is one "ice box" patent, in 1867, and one "Ice and coal box," in 1866. On the other hand, there are over 190 "refrigerators," beginning I think in 1837, plus one "ice refrigerator," one "ice-box refrigerator," plus a score of "refrigerating devices," "... chambers," "...cupboards," etc. The term "fridge," still in wide usage in parts of the country, actually is a shortened brand-name: Frigidaire," and probably originated in the 1920s. The company that became Frigidaire began in 1916 as the Guardian Frigerator Co.

XV-1. Freezer. *The trade name for it became a generic term for home freezers: "Deepfreeze." Two cylinders, each 18" diam. x 30" deep. You used all food in one unit & turned it off, then switched over to food in 2nd unit. Deepfreeze Division, Motor Products Corp., North Chicago, IL. Country Gentleman ad, 1945.* **$125+**

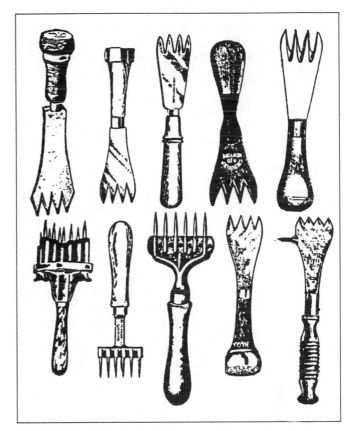

XV-3. Ice chisels. *Most are versions of 4-toothed style. Those with flat-ended handles were used by hitting with mallet. Top left to right:* **(1)** *Polished steel blade, iron band around handle kept it from splitting when hit. Matthat-Ingram, c.1890.* **(2)** *Steel blade, tinned "cap" to wood handle, 10-1/2"L. Sexton catalog, 1930s (may be LF&C)* **(3)** *Steel blade, wood handle, choice of 6", 8" or 10" blades, with 8", 10" or 12" handles, 12" handle. Landers, Frary & Clark. Sexton catalog, 1930s.* **(4)** *Steel, iron ferrule, C. W. Dunlap & Co., NYC. c.1904-1910.* **(5)** *Steel & wood. Heinz & Munschauer, 1882. Lower left to right:* **(6)** *Galvanized iron, hardwood handle, steel points "securely fastened & interchangeable." 9", 11-1/2" or 48"L. Sold by Albert Pick, 1909.* **(7)** *"Gilchrist's Needle Point Ice Chipper No.50," also for "caked salt, sugar, etc." Sexton catalog, 1930s.* **(8)** *"Ice Pick Chipper," tinned steel, 9-1/2"L x 3"W. Pick, 1909.* **(9)** *"Four-Point Ice Shaver," tempered steel, nickeled iron band & ferrule to wood handle. On cap: "N. White City & Co." (?) Pick, 1909.* **(10)** *Combo shave & pick, nickeled malleable iron. 6-1/2"L blade; 12"L overall. Pick, 1909.* **$5-$25**

XV-2. Ice chippers. (B-L) & **(B-R)** *"Lightning" and* **(T)** *"Crown." Both mfd. by North Brothers Mfg. Co., Philadelphia. "They take the place of the old-time bag and hatchet, and quickly reduce the ice to uniformly small pieces, about the size of a peanut." Lightning was made in No.1, for families; and No.2, with 48"L handle, for confectioners, hotels, restaurants. North's promo-cookbook* Dainty Dishes For All the Year Round, *by Mrs. S. T. Rorer.* **$15-$25**

Ice breakers – See Ice crushers

Ice buckets. I'm not considering these in this book, but they are becoming quite collectible, especially aluminum ones (collected by aluminists, and any in the shape of something which might make it a theme collectible. Not all are lined with vacuum-sealed mercury glass, but those that are may be older and more valuable. Price range generally. .... **$5-$35**

Ice chipper, cast iron, "Gilchrist #50," Newark, NJ, 20th C. .... **$20+**

Ice chipper, cast iron, brass ferrule, wood handle, "Briddell #60," Charles D. Briddell, Inc., Crisfield, MD, late 19th or early 20th C. .... **$10+**

Ice chipper, steel with wood handle, wicked looking, "Crown," mfd. by North Brothers, Philadelphia, PA, c.1900. .... **$15+**

Ice chipper & bottle opener combo, iron, wood handle, "Coolerator," Duluth Refrigerator Corp., Duluth, MN, early 20th C. .... **$15+**

Ice chisel, steel, turned wood handle, down-turned chisel head fitted on back with a much shorter head with 4 very broad sharp teeth, "Crown Ice Chipper," mfd. by American Machine Co., Philadelphia, PA, pat'd. April 8, 1884. .... **$15+**

Ice chisel, polished steel blade, turned wooden handle with iron band to keep it from splitting when hit with mallet, 4 wicked sharp beveled teeth, Matthai-Ingram Co., c.1890s. .... **$15+**

Ice chopper & container – heavy clear glass tumbler with 3 red bands & 2 black bands indicating ounce measurements, chromed lid, fitted with heavily weighted nickeled metal cross bladed chopper with knob handle, blades have teeth, Amerian, 20 oz. capacity, 9"H, c.1930s to 1940s. .... **$20+**

XV-4-A. Ice cream freezers. (L) Cedar tub with can & stirrer. Note bung hole. Dubois, Patisserie d'Aujourd'hui, 1860s-70s. (R) "Patent Ice Cream Freezer & Mould. – By which Creams, Ices &c., can be frozen and fit for table use in a very few minutes. The forms are easily managed and now coming into general family use." American Home Cook Book, 1854. This freezer also has bung hole at bottom for draining off melted ice. Bail handle, interesting double-ended, knobbed horizontal twisting stirrer for can. In 1854, when this cookbook was published, there were only five pat'd. American ice cream freezers; another was pat'd in Sept. 1854. (L) $65+; (R) $150+

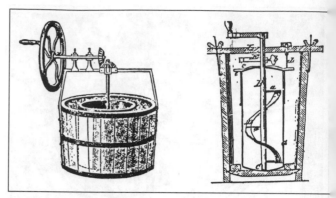

XV-4-B. Ice cream or sorbétière freezer, freezer patent. (L) Cedar tub, large cranked wheel with bevel gears. It is called a turbine in the book it's in – Dubois, Patisserie d'Aujourd'hui, c.1860s-70s. (R) Pat'd. June 10, 1856, by Joseph Parisette, Indianapolis, IN, #15,083. Features spiral scraper, which revolves & scrapes sides of can, as well as forcing to the bottom the frozen cream so that the unfrozen will "rise to the top to be mixed and equally frozen." Official Gazette. (L) $125+; (R) if it exists: $65+

Ice cracker, long springy chromed steel handle with plastic grip and with heavy round head, used with ice in palm of hand or on towel, "Tap-Icer," Williamsport, PA, c.1960. .... **$3+**

Ice cream can, gray graniteware, container for ingredients, which could be put into some kinds of ice cream freezers. 1 qt. size, late 19th C. .... **$70+**

Ice cream carrier, for picnics, oak box, zinc lining, side door swings open to put in block of ice cream, then you lift off top & pack in ice, "The Bradley Ice Cream Cabinet, Patented," mfd. by the Bradley Mfg. Co., New Haven, CT, 8-1/2"H x 11" x 9", late 19th C.
• Ice cream is a high ticket area of specialization in kitchen collections. For collector club, see Ice cream molds in Chapter IV, Molds. .... **$225-$275**

Ice cream freezer, "North Pole," Alaska Freezer Co., Winchendon, MA, 20th C. .... **$45+**

❖ NOTES ❖

Patents for Ice Cream Freezers – Between 1790 and 1873 there were only about 60 patentees for ice cream freezers. Lots of searching has not uncovered a patent between 1790 and 1843, although ice cream was known in America supposedly by the 1740s. As far as I can tell, the **(1)** first patent was granted Nancy M. Johnson, Philadelphia, Sept. 9, 1843 (#3254); **(2)** William G. Young, Baltimore, May 30, 1848 (#5,601). Young alluded to Johnson's patent, misquoting her name as Johnston. (I have a note in my files that Edward M. Manigle of Philadelphia also got one on May 30, 1848, but have no idea where that came from – the name with that date is not in the *Subject Index of Patents*. Manigle did get a patent for an improved "bottom for ice-cream freezers" on Dec. 12, 1868. He mentioned in that claim that previous freezers were made with a heavy inner bottom meant to withstand wear, and also a lead bottom under that to protect from wear.) **(3).** Anthony H. Austin, Baltimore,

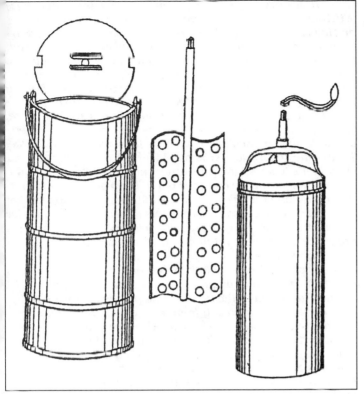

XIV-5-A. Ice cream freezer patent. an "artificial freezer" pat'd. by **Nancy M. Johnson**, Philadelphia, PA, Sept 9, 1843 (#3254). Johnson wrote, "Instead of causing the freezer or vessel which contains the substance to revolve as heretofore has been practiced, within the ice and salt mixture, by the hands of the operator, I place within it a vertical shaft reaching to the bottom, and coming up a short distance above the cover. ... After the lid is placed over the freezer a crank having a wooden or other nonconducting handle can be placed to give motion to the shaft (thereby rotating the curved 'wings'). When the revolutions are made [clockwise] the vertical edges of the beater tend constantly to carry the liquid or semi-fluid mass from the center to the circumference of the cylinder ... and when the operator turns the crank counter-clockwise, the vertical edges will tend to cut off any frozen matter from the inner surface and to gather it toward the central parts, thus constantly allowing fresh portions of the cream or other substances to be frozen to come in contact with the refrigerating surface. ... I do not confine myself to any particular material in the construction of the freezer or beater. For lemon, orange and other juices containing acid which might react slightly upon tinned iron, I prefer glass cylinders for freezers and hard wood or ivory for the wings of my beater; for cream and other substances which are not acid, the thickest of tinned iron is the most suitable material of which to form the beater. ... In seasons and at places where the economy of ice and salt is important, I make use of a tub or box whose diameter is only three or four inches larger than the freezer cylinder, and by wrapping it in thick woolen blanket, or blanket padded with wool, fur, or other material having a low conducting power for heat, I can defend the contents from external heat and greatly diminish the quantity of [salt and ice] needed. When the economy of salt is particularly important, I evaporate the salt water derived from the salt and ice, thus making a very limited quantity of salt" available for an indefinite number of re-uses. We know this was mfd. because the next patentee mentions it (albeit with wrong spelling, as Johnston's freezer.)

Sept. 19, 1848 (#5,775); **(4)** H. B. Masser, Sunbury, PA, Dec. 12, 1848 (#5,960) (Note that Masser got four patents between 1848 and 1867); **(5)** John Decker, Bel Air, MD, Aug. 21, 1849 (#6,661); **(6)** Goldsmith Coffeen, Jr., Warren, County, OH, Nov. 13, 1849 (#6,865); **(7)** Thomas M. Powell, Baltimore, MD, Sept. 5, 1854, (#11,651); **(8)** Joseph Parisette, Indianapolis, IN, June 10, 1856 (#15,083); **(9)** H. B. Masser, Jan. 19, 1858 (#19,147); **(10)** E. P. Torrey, Jersey City, NJ, Jan. 17, 1860 (#26,867). • **Baltimore:** There must be a reason besides the summertime humidity and heat why the city known for canned peaches and oysters, and not a few other kitchen-related inventions, was so into ice cream; even today it's supposed to be America's number one ice cream city!!

• • •

Makers of Ice Cream Freezers. In the *Thomas' Register of American Manufacturers*, for **1905-06**, there are but 14 makers of ice cream freezers listed: • White Mountain, Nashua, NH; • Treman, King & Co., Ithaca, NY; • Cordley & Hayes, NYC, who made them of Indurated Fibre ware; • Crandall & Godley, NYC; • Slotkin & Praglin, NYC; • E. C. Stearns & Co., Syracuse, NY; • Dana Mfg.; • H. Day & Co.; • Kingery Mfg. Co., and • The Samuel C. Tatum Co., all of Cincinnati, OH; • J. P. Anderson & Co.; • Thomas Mills & Brother; • North Brothers Mfg. Co.; • Charles W. Packer, all four

in Philadelphia, **1909**. In the *House Furnishing Review Buyer's Directory*, which gives brand names too: • Alaska Freezer Co., Winchendon, MA, "Alaska," "North Star," "Iceberg"; • Columbus Brass Co., Columbus, OH; • Commercial Can & Mfg. Co., Chicago, "Ideal"; • Consolidated Mfg. Co., Hartford, CT, "Sanitary Crystal Glass"; • Cordley & Hayes, NYC, "Fibrotta"; • Dana Mfg. Co., Cincinnati, OH, "Dana Peerless"; • J. B. Foote Foundry Co., Frederickstown, OH, "Crystal"; • North Bros. Mfg. Co., Philadelphia, "Lightning," "Jumbo Lightning," "Gem," "Blizzard," "Double Action Crown," "American Twin," Improved Philadelphia Seaman," "Combination Improved Seaman," "Improved Lightning"; • Reid-Edelmuth Mfg. Co., Brooklyn, NY, "Champion"; • Richmond Cedar Works, Richmond, VA, "Snow-ball," "Double Quick," "Frost King," "Steel Frame"; • Smith & Hemenway Co., NYC, "Polar Star"; • Sturges & Burn Mfg. Co., Chicago, IL, "Jack Frost"; • William J. Tate, Philadelphia; • Treman, King & Co., Ithaca, NY, "Automatic"; • John W. Wallace Co., NYC, "Philadelphia," "Champion," "Cincinnati"; • White Mountain Freezer Co., Nashua, NH, "White Mountain," "Arctic." *1915 HFR Buyer's Directory.* • Acme Freezer Co. (metal freezers), Philadelphia. • Alaska Freezer Co. (metal & wood), Winchendon, MA, added "North Pole"; • Automatic Ice Cream Freezer Co., Omaha, NE; • Cardington Cabinet Co., Cardington, OH, "Diamond,"

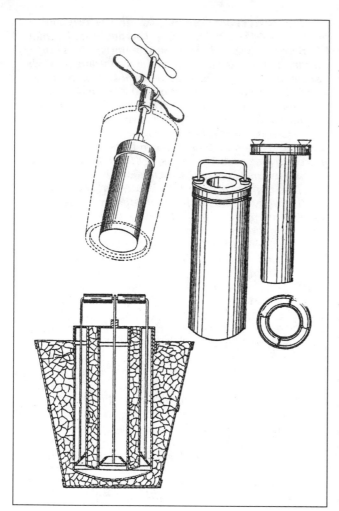

XIV-5-B. Ice cream freezer patents. *Clockwise from top:* **(1) William G. Young**, *Baltimore, MD, May 30, 1848 (#5,601), an "Improvement ... ." "Many devices have been resorted to for freezing ice cream but all have been found defective. The best now in use is that known as 'Johnston's," [sic] which is, like the ordinary freezer, with a revolving shaft inside it, on which are two curved wings. ... I find the operating is greatly facilitated by causing the freezer itself to move rapidly as well as the cream inside."* **(2) Anthony H. Austin**, *Baltimore, MD, Sept 19, 1848 (#5,775). At left is the freezer assembled, at right is the inner cylinder, which is filled with the salt & ice. To use, the small cylinder is filled with ice & salt, the cap put on, and it's inserted into the larger cylinder; then cream and ingredients for the ice cream is put in the outer cylinder, and the cap locking the two together is put on. A "common tub" of ice and salt is necessary to complete the set-up. The cylinder holding the cream has four circular "planes" (see rings) which are concentric rings, and fit around the inner cylinder; they are connected, and moved, by the vertical rod-handle. The operator puts the assembly into the common tub, then moves everything up and down, at the same time moving the "planes" attached to the handle. The planes scrape off congealed cream continuously from the walls of the cylinders and also cuts through the congealed cream inside "into very small particles, and thus render it soft and pleasant to the palate, and light and frothy, as termed by confectioners."* **(3) Thomas M. Powell**, *Baltimore, MD, Sept 5, 1854 (#11,651). Mr. Powell loved drawing ice and salt crystals! His patent shows the tub or bucket of ice & salt, as well as his invention: an ice cream freezer "with three cylindrical chambers – two of which – the center and outer ones serving for the cream, the intermediate one for the ice. By ... surrounding the freezer with ice, and filling the intermediate chamber with the same, the cream will be exposed to three freezing surfaces instead of two, as in other freezers."* All **Baltimore!**

"Crystal"; • Andrew A. Clifford, NYC, "Auto Vacuum"; • Consolidated Mfg. Co., Hartford, CT; • Culinary Mfg. Co., Orange, NJ; • Dazey Churn Mfg. Co. (glass), St. Louis, MO, "Dazey"; • C. H. & E. S. Goldberg, NYC; • Horizontal Freezer Co., Chicago, IL, "Horizontal"; • Thomas W. Houchin (metal), NYC, "Glacier"; • H. G. Kaufman, NYC; • Kingery Mfg. Co., Cincinnati, OH; • Henry G. Lang, Chicago, IL; • New England Enameling Co., Middletown, CT, "Ideal"; • North Bros. Mfg. Co., Philadelphia, added "Joy"; • Peerless Freezer Co., Winchendon, MA, "Peerless," "Freezo"; • Richmond Cedar Works, Richmond, VA; • Rice & Danziger, NYC; • Shapleigh Hardware Co., St. Louis, MO, "Jersey"; • Simmons Hardware Co., St. Louis, MO, "Wonder"; • Steinfeld Bros., NYC, "Simplex," "Duplex," "Triplex," "Acme"; • Thomas-Peters Co., Canton, OH, "Little Dandy"; • Thomas King & Co., Ithaca, NY; • Walker & Pratt Mfg. Co., Boston, MA; • James Y. Watkins & Son, NYC; • White Mountain Freezer Co., Nashua, NH, added "Nashua"; • F. E. Whitney, Boston, MA.

Ice cream freezer, all metal, galvanized iron outer box, "reinforced cover," heavy tin round "paint can" cylinder inside with a "friction cover which is absolutely water tight," tinned iron dasher and crank with wooden knob, the crank being outside the box's side, "The Snow Flake Freezer" stenciled on side, mfd. by Snow Flake Mfg Co., came in 1, 2, 3 and 4 qt. sizes, c.1907-1908. With tin ones, condition must be very, very good, especially of stencils or paper labels. .... **$60+**

Ice cream freezer, clamps to table, "Liberty Can Co.," Lancaster, PA, 2 qt. size, pat'd. 1920 & 1921.. **$50+**

❖ NOTES ❖

Doughboys Love Ice Cream – "Ice cream has played a great part in this war [WWII] and is recognized as a morale builder, unsurpassed. The importance of ice cream has been testified to by the enormous amounts of prepared mix and portable equipment for freezing provided by the army and used so close to combat lines that battle weary men just back of the front have been able to have a dish of ice cream in the protection of the nearest foxhole." Dr. H. A. Ruehe, *American Butter Institute, The Sealtest Food Adviser*, Fall 1945.

Ice cream freezer, galvanized metal canister, snug fitting lid, vertical crank with wooden knob, wire bail handle, "Glacier Freezer Triple Action," mfd. by Sunburst Alcohol Stove Co., T. W. Houchin, NYC, NY, c.1912.. **$55+**

Ice cream freezer, galvanized tin, blue painted lid, outer body, crank, paper label says "Kwik Freeze," 20th C. .... **$45+**

ce cream freezer, horizontal heavy tin duplex-style cylinder with stationary dasher blade inside each half, cylinder (which fits into malleable cast iron screw clamp frame) turns freely when cranked, while the dashers remain stationary, oblong hinged hatch in middle for putting in salt & ice, close-fitting caps at each end for adding ingredients for doing 2 flavors of ice cream at the same time, "Acme," mfd. by Palmer Hardware Mfg. Co., Troy, NY, c.1892 .... **$100+**

Ice cream freezer, japanned & stenciled tin canister, with imitation graining & bronze decorations and label. Heavy porcelain knob with gilding on close-fitting lid, galvanized interior, long cone-shaped insert to hold ingredients with salt packed around, cast iron side handles, "Automatic Ice Cream Freezer," mfd. by Treman King & Co, "System Dr. Meidinger" (refers to a foreign patent?), Ithaca, NY, 13-1/2"H x 6" diam., c.1880s; still in business 1905. ...... **$165+**

Ice cream freezer, looks like horizontal barrel churn with straight cylindrical sides, on A-frame, all wood but for iron bands on freezer, iron crank in end. A small size one is tabletop & mounted to board. "Tingley's Patent Horizontal," mfd. by the churn maker Charles G. Blatchley as "Blatchley's Horizontal," Philadelphia, PA, sizes from 3 to 40 qts. Pat'd. by J. Tingley of Philadelphia, Feb. 11, 1868 (#74,259) & June 6, 1871 (#115,657). Advertised by Blatchley in 1874, and as late as 1911............................ **$125+**

❖ NOTE ❖

Directions for Freezing Ice-Creams and Custards *– Ice-creams, custards and water are so delightful and refreshing for summer desserts and tea, it is to me a matter of astonishment that every family is not supplied with a patent ice-cream freezer, of which there are many in the market. By the use of one of these, the process of freezing is rendered so much more expeditious and satisfactory as to more than compensate for the trifling expense involved in its purpose. If not provided with this convenience, a small quantity of ice-cream can be frozen in a tin bucket, taking care that there are no holes in it to let in the water, and spoil the cream. Set this bucket in a wooden tub or bucket several inches larger. On the bottom of this place a layer of pounded ice and salt; set in the bucket containing the cream, or custard, and pack closely around its sides a mixture of pounded ice and salt (mixed in the proportion of six pounds of ice to one of salt), extending to within two inches of the top of the freezer. Cover the freezer, and keep it in constant motion, removing the cover frequently to scrape the congealed cream from the sides with a silver spoon or wooden paddle, taking care to keep the sides clear, and stirring it well to the bottom. Keep the tub well filled with salt and ice outside the freezer, and take great care that none of the salt water gets in to spoil the cream. The outside tub or bucket should have a hole in or near the bottom, from which the bung can be removed to allow the water to pass out as the ice melts. After the cream is well frozen, it may be packed in moulds, and set in salt and pounded ice. When you wish to serve it, wrap the mould with a hot cloth, turn out the cream and serve immediately.*

"For making ice-cream, genuine cream is, of course, preferable. But in the absence of this, equal parts of milk and cream may be used; or, the milk may be heated, and, while hot, perfectly fresh sweet butter added to it in sufficient quantity to give it the richness of cream. Boiled milk or custards must be allowed to become perfectly cold before putting them in the freezer. Sour cream or buttermilk may be used by stirring into them enough soda to correct their acid before sweetening and flavoring. Custards and creams for freezing should be sweetened and flavored more highly than when not frozen." Mrs. A. P. Hill, Mrs. Hill's New Family Receipt Book. NY: 1870.

Ice cream freezer, pail shaped, crank on top, frame of malleable cast iron, pail is tinned wrought sheet iron, Isaac S. Williams & Co., Philadelphia, pat'd. June 21, 1881 .... **$55+**

Ice cream freezer, staved wooden bucket with wire bail handle, tinned cast iron works, crank turns numerous horizontally-fixed beater blades, "Rapid," Clement & Dunbar, Philadelphia, 4 gal. capacity, c.1880s.... **$55+**

Ice cream freezer, tin, "Kress," poss. Philadelphia, pat'd. July 23, 1912.. **$30+**

Ice cream freezer, tin cylinder, wooden crank top, "Acme," mfd. by Ritter, Philadelphia, 2 gal. capacity, pat'd. Feb. 15, 1910. Later patent shown on other Acmes is July 3, 1912. .... **$35+**

Ice cream freezer, wood bucket with cast iron works, "Arctic," mfd. by White Mountain Freezer Co., Nashua, NH, pat'd. 1889. They were still in business 1915. .... **$35+**

Ice cream freezer, wood & galvanized metal, "Frost King," Richmond Cedar Works, Richmond, VA, 20th C. (Still making them in 1930s.) .... **35+**

XV-6. Ice cream freezer. *"Automatic Ice Cream Freezer, Treman King & Co., System Dr. Meidinger, Ithica, NY 1 & 3 East State Street." Japanned tin, imitation graining, galvanized inside, gold & bronze decorations & label. Heavy porcelain knob with gilding on close-fitting lid. Conical insert that holds ingredients lifts out, with a "bayonet' twist" – to pack salt & ice in. 13-1/2"H x 6" diam. 1870s? Collection of Meryle Evans.* **$165+**

XV-7. Ice cream freezer. *"Jack Frost," 2 quart size. Wood & cast iron. With litho'd depiction of winter play scene inside lid. "It takes very little ice and salt, being constructed on an entirely new principle. Instead of having the ice and salt on the outside of the can, the can is on the outside, and the ice and salt inside." The Housewife, July 1891.* **$100-$150**

❖ NOTES ❖

"**A Freezing Tub** must be made oblong or oval, the sides to be as upright as possible; may be made to hold two or three sabbatiers, or freezing pots, in length, leaving a sufficient space for the ice; it must have a false bottom with some holes in it; in the side of the tub, near the bottom, make a hole for a peg, by which means you may constantly draw off the water, a precaution highly necessary when freezing, to prevent the water from ever getting into the sabbatier. Sabbatiers, ice moulds, and ice spoons, may be supplied by any experienced pewterer." Joseph Bell, *A Treatise on Confectionary*, Newcastle, England, 1817.

❖ NOTE ❖

To freeze Ices – *If only one sort of ice, set the freezing pot in a small upright pail, made as above, with two bottoms, &c.; if two or three sorts, set your pots at a proper distance in the long pail; fill up the space with ice well beat, mix in three or four handfuls of salt, and press both well down; then take a clean cloth and make the tops of the pots clear of ice and salt; take off the tops; and put into each the creams or waters previously mixed for them; please to observe, that pots must not be more than half full; then replace the top to each; draw the tub a little to one side, and turn each pot as quickly, as possible; if you have two pots in, turn one with each hand; if three, let one stand alternately; when you have turned the pots ten minutes, take off the tops, and scrape the frozen cream down from each with an ice spoon; if the cream appears hard and flinty, you may conclude*

it is not rich enough mixed; if, on the other hand, it does not freeze, it is over rich, and in either case must be rectified; if right, proceed as before directed, and every ten minutes, scrape it down; when the cream in the pots appears nearly frozen, keep off the covers, and work well with the ice spoon, making the pots turn round in the ice, this will make the cream both smooth and light; as soon as it appears pretty stiff, put on the tops, and cover the pots well up with more ice and salt, until you prepare your moulds to receive it. N.B. It may be necessary here to note, that you must have an ice spoon for each pot; or must be careful to wash it every time, to prevent a mixture of tastes." Joseph Bell, A Treatise on Confectionary. Newcastle, England, 1817. • For Bell's tips on molding ice cream, see an Ice cream mold entry in Chapter IV.

Ice cream freezer, wood, metal, "Auto Vacuum," Auto Vacuum Freezer Co., NYC, pat'd. Jan. 2, 1912. .... **$35+**

Ice cream freezer, wood with cast iron crank & frame, 2 gal. size, dated 1858 – probably one pat'd. by H. B. Masser of Sunbury, PA, on Jan. 19, 1858. This is an early patent... **$125+**

Ice cream freezer, wooden tub/bucket, bail handle, iron crank & frame, "American," American Machine Co., Philadelphia, c.1880s. .... **$45+**

Ice cream freezer, glass canister with fitted glass lid, looks like churn or egg whip: it is! "Dazey Ice Cream Freezer Whip, Egg Beater Butter Churn Mold" and "Dazey Churn & Mfg. Co. St. Louis MO" on bottom. Metal whip with holes & vertical handle up through lid to push/pull. 11"H x 4" diam.................. **$900+**

Ice cream maker, glass canister with feet, wire frame, with original recipe & instruction folder inside, "Sanitary Crystal Glass Ice Cream Freezer," mfd. by "Consolidated Mfg. Co.," American (poss. Dayton, OH; poss. Quincy, IL), early 20th C. .... **$70+**

XV-8. Ice cream freezer. *"Horizontal Ice-Cream Freezer," cedar, oak frame, has perforated metal "bucket" inside the churn-like body, cast iron crank. "Tingley's Patent," mfd. by Chas. G. Blatchley, Philadelphia. Picture from ad in Harpers magazine, April 6, 1872.* **$125+**

ce cream mixer, cast aluminum, used with CO_2 cartridges, that came in boxes of 5, then put in freezer tray after mixing, "One Smoothie Whip is required for making. ... When the Whip has been discharged and removed from the holder it can be thrown out, as it cannot be used again." Marked with decal of name "Smoothie" superimposed over a green sundae dish with ice cream in it, "The Smoothie. The Instant Home Mixer of 'Satin Smooth' Ice Cream," mfd. by Ralmac Corp., Grand Rapids, MI, no date, c. 1950s **$35**

Ice cream molds & ice cream dishers – See Chapter IV (Molds)

Ice cream packing tins, set of 4, tin, American, 4 qt., 1 pt., 1/2 pt. & 1/4 pt. capacity, early 20th C. ...... **$35-$50**

Ice crusher, also called ice cube breaker, or ice grinder, mechanical, cream-colored painted cast metal, wood handle crank, on a stand with place for a tumbler, "National Ice-Crusher," 9"H, pat'd. 1936. .... **$20+**

Ice crusher, all cast iron, oblong jaws with "waffled" treads inside, "Stover Ice Cube Kracker," Stover, Freeport, IL, 7-3/4"L, early 1900s. **$15**

Ice crusher, mechanical, malleable cast iron, "Alaska #1," Alaska Freezer Co., Winchendon, MA, 1880s (?) to 1930s. .... **$35+**

Ice crusher, mechanical, malleable iron hopper & housing on decorative cast iron double "A" base, side crank, 12"H, marked "Chandler's Ice Cutting Machine," on handle: "pat'd. Nov. 16, 1880." .... **$150+**

Ice crusher or breaker, mechanical, sheet metal hopper above 4-legged cast iron stand on plinth, with lion-head knees to each leg, large wheel crank turns two gears in side. Four sizes, the first two available with a receiver drawer. Size No. 3 "will take a piece of ice about 5" by 8", breaking it into pieces about the size of chestnuts." Advertised in Mrs. Marshall's cook-books as a "household machine for crushing ice," but in a catalog as for "hotel keepers, ships' cabins, Butlers' pantries," etc. Marked on hopper "Mrs. A. B. Marshall, London." .... **$175+**

Ice crusher, mechanical, cast iron base, with green glass ice hopper, "Lightning," North Brothers Mfg. Co., Philadelphia, PA, Mar. 29, 1932 design patent #86599, by Thomas J. Fegley & George O. Leopold, Philadelphia & assignors to North Bros. Green glass adds some value. .... **$75+**

Ice crusher, mechanical, enameled steel frame and platform, fitted with square green Depression glass container, hopper above with crank, "Lightning," North Brothers, Nov. 13, 1934 patent #1980952, which was filed over three years before by Fegley & Leopold. Crossover interest from glass people. **$75+**

Ice crusher, mechanical, nickel plated brass, "Coolerator," Duluth Refrigerators, Duluth, MN, 20th C. .... **$25+**

Ice crusher, mechanical, cast metal alloy, Dazey, the churn people, St. Louis, MO, 1940s. .... **$20+**

Ice cube tray, aluminum, dividers so niftily jointed it looks like a millipede, no maker mark, 12-1/8"L, marked with patents #214,795, #2,265,705, #2,212,424, & #2,212,425, the first 2 numbers are incorrect; I'm not so sloppy that I get so many numbers wrong in transcription; I think a number was just put on in anticipation of getting a patent, or the die-cutter made a mistake............................ **$5-$8**

Ice cube tray, green rubber with metal wire puller or grip, "FlexoTray," mfd. by Inland Mfg. Co., Dayton, OH, 10-1/2"L, April 23, 1929 reissue patent #17278, pat'd. by Lloyd G. Copeman, Flint, MI, assignor to Copeman Laboratories Co. of Flint. The original patent was #274,717 of July 1928. • According to a 1931 ad, the "FlexoTray" was made for Westinghouse, Kelvinator, Leonard, Electrolux, Servel, Copeland, Universal & other refrigerators. Inland also made the "Quickube Tray" for Frigidaire (o.1937), and the "DuFlex" for General Electric. These various flexible rubber trays were "supplied by all leading automatic refrigerator makers." .... **$6+**

Ice cube tray, natural colored brownish rubber, very flexible, makes 21 cubes, each cup has interconnecting hole in inner walls, "FlexoTray," mfd. by The Inland Mfg. Co., Dayton, OH, 1-3/4" deep x 12-1/4"L x 3-3/4"W, 1929 reissue patent #s 17278 & 17279. .... **$8+**

Ice pick, also called an ice awl, long pointed steel with rounded knobby turned wooden handle, deep ferrule, made by many companies, one being C. W. Dunlap Mfg. Co., NYC, N.Y., c.1890s & later. .... **$5+**

Ice pick, all metal, steel pick, cast heavy metal handle, adv'g. "Coca-Cola," 20th C. .... **$8+**

Ice pick, iron & steel, "Arcade," Freeport, IL, early 20th C. .... **$10+**

Ice pick, iron with turned wood knob handle, spring action, punch it down & shaft telescopes to increase pounds-per-square inch force, in F. A. Walker catalog, c.1870s. .... **$35+**

Ice pick, steel prickers, nicely shaped turned wood handle, cup-like aluminum housing for prickers when not in use, push up & lock aluminum cup with bayonet lock, not marked, 8"L, late 19th or early 20th C. .... **$30-$40**

Ice pick, steel with cast iron drop weight that slides down shank & hits bottom piece to add power to your punch, American, 11 5/8"L, late 19th C. .... **$35+**

Ice pick, wood handle, motto, "Use Ice Year Around," early 20th C. .... **$5+**

Ice pick, cast aluminum & steel, handle is shapely woman's leg, probably not a production piece but made by an artist/craftsman. 11"L, c.1920s-30s. (See a stove lid lifter in Chapter XI.)................ **$75+**

Ice pick & bottle opener combined, cast iron, steel, "Watertown Ice Co.," c.1890s-1910. .... **$5+**

Ice pick or chipper, 4 steel points in fork shape, brass ferrule, turned wooden handle, "Crawford," Newark, NJ, 7-1/2"L, late 19th C................................. **$15+**

Ice pick or hammer, brass, long rod handle with ruffled cuff ferrule and small cast fist holding large tack-shaped thing with point & flat top, English or Continental, 10"L overall, with fist about 3"L, prob. mid 19th C. .... **$150+**

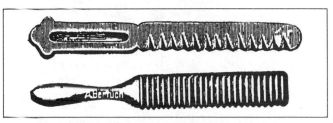

XV-9. Ice-breaking knives. *Iron or steel. Two types from* A. Bertuch *catalog of specialties mainly for ice cream makers & confectioners. Berlin, Germany, c.1904.* **$15+**

Ice pick & scraper, nickeled iron with wooden handle, a sort of fork with a frame over top of tines, has a small maw to catch shavings, mfd. by & adv'g. "Coolerator. The Air Conditioned Refrigerator," Coolerator Co., Duluth, MN, 12"L, 20th C. .... **$15+**

Ice scoop, corrugated galvanized tin with wooden handle, long bowl with high slightly rounded sides, flat heel, American, 9"L, c.1890s. .... **$8+**

Ice scraper & chipper, cast iron with wooden handle, "White Mountain," Nashua, NH, late 19th or early 20th C. .... **$10+**

Ice shaver, cast iron, "Arctic Ice Shave #33," Grey Iron Casting Co., Mount Joy, PA, late 19th C. .... **$15+**

Ice shaver, cast iron, steel, Griswold, Erie, PA, late 19th or early 20th C. .... **$35+**

Ice shaver, cast iron & steel, hand-cranked rotary type, Clawson Machine Co., Flagtown, NJ, early 20th C. .... **$75+**

Ice shaver, heavy cast iron, tinned, lid has a monogram, "ACW" for A. C. Williams Co., Ravenna, OH, 7-5/8"L, c.1890s-1910. .... **$15+**

Ice shaver, nickeled cast iron, hinged hopper, removeable blade, "Gem," mfd. by North Brothers Mfg. Co., Philadelphia, patent applied for. .... **$15+**

Ice shaver, cast metal, big cup with adjustable and sharpenable steel blade, "Logan-Strowbridge Iron Co. #12," New Brighton, PA, pat'd. Dec. 21, 1897 by John H. Logan as a "self emptying ice shredder." .... **$20+**

Ice shaver, cast iron base with steel shaving table, stands high on four beautiful scrolled cabriole legs, mid 19th C. .... **$175+**

Ice shaver, wood with four turned 'piano' legs, steel shaver set into top, used with a tumbler or other vessel to catch shavings underneath, called an Ice Plane by maker, mfd. by a Mr. Keith, London, England, c.1850. .... **$125+**

XV-10. Ice crusher or breaker. No.1 of 4 sizes. This one "for hotel keepers, confectioners, wine merchants, refreshment rooms, ships' cabins, butlers' pantries, &c." Cast iron, cast iron legs with lion's head knees. Circular ring underneath is for pan to catch the ice. Largest styles had drawers underneath. No. 3 "will take a piece of ice about 5" x 6" x 8", breaking it into pieces about the size of a chestnut." Ad in Mrs. A. B. Marshall's Cookery Book, *London, c.1900.* **$175+**

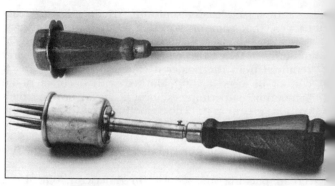

XV-11. Ice picks. (T) Needle point, wood handle with scalloped cap of metal which is a crusher head. 7-5/8"L. Probably Androck, c.1930s. *(B)* Mechanical one, with protective housing when not in use. Wood handle with flat top for mallet, steel prickers & shank, aluminum housing. To reveal pick points, you push aluminum cup up shaft & twist it. Bayonet locking device. 8"L. Located by Primitive Man, Bob Cahn, Carmel, NY. (A similar newer one is fixed-position with 5 points, square wood handle, marked "Chip Chop," "Pat Pend, Apex Products Corp, N.Y.C." worth $5+.) **$5-$15; $30-$45**

Ice shaver or plane, galvanized cast iron (they also made one of cast aluminum) with double edged tool steel blade, hinged angled top that encloses compartment that catches the shavings, looks almost identical to one made by Stover, "No. 77," Gilchrist Co., Newark, NJ, c.1906. .... **$10**

Ice shaver, tongs & hammer combined, cast iron, American, 13-1/4"L, pat'd. June 1878. .... **$75+**

Ice shaver – See Meat tenderizer combo tool, Chapter I

Ice shredder, tinned cast iron, cone-shaped with lid, shaving blade is in lid so held cone tip up to work, slightly curved double handles hinged at end, one attached to cone, one to lid, held together while scraping, "after the Shredder is scraped full of ice, tap the small end of cone so as to make contents solid," after which you release handle to reveal snow cone, which fits then into paper holder, "especially adapted for the use of vendors selling 'Snow Balls,' as by hole in the small end of cone the ball can be readily flavored and easily ejected." "Enterprise Hardware Co. #43," Philadelphia, c.1890s, sold into 20th C. .... **$30+**

Ice shredder or shaver, tinned cast iron cup with curved handle, looks like little saucepan with hinged lid, steel shaver teeth inside, makes snow balls for snow cones, or ice for icing oysters on the half shell, or celery, fruits, drinks, marked "Enterprise Mfg. Co. #33" on lid, 7-3/4"L overall, cup is 3-1/2" diam. x 2-1/2" deep, sold at least by July 1892; pat'd. July 4, 1893, lucky patent date for ice cold treat! • The same size #34 was nickeled, & cost 3 times as much when new, but not now. .... **$30+**

❖ NOTES ❖

Ice tongs – All depend on the weight of the ice block itself to pull the two "scissor"-action, upward-curving hooks inward toward each other to grip the ice when it's ifted. The handles, which are spread apart while positioning around the block, are brought back to starting position for carrying, and the act of lifting seats the hooks' points on opposite sides of the block of ice. Depending on the type, handles may have a starting position that's either very close together, or a hand's breadth apart. A block of ice might weigh 50 pounds or more. A strong man could hold closed the two rubber or wooden grips found on many late 19th & early 20th C tongs with one hand. Likewise for those with simple loop handles. But the best and most valuable tongs have a kind of bail handle connecting the two upper ends of the pivoting hooks, so that the ice can be carried as easily as a suitcase. The bail may be a curve of iron rod, or may be a shapely grip of forged iron.

Ice tongs, cast handles & forged iron hooks, American, 21"L, c.1880s-1900.. **$25+**
Ice tongs, iron, "Butler Ice Co.," 14"L, c.1900. ..... **$15+**
Ice tongs, iron with wooden grips, adv'g. "Dixie Gem Coal, Ice & Fuel Co.," 14"L, early 20th C. There were many dealers who sold both ice and coal......... **$25+**
Ice tongs, all forged iron, including 2 looped handle grips, 12"L, late 19th C. .... **$55+**
Ice tongs, forged iron, pointed tips are bifurcated to seize the ice better, 12"L, probably mid-1800s, ... **$65+**

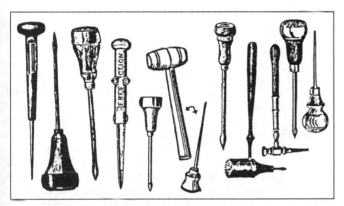

XV-12. Ice picks. Left to right: **(1)** "Unique," steel needlepoint, malleable cast iron handle slides up & down, serves as a hammer. 8-1/2"L. Albert Pick catalog of kitchen supplies, mainly for hotels, 1909. **(2)** Patented, iron bound wood handle, pick with slight "arrowhead" or spear point – the other type of pick point. John Van Range Co., 1914. **(3)** 5"L pick. Sexton, c.1930. **(4)** "Perfection," all iron handle. Mfd. by W. G. Browne Mfg. Co. 1910. **(5)** "Ice Pick – Steel Awl," 8-3/4"L, tinned cap. Sexton, c.1930. **(6 & 7)** connected by arrows, "Ice mallet with pick that slides into the handle" of the mallet. Most valuable one here. American Home Cook Book, 1854. **(8)** Steel point, wood handle. Without iron band. Matthai-Ingram, c.1890. **(9)** "Steak pounder & ice mallet No4." Steel pick in head of hammer. Heinz & Munschuuer, 1882. **(10)** Ice hammer & pick, rosewood handle, tempered steel point, silver-plated hammer & shank. 2nd most valuable. 8-1/2"L x 2-7/8"W. **(11)** "Spear point" steel pick, nickeled iron band & ferrule. 8-1/2"L. Has "N. White City & Co." cap mark. **(12)** Needle pick, steel, hardwood knob handle, 9-1/4"L. Last 3 all Albert Pick catalog 1909. **$5-$65**

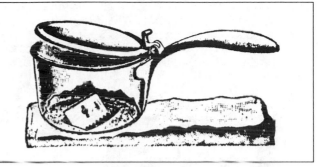

XV-13. Ice shaver or shredder. Tinned or nickeled cast iron cup-like saucepan, hinged lid. Cutaway view shows adjustable (& removable) blade inside. Enterprise Mfg. Co., Philadelphia. It is "only necessary to draw the blade upon the ice, the pressure applied producing fine or coarse pieces, as desired. To remove the finely cut ice from the cup the shredder is grasped firmly in the right hand, striking it inverted upon the left, being careful to keep the lid closed. The ice is then scraped into some convenient receptacle. It is not necessary to take the ice out of the refrigerator, as the cup may be filled from the side or top of the cake." **$30+**

Ice tongs, forged iron, with simple rod bail handle connecting 2 handles, 14"L, look like calipers more than most, mid-19th C... **$65+**
Ice tongs, forged iron with decorative twisting for tensile strength, American, 14-1/2"L, 19th C. ..... **$75+**
Ice water bottle, green glass, oblong with big rounded top, embossed pebbly surface with depiction of Monitor Top refrigerator, & words "WATER ... for use with the GENERAL ELECTRIC REFRIGERATOR" on the front, measures from 1 cup (1/2 pt.) to 3 cups (1/2 pts.) on back, GE, 8-1/2"H x 5"W, 1927........................ **$75+**
Refrigerator for nursery, japanned sheet steel chest with lifting handles at each end, looks like oak graining with pin striping, hasped lid lifts to reveal one compartment of porcelainized steel for ice water or other cold liquid, another compartment for food, insulated with mineral wool (asbestos), mfd. by James R. Wotherspoon, Philadelphia, PA, very early 20th C. • Fries & McAleer made these too, almost identical in appearance. **$35**
Refrigerator (icebox), ash, enameled metal interior, 2 door, 57"H, c.1890s-1910. .... **$175+**
Refrigerator (icebox), oak, 4 doors, "Northey Duplex," 6 feet 2-1/2"H x 4 feet 1-1/2"W x 2-1/2 feet deep, c.1890s-1910. .... **$350+**
Refrigerator (icebox), oak, porcelainized interior, lift top lid with zinc-lined box, one door, wire shelves, 47"H x 27-1/2"W, c.1900. .... **$175+**
Refrigerator (icebox), unusual tall cupboard type, door over door, oak with paneled sides, bracket feet, M. M. Whitman & Co., Worcester, MA, 60"H x 28-1/2"W x 23-1/2" deep, c.1890s-1910. Oak: $$$; pine: $. .... **$400+**
Refrigerator (icebox), which could be converted to electricity with a compressor, motor & gas coils, large boxy enameled (ivory, grey, blue or green) steel cabinet on casters, 4 hinged doors, lined with white "quarried" stone, "White Mountain," Maine Mfg. Co., Nashua, NH, c.1927. .... **$100+**

XV-15. Ice scoop. *Galvanized crimped tin, wood handle, 9"L, c.1890-1920. Other prettier ones of the period, with turned wood handles, were made of nickeled copper & cast aluminum.* **$8+**

XV-14. Ice planes. (T-R) *Nickeled iron legs, steel top & blade, wood base. 7-1/2"H x 14-1/2"L x 6-1/4"W. Albert Pick, 1909 catalog.* **(B-L)** *"Keith's Registered Plane," English. "The ice plane is as simple in its construction as its application, being merely rubbing the ice to and fro rapidly upon the surface, when the snowlike flakes will descend into the vessel below. Sherry Cobblers, Mint Juleps, &c. – It will be found of great utility wherever ice is used (more especially the Wenham Lake ice), as it is rendered into a more elegant, agreeable, and useful form at table than the irregular masses which are less sightly. It will be found indispensable for the preparation of the American beverages, sherry cobblers, mint juleps, &c. Mr. Keith is decidedly at the head of the ice department in this country, and has been so spirited in his enterpises as to keep completely at bay his numerous imitators." The Lady's Newspaper, June 15, 1850. Ice from "Wenham Lake" (on which I could find no information) presumably was very fine, as it was contrasted with "common rough ice."* **$45+; $125+**

Refrigerator (ice box), white enamel-painted steel inside and out, insulated with cork, 4 stumpy bathtub-like legs with casters, lid lifts off top part where ice goes, hinged door in side reveals 2 (1916 one seems to have 3) round revolving nickel plated shelves inside, later ones had a spigot on side of top part to draw off ice cold water for drinking (you'd have to trust your ice man!), in 1920 ad, glass water cooler with removable top shown adjacent to the ice compartment, "White Frost," mfd. by Metal Stamping Co., Jackson, MI, 43"H x 23" diam., pat'd. Sept. 11, 1906, Nov. 6, 1906 and June 23, 1908. Advertisements claimed that the White Frost was used by the government during work on the Panama Canal. By 1916 the company was called White Frost Refrigerator Co., and by 1920 it was the Home Products Corporation. It was still selling in 1920, in nearly the same form. Condition of original baked-on enamel paint, and condition of inside affects value. .... **$55-$100+**

Refrigerator (icebox), zinc alloy, nickeled brass hardware, 2 doors with wire shelves, 4 legs, c.1890s-1910. .... **$150+**

Refrigerator (icebox), "side board & china closet" combined. "Antique" ash, with decorative carving, china closet with 4 shelves, glass front, decorative molding on top; drawers for silverware and linen – raised above top of refrigerator, affording a small sideboard serving area. Included a water cooler. About 68"H x 28"W. "Old Maid Refrigerator," "for people desiring the comforts of life in small rooms." "Leonard Cleanable Refrigerators," mfd. by Grand Rapids Refrigerator Co., Grand Rapids, MI, c.1892. .... **$550+**

Refrigerator (icebox), in sideboard style, carved ash "finished in antique oak," with beveled mirror above, fancy hardware, meant for dining room. Included water cooler with faucet. "The Siberia," Simmons Hardware Co., St. Louis, MO, 83"H x 45-1/2"W x 23" deep, c.1900. .... **$700+**

Refrigerator (electric), box on short cabriole legs, motor housing on top is shaped like the Capitol dome in Washington, DC, white enameled steel, "Ice-O-Matic" in Capitol Model, mfd. by Williams Oil-O-Matic Heating Corp., Bloomington, IL, small, c.1930. • **It's What's On Top That Counts.** – The most famed refrigerator with motor housing on top is the **GE Monitor Top**, but it is also the most commonly found. According to a 1930 ad, you can have the motor "unit on top of its good-looking cabinet; in the lower compressor compartment or in the basement." .... **$100+**

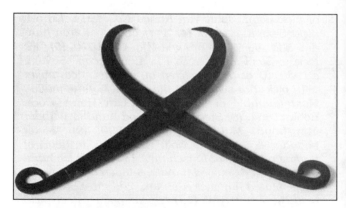

XV-16. Ice tongs. *Forged iron, handles have what cataloguer called "pigtail ends." 19"L. Photo courtesy Litchfield Auction Gallery, Litchfield, CT. Ex-Harold Corbin Collection, auctioned Jan. 1, 1989.* **$75+**

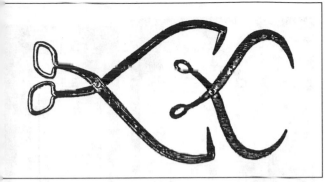

XV-17. Ice tongs. *"Wrought iron," but not black-smith-made like previous pair. Medium & large size from catalogs c.1900-1910.* **$15+**

Refrigerator (electric), but looks just like large icebox, white enameled steel, tall box with nickeled-steel binding around each of 6 doors, plated hinges & handles, louvered motor compartment underneath, upper right door reveals ice cube tray, glass in all doors makes this look like professional restaurant refrigerators sold today to upscale housewives, Servel Corp. (soon Electrolux Servel), factories in Evansville, IN, Carteret, NJ, Newburgh, NY, c.1925. .... **$75**

Refrigerator (electric), white enameled steel, stepped streamline shape, black base, bin compartment with pull-down door at bottom, main door reveals small central freezer compartment, several shelves, many nickeled wire shelves built into drawer, amazing part is the radio built into the top front of the refrigerator, WOW!!! "Crosley Shelvador," Crosley Radio Corp., Cincinnati, OH, c.1938. Because of the radio this has great crossover collector value, even if the radio needs tubes. .... **$425+**

Refrigerator bottle, green glass, pat'd. Sept. 15, 1931. .... **$35+**

XV-18. "Closet or Upright Refrigerator." (L) *"The door on the side insures ventilation, and the closet form is most convenient to arrange dishes."* Ameri-can Home Cook Book, 1854. *The form of this looks as if ice were in it, but there is no textual evidence of ice.* **(R)** *"Glacier Refrigerator," mfd. by Northern Refrigerator Co., Grand Rapids, MI. Their motto: "As far ahead of all others as the electric light excels the candle." Work had probably begun to make an elec-tric refrigerator. Century, May 1892.*

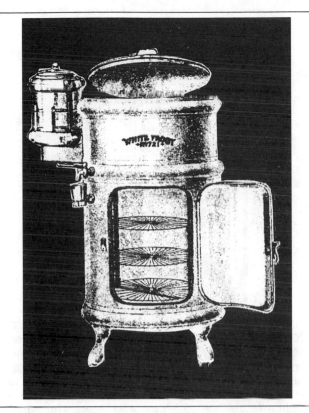

XV-19. Refrigerator – Ice box. *"White Frost Sani-tary," cylindrical in shape, mfd. by C. A. Carey, Home Products Corp., Jackson, MI. Ladies' Home Journal ad, May 1920: "Our iceman says, 'This is the only refrigerator in town. People could afford to throw their ice boxes away and save the price of a White Frost in ice." A doctor says, "From a sanitary standpoint, it cannot be beaten." Steel, granulated cork insulation, nickel trim, white glass water cooler, removable top. After 80+ years without another round or cylindrical refrigerator, a new one appears in the 21st Century: East German company Foron has one that runs on hydrocarbons (environment smiles), and as of 2002 is being manufactured in the U.S. by Equator. Wait'll you see it – it's super! For the old one:* **$300+**

Refrigerator container, pale blue "crystal" glass, with lid, "Fire-King," Anchor Hocking Glass Corp., 4-1/2" x 5", 1940s-50s. .... **$30+**

Refrigerator container, glass, "Westinghouse," 1930s. .... **$10-$15+**

Refrigerator defroster attachment, electric, enameled steel housing to a timing device, which could be set almost like a thermostat, you'd plug the refrigerator into it, and it into the outlet. "Magic Defroster," "makes old refrigerators into modern automatic defrosters." Mfd. by Maxilume Co., Chicago, c.1950. .... **$5+**

Refrigerator ice water dispenser, glass with fired-on opaque pastel green finish, chrome spigot with red rubber gasket, clear glass (called "crystal") lid molded with concentric rings, sort of a glass shoebox that lies on its side with spigot at one end, for getting cold water. In old refrigerators this might fit under the tiny freezer compartment, mfd. by Hall, 12"L, c.1930s. .... **$65+**

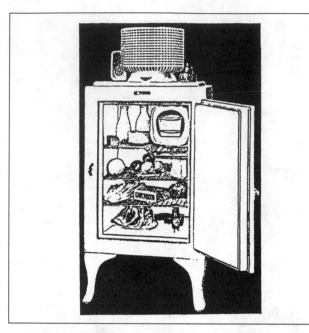

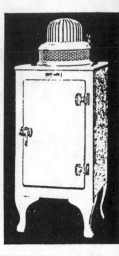

XV-20. Refrigerator classic. *A General Electric "Monitor Top." 1927* Ladies' Home Journal *ad reads: "Here is a new development in electric refrigerators for the home. ... It marks an entirely new conception. ... an entirely new type of icing unit – unlike any other you have ever seen. The entire mechanism of the GE Icing Unit is housed on top of the cabinet in one hermetically sealed casing. That is all the mechanism – none below the box. None in the basement. There are no pipes, no drains, no attachments. All bulky machinery is eliminated – virtually no servicing. The result of fifteen years of intensive research." Electric Refrigeration Dept., GE Co., Cleveland, OH. It lasted forever too – a lesson for today. In 1929 there were six Monitor-top styles, including doublewide ones.* **$175+**

XV-21. Refrigerators. (L) *From 1935 ad comes this "New G-E Model X-4" designed for small homes and apartments.* **(R)** *"Ice-O-Matic Capitol Model," mfd. by Williams Oil-O-Matic Heating Corp., Bloomington, IL. You could have the motor "on top" as illustrated; "in the lower compressor compartment or in the basement."* Country Life, *1930. It's a toss-up between which you'd want the most. The only problem with the Ice-O-Matic is that you lose a horizontal storage space on top! I need every surface I can find.* **$175+**

❖ NOTES ❖

"Jadite" generally is used by collectors/dealers to refer to a color, most usually, a pale green that can be opaque "milk" glass, but Jadite is also specifically a trade name for an opaque green that Jeannette Glass Co. (Jeannette, PA) made; the name "Jade-ite" was used by Anchor Hocking. Other pieces in opaque green were made by Fenton Glass Co., who used simply "Jade"; and McKee Glass Co. used "Jade Green." Collectors tend to use it for a wide range of very pale to rather richly green opaque but translucent glass. When used in ads it often doesn't mean the Jeannette brand name.

Refrigerator ice water dispenser, pebbly-textured clear, or "crystal," glass body, plain "crystal" lid, white rubber gasket, c.1930s. .... **$30+**
Refrigerator jar, saltglazed stoneware, small size, Red Wing, MN, 20th C. .... **$100+**
Refrigerator jar, saltglazed stoneware with 2 blue bands, bail handle, "Red Wing Refrigerator Jar, Compliments of Semon's Fair Store, Athens, Wisc.," mfd. in MN, 5-3/4"H, early 20th C. .... **$95+**

XV-22. Refrigerator with radio. *"Shelvado ... just open the door. There, at your fingertips, are your most-often-needed foods. No reaching. No searching." This model with "built-in radio." Crosley Electric Refrigerators, mfd. by Crosley Radio Corp., Cincinnati, OH.* McCall's, *June 1938. (Shelvadors introduced c.1936.)* **$425+**

XV-23. Water cooler. *Stoneware with cobalt flower decoration, rare exagerated ovoid shape, 2 handles. Made by I. Seymour, Troy, NY, 18"H, 19th C. A perfectly beautiful form, sensual & almost figural. Photo courtesy Litchfield Auction Gallery, Litchfield, CT. Ex-Harold Corbin Collection. Auctioned Jan. 1, 1990 for:* **$6,000**

XV-24. Water filter & water coolers. (T-L) *Stoneware filter, for "purifying cistern water for cooking or table use." (T-R) "Water cooler, filled in with charcoal, preserves the ice and keeps water icy cold. – The water is kept cooler than the atmosphere without ice." The cooler looks like japanned sheet metal, but may be stoneware. Both pictures from American Home Cook Book, 1854. Often coolers and filters were combined. (B-L) "Improved Sanitary," gray stoneware, blue bands, mfd. by Fulper Pottery Co., Flemington, NJ. House Furnishing Review, April 1908. [Fulper was established in 1805.] (B-R) Stoneware with leaf decoration, nickeled faucet. 12 sizes, from 2 gallons to 50 gallons. Albert Pick catalog, 1909.* **$75+**

Refrigerator pan, galvanized steel, looks like dog feeding dish for a St. Bernard, round with bowl bottom set in side, 2 side ear handles, catches drips from melting ice, New England Enameling Co., Middletown, CT, c.1890s-1910. • "A strictly modern newspaper item tells of a bride who declined an invitation to a picnic because she could never be away from the apartment for more than five hours and twenty minutes at a stretch. Her inquisitive friends asked why. 'Well,' she explained reluctantly, 'you see, every five hours and twenty-one minutes, the refrigerator-pan overflows.'" Frances Lester Warner, "When Equipment Overflows," *House Beautiful*, Feb. 1927........................... **$10+**

Refrigerator water bottle, rich green Depression glass, embossed design of old-fashioned well, American, 1930s.. **$35+**

Refrigerator water jug, swirled cobalt blue Depression glass, with spigot, 20th C. .... **$145+**

Water cooler, japanned tin urn, stenciled "Ice Water," with cast iron finial to ridged, domed tin lid & cast iron spigot, in F. A. Walker catalog, came in 8 sizes: 2, 3, 6, 8, 10, 15 & 20 gal., c.1870s. This also came with porcelain liner, in 2, 3, 4, 6, 8 & 10 gallon sizes.. **$45+**

Water cooler, saltglazed stoneware jug, ear handles, on wonderful turned stoneware pedestal base, metal spigot, gray with cobalt blue birds on branches, incised & colored, capacity "4" (gallons), PA, 21-1/2"H, mid 19th C...................................... **$4,250+**

Water cooler, saltglazed stoneware with cobalt blue flower design, pewter spigot, no lid, 4 gal. size, 19th C. .... **$350+**

XV-25. "Lady Franklin Family Ice Urns." *"Perfection" granite ironware & "Pearl Agateware" with quadruple silverplate fittings, mfd. by Manning, Bowman & Co., 1892 catalog. (L) & (M) show detached parts – including "shell" which fit down over handled reservoir, and footed stand. Two sizes, for 6 pints or 8, and had matching footed goblets. (R) "Assorted decorations in winter scenes," 9-pint size with goblets to match, you could order "plain silver band just above the faucet" engraved however you liked.* **$400-$1,000**

Water cooler, white & blue spongeware, "Avery & Winter Pottery Co. #6," NYC, NY, 19th C. .... **$350+**

Water filter & cooler, blue & white glazed pottery with relief floral and scroll designs, shapely breasted container with spigot hole near bottom, "The Allen Germ-Proof Filter," Toledo, OH, 13-1/2"H x 10-1/4" diam., late 19th C. • When I lived in Toledo I saw only one of these, the lidless one I bought. Since then, at flea markets all over, I've seen a number of them, all without lids, most chipped. (See the one on the cover.) .... **$125-$300**

FOR MORE INFORMATION

ICE CREAM HISTORY

Linda Stradley

The author of cookbooks *What's Cooking America, and I'll Have What They're Having – Favorite Regional Foods of America*, has this interesting Web site outlining the history of ice cream.

Web site: www.geocities.com/NapaValley/4079/History/IceCream/IceCreamHistory.htm

CLUBS

The Ice Screamers

If you love ice cream and/or other soda fountain collectibles, and all the tools used to advertise it, make it, or deliver it to your waiting mouth, this is the club for you. They cover everything from cone holders to straw holders, from dippers to mixers. They have a newsletter and a convention every year.

Contact: Don & Judy Snyder, Membership
P.O. Box 465
Warrington, PA 18976
Phone: (215) 343-2676
E-mail: smoothsail@aol.com
Web site: www.icescreamers.com
Web site of club contacts: www.ices creamers.com/Contacts.html

RESTORATION & REPRODUCTION PARTS

Constantine's
1040 E. Oakland Park Blvd.
Ft. Lauderdale, FL 33334
Phone: (954) 561 1716
E-mail: info@constantines.com
Web site: www.constantines.com

Phyllis Kennedy Hardware

Hardware for furniture, Hoosier cabinets, iceboxes, etc.

Contact: Phyllis Kennedy
10655 Andrade Dr.
Zionsville, IN 46077
Phone: (317) 873-1316
E-mail: philken@kennedyhardware.com
Web site: www.kennedyhardware.com

Muffs Restoration Hardware
For Hoosiers, furniture, iceboxes, etc.
Orange Plazai
135 S. Glassell
Orange, CA 92866-1421
Phone: (714) 997-0243
E-mail: muffs@earthlink.net
Web site: www.muffshardware.com

Northland Furniture & Restoration

For Hoosiers, iceboxes; also pie safe tins.

7118 NW Eastside Dr.
Kansas City, MO 64152
Phone: (877) 258-3876
E-mail: sales@northlandrestoration.com
Web site: www.northlandrestoration.com/hardware.htm

COPPER, BRASS, NICKEL, TIN, & CHROME FINISHES

There are many places listed on the Internet, and in the Yellow Pages of telephone directories, who do plating; although many are for machine parts, tool & die companies, motorcyclists, musicians, & golfers, others cater to collectors of various kinds – from toy cars to guns to stove parts & hardware. For tinning, see also end of Chapter XII (Pots & Pans).

Plateworld Directory

An online site with links to platers in all the states.

Web site: www.plateworld.com/shops.htm

Industrial Resource Network

This international online site is a "power sourcing" site where everyone from individuals to manufacturers can find what they need in reference to their own regions of the world. This one might be of help to you.

Web site: www.powersourcing.com/se/plating serviceonceramic-pliers.htm

Victrola Repair Service

Their main business is nickel-plating old Victrola parts, but they plate smallish things. Perfect for kitchen tools.

Contact: Les Royer & Rod Lauman
206 Cliff St.
St. Johnsbury, VT 05819
Phone: (802) 748-4893
E-mail: victrola@together.net
Web site: www.together.net/~victrola/index.html

New England Chrome Plating

This company plates stoves, lamps, fireplace equipment, hardware, housewares, piano parts, etc., in brass, chrome, zinc, nickel, copper & even gold (in case you want to make a special treasure out of a kitchen utensil!). They have locations in Connecticut, Florida, and Arkansas.

63 Thomas St.
East Hartford, CT 06108
Phone: (860) 528-7176
E-mail: necpl@msn.com
Web site: www.newenglandchrome.com/antique.shtml

Color Cabinet

Plate 1. "The New Aspinwall Double Action Churn" *chromolithograph advertising flyer, c. 1900. Such flyers were available to churn dealers all over the country to imprint with their own names and addresses.*

Utensil Cupboard in the MIRRO Test Kitchen

Plate 2. 1920's recipe brochure for Mirro *aluminum ware, showing storage cupboard full of Mirro wares. Kitchen with typical period two-checkered tiles, and Colonial Revivalist braided rag rug.*

Plate 3. Trade card for "Raven Paste" *stove polish. Chromolithographic, c. 1880s.*

Plate 4. Meat chopper chromolith trade card, *c. 1900, shows copper water heater at left of the brickset range. Often such trade cards give glimpses of historically correct interiors that we wouldn't be able to see otherwise.*

Plate 5. Trade card for Taylor's Baking Powder, *Chromolithographed advertising. The cook is dismayed because whereas in the past she had to use more baking powder, here she used too much Taylor's, resulting in a sort of "I Love Lucy" incident: The quick bread rising so much in the oven that it lifts the top off her cookstove! 1880s.* **$15**

Plate 6. "Food Surprises from the Mirro Test Kitchen" *recipe brochure, 1920s. Often manufacturers of stoves, refrigerators, or kitchen utensils published recipe books from test kitchens at the manufacturing plant.*

Plate 7. Ad for Nairn Gold Seal Inlaid linoleum – *showing housewife at Hoosier-like cabinet with two yellowware bowls in pretty blue and yellow kitchen. From Ladies Home Journal, April 1926.*

Plate 8. Trade card for Grand Rapids Refrigerator, *showing snug family eating supper, with the ice box in a louvered "storm house" structure built off the back of the house. C. 1880.* **$15**

Plate 9. Lithograph by L. Prang & Co., *showing pastry making, and beautiful kitchen interior of c.1874. Note the large kitchen "piano" (as large ranges were nicknamed). This brickset range, in original fireplace or hearth opening, may be a Kitchener.*

It is a GOOD Gas Range   That Has This RED WHEEL

Plate 10. "Magic Chef" ad from a 1931 *Ladies' Home Journal*. *The marbleized enamel finish of the stove is "Italian Grand Antique Marble" with ivory trim. Note red and green décor of kitchen.*

Plate 11. Pastry jagger, *marbleized asparagus green Catalin plastic. 1930s.*

Plate 12. Pastry jagger – pie wheel, *turned & carved wood, pewter wheel. Probably the red paint is over even older dark green. Early to mid 18th C.*

Plate 17. Apple parer, painted straddle type, *Pennsylvania German, mid 19th C. Formerly in The Keillor Family Collection.*

Plate 18. Toy tea kettle, *nickeled iron, Wagner Ware, Sidney, OH. Even has heat-dispensing coil handle. 3-3/4" H. Collection of Bonnie Myers.*

Plate 19. Miniature cake server *or turner, tin, tubular handle. Possibly from toy Nuremberg kitchen. 5-1/2" L, 19th C.*
20th C. pie

Plate 20. Stove paint advertising model. *What looks like a toy stove is an advertising model used by Sapolin Hot Pipe Aluminum paint. The color scheme of yellow, cream and turquoise was common in late 1920s, early '30s kitchens.*
$125+

All photos of electric toasters are courtesy Jens Veerbeck, Essen-Ketwig, Germany. His collection is featured at his virtual museum, at **www.toastermuseum.com.**

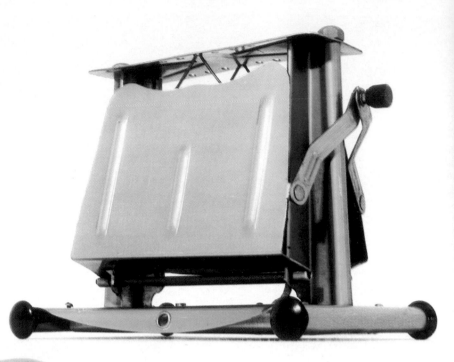

Plate 21. "Sanda" toaster, anodized blue aluminum, *black Bakelite knobs & disc feet. English, 1930s-40s .*

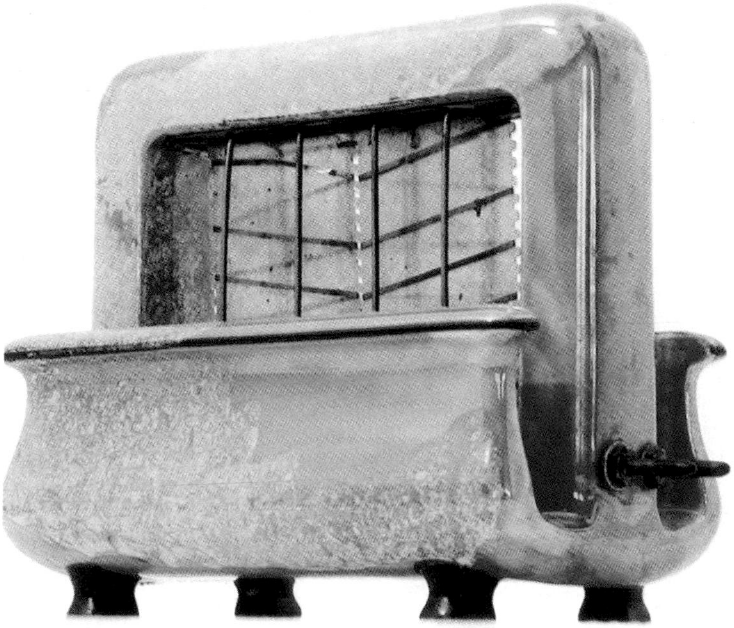

Plate 22. "Toastrite" by Pan Electric Mfg. Co., *Cleveland, OH, iridescent orange-glazed porcelain, c. 1920s-30s.*

Plate 23. "Filrouge" in anodized aluminum, *big wooden plinth-like feet. French, c. 1940s.*

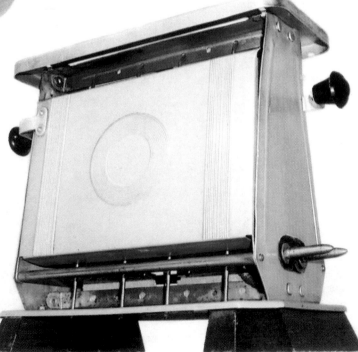

Plate 24. "Clem" – a green British *anthropomorphic design with painted iron body, chrome doors, Bakelite knobs, c. 1920s-30s.*

Plate 25. "OSI" Model 3, *German nickel-plated, gear-mechanism toaster from c. 1922. Mfd. by* Offenbacher Schrauben Industrie *("OSI").*

Plate 26. Bottle whimsy with 3-D scene of carved & painted men, *tables & little hams. Carved by Jim Cave, one of collectors' favorite carvers. Photo & collection of Susan D. Jones.*

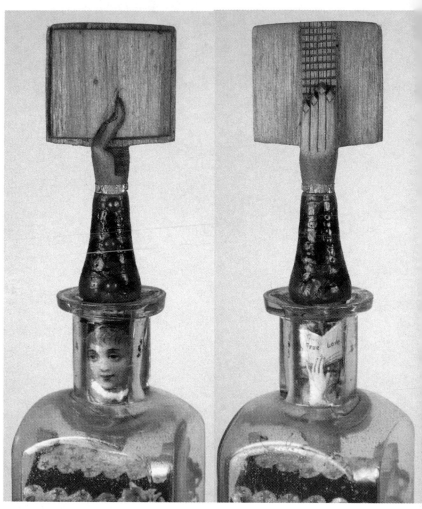

Plate 27. Carved & painted bottle stopper of hand holding book. *The contents of the bottle whimsy and finial were carved & decorated by the same artist. Such bottles, with miniature objects inserted with tweezers & glued into position, are related to more familiar ship-in-a-bottle puzzle bottles. Photo & collection of Susan D. Jones. See end of Chapter VII for more information. Web site:* **http://sdjones.net/FolkArt/bottlestory.html**

Plate 28. Cover & page from a crochet how-to pot holders booklet, *published by Coats & Clark, Book No. 312, 1955. "Funny Faces" on the cover; and three versions of "Merry Menangerie" animal heads, a "Tick-Tack-Toe," "Home, Sweet Home," and "Woven Plaid" in green.*

Plate 29. Miniature enamelware tea kettle *in sky blue, with wire bail handle. Even knob on lid is porcelainized. 3-1/4" diam., c. 1900. Bonnie Myers collection.* **$75+**

Plate 30. "Rice á la Parisienne" – dessert as sculpture *from* Katherine Mellish's Cookery & Domestic Management *cookbook. London & NY: E. & F. N. Spon, 1901.*

PLATE 8.

RICE À LA PARISIENNE.

Plate 31. Hand-painted plate of Bavarian porcelain *is very unusual for its ear of Indian corn. 7-1/4", c. 1900. The vegetable garden rug in the background was designed by me, and hooked by my mother, the late Mary Mac Franklin.* **$30**

Plate 32. Repaired cherry stoner, *cast iron with wooden leg. Scott Mfg. Co., Baltimore, MD, marked "patent pending."* $35+

Plate 33. Chesterman's Coffee Pot, *pat'd. July 19, 1859. A biggin style pot of tin, with cast white metal handle. Cork stopper keeps steam inside.* **$175+**

Plate 34. Nutmeg grater, *pat'd. by Nathan Ames, Oct 13, 1857. Tin with some remaining blue paint, wood spring-activated foller or pusher. This was probably made later, maybe as late as 1871, because advertising pictures of this grater from then show the strap-like cup handle of tin.* **$500+**

Plate 35. Reamer for juicing citrus fruit, *of mottled green phenolic plastic. Named the "Ex-squeeze-it", it's also marked "B.C.M.", "Pat. No. 362187", and "D.R.G.M." Circa. 1930s.* **$30+**

Plate 36. Egg slicer with orange-glazed porcelain plate-tray, *marked on base "Wales Slicer Belmet Products." 3"H x 8" diam. 1930s-40s. Photo courtesy eBayer Judyjester.*

PRESERVING

——— XVI. CAN & DRY ———

The collectible objects in this chapter were for home use. It seems a bit funny, etymologically, that practically everything in this category has to do with glass jars, not tin cans. But that is only because the so-called fruit jars (also called canning jars) are the most widely-collected food-preserving items, and old food cans don't have the potential to become that. Occasionally, you see a very old can, contents intact if not edible, and there are some collectors for them – mainly identifying themselves with country store and/or advertising collectors. It is true that people could buy ready-to-fill tin cans directly from the can manufacturers, to put up produce in their own kitchens. The cans had different features and selling points, but those with lids already in place, with openings in the center of the lids were probably favored. The holes, generally speaking, were about 2-1/4" diameter, and were closed by a cap soldered in place, using a "capping steel," and a "tipping copper." To open those cans, people did not melt the solder and take the cap off: a can opener was necessary. See Chapter VIII (Open & Close).

For decades, bottle and glass collectors have been digging up **glass fruit jars** and also **glass jellies**, then cataloguing them, trading, and selling them. Both are always in evidence at local and regional bottle shows, some of which convene almost every month, and sometimes fruit jars make headlines in generalist collector newspapers when rarities sell for a high price. Fruit jars constitute a very specialized field with a strong resale market, and ever-changing market prices, as rarities are discovered, and as other rarities are found not to be so rare after all.

Knowledge is widely shared about the jars themselves, closures, seals, marks & colors, and mysterious sightings and reportings of hitherto unknown jars. But unless you are prepared to study them, buy only for decorative or useful value. Obviously, very very large ones, or very early ones, or those with odd closures, or those in unusually-colored glass, or with figural embossing, or just those known to be extremely rare, will usually be worth the most, but you have to get into the "loop" of other collectors and dealers so that information on repros will get to you in time to save an expensive mistake. Many reproductions, fakes, and altered jars are on the market, especially now on eBay, where at any given time over 750 jars are for sale. Some Web sites at the end of this chapter help you find out about fakes.

My personal favorites in this chapter are the Kerr "Angel & Crown" jelly glasses. As a collector of 20th century folk art, I find the simple, embossed line "drawings" of angels irresistible; I wish I could have a leaded window made from them. (And another made from the opalescent lid inserts for some canning jars.)

Can openers is so large a category that I put them in their own section in the chapter on "Holding & Handling," Chapter VIII, which also has a few pictures of old cans. The mechanical go-withs for fruit jars are included in this chapter; see **fruit jar wrenches** and **lifters**; and **tipping coppers**. A man in Illinois has over 600 different tipping coppers or soldering irons; the variety is endless, and they are handsome. (And not all of them are copper, or copper-plated; some are brass.) He's a man after my own heart, concentrating now on one-of-a-kind homemade examples.

Can openers – See Chapter VIII (Open & Close)

Canner, tin & cold-rolled copper, 2 canisters (they came in other sizes & numbers of canisters) of tin set down into rectangular water reservoir, glass canning jars were set, lidless, into the metal cans for heating. Expensive models had copper bottoms, came with wood, iron & leather strap jar wrench, also booklet of recipes & instructions, "Mudge Patent Processor," mfd. by John L. Gaumer Co., Philadelphia, PA, 14-3/4"H x 13-1/4"L x 8"W, box is 4"H, pat'd. July 27, 1886. .... **$175+**

❖ NOTES ❖

Using the Mudge – Self-proclaimed as a "household necessity. ... The cheapest, most efficacious, most economical system of putting up high standard goods." It

came in several models, which ranged in price from $3 to $12 before the turn of the century, and differed in size, number of canners, quality and quantity of the "tin plate, cold-rolled copper bottoms, copper tops and steam whistles." You put the processor box on the range, added water, then the carefully-filled cans into the water with the covers placed over them. • "Have water boiling to generate steam before using. Keep well boiling vigorously while using the canner as you must have sufficient steam to do good work. Put fruit or vegetables in the jar raw. Place jar on a dry folded towel while pouring in the hot syrup or water to prevent breakage. Pour in slowly. In cooking or canning dry, be careful to temper glass jars before subjecting to the action of the steam. Place wooden blocks on the canner under the jars to prevent breaking. Do not put the lids on the jars while processing. ... Be careful to sterilize lids and rubbers before sealing. Never allow water to boil away. If steam escapes through the whistle, it is time to refill [the well] to keep the bottom from burning. ... Be sure to wipe the canner dry after using before putting away. Read Mrs. Rorer's directions carefully." Finally, to catch every possible purchaser, the booklet claimed "While this apparatus is called a cannery, it is an admirable contrivance for cooking vegetables, meats and making tea and coffee. It saves time and fuel and preserves flavor and color." The jar holder (original cost 25¢) that came with the canner claimed "Our adjustable jar holder will be appreciated by those who have burnt their fingers in lifting hot jars. They are leather lined, strongly bound by tin with wooden handles. The adjustment is made so they will fit any size jar. Handy for sealing and removing jar lids too." *Mudge booklet.*

Canning jar – See Fruit jar; also Preserve jar

Canning rack, wire, rectangular & meant for use in a 2-hole boiler, late 19th or early 20th C. .... **$10+**

Corn dryer, all twisted wire, the sharp points were made by clipping the wire at an angle. Hanging ring at top, American, c.1910. .... **$10+**

Corn dryer, or seed corn tree, wooden rod with short iron pins stuck crosswise through it to hold 28 ears

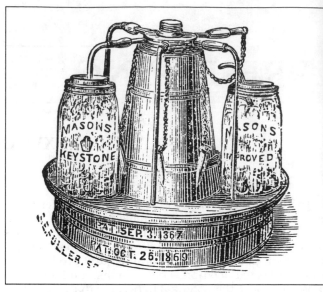

XVI-2. Fruit preserving apparatus. *"Payne's 'Common Sense' Fruit Preserver," sold through Williams & Chase, NYC. The "approved apparatus for preserving by steam, an arrangement regarded by scientific judges as the most complete ever offered to the public. Its construction is perfectly simple and easy to manage. Six or more jars can in as many minutes be preserved, with one-fourth the labor and fuel. The fruits retain all their Solidity, Flavor & Beauty, requiring no sugar, unless preferred. When perfect jars are used (those represented in the cut, also Mason's Union and Standard, are regarded by the inventor as among the best." Came in 1-pipe, 2-pipe, 4-pipe and 6-pipe sizes. Pat'd. Sept. 3, 1867; and Oct. 26, 1860. Peterson's Ladies' Magazine, 1870 ad.* **$40-$75+**

XVI-1. Canner. *"Mudge Patent Processor, for Canning and Cooking Fruit & Vegetables," John L. Gaumer Co., Philadelphia, PA. A two-vessel style with iron wire bail handles. Cold-rolled copper bodies and tin lids, 14-3/4"H overall x 13-1/4"L x 8"W. Included here is the all wood jar wrench, 9"L, and Mrs. Sara T. Rorer's instruction & recipe booklet. Note steam whistle lower left corner of box's top. Original prices ranged from $3 to $12, depending on number of cans, size, and the amount of copper. Collection of Meryle Evans. Collector Dolores Thomas sent me pictures of her 4-can completely tinned set, including recipe booklet. Her cans have no bails, but the lids have bracket strap handles. Value for either about evens out:* **$175-$300+**

of corn, iron T-handle, American, about 20"L, pat'd. Feb. 4, 1908 by James C. Blackford. .... **$35+**

Corn dryer, forged iron with 10 long sharp chiseled hooks, eye hole at top, hangs from ceiling hook, looks like a fish backbone, American, 20"L with 4"L hooks at a 40-degree angle from vertical, very early 19th C. .... **$100+**

Cup, for jellies & jams, pressed wood fiber with impressed design of Classical Greco-Roman woman next to tall stand, lid, & "although the Kleen Kup is made of wood fibre, it may be filled with heated jam, marmalade, jelly, or the like as any glass tumbler may be filled, and under the same conditions. The jelly may be heated to almost any degree Fahrenheit, and during the filling process it is unnecessary to immerse the kup in cold water, or wrap it in cold, wet cloths. ... The use of paraffine wax on top of the cooled jelly is optional." Called the "Wedgewood [sic] Kleen Kup," mfd. by Mono-Service Co., Newark, NJ, 1918. Came originally in a cardboard box of one dozen. See also Jelly glasses. For one: $3+; set in box: .... **$10-$15+**

Fruit dryer, galvanized tin base to set over stove top, wooden frame with 8 wood drawers with wire screening for bottoms. Used to dry sliced fruit or pitted, halved apricots, pears, etc. paper label mostly gone, American, 25-1/4"H x 18-1/2"L x 14"W, c.1900.. **$75+**

Hard to tell age of **corn dryers**. Late 19th and 20th C examples may also be wrought iron, but they look machine-made perfect. There are modern reproductions being made and sold today. I won't spend my money to write off for one, so can't describe it minutely. Value of late 19th or early 20th C examples of forged iron, with some aesthetic merit, would be up to $35. Wire ones shouldn't be more than $15.

Fruit dryer, tin frame with wire screen, 3 shelves, removeable trays, for drying sliced apples & other fruits, "Arlington Oven Dryer" on brass ID plate, Arlington, MA, 9"H x 14" x 10-1/2." 19th C. .... **$110+**

❖ NOTES ❖

Fruit jar colors – Fruit jars, or canning jars of blow-molded glass were made in many colors, by far the most common of which are light aqua and clear (or "crystal"). Colors I've seen on price tags, or in articles and books, also include: opaque white; opalescent; smoke; light & dark amber; reddish amber; streaked amber; citron; straw yellow; yellow green; emerald green; light & dark olive green; apple green; amethyst – like the color sunned glass becomes; dark aqua; "Ball blue"; cornflower blue; light, medium & dark cobalt blue; dark greenish blue; brown; even black. Creswick mentions a "dark puce," but I get confused between mauve and puce. I've read of red, pink, and dark purple jars, but I know they are such rare colors that they are prime pieces for fakers. **Determining color.** – Color is so important to this field that experienced collectors go to great lengths to describe the colors. Collectors can buy a "SPEC-TRU Standard Color Reference for

Transparent Glass" at www.fruitjars.com/store/products.asp?id=59&cat=Books. Photographs of jars is not a hit-or-miss thing, especially when posting to an auction online. Experienced sellers will sometimes go to the trouble, and added expense, of putting a link to a photo of the jar they're selling with explicit lighting conditions. Color shown in the photos will usually be for window- or backlit-display, or on a perfectly white background (even the faintest off-white piece of cardboard will affect the way the color looks). **Fake color.** – In case you are new to the hobby, you may not know about the fruit jars on the market since 1994 that have had their color artificially induced by irradiation. Several thousand otherwise common clear jars were done by a man in Indiana in amber and in purple and sold cheaply by the man who figured out how to do it. When he quit, a person in Florida began doing it. There are **two clues**, which are not sure-fire. One of which wouldn't help you anyway if you had already bought something. (1) The color seems a bit cloudy or smoky, maybe like looking through glasses that haven't been cleaned in a while. (2) The color seems to fade under normal room-temperature conditions – sometimes as quickly as in two months or so. (Makes you wonder if the faker is keeping them refrigerated before seeding them into the market. And one trouble with the Florida origin is that seeding is easy from there because there are so many generalist dealers from all over the country who include Florida on their show circuit. It's easy for them to innocently acquire a jar or two, and take them back to their home communities, like roaches take poison back to their nests.)

XVI-4. Canner. *"Iron Horse Cold Pack" canner, mfd. by Rochester Can Co., Rochester, NY, c.1930. • "With this the uncooked fruit can be placed directly in the jars, the syrup added and the cooking done directly in the jars, practically eliminating the labor formerly required." Made of charcoal (blackened) tin, bottom double-seamed, wood handle grips at side. Rack for 7 quart jars, and a wire jar lifter. 9"H x 13-3/4" diam. They also made them of copper or galvanized steel. I believe the picture is probably a printed paper label – most desirable to have and key to value.* **$30-$60**

XVI-3. Pressure cooker for canning. *Heavy aluminum, with lid fastened on with wing-nuts. Note pressure gauge. Picture originally provided by The Pressure Cooker Co., to Science & Invention magazine, May 1930.* **$15-$25.** *See also p. 653.*

"Whittle" marks – A lot of fruit jars put up for sale are described with the notation that "whittle marks" can be seen on the surface of the glass. Of course, at least some mold-blown jars were formed inside molds made over a carved-wood model, which might show whittling marks if it weren't finely finished. I believe that later molds would have been made over a first generation jar itself, thus making it a second-generation mold, less finely-detailed, which would show up on surface and embossed marks.

Lids & Closures – Fruit jar lids may be clear glass or opalescent glass or vitreous pottery or metal. A few 19th century patents are behind most of the jars & lids that were made well into the 20th century (some still being made). Maybe the most famous patent is John Mason's of Nov. 30, 1858; his lids are threaded bands or full caps, and utilized a rubber gasket. Many lids have a threaded metal band that holds the insert in place: zinc, and most recently those "brass"-plated tin bands used today. There are also full caps with glass liners – zinc, plated steel threaded cap, aluminum, etc. To secure them, some have spring wire attachments – like the 1875 "Lightning" patent – that worked to clamp & lock the lid in place, or spring steel clamps, or iron yokes, that make the fit of the lid snugger. Some lids, of glass or metal, worked like stoppers in the mouth of the jar. An unusual lid is one of the "Squire's Patent" lids, which utilized small knobs on lid and jar to anchor an elastic band that acted sort of like a bungee cord to lace jar and lid together! Another extremely unusual jar & lid is the "New Windsor," which has a cylindrical body but a square mouth and lid!

Lid straighteners & reformers – Another sort of tool came into use to fix metal jar lids which had been bent or distorted during opening of the jar. These worked best with relatively soft zinc lids, and some of them could actually re-tool the screw threads to some extent. The reformers may look like jar wrenches, with a band that can be tightened around lid, then pulled around (like a clock hand) circumference to press the metal against the jar's neck or lip. Others look something like biscuit cutters, with a wooden grip raised above a circle of iron. This type fitted down around the band or threaded side of the lid and was firmly rotated. Another type was a cranked machine, screw-clamped to table. The jar lid was fitted onto the threaded chuck, and held firmly while the user cranked the chuck around.

Lid openers or "jar wrenches" became necessary with screw caps or screw bands, and were used to screw the caps on as well as off. If properly and tightly sealed, the jars were hard to open. Many wrenches utilized wood, leather or rubber to cushion the tool.

❖ NOTES ❖

Turn of Century Jar Makers – According to *Thomas' Register of American Manufacturers*, 1905-06, quite a number of companies made glass fruit jars at the beginning of the 20th Century. As listed, they are:

Ball Brothers Glass Mfg. Co., Muncie, IN;
Consolidated Fruit Jar Co., New Brunswick, NJ;
Co-operative Flint Glass Co., Ltd., Beaver Falls, PA;
Crystal Glass Co., Bridgeport, OH;
Cumberland Glass Mfg. Co., Bridgeton, NJ;
D. Cunningham Glass Co., Pittsburg, PA;
S. George Co., Wellsburg, WV;
Gilchrist Improved Jar Co., Philadelphia, PA & Elmer, NJ;
W. Glenny Glass Co., Cincinnati, OH;
Greenfield Fruit Jar & Bottle Co., Greenfield, IN;
Hazel-Atlas Glass Co., Wheeling, WV, & Washington, PA;
Hemingway Glass Co., Covington, KY;
Hero Fruit Jar Co., Philadelphia, PA;
Hermetical Closure Co., San Francisco, CA;
Louis Hollweg, Indianapolis, IN;
Illinois Glass Co., Alton, IL;
Kearns-Gorsuch Bottle Co., Zanesville, OH;
J. A. Landsberger Co., San Francisco, CA;
Marion Fruit Jar & Bottle Co., Marion, IN;
Moore Brothers Glass Co., Clayton, NJ;
National Glass Co., Pittsburg, PA;
F. H. Palmer, Brooklyn, NY;
Penna Glass Co., Anderson, IN;
Port Glass Works, Bellville, IL;
Poughkeepsie Glass Works, Poughkeepsie, NY;
Red Key Glass Co., Red Key, IN;
Safe Glass Co., Upland, IN, & Chicago, IL;
Skillin-Goodin Glass Co., Yorktown, IN;
A. G. Smalley & Co., Boston;
Sneath Glass Co., Hartford City, IN;
Swayzee Glass Co., Swayzee, IN;
Terre Haute Glass Mfg. Co., Terre Haute, IN;
Upland Co-Operative Glass Co. [which may have included Safe Glass Co.], Upland, IN;
Vacuum Jar & Fruit Package Co., San Francisco, CA;
Victor Jar Co., Detroit, MI;
Weightman Glass Co., Pittsburg, PA;
Western Flint Glass Co., Eaton, IN;
Weston Glass Co., Weston, WV;
Woodbury Bottle Works, Woodbury, NJ;
Wormser Glass Co., Pittsburg, PA;
R. G. Wright & Co., Buffalo, NY

Many of the same companies were still making jars in the early 1930s. • The name "Hemingway" may confuse. By the 1930s, there was a company in Muncie, IN, Hemingray, that made insulators, and also jars. And a Hemingway Glass Co. in Syracuse, NY.

Fruit jar, also called a canning jar, yellow amber glass, wax sealer, no lid, "Putnam Glass Works," Zanesville, OH, 1 qt. size. • According to Alice Creswick, there are two different ambers for this jar: a "deep olive amber" and a "deep yellow amber." This one is a rich color, but not what I'd call "deep." ...... **$350+**

Fruit jar, amber glass, square base & sides with arched shoulders & screw-on metal lid has milky, almost opalescent, insert, jar marked with large monogram of intertwined "A, G & S" and "Full Measure," mfd. by A. G. Smalley & Co., Boston, MA, 1 qt. size, also has 2 patent dates: Dec. 13, 1892, and April 7, 1896. .... **$50+**

Fruit jar, aqua glass, cylindrical body goes in at abruptly rounded shoulder, then goes out again at mouth, wax sealer type with rather deep moat for melted wax, glass stopper lid, missing the iron yoke clamp with hooked-under arms, that was tightened by wing nut to hold lid in place, marked "Millville Atmospheric," also "Whitall's Patent," with date. Inventor J. M. Whitall was from Philadelphia. 1 qt. size, "Preserve-jar" patent granted June 18, 1861. Whitall got a patent for a "Fruit-jar Stopper" on April 11, 1865 • A cobalt blue example of this sold for $10,000 in 1982. Wow! .... **$35+**

Fruit jar, aqua glass, cylindrical with abruptly rounded shoulder, glass & metal stopper, best thing about this is it's stopper. A much more valuable "Lafayette" has an embossed portrait profile bust of the French hero of the American War of Independence. "Lafayette" in signature script, 1 qt. size. 1880s. .... **$125+**

Fruit jar, aqua glass, iron yoke clamp & glass lid. The yoke clamp, with 2 curved arms that hook under flange just below rim of jar, acts as a press to hold lid against rim, and is tightened by a thumbscrew rather than a wing nut like on the Millville Atmospheric. It doesn't have a spring like the Earle patent, but looks somewhat similar. Jar marked "Eagle" in nice serif cap letters, along with dates, "patd Dec. 28th, 1858. Reisd [reissued] June 16, 1868." • I guess this is the J. K. Jenkins patent for "preserving fruit." I can't find anything else that fits the date & the classification. .... **$125+**

Fruit jar, aqua glass, shaped like a Mason, embossed "Swayzee's Improved Mason," Swayzee Glass Co., Swayzee, IN, c.1900. .... **$10+**

Fruit jar, aqua glass, slowly sloping shoulder, screw-on cap, the top rim is slightly beveled out, there is no wider flange or ring below the screw threads on the

XVI-6. Fruit dryer. *Wood with galvanized tin base & wire mesh screening in each of eight drawers. Used on top of range to dry sliced fruit or pitted, halved apricots, etc. 26"H, early 20th C.* **$75+**

glass, marked "Mason's Patent," 1 qt. size, pat'd. Nov. 30, 1858, but made for a long time after that.. **$8+**

❖ NOTES ❖

Masons by many makers. The above is only one of hundreds of various "Mason" jars made by all kinds of glass-makers. Mason himself was a metal-worker, and his patent was for the hermetic lid and ground lip. Through licensing, scores of manufacturers made the jars. And the very name "Mason" is sometimes used as a generic term for fruit jar, so well is it known. The best of these, although they are all well-formed and simply functional, are the biggest, the smallest, those in unusual colors (various blues, citron, even black), and those with rare embossed marks. You will have to study, study and go to every show and talk to dealers and other collectors if you want to get into this field. I don't know how many collectors still depend on bottle digs for great finds, but they are about the closest to old-fashioned archaeology as we find in the collecting world. • **Mason 1858 fakes are prevalent.** Huge ones and little ones, made mainly in China and sold as a decorative storage item for the kitchen in the first market, and after that, who knows!

XVI-5. Cup for jellies or jams. *"The Wedgwood Kleen Kup," mfd. by Mono Service Co., Newark, NJ. "Decorated wood fibre with classical Greco-Roman lady. The jelly may be heated to almost any degree Fahrenheit, and during the filling process it is unnecessary to immerse the kup in cold water, or wrap it in cold, wet cloths. It is suggested, however, that the filled kups be allowed to stand over night, or until thoroughly cold, before the lids are inserted. The use of paraffine wax on top of the cooled jelly is optional." House Furnishing Review ads, 1918. Per cup:* **$3+**

Fruit jar, aqua glass, wire bail clip handle, "Trademark Lightning Putnam #31." Pat'd. by Henry W. Putnam, April 25, 1882. (Earlier patents 1875 & 1877.).. **$45+**

Fruit jar, aqua glass, zinc screw-on lid, embossed "Mason's Patent," so-called "midget" 1 pint, Nov. 30, 1858. There's an even smaller one, the 1/2 pint size. Please investigate this field carefully before assuming you've got the $$$ jar. This might be worth: **$500**

Fruit jar, bluish-aqua glass (color called "Ball Blue" by Creswick), uses the "Lightning" wire bail lid clip, glass lid, "McDonald New Perfect Seal," pat'd. July 14, 1908. .... **$8-$15+**

Fruit jar, very pale aqua glass, embossed "WOODBURY," on bottom and "Woodbury Glass Works – Woodbury NJ" and "8" Glass lid has raised center, a knob-like protrusion which is threaded; bracket lid clamp fits over it, and brass cap secures it by screwing onto the "knob." 7-1/2"H x 3-1/2" diam. Lid embossed: "PATd NOV 25th 1884 MAR.3d 85." .... **$65+**

Fruit jar, clear, embossed "American Improved Preserve Can," on one side, and lo-and-behold a favorite egg-beater inventor's name and patent date on the other side, arched over & under a star: "Earle's Patent Feb 2d 1864." Timothy Earle, Valley Falls, RI. His patent was actually for the C-shaped curved iron clamp: "This device consists of a yoke, the ends of which are curved so as to fit under a lip or projection on the neck. The yoke turns upon a spindle, and the latter is provided with a coiled spring, which serves to press the cover upon the jar; the object being to dispense with the inclined lips on the lip or projection of the neck of the jar." **$850**

Fruit jar, pale green ("Jersey" green) glass with glass lid secured with wire clamp, embossed around lid "Cohansey Manufacturing Co Philadelphia PA Patented Jan 18, 1876" with a "Y" in center of lid. "8" on bottom of jar. 1 quart size............................... **$35**

Fruit jar, clear or "crystal" glass with wax seal groove in lip, "Rau's Improved Groove," American, c.1900.. **$35-$45**

Fruit jar, heavy crystal clear glass jar with paneled (almost gadrooned) sides, lid has large high knobby ribbed ball finial (so your hand wouldn't slip) that's hollow on the inside so a spoon could be kept in the jar after opening. For crushed fruit. Heisey, with "H" inside diamond mark, 10"H with lid on, jar itself 6"H x 5-3/8" diam. base. with embossed "PATENTED JULY 7, 1908."... **$200+**

Fruit jar, glass, rubber, dried clay, American, c.1880. I assume this was made; has anyone seen one? It was described in the pages of the Oct. 1880 *Scribner's Monthly* magazine as "A new device for preserving fruit in its natural condition [that] consists of a glass jar or tumbler, having a cover with a rubber packing-ring, secured to the jar by a screw clamp. At the bottom of the jar is a hole, designed to be closed airtight by a suitable stopper, and inside the jar is placed a layer of dried clay, to absorb the moisture that may escape from the fruit. The grapes or other fruits are hung up inside the jar, the cover is put on, and air is withdrawn by means of an air-pump, when the opening in the bottom is closed and sealed." If it exists: .... **$85+**

Fruit jar, medium cobalt blue glass, glass lid has little notch in its high thick dorsal "fin," wire bail clip, "The Canton Electric Fruit Jar," 1880s. • You probably won't see one of these, they're so extremely rare, but it's nice to dream that you might find one at a yard sale! Of course, cobalt blue is a choice color for wretched fakes. So far as I know, the "Canton Electric" hasn't been replicated............. **$2,500-$4,000**

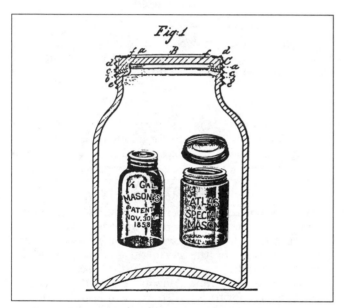

XVI-7. Fruit jar patent, *framing examples of two Mason jars. In this collage of pictures, the outer drawing is John L. Mason's patent drawing for #102,913, issued to him on May 10, 1870 for an improvement in his earlier fruit jar closure. He sold the patent to Consolidated Fruit-Jar Co., who sued another maker, Wright, for using the patent. The case went to the U.S. Supreme Court, who decided the merits of the suit on the basis of the patentee [Mason] forfeiting his "right to the invention if he constructs it and vends it to others to use, or if he uses it publicly himself in the ordinary way" up to two years before applying for a patent. Poor Mr. Mason had "completed his invention in June 1859, at which time he had at least two dozen jars made. Some of the jars he gave away; others he sold to get the money they yielded and to test salability in the market. Mason failed to file a patent application until January 15, 1868," almost 10 years later! The case was decided against Consolidated and Mason in favor of Wright. Information & patent drawing adapted from a 1947 book by C. D. Tuska,* Patent Notes for Engineers, *from Official Gazette records.*

❖ NOTES ❖

Buying fruit jars on eBay. This isn't a hobby for the faint of heart. The more the prices have gone up, the more you have to worry about fakes, repros, and altered-color jars. At the same time, because of the great popularity of this field of collecting, and the great numbers of jars manufactured over a century or so, eBay has turned out to be a good place to sell and buy jars. You just have to know what you're doing. I suggest buying the books (see the Bibliography entries for XVI); audit the auctions without bidding for a while; join a club; look at what established collectors and dealers are selling at shows, auctions, and on their own Web sites. Then plunge into eBay. One thing you'll be tracking as you visit the online auctions is how many people bid. A jar that goes for, say, $450, and had 20 bids, means that at least two bidders were working the sale, very aware of and assured of real value, and therefore bidding in small increments to the current market value. Of course, one joker could throw this off, say a very wealthy beginner determined to bag a prize no matter the cost or value. But you can inspect the bidding record after the sale is complete, and you'll see the eBay names of the bidders, and all the bids up to the winning one. (What you won't know is if the winner bid a lot more than the bid which won the auction. But you wouldn't need to know that unless you planned to bid against that bidder in future.) If I were a beginning fruit jar collector, I'd make it a practice to look at the auctions every week, doing searches for what I was particularly interested in. I'd also print out auction results periodically, perhaps with highest prices first, and keep them in a notebook. • Note that almost all those listed below had original, or at least appropriate, lids.

April 2002 Fruit Jars on eBay. Just for fun, here are the **jars over $100** sold from April 21 to May 7, 2002, with the number of bids in parentheses. I've pretty much used only the sellers' descriptions as found in titles of auctions. • $10,100, Mason's 1858, bottom marked Nov 20 67 PAT 78, 3-part mold cobalt (15). • $1,475, Flaccus Bros. emerald green, pint (6). $800, Hemingray push-down wax sealer, 1/2-gallon (2). • $795, Potter & Bodine, push-down wax sealer airtight, quart (13). • $795, Union Stoneware, Red Wing, MN, stoneware, mason cap, bottom marked PAT JAN 24 1899, 1-gallon (19). $545, Mason's, 1858, aqua, gallon (14). • $384, The Dandy, on bottom: GILBERDS 9, #5, PAT OCT. 13TH 1885, honey amber (21). • $358.03, John M. MOORE & Co. Manufacturers N.J. &. PATENTED DEC. 3rd 1861, Fislerville, quart (23). • $356.13, Mason's 1858, green with amber swirls, pint (20). • $333.50, CHICAGO CFPJ immerser insert, [Australian], green (21). • $330, Van Vliet 1881, 1-quart (12). • $325, John BELL, Waynesboro, stoneware, 1-1/2-quart (7). • $300.50, PEERLESS, glass lid, iron closure, quart (18). • $261, MASON'S, #5, dark amber, quart (20). • $256.99, Union Stoneware, Red Wing, MN, Mason cap, 1/2-gallon (11). • $220, LIGHTNING, yellow amber, pint (14). • $212.50, E. BENNETT'S Patent Dec. 2, 1856, stoneware, wax sealer (17). • $210.29, GOW'S Syrups & Crushed Fruits, [Australian], aqua, quart (7). • $204, ECLIPSE 8, aqua, quart. • $202.50, 2 jars: B B WILCOX, PATD MARCH 26th 1867, with "fin back" glass lid, aqua, quart; & ST. JOHNSBURY VT Maple Products Co. Towle Ball Sure Seal with lid "Lightning Pat Apr 25 82," ice blue, quart (24). • $187.50, Union Stoneware, Red Wing, Mason cap, 1-quart (10). • $181, CFJC [The Consolidated Fruit Jar Co.] Queen, Mason's imp. lid "REGISTERED MAY 23d 1871," light aqua-green, pint (4). • $177.51, BEEHIVE, embossed with beeskip & bees, aqua, quart (11). • $173.50, LIGHTNING, yellow amber, quart (12). • $171, HEMINGRAY, cylinder, deep blue-aqua, replica cap, 1-1/2-quart • $166.51, MASON'S BG Co. Improved, pint (4). • $158.05, GILBERD'S Improved Star, aqua, quart (6). • $143.50, 3 jars: LIGHTNING, bottom: "PUTNAM 327" or "190," clear glass Lightning lids, amber (17). • $132.50, GLOBE, original glass lid with iron clamp, bright orangey amber, 1/2-gallon (4). • $130, JAS HAMILTON & CO Manufacturers, Greensboro, PA, adv'g. crock, wax sealer (?), stoneware (2). • $129.01, GLOBE, original clamp & lid, deep reddish amber, quart (9) •$127.50, SUN, aqua (13). • $125, LIGHTNING, PUTNAM II, cornflower blue, quart (4). • $121.23, NEWBON Approved [this one sold from Australia] (8). • $115.49, GLOBE, amber, quart (9). • Reserve of $112.50 not met, 3 "pictorial" [Australian], a FEDERAL

with flag; a QUEENSLAND with map & pineapple, and the AMERICAN with eagle. (4). • $111.11, The Champion (6). • $107.51, CANTON Domestic, lid with patent DEC. 31 1889, quart (13).• $107.50, CLIMAX, aqua, 1/2-pint (21). • $105.06, J. T. KINNEY, lid marked A. KLINE Pat'd Oct. 27, 1863, pale green (9). • $102.50, GLOBE, base marked 18, honey amber, quart (37). • **Just under $100:** To list just a few: a Beaver 1/2-gallon; a Winslow; Yarraville Colonial Sugar Refining Coy Limtd [Australian, by Melbourne Glass Bottle Co.] quart; The Canton; Glass Bros. brown stoneware Imperial quart [London, Ontario]; Woodbury; and many more.

Fruit jar holder, wire, looks like a doll stand, only the arms come around neck of jar, not waist of doll, 6"H, c.1900.. **$10+**

Fruit jar holder & wrench, 2 tools of steel. Holder is a band of steel with a number of holes (like a belt) to clamp around jar for perfect sizing; the wrench has a shallow cap, divided in 2 unequal parts to make gross adjustments to fit different size lids. "The T. & B.," Tarbox & Bogart Mfg. Co., Cleveland, OH, pat'd. Dec. 3, 1901 by Henry W. Bogart. Ad copy: "Don't be balked by the cap, serve plums when you want plums, no matter whether Jack's at home or not." The pair: .... **$55+**

XVI-8. Fruit jar patent. *"Squire's Patent," mfd. by John B. Bartlett, NYC. Undated flyer from 1860s. The jars shown are quite interesting to a collector, and very valuable. There are three tiny knob "feet" on the bottom, which allowed water to circulate entirely around the jar. Creswick lists five Squire jars: (1) has 3 feet, pat'd. Oct. 18, 1864, "two metal crossbars, fitting over the center hub of the lid." (2) Same date & closure, but has 4 feet. (3) Additional patent of March 7, 1865, 3 feet, and has an "opening on lip." New patent calls for a single "locking bar, turning on a central hub on the lid." (4) Like (3) except has two side openings in lip. And (5), jar has 3 feet, and 4 knobs on lip, and has a glass lid that also has 4 knobs around the circumference, with a vent hole in the middle. The woman in the picture is "lacing" on the elastic bands. According to Creswick, these Squire jars were all made in aqua, and are worth a lot of money:* **$750+**

Fruit jar lids. These are very collectible in their original boxes, especially with original sheet of instructions. It's partly the lids themselves, but partly the graphics. Boxes that are collectible contain the lid discs, the rings (ring-shaped screw-on part), both lids and rings, caps that are the rings and discs all-in-one, or jar lid rubbers – gaskets for the lids. The sizes are noted on the boxes – regular size, #50, #56, midget or small-mouth #63s, and boxes came with different quantities – usually one or two dozen. • Some **makes/models** are "Anchor Flex-Lids Wide Mouth" (Anchor Cap & Closure Corp. of Canada); "Atlas Glass Discs"; "Ball Dome Lids"; "Ball Good Luck" jar rubbers; "Ball Zinc Caps" (porcelain-lined); "BerNARdin Snap Lids"; "Boyd's Caps"; "Clear-Vu"; "Columbia"; "CFJCO (Consolidated Fruit Jar Co.); "Crown Mason Caps"; "Dymond Glass Co."; "E-Z Seal"; "Economy Caps" (for Kerr Economy jars); "Hazel Atlas"; "Kerr Mason Caps"; Jeannette Mason"; "Perfect Seal"; "Presto Glass Lids"; "Pyramid Mason Caps"; "Rayl Mason"; "Samco"; "Sherwood"; "A. G. Smalley & Co."; "Viceroy" rubber rings; "Weir" lids. Some lids are discs of glass, metal, or ceramic, used with a threaded band of metal (usually zinc). Others are caps complete in one piece. Of course the oldest are the most desirable; condition of the box is important too. For a boxful the value can be: $3 up to $15+ • **Orphaned parts.** I might add that personally I'd consider collecting un-boxed examples of all kinds of screw rings, lids, insert discs, because there are so many varieties of color, size, marking, patent info, style. These are sold on eBay. Individual pieces: .... **$1+**

❖ NOTES ❖

"**Rubber rings** somewhat perish after being on the bottles a few months. If used again they may break, air will enter the bottles, and then the contents will be lost. Spare rubber rings and washers should be kept in a vacuum bottle with a piece of wet cotton wool or muslin, the bottle being closed with a cover, ring and clip. The damp cotton wool is very necessary in India and other tropical climates, and the bottle containing the rings should be kept in a rather dark, cool place." Geo. Fowler, *How to Bottle Fruit, Vegetables, Game, Poultry, Milk, &c.* Reading, England: Fowler, n.d., revised edition c. 1922.

Round Ring Boxes. These are early 20th C round boxes in which rubber seal rings were sold. If you read this article, you're well on your way to a total desire to find some for your collection. "*Round Ring Boxes,*" by Tom Caniff & Tammy Johnson. Go to: www.fruit jars.com/ref/articles/news.asp?article=15.

❖ NOTES ❖

1909 maker of rubber fruit jar rings, with all the trade names, as found in the *House Furnishing Review Buyers Guide* for 1909: Boston Woven Hose & Rubber Co., Cambridge, MA, "American Beauty," "Arab," "Perfection," "Pomona," "Sterling," "Brazilian," "Blue Ribbon," and "Purity."

Fruit jar lifter, iron, "E-Z Lift." **$5**
Fruit jar lifter, little one-jar basket, with loop-de-loop sides that form feet for carrier, twisted side pieces with wire bail handle, wooden grip, American, about

5"H, 19th C. • **Reproduction alert.** – An exact copy is made by Mathews Wire, of Frankfort, IN. Only the turned wooden handle looks too new, and there are no dings, sags, shrugs, or banged-up bends in the wire. • A number of **bent-wire, one-jar holders** with wire bail (but no wood grip) attached to two twisted-wire side pieces, are showing up on eBay. I don't know if they're old. Old:............................. **$10-$20+**
Fruit jar lifter, metal, "Simplex," Gorman Mfg. Co., Boston, MA, late 19th C. **$15**
Fruit jar opener, works like pliers, metal with rubber grips, "The Gunnard Co.," Minneapolis, MN, pat'd. 1936. (I've seen this called a "Gunnard Reliner," in which case it means it's a lid realigner or straightener. .... **$15+**
Fruit jar opener, rubber, "Cupples Presto Wrench" is not really a wrench, it's a cap-shaped rubber gripper put over the cap to make it easier to grip with the hand and turn the cap. A similar rubber one is the "Swenson Jar Opener." .... **$5-$10**
Fruit jar opener, red rubber over heavy wire, "Daisy Jar Opener," 20th C. .... **$5-$8**
Fruit jar reformer, plated iron, adjustable, using screw driver, small wheel set at angle runs around edge of glass jar, American, 7-3/8"L, pat'd. Mar. 5, 1907. .... **$10-$15+**
Fruit jar sealer & wrench, nickeled malleable cast iron, plier handle, looks like a short-handled snake catcher with wire hoop that adjusts to fit, one side marked "Up for wrench," mfd. by Stockland, Minneapolis, MN, 6-5/8"L, no date, but early 20th C. This is similar to the one by the Best Co., seen in XVI-17, except it has 2 handles............................. **$15-$20**
Fruit jar wrench, iron & wire, cast iron grip & edge frame, with lasso-like spring steel wire which tightens when grip is cocked. Marked with "on" and "off" position, "Best S. Co.," Lancaster, PA, 7-3/4"L, pat'd. May 8, 1917. .... **$10-$15+**
Fruit jar wrench, cast iron, "Wilson's," Wilson Mfg. Co., Niles, OH, early 20th C (?). .... **$25+**
Fruit jar wrench, green painted iron, 2 sets of arms, the lower pair has white rubber sleeves to hold jar safely, upper metal arms swivel or pivot and turn the lid without the lower arms moving. Very ingenious, 8-1/4"L, 20th C. .... **$15-$25**
Fruit jar wrench, plier-like, tinned iron, in original box, "Presto," mfd. by Cupples, (possibly Cupples Co., St. Louis, MO), 20th C. .... **$5-$10**
Fruit jar wrench, iron, "C. A. Powell, Cleveland, OH," "pat appl for," c. 1910s. .... **$10-$15**
Fruit jar wrench, metal, "Triumph Fruit Can Wrench," mfd. by Benjamin P. Forbes [Chocolate] Co., Cleveland, OH, 6-1/2"L x 2-1/4"W, "patent pending." Some are seen with the patent date Nov. 3, 1903. And it's in 1932-33 *Thomas' Register.* • Note: When patented, the manufacturer was given as "Benj. P. Forbes, Cleveland, O." I don't know when "Chocolate" came into the name. • Forbes also made, c.1903, the "Perfection Fruit Jar Wrench" and the "Perfection Fruit Jar Holder," meant to fit "any Mason jar made." Wrench is flat steel, with handle used to adjust size of flat ring that goes on lid; holder has a band of metal that holds the jar, & cast iron plier handles. .... **$15-$35+**
Fruit jar wrench, nickeled steel, adjustable, "Winchester's of Carthage," Carthage, MO. **$15**

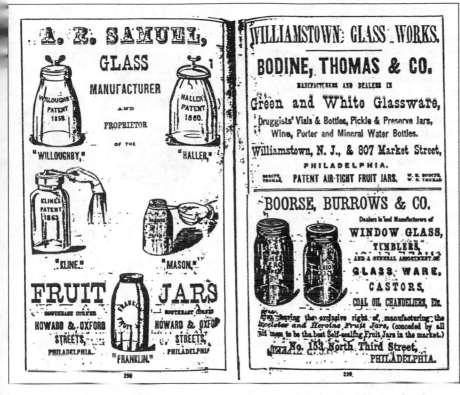

XVI-9. Fruit jars. *Facing pages from an 1860's book:* Philadelphia and Its Manufactures. *See the "Willoughby," the "Kline," the "Franklin," the "Mason" and the "Haller" in A. E. Samuel's ad; and the "Heroine," and "Excelsior," jars of Boorse, Burrows & Co. As well as Bodine patent "pickle and preserve jars."* (1) "H. & S. Willoughby's Patent," pat'd. Jan. 1, 1859, has metal stopper which was set into mouth, with some "gum," and then tightened to become air-tight by screwing the wing-nut. "To open the Jar, apply warm water around the gum ring, partially unscrew, and draw out the stopper." Three sizes: 1 pt., 1 qt., and 1 half gallon. (2) "Kline's Patent," pat'd. Oct. 27, 1863. Directions were to "Place the gum over the small end of the stopper, insert it into the mouth of the jar, the gum resting on the shoulder (if the mouth of the Jar is wet the Stopper should also be wet); then by screw action force the Stopper down. Immediately after closing the jar, force a pin in between the Stopper and the gum, for the escape of the air compressed, occasioned in putting in the Stopper. Withdraw the pin in a few seconds. Examine the Jar an hour after closing. If the Stopper has sunk in the Jar is air tight." To open it, you forced a pin in, to admit air, then applied warm water around the gum. (3) "Franklin's Patent," pat'd. Aug. 8, 1865. Had a very modern lid: with a threaded rim and a threaded metal band which held on the glass lid. (4) "Haller's Patent," pat'd. Aug. 7, 1860. Has a metal stopper & rim, tightened with the wing-nut visible in picture. (5) "Mason's Patent," pat'd. Nov. 30, 1858. Beyond that, I can't tell from picture how this one distinguishes itself from the hundreds of Mason jars of that patent. Did A. R. Samuel really manufacture this Mason? Various glass companies did. (6) "The HERO ine," pat'd. Nov. 26, 1867, with 8 patents on the glass lid insert from 1856 to 1869. The first of these were "The HERO," but obviously something interesting happened to make them add, on a line below "HERO" a smaller "INE". (7) "Excelsior," about which I can tell nothing. The ad states that the advertiser, Boorse, Burrows & Co., Philadelphia, have "the exclusive right of manufacturing the Excelsior and Heroine Fruit Jars, (conceded by all fruit men to be the best Self-sealing Fruit Jars in the market.)" Values for quart jars – big ones may be worth 20 times as much; little ones 4 or 5 times as much.
(1) $50+ ; (2) $30+; (3) $75+; (4) $950+; (5) $25-$100+; (6) $125+; (7) prob. $20+

Fruit jar wrench, tinned iron, flat metal, adjustable diameter loop, mfd. by A. C. Williams, Ravenna, OH, 8"L, c.1910. .... **$7+**

Fruit jar wrench & can opener combined, cast iron frame, steel blade, adjustable leather strap, "Mason Jar Sealer and Opener," c.1912. .... **$15+**

Fruit jar wrench & can opener combined, steel, has flat loop that fits over lid, tightened by "cocking" the handle. The handle has a sharp point on tip (to start hole for opener), and a sliding adjustable blade. J. C. Forster (or Forester?) & Son, Pittsburgh, PA, Pat'd. Sept. 13, 1910. Note spelling of Pittsburgh with an "h." Up to 1890, the official spelling had a final "h"; from 1890 to 1911 the spelling was Pittsburg and then it reverted again. .... **$20-$30**

Funnel or fruit jar filler – See Chapter V (Measures)

Herb drying rack, wood with original old blue paint, 28"L, 19th C. Auction notices are always mentioning "Shaker herb drying rack," but probably very few (if any) are Shaker. • The price on this is determined more than anything else by the blue paint. .... **$350-$500+**

Jars – See also Chapter VII

Jelly cup – See Cup, for jellies & jams

❖ NOTES ❖

Jelly glasses, also called **jellies, jelly jars, jam jars,** and **jelly tumblers,** blown or press-molded glass, mostly in clear ("crystal"), but also medium blue, light & dark green, and "Ball Blue," to borrow from fruit jar-collecting. They are usually the size and shape of small tumblers, with slightly slanted sides. But others are bell-shaped, some like cups, some are footed and have stems like goblets. Some are half-size, like low-walled custard cups. The most collectible have a design of some sort – from flutes or "thumb-prints" to very detailed fruit, berries, flowers or patriotic patterns. Although some old jelly glasses were used as molds, and the jelly turned out onto a serving dish in all its quivery beauty, often as not the design is not on the inside (where it would impress the gelatin), but on the outside. There are also jelly glasses known as **table jellies,** which are among the oldest types (late 18th C. in this country), and were individual dessert glasses. Lids are not often present, and for some jellies (as the collectors call them), it is not known what kind of lid was original – metal or glass – or even if there were a lid at one time, because some were just sealed with wax or paraffin, then protected with a circle of cloth tied tightly on. For such an ubiquitous household object, it amazes me how few I see at even the largest of flea markets. I feel even less qualified to write anything about jellies than I do about fruit jars, although they both are related to kitchen collectibles. Bottle shows almost always include not only fruit jars but at least a few jellies. • For the most information about American jellies, I highly recommend a charming and reliable self-published looseleaf book by the late Barbara Bowditch (see the Bibliography). Very clear, enticing line drawings by the late George Bowditch, as well as color pictures, show us side views as well as patterns on the bottom or lid. For me, the most delightful and desirable of all the jellies are the Kerr "Angel & Crown," (sometimes nicknamed "Bee & Crown"), names referring to a figural trademark embossed on the outside bottom of what would otherwise be rather plain glasses. There are many variations, as each mold-carver made his own version of the angel & crown element in the Kerr family coat-of-arms. I have at least 12 different ones – the first was a gift from Betty Landis. Mark-rubbings by Dennis Smith, for Barbara Bowditch's book, show many more. • Rare jellies may bring much more, but most jellies are at low end of this range: **$3-$50**.

XVI-11. Preserved foods in original jars. (L) Hermetically sealed glass jar for "soft, rich" cheese. "American Club House Cheese," Chandler & Rudd Co., Cleveland, OH. "A full size jar will be sent to any point in the United States, charges prepaid, on receipt of 50¢." Picture and words probably printed on paper label. (M) & (R) "Preserved Strawberries" in the nifty jar, and "Red Currant Jelly" in the jelly glass. Curtice Brothers Co., Rochester, NY. Both are ads from Century Magazine, Dec. 1891. $5-$35+

Meat curing pump, metal, in original cardboard tube with instructions, "Morton Salt," American, 20th C. .... **$20-$25**

Preserve can – See Fruit jar. I've put all glass canning jars under "Fruit jar," and ceramic canning jars here under "Preserve jar."

❖ NOTES ❖

Several companies made **earthenware** or **stoneware canning jars** at the turn of the century. The only two listed in *Thomas' Register of American Manufacturers,* **1905-06,** are Chicago Pottery Co., Chicago, IL; and Weir Pottery Co., Monmouth, IL. • *1932-33 Thomas's* includes: Robinson Clay Product Co., of NY, NJ, CT, OH; Western Stoneware Co., Monmouth, IL; White Hall Pottery Works, White Hall, IL; Louisville Pottery Co., Louisville, KY; Dorchester Pottery Works, Boston, MA; Red Wing Union Stoneware Co., Red Wing, MN; United States Stoneware Co., Akron, OH; Logan Pottery Co., Logan, OH; Hyssong Pottery Co., Bloomsburg, PA; and Sherwood Brothers Co., New Brighton, CT.

❖ NOTES ❖

Brown saltglaze was made like gray or buff stoneware, with one extra step. Instead of firing the plain clay vessel, and throwing salt in to vaporize as a glaze, a brown slip was brushed on or the vessel was dipped in it, allowed to dry, then fired just like other pieces, and at the right time the salt was thrown in.

XVI-10. Fruit jars. (L) "Mason's Improved Butter Jar," and (R) the highly desirable "Millville Atmospheric Fruit Jar." The Mason's has a metal screwband seal and glass lid, and probably dates to the turn of the 20th century. The Millville, with a glass lid held by yoke and thumbscrew, was made with the J. M. Whitall patent of June 18, 1861. Picture courtesy of the National Museum of American History, Smithsonian Institution.

Preserve jar, brown saltglazed stoneware, wax seal type with ridged flat rim into which wax or paraffin was melted; then the lid was pushed down before wax solidified, "Minnesota Stoneware," MN, 1-1/2 quart size, late 19th C. .... **$125+**

Preserve jar, redware, "Galena," Illinois (?), 9"H, late 19th C. .... **$100+**

Preserve jar, saltglazed stoneware, with double rim with recess for wax, called a "wax sealer," with original lid, some nicking where sharp tool has been used over years of use to dig out hardened wax, American (?), 1 qt. size, late 19th C. **$60**

Preserve jar, saltglazed stoneware with blue flowers, and stenciled blue capacity number "1," "Hamilton & Jones," Greensboro, PA, one gal. capacity, c.1870s .... **$130+**

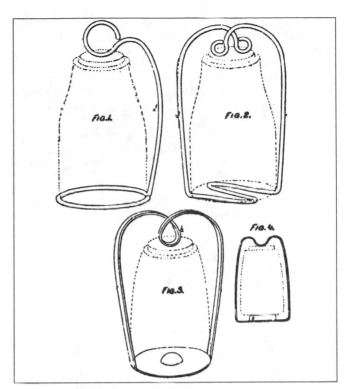

XVI-13. Jar holder patent, *actually called by inventor a "dish holder," but obviously with fruit jars sketched in. Pat'd. Apr. 26, 1870, by W. P. Walter. Spring wire bails of different types to fit different shapes of fruit jars.*

Preserve jar, saltglazed stoneware, stoneware lid, wire clamp-on lever to hold lid on, top of jar, like a jug, slants up, to only about 1/3 diam. of jar itself, "The Weir Stone Fruit Jar," mfd. by Weir Pottery Co., Monmouth, IL, 1 qt. size, (sizes: 1 pint, 1, 2, 4 & 8 qts. up to 10 gal., pat'd. Mar. 21,1892; made into early 20th C. .... **$55+**

Preserve jar, stoneware, saltglazed in shades of brown, 12 paneled sides, Peoria Pottery Co., Peoria, IL, 7"H x 4-1/2" diam., last quarter 19th C. .... **$55+**

XVI-12. Fowler's Vacuum Bottles for putting up food. *The spring steel clips were removed when the bottles were cold. The lids were lacquered metal. There was "no screwing down of hot bottles, these are self-closing. They seal every time without any trouble." Clockwise from top: (1) #31 bottle with "very little shoulder and may be emptied without the contents being broken" for a "brace of grouse, partridges, best portions of large birds, etc., excellent for half-pears, peaches, short asparagus, etc." 6-1/2"H holds 1-1/2 pound of fruit. (2) #41, for the same things as #31, but more. 6-1/2"H holds 2 pounds fruit. (3) Oval mould, which came in 5 sizes: 3", 4", 5", 6", and 7-1/2" diam., and therefore held from 1/4 pound to 4 pounds. Shown is the 7-1/2" x 5" oval, 4-pound size. Major P. J. W–, of Pitlochry, UK, wrote Fowler's in 1921: "I may tell you a bottle of Partridge done last January which I took to a picnic was excellent, and people would hardly credit it being 6 months old. I am doing Game and Chicken now and telling people about the process." (4) Example of a 1-1/2 pound mould for potted meat or fruit jelly and "special for Xmas Puddings." Fowler had vacuum bottles from "squat" to 10"H. Geo. Fowler, How to Bottle Fruit, Vegetables, Game, Poultry, Milk, &c. Reading, England: Fowler, n.d., revised edition c.1922.*

✤ RECIPE ✤

Tomato Chutney *– Ingredients: 6 lbs. Green or Ripe Tomatoes, 3 lbs. Cooking Apples, 4 ozs. Salt, 8 ozs. Brown Sugar, 1-1/2 pints Vinegar, 6 Cloves of Garlic, 6 ozs. Ground Ginger, 1 oz. Mustard Seed. Method: Wash and peal the tomatoes, wash, peel and slice the apples, put them into bottles, which should be closed with rubber rings, covers and clips, and sterilize for 2 hours at a temperature above 200 degrees. Whenn the tomatoes and apples are soft rub as much as possible through a sieve, add the sugar, ginger and mustard seed, also the garlic – chopped finely – mix ingredients thoroughly and whilst hot pour them into vacuum bottles or pickle jars and sterilize at a temperature above 200 degrees for two hours. Tomato Sauce, Chutney and other preparations, when sterilized in the vacuum bottles, will keep for an indefinite period." Geo. Fowler, How to Bottle Fruit, Vegetables, Game, Poultry, Milk, &c. Reading, England: Fowler, n.d., revised edition c.1922.*

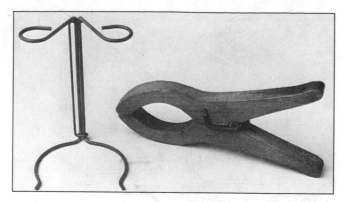

XVI-14. Jar holders. *These were used for handling hot jars – the one at left, for lifting from canner, were left in the kettle while canning.* **(L)** *All wire, like a doll stand, 9"H.* **(R)** *Other one like blanket pin is mostly wood and grips really tight. See Mudge canner XVI-1.* **$5-$15+**

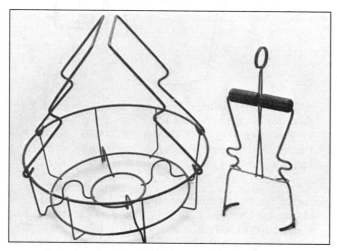

XVI-15. Jar rack & lifter. (L) *Wire, rack holds 4 jars for sterilizing. Basket part is 3-1/4"H x 10-1/4" diam.* **(R)** *The lifter works with one hand; your thumb goes through hole at top while fingers pull up on wooden grip. 10"H, early 20th C.* **$15-$35**

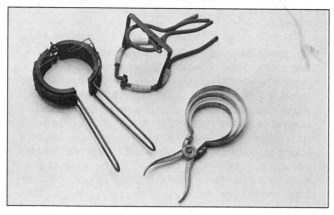

XVI-16. Jar wrenches. (L) *Wood with heavy wire handles.* **(T-R)** *Wire with leather. A double gripper that grips the jar with the bigger wrench and the lid with the pivoting upper wrench. 9-1/2"L.* **(B-R)** *with 3 bands is copper. The band can be selected to fit the circumference of the jar to be opened. 9-1/2"L. All located by The Primitive Man, Bob Cahn, Carmel, NY.* **$25-$65**

Tin cans – See Chapter VIII (Open & Close)

Tipping coppers, or soldering irons – copper bullet-like or wedge-shaped pointed head, sometimes with hexagonal sides like a large copper crystal, usually have heavy iron wire shaft or handle, sometimes with wooden grip at end, used to solder closed the vent hole left in the top of the early cans. About 8" to 10"L, 19th & 20th C. Such tools are still made. The tin cans were boiled, filled with hot food, and the top soldered on (or a cap in center of top was soldered into place). Then a steam hole was punched in the lid and the can boiled again, and steam escaped from the hole, after which it was immediately soldered closed, using a heated tipping copper and solder. If a can was found with 2 small holes, both soldered up, it indicated that someone had taken a spoiled batch of food, re-heated and re-sealed the can.. **$5-$15**

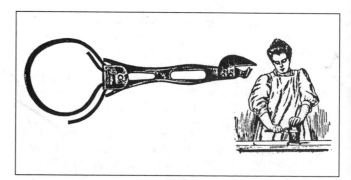

XVI-17. Mason Jar Sealer & Can Opener combined. *Made of "New Process White Metal," which is "strong, will not break, takes a high polish, and will last a lifetime." Leather strap and malleable cast iron frame. I believe it really was called "The Mason," but don't know who had the license to use the Mason name. From F. W. Seastrand drummers' catalog, c.1912.* **$20-$35**

XVI-18. Other folk art angels & crowns. These greatly reduced drawings are done from a fraktur-like drawing (top) of the Pennsylvania Germans, and from four gravestone carvings from the mid-to-late 18th C., in Connecticut. There are many other New England gravestone carvings of similar subjects. The A. H. Kerr glass company, of Oklahoma, supposedly took the angel & crown motif from the family coat of arms, but I have no confirmation of that. Interesting how almost Mayan or Aztec the angels look here! For further reading, see Allan I. Ludwig's Graven Images. New England Stonecarving and its Symbols, 1650-1815. *Middletown, CT: Wesleyan University Press. And Scott T. Swank, et al, Arts of the Pennsylvania Germans. Wilmington, DE: Winterthur, 1983.*

XVI-19. "Angel & crown" Kerr jelly glass bottoms. *Also known as "Bee & crown." Pure folk art. These are only five of an estimated 58 different patterns molded in bottom (inside of the glasses, outside of the tumblers) of the "jellies." Tumblers are 3-3/4"H x 2-7/8" diam. at top. The smaller glasses, with fluted sides, range from about 2-1/4"H x 3-1/4" diam. to 2-3/8"H x 3-1/2" diam. The mold-makers at Kerr interpreted the crown and angel, seemingly a different way each time they carved a new model. I am deeply indebted to the Jelly Jammers club, and to Betty Landis for giving me my first one, and setting me off. Especial thanks go to the late Barbara Bowditch, author of a remarkable book American Jelly Glasses, which includes rubbings done by Dennis Smith, of 58 of the angel and crown, as well as much more. (See Bibliography.) I couldn't do rubbings. Bottoms shown here were done on photo copy machine with a disk of black paper inside tumbler, and a white piece of paper with circle cut out, laid on top of copier's glass. I've collected folk art for 30 years, and this is the first time I've ever seen anything like these angels on a mass-produced object. The various treatments of hair, wings, face-shape, gown, star, and crown are remarkable. See XVI-21 for some parallel angels. Recent searches on eBay have turned up none of these glasses.* **$2-$10**

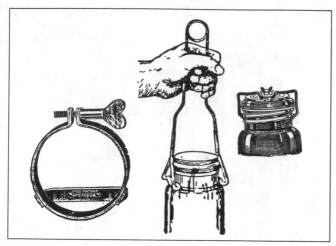

XVI-20 Fowler's bottling tools. (L) *Screw top bottle band remover. It is screwed to a door or wall through the horizontal band; the "hoop is tightened on the jar's band by the thumb screw, leaving both hands free to turn the bottle to slacken the band, which may afterwards be removed." I think I'd want to mount this horizontally! **(M)** Bottle tongs for lifting hot bottles from the Sterilizer. Also useful "for immersing Peaches and Tomatoes in hot water for removing the skins." **(R)** Fowler's patent clips for screw top bottles. "By using these instead of the screw band, the glass covers, if they are not faulty, seal during sterilizationn, thus avoiding screwing down covers while the bottles are hot. The clips are removed when the bottles are cold."* **$5+**

XVI-21. Fruit jar wrenches. (T) *Unmarked one of nickeled metal. Note bottle crown cap opener at top.* **(M)** *Looks like a lariat – wire & malleable cast iron. Best & Co., pat'd. 1917.* **(B)** *Nickeled steel, mfd. by A. C. Williams, New Jersey, c.1900. They specialized in corkscrews and bottle openers.* **$8-$25**

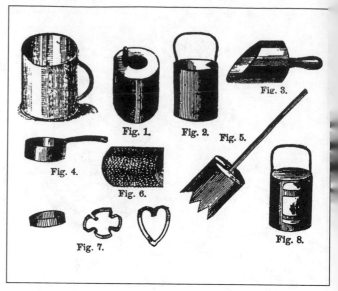

XVI-22. "Uses for Old Fruit Cans." Make-dos, *mostly from article in American Agriculturist, Jan. 1875.* **(T-L)** *Cup at top left was from AA, 1880. "Take round fruit, or vegetable, cans and melt off the top; bend a hickory withe for a handle, as shown in the engraving, and fasten it with wire or rivets. This makes a useful dipper, pitcher, measure, or vessel for many purposes about the barn or house; one may be made for the flour barrel; another for sugar; others for feed, grain, etc." Others:* **(Fig. 1)** *Emptied can, showing old-type hole in top which was soldered on after canning. You would melt other solder and flatten the tin, which is useful for "covering mouse and rat-holes," etc. If you lived in an old apartment in NYC, you'd find tin can lids nailed down over holes in the floor and wall.* **(Fig. 2)** *"Little bucket or paint pot."* **(Fig. 3)** *Scoop.* **(Fig. 4)** *Saucepan "for small messes."* **(Fig. 5)** *A fruit-picker.* **(Fig. 6)** *Coarse grater "for crackers, dry bread, horseradish, and the like." The tin is tacked to board.* **(Fig. 7)** *"Muffin and cakerings." Strips cut and held by rivets.* **(Fig. 8)** *Lantern, with a piece of "stove mica" set into side."*

XVI-23. Tipping copper, for soldering can lids in home canning, or for mending tinwares. *The sharp long tip was copper, which conducted heat very well; held in iron cleft, wood handle. The "pointed portion is to be 'tinned,' as the workmen say, which means that it is to be coated with solder. To tin the point, file it smooth, heat the tool hot enough to melt solder, then quickly file the surface bright, and rub it on a small lump of solder that has been placed on a board for the purpose, using rosin, or a few drops of a zinc solution." American Agriculturist, Feb. 1870.* **$15-$25+**

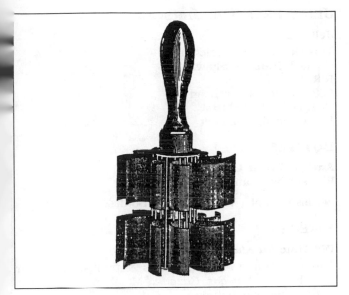

XVI-25. Fruit can soldering machine, sometimes described as a cylinder-scraper for automobiles, which for all I know it may have been used for. "Allens'," mfd. by Hull Brothers, Webster & Co., Cleveland, OH. "The only machine ever made which will finish the can completely with one handling. By the use of it the can only requires one handling to finish soldering. Adjusts to size of both top and bottom; they will not spring off while being soldered." I've seen one – it's about 9" or 10"L, nice wooden handle, and it rattles when turned quickly back and forth, so it may also be mistaken for some kind of noisemaker. The Metal Worker, July 8, 1882. **$75+**

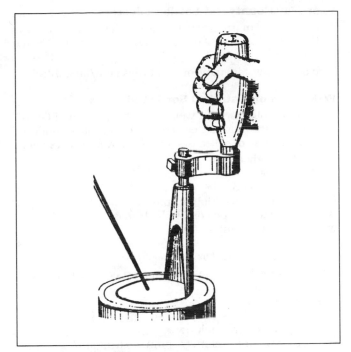

XVI-24. Soldering tool patent. Pat'd. Jan. 13, 1880, by William Painter, Baltimore, MD, assignor of 1/2 of right to Louis B. Keizer. A "hand soldering device for capping cans, the combination of a soldering tool whose edge is curved to conform to the groove in the can-top, and is the sole guide of the tool, with a handle." I don't know if it was ever made.

FOR MORE INFORMATION

PUBLICATIONS

Fruit Jar Annual

Indispensable annual with price guide, auction reports, fruit jar collector directory, special articles on one aspect, etc

Editor/author: Jerry McCann
5003 W. Berwyn Ave.
Chicago, IL 60630
Phone: (773) 777-0443
E-mail: fjar@aol.com

Fruit Jar News

This monthly is the successor to the late Dick Roller's newsletter.
Editor: Tom Caniff
FJN Publishers, Inc.
364 Gregory Ave.
West Orange, NJ 07052-3743
Caniff's e-mail: tomcaniff@aol.com

FRUIT JAR WEB SITES

Midwest Antique Fruit Jar & Bottle Club

Meetings, semi-annual shows, monthly newsletter, etc.
Contact: Norman & June Barnett
PO Box 38
Flat Rock, IN 47234

Phone: (812) 587-5560
E-mail: jbarnett@fruitjar.org
Web site: http://fruitjar.org

New Zealand Antique Bottle & Collectables

Links to clubs, research archive, etc.
Web site: http://nzbottle.homestead.com/files/page7.htm

Fruit Jars.Com

A fun site with good articles & lots of pictures. One shows fruit jar patents up to 1926. Greg Spurgeon's "Jar Colors" will be very useful to beginners; Spurgeon's own site is www.hoosierjar.com/. Tom Caniff & Tammy Johnson's historical "Round Ring Boxes" is about the early round boxes that held rubber jar rings.

Contact: Mike Sollars
E-mail: mike@fruitjars.com
Web site: www.fruitjars.com/index.asp

Fruit Jar Collector

Collector Bob Clay, highly regarded in the fruit jar world, who worked for Ball Glass for almost 20 years, has an "About Me" page on eBay, with links to articles he's written.

E-mail: raclay@earthlink.net
eBay Web site: http://members.ebay.com/aboutme/bobclay/

Cape May County, NJ Bottle Collectors

This site has many great links to collectors & clubs in the USA, Canada, Australia, Denmark, & the United Kingdom.

Web site: www.capemaycountybottles.com/links.html

Federation of Historical Bottle Collectors

Individual collectors as well as clubs can join FOHBC, and get the newsletter. The Web site has wonderful links to sites of collectors, clubs all over, dealers, etc.

Contact: Wendy Smith
2230 Toub St.
Ramona, CA 92065
E-mail: membership@fohbc.com
Web sites: www.fohbc.com/links.htm & www.fohbc.com/clubs.htm

The Fruit Jar Collector

This collector has some good tips on collecting.
Contact: Phil Murphy
322 Brown Ave.
Collinsville, IL 62234
E-mail: pmurfe@intertek.net
Web site: www.intertek.net/~pmurfe/fruitjars/main.html

Info on Irradiated Glass & Color Changes

Sometimes fruit jars sold in a rare color are actually old jars that have had their color altered by irradiation. A site for glass insulators' has an article by Dwayne Anthony that will help you learn about this fraud.

Web site: www.nia.org/altered/

JELLY PRESERVE JARS

Jelly Jammers

This club has a newsletter.
Contact: Margaret Shaw
R.R. 1
6086 W. Boggstown Road
Boggstown, IN 46110
E-mail: emshaw@in.net

BOTTLES

Antique Bottle Collector's Haven

Web site: www.antiquebottles.com/

See also Chapter VII for more on Bottles

VINEGAR

Old Time Vinegar Society

This organization has meetings & publishes a quarterly, the *Vinegar Gazette*. Members also collect other types of bottles.

Contact: Teddy Speas
745 Beth-Rural Hall Rd.
Rural Hall, NC 27045
Phone: (336) 969-4616
E-mail: speas@triad.rr.com
Web site: www.antiquebottles.com/vinegarclub

White House – The Collection of Charles Perry - Bottles, Jugs, and Jars (Book)

Author: Charlie Perry
Route 2, Box 102-B
Norlina, NC 27563
Phone: (252) 257-4008

FURNISHING

XVII. CHAIRS, TABLES, CUPBOARDS, & CABINETS

You may doubt that there are "collectors" of furniture. But, like a surprising number of people, I happen to collect chairs (mostly not kitchen chairs, however), and I have good friends in Massachusetts who collect wall-hung wooden cupboards, most of which are a couple of centuries old. Many people are constrained by money and room, and find it hard to visualize a collection of tables, for example, arranged anywhere in the house. (Some of my chairs are hung on the wall; some are in storage against the time when one of my dreams – a Chair Room – can be made real.)

A good percentage of collectors of kitchen implements of the 20th century own, or would like to own, at least one period piece of furniture which helps set the smaller pieces in a natural context. The most popular item is a **Hoosier cabinet**, made by Hoosier Mfg. Co. of Indiana, or similar ones by one of many other companies, frequently located in Indiana. Lots of Hoosier or Sellars cabinet accessories – flour sifters, sugar canisters, spice jars, etc., are frequently auctioned on eBay. Spare parts are available too: see the end of this chapter and Chapter XV.

For collectors of 19th century implements and hollowware, a scrubbed-top table, a pie safe, or some Windsor-style kitchen chairs are goals. Hutch tables and wall cupboards with forged iron hardware are favored by collectors of 18th- and early 19th-century wares. These pieces help set the scene.

What makes up a collection of furniture? Some people say you have to have at least two pieces; others say three or more are needed; I tend to agree with the latter. A pair of something, even an unmatched pair, isn't really a collection. Various assembled pieces of furniture, all in original green paint, or all made of bird's-eye maple, or all with turned legs, or all made in North Carolina – now that's a collection!

A lot of furniture is auctioned on eBay, including at least a few Hoosiers every month or so. The real disadvantage is that you are bidding on something quite large, and even with a good digital photo, even with detail shots, on the auction site, you still don't get the full effect of finish, mars, scratches, and especially soundness. So really be sure before you bid. The same holds true for catalog sales at which you can't be present.

Baker's cupboard, very like a pie safe, pine with one large door, slatted shelves & screened sides, for cooling fresh-baked bread loaves, c.1890s-1910. .... **$400+**

Baker's rack, iron, sides look like intertwined grapevines, 5 shelves, European or poss. American, 6-1/2 ft. H x 5 ft. W, early 20th C. .... **$575+**

Butcher block, deep, solid maple on strong thick turned legs, worn & scarred, 20" square, 19th C. **$400**

Cabinet, also called a kitchen piano by the Hoosier Mfg. Co. because it put "everything at her fingers' ends," varnished wood, porcelainized iron counter top, original sifter and bin, revolving spice rack for 7 containers with shaker tops, flour & sugar containers, perfect condition, "Hoosier," New Castle, IN, very early 20th C. .... **$800+**

❖ NOTES ❖

Hoosier kitchen cabinets in the ads. Ads in a 1901 and 1902 *Ladies' Home Journal* said that "Does away with tiresome walking around a hot kitchen"; and, "Household Economy is as much a matter of saving your steps as of thrifty living. There is more time and strength left for these things if you have a Hoosier Kitchen Cabinet. Convenient, compact, orderly ... can be put where you wish." Another ad, in *House Furnishing Review*, Jan. 1908, said that the "Hoosier kitchen cabinet saves as many steps as a bicycle. It is as necessary a convenience as a sewing machine." 1908 *Ladies' Home Journal* ads stress **handiness:** "Every bit of working space on the Hoosier Cabinet is available. The flour can be sifted by a turn of the hand – the sugar is in the dust-proof bin at the right – the spices in the cans at the left – package goods in the cupboard above – all utensils are before you or in the pantry below – everything is at your fingers' ends, leaving the big aluminoid table top free for your work. Hoosier Cabinets save one-half the time and one-half the labor by grouping every article at your fingers' ends – saving unnecessary steps – they give you more time for other things."
Efficiency was a word well-known to housewives by 1908. People as disparate as the Beecher sisters and all manner of inventors, throughout the last half of the 19th century, claimed that their method or gadget would economize effort and save labor. Daughters of a crusading anti-slavery minister, Catharine E. Beecher and sister, Harriet Beecher Stowe (who wrote Uncle Tom's Cabin) wrote their instructive *The American Woman's Home: or, Principles of Domestic Science in 1869*. In Chapter II, they wrote that their aim was to present "modes of economizing time, labor, and expense by the close packing of conveniences."

A man named Frederick Winslow Taylor, who died in 1915, was an early **efficiency spokesman;** his paper, "*The Principles of Scientific Management*," was

XVII-1. "A Method of Arranging a Kitchen," *from the* American Agriculturist, *April 1876. A farmhouse kitchen designed by L. D. Snook to suit the farmer's wife – as a complement to city kitchens "arranged with great care to facilitate the work of servants."* **(E)** *is a wood or iron sink, and if wood, treated with linseed oil inside. "An iron pump is placed in at the end near the wall and connects with the cistern. The outlet pipe is at the opposite end near the window." Below the sink is a "closet" with two doors, and to the right of that is a china closet* **(H)** *and a lower "closet" for kettles, tinware, and the various cooking utensils. The oiled wooden rack* **(B)** *below the window is slatted, and for draining dishes.* **(F)** *is a pass-through to the pantry seen through the door. On the lowest shelf in the pantry appears to be a bread dough raiser. What about the stove? "For convenience the stove should be placed upon the side of the room occupied by the closets [cupboards], or near where the table stands in the illustration." The next picture in the article showed how a pantry should be arranged. We think of a pantry as a place for storing food, but remember the root word: pan. "In houses of old style there was either no pantry at all, the kitchen being furnished with a dresser and shelves, or it was merely a small closet to hold the articles in less common use. In modern houses the pantry is next in importance to the kitchen, and it should be so arranged as to accommodate all the appliances used in cookery, as well as the china, glass-ware, cutlery, and other articles for the table."*

published in 1911 – the same year as the Gilbreth book, mentioned below, was published. Taylor did not rise out of a muddled world as its efficiency savior. His efforts, along with Henry Ford, unheralded inventors, cookbook author Fannie Farmer, and other pioneers of efficiency, helped formalize the movement.

Frank and Lillian Gilbreth are probably more famous than Taylor because of their concept of therbligs ("Gilbreth" spelled backwards except for the "th.") **Therbligs** were a sort of graphic unit so that tasks could be broken down from start to finish into various motions – or therbligs – such as select, grasp, transport, hold, etc. This therblig system wasn't really known until some 15 years after the Hoosier ads quoted above. Frank Gilbreth, and later he and his wife, published several books on **motion study** – the

first a book titled *Motion Study, a Method for Increasing the Efficiency of the Workman in 1911.* [See also the breakdown of the steps required by a tinsmith and a factory worker to make a coffee pot, outlined in Chapter XIV (Coffee, Tea).] Lillian Gilbreth received patents on several household tools, including an electric mixer, and a step-pedal trash can. By the way, the beloved 1948 biography-memoir *Cheaper By the Dozen,* by two of their children, is about the Gilbreths raising of their big family,

Efficiency experts used stopwatches and long-exposure photographs that caught serial movements with flash lighting like stroke lights. The motions could be precisely timed, making possible "time-and-motion" studies of all steps required to do a specific job (in factories). The photos allowed diagramming of "better" hand and body movements to follow smaller arcs and shorter pathways. Managers loved it, workers didn't because they had often approached their work as individual craftsmen-artisans, and they were, they thought, being turned into machines, tools of managers who couldn't do the actual jobs themselves. Although the scientific methods used to increase efficiency seemed unnatural and were unwelcome by so many people, the word "efficiency" itself had a positive meaning.

Any of you who have been faced with a repetitive task, whether it's stuffing envelopes or slicing zucchini, have probably experimented with which side to place the stacks or the bowl to get the job done quickly. That's motion study in action.

Cabinet, all original finish, double doors above, flanking flour bin with oval glass window, slightly arched top, bins below, 4 drawers, sifter, spice rack, etc., "Hoosier Mfg. Co.," early 20th C. .... **$600+**

XVII-2. "Plate dresser" & work table, *as depicted in a wood engraving from an 1833 edition of a chapbook,* Mother Goose's Melodies, *published in England. The caption reads "Sing, Sing! – What shall I sing? The Cat's run away with the Pudding-Bag String." "Chapbook" is an elided "cheapbook," because typically these cheaply-printed little books were sold as comic books were in the 1950s, and had poems, moralizing tales, and lots of woodcut or wood engraving illustrations.*

Cabinet, oak in original finish, flour bin & sifter, roll front that works very well, "Hoosier," early 20th C. .... $550+

Cabinet, painted wood, doors above, bins, pull out pastry board, "Sellers," early 20th C............. $475+

Cabinet, step-back hutch top, 2 doors above, 2 utility drawers over bin, nice legs, Larkin, early 20th C. .... $575+

Cabinet, maple, bottom has 2 bins, 2 drawers & 2 molding boards for rolling out dough, top section has 8 drawers flanking small cupboard with door, American, 48"W, late 19th C. .... $750+

Cabinet, painted green with green & black marbleized enameled-iron work surface, casters on legs, arched doors, clock set in frame at top, wonderful looking, "Keystone Cabinet Co." with truncated arrowhead-like keystone logo, Littlestown, PA, 39-3/4"W, pat'd. Feb. 2, 1922. • A spectacular greenie piece for a Depression glass kitchen. Or for any other room; this is a beauty. .... $2,500+

XVII-3. "A Corner Cupboard." You've seen in illustrations XVII-1 and -2 precursors of multi-purpose cabinets – the cupboard for utensils, the pantry, and the combination dresser & table. This one shows how an awkward corner between doors leading to a dining room and to a pantry was made to "be comprehensive, compact, capacious, and convenient." **(A)** covers a flour barrel and is a swing-out curved door. **(B)** is the hinged top lid or cover. **(C)** is the top of a "case of drawers" **(F)** & **(G)**, but just under it, in **(E)**, is "a space for the bread pan and the molding-board, which slides in on cleats; these are reached by the door **(D)**, which lifts, and is provided with a spring-catch. Above, **(H)** are cupboards up to the ceiling. This kind of built-in, from 1876, predates the built-in kitchen cupboards we are used to from the last half of the 20th C. American Agriculturist, April 1876.

Cabinets, sometimes called **cabinet tables,** or baker's cupboards, of the **"Hoosier"-type,** with shelves, drawers, bins, dough-boards, sifters, and work counter, are a mass-produced elaboration of a much earlier free-standing cupboard or dresser dating back hundreds of years ago, especially in Europe. Some from the early 19th century, with drawers, bins, and shelves for staples, are obvious predecessors – especially Shaker cupboards.

The c.1890s-1920s cabinet-cupboards, to which we've given the generic "Hoosier" name were marketed aggressively as aids to the "science" of cookery, and helped housewives see themselves as efficient professionals, with their own offices or places of business that were as important as the offices to which their husbands went every day. Practicality and efficiency were buzzwords appealing to women who perhaps appreciated having their housework recognized as a career, even a scientific career. An article by Mary Jane Hill ("The Changing Kitchen Cabinet," *Antique Trader,* Jan. 10, 1979) tells of an efficiency survey of women's kitchen work done by expert Harrington Emerson in the 1920s. He concluded that "The housewife was taking 2,113 steps to prepare three meals a day," but that "only 520 steps were actually necessary" if a cabinet such as the "Napanee Dutch Kitchenet" were used.

By the 1920s, there were porcelainized metal cabinets, which were more sanitary than wood, but most of the ones collected now are wood, either varnished natural finish or painted white, some with enameled or porcelainized iron work surface. They have varying numbers of built-in accessories -- from spice containers & flour sifters & coffee grinders to clocks, shopping aids and a filing compartment for household bills -- and were made by many companies besides Hoosier, in various states, but mostly Indiana, from the turn of the 20th century on for about three decades. (Hoosier closed down in 1942. Coppes, Zook & Mutschler', of Nappanee, IN, are considered the oldest – founded in 1876 – and Coppes is still in business making kitchen cabinets in 2002.) A 1902 ad for a large "#20 Hoosier," with drawers on the side, the front, and in the upper half, as well as loads of shelves, said it was "often used instead of a 'built-in' cupboard." But most of these factory-made movable cabinets date after 1910s but before built-in cabinets in 1940s. Value ranges widely; those at the low end are plain or in poor condition. Rather expensive manufactured ones are "possum bellies" – large, with rounded bins, built-in sifters, racks & extra details.

Avoid the overly refinished, and remember that, originally, many cabinets were painted, and all cabinets made of several different woods were painted. Oak was considered the superior wood because it is hard and wouldn't tend to "absorb odors" and get musty-smelling. You will sometimes find cabinets with their original grain-painted finish. Ariel's cabinets were unusual because they used colored stains through which the grain would show. Green was the most popular color. Wide value range of all cabinets due to condition, features, appearance.

• • •

Makers of kitchen cabinets and/or kitchen safes in the early 1900s are listed. Only a few advertised nationally. The generic name "hoosier" often applied to all movable kitchen cabinets comes from Hoosier Mfg. Co., New Castle, IN. Others include: Acme, Wilkinson, IN; Acme Kitchen Furn. Co., Chattanooga, TN; Alles Bros. (made kitchen safes), Henderson, KY; Andrews, in Andrews, IN; Ariel** Cabinet Co., Peru, IN; Aude Furn. Co., St. Louis, MO; Bagby Furn. Co. (safes), Baltimore, MD; Bisk Corp., Brockton, MA; Bryant Furn. Co., Truxton, NY; Campbell, Smith & Ritchie's "Boone," Lebanon, IN; Cardinal's "Mother Hubbard's," Wabash, IN; Coppes, Zook & Mutschler's "Napanee," and "Napanee Dutch Kitchenet," Nappanee, IN; A. D. Deemer Furn. Co., Brookville, PA; Dubuque Cabinet Makers' Assoc., Dubuque, IA; Evansville Furn. Co. (safes), Evansville, IN; Fitts-Crabtree Mfg. Co. (safes), Sanford,

XVII-5. "Possum-belly" cabinet tables. *With their original prices!* **(T-L)** *"Princess," made mostly of ash, with sanded top – what became known as a scrub-top. Base finished "antique oak." 27" x 47"L. Two "sliding extension boards; two partitioned sliding bins which may be used for potatoes, etc." $5.65.* **(T-R)** *"Domestic new-style Combination Kitchen Cabinet," made of ash, 18" x 45" with drop leaf shown up; sliding bins and extension carving boards. $6.90.* **(B-L)** *"Convenient," ash, plain top, "antique color" base, 27" x 42" top, two 50-lb bin drawers," $5.90.* **(B-R)** *"Kitchen Queen," seasoned white wood. One large drawer above sliding flour bin. Top unfinished; rest "golden oak." $2.95. All from Albert Pick mail order catalog, 1909.* **$150-$350+**

XVII-4. Butcher blocks. (T-L) *"Made from 1-1/2 strips of best grade white maple, glued & bolted together," turned legs. Seven sizes: from 15" square to 30" x 40". S. D. Sexton catalog, Baltimore, c.1930s.* **(T-R)** *Not so described, but looks like section of tree trunk. Five diameters, from 18" to 30"; and* **(M-L)** *"Butcher Bench," thick plank 24"W x any length. Braced with iron rods, on heavy turned trestle legs.* **(M-R)** *"Square sectional" block in 3 sizes, from 20" x 25" to 25" x 30", bolted through, on turned legs. Last three all from Duparquet, Huot & Moneuse suppliers' catalog, c.1904-1910.* **(B)** *A high "sectional maple block," that looks like a work table & is called a* **chef block.** *18" x 18" x 10" deep; 34"H overall. Also Sexton, c.1930s. Most surface distress from use & age don't devalue. The top may even have a deep depression from long heavy use, but with good color and interesting legs, it may still have decorative value. In fact, most old ones bought today are stage-setting pieces not true collectibles. (B) is the most valuable, and might bring $1,000+. The rest:* **$90-$500+**

NC; Ft. Smith Folding Bed & Table Co., Ft. Smith, AR; Globe Furn. Co., Evansville, IN; Goshen Pump Co. (latter also made safes), Goshen, IN; Greencastle Cabinet Co., Greencastle, IN; Helmers Mfg. Co., Leavenworth, KS; High Point Mantel & Table Co. (safes), High Point, NC; House & Herrmann, Wheeling, WV; C. A. Hubbard, Martinsville, IN; Ideal Cabinet Co., Evansville, In.; Indiana Furn. Co., Evansville, IN; I-X-L, Goshen, IN; L. A. Jennings, New Castle, IN; Kesslers & Sons (safes), Logan, OH; Klanke, --?--*; Koenig Furn. Co. (safes), St. Louis, MO; Kompass & Stoll, Niles, MI; Jonathan Koontz Sons, Union City, IN; Larkin, --?--*; R. E. Lasher & Co. (safes), St. Louis, MO; Lebanon Mfg. Co., Lebanon, IN; Marysville Cabinet Co., Marysville, OH; McCure Mfg. Co., Marion, IN; G. P. McDougall, Indianapolis & Frankfort, IN, who made "Plainview" for Montgomery Ward; McLoud & Sparks (also safes), Ft. Smith, AR; McNown Mfg. Co., Columbia, IN; A. H. Meyer, Lebanon, IN; Minnesota Furn. Co.'s "Elwell Kitchen Cabinet," Minneapolis, MN; Mound City Furniture Co. (safes), Mound, IL; Parker-Battle-Talbot Mfg. Co. (safes), Tullohoma, TN; Paul Mfg. Co., Ft. Wayne, IN; Queen Cabinet Co., Chicago, IL; G. I. Sellers & Sons Co., Elwood, IN; Charles Sueme (safes), St. Louis, MO; Tillman Bros. (safes), La Crosse, WI; Tipp Bldg. & Mfg. Co., Tippecanoe City, OH; Union Cabinet Co., Marion, IN; Ware Mfg. Co. (safes), Atlanta, GA; Wasmuth-Endicott Co.'s "Kitchen Maid," Andrews, IN; Wilson Co., Grand Rapids, MI; Winter Lumber Co., Sheboygan, WI.

*I couldn't find addresses for Larkin or Klanke. I do wonder if maybe Larkin Mfg Co., Buffalo, NY, who made soap and had a premium program, might not have had cabinets made by another company.

** The name "Ariel" was chosen, reportedly, by the company president, Charles Morrice, who said he was once an aerialist in the circus.

• • • •

Hoosier Cup Race on eBay, August 17-27, 2001. Hannah-house-antiques, eBay sellers of Lancaster, OH, put up a restored, 1940s kitchen cupboard/pantry set of 3 units, consisting of the centerpiece of step-back cupboard with white porcelain, pull-out work surface, complete with original flour sifter and flour bin, a single-width two-door (over and under) pantry cupboard on the left side, and a double-width four-door pantry cupboard on the right.

Its complete restoration included repainting in a specially-mixed paint made to match a paint sample from the cupboard, re-backing the tambour pull-down cover, replacing two of the three "Hoosier" name plates, and papering the inside with reproduction Hoosier paper. Red Bakelite handles on all doors were original. The set is 68"H x 86"W overall. Hannah-house-antiques also threw in various period kitchen utensils and appliances. The seller included numerous photos, carefully described each element, and any and all replacements and repairs.

Hannah-house-antiques started the auction off at $250, and stated that freighting it anywhere in the US would be $450. The first bid was placed a mere 2-1/2 minutes after the cabinet was posted. Over the next seven hours, three bidders bid it up to $800, which held for almost two days. Over the 10 days of the auction, there were 39 bids, from seven bidders, including a long string of bids from $1,025 to $2,000 by one person (let's call her W), over a period of seven minutes, trying to top the existing (although unknown) bid of another bidder (let's call him X) of $3,000, but ultimately failing.

For three more days X's $3,000 bid held as the highest. Then a new bidder (let's call her Y) came in with a bid of $3,500, which held for about 12 hours. Back came X at $4,000; then Y with $4,008, and then eight minutes later X bid $4,500. Then a brand new bidder (Z) stepped in and tried, not knowing about the $4,500 bid because it hadn't been necessary to reveal the highest bid level up to that point. This new bidder Z tried to inch up from the $4,008, being topped by X's automatic $250 increment bids each time, because of X's prevailing high bid of $4,500. Suddenly Y was over, with a bid of $4,508, but feeling insecure, or rethinking the matter, Y then raised the bid to $4,658, which held for 28 seconds, which was a mere 18-1/2 minutes before the end of the auction.

Suddenly, up the track comes X again, trying, trying, with three bids in one minute, trying to win the Hoosier Race: $5,000; $5,500; gosh, then $6,000! But the thing X didn't know was that the sleeper, Y, had already bid $6,000 four minutes before. It was like racing against an invisible horse with an invisible jockey!

Finally, two minutes later, Y bid $6,100, and 14 minutes and three seconds later the Hoosier belonged to Y for $6,100 plus $450 shipping, unless the winner was picking it up herself. The bidding record, available to everyone after the auction is over, showed that four bidders had been willing to pay over $2,000, and three bid over $4,000. What it didn't show was if the winner, Y, had bid any higher than $6,100. Since the amount was over $5000, $100 was the automatic increment at that point, but I suspect that Y had bid $6,250 or even higher.

XVII-6. Combination table & cabinet. *Upper part is an open dresser mainly for keeping & displaying china. There is a drop-down hinged door for what appears to be a spice shelf on top. Lower table part was called a **cabinet table**, with cutlery drawer & two bin drawers. Unidentified English illustration, c.1900-1910.* **$450-$700+**

Anyone who has priced new kitchen cabinets knows that this isn't too bad a price for something decorative, functional, and historically interesting.

The curious thing to me, because I engage in a lot of last minute bidding, is that not a single bidder added odd cents to their bids. The rules on eBay are that tie bids are won by the bidder who has bid that amount first. Most eBaying experts suggest adding odd cents, such as $5.27 instead of $5.25; or $131.69 instead of $129.99. Anyway, it is a good idea to print out and analyze the strategic bidding for multi-bidder big-ticket items of a type you might be interested in. Like people who can read score sheets for baseball games, you can become a more skillful bidder.

Cabinet table, elm with maple top, cast iron handles, zinc bin drawer at bottom, 3 drawers at left, door on right half reveals 2 shelves, paneled sides, McDougal's "Plainview," from Montgomery Ward catalog, 2 ft. 8"H x 4 ft. 4"L x 2 ft. 4" deep, c.1895. • When the bins' curved fronts show, a popular name for these tables is possum belly tables; the name also applies to bin tables with cabinets above.................. **$350+**

Cabinets or chests for spice – See Chapter VII (Storage)

Cupboard, also called a pantry cupboard, wall hung, primitive pine, stripped, alas, of original paint, hence much lower in value. It's possibly English – countless (except by U.S. Customs) container loads of stripped pine "country" pieces are imported each year. American, Scandinavian or English, 19th C. **$400**

Cupboard, brown painted wood, top has crested back & side board and a pair of drawers with turned wood knobs, overhanging lower part by a little over an inch, scalloped apron, very short feet, 2 doors with 2 tins each in punctured star-in-circle design, West VA, 19th C. .... **$2,500+**

Cupboard, cherry in original finish, step-back consisting of a blanket chest or bin with hinged board lid on bottom, 2 shelf cupboard above with molded cornice, 2 doors with 3 punctured tins each door, footed basket with droopy flowers design, PA (?), 19th C. .... **$3,500+**

Cupboard, red painted walnut(?) with molded cornice, 2 top doors glazed with 6 panes each, 2 drawers in middle with wooden knobs, scalloped apron & bracket feet, 2 lower doors with punctured tins painted green, American, 94"H x 60"W, 19th C. .... **$3,200+**

Cupboard, red painted wood, tall, scalloped apron in front and sides almost to floor, 2 tall doors with 4

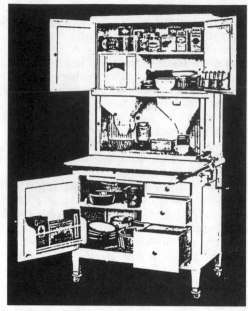

XVII-8. "Hoosier cabinet," *this one really mfd. by Hoosier. Called by them their "Thirty-Six-Inch Hoosier." 71-1/2"H x 37"W, finished in white enamel, or available in "light golden oak." "Equipment includes white* Porceliron *top; mouse-proof construction; ant-proof casters; shaker flour sifter; 9-piece glassware set; package rack on lower door; shallow utensil tray suspended from work-table." Has a meat grinder clamped to work surface, and you can see the spice rack on upper right door. Hoosier Mfg. Co., Newcastle, IN, 1922 catalog. Value range is for unrefinished white original finish, which just a few years ago was not as highly prized as the wood. (See paragraph in text on the "Hoosier Cup Race.")* **$550-$1,500+**

XVII-7. Combination cabinet tables. *All from a 1909 supplier's catalog. (L) to (R) from top: (1) "Ever Ready Table and Shelf." Overall it's 66"H; table 28-1/2"H x 42" x 26" deep. Bass or cottonwood, light or dark finish. Identical to one in previous picture, although that one was supposedly English. (2) "Locker," of oak, with base consisting of one tin-lined tilting bin, 2 drawers, 2 pull-out molding boards, 2 compartments. 83"H overall, "golden oak" finish. (3) "Triumph," with more drawers than the others, glass-fronted cupboard, 81"H overall. Bass or cottonwood, light or dark finish. (4) "Winner," of oak, sanded table top, tilting 100-lb flour bin with tin lining, glass & wood-panelled cupboard doors, 83"H x 48"W. (5) "Handy," for china, glass, cutlery, linens, but with no work surface. 79"H. (6) "Utility," with all sizes of drawers, many features not in any others, including drawers on side, and removable extension boards "for many purposes." Oak, in "golden oak" finish. 75-1/2"H x 42"W. Originally this was the most expensive at $17.25; others ranged from $6.95 to $16.80. Albert Pick catalog, 1909.* **$200-$2,000+**

punctured tins each door plus 4 tins on each side, flat board top; punctured design is X with 2 hearts & 2 diamonds filling in spaces between the crossed lines, Ohio (?), 60"H x 42"W x 17"D, 19th C. • Dealers Robb & Alice Guss, Youngsville, NY, sold this in 1984. Price range mine................... **$3,000+**

Cupboard, step-back, of curly cherry – highly figured wood, bottom has scalloped apron, 2 doors, long drawer below counter top, above has molded cornice, 2 doors with 3 punctured tins each, simple concentric curved lines of quarter circles, made by John Richey, Hammersville, OH, 19th C. • Sold at Garth's, Nov. 1983, at the Ron Klapmeir Sale, for $2,300. Now?... **$3,500+**

Cupboard, walnut, 2 pieces, 12 small glass windows & 3 spice drawers of tiger maple in top, 3 tiger maple drawers for cutlery in 2 door base, Pennsylvania, 19th C. .... **$2,800+**

Cupboard or meat safe, hung from beam, tan painted wood frame has short feet, but at top the sides extend like upside down legs, each having a hole for bolting to a beam, 2 shelves, 4 tins with slits in 10 concentric circles, corners with odd X marks, Ohio, mid to 3rd quarter of 19th C. .... **$800+**

Dry sink, child size and well-made, wood with cupboard underneath with 2 doors with knobs, sea green paint inside sink, counter & splash board, brown & ochre grain-painted outside, American, 20"H x 22"W, c.1860s. .... **$450+**

Dry sink, painted pine, zinc lining, one drawer, cupboard below with 2 doors, prob. American, 19th C. • Value ranges widely due to paint color & appearance, style, details such as drainboard and drawer, origin, and size. Even a gnawed rathole may add value for some collectors (such as mot.). .... **$250-$1,500**

Dry sink, pine with cast iron well liner, traces of old gray paint, very plain & handsome, 19th C. • The iron liner is unusual; most are zinc or tin or painted wood. .... **$700+**

Dry sink, wood painted olive drab underneath, sink painted white inside, original tacked-on sink lining, probably metal, probably zinc, now missing, small drawer to right for scouring materials, square drawer knob replaced, American, prob. PA, 43-3/4"W, c.1860s or 1870s. .... **$1,000+**

Dry sink & cupboard, beautiful glowing old red paint, zinc sink, compartment with lid at left of sink for cleaning materials, cupboard was built-in & upper shelves have no back, taken out of an old Easton, PA home, 9 feet high, 19th or very early 20th C. • Dealers Jack & Vicky Pilarski had this superb piece. Wish I'd bought it!............................. **$6,500+**

Flour bins – See Chapter VII (Storage & Containers)

Hanging cupboard, old green paint over pine, 3 shelves, one door, simple iron latch, about 37"H x 26"W x 8" deep, Maine, 19th C. .... **$550+**

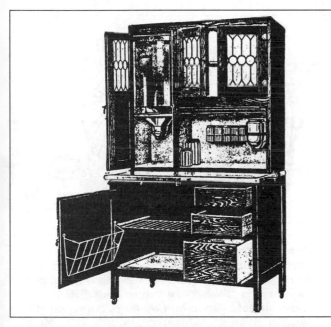

XVII-9. Cabinet. "I-XL" Co., Goshen, IN. All white enameled, nickeled hardware, "drop roll curtain" in middle right section. Glass jar equipment includes "swinging sugar bin with metal cap and cut-off, one coffee, one tea, and five spice jars." Tilting metal sifter flour bin with glass front. Slide-out top of "polished metal or white porcelain." "Special bracket and block for food grinder." Sliding bread board, metal-lined drawers. 70"H x 40"W. Also available in golden oak finish." From c.1916 I-XL catalog. Note classy leaded glass panels, resembling house fenestration of the time. **$650-$1,000**

XVII-10. Barrel chair. "Homemade easy chair," reads heading in American Agriculturist, Mar. 1865. Quite possibly not for the kitchen, but it's made from "a good flour barrel," with a few staves cut away. "A small opening or door can be made under the seat, which will furnish a convenient work box" (perhaps sewing, darning or knitting materials). The article advises nailing the hoops to each stave before commencing the making of such a chair! Value would depend on age of original barrel, its patina or finish, skill of making, and possibly the upholstered cushion. **$100-$250**

Hanging cupboard, pine with grayish blue old paint, one simple paneled door, no molding, brass keyhole probably adapted from another piece of furniture, simple door latch, American c.1830s to 1850s............. **$575+**

Hanging cupboard, simple pine butt joints, blue milk paint, 2 door, 2 shelves, prob. PA, European heritage, 1870s or 1880s.................................. **$450+**

Hutch table, 2-plank top, red over old blue paint, rosehead nails and turned pegs, butterfly cleats on underside hold planks together. Tabletop made to be lifted into upright position to provide a seat when not serving as a table. Really convertible furniture! American, 37-1/2" diam., this one c.1830s, but the form is much older. .... **$5,500+**

❖ NOTES ❖

Hutch – The "hutch" in hutch cupboard is probably from words in Middle English and Latin that mean "care, keeping, guard," and would therefore be related to a hutch in the sense of a storage chest or coffer, or a "box or box-like pen or 'house' in which an animal is confined." *Oxford English Dictionary*, or a hutch as a kneading trough for dough op cit. "Hutch" in hutch table is probably from other words, and is related to what the *OED* calls an "obsolete phonetic variant of hulch ... meaning hunched or humped, as in "hutch back." When the tabletop of a hutch table is in its vertical position, the already anthromorphic shape of the bench or chair underneath takes on a round-shouldered, even "hunch-backed" appearance. • *Huck.* – Mountain or Piedmond Virginians say to this day "huck," as in "huck table" or "huck chair."

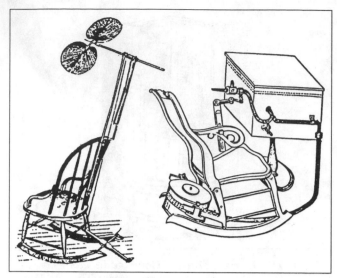

XVII-11. Rocking chair patents. (L) *"Fly Fan and Rocking Chair" pat'd. in 1899, by James T. Cowan, Boston, MA. Patent #622,123.* **(R)** *"Ventilating Rocking Chair," pat'd. Nov. 24, 1857, by D. Kahnweiler, Wilmington, DE. #18,696. It compressed air within the box to blow out on the hot rocker. Official Gazette. A new combination rocking chair & fan was patented about every seven years. Other combos included rocking chairs with churns, with cradles & even one that was also a trunk, and one that played music. The one on the left was actually made – I don't know how many were made, but it's safe to say they're scarce.* **$700+**

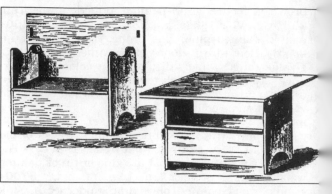

XVII-13. "A Useful Piece of Furniture." *"In many rural households, the space allotted to the kitchen is often cramped and narrowed too much. A piece of kitchen furniture that will answer three distinct purposes is a great convenience. Here is one that is at once a settee, trunk, and an ironing table or bake board. There is a box or trunk, in which one may stow away many things that usually lie about, having no special place otherwise. The lid of this trunk forms the seat of the settee. The ends are raised up, forming the arms. The back of it is pivoted upon one side of the ends, and when it is turned down it forms a table. When it is turned down, it is held in place by two small hooks."* American Agriculturist, Nov. 1874. *A vast number of these were made up through the 1950s to supply neo-Colonial decorative schemes.* **$250-$1,000**

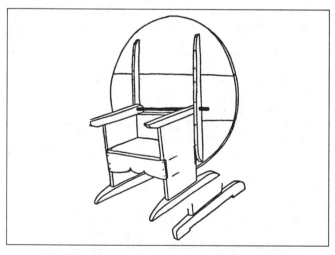

XVII-12. Hutch table. *Trestle-footed (with a foot variation shown next to it), with 3-board round top. Pin goes all the way across (shown in black here). Other hutch tables have other types of legs or feet, including, most rarely, four turned legs. They also have square, oblong or oval tops, though most are round. Some have storage in the seat, accessible through drawer or lifting lid. Many have two much shorter pivoting pins that don't go all the way across. The rarest, and oldest, were made from such huge trees that a single board, or at most two, was wide enough to make even a 50" top. Late 18th or very early 19th C.* **$2,000-$10,000+**

XVII-14. Kitchen lamps. (L) *The designation "kitchen lamp" is not commonly found in old ads, but the lamp at left, of an old type, was so named. The ad reads "Tin kitchen lamps. Strong, neat, well made, durable. Made by Geuder & Paeschke Mfg. Co. Tin Wares, Milwaukee, Wis."* The Metal Worker, Jan. 9, 1892. *Note horizontal cylindrical reservoir for fuel, with star on end, and the reflector that would put more light where it was needed. It could be set down on a work surface, even a shelf or windowsill, or hung on wall where needed.* **(R)** *"Jaxon" reflector lamp, "made from one piece of 7-gauge steel wire very strong and springy, complete with 7-inch bright tin reflector and 4-1/2-inch front, made for No. 2 burner. New and a ready seller."* In mail order catalog of Butler Brothers, 1899. *You will find some that were converted to electricity.* **$95-$125+**

Hutch table, pine & maple in original red stain, circular top above bench base, New England, 27"H x 45-1/4" diam. top, late 18th C. .... **$5,000+**

Jam cupboard, bootjack ends, 5 shelves with 2 doors, stripped exterior, alas, but possibly original light blue inside, American, 50"H, c.1890s-1910.. **$750+**

Kitchen cabinet – See the Hoosier-type cabinets above.

Kitchen tables – See Cupboard table; also Table.

Lamp, tin & glass, wall mounted reflector oil lamp, American, 1860s-70s. We tend to overlook lamps for the kitchen; ones like this were mounted above work tables, sink, and cook stove. Some have mirrored reflectors. .... **$125+**

Lamps, nickeled brass, double light, reflectors painted white inside, outside enameled dark green, reflector angled light down onto stove, and could be set on the hob shelves, Boston, MA (?), 18"H, c.1840s..................................... **$250+**

Meat safe, "a back porch piece" according to dealer, green painted wood, tall legs, 18 punctured tins in geometric design with rough side out, bottom of legs dipped in tar for setting in pans of water to keep ants out, brass catch on door, once had keyhole, iron catch inside, from New Berne, Craven County, NC, 71-1/2"H x 36-1/2"W x 26-1/2" deep, c.1830s to 1860. .... **$3,500+**

Meat safe hook, cast iron, long screw for beam or ceiling with curvy hook at bottom & cup in middle for bug deterring water (ever see a roach that couldn't swim an inch?), patented by Joseph C. Moulton as a "suspension hook & insect insulator," Fitchburg, MA, pat'd.. Oct. 28, 1859. You know what a cup hook looks like? That little piece that fits against the wood with the hook coming out of it? That's what this looks like, only much larger, and it's iron.................. **$35+**

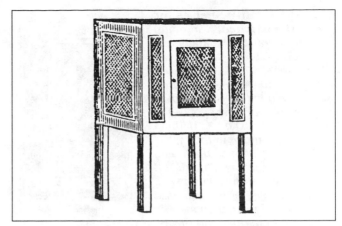

*XVII-16. **Meat safe.*** *Wood and wire, "to protect food from mice, insects, &c." Wood with wire gauze screens. No. 79 in list of kitchen requisites given in* American Home Cook Book, *by an American Lady. NYC: Dick & Fitzgerald, 1854. This would probably have almost no value unless something interesting had been done to the surface (carving or painting), or unless the iron wire gauze had rusted out and been replaced by homemade punctured tins, which may or may not have predated metal screening. Looks like a rabbit hutch!*

Milk cupboard, also called a milk or cheese safe, tall wooden case, square top, louvered sides and door, lined with thin muslin, central shaft or axle, around which revolve the 8 round shelves, for holding milk pans, meat or other food needing a safe, pat'd. by E. H. Nash, Westport, CT, about 50"H x 22" square, pat'd. July 27, 1858. .... **$250+**

Milk cupboard, wood with original mustard color paint, 6 shelves, open back & front for air circulation, prob. PA-European heritage, 70"H, 19th C. .... **$1,700+**

*XVII-17. **"Wooden Meat Screen,*** *lined with tin." Trestle feet with what appears to be casters. Note iron handle on right side for pulling it. The measurement is given as 3-ft., 9", but whether that is height or length I don't know. London dealers William S. Adams & Son, "Outfitters for Kitchens," advertised this in small booklet called* Francatelli's Cook's Guide Advertiser, *c.1860-61.*

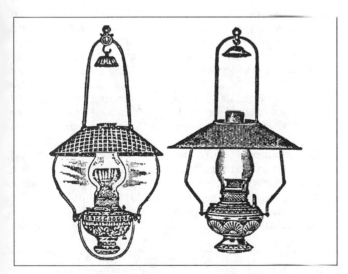

*XVII-15. **Suspension lamps,*** *suitable for many locations, including a kitchen.* **(L)** *"Pittsburgh' store or hall lamp, absolutely non-explosive. Burns over 10 hours without refilling." 20" diameter tin shade.* **(R)** *"Banner' store lamp, with extra feeder wick and oil drip cup on inside of tube to carry any overflow back to the wick." 20" tin shade, No. 3 burner, font wick and chimney." The second would have been nice for a kitchen, but probably only very rarely used for one, at least in a private home. Both also in* Butler Brothers *catalog, 1899.* **$150+**

XVII-18. "Milk Shelves for the Kitchen." *"In many farm-houses the kitchen is obliged to ... serve as the dairy, in which the milk is set, and the cream is kept, especially in the winter, when it is the warmest spot in the house. There is nothing objectionable in this, if the kitchen is kept scrupulously clean, and well ventilated. But a well-contrived cupboard, kept specially for the milk and cream, where they may be safe from dust and drafts,*

and yet have proper ventilation, will be a great advantage." This one is six-sided, and *"wide enough to hold two ten-quart pans across it, or four upon each shelf. This will be nearly or quite 3 feet outside measure. This will be ample for winter use, where ten cows are kept."* There's a center post that turns, having a pointed bottom that fits into a small socket in which is put some *"fine chips of soap, or a little powdered black lead."* Five round shelves are fixed to it. Under the shelves, which are rather close together, is space for two *"cream crocks,"* of stoneware. American Agriculturist, Dec. 1875.

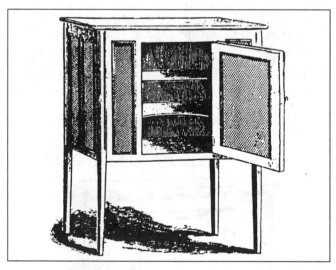

XVII-19. Meat safe. *Wood with wire screening. L. H. Mace catalog, 1880s. Value would depend on appearance, condition & finish.* **$100-$300+**

Milking stool, cast iron, 3 sproingy insect-like legs, doughnut seat with big hole in center, "E. A. Kaestner Co.," Baltimore, MD, 12"H, 19th or early 20th C. **$50**

❖ **NOTES** ❖

Punched & "Punctured – The adjective "punched" is slightly misleading. Pie safes have punctured holes in their "punched tins"; that is, the holes were punched [verb] all the way through. I feel there is a need to differentiate between punched and punctured because

the word **punched** is used specifically to describe a certain kind of tinsmith's decorative work, usually on coffee pots, where a punch [the tool] has been used to make a raised or pimply mark that could be used to make a textured design. A grater (of tin or brass, for example) can have both **punctured holes** and pierced holes or perforations. The latter two do not have the rough, ragged edge of a punctured hole. The tools used to punch and to puncture are different in that the former are used to make a mark and have a flattened or rounded tip, perhaps even one cast with a letter or symbol or other mark, and the latter must have a point sharp enough to go through the metal. Dealers, & authors of auction catalogs & articles describe the tins in pie safes as "punched." They also use "punched" when describing a kind of tin ware decoration where a punch is used to make a dimple or tiny bump. I will fly in the face of common and widely-accepted usage and use the slightly clumsy "punctured" in this book. I'm not really being stubborn about this, though I expect to get some pooh-pooh reaction. Part of my reason is based on the ease of retrieving exact information when searching the computer; part of it is to make clear what I mean, with no further explanation needed. I do not expect to change common usage, nor do I want you to think that only an ignoramus would say "punched tins." • For more on the tins, see separate short article at the end of this chapter.

Pie safe, almost Biedermeier or Empire in form, with paneled pilasters flanking the 2 doors, 2 drawers above, with keyholes, very short round feet, poss. cut down, 4 tins with punctured pattern of sort of fattened & straightened-out fylfot (pinwheels) & triangular corner spandrels, Southwest VA or East TN, mid 19th C. .... **$1,450+**

Pie safe, black painted wood, 2 drawers, 2 three tin doors with punctured 8 point stars & quarter-round spandrels in corners, latches on both doors, stenciled inside one drawer "J. Zitzer & Son, Furniture Dealer & Undertaker," West Alexandria, OH, late 19th C. .... **$1,000+**

Pie safe, folding, oak with wire screening, sides fold in half, patented but no legible mark, American, late 19th C. • Aaron Osborne, of Georgetown, CT, patented this July 5, 1881, "as a new article of manufacture, a provision-safe having its sides hinged, and adapted to fold together without being detached one from the other ... in combination with a collapsible body ... a board or stretcher adapted to fit within the body and to hold the same in an expanded condition. ..." .... **$650+**

❖ **NOTES** ❖

Cold Basement. An 1891 *Ladies' Home Journal* ad reads: "Mother wants it. Wright's Kitchen Safe, Refrigerator and dumb Waiter combined or separate. Can be instantly lowered into cellar from any part of room floor. – Cochran Safe Co., Cochran, IN."

Pie safe, green painted wood, 12 tins, 3 on each side, 3 on both doors, punctured holes & slits, depicting footed bowls with tulips, from MD (?), 42-3/4"W, c.1860s. **$2,000**

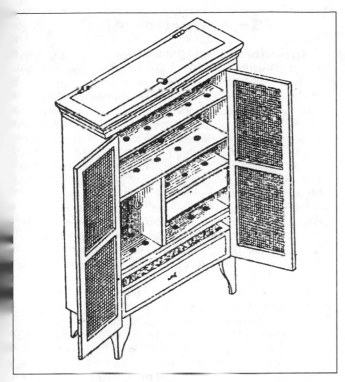

XVII-20. "Insect-proof Closet & Safe" patent. Pat'd. Aug. 30, 1881, by Charles H. Larrabee, Napa City, CA, assignor to Hamilton W. Crabb, same place. Bottom drawer serves as a "water-containing tank." Holes served to circulate air from shelf to shelf. Official Gazette. **$100-$200**

Pie safe, low counter height cupboard, short bracket feet, one shelf, 2 doors with single oblong punctured tin in each door, double repeat pattern of 6-point flower in circle with 6 bull's eyes in each door, PA, 40"H x 54"W, mid to late 19th C............... **$1,250+**

Pie safe, painted wood, 8 tins, 2 on each side, 2 in each door, long drawer at bottom, long straight legs, simple punctured geometric design, marked "John M. Smythe Co.," Chicago, IL, c.1890s-1910....... **$700+**

Pie safe, painted wood case in dark greenish black, scalloped apron, interesting long legs with 2 turned bands slightly thicker than legs, flat top, one central door with odd old hardware, screen & mesh panel openings framed with molding – 6 in door, 3 flanking each side of door, almost looks like some kind of hutch or bird cage, but no place for feeding the animals, American, 52"H x 39-1/2"W x 17-1/2" diam., mid 19th C. • NYC's Ricco-Johnson Gallery, which often comes up with interesting folk art pieces, had this for sale in early 1984. Value is mine, based on the strong folk art appeal of this piece....... **$5,500+**

Pie safe, painted wood frame, hangs from beams – the corner pieces project above the top about 5", and have fairly large holes so that they'd be easy to lift up onto nails driven in the beams, sides & front with slit pierced tin panels, single door, 5-point stars or 6-point petals within circles, very free & graphic, perhaps Lancaster, PA, mid 19th C. .... **$1,200+**

Pie safe, pine, 12 panels of punctured tin in front & sides, unexceptional concentric circles, etc., geometric pattern, 2 doors, American, 58"H x 37"W, late 19th C or early 20th C. **$750**

XVII-21. Sideboard & provision safe. Wood (probably poplar) with punctured tin panels for decoration & ventilation. Sideboard is 4ft., 6"H x 3ft., 1"W x 1ft., 2" deep. "Tin provision safe" is 4ft., 9"H x 2ft., 6" W x 1ft., 2-1/2" deep. Bagby & Rivers, Baltimore, 1882 catalog. Baltimore, by the way, is still famous for painted window & house door screens, usually a form of rural landscape with a pond & swans. These paintings do not obstruct the vision from the inside looking out, but serve both to decorate the outside, and to a small extent, make less visible the interior. I have never seen a pie safe with painted screening in its doors or sides. However, the hardware company, John Duer & Sons, of Baltimore, offered two interesting things in their 1878 catalog: (1) "wire cloth" with a printed design of a stylized 4-petal flower surrounded by an abstract pattern resembling basketweave. Offered in "green, or plain colors," and (2) "punched tin," 10" x 14", in the "Baltimore pattern," similar to **G** shown in picture XVII-24, except that it has 3 lobes on each side. Duer was the "Sole Manufacturers of this pattern." The pattern shown in these Bagby & Rivers cabinets looks quite similar also, except the diamond is more attentuated. **$400-$1,400+**

❖ NOTES ❖

Wythe or wythout – Because of scholarship that's been done on regional pie safes, you shouldn't say only "American" now. Try to locate Roddy Moore's well-illustrated "Wythe County, Virginia, punched tin: its influence and imitators," *The magazine ANTIQUES*, Sept. 1984. I can't make a more complete study myself, and urge you to read everything you can before plunking down big money. Fine Wythe County safes deserve praise, and Moore's article gave them added cachet, translating to much increased prices. • An urn of the type frequently seen in Wythe County pieces has a nice rounded bowl body, flared stem, pedestal base, & two vertical handles, and is sometimes called a chalice. I recently saw a graphite drawing of what I would have thought was a cast iron or stone urn, with several doves drinking from it or flying about it, and the dealer described it as "doves and chalice," which somehow seems to have a much more religious context than a simple garden scene with an "urn" would have. • Pennsylvania and Ohio pie safes are also avidly collected.

Pie safe, pine, 12 panels of punctured tins, front & sides, stars & crescent moons, 2 door, American, 55"H, late 19th C. .... **$1,200+**

Pie safe, pine, 3 punctured tin panels on each side & 3 panels on both front doors, whirligig design with quarter-circle spandrels (designs filling each corner of tins), 3 shelves, clean & not refinished, 4 legs all in good condition at bottom, not rat chewed or water rotted, American, 47"H, mid to late 19th C. .... **$1,500+**

❖ NOTES ❖

To Get Rid of Ants – Wash the shelves with salt and water; sprinkle salt in their paths. To keep them out of safes: Set the legs of the safe on tin cups; keep the cups filled with water." Mrs. A. P. Hill, *Mrs. Hill's New Family Receipt Book*, NY: 1867, 1870.• "If ants are troublesome, set legs in cups of water." Catherine Beecher & Harriet Beecher Stowe, *American Woman's Home*, 1869. (See the Meat safe hook above.)

Pie safe, pine, 6 punctured tins, star designs on doors only, wood on sides, 4 very long legs, 2 shelves, American, 50"H, mid to late 19th C. **$850**

Pie safe, red painted wood, 12 tins, 3 on each side, 3 on both doors, punctured petaled-flower design adapted to fit rectangular shape (sometimes called a butterfly pattern), white porcelain knobs (could be original or not), southern IL, mid 19th C. .... **$1,200-$1,800**

Pie safe, red-stained sycamore & maple, straight case with medium-length legs, long single drawer at bot-

XVII-22. Pie safe. *It is not upside down; it's meant to be bolted or hung from rafters. Painted wood case with punctured tins on all four sides, larger than most. Three shelves inside. Front door has flower-stars in the corners to match the center; the sides have fan-shaped, rayed spandrels in the corners. 34"H x 36"W x 22" deep. Ex-collection of Earl F. & Ada F. Robacker, auctioned by T. Glenn Horst, Horst Auctions, Farmersville, Lancaster County, PA, on June 23-24, 1989. Price realized was very low – $475, but apparently other examples of this safe exist.* **$450-$650**

Reproduction Alert

Reproduction or Fake Tins – Beware the faked country-look tins. An old pine safe can be stripped of its old tins, then be gussied up with distressed tin pierced with valuable eagle, animal, flag, human forms. I saw such a one the summer of 1987 in Charlottesville. The body was old, nice long legs and small 2 shelf box, with 4 front panels and 2 on each side. The tins had coffee cups, forks, spoons, dogs, birds, flowers ... just too too TOO. Over it all was a layer of what looked like old blue milk paint, scratched and distressed. The price of $1,800 was high enough to almost seem OK, but too low if this were for real. You must develop a sixth sense about the look of the tins. Newly-made punctured tins have been used to make an old all-wood cupboard into a more desirable pie safe; they have also been used to replace very simple designs with designs that seem folk art-y and unique. Beware especially of any pie safe with figural or zoomorphic, or pictorial tins, such as men in stovepipe hats, forks and spoons, cows, pigs, dogs, flags, and eagles. Know your dealer, ask about provenance, inspect tins carefully on both sides with a magnifying glass. For people who want to make their modern kitchen cupboards into mini pie safes, new punctured tin panels may save some trouble. Look online for sources.

---

tom, overhanging board top, 2 interesting doors, each with 3 punctured tins in design of clock face with Arabic numerals & curved horn, the time reading 12 minutes to 12 on each one, crescent moons in corners, dealers have called such designs "New Year" tins, maybe OH, late 19th or early 20th C. • Dealers Tim & Barb Martien, Western Reserve Antiques, Burton, OH, had this for sale in 1984. Value mine. **$3,200**

Pie safe, red stained wood, turned feet but straight case and board top, 2 large doors with single tin panel each, punctured with characteristic urn with ear handles & tall multi-stemmed tulip design, star spandrels in corners, side panels punctured too, southwestern VA, classic Wythe County design, mid 19th C. .... **$2,500+**

Pie safe, refinished wood, alas, straight-sided case with turned feet, flat board top, 2 large doors with single large tin on each, punctured as if with 4 panels each, centered pinwheels (fylfot), round spandrels in corners, keyhole in door, Wythe County, VA, 54"W, late 19th C. • Refinished wood reduces value of pie safes. .... **$800+**

Pie safe, simple wooden case with straight medium-length legs, molded top, fancy scalloped apron or skirt, 2 doors, each with 2 punctured tins, design an 8 petaled flower within circle, 2 shelves, 2 drawers at top with wooden knobs, PA (?), early to mid 19th C. .... **$1,250+**

Pie safe, tall elegant piece, dark varnish, with molded cornice, 2 doors, each with one square tin in center

Reproduction Alert

Reproduction Pie Safes. Not only the tins are reproduced. There are also cabinet-makers producing distressed, worn-looking pie safes with marring and scratches and scrubbed-off paint to simulate antiques. Most of these have at least two layers of paint, with the outer layer scumbled and rubbed to reveal the one underneath. Some makers use old-fashioned milk paint. Popular colors include dark barn reds, ochres & mustard yellows, soft greens, blues, gray, black, and cream. One company has been making repro pie safes for over 25 years, adding even more to the possibility that someone will be fooled.

with punctured rectangular tins above & below, bull's eye (one in square, 2 in rectangles) framed with quarter- & half-round spandrels, plus 6 narrow oblong punctured tins in panels flanking doors, in ad of Georgia dealer, perhaps GA provenance, about 80" to 90"H, late 19th C. .... **$2,000+**

Pie safe, tall simple wood case, flat board top, straight legs, long drawer across top, 2 doors, each with 3 tins, punctured design of a footed sugar bowl with ear handles & domed lid with large round finial & footed cream jug, both with concentric rings forming body, the decoration making you think this might be a cupboard for dairy products, a cheese or butter safe, found in Arkansas, late 19th or early 20th C. • Dealer Joan Gould, Summer Kitchen Antiques of Little Rock, said another in this pattern was found in Arkansas. At $595 in 1984, it seemed way under the money... **$2,750+**

❖ NOTES ❖

Butter cupboards – According to Carl W. Drepperd's *A Dictionary of American Antiques*, the butter cupboard dating to 15th century England or the Continent, was for storing butter or cheese. Made entirely of oak (or other woods), they had pierced doors for air circulation. In *Primer of American Antiques*, Drepperd said that pie safes or butter cupboards were known in 17th century America, and probably were first offered as a commercial product in the 1880s. Related are the meat safe or meat keep, and the French gard-manger. • An antique store in NYC advertised in 1993 a 19th century "Chinese Provincial" kitchen cabinet of "pine." Just over 6 feet high, it stands on 4 long legs, and has an airy compartment with carved fretwork doors; three drawers above that; and another compartment with fretwork doors. It's strange to see our pie safes in another guise! • In 2002, I saw a **food safe from France** in a dealer's booth filled with otherwise American primitives. It was in two parts: on a stand of four square-post legs was a heavy woven-wire boxy piece with a latched door and shelves inside. On top of that was a slightly smaller boxy upper part with door and shelves. The wire was very thick, and had been painted and repainted in creamy white paint a number of times. It was wonderful.

❖ NOTES ❖

"A **closet, called a safe,** for keeping food in the cellar, is an important convenience for keeping meat, milk, bread and various articles in daily use." Mrs. Cornelius, *The Young Housekeepers Friend*, or, *A Guide to Domestic Economy & Comfort*, Boston & NY: 1846

Pie safe, varnished pine, straight board top, straight simple case & medium length legs, single drawer below cupboard, 2 doors with 3 punctured tins, design of each is a 5 point star within circle, plus 4 smaller stars around circle, smallest star within big star, with 3 straight rows of holes for border, Colorado, 55-1/8"H, c.1875. • Described from picture of one in collection of the State Historical Society of Colorado. The value range is mine, not the Society's... **$1,200-$1,500**

Pie safe, walnut, 12 tins with tulip & vase (or basket) design, 2 shelves, 2 drawers, short turned wooden legs, not refinished but cleaned up, simple iron latch, American, poss. PA (?), 54"H, mid 19th C. Walnut is a cachet wood............................. **$2,500+**

Pie safe, walnut & poplar, straight case with flat board top, shortish straight legs, long dovetailed drawer across top, 2 three tin doors, punctured design of many petaled flower or butterfly, in horizontal rect angles, poss. from the South, or IL, mid 19th C. **$2,200**

Pie safe, wood with traces of green paint, 2 shelves above double drawers, 2 doors with 3 punctured tin panels, base constructed of cutout boards instead of legs, American, 53"H x 40"W, mid to late 19th C. .... **$800+**

Portable pantries – See Chapter VII (Storage)

Shelf paper, various patterns & colors, also shelf edge papers printed, scalloped, pleated, or lace. All these are collectible, if unnoticed to this time, and nothing adds a more authentic touch to a shelf with a collection of 1920s or 30s or 40s gadgets and implements than authentic shelf paper, or at least edge papers, thumb-tacked neatly in place with colored tacks. 1910s to 1950s. (Another thing to do, which I did for my 1870's cupboard, is to cut fancy-edge shelf border strips from colorful comic strip newspaper section.)..................................... **$2-$8+**

❖ NOTES ❖

Yo, Bounty! – "The uses of paper in the home are not so many. Shelving in the pantry or kitchen can be kept in renewed health with paper laces. The bungalow, motor trip or picnic can well be supplied with paper or fibre plates. Rather would we warn you against paper uses; such as wrapping up your ice to preserve it, for it doesn't; wrapping up your food stuff in paper in refrigerator; greasing muffin pans with paper, for which you should use a brush. Sometimes, however, a piece of paper will clean off the top of the stove very efficiently, yet even here a brush would be far better. Clean brown paper to absorb French fried potatoes is quite indispensable. The paper napkin has made its place even in the homes of wealth. Wax paper is a delight to wrap up sandwiches and keep bread-stuffs and cakes fresh for touring or picnics. Paper lining for drawers is necessary. The pretty paper lace doily for under finger bowls, cake and bread is delightfully pretty and saves the linen, the laundress and the laundry list." Ethel R. Peyser, "Tinware, Rubber and Paper for the Kitchen," *House & Garden*, June 1922.

Shopping list aid, also called a daily reminder or household reminder, tin, lithographed in blue & white with flowers, flat oblong device, with tabs along left & right sides that are pulled out to mark those things on the printed lists to be bought, such as Rice & Sago, Lemons, Blacking, Oatmeal or Wash Blue, named "The Housekeeper's Friend," this one prob. European, c.1908. .... **$35+**

Shopping list aid, lithographed cardboard, adv'g. "Doe-Wah-Jack" stoves, c.1890s-1910. .... **$35+**

Shopping list aid, paper, meant for a Hoosier cabinet & marked "Hoosier," early 20th C. .... **$35+**

Shopping list aid, plastic disc with tiny blue plastic knobs to indicate which of the many things printed around the circumference are needed, adv'g. "Watkins Awning & Sign Co., Farmville, VA," maker name not shown, 3-3/8" diameter not counting little knobs, c.1948. .... **$25+**

XVII-24. Convertible step ladders. (T-L &-R) *Folding step ladder chair, shown in both positions, were manufactured by Tucker & Dorsey Mfg. Co., Indianapolis, who made all kinds of woodenwares including ironing boards and pastry boards. Advertised in* The Metal Worker, *June 21, 1890. Same linecuts used in 1909 Albert Pick wholesale catalog, advertised as "solid and substantial; it is a good hall chair. As a step ladder it is heavy enough to be used wihtout danger of upsetting. Finished in oak."* **(B)** *Called "utility steps" in F. A. Walker wholesale catalog, Boston, 1870s. Instead of folding, the steps slid under the stool. Finish and condition account for value.* **$40-$125+**

Step stool or folding stool, painted wood, 3 steps, slightly cutout step shape, very attractive, American, about 1910-1920. .... **$15+**

❖ NOTES ❖

Work Perch – One offspring of the new style of kitchen work was the kitchen stool, with or without a back, but always with a rung or footrest, which could be pulled up to the desk-like cabinet table, affording the housewife a comfortable seat while she worked. It was claimed, of course, that from one spot the housewife could reach everything she needed without the trudgery of walking all over the kitchen to do something like make an apple pie! Some cabinet companies also made stools, and some were combo stepladders & stools. Most:$15-$65

• • • •

Celebrity Silliness – In the middle 1980s, a For Sale ad appeared in a collector newspaper for a "Folding

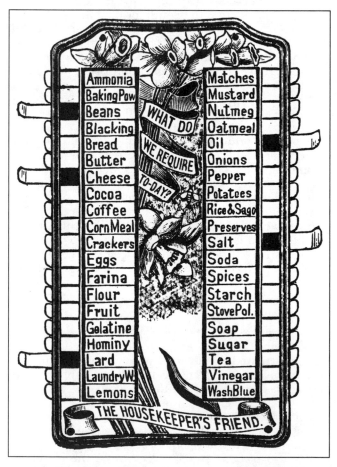

XVII-23. Shopping list aid or reminder. *"The Housekeeper's Friend." Probably printed celluloid. Advertised by wholesale importer G. M. Thurnauer & Brother who supplied kitchenwares to the trade. The NYC firm imported from Germany and France. Ad in* House Furnishing Review, *Nov. 1909.* **$35+**

kitchen stool used by James Dean before his movie fame; from Fairmount, IN. personal friend. Offers considered, collectors only." I don't know what eventually happened, but this is an example of the Absurd Rub-Off Theory of Collectible Objects which is behind the very high prices of things once belonging to a famous person. Andy Warhol's cookie jars went for 10 times market price, and it's quite possible he never even touched them, merely pointed to them before buying. When James Beard's cookbooks were auctioned, the auction house glued in cheapo copies of his bookplate, despite the fact that Beard himself had chosen to put bookplates in very few books. (At that sale, a box of tatty old dirty bowties sold for hundreds of smackeroos.) While fabulous prices are being paid for Van Gogh's and Picasso's and Frank Stella's paintings, works that were actually created by and intimately touched by the masters, objects supposed to have been touched by, or known to have been owned by, famous people who had nothing to do with the objects' creation, are selling for outrageous prices. Auras don't rub off.

Table and 4 chairs, enamelware top, drop leaf & extension, nice geometric or abstract floral design on top in red or black, American, c.1910-1940s. • These have gone up greatly in popularity. Sets, with four kitchen chairs and a table (often without extension leaves), varnished or painted in snowy white, show up at every big antique show and sell for many hundreds of dollars. They are in with the modern & Deco stuff at the big shows in NYC. .... **$400-$1,500+**

Table, birch with single wide birch plank top, 2 side drawers, turned legs, late 19th C, Memphis, TN, 28-7/8"H x 59-1/2"L x 30"W, c.1890s-1910. • My Franklin grandfather worked for a lumber mill in Memphis, calculating board feet from standing trees, and he had this table made with an extraordinarily wide single plank top just shy of 1" thick. Unfortunately refinished – with colored stain over what was a won-

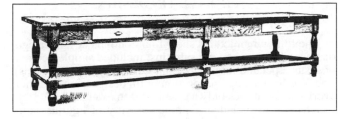

XVII-25. Cooks' Table. *Meant for hotel or restaurant kitchen, but could have been used in large household kitchen. "Securely and neatly constructed of natural wood, resting on heavy turned legs, with dish shelf below. Tops are of three strips, tongued and grooved, leaded and securely bolted together. Tables up to 8' in length have one drawer and four legs; those 10ft. to 16ft. have two drawers and three sets of legs. Came in choice of 3 widths – 30", 36", and 42", and in 8 lengths – 5ft., 6ft., 7ft., 8ft., 10ft., 12ft., 14ft., and 16ft. L. Catalog of S. B. Sexton Stove & Mfg. Co., Baltimore, c.1930s.* **$400-$1,200+**

derful scrubbed finish. De-valued by refinishing.. **$400+**

Table, wide plank pine drop-leaf top, turned sturdy legs, pull out bread boards each end, with utility drawers for implements at each end. At each end of this tea-cake-for-two working table is a big possum belly flour or meal bin. All drawers, including bins, have single cast iron dog's head pull, American, c.1880 to 1900. • The **dog's head pulls** are what give this table that extra punch & even crossover value to dog collectors. .... **$850+**

Table, child's, wood with blue & white porcelainized top, American, early 20th C......................... **$250+**

Table, drop leaf, green paint, very deep overhang at ends, American, 36"L, mid 19th C. .... **$200+**

FOR MORE INFORMATION

"HOOSIER"-TYPE CABINETS

See also the plating resources at the end of Chapter XV.

Philip Kennedy Hardware, Inc.

Philip D. Kennedy wrote the book on Hoosiers.

10655 Andrade Drive
Zionsville, IN 46077
Phone (317) 873-1316
E-mail: philken@kennedyhardware.com
Web site: www.hoosiercabinets.com/

EFFICIENCY & HOUSEWORK

There are several Web sites related to these subjects. They'll give you a historic overview that may focus on society at large or on women and housekeeping. Do a Google search with key words.

Iowa State University
www.public.iastate.edu/~history/380hoec.htm

Web sites devoted to the subject of the Gilbreths, early time and motion experts; & Frederick Winslow Taylor, early management-efficiency expert.

Gilbreths
Material on this Web site was prepared by the staff of the Business Library at the University of Western Ontario. Links to many books.
www.lib.uwo.ca/business/gilbreths.html

The Gilbreth Network
This site coordinated by David Ferguson.
http://gilbrethnetwork.tripod.com/front.html

THE SCIENCE OF WORK

This Access Tucson site outlines differences in Gilbreths' & Taylor's work.
http://access.tucson.org/~michael/g_1.html

PIE SAFE TIN DESIGNS
Filling Empty Rectangles with Patterns

The following pictures show four common design categories used for punched pie safe tins, included simple geometrics, stars, petaled-flower-like shapes, and fylfot (pinwheels). The four form a large proportion of tin designs, but this short overviews describes only a couple dozen examples.

I have also included a single category of figurals—urn-and-flower designs (XVII-36)—although many more figurals are to be found, including horsemen, chickens, and cups and saucers. The urn-and-flowers are included because of Wytheville-area safes, which are at the time of writing the only ones to have been written about in a scholarly way (Roddy Moore, "Wythe County, Virginia, punched tin: its influence and imitators," The Magazine ANTIQUES, September, 1984), and they are advertised rather frequently.

Before I began collecting and arranging pictures by pattern type, I theorized that the obvious similarities to other repeating geometric patterns were meaningful rather than coincidental, even to the extent that comparison would prove that pie safe tin punchers copied their designs from something previously existing. I assumed that such post hoc likenesses would become expecially evident when pie safe designs were compared with quilts and jacquard coverlets. I thought that I would be able therefore to offer names for the designs, based on established quilt design names.

This turne dout to be impossible, except in the most simplistic way, matching a star to a star, for example. I was surprised and pleased to find close similarities between stitch-like slits and holes and quilting stitches (which subtly overlay more easily visible pieces, patches or appliqués, and hold batting or lining in place)—especially in fan and petal motifs.

Although both quilters and tin-punchers were concerned with filling up squares or rectangles with patterns, the methods involved in ventilating a sheet of tin and making a quilt are very different. Tin-punchers break up the surface of a square or oblong blank with rounded or angular shapes defined by holes or slits. Quilters assemble a whole by fitting cut shapes, most of which are straight-edged and angular, together.

XVII-26. "Perforated plate for kitchen-safes" patent.
Pat'd Nov. 11, 1884, by George W. Knapp, Baltimore, MD. No. 307,959, Knapp's claim was for "The method of ornamenting perforated plates for safes, consisting in first applying a colored design to a surface of the plate, and then making the ventilating-perforations with respect to the features of the said colored design, and producing on the same surface a burr projecting about each perforation, so located as to avoid marring the said colored design." Official Gazette. (I've seen only one pie safe with the punctured tins painted in other than the same or contrasting color to the case—not that the idea is odd. That was Pl. VIII, a pie safe from Tennessee, in the 1984 article by Roddy Moore, ANTIQUES magazine.) If it were ever made, value dependent upon patina and original polychromed tins. **$500 - $900+**

The elements of geometric designs include circles, diamonds, triangles, squares, and lines, which may be connected or not (i.e., may be parallel or divergent/convergent, such as rays). Petals and pie wedges are formed by combining triangles and circles. All geometric designs, and parts of figural ones, can be laid out with tools no more complex than a pair of dividers, probably found in nearly every nineteenth-century homeowner's toolbox, a straight-edge of some kind, and a scribe or pencil. Fan-shaped spandrels filling the corners of so many tins are easy to do with a compass or dividers. One point is placed at the corner, the other leg is adjusted, and a curve is lightly scratched onto the tin, to be traced with holes.

The several tins of one pie safe may be so alike that you know a tracing of some kind was done. One way would be with a set of cutout tin templates like those for making identical multiple quilt pieces. Another way would be to use heavy paper, rubbed with powdered graphite on the side against the tin, with the design on top traced again and again. Although each tin has the same overall design, all were executed individually, and have obvious differences in measurement or placement.

Probably a majority of geometric designs are a consequence of the tools used and the given shape of the tins, as well as the need to make the tin function as a ventilated screen. For corroborating evidence, look at wood-frame footwarmers with tin sides punctured for ventilation. A motif vocabulary of 5-, 6-, or 8-point stars, hearts, and stylized geometric flowers was available to most people, no matter whether they were making blanket chests, fraktur, candlewick spreads, pie safes, or quilts, but each motif may or may not have any special meaning for its user. In other words, it may be subjective and hence figural, or it may be a pleasing gap-filler. A start may be patriotic or heavenly, or it may be there because it could be made to fit an empty space, or simply because it was easy to do by means of a tool. Not every artisan is an "artist" also.

Generally speaking most pie safe tin designs, like patterns filling any empty rectangles or squares, are not culture-specific, but are found on ancient tiles, pattern glass, Amerindian as well as Persian rugs, and architectural friezes from Abyssinia to China.

It is arguable that some pie safe tin designs are expanded doodles! Flipping through my old high school notebooks, I see page corners and blank spaces filled with pattern-making dots, lines, triangles, circles, fan, tendrils, and even fylfot-like squiggles.

The more figural designs are in a way culture-specific, although more than one culture may claim such figures as hearts, tulips, lilies, grapes, urns, horses, etc., and probably would assign different symbolic meaning to them (just as they do the simpler geometrics).

By conducting this small survey and studying quilt books throughout, I've learned that when comparing different classes of objects, <u>similarity of final appearance does not prove similitude of intent or technique.</u> Patterns of some pie safe tins and some quilts may be strikingly similar when the two are viewed together, but it's sophistry to therefore assume that one was a model and the other a copy. Instead, it seems more nearly true to say that all decorative arts draw on a large but nevertheless finite "dictionary" of design elements.

NOTE: All drawings here are of pie safe tins, and were done by me as photo-tracings or from actual safes. The former are generally more accurate, although often the perspective is very slightly skewed off from a perfect rectangle, and occasionally the photo may have misled me with small shadows or scratches. I've used dashes)- ===_ for slits or slots, and dots, big or little *==== for nail holes or other basically round holes. An X represents crossed slits in the original. All dealer or collector sources are noted in individual captions.

Portable pantries—See Chapter VII

XVII-27. Pie Safe Tins: *Simple Geometrics. (L) to (R), top row then bottom.* **(A)** *Calico Cat Antiques, Ann & Dick Wardrop, Wexford, PA, (8), shaped apron, [Ohio] Antique Review, May, 1990.* **(B)** *Loy's Auction Sales, Kernsville, NC, Jean Craddock photo, (4), 2 drawers above doors, AntiqueWeek, March 27, 1989.* **(C)** *Vicki & Bruce Waasdorp, Clarence, NY, (6), long drawer below doors, long legs. New York-Pennsylvania Collector, November 1989.* **(D)** *Robb & Alice Guss, Youngsville, NY (8), cupboard has shaped apron, very short legs, Antiques & Arts Weekly, July 20, 1984.* **(E)** *In "Antiques in Dutchland," by Earl & Ada Robacker, Pennsylvania Folklife, Fall 1961. (6), shallow drawer beneath doors, long legs.* **(F)** *Made by John Rickey of Hammersville, OH, Garth's Auctions, Inc., Delaware, OH, Ron Klapmeir Sale Plus Additions, November 25 26, 1988, (6), step back cupboard, with tins for upper doors, [Ohio] Antique Review, January, 1984.* **(G)** *Sheppheards, Schellsburg, PA, (6), drawer below doors [Ohio] Antique Review, October 1990.* **(H)** *Collection of John Little Jr., Fig 23 in article by Roddy Moore, from Sullivan County, TN, (8), Empire style 1840-60 cupboard with four tins on both of two doors in lower part of cupboard. A full circle is formed in the center of each door by the conjunction of four spandrels. The tins are not divided by wood molding or framework. The elongated hexagonal design in the center of each of the 8 tins are marked in the sort of diapered, or diamond, pattern formed with parallel lines of holes. This was a very popular filler pattern for cut glass and later pressed glass. The magazine ANTIQUES, September 1984.*

XVII-28. Pie Safe Tins: Stars. *(L) to (R) from top:* **(A)** *Tim Martien, Burton, OH, (4), Odd cupboard/safe with top*

half having 2 doors with the tins, divided from lower half by drawer. Lower half was wood paneled doors. Each side has 4 stacked tins over single wood panel. Thought to be from Tennessee. [Ohio] Antique Review, clipping not dated. **(B)** *Antique Associates, at West Townsend & Joslin Tavern (group shop), (8), 70"H cupboard, 4 over 4, with long drawer in middle, between 2 sets of doors. New York Pennsylvania Collector, May, 1990.* **(C)** *Muleskinner, Clarence, NY (6), long drawer under 2 doors. Maine Antique Digest, August, 1989.* **(D)** *Collection State Historical Society of Colorado, (6), very shallow drawer below 2 doors. Sides not tinned. Unidentified clipping, probably from the magazine ANTIQUES.* **(E)** *Labeled inside "J. Zitzer & Son, Furniture Dealer and Undertaker, West Alexandria, Ohio." Ohio collector's consignment to Garth's Auctions, Inc., Delaware, OH, January 6, 1984 sale. (6), long drawer under 2 doors. [Ohio] Antique Review, February 1984.* **(F)** *The Blue Door, Mudge Saver, Sunbury, OH, (6), drawer above 2 doors. [Ohio] Antique review, October 1990. NOTE: Charles A. Muller, the editor of the [Ohio] Antique Review (name was changed to Antique Review in the mid-1980s), is knowledgeable about pie safes himself, and his collector paper has the most pie safe ads of any. Perhaps this is because the majority of pie safes seem to come from the Midwest.*

XVII-29. Pie Safe Tins: Pinwheels or Fylfots. *(L) to (R) from top:* **(A)** *Thomas C. Queen, (3), this is actually a sideboard with 3 doors side by side. From Lee County, VA, c.1859. Maine Antique Digest, undated clip.* **(B)** *Wiltshire Antiques, Milford, OH, (8), 2 drawers above 2 doors, shallow shaped apron, tapered legs. [Ohio] Antique Review, April 1986.* **(C)** *Kenneth W. Farmer auction, each with 4 tins not divided by molding or framework. [Ohio] Antique Review, April 1985.* **(D)** *Mary Mac & Robert Franklin, VA (6), short turned legs, found in central VA.* **(E)** *Muleskinner, Ronald Korman, prop., Clarence, NY, (4) long drawer under 2 doors, tall turned legs, believed to be of Southern origin. Maine Antique Digest, April 1987.*

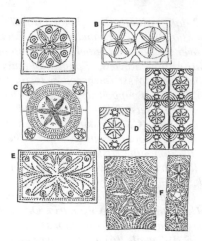

XVII-30. Pie Safe Tins: Petals, Flowers, Butterfly. *(L) to (R) from top: (A) Belmont Antiques, Belmont, VT, (4), low, bracket-foot cupboard with 2 almost square tins on both of 2 doors, the tins not divided by molding or framework. Pennsylvania origin. Unidentified clipping, probably from New York-Pennsylvania Collector. (B) Private collector, Long Beach, CA (6) short legged cupboard with exceptionally oblong tins, 3 on each door. Wonderful use of doubled design to fill otherwise awkward space. Safe found in Michigan. (C) Ex-Collection Earl F. & Ada F. Robacker. (1), single large panel on front of wall or rafter-hung safe, which probably has tins on other 3 sides also. Two oblong sheets of tin are joined along the horizontal axis to form one outside tin about 3-1/2 feet wide. From Pennsylvania Folklife, Spring 1961. Next is a design very similar to (A) and (C), in the Bybee Collection, in the von Rosenberg kitchen, at Round Top, TX. (D) Charles Gerhardt Antiques, Lebanon, OH, (10), but arranged in what may be a unique fashion—with 4-1/2 panels on each of 2 doors. See the larger drawing at the right that shows how the parts are assembled. [Ohio] Antique Review, January 1990. (E) Dogwood Antiques, Sparta, TN, (6), shallow drawer above 2 doors. Unidentified clipping, possibly Mid-Atlantic Antiques, or Antiques Gazette. (F) Gus Knapp, Hudson, OH, (3), large hanging safe with large tin on door and a narrower panel (with a star in the center) on either side. Undated [Ohio] Antique Review clipping.*

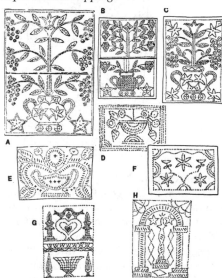

XVII-31. Pie Safe Tins: *Urns, Flowers, Columns. Virginia, Pennsylvania, and possibly Ohio safes. The first three drawings are beautiful examples of classic Wythe County area urn & flower or urn & grape designs, with stars (or starflowers). Here the stars are separate from the stems; in some similar*

examples, pinwheels or stars may take the place of some of the grapes or flowers. Sometimes hearts take the place of or are used along with stars, grapes, or flowers. In the lower, and sometimes upper corners, one finds stars, pinwheels, flowers, or columns resembling candles, which may relate to the Fraternal Order of Masons. One constant, in all the examples I saw but one, is that the vertical stalk/stem is made with 3 lines, possibly signifying the Trinity. (A) From article about Roddy Moore's research into Southwest VA and East TN safes, prior to the ANTIQUES article. Antique Gazette, March 1984. (B) Just Us, J & S. Schneider, Tucson, AZ, (4), 2 doors with 2 short drawers above, short turned legs. Wythe County area. The 2 tins on each door are joined (and obviously not lined up) horizontally across center, with no molding or framework. Note diapered checker design inside urn. Maine Antique Digest, October 1984. (C) Kenneth Farmer auctioneer, Radford, VA, Feburary 2, 1985 sale. (4 tins joined to make 2), with side panels. Wythe County area. This is a drawing of the side tin, showing the star flowers; interior decoration of the urn is the same. Note how the "kite"-like shapes attached to the lower part of the flowers resemble those in the upper part of the urn/vase in (A). Main Antique Digest, April 1985. (D) Don and Janie Noyes, Glenford, OH. (6), a stepback cupboard, extremely severe case design, lower part being a lift-top chest. Tins set into 2 upper doors. Probably Pennsylvania. Maine Antique Digest, March 1986. (E) Leland Schmidt, Rockford, IL, number of tins not shown, possibly (6), unidentified clipping, New York-Pennsylvania Collector, or [Ohio] Antique Review. (F) Carol Ann & Ed Mathias, Bexley, OH, (6), [Ohio] Antique Review, June 1988. (G) Collection of Carl & DeEtta Pace, fig. 16 in Moore's ANTIQUES article. (2), long drawer above 2 doors. Depiction of footed compote, possibly meant to represent on in pressed glass. Garlands, lovebirds, hearts, a diamond, 2 candles and 2 trees resembling Cedars of Lebanon complete the striking design. The magazine ANTIQUES, September 1984. (H). K & K Antiques, Springfield, OH. (8), 4 tins joined without molding or framework to create effect of one large tin for each door. Short turned legs, sideboard type of safe with low gallery backplate on side & back of the top. Siever County, TN origin. Maine Antique Digest, April 1989.

XVII-32. Pie Safe Case Types. *Showing fronts only; many, even most, pie safes also have tins on the side. (L) to (R) from top: (A) Four tins in 2 doors, tins separated by framework (or molding), with 2 drawers above doors, short legs. (B) Six tins in 2 doors, bracket feet, shaped apron. (C) Hanging safe with large tin (or joined tins) on single door. Other tins usually on other vertical sides. Hung from rafters. (D) Six tins in 2 doors, above long drawer, long tapered legs. (E) Twelve tins joined without framework or molding to form 2 large tins in 2 doors, turned feet. (F) Wythe County (and neighboring counties), Virginia-type case with 2 drawers above 2 doors, and distinctive urn & grapes (urn & flowers, urn & stars) pattern. Turned feet not always found on type. Single drawer sometimes found. All drawings are of composite types not taken from any single model.*

ELECTRIFYING WORK

XVIII. GADGETS AND APPLIANCES

Most interesting to me about this category is the **social history** behind it. First, there were the marketing efforts of power companies who could see the Future and knew it had to be Electric for their own survival. Power companies in the first quarter of the 20th century drummed up business by actively selling an "Electric Future." It's amusing to read articles written for their own trade journals. One such article is transcribed in this chapter; they offer background to our understanding of public ad campaigns of the 1910s to 1930s.

For example, an article in *Edison Electric Institute Bulletin*, September 1934, tells about the development of a "distinctive and appealing character" – "**Reddy Kilowatt, the Electrical Servant**." Reddy, also spelled "Ready" by some electric power supply companies, formed the basis for a "program ... to humanize the utility approach to the public by translating ... the complicated business of serving electricity to all types of customers." Reddy's appeal holds strong today, although it is the rare customer who has a choice about whether or not to buy electricity. Reddy danced on pot-holders and aprons as well as in print ads and company cookbooks.

Nowadays, power companies issue occasional brochures on "saving energy," and then spend the rest of their time lobbying before state assemblies for rate increases because of decreased usage; or fighting people who want to sell them excess power generated by privately-owned windmills; or succumbing to financial witchcraft like Enron's. They are otherwise mired in a bureaucracy of meter-reading and kilowatt hours. According to Charles Fisher, author of *Hazelcorn's Book On Toasters*, writing about the potential dangers of plugging very old low-voltage toasters into modern power supplies, "many locations [today] have 123 volts; this is your power company's way of making you buy more power than you actually need! All appliances will work on 117 volts ... 10% less in power and cost." How do you like that? Obviously power companies today don't need to fund their own test kitchens as in the old days, or pay well-known cookbook authors to prepare promotional cookbooks. And thankfully they have not resurrected old Reddy to try to humanize nuclear power plants and high tension electric lines. Talk about zap!

The second aspect of the social history of household electricity is the utopian view that it would replace what was a dwindling supply of cheap servants and make homemakers' lives easier. For the majority of plugged-in households in the teens and early 1920s, life in general was pretty trig, and electricity only made it more so. One writer, in *Truth* magazine in the UK, trilled "Fancy cooking cutlets and frying pancakes with captured lightning! It really seems tremendous ... you would have fallen in love with the exquisite cleanliness of the process!" You giggle at the retouched, vignette photographs in old power-company booklets, showing cute young things, in flimsy peignoirs, sitting at their dressing tables curling their hair, or standing at a tea table, ogled by admiring friends while making waffles, or posing beside tabletop washing machines in which you can be sure there were some dainty silk stockings.

Once electricity was available in a community, probably the biggest problem in selling electrical appliances in the early days was that there was virtually **no one to do repairs**; and undoubtedly many people were afraid of shocks and electrocution. Find a copy of James Thurber's story "The Car We Had to Push," which appears in a collection of stories published in 1933 called *My Life and Hard Times*. In the story, Thurber tells about one of "the victims and martyrs of the wild-eyed Edison's dangerous experiments" – his mother's mother, who "lived the latter years of her life in the horrible suspicion that electricity was dripping invisibly all over the house. It leaked, she contended, out of empty sockets if the wall switch had been left on." In fact, if you want to be charmed completely, get copies of all of Thurber's wonderful stories and read them again.

The other thing I love about old electric appliances is **design**: pure and simple, or tacky and gawd-awful. From the beginning, small electrical appliances were the way a sense and appreciation of industrial design was domesticated. Sometimes the design factor was assumed to be so important that ads mentioned the industrial designer, such as Henry Dreyfuss, Russel Wright, or Raymond Loewy, by name; in the 1970s on, we became used to seeing, knowing, and seeking the work of product designers/architects such as Michael Graves, Richard Sapper, etc.

Toasters are the big thing here, as you are well aware. I use an old (c.1941) toaster myself, with perfect satisfaction. It's not very outré to look at, but it's easy to use, easy to fix, and easy to clean. Some collectors use a vintage toaster; others prefer a new British "Dualit." In selecting the couple dozen toasters listed here, I tried to pick out some aesthetic or techno-historical winners; also a number that aren't rare but which add breadth (and perhaps a bit of cheapth) to a collection. I believe that European toasters should enjoy higher value in this country. We embrace every other kind of collectible from abroad. European toasters are absolutely gorgeous – see the color section. In the US we are often very stubborn about buying only "made in USA," when in reality, since the beginning of this country filled with immigrants, we have brought, bought, inherited, imported, and used kitchen things from all over the world.

Mixers are moving up very quickly in popularity as an electrible collectric. Although a few long-time collectors were disposing of their huge collections in the early "otts" (as some people call the first few years of the 21st century), scores of new collectors began to build collections. See end of chapter.

In the last few years, **other small appliances**, some dating well into the 1960s, have become increasingly collectible. Anything slightly kitschy is collected, as are things that look like space ships or flying saucers. I have even succumbed to the design of 1960s-70s sandwich grills, the ones that store up on edge like a briefcase. At the local Salvation Army one day, I found seven; all different, though most were made by Singer, only $5 each. They were the type that make a sealed-edge melted cheese sandwich with a sealed diagonal line on which you cut.

Good news or bad? Many electric appliances are sold on the Internet; eBay is good over the very long haul for building a collection, especially if you want to pay true market value. Meanwhile, there's still time to scout them out at fleas, rummage sales, and thrift shops. One thing I've noticed is that out of 125 electric kitchen things up for auction on a day you do the search, possibly as few as 10 will actually be sold. If you do an eBay search for completed electric mixers, for example, about 50 auctions will come up. About half, even of wonderful-seeming items, never got a bid at all even if they started at 99¢. Others remained unsold because the seller put an unrealistic reserve on the item. Shipping is often many times the cost of the thing. Rarities rarely appear on eBay, which means you have to stake out a subject

XVIII-1-A. Electric kitchen of 1894, *of Mr. H. J. Dowsing, England. "In 1891 Mr. H. J. Dowsing, one of the pioneers of heating and cooking and founder of the Dowsing Radiant Heat Co., had a stand at the Crystal Palace Electrical Exhibition [see paragraph in the text] at which were shown Electric cookers and heaters. He certainly had far-seeing ideas. Certainly Messrs. Crompton, who were responsible for the manufacture of these articles, fully grasped the possibilities of Electricity being applied for perfect cooking in the future. "Not only the stove and wall oven are electric, but also the saucepan or frying pan at far right, placed on the market in England in 1893-94 by Dowsing. From* Electric Cooking, Heating & Cleaning. A Manual of Electricity in the Service of the Home, *by Maud Lancaster, 1914. This book will be referred to in subsequent captions as* Lancaster, Electric Cooking, 1914.

field where there's some hope of finding things with little competition. My advice, as always when intending to collect online, is to print out pages of completed sales, highest price first; also to select to print, single items of special interest to you. Buy a hole-punch and keep the pages in a notebook.

An eBay collector by the name of "popsup" says that "**toaster collectors** cross-collect in three main ways. Many collect other electrical items (waffle irons, radios, electric clocks). Fewer cross-collect with kitchen items; many vintage toaster buyers just get one item to go with a display or for décor in a vintage kitchen. A third category cross-collects with other period items, usually collecting chrome, Bakelite, art deco, or streamline."

Jeff Smith, of Evanston, IL, going by the eBay name "jeffjunk," says that in 1998 he "discovered on eBay any given day you could find about 200 old toasters for sale ... probably 20 ended per day. I kind of went overboard on bidding and buying toasters online." Unfortunately, this isn't true four or five years later; most of the 20-30 toasters listed are fairly common if pre-1940, or very common if post-1940. Jeff goes on to say, "I also started hunting in places where sellers told me *they* found toasters – rummage, garage, and estate sales, thrift shops, and flea markets. I often would find no toasters at these other venues, but as a 'consolation prize' I often dragged home waffle irons, electric fans, percolators, blenders, mixers, all manner of kitchen gadgets. Eventually I was so overloaded that I had to sell some excess out of necessity. It proved fun and a way of weeding out, improving my own collection. Note that eBay calls itself a **'trading community'** and I think for most people that's what it is; you trade stuff you have and don't want for stuff you do want." Remember, everyone, what comedian George Carlin said about houses: "Houses are places where you keep your stuff."

Bakelite & Catalin. You'll see one of these with most electric appliances that have a handle, knob, or cord plug. Probably most of the dark, dense, brown or nearly black plastic is actually **Bakelite**, which is a mixture of phenol and formaldehyde and fibers or roughage, like sawdust, and it has to be pressure-molded with heat. The fibers make it strong, and heavier than Catalin, but it is very easy to ruin the shiny surface, which I did out of total stupidity years ago.

Colored molded plastics, somewhat translucent, and usually in colors or marbelized colors, are practically sure to be **Catalin** or another, similar (also a mixture of phenol and formaldehyde) molded thermoset resin (meaning it sets after being heated in its mold). Catalin did make a black opaque plastic.

"Bakelite" has been a buzz-word meant more to attract attention and imply quality from the beginning. Some old electric appliances were advertised as having "Bakelite™" handles, but as far as I know they never told consumers how to take care of it. The two materials are very different in qualities that impact cleaning and care. See the end of this chapter for two sites to help. • Throughout this book I've used a phrase "Bakelite™ (or other molded phenolic resin)" to cover my ignorance. So I too am guilty of using the buzzword.

Wiring is the major caveat attached to buying old electric appliances. You must, somehow, make absolutely sure that whatever you plug in, especially if you plan to use it, has safe wiring. Never plug in something with a brittle, crumbling, rubber cord cover. Never plug in something that's badly frayed with exposed wire.

XVIII-1-B. Electric kitchen of 1894, *"sketched from one in operation in a private home in 1894."* The *Woman's Book: Dealing Practically with the Modern Conditions of Home Life.* ... NY: Charles Scribner's Sons, 1894. *Note all the electric outlets with things plugged in on an upper shelf and the work surface: kettle, pot, saucepan, frying pan, and what appears to be a toaster oven (!) on the right.*

Never leave a new old appliance plugged in, no matter how good the cord looks, and leave the room.

Modest & Humble Disclaimer. Yes, this is the first and only time I've been both modest and humble in this book. This field is growing rapidly each day, and I feel misgivings about even trying to evaluate and describe some of the things here. It's true of all the specialties, but you must read all you can, and join any and all groups. There are some very good books and Web sites. The one thing I can offer is certain background information not always included in other

books. See if you can resist starting a collection of mixers, toasters, or even hot plates! I dare you!

Appliance abbreviations used below:

auto. = automatic
b = broilers
bw = bottle warmers
c-d = chafing dishes
cg = coffee mills or grinders
ck = cookers
cma = coffee makers
cp = coffee percolators
cp/tp = coffeepots/teapots
crnp = corn poppers
ds = disc stoves
eb & cw = eggbeaters & cream whips
EH&U = "Electric Housewares & Utilties" (1930 only)
fmx = food mixers
gd = griddles
gr = grills
gre = grilles
hp = hot plates
ih = immersion heaters
jc = juicers
je = juice extractors
mx = mixers
o = ovens
port. = portable
prs = pressure cookers
pw = plate warmers
res. = restaurant and/or hotels, etc.
ro = roasters
sat = sandwich toasters
sg = sandwich grills
sgr = sandwich grilles
sto = stoves
tab. = table (used before particular item)
tk = tea kettles
tos = toasters
tp = teapots
unsp. = unspecified
u = urns
waf = waffle
wh = water heaters
wi = waffle irons (will spell out when variant)

Electric Appliance Makers

The following lists come from two basic sources. The listings are as complete as I could make them; I believe that omissions or errors are probably present in the sources I used. Note that some manufacturers given in individual listings are not in the list here, but it's because they weren't in *Thomas'* or *House Furnishing Review*. Abbreviations of products are given above. • From *1905-06 Thomas' Register of American Manufacturers:* • Simplex Electrical Co., Cambridgeport, MA (b) (A 1904 Simplex product catalog shows flat-bed gd/tos; also c-d & tp); American Electrical Heater Co., Detroit, MI (b). • **1909** *House Furnishing Review Buyers' Directory;* • American Electric Heater Co., Detroit, MI (b; c-d; gd; curling iron heaters; hp; tk; o; cp; tos); • Simplex Heating Co., Cambridge, MA (tos, & unsp. kitchen utensils); • **1915** *House Furnishing Review Buyers' Directory,* with trade-names; • American Electrical

Heater Co., Detroit, MI (cp/tp, tos); • Berkeley Electric Cooker Co., Berkeley, CA (ck – "Sav-R"; hp; o); • Anglo-American Co., Pittsburg, PA (unsp.); • Birtman Electric Co., Chicago, IL (unsp. – "Bee" & "Bee-Vac"); • Copeman Electric Stove Co., Flint, MI (hp "Double and Single," tos); • Current Electric Co., Chicago (unsp.); • Excel Electric Heating Co., Newark, NJ (cp, cp/tp); • General Electric Co., Schenectady, NY (crnp); • Globe Stove & Range Co., Kokomo, IN (o; crnp); • Hot-point Electric Heating Co., NYC (hp; cp; cp/tp); • Hughes Electric Heating Co., Chicago (hp – "Hughes"); • Insto Electric Heater Co., Buffalo, NY (hp – "Vulcan"); • Pacific Electric Heating Co., Ontario, CA (cp &cp/tp - "El Perco," tos - "El Tosto") • Presto Electrical Mfg. Co., San Francisco, CA (cp & cp/tp - "Presto"); Simplex Electric Heating Co., Cambridge, MA (cp & cp/tp); • Union Electro Products Co., Detroit, MI (crnp); • Utilities Supply Co., Cincinnati, OH (cp & cp/tp - "Tusco"); • Vulcan Electric Heating Co., Buffalo, NY (crnp); • Western Electric & Mfg. Co., East Pittsburg, PA (hp); • Westinghouse Electric & Mfg. Co., East Pittsburg, PA (cp; cp/tp); • *1930 House Furnishing Review Buyers' Directory*, with products & trade-names. (Note that under the heading "Electric Housewares & Utilties" 12 companies were listed, without specifying. These are noted as EH&U.) • Allen Brothers Co., Hartford, CT (gd, gr, hp, mx, pw, tos, wi); • Bersted Mfg. Co., Chicago, IL (EH&U, hp, cp, tab. sto, tos, wi); • Birtman Electric Co., Chicago (EH&U, tos); • A. F. Dormeyer Mfg. Co., Chicago, IL (eb & cw, mx); • Dover Mfg. Co., Dover, OH (cp); • Everts & Zuver, NYC (EH&U, cp, tos, wi); • Fargo Aluminum Co., Taunton, MA (mx); • Fitzgerald Mfg. Co., Torrington, CT (EH&U, gd, gr, hp, mx, tab. sto, tos, wi – "Star-Rite"); • The A. C. Gilbert Co., New Haven, CT (eb & cw, mx); • Griswold Mfg. Co., Erie, PA (gd, hp, o, wi); • Hinkle Leadstone Co., Chicago [crnp (?), gr, mx, crnp, tp, tos, wi]; • Janusch Mfg. Co., NYC (EH&U); • Knapp-Monarch Co., St. Louis, MO [crnp (?), EH&U, gr, hp, tab. sto, tos, wi]; • Landers, Frary & Clark, New Britain, CT [b, churns, crnp (?), EH&U, gd, gr, hp, mx, o, crnp, pw, tab. sto, tp, tos, wi – "Universal"]; • Francis Leffler, NYC, possibly an agent, (EH&U, hp, tos); • Ben S. Loeb, Inc., NYC [b, crnp (?), EH&U, gd, gr, hp, mx, tos, wi – "Master"]; • Master Bake Pot Co., Bloomfield, NJ (o); • National Enameling & Stamping Co., Milwaukee, WI (gr, tos, tp); • National Stamping & Electric Works, Chicago [b, c-d, crnp (?), EH&U, gd, gr, hp, o, pw, tab. sto, tos, wi]; • Patent Novelty Co., Fulton, IL (wh); • Polar Ware Co., Sheboygan, WI (cp); • Salmanson & Baumritter, NYC (EH&U, gr, hp, cp, tos, wi); • Samson-United Corp. Rochester, NY (wi); • Savory Inc., Buffalo, NY (tos); • Vollrath Co., Sheboygan, WI (cp, tp); • Waage Electric Co., Chicago (cp, tos, wi); • Westinghouse Electric & Mfg. Co., Domestic Appliance Dep't., Mansfield,

XVIII-1-C. "Preparing dinner with Electric Cooker." *These are called "electric cookers" in England, but they function like stoves. General Electric Co. of Great Britain photo, in* Electric Cooking, *1914.*

OH (EH&U, gd, gr, hp, o, cp, pw, tab. sto, tos - "Turn over," wi). • *1932 Thomas' Register of American Manufacturers, Buyers' Guide*. (Note that many of these companies made such things as curling irons & sad irons, outside purview of this book.) • Acme Electric Heating Co., Boston, MA (b, hp, wi, sat, sto, tos, u); All-Rite Co., Rushville, IN (tos, res. tos, sat; • Aluminum Goods Mfg. Co., Manitowoc, WI (aluminum cp, waf moulds, bw, hp); • Armstrong Appliance Corp, Huntington, WV (tab. gre, wi, tos, crnp); • Beardsley & Wolcott Mfg. Co., Waterbury, CT (wi, tab. sto, tos, nursing bw); • Bersted Mfg. Co., Chicago, IL & Fostoria, OH (wi, hp, tos, res. tos, cp, u); • Betsy Ross Electric Products Corp, Johnson City, NY (tos); • Bridgeport Engineering Co., Bridgeport, CT (cookers for "wienies"); • Buckwalter Stove Co., Royersford, PA (hp); • Camman Mfg. Co., Waltham, MA (combined mixer, beater, kneader, grinder, etc.); • Cannon Oiler Co., Keithsburg, IL (crnp); • Century Mfg. Co., Elizabethtown, PA (tos); • Chicago Flexible Shaft Co., Chicago (auto. & non-auto. tos); • Club Aluminum Utensil Co., Chicago (wi, mx); • Coleman Lamp & Stove Co., Wichita, KS (cp, wi, tos, hp); • Cornwall & Patterson Mfg. Co., Bridgeport, CT (res. tos, hp); • C. Cretors & Co., Chicago (crnp); • Detroit Electric Stove Co., Detroit, MI (port. hp); • Diamond Appliance Co., South Bend, IN (gre, tos); • A. T. Dietz, Toledo, OH (crnp); • Dominion Electrical Mfg. Co., Minneapolis, MN (wi, tab. sto, tos, crnp); • A. F. Dormeyer Mfg. Co., Chicago (fmx); • Dos Mfg. Co., Fortville, IN (crnp); • Double Action Mfg. Corp., Grand Rapids, MI (tos); • Dover Mfg. Co., Dover, OH (cp); • Drake Mfg. Co., Milwaukee, WI (hp, rotary tos, weiner & marshmallow ro); • Duparquet, Huot & Moneuse Co., NYC (b, res. tos, res. sto); • Thomas A. Edison, Inc., Edicraft Div., Orange, NJ (tos, sat, waf bakers); • H. Ehrlich & Sons Mfg. Co., St. Joseph, MO (coffee grinders); • Electrahot Mfg. Co., Minneapolis, MN (unspec., tos); • Eureka Tool & Machine Co., Newark, NJ (tos); • Enterprise Mfg. Co. of Pennsylvania, Philadelphia (cg); • Estate Stove Co., Hamilton, OH (port. hp, tos?); • Ev'ryday Electric Co., Marion, IN (tos, gre, hp); • Excel Electric Co., Muncie, IN (ck, crnp, toy tos); • Fitzgerald Mfg. Co., Torrington, CT (wi, drink mx, urn sets, tos, hp); • G. R. Electric Mfg. Co., Manhattan, KS (hp); • General Mfg. Co., Dayton, OH (wi); • Graybar Electric Co., NYC (jobbers of "everything electrical for the house," cp, tos, res. tos); • Great Lakes Pressed Steel Corp., Buffalo, NY (res. weiner [bun] tos); • Griswold Mfg. Co., Erie, PA (hp, waf bakers, gd, tos); • Hankscraft Co., Madison, WI (nursing bw; also made electric heaters that could be used to convert fireless cookers & ovens); • Havell Mfg. Co., Irvington, NJ (res. tos); • Hevi-Duty Electric Co., Milwaukee, WI (hp); • Hobart Mfg. Co., Troy, OH ("food preparing & dish washing machinery"); • Holcomb & Hoke Mfg. Co., Indianapolis, IN (crnp); • Hot Glow Electric Mfg. Co., Buffalo, NY (hp, coffee urn heaters); • W. E. Kautenberg Co., Freeport, IL (tos); • O. S. Keene Machine Co., Chicago (pancake gre, crnp); • KitchenAid Mfg. Co., Troy, OH (food preparers), see: Hobart also; • Knapp-Monarch Co., Belleville, IL (wi, gre, sto, crnp); • Landers, Frary & Clark, New Britain, CT (c-d, wi, tk, cp, tos, milk warmers); • Lewis Electric Mfg. Co., Cleveland, OH (tos, gr, hp, pancake gd); • A. J. Lindemann & Hoverson Co., Milwaukee, WI (wi, hp, tab. sto, tos); • Made-Rite Mfg. Co., Sandusky, OH (sat, gr, tos); • Majestic Electric Appliance Co., San Francisco, CA (unsp., tos); • Manning, Bowman & Co., Meriden, CT (wi, tk, cp, kitchen mx, tos, tab. ck); • Mabey Electric & Mfg. Co., Indianapolis, IN (res. hp, sat, gre, crnp); • Mattatuck Mfg. Co., Waterbury, CT (auto. tos, res. tos, 2-slice tos.); • McCurdy Mfg. Co., Louisville, KY (tos); • McKenney & Waterbury Co., Boston, MA (tab. gre, tos); • Metal Ware Corp., Two Rivers, WI (wi, cp, tos); • Metropolitan Electric Mfg. Co., Long Island City, NY ("electric specialties," unsp. appliances); • Fred J. Meyers Mfg. Co., Hamilton, OH (crnp); • National Enameling & Stamping Co., Milwaukee, WI (hp); • National Stamping & Electric Works, Chicago (tab. gre, tos); • Northwest Metal Products, Seattle, WA (hp); • National Enameling & Stamping Co., Milwaukee, WI (ck, casseroles, hp); • New Delphos Mfg. Co., Delphos, OH (crnp); • The Ohio Stamping & Engineering Co., Dayton, OH (1- & 2-hole hp); • Pelouze Mfg. Co., Chicago (tos); • Prometheus Electric Corp., NYC (gd, u, hp); • Poughkeepsie Gold Seal Electric Co., Poughkeepsie, NY (wi, cp, tos); • Reimers Electric Appliance Co., North Bergen, NJ (hp, baby bw); Rock Island Mfg. Co., ("RIMCO"), Chicago, IL, Rock Island, IL (waf moulds, tos); • Robeson-Rochester Corp, Rochester, NY (cp, tos, u, wi); • Rosedale Mfg. Co., Kansas City, KS (wi, sat); • Rutenber Electric Co., Marion, IN (hp, tab. sto, tos, wi); • Samson-United Corp., Rochester, NY (hp, tab. sto, res. tos, wi); • Savory, Inc., Buffalo, NY (wiener ro, ro); • Schwartz & Steinberg, NYC (tos); • Schwartzbaugh Mfg. Co., Toledo, OH (hp, ck, wi); • Albert Sechrist Mfg. Co., Denver, CO (prs); • Serelco, Inc., NYC (b, hp, steamers, etc.); • Standard Electric Stove Co., Toledo, OH (hp, u); • Star Mfg. Co., St. Louis, MO (crnp, sat, tos, hot dog ck, res. gre); • Superior Electric Products Corp., St. Louis, MO (cp, tos, wi); • Harold E. Trent Co., Philadelphia, PA (hp); • Uneek Utilities Corp., Chicago (ck for "weenies," crnp); • Utility Electric Co., St. Louis, MO (tos, res. tos); • Waage Electric Co., Chicago & NYC (wi, cp, ih, u, sto, ds, tos, res. tos); • Waters-Genter Co., Minneapolis, MN (auto. tos, waf bakers); • West Coast Specialties, Ltd., Los Angels, CA (sat); • Westinghouse Electric Mfg. Co., East Pittsburgh, PA (sg, wi, cp, hp, tos sto, tos, ds, res. tos); • White Beauty Electric Co., Chicago (cp). • **1945** Thomas' Register of American Manufacturers, Buyers' Guide. (With products if given. Note the Register shows many "etc."). • Acme Electric Heating Co., Boston, MA (b, wi, sto, tos, res. sat, u); • Adel Precision Products Corp., Burbank, CA; • All-Rite Co., Rushville, IN (tos, sat, res. tos); • Aluminum Goods Mfg. Co., Manitowoc, WI (aluminum cp, bw, small appliances); • Armstrong Products Corp., Huntington, WV (tab. gre, sto); • Bendix Aviation Corp., North Hollywood, CA; • Bersted Mfg. Co., Chicago, IL & Fostoria, OH (wi, hp, tos, res. sat, crnp, u); • Camfield Mfg. Co., Grand Haven, MI ("two-slice fully auto. tos"); • Chicago Electric Mfg. Co., Chicago, IL (wi, tos, fans); • Chicago Flexible Shaft Co., Chicago (fmx, cma, tos, cord & plug sets); • Diehl Mfg. Co., Electrical Div. of The Singer Co., Somerville, NJ (fans); • Dominion Electrical Mfg., Mansfield, OH (wi, tab. sto, tos, sandwich gre); • Dormeyer Corp., Chicago (fmx, je); • Duparquet-Dubois, Inc., NYC (b, sto, res. tos); • Eastern Metal Spinning Co., NYC (tab. b); • Enterprise Mfg. Co., Philadelphia (meat choppers & cg); • Eureka Tool & Machine Co., NYC (tos); • Faraday Electric Corp., Adrian, MI (b, gr); • Finders Mfg. Co., Chicago (tab. b); • Forestek Plating & Mfg. Co., Cleveland, OH (res. sat); • General Electric Co., Bridgeport, CT, & Schenectady, NY (tos, res. tos,

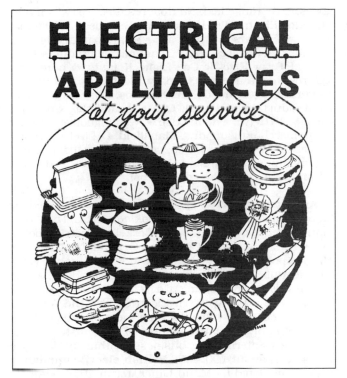

Illustration by Eric Nitsche, *for article in* House Beautiful, *May 1937. From sandwich toaster to mixer to beanery slow cooker.*

etc.); • GO Electric, NYC ("rangette"); • Graybar Electric Co., NYC, jobber for "all types of port. & stationary appliances"; • Hamilton Machine Mfg., Syracuse, NY (res. tos); • Hankscraft Co., Madison, WI (baby bw); • A. J. Holmes Electric Co., Tacoma, WA (res. tos); • International Sales Corp., Indianapolis, IN (auto. res. tos); • Knapp-Monarch Co., St. Louis, MO (wi, gr, sto, tos, mx, whippers, sat); • Landers, Frary & Clark, New Britain, CT (c-d, waf makers, tk, cg, coffee precipitators, hp, urn sets, ranges); • Mabey Electric Co., Peoria, IL (hp, sat, gre, for restaurants); • Majestic Electric Appliance Co., Mansfield, OH; • Manning, Bowman & Co. (wi, cp, tos, tab. ck); • Marlun Mfg. Co., NYC (b, ro); • Mason Can Co., East Providence, RI (res. tos); • McGraw – see Toastmaster; • McKenney & Waterbury Co., Boston, MA (tab. gre, tos); • Metal Ware Corp., Two Rivers, WI (wi, crnp, tos, sat); • Miracle Products Co., Chicago, IL (tos, fmx, ro); • National Stamping & Electric Works, Milwaukee, WI & Chicago, IL (casseroles, tab. gre, tos, wi, hp, sto, sat); • Naxon Utilities Corp., Chicago (gd, b, ro); • Noblitt-Sparks Industries, Inc., Columbus, IN; • Perfect Automatic Egg Timer & Mfg. Co., Chicago (auto. & non-auto. res. tos, res. sat, etc.); • Precision Mfg. Co., Dover, NJ (tos, res. tos, sat, b, hp, wi); • Prevore Electric Mfg. Co., Brooklyn, NY (wi, sge, sto, res. tos, tos, b, ro, hp); • Proctor Electric Co., Philadelphia, PA (auto. & non-auto. tos, res. tos, wafflers, "Roast-Or-Grilles"); • Prometheus Electric Corp., NYC (gd, u, hp); • Rock Island Division, Chicago, IL (waf moulds); • Samson-United Corp., Rochester, NY; • Savory Equipment, Newark, NJ (res. tos); • Sheridan Electronics Corp., Chicago, IL (tos); • Singer – See Diehl; • Son Chief Electrics, Winsted, CT (tos, hp, wi); • Starr Bros. Bell Co., East Hampton, CT (res. tos); • Sta-Warm Electric Co., Ravenna, OH (pots, kettles); • Sun Flame Appliances, Ltd., Ridgefield, NJ (tos, res. tos, sto, wi, cma); • Superior Electric Products, Cape Girardeau, MO (cma, tos, bowl heaters, wi, hp, sat); • Swartzbaugh Mfg. Co., Toledo, OH (hp, ck, ro); • Toastmaster Products Division, McGraw Electric Co., Elgin, IL (auto. & non-auto. tos, res. tos, auto. wi); • Utility Electric Co., St. Louis, MO (toasted waf molds, tos, res. tos, sg); • Victor Electric Products, Cincinnati, OH; • Waage Mfg. Co., Chicago & NYC (wi, gd, ih, ds); • Westinghouse Electric Corp., merchandising div., Mansfield, OH (refrigerators, ranges, dishwashers, wi, cp, cma, tos, res. tos, roaster-o, fans, hp, sg); • Winsted Hardware Mfg. Co., Winsted, CT (auto. hp, pancake gd, mx, tos).

• • •

American electric appliance makers as listed by **Maud Lancaster** in *Electric Cooking*, **1914**: The Automatic Electric Cook Co. • The Berkeley Electric Cooker Co. • The Cook Stove Co. • The General Electric Co. • The Hotpoint Electric Heating Co. • The Hughes Electric Heating Co. • The Prometheus Electric Co. • The Simplex Electric Heating Co. • The Vulcan Electric Heating Co. • The Western Electric Co. • The Westinghouse Electric Co. • She does not mention Edison Electric, probably because most of her list was of companies entering the business "within the last five years" (i.e., about 1907-08). **British electric appliance makers** as listed by Maud Lancaster in **1914**: • Amorduct Mfg. Co. • Benham & Sons • A. F. Berry, "Tricity" • British Prometheus Co. (founded 1892) • The Carron Co. • Dowsing Radiant Heat Co. • Messrs. Crompton & Co. • Eastman & Warne • "Eclipse" – The Electric & Ordnance Accessories Co. • The Electrical Co. • The Falkirk Iron Co. • Ferranti • General Electric of Great Britain • Jackson Electric Stove Co. • Phoenix Electric Heating Co. (founded 1894) • Purcell & Nobbs • Simplex Conduits • Spagnoletti • The British Thomason-Houston Co.

XVIII-2. Reddy Kilowatt, with added avoirdupois. This version is a painted cutout plywood sign, probably unique, used as window advertising. "Meet Reddy Kilowatt. You will like him – he is a genius of accomplishment – capable, infinitely willing, infinitely powerful. ... He is YOUR servant." About 28"H. 1930s-40s. Sort of folk art. **$100+**

Toaster Makers in collector books on toasters which aren't in the above lists or which didn't mention toasters as a product, or with broader production date info, with estimated date in parentheses. As you see they are all North American companies, but double what would otherwise be known about toaster manufacturers! • All-Rite Co., Rushville, IN, "Hostess" (porcelain sandwich toasters), (c.1920s-30s?); • Armstrong Electric & Mfg. Corp., Huntington, WV, "Perc-O-Toaster" (c.1918); • Arvin Industries Inc., Columbus, IN (c.1950s); • Brust-Haris [sic] Mfg. Co., Chicago (c.1930s); • Butler Bros., Chicago (c.1930s-40s); • Chicago Electric Mfg. Co., Chicago, "Handy Hot" also "Handyhot" (c.1920s); • Calkins Appliance Co., Niles, MI, "Breakfaster" (c.1930s-40s?); • Capitol Products, Winsted, CT (c.1930s-40s); • Chicago Flexible Shaft Co., Chicago, "Sunbeam" (pat'd. 1924); • Connecticut Appliance Co., Winsted, CT, "Coronet" (c.1930s); • Curtainless, NY, "Reddy Toaster Range" (c.1920s); • Deree Co., Chicago (c.1930s); • Electro Weld Co., n.p. (c.1920s); • Edison Electric Appliance Co., NY, Chicago, Ontario, CAN, "Hot-point" (c.1915); • Electroweld, prob. Lynn, MA, "Electroweld" (c.1919); • Empire, The Metal Ware Corp., Two Rivers, WI, "Empire" (c.1930s) & "Travl-Mate" (1960s?); • Estate Stove Co., Hamilton, OH, "Estate" (c.1925); • "Full Vision," no maker's name (c.1940s); • General Mills Inc., Minneapolis, MN (c.1950s); • Girard, n.p., "Girard" (c.1910s+); • H & S, Montreal, CAN (may be Toastess Corp.) (c.1930s); • John H. Graham, NYC, later Rock Island Mfg. Co., Rock Island, IL (c.1923); • Great Northern Mfg. Co., Chicago, "Quality Brand" (c.1929), later made by Metal Ware Corp. as "Empire"; • Hoskins Mfg. Co., Detroit, MI, "Cheerie Toastove," (1909 patent & according to C. Fisher, "first appliance advertised using the Marsh 1906 patent for Nichrome"); • Hotpoint Electric Heating Co., NY, Chicago, Ontario, CAN, Vancouver, "El Tosto" (c.1914); • Montgomery Ward & Co., Chicago, "Twin Oven" (pat'd. 1923); • Electro Mfg. Co. of America, Philadelphia, "Electro Automatic" (c. 1930s?); • Justrite Electric & Mfg. Co., Minneapolis, MN (c.1930s); • Kwik-Way Co., St. Louis, MO, "Kwik-Way" (c.1940s); • Lasko Metal Products Inc., (sometimes reported as Lasco Metal Products), West Chester, PA (c.1940s-50s?); • Lexington Machinery Development Co., Clifton, NJ, "Toast Queen" (c.1930s); • Liberty Gauge & Instrument Co., Cleveland, OH (c.1929); • Magic Maid Division Son-Chief Electrics, Winsted, CT, "Magic Maid" (c.1950s); • Malda Electric Mfg. Co., Chicago (c.1930s); • Manhattan Electical Supply Co., NYC, "MESCO" (c.1914-15); • Mecky Co., Philadelphia, "Ledig" (c.1920s); • Merit Made, Buffalo, NY, "Merit Made" (c.1940s); • MESCO – See Manhattan Electical; • Miracle Electric Co., Chicago, "Miracle" (c.1940s); • Monitor Equipment Corp., n.p. (1950s?); • Nelson Machine & Mfg. Co., Cleveland, OH (c.1930s); • Novelty Mfg. Co., Waterbury, CT, "Wilwear" (c.1910s); • Oatlin Mfg. Co., Oatlin, IL (c.1920s); • Pelouze Mfg. Co., Chicago (c.1918); • Porcelier Mfg. Co., Greensburg, PA (porcelain) (c.1930s-40s); • Penna Aircraft Works, Philadelphia, PA, "Penn-Air" (c.1930s); • Perfection Electric Products Co., New Washington, OH, "Excelsior Twin Reversible" (c.1920s-30s); • Pittsburgh Electrical Specialties Co., Pittsburgh, PA, "Victory" (c.1919); • Precision Mfg. Co., Dover, NJ, "Rainbow" (1930s); • Proctor & Schwartz, Inc., Philadelphia, "Proctor Thermostatic" [pat'd. 1925); • Red Seal Appliance Co., Rochester, NY, "Red Seal" (1936 patent); • Renfrew Electric & Refrigerator Co., Ltd., n.p. (Canadian?) (c.1920s); • Rex-Ray Appliances, St. Louis, MO (c.1930s); • Riverside Mfg. Co., Ypsilanti, MI, "The Junior Toaster" (c.1930s?); • Rochester Stamping Co., (later Robeson Rochester Corp.), Rochester, NY, "Royal Rochester" (c.1910s); • Rock Island Mfg. Co., Rock Island, IL, "RIMCO" (c.1920s), see also Graham; • Russell Electric, Chicago, IL; • Royal Brand Products, NYC, "Energex" (c.1920s); • Samson-United Corp., Rochester, NY, "Samson Tri-Matic" (c.1938); • Sears & Roebuck, Chicago, IL, "Auto-Toastmaker"; "Heatmaster") (c.1930s-1940s); • Security Electric Mfg. Co., Chicago, "Security" (c.1940s?); • Seneca Co., Brighton, NY (c.1930s); • Son-Chief Electric Inc., Winsted, CT, "Son-Chief" (c.1940s?); • Standard Appliance Mfg. Co., Ltd., Toronto, CAN (c.1930s); • Standard Stamping Co., Huntington, WV (1918 patent); • Steelcraft, Kansas City, MO (c.1940s wartime?); • Superior Electric Products, St. Louis, MO, "Super Lectric" (c.1930s?); • Superstar, Long Island City, NY, "Thermo Mastergrill," "Toastrite Pop-Up" (c.1930s, '40s); • Superior Electric Products Corp., St. Louis, MO (c.1920s-30s); • Toastess Corp., Montreal, Canada, "Sturdy" (c.1930s?); • Toast-O-Lator Co., Long Island City, NY, "Toast-O-Lator" (c.1939-1952); • Toastwell Co., St. Louis, MO (c. late 1930s-40s); • Triangle Appliance Mfg. Co., Chicago, IL, "Tamco" (c.1910s-20s?); • United Drug Co., Boston, MA, "Electrex" (1920 & 1927 patents); • Waters-Genter Co., McGraw Electric, Minneapolis, MN, "Toastmaster" (c.1920s-30s); • Watts Electro Mfg. Co. of America, Philadelphia, (c.1920s-30s); • West Bend Co., West Bend, WI (c.1960s?); • Wharton Mfg. Co., Philadelphia, PA, "Commander" (c. 1929).

A FEW THINGS A CENT'S WORTH OF ELECTRICITY WILL DO

It will bring to a boil two quarts of water.
It will run the electric boiler for six minutes.
It will operate a twelve-inch fan for ninety minutes.
It will operate an electric griddle for eight minutes
It will operate a luminous radiator for eight minutes.
It will make a Welsh rarebit in an electric chafing dish.
It will operate a sewing machine motor for three hours.
It will keep an eight-inch disc stove hot for seven minutes, or long enough to cook a steak.
It will operate a seven-inch frying pan for twelve minutes.
It will make four cups of coffee in an electric coffee percolator.
It will keep a foot-warmer hot for a quarter of an hour.
It will keep a six-pound electric flatiron hot for fifteen minutes.
It will heat an electric curling iron once a day for two weeks.
It will clean seven pairs of boots on a boot polisher.
It will clean five hundred knives on a knife cleaner.
It will carry a passenger up and down about three times in an eighty-foot house elevator.
It will run an electric clock one year.
It will run a small office ventilating fan about two hours.
It will warm sufficient water for shaving three mornings.
It will light three hundred cigars.
It will iron three silk hats.
It will fill and cork twenty-five dozen pint bottles.
It will pump ten gallons of water to a height of twenty-five feet.
It will run or operate an electric piano for one hour.

XVIII-3. One cent of electricity – *what it would do in 1914. You can see from the list that much was done by electricity, at what may seem a very early date. I love the juxtaposition of old & new fangles – silk hats to ventilating fans! Lancaster,* Electric Cooking, *1914.*

❖ NOTES ❖

Prometheus was a Greek god who, in defiance of Zeus' wishes, stole fire to give it to humans. In retaliation, Zeus created Pandora and sent her down to cause trouble. We've been cookin' (and playing with fire) ever since – and we've also been opening boxes and jars that maybe aren't our business! Fortunately, hope remains in that box that Pandora opened. By the way, "**Lucifer**" means "light-bringer" or "light-bearer" – not all that different from Prometheus, and, for that matter, St. Lucy.

• • •

Mica is a translucent, silkily-shiny mineral, a silicate crystal, that is composed of very thin flat sheets or layers (like French pastry!) which can be separated; the thinnest sheets are transparent. Five hundred years ago it was called "muscovy-glass" because of its use as a glass substitute in Muscovy, part of Russia. It became very useful in making windows in stove fireboxes because heat didn't melt it; it was early used for translucent panels in oven doors, heating stoves & lanterns. Later it became useful as an insulating material, or a heat shield, in electric appliances, or for small viewing windows in the doors of toasters, etc. In the *1945 Thomas' Register* is an ad by Ford Radio & Mica Corp., Brooklyn, NY. "Fabricated mica parts for every radio, electrical, and electronic purpose."

• • •

Masters of Electricity. "Master" was a popular name for all kinds of appliances. There is "Mixmaster" (Sunbeam); "Toastmaster" (Waters-Genter); the "Chef Master" doughnut maker; the "Drinkmaster" (Hamilton Beach); "Speed Master" (Son-Chief); "Powermaster" (Sears); "Heatmaster" (no mark); and the funny thing is, the Master Electric Co., Dayton, OH, seems not to have used this powerful word for their products. Maybe they were too late!

Baby food warmer, small pitcher-like vessel set on electric base, gray & white enamelware looks like moss agate, 4 wood button feet screwed on to base, odd plug with flat prongs, many marks, "AGL, #2510," "Triangle Lektrik Baby Food Warmer," American Electrical Heater Co., Detroit, MI, 4-1/2"H, early 20th C...................... **$30+**

Baker, round-cornered oblong chromium box like a big shoe box, with slide out baking tray drawer, black plastic handle on drawer, 4 little feet, temperature dial on top, "Redi-Baker," mfd. by Knapp Monarch NESCO, St. Louis, MO, c.1963. .... **$15+**

Bar mixer, stainless steel body shaped like pencil stub, diamond-shaped beater to insert, battery-operated, "Marbo." 1960s. .... **$3+**

Beaters – See in "M" listings a section on Mixers - Beaters - Drink Mixers - Milkshake Mixers

Bottle warmer, chromed metal, plastic knobs, temperature gauge on top, "Sunbeam," Chicago Flexible Shaft, 12-15/16"H, developed 1951; this one early 1950s. **$15**

Bread-maker, cast aluminum with many accessories, dough hooks, dough paddles, plus grinding & slicing pieces, KitchenAid, Troy, OH, c. late 1940s. .... **$15+**

Butter keeper, countertop, plastic & metal, 4-3/4"H x 9-1/4"L x 4-1/2"W, controls from "soft" to "hard," Nash-Kelvinator, 1930s? .... **$20+**

Carriage stove – See Hot plate

Casserole, tan, brown & black enameled body with chrome & red Art Deco design of woman serving steaming casserole dish on front, 2 Bakelite Deco black handles & lid knob, inner bowl, electric cord, high & low settings for heat, "NESCO Thrifty Cook Casserole #B40," National Enamel & Stamping Co., Milwaukee, WI, c.1940s. .... **$60+**

Casserole or chafing dish, chromed metal, ivory-color molded phenolic resin curved side handles & lid knob, divided Pyrex™ glass liner, detachable cord, underside marked "Chase Brass & Copper Co Model 90115," "pat. applied for," centaur logo, Waterbury, CT, 9-3/4" diam. Has original papers, including mini catalog "Table Electrics by Chase," which adds value. 1940s. .... **$55+**

Chafing dish, nickeled brass & iron, turned wood handle, well-shaped frame & pan, lion's paw feet, domed lid, "Type ECD," mfd. by General Electric, c.1918 or 1919. .... **$30+**

Churn – See in "M" listings a section on Mixers - Beaters - Drink Mixers - Milkshake Mixers

Clocks – See Chapter V (Measure)

XVIII-4. Chafing dishes. Styled exactly like traditional ones using alcohol lamps, these were touted for making "dainty dishes" right on the table. (L) General Electric Co., Schenectady®; Landers, Frary & Clark "Universal." Both have ebonized wooden handles and finials, and are somewhat in the Georgian mode of the 1830s. Pictures from Electric Cooking, 1914. **$35-$55+**

The World is Led to an Electric Kitchen

"The **Great Exhibition of the Works of Industry of All Nations," 1851**, was held in a beautiful glass building 1,848 feet long, 408 feet wide, and 108 feet high, with hundreds of thousands of glass panes in a wrought iron frame, like a beautiful, big greenhouse. Nicknamed in the press "the Crystal Palace," it was built in Hyde Park, London, and was a modern wonder of the world. Despite all the amazing things on display at this international trade fair (particpants included France, Germany, Austria, Belgium, Russia, Turkey, Switzerland, the Netherlands, Egypt, Spain, Portugal, Brazil, Mexico, China, Arabia, Persia, Africa, India, and North America), the building itself was the main attraction for many fair-goers. Displays were in four broad categories: Raw Materials, Machinery and Mechanical Invention, Manufactures, and Art. As with all world's fairs, countries competed for prize medals bestowed on the best displays. This was partly out of pride, and partly because these medals and awards were used as part of advertising campaigns, by being mentioned and depicted in any print advertising, and sometimes on packaging. • After the fair, the Crystal Palace was dismantled and rebuilt in 1854 as a much larger building in Sydenham Hill, south of London, England, and served as the venue for all kinds of events, including electric lights in 1882. In **1891** there was another exhibition "the **Crystal Palace Electrical Exhibition**, where among others, Dowsing Radiant Heat Co. took part, and Crompton & Co. exhibited an electric kettle." • **Note:** There are many interesting sites on the Web relating to all aspects of the Crystal Palace in both of its incarnations. • One of my favorite books of all time is *The Young Visiters*, written by Daisy Ashford, supposedly when she was only nine. It is, as Daisy would have said, "rarther wonderful." The book is a more than "rarther wonderful" tale of Mr. Salteena who visits the "Crystale Pallace," among other adventures. Amazingly, you can still buy the book, or you can read it, or print it out, from the Stone Soup Web site: www.stonesoup.com/ash2/ash1.html. • The **Philadelphia International Electrical Exhibition, 1884**, under the auspices of the Franklin Institute of the State of Pennsylvania for the Promotion of the Mechanic Arts. The Franklin Institute stated in their proposal for the event that "The subject of electricity and its applications is at present attracting an unusual amount of attention, and the exhibition, side by side, of the best achievements of Europe and America cannot fail to be of the highest interest." *The Manufacturer & Builder*, Oct. 1883. It was true; the world's air fairly crackled with interest: The **Paris Electrical Exposition** had been held in **1881**; **Vienna** had had an electrical exhibition in **1883**, as had Berlin. Light & Communication were thought to be the best application of electricity. Thomas Alva Edison's companies showed lamps, and batteries to use in household work, telegraphy, telephones, etc. • The **World's Columbian Exposition in Chicago, 1893**. Among many glorious departments, in buildings and walkways illuminated by electricity, the major uses of electricity were still seen at the time as ighting, telegraphy, and transportation. Among the showcase buildings was the Electrical Hall, wherein was the world's introduction to a new concept – cooking everything with electricity. The chief of the Electrical Hall was quoted as saying that the aim of the exhibits was "the enlightenment of the people as to the progress of a branch of science and industry yet scarcely out of its cradle, and to foreshadow the possibilities of its future." A German display included heating and cooking appliances. A model kitchen was set up in the North Hall, with electric ovens, electrically-heated griddles, kettles, etc., whose current was regulated by switches. The kitchen was hardly what you might expect – it looked like an old-fashioned kitchen with wooden cupboards, retro-fitted with a flat, large electrical panel on the wall behind the wooden (non-conducting) work-station, on which sat individual cooking utensils, including a chafing dish, a frying pan, and a coffee urn. A chandelier hung from the ceiling. The 1894 Dowsing mansion kitchen in XVIII-1-A actually looks a lot more modern because of the checkerboard tiled floor, and the built-in oven. • Hubert Bancroft, in his large, photographically-illustrated *The Book of the Fair* [Chapter 14], wrote that "the principle that heat is generated by resistance to the electric current is illustrated" by the "coffee-pots, tea-pots, flat-irons, and all other utensils having enamelled bottoms, in which are imbedded small copper wires. When the current is turned on and passes along the wires, the resistance offered by the enamel produces heat, which can be easily regulated and directed." *The Book of the Fair, an Historical and Descriptive Presentation,* by Hubert Howe Bancroft. Chicago: Bancroft Co., 1893. • A **bibliography** to get you started if you want to read about worlds' fairs, progress, etc., is at this Smithsonian Institution URL: www.sil.si.edu/silpublications/worlds-fairs-2000.htm.

•　　•　　•

'Wire Your Home Time' and Electrical Housewares – "From April 1 to May 15, 1917, will be known as 'Wire Your Home Time' throughout the country, and the Society of Electrical Development tell us that there are fifteen million homes in America yet to be wired for electric service.

"Here are some facts that are interesting to dealers having Electrical Houseware Departments or who have facilities for handling wiring contracts or sell electrically heated or operated devices: 20,500,000 homes in U.S. 5,500,000 wired for electric service. 15,000,000 yet to be wired, now lighted by other means than electricity. 5,000,000 sockets empty. 1075 per cent more electric light obtainable for the same money than 20 years ago. 110,000,000 incandescent lamps now sold yearly. Only one in three of the homes on the existing distribution lines of electric companies are wired. Far less than one per cent of the homes of the country are wired for complete electric service.

"Of course, not all these homes will be wired, but a number of them will, which means that thousands will be able to enjoy the pleasures of electric lighting, cooking, cleaning, sewing, ironing, washing, and the many other forms of electric service.

"The development of the servant question in this modern home is very important to the dealer selling Electrical Housewares. Years ago, when all families boasted and enjoyed an entire house for themselves,

servants were a necessity. In later years, when the apartment or 'flat' came into vogue and the servant in the house was changed to the 'living-out girl' or the one who 'worked by the day,' electricity first received the attention that it deserved. As the family's living quarters became smaller, the necessity of having outside help became less, and the advantages of electrically operated devices became more prominent.

"Then the servant, seeing that eventually she would be supplanted by the 'housekeeping by wire' method, demanded increased wages all out of proportion to the services performed, with the result that electricity again received additional impetus until today it is a recognized factor in the operation of the modern home.

"When munition plants offered to women, even those unskilled in mechanics, large salaries which daily oftentimes equaled their weekly wages, the domestic forsook her pots and pans, the broom and the wash tub, to take her place among the ranks of those employed in making explosives and other necessities for the continuing of the war.

"In despair, the housewife turned a hopeless face toward carrying on the home duties by herself or with less help; and when the alert merchant called her attention to the modern way of washing clothes with the Electric Washer instead of the 'elbow-grease' way of the laundress, she listened carefully, tested thoroughly – and bought. Now many thousands of housewives all over the country sing the praises of the Electric Washing Machine.

"It was the same way with the Electric Vacuum Cleaner. When its efficiency in removing – not merely scattering – the dust and dirt was demonstrated to her, she immediately became a convert to the dustless method, the Vacuum Cleaner way. Now she does not have to spend many weary hours dusting, as the Vacuum Cleaner catches and holds the dust.

"Then when the beauty, convenience, and usefulness of electrically operated cooking utensils were shown her, she appreciated their many points of advantage. The Electric Percolator, the Electric Stove, the Electric Egg Boiler, the Electric Chafing Dish, the Electric Toaster, etc., etc. – all of these she bought and found useful.

"In the kitchen she placed an Electric Dish Washer, which eliminated all the dreary drudgery of dish washing. Three times a day, year in and year out, the dishes must be washed. The clothes may be washed once a week, but the dishes cannot wait. The hands of the housewife were saved from this disagreeable task and the electric machine eagerly took up the work, which it performed automatically, efficiently as well as thoroughly and cleanly. Again, the chinaware or glassware does not suffer when the Electric Dish Washer is employed like it does when 'Mamie' does the work.

"The handy 'power unit' was another large factor in cutting down the kitchen labor. It polished the silver, it ground the coffee, turned the ice cream freezer, the egg beater and the grindstone in a business-like way, and at a small cost for current.

"The laundry next received attention, and with the Electric Washing Machine safely installed the Electric Iron was added and the Electric Mangle, perhaps.

"For the rooms of the house there were suitable Electric Lamps in a multitude of styles and sizes, while for Milady's room the Electric Curling Iron, Electric Heating Pad, etc., were found of more than ordinary use.

"Today, more than ever before, the Electric Fan is gaining a foothold in the home and rightly so. For years it was found only in the business office, the store or the factory, but now it is a recognized necessity even in the winter months.

"Although the writer has not touched deeply on the many and different uses of Electrical Housewares, the average alert merchant has already seen the light and has contemplated stocking and selling Electrical Housewares. As the days get longer and the day warmer, these labor and time saving devices should be brought to the attention of the buying public, as the summer time is the season when all of these conveniences are more than ever appreciated." "Electrical Housewares" section, *House Furnishing Review*, March 1917.

Coffee makers & percolators – See Chapter XIV (Coffee, Tea)

Coffee grinders – See Chapter XIV (Coffee, Tea)

❖ NOTES ❖

Cookbooklets & Appliances. Lots of food companies and utensil companies put out instructive cookbooks to go with them. There are also many cookbooklets or advertising cookbooks for electric appliances, from mixers to stoves to freezers, from the 1910s on. Most are part instruction booklet, part recipes. Sunbeam Mixmaster; KitchenAid; Hamilton Beach Mixer; Presto; Mirro-Matic; Waring Blender; Osterizer; Servel; General Electric; Hot-point; Kelvinator; etc. The colorful graphics on the covers, especially c.1920-1940, make them worth framing. A Schiffer collectors' book for these is Sandra J. Norman's *Vintage Cookbooks and Advertising Leaflets*.

Cooker, double-pan, the upper one probably for keeping food hot, or slowly cooking (as the food in lower pan cooked). Nesco Roaster®, plain white enamelware. National Enameling and Stamping Company, 1950s, or possibly 1940s. See Crock-Pot®. ..... **$10+**

Corn popper, aluminum pan on aluminum electrified coil-heating base, black wood handles & lid knob, glass dome cover, came with measuring cup for corn, "Knapp-Monarch Co.," St. Louis, MO, c.1940s.. **$10+**

Corn popper, aluminum saucepan shape with long black wood handle, sets onto ventilated aluminum coil-heater base, "West Bend Aluminum Co.," West Bend, WI, 1950s (?)... **$5+**

Corn popper, heavy, blackened tin, short cylindrical drum steel body, crank in top with a bent blade of heavy wire, like a dough mixer, green wood side handles & crank knob, mark stamped on bottom but illegible, American, 8-1/2"H x 8" diam., c.1928 to 1935. A similar one almost looks like copper. ... **$15+**

Corn popper, chrome-plated steel drum body on three curvy sheet metal cabriole legs, green-painted wood side handles & top crank knob out of center of ventilated flat metal lid, 7"H x 8-1/4" diam., lid embossed "Excel Electric Corn Popper," mfd. by Excel Electric Co., Muncie, IN, 1940s. Simpler model just has strap handles, no wood. .... **$15+**

Corn popper, blackened steel drum body, set within 3 tall columnar legs (like broom handle) of red painted wood, crank top domed lid, with wooden disk-knob out of which comes crank with red knob, "Jolly Time" (sometimes "U.S. Electric Corn Popper"), "U. S. Mfg. Corp. Decatur, IL." Detachable cord with red-light unit about 18" from body. Space station styling. (Note: The design evolved slightly; the next version has the lid in red to match the legs & knob, but the disc on top is black. Drum body slightly heavier weight. Marked "No. 7, 41" on bottom, along with U.S. Mfg.) 1940s. Look for one in original red & blue pop-open hexagonal box! Fun graphics........... **$15+**

Corn popper, metal drum body on short legs, 2 handles, lid, heating element inside at bottom, perforated with band of holes, "Dominion Electric Co.," Minneapolis, MN, 1930s.................................. **$25**

Corn popper, nickeled steel with perforations, straight-sided basket pan on heating stand with 3 legs, wooden side handle, lid through which top crank comes, green wood & green cord, "Betsy Ross," mfd. by Central Flat-iron Mfg. Co., Johnson City, NY, 6-1/2"H x 8-1/2" diam., introduced June 1930. .... **$20+**

Corn popper, chrome, slant-sided vessel with pointy black plastic legs, & spectacular space-needle black high pointy finial on flat lid, angular handle, mfd. by Regal, c.1950s. Great look............................ **$10+**

Corn popper, big chrome vessel with black plastic legs and handles, "Jolly Time," mfd. by Mirro. 9"H x 8" diam. c.1970s (?). Value because it can be used & looks spacey.. **$35+**

Corn popper, clear & red plastic & cast metal, shaped like circus wagon with many-spoked well made turning wheels, embossed in red on side "The Great American Popcorn Machine," "4 Qt. - Self Buttering," 10-1/4"H x 12"L, mfd. by Sunbeam, 1976. In original colorfully printed box ready to be assembled... **$15+**

❖ NOTES ❖

Crock-Pot®, as most electric slow-cookers are popularly known & made by various companies, may soon become collectible. On the outside, some are ceramic; some are enamelware, but most do have crockery liners that are usually removable, and are heated from below by heating units in the outer housing. • Rival claims that they evolved from an appliance for cooking beans, called the "Beanery," made by Naxon Utilities Corp., which was acquired by Rival Mfg. in 1970. An early adv'g. slogan of Rival's was "Cooks all day while the cook's away." • I believe they evolved much earlier from the Nesco® Roaster, which was an enamelware double-boiler made by National Enameling and Stamping Company, that was electrified in the early 1930s by wiring the lower pan to make a portable oven, and patented as a "heat insulated cooking vessel" by the well-named Alva T. Smith, Jan. 24, 1933, #1,895,212. Smith, of Milwaukee, claimed that "one of the primary objects of this invention is to provide an electrically heated [and insulated] cooking vessel of extremely light weight, and which can be handled and cleaned similar to kitchen cooking vessels, and which is particularly adapted for use as a bean pot, but which is susceptible for other cooking purposes, which will readily suggest themselves to a housewife." The heating elements were "wound around the insulating" material inside the walls. • The Nesco slow cookers are sometimes plain enamelware, or sometimes have a decoration such as a colorful 1930's design of a young woman tending pots of tulips & houseplants [instead of cooking?]. Most of the Rival ones from the 1970s have typical kitchen-y decoration, such as vegetables or roosters, making them very homey-looking, even corny to today's eyes. West Bend made a bean pot that's a slow cooker. A white ceramic West Bend, that sits on a chrome heating base (see also Pot warmer), is decorated with 1960s modernistic measuring spoons & serving fork. • Slow cookers are coming back, as are fondue pots, more as a lifestyle thing than as a collectible. See also Cooker above.

Defroster, for refrigerators, aluminum with wood handle, pan-shaped, heating coils inside aluminum pan body, thing set inside freezer to defrost accumulated ice. "Heatflo," mfd. by Chromalox Co., Murfreesboro, TN, 1950s. In original graphic box: .... **$7+**
Disc stoves – See Hot plate.
Doughnut maker, electric, oval black sheet metal base, 2 round lids, sort of works like waffle maker, only it makes 7 "donuts," the base & upper molds having the 7 rings with convex centers which touch when closed to create the hole, Wallace Ray Co., Waseca, MN, 1968 ad in McCall's Needlework & Crafts magazine. Just 20+ years ago, but the ad copy seems so dated & funny today. The screaming headlines, above the smiling bob-haired woman gazing upon the maker, is "MAKE MONEY MAKING DONUTS. - New! - Greaseless! - Different! No experience needed! New electric machine bakes 14 dozen per hour, all kinds: Plain, Iced, Raisin, etc. Costs you only 16¢ per doz. YOU earn up to $125 a month SPARE TIME ... MUCH MORE FULL TIME! Start in own kitchen. Sell to restaurants, grocers, drugstores, cafeterias, plants, etc. No bookkeeping! Collect cash profits daily! Machine guaranteed. Add more as needed. Write today for Free Recipes, details. No obligation." .... **$35+**
Donut maker, cast & stamped metal with no-stick interior, makes 6 "donuts," "Master Chef," 9-1/2" diam., c.1960s. .... **$12+**

XVIII-5. **Dining room set,** *consisting of chafing dish (ECD), a type of hot plate called a "stove" (ES) (sometimes a "disc stove"), & a coffee percolator urn (ECP) with glass top. General Electric, 1918-1919. ECD.* **$45+;** *ES* **$25+;** *ECP* **$80+**

XVIII-6. **Egg cooker.** *Ceramic bottom by "Fiesta Ware," chromed metal parts including lid and poaching rack mfd. by Hankscraft Co., Madison, WI. Ceramic came in variety of colors; cream or pastel green is most common, bright Fiesta red most desirable. A small "casserole dish" came with this unit, for making coddled eggs or custards, but I've never seen one for sale with that. They do work, but they're a nuisance to clean and maintain. Electric Home, 1936. Hankscraft also made a bottle warmer along the same lines.* **$65+**

Drink Mixers – See in "M" listings a section on Mixers - Beaters - Drink Mixers - Milkshake Mixers
Egg boiler, electric, metal, "El Eggo," mfd. by Pacific Electric Heating Co., Ontario (?), CAN, late 1890s. ..... **$15+**
Egg cooker, all chrome Deco body & lid with little black knob, top opens with little lever button, marked "Samson No. 187C, Samson-United Corp. Rochester, N.Y., 85773 8 Pat's Pend." 6"H x 6-2/3" diam., 1930s. .... **$45+**
Egg cooker, red ceramic, chrome lid, metal poaching rack inside & ceramic insert, includes instruction booklet, Fiesta Ware ceramic; 6"H x 5-1/2" diam., cooker itself "#599," Hankscraft Co., Good Housekeeping Institute Seal of Approval, Madison, WI, c.1930s. • The same cooker, in orange or light blue, about the same price; in yellow, slightly less; in pale sea foam green, about $10 less. Crossover interest in ceramics. .... **$65+**
Egg cooker & poacher, aluminum body with domed, stepped lid with a horizontal clear-plastic cylindrical handle/gauge device on top – a water-measure for soft-boiling & poaching. Inserts: shallow poaching pan with 3 divisions, & a flat plate with 6 egg-size holes for boiling in shell. Model E2, Sunbeam, Chicago, IL, 8"H x 6"W, looks 1940s. With all parts & intact plastic measurer: .... **$10+**
Eggbeater – See in "M" listings a section on Mixers - Beaters - Drink Mixers - Milkshake Mixers
Flour sifter, tin cylindrical body like many sifters, screen & moving agitator inside, blue & white decal on side says: "The Miracle Electric Flour Sifter. Do not immerse in water." 6"H x 3-3/4" diam., Mfd. by Miracle Electric Mfg. Co., Chicago, IL, c.1930s (?) "patent pending." .... **$20+**
Fondue pot, red-finished "Flame" color, stamped metal pot with encircling white designs & long black plas-

tic handle sits on heating plate of the base, black lid, fork holder fits onto pot edge & holds 6 pointy wood-handled forks each of which has nub of different color on end so users could keep track of their own, recipe book, Oster Electric Fondue Pot, Model 691, 1976. (Notes: The same forks seem to have come with Regal's "Mardi Gras" pot also, & maybe others? Longer handled ones came with Presto.) Pot came in other colors: pale green, yellow, even black I think. .... **$18+**

Fondue pot, red & black spaceship-like design, stainless pot with Teflon™ lining, orangey-red drip ring, wire ring, small black lid with handle pointing up, black disc base has holes to hold 8 color-coded wooden-handled long forks, 6-1/4"H x 11" diam. at widest, "Presto" automatic model "PEO5A," mfd. by Presto, Eau Claire, WI, 1960s? **Fashion warning:** expect to find '60s fondue pots in avocado & harvest gold, too. .... **$20+**

Food preparer, enameled metal base and bowl, lid has large central opening, blades inside, "mixes batter, juices fruits, whips, shreds, slices, chops, grinds. Eliminates the uncertainty & fatigue of food preparation." "Culinaire," mfd. by P. A. Geier Co. & affiliate Continental Electric Co., Ltd., Cleveland, OH, and Toronto, Canada, c.1934. Two years later Geier had a new "Royal Culinaire," with chromium plated bowl & a juicer attachment. .... **$50+**

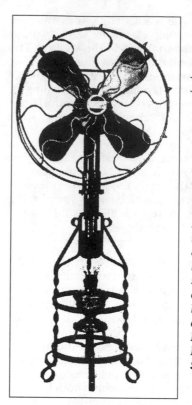

XVIII-8. Hot air, kerosene lamp fan. *The famous "Lake Breeze" floor-standing fan with wrought iron base. This looks like many items of the same period for use on the porch – plant stands and furniture, and its independence of electricity or water meant that it could be used outdoors. The kerosene lamp below caused rising hot air, which eventually caused the blades to turn. It is considered a very desirable collectors' fan, and brings thousands of dollars at auction. Lake Breeze Motor, Chicago, IL. Mfd. c. 1914-20.* **$2,500+**

XVIII-7. Table fans. (L) *White Cross Breezer Fan No. 60, nickel-plated, "especially adapted for use in small rooms, offices, state rooms, telephone booths, by the bed-side, on the desk and enclosed motor boats and automobiles. It is equipped with starting and speed-regulating device and is particularly adapted as a portable electric fan, from the fact of it being lighter in weight than the average eight inch fan. Angle adjustable. Nickeled or oxidized copper cast iron & tool steel." **(R)** White Cross Table Fan No. 289, "for use on table as a center piece." The bowl didn't revolve, but I'd hate to reach carelessly for a summer peach & miss the bowl. AC or DC, any cycle, and was furnished for any voltage from 100 to 220. Three speeds. Nickeled cast iron, brass blades, removable pressed glass bowl on top. 10-1/2"H x 9-1/2" diam. Both mfd. by Lindstrom-Smith Co., Chicago. Editorial note in House Furnishing Review, May 1915.* **(L) $65+; (R) $500+**

Food warmer, copper with black molded phenolic resin, probably Bakelite, handles, 3 compartments, Chase Brass & Copper, with centaur logo, 1940s. ...... **$30+**

Frittering pan – like a frying pan but without typical long handle, aluminum 2-tone, pinkish-copper anodized lid & underside & silvery-aluminum band around the flying saucer shape with elongated triangular landing pods (feet), sprouty side handles, domed lid with knob, detachable cord plugs into porthole inside, so space ship can land on the buffet table, mfd. by Cory Corp., Chicago, IL (most noted for coffee-making stuff: they started out as Cory Glass Coffee Brewer Co.), 1950s. .... **$15+**

Frying pan, heavy cast aluminum, large & round, nearly flat lid with knob, black pointy feet sets it high above surface, heating is in closed channel encircling underside of pan, fantastic drop-set substantial black plastic handle with the control knob on end – "off" to 400 degrees! Below knob are 2 prongs for plug. 11-1/2" diam., 20"L overall. General Electric, Canada. 1950s. .... **$15+**

Frying pan, cast iron, with lid that has drip nipples on inside, looks like most fairly short handled iron skillets, 12" diam., marked "Country Charm Skillet Model No. S-60," "The House of Webster - Rogers, Arkansas." With booklet of recipes, *Our Treasury of Old Fashioned Recipes.* Thermostat by American Thermostat Corp., electrified base with separate cord. Late 1950s. .... **$45+**

❖ NOTES ❖

House of Webster, in Rogers, Arkansas, was established in 1934. Right from the beginning they put up their food gifts in containers that were replicas of things from the old times – like an old butter churn, a cast iron kettle, and a cream can. In 1957, they intro-

Griddle, chromed metal, small rectangle on short legs, "Electrahot" Style 512, Electrahot Mfg. Co., Minneapolis, MN, c.1930s. .... **$15+**

Hand mixer – See in "M" listings a section on Mixers - Beaters - Drink Mixers - Milkshake Mixers

Hot dog cooker, black metal base, green pottery insert with side cup handle & 4 brass feet that fit into holes in metal base, probably something to do with the electrical connection, black plastic handle, "The Lightning Wiener Cooker," mfd. by Lightning Cooker Co., Cleveland, OH, holds 3 hot dogs, c.1920s or 1930s. No patent numbers............................. **$25+**

Hot dog steamer, white enameled metal house with heavy-duty molded red plastic peaked roof with steam vent chimneys, marked "Dog House" on front, "Sunbeam," Chicago Flexible Shaft Co., 7"H x 7-3/4"L, 1980s. Perfect example of an almost-instant collectible. It is not a "Snoopy" item, but plays only on word "Dog." Faddish, figural & extremely well-made.............................. **$20+**

Hot plate, tinned sheet iron & cast iron, triangular base with insulated round button feet, round top with center hole, toggle switch on side with "DOUX" ("soft," or, prob., "low"), embossed under switch, embossed "ALS THOM VIVALOX 800W 120V," prob. French Canadian, 1920s. Very handsome & collectible; like very few hot plates. .... **$15+**

Hot plate, enamelware, 5"H x 11-1/2" x 11" square, "Model C," mfd. by Chromalox. **$15**

XVIII-9. Frypan & "frittering pan." "Eclipse" deep frying pan, made by the Electric & Ordnance Accessories Co., Birmingham, England, & unidentified frittering (deep frying) pan, heating elements in their bases. Pictures from a book that combines American and English appliances, cooking techniques and vocabulary: Maud Lancaster's Electric Cooking, Heating & Cleaning, 1914. The indistinct picture of the frittering pan appears to show glass marbles forming the feet. • Lancaster gives a list of electrical appliance makers – see directory at beginning of this chapter. The values could go way up. **$30-$55+**

XVIII-10. Hotdog or wiener cooker. "Here we have the use of electricity in its simplest form where the 'hot dogs' are cooked by running the electricity through them. Alternating current should be used. The electricity boils the water contained in the food and causes it to do its own cooking. Such a cooker has another automatic feature inasmuch as the carrying handle also controls the switch. When the handle is in its vertical position the current is on, and when the wieners are cooked the handle is put to one side or the other of the device, automatically shutting off the current and leaving free space for handling the wieners. These devices are furnished in different sizes and colors to suit one's fancy." Electric Home, 1936. • **Alternating versus Direct Current.** This is uncomfortably like a description of electrocution, which had been in use to execute criminals since 1889, when current generated by a Westinghouse alternating-current power plant in New York state provided the electricity. One of the brouhahas at the time of the first electrocution was over whether alternating or direct current would be most efficient. Thomas Edison and others felt that direct current would not work as well as alternating; George Westinghouse, who had developed the first alternating current power plant, protested on general grounds because electricity was already regarded as dangerous, and on specific grounds, because of the 'bad press' his kind of electricity would receive. **$45+**

Hot plate, gray graniteware square base with wonderful rounded pylon corner feet, round concentric heating rings, 7-1/4" square, Canadian (?), c.1920s. . **$25+**

Hot plate, nickel-plated square top with simple scrolled & other cutouts, central round heating part, 4 small feet, only 6" square. Stamped underneath "Electric Trivet, Model N-1, UL," no maker mark, detachable cord. Very attractive. early 1920s. .... **$20+**

Hot plate or table stove, nickel-plated sheet steel, wonderful girder-like sheet metal legs with cutouts, riveted to square body, "Hold Heet," mfd. by Russell Electric Co., Chicago, IL, 3"H x 5" square, 2 twisted cloth-covered wires – one plug but each wire attached to 2 widely-separated terminals, direct current, late 1920s.............................. **$30+**

Hot plate, medium green enamelware, 3"H x 7-1/2" square, round heating element centered on top, 2 wooden grip side handles, French. .... **$20+**

Hot plate, nickel-plated round heater with heating coils set in ceramic, 3 wonderful heavy curved iron cabriole-like legs, "Cat. No. 350," mfd. by "Knapp-Monarch Co., Webster City, IA," 4-1/8"H x 7-3/8" diam. Early 1930s. .... **$28+**

Hot plates – See also Pot warmer

Ice cream mixers, electric – See Chapter XVI (Chill)

Immersion heater, chromed heating cylinder with long cord, "Lightning Speed Portable Electric Hot Water Heater," in original box. Meant to be used by travelers, students, roomers, etc., and dunked right into the soup or coffee or mug of water for shaving. 1930s. .... **$10+**

Insect killer, chromed metal canister, hangs from ceiling, with removable base (for taking out dead insects), alternating current only. "Vaporizer," mfd. by Manning-Bowman, 1930s. • The description of this peculiar item in E. S. Lincoln's 1936 book, *The Electric Home*, says it "looks like an ordinary birdcage, but instead of containing a canary it contains an ordinary light bulb. The small vertical wires that surround the bulb are charged with electricity and when any insect comes in contact with these wires it is instantly killed." The caption is even weirder: "Electrically heated vaporizor for exterminating moths and other flying insects." **The Good Die Young.** – This vaporizer killed flies in the house; but the electric bug zappers that sound so annoying and frenetic on summer evenings, when your neighbors leave them on 24 hours a day, are killing useful insects. Few mosquitoes are killed, and flies sleep at night. Night birds compete with the zappers, and many people have found rare & beautiful moths (not clothes-eating varieties) dead in their killing

XVIII-12. Combination tabletop appliance. *For grilling, making pancakes, poaching eggs, heating liquids. Nickeled steel with black-painted wooden handles. 3 feet pads of nonconducting "fibre." Three heat levels with "snap switch," a removable rack with 4 separate pans for egg poaching. Shape and size (8" diam.) of stove plate permits use of round aluminum vessels. Depths of the 3 utensils are 1/4" (the griddle), 1-1/4", and 2". D. J. Barry jobber catalog, 1924. Manufacturer not given, but probably "Universal" (Landers, Frary & Clark).* **$35+**

machines. Kindly turn yours off; you will do Nature a favor. .... **$20+**

Juicer, green Jadite glass, tall base straddles container, on top is dark green enameled motor housing with chrome trim, cream ceramic reamer, alternating current only, 17-1/2"H, "Sunkist Juicit," mfd. by Chicago Electric Mfg. Co., "Handy Hot®" Product, Chicago, IL, 8-3/4"H, 1934 patents #1943270 and #1962856. .... **$55+**

Juicer, electric, footed metal cylinder, pump-like spout near top, white glass (maker called "alabaster") bowl & reamer. 1929 ad copy makes us giggle now: "To meet Fresh Fruit Juice speed requirements comes along the perfected and proved Orange and Lemon go-getter known far & near as Sunkist Junior Electric Extractor. ... Not only a handsome donation [sic], but much wanted because it snaps out a glass or a gallon of juice for breakfast – or other purposes – with alacrity equaled by no other method. ... [The] whizzing cone gets all the Orange or Lemon Juice without the usual work – and mess. Two instantly removable parts to wash under faucet." Obviously written by one of the Poets of Electricity!" "Sunkist Jr," mfd. by California Fruit Growers' Exchange, Chicago, 10"H, late 1920s. .... **$45+**

Kettle, chrome-plated with quadrant-curved black molded phenolic resin handle from base up over top, short thrusting-lipped filling-and-pouring spout, extremely sleek modern design, 2-1/2 quart capacity, 9-1/2"H x 8" diam., detachable cord out of base of handle, Model "K48B," Canadian General Electric Ltd., Barrie, Ontario, c. late 1950s. Another came with a ivory-color handle & base (K49FM 3706), which I prefer. .... **$55+**

Liquid mixers – See in "M" listings a section on Mixers - Beaters - Drink Mixers - Milkshake Mixers

Malted milk or Milk shake mixers – See in "M" listings a section on Mixers - Beaters - Drink Mixers - Milkshake Mixers

XVIII-11. Juicer. *"Sunkist Juicit" deluxe model No. BM-21, in the "Handy Hot®" line, by Chicago Electric Mfg. Co. "Included in its construction is a Magic Automatic Strainer that oscillates rapidly back and forth, whipping the juice cells of the pulp against sharpened edges of strainer holes, first releasing every drop of juice, and, secondly, cutting the health-giving pulp into tiny particles." Chrome with "French Ivory" glass juice collector bowl and reamer. "Powerful induction type motor does not interfere with radio reception and operates only on 110-120 volts, 50-60 cycle alternating current. Toggle switch. Cord and plug cap attached." Handy Hot® catalog AA, 1940.* **$55+**

Microwave oven, countertop, sheet metal drop front oven with 2 buttons "start" & "light," and 2 knobs to control time on right (one for up to 5 minutes; one for 5-25 minutes). First countertop microwave. (According to J. Carlton Gallawa, Tappan Stove Co., Bellaire, OH, made the first home model, a floor-standing behemoth the size of a refrigerator, in the early 1950s.) "Radar Range," mfd. by Amana Refrigeration Inc., Div. of Raytheon, Amana, IA, 1967. Hardly any collector interest, yet, in any microwaves, but someday? .... **$10+**

❖ NOTES ❖

Women & Machines – In a 1919 speech, Raymond Marsh, Secretary of the American Washing Machine Manufacturers' Association, said "A wonderful story could be told about how women went into factories and recovered entirely from their awe and fear of machinery. Experience has shown that women are and can be efficient at running machinery. ... During the war, women rendered efficient service working hydraulic presses, heating and charging furnaces, welding brass, forging chains, molding bricks, constructing compasses ... and a thousand and one other important and necessary tasks." Marsh's point was that WWI encouraged the use of labor saving devices in the kitchen because women had lost their fear of machines and they had no household servants when every able-bodied woman in the U.S., England and France (and probably Germany too) went to work in war-industry factories.

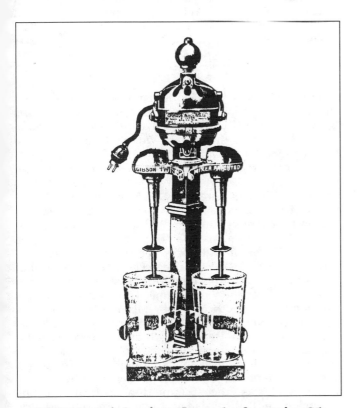

XVIII-13. Drink mixer for soda fountain. Gibson "Twin-Mixer," H. B. Gibson Co., NYC, hooked up to a Hamilton-Beach motor, Racine, WI. Could be had quadruple silver-plated, or nickel-plated. June 1919 ad in The Soda Fountain. **$300+**

XVIII-14. Drink mixer – electric. "Arnold Sanitary Mixer No. 12," nickeled. In suppliers' catalog of 1921. **$125+**

❖ NOTES ❖

Cucumbers — "He had been eight years upon a project for extracting sunbeams out of cucumbers, which were to be put into phials hermetically sealed, and let out to warm the air in raw inclement summers." Jonathan Swift, Voyage to Laputa, from *Gulliver's Travels*, 1726. Actually he should probably have tried to extract cucumbers from Sunbeams!

❖ RECIPE ❖

Cucumber Sauce. 3 medium-sized cucumbers. 2 oz. of butter. 1 oz. of flour. 1/2 pint of white stock. Cayenne. A few drops of lemon juice. Salt. – Peel the cucumbers, and take out the seeds. Cut the cucumber into small pieces. Put the pieces into a stewpan with one ounce of butter, and cover closely with a lid. Draw to the side of the stove, and cook gently until quite tender. Melt the remaining ounce of butter in a saucepan; stir in the flour. Add to this the white stock (or milk, if stock is not available). Season with cayenne pepper and salt. Add this to the cucumber and then rub the whole through a hair sieve. Re-warm and just before serving add a few drops of lemon juice. The same saucepan that the cucumbers are cooked in will do for making the sauce, provided it is not too large, as it can be made after the cucumbers are cooked." Katharine Mellish's Cookery Book, London: E. & F. N. Spon, 1901. • *You can probably get the same effect by putting the cooked mixture into a mixer, instead of rubbing through a "hair sieve."*

Beaters or Small Mixers with Beater Jars, Containers, Measuring Cups

Beater, stainless steel blade, white glass jar, red knob, "K-M" Knapp-Monarch Co., St. Louis, MO, 9-1/2"H, 1931+. .... **$15-$25**

Beater, white motor housing in stepped, rounded rings. Air vents on top only, lid fitted to clear glass jar with 4 paneled corners, "Handy Hot Whipper," Chicago Electric Division of The Silex Co., 8-1/4"H x 4-3/4" diam. Pat. #2,179,383, by Frank Rodwick, Nov. 7, 1939, assigned to Chicago Electric Mfg. Co. Brand name often seen as "Handyhot." .... **$25-$30**

Beater, white motor housing with many air vents side & top, red wood knob on top, opaque white glass jar like above, triangle blade, "Challenge," 1940s. .... **$15-$25**

Beater, white motor housing, bracket handle, lid fits onto 6-sided glass container embossed with "O" in diamond (Owens Glass Co.), "Sterling," mfd. by CEM – Chicago Electric Mfg. Co. "9-41," "Patent #1,917,289" is for a "self-starting induction motor." July 11, 1933, by Bernhart A. Benson, assignor to CEM. Instructions on "How to Whip Cream Successfully." .... **$15-$25**

Beater, heavy metal motor housing with black wood knob on top, sets down in Vidrio opaque glass bowl with green & rusty pumpkin swirls, original wiring, "WM-40," Whip-Mix, bowl is 4-1/2"H, overall height including knob is 7-5/8"H, 20th C. Dennis Thompson has three of the "rarest **Vidrio** pieces": glass lids to this mixer's bottom, provided so that the container could be used as a refrigerator jar. To find the mixer, a matching lid, and the beater itself would probably triple the value. **$65**

Beater, paneled custard slag glass container, with ivory-painted metal motor housing with shaped knob, simple beater blades, Eugene Newham patent #1,790,242, Jan. 27, 1931, for the motor & simple stand. (See the "K-M" also.) "Vidrio," Vidrio Products Corp. (the glass parts), Cicero, IL, 1930s. .... **$35+**

Beater, cobalt blue paneled glass container 4-1/2"H fitted with single squiggly beater blade attached to housed motor, strap handle, lid has hole for pouring ingredients in with funnel, "Vidrio Products Corp.," Catalog #E20, Chicago, IL, 2-cup capacity, 1933 patent #1,935,857. (This also came with a

XVIII-15. Eggbeater. Electric *"Challenge," mfd. by CEM Co., "Tyre" model "AVUB". Simple single dasher blade, works perfectly, even hums. 3 cup capacity, 8-1/2"H, 110-120 volts.* **$10+**

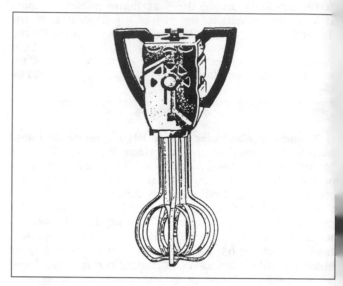

XVIII-16. Eggbeater & food mixer. *"Dormeyer," mfd. by A. F. Dormeyer Mfg. Co., Chicago.* American Cookery *magazine, 1930.* **$20+**

Depression green glass jar with pale green-painted metal lid & motor housing & fat turned-wood side handle. That one is valued at about 1/4 to 1/3 of value of blue one. Yet another, much rarer than either, has an ultramarine glass container.) The cobalt blue: .... **$120+**

❖ NOTES ❖

Vidrio Mystery. The Vidrio name is usually seen on small electric appliances with glass. It even means "glass" in Spanish. According to *Thomas' Directory, 1932-33,* glass products were Vidrio's beat. They were listed under "Glassware: table, blown, flint, pressed, etc." *The Housefurnishing Review,* that I depend on so much, does not list Vidrio at all in their 1930 Buyer's Guide. In *Thomas' Directory, 1945-46,* there's a listing under "trade names" but not for "manufacturers" for "Vidrio Hair Dryers," mfd. by Vidrio Products Co., Chicago, IL"; also, as manufacturer of "portable clothes washer." Objects from table & floor lamps, clocks, ashtrays, cigarette lighters, desk accessories & gear-shift knobs to hand mixers, countertop washing machines & hair dryers bear the Vidrio name. The mystery remains: who made the electrical parts? Mixer-collector Dennis Thompson, who specializes in Vidrio, has collected many Vidrio items. He believes that they had mechanical/electrical designers as well as glass designers because they "had styles that are unique to Vidrio items, and they marketed a number of items without glass parts, such as their countertop clothes washing machines and dishwashers, hairdriers, etc." Vidrio made a 2-piece reamer in transparent green that is listed in juicer guides as rare. Also a rare hand-cranked metal juicer on a slag glass bottom called the "Gem Squeezer." Both are in Gene Florence's kitchenware book. A version – still called the Gem Squeezer – was made by Quam-Nichols entirely in metal. The most elusive evidence is that Vidrio received a "patent for a full-ized Vidrio mixer of unique style, but none is known to the mixer-community. That patent was granted in 1938." Dennis Thompson went to Cicero, IL, in mid-2002, and found Vidrio listed in the telephone directory at least from 1928 to the mid-1930s, but by the time that mixer patent was granted in 1938, they were no longer in the directory, and had moved (?) to Chicago. If you have any information valuable to Thompson's research, e-mail him at dthomp@core.com, or write him at address listed at end of this chapter.

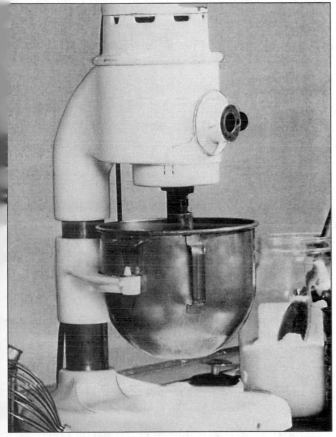

*XVIII-17. Mixer on stand. Hobart Corporation's "KitchenAid" Model H 1918. This mixer, meant for home use, followed by three years the first commercial electric mixer – for restaurants & hotels – that was introduced in 1915. Picture courtesy of Hobart Corp. Hobart, founded in 1897, was innovative from the beginning. To quote from a short history of the company, "During the period from 1905 to 1910, peanut butter and hamburger were becoming popular items in the American diet, and Hobart introduced an electric meat chopper and a peanut butter machine. To build sales for these products, Hobart pioneered time-payment selling." In another publication, a Newcomen Address given by President David Meeker in 1960, the story is related of Hobart's dishwasher. Hobart & the Crescent Washing Machine Co. joined in 1926. To quote: "The history of [Crescent] dates back to the 1880s when an imaginative and purposeful lady, Mrs. Josephine Garis Cochrane, built a machine for the purpose of doing her own dishes." **Note:** This caption was incorrect in 3rd & 4th editions. This is the correct caption, finally. Note: for info on the 1937 Model "K," go to: www.idsa.org/whatis/100yr/kitchenaid.htm.* **$175+**

Beater, iron housing lid with strap handle, looks like part of an old hair dryer, activates 2 wing blade, glass jar, works perfectly, hums quietly, "Challenge," mfd. by CEM Co., "Tyre AVUB" (Whur's this, hey! Sounds like a Biblical land of gluttony & sloth. Actually it's a model code.). "CEM" is Chicago Electrical Mfg. Co., Chicago, IL, 8-1/2"H, with 3-cup capacity, 1930s? (CEM established c.1903.)..................... **$15+**

Beater, enameled tan metal motor housing/lid, strap handle, glass container, "Model AVUB 110-120 volts," Chicago Electric Mfg. Co., 7-1/2"H x 3-1/2" diam. motor housing, 3-cup, 24-oz. container is 4-3/4"H x 5" diam. at top. 1940s?.............................. **$10-$25**

Beater, sheet metal motor housing painted green with bracket strap handle & off-white fitted lid & single loop blade, 3-cup glass measuring bowl is 4-3/4"H x 5" diam., "Electric Mixer" mfd. by The Master Electric Co., Dayton, OH, late 1930s................ **$10-$25**

Beater, enameled pale yellow motor housing, slightly offset of center on fitted lid, nickeled strap bracket handle, single beater, clear glass 2-cup capacity container with 4 foot-like projections, embossed on bottom "Meljax Manufacturing Corp., Chicago 54 Illinois," 8"H x 4-1/2" diam. Prob. successor to CEM, c.1950. .... **$10+**

Beater, chrome motor housing & lid fitted to glass measure that has three little feet, angled black modern tiller handle on top, beater detaches, "Dorby" on underside of motor, glass embossed on bottom: "Grand Sheet Metal Products Co. Home Appliance Division Melrose Park, Illinois," 9"H overall x 4-1/2" diam. 1940s. .... **$15+**

Beater, white-finished metal motor housing fits onto white glass receptacle that has 4 streamlined feet, bright red bird-beak handle curves over motor, "Knapp-Monarch," St. Louis, MO. This one, sold by eBayer "vandyk" from his collection, is especially nice because of its original colorful hang-tag: "Electrical Servants" "K-M" with "Guarantee." .... **$25+**

Beater, stamped sheet metal motor housing & lid fits onto slant-sided, 4-side, 3-cup capacity clear glass container. "Kwik-Way No. K-107," Kwik-Way Co., St. Louis, MO. Pat. #1,938,857 given to Greenleaf Whittier Pickard for electrical condensor, Dec. 12, 1933. Patent application was filed back in 1922. In 1933, he assigned his patent to General Electric, but Knapp-Monarch, and Kwik-Way both used it for their mixers. .... **$10+**

❖ NOTES ❖

Mixer Uses. "Use Electric Mixer to WAX, POLISH, SAND" – so advertised Towle Mfg. Co., Walnut Creek, CA, in Sept. 1960. Their device, a "slip-on TOOLZON," was fitted on the shaft of "any mixer" so that you could "let your kitchen mixer wax furniture, floors, auto; polish silver, glass, brass; sand wood, metal, ceramics." (I can just see the product liability disclaimers.) In theory it's a great idea.

XVIII-18. Mixer & food preparer. *The "Kitch-enAid" for home use – showing the whipping blades. The detachable funnel lying on the right of the work stand.* "The kitchen is too often a drab kind of place. Yet surely, considering the hours spent there, ... it ought to be the cheerfullest room in the house. In KitchenAid homes, the kitchen has come into its own. It is **Mother's workshop** – a place where drudgery has given way to self expression – where cooking and baking has become a joy – new recipes a real sport. It is no longer a lonely place. Dad, who admires mechanical ingenuity, likes to watch KitchenAid's deft, steel hands at work – or to 'run' it himself, especially in freezing ice cream. You will find 'Junior' and 'sister' there, too, and very often a guest." *Hobart Corp., Troy, OH, "KitchenAid" catalog, 1928. This mixer for home use followed by three years the first commercial electric mixer, for restaurants and hotels. Hobart Corp., founded in 1897, was innovative from the beginning. To quote from a short company history, "During the period from 1905 to 1910, peanut butter and hamburger were becoming popular items in the American diet, and Hobart introduced an electric meat chopper and a peanut butter machine. To build sales for these products, Hobart pioneered time-payment selling."* **$175+**

Churns

Churn, heavy sheet metal motor housing, with shaft & wooden paddles, clamp fits onto barrel-shaped large clear glass body embossed with cow, bail handle with wood grip, "Gem Dandy," "Standard Electric Churn," 22-1/2"H overall, body 16"H, 2-1/2 gal., mfd. by Alabama Manufacturing Co., Birmingham, AL, 1940s. .... **$45+**

Drink or Liquid Mixers

Drink mixer, various metals, some enameled, "Drinkmaster," Hamilton Beach, Racine, WI, 1926. ... **$60+**

Drink mixer, etc., chromed motor housing on black stand, original tall, silver-striped glass tumbler or container with it's ringed splash lid, "MIXALL" or "MIX-ALL," mfd. Chronmaster Electric Corp., New York & Chicago, pat'd. Jan. 9, 1934. With original recipe booklet 14"H. The patent # on it says "License Pat. 1943270" but I can't get it on the US Patent Office site as a utility, reissue or design patent. Nancy Platnick of WACEM says the patent is Ameri-

can & is for a "shaded-pole induction motor" granted to James J. Gouge & assigned to Chicago Electrical Mfg. **$25**

Liquid mixer, enameled iron base for motor, glass top, base looks like a streamlined locomotive front, Holliwood Liquefier Co. (sometimes seen as Hollywood Liquefier), South Pasadena, CA, 1930s. Stylin' name! **$200**

Malted Milk & Milk Shake Mixers

Malted milk mixer, metal & glass, 17-1/2"H, "Arnold #15," Arnold Electric Co., Hamilton Beach subsidiary, 1923+. **$100**

Milk shake mixer, white porcelain base, glass, metal, Arnold Mfg Co., adv'g. "Horlicks, The Original Malted Milk," c.1930s. **$300**

Milk shake mixer, metal & glass, "Gilchrist," Newark, NJ. Raymond Gilchrist's patent was granted Aug. 21, 1923. .... **$100**

Malted milk mixer, also called a malt mixer, a stand with mounted motor-head, single spindle mixing blade, "Hamilton Beach #51," Racine, WI, c.1911.............................. **$100+**

Malted milk machine, green porcelainized cast iron, 2 containers, Hamilton Beach Mfg. Co., Racine, WI, 1930s-40s.............................. **$150+**

Milk shake mixer, triple head & 3 speed, green or cream enameled steel, glass, this triple head type was for a soda fountain, not the home, Hamilton Beach, 1930s. .... **$165+**

Hand Mixers, without Fitted Bowls

Hand-held mixers weren't viable until the weight of the motor was light enough for the unit to be held with one hand. A lot of stand mixers have detachable motor housings with handgrips; those could be used both ways, but are listed under Stand mixers.

Mixer, hand-held, streamlined motor housing with handle attached front & back, takes 2 beater blades, "Dormey," "Model 7500," mfd. by Dormeyer. Original box & recipes. 1950s. .... **$20+**

Mixer, hand-held, streamlined chrome bullet body with black handle, marked on end-plate: "Fostoria F [in shield] McGraw Electric Co. – Bersted Mfg. Div. Boonville, MD – Model 50X." Looks 1950s. ..... **$10+**

Mixer or beater, hand-held with simple, self-assembled optional stand, black finish, steel motor housing,

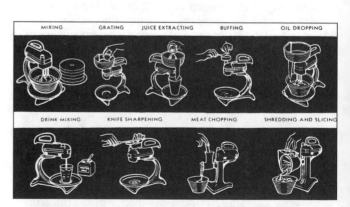

XVIII-19. Mixer in many roles. *Page decorations for the G-E "Hotpoint Portable Mixer." 1935-36 catalog. Sunbeam and KitchenAid mixers also had multiple uses.*

fattish easy-grip handle, "Polar Cub," A. C. Gilbert Co., New Haven, CT. In original box with glorious graphics, including housewife mixing while 2 tiny polar bear cubs wrestle on table. 1920s+. .... **$75+**

Mixer, hand-held, streamlined white-finish body, detachable double blades, "Osterett" Model 400, John Oster Mfg. Co., box says "mixes, mashes, whips, beats, creams," 1950s............................ **$15-$20+**

Tabletop or Stand Mixers

Stand mixers were an easy segue from rotary egg-beaters with stands. At a glance, some of them look very like each other. According to Don Thornton, in *Beat This, The Eggbeater Chronicles*, p. 209, the first electric mixer-beater was probably patented in 1885; the inventor, Rufus M. Eastman, claimed that his device was to be connected to the work surface and "operated by a motor." Probably the earliest really recognizable stand mixer patents were in 1909 and 1910. Most stand mixers take up a lot of counter space, but the first one here is almost the size of one of the cute beater/mixers with a container. You won't find blenders in here, but they were and are a sort of combined drink mixer and food puréer.

Mixer, white-enameled motor housing (with wooden handle), & cast iron pivoting stand with very small footprint, white opaque glass bowl, 4-3/8"H x 6" diam., is marked "McKee." "Type AVUD, 60 cycles," "Mary Dunbar Handymix," Chicago Electric Mfg. Co. Has design patent from 1940. 11-1/2"H; base 5-3/4"W x 8-1/4"L. Not common. .... **$20-$40**

Mixer, white-enameled cast iron stand & 3-speed metal motor housing/body. Ad in *American Home* says

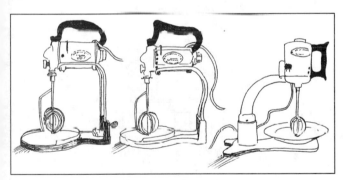

*XVIII-20. Old stand mixers. Lucky I have some self-control left after doing this 5th edition. These three early mixers are just wonderful in design. (L) Very rare Hamilton Beach "Combination Food Mixer and Extractor" Model A with the **red badge** name plate, which says "FM 54095" & shows Pat. #1,738,112. Introduced 1925. Note upright support (actually two L-shaped rods). (M) The **green badge** Hamilton Beach, #–3452, with the curved rod uprights, and a slight modification in the handle – both are types of handles often seen on big coffee pots. Drawings done from photos by Adrian Van Dyk, eBayer "vandyk" who by the time this book is out will probably have sold all of his large collection of mixers. (R) "Depression green"-colored "DeLuxe Royal Dormeyer Mixer, 3 speeds, 13"H, 1930s. Drawing from sale by eBayer "romans10." All three eBay auctions 2002. (L) & (M) $175+, (R) $100+*

*XVIII-21. **Mixer beater.** "Quick-Mix" with one speed & one beater. The eye at left of motor housing is for hanging it on a hook when not in use. Manufacturer's name not in Thomas' Register of American Manufacturers of the 1930s. Pictured in Electric Home, 1936. Vidrio & mixer-collector Dennis Thompson has two versions of this mixer. One is like this; the other has an oval shape and is marked "Royal Rochester Quick Mix, Rochester, NY." The rivets, handle & beater style are the same. Royal Rochester also made toasters. **$35+***

"now, in addition to portable one-hand operation, bowl control and the many other time-tested and exclusive features, the New Model 'C' has 57% more power, no radio interference, and new streamline beauty – yet it costs you no more. The exclusive 'Bowl Control' feature regulates the revolving speed of the bowl – and allows it to be shifted to prevent the mixture from piling up in the middle or around the edge." Attachments included "juice extractor, meat grinder, slicer-shredder, coffee grinder and potato peeler" bought separately. "Hamilton Beach Model C," Hamilton Beach Mfg Co., Racine, WI, new in 1934. Without extra attachments: **$45**

Mixer, cast metal base with detachable mixer, juicer attachment, set of ceramic, heat-proof mixing bowls & lids could be put in oven, Sears' "Powermaster DeLuxe," late 1930s. .... **$45+**

Mixer, cast metal stand with curved & angled upright painted pale yellow; motor housing yellow with green band, matching yellow & green-banded bowl on stand, Landers, Frary & Clark, green cartouche decals: "For Food Chopper" "Universal" "For Mixer & Beater," 14"H upright, early 1920s. Also, according to Nancy Platnick, "the green trim and LFC monogram decal are really susceptible to fading; if the logo is in great condition, this could go for much more." .... **$60-$95**

Mixer, cast & sheet metal, nickel plated, with turned wood spade handle; a portable food mixer in its own heavy wire stand (rather like a doll stand), that allowed it to be used in vertical position with a tumbler or other fairly low container. They advertised "Used on stand or in the hand." To be plugged into lamp socket. "Whip-All," mfd. by Air-O-Mix, Wilmington, DE, 1923 to about 1926-27. Short-lived, hence very rare. .... **$400+**

Mixer, cast metal base with mixer that, when first introduced, came with 2 stainless steel mixing bowls, and somewhat later, one attachment: a juicer. That was soon to be joined by other attachments: a food chopper, grater, potato peeler, knife sharpener, polisher, can opener, drink mixer & coffee grinder. "Mixmaster," mfd. by the Chicago Flexible Shaft Co. (later Sunbeam), Chicago, IL, 1930-31. (By 1936, all the other attachments were available.) According to Earl Lifshey, author of *The Housewares Story* (see Bibliography), "By 1936 "Mixmaster sales reached to more than 300,000 units." By 1957, "over twelve million homemakers are saving time and arm-work" with their Mixmasters. So there are plenty of old & older ones out there for collectors; the trick is finding the attachments. An early Model M4 with 6 attachments: .... **$200-$250**

Mixer, with instruction booklet and many attachments, including ricer, meat grinder, mixing bowls of creamy green glass, "Sunbeam Model M4C." [I had a note that it was "FC4" if that means anything.] Chicago Flexible Shaft Co., 1934 patent #1926910 is latest patent number. Their first "Mixmaster" was 1930. .... **$80+**

Mixer, stainless steel/chrome & black, base of stand, handle & back end of mixer housing of black plastic, very streamline shape – in horizontal position it actually resembles space-ship/bullet-shape tail lights on some 1950s finned cars; 2 "Glasbake" mixing bowls, "Sunbeam Mixmaster Model 12C," Chicago, c.1957. .... **$50-$100**

Mixer, fantastic pink paint-enamel finish on stand & motor housing, black plastic trim. Even "Glasbake" bowl has fired-on pink finish Small bowl has pouring lip, is 5"H x 6-1/2" diam., embossed on bottom "Glasbake Made for Sunbeam No. 20 20CJ." Finned "Mix-Finder Dial" knob on back of motor housing changes 12 speed settings. "Sunbeam Mixmaster," Chicago, late 1950s. Color adds value! The Model 11 & the Model 12 were available in white, chrome, pink, yellow, and turquoise. In their manual/cook-

XVIII-23. Mixer. *Single stainless steel blade, red wooden knob, white glass ribbed beater jar was press-molded with 4-strut rocket-fin designs – for stability and style. 9-1/2"H. "K-M," Knapp-Monarch Co., St. Louis, MO. Patent same as one used with Vidrio beaters: #1,935,857. Jan. 27, 1931.* **$15-$25**

book of 1957, Sunbeam lists all the available parts, attachments & bowls. The juicer attachment came only in white & clear glass; for a "Deluxe" you could get the large & small bowls in aluminum, white glass, turquoise, pink or yellow glass............ **$135+**

Mixer, enameled cast metal motor housing in yellow-cream with green trim, black handle on side, stand is green, opaque green glass reamer bowl, & mixing bowl marked "Manning-Bowman" on bottom, tur-

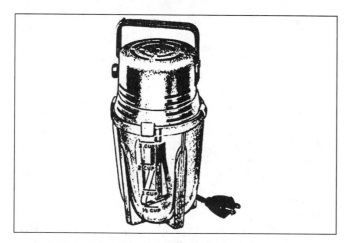

XVIII-22. Mixer beater "whipper." *"Handy Hot" deluxe combination mixer, clear glass beater jar with graduated markings for 3 cups. White motor housing with nickeled handle. 110-120 volts, 50-60 cycle AC current. Chicago Electric Manufacturing Co. (Chicago Electric Division of the Silex Co.), 8-1/4"H, 1938 catalog. See patent in XVIII-24.* **$25+**

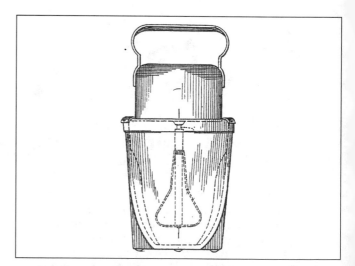

XVIII-24 . Whipper patent for "Handy Hot." *This "whipper" was pat'd. Nov. 7, 1939, by Frank Rodwick, Chicago, assignor to Chicago Electric Mfg. Co. Pat. #2,179,383, Serial No. 259,583. (Serial numbers were assigned by the Patent Office, and sometimes appear on products.) "The present invention relates to an agitator, beater, or whipping member and its manner of juncture with a drive shaft. ... This member must be subjected to cleansing after use, a treatment which is not applicable to the associated control and drive means which is normally electrical in nature." Rodwick's invention provided a latch that was "means for realeasability and positively securing a driven element to a drive shaft element."*

bine combines 4 outer blades with 2 small ball-shaped blades inside, Model 8, Manning-Bowman & Co., Meriden, CT. Patent #01,938,857 is for an electrical condensor, pat'd. by Greenleaf Whittier Pickard, Dec. 12, 1933 (filed 11 years before in 1922), and assigned to GE........................... **$125-$250**

Mixer, green cast iron frame, green Jadite bowl, green wooden handle, like a small KitchenAid, "Mixette," mfd. by F. A. Smith Mfg. Co., Rochester, NY, c.1930s... **$80+**

Mixer, plated metal stand has tall post to which multispeed beater motor clamped at any height, revolving metal mixing bowl, "Star-Rite Magic Maid," Fitzgerald Mfg. Co., Torrington, CT, c.1931.............. **$125**

Mixer & food processor, enameled cast iron base and motor housing, holder for mixing bowls, 3 speeds & attachments to beat eggs or mix batters, whip cream, mix dough, strain fruits, sieve & puree vegetables, slice potatoes, chop meats or nuts, make ice cream, grind coffee, shred or grate, extract citrus fruit juice, make applesauce (yep, sounds like a you-know-what), KitchenAid division of Hobart Mfg. Co., Troy, OH, early model introduced c.1920; this large one c.1930... **$175-$300**

Outlet, cast iron, figural with 3 outlets & 2 lions' heads, American or English, 3"L, late 19th C (?)......... **$65+**

Outlet, twin outlet porcelain plug for appliances, in original box depicting woman demonstrating the plug hanging from a ceiling fixture (shades of George Booth cartoons). "Permits the Use of Two Electrical Conveniences at the Same Time." "GE," General Electric, Schenectady, NY, 4"L, 1916............... **$15+**

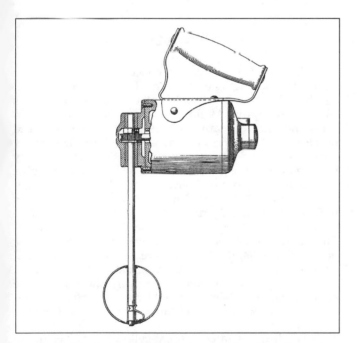

XVIII-25. "Motor-driven beater" pat'd. Dec. 3, 1929, by Thomas B. Myers, Racine, WI, assignor to Hamilton Beach, same place. Pat. #1,738,112, Serial #383,623, is a "portable unitary structure" for beating eggs, whipping creams, and for other purposes." To avoid the danger of "wetting the motor," Myers provided his own version of "removably mounted" beater elements which could be slipped off the rods and wiped with a cloth.

Lookalike Alarm

KitchenAid has put out a retro "classic" mixer with stainless steel bowl styled to look very like the 1937 Model "K" designed by Egmont Arens. The original "K" was $55; this one is $250!!!

❖ NOTES ❖

The best information on the development of **electrical plugs** is found in the July 1986 issue of *Technology and Culture* quarterly of the Society for the History of Technology, in an article by Dr. Fred E. H. Schroeder of the University of Minnesota, entitled "More 'Small Things Forgotten': Domestic Electrical Plugs and Receptacles, 1881-1931." At that time this was published by The University of Chicago Press, but now the Johns Hopkins University Press, POB 19966, Baltimore, MD 21211-0966, is the publisher. Back issues of T&C are $12 + postage; we can't guarantee this issue will be in print. E-mail jlorder@jhupress.jhu.edu or phone (US & CAN) 800-548-1784 to check availability. For anyone interested in electrical appliances, I would highly recommend this if you can locate a copy. • For information on joining the **Society for the History of Technology** (SHOT), write JHU Press, at the above address; call (800) 548-1784; e-mail: tac@chaos. press.jhu.edu; or go to: http://shot.jhu.edu/member ship.htm. • Great news! The article has been included in a book of selected readings; see Bibliography, Lafol lette, Marcel. C., & Jeffery K. Stine. Also see Schroeder, Fred E. H.

• • •

Direct current & alternating current (DC and AC). Electricity was delivered by direct current into the 1880s and beyond. It could be produced in little power stations and sent along wires for relatively short distances. Alternating current could be sent much much further. In NYC, electric current was DC everywhere until 1886, when AC became available to more and more customers. When I lived in an 1892 building on E. 20th St., the 1892 elevator was powered by DC; pockets throughout the lower part of Manhattan used DC power. Just off 20th St., on Irving Place I believe, a shoe repair shop had to close in the 1970s because all their turn of the century machines operated on DC, and improvements to the neighborhood had brought AC exclusively to the building. • You will find many old electric kitchen appliances, and other items, with a reference to DC or AC power on the plate or "badge" as collectors may call it. I suspect that some companies made appliances both ways in the early part of the 20th century because not to do so would have meant losing a large number of potential customers.

Popcorn popper – See Corn popper

Pot warmer, stamped sheet steel, round footed base, curved top snuggles pot, ringed heating elements, "#2619," "Electric Heaters & Engineering Toronto Canada," 1930s-40s (?). .... **$5+**

Potato baker, insulated oven in casserole or chafing dish shape, on 3 sheet metal legs, molded phenolic

XVIII-26. Tabletop oven. *Chrome-plated, 3 cabriole legs, rack inside over holes to let heat rise, high
cover, wooden knob, plated metal, temperature
gauge on side, "Stanley Ovenette," mfd. by Stanley
Savage Mfg. Co., Chicago, IL, 8" diam., 1930s,
1935 ad.* **$35+**

resin side handles & lid knob, heating element in
bottom part, "Knapp-Monarch," St. Louis, MO,
1930s. .... **$25+**
Sandwich grill, oblong streamlined body, thick, heavy lid
is removable (for washing) grill surface, inside is
smooth, of course, 4 legs, "tassel-like" pendant
molded phenolic resin "Bakelite" lid handle, also has
accessory broiling and frying grids, "Edicraft," Edison
Electric, NJ, 1930s. With all grids & grills:........ **$35+**
Sandwich grill, chrome finish, oblong flat grilling surfaces inside, grills removable, to be used with or
without the lid down, the appearance is of a grill on
a footed tray, but it's all connected, molded phenolic
resin handles at sides & lid front, "General Electric,"
Bridgeport, CT & Ontario, CAN, 4"H x 14-1/2"L x
9"W, late 1940s.. **$15**
Skillet – See Frying pan
Slow cookers – See Cooker; also Crock-Pot®
Stoves, electric – See Chapter XI (Stoves)
Stovetop toaster – See XI-50 in Chapter XI (Stoves)
Teapots, coffee pots, electric – See Chapter XIV
(Coffee & Tea)

❖ NOTES ❖

Heating Element is the name given to that portion of
a cooker or heater which gives out the heat. ... It consists
of some material which is more or less a bad conductor
of electricity, and when current is taken through it by making it a portion of an electrical circuit, it becomes hot
owing to the resistance it sets up to the wave of current.
The greater the resistance, the more intense the heat, but
great heat can be set up by employing an element of lower
resistance and using more of it. If a wire is used as the
heating unit, the thinner it is, the greater is its resistance,
but much depends upon the kind of wire and its length.
... The wire may be laid over strips of mica in the form of
a close winding, mica being an excellent insulator, capable of withstanding great heat; it may be in the form of a
spiral threaded through tubes of quartz glass ...; or it
may be wound in the form of a flat helix, with mica separating adjacent turns; a sheet of mica or of quartz being
used on one or both sides. In other cases the wire is

exposed, and wound in long lengths over insulating supports, or in coils supported by porcelain insulators fixed
in the cooker frame. The length and diameter of the wire
are adjusted for the supply pressure (voltage) with which
the apparatus is intended to work. ... It is not necessary
to use a wire for a heating element, alternatives being an
extremely thin deposit on a mica base, of an alloy of copper, gold and other metals having 'royal' characteristics,
i.e., those which do not rust or oxidize by exposure to
moisture or at high temperatures; or blocks of metallifer-
ous earth, a material which has lately been introduced
and for which great advantages are claimed. It is possible
in certain circumstances, to generate very considerable
heat by the influence of an electrical current passing
through a coil of wire laid over strips of copper in conjunction with a core formed of thin plates of iron, but this
system, while quite practicable for cookers, has been
abandoned commercially, because it can only be adopted
on alternating current circuits. A heating element may be
formed from any material which offers a resistance to the
passage of current, but its value for practical purposes
depends upon many conditions, which have been found
by prolonged experiment to be met most thoroughly by a
wire of **special nickel alloy [Nichrome].**" Maud Lancaster, *Electric Cooking, Lighting & Heating,* 1914 American edition, with some revision by the American Stephen
L. Coles, former editor of "Electrical Review." Theoreti-
cally, speaking as a collector, it is quite possible that a
fully-functioning bread toaster was made well before
Nichrome, especially given that several companies used
ceramic, and the "Eclipse" shown in the picture obviously
has a ceramic base, and the 1890 element shown in Lancaster's chart at XVIII-28 is wire embedded in enamel.

Toasters

You'll find that toaster-collectors refer to their
charges as belonging to different "families and species,"
as Charles Fisher put it in his pioneer book on toasters
(see Bibliography). As far as I know, he came up with
the wonderful, evocative names for these families and
species: Prototoasters, Perchers & Pinchers, Turners &
Floppers, Swingers & Sidewinders. You have to buy
this book, it's the only one with lots of knowledgable
technical background. Collectors still use such categories, expanded in E. Townsend Artman's book to
include Flat Beds, Turners, Sliders & Drive Thru's, Tip-
pers, Floppers, Droppers, and Pop Ups. I won't, merci-
fully, add any categories. All I want to say is that *de
gustibus non disputandum,* "there is no disputing taste"
or, *de tostaros non disputandum* (you got it). I don't
know if I'm being perverse, but I really like some of the
simple "cheap" toasters decried by some writers. Spare,
cheap and functional – the category: Linda's Likables.

Toaster, chrome-plated vertical cylinder, revolves on its
base and was probably used in center of breakfast
table, big black plastic knob on top & 3 oblong feet,
4 wire-frame swingout 'car' doors with slot for toast
(where car window would be), heating element in
central core, "ELEM" German, 1958. I've seen only
two, both in photos, with no further information. It
looks like it's about 13" to 15"H. Lots 613 & 621, in
auction, June 10, 1989, at Breker, Auction Team
Köln, Germany.. **$500+**

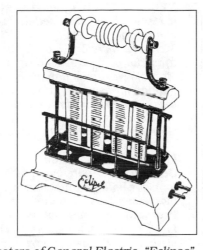

XVIII-27. Early English electric toaster the "Eclipse." *The first toaster according to the Cologne, Germany, auction house Auction Team Breker, which sold this "Eclipse" toaster at auction, April 28, 1990. The catalog description says "1893," but that date seems unlikely, although it is very antique in style & relates to the D-12 toasters of General Electric. "Eclipse" was the trade name used by the Electric & Ordnance Accessories Co., Birmingham, England, but according to the Lancaster book of 1914, E&O didn't get into the business of electrical appliances until after about 1905. They also made table stoves, electric "cookers" (stoves), saucepans, and the frypan & stewpan shown in XVIII-9. Maud Lancaster's book on electrical housekeeping, published in 1914, had the chart in the next picture, that showed state-of-the-art heating elements for toasters, etc. The "Eclipse" element, fifth down, has crimped "high resistance ribbon ... wound over mica strips." One of the mysteries of dating toasters has been how much collectors should depend on dating toasters by the prevalent, but not exclusive, use of* **Nichrome** *– the high resistance wires which wouldn't melt when heated. Marsh's famous patent of Feb. 6, 1906, was for an alloy of chromium & nickel, dubbed Nichrome. This is an English toaster, so was there an English inventor who found another alloy? Was an alloy with Nichrome's particular qualities even necessary? Read the Elements chart info and decide for yourself. The price realized for the "Eclipse" at the 1990 auction was $2,165. According to Dave Woodcock, curator of "Secret Life of the Home" display (see end of chapter), the "Eclipse" has also been attributed to the Crompton Co., but definitely not that early. Dave says "I have yet to find an English-made electric toaster that pre-dates the Edwardian period; you begin to get them about 1911-1914, though any electric toaster in Britain was rare until the early '20s." According to German expert collector Jens Veerbeck, a German kitchen book showed the "Eclipse" and repeated the "1893" date. Jens writes, "I don't think that the Eclipse is from 1893. Maybe a patent, but not the toaster. Some collectors in America bought some Eclipses from a Dutch collector in 2000 for a whole bunch of money. A friend of mine from NYC bought a black & white version. I think, and some American collectors do too, that they are fakes. The Dutch guy sold four or five of them within one year in nearly mint condition" Well, in the US we have a tradition of "warehouse finds" opening like a Pandora's box of questions (fake? real? new? old?), but also hope that the real thing may come along. Anyone out there know anything? If real:* **$2,000+**

Toaster, nearly square chromed box with slightly sloped sides, interlocking diamond cutouts on doors, 4 corner columns rise from black stepped molded phenolic resin base, what the manufacturer called "artistic" black pendent handles on 2 ends, black triangle door handles, lever to cause toast to pop up, 2 slices, automatic switch-off with bell, adjustable for doneness, "Auto-Toastmaker," Bersted Mfg. Co., Chicago, IL, new in 1930. .... **$45+**

Toaster, chrome & black-painted sheet metal, oblong on black tray base, flip down doors with black triangular handles, does 4 slices, "Victorian, Model A55" (virtually the same as A65), Bersted Mfg. Co., Chicago, IL, 6-3/8"H x 12"L x 6-3/4"W, prob. late 1930s. A 1940s model with brown reeded Bakelite handles is "Fostoria Bersted Mfg. Co. Model 60." .... **$175+**

Toaster, gorgeously simple open-sided metal box on base with curled strap metal legs, black baked enamel finish, toasting elements visible like a modern art sculpture, "Cookenette," no mfr.'s name, prob. 1920s or '30s, but not in **1930** *House Furnishing Review Buyer's Guide.* I wonder if it might have been made by American Electric Heater Co., which also took a very simple design approach. .... **$250+**

Toaster, heavy aluminum, streamlined curved body, 2 slots on top, but the toast pops down!! It actually comes out a slide opening. molded phenolic resin push-down timer-set is also handle matching stationary one at other end, knob at bottom to set from D[ark] to L[ight], "Delta 280" "Pop-Down" automatic, 8-3/4"H x 9-1/4"L x 7-1/2"W, mfd. by A.B.C. Electric, Winnipeg , Manitoba, Canada, 1940. Another manufacturer was Delta Mfg. Corp., Philadelphia, PA. • Note: also made in chrome finish, ... **$100+**

Toaster, nickel-plated, pull lever & it opens like a book, makes 2 pieces of toast, has 6 toasting darkness degrees, "Edicraft Automatic," or "Edicraft Speed Toaster," mfd. by Thomas A. Edison Inc., Orange, NJ, 7-1/8"H x 10-1/4"L, late 1920s. Called in advertisements the "automaticrat of the breakfast table," echoing Westinghouse's slogan. They'd have a lawsuit these days. .... **$600+**

❖ NOTES ❖

Star Wars Go-With. Ernie Fosselius, San Francisco filmmaker, made a one-minute pseudo-trailer for Star Wars in 1978. It's called *Hardware Wars.* The special effects, in Lucas's film, are boldly faked using mixers, toasters, eggbeaters, etc., as spaceships and weaponry. There's now an updated special edition; also a new 60-minute DVD edition. You can buy the video on Amazon.com, new or used. The cover is often missing, but you could always keep a stack of them under a toaster cover!

• • •

Toasting patterns. Artman's book on toasters shows how a piece of white bread looks after being toasted in each of his categories. Anytime the piece of bread rested on a patterned piece of metal, the radiant heat beamed at it would effect the bread differently when there was no interference from a piece of metal and where there was. It's a new way to look at the "Percher" and "Pincher" and "Turner & Swinger" types especially. • In the 1980s & '90s, bread stamps were sold that were to be pressed onto the bread before toasting, in order to

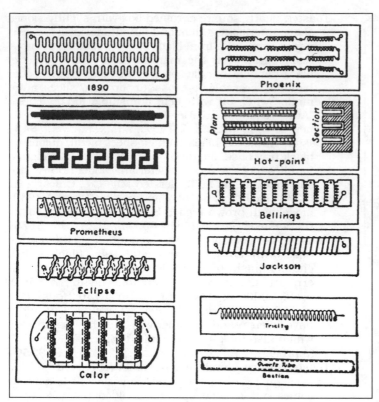

XVIII-28. Electric heating elements from 1890-c.1914. *I have assumed that these are in somewha[t] chronological order. Not until "Hot-point" used it is Nichrome mentioned, and then all the companies after Hot-point are listed as using it specifically. Marsh's Nichrome patent was applied for in 1905, making it possible that it could have actually been used earlier than that.* • *"Early [1890] electric heating elements were made up in spiral form of iron, German silver, and other resistance wires and were similar in form to resistances used for motor and lamp regulation. For self-contained utensils, fine German silver wire was embedded in enamel; [and] for cigar lighters and other very small heaters, German silver wire was threaded in thin mica."* • **Prometheus:** *Three forms introduced by the Prometheus Co. (American). (1) Strip element "consisting of a deposit of gold and platinum on strips of mica"; (2) ribbon in the "key pattern form used for flat irons, hot-plates, etc."; (3) finally, "oven elements took the form of special high resistance wire or tape wound over mica, varnished and encased with thin steel."* • **Eclipse:** *"High resistance ribbon crimped to give greater length and free-air space, wound over mica strips with the ends connected to heavy eyelet terminals."* • **Calor:** *"A base of fireclay with grooves into which spirals of fine high resistance wire are placed."* • **Phoenix:** *"Spiral wire coils held lightly at short intervals by porcelain insulators mounted on a suitable base."* • **Hot-point:** *"Nichrome wire or ribbon, wound lightly around thin strips of mica; further covered with a thin mica covering and inserted very tightly into grooves or slots made in the hot-plate or iron base to receive the finished strips."* • **Bellings:** *"Fireclay strip with spirals of nichrome wire stretched across width of base, notches being provided in the base for receiving ends of the spiral and holding them tightly in position."* • **Jackson:** *"Has a different class of fireclay base with quite a smooth surface, the section of the strips, being a flat oval, wire or ribbon of nichrome, is wound tightly over the strip in one continuous length and clamped between heavy terminals at each end."* • **Tricity:** *"Nichrome ribbon wound over thin mica and clamped between thin sheets of mica and metal. The method of winding provides for uniform distribution of heat at any loading."* • **Bastian** *or* **Quartzalite:** *"A spiral of nichrome wire or ribbon coated with a film of oxide insulation. The spiral is held in or on a quartz tube. The turns of the spiral may be close together without fear of short circuit. This gives it a 'hot-rod' appearance."* *Elements used by* **General Electric Co. of America** *are in the text, but not diagramed. "Cartridge elements are used in the cast-iron disc-stoves, grids, broilers, etc. For 110-volt circuits German silver is used, and for 220-volt circuits colorite is used. The element is one and one-fourth inches in diameter by five inches long; resembles a cartridge, and is usually inserted in a close-fitting chamber bored into a casting. It is a thin tape of resistor (about 1/8″ wide) coiled to form a hollow cylinder. Between the turns is an insulating cement, which binds the whole into a solid tube. This cylinder of wound calorite is inserted in a mica-lined metal cartridge shell which in turn is inserted into the bore of the appliance."* **GE** *"Encased disc heating elements are used in small water heaters, chafing dishes, coffee percolators, teakettles and small disc stoves.* **The Ferranti element** *is made up of nichrome wire coiled in disc form with thin insulating matrial between adjoining turns ... the whole is tightly enclosed in a sheathing of metal.* **Dowsing's 'Hot-Bar' element** *is a fire-clay base with longitudinal grooves into which are tightly pressed long spirals of nichrome wire, which when heated has the appearance of a 'hot-bar.'"* From Electric Cooking and Heating, 1914.

---

condense the bread and create an obvious design (a teddy bear, or "Good Morning," for example) when the bread was toasted. They don't seem to work on the bread I eat (Alvarado Street Bakery, Protein Bread), but I'm sure it works on air-fluffed white bread.

• • •

Jazzy Vented Toaster Doors. The fancy or plain cutouts in toaster doors are vents. The practical need to disperse heat and moisture from the bread to make the preferred crisp toast also gave designers the opportunity to be very imaginative, or imitative, or bold in designing the slots, vents, etc., in toaster doors and tops. Because electric toasters first came in during the demise of Art Nouveau styling, and the birth of Art Deco, designers created cut-outs in curving or angular or geometric forms, sometimes combining all, with Deco vents and Nouveau imitation chased flowers. While vents were totally practical and necessary in early toasters, they also had a symbolic significance. They implied that a lot of "heat" was being generated by the progress of modern conveniences, energy generated by the appliance, not the housewife! Sizzle! Later, car designers used the same symbolic trick, although again with a practical purpose to help release the engine's heat. We can look back and construct another layer of meaning too: these designs were COOL!!! The word was known, it was a jazz word, a state of being. And if electricity meant anything to the consumer, it meant a new state of being.

•   •   •

Raymond Loewy on product design in the 1920s. Designer Loewy thought that most toasters were good products with horrible design. He said he was "disappointed" at their "poor physical appearance ... and their design vulgarity." He even called the combination of production quality and ugly design an "unholy alliance," citing as proof a schmaltzy "mess of stripes, moldings, and decalcomania curlicues." I'm sure we all can figure out which toasters he would like and which he wouldn't.

Toaster, plain white porcelain base, high-frame wire basket rack with 11 upright wires on both sides, with heating elements in center, "General Electric D-12," Oct. 20, 1908, patent is for heating element. c.1910 according to C. Fisher. This was, he says, 2nd version of "D-12." Subtract $75+ for missing detachable wire warming rack; add $200+ for hand-painted, floral-decorated porcelain base. .... **$200+**

Toaster, white porcelain base, wire basket with low sides and 6 vertical wires, with detachable wire warming rack above, "General Electric D-12" (3rd version, according to Fisher), 2 patent dates, for heating elements, 1908 & 1909. Toaster c.1912 until (?). .... **$250+**

Toaster, simple heavy wire frame with finer wires crisscrossing inside, "General Electric X-2," pat'd. Nov. 9, 1915. • Mr. Charles P. Fisher corrects GE's own misinformation that this one was patented in 1905; the patent date is actually 1915. This is the value of specialization in research. More than "rare"; as recently as 1998, only one was known – it belongs to a couple in Sylvania, OH. .... **$1,000+**

Toaster, green baked-on enameled sheet metal with cream-color cutout doors, 7"H, "The Handy Hot" or "Handyhot," Chicago Mfg. Co., (or Chicago Electric Mfg. Co.), Chicago, IL, c.1930s. (Some ads & boxes showed "HandyHot." .... **$45+**

Toaster, chrome, black Bakelite™ handles, leaping deer or gazelle Art Deco decoration on door, does only one piece of toast at a time, toast holder controlled by lever handle, tilt down to insert bread, push up to insert holder in toaster, dial on side for degree of toastedness, using letters of alphabet from A to K instead of numbers, Hotpoint "A General Electric Organization." 6-3/4"H, late 1920s. (Another had a leaping gazelle toaster with black Bakelite stepped base, marked "Edison General Electric Appliance Co., Inc., Chicago." c.1931. It's worth $400+). Chrome: .... **$200+**

Toaster, fabulous 3 slicer, black baked enameled steel 3-sided box frame and base, 3 decorated chrome doors, triangular top of chrome with knob, mica in heating element, "Delta," mfd. by Kamco Inc., Unionville, CT, c.1935. Collector Carl Roles has one that appears to be all chrome & is called the "Great Northern." He says that the construction of it is very poor. Original price: $2.39; where, oh, where is that time machine! .... **$950+**

Toaster, enameled black metal base and top, very boxy, chromium body has 2 sets of 4 vertical stamped

lines or stripes on both sides (design is "Beaumonde Pattern"), low molded phenolic resin knob on end door, end-loading for 2 slices, 7-7/8"H, "Double-Quick," Universal Electric Model E 7542, mfd. by Landers, Frary & Clark, c.1935. Another version was all chrome. .... **$75+**

Toaster, chromed-brass pedestal base with ball feet not at corners, very Deco, like the Chrysler Building in NY (erected 1928-1931). Embossed fancy decoration on sides, pendent handles at each end, toasting frame is like an abstract slice of toast turned diamond-wise, arched top, 2 push-buttons – one for each side; push & bread carrier or "basket" swings out. Push again & basket pivots back to toast other side. Called by collectors either the "Diamond & Earrings" or "Sweetheart" toaster. "Universal E-9410," mfd. by Landers, Frary & Clark, New Britain, CT, design pat'd. by George Curtiss in 1929. .... **$450+**

Toaster, boxy body, almost as long as high (came with choice of nickel or chrome finish), on wide base with 4 small button feet, embossed on sides with decorative border & medallion that looks for all the world like a Georgian wall mirror, toast holder for one slice pulls out of end, holds bread vertically, clockwork timer, adjustable for brownness; a gussied-up & automatic version of the simpler E942. "Universal E9422," Landers, Frary & Clark, New Britain, CT, late 1920s to 1930. This style looks so neo-Georgian/Victorian, it is hard to believe that it was being made at the same time as much more streamlined electric toasters. .... **$45+**

Toaster, nickel-plated, fold-down doors have pattern of 7 popsicle-stick like vertical slots; best part is open-book rack above with same pattern of narrow slots. Flat base with disc feet, 7"H. The "Thermax E 1942," mfd. by Landers, Frary & Clark. Simple & beautiful as a garden gate, c.1913-1917 according to Hazelcorn's. .... **$95+**

Toaster, brightly nickel-plated, squarish on truncated oblong flat base, 7 vertical cutouts in both drop down doors, arched curves on top (one arch is configured to also be a handle) keeps 6 slices toast warm, "Universal," Landers, Frary & Clark, underneath stamped "Pat. Dec. 9, 13, Oct. 5, 15, CT BTN. 15961, 1912, 22258, 1912, Canada, June 1, 1915; BTE S.C.D.C. No. 446548." .... **$125+**

I never had a piece of toast,
Particularly long and wide,
But fell upon the sanded floor,
And always on the buttered side.

–Anonymous, Parody of a soppy stanza by poet Thomas Moore from the 19th century. The parody was published in Walter Hamilton's Parodies, *Vol. 3, date unknown.*

Toaster, toast warmer rack above for 6 slices, put bread in wire frame of spring-loaded gate, it comes down on a spring, you flip it & push it back up to the heating elements, 7-3/8"H, "The Reversible Toaster," #9-25, Manning-Bowman Co., Meriden, CT, pat'd. Dec. 28, 1920, & Dec. 4, 1923. The Feb. 6, 1906, patent is for Albert Marsh's patent for "nichrome," the alloy of chromium & nickel, used for the heating wires called "resistance" wires. .... **$125+**

MAKING TOAST WITH STYLE

Toaster-collecting is now an international pursuit, as is much of kitchen-collecting. No longer content with the mechanical fantasies of toaster-designers of their own countries, Americans, Canadians, Germans, Australians, Italians, British, and other collectors go on toaster-collecting jaunts whenever they are traveling abroad to look for interesting old designs. The Internet and eBay help this international search. The styles of bread sold in supermarkets all over the world are a lot more uniform nowadays than they were 70 or 80 years ago. Bread sold by bakers in Europe was found in variety of configurations – here in the USA we nov finally, have a good selection of round, oval, and squar breads in any big grocery. The few mostly-electri toasters on these two pages are some of my favorite from the collection of Jens Veerbeck, a graphic designe and architectural designer from Germany. See book by Artman, and Greguire in Bibliography, and see en of this chapter for more information. Estimation of val ues varies wildly so I am not reporting here.

XVIII-Toaster-A. *"The Rangette" – a gas toaster by Tobias Heater, USA. Nickeled cast iron, steel, white porcelain gas-cock handle. Pat'd. April 14, 1914. Very rare. Photo by Jens Veerbeck.*

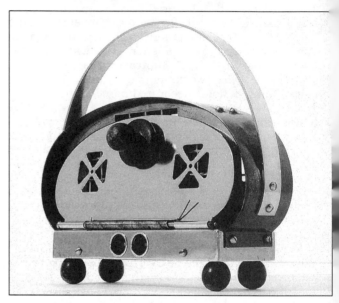

XVIII-Toaster-C. *"Siemens Schuckert" pocketbook style, nickel-plated with slightly bronzed tone. Black wood round knobs. German, c. 1920s-30s. There were two versions, with different cutouts. This is the wider one. Photo by Jens Veerbeck.*

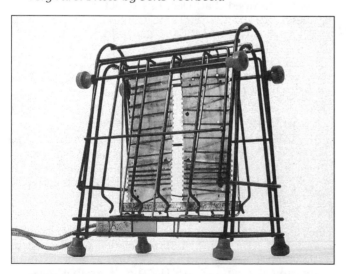

XVIII-Toaster-B. *"Steelcraft" all wire toaster, with little red turned-wood feet & knobs. Wire is painted black (also came in blue, green or red). Two oblongs of mica insulate the heating elements. Sculpture of the Calder type. Photo by Jens Veerbeck.*

XVIII-Toaster-D. *"SEM Universel," small & narrow, nickel-plated, black Bakelite knobs, marked on handles & on original 3-plug cord. French, early 1920s. Very rare. Photo by Jens Veerbeck.*

XVIII-Toaster-E. *"HUZA" nickel-plated Dutch toaster by Huza. c.1930s. Photo by Jens Veerbeck.*

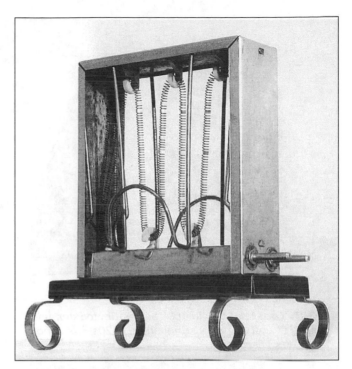

XVIII-Toaster-G. *"Pelouze" with decorative cabriole legs, nickel-plated version 2 with more solid toast & warmer top (#1 had wire rack & no end handles). Design patent from 1912 is of version 1. Mfd. by Pelouze, Chicago, IL. c.1918+. Photo by Jens Veerbeck.*

XVIII-Toaster-F. *"Cookenette" on scrolled legs. Elegant chrome-plated toaster; base-plinth painted black. No marks. Photo by Jens Veerbeck.*

XVIII-Toaster-H. *"SEM" 01 with peg-like legs. Nickel-plated with bread clamps that have black wood knobs, spring-activated at top. French, early 1920s. Rare. Photo by Jens Veerbeck.*

 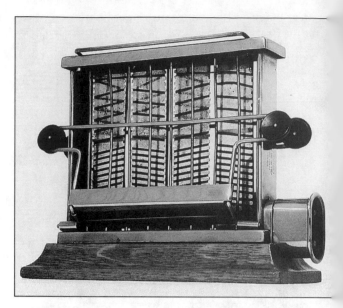

XVIII-Toaster-I. *"Colombo" aluminum toaster, with big "H" cutout doors. English, c.1920s-30s. Photo by Jens Veerbeck.*

XVIII-Toaster-J. *"Epeha 90050." Nickel-plated with wood base, German, 1920s. Photo by Jens Veerbeck.*

oaster, black bottom chrome upper 2-slicer pop-up, plump but sleek, with brown plastic handles each end, one is also the pushdown, tiny dial at bottom, about 7"H. This is the toaster I use every day, since buying it at a thrift shop in the 1970s. And I can fix it myself if something goes wrong. "Toaster with the Tester," Manning-Bowman, Division McGraw-Edison Co., Boonville, MO, prior to WWII, suspended, then in production again.. **$10+**

❖ NOTES ❖

After the War – A 1944 ad in *House & Garden* is interesting because of insight into effects of war on domestic appliance production. "Watch for the return of the famous 'Toaster with the Tester' and other top-quality Manning-Bowman appliances. They'll be back soon we hope) when our production facilities are no longer needed by the armed forces... . Manning-Bowman – Means Best. Keep on buying war bonds!"

Toaster, nickeled metal, flip-down doors perforated with 7 long popsicle stick vertical slots, warming platform on top, "patented attachment turns the toast automatically" is activated by touching door handles, "Electric Flipflop Model 65" (by 1922 called the "Marion Flipflop"), pat'd. July 26, 1914, mfd. by Rutenber Electric

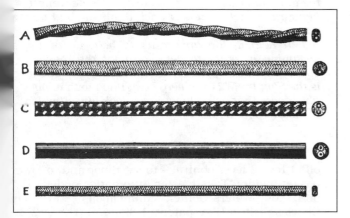

***XVIII-29. Typical flexible electric cords**, as depicted in* The Electric Home, *1936. The two general types are heater cord and lamp cord. Heater cord has an asbestos covering over each conductor [wire] to prevent any burning and is used [for] ... the iron, toaster, stove, etc. " **(A)** Twisted conductor, cotton-covered. **(B)** Portable show cord, but reinforced with a common cotton, rayon or silk covering. **(C)** Portable heater cord, where each conductor is covered with asbestos to prevent burning. This type of cord should be used with all heating appliances, such as irons, heaters, toasters, etc. **(D)** Rubber-covered cord, which is more durable than those previously described. Heavy-duty cord of this type has a thicker covering than ordinary cord. **(E)** Decorative form of cord, usually oval in shape and covered with silk, rayon, cotton or rubber in several common colors." The book also explains the importance of looking at the "safe" tag wrapped around the cord every five feet, declaring that the cord has been inspected by the Underwriters' Laboratories.*

Co., Marion, IN. (The Model 66, the "Marion Giant Flip-flop" has slogan on side: "Make Toast Your Breakfast Food." c.1914+.................................... **$50+**

Toaster, chrome & black Bakelite, high 3/4-quarter-round top body with flat sides & flat bottom, shapely black base, antenna-like device sticks out of top & you push to open both side doors at once, handles on both ends, Model Z, Merit-Made Co., Buffalo, NY, late 1930s-early 1940s. • **Half-round body toasters** were made by Knapp-Monarch (21-501), Sunbeam (T-9), Prometheus (WRO); and an almost quarter-round toaster was CEM's Handy Hot. • Merit-Made:.. **$70+**

Toaster, chrome & black painted tin, very angled truncated pyramid shape, pluperfect Deco, red Bakelite™ (or other molded phenolic resin) double knobs on the 2 doors, engraved with wheat design, 4 little button feet, Nelson Machine & Mfg. Co., Cleveland, OH, c.1930s....................................... **$125+**

Toaster, shapely ceramic body, with resemblance to Oriental temple, 4 feet, mica, outstanding under-glaze decoration in version of "Blue Willow" pattern, with the typical arched footbridge, 2 figures on bridge, temples & trees, "Toastrite," Pan Electrical Mfg. Co., Cleveland, OH, c.1920s. (Also came in dark rosy pink pattern.) .... **$2500+**

Toaster, rounded pyramidal shape, nickeled-plated stamped aluminum, interesting little decorative corner slits at top which allowed the sheet metal pattern to be bent down to form the shape without crimping the corners, 2 slices, black painted base, 6-5/8"H, black handles, "Riverside Mfg. Co.," Ypsilanti, MI, 1930s................................. **$85**

Toaster, chromed sheet metal, peaked tent shape with pull down doors decorated with 2 vertical bands with sort of wheat berry design, the dished tray on top – for buttering prepared toast or keeping it warm – lifts off for cleaning, dial control for light, brown or medium sticks out under one side, "Serv-Hot Toast Tray" & "Queen Mary" pattern, "Royal-Rochester" toaster, mfd. by Robeson-Rochester Corp, Rochester, NY, c.1937. .... **$55+**

Toaster, moderately interesting Art Deco design, in original box, "Speed Master," mfd. by Son-Chief Electric Co., Winsted, CT, 1930s. .... **$25+**

Toaster, brightly chromed, Deco design, side-loading manual, doors with wood handles, "Son-Chief," Series 680, Son Chief Electronics, Winsted, CT, 1920s-30s...................................... **$55**

Toaster, high & skinny, porcelain base, nickel-plated openwork metal with 6 small cutout stars on top, 2 toast doors are loaded, then you turn to other side, 2 knobs of knurled plastic stick up on top, you use to turn bread slices around. Carrying grips at both ends, "Star-Rite Reversible, the Star Electric Toaster," "patented," mfd. by Fitzgerald Mfg Co., Torrington, CT, 9"H, c.1928-29. • Just one of a number of "Star-Rite" toasters; some automatic........................ **$60+**

Toaster, chrome half-round body, flat sides, black Bakelite base & handles, red signal light on one side, near base, hinged crumb tray, could be set for "pops toast up" or "keeps toast warm," 2 slices, styling by George Scharfenberg, "Sunbeam" Model T-9, Chicago Flexible Shaft Co., Chicago, IL, 1940. .... **$95+**

Toaster, chrome body, black Bakelite base, does only one piece at a time, bread is inserted in one end & comes out other end of narrow body (which is an elongated oval seen from above), after a rather jerky trip through the length of the toaster ... a trip you can observe through a very small porthole in the side. Adjustable light & dark lever. Has a fan inside that cools the works (but not the toast). 11"H. "Toast-O-Lator, Model J," pat'd. by Alfredo DeMatteis, mfd. by Toast-O-Lator Corp., Long Island City, NY, about 11"H, c.1938. (Note: manufacturer's name, earlier? later? is Crocker-Wheeler Electrical Mfg. Co.) .... **$250+**

Toaster, pop-up, chrome-plated, interesting one slice top-loader with 6 horizontal venting louvers on each side, one end squared neatly, the other end rounded

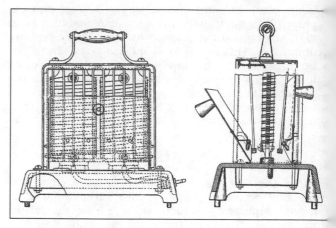

XVIII-31. Patent for electric toaster by James I. Ayer, Cambridge, MA, assignor to Simplex Electric Heating Co., Boston. Patent #951,765, granted Mar. 8, 1910. Mr. Ayer said that "I have found that by inclosing the heating element against the free passage of air...the heat is kept in rather than disseminated, [and] the apparatus is enabled to attain great efficiency." The doors he designed terminated "somewhat short of the top so as to leave a space for the necessary escape of steam or moisture as it is driven off from the bread." These doors were "preferably ... removable to permit the ready cleaning of the inside." He also described the need for the inner walls and the doors to have "inner reflecting surfaces which reflect back the heat" and that those surfaces inside the doors were "of material aid in helping the apparatus to heat up at the beginning in order to get ready for the toasting operation." One of the toasters bearing this patent is the Simplex T-211, a very boxy thing with removable doors that actually makes it look like a heater. It's worth over $400.

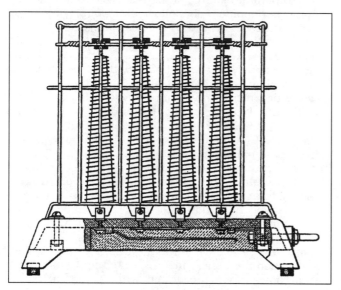

XVIII-30. Patent for "electric heater" by Frank E. Shailor, Detroit, assignor to General Electric, NYC. #950,058, Feb. 22, 1910. Shailor refers to the "application of Parkhurst, [serial] number 436,620, filed Nov. 20, 1908 (about 8 months before Shailor filed his) and described that inventor's arrangement of the "bare high resistance wires arranged vertically on a base and surrounded by a metallic cage. This cage has a pocket on each side for receiving the material to be toasted." Shailor claims that he had found that the coils may be arranged in a much more rigid manner by winding the ... wire upon a core or support of insulating material and securing the support to the base, ... and by tapering the coils from one end and having the large end at the bottom." Shailor's "heater" or toaster was to have a base of "insulating material, such as porcelain, slate or the like." His patent also refers to a particular **high-resistance wire** that had been pat'd. for General Electric by John T. H. Dempster in order **to get around the Marsh patent** for a nickel-chrome alloy of 1906. Dempster had come up with an alloy that is "heat refractory to an extraordinary degree and does not easily oxidize." He proposed that his alloy would, by weight, have 62 parts nickel, 20 parts iron, 13 parts chromium, 5 parts manganese, and about 13/100 of a part of silicon, about 4/100 of a part of carbon, and 2/100 of a part of phosphorus. By the way, GE didn't get away with it, but the **D-12** based on Shailor's patent is a collector's favorite.

off at top, 2 lever control – to set timer and to lower basket inside, "Toastmaster Automatic, Model 1A1," mfd.. by Waters-Genter, Minneapolis, MN, has Charles Strite's 1926 patent, 1,394,450. The "A 2" 2-slice model was also made.............................. **$65+**

❖ NOTES ❖

Charles P. Strite, major toaster patentee and McGraw-Edison mechanic, of Minneapolis, MN, received patent # 1,394,450, October 18, 1921, serial # 390,706, for a "bread-toaster" for commercial restaurant use. (The application was filed June 22, 1920.) Five years later, he got a patent for a pop-up made by Waters-Genter ("Toastmaster 1A 1"). (There were many toaster patents before Strite, but I like his language.) Strite claimed 1. "a bread toaster comprising an oven ... and means for automatically moving the toasted bread ...when the toasting operation is completed." 2. "... means for automatically cutting off the supply of heat ... ." 3. "... bread carriers adapted to occupy an inward position within said oven ... ." 4. "... oven having slots for insertion of slices of bread. ..." 5. "... means for automatically cutting off the supply of heat and moving the toasted bread outwardly through said lots ... ." 6. "A bread toaster comprising a frame, an oven mounted on said frame, electrical heating means associated with said oven, a support slidably mounted in said frame, a switch ... attached to said support ... ." 7. "... means for controlling the sliding movement of said support ... ." 8. "... an oven including a skeleton frame having windows mounted therein ... ." 9. "... carriers for slices of bread mounted for vertical movement in said oven ... ." 10. "... sheets of insulating material mounted in said to oven adjacent said carriers, heating wires wrapped on said sheets, metallic binding strips secured upon said sheets, ... and means for supplying electrical current to said strips." 11. "... bus-bars mounted adjacent said oven ... elements engaging sets of lugs so as to be held in slightly bent position ... ." 12. "... means for separately controlling ... current to a member of said bus-bar, and means for causing said switch to open simultaneously with the upward movement of said carriers." 13. "... an oven having walls of material which is non-heat-absorbing ... ." Strite also writes, "My invention relates to bread toasters. An object is to provide an automatic electric bread toaster in which the heating current will be automatically cut off after the bread has been toasted for a predetermined length of time, which may be varied according to the amount of moisture in the bread and the degree of crispness desired for the toast. Another object is to provide a toaster in which the bread is toasted in a substantially closed casing or oven having windows through which the bread may be observed while it is being toasted. Another object is to provide a device in which the toast is automatically removed from the oven. Another object is to provide a toaster in which a number of slices of bread may be toasted and in which

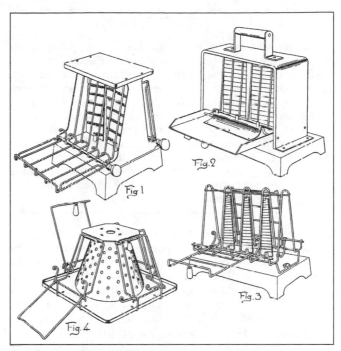

XVIII-32-B. Four drawings from the patent for a "Toast Turner" by Hazel B. Copeman, herself, Aug. 25, 1914, #1,108,552. A very widely-reaching patent that "relates to devices for turning bread which is in the process of toasting. It is applicable to toasters in general, including electric and gas toasters." She shows **(1)** a "well known form of vertical toaster ... [with a] grid supported ... at an inclination to the heating coils." "A turning rod is journaled in the lower ends of the grid bars." **(2)** is "a form of toaster in which, in place of turning the grid, a turning plate is employed ... journaled in the side standards by wire trunnions." **(3)** This toaster has "the bars of the toaster-grid bent to the horizontal at their lower ends to form a retaining sill and then are bent up again to form a sort of fence at the outside to hold the bread upon the sill." Hazel Copeman said that her invention could be used to turn the toast on this type also. And finally, **(4)** is a non-electric "gas toaster" used on a stove top, and Copeman explained how her turner would work with this one too. In all cases, presumably anyone could have their particular toaster retro-fitted with a Copeman turning device. See also XII-31, -32

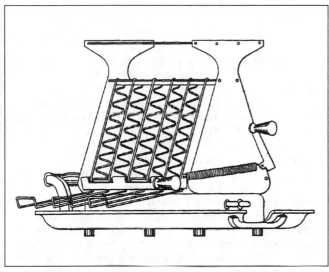

XVIII-32-A. Patent by Spencer A. Wiltsie, Erie, PA, assignor to Copeman Electric Stove Co., Flint, MI. #1,105,230, July 28, 1914. One of his concerns was to keep the bread from sliding off the carrier, and he also left space so that "the operator may grasp the bread or toast ... thus readily removing it." There were no doors, just the wire grids, which Wiltsie called "reversing carriers, covers or pressure grids," so evidently he wasn't concerned like Ayer was about providing a reflective surface that would heat the toaster up in order to use it.

current may be supplied to all of the heating elements or only a portion of the same, depending upon the number of slices which it is desired to toast at any one time. [From two to four slices!] Another object is to provide ... [a] toasting operation performed electrically in an economical manner by means which is not liable to get out of order." He includes a number of drawings too confusing for this book, and indicates a "clockwork mechanism ... of any usual or well-known construction." Finally, he says "When the toaster is first started one or two trials will be sufficient to determine the proper setting for the particular kind of bread which is being toasted. If the bread is drier than usual, a less time will be required."

Limp versus Crisp – Charles Fisher, who wrote what is now called *Hazelcorn's ... Old Electric Toasters*, told me that because of the greater air intake through toaster doors with a lot of openwork, toast was crisper when made in them, although it took longer. Toaster doors without openwork, or with very little, was in aid of faster, less crispy toasting. In England, people are accustomed to, and prefer, crisp toast. Perhaps early in the 20th C, Americans preferred it the English way, whereas later in the century maybe they were looking for ways to save electricity, and persuaded themselves to prefer limper toast!

Toaster, nickel plated, blue wooden knobs, swing-out baskets with pivoting hinges so that toast could be "turned over" by pushing the baskets back in the opposite way. This pivoting action is interesting relative to pivoting toe toasters of hearth cooking times. Sold as "Electrex," United Drug Co.; or "Torrid Push-omatic," by Frank E. Wolcott Mfg. Co.; or Beardsley-Wolcott, so Boston, MA or Waterbury, CT, 7"H x 8"L x 4-1/4"W, 1920 & 1927 patents, Fisher says name "Pushomatic" used 1928 to c.1930. Knobs also came in black, green, & red...................................... **$45+**

Toaster, chrome oblong body with control end slightly truncated at top corner, one slice capacity (they also made a 2-slice model), Bakelite handles at each end, 5 fluted vertical panels on both sides, Deco-né-Clas-

sical beautiful design, integral cord, "Toastmaste
Model 185," mfd. by Waters-Genter Co., division
McGraw Electric Co., Minneapolis, MN, 1930s. • Fc
designer info, go to: www.idsa.org/whatis/100yr
water-genter.htm. **$55**

XVIII-34. Toasters & other appliances. *From bottom left: (1) Early toaster with high sided basket (like the "Eclipse"), flower-decorated white porcelain base. General Electric. According to engineer Charles P. Fisher, this is the second version of the GE D-12, dating to "about 1910." Note the high 'railing' of the toast-holding basket. The third version, says Fisher, looks almost the same but has considerably lower sides. It probably dates to about 1912. By the way, an even rarer decorated porcelain toaster would be the $1000+ Blue Willow pattern (which came in blue & white, or rosy pink & white) made by Pan Electrical Mfg. Co., Cleveland, OH, c.1925. (2) Above, seemingly floating in air [but on Plexiglas] is a nickel-plated "Universal E947" made by Landers, Frary & Clark, pat'd. Jan. 31, 1922. Fisher describes this toaster as "the loveliest and most durable of swingers," and I agree. The base alone is beautiful; it's worth buying the toaster for those angled non-conductive disks forming the feet. This dates to between 1922-29. (3) Center is an "Angelus Campfire Bar-B-Q Marshmallow Toaster," red rubber feet on wire legs. 3-1/2"H x 3" square with a truncated insert in top – some very low, others very high. Came with marshmallow forks. "Pat. Appl. For," some of these look somewhat older than others, even as early as the 1920s; when found in a box, the graphics change – from late 1920s to 1950s. The rubber feet are white on later ones. At least early on, canned marshmallows were also sold, "Campfire the original food Marshmallows," "The Campfire Co." Milwaukee, WI. (4) The pedestal base waffle iron is heavily chromed and has a decorative porcelain insert in the lid. It is undated, but is probably about 1930. Collector Susan Lewis wrote me about hers, similar but with lovebird design, made by "SuperLectric." Hers is also undated. The electric iron is not described by G-E, who provided the photograph. Three value ranges are for the 2 toasters and the waffle iron. (1) $250-$350; (2) $45+; (3) $45+; (4) $85-$150*

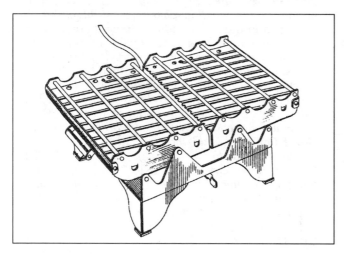

XVIII-33. Patent for the "Edicraft" speed toaster *that opens like a book, which would be entitled "Brunhilda & the Reinking Have Breakfast." George E. Reinking, Fort Wayne, IN, received patent #1,194,663, Aug. 15, 1916, for his "combined electric stove and toaster." He wanted a toaster having "co-acting grate sections which may be moved to horizontal position so that articles may be placed thereon to be heated and wherein the said grate sections may be moved to upstanding position to confront each other for receiving an article of food therebetween so that the said article may be toasted simultaneously upon opposite sides thereof." He provided that the sections would lock into position, and could be manually released. The resulting toaster, as manufactured, is quite different, and is worth over $550.*

XVIII-35. Toaster, *with flat bed. Bread held in horizontal basket, rather than vertical. Not a very efficient toaster for the time, but rather stylish in appearance. This one is relatively late, but the earliest bread toasters were this style. Picture from Louise J. Peet & Lenore E. Sater's* Household Equipment, *1934, 1940.* **$15+**

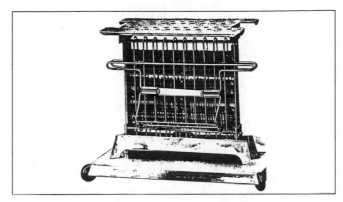

XVIII-38. Toaster. *"Universal" E941N [nickel] or E941S [German silver], by Landers, Frary & Clark with perforated top plate for keeping toast warm. This is a primitive "flipdown" door type for two slices. Note the angled feet disks – terrific styling. Came with 6ft.L "mercerized silk finish flexible cord, triple contact terminal plug." 1914 catalog. LF&C also offered a "twin" style (E943, which had the top of this E941, but the doors of the Thermax E3941), with two identical toasters mounted to a single oblong flat base!* **$25+**

XVIII-36. Toaster. *General Electric, Model X-2, pat'd. Nov. 9, 1915 (not 1905 as stated in 2nd edition. I thank Charles P. Fisher, again, for correcting this error, which resulted because GE itself gave me a 1905 date.) According to Fisher, it may never have been marketed, although obviously the toaster itself exists or GE couldn't have sent me a picture! A collector in Sylvania, Ohio bought the only one known sometime in the 1990s. If more exist, the value would be very high.* **$2,000+**

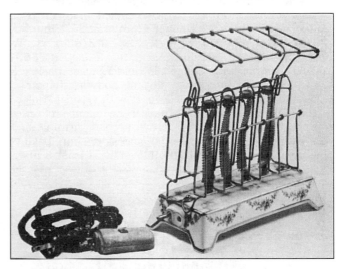

XVIII-37. Toaster. *General Electric, 2nd version of D-12, pat'd by Frank Shailor of GE in July 1909 & Feb. 1910. Detachable wire warming rack in place. Painted porcelain base. Picture courtesy GE shows plug and cord which I am not sure are original because I don't think they had the black cloth-wrapped cords with white dots, as shown here, at the time. Note how the outer wires of the bread holder are quite high. A D-12 sold on eBay in May 2002 that had the low sides & didn't have the warming rack on top, and the white porcelain base wasn't decorated, but it had the original detachable, tan-cloth-wrapped cord. On the end that plugged onto the prongs on the toaster, the cord has a long part with two holes, individually insulated. It also came with an adapter, which was screwed into a lamp socket instead of a bulb, and then became an outlet for the hard rubber plug. This one was embossed on the bottom of the porcelain "Pat. Dec. 28 1909" (looks like 1908), and "G.E. Co. USA Type D-12." See XVIII-30, for Shailor's patent. Plain high side:* **$475+**; *plain low side:* **$325+**; *decorated:* **$950+**

Toaster, nickel-plated, straight-lined base, 2 openwork (interlocking long ellipses) flip-down doors, oblong openwork warming shelf above, mica & wire elements, 4 knurled Bakelite knobs at bottom corners of doors, 7-1/2"H. "Westinghouse Turnover Toaster, Model S372788B," known as "The Aristocrat of the Breakfast Table," mfd. by Westinghouse Electric Mfg. Co., Mansfield, OH, model dates to c.1925. • Westinghouse made several "Turnover" toasters from 1914 on; patent dates "July 28, 1914" and "Aug. 25, 1914. The c.1920 TT-3, according to jeffjunk has compressed-fibre handles (2 to each drop-down door) shaped like skate keys. Earlier ones had wire doors; the very earliest had ceramic heating elements; later ones have doors with less openwork. .... **$55+**

Toaster combo: with egg cooker & bacon cooker; "Triplex Grill," chrome, 3-tiered appliance only 6-3/4"H, cooks 4 eggs on the bottom, toast in the middle, bacon on the top, all slide-in cooking parts have tapered black handles, vented base, stamped "Hotpoint," Catalog "#116G10, W660 V110," mfd. by Edison Electric Appliance Co., pat'd. Nov. 4, 1913. .... **$200+**

Toaster combo: with hot plate & warming oven, cast iron base, white enameled metal with black trim, black Bakelite handles, "darker" & "lighter" switch, push down lever for toast, nickeled plate on oven door says "LASCO Toaster Combination," mfd. by Lasco Toaster Co., 7-1/2"H x 9-3/8" x 13"W, c.1930s. .... **$85+**

Toaster combo: with sandwich holder, toast basket & butter melter; handsome chrome body in shape of 2 near-halves of ball spread apart with vertical "valley," the convex halves look like 2 headlamp reflectors opposite each other. Zigzag wire toast warming shelf above, long black handle on one side, short balance handle for other hand on other side, at least 3 insert

XVIII-40. Toaster. *Nickel plated, blue wooden knobs, 7"H x 8"L x 4-1/4"W, 1920 & 1927 patents. "Electrix" by United Drug Co. Very close to design of LF&C Universal E947.* **$45+**

trays, each with long tapered black handles: (1) one with wire arches to hold a piece of toast, (2) butter-melter is a shallow oblong tray or cradle with arched sides, (3) sandwich holder is a very elegant box with pattern of holes that would fit sideways into the toaster. "Ledig Toaster-Cooker, No. 500 A," mfd. by "Mecky Co., Philadelphia, PA, pat'd. Aug. 1921." (Also has Marsh nichrome patent of 1906.) .... **$850+**

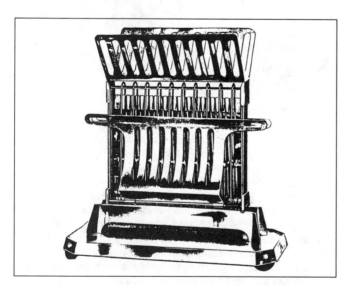

XVIII-39. Toaster. *"Thermax" No. E1942, by Landers, Frary & Clark. Although it could be ordered through LFC's "Universal" catalog of 1914, this toaster was in their not-so-well-known "Thermax" line. Available like the previous one in nickel or silver plate, but with 6'L "flexible cord." Triple contact terminal plug. Note slotted V-shape warming rack above and the nifty sleek slotted doors.* **$100+**

XVIII-41. Toaster. *"Marion Giant Flipflop #66," mfd. by Rutenber Electric Co., Marion, IN. According to Charles Fisher, many versions of this were made, with vertical cutouts in the door, cutouts in the bases, different flat tops. Nickel plated, c.1917. From unidentified catalog page. What a name for a marketing director to fuss with, and I bet no American politician would have been caught using one!* **$50+**

XVIII-42. Toaster.

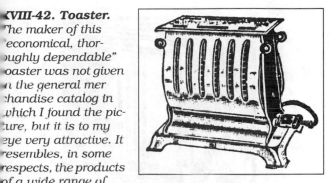

The maker of this "economical, thoroughly dependable" toaster was not given in the general merchandise catalog in which I found the picture, but it is to my eye very attractive. It resembles, in some respects, the products of a wide range of manufacturers', but I couldn't find it in Fisher's, Greguire's or Artman's books, nor in any of my catalogs. "Sparkling nickel plate," 7-1/2" x 7-1/2" x 4-1/4", 6ft.L cord, 2-piece plug. "All complicated and fragile moving parts are eliminated. Being standard size, it takes a full slice of bread without trimming. Women appreciate its artistic design and quiet elegance." Possibly Lindemann & Hoverson, of Milwaukee, or possibly Russell Electric, Chicago. From Slack Mfg. Co., Chicago, c.1925 catalog. I don't think they actually made electric appliances. **$35+**

XVIII-43. Toaster, for one slice, automatic. Toastmaster 1A1, 1926. This was Waters-Genter/McGraw-Edison's first domestic toaster, and was the design of factory superintendent Murray Ireland. Its innards were a result of McGraw-Edison mechanic Charles Strite's inventiveness. In 1918, Mr. Strite built the first automatic pop-up toaster, and the principle of its operation, using a spring motor and switch, was patented in 1919. See the Charles P. Strite paragraph in the text. Commercial toasters were made soon after, for restaurants and lunch counters, and sold under the Strite name. There were models for lunchrooms & hotels, such as the "Eight Slice Strite Automatic," which actually could do 12 small slices, or 360 per hour! There was also a "Three Slice Strite," 3 slices every 1-1/4 minutes! But it was not until 1926 that this first home model automatic pop-up appeared in housewares departments. The switch was pat'd. by Thomas C. Forbes, Hopkins, MN, assignor to W-G, July 10, 1928, #1,676,257. Forbes wrote that the switch could be "engaged and disengaged with a quick, snappy movement even when the initial operating means for the switch is moved very slowly." Sounds like some toasters I know! The 1A1 sold in 1926 for the then-whopping $12.50. Waters-Genter was founded in 1921 & it was acquired by McGraw Electric Co. (later McGraw-Edison). **$65+**

XVIII-44. Toaster. The "new and improved" 1930 pop-up "Toastmaster." "It comes in 1 and 2-slice sizes and is a revelation in simplicity and smartness. Of the hundreds of thousands who saw the remarkable first model, which revolutionized toastmaking in America, not one would have believed it could ever have been improved on. Yet – that has been done! With the new model, all you do is drop in the bread and press but a single lever. And forget about it!" Waters-Genter Co., Division of McGraw Electric Co., Minneapolis, MN. Oct. 1930 ad in Good Housekeeping. The one-slice, which I use, is called a "bachelor toaster." **$55+**

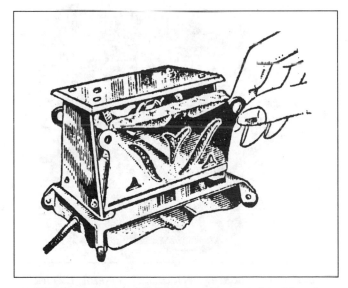

XVIII-45. Toy toaster. Note the disc feet like the Universal. This was described in the June 1930 House Furnishing Review, shortly after they began covering the toy market. "The Excel Electric Co., Muncie, IN, makes the Excel Toastoy, a toy electric toaster, for toasting half slices of bread. Nickeled throughout, with 'nichrome' heating element, 150-watt capacity, complete with plug and silk cord. Retails at $1." Nickel finish; 5"H x 6"L x 3"W. (One sold on eBay was measured as 4"H x 5"L.) The "Toastoy" had apparently been for sale in 1929 also, and they continued making them for several years, at least until 1933. **$75+**

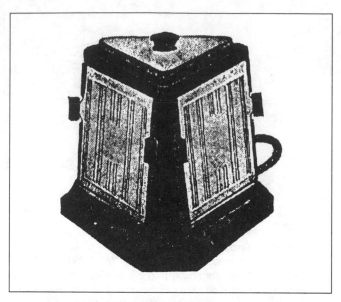

XVIII-46. Toaster. *"Delta," mfd.. by Kamco Inc., Unionville, CT, c.1935. Chrome doors in black-enameled frame. Originally only $2.39. House Furnishing Review, July 1935. One of the most sought-after of all toasters.* **$950+**

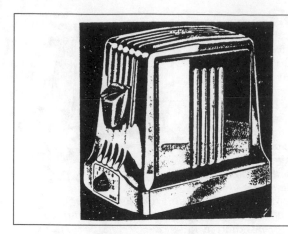

XVIII-48. Toaster. *"The Hotpointer" No. 129T41, automatic, 2 slices, General Electric. "The thermostat, placed right against one slice of the bread, regulates the color of the toast as determined by the setting of the Control Knob. ... Hotpointer signal light, on top, glows a ruddy red when the current is on, and fades out when the current turns off. Tiny bell concealed in base of toaster chimes gently when toast is done. The Hotpointer is absolutely silent in operation, except for this soft musical chime note." Chromed finish, black Calmold™ plastic knob and handle, nichrome wire with mica, 6ft.L detachable cord set with G-E moulded rubber attachment plug and miniature Calmold appliance plug. 850 watts, 115, 125 volts. 1935-36.* **$30+**

XVIII-47. Toaster. *"Hotpoint General Electric," mfd. by Edison General Electric Appliance Co., Chicago, IL, 1931. "Non-tarnishing Chromeplate, with lustrous black Calmold base and trim." "It does more than automatic oven-type toasters have done before," says an ad in* Good Housekeeping, *April 1931, "not only toasts any size bread, but crackers and biscuit halves, too. Instantly adjustable for any degree of brownness. ... Here is beauty to match lovely damask linens and fine silver, yet it costs only $12.50 – at your electric company or dealer's store." Note Art Deco leaping gazelle design in center of side. Ad from* Ladies' Home Journal, *March 1931.* **$200+**

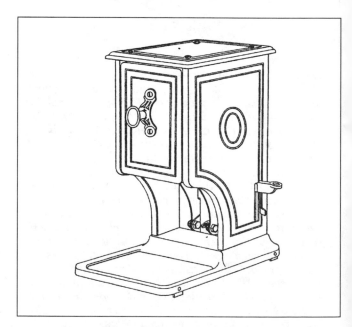

XVIII-49. Toaster patent *for what became the "Universal Model E7732" by Landers, Frary & Clark. Design patent #87,297, granted July 5, 1932, to Oscar M. Anderson & Fred W. Juengst, New Britain, CT., assignors to Landers, Frary & Clark. The finished toaster in production is chrome with black plastic handles & knobs, and is 10-1/2"H x 10"L x 6"W. Very solid!* **$65+**

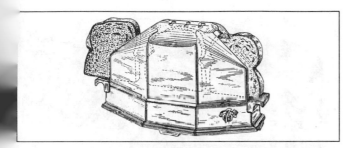

XVIII-50. Toaster patent *granted to William M. Anderson, Minneapolis, assignor to F. J. Kerner & to himself, of Minneapolis. Application was made Oct. 18, 1937; the patent itself was not granted until Apr. 2, 1940, #2,195,638. (It certainly seems to be the precursor to the wonderful "Toast-O-Lator" toaster that toasts bread as it passes through the tunnel of heat. But the patents credited on the "Toast-O-Lator" are in the next picture.) From Anderson's claim: "my present invention ... consists in novel device, combinations of devices and arrangements of parts ... [to] automatic controls, ... and has, as an important object, the provision of an automatic electric toaster in which each slice of bread or analogous sheet material progressively subjected to heat within the toaster, starting from the first piece treated after energization of the heating element ... will be automatically uniformly heat-treated entirely without manual control." Note the three sets of vents on the top.*

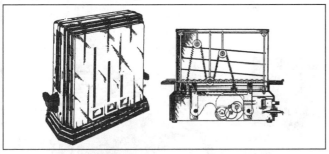

XVIII-51. Toaster patents that were the "Toast-O-Lator." (L) *Stylish toaster body, as envisioned by inventor William A. Pentecost, pat. #2,188,309, granted Jan. 30, 1940 (but filed March 8, 1934). Pentecost's patent also included drawings of the inner workings very like the* **De Matteis patent at right.** *Pentecost claimed "a toaster comprising an elongated casing providing a cooking zone, an adjustably fixed support member arranged to directly engage an edge of a mass of toastable material ... a pair of heating elements." ®Pat. #2,112,075, granted Mar. 22, 1938 (applied for Nov. 14, 1935 – after Pentecost's & before Anderson's), to Alfredo De Matteis, Valley Stream, NY, and Alvin C. Goddard, Forest Hills, Long Island, NY, assignors to Toastolator Co., NYC. Basically their claim was "In household toasters ... as heretofore constructed, the slice of bread ... has been held stationary between a pair of fixed heating elements. In some cases the bread is automatically ejected ... after a predetermined time, which may be adjusted. ... [The disadvantage is] that parts of the bread may be subjected to a more intense heating than others and also that parts shielded by holding members may not be toasted or browned at all. Moreover, in case the ejecting device may fail to work, the bread will be toasted too much or not enough."*

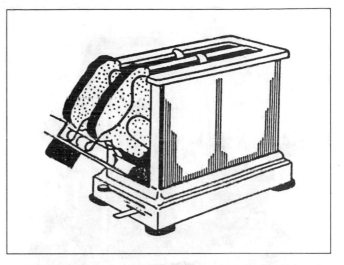

XVIII-52. Toaster. *Neat tipping action. Safe retrieval of non-pop-up toast was a concern of consumers and manufacturers. Chromium "Universal Moderne" automatic model by Landers, Frary & Clark, catalog #E7822, c.1937. Has composition handles & feet. Picture from Peet's book* Household Equipment, *1940.* **$50+**

XVIII-53. Toaster. *Two views. Spider web design desirable extra for collectors. General Electric 119T46, 1940.* **$55+**

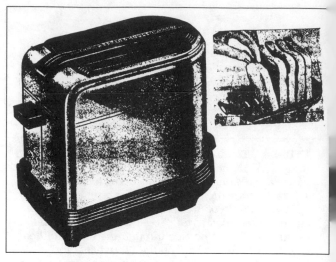

XVIII-56. Toaster & toast server-top. *Westinghouse "Pop-Up," Model TD 414, automatic "crisper for regular or Melba toast." Streamline design rounded at far end, chrome finish, Bakelite™ base & handles, curved end for easy parking. Bakelite cover-server fits down into slot "preventing dust from getting into wells" as barely visible in (L) this catalog photo, and being used inverted as toast server at ® that "prevents toast from absorbing moisture from cold plates" – a really excellent idea. In Dearborn catalog, 1940. With the two-way cover/rack:* **$65+**

XVIII-54. Toaster. *"Universal Turn-Easy" model E1321 in the Coronet pattern. "Second to none in styling. Its design follows the modern trend with artistic chasing." Came with matching percolator, waffle iron, etc. Chrome plated, "smart black handles & feet" [they don't mention Bakelite, used in describing others on same page], 6ft.L cord and plug. Lowering doors turns toast over. From Ft. Dearborn Mercantile catalog, 1942.* **$35+**

XVIII-55. Toaster. *"Toastwell," manufactured by Utility Electric Co., St. Louis. It's completely automatic "pop-out" type, and "super silent – no 'ticking' annoyance found in the ordinary toasters." I bet he got a bad burn on his cheek! Pop-up, chrome plated with Bakelite™ handles & base. 7"H x 11-1/2"L. 725 watts; 110-125 volts AC or DC, detachable cord & plug. It also came in a 4 slice style, which was simply elongated to 13-3/8"L, and 7-1/4"H. Pictures from Dearborn catalog, 1942. The 4-slice style would bring more.* **$45+**

XVIII-57. Toaster. *"Sunbeam," by Chicago Flexible Shaft Co. "The lovely oval design [is] the last word in modern styling by George Scharfenberg." [Imagine a 1990's toaster ad giving the designer's name, unless it was a famous architect and the toaster was $250.] Ad claimed "every slice of toast the identical shade of every other slice, whether it's first or last." That was useful when making party canapes, I guess. Could be had also as part of a "stunning buffet set including four new intaglio crystal lap trays, 3-compartment appetizer dish and large, roomy walnut tray." The really nifty feature was you could set this one to pop-up or to keep the toast inside until wanted. Saturday Evening Post, 1940.* **$55+**

XVIII-58. Toasters for big families or diners.
When time was of the essence, these two commercial toasters did the trick. **(L)** The "Three Slice Strite Automatic" was advertised in the 1924 Barry's jobber catalog: "it will turn out three slices every minute and a quarter, and it will produce a dozen orders every ten minutes. 12"L x 10"W, 2,200 watts! Originally cost $105.00. "Eight Slice Strite Automatic," advertised as alternatively making 12 "small slices." Barry's catalog said "This machine will make its full capacity of toast every minute and a quarter, and will supply in an hour 360 large slices of toast or over 500 slices, if each slice measures not over 3-1/4"W." 5,500 watts. 17"H x 15"L x 12-1/2"W. Original price: $270.00. **$200+**

Toaster combo: with oven & coffee pot warmer plate & fitted coffee-pot, nickel-plated, low square oven on cabriole feet with insulators, toasting rack/tray with stubby handle inserts into oven, top curves up like plinth to hold a coffee-pot with gooseneck spout & its own low square flat base that fits down over heating elements to ensure every watt was used. "Perc-O-Toaster Model PT" mfd. by Armstrong Electric Mfg. Corp., Huntington, WVA. 1920s. With pot: $250+; with waffle iron attachment that slips into the oven part: .... **$600+**

Toaster stove, nickel-plated, little rectangular cooker on cabriole legs, tray and comfit mesh screen, Westinghouse Electric & Mfg. Co., East Pittsburg, PA, early 1920s. **$65**

Toasters, non-electric – See Chapter X (Hearths); also Chapter XI (Stoves)

Waffle irons, electric – See Chapter IV (Mold & Form)

Water bottle heater, flexible metal wand-like rod, 12"L, attached by thick cloth-wrapped cord to control unit (?), that has much longer twisted 2-strand conductor cord with lamp-socket plug end. "An electrical device made for heating a rubber water-bag. Fits

XVIII-60. Hot water or immersion heater. Unit for heating a pail of water. The "Premier" by the National Ideal Co., Toledo, OH. Ad from Farm Journal, Nov. 1947. **$10**

XVIII-59. Hot water urns. (L) Edison Electric Co. hot water urn, of nickeled heavy spun copper. Heating disk is in base above little legs. 19"H x 9"W. "Instantaneous"® hot water heater, mfr. unknown. Copper, capacity of 4 pints, 15"H x 7"W. Note the claw & ball feet, which may be glass marbles, although it doesn't say so. 1906. Note the "lamp socket plug" that screws into light bulb socket. Both from Albert Pick Hotel Supplies catalog, 1909. **$50-$100+**

any size or style of bag made. Can be regulated for any temperature desired, low, medium and high." "Christian Water-Bottle Heater" mfd. by Hansen & Moist, Long Beach, CA. Prob. early 1920s. Up for sale on eBay by kathysdolls1 in 2002. .... **$15+**

Water kettle - See Kettle

FOR MORE INFORMATION

SMALL APPLIANCES

The Old Appliance Club

Big & small appliances. A large, active, friendly membership. Fact-filled back issues of the newsletter "*The Old Road Home*" available, and catalogued on Web site. TOAC was founded by Jack Santora, who calls himself an American Antique Appliance Archaeologist. TOAC helps locate parts & service, and will offer advice on phone about whether to buy or walk.
Contact: Gina Thompson
J.E.S. Enterprises
POB 65
Ventura, CA 93002
Phone: (805) 643-3532

E-mail: jes@west.net
Web site: www.antiquestoves.com/toac/oldroad.htm

Decodan

Dan reconditions small appliances (mainly mixers), colors to suit you; cleans motors & oils them; replaces or repairs major parts; and sells on eBay as decodan.
Contact: Dan McQuade
POB 770535
Memphis, TN 38177-0535
Phone: (901) 272-1183
E-mails: decodan@decodan.com or sales@decodan.com
Web site: www.decodan.com/

Twentieth Century Appliance Restorations

Arnold says cords can be replaced, whether directly wired or detachable. He needs to have the old detachable cord sent to him so that he can match the plug. "My best customers are my educated customers. It is worth the price of a phone call to know whether you've found a beauty or a beast!" Sales, parts, service, literature, historically accurate cloth cords, functional & cosmetic restoration of small appliances to refrigerators to radios. Visit frequently!
Contact: Mike Arnold
49 Christie St.
Troy, NY 12180
Phone: (518) 272-7916
E-mail: monitortop@monitortop.com
Web site: www.monitortop.com

Park Electric Repair Co.

Bill Schoenhoefer, and before him, his father Ralph, have fixed old electric appliances in St. Louis since 1947. The elder even made house calls for poorly toasters. According to an article by Jeannette Batz, "*Best of St. Louis*," Schoenhoefer's personal favorite appliance is a Model 5 Sunbeam Mixmaster!
9796 Clayton Rd.
St. Louis, MO 63124-1504
Phone: (314) 993-6711

ELECTRICAL APPLIANCE AUCTIONS

Auction Team Köln – Breker

In all these years, I've never found but one auction house that has large, important auctions of old technological items, except this one German house, Auction Team Köln. Their "Technical Antiques" sales (not spe-cialty one-subject auctions) are generally titled "Clocks & Old Technology" (*Uhren & Alte Technik*), and cover clocks, phonographs, automata, scientific & medical instruments, drawing instruments, lab apparatus, optical devices, tools, radios and TVs, electrical appliances, sewing machines, flat irons, toasters, household & kitchen antiques, automobilia, bicycles, vending machines, industrial design, etc. There are international representatives in the US, Japan, Argentina, France, Australia/New Zealand. Click on "Addresses" on Web page. You can also subscribe to catalogs, which will probably show things you've never seen before. No e-mail orders of catalogs.
Bonner Strasse 528-530
D-50968
Köln (Bayenthal/South)
Phone: /49/221/38 70 49
Fax: /49/221/37 48 78
E-mail: auction@breker.com
Web site: www.breker.com

COMPANY & DESIGN HISTORIES

Hamilton-Beach/Proctor-Silex

Go to this Web site, read, then click on "Company History" and "Antiques Museum" for a "trip down memory lane" from 1910 to 1980!! Minimal text with pictures of everything.
Web site: www.hamiltonbeach.com/hb

Sunbeam

Just a blip of history.
Web site: www.sunbeam.com/products/mixers_history.htm

100 Years of Design

Interesting site of the Industrial Designers Society of America, with what they describe as "monthly excerpts" from a proposed book, *100 Years of Design – A Chronology 1900-2000*, by Carroll Gantz. Good to know more about the talented designers who designed products we still admire.
Web site: www.idsa.org/whatis/100yr/100yearsofdesign.htm

Bakelite & Catalin

To read about these two related but different cast plastics, here's a good Web site by Lloyd Fadem & Stephen Z. Fadem.

An excellent page on caring for & cleaning set up by C. E. "Sonny" Clutter on his fascinating old radio Web site & virtual museum.
Web site: www.deco-echoes.com/bakelite.html
Web site: www.radiolaguy.com/clean-shine.htm

MIXERS

WACEM

We Actually Collect Electric Mixers was founded in 1999. A lot of very knowledgeable people belong. A very fun site.
Contact/founder: Nancy Platnick
50 Brentwood Rd.

Bay Shore, NY 11706
E-mail: electrickook@yahoo.com
Web site: http://groups.yahoo.com/group/WACEM

Mixmaster Site

Sunbeams – poetry in motion on this extraordinary 23-page site for Sunbeams & some other electric mixers. It's the most detailed, joyful collector site I've ever seen. As the sleuth-poet who started the site says, the Mixmaster "... plays you a kind of chamber music in soft, sustained chords." Jeff Kallman praises the "distinctive fragrance from the motor lubricants," & has put a book's worth of facts & links onto this site, with a healthy dose of comment on corporate mentality.
Contact: Jeff Kallman
4302 Pickwick Circle
Huntington Beach, CA 92649
E-mail: kallman@cts.com
Web site: www.angelfire.com/home/flexibleshaft/
Sunbeam1.html

Vidrio Items & Mixers

This collector wrote a book on Watt Pottery (Schiffer, 1994, and collects all Vidrio glass products; they specialized in electrical appliances with glass parts. Also pre WWII electric mixers & juicers. He'd like to hear from people regarding Vidrio or electric mixers in general.
Contact: Dennis Thompson
E-mail: dthomp@core.com
Web site: http://my.core.com/~dthomp/index.html

BOOKS

Beat This

For a long time, there was nothing much in print about electric mixers, except in *The Eggbeater Chronicles, The Stirring Story of America's Greatest Invention*, by Don Thornton. A very short chapter in this great book on eggbeaters, includes patent info. See Bibliography, or order online.
Web site: www.thorntonhouse.com

TOASTERS

Toaster Collector Association

Annual meetings, occasional newsletter.
Contact: Chris Steiner, President
2822 S. Park Drive
Silver Lake OH 44224
E-mail: pres@toastercollector.com
Web site: www.toastercollector.com/index.html

TOASTER COLLECTOR

Toasters Galore

Contact: Carl Roles
POB 529
Temecula, CA 92593
E-mail: rocknroles@yahoo.com

TOASTER MUSEUMS

Undoubtedly, someday there will be a real toaster museum open again to the public. For now, my favorites are virtual.

The International Central Services Toaster Museum

A graphic & media designer & consultant, Jens Veerbeck has assembled a beautiful collection of toasters, European, Australian, American, & Canadian. It will help you navigate this great virtual museum if you give it your full screen, as many buttons show up to right of center, (I usually work with two windows at a time.) When you go to the Web site, click on the "start" button. From there, you can choose permanent or special exhibitions, for sale, links, collectors. Veerbeck has alphabetized all by companies, with thumbnails. See some of my favorites of Veerbeck's collection in the color section of this book.
Contact: Jens Veerbeck
Central Services
Promenadenweg 23
45 219 Essen-Kettwig
Germany
Phone: +49 (0)2054 - 87 42 98
Phone: ++49 (0)208 - 388 18 68
E-mail: veerbeck@central-services.de
Web site: www.central-services.de/toastermuseum

Www.Toasters.De

A site of one collector's many pages (some in 8 languages, German, English, French, Spanish, Italian, Danish, Norwegian, Swedish), for seeing, selling, buying, history, links, recipes & more. And not just toasters, but other small appliances.
Contact: Michael Trautmann
eBay name: tosti
Munich, Germany
E-mail: michael_trautmann@t-online.de
Phone: ++49-172-9941140
Web site: www.toasters.de/Framese.html

Toaster Museum Foundation

Here you can see the Cyber Toaster Museum, & buy fun toaster-related stuff. You can also link to "Unusual Museums of the Internet."

The couple who started this once had a toaster museum in Seattle, moved to Charlottesville, VA, and hope to open one again. Tom Richardson has created a valuable index to the site, with links to other sites. A newsletter, *Hotwire*, with contributions by collectors from all over can be ordered (long with back issues) from the Foundation.
1003 Carlton Ave., Suite B
Charlottesville, VA 22902-5974
Web site: www.toaster.org/
Index Web site: www.greencoast.ca/sitez/
toaster/my_index.html

TOASTER-RELATED COLLECTIBLES

This isn't, strictly speaking, a museum, but it's a wonderful site to see scores of things in the toaster shape such as cookie jars, teapots & S&Ps, toys, greeting cards, etc., plus a few real toasters. Beverly & Jack do not collect, nor can they answer questions about, real toasters.
E-mail: bright.bytes@verizon.net
Web site: http://brightbytes.com/collection/
toaster.html

ELECTRIC KITCHENS, ETC.

Period kitchens set up with electrical appliances are viewable here.

London Science Museum

Collection of domestic appliances, "The Secret Life of the Home," open to public. Electric cookers, mixers, choppers, blenders. Electric toasters, kettles, and much more. This exhibit was devised by cartoonist/engineer Tim Hunkin & David Woodcock in 1995.
Contact: David Woodcock, Curator
Exhibition Rd.
South Kensington
London SW7 2DD England
Phone: +44 0207 942 4214
E-mail : d.woodcock@nmsi.ac.uk
Web site: http://www.sciencemuseum.org.uk/gallery

Museum of Science and Industry
Liverpool Rd.
Manchester M3 4JP
England
Phone: (0161) 832-2244

Simply Switch On...!

URL for toasters: http://homepage.dtn.ntl.com/paul.linnell/electricity/toasters.html

URL for everything:

Small electric appliances virtual museum established by Paul Linnell. I hope this site stays up for a long time; it's full of information & pictures of all kinds of United Kingdom small electric appliances. Lots of history, virtual exhibits, pictures. Also links to some Web sites of interest.

http://inventors.about.com/gi/dynamic/offsite.htm?once=true&site=http://homepage.dtn.ntl.com/paul.linnell/electricity/kettles.html

MICROWAVE OVENS

J. Carlton Gallawa

"The complete microwave oven repair & information network," with history outline.
Microtech
POB 940
Gonzalez, FL 32560
E-mail: microtech@gallawa.com
Web site: www.gallawa.com/microtech/history.html

FANS

Collector Club

The Antique Fan Collectors Association has events & a newsletter.
Contact: Membership
POB 5473
Sarasota, FL 34277-5473
E-mail: membership@fancollectors.org
Web site: www.fancollectors.org/

American Fan Museum

The Fan Man himself, founder of the AFCA, author of several books, formerly of Dallas. (The Fan Man Fan Museum is run by his former manager, who bought the Dallas business.) House is now active in collecting, & writing about, cowboy & western memorabilia. See Bibliography for fan books.
Kurt House
218 Country Wood
San Antonio, TX 78216

Phone: (210) 490-2433
E-mail: cowboyhous@aol.com

The Fan Man Fan Museum

James Denoyer's collection of fans is mostly electric, with a few kerosene, gas, etc. And this is the kind of museum we wish we could always visit as collectors: except for few rare models, all of the fans in the museum are for sale! Because Denoyer's wife loves old waffle irons & toasters, they and some other kitchen appliances are also on view.
1914 Abrams Pkwy. at Gaston Ave.
Dallas, TX 75214-6218
Phone: (214) 826-7700 or 826-7721

Fan Restoration

This site for the Antique Fan Collectors Association with a number of leads to restoration/reproduction parts for fans, including that most important service motor rewinding.
Contact: Dave Friedlund
E-mail: davefr@pacifier.com
Web site: www.fancollectors.org/info/source.htm

WINDMILLS

Windmillers' Gazette

This quarterly newsletter of water-pumping windmills & wind power history is for collectors of wind machines & farm implements, technology fans [!], and, in the words of the editor, "people with romantic, artistic, and sentimental interest in windmills." Articles on mills, how-to repair, even kitchen items made by such a windmill company as Stover.
Publisher/founder: T. Lindsay Baker
PO Box 507
Rio Vista, Texas 76093
Web site: http://windmillersgazette.com/index.html

Windmill World

A site covering world-wide traditional windmills, & watermills, events, even mills for sale. Annual events include amateur radio stations broadcasting from various mills! Also has tons of info on foreign mills & organizations, with links. Unique in all the sites I've visited on anything is Berry's conscientious noting of broken links.
Contact: Mark Berry
Web site: www.windmillworld.com/

International Molinological Society

This & the next society cover mills for pumping water, grinding grain, etc.
Contact: Michael Harverson
125 Parkside Drive
Watford, Hertfordshire
WD1 3BA, England

Society for the Preservation of Old Mills
Contact: Dick Sullin, Treasurer SPOOM
111 South Main
Rockford, MI 49341

Vereniging De Hollandsche Molen

Site for Dutch mills, in Dutch only, with information on National Mill Day. You can e-mail from the site.
Web site: www.molens.nl/index.html

RESEARCHING

XIX. RESEARCHING PATENTS FOR KITCHEN COLLECTIBLES

Finding the Geniuses Behind It All

Thomas Alva Edison defined genius as "1% inspiration and 99% perspiration." It's also the secret of successful invention, but just when we collectors begin a litany of thanks for the ingenious gadgets we love, we notice that Edison also wrote "there is no substitute for hard work." Oh, but, praise be, there is, if you think hard is fun! Tracing inventions from the U.S. Patent Office's first century is profitable fun, although the search needs inspiration and perspiration in the same ratio as genius. As a break from the hard work, we love serendipitous finds of funny-looking inventions found by browsing *Gazettes*. Fortunately, kitchen inventions are numerous throughout the over 210+ years the United States has been granting patents.

An early Patron Saint of Kitchen Substitutes for Hard Work (i.e., Labor-Saving) was **Moses Coates**, a mechanic from Chester County, PA, who on Feb. 4, 1803, got the first apple parer patent. No exact Coates are known, but early handmade wooden parers of that type exist from the first third of the 19th century. Mass production (and interchangeability) of cast iron gears by 1850 set off a "furious battle to perfect the paring machine," **says** John Lambert, founder of Apple Parer Enthusiasts.

Many **parer patents** were granted in 1857, with no corresponding leap in pie pan or pie trimmer patents. You do wonder if All-American Apple Pies didn't come of age in 1857, although a new recipe was needed in 1867, when nutmeg graters had their great year! In 1857, baseball was already the All-American sport, and the country was in turmoil over slavery, the "Mormon War," and a financial panic. Lambert suspects that 1855-56's crop of really "great designs" (including the turntable parer) spurred others to "top that" if they could. In 1867, Reconstruction Acts were the aftermath of the Civil War, Charles Dickens visited the U.S., and Russia sold Alaska to the U.S.

By 1890, when there were over 100 parer patents, the market had a "shake-out" and a few – including the Reading '78, Little Star, and White Mountain – were left, featured for many decades in hardware stores and mail-order catalogs. A newish variation of the "White Mountain" – Model #300 – is still manufactured today by the White Mountain Freezer Co.

U.S. patent records hint at a **booming canning industry** that may have precipitated the decline of home-use apple parer patents. Peeled apple segments were ready in a jiffy with a **can opener**; hundreds of those were patented, beginning with one in 1858, then skipping past most of the Civil War to 1864. The canning industry itself, which began circa 1840, was the biggest labor-saving "device" between the wheel and 1930, when Clarence Birdseye began to freeze food in little boxes.

Instead of having a parer clamped to the kitchen counter all fall – not to mention mechanical pineapple eyesnips, tomato corers, corn shellers, raisin seeders, wheat berry grinders, peach parers, meat tenderizers, cabbage cutters, bean slicers, pea shellers, and the like – you could bypass picking, sorting, washing, and parboiling with boxes or tins of food ready to cook or serve straight out of the can! You could even buy extremely large cans of berries or fruit or vegetables, and then re-can them in your own meal-sized fruit jars.

Patented Progress – Established by act of Congress on April 10, 1790, "to promote the progress of useful arts," the Patent Office granted only three patents the first year because almost no inventions met the test of being "sufficiently useful and important." My figures are from looking at the chronology of unnumbered patents in the "Early Unnumbered Patents" ... 1790 to 1836 (see Bibliography). In fact, until a new act of February 24, 1793, took away the power of rejection, or judging of worthiness, there were only seven patents granted – for spinning cotton, type punches, and cloth shearing machines. The first one under the new law was Eli Whitney's first patent for a cotton gin. Whitney got all three of the patents granted in 1794; and in 1795 and 1796 only three patents were granted each year. After that, the pace picked up considerably so that eventually some 8,500 to 10,000 unnumbered patents were granted through 1835. We have only sketchy information on many of them. The **first Superintendent** of the Patent Office was a **Dr. Thornton**, appointed by President Thomas Jefferson; he took over from a clerk in the Department of State (who had previously issued patents) in 1803 and issued patents for the next 24 years until he died in 1827. A glimpse of his kindly personality, and his eagerness to help inventors, may be found in some correspondence that is on the Web at www.myoutbox. net/poar1830.htm. Also on that in-progress site is a chart of the numbers of patents issued in those early years; there is a considerable discrepancy between those numbers and the ones cited above. For example, the 1829 document quoted on the site says that 22 patents were reported to Congress in 1793; although only 20 were registered. Also, it says that for the years 1790, 1791, and 1792, 47 patents were issued.

From 1836 to 1882, the Patent Office issued 269,819 numbered patents, 13,507 design patents, 10,264 reissues, and 9,919 trademarks (reflecting the burgeoning of brand marketing). We laugh to read what is sometimes reported to be an apocryphal remark, that in 1833 Patent Office Commissioner John D. Craig wanted to resign because he believed that everything "seems to have been done." Another pessimist, W. P. N. Fitzgerald, who was the Patent Examiner in charge of inventions of mills, land conveyances, lumber machinenry, hydraulics, pneumatics, and textiles, wrote in his 1849 report to Thomas Ewbanks, the Commissioner of Patents, his belief that "The field of invention in many of its departments is limited; and every year must necessarily circumscribe it still more narrowly, leaving little to be invented except what has been invented previously."

Worse Than Useless – For the first 60 years many, shall-we-say, undeserving inventions were granted patents. Even if well-intentioned, many neither claimed something truly new, nor even described something that would work, let alone save labor. Those silly if imaginative inventions, which patent collectors love to find and photocopy, didn't satisfy what Judge Learned Hand called a requisite for a valid subject for patent: "a new display of ingenuity." In an 1838 *Franklin Institute Journal*, the editor chastised one patentee thusly: "We cannot well conceive of a less promising affair than the foregoing, but things are not stopped in the Patent Office merely because they are trifling." It was relatively cheap and easy to get a patent, and there was a slim chance to make a fortune. I've seen no evidence that any early inventors did any kind of patent searching such as is done by patent lawyers today, so many self-styled inventors entered what they saw as a sort of lottery for fortune by applying patents for just about anything.

The problem was not a new one. According to an article on the history of the Patent Office, in the *Official Gazette*, Oct. 9, 1877, "From 1790 to the re-organization of the Patent Office in 1836 there were granted 11,348 patents, a large number of which, on account of lack of novelty or usefulness, were valueless. The abuses which grew out of the promiscuous granting of patents without further inquiry than as to the payment of the fee and the form of the application attracted public attention in the early part of the present [19th] century," but it wasn't until July 4, 1836, that Congress passed a bill to improve the system of awarding patents. Apparently, the main fraud was by **patent pirates**, who would go into the model room, draw a patent drawing from the model, copy the specifications, make a few little changes, and automatically, upon payment of the required fee they would get a patent, for which they would then sell the rights to unsuspecting individuals and companies who wanted to manufacture these inventions.

Women Inventors – *The New York Times* reported Dec. 14, 1890, that: "2,400 women have secured patents but very few have made much money with them with the exception of the lady who was so fortunate as to hit upon the **fluting iron**. ... The women who have secured patents have been mostly thrifty housewives, and their inventions have been generally in the nature of kitchen utensils and domestic articles."

The Times article was based on a Patent Office publication, an 1809-1888 chronological listing of "Women Inventors," giving names, patent numbers, inventions, and dates. Among women's patents we find cookstoves, ice-cream freezers, butter-workers, washing-machines, a combination of sofa and bathing tub, vegetable-graters, culinary boilers, and – beginning in the 1840s – a lot of "improvements on" mincing-knives, sieves, pie-tubes, bathroom racks, pastry-rollers, dish-washers, strawberry-hullers, flour-sifters, cake-stirrers, &c.

The 1870s brought a spate of housekeeping helpers including a canning funnel, an egg-poaching pan, a fruit-fork, and an ever-useful "pantaloon tree," for drying those voluminous unmentionables. Sarah Sewell, Mark Centre,

OH, patented a combined washing-machine and teeter or seesaw (#330,626), Nov. 17, 1885. A lot of today's day care centers could use one of those.

Predominate in most years were inventions relating to sewing, clothing, corsetry and – as an indication of the hard work involved – laundering and ironing. Many women besides famous Mrs. Potts (the probable "fortunate" lady cited by the *The New York Times*) got patents on sad irons and fluting irons.

Hundreds of women's patents, including domestic-science ones, were little machines. Sarah Cooper Morrisonville, PA, patented (#196,743) an "Improvement in apple quartering and coring machines" on Nov. 6, 1877; Emma Orendorff, Delavan, IL, patented (#199,704) an "Improvement in apple-corers" on Jan. 8, 1878. Another collecting specialty – eggbeaters – is represented by Sarah A. Ulmer, Portland, ME, whose tin churn-like eggbeater (#224,117) was patented Feb. 3, 1880. Ulmer's beater was manufactured, and is in at least one collection. Scores of them may be out there. Others patentees include Katherine Livingood, Womelsdorf, PA, eggbeater (#282,738) on on Aug. 7, 1883; Hannah Zephyrene Gibson, Oberlin, OH, eggbeater (#293,648), Feb. 19, 1884; Eugenia Kilborn, Cedar Rapids, IA, eggbeater (#303,022), Aug. 5, 1884; and Edith A. Marsh, New Albany, IN, eggbeater (#345,709), July 20, 1886. All are possible finds, especially in or near patentees' hometowns.

An article in *House Furnishing Review* of January 1903 noted inventions recently viewed at the Woman's Department of the Mechanics' Fair in Boston. Described as "the most original and unique invention" was Philadelphian Lydia C. Sharples' bread-making machine. It was already being manufactured by The Scientific Bread Machine Co., Philadelphia. It took her three years, but Sharples made her own working patent model, of cardboard, tin and wood, and I bet her dyspeptic husband, for whom she wished to make digestible bread, was a happy man!

Publication of Patents – Brief note was made of some out-of-the-ordinary inventions in some 19th century scientific journals (such as the *Journal of the Franklin Institute*, Philadelphia), agricultural newspapers from the 1840s on, *Scientific American*, and some English gentlemen's magazines published in American editions from the late 1700s on, and a few patents of particular interest might be mentioned in newspapers, especially those of local inventors. But illustrations were rare. The Patent Office had to supply a drawing of a patent if someone wrote to ask for one, and by 1861, photographic reproduction of patent drawings was being experimented with. The Civil War intervened, but starting July 1, 1869, twelve copies of each patent were being made as a matter of course, with the drawings and the specs. A year later, photolithographic copies were being made: 300 of each patent, but they decided that was in excess of the demand, so the number was cut to 150 for many years. Specifications and drawings were sent to the 50 depository libraries around the country from 1871 to at least 1873. The weekly *Official Gazette* was begun in 1873 (although one source I've seen says 1872), and at first was bound three or four months per volume. Many American inventors didn't live in or near a city with a depository library of patent records, and few lived in Washington, D.C., where anyone could go to the Patent Office and look at file copies of the patents, or at the thousands of meticulous working models that were submitted as required with most primary patents until about 1881.

Patent Models Galore & On Fire – The galleries at the Patent Office, with huge glass cases full of wonderful models, were a popular tourist site in the nineteenth century – and would be today, if the powers that be had thought enough of our inventive history to keep the models that survived two devastating fires.

The editor of the "Mechanics Register" section of the *Journal of the Franklin Institute* wrote after the December 15, 1836 fire: "Our readers need not be informed of the great national loss consequent upon the burning of the Patent Office." A precis of the losses included "the records, originals, drawinngs, models, &c., ... [that] embraced the whole history of American invention for nearly half a century." "168 large folio volumes of records, and 26 large portfolios, containing 9,000 drawings," "230 volumes of books ... of scientific subjects," "about seven thousand models [that] displayed great talent, ingenuity, and mechanical science" were all lost. A new, so-called "fire-proof" building was erected in 1840, and in just nine years 200 patent models had been rebuilt, and 14,997 new models, half for patents granted, half for rejects, were stored. Most, if not all patent models that didn't perish in the 1836 fire in the Office's first building, succumbed to the September 24, 1877 fire. A blow-by-blow account of the progress of the fire that raged through the third floor, wood-raftered and therefore perfect tinder, was published in the *Official Gazette* of October 9, 1877. Firemen from the District were aided by four engine companies rushed from Baltimore on railroad flatcars, and soldiers and policemen studded the Mall to guard the treasures that could be rescued. The third floor display galleries, "visited yearly by thousands of people, both for profit and pleasure ... contained about 200,000 models of American invention." The fire destroyed "about 12,000 rejected models," and another 75,000 models ... among them were several thousand known as "pending" and "issue" cases. The rejects were not considered a loss, and in fact "the propriety of breaking them up and selling them for old metal had recently been seriously discussed." If the rejects and the other pending and issue patent models were for sale today, we could practically retire the national debt, so greatly are all patent models valued by collectors.

As if the lessons of fire had never been taught, in 1888 Congress decided to sell the models, and inventors were notified. They claimed about 2,000 models, and the rest were packed up higgledy-piggledy in crates. Around 1907, the Smithsonian curators were asked if they wanted any – and they unpacked crates and took about 4,000 models. Curators at the Henry Ford Museum in Dearborn, Michigan, also acquired several thousand. According to an article by R. James Aber, in the *Early American Industries Association* magazine, *The Chronicle*, of April 1974, an English businessman, Sir Henry Wellcome, bought the remainder of the collection – an estimated 175,000 models packed in about 3500 crates – in 1925, for under $10,000. He wanted to build a museum, but died before it could be done. Crosby Gaige bought them next, and sold them to a business consortium. They sat in storage for years, and in 1941 or 1942, O. Rundle Gilbert, a well-known auctioneer of Garrison, NY, bought the collection, which was in uncatalogued crates, for an undisclosed amount. Fire destroyed about 20,000 models in one of Gilbert's barns. Extremely important models of every description were unpacked in dribs and drabs over the next three decades, and individual models were sold to collectors, usually for a couple of hundred dollars or less. Models still show up on the market – usually for many hundreds or even thousands of dollars.

Patent Research – Probably the most inexpensive, tantalizing pursuit for collectors of cooking or housekeeping tools is patent research. Especially now with access to patents on the Internet. It's so absorbing that more time can be spent researching the genius behind the tool than in finding it (or earning the money to buy it). One devoted patent collector is Don Thornton, whose remarkable eggbeaters compelled him to search out their inventors' thought processes – as revealed in application specifications. Thornton says that "The *Official Gazette* is the history of America in the form of millions of illustrated short stories!" He recommends hanging out at a patent depository library, preferably one with patents on microfilm and also hardbound copies of indices and *Official Gazettes*, which have pictures and short descriptions of every patent, including design patents and trademarks. The good ones don't stop at 1900, either; Don has made great finds in 1940s and '50s *Gazettes*.

Pictures and claims help determine what, if any, parts are missing from a piece, or how something is supposed to work. And monetary value is affected by patent knowledge in other ways. About twenty years ago I bought a humorously waggly sheet brass and iron wire eggbeater which screw-clamped to a shelf edge. I paid more than I'd ever paid before, but the dealer said it would have been more if it had been a patented piece. A few years later, the patent drawing for it was found. Now the somewhat rough sawn edges of heavy sheet brass seemed a sign that it might be a production prototype, not a one-off piece. The value went up 300% and I sold it. Us patent junkies get hooked by suspenseful searches for patents for things we have – or think we have. At an auction, I bought a cast iron gadget billed as a "pea sheller." The only mark was "Dec. 4, 1855"; it had felt-covered wringer-like rollers, and a trough. Pop them ol' peapods, thought I. A year later, by chance, I was browsing the *Gazette*'s precursor (see Research), the patent report for 1855, and there was a picture of my gadget! It's a knife scourer. The felt pads held scouring powder or pumice, and the trough caught the pasty mess of pumice and water. I don't know if the value went up or down – depends on which class of gadget is most sought-after. An embossed "patent" date on a gear may actually be the date an impatient inventor sent an application to Washington; or it may have been made up so that a gadget already in production would seem patent-protected. Always check a perpetual calendar to confirm that a date found on an object fell on Tuesday. As a break from the "hard work" we love serendipitous finds of funny-looking inventions found by browsing *Gazettes*. Lucky Don Thornton lives near a patent library where he searches a year's index, sees how interesting the drawing looks in the *Gazette*, puts a microfilm reel on a machine, spins the crank to his target patent, and makes a photocopy right then. Instant gratification!

You can also be a P.I. [Patent Investigator] by (A) using your own three-volume *Subject-Matter Index of Patents*, (B) consulting the *Official Gazette of the Patent and Trademark Office (P.T.O.)*, at regional patent depository libraries, and (C) ordering photocopies of specific patents (typically you'll get a full-page drawing, plus one to four pages of inventor's claims). Order photocopies from the P.T.O. (PS Center, CPK-1, Washington, DC 20231, or online at the Patent Office Web site – see how-to article at the end of this chapter). For years I got patent copies from the P.T.O. by sending an object's name and date, and sometimes the inventor. Now this germane information is called "narrative comment" by P.T.O, which will only fill an order by patent number. Your local library can advise you on the closest of over 50 depository libraries around the U.S. that have bound (or microfilmed) issues of the weekly *Official Gazette* from 1873 on, or others that have at least som years on microfilm.

Tracking down the thoughts and hopes of inventors no matter how deluded they were, is a hobby in itself It's a form of virtual reality for the browser – wha might have been, what could be out there. If you ar feeling jaded about finding a rare apple parer, or ar idiosyncratic eggbeater, or a brilliantly efficient car opener to add to your collection, consider taking ar *Official Gazette* sabbatical!

FOR MORE INFORMATION

BOOKS & JOURNALS

See entries in the Bibliography next to the code INV. Also:

Journal of the Franklin Institute, Franklin Institute, Philadelphia, 1820s to 1850s. A large section entitled "Mechanics' Register" disseminated details of American patents, often with pithy remarks. Editor Thomas P. Jones became Commissioner of Patents in 1828/29.

Report of the Commissioner of Patents for the Year _____. Arts and Manufacturers. Published as a report to the House of Representatives, about 40,000 copies were printed each year – some for the use of the Congressmen. I believe these bound, 2- and 3-volume reports started in the 1840s. One volume each year has illustrations; another has claim précis. Very rare and expensive.

Official Gazette of the U.S. Patent & Trademark Office, Washington, DC. Began 1873; continues today. Contains brief patent claims & pictures, plus indices of inventor, object and assignor. Individual volumes occasionally show up for sale at antiquarian booksellers for hundreds of dollars.

British patents dating back to 1617 A.D. are represented by specifications and abstracts by the Science Reference & Information Service of the Patent Office Library. I've bought through antiquarian booksellers 115pp-150pp illustrated tri-annual "Abridgments" for Class 28, Cooking and Kitchen Appliances, Breadmaking, and Confectionery patents. In 1900, the British Patent Office was preparing illustrated abridgements for some 146 classes, covering the period 1617 to 1854. I've never seen them. Reference materials at the Library are open to the public, but our kind of historical research cannot be undertaken by SRIS staff. For services available from the B.P.O., write Head of Marketing & Publicity, The Patent Office, State House, 66-71 High Holborn, London WC1R 4TP, England. By the way, it's frustrating to work with British patents because in their system, it's the application that gets the number! Copies of some British and other foreign patents can be ordered through RPS.

Books relating to invention include Mechanical dictionaries: Various late–1800s, early–1900s books with 1,000s of mechanical drawings of gears, parts and motives to use in making or inventing a gadget or machine. Patent process books are more or less detailed, about developing ideas, applying for patents, and defending claims. One is Munn & Co.'s *The U.S. Patent Law. Instructions How to Obtain Letters Patent*, 1867.

BIBLIOGRAPHY

An extensive list of online books on invention and technology are at this site of the Lemelson Center. (See entry below.)

Web site: www.si.edu/lemelson/dig/bibliography.html

MUSEUMS

The Rothschild Petersen Patent Model Museum

Most of the 4,000 models were acquired by Rothschild from Cliff Petersen of California, in the 1990s; others are from smaller collections from around the U.S., including all models from Carolyn Pollan's Patent Model Museum in Fort Smith, Arkansas. The Museum is in crowded quarters now, viewable by appointment only. Mr. Rothschild hopes to establish a national patent model museum. Models have gone out in traveling exhibitions. Imput from individuals or organizations interested in helping to establish a national Patent Model Museum is welcome.

Contact: Alan W. Rothschild
4796 West Lake Road
Cazenovia, NY 13035
E-mail: maxertaxer@aol.com
Web site: www.patentmodel.org/museum.html
To see some models: www.patentmodel.org/models.html

The Jerome and Dorothy Lemelson Center for the Study of Invention and Innovation

This is part of the Smithsonian's National Museum of American History, Behring Center, in Washington, D.C. In 1995, the Lemelson Foundation (the late Jerome Lemelson, an inventor who held over 550 patents, and his wife Dorothy) gave $14.5 million to permanently endow the Smithsonian's program promoting invention and creativity. The Smithsonian has about 10,000 patent models. Exhibitions, including traveling exhibits, are planned that will utilize various categories of the models.

Web sites: http://americanhistory.si.edu/
www.si.edu/lemelson/

The Museum of Science & Industry

This great museum was one of my childhood favorites. I'll never forget riding down in a cage that simulated a miner's experience. It's in Hyde Park, just south of Chicago, where the Columbian Exposition of 1893 took place.

57th Street and Lake Shore Drive
Chicago, IL 60637
Phone: (773) 684-1414 or (800) 468-6674
E-mail: msi@msichicago.org
Web site: www.msichicago.org

The Franklin Institute

Yes, this is the oldest ongoing organization that celebrates and encourages invention.

222 North 20th St.
Philadelphia, PA 19103
Phone: (215) 448-1200
Web site: http://sln.fi.edu

Inventure Place

Home of the National Inventors Hall of Fame, and dedicated to creative and inspired invention. As of mid-2002, and somewhat off-puttingly, you need Flash version 5 to access Web site.

221 South Broadway St.
Altron, OH 44308
Phone: (800) 968-4332
Web site: www.invent.org/index.asp

United Kingdom & European Sites

Links to museums in Munich, Bonn, Paris, Florence and London are at this Lemelson Center site.

Web site: www.si.edu/lemelson/dig/links.html

ORGANIZATIONS

Formerly the: U.S. Patent Model Foundation, has a publication *Invent America!* and a newsletter. Also sponsor of a Web site for encouraging invention and problem-solving among children.

Invent America!

Contact: Nancy Metz, Exec. Director
510 King St., Suite 420
Alexandria, VA 22314
Phone: (703) 684-1836
Web site: www.inventamerica.com

Web sites of Interest

Inventor Organizations and Associations

Many links to sites for practicing inventors and those interested.

Web site: www.nal.usda.gov/ttic/misc/invassn.htm

Association of Science-Technology Centers

A way to find resources related to invention, including "Invention at Play" for children and adults.

Web site: www.astc.org/exhibitions/invention/dinvention.htm

Museum of Unworkable Devices

This delightful and fascinating site, mounted by Donald Simanek, is a good overview of that most perpetual and perplexing invention problem: perpetual motion machines. You'll love it.

Web site: www.lhup.edu/~dsimanek/museum/unwork.htm

Eric's History of Perpetual Motion and Free Energy Machines

Another amusing & fine site, by Eric Krieg, with information on the long history of this elusive goal pursued by thousands, from da Vinci to Congreve to an amazing number of 20th C inventor-dreamers.

Web site: www.phact.org/e/dennis4.html

RESEARCHING PATENTS ON THE WEB

The whole long, glorious history of the U.S. Patent & Trademark Office is right there on the Web, and you have to learn how to use it. This is probably true for the patent offices of many countries. The only URL I have is for the British Library's site from where you can do some patent research, which is at http://vincent.bl.uk/cgi.bin/dialog server. I suspect the possible search dates are limited. See the Bibliography for information on indices to British patents.

The major disappointment for collectors is that before about 1996, it's the **Number or Nothing**. Number indices can be found at libraries that were or still are patent depositories; these libraries got the weekly record of patents granted that week from the Patent Office. Many libraries have gotten rid of the actual *Patent Gazettes*, which is horrible in my view, but space is at a premium. But taking their place are microfilm or microfiche copies that will show you the wonderful pictures and short description. And, best of all, there are bound subject indices for each year. There's one volume that covers 1790-1836 unnumbered patents; there's a three-volume subject index from 1836-1873; then starting in 1874 there are individual volumes. In those, there are alphabetical listings of the inventors and companies that have received utility patents in that year, the same for design patents, reissues, and trademarks. Starting in 1931, they start listing plant patents.

I advise you to **bookmark the patent number search page**, http://164.195.100.11/netahtml/srchnum.htm, and you'll soon be doing number searches. You'll discover that some times of day are better than others. In a high traffic time (say, mid-afternoon EST during the week, when patent research by law offices are going on, you may be terminated after a fairly short time), but 3 a.m. EST on Saturday might be clear for hours for searching.

The **USPTO home page** for patent searches is found at: www.uspto.gov/patft/index.html. Go to it to read all about it. I also recommend the site that the University of Chicago has that helps explain the U.S. patent system. It's at www.lib.uchicago.edu/e/su/sci/patents.html.

There is a very short, one page introduction on conducting manual searches which tells about searching by patent numbers, inventor's name, and dates of issue. There are different "fields" – which are, in effect, little fenced-in areas in the database, each of which holds a different kind of information. One field has only inventor names; another has only subjects; another has only assignees; etc., etc. There are pages of back-up help entries for you linked from the site, so you can read how to enter the correct field code. A chart of field codes is provided. Patent classification numbers change over the years. Especially after 1836. Just for fun, here's a comparison of the class numbers for Class number 5: from 1790-1836, "5" was cooking stoves, kitchen ranges, roasters, asbestos, bakers, boilers, bricks, burners, candlesticks, chandeliers, chimneys, roasting jacks, spark catchers, steam engines, ventilating, and wood. In 1963, "5" was, simply, beds. And cooking, illuminating, fuel, heating, ventilation, were all split up into various classes. From 1790-1836 there were 22 classes; in 1963, there were 431 classes, some deliberately left blank so that related classes could be eased into a logical order. You can access the part of the site that supposedly makes other searches possible, including the "Manual of Patent Classification" and "Locate Patent & Trademark Depository Libraries," by going to http://www.uspto.gov/web/menu/search.html.

Supposedly any patent since 1790, for which a paper copy exists, can be accessed on a computer. But **numbers weren't issued until 1836**. My experience is that doing classification searches to find a patent doesn't work. A librarian at NYC's patent library (fabulous Science & Technology division is in the old B. Altman's store building at 34th and Madison Avenue, NYC), tried to do a classification-based search for eggbeaters. We got one hit before the 1990s, and while I didn't pursue it, I suspect that was a reference patent used in a much later patent. So, it's the Number or Nothing. Another temporary hitch is when your particular computer can't "read" the TIFF files. Mac OS users, like me, have to buy **a plug-in image-enabler.** Yes! One exists. I found mine – Accel View TIFF – which supports Mac OS 7 or above on 68030, 6840, and all PowerPCs. It's reasonably priced and can be bought from the maker, Acordex Imaging Systems, as a download at http://www.acordex.com. They do have updates, but I haven't found I needed that. Versions of Accel View TIFF is designed to be used with Netscape Navigator, Internet Explorer, and other compatible Web browsers, so you have a choice for Mac or Windows.

When you do find the patent you are interested in you can print it out. Free! The TIFF format means you do your click right on the image itself, and choose one from a number of choices, including "Print."

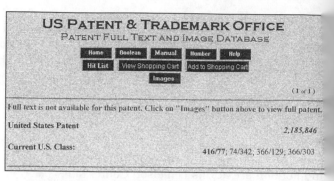

XIX-3. The "Images" button is on the third window that comes up. Click on it to see your patent. Note that current class numbers are at the right.

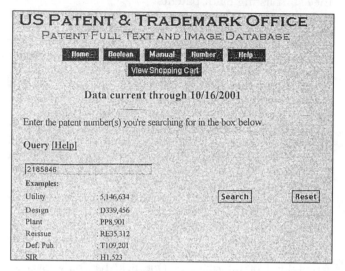

XIX-1. Opening page or window for doing a patent number search, at http://164.195.100.11/ netahtml/srchnum.htm. You type in your patent number. As you see, for utility patents you don't need a prefix, nor do you need commas. Enter the number and click on SEARCH.

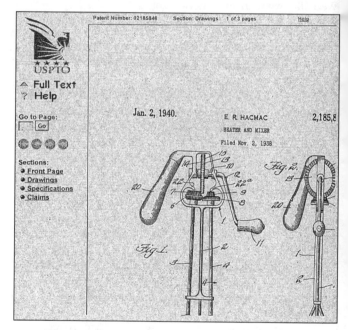

XIX-4. Fourth window has column at left that lets you navigate the data on a particular patent. Note along top is the patent number, the number of pages (here, 3). This is a TIFF document. You don't have to read the specs or go to another page, you can just click on the image and select "print" or go to another page. Some claims are quite long, so you may want to do a "Go to Page" as on left side here.

XIX-2. Next window where you click on the patent number of your choice (it's at the bottom, in blue, under PAT. NO). It is also where you can return to put in a new number, instead of the first page, but only if your preceding search was successful. Otherwise, it seems to mess up your search. Note the black buttons at the top where you can get to other parts of the Patent Office site.

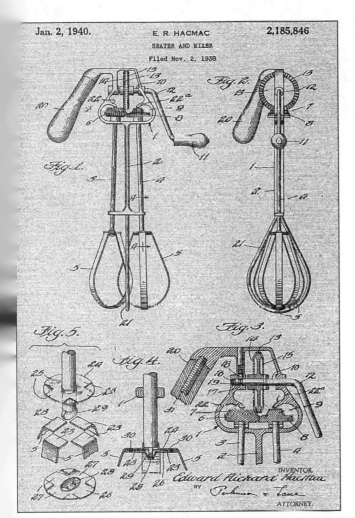

UNITED STATES PATENT OFFICE

2,185,846

BEATER AND MIXER

Edward Richard Hacmac, Hollywood, Calif., assignor to Na-Mac Products Company, a corporation of California

Application November 2, 1938, Serial No. 238,454

1 Claim. (Cl. 259—131)

The present invention relates to a novel construction of beater and mixer and more particularly to a novel means for securing the mixing and beating elements to their shafts.

Among the objects of the present invention is the provision of a strong, sturdy device of the kind described having far less number of parts than the devices now on the market. Another object is to provide a novel gearing arrangement for an interdigitating beater and mixer so constructed as to provide quick adjustment for different speeds as required in the operation of such a device.

The present invention is an improvement on the beater and mixer shown in my pending application Serial No. 208,137, filed May 16, 1938.

Further objects, advantages and capabilities will be apparent from the disclosure or are inherent in the device.

In the drawing:

Fig. 1 is a view in side elevation of my novel beater and mixer;

Fig. 2 is a front elevational view thereof.

Fig. 3 is an enlarged fragmentary view in vertical cross section of the main portion of the frame and the gearing device therein;

Fig. 4 is an enlarged fragmentary view of the lower end of a shaft for my novel beating and mixing element;

Fig. 5 is a fragmentary view in perspective of the parts providing a connection for my beating and mixing element and a shaft therefor.

Referring more particularly to the disclosure in the drawing, there is shown a novel construction of mixer and beater provided with a skeleton or cut-away frame 1 depending from which is an elongated inverted T-shaped member 2, the cross piece of this member and the lower portion of the frame both being provided with suitable openings to receive and provide bearings for rotatable driven shafts 3 and 4 at the lower end of which are secured the novel interdigitating beating and mixing elements 5. Secured or pinned to the shaft 3 adjacent its upper end is gear 6 having a fixed bevel gear or pinion 7 on its upper surface. The gear 6 meshes with the gear 8 secured or keyed on the shaft 4, this gear 8 having secured on its upper surface a bevel gear or pinion 9. The bevel gears or pinions 7 and 9 are shown of different diameters for the purpose of providing different speeds of rotation of the driven gears 6 and 8 and their respective shafts and beating and mixing elements.

Rotatably mounted in the bearings formed in the skeleton frame 1 is a rotatable drive shaft 10 integrally provided with a crank arm 12 having a handle 11 on its outer end for manual rotation of the drive shaft. The rotatably mounted shaft 10 is longitudinally slidable in these bearings. Secured or keyed to this shaft is a gear 13 having gear faces 14 and 16 on its opposite sides, the teeth of the faces 14 and 16 being adapted to be moved into driving engagement with the bevel gears or pinions 7 and 9, respectively. When the teeth on the face 14 are in driving engagement with the teeth on the bevel gear or pinion 7, the gear 13 will drive the bevel gear or pinion 7, gear 6 and gear 8 so as to rotate the shafts 3 and 4 and their beating and mixing elements 5 in opposite directions.

In order to retain the bevel drive gear 13 in meshing engagement with the gear or pinion 7 or with the gear or pinion 9, means are provided for locking the shaft 10 in either position of adjustment. This is accomplished by means of a pair of spaced annular races 16 and 17 formed in the shaft adapted to interlock with a spring-pressed ball or detent 18. This ball or detent will permit ready manual shifting of the shaft but prevent unintentional accidental displacement or operation of the intermeshing bevel gears after the driving gear 13 has been moved into driving engagement with either of the gears or pinions 7 and 9. The section 19 between the races 16 and 17 in my improved construction is of substantially conical construction whereby to prevent the ball or detent 18 from coming to rest in dead center or in inoperative position between the bevel gears 7 and 9.

In order to securely hold the beating and mixing elements in operative position the invention comprehends a handle 20 suitably attached or threaded to a projection 22 extending from the upper portion of the frame 1 whereby to provide sufficient clearance between the handle and the frame for insertion of the hand of the user. In order that the beating and mixing elements 4 do not contact or scrape the bottom of the container in which the device is to be used, I provide a U-shaped member or stirrup 21 extending beyond the outer ends of the beaters so as to maintain them spaced from the bottom of the container. To limit upward movement of the shafts 3 and 4, I provide extensions 22 and 22a integrally formed with the inner sides of the skeleton frame 1 and terminating just above the tops of the bevel gears 7 and 9.

My invention also relates to the novel stirring and beating elements and the means for attaching them to their shafts, shown in detail in Figs.

XIX-5. *The image of the HacMac* beater and mixer, patented by Edward HacMac. Why did I choose this patent? I was taken with the name, and figured that since this entire book has been written on a Mac, and I felt almost like a clever hans hacker getting to do all this from the comfort of my home, so it was a natural!

XIX-6. *The next window,* which is the **first of two spec pages** for the HacMac. I got to it by clicking on "next page" on the pull-down menu accessed right on the image page.

XX. U.S. PATENT TUESDAYS, OR... 1790 TO 1974 IN 14 CALENDARS

I, and other patent devoteés, have at a late date come to a rude awakening concerning the so-called "patent Tuesdays," referred to throughout this book. Unfortunately, my bottom-line dogmatic statement that "If your embossed or printed date is *not* a Tuesday then it's not an American patent date," is dead wrong. And even after the onset of Tuesday grants, some American objects bear dates which weren't Tuesdays, but may have been application dates or some other date put on for the appearance of protection by the maker. (NOTE: The two listings most affected by this subject are the "Union" apple parer in Chapter I, and a cracker pricker & cutter in Chapter IV.)

Pessimism, or perhaps an excess of optimism, in the Patent Office – from 1790 on – contributed to 46+ years of a cavalier, careless attitude toward the worth of inventions, prevention of fire, protection of patents, and even the institution of a numbering system! Numbers weren't assigned until *after* the big fire in December 1836. And even then, patents were not, as I had thought from spot checks, given out on Tuesdays in a regular way for quite a while. Newspapers and journals printed patent news on Wednesdays, after the high lights of patents granted the previous day were tele graphed to the editors.

We are giving you perpetual "Tuesday-only" calen dars, to check dates that appear in old ads, or marked on utensils. But remember that before about 1846 even though patents had been numbered for a decade, a Tuesday grant was, seemingly, no more likely than a Monday, Thursday or Saturday grant.

The Index below covers 1836 to 1976. The roman numeral next to each year refers you to the specific cal endar table you need out of the fourteen. **Leap Years** have their own seven tables: VIII, IX, X, XI, XII, XIII, XIV.) The first year of *numbered* U.S. patents shows up as <u>1836 - XIII</u>; refer to <u>Table XIII</u> (a leap year) to see 1836's Tuesdays, from January 5 to December 27.

	1836 - XIII	1837 - I	1838 - II	1839 - III
1840 - XI	1841 - VI	1842 - VII	1843 - I	1844 - IX
1845 - IV	1846 - V	1847 - VI	1848 - XIV	1849 - II
1850 - III	1851 - IV	1852 - XII	1853 - VII	1854 - I
1855 - II	1856 - X	1857 - V	1858 - VI	1859 - VII
1860 - VIII	1861 - III	1862 - IV	1863 - V	1864 - XIII
1865 - I	1866 - II	1867 - III	1868 - XI	1869 - VI
1870 - VII	1871 - I	1872 - IX	1873 - IV	1874 - V
1875 - VI	1876 - XIV	1877 - II	1878 - III	1879 - IV
1880 - XII	1881 - VII	1882 - I	1883 - II	1884 - X
1885 - V	1886 - VI	1887 - VII	1888 - VIII	1889 - III
1890 - IV	1891 - V	1892 - XIII	1893 - I	1894 - II
1895 - III	1896 - XI	1897 - VI	1898 - VII	1899 - I
1900 - II	1901 - III	1902 - IV	1903 - V	1904 - XIII
1905 - I	1906 - II	1907 - III	1908 - XI	1909 - VI
1910 - VII	1911 - I	1912 - IX	1913 - IV	1914 - V
1915 - VI	1916 - XIV	1917 - II	1918 - III	1919 - IV
1920 - XII	1921 - VII	1922 - I	1923 - II	1924 - X

1925 - V	1926 - VI	1927 - VII	1928 - VIII	1929 - III
1930 - IV	1931 - V	1932 - XIII	1933 - I	1934 - II
1935 - III	1936 - XI	1937 - VI	1938 - VII	1939 - I
1940 - IX	1941 - IV	1942 - V	1943 - VI	1944 - XIV
1945 - II	1946 - III	1947 - IV	1948 - XII	1949 - VII
1950 - I	1951 - II	1952 - X	1953 - V	1954 - VI
1955 - VII	1956 - VIII	1957 - III	1958 - IV	1959 - V
1960 - XIII	1961 - I	1962 - II	1963 - III	1964 - XI
1965 - VI	1966 - VII	1967 - I	1968 - IX	1969 - IV
1970 - V	1971 - VI	1972 - XIV	1973 - II	1974 - III
1975 - IV	1976 - XII			

TABLE I.
JAN 3, 10, 17, 24, 31
FEB 7, 14, 21, 28
MAR 7, 14, 21, 28
APR 4, 11, 18, 25
MAY 2, 9, 16, 23, 30
JUN 6, 13, 20, 27
JUL 4, 11, 18, 25
AUG 1, 8, 15, 22, 29
SEP 5, 12, 19, 26
OCT 3, 10, 17, 24, 31
NOV 7, 14, 21, 28
DEC 5, 12, 19, 26

TABLE II.
JAN 2, 9, 16, 23, 30
FEB 6, 13, 20, 27
MAR 6, 13, 20, 27
APR 3, 10, 17, 24
MAY 1, 8, 15, 22, 29
JUN 5, 12, 19, 26
JUL 3, 20, 27, 24, 31
AUG 7, 14, 21, 28
SEP 4, 11, 18, 25
OCT 2, 9, 16, 23, 30
NOV 6, 13, 20, 27
DEC 4, 11, 18, 25

TABLE III.
JAN 1, 8, 15, 22, 29
FEB 5, 12, 19, 26
MAR 5, 12, 19, 26
APR 2, 9, 16, 23, 30
MAY 7, 14, 21, 28
JUN 4, 11, 18, 25
JUL 2, 9, 16, 23, 30
AUG 6, 13, 20, 27
SEP 3, 10, 17, 24
OCT 1, 8, 15, 22, 29
NOV 5, 12, 19, 26
DEC 3, 10, 17, 24, 31

TABLE IV.
JAN 7, 14, 21, 28
FEB 4, 11, 18, 25
MAR 4, 11, 18, 25
APR 1, 8, 15, 22, 30
MAY 6, 13, 20, 27
JUN 3, 10, 17, 24
JUL 1, 8, 15, 22, 29
AUG 5, 12, 19, 26
SEP 2, 9, 16, 23, 30
OCT 7, 14, 21, 28
NOV 4, 11, 18, 25
DEC 2, 9, 16, 23, 30

TABLE V.
JAN 6, 13, 20, 27
FEB 3, 10, 17, 24
MAR 3, 10, 17, 24, 31
APR 7, 14, 21, 28
MAY 5, 12, 19, 26
JUN 2, 9, 16, 23, 30
JUL 7, 14, 21, 28
AUG 4, 11, 18, 25
SEP 1, 8, 15, 22, 29
OCT 6, 13, 20, 27
NOV 3, 10, 17, 24
DEC 1, 8, 15, 22, 29

TABLE VI.
JAN 5, 12, 19, 26
FEB 2, 9, 16, 23
MAR 2, 9, 16, 23, 30
APR 6, 13, 20, 27
MAY 4, 11, 18, 25
JUN 1, 8, 15, 22, 29
JUL 6, 13, 20, 27
AUG 3, 10, 17, 24, 31
SEP 7, 14, 21, 28
OCT 5, 12, 19, 26
NOV 2, 9, 16, 23, 30
DEC 7, 14, 21, 28

TABLE VII.
JAN 4, 11, 18, 25
FEB 1, 8, 15, 22
MAR 1, 8, 15, 22, 29
APR 5, 12, 19, 26
MAY 3, 10, 17, 24, 31
JUN 7, 14, 21, 28
JUL 5, 12, 19, 26
AUG 2, 9, 16, 23, 30
SEP 6, 13, 20, 27
OCT 4, 11, 18, 25
NOV 1, 8, 15, 22, 29
DEC 6, 13, 20, 27

TABLE VIII.
JAN 3, 10, 17, 24, 31
FEB 7, 14, 21, 28
MAR 6, 13, 20, 27
APR 3, 10, 17, 24
MAY 1, 8, 15, 22, 29
JUN 5, 12, 19, 26
JUL 3, 10, 17, 24, 31
AUG 7, 14, 21, 28
SEP 4, 11, 18, 25
OCT 2, 9, 16, 23, 30
NOV 6, 13, 20, 27
DEC 4, 11, 18, 25

TABLE IX.
JAN 2, 9, 16, 23, 30
FEB 6, 13, 20, 27
MAR 5, 12, 19, 26
APR 2, 9, 16, 23, 30
MAY 7, 14, 21, 28
JUN 4, 11, 18, 25
JUL 2, 9, 16, 23, 30
AUG 6, 13, 20, 27
SEP 3, 10, 17, 24
OCT 1, 8, 15, 22, 29
NOV 5, 12, 19, 26
DEC 3, 10, 17, 24, 31

TABLE X.	TABLE XI.	TABLE XII.
JAN 1, 8, 15, 22, 29	JAN 7, 14, 21, 28	JAN 6, 13, 20, 27
FEB 5, 12, 19, 26	FEB 4, 11, 18, 25	FEB 3, 10, 17, 24
MAR 4, 11, 18, 25	MAR 3, 10, 17, 24, 31	MAR 2, 9, 16, 23, 30
APR 1, 8, 15, 22, 29	APR 7, 14, 21, 28	APR 6, 13, 20, 27
MAY 6, 13, 20, 27	MAY 5, 12, 19, 26	MAY 4, 11, 18, 25
JUN 3, 10, 17, 24	JUN 2, 9, 16, 23, 30	JUN 1, 8, 15, 22, 29
JUL 1, 8, 15, 22, 29	JUL 7, 14, 21, 28	JUL 6, 13, 20, 27
AUG 5, 12, 19, 26	AUG 4, 11, 18, 25	AUG 3, 10, 17, 24, 31
SEP 2, 9, 16, 23, 30	SEP 1, 8, 15, 22, 29	SEP 7, 14, 21, 28
OCT 7, 14, 21, 28	OCT 6, 13, 20, 27	OCT 5, 12, 19, 26
NOV 4, 11, 18, 25	NOV 3, 10, 17, 24	NOV 2, 9, 16, 23, 30
DEC 2, 9, 16, 23, 30	DEC 1, 8, 15, 22, 29	DEC 7, 14, 21, 28

TABLE XIII.	TABLE XIV.	
JAN 5, 12, 19, 26	JAN 4, 11, 18, 25	
FEB 2, 9, 16, 23	FEB 1, 8, 15, 22, 29	
MAR 1, 8, 15, 22, 29	MAR 7, 14, 21, 28	
APR 5, 12, 19, 26	APR 4, 11, 18, 25	
MAY 3, 10, 17, 24, 31	MAY 2, 9, 16, 23, 30	
JUN 7, 14, 21, 28	JUN 6, 13, 20, 27	
JUL 5, 12, 19, 26	JUL 4, 11, 18, 25	
AUG 2, 9, 16, 23, 30	AUG 1, 8, 15, 22, 29	
SEP 6, 13, 20, 27	SEP 5, 12, 19, 26	
OCT 4, 11, 18, 25	OCT 3, 10, 17, 24, 31	
NOV 1, 8, 15, 22, 29	NOV 7, 14, 21, 28	
DEC 6, 13, 20, 27	DEC 5, 12, 19, 26	

RESEARCHING

XXI. UNITED STATES PATENT NUMBERS

This table shows numbered patents only (there were over 7,000 unnumbered Patents and Design Patents issued between 1790 and 1836). I've given the number of the first patent issued each year for four different kinds of patents from 1836 through 1970. Listed are numbered Patents (also known as Utility Patents), Design Patents (given for the look of something, not its mechanics), Reissued Patents, and Trademark Patents. A Reissue Patent is meant to correct a "defective" patent that – by inadvertence, accident, or mistake – either claimed too much as new, or for which the specifications were incorrect or insufficient. According to patent law, no new matter could be introduced into the patent except to correct omissions; however, drawings could be remade to conform to the specifications, or the specifications might be rewritten to conform to the drawings. If granted by the Patent Office, a Reissue Patent is only for the unexpired term of the original patent and doesn't extend it.

If a patent number is marked on your mystery gadget, you can at least find out what year it was patented (assuming the number is correct). A cast embossed "patent" date on a gear may actually be the date an impatient inventor sent an application to Washington; or it may have been made up so that a gadget already in production

would seem patent-protected. For patents after about 1846, you can check the perpetual calendar in this book to confirm that a date found on an object fell on Tuesday (although there are pitfalls in that also, as you will read). A patent number, permanently marked on a manufactured item, was required by law as of April 1, 1927, but many older patents also included the number.

Sometimes a number will appear which is not designated as a Design or Reissue Patent. Then you must decide for yourself, from the appearance of the object, what the approximate age is. For example, let's say the item is marked "Pat. # 10,365." That number could be a Utility Patent of the year 1854, a Design Patent of 1878, or a Reissue Patent of 1883. This is where you must bring into play any and all knowledge and feel you have for the thing itself, including the method of manufacture, the purpose of the gadget, the shape of the handle, the material from which it's made, how it relates to objects of known date. This can be confusing, especially for things made in the third or fourth quarter of the 19th century, but at least you've narrowed it down – in this case, to three years: 1854, 1878, or 1883. (Very few objects or tools – if any – would bear a Trademark Patent number, although advertising for the objects might.)

UNITED STATES PATENT NUMBERS
Table Showing the First Number of Utility Patents, Design Patents, Reissues & Trademarks (up to 1955) Issued Each Year from 1836 to 1976

DATE	PATENT	DESIGN	REISSUE	TRADEMARK
1836	1			
1837	110			
1838	546		1	
1839	1,061		7	
1840	1,465		20	
1841	1,923		30	
1842	2,413		36	
1843	2,901	1	49	
1844	3,395	15	60	
1845	3,873	27	67	
1846	4,348	44	78	
1847	4,914	103	91	
1848	5,409	163	105	
1849	5,993	209	128	
1850	6,981	258	158	
1851	7,865	341	184	
1852	8,622	431	209	
1853	9,512	540	229	
1854	10,358	626	258	
1855	12,117	683	286	
1856	14,009	753	337	
1857	16,324	860	420	

DATE	PATENT	DESIGN	REISSUE	TRADEMARK
1858	19,010	973	517	
1859	22,477	1,075	643	
1860	26,642	1,183	674	
1861	31,005	1,366	1,106	
1862	34,045	1,508	1,253	
1863	37,266	1,703	1,369	
1864	41,047	1,879	1,596	
1865	45,685	2,018	1,844	
1866	51,784	2,239	2,140	
1867	60,658	2,533	2,430	
1868	72,959	2,858	2,830	
1869	85,503	3,304	3,250	
1870	98,460	3,810	3,784	1
1871	110,617	4,547	4,223	122
1872	122,304	5,452	4,687	608
1873	134,504	6,336	5,216	1,099
1874	146,120	7,083	5,717	1,591
1875	158,350	7,969	6,200	2,150
1876	171,641	8,884	6,831	3,288
1877	185,813	9,686	7,452	4,247
1878	198,733	10,385	8,020	5,463
1879	211,078	10,975	8,529	6,918
1880	223,211	11,567	9,017	7,790
1881	236,137	12,082	9,523	8,139
1882	251,685	12,647	9,994	8,973
1883	269,820	13,508	10,265	9,920
1884	291,016	14,528	10,432	10,822
1885	310,163	15,678	10,548	11,843
1886	333,494	16,451	10,677	12,910
1887	355,291	17,046	10,793	13,939
1888	375,720	17,995	10,892	15,072
1889	395,305	18,830	10,978	16,131
1890	418,665	19,553	11,053	17,360
1891	443,987	20,439	11,137	18,775
1892	466,315	21,275	11,217	20,537
1893	486,976	22,092	11,298	22,274
1894	511,744	22,994	11,397	23,951
1895	531,619	23,922	11,461	25,757
1896	552,502	25,037	11,520	27,586
1897	574,369	26,482	11,581	29,399
1898	596,467	28,113	11,646	31,070
1899	616,871	29,916	11,706	32,308
1900	640,167	32,055	11,798	33,957
1901	664,827	33,813	11,879	35,678
1902	690,385	35,547	11,960	37,606
1903	717,521	36,187	12,070	39,612
1904	748,567	36,723	12,189	41,798
1905	778,834	37,280	12,299	43,956
1906	808,618	37,766	12,428	48,446
1907	839,799	38,391	12,587	59,014
1908	875,679	38,980	12,738	66,892
1909	908,436	39,737	12,906	72,083
1910	945,010	40,424	13,066	76,267
1911	980,178	41,063	13,189	80,506
1912	1,013,095	42,073	13,346	84,711
1913	1,049,326	43,425	13,504	89,731
1914	1,083,267	45,098	13,668	94,796
1915	1,123,212	46,813	13,858	101,613
1916	1,166,419	48,358	14,040	107,875

DATE	PATENT	DESIGN	REISSUE	TRADEMARK
1917	1,210,389	50,177	14,238	114,666
1918	1,251,458	51,629	14,417	120,005
1919	1,290,027	52,836	14,582	124,066
1920	1,326,899	54,359	14,785	128,274
1921	1,364,063	56,844	15,018	138,556
1922	1,401,948	60,121	15,257	150,210
1923	1,440,362	61,478	15,513	163,003
1924	1,478,996	63,675	15,739	177,848
1925	1,521,590	66,346	15,974	193,596
1926	1,568,040	69,170	16,240	207,437
1927	1,612,790	71,772	16,515	222,401
1928	1,654,521	74,159	16,841	236,987
1929	1,696,897	77,347	17,176	251,129
1930	1,742,181	80,254	17,550	265,655
1931	1,787,424	82,966	17,917	278,906
1932	1,839,190	85,903	18,312	290,313
1933	1,892,663	88,847	18,705	299,926
1934	1,941,449	91,258	19,038	309,066
1935	1,985,878	94,179	19,409	320,441
1936	2,026,516	98,045	19,804	331,338
1937	2,066,309	102,601	20,226	342,070
1938	2,104,004	107,738	20,610	353,324
1939	2,142,080	112,765	20,959	363,536
1940	2,185,170	118,358	21,311	374,062
1941	2,227,418	124,503	21,683	384,047
1942	2,268,510	130,989	21,992	392,581
1943	2,307,007	134,717	22,242	399,378
1944	2,338,081	136,916	22,415	404,974
1945	2,366,154	139,862	22,585	411,001
1946	2,391,856	143,386	22,706	418,494
1947	2,413,675	146,165	22,827	426,610
1948	2,433,824	148,267	22,957	435,590
1949	2,457,797	152,235	23,068	441,712
1950	2,492,944	156,686	23,186	443,654
1951	2,536,016	161,404	23,315	444,377
1952	2,580,379	165,568	23,449	444,623
1953	2,624,046	168,527	23,612	444,746
1954	2,664,562	171,241	23,763	444,794
1955	2,698,434	173,777	23,918	444,807
1956	2,728,913	176,490	24,105	
1957	2,775,762	179,467	24,263	
1958	2,818,567	181,829	24,413	
1959	2,866,973	184,204	24,584	
1960	2,919,443	186,973	24,761	
1961	2,966,681	189,516	24,918	
1962	3,015,103	192,004	25,107	
1963	3,070,801	194,304	25,309	
1964	3,116,487	197,269	25,507	
1965	3,163,865	199,955	25,707	
1966	3,226,729	203,379	25,953	
1967	3,295,143	206,567	26,132	
1968	3,360,800	209,732	26,328	
1969	3,419,907	213,084	26,515	
1970	3,487,470	216,419	26,749	
1971	3,551,909	219,637	27,018	
1972	3,631,539	222,793	27,264	
1973	3,707,729	225,695	27,540	
1974	3,781,914	229,729	27,856	
1975	3,858,241	234,033	28,292	
1976	3,930,271	238,315	28,671	

RESEARCHING

XXII. BIBLIOGRAPHY
Publications Recommended and/or Consulted

This extensive bibliography is meant to help you to do research in **primary and secondary sources** – as I have done. (Primary is an original publication, such as an old magazine or a technical book, or patent records. Secondary is "digested" primary information, analyzed and/or synthesized by the author.)

Most listings are books; some are journals, magazines, collector newspapers or club publications. Many books include valuable bibliographies of their own; I like authors who list sources, and I urge you to assemble book lists on your own special subjects. Oddly, considering the scope and acclaim of this book, it is often excluded from bibliographies in books on the same subject! But I want to give the reader the choice of many books to use.

Many of the listed books are outstanding works – readable, informative, obsessive in detail, and well-illustrated. I can't recommend all, except as picture sources. Some books contain information that is incorrect or romanced from thin air, but may be useful to zero-in on facts. Many valuable secondary research sources are articles published in periodicals. They have been credited throughout the text, and the periodicals are listed in alphabetical order here. Newsletters are here (I hope I got them all), or in their particular chapters – often in the introductory paragraphs. Trade catalogs are invaluable and irrefutable. The few hundred I have collected since 1970 are my treasure trove. The ones I have used most are here in this listing. Some sources for trade catalogs are listed below. Look at the Introduction at the beginning of this book also for other research resources.

Alas, many books are out of print and hard to find. They are worth searching for, and there are now a number of specialized dealers in new, out of print, and antiquarian books on the decorative arts, practical arts, antiques and collectibles, and cookery.

A huge source for new, and out-of-print, items is the Web, with a number of **searchable virtual bookstores** which either have individual Web sites to order from, or are in databases drawing from 500 or more booksellers here and abroad. Among the ones I've used are: abe books.com; advancedbooksearch.com; bibliofind.com; half.com; hamiltonbook.com; amazon.com; zubal.com; wonderbks.com; powells.com; and daedalusbooks.com. A really friendly, and helpful, source for new or newish books is **Martin J. Donnelly Antique Tools;** (800) 869-0695; e-mail: mjd@mjdtools.com; Web site: www.mjd-tools.com/ and the eBay™ name is: greatcatalogue (and it is!). Another multi-tool book source, hosted by the publisher of the books, is **Astragal Press** in Mendham, New

Jersey. Several of their books are listed below. Web site www.astragalpress.com/astragal_catalog.html. E-mail: astragalpress@attglobal.net. A useful Web site with addresses of many bookshops in 16 countries around the world that specialize in cookbooks is **Henry Notaker's Old Cookbooks and Food History** site www.notaker.com/bib liogr/biblbibl.htm. Links to libraries, clubs, etc., are at **Food and Culinary History Links** at www.foodbooks. com/foodlink.htm#Newsletters. There are sites for searching non-English language titles abroad. You can also search the catalogs of some libraries, such as the Library of Congress, online. Least frustrating is to use the computer in a public or university library system and look at various countries' **Books in Print,** and also the enormous database known as WorldCat (world catalog), which cannot be subscribed to privately.

A few titles – probably foreign or self-published – have incomplete listings because I cannot find any more information about the author, publisher, or date of publication. Where it appears in listings, "N.p." means no place is known or given; "n.d." means no date is known or given; any publication information appearing in brackets [ ] was guessed at from clues gleaned from inside the books. The titles of older books and magazines have been presented as they were then printed regardless of whether or not they are correct; bear in mind that typographical and grammatical inconsistencies abounded in the early days of printing.

This bibliography is long, and in many ways is most useful as a straight alphabetical listing. You might get ideas for something new to collect by browsing the bibliography.

To aid those interested only in books related to their subject, or items from a particular chapter, there are chapter numbers (in Roman numerals) or abbreviations of very general subjects in caps, at the left of each entry. Run your finger down the line for your subject:

CAT = trade catalogs (except those entirely on one subject, such as molds) which go in their appropriate chapter)
CBK = Cookbook
CSTi = Cast iron wares
GEN = general history or broad coverage of many types of kitchen things, social history, kitchens & their utensils
HIS = historical treatment of kitchens & cooking, especially pre-1700
INV = invention or patent records or history
KIT = kitchens and kitchen design
MET = assorted metalworking histories, and mixed metalwares, except resources on cast iron
PAP = paper or ephemera resources other than catalogs

OY = toy or play kitchenwares
WWW = books/magazines on how to collect on the Internet. Clubs are coded by their subject chapter.

E-mail addresses and Web site addresses (in bold) can and do change; if what you find here seems outdated, use a search engine to help find new sources. Also, none of the e-mail or Web addresses use a period, semicolon or comma at the end, no matter where you find the listing. Addresses and zip codes, along with contact names, etc., appear in parentheses at the end of a listing for your ordering and information-gathering convenience. If new books in your special field are published, please write to me, care of Krause Publications. Happy studies!

CAT   A & J Mfg. Co. *Colorful Kitchen Tools.* Catalog. Binghampton, NY & Chicago: Edward Katzinger Co., A & J Division, 1930.

NV   *Abridgements of Specifications Relating to Cooking, Bread-Making, and Confectionery, A.D. 1634-1866.* London: Office of the Commissioner of Patents, 1873.

GEN   Adams & Son, *William S. Francatelli's Cook's Guide Advertiser.* London, England: Richard Bentley, 1861.

GEN   Adamson, Gareth. *Machines at Home.* London: Lutterworth, 1969.

XI   Adkins, Jan E. *Art & Ingenuity of the Woodstove.* W. Clement Stone, PMA Communications, Inc., 1980.

MET   Agricola, Georgius. *De Re Metallica.* Translated by Herbert Hoover. Ancient classic on metals. Reprint by Dover Books, NYC, of the 1912 edition, 1990.

VII   Aikins, Larry. *Pictorial Price Guide to Metal Lunch Boxes & Thermoses.* Gas City, IN: L-W Book Sales, 1992; 1994.

GEN   Alcott, William Alexander. *The Young House-Keeper, or Thoughts on Food and Cookery.* Boston: G. W. Light, 1838; 1842.

GEN   Allemagne, Henry René d'. *Les Accessoires du Costume et du Mobilier: Vol. 2. Outils & Instruments de Précision.* Paris: Schemit, 1928. Decorative & utilitarian objects.

CBK   Allen, Colonel Bob. *Cook Book Gossip over the Back Fence.* St. James, MO: Cookbook Collectors Club of America, 1997. 650 pp. Newsletter columns 1990-1996. (POB 56, zip 65559)

CBK   ———. *A Guide to Collecting Cookbooks.* Paducah, KY: Collector Books, 1990; rev. 1993; rev. 1995.

CBK   ———. *A Guide to Collecting "Jell-O" Cookbooklets.* St. James, MO: 1997. See also *Cook Book Collectors Club.*

XVIII   Allen, Edith Louise. *Mechanical Devices in the Home.* Peoria, IL: Manual Arts Press, 1922. Includes household appliances.

XVIII   Alphin, Elaine Marie. *Toasters.* (Household History series.) Minneapolis, MN: Carolrhoda Books, 1998. For children.

I   Althof, Ken. *The Nutcracker Collectors Guide.* N.p. [U.S.]: Midwest of Cannon Falls, 1995. History of the Erzgebirge nutcrackers of Germany: painted, carved, and wooden nutcrackers.

VII   *Aluminist, The.* Bimonthly newsletter of Hammered Aluminum Collectors Assoc. (Dannie Woodward, POB 1346, Weatherford, TX 76086. E-mail: al1310@aol.com)

GEN   *American Agriculturist.* Monthly. NYC: Orange Judd & Co., 1840s-1880s.

INV   *American Artisan and Patent Record.* NYC: 1864-1875. Vols. 1-17 were weekly; Vols. 18, 19, monthly.

VIII   *American Collectors of Infant Feeders.* Publication. (5161 W. 59th St., Indianapolis, IN 46254)

VIII   *American Dream Collectibles.* Quarterly newsletter. Hammered aluminum by the Continental Company. (Ed Gangawere, 5128 Schultz Bridge Rd., Zionsville, PA 18092-2542)

GEN   *American Heritage Cookbook and Illustrated History of American Eating and Drinking.* NYC: American Heritage Pub. Co., 1964. Incomparable illustrations and invaluable biographies. Reprinted, © 1880s.

CBK   *American Home Cook Book, by an American lady.* NYC: Dick & Fitzgerald, 1854.

CSTi   Ames, Alex. *Collecting Cast Iron.* England: Moorland Pub., 1980.

GEN   Andrews, Edward Deming. *The Community Industries of the Shakers.* Handbook 15. Albany, NY: NY State Museum, 1932.

VII   Andrews, Jack. *Samuel Yellin, Metalworker.* Reprint of earlier edition. Berlin, MD: Skipjack Press, 6 Laport Court, Ocean Pines, 21811. 1-800-247-6553. Skipjack has many books on blacksmithing.

IV   Anthoine, A. *Moules à Glaces en Étain.* Catalog. Paris: c. 1900. May have been jobbers, not manufacturers. Tin ice cream molds.

PAP   *Antiquarian Bookman's Weekly (AB Weekly).* Closed up shop in 2000, after helping book lovers for 52 years. Their special interest issues throughout the year, (Cookbooks, Technology & Science, etc.) are collectible.

GEN   *Antique & Collectors Reproduction News (ACRN).* Monthly. (ACRN, POB 71174, Des Moines, IA 50325. 800-227-5531)

VII   *Antique Bottle & Glass Collector.* Magazine. (Jim Hagenbuch, POB 180, East Greenville, PA 18041. E-mail: glswrk@enter.net; Web site: www.glswrk-auction.com)

PAP   *Antique Label Collecting: A Primer.* Society of Antique Label Collectors, 1992. Including baking soda, citrus, other fruits & vegetables. (POB 24811, Tampa, FL 33623)

MET   *Antique Metalware. Brass, Bronze, Copper, Tin, Wrought & Cast Iron.* Edited by James R. Mitchell. NYC: Universe Books, 1976. Anthology of metal-related articles from the magazine *Antiques*, 1922-1976.

MET   *Antique Metalware Society.* Publication. (34 Highfield Ave., Headington, Oxford OX3 7LR Great Britain 01865.761441)

GEN   *Antique Trader Weekly.* This incredible weekly was close to a paper eBay ... thousands of ads every week. (For current subscription information, contact: Krause Publications, 700 E. State St., Iola, WI 54990; 888-457-2873)

GEN   *Antiques & the Arts Weekly.* Bee Pub. Co. (5 Church Hill Rd., Newtown, CT 06470)

XI   *Antique Stove Assoc.* Newsletter. (Macy Stern, 2617 Riverside Dr., Houston, TX 77004. E-mail: Help@AntiqueStoveAssoc.org; Web site: www.antiqueStoveAssoc.org)

GEN   *AntiqueWeek.* Tabloid newspaper; several regional offices & editions. (POB 90, Knightstown, IN 46148-9900, or 525-K East Market St., Leesburg, VA 22075. Info: 800-876-5133)

I   *APEs* newsletter – See: International Society of Apple Parer Enthusiasts.

GEN   Arminjon, Catherine. *From the Hearth to the Table: Kitchen & Fireplace Utensils, Three Centuries of Craftsmanship.* Montreal, CAN: Musée David M. Stewart, 1986.

GEN   ———. *De la Crémaillère à la table: ustensiles de cuisine et d'âtre, trois siècles d'artisanat.* Montreal, CAN: 1986.

GEN   Arnold, Eleanor, ed. *Voices of American Homemakers.* Oral History Project of the National Extension Homemakers Council. Bloomington, IN: Indiana Univ. Press, 1993.

XVI   Arnold, Ken. *Australian Preserving & Storage Jars pre-1920.* © Australia, 1983. (Available from Phoenix Press, 5003 W. Berwyn Ave., Chicago, IL 60631-1501)

GEN   Arnold, Ken. *Kitchenalia: Valuation Guide.* Golden Square, Vic., Australia: Crown Castleton Pub., 1993.

MET   Art Gallery of Ontario. *Wrought Iron: European Household Utensils from the 17th to the 19th Century: From the Macdonald Stewart Collection, Montreal Military & Maritime Museum, St. Helen's Island.* Toronto, CAN: The Gallery, 1975. Exhibit catalog with bibliography.

MET   Arthur, Eric & Thomas Ritchie. *Iron. Cast & Wrought Iron in Canada from the Seventeenth Century to the Present.* Toronto, CAN: Univ. of Toronto Press, 1982.

XVIII   Artman, E. Townsend. *Toasters, 1909-1960: A Look at the Ingenuity and Design of Toaster Makers.* Atglen, PA: Schiffer Pub. Co., 1996.

GEN   *Arts & Culture.* Box 1333, Gracie Square Station, NYC, 10028.

VII   Alsford, Denis. *Match Holders. 100 Years of Ingenuity.* Atglen, PA: Schiffer Pub. Co., 1994.

CER   Atterbury, Paul. *Cornish Ware Kitchen and Domestic Pottery by T. G. Green of Church Gresley.* N.p. [England]: R. Dennis, 1996.

GEN   Atwater, Helen. *Selection of Household Equipment.* Washington, D.C.: U.S. Government Printing Office, 1915.

XVIII   Auction Team Köln. Founded by Uwe Breker. Various catalogs since the 1980s provide some information to researchers. Auction catalogs in category "clocks and old technology" sometimes include flat irons, toasters, electrical kitchen gadgets, etc. (POB 50.1119, D-50971, Koeln, Germany. E-mail: auction@breker.com; Web site: www.Breker.com)

GEN, VI   *Australian Bottle & Collectibles Review.* Quarterly. Wide variety, including kitchenwares. (c/o Whittlesea Post Office, Whittlesea, Vic., 3757, Australia)

V   Azimov, Isaac, *Realm of Measure.* Greenwich, CT: Fawcett, 1960.

GEN   Babcock, Emma Whitcomb. *Household Hint* Vol. II, Appleton's Home Books. NYC: Appleton, 1881.

VIII   *Bacchus Corkscrew Collection, The.* N.p., 198_. 1987.

GEN   Bacon, Elizabeth Mickle. *The Growth of Household Conveniences in the U.S. from 1865* _ *1900.* Cambridge, MA: 1942. Harvard Univ. dissertation thesis.

VII   Baird, James S. *Hoard's Dairyman Dairy Collectibles.* Ft. Atkinson, WI: W. D. Hoard & Sons Co 1994. (28 Milwaukee Ave. W., 53538-0801)

GEN   Baker, Elizabeth F. *Technology and Women' Work.* NYC: Columbia Univ. Press, 1964.

INV   Baker, Eric, & Jane Martin. *Great Inventions/Good Intentions. An Illustrated History of American Design Patents.* San Francisco Chronicle Books, 1990. Great fun!

V   Baker, John. *Mauchline Ware.* Aylesbury England: Shire, 1998.

INV   Baker, Ronald. *New and Improved: Inventors and Inventions That Have Changed the Modern World.* London: British Museum, 1976 Aspirins to zippers, illustrated with patent drawings.

I   *Bang Board, The.* Newsletter for the Corn Items Collectors Assoc. All kinds of corn-related items: dryers, graders, sacks, signs, shellers, nubbers, and popcorn stuff! (Robert Chamberlain, 9288 Poland Rd., Warrensburg, IL 62573. E-mail: bob@burrusseed. com)

CBK   Barile, Mary. *Cookbooks Worth Collecting.* Radnor, PA: Chilton Books, 1993.

GEN   Barlow, Ron. *Victorian Houseware: Hardware and Kitchenware.* El Cajon, CA: Windmill Pub. Co., 1992; NYC: Dover Pub., 2001. Catalog linecuts of objects for 19th century homes.

PAP   Barlow, Ron, & Ray Reynolds. *The Insider's Guide to Old Books, Magazines, Newspapers and Trade Catalogs.* El Cajon, CA: Windmill Pub. Co., #2147. 1995. (Windmill View Dr., zip 92020)

GEN   Barnes, Frank T. *Hooks, Rings & Other Things. ... N.E. Iron, 1660-1860.* Hanover, MA: Christopher Pub., 1988. New England bygones.

X   Barons, Richard. *The American Hearth.* N.p. [Binghamton, NY]: Broome County Historical Society, 1976. Covers 1600-1775.

CAT   Barry, D. J., & Co. *Hotel Supplies.* Catalog. NYC: 1924. Manufacturers, jobbers, importers of house furnishings.

GEN   Barton, Stuart. *Kitchenalia, 1620-1920.* Tenterden: MJM, 1982.

GEN   Batz, Jeannette. *The Broom Closet: Secret Meanings of Domesticity in Postfeminist Novels.* NYC: Peter Lang Pub. Group, 1996. Housekeeping in American literature.

GEN   Beard, James, Milton Glaser, ed., et al. *The Cook's Catalogue.* NYC: Harper & Row, 1975. Rev. & expanded *The New Cook's Catalogue. The Definitive Guide to Cooking Equipment,* ed. by Burt Wolf, Emily Aronson, & Florence Fabricant. NY: Alfred Knopf, 2000.

GEN   Beard, James, intro. *The International Cooks' Catalogue.* NYC: Random House, 1977. Useful because it shows today's exotic utensils we might think are much older.

VIII — Beauchamp, K. G. *Exhibiting Electricity*. London, England: Institution of Electrical Engineers, 1997. History of Technology series. History of public & technical exhibitions since 18th C. 352 pp. Order from: IEE, Savoy Place, London, WC2R OBL, UK, or www.iee.org/Publish/Ordering/

INV — Beckmann, Johann. *Concise History of Ancient Institutions, Inventions and Discoveries in Science and Mechanic Art*. Translated from German. 3 vols. London: J. Bell, et al., 1797.

GEN — Beitz, Les. *Treasury of Frontier Relics*. NYC: Edwin House, 1966.

GEN — Benker, Gertrud Schmittinger. *Kuchlgschirr und Essensbräuch*. Regensburg, GERMANY: Pustet, 1977. German kitchen history.

GEN — Bent, Silas. *Slaves by the Billion: the Story of Mechanical Progress in the Home*. NY, Toronto: Longmans, Green, 1938.

V, VII — Bercovici, Ellen, Bobbie Zucker Bryson, and Deborah Gillham. *Collectibles for Kitchen, Bath & Beyond. A Pictorial Guide*. Norfolk, VA: Antique Trader Books (Landmark Specialty Pub.), now Krause Publications, 1998. Also: 2nd ed. Krause Publications, 2001.

V — Berning, Bill, & Jan Berning. *Scales: A Collector's Guide*. Atglen, PA: Schiffer. (Autographed copies directly from the Bernings: 135 W. Main St., Genoa, IL 60135. Phone: 815-84-3134. E-mail: IweighU@yahoo.com)

VIII — Bernston, Buster, & Per Ekman. *Scandinavian Corkscrews*. Taby, Sweden: Tryckerförlaget, 1994.

IV — Bertuch, A. *Katalog A*. Berlin, Germany, 1904. Molds for cake, ice cream, pudding, candy, nougat.

INV — Besterman, Theodore. *Technology, Including Patents. A Bibliography of Bibliographies*. 2 vols. © 1939. Totowa, NJ: Rowman & Littlefield, 1971.

PAP — *Biblio*. Bimonthly for collectors of books, mss, and ephemera. Aster Pub. Corp., (845 Williamette St., Eugene, OR 97401)

VIII — Bidault, Gérard. *Les Fabriques Francais de Tier-Bouchon 1820-1970*. France: Bidault, 2000.

MET — Biringuccio, Vannoccio. *The Pirotechnia (The Classic Sixteenth-Century Treatise on Metals and Metallurgy)*, first published 1540. With introduction, forewords, & bibliography. Reprint NYC: Dover Books, 1990.

GEN — Bishop, Christina. *Collecting Kitchenware* (Miller's series). Wappingers Falls, NY: Antique Collectors Club, Millers Publications, 1995; 1999. Mainly English.

GEN — Bishop, John Leander. *A History of American Manufacturers from 1608-1860*. Philadelphia: E. Young & Co., 1861.

XVI — Bitting, A. W. *Appertizing, or the Art of Canning: Its History and Development*. San Francisco: priv. pub., 1937.

VII — Bivins, John, Jr. *The Moravian Potters in North Carolina*. Chapel Hill: Univ. of N.C. Press, 1972.

VIII — Blake, Philos [pseud.]. *For Openers: Illustrated Catalogue of American Patented Corkscrews and Can-openers ... Exhibition at CHS Oct. 10, 1980 to Jan. 5, 1981*. [Hartford, CT]: CT Historical Society, 1980.

VIII — Blake, Philos. [pseud] *Guide to American Corkscrew Patents*. Vol. 1, *1860-1895*; Vol. 2: *1896-1920*. New Castle, DE: Bottlescrew Press, 1978; 1981.

XV — Blankenship, Victor A., Sr. *Frigidaire Memorabilia and Advertising Collectibles*. Dayton, OH: Victor Pub., 1991. No pictures, just listings. (POB 417, zip 45449)

I — Bohn, Carol. *American Patented Nutmeg Graters: A Working Handbook*. Mifflinburg, PA: author. Complete patent records with lots of photos & collecting information. Due out late 2003. (501 Market St., zip 17844)

MET — Bolton, J. W., comp. *Bibliography on Cast Iron ... For the Use of the Committee On Cast Iron of the A.F.A.* [Chicago]; American Foundrymen's Association, 1927.

XVI — Bond, Ralph. *Fruit Jar Patents Vol. I, Early 1800s-1869*. N.p.; n.d. Long out of print, but plans are to expand and publish this soon as part of Dick Roller's series for Phoenix Press.

MET — Booher, Fred. *Graniteware: Identification & Value Guide*. Paducah, KY: Collector Books, 1977.

XI — Boram, Clifford. *How to Get Parts Cast for Your Antique Stove: Dealing with a Foundry Is Easier Than You Think*. Monticello, IN: Autonomy House, 1982. (417 N. Main, zip 47960)

VII — Bosker, Gideon. *Great Shakes: Salt & Pepper for All Tastes*. NYC: Abbeville, 1986.

VII — Bosker, Gideon, & Lena Lencek. *Salt and Pepper Shakers: Identification and Price Guide*. NY: Avon Paperbacks, 1994.

Bossche, Willy Van den – See: Van den Bossche, Willy.

VII — *Bottles & Bygones Club of Great Britain*. Quarterly e-zine – magazine on the Web, with membership. (Mike Sheridan, 30 Brabant Rd., Cheadle Hulme, Cheadle Cheshire SK8 7AU, England. Web site: www.bygones.demon.co.uk/bottle.htm)

VII+ — *Bottles & Extras*. Monthly magazine of The Federation of Historical Bottle Collectors. (Web site: www.fohbc.com/)

XVI — Bowditch, Barbara. *American Jelly Glasses: A Collector's Notebook*. Drawings by George Bowditch. Hilton, NY: author, 1986. Wonderful book now permanently out of print. The few copies left can be bought from the Shaws, listed at the end of Chapter XVI.

GEN — Bradley, Rose. *The English Housewife in the Seventeenth and Eighteenth Centuries*. London: Edward Arnold, 1912.

XIV — Bramah, Edward, & Joan Bramah. *Coffee Makers: 300 Years of Art and Design*. N.: Cimino Pub. Group, 1992.

XVI — Brantley, William F. *A Collector's Guide to Jars*. Muncie, IN: Ball Corporation, 1975.

IV — Braun, Ludwig, & Jörg Paczkowski. *Weimer Backmodel: zur Ausstellung*. Wertheim, Germany: Historisches Museum für Stadt und Grafschaft, 1983. German carved wood cookie molds exhibition catalog.

VII — Brazer, Esther Stevens. *Early American Decoration*. Springfield, MA: Pond-Ekber, 1940. Tole ware.

GEN — Breazeale, James F. *Economy in the Kitchen.* NYC: Frye Pub. Co., 1918.

CAT — Breck, Joseph & Sons. *Agricultural Hardware, Implements, Woodenware.* Catalog. Boston: 1903; 1905.

XVIII — Breuer, Gerda & Kerstin Plüm. *Design: Sammlung Stiftung Schriefers*, Wienand, Germany: 1998. Catalog of private design collection of Werner Schriefers.

WWW — Brewster, Michael S. *Amazon, and Other Online Auctions.* MSB Publishing, 2000.

GEN — Bridge, Fred, & Jean F. Tibbetts. *The Well-Tooled Kitchen.* NYC: William Morrow & Co., 1991; NY: Morrow-Avon, 1992.

VII — *British Novelty Salt and Pepper Collectors Club.* Quarterly newsletter. (Ray Dodd, Coleshill Clayton Rd, Mold Flintshire CH7 1SX, England. Web site: www.ezeeweb.co.uk/shakers)

GEN — Brooke, Sheena. *Hearth and Home: A Short History of Domestic Equipment.* London: Mills & Boon, 1973.

INV — Brown, Henry T. *Five Hundred and Seven Mechanical Movements...Including Many Movements Never Before Published, and Several Which Have Only Recently Come Into Use.* NYC: Brown, Coombs & Co., 1869 ...; 1896; ...1911; Reprint: Mendham, NJ: Astragal Pr, 1995. (5 Cold Hill Road, S., Suite 12, POB 239, Mendham, NJ 07945. E-mail: astragalpress@attglobal.net)

INV — ———. *Manual of Mechanical Movements.* © 1868; renewed 1896. Reprinted: South Orange, NJ: W. M. Clark, 1933. These were published for inventors, but can help us identify mechanical movements in odd gadgets.

INV — Brown, J. J. *Ideas in Exile: A History of Canadian Invention.* Toronto, CAN: McClelland & Stewart, 1967.

INV — Brown, Travis. *Popular Patents: America's First Inventions from the Airplane to the Zipper.* Metuchen, NJ: Scarecrow Press, 2000.

VII — Bull, Donald A. *Beer Advertising Openers – A Pictorial Guide.* Trumbell, CT: author, 1978.

VIII — ———. *Boxes Full of Corkscrews.* Schiffer, 2000.

VIII — ———. *Pocket Guide to Corkscrews.* Schiffer, 1999.

VIII — Bull, Donald. *A Price Guide to Beer Advertising Openers & Corkscrews.* Trumbull, CT: author, 1981.

VIII — ———. *The Ultimate Corkscrew Book.* PA: Schiffer, 1999.

VIII — Bull, Donald, & John R. Stanley. *Just for Openers – A Guide to Beer, Soda, & Other Openers.* Schiffer, 1999.

VIII — ———. *Soda Advertising Openers.* Schiffer, 2000.

KIT — Bullock, Helen Claire Duprey. *Kitchens in Colonial Virginia.* Williamsburg, VA: Colonial Williamsburg Foundation, 1931.

BK — Bullock, Helen. *A National Treasury of Cooking. Recipes of: Ante Bellum America; Early America; Victorian America; The Young Republic; The Westward Empire.* 5 vols. NYC: Heirloom Pub., 1967.

IV — Bunn, Eleanor. *Metal Molds, Ice Cream, Chocolate, Barley, Sugar, Cake.* Paducah, KY: Collector Books, 1981.

GEN — Burgess, Fred. W. *Chats on Household Curic*. NYC: F. A. Stokes Co., 1914.

MET — Burgess, F. W. *Chats on Old Copper & Bras*. NYC: F. A. Stokes, 1914.

CAT — Butler Brothers. *Christmas Catalog.* Chicag 1899. Thousands of mail order househo. items.

VIII — Butter, Robin, & Gillian Walking. *Book of Wir Antiques.* Wappingers Falls, NY: Antique Co lectors Club, 1994. (Market St., Industri. Park, 12590)

XVIII — Byers, Anthony. *Centenary of Service: A Hi tory of Electricity in the Home.* London: Ele tricity Council, 1981.

MET — Campbell, Bonita J. *Depression Silve Machine Age Craft and Design in Aluminun* Granada Hills, CA: author, n.d. (POB 315 zip 91394)

XVIII — Campbell, Edward A. *How to Repair Washin Machines..., Refrigerators, ...Mixers, Toas ers, ...*. NYC: Arco, 1937.

GEN — Campbell, Susan. *Cooks' Tools. Complete Mar ual of Kitchen Implements & How to Us Them.* NYC: William Morrow, 1980. Moder: tools; old uses.

VII — Campbell's Soup Collector Club. (David & Micki Young, 414 Country Lane Ct., Wau conda, IL 60084)

Canadian Corkscrew Collectors Club – See: *Quarterly Worme.*

IV — *Candy Gram*, newsletter of Candy Containe Collectors of America. (Betty MacDuff, 2711 De La Rosa St., The Villages, FL 32159. Web site: www.candycontainer.org/)

VII — Caniff, Tom. *Label Space, The Book.* Chicago, IL: Phoenix Press, 1996. Columns from "Bottles & Extras." All about labeled product or packer jars. See also: McCann, Jerry. (E-mail: tomcaniff@aol.com)

VII — Carey, Larry, & Sylvia Tompkins. *1001 Salt & Pepper Shakers.* Atglen, PA: Schiffer Pub. Co. Also *1002 Salt & Pepper Shakers; 1003 Salt & Pepper Shakers, 1996; 1004....; 1005..., 1999; 1006..., 2001.* And can you believe it? They're all different! Includes (*1001*),: Black Americana, cats, mermaids, Niagara Falls, etc; (*1002*),: nodders; (*1003*),: characters, mascots, symbols; (*1004*),: nursery rhymes, children's literature; (*1005*),: miniatures; (*1006*),: advertising motifs.

X — Carlo, Joyce W. *Trammels, Trenchers & Tartlets.* Peregrine Press, 1982. Cooking & Kitchens, USA, to 1775.

CBK — Carson, Jane. *Colonial Virginia Cookery.* Williamsburg, VA: Williamsburg Research Studies, 1968. Good on colonial kitchens & early cookbooks.

INV — Carter, Ernest Frank. *Dictionary of Inventions and Discoveries.* London: F. Muller, 1966.

GEN — Carter, Mary R. *Kitchen Junk.* NY: Viking Penguin, 1999. By the self-proclaimed "Queen of Junk" – but, hey: that's me and my domain!

MET — *Cast Iron: Architecture and Ornament, Function and Fantasy.* London: John Murray, 1987.

CSTi — *Cast Iron Collectors*, Southern chapter. (Jim Bell, POB 355, Swainsboro, GA 30401)

STi   *Cast Iron Marketplace.* (Craig C. Leverenz, 465 Cemetery Rd., Kinnickinnick Twsp, WI 54022. Phone: 715-425-7981)

IT   *The Kitchen Catalogue.* York, England: Castle Museum, 1979.

NV   *Catalogue of the Machines, Models, etc., In the Patent Museum, South Kensington.* London: HMSO, 1863.

GEN   Celehar. Jane. *Kitchens & Gadgets. 1920 to 1950.* Des Moines, IA: Wallace-Homestead, 1982. Handle shapes; dates, company histories good.

GEN   ———. *Kitchens & Kitchenware.* Lombard, IL: Wallace-Homestead, 1985.

CAT   Central Stamping Co. *Catalog No. 43.* NYC: 1920.

VII   Chase Collectors Society. (Barry L. Van Hook, 2149 W. Jibsail Loop, Mesa, AZ 85202-5524. Web site: www.public.asu.edu/~icblv/chase. htm)

XV   Cherry-Bassett Co. *Complete Catalog of Equipment for Milk Plants, Ice Cream Plants ... No. 53.* Baltimore, Philadelphia: 1921.

CAT   Chiurazzi, J. & Fils / S. De Angelis & Fils. *Artistic Founding.* Catalog. Naples, Italy: 1910-11. Reproductions of ancient metalwares found at Pompei & Herculaneum.

GEN   Christensen, E. O. *The Index of American Design.* NYC: Macmillan, 1950.

GEN   *Chronicle, The.* Quarterly journal of Early American Industries Association (EAIA). Since 1933. Organization dedicated to studying & preserving all tools, including household & kitchen tools. (E. W. Hall, EAIA, 167 Bakerville Rd., So. Dartmouth, MA 02748. Web site: www.eaiainfo.org)

XV   Clad, V. & Sons, Inc. Clad's Advertising Pamphlet. Philadelphia: c. 1890-1900.

XVI   Clark, Hyla. *The Tin Can Book.* NYC: New American Library, 1977.

VII   Clements, Monica Lynne, & Patricia Rosser Clements. *An Unauthorized Guide to Fire-King Glasswares.* Atglen, PA: Schiffer Pub. Co., 1999.

MET   Coffin, Margaret. *The History & Folklore of American Country Tinware, 1700-1900.* Camden, NJ: Thomas Nelson & Sons, 1968.

VIII   Coldicott, Peter. *A Guide to Corkscrew Collecting.* Over Wallop, Stockbridge: BAS Printers Ltd., Hants, UK: author, 1993.

GEN   *Collectormania Australia P/L.* Monthly tabloid newspaper. Ian Welsh, ed. Largest Australian collector; periodical has international subscriptions. (POB 112, Campbells Creek, Vic., 3451 Australia)

GEN   *Collectors.org.* This is like a huge newsletter, updated weekly, right on the Web. Lists collector clubs, flea markets, auctioneers, conventions, workshops, appraisals, restoration experts, etc. Click on a selection from the club directory of "Kitchen" or "Metals" or "Ceramics," etc. (Web site: www.collectors. org/)

WWW   Collier, Marsha, et al. *eBay™ for Dummies®.* 2nd ed. NYC, Cleveland: Hungry Minds, 2001. Includes packing advice.

GEN   Colvin Run Mill Park. *Before Cuisinart®: An Exhibit of Early American Kitchenware.* [VA], Fairfax Cty Parks: 1983.

GEN   Congdon-Martin, Douglas, with Bob Biondi. *Figurative Cast Iron, a Collector's Guide.* Atglen, PA: Schiffer Pub. Co., 1995. Good pix, but very short on info.

GEN   Consentino, Geraldine, & Regina Stewart. *Kitchenware: A Guide for the Beginning Collector.* NYC: Golden Press, 1977.

KIT   Cook, Mary Alexander. *The Cape Kitchen; a Description of Its Position, Lay-out, Fittings and Utensils.* Stellenbosch, South Africa: Stellenbosch Museum, [1970s]. Beautiful metalwares.

XVIII   Cook, Patricia & Catherine Slessor, Bakelite: *An Illustrated Guide to Collectible Bakelite Objects.* England: The Apple Press, a Quintet Book, 1992.

CBK   *Cook Book Collectors Club of America.* (Col. Bob Allen, POB 56, St. James, MO 65559)

CBK   *Cookbook Collectors' Exchange.* Quarterly. (Sue Erwin, POB 89, Magalia, CA 95954)

IV   *Cookie Crumbs.* Quarterly newsletter. Cookie Cutter Collectors Club. (Joyce Moorhouse, 2763 310th St., Cannon Falls, MN 55009)

IV   *Cookies Newsletter.* (Rosemary Henry, 9610 Greenview Lane, Manassas, VA, 20109-3320. E-mail: editor@cookiesnewsletter. com; Web site: www.cookiesnewsletter.com)

GEN   Cooley, Anna Maria, & Wilhelmina H. Spohr. *Household Arts for Home and School.* 2 vols. NYC: The Macmillan Co., 1920.

GEN   Cooper, Carolyn C. "The Ghost in the Kitchen: Household Technology at the Brattleboro Museum, Vermont." Article in *Technology and Culture*, Vol. 28, No. 2. Chicago: Univ. of Chicago Press, 1991.

GEN   Cope, Kenneth L. *Kitchen Collectibles: An Identification Guide.* Mendam, NJ: The Astragal Press, 2000. (E-mail: astragalpress@attglobal. net)

XVIII   Corley, Thomas Anthony Buchanan. *Domestic Electrical Appliances.* London: Jonathan Cape, 1966.

GEN   Cowan, Ruth Schwartz. *More Work for Mother. The Ironies of Household Technology from the Open Hearth to the Microwave.* NY: Basic Books, 1983.

VIII   Crestin-Billet, Frederique. *Collectible Corkscrews.* Paris, et al: Flammarion et Cie, 2001. In English.

XVI   Creswick, Alice. *The Collector's Guide to Old Fruit Jars.* Grand Rapids, MI: author, 1st through 6th editions, through 1991. Also called the *"Red Book of Fruit Jars."* All editions desirable. Drawings by Howard Creswick are exquisitely done. See also: Leybourne.

PAP   Crom, Theodore R. *Trade Catalogues* – 1542 to 1842. Hawthorne, FL: author, n.d. (Rt. 2, Box 212, zip 32640)

MET   Curtis, Tony. *Copper & Brass.* Galashiels, Scotland: Lyle Publications, 1982.

GEN   ———. *Kitchen Equipment.* Galashiels, Scotland: Lyle Publications, 1978, rev. 1982. Mostly illustrated price guide.

XI   Curtis, Will, & Jane Curtis. *Antique Wood-stoves.* Ashville, ME: Cobblesmith, 1975.

I   *Cutting Edge, The.* Quarterly newsletter of Glass Knife Collectors Club. (Adrienne Escoe, POB 342, Los Alamitos, CA 90720) d'Allemagne – See: Allemagne.

XVIII   Dahlman, Albert-Friedrich. *Vom Kochtopf zur High-Tech: Entwicklung der Deutschen Gross-geräte-Industrie.* Munich: R. Oldennbourg, 1992.

VII   Davern, Melva. *The Collectors Encyclopedia of Salt and Pepper Shakers, Figural and Novelty.* Paducah: Collector Books, 1991. She's also done a "second series." (Author: POB 81914, Pittsburgh, PA 15217)

KIT   Davidson, Alan. *The Cook's Room: A Celebration of the Heart of the Home.* Sydney, Australia: Doubleday, 1991. Utensils +.

GEN   Davidson, Caroline. *A Woman's Work Is Never Done: A Social History of Housework, 1630-1950.* London: Chatto & Windus, 1982.

GEN   Davies, Jennifer. *The Victorian Kitchen.* London: BBC, 1989.

GEN   de Haan, David. *Antique Household Gadgets and Appliances, c. 1860 to 1930.* Poole, England: Blandford, 1977; Woodbury, NY: Barron's, 1978.

VII   DePasquale, Dan, & Gail DePasquale, & Larry Peterson. *Red Wing Collectibles.* Paducah, KY: Collector Books, 1986.

VII   ——. *Red Wing Stoneware.* Paducah, KY: Collector Books, 1983, prices updated 1990.

VIII   D'Errico, Nicholas F. *American Corkscrews Patents 1921-1992.* CT: author, 1993.

VIII   De Sanctis, Paolo, & Maurizio Fantoni. *I Cavatappi/Corkscrews.* Milan, Italy: Be-Ma Editrice, 1988. In Italian & English.

VIII   ——. *Le Collezioni Cavatappis. Milan: Mailand,* 1993.

VIII   ——. *The Corkscrew, a Thing of Beauty.* Milan: Marzorati Editore, 1990.

VIII   ——. *Schiaccianoci/Nutcrackers.* Milan: Italy: Be-Ma Editrice, 1990. In Italian & English.

MET   DeVoe, Shirley Spaulding. *The Art of the Tinsmith, English and American.* Exton, PA: Schiffer Publishing, 1981.

MET   ——. *The Tinsmiths of Connecticut.* Middletown, CT: Wesleyan Univ. Press, 1968.

VII   Dezso, Douglas M., J. Leon Poirier, Rose D. Poirier. *Collector's Guide to Candy Containers; Identification & Values.* LW Publishing & Book Sales, 1996.

XV   Dickson, Paul. *The Great American Ice Cream Book.* NYC: Atheneum, 1972.

X   di Meglio, Jean. *Irons in the Fire: A Brief Look at the Open Hearth Cooking on Which Young America Grew Up.* Early Trades & Crafts Society, 1973.

XVIII   DiNoto, Andrea. *Art Plastic.* NYC: Abbeville Press, 1984. Glorious, colorful things for the entire house.

VIII   Dippel, Horst. *Korkenzieher.* Hamburg, Germany: Ellert & Richter, 1988. Corkscrews.

IV   Divone, Judene. *Chocolate Moulds. A History & Encyclopedia.* Oakton, VA: Oakton Hills Pub., 1987. Profusely illustrated. Divone also compiled & reprinted an Anton Reich catalog of *schokoladenformen.*

INV   Dobyns, Kenneth W. *The Patent Office Pony. History of the Early Patent Office.* Spotsylvania, VA: Sergeant Kirkland's Press, 1994. Yakama Trail, 22553. Related Web sit www.myoutbox.net/pohome.htm. This boo is a must for an understanding of the impotance of the Patent Office.

GEN   *Domestic Utensils: Index of American Desig Part 5.* Teaneck, NJ: Somerset House, 1979

VIII   Doornkaat, Heinz ten. *Korkenzieher.* German author, 1991.

IV   Dorchy, Henry. *Le Moule a Chocolat. Un nouv objet de collection.* Paris: Les Editions d l'Amateur, n.d. [1980s]. Copious illustration from catalogs, factory scenes, and chocolat molds themselves.

CAT   *Dover Stamping Co. Catalog, 1869.* Facsimile Princeton, NJ: American Historical Catalo Collection, The Pyne Press, 1971.

CBK   Dover Stamping Co. *Cook Book.* Boston: 1899.

GEN   Dow, George Francis. *The Arts & Crafts in Ne England, 1704-1775. Gleanings from Bosto Newspapers.* Topsfield, MA: Wayside Pr., 1927.

KIT   Downing, Frances Stade von. *How the Nine teenth-Century American Kitchen, Its Archi tecture and Objects, Influenced the Role o Women in Society.* Dissertation thesis. NYC Cooper-Hewitt Museum & Parson's School o Design, 1984.

MET   Dragowick, Marilyn, ed. *Metalwares Price Guide* Dubuque, IA: Antique Trader Books, 1997.

CBK   Dubois, Urbain. *La Patisserie D'Aujourd'hui.* 7th ed. Paris: © 1890-93. Most illustrations date to © 1860s-70s.

IV   Dudrear, Albert C., Jr. *Clear Toy Candy: History, Mould-Makers, Recipes.* 2nd ed. Brochure, 1983.

CAT   Duparquet & Huot. *Catalog of ... the Imperial French Cooking Range and Broiler: Also, Coffee and Tea Urns, Oyster and Cast-Iron Steam Kettles, Cast-Iron, Tin, and Copper Cooking Utensils.* NYC: 1885.

CAT   Duparquet, Huot & Moneuse. *Catalog.* House furnishings mainly for hotels & restaurants. NYC: © 1904-1910.

CBK   DuSablon, Mary A. *America's Collectible Cookbooks: The History, the Politics, the Recipes.* Athens, OH: Ohio Univ. Press, 1994.

GEN   Duval, Gaston. *Musée Rétrospectif du Groupe X, Alimentation, à l'Exposition universelle internationale de 1900 à Paris.* [Paris?]: 1900. For the International Exposition of 1900.

GEN   Dwight, Timothy. *Travels in New England and New York – 1796-1815.* 4 vols. London: W. Baynes & Son, 1823.

GEN   Earle, Alice Morse. *Home Life in Colonial Days.* NYC: Macmillan, 1899.

GEN   Early American Industries Association – See: *Chronicle, The.*

GEN   *Early American Life.* Harrisburg, PA: Cowles. Look for back issues.

INV   *Early Unnumbered Patent Index.* Woodbridge, CT: Research Publications, 1980. Used to be available from Rapid Patent Service, Arlington, VA; now seems to be out of print.

EN Eaton, Allen Hendershott. *Handicrafts of New England*. NYC: Harper, 1949. Also one on the *Southern Highlands*. NYC: Russell Sage Foundation, 1937.

II *Eggcup Collectors' Corner*. Quarterly newsletter for the club. (Joan George, 67 Stevens Ave., Old Bridge, NJ 08857)

II Eikelberner, George, & Serge Agadjanian. *The Compleat American Candy Containers Handbook*. Mentor, OH: Bowden Pub. Revised ed. 1986. (6252 Cedarwood Rd., zip 44060)

XVIII Electrical Assoc. for Women. *The Electrical Age for Women*. Quarterly. London: Electrical Assoc. for Women, 1926-1978. Continued by: *Electric Living*.

XVIII *Electrical Dealer*. Monthly. Chicago, IL: Haywood Pub., 1928.

XII *Enchantment of Enameled "Cook Ware."* Kermit, TX: Collectors Weekly Books, 1974.

CAT *Enterprise Mfg. Co. Catalog*. Philadelphia: © 1900-1910. Another, 1881.

PAP *Ephemera Society Quarterly*. Journal. The English Ephemera Society was first. (8 Galveston Rd., Putney, London SW15 2SA, England)

PAP *Ephemera Society Journal*. The Ephemera Society of Australia. (Edwin Jewell, POB 479, Warragul, Vic. 3820, Australia)

PAP *Ephemera Society Journal*. The Ephemera Society of Austria [Ephemera Gesellschaft Osterreich]. (Friedl Wolaskowitz, Baumlegarten 5, A-6973, Hoehst, Austria)

PAP *Ephemera Society Journal*. The Ephemera Society of Canada. (Barbara Rusch, 36 Macauley Dr., Thornhill, Ontario L3T 5S5, CAN)

V *Equilibrium*. Quarterly. Chicago, IL: International Society of Antique Scale Collecting. (Bob Stein, 300 W. Adams, Ste. 821, Chicago, IL 60606)

GEN Ettlinger, Steve R. *The Kitchenware Book*. NY: Macmillan, 1992.

X Eveleigh, David J. *Brass and Brassware*. Aylesbury, England: Shire Books, 199-.

X, XI ———. *Firegrates and Kitchen Ranges*. Aylesbury, England: Shire Books, 199-.

GEN ———. *Old Cooking Utensils, 1600-1900*. Princes Risborough: Shire Books, 1986.

IV Evertz, Leonhard. *Aachenner Backformen der Sammlung van den Daele*. Aachenn, Germany: Mayer, 1975. Bread molds in collection of Leo van den Daele.

MET Fairbairn, Sir William. *Iron; Its History, Properties and Process of Manufacture*. Edinburgh: A. & C. Black, 1865.

GEN *Fakes & Reproductions of 1996*. Des Moines, IA: Antique & Collectors Reproduction News. (POB 12130, zip 50312-9403)

I Fantoni, Maurizio. *Nutcrackers*. Milano, Italy: BE-MA, c. 1990.

VIII Fantoni, Maurizio, & de Sanctis. *Corkscrews. I Cavatappi*. Milano, Italy: BE-MA, 1988. 138 pp, color illustrations.

GEN Faulkner, Wendy, & Erik Arnold, eds. *Smothered by Invention: Technology in Women's Lives*. London: Pluto Press, 1985.

HIS Faure-Boucharlat, E. *A la Fortune du Pot: la cuisine et le table à Lyon et à Vienne, Xe-XIXe siè-*

cles. Lyon, France: Musée de la Civilisation Gallo-Romaine, 1990. Gallo-Roman archaeological finds related to kitchen utensils, etc.

GEN Fearn, Jacqueline. *Domestic Bygones*. Aylesbury, England: Shire, 1977.

VII *Feeding Baby through the Ages*. N.p.: Mead Johnson Laboratories, n.d. [c. 1976]. Photos collaged with genre scenes of baby feeders from ancient Rome on.

VI Fehling, Loretta Smith. *More Terrific Tablecloths*. Atglen: Schiffer, 1999.

GEN Feild, Rachel. *Irons in the Fire. A History of Cooking Equipment*. London: Crowood Press, 1984. History to 1983.

MET Fennimore, Donald L. *Metalwork in Early America: Copper and Its Alloys from the Winterthur Collection*. Winterthur Museum; 1996.

IV *Festliches Backwerk. Holzmodel, Formen aus Zinn, Kupfer und Keramik, Waffel- und Oblateneisen*. Nurnberg, Germany: Germanisches National Museum, 1981. Baking molds in tin, copper, ceramic, cast iron.

V Fields, Linda. *Four & Twenty Blackbirds, A pictorial identification & price guide for pie birds*. Vol. I. Paducah, KY: Image Graphics, 1998; Vol. II, 2002. Available from author: 158 Bagsby Hill Lane, Dover, TN 37058. E-mail: fpiebird@compu.net ; Web site: www.festivalusa.com/my-picbird. Lots of photos of US & foreign pie birds & funnels.

VII *Fiesta Collector's Quarterly*. Newsletter of Fiesta Collector's Club. (Joel Wilson, Jr. POB 471, Valley City, OH 44280. Web site: www.chinaspecialties.com/fiesta.html)

VIII *Figural Bottle Openers, Identification Guide*. Available through Figural Bottle Opener Collectors. See the entry *Opener* in the Bibliography.

GEN *Fine Tool Journal, The*. Bimonthly focusing on carpenters' tools, with some info at times on household tools. (Founder & editor, Vernon U. Ward; owner now Clarence Blanchard. 27 Fickett Rd., Pownal, ME 04069. E-mail: ceb@finetoolj.com; Web site: www.Finetoolj. com)

VII *Fire-King News*. (Dale Kilgo, POB 473, Addison, AL 35540, E-mail: dkilgo-1069@aol. com)

XVIII Fisher, Charles. *Early American Electric Toasters. 1906-1940*. Teaneck, NJ: H.J.H Publications, c. 1987; 1994; updated 1996. Now known as *Hazelcorn's Price Guide to Old Electric Toasters*.

PAP Fitzsimmons, Ada. *American Collectibles as Advertised, 1860-1899*. San Anselmo, CA: Paper Pile Enterprises, n.d. (Available through author at Paper Pile [see], or eBay. Her eBay name: paper-mountain)

VII Florence, Gene. *Kitchen Glassware of the Depression Years*. 1st through 6th editions. Paducah, KY: Collector Books, 1981; 1983; 1987; 1990; 1997, 2001. One of his incomparable books on Depression glass.

VI Florence, Judy. *Aprons of the Mid-Twentieth Century*. Schiffer, n.d.

MET Flower, Philip William. *A History of the Trade in Tin; ... Tin Mining and Metallurgy; ... the Tin-plate Trade. ... Ancient and Modern Processes of Manufacturing Tin-Plates*. London, Eng: George Bell & Son, 1880.

VII   Forty, Anne. *Treen & Earthenware*. Midas Books, 1979.

CBK   Fowler, George. *How to Bottle Fruit, Vegetables, Game, Poultry, Milk, &c.* Reading, England: Fowler, n.d., revised edition c. 1922

KIT   Frampton, Alyse. *The Habitant Kitchen in New France, 1700-1750*. Master's thesis. Toronto, CAN: 1977.

PAP   Franklin, Linda Campbell. *Bibliography of Antiques & Collectibles. Books in the English Langauge, 1570-1976*. Metuchen, NJ: Scarecrow Books, 1978.

GEN   Franklin, L. C. *From Hearth to Cookstove: An American Domestic History of Gadgets & Utensils ... 1700-1930*. Florence, AL: *House of Collectibles*, 1976, 1978. There's a so-called "3rd edition" – with my name removed & replaced by the publisher's son's name, "Mark Hudgeons," as editor.

GEN   ———. *300 Years of Housekeeping Collectibles*. Florence, AL: Books Americana.

GEN   ———. *300 Years of Kitchen Collectibles*. Florence, AL: Books Americana, 1st through 4th editions: 1981, 1984, 1991, 1997.

GEN   Franklin, L. C., ed. *Kitchen Collectibles News*. NYC: 1984-86. 18 issues. Americana, 1992.

VIII   Fredericksen, Paul. *Corkscrews That Work*. San Francisco, CA: The Wine Institute, 1946. Typescript of report done by Wine Advisory Board & Wine Institute.

XVIII   Fredgant, Don. *Electrical Collectibles: Relics of the Electrical Age*. San Luis Obispo, CA: Padre Productions, 1981.

XII   Freeman, Larry. *Collecting Old Graniteware; Porcelain on Steel, a Forerunner of Aluminum Kitchenware*. Watkins Glen, NY: Century House, 1978.

XIV   Friend, Terry. *Coffee Mills. An Illustrated Price Guide*. Paducah, KY: Collector Books, 1982. 78 pp with 145 mills.

XVI   *Fruit Jar News, The.* (FJN Publishers, 364 Gregory Ave., West Orange, NJ 07052-3743. Tom Caniff, ed., 1223 Oak Grove Ave., Steubenville, OH 43952-1649. E-mail: tomcaniff@aol.com)

GEN   Fuentes, Cecilia, & Darla Hernández. *Fogones y Cocinas Tradicionnales de Venezuela*. Caracas, Spain: Ediciones Cavendes, 1993.

INV   Fuller, Edmund. *Tinkers and Geniuses, the Story of the Yankee Inventors*. NYC: Hastings House, 1955.

MET   Fuller, John, Sr. *Art of Coppersmithing: A Practical Treatise on Working Sheet Copper into All Forms*. NYC: David Williams Co., 1894, then 1911. Published serially, 1889-90. Reprinted: Mendham, NJ: Astragal Press, 1993. (E-mail: astragalpress@attglobal.net)

XIV   Fumagalli, Ambrogio. *Coffeemakers. Macchine da Caffe, 1800-1950, American & European*. San Francisco: Chronicle Books, Bella Cosa Series, 1995. Vintage instruments from tin pots to fancy machines.

VII   Gallo, John. *Nineteenth and Twentieth Century Yellow Ware*. Richfield Springs, NY: Heritage Press. 1985.

XVII   Garth's Auctions. *Paustenbach Collection P Safes*. Auction catalog for October 18-19 1996 auction. The Paustenbachs were goin to write a book; but this may be the on "book" published on the subject. (Garth Auctions, 2690 Stratford Rd., Delaware, O 43015. Web site: www.garths.com/)

MET   Gaston, Mary Frank. *Antique Brass*. Paducah Collector Books, 1985.

XVIII   General Electric Co. *The Home of a Hundre Comforts*. Bridgeport, CT: GE Co., 1920.

GEN   Genêt, Nicole, Louise Décarie-Audet, & Luce Ver mette. *Les Objets Familiers de Nos Ancêtres* Montreal, CAN: Editions de l'Homme, 1974 French Canadian kitchen utensils, etc.

MET   Gentle, Rupert, & Rachael Feild. *Englis Domestic Brass, 1680-1810*. NYC: E. P. Dut ton, 1975. Revised by Belinda Gentle, fo Antique Collector's Club, 1994. New on expands date range: 1640-1920, an includes some continental European, som iron, steel, and copper.

CAT   Geuder, Paeschke & Frey Co. *Cream Cit Ware*. Catalog. Milwaukee, WI: 1925.

VII   Giarde, Jeffrey L. *Glass Milk Bottles: Their Makers and Marks*. Bryn Mawr, CA: Time Travelers Press, 1980.

INV   Giblin, James C. *From Hand to Mouth: Or, Hou We Patented Knives, Forks, Spoons, & Chopsticks, & the Table Manners to Go with Them.* NYC: Harper Collins Children's Books, 1987.

INV   Giedion, Siegfried. *Mechanization Takes Command, A Contribution to Anonymous History.* NYC: Oxford Univ., 1948. One section of great interest is "Mechanization Encounters the Household."

GEN   Gilbreath, Lilian. *The Home-Maker and Her Job*. NYC: D. Appleton, 1927.

GEN   Gilman, Charlotte Perkins. *The Home: Its Work and Influence*. NYC: McClure Phillips, 1903. Reprint: Urbana, IL: Univ. of Illinois Press, 1972.

GEN   Girard, Sylvie. *Histoire des Objets de Cuisine et de Gourmandise*. [Paris]: J. Grancher, 1991.

GEN   ———. *Les Ustensils de Cuisine et Leurs Recettes*. Paris: MA Editions, 1986. Utensils & cookery.

VIII   Giulian, Bertrand B. *Corkscrews of the Eighteenth Century; Artistry in Iron and Steel*. Yardley, PA: White Space Pub., 1967, 1995. (769 Sumter Dr.)

PAP   Gobright, John Christopher. *The New York Sketchbook and Merchants Guide, A Directory*. NYC: J. C. Gobright, 1859.

VIII   Goins, John. *Encyclopedia of Cutlery Markings*. Knoxville, TN: Knife World Pub., 1986.

GEN   Goldberg, Michael J. *Collectible Plastic Kitchenware & Dinnerware, 1935-1965*. Atglen, PA: Schiffer Pub. Co., 1995. Mostly post WWII wares.

GEN   ———. *Groovy Kitchen Designs for Collectors, 1935-1965: With Value Guide*. Atglen, PA: Schiffer Pub., 1996. Includes appliances.

VII   Gonzalez, Mark. *Collecting Fiesta, Lu-Ray & Other Colorware*. L-W Book Sales, 2000.

EN Goodholme, Todd S. *Domestic Encyclopedia of Practical Information.* NYC: Henry Holt & Co., 1877.

XVIII Gordon, Bob. *Early Electrical Appliances.* Aylesbury, England: Shire Books, 1984. Created the Milne Museum of electrical relics at Tonbridge, Great Britain.

GEN Gottesman, Rita Susswein. *The Arts & Crafts in New York, 1726-1776.* NYC: New-York Historical Society, 1938. Also, *1777-1799:* 1954.

MET Gould, Mary Earle. *Antique Tin & Tole Ware.* Rutland, VT: Charles E. Tuttle, 1962.

V, VII Gould, M. E. *Early American Wooden Ware & Other Kitchen Utensils.* Rutland, VT: Tuttle, 1962.

WWW Graf, Annette E. *How to Sell on eBay and Other On-Line Auctions.* Graf Publishing, 1999.

V Graham, J. T. *Scales & Balances. A Guide to Collecting.* Aylesbury, England: Shire, 1981.

GEN Gray, Dorothy. *Gone with the Hearth.* Millbrae, CA: Celestial Arts/Les Femmes, 1976. Utensils, cookbooks, food.

IV Greaser, Arlene & Paul H. *Cookie Cutters & Molds.* Allentown, PA: 1969.

XVIII *Greatest Achievements: Household Appliances.* N.p.: National Academy of Engineering (?), n.d. [after 1955.]

GEN Green, Harvey, with assistance of Mary-Ellen Perry. *The Light of the Home: An Intimate View of the Lives of Victorian Women in America.* NYC: Pantheon, 1983. Illustrated with artifacts from the incredible Margaret Strong Museum.

CER Green, T. G. *Cornish Ware. Kitchen & Domestic Pottery.* Wappingers Falls, NY: Antique Collectors Club, 1996.

XII Greguire, Helen. *The Collector's Encyclopedia of Graniteware.* Paducah, KY: Collector Books, 1990. Full color.

XII ———. *Collector's Encyclopedia of Graniteware: Colors, Shapes and Values, Book 2.* Collector Books, 1993; prices updated 2000.

XVIII ———. *Collector's Guide to Toasters & Accessories Identification & Values.* Paducah, KY: Collector Books, 1997.

GEN Grigson, Geoffrey, & Charles H. Gibbs-Smith, eds. *Things. A Volume about the Origin and Early History of Many Things, Common and Less Common, Essential and Inessential.* London: Waverley Book Co., 1954. (Vol. 3 of 4 books: *People; Places; Ideas.*)

XIV *Grinder Finder.* Newsletter of Assoc. of Enthusiasts. Coffee mills. (Lucy Fullinwider, POB 5761, Midland, TX 79704, or Judith A. Sivonda, 375 Congdon St., Middleton CT 06457. Web site: www.millmania.com/ ACME.html)

MET Grist, Everett. *Collectible Aluminum. Hammered, Wrought, Forged & Cast.* Paducah, KY: Collector Books, 1993.

GEN *Gristmill.* Magazine for Mid-West Tool Collectors Assoc. (John G. Wells, POB 8016, Berkeley, CA 94707-8016. Web site: www.mwtca.org)

CSTi *Griswold & Cast Iron Collectibles.* Web newsletter, with message boards, Q & A, things for sale, etc. (Editor Gregory L. Stahl has a nice attitude toward new & old collectors. Web site: http://griswold.auctiondesk.net)

CSTi Griswold & Cast Iron Cookware Association. (Joanie Baldini, 3007 Plum St., Erie, PA 16508. E-mail: thespider@aol.com; her Web site: www.griswoldcastiron.com. Association Web site as of 1/2001: http://208.55.238.143/. In process of moving, but if you can't find it, e mail Ms. Baldini.)

CSTi Griswold Mfg. Co. *1928 Catalog Reprint.* 1985. (Chuck Wafford, 1936 "H" St., Springfield, OR 97477)

CSTi *Griswold Cast Iron. A Price Guide.* Neil Wood, ed. Gas City, IN: L-W Book Sales, 1993.

CSTi *Griswold Vol. II. Cast Iron, Porcelain, Aluminum.* Gas City, IN: L-W Book Sales, 1995.

XI Groft, Tammis Kane. *Cast with Style. Nineteenth Century Cast-Iron Stoves from the Albany Area.* Rev. ed. Albany, NY: Albany Institute of History, 1984.

XVIII Großkopf, Arne. *Brotröster und Toaster, 1910-1966.* Germany: author, 1989.

CER Guappone, Carmen A. *United States Decorated Stoneware.* McClellandtown, PA: Guappones Publications, 1993. (RD#1, Box 10, zip 15458)

VII Guarnaccia, Helene. *Salt and Pepper Shakers, Volumes I, II, III, IV.* Paducah, KY: Collector Books, 1985, 1989, 1991, 1995.

CER Guilland, Harold F. *Early American Folk Pottery.* Radnor, PA: Chilton Books, 1971.

XI Haines, Leland M. *Round Oak Stoves, Ranges and Furnaces.* Houston: Macy's Texas Stove Works, 1994. 272 pp, many illustrations. (5515 Almeda Rd, zip 77004)

VIII *Handbook of U.S. Beer Advertising Openers & Corkscrews. 1997.* Chapel Hill, NC: Just For Openers, 1997. (POB 64, zip 27514-0064)

MET *Handwrought Object, 1776-1976, The.* Exhibit catalog, curated by Nancy Neumann Press. Ithaca, NY: Herbert F. Johnson Museum, Cornell, 1976.

VI Hankenson, Dick. *Trivets.* Bound with a later dated supplement. Maple Plain, MN: author, 1963.

VI ———. *Trivets, Book 1.* Des Moines, IA: Wallace-Homestead, 1972.

VI ———. *Trivets. Old and Re-Pro.* (Or *Trivets, Old and New Reproductions.*) Maple Plain, MN: 1972.

V Hannay, H. Ford, *From Cubits to Size Blocks.* N.p. [CT ?], 1958. Interesting info on "units of the flesh" – thumbs and feet.

HIS Harcum, Cornelia Gaskins. *Roman Cooking Utensils in the Royal Ontario Museum of Archaeology.* N.p. (USA): 1921. Reprint from *American Journal of Archaeology*, Vol. 20, #1, 1921.

GEN Hardyment, Christina. *From Mangle to Microwave. The Mechanization of Household Work.* Oxford, England: Polity Press, 1988.

GEN Harland, Marion [Mary Virginia Hawes Terhune]. *House and Home, A Complete Housewife's Guide.* Philadelphia: Franklin News Co., 1889.

CSTi Harned, Bill & Denise. *Griswold Cast Collectibles.* Edinboro, PA: Globe Printing, 1985. (POB 340, 18412) (conflicting info on Amazon).

CBK Harris, Hester. *Cast Iron Cookbook.* Concord, CA: Nitty Gritty Productions, 1969.

KIT Harrison, Molly. *The Kitchen in History.* NYC: Charles Scribner's, 1972.

IV Haussler, Jon B. *Griswold Muffin Pans.* Atglen, PA: Schiffer, 1997.

GEN Hayden, Dolores. *The Grand Domestic Revolution: A History of Feminist Designs for American Homes, Neighborhoods, and Cities.* Cambridge, MA, & London: The MIT Press, 1981.

XVIII *Hazelcorn's Price Guide to Old Electric Toasters, 1908-1940.* See: Fisher, Charles.

GEN Heath, Adrian, Ditte Heath, and Aage Lund Jensen. *300 Years of Industrial Design: Function, Form, Technique 1700-2000.* NYC: Watson-Guptill Pub., 2000.

VIII Heckmann, Manfred, *Korkenzieher.* Berlin, Germany: Fasanen Editions, 1979.

VIII ———. *Corkscrews: An Introduction to Their Appreciation.* San Francisco, CA: The Wine Appreciation Guild, 1996. (155 Connecticut St., 94107)

VII Hedges, A. A. C. *Bottles and Bottle Collecting.* Aylesbury, England: Shire Books, reprint 2002.

X Hempel, Gudrun. *Herd- und Küchengerät aus der Metallsammlung des Österreichischen Museums für Volkskunde.* Vienna, Austria: Das Museum, 1989. Hearth Tools and utensils and metalworking.

Henry, Rosemary – See: Wetherill, Phyllis.

CBK Herman, Judith, & Marguerite Shallett Herman. *The Cornucopia: Being a Kitchen Entertainment and Cook Book ... 1390-1899.* NYC: Harper & Row, 1973. A salmagundi of recipes, folklore, & tidbits.

GEN Herrick, Christine Terhune. *Kitchen Experience.* NY: National Enamelling & Stamping Co., 1903. Cooking hints.

I Heuring, Jerry & Elaine. *Keen Kutter. Illustrated Price Guide.* Paducah, KY: Collector Books, 1984.

CER Hill, Ozella, & D. L. Hill. *Sleepy Eye Update.* Tulsa, OK: author, 1979. Stoneware bottles. See: Meugniot, E. (POB 50415, zip 74150)

INV Hindle, Brooke, & Steven Lubar. *Engines of Change: The American Industrial Revolution 1790-1860.* Washington D.C.: Smithsonian Institution, 1986.

VII Hine, Thomas. *The Total Package. The Evolution and Secret Meanings of Boxes, Bottles, Cans, and Tubes.* NY: Little Brown, 1994. From the advertising psych viewpoint.

IV Hipp, Hans. *Lebzelten, Wachsstöcke, Votivgaben: Handwerk un Brauch.* Pfaffenhofenn, Germany: W. Ludwig, 1983. Carved wood cookie molds, etc., in Bavaria.

INV Hiscox, Garner Dexter. *Mechanical Movements; ...Commencing with a Rudimentary Description of the Early Known Mechanical Powers...to the Present Time.* NYC: Munn & Co., 1899.

XVIII Hofmann, Andrés Alfaro. *Mecanització. Una Història de L'Electrodomèstic.* Valenciana, Col. Lecció Alfaro Hofmann. València, Spain: Generalitat Valenciana, Conselleria de Cultura, Educacio I Ciencia, 1995. Exhibit of domestic mechanization, history of electrical appliances, curated by Mr. Hofmann from his collection. Has English translation.

GEN Holloway, Laura C. *The Hearthstone; or, Life [at] Home, a Household Manual.* N.p., 1883.

GEN Hooker, Richard J. *Food & Drink in America, [a] History.* Indianapolis & NY: Bobbs-Merril[l], 1981.

GEN Hosley, William. *The Japan Idea: Art and Life [in] Victorian America.* Catalog of exhibit in 1990 a[t] Wadsworth Atheneum, Hartford, CT. 1990.

IV Hörandner, Edith. *Model: Geschnitzte forme[n] für Lebkuchen, Spekulatius und Springerle[.]* Munich, Germany: Callwey, 1982. Cooki[e] molds for Lebkuchen, etc.

XVIII Hospitalier, Édouard, with additions by C. J[.] Wharton. *Domestic Electricity for Amateurs[.]* London, NY: E. & F. N. Spon, 1885. Translated from French with additions by Wharton[.] Electric household appliances.

GEN Hotra, Lynda McCurdy. *Better Quality: A[n] Illustrated History of the Lisk Mfg. Co[.]* Canandaigua, NY: Ontario County Historical Society, 1987.

XVIII *Hotwire: the Newsletter of the Toaster Museum Foundation.* Portland, OR: The Foundation, 1997-. (The Foundation is now located at: 1003 Carlton Ave., Ste B, Charlottesville, VA, 22902-5974. E-mail: eric@toaster.org. Web site: www.toaster.org)

X, XI Hough, Walter. *Collection of Heating and Lighting Utensils in the U.S. National Museum* [Smithsonian]. Washington, DC: GPO, 1928.

GEN *House & Garden.* NYC: Conde Nast Pub., 1901-1921+. Monthly. See: *These Simple Things.*

XVIII House, Kurt D. *Antique Mechanical Fans.* San Antonio, TX: Trade Routes Antiques/The Fan Man, Inc., 2nd rev. ed. 199-. (218 Country Wood Dr., San Antonio, TX, 78216-1607. E-mail: cowboyhous@aol.com)

GEN *House Furnishing Review.* NYC: © 1890-1930. Trade journal for buyers in hardware stores & home furnishings departments.

IV Hueg, Henry & Co. *Book of Designs for Bakers & Confectioners.* Catalog. NYC: 1896.

IV Hueg, Henry & Co. *The Little Confectioner.* NYC: 1921.

XVI Hughes, Therle. *Sweetmeat & Jelly Glasses.* Guildford, England: Lutterworth Press, 1981.

GEN Hume, Ivor Noël. *Historical Archaeology.* NYC: Alfred A. Knopf, 1968.

XVIII Hunter, Allan. *A Comparison of Electric Toasters.* Thesis for Univ. of Utah, Dept. of Electrical Engineering. [Salt Lake City]: 1948. Not a collector book, but useful.

VII Husfloen, Kyle, ed. *Black Americana Price Guide.* Dubuque, IA: Antique Trader Books, 1996.

GEN Hutchinson, Elsie Lillian. *The Housefurnishings Department – Department Store Merchandise Manual.* NYC: NYU, The Ronald Press Co., 1918, 1922.

GEN Hutson, N. Joan. *Heirlooms from the Kitchen.* Huntsville, AL: Dajan Enterprises, 1985. (1908 Waxleaf Garden S.E., 35803-1232)

IV, XV *Ice Screamer, The.* Newsletter for The Ice Screamers organization for collectors of ice cream and soda fountain memorabilia and "hardware." (Duvall Sollers, POB 465, Warrington, PA 18976. E-mail: smoothsail@aol.com; Web site: www.icescreamers.com)

IV   *In Praise of Hot Liquors: The Study of Chocolate, Coffee and Tea-Drinking 1600-1850.* York, England: York Civic Trust, 1995. Catalog of an exhibition. (Fairfax House, Castlegate, YO1 1RN)

VII   *Indiana Cabinets, including Hoosier, Sellers, McDougall, Napanee, Etc.* Reprint of catalog pages. Gas City, IN: L-W Books, 1997.

Ingram, Arthur W. W. *Dairying Bygones.* Aylesbury, England: Shire Books, 198-?

International Cooks' Catalogue – See: Beard, James, intro.

VII   *International Match Safe Association.* Quarterly newsletter. (George Sparacio, POB 791, Malaga, NJ 08328. E-mail: IMSAoc@aol.com)

International Society of Apple Parer Enthusiasts. Newsletter. (Gerald W. Laverty, 735 Cedarwood Terr., Apt. 735B, Rochester, NY 14609. Web site: www.collectoronline.com/clubs/ISAPE/)

VII   Ito, Teiji. *Wabi, Sabi, Suki: The Essence of Japanese Beauty.* Hiroshima, Japan: Mazda Motor Co., 1993.

IV   Jaburg Brothers. *Best of Everything for Bakers.* NYC: 1908. Catalog.

VII   Jacobs, Sharon Ray. *String along with Me: A Collector's Guide to Stringholders with Prices.* Gas City, IN: L-W Book Sales, 1996.

INV   James, P., & N. Thorpe, *Ancient Inventions.* NY: Ballantine, 1995.

MET   Jarrett, John. *A Treatise upon Tin Plate Manufacture in the United States.* [U.S.]: American Tinned Plate Association, 1884.

GEN   Jekyll, Gertrude, & Sydney R. Jones. *Old English Household Life: Some Accounts of Cottage Objects and Country Folk.* London: B. T. Batsford, 1933. Various country bygones.

XVI   *Jelly Jammers Journal.* Jelly Jammers club. (Deena Caniff, 1223 Oak Grove Ave., Steubenville, OH 43952. E-mail: emshaw@in.net)

GEN   Jenkins, J. Geraint. *Traditional Country Craftsmen.* London: Routledge & Kegan Paul, 1965. Great Britain stuff.

MET   Jenkins, Paul. *Twenty by Fourteen: A History of the South Wales Tinplate Industry, 1700-1961.* Llandysul, Wales: Gomer, 1995.

V   Jewell, Brian. *Veteran Scales & Balances.* Tunbridge Wells, England: Midas Books, 1978.

MET   John, W. D., & Anne Simcox. *Pontypool and Usk Japanned Wares, with the Early History of the Iron and Tinplate Industries at Pontypool.* Newport, England: Ceramic Book Co., 1953; 1966.

VII   Johnson, Donald-Brian. *The Chase Era: 1933 and 1942 Catalogs of the Chase Brass & Copper Co.* Atglen: Schiffer, n.d.

MET   Johnson, Frances. *Aluminum Giftware.* Atglen: Schiffer, 1996.

GEN   ———. *Kitchen Antiques.* Atglen: Schiffer, 1996.

GEN   Johnson, Lawrence A. *Over the Counter and on the Shelf.* Rutland, VT: Charles C. Tuttle Co., 1961.

XV   Jones, Joseph C., Jr. *American Ice Boxes.* Humble, TX: Jobeco Books, 1981.

INV   Jones, Stacy V. *Invention's Necessity is Not the Mother of Patents Ridiculous and Sublime.* NYC: Quadrangle, 1973; London: Allen & Unwin, 1975.

CAT   Joseph, S. Co. *Hotel, Bakery & Restaurant Supplies .... Catalog.* NYC: © 1927.

VII   *Journal of the Antique Metalware Society, The* yearly journal; and *Base Thoughts,* the newsletter. Antique Metalware Society, POB 63, Honiton. Devonshire, EX14 1HP England. Lots of technical stuff included, for those who want to know important background facts.

GEN   *Journal of Early Southern Decorative Arts, The.* Biannual publication of MESDA. Winston-Salem, NC: MESDA. (POB 10310, zip 27108)

GEN   *Journal of Domestic Appliances.* London: Sewell, 1881- . Formerly was *Sewing Machine Gazette,* 1874-1881.

VIII   *Just for Openers.* Newsletter of collectors' organization. Contact John Stanley, POB 64, Chapel Hill, NC 27514. Web site: www.just foropeners.org/. Emphasis on beer & soda adv'g. openers & corkscrews.

WWW   Kaiser, Laura Fisher, Michael B. Kaiser, and Pierre Omidyar. *The Official eBay Guide to Buying, Selling and Collecting Just About Anything.* Fireside Press, 1999.

KIT   Kalman, Bobbie. *The Kitchen.* Crabtree Pub. Co., 1990. Historic Communities Series. For children.

INV   Kane, Joseph Nathan. *Necessity's Child: The Story of Walter Hunt, American's Forgotten Inventor.* Jefferson, NC & London: McFarland & Co., Inc. Publishers, 1997. Hunt patented the safety pin, a great fountain pen, the first sewing machine, and a knife sharpener. (Box 611, zip 28640)

GEN   Kate-von Eicken, Brigitte ten. *Kuchengerate um 1900.* Stuttgart: Walter Hadecke Verlag, [1979?]. (7252 Weil der Stadt, Stuttgart, Germany)

CAT   Katzinger Co., Edward. *Katzinger Co.* Price List 53. Chicago: 1940.

XVIII   Katzwedel, Lothar. *Elektro-Haushaltgeräte.* Leipzig, Germany: Fachbuchverlag, 1961. Domestic electric appliances, etc.

MET   Kauffman, Henry J. *American Copper & Brass.* NYC: Thomas Nelson & Sons, 1968. Reprint. NYC: Crown, 1979.

MET   ———. *Early American Ironware, Cast & Wrought.* Rutland, VT: Charles E. Tuttle, 1966.

X   ———. *The American Fireplace: Chimneys, Mantelpieces, Fireplaces & Accessories.* NYC: Galahad Books, 1972.

X   Kauffman, Henry J., & Quentin H. Bowers. *Early American Andirons and Other Fireplace Accessories.* NYC: Thomas Nelson, 1974.

VIII   Kaye, Edward R. *The Handbook of Beer Advertising Openers and Corkscrews.* Sanibel Island, FL: Kaye, 1984. (968 Greenwood Ct., zip 33957)

VII   *"Keeping Abreast."* Quarterly newsletter of American Collectors of Infant Feeders. Contact: JoAnn Gifford, Sec'y., 1849 Ebony Dr., York, PA 17402-4706. Website: www.acif.org/home.htm

GEN   Ketels, Sophus. *Fachwissenschaftliche Studie der Haus- und Küchengeräte-, Glas-, Porzellan-, Steingut-, Eisen- und Gusswaren-Branche.* Erfurt, Germany: 1909. House-

GEN   hold & kitchen utensils & cookware, glass, ceramic, stoneware, etc.

GEN   Kellogg, Ella Ervilla Eaton. *Science in the Kitchen*. Battle Creek, MI: Good Health Pub. Co., 1910. First published in 1893.

VI   Kelly, Rob Roy, and James Ellwood, in conjunction with Shelburne Museum, Vt. *Trivets & Stands*. Lima, OH: Golden Era Publications, 1990. Thousands pictured. (POB 934, zip 45802)

XVII   Kennedy, Phillip D. *Hoosier Cabinets*. Indianapolis, IN, [1990?]. (9256 Holyoke Ct., zip 46268)

CSTi   *Kettles 'n Cookware Newsletter*. Bimonthly. (David G. Smith, ed. 11918 2nd St, POB B, Perrysburg, NY, 14129. E-mail: panman@ utec.net; Web site: www.panman.com)

IV   Kevill-Davies, Sally. *Jelly Moulds*. Guildford, England: Lutterworth Press, 1983.

MET   Kilbride, Richard J. *Art Deco Chrome, The Chase Era, Vol. I*. Stamford, CT: Jo-D Books, 1988.

MET   ———. *Art Deco Chrome Book #2, Collectors Guide: Industrial Design in the Chase Era*. Stamford, CT: Jo-D Books, 1992. (Chase Brass & Copper.)

IV   Kindig, Paul E. *Butter Prints & Molds*. West Chester, PA: Schiffer, 1986. Near perfect: well illustrated, info, opinions & history.

I   King, Alan. *Corn Huskers & Shellers, 1900-1953*. [Canada?]

    Kitchen Collectibles News – See: Franklin, L. C.

GEN   Klever, Ulrich. *Alte Kuchengerate, Backen und Kochen*. Munich: Wilhelm Heyne Verlag, 1979. Cooking & baking utensils & molds.

INV   Knight, Edward H. *American Mechanical Dictionary*. 2 vols. NYC: J. B. Ford & Co., 1874; NYC: Riverside Press, 1876. Terrific!

INV   ———. *The Practical Dictionary of Mechanics, 1874-1877*. Supplement. Boston: Houghton, Mifflin, 1884.

GEN   Königer, Maribel. *Küchengerät des 20. Jahrhunderts. Kochen mit Stil und Styling*. Germany: Klinkhardt & Biermann, 1994. 20th century kitchen style & inventions. Some toasters.

GEN   *KOOKS*, newsletter of Kollectors of Old Kitchen Stuff. (Contact with SASE: Carol Bohn, 501 Market St., Mifflinburg, PA 17844)

VII   Koren, Leonard. *Wabi-Sabi for Artists, Designers, Poets & Philosophers*. Berkeley, CA: Stone Bridge Press, 1994.

VII   *Kovels' Bottles Price List*. Ralph & Terry Kovel, comp. 11th ed., 2000.

GEN   *Kovels' on Antiques and Collectibles*. Newsletter. The Kovels have earned their fame with years of hard work! (Ralph & Terry Kovel POB 420235, Palm Coast, FL 32142-0235)

IV   Kronberger, Hanna Frentzen. *Die alte Kunst der süssen Sachen; Backformen und Waffeleisen vergangener Jahrhunderte*. Hamburg, Germany: Broschek, 1959. Cookie molds & waffle irons.

GEN   Kruger, Laura. *Vom Zauber Alten Hausgerats*. Freiburg im Breisgau: Rombach & Co., 1981.

GEN   *Küchengeräte*. Basel, Germany: Museum für Völkerkunde und Schweizerisches Museum für Volkskunde Basel, 1963.

IV   Kulturgeschichtiches Museum Osnabrück. *Festliches Backwerk im Jahreslauf: Osnabrück 20. Jahrhundert*. Osnabrück, Germany: the Museum, 1975. Bake molds & history.

VII   Kurlansky, Mark. *Salt: A World History – the magnificent story of how a common rock has shaped civilization*. NYC: Walker & Co., 2001; London, UK: Jonathan Cape, 2002. 482 pages with illustrations.

IV   Kürth, Herbert, & Joachim Petri. *Kunst der Model: Kulturgeschichte der Back- und Hohlformen*. Gütersloh, Germany: Prisma Verlag, 1981. European cookie molds as folk art & various other molds.

GEN   Kurtis, Wilma, & Anita Gold. *Prairie Recipes and Kitchen Antiques*. Chicago: Bonus Books, 1992. Frontier cookery.

XIV   Kvetko, Edward, & Douglas Congdon-Martin. *Coffee Antiques*. Atglen: Schiffer, 2000.

PAP   *Ladies' Home Journal*. Monthly. Philadelphia: Curtis Pub. Co., 1887-1920 consulted.

XVIII   Lafollette, Marcel C., & Jeffery K. Stine, eds. *Technology and Choice*. Chicago, IL: University of Chicago Press, 1991. Contains plug article by Fred Schroeder.

CAT   Lalance & Grosjean Mfg. Co. *Catalog*. NYC: 1890. 360 pp of assorted utensils.

MET   *Lamprecht Collection of Cast Iron Art, The*. Small catalog. Birmingham, AL: American Cast Iron Pipe Co., 1941. Famous collection that needs a better book.

XVIII   Lancaster, Maud. *Electric Cooking, Heating & Cleaning*. NYC: D. Van Nostrand, 1914.

X   Landis, Henry Kinzer. *Early Kitchens of the Pennsylvania Germans. A Paper Read in 1935*. Norristown, PA: Pennsylvania German Society, 1939.

GEN   Lantz, Louise K. *Old American Kitchenware, 1725-1925*. NYC: Thomas Nelson, 1970. Separate small price guide booklets were updated periodically by author, Hydes, MD.

GEN   Larkin, Jack. *The Reshaping of Everyday Life, 1790-1840*. NYC: Harper & Row, 1988. By the historian at Old Sturbridge Village in MA.

CER   Lasansky, Jeannette. *Central Pennsylvania Redware Pottery 1780-1904*. Lewisburg, PA: Union County Oral Traditions Project, 1979; reprint 1989.

CER   Lasansky, J. *Made of Mud. Stoneware Potteries in Central Pennsylvania, 1831-1929*. Lewisburg, PA: Oral Traditions, 1979. All Lasansky's books are extremely informative & attractive; copious duotone illustrations.

MET   ———. *To Cut, Piece, & Solder. Work of the Rural Pennsylvania Tinsmith 1778-1908*. Lewisburg, PA: Oral Traditions, 1982.

MET   ———. *To Draw, Upset, & Weld. Work of the Pennsylvania Rural Blacksmith 1742-1935*. Lewisburg, PA: Oral Traditions, 1980.

VII   ———. *Willow, Oak & Rye. Basket Traditions in Pennsylvania*. Lewisburg, PA: Oral Traditions, 1979.

IV   *Lebzeltmodel aus dem Liszt Ferenc Múzeum, Sopron, und dem Burgenländischen Landesmuseum*. [Austria]: 1980. Catalog for Hungary & Austria exhibitions of cookie molds.

VII   Lechler, Doris Anderson. *Children's Glass Dishes, China, and Furniture. Vol. II*. Paducah, KY: Collector Books, 1986.

VII   Lechner, Mildred, & Ralph Lechner. *The World of Salt Shakers*. Paducah, KY: Collector Books, 1992. Not the kitsch figurals.

GEN   Lee, Darlene. *Thing-a-Ma-Jigs: a Book of 18th Century Necessities and Niceties*. Charlotte, MI: author, 1988.

GEN   ———. *What-Cha-Ma-Callits: More 18th Century Necessities and Niceties*. Charlotte, MI: Eaton Graphics for author, 1988.

CER   Leibowitz, Joan. *Yellow Ware. The Transitional Ceramic*. Exton, PA: Schiffer, 1985.

XII   LeMieux, Linda D. *A History in Pots and Pans, 1674-1800*. [Deerfield, MA]: Historic Deerfield Fellowship Program, 1974.

GEN   Lena, Birte, & Günter Herburger. *Schöner kochen: in 52 Arten*. Düsseldorf: Verlag Eremiten-Presse, 1974. 52 works of art showing kitchen utensils.

GEN   Lepistö, Vuokko. *Joko Teillä on primuskeitin? kotitalousteknologian saatavuus ja tarjonta Helsingissä 1800-luvun puolivälistä 1910-luvun lopulle*. Helsinki: SHS, 1994. Finnish with English summary. Finnish utensils.

VIII   Lesser, Charles. *Guidebook to Figural Bottle Openers*. Harrington, DE: 1953, c.1990s. (Sugar Stick Rd., zip 19952)

XVI   Leybourne, Douglas M., Jr. *The Collector's Guide to Old Fruit Jars, Redbook #7... 7th ed.; 8th ed.; 9th ed*. North Muskegon, MI: author, 1994; 1997, 2001. Mr. Leybourne is carrying on from six amazing editions done by Alice Creswick. (POB 5417, zip 49445)

XVI   ———. *The Fruit Jar Works, Vol. I; Vol. II*. North Muskegon, MI: author, back in print 1996. (Box 5417, zip 49445)

GEN   Lifshey, Earl. *The Housewares Story: A History of the American Housewares Industry*. Chicago, IL: Nat'l Housewares Mfrs. Assoc., 1973. An incredibly useful trade-sponsored history with copious illustrations.

XVIII   Lincoln, Edwin Stoddard, & Paul C. Smith. *The Electric Home. A Standard Ready Reference Book*. NYC: Electric Home Pub., 1933; 1934; 1936.

VII   Lindenberger, Jan. *Black Memorabilia for the Kitchen, a Handbook & Price Guide*. Atglen, PA: Schiffer Pub., 1992.

GEN   Lindenberger, Jan. *The 50s & 60s Kitchen: A Collector's Handbook & Price Guide*. Atglen, PA: Schiffer Pub., 1994; 1999.

GEN   ———. *Fun Kitchen Collectibles. A Handbook & Price Guide*. Atglen, PA: Schiffer Pub., 1996.

MET   Lindsay, J. Seymour. *Iron & Brass Implements of the English & American House*. Boston: Medici Society, 1927. New edition. Bass River, MA: C. Jacobs, 1964.

GEN   Lord, Priscilla Sawyer, & Daniel J. Foley. *The Folk Arts and Crafts of New England*. NYC: Chilton, 1965.

VII   Lupton, E. & J. A. Miller. *The Bathroom, the Kitchen, and the Aesthetics of Waste*. New expanded edition. Princeton Architectural Press, 1996.

CAT   *L. H. Mace & Co. 1883 Catalog*. Facsimile. Princeton, NJ: American Historical Catalog Collection, Pyne Press, 1971. Woodenware; meat safes.

   Mc-names – See: in strict letter-by-letter alphabetical order.

INV   Macdonald, Anne L. *Feminine Ingenuity: Women and Invention in America*. NYC: Ballantine Books, 1992. Author is herself a patent-holder.

VIII   MacLean, Ron. *Common Corkscrews V. Star Brown Mfg Co*. Mississauga, Ontario, CAN, 1994. Also #I, 198-; #II, 1989; #III, 1990; #IV, 199-. (Ron MacLean, 4201 Sunflower Dr., L5L 2L4)

VIII   ———. *A Guide to Canadian Corkscrew Patents*. Mississauga, Ontario: R. MacLean, 1985.

XIV   MacMillan, Joseph E. *The MacMillan Index of Antique Coffee Mills*. Marietta, GA: author, 1995. Definitive, 1,322 pp book primarily of patent history, with biographies and copious illustrations & photographs. (657 Old Mountain Rd., zip 30064)

MET   *Made of Iron*. Catalog of an exhibition, Sept.-Dec., 1966. Dominique de Menil, Curator; Stephen V. Grancsay, Introduction. Houston, TX: Univ. of St. Thomas Art Department, 1966. I've treasured this profusely-illustrated, impeccably-written catalog for over 30 years.

GEN   *Maine Antique Digest*. Still wonderful in the real & virtual worlds. (POB 1429, Waldoboro, ME 04572-1429. Phone: 800-752-8521. Web site: www.maineantiquedigest.com)

GEN   *Maloney's Antiques & Collectibles Resource Directory*. 6th edition published by Krause, 2001. (Maloney's, POB 2049, Frederick, MD 217-1049. Web site: www.maloneysonline.com/)

MET   Manning, Bowman & Co. *Perfection Granite Ironware. Decorated Pearl Agateware*. Catalog. Meriden, CT: © 1892.

IV   Marque C. C. *Fabrique Spéciale de Moules en Etain*. Catalog. Paris: 1900.

GEN   Marshall, Jo. *Kitchenware. Collecting for Tomorrow*. London: BPC Publishers, 1976.

CBK   Marshall, Mrs. A. B. *Cookery Book*. London: © 1900. 45k printed. Most of it dates to © 1887.

CBK   ———. *Larger Cookery Book of Extra Recipes*. 10k printed. London: © 1902.

XV   Marshall, Mrs. A. B. *The Book of Ices. Including Cream & Water Ices, Sorbets, Mousses, Iced Soufflés*. 14th ed. London: © 1900-1902.

IV   Martin, Andreas. *Pfefferküchler: seltenes Handwerk in Sachsen; mid...Back- und Anleitungsbuch für die Pfefferküchlerei aus dem Jahre 1845*. Dresden, Germany: Sächsisches Druck- und Verlagschaus, 1996. Bread & Gingerbread molds.

CBK   Mason, Charlotte. *The Ladies' Assistant for Regulating & Supplying the Table*. London: Printed for J. Walter, 1787.

XV   Masters, Thomas. *A Short Treatise Concerning Some Patent Inventions for the Production of Ice, Artificial Cold, etc. Also the Newly Improved Culinary Utensils*. London: 1850.

   Martin, Jane – See: Baker, Eric.

CAT   Matthai-Ingram Co. *Illustrated Catalogue of Sheet Metal Goods. Catalog 41*. Baltimore: © 1890.

GEN   Matthews, Mary Lou. *American Kitchen Collectibles*. Gas City, IN: L-W Promotions, 1973. Some good catalog pix, negligable text.

GEN   Matwiejczyk, Marian Ann. *American Kitchen Utensils for Food Preparation and Their Progressional Development, 1876-1917.* Cornell University Master's thesis, 1982.

V   *Mauchline Ware Collectors Club Newsletter.* (Barry Kottler, Unit 17, Romsey Industrial Estate, Greatbridge Road, Romsey Hantshire S051 HR, England)

XVIII   Mauzy, Barbara. *Bakelite in the Kitchen.* Atglen: Schiffer, 1998; 2nd ed. 2001.

GEN   ———. *The Complete Book of Kitchen Collecting.* Atglen, PA: Schiffer, 1997. 1920s-1950s.

VII   Mauzy, Barbara. *Depression Era Kitchen Shakers.* Atglen: Schiffer, 1998.

XVIII   *Maytag Collector's Club* newsletter. (Nate Stoller, 960 Reynolds Ave., Ripon, CA 95366. E-mail: multimotor@aol.com; Web site: wwwmaytagclub.com)

CER   McAllister, Lisa S., & John L. Michel. *Collecting Yellow Ware, an Identification & Value Guide.* Paducah, KY: Collector Books, 1993.

XVI   McCann, Jerry, comp. & ed. *The Guide to Collecting Fruit Jars. Fruit Jar Annual, 1996; 1997; 1998; 2002.* Chicago, IL: Phoenix Press, 1996-98; 2001. We hope lib infinitum! 100s of jars with values; clear drawings; readable articles; collector directory; ad space for collectors & dealers. (5003 W. Berwyn Ave., zip 60630-1501. Web site: www.antiquebotl.com/mccann.htm)

CSTi   McNerney, Kathryn. *Antique Iron. Identification & Values.* Paducah, KY: Collector Books, 1984.

XI   Meckley, Jim. *Flue Covers.* Paducah, KY: Collector Books, 1998.

CBK   Mendelson, Anne. *Stand Facing the Stove. The Story of the Women Who Gave America "The Joy of Cooking."* NYC: Henry Holt & Co., 1996. Author of this yummy book on the Rombauers claims America is a "society where cookbooks are replacing cooking."

X, XI   Mercer, Henry C. *The Bible in Iron.* Doylestown, PA: Bucks County Historical soc., © 1914. 3rd edition with additions by Joseph E. Sandford, 1961. Cast iron 5-, 6- and 10-plate stoves, also firebacks.

MET   *Metalwork in Early America – Copper & Its Alloys; Selections from the Winterthur Collection.* Wappingers Falls, NY: Antique Collectors Club, 1996.

MET   *Metal Worker, Plumber & Steam Fitter, The.* NYC: 1882. Trade journal. Assorted dates consulted.

CER   Meugniot, Elinor. *Old Sleepy Eye.* Tulsa, OK: author, 1973. Stoneware bottles. See also: Hill, Ozella. (POB 50415, zip 71450)

GEN   *MidAtlantic Antiques Magazine, The.* (P.O. Box 908, Henderson, NC: 27536-0908. Phone: 800-326-3894)

I   Miles, Elizabeth B. *The English Silver Pocket Nutmeg Grater; A Collection of Fifty Examples from 1693 to 1816.* [Shaker Heights?] OH, 1966. The fancy ones carried by the gentry.

VII   *Milkroute, The.* Monthly newsletter of National Assoc. of Milk Bottle Collectors. (Box 105, Blooming Grove, NY 10914. Or, 4 Ox Bow Rd, Westport, CT 06880. E-mail: milkroute@yahoo.com)

I   Mills, Robert. *Nutcrackers.* Aylesbury, England: Shire Books, 199-.

XVIII   Miller, Gary, & K. M. Scotty Mitchell. *Price Guide to Collectible Kitchen Appliances.* Des Moines, IA: Wallace-Homestead, 1991.

GEN   Miller, Robert William. *American Primitives.* Des Moines, IA: Wallace-Homestead, 1972. Collection of Museum of Appalachia, Norris, TN.

XV   Mills, Thomas & Bro. *Ice Cream Manufacturers' Equipment. Catalog 31.* Philadelphia: © 1915. A larger one dates to 1930.

VII   Milton, Giles. *Nathaniel's Nutmeg: Or, the True and Incredible Adventures of the Spice Trader Who Changed the Course of History.* London: Hodder & Stoughton, Ltd., and Sceptre Press, 1999; NYC: Farrar, Strauss & Giroux, 1999. (Title slightly different in UK.) 400 pages. (And no mention of nutmeg graters or spice boxes in the index!)

   Mitchell, James R., ed. – See: *Antique Metalware.*

IV   Mockershoff, Barbara, Achim Hubel, & Hermann Reidel. *Das Werk der fleissigen Bienen: geformtes Wachs aus einer alten Lebzelterei.* Munich, Germany: Schnell & Steiner, 1984. Cookie molds of carved wood.

I   Moffet, Jim. *American Corn Huskers. A Patent History.* Sunnyvale, CA: Off Beat Books, 1996. 262 patent drawings, patentor index. (1345 Poplar Ave., zip 94087)

CAT   *Montgomery Ward 1895 Catalogue* reprint. NYC: Dover Publications, 1970s.

MET   Moore, Jan. *Antique Enameled Ware.* Paducah, KY: Collector Books, 1975.

MET   Moore, N. Hudson. *Old Pewter, Brass, Copper & Sheffield Plate.* Garden City, NY: Garden City Pub. Co., 1933.

PAP   Morse, Sidney. *Household Discoveries: An Encyclopedia of Practical Recipes and Processes.* Petersburg, NY: The Success Co., 1909.

GEN   Müller, Renate, & Gerhard Kaufmann. *Licht und Feuer im ländlichen Haushalt: Lichtquellen und Haushaltsgeräte.* Hamburg, Germany: Altonaer Museum, 1994. Lighting, hearth cooking, utensils, etc.

GEN   Mumford, Lewis. *The Myth of the Machine.* NYC: Harcourt Brace, 1966.

IV   Münchner Stadtmuseum. *Wachszieher und Lebzelter im alten München.* Munich: Germany, 1981. Exhibition catalog of cookie molds, wax figures, etc.

MET   Mundey, Alfred Holley. *Tin and the Tin Industry.* London: I. Pitman, 1926.

GEN   Museum fur Volkerkunde und Schweizerisches Museum fur Volkskunde Basel. *Catalog.* Basel, Switzerland: Das Museum, 1963. 32 pp, illustrated.

GEN   Museum of Modern Art. *Useful Objects in Wartime: Fifth Annual Exhibition of Useful Objects Under $10.00.* NYC: MOMA, 1943.

GEN   Mussey, Barrows, ed. *Yankee Life by Those Who Lived It.* NYC: Alfred Knopf, 1947. Excerpts from journals, autobiographies, letters, etc.

GEN   Myerson, Jeremy, & Sylvia Katz. *Kitchenware. Conran Design Guides.* NYC: Van Nostrand Reinhold, 1990. The last 50+ years of kitchen collectibles from the industrial design view; includes designer bios.

NV   Nagler, Bernard. *Patent Pending*. London & Los Angeles, CA: Price Stern, 1968.

GEN   Narumo, Kinjiro. *Domestic Japan*. Yokohama: Yokohama Seishi Bunsha, 1895. Illustrated everyday utensils in Japan.

XII   *National Graniteware Society Newsletter*. Quarterly. (Contact: James Cox, POB 9248, Cedar Rapids, IA 52409-9248. E-mail: info@graniteware.org. Web site: www.graniteware.org)

I   *National Reamer Collectors Association* quarterly newsletter. (Larry Branstad, 405 Benson Rd N., Frederic, WI 54837)

IV   Neuber, Wolf. *Das hölzerne Bilderbuch: Lebzeltermodeln: mit traditionellen Lebkuchenrezepten*. Vienna: Brandstätter, 1997. Cookie molds & woodcarving, plus ginger cookery.

XVIII Newman, Geoffrey, & Adrian Forty. *British Design (1915-1939)*. [England] Milton Keynes: Open Univ. Press, 1975. A survey of design, and a study of the development of the "electric home" in the UK between WWI and WWII.

I   Newman, S. F. *Some Notes on the Nutmeg Graters Used in Folk Medicine*. Reprint from *Folklore*, Vol. 54. London: W. Glaisher, 1943.

VII   Nichols, Harold. *McCoy Cookie Jars from the First to the Last*. Ames, IA: Nichols Wrestling Products, Inc., 1992. For those wrestling with the important question: To eat a cookie, or not to eat. (POB 1067, zip 50010)

VII   Nishida, Masayoshi. *Rikyu to Basho: "Wabi" to "Sabi" No Genryu*. Tokyo, Japan: Ofusha, 1975. Supposed to be best book on the Japanese aesthetic of the imperfect.

CBK   Norman, Sandra J. *Vintage Cookbooks & Advertising Leaflets*. Schiffer, 1998.

CAT   North Bros. Mfg. Co. *Dainty Dishes for All the Year Round*, by Mrs. S. T. Rorer. Philadelphia: 1912. Cookbooklet with catalog pages. See also Ward, Joe.

VII   *Novelty Salt & Pepper Shakers Club Newsletter*. (Lulu Fuller, POB 677388, Orlando, FL 32667-7388. E-mail: jlfuller1@aol.com)

I   *Nutcracker Collectors' Club newsletter*. (Susan Otto, 12204 Fox Run Dr., Chesterland, OH 44026. E-mail: nutsuc@core.com)

XVIII Nye, David. *Electrifying America: Social Meanings of a New Technology*. Cambridge, MA: MIT Press, 1988.

GEN   Oakley, Ann. *The Sociology of Housework*. London: Martin Robertson, 1974.

GEN   *Objects for Preparing Food*. Exhibit catalog, with intros by curator Sandra Zimmerman, & Mimi Shorr (Sheraton). Washington, DC: Renwick Gallery, 1972. Done in conjunction with the Museum of Contemporary Crafts of the American Crafts Council, NYC.

CBK   O'Connor, Hyla. *The Early American Cookbook*. NYC: Rutledge Press, 1974. Includes utensils and food.

GEN   Oehme, Ursula, Brigitte Richter, & Katrin Sohl. *Eigener Herd ist Goldes wert: Küche und Kochen in Leipzig*. Leipzig: Stadtgeschichtliches Museum, 1995. Kitchens & cookery.

INV   *Official Gazette*. Washington, DC: U.S. Patent Office, 1872 -.

GEN   *Ohio Tool Box*. Quarterly newsletter of Ohio Tool Collectors Assoc. (George E. Woodard, POB 261, London, OH 43140-0261)

VII   *Old Bottle Club of Great Britain*. Quarterly magazine of a club that is part of an umbrella organization: BBR. (BBR, c/o Elsecar Heritage Centre, Nr Barnsley S, Yorkshire S74 8HJ)

XVIII *Old Road Home*. Quarterly magazine for the Old Appliance Club. (Gina Thompson, POB 65, Ventura, CA 93002. E-mail: jes@west. net. Web site: www.theoldapplianceclub. com)

VIII O'Leary, Fred. *Corkscrews: 1000 Patented Ways to Open a Bottle*. Atglen, PA: Schiffer Pub. Co., 1996. Many photos.

VIII Olive, Guy. *Tire-Bouchon Francais Brevets 1828-1974*. France: 1995.

VIII *Opener*. Newsletter of Figural Bottle Opener Collectors. (Sec'y.: Mary Link, 1774 N. 675E., Kewanna, IN 46939. Web site: http://home. att.net/~fbocclub/clubinfo.htm.

CER   Osgood, Cornelius. *The Jug and Related Stoneware of Bennington*. Rutland, VT: Charles Tuttle, 1971.

IV   Ott, Ernst. *Der Tirggelbäcker*. Basel, Switzerland: Druck G. Krebs, 1967. Swiss cookie molds, bakeries, etc.

GEN   Palmer, Phyllis. *Domesticity & Dirt. Housewives & Domestic Servants in the U.S., 1920-1945*. Philadelphia, PA: Temple Univ. Press, 1989.

PAP   *Paper and Advertising Collector, The. (P.A.C.)* Monthly. (Denise M. Sater, ed., POB 500, Mt. Joy, PA, 17552. E-mail: pac@engleonline. com and Web site: www.engleonline.com)

PAP   *Paper Collectors' Marketplace*. Monthly. (POB 128-W, Scandinavia, WI 54977-0128. E-mail: pcmpaper@gglbbs.com)

PAP   *Paper Pile Quarterly, The*. (Ada Fitzsimmons, ed. POB 337, San Anselmo, CA 94979. E-mail: apaperpile@aol.com)

VIII Paradi, Joseph C. *French Corkscrew Patents*. Ontario, CAN: author, 1988.

VIII Paradi, Monika. *Cookbook for Corkscrew Collectors*. Mississauga, Ontario, CAN: Canadian Corkscrew Collectors Club, 1991.

CBK   Parloa, Miss Maria. *Kitchen Companion. A Guide for All Who Would Be Good Housekeepers*. Boston: Estes & Lauriat, 1887. By founder of the Original Cooking School in Boston.

XVII Paustenbach, Dennis, & Louise Paustenbach. *Pie Safes*. The Paustenbachs wrote in-depth articles on pie safes for Antique Review, an Ohio monthly. Collection auctioned October 18-19, 1996. See: Garth's Auctions.

GEN   Pearsall, Ronald. *Collecting Mechanical Antiques*. (1830-1880.) Newton Abbot: David & Charles; NYC: Arco, 1973.

MET   Pearse, John Barnard. *A Concise History of the Iron Manufacture of the American Colonists up to the Revolution*. Philadelphia: Allen, Lane & Scott, 1876.

XVI   Pearson, Stanley E. *Just Jarring Around*. Strafford, NH: author, 1971.

CAT   Pearson-Page Co., Ltd. *New Catalogue*. Birmingham & London, England: 1925. Cast brass reproductions of 1000s of household items & decorations.

IV Pechstein, Klaus, & Ursula Ellwart. *Festliches Backwerk: Holzmodel, Formen aus Zinn, Kupfer und Keramik, Waffel-und Oblate-neisen.* Nürnberg, Germany: Das Germanis-chen Nationalmuseums, 1981. Molds & cookie molds of wood, tin, ceramic, etc.

GEN Peet, Louise Jenison, & Lenore E. Sater. *Household Equipment.* NYC: John Wiley & Sons, 1934; 1940.

X Peirce, Josephine H. *Fire on the Hearth. Evolution ... of the Heating-Stove.* Springfield, MA: Pond-Ekberg, 1951.

GEN *Pennsylvania German Folklore Society,* various publications. Allentown, PA: The Society, 1936–.

MET Perry, Evan. *Collecting Antique Metalware.* NYC: Doubleday, 1974.

VIII ———. *Corkscrews & Bottle Openers.* Ayles-bury, England: Shire Pub., 1980; 2nd rev. ed., 1995; 3rd ed., 1998.

VIII Peters, Ferd. *German Corkscrew Patents & Registrations, 1877-1945.* Holland: author, 1996.

VIII ———. *German Corkscrew Patents & Registrations, 1891-1945.* 2nd ed. Holland: author, 1997.

VIII ———. *Mechanical Corkscrews, Their Evolution, Actions, and Patents.* Holland: author, 1999.

INV Petroski, Henry. *The Evolution of Useful Things.* NYC: Vintage Books, 1994.

GEN Peyser, Ethel R. *Cheating the Junk-Pile; the Purchase and Maintenance of Household Equipments.* NY: E. P. Dutton, 1922. A 400-page classic, with illustrations. New enlarged edition, 1930.

GEN Phipps, Frances. *Colonial Kitchens, Their Furnishings, and Their Gardens.* NYC: Hawthorne Books, 1972. Still one of the best.

CAT Pick, Albert & Co. *E-6 General Catalog. Hotel, Restaurant, Bar, Fountain Furnishings & Kitchen Utensils.* Chicago: 1905; 1909. Jobber & wholesaler with 1000s of items.

CAT Pick-Barth Co. *General Catalog E-32.* Chicago: 1929.

V *Piebirds Unlimited.* Newsletter. (Patricia Donaldson, POB 192, Acworth, GA 30301-0192. E-mail: pldonaldson@mindspring.com)

MET Pikul, David T., & Ellen M. Plante. *Collectible Enameled Ware: American & European.* Atglen: Schiffer, 2000.

GEN Pinto, Edward H. *Treen & Other Wooden Bygones.* London: Bell & Hyman, 1969. Reprinted in 1979. Huge & informative, although mostly British & European wares, and many of them now 200-300 years old and not available to collectors.

GEN Plante, Ellen M. *The American Kitchen 1700 to the Present. From Hearth To Highrise.* NYC: Facts on File, 1995.

GEN ———. *Kitchen Collectibles.* Radnor, PA: Wallace-Homestead, 1991.

MET Player, John. *The Origins and Craft of Antique Tin & Tôle.* Available as of 1997 from Christie & Christie Associates. (POB 392, Cookstown, Ontario L0L 1L0, CAN)

VII Polak, Michael. *Bottles: Identification & Price Guide.* Avon Books, 1997; 3rd ed., 2000. No,

not Avon bottles: soda, beer, medicine, po[i]son, ink, and miniatures.

XVIII Poletti, Raffaella. *La Cucina Elettrica: I picc[o] elettrodometici da cucina dalle origini agli an[n] settanta/Small kitchen appliances from the[ir] invention to the seventies.* Milan, Italy: Cruis[i] nallo, 1994. The Phillips project by Alessi.

GEN Porter, Enid M. *The Hearth and the Kitchen.* 1[?] pp guidebook. Cambridge, Eng: Cambridg[e] & County Folk Museum, 1971.

CAT Porter Co., C. B. *Catalogue Illustrating &[?] Describing Plain Enameled Tinware, ... Wate[r] Coolers.* Philadelphia: 1920.

MET Powers, Beatrice F., & Olive Floyd. *Early Amer ican Decorated Tinware.* NYC: Hastings House, 1957.

GEN Prime, Alfred Coxe. *The Arts & Crafts in Philadel phia, Maryland, and South Carolina, 1720-1785.* Topsfield, MA: Walpole Society, 1929. Also: *The Arts & Crafts ... 1786-1800;* 1932.

VIII Pumpenmeier, Klaus. *Deutscher Gebrauch-musterschutz für Korkenzieher, 1891-1945.* Bad Salzuflen, Germany: author, 1997.

TOY Punchard, Lorraine May. *Playtime Kitchen Items & Table Accessories.* Bloomington, MN: author, 8201 Pleasant Ave. So., 55420, 1993.

TOY ———. *Playtime Pottery & Porcelain from the United Kingdom and the United States.* Atglen, PA: Schiffer Pub., 1996.

X Putnam, J. Pickering. *The Open Fireplace in All Ages.* Boston: J. R. Osgood, 1881; Boston: Ticknor & Co., 1886.

VIII *Quarterly Worme.* Newsletter of the Canadian Corkscrew Collectors club. (Milt Becker, One Madison St., E. Rutherford, NJ, 07073. E-mail: clarethous@aol.com)

GEN Quennell, M., & C.H.B. Quennell. *A History of Everyday Things in England. Part 3: The Rise of Industrialism, 1733-1851.* London: Batsford, 3rd ed., 1945.

GEN Ravenhill, Alice. *Labor-Saving Devices in the Household.* Logan: Utah Agricultural College, 1912.

GEN Rawson, Marion Nicholl. *Handwrought Ancestors.* NYC: E. P. Dutton, 1936.

INV Ray, William, & Marlys Ray. *The Art of Invention; Patent Models and Their Makers.* Princeton, NJ: Pyne Press, 1974.

GEN Raycraft, Don. *Price Guide to Kitchen Antiques, Vols. 1 & 2.* Des Moines, IA: Wallace-Homestead, 1977. 6-pp prices.

GEN Raycraft, Don, & Carol Raycraft. *The Collector's Guide to Kitchen Antiques.* Paducah, KY: Collector Books, 1980.

GEN ———. *Early American Kitchen Antiques.* Des Moines, IA: Wallace-Homestead Book Co., 1977.

CER *Redwing Collectors Club Newsletter.* (Box 50, Red Wing, MN 55066)

CAT Reed Mfg. Co. *Matchless Metalware.* Catalog 27. Newark, NY & Canandaigua, NY: 1927.

IV Reichen, Quirinus. *Spuren in Holz geschnitten: reiche Volkskunst auf Buttermodeln = Souve-nances de bois gravé: richesse folklorizue des moules á beurre.* Kiesen, Germany: Milch-wirtschaftliches Museum, 1989. Butter molds, at a dairy museum. Text in German & French.

'OY   Reinelt, Sabine. *Puppenküche und Puppenherd in drei Jahrhunderten.* Ludwigsburg, Germany: Kunstverlag Weingarten, 1985. Copious illustrations of kitchen toys.

VIII   Reichler, Mel, & Jim Egan. *Corkscrews.* NYC: author, 1996.

IIS   Renfrew, Jane, Maggie Black, Peter Brears, & Jennifer Stead. *Food & Cooking in Britain.* 7 vols: Great Britain's cooking & food in various periods: prehistoric, Roman, Middle Ages, 16th through 19th centuries. [England]: English Heritage, 1985.

MET   Revi, Albert Christian, ed. *Spinning Wheel's Collectible Iron, Tin, Copper & Brass.* Castle Books, 1974. Anthologized articles from lamentably defunct magazine. Mr. Revi, bless you for starting so many of us on our collecting paths!

VII   Reynolds, Martin F. *CUPS – Collapsible, Collapsion or Telescopic.* Crosswicks, NJ: Author, 2002. Available from author, 425 Ellisdale Rd., POB 2, Crosswicks 08515. 35-pp booklet on wide variety of these cups.

GEN   Richman, Irwin *Pennsylvania German Arts: More Than Hearts, Parrots and Tulips (Lancaster Heritage).* Atglen: Schiffer, 2000.

MET   Rickard, T. A. *Man and Metals.* NYC: McGraw-Hill, 1932.

PAP   Rickards, Maurice. *Encyclopedia of Ephemera.* NY: Routledge, 2000.

I   Ricketts, Linda, & Kenneth Ricketts. *Citrus Juice Reamers.* Laurel, MD: authors, 1970; 1979.

I   Rittenhouse, Judith A. *Ornamental & Figural Nutcrackers.* Paducah, KY: Collector Books, 1993.

CAT   Ritzinger & Grasgreen. *Catalog of Household Goods & Novelties.* NYC: c. 1906-07. Importers & jobbers for door-to-door sales persons.

GEN   Robacker, Earl F. *Pennsylvania Dutch Stuff, a Guide to Country Antiques.* NYC: A. S. Barnes, 1944.

IV   ———. *Pennsylvania German Cooky Cutters & Cookies, Home Craft Course.* Plymouth Meeting, PA: 1946. 20 pp booklet.

GEN   Robacker, Earl F. *Touch of the Dutchland.* NY: A. S. Barnes, 194-; 2nd ed., 1965.

XVIII   Roberts, Evelyn Hortense. *Utensils for the Electric Range.* Pullman, WA: State College of Washington, 1933.

X, XI   Roberts, Hugh D. *Downhearth to Bar Grate: An Illustrated Account of the Evolution in Cooking Due to the Use of Coal Instead of Wood.* Avebury, Marlborough, Wilts., England: Wiltshire Folk Life Society, 1981.

VII   Roerig, Fred, & Joyce Roerig. *Collector's Encyclopedia of Cookie Jars, Vol. I.* Paducah, KY: Collector Books, 1991. *Vol. II,* 1993. Copious illustrations.

CAT   Rogers, Henry, Sons & Co. *Book No. E5528.* Wolverhampton, England: 1914.

VII   Rogove, Susan T., & Marcia B. Steinhauer. *Pyrex by Corning: A Collectors Guide.* Marietta, OH: Antique Publications. (POB 553, 45750. 1993)

I   Rollband, James. *American Nutcrackers: A Patent History and Value Guide.* Sunnyvale, CA: Off Beat Books, 1996. 180 pp, 537 patent illustrations. Inventor index only. (1345 Poplar Ave., 94087)

XVI   Roller, Dick. *Fruit Jar Patents, Vol. I, 1853-1869.* Chicgo: Phoenix Press, 1998. (To order Roller's patent books: Jerry McCann, 5003 W. Berwyn Ave, Chicago, IL 60630, or Web site: www.antiquebotl.com/mccann.htm)

XVI   Roller, Dick. *Fruit Jar Patents, Vol. II, 1870-1899.* Chicago: Phoenix Press, 1980s; reprint 1997. 700+ pp. (5003 W. Berwyn Ave., 60630-1501) See also: Bond, Ralph.

XVI   ———. *Fruit Jar Patents, Vol. III, 1900-1942.* Chicago: Phoenix Press, 1996. 500 pp, 4 cross-reference indices for foolproof identification.

XVI   ———. *Indiana Glass Factories Notes.* Paris, IL: Acorn Press, 607 Driskell St., Paris, IL 61944. ©1994.

XVI   ———. *The Standard Fruit Jar Reference.* Paris, IL: Acorn Press, 1983.

PAP   Romaine, Lawrence B. *Guide to American Trade Catalogs 1744-1900.* NYC: R.R. Bowker, 1960. Reprinted by Dover Books, NYC, 1990. Each of 60+ categories has many listings of trade catalogs, with locator guide.

XVIII   Rubin, Susan Goldman. *Toilets, Toasters & Telephones: the How and Why of Everyday Objects.* San Diego, CA: Harcourt, Inc., 1998. For children! Nice photographs.

GEN   Ruempol, A. P. E., & A. G. A. van Dongen. *Preindustriële Gebruiksvoorwerpen = Pre-industrial Utensils: 1150-1800.* Amsterdam, Holland: De Bataafsche Leeuw, 1991. Dutch & English. Kitchen & tablewares at decorative arts museum.

X, XI   Rumford, Benjamin Graf von. *On the Construction of Kitchen Fire-places and Kitchen Utensils. Together with remarks ... on cookery; and proposals for improving [cookery].* London: printed by A. Strahan, for T. Cadell Jr. & W. Davies, 1799. [Third edition of my 300 Years book had chapter on Count Rumford's designs, with illustrations.]

X, XI   ———. *The Complete Works of Count Rumford.* 4 volumes. Boston: American Academy of Arts & Sciences, 1870; 1875; or London: Macmillan, 1875. Translated into English; Rumford was an expatriate American who invented improvements for stoves and fireplaces to improve the lot of the poor. Many translations & editions.

VII   Runkewich, Fred. *Fred's Price Guide to Modern Bottles.* Cheyenne, WY: author, n.d. (POB 1423, zip 82003)

XI   Russell, Robert. *Leave the Wood by the Kitchen Door: Kitchenware, 1880-1930: A Guide Book Containing Information for Teachers and Suggested Related Activities ... for Students.* [Etobicoke, Ontario] CAN: Bd of Education, 1972. Probably available in French.

CAT   Russell & Erwin Mfg. Co. *Illustrated Catalog of American Hardware.* New Britain, CT: 1865. A facsimile reprint was published by Assoc. for Preservation Technology, 1980.

GEN   Russell, Loris S. *Handy Things to Have Around the House. Oldtime Domestic Appliances of Canada and the U.S.* NY: McGraw-Hill Ryerson Ltd., 1979.

GEN   Rybczynski, Witold. *Home.* NYC: Viking Press, 1986. The best.

IV   Rycraft, Carol, & Paul Rowton. *The Rycraft Cookie Stamp Collector's Handbook; A Price Guide & History of the Cookie Stamps Grandma Used.* Rycraft, Inc., 1998.

IV   Sánchez Marcos, Marta, & Maria José Frades. *Catálogo de los sellos de pan del Museo de Salamanca: industria panadera tradicional salmantina.* Salamanca, Spain: Junta de Castilla y León, 1995.

GEN   Scammell, Henry B., comp. *Treasure House of Useful Knowledge; an Encyclopedia of Valuable Receipts in the Principal Arts of Life.* St. Louis, MO: Buckland Pub. Co., 1885, 1891. Fascinating stuff, uncredited excerpts from books by authorities "whose name is legion."

HIS   Scheffer, Charlotte. *Cooking and Cooking Stands in Italy, 1400-400 B.C.* Stockholm, Denmark: P. Aström, 1981.

VII   Schiffer, Nancy. *Baskets with Price Guide.* Schiffer, n.d.

MET   Schiffer, Peter, Nancy, & Herbert. *Antique Iron. Survey of American & English Forms, Fifteenth through Nineteenth Centuries.* Exton, PA: Schiffer, 1979. Excellent pictures as usual but scant information.

MET   ———.. *The Brass Book, American, English & European, 15th Century to 1850.* Exton, PA: Schiffer, 1978.

GEN   Schipper, Elizabeth de. *Quintessens: wetenswaardigheden over acht eeuwen kookgerei.* Exhibition catalog. Rotterdam: Museum Boymans-van Beuningen, 1992. Netherlands kitchen utensils.

IV   Schmidt, Leopold. *Ausstellung Lebzeltenmodel aus Österreich.* Vienna, Austria: Im Selbstverlag des Österreichischen Museums für Volkskunde, 1972. Folk museum exhibit of cookie molds.

VII   Schneider, Mike. *The Complete Cookie Jar Book.* Atglen, PA: Schiffer, 1991; 3rd revised ed., 199- (?)

VII   Schneider, Mike. *The Complete Salt & Pepper Shaker Book.* Atglen, PA: Schiffer Pub., 1993.

IV   Schnyder, Rudolf. *Alte Zürcher Gebäckmodel.* Zürich: Buchdruckerei Berichthaus, 1970. Cookie molds.

XVI   Schroeder, Bill. *One Thousand Fruit Jars Priced.* Paducah, KY: Collector Books, 1983.

INV   Schroeder, Fred E. H. *Twentieth Century Everyday Inventions.* Greenwood Press, 2002. Including 2 chapters on kitchen appliances.

PAP   *Scientific American.* Weekly. NYC: Munn & Co., 1845-1859. These 19th century issues almost always contain something on household improvement.

PAP   *Scientific Artisan; A Journal of Patents, Science, Art, Discovery, Inventions, Etc.* Cincinnati, OH: American Patent Co., Nov. 1858-April 1860. Weekly treasure for the curious – then and now.

CAT   *Sears, Roebuck & Co., 1902 Catalog.* Facsimi_ edition by: NYC: Crown Publishers, 196_ Badly printed. See also: Montgomery Ward.

GEN   Séguin, Robert-Lionel. *Les Ustensiles en No_ velle-France.* Montreal, CAN: Leméac, 197_ French Canadian utensils.

GEN   Seymour, John. *The National Trust Book_ Forgotten Household Crafts.* London: Dorlir Kindersley, 1987.

MET   Sferrazza, Julie. *Farber Bros. Krome-Kraft: Guide for Collectors.* Marietta, OH: Antiqu_ Publications, 1988. (POB 553, zip 45750)

MET   Sferrazza, Julie. *Farber Bros. 1941 Catalo_ reprint.* Marietta, OH: Antique Publications 1988. (POB 553, zip 45750)

CAT   Silver & Co. *Silver's House Furnishings. Cata_ log No. 18.* Brooklyn, NY: 1910.

MET   Simpson, Bruce L. *Development of the Meta_ Castings Industry.* Chicago, IL: America_ Foundrymen's Association, 1948. From pre_ historical use through the mechanization o_ foundries, from jewelry to cannons. Pro_ fusely illustrated. If you love iron, you've go_ to track this down.

WWW   Sinclair, Joseph T. *eBay the Smart Way: Sell_ ing, Buying, and Profiting on the Web's #1_ Auction Site.* 2nd ed. AMACOM, 2001.

MET   Sipe, Brian M. *Coppersmithing in Nineteenth Century Philadelphia – the Bentley Shop._* Thesis. Univ. of Delaware, 1987.

GEN   Skougaard, Mette. *Bondens køkken: madlavning og maltider I 1800-tallets landbosamfund.* Copenhagen, Denmark: Nationalmuseet, 1984. Danish kitchen utensils.

CER   Slesin, Suzanne, Stafford Cliff, & Daniel Rozensztroch. *Kitchen Ceramics.* NYC: Abbeville Press, 1997.

VII   Slesin, Suzanne, & Daniel Rozensztroch. *Wire.* NYC: Abbeville Press, 1994. Fabulous pictures & objects, hardly any info.

VII   Smith, Darrell A. *Black Americana, a Personal Collection.* Tempe AZ: Black Relics, Inc., 1989. (POB 24954, zip 85282)

CSTi   Smith, David G., & Chuck Wafford. *The Book of Griswold & Wagner. Favorite Piqua, Sidney Hollow Ware, Wapak.* Atglen, Known as the "Blue Book." PA: Schiffer Pub., 1995; rev. ed.

CSTi   ———. *The Book of Wagner & Griswold.* Atglen, PA: Schiffer, 2001. Known as the "Red Book," this illustrates 100s of items not in other book; has histories, catalog list numbers, prices, etc.

IV   Smith, Elmer Lewis, ed. *Early American Butter Prints.* Witmer, PA: Applied Arts, 1971.

MET   Smith, Elmer, & Mel Horst. *Early Iron Ware.* Lebanon, PA: Applied Arts, 1971. Other books: *Household Tools & Tasks;* and *Tinware, Yesterday & Today.*

IV   Smith, Richard Flanders. *Pennsylvania Butter Prints.* Ephrata, PA: Science Press, 1970.

IV   Smith, Wayne. *Ice Cream Dippers. An Illustrated History & Collector's Guide.* Author, 1986. Beautifully photographed & well-researched. *Price Guide* available too. (POB 418, Walkersville, MD 21793)

CER   Snyder, Jeffery B. *Fiesta Colorful Dinner Ware with Values.*

MET   Sonn, Albert H. *Early American Wrought Iron.* 3 vols. NYC: Charles Scribner's, 1928. Reprinted in 1979. Vol. 3 is *Andirons, Broilers, Trammels, Etc.*

V   Soslau, Eric, & Judy Soslau. *Bibliography of Weighing Instruments.* Chicago: International Society of Antique Scale Collectors, 1995.

GEN   Soyer, Alexis. *The Pantropheon; or, History of Food, and Its Preparation* ... London: Simpkin, Marshall, 1853. Has 3000 references to various authors.

XVIII   Sparke, Penny. *Electrical Appliances. Twentieth Century Design.* London: Unwin Hyman, 1987.

XXIII   Sparreboom, Jos, & Marg Sparreboom. *Food Lexicon.* A multi-language dictionary of food terms, including some tools. (Web site: www.xs4all.nl/~margjos/index.html, and/or www.foodlexicon.net for English text.)

IV   Spielman, George B. *Masonic Collectables.* Knoxville, MD: author, n.d. 19604 Rohrersville Rd., zip 21758)

GEN   *Spinning Wheel.* Albert Christian Revi, ed. Hanover, PA: Everybodys Press, 1950s–1970s. Wonderful source of information on kitcheny subjects. Look for back issues.

GEN   Sprackling, Helen. *Customs on the Table Top. How New England Housewives Set Out Their Tables.* Sturbridge, MA: Old Sturbridge Village, 1958, 1966.

GEN   Squirrell, M. P. *Has Machinery Lessened the Labour of Mankind?* Norwich, England: Norwich Democratic Assoc., 1885.

IV   Stahl, Ernst. *Holzmodeln aus dem Thüringer Raum.* Leipzig, Germany: Prisma-Verlag, 1990. Wooden baker's molds.

INV   Stanley, Autumn. *Mothers & Daughters of Invention. Notes for a Revised History of Technology.* Metuchen, NJ: Scarecrow Press, 1993. About the 2000 19th century women inventors (1790-1872); the Patent Office published a list of these women inventors in the *Official Gazette.*

VIII   Stanley, John R. *The 1994 Handbook of Beer Advertising Openers and Corkscrews.* Durham, NC: Stanley, 1994. 2nd ed. with Edward R. Kay, Donald A. Bull. *The 1998 Handbook* .... Chapel Hill, NC: Stanley, 1998.

IV   Stephenson, Lee, & Byrna Fancher, comp. *A Guide to Hallmark Cookie Cutters.* N.p. [Ohio], 1994

IV   Stephenson, Milli Simerl. Wilton *Cookie Cutters.* N.p. [Ohio]: Lee Stephenson, 1998.

GEN   Stewart, Regina, & Geraldine Cosentino. *Kitchenware.* Western Publishing Co., 1977.

GEN   ———. *Stoneware.* Western Publishing Co., 1977.

TOY   Stille, Eva. *Doll Kitchens, 1800-1980.* Tr. by Edward Force. English edition: West Chester, PA: Schiffer Pub., 1988. Fabulous source, with great pictures by Severin Stille. Eva has done it – how could anyone improve this book? (German edition: Eva Stille & Peter Beitlich. *Aus der Küche um 1900.* Munich: Kochbuchverlag Heimeran, 1978.)

GEN   Stoneback, Diane. *Kitchen Collectibles: The Essential Buyer's Guide.* Radnor, PA: Chilton Book Co., 1994.

GEN   Stoudt, John Joseph. *Early Pennsylvania Arts & Crafts.* NYC: A. S. Barnes, 1964.

GEN   ———. *Sunbonnets and Shoofly Pies. A Pennsylvania Dutch Cultural History.* Cranbury, NJ: A. S. Barnes, 1973.

VIII   Street, Julian. *Wines, Their Selection, Care and Service ... and on Wineglasses, Cradles, Corkscrews, and Kindred Matters.* NYC: Knopf, 3rd ed., 19–; 4th printing, 1966.

MET   Stuart, Peterson & Co. *Celebrated Tinned, Enameled, Turned & Plain Hollow Ware.* NYC: 1975. Also 1866; 1876 & 1888.

XVIII   Sturm, Hermann. *Gestalten Gebrauchen Erinnem.* Germany: author, Univ. Essen. 1994. Design collection of author, with some European toasters.

INV   *Subject-Matter Index of Patents for Inventions. Issued by the U.S. Patent Office, 1790 to 1873, Inclusive.* 3 vols. NYC: Arno Press, 1976. Then available from Ayer Co. Pubns, Salem, NH. Now set is nearly impossible to find. Supposed to be a US Gov't. Printing Office document: *Doc C21.5/2: 1790-1873,* but I can find no trace of it. Regional patent depository libraries in US will have more for research.

VII   Sullivan, Audrey. *A History of Match Safes in the United States.* Ft. Lauderdale, FL: Riverside Press, Inc., 1978.

VII   Supnick, Mark, & Ellen Supnick. *The Wonderful World of Cookie Jars.* Revised ed. Gas City, IN: L-W Book Sales, 1997.

IV   Suppan, Rudolf. *Geschnitzte Pracht aus alten Zeiten.* Graz, Germany: Verlag f. Sammler, 1979. Cookie molds of wood.

MET   Swank, James M. *History of the Manufacture of Iron in All Ages .... Particularly in the U.S. for Three Hundred Years. From 1585-1885.* Philadelphia, PA: for the author, 1882. I guess I could call my book *400 Years of Kitchen Collectibles!*

GEN   Swank, Scott T., Benno M. Forman, et al. *Arts of the Pennsylvania Germans.* NYC: Norton, for the Henry Francis du Pont Winterthur Museum, 1983.

GEN   *"Technology and Culture."* Quarterly journal of the Society for the History of Technology. Chicago, IL: Univ. of Chicago Press. Started c. 1960.

CER   Tefft, Gary, & Bonnie Tefft. *Red Wing Potters & Their Wares.* Locust Enterprises, first published 1981. New edition & also a price guide. (Tefft, W174 N9422 Devonwood Rd., Menomonee Falls, WI 53051)

CAT   Thayer, W. H. *Thayer's Household Combination.* [Boston]: 1881. Advertising flyer for kitchenwares.

GEN   *These Simple Things: Some Appreciation of the Small Joys in Daily Life From House & Garden.* Charming essays by Elizabeth Bowen, Marianne Moore, and Rumer Godden, etc.; first appeared in *H&G* magazine. NYC: Simon & Schuster, 1962, 1963, 1965.

IV   Thiele, Ernst. *Waffeleisen und Waffelgebäcke in Mitteleuropa.* Köln, Germany: Oda-Verlag, 1959. Molds and waffles and religious cakes, etc., in central Europe.

GEN   *Thomas' Register of American Manufacturers and First Hands in All Lines. The Buyers' Guide 1905-1906.* Reprint of 1905-06 edition, probably by Thomas Pub. Co., NY, whose registers are now many volumes per edition. Any old ones you find at library book sales or whatever will reward you in fascinating business history.

X, XI   Thompson, Sir Benjamin (Count Rumford). *Complete Works.* 4 vols. Boston, MA: American Academy of Arts & Sciences, 1870-1875. Reprint: Cambridge, MA: Belknap Press, 1968-1970. Inventor and social engineer Count Rumford designed and wrote about many things – notably for us, coffee pots and chimneys.

GEN   Thompson-Johnson, Frances. *Antiques from the Country Kitchen.* Des Moines, IA: Wallace-Homestead, 1985.

GEN   Thompson, Frances. *Mountain Relics.* Cranbury, NJ: A. A. Barnes, 1976.

GEN   ———. *The Enchantment of Enameled Cookware: An Illustrated Price Guide.* Kermit, TX: Collectors Weekly, 1974.

VII   Thornburg, Irene. *Salt & Pepper Shakers in Series.* Battle Creek, MI: author, 1998. Book now through Schiffer. Ms. Thornburg runs a club for collectors & publishes a quarterly newsletter. (581 Joy Rd., zip 49014-8450)

I   Thornton, Don. *Apple Parers.* Moss Beach, CA: Thornton House, 1997. Copious illustrations, including patents, fully indexed. (POB 57, Moss Beach, CA 94038-0057)

II   ———. *The Eggbeater Book. The First and Last Word about Man's Greatest Invention.* NYC: Arbor House, 1983. Terrific book which publisher cut too short.

II   ———. *Beat This. The Eggbeater Chronicles. The Stirring Story of America's Greatest Invention.* Sunnyvale, CA: Off Beat Books, 1994. (Now Thornton House, POB 57, Moss Beach, CA 94038-0057)

II   ———. *Beat This. The Eggbeater Chronicles. The Stirring Story of America's Greatest Invention.* 2nd, enlarged ed. Moss Beach, CA: Thornton House, 1999. Copious illustrations, including patents, fully indexed, and the end-all to beat-all. (POB 57, zip 94038-0057)

GEN   Thuro, Catherine M. V. *Oil Lamps Vol. I. Kerosene Era in North America.* Des Moines, IA: Wallace-Homestead, 1993. *Vol. II,* 1995.

XVI   Tice, Patricia M. *Ice Cream for All. Social History & Recipes.* Rochester, NY: Strong Museum, 1990.

VII   *Tin Container Collectors Association.* Newsletter. (POB 440101, Aurora, CO 80044)

TOY   *Tiny Times, The.* Quarterly newsletter for Collectors of Toy Dishes and Children's Furniture Club. (Shelley Smith, POB 159, Bethlehem, CT 06751)

XVIII   *Toast to You, A.* Quarterly publication of Upper-Crust: Toaster Collectors Assoc. (Carl Roles, Toasters Galore, POB 529, Temecula, CA 92593)

XVIII   *Toaster Collectors Association.* Newsletter. (Jim Barker, POB 746, Allentown, PA 18105)

XVIII   *Toasters and Small Kitchen Appliances: A Price Guide.* Gas City, IN: L-W Book Sales, 1995.

GEN   *Today's Collector. The Marketplace for Antiques and Collectibles.* Monthly. (Iola, WI: Krause Publications, 700 E. State St., 54990-0001. Phone: 715-445-3776)

GEN   Toller, Jane. *Turned Woodware for Collectors. Treen & Other Objects.* Cranbury, NJ: A. S. Barnes, 1975.

VII   Tompkins, Sylvia, & Irene Thornburg. *America's Salt & Pepper Shakers.* Atglen: Schiffer.

GEN   *Tool Shed.* Newsletter of Collectors of Rare & Familiar Tools Society. (Web site: hometown. aol.com/craftsofnj)

XVI   Toulouse, Julian Harrison. *A Collectors' Manual: Fruit Jars.* Hanover, PA: Everybody's Press, 1969. A pioneer in the field.

PAP   *Trade Card Journal.* Publisher Kit Barry. For collectors seeking late 19th century ephemera that relates to their collecting field. (109 Main St., Brattleboro, VT 05301)

GEN   Tremblay, Yves. *Les Ustensiles, les objets de couture et le luminaire de Place-Royale.* [Quebec]: Ministry of Culture, 1995. Lighting & cooking tools & utensils.

IV   Trice, James E. *Butter Molds; an Identification & Value Guide.* 2nd edition. Paducah, KY: Collector Books, 1980. Great variety pictured; little information.

VII   Turner, Jean W. *Collectable Aunt Jemima.* Atglen, PA: Schiffer Pub., 1994.

GEN   Tryon, Rolla Milton. *Household Manufacturers in the U.S., 1640-1860.* Chicago: Univ. of Chicago Press, 1917; reprint. NYC: Johnson Reprint, 1966.

XII   Tyler, John Dewey. *18th- and 19th-Century Cast-Iron Cooking Utensils.* Gettysburg, PA: Early American Society, 1978.

VII   Tyne & Wear County Council Museums. *Pyrex. 60 Years of Design.* Exhibition catalog from Sunderland Museum. Sunderland, UK: 1983.

GEN   Ure, Andrew. *A Dictionary of Arts, Manufactures & Mines.* 2 vols. England: 1839. NYC: D. Appleton, 1854. Fascinating!

INV   Usher, Abbott Payson. *A History of Mechanical Inventions.* NYC: McGraw Hill, 1929. Rev. ed. Cambridge, MA: Harvard Univ. Press, 1954.

VII   Van den Bossche, Willy. *Antique Glass Bottles: Their History and Evolution (1500-1850). A Comprehensive Illustrated Guide with a Worldwide Bibliography of Glass Bottles.* Wappingers Falls, NY: Antique Collectors Club, 2001.

INV   Van Dulken, Stephen. *British Patents of Invention 1617-1977: A Guide for Researchers.* London, England: British Museum, 1999. Tells how patents can reveal history, and gives info on patent specs, searching for patents, etc.

INV   ———. *Introduction to Patents Information.* 3rd ed. London: British Museum, 1998. Step-by-step how-to on researching UK and overseas patent info; includes printed sources, CD/ROM databases, etc. Europe, Japan, UK, US.

INV   Van Dulken, Stephen. *Inventing the 20th Century; 100 Inventions That Shaped the World: From the Airplane to the Zipper.* NYC: N.Y. Univ. Press, 2000.

Van Vleck, Richard. *History of Agriculture, Hand & Box Mounted Corn Shellers.* Vol. 1 on CD/ROM. Includes US patents, journal articles from the 19th century, etc. Taneytown, MD: n.d. (American Artifacts, POB 412, 21787. Web site: www.americanartifacts.com)

IV Van Vuren, Barbara, & Robert E. Van Vuren. *Butter Molds & Stamps: A Guide to American Manufacturers.* Napa, CA: Butter Press, 2000. POB 5782, Napa, 94581. Photos & catalog reprints; separate price guide. Web site: www.buttermold.net/print.html; e-mail: vanvurens@buttermold.net .

VII Van Wieren, Dale. *American Breweries II.* c. 1996. For identifying beer can openers. (Order from John Stanley, POB 64, Chapel Hill, NC 27514-0064)

INV Varc, Ethlie Ann, & Greg Ptacek. *Mothers of Invention. From the Bra to the Bomb: Forgotten Women & Their Unforgettable Ideas.* NYC: Quill/William Morrow, 1987.

MET Verdier, Roger. *La Dinanderie: objets en cuivre, laiton et bronze due XVIe au XIXe Siècle.* Saint-Martin-de-la-Lieue, Lisieux: R. Verdier, 1986. Brass, bronze utensils, etc.

HIS Vermeersch, Valentin. *Cuisines Anciennes.* Bruges, Belgium: Arnis des Musées communaux Bruges, 1990. Belgian kitchens & utensils in art.

CER Viel, Lyndon C. *The Clay Giants. The Stoneware of Red Wing, Goodhue County, Minnesota. Book 2.* Des Moines, IA: Wallace-Homestead, 1980.

VII *Vinegar Gazette.* Newsletter of the Ole Time Vinegar Society. (E-mail: vnicgar@mindspring. com [yes, mixed-up spelling is correct])

VIII Vizakay, Stephen. *Vintage Bar Ware Identification & Value Guide.*

MET Vogelzang, Vernagene, & Evelyn Welch. *Graniteware. Collectors' Guide with Prices.* Wallace-Homestead, 1981. *Book II,* 1986. Great pictures and storehouse of in-depth information.

MET Vosburgh, H. K. *The Tinsmith's Helper and Pattern Book.* Unionville, CT: Union Printing Co., 1879; 1911. Reprint: Mendham, NJ: Astragal Press, 1994. (E-mail: astragalpress@attglobal. net)

Wafford, Chuck – See: Smith, David G. & Chuck Wafford.

CSTI *Wagner Ware, Catalog No. 20, 1915,* reprint. Originally published Sidney, OH: Wagner Mfg. Co.; reprint Corvallis, OR: Gary Franzen, 1995. Cast aluminum, polished iron, and nickel-plated cooking utensils.

CSTi *Wagner Ware 1931 Catalog* reprint. Sacramento, CA: Cast Iron Connection, n.d. (3084 Yellowstone Lane, zip 95821-2360)

GEN Währen, Max, Christoph Schneider, Sylvia Fünfschilling, & Alex R. Furger. *Die Puls: römischer Getreidebrei.* Augst, Germany: Römermuseum, 1995. Ancient Roman utensils.

CAT Walker, F. A. Various catalogs & flyers. Boston: c. 1870s-90s. Large, undated catalog of housewares, many imported from France & England; some mfd. by Walker.

I Walker, Mary. *Reamers (200 Years): Price Guide 1980/81.* Sherman Oaks, CA: Muski, 1980.

GEN Wallance, Don. *Shaping America's Products.* NYC: Reinhold, 1956.

VIII Wallis, Fletcher. *British Corkscrew Patents From 1795.* Limited edition of 1000 copies. Brighton, England: Vernier Press, n.d. (18 Gerard Street, Brighton BN1 4NW, UK. E-mail: pipes@brighton.co.uk; North American source: Ron MacLean, e-mail: rmaclean@ netcom.ca)

IV Walzer, Albert. *Liebeskutsche, Reitersmann, Nikolaus und Kinderbringer.* [Konstanz]: Thorbecke, 1963. Cookie molds and decoration.

CAT *Wapak c.1910 Catalog* Reprint. Ohio: Combs Pub. Co., 1991.

XV Ward, Joe. *North Brothers Mfg. Company Product Guide. "Yankee," "Handyman, Shepard, Gem, Lightning, Etc."* Assembled history, catalog pages, tools & kitchen tools, price guide. Covers 1880-1946. Baraboo, WI: author, 354 Inverness Trail Ct., Unit 2, 53913. E-mail: joeward@midplains.net.

CBK *Warne's Model Cookery & Housekeeping Book,* compiled & edited by Mary Jewry. People's Edition. London: Frederick Warne & Co., 1868.

GEN Warren, Geoffrey. *Kitchen Bygones.* London: Souvenir Press, 1984.

CAT Washburn Co. *Sno-Cap. The New Androck Line of Kitchen Equipment.* Worcester, MA & Rockford, IL: 1927.

CAT Washburn Co. *The Androck Line. Balanced Kitchenware.* No.225. 1936.

VIII Watney, Bernard M., & Homer D. Babbidge. *Corkscrews for Collectors.* London, Eng: Sotheby's, 1981. Revised by B. Watney, 1993. Gorgeous, informative book.

GEN Wddyn, Ieuan. *Cerdd Dodrefn Ty.* [Wales], 1899 (?). Welsh kitchen utensils & dowry.

IV Weaver, William Woys. *America Eats. Forms of Edible Folk Art.* NYC: Harper & Row, 1989. Cookbook profusely & beautifully illustrated with utensils & decorated, molded food.

IV Weaver, W. W. *The Christmas Cook. Three Centuries of American Yuletide Sweets.* NYC: Harper & Row, 1990. Molded & painted cookies.

MET Weeks, Joseph Dame. *Tin and Tin Plate. Their History, Production and Statistics.* Pittsburgh, PA: American Manufacturer and Iron World, 1892. 44 pp supplement to the trade periodical.

IV Weiner, Piroska. *Carved Honeycake Moulds.* Budapest, Hungary: Corvina Kiado, 1964; 2nd ed. enlarged 1981. London: Collet, 1964. Hungarian "folk arts and crafts" books are excellent, with wonderful pictures.

GEN Weiss, Jeffrey, Susan Osborn, & David Leach, et al. *Kitchen Antiques.* NNY: Harper & Row, 1980.

Welch, Evelyn – See: Vogelsang.

INV Welsh, Peter C. *United States Patents 1790 to 1870: New Uses for Old Ideas.* Bulletin. Washington, D.C.: Museum of History & Technology, Smithsonian Institution, 1964.

VII Westfall, Ermagene. *Cookie Jars.* Paducah, KY: Collector Books, 1983; Book II, 1993.

IV Wetherill, Phyllis Steiss. *Cookie Cutters & Cookie Molds.* Exton, PA: Schiffer, 1985. Encyclopedic for more modern cutters; much detail.

IV   Wetherill, Phyllis S., & Rosemary Henry. *A Cookie Shapers' Bible.* 1998. Alphabetical encyclopedia of American & foreign cutter & mold makers, emphasis on 20th century, profusely illustrated. (For ordering information: SASE to Mrs. Henry, 9610 Greenview Ln., Manassas, VA 20109) See *Cookies.*

IV   ————. *Encyclopedia of Cookie Shaping.* Washington, D.C.: author, 1981. The late, great Phyllis' first.

XVI   Wetzel, Keri S. *Rings and Things. Guide to Jar Rings, Lid Boxes, etc.* Vol. 2 of *Fruit Jar Ring Boxes.*

XIV   White, Michael L., & Judith A. Sivonda. *Antique Coffee Grinders. American, English, and European.* Atget, PA: Schiffer, 200-? Order from Sivonda: 375 Congdon St., Middletown, CT 06457.

XIV   White, Michael L., & Derek S. White. *Early American Coffee Mills. Patent History & Guide for Collectors.* Yardley, PA: WhiteSpace Publishing, 769 Sumter Dr., 19067. 1994.

X   Wilby, Viola. *Kitchen Fireplaces in Deerfield.* [Deerfield, MA]: Historic Deerfield, Inc., 1973. Cooking hearths.

GEN   Wildhaber, Robert. "*Küchengerate. Wechselausstellung im Schweizerischen Museum fur Volkskund Basel, Dezember 1962 bis Mai 1963.*" In *Schweizer Volkskunde Korrespondenzblatt der Schweizerischen. Gesselschaft fur Volkskunde,* No. 5/6, pp. 65-92, 1962.

INV   Willich, Antony Florian M. *The Domestic Encyclopedia. Inventions and Improvements Chiefly Applicable to Rural and Domestic Economy.* 5 vols. Philadelphia: W. Y. Birch & A. Small, 1803-04 (1st American edition); 3 vols., with additions by Dr. Thomas Cooper: Philadelphia, PA: A. Small, 1821. Try to get a set – or even just one volume!

MET   Wills, Geoffrey. *Collecting Copper & Brass.* NYC: Bell Pub. Co., 1962.

CAT   Wire Goods Co. "*Sherwood*" *Wire Hardware. Wire Kitchen Ware. Catalog 7.* Worcester, MA: 1915. Also a supplement, 1915.

XVIII   Witt, John M. *Collector's Guide to Electric Fans.* Paducah, KY: Collector Books, 1996.

GEN   Wolf, Burt, Emily Aronson, & Florence Fabricant, eds. *The New Cooks' Catalogue.* NYC: Knopf, 2000. See also: Beard, James.

GEN   Woman's Book, The. *Dealing Practically with the Modern Conditions of Home Life.* NYC: Charles Scribner's Sons, 1894.

GEN   *Woman's Home Companion.* NYC & Springfield, OH: Crowell & Collier Co., 1897-1902. Monthly, formerly *Ladies' Home Companion.*

VII   Woodall, Allen & Sean Brickell. *Illustrated Encyclopedia of Metal Lunch Boxes.* Atglen, PA: Schiffer Pub., 1992.

GEN   Woodforde, John. *The Observer's Book of Kitchen Antiques.* London: Warne Books, Observer's Pocket Series, 1982.

X, XI   Wright, Lawrence. *Home Fires Burning. History of Domestic Heating & Cooking.* London: Routledge & Kegan Paul, 1964.

GEN   Wright, Richardson. *Hawkers & Walkers in Early America, Strolling Pedlers, Preachers, Lawyers ... and Others; from the Beginning to*

the Civil War. Philadelphia, PA: J. B. Lippincott, 1927.

GEN   *Wrinkles & Recipes,* Compiled from Scientific American. NYC: Scientific American Publishing Co., 1875. Many household tool tips.

GEN   Wuhr, Hans. *Alte Küchen und Küchengeräte.* Darmstadt, Germany: F. Schneekluth, 1955. 1978. 32 pp, illustrated.

GEN   *Yankee's Book of Whatsits: ...100 Ingenious Old-Time...Labor Savers...How Many Can You Identify?* Dublin, NH: Yankee, 1975.

GEN   Yarwood, Doreen. *500 Years of Technology in the Home.* London: Batsford, 1983.

HIS   Yarwood, Doreen. *The British Kitchen. Housewifery Since Roman Times.* London: Batsford, 1981.

XIV   Yena, Louise. *The Handbook of Antique Coffee and Tea Collectibles; a Price Guide.* Vol. I. San Antonio, TX: author, 1971.

VII   Young, Jackie. *Black Collectables. Mammy and Her Friends.* West Chester, PA: Schiffer Pub., 1988; Atglen, PA: rev. ed., 1991.

GEN   Young, Norman S. *Fabulous But Fake. Vol. I. The Professional's Guide to Fake Antiques.* Albany, NY: Fake Publications, Inc., 1994. For dealers and collectors of tin, ironware, toys, lighting devices, folk art and weathervanes. (POB 887, zip 12201)

IV   Zogg, Annemarie, & Robert Hirt. *Zürcher Gebäckmodel.* Bern, Switzerland: Paul Haupt, 1970. Swiss folk art bread molds.

IV   ————. *Zuri-Tirggel.* Zurich: Zurcher Kantonalbank, 1992. Cake boards & the cakes baked in them.

RESEARCHING

XXIII. GERMAN KITCHEN UTENSIL GLOSSARY

I've provided this glossary for four reasons: (1) many kitchen things were imported from Germany to the U.S. in the late 1800s and early 1900s; (2) many of the foreign-language books on kitchen antiques now available are in German; (3) the old Gothic typeface in all German books of the nineteenth century and before, and many from the early twentieth century, make many letters virtually unrecognizable to non-German readers, but if a word can be compared to a word transcribed in a modern font, many mysteries can be solved; and finally because (4) German can be so hard (although fun) to translate.

Often the words are compounds made up to describe the function; for example, one word for colander actually translates "to slip through" – *Durchschlag*. Or the compound may denote the material from which the gadget or utensil is made.

Furthermore, different dictionaries and different authors give different ways of compounding many words – sometimes all run together, sometimes hyphenated, and, even more confusing – sometimes in different order! Some words are capitalized, some aren't; and plurals have different endings.

Words listed here are mostly nouns, with a few useful adjectives. For the casual browser, one of the most disconcerting things in a German-language book is a character that looks like a capital "B" that stands for a double ess (although not all instances where a double ess appears). One of our favorite words as kitchen collectors is **Gusseisen** or **Gußeisen:** cast iron!

An interesting and **useful Web site** is found at: www.xs4all.nl/~margjos/dehead.htm, with a multi-language food terms glossary, including some utensils. As of October 2001, it included German, English, French, Danish, and Dutch. The compilers, Jos and Marg Sparreboom, are from the Netherlands. They are planning to add other languages to the site.

English to German Listing:

All-in-one baking tool — *Alle Hilfsgeräte beim Backen in einem*
Aluminum foil — *Alufolie*
Angel food cake pan — *Biskuitkuchenform*
Apple corer — *Apfelbohre or Apfelausstechen*
Apple parer — *Apfelschälmaschine*
Appliance — *Vorrichtung or Gerät*
Apron — *Schürze*
Asparagus cooker — *Spargelkocher*
Aspic mold — *Aspikform or Geleeform*
Aspic mold in fish shape — *Sülzform für Fischsülze*
Bain marie (water bath pan) — *Wasserbad*
Baking dish — *Auflauf* [Oven dish – *Gratinform*]
Baking mold — *Backform*
Baking pan (such as a clay muffin pan) — *Muldenpfanne für Gebäck*
Baking sheet or tin — *Backblech, Plätzchenblech, Backtisch, Herdbackblech* (for fireplace)
Basket spit — *Korbförmigem Bratspieß*
Bean cutter — *Bohnenschneidemaschine*
Beetle or pestle — *Gemüsestampfe or Stampfer*
Biscuit breaker — *Teigklopfer*
Blender — *Mixer*
Bottle — *Flasche*
Bottle opener — *Flaschenöffner or Kapselheber*
Brass — *Messing*
Brazier — *Kohlenfeuer*
Breadbox — *Brotbüchse or Brotkasten*
Bread cutter — *Brotschneider*
Bread knife — *Brotmesser*
Bread peel — *Teigspaten*

Bread pudding mold — *Brotpuddingform*
Bread stamp — *Brotstempel*
Broiler — *Bratrost*
Bronze — *Bronzeguß or Bronze*
Butter hands — *Butterformer*
Butter machine — *Buttermaschine*
Butter mold — *Buttermodel or Butterform*
Butter stamp — *Butterstempel*
Butter stamp, wood with relief design — *Butterstempel aus Holz mit Reliefmuster*
Butter-shaping ladle — *Butterformlöffel*
Cabbage cutter — *Kräutschneider or Kohlschneider*
Cabbage cutter or plane — *Kräuterhackmesser mit Brett*
Cabbage cutting machine — *Kohlschneidemaschine*
Cabbage plane — *Krauthobel*
Cake icer — *Sprizbeutel*
Cake mold — *Küchenform or Biskuitform*
Cake tin or pan — *Kastenkuchenform or Napfkuchenform*
Cake turner — *Pfannenwender*
Can or tin — *Dose or Kanister*
Can opener — *Konservendosenöffner or Dosenöffner*
Can opener (tin box opener) — *Büchsenöffner*
Candy droppers, or pouring pans — *Gießpfannen*
Candy droppers with spouts — *Gießpfannen feststehenden Rohren*
Candy mold — *Konditorförmchen*
Canning jar — *Konfitürengläser or Einweckglas or Weckglas*
Caraway seed mill — *Kümmelmühle*

Carved wood — *Holzgeschnitzter*
Carving board — *Schneidebrett*
Carving knife — *Vorlegemesser* or *Tranchiermesser*
Cast iron — *Gußeisen*
Cast iron pot — *Gußeisen Töpf*
Ceramic — *Keramik (n.); Keramisch* (adj.)
Cheese board — *Käsebrett*
Cheese press — *Käsepresse*
Cheese slicer or cheese plane — *Käsehobel*
Cherry pitter — *Kirschenentkerner*
Cherry pitter, mechanical — *mechanischer Kirschenentkerner*
Chocolate mill — *Kakaomühle*
Chocolate mold — *Form für Schokolade* or *Schokoladeform*
Chocolate mold, Easter bunny — *Osterhase Form für Schokolade*
Chopper for vegetables — *Hackbeil für Gemüse*
Chopper or cleaver — *Hackbeil*
Chopping board — *Holzbrett* or *Schneidebrett*
Chopping bowl for vegetables — *Gemüsespülschüssel*
Chopping knife — *Hackmesser*
Chopping knife with curved blade — *Wiegemesser*
Churn — *Butterstampfer*
Churn — *Butterfaß* or *Butterstampfer*
Cider press — *Apfelpresse*
Cleaver — *Hackbeil*
Clock for kitchen — *Küchenuhr*
Coffee filter — *Kaffeefilter*
Coffee mill or grinder — *Kaffeemühle*
Coffee mill, wall-mounted — *Wandkaffeemühle*
Coffee pot — *Kaffeekanne*
Coffee roaster — *Kaffeerostmaschine* or *Kaffeebrenner* or *Kaffeeröster*
Coffee roaster, globe-shaped — *kugelförmiger Kaffeeröster*
Colander — *Durchschlag* (literally to slip through) or *Seiher* or *Sieb*
Combination knife tool — *Kombinationsmesser*
Combination baking tool — *Alle Hilfsgerate beim Backen in einem* (in einem means "in one")
Combination or all purpose tool — *Allzweckgerät*
Cookbook — *Kochbüch*
Cookie or cake cutter — *Ausstechform*
Cookie cutter, Christmas Eve — *Ausstechform für Weihnachtsgebackerie*
Cookie sheet — *Kuchenblech*
Cooking pot — *Kochtopf*
Cooking spoon — *Küchenlöffel* or *Kochlöffel* (primarily for wooden spoon)
Cooking stove or cooker — *Kochmaschine* or *Küchenmaschine*
Cook's knife — *Küchenmesser*
Copper — *Kupfer*
Copper mold — *Kupferform*
Cork drawer — *Korkzieher* or *Korkenzieher* or *mechanischer Korkenzieher*
Cork press — *Korkenverkleinerungsappart* or *Kork-Handpresse*
Corking machine or cork driver — *Korkmaschine*
Corkscrew — *Korkenzieher*
Cream whip or eggbeater, mechanical — *mechanischer Schneebesen*
Crinkle cutter — *Buntschneidemesser*
Crock — *Krug* or *Topf*
Crockery — *Töpferware* or *Geschirr*
Crumb grater — *Reibe für Brösel* or *Reibe für Krümel*

Cucumber slicer — *Gurkenhobel*
Cup spoon (ladle) — *Schöpflöffel* or *Suppenkelle*
Cupboard — *Schrank*
Cutlery — *Besteck*
Cutlery cleaner — *Besteckputzmaschine*
Decorating stencils (for cake tops) — *Schablonen*
Dish cover, wire — *Drahtglocken*
Dishwashing pan — *Spülschüssel*
Dough or pastry knife — *Teigmesser*
Dough or pastry wheel — *Teigrad* or *Teigrädchen*
Dough scraper — *Teigschaber*
Dough tray — *Backmulde*
Dough trough — *Backtrog*
Draining basket for deepfry — *Drahteinsatz*
Earthenware — *Töpferwaren* or *Tongeschirr*
Egg pan — *Eierpfanne* or *Eierkuchleinpfanne;* also (probably dialectical) *Poffertjes-Pfanne*
Egg slicer — *Eierteiler* or *Eierschneider*
Egg timer — *Eieruhr*
Eggbeater or whisk — *Schneebesen* or *Schläger* or *Schneeschläger*
Electric — *Elektrisch* (adj.)
Enameled — *emaillierte* (adj.)
Enamelware — *Emailwaren*
Figural (adj.) — *Plastischen Figur*
Filleting knife — *Aussbeinmesser* or *Filetiermesser*
Fireless cooker (hay box) — *Kochkiste*
Fireplace, for the — *fur die Herdplatte* or *für den Herd* or *für die Feuerstelle*
Fish lifter — *Fischheber* or *Fischvorlegemesser*
Fish slice — *Bratmesser*
Flour dredger or shaker — *Mehlstreuer*
Flour scoop — *Mehlschaufel*
Flour sifter — *Mehlsieb*
Fondue pot — *Fonduetopf*
Food cupboard or meat safe — *Speiseschrank*
Food mill — *Passiermaschine*
Food processor — *Küchenmaschine*
Footed base — *Standring*
Form or shape cutter — *Ausstechform*
Frosting tube — *Zuckergußpritzen*
Fruit parer — *Obstschälmaschine* or *mechanische Obstschälmaschine*
Fruit press — *Fruchtpresse*
Fruit scraper — *Obstschaber*
Fruit stoner — *Obstentkerner*
Frying pan — *Bratpfanne* or *Frittierpfanne*
Frying pan with lid — *Stieltopf mit Deckel*
Funnel — *Trichter*
Garlic press — *Knoblauchpresse*
Garnishing knife — *Garniergeräte*
Gingerbread mold — *Ingwerkuchenmodel*
Glass (the material) — *Glas*
Graniteware — *Granitemaille*
Grater — *Reibe* or *Raspel*
Grater, tinned iron — *Reibeisen*
Grating machine — *Reibmaschine*
Griddle — *Backblech*
Griddle plate or grill (top of stove) — *Kontaktgrill*
Gridiron, enameled white inside — *Bratrost innen weiss emailliert*
Grill — *Grill* or *Bratrost*
Handle — *Henkel* or *Stiel* or *Griff*
Hash machine or chopping machine — *Hackmaschine*
Hearth — *Herd* (See also Fireplace)
Hearth tools — *Herdbesteck*

Hearth-hanging saucepan — *Kaminhangetopf* or *Stielkasserolle*

Hot plate — *Backhaube* or *Heizplatte* or *Kochplatte*

Ice box — *Eisfach* or *Eisschrank* or *Kühltasche*

Ice-breaking knife — *Eisdressiermess*

Ice cream "bomb" mold — *Eisbombeform* or *Eisförmchen*

Ice cream mold — *Eisförmchen*

Ice cube tray — *Eiswurfelschale* or *Eiswurfellade*

Ice machine or ice cream freezer — *Eismaschine*

Ice pick — *Eispickel*

Iron pot or saucepan — *Eisenhäfen*

Jagger — *Teigrad*

Jar lid wrench — *Schraubdeckelöffner*

Jelly glass — *Geleeglas* or *Glas*

Jelly mold — *Geleeform*

Jug — *Krug* or *Kanne*

Juicer — *Entsafter* or *Fruchtpresse* (See Lemon squeezer also)

Kettle — *Kessel*

Kettle, brass — *Messingen Kessel*

Kettle, iron — *Eisener kessel*

Kettle holder — *Topflappen*

Kitchen — *Küche*

Kitchen cloth — *Küchenschürze*

Kitchen cupboard — *Kuchenschrank*

Kitchen utensils — *Küchengeschirr* or *Küchengeräte*

Kitchen scales — *Küchenwaage*

Kneading machine — *Knetmaschine*

Knife — *Messer*

Knife scouring board with sand box — *Schmirgelbrett mit Sandkasten*

Knife-cleaner — *Messerputzmaschine*

Knife sharpener — *Messerschärfer*

Ladle — *Schöpflöffel* or *Suppenkelle* or *Schöpfkelle*

Larding needle — *Spicknadeln*

Lemon press or squeezer or juicer — *Zitronenpresse*

Lemon zester or grater — *Zitronenreibe*

Lenten dough baby mold — *Form für Fatschenkind* (or *Wickelkinder*)

Lid — *Deckel* or *Topfdeckel*

Lobster cracker — *Hummerknacker*

Marchpane — *Marzipan*

Marzipan mold — *Marzipanform*

Mayonnaise maker — *Mayonnaiseschläger*

Meal sifter — *Mehlsieb*

Measuring beaker or cup — *Meßbecher*

Measuring spoon set — *Messlöffel*

Meat chopper — *Fleischhacker*

Meat grinder — *Fleischwolf*

Meat press — *Fleischpresse*

Meat tenderizer — *Fleischklopfer* or *Fleischhammer*

Melon baller — *Melonenstech* or *Kugelausstecker*

Metal — *Metall* (n.); *Metalllen* or *metallish* (adj.)

Milk cooker (a sort of double boiler) — *Milchkocher*

Mill — *Mühle*

Mincer — *Fleishwolf*

Mincing knife — *Wiegemesser*

Mincing machine (for meat) — *Fleischmaschine*

Mixing appliance or Mixer — *Rührapparat* or *Mischer* or *Mixer* or *Rührmaschine*

Mixing bowl — *Rührschlüssel*

Mixing bowls for eggs — *Schneekessel*

Mixing spoon — *Rührlöffel*

Mold (mould) — *Form* or *Gußform*

Mold, clay or ceramic — *Tonform*

Mold, iron — *Eisenguß* or *Gußeisen*

Mortar, brass — *Messingmer*

Mortar & pestle — *Mörser und Stößel*

Mortar with pestle — *Mörser mit Pistill*

Mortar, wooden — *Holzmörser*

Noodle roller, wooden — *Nudelrolle aus Holz* or simply *Nudelholz* or *Nudelwalker*

Nutcracker — *Tannenhher* or *Nußknacker*

Nutmeg grater — *Muskatreibe*

Oatmeal cooker — *Haferflockenkocher* or *Hafermehlkocher*

Opener — *Öffner*

Oven — *Bakröhre* or *Backofen*

Pan — *Pfanne*

Pan or pot trivet — *Pfannenhalter*

Pancake pan — *Plett kaker* or *guß eiserne Platte zum Pfannkuchenbacken*

Pancake turner — *Pfannenwender*

Paring knife — *Tourniermesser* or *Schälmesser*

Paring machine — *Schälmaschine*

Pastry cutter — *Ausstechform* or *Ausstechformchen*

Pastry jagger or wheel — *Teigrädchen* or *Kuchen-Teigrad*

Pastry knife — *Teigmesser*

Pastry or pie rimmer — *Rändel*

Pastry sheet (for baking) — *Pastetenblech*

Pastry tube — *Teigspritzen*

Peppermill — *Pfeffermühle*

Pestle — *Stäßel* or *Gemüsestampfe* or *Mörserkeule*

Pewter marzipan lily mold — *Zinnform für Marzipanblume zur Tortendekoration Lilie*

Pie funnel — *Pastetenschornsteine*

Pie jagger — *Teigrad*

Pie mold — *Pastete Form*

Plum pudding mold — *Plumpuddingform* or *Pflaumepuddingform*

Popover pan — *Poffertjes-pfanne*

Poppyseed mill — *Mohnmühle*

Pot — *Topf* or *Kochtopf*

Pot lid — *Topfdeckel*

Pot with three legs — *Dreibeinigtopf*

Potato ricer — *Kartoffelpresse*

Potato steamer or boiler — *Kartoffeldampftopf*

Potholder — *Topflappen*

Poultry shears — *Geflügelschere*

Poundcake mold — *Napfkuchen*

Pounder — *Stampfer*

Pressure cooker — *Dampfkochtopf, Umbachschen Dampftopf, Dampfdrucktopf* or *Schnellkochtopf*

Pressure cooker (Papin's Digester) — *Papinscher Topf*

Pudding mold — *Puddingform* or *Kochpuddingform*

Pudding steamer, or steamed-pudding mold — *Dampfpuddingform*

Rack (for roast pan) — *Gitterrost*

Refrigerator — *Kühlschrank*

Revolving grill — *Drehgrill*

Rice ball — *Reisbäll*

Rice cooker (a double boiler steamer) — *Reiskocher*

Rice mold, ring-shaped — *Reisrandform*

Roasting pan or tin (also frying pan) — *Bratpfanne*

Rocking mincer or chopper — *Wiegemesser*

Rolling pin — *Wellholz* or *Rollholz* or *Teigrolle* or *Plätzchentrommel* or *Kuchenroller*

Rolling pin, with longitudinal ribbing — *Nudelholz* or *Nudelwalze* or *Nudelwalker*

Rusk cutter or divider (for rusk biscuit) — *Zwiebackschneider*

Salad dryer — *Salatschwinge*
Salt — *Salz*
Salt box — *Wandsalzfässer*
Saucepan — *Topf* or *Tiegel* or *Stielkasserolle* or *Kochtopf* or *Schmortopf*
Sausage grinding & stuffing machine — *Würstfullmaschine*
Scale, household or kitchen — *Haushaltswaage*
Scales — *Waage*
Scales (literally quick scale) — *Schnellwaage*
Scaler for fish — *Schupper*
Sharpening steel — *Wetzstahl*
Sieve or colander — *Sieb*; a big round sieve: *Großes Sieb*
Skewer — *Bratspieß* or just *Spieß*
Skillet for oven — *Bratentopf*
Soufflê mold — *Soufflêförmchen*
Soup strainer — *Bouillonsieb*
Spatula — *Backshaufel* or *Spatel* or *Spachtel* or *Bratenwender* or *Pfannenlutscher* or *Wender*
Speculas mold (a carved board) — *Spekulatiusbrett*
Spice box — *Gewürzdose*
Spice box or chest — *Gewürzkasten*
Spice grater — *Gewugreibe*
Spice mill — *Gewürzmühle*
Spice rack — *Gewürzregal*
Spit — *Bratspieß* or *Drehspieß* or *Spieß* or *Grillspieß*
Spoon — *Löffel*
Spoons, set of wooden — *Kochlöffelgarnitur*
Spring balance scale — *Federwaage*
Spring form baking pan — *Springform*
Springerle mold — *Holzmodel zum Backen von Springerle*
Stainless steel — *rostfreier Stahl*
Stamper (like a beetle or pestle) — *Stampfe*
Steamer — *Dampfkessel* or *Dampfkochtopf*
Steel — *Stahl*
Steelyard — *Schnellwaage* or *Handwaage*
Stew pan — *Tiegel* or *Kasserolle* or *Bratentopf*
Stove or range — *Küchenherd* or *Kochmaschine* or *Ofen* or *Herd*
Stove plate — *Ofenplatte*
Strainer — *Filtriertrichter*

Strainer (also colander) — *Seihe* or *Seiher* or *Sieb*
Sugar loaf cutter — *Zange zum Zerkleinern von Hutzucker*
Sugar nippers — *Zuckerzangen* or *Zuckerknieper*
Sugar shaker or castor — *Zuckerstreuer*
Syllabub churn — *EiweiBchlägen*
Tea ball — *Tee-Eier*
Tea kettle — *Teekessel*; also *Wasserkessel*
Teapot — *Teekanne*
Tea strainer — *Teesieb*
Tin — *Blech* or *Zinn* (which is also pewter)
Tin can — *Blechdose* or *Blechbüsche*
Tin kettle — *Weißblechkessel*
Tin opener or can opener — *Büchsenöffner* or *Dosenöffner*
Tinned copper — *verzinntem Kupfer*
Tinware — *blechen Geschirr* or *Blechwaren*
Toaster — *Toaster* or *Brotröster*
Tongs — *Zange*
Trammel, sawtooth — *Kesselhake in Sägeform*
Trivet or stand — *Dreifuß* or *Untersetzer*
Tub — *Zuber* or *Bottich* (for coopered ware)
Tub, small — *Kleine Zuber*
Turning spit — *Bratenwender*
Vegetable chopper — *Wiegemesser* (although word for vegetable is Gemüse)
Vegetable chopping machine — *Hackmaschine* or *Gemüse-Zerkleinerungsmaschine*
Wafer iron (literally wafer bake tongs) — *Oblaten-Backzange*
Wafer iron or waffle iron — *Waffeleisen*
Waffle iron, electric — *Waffelautomat*
Waffle iron for stovetop — *Waffeleisen für die Herdplatte*
Water glass or tumbler — *Wasserglas*
Water kettle — *Wasserkessel* (especially one that whistles)
Whisk or eggbeater — *Schneebesen* or *Schläger* or *Schneeschläger* or *Schlägbesen* or *Eieruhr*
Wooden — *hölz-* (adj.)
Wrought iron — *Schmiedeeisen* (n. or adj.) or *Schmiedeeisern* (adj.)
Zester — *Zestenreisser* or *Zitronenreibe*

German to English Listing:

Alle Hilfsgerate beim Backen in einem — *All-in-one combination baking tool*
Allzweckgerät — *Combination tool or all-purpose tool*
Alufolie — *Aluminum foil*
Apfelbohre or Apfelausstechen — *Apple corer*
Apfelpresse — *Cider press*
Apfelschälmaschine — *Apple parer*
Aspikform — *Aspic mold*
Auflauf — *Baking dish*
Aussbeinmesser — *Filleting knife*
Ausstechform — *Cookie or cake cutter, or form or shape or pastry cutter*
Backform — *Baking mold*
Backhaube — *Hot plate*
Backblech — *Baking tin, or griddle*
Backmulde — *Dough tray*
Backofen — *Bake oven*
Backshaufel — *Spatula* (literally bake shovel)
Backtisch — *Baking sheet*
Backtrog — *Dough trough* or *kneading tray*

Besteckputzmaschine — *Cutlery-* or *knife-cleaning machine*
Blech — *Sheet metal* (thus, usually, tinned sheet iron); also *sheet pan* (a pan made of same)
Blechen Geschirr or Blechwaren — *Tinware* or *metal pots and pans*
Bohnenhobel — *Bean slicer*
Bohnenschneidemaschine — *Bean cutter*
Bouillonsieb — *Soup strainer*
Bratpfanne — *Frying pan*; also *roasting pan* or *tin*
Bratentopf — *Oven skillet*
Bratenwender — *Turning spit*; also *fish slice* (!?); also *spatula*
Bratmesser — *Fish slice*
Bratpfanne — *Frying pan*
Bratrost — *Broiler* or *grill*
Bratrost innen weiss emailliert — *Gridiron, enameled white inside*
Bratrost über offenem Feuer auch — *Gridiron for hearth*

Bratspiessen — *Spit* or *Skewer*
Bronzeguß — *Bronze*
Brotbüch or Brotkasten — *Bread box*
Brotmesser — *Bread knife*
Brotpuddingform — *Bread pudding mold*
Brotroster — *Toaster for bread*
Brotschneider — *Bread cutter*
Brotstempel — *Bread stamp*
Büchsenöffner — *Tin opener* or *can opener*
Buntschneidemesser — *Crinkle cutter*
Butterfaß — *Churn*
Butterformer — *Butter hands*
Butterformlöffel — *Butter-shaping ladle*
Buttermaschine — *Butter machine*
Buttermodel or Butterform — *Butter mold*
Butterstampfer — *Churn*
Butterstempel — *Butter stamp*
Dampfkessel — *Steamer*
Dampfkochtopf or Dampfdrucktopf — *Pressure cooker*
Dampfpuddingform — *Pudding steamer*
Deckel — *Lid*
Drahteinsatz — *Draining basket for deep fry*
Drahtglocken — *Dish cover of wire*
Drahtsieb — *Wire sieve*
Drehgrill — *Revolving grill*
Dreibeinigtopf — *Pot with three legs*
Dreifuß — *Trivet*
Durchschlag — *Colander or sieve or strainer*
Eierkuchleinpfanne or Eierpfanne — *Egg-cooking pan*
Eierschneebese — *Eggbeater*
Eierteiler or Eierschneider or Eierköpfer — *Egg slicer*
Eieruhr — *Egg timer*
Einweckglas — *Preserving jar*
Eisbombeform — *Ice cream "bomb" mold*
Eisdressiermess — *Ice-breaking knife*
Eisene Hafen — *Iron pots*
Eisener kessel — *Kettle, iron*
Eisenguß — *Mold of iron*
Eisförmchen — *Ice cream mold*
Eismaschine — *Ice machine* or *ice cream freezer*
Eiswaffeleisen — *Ice cream cornet* or *waffle iron*
Eiswürfelschale or Eiswürfellade — *Icecube tray*
Eiweißchlägen — *Syllabub churn*
Elektrisch — *Electric* (adj.)
Emaillierte — *Enameled*
Entsafter or Fruchtpresse — *Juicer*
Fatschenkind or Wickelkinder — *Lenten dough baby*
Federwaage — *Spring balance scale*
Filtriertrichter — *Strainer*
Fischheber — *Fish lifter*
Flasche — *Bottle*
Flaschengestell — *Bottle rack*
Flaschenöffner — *Bottle opener*
Fleischklopfer or Fleischhammer — *Meat tenderizer or pounder*
Fleischmaschine — *Mincing machine* (for meat)
Fleischpress — *Meat press*
Fleischwolf — *Meat grinder* or *mincer*
Fonduetopf — *Fondue pot*
Form — *Mold*
Formchen — *Small mold*
Form für Schokolade — *Chocolate mold*
Frittierpfanne — *Frying pan*
Fruchtpresse — *Fruit press* or *juice press*
Fur di Herdplatte — *for the fireplace*
Gang — *Gear*

Garniergeräte — *Garnishing knife*
Gefügelschere — *Poultry shears*
Geleeform — *Jelly mold*
Geleegläs — *Jelly glass*
Gemüsesieb — *Colander*
Gemüsespülschüssel — *Chopping bowl for vegetables*
Gemüsestampfe — *Beetle* or *pestle*
Gemüse-Zerkleinerungsmaschine — *Vegetable chopping machine*
Gerät — *Device* or *gadget*
Geschmiedetem Eisen — *forged iron* (adj.)
Gewugreibe — *Spice grater*
Gewürzdose — *Spice box*
Gewürzkasten — *Spice box* or *chest*
Gewürzmühle — *Spice mill*
Gießform — *Candy mold*
Gießpfannen — *Candy droppers*, or *pouring pans*
Gitterrost — *Rack (for roast pan)*
Gratinform — *Oven dish*
Griff — *Grip* or *handle*
Grillrost — *Grill*
Gußform — *Mold*
Gurkenhobel — *Cucumber slicer*
Gußeisen — *Cast iron*
Gußeisen mit reichem Dekor — *Cast iron with raised decoration*
Gußeisentöpf — *Cast iron pot*
Hackbeil — *Chopper* or *cleaver*
Hackbeil für Gemüse — *Chopper for vegetables*
Hackbrette — *Chopping* or *cutting board*
Hackmaschine — *Hash machine* or *chopping machine*
Hackmesser — *Chopping knife*
Haferflockenkocher — *Oatmeal [flake] cooker*
Haushaltswaage — *Household* or *kitchen scale*
Hebelkorkenzieher — *Corkscrew with levers*
Henkel — *Handle*
Henkeltopf — *Pot or pan with handle(s)*
Herd — *Hearth* or *stove*
Herdbackblech — *Baking tin for fireplace/hearth*
Herdbesteck — *Hearth tools*
Hobel — *Plane slicer*
Holzbrett — *Chopping board*
Hölzern — *Wooden* (adj.)
Holzgeschnitzter — *Carved wood*
Holzmodel zum Backen von Springerle — *Wooden springerle mold*
Holzmorser — *Mortar, wooden*
Hummerknacker — *Lobster cracker*
Ingwerkuchenmodel — *Gingerbread mold*
Kaffeefilter — *Coffee filter*
Kaffeekanne — *Coffee pot*
Kaffeemühle — *Coffee mill* or *grinder*
Kafeewärmer — *Cosy for coffee pot*
Kakaomühle — *Cocoa* or *chocolate mill*
Kaffeerostmaschine or Kaffeebrenner or Kaffeeröster — *Coffee roaster*
Kamin — *Fireplace*
Kaminhangetopf — *Hearth-hanging saucepan*
Kannchen — *Jug* or *pot*
Kanne — *Can* or *pot*
Kapselheber — *Bottle opener*
Kartoffeldampftopf — *Potato steamer* or *boiler*
Kartoffelkäfer or Kartoffelstampfe — *Potato beetle or pestle*
Kartoffelpresse — *Potato ricer*

Kartoffelschäler — *Potato peeler*
Kartoffelstampfer — *Potato masher*
Käsebrett — *Cheese board*
Käsehobel — *Cheese slicer* or *cheese plane*
Käsepresse — *Cheese press*
Kelle — *Ladle*
Keramisch — *Ceramic* (adj.)
Kessel — *Kettle*
Kesselhake in Sägeform — *Trammel, sawtooth*
Kirschenentkerner — *Cherry pitter*
kleine Zuber — *Small tub*
Kleinküchenmaschine — *Mixer*
Knetmaschine — *Kneading machine*
Knoblauchpresse — *Garlic press*
Kochkiste — *Fireless cooker* (hay box)
Kochmaschine — *Cooking stove*
Kochbüch — *Cookbook*
Kochlöffel — *Cooking spoon* (usually wooden?)
Kochpuddingform — *Pudding mold*
Kochtopf — *Cook pot*
Kohlenfeuer — *Brazier*
Kohlschneidemaschine — *Cabbage cutting machine*
Kombinationsmesser — *Combination knife tool*
Konditorförmchen — *Candy mold*
Konfitürengläser —*Canning jar* or *jam jar*
Konservendose — *Tin can*
Konservendosenöffner — *Can opener*
Kontaktgrill — *Griddle plate* or *grill* (top of stove)
Korbförmigem Bratspieß — *Basket spit*
Korkenverkleinerungsappart or Korkhandpresse — *Cork press*
Korkenzieher — *Corkscrew*
Korkmaschine — *Corking machine* or *cork driver*
Korkzieher or Korkenzieher or mechanischer Korkenzieher — *Cork drawer*
Kräuterhackmesser mit Brett or Krauthobel — *Cabbage cutter* or *plane*
Kräutschneider — *Cabbage cutter*
Krug — *Jug* or *crock* or *pitcher*
Küche — *Kitchen*
Kuchenblech — *Cookie sheet*
Küchenform — *Cake mold*
Kuchengabel — *Pastry fork*
Küchengeschirr or Küchengeräte — *Kitchen utensils* or *kitchenware*
Kuchenheber — *Cake lifter* or *turner*
Küchenherd — *Stove* or *range*
Küchenhobel — *Kitchen plane* (slicer)
Küchenlöffel — *Cooking spoon*
Küchenmaschine — *Food processor*
Küchenmesser — *Cook's knife*
Kuchenroller — *Rolling pin*
Küchenschrank — *Kitchen cupboard*
Küchenschürze — *Kitchen cloth*
Kuchen-Teigrad — *Paste jagger*
Küchentisch — *Kitchen table*
Küchenwaage — *Kitchen scales*
Kugelausstecker — *Melon baller*
Kugelform — *Round mold*
Kugelförmiger Kaffeeröster — *Globe-shaped coffee roaster*
Kühlschrank — *Refrigerator* (literally cold cupboard)
Kümmelmühle — *Caraway seed mill*
Kupfer — *Copper*
Kupferform — *Copper mold*
Löffel — *Spoon*
Marzipanform — *Marzipan mold*

Mayonnaiseschläger — *Mayonnaise beater* or *make[...]*
Mechanische Schneebese — *Cream whip* or *eggbeater, mechanical*
Mechanischer Kirschenentkerner — *Cherry pitter, mechanical*
Mehlschaufel — *Flour scoop*
Mehlsiebe — *Flour* or *meal sifter*
Melonenstech — *Melon baller*
Messer — *Knife*
Messerputzmaschine — *Knife-cleaner*
Messing — *Brass*
Messingerkessel — *Kettle, brass*
Messingmer — *Mortar, brass*
Messingschild — *Brass plate* (the metal)
Meßbecher — *Measuring beaker* or *cup*
Messlöffel — *Measuring spoon set*
Metall — *Metal*
Model — *Wooden mold* (such as for Springerle or Speculas)
Mohnmühle — *Poppyseed mill*
Morser mit Pistill — *Mortar with pestle*
Mörser und Stößel (Stöß) — *Mortar and pestle*
Muhle — *Mill*
Muldenpfanne für Gebäck — *Baking pan* (such as a clay muffin pan)
Muskatreibe — *Nutmeg grater*
Napfkuchenmold — *Poundcake mold in ring-shape*
Nudelbrett — *Pastryboard* or *doughboard*
Nudelrolle aus Holz or Nudelholz or Nudelwalze — *Rolling pin, with longitudinal ribbing, a wooden noodle roller*
Nußknacker — *Nutcracker*
Oblaten-Backzange — *Wafer iron* (literally wafer bake tongs)
Obstentkerner — *Fruit stoner*
Obstschälmaschine or Mechanische Obstschälmaschine — *Fruit parer*
Ofen — *Cooking stove*
Ofenplatte — *Stove plate*
Öffner — *Opener*
Osterhasen Form für Schokolade — *Chocolate mold of Easter bunny*
Papinscher Topf — *Pressure cooker* (Papin's Digester)
Passiermaschine — *Food mill*
Passiersieb — *Strainer*
Pastete Form — *Pie mold*
Pastetenblech — *Pastry sheet*
Pastetenschornsteine or Pastetchen — *Pie funnel* or *chimney*
Pfanne — *Pan*
Pfannenhalter — *Pan* or *pot trivet*
Pfannenlutscher — *Spatula*
Pfannenwender — *Pancake* or *cake turner*
Pfeffermühle — *Peppermill*
Plastischen Figur — *Figural*
Plätzchentrommel — *Rolling pin*
Plätzchenblech — *Baking sheet*
Plettkakerpfanne — *Pancake pan*
Plumpuddingform — *Plum pudding mold*
Poffertjes-pfanne — *Popover pan* or *egg pan*
Puddingform — *Pudding mold*
Rändel — *Pastry* or *pie rimmer*
Reibe — *Grater*
Reibe für Brösel — *Crumb grater*
Reibeisen — *Grater, tinned iron*
Reibmaschine — *Grating machine*
Reisbäll — *Rice ball*

Reiskocher — *Rice cooker* (a double boiler steamer)
Reisrandform — *Rice mold* or *ring mold for rice*
Rollholz — *Rolling pin*
Rostfreies Besteck — *Stainless steel cutlery*
Rührapparat or Rührmaschine or mixer — *mixing appliance* or *mixer*
Rührlöffel — *Mixing spoon*
Rührschlüssel — *Mixing bowl*
Salatschleuder — *Salad drainer*
Salatschwinge — *Salad dryer* (swinging)
Salz — *Salt*
Salzfäßchen — *Salt cellar*
Schablonen — *Decorating stencils* (for cake tops)
Schälmaschine — *Paring machine*
Schälmesser — *Paring knife* or *peeler*
Schmiedeeisen — *Wrought iron*
Schmirgelbrett mit Sandkasten — *Knife scouring board with sand box*
Schmortopf — *Saucepan*
Schneebesen or Schlager — *Whisk* or *eggbeater*
Schneekessel — *Mixing bowls for eggs*
Schneidebrett — *Carving board*
Schnellkochtopf — *Pressure cooker*
Schnellwaage — *Steelyard*
Schokoladeform — *Chocolate mold*
Schöpflöffel or Schöpfkelle — *Ladle* or *cup spoon*
Schrank — *Cupboard*
Schraubdeckelöffner — *Jar lid wrench* (for screw-on lid)
Schupper — *Fish scaler*
Schürze — *Apron*
Seihe or Sieher — *Strainer* or *colander*
Sieb — *Sieve* or *colander*
Soufflêförchen — *Soufflê mold*
Spargelkocher — *Asparagus cooker*
Spalter — *Cleaver*
Spatel — *Spatula*
Speiseschrank — *Food cupboard* or *meat safe*
Spekulatiusbrett — *Speculas mold* (a carved board)
Spicknadeln — *Larding needle*
Spieß — *Spit*
Springform — *Springform baking pan*
Sprizbeutel — *Cake icer*
Spülschüssel — *Dishwashing pan*
Stahl — *Steel*
Stampfer — *Stamper* or *pounder* (a beetle or pestle)
Standring — *Footed base*
Stiel — *Handle*
Stielpfanne — *Frying pan with long handle*
Stieltopf mit Deckel — *Frying pan with lid* (or saucepan with lid)
Stößel or Morserkeule — *Pestle*
Sulzform für Fischsülze — *Aspic mold in fish shape*
Tannenhher or Nußknacker — *Nutcracker*
Tee-Eier — *Tea ball*
Teekessel — *Tea kettle*
Teelöffel — *Teaspoon*
Teesieb — *Tea strainer*
Teigklopfer — *Biscuit breaker*
Teigmesser — *Dough* or *pastry knife*
Teigräd or Teigrädchen — *Dough* or *pastry wheel* or *pie jagger*
Teigrolle — *Rolling pin*
Teigschaber — *Dough scraper*

Teigspaten — *Bread peel*
Teigspritzen — *Pastry tube*
Tiegel — *Stew pan* or *saucepan*
Toaster or Brotröster — *Toaster*
Topflappen — *Kettle holder*
Tonform — *Clay* or *ceramic mold*
Topf — *Pot* or *saucepan*
Topfchen — *Small pot*
Topfdeckel — *Pot lid*
Töpferware — *Earthenware* or *crockery*
Tourniermesser — *Paring knife*
Trichter — *Funnel*
Umbachschen Dampftopf — *Pressure cooker*
Untersetzer — *Trivet* or *stand*
Verzinntcm Kupfer — *Tinned copper*
Vorlegemesser — *Carving knife*
Vorrichtung — *Appliance* or *gadget* or *device*
Waage — *Scales for weighing*
Waffeleisen — *Wafer iron* or *waffle iron*
Wandkaffeemühle — *Coffee mill, wall-mounted*
Wandsalzfässer — *Salt box* (to hang on wall)
Wasserbad — *Bain marie* (water bath pan)
Wasserglas — *Water glass* or *tumbler*
Wasserkessel — *Water kettle* (word also used for tea kettle)
Weckglas — *Preserving jar*
Weißblechkessel — *Tin kettle* (weiB is white; Weißmetal is white metal)
Wellholz — *Rolling pin with corrugated ribs*
Wender — *Spatula*
Wetzstahl — *Sharpening steel*
Wiegemesser — *Vegetable mincing knife, also a rocking chopper with curved blades*
Zange zum Zerkleinern von Hutzucker — *Sugar loaf cutter* (Zange is pliers)
Zestenreisser — *Zester*
Zinnform — *Pewter mold*
Zitronenpresse — *Lemon press*
Zitronenreibe — *Lemon zester* or *grater*
Zuber — *Washtub*
Zubereitung — *Cooking instructions*
Zuckergußpritzen — *Frosting tube*
Zuckerknieper or Zuckerzangen — *Sugar nippers*
Zuckerstreuer — *Sugar shaker*
Zwiebackschneider — *Rusk cutter* or *divider* (rusks arc a sort of biscuit)

Sources: Ulrich Klever's *Alte Küchengeräte*; Laura Krüger's *Vom Zauber alten Hausgeräts*; and Brigitte Kate-von Eicken's *Küchengeräte Um 1900*. Also a number of German language old trade catalogs. Also the following German/English dictionaries: *Langenscheidt's Standard German Dictionary* (1970); K. Wichmann's *German-English ... Dictionary* (1971); *The Oxford-Duden German Dictionary* (1997); *The Oxford-Duden Pictorial German and English Dictionary* (1994); *Langenscheidt's New College German Dictionary* (1995); and, one of the easiest and most helpful dictionaries I've used, the unabridged *Harper-Collins German Dictionary* (1997). Additional words came from 19th and early 20th century trade catalogs. And finally, I am indebted to people at Krause for correcting many of my mistakes especially umlauts and the endings of words.

VISUAL GLOSSARY INDEX

VISUAL GLOSSARY

PARTS, SHAPES, HANDLES, LEGS, SPOUTS, Etc.

The drawings on these two pages illustrate terms used throughout the book. The terms are alphabetical in one list; numerical in the other.

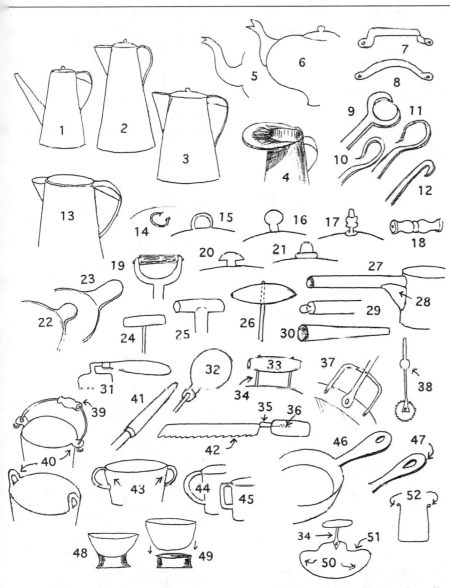

20. *Mushroom* finial
21. *Acorn* finial
22. *Tab* handle
23. Elongated tab handle, or *porringer handle*
24. T-handle
25. *Tubular* T handle
26. *Torpedo* or *cigar* handle with *tang* through it
27. *Tubular* handle
28. *Boss* [a brace]
29. Tubular handle with *hanging ring*
30. *Tapered* tubular handle; this one open at end: a *socket handle*
31. *Tiller* handle parallel to blade
32. *Bulb* or round handle
33. *Cigar* handle
34. A *tang*, one of two, also called a *shank*
35. *Ferrule*
36. *Tang* into wooden handle
37. *Braced* handle, usually wrought iron with copper pan, found on most *Turkish & Middle Eastern* pans
38. *Knop* (Like a knob, only not on end)
39. *Grip* on *falling bail* handle
40. *Ear* for *bail* handle, also called a *lug handle* for a bail
41. *Bullet* handle
42. *Serrated* or *saw-edge* blade
43. *Ear* handles
44. *Curved mug* handle
45. Squared or *bracket mug handle*
46. *Skillet* or *frying pan handle*, oval *hanging hole*
47. *Teardrop* hanging hole
48. *Fixed foot* on vessel
49. *Loose foot* on vessel (hence, expression *"footloose"*)
50. Curved *rocker blade* (*"carpet cutter"*)
51. *Shoulder*
52. *Rolled rim*
53. *Lug handle* on bulbous pot, or *bulge pot*, with longish *peg feet*
54-A. *Plier*, a levered mechanical action with the *fulcrum* partway back from business end
54-B. *Offset jaw* plier
55. *Fulcrum*, or *pivot point* for *lever*(s)

1. Coffee pot, *lighthouse* shape, straight spout, *braced strap* handle
2. Coffee pot, long *pocket spout*, strap handle
3. *Coffee boiler* shape
4. Pitcher or vessel with *wrap-around lip*
5. *Gooseneck spout* on teapot
6. *"Duckneck" spout* in my coinage, on *pigeon-breasted* teapot
7. *Strap* handle, *bracket*-shape [square parenthesis]
8. *Strap* handle, *parenthesis* shape ( )
9. *Ram's horn* wrought iron handle
10. *Rat-tail* wrought handle
11. *Rat-tail* handle with *twist* for strength
12. Handle with *hooked* end
13. Coffee *boiler* with *pocket spout* or pouring lip
14. *Ring* handle, *loose*
15. *Ring* handle, *fixed*
16. *Ball* or round *finial* knob
17. *Turned finial* knob
18. *Turned* or *shaped* handle, or *grip*
19. *Spade* or D handle, with wood grip

78-B. The *concave*, sunken shape

79. *Ogee* shape [with lines], the *negative shape* is a *reverse-ogee*. Usually of carved wood molding, but can describe other materials in other usages.

80. *Bulbous* jar or shape, the *bulg* is termed the *breast*

81. *Neck* of vessel

82. *Shoulder* of vessel

83. *Foot* of vessel

84. *Turned* (metal or wood) with a narrow *bead* or *beading* (doesn't have to actually look like beads)

85. *Scalloped* line

86. *Sawtooth*, *serrated*, or *zigzag* lin

87. *Crenelated* line, like top of *cas tle* turret

88. *Spiral*

89. *Bull's-eye*, or *target*

90. *Coiled* line, like a *spring*

91. Mold with *scalloped* or *gadrooned* sides

92. *Pinwheels* or *fylfots*. Very close to ancient *swastika*

93. *Bowler* or *derby* hat shape

94. *Tubular*, long thin *cylinder*

95. *Pear* shape

96. *Tulip* shape

97. *Elongated tulip* shape

98. *Egg* shape, or *ovoid*

99. *Oval* shape

100. *Cartouche*, or an *ellipse* with rounded ends; said of a shape that encloses a mark or signature

101. *Kidney* shape, or sometimes *bean* shape

102. *Hotdog* or *sausage* shape

103. *Puck* shape

104. *Cigar* shape with *truncated* ends

105. *Rectangle*

106. *Oblong*, which is also a *rectangle*, but I use *oblong* to imply somewhat longer sides

107. *Cylinder* with *truncated* end

108. *Cylinder*

109. *Tapered cylinder*

110. *Bulbous* vase shape with *flared neck* & *flared foot* with *beaded* edge

111. U-shaped *trough*

112. V-shaped *trough*

113. *Ellipse*

114. *Wedge* shape, *triangle*, *piece of pie*

115. *Ribbed cone*, *conical* shape

116. *Fluted cone*

117. *Dogleg*, said of a crank or leg, because of the compound angles

56. *Nutcracker*, *levered* mechanical action, *hinged fulcrum* at business end

57. *Tong*, *levered* mechanical action, *fulcrum opposite* the business end

58. *Scissor*, *levered* mechanical action, *fulcrum* further back from business end

59. *Lapped two-finger joint*, on *bentwood*

60. *Dovetail* joint, on metal (not as strictly shaped as on wood). Adds soldering strength.

61. *Elongated casting gate* on bottom of cast iron cooking pot

62. Filed-off *casting sprue* (served same purpose as casting gate) but is more tube-like

63. *Truncated* corners or ends on a *rectangle*. Any kind of corners can be truncated or cut short

64. *Tubed*, or sealed at one end of a *tapered tube* in mold (it wouldn't spout!)

65. *Spouted*, or open at both ends of a *tapered spout* in mold (it would spout!)

66. *Raised flange* on lid of cast iron *Dutch oven*

67. *Peg* feet, short

68. *Peg* feet, long

69. *Shoe foot* (on furniture)

70. *Plinth*, or relatively low *base*, for something. In this case a dog nutcracker.

71. *Slanted*, *canted*, or *sloped* sides to a vessel

72. *Flared* or *curved* sides to a vessel

73. Way of illustrating *wood*, here with *knots* & *graining* that make up what's called the wood's "*figure*"

74. *Spiraled coil* wire, used for *heat sink handle* grips

75. *Cabriole* leg (sometimes called "Queen Anne")

76. *Penny foot* on forged leg

77. *Snake foot* on forged leg

78-A. The *convex* bulging shape that fits into

INDEX

SUBJECTS & RECIPES

If you wonder about some strange old term used by cooks or tinsmiths, or a metal or unusual material, I hope it's here. I have put in the kind of odd things I tend to want to look up.

A subject that starts on, for example, page 222 will either be listed as 222-28, or 222+, the latter used most often when the subject pops up repeatedly over the next few pages after 222. A subject that appears unexpectedly in another chapter will have that specific page listed.

I suggest you personalize the Index while you read by making notes and additions in the margins.

All recipes are alphabetical under the heading Recipes. Most clubs and museums, resources and Web sites will be found at the end of their respective chapters; a few are within chapters or in the Bibliography.

Knife, Boxes, 472; Cleaners & scouring boxes, 551-52; Eating with, 170; Sharpeners, 552; Knives, 24-27, 32, 27, 68, 69, 90

Knop, defined, 300, 888-89

Kraut cutters, planes – See Cabbage cutters

Kugelhopf mold, 311, 321

Ladies' clothing, burning, 589

"Ladle" or "Dipper," which term, 674-75; Ladles, 175

Lady finger molds, 307, 309-10

Lady's legs motif, 75-76. (See also Bawdy legs)

Lamb cake molds, 218

Lamps, 792-93; Fillers, 703, 704; Heaters, 730

Landis Valley Museum, 90

Lap mill, 685

Lard, Jar, 479; Press, 47, 68; Skimmer, strainer, 168; Larding needles, 143

Latten, 681

Laundry blueing, 101

Lava wafers for tourists, 366

Lazy elbows or tongs, 543, 583

Lead, 285; Glaze, 146, 486; Jug, 478; Molds, 186

Lebkuchen cookies, 240

Left-hand or right-hand stoves, 615

Leg of mutton holder, 676

Lehnware, Joseph Lehn, 459, 462, 476

Lemon & lime juicers, squeezers, 52-68; Lemons, well rolled, 62

Lenten child pastry, 317

Lettuce baskets, 170

Liberty cap, 217

Lid, Lifters, 621-24, 633; Reformers, 772; Lids, for pans, 650, 654

Lignum vitae, 74

Linoleum, 755

Lions, 251

Liquid measures, 416+

Loaf pans, 310

Lollipop or sucker molds, 310

Love spoon, 676

Lozenge shape, 207

Lucifer, 809; Lucifers, 483

Lug poles, 567, 569, 588

Lunch & dinner boxes, carriers, pails, 479-82

Lute, mending with, 716

Macaroni spoon, 677

Mace, 499

Macedoine molds, 310

Machine vs. man-made, 712-13

Madeline molds, 311-12

Make-dos, 29, 30, 449, 478, 482, 490-91, 716

Malleable cast iron, 524

Malted milk mixers, 122, 820

Mandelplaettchen cookies, 240

Manos, John, 282

Maple, Sugar, Molds, 311-13; Sap spouts, 423; Skimmers, 167

Marchpane, 202

Marks – See French; German; Inventory; Molds; Patents

Marmalade, Cutters, 69; Molds, 263

Marrow spoons, 677

Marshmallow cooker, 834

Mary Ann cake pan, 218, 219

Marzipan, marchpane, etc., 202; Molds, 199, 313

Masher, 24

Masonic or Freemason symbols, 195-96

Match holders & safes, 481-85; Matches, History of, 483-84

"Mauve," 709

Mayonnaise mixers, 135, 143-45

McKinley Tariff Act, 668, 733

Measure, Units of, 406-07; Measures, Dry & Liquid, tables for, 406-07; Measuring cups, 419; Pitchers, 420; Spoons, 420. (See also Coffee)

Meat, Against eating, 358, etc.; Choppers, 44-45, 69-70, 754; Curing pump, 778; Cutter's glove, 70; Fret, 24; Grinders, 44-45, 69-70; Juicer, 59, 70; Presses, 47, 70, 71; Safes, 790, 793; Screens, 590-91; Tenderizers, 36, 71-73, 356. (See also Chopping knives)

Melon molds, 326, 330-31

Mending – See Repaired wares

Mennonite kitchens, 615

Metal, Drives, 153; Polishing, 555, 601. (See also individual metals)

Mica, 809

Microwave, 817

Milk, Bottles, 485; Bottle openers, 545; Can server, 485; -House, 115; or Cheese cupboards, 793-94; Pail, 486; Shake mixers, 820; Skimmers, 168; Milking stool, 794

Mill, Chocolate, 31, 85; Coffee, 685+; Pepper, 91-92; Wheat berry, 104

Mincers – see Chopping knives

Miniature, Cake server, 761; Dish drainer, 550; Nutcracker, 78; Sifter, 163; Tea kettles, 760, 765; Teapot, 726

Mixers, 145; Electric, 693; Mixing, Bowls, 145-48; Spoons, 148-49

Moiree metallique, 507

Molasses, 169; Cans, 169; Faucets, 169, 438; Pitcher, 486; Skimmers, 168, 169

Mold or mould parts, 314; Molding boards, 262; Molded food, Victorian style, 179, 313-15, 758, 766; Molds, 314-15; Copper, marks on, 320; Parts of, 314. (See also specific molds under Butter, Cake, etc.)

Molinillo, 684

Monitor Top, Refrigerator, 748, 750; Clocks, 409

Monsieur Vieux Bois, 572

Moon cakes, 275

Moravian, Christmas Cakes, 256-57; Coffee pot, 700

Mortars & pestles, 73-74

"Mother's helper," 711

Motifs and designs, Angels, 781; Catchpenny prints, 359; Chinese, 469; Christmas, 243; Dogs, 244; Fancy, 35; Fraternal orders, 195-96; Japanese, 468; Masonic, 195-96; New Year's, 243; Nutcrackers, 75; Pinwheel or fylfot, 195; Pressed glass, 211, 800; Springerle, 359; Stars, 194, 207, 262, 367; Tradesmen, 359; Trees, 196-97, 243; Twins, 256; Zoomorphic, 284

Motion studies, 785-86

Mousses, 313-14

Muddler, Chocolate, 684

Muffin pans, 332+, 381+

Muffineer, 157

Mullers, 684

Mulling iron, 583

Mummers, 245

Museums: See at end of each chapter

Music & musical, 28, 44, 104, 355, 552, 581

Mustard pot, 486

Nailsea glass, 353

Nambu ironware, 726, 729

Napkin rings, 486

Nappies, 487

Necromancer, 608

New Year's, Cakes, 201-02, 362

New York City, 19th century, 202-05

Newfoundland dogs, 244

Newspaper rack, 487

Niblo's, 185

Nichrome, 824

Nickel plating & nickel, 616, 648

Nipper, 244

Nirosta, 648

Noah's Ark, 255

Nomenclature -- specialty words, 39, 46, 120, 128, 131, 153, 179-80, 193, 196, 202, 239, 284-85, 313-14, 319, 321, 348, 366, 440, 507, 513, 559, 586, 604, 611, 614-15, 664, 665, 674-75, 702, 710, 728, 794

Noodle cutters, 339-40, 356

Nougat, molded, 226, 318

Nursing bottle, 487

Nut roaster, 607

Nutcrack Night, 82; Nutcrackers, 75-83; Nut-grinders or choppers, 83-84, 103

Nutmeg graters, 11, 48, 84-89, 308, 768; Nutmegs, 11, 499; How to grate, 88

Oble iron, 366

Odd Fellows symbols, 195-96

Official Gazette, 846, 847

Oil, Spills, 175; Stove, 622

Oiler cans, 487

Olive forks, 677

Omelet pan, 650

One-handed devices, 137, 162

Onion. Peelers, 89-90; Juicer, 59

"Openwork," 128

Orange, Juicers, 54+; Peelers, 90

Organizations, 10. Also at end of each chapter

Outlets, electrical, 823

Ovens, Doors for, 611; Electric tabletop, 82; Stovetop, 626; Thermometers, 438

Oyster, Broiler, 650; Knives, 90

Pails, 487+

Pain d'epices, 247

Paint, Gray, 459; Green, 462; Old finish, 48; Stove, 761

Pancake, Bells, 664; Pan, 340, 345, 650; Turner, 664-69. (See also Ebelskiver pan; Plett kaker)

Pantry boxes, 487

Paper, Candy cases, 466-67; Kitchen uses, 45; 797

Papin, Denis, 653, 660 [Denis Papin, no Jacques.]

Parers -- See Apple parers; Peach -- ; Potato –

Paring knives, 90

Parrots, 180

Pasta, Cabinet, 501, 503; Maker, 340; Spoon 677

Pastry, Blenders, 149; Boards, 340-41, 35; 354; Grate, 448; Jaggers, 296-307; Lenten 317; Pinchers, 298; Tubes, 341

Pâte molds, 275, 324

Patent, Models, 847; Office, 845-47

Patents, Dates, 89, 91; Disputes, 21-22; Interne research, 61 ; Marks, French, 49, 286 Marks, German, 49, 286; Marks, Italian, 49 Numbers, 855-57; Silly, 51 "Pat. appl. mark, 88, 544; Research, 61, 845-58; Tues days, 852-54; Women, holders of, 142, 151 183, 304, 741, 833

Pattern glass motifs, 211, 800; Patterns, Pie safe tins, 800-02; Toast, 825-26

Patty, Bowls & irons, 650; Pans, 312. See Tim bale irons, 341-43

Peas, Eating, 170; Ladles, 170; Shellers, 24, 90-91; Skimmers, 170

Peach, Canning, 91; Parers & stoners, 18, 91; Pitter, 91

Peanut, Shucker, 91; Butter machine, 91; Roaster, 650

Pease, Hiram, & Peaseware, 506

Peddlers, 249

Peelers – See various Parers

Peels, 39, 664, 677-78

Peg & worm, 542

"Pennsylvania Dutch" & "Pennsylvania German," Definitions of, 179-80; Cookies, 240; Motifs, 180; Vocabulary, 179

Pepper, Boxes, 487-88, 493; Mills, 91-92; Shakers, 493

Percolators, 713

Periodical research, 261

Perpetual calendar, 852-54

Pestles -- See Mortars & pestles

Petite Marmite, 654

Petits fours molds, 312

Pewter, 284, 285, 290

Phrygian cap, 217

Piccolo mold, 331

Pickles, 36; Jars for, 456, 488

Picnic, Baskets, 488; forks & spoons, 678

Pie, Birds, 422-23; Carriers, racks, 489; Cornerfold, 307; Crimpers, 296-97, 302-05, 306, 307; Cutter, 343, 679; Fillers, 416; Funnels, 422-23; Lifters, 678-79; Markers or Printers, 343-44 ; Pans or plates, 344-45; Racks, 489; Safes, 794-97, 800-02; Segmenter, 343, 679 Trimmers or wheels, 302, 757 (See Jaggers); Pies, 302

Pieced tin, 497

Pierced, 794

Pig sanctuary, 358

Piggins, 490, 493

Pin feather pullers, 100

Pineapple eye snips, 92

Pinwheel motif, 195, 800-02

Pit bottom, defined, 728

Pitchers, 490

Pizza cutters or wheels, 104, 307

Pizzelle irons, 368